CANADA

Lake Superior
Lake Huron
Lake Michigan
Lake Erie
Lake Ontario

WISCONSIN
Green Bay
Madison ★
Milwaukee

MICHIGAN
Grand Rapids
Lansing ★
Detroit

Rockford
Chicago
Gary
Fort Wayne

OHIO
Toledo
Cleveland
Akron
Wheeling
Columbus ★

INDIANA
Indianapolis ★
Cincinnati

Peoria
Springfield ★
ILLINOIS

CENTRAL
PLAINS

St. Louis
Jefferson City ★

MISSOURI

ARKANSAS
Little Rock ★
Pine Bluff

Memphis

TENNESSEE
Nashville ★
Knoxville

KENTUCKY
Frankfort ★
Louisville
Lexington

WEST VIRGINIA
Huntington
Charleston ★

VIRGINIA
Richmond ★
Newport News

WASHINGTON, D.C. ⊛

MARYLAND
Baltimore
Annapolis ★

DELAWARE
Dover ★
Wilmington

NEW JERSEY
Trenton ★
Newark
Jersey City

Philadelphia
Harrisburg ★

PENNSYLVANIA
Pittsburgh

NEW YORK
Buffalo
Rochester
Syracuse
Albany ★

MAINE
Augusta ★
Lewiston
Portland

VT
Burlington
Montpelier ★

NH
Concord ★
Manchester

MA
Worcester
Boston ★
Cape Cod

CT ★ Hartford
Bridgeport

RI Providence ★

New York City
LONG ISLAND

ADIRONDACK MTS.
St. Lawrence River
Bay of Fundy

ALLEGHENY MTS.
Susquehanna River
Hudson River
Mohawk River

DELMARVA PENINSULA
Chesapeake Bay
Norfolk

James River
Ohio River
Mississippi River
Tennessee River

Mt. Mitchell ▲
6,684 ft.
(2,030 m)

NORTH CAROLINA
Winston-Salem
Greensboro
Raleigh ★
Charlotte
Greenville

SOUTH CAROLINA
Columbia ★
Charleston

BLUE RIDGE MTS.
PIEDMONT

COASTAL PLAIN

Cape Hatteras
Cape Fear

GEORGIA
Atlanta ★
Macon
Columbus
Savannah

ALABAMA
Montgomery ★
Birmingham

MISSISSIPPI
Jackson ★
Meridian

Huntsville

LOUISIANA
Shreveport
Baton Rouge ★
New Orleans
Biloxi
Mobile

Tallahassee ★

Jacksonville

FLORIDA
Cape Canaveral
Tampa
St. Petersburg
Lake Okeechobee
Fort Lauderdale
Miami

Florida Keys
Straits of Florida

Mississippi Delta

ATLANTIC OCEAN

35°North Latitude
70° West Longitude

Mexico

CANADA

ATLANTIC OCEAN

PUERTO RICO (U.S.)
San Juan

0   100 Miles
0   100 Kilometers

CUBA

0   200 Miles
0   200 Kilometers

The United States: Physical-Political

Land Elevation

Feet	Meters
10,000	3,000
7,000	2,000
3,000	1,000
700	200
(Sea Level) 0	0 (Sea Level)
Below Sea Level	Below Sea Level

▭ International boundaries

▭ State boundaries

⊛ National capital

★ State capital

Would your life be easier if you had an electronic version of your textbook?

MyHistoryLab contains **the complete text** with **icons** that link to selected sources. You can print sections of the text to read anytime, anywhere.

Are you overwhelmed by the time it takes to find primary source documents, images, and maps for your research papers?

MyHistoryLab contains over **1,100 documents, images, maps, and video clips**—all in one place—to help make writing your research paper easier and more effective, and to help you better understand the course material.

Charleston Chain Gang

Are you sometimes overwhelmed when you study for exams?

MyHistoryLab gives you a **quizzing and testing program** that shows what you've mastered, as well as where you need more work. Look for these icons on MyHistoryLab:

Did your professor assign other books to read?

50 FREE BOOKS! MyHistoryLab allows you to read, download, or print fifty of the most commonly assigned works for this course – all at no additional cost!

History Bookshelf Listing.

1. Thomas Hariot A Brief and True Report of the New Found Land of Virginia (1588)
2. Mary White Rowlandson Narrative of the Captivity and Restoration of Mrs. Mary Rowlandson (1682)
3. Phillis Wheatley Religious and Moral Poems (1773)
4. Thomas Paine Common Sense (1776)
5. Alexander Hamilton, John Jay, and James Madison The Federalist Papers (1787-1788)
6. Benjamin Franklin, The Autobiography of Benjamin Franklin (1788)
7. Thomas Malthus Essay on Population (1798)
8. James Fennimore Cooper The Last of the Mohicans (1826)
9. Black Hawk Autobiography of Ma-ka-tai-me-she-kia-kiak, or Black Hawk (1833)
10. Alexis De Tocqueville Democracy in America (Two Volumes) (1835)
11. Angelina Emily Grimke An Appeal to the Christian Women of the South (1836)
12. Frances Anne Kemble Journal of a Residence on a Georgia Plantation (1838)
13. Richard Henry Dana Two Years Before the Mast (1840)
14. Frederick Douglass, The Narrative of the Life of Frederick Douglass, An American Slave (1845)
15. Francis Parkman The Oregon Trail: Sketches of Prairie and Rocky-Mountain Life (1847)
16. Henry David Thoreau Civil Disobedience (1849)
17. Sojourner Truth The Narrative of Sojourner Truth (1850)
18. Harriet Beecher Stowe Uncle Tom's Cabin (1852)
19. Henry David Thoreau Walden (1854)
20. Harriet Jacobs Incidents in the Life of a Slave Girl (1861)
21. John Stuart Mill The Contest in America (1862)
22. Carl Schurz Report on the Condition of the South (1865)
23. Excerpts from Recollections and Letters of General Robert E. Lee by Captain Robert E. Lee, His Son (1904)
24. Catharine Esther Beecher American Woman's Home (1869)
25. Mark Twain The Adventures of Huckleberry Finn (1885)
26. Edward Bellamy Looking Backward, 2000-1887 (1888)
27. John Muir The Yosemite (1890)
28. Rudyard Kipling American Notes (1891)
29. Charlotte Perkins Gilman The Yellow Wallpaper (1892)
30. Stephen Crane The Red Badge of Courage (1895)
31. Ida B. Wells-Barnett The Red Record (1895)
32. Kate Chopin The Awakening and Selected Short Stories (1899)
33. Thorstein Veblen Theory of the Leisure Class (1899)
34. Jacob Riis The Making of an American (1901)
35. Booker T. Washington Up From Slavery (1901)
36. W.E.B. Du Bois The Souls of Black Folk (1903)
37. George Washington Plunkitt Plunkitt of Tammany Hall (1905)
38. Upton Sinclair The Jungle (1906)
39. Frederick Jackson Turner Rise of the New West (1906)
40. Gifford Pinchot The Fight for Conservation (1910)
41. Frederick Winslow Taylor The Principles of Scientific Management (1911)
42. Jane Addams Twenty Years at Hull House (1912)
43. James Weldon Johnson The Autobiography of an Ex-Colored Man (1912)
44. Emma Goldman Anarchism and Other Essays (1917)
45. Carter G. Woodson A Century of Negro Migration (1918)
46. F. Scott Fitzgerald This Side of Paradise (1920)
47. Margaret Sanger Woman and the New Race (1920)
48. Zitkala-Sa (a.k.a. Gertrude Bonnin) American Indian Stories (1921)
49. Walter Lippmann Public Opinion (1922)
50. Sinclair Lewis Babbitt (1922)

Need extra help during evening hours?

Get help from The Tutor Center when your instructor is often unavailable — 5 pm to midnight, Sunday through Thursday, Spring and Fall terms (Sunday through Wednesday, Summer term). Tutors can help you navigate MyHistoryLab or review your paper for organization, grammar, and mechanics.

The **Tutor Center**

Benjamin Cummings • Longman • Addison-Wesley • Allyn & Bacon

Now, flip through this text. You will find the icons shown on the next page. Each icon will direct you to a place in MyHistoryLab to help you better understand the material. For example, when reading about the 1700's, you will find an icon that links you to a letter by an indentured servant; when reading about the 20th century, you will find an icon that links you to a video clip about the Cold War.

VIDEO CLIP.

Historical and political video clips from the last century bring history to life.

AUDIO CLIP.

Hear the sounds of the past by listening to historical music in original recordings, or more contemporary performances of original works.

MAP.

Interactive maps will help you visualize the geography you are exploring in this course. You will also find printable map activities from one of Longman's workbooks, along with atlas maps.

IMAGE.

You'll find photos, cartoons, and art work that relate to the topic you're reading.

DOCUMENT.

This icon will lead you to primary source documents, so you can see the original documents that pertain to the people and events you're studying.

The American People

THE AMERICAN PEOPLE

Creating a Nation and a Society

Seventh Edition

General Editors

Gary B. Nash
University of California, Los Angeles

Julie Roy Jeffrey
Goucher College

John R. Howe
University of Minnesota

Peter J. Frederick
Heritage University

Allen F. Davis
Temple University

Allan M. Winkler
Miami University of Ohio

Charlene Mires
Villanova University

Carla Gardina Pestana
Miami University of Ohio

PEARSON
Longman

New York   San Francisco   Boston
London   Toronto   Sydney   Tokyo   Singapore   Madrid
Mexico City   Munich   Paris   Cape Town   Hong Kong   Montreal

Executive Editor:	*Michael Boezi*
Senior Development Editor:	*Betty Slack*
Media and Supplements Editor:	*Kristi Olson*
Executive Marketing Manager:	*Sue Westmoreland*
Production Manager:	*Eric Jorgensen*
Project Coordination, Text Design, and Electronic Page Makeup:	*Elm Street Publishing Services, Inc.*
Cover Design Manager:	*John Callahan*
Cover Illustration/Photo:	*Left image: courtesy of Getty Images. Right image: Bust of Dr. Mary Harris Thompson [1829–1895]. DN-0001130, Chicago Daily News negatives collection, Chicago Historical Society.*
Photo Researcher:	*Photosearch, Inc.*
Manufacturing Buyer:	*Roy L. Pickering, Jr.*
Printer and Binder:	*Quebecor World / Versailles*
Cover Printer:	*Coral Graphics*

For permission to use copyrighted material, grateful acknowledgment is made to the copyright holders on pp. C-1–C-2, which are hereby made part of this copyright page.

Library of Congress Cataloging-in-Publication Data

    The American people: creating a nation and a society / general editors, Gary B. Nash . . .
      [et al.].—7th ed.
        p. cm.
      Includes bibliographical references and index.
      ISBN 0-321-33765-4 (Single Volume Edition)
        1. United States—History. I. Nash, Gary B.

    E178.1.A49355 2006b
    973—dc22   2005048870

Please visit us at http://www.ablongman.com

ISBN 0-321-33765-4 (Single Volume Edition)
ISBN 0-321-33776-X (Volume One)
ISBN 0-321-33775-1 (Volume Two)

2 3 4 5 6 7 8 9 10—QWV—08 07 06

Brief Contents

Detailed Contents

Features

RECOVERING THE PAST

ANALYZING HISTORY

AMERICAN VOICES

How Others See Us

MAPS

FIGURES

TABLES

Preface

The Yoruba people of West Africa have an old saying: "However far the stream flows, it never forgets its source." Why, we wonder, do such ancient societies as the Yoruba find history so important, whereas today's American students question its relevance? This book aims to help students appreciate the usefulness of history.

In a twenty-first century marked by the increasing ethnic and racial diversity of American society, history is of central importance in preparing us to exercise our rights and responsibilities as free people in an increasingly interdependent global world.

History cannot make good citizens, but without history we cannot understand the choices before us and think wisely about them. Lacking a collective memory of the past, we would be unaware of the human condition and the long struggles of men and women everywhere to deal with the problems of their day and to create a better society. Without historical knowledge, we deprive ourselves of knowing about the full range of approaches people have taken to political, economic, social, and cultural life; to solving human problems; and to conquering the obstacles in their way. With knowledge of how events beyond our national boundaries have affected our own history, we are better able to deal with the challenges of contemporary globalism.

History has a deeper, even more fundamental importance: the cultivation of the private person whose self-knowledge and self-respect provide the foundation for a life of dignity and fulfillment. Historical memory is the key to self-identity, to seeing one's place in the long stream of time, in the story of humankind.

When we study our own history, that of the American people, we see a rich and extremely complex human story that stretches back to the last ice age when nomadic hunters arrived in the Americas from Siberia. This country, whose written history began thousands of years later with a convergence of Native Americans, Europeans, and Africans, has always been a nation of diverse peoples—a magnificent mosaic of cultures, religions, and skin shades. This book explores how American society assumed its present shape and developed its present forms of government; how as a nation we have conducted our foreign affairs and managed our economy; how as individuals and in groups we have lived, worked, loved, married, raised families, voted, argued, protested, and struggled to fulfill our dreams and the noble ideals of the American experiment.

Several ways of making the past understandable distinguish this book from the old textbooks, which provided a "master narrative" of a mostly white, rich, powerful, male-dominated American history. While this book covers significant public events such as presidential elections, wars and diplomatic treaties, and economic legislation, we have integrated this familiar national narrative with the private human stories that describe and give meaning to our shared past.

Within a chronological framework, we have woven together our history as a nation, as a people, and as a society. When, for example, national political events are discussed, we analyze their impact on social and economic life at the state and local levels. Wars are described not only as they unfolded on the battlefield and in the salons of diplomats but also on the home front, where they are history's greatest motor of social change. The interaction of ordinary Americans with extraordinary events runs as a theme throughout this book.

Above all, we have tried to show the "humanness" of our history as it is revealed in people's everyday lives. This textbook is marked by the words of ordinary Americans, the authentic human voices of those who participated in, responded to, and helped shape epic events such as war, slavery, industrialization, and reform movements.

SIX RECURRING THEMES

Our primary goal is to provide students with a rich, balanced, and thought-provoking treatment of the American past. By this, we mean a history that treats the lives and experiences of Americans of all national origins and cultural backgrounds, at all class levels of society, and in all regions of the country. It also means a history that seeks connections among the many factors—political, economic, technological, social, religious, intellectual, and biological—that have molded and remolded American society over four centuries. And, finally, it means a history that encourages students to think about how they share an inherited and complex past filled with both notable achievements and thorny problems.

The only history befitting a democratic nation is one that inspires students to initiate a frank and searching dialogue with their past. Historians continually revise their understanding of what happened in the past. Historians reinterpret history because they find new evidence on old topics, add new voices, and are inspired by new sensibilities to ask questions about the past that did not interest earlier historians. Therefore, we hope to promote class discussions and inquiry organized around six recurring themes we see as basic to the American historical experience:

1. **The peopling of America**   How has this nation been peopled diversely from native inhabitants of the Americas to those voluntarily coming from Britain and Europe or forced from Africa in chains in the colonial era, to more diverse European immigrants a century ago, to the many recent migrants from Asia, the Pacific Islands, Africa, and Latin America? How have these successive waves of newcomers contributed to the American cultural mosaic by preserving their ethnic, racial and religious heritages? How have the tensions between cultural assimilation and cultural preservation been played out, in the past and today?

2. **Developing American democracy**   To what extent have Americans developed a stable, democratic political system flexible enough to address the wholesale changes occurring in the last two centuries, and to what degree has this political system been consistent with the principles of our nation's founding?

3. **Environmental, economic, and technological change**   How have environmental, economic, and technological changes affected the American landscape; attitudes toward nature, work, family life, leisure, and sexual behavior; the division of wealth; and community relations throughout the land?

4. **Religion and reform in American life**   What role has American religion played in the development of the nation? How have religion and religious values affected social change in our history? Whatever their varied sources, how have the recurring reform movements in our history dealt with economic, political, social, and cultural problems in attempting to square the ideals of American life with the reality?

5. **America and the world**   In what ways have global events and trends had an impact on the shape and character of American life? How has the United States affected the rest of the world? To what extent has the United States served as a model for other peoples, as an interventionist savior of other nations around the globe, and as an interfering expansionist superpower in the affairs of other nations?

6. **Diversity, values, and American dreams**   In the pursuit of American dreams, how have American beliefs and values changed over more than four hundred years of history, and how have they varied among different groups—women and men; Americans of many colors and cultures; and people of different regions, religions, sexual orientations, ages, and classes?

In writing a history that revolves around these themes, we have tried to convey two dynamics that operate in all societies. First, as we observe people continuously adjusting to new developments, such as industrialization, urbanization, and internationalism, over which they seemingly have little control, we realize that people are not paralyzed by history but are the fundamental creators of it. People retain the ability, individually and collectively, to shape the world in which they live and thus in considerable degree to control their own lives.

Second, we emphasize the connections that always exist among social, political, economic, and cultural events. Just as our individual lives are never neatly parceled into separate spheres of activity, the life of a society is made up of a complicated and often messy mixture of forces, events, and accidental occurrences. In this text, political, economic, technological, and cultural factors are intertwined like strands in a rope as ordinary and extraordinary American people seek to fulfill their dreams.

STRUCTURE OF THE BOOK

The chapters of this book are grouped into six parts that relate to major periods in American history. The title of each part suggests a major theme that helps characterize how the American people changed over time: from a colonizing to revolutionary to expanding to industrializing people, and in the last hundred years a modernizing and, most recently, a "resilient" people, adapting to challenging new forces in the world.

Each chapter begins with an *outline* that provides an overview of the chapter's organization. Next, a personal story, called "American Stories," recalls the experience of an ordinary or lesser-known American. The story puts a human face on history, suggesting that our past was shaped by ordinary as well as extraordinary people. Chapter 3, for example, is introduced with an account of the life of Anthony Johnson, who came to Virginia as a slave but who managed to gain his freedom along with his wife, Mary, and in the face of racial prejudice lost his hard-earned land. This brief anecdote introduces the overarching themes and major concepts of the chapter and its organizing structure.

Following the personal American story, a *brief chapter overview* links the story to the text. Each overview includes three recurring ways we seek to help students better understand, remember, and more permanently learn the significant history in the chapter; for example, in Chapter 3:

1. The overview connects Anthony and Mary Johnson's story to the *overarching themes and major concepts* of the chapter, in this case the multiracial peopling and character of American society, how enslaved Africans, Native Americans, and European immigrants interacted and coped with diversity and change, and the violent instability of late-seventeenth-century colonial economic, social, and political life.

2. These themes recall the *six recurring themes* from the Preface, in this case the multiethnic peopling of America, how diverse Americans responded to the stresses of daily life in an effort to achieve their dreams, and how the American people sought to

turn their religious and political ideals into reality amidst conflicting pressures and forces.

3. Third, the overview lays out the *organizational structure* of the chapter, in this case the comparisons among six regional areas of early colonization and how each developed a different pattern of life in an effort to implement ideal goals.

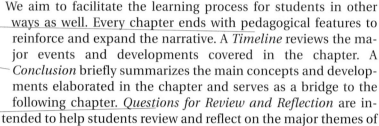

We aim to facilitate the learning process for students in other ways as well. Every chapter ends with pedagogical features to reinforce and expand the narrative. A *Timeline* reviews the major events and developments covered in the chapter. A *Conclusion* briefly summarizes the main concepts and developments elaborated in the chapter and serves as a bridge to the following chapter. *Questions for Review and Reflection* are intended to help students review and reflect on the major themes of the chapter and to connect them to the six major recurring themes and questions. The *Recommended Readings* posted on the Web site for the book (www.ablongman.com/nash) are supplementary sources for further study or research on topics discussed in the chapter. The annotated selection of novels and films, under the heading *Fiction and Film,* directs students to additional sources, both from and about the period. Finally, a special annotated section of suggested Web sites, *Discovering U.S. History Online,* offers students information on electronic sources relating to chapter themes.

SPECIAL FEATURES

Several distinctive features help contribute to student learning of history.

- **Recovering the Past** A distinctive feature of this book is the two-page "Recovering the Past" essay in each chapter. These RTPs, as the authors affectionately call them, introduce students to the fascinating variety of evidence—ranging from household inventories, folk tales, and diaries to tombstones, advertising, and popular music—that historians have learned to employ in reconstructing the past. Each RTP gives basic information about the source and its use by historians and then raises questions, under the heading "Reflecting on the Past," for students to consider as they study the example reproduced for their inspection.

- **NEW! American Voices** Every chapter contains one or two brief passages from a wide variety of public and personal primary sources capturing the voices of the American people. Each statement will be prefaced by a short introduction putting the "voice" into context and posing two or three questions to explore about the passage. Here readers will "hear" the voices of both extraordinary and ordinary Americans, men and women, and people from many diverse cultures and classes: white ministers, teachers, and reformers; Native American orators; African American slaves and white slaveholders; newly arrived European, Chinese, and Mexican immigrants; soldiers from American wars; athletes, inventors, politicians, urban garment factory workers, and southern civil rights workers; and many others.

- **NEW! How Others See Us** Less frequently but included in each section of the textbook are brief passages or, on occasion, illustrations such as posters or cartoons from non-Americans, commenting on "how others see us." This feature is in keeping with our aim of putting American history into a global context and illustrating that those outside the United States (and often the "outsiders" within) sometimes know us better than we know ourselves.

- **Analyzing History** This feature brings together, in visually engaging ways, a variety of socioeconomic data that illustrates the ways in which complex changes are closely intertwined at particular moments in American history. One chart, for example, suggests how new methods of steel production during the late nineteenth century affected prices, working and living conditions, and investment in industry. Our goal is not only to show connections but also to encourage visual literacy by helping students read and interpret statistics and graphs. We have written captions for this feature to assist students in analyzing these materials and have posed "Reflecting on the Past" questions to encourage them to think about the implications of the data presented.

- **An international context for American history** Believing that in today's global society it is particularly important for students to think across national boundaries and to understand the ways in which our history intersects with the

world, we have provided an international framework. Rather than developing a separate discussion of global events, we have woven an international narrative into our analysis of the American past. Chapter 13, for example, discusses the international context for American expansionism. Chapter 10 examines the international character of reform. We have shown the ways in which the United States has been influenced by events in other parts of the world and the connection between the history of other nations and our own. We have also drawn attention to the aspects of our history that appear to set the nation apart. New tables, charts, and maps with a global focus provide an additional dimension for this international context.

- **MyHistoryLab** Complementing the text of *The American People,* Seventh Edition, is a diverse array of assets found on the accompanying premium Web site, www.myhistorylab.com, an online package containing the entire textbook,

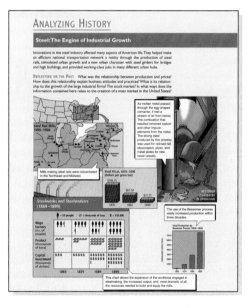

numerous study aids, course management, and hundreds of assets. Icons throughout the pages of the text identify the type of asset and its specific content, enriching the text's presentation of history with multimedia material, including primary source documents, images, audio and video clips, and interactive maps.

Document Primary source documents, each with its own introductory headnote and questions for study and reflection.

Image Paintings, historical photographs, cartoons, and other types of images, each with a brief explanatory note and accompanied by thought questions.

Audio Audio recordings of works from the Library of Congress and the Smithsonian Folkways collections.

Video Video clips from the beginning of the twentieth century to the present.

Map Interactive maps with detailed captions. The Web site also contains an extensive collection of still maps and map exercises.

- **Discovering U.S. History Online**
  Suggested Web sites, carefully evaluated for this edition, allow students to explore particular areas that relate to each chapter. These sites can also provide the basis for written evaluations, essays, and other learning activities.

- **Illustration Program** Color illustrations—paintings, cartoons, photographs, maps, and figures—amplify important themes while presenting visual evidence for student reflection and analysis. Captions on all photographs, maps, and figures are designed to help students understand and interpret the information presented. Many captions pose questions for students to think about. Summary tables, which we refer to as "talking boxes," recap points discussed in the narrative, pulling the material together in a format designed for ease of study. Examples of such "talking boxes" include "Significant Factors Promoting Economic Growth, 1820–1860" in Chapter 10 and "Conflicting Aims During the Cold War" in Chapter 27.

New Publications for Women The women's movement spawned a number of publications that attempted to give women greater control over various aspects of their own lives. The book *Our Bodies, Ourselves* and *Ms.* magazine were two important sources in that effort. What do you think this cover picture was trying to convey? Is it successful? *(Reprinted by permission of Ms. Magazine, © 1982.)*

CHANGES IN THE SEVENTH EDITION

The seventh edition of *The American People* has benefited from the helpful comments of scholars as well as the experience of instructors and students who have used previous editions of the textbook. To address their comments we have made the following adaptations in the seventh edition: we have added many first-person voices from both inside and outside the American experience, and we have tried to situate American history in a global context. We have identified six significant themes to help students ask questions about the American past.

Our aim has been to write a balanced and vivid history of the development of the American nation and its society. We also provide a variety of support materials to help make teaching and learning enjoyable and rewarding. The reader will be the judge of our success. We welcome your comments.

GARY B. NASH
JULIE ROY JEFFREY

INSTRUCTOR SUPPLEMENTS FOR QUALIFIED COLLEGE ADOPTERS

MyHistoryLab provides students and instructors with an online package complete with the entire textbook, numerous study aids, and course management. With more than 1,000 primary sources, images, audio clips, and video clips, as well as more than 150 map activities with gradable quizzes, geographic case studies, map workbook activities, and atlas maps, the site offers students a unique, interactive experience that brings history to life. The comprehensive site also includes a History Bookshelf with 50 of the most commonly assigned books in history classes and a History Toolkit with tutorials and helpful links.

LongmanAmericanHistory.com provides students with the same resources as MyHistoryLab, but without the e-book or course management features.

History Digital Media Archive CD-ROM The Digital Media Archive CD-ROM contains electronic images and interactive and static maps, along with media elements such as video. These media assets are fully customizable and ready for classroom presentation or easy downloading into your PowerPoint presentations or any other presentation software. ISBN: 0-321-14976-9.

Visual Archives of American History, Updated Edition Available on two CD-ROMs and with added content, this encyclopedic collection of instructor resources contains dozens of narrated vignettes and videos as well as hundreds of photos and illustrations ready for use in PowerPoint presentations, course Web sites, or online courses. ISBN:0-321-18694-X.

Companion Web site, www.ablongman.com/nash Instructors can take advantage of the Companion Web site that supports this text. The instructor section of the Web site includes the Instructor's Manual, teaching links, and downloadable maps and images from the text in PowerPoint™.

PowerPoint™ Presentations These presentations contain an average of 15 PowerPoint slides for each chapter. These slides may include key points and terms for a lecture on the chapter, as well as full-color slides of some important maps, graphs, and charts within a particular chapter. The presentations are available for download at www.ablongman.com/nash and www.ablongman.com/irc.

Instructor Resource Center www.ablongman.com/irc As part of Pearson Education's commitment to helping you maximize your time at every stage of course preparation, we are delighted to offer you access to our Instructor Resource Center (IRC). Once you have registered for this instructor-only resource, you can log in to premium online products, browse and download book-specific instructor resources, and receive immediate access and instructions to installing course management content to your campus server . . . all from your book's Web page in our online catalog. If you already have access to CourseCompass or Supplements Central, you can log in to the IRC immediately using your existing login and password. Otherwise, visit the Instructor Resource Center welcome page at www.ablongman.com/irc to register for access today.

Instructor's Manual, prepared by Mark Simon, York College. This guide was written based on ideas generated in "active learning" workshops and is tied closely to the text. In addition to suggestions on how to generate lively class discussion and involve students in active learning, this supplement also offers a file of exam questions and lists of resources, including films, slides, photo collections, records, and audiocassettes. ISBN:0-321-39894-7.

Test Bank This test bank, prepared by Jennifer Fish Kashay, California State University, San Bernadino, contains more than 3,500 objective, conceptual, and essay questions. All questions are keyed to specific pages in the text. ISBN:0-321-39661-8.

TestGen-EQ Computerized Testing System This flexible, easy-to-master computerized test bank on a dual-platform CD includes all of the items in the printed test bank and allows instructors to select specific questions, edit existing questions, and add their own items to create exams. Tests can be printed in several different formats and can include figures, such as graphs and tables. ISBN:0-321-39896-3.

Text-specific Transparency Set A set of four-color transparency acetates showing maps from the text. ISBN:0-321-39346-5.

Discovering American History Through Maps and Views Transparency Set Created by Gerald Danzer of the University of Illinois at Chicago, the recipient of the AHA's James Harvey Robinson Prize for his work in the development of map transparencies, this set of 140 four-color acetates is a unique instructional tool. It contains an introduction to teaching history through maps and a detailed commentary on each transparency. The collection includes cartographic pictorial maps, views, photos, urban plans, building diagrams, and works of art.

STUDENT SUPPLEMENTS FOR QUALIFIED COLLEGE ADOPTERS

MyHistoryLab provides students with an online package complete with the entire textbook, numerous study aids, and course management. With more than 1,000 primary sources, images, audio clips, and video clips, as well as more than 150 map activities with gradable quizzes, geographic case studies, map workbook activities, and atlas maps, the site offers a unique, interactive experience that brings history to life. The comprehensive site also includes a History Bookshelf with 50 of the most commonly assigned books in history classes and a History Toolkit with tutorials and helpful links.

LongmanAmericanHistory.com provides students with the same resources as MyHistoryLab, but without the e-book or course management features.

Study Card for American History Colorful, affordable, and packed with useful information, Longman's Study Cards make studying easier, more efficient, and more enjoyable. Course information is distilled down to the basics, helping students quickly master the fundamentals, review a subject for understanding, or prepare for an exam. Because they're laminated for durability, students can keep these Study Cards for years to come and pull them out for a quick review.

Companion Web site for The American People, **Seventh Edition**
www.ablongman.com/nash. The online course companion provides a wealth of

resources for students using *The American People,* Seventh Edition. Students can access chapter summaries, interactive practice test questions, and Web links for every chapter. The Web site is a comprehensive online study guide for students.

Study Guide This two-volume study guide, prepared by Thomas F. Jorsch, Ferris State University, includes chapter outlines, significant themes and highlights, a glossary, learning enrichment ideas, sample test questions, exercises for identification and interpretation and geography exercises based on maps in the text. Volume One ISBN: 0-321-39321-X, Volume Two ISBN: 0-321-39345-7.

Research Navigator Guide This guidebook includes exercises and tips on how to use the Internet in your study of U.S. history. It also includes an access code for Research Navigator—the easiest way for students to start a research assignment or research paper. Research Navigator is composed of three exclusive databases of credible and reliable source material, including EBSCO's ContentSelect Academic Journal Database, the *New York Times* Search by Subject Archive, and the "Best of the Web" Link Library. This comprehensive site also includes a detailed help section.

Longman American History Atlas A four-color reference tool and visual guide to American history that includes almost 100 maps and covers the full scope of history. Atlas overhead transparencies available to adopters. *Only $3.00 when bundled in advance with a new book.*

Mapping American History: Student Activities Written by Gerald Danzer of the University of Illinois at Chicago, this free map workbook for students features exercises designed to teach how to interpret and analyze cartographic materials as historical documents. Available free to qualified college adopters when bundled in advance with the textbook.

Mapping America: A Guide to Historical Geography, Second Edition Written by Ken Weatherbie of Del Mar College, this two-volume workbook contains 35 exercises correlated to the text that review basic American historical geography and ask students to interpret the role geography has played in American history. *Mapping America* is available free to qualified college adopters when bundled with the text.

American History in a Box Created by editors Julie Roy Jeffrey and Peter Frederick, this unique "reader in a box" is designed to give students an up-close-and-personal view of history. The collection includes loose facsimiles of written documents, visual materials and artifacts, songs and sheet music, portraits, cartoons, film posters, and more, so that students can learn firsthand what history is and what historians do. "Placing the Sources in Context" and "Questions to Consider" accompanying each set of materials in the collection help guide students through the practice of historical analysis.

Voices of the American People This collection of primary documents reflects the rich and varied tapestry of American life and is correlated directly to the content and organization of *The American People.* It is available to qualified college adopters at no charge when bundled with a new book.

Sources of the African American Past, Second Edition Edited by Roy Finkenbine of the University of Detroit at Mercy, this collection of primary sources covers key themes in the African American experience from the West African background to the present. Balanced between political and social history, it offers a vivid snapshot of the lives of African Americans in different historical periods and includes documents representing women and different regions of the United States. Available at a minimum cost to qualified college adopters when bundled with the text.

Women and the National Experience, Second Edition Edited by Ellen Skinner of Pace University, this primary source reader contains both classic and unusual documents describing the history of women in the United States. The documents provide dramatic evidence that outspoken women attained a public voice and participated in the development of national events and policies long before they could vote. Chronologically organized and balanced between social and political history, this reader offers a striking picture of the lives of women across American history. Available at a minimum cost to qualified college adopters when bundled with the text.

Reading the American West Edited by Mitchel Roth of Sam Houston State University, this primary source reader uses letters, diary excerpts, speeches, interviews, and newspaper articles to let students experience how historians do research and how history is written. Every document is accompanied by a contextual headnote and study questions. The book is divided into chapters with extensive introductions. Available at a minimum cost to qualified college adopters when bundled with the text.

A Short Guide to Writing About History, Fourth Edition Written by Richard Marius and Melvin E. Page, this practical text teaches students how to incorporate their own ideas into their papers and to tell a story about history that interests them and their peers. Focusing on more than just the conventions of good writing, this text shows students how first to think about history, and then how to organize their thoughts into coherent essays. The ***Short Guide*** covers both brief essays and the document resource paper as it explores the writing and researching processes; examines different modes of historical writing, including argument; and concludes with guidelines for improving style.

Library of American Biography Series Each concise biography in this distinguished series focuses on an individual whose actions and ideas significantly influenced American history and relates the life of the subject to the issues and events of the time period. Now featuring the guiding hand of series editor Mark C. Carnes, the series is being revised and updated with today's students in mind. Each volume is offered at a lower price, and study and discussion questions have been added at the end of each new volume to encourage students to reflect on the role of the subject in the shaping of American history. Classic books in the series include Edmund S. Morgan, *The Puritan Dilemma: The Story of John Winthrop;* Harold C. Livesay, *Andrew Carnegie and the Rise of Big Business;* William T. Youngs, *Eleanor Roosevelt: A Personal and Public Life;* Allan Winkler, *Franklin D. Roosevelt and the Making of Modern America;* and Dan LaBotz, *César Chávez and La Causa.*

Penguin Books The partnership between Penguin Putnam USA and Longman Publishers offers your students a discount on many titles when bundled with any Longman survey. Available titles include *Narrative of the Life of Frederick Douglass* by Frederick Douglass, *Why We Can't Wait* by Martin Luther King, Jr., *Beloved* by Toni Morrison, and *Uncle Tom's Cabin* by Harriet Beecher Stowe. For a complete listing of titles, go to **www.ablongman.com/penguin**.

Acknowledgments

The authors wish to thank the following reviewers who gave generously of their time and expertise and whose thoughtful and constructive comments have contributed greatly to this edition:

Thomas Appleton, *Eastern Kentucky University*

Daniel Ashyk, *Cleveland State University*

Eirlys Barker, *Thomas Nelson Community College*

Mathias Bergmann, *Randolph-Macon College*

Troy Bickham, *Texas A&M University*

John Boswell, *San Antonio College*

Roger Bromert, *Southwestern Oklahoma State University*

Jerry Brookshire, *Middle Tennessee State University*

Sharon Carlson, *Western Michigan University*

Kevin Chambers, *Gonzaga University*

Jane E. Dabel, *California State University, Long Beach*

Walter Dabrowski, *Burlington County College*

Salvador Diaz, *California State University, Fresno*

Herbert Ershkowitz, *Temple University*

Vallye Ezell, *Richland College*

Michael Flores, *Cypress College*

Raymond Frey, *Centenary College*

Karen Garner, *Florida International University*

Loretta Goldy, *Portland Community College*

Lesley J. Gordon, *University of Akron*

Stuart Graybill, *Sacramento City College*

J. R. Green, *Central Michigan University*

David Groeninger, *College of Lake County*

Gerhard Grytz, *University of Texas at Brownsville*

Mark Hagy, *Virginia Highlands Community College*

David Halahmy, *Cypress College*

Timothy Hall, *Central Michigan University*

David Hansen, *University of Texas at San Antonio*

Tim Herrmann, *Northern Kentucky University*

David Hudson, *California State University, Fresno*

Marla Hughes, *University of Maryland*

Cherisse R. Jones, *Arkansas State University*

Errol D. Jones, *Boise State University*

Thomas F. Jorsch, *Ferris State University*

Jennifer Fish Kashay, *California State University, San Bernardino*

Stephen Katz, *Community College of Philadelphia*

Suzanne Katz, *Saddleback College*

Ken Kirkland, *Colorado State University*

Renee Laegreid, *Hastings College*

Alan K. Lamm, *Mount Olive College*

Tonya Thames Leonard, *West Chester University*

Mike Light, *Grand Rapids Community College*

Marian Macbeth, *J. Sargeant Reynolds Community College*

Thomas Mays, *Humboldt State University*

Marcella McCoy, *Philadelphia University*

Constance M. McGovern, *Frostburg State University*

Amy McKinney, *University of Montana—Western*

Debra Meyers, *Northern Kentucky University*

James Mills, *University of Texas at Brownsville*

John Monroe, *Spokane Falls Community College*

Christine Moore, *Southwestern College*

Christopher Mortenson, *Texas A&M University*

William Mugleston, *Floyd College*

Tom Murphy, *Bemidji State University*

Steven Noll, *University of Florida*

Jimmy Norris, *North Dakota State University*

Ray O'Brien, *Bucks County Community College*

Richard Oestreicher, *University of Pittsburgh*

John Oriji, *California Polytechnic State University*

Chris Paine, *Lake Michigan College*

Anne Paulet, *Humboldt State University*

Linda C. Powell, *Amarillo College*

Mary Pratt, *Southwest Tennessee Community College*

Marguerite Renner, *Glendale Community College*

William Roba, *Scott Community College*

Tara Ross, *Onondaga Community College*

Marion Roydhouse, *Philadelphia University*

Maryann Rubino, *Sussex County Community College*

Nancy Rupprecht, *Middle Tennessee State University*

Robert Sawrey, *Marshall University*

Bryan Seiling, *Cypress College*

Donald Shaffer, *University of Northern Colorado*

Steve Shone, *University of Montana—Western*

Shirley Stephens, *Central Washington University*

Barbara Stites, *Los Angeles City College*

Carl Swanson, *East Carolina University*

Mary Swilling, *University of Mississippi*

Alexander Thomson, *Schoolcraft College*

Steve Tripp, *Grand Valley State University*

Loren Whetsell, *St. Charles Community College*

Mickey White, *Temple College*

Larry Wilson, *San Jacinto College—Central*

Robert Young, *Carroll Community College*

Charles Zappia, *San Diego Mesa College*

About the Authors

GARY B. NASH received his Ph.D. from Princeton University. He is currently Director of the National Center for History in the Schools at the University of California, Los Angeles, where he teaches colonial and revolutionary American history. Among the books Nash has authored are *Quakers and Politics: Pennsylvania, 1681–1726* (1968); *Red, White, and Black: The Peoples of Early America* (1974, 1982, 1992, 2000); *The Urban Crucible: Social Change, Political Consciousness, and the Origins of the American Revolution* (1979); *Forging Freedom: The Formation of Philadelphia's Black Community, 1720–1840* (1988); *First City: Philadelphia and the Forging of Historical Memory* (2002); and *The Unknown American Revolution: The Unruly Birth of Democracy and the Struggle to Create America* (2005). A former president of the Organization of American Historians, his scholarship is especially concerned with the role of common people in the making of history. He wrote Part 1 and served as a general editor of this book.

JULIE ROY JEFFREY earned her Ph.D. in history from Rice University. Since then she has taught at Goucher College. Honored as an outstanding teacher, Jeffrey has been involved in faculty development activities and curriculum evaluation. She was Fulbright Chair in American Studies at the University of Southern Denmark, 1999–2000. Jeffrey's major publications include *Education for Children of the Poor* (1978); *Frontier Women: The Trans-Mississippi West, 1840–1880* (1979, 1997); *Converting the West: A Biography of Narcissa Whitman* (1991); and *The Great Silent Army of Abolitionism: Ordinary Women in the Antislavery Movement* (1998). She collaborated with Peter Frederick on *American History in a Box*, two volumes (2002). She is the author of many articles on the lives and perceptions of nineteenth-century women. Her research continues to focus on abolitionism as well as on history and film. She wrote Parts 3 and 4 in collaboration with Peter Frederick and acted as a general editor of this book.

JOHN R. HOWE received his Ph.D. from Yale University. At the University of Minnesota, he has taught the U.S. history survey and courses on the American revolutionary era and the early republic.

His major publications include *The Changing Political Thought of John Adams* (1966), *From the Revolution Through the Age of Jackson* (1973), *The Role of Ideology in the American Revolution* (1977), and *Language and Political Meaning in Revolutionary America* (2003). His present research deals with the social politics of verbal discourse in late eighteenth- and early nineteenth-century Boston. He has received a Woodrow Wilson Graduate Fellowship, a John Simon Guggenheim Fellowship, and a Research Fellowship from the Charles Warren Center for Studies in American History. Howe wrote Part 2 of this book.

PETER J. FREDERICK received his Ph.D. in history from the University of California, Berkeley. Currently a Distinguished Professor of American History and Culture at Heritage University on the Yakima Nation reservation in Washington, his career of innovative teaching began at California State University, Hayward, in the 1960s and continued at Wabash College (1970–2004) and Carleton College (1992–1994). Recognized nationally as a distinguished teacher and for his many articles and workshops on teaching and learning, Frederick was awarded the Eugene Asher Award for Excellence in Teaching by the AHA in 2000. He has also written several articles on life-writing and a book, *Knights of the Golden Rule: The Intellectual as Christian Social Reformer in the 1890s*. With Julie Jeffrey, he recently published *American History in a Box*. He coordinated and edited all the "Recovering the Past" sections and coauthored Parts 3 and 4.

ALLEN F. DAVIS earned his Ph.D. from the University of Wisconsin. A former president of the American Studies Association, he is a professor of history at Temple University and editor of *Conflict and Consensus in American History* (9th ed, 1997). He is the author of *Spearheads for Reform: The Social Settlements and the Progressive Movement* (1967); *American Heroine: The Life and Legend of Jane Addams* (1973); and *Postcards from Vermont: A Social History* (2002). He is coauthor of *Still Philadelphia* (1983); *Philadelphia Stories* (1987); and *One Hundred Years at Hull-House* (1990). Davis wrote Part 5 of this book.

ALLAN M. WINKLER received his Ph.D. from Yale University. He has taught at Yale and the University of Oregon, and he is now Distinguished Professor of History at Miami University of Ohio. An award-winning teacher, he has also published extensively about the recent past. His books include *The Politics of Propaganda: The Office of War Information, 1942–1945* (1978); *Home Front U.S.A.: America During World War II* (1986, 2000); *Life Under a Cloud: American Anxiety About the Atom* (1993, 1999); and *The Cold War: A History in Documents* (2000), and *Franklin D. Roosevelt and the Making of Modern America* (2006). His research centers on the connections between public policy and popular mood in modern American history. Winkler wrote Part 6 of this book.

CARLA GARDINA PESTANA received her Ph.D. from the University of California at Los Angeles. She taught at Ohio State University, where she served as a Lilly Teaching Fellow and launched an innovative on-demand publishing project. Currently she holds the W. E. Smith Professorship in History at Miami University. Her publications include *Liberty of Conscience and the Growth of Religious Diversity in Early America* (1986), *Quakers and Baptists in Colonial Massachusetts* (1991), and *The English Atlantic in an Age of Revolution, 1640–1661* (2004). She is also the co-editor, with Sharon V. Salinger, of *Inequality in Early America* (1999). At present, she is completing a book on religion in the British Atlantic world to 1830 for classroom use. She contributed to Part 1 of this edition of *The American People.*

CHARLENE MIRES earned her Ph.D. in history at Temple University. At Villanova University, she teaches courses in nineteenth- and twentieth-century U.S. history, public history, and material culture. She is the author of *Independence Hall in American Memory* (2002) and serves as editor of the Pennsylvania History Studies Series for the Pennsylvania Historical Association. A former journalist, she was a co-recipient of the Pulitzer Prize for general local news reporting with other staff members of the Fort Wayne (Indiana) *News-Sentinel.* She contributed to Part 5 of this edition of *The American People.*

THE AMERICAN PEOPLE

CHAPTER 1
Ancient America and Africa

Portuguese troops storm Tangiers in Morocco in 1471 as part of the ongoing struggle between Christianity and Islam in the mid-fifteenth century Mediterranean world. *(The Art Archive/Pastrana Church, Spain/Dagli Orti)*

American Stories

Four Women's Lives Highlight the Convergence of Three Continents

In what historians call the "early modern period" of world history—roughly the fifteenth to the seventeenth century, when peoples from different regions of the earth came into close contact with each other—four women played key roles in the convergence and clash of societies from Europe, Africa, and the Americas. Their lives highlight some of this chapter's major themes, which developed in an era when the people of three continents began to encounter each other and the shape of the modern world began to take form.

Born in 1451, Isabella of Castile was a banner bearer for *reconquista*—the centuries-long Christian crusade to expel the Muslim rulers who had controlled Spain for centuries. Pious and charitable, the queen of Castile married Ferdinand, the king of Aragon, in 1469. The union of their kingdoms forged a stronger Christian Spain now prepared to realize a new religious and military vision. Eleven years later, after ending hostilities with Portugal, Isabella and Ferdinand began consolidating their power. By expelling Muslims and Jews, the royal couple pressed to enforce Catholic religious conformity. Their religious zeal also led them to sponsor four voyages of Christopher Columbus as a means of extending Spanish power across the Atlantic. The first was commissioned in 1492, only a few months after what the Spanish considered a "just and holy war" against infidels culminated in the surrender of Moorish Granada, the last stronghold of Islam in Christian Europe. Sympathizing with Isabella's fervent piety and desire to convert the people of distant lands to Christianity, Columbus after 1493 signed his letters "Christopher Columbus, Christ Bearer."

On the other side of the Atlantic resided an Aztec woman of influence, also called Isabella by the Spanish, who soon symbolized the mixing of her people with the Spanish. Her real name was Tecuichpotzin, which meant "little royal maiden" in Nahuatl, the Aztec language. The firstborn child of the Aztec ruler Moctezuma II and Teotlalco, his wife, she entered the world in 1509—before the Aztecs had seen a single Spaniard. But when she was 11, Tecuichpotzin witnessed the arrival of the conquistadors under Cortés. When her father was near death, he asked the conqueror to take custody of his daughter, hoping for an accommodation between the conquering Spanish and the conquered Aztecs. But Tecuichpotzin was reclaimed by her people and soon was married to her father's brother, who became the Aztec ruler in 1520. After he died of smallpox within two months, the last Aztec emperor claimed the young girl as his wife.

But then in 1521, the Spanish siege of Tenochtitlán, the Aztec island capital in Lake Texcoco, overturned the mighty Aztec Empire and soon brought Tecuichpotzin into the life of the victorious Spanish. In 1526, she learned that her husband had been tortured and hanged for plotting an insurrection against Cortés. Still only 19, she soon succumbed to the overtures of Cortés, agreeing to join his household and live among his Indian mistresses. Pregnant with Cortés's child, she was married off to a Spanish officer. Another marriage followed, and in all she bore seven children, all descendants of Moctezuma II. All became large landowners and figures of importance. Tecuichpotzin was in this way a pioneer of *mestizaje*—the mixing of races—and thus one of the leading Aztec women who launched the creation of a new society in Mexico.

Elizabeth I—daughter of Henry VIII, who had established the Church of England and rejected the authority of the Catholic pope in Rome—became the key figure in encouraging English expansion overseas. Through her long rule of nearly a half-century, she inspired Protestant England to challenge Catholic Spain and France. Even Pope Sixtus V acknowledged that she was "a great woman, and were she only Catholic she would be without her match." He also remarked, "She is only a woman, yet she makes herself feared by Spain, by France, by the Emperor, by all." Commissioning buccaneers such as John Hawkins and Francis Drake, and sponsoring promoters of colonization such as Walter Raleigh and the Richard Hakluyts (both uncle and nephew), Elizabeth assured the planting of English colonies in North America. They would grow mightily after her death in 1603 and eventually challenge the Dutch, French, and Spanish, who also saw the Americas as a source of great wealth and power.

Elizabeth I's vitality, ambition, and wit suited her perfectly to lead England forward, even though her nation, when she assumed the throne in 1558, was weak in comparison to France, Spain, and even Portugal. Investing her own money in voyages of exploration and settlement, she encouraged others from the middle and upper classes to do the same. In backing a 20-year conflict with the Spanish—a religious conflict and also a struggle for maritime power—she opened a gateway to the Americas for the English.

On the west coast of Africa was another powerful woman. Born around 1595 and named because she entered the world with the umbilical cord wrapped around her neck (which was believed to foretell a haughty character), Queen Njinga led fierce resistance to the Portuguese slave trade and the Portuguese attempts to control Angola. She knew that the Portuguese had been trading for slaves in Angola and had even converted King Affonso I of the Kongo Kingdom to Catholicism in the 1530s. She also knew that by the time Queen Elizabeth came to power in 1558 in England, the Portuguese had trapped her people into incessant wars in order to supply slaves to their Portuguese trading partners. Only when she assumed the throne of Ndongo (present-day Angola) in 1624 did Queen Njinga's people begin to resist Portuguese rule. Leading her troops in a series of wars, she gave a fierce battle cry that legend says was heard for miles, making her a heroic figure in Angolan history.

In opening this book, the stories of Queen Isabella of Castile, Aztec princess Tecuichpotzin, Queen Elizabeth I of England, and Angola's Queen Njinga set the scene for the intermingling of Europeans, Africans, and Native Americans in the New World, what Europeans called North and South America, by examining the backgrounds of the peoples of three continents and glimpsing the changes occurring with each of their many societies as the time for a historic convergence neared. This allows us to better understand the advent of colliding cultures among societies rimming the Atlantic Ocean.

In narrating this historic meeting of societies previously distanced from each other, historians have too often portrayed Europeans reaching the Americas as the carriers of a superior culture that inevitably vanquished people living in a primitive if not "savage" state. Such a view renders Native Americans and Africans passive and static people—so much dough to be kneaded by advanced Europeans. Modern historical scholarship, however, tells us that Africans and Native Americans played critically important roles in a complex intercultural birthing of a "new world." Thus we examine the complexities of West African societies, delve into the societies of some of the peoples of North and South America, and study Western Europeans of the late fifteenth century. In drawing comparisons and contrasts, we equip ourselves to see three worlds meet as a new global age began.

THE PEOPLES OF AMERICA BEFORE COLUMBUS

Thousands of years before the European exploratory voyages in the 1490s, the history of humankind in North America began. Thus, American history can begin with some basic questions: Who were the first inhabitants of the Americas? Where did they come from? What were they like? How had the societies they formed changed over the millennia that preceded European arrival? Can their history be reconstructed from the mists of prehistoric time?

Migration to the Americas

Almost all the evidence suggesting answers to these questions comes from ancient sites of early life in North America. Archaeologists have unearthed skeletal remains, pots, tools, ornaments, and other objects to reach a tentative date for the arrival of humans in America of about 35,000 B.C.E.—about the same time that humans began to settle Japan and Scandinavia.

Nearly every Native American society has its own story about its origins in the Americas. For example, many believe that they were the first people in North America, people who emerged out of the earth or from underneath the waters of a large lake. However, paleoanthropologists, scientists who study ancient peoples, generally agree that the first inhabitants of the Americas were nomadic bands from Siberia, hunting big-game animals such as bison, caribou, and reindeer. These sojourners from Asia began to migrate across a land bridge connecting northeastern Asia with Alaska. Geologists believe that this land bridge, perhaps 600 miles wide, existed most recently between 25,000 and 14,000 years ago, when massive glaciers locked up much of the earth's moisture and left part of the Bering Sea floor exposed. Ice-free passage through Canada was possible only briefly at the beginning and end of this period, however. At other times, melting glaciers flooded the land bridge and blocked foot traffic to Alaska. Scholars are divided on the exact timing, but the main migration apparently occurred between 11,000 and 14,000 years ago, although possibly much earlier. Some new archaeological finds suggest multiple migrations, both by sea and land, from several regions of Asia and even from Europe.

DOCUMENT

Iroquois Creation Story; Pima Creation Story; Ottawa Origins Story (recorded ca. 1720)

Migration Routes from Asia to the Americas

The red arrows indicate the general flow of migrating societies over thousands of years before Europeans reached the Americas. Based on fragile archaeological evidence, these migratory patterns are necessarily tentative, and new discoveries support the theory of early Stone Age arrivals by boat. **Reflecting on the Past** Can you reconcile Native American creation myths with archaeological evidence of the first humans reaching the Americas by crossing the Bering Straits land bridge? If so, how?

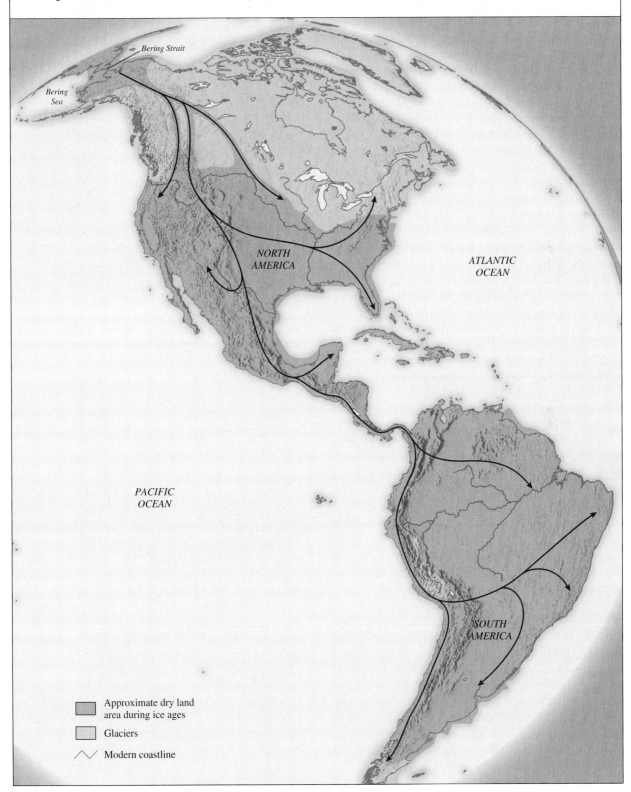

Hunters, Farmers, and Environmental Factors

Once on the North American continent, these early wanderers began trekking southward and then eastward, following vegetation and game. In time, they reached the tip of South America—some 15,000 miles from the Asian homeland to Tierra del Fuego, the southernmost limit of South America. Moving eastward, they traversed some 6,000 miles from Siberia to the eastern edge of North America. American history has traditionally emphasized the "westward movement" of people, but for thousands of years before Columbus's arrival, the frontier moved southward and eastward. Thus did people from the "Old World" discover the "New World" thousands of years before Columbus.

Archaeologists have excavated ancient sites of early life in the Americas, unearthing tools, ornaments, and skeletal remains that allow them to reconstruct the dispersion of these first Americans over an immense land mass. Although much remains unknown, archaeological evidence suggests that as centuries passed and population increased, the earliest inhabitants evolved into separate cultures, adjusting to various environments in distinct ways. Europeans who rediscovered the New World thousands of years later would lump together the myriad societies they found. But by the late 1400s, the "Indians" of the Americas were enormously diverse in the size and complexity of their societies, the languages they spoke, and their forms of social organization.

Archaeologists and anthropologists have charted several phases of Native American history. The Beringian period of initial migration ended about 14,000 years ago. During the Paleo-Indian era, 14,000 to 10,000 years ago, big-game hunters flaked hard stones into spear points and chose "kill sites" where they slew herds of Pleistocene mammals. This more reliable food source allowed population growth, and nomadism began to give way to settled habitations or local migration within limited territories.

Then during the Archaic era, from about 10,000 to 2,500 years ago, great geological changes brought further adaptations to the land. As the massive Ice Age glaciers slowly retreated, a warming trend turned vast grassland areas from Utah to the highlands of Central America into desert. The Pleistocene mammals were weakened by more arid conditions, but human populations ably adapted as they learned to exploit new sources of food, especially plants.

About 9,000 to 7,000 years ago, a technological breakthrough took place, probably independently in widely separated parts of the world, as humans

An Ancient Skeleton The skeleton shown here of a saber-tooth cat was recovered from a tar pit in downtown Los Angeles, where excavation of the pits began in 1908. Roving animals, including dinosaurs, giant sloths, and wolves, were trapped in the sticky asphalt bog and preserved for as long as 40,000 years. *(Ed Ikuta/Courtesy of the George C. Page Museum)*

learned how to plant, cultivate, and harvest. This development, which historians call the agricultural revolution, allowed humans to gain control over once-ungovernable natural forces. Agriculture slowly brought dramatic changes in human societies everywhere.

Historians have sometimes imagined that the early peoples of the Americas lived in a primordial paradise in harmony with their surroundings. But recent archaeological evidence points to examples of environmental devastation that severely damaged the biodiversity of the Americas. The first wave of intruders found a wilderness teeming with so-called megafauna: saber-toothed tigers, woolly mammoths, gigantic ground sloths, huge bison, and monstrous bears. But by about 10,000 years ago, overhunting and a massive shift of climate deprived these huge beasts of their grazing environment.

The depletion of the megafauna left the hemisphere with a much restricted catalogue of animals. Left behind were large animals such as elk, buffalo, bear, and moose. But the extinction of the huge beasts forced people to prey on new sources of food such as turkeys, ducks, and guinea pigs, and this may have gradually reduced their population.

Over many centuries in the Americas, salinization and deforestation put the environment under additional stress. For example, in what is today central Arizona, the Hohokam civilization collapsed hundreds of years ago, much like that in ancient Mesopotamia, when the irrigation system became too salty to support agriculture. At New Mexico's Chaco Canyon, the fast-growing Anasazi denuded a magnificently forested region in their search for firewood and building materials. This resulting soil erosion impoverished the region for the Anasazi.

As Native Americans learned to domesticate plant life, they began the long process of transforming their relationship to the physical world. Like all living organisms, human beings depend on plants to survive. For both humans and animals, plants are the source of life-sustaining fuel. The ultimate source of this energy is the sun. But in tapping solar energy, humans and animals had to rely on plants because they are the only organisms capable of producing significant amounts of organic material through the photosynthetic process. Plant life was—and still is—the strategic element in the chain of life.

Dating the advent of agriculture in the Americas is difficult, but archaeologists estimate it at about 5000 B.C.E. Agriculture had already been developed in southwestern Asia and in Africa and spread to Europe at about the time people in the Tehuacán valley of central Mexico first planted maize and squash. Over the millennia, humans progressed from doorside planting of a few wild seeds to systematic clearing and planting of fields. As the production of domesticated plant food ended dependence on gathering wild plants and pursuing game, settled village life began to replace nomadic existence. Increases in food supply brought about by agriculture triggered other major changes. As more ample food fueled population growth, large groups split off to form separate societies. Greater social and political complexity developed because not everyone was needed as before to secure the society's food supply. Men cleared the land and hunted game while women planted, cultivated, and harvested crops. Many societies empowered religious figures, who organized the common followers, directed their work, and exacted tribute as well as worship from them. In return, the community trusted them to ward off hostile forces.

Pre-Columbian Societies of the Americas

Everywhere in the Americas, regional trading networks formed. Along trade routes carrying commodities such as salt for food preservation, obsidian rock for projectile points, and copper for jewelry also traveled technology, religious ideas, and agricultural practices. By the end of the Archaic period, about 500 B.C.E., hundreds of independent kin-based groups, like people in other parts of the world, had learned to exploit the resources of their particular area and to trade with other groups in their region. For centuries thereafter, native societies grew in size, developed more sophisticated agricultural techniques, and in some areas adopted a sedentary life.

Mesoamerican Empires

Of all the large-scale societies developing in the Americas during Europe's medieval period, the most impressive were in Mesoamerica—the middle region bridging the great land masses of South and North America. The Valley of Mexico, now

An Aztec Pictograph At the bottom of this pictograph, the Aztecs displayed the conquest of two villages—Colhuacan pueblo and Tenayucan pueblo—on the western side of Lake Texcoco. These were the first two victories that marked the beginning of the consolidation of Aztec power in central Mexico less than a century before Columbus's voyages. Note the importance of corn in the upper part of the pictograph and the prickly pear cactus, the meaning of Tenochtitlán, and the eagle, symbol of their war god, in the center. *(Bodleian Library, University of Oxford [MS Arch. Seld.A.1. fol. 2r])*

Expansion of the Aztec Empire, 1427–1519

In the century before Europeans breached the Atlantic to find the Americas, the Aztecs' rise to power brought 10 to 20 million people under their sway—more than the entire population of Spain and Portugal at this time.

1427–1440
1440–1468
1469–1481
1486–1502
1502–1519

dominated by Mexico City, became the center of the largest societies that emerged in the centuries before the Spanish arrived early in the sixteenth century. In less than two centuries, the Aztecs, successor to the earlier Olmec and Toltec civilizations, built a mighty empire rivaling any known over the centuries in Europe, Asia, and Africa by using their warrior skills to subjugate smaller tribes. By the time of Columbus's first voyage in 1492, the Aztecs, with a population estimated at 10 to 20 million people, controlled most of central Mexico. Extracting tribute from conquered peoples—beans, maize, and other foodstuffs; cotton fabrics; bird feathers for war costumes; animal furs; and labor on state projects such as canals, temples, and irrigation—the Aztecs built a great capital in Tenochtitlán ("Place of the Prickly Pear Cactus"), a canal-ribbed city island in the great lake of Texcoco. Connected to the mainland by three broad causeways and supplied with drinkable water by an impressive aqueduct, Tenochtitlán boasted a population of perhaps 150,000, comparable to the medieval city–state of Venice and certainly one of the world's greatest cities on the eve of the Columbian voyages.

Aztec society was as stratified as any in Europe, and the supreme ruler's authority was as extensive as that of any European or African monarch. Every

Aztec was born into one of four classes: the nobility, including the emperor's household, priests, and military officers; free commoners with rights to land and organized in precincts with temples and schools; serfs, who like those in Europe were bound to the soil and toiled on the lands of nobles; and slaves, who had rights akin to those of slaves in ancient Rome or Greece.

When they arrived in 1519, Spaniards could hardly believe the grandeur they saw in the immense Aztec capital, which covered about 10 square miles and boasted some 40 towers—one of them, according to the first Spaniards entering the city, higher than the cathedral of Seville, the largest in Spain. "When we saw so many cities and villages built in the water and other great towns on dry land and that straight and level causeway going towards Mexico," wrote one Spaniard in the army of Cortés, "we were amazed and said that it was like the enchantments they tell of in the legend of Amadis. . . . Some of our soldiers even asked whether the things that we saw were not a dream." Indeed, they had found their way to the most advanced civilization in the Americas, where through skilled hydraulic engineering, the Aztecs cultivated chinampas, or "floating gardens," around their capital city in which grew a wide variety of flowers and vegetables. The Spaniards were unprepared for encountering such an advanced civilization built by what they considered savage people.

Regional North American Cultures

The regions north of Mesoamerica were never populated by societies of the size and complexity of the Aztecs, though some of them, particularly in what is now the American Southwest, felt the Aztec influence. Throughout the vast expanses of North America in the last epoch of pre-Columbian development—the so-called post-Archaic phase—many distinct societies evolved through a complex process of growth and environmental adaptation. In the southwestern region of North America, for example, Hohokam and Anasazi societies (the ancestors of the

Tenochtitlán The plan of Tenochtitlán, later Mexico City, is from the Latin edition of Cortés's "Second Letter," on his conquest of the Aztecs. Cortés's account was widely published in Europe, where the Germans, French, and English were astounded to hear of such an extraordinary Aztec metropolis with floating gardens, causeways, and monumental architecture. How would this city compare with those in Europe? *(The Granger Collection, New York)*

The First Americans: Major Indian Groups and Culture Areas in the 1600s

present-day Hopi and Zuñi) had developed a sedentary village life thousands of years before the Spanish arrived in the 1540s.

By about 1200 C.E., these "Pueblo" people, as the Spanish later called them, were developing planned villages composed of large, terraced, multistoried buildings, each with many rooms and often constructed on defensive sites that would afford the Anasazi protection from their northern enemies. The largest of them, containing about 800 rooms, was at Pueblo Bonito in Chaco Canyon. By the time the Spanish arrived in the 1540s, the indigenous Pueblo people were using irrigation canals, dams, and hillside terracing to water their arid maize fields. In its agricultural techniques, skill in ceramics, use of woven textiles for clothing, and village life, Pueblo society resembled that of peasant communities in many parts of Europe and Asia. Don Juan de Oñate reported home in 1599 after reaching the Pueblo villages on the Rio Grande that the Native Americans "live very much the same as we do, in houses with two and three terraces. . . . "

Far to the north, on the Pacific coast of the Northwest, native Tlingit, Kwakiutl, Salish, and Haida people lived in villages of several hundred, drawing their sustenance from salmon and other spawning fish and living in plank houses displaying elaborately

Cliff Palace in Colorado

carved red cedar pillars and guarded by gigantic totem poles depicting animals with supernatural power. Reaching this region much later than most other parts of the hemisphere, early European explorers were amazed at the architectural and artistic skills of the Northwest indigenous people. "What must astonish most," wrote one French explorer in the late eighteenth century, "is to see painting everywhere, everywhere sculpture, among a nation of hunters."

Carving and painting soft wood from deep cedar forest surrounding their villages, Northwest native people defined their place in the cosmos with ceremonial face masks, which often represented animals, birds, and fish—reminders of magical ancestral spirits that inhabited what they understood as the four interconnected zones of the cosmos: the Sky World, the Undersea World, the Mortal World, and the Spirit World.

Ceremonial masks played a pivotal place in the Potlatch, a great winter gathering with song, dance, and ritual. In the Potlatch ceremonial dances, native leaders honored their family lineage and signified their chiefly authority in the tribe. By giving away many of their possessions, chiefs satisfied tribe members and in this way maintained their legitimacy, a largesse that mystified and often disturbed material-minded Europeans. Attempts by American and Canadian authorities to suppress

An Anasazi Village   The ruins of Pueblo Bonito in Chaco Canyon, New Mexico, mark the center of Anasazi culture in the twelfth century C.E. This San Juan River basin town may have contained a thousand people living in apartment-like structures larger than any built in North America until the late nineteenth century. *(© David Muench)*

Potlatch ceremonies in the late nineteenth century never succeeded.

Far to the east, Native American societies have been traced as far back as about 9000 B.C.E. From the Great Plains of the midcontinent to the Atlantic tidewater region, a variety of tribes came to be loosely associated in four main language groups: Algonquian, Iroquoian, Muskhogean, and Siouan. Like other tribal societies, they had been transformed by the agricultural revolution, gradually adopting semifixed settlements and developing trading networks that linked societies occupying a vast region.

Among the most impressive of these societies were the mound-building societies of the Mississippi and Ohio valleys. When European settlers first crossed the Appalachian Mountains a century and a half after arriving on the continent, they were astounded to find hundreds of ceremonial mounds and gigantic sculptured earthworks. Believing all "Indians" to be forest primitives, they reasoned that these were the remains of an ancient civilization that had found its way to North America—perhaps Phoenicians, survivors of the sunken island of Atlantis, or the Lost Tribes of Israel spoken of in European mythology.

Archaeologists now conclude that the "Mound Builders" were the ancestors of the Creek, Choctaw, and Natchez. Their societies, evolving slowly over the centuries, had developed considerable complexity by

the advent of Christianity in Europe. In southern Ohio alone about 10,000 mounds used as burial sites have been pinpointed, and archaeologists have excavated another 1,000 earth-walled enclosures, including one enormous fortification with a circumference of about 3½ miles, enclosing 100 acres, or the equivalent of 50 modern city blocks. From the mounded tombs, archaeologists have recovered a great variety of items that have been traced to widely separated parts of the continent—evidence that the Mound Builders participated in a vast trading network linking hundreds of Native American villages across the continent.

The mound-building societies of the Ohio valley declined many centuries before Europeans reached the continent, perhaps attacked by other tribes or damaged by severe climatic changes that undermined agriculture. By about 600 C.E., another mound-building agricultural society arose in the Mississippi valley. Its center, the city of Cahokia with at least 20,000 (and possibly as many as 40,000) inhabitants, stood near present-day St. Louis. Great ceremonial

Carved Mask   For thousands of years, indigenous people in the Northwest have carved masks to be used by dancers who commemorate ancient family and clan history. Because they were carved of soft wood, most very old masks have not survived. This mask was carved by a Bella Colla artist in the nineteenth century. *(Erich Lessing/Art Resource, NY)*

Reconstructed View of Cahokia

plazas, flanked by a temple that rose in four terraces to a height of 100 feet, marked this first metropolis in America. This was the urban center of a far-flung Mississippi culture that encompassed hundreds of villages from Wisconsin to Louisiana and from Oklahoma to Tennessee.

Before the mound-building cultures of the continental heartlands mysteriously declined, their influence was already transforming the woodland societies along the Atlantic. The numerous small tribes that settled from Nova Scotia to Florida never equaled the larger societies of the midcontinent in earthwork sculpture, architectural design, or development of large-scale agriculture. But they were far from the "savages" that the first European explorers described. They had added limited agriculture to their skill in using natural plants and had developed food procurement strategies that exploited all the resources around them.

In the far north were the Abenaki, Penobscot, Passamaquoddy, and others, who lived by the sea and supplemented their diet with maple sugar and a few foodstuffs. Farther south, in what was to become New England, were the Massachusetts, Wampanoag, Pequot, Narragansett, Niantic, Mahican, and others—small tribes occupying fairly local areas and joined together only by occasional trade. In the mid-Atlantic area were the Lenape, Susquehannock, Nanticoke, Pamunkey, Shawnee,

Pre-Columbian Societies of the Americas

Once described as nomadic hunter–gatherers, indigenous peoples in the Americas were agriculturalists and urban dwellers in many areas and populated the land as densely as did people in many other parts of the world.

Great Serpent Mound

One of the hundreds of symbolic mounds built by people of the Hopewell culture, this mound, in the shape of a serpent, is near present-day Cincinnati. Nearly a quarter-mile long and about 20 feet across, the coiled earthen serpent is devouring a frog or an egg. In 1887, Frederick Putnam, a Harvard archaeologist, saved the mound from destruction. Can you estimate how much labor was required to construct this earthworks with simple tools? *(Courtesy, National Museum of the American Indian, Smithsonian Institution, P18523. Photo by Major Dache M. Reeves.)*

RECOVERING THE PAST

Archaeological Artifacts

The recovery of the past before extensive written records existed is the domain of archaeology. Virtually our entire knowledge of native societies in North America before the arrival of European colonizers is drawn from the work of archaeologists who have excavated the ancient living sites of the first Americans. Many Native Americans today strongly oppose this rummaging in the ancient ancestral places; they particularly oppose the unearthing of burial sites. But the modern search for knowledge about the past goes on.

Archaeological data have allowed us to overcome the stereotypical view of Native Americans as a primitive people whose culture was static for thousands of years before Europeans arrived in North America. This earlier view allowed historians to argue that the tremendous loss of Native American population and land accompanying the initial settlement and westward migration of white Americans was more or less inevitable. When two cultures, one dynamic and forward-looking and the other static and backward, confronted each other, historians have frequently maintained, the more advanced or "civilized" culture almost always prevailed.

Much of the elaborate early history of people in the Americas is unrecoverable. But many fragments of this long human history are being recaptured through archaeological research. Particularly important are studies that reveal how Indian societies were changing during the few centuries immediately preceding the European arrival in the New World. These studies allow us to interpret more accurately the seventeenth-century interaction of Native Americans and Europeans because they provide an understanding of Native American values, social and political organization, material culture, and religion as they existed when the two cultures first met.

One such investigation has been carried out over the last century at the confluence of the Mississippi and Missouri rivers near modern-day East St. Louis, Illinois. Archaeologists have found there the center of a vast Mississippi culture that began about 600 C.E., reached its peak about 300 years before Columbus's voyages, and then declined through a combination of drought, dwindling food supplies, and internal tensions. Cahokia is the name given to the urban center of a civilization that at its height dominated an area as large as New York State. At the center of Cahokia stood one of the largest earth constructions built by ancient humans anywhere on the planet. Its base covering 16 acres, this gigantic earthen temple, containing 22 million cubic feet of hand-moved earth, rises in four terraces to a height of 100 feet, as tall as a modern 10-story office building. The central plaza, like those of the Aztecs and Mayans, was oriented exactly on a north–south axis in order to chart the move-

Pottery effigy vessels in the shape of human heads. *(National Museum of the American Indian, Smithsonian Institution [17/3277 and 23/0980])*

A reconstructed view of Cahokia, the largest town in North America before European arrival, painted by William R. Iseminger. The millions of cubic feet of earth used to construct the ceremonial and burial mounds must have required the labor of tens of thousands of workers over a long period of time. *(Cahokia Mounds State Historic Site)*

ment of celestial bodies. The drawing shown above indicates some of the scores of smaller geometric burial mounds near this major temple. Notice the outlying farms, a sure sign of the settled (as opposed to nomadic) existence of the people who flourished 10 centuries ago in this region. How does this depiction of ancient Cahokia change your image of Native American life before the arrival of Europeans?

By recovering artifacts from Cahokia burial mounds, archaeologists have pieced together a picture, still tentative, of a highly elaborate civilization along the Mississippi bottomlands. Cahokian manufacturers mass-produced salt, knives, and stone hoe blades for both local consumption and export. Cahokian artisans made sophisticated pottery, ornamental jewelry, metalwork, and tools. They used copper and furs from the Lake Superior region, black obsidian stone from the Rocky Mountains, and seashells from the Gulf of Mexico, demonstrating that the people at Cahokia were involved in long-distance trade. In fact, Cahokia was a crucial crossroads of trade and water travel in the heartland of North America.

The objects shown opposite, unearthed from graves by archaeologists, are an example of the culture of the Mississippi Mound Builders. The round-faced pottery bottles in the form of heads, each about 6 inches tall and wide, show a sense of humor in early Mississippi culture. Holes in the ears of the bottles once held thongs so that the objects could be hung or carried. Other objects, such as a figure of a kneeling woman found in Tennessee, had holes under the arms for a similar purpose.

Some graves uncovered at Cahokia contain large caches of finely tooled objects while other burial mounds contain many skeletons unaccompanied by any artifacts. From this evidence archaeologists conclude that this was a more stratified society than those encountered by the first settlers along the Atlantic seaboard. Anthropologists believe that some of the Mississippi culture spread eastward before Cahokia declined, but much mystery still remains concerning the fate and cultural diffusion of these early Americans.

REFLECTING ON THE PAST What other conclusions about Cahokian culture can you draw from figures such as these? Are there archaeological sites in your area that contain evidence of Native American civilization?

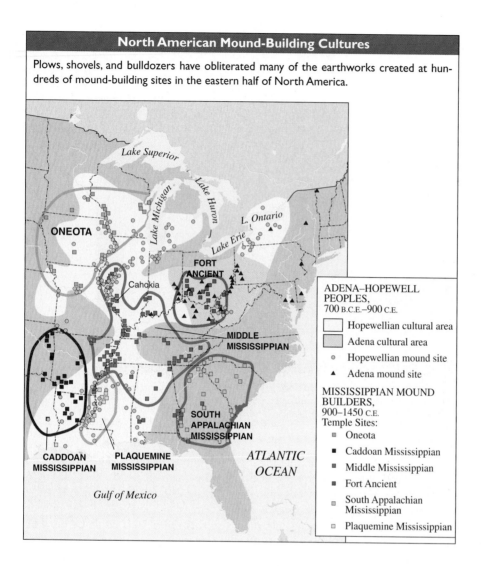

North American Mound-Building Cultures

Plows, shovels, and bulldozers have obliterated many of the earthworks created at hundreds of mound-building sites in the eastern half of North America.

Tuscarora, Catawba, and other peoples, who added limited agriculture to their skill in using natural plants for food, medicine, dyes, and flavoring. Most of these eastern woodland tribes lived in waterside villages. Locating their fields of maize near fishing grounds, they often migrated seasonally between inland and coastal village sites or situated themselves astride two ecological zones. In the Northeast, their birchbark canoes, light enough to be carried by a single person, helped them trade and communicate over immense territories.

In the Southeast were densely populated rich and complex cultures, which traced their ancestry back at least 8,000 years. Belonging to several language groups, some of them joined in loose confederacies. Called "Mississippian" societies by archaeologists, the tribes of the Southeast created elaborate pottery and basket weaving and conducted long-distance trade. These cultures also were influenced by Hopewell burial mound techniques, some of which involved earthmoving on a vast scale. A global warming trend that increased the annual average temperature by a few degrees for about four centuries after 900 helped agriculture flourish in this region, leading in some cases, as with the Natchez, to the development of highly stratified societies in which chiefs and commoners were sharply divided and priests led ritual ceremonies. These people were the ancestors of the powerful Creek and Yamasee in the Georgia and Alabama regions; the Apalachee in Florida and along the Gulf of Mexico; the Choctaw, Chickasaw, and Natchez of the lower Mississippi valley; the Cherokee of the southern Appalachian Mountains, and several dozen smaller tribes scattered along the Atlantic coast. However, after the "Little Ice Age," which spanned several centuries after about 1300, they abandoned their mounded urban centers and devolved into less populous, less stratified, and less centralized societies.

AMERICAN VOICES

The Legend of the Great League of the Iroquois

The legend of the Great League of the Iroquois, formed about 1450 by the mythical figure Dekanawidah to bind the five separate nations of the Iroquois together, was passed down orally from generation to generation. Here is an excerpt.

We bind ourselves together by taking hold of each other's hands so firmly and forming a circle so strong that if a tree should fall upon it, it could not shake nor break it, so that our people and grandchildren shall remain in the circle in security, peace, and happiness. Be of strong mind, O chiefs! Carry no anger and hold no grudges. Think not forever of yourselves, O chiefs, nor of your own generation. Think of continuing generations of our families, think of our grandchildren and of those yet unborn, whose faces are coming from beneath the ground.

- *Does this account of forming an ethnic confederacy seem distinctly Native American, or might it have resonated among Europeans of different ethnic backgrounds?*

- *What values are stressed in this legend?*

The Iroquois

Far to the north of the declining southeastern mound-building societies, between what would become French and English zones of settlement, five tribes composed what Europeans later called the League of the Iroquois: the Mohawk, Oneida, Onondaga, Cayuga, and Seneca. The Iroquois Confederation began as a vast extension of the kinship group that characterized the northeastern woodland pattern of family settlement and embraced perhaps 10,000 people at the time Europeans began to build northeastern settlements in the sixteenth century.

DOCUMENT

Dekanawida Myth and the Achievement of Iroquois Unity

Not long before Europeans began coming ashore in eastern North America, the loosely organized and strife-ridden Iroquois strengthened themselves by creating a more cohesive political confederacy. As they learned to suppress intra-Iroquois blood feuds, villages gained stability, population increased, and the Iroquois developed political mechanisms for solving internal problems and presenting a more unified front in parlaying with their Algonquian neighbors for the use of hunting territories to the north or in admitting dependent tribes to settle in their territory. This facilitated the development of a coordinated Iroquois policy for dealing with the European newcomers.

Work in the palisaded villages of Iroquoia, some bustling with more than a thousand people, was performed communally and land was owned not by individuals but by all in common. While there might be individual farming or hunting efforts, it was understood that the bounty was to be divided among all. Similarly, several families occupied a longhouse, but the house itself, like all else in the community, was common property. "No hospitals [poorhouses] are needed among them," wrote a French Jesuit in 1657, "because there are neither mendicants nor paupers as long as there are any rich people among them.

A European View of Indian Women   When the Frenchman Jacques Le Moyne arrived in what is now South Carolina in 1565, he painted Indian women cultivating the soil and planting corn. Le Moyne's painting did not survive, but it was rendered as shown here by the Flemish engraver Theodor de Bry, who purchased it from Le Moyne's widow in 1588. De Bry took some liberties; for example, he put European-style hoes with metal blades into the hands of the women, whereas they tilled with large fish bones fitted to sticks. Did Iroquois women play the same role in agriculture?

15

Native American Trade Networks in 1400

By recovering objects such as shell necklaces, stone tools, and decorative copper from ancient sites of Indian habitation, and by determining their place of origin, anthropologists have developed this approximate map of Native American trading networks in the century before the arrival of Europeans.

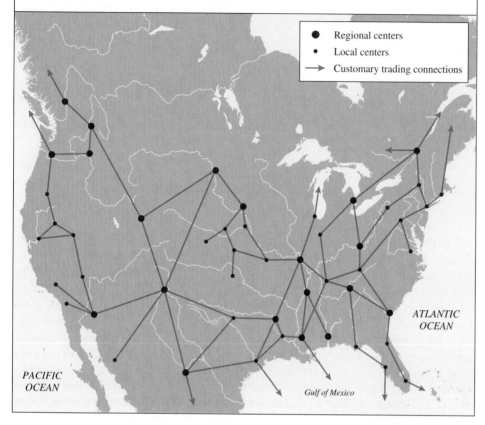

● Regional centers
• Local centers
→ Customary trading connections

ATLANTIC OCEAN

PACIFIC OCEAN

Gulf of Mexico

Their kindness, humanity, and courtesy not only makes them liberal with what they have, but causes them to possess hardly anything except in common. A whole village must be without corn, before any individual can be obliged to endure privation." One historian has called this "upside down capitalism," in which the goal was not to pile up material possessions but to reach the happy situation in which they could give what they had to others.

Out of extended kinship groups, the Iroquois organized village settlements. Like many Africans, the Iroquois had matrilineal families with family membership determined through the female rather than male line. A typical Iroquois family comprised an old woman, her daughters with their husbands and children, and her unmarried granddaughters and grandsons. Sons and grandsons remained with their kinship group until they married; then they joined the family of their wife or the family of their mother's brother. If these arrangements puzzled Europeans, whose men controlled women strictly, so did the Iroquois woman's prerogative of divorce;

if she desired it, she merely set her husband's possessions outside the longhouse door.

Iroquois society also invested the community's women with a share of political power in ways the Europeans found strange. Political authority in the villages derived from the matrons or senior women of the *ohwachiras*—a group of related families. These women named the men representing the clans at village and tribal councils and appointed the 49 sachems or chiefs who met periodically when the confederated Five Nations met. These civil chiefs were generally middle-aged or elderly men who had gained fame earlier as warriors but now gained their prestige at the council fires. The political power of the women also extended to the ruling councils, in which they caucused behind the circle of chiefs and made sure that the tribal council did not move too far from the will of the women who appointed them. The male chiefs were secure in their positions only as long as they could achieve a consensus with the women who had placed them in office.

The tribal economy and military affairs further demonstrated the division of power between men and women. While men did most of the hunting and fishing, the women were the community's primary agriculturists. In tending the crops, they became vital to sustaining the community. When men were away on weeks-long hunting expeditions, women were left entirely in charge of village daily life. If "the forest belonged to the men," one historian explains, "the village was the woman's domain." In military affairs women played a significant role, for they supplied the moccasins and food for warring expeditions. A decision to withhold these supplies was tantamount to vetoing a military foray. Clan matrons often initiated war by calling on the Iroquois warriors to bring them enemy captives to replace fallen clan members.

In raising children, Iroquois parents were more permissive than Europeans. They did not believe in harsh physical punishment, encouraged the young to imitate adult behavior, and were tolerant of fumbling early attempts. The mother nursed and protected the infant while hardening it by baths in cold water. Weaning ordinarily began at age three or four. Childhood interest in the anatomy and in sexual experimentation was accepted as normal. All this contrasted with European child-rearing techniques, which stressed accustoming the child to authority from an early age through frequent use of physical punishment, condemning early sexual curiosity, and emphasizing obedience and respect for authority.

The approach to authority in Iroquois society, as in most other native societies in North America, lacked most of the complicated machinery developed by Europeans to direct individual lives. No laws and ordinances, sheriffs and constables, judges and juries, or courts or jails—the apparatus of authority in Europe—existed in pre-contact North America. Yet the Iroquois set boundaries of acceptable behavior firmly. They prized the autonomous individual yet maintained a strict code of right and wrong. They governed behavior by imparting a sense of tradition and attachment to the group through communally performed rituals. Europeans dealt with crime through investigation, arrest, prosecution, and sentencing. But in Native American society, those who stole food, to take one example, were "shamed" and ostracized until the culprits atoned for their actions and proved ready for re-entry into village communal life.

Pre-Contact Population

For many decades, anthropologists and historians estimated that the population of the Americas, and especially North America, was small, only about 10

Native Population of the Americas in World Context, 1500

Because they are from a time when censuses were rare in most parts of the world, all these population figures are estimates. Some demographers believe that 100 million people inhabited the Americas in 1500. New research and lively debate will no doubt alter these figures. **Reflecting on the Past** What is the population today of the areas listed here, and how do you account for differing distribution of the world's population?

China	100–150 million
India	75–150 million
Southwest Asia	20–30 million
Japan and rest of Asia	30–50 million
Europe (including Russia)	70–90 million
Africa	50–70 million
Americas	50–70 million

percent of Europe's population at the time of Columbus's first voyage in 1492. Only recently have scholars conceded that most estimates made in the past were grossly understated due to the conventional view that Native American societies peopled by nomadic hunters and gatherers could not be very large.

However, archaeological research in recent decades has indicated that the sophisticated agricultural techniques of Native American societies allowed the sustaining of large societies. Therefore, population estimates have soared, with today's scholars estimating the pre-contact population north of the Rio Grande to be at least 4 million people, of whom perhaps half lived east of the Mississippi River and some 700,000 settled along the eastern coastal plain and in the piedmont region accessible to the early European settlers. Though estimates vary widely, the most reliable suggest that about 50 to 70 million people lived in the entire hemisphere when Europeans first arrived, contrasting with some 70 to 90 million in Europe (including Russia) around 1500, about 50 to 70 million in Africa, and 225 to 350 million in Asia. The European colonizers were not coming to a "virgin wilderness," as they often described it, but to a land inhabited for thousands of years by people whose village existence in some ways resembled that of the new arrivals.

In some important ways, however, Native American culture differed sharply from that of Europeans. Horses and oxen, for example, did not exist in the New World. Without large draft animals, Native Americans had no incentive to develop wheeled vehicles or, for that matter, the potter's wheel. Many inventions—such as the technology for smelting iron, which had diffused widely in the Old World—had not crossed the ocean to reach the

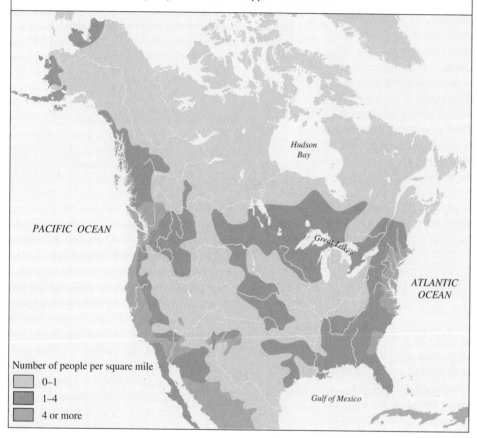

Native American Population Density in North America, ca. 1500

Historical demographers have devised estimates of Native American population density in North America before the arrival of Europeans. Estimates are based on the "carrying capacity" of different ecological regions: rainfall, access to fish and animals, soil fertility, and length of growing season are all factors in the capacity of the land to support human life.

Hudson Bay

PACIFIC OCEAN

Great Lakes

ATLANTIC OCEAN

Number of people per square mile
- 0–1
- 1–4
- 4 or more

Gulf of Mexico

New World. The opposite was also true: valuable New World crops, such as corn and potatoes developed by Native American agriculturists, were unknown in the Old World before Columbus.

Contrasting Worldviews

Having evolved in complete isolation from each other, European and Native American cultures exhibited a wide difference in values. Colonizing Europeans called themselves "civilized" and typically described the people they met in the Americas as "savage," "heathen," or "barbarian." Lurking behind the physical confrontation that took place when Europeans and Native Americans met were latent conflicts over humans' relationship to the environment, the meaning of property, and personal identity.

Europeans and Native Americans conceptualized their relationship to nature in starkly different ways.

Regarding the earth as filled with resources for humans to use and exploit for their own benefit, Europeans separated the secular and sacred parts of life, and they placed their own relationship to the natural environment mostly in the secular sphere. Native Americans, however, did not distinguish between the secular and sacred. For them, every aspect of the natural world was sacred, inhabited by a variety of "beings," each pulsating with spiritual power and all linked together to form a sacred whole. Consequently, if one offended the land by stripping it of its cover, the spiritual power in the land—called "manitou" by some eastern woodland tribes—would strike back. If one overfished or destroyed game beyond one's needs, the spirit forces in fish or animals would take revenge, because humans had broken the mutual trust and reciprocity that governed relations between all beings—human or nonhuman. To neglect reciprocal obligations in nature's domain was to court sickness, hunger, injury, or death.

Pelican This figure of a pelican was extracted in the 1890s from deep muck on Key Marco, Florida. It is dated through carbon-14 tests to about 1000 C.E. Anthropologists believe that the figure was part of a shrine. *(University of Pennsylvania Museum [40708 Neg No. T4-303])*

Europeans believed that land, as a privately held commodity, was a resource to be exploited for human gain. They took for granted property lines, inheritance of land, and courts to settle resulting land disputes. Property was the basis not only of sustenance but also of independence, wealth, status, political rights, and identity. The social structure directly mirrored patterns of land ownership, with a land-wealthy elite at the apex of the social pyramid and a propertyless mass at the bottom.

Native Americans also had concepts of property and boundaries. But they believed that land had sacred qualities and should be held in common. As one German missionary explained the Native American view in the eighteenth century, the Creator "made the Earth and all that it contains for the common good of mankind. Whatever liveth on the land, whatsoever groweth out of the earth, and all that is in the rivers and waters ... was given jointly to all and everyone is entitled to his share."

Communal ownership sharply limited social stratification and increased a sense of sharing in most

Native American communities, much to the amazement of Europeans accustomed to wide disparities of wealth. Not all Europeans were acquisitive, competitive individuals. The majority were peasant farmers living from the soil, living in kin-centered villages with little contact with the outside world, and exchanging goods and labor through barter. But in Europe's cities, a wealth-conscious, ambitious individual who valued and sought wider choices and greater opportunities to enhance personal status was coming to the fore. In contrast, Native American traditions stressed the group rather than the individual and valor rather than wealth.

There were exceptions. The empires of the Aztec in Central America and the Inca in South America were highly developed, populous, and stratified. So, in North America, were a few tribes such as the Natchez. But on the eastern and western coasts of the continent and in the Southwest—the regions of contact in the sixteenth and seventeenth centuries—the European newcomers encountered a people whose cultural values differed strikingly from theirs.

European colonizers in North America also found the matrilineal organization of many tribal societies contrary to the European male-dominated sexual hierarchy. Family membership among most tribes was determined through the female line and divorce was the woman's prerogative. Clans were composed of several matrilineal kin groups related by a blood connection on the mother's side.

In Native American societies, women also held subordinate positions, but not nearly to the extent found among European women. While European women were excluded almost entirely from political affairs, senior women in many Native American villages designated the men who sat in a circle to deliberate and make decisions and stood behind them to lobby and instruct. Village chiefs were male, but they were often chosen by the elder women of their clans. If the men moved too far from the will of the women who appointed them, these chiefs were removed or "dehorned." "Our ancestors," the Oneida chief Good Peter explained, "considered it a great transgression to reject the counsel of their women, particularly the female governesses. Our ancestors considered them mistresses of the soil. ... The women, they are the life of the nation."

The role of women in the tribal economy reinforced the sharing of power between male and female. Men hunted, fished, and cleared land, but women controlled the cultivation, harvest, and distribution of crops, supplying probably three-quarters of their family's nutritional needs. When the

Mississippian Culture Shrine Figures   Carved from marble 700 to 800 years ago, these shrine figures, male and female, were found in a tomb in northwestern Georgia. The Native American carvings, known to us only as part of a South Appalachian Mississippi culture, are thought to be representations of ancestor gods. Are similar shrine figures found in African and European societies? *(Lynn Johnson/Aurora & Quanta Productions)*

men were away hunting, the women directed village life. Europeans, imbued with the idea of male superiority and female subordination, perceived such sexual equality as another mark of "savagery."

In economic relations, Europeans and Native Americans differed in ways that sometimes led to misunderstanding and conflict. Over vast stretches of the continent, Native Americans had built trading networks for centuries before Europeans arrived, making it easy for them to trade with arriving Europeans and incorporate new metal and glass trade items into their culture. But trade for Indian peoples was also a way of preserving interdependence and equilibrium between individuals and communities. This principle of reciprocity displayed itself in elaborate ceremonies of gift giving and pipe smoking that preceded the exchange of goods. Europeans saw trade largely as economic exchange, with the benefit of building goodwill between two parties sharply limited in comparison with the Native American view.

The English saw a final damning defect in the religious beliefs of Native Americans. Europeans built their religious life around the belief in a single divinity, written scriptures, a trained and highly literate clergy, and churches with structured ceremonies. Native American societies, sharing no literary tradition, had less structured religious beliefs. Believing that human life could be affected, positively or negatively, by the mysterious power pervading everything in nature—in rocks, water, the sun, the moon, and animals—Native American people sought to conciliate these spirits and maintain proper relationships with them, even the spirits of the fish, beaver, and deer they hunted. Pueblo people, for example, living in arid lands where rainfall dictated their well-being, expressed their thanks for rain by performing frequent ritual dances.

For Europeans, the Native Americans' polytheism, or belief in several gods, was pagan and devilish. Native religious leaders, called shamans, used medicinal plants and magical chants to heal the sick and facilitated the people's quests to communicate with the spiritual world. But Europeans regarded the shamans as especially dangerous because they occupied powerful roles among a spiritually misled people. Their fear and hatred of infidels intensified by the Protestant Reformation, Europeans saw a holy necessity to convert—or destroy—these enemies of their God.

AFRICA ON THE EVE OF CONTACT

Half a century before Columbus reached the Americas, a Portuguese sea captain, Antam Gonçalves, made the first European landing on the west coast of sub-Saharan Africa. If he had been able to travel the length and breadth of the immense continent, he would have encountered a rich variety of African states, peoples, and cultures that had developed over many millennia. What Europeans considered African backwardness and cultural impoverishment was a myth perpetuated after the slave trade had begun transporting millions of Africans to the New World. During the period of early contact with Europeans, Africa, like pre-Columbian America, was recognized as a diverse continent with a long history of cultural evolution.

The Spread of Islam

"The seat of Mansa Sulayman [the sultan, or ruler] was a sprawling, unwalled town set in a 'verdant and

Spread of Islam in Africa, ca. 1500

This map shows the extensive reach of Islam in Africa by 1500. On most of the North African Mediterranean coast and in the powerful Mali and Songhai kingdoms, the Muslim faith predominated. **Reflecting on the Past** Do you think enslaved Africans who had converted to Islam practiced their faith after arriving in the American colonies? How would they do so on slave plantations?

hilly' country," wrote Arab geographer Abu Abdallah Ibn Battuta in 1351 after visiting the capital of the Mali Kingdom at about the same time that the Aztecs rose to eminence in Mesoamerica. "The sultan had several enclosed palaces there . . . and covered [them] with colored patterns so that it turned out to be the most elegant of buildings." The 47-year-old Ibn Battuta, born into a family of Muslim legal scholars in Tangier, Morocco, on the southern shore of the Mediterranean Sea, was struck with Mali's splendor. "Surrounding the palaces and mosques were the residences of the citizenry, mud-walled houses roofed with domes of timber and reed." Keenly interested in their laws, Ibn Battuta wrote, "Amongst their good qualities is the small amount of injustice amongst them, for of all people they are the furthest from it. Their sultan does not forgive anyone in any matter to do with injustice. . . . There is also the prevalence of peace in their country, the traveler is not afraid in it nor is he who lives there in fear of the thief or of the robber." With Ibn Battuta traveled the Muslim faith, or commitment to Islam (meaning "submission to Allah").

Portuguese Attack on Tangiers In this beautiful tapestry hanging in the Collegiate Church of Pastrana in Spain, we can see Dom Affonso V, the Portuguese king, leading his troops in 1471 in an attack on Tangiers, a Muslim stronghold in North Africa. The Portuguese campaigns of conquest in North Africa from the 1450s to the 1470s were a response to the fall of Constantinople to the Ottomans in 1453, a terrible blow to the Catholic world in its prolonged struggle with Islam. *(Bettmann/CORBIS)*

This account of the greatest traveler of premodern times opens a window to the two themes of this section: the spread of Islam and the rise of great empires in West and Central Africa—a region then called the Sudan (the word comes from *al-Sudan,* the Arabic term for "black people"). Ibn Battuta had traveled for more than 20 years through much of the Eastern Hemisphere before reaching Mali, visiting territories equivalent to some 44 present-day countries and traversing 73,000 miles.

Spreading rapidly in Arabia after Muhammad, the founder of Islam, began preaching in 610 C.E., Islam rose to global eminence after several centuries. By the tenth century, Egypt was predominantly Muslim, and Islam was spreading southward from Mediterranean North Africa across the Sahara Desert into northern Sudan, where it took hold especially in the trading centers. In time, Islam encompassed much of the Eastern Hemisphere and became the main intermediary for exchanging goods, ideas, and technologies across a huge part of the world. When Portuguese traders initiated the slave traffic in West Africa in the 1400s, they found that many of the Africans they forced onto slave ships were devout Muslims.

The Kingdoms of Central and West Africa

The vast region of West Africa, to which Islam was spreading by the tenth century, embraced widely varied ecological zones—partly a vast desert, partly

grasslands, and partly tropical forests. As in Europe and the Americas at that time, most people tilled the soil, and by the time of first contact with Europeans were practicing sophisticated agricultural techniques and livestock management. Part of their skill in farming derived from the development of iron production, which began among the Nok in present-day Nigeria about 450 B.C.E., long before it reached Europe. Over many centuries, more efficient iron implements for cultivating and harvesting increased agricultural productivity, in turn spurring population growth. With large populations came greater specialization of tasks and thus greater efficiency and additional technical improvements. The pattern was similar to the agricultural revolution that occurred in the Americas, Europe, the Far East, the Middle East, and elsewhere.

Cultural and political development in West Africa proceeded at varying rates, largely dependent on ecological conditions. Regions blessed by good soil, adequate rainfall, and abundance of minerals, as in coastal West Africa, began engaging in interregional trade. This in turn brought population growth and cultural development. But where deserts were inhospitable or forests impenetrable, social systems remained small and changed slowly. The Sahara Desert, once a land of flowing rivers and lush green pastures and forests, had been depopulated by climate changes that brought higher temperatures and lower rainfall. As desertification occurred between about 4000 B.C.E. and 2500 B.C.E.,

Sahara people moved southward in search of more fertile land, first to oases situated along a strip of grasslands, or savanna, on the desert's southern border, then farther south to the fertile rain forests of the Niger River basin where they built some of Africa's greatest empires.

The Ghana Empire The first of these empires was Ghana. Developing between the fifth and eleventh centuries, when the Roman Empire collapsed and medieval Europe stagnated, it occupied an immense territory between the Sahara and the Gulf of Guinea and stretched from the Atlantic Ocean to the Niger River. Though mostly a land of small villages, it became a major empire noted for its extensive urban settlement, sculpture and metalwork, long-distance commerce, and complex political and military structure. Ideally positioned for trade, Ghana became a wealthy empire built primarily on trade rather than military conquest, partly because of trading contacts

Niger Region Archer This terra cotta sculpture from the Niger River delta region shows an archer. In the collection of the Smithsonian Institution's National Art Museum of African Art, it is dated to the thirteenth–fifteenth century. *(Archer Figure, Inland Niger Delta Style, Mali, 13th–15th century, Ceramic H x W x D: 61.9 x 16.5 x 16.5 cm, Museum Purchase 86-12-1, Photograph by Franko Khoury, National Museum of African Art, Smithsonian Institution.)*

with Muslim Arabs, who had crossed the Sahara Desert in camel caravans to control the region by the eleventh century. From the south came kola nuts, palm oil, copper, and gold. From the north came imported items such as ceramics, glass, oil lamps, and—absolutely essential—the salt from Saharan mines that preserved and flavored food. By the late 900s, Ghana controlled more than 100,000 square miles of land and hundreds of thousands of people. Gold was so plentiful that a pound of gold was traded for a pound of salt.

A thriving caravan trade with Arab peoples across the Sahara to Morocco and Algeria brought extensive Muslim influence by the eleventh century, when the king of Ghana boasted an army of 200,000 and maintained trading contacts as far east as Cairo and Baghdad. Gold made Kumbi-Saleh, Ghana's capital, the busiest and wealthiest marketplace in West Africa. By Europe's Middle Ages, two-thirds of the gold circulating in the Christian Mediterranean region was coming from Ghana.

As trade in Ghana grew more profitable, Arab merchants came to live in the empire, especially in the capital city of Kumbi-Saleh. With the trading of goods came the exchange of ideas. Arabs brought the first system of writing and numbers to West Africa, and the Ghanaian kings adopted Arab script and appointed Arabs to government positions. As these Arabs gained influence in Ghana, they spread the Islamic faith. Most of Ghana's rulers held tightly to their traditional religion and rejected the Muslim principle of patriarchy in which royal succession would follow the father's lineage. But many Ghanaians, especially in the cities, converted to Islam. By 1050, Kumbi-Saleh boasted 12 Muslim mosques.

The Mali Empire An invasion of North African Muslim warriors beginning in the eleventh century introduced a period of religious strife that eventually destroyed the kingdom of Ghana. Rising to replace it was the Islamic kingdom of Mali, dominated by the Malinke, or Mandingo, people. Through effective agricultural production and control of the gold trade, Mali flourished. The cultivation of rice and harvesting of inland deltas for fish helped support the thriving trade for salt, gold, and copper. Under Mansa Musa, a devout Muslim who assumed the throne in 1307, Mali came to control territory three times as great as the kingdom of Ghana. Famed for his 3,500-mile pilgrimage across the Sahara and through Cairo all the way to Mecca in 1324 with an entourage of some 50,000, Mansa Musa drew the attention of Mediterranean merchants. Dispensing lavish gifts of gold as he proceeded east, he made Mali gold legendary.

The Empires of Ghana, Mali, and Songhai

These ancient empires, each in their turn, controlled vast areas of West Africa. Ghana, which built its wealth on trade, was at its height from about 900 to 1100 C.E. Mali's devout Muslim leader, Mansa Musa, commissioned large mosques and turned Timbuktu into a center of Islamic learning. Songhai began its rise to power after the death of Mansa Musa. **Reflecting on the Past** Why would some Europeans send their sons to Timbuktu to study? What evidence can you find that Muslim ideas contributed to European scientific and cultural knowledge?

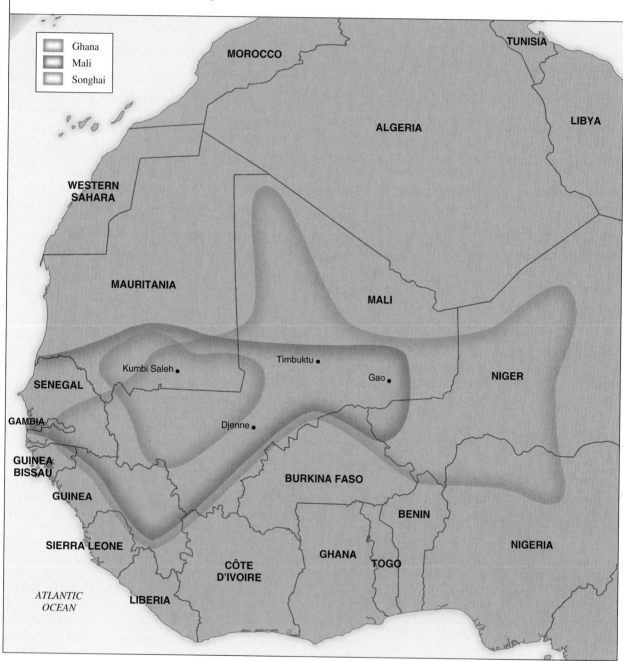

Coming home, Mansa Musa brought Muslim scholars and artisans with him who were instrumental in establishing Timbuktu, at the center of the Mali Empire, as a city of great importance. Noted for its extensive wealth, Timbuktu's Islamic university developed a distinguished faculty, who instructed North Africans and southern Europeans who came to study. Traveling there in the 1330s, Ibn Battuta wrote admiringly of "the discipline of its officials and provincial governors, the excellent condition of public finance, and . . . the respect accorded to the decisions of justice and to the authority of the sovereign."

The Songhai Empire After Mansa Musa died in 1332, power in West Africa began to shift to the Songhai, centered on the middle Niger River. A mixture of farmers, traders, fishermen, and warriors, the Songhai declared independence from Mali in 1435. Just as Mali had grown out of a state in the empire of Ghana, the new Songhai Empire grew out of a region that had once been part of Mali. By the time Portuguese traders in the late 1400s were establishing firm commercial links with the Kongo, far to the south, the Songhai Empire was at its peak under the rule of Sonni Ali (1464–1492) and Muhammad Ture (1493–1528).

Yet Songhai, too, collapsed, as some tribes that were resentful of Muslim kings began to break away. But the most dangerous threat came from Morocco, in North Africa, whose rulers coveted Songhai's sources of salt and gold—the two critical commodities in the African trade. Equipped with guns procured in the Middle East, Morocco's ruler conquered Timbuktu and Gao in 1591. The North Africans remained in loose control of western Sudan for more than a century, as the last great trading empire of West Africa faded. At a time when England, France, Spain, and other centralized kingdoms in Europe were emerging, the great empires of West Africa slowly devolved into smaller states. Looking back over the long centuries of the tragic Atlantic slave trade, it seems that by a melancholy quirk of history, local West African conflicts made it easier for European slave traders to persuade tribal leaders to send out warrior parties to capture tradeable slaves.

The Kingdoms of Kongo and Benin Farther south along the Atlantic coast and in Central Africa lay the vast kingdom of Kongo. The first European to encounter these people was the Portuguese ship captain Diego Cao, who in 1482 anchored in the mouth of the mighty Kongo River. Kongo's royal capital, Mbanza, was a trade center for a kingdom of several million people and also became a center of trade relations with the Portuguese, who by the 1490s were sending Catholic missionaries to the court of King Mani-Kongo. Thus was Mani-Kongo's son baptized Affonso I, and under Affonso's rule in the early 1500s, a flourishing trade in slaves with the Portuguese began.

Like Kongo, the kingdom of Benin developed long before seaborne Europeans reached western Africa. Benin, which became so important in the English slave trade, was formed in about 1000 C.E. west of the Niger Delta. When Europeans reached Benin City hundreds of years later, they found a walled city with broad streets and hundreds of buildings. Thousands of slaves procured in the interior passed through

Benin Leopards In the Benin kingdom of West Africa, people celebrated the leopard as "king of the bush." Copper alloy leopards of this kind were usually placed at the king's side when he sat in state to symbolize the king's ominous power combined with prudent reserve. *(Photograph © 1978 Dirk Bakker)*

Benin City on their way for exchange with the Portuguese, and later the English, at coastal Calabar, where one of the main slave forts stood. One of Benin's most important chroniclers, Olaudah Equiano, endured just such a trip. He was born in a village in "a charming fruitful vale," far into the interior of the kingdom of Benin, which he regarded as "the most considerable" of "a variety of kingdoms" in the "part of Africa known by the name of Guinea." Equiano's story has a timelessness that allows it to stand for the experiences over several centuries of millions of Africans who were born in western Africa, the ancestral homelands of most of today's African Americans.

African Slavery

The idea that slavery was a legitimate social condition in past societies offends modern values, and it is difficult for many Americans to understand why Africans would sell fellow Africans to European traders. But there were no people who identified themselves as Africans four centuries ago; rather, they thought of themselves as Ibos or Mandingos, or Kongolese, or residents of Mali or Songhai. Moreover, slavery was not new for Africans or any other people in the fourteenth century. It had flourished in ancient Rome and Greece, in large parts of eastern Europe, in southwestern Asia, and in the

Mediterranean world in general. In times of pillage and conquest, invading people everywhere sold prisoners into slavery. Conquerors could not tolerate holding massive numbers of the enemy in their midst and therefore often sold them to distant lands as slaves, where their threat would be neutralized. This seemed more merciful than mass execution—and more profitable.

Slavery had existed in Africa for centuries, but it had nothing to do with skin color. Like other peoples, Africans accepted slavery without question as a condition of servitude and slaveholding as a mark of wealth. To own slaves was to be wealthy; to trade slaves was a way of increasing one's wealth. Olaudah Equiano described how his tribe traded slaves to "mahogany-coloured men from the south west" of his village: "Sometimes we sold slaves to them but they were only prisoners of war, or such among us as had been convicted of kidnaping, or adultery, and some other crimes which we esteemed heinous." In this way, African societies for centuries conducted an overland slave trade that carried captured people from West Africa across the vast Sahara Desert to Christian Roman Europe and the Islamic Middle East.

From the tenth to fifteenth century, about 5,000 West Africans were sold eastward as sugar workers in Egypt, as domestic servants and craftspeople throughout the Arabic world, and as soldiers in North Africa. Islam had facilitated this process by establishing secure trade routes connecting West Africa with the Mediterranean world and the lands east of it. By the time Songhai rose to prominence in West Africa, the kingdom became a major supplier of enslaved captives across the Sahara to North Africa. This trade gave Songhai's elite access to European trade goods—Venetian beads, fine cloth, and horses, the latter especially important to Songhai warriors who were waging war against neighboring peoples. Though this slave traffic was on the rise, it was still an occasional rather than a highly organized trade, and it was carried out to provide Mediterranean trading partners with soldiers, household servants, and artisans rather than gangs of field workers.

In this way, the peoples of West Africa held to a conception of slavery very different from the one that would develop in the European colonies of the Americas. "Those prisoners which were not sold or redeemed," remembered Equiano, "we kept as slaves; but how different was their condition from that of slaves in the West-Indies! With us, they do no more work than other members of the community, even their master. Their food, clothing, and lodging were nearly the same as theirs, except they were not permitted to eat with the free-born." Most important in the African practice of slavery was that the enslaved served as soldiers, administrators, sometimes as royal advisers, and even occasionally as royal consorts. Also key was the possibility of freedom: the status of slave was not necessarily lifelong but was revocable, and slavery did not automatically pass on to the female slave's children.

The African City of Loango The city of Loango, at the mouth of the Congo River on the west coast of Africa, was larger at the time of this drawing in the mid-eighteenth century than all but a few seaports in the British colonies in North America. What can you discern from the figures in the foreground? *(The Granger Collection, New York)*

The African Ethos

Many of Africa's peoples—Ashanti, Mandingo, Coromantee, Yoruba, Fon, Hausa, Ibo, Whydah, Ga, and others—eventually became African Americans. Indeed, they would become at least two-thirds of all the immigrants who crossed the ocean to the Western Hemisphere in the three centuries after Europeans began colonizing there. They came from a rich diversity of cultures, but most of them shared certain ways of life that differentiated them from Europeans.

As in Europe, the family was the basic unit of social organization. By maintaining intimate connections between man and woman, parent and child, sister and brother, enslaved Africans developed an important defense against the cruelties of slavery. Unlike Europeans, however, where patriarchy put the father and husband at the center of family life, Africans organized themselves in a variety of kinship systems. In many African societies, as in many Native American ones, the family was matrilineal, with property rights and political inheritance descending through the mother rather than the father. When a chief died, the son of his sister inherited his position. Upon marrying, a man joined his wife's people. This matrilineal tradition carried over into slavery, as African women continued to have an influence not typical in European family organization. In Africa, each person was linked to others in the village, his or her identity defined by family relationships. Individualism, which would become so prized in English society transplanted to North America, was an alien, distasteful, and nearly meaningless concept to Africans.

Africans brought a complex religious heritage with them to the Americas, which no amount of desolation or physical abuse could wipe out. Widespread across Africa was a belief in a supreme Creator of the cosmos and in a pantheon of lesser deities associated with natural forces, such as rain, animals, and the fertility of the earth, that could intervene in human affairs and were, therefore, elaborately honored. West Africans, like most native North Americans, held that spirits dwelt in the trees, rocks, and rivers around them, and hence they exercised care in their treatment.

Africans also worshiped ancestors, who they believed mediated between the Creator and the living. Relatives held elaborate funeral rites to ensure the proper entrance of a deceased relative into the spiritual world. The more ancient an ancestor, the greater this person's power to affect the living; thus the "ancient ones" were devoutly worshiped. Deep family loyalty and regard for family lineage flowed naturally from ancestor worship.

Finally, West Africans believed in spirit possession, in which the gods spoke to men and women through

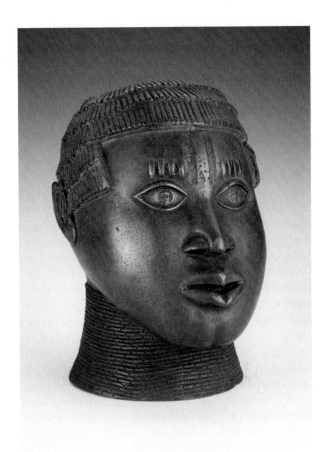

Edo Sculpture This commemorative head, probably of a queen mother, was made by an Edo of the Benin kingdom about the time Columbus was making his first voyage across the Atlantic. The elaborate headdress and collar of beads are fashioned from copper alloy with iron inlay. Would ordinary Ibo women be dressed like this? *(Commemorative trophy head. Edo peoples, Nigeria, Late 15th–early 16th century, Copper alloy, iron inlay, H x W x D: 23.2 x 15.9 x 20 cm, Purchased with funds provided by the Smithsonian Collections Acquisition Program, 85-5-2. Photograph by Franko Khoury, National Museum of African Art, Smithsonian Institution.)*

priests and other religious figures. "Though we had no places of public worship," Equiano remembered, "we had priests and magicians, or wise men . . . held in great reverence by the people. They calculated time, foretold events, . . . and when they died, they were succeeded by their sons."

While their religious beliefs differed from those of their European slave owners, Africans shared some common ground, including a belief in an invisible "other world" inhabited by the souls of the dead who could be known through revelations that spiritually gifted people could interpret. These roughly shared foundations of religious feeling fostered the development of a hybrid African Christianity. In fact, in the kingdom of Kongo and several small kingdoms close to the Niger Delta, extensive contact with the Portuguese had allowed Christianity to graft itself onto African religious beliefs by the time English colonies were planted in North America in the seventeenth century. African religious customs, funeral rites, sacred images, and charms for protection against evil spirits lost some of their power during enslavement, though how fast this happened is murky and clearly varied from place to place. But even to the present day, African religious beliefs and practices still hold at least partial sway among some African Americans.

Social organization in much of West Africa by the time Europeans arrived was as elaborate as in fifteenth-century Europe. At the top of society stood the king, supported by nobles and priests, usually elderly men. Beneath them were the great mass of people, mostly cultivators of the soil in innumerable villages. "Agriculture is our chief employment," recalled Equiano, "and everyone, even the children and women, are engaged in it. Thus we are habituated to labour from our earliest years" and "everyone contributes something to the common stock." In urban centers, craftspeople, traders, teachers, and artists lived beneath the ruling families. At the bottom of society toiled the slaves. As in ancient Greece and Rome, they were "outsiders"—war captives, criminals, or sometimes people who sold themselves into servitude to satisfy a debt. [The rights of slaves were restricted, and their opportunities for advancement were narrow. Nevertheless, as members of the community, they were entitled to protection under the law and allowed the privileges of education, marriage, and parenthood.] Their servile condition was not permanent, nor was it automatically inherited by their children, as would be the fate of Africans enslaved in the Americas.

EUROPE ON THE EVE OF INVADING THE AMERICAS

In the ninth century, about the time that the Mound Builders of the Mississippi valley were constructing their urban center at Cahokia and the kingdom of Ghana was rising in West Africa, western Europe was an economic and cultural backwater. The center of political power and economic vitality in the Old World had shifted eastward to Christian Byzantium, which controlled Asia Minor, the Balkans, and parts of Italy. The other dynamic culture of this age, Islam, had spread through the Middle East, spilled across North Africa, and penetrated Spain and West Africa south of the Sahara.

Within a few centuries, an epic revitalization of western Europe occurred, creating the conditions that enabled its leading maritime nations vastly to extend their oceanic frontiers. By the late fifteenth century, a 400-year epoch of militant overseas

European expansion was underway. Not until the second half of the twentieth century was this process of Europeanization reversed; then colonized people began to regain their autonomy and cultural identity through wars of national liberation—a process now nearing completion.

The Rebirth of Europe

The rebirth of western Europe, which began around 1000 C.E., owed much to a revival of long-distance trading from Italian ports on the Mediterranean and to the rediscovery of ancient knowledge that these contacts permitted. The once mighty cities of the Roman Empire had stagnated for centuries, but now Venice, Genoa, and other Italian ports began trading with peoples facing the Adriatic, Baltic, and North seas. These new contacts brought wealth and power to the Italian commercial cities, which gradually evolved into merchant-dominated city–states that freed themselves from the rule of feudal lords in control of the surrounding countryside. By the late 1400s, sailing ships were crossing all the sea basins of the Eastern Hemisphere—the China Sea, the Indian Ocean, the Persian Gulf, the Red and Black seas, and the Mediterranean, thus creating a zone of intercultural communication never before achieved.

While merchants led the emerging city–states, western Europe's feudal system gradually weakened. For centuries, warrior aristocrats, not kings, had exercised the normal powers of the state: the power to tax, wage war, and administer the law. In the thirteenth and fourteenth centuries, however, kings began to reassert their political authority and to undertake efforts to unify their realms. One of their primary goals was to curb the power of the great feudal lords who dominated entire regions and to force lesser nobles into dependence on and obedience to the crown.

Concurrently in the fourteenth century, the mass of peasant people suffered greatly. Famine struck many parts of Europe after 1300 because the production of food did not keep up with population increases. Malnutrition reduced the resistance of millions when the Black Death (bubonic plague) struck with fury. It first devastated China, wiping out nearly one-third of the population, and then moved eastward following trade routes to India and the Middle East, hitting hardest in the cities. Then in 1348 it reached western Europe and North Africa. Over the next quarter century, some 30 million Europeans died, a blow from which Europe did not recover demographically for centuries. This unprecedented human misery produced economic disruption, violent worker strikes, and peasant uprisings. Yet the

A Chapel Made of Bone   The Black Death of the mid-fourteenth century killed nearly 40,000 people in the region of Prague. Five centuries later, a Czech wood-carver fashioned the bones of thousands of Black Death victims into a chapel where visitors are astounded to see a bone altar, bone chalices, the bone chandelier that is pictured here, and gigantic bone bells. Every bone in the human body is used in the chandelier. How does the Black Death compare with modern-day scourges such as AIDS? *(Photograph © Lubomir Stiburek)*

a more unified state, with the English kings wielding less political power than their counterparts on the European continent.

Economic changes of great significance also occurred in England during the sixteenth century. To practice more profitable agriculture, great landowners began to "enclose" (consolidate) their estates, throwing peasant farmers off their plots and turning many of them into wage laborers. The formation of this working class was the crucial first step toward industrial development.

Continental Europe lagged behind England in two respects. First, it was far less affected by the move to "enclose" agricultural land because continental aristocrats regarded the maximization of profit as unworthy of gentlemen. Second, continental rulers were less successful in engaging the interests of their nobilities, and these nobles never shared governance with their king, as did English aristocrats through their participation in Parliament. In France, a noble faction assassinated Henry III in 1589, and the nobles remained disruptive for nearly another century. In Spain, the final conquest of the Muslims and expulsion of the Jews, both in 1492, strengthened the monarchy's hold, but regional cultures and leaders remained strong. The continental monarchs would thus warmly embrace the doctrine of royal absolutism—the unqualified authority of the king or queen—that developed in the sixteenth century.

Black Death promoted the unification of old realms into early modern states. The nobilities with which monarchs had to contend were reduced in size, for the plague defied class distinction. Ironically, feudal lords treated their peasants better for a time because their labor, tremendously reduced by the plague, became more valuable.

Early developments in England led to a distinctive political system. In 1215, the English aristocracy curbed the powers of the king when they forced him to accept the Magna Carta. On the basis of this charter, a parliament composed of elective and hereditary members eventually gained the right to meet regularly to pass money bills and therefore act as a check on the Crown. During the sixteenth century, the Crown and Parliament worked together toward

The New Monarchies and the Expansionist Impulse

In the second half of the fifteenth century, ambitious monarchs coming to power in France, England, and Spain sought social and political stability in their kingdoms by creating armies and bureaucracies strong enough to quell internal conflict and raising taxes sufficient to support their regimes. In these countries, and in Portugal as well, economic revival and the reversal of more than a century of population decline and civil disorder nourished the impulse to expand. This impulse was also fed by Renaissance culture. Ushering in a new, more secular age, the Renaissance (Rebirth) encouraged innovation (in science as well as in art and music), freedom of thought, richness of expression, and an emphasis on human abilities. Beginning in Italy and spreading northward through Europe, the Renaissance peaked dramatically in the late fifteenth century when the age of overseas exploration began.

The exploratory urge had two initial objectives: first, to circumvent overland Muslim traders by finding an eastward oceanic route to Asia; second, to tap the African gold trade at its source, avoiding Muslim intermediaries in North Africa. Since 1291, when Marco Polo returned to Venice with tales of Eastern treasures such as spices, silks, perfumes, medicines, and jewels, Europeans had bartered with the Orient via a long eastward overland route through the Muslim world. Eventually, Europe's mariners found they could voyage to Cathay (China) by both eastward and westward water routes.

Portugal seemed the least likely of the rising nation–states to lead the expansion of Europe outside its continental boundaries, yet it forged into the lead at the end of the fifteenth century. A poor country of only 1 million inhabitants, Portugal had gradually overcome Moorish control in the twelfth and thirteenth centuries and, in 1385, had wrenched itself free of domination by neighboring Castile. Led by Prince Henry the Navigator, for whom trade was secondary to the conquest of the Muslim world, Portugal breached the unknown. In the 1420s, Henry began dispatching Portuguese mariners to probe the unknown Atlantic "sea of darkness." Important improvements in navigational instruments, mapmaking, and ship design aided his intrepid sailors. Symbolizing the increasingly interconnected world, the compass, invented by the Chinese, was copied by Middle Eastern Arabs, then by the Portuguese.

Portuguese captains operated at sea on three ancient Ptolemaic principles: that the earth was round, that distances on its surface could be measured by degrees, and that navigators could "fix" their position at sea on a map by measuring the position of the stars. The invention in the 1450s of the quadrant, which allowed a precise measurement of star altitude necessary for determining latitude, represented a leap forward from the chart-and-compass method of navigation. Equally important was the design of a lateen-rigged

AMERICAN VOICES

In 1444, Gomes Eannes de Zurara, a representative of Portugal's Prince Henry, described the arrival by ship of enslaved Africans at Lagos, Portugal.

What heart could be so hard as not to be pierced with piteous feeling to see that company? For some kept their heads low, and their faces bathed in tears, looking one upon another. Others stood groaning very dolorously. Looking up to the height of heaven, fixing their eyes upon it, crying out loudly, as if asking help from the Father of nature; others struck their faces with the palms of their hands, throwing themselves at full length upon the group; while others made lamentations in their manner of a dirge, after the custom of their country . . . But to increase their suffering still more there now arrived those who had charge of the division of the captives, and . . . then was it needful to part fathers from sons, husbands from wives, brothers from brothers. No respect was shown to either friends or relations, but each fell where his lot took him.

- *Does the wording and tone of this passage indicate that Eannes de Zurara was opposed to the slave trade?*

- *Why would a courtier of Prince Henry write this?*

caravel, adapted from a Moorish ship design. The triangular sails permitted ships to sail into the wind, allowing them to travel southward along the African coast—a feat the square-rigged European vessels could never perform—and return northward against prevailing winds.

By the 1430s, the ability of Prince Henry's captains to break through the limits of the world known to Europeans had carried them to Madeira, the Canary Islands, and the more distant Azores, lying off the coasts of Portugal and northwestern Africa. These were soon developed as the first European-controlled agricultural plantations, located on the continent's periphery and designed to produce cash crops such as sugar that could be marketed in Europe. Thus, the Madeiras, Canaries, and Azores became a kind of laboratory for much larger European colony building much farther from the colonizers' homelands.

From islands off the West African coast, the Portuguese sea captains pushed farther south, navigating their way down the west coast of Africa by 1460. While carrying their Christian faith to new lands, they began a profitable trade in ivory, slaves, and especially gold. Now, they were poised to capitalize on the connection between Europe and Africa, though not yet knowing that a stupendous land mass, to become known as America, lay far across the Atlantic Ocean.

Astrolabe In Columbus's era, the astrolabe was the most important astronomical computer, in which the celestial sphere was projected onto the equator's plane. Once the movable arm was set, the entire sky was visible. Europeans adopted it in the twelfth century from the Islamic world, where it had been used for centuries. *(Courtesy of Adler Planetarium & Astronomy Museum, Chicago, Illinois)*

TIMELINE

35,000 B.C.E.	First humans cross Bering Land Bridge to reach the Americas
12,000 B.C.E.	Beringian epoch ends
8000 B.C.E.	Paleo-Indian phase ends
500 B.C.E.	Archaic era ends
500 B.C.E.–1000 C.E.	Post-Archaic era in North America
600 C.E.–1100	Rise of mound-building center at Cahokia
632–750	Islamic conquest of North Africa spreads Muslim faith
800–1026	Kingdom of Ghana controls West Africa's trade
1000	Norse seafarers establish settlements in Newfoundland. Kingdom of Benin develops
1000–1500	Kingdoms of Ghana, Mali, Songhai in Africa
1200s	Pueblo societies develop village life in southwestern North America
1235	Defeating the Ghanaian king, Mali becomes a West African power

1291	Marco Polo's return from East Asia to Venice quickens European trade with Eastern Hemisphere
1300s	Rise of Aztec society in Valley of Mexico
1300–1450	Italian Renaissance
1324	Mansa Musa's pilgrimage to Mecca expands Muslim influence in West Africa
1420s	Portuguese sailors explore west coast of Africa
1435	Kingdom of Songhai declares independence from kingdom of Mali
1450–1600	Northern European Renaissance
1460s–1590s	Kingdom of Songhai controls West Africa's trading societies
1469	Marriage of Castile's Isabella and Aragon's Ferdinand creates Spain
1500s	Quickening of western European trade and production of consumer goods

Conclusion

The Approach of a New Global Age

All the forces that have made the world of the past 500 years "modern" began to come into play by the late fifteenth century. As the stories about four important women of this era demonstrate, deep transformations were underway in West Africa, in southern and western Europe, and in the Americas. West African empires had reached new heights, some had been deeply influenced by the Islamic faith, and many had become experienced in transregional trade. Muslim scholars, merchants, and long-distance travelers were becoming the principal mediators in the interregional exchange of goods, ideas, and technical innovations. Meanwhile the Renaissance, initiated in Italy, worked its way northward and brought new energy and ambition to a weakened, disease-ridden, and tired Europe. Advances in maritime technology also allowed Europeans to make contact with the peoples of West Africa and develop the first slave-based plantation societies in tropical islands off the West African coast. In the Americas, large empires in Mexico and—as we will see in Chapter 2, Peru—were growing more populous and consolidating their power while in North America the opposite was occurring: a decay of powerful mound-building societies and a long-range move toward decentralized tribal societies. The scene was set for the great leap of Europeans across the Atlantic, where the convergence between the peoples of Africa, the Americas, and Europe would occur.

Questions for Review and Reflection

1. To what do you attribute the remarkable diversity of cultures in the Americas in the centuries prior to contact with Europeans? What are the most marked examples of that diversity?

2. What were the major features of western African society and culture prior to contact with European traders?

3. What were the causes and major consequences of the revitalization of western Europe in the period after 1000 C.E.?

4. Africa, Europe, and the Americas at the start of the "early modern period" are often treated as dramatically different in every way, yet commonalities existed. What were the most striking of these common features?

5. Why did western Europeans expand out of their geographical confines to explore, conquer, and colonize the Americas? What factors were not present in Africa or the Americas to foster expansion into the Atlantic basin from those areas?

Recommended Reading

Recommended Readings are posted on the Web site for this textbook. Visit www.ablongman.com/nash

Fiction and Film

Peter Forbath's *Lord of the Kongo* (1996) tells the dramatic story of a young Portuguese sailor counted among those interacting with the Kongo people of West Africa in the early 1500s. Chinua Achebe's *Things Fall Apart* (1958) is already a classic—an unsentimental depiction of tribal life in Nigeria before and after the arrival of Europeans. Barbara Tuckman's *A Distant Mirror* (1978) is the most engaging novel ever written about the European Middle Ages—and particularly about the calamitous fourteenth century when England and France waged the Hundred Years' War (1337–1429). In *The Man on a Donkey* (1952), H. F. M. Prescott brings alive the tumultuous English era of Henry VIII.

Search of the First Americans (1992), part of the Nova series produced by the Public Broadcasting System (PBS), provides a fascinating introduction to the peopling of the Americas before the Columbian voyages. *Secrets of the Lost Red Paint People,* also in this series, shows how archaeologists have reconstructed—always tentatively—the ancient world of the Americas. Films for the Humanities and Sciences in Princeton, New Jersey, has produced a five-part series of short films to recreate the history and culture of some of the great West African societies, particularly those from which today's African Americans in North America and the West Indies have derived. In *The Agony and the Ecstasy* (1965), derived from Irving Stone's biography of Michelangelo, Charlton Heston and Rex Harrison bring alive the Italian Renaissance. *Luther,* John Osborne's play that captivated London theatergoers, appeared on film, with Stacy Keach playing Luther, in 1974. *The Return of Martin Guerre* (1982), called by some the best historical movie ever made, depicts French peasant life in the era when Europeans were awakening to overseas exploration and settlement.

Discovering U.S. History Online

Ancient Mesoamerican Civilizations

www.angelfire.ca/humanorigins

This page supplies information regarding Mesoamerican civilizations with well-organized essays, links, and photos.

Cahokia Mounds

www.medicine.wustl.edu/~mckinney/cahokia/cahokia.html

This online presentation of the historical Cahokia Mounds offers background information, an interactive map of the site, a satellite map, and other photos.

Pre-Contact Cultural Areas
www.kstrom.net/isk/maps/houses/housingmap.html
www.kstrom.net/isk/maps/cultmap.html
These clickable maps give regional cultural information about pre-contact native peoples of North America.

Vikings in the New World
www.emuseum.mnsu.edu/prehistory/vikings/vikhome.html
This site explores the history of some of the earliest European visitors to the Americas.

Civilizations in Africa
www.wsu.edu:8080/~dee/CIVAFRCA/CIVAFRCA.HTM
This site offers a region-by-region, broad overview of the pre-conquest civilizations in Africa.

The Slave Kingdoms
www.pbs.org/wonders
Part of the PBS online exhibition "Wonders of the African World," this section describes the West African cultures during the slave trade as well as both African and European participation in the slave trade.

The Ancient West African City of Benin
www.nmafa.si.edu/exhibits/beninsp.htm
A brief description and exhibit example from each of the three sections of this Smithsonian Institution exhibit give a view through art of the extent of cultural development at the time of European contact and subsequent slave trade.

Life in Elizabethan England
www.renaissance.dm.net/compendium/home.html
This site provides a compendium of information about everyday life, politics, and religion in England prior to "the westward fever."

Life in Sixteenth-Century France
www.lepg.org/index.html
This detailed site offers "a guide to the history, culture, and daily life of 16th century France."

Renaissance
www.learner.org/exhibits/renaissance
An exploration of the European Renaissance, this interactive site seeks to discover and describe "the forces that drove this rebirth in Europe, and in Italy in particular."

CHAPTER 2

Europeans and Africans Reach the Americas

Slave Deck of the Albanez, watercolor done by a young naval officer in a Spanish slave ship captured by the HMS *Albanez*. *(Francis Meynell, View of the Deck of the Slave Ship Albanez. © National Maritime Museum, London)*

American Stories

Old World Sojourners Mingle with New World Inhabitants

Just 15 years after conquistadors led by Hernán Cortés toppled the Aztec Empire in Mexico, Spanish horsemen, searching for Native Americans to capture as slaves, happened upon some 600 of them in northwestern Mexico. Traveling with the natives were an African and three Spaniards, all dressed in native garb. The horsemen were "thunderstruck to see me so strangely dressed and in the company of Indians," noted Álvar Núñez Cabeza de Vaca, one of the three Spaniards accompanying the natives. "They went on staring at me for a long space of time, so astonished that they could neither speak to me nor manage to ask me anything."

De Vaca, his two Spanish companions, and the African had been lost for eight years and were presumed dead. They had been part of the 1528 expedition that had tried to plant a permanent Spanish settlement in what the Spanish called La Florida. Establishing themselves near the swamplands of Tampa Bay, the Spanish adventurers encountered starvation, disease, a leadership crisis, and hostile Native Americans. Captured by the Apalachee, who enslaved them, de Vaca and his companions soon adopted Native American ways, adapted to a new environment, and used their cleverness to convince their captors that they possessed magical healing power. The African, already a slave of one of the captured Spaniards and known as Estevan (sometimes called Estanvanico or Esteban), became an accomplished linguist, healer, guide, and negotiator. When they fled their captors, the four fugitives plunged into the wilderness and headed west. Paddling crude boats across the Gulf of Mexico, they shipwrecked on the Texas coast and took refuge among merciful Native Americans.

DOCUMENT

Alvar Núñez de Vaca, "Indians of the Rio Grande"

Such forays into a rugged and uncharted territory cast the Spanish and African adventurers into unaccustomed roles and sorely tested their ability to survive among the indigenous people, who generally opposed their intrusion into their homelands. De Vaca, a conquistador experienced in enslaving Native Americans, had become a slave himself before the flight to Texas. Estevan's status as the slave of a Spanish conquistador all but dissolved in the process of becoming a Native American slave and then a refugee from enslavement. In his journal, de Vaca described Estevan as "a black," "a Moor," and "an Arabian." But these were only words describing his skin color (dark), his religion (Islam), and his geographical homeland (Morocco). What mattered in this strange and often hostile land was not Estevan's blackness or even his slave status. What counted, in this time before the idea of racial categories, were his linguistic abilities, his fortitude, and his cleverness as a go-between. Estevan, an Atlantic creole—a man who originated on one land bordering the Atlantic—became a new man in the process of the cultural, linguistic, and social braiding that was occurring throughout the sixteenth-century Atlantic world.

For five years, Estevan, his master Andrés Dorantes, de Vaca, and another Spaniard traveled for about 2,500 miles. Often following friendly Native American guides, the four travelers came to be regarded as holy men, possessing the power to heal. Reaching present-day New Mexico, they found Native Americans who, according to de Vaca, described them as "four great doctors, one of them black, the other three white, who gave blessings [and] healed the sick." On one occasion, the natives gave Estevan a sacred gourd rattle. Then, in 1536, the foursome stumbled upon the Spanish expedition in northern Mexico. Three years later, after joining a new Spanish expedition, Estevan blazed a trail for Francisco Vásquez de Coronado's *entrada* (incursion) of 1540. In what would later be called Arizona, Estevan was selected to forge ahead into Zuñi country with Native American guides, in search of the fabled seven gold-filled cities of Cibola. His gift for acquiring native languages and his long experience with peoples of the vast territory north of New Spain made him the logical choice. But on this trip, Estevan met his death at the hands of Zuñi warriors, perhaps angry at his consorting with Zuñi women.

The four voyages of Christopher Columbus from 1492 to 1504, conducted on the eve of religious conflict and reformation in Europe, brought together people like Estevan and de Vaca from three previously unconnected continents. Together, they made a new world, their lives intersecting, their cultural attributes interacting. Here was the beginning of creating an Americas-wide cultural mosaic.

In this chapter, we follow the epoch-making voyages of Columbus, the arrival of Spanish conquistadors, their remarkable conquest of vast territories in Mesoamerica and the southern regions of North America, and the momentous effect of plants, animals, and germs as they traveled westward and eastward across the Atlantic.

We will also see how the phenomenal exploits of Hernán Cortés and Francisco Pizarro, and the discovery of immense quantities of silver, attracted the attention of other Europeans—first the French, then the Dutch and English. Latecomers in the race to exploit the treasures of the Americas while providing a place for the downtrodden and opportunity-blocked settlers of Europe, the English, as we will see, finally appeared on the scene in the Americas a century after the Columbian voyages. Their presence, while escalating the rivalries among emerging European nation–states as they jumped across the Atlantic, planted the seeds of an English-dominated American nation.

BREACHING THE ATLANTIC

When Ferdinand and Isabella married in 1469 to unite the independent states of Aragon and Castile, they launched this new Spanish nation into its golden age, beginning with the four voyages of Christopher Columbus to the Americas between 1492 and 1504. Meanwhile, the Portuguese extended their influence along the west coast of Africa and all the way to East Asia. In a short period, contact between peoples in different parts of the world increased markedly, shrinking the globe. Then came the great leap across the Atlantic Ocean, triggering global changes of unimaginable significance. Western Europeans were becoming the most dynamic force in the world and were on the verge of exerting a greater global influence than the people of any single region had ever done before.

The Columbian Voyages

Leading the way for Spain was an Italian sailor, Christopher Columbus. The son of a poor Genoese weaver, Columbus had married into a prominent family of Lisbon merchants, thus making important contacts at court. Celebrated for hundreds of years as a heroic discoverer and now often attacked as a ruthless exploiter of Native American peoples and lands, Columbus is best understood in the context of his own times—an age of great brutality and violence and also an age in which Catholic Spain was engaged in the final stages of expelling the Moorish people who had controlled southern Spain for centuries. Columbus's urge to explore was nourished by ideas and questions about the geographic limits of his world, and he was inspired by notions of contributing to the reconquest of Moorish Spain. The Latin inscription on the tomb of his monarchs, Isabella and Ferdinand, captures the missionary mood of the era: "Overthrowers of the Mahometan sect and repressors of heretical stubbornness."

Like many sailors, Columbus had listened to sea tales about lands to the west. He may have heard Icelandic sagas about the voyages of Leif Eriksson and several thousand Norse immigrants who had reached Newfoundland five centuries earlier during an era of global warming that allowed them to cross unexplored expanses of water. Other ideas circulated that the Atlantic Ocean stretched to India and eastern Asia. Could one reach the Indies by sailing west rather than by sailing east around Africa, as the Portuguese were attempting? Columbus hungered to know.

DOCUMENT

Privileges and Prerogatives Granted to Christopher Columbus

For nearly 10 years, Columbus unsuccessfully sought financial backing and royal sanction in Portugal for exploratory voyages. Many mocked his modest estimates of the distance westward from Europe to Japan, which he reckoned at 3,500 miles rather than contemporary estimates of 10,000 to 12,000 miles—far beyond the limit of small European ships, which could not carry enough food and water to keep sailors alive over such distances. Finally, in 1492, Spain's Queen Isabella commissioned him, and he sailed west with three tiny ships and a crew of about 90 men. In the fifth week at sea—longer than any European sailors had been out of the sight of land—mutinous rumblings swept through the crews. But Columbus pressed on. On the seventieth day, long after Columbus had calculated he would reach Japan, a lookout sighted land about 3,000 miles from Seville. On October 12, 1492, the sailors clambered ashore on a tiny island in the Bahamas (just east of Florida), which Columbus named San Salvador (Holy Savior). Grateful sailors "rendered thanks to Our Lord, kneeling on the ground, embracing it with tears of joy."

DOCUMENT

From the Journal of Christopher Columbus

Columbus's Second Voyage In this fanciful depiction of Columbus's second voyage across the Atlantic, a large fleet is propelled by oars as well as wind. Waving goodbye are Queen Isabella and King Ferdinand (upper right). A sea monster (upper left) may threaten the expedition. What is the meaning of the emblems on the flags flown on Columbus's ship (top center) and a priest's ship (center left)? *(Courtesy, American Antiquarian Society)*

Believing he had reached Asia, Columbus explored the island-speckled Caribbean for 10 weeks.

DOCUMENT
Columbus, Letter to Luis de Sant' Angel (1493)

After landing on a heavily populated island that he named Hispaniola (shared today by Haiti and the Dominican Republic) and on Cuba (which he thought was the Asian mainland), he set sail for Spain with cinnamon, coconuts, a bit of gold, and several kidnaped natives. Homeward bound, he penned a report of what he believed were his Asian discoveries: hospitable people, fertile soils, magnificent harbors, and gold-filled rivers. When he landed, his report was quickly distributed throughout Europe

Columbus's report brought him financing between 1494 and 1504 for three much larger expeditions to explore the newfound lands. The second voyage, carrying more than 1,200 Spaniards in 17 ships, initiated the first extended contact between Europeans and Native Americans. In an ominous display of what was to come, Columbus's men captured some 1,600 Taínos on Hispaniola and carried 550 of them back to Spain as slaves in 1495. Only 350 survived the stormy voyage to Spain. Here began the Atlantic slave trade that would alter the history of the world, though it began in the reverse direction of what would soon become its dominant flow. Although his discoveries seemed less significant than the Portuguese exploits in the South Atlantic, Columbus had led Spain to the threshold of a mighty empire. He died in 1506, to the end believing that he had found the water route to Asia.

While Spain began to project its power westward across the Atlantic, the Portuguese extended their influence in different directions—southward toward West Africa and then eastward to East Asia. In 1497, Vasco da Gama became the first European to sail around the cape of Africa; he picked up a Hindu pilot in East Africa who guided him all the way across the Indian Ocean in 1498. This allowed the Portuguese to colonize the Indian Ocean region and to reach modern Indonesia and southern China by 1513. By forcing trade concessions in the islands and coastal states of the East Indies, the Portuguese unlocked the fabulous Asian treasure houses that, since Marco Polo's time, had whetted European appetites. By 1500, they had captured control of the African gold trade monopolized for centuries by North African Muslims. The gleaming metal now traveled directly to Lisbon by sea rather than by camel caravan across the Sahara to North African Muslim ports such as Tunis and Algiers.

AMERICAN VOICES

Christopher Columbus, The Encounter with the Taíno

Columbus's journals describing his first encounters with Taíno people in the West Indies give insight into both the natives themselves as well as European perceptions of them. This description is from Columbus's first voyage to the Americas in 1492.

In order that they might feel great amity towards us, . . . [I] gave to some among them some red caps and some glass beads, which they hung round their necks. . . . At this they were greatly pleased and became so entirely our friends that it was a wonder to see. Afterwards they came swimming to the ships' boats, where we were, and brought us parrots and cotton thread in balls, and spears and many other things, and we exchanged for them other things, such as small glass beads and hawks' bells. . . . They all go naked as their mothers bore them, and the women also. . . . They do not bear arms, or know them, for I showed them swords and they took them by the blade and cut themselves out of ignorance. They have no iron. Their spears are certain reeds, without iron, and some of these have a fish tooth at the end, while others are pointed in various ways. They are generally fairly tall, good looking, well proportioned. . . . They should be good servants and of quick intelligence, . . . and I believe that would easily be made Christians, for it appeared to me that they had no creed.

- *In what ways does Columbus believe the native peoples of the Americas could be useful to Europeans?*

- *Do you think Columbus was right in believing that the Taínos would agree to be servants and adopt Christianity?*

Columbus's Four Voyages

The different courses taken by Columbus on his four Atlantic crossings were prompted by his desire to explore the island-rich Caribbean Sea. He departed on his second voyage only months after reaching Seville with news about the first epic voyage.

First voyage (1492–1493)
Second voyage (1493–1496), inset only
Third voyage (1498–1500), inset only
Fourth voyage (1502–1504)

Portuguese Voyages of Exploration

The four voyages by Portuguese sea captains between 1482 and 1500 show how those who sailed southward and eastward opened up distant parts of the world to Europeans in the same era when Columbus was sailing westward to the Americas. **Reflecting on the Past** Did Columbus share his Atlantic Ocean experiences with the Portuguese sea captains who reached the Indian Ocean? If so, how? What did Columbus learn from the Indian Ocean voyagers that helped him in his Atlantic Ocean voyages?

Religious Conflict During the Era of Reconnaissance

The expansion of Spain and Portugal into new areas of the world profoundly affected patterns of economic activity in Europe. Its commercial center now shifted away from the ports of the Mediterranean to the Atlantic ports facing the New World. But this fast-growing commercial power also had a deeply religious aspect since it occurred in the midst of, and magnified, an era of religious conflict and reformation.

Shortly after Columbus's Atlantic voyages, the people of western Europe were torn by religious schisms that escalated national rivalries. At the heart of Europe's religious strife was a continental movement to return the Christian church to the purity of early Christianity. Criticism of the worldliness of the Catholic church mounted during the Renaissance. Then a German monk, Martin Luther, became the

first to break successfully with Rome, initiating the Protestant Reformation that changed both theology and practice. As Protestant sects multiplied, Catholics began to reform their Church, and the two groups began a long battle for the souls of Europeans.

Luther was preparing for a legal career in 1505 when a bolt of lightning nearly struck him during a violent thunderstorm. Trembling with fear, he vowed to become a monk. But he lost faith in the power of the age-old rituals and sacraments of the Church—the Mass, confession, pilgrimages to holy places, even crusades against Muslim infidels. He believed that salvation came through an inward faith, or "grace," that God conferred on those he chose. Good works, Luther believed, did not earn grace but were the external evidence of grace won through faith. Insisting on "justification by faith," Luther had taken the revolutionary step of rejecting

Martin Luther The young Martin Luther pictured here had entered a monastery against his father's will at age 22. Twelve years later he began his revolt against the Catholic church and was excommunicated by Pope Leo X when Luther was 38. *(Cranach, Lucas, the Elder (1472–1553), Portrait of Martin Luther (1483–1546) (oil on panel), Germanisches National Museum, Nuremberg, Germany/Bridgeman Art Library)*

the Church's elaborate hierarchy of officials, who presided over the rituals intended to guide individuals to salvation.

Luther's doctrine of "justification by faith" did not threaten the Church until 1517, when he openly attacked the sale of "indulgences." By purchasing these indulgences, or pardons for sins, individuals had been told, they could reduce their time of penance (or that of a deceased relative) in purgatory. The pope used the money raised from the sale of indulgences for the building of St. Peter's in Rome. Luther drew up 95 arguments against indulgences and their sale and called on Christians to practice true repentance. Printing, invented less than 70 years earlier, allowed the rapid circulation of Luther's protest. The printed word and the ability to read it were to become revolutionary weapons throughout the world.

Luther's cry for reform soon inspired Germans of all classes. He denounced five of the seven sacraments of the Church, calling for a return to baptism

and communion alone. He attacked the upper clergy for luxurious living and urged priests, who were nominally celibate but often involved in irregular sexual relations, to marry respectably. He railed against the "detestable tyranny of the clergy over the laity" and called for a priesthood of all believers. He urged people to seek faith individually by reading the Bible, which he translated into German and made widely available for the first time in printed form. Most dangerously, he called on the German princes to assume control over religion in their states, directly challenging the authority of the pope in Rome and further undermining the functions of the clergy.

The basic issue dividing Catholics and Protestants thus centered on the source of religious authority. To Catholics, religious authority resided in the organized Church, headed by the pope. To Protestants, the Bible was the sole authority, and access to God's word or God's grace did not require the mediation of the Church.

Building on Luther's redefinition of Christianity, John Calvin, a Frenchman, brought new intensity and meaning to the Protestant Reformation. In 1536, at age 26, he published a ringing appeal to every Christian to form a direct, personal relationship with God. By Calvin's doctrine, God had saved a few souls at random before Creation and damned the rest. Human beings could not alter this predestination, but those who were good Christians must struggle to understand and accept God's saving grace if he chose to impart it. Without mediation of ritual or priest but by "straight-walking," one was to behave as one of God's elect, the "saints." This radical theology, even more insistent on individual godliness than Luther's, spread among all classes throughout Europe.

Calvin proposed reformed Christian communities structured around the elect few. To remake the corrupt world and follow God's will, communities of "saints" must control the state, rather than the other way around. Elected bodies of ministers and dedicated laymen, called presbyteries, were to govern the church, directing the affairs of society so that all, whether saved or damned, would work for God's ends.

Calvinism, as a fine-tuned system of self-discipline and social control, was first put into practice in the 1550s in the city–state of Geneva, between France and Switzerland. Here the brilliant and austere leader established his model Christian community. A council of 12 elders drove nonbelievers from the city, rigidly disciplined daily life, and stripped the churches of every appeal to the senses—images, music, incense, and colorful clerical gowns. Religious reformers from all over Europe flocked to the new holy community, and Geneva soon became the continental center of the reformist Christian movement. The city was, wrote John Knox of Scotland in 1556, "the most perfect school of Christ that ever was in the earth since the days of the apostles."

Calvin's radical program converted large numbers of people to Protestantism throughout Europe. Like Lutheranism, it recruited most successfully among the privileged classes of merchants, landowners, lawyers, and the nobility and among the rising middle class of master artisans and shopkeepers.

Sixteenth-century monarchs initially regarded attacks on the Catholic church with horror. But many local princes adopted some version of the reformed faith. The most important monarch to break with Catholicism was Henry VIII of England. When Pope Clement VII refused him permission to divorce and remarry, Henry declared himself head of the Church of England, or Anglican church. Although it retained many Catholic features, the Church of England moved further in a Protestant direction under Henry's son Edward. But when Mary, Henry's older Catholic daughter, came to the throne, she vowed to reinstate her mother's religion by suppressing Protestants. Her policy created Protestant martyrs, and many were relieved when she died in 1558, bringing Henry's younger Protestant daughter, Elizabeth, to the throne. During her long rule, the flinty Elizabeth steered Anglicanism along a middle course between the radicalism of Geneva and the Catholicism of Rome.

Some of the countries most affected by the Reformation—England, Holland, and France—were slow in trying to colonize the New World, so Protestantism did not gain as early a foothold in the Americas as Catholicism, which in Spain and Portugal remained almost immune from the Protestant Reformation. Thus, Catholicism swept across the Atlantic virtually unchallenged in the colonies of Spain and Portugal during the century after Columbus's voyages.

THE SPANISH CONQUEST OF AMERICA

From 1492 to 1518, Spanish and Portuguese explorers opened up vast parts of Asia and the Americas to European knowledge. Yet during this age of exploration, only modest attempts at settlement were made, mostly by the Spanish on the Caribbean islands of Cuba, Puerto Rico, and Hispaniola. The three decades after 1518, however, became an age of conquest. In some of the bloodiest chapters in recorded history, the Spanish nearly exterminated

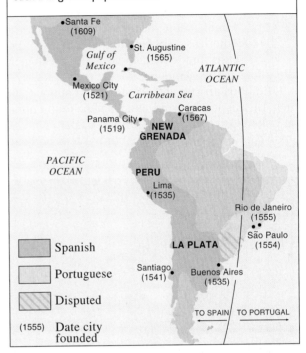

Treaty of Tordesillas

The Treaty of Tordesillas, promulgated by Pope Alexander VI, drew a line dividing all claims to land in the Americas between Portugal and Spain. Until the arrival of the Spanish and Portuguese in the Americas, never before had such small numbers of people established their dominance over such a large and populous area.

the native peoples of the Caribbean islands, toppled and plundered the great inland Aztec and Inca empires in Mexico and Peru, gained control of territories 10 times as large as their Spanish homeland, discovered fabulous silver mines, and built an oceanic trade. This short era of conquest had immense consequences for global history.

Portugal, meanwhile, concentrated mostly on building an eastward oceanic trade to southeastern Asia. In 1493, the pope had demarcated Spanish and Portuguese spheres of exploration in the Atlantic. Drawing a north–south line 100 leagues (about 300 miles) west of the Azores, the pope confined Portugal to the eastern side. One year later, in the Treaty of Tordesillas, Portugal obtained Spanish agreement to move the line 270 leagues farther west. These were some of the most significant lines ever drawn on a map. Nobody knew at the time that a large part of South America, as yet undiscovered by Europeans, bulged east of the new demarcation line and therefore fell within the Portuguese sphere. In time, Portugal would develop this region, Brazil, into one of the most profitable areas of the Americas.

Caribbean Experiments

Columbus's second Atlantic expedition in 1493 established the first Spanish colony in the New World on the island of Hispaniola (or Santo Domingo). The inhabitants, the Taíno, were the first New World indigenous people to encounter Europeans, and the encounter provided a preview of what would soon occur elsewhere in the Americas: subjugation, biological disease, and eventually immense ecological alterations to the island.

Columbus Landing at Hispaniola— Woodcut

Columbus arrived with 17 ships and about 1,200 men. He was seeking gold, and when he found none, he visited Cuba and then returned to Spain with six Taíno captives. What he left behind—seeds and cuttings for propagating European crops, livestock, and, hidden in sacks of seed, weeds—would prove to be the agents of ecological change. Meantime, once the Spanish saw that the island was teeming with as many as 3 million Taíno, they used military force to subdue them and turn them into a captive labor force. Similar conquests brought the people of Puerto Rico under Spanish control in 1508 and the people of Cuba in 1511. Spanish diseases soon touched off a biological holocaust that killed most of the Native Americans on these islands within a single generation. Some Taíno women married Spanish men and produced the first mestizo society in the Americas, but by 1550, the Taíno no longer existed as a distinct people.

Spanish immigration to the Caribbean islands was underway by 1510, closely followed by the importation of enslaved Africans who were put to work on the first sugar plantations created in the Americas. Over the course of the sixteenth century, about a quarter million Spaniards—most of them young, single men—emigrated to the Americas. But the islands dotting the Caribbean did not reach their potential as cash-crop economies until much later. For now, they served as laboratories for larger experiments in Mexico and South America, launching pads from which to mount invasions of the Mesoamerican mainland, and places to build fortified ports such as San Juan, Puerto Rico, and Havana, Cuba.

The Conquistadors' Onslaught at Tenochtitlán

Within a single generation of Columbus's death in 1506, Spanish conquistadors explored, claimed, and conquered most of South America except Brazil, as well as Central America and the southern parts of North America from present-day Florida to California. Led by audacious explorers and soldiers, and usually accompanied by enslaved Africans, they established Spanish authority and Catholicism over an area that dwarfed their homeland in size and population. They were motivated by religion, pride of nation, and dreams of personal enrichment. "We came here," explained one Spanish foot soldier, "to serve God and the king, and also to get rich."

In two bold and bloody strokes, the Spanish overwhelmed the ancient civilizations of the Aztecs and Incas. In 1519, hearing of a great empire in Mexico's interior, Cortés set out from Cuba, unauthorized by its governor, with 11 ships, 550 Spanish soldiers, several hundred native Cubans, some enslaved Africans, and well-fed mounts and pack horses. Reaching the coast of Mexico at Veracruz, he marched over rugged

A Taíno Carving   The crouching male figure shown here was fashioned from wood by a Taíno carver on Hispaniola (now the Dominican Republic). The stern visage may have been intended to warn Taínos not to drink the poisonous cassava juice extracted from the tuber that provided them with their main flour for bread. *(Nelson A. Rockefeller Collection/Boltin Picture Library)*

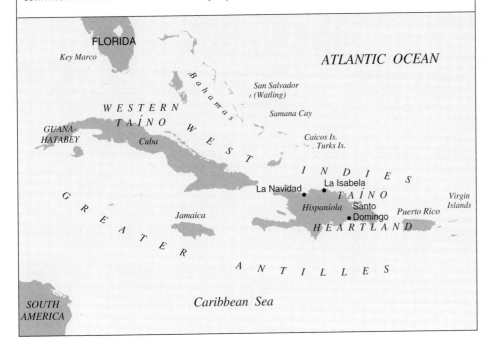

Greater Antilles in 1520

In the West Indies explored by Columbus, most of the inhabitants, as shown on this map, were Taíno. Columbus's knowledge that Marco Polo had found 7,448 islands dotting the China Sea convinced him that the Taíno were "the people of the Great Khan [of China]."

mountains to attack Tenochtitlán (now Mexico City), the capital of Moctezuma II's Aztec Empire. Seizing towns subject to Aztec rule, Cortés enlisted Native American support against their hated overlords. Following two years of sparring with the Aztecs and their subject people, Cortés assaulted Tenochtitlán and, after a four-month siege, dramatically brought the Aztec Empire to its knees.

The Spanish use of horses and firearms provided an important advantage; so did a murderous small-pox epidemic in 1520 that felled thousands of Aztecs. Support from local peoples oppressed by Moctezuma's tyranny was also important in over-throwing the Aztec ruler. Cortés was exceedingly lucky in being given a Nahuatl woman named Malinche, whom the Spanish would rename Doña Marina. Fluent in both Mayan and Nahuatl, the Aztec language, Malinche became Cortés's interpreter, giving him an advantage over the natives he encountered. Native peoples regarded Malinche as a traitor, and so her name passed down in the Mexican vocabulary as *malinchista*—a person betraying his or her people. In two years, the conquistadors had destroyed the empire that had brought Mesoamerica to the peak of thousands of years of development.

In the next few decades, foraying from the Valley of Mexico, the Spanish extended their dominion

Indian Resistance In this engraving by Theodor de Bry, who provided Europeans with some of their first images of what awaited them in the Americas, a Spanish attack on indigenous people provokes a spirited response from the heights of a spreading tree. What tactics do the native people employ? Were they likely to be effective? *(The Art Archive/Biblioteca Nazionale Marciana Venice/Dagli Orti)*

AMERICAN VOICES

Titu Cusi Yupangui, The Inca Attempt to Repulse the Spanish at Cuzco

In one of the rare native accounts of the Spanish conquest, Titu Cusi Yupanqui, son of the Inca ruler, describes his father's attempt to repulse the Spanish at Cuzco in 1537.

All the Spaniards were organized into squadrons in the plaza of Cuzco, their numbers not being known except that it is said that there were many men and that they had many blacks with them. Then there came into view all around Cuzco, a huge number of Indians, blowing whistles and trumpets and shouting loudly enough to terrify the whole world. In all, there were more than 400,000 Indians . . . . And when the Spaniards saw so many Indians following them, they turned their horses and made a circuit around a mountain that was called Queancalla, attacking the Indians in the rear where Vila Oma [an Inca commander] was, the latter having climbed up with all his men and fortified himself in the fortress of Cuzco . . . .

There they fought strongly and took the four gates of the fortress, while from the walls, which are very strong, the Indians threw down many boulders and launched arrows, darts, and lances, which badly injured the Spaniards. With these boulders, they killed Juan Pizarro and two blacks as well as many of the Indians who were helping them. When Vila Oma's men ran out of boulders and other ammunition, the Spaniards were able with divine assistance to enter the fortress and seize it, killing many of the Indians inside, while others threw themselves from the walls.

■ *How were several hundred Spaniards able to defeat so many Incas?*

■ *Why do you think the Inca leader believed Pizarro won the battle "with divine assistance"?*

The Decapitator
Anthropologists who discovered the Royal Tombs of the Moche people found many small sculptures of what they called the "Decapitator." Why do you think "Decapitator" replicas are so popular today in museum shops? *(Photograph by Susan Einstein, Courtesy of UCLA Fowler Museum of Cultural History)*

over the Mayan people of the Yucatán, Honduras, and Guatemala. Disease was always their forerunner, mowing down the native peoples even before the Spanish arrived.

In the second conquest, Francisco Pizarro, marching from Panama through the jungles of

Ecuador and into the towering Andes mountains of Peru with a mere 168 men, most of them not even soldiers, toppled the Inca Empire. Like the Aztecs, the populous Incas lived in a highly organized social system. But also like the Aztecs, they were riddled by smallpox and weakened by violent internal divi-

The Inca Empire in 1500

The Inca Empire in 1500 was gigantic, extending along the west coast of South America for some 2,600 miles and containing an estimated 14 million people. Only the Ottoman and Chinese empires in the Old World controlled more land than the Inca.

Guaca
Quito
Ingapirca (Hatun Cañar)
Tomebamba (Cuenca)
Tumbes
MOCHE
Cajamarca
REGION
Chiquitoy
Viejo
Chan Chan
Huánuco Pampa
Jauja
Pachacamac
Inkawasi
Tambo Colorado
Ica
Nazca
Atico

Orinoco R.
Magdalena R.
Japurá R.
Amazon R.
Juruá R.
Madeira R.

SOUTH
AMERICA

Machu Picchu
Cuzco
Vilcas Huaman
Lake Titicaca
Chucuito
Chuquiabo
(La Paz)
Tiwanaku
Paria

Pica
Tuplza
Catarpe
Tilcara
Mt. Acay
La Paya
Pucara de
Andagala
Chilecito

COLOMBIA
Equator
ECUADOR
SOUTH
AMERICA
PERU
BOLIVIA
CHILE
ARGENTINA

Ranchillos
Santiago

Paraná R.

PACIFIC
OCEAN

ATLANTIC
OCEAN

*Falkland
Islands*

▢ Inca Empire
● Inca town
— Inca road

*Tierra del
Fuego*

sions. These conditions ensured Pizarro's success in capturing their capital at Cuzco in 1533, and soon other gold- and silver-rich Inca cities. Further expeditions into Chile, New Granada (Colombia), Argentina, and Bolivia in the 1530s and 1540s brought under Spanish control an empire larger than any in the Western world since the fall of Rome.

By 1550, Spain had overwhelmed the major centers of native population in the Americas. Spanish ships carried gold, silver, dyewoods, and sugar east across the Atlantic and transported African slaves, colonizers, and finished goods west. In a brief half century, Spain had exploited the advances in geographic knowledge and maritime technology of its Portuguese rivals and brought into harsh but profitable contact with each other the people of three continents. The triracial character of the Americas was already firmly established by 1600.

For nearly a century after Columbus's voyages, Spain enjoyed almost unchallenged dominion over the fabulous hemisphere newly revealed to Europeans. Greedy buccaneers of various nations snapped at the heels of homeward-bound Spanish treasure fleets, but this was only a nuisance. France tried to contest Spanish or Portuguese control by planting small settlements in Brazil and Florida in the mid-sixteenth century, but these were quickly wiped out. England remained island-bound until the 1580s. Until the seventeenth century, only Portugal, which staked out important claims in Brazil in the 1520s, challenged Spanish domination of the Americas.

The Great Dying

Spanish conquest of major areas of the Americas triggered a biological disaster, setting in motion one of the most dramatic population declines in recorded history. The population of the Americas on the eve of European arrival had grown to an estimated 50 to 70 million. In central Mexico, the highlands of Peru, and certain Caribbean islands, population density exceeded that of most of Europe. Though less populous than the peoples of the Americas, the European colonizers had one extraordinary advantage: over the centuries Europeans had built up immunities to nearly every lethal microbe that infects humans on an epidemic scale. Such biological defenses did not eliminate smallpox, measles, diphtheria, and other afflictions, but they limited their deadly power. Geographic isolation, however, had kept these diseases from the peoples of the Americas. So, too, did their lack of large domesticated animals, which

AUDIO

Two-Step:
Inform Your
Grandma

were the major disease carriers. Arriving Europeans therefore unknowingly encountered a huge component of the human race that was utterly defenseless against the "domesticated" infections the Europeans and their animals carried.

The results were catastrophic. In 1518, the smallpox virus erupted on Hispaniola. The Spanish priest

DOCUMENT

Bartolomé de Las Casas, "Of the Island of Hispaniola" (1542)

Bartolomé de las Casas recorded that "of that immensity of people that was on this island and which we have seen with our own eyes" only about a thousand were spared among a population of between 1 and 3 million that had existed when Columbus arrived. Of some 15 million inhabitants in central Mexico before Cortés's arrival, nearly half perished within 15 years. In the Valley of Mexico, where the Aztec capital of Tenochtitlán stood, the estimated population was 1.5 to 3 million before the conquistadors arrived. Eighty years later, in 1600, only 70,000 native people could be counted.

Demographic disaster also struck the populous Inca peoples of the Peruvian Andes, speeding ahead of Pizarro's conquistadors. Smallpox "spread over the people as great destruction," an old Native American told a Spanish priest in the 1520s. "There was great havoc. Very many died of it. They could not stir, they could not change position, nor lie on one side, nor face down, nor on their backs. And if they stirred, much did they cry out. . . . And very many starved; there was death from hunger, [for] none could take

care of [the sick]." Such terrifying sickness led many natives to believe that their gods had failed them, and this belief left them ready to acknowledge the greater power of the Spaniards' God.

In most areas where Europeans intruded in the hemisphere for the next three centuries, the catastrophe repeated itself. Every European participated accidentally in the spread of disease that typically eliminated, within a few generations, at least two-thirds of the native population. The first historian to appreciate the role played by disease in the Spanish conquest, writing more than a half century ago, accurately described the role of the pathogens unleashed in the

MAP

Native American Population Loss,

New World: these "forerunners of civilization, the companions of Christianity, the friends of the invader" were "more terrible than the conquistadors on horseback, more deadly than sword and gunpowder, they made the conquest . . . a walkover compared with what it would have been without their aid."

The enslavement and brutal treatment of the native people intensified the lethal effects of European diseases. Having conquered the Incas and Aztecs, the Spanish enslaved thousands of native people and assigned them work regimens that severely weakened their resistance to disease. Bartolomé de las Casas and some other priests waged lifelong campaigns to reduce the exploitation of the Native Americans, but they had only limited power to control the actions of their colonizing compatriots.

The Columbian Exchange

Much more than lethal microbes crossed the Atlantic with the Spaniards as they conquered the Caribbean islands and then large parts of Central and South America. With them came animal and plant life that altered ecosystems and transformed the landscape. Westward-bound Spanish ships brought wheat, rye, barley, oats, and other European grains; fruits such as cherries, peaches, pears, lemons, oranges, melons, and grapes; vegetables such as radishes, salad greens, and onions. All of these, unknown in the New World, perpetuated European cuisine and were gradually incorporated into Native American diets. Even more important were the herd animals of the Europeans. Cattle, goats, horses, burros, pigs, and sheep caused the greatest transformation, flourishing as they grazed in the vast grasslands of the Americas safe from the large carnivores that attacked them in the Old World. Cattle reproduced so rapidly that feral livestock

IMAGE

Cattle Arrive in the New World

Smallpox Victims   Aztec victims of smallpox, contracted during Cortés's invasion of Tenochtitlán in the 1520s. The woodcut is from the sixteenth-century work *Historia de las Casas de Nueva Espana* by Fray Bernardo de Sahagun. According to the account of the disease, "The sores were so terrible that the victims could not lie face down, . . . nor move from one side to the other. And when they tried to move even a little, they cried out in agony." *Firenze, Biblioteca Medicea Laurenziana (ms. Med. Palat. 220, c. 460v) Su concessione del Ministero per i Beni e le Attivitá Culturali Évietata ogni ulteriore riproduzione con qualsiasi mezzo.*

ANALYZING HISTORY

The Columbian Exchange

In the last several millennia of world history, the Columbian Exchange, as historian Alfred Crosby has termed it, stands as the most significant geographical rearrangement of organisms with profound environmental and human consequences.

REFLECTING ON THE PAST   Can you determine why inhabitants of the Americas had few domesticated animals before the arrival of Europeans? Why were infectious diseases rare in the pre-Columbian Americas? What is the relationship between the lack of domesticated animals and the general absence of infectious diseases?

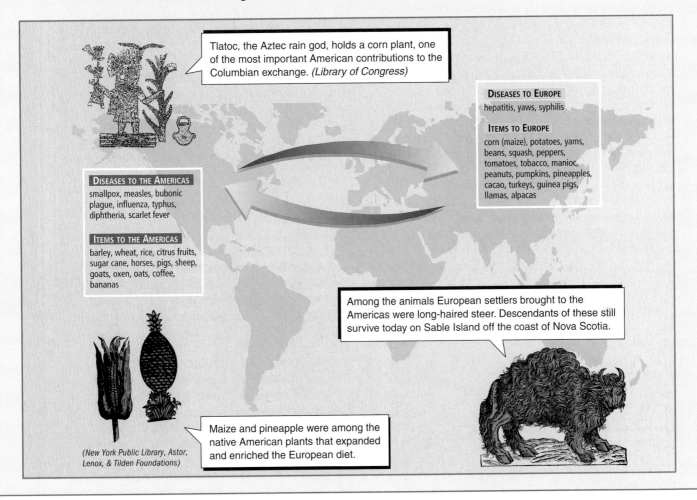

Tlatoc, the Aztec rain god, holds a corn plant, one of the most important American contributions to the Columbian exchange. *(Library of Congress)*

DISEASES TO EUROPE
hepatitis, yaws, syphilis

ITEMS TO EUROPE
corn (maize), potatoes, yams, beans, squash, peppers, tomatoes, tobacco, manioc, peanuts, pumpkins, pineapples, cacao, turkeys, guinea pigs, llamas, alpacas

DISEASES TO THE AMERICAS
smallpox, measles, bubonic plague, influenza, typhus, diphtheria, scarlet fever

ITEMS TO THE AMERICAS
barley, wheat, rice, citrus fruits, sugar cane, horses, pigs, sheep, goats, oxen, oats, coffee, bananas

Among the animals European settlers brought to the Americas were long-haired steer. Descendants of these still survive today on Sable Island off the coast of Nova Scotia.

(New York Public Library, Astor, Lenox, & Tilden Foundations)

Maize and pineapple were among the native American plants that expanded and enriched the European diet.

swarmed across the countryside, often increasing tenfold in three or four years. In time they ate themselves out of their favorable environment, stripping away plant life, which soon led to topsoil erosion and eventually to desertification.

Pigs were even harder on the environment. Reproducing at staggering rates, they tore into the manioc tubers and sweet potatoes in the Greater Antilles where Columbus first introduced eight of them in 1493. They devoured guavas and pineapples,

ravaged lizards and baby birds, and stripped the land clean. Similar swine explosions occurred on the mainland of Mexico and Central America, where along with cattle they devastated the grasslands. Old World hoofed animals took to the savannas and meadows of the Americas "like Adam and Eve returning to Eden," as the main historian of the Columbian Exchange explains.

Spaniards brought the flora and fauna that they prized most to the Americas, but also traveling with them were unwelcome passengers. Among the most destructive were weeds, their seeds hidden in sacks of fruit and vegetable seed. Once they took root, weeds proved hard to control in an age lacking the chemicals used today. Therefore, invasive weeds, including clover that crowded out native flora, entered the Americas. So did rats and rabbits, pesky stowaways that reproduced as fast as pigs. They decimated native small animals, spread diseases, and added a new dimension to the human struggle for life.

New World Plants

The "Columbian Exchange" had its eastbound dimension but mainly this advantaged European, African, and eventually Asian recipients. Syphilis and yaws, diseases apparently unknown in Europe until about 1500, were afflictions of the Americas that created misery in the Old World as they traveled eastward, although they were never remotely on the scale of the scathing smallpox epidemics. On the other hand, table foods from the Americas such as pumpkins, pineapples, squash, peanuts, and beans enriched the European diet. So did guinea pigs and turkeys. Tomatoes, known as "love apples" for their supposed stimulus to sexual potency, became a staple of European cuisine. Llamas and alpacas produced wool for warmth. Over time, the most important food transfers proved to be maize and potatoes. The potato, with its fundamental advantage over Old World grains, slowly spread from its point of introduction in northern Spain northward and eastward through Europe. From the North Sea to the Ural Mountains, farmers on the northern European plain learned slowly that by substituting potatoes for rye—the only grain that would thrive in the short and often rainy summers—they could quadruple their yield in calories per acre. The transition to the New World potato allowed for population growth and strengthened the sinew of Europe's diet.

Likewise, Native American maize (to be renamed corn) could be cultivated in mountain valleys, such as in Spain, Greece, and the Balkans, where it became the staple grain. Maize also reached Africa and China as early as the 1550s; the New World sweet potato also made its entry into China.

Aztec Corn Myth In this pictograph of an ancient Aztec myth, maize plays a central role; the first female spreads kernels of maize, or corn, while her husband tries to divine the future. Can you decipher some of the border figures? *(Bibliothèque de l'Assemblée Nationale, Paris [Plate No. 20, Codex Borbonicus])*

Silver, Sugar, and Their Consequences

The small amount of gold that Columbus brought home from the Caribbean islands raised hopes that this metal, which along with silver formed the standard of wealth in Europe, might be found in the transatlantic paradise. Though some gold was gleaned from the Caribbean islands and later from Colombia, Brazil, and Peru, it would be more than three centuries before anyone would discover gold in windfall quantities in North America.

Silver was another matter. It proved most abundant—so plenteous, in fact, that when bonanza strikes were made in Bolivia in 1545 and then in northern Mexico in the 1550s, much of Spain's New World enterprise focused on its extraction. For most of the sixteenth century, the Spanish Empire in America was a vast mining community. Sixteen thousand tons of silver were scooped from Spain's colonies in the Americas between 1500 and 1650.

West Indies Slave Labor In this 1823 lithograph by William Clark, we see West Indies gang laborers preparing the ground for sugar planting. A black overseer directs the workforce of both women and men. Has the artist romanticized slave labor in the cane fields? If so, in what ways? *(By permission of the British Library, Shelfmark 1786.c.9)*

Native people, along with some African slaves, provided the first labor supply for the mines. The Spaniards permitted the highly organized Native American societies to maintain control of their own communities but exacted from them huge labor drafts for mining. At Potosí, in Bolivia, 58,000 workers labored at elevations of up to 13,000 feet to extract the precious metal from a fabulous sugarloaf "mountain of silver." The town's population reached 120,000 by 1570, making it much larger than any in Spain at the time. Thousands of other workers toiled in the mines of Zacatecas, Taxco, and Guanajuato. By 1660, they had scooped up more than 7 million pounds of silver from the Americas, tripling the entire European supply.

The flood of bullion from the Americas to Europe triggered profound changes. It financed further conquests and settlement in Spain's American empire, spurred long-distance trading in East Asian silks and spices, and capitalized agricultural development in the New World of sugar, coffee, cacao, and indigo. The bland diet of Europeans gradually changed as items such as sugar and spices, previously luxury articles for the wealthy, became accessible to ordinary people.

The enormous increase of silver in circulation in Europe after the mid-sixteenth century also caused a "price revolution." The supply of silver increased faster than the demand for goods and services that Europeans could produce, so the value of silver coins declined. Put differently, prices rose, doubling between 1550 and 1600 in many parts of Europe and rising another 50 percent in the next half century. Farmers got more for their produce, and merchants thrived on the increased circulation of goods. Artisans, laborers, and landless agricultural workers (the vast majority of the population) suffered when wages did not keep up with rising prices. As one of the first English immigrants to America lamented, skilled artisans "live in such a low condition as is little better than beggary."

Overall, the price revolution brought a major redistribution of wealth and increased the number of people in western Europe living at the margins of society. It thus built up the pressure to immigrate to the Americas, Europe's new frontier. At the same time, rising prices stimulated commercial development. Expansion overseas fed expansion at home and intensified changes toward capitalist modes of production already underway in the sixteenth century.

While the Spaniards organized their overseas empire around the extraction of silver from the highlands of Mexico, Bolivia, and Peru, the Portuguese staked their future on sugar production in Brazil. Spanish colonial agriculture supplied the huge mining centers, but the Portuguese, using cultivation techniques developed earlier on their Atlantic islands off the coast of Africa, produced sugar for export markets.

Whereas Spanish mining operations rested primarily on the backs of the native labor force, the lowland Portuguese sugar planters scattered the indigenous people and replaced them with platoons of African slaves. By 1570, this regimented workforce was producing nearly 6 million pounds of sugar annually; by the 1630s, output had risen to 32 million pounds per year. High in calories but low in protein, the sweet "drug food" revolutionized the tastes of millions of Europeans and stimulated the oceanic transport of millions of African slaves across the Atlantic.

From Brazil, sugar production jumped to the Caribbean islands. Here, in the early seventeenth century, England, Holland, and France challenged Spain and Portugal. Once they secured footholds in the West Indies, Spain's enemies stood at the gates of the Hispanic New World empire. Through contraband trading with Spanish settlements, piratical attacks on Spanish treasure fleets, and outright seizure of Spanish-controlled islands, the Dutch, French, and English in the seventeenth century gradually sapped imperial Spain's strength.

Spain's Northern Frontier

The crown jewels of Spain's New World empire were silver-rich Mexico and Peru, with the islands and coastal fringes of the Caribbean representing lesser, yet valuable, gemstones. Distinctly third in importance were the northern borderlands of New Spain—the present-day Sun Belt of the United States. Yet the early Spanish influence in Florida, the Gulf region, Texas, New Mexico, Arizona, and California indelibly marked the history of the United States. Spanish control of the southern fringes of North America began in the early 1500s and did not end for three centuries, when Mexico wrested independence from Spain in 1821. Far outlasting Spanish rule were the plants and animals they introduced to North America, ranging from sheep, cattle, and horses to various grasses and weeds that crowded out native plants.

Horses were of special importance. They had arrived with Columbus in 1493 but did not thrive in the tropical climate of the Greater Antilles. But once the Spanish reached the three great temperate grasslands of the Americas—the Argentine pampas, the Venezuelan llanos, and the North American Great Plains stretching all the way from southern Canada to northern Mexico—horses flourished. Flourishing with them were cattle, which were the foundation of the Spanish economy on their northern frontier. Horses and cattle were both tough on the grasslands, destroying ground cover and clearing the way for an invasion of European weeds and less nutritious grasses.

Spanish explorers began charting southeastern North America in the early sixteenth century. First came Juan Ponce de León's expeditions to Florida in 1515 and 1521 and Lucas Vasquez de Ayllón's short-lived settlement at Winyah Bay in South Carolina in 1526. For the next half century, Spaniards planted small settlements along the coast as far north as the Chesapeake Bay, where their temporary encampment included enslaved Africans. The Spanish traded some with the natives, but the North American coast, especially Florida, was chiefly important to the Franciscan friars, who attempted to gather the local tribes into mission villages and convert them to Catholicism.

The Spanish made several attempts to bring the entire Gulf of Mexico region under their control. From 1539 to 1542, Hernán de Soto, a veteran of Pizarro's conquest of the Incas a few years before, led a military expedition deep into the homelands of the Creek and Choctaw. Yearning to find another Tenochtitlán or Cuzco, he explored westward from Tampa Bay across the Mississippi River to present-day Arkansas and eastern Texas. But he found only

Spanish Vaqueros
James Walker's *Vaqueros in a Horse Corral* speaks beautifully of the Spanish origins of the cowboy in the American West. Can you identify Spanish elements in the vaqueros' outfits? (*James Walker*, Vaqueros in a Horse Corral *1877, Gilcrease Museum of Art, Tulsa, OK [01236.1480]*)

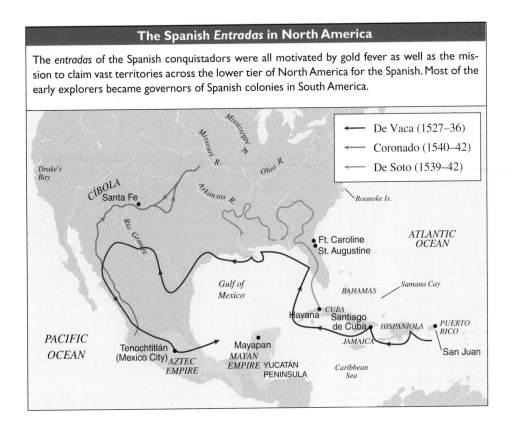

The Spanish *Entradas* in North America

The *entradas* of the Spanish conquistadors were all motivated by gold fever as well as the mission to claim vast territories across the lower tier of North America for the Spanish. Most of the early explorers became governors of Spanish colonies in South America.

De Vaca (1527–36)
Coronado (1540–42)
De Soto (1539–42)

agricultural-based tribes, influenced by Mayan and Aztec people, who lived in sizable villages and built ceremonial pyramids.

De Soto's expedition could not provide what the Spanish most wanted—gold. Pillaging thickly settled native villages for furs and freshwater pearls, seizing food supplies, and enslaving Native Americans to serve as human pack animals, de Soto's men cut a brutal swath as far north as North Carolina and as far west as Arkansas. Death preceded them and intensified in their wake. De Soto never conquered the peoples he encountered; instead, the environment and tenacious Native American resistance conquered him. After seeing their leader die a miserable death, de Soto's men and enslaved Africans limped back to Mexico with what was left of their forces. Little could the English know that their Spanish enemies were paving the way for them in North America's southeastern sector by spreading lethal microbes that devastated Native American societies and breaking up the great chiefdoms of the lower South.

In 1559, Spaniards again marched northward from Mexico in an attempt to establish their authority in the lower Gulf region. Everywhere they went, they enslaved Native Americans to carry provisions. In 1565, they sought to secure Florida. Building a fort at St. Augustine, they evicted their French rivals at Fort Caroline, 40 miles to the north. St. Augustine

became the center of Spain's northeastern frontier, and Florida remained a Spanish possession for more than two centuries.

The Southwest became a more important region of early Spanish activity in North America. Francisco Vásquez de Coronado explored the region from 1540 to 1542, leading an expedition of several hundred Spanish soldiers, a number of Africans, and a baggage train of some 1,300 friendly Native Americans, servants, and slaves. Coronado never found the Seven Cities of Cíbola, reported by earlier Spanish explorers to be fabulously decorated in turquoise and gold; but he opened much of Arizona, New Mexico, and Colorado to eventual Spanish control, happened upon the Grand Canyon, and probed as far north as the Great Plains. His interior explorations, together with the nearly simultaneous expedition of de Soto in the Southeast, established Spanish claims to the southern latitudes of North America.

The Southwest, like Florida and the Gulf region, had no golden cities. In New Mexico, however, Franciscan friars tried to harvest souls. A half century after Coronado's exploratory intrusions, Don Juan de Oñate led 129 soldiers, about 500 Spanish settlers, and 10 Franciscan friars up the Rio Grande in 1598 to find some 60,000 Pueblo gathered in scores of settled towns where for centuries they had been practicing agriculture. For the next 80 years, the Franciscans tried to graft Catholicism onto Pueblo culture by building churches on the edges of ancient native villages. As long as the priests were content to overlay Native American culture with a veneer of Catholicism, they encountered little resistance because the Pueblo found advantage in Spanish military protection from their Apache enemies and valued access to mission livestock and grain during years of drought. So outwardly they professed the Christian faith, while secretly adhering to their traditional religion. Meanwhile, Spanish settlers—never more than a thousand in 1680—carved out cattle ranches and built small towns.

ENGLAND LOOKS WEST

By the time England awoke to the promise of the New World, Spain and Portugal were firmly entrenched there. But by the late sixteenth century, the conditions necessary to propel England overseas had ripened. During the early seventeenth century, the English, as well as the Dutch and French, began overtaking their southern European rivals. For the English, the first challenge came in the Caribbean, where between 1604 and 1640 the English planted several small colonies producing tobacco and later sugar. Few guessed that some secondary and relatively unproductive settlements then being planted on the North American mainland would in time be among England's most prized possessions.

England Challenges Spain

England was the slowest of the Atlantic powers to begin exploring and colonizing the New World. Although far more numerous than the Portuguese, the English in the fifteenth century had little experience with long-distance trade and few contacts with cultures beyond their island aside from the French, against whom they had waged the Hundred Years' War (1337–1453). Only the voyages of John Cabot (the Genoa-born Giovanni Caboto) gave England any claim in the New World sweepstakes. But England never followed up on Cabot's voyages to Newfoundland and Nova Scotia—the first northern crossing of the Atlantic since the Vikings.

DOCUMENT

Henry VII, Letters of Patent Granted to John Cabot

At first, England's interest in the far side of the Atlantic centered primarily on fish. This high-protein food, basic to the European diet, was the gold of the North Atlantic. Early North Atlantic explorers found the waters off Newfoundland and Nova Scotia teeming with fish—not only the ordinary cod but also the delectable salmon. In the 1520s, it was the fishermen of Portugal, Spain, and France, more than those of England, who began making annual spring trips to the offshore fisheries. Not until the end of the century would the French and English drive Spanish and Portuguese fishermen from the Newfoundland banks.

Exploratory voyages along the eastern coast of North America hardly interested the English. It was for the French that Cartier and Verrazano sailed between 1524 and 1535. They sought straits so that India-bound ships could sail around the northern land mass (still thought to be a large island). The two navigators encountered many Indian tribes, charted the coastline from the St. Lawrence River to the Carolinas, and realized that the northern latitudes of North America were suitable for settlement. However, Europeans were not yet interested in settlements, so their discoveries had no immediate value.

DOCUMENT

Jacques Cartier, First Contact with the Indians (1554)

Changes in the late sixteenth century, however, propelled the English overseas. The rising production of woolen cloth, a mainstay of the English economy, had sent merchants scurrying for new markets after 1550. Their success in establishing trading companies in Russia, Scandinavia, the Middle East, and India vastly widened England's commercial orbit and raised hopes for developing still other spheres. Meanwhile, population growth and rising prices depressed the economic conditions of ordinary people and made them look across the ocean for new opportunities.

The cautious policy of Queen Elizabeth I, who ruled from 1558 to 1603, did not at first promote overseas colonies. She favored Protestantism as a vehicle of national independence rather than a missionary project. Ambitious and talented, she had to contend with Philip II, the fervently Catholic king of Spain. Regarding Elizabeth as a Protestant heretic, Philip plotted incessantly against her. The pope added to Catholic–Protestant tensions in England by excommunicating Elizabeth in 1571 and absolving her subjects from paying her allegiance—in effect, inciting them to overthrow her.

The smoldering conflict between Catholic Spain and Protestant England broke into open flames in 1587. Two decades before, Philip II had sent 20,000 Spanish soldiers into his Netherlands provinces to suppress Protestantism. Then, in 1572, he had helped arrange the massacre of thousands of French Protestants. By the 1580s, Elizabeth was providing covert aid to the Protestant Dutch revolt

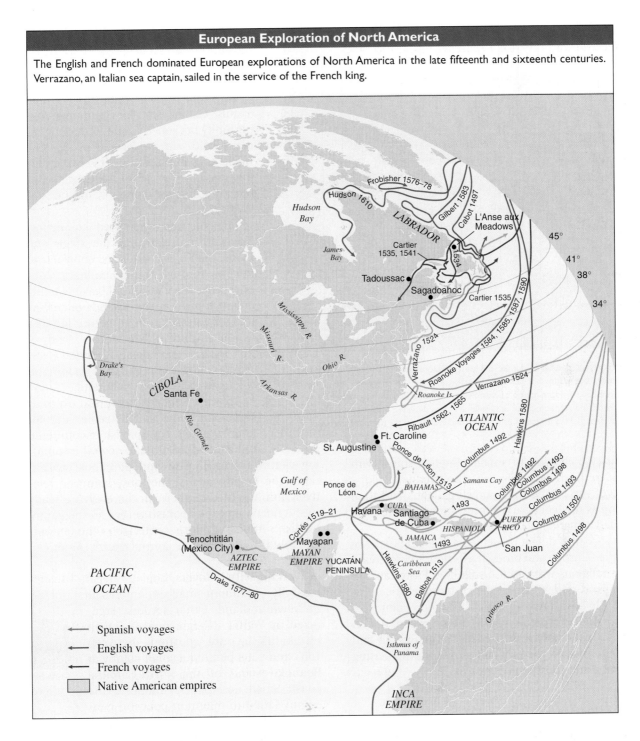

European Exploration of North America

The English and French dominated European explorations of North America in the late fifteenth and sixteenth centuries. Verrazano, an Italian sea captain, sailed in the service of the French king.

against Catholic rule. Philip vowed to crush the rebellion and decided as well to launch an attack on England to wipe out this growing center of Protestant power.

Elizabeth fed the flames of the international Catholic–Protestant conflict in 1585 by sending 6,000 English troops to aid the Dutch Protestants. A year later, the colorful sea dog Francis Drake, who had been raiding Spanish shipping on the coasts of Mexico and Peru, bombarded Spanish St. Augustine

in Florida, looted the city, and touched off an epidemic that the Florida Indians attributed to the "English God that made them die so fast." Two years later, infuriated by Drake's piracy and support of Protestant rebels in the Netherlands, Philip dispatched a Spanish armada of 130 ships carrying 30,000 men and 2,400 artillery pieces. Sails blazing with crusaders' crosses, the fleet set forth to conquer Elizabeth's England. For two weeks in the summer of 1588, a sea battle raged off the English coast.

Queen Elizabeth I   Under the leadership of Elizabeth I, here displayed in royal finery and resting her hand on the globe, England challenged and ultimately overturned Spain's domination of worldwide sea trade. Behind the placid face was a determined and sometimes ruthless ruler. What is depicted outside the window? *(By kind permission of the Marquess of Tavistock and Trustees of the Bedford Estate)*

A motley collection of smaller English ships, with Drake in the lead, defeated the armada, sinking many of the lumbering Spanish galleons and then retiring as the legendary "Protestant wind" blew the crippled armada into the North Sea.

The Spanish defeat prevented a crushing Catholic victory in Europe and brought a temporary stalemate in the religious wars. It also solidified Protestantism in England and brewed a fierce nationalistic spirit there. Shakespeare's love of "this other Eden, this demi-paradise" spread among the people; and with Spanish naval power checked, both the English and the Dutch found the seas more open to their rising maritime and commercial interests.

The Westward Fever

In the last decades of the sixteenth century, the idea of overseas expansion began to capture the imagination of important elements of English society. Urging them on were two Richard Hakluyts, uncle and nephew. In the 1580s and 1590s, they devoted themselves to advertising the advantages of colonizing across the Atlantic. For nobles at court, colonies offered new baronies, fiefdoms, and estates. For merchants, the New World promised exotic produce to sell at home and a new outlet for English cloth. For militant Protestant clergy, there awaited a continent filled with heathens to be saved from devilish savagery and Spanish Catholicism. For commoners, opportunity beckoned in the form of bounteous land, almost for the taking. The Hakluyts' pamphlets publicized the idea that the time was ripe for England to break the Iberian monopoly on the New World riches.

England first attempted colonizing, however, in Ireland. In the 1560s and 1570s, the English extended control over Ireland through brutal military conquest. The emerald island became a turbulent frontier for thousands of career-hungry younger sons of gentry families as well as landless commoners. Many of the leaders of England's initial New World colonization got their training in subjugating "savages" in Ireland.

The first English attempts at overseas settlement were small, feeble, and ill-fated. Whereas the Spanish encountered unheard-of wealth and scored astounding victories over ancient and populous civilizations, the English at first met only failure in relatively thinly settled lands. With the French already to the north, and the Spanish settled in the south, English settlement efforts centered on the temperate middle zone of the central North American coast.

Working with leftovers, England began—unsuccessfully—to mount small settlements, first in 1583 in Newfoundland. Other settlers, organized by Walter Raleigh, one of Queen Elizabeth's favorite courtiers, between 1585 and 1588 planted a small colony at Roanoke Island, off the North Carolina coast. Small and poorly financed, the colony failed to maintain peaceful relations with the local natives. By the time a relief expedition arrived in 1591, the Roanoke colonists had vanished. It was an ominous beginning for England's overseas ambitions.

Discouraged Englishmen waited another generation before trying again. Small groups of men sent out to establish a tiny colony in Guiana, off the South American coast, failed in 1604 and 1609. Another group, set down in Maine in 1607, lasted

DOCUMENT

Thomas Harriot, The Algonquian Peoples of the Atlantic Coast

A Blue-Skinned Pict Male John White, whose watercolors on Roanoke Island provided fascinating ethnographic detail of Native Americans, also painted this mythical Pict male with blue skin to accompany his Roanoke drawings. The Picts were an ancient people—the ancestors of seventeenth-century Britons. White pictured them as tattooed, savage, bloodthirsty people. Here a male holds the head of a slain enemy. If Britons could evolve from such savages, suggested White, then the natives of North America could be patiently schooled in English ways. (© British Museum [1906-5-9-1(24)/ PS211689])

only one year. Although they would flourish in time, even the colonies founded in Virginia in 1607 and Bermuda in 1612 floundered badly for several decades.

English merchants, sometimes supported by gentry investors, undertook these first tentative efforts, risking capital in the hope of realizing profits similar to their other overseas commercial ventures. The Spanish and Portuguese colonizing efforts were national enterprises that were sanctioned, capitalized, and coordinated by the crown. By contrast, English colonies had their queen's blessing, but were private ventures without royal subsidies or naval protection.

English colonization could not succeed until these first merchant adventurers solicited the wealth and support of the prospering middle class. This support grew steadily in the first half of the seventeenth century, but even then investors were drawn far more to the quick profits promised in West Indian tobacco production than to the uncertainties of mixed farming, lumbering, and fishing on the North American mainland. In the 1620s and 1630s, most of the English capital invested overseas went into establishing tobacco colonies in tiny Caribbean islands, including St. Christopher (1624), Barbados (1627), Nevis (1628), Montserrat (1632), and Antigua (1632).

DOCUMENT
Thomas Harriot, On Tobacco (1588)

Apart from the considerable financing required, the vital element in launching a colony was a suitable body of colonists. The changing agricultural system, combined with population growth and the unrelenting increase in prices caused by the influx of New World silver, produced a surplus of unskilled labor, squeezed many small producers, and spread poverty and crime. By the late 1500s, wrote Richard Hakluyt, the roads were swarming with "valiant youths rusting and hurtful for lack of employment," and the prisons were "daily pestered and stuffed full of them." Pushed in response to these conditions, about 80,000 streamed out of England between 1600 and 1640, at the same time that dreams of opportunity and adventure pulled them westward. In the next 20 years, another 80,000 departed.

A generation later, beginning in 1618, the renewed European religious wars between Protestants and Catholics devastated the continental market for English woolen cloth, bringing unemployment and desperate conditions to the textile regions. Probably half of England's households lived on the edge of poverty. "This land grows weary of her inhabitants," wrote John Winthrop of East Anglia, "so as a man, which is the most precious of all creatures, is near more vile among us than a horse or a sheep."

Religious persecution and political considerations intensified the pressure to emigrate from England in the early seventeenth century. For the first time in their history, large numbers of English people were abandoning their island homeland to carry their destinies to new frontiers. The largest number went to the West Indies, about one-third migrated to the North American mainland, and fewer went to the plantations in northern Ireland.

The East Coast of North America John White's chart, from the Chesapeake Bay to the tip of Florida, drew upon knowledge of French and Spanish attempts at colonization. Small red dots indicate places where White believed Europeans had made landfalls. Dolphins, flying fish, and spouting whales decorate the map, along with the coat of arms of Walter Raleigh. (© British Museum [1906-5-9-1(2)/PS225251])

Anticipating North America

The early English settlers in North America were far from uninformed about the indigenous people of the New World. Beginning with Columbus's first description of the New World, published in several European cities in 1493 and 1494, reports and promotional accounts circulated among the participants in early voyages of discovery, trade, and settlement. This literature became the basis for anticipating the world that had been discovered beyond the setting sun.

Colonists who read or listened to these accounts got a dual image of the native people. On the one hand, Native Americans were depicted as a gentle people who eagerly received Europeans. Columbus had written of the "great amity toward us" that he encountered in San Salvador in 1492 and had described the Arawak there as "a loving people" who "were greatly pleased and became so entirely our friends that it was a wonder to see." Verrazano, the first European to touch the eastern edge of North America, wrote optimistically about the native people in 1524. The natives, graceful of limb and tawny-colored, he related, "came toward us joyfully uttering loud cries of wonderment, and showing us the safest place to beach the boat."

This positive image of Native Americans reflected both the friendly reception that Europeans often actually received and the European vision of the New World as an earthly paradise where war-torn, impoverished, and persecuted people could build a new life. The strong desire to trade with the native people also encouraged a favorable view because only a friendly Native American could become a suitable partner in commercial exchange.

Early North American travel literature also portrayed a counterimage of a savage, hostile Indian. As early as 1502, Sebastian Cabot had paraded in England three Eskimos he had kidnaped on an Arctic voyage, describing them as flesh-eating savages and "brute beasts" who "spake such speech that no man could understand them." Many other accounts portrayed the New World natives as crafty, brutal, loathsome half-men, who lived, as Amerigo Vespucci put it, without "law, religion, rulers, immortality of the soul, and private property."

How the Savages Roast Their Enemies (1575)

The English had another reason for believing that all would not be friendship and amiable trading when they came ashore. For years they had read accounts of the Spanish experience in the Caribbean, Mexico, and Peru—and the story was not pretty. Many books described in gory detail the wholesale violence that occurred when Spaniard met Mayan, Aztec, or Inca. Accounts of Spanish cruelty, even genocide, were useful to Protestant pamphleteers, who labeled the Catholic Spaniards "hell-hounds and wolves." Immigrants embarking for North America

Conquistadores Torturing Native Americans

Pomeiock Noblewoman and Daughter John White, governor of the second expedition to Virginia in 1587, rendered the first pictorial records of native life in the Americas. This watercolor of a tattooed noblewoman of Pomeiock shows her right arm resting in a chain of pearls or copper beads. Her young daughter holds a prized English doll in an Elizabethan dress. Do you think English colonizers would have found tattooing attractive? (© *British Museum*)

wondered whether similar violent confrontations awaited them.

Another factor nourishing negative images of Native Americans stemmed from their possession of the land necessary for settlement. For Englishmen, rooted in a tradition of the private ownership of property, this presented moral and legal, as well as practical, problems. As early as the 1580s, George Peckham, an early promoter of colonization, had admitted that the English doubted their right to take the land of others. In 1609, Anglican minister Robert Gray wondered, "By what right can we enter into the land of these savages, take their rightful inheritance from them, and plant ourselves in their places, being unwronged or unprovoked by them?"

The problem could be partially solved by arguing that English settlers did not intend to take the natives' land but wanted only to share it with them. In

return, they would offer the advantages of a more advanced culture and, most important, the Christian religion—a claim that would be repeated for generations. As the governing council in Virginia put it in 1610, the settlers "by way of merchandizing and trade, do buy of [the Native Americans] the pearls of earth, and sell to them the pearls of heaven."

A more ominous argument also justified English rights to native soil. By denying the humanity of the Native Americans, the English, like other Europeans, claimed that the native possessors of the land disqualified themselves from rightful ownership of it. "Although the Lord hath given the earth to children of men," one Englishman reasoned, "the greater part of it [is] possessed and wrongfully usurped by wild beasts and unreasonable creatures, or by brutish savages, which by reason of their godless ignorance and blasphemous idolatry, are worse than those beasts which are of the most wild and savage nature."

Defining the Native Americans as "savage" and "brutish" did not give the English arriving in the New World the power to dispossess them of their soil, but it armed the settlers with a moral justification for doing so when their numbers became sufficient. Few settlers arriving in North America doubted that their technological superiority would allow them to overwhelm the indigenous people. For their part, the natives probably perceived the arriving Europeans as impractical, irreligious, aggressive, and strangely intent on accumulating things.

AFRICAN BONDAGE

For almost four centuries after Columbus's voyages, European colonizers, in the largest forced migration in human history, transported Africans from their homelands and used their labor to produce wealth. Estimates vary widely, but at least 9.6 million Africans were brought to the Americas, and millions more perished on the long, terrible journey. Nearly as many were traded across the Sahara to Red Sea and Indian Ocean slave markets during the centuries from 650 to 1900.

Once the slave trade began, locales for producing desired commodities such as sugar, coffee, rice, and tobacco moved from the Old World to the Americas, building the first transoceanic European colonial empires. This gradually shifted Europe's orientation from the Mediterranean Sea to the Atlantic Ocean, with African forced labor an essential part of the immense Atlantic-basin system of trade and the success of the overseas colonies of European nations. Without African labor, the overseas colonies of European nations would never have flourished as they did.

RECOVERING THE PAST

Illustrated Travel Accounts

English travel accounts of New World settlements had a threefold purpose: first, to convince investors that purchasing stock issued by colonizing companies would reward them richly; second, to attract colonists through promotional descriptions of an exotic new world; and third, to serve as a Protestant weapon against colonizing Catholic countries, especially Spain. These pamphlets have furnished historians with rich ethnographic evidence of Native American lifeways in the Americas, a source of information on English attitudes toward Native Americans, and insights into how new technologies in book publishing fed the Protestant–Catholic conflict.

In 1588, Thomas Harriot (1560–1621), a minister, mathematician, and scientist trained at Oxford, published the first popular pamphlet describing and promoting English colonization. It came off the press as the English were repelling the Spanish Armada trying to destroy the English navy. In *A Briefe and True Report of the New Found Land of Virginia, directed to the Investors, Farmers and Wellwishers of the project of Colonizing and Planting there,* Harriot described what he had seen in eastern North America as a member of the second expedition to the Roanoke colony in 1585. Harriot enthusiastically described the pleasant climate and fertile land that would make farming easy, while boasting the commodities that English colonists could easily procure in Virginia—furs, pearls, iron, timber, precious metals, and more. Also on this voyage was a talented watercolorist, John White, whose many paintings depicted Native Americans living in villages, practicing agriculture, and engaging in dances, religious activities, and child rearing—a people who seemed to be ones with whom the English could settle peacefully (see figure opposite).

Harriot's *Briefe and True Report* became a model for English colonial promotional pamphlets. In 1589, he teamed up with Théodore de Bry, a Protestant engraver who in 1570 had fled Liège, his Belgian hometown, to escape the Spanish Inquisition, and taken refuge in Strasbourg, a Protestant stronghold and a center of engraving and the book trade. Once in London, de Bry created new copperplate engravings of White's watercolor paintings for a second edition of the *Briefe and True Report.* Taking artistic liberties, de Bry made the Native Americans seem more civilized to the English (see figures at top of next page). In 1590, Harriot's reissued, illustrated *Briefe Report* attracted great attention, appearing as the first volume of a series of European travel accounts gathered by de

Bry and advertised as *The Grand Voyages to America.* When John Smith published his *Generall Historie of Virginia, New England, and the Summer Isles* in 1624, the first lengthy eyewitness account of early English settlement in North America, it used many of de Bry's engravings, copied from John White's watercolors.

De Bry's engravings introduced large numbers of Europeans to images of Native American life and to impressions of the first encounters of Europeans with the indigenous people. A few Europeans had seen crude woodcuts of native life in the Americas in earlier sixteenth-century travel accounts. But not until de

English viewers of this watercolor of a Native American town on the bank of the Pamlico River (in present-day Beaufort County, North Carolina) might see that though they called them "savages," the Eastern Woodlands natives tilled their maize fields (shown on the right), enjoyed dancing (lower right), and buried their chiefs (see tomb in lower left) in ways familiar to Europeans. At the upper right is a small, elevated watchman's hut. (© *British Museum*)

John White's picture of a man and woman squatting on a mat at a meal of soaked maize. Harriot noted that "they are very sober in their eating and drinking, and consequently very long lived because they do not oppress nature." In de Bry's reinterpretation of this image, the man's and woman's posture, with legs extended, is much like that of Europeans at a picnic. Both figures have much lighter skin than in White's watercolor. The woman's face has been prettified by European standards, while the man has acquired musculature familiar to Europeans through Leonardo da Vinci paintings. De Bry has added fish, nuts, and a gourd to the scene. *(Left: British Museum [1906-5-9-1(20)/PS207965]; right: © The Mariners' Museum/Corbis)*

Bry's copperplate engravings, which offered clear, precise details, did book illustration advance to the point at which a panoramic view of the European colonization of the Americas become available to the many. The great Catholic–Protestant conflict in sixteenth- and seventeenth-century Europe, being played out in the Americas, could thus be presented to a wide audience through the de Bry–illustrated travel accounts.

Théodore de Bry's illustrations were based on Las Casas's accounts of actual incidents, but his imagination ran free in creating chilling images. In this engraving, a huge conquistador holds a child by the legs and prepares to dash its brains out against a rock. Another Spaniard ignites a fire to burn thirteen Native Americans hanging from a crude gallows, while other conquistadors (in the background) hunt down fleeing natives. *(From the Collections of the James Ford Bell Library, University of Minnesota, Minneapolis, Minnesota)*

Just before he died in 1598, de Bry published a Latin version of Bartolomé de Las Casas's *Short Account of the Destruction of the Indies,* first published in 1541 by the Spanish Dominican friar, who had lived for nearly 40 years in New Spain. Las Casas gave his life to converting the Native Americans to Catholicism and was intent on stopping the cruel Spanish treatment of them. His book was filled with details on horrific Spanish torture and killing of Native American women and children as well as adult males. Protestants had earlier republished Las Casas's exposé in French, English, and other languages, eager to offer proof of Catholic Spain's depravity in the Americas. But de Bry's illustrations for the 1598 edition published in Frankfurt showed Spanish ruthlessness with such graphic horror as to terrify the reader.

After their father's death, Jean-Théodore and Jean-Israël de Bry published another 22 illustrated volumes of voyages to the Americas, including 8 volumes with illustrations emphasizing how the Spanish Catholics brutalized the native people. Published in English, German, French, and Latin editions, the illustrated books promoted the idea of English superiority while providing Europeans with graphic material on the exotic peoples on the other side of the Atlantic.

REFLECTING ON THE PAST Look at these four illustrations and imagine that you saw them in England as you prepared to cross the Atlantic among a group of colonists. Having never lived outside the small village where you had been born, how do you see the Native Americans? How will you prepare yourself for encounters with them? How will you be able to avert the violence of the Spanish colonists?

While the economic importance of enslaved Africans can hardly be overstated, it is equally important to understand the cultural interchange that occurred. From 1519 to the early nineteenth century, African newcomers probably outnumbered Europeans two or three to one. As a result, African slavery became the context in which European life would evolve in many parts of the Americas. At the same time, the slave trade etched lines of communication for the movement of crops, agricultural techniques, diseases, and medical knowledge among Africa, Europe, and the Americas.

North America remained a fringe area for slave traders until the early eighteenth century. Yet those who came to the American colonies, about 10,000 in the seventeenth century and 350,000 in the eighteenth century, profoundly affected the destiny of North American society. In a prolonged period of labor scarcity, their labor and skills were indispensable to colonial economic development, while their African customs mixed continuously with those of their European masters. Moreover, the racial relations that grew out of slavery so deeply marked society that the problem of race has continued to be one of this nation's most difficult problems.

The Slave Trade

The African slave trade began as an attempt to fill a labor shortage in the Mediterranean world. As early as the eighth century, Arab and Moorish traders had driven slaves across Saharan caravan trails for delivery to Mediterranean ports. Seven centuries later, Portuguese merchants became the first European slave traders.

When Portuguese ship captains reached the west coast of Africa by water, they tapped into a slave-trading network that had operated in central and west Africa for many generations. For Africans, the Portuguese were nothing more than a new trading partner, one that could provide guns, horses, copper and brass, and especially textiles. Slaveholding was deeply rooted in African societies, regarded as a natural part of human organization, and was important in enhancing one's status and augmenting one's ability to produce wealth. However, slaves were employed in a wide variety of occupations, often serving as soldiers, administrators, and even occasionally as royal advisers.

Many Africans were relegated to slavery by judicial decree for crimes they had committed, but far more were captives in the wars between the numerous states of central and western Africa. Songhai—the largest state in Africa in the 1500s—waged several wars of territorial conquest, capturing slaves as it expanded its empire. The economy of the kingdom of Dahomey depended heavily for several centuries on commerce in slaves. One former slave, Francisco Feliz de Sousa, came to own a fleet of slave ships. But the early trade in human flesh was mainly in the hands of the Spanish and Portuguese, who carried some 100,000 enslaved Africans to the

Africans Being Taken to Slave Ships
This rare depiction of enslaved Africans being ferried out to European slave ships was first published in Jean Barbot's *A description of the coasts of north and south-Guinea* (1688). At the right is the slave fort of Manfroe while three other slaving stations appear to the left of it. (*New York Public Library, Rare Book Collection, Astor, Lenox and Tilden Foundations/Art Resource, NY*)

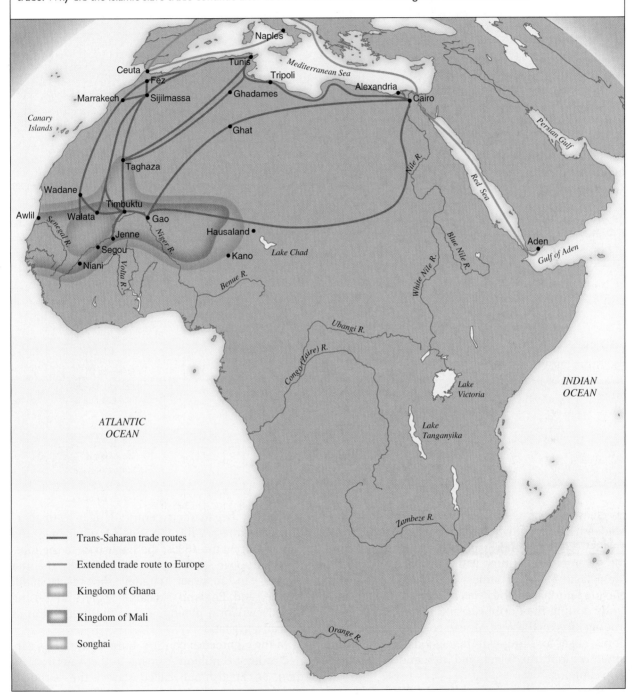

The Islamic Slave Trade

Though much less noticed than the Atlantic slave trade, the Islamic slave traffic across the Sahara Desert, Red Sea, and Indian Ocean was equally important numerically. The Islamic slave trade continued long after the Atlantic slave trade came to a halt in the late nineteenth century. **Reflecting on the Past** Why has the Islamic slave trade received less attention than the Atlantic slave trade? Why did the Islamic slave trade continue after abolitionists succeeded in ending the Atlantic slave trade?

Iberian peninsula before Columbus's first voyage across the Atlantic.

More than anything else, sugar transformed the African slave trade. For centuries, sugarcane had been grown in the Mediterranean countries to sweeten the diet of the wealthy. As sugar's popularity grew, the center of production shifted to Portugal's Atlantic islands of Madeira and São Tomé, off the west coast of Africa. Here in the 1460s, a European nation for the first time established an

West African Slaving Forts

Europeans fought lustily for control of slaving forts on the West African coast, and many forts changed hands several times during the long period of the Atlantic slave trade. **Reflecting on the Past** How did West Africans participating in the slave trade adjust to the languages of different European slave traders? Or did the European slave traders learn a variety of African languages in order to trade at the coastal forts?

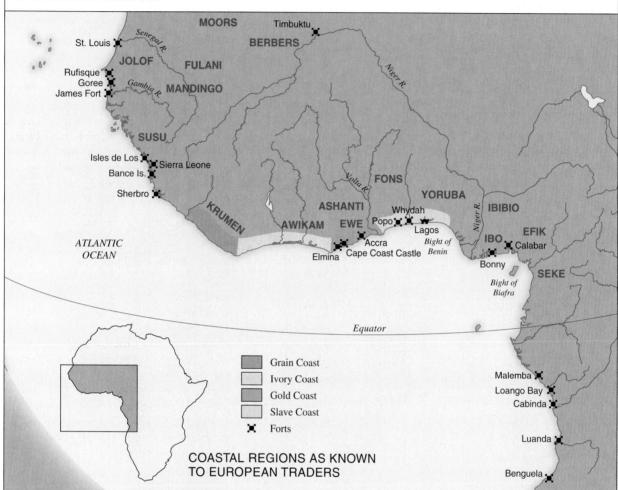

COASTAL REGIONS AS KNOWN
TO EUROPEAN TRADERS

overseas colony organized around slave labor. From Madeira, the cultivation of sugar spread to Portuguese Brazil and Spanish Santo Domingo. By the seventeenth century, with Europeans developing a taste for sugar almost as insatiable as their craving for tobacco, they vied fiercely for the tiny islands dotting the Caribbean and for control of the trading forts on the West African coast. African kingdoms, eager for European trade goods, fought each other to supply the "black gold" demanded by white ship captains.

European nations competed for West African trading rights. In the seventeenth century, when slave traders brought about 1 million Africans to the New World, the Dutch replaced the Portuguese as the major supplier. The English, meanwhile, hardly counted in the slave trade. Not until the 1690s,

when they began their century-long rise to maritime greatness, did the English challenge the Dutch. But by the 1690s, the English were the foremost European slave traders. Paradoxically, the first nations to forswear chattel slavery—Holland, France, and England—became leaders in raising their New World plantations on the foundation of African slave labor.

In the eighteenth century, European traders carried at least 6 million Africans to the Americas. By then, an Englishman called slavery the "strength and the sinews of this western world."

Once established on a large scale, the Atlantic slave trade dramatically altered slave recruitment in Africa. When criminals and "outsiders" were insufficient in number to satisfy the growing European demand, African kings highly desirous of European goods and others imported from Asia waged war against neighboring tribes. European guns abetted the process. By 1730, Europeans were providing some 180,000 weapons a year, spreading kidnaping and organized violence while strengthening the most militarily effective kingdoms. Again and again, coastal and interior kings invaded the hinterlands of western and central Sudan to procure slaves. Perhaps three-quarters of the slaves transported to English North America came from the part of western Africa that lies between the Senegal and Niger rivers and the Gulf of Biafra.

In this forcible recruitment of slaves, young males—most of them 10 to 24 years old—were preferred over women. This demonstrated the preference of New World plantation owners for male field laborers, and it also reflected the decision of vanquished African villagers to yield more men than women to raiding parties because women were the chief agriculturists in their society and, in matrilineal and matrilocal kinship systems, were too valuable to be sacrificed.

The Middle Passage

Even the most vivid accounts of the slave trade cannot convey the pain and demoralization that accompanied the initial capture and subsequent march to slave-trading forts on the West African coast or the dreaded "middle passage" across the Atlantic. Olaudah Equiano, an eighteenth-century Ibo from what is now Nigeria, described how raiders from another tribe kidnaped him and his younger sister when he was only 11 years old. He passed from one trader to another while being marched to the coast. Many slaves attempted suicide or died from exhaustion or hunger on these forced marches. But Equiano survived. Reaching the coast, he encountered the next humiliation—confinement in barracoons, or fortified enclosures on the beach, where a surgeon from an English slave ship inspected him. Equiano was terrified by the light skins, language, and long hair of the English and was convinced that he "had got into a world of bad spirits and that they were going to kill me."

IMAGE

Diagram of a Slave Ship Outfitted for the Middle Passage

DOCUMENT

Olaudah Equiano, The Middle Passage (1788)

More cruelties followed. European traders often branded the African slaves with a hot iron to indicate which company had procured them. The next trauma came with the ferrying of slaves in large canoes to the ships anchored in the harbor. An English captain recounted the desperation of Africans who were about to lose touch with their ancestral homeland and embark on a vast unknown ocean. "The Negroes are so loath to leave their own country," he wrote, "that they have often leaped out of the canoes, boat and ship, into the sea, and kept under the water till they were drowned."

Conditions aboard the slave ships were miserable, even though the traders' goal was to deliver alive as many slaves as possible to the other side of the Atlantic. Manacled slaves belowdecks were crowded together like corpses in coffins. "With the loathsomeness of the stench, and crying together," said Equiano, "I became so sick and low that I was not able to eat, nor had I the least desire to taste anything." The refusal to take food was so common that ship captains devised special techniques to cope with slaves who were determined to starve themselves to

A Slave Coffle   The pain of a slave coffle, in which enslaved Africans were tied together with forked branches and bark rope, shows in this eighteenth-century print. About one-eighth of the slaves marched toward coastal holding pens were children. *(Time Life Pictures/Getty Images)*

DOCUMENT
Alexander
Falconbridge,
The African
Slave Trade
(1788)

death rather than reach the New World in chains. Slavers flogged their captives brutally and applied hot coals to their lips. If this did not suffice, they force-fed the slaves with a mouth wrench. Yet for all the attempts to terrify the Africans into passive commodities, the slaves rebelled on about one-tenth of slave ships crossing the Atlantic.

The Atlantic passage usually took four to eight weeks, and one of every seven captives died en route. Many others arrived in the Americas deranged or dying. In all, the relocation of any African may have averaged about six months from the time of capture to the time of arrival at the plantation of a colonial buyer. During this protracted personal crisis, the slave was completely cut off from the moorings of a previous life—language, family and friends, tribal religion, familiar geography, and status in a local community. Ahead lay endless bondage.

Slavery in Early Spanish Colonies

Before a single enslaved African touched soil in the English colonies, thousands of slaves were already present in North America. They came first with fifteenth-century Spanish explorers such as Ponce de Leon, Vasquez de Ayllón, de Soto, and Coronado. The Morocco-born Estevan was indispensable to Coronado's expedition in North America's Southwest, serving as guide, healer, linguist, and diplomat to Native American tribes. The importance of Africans on these arduous expeditions gave slavery a distinct character in the early Spanish colonies. Laboring in fields, in fort and church construction, and on supply trains, they were also valuable as soldiers, guides, and linguistic go-betweens with Native American people. In this way, slavery had little of the caste-like character it developed in the English colonies. Also contributing to the greater flexibility of Spanish slavery was the frequent crossing of blood among Spaniards, Native Americans, and Africans.

TIMELINE

1440s	Portuguese begin kidnaping Africans and trading with them for slaves on Africa's western coast
1460s	Using African labor, sugar plantations in Portuguese Madeira become major exporters
1492	Christopher Columbus lands on Caribbean islands Spanish expel Moors (Muslims) and Jews
1493–1504	Columbus makes three additional voyages to the Americas
1493	Spain plants first colony in Americas on Hispaniola
1494	Treaty of Tordesillas
1497–1585	French and English explore northern part of the Americas
1498	Vasco da Gama reaches India after sailing around Africa
Early 1500s	First Africans reach the Americas with Spanish
1508–1511	Spanish conquistadors subjugate native people on Puerto Rico and Cuba
1513	Portuguese explorers reach China
1517	Luther attacks Catholicism and begins Protestant Reformation

1520	First disease contracted from Spanish devastates Aztec people
1521	Cortés conquers the Aztecs
1528	Spain plants first settlement on Florida coast
1527–1536	Cabeza de Vaca *entrada* across southern region of North America
1530s	Calvin calls for religious reform
1533	Pizarro conquers the Incas
1534	Church of England established
1539–1542	De Soto expedition explores the Southeast
1540–1542	Coronado explores the Southwest
1558	Elizabeth I crowned queen of England
1585	English plant settlement on Roanoke Island
1588	English defeat the Spanish Armada
1590	Roanoke settlement fails
1603	James I succeeds Elizabeth I

Conclusion

Converging Worlds

The Iberian voyages of the late fifteenth and early sixteenth centuries, linking Europe and Africa with the Americas, brought together people such as the Spanish conquistador Alvar Núñez Cabeza de Vaca, the Moroccan captive Estevan, and chiefs of Creek villages in the southeastern sector of North America. Here were the beginnings of a communications network that ultimately joined every region of the globe and linked the destinies of widely disparate peoples living on many parts of the immense Atlantic basin. Other nations would follow Spain, but it was the Spanish who first erected colonial regimes that drew on homeland traditions of law, religion, government, and culture. The Spanish also initiated maritime and commercial enterprises profoundly affecting patterns of production, with the Americas destined to become the great producer of foodstuffs to be exported to Europe. Part of this fledgling global economy was the trade in human beings—Africans carried to Spain and Portugal, then to the Atlantic islands off the west coast of Africa, and finally to the Americas in one of the most tragic chapters of human history. Accompanying this, and paving the way for European settlement, was the greatest weapon possessed by Europeans—the germs carried in their bodies that decimated the indigenous people of the Americas in the greatest biological holocaust in the annals of history.

The English immigrants who began arriving on the eastern edge of North America in the early seventeenth century came late to a New World that other Europeans had been colonizing for more than a century. The first English arrivals, the immigrants to Virginia, were but a small advance wave of the large, varied, and determined fragment of English society that would flock to the western Atlantic frontier during the next few generations. Like Spanish, Portuguese, and French colonizers before them, they would establish new societies in the newfound lands in contact with the people of two other cultures—one made up of ancient inhabitants of the lands they were settling and the other composed of those brought across the Atlantic against their will. We turn now to the richly diverse founding experience of the English latecomers in the seventeenth century and their contests with French, Dutch, and Spanish contenders for control of North America.

Questions for Review and Reflection

1 How did the religious changes in Europe affect European expansion into the Americas?

2 What was the Columbian Exchange, and what impact did it have on Europe and the Americas?

3 Why was England slow to become involved in exploration and colonization? How did the late arrival of the English affect their history in the New World?

4 What were the causes and consequences of the African slave trade with the European colonies in the Americas?

5 What was the impact of the collision of cultures that occurred in the Americas in the early colonial period?

Recommended Reading

Recommended Readings are posted on the Web site for this textbook. Visit www.ablongman.com/nash

Fiction and Film

In the feature film *Conquest of Paradise* (1992), Gerard Depardieu plays Christopher Columbus, but Boston's WGBH seven-part *Columbus and the Age of Discovery* (1991) is much more comprehensive and authentic. In the miniseries *Roanoke*, PBS explores the friction between Indians and colonizers in the first attempt of the English to plant a North American settlement. Louise Erdrich's poem titled "Captivity," which can be found in her *Jacklight* collection (1984), is a valuable Native American–centered reading of one of the most popular Native American captivity accounts ever published—Mary Rowlandson's *A Narrative of the Captivity, Sufferings and Removes of Mrs. Mary Rowlandson,* first published in 1682. Boston's WGBH has produced a superb four-part video series on *Africans in America* (1998). The first two parts cover slavery and slave culture in the seventeenth and eighteenth centuries. Much shorter is the BBC production *A Son of Africa: The Slave Narrative of Olaudah Equiano,* a half-hour video of the only eighteenth-century slave who wrote an autobiography.

Discovering U.S. History Online

1492: An Ongoing Voyage
www.lcweb.loc.gov/exhibits/1492/intro.html
An exhibit of the Library of Congress in Washington D.C., this site provides brief essays and images about early civilizations and contact in the Americas.

The European Voyages of Exploration
www.ucalgary.ca/applied_history/tutor/eurvoya
This site has images and texts for nearly every facet of European exploration.

Jamestown
www.iath.virginia.edu/vcdh/jamestown/images/white_debry_html/introduction.html
This site presents Theodor de Bry's engravings of America alongside John White's original drawings, giving "the opportunity to use this material as a pedagogical resource on English views of native people."

Spain, the United States, and the American Frontier
www.international.loc.gov/intldl/eshtml/
A joint effort of American and Spanish national libraries, this bilingual site presents primary materials and several exhibits about the pre-conquest to contact period between the two countries.

The Columbus Doors
www.xroads.virginia.edu/~CAP/COLUMBUS/colhome.html
Via the topics covered by the panels on the Capitol Columbus doors, historians discuss the Columbus myth and how it has changed over time.

Florida History Timeline
www.palmm.fcla.edu/fh/outline/outline.html
This Web site gives an overview of pre- and postcolonial Florida.

Sir Francis Drake
www.mcn.org/2/oseeler/drake.htm
This comprehensive site covers much of Drake's life and voyages.

John Cabot
www.heritage.nf.ca/exploration/cabot.html
Giovanni Caboto, or John Cabot, sailed for England to the New World in the late fifteenth century. This site describes his voyages as well as England's goals.

Africans in America
www.pbs.org/wgbh/aia/part1/1narr2.html
This site offers a brief background and a few illustrations of the English foray into slavery and colonization in the Americas.

African American Odyssey: Slavery—The Peculiar Institution
lcweb2.loc.gov/ammem/aaohtml/exhibit/aopart1.html
A Web exhibit that includes paintings, original documents, engravings, and broadsides, along with background information on each.

Slave Movement During the Eighteenth and Nineteenth Centuries
dpls.dacc.wisc.edu/slavedata/index.html
This site provides downloadable primary source data from the slave trade.

Afro-Louisiana History and Genealogy
www.ibiblio.org/laslave/
The author has compiled a thorough database of "African slave names, genders, ages, occupations, illnesses, family relationships, ethnicity, places of origin, prices paid by slave owners, and slaves' testimony and emancipations" from slave inventories recorded by the French and Spanish proprietors in Louisiana.

Colonizing a Continent in the Seventeenth Century

Cecil Calvert grasping a map of Maryland held by his grand-father, the second Lord Baltimore; detail of a painting by Gerard Soest, court painter to Charles II. *(Enoch Pratt Free Library, Baltimore)*

American Stories

An African on the Virginia Frontier

Anthony Johnson, an African, arrived in Virginia in 1621 with only the name Antonio. Caught as a young man in the Portuguese slave-trading net, he had passed from one trader to another in the New World until he reached Virginia. There he was purchased by Richard Bennett and sent to work at Warrasquoke, Bennett's tobacco plantation on the James River. In the next year, Antonio was brought face-to-face with the world of triracial contact and conflict that would shape the remainder of his life. On March 22, 1622, the Powhatan tribes of tidewater Virginia fell on the white colonizers in a determined attempt to drive them from the land. Of the 57 people on the Bennett plantation, only Antonio and four others survived.

Antonio—his name anglicized to Anthony—labored on the Bennett plantation for some 20 years, slave in fact if not in law, for legally defined bondage had not yet fully taken hold in the Virginia colony. During this time, he married Mary, another African trapped in the labyrinth of servitude, and fathered four children. In the 1640s, Anthony and Mary Johnson gained their freedom after half a lifetime of servitude. Probably at this point they chose a surname, Johnson, to signify their new status. Already past middle age, the Johnsons began carving out a niche for themselves on Virginia's eastern shore. By 1650, they owned 250 acres, a small herd of cattle, and two black servants. In a world in which racial boundaries were not yet firmly marked, the Johnsons had entered the scramble of small planters for economic security.

By schooling themselves in the workings of the English legal process, carefully cultivating white patronage, and working industriously on the land, the Johnsons gained their freedom, acquired property, established a family, warded off contentious neighbors, and hammered out a decent existence. But by the late 1650s, as the lines of racial slavery tightened, the customs of the country began closing in on Virginia's free blacks.

In 1664, convinced that ill winds were blowing away the chances for their children and grandchildren in Virginia, the Johnsons began selling their land to white neighbors. The following spring, most of the clan moved north to Maryland, where they rented land and again took up farming and cattle raising. Five years later, Anthony Johnson died, leaving his wife and four children. The growing racial prejudice of Virginia followed Johnson beyond the grave. A jury of white men in Virginia declared that because Johnson "was a Negroe and by consequence an alien," the 50 acres he had deeded to his son Richard before moving to Maryland should be awarded to a local white planter.

Johnson's children and grandchildren, born in America, could not duplicate the modest success of the African-born patriarch. By the late seventeenth century, people of color faced much greater difficulties in extricating themselves from slavery. When they did, they found themselves forced to the margins of society. Anthony's sons never rose higher than the level of tenant farmer or small freeholder. John Johnson moved farther north into Delaware in the 1680s, following a period of great conflict with Native Americans in the Chesapeake region. Members of his family married local Native Americans and became part of a triracial community that has survived to the present day. Richard Johnson stayed behind in Virginia. When he died in 1689, just after a series of colonial insurrections connected with the overthrow of James II in England, he had little to leave his four sons. They became tenant farmers and hired servants, laboring on plantations owned by whites. By now, slave ships were pouring Africans into Virginia and Maryland to replace white indentured servants, the backbone of the labor force for four generations. To be black had at first been a handicap. Now it became a fatal disability, an indelible mark of degradation and bondage.

Anthony and Mary Johnson's story is one of thousands detailing the experiences of seventeenth-century immigrants who arrived in North America. Their story is not about those European immigrants who sought both spiritual and economic renewal in the New World. But their lives became intertwined with those who were trying to escape European war, despotism, material want, and religious corruption. Like free immigrants and indentured servants from Europe, the Johnsons had to cope with new environments, new social situations, and new mixings of people who before had lived on different continents. Mastering the

North American environment involved several processes that would echo down the corridors of American history. Prominent among them were the molding of an African labor force and the gradual subjection of Native American tribes who contested white expansion. Both developments occurred in the lifetimes of Anthony and Mary Johnson and their children. Both involved a level of violence that made this frontier of European expansion not a zone of pioneer equality and freedom but one of growing inequality and servitude.

This chapter reconstructs the manner of settlement and the character of immigrant life in six areas of early colonization: Chesapeake Bay, southern New England, the French and Dutch area from the St. Lawrence River to the Hudson River, the Carolinas, Pennsylvania, and the Spanish toeholds on the southern fringe of North America. A comparison of these various colonies will show how the colonizers' backgrounds, ideologies, modes of settlement, and uses of labor—free, slave, and indentured—produced distinctly different societies in North America in the seventeenth century. The chapter also shows how these regional societies changed over the course of the seventeenth century and how they experienced internal strain, a series of Native American wars, a destructive and community-shattering witchcraft craze, and reactions to England's attempts to reorganize its overseas colonies.

The Colonies to 1740

THE CHESAPEAKE TOBACCO COAST

In 1607, a group of merchants established England's first permanent colony in North America at Jamestown, Virginia. But for the first generation, its permanence was anything but assured; even into the second and third generation of settlement along the waters flowing into the Chesapeake Bay, the English colonizers were plagued with internal discord and violent clashes with the native peoples.

Jamestown, Sot Weed, and Indentured Servants

Under a charter from James I, the Virginia Company of London operated as a joint-stock company, an early kind of modern corporation that sold shares of stock and used the pooled capital to outfit and supply overseas expeditions. Although the king's charter to the company began with a concern for bringing Christian religion to native people who "as yet live in darkness and miserable ignorance of the true knowledge of God," most of the settlers probably agreed with Captain John Smith, who wrote that "We did admire how it was possible such wise men could so torment themselves with such absurdities, making religion their colour, when all their aim was profit."

Profits in the early years proved elusive, however. Expecting to find gold, a rewarding trade with Native Americans for beaver and deer skins, and a water route to China, the original investors and settlers got a rude shock. Dysentery, malaria, drought, and malnutrition carried off most of the first colonists. More than 900 settlers, mostly men, arrived in the colony between 1607 and 1609; only 60 survived.

Seeking occupational diversity, the Virginia Company sent French silk artisans, Italian glassmakers, and Polish potash burners to Jamestown.

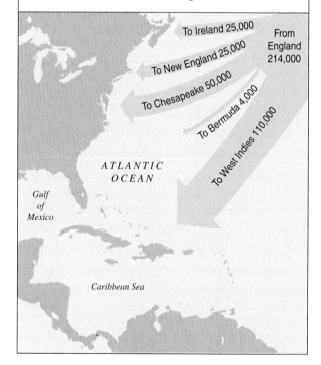

The Great English Migration, 1630–1660

This map shows that more than half of all the early English immigrants to the Americas went to the West Indies. Even a larger proportion of the Africans brought to the English colonies found themselves sold in England's Caribbean Islands.

To Ireland 25,000

To New England 25,000

From England 214,000

To Chesapeake 50,000

To Bermuda 4,000

To West Indies 110,000

ATLANTIC OCEAN

Gulf of Mexico

Caribbean Sea

Jamestown Excavation A major archaeological research project has been underway at Jamestown for several years in preparation for the 400-year anniversary of the founding of Jamestown in 1607. What do you think the foundations marked in this view represent? (Ira Block/National Geographic Image Collection)

Still, the Virginia Company of London poured in more money and settlers, many enticed with promises of free land after seven years' labor for the company. In 1618, the company even offered 50 acres of land outright to anyone journeying to Virginia. To people on the margins of English society, the promise of free land seemed irresistible. More than 9,000 crossed the Atlantic between 1610 and 1622. Yet only 2,000 remained alive at the end of that period. "Instead of a plantation," wrote one English critic, "Virginia will shortly get the name of a slaughter house."

Beside the offer of free land, a crucial factor in the migration was the discovery that tobacco grew splendidly in Chesapeake soil. Francis Drake's boatload of the "jovial weed" (so named for its intoxicating effect), procured in the West Indies in 1586, popularized it among the upper class and launched an addiction that continues to this day.

But one-third of the first immigrants were gold-seeking adventurers with unroughened hands, a proportion of gentlemen six times as great as in the English population. Many others were unskilled servants, some with criminal backgrounds, who (according to John Smith) "never did know what a day's work was." Both types adapted poorly to wilderness conditions, and Smith got few of the carpenters, fishermen, blacksmiths, and farmers he wanted.

The colony was also hampered by the assumption that Englishmen could exploit the Native Americans as Cortés and Pizarro had done. But the English found that the some 24,000 local Powhatan were not densely settled and could not be easily subjugated. Unlike Spain, England had sent neither an army of conquistadors nor an army of priests to subdue the natives. Instead, relations with the small groups that the able Powhatan had united into a confederacy turned bitter almost from the beginning. The Powhatan brought supplies of maize to the sick and starving Jamestown colony during the first autumn. However, John Smith, whose military experience in eastern Europe had schooled him in dealing with people he regarded as "barbarians," raided Native American food supplies and tried to cow the local tribes. Amid one of the most severe droughts in centuries, which reduced the maize supply, the Powhatan withdrew from trade with the English and sniped at their flanks. Many settlers died in the "starving times" of the first years.

DOCUMENT

Powhatan to John Smith (ca. 1609)

DOCUMENT

John Smith, "The Starving Time" (1624)

Early Chesapeake Settlement

Only the major Native American villages in the early 1600s are indicated on this map. Note that the town sites are all oriented to the rivers—the source of both food and transportation.

Rappahannock R.

Potomac R.

Approximate boundary of Powhatan Confederacy

Chesapeake Bay

⌂ Powhatan   ⌂ Werowocomoco

York R.

⌂ Henrico   Paspahegh ⌂

● Jamestown

James R.   ⌂ Kecoughtan   ATLANTIC OCEAN

⌂ Nansemond

● = English settlement
⌂ = Native American settlement

A History of Virginia A small caption in the middle of this set of panels reads, "A description of part of the adventures of Cap: Smith in Virginia." The images were rendered by Robert Vaughan, an English engraver, and were published in *The Generall Historie of Virginia, 1624, by Captain John Smith*. In the lower right panel, an oversized Pocahontas (at the right) begs for the life of Smith, whose head is on a block, ready for dismemberment by an Indian executioner. What overall effect would this engraving have on readers of John Smith's history in England?

Even James I's denunciation of smoking as "loathsome to the eye, hateful to the nose, harmful to the brain, and dangerous to the lungs" failed to halt the smoking craze. The "sot weed" became Virginia's salvation. Planters shipped the first crop in 1617, and tobacco cultivation spread rapidly. Tobacco yielded enough profit for settlers to plant it even in the streets and marketplace of Jamestown. By 1624, Virginia exported 200,000 pounds of the "stinking weed"; by 1638, though the price had plummeted, the crop exceeded 3 million pounds. Tobacco became to Virginia in the 1620s what sugar was to the West Indies and silver to Mexico and Peru. In London, men joked that Virginia was built on smoke.

Because tobacco required intensive care, Virginia's planters had to find a reliable supply of cheap labor. They found it by recruiting mostly English and Irish laborers to be indentured servants, who willingly sold years of their working lives in exchange for free passage to America. Nearly three-quarters of them were male, mostly between 15 and 24 years old, and nearly all came from the lower rungs of the social ladder at home.

Life for indentured servants often turned into a nightmare. Only about one in 20 realized the dream of freedom and land. If malarial fever or dysentery did not quickly kill them, they often succumbed to brutal work routines. Even by the middle of the seventeenth century, about half died during the first few years of "seasoning." Masters bought and sold their servants as property, gambled for them, and worked them to death, for there was little motive for keeping them alive beyond their term of service. "My Master Adkins," wrote one servant in 1623, "hath sold me

DOCUMENT

James I, "A Counterblaste to Tobacco"

DOCUMENT

Wessell Webling, His Indenture (1622)

for £ 150 like a damned slave." When servants neared the end of their contract, masters found ways to add time and were backed by courts that they controlled.

Contrary to English custom, masters often put women servants to work at the hoe. Sexual abuse was common, and servant women paid dearly for illegitimate pregnancies. The courts fined them heavily and ordered them to serve an extra year or two to repay the time lost during pregnancy and childbirth. They also deprived mothers of their illegitimate children, indenturing them out at an early age. Many servant women accepted the purchase of their indenture by any man who suggested marriage as the best release from this hard life.

Expansion and Indian War

As tobacco production caused Virginia's population to increase, violence mounted between white colonizers and the Powhatan tribes. In 1614, the sporadic hostility of the early years ended temporarily

A Cult of Smokers By the end of the 1600s, most young European males were addicted to tobacco. Like the young Dutchmen shown in this painting, they practiced various tricks such as the "ring," "whiffle," "gulp," and "retention" as part of the smoking cult. Is smoking still a cult today? *(Adriaen Brouwer,* The Smokers, *The Metropolitan Museum of Art, Bequest of Michael Friedsam, 1931, The Friedsam Collection [32.100.21] © 1989 The Metropolitan Museum of Art)*

Ætatis suæ 21. A°. 1616.

Matoaks als Rebecka daughter to the mighty Prince Powhatan Emperour of Attanoughkomouck als Virginia converted and baptized in the Christian faith, and Wife to the Wor.ⁿ Mr. Tho: Rolff.

Pocahontas Painted at the time she was presented to the court of King James I, Pocahontas appears in a red velvet jacket over a dark dress with gold buttons. She holds a fan of three ostrich feathers. We can only imagine how her elaborate shoulder collar of white lace must have felt for a 22-year-old woman accustomed to loose-fitting, comfortable clothes. *(Anonymous,* Pocahontas, *c. 1595–1617, daughter of Powhatan chief. National Portrait Gallery, Smithsonian Institution/Art Resource, NY)*

with the arranged marriage of Chief Powhatan's daughter, the fabled Pocahontas, to planter John Rolfe. However, the profitable cultivation of tobacco continued to create an intense demand for land. With settlers pushing inland, the local tribes pondered their future.

In 1617, when Powhatan retired, leadership of the Chesapeake tribes fell to Opechancanough. This proud and talented leader began preparing an all-out attack on his English enemies. The English murder of Nemattanew, a Powhatan war captain and religious prophet, triggered a fierce Native American assault in 1622 that dealt Virginia a staggering blow. More than one-quarter of the white population fell, and the casualties in cattle, crops, and buildings were equally severe.

The devastating attack bankrupted the Virginia Company. The king annulled its charter in 1624 and established a royal government, allowing the elected legislative body established in 1619, the House of Burgesses, to continue lawmaking in concert with the royal governor and his council.

The Native American assault of 1622 fortified the determination of the surviving planters to pursue a ruthless new Native American policy. John Smith, writing from England two years later, noted the grim satisfaction that had followed the attack. Many, he reported, believed that "now we have just cause to destroy them by all means possible." Bolstered by instructions from London to "root out [the Native Americans] from being any longer a people," the Virginians conducted annual military expeditions against the native villages.

IMAGE

Scene from John Smith's Memoirs

Population growth after 1630 and settlers' perpetual need for fresh acreage because tobacco quickly exhausted the soil intensified the pressure on Native American land. The tough, ambitious planters soon encroached on Indian territories, provoking war in 1644. The Chesapeake tribes, Virginians came to believe, were merely obstacles to be removed from the path of English settlement.

Proprietary Maryland

By the time Virginia had achieved commercial success in the 1630s, another colony on the Chesapeake took root. The founder's main aim was not profit but rather a refuge for Catholics and a New World version of England's manor-dotted countryside.

George Calvert, an English nobleman, designed and promoted the new colony. Closely connected to England's royal family, he had received a huge grant of land in Newfoundland in 1628, just three years after James I had made him Lord Baltimore. In 1632, Charles I, James's son, prepared to grant him a more hospitable domain of 10 million acres, which Calvert named Terra Maria, or Maryland, to honor the king's Catholic wife, Henrietta Maria.

Catholics were an oppressed minority in England, and Calvert planned his colony as a haven for them. But knowing that he needed more than a small band of Catholic settlers, the proprietor invited others, too. Catholics, never a majority in his colony, were quickly overwhelmed by Protestants who jumped at the offer of free land with only a modest yearly fee to the Calverts.

DOCUMENT

The Charter of Maryland (1632)

Lord Baltimore died in 1632, leaving his 26-year-old son, Cecilius, to carry out his plans. The charter guaranteed the proprietor control over all branches of government, but young Calvert learned that his colonists would not be satisfied with fewer liberties than they enjoyed at home or could find in other

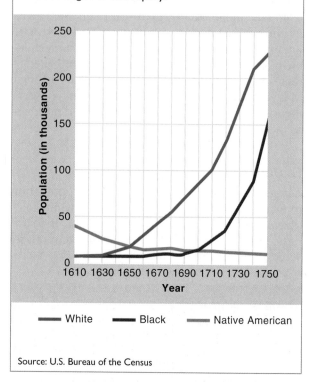

Population of the Chesapeake Colonies, 1610–1750

As indicated in this chart, it was not until the 1690s, when Chesapeake planters began turning to Africa for their labor, that the black population in the Chesapeake colonies began to rise rapidly.

Population (in thousands) — Year: 1610 1630 1650 1670 1690 1710 1730 1750

— White   — Black   — Native American

Source: U.S. Bureau of the Census

colonies. Hence, the Lords Baltimore gave up their charter-given right to initiate all colonial laws, subject only to the advice and consent of the people.

Arriving in 1634, immigrants ignored Calvert's plans for 6,000-acre manors for his relatives and 3,000-acre manors for lesser aristocrats, each to be worked by serflike tenants. The settlers took up their free land, imported as many indentured servants as they could afford, maintained generally peaceful relations with local native tribes, grew tobacco on scattered riverfront plantations like their Virginia neighbors, and governed themselves locally as much as possible. Although Maryland grew slowly at first—in 1650, it had a population of only 600—it developed rapidly in the second half of the seventeenth century. By 1700, its population of 33,000 was half that of Virginia.

Daily Life on the Chesapeake

Though immigrants to the Chesapeake Bay region dreamed of bettering the life they had known in England, most found life dismal. Only a minority could marry and rear a family, because marriage had to be deferred until the indenture was completed. And there were three times as many men as women. Marriages were fragile. Either husband or wife was likely to die of disease within about seven years. The vulnerability of pregnant women to malaria frequently terminated marriages, and death claimed half the children before they reached adulthood. Few children had two living parents while growing up. Grandparents were almost unknown.

In a society so numerically dominated by men, widows were prized and often remarried quickly. Such conditions produced complex families, full of stepchildren, stepparents, half-sisters, and half-brothers.

The household of Robert Beverley of Middlesex County illustrates the tangled family relationships in this death-filled society. When Beverley married Mary Keeble in 1666, she was a 29-year-old widow who had borne seven children during her first marriage. At least four of them were still alive to join the household of their mother's new husband. They gained five half-brothers and half-sisters during their mother's 12-year marriage to Beverley. When Mary Keeble Beverley died at age 41, her husband quickly remarried a recent widow, Katherine Hone. Beverley's second wife brought her son into the household and in the next nine years produced four more children with Beverley before his death in 1687. Thus, between 1666 and 1687, Beverley had married two widows who bore him nine children and had been stepfather to the eight children his two wives had produced with previous husbands. Not one of these 17 children, from an interlocking set of four marriages, reached adulthood with both a living mother and father.

Plagued by horrendous mortality, the Chesapeake remained, for most of the seventeenth century, a land of immigrants rather than a land of settled families. Churches and schools took root very slowly. The large number of indentured servants further destabilized community life. Strangers in a household, they served their time and moved on, or died, replaced by other strangers, purchased fresh from England.

The region's architecture reflected the difficult conditions. Life was too uncertain, the tobacco economy too volatile, and the desire to invest every available shilling in field labor too great for men to build grandly. At first they lived in primitive huts and shanties, hardly more than windbreaks. Even by the early eighteenth century, most Chesapeake families lived in crude houses without interior partitions. Eating, dressing, working, and loving all took place with hardly a semblance of privacy. For nearly two centuries, most ordinary Virginians and Marylanders were "pigg'd lovingly together," as one planter put it. Even prosperous planters did not begin constructing fully framed, substantial homesteads until a century after the colony was founded.

The crudity of life also showed in the household possessions of the Chesapeake colonists. Struggling farmers and tenants were likely to own only a straw mattress, a simple storage chest, and the tools for food preparation and eating—a mortar and pestle to grind corn, knives for butchering, a pot or two for cooking stews and porridges, and wooden trenchers and spoons for eating. Most ordinary settlers owned no chairs, dressers, plates, or silverware. Among middling planters, the standard of living was raised only by possession of a flock mattress, coarse earthenware for milk and butter, a few pewter plates and porringers, a frying pan or two, and a few rough tables and chairs. To be near the top of Chesapeake society meant having three or four rooms, sleeping more comfortably, sitting on chairs rather than squatting on the floor, and owning such ordinary decencies as chamber pots, candlesticks, bed linen, a chest of drawers, and a desk. Only a few boasted such luxuries as clocks, books, punch bowls, wineglasses, and imported furniture. Four generations elapsed in the Chesapeake settlements before the frontier quality of life slowly gave way to more refined living.

Bacon's Rebellion Engulfs Virginia

The rough and crooked road that the Chesapeake colonies had followed in the seventeenth century reached an explosive point in 1675–1676 when a war fought both between the native and white populations and among the colonizers occurred. Before it all ended, hundreds of whites and Native Americans lay dead in Virginia and Maryland, Virginia's capital of Jamestown lay smoldering, and English troops were crossing the Atlantic to suppress what the king labeled an outright rejection of his authority. This tangled conflict was called Bacon's Rebellion after the headstrong Cambridge-educated planter Nathaniel Bacon, who arrived in Virginia at age 28.

Bacon and many other ambitious young planters detested the Native American policy of Virginia's royal governor, Sir William Berkeley. In 1646, after the second Native uprising against the Virginians, the Powhatan tribes had been granted exclusive rights to territory beyond the limits of white settlement. Stable Native American relations suited the established planters, some of whom traded profitably with the natives, but became obnoxious to new settlers. Nor did harmonious conditions please

RECOVERING THE PAST

Houses

Homesteading is central to our national experience. For 300 years after the founding of the first colonies, most Americans were involved in taming and settling the land. On every frontier, families faced the tasks of clearing the fields, beginning farming operations, and building shelter for themselves and their livestock. The kinds of structures they built depended on available materials, their resources and aspirations, and their notions of a "fair" dwelling. The plan of a house and the materials used in its construction reveal much about the needs, resources, priorities, and values of the people who built it.

By examining archaeological remains of early ordinary structures and by studying houses that are still standing, historians are reaching new understandings of the social life of pioneering societies. Since the 1960s, archaeologists and architectural historians have been studying seventeenth-century housing in the Chesapeake Bay and New England regions. They have discovered a familiar sequence of house types—from temporary shanties and lean-tos to rough cabins and simple frame houses to larger and more substantial dwellings of brick and finished timber. This hovel-to-house-to-home pattern existed on every frontier, as sodbusters, gold miners, planters, and cattle raisers secured their hold on the land and then struggled to move from subsistence to success.

What is unusual in the findings of the Chesapeake researchers is the discovery that the second phase in the sequence—the use of temporary, rough-built structures—lasted for more than a century. Whereas many New Englanders had rebuilt and extended their temporary clapboard houses into timber-framed, substantial dwellings by the 1680s, Chesapeake settlers continued to construct small, rickety buildings that had to be repaired continually or abandoned altogether every 10 to 15 years.

William Boardman house, Saugus, Massachusetts, ca. 1687; a floor plan of the house is shown above. *(Courtesy of the Society for the Preservation of New England Antiquities)*

78

Reconstructed Chesapeake planter's house, typical of such simply built and unpainted structures in the seventeenth century. *(Photograph by Julie Roy Jeffrey)*

The William Boardman house shown opposite, built around 1687, is an example of the "orderly, fair, and well-built" houses of late-seventeenth-century Massachusetts. Its plan shows a typical arrangement of space: the hall, used for cooking, eating, working, and socializing; the parlor; a sleeping room for the parents; and a lean-to for kitchen chores and activities such as dairying. The great central chimney warmed the main downstairs room. Upstairs were two rooms used for both storage and sleeping. As you examine the exterior of the building, note the materials that have been used and the arrangement and treatment of windows, doors, and chimney. What impression of the Boardman family might visitors have as they approached the house? What kind of privacy and comfort did the house provide for family members?

The house shown above is a typical reconstructed tobacco planter's house. It has some of the same features as the Boardman house, for both are products of an English building tradition. But there are some major differences between the two. In the Chesapeake house, the chimney is built not of brick but of mud and wood, and there is no window glass, only small shutters. The exterior is rough, unfinished planking. The placement of doors and windows and the overall dimensions indicate that this house has only one room downstairs and a loft above. The builders of this house clearly enjoyed less privacy and comfort than the Boardmans.

Historians have puzzled over this contrast between the architecture of the two regions. Part of the explanation may lie in the different climatic conditions and different immigration patterns of New England and the Chesapeake. In the southern region, disease killed thousands of settlers in the early decades. The imbalance of men and women produced a stunted and unstable family life, hardly conducive to

an emphasis on constructing fine homes. In New England, good health prevailed almost from the beginning, and the family was at the heart of society. It made more sense, in this environment, to make a substantial investment in larger and more permanent houses. Some historians argue, moreover, that the Puritan work ethic impelled New Englanders to build solid homes—a compulsion unknown in the culturally backward, "lazy" South.

Archaeological evidence combined with data recovered from land, tax, and court records, however, suggests another reason for the impermanence of housing in the Chesapeake region. Living in a labor-intensive tobacco world, it is argued, planters large and small economized on everything possible in order to buy as many indentured servants and slaves as they could. Better to live in a shanty and have 10 slaves than to have a handsome dwelling and nobody to cultivate the fields. As late as 1775, the author of *American Husbandry* calculated that in setting up a tobacco plantation, five times as much ought to be spent on purchasing 20 black fieldhands as on the "house, offices, and tobacco-house."

Only after the Chesapeake region had emerged from its prolonged era of mortality and gender imbalance and a mixed economy of tobacco, grain, and cattle had replaced the tobacco monoculture did the rebuilding of the region begin. Excavated house sites indicate that this occurred in the period after 1720. New research reveals that the phases of home building and the social and economic history of a society were closely interwoven.

REFLECTING ON THE PAST What do houses today reveal about the resources, economic livelihood, priorities, and values of contemporary Americans? Do class and regional differences in house design continue?

the white ex-indentured servants who hoped for cheap frontier land.

Land hunger and dissatisfaction with declining tobacco prices, rising taxes, and lack of opportunity erupted into violence in the summer of 1675. A group of frontiersmen used an incident with a local tribe as an excuse to attack the Susquehannock, whose rich land they coveted. Governor Berkeley denounced the attack, but few supported his position. As he explained, he faced "a people where six parts of seven at least are poor, indebted, discontented, and armed." The badly outnumbered Susquehannock prepared for war as rumors swept the colony that they were offering large sums to gain western native allies or that New England tribes would support them.

Thirsting for revenge, the Susquehannock attacked during the winter of 1675–1676 and killed 36 Virginians. That spring, the hot-blooded Nathaniel Bacon became the frontiersmen's leader. Joined by

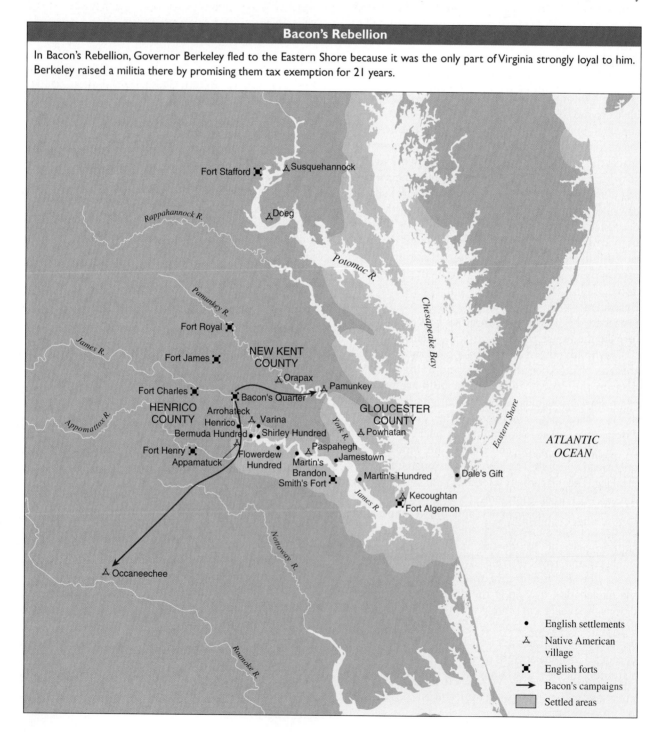

Bacon's Rebellion

In Bacon's Rebellion, Governor Berkeley fled to the Eastern Shore because it was the only part of Virginia strongly loyal to him. Berkeley raised a militia there by promising them tax exemption for 21 years.

hundreds of runaway servants and some slaves, he attacked friendly and hostile Native Americans alike. Governor Berkeley refused to sanction these attacks and declared Bacon a rebel, sending 300 militiamen to drag him to Jamestown for trial. Bacon recruited more followers, including many substantial planters. Frontier skirmishes with Native Americans had turned into civil war. During the summer of 1676, Bacon's and Berkeley's troops maneuvered, while Bacon's men continued their forays against local tribes. Then Bacon boldly captured and razed Jamestown, forcing Berkeley to flee across Chesapeake Bay.

DOCUMENT

Nathaniel Bacon's Declaration (July 30, 1676)

Virginians at all levels had chafed under Berkeley's rule. High taxes, an increase in the governor's powers at the expense of local officials, and the monopoly that Berkeley and his friends held on the Native American trade were especially unpopular. This opposition surfaced in the summer of 1676 as Berkeley's and Bacon's troops pursued each other through the wilderness. Berkeley tried to rally public support by holding new assembly elections and extending the vote to all freemen, whether they owned property or not. But the new assembly turned on the governor, passing laws to make government more responsive to the common people and to end rapacious officeholding. It also legalized enslaving Native Americans.

Time was on the governor's side, however. Having crushed the Native Americans, Bacon's followers began drifting home to tend their crops. Meanwhile, 1,100 royal troops were dispatched from England. By the time they arrived in January 1677, Nathaniel Bacon had died of swamp fever and most of his followers had melted away. Berkeley hanged 23 rebel leaders without benefit of trial.

DOCUMENT

Declaration Against Nathaniel Bacon (1676)

Royal investigators afterward reported that Bacon's followers "seem[ed] to wish and aim at an utter extirpation of the Indians." This hatred of Native Americans, along with hopes of land ownership and independence, became a permanent feature of Virginia life. Even a royal governor could not restrain such men. A generation later, in 1711, the legislature spurned the governor's plea for quieting the Native American frontier with educational missions and regulated trade, instead voting military appropriations of £20,000 "for extirpating all Indians without distinction of Friends or Enemys." The remnants of the once populous Powhatan Confederacy lost their last struggle for the world they had known. Now they moved farther west or submitted to a life on the margins of white society as tenant farmers, day laborers, or domestic servants.

After Bacon's Rebellion, an emerging planter aristocracy annulled most of the reform laws of 1676. By making new land available, the war relieved much of the social tension among white Virginians. Equally important, Virginians with capital to invest were turning from the impoverished rural villages of England and Ireland to the villages of West Africa to supply their labor needs. This halted the influx of poor white servants who, once free, had formed a discontented mass at the bottom of Chesapeake society. A racial consensus, uniting whites of different ranks in the common pursuit of a prosperous, slave-based economy, began to take shape.

Bacon's Rebellion caused rumblings outside Virginia. Many of his followers fled to North Carolina, joining disgruntled farmers there, who were distressed by recent Native American uprisings, export duties on tobacco, and quitrents controlled by a mercenary elite. Led by George Durant and John Culpeper, they drove the governor from office and briefly seized power.

In Maryland, Protestant settlers chafed under high taxes, quitrents, and officeholders regarded as venal, Catholic, or both. Declining tobacco prices and a fear of Indian attacks increased their touchiness. A month after Bacon razed Jamestown, insurgent small planters tried to seize the Maryland government. Two leaders were hanged for the attempt. In 1681, Josias Fendall and John Coode, "two rank Baconists" according to Lord Baltimore, led another abortive uprising.

In all three southern colonies, the volatility of late-seventeenth-century life owed much to the region's peculiar social development. Where family formation was retarded by imbalanced gender ratios and fearsome mortality, and where geographic mobility was high, little social cohesion or attachment to community could grow. Missing in the southern colonies were the stabilizing power of mature local institutions, a vision of a larger purpose, and the presence of experienced and responsive political leaders.

The Southern Transition to Slave Labor

English colonists on the mainland of North America at first regarded Native Americans as the obvious source of labor. But European diseases ravaged native societies, and the native people, more at home in the environment than the white colonizers, were difficult to subjugate. Indentured white labor proved the best way to meet the demand for labor during most of the seventeenth century.

ANALYZING HISTORY

The Atlantic Slave Trade

The enslavement of Africans and their forced migration to many parts of the world has no precedent in human history.

REFLECTING ON THE PAST   To what degree did climate and other environmental factors determine the development of slave-based societies in the Americas? What differences marked the Atlantic slave trade from the slave trade across the Sahara and through the Red Sea and Indian Ocean?

Most slaves came from coastal West Africa.

DESTINATION OF ENSLAVED AFRICANS

British North America	427,000
Mexico and Central America	224,000
British/French West Indies	4,040,000
Spanish America	746,000
Portuguese America	3,647,000

SOURCE: Data from Phillip D. Curtin, *The Atlantic Slave Trade*

The transport of Africans to Portuguese Brazil dwarfed that of all other colonies.

Area of origin of slaves
Area of slave settlement
Slave shipping (in thousands)
Routes for movement of slaves to the coast
Walo   Supplier tribe
•   Major slave ports

UNITED STATES — CANADA — New Orleans — Baltimore — Charleston — Jamestown — Havana — Domingo — Puerto Rico — Maracaibo — Georgetown — Ceará — BRAZIL — Bahia

ATLANTIC OCEAN — EUROPE — Mediterranean Sea — AFRICA — Sahara

British Caribbean 1,665 — French Caribbean 1,600 — Danish Caribbean 28 — Dutch Caribbean 500 — 399 — 50 — 1,552 — 3,646

Arguin — St. Louis — Gorée — Walo — Cayor — Baol — Manding — Fante — Pula — Susu — Anamabu — Lagos — Benin — Bobangi — Axim — Elmina — Cape Coast — Ouidan — Porto Novo — Forcados — Bonny — Calabar — Teke — Loango — Molembo — Cabinda — Luanda — Kongo — Benguela — Angola — Ndongo

From East Africa (numbers uncertain)

The illustration above, from an eighteenth-century pamphlet, demonstrates British regulations for stowing the human cargo aboard slave ships. *The Brooks*, a 320-ton slave-trading ship, was built to accommodate 451 people. However, because it was expected that many slaves would die en route, ship captains sometimes attempted to increase their profits by crowding even more slaves into the hold than regulations allowed (*The Library of Congress*).

SLAVE IMPORTATIONS, 1526–1810

Thousands of slaves
4,500
4,000
3,500
3,000
2,500
2,000
1,500
1,000
500
0

British N. America — British/French West Indies — Spanish America — Portuguese America

For every African brought to North America, more than nine were sold as slaves in the West Indies and more than eight in Brazil.

However, beginning in 1619, a few Africans entered the Chesapeake colonies to labor in the tobacco fields alongside white servants. But as late as 1671, when some 30,000 slaves toiled in English Barbados, fewer than 3,000 served in Virginia. They were still outnumbered there at least three to one by white indentured servants.

Only in the last quarter of the seventeenth century did the southern labor force begin to shift to a black slave majority. Three reasons explain this shift. First, the rising commercial power of England, at the expense of the Spanish and Dutch, swelled English participation in the African slave trade. This allowed southern planters, beginning in the 1680s, to purchase slaves more readily and cheaply than before. Second, the supply of white servants from England began drying up. Third, Bacon's Rebellion, involving rebellious former servants seeking land, led white planters to seek a more pliable labor force. Consequently, by the 1730s, the number of white indentured servants dwindled to insignificance. Black hands, not white, tilled and harvested Chesapeake tobacco and Carolina rice, and slave labor became the priority in starting a plantation.

In enslaving Africans, English colonists in North America merely copied their European rivals in the New World and emulated their countrymen on Barbados, Jamaica, and the Leeward Islands. There, from the 1630s on, the English had used brutal repression to mold Africans into a sugar- and tobacco-producing slave labor force. Human bondage would later become the subject of intense moral debate, but in the seventeenth century, all but a few whites accepted it without question.

The System of Bondage

The first Africans brought to the American colonies were probably sold as bound servants, who served their term and then, like Anthony and Mary Johnson, gained their freedom. Once free, they could buy land, hire out their labor, and move as they pleased. Their children, like those of white indentured servants, were born free. But gradually, Chesapeake planters drew tighter lines around the activities of black servants. By the 1640s, Virginia forbade blacks, free or bound, to carry firearms. In the 1660s, marriages between white women and black servants were banned as "shameful matches" and the "disgrace of our Nation." By the end of the century, when incoming Africans increased from a trickle to a torrent, even the few free blacks found themselves pushed to the margins of society. Slavery, which had existed for centuries in many societies as the lowest social status, was now becoming a caste reserved for those

Equiano This portrait, painted about 1780 after Equiano had purchased his freedom, shows him as a successful Londoner with hair and clothes in the style of a fashionable Englishman. In 1792, Equiano married an English woman and had two daughters with her. He died five years later. Do you think white Londoners in the 1790s accepted mixed-race marriages calmly? (Portrait of a Negro Man, Olaudah Equiano, 1780s, Robert Albert Memorial Museum, Exeter, Devon England/The Bridgeman Art Library)

with black skin. Step by step, white society turned the black servant from a low-status human being into a chattel, or commodity.

In this dehumanization of Africans, which the English largely copied from their colonial rivals, the key step was instituting hereditary lifetime service. Once servitude ended only by death, other privileges quickly vanished. When a mother's slave condition legally passed on to her newborn black infant (which was not the case in slavery in Africa), slavery became self-perpetuating, passing automatically from one generation to the next.

Slavery became not only a system of forced labor but also a pattern of human relationships legitimated by law. By the early eighteenth century, most provincial legislatures limited black rights. Borrowed largely from England's Caribbean colonies, "Black codes" forced Africans into an ever narrower world. Slaves could not testify in court, engage in commercial activity, hold property, participate in the political process, congregate in public, travel without permission, or legally marry or be parents. Nearly stripped of human status, they became defined as

DOCUMENT

Laws of Virginia (1661, 1662, 1691, 1705)

property, and gradually all legal restraints on the masters' treatment of them disappeared.

Eliminating slave rights did not eliminate slave resistance. With every African in chains a potential rebel, the rapid increase in the slave population brought anxious demands for strict control and justifications for brutality. "The planters," wrote one Englishman in Jamaica, "do not want to be told that their Negroes are human creatures. If they believe them to be of human kind, they cannot regard them as no better than dogs or horses." Thus occurred one of the great paradoxes of modern history. Many Old World immigrants imagined the Americas as a liberating and regenerating arena. Yet the opportunity to exploit its resources led to a historic process by which masses of Africans were wrenched from their homelands and forced into a system of slavery that could be maintained only by increasing intimidation and brutality.

MASSACHUSETTS AND ITS OFFSPRING

While some English settlers in the reign of James I (1603–1625) scrambled for wealth on the Chesapeake, others in England looked to the wilds of North America as a place to build a tabernacle to God. The society they fashioned aimed at unity of purpose and utter dedication to reforming the corrupt world. American Puritanism would powerfully affect the nation's history by nurturing a belief in America's special mission in the world. But the "New England way" also represented an attempt to banish diversity on a continent where the arrival of streams of immigrants from around the globe was destined to become the primary phenomenon.

Puritanism in England

England had been officially Protestant since 1558. Many English in the late sixteenth century, however, thought the Church of England was still riddled with Catholic vestiges. Some demanded the end of every taint of "the Bishop of Rome and all his detestable enormities." Because they wished to purify the Church of England, they were dubbed Puritans.

Religious reformers as well as men and women hoping to find in religion an antidote to the unsettling changes sweeping over English society were attracted to the Puritan movement. The growth of turbulent cities, the increase of wandering poor, rising prices, and accelerating commercial activity made them fear for the future and long for restraining old institutions such as the church, guilds, and local government.

While the concept of the individual operating as freely as possible, maximizing both opportunities and personal potential, is at the core of our modern system of beliefs, many in Elizabethan England dreaded the crumbling of traditional restraints. They wanted to preserve the ideal of community and the belief that people were bound together by reciprocal rights and responsibilities. Symptoms of the "degeneracy of the times" included the defiling of the Sabbath by Maypole dancing, card playing, fiddling, bowling, and all the rest of the roistering and erotic behavior reflected in Shakespeare's dramatic portrayals of "Merrie England." Puritans vowed to reverse the march of disorder by imposing a new discipline.

One part of their plan was a social ethic stressing work as a primary way of serving God. This emphasis on work made the religious quest of every member of society equally worthy. The labor of a mason was just as valuable in God's sight as that of a merchant, and so was his soul. The "work ethic" would banish idleness and impart discipline throughout the community. Second, Puritans organized themselves into religious congregations in which each member hoped for personal salvation but also supported all others in their quest. Third, Puritans assumed responsibility for coercing and controlling "unconverted" people around them.

In 1603, when King James VI of Scotland became James I of England, he claimed to be responsible only to God. This assertion led to his collision with the rising power of the Puritans, who occupied the pulpits in hundreds of churches, gained control of several colleges at Oxford and Cambridge, and obtained many seats in Parliament where they challenged the king's power. In response, James harassed them, removed dozens of Puritan ministers from their pulpits, and threatened many others. "I will harry them out of the land," he vowed, "or else do worse."

When Charles I succeeded to the throne in 1625, the situation for Puritans became worse. Determined to strengthen the monarchy and stifle dissent, the king summoned a new Parliament in 1628 and one year later adjourned this venerable body (which was the Puritans' main instrument of reform) when it would not accede to royal demands. The king then appointed William Laud, the bishop of London, to high office and turned him loose on the Puritans, whom Laud called "wasps" and the "most dangerous enemies of the state."

By 1629, as the king began ruling without Parliament, many Puritans were turning their eyes to northern Ireland, Holland, the Caribbean, and, especially, North America. They were convinced that God intended them to carry their religious and social reforms beyond the reach of persecuting authorities. A declining economy added to their discouragement about England. Many Puritans decided that they should transport a fragment of English society to some distant shore and complete the Protestant Reformation.

Puritan Predecessors in New England

Puritans were not the first European colonizers to reach northeastern North America. Since the early 1500s, fishermen from several European nations had dried their Newfoundland catches on the coast of Cape Cod and Maine, frequently encountering Algonquian-speaking natives. A short-lived attempt at settlement in Maine had been made in 1607. Seven years later, the aging Chesapeake war dog John Smith, hired to hunt whales off the North American coast, coined the term "New England."

No permanent settlement took root, however, until the Pilgrims—actually outnumbered by non-Pilgrims—arrived in Plymouth in 1620. Unlike the Puritans who followed, these humble Protestant farmers did not expect to convert a sinful world. Rather, they wanted to be left alone to realize their radical vision of a pure and primitive life. Instead of reforming the Church of England, they were Separatists who left it, first fleeing from England to Amsterdam in 1608, then to Leyden, Holland, and, finally, in 1620, to North America.

AUDIO
Plymouth Colony

Arriving at Cape Cod in November 1620, the Pilgrims were weakened by a stormy nine-week voyage and were ill-prepared for the harsh winter ahead. Misled by John Smith's glowing report of a warm, fertile country, they discovered instead a severe climate and a rockbound coast. By the following spring, half the *Mayflower* passengers were dead, including 13 of the 18 married women.

The survivors, led by the staunch William Bradford, settled at Plymouth. Squabbles soon erupted with local Native Americans, whom Bradford considered "savage and brutish men." In 1622, they found themselves nearly overwhelmed by the arrival of 60 non-Pilgrims, sent out by the London Company, which had helped the Pilgrims finance their colony. For two generations, the Pilgrims tilled the soil, fished, and tried to keep intact their religious vision. But with the much larger Puritan migration that began in 1630, the Pilgrim villages nestled around Cape Cod Bay became a backwater of

DOCUMENT
William Bradford, from *History of Plymouth Plantation*

Pilgrim Kitchen This scene of a woman in early seventeenth-century dress at Plimoth Plantation recreates life in the interior of one of the first crude houses erected by the Pilgrims. *(AP/Wide World Photos)*

the thriving, populous Massachusetts Bay Colony, which absorbed them in 1691.

Errand into the Wilderness

In 11 ships, about 1,000 Puritans set out from England in 1630 for the Promised Land—the vanguard of a movement that by 1642 brought about 18,000 colonizers to New England. Led by John Winthrop, a talented, Cambridge-educated member of the English gentry, they operated under a charter from the king to the Puritan-controlled Massachusetts Bay Company. The Puritans set about building their utopia convinced they were carrying out a divine task. "God hath sifted a nation," wrote one Puritan, "that he might send choice grain into this wilderness."

Their intention was to establish communities of pure Christians who collectively swore a covenant with God. Dreaming of homogeneous communities where the good of the group outweighed individual interests, Winthrop counseled that "We must delight in each other, make others' conditions our own, rejoice together, mourn together, labor and suffer together."

DOCUMENT
John Winthrop, "A Model of Christian Charity" (1630)

Puritans willingly gave up freedoms that other English settlers sought. An ideology of rebellion in England, Puritanism in North America became an ideology of control, suffused with a powerful sense of mission that still remains part of American thinking. As Winthrop reminded the first settlers, "we shall be as a city upon a hill [and] the eyes of all people are upon us."

As in Plymouth and Virginia, the first winter tested the strongest souls. More than 200 of the first

John Winthrop Always searching himself as well as others for signs of weakness, John Winthrop became the first governor of the Massachusetts Bay Colony. Do you think this portrait was painted in England or in Massachusetts? Explain your answer. *(Charles Osgood, John Winthrop (1588–1649) 1834, © Massachusetts Historical Society, Boston, MA, USA/Bridgeman Art Library)*

700 settlers perished, and 100 others, disillusioned and sickened by the forbidding climate, soon returned to England. But Puritans kept coming, settling along the rivers that emptied into Massachusetts Bay. A few years later, they pushed south into what became Connecticut and Rhode Island, as well as northward along the rocky coast.

Motivated by their militant work ethic and sense of mission, and led by men experienced in local government, law, and exhortation, the Puritans thrived. The early leaders of Virginia were soldiers of fortune or roughneck adventurers with predatory instincts, men who had no families or had left them at home; ordinary Chesapeake settlers were mostly young men with little stake in English society who sold their labor to cross the Atlantic. But the early leaders in Massachusetts were university-trained ministers, experienced members of the lesser gentry, and men with a compulsion to fulfill God's prophecy for New England. Most ordinary settlers came as free men and women in families. Artisans and farmers from the middle ranks of English society, they established tight-knit communities in which, from the outset, the brutal exploitation of labor rampant in the Chesapeake had no place.

Relying mostly on free labor, the Puritans built an economy based on agriculture, fishing, timbering, and trading for beaver furs with local Native Americans. Even before leaving England, the directors of the Massachusetts Bay Company transformed their commercial charter into a rudimentary government. In North America, they laid the foundations of self-government. Free male church members annually elected a governor and deputies from each town, who formed one house of a colonial legislature, the General Court. The other house was composed of the governor's assistants, later to be called councillors. Consent of both houses was required to pass laws.

The Puritans established the first printing press in the English colonies and founded Harvard College, which opened its doors in 1636 to train clergymen. The Puritan leaders also launched a brave attempt in 1642 to create a tax-supported school system, open to all wanting an education.

In spite of these accomplishments, the Puritan colony suffered many of the tensions besetting people bent on human perfection. Nor did Puritans prove any better at reaching an accommodation with the Native Americans than their less pious countrymen on the Chesapeake. Surrounded by seemingly boundless land, Puritans found it difficult to stifle acquisitive instincts and to keep families confined in compact communities. "An over-eager desire after the world," wrote an early leader, "has so seized on the spirits of many as if the Lord had no farther work for his people to do, but every bird to feather his own nest." Those remaining at the nerve center in Boston agitated for broader political rights and even briefly ousted Winthrop as governor in 1635, when the colony's clergy backed the stiff-necked Thomas Dudley. After a few years, Governor Winthrop wondered whether the Puritans had not gone "from the snare to the pit."

Winthrop's troubles multiplied in 1633 when Salem's Puritan minister, Roger Williams, began to voice disturbing opinions. The contentious and visionary young man argued that the Massachusetts Puritans were not truly pure because they would not completely separate from the polluted Church of England (which most Puritans still hoped to reform). Williams also denounced mandatory worship and argued that government officials should confine themselves to civil affairs and not interfere with religious matters. "Coerced religion," he warned, "on good days produces hypocrites, on bad days rivers of blood." Today honored as the earliest spokesman for the separation of church and state, Williams in 1633 seemed to strike at the heart of the Bible commonwealth, whose leaders regarded civil and religious affairs as inseparable. Williams also charged the Puritans with illegally intruding on Native American land.

For two years, Puritan leaders could not quiet the determined young Williams. Convinced that he would split the colony into competing religious groups and undermine authority, the magistrates vowed to deport him to England. Warned by Winthrop, Williams fled southward through winter snow with a small band of followers to found Providence in what would become Rhode Island.

Even as they were driving Williams out, the Puritan authorities confronted another threat: a devout and magnetic woman of extraordinary talent and intellect who arrived in 1634 with her husband and seven children. Quickly gaining respect among Boston's women as a midwife, healer, and spiritual counselor, Anne Hutchinson soon began to discuss religion and suggested that the "holy spirit" was absent in the preaching of some ministers. Before long Hutchinson was leading a movement labeled *antinomianism,* which stressed the mystical nature of God's free gift of grace while discounting the efforts the individual could make to gain salvation.

By 1636, Boston was dividing into two camps—those who followed the male clergy and those drawn to the theological views of a gifted though untrained woman without official standing. Her followers included most of the community's malcontents—merchants and artisans who chafed under the price controls the magistrates imposed in 1635 to stop inflation, young people resisting the rigid rule of their elders, and women disgruntled by male authority. Hutchinson doubly offended the male leaders of the colony because she boldly stepped outside the subordinate position expected of women. "The weaker sex" set her up as a "priest" and "thronged" after her, wrote one male leader. Another described a "clamour" in Boston that "New England men . . . usurp over their wives and keep them in servile subjection."

Determined to remove this thorn from their sides, the clergy and magistrates put Hutchinson on trial in 1637. After long interrogations, they convicted her of sedition and contempt in a civil trial and banished her from the colony "as a woman not fit for our society." Six months later, the Boston church excommunicated her for preaching 82 erroneous theological opinions. She had "highly transgressed and offended and troubled the church," pronounced the presiding clergyman, and "therefore in the name of our Lord Jesus Christ, I do cast you out and deliver you up to Satan and account you from this time forth to be a heathen and a leper." In the last month of her eighth pregnancy,

A Monument to Defiance   No likeness of Anne Hutchinson was ever painted, so her face in this sculpture standing outside the Massachusetts Statehouse in downtown Boston is entirely the work of the artist. The monument was erected in 1922. The sculptor, Cyrus E. Dallin, is famous for his "Appeal to the Great Spirit," a Native American figure showing desperation but defiance, much like Anne Hutchinson. *(Kevin Fleming/Corbis)*

Hutchinson, with a band of supporters, followed Roger Williams's route to Rhode Island in 1638.

Ideas proved harder to banish. The magistrates could never enforce uniformity of belief nor curb the appetite for land. Growth, geographic expansion, and commerce with the outside world all eroded the ideal of integrated, self-contained communities vibrant with piety. Leaders faced the nearly impossible task of containing land-hungry immigrants in an expansive region. By 1636, groups of Puritans had swarmed not only to Rhode Island but also to Hartford and New Haven, where Thomas Hooker and John Davenport led new Puritan settlements in what became Connecticut.

New Englanders and Indians

Though the charter of the Massachusetts Bay Company spoke of converting "the natives to the knowledge and obedience of the only true God and Saviour of mankind and the Christian faith," the instructions that Governor John Winthrop carried from England reveal other Puritan thoughts about

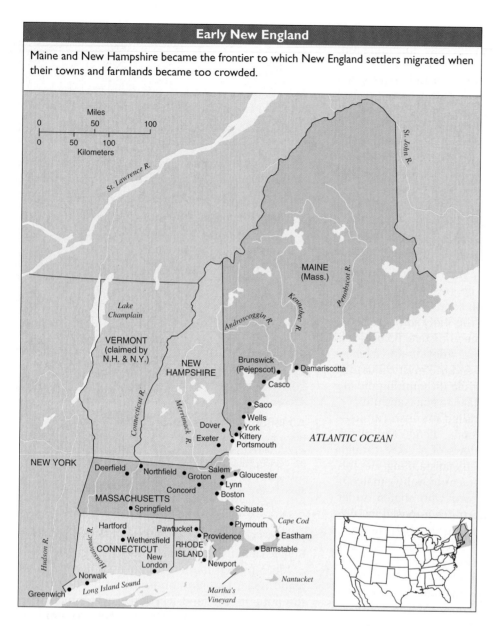

Early New England

Maine and New Hampshire became the frontier to which New England settlers migrated when their towns and farmlands became too crowded.

the native inhabitants. According to Winthrop's orders, all men were to receive training in the use of firearms, a reversal of the sixteenth-century English policy of disarming the citizenry in order to quell public disorders. New England magistrates prohibited Native Americans from entering Puritan towns and threatened to deport any colonist selling arms to a native or instructing one in their use.

Only sporadic conflict with local tribes occurred at first because disease had left much of New England vacant. In 1616, visiting English fishermen had triggered a ferocious outbreak of respiratory viruses and smallpox that wiped out three-quarters of some 125,000 Native Americans. Five years later, an Englishman exploring the area described walking through a forest where human skeletons covered the ground. The Puritans believed that God

had intervened on their side, especially when smallpox returned in 1633, killing thousands more natives and allowing new settlers to find land. Many surviving natives welcomed the Puritans because they now had surplus land and through trade hoped to gain English protection against tribal enemies to the north.

The settlers' pressure for new land, however, soon reached into areas untouched by disease. Land hunger mingled with the Puritan sense of mission made an explosive mix. To a people brimming with messianic zeal, the Native Americans represented a challenge to the building of a religious commonwealth that would "shine as a beacon" back to decadent England. Puritans believed that God would blame them for not civilizing and Christianizing the natives and would punish them with his wrath, so they tried to make the "savages" of New England strictly accountable to their ordinances. They succeeded with the smaller, disease-ravaged tribes of eastern Massachusetts, but control over the stronger Pequot led to a bloody war in 1637. The Puritan victory assured English domination over all the tribes of southern New England except the powerful Wampanoag and Narragansett of Rhode Island and removed the last obstacle to expansion into the Connecticut River valley. Missionary work, led by John Eliot, began among the remnant tribes in the 1640s. After a decade of effort, about 1,000 Native Americans had been settled in four "praying villages," learning to live according to the white settlers' ways.

The Web of Village Life

Unlike the dispersed Chesapeake tobacco planters, the Puritans established small, tightly settled villages that were vital centers of life. Most were "open field" agricultural communities where farmers trudged out from the village each morning to cultivate narrow strips radiating out from the town. They grazed their cattle on common meadowland and cut firewood on common woodland. In other towns, Puritans employed the "closed field" system of self-contained farms that they had known at home. Both systems re-created common English patterns of agriculture with families living close together in towns built around a common, with a meetinghouse and tavern. These small, communal villages kept families in close touch so that each could be alert not only to its own transgressions, but also to those of its neighbors. "In a multitude of counsellors is safety," Puritan ministers were fond of advising, and the little villages of 50 to 100 families perfectly served the need for moral surveillance, or "holy watching." To achieve godliness and communal unity, Puritans also prohibited single men and women from living by themselves, beyond patriarchal authority and group observation. Left to themselves, men and women would stray from the path, for, as Thomas Hooker put it, "every natural man and woman is born full of sin, as full as a toad of poison." Virginia planters counted the absence of restraint as a blessing. New Englanders feared it as the Devil.

At the center of every Puritan village stood the meetinghouse. These plain wooden structures, sometimes called "Lord's barns," gathered in every soul in the village twice a week. No man stood higher in the community than the minister, the spiritual leader in these small, family-based, community-oriented settlements, which viewed life as a Christian pilgrimage.

In Commemoration of Lydia Minot Funeral testimonies like this one were cheaply printed as broadsides and were passed out to mourners. When Lydia Minot died in 1667 while giving birth to her sixth child, she was memorialized with anagrams and acrostics—popular literary exercises in the seventeenth century. What do the hourglass, coffin, and shovel, at the middle of the broadside, symbolize? *(Courtesy of the Massachusetts Historical Society)*

The unique Puritan mixture of strict authority and incipient democracy, of hierarchy and equality, can be seen in the way the Massachusetts town distributed land and devised local government. After receiving a grant, townsmen met to parcel out land. They awarded individual grants according to the size of a man's household, his wealth, and his usefulness to the church and town. Such a system perpetuated existing differences in wealth and status. Yet some towns wrote language into their covenants that to the modern ear has an almost socialistic ring. "From each according to his ability to each as need shall require," read one. But it was not socialism that the Puritans had in mind; rather, they believed that the community's welfare transcended individual ambitions or accomplishments and that

How Others See Us

John Josselyn of Kent, England, on his second trip across the Atlantic, described New Englanders in the 1660s in this way.

The great masters [magistrates] as also some of their merchants, are damnable rich, generally all of [them] inexplicably covetous and proud. They receive your gifts but as an homage or tribute due to their transcendancy [high social position], which is a fault their clergy are also guilty of, whose living is upon the bounty of their hearers . . . . But . . . there are many sincere and religious people amongst them, descried by their charity and humility . . . by their hearty submission to their sovereign, the king of England, by their diligent and honest labor in their callings . . . . There are none that beg in the country, but there be witches too many—bottle-bellied witches amongst the Quakers and others that produce many strange apparitions (if you will believe reports of it): of a shallop [small ship] at sea manned with women; of a ship and a great red horse standing by the main mast; a ship being in a small cove to the eastward vanished of a sudden; of a witch that appeared aboard a ship twenty leagues to sea; of a mariner who took up the carpenter's broad axe and cleft her head with it; the witch dying of the wound at home.

■ *Does Josselyn believe in witches?*

■ *What do the many reports of apparitions tell you about the Salem witchcraft trials 30 years after this account was written?*

Source: John Josselyn, *Two Voyages to New England* (London, 1674), excerpted in James Axtell, *America Perceived: A View from Abroad in the 17th Century* (West Haven, Conn.: Pendulum Press, 1974), 102–103. Spelling and punctuation have been modernized.

---

unity demanded limits on the accumulation of wealth. Every family should have enough land to sustain it, and prospering men were expected to use their wealth for such community projects as repairing the meetinghouse, building a school, or aiding a widowed neighbor.

Having felt the sting of centralized power in church and state, Puritans emphasized local exercise of authority. Until 1684, only male church members could vote, and as the proportion of males who were church members declined, so did the proportion of men who could vote. These voters elected selectmen, who allocated land, passed local taxes, and settled disputes. Once a year, all townsmen gathered for the town meeting, which Thomas Jefferson later called the "wisest invention ever devised by the wit of man for the perfect exercise of self-government." At town meetings the citizens selected town officers for the next year and decided matters large and small. The appointment of many citizens to minor offices—surveyors of hemp, informers about deer, purchasers of grain, town criers, measurers of salt, fence viewers, and others—bred the tradition of local government. About one of every 10 adult males in many towns was selected each year for some office, large or small.

The predominance of families also lent cohesiveness to Puritan village life. Strengthening this family orientation was the healthy environment of the

Population of the New England Colonies, 1620–1750

The fact that white population growth was far more rapid in New England than in the Chesapeake region reflected higher birthrates, a healthier environment, and a reliance on free labor.

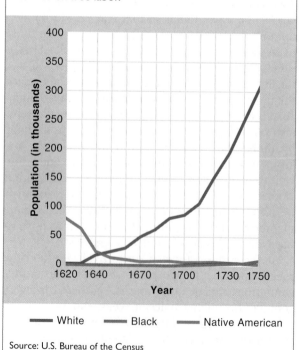

Source: U.S. Bureau of the Census

90

The Mason Children Three of Arthur and Joanna Mason's five children were captured in this 1670 painting. The nine-year-old boy on the left holds a silver-headed walking stick, signifying his status as male heir. His six-year-old sister in the middle holds a yellow fan and red and yellow ribbons. The four-year-old sister to the right holds a rose, which Puritans used as a symbol of innocence associated with childhood. Why do you think the artist portrayed these children with faces typical of older boys and girls? *(The Freake-Gibbs painter,* The Mason Children: David, Joanna, and Abigail, *1670. Fine Arts Museum of San Francisco, Gift of Mr. and Mrs. John Rockefeller 3rd, 1979 .7.3)*

in England because of the healthier climate and better diet. In most of Europe, only half the babies born lived long enough to produce children themselves. Life expectancy for the population at large was less than 40 years. In New England, nearly 90 percent of the infants born in the seventeenth century survived to marriageable age, and life expectancy exceeded 60 years—longer than for the American population as a whole at any time until the early twentieth century. About 25,000 people immigrated to New England in the seventeenth century, but by 1700, they had produced a population of 100,000. By contrast, some 75,000 immigrants to the Chesapeake colonies had yielded a population of only about 70,000 by the end of the century.

Women played a vital role in this family-centered society. The Puritan woman was not only a wife, mother, and housekeeper; she also kept the vegetable garden; salted and smoked meats; preserved vegetables and dairy products; and spun yarn, wove cloth, and made clothes.

Puritans' "New Israel." Whereas the germs carried by English colonizers devastated neighboring Native American societies, the effect on the newcomers of entering a new environment was the opposite. The low density of settlement prevented infectious diseases from spreading, and the isolation of the New England villages from the avenues of Atlantic commerce, along which diseases as well as cargo flowed, minimized biological hazards.

The result was a spectacular natural increase in the population and a life span unknown in Europe. At a time when the population of western Europe was barely growing—deaths almost equaled births—the population of New England, discounting new immigrants, doubled every 27 years. The difference was not a higher birthrate. New England women typically bore about seven children during the course of a marriage, but this barely exceeded the European norm. The crucial factor was that chances for survival after birth were far greater than

The presence of women and a stable family life strongly affected New England's regional architecture. As communities formed, the Puritans converted early economic gains into more substantial housing rather than investing in bound labor as Chesapeake colonists did, a practice that retarded family formation and rendered the economy unstable. In New England, well-constructed one-room houses with sleeping lofts quickly replaced the early "wigwams, huts, and hovels." Families then added parlors and lean-to kitchens as soon as they could. Within a half century, New England immigrants accomplished a general rebuilding of their living structures, whereas Chesapeake residents lagged far behind.

A final binding element in Puritan communities was the stress on literacy and education, eventually to become a hallmark of American society. Placing religion at the center of their lives, Puritans emphasized the ability to read catechisms, psalmbooks, and especially the Bible. In literacy and education, Puritans saw guarantees for preserving their central values.

Though eager to be left alone, Puritans could not escape events in England. In 1642, King Charles I pushed England into revolution by violating the country's customary constitution and continuing earlier attacks against Puritans. By 1649, the ensuing civil war climaxed with the trial and beheading of the king. Thereafter, during the so-called Commonwealth period (1649–1660), Puritans in England could complete the reform of religion and society at home. Meanwhile, migration to New England abruptly ceased.

Page from *The New England Primer*

The 20,000 English immigrants who had come to New England by 1649 were scattered from Maine to Long Island. Governor Winthrop of Massachusetts and Roger Williams of Rhode Island deplored this dispersion and condemned the "depraved appetite" for new and better land. Yet in a terrain so rock-strewn that its pastures were said to produce Yankee sheep with sharpened noses, it was natural that farmers should seek better plow land.

In 1643, to combat the problems of dispersion, Puritan leaders established the Confederation of New England, intended to coordinate government among the various Puritan settlements (Rhode Island was pointedly excluded) and to provide more effective defense against the French, the Dutch, and the Native Americans. This first American attempt at federalism functioned fitfully for a generation and then dissolved.

Although the Puritans fashioned stable communities, developed the economy, and constructed effective government, their leaders, as early as the 1640s, complained that the founding vision of Massachusetts Bay was faltering. Material concerns seemed to transcend religious commitment; the individual prevailed over the community. In 1638, the General Court declared a day of humiliation and prayer to atone for the colony's "excess idleness and contempt of authority." A generation later, the synod of 1679—a convention of Puritan churches—cried out that the "church, the commonwealth and the family are being destroyed by self-assertion." If social diversity increased and the religious zeal of the founding generation waned, that was only to be expected. One second-generation Bay colonist put the matter bluntly. His minister had noticed his absence in church and found him later that day at the docks, unloading a boatload of cod. "Why were you not in church this morning?" asked the clergyman. Back came the reply: "My father came here for religion, but I came for fish."

King Philip's War in New England

For religious leaders concerned about declining piety, continued difficulties with native tribes of southern New England signaled new evidence of God's displeasure. Following the Pequot War of 1637, the Wampanoag and Narragansett tried to keep their distance from the Puritans who coveted their territories. As New Englanders quarreled among themselves over provincial boundaries, they gradually reduced the natives' land base.

By the 1670s, when New England's population had grown to about 50,000, the Native American leader was Metacomet (called King Philip by the English), the son of Massasoit, the Wampanoag chief who had allied with the first Plymouth settlers in 1620. Metacomet had watched his older brother preside over the deteriorating position of his people after their father's death in 1661. Becoming chief in his turn, Metacomet faced one humiliating challenge after another, climaxing in 1671, when leaders of the Plymouth colony forced him to surrender a large stock of guns and accept his people's subjection to English law.

Metacomet began organizing a resistance movement fed by the rising anger of the young Wampanoag males, who refused to imitate their fathers, who had acquiesced to the colonizers' encroachments and abridgment of their sovereignty. For the young tribesmen, revitalization of their ancient culture through war became as important a goal as defeating the enemy. Rather than submit further, they attempted a pan-Indian offensive against an ever-stronger intruder.

In 1675, Puritans executed three Wampanoag for murdering John Sassamon, a Christianized Native American educated at Harvard who had allegedly warned Plymouth colony of an impending native attack. The execution sparked insurrection. That summer the Wampanoag unleashed daring hit-and-run attacks on villages in the Plymouth colony. By autumn, many New England tribes, including the powerful Narragansett, had joined Metacomet. Towns all along the frontier reeled under Native American attacks. By November, native warriors had devastated the entire upper Connecticut River valley, and by March 1676, they were less than 20 miles from Boston and Providence. As assumptions about English military superiority faded, New England officials passed America's first draft laws. Widespread draft evasion and friction among the colonies hampered a counteroffensive.

Metacomet's offensive faltered in the spring of 1676, sapped by food shortages, disease, and the refusal of the powerful Mohawk to join the New England tribes. Then Metacomet fell in a battle near the Wampanoag village where the war had begun.

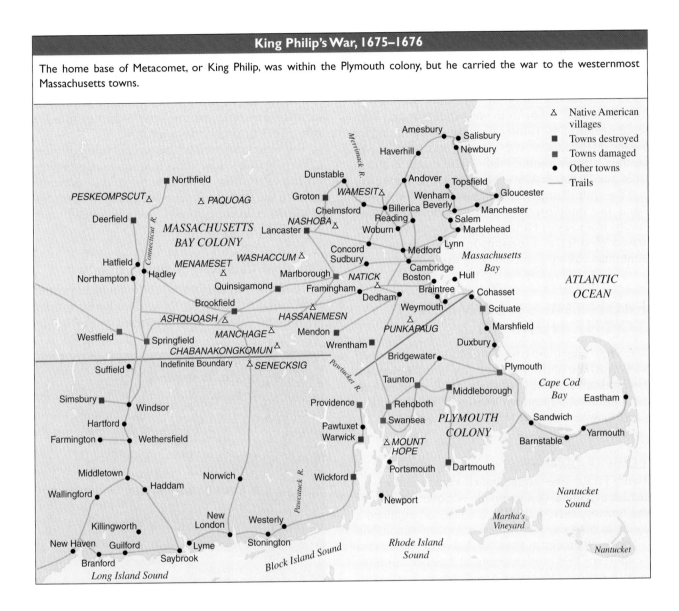

King Philip's War, 1675–1676

The home base of Metacomet, or King Philip, was within the Plymouth colony, but he carried the war to the westernmost Massachusetts towns.

The head of this "hell-hound, fiend, serpent, caitiff and dog," as one colonial leader branded him, was displayed in Plymouth for 25 years.

At war's end, several thousand colonists and perhaps twice as many Native Americans lay dead. Of some 90 Puritan towns, 52 had been attacked and 13 completely destroyed. Some 1,200 homes lay in ruins and 8,000 cattle were dead. The estimated cost of the war exceeded the value of all personal property in New England. Not for 40 years would the frontier advance beyond the line it had reached in 1675. Native American towns were devastated even more completely, including several inhabited by "praying Indians" who had converted to Christianity and allied with the whites. An entire generation of young men had been nearly annihilated. Many of the survivors, including Metacomet's wife and son, were sold into slavery in the West Indies.

Slavery in New England

The Wampanoag captives sold as slaves in the West Indies continued New England's involvement in the dirty business of slavery. New England's crops were not labor-intensive, so coerced labor never became the foundation of New England's workforce. Slavery did take root in the cities, though, where slaves worked as artisans and domestic servants. Northern colonial economies also became enmeshed in the Atlantic commercial network, which depended on slavery and the slave trade. New England's merchants eagerly pursued profits in the slave trade as early as the 1640s. By 1676, New England slavers were packing their holds with slaves from Madagascar, off the coast of East Africa, and transporting them 6,000 miles to the western side of the Atlantic. By 1750, half the merchant fleet of Newport, Rhode Island, reaped profits from carrying human cargo. In New York and

Philadelphia, building and outfitting slave vessels proved profitable.

New England's involvement in the international slave trade deepened with the growth of its seaports as centers for distilling rum—the "hot, hellish and terrible liquor" made from West Indian sugar. Rum became one of the principal commodities traded for slaves on the African coast. As the number of slaves in the Caribbean multiplied—from about 50,000 in 1650 to 500,000 in 1750—New England's large fishing fleet found important markets for its cod. Wheat from the middle colonies and barrel staves and hoops from North Carolina also serviced the slave-based West Indies economy. In short, every North American colony participated in the slave business.

FROM THE ST. LAWRENCE TO THE HUDSON

The New Englanders were not the only European settlers in the northern region, for both France and Holland created colonies there. While English settlers founded Jamestown, the French were settling Canada, where they had failed in the 1540s.

France's America

Henry IV, the first strong French king in half a century, sent Samuel de Champlain to explore deep into the territory even before the English had obtained a foothold on the Chesapeake. Champlain established a small settlement in Port Royal, Acadia (later Nova Scotia), in 1604 and another at Québec in 1608. French trading with Native Americans for furs had already begun in Newfoundland, and Champlain's settlers hoped to keep making these easy profits. But the holders of the fur monopoly in France did not encourage immigration to the colony, fearing that settlement would reduce the forests from which the furs were harvested. New France therefore remained so lightly populated that English marauders easily seized and held Québec from 1629 to 1632.

In 1609–1610, Champlain allied with the Algonquian Indians of the St. Lawrence region in attacking their Iroquois enemies to the south, earning their enmity. This drove the Iroquois to trade furs for European goods with the Dutch on the Hudson River; when the Iroquois exhausted the furs of their own territory, they turned north and west, determined to seize the forest-rich resources from the Huron, French allies in the Great Lakes region.

When the Iroquois descended on them in the 1640s, the Huron were already decimated by a decade of epidemics that spread among them as Jesuit priests entered their villages. In the "beaver wars" of the 1640s and 1650s, the Iroquois used Dutch guns to attack Huron parties carrying beaver pelts to the French. By midcentury, Iroquois attacks had scattered the Huron, all but ending the French fur trade and reducing the Jesuit influence to a few villages of Christianized Huron.

The bitterness bred in these years colored future colonial warfare, driving the Iroquois to ally with the English against the French. By the mid-seventeenth century, the English remained unhindered by the beleaguered French colonists, who numbered only about 400.

England Challenges the Dutch

By 1650, the Chesapeake and New England regions each contained about 50,000 settlers. Between them lay the mid-Atlantic area controlled by the Dutch,

A Young Dutch Girl in America An anonymous artist painted Megdalena Down as a young girl living in the Hudson River region in the 1740s. Does her apparel suggest she is the daughter of a Dutch family? (John Heaten, Magdalena Douw (Ganesvoort), c. 1740, Courtesy, Winterthur Museum, gift of Henry Francis du Pont)

New Amsterdam in 1644 The fort at the tip of Manhattan, flying an English flag, shows prominently in this 1664 map of Dutch New Amsterdam just after it had been bloodlessly conquered by a small English fleet. The park-filled city and the Governor's garden fronting on the Hudson River were separated by a wall from the farmlands of "upper" Manhattan. *(By Permission of the British Library, Shelfmark Maps.K.Top.121.35)*

who planted a small colony named New Netherland at the mouth of the Hudson River in 1624. In the next four decades they extended their control to the Connecticut and Delaware river valleys. South of the Chesapeake lay a vast territory where only the Spanish, from their mission frontier in Florida, challenged the power of Native American tribes.

Although for generations they had been the Protestant bulwarks in a mostly Catholic Europe, England and Holland became bitter commercial rivals in the mid-seventeenth century. By the time the Puritans arrived in New England, the Dutch had become the mightiest carriers of seaborne commerce in western Europe. By one contemporary estimate, Holland owned 16,000 of Europe's 20,000 merchant ships. The Dutch had also muscled in on Spanish and Portuguese transatlantic commerce, trading illegally with Iberian colonists who gladly violated their government's commercial policies to obtain cloth and slaves more cheaply. By 1650, the Dutch had temporarily overwhelmed the Portuguese in Brazil, and soon their vast trading empire reached the East Indies, Ceylon, India, and Formosa (now Taiwan). The best shipbuilders, mariners, and businessmen in western Europe, they validated the dictum of Sir Walter Raleigh that "whosoever commands the sea commands the trade; whosoever commands the

trade of the world commands the riches of the world, and consequently the world itself."

In North America, the Dutch West India Company's New Netherland colony was small, profitable, and multicultural. Agents fanned out from Fort Orange (Albany) and New Amsterdam (New York City) into the Hudson, Connecticut, and Delaware river valleys, establishing a lucrative fur trade with local tribes by hooking into the sophisticated trading network of the Iroquois Confederacy, which stretched to the Great Lakes. The Iroquois welcomed the Dutch presence, who were few in number, did not have voracious appetites for land, and willingly exchanged desirable goods for the pelts of animals plentiful in the vast Iroquois territory. At Albany, the center of the Dutch–Iroquois trade, relations remained peaceful and profitable for several generations.

Although the Dutch never settled more than 10,000 people in their mid-Atlantic colonies, their commercial and naval powers were impressive. The Virginians learned this in 1667 when brazen Dutch raiders captured 20 tobacco ships on the James River and confiscated virtually the entire tobacco crop for that year.

By 1650, England was ready to challenge Dutch maritime supremacy. War broke out three times between 1652 and 1675, as the two Protestant nations competed to control the emerging worldwide capitalist economy. In the second and third wars, New Netherland became an easy target for the English. They captured it in 1664 and then, after it fell to the Dutch in 1673, recaptured it almost immediately. By 1675, the Dutch had been permanently dislodged from the North American mainland. But they remained mighty commercial competitors of the English around the world.

New Netherland—where from the beginning Dutch, French Huguenots, Walloons from present-day Belgium, Swedes, Portuguese, Finns, English, refugee Portuguese Jews from Brazil, and Africans had commingled in a babel of languages and religions—now became New York, so named because Charles II gave it (along with the former Dutch colonies on the Delaware River) to his brother the duke of York, later King James II. Under English rule, the Dutch colonists remained ethnically distinct for several generations, clinging to their language, their Dutch Reformed Calvinist churches, and their architecture. In time, however, English immigrants overwhelmed the Dutch, and gradual intermarriage among the Dutch, the French Huguenots (Protestants), and the English diluted ethnic loyalties. New York retained its polyglot, religiously tolerant character, and its people never allowed religious concerns or utopian plans to interfere with the pragmatic conduct of business.

Father Isaac Jogues, Description of New York (1646)

PROPRIETARY CAROLINA: A RESTORATION REWARD

In 1663, three years after he was restored to his father's throne, England's Charles II granted a vast territory named Carolina to a group who supported him during his exile. Its boundaries extended from Virginia southward to central Florida and westward to the Pacific. Within this potential empire, eight London-based proprietors, including several involved in Barbados sugar plantations, gained governmental powers and semifeudal rights to the land. The system of governance planned for Carolina had both feudal and modern features. To lure settlers, the proprietors promised religious freedom and offered land free for the asking. However, this generous land offer included a scheme for a semimedieval government in which they, their deputies, and a few noblemen would monopolize political power. Reacting to a generation of revolutionary turbulence in England, they designed Carolina as a model of social and political stability

in which a hereditary aristocracy would check boisterous small landholders.

Carolina realities bore faint resemblance to these hopes. The rugged sugar and tobacco planters who streamed in from Barbados and Virginia, where depressed economic conditions made a new beginning seem attractive, claimed their 150 acres of free land, as well as additional acreage for each family member or servant they brought. They ignored proprietary regulations about settling in compact rectangular patterns and reserving two-fifths of every county for an appointed nobility. In government, they also did as they pleased. Meeting in assembly for the first time in 1670, they refused to accept the proprietors' Fundamental Constitutions of 1667 and ignored orders from the proprietors' governor. Most of the settlers already knew how to run a slave society from having lived in Barbados, and they shaped local government from that experience.

The Indian Debacle

Carolina was the most elaborately planned colony in English history yet the least successful in achieving the harmony the proprietors had intended. Mindful of the violence that had plagued other settlements, they projected a well-regulated Native American trade, run exclusively by their appointed agents. By drawing the major tribes of the Southeast—the Cherokee, Creek, and Choctaw—into trade they might reap vast wealth, which the Spanish in Florida had failed to tap. But the aggressive settlers from the West Indies and the Chesapeake flouted all this.

To the consternation of the London proprietors, capturing Native Americans for sale in New England and the West Indies became the cornerstone of commerce in Carolina in the early years, plunging the colony into a series of wars. Planters and merchants selected a small tribe, armed it, and rewarded it handsomely for bringing in enemy captives. But even strong tribes found that after they had used English guns to enslave their weaker neighbors, they themselves were scheduled for elimination. The colonists claimed that "thinning the barbarous Indian natives" was needed to make room for white settlement, and the "thinning" was so thorough that by the early eighteenth century the two main tribes of the coastal plain, the Westo and the Savannah, were nearly extinct.

Early Carolina Society

Carolina's fertile land and warm climate convinced many that it was a "country so delicious, pleasant, and fruitful that were it cultivated doubtless it

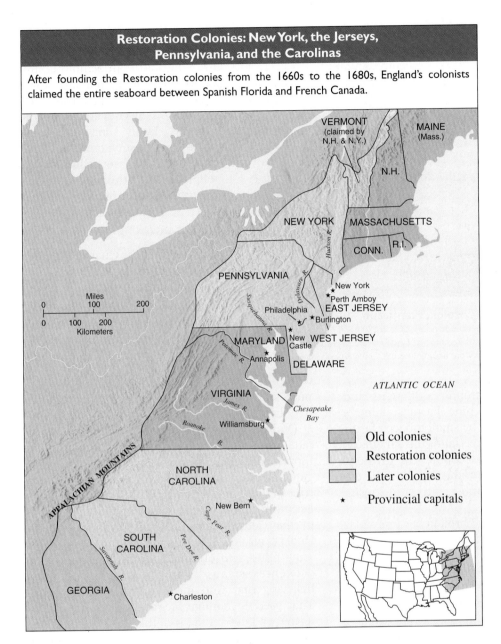

Restoration Colonies: New York, the Jerseys, Pennsylvania, and the Carolinas

After founding the Restoration colonies from the 1660s to the 1680s, England's colonists claimed the entire seaboard between Spanish Florida and French Canada.

would prove a second Paradize." In came Barbadians, Swiss, Scots, Irish, French Huguenots, English, and migrants from northern colonies. But far from creating paradise, they clashed abrasively in an atmosphere of fierce competition, ecological exploitation, brutal race relations, and stunted social institutions. Decimating the coastal Native Americans made it easier to expand the initial settlements around Charleston.

After much experimentation, planters found a profitable staple crop that would flourish in this forbidding environment: rice. Its cultivation required backbreaking labor to drain swamps, build dams and levees, and hoe, weed, cut, thresh, and husk the crop. Many early settlers had owned African slaves in Barbados, so their reliance on slave labor came

naturally. On widely dispersed plantations, black labor came to predominate. In 1680, four-fifths of South Carolina's population was white. But by 1720, when the colony had grown to 18,000, black slaves outnumbered whites two to one.

As in Virginia and Maryland, the low-lying areas of coastal Carolina were so disease-ridden that population grew slowly in the early years. "In the spring a paradise, in the summer a hell, and in the autumn a hospital," remarked one traveler. Malaria and yellow fever, especially dangerous to pregnant women, were the main killers that retarded population growth, and the scarcity of women further limited natural increase. Like the West Indies, the rice-growing region of Carolina was at first more a place to accumulate a fortune than to rear a family.

Slave Quarters on a South Carolina Plantation   This painting of Mulberry Plantation in South Carolina shows the mansion house, built in 1708, and rows of slave huts constructed in an African style. Most enslaved Africans lived in far more primitive structures in the eighteenth century. *(Mulberry Plantation, Gibbes Museum/Carolina Art Association)*

In healthier northern Carolina, a different kind of society emerged amid pine barrens along a sandy coast. Settled largely by small tobacco farmers from Virginia seeking free land, the Albemarle region developed a mixed economy of livestock grazing, tobacco and food production, and the extraction of naval stores—lumber, turpentine, resin, pitch, and tar.

In 1701, North and South Carolina became separate colonies, but their distinctiveness had already emerged. Slavery took root only slowly in North Carolina, which was still 85 percent white in 1720. A land of struggling white settlers, its healthier climate and settlement by families rather than by single men with servants and slaves gave it a greater potential for sustained growth. But in North as well as South Carolina, scattered settlements, ethnic and religious diversity, and a lack of shared assumptions about social and religious goals inhibited the growth of a strong colony-wide identity.

THE QUAKERS' PEACEABLE KINGDOM

Of all the utopian dreams imposed on the North American landscape in the seventeenth century, the most remarkable was the Quakers'. During the English civil war, the Society of Friends, as the Quakers called themselves, had sprung up as one of the many radical sects searching for a juster society and a purer religion. Their visionary ideas and defiance of civil authority cost them dearly in fines, brutal punishment, and imprisonment. After Charles II and Parliament stifled radical dissent in the 1660s, they, too, sent many converts across the Atlantic. More than any other colony, the society they founded in Pennsylvania foreshadowed the religious and ethnic pluralism of the future United States.

The Early Friends

Like Puritans, the Quakers regarded the Church of England as corrupt. But Quakers went much further, rejecting all Church officials and institutions and holding that every believer could find grace through the "inward light," a redemptive spark in every human soul. Rejecting original sin and eternal predestination, Quakers offered a radical alternative to Calvinism.

Other Protestants, regarding them as dangerous fanatics, persecuted Quakers in England after their movement, led by George Fox and Margaret Fell, gathered momentum in the 1650s. The Quaker doctrine of the "light within" took precedence even over Scripture and elevated all laypeople to the position of the clergy. Practicing civil disobedience, the Quakers also threatened social hierarchy and order. They refused to observe the customary marks of deference, such as doffing one's hat to a superior, believing that God made no social distinctions. They used the familiar *thee* and *thou* instead of the formal and deferential *you*, they resisted taxes supporting the Church of England, and they refused to sign witnesses' oaths on the Bible, regarding this as profane. Most shocking, they renounced the use of force in human affairs and therefore refused to perform militia service.

Quakers also affronted traditional views when they insisted on the spiritual equality of the sexes and the right of women to participate in church matters on an equal, if usually separate, footing with men. Quaker leaders urged women to preach and to establish separate women's meetings. Among Quakers who fanned out from England to preach the doctrine of the inward light, 26 of the first 59 to cross the Atlantic were women. All but four of them were unmarried or without their husbands and therefore living, traveling, and ministering outside male authority.

Intensely committed to converting the world, Quakers ranged westward to North America and the Caribbean in the 1650s and 1660s. Nearly everywhere, they faced jeers, prison, mutilation, deportation, and death. Puritan Massachusetts warned them "to keep away from us and such as will come to be gone as fast as they can, the sooner the better." Hungering to serve in what they called "the Lamb's War" (the crusade of the meek), the Quakers vowed to test the Puritans' resolve and kept coming. To enforce religious conformity, the Bay Colony magistrates in 1659 hanged two Quaker men on the Boston Common and threatened to do the same to Mary Dyer, an old woman who had followed Anne Hutchinson a quarter century before. Led from the colony, Dyer returned the next year, undaunted, to meet her death at the end of a rope in 1661.

Early Quaker Designs

By the 1670s, the English Quakers were looking for a place in the New World to carry out their millennial dreams and escape severe repression. They found a leader in William Penn. His decision to identify with this radical and persecuted sect was surprising, for he was the son of Sir William Penn, the admiral who had captured Jamaica from Spain in 1654. In 1666, the 23-year-old Penn adopted the Quaker creed and thereafter devoted himself to the Friends' cause.

In 1674, Penn joined other Friends in establishing a North American colony, West Jersey. They had bought the land from one of the proprietors of New Jersey, itself a new English colony recently carved out of the former New Netherland. For West Jersey, Penn helped fashion a constitution extraordinarily liberal for its time that allowed virtually all free males to vote for legislators and local officials. Settlers were guaranteed freedom of religion and trial by jury. As Penn and the other trustees of the colony explained, "We lay a foundation for [later] ages to understand their liberty as men and Christians, that they may not be brought in bondage, but by their own consent; for we put the power in the people."

The last phrase, summing up the document, would have shocked anyone of property and power in England or North America at the time. Most regarded "the people" as ignorant, dangerous, and certain to bring society to a state of anarchy if allowed to rule themselves. Nowhere in the English world had ordinary citizens, especially those who did not own land, enjoyed such extensive privileges. Nowhere had a popularly elected legislature received such broad authority.

William and Hannah Callowhill Penn The likenesses of William Penn and Hannah Callowhill Penn, his second wife, were done by Francis Place, an amateur artist. After Penn died in 1718, his widow became an absentee director of the family affairs in Pennsylvania until she died in 1726. Does Hannah Penn's clothing suggest that she is a Quaker? *(Top: Francis Place, William Penn. The Historical Society of Pennsylvania [1957.8]; bottom: Francis Place, Hannah Callowhill Penn. The Historical Society of Pennsylvania [1957.7])*

West Jersey sputtered at first. Only 1,500 immigrants arrived in the first five years, and for several decades the colony was caught up in tangled claims to the land and government. The center of Quaker hopes lay across the Delaware River, where in 1681, Charles II granted William Penn a territory almost as large as England, paying off a large royal debt to Penn's father. Charles II also benefited by getting the pesky Quakers out of England. Thus Penn and the Quakers came into possession of the last unassigned segment of the eastern coast of North America, and one of the most fertile.

Pacifism in a Militant World: Quakers and Native Americans

On the day Penn received his royal charter for Pennsylvania, he wrote a friend, "My God that has

DOCUMENT

William Penn, Description of Pennsylvania (1681)

given it to me will, I believe, bless and make it the seed of a nation." The nation that Penn envisioned was unique among colonizing schemes. Penn intended to make his colony an asylum for the persecuted and a refuge from arbitrary state power. Puritans had strived for social homogeneity and religious uniformity, excluding all not of like mind. In the Chesapeake and Carolina colonies, aggressive, unidealistic men had

sought to exploit their lands and bondspeople. But Penn dreamed of inviting to his forested colony people of all religions and national backgrounds, offering them peaceful coexistence. His state would neither claim authority over citizens' consciences nor demand military service of them.

The Quakers began streaming into Pennsylvania in 1682, quickly absorbing earlier Dutch, Finnish, and Swedish settlers. They participated in the government by electing representatives who initiated laws. They were primarily farmers, and like colonists elsewhere, they avidly acquired land, which Penn sold at reasonable rates. Unlike other colonizers, the Quakers practiced pacifism, holding the ethic of love and nonresistance embodied in the Sermon on the Mount as literally binding on them.

Even before arriving, Penn laid the foundation for peaceful relations with the Delaware tribe inhabiting his colony. "The king of the Country where I live, hath given me a great Province," he wrote to the Delaware chiefs, "but I desire to enjoy it with your Love and Consent, that we may always live together as Neighbors and friends." In this single statement Penn dissociated himself from the entire history of European colonization in the New World and from the widely held negative view of Native Americans. Recognizing the natives as the rightful owners of the land included in his grant, Penn pledged not to sell

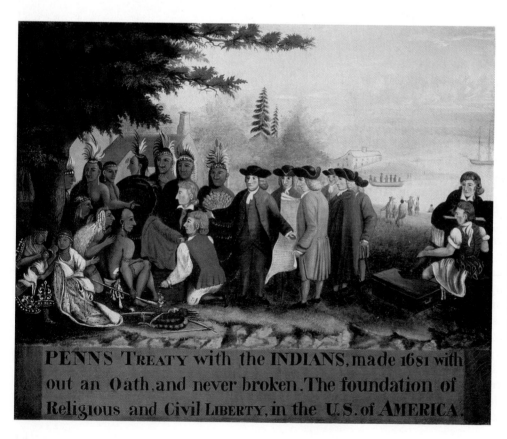

Concluding a Treaty with the Indians

Edward Hicks painted *Penn's Treaty with the Indians* in the nineteenth century. It is a romanticized version of the Treaty of Shackamaxon by which the Lenape chiefs ceded the site of Philadelphia to Penn. The treaty was actually made in 1682, but Hicks was correct in implying that the Lenape held Penn in high regard for his fair treatment of them. What evidence of Quaker pacifism do you find in this painting? *(Edward Hicks, Penn's Treaty with the Indians, Gift of Edgar William and Bernice Chrysler Garbisch, © 2000 Board of Trustees, National Gallery of Art, Washington)*

AMERICAN VOICES

William Penn, To the Delaware Chiefs

Addressing them as "My Friends in 1681," William Penn wrote the Delaware (Lenape) chiefs the following letter as Quaker colonists were preparing to leave England for Pennsylvania. Penn signed the letter "I am your friend, William Penn."

There is one great God and power that has made the world and all things therein, to whom you and I and all people owe their being and well-being, and to whom you and I must one day give an account for all that we do in this world. This great God has written his law in our hearts, by which we are taught and commanded to love and help and do good to one another, and not to do harm and mischief one unto another. Now this great God has been pleased to make me concerned in our parts of the world, and the kind of the country where I live has given unto me a great province therein, but I desire to enjoy it with your friends, else what would the great God say to us, who has made us not to devour and destroy one another, but live soberly and kindly together in the world. . . . I am very sensible of the unkindness and injustice that has been too much exercised towards you by the people of these parts of the world, who have sought themselves, and to make great advantages by you, rather than be examples of justice and goodness unto you; which I hear has been matter of trouble to you and caused great grudgings and animosities, sometimes to the shedding of blood, which has made the great god angry. But I am not such a man, as is well known in my own country. I have great love and regard toward you and I desire to win and gain your love and friendship by a kind, just, and peaceable life; and the people I send are of the same mind, and shall in all things behave themselves accordingly. And if in anything any shall offend you or your people, you shall have a full and speedy satisfaction for the same by an equal number of honest men on both sides, that by no means you may have just occasion of being offended against them.

- To what extent does Penn's Quaker pacifism explain this letter?

- Was there any precedent for what he mentions at the end of the letter: mediation of European–Native American disputes by an equal number of native and white males?

---

one acre until he had first purchased it from local chiefs. He also promised to regulate strictly the Native American trade and to ban alcohol sales.

The Quaker accomplishment is sometimes disparaged with the claim that there was little competition for land in eastern Pennsylvania between the natives and the newcomers. However, a comparison between Pennsylvania and South Carolina, both established after the restoration of Charles II to the English throne in 1660, shows the power of pacifism. A quarter century after initial settlement, Pennsylvania had a population of about 20,000 whites. Penn's peaceful policy had so impressed Native American tribes that native refugees began migrating into Pennsylvania from all sides. During the same 25 years, South Carolina had grown to only about 4,000 whites, many of them involved in wholesale violence employed to enslave thousands of Native Americans and lay waste to the Spanish mission frontier in Florida.

As long as the Quaker philosophy of pacifism and friendly relations with the local Native Americans held sway, interracial relations in the Delaware River valley contrasted sharply with those in other parts of North America. But ironically, the Quaker policy of toleration, liberal government, and exemption from military service attracted thousands of immigrants to the colony (especially in the eighteenth century) whose land hunger and disdain for Native Americans undermined Quaker trust and friendship. Driven from their homelands by hunger and war, Germans and Scots–Irish flooded in, swelling the population to 31,000 by 1720. Neither shared Quaker idealism about racial harmony. They pressed inland and, sometimes encouraged by the land agents of Penn's heirs, encroached on the lands of the local tribes. By the mid-eighteenth century, white immigrants were spilling blood with the natives who also sought sanctuary in Pennsylvania.

Building the Peaceable Kingdom

Although Pennsylvania came closer to matching its founder's goals than any other European colony, Penn's dreams never completely materialized.

101

Unable to persuade people to settle in compact villages, which he believed necessary for his "holy experiment," they instead created open country networks without any particular centers or boundaries.

Still, because Quaker farmers prized family life and immigrated almost entirely in kinship groups, a sense of common endeavor persisted. This helped them maintain their distinctive identity. So did other practices such as allowing marriage only within their society, carefully providing land for their offspring, and guarding against too great a population increase (which would cause too rapid a division of farms) by limiting the size of their families.

Settled by religiously dedicated farming families, Pennsylvania boomed. Its countryside became a rich grainland. By 1700, the port capital of Philadelphia overtook New York City in population, and a half century later, it was the largest city in the colonies, bustling with artisans, mariners, merchants, and professionals.

The Limits of Perfectionism

Despite commercial success and peace with Native Americans, not all was harmonious in early Pennsylvania. Politics were often turbulent, in part because of Pennsylvania's weak leadership. Penn was a much-loved proprietor, but he returned to England in 1684, revisiting his colony briefly in 1700. Penn's absence created a leadership vacuum.

A more important cause of disunity resided in the Quaker attitude toward authority. In England, balking at authority was almost a daily part of Quaker life. But in Pennsylvania, the absence of persecution eliminated a crucial binding element from Quaker society. The factionalism that developed among them demonstrated that people never unify as well as when under attack. Rather than looking inward and banding together, they looked outward to an environment filled with opportunity. Their squabbling filled Penn with dismay. Why, he asked, were his settlers so "governmentish, so brutish, so susceptible to scurvy quarrels that break out to the disgrace of the Province?"

Meanwhile, Quaker industriousness and frugality helped produce great material success. After a generation, social radicalism and religious evangelicalism began to fade. As in other colonies, settlers discovered the door to prosperity wide open, and in they surged. Pennsylvania, it is said, was the first community since the Roman Empire to allow people of different national origins and religious persuasions to live together under the same government on terms of near equality. English, Highland Scots, French, Germans, Irish, Welsh, Swedes, Finns, and Swiss all settled in Pennsylvania. This ethnic mosaic was further complicated by a medley of religious groups, including Mennonites, Lutherans, Dutch Reformed, Quakers, Baptists, Anglicans, Presbyterians, Catholics, Jews, and a sprinkling of mystics. Their relations may not always have been friendly, but few attempts were made to discriminate against dissenting groups. Pennsylvanians thereby laid the foundations for the pluralism that was to become the hallmark of American society.

NEW SPAIN'S NORTHERN FRONTIER

Spain's outposts in Florida and New Mexico, preceding all English settlements on the eastern seaboard, fell into disarray between 1680 and the early eighteenth century just as the English colonies were sinking deep roots. Trying to secure a vast northern frontier with only small numbers of settlers, the Spanish relied on forced Native American labor. This reliance proved to be their undoing in Florida and New Mexico.

Popé's Revolt

During the 1670s, when the Franciscans developed a new zeal to root out traditional Native American religious ceremonies, the Pueblo people turned on the Spanish intruders. In years of harsh rule, the Spanish had extracted tribute labor from the Pueblo, who at the same time suffered the ravaging effects of European diseases. Both of these punishing long-term effects contributed to Pueblo alienation, but an assault on their religion pushed the Pueblo to the edge. Launching a campaign to restrict native religious ceremonies in the 1670s, the Spanish friars seized the Pueblo kivas (underground ceremonial religious chambers), forbade native dances, and destroyed priestly masks and prayer sticks.

In August 1680, Popé, a much-persecuted medicine man from San Juan pueblo, responded by leading about two dozen Pueblo villages scattered over several hundred miles to rise up in fury. They burned Spanish ranches and government buildings, systematically destroyed Spanish churches, lay waste to Spanish fields, and killed half of the friars. As the Spanish governor in Santa Fe watched the church go up in flames, he reported his shock at the "scoffing and ridicule which the wretched and miserable Indian rebels made of the sacred things, intoning . . . prayers of the church with jeers."

Spanish settlers, soldiers, and friars streamed back to El Paso, abandoning their northern frontier in the Southwest for more than a decade. Only in 1694 did a

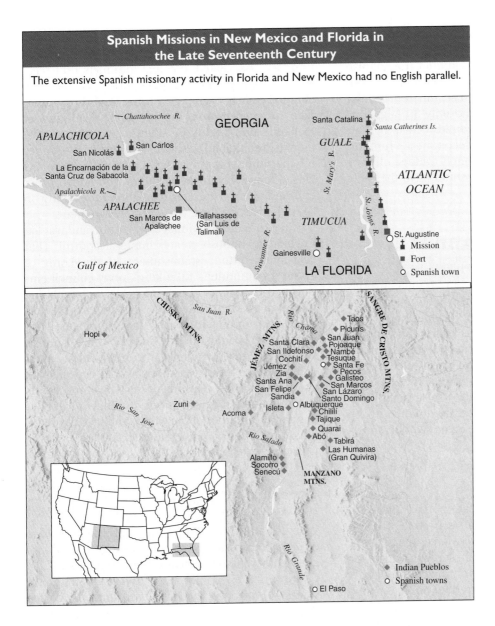

Spanish Missions in New Mexico and Florida in the Late Seventeenth Century

The extensive Spanish missionary activity in Florida and New Mexico had no English parallel.

DOCUMENT

Legal Statement of Pedro Hidalgo, Soldier, Santa Fe (1680)

new Spanish governor, the intrepid Diego de Vargas, regain Santa Fe and gradually subdue most of the Pueblo. Learning from Popé's rebellion, the Spanish declared a cultural truce, easing their demands for Pueblo labor tribute and tolerating certain Pueblo rituals in return for nominal acceptance of Christianity. Periodic tension and animosity continued, but the Pueblo had to come to terms with the Spanish because of their need for defense against their old enemies—the Navajo, Ute, and Apache.

Decline of Florida's Missions

The Franciscan missions established in Florida along the Atlantic coast and inland to the west in

the Florida panhandle had firmed up New Spain's grip of the southeast corner of North America. Yet few Spanish settlers could be persuaded to settle in Florida. As the governor of Cuba put it frankly in 1673, "It is hard to get anyone to go to St. Augustine because of the horror with which Florida is painted. Only hoodlums and the mischievous go there from Cuba."

Much devastated by disease, the Florida Indians and their Franciscan spiritual shepherds were as severely pummeled as those in New Mexico in the late seventeenth century. English settlers in neighboring South Carolina were eager to use Native American allies to attack the Spanish Indian villages and sell the captives into slavery. The attacks of Carolinians in the early 1680s destroyed a number of Spanish missions. When England and Spain went to war in

1701—called Queen Anne's War in the colonies—the Carolinians attacked Florida. Burning mission villages to the ground, they slaughtered the Spanish friars and captured some 4,000 women and children to be sold as slaves. The Spanish mission frontier was thoroughly devastated, and only St. Augustine remained as a Spanish stronghold. Unlike in New Mexico, there was no Spanish reconquest. From this time onward, English and French traders, offering more attractive trade goods, would have the main influence over Florida Indians.

AN ERA OF INSTABILITY

A dozen years after King Philip's War in New England and Bacon's Rebellion in Virginia, a series of insurrections and a searing witchcraft incident convulsed colonial society. The Revolution of 1688 triggered the rebellions and was known thereafter to English Protestants as the Glorious Revolution since it ended forever the notion that kings ruled by "divine right." Marking the last serious Catholic challenge to Protestant supremacy, it also signified a struggle for social and political dominance in the expanding colonies, as did the Salem witchcraft trials in Massachusetts.

Organizing the Empire

From the beginning of colonization, the English assumed that overseas settlements existed to promote the national interest at home. Mercantilist theory held that colonies were meant to serve as outlets for English manufactured goods, provide foodstuffs and raw materials, stimulate trade (and hence promote a larger merchant navy), and fill royal coffers by exporting commodities such as sugar and tobacco on which duties were paid. In return, colonists received English military protection and guaranteed markets.

Beginning with a small step in 1621, when the king's council forbade tobacco growers to export their crop to anywhere but England, the Crown slowly began to regulate its colonies in order to mold them into a unified empire. However, not until 1651, when the colonists traded freely with the commercially aggressive Dutch, did Parliament consider regulating colonial affairs. It passed a navigation act requiring that English or colonial ships, manned by English or colonial sailors, carry all goods entering England, Ireland, and the colonies, no matter where those goods originated. These first steps toward a regulated empire were also the first steps to place England's power behind national economic development.

In 1660, after the monarchy was restored, Parliament passed a more comprehensive navigation act that listed colonial products (tobacco, sugar, indigo, dyewoods, and cotton) that could be shipped only to England or other English colonies. Like its predecessor, the act took dead aim at Holland's domination of Atlantic commerce, while increasing England's revenues by imposing duties on the enumerated articles. Later navigation acts closed loopholes in the 1660 law and added other enumerated articles. This regulation bore lightly on the colonists, for the laws lacked enforcement.

After 1675, international competition and war led England to impose greater imperial control. That year marked the establishment of the Lords of Trade, a committee of the king's privy council empowered to make and enforce decisions regulating the colonies. Their chief aim was to create more uniform governments in North America and the West Indies that would do the Crown's will. Although movement toward imperial centralization often sputtered, the trend was unmistakable, especially to colonists who felt the sting of royal customs agents sent to enforce the navigation acts. England was becoming the shipper of the world, and its state-regulated policy of economic nationalism was essential to commercial greatness.

The Glorious Revolution in North America

When Charles II died in 1685, his brother, the duke of York, became King James II. This set in motion a chain of events that nearly led to civil war. Like Charles, James II professed the Catholic faith. Charles II, however, had disclosed this only on his deathbed, while the new king announced his faith immediately on assuming the throne. Consternation ensued. Protestant England recoiled when James issued the Declaration of Indulgence, which granted liberty of worship to all. Belief that the declaration was primarily a concession to Catholics hardened when the king began creating Catholic peerages to fill the House of Lords, appointed Catholics to high government posts, and demanded that Oxford and Cambridge open their doors to Catholic students. In 1687, the king dismissed a resistant Parliament. When his wife, supposedly too old for childbearing, bore a son in 1688, a Catholic succession loomed.

Convinced that James aimed at absolute power, Protestant leaders in 1688 invited a Dutch prince, William of Orange, to seize the throne with his wife, Mary, who was James's Protestant daughter.

DOCUMENT

English Bill of Rights (1689)

James abdicated rather than fight. It was a bloodless victory for Protestantism, for parliamentary power and the limitation of kingly prerogatives, and for the merchants and gentry of England.

The response of New Englanders to these events stemmed from their previous experience with royal authority and their fear of "papists." In 1676, New England became a prime target for efforts to reorganize the empire and crack down on smuggling, which had prevailed there for two generations. Charles II annulled the Massachusetts charter in 1684, and two years later James II appointed Sir Edmund Andros, a crusty professional soldier and former governor of New York, to rule over the newly created Dominion of New England. Soon the dominion gathered under one government all the English colonies from Maine to New Jersey. Puritans now had to swallow the bitter fact that they were subjects of London bureaucrats who cared more about shaping a disciplined empire than about New England's special religious vision.

At first, New Englanders accepted Andros, though coolly. But he soon earned their hatred by invading freedoms they cherished. He imposed taxes without legislative consent, ended trial by jury, abolished the General Court of Massachusetts (which had met annually since 1630), muzzled Boston's town meetings, and challenged land titles. He also mocked the Puritans by converting a Boston Puritan meeting-house into an Anglican chapel, held services there on Christmas Day—a gesture that to Puritans stank of popery—and insisted on religious toleration.

When news reached Boston in April 1689 that William of Orange had landed in England, Bostonians streamed into the streets. They imprisoned Andros, a suspected papist, and overwhelmed the fort in Boston harbor, which held most of the governor's small contingent of red-coated royal troops. Andros escaped, disguised in women's clothing, but was quickly recaptured. Boston's ministers, along with merchants and former magistrates, led the rebellion, but city folk of the lower orders supplied the foot soldiers. For three years, an interim government ruled Massachusetts while the Bay colonists awaited a new charter and a new royal governor.

Although Bostonians had dramatically rejected royal authority and the "bloody devotees of Rome," no internal revolution occurred. However, growing social stratification and the emergence of a political elite caused some citizens to argue that men of modest means but common sense might better be trusted with power. "Anarchy" was the word chosen by Samuel Willard, minister of Boston's Third Church, to tar the popular spirit he saw unloosed in Boston in the aftermath of Andros's ouster. But such egalitarian rumblings came to little.

In New York, the Glorious Revolution was similarly bloodless at first but far more disruptive. Royal government melted away on news of James's abdication. Displacing the governor's "popishly affected dogs and rogues," German-born militia captain Jacob Leisler established an interim government and ruled with an elected Committee of Safety for 13 months until a governor appointed by King William arrived.

Leisler's government enjoyed popularity among Dutch small landowners and urban laboring people who had resented the English seizing their colony and crowding them out of the society they had built.

Most of the upper Dutch echelon, however, had adjusted to English rule and many incoming English merchants had married into Dutch families. These New Yorkers detested Leisler as an upstart—a common foot soldier of the Dutch West India Company who arrived in 1660 and had leapfrogged into the merchant class by marrying a wealthy widow. After the English seized the Dutch colony in 1664, he was often at odds with English leaders.

The Glorious Revolution ignited this smoldering social conflict. Leisler shared Dutch hostility toward New York's English elite, and his sympathy for the common people, mostly Dutch, earned him the hatred of the city's oligarchy. Leisler freed imprisoned debtors, planned a town-meeting system of government for New York City, and replaced merchants with artisans in important offices. By the autumn of 1689, Leislerian mobs were attacking the property of some of New York's wealthiest merchants. Two merchants, refusing to recognize Leisler's authority, were jailed.

Leisler's opponents were horrified at the power of the "rabble." They believed that ordinary people had no right to rebel against authority or to exercise political power. When a new English governor arrived in 1691, the anti-Leislerians embraced him and charged Leisler and seven of his assistants with treason for assuming the government without royal instructions.

In the ensuing trial, an all-English jury convicted Leisler and Jacob Milbourne, his son-in-law and chief lieutenant, of treason and ordered them hanged. Leisler's popularity among the artisans of the city was evident when his wealthy opponents could find no carpenter in the city who would make a ladder for the scaffold. After his execution, peace gradually returned to New York, but for years provincial and city politics reflected the deep rift between Leislerians and anti-Leislerians.

The Glorious Revolution also focused dissatisfactions in several southern colonies. Because a Catholic proprietor ruled Maryland, the Protestant majority seized power in July 1689 on word of the Glorious Revolution, using it for their own purposes. They vowed to cleanse Maryland of popery and to reform a corrupt customs service, cut taxes and fees, and extend the rights of the representative assembly. The militant Protestant John Coode, formerly a fiery Anglican minister who had been involved in a brief rebellion in 1681, assumed the reins of government and held them until the arrival of Maryland's first royal governor in 1692.

In neighboring Virginia, the wounds of Bacon's Rebellion were still healing when word of the Glorious Revolution arrived. The fact that Virginia lived under a Catholic governor, Lord Howard of Effingham, and a number of Catholic officials, fostered rumors of a Catholic plot. News of the revolution in England led a group of planters, suffering a prolonged drop in tobacco prices, to try to overthrow the governor, but the governor's council defended itself, partly by removing Catholics from positions of authority.

The Glorious Revolution brought lasting political changes to several colonies. The Dominion of New England collapsed. Connecticut and Rhode Island regained the right to elect their own governors, but Massachusetts (now including Plymouth) and New Hampshire became royal colonies with governors appointed by the king. In Massachusetts, a new royal charter in 1691 eliminated Church membership as a voting requirement. The Maryland proprietorship was abolished (to be restored in 1715 when the Calverts became Protestant), and Catholics were barred from office. Everywhere Protestant Englishmen celebrated their liberties.

The Social Basis of Politics

The colonial insurrections associated with the Glorious Revolution revealed social and political tensions that accompanied the transplanting of English society to the North American wilderness. Colonial societies were hardly beyond the frontier stage, still fluid, unruly, competitive, and lacking the stable political systems and acknowledged leadership class thought necessary for social order.

The emerging colonial elite tried to foster stability by upholding a stratified Old World–style society in which children were subordinate to parents, women to men, servants to masters, and the poor to the rich. Hence, leaders everywhere tried to maintain social gradations and subordination. Puritans did not file into church on Sundays and occupy the pews randomly; seats were "doomed," or assigned according to customary yardsticks of respectability—age,

parentage, social position, wealth, and occupation. Even in fluid Virginia, lower-class people were hauled before courts for horse racing because this was a sport legally reserved for men of social distinction.

These social distinctions proved difficult to maintain. Regardless of previous rank, settlers rubbed elbows so frequently and faced such raw conditions together that those without pedigrees often saw little reason to defer to men of superior rank. "In Virginia," explained John Smith, "a plain soldier that can use a pickaxe and spade is better than five knights." Colonists everywhere gave respect not to those who claimed it by birth but to those who earned it by deed. A native elite gradually formed, but it had no basis as in Europe in legally defined and hereditary social rank. Planters and merchants, accumulating large estates, aped the English gentry by cultivating the arts, building fine houses, and acquiring symbols of respectability such as libraries, coaches, and racehorses. Yet their place was rarely secure. New competitors nipped constantly at their heels.

Amid such social flux, the elite never commanded general allegiance to the ideal of a fixed social structure. Ambitious men on the rise such as Nathaniel Bacon and Jacob Leisler, and their discontented followers, rose up against the constituted authorities, which they almost certainly would not have dared to do so in their homelands. When they gained power during the Glorious Revolution, in every case only briefly, the leaders of these uprisings linked themselves with a tradition of English struggle against tyranny and oligarchical power. They vowed to make government more responsive to the ordinary people, who composed most of their societies.

Witchcraft in Salem

The ordinary people in the colonies, for whom Bacon and Leisler tried to speak, could sometimes be misled, as the tragic events of the Salem witch hunts demonstrated. In Massachusetts, the deposing of Governor Andros left the colony in political limbo for three years, and this allowed what might have been a brief outbreak of witchcraft in the little community of Salem to escalate into a bitter and bloody battle. The provincial government, caught in transition, reacted only belatedly.

DOCUMENT

Ann Putnam's Deposition (1692)

On a winter's day in 1692, 9-year-old Betty Parris and her 11-year-old cousin Abigail Williams began to play at magic in the kitchen of a small house in Salem, Massachusetts. They enlisted the aid of Tituba, the slave of Betty's father, Samuel Parris,

What Witches Can Do On both sides of the Atlantic, most people took witches seriously. The book *Full and Plain Evidence Concerning Witches and Apparitions*, published in London in 1681, showed devil-inspired witches flying over a house, entering an attic window, and hovering in one of the rooms. *(By permission of the Houghton Library, Harvard University)*

the minister of the small community. Tituba told voodoo tales from her Caribbean past and baked "witch cakes." The girls soon became seized with fits and began making wild gestures and speeches. Soon other young girls in the village were behaving strangely. Village elders extracted confessions that they were being tormented by Tituba and two other women, both social outcasts.

What began as young girls' play turned into a ghastly rending of a farm community capped by the execution of 20 villagers accused of witchcraft. In the seventeenth century, people still took literally the biblical injunction "Thou shalt not suffer a witch to live." For centuries throughout western Europe, people had believed that witches followed Satan's bidding and did evil to anyone he designated. Communities had accused and sentenced women to death for witchcraft far more often than men. In Massachusetts, more than 100 people, mostly older women, had been accused of witchcraft before 1692, and more than a dozen had been hanged.

In Salem, the initial accusations against three older women quickly multiplied. Within weeks, dozens had been charged with witchcraft, including several prominent figures. Formal prosecution of the accused witches could not proceed because neither the new royal charter of 1691 nor the royal governor to rule the colony had yet arrived. For three months, while charges spread, local authorities could only jail the accused without trial. When Governor William Phips arrived from England in May 1692, he ordered a special court to try the accused. By then, events had careened out of control.

All through the summer, the court listened to testimony. By September it had condemned about two dozen villagers. The authorities hanged 19 of them on barren "Witches Hill" outside the town and crushed 80-year-old Giles Corey to death under heavy stones. The trials rolled on into 1693, but by then, colonial leaders, including many of the clergy, recognized that a feverish fear of one's neighbors, rather than witchcraft itself, had possessed the little village of Salem.

DOCUMENT
The Conclusions of the Massachusetts Bay Elders (1695)

Many factors contributed to the hysteria. Among them were generational differences between older Puritan colonists and the sometimes less religiously motivated younger generation, old family animosities, population growth and pressures on the available farmland, and tensions between agricultural Salem Village and the nearby commercial center called Salem Town. An outbreak of

AUDIO
Lookie There!

food poisoning may also have caused hallucinogenic behavior, and a new Native American war on the Massachusetts–Maine frontier caused near-hysteria. Probably nobody will ever fully understand the exact mingling of causes, but the fact that most of the individuals charged with witchcraft were women underscores the relatively weak position of women in Puritan society. The relentless spread of witchcraft accusations suggests the anxiety of this tumultuous era of war, economic disruption, the political tension, and the erosion of the early generation's utopian vision.

TIMELINE

1607	Jamestown settled
1616–1621	Native American population in New England decimated by European diseases
1617	First tobacco crop shipped from Virginia
1619	First Africans arrive in Jamestown
1620	Pilgrims land at Plymouth
1622	Powhatan tribes attack Virginia settlements
1624	Dutch colonize mouth of Hudson River
1630	Puritan immigration to Massachusetts Bay
1632	Maryland grant to Lord Baltimore (George Calvert)
1633–1634	Native Americans in New England again struck by European diseases
1635	Roger Williams banished and flees to Rhode Island
1637	New England wages war against the Pequot people
1638	Anne Hutchinson exiled to Rhode Island
1640s	New England merchants enter slave trade Virginia forbids blacks to carry firearms
1642–1649	English civil war ends great migration to New England
1643	Confederation of New England
1650–1670	Judicial and legislative decisions in Chesapeake colonies solidify racial lines
1651	Parliament passes first navigation act
1659–1661	Puritans hang three Quaker men and one Quaker woman on Boston Common
1660	Restoration of King Charles II in England
1663	Carolina charter granted to eight proprietors
1664	English capture New Netherland and rename it New York Royal grant of the Jersey lands to proprietors
1673–1685	French expand into Mississippi valley
1675–1677	King Philip's War in New England
1676	Bacon's Rebellion in Virginia
1680	Popé's revolt in New Mexico
1681	William Penn receives Pennsylvania grant
1684	Massachusetts charter recalled
1688	Glorious Revolution in England, followed by accession of William and Mary
1689	Overthrow of Governor Andros in New England Leisler's Rebellion in New York
1690s	Transition from white indentured servitude to black slave labor begins in Chesapeake region
1692	Witchcraft hysteria in Salem

Conclusion

The Achievement of New Societies

Nearly 200,000 immigrants who had left their European homelands reached North America in the seventeenth century. Coming from a variety of social backgrounds and spurred by different motives, they represented the rootstock of distinctive societies that would mature in the North American colonies of England, France, Holland, and Spain. For three generations, North America served as a social laboratory for religious and social visionaries, political theorists, fortune seekers, social outcasts, and, most of all, ordinary men and women seeking a better life than they had known in Europe.

By the end of the seventeenth century, 12 English colonies on the eastern edge of North America (and several others in the West Indies) had secured footholds in the hemisphere and erected the basic scaffolding of colonial life. So had Spanish and French colonies lying north, south, and west of the English. The coastal Native American tribes were reeling from disease and a series of wars that secured the English colonists' land base along 1,000 miles of coastal plain. Though never controlling the powerful tribes of the interior, the colonists had established a profitable trade with them. English settlers had overcome a scarcity of labor by copying the other European colonists in the hemisphere, who had linked the west coast of Africa to the New World through the ghastly trade in human flesh. Finally, the English colonists had engaged in insurrections against what they viewed as arbitrary and tainted governments imposed by England.

The embryo of British America carried into the eighteenth century contained peculiarly mixed features. Disease, stunted family life, and the harsh work regimen imposed by the planters who commanded the labor of the vast majority ended the dreams of most who came to the southern colonies. Yet population inched upward, and the bone and sinew of a workable economy formed. In the northern colonies, to which the fewest immigrants came, life was more secure. Organized around family and community, favored by a healthier climate, and motivated by religion and social vision, the Puritan and Quaker societies thrived.

Still physically isolated from Europe, the colonists developed a large measure of self-reliance. Slowly, they began to identify themselves as the permanent inhabitants of a new land rather than as transplanted English, Dutch, or Scots-Irish. Viewing land and labor as the indispensable elements of a fruitful economy, they learned to exploit without apologies the land of one dark-skinned people and the labor of another. Yet even as they attained a precarious mastery in a triracial society, they were being culturally affected by the very people to whose land and labor they laid claim. Although utopian visions of life in North America still preoccupied some, most colonists had awakened to the reality that life in the New World was a mixture of unpredictable opportunity and sudden turbulence, unprecedented freedom and debilitating wars, racial intermingling and racial separation. It was a New World in much more than a geographic sense, for the people of three cultures who now inhabited it had remade it. And, while doing so, people like Anthony and Mary Johnson (whom we met at the beginning of the chapter) were remaking themselves.

Questions for Review and Reflection

1. What factors most shaped the development of the colonial Chesapeake region in the seventeenth century?

2. Early Massachusetts was organized around shared religious goals, yet it was riven by strife. How do you explain the tensions within this colony?

3. Seventeenth-century North America included a wide variety of colonial endeavors. What were the main regional divisions and distinguishing features of each area?

4. What were the causes and consequences of King Philip's War and Bacon's Rebellion? In what ways were the two conflicts similar or different?

5. What were the effects of the Glorious Revolution on the colonies and the empire?

6. Despite differences between colonial regions, it appears that prejudicial attitudes toward Africans and Native Americans were a common thread running through all colonial societies.

   Do you agree, and if so do you see any exceptions to this rule?

Recommended Reading

Recommended Readings are posted on the Web site for this textbook. Visit www.ablongman.com/nash

Fiction and Film

Nathaniel Hawthorne's *The Scarlet Letter* (1850) is an American classic on Puritan love, infidelity, and morality; Hollywood's version, by the same title, features Demi Moore and Gary Oldman (1995). John Barth's *The Sotweed Factor* (1960) is a rollicking and ribald novel about indentured servitude, tobacco planting, love, and brutishness in seventeenth-century Maryland. *Black Robes* (1991), a gripping film made in Canada, evokes all the cruelty of the contact between early French Jesuit missionaries and the Iroquois people. The film is based on Brian Manning's novel of the same name. Werner Herzog's *Aguirre: The Wrath of God* (1972) is a surreal film about the early Spanish conquest of much of the

Americas in the sixteenth century. A much milder film on early Indian–European contact is *Squanto: A Warrior's Tale* (1994), featuring Adam Beach. *Three Sovereigns for Sarah* (1985), a PBS miniseries starring Vanessa Redgrave, stunningly dramatizes the Salem witchcraft trials. Arthur Miller's play *The Crucible* (1953), on the same topic, is as engaging today as it was three decades ago when it played on stages around the country. Wayne Carlin's *The Wished For Country* (2002) is a compelling historical novel about the indentured servants, Africans, and Native Americans who met each other in early Maryland and how, from their intermingling, the triracial Wesort people emerged.

Discovering U.S. History Online

Jamestown

www.nps.gov

Using the search facility on the main page, search for Jamestown. Essays on the historical significance of Jamestown, some of the personalities, manufacturing and industries, timelines, and bibliographies make up this informative site.

Jamestown Rediscovery

www.apva.org

This site has excellent material on the archaeological excavation of Jamestown.

Plymouth Colony, 1620–1691

www.etext.virginia.edu/users/deetz

This collection of searchable texts, mostly primary sources, provides information about the late seventeenth-century Plymouth colony.

The Pilgrim Story

www.pilgrimhall.org/museum.htm

Well-illustrated with images from the museum, this online exhibit gives an overview of the pilgrims' origins and their settlement in the New World.

Colonization—New England

www.usahistory.info/New-England/
www.usahistory.info/NewEngland/

A history of colonization of New England, including the Massachusetts Bay Colony, King Philip's War, and Puritan laws and character, is presented via a reprint of a turn-of-the-century textbook with links to definitions and illustrations.

Divining America: Religion and the National Culture

www.nhc.rtp.nc.us:8080/tserve/eighteen/ekeyinfo/puritan.htm

An illustrated essay on Puritan ideas and how they intersected with American history.

Long Island

www.lihistory.com/3/chap3cov.htm

This is one chapter of a well-organized site on the history of Long Island, New York, originally published as a series of articles in a local newspaper.

The People of Colonial Albany

www.nysm.nysed.gov/albany/index.html

This site gives detailed information about the settlers of Albany using essays, biographical information, portraits, maps, architecture, and more. Some information is presented about the pre-European native settlers of the area.

Investigations in the Richard B. Russell Dam and Lake Area

www.cr.nps.gov/seac/brochure3/front.htm

This brochure, adapted for the Web, presents prehistoric and historical cultural findings from this Georgia/South Carolina archaeological site.

History of North Carolina and South Carolina

www.usahistory.info/southern/North-Carolina.html
www.usahistory.info/southern/South-Carolina.html

Histories of the Carolinas are presented via a reprint of a turn-of-the-century textbook with links to illustrations and other documents.

William Penn

www.xroads.virginia.edu/~CAP/PENN/pnhome.html

William Penn was an extraordinary colonial figure, and this site is a good introduction to the man and some of his achievements.

Cultural Readings: Colonization and Print in the Americas

www.library.upenn.edu/special/gallery/kislak/index/cultural.html

This site presents primary sources—including books, manuscripts, illustrations, and maps—from the colonial period.

The Golden Crescent: Crossroads of Florida and Georgia

www.cr.nps.gov/goldcres/

This site presents the cultural history and prehistory of the European, African, and native inhabitants of the region.

New Spain: The Frontiers of Faith

www.humanities-interactive.org/newspain/

An illustrated exhibit of documents from the Thomas Gilcrease Institute pertaining to the Spanish colonies in the New World.

Salem Witchcraft Trials, 1692

www.law.umkc.edu/faculty/projects/ftrials/salem/salem.htm

Images and primary documents compose this account of the events in Salem.

Salem Witch Trials: Documentary Archive and Transcription Project

etext.lib.virginia.edu/salem/witchcraft/

Richly illustrated with documents and map images, this site presents both primary and secondary source material on the Salem witch trials.

The Maturing of Colonial Society

Joseph Beekman Smith, *Wesley Chapel on John Street, New York City—1768* (detail), completed 1817–1844 (based on earlier sketches). *(Joseph Beekman Smith, Wesley Chapel on John Street New York City-1768. Old John Street United Methodist Church)*

American Stories

A Struggling Farmer's Wife Finds True Religious Commitment

In 1758, 37-year-old Hannah Cook Heaton stood trial for her refusal to attend her local congregationalist church. A resident of North New Haven, Connecticut, Hannah was required by Connecticut law to attend Sunday worship services—a law derived from the belief that religious uniformity was a social good. Hannah did not object to churchgoing; in fact, she was a fervent Christian. She had been a member of Isaac Stiles's church—indeed, he had performed her marriage to Theophilus Heaton, Jr., in 1743. But later in that decade, after she had been caught up in the enthusiasm of the Great Awakening, a series of religious revivals that rocked New England in the 1740s, Hannah ceased to attend Sunday worship. Thereafter, finding that her minister's preaching and church admission policies left her cold and dissatisfied, Heaton quit the church, arguing that Stiles had never himself undergone conversion and was therefore a "blind guide" leading his flock astray.

Hannah's decision to leave the village church was prompted by the preaching of men she believed were imbued with the spirit. Hearing touring evangelists George Whitefield, James Davenport, and Gilbert Tennant sparked a profound conversion experience. As she later recorded in her diary, she "thought I see Jesus with the eyes of my soul." This religious transformation led her to join a small congregation headed by Benjamin Beach, a lay preacher. Uneducated and unlicensed, he was precisely the kind of man whom Harvard- and Yale-trained ministers regarded as a threat to well-ordered New England communities. Yet many like Hannah Heaton found him spiritually gifted, and so they separated themselves from the established church to meet regularly at Beach's home for worship and prayer.

Because she abandoned the established church for this community of believers, who called themselves Separatists, Hannah was pressured by both members of Stiles's church and local officials and then finally brought to trial. She remained defiant, telling the justice at her trial that "there was a day a-coming when justice would be done . . . there is a dreadful day a-coming upon them that have no Christ." Declaring that Hannah "talked sass," the justice convicted her of breaking the law and fined her twelve shillings.

To Hannah's dismay and despite her efforts, her husband never shared her commitment to the dissenters. He remained a member of Stiles's church, urged Hannah to rejoin it, and, against Hannah's wishes, paid her fine in the trial of 1758. Resenting his wife's involvement with the Separatists, he hid her spectacles so she could not read her Bible or write in her diary, threw her diary in the mud, and refused to provide her with a horse to ride to the Separatists' meetings. Hannah worried about his immortal soul, disheartened that even on his deathbed she could not persuade him to repent and seek after the Lord.

Hannah Cook Heaton was in many ways a typical colonial woman, married to a farmer and the mother of numerous children. Her life would be virtually unknown to us except that she kept a diary of her spiritual experiences, in which she revealed a life that was dramatically reshaped by the Great Awakening. Her identity as a Separatist was fundamental to her life, affecting her marriage and her intimate relationships. Her separatism also brought her briefly into public prominence, as one of the few members of her movement to be prosecuted in court in Connecticut in the 1750s. Her life suggests the significance of revivalism in the lives of many eighteenth-century colonists. Her religious convictions motivated her to defy various authorities in her life, including her husband, her minister, and the local magistrate.

The religious revivals that transformed Hannah Heaton's life were just one of the forces affecting colonial life during the eighteenth century. Between 1680 and 1750, a virtual population explosion occurred in the English colonies, swelling the number of settlers from 150,000 settlers in 1680 to more than 1 million at midcentury. Such growth staggered English policymakers, who uneasily watched the population gap between England and its American colonies closing rapidly. A high marriage rate, large families, lower mortality than in Europe, and heavy immigration accounted for much of the population boom.

This chapter's first, second, and fourth sections explain how population growth and economic development gradually transformed eighteenth-century British America. Three variations of colonial society emerged: the farming society of the North, the plantation society of the South, and the urban society of the seaboard commercial towns. Although they shared some important characteristics—growing class differences and a deepening involvement with slavery except on the frontier—each region had distinctive features. Even within regions, diversity increased as incoming streams of immigrants, mostly from Germany, Ireland, and France, and especially from Africa, added new pieces to the shifting American mosaic.

Until the late seventeenth century, the Spanish, French, and English settlements in North America were largely isolated from one another. But when a long period of war erupted in Europe among these colonizing nations, North America and the Caribbean became important theaters of international conflict—a development that would reach a climax in the second half of the eighteenth century.

This chapter also explores the commercial orientation that spread from north to south, especially in the towns and their immediate hinterlands, as local economies matured and forged sturdier links within the Atlantic basin trade network. We will also see how colonists such as Hannah Heaton experienced a deep-running religious awakening that established evangelical religion as a hallmark of American society. Connected to this democratization of religion was the changing exercise of political power. From increasingly powerful legislative assemblies and local instruments of governance emerged seasoned leaders, a tradition of local autonomy, and a widespread belief in a political ideology stressing the liberties that freeborn Englishmen should enjoy. In these ways, raw frontier settlements developed into mature provincial societies.

THE NORTH: A LAND OF FAMILY FARMS

Although New England strove to maintain its homogeneity by making non–English immigrants unwelcome, the mid-Atlantic colonies swarmed with waves of immigrants from the Rhineland and Ireland, showing how connected were the destinies of people on opposite sides of the Atlantic. About 90,000 Germans flocked in during the eighteenth century, many fleeing "God's three arrows": famine, war, and pestilence. They settled where promoters promised cheap and fertile land, low taxes, and freedom from military duty. Coming mostly in families, they turned much of the mid-Atlantic hinterland into a German-speaking region. Place names still mark their zone of settlement: Mannheim, New Berlin, and Herkimer, New York; Bethlehem, Ephrata, Nazareth, and Hanover, Pennsylvania; Hagerstown and Frederick, Maryland; Mecklenberg and New Hanover, North Carolina. Even more Protestant Scots–Irish arrived. Mostly poor farmers, they streamed into the same backcountry areas where Germans were settling, especially New York and Pennsylvania, and many went farther, into the mountain valleys of the Carolinas and Georgia.

Northern Agricultural Society

In the mid-eighteenth-century northern colonies, especially New England, tight-knit farming families that were organized in communities of several thousand people dotted the landscape. New Englanders staked their future on a mixed economy. They cleared forests for timber used in barrels, ships, houses, and barns. They plumbed the offshore waters for fish that fed both local populations and the ballooning slave population of the West Indies. And they cultivated and grazed as much of the thin-soiled rocky hills and bottomlands as they could recover from the forest.

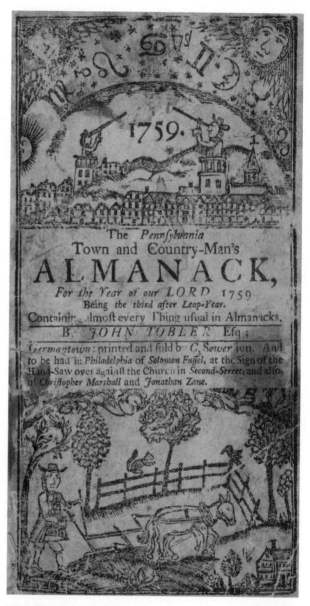

The Farmer's Guide Other than a Bible, an almanac was often the only book in a farmer's house. What did farmers find in almanacs that made them so valuable? (*The Library Company of Philadelphia*)

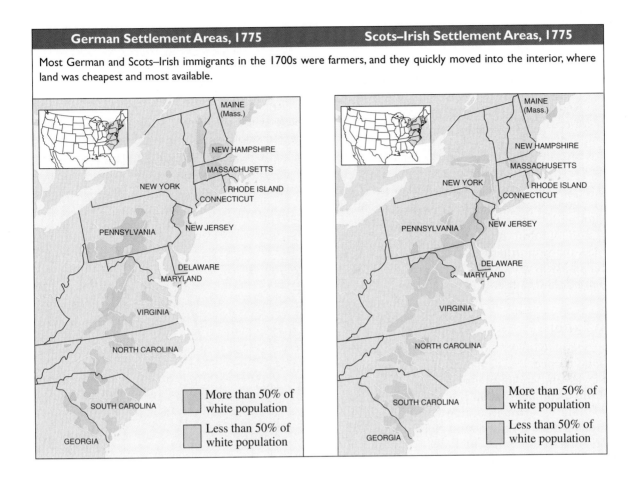

German Settlement Areas, 1775

Scots–Irish Settlement Areas, 1775

Most German and Scots–Irish immigrants in the 1700s were farmers, and they quickly moved into the interior, where land was cheapest and most available.

More than 50% of white population

Less than 50% of white population

The farmers of the middle colonies—Pennsylvania, Delaware, New Jersey, and New York—drove their wooden plows through much richer soils than New Englanders. They enjoyed the additional advantage of settling an area cleared by Native Americans who had relied more on agriculture than New England tribes. Thus favored, mid-Atlantic farm families produced modest surpluses of corn, wheat, beef, and pork. By the mid-eighteenth century, New York and Philadelphia ships were carrying these foodstuffs not only to the West Indies, always a primary market, but also to England, Spain, Portugal, and even New England. In this way, they strengthened ties within the Atlantic basin.

In the North, the broad ownership of land distinguished farming society from every other agricultural region of the Western world. Although differences in circumstances and ability led gradually toward greater social stratification, in most communities, few were truly rich or abjectly poor. Except for indentured servants, most men lived to purchase or inherit a farm of at least 50 acres. With their family's labor, they earned a decent existence and provided a small inheritance for each of their children. Settlers valued land highly, for freehold tenure ordinarily guaranteed both economic independence and political rights.

By the eighteenth century, with widespread property ownership, a rising population pressed against a limited land supply especially in New England. Family farms could not be divided and subdivided indefinitely, for it took at least 50 acres (of which only a quarter could usually be cropped) to support a family. In Concord, Massachusetts, for example, the founders had worked farms averaging about 250 acres. A century later, in the 1730s, the average farm had shrunk by two-thirds, as farm owners struggled to provide an inheritance for the three or four sons that the average marriage produced.

Decreasing soil fertility compounded the problem of dwindling farm size. When land had been plentiful, farmers planted crops in the same field for three years and then let it lie fallow seven years or more until it regained its strength. But on the smaller farms of the eighteenth century, farmers reduced fallowing to only a year or two, reducing crop yields and forcing farmers to plow marginal land or shift to livestock production. Thus, Jared Eliot, New England's first agricultural essayist, referred to "our old land which we have worn out."

The diminishing size and productivity of family farms drove many New Englanders to the frontier or out of the area. "Many of our old towns are too full of inhabitants for husbandry, many of them living on small shares of land," bemoaned one Yankee. In Concord, one of every four adult males migrated from town every decade from the 1740s on. In many towns out-migration was even greater, with some drifting to New York and Pennsylvania, and others going to western Massachusetts, New Hampshire, Maine, and Nova Scotia. Still others sought opportunities as artisans in the coastal towns or took to the sea.

Northern farming was less intense than in the South. The growing season was shorter, and cereal crops required incessant labor only during spring planting and autumn harvesting. This seasonal rhythm led many northern cultivators to fill out their calendars with work as clockmakers, shoemakers, carpenters, and weavers.

Unfree Labor

In the northern colonies, though the shorter growing seasons curbed the demand for labor in the North, slaves and indentured servants made up much of the incoming human tide after 1713. The westward traffic in servants became a regular part of the commerce linking Europe and North America.

Despite official attempts to reduce the "tight packing" of indentured immigrants, shipboard conditions for both slaves and servants worsened in the eighteenth century. Crammed between decks in stifling air, they suffered from smallpox and fevers, rotten food, impure water, cold, and lice. "Children between the ages of one and seven seldom survive the sea voyage," lamented one German immigrant, "and parents must often watch their offspring suffer miserably, die, and be thrown into the ocean." As one Virginia observer remarked of an incoming troop of servants in 1758, "I never see such parcels of poor wretches, some almost naked and what had clothes was as black as chimney sweepers and almost starved." The shipboard mortality rate of about 15 percent in the colonial era made this the unhealthiest of all times to seek American shores.

Most indentured servants, especially males, found the labor system harsh. Merchants sold them, one shocked Britisher reported in 1773, "as they do their horses, and advertise them as they do their beef and oatmeal." Every servant's goal was to secure a foothold on the ladder of opportunity. However, many died before finishing their time; others won freedom only to toil for years as poor day laborers and tenant farmers. The chief beneficiaries of the system of bound white labor were the masters.

DOCUMENT

Gottlieb Mittelberger, "The Passage of Indentured Servants"

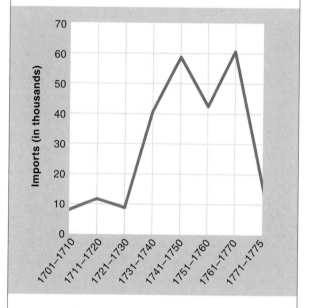

Slaves Imported to North America, 1701–1775

Overwhelmingly, Africans transported to the American colonies arrived from the 1730s to the 1770s. Rapid natural increase, as well as importation, swelled the African population to about 500,000 by the outbreak of the American Revolution.

Source: R. C. Simmons, *The American Colonies: From Settlement to Independence,* 1976.

The number of enslaved Africans in the northern colonies grew in the eighteenth century but not nearly as fast as the indentured servant population. Slaves made up less than 10 percent of the population in all northern colonies and in most only 3 to 4 percent. Since in the North the typical slave labored alone or with only a few others while living in the same house as the master, slaves adapted to European ways much faster than in the South. Slavery was also less repressive in the North.

Along with occasional Native American slaves, enslaved Africans typically worked as artisans, farmhands, or personal servants. Slavery grew fastest in the northern ports. Artisans invested profitably in slaves; ship captains purchased them for maritime labor; and an emerging urban elite of merchants, lawyers, and landlords displayed its wealth with slave coachmen and personal servants. By the beginning of the eighteenth century, more than 40 percent of New York City's households owned slaves. Even in Quaker Philadelphia, slaveholding increased sharply in the eighteenth century. Struggling white artisans resented slave workers for undercutting their wages, and the white citizenry feared black arsonists and rebels. Yet high labor demand outweighed these reservations, and the advantage of purchasing life-long servants for just two years' worth of a free white laborer's wages was obvious.

Changing Values

Boston's weather on April 29, 1695, began warm and sunny, noted the devout merchant Samuel Sewall in his diary. But by afternoon, lightning and hailstones "as big as pistol and musket bullets" pummeled the town. Sewall dined that evening with Cotton Mather, New England's prominent Puritan clergyman. Mather wondered why "more ministers' houses than others proportionately had been smitten with lightning." The words were hardly out of his mouth before hailstones began to shatter the windows. Sewall and Mather fell to their knees in prayer "after this awful Providence." These two third-generation Massachusetts Puritans understood that God was angry with them as leaders of a people whose piety was giving way to worldliness. Massachusetts was becoming "sermon-proof," explained one dejected minister.

In other parts of the North, the expansive environment and the Protestant emphasis on self-discipline and hard work were also breeding qualities that would become hallmarks of American culture: ambitiousness, individualism, and materialism. One colonist remarked, "Every man expects one day or another to be upon a footing with his wealthiest neighbor." Commitment to religion, family, and community did not disappear, but fewer people saw daily existence just as a preparation for the afterlife. Land was not simply a source of livelihood but as a commodity to be bought and sold for profit.

A slender almanac, written by the twelfth child of a poor Boston candle-maker, captured the new outlook with wit and charm. Born in 1706, Benjamin Franklin climbed the ladder of success spectacularly. Running away from a harsh apprenticeship to an older brother when he was 16, he abandoned a declining Boston for a rising Philadelphia. By 23, he had learned the printer's trade and was publishing the *Pennsylvania Gazette*. Three years later, he began *Poor Richard's Almanack*, which, next to the Bible, was the most widely read book in the colonies. Franklin filled it with quips, adages, and homespun philosophy: "The sleeping fox gathers no poultry." "Lost time is never found again." "It costs more to maintain one vice than to raise two children." "Sloth makes all things difficult but industry all easy." Franklin caught the spirit of the rising secularism of the eighteenth century and preached the utilitarian doctrine that good is whatever is useful. For Franklin, the community was best served through individual self-improvement and accomplishment.

Women and the Family in the Northern Colonies

In 1662, Elnathan Chauncy, a Massachusetts schoolboy, copied into his writing book that the soul "consists of two portions, inferior and superior; the superior is masculine and eternal; the feminine inferior and mortal." Generations on both sides of the Atlantic had taught such ideas as part of a larger conception of God's design that assigned degrees of status and stations in life to all individuals. In that world, women were subordinate, taught from infancy to be modest, patient, and compliant. Regarded by men as weak of mind and large of

Rebecca Jones's Sampler Part of becoming the "ideal" woman was learning patience and artistic exactitude. Rebecca Jones, a Philadelphia teenager, spent hundreds of hours working birds, animals, and sprigs of flowers into her compartmented sampler, which also recorded the exact time of her birth. *(Courtesy of the Atwater Kent Museum of Philadelphia)*

heart, they existed for and through men, subject first to their fathers and then to their husbands.

Colonial women usually accepted these narrowly circumscribed roles and few complained openly that their work was generally limited to housewifery and midwifery. They silently accepted exclusion from the early public schools, laws that transferred to their husbands any property or income they brought into a marriage, and customs prohibiting them from speaking in their churches or participating in governing them (except in Quaker meetinghouses).

In a society in which producing legal heirs was the means of transmitting property, parental guidance prevailed over love in choosing a husband. Once wed, women expected to remain so until death, for they could rarely obtain a divorce. But young colonial women slowly gained the right of consenting to a marriage partner—a right that came by default to the thousands of female indentured servants who completed their labor contracts and had no parents within 3,000 miles to dictate to them.

On the colonial frontier, women's lives changed in modest ways. One in 10 European women did not marry. But in the colonies, where men outnumbered women for the first century, a spinster was almost unheard of, and widows remarried with astounding speed. "A young widow with 4 or 5 children, who among the middling or inferior ranks of people in Europe would have little chance for a second husband," observed one Englishman, "is in America frequently courted as a sort of fortune." *Woman* and *wife* thus became nearly synonymous.

Another change concerned property rights. As in England, single women and widows in the colonies could make contracts, hold and convey property, represent themselves in court, and conduct business, though a woman forfeited these rights, as well as all property, when she married. In the colonies, however, legislatures and courts gave wives more control over property brought into marriage or left at their husbands' death. They also enjoyed broader rights to act for and with their husbands in business transactions.

DOCUMENT
Prenuptial Agreement (1653)

Although colonial society did not encourage or reward female individuality, women worked alongside their husbands in competent and complementary ways. Women had limited career choices and rights but broad responsibilities. The work spaces and daily routines of husband and wife overlapped and intersected far more than today. Farm women as well as men worked at planting, harvesting, and milking cows. Women also made candles and soap, butter and cheese, and smoked meat; they made

Deborah Franklin For much of her marriage, Deborah Read Franklin saw little of her famous husband. In the last eighteen years of her life, from 1756 to 1774, she saw Benjamin for less than three years because he stayed in London for extended periods. Can you use Internet resources and Deborah's published letters to find out how she coped with such absences? *(Benjamin Wilson,* Deborah (Read) Franklin, *1759, American Philosophical Society)*

cloth and sometimes marketed farm products. A merchant's wife kept shop, handled accounts when her husband voyaged abroad, and helped supervise the servants and apprentices. "Deputy husbands" and "yoke mates" were revealing terms used by New Englanders to describe eighteenth-century wives.

Despite conventional talk of inferiority, women within their families and neighborhoods nevertheless shaped the world around them. Older women modeled the behavior of young women, aided the needy, and subtly affected menfolk, who held formal authority. Women outnumbered men in church life and, like Hannah Heaton, worked within their families to promote religion in outlying areas, to seat and unseat ministers, and to influence morals. Periodically, they appeared as visionaries and mystics.

Until the late eighteenth century, the "obstetrick art" was almost entirely in their hands. Midwives counseled pregnant women, delivered babies, supervised postpartum recovery, and participated in infant baptism and burial ceremonies. Mrs. Phillips, an immigrant to Boston in 1719, was a familiar figure as she hurried through the streets to attend the lying-in of about 70 women each year. In her 42-year career, she delivered more than 3,000 infants. Because colonial women were pregnant or nursing infants for about half the years between ages 20 and 40 and because childbirth was dangerous, the circle of female friends and relatives attending childbirth created strong networks of mutual assistance.

In her role as wife and mother, the eighteenth-century northern woman differed somewhat from her English counterpart. Whereas English women married in their midtwenties, American women typically took husbands a few years earlier, increasing their childbearing years. Hence, the average colonial family included five children (two others typically died in infancy), whereas the English family contained fewer than three. Gradually, the marriage age crept up and the number of children per family inched down.

Northern child-rearing patterns varied widely. In the seventeenth century, stern fathers dominated Puritan family life, and few were reluctant to punish unruly children. "Better whip'd than damn'd," advised Cotton Mather, reinforcing the belief that breaking the young child's will created a pious and submissive personality. Quaker mothers, however, tended to use love rather than guilt to mold their children. Puritan parents usually arranged their children's marriages but allowed them the right to veto. Young Quaker men and women made their own matches, subject to parental veto. These differences aside, all children played roles, from an early age, in contributing to the family economy.

The father-dominated family of New England gradually declined in the eighteenth century, replaced by the mother-centered family, in which affectionate parents encouraged self-expression and independence in their children. This "modern" approach, on the rise in Europe as well, brought the colonists closer to the methods of parenthood found among the coastal Native Americans, who initially had been disparaged for their lax approach to rearing their young.

Ecological Transformation

Wherever Europeans settled in the Americas, they brought with them animals, plant life, diseases, and ways of viewing natural resources—all with enormous consequences. In England's North American colonies, the rapid increase of settlers after 1715 affected the environment rapidly. First, the demand for wood—for building and heating houses, for producing the charcoal necessary for ironmaking, for shipbuilding and barrelmaking—swiftly depleted coastal forests. Rapid and often wasteful harvesting of the forests had many ill effects. Without the forest canopy,

summers became hotter and winters colder. Early-melting snow caused watersheds to empty faster, and, in turn, triggered soil erosion and drought.

A second ecological transformation occurred when animals brought by Europeans began to replace animals already in North America. European colonists were a livestock people, skilled in mixed farming and herding of domesticated cattle, horses, pigs, sheep, and goats. Multiplying rapidly in a favorable environment, pigs and cattle "swarm like vermin upon the earth," reported one Virginia account as early as 1700. In an environment generally free of animal predators, the grazing animals devoured the tall grasses and most palatable plant species. With little or no ground cover, new unwelcome plant species took hold: stinging nettles, dandelions, and nightshade. Native grasses and shrubs disappeared so quickly that the European livestock began to die for lack of grazing land.

Meanwhile, native fur-bearing animals—beaver, deer, bear, wolf, raccoon, and marten—rapidly became extinct in the areas of settlement. Prizing their pelts or hating them as predators of domesticated animals, colonists and Native Americans hunted these species relentlessly. One broken link in the ecological chain affected others. For example, the dams and ponds of the beaver, which had been breeding grounds for many species of wild ducks, soon were drained and converted to meadows for cattle. Animals prized for dinner-table fare also quickly reached extinction along the East Coast. Wild turkeys were a rarity in Massachusetts by the 1670s and deer disappeared by the early 1700s in settled areas. "Hunting with us exists chiefly in the tales of other times," wrote Yale's president in the late eighteenth century.

All these environmental changes were linked not only to the numbers of Europeans arriving in North America but also to their ways of thinking about nature. Transplanted Europeans saw only the possibility of raising valuable crops as if the ecosystem were composed of unconnected elements, each ripe for exploitation. Land, lumber, fish, and fur-bearing animals could be converted into sources of cash that would buy imported commodities that improved one's material condition. Coming from homelands where land was scarce, the settlers viewed their ability to reap nature's abundance in North America as proof of their success. Yet the "rage for commerce" and for an improved life produced wasteful practices on farms and in forests and fisheries. "The grain fields, the meadows, the forests, the cattle, etc.," wrote a Swedish visitor in the 1750s, "are treated with equal carelessness." Once the native peoples had been driven from the land, and seeing no limits to the land that was available, the colonists embarked on ecologically destructive practices that over a period of many generations profoundly altered the natural world of North America.

THE PLANTATION SOUTH

Between 1690 and 1760, the southern white tidewater settlements changed from a frontier society with high immigration, a surplus of males, and an unstable social organization to a settled society composed mostly of native-born families. But while a mature southern culture took form from the ocean to the piedmont, after 1715 Scots–Irish and German immigrants flooded into the backcountry of Virginia, the Carolinas, and the new colony of Georgia, which was founded in 1732 as a debtors' haven and a buffer between Spanish Florida and the Carolinas. The fast-growing slave population accounted for swifter population growth than in the North. Virginia, with a population of nearly 340,000 by 1760, remained by far the largest colony in North America.

DOCUMENT

James Oglethorpe, "Establishing the Colony of Georgia" (1733)

The Tobacco Coast

Tobacco production in Virginia and Maryland expanded rapidly in the seventeenth century, with exports reaching 25 million pounds annually during the 1680s. Then, two decades of war in Europe made Atlantic-basin commercial traffic more dangerous, drove up transportation costs, and dampened the demand for tobacco. Stagnation in the tobacco market lasted from the mid-1680s until about 1715.

During this period the Upper South underwent a profound social transformation. First, African slaves replaced European indentured servants so rapidly that by 1730 the unfree labor force was overwhelmingly black. Second, planters responded to the depressed tobacco market by diversifying their crops. They shifted some tobacco fields to grain, hemp, and flax; increased their herds of cattle and swine; and became more self-sufficient by developing local industries to produce iron, leather, and textiles. By the 1720s, when a profitable tobacco trade with France created a new period of prosperity, the economy was much more diverse and resilient. Third, the population structure changed rapidly. African slaves grew from about 7 percent to more than 40 percent of the region's population between 1690 and 1750, and the drastic imbalance between white men and women disappeared. Families rather than single men now predominated. The earlier frontier society of white immigrants, mostly living short, unrewarding lives as indentured servants, grew into an

eighteenth-century plantation society of native-born freeholder families.

Notwithstanding the influx of Africans, slave owning was far from universal. As late as 1750, a majority

The Carters of Virginia Charles Carter and his wife Anne Byrd Carter are pictured here as of about 1730–1735. The Carter and Byrd families were among Virginia's wealthiest owners of land and slaves. What is the artist trying to convey in the background of the paintings? *(Top: Portrait of Charles Carter of Cleve, artist unidentified, ca. 1725–1730, Colonial Williamsburg Foundation; bottom: Portrait of Mrs. Charles Carter of Cleve, William Dering, 1735–1740, Colonial Williamsburg Foundation)*

of families owned no slaves at all. Not more than one-tenth of slaveholders held more than 20 slaves. Nonetheless, the common goal was the large plantation where slaves made the earth yield up profits to support an aristocratic life for their masters.

The Chesapeake planters who acquired the best land and accumulated enough capital to invest heavily in slaves created a gentry lifestyle that set them apart from ordinary farmers. By the eighteenth century, the development of the northern colonies had produced prosperous farmers worth several thousand pounds. But such wealth paled alongside the estates of men who counted their slaves by the hundreds, their acres by the thousands, and their fortunes by the tens of thousands of pounds.

Ritual display of wealth marked southern gentry life. Racing thoroughbred horses and gambling on them recklessly, sometimes for purses of £100 (at a time when a laboring man earned £40 per year), became common sport for young gentlemen, who had often been educated in England. Planters began to construct stately brick Georgian mansions, filled with imported furniture, attended by liveried black slaves, and graced by formal gardens and orchards. The emerging Chesapeake planter elite controlled the county courts, officered the local militia, ruled the parish vestries of the Anglican church, made law in their legislative assemblies, and passed to their sons the mantle of political and social leadership.

For all their airs, these southern squires were essentially agrarian businessmen. They spent their days haggling over credit, land, slaves, and tenant leases; scheduling planting and harvesting; conferring with overseers; and disciplining slaves. Tobacco cultivation (unlike that of wheat and corn) claimed the planter's year-round attention. A planter's reputation rested on the quality of his crop. To personalize their tobacco, planters stamped their hogsheads of leaf with their initials or emblem. "Question a planter on the subject," explained one observer, "and he will tell you that he cultivates such or such a kind [of tobacco], as for example, Colonel Carter's sort, John Cole's sort or [that of] some other leading crop master."

Planters' wives also shouldered many responsibilities. They superintended cloth production and the processing and preparation of food while ruling over households crowded with children, slaves, and visitors. An aristocratic veneer gave the luster of gentility to plantations from Maryland to North Carolina, but in fact these were large working farms, often so isolated from one another that the planter and his wife lived a "solitary and unsociable existence," as one phrased it.

The Rice Coast

The plantation economy of the Lower South in the eighteenth century rested on rice and indigo. Rice exports surpassed 1.5 million pounds per year by 1710 and reached 80 million pounds by the eve of the Revolution. Indigo, a smelly blue dye obtained from plants for use in textiles, became a staple crop in the 1740s after Eliza Lucas Pinckney, a wealthy South Carolina planter's wife, experimented successfully with its cultivation. Within a generation,

Slaves on an Indigo Plantation Indigo production, mostly the work of enslaved Africans in South Carolina, was dirty, smelly, and debilitating. This eighteenth-century engraving shows each step, from the indigo plant at lower right to slaves tending vats of boiling water. An overseer (top right) supervises the slaves. (*The Folger Shakespeare Library*)

The Charleston Waterfront This engraved view of Charleston's waterfront a few decades before the American Revolution shows that it was little more than a waterside village, yet it was the southern colonies' busiest seaport. What are the two tallest buildings in the city? *(Courtesy, American Antiquarian Society)*

indigo production had spread into Georgia, ranking among the leading colonial exports.

The expansion of rice production, exported to the West Indies and Europe, transformed the swampy coastal lowlands around Charleston, where planters imported thousands of slaves after 1720. By 1740, slaves composed nearly 90 percent of the region's inhabitants. White population declined as wealthy planters entrusted their estates to resident overseers. They wintered in cosmopolitan Charleston and summered in Newport, Rhode Island, their refuge from seasonal malaria along the rice coast. At midcentury,

a shocked New England visitor described it as a society "divided into opulent and lordly planters, poor and spiritless peasants, and vile slaves."

Throughout the plantation South, the courthouse became a central male gathering place. All classes came to settle debts, dispute over land, and sue and be sued. When court was over, a multitude lingered on, drinking, gossiping, and staging horse races, cockfights, wrestling matches, footraces, and fiddling contests—all considered tests of male prowess.

The church, almost always Anglican in the South before 1750, also became a center of community gathering. A visiting northerner described the animated socializing before worship: men "giving and receiving letters of business, reading advertisements, consulting about the price of tobacco and grain, and settling either the lineage, age, or qualities of favourite horses." Then people filed into church, with lesser planters entering first and standing attentively until the wealthy gentry, "in a body," took their pews at the front. After church, socializing continued, with young people strolling together and older ones extending invitations to Sunday dinner. New England's pious Sabbath was little in evidence.

The Backcountry

While the southern gentry matured along the tobacco and rice coasts, settlers poured into the upland backcountry. As late as 1730, only hunters and Native American fur traders had known this vast expanse of hilly red clay and fertile limestone soils from Pennsylvania to Georgia. Over the next four decades, it attracted some 250,000 inhabitants, nearly half the southern white population.

Thousands of land-hungry German and Scots–Irish settlers spilled into the interior valleys along the eastern side of the Appalachians. They squatted on land, lived tensely with neighboring Indians in a region where boundaries were shadowy, and built a subsistence society of small farms. This "mixed medley from all countries and the off scouring of America," as one colonist described

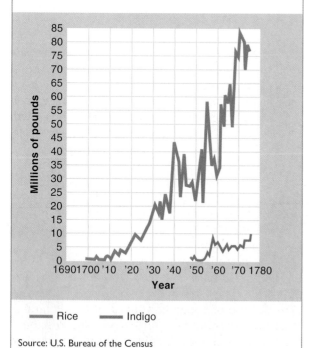

Rice and Indigo Exports from South Carolina and Georgia, 1698–1775

Just as Virginia had been built on tobacco, South Carolina and Georgia were built on rice. Much of it was sent to the West Indies to feed the huge population of enslaved Africans there.

Millions of pounds

16901700 '10 '20 '30 '40 '50 '60 '70 1780

Year

—— Rice　　—— Indigo

Source: U.S. Bureau of the Census

AMERICAN VOICES

Charles Woodmason, A Congregation in the Southern Backcountry

Planter, merchant, and then clergyman, Charles Woodmason preached extensively in the southern backcountry, always struggling to understand the crudity of frontier life.

It would be a great novelty to a Londoner to see one of these congregations. The men with only a thin shirt and a pair of breeches or trousers on—barelegged and barefooted. The women bareheaded, barelegged, and barefooted, with only a thin shift and under petticoat.... The young women have a most uncommon practice, which I cannot break them of. They draw their shift as tight as possible to the body and pin it close to show the roundness of their breasts and slender waists (for they are generally finely shaped) and draw their petticoat to their hips to show the fineness of their limbs so that they might as well be in *puri naturalibus*. Indeed, nakedness is not censurable or indecent here, and they expose themselves often quite naked without ceremony, rubbing themselves and their hair with bear's oil and tying it up behind in a bunch like the Indians (being hardly one degree removed from them). In a few years, I hope to bring about a reformation, as I have already done in several parts of the country.

- *Why do you think young frontier women adopted Native American customs?*

- *Did the men and women go barefooted by choice or necessity?*

---

them, remained isolated from the coastal region for several generations, which helped these pioneers cling fiercely to folkways they had brought across the Atlantic.

Crude backcountry life appalled visitors from the more refined seaboard. In 1733, William Byrd described a large Virginia frontier plantation as a "poor, dirty hovel, with hardly anything in it but children that wallowed about like so many pigs." Charles Woodmason, a stiff-necked Anglican minister who tramped between settlements in the Carolina upcountry, was shocked. "Through the licentiousness of the people many hundreds live in concubinage—swopping their wives as cattle and living in a state of nature more irregularly and unchastely than the Indians."

These comments reflected the poverty of frontier life and the lack of schools, churches, and towns. Most families plunged into the backcountry with only a few crude household possessions, tools, a few chickens and swine, and the clothes on their backs. They lived in rough-hewn log cabins and planted their corn, beans, and wheat between tree stumps. Women toiled alongside men. For a generation, everyone endured a poor diet, endless work, and meager rewards.

By the 1760s, the southern backcountry had begun to emerge from the frontier stage. Small marketing towns such as Camden, South Carolina; Salisbury, North Carolina; Winchester, Virginia; and Fredericktown, Maryland, became centers of craft activity, church life, and local government. Farms began producing surpluses for shipment east. Density of settlement increased, creating a social life known for harvest festivals, log-rolling contests, horse races, wedding celebrations, dances, and prodigious drinking bouts. Class distinctions remained narrow compared with the older seaboard settlements, as many backcountry settlements acquired the look of permanence.

Family Life in the South

As the South emerged from the early era of withering mortality and stunted families, male and female roles gradually became more physically and functionally separated. In most areas, the white gender ratio reached parity by the 1720s, depriving women of their leverage in the marriage market. The growth of slavery also changed white women's work role, with the wealthy planter's wife becoming a domestic manager in "the great house." In a description of his daughters' daily routine, William Byrd II pointed to the emerging female identity: "They are every day up to their elbows in housewifery, which will qualify them effectually for useful wives and if they live long enough for notable women."

The balanced gender ratio and the growth of slavery also brought changes for southern males. The planters' sons had always been trained in horsemanship, the use of a gun, and the rhythms of agricultural life. Learning how to manage and discipline slaves was as important as lessons with tutors. Bred to command, southern planters' sons developed a self-confidence and authority that propelled many of them into leadership roles during the American Revolution.

On the small farms of the tidewater region and throughout the back settlements, women's roles closely resembled those of northern women. Women labored in the fields alongside their menfolk. "She is a very civil woman," noted an observer of a southern frontierswoman, "and shows nothing of ruggedness or immodesty in her carriage; yet she will carry a gun in the woods and kill deer and turkeys, shoot down wild cattle, catch and tie hogs, knock down beeves with an ax, and perform the most manful exercises as well as most men in those parts."

Marriage and family life were more informal in the backcountry. With vast areas unattended by ministers and with courthouses out of reach, most couples married or "took up" with each other until an itinerant clergyman on horseback appeared to bless the marriages and baptize the children.

Enslaved Africans in the Southern Colonies

From the late seventeenth century, the slave population grew rapidly—from about 15,000 in 1690 to 80,000 in 1730 and 325,000 in 1760. By then, when they composed one-fifth of the colonial population, Africans were growing in number far more from natural increase than from importation. The generation after 1730 witnessed the largest influx of African slaves in the colonial period, averaging about 5,000 a year. In the entire period from 1700 to 1775, more than 350,000 African slaves entered the American colonies.

Most of these miserable captives were auctioned off to southern planters, but some landed in the northern cities, especially New York and Philadelphia. Merchants sold them there to artisans, farmers, and upper-class householders seeking domestic servants.

The basic struggle for Africans toiling on plantations 5,000 miles from their homes was to create strategies for living as satisfactorily as possible despite horrifying treatment. The master hoped to convert the slave into a mindless drudge who obeyed every command and worked efficiently for his profit. But attempts to cow slaves rarely succeeded completely. Masters could set the external boundaries of existence for their slaves, controlling physical location, work roles, diet, and shelter. But the authority of the master class impinged far less on how slaves established friendships, fell in love, formed kin groups, reared children, worshiped their gods, buried their dead, and organized their leisure time.

In these aspects of daily life, slaves in the Americas drew on their African heritage to shape their existence to some degree, thus laying the foundations for an African American culture. At first, this culture had many variations because slaves came from many areas in Africa and lived under different conditions in the colonies. But common elements emerged, led by developments in the South, where about 90 percent of American slaves labored in colonial times.

Indian Traders at New Orleans Visiting French Louisiana in 1735, Alexander de Batz painted members of the Illinois tribe who traded at New Orleans. Note the hatted African, who apparently has been adopted by the Illinois. What do you think the barrels and boxes in the foreground contain? *(Peabody Museum, Harvard University, Photography by Hillel Burger)*

Arriving in North America, Africans entered a relatively healthy environment compared with other slave-labor areas in the Western Hemisphere. In the southern colonies, where the ghastly mortality of the early decades had subsided by the time Africans were arriving in large numbers, the slave's chance for survival was much better than in the West Indies or Brazil. This, as well as a more even gender ratio, led to a natural increase in the North American slave population unparalleled elsewhere.

Although slave codes severely restricted the lives of slaves, the possibility for family life increased as the southern colonies matured. Larger plantations employed dozens and even hundreds of slaves, with many of the men laboring in skilled crafts, and the growth of roads and market towns permitted them greater opportunities to forge relationships beyond their own plantation. By the 1740s, a growing proportion of Chesapeake slaves were American-born, had established families, and lived in plantation outbuildings where from sundown to sunup they could fashion personal lives.

In South Carolina, African slaves drew on agricultural skills practiced in Africa and made rice the keystone of the coastal economy by the early eighteenth century. Their numbers increased rapidly, from about 4,000 in 1708 to 90,000 by 1760. Working mostly on large plantations in swampy lowlands, they endured the most life-sapping conditions on the continent. But they outnumbered whites three to one by 1760 and hence could maintain more of their African culture than slaves in the Chesapeake region. Many spoke Gullah, a "pidgin" mixing several African languages. They often gave African names to their children and kept alive African religious customs.

Resistance and Rebellion

Slaves not only adapted to bondage but also resisted and rebelled in ways that constantly reminded their masters that slavery's price was eternal vigilance. Slaveowners interpreted rebelliousness as evidence of the "barbarous, wild savage natures" of Africans, as a South Carolina law of 1712 phrased it. Some planters, like Virginia's Landon Carter, believed that "slaves are devils and to make them free is to set devils free." But from the African point of view, resistance was essential to maintaining meaning and dignity in a life of degrading toil. Resisters' goals varied: to rejoin family members, to flee, to persuade masters to improve their condition, or to avenge sadistic overseers.

"Saltwater" Africans, fresh from their homelands, often fought slavery fiercely. "They often die before they can be conquered," said one white planter. Commonly, initial resistance took the form of fleeing—to renegade frontier settlements, to interior Native American tribes (which sometimes offered refuge), or to Spanish Florida. Rebellions, such as those in New York City in 1712 and at Stono, South Carolina, in 1739, mostly involved newly arrived slaves. There was no

DOCUMENT
James Oglethorpe, "The Stono Rebellion" (1739)

Advertisement for a Runaway Slave
Colonial newspapers, from Boston to Charleston, were filled with ads for runaway slaves. This ad, from the *Pennsylvania Gazette* (August 26, 1762), indicates that Joe (who has renamed himself Joseph Boudron) is an accomplished linguist who speaks English, French, Spanish, and Portuguese. Read the description of the clothes worn by the runaway slave and speculate why he chose these garments. *(The Historical Society of Pennsylvania [Pennsylvania Gazette, 8/26/1762])*

Philadelphia, August 24, 1762.

RUN away from the Subscriber Yesterday, a Mulattoe Man Slave, named Joe, alias Joseph Boudron, a middle-sized Man, a brisk lively Fellow, about 23 Years of Age, was born at Guadaloupe, has lived some Time in New-York, and Charles-Town, in South-Carolina, speaks good English, French, Spanish, and Portuguese: Had on when he went away, an old whitish coloured Broadcloth Coat, faced with Plush, and Metal Buttons, a Calicoe Jacket, black knit Breeches, blue Worsted Stockings, new Shoes, with large Brass Buckles, Check Shirt, an old laced Hat, and has other Things not known; he is a good Cook, and much used to the Seas, where it is thought he intends, or for New-York. Any Person that takes up said Runaway, and brings him to me, or secures him in any Goal in this Province, shall have Two Pistoles Reward, and if in any other Province, Four Pistoles, and reasonable Charges, paid by me

THOMAS BARTHOLOMEW, junior.

N. B. All Masters of Vessels and others are desired not to carry him off, or harbour him, on any Account.

North American parallel, however, for the massive slave uprisings of the West Indies and Brazil, where Africans vastly outnumbered their masters and therefore had a special incentive for rebelling.

The relatively small rebellions that did occur (or were feared) led to atrocious repression. Near Charleston in 1739, officials tortured and hanged 50 black rebels. Their decapitated heads, impaled on posts, warned other potential insurrectionists. In New York City a year later, rumors of a planned insurrection caused the hanging of 18 slaves and 4 white allies and the burning of 13 other slaves.

As slaves learned English, adjusted to work routines, and began forming families, they practiced more subtle forms of resistance. Dragging out jobs, pretending illness or ignorance, and breaking tools were ways of avoiding physical exhaustion and indirect forms of opposing slavery itself. More direct resistance included truancy, arson directed against the master's barns and houses, crop destruction, pilfering to supplement their food supply, and direct assaults on masters, overseers, and drivers. Overall, slave masters did extract labor and obedience from their slaves, but they did so only with difficulty. To push slaves too hard could be costly. One South Carolina planter drove his slaves late into the night cleaning and barreling a rice crop in 1732. When he awoke in the morning, he found his barn, with the entire harvest in it, reduced to ashes.

Black Religion and Family

The balance of power was always massively stacked against the slaves. Only the most desperate challenged the system directly. But as slaves struggled to find meaning and worth in their existence, religion and family became especially important.

Africans brought to the New World a complex religious heritage that no desolation or physical abuse could crush. People enduring the daily travail that accompanied slavery typically turned for relief to their deepest emotional sources. Coming from cultures where the division between sacred and secular activities was less clear than in Europe, slaves made religion central to their existence. Most slaves died strangers to Christianity until the mid-eighteenth century. Then they began to blend African religious practices with the religion of the master class, using this hybrid religion both to light the spark of resistance and to find comfort from oppression.

The religious revival that began in the 1720s in the northern colonies and spread southward thereafter made important contributions to African American religion. Evangelicalism stressed personal rebirth, used music and body motion, and produced an intense emotional experience. The dancing, shouting, rhythmic clapping, and singing that came to characterize slaves' religious expression represented a creative mingling of West African and Christian religions.

Besides religion, the slaves' greatest refuge from their dreadful fate lay in their families. In West Africa, all social relations were centered in kinship, which included dead ancestors. Torn from their native societies, slaves placed great importance on rebuilding extended kin groups.

Most English colonies prohibited slave marriages. But in practice, slaves and masters struck a bargain. Slaves desperately wanted families, and masters found that slaves with families would work harder and be less inclined to escape or rebel.

Slaves fashioned a family life only with difficulty, however. The general practice of importing three male slaves for every two females stunted family formation. Female slaves, much in demand, married in their late teens, but males usually had to wait until their mid- to late twenties. But as natural increase swelled the slave population in the eighteenth century, the gender ratio became more even.

Slave marriages were rarely secure because they could be abruptly severed by the sale of either husband or wife. This happened repeatedly, especially when a deceased planter's estate was divided among his heirs or his slaves were sold to his creditors to satisfy debts. Children usually stayed with their mothers until about age 8; then they were frequently torn from their families through sale, often to small planters needing only a hand or two. Few slaves escaped separation from family members at some time during their lives.

White male exploitation of black women represented another assault on family life. How many black women were coerced or lured with favors into sexual relations with white masters and overseers cannot be known, but the sizable mulatto (mixed-race) population at the end of the eighteenth century indicates that the number was large. Interracial liaisons, frequently forced, were widespread, especially in the Lower South. In 1732, the *South-Carolina Gazette* called racial mixing an "epidemical disease." It was a malady that had traumatic effects on slave attempts to build stable relationships.

In some interracial relationships, the coercion was subtle. In some cases, black women sought the liaison to gain advantages for themselves or their children. These unions nonetheless threatened both the slave community and the white plantation ideal. They bridged the supposedly unbridgeable gap between slave and free society and produced children who did not fit into the plantation ideal of separate racial categories.

Despite such obstacles, slaves fashioned intimate ties as husband and wife, parent and child. If monogamous relationships did not last as long as in white society, much of the explanation lies in slave life: the shorter life span of African Americans, the shattering of marriage through sale of one or both partners, and the call of freedom that impelled some slaves to run away.

Whereas slave men struggled to preserve their family role, many black women assumed a position in the family that differed from that of white women. Plantation mistresses usually worked hard in helping manage estates, but nonetheless the ideal grew that they should remain in the house guarding white virtue and setting standards for white culture. In contrast, the black woman remained indispensable to both the work of the plantation and the functioning of the slave quarters. She toiled in the fields and slave cabins alike. Paradoxically, black women's constant labor made them more equal to men than was the case of women in white society.

Above all, slavery was a set of power relationships designed to extract the maximum labor from its victims. Hence, it regularly involved cruelties that filled family life with tribulation. Still, slaves in North America toiled in less physically exhausting circumstances than slaves on sugar and coffee plantations and were better clothed, fed, and treated than Africans in the West Indies, Brazil, and other parts of the hemisphere. Therefore, they were unusually successful in establishing families. Slave family life in the American colonies brimmed with uncertainty and sorrow but was nonetheless the greatest monument to slaves' will to endure captivity and eventually gain their freedom.

CONTENDING FOR A CONTINENT

By 1750, when English colonists numbered about 1.2 million, only a small fraction of them, along with their African slaves, lived farther than 100 miles from the Atlantic Ocean. Growing rapidly, the English colonies were beginning to elbow up against the French and Spanish settlements in the rich river valleys of the Ohio and Mississippi and beyond. France posed the greatest threat to English colonists in the interior of North America, while the Spanish presented another challenge on their southern flank. On the other side of the continent,

the Spanish were moving northward up the California coast until they reached the limits of Russian settlement in northern California.

France's Inland Empire

In 1661, France's Louis XIV, determined to make his country the most powerful in Europe, looked with keen interest to North America and the Caribbean. New France's timber would build the royal navy, its fish would feed the growing mass of slaves in the French West Indies, and its fur trade, if greatly expanded, would fill the royal coffers. From French Caribbean islands came precious sugar.

New France grew in population, economic strength, and ambition in the late seventeenth century. In 1673, Louis Joliet and Father Jacques Marquette, a Jesuit priest, explored an immense territory watered by the Mississippi and Missouri rivers. A decade later, military engineers and priests began building forts and missions in the Great Lakes region and the Mississippi valley. In 1682, René Robert de La Salle canoed down the Mississippi all the way to the Gulf of Mexico and planted a settlement in Texas at Matagorda Bay. The French solidified their claim to the North American heartland and the lower Mississippi valley when Pierre le Moyne d'Iberville established a small settlement at Biloxi in 1699 and then three years later a settlement at Mobile.

In the first half of the eighteenth century, the French developed a system of forts, trading posts, and agricultural villages throughout the heart of the continent, threatening to pin the English to the seaboard. French success in this vast region hinged partly on shrewd dealing with the Native American tribes, which retained sovereignty over the land but gradually succumbed to French diseases, French arms, and French-promoted intertribal wars.

Because France's interior empire was organized primarily as a military, trading, and missionizing operation, male French settlers arrived with few French women. Thus, for a long time, French men were in a state of need when they encountered Native Americans—not only for trading partners, allies, and religious converts but also for wives. These needs produced a mingling of French and Native American peoples—what the French called *metissage*—in the North American interior. Such interracial marriages, called "the custom of the country," were welcomed by the natives as well as the French. Marital alliances cemented trade and military relations. French traders entered Native American kinship circles, making trade flow smoothly, while natives gained protection against

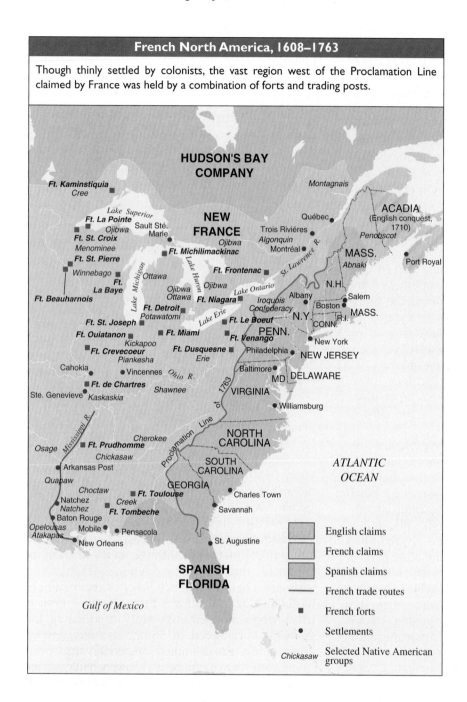

French North America, 1608–1763

Though thinly settled by colonists, the vast region west of the Proclamation Line claimed by France was held by a combination of forts and trading posts.

their enemies and access to provisions and weapons at French trading posts.

The French presence in the continent's vast heartland, thinly dotted with small farming communities, created a shield against the expansive British. As the French population grew to about 70,000 by 1750, they demonstrated how European settlers and Native American peoples could coexist. Almost all French settlements in North America's interior were mixed-race, or *meti*, communities—a sharp contrast to the English colonies.

In 1718, French pioneers of the interior and those along the Gulf of Mexico were inundated when

France settled New Orleans at great cost by transporting almost 7,000 whites and 5,000 African slaves to the mouth of the Mississippi River. Disease rapidly whittled down these numbers, and an uprising of the powerful Natchez in 1729 discouraged further French immigration. Most of the survivors settled around the little town of New Orleans and on long, narrow plantations stretching back from the Mississippi River. While New Orleans' economy and society resembled early Charleston, South Carolina, it was run and financed by royal government and knew nothing of representative political institutions such as elections, legislative assembly, newspapers, or taxes.

New Orleans Parish, 1723   This map of New Orleans Parish in 1723, when the colony was still struggling, shows every plantation fronting on the Mississippi River. How do you think this arrangement of property affected social relations? *(Courtesy of The Newberry Library, Chicago)*

French slaves were critically important to the development of Louisiana. Arriving with skills as rice growers, indigo processors, metal workers, river navigators, herbalists, and cattle keepers, Africans became the backbone of the economy. Like male slaves in the Spanish colonies, they mingled extensively with Native American women, producing mixed-race children known locally as *grifs*. African women also made interracial liaisons with French immigrants, often soldiers in search of partners. By 1765 black Louisianans, outnumbering whites, served as militiamen and sometimes received freedom for military service. Paternalistic French law also gave slaves some protection in courts. All in all, the chance of gaining freedom in fluid French Louisiana exceeded that of any other colony in North America's Southeast, and the absorption of free blacks into white society, particularly if they were of mixed-race descent, was shockingly common from the English point of view. When the Spanish took over the colony in 1769, they guaranteed slaves the right to buy freedom with money earned in their free time. Soon a free black class emerged. When Americans acquired the colony in 1803, they suppressed freedom purchase and discouraged manumission.

A Generation of War

The growth of French strength and ambitions brought British America and New France into deadly conflict beginning in the late seventeenth century. Protestant New Englanders regarded Catholic New France as a satanic challenge to their divinely sanctioned mission. When the European wars began in 1689, precipitated by Louis XIV's territorial aggression in western and central Europe, conflict between England and France quickly extended into every overseas theater where the two powers had colonies. In North America, the battle zone included New York, New England, and eastern Canada.

In two wars, from 1689 to 1697 and 1701 to 1713, the English and French, while fighting in Europe, also sought to oust each other from the Americas. The zone of greatest importance was the Caribbean, where slaves produced huge sugar fortunes. But both home governments valued the North American settlements greatly as a source of the timber and fish that sustained the sugar-producing West Indian colonies.

The English struck three times at the centers of French power—at Port Royal, which commanded the access to the St. Lawrence River, and at Quebec, the capital of New France. In 1690, during King

Queen Anne's War: Major Battles and Territorial Changes

Like every other Anglo-French conflict in the seventeenth and eighteenth centuries, Queen Anne's War was fought in the Caribbean as well as in North America. The sugar- and coffee-rich islands of the West Indies, teeming with enslaved Africans, made them prizes in the competition for empire.

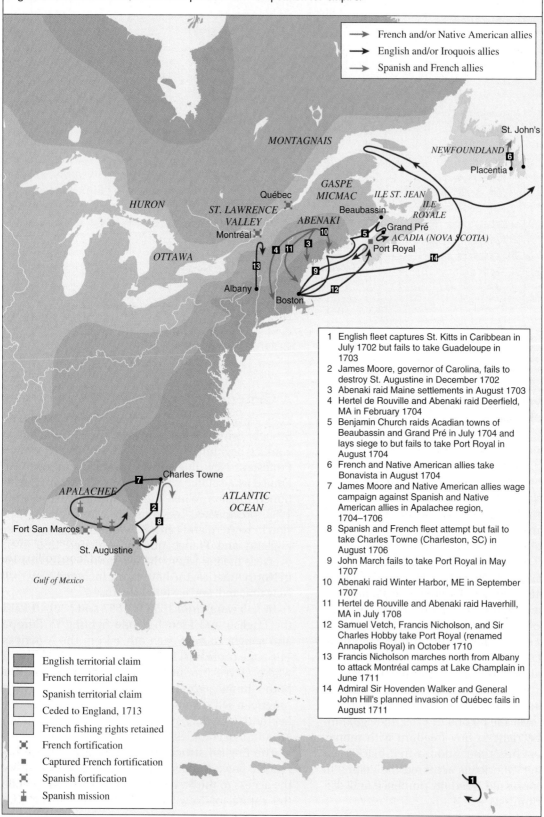

French and/or Native American allies
English and/or Iroquois allies
Spanish and French allies

1 English fleet captures St. Kitts in Caribbean in July 1702 but fails to take Guadeloupe in 1703
2 James Moore, governor of Carolina, fails to destroy St. Augustine in December 1702
3 Abenaki raid Maine settlements in August 1703
4 Hertel de Rouville and Abenaki raid Deerfield, MA in February 1704
5 Benjamin Church raids Acadian towns of Beaubassin and Grand Pré in July 1704 and lays siege to but fails to take Port Royal in August 1704
6 French and Native American allies take Bonavista in August 1704
7 James Moore and Native American allies wage campaign against Spanish and Native American allies in Apalachee region, 1704–1706
8 Spanish and French fleet attempt but fail to take Charles Towne (Charleston, SC) in August 1706
9 John March fails to take Port Royal in May 1707
10 Abenaki raid Winter Harbor, ME in September 1707
11 Hertel de Rouville and Abenaki raid Haverhill, MA in July 1708
12 Samuel Vetch, Francis Nicholson, and Sir Charles Hobby take Port Royal (renamed Annapolis Royal) in October 1710
13 Francis Nicholson marches north from Albany to attack Montréal camps at Lake Champlain in June 1711
14 Admiral Sir Hovenden Walker and General John Hill's planned invasion of Québec fails in August 1711

English territorial claim
French territorial claim
Spanish territorial claim
Ceded to England, 1713
French fishing rights retained
French fortification
Captured French fortification
Spanish fortification
Spanish mission

William's War (1689–1697), their small flotilla captured Port Royal, the hub of Acadia (which was returned to France at the end of the war). The English assault on Quebec, however, failed disastrously. In Queen Anne's War (1701–1713), New England attacked Port Royal three times before finally capturing it in 1710. A year later, when England sent a flotilla of 60 ships and 5,000 men to conquer Canada, the land and sea operations foundered before reaching their destinations.

With European-style warfare miserably unsuccessful in America, both England and France attempted to subcontract military tasks to their Native American allies. This policy occasionally succeeded, especially with the French, who gladly sent their own troops into the fray alongside Native American partners. In both wars, the French and their Native American allies wiped out the frontier outpost of Schenectady, New York, in 1690; razed Wells, Maine, and Deerfield, Massachusetts, in 1703; and battered other towns along the New England frontier during both wars.

Retaliating, the English-supplied Iroquois left New France "bewildered and benumbed" after a massacre near Montreal in 1689. Assessing their own interests and too powerful to be bullied by either France or England, the Iroquois sat out the second war in the early eighteenth century. Convinced that neutrality served their purposes better than acting as mercenaries for the English, they held to the principle that "we are a free people uniting ourselves to whatever sachem [chief] we wish."

Though England had rebuffed France after a generation of war, New England suffered grievous economic and human losses. Massachusetts bore the heaviest burden. Probably one-fifth of all able-bodied males in the colony participated in the Canadian campaigns, and of these, about one-quarter never lived to tell of the terrors of New England's first major experience with international warfare. The war debt was £50,000 sterling in Massachusetts alone, a greater per capita burden than the national debt today. At the end of the second conflict, in 1713, war widows were so numerous that the Bay Colony faced its first serious poverty problem. In addition, wartime taxes and price inflation had eaten deeply into the pocketbooks of most working families.

The colonies south of New England remained on the sidelines during most of the two wars. But war at sea between European rivals affected even those who sat out the land war. New York lost one of its best grain markets when Spain, allied with France, outlawed American foodstuffs in its Caribbean colonies. The French navy plucked off nearly one-quarter of the port's fleet and disrupted Philadelphia grain merchants' access to the Caribbean.

The burdens and rewards fell unevenly on the participants, as usually happens in wartime. Some lowborn men could rise spectacularly. William Phips, the twenty-sixth child in his family, had been a poor sheep farmer and ship's carpenter in Maine who seemed destined to go nowhere. He then won a fortune by recovering a sunken Spanish treasure ship in the West Indies in 1687 and was given command of the expedition against Port Royal in 1690. Victory there catapulted him to the governorship of Massachusetts in 1691; thereafter his status was secure.

Other men, already rich, got richer. Andrew Belcher of Boston, who had grown wealthy on provisioning contracts during King Philip's War, supplied warships and outfitted the New England expeditions to Canada. He became a local titan, riding in London-built coaches, erecting a handsome mansion, and purchasing slaves.

Most men, especially those who did the fighting, gained little, and many lost everything. The least securely placed New Englanders—indentured servants, apprentices, recently arrived immigrants, unskilled laborers, fishermen, and ordinary farmers—supplied most of the voluntary or involuntary recruits, and they died in numbers that seem staggering today. Antipopery, dreams of glory, and promises of plunder in French Canada lured most of them into uniform. Having achieved no place on the paths leading upward, they grasped at straws and usually failed again.

In 1713, the Peace of Utrecht, which ended Queen Anne's War, capped the century-long rise of England and the decline of Spain in the rivalry for the sources of wealth outside Europe. England, the big winner, received Newfoundland and Acadia (renamed Nova Scotia), and France recognized English sovereignty over the fur-rich Hudson Bay territory. France retained Cape Breton Island, controlling the entrance to the St. Lawrence River. In the Caribbean, France yielded St. Kitts and Nevis to England. Spain lost its provinces in Italy and the last of its holdings in the Netherlands to the Austrian Hapsburgs. Spain also surrendered Gibraltar and Minorca to England and awarded the English the lucrative privilege of supplying the Spanish empire in the Americas with African slaves.

Spain's Frail North American Grip

Spain's grip on its colonies in North America had always been tenuous. On the East Coast, the growth of South Carolina's slave-based plantation society in the late seventeenth century stemmed partly from the

A Chart of Mixed-Race Families   The mixing of races in Spain's New World colonies is vividly displayed in paintings of interracial families, widely produced in Mexico in the eighteenth century. In each painting shown here, the mother and father of different racial ancestries produces a child with a different racial term. In panel 5, for example, the mulatto mother and Spanish father produce a "Morisco" child. Paintings such as these spread the view that interracial mixing was the natural path of human affairs when people of different racial backgrounds converged. *(Anonymous,* Human Races (Las Castas), *18th century, Schalkwijk/Art Resource, NY)*

Hispanics, mestizos, and detribalized Native Americans began to increase modestly in Texas, New Mexico, and California in the first half of the eighteenth century, but by 1745 in Florida they had only one-tenth the population of the English in South Carolina. New Mexico's Hispanic population of about 10,000 at midcentury could defend the vast region only because no European challenger appeared.

As in New France, racial intermixture and social fluidity were more extensive in New Spain than in the English colonies because Spanish male colonizers greatly outnumbered Spanish women. Precisely how much intermixing occurred is uncertain because the Spanish never defined racial groups as distinctly as the English. The word *Spaniard* on a census might mean a white immigrant from Mexico or a part–Native American person who "lived like a Spaniard." Social mobility was considerable because the Crown was willing to raise even a common person to the status of *hidalgo* (minor nobleman) as an inducement to settle in New Spain's remote northern frontier. Most of the immigrants became small ranchers, producing livestock, corn, and wheat for export to southward Spanish provinces.

Native Americans had mixed success in resisting Spanish domination. In New Mexico, an early nineteenth-century Spanish investigator saw the key to Pueblo cultural autonomy as the underground kivas, which were "like impenetrable temples, where they gather to discuss mysteriously their misfortunes or good fortunes, their happiness or grief. The doors of these *estufas* are always closed to us." However, California tribes had difficulty in maintaining cultural cohesion. In the 1770s, the Spanish rapidly completed their western land and sea routes from San Diego to Yerba Buena (San Francisco) to block Russian settlement south of their base in northern California. California's Spanish pioneers were Franciscan missionaries, accompanied by royal soldiers. The priests would choose a good location and then attract a few Native Americans to be baptized and resettled around the missions, which they helped build. Visiting relatives would then be induced to stay. These Native Americans lived under an increasingly harsh regimen until they were reduced to a condition of virtual slavery. The California mission, with

English use of Native American allies to attack Spanish Indian missions and outposts and sell the captives into slavery. From this time forward, English and French traders, with more attractive trade goods to offer, held sway over Florida Indians.

After the Peace of Utrecht in 1713, Spain maintained a fragile hold on the southern tier of the continent. However, Spain learned how easily its thinly peopled missions and frontier outposts could be crippled or destroyed by chafing Native Americans and invading English. In the first half of the eighteenth century, the Spanish settlements stagnated, suffering from Spain's colonial policy that regarded them as marginal, money-losing affairs, useful only as defensive outposts.

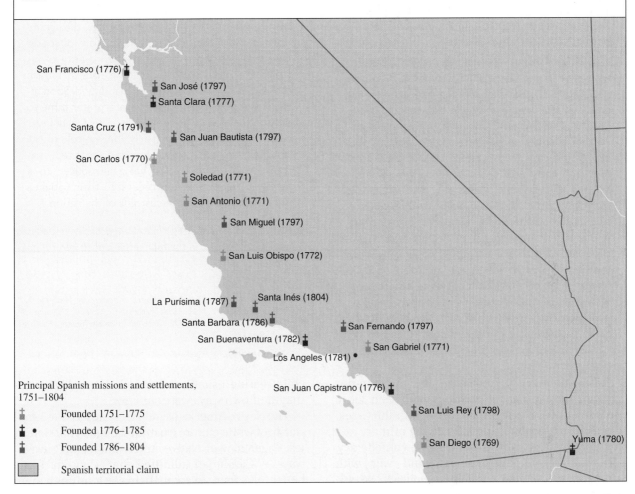

Spanish Missions in California

As colonists in the British colonies on the eastern seaboard careened toward revolution, Spanish Franciscan priests were building a string of missions on the other side of the continent, hoping to convert Native Americans to Catholicism while capturing their labor.

San Francisco (1776)
San José (1797)
Santa Clara (1777)
Santa Cruz (1791)
San Juan Bautista (1797)
San Carlos (1770)
Soledad (1771)
San Antonio (1771)
San Miguel (1797)
San Luis Obispo (1772)
La Purísima (1787)
Santa Inés (1804)
Santa Barbara (1786)
San Fernando (1797)
San Buenaventura (1782)
San Gabriel (1771)
Los Angeles (1781)
San Juan Capistrano (1776)
San Luis Rey (1798)
San Diego (1769)
Yuma (1780)

Principal Spanish missions and settlements, 1751–1804

Founded 1751–1775
Founded 1776–1785
Founded 1786–1804
Spanish territorial claim

its extensive and profitable herds and grain crops, theoretically belonged to the Native American converts, but they did not enjoy the profits. Ironically, the spiritual motives of the priests brought the same degradation of tribal Americans as elsewhere.

Cultural and Ecological Changes Among Interior Tribes

During the first half of the eighteenth century, the inland tribes proved their capacity to adapt to the contending European colonizers in their region while maintaining political independence. Yet extensive contact with the French, Spanish, and English slowly brought ominous changes to Native American societies. European trade goods, especially iron implements, textiles, firearms and ammunition, and alcohol, altered Native American ways of life. Subsistence hunting turned into commercial

hunting, restricted only by the quantity of trade goods desired. Native American males, gradually wiping out deer and beaver east of the Mississippi River, spent more time away from the villages trapping and hunting. Women were also drawn into the new economy, skinning animals and fashioning pelts into robes. Among some tribes, these commercial activities became so time-consuming that they had to procure food from other tribes.

The fur trade greatly altered traditional Native American life. Spiritual beliefs that the destinies of humans and animals were closely linked eroded when trappers and hunters declared all-out war on the beaver and other fur-bearing animals in order to exchange pelts for attractive trade goods. Competition for furs sharpened intertribal tensions, often to the point of war. The introduction of European weaponry, which Native Americans quickly mastered, intensified these conflicts.

AMERICAN VOICES

Susanna Johnson, Adoption into a Native American Tribe

Susanna Johnson, who had been captured by Abenaki in 1754, describes her adoption into the tribe and her assignment to a Native American "master."

I, with my infant, was taken to the grand parade, where we found a large collection of the village inhabitants. An aged chief stepped forward into an area, and after every noise was silenced and every one fixed in profound attention he began his harangue: his manner was solemn; his motions and expression gave me a perfect idea of an orator. Not a breath was heard, and every spectator seemed to reverence what he said. After the speech my little son was brought to the opposite side of the parade, and a number of blankets laid by his side. It now appeared that his master and mine intended an exchange of prisoners. My master, being a hunter, wished for my son to attend him on his excursions. Each delivered his property with great formality; my son and blankets being an equivalent for myself, child, and wampum. I was taken to the house of my new master, and found myself allied to the first family. My master, whose name was Gill, was son-in-law to the grand sachem, was accounted rich, had a store of goods, and lived in a style far above the majority of his tribe. He often told me that he had an English heart, but his wife was true Indian blood. Soon after my arrival at his house the interpreter came to inform me that I was adopted into his family. I was then introduced into his family, and was told to call them brothers and sisters. I made a short reply, expressive of gratitude for being introduced to a house of high rank, and requested their patience while I should learn the customs of the nation.

■ *Do you believe captured Native Americans were adopted into white families in the manner described here? If not, why?*

Source: *Indian Narratives: Containing a Correct and Interesting History of the Indian Wars* (Claremont, N.H.: 1854), excerpted in Colin G. Calloway, *First Peoples: A Documentary Survey of American Indian History* (Boston: Bedford Books, 1999), 176–177.

Tribal political organization in the interior changed too. Earlier, most tribes had been loose confederations of villages and clans with the Creek, Cherokee, and Iroquois peoples giving primary loyalty to the village, not to the tribe or confederacy. But trade, diplomatic contact, and war with Europeans required coordinated policies, so villagers gradually adopted more centralized leadership. For example, the basic unit of Cherokee political authority was the nearly autonomous village. But tension with Creek neighbors and intermittent hostilities with the English pressed home the need for coordinated decision making. By 1750, the Cherokee had formed an umbrella political organization that gathered together the fragmented authority of the villages and formed a more centralized tribal "priest state." When this proved inadequate, warriors began to assume the dominant role in tribal councils, replacing the civil chiefs.

While incorporating trade goods into their material culture and adapting their economies and political structures to new situations, the interior tribes held fast to many traditions. They saw little reason to replace what they valued in their own culture. What they saw of the colonists' law and justice, religion, education, family organization, and child rearing usually convinced Native Americans that their own ways were superior.

The Native Americans' refusal to accept the superiority of white culture frustrated English missionaries, eager to win Native Americans from "savage" ways. A Carolinian admitted that "they are really better to us than we are to them. We look upon them with scorn and disdain, and think them little better than beasts in human shape, though if well examined, we shall find that, for all our religion and education, we possess more moral deformities and evils than these savages do."

Overall, interior tribes suffered from contact with the British colonizers. Decade by decade, the fur trade spread epidemic diseases, intensified warfare, depleted game animals, and drew Native Americans into a market economy in which their trading partners gradually became trading masters.

THE URBAN WORLD OF COMMERCE AND IDEAS

Only about 5 percent of the eighteenth-century colonists lived in towns as large as 2,500, and no city boasted a population above 16,000 in 1750 or 30,000

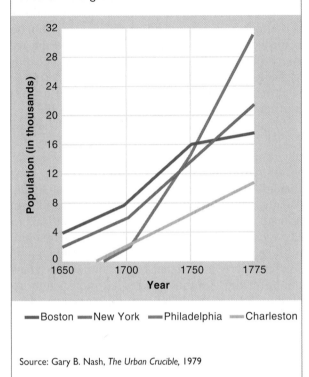

Urban Population Growth, 1650–1775

By 1755, Boston had lost its lead as British North America's largest city. Plagued by costly wars and economic difficulties, its population leveled off, whereas that of other cities grew.

■ Boston ■ New York ■ Philadelphia ■ Charleston

Source: Gary B. Nash, *The Urban Crucible,* 1979

Cities were trade centers. Through them flowed colonial export staples (tobacco, rice, furs, wheat, timber products, and fish) and the imported goods that colonists needed: manufactured and luxury goods from England (glass, paper, iron implements, and cloth); wine, spices, coffee, tea, and sugar from other parts of the world; and the human cargo to fill the labor gap. The pivotal seaport figure was the merchant, often engaging in both retail and wholesale trade, usually the moneylender (for no banks yet existed), and frequently the shipbuilder, insurance agent, land developer, and coordinator of artisan production.

By the eighteenth century, the American economy was integrated into an Atlantic trading system that connected settlers to Great Britain, western Europe, Africa, the West Indies, and Newfoundland. Great Britain, like other major trading nations of western Europe, pursued mercantilist trade policies. Mercantilism's core idea was that a country must gain wealth by increasing exports, taxing imports, regulating production and trade, and exploiting colonies. These policies governed British treatment of their North American and Caribbean colonies.

Colonial Products

The colonists could never produce enough exportable raw materials to pay for the imported goods they craved, so they had to earn credits in England by supplying the West Indies and other areas with foodstuffs and timber products. They also accumulated credit by providing shipping and distribution services. Sailing from Boston, Salem, Newport, and Providence, New Englanders became the most ambitious participants in the carrying trade.

The Artisan's World

Although merchants stood first in wealth and prestige in the colonial towns, artisans were far more numerous. About two-thirds of urban adult males (slaves excluded) labored at handicrafts. By the mid-eighteenth century, the colonial cities contained scores of specialized "leather apron men" besides the proverbial butcher, baker, and candlestick maker. Handicraft specialization increased as the cities matured, but every artisan worked with hand tools, usually in small shops.

Work patterns for artisans were irregular, dictated by weather, length of daylight, erratic delivery of raw materials, and shifting consumer demand. When ice blocked northern harbors, mariners and dockworkers endured slack time. If prolonged rain delayed the slaughter of cows in the country or

in 1775. Yet urban societies were at the leading edge of the transition to "modern" life. There, a barter economy first gave way to a commercial economy, a social order based on assigned status turned into one based on achievement, rank-conscious and deferential politics changed to participatory and contentious politics, and small-scale artisanship was gradually replaced by factory production. Into the cities flowed European ideas, which radiated outward to the hinterland.

The Connecticut Peddler

Sinews of Trade

In the half century after 1690, Boston, New York, Philadelphia, and Charleston blossomed into thriving commercial centers. Their growth accompanied the development of the agricultural interior, to which the seaports were closely linked. As the colonial population rose and spread out, minor seaports such as Salem, Newport, Providence, Annapolis, Norfolk, and Savannah gathered 5,000 or more inhabitants.

Nathaniel Hurd, Boston Engraver   Not many Boston artisans became prosperous enough to have their portrait painted. But a few did, including Paul Revere and Nathaniel Hurd, the engraver shown here. Hurd came from a long line of artisans: his great-grandfather was a tailor, his grandfather a joiner, and his father a silversmith. Hurd's open collar and rolled-up sleeves show him in his working outfit. This unfinished portrait was probably a study for a more elegant portrait that showed Hurd in an embroidered silk blouse. *(John Singleton Copley,* Unfinished painting of engraver Nathaniel Hurd. *Memorial Art Gallery of the University of Rochester, Marion Stratton Gould Fund)*

made impassable the rutted roads into the city, the tanner and the shoemaker laid their tools aside. The hatter depended on the supply of beaver skins, which could stop abruptly if disease struck a Native American tribe or war disrupted the fur trade. Every urban artisan knew "broken days," slack spells, and dull seasons. Ordinary laborers dreaded winter, for it was a season when cities had "little occasion for the labor of the poor," and firewood could cost several months' wages.

Urban artisans took fierce pride in their crafts. While deferring to those above them, they saw themselves as the backbone of the community, contributing essential products and services. "Our professions rendered us useful and necessary members of our community," the Philadelphia shoemakers asserted, "Proud of that rank, we aspired to no higher." This self-esteem and desire for community recognition sometimes jostled with the upper-class view of artisans as "mere mechanicks," part of the "vulgar herd."

Striving for respectability, artisans placed a premium on achieving economic independence. Every artisan began as an apprentice, spending five or more teenage years in a master's shop, then, after fulfilling his contract, becoming a "journeyman," selling his labor to a master and frequently living in his house where he ate at his table and sometimes married his daughter. He hoped to complete within a few years the three-step climb from servitude to self-employment. After setting up his own shop, he could control his work hours and acquire the respect that came from economic independence. But in trades requiring greater organization and capital, such as distilling and shipbuilding, the rise from journeyman to master often proved impossible.

In good times, urban artisans did well. They expected to earn a "decent competency" and eventually to purchase a small house. But success was far from automatic, even for those following Poor Richard's advice about hard work and frugal living. An advantageous marriage, luck in avoiding illness, and an ample inheritance were often critical. In Philadelphia, about half the artisans in the first half of the eighteenth century died leaving enough personal property to have ensured a comfortable standard of living. Another quarter left more, often including slaves and indentured servants. New England's artisans did not fare so well because their economy was weaker.

Urban Social Structure

Population growth, economic development, and war altered the urban social structure between 1690 and 1765. Stately townhouses displayed fortunes built through trade, shipbuilding, war contracting, and—probably most profitable of all—urban land development. "It is almost a proverb," a Philadelphian observed in the 1760s, "that every great fortune made here within these 50 years has been by land." A merchant's estate of £2,000 sterling was impressive in the early eighteenth century. Two generations later, North America's first millionaires were accumulating estates of £10,000 to £20,000 sterling.

The rise of Thomas Hancock, on whose fortune his less commercially astute nephew, John Hancock, would later construct a shining political career, shows how war could catapult an enterprising trader to affluence. An opportune marriage to the daughter of a prosperous merchant provided bookseller Hancock with a toehold in commerce and enough capital to invest in several vessels. By 1735, he had made enough money, much of it from smuggling tea, to build a mansion on Beacon Hill. When war broke out with Spain in 1739, Hancock obtained lucrative supply contracts for military expeditions to the Caribbean and Nova Scotia. He also invested

Wealth Distribution in Colonial America

Percentage of wealth held by the richest 10% and the poorest 30% of the population in two cities and one rural area.

Year	Richest 10%	Poorest 30%
Boston		
1684–1699	41.2	3.3
1700–1715	54.5	2.8
1716–1725	61.7	2.0
1726–1735	65.6	1.9
1736–1745	58.6	1.8
1746–1755	55.2	1.8
1756–1765	67.5	1.4
1766–1775	61.1	2.0
Philadelphia		
1684–1699	36.4	4.5
1700–1715	41.3	4.9
1716–1725	46.8	3.9
1726–1735	53.6	3.7
1736–1745	51.3	2.6
1746–1755	70.1	1.5
1756–1765	60.3	1.1
1766–1775	69.9	1.0
Chester County, Pennsylvania		
1693	23.8	17.4
1715	25.9	13.1
1730	28.6	9.8
1748	28.7	13.1
1760	29.9	6.3
1782	33.6	4.7

Source: Gary B. Nash, *The Urban Crucible*, 1979.

enable them to contribute to their own support through spinning and weaving. Despite the warnings of Boston's ministers that "if any would not work, neither should they eat," they refused to leave their children at home to labor in America's first textile factory.

Urban eighteenth-century tax lists reveal the increasing gap between the wealthy and the poor. The top 5 percent of taxpayers increased their share of the cities' taxable assets from about 30 to 50 percent between 1690 and 1770. The bottom half of the taxable inhabitants saw their share of the wealth shrink from about 10 to 4 percent. Except in Boston, the urban middle classes continued to gain ground. Still, the growth of princely fortunes amid increasing poverty made some urban dwellers reflect that Old World ills were reappearing in the New.

The Entrepreneurial Ethos

As the cities grew, new values took hold. In the traditional view of society, economic life was supposed to operate according to what was fair, not what was profitable. Regulated prices and wages, quality controls, supervised public markets, and other such measures seemed natural because a community was defined as a single body of interrelated parts, where individual rights and responsibilities formed a seamless web.

In their commercialized cities, most urban dwellers grew to regard the subordinating of private interests to the commonweal as unrealistic. Prosperity required the encouragement of acquisitive appetites rather than self-denial, for ambition would spur economic activity as more people sought more goods. The new view held that if people were allowed to pursue their material desires competitively, they would collectively form a natural, impersonal market of producers and consumers that would advantage everyone.

Hence, as the colonial port towns became imbedded in the Atlantic world of commerce, merchants began to make decisions according to the emerging commercial ethic that rejected traditional restraints on entrepreneurial activity. If wheat fetched eight shillings a bushel in the West Indies but only five in Boston, a grain merchant felt justified in sending all he could purchase from local farmers to the more distant buyer. Indifferent to individuals and local communities, the new transatlantic market responded only to the invisible laws of supply and demand.

Tension between the new economic freedom and the older concern for the public good erupted only with food shortages or galloping inflation. Because

heavily in privateers, who engaged in private warfare against enemy shipping and auctioned the enemy vessels they overpowered. When peace returned in 1748, Hancock was riding through Boston in a London-built four-horse chariot emblazoned with a heraldic shield.

Alongside urban wealth grew urban poverty. From the beginning, every city had its disabled, orphaned, and widowed who required aid. But after 1720, poverty marred the lives of many more city dwellers, including war widows with no means of support, rural migrants, and recent immigrants. Boston was hit especially hard. Its economy stagnated in the 1740s, and taxpayers groaned under the burden of paying for heavy war expenditures. Cities devised new ways of helping the needy, such as building large almshouses where the poor could be housed and fed more economically. But many of the indigent preferred "to starve in their homes" rather than endure the discipline and indignities of the poorhouse. Boston's poor women also resisted laboring in the linen factory that was built in 1750 to

RECOVERING THE PAST

Household Inventories

Historians use probate records to examine social changes in American society. They include wills, the legal disposition of estates, and household inventories taken by court-appointed appraisers that detail the personal possessions left at death. Inventories have been especially valuable in tracing the transformation of colonial communities.

Like tax lists, inventories can be used to show changes in a community's distribution of wealth. But they are far more detailed than tax lists, providing a snapshot of how people lived at the end of their life. Inventories list and value almost everything a person owned—household possessions, equipment, books, clothes and jewelry, cash on hand, livestock and horses, crops and stored provisions. Hence, through inventories, we can measure the quality of life at different social levels. We can also witness how people made choices about investing their savings—in capital goods of their trade such as land, ships, and equipment; in personal goods such as household furnishings and luxury items; or in real property such as land and houses.

Studied systematically (and corrected for biases, which infect this source as well as others), inventories show that by the early 1700s, ordinary householders were improving their standard of living. Finished furniture such as cupboards, beds, tables, and chairs turn up more frequently in inventories. Pewter dinnerware replaces wooden bowls and spoons, bed linen makes an appearance, and books and pictures are sometimes noted.

Among an emerging elite before the Revolution, much more fashionable articles of consumption appear. The partial inventory of Robert Oliver, a wealthy merchant and officeholder living in a Boston suburb, is reproduced here. You can get some idea of the dignified impression Oliver wished to make by looking at his furniture and dishes and by noticing that he owned a mahogany tea table, damask linen, and a bed with curtains. The inventory further suggests the spaciousness of Oliver's house and shows how he furnished each room.

It is helpful when studying inventories to categorize the goods in the following way: those that are needed to survive (basic cooking utensils, for example); those that make life easier or more comfortable (enough plates and beds for each member of the family, for example); and those that make life luxurious (slaves, silver plates, paintings, mahogany furniture, damask curtains, spices, wine, and so forth). Oliver had many luxury goods as well as items that contributed to his use of leisure time and his personal enjoyment. Which items in his inventory do you think were needed only to survive comfortably? Which were luxuries? What other conclusions can you draw about the lifestyle of rich colonial merchants like Oliver?

Beyond revealing a growing social differentiation in colonial society, the inventories help the historian understand the reaction during the Great Awakening to what many ordinary colonists regarded as sinful pride and arrogance displayed by the elite. By the 1760s, this distrust of affluence among simple folk had led to outright hostility toward men who surrounded themselves with the trappings of aristocratic life. Even the ambitious young John Adams, a striving lawyer, was shocked at what he saw at the house of a wealthy merchant in Boston. "Went over the House to view the furniture, which alone cost a thousand Pound sterling," he exclaimed. "A seat it is for a noble Man, a Prince. The Turkey Carpets, the painted Hangings, the Marble Tables, the rich Beds with crimson Damask Curtains . . . are the most magnificent of any Thing I have ever seen."

Such a description takes on its full meaning only when contrasted with what inventories tell us about life at the bottom of society. The hundreds of inventories for Bostonians dying in the decade before the American Revolution show that fully half of them died with less than £40 personal wealth and one-quarter with £20 or less. The inventories and wills of Jonathan and Daniel Chandler of Andover, Massachusetts, show the material circumstances of less favored Americans who suffered from the economic distress afflicting New England since the 1730s. Note that Daniel Chandler was a shoemaker.

REFLECTING ON THE PAST How do the possessions of these brothers compare with Oliver's partial inventory? An examination of these contrasting inventories helps explain the class tension that figured in the revolutionary experience.

Household Inventory of Robert Oliver, Wealthy Merchant

Dorchester Jan.ry 11.th 1763.

Inventory of what Estates Real & Personall, belonging to Coll.o Robert Oliver [Esquire] late of Dorchester Deceased, that has been Exhibited to us the Subscribers, for Apprizement. Viz.t

In the Setting Parlour Viz.tt

a looking Glass		£4.—.—
a Small Ditto		0.6.0
12 Metzitens pictures Glaz'd	@6/	3.12.—
8 Cartoons D.o Ditto		4.—.—
11 small Pictures		—.4.—
4 Maps		—.10.—
1 Prospect Glass		—.10.—
2 Escutchons Glaz'd		—.4.—
1 pair small hand Irons		—.6.—
1 Shovel & Tongs		—.8.—
1 Tobacco Tongs		—.1.—
1 pair Bellowes		—.2.—
1 Tea Chest		—.2.—
2 Small Waters		—.1.—
1 Mehogony Tea Table		1.—.—
8 China Cups & Saucers		—.2.—
1 Earthen Cream Pott		—.—.1
1 Ditto. Sugar Dish		—.—.4
1 Black Walnut Table		1.—.—
1 Black Ditto Smaller		0.6.—
1 Round painted Table		0.1.—
7 Leather Bottom Chairs @ 6/		2.2.—
1 Arm.d Chair Common		1.3.—
1 Black Walnut Desk		1.12.—
1 pair Candlesticks snuffers & Stand Base Mettle		—.4.—
6 Wine Glasses 1 Water Glass		—.1.—
a parcell of Books		1.—.—
a Case with Small Bottles		0.4.—
		22.1.5

In the Entry & Stair Case Viz.t

17 pictures		£0.10.—
		0.10.0

In the Kitchen Chamber Viz.t

a Bedstead & Curtains Compleat		£4.—.—
a Bed Bolster & 2 pillows		5.—.—
a Under Bed & 1 Chair		0.1.—
2 Rugs & 1 Blankett @ 6/		0.18.—
		09.19.0

In the Dining Room Viz.t

1 pair of andirons		£0.3.—
7 Bass Bottoms Chairs		0.7.—
1 Large Wooden Table		0.3.—
1 Small Ditto Oak		0.1.—
1 Small looking Glass		0.6.—
1 Old Desk		0.6.—
1 Case with 2 Bottles		0.2.—
1 Warming pan		0.12.—
		2. 0. 0

In the Marble Chamber Viz.t

1 Bedstead & Curtains Compleat		£8.—.—
1 feather Bed, Bolster & 2 pillows		8.—.—
1 Chest of Drawers		2.8.—
1 Buroe Table		1.—.—
6 Chairs Leather'd Bottoms	@ 6/	1.16.—
1 Small dressing Glass		—.6.—
1 Small Carpett		1.—.—
1 White Cotton Counterpin		—.18.—
1 pair Blanketts		1.12.—
1 pair holland Sheets		1.4.—
3 pair Dowlases D.o New	@ 12^s/p.^{r}	1.16.—
3 pair & 1 Ditto Coarser	@ 4/	0.14.—
3 pair Cotton & Linnen D.o	@ 3/	0.9.—
4 pair Servants Ditto	@ 2/	0.8.—
4 Coarse Table Cloths	@ 1/	0.4.—
10 Ditto Kitchen Towels	@ 1/	0.1.—
5 Diaper Table Cloths	@ 12/	3.—.—
6 Damask Table Cloths	@ 18/	5.8.—
4 N: England Diaper D.o	@ 3	0.12.—
4 pair Linnen pillow Cases	@ 2/	0.8.—
5 Coarser Ditto	@ 1/	0.5.—
6 Diaper Towels	@ 6^d	0.3.—
7 Damask Ditto	@ 2/	0.14.—
2 doz.n & 9 Damask Napkins	@ 24/doz.^{n}	3.6.—
1 Gauze Tea Table Cover		0.1.—
		£43.13.0

Household Inventory of Jonathan Chandler (d. 1745)

Cash	£18p
Gun	1p
Psalmbook	8p
	£19p
Debts	£5p
Total	£14p

Household Inventory of Daniel Chandler (d. 1752), Shoemaker

Bible
Shoe knife
Hammer Total   £12
Last (shoe shaper)
Various notes

The Differing Layouts of Philadelphia and Boston
The grid pattern of Philadelphia's straight streets contrasts sharply with Boston's crooked and irregular roads and alleys. Topography had everything to do with this. Surrounded by water, which created an irregular shoreline, and dominated by three high hills (leveled in the nineteenth century) Boston's streets were laid out in the manner of goat paths. *(Left: Engraving by R. Scot and S. Allardice, "Plan of the City and Suburbs of Philadelphia" 1794. Humanities and Social Sciences Library, Map Division, The New York Public Library/Art Resource, NY; right: Library of Congress Geography & Maps Division)*

the American colonies experienced none of the famines that ravaged Europe in this period, such crises were rare, usually occurring during war, when demand for provisions rose sharply. Such a moment struck in Boston during Queen Anne's War. Merchant Andrew Belcher contracted to ship wheat to the Caribbean, where higher prices would yield greater profit than in Boston. Ordinary neighbors, threatened with a bread shortage and angered that a townsman would put profit ahead of community needs, attacked one of Belcher's grain-laden ships and tried to seize the grain. The grand jury, composed of substantial members of the community, hinted its approval of the violent action against Belcher by refusing to indict the rioters.

The two conceptions of community and economic life continued to rub against each other for decades. Urban merchants, shopkeepers, land speculators, and ambitious artisans cleaved more and more to the new economic formulas, while many clergymen continued to preach the traditional message: "Let no man seek his own, but every man another's wealth." By the mid-eighteenth century, the pursuit of profits was winning out over the old community-oriented social compact.

The American Enlightenment

Ideas not only about economic life but also the nature of the universe and the improvement of the human condition filtered across the Atlantic. In the eighteenth century, an American version of the European intellectual movement called the Enlightenment came into focus.

In what is called the Age of Reason, European thinkers rejected the pessimistic Calvinist concept of innate human depravity, replacing it with the optimistic notion that a benevolent God had blessed humankind with the supreme gift of reason. Thinkers like John Locke, in his influential *Essay Concerning Human Understanding* (1689), argued that God had not predetermined the content of the human mind but had instead given it the capacity to acquire knowledge. All Enlightenment thinkers prized this acquisition of knowledge, for it allowed humankind to improve its condition. As the great mathematician Isaac Newton demonstrated, systematic investigation could unlock the secrets of the physical universe. Moreover, scientific knowledge could be applied to improve society.

The scientific and intellectual advances of the seventeenth and eighteenth centuries encouraged a

HOW OTHERS SEE US

Andrew Burnaby, On the Pennsylvanians

The English clergyman Andrew Burnaby toured the mid-Atlantic English colonies in 1759–1760, just a few years before relations between England and its North American colonies became severely strained. Here are some of his judgments on the Pennsylvanians he visited.

The Pennsylvanians, as to character, are a frugal and industrious people: not remarkably courteous and hospitable to strangers unless particularly recommended to them; but rather, like the denizens of most commercial cities, the reverse. They are great republicans, and have fallen into the same errors in their ideas of independency as most of the other colonies have. They are by far the most enterprizing people upon the continent. As they consist of several nations, and talk several languages, they are aliens in some respect to Great Britain; nor can it be expected that they should have the same filial attachment to her which her own immediate offspring have. However, they are quiet and concern themselves but little, except about getting money.

The women are exceedingly handsome and polite; they are naturally sprightly and fond of pleasure; and, upon the whole, are much more agreeable and accomplished than the men. Since their intercourse with the English offices, they are greatly improved; and, without flattery, many of them would not make bad figures even in the first assemblies in Europe. Their amusements are chiefly dancing in the winter; and, in the summer, forming parties of pleasure upon the Schuylkill [River] and in the country.

■ *What does Burnaby mean by calling the Pennsylvanians "great republicans"?*

■ *Do you think he finds a connection between money-grubbing and his comments on the superiority of American women?*

Source: Andrew Burnaby, *Travels Through the Middle Settlements in North-America in the Years 1759 and 1760* (London, 1762; reprint, Ithaca, N.Y.: Cornell University Press, 1960), p 61.

Animals of North America   In two trips to the Americas between 1712 and 1726, the Englishman Mark Catesby captured the flora and fauna of the British colonies, both on the North American mainland and in the West Indies. His work, published in 1747 as *Natural History of Carolina, Florida, and the Bahama Islands,* became the first illustrated natural history of the British colonies. Portrayed here is the American bison, unknown in Europe, and chiggers, heron, and eft (the latter held in the heron's beak). *(Colonial Williamsburg Foundation)*

The Quaker Benjamin Lay Benjamin Lay was regarded as eccentric and a troublemaker, even by his fellow Quakers. Known primarily as a fervent opponent of slavery and the slave trade as early as the 1730s, he was also in the vanguard of many reform movements such as temperance and vegetarianism. The portrait shows Lay's dwarflike stature. What does the basket at bottom left symbolize? *(William Williams,* Portrait of Benjamin Lay, *1750. National Portrait Gallery, Smithsonian Institution/Art Resource, NY)*

belief in "natural law" and fostered debate about the "natural" human rights. In Europe, French philosophers Voltaire and Denis Diderot explored the issue of equality. From 1750 to 1772, Diderot published his *Encyclopedia,* which treated such topics as equality, liberty, reason, and rights. These ideas spread in Europe and the Americas, eventually finding expression in movements for reform, democracy, and liberation—all of deep interest to those beginning to oppose slavery and the slave trade as abominations. Even as the traffic in slaves peaked, religious and humanitarian opposition to slavery arose. The idea grew in the 1750s that slavery contradicted the Christian concept of brotherhood and the Enlightenment notion of the natural equality of all humans. Abolitionist sentiment was also fed by the growing belief that a slave master's authority "depraved the mind," as the Quaker John Woolman argued. An introspective tailor from New Jersey, in the 1750s Woolman dedicated his life to a crusade against slavery. He traveled thousands of miles on foot to convince every Quaker slaveholder of his or her wrongdoing. Only a few hundred masters freed their slaves in the mid-eighteenth century, but men such as Woolman had planted the seeds of abolitionism.

Eighteenth-century Americans began to make significant contributions to the advancement of science. Naturalists such as John Bartram of Philadelphia gathered and described American plants from all over eastern North America as part of the transatlantic attempt to classify all plant life into one universal system. Professor John Winthrop III of Harvard made an unusually accurate measurement of the earth's distance from the sun. Foremost of all was Benjamin Franklin, whose spectacular (and dangerous) experiments with electricity, the properties of which were just becoming known, earned him an international reputation.

Franklin's true genius as a figure of the Enlightenment came in his practical application of scientific knowledge. Among his inventions were the lightning rod, which nearly ended the age-old danger of fires when lightning struck wooden buildings; bifocal spectacles; and a stove that heated rooms more cost-effectively than the open fireplace. Franklin made his adopted city of Philadelphia a center of the American Enlightenment by helping found America's first circulating library in 1731, an artisans' debating club for "mutual improvement," and an intercolonial scientific association that in 1769 became the American Philosophical Society.

Most colonists were not educated enough to participate actively in the American Enlightenment, and only a handful read French Enlightenment authors such as Voltaire. But the efforts of men such as Franklin exposed thousands, especially in the cities, to new currents of thought. This kindled hopes that Americans, blessed by an abundant environment, might achieve the Enlightenment ideal of a perfect society.

THE GREAT AWAKENING

Many of the social, economic, and political changes occurring in eighteenth-century colonial society converged in the Great Awakening, the first of many religious revivals that would sweep America during the next two centuries. Though the timing and character of the Awakening varied from region to region, this quest for spiritual renewal challenged old sources of authority and produced patterns of thought and behavior that helped fuel a revolutionary movement in the next generation.

Fading Faith

Early eighteenth-century British America remained an overwhelmingly Protestant culture. Puritanism—that is, the Congregational church—dominated all of New England except Rhode Island. Anglicanism held sway in much of New York and throughout the South except the backcountry. In the mid-Atlantic and in the back settlements, German Mennonites, Dunkers, Moravians, and Lutherans; Scots–Irish Presbyterians; and English Baptists and Quakers all mingled. Even so, two-thirds of the colonists went to no church at all, partly because in many areas, ministers and churches were simply unavailable. In the most populous colony, Virginia, only 60 parsons in 1761 served a population of 350,000—one for every 5,800 people.

Most colonial churches were voluntary ("congregated") groups, formed for reasons of conscience rather than government compulsion. Though Catholics, Jews, and nonbelievers could not vote or hold office, the persecution of Quakers and Catholics had largely passed, and by 1720 some dissenting groups had gained the right to use long-obligatory church taxes to support their own congregations.

The clergy often administered their congregations with difficulty. Anglicans and several German sects maintained close ties to mother churches across the Atlantic, whereas other denominations attempted to centralize authority. However, most efforts to tighten organization and discipline failed. For example, Anglican ministers had to be ordained in England and regularly report to the bishop of London. But in his Chesapeake parish, an Anglican priest faced wealthy planters who controlled the vestry (the local church's governing body), set his salary, and would drive him out if he challenged them too forcefully. In Connecticut, the Saybrook Platform of 1708 created a network, or "consociation," of Congregational churches, but individual churches still preserved much of their autonomy.

Though governing their churches frustrated many clergymen, religious apathy was a more pressing problem. As early as the 1660s, New England's Congregational clergy had adopted the Half-Way Covenant in order to combat religious indifference. It allowed children of church members, if they adhered to the "forms of godliness," to join the church even if they could not demonstrate that they had undergone a conversion experience. They could not, however, vote in church affairs or take communion.

Such compromises and innovations could not halt the creeping religious apathy that many ministers observed. An educated clergy, its energies often drained by doctrinal disputes, appealed too much to the mind and not enough to the heart. As one Connecticut leader remembered it, "the spirit of God appeared to be awfully withdrawn."

The Awakeners' Message

The Great Awakening was not a unified movement; rather it was a series of revivals that swept different regions between 1720 and 1760 with varying degrees of intensity. The first stirrings came in the 1720s in New Jersey, where a Dutch Reformed minister, Theodore Frelinghuysen, excited his congregation through emotional preaching about the need to be "saved" rather than offering the usual theological abstractions. A neighboring Presbyterian, Gilbert Tennent, soon took up the Dutchman's techniques, with similar success.

From New Jersey, the Awakening spread to Pennsylvania in the 1730s, especially among Presbyterians, and then broke out in the Connecticut River valley. There its greatest leader was Jonathan Edwards in Northampton, Massachusetts. Later a philosophical giant in the colonies, as a young man Edwards gained renown by frightening his parishioners with the fate of "sinners in the hands of an angry God." "How manifold have been the abominations of your life!" Edwards preached. "Are there not some here that have debased themselves below the dignity of human nature, by wallowing in sensual filthiness, as swine in the mire . . . ?" Edwards paraded one sin after another before his trembling congregants and drew such graphic pictures of the hell awaiting the unrepentant that his Northampton neighbors were soon preparing frantically for the conversion by which they would be "born again." His *Faithful Narrative of the Surprizing Work of God* (1736), which described his town's awakening, was the first published revival narrative. This literary form would be used many times in the future to fan the flames of evangelical religion.

DOCUMENT

Jonathan Edwards, "Sinners in the Hands of an Angry God" (1741)

In 1739, these regional brushfires of evangelicalism were drawn together by a 24-year-old Anglican priest from England, George Whitefield. Inspired by John Wesley, the founder of English Methodism, Whitefield used his magnificent speaking voice in dynamic open-air preaching before huge gatherings. Whitefield barnstormed seven times along the American seaboard, beginning in 1739. In Boston, he preached to 19,000 in three days and at a farewell sermon left 25,000 writhing in fear of damnation. In his wake came American preachers whom he had inspired, mostly young men.

DOCUMENT

Benjamin Franklin on George Whitefield (1771)

Jonathan Edwards   Jonathan Edwards (1703–1758) was the first major philosopher in the American colonies. A leader of the Great Awakening in Massachusetts, he was ousted by his congregation for reprimanding the children of church members for reading *The Midwife Rightly Instructed,* an obstetric guide that was as close as curious children could come to learning about sex. *(Joseph Badger,* Reverend Jonathan Edwards (1703–1758), *c. 1750–1755. Yale University Art Gallery, New Haven, Conn., bequest of Eugene Phelps Edwards)*

Samson Occom
Samson Occom, a Mohegan born in Connecticut, was attracted to Christianity, like so many others who were "outsiders," by the emotional and populistic appeal of the Great Awakening preachers. On a trip to England, Occom raised £12,000 for an evangelical school for Native Americans, later to become Dartmouth College. What did the artist men to convey by the oversize book Occom points at? *(Courtesy of the Boston Public Library, Print Department)*

George Whitefield
George Whitefield, who first toured the American colonies in 1739 and 1740, sent thousands of souls "flying to Christ" with his emotional sermons. More Americans heard Whitefield on his many seaboard itinerancies than any other figure in the eighteenth century. *(John Wollaston,* George Whitefield, *1742. National Portrait Gallery, London)*

The appeal of the Awakeners lay both in the medium and the message. They preached that the established, college-trained clergy was too intellectual and tradition-bound. Congregations were dead, Whitefield declared, "because dead men preach to them." "The sapless discourses of such dead drones," cried another Awakener, were worthless. The fires of Protestant belief could be reignited only if individuals assumed responsibility for their own conversion.

An important form of individual participation was "lay exhorting," which meant that anyone— young or old, female or male, black or white—could defy assigned roles and spontaneously recount a conversion experience and preach "the Lord's truth." This horrified the trained clergy and shattered their monopoly. The oral culture of common people gained new importance, their impromptu outpourings contrasting sharply with the controlled literary culture of the gentry.

How religion, social change, and politics became interwoven in the Great Awakening can be seen by examining two regions swept by revivalism. Both Boston, the heartland of Puritanism, and interior Virginia, a land of struggling small planters and slave-rich aristocrats, experienced the Great Awakening, but in different ways and at different times.

Revivalism in the Urban North

In Boston, Whitefield-inspired revivalism blazed up amid political controversy about paper money and land banks, which pitted large merchants against local traders, artisans, and the laboring poor, who preferred the fiscally liberal land bank over the merchants' fiscally conservative silver bank.

Whitefield's arrival in Boston coincided with the currency furor. At first, Boston's elite applauded his ability to call the masses to worship. It seemed that the master evangelist might restore social harmony by redirecting people from earthly matters such as the currency dispute toward concerns for their souls. But when he left Boston in 1740, others followed him who were more critical of the "unconverted" clergy and the self-indulgent accumulation of wealth. One was 25-year-old James Davenport, who appeared anything but respectable to the elite.

Finding every meetinghouse closed to him, even those whose clergy had embraced the Awakening, Davenport preached daily on the Boston Common, aroused religious ecstasy among thousands of people like Hannah Heaton, and stirred up feeling against the city's leading figures. Respectable people decided that revivalism had gotten out of hand when ordinary people began verbally attacking opponents of the land bank in the streets as "carnal wretches, hypocrites, fighters against God, children of the devil, [and] cursed Pharisees." A revival that had begun as a return to religion among backsliding Christians had overlapped with political affairs. Hence, it threatened polite culture, which stressed order and discipline from ordinary people.

Southern Revivalism

Although aftershocks continued for years, by 1744 the Great Awakening was ebbing in New England and the middle colonies. But in Virginia, where the initial religious earthquake was barely felt, tremors of enthusiasm rippled through society from the mid-1740s onward. As in Boston, the Awakeners challenged and disturbed the gentry-led social order.

Whitefield stirred some religious fervor during his early trips through Virginia. Traveling "New Light" preachers, led by the brilliant orator Samuel Davies, were soon gathering large crowds both in the backcountry and in the traditionally Anglican parishes of the older settled areas. By 1747, worried Anglican clergymen persuaded the governor to issue a proclamation restraining "strolling preachers." As in other colonies, Virginia's leaders despised traveling evangelists, who, like lay exhorters, conjured up a world without properly constituted authority. When the Hanover County court gave the fiery James Davenport a license to preach in 1750, the governor ordered the suppression of all circuit riders.

New Light Presbyterianism, challenging the gentry-dominated Anglican church's spiritual monopoly, spread in the 1750s. Then, in the 1760s, came the Baptists. Renouncing finery and ostentatious display and addressing each other as "brother" and "sister," the Baptists reached out to thousands of unchurched people. Like northern revivalists, they focused on the conversion experience. Many of their preachers were uneducated farmers and artisans who called themselves "Christ's poor" and insisted that heaven was populated more by the humble poor than by the purse-proud rich. Among the poorest of all, Virginia's 140,000 slaves in 1760, the evangelical message began to take hold.

The insurgent Baptist movement in rural Virginia became both a quest for a personal, emotionally satisfying religion among ordinary folk and a rejection of gentry values. Established Anglican pulpits denounced the Awakeners as furiously as had respectable New England divines. In both regions, social changes had weakened the cultural authority of the upper class and, in the context of religious revival, produced a vision of a society drawn along more equal lines.

Legacy of the Awakening

By the time George Whitefield returned to North America for his third tour in 1745, the revival had burned out in the North. Its effects, however, were long-lasting. Notably, it promoted religious pluralism and nourished the idea that all denominations were equally legitimate. Whitefield had anticipated this tendency when he sermonized: "Father Abraham, whom have you in heaven? Any Episcopalians? And the answer came back, No! Any Presbyterians? No! Any Independents or Methodists? No, no, no! Whom have you there? And the final answer came down from heaven, We don't know the names here. All who are here are Christians."

By legitimizing the dissenting Protestant groups that had sprung up in seventeenth-century England, the Great Awakening gave them all a basis for living together in relative harmony. From this framework of denominationalism came a second change—the separation of church and state. Once a variety of churches gained legitimacy, it was hard to justify one denomination claiming special privileges. In the seventeenth century, Roger Williams had tried to sever church and state because he believed that ties with civil bodies would corrupt the Church. But during the Awakening, groups such as the Baptists and Presbyterians in Virginia constituted their own religious bodies and broke the Anglican monopoly as *the* Church in the colony. This undermining of the church–state tie would be completed during the Revolutionary era.

A third effect of the revival was to legitimize community diversity. Almost from their beginnings,

Rhode Island, the Carolinas, and the middle colonies had recognized this. But uniformity had been prized elsewhere, especially in Massachusetts and Connecticut. There, the Awakening split Congregational churches into New Lights and Old Lights. Mid-Atlantic Presbyterian churches faced similar schisms. In hundreds of rural communities by the 1750s, two or three churches existed where only one had stood before. People learned that the fabric of community could be woven from threads of many hues.

New eighteenth-century colonial colleges reflected the religious pluralism. Before 1740, there existed only Puritan Harvard (1636) and Yale (1701) and Anglican William and Mary (1693). But between 1746 and 1769, six new colleges were added: Dartmouth, Brown, Princeton, and what are now Columbia, Rutgers, and the University of Pennsylvania. None was controlled by an established church, all had governing bodies composed of men of different faiths, and all admitted students regardless of religion. Eager for students and funds, they made nonsectarian appeals and combined the traditional Latin and Greek curricula with natural sciences and natural philosophy.

Last, the Awakening nurtured a subtle change in values that crossed over into politics and daily life. Especially for ordinary people, the revival experience created a new feeling of self-worth. People assumed new responsibilities in religious affairs and became skeptical of dogma and authority. Many, especially the fast-growing Baptists, decried the growing materialism and deplored the new acceptance of self-interested behavior. He who was "governed by regard to his own private interest," Gilbert Tennent preached, was "an enemy to the public," for in true Christian communities, "mutual love is the band and cement." By learning to oppose authority and create new churches, thousands of colonists unknowingly rehearsed for revolution.

POLITICAL LIFE

"Were it not for government, the world would soon run into all manner of disorders and confusions," wrote a Massachusetts clergyman early in the eighteenth century. "Men's lives and estates and liberties would soon be prey to the covetous and the cruel," and every man would be "as a wolf" to his neighbors. Few colonists or Europeans would have disagreed. Government existed to protect life, liberty, and property.

How should political power be divided—in England, between the English government and the American colonies, and within each colony? Colonists naturally drew heavily on inherited political ideas and institutions—almost entirely English ones, for it was English charters that sanctioned settlement, English governors who ruled, and English common law that governed the courts. But meeting unexpected circumstances in a new environment, colonists modified familiar political forms.

Structuring Colonial Governments

All societies consider it essential to determine the final source of political authority. In England, the notion of the God-given, supreme monarchical authority was crumbling even before the planting of the colonies. In its place arose the belief that stable government depended on blending and balancing the three pure forms of government: monarchy, aristocracy, and democracy. Unalloyed, each would degenerate into oppression. Monarchy, the rule of one, would become despotism. Aristocracy, the rule of the few, would turn into corrupt oligarchy. Democracy, the rule of the many, would descend into anarchy or mob rule. Most colonists believed that the Revolution of 1688 in England had vindicated and strengthened a carefully balanced political system.

In the colonies, political balance was achieved somewhat differently. The governor, as the king's agent (or, in proprietary colonies, the agent of the proprietor to whom the king delegated authority), represented monarchy. Bicameral legislatures arose in most of the colonies in the seventeenth century, and in most provinces they had upper houses of wealthy men appointed by the governor; as a pale equivalent of Britain's House of Lords, it formed a nascent aristocracy. The assembly, elected by white male freeholders, replicated the House of Commons and was the democratic element. Every statute required the governor's assent (except in Rhode Island and Connecticut), and all colonial laws required final approval from the king's privy council. This royal check operated imperfectly, however. A law took months to reach England and months more before word came of its final approval or rejection. In the meantime, the law took force in the colony.

Behind the formal structure of politics stood rules governing who could participate as voters and officeholders. In England, land ownership conferred political rights (women and non-Christians were uniformly excluded). Only men with property producing an annual rental income of 40 shillings or more could vote or hold office. The colonists closely followed this principle, except in Massachusetts, where until 1691 Church membership was the basic

Colonial Foundations of the American Political System

1606 Virginia companies of London and Plymouth granted patents to settle lands in North America.

1619 First elected colonial legislature meets in Virginia.

1634 Under a charter granted in 1632, Maryland's proprietor is given all the authority "as any bishop of Durham" ever held—more than the king possessed in England.

1635 The council in Virginia deports Governor John Harvey for exceeding his power, thus asserting the rights of local magistrates to contest authority of royally appointed governors.

1643 The colonies of Massachusetts, Plymouth, Connecticut, and New Haven draw up articles of confederation and form the first intercolonial union, the United Colonies of New England.

1647 Under a charter granted in 1644, elected freemen from the Providence Plantations draft a constitution establishing freedom of conscience, separating church and state, and authorizing referenda by the towns on laws passed by the assembly.

1677 The Laws, Concessions, and Agreements for West New Jersey provide for a legislature elected annually by virtually all free males, secret voting, liberty of conscience, election of justices of the peace and local officeholders, and trial by jury in public so that "justice may not be done in a corner."

1689 James II deposed in England in the Glorious Revolution and royal governors, accused of abusing their authority, ousted in Massachusetts, New York, and Maryland.

1701 First colonial unicameral legislature meets in Pennsylvania under the Frame of Government of 1701.

1735 John Peter Zenger, a New York printer, acquitted of seditious libel for printing attacks on the royal governor and his faction, thus widening the freedom of the press.

1754 First congress of all the colonies meets at Albany (with seven colonies sending delegates) and agrees on a Plan of Union (which is rejected by the colonies and the English government).

1765 The Stamp Act Congress, the first intercolonial convention called outside England's authority, meets in New York.

requirement. As in England, the poor and propertyless were excluded, for they lacked the "stake in society" that supposedly produced responsible voters.

In England the 40-shilling freehold requirement kept the electorate small, but in the colonies, where land was cheap, it conferred the vote on 50 to 75 percent of free adult males. However, as the proportion of landless colonists increased in the eighteenth century, the franchise contracted.

Though voting rights were broadly based, most men assumed that the wealthy and socially prominent should hold the main political positions. Balancing this elitism, however, was the notion that the entire electorate should periodically judge the performance of those entrusted with political power and reject those who were found wanting. Following the precedent of England's Glorious Revolution, in British America the people were assumed to have the right to badger their leaders, to protest openly, and, in extreme cases of abuse of power, assume control and put things right. Crowd action, frequently effective, gradually achieved a kind of legitimacy.

The Crowd in Action

What gave special power to the common people when they assembled to protest oppressive authority and the trampling of traditional English liberties was the general absence of effective police power. In the countryside, where most colonists lived, only the county sheriff insulated civil leaders from angry farmers. In the towns, the sheriff had only the night watch to keep order. As late as 1757, New York's night watch was described as a "parcel of idle, drinking vigilant snorers, who never quelled any nocturnal tumult in their lives." In theory, the militia stood ready to suppress public disturbances, but crowds usually included many militiamen.

Boston's Impressment Riot of 1747 vividly illustrates the people's readiness to defend their inherited privileges and the weakness of law enforcement. It began when Commodore Charles Knowles brought his royal navy ships to Boston for provisioning—and to replenish the ranks of mariners thinned by desertion. When Knowles sent press gangs to fill the crew vacancies from Boston's waterfront population, they scooped up artisans, laborers, servants, and slaves, as well as merchant seamen from ships riding at anchor in the harbor.

But before the press gangs could hustle away their victims, a crowd of angry Bostonians seized several British officers, surrounded the governor's house, and demanded the release of their townsmen. When the sheriff and his deputies tried to intervene, the mob mauled them. The militia refused to respond. An enraged Knowles threatened to bombard the town, but negotiations amid further tumult averted a showdown. Finally, Knowles released the impressed Bostonians. After the riot, a young politician named Samuel Adams defended

The "Paxton Boys" in Philadelphia   When frontier farmers marched on Philadelphia in 1763 to demand more protection on the frontier, a miniature civil war was narrowly averted. Philadelphians had little use for the "Paxton Boys," who had murdered 20 harmless Christian Indians in retaliation for frontier raids. Why are soldiers and mounted men commanding the public space? *(The Library Company of Philadelphia)*

Boston's defiance of royal authority. The people, he argued, had a "natural right" to band together against press gangs that deprived them of their liberty. He labeled local magnates who supported the governor in this incident "tools to arbitrary power."

The Growing Power of the Assemblies

While the Impressment Riot of 1747 was dramatic, a more gradual and restrained change was underway—the growing ambition and power of the legislative assemblies. For most of the seventeenth century, royal and proprietary governors had exercised greater power in relation to the elected legislatures than did England's king in relation to Parliament. Governors could dissolve the lower houses and delay their sitting, control the election of their speakers, and in most colonies initiate legislation with their appointed councils. They had authority to appoint and dismiss judges at all levels of the judiciary and to create chancery courts, which sat without juries. Governors also controlled the expenditure of public monies and had authority to grant land to individuals and groups, which they sometimes used to confer vast estates on their favorites. They lacked, however, the extensive patronage power that enabled ministers of

government in England to manipulate elections and buy off opponents.

Since the seventeenth century, Virginia, Massachusetts, and New York had been royal colonies, with crown-appointed governors. In the eighteenth century, royal government came to New Jersey (1702), South Carolina (1719), and North Carolina (1729), replacing proprietary regimes.

Many royal governors were competent military officers or bureaucrats, but some were corrupt recipients of patronage posts. Some never even came over, preferring to pocket the salary and pay part of it to another man who went to serve as lieutenant governor. One committed suicide a week after arriving. Most, however, were merely mediocre.

Eighteenth-century legislatures challenged the swollen powers of the colonial governors. Bit by bit, they won new rights: to initiate legislation, to elect their own speakers, to settle contested elections, to discipline members, and to nominate provincial treasurers who disbursed public funds. Most important, they won the "power of the purse"—the authority to initiate money bills, specifying how much money should be raised by taxes and how it should be spent. Thus, the elected assemblies gradually transformed themselves into governing bodies reflecting the interests of the electorate. Governors complained bitterly about the "levelling spirit" and "mutinous and disorderly behavior" of the assemblies, but they could not stop their rise.

Local Politics

Binding elected officeholders to their constituents became an important feature of the colonial political system. In England, the House of Commons claimed to represent the entire nation rather than narrow local interests, yet was filled with representatives from "rotten boroughs" (ancient places left virtually uninhabited by population shifts) and with men whose vote was controlled by the government because they had accepted offices, contracts, or gifts. American assemblies, by contrast, contained mostly representatives sent by voters who instructed them on particular issues and held them accountable.

Royal governors and colonial grandees who sat as councilors often deplored this localist, popular orientation. Sniffed one aristocratic New Yorker, the assemblies were crowded with "plain, illiterate husbandmen [small farmers], whose views seldom extended farther than the regulation of highways, the destruction of wolves, wildcats, and foxes, and the advancement of the other little interests of the particular counties which they were chosen to represent." In actuality, most lower-house members were merchants, lawyers, and substantial planters and farmers, who by the mid-eighteenth century constituted the political elite in most colonies. They took pride in upholding their constituents' interests, for they saw themselves as bulwarks against oppression and arbitrary rule, which history taught them were most frequently imposed by monarchs and their appointed agents.

Local government was usually more important to the colonists than provincial government. In the North, local political authority generally rested in the towns (which included surrounding rural areas). The New England town meeting decided a wide range of matters, arguing until it could express itself as a single unit. "By general agreement" and "by the free and united consent of the whole" were phrases denoting a collective assent rather than a democratic competition among differing interests and points of view.

In the South, the county was the primary unit of government, and by the mid-eighteenth century, a landed squirearchy of third- and fourth-generation families had achieved political dominance. They ruled the county courts and the legislature, and substantial farmers served in minor offices such as road surveyor and deputy sheriff. At court sessions,

usually four times a year, deeds were read aloud and then recorded, juries impaneled and justice dispensed, elections held, licenses issued, and proclamations read aloud. On election days, gentlemen treated their neighbors (on whom they depended for votes) to "bumbo," "kill devil," and other alcoholic treats.

The Spread of Whig Ideology

Whether in local or provincial affairs, a political ideology called Whig, or "republican," had spread widely by the mid-eighteenth century. This body of thought, inherited from England, rested on the belief that concentrated power was historically the enemy of liberty and that too much power lodged in any person or group usually produced corruption and tyranny. The best defenses against concentrated power were balanced government, elected

Stopping the Freedom of the Press John Peter Zenger symbolized freedom of the press, but it wasn't until the nineteenth century that his image was ever created. This engraving showing the burning of Zenger's newspaper, and the stocks awaiting him, is a modern re-creation of the scene. What betrays this image as a nineteenth-century creation? *(Bettmann/CORBIS)*

1662	Half-Way Covenant in New England
1682	La Salle canoes down Mississippi River and claims Louisiana for France
1689–1697	King William's War
1700	Spanish establish first mission in Arizona
1701–1713	Queen Anne's War
1704	*Boston News-Letter*, first regular colonial newspaper, published
1712	First northern slave revolt erupts in New York City
1713	Peace of Utrecht
1714	Beginning of Scots–Irish and German immigration
1715–1730	Volume of slave trade doubles
1718	French settle New Orleans
1720s	Natural increase of African population begins
1732	Benjamin Franklin publishes first *Poor Richard's Almanack*

1734–1736	Great Awakening begins in Northampton, Massachusetts
1735	Zenger acquitted of seditious libel in New York
1739	Slave revolt in Stono, South Carolina
1739–1740	Whitefield's first American tour spreads Great Awakening
1740s	Slaves compose 90 percent of population on Carolina rice coast Indigo becomes staple crop in Lower South
1747	Impressment Riot in Boston
1750s	Quakers initiate campaign to halt slave trade and end slavery
1760	Africans compose 20 percent of colonial population
1760s–1770s	Spanish establish California mission system
1769	American Philosophical Society founded at Philadelphia

legislatures adept at checking executive authority, prohibition of standing armies (almost always controlled by tyrannical monarchs to oppress the people), and vigilance by the people in watching their leaders for telltale signs of corruption.

Much of this Whig ideology reached the people through some 23 newspapers circulating in the colonies by 1763. Many papers reprinted pieces from English Whig writers railing against corruption and creeping despotism. Though limited to a few pages and published only once or twice a week, the papers passed from hand to hand and were read aloud in taverns and coffeehouses, so that their contents probably reached most urban households and a substantial minority of rural farms.

The new power of the press and its importance in guarding the people's liberties against would-be tyrants (such as haughty royal governors) were dramatically illustrated in the Zenger case in New York.

Young John Peter Zenger, a printer's apprentice, had been hired in 1733 by the anti-government faction of Lewis Morris to start a newspaper, the *New-York Weekly Journal*, that would publicize the tyrannical and corrupt actions of Governor William Cosby.

Arrested for seditious libel, Zenger was defended brilliantly by Andrew Hamilton, a Philadelphia lawyer hired by the Morris faction to convince the jury that Zenger had been simply trying to inform the people of attacks on their liberties. Although the jury acquitted Zenger, the libel laws remained very restrictive. But the acquittal did reinforce the notion that the government was the people's servant, and it brought home the point that public criticism could keep people with political authority responsible to the people they ruled. Such ideas about liberty and corruption, raised in the context of local politics, would shortly achieve a much broader significance.

Conclusion

America in 1750

The English colonies in North America, robust and expanding, matured rapidly between 1690 and 1750. Transatlantic commerce linked them closely to Europe, Africa, and other parts of the Americas.

Churches, schools, and towns—the visible marks of the receding frontier—appeared everywhere. And everywhere, people like Hannah Heaton had been energized by the Great Awakening and were introduced to the idea of ordinary people helping to shape the future. A balanced gender ratio and stable family life had been achieved throughout the colonies. Many men were able to move up in society despite frequent obstacles. Seasoned political leaders and familiar political institutions functioned from Maine to Georgia.

Yet the sinew, bone, and muscle of American society had not yet fully knit together. The polyglot population, one-fifth of it bound in chattel slavery and its Native American component still unassimilated and uneasily situated on the frontier, was a kaleidoscopic mixture of ethnic and religious groups. While developing rapidly, its economy showed weaknesses, particularly in New England, where land resources had been strained. The social structure reflected the colonizers' emergence from a frontier stage, but the consolidation of wealth by a landed and mercantile elite was matched by pockets of poverty appearing in the cities and some rural areas. Full of strength, yet marked by awkward incongruities, colonial America in 1750 approached an era of strife and momentous decisions. Much of that strife involved the growing power of France's inland empire in North America and the way that wars in Europe were becoming globe-encircling conflicts.

Questions for Review and Reflection

1. Regional variations within colonial society created different social and economic systems in areas of North America. What were the key regional divisions, and what differences characterized the societies and economies in each?

2. Why did slavery become a widespread institution in eighteenth-century colonial North America, and how did it shape society?

3. Was the Great Awakening compatible with other changes occurring in the society, or did it contradict most other trends? How do you see religious change relating to social, political and intellectual changes?

4. Was colonial America more affected by transatlantic trends or local influences in the areas of politics, ideas and social life?

5. What were the most important aspects of colonial society that enabled it to mature? Why do you think these particular factors most significant?

Recommended Reading

Recommended Readings are posted on the Web site for this textbook. Visit www.ablongman.com/nash

Fiction and Film

Kenneth Roberts, king of historical novelists on eighteenth-century America, movingly describes the Seven Years' War in *Northwest Passage* (1937); Spencer Tracy starred in the Hollywood version with the same title. James Fenimore Cooper's *The Last of the Mohicans* (1836) is another American classic, but much more to the taste of today's students is Hollywood's movie by the same title (1992), starring Daniel Day-Lewis and Madeleine Stowe.

Discovering U.S. History Online

History Buff's Reference Library
www.historybuff.com/library/refseventeen.html
This site offers brief journalistic essays on newspaper coverage of sixteenth- to eighteenth-century American history.

Bethlehem, Pennsylvania
www.bdhp.moravian.edu
A cooperative effort of area libraries, this site examines the history of the Moravian community of Bethlehem, Pennsylvania.

Martha Ballard's Diary
www.dohistory.org
Focusing on the life of Martha Ballard, a late eighteenth-century New England woman, this site employs selections from her diary, excerpts from a book and film about her life, and other primary documents that enable students to conduct their own historical investigation.

Colonial Williamsburg

www.history.org/Almanack/almanack.cfm

Sections of this view of colonial Williamsburg include "Meet the People," "See the Places," and "Colonial Life."

Excerpts from Slave Narratives

www.vgskole.net/prosjekt/slavrute/primary.htm

This site offers online access to slave narratives dating from the seventeenth century.

Two Centuries of Louisiana History

lsm.crt.state.la.us/cabildo/cabildo.htm

This state-run site focuses on the diverse ethnic heritage of Louisiana's people. The early sections cover pre-contact and colonial Louisiana.

Military Artifacts of Spanish Florida, 1650–1821

www.artifacts.org/default.htm

Along with an extensive display of military artifacts, this "Internet Museum" also provides background information on the age of Spanish exploration and settlement as well as details about its rival, Bourbon France.

Colonial Currency

etext.lib.virginia.edu/users/brock

This site includes useful primary and secondary documents on early American currency.

North American Women's Letters and Diaries

www.lib.uchicago.edu/efts/asp/NAWLD

At this site, students can find rich firsthand accounts of colonial life from women's perspectives.

White Oak Fur Post

www.whiteoak.org

This site documents an eighteenth-century fur trading post among Native Americans in the region that would become Minnesota.

Religion in Eighteenth-Century America

www.lcweb.loc.gov/exhibits/religion/rel02.html

Providing an overview of eighteenth-century religion in the American colonies, this site draws on primary source material such as paintings of clergymen, title pages of published sermons, and other artifacts.

Benjamin Franklin

www.english.udel.edu/lemay/franklin

This richly illustrated site relates the story of Franklin's life and political involvement in seven parts.

The Trial of John Peter Zenger

www.jurist.law.pitt.edu/trials20.htm

This site provides a thorough essay on the trial, with links to primary documents.

The Strains of Empire

A View of the Town of Concord (April 1775), attributed to Ralph Earle. *(Attributed to Ralph Earle, View of the town of Concord (April 1775) Concord Museum, Concord, MA)*

American Stories

A Shoemaker Leads a Boston Mob

In 1758, when he was 21 years old, Ebenezer MacIntosh of Boston laid down his shoemaker's awl and enlisted in the Massachusetts expedition against the French on Lake Champlain—one battle in the war that was raging between England and France in North America, the Caribbean, and Europe. The son of a poor Boston shoemaker who had fought against the French in a previous war, MacIntosh had known poverty all his life. Service against the French offered the hope of plunder or at least an enlistment bounty worth half a year's wages. One among thousands of colonists who fought against the "Gallic menace" in the Seven Years' War, MacIntosh contributed his mite to the climactic struggle that drove the French from North America.

But a greater role lay ahead for the Boston shoemaker. Two years after the Peace of Paris in 1763, England imposed a stamp tax on the American colonists. In the massive protests that followed, MacIntosh emerged as the street leader of Boston's ordinary people. In two nights of the most violent attacks on private property ever witnessed in North America, a crowd nearly destroyed the houses of two of the colony's most important officials. On August 14, they tore through the house of Andrew Oliver, a wealthy merchant and the appointed distributor of stamps for Massachusetts. Twelve days later, MacIntosh led the crowd in attacking the mansion of Thomas Hutchinson, a wealthy merchant who served as lieutenant governor and chief justice of Massachusetts. "The mob was so general," wrote the governor, "and so supported that all civil power ceased in an instant."

For several months, the Boston shoemaker's power grew. Called "General" MacIntosh and "Captain-General of the Liberty Tree," he soon sported a militia uniform of gold and blue and a hat laced with gold. Two thousand townsmen marched behind him in orderly ranks through the crooked streets of Boston on November 5 to demonstrate their solidarity in resisting the hated stamps.

Five weeks later, a crowd humiliated stamp distributor Oliver. Demanding that he announce his resignation before the assembled citizenry, they marched him across town in a driving December rain. With MacIntosh at his elbow, he finally reached the "Liberty Tree," which had become a symbol of resistance to England's new colonial policies. There the aristocratic Oliver ate humble pie. He concluded his resignation remarks with bitter words, hissing sardonically that he would "always think myself very happy when it shall be in my power to serve the people."

"To serve the people" was an ancient idea embedded in English political culture, but it assumed new meaning in the American colonies during the epic third quarter of the eighteenth century. Few colonists in 1750 held even a faint desire to break the connection with England, and fewer still might have predicted the form of government that 13 states in an independent nation might fashion. Yet 2 million colonists moved haltingly toward a showdown with mighty England. Little-known men such as Ebenezer MacIntosh as well as his historically celebrated townsmen Samuel Adams, John Hancock, and John Adams were part of the struggle. Collectively, ordinary people such as MacIntosh influenced—and sometimes even dictated—the revolutionary movement in the colonies. Though we read and speak mostly of a small group of "founding fathers," the wellsprings of the American Revolution can be fully discovered only among a variety of people from different social groups, occupations, regions, and religions.

This chapter addresses the tensions in late colonial society, the imperial crisis that followed the Seven Years' War (in the colonies, often called the French and Indian War), and the tumultuous decade that led to the "shot heard round the world" fired at Concord Bridge in April 1775. It portrays the origins of a dual American Revolution. Ebenezer MacIntosh, in leading the Boston mob against Crown officers and colonial collaborators who tried to implement a new colonial policy after 1763, helped set in motion a revolutionary movement to restore ancient liberties thought by the Americans to be under deliberate attack in England. This movement eventually escalated into the war for American independence.

But MacIntosh's Boston followers were also venting years of resentment at the accumulation of wealth and power by Boston's aristocratic elite. Behind every swing of the ax, every shattered crystal goblet, and every splintered mahogany chair lay the fury of Bostonians who had seen the conservative elite try to dismantle the town meeting, had suffered economic hardship, and had lost faith that opportunity and just relations still prevailed. This sentiment, flowing from resentment of what many believed was a corrupt, self-indulgent, and elite-dominated society, produced a commitment to reshape American society even while severing the colonial bond. As distinguished from the war for independence, this was the American Revolution.

THE CLIMACTIC SEVEN YEARS' WAR

After a brief period of peace following King George's War (1744–1748), France and England fought the fourth, largest, and by far most significant of the wars for empire that had begun in the late seventeenth century. Known variously as the Seven Years' War, the French and Indian War, and the Great War for Empire, this global conflict in part represented a showdown for control of North America's interior between the Allegheny Mountains and the Mississippi River. In North America, the Anglo-American forces ultimately prevailed, and their victory dramatically affected the lives of all the diverse people living in the huge region east of the Mississippi—English, German, and Scots–Irish settlers in the English colonies; French and Spanish colonizers in Canada, Florida, and interior North America; African slaves in a variety of settlements; and, perhaps most of all, the powerful Native American tribes of the interior.

War and the Management of Empire

England began constructing a more coherent administration of its far-flung colonies after the Glorious Revolution of 1688. In 1696, a professional Board of Trade replaced the old Lords of Trade; the Treasury strengthened the customs service; and Parliament created overseas vice-admiralty courts, which functioned without juries to prosecute smugglers who evaded the trade regulations set forth in the Navigation Acts. Parliament began playing a more active role after the reign of Queen Anne (1702–1714) and continued to do so when the weak, German-speaking King George I came to the throne. Royal governors received greater powers, got more detailed instructions, and came under more insistent demands from the Board of Trade to enforce British policies. England was quietly installing the machinery of imperial management tended by a corps of colonial bureaucrats.

The best test of an effectively organized state is its ability to wage war. Four times between 1689 and 1763, England matched its strength against France, its archrival in Europe, North America, and the Caribbean. These wars of empire had tremendous consequences for the home governments, their colonial subjects in the Americas, and the native North American tribes drawn into the bloody conflicts.

The Peace of Utrecht (see Chapter 4), which ended Queen Anne's War (1702–1713), brought victor's spoils of great importance to England. The generation of peace that followed was really only a time-out, during which both England and France strengthened their war-making capacity. Britain's productive and efficiently governed New World colonies made important contributions. Though known as a period of "salutary neglect," this was actually an era when the king and Parliament increased their control over colonial affairs.

Concerned mainly with economic regulation, Parliament added new articles such as fur, copper, hemp, tar, and turpentine to the list of items produced in the colonies that had to be shipped to England before being exported to another country. Parliament also curtailed colonial production of articles important to England's economy: woollen cloth (1699), beaver hats (1732), and finished iron products (1750). Most important, Parliament passed the Molasses Act in 1733, an attempt to stop New England from trading with the French West Indies for molasses to convert into rum. Parliament imposed a prohibitive duty of six pence per gallon on French slave-produced molasses. This turned many of New England's largest merchants and distillers into smugglers, for a generation schooling them, their ship captains, crews, and allied waterfront artisans in defying royal authority.

The generation of peace ended abruptly in 1739 when England declared war on Spain. The immediate cause was the ear of an English sea captain, Robert Jenkins, which had been cut off eight years earlier when Spanish authorities caught him smuggling. Encouraged by his government, Jenkins publicly displayed his pickled ear in 1738 to whip up war fever against Spain. The real cause, however, was England's determination to continue its drive toward commercial domination of the Atlantic

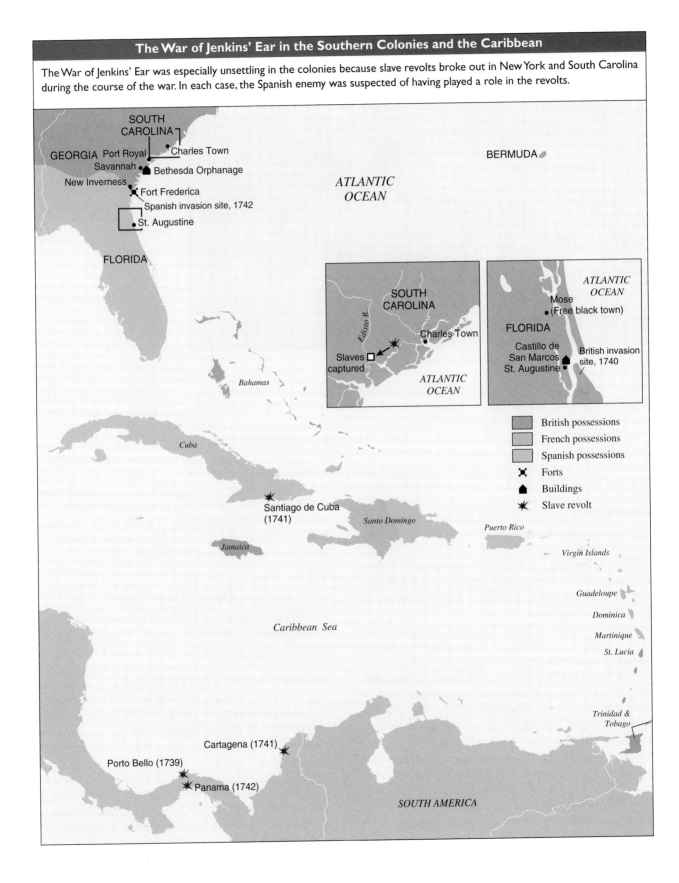

The War of Jenkins' Ear in the Southern Colonies and the Caribbean

The War of Jenkins' Ear was especially unsettling in the colonies because slave revolts broke out in New York and South Carolina during the course of the war. In each case, the Spanish enemy was suspected of having played a role in the revolts.

SOUTH CAROLINA

GEORGIA Port Royal
Charles Town

Savannah Bethesda Orphanage

New Inverness
Fort Frederica

Spanish invasion site, 1742

St. Augustine

FLORIDA

BERMUDA

ATLANTIC OCEAN

SOUTH CAROLINA

Edisto R.

Charles Town

Slaves captured

ATLANTIC OCEAN

ATLANTIC OCEAN

Mose (Free black town)

FLORIDA

Castillo de San Marcos
St. Augustine

British invasion site, 1740

Bahamas

Cuba

Santiago de Cuba (1741)

Santo Domingo

Jamaica

Puerto Rico

Virgin Islands

Guadeloupe

Dominica

Martinique

St. Lucia

Caribbean Sea

Trinidad & Tobago

Cartagena (1741)

Porto Bello (1739)

Panama (1742)

SOUTH AMERICA

British possessions
French possessions
Spanish possessions
Forts
Buildings
Slave revolt

The Assault on Fort Louisbourg In this dramatic painting, colonial assault groups prepare to go ashore on Cape Breton Island to capture the nearby Fort Louisbourg. The colonial forces were commanded by William Pepperell, a merchant, shipbuilder, and land speculator who—for capturing the French fortress—was the first American to be knighted by the English. *(Anne S. K. Brown Military Collection, Brown University Library)*

basin. The British Navy captured Porto Bello in Spanish Panama in 1739, but four expeditions against Spanish strongholds in 1740–1742 were disasters. Admiral Edward Vernon recruited some 3,500 American colonists for these attacks, enticing them with dreams of capturing mountains of Spanish silver and gold. But the Spanish withstood attacks against St. Augustine in Florida; Havana, Cuba, Cartagena, and Colombia; and Panama. Most of the American colonists died of yellow fever, dysentery, and outright starvation, and those who limped home, including George Washington's father, Lawrence Washington, who renamed his Virginia plantation after Admiral Vernon, had little booty to show for their efforts.

From 1744 to 1748, the Anglo-Spanish war merged into a much larger Anglo-French conflict, called King George's War in North America and the War of Austrian Succession in Europe. Its scale far exceeded that of previous conflicts, highlighting the need for increased discipline within the empire. Unprecedented military expenditures led Britain to ask its West Indian and American colonies to share in the costs of defending—and extending—the empire and to tailor their behavior to home country needs. But for American colonists, except for war contractors such as Boston's Thomas Hancock, the war was costly. All New Englanders swelled with pride in June 1745 after Massachusetts volunteers, coordinating their attacks with British naval forces, captured the massive French fortress of Louisbourg on Cape Breton Island, guarding the approach to the St. Lawrence River, after a six-week siege. But

the losses were staggering. "One half of our militia [died] like rotten sheep," reported one Boston leader, who believed that one-fifth of all Massachusetts adult males had perished, leaving thousands of widows and orphaned children. New Englanders were bitter when at war's end in 1748, the British government handed the prized Fort Louisbourg back to France in exchange for French withdrawal from conquests in parts of British-controlled India and an agreement to spare the British army trapped in Europe.

Outbreak of Hostilities

The return of peace in 1748 did not relieve the tension between English and French colonists in North America. Reaching back to the early seventeenth century and fueled by religious hatred, it was intensified by the spectacular population growth of the English colonies: from 250,000 in 1700 to 1.25 million in 1750, and to 1.75 million in the next decade. Three-quarters of the increase came in the colonies south of New York, propelling thousands of land-hungry settlers westward.

Fur traders and land speculators promoted this westward rush. The fur traders were penetrating a French-influenced region, where they offered native trappers and hunters better prices and, sometimes, higher-quality goods than the French. In the 1740s and 1750s, speculators (including many future revolutionary leaders) formed land companies to capitalize on the seaboard population explosion. The farther west the settlement line moved, the closer it came to the western trading empire of the French and their Native American allies.

Colonial penetration of the Ohio valley in the 1740s established the first English outposts in the continental heartland and challenged the French where their interest was vital. While the English controlled most of the eastern coastal plain of North America, the French had nearly encircled them to the west by building a chain of trading posts and forts along the St. Lawrence River, through the Great Lakes, and southward into the Ohio and Mississippi valleys all the way to New Orleans.

Confronted by English intrusions, the French resisted. They attempted to block further English expansion west of the Alleghenies by constructing new forts in the Ohio valley and by prying some tribes loose from their new English connections. By 1753, the French were driving the English traders out of the Ohio River valley and establishing a line of forts between Lake Erie and the forks of the Ohio River, near present-day Pittsburgh. There, near Fort Duquesne on May 28, 1754, the French smartly rebuffed an ambitious 21-year-old Virginia militia colonel named George Washington, dispatched by his colony's government to expel them from the region and drive them from the very site where the Ohio Company, a syndicate of wealthy Virginia speculators, had built a Native American trading post. The skirmish produced only a few casualties, but it quickly escalated into a global war that rearranged the balance of power not only in North America but in Europe and the entire Atlantic world.

The Seven Years' War

Men in the capitals of Europe, not in the colonies, decided to force a showdown in the interior of North America. England's powerful merchants, supported by American clients, had been emboldened by English success in overwhelming the mighty French fortress at Louisbourg. Now, they argued, the time was ripe to destroy the French overseas trade. Convinced, the English ministry ordered several thousand troops to North America in 1754; in France, 3,000 regulars embarked to meet the English challenge.

With war looming, the colonial governments attempted to coordinate efforts. Representatives of seven colonies met at Albany, New York, in June 1754 to plan a colonial union and rewin the allegiance of the Iroquois, whose grievances had grown sharply after a group of land speculators had tried to grab nearly a million acres of Mohawk land. Both failed. The 150 Iroquois chiefs left with 30 wagonloads of gifts but made no firm commitment to fight the French. Benjamin Franklin designed a plan for an intercolonial government to manage Native American affairs, provide for defense, and have the power to pass laws and levy taxes. But even the clever woodcut displayed in the *Pennsylvania Gazette* that pictured a chopped-up snake with the insignia "Join or Die" failed to overcome the long-standing jealousies that had thwarted previous attempts at intercolony cooperation, and the colonies rejected his plan.

"Join or Die" Cartoon

"Old Hendrick" The Americans and British relied heavily on the Iroquois in attempting to vanquish the French in the Seven Years' War. "Old Hendrick," the Mohawk chief pictured here, is shown in elaborate European apparel given him by King George II in 1740 to help seal a diplomatic alliance. Chief Hendrick died at the Battle of Lake George in 1755, fighting alongside the British against the French. Which articles of his clothing are distinctly English? *(Courtesy of the John Carter Brown Library at Brown University)*

With his newly arrived British regiments and hundreds of American recruits, General Edward Braddock slogged across Virginia in the summer of 1755, each day cutting a few miles of road through forests and across mountains. A headstrong professional soldier who regarded his European battlefield experience as sufficient for war in the American wilderness, Braddock had contempt for the woods-wise French regiments and their stealthy Native American allies.

As Braddock neared Fort Duquesne, the entire French force and the British suddenly surprised one another in the forest. The French had 218 soldiers and Canadian militiamen and 637 Native American allies, while Braddock commanded 1,400 British regulars, supported by 450 Virginians and a few Native American scouts commanded by Washington. Pouring murderous fire into Braddock's tidy lines, the French and their Native American allies won.

Braddock perished, and two-thirds of the British and Americans were killed or wounded. Washington, his uniform pierced by four bullets, had two horses shot from beneath him. Although it had 1,000 men in reserve down the road, the Anglo-American force beat a hasty retreat.

Braddock's ignominious retreat brought almost every tribe north of the Ohio River to the French side. Throughout the summer, French-supplied Native American raiders torched the Virginia and Pennsylvania backcountry. "The roads are full of starved, naked, indigent multitudes," observed one officer. One French triumph followed another during the next two years. Never was disunity within the English colonies so glaring. With its Native American allies, French Canada, only 70,000 inhabitants strong, had badly battered 1.5 million colonists supported by the British army.

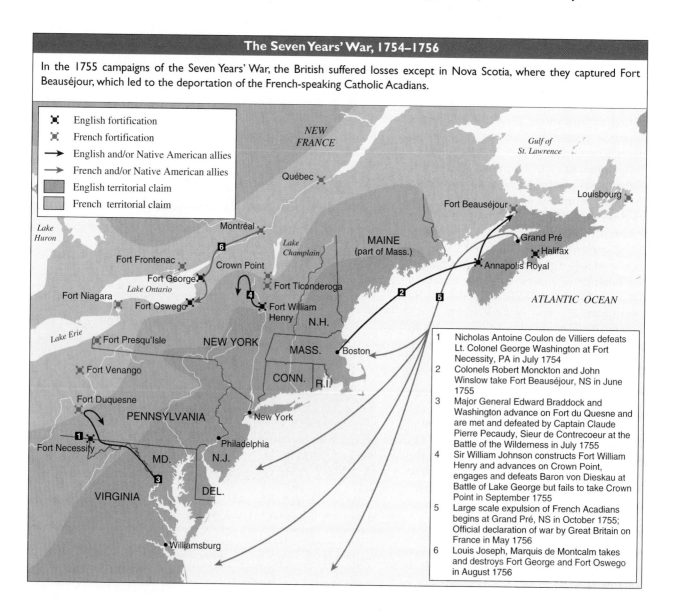

The Seven Years' War, 1754–1756

In the 1755 campaigns of the Seven Years' War, the British suffered losses except in Nova Scotia, where they captured Fort Beauséjour, which led to the deportation of the French-speaking Catholic Acadians.

- ☒ English fortification
- ☒ French fortification
- → English and/or Native American allies
- → French and/or Native American allies
- ▪ English territorial claim
- ▫ French territorial claim

1. Nicholas Antoine Coulon de Villiers defeats Lt. Colonel George Washington at Fort Necessity, PA in July 1754
2. Colonels Robert Monckton and John Winslow take Fort Beauséjour, NS in June 1755
3. Major General Edward Braddock and Washington advance on Fort du Quesne and are met and defeated by Captain Claude Pierre Pecaudy, Sieur de Contrecoeur at the Battle of the Wilderness in July 1755
4. Sir William Johnson constructs Fort William Henry and advances on Crown Point, engages and defeats Baron von Dieskau at Battle of Lake George but fails to take Crown Point in September 1755
5. Large scale expulsion of French Acadians begins at Grand Pré, NS in October 1755; Official declaration of war by Great Britain on France in May 1756
6. Louis Joseph, Marquis de Montcalm takes and destroys Fort George and Fort Oswego in August 1756

Farther north, the Anglo-American forces had more success, overpowering Fort Beauséjour, the French fort on the neck of land that connected Nova Scotia, held by the English since the Peace of Utrecht, and the French Canadian mainland. This quickly led to the expulsion of the French Acadians, who had been promised the right to practice Catholicism and keep their land while promising neutrality in any war between the English and French. When they refused to swear oaths of unqualified allegiance to the English king, which would revoke their religious freedom and oblige them to fight against fellow Frenchmen on the Canadian mainland, the British rounded up about 6,000 Acadians, herded them aboard ships, and dispersed them among the English colonies, giving their confiscated land to New Englanders. Another 7,000 to 10,000 Acadians escaped to the Canadian mainland, and in time, about 3,000 of those deported to the English colonies made their way to French Louisiana. The English justified their ethnic cleansing—the first time they had relocated a civilian population by force—as a wartime security measure.

The French won most of the battles in 1756, including a victory at Fort William Henry on Lake George, where the Native American allies of the French proved essential. At this point, Britain declared war on France, and the French and Indian War in North America turned into a world war with France, Austria, and Russia pitting themselves against England and Prussia. The turning point in the war came after the energetic William Pitt became England's secretary of state in 1757. "I believe that I can save this nation and that no one else can," he boasted, abandoning Europe as the main theater of action against the French and throwing his nation's military might into the American campaign. The forces he dispatched to North America in 1757 and 1758 dwarfed all preceding commitments: about 23,000 British troops and a huge fleet with 14,000 mariners. But even forces of this magnitude, when asked to engage the enemy in the forests of North America, were not necessarily sufficient to the task without Native American support, or at least neutrality. "A doubt remains not," proclaimed one English official in the colonies, "that the prosperity of our colonies on the continent will stand or fall with our interest and favour among them."

Tribal Strategies

The Iroquois knew that their interest lay in playing off one European power against the other. "To preserve the balance between us and the French," wrote a New York politician, "is the great ruling principle of modern Indian politics."

Anglo-American leaders knew that the support of the Iroquois and their tributary tribes was crucial and could be secured in only two ways: through purchase or by a demonstration of power that would convince the tribes that the English would prevail with or without their assistance.

The first English stratagem failed. In 1754 colonial negotiators heaped gifts on the Iroquois chiefs at the Albany Congress but received only tantalizing half-promises of support against the French. The second alternative fizzled because the English proved militarily inferior to the French in the first three years of the war. Hence, the westernmost of the Iroquois Six Nations, the Seneca, fought on the side of the French in the campaigns of 1757 and 1758, while the Delaware, a tributary tribe, harassed the Pennsylvania frontier.

However, in 1758, the huge English military buildup began to produce victories. The largest army ever assembled in North America to that point, some 15,000 British and American soldiers, including Bostonian Ebenezer MacIntosh, suffered terrible casualties and withdrew from the field after attempting to storm Fort Ticonderoga on Lake Champlain in June 1758. Then the tide turned. Troops under Sir Jeffrey Amherst captured Louisbourg, on Cape Breton Island, and Fort Duquesne fell to another army of 6,000. The resolute Pitt had mobilized the fighting power of the English nation and put more men in the field than existed in all of New France. The colonists, in turn, had put aside intramural squabbling long enough to overwhelm the badly outnumbered French.

The victories of 1758 finally moved the Iroquois away from neutrality. Added incentive to join the Anglo-American side came when the English navy bottled up French shipping in the St. Lawrence River, cutting the Iroquois off from French trade goods. By early 1759, foreseeing a French defeat in North America, the Iroquois pledged 800 warriors for an attack on Fort Niagara, the strategic French trading depot on Lake Ontario.

Dramatic Anglo-American victories did not always guarantee Native American support. Backcountry skirmishes with the Cherokee from Virginia to South Carolina turned into a costly war from 1759 to 1761. In 1760, the Cherokee mauled a British army of 1,300 under Amherst. The following summer, a much larger Anglo-American force invaded Cherokee country, burning towns and food supplies. English control of the sea interrupted the Native Americans' supply of French arms. Beset by

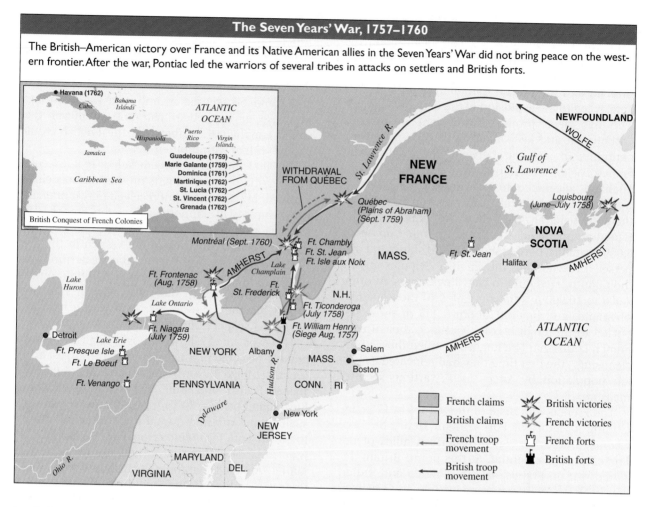

The Seven Years' War, 1757–1760

The British–American victory over France and its Native American allies in the Seven Years' War did not bring peace on the western frontier. After the war, Pontiac led the warriors of several tribes in attacks on settlers and British forts.

food shortages, lack of ammunition, and a smallpox epidemic, the Cherokee finally sued for peace.

Other Anglo-American victories in 1759, the "year of miracles," decided the outcome of the bloodiest war yet known in the Americas. The capture of Fort Niagara, the critical link in the system of forts that joined the French inland empire with the Atlantic, was followed by the conquest of sugar-rich Martinique in the West Indies. The culminating stroke came at Québec. Led by 32-year-old General James Wolfe, 5,000 troops scaled a rocky cliff and overcame the French on the Plains of Abraham. The capture of Montréal late in 1760 completed the shattering of French power in North America. While fighting continued for three more years in the Caribbean and in Europe, in the American colonies the old English dream of destroying the Gallic menace had finally come true.

Consequences of the Seven Years' War

The Treaty of Paris, ending the Seven Years' War in 1763, brought astounding changes to European and Native peoples in North America. Spain acquired New Orleans, the vast Louisiana territory west of the Mississippi, and Havana, and in turn surrendered Spanish Florida to the British. The interior Native American tribes, which had adeptly forced Britain and France to compete for their support, suffered a severe setback when the French disappeared and the British became their sole source of trade goods. Iroquois, Cherokee, Creek, Ojibwa, Shawnee, and scores of other interior tribes were now forced to adjust to this reality.

After making peace, the British government launched a new policy designed to separate Native Americans and colonizers by creating a racial boundary roughly following the crestline of the Appalachian Mountains from Maine to Georgia. The Proclamation of 1763 reserved all land west of the line for Native American nations. White settlers who were already there were told to withdraw.

This well-meaning attempt to legislate interracial accord failed completely. Even before the proclamation was issued, the Ottawa chief Pontiac, concerned that the elimination of the French threatened the old treaty and gift-giving system, had gathered together many of the northern tribes that

The Taking of Québec   The storming of French Québec in 1759 was the decisive blow in England's campaign to end the French domination of Canada and the lands west of the Appalachians. The exploits of General James Wolfe made him a hero throughout England and the colonies. (*National Army Museum, London*)

had aided the French assaults on the English forts during the Seven Years' War. Although Pontiac's pan-Indian movement to drive the British out of the Ohio valley collapsed in 1764, it served notice that the interior tribes would fight for their lands.

London could not enforce the Proclamation of 1763. Staggering under an immense wartime debt, England decided to maintain only small army garrisons in America to regulate the interior. Nor could royal governors stop land speculators and settlers from privately purchasing land from trans-Appalachian tribes or simply encroaching on their land. Under such circumstances, the western frontier seethed after 1763.

Not only did the epic Anglo-American victory redraw the map of North America, but the war also had important social and economic effects on colonial society. It convinced the colonists of their growing strength, yet left them debt-ridden and weakened in manpower. The wartime economy spurred economic development and poured British capital into the colonies, yet rendered them more vulnerable to cyclic fluctuations in the British economy.

Military contracts, for example, brought prosperity to most colonies during the war years. Huge orders for ships, arms, uniforms, and provisions enriched northern merchants and provided good prices for farmers as well. Urban artisans enjoyed full employment and high wages, as tailors' needles flashed to meet clothing contracts, shoemakers stitched for an unprecedented demand for shoes, and bakers found armies clamoring for bread. Privateers—privately outfitted ships licensed by colonial governments to attack enemy shipping—enriched the fortunate few. On a single voyage in 1758, John MacPherson snared 18 French ships. The prize money was lavish enough to allow this son of a Scottish immigrant to pour £14,000 into creating a country estate outside Philadelphia, to which he retired in splendor.

The war, however, required heavy taxes and took a huge human toll. Privateering carried many fortune seekers to a watery grave, and the wilderness campaigns from 1755 to 1760 claimed thousands of lives. Garrison life brought wracking fevers (which claimed more victims than did enemy weapons), and battlefield medical treatment was too primitive to save many of the wounded. Boston's Thomas Hancock predicted at the beginning of the war that "this province is spirited to [send] every third man to do the work of the Lord." But the Lord's work was expensive. Thomas Pownall, assuming the governorship of Massachusetts in August 1757, found not the "rich, flourishing, powerful, enterprizing"

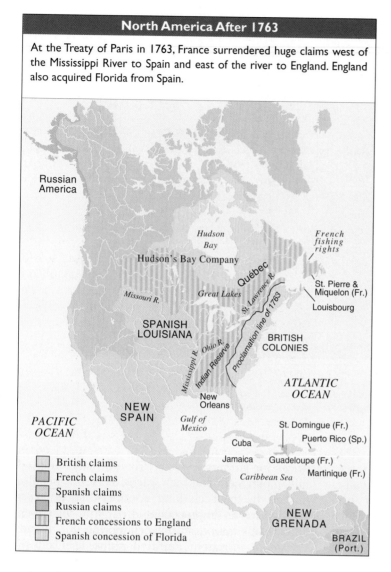

North America After 1763

At the Treaty of Paris in 1763, France surrendered huge claims west of the Mississippi River to Spain and east of the river to England. England also acquired Florida from Spain.

Russian America

Hudson Bay

Hudson's Bay Company

French fishing rights

Québec

Missouri R.

Great Lakes

St. Lawrence R.

St. Pierre & Miquelon (Fr.)

Louisbourg

SPANISH LOUISIANA

Mississippi R. *Ohio R.* *Indian Reserve* *Proclamation line of 1763*

BRITISH COLONIES

ATLANTIC OCEAN

New Orleans

NEW SPAIN

Gulf of Mexico

PACIFIC OCEAN

St. Domingue (Fr.)

Cuba

Puerto Rico (Sp.)

Jamaica

Guadeloupe (Fr.)

Caribbean Sea

Martinique (Fr.)

NEW GRENADA

BRAZIL (Port.)

British claims
French claims
Spanish claims
Russian claims
French concessions to England
Spanish concession of Florida

badly, especially in the coastal towns. "The tippling soldiery that used to help us out at a dead lift," mused a New York merchant, "are gone to drink [rum] in a warmer region [the Caribbean], the place of its production."

Although even some wealthy merchants went bankrupt, the greatest hardships after 1760 fell on laboring people. Those with the smallest wages had the thinnest savings to cushion them against hard times. How quickly their security could evaporate showed in Philadelphia, where early in the contractionary cycle many poor people, unable to pay their property taxes, were "disposing of their huts and lots to others more wealthy than themselves." Established artisans and shopkeepers were caught between rising prices and reduced demand for their goods and services. A New York artisan expressed a common lament in 1762. Thankfully, he still had employment, he wrote in the *New-York Gazette*. But despite every effort at unceasing labor and frugal living, he had fallen into poverty and found it "beyond my ability to support my family . . . [which] can scarcely appear with decency or have necessaries to subsist." His situation, he added, "is really the case with many of the inhabitants of this city."

The Seven Years' War paved the way for a far larger conflict in the next generation. The legislative assemblies, for example, which had been flexing their muscles at the expense of the governors in earlier decades, accelerated their bid for political power. During wartime, knowing that their governors must obtain military appropriations, they extracted concessions as the price for raising revenues. The war also trained a new group of military and political leaders. In carrying out military operations on a scale unknown in the colonies and in shouldering heavier political responsibilities, men such as George Washington, Samuel Adams, Benjamin Franklin, Patrick Henry, and Christopher Gadsden acquired the experience that would serve them well in the future.

In spite of severe costs, the Seven Years' War left many colonists buoyant. New Englanders rejoiced at the final victory over the "Papist enemy of the North." Frontiersmen, fur traders, and land speculators also celebrated the French withdrawal, for the West now appeared open for exploitation. The colonists also felt a new sense of identity after the

colony he expected but a province "ruined and undone."

The human cost of the war was high, especially in New England, which bore the brunt of the fighting. Probably half of all New England men of military age served in the war and perhaps three-quarters of those between ages 17 and 24. The magnitude of human loss in Boston was probably greater than in any war fought by Bostonians up until this time or in the future. The wartime muster lists show that nearly every working-class Bostonian tasted military service at some point during the long war. When peace came, Boston had a deficit of almost 700 men in a town of about 2,000 families. The high rate of war widowhood feminized poverty and required expanded poor relief to maintain husbandless women and fatherless children.

Peace ended the casualties but also brought depression. When the bulk of the British forces left North America in 1760, the economy slumped war. Surveying a world free of French and Spanish threats, they began reassessing subordination to England and the advantages of standing alone. As a French diplomat predicted at the war's end, the colonists would soon discover "that they stand no longer in need of your protection. You will call on them to contribute towards supporting the burden which they have helped to bring on you; they will answer you by shaking off all dependence."

The British, however, viewed the matter differently at the end of the Seven Years' War. From their perspective, the colonists were unreliable, had fought poorly, and were "an obstinate and ungovernable people, utterly unacquainted with the nature of subordination," as one British officer put it. Many royal army officers who had fought alongside the Americans had little but contempt for the "martial virtue" of the colonists. "He could take a thousand grenadiers to America," boasted one officer, "and geld all the males, partly by force and partly by a little coaxing."

THE CRISIS WITH ENGLAND

At the end of the Seven Years' War, George Grenville became the chief minister of England's 25-year-old king, George III. He inherited a national debt that had billowed from £75 million to £145 million and a

nation of wearied taxpayers. Grenville proposed new taxes in America, asking the colonists to bear their share of running the empire. His particular concern was financing the 10,000 British regulars left in North America after 1763 to police French-speaking Canada and the Native Americans—and to remind unruly Americans that they were still subjects. In so doing, he opened a rift between England and its colonies that in a dozen years would ripen into revolution.

Sugar, Currency, and Stamps

In 1764, Grenville pushed through Parliament several bills that in combination pressed hard on colonial economies. First came the Revenue Act (or Sugar Act) of 1764. While reducing the tax on imported French molasses from six to three pence per gallon, it added various colonial products to the list of commodities that could be sent only to England. It also required American shippers to post bonds guaranteeing observance of the trade regulations before loading their cargoes. Finally, it strengthened the vice-admiralty courts to prosecute violators of the trade acts.

Many colonial legislatures grumbled about the Sugar Act because a strictly enforced duty of three pence per gallon on molasses pinched more than the loosely enforced six-pence duty. But only New York objected that any tax by Parliament to raise revenue (rather than to control trade) violated the rights of overseas English subjects who were unrepresented in Parliament.

Next came the Currency Act. In 1751, Parliament had forbidden the New England colonies to issue paper money as legal tender, and now it extended that prohibition to all the colonies. In a colonial economy chronically short of hard cash, this measure constricted trade.

The move to tighten up the machinery of empire confused the colonists because many of the new regulations came from Parliament. For generations, colonists had viewed Parliament as a bastion of English liberty. Now Parliament began to seem like a violator of colonial rights. Colonial leaders were uncertain about where Parliament's authority began and ended. The colonists had always implicitly accepted parliamentary power overseas because it was easier to evade distasteful trade regulations

Benjamin Franklin in London In 1774, Benjamin Franklin, shown standing silently in this oil painting, stood before members of the English Parliament in London to receive a dressing down in the "Cockpit," named for the cockfights staged there in the day of Henry VIII. Franklin was accused of releasing copies of letters from Governor Thomas Hutchinson of Massachusetts to British officials that would intensify the friction between Britain and its American colonies. (*Christian Schussele*, Benjamin Franklin Appearing Before the Privy Council, *1867. © Huntington Library/SuperStock*)

than to contest this power. But the exact limits of that authority were vague.

After Parliament passed the Sugar Act in 1764, Grenville announced his intention to extend to America the stamp duties—already imposed in England—on every newspaper, pamphlet, almanac, legal document, liquor license, college diploma, pack of playing cards, and pair of dice. He gave the colonies a year to suggest alternative ways of raising revenue. The colonies objected, but none provided another plan. Knowing that colonial property taxes were slight compared with those in England, Grenville dismissed the petitions that poured in from the colonies and drove the bill through Parliament. The Stamp Act became effective in November 1765.

Colonial reaction to the Stamp Act ranged from disgruntled submission to mass defiance. The breadth of the reaction shocked the British government—and many Americans as well. Lieutenant Governor Hutchinson of Massachusetts believed that "there is not a family between Canada and Pensacola that has not heard the name of the Stamp Act and but very few . . . but what have some formidable apprehensions of it." In many cases, resistance involved not only discontent over England's tightening of the screws on the American colonies but also internal resentments born out of local events. Especially in the cities, the defiance of authority and destruction of property by people from the middle and lower ranks redefined the dynamics of politics, setting the stage for a 10-year internal struggle for control among the various social elements alarmed by the new English policies.

Stamp Act Riots

In late 1764, Virginia's House of Burgesses became the first legislature to react to the news of the Stamp Act. It strenuously objected to the proposed stamp tax, citing the economic hardship it would cause. Virginians were already worried by a severe decline in tobacco prices and heavy war-related taxes, which mired most planters in debt. Led by 29-year-old Patrick Henry, a fiery lawyer newly elected from a frontier county, the House of Burgesses in May 1765 debated seven strongly worded resolutions. Old-guard burgesses regarded some of them as treasonable. The legislature finally adopted the four more moderate resolves, including one proclaiming that it was their "inherent" right to be taxed only by their own consent.

Many burgesses had left for home before Henry introduced his resolutions, so less than a quarter of Virginia's legislators voted for the four moderate resolves. But within a month, newspapers of other colonies published all seven resolutions, which included a defiant assertion that Virginians did not have to pay externally imposed taxes and branded as an "enemy to this, his Majesty's colony" anyone who denied Virginia's exclusive right to tax itself.

Hutchinson Family House

Thomas Hutchinson inherited the family house in Boston's North End. Every window shown here was smashed on August 26, 1765. Some in the furious crowd also reached the roof by midnight and worked until daylight in cutting down a large cupola. By dawn, according to one account, the mansion was "a mear Shell." Why did Boston authorities not stop the rampaging crowd? (*Photograph courtesy of the Society for the Preservation of New England Antiquities [#10600-A]*)

Henry and the aggressive young burgesses had hurled words of defiance at Parliament for other colonies to reflect on and match.

Governor Francis Bernard of Massachusetts called the Virginia resolves an "alarm bell for the disaffected." Events in Boston in August 1765 amply confirmed his view. On August 14, Bostonians hung a rag-dressed effigy of stamp distributor Andrew Oliver from an elm tree in the south end of town. When the sheriff tried to remove it at the order of Lieutenant Governor Thomas Hutchinson, Oliver's brother-in-law, a hostile crowd intervened. In the evening, workingmen cut down Oliver's effigy, shouting boisterously as they carried it through the streets, leveled his new brick office, and reduced his luxurious mansion to a shambles. The stamp distributor promptly asked to be relieved of his commission. Twelve days later, MacIntosh led the crowd again in an all-night bout of destruction of the handsomely appointed homes of two British officials and

1765 Stamp Act Protest

Hutchinson, a haughty man, who was as unpopular with the common people as his great-great-grandmother, Anne Hutchinson, had been popular. Military men "who have seen towns sacked by the enemy," one observer reported, "declare they never before saw an instance of such fury."

In attacking the property of men associated with the stamp tax, the Boston crowd demonstrated not only its opposition to parliamentary policy but also its resentment of a local elite. For decades, ordinary Bostonians had aligned politically with the Boston "caucus," which led the colony's "popular party" against conservative aristocrats such as Hutchinson and Oliver. They had also read in the *Boston Gazette* that the new parliamentary legislation had been proposed by "mean mercenary hirelings among yourselves, who for a little filthy lucre would at any time betray every right, liberty, and privilege of their fellow subjects."

But the "rage-intoxicated rabble" had suddenly broken away from the leaders of the popular party

Steps on the Road to Revolution

1763 Treaty of Paris ends Seven Years' War between England and France; France cedes Canada to England.
Proclamation of 1763 forbids white settlement west of Appalachian Mountains.

1764 Sugar Act sets higher duties on imported sugar and lower duties on molasses and enlarges the power of vice-admiralty courts.
Currency Act prohibits issuance of paper money by colonies.

1765 Stamp Act requires revenue-raising stamps purchased from British-appointed stamp distributors on printed documents.
Stamp Act Congress meets in New York.
Quartering Act requires colonies to furnish British troops with housing and certain provisions.
Sons of Liberty formed in New York City and thereafter in many towns.

1766 Declaratory Act asserts Parliament's sovereignty over the colonies after repealing Stamp Act.
Rent riots by New York tenant farmers.

1767 Townshend Revenue Acts impose duties on tea, glass, paper, paints, and other items.
South Carolina Regulators organize in backcountry.

1768 British troops sent to Boston.

1770 British troops kill four and wound eight American civilians in Boston Massacre.

1771 Battle of Alamance pits frontier North Carolina Regulators against eastern militia led by royal governor.

1772 British schooner *Gaspee* burned in Rhode Island.
Committee of Correspondence formed in Boston and thereafter in other cities.

1773 Tea Act reduces duty on tea but gives East India Company right to sell directly to Americans.
Boston Tea Party dumps £10,000 of East India Company tea into Boston harbor.

1774 Coercive Acts close port of Boston, restrict provincial and town governments in Massachusetts, and send additional troops to Boston.
Québec Act attaches trans-Appalachian interior north of Ohio River to government of Quebec.
First Continental Congress meets and forms Continental Association to boycott British imports.

1775 Battles of Lexington and Concord cause 95 American and 273 British casualties; Americans take Fort Ticonderoga.
Second Continental Congress meets and assumes many powers of an independent government.
Dunmore's Proclamation in Virginia promises freedom to slaves and indentured servants fleeing to British ranks.
Prohibitory Act embargoes American goods.
George III proclaims Americans in open rebellion.

1776 Thomas Paine publishes *Common Sense*.
British troops evacuate Boston.
Declaration of Independence.

and gone farther than they had intended. Hutchinson was one of their main targets. Characterized by young lawyer John Adams as "very ambitious and avaricious," Hutchinson was, in the popular view, chief among the "mean mercenary hirelings" of the British. The more cautious political leaders now realized that they would have to struggle to regain control of the protest movement.

Protest took a more dignified form at the October 1765 Stamp Act Congress in New York. English authorities branded this first self-initiated intercolonial convention a "dangerous tendency." The delegates formulated 12 restrained resolutions that accepted Parliament's right to legislate for the colonies but denied its right to tax them directly.

Violent protests against the Stamp Act also wracked New York and Newport, Rhode Island. Leading the resistance were groups calling themselves the Sons of Liberty, composed mostly of artisans, shopkeepers, and ordinary citizens. By late 1765, effigy-burning crowds all over America persuaded stamp distributors to resign. Colonists defied English authority even more directly by forcing most customs officers and court officials to open the ports and courts for business after November 1 without using the hated stamps required after that date. This often took months of pressure and sometimes mob action, but the Sons of Liberty, often led by new faces in local politics, got their way by going outside the law.

DOCUMENT

Benjamin Franklin, Testimony Against the Stamp Act (1766)

In March 1766, Parliament debated the furious American reaction to the Stamp Act. Lobbied by many merchant friends of the Americans, Parliament voted to repeal it, bowing to expediency but also passing the Declaratory Act, which asserted Parliament's power to enact laws for the colonies in "all cases whatsoever."

The crisis had passed, yet nothing was solved. Americans had begun to recognize a grasping government trampling its subjects' rights. The Stamp Act, one New England clergyman foresaw, "diffused a disgust through the colonies and laid the basis of an alienation which will never be healed." Stamp Act resisters had politicized their communities as never before. The established leaders, generally cautious in their protests, were often displaced by those lower on the social ladder. Men such as New York ship captains Alexander McDougall and Isaac Sears mobilized common citizens and raised political consciousness, employing mass demonstrations and street violence to humble stamp distributors and force open the courts and seaports. Scribbled John Adams in his diary: "The people have become

more attentive to their liberties, . . . and more determined to defend them. . . . Our presses have groaned, our pulpits have thundered, our legislatures have resolved, our towns have voted; the crown officers have everywhere trembled, and all their little tools and creatures been afraid to speak and ashamed to be seen."

Gathering Storm Clouds

Ministerial instability in England hampered the quest for a coherent, workable American policy. Attempting to be a strong king, George III chose ministers who commanded little respect in Parliament. This led to strife between Parliament and the king's chief ministers and a generally chaotic political situation just as the king was trying to overhaul the empire's administration.

To manage the colonies more effectively, the Pitt-Grafton ministry appointed by the king in 1767 obtained new laws to reorganize the customs service, establish a secretary of state for American affairs, and install in the port cities three new vice-admiralty courts, which did not use juries to try accused smugglers. Still hard-pressed for revenue—for at home the government faced severe unemployment, tax protests, and riots over the high price of grain—the ministry pushed through Parliament the relatively small Townshend duties on paper, lead, painters' colors, and tea. A final law suspended New York's assembly until that body ceased defying the Quartering Act of 1765, which required public funds for support of British troops garrisoned in the colony since the end of the Seven Years' War. New York knuckled under in order to save its legislature.

Massachusetts led the colonial protests against the Townshend Acts. Its House of Representatives sent a circular letter written by Samuel Adams to each colony objecting to the new Townshend duties as unconstitutional because they would be used to underwrite salaries for royal officials in America. Under instructions from England, Governor Bernard dissolved the legislature after it refused to rescind the circular letter. "The Americans have made a discovery," declared Edmund Burke before Parliament, "that we mean to oppress them; we have made a discovery that they intend to raise a rebellion. We do not know how to advance; they do not know how to retreat."

Showing more restraint than they had in resisting the Stamp Act, most colonists only grumbled and petitioned. But Bostonians protested stridently. In the summer of 1768, after customs officials seized a sloop owned by John Hancock for a violation of the trade regulations, an angry crowd mobbed them.

For months the officials took refuge on a British warship in Boston harbor. Newspapers warned of new measures designed to "suck the life blood" from the people and predicted that troops would be sent to "dragoon us into passive obedience." To many, the belief grew that the English were plotting "designs for destroying our constitutional liberties."

Troops indeed came. The attack on the customs officials convinced the English that the Bostonians were insubordinate and selfish. The ministry dispatched two regiments from England and two more from Nova Scotia, meant to bring the Bostonians to a proper state of subordination and make them an example. Cries went up against maintaining standing armies in peacetime, but radical Bostonians who proposed force to prevent the troops from landing got little support from delegates called to a special provincial convention. On October 1, 1768, red-coated troops marched into Boston without resistance.

Thereafter, the colonists' main tactic of protest against the Townshend Acts became economic boycott. First in Boston and then in New York and Philadelphia, merchants and consumers adopted nonimportation and nonconsumption agreements, pledging neither to import nor to use British goods. These measures promised to bring the politically

influential English merchants to their aid, for half of British shipping was engaged in commerce with the colonies, and one-quarter of all English exports were consumed there. When the southern colonies also adopted nonimportation agreements in 1768, a new step toward intercolonial union had been taken.

Many colonial merchants, however, especially those with official connections, saw nonimportation agreements as lacking legal force and refused to be bound by them. They had to be persuaded otherwise by street brigades, usually composed of artisans for whom nonimportation was a boon to home manufacturing. Crowd action welled up again in the seaports, as patriot bands attacked the homes and warehouses of offending merchants and "rescued" incoming contraband goods seized by customs officials.

England's attempts to discipline its American colonies and oblige them to share the costs of governing an empire lay in shambles by the end of the 1760s. Using troops to restore order undermined the very respect needed for colonial acceptance of parliamentary authority. Newspapers denounced new extensions of British control. Colonial governors quarreled with their legislatures. Customs officials met with determined opposition and were widely accused of arbitrary actions and excessive zeal in

British Troops Arriving in Boston Rather than quelling the disorder as King George III hoped, the occupation of Boston by British troops in 1768 increased tensions. In this engraving by Paul Revere, the red-coated troops are debarking at the Long Wharf. *(Paul Revere,* British Troops Land at Long Wharf, Boston. *Courtesy Winterthur Museum)*

Massachusetts's Militia Ralph Earle's battle paintings were turned into engravings by Amos Doolittle and widely sold. This engraving shows Massachusetts militiamen confronting the redcoated British soldiers. Is this engraving propagandistic? *(John Warner Barber, engraved by A. Doolittle after Ralph Earle,* The Battle of Lexington, April 19th 1775, *from 'Connecticut Historical Collections,' 1832, Private Collection/Bridgeman Art Library)*

The Growing Rift

In June 1772, England created a new furor by announcing that it, rather than the provincial legislature, would henceforth pay the salaries of the royal governor and superior court judges in Massachusetts. Even though the measure saved the colony money, it looked like a scheme to impose a despotic government and thus undermine a right set forth in the colony's charter. Judges paid from London presumably would obey London.

Boston's town meeting protested loudly and created a Committee of Correspondence to win other colonies' sympathy. Crown supporters called the committee "the foulest, subtlest, and most venomous serpent ever issued from the egg of sedition." By the end of 1772, another 80 towns in Massachusetts had created committees. In the next year, all but three colonies established Committees of Correspondence in their legislatures.

Samuel Adams was by now the leader of the Boston radicals, for the influence of laboring men like Ebenezer MacIntosh had been quietly reduced. Adams was an experienced caucus politicker and a skilled political journalist, and (despite his Harvard degree) he had deep roots among the laboring people. He organized the working ranks through the taverns, clubs, and volunteer fire companies and secured the support of wealthy merchants such as John Hancock, whose ample purse financed patriotic celebrations and feasts that kept politics on everyone's mind and helped build interclass bridges. In England, Adams became known as one of the most dangerous firebrands in America.

In 1772, Rhode Islanders gave Adams a new issue. The commander of the royal ship *Gaspee* was roundly hated for hounding the fishermen and small traders of Narragansett Bay. When his ship ran aground while pursuing a suspected smuggler, Rhode Islanders burned the stranded vessel to the waterline. A Rhode Island court then convicted the *Gaspee*'s captain of illegally seizing what he was convinced was smuggled sugar and rum. London reacted with cries of high treason. Investigators found the lips of Rhode Islanders sealed. The event was tailor-made for Samuel Adams, who used it to "awaken the American colonies, which have been too long dozing upon the brink of ruin."

The final plunge into revolution began when Parliament passed the Tea Act in early 1773, allowing

enforcing the Navigation Acts. The Townshend duties had failed miserably, yielding less than £21,000 by 1770 while costing British business £700,000 through the colonial nonimportation movement.

On March 5, 1770, Parliament repealed all the Townshend duties except the one on tea (which the new minister of state, Lord North, explained was retained "as a mark of the supremacy of Parliament and an efficient declaration of their right to govern the colonies"). On that same evening in Boston, British troops fired on an unruly crowd of heckling citizens. When the smoke cleared, five bloody bodies, including that of Ebenezer MacIntosh's brother-in-law, stained the snow-covered street. Bowing to furious popular reaction, Thomas Hutchinson, recently appointed governor, ordered the British troops out of town and arrested the commanding officer and the soldiers involved. They were later acquitted, with two young patriot lawyers, John Adams and Josiah Quincy, Jr., providing a brilliant defense.

IMAGE

Handbill "On the Death of Five Young Men"

In spite of the potential of the "Boston Massacre" for galvanizing the colonies into further resistance, opposition to English policies, including boycotts, subsided in 1770. Popular leaders such as Samuel Adams in Boston and Alexander McDougall in New York, who had made names for themselves as the standard-bearers of American liberty, had few issues left, especially when the economic depression that had helped sow discontent ended. Yet the fires of revolution had not been extinguished but merely dampened.

DOCUMENT

Boston Gazette Description of the Boston Massacre (1770)

A Sedate Portrait of a Colonial Firebrand Royal Governor Thomas Hutchinson called Sam Adams "[the greatest] incendiary in the King's dominion" whereas his cousin, John Adams, called him "a plain, simple, decent citizen of middling stature, dress, and manners." Boston's premier painter, John Singleton Copley, painted Samuel Adams in just this way—in a simple wool suit with no embroidery and a partially unbuttoned waistcoat, suggesting the patriot leader's disdain for proper appearances. What is Adams pointing at? (*John Singleton Copley, American [1738–1815], Samuel Adams, about 1772; Oil on canvas; 49 1/2 x 39 1/2 in [125.7 x 100.3 cm], Deposited by the city of Boston, 30.76c. Courtesy of the Museum of Fine Arts, Boston. Reproduced with permission. © 1999 The Museum of Fine Arts, Boston. All Rights Reserved.)*

the practically bankrupt East India Company to ship its tea directly to North America with the colonists paying only a small tax. Americans would get inexpensive tea, the Crown a modest revenue, and the East India Company a new lease on life. But colonists reacted furiously because their smuggled Dutch tea would be undersold. American merchants who competed with the East India Company bitterly denounced the monopoly, warning that other monopolies would follow and intermediaries of all kinds eliminated. The colonists also objected that the government was shrewdly trying to gain acceptance of Parliament's taxing power. As Americans drank the taxed tea, they would also be swallowing the English right to tax them. Showing that their principles were not entirely in their pocketbooks, Americans staged

mass meetings that soon forced the resignation of East India Company's agents, and citizens vowed to stop the obnoxious tea at the water's edge.

Governor Hutchinson of Massachusetts brought the tea crisis to a climax, convinced that to yield again to popular pressure would forever cripple English sovereignty in America. The popular party led by Samuel Adams had been urging the citizens to demonstrate that they were not yet prepared for the "yoke of slavery" by sending the tea back to England. When Hutchinson refused, 5,000 Bostonians packed Old South Meeting House on December 16, 1773, noisily passing resolutions urging the governor to grant the tea ships clearance papers to return to England with their cargoes. But Hutchinson was not swayed. "This meeting," despaired Samuel Adams, "can do no more to save the country."

IMAGE
1774
Illustration, List of Crimes by the Massachusetts Governor

At nightfall, a band of Bostonians dressed as Native Americans boarded the tea ships, broke open the chests of tea, and flung £10,000 worth of the East India Company's property into Boston harbor. George Hewes, a 31-year-old shoemaker, recalled how he had garbed himself as a Mohawk, blackened "face and hands with coal dust in the shop of a blacksmith," and joined men of all ranks in marching stealthily to the wharves to do their work. In time, this event would be remembered as the Boston Tea Party.

DOCUMENT
John Andrews to William Barrell, Boston Tea Party (1773)

Now the die was cast. Lord North, the king's chief minister, argued that the dispute was no longer about taxes but about whether England had any authority over the colonies. George III put it succinctly: "We must master them or totally leave them to themselves and treat them as aliens."

Thoroughly aroused, Parliament passed the Coercive Acts, stern laws that Bostonians promptly labeled the "Intolerable Acts." The acts closed the port of Boston to all shipping until the colony paid for the destroyed tea and barred local courts from trying British soldiers and officials for acts committed while suppressing civil disturbances. To hamstring the colony's belligerent political assemblies, Parliament amended the Massachusetts charter to transform the council from an upper legislative chamber, elected by the lower house, to a body appointed by the governor. This amendment stripped the council of its veto power over the governor's decisions.

The act also struck at local government by authorizing the governor to prohibit all town meetings except for one annual meeting to elect local officers of

City Plan of Boston, 1772

Boston's many churches became important political meeting places in the tumultuous decade leading to the outbreak of war in 1775. Old South Meeting House, holding as many as 5,000 people, became the gathering place of "body of the people." Faneuil Hall was the usual site of town meetings, but when crowds exceeded its capacity of 1,200, meetings were adjourned and reconvened at Old South Meeting House.

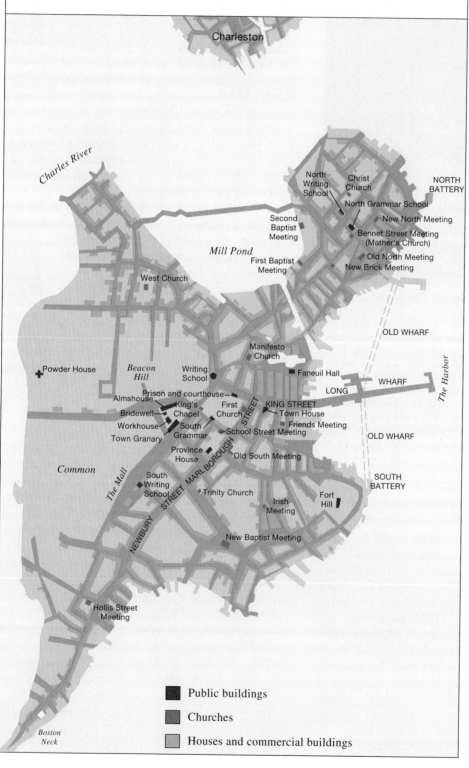

Charleston

Charles River

NORTH
BATTERY

North
Writing
School

Christ
Church

North Grammar School

New North Meeting

Second
Baptist
Meeting

Bennet Street Meeting
(Mather's Church)

Mill Pond

First Baptist
Meeting

Old North Meeting
New Brick Meeting

West Church

OLD WHARF

Manifesto
Church

The Harbor

Powder House

*Beacon
Hill*

Writing
School

Faneuil Hall

WHARF

LONG

Prison and courthouse

Almshouse

King's
Chapel

First
Church

KING STREET

Town House

Bridewell

STREET

Friends Meeting

Workhouse

South
Grammar

School Street Meeting

OLD WHARF

Town Granary

Province
House

Old South Meeting

Common

South
Writing
School

MARLBOROUGH STREET

SOUTH
BATTERY

The Mall

Trinity Church

Irish
Meeting

Fort
Hill

NEWBURY STREET

New Baptist Meeting

Hollis Street
Meeting

*Boston
Neck*

■ Public buildings

■ Churches

■ Houses and commercial buildings

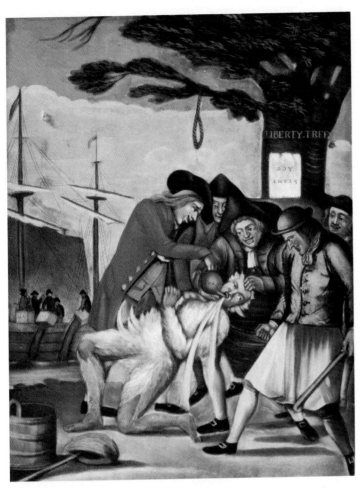

The Bostonians Paying the Excise-Man Public sentiment against the importation of tea and other British goods often found expression in a coat of tar and feathers applied to the bare skin of the offending importer. Note the symbols in *The Bostonians Paying the Excise-Man:* the Liberty Tree with a hangman's noose and the overturned copy of the Stamp Act. What is happening in the background? *(Library of Congress)*

government. Finally, General Thomas Gage, commander in chief of British forces in America, replaced Thomas Hutchinson as governor. "This is the day, then," declared Edmund Burke in the House of Commons, "that you wish to go to war with all America, in order to conciliate that country to this."

Lord North's plan to strangle Massachusetts into submission and hope for acquiescence elsewhere in the colonies proved popular in England. Earlier, the colonies had gained supporters in Parliament for their resistance to what many regarded as attacks on their fundamental privileges. Now this support evaporated, and the colonists found their maneuvering room severely narrowed. When the Intolerable Acts arrived in May 1774, Boston's town meeting urged all the colonies to ban trade with England. While this proposal met with faint support, a second call, for a meeting in Philadelphia of

delegates from all colonies, received a better response. Called the Continental Congress, it began to transform a 10-year debate conducted by separate colonies into a unified American cause.

In September 1774, 55 delegates from all the colonies except Georgia converged on Carpenters' Hall in Philadelphia. The discussions centered not on how to prepare for a war that many sensed was inevitable but on how to resolve sectional differences that most delegates feared were irreconcilable. Overcoming prejudices and hostilities was as important as the formal debates. New Englanders were eyed with suspicion especially for their reputed intolerance and self-interest. "We have numberless prejudices to remove here," wrote John Adams from Philadelphia. "We have been obliged to keep ourselves out of sight, and to feel pulses, and to sound the depths; to insinuate our sentiments, designs, and desires by means of other persons, sometimes of one province, and sometimes of another."

The Continental Congress was by no means a unified body. Some delegates, led by cousins Samuel and John Adams from Massachusetts and Richard Henry Lee and Patrick Henry of Virginia, argued for outright resistance to Parliament's Coercive Acts. Moderate delegates from the middle colonies, led by Joseph Galloway of Pennsylvania and James Duane of New York, urged restraint and further attempts at reconciliation. After weeks of debate, the delegates agreed to a restrained Declaration of Rights and Resolves, which attempted to define American grievances and justify the colonists' defiance of English policies and laws by appealing to the "immutable laws of nature, the principles of the English constitution, and the several [colonial] charters and compacts." Congress had a more concrete plan of resistance. If England did not rescind the Intolerable Acts by December 1, 1774, all imports and exports between the colonies and Great Britain, Ireland, and the British West Indies would be banned. To keep reluctant southern colonies in the fold, some exceptions were made for the export of southern staple commodities.

By the time the Congress adjourned in late October, leaders from different colonies had transformed Boston's cause into a national movement. "Government is dissolved [and] we are in a state of nature," Patrick Henry argued dramatically. "The

Portrait of a Participant in the Boston Tea Party
This portrait of George Robert Twelve Hewes was painted in 1835 when the last survivor of the Boston Tea Party was called "The Centenarian," though he was 93 years old. A biography of the poor shoemaker, written by Benjamin Bussey Thatcher, came off the press in the same year. *(Joseph G. Cole, The Centenarian, 1835: Portrait of George Robert Twelve Hewes. Courtesy of The Bostonian Society/Old State House)*

distinctions between Virginians, Pennsylvanians, New Yorkers, and New Englanders are no more. I am not a Virginian, but an American." Many other delegates were a long way from his conclusion; still the Congress agreed to reconvene in May 1775.

By the time the Second Continental Congress met, the fabric of government was badly torn in most colonies. Illegal revolutionary committees, conventions, and congresses were replacing legal governing bodies. Assuming authority in defiance of royal governors, who suspended truculent legislatures in many colonies, they often operated on instructions from mass meetings where everyone, not just those entitled to vote, gave voice. These extralegal bodies created and armed militia units, bullied merchants and shopkeepers refusing to obey popularly authorized boycotts, levied taxes, operated the courts, and obstructed English customs officials. By the end of 1774, all but three colonies had defied their own charters by appointing provincial assemblies without royal authority. In the next year, this independently created power became evident when trade with England practically ceased.

The Québec Act of 1774

Most colonists hated the Québec Act, which attached the trans-Appalachian interior north of the Ohio River to the British government in Québec, because they believed this act passed by Parliament, like others during the prewar years, was aimed at the heart of colonial liberty. It not only sealed off the western lands from colonial speculators but guaranteed the right of French Catholics to practice their religion freely—an offense, especially, to New England Puritans.

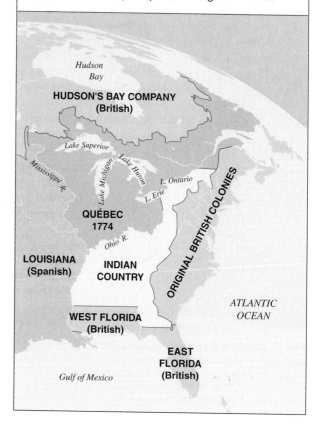

THE IDEOLOGY OF REVOLUTIONARY REPUBLICANISM

In the tumultuous years between 1763 and 1774, the colonists had been expressing many reactions to the crisis with Britain. Mostly these took the form of newspaper articles and pamphlets written by educated lawyers, clergymen, merchants, and planters. But the middling and lower ranks of society had also expressed themselves in printed broadsides, appeals in the newspapers, and even ideologically laden popular rituals such as tarring and feathering and burning in effigy. Gradually, the colonists pieced together a political ideology, borrowed partly from English political thought, partly from the theories of the Enlightenment, and partly from their own experiences. Historians call this new ideology "revolutionary republicanism," but no single coherent ideology united all the colonists' varied interests and experiences.

A Plot Against Liberty

Many American colonists agreed with earlier English Whig writers who charged that corrupt and power-hungry men were slowly extinguishing the lamp of liberty in England. The so-called "country" party represented by these Whig pamphleteers proclaimed itself the guardian of the true principles of the English constitution and opposed the "court" party—the king and his appointees. From this perspective, every ministerial policy and parliamentary act in the decade after the Stamp Act appeared as a subversion of English liberties. Most Americans regarded resistance to such blows against liberty as wholly justified.

The belief that England was carrying out "a deep-laid and desperate plan of imperial despotism . . . for the extinction of all civil liberty," as the Boston town meeting expressed it in 1770, spread rapidly in the next few years. By 1774, John Adams was writing of the "conspiracy against the public liberty [that] was first regularly formed and begun to be executed in 1763 and 1764." From London, America's favorite writer, Benjamin Franklin, described the "extreme corruption prevalent among all orders of men in this old rotten state." Another pamphleteer reached the conclusion that England was no longer "in a condition at present to suckle us, being pregnant with vermin that corrupt her milk and convert her blood and juices into poison."

Among many Americans, especially merchants, the attack on constitutional rights blended closely with the threats to their economic interests contained in the tough new trade policies. Merchants saw a coordinated attack on their "lives, liberties, and property." If a man was not secure in his property, he could not be secure in his citizenship, for it was property that gave a man the independence to shape his identity.

Revitalizing American Society

The continuing crisis over the imperial relationship by itself inspired many colonists to resist impending tyranny. But for others, the revolutionary mentality was also fed by a belief that an opportunity was at hand to revitalize American society. They believed that the growing commercial connections with a decadent and corrupt England had injected poison into the American bloodstream. They worried about the luxury and vice they saw around them and came to believe that resistance to England would return American society to a state of civic virtue, spartan living, and godly purpose.

Britannia Dismembered This cartoon, originally published in London and re-engraved in Philadelphia shows Britannia dismembered. Can you translate the motto—"Date Obolum Bellisario"—and track its origin? *(The Granger Collection, New York)*

The colonial protest movement got much of its high-toned moralism from its fervent supporters, the colonial clergy. This was especially true in New England, where so secular a man as John Adams groaned at the "universal spirit of debauchery, dissipation, luxury, effeminacy and gaming." As in most revolutionary movements, talk of moral regeneration, of a society-wide rebirth through battle against a corrupt enemy, ennobled the cause, inspiring people in areas that had been stirred a generation before by the Great Awakening.

THE TURMOIL OF A REBELLIOUS PEOPLE

The long struggle with England over colonial rights between 1763 and 1774 did not occur in a unified society. Social and economic change, which accelerated in the late colonial period, brought deep unrest and calls for reform from many quarters. By the 1760s, many colonists had lost faith in the internal social systems of the colonies, just as allegiance to England and to the British mercantile system had worn thin.

Many of the colonists who struggled for security in the aftermath of the Seven Years' War hoped that migration to frontier land would improve their fortunes. A flood of new immigrants from Ireland and Germany after the Treaty of Paris in 1763 added to the pressure to reach the trans-Appalachian river valleys. However, the western option involved much violence with Native American tribes. Therefore, most colonists chose to work out their destinies at home or in other communities along the coastal plain to which they migrated in search of opportunity.

RECOVERING THE PAST

Poetry

Poetry is one of the most ancient and universal of the arts. Making its effect by the rhythmic sound and imagery of its language, poetry often expresses romantic love, grief, and responses to nature. But other kinds of poetry interest historians: reflections of human experience, often expressed with deep emotion, and political verses, often written to serve propagandistic goals. For generations, American historians have drawn on poetry to recapture feelings, ideas, and group experiences. For example, Native American creation myths have often taken poetic form; the poems of Anne Bradstreet and Michael Wigglesworth in seventeenth-century Massachusetts tell us much about Puritan mentality and attitudes on topics running from marriage to death; the poetry of the American Transcendentalists tells us about nineteenth-century notions of heroism and who was admired; and Langston Hughes, Arna Bontemps, and other poets of the Harlem Renaissance have expressed through poetry the bittersweet nature of the African American experience. All this material is grist for the historian's mill.

DOCUMENT
Anne Bradstreet, Before the Birth of One of Her Children

The revolutionary generation created poetry of great interest to historians. The newspapers of several port cities published weekly "Poet's Corner" satires, drinking songs, and versed commentary on the issues of the day. Verse was widely used to provoke public discussion; in 1767 poets prompted the boycott of British goods to obtain Parliament's reversal of the hated Townshend duties.

A year later, Philadelphia's John Dickinson composed a "Liberty Song" that became the first set of verses learned in all the colonies. Boston's Sons of Liberty began using this "Liberty Song" in annual ceremonies celebrating their resistance to the Stamp Act. Soon the verses were printed in newspapers throughout the colonies and were used widely in public gatherings. Set to music and easily learned, the verses cultivated anti-British feeling and a sense of the need for intercolonial cooperation:

AUDIO
The Liberty Song

> COME join Hand in Hand, brave AMERICANS all,
> And rouse your bold Hearts at fair LIBERTY'S Call;
> No tyrannous Acts shall suppress your just Claim,
> Or stain with Dishonor America's Name.

Of all the poets of the revolutionary era, none has fascinated today's historians more than Phillis Wheatley, a young slave in Boston who wrote her first poem at age 14 in 1767. Within six years, she became North America's first published black poet. Boston's "Ethiopian poetess" had been brought from Africa to Boston at age 7 and purchased by a prospering tailor named John Wheatley. Soon her master and his wife discovered that she was a prodigy. After learning English so well in 16 months that she could read the most difficult passages of the Bible, she soon showed an uncanny gift for writing. Much of her writing was inspired by deep religious feelings, but she soon was caught up in the dramatic events in Boston that were bringing revolution closer and closer. In her poem entitled "To the King's Most Excellent Majesty," she saluted King George III for repealing the Stamp Act; in "On the Death of Mr. Snider [Seider], Murder'd by Richardson," she lambasted the British customs officer who murdered a teenage member of a crowd protesting the British soldiers who occupied Boston in 1768.

Wheatley was anything but radical. She had so thoroughly imbibed Christianity from her master and mistress that she wrote in one of her first poems that "Twas mercy brought me from my *Pagan* land." Many times she used poetry to implore slaves to "fly to Christ." But by 1772, she was inserting a muffled plea for an end of slavery in her odes to American rights and American resistance to British policies.

That Wheatley's poems were published in London in 1773 is remarkable. Women were not supposed to write publicly in the eighteenth century, and certainly not black women. Nonetheless, her master, supported by Boston friends and proud of his slave prodigy, shipped a sheaf of poems to a bookseller in England, who obtained the support of the Countess of Huntingdon for publishing them. They appeared under the title *Poems on Various Subjects, Religious and Moral.* Even more remarkable was that Wheatley, only 20 years old, took a ship to London to see her book come off the press. Her master and mistress financed the trip, hoping that sea air would clear her clogged lungs. There she was introduced to important reformers and public dignitaries, received a copy of Milton's *Paradise Lost* from the lord mayor of London, and met with Benjamin Franklin. She returned to Boston in 1774.

REFLECTING ON THE PAST Read the two poems that follow: Wheatley's "On the Death of Mr. Snider [Seider], Murder'd by Richardson," composed in 1770, and her poem addressed to the king's minister in charge of colonial affairs, penned two years later. As modern readers, you may find the poetry stilted, but

POEMS

ON

VARIOUS SUBJECTS,

RELIGIOUS AND MORAL.

BY

PHILLIS WHEATLEY,

NEGRO SERVANT to Mr. JOHN WHEATLEY,

of BOSTON, in NEW ENGLAND.

L O N D O N:

Printed for A. BELL, Bookseller, Aldgate; and sold by
Messrs. COX and BERRY, King-Street, *BOSTON.*

M DCC LXXIII.

Published according to Act of Parliament, Sept.ʳ 1, 1773 by Archᵈ Bell,
Bookseller Nº 8 near the Saracens Head Aldgate.

Wheatley worshiped at Old South Meeting House, which held some 5,000 people. In the 1770s, people frequently gathered there for political rallies and deliberations. This partly explains Wheatley's growing interest in the political battles raging in Boston. Wheatley's patroness in England specifically requested a drawing of Phillis for the frontispiece of this volume of poetry. Scipio Moorhead, slave of Boston's Presbyterian minister, did the drawing. Wheatley's mistress, Susannah Wheatley, called it a fine likeness. *(From the copy in the Rare Book Collection, The University of North Carolina at Chapel Hill)*

Wheatley's style was modeled on poetic conventions of the eighteenth century. What change can you discern in Wheatley's political consciousness between 1770 and 1772? Do you consider her poem on Seider's murder by a British customs officer propagandistic? How does she relate the plight of enslaved Africans to the American colonists' struggle? More generally, how effective do you think poetry is in arousing sentiment and mobilizing political energy? Can you think of verse serving as lyrics in popular protest music today?

On the Death of Mr. Snider, Murder'd by Richardson (1770)

In heaven's eternal court it was decreed
How the first martyr for the cause should bleed
To clear the country of the hated brood
We whet his courage for the common good.
Long hid before, a vile infernal here
Prevents Achilles in his mid career
Wherev'r this fury darts his Poisonous breath
All are endanger'd to the shafts of death

To the Right Honourable William, Earl of Dartmouth, His Majesty's Principal Secretary of State for North America (1772)

HAIL, happy day, when, smiling like the morn,
Fair Freedom *rose* New-England *to adorn:*
The northern clime beneath her genial ray,
Dartmouth, congratulates thy blissful sway:
Elate with hope her race no longer mourns,
Each soul expands, each grateful bosom burns,
While in thine hand with pleasure we behold
The silken reigns, and Freedom's *charms unfold.*
No more, America, in mournful strain
Of wrongs, and grievance unredress'd complain,
No longer shalt thou dread the iron chain,
Which wanton Tyranny with lawless hand
Had made, and with it meant t' enslave the land.
Should you, my lord, while you peruse my song,
Wonder from whence my love of Freedom *sprung,*
Whence flow these wishes for the common good,
By feeling hearts alone best understood,
I, young in life, by seeming cruel fate
Was snatch'd from Afric's fancy'd happy seat:
What pangs excruciating must molest,
What sorrows labour in my parent's breast?
Steel'd was that soul and by no misery mov'd
That from a father seiz'd his babe belov'd:
Such, such my case. And can I then but pray
Others may never feel tyrannic sway?

177

Tarring and Feathering a Customs Official   In January 1774, after British customs officer John Malcolm bullied a small boy and then beat George Robert Twelve Hewes (who had intervened), a Boston crowd tarred and feathered Malcolm. As shown here, Bostonians force Malcolm into a cart, which was dragged through town to the hoots of the crowd. What is the origin of tarring and feathering? *(CORBIS)*

As agitation against English policy intensified, previously passive people took a more active interest in politics. In this charged atmosphere, the constitutional struggle with England spread quickly into uncharted territory. Groups emerged—slaves, urban laboring people, backcountry farmers, evangelicals, women—whose enunciated goals were sometimes only loosely connected to the struggle with England. The stridency and potential power of these groups frightened many in the upper class. Losing control of the protests they had initially led, many would abandon the resistance movement.

Urban People

Although the cities contained only about 5 percent of the colonial population, they were the core of revolutionary agitation. As centers of communications, government, and commerce, they led the way in protesting English policy, and they soon contained the most politicized citizens in America. Local politics could be rapidly transformed as the struggle against England meshed with calls for internal reform.

Philadelphia offers a good example of popular empowerment. Before the Seven Years' War, artisans had usually acquiesced to local leadership by merchant and lawyer politicos. But economic difficulties in the 1760s and 1770s led them to band together within their craft and community. Artisans played a central role in forging and enforcing a nonimportation agreement in 1768. They called public meetings, published newspaper appeals, organized secondary boycotts against foot-dragging merchants, and tarred and feathered their opponents. Cautious merchants complained that mere artisans had "no right to give their sentiments respecting an importation" and called the craftsmen a "rabble." But artisans, casting off their customary deference, forged ahead. By 1772, they were filling elected municipal positions and insisting on their right to participate equally with their social superiors in nominating assemblymen and other important officeholders. They also began lobbying for reform laws, calling for elected representatives to be more accountable to their constituents. Genteel Philadelphians muttered, "It is time the tradesmen were checked—they ought not to intermeddle in state affairs—they will become too powerful."

By 1774, the meddling of the Philadelphia working class in state affairs reached a bold new stage—de facto assumption of governmental powers by committees created by the people at large. Artisans had first assumed such extralegal authority in policing the nonimportation agreement in 1769. Now, responding to the Intolerable Acts, they proposed a radical slate of candidates for a committee to enforce a new economic boycott. Their ticket drubbed one nominated by conservative merchants.

AMERICAN VOICES

A Petition from Massachusetts Blacks to Governor Thomas Gage

More than two years before the Declaration of Independence, "a great number of blacks" of Massachusetts petitioned Thomas Gage, captain general and governor in chief of the colony, and the legislature to free them from slavery.

Your petitioners apprehend we have in common with all other men a natural right to our freedoms, without being deprived of them by our fellow men, as we are a freeborn people and have never forfeited this blessing by any compact or agreement whatever. But we were unjustly dragged by the cruel hand of power from our dearest friends and some of us stolen from the bosoms of our tender parents and from a populous, pleasant, and plentiful country and brought hither to be made slaves for life in a Christian land. Thus we are deprived of everything that has a tendency to make life even tolerable; the endearing ties of husband and wife we are strangers to, for we are no longer man and wife than our masters or mistresses think proper.... Our children are also taken from us by force and sent many miles from us where we seldom or ever see them again, there to be made slaves of for life, which sometimes is very short by reason of being dragged from their mother's breast.... We therefor beg your excellency and honors will give this its due weight and consideration and that you will accordingly cause an act of the legislative to be passed that we may obtain our natural right, our freedoms, and our children be set at liberty at the year of twenty one....

- *How did these enslaved petitioners acquire the idea of "our natural right" invoked at the beginning and end of this petition?*

- *Is it borrowed or found in their own African cultural heritage?*

Source: Massachusetts Historical Society *Collections*, 5th Series, III (Boston, 1877), excerpted in Herbert Aptheker, ed., *A Documentary History of the Negro People of the United States*, Vol. 1 (New York: Citadel Press, 1968), 8–9. Spelling and punctuation have been modernized.

The political support of the new radical leaders centered in the 31 companies of the Philadelphia militia, composed mostly of laboring men, and in the extralegal committees now controlling the city's economic life. Their leadership helped overcome the conservatism of the regularly elected Pennsylvania legislature, which was resisting the movement of the Continental Congress toward independence. The new radical leaders also demanded internal reforms: curbing the accumulation of wealth by "our great merchants ... at the expense of the people"; abolishing the property requirement for voting; allowing militiamen to elect their officers; and imposing stiff fines, to be used for the support of the families of poor militiamen, on men who refused militia service.

Philadelphia's radicals never controlled the city. They always jostled for position with prosperous artisans and shopkeepers of more moderate views and with cautious lawyers and merchants. But mobilization among artisans, laborers, and mariners, in other cities as well as Philadelphia, became part of the chain of events that led toward independence. Whereas most of the patriot elite fought only to change English colonial policy, the people of the cities also struggled for internal reforms and raised notions of how an independent American society might be reorganized.

Patriot Women

Colonial women also played a vital role in the movement toward revolution, and they drew on revolutionary arguments to define their own goals. They signed nonimportation agreements, harassed noncomplying merchants, and helped organize "fast days," on which communities prayed for deliverance from English oppression. But the women's most important role was to facilitate the boycott of English goods. The success of the nonconsumption pacts depended on substituting homespun cloth for English textiles on which colonists of all classes had always relied. From Georgia to Maine, women and children began spinning yarn and weaving cloth. "Was not every fireside, indeed a theatre of politics?" John Adams remembered after the war. Towns vied patriotically in the manufacture of cotton, linen, and woollen cloth, with the women staging open-air spinning contests to publicize their commitment.

After the Tea Act in 1773, the interjection of politics into the household economy increased as patriotic women boycotted their favorite drink. Newspapers carried recipes for tea substitutes and recommendations for herbal teas. In Wilmington, North Carolina, women paraded solemnly through the town and

Women Signing an Anti-Tea Agreement

TO THE
Delaware Pilots.

WE took the Pleafure, fome Days fince, of kindly admonifhing you *to do your Duty*; if per-chance you fhould meet with the *(Tea,)* SHIP POLLY, CAPTAIN AYRES; a THREE DECKER which is hourly expected,

We have now to add, that Matters ripen faft here; and that *much is expected from thofe Lads who meet with the Tea Ship.*----There is fome Talk of A HANDSOME REWARD FOR THE PILOT WHO GIVES THE FIRST GOOD ACCOUNT OF HER.----How that may be, we cannot *for certain* determine: But ALL agree, that TAR and FEATHERS will be his Portion, who pilots her into this Harbour. And we will anfwer for ourfelves, that, whoever is committed to us, as an Offender againft the Rights of *America*, will experience the utmoft Ex-ertion of our Abilities; as

THE COMMITTEE FOR TARRING AND FEATHERING.

An Exhortation to Action Not only Bostonians took action against the Tea Act. This Philadelphia broadside from "The Committee for Tarring and Feathering," issued several weeks before the Boston Tea Party, exhorts pilots on the Delaware River to watch for an arriving tea ship. *(Library of Congress)*

then made a ritual display of their patriotism by burning their imported tea.

Colonial protests and petitions against England's arbitrary uses of power changed women's perception of their role. The more male leaders talked about England's intentions to "enslave" the Americans and England's callous treatment of its colonial "subjects," the more American women began to rethink their own domestic situations. The language of protest against England reminded many American women that they too were badly treated "subjects" of their husbands, who often dealt with them cruelly and exercised power over them arbitrarily.

Most American women, still bound by the social conventions of the day, were not ready to occupy such new territory. But the protests against England had stirred up new thoughts about what seemed "arbitrary" or "despotic" in their own society. Hence, many agendas for change appeared and with them a new feeling that what had been endured in the past was no longer acceptable.

Protesting Farmers

In most of the agricultural areas of the colonies, where the majority of settlers made their livelihoods, passions over English policies awakened only slowly. After about 1740, farmers had benefited from a sharp rise in the demand for foodstuffs in England, southern Europe, and the West Indies. Rising prices and brisk markets brought a higher standard of living to thousands of rural colonists, especially south of New England. Living far from harping English customs officers, impressment gangs, and occupying armies, the colonists of the interior had to be drawn gradually into the resistance movement by their urban cousins. Even in Concord, Massachusetts, only a dozen miles from the center of colonial agitation, townspeople found little to protest in English policies until England closed the port of Boston in 1774.

Still, other parts of rural America seethed with social tension before the war. The dynamics of conflict, shaped by the social development of particular regions, eventually became part of the momentum for revolution. In three western counties of North Carolina and in the Hudson River valley of New York, for example, widespread civil disorder marked the prerevolutionary decades.

For years, the small farmers of western North Carolina had suffered exploitation by corrupt

Sarah Franklin Bache The daughter of Benjamin and Deborah Franklin, Sarah Franklin Bache went door to door to raise money to buy linen from which Philadelphia women made 2,200 shirts for the nearly naked soldiers of Washington's army. *(John Hoppner (English, 1758–1810), Mrs. Richard Bache (Sarah Franklin, 1743–1808), 1793. The Metropolitan Museum of Art, Catharine Lorillard Wolfe Collection, Wolfe Fund, 1901. (01.20) Photograph © 1998 The Metropolitan Museum of Art)*

AMERICAN VOICES

George Sims, from "An Address to the Inhabitants of Granville County"

George Sims, a farmer and schoolmaster, became a spokesman for poor frontiersmen in North Carolina. This is an excerpt from Sims's "An Address to the People of Granville County," complaining of oppression of small farmers.

Does not daily experience show us the gaping jaws of ruin, open and ready to devour us? Are not your lands executed [seized by the sheriff], your Negroes, horses, cattle, hogs, corn, beds, and household furniture? Are not these things . . . taken and sold for one tenth of their value? Not to satisfy the just debts which you have contracted; but to satisfy the cursed exorbitant demands of the clerks, lawyers, and sheriffs. Here they take your lands, which perhaps are worth four or five hundred pounds, and sell them at public vendue [auction] for about forty or fifty pounds. And who buys? Why the same villains who have taken your Negroes and other personal estate, and have the county's money in their hands. . . . It would be enough to make us turn rebels and throw off all submission to such tyrannical laws. For if these things were tolerated, it would rob us of the very means of living, and it would be better for us to die in defense of our privileges, than to live slaves to a handful of scapegallows or perish for want of the means of subsistence. . . . [We should] combine as one man to throw off the heavy yoke, which is cast upon our necks, and resume our ancient liberties and privileges as free subjects.

■ *Do you think the claims of George Sims are exaggerated–that "clerks, lawyers and sheriffs" put a "heavy yoke" on the necks of small farmers and deprived them of their "ancient liberties and privileges?"*

■ *Is Sims a trouble maker or is he the fearless leader of truly oppressed small farmers?*

county officials appointed by the governor and a legislature dominated by eastern planter interests. Sheriffs and justices, allied with land speculators and lawyers, seized property when farmers could not pay their taxes and sold it, often at a fraction of its worth, to their cronies. The legislature rejected western petitions for lower taxes, paper currency, and lower court fees. In the mid-1760s, frustrated at getting no satisfaction from legal forms of protest, the farmers formed associations—the so-called Regulators—that forcibly closed the courts, attacked the property of their enemies, and whipped and publicly humiliated judges and lawyers. When their leaders were arrested, the Regulators stormed the jails and released them.

In 1768 and again in 1771, Governor William Tryon led troops against the Regulators. Bloodshed was averted on the first occasion, but on the second, at the Battle of Alamance, two armies of more than 1,000 fired on each other. At least nine men died on each side before the Regulators fled the field. Six leaders were executed in the ensuing trials. Though the Regulators lost the battle, their protests became part of the larger revolutionary struggle. They railed against the self-interested behavior of a wealthy elite and asserted the necessity for people of humble rank to throw off deference and assume political responsibilities.

Rural insurgency in New York flared up in the 1750s, subsided, and then erupted again in 1766. The conditions under which land was held precipitated the violence. A few wealthy families with enormous landholdings, acquired as virtually free gifts from royal governors, controlled the Hudson River valley. The Van Rensselaer manor, for example, totaled a million acres. Hundreds of tenants with their families paid substantial annual rents for the right to farm on these lands. When tenants resisted rent increases or purchased land from Native Americans who swore that manor lords had extended the boundaries of

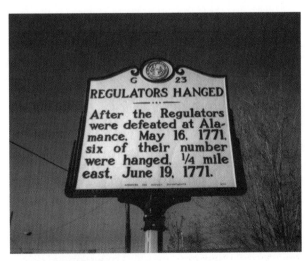

Commemoration of the Battle of Alamance A road sign in North Carolina is one of the few reminders that a bloody battle was fought at Alamance between small farmers and a militia commanded by the colony's governor in 1771. (© 2002 Steven H. J. Rankin)

their manors by fraud, the landlords began evicting them.

As the wealthiest men of the region, the landlords had the power of government, including control of the courts, on their side. Organizing themselves and going outside the law became the tenants' main strategy, as with the Carolina Regulators. By 1766, while New York City was absorbed in the Stamp Act furor, tenants led by William Prendergast began resisting sheriffs who tried to evict them from lands

they claimed. The militant tenants threatened landlords with death and broke open jails to rescue friends. British troops from New York were used to break the tenant rebellion. Prendergast was tried and sentenced to be hanged, beheaded, and quartered. Although he was pardoned, the bitterness of the Hudson River tenants endured through the Revolution. Most of them, unlike the Carolina Regulators, fought for the British because their landlords were patriots.

TIMELINE

1696	Parliament establishes Board of Trade
1701	Iroquois set policy of neutrality
1702–1713	Queen Anne's War
1713	Peace of Utrecht
1733	Molasses Act
1739–1742	War of Jenkins' Ear
1744–1748	King George's War
1754	Albany conference
1755	Braddock defeated by French and Indian allies Acadians expelled from Nova Scotia
1756–1763	Seven Years' War
1759	Wolfe defeats the French at Québec
1759–1761	Cherokee War against the English
1760s	Economic slump
1763	Treaty of Paris ends Seven Years' War Proclamation Line limits westward expansion

1764	Sugar and Currency acts Pontiac's Rebellion in Ohio valley
1765	Colonists resist Stamp Act Virginia House of Burgesses issues Stamp Act resolutions
1766	Declaratory Act Tenant rent war in New York Slave insurrections in South Carolina
1767	Townshend duties imposed
1768	British troops occupy Boston
1770	"Boston Massacre" Townshend duties repealed (except on tea)
1771	North Carolina Regulators defeated
1772	*Gaspee* incident in Rhode Island
1773	Tea Act provokes Boston Tea Party
1774	"Intolerable Acts" First Continental Congress meets in Philadelphia

Conclusion

On the Brink of Revolution

The colonial Americans who lived in the third quarter of the eighteenth century participated in an era of political tension and conflict that changed the lives of nearly everyone. The Seven Years' War removed French and Spanish challengers and nurtured the colonists' sense of separate identity. Yet it left them with difficult economic adjustments, heavy debts, and growing social divisions. The colonists heralded the Treaty of Paris in 1763 as the dawning of a new era, but it led to a reorganization of England's triumphant yet debt-torn empire that had profound repercussions in America.

In the prerevolutionary decade, as England and the colonies moved from crisis to crisis, a dual disillusionment penetrated ever deeper into the colonial consciousness. Pervasive doubt arose concerning both the colonies' role, as assigned by England, in the economic life of the empire and the sensitivity of the government in London to the colonists' needs. Meanwhile, the colonists began to perceive British policies—instituted by Parliament, the king, and his advisers—as a systematic attack on the fundamental liberties and natural rights of British citizens in North America.

The fluidity and diversity of colonial society and the differing experiences of Americans during and after the Seven Years' War evoked varying responses to the disruption that accompanied the English reorganization of the empire. In the course of resisting English policy, many previously inactive colonists, such as the humble shoemaker Ebenezer MacIntosh, entered public life to challenge gentry control of political affairs. Often occupying the most radical ground in opposing England, they simultaneously challenged the growing concentration of economic and political power in their own communities. What lay ahead was not only war with England but protracted arguments about how the American people, if they prevailed in their war for independence, should refashion their society.

Questions for Review and Reflection

1. What roles did Native Americans play in the imperial conflicts of the eighteenth century?

2. How did the Seven Years' War help pave the way for the colonies' break with Britain?

3. The British government pursued policies toward its colonies that it thought reasonable and just in the aftermath of the Treaty of Paris. Why did many colonists see these policies in an entirely different light?

4. What was the contribution of "republican ideology" to the revolutionary movement?

5. What does it mean to say that there were two American revolutions? How were the two related?

Recommended Reading

Recommended Readings are posted on the Web site for this textbook. Visit www.ablongman.com/nash

Fiction and Film

Americans have written novels about the American Revolution almost from the day the firing stopped. James Fenimore Cooper's *The Spy: A Tale of the Neutral Ground* (1822) is the best of the early ones. Historian Paul Leicester Ford's *Janice Meredith: A Story of the American Revolution* (1899) remains absorbing a century after its publication. In the modern period, Kenneth Roberts's four novels on the Revolution have entertained American readers for two generations: *Arundel* (1933), *Oliver Wiswell* (1940), *Rabble in Arms* (1953), and *The Battle of Cowpens: The Great Morale-Builder* (1958). *Oliver Wiswell* is especially notable for its recreation of a Loyalist's view of the Revolution. *Mary Silliman's War* (Heritage Film and Citadel Film, 1993) shows the Revolution through the eyes of a Connecticut family in which husband and wife must reconcile their differing views on the Patriots and Loyalists. The English film on George III *The Madness of King George* (1994) brings alive the era of the American Revolution and turns the king into the deeply psychotic ruler that some at the time believed he was. *Liberty* (Middlemarch Films, 1997) is a docudrama produced for television that has many high moments but neglects the internal struggles within the patriot ranks for reforming American society.

Discovering U.S. History Online

Exploring the West from Monticello: An Exhibition of Maps and Navigational Instruments
www.lib.virginia.edu/exhibits/lewis_clark/home.html
Maps and charts reveal knowledge and conceptions about the known and the unknown. This site includes a number of eighteenth-century maps.

Maps of the French and Indian War
www.masshist.org/maps/MapsHome/Home.htm
In addition to contemporary maps, this site explains the political significance of the maps and gives a background of the wars.

1755: The French and Indian War

www.web.syr.edu/~laroux/

This amateur site presents information about French soldiers who came to New France between 1755 and 1760 to fight in the French and Indian War as well as a list of key places.

A Century of Lawmaking

www.memory.loc.gov/ammem/amlaw/lwjc.html

A searchable version of "the daily proceedings of the Congress as kept by the office of its secretary, Charles Thomson."

Phillis Wheatley (1753–1784)

www.csustan.edu/english/reuben/pal/chap2/wheatley.html

This online essay on Phillis Wheatley includes samples of her poetry and a bibliography.

Thomas Paine

www.thomaspaine.org

This official site contains a large archive of Paine's work, including *Common Sense,* and information about the association.

The Freedom Trail

www.freedomtrail.org/index.html

This site presents the story of colonial protest via Boston historical sites.

Georgia's Rare Map Collection

www.scarlett.libs.uga.edu/darchive/hargrett/maps/revamer.html

This site contains maps of colonial and revolutionary America.

C H A P T E R **6**

A People in Revolution

William Mercer, *Battle of Princeton*, ca. 1786–1790. Because infantry weapons were inaccurate at long distance, lines formed in close proximity, where fire was more deadly and combat intensely personal. What must the sounds of such close-in combat been like? *(William Mercer, Battle of Princeton, c. 1786–1790. Atwater Kent Museum of Philadelphia, The Historical Society of Pennsylvania Collection)*

American Stories ─────────────

Among the Americans wounded and captured at the Battle of Bunker Hill in the spring of 1775 was Lieutenant William Scott of Peterborough, New Hampshire. Asked by his captors how he had come to be a rebel, "Long Bill" Scott replied:

> The case was this Sir! I lived in a Country Town; I was a Shoemaker, & got [my] living by my labor. When this rebellion came on, I saw some of my neighbors get

into commission, who were no better than myself. . . . I was asked to enlist, as a private soldier. My ambition was too great for so low a rank. I offered to enlist upon having a lieutenant's commission, which was granted. I imagined my self now in a way of promotion. If I was killed in battle, there would be an end of me, but if my Captain was killed, I should rise in rank, & should still have a chance to rise higher. These Sir! were the only motives of my entering into the service. For as to the dispute between Great Britain & the colonies, I know nothing of it; neither am I capable of judging whether it is right or wrong.

Scott may have been trying to gain the sympathy of his captors, but people fought in America's Revolutionary War out of fear and ambition as well as principle. We have no way of knowing whether Long Bill Scott's motives were typical. Certainly many Americans knew more than he about the colonies' struggle with England, but many did not.

In the spring of 1775, the Revolutionary War had just begun. So had Long Bill's adventures. When the British evacuated Boston a year later, Scott was transported to Halifax, Nova Scotia. After several months' captivity, he managed to escape and make his way home to fight once more. He was recaptured in November 1776 near New York City, when its garrison fell to a surprise British assault. Again Scott escaped, this time by swimming the Hudson River at night with his sword tied around his neck and his watch pinned to his hat.

During the winter of 1777, he returned to New Hampshire to recruit his own militia company. It included two of his eldest sons. In the fall, his unit helped defeat Burgoyne's army near Saratoga, New York, and later took part in the fighting around Newport, Rhode Island. When his light infantry company was ordered to Virginia in early 1778, Scott's health broke, and he was permitted to resign from the army. After a few months' recuperation, however, he was at it again. During the last year of the war, he served as a volunteer on a navy frigate.

For seven years, the war held Scott in its harsh grasp. His oldest son died of camp fever after six years of service. In 1777, Long Bill sold his New Hampshire farm to meet family expenses. He lost a second farm in Massachusetts shortly afterward. After his wife died, he turned their youngest children over to relatives and set off to beg a pension or job from the government.

Long Bill's saga was still not complete. In 1792, he rescued eight people when their boat capsized in New York harbor. Three years later, General Benjamin Lincoln took Scott with him to the Ohio country, where they surveyed land that was opening for white settlement. At last he had a respectable job and even a small government pension as compensation for his nine wounds. But trouble would still not let him go. While surveying on the Black River near Sandusky, Scott and his colleagues contracted "lake fever." Though ill, he guided part of the group back to Fort Stanwix in New York, then returned for the others. It was his last heroic act. A few days after his second trip, on September 16, 1796, he died.

American independence and the Revolutionary War that achieved it were not as hard on everyone as they were on Long Bill Scott, yet together they transformed the lives of countless Americans. The war lasted seven years, longer than any other of America's wars until Vietnam nearly two centuries later. And unlike the nation's twentieth-century conflicts, it was fought on American soil, among the American people, disrupting families, destroying communities, spreading disease, and making a shambles of the economy. The war also had far different consequences for men than women, black slaves than their white masters, Native Americans than frontier settlers, and overseas merchants than urban workers. This chapter examines each of these issues, as well as the war's military progress.

The chapter also explains why America's struggle for independence became internationalized as France, Spain, and other nations, driven by their own imperial ambitions and the realities of European power politics, joined in the conflict against England. The war and the Treaty of Paris (1783) that ended it not only secured American independence, but also redrew the contours of imperial ambition in North America and recast relations between England and the nations of western Europe. More than that, America's fight for independence ushered in an extended Age of Revolution that over the following half century would see a king toppled and aristocratic privilege overthrown in France, political reforms erupt throughout much of Europe, and independence movements undercut European imperialism in Haiti and Latin America.

As activity quickened under the pressure of war and revolution, the American people mounted a

political revolution of profound importance, another important topic of Chapter 6. Politics and government were transformed in keeping with republican principles, the clash of opposing interests, and the rapidly changing circumstances of public life. How much power should the new state governments have, and how democratic could they safely be? Could individual liberty be reconciled with the need for public order? Should women as well as men, and free blacks as well as whites, be considered American citizens? And what should the national government be like? Seldom has the nation's political agenda been more important, or more sharply contested, than during these critical years.

Our understanding of the experience out of which the American nation emerged must begin with the Revolutionary War, for as Long Bill Scott understood all too well, liberty came at a high cost.

BURSTING THE COLONIAL BONDS

By the spring of 1775, tension between the colonies and England was at the breaking point. In each of the colonies extralegal committees and assemblies organized continuing resistance to the Intolerable Acts, while in England, Parliament and the king's ministers prepared to crush the colonial rebellion. The outbreak of fighting at Lexington and Concord decisively transformed the imperial crisis. No longer was it limited to a struggle over competing theories of parliamentary authority and colonial rights, for now the firing had commenced and men on both sides lay dying. Within little more than a year of that fateful event, England's empire was severed.

The Final Rupture

The final spark to the revolutionary powder keg was struck in April 1775. The government in London ordered General Gage, commander of the British troops occupying Boston, to arrest "the principal actors and abettors" of insurrection. Under cover of night, he sent 700 redcoats out of Boston to seize colonial arms in nearby Concord. But Americans learned of the plan, and when the troops reached Lexington at dawn, 70 armed "Minutemen"—townsmen available on a minute's notice—were waiting. In the ensuing skirmish, 18 Massachusetts farmers fell, 8 of them mortally wounded.

Marching farther west to Concord, the British encountered another firefight. Withdrawing, the redcoats made their way back to Boston, harassed by militiamen firing from farmhouses and from behind stone walls. Before the bloody day ended, 273 British and 95 Americans lay dead or wounded. News of the bloodshed swept through the colonies. Within weeks, thousands of men besieged the British troops in Boston. According to one colonist, everywhere "you see the inhabitants training, making firelocks, casting mortars, shells, and shot."

DOCUMENT

Joseph Warren, "Account of the Battle of Lexington" (1775)

As fighting erupted around Boston, the Second Continental Congress assembled in May 1775 in Philadelphia. Many delegates knew one another from the earlier Congress. But fresh faces appeared, including Boston's wealthy merchant, John Hancock; a young planter-lawyer from Virginia, Thomas Jefferson; and Benjamin Franklin, who had recently arrived from London.

Meeting in the statehouse, where the king's arms hung over the entrance and the inscription on the tower bell read "Proclaim liberty throughout the land unto all the inhabitants thereof," the Second Congress set to work. Though its powers were unclear and its legitimacy uncertain, the desperate situation required that it act. After a spirited debate, Congress authorized a continental army of 20,000 and, partly to cement Virginia to the

IMAGE

Independence Hall

cause, chose George Washington as commander in chief. Over succeeding weeks, it issued a "Declaration of Causes of Taking-up Arms," sent the king an "Olive Branch Petition" humbly begging him to remove the obstacles to reconciliation, made moves to secure the neutrality of the interior Native American tribes, issued paper money, and approved plans for a military hospital.

While debate continued over whether the colonies ought to declare themselves independent, military action grew more intense. The fiery Ethan Allen and his Green Mountain Boys from eastern New York captured Fort Ticonderoga, controlling the Champlain valley, in May 1775. On New Year's Day in 1776, the British shelled Norfolk, Virginia. Still, many members of the Congress dreaded a final rupture and hoped for reconciliation. Such hopes finally crumbled at the end of 1775 when news arrived that the king, rejecting the Olive Branch Petition and proclaiming the colonies in "open and avowed rebellion," had dispatched 20,000 additional British troops to quell the insurrection. Those fatal words made Congress's actions treasonable and turned all who obeyed the Congress into traitors.

Royal Proclamation of Rebellion (1775)

Thomas Paine's *Common Sense*

As the crisis deepened, a pamphlet appeared that would speed the move toward independence. Published in Philadelphia on January 9, 1776, Thomas Paine's *Common Sense* soon appeared in bookstalls all over the colonies. In scathing language, Paine denied the very legitimacy of monarchy. "Of more worth is one honest man to society," he scoffed, "than all the crowned ruffians that ever lived." It was Paine's unsparing rejection of monarchy that made his pamphlet seem so radical. From there it was a logical step to call openly for Americans to act in defense of their liberties. "O ye that love mankind," he declared. "Ye that dare oppose not only the tyranny, but also the tyrant, stand forth!" Paine's ringing challenge had the desired effect.

The pamphlet's astounding popularity—it went through 25 editions in 1776 and sold more copies than any printed piece in colonial history—stemmed not only from its argument but also from its style. Shunning the elaborate, legalistic language of most pamphlets written by lawyers and clergymen, Paine wrote for the common people who read little more than the Bible. Using biblical imagery and plain language, he appealed to their Calvinist heritage and millennial yearnings: "We have it in our power to begin the world over again," he exulted. "The birthday of a new world" was at hand. It was language that could be understood on the docks, in the taverns, on the streets, and in the farmyards.

Many Whig leaders found his pungent rhetoric and egalitarian call for ending hereditary privilege and concentrated power too strong. They denounced the disheveled immigrant as a "crack-brained zealot

Thomas Paine and the Title Page of *Common Sense* In *Common Sense*, Thomas Paine took the radical step of attacking George III and the entire concept of monarchy in plain but muscular language that common folk could understand. Why do you suppose Paine did not put his name on the title page? *(Left: Copy by Auguste Millère, after an engraving by William Sharp, after George Romney, Thomas Paine, National Portrait Gallery, London; right: Library of Congress)*

for democracy" who appealed to "every silly clown and illiterate mechanic." But thousands who read or listened to *Common Sense* were radicalized by it and came to believe not only that independence could be wrestled from England, but also that a new social and political order could be created in North America.

Declaring Independence

By the time Paine's hard-hitting pamphlet appeared, members of Congress were talking less gingerly about independence. When England embargoed all trade to the colonies and ordered the seizure of American ships, the Congress declared American ports open to all countries. "Nothing is left now," Joseph Hewes of North Carolina admitted, "but to fight it out." It was almost anticlimactic when Richard Henry Lee introduced a congressional resolution on June 7 calling for independence. After two days of debate, the Congress ordered a committee chaired by Jefferson to begin drafting such a document.

Though it would become revered as the new nation's birth certificate, the Declaration of Independence was not a highly original statement. It drew heavily on the Congress's earlier justifications of American resistance, and its theory of government had already been set forth in scores of pamphlets over the previous decade. The ringing phrases that "all men are created equal, that they are endowed by their Creator with certain unalienable Rights, that among these are Life, Liberty, and the pursuit of Happiness" were familiar in the writing of many American pamphleteers.

Jefferson, "Rough Draft" of the Declaration of Independence

Jefferson's committee presented the declaration to Congress on June 28, and Congress began to debate the document on July 1. The following day 12 delegations voted "yes," with New York abstaining, thus allowing the Congress to say that the vote for independence was unanimous. Two more days were spent polishing the document. The major change was the elimination of a long argument blaming the king for slavery in America. On July 4, Congress sent the document to the printer.

Four days later, Philadelphians thronged to the state house to hear the Declaration of Independence read aloud. They "huzzahed" the reading, tore the plaque of the king's arms from above the statehouse door, and later that night, amid cheers, toasts, and clanging church bells, hurled this symbol of more than a century and a half of colonial dependency on England into a roaring fire.

Signing of the Declaration of Independence

Jefferson's Draft of the Declaration of Independence As this page from an early draft of the Declaration indicates, Jefferson worked hard to get the language just right. Read the finished document in the Appendix of this book (see pp. A-2–A-3). Which parts of the document do you think gave Jefferson the most trouble? *(Manuscript Division, Library of Congress)*

Across the land, people raised toasts to the great event: "Liberty to those who have the spirit to preserve it," and "May Liberty expand sacred wings, and, in glorious effort, diffuse her influence o'er and o'er the globe." Independence had been declared; the war, however, was yet to be won.

THE WAR FOR AMERICAN INDEPENDENCE

The war began in Massachusetts in 1775, but within a year its focus shifted to the middle states. After 1779, the South became the primary theater. Why

Military Operations in the North, 1776–1780

During the early years of the war, fighting was most intense in upper New York and the mid-Atlantic states. There, as in the South (see the map on p. 194), the British and their Native American allies opened a second front far to the interior. Why did they do so, and how did this complicate American strategy?

did this geographic pattern develop, what was its significance, and why did the Americans win?

The War in the North

For a brief time following Lexington and Concord, British officials thought of launching forays out from Boston into the surrounding countryside. They soon reconsidered, however, for the growing size of the continental army and the absence of significant Loyalist strength in the New England region urged caution. Even more important, Boston became untenable after the Americans placed artillery on the strategic Dorchester Heights. On March 7, 1776, the British commander General William Howe decided to evacuate the city.

Fearing retaliation against Loyalists and wishing not to destroy lingering hopes of reconciliation, Howe spared the city from the torch, but the departing troops left it in a shambles. "Almost everything here, appears Gloomy and Melancholy," lamented one returning resident.

For a half dozen years after Boston's evacuation, British ships prowled the New England coast, confiscating supplies and attacking coastal towns. Yet away from the coast, there was little fighting. Most New Englanders had reason to be thankful for their good fortune.

The British established their new military headquarters in New York City, a site that offered important strategic advantages: a central location, a spacious harbor, control of the Hudson River route to the interior, and access to the abundant grain and livestock of the Middle Atlantic states. In addition, Loyalist sentiment ran deep among the inhabitants of the city and its environs.

In the summer of 1776, Washington moved his troops south from Boston, determined to challenge the British for control of New York City. It proved a terrible mistake. Outmaneuvered and badly outnumbered, he suffered defeat on Long Island and then in Manhattan itself. By late October, the city was firmly in British hands. It would remain so until the war's end.

In the fall of 1776, King George III instructed his two chief commanders in North America, the brothers General William and Admiral Richard Howe, to make a final effort at reconciliation with the colonists. In early September, they met with three delegates from the Congress on Staten Island, in New York harbor. But when the Howes demanded revocation of the Declaration of Independence before negotiations could begin, all hope of reconciliation vanished.

For the next two years, the war swept back and forth across New Jersey and Pennsylvania. Reinforced by German mercenaries hired in Europe, the British moved virtually at will. Neither the state militias nor the continental army—weakened by losses, low morale, and inadequate supplies—offered serious opposition. At Trenton in December 1776 and at Princeton the following month, Washington surprised the British and scored victories that prevented the Americans' collapse. Survival, however, remained the rebels' primary goal.

American efforts during the first year of the war to invade British Canada and bring it into the rebellion also fared badly. In November 1775, American forces had taken Montréal. But the subsequent assault against Québec ended with almost 100 Americans killed or wounded and more than 300 taken prisoner. The American cause could not survive many such losses.

Washington had learned the painful lesson at New York that his troops were no match for the British in frontal combat. He realized, moreover, that if the continental army was defeated, American independence would certainly be lost. Thus, he decided to harass the British, making the war as costly for them as possible, and protect the civilian population as best he could while avoiding major battles. He would follow that strategy for the rest of the war.

As a consequence, the war's middle years turned into a deadly chase that neither side proved able to win. In September 1777, the British took Philadelphia, sending the Congress fleeing into the countryside, but then hesitated to press their advantage. On numerous occasions British commanders failed to act decisively, either reluctant to move through the hostile countryside or uncertain of their instructions. In October 1777, the Americans won an important victory at Saratoga, New York, where General John Burgoyne surrendered with 5,700 British soldiers. That victory prompted France to join the struggle against England.

Congress and the Articles of Confederation

As war erupted, the Continental Congress turned to the task of creating a more permanent and effective national government. It was a daunting assignment, for prior to independence the colonies had quarreled repeatedly over conflicting boundaries, control of the Native American trade, and commercial advantage within the empire. The crisis with England had forced them together, and the Congress embodied that tenuous union.

As long as hopes of reconciliation with England lingered, the Congress's uncertain authority posed no serious problems. But as independence and the prospects for an extended war loomed, pressure to establish a more durable government increased. On June 20, 1776, shortly before independence was declared, Congress appointed a committee, chaired by John Dickinson of Pennsylvania, to draw up a plan of perpetual union. So urgent was the crisis that the committee responded in a month's time, and debate on the proposed Articles of Confederation quickly began.

The delegates promptly clashed over whether to form a strong, consolidated government or a loose confederation of sovereign states. As the debate went on, those differences sharpened. Dickinson's draft, outlining a government of considerable power, generated strong opposition. American experience with a "tyrannous" king and Parliament had revealed the dangers of a central government unmindful of the people's liberties.

As finally approved, the Articles of Confederation represented a compromise. Article 9 gave the Congress

Western Land Claims Ceded by the States, 1782–1802

Seven of the original states laid claim, based on their colonial charters, to lands west of the Appalachian Mountains. Eventually the states ceded those lands to Congress, thus making ratification of the Articles of Confederation and the creation of new western states possible. Why were the western claims such a problem?

sole authority to regulate foreign affairs, declare war, mediate boundary disputes between the states, manage the post office, and administer relations with Native Americans living outside state boundaries. The Articles also stipulated that the inhabitants of each state were to enjoy the "privileges and immunities" of the citizens of every other state. Embedded in that clause was the basis for national, as distinguished from state, citizenship.

At the same time, the Articles sharply limited what the Congress could do and reserved broad governing powers to the states. For example, the Congress could neither raise troops nor levy taxes but could only ask the states for such support. Article 2 stipulated that each state was to "retain its sovereignty, freedom and independence," as well as "every power . . . which is not by this confederation expressly delegated to the United States in Congress assembled." Nor could the Congress's limited powers be easily expanded, because the Articles could be amended only by the unanimous agreement of all 13 states.

Though the Congress sent the Articles to the states for approval in November 1777, they were not ratified until March 1781. Ratification required approval by all the states, and that was hard to obtain. The biggest impediment was a bitter dispute over control of the lands west of the Appalachian Mountains. Some states had western claims tracing back to their colonial charters, but other states, such as Maryland and New Jersey, did not. In December 1778, the Maryland assembly announced that it would not ratify until all the western lands had been ceded to Congress. For several years, ratification hung in the balance while politicians and land speculators jockeyed for advantage. Finally, in 1780, New York and Virginia agreed to give up their western lands. Those decisions paved the way for Maryland's ratification in early 1781. Approval of the Articles was now assured.

Meanwhile, Congress managed the war effort as best it could, using the unratified Articles as a guide. Events quickly proved its inadequacy, because Congress could do little more than pass resolutions and implore the states for support. If they refused, as they frequently did, Congress could only protest and urge cooperation. Its ability to function was further limited by the stipulation that each state's delegation cast but one vote. Disagreements within state delegations sometimes prevented them from voting at all. That could paralyze Congress, because most important decisions required a nine-state majority.

As the war dragged on, Washington repeatedly criticized Congress for its failure to support the army. Acknowledging its own ineffectiveness, Congress in 1778 temporarily granted Washington extraordinary powers, asking him to manage the war on his own. In the end, Congress survived because enough of its members realized that disaster would follow its collapse.

The War Moves South

As the war in the North bogged down in a costly stalemate, British officials adopted an alternative strategy: invasion and pacification of the South.

Royal officials in the South encouraged the idea with reports that thousands of Loyalists would rally to the British standard. The southern coastline with its numerous rivers, moreover, offered maximum advantage to British naval strength. Moreover, if the countless slaves could be lured to the British side, the balance might tip in Britain's favor. Even the threat of slave rebellion would weaken white southerners' will to resist. Persuaded by these arguments, the British shifted the war's focus to the South during the final years of the conflict.

Georgia—small, isolated, and largely defenseless—was the initial target. In December 1778, Savannah, the state's major port, fell to a seaborne attack. For nearly two years, the Revolution in the state virtually ceased. Encouraged by their success, the British turned to the Carolinas, with equally impressive results. On May 12, 1780, Charleston surrendered after a month's siege. At a cost of only 225 casualties, the British captured the entire

Military Operations in the South, 1778–1781

The war in the South, as in the North (see the map on p. 191), was fought along the coast and in the interior, while British and French forces battled as well in the West Indies. Important water routes shaped the course of the war from its beginning to the end. Why was this so?

Cornwallis's Surrender at Yorktown Though this painting by John Trumbull captures the drama of the British surrender at Yorktown, it misrepresents one interesting fact. Asserting that he was ill, Lord Cornwallis sent a subordinate officer to yield the symbolic sword of surrender. *(John Trumbull,* The Surrender of Lord Cornwallis at Yorktown, *19 October 1781, Architect of the Capitol)*

5,400-man American garrison. It was the costliest American defeat of the war.

After securing Charleston, the British quickly extended their control north and south along the coast. At Camden, South Carolina, the British killed nearly 1,000 Americans and captured 1,000 more, temporarily destroying the southern continental army. With scarcely a pause, the British pushed on into North Carolina. There, however, British officers quickly learned the difficulty of extending their lines into the interior: distances were too large, problems of supply too great, the reliability of Loyalist troops too uncertain, and popular support for the revolutionary cause too strong.

In October 1780, Washington sent Nathanael Greene south to lead the continental forces. It was a fortunate choice, for Greene knew the region and the kind of war that had to be fought. Determined, like Washington, to avoid large-scale encounters, Greene divided his army into small, mobile bands. Employing what today would be called guerrilla tactics, he harassed the British and their Loyalist allies at every opportunity, striking by surprise and then disappearing into the interior. Nowhere was the war more fiercely contested than through the Georgia and Carolina backcountry. Neither British nor American authorities could restrain the violence. Bands of private marauders, roving the land and seizing advantage from the war's confusion, compounded the chaos.

In time, the tide began to turn. At Cowpens, South Carolina, in January 1781, American troops under General Daniel Morgan won a decisive

victory, suffering fewer than 75 casualties to 329 British deaths and taking 600 men prisoner. In March, at Guilford Court House in North Carolina, Cornwallis won, but at a cost that forced his retreat to Wilmington, near the sea.

In April 1781, convinced that British authority could not be restored in the Carolinas while the rebels continued to use Virginia as a supply and staging area, the British commander Cornwallis moved north. With a force of 7,500, he raided deep into Virginia, sending Governor Jefferson and the Virginia legislature fleeing from Charlottesville into the mountains. But again Cornwallis found the costs of victory high, and again he turned back to the coast for protection and resupply. On August 1, he reached Yorktown.

Cornwallis's position was secure as long as the British fleet controlled Chesapeake Bay, but that advantage did not last long. In 1778, the French government, still smarting from its defeat by England in the Seven Years' War and buoyed by the American victory at Saratoga in 1777, had signed an alliance with the Congress, promising to send its naval forces into the war. Initially, the French concentrated their fleet in the West Indies, hoping to seize some of the British sugar islands. But on August 30, 1781, after repeated American urging, the French admiral Comte de Grasse arrived off Yorktown. Reinforced by a second French squadron from the North, de Grasse established naval superiority in Chesapeake Bay. At the same time, Washington's continentals, supplemented by French troops, marched south from Pennsylvania.

As Washington had foreseen, French entry turned the tide of war. Cut off from the sea and pinned down on a peninsula between the York and James Rivers by 17,000 French and American troops, Cornwallis saw his fate sealed. On October 19, 1781, near the hamlet of Yorktown, he surrendered. While a military band played "The World Turned Upside Down" and hundreds of

The American Revolution

civilians looked on, nearly 7,000 British troops laid down their arms.

Learning the news in London a month later, Lord North, the king's chief minister, exclaimed, "Oh, God! It is all over." On February 27, 1782, the House of Commons cut off further support of the war. North resigned the following month. In Philadelphia, citizens poured into the streets to celebrate while the Congress assembled for a solemn ceremony of thanksgiving. Though the preliminary articles of peace were not signed until November 1782, everyone knew after Yorktown that the Americans had won their independence.

Native Americans in the Revolution

The Revolutionary War drew in countless Native Americans as well as colonists and Englishmen. It could hardly have been otherwise, for the lives of all three peoples had been intertwined since the first English settlements more than a century earlier.

By the time of the revolution, the major coastal tribes had been decimated by warfare and disease, their villages displaced by white settlement. Powerful tribes, however, still dominated the interior between the Appalachians and the Mississippi River. The Iroquois Six Nations, a confederation numbering 15,000 people, controlled the area from the Hudson River to the Ohio valley. In the Southeast, five tribes—the Choctaw, Chickasaw, Seminole, Creek, and Cherokee, 60,000 people in all—dominated the interior.

The interior tribes were more than a match, militarily and diplomatically, for the few white settlers who had pushed across the Appalachians. As the imperial crisis between England and its colonies deepened, Native and European Americans eyed each other warily across this vast "middle ground."

When the Revolutionary War began, British and American officials urged the Native Americans to remain neutral. The Native Americans, however, were too important militarily for either side to ignore. By the spring of 1776, both were seeking Native American alliances. Recognizing their stake in the conflict, Native Americans up and down the interior debated their options.

Alarmed by encroaching white settlement and eager to take advantage of the colonists' troubles with England, a band of Cherokee, led by the warrior Dragging Canoe, launched a series of raids in July 1776 in what is today eastern Tennessee. In retaliation, Virginia and Carolina militias laid waste a group of Cherokee towns. Thomas Jefferson expressed satisfaction at the outcome. "I hope that the Cherokees will now be driven beyond the Mississippi," he wrote. "Our contest with Britain is too serious . . . to permit any possibility of [danger] . . . from the Indians." The Cherokee never again mounted a sustained military effort against the rebels. Seeing what had befallen their neighbors, the Creek stayed aloof. Their time for resistance would come in the early nineteenth century, when white settlers began to push onto their lands.

In the Ohio country, the struggle lasted longer. For several decades before the Revolution, explorers such as Daniel Boone had contested with the Shawnee and others for control of the region bordering the Ohio River. The Revolutionary War intensified these conflicts. In February 1778, George Rogers Clark led a ragtag band of Kentuckians through icy rivers and across 180 miles of forbidding terrain to attack a British outpost at Vincennes, in present-day Indiana. Though heavily outnumbered, Clark fooled the British troops and their Native American allies into believing that his force was much larger, and the British surrendered without a shot. Though skirmishes between Native Americans and marauding American forces continued for several years, Clark's victory tipped the balance in the war's western theater.

The Devastation of the Iroquois

To the northeast, an even more deadly scenario unfolded. At a council in Albany, New York, in August 1775, representatives of the Iroquois Six Nations listened while American commissioners urged them to remain at home and keep the hatchet buried deep. "The determination of the Six Nations,"

Joseph Brant   Mohawk chief Joseph Brant (Thayendanegea) played a major role in the Iroquois's decision to enter the war on the side of Britain. Can you identify the symbols of authority in his dress? *(National Gallery of Canada)*

replied Little Abraham, a Mohawk leader, "[is] not to take any part; but as it is a family affair, to sit still and see you fight it out." Iroquois neutrality, however, did not last long.

After U.S. troops raided deep into Mohawk territory west of Albany, the British urged the Iroquois to join them against the rebels. Most did so in the summer of 1777, at the urging of Joseph Brant, a Mohawk warrior who had visited England several years earlier and proclaimed England's value as an ally against American expansion.

It was a fateful decision for Native Americans and whites alike. Over the next several years, the Iroquois and their British allies devastated large areas in central New York and Pennsylvania. An officer of the Pennsylvania militia reported somberly, "Our country is on the eve of breaking up. There is nothing to be seen but disolation, fire & smoak."

The Americans' revenge came swiftly. During the summer of 1779, General John Sullivan led a series of punishing raids into the Iroquois country, burning villages; killing men, women, and children; and destroying fields of corn. His motto was blunt: "Civilization or death to all American savages." By war's end, the Iroquois had lost as many as one-third of their people as well as countless towns. Their domination of the northeastern interior was permanently shattered.

Not all the Eastern Woodland tribes sided with England in the Revolutionary War. The Oneida and the Tuscarora, members of the Iroquois confederation, fought with the Americans, their decision driven by intertribal politics and effective diplomacy by emissaries of the Continental Congress. In New England, the Stockbridge, a small tribe surrounded by a sea of white settlement, contributed warriors and scouts, while farther to the south the Catawba, similarly dependent on the Americans for trade and diplomacy, also signed on. The Native Americans who fought for American independence, however, reaped little reward. Though General Sullivan spared the Oneida and Tuscarora villages, the British and their Iroquois allies destroyed them in turn. And although a number of Native American warriors were compensated by grateful state governments once the war was over, tribes allied with the victorious American cause enjoyed no protection from the accelerating spread of white settlement.

Most Native Americans had sound reason for opposing American independence, because England provided them with trade goods, arms, and markets for their furs. England, moreover, had promised protection against colonial expansion, as the Proclamation Line of 1763 had demonstrated. Yet at the peace talks that ended the Revolutionary War, the British ignored their Native American allies. They received neither compensation for their losses nor guarantees of their land, for the boundary of the United States was set far to the west, at the Mississippi River.

Though the Native Americans' struggle against white expansion would continue, their own anticolonial war of liberation had failed. The American Revolution, declared a gathering of Native American chiefs to the Spanish governor at St. Louis in 1784, had been "the greatest blow that could have been dealt us."

Negotiating Peace

In September 1781, formal peace negotiations began in Paris between the British commissioner, Richard Oswald, and the American emissaries—Benjamin Franklin, John Adams, and John Jay. The negotiations were complicated by the involvement in the war of several European countries seeking to weaken Great Britain. The Americans' main ally, France, had entered the war in February 1778. Eight months later, Spain declared war on England, though it declined to recognize American independence. Between 1780 and 1782, Russia, the Netherlands, and six other European countries joined in a League of Armed Neutrality aimed at protecting their maritime trade against British depredations. America's Revolutionary War had quickly become internationalized. It could hardly have been otherwise, given England's centrality to the European balance of power and the long-standing competition among European powers for colonial dominance in North America.

Dependent on French economic and military support, Congress instructed the American commissioners to follow the advice of the French foreign minister Charles Vergennes. But as the American commissioners soon learned, Vergennes was prepared to let the exhausting war continue in order to weaken England and tighten America's dependence on France. Even more alarming, Vergennes suggested that the new nation's boundary should be set no farther west than the crest of the Appalachian Mountains, and he hinted that the British might retain areas they controlled at the war's end. That would have left New York City and other coastal enclaves in British hands.

In the end, the American commissioners ignored their instructions and, without a word to Vergennes, arranged a provisional peace agreement with the British emissaries. It was fortunate that they did so, for the British were prepared to be generous. In the Treaty of Paris signed in September 1783, England

American Peace Commissioners John Jay, John Adams, and Benjamin Franklin (the three figures on the left in the unfinished painting by Benjamin West) meet with the British commissioners in Paris to negotiate preliminary conditions of peace in 1783. *(Benjamin West, Commissioners of the Preliminary Peace Negotiations with Great Britain, c. 1783/Courtesy, Winterthur Museum)*

recognized American independence and agreed to set the western boundary of the United States at the Mississippi River. Britain promised as well that U.S. fishermen would have the right to fish the waters off Newfoundland and that British forces would evacuate American territory "with all convenient speed." In return, Congress would recommend that the states restore the rights and property of the Loyalists. Both sides agreed that prewar debts owed the citizens of one country by the citizens of the other would remain valid. Each of these issues would trouble Anglo-American relations in the years ahead, but for the moment it seemed a splendid outcome to a long and difficult struggle.

The Ingredients of Victory

In spite of English fears and congressional hopes, only half of Britain's New World colonies (13 out of 26) joined the rebellion against British authority. Congressional efforts to enlist Canadian support foundered. Canada's location at the western end of the North Atlantic sea routes made it a center of British military force. The colony's French Catholic majority, moreover, harbored bitter memories of conflicts during the Seven Years' War with England's Protestant colonists to the south.

Congress made overtures as well to white planters on Jamaica and other British sugar islands in the Caribbean. But the islands' sugar economies were heavily dependent on British markets. Planters depended as well on British military force for protection against Spanish and Dutch raiders, to say nothing of the slave majorities in their midst. Reports that slavery was being questioned in some of the rebellious colonies struck fear into planters' hearts.

Even without the support of Canada and the Caribbean islands, the 13 weak and disunited North American states were able to defeat Great Britain, the most powerful nation in the Atlantic world. How was that so? Certainly Dutch loans and French military resources were crucially important. At the height of the war, France fielded a force of more than 10,000 men in North America.

More decisive, though, was the American people's determination not to submit. Often the Americans were disorganized and uncooperative. Repeatedly, the war effort seemed about to collapse as continental troops drifted away, state militias refused to march, and supplies failed to materialize. Neither Congress nor the states proved capable of providing consistent direction to the struggle. Yet as the war progressed, the people's estrangement from England deepened and their commitment to the "glorious cause" grew stronger. To subdue the colonies, England would have had to occupy the entire eastern third of the continent, and that it could not do.

Even though state militias frequently refused to go beyond their own borders and after the first months of the war engaged in relatively few battles, they provided a vast reservoir of manpower capable of intimidating Loyalists, gathering intelligence, and harassing British forces that would otherwise have been free to engage the continental army. And though Washington frequently disparaged the militia's fighting qualities, he gradually learned to utilize them in the war effort.

The American victory owed much as well to Washington's organizational talents. Against massive odds,

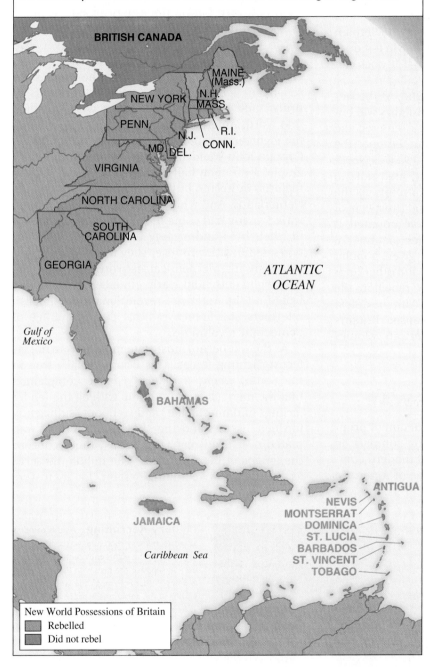

England's American Empire Divides

The majority of England's New World colonies did not rebel in 1776. **Reflecting on the Past** What difference would it have made if Canada and England's Caribbean colonies had joined the 13 North American colonies in throwing off English rule?

New World Possessions of Britain
- Rebelled
- Did not rebel

enjoyed clear military superiority over the Americans. Its troops were more numerous, better armed and supplied, and more professional. Until the closing months of the contest, Britain enjoyed naval superiority as well, enabling its forces to move up and down the coast virtually at will.

Britain, however, could not capitalize on its advantages. It had difficulty extending its command structures and supply routes across several thousand miles of ocean. As a result, decisions made in London were often based on faulty or outdated intelligence. Given the difficulties of supply, British troops often had to live off the land, thus reducing their mobility and increasing the resentment of Americans whose crops and animals they commandeered.

Faced with these circumstances, British leaders were often overly cautious. Burgoyne's attempt in 1777 to isolate New England by invading from Canada failed because Sir William Howe decided to attack Philadelphia rather than move northward up the Hudson River to join him. Similarly, neither Howe nor Cornwallis pressed his advantage in the central states during the middle years of the war, when more aggressive action might have crushed the continentals.

Just as important, British commanders generally failed to adapt European battlefield tactics to the realities of the American war. They were willing to fight only during specified times of the year and used formal battlefield maneuvers, even though the wooded American terrain was better suited to the use of smaller units and irregular tactics.

often by the sheer force of his will, he held the continental army together and created a military force capable of winning selected encounters and surviving over time. Had he failed, the Americans could not possibly have won.

In the end, however, it is as accurate to say that Britain lost the war as that the United States won it. With vast economic and military resources, Britain

Washington and Greene were more flexible, often employing a patient strategy of raiding, harassment, and strategic retreat. Guiding this strategy was a willingness, grounded in necessity, to allow England control of territory along the coast. But it was based as well on the conviction that popular support for the revolutionary cause would grow and that the costs of subduing the colonial rebellion would become greater than the British government could bear. As a much later American war in Vietnam would also reveal, a guerrilla force can win if it does not lose, while a regular army loses if it does not consistently win.

The American strategy proved sound. As the war dragged on and its costs escalated, Britain's will began to waver. After France and Spain entered the conflict, Britain had to worry about Europe, the Caribbean, and the Mediterranean as well as North America, while unrest in Ireland and food riots in London tied down additional English troops. As the cost in money and lives increased and prospects of victory dimmed, opposition to the war mounted. It was spearheaded by longtime critics of imperial policy such as Edmund Burke and given popular voice by the followers of John Wilkes and other English radicals who saw in America's rebellion the promise of political reform at home. With the defeat at Yorktown, support for the war collapsed. Britain's effort to hold on to its 13 North American colonies had failed.

THE EXPERIENCE OF WAR

In terms of the loss of life and destruction of property, the Revolutionary War pales by comparison with America's more recent wars. Yet modern comparisons are misleading, for the War of American Independence proved terrifying to the people caught up in it.

Recruiting an Army

Estimates vary, but on the American side as many as 250,000 men may at one time or another have borne arms. That amounted to one out of every two or three adult white males. Though a majority of recruits were native born, many who fought for American freedom came from the thousands of British and European immigrants who streamed into North America during the middle decades of the eighteenth century. Of the 27 men enrolled in Captain John Wendell's New York company, for example, more than half had been born abroad, the majority in Ireland but others in Germany and the Netherlands. And while the motives of these men varied, many had come to America seeking to better their lives and eagerly embraced the Revolution's democratic promise. They were the vanguard of a transatlantic political network that, over the late eighteenth and early nineteenth centuries, would tie the American revolutionaries to English reformers and French radicals during the age of democratic revolutions.

As the war began, most state militias were not effective fighting forces. This was especially true in the South, where Nathanael Greene complained that the men "came from home with all the tender feelings of domestic life" and were not "sufficiently fortified . . . to stand the shocking scenes of war, march over dead men, [or] hear without concern the groans of the wounded." The militia did serve as a convenient recruiting system, for men were

Military Recruiting   As this painting suggests, military recruiting was a community affair in the eighteenth century. What do you suppose the man with upraised arms is doing? What role might the women be playing in the recruitment process? *(William T. Ranney, Recruiting for the Continental Army, c. 1857–59, oil on canvas, 53³/₄ x 82¹/₄ in. Munson-Williams-Proctor Art Institute, Museum of Art, Utica, New York, [58.284])*

American Uniforms This watercolor painting offers a humorous, even mocking, depiction of the variety of uniforms worn by American troops. *(Anne S. K. Brown Military Collection, Brown University)*

already enrolled and arrangements were in place for calling them into the field on short notice. Given its grounding in local community life, the militia also legitimated the war among the people and secured their commitment to the revolutionary cause. And what better way to separate Patriots from Loyalists than by mustering the local company and seeing who turned out?

During the early years of the war, when enthusiasm ran high, men of all ranks—from the rich and middle classes as well as the poor—volunteered to fight the British. But as the war went on, casualties increased, enlistment terms grew longer, military discipline became harsher, and the army filled with conscripts. Eventually, the war was transformed, as wars so often are, into a poor man's fight as wealthier men hired substitutes and communities filled their quotas with strangers lured by enlistment bonuses. Convicts, out-of-work laborers, free and unfree blacks, and even British deserters filled the continental army with an array of "Tag, Rag, and Bobtail" soldiers.

For the poor and the jobless, whose ranks the war rapidly swelled, military bonuses and the promise of board and keep proved attractive. But often the bonuses failed to materialize, and pay was long overdue. Moreover, life in the camps was harsh, and soldiers frequently learned of their families' distress. As the war dragged on and desertion rates rose as high as 25 percent, Washington imposed harsher discipline in an effort to hold his troops in line.

Occasionally, frustration spilled over into open revolt. In 1779, Sergeant Samuel Glover and a group of soldiers from the North Carolina line, who had been unpaid for 15 months, refused to obey the commands of their superior officer "until they had justice done them." Glover was executed for insubordination. His widow later apologized to the North Carolina assembly for her husband's conduct but asked sorrowfully, "What must the feeling of the man be who . . . with poverty staring him full in the face, was denied his pay?"

Throughout the war, soldiers suffered from shortages of supplies. At Valley Forge during the terrible winter of 1777–1778, men went without shoes or coats. Declared one anguished soul, "I am sick, discontented, and out of humour. Poor food, hard lodging, cold weather, fatigue, nasty cloathes, nasty cookery, vomit half my time, smoked out of my senses. The Devil's in't, I can't Endure it. Why are we sent here to starve and freeze?"

George Washington at Valley Forge

Neither state governments nor Congress could effectively administer a war of such magnitude. Though many individuals served honorably as supply officers, others exploited the army's distress. Washington commented bitterly on the "speculators, various tribes of money makers, and stock-jobbers" whose "avarice and thirst for gain" threatened the country's ruin.

Swarms of camp followers further complicated army life. Wives and prostitutes, personal servants

RECOVERING THE PAST

Military Muster Rolls

In almost all of America's wars, patriotism has run high and bombastic rhetoric has inspired citizens to arms. The American Revolution was no exception. But people fought for other than patriotic reasons, as the account of "Long Bill" Scott makes clear. It is always difficult to assess human motivations in something as complex as war. If we knew which Americans bore arms, however, it would help us understand why people fought and perhaps even understand what the war meant to them.

The social composition of the revolutionary army changed markedly as the war went along. At the beginning, men from all walks of life and every class fought in defense of American liberty. However, as the war lengthened and its costs increased, men who could afford to do so hired substitutes or arranged to go home, whereas men of less wealth and influence increasingly carried the burden of fighting. Many of them did so out of choice, for the army promised adventure, an escape from the tedium of daily life, a way to make a living, and even, as for "Long Bill" Scott, the chance to rise in the world. Thus thousands of poorer men hired out to defend American liberty. Such a decision was attractive to them because their opportunities were limited.

Enlistment lists of the continental army and the state militias offer one important source for studying the social history of the Revolutionary War. Although eighteenth-century records are imperfect by modern standards, recruiting officers did keep track of the men they signed up so that bounties and wages could be paid accurately. These lists usually give the recruit's name, age, occupation, place of birth, residence, and length of service.

Such lists exist for some of America's earliest wars. The muster rolls for New York City and Philadelphia during the Seven Years' War, for example, show that these two cities contributed 300 and 180 men per year, respectively, to the war effort. Most of the enlistees in that earlier war were immigrants—about 90 percent of New York's recruits and about 75 percent of Philadelphia's. Their occupations—mariner, laborer, shoemaker, weaver, tailor—indicate that they came primarily from the lowest ranks of the working class. Many were former indentured servants and many others were servants running away from their masters to answer the recruiting sergeant's drum. In these Middle Atlantic port towns, successful, American-born artisans left the bloody work of bearing arms against the French to those beneath them on the social ladder. Enlistment lists for Boston, however, reveal that soldiers from that city were drawn from higher social classes.

A comparison of the Revolutionary War muster rolls from different towns and regions provides a view of the social composition of the revolutionary army and how it changed over time. It also offers clues to social conditions in different regions during the war and how they might have affected military recruitment.

The lists shown here of Captain Wendell's and Captain White's companies from New York and Virginia give "social facts" on 81 men. What kind of group portrait can you draw from the data? Some occupations, such as tanner, cordwainer, and chandler, may be unfamiliar, but they are defined in standard dictionaries. How many of the recruits come from middling occupations (bookkeeper, tobacconist, shopkeeper, and the like)? How many are skilled artisans? How many are unskilled laborers? What proportions are foreign and native born? Analyze the ages of the recruits. What does that tell you about the kind of fighting force that was assembled? How do the New York and Virginia companies differ in terms of these social categories and occupations? How would you explain these differences?

To extract the full meaning of the soldiers' profile, you would have to learn more about the economic and social conditions prevailing in the communities from which these men are drawn. But already you have glimpsed how social historians go beyond the history of military strategy, tactics, and battles to understand the "internal" social history of the Revolutionary War.

REFLECTING ON THE PAST   How would social historians describe and analyze more recent American wars? What would a social profile of soldiers who fought in Vietnam or Iraq, including their age, region, race, class, extent of education, and other differences, suggest to a social historian of these wars?

New York Line—1st Regiment

Captain John H. Wendell's Company, 1776–1777

Men's Names	Age	Occupation	Place of Birth	Place of Abode
Abraham Defreest	22	Yeoman	N. York	Claverack
Benjamin Goodales	20	do [ditto]	Nobletown	do
Hendrick Carman	24	do	Rynbeck	East Camp
Nathaniel Reed	32	Carpenter	Norwalk	Westchester
Jacob Crolrin	29	do	Germany	Bever Dam
James White	25	Weaver	Ireland	Rynbveck
Joseph Battina	39	Coppersmith	Ireland	Florida
John Wyatt	38	Carpenter	Maryland	
Jacob Reyning	25	Yeoman	Amsterdam	Albany
Patrick Kannely	36	Barber	Ireland	N. York
John Russell	29	Penman	Ireland	N. York
Patrick McCue	19	Tanner	Ireland	Scholary
James J. Atkson	21	Weaver	do	Stillwater
William Burke	23	Chandler	Ireland	N. York
Wm Miller	42	Yeoman	Scotland	Claverack
Ephraim H. Blancherd	18	Yeoman	Ireland	White Creek
Francis Acklin	40	Cordwainer	Ireland	Claverack
William Orr	29	Cordwainer	Ireland	Albany
Thomas Welch	31	Labourer	N. York	Norman's Kill
Peter Gasper	24	Labourer	N. Jersey	Greenbush
Martins Rees	19	Labourer	Fishkill	Flatts
Henck Able	24	do	Albany	Flatts
Daniel Spinnie	21	do	Portsmouth	
Patrick Kelly	23	Labourer	Ireland	Claverack
Richd James Barker	12	do	America	Rynbeck
John Patrick Cronkite	11			Claverack
William Dougherty	17		Donyal, Ireland	Sch^ty

Virginia Line—6th Regiment

Captain Tarpley White's Company, December 13th, 1780

Name	Age	Trade	Where Born State or Country	Town or County	Place of Residence State or Country	Town or County	Name	Age	Trade	Where Born State or Country	Town or County	Place of Residence State or Country	Town or County
Win Bails, Serjt	25	Baker	England	Burningham	Virg.	Leesburg	Joseph Holburt	33	Tailor	"	Middlesex	"	Federickb^g
Arthur Harrup"	24	Carpenter	Virg.	Southampton	"	Brunswick	Henry Willowby	19	Planter	Virg.	Spotsylvania	"	Spotsylvania
Charles Caffatey"	19	Planter	"	Caroline	"	Caroline	Thos Pearson	22	Planter		Pennsylvany	"	Loudon
Elisha Osborn"	24	Planter	New Jersey	Trenton	"	Loudon	Jno Scarborough	19	Planter	Virg.	Brunswick	"	"
Benj Allday	19	"	Virg.	Henrico	"	Pawhatan	Chas Thacker	21	Planter	"	"	"	"
Wm Edwards Senr	25	"	"	Northumberland	"	Northumberland	Nehemiah Grining	20	Planter	Virg.	Albemarle	Virg.	Albemarle
James Hutcherson	17	Hatter	Jersey	Middlesex	"	P.Williams	Ewing David	19	Planter	"	King W^m	"	Brunswick
Robert Low	31	Planter	"	Powhatan	"	Powhatan	Isaiah Ballance	17	Shoemaker	"	Norfolk	"	Norfolk
Cannon Row	18	Planter	Virg.	Hanover	Virg.	Louisa	Wm Alexander	20	Planter	Virg.	Northumbl^d	Virg.	Northumbl^d
Wardon Pulley	18	"	"	Southampton	"	Hallifax	Wm Harden	26	Planter	"	Albemarle	"	Albemarle
Richd Bond	29	Stone Mason	England	Cornwell	"	Orange	John Ward	20	Sailor	England	Bristol	"	Northumbl^d
Tho Homont	17	Planter	Virg.	Loudon	"	Loudon	Daniel Cox	19	Planter	Virg.	Sussex	"	Sussex
Tho Pope	19	Planter	"	Southampton	"	Southampton	George Kirk	21	Planter	"	Brunswick	"	Brunswick
Tho Morris	22	Planter	"	Orange	"	Orange	John Nash	19	Planter	"	Northumbl^d	"	Northumbl^d
Littlebury Overby	24	Hatter	"	Dinwiddie	"	Brunswick	Wm Edward, Jr.	19	Planter	"	Northumbl^d	"	Northumbl^d
James [Pierce]	27	Planter	"	Nansemond	"	Nansemond	John Fry	20	Turner	"	Albemarle	"	Albemarle
Joel Counsil	19	Planter	"	Southampton	"	Southampton	Jno Grining	25	Hatter	"	Albemarle	"	"
Elisha Walden	18	Planter	"	P.William	"	P.William	Daniel Howell	30	Planter	"	Loudon	"	Loudon
Wm Bush	19	S Carpenter	Virg.	Glocester	Virg.	Glocester	Milden Green	25	Planter	"	Sussex	"	Sussex
Daniel Horton	22	Carpenter	"	Nansemond	"	Nansemond	Matthias Cane	32	Planter	"	Norfolk	"	Norfolk
John Soons	25	Weaver	England	Norfolk	"	Loudon	Wm Mayo	21	Joiner	"	Dinwiddie	"	Dinwiddie
Mara Lumkin	18	Planter	Virg.	Amelia	"	Amelia	Jas Morgan	25	Shoemaker	England	Shropshire	"	Stafford
Wm Wetherford	27	Planter	"	Goochland	"	Lunenburg	Mathew Catson	19	Planter	Pennsylvania	York	"	Berkly
John Bird	16	Planter	"	Southampton	"	Southampton	Wm B[rown]	22	Planter	"	"		
Tho Parsmore	22	Planter	England	London	"	Fairfax	Richd Loyd	42	Planter	Virg.	Surry	Virg.	Surry
Josiah Banks	27	Planter	Virg.	Gloucester	"	Gloucester	Abram Foress	33	Planter	"	Gloster	Virg.	Gloster
Richd Roach	28	Planter	England	London	"	Culpeper	Wm White	19	Planter	"	"		Gloster

203

and slaves, con men, and civilian provisioners swarmed around the continental army camps. While often providing essential services, they slowed the army's movement and threatened its discipline.

The Casualties of Combat

The death that soldiers dispensed to each other on the battlefield was intensely personal. Because the effective range of muskets was little more than 100 yards, soldiers came virtually face-to-face with the men they killed. According to eighteenth-century practice, armies formed on the battlefield in ranks and fired in unison. After massed volleys, the lines often closed for hand-to-hand combat with knives and bayonets. Such encounters were indelibly etched in the memory of individuals who survived them. Partisan warfare in the South, with its emphasis on ambush and cyclic patterns of revenge, personalized combat even more.

British officers expressed shock at the "implacable ardor" with which the Americans fought. The Americans' ferocity is attributable in part to the fact that this was a civil war. Not only did Englishmen fight Americans, but American Loyalists and Patriots fought each other as well. As many as 50,000 Americans fought for the king in some of the war's most bitter encounters. "The rage of civil discord," lamented one individual, "hath advanced among us with an astonishing rapidity. The son is armed against the father, the brother against the brother, family against family."

DOCUMENT

Letter from a
Revolutionary
War Soldier

The passion with which American Patriots fought derived as well from their belief that the very future of human liberty depended on their success. In such a historic crusade, nothing was to be spared that might bring victory.

Medical treatment, whether for wounds or the diseases that raged through military camps, frequently did more harm than good. Casualties poured into hospitals, overcrowding them beyond capacity. Dr. Jonathan Potts, the attending physician at Fort George in New York, reported that "we have at present upwards of one thousand sick crowded into sheds & labouring under the various and cruel disorders of dysentaries, bilious putrid fevers and the effects of a confluent smallpox. . . . " Surgeons, operating without anesthetics and with the crudest of instruments, threatened life as often as they preserved it. Few understood the causes or proper treatment of infection. Doctoring consisted mostly of bleeding, blistering, and vomiting. One doctor reported that "we lost no less than from 10 to 20 of camp diseases, for one by weapons of the enemy."

No one kept accurate records of how many soldiers died, but the most conservative estimate runs to more than 25,000, a higher percentage of the total population than for any other American conflict except the Civil War. For Revolutionary War soldiers, death was an imminent reality.

Civilians and the War

While the experience of war varied from place to place, it touched the lives of virtually every American. Noncombatants experienced the realities of war most intensely in densely settled areas along the coast. The British concentrated their military efforts there, taking advantage of their naval power and striking at the political and economic centers of American life. At one time or another, British troops occupied every major port city.

Urban dwellers suffered profound dislocations. About half of New York City's inhabitants fled when the British occupation began. They were replaced by an equal number of Loyalists from the surrounding countryside. An American officer somberly reported what he found as his troops entered New York at the war's end: "Close on the eve of an approaching winter, with an heterogeneous set of inhabitants, composed of almost ruined exiles, disbanded soldiery, mixed foreigners, disaffected Tories, and the refuse of the British army, we took possession of a ruined city."

In Philadelphia, the occupation was shorter and disruptions were less severe, but the shock of invasion was no less real. Elizabeth Drinker, living alone after local Patriots had exiled her Quaker husband, found herself the unwilling landlady of a British officer and his friends. Though the officer's presence may have protected her from the plundering that went on all around, she was constantly anxious, confiding to her journal that "I often feel afraid to go to Bed." During the occupation, British soldiers frequently tore down fences for their campfires and confiscated food to supplement their own tedious fare. Even Loyalists complained of the "dreadful consequences" of British occupation.

Along the entire coastal plain, British landing parties descended without warning, seizing supplies and terrorizing inhabitants. In 1780 and 1781, the British mounted punishing attacks along the Connecticut coast. More than 200 buildings in Fairfield were burned, and much of nearby Norwalk was destroyed. The southern coast, with its broad, navigable rivers, was even more vulnerable. In December 1780, Benedict Arnold, the American traitor who was by then fighting for the British, ravaged Virginia's James River valley, uprooting tobacco, confiscating slaves, and

New York City Burning In 1776, as the British took control of New York, nearly a quarter of the city was consumed by a fire apparently set by a defiant Patriot woman. Among the gutted buildings was the elegant Trinity Church, the tallest structure in the city. Not until the British evacuated in 1783 did reconstruction of the city begin. (*Library of Congress*)

creating panic among whites. Similar devastation befell the coastal regions of Georgia and the Carolinas.

Such punishing attacks sent civilians fleeing into the interior. During the first years of the war, the port cities lost nearly half their population, while inland communities struggled to cope with problems of housing, social order, and public health generated by the thousands of refugees who streamed into them.

Not all refugee traffic moved inland, away from the coast. Settlers from the interior fled eastward for safety as Loyalist rangers and their Native American allies fought Patriot militias in a violent, often chaotic struggle. According to one observer, after nearly five years of warfare in Tryon County in western New York, 12,000 farms had been abandoned, 700 buildings burned, thousands of bushels of grain destroyed, nearly 400 women widowed, and perhaps 2,000 children orphaned. Similar disasters unfolded up and down the backcountry from Maine to Georgia.

Wherever the armies went, they generated a swirl of refugees, who spread vivid tales of the war's devastation. This refugee traffic, together with the constant movement of soldiers between army and civilian life, brought the war home to countless people who did not experience it firsthand.

As they moved across the countryside, the armies lived off the land, taking what they needed. In New Jersey, Britain's German mercenaries raised additional fears, particularly among women. A committee of the Congress, taking affidavits from women in April 1777, reported that it had "authentic information of many instances of the most indecent treatment, and actual ravishment of married and single women." Such was the nature of that "most irreparable injury," however, that the women suffering it, "though perfectly innocent, look upon it as a kind of reproach to have the facts related and their names known." Whether the report had any effect is unknown.

Disease spread by the movement of people across the landscape ravaged populations as well. During the 1770s and 1780s, a smallpox epidemic surged across Mexico and North America, wreaking its devastating effects from the Atlantic coast to the Pacific, and from the Southwest to Hudson's Bay in Canada.

The human toll is impossible to measure exactly, but before the virus was spent it may have killed more than 130,000 people—Native Americans and Englishmen, African Americans and European Americans among them. Because a crash program of inoculation launched by Washington in 1777 (the first large-scale immunization program in American history) protected the continental army, and because many English troops carried immunity from earlier exposure to the disease at home, the plague did not significantly affect the war's outcome. Still, it took a terrible toll. In New England and the mid-Atlantic states it was spread by returning soldiers and Britain's disease-infested prison ships. In the Chesapeake, thousands of black Loyalists succumbed, while in the backcountry the virus raced through Native American populations, reducing their capacity to resist the rebels. Beyond the Mississippi, agricultural tribes such as the Mandan, Hidatsa, and Arikara were virtually wiped out. The pox, declared one observer gloomily, "spread its destructive and desolating power, as the fire consumes the dry grass of the field."

The Loyalists

Among the Americans suffering losses were those who remained loyal to the Crown. Though many Loyalist émigrés established successful lives in England, the Maritime Provinces of Canada, and the British West Indies, others found the uprooting an ordeal from which they never recovered. On September 8, 1783, Thomas Danforth, formerly a prosperous lawyer from Cambridge, Massachusetts, appeared in London before the official commission appointed to receive Loyalist claims. In explaining the consequences of his loyalty, Danforth declared that after devoting his whole life to "preparing himself for future usefulness," he was now "near his fortieth year, banished under pain of death, to a distant country, where he has not the most remote family connection … cut off from his profession, from every hope of importance in life." Without assistance he would sink to "a station much inferior to that of a menial servant," his financial affairs in disarray, his future uncertain. Many of the several thousand Loyalists who appeared before the king's commission gained partial reimbursement for their losses, though it proved meager compensation for the loss of house and property, expulsion from their communities, and relocation in a distant land. The vast majority of Loyalists never had the opportunity to make their case before the commission, and thus secured nothing.

Although we do not know how many colonists remained loyal to England, tens of thousands evacuated with British troops at the end of the war. At least as many slipped away to England, Canada, or the West Indies while fighting was still underway. Additional thousands who wished the Revolution

had never occurred stayed on in the new nation, struggling to rebuild their lives. The number of Loyalists varied from region to region. They were fewest in New England and most numerous around New York City, where British authority was most stable.

In each state, revolutionary assemblies exacted revenge against those who had rejected the revolutionary cause by enacting laws depriving Loyalists of the vote, confiscating their property, and banishing them from their homes. In 1778, the Georgia assembly declared 117 people guilty of treason, expelled them from the state on pain of death, and declared their possessions forfeit. Two years earlier, the Connecticut assembly had passed a remarkably punitive law threatening anyone who criticized either the assembly or the Continental Congress with immediate fine and imprisonment. Probably not more than a few dozen Loyalists actually died at the hands of the revolutionary regimes, but thousands found their livelihoods destroyed, their families ostracized, and themselves subject to physical attack.

The Tory's Day of Judgment

Punishing Loyalists—or people accused of being Loyalists, a distinction that was often unclear in the confusion of the times—was politically popular. Most Patriots argued that such "traitors" had put themselves outside the protection of American law. Others, however, argued that republics were intended to be "governments of law and not of men" and worried that no one's rights would be safe when the rights of any were disregarded. No other wartime issue raised so starkly the troubling question of balancing individual liberty against public security. That issue would return to trouble the nation in the years ahead.

Why did so many Americans remain loyal to the Crown, often at the cost of personal danger and loss? Royal appointees such as customs officers, members of the governors' councils, and Anglican clergy often remained with the king, as did members of groups dependent on British authority—for example, settlers on the Carolina frontier who believed themselves mistreated by the planter elite along the coast, and ethnic minorities such as Germans who feared domination by the Anglo-American majority. Other Loyalists made their choice because they believed it futile to oppose English power and doubted that independence could be won.

Still others based their decision on principle. "Every person owes obedience to the laws of the government," insisted Samuel Seabury, "and is obliged in honour and duty to support them. Because if one has a right to disregard the laws of the society to which he belongs, all have the same right;

AMERICAN VOICES

Anna Rawle, from her Diary, October 25, 1781

Anna Rawle was born to a Quaker family in Philadelphia. Her stepfather was a well known Loyalist, but she appears to have had a political mind of her own. She married a local merchant and remained in Philadelphia after the American Revolution. As her experience reveals, however, town residents who failed to join in the tumultuous celebration of the peace treaty ending the war risked hard handling by Patriot mobs.

I . . . would not have imagined . . . (our) house to be illuminated last night, but it was. A mob surrounded it, broke the shutters and the glass of the windows, and were coming in, none but forlorn women here. We for a time listened for their attacks in fear and trembling till, finding them grow more loud and violent . . . ran into the yard . . . . We had not been there many minutes before we were drove back by the sight of two men climbing the fence. We thought the mob were coming in . . . but it proved to be Coburn and Bob. Shewell, who called to us not to be frightened, and fixed lights up at the windows, which pacified the mob, and after three huzzas they moved off . . . . Even the firm Uncle Fisher was obliged to submit to have his windows illuminated, for they had pickaxes and iron bars with which they had done considerable injury to his house . . . . In short it was the most alarming scene I ever remember. For two hours we had the disagreeable noise of stones banging about, glass crashing, and the tumultuous voices of a large body of men, as they were a long time at the different houses in the neighborhood. At last they were victorious, and it was one general illumination throughout the town.

- *What do you make of her experience?*

- *Is it understandable, even justifiable given the circumstances?*

and then government is at an end." Another Loyalist worried about the kind of society independence would bring when revolutionary crowds showed no respect for the rights of dissenters such as he. "If I differ in opinion from the multitude," he asked, "must I therefore be deprived of my character, and the confidence of my fellow-citizens; when in every station of life I discharge my duty with fidelity and honour?" Such individuals claimed to be upholding reason and the rule of law against revolutionary disorder. Their defeat weakened conservatism in American society and promoted revolutionary change.

African Americans and the War

The revolution caught up thousands of American blacks in its toils. In the northern states, free and enslaved blacks were enlisted in support of the revolutionary cause. The South's nearly 400,000 slaves were viewed by the British as a resource to be exploited and by southern whites as a source of vulnerability and danger. Sizing up the opportunities provided by the war's confusion, southern blacks struck out for their own freedom by seeking liberty behind British lines, journeying to the north, or fleeing to mixed-race settlements in the interior. Before the war was over, the conflict generated the largest slave rebellion in American history prior to the Civil War.

Hearing their masters' talk about liberty, growing numbers of black Americans questioned their own

James Lafayette James Armistead Lafayette, a Virginia slave, served as a spy against the British for the French general Lafayette. In recognition of his service, the Virginia General Assembly granted him his freedom in 1786. *(James Armistead Lafayette, Valentine Museum, Richmond, VA)*

Resettlement of Black Loyalists After the Revolution

Thousands of American blacks departed the new nation with British troops at the end of the Revolutionary War. As the map indicates, their destinations varied. **Reflecting on the Past** How did resettlement outside the United States reshape the lives of black Loyalists?

oppression. In the North, slaves petitioned state legislatures for their freedom, while in the South, pockets of insurrection appeared. In 1765, more than 100 South Carolina slaves, most of them young men in their 20s and 30s, fled their plantations. The next year, slaves paraded through the streets of Charleston chanting, "Liberty, liberty!"

In November 1775, Lord Dunmore, Virginia's royal governor, issued a proclamation offering freedom to all slaves and servants "able and willing to bear arms" who would leave their masters and join the British forces at Norfolk. Within weeks, 500 to 600 slaves responded.

DOCUMENT

Proclamation of Lord Dunmore (November 14, 1775)

Among them was Thomas Peters, an African who had been kidnaped from the Yoruba tribe in what is now Nigeria and brought to Louisiana by a French slave trader in 1760. Peters resisted enslavement so fiercely that his master sold him into the English

colonies. By 1770, he was toiling on William Campbell's plantation on the Cape Fear River, near Wilmington, North Carolina.

Peters's plans for his own declaration of independence may have ripened as a result of the rhetoric of liberty he heard around his master's house, for William Campbell was a leading member of Wilmington's Sons of Liberty and talked enthusiastically about inalienable rights. By mid-1775, the Cape Fear region, like many areas of the coastal South, buzzed with rumors of slave uprisings. After the British commander of Fort Johnston encouraged Negroes to "elope from their masters," the state assembly banned the importation of new slaves, dispatched patrols to disarm all blacks, and imposed martial law. When 20 British ships entered the Cape Fear River in March 1776 and disembarked royal troops, Peters seized the moment to redefine himself as a man, instead of William Campbell's property, and escaped. Before long, he would fight with the British-officered Black Pioneers.

How many African Americans sought liberty behind British lines is unknown, but as many as 20 percent may have done so. Unlike their white masters, blacks saw in England the promise of freedom, not tyranny. As the war dragged on, English commanders pressed blacks into service. A regiment of black soldiers, formed from Virginia slaves who responded to Dunmore's proclamation, marched into battle, their chests covered by sashes emblazoned with the slogan "Liberty to Slaves."

Some of the blacks who joined England achieved their freedom. At the war's end, several thousand were evacuated with the British to Nova Scotia. Their reception by the white inhabitants, however, was generally hostile. By 1800, most had left Canada to help establish the free black colony of Sierra Leone in West Africa. Thomas Peters was a leader among them.

Many of the slaves who fled behind British lines, however, never won their freedom. Under the terms of the peace treaty, hundreds were returned to their American owners. Several thousand others, their value as field hands too great to be ignored, were transported to harsher slavery on West Indian sugar plantations.

Other blacks took advantage of the war's confusion to flee. Some went north, following rumors that slavery had been abolished there. Others sought refuge among Native Americans in the southern interior. The Seminole of Georgia and Florida generally welcomed black runaways and through intermarriage absorbed them into tribal society. Blacks met a more uncertain reception from the Cherokee and Creek. Some were taken in, others were returned to their white owners for bounties, and still others were held in slavelike conditions by new Native American masters.

Fewer blacks fought on the American side than on England's, in part because neither Congress nor the states were eager to see them armed. Faced with the increasing need for troops, however, the Congress and each of the states except Georgia and South Carolina eventually relented, pressing blacks into service. Of those who served the Patriot cause, many received the freedom they were promised. The patriotism of countless others, however, went unrewarded.

THE FERMENT OF REVOLUTIONARY POLITICS

The Revolution altered people's lives in countless ways that reached beyond the sights and sounds of battle. No areas of American life were more powerfully changed than politics and government. Who would have a voice in revolutionary politics, and who would be excluded? How vigorously would political equality be pursued, or how tenaciously would people cling to the traditional belief that citizens should defer to their political leaders? And how would the new state governments balance the need for order and the security of property against demands for democratic openness and accountability? These were some of the explosive questions that had to be addressed. Seldom has American politics been more heated; seldom has it struggled with more daunting problems than at the nation's founding.

Mobilizing the People

Under the pressure of revolutionary events, politics absorbed people's energies as never before. The politicization of American society was evident in the flood of printed material that streamed from American presses. Newspapers multiplied and pamphlets by the thousands fanned political debate. Declared one contemporary in amazement, it was

> a spectacle . . . without a parallel on earth. . . . Even a large portion of that class of the community which is destined to daily labor have free and constant access to public prints, receive regular information of every occurrence, [and] attend to the course of political affairs. Never were political writings so cheap, so universally diffused, so easy of access.

Pulpits rocked with political exhortations as well. Religion and politics had never been sharply separated in colonial America, but the Revolution drew them more tightly together. Some believed that God had designated America as the place of Christ's Second Coming and that independence foretold that glorious day. Others of a less millennial persuasion thought of America as a "New Israel"—a covenanted people specially chosen by God to preserve liberty in a threatening world. Giving the metaphor a classical twist, Samuel Adams called on Bostonians to join in creating a "Christian Sparta."

In countless sermons, Congregational, Presbyterian, and Baptist clergy exhorted the American people to repent the sins that had brought English tyranny upon them and urged them to rededicate themselves to God's purposes by fighting for American freedom. It was language that people nurtured in Puritan piety and the Great Awakening instinctively understood.

The belief that God sanctioned their revolution strengthened Americans' resolve. It also encouraged them to equate their own interests with divine intent

AMERICAN VOICES

Timothy Dwight, "Columbia, Columbia, To Glory Arise"

Many Americans believed that their revolution and the new nation that emerged from it were parts of a Providential plan for ushering in a dramatic new era of liberty, not only in North America but in Europe and other parts of the world as well. Timothy Dwight, New England clergyman, chaplain of a Connecticut Continental Brigade, and future president of Yale College, believed this to be true, as these excerpts from one of his poems clearly show.

"Columbia, Columbia, To Glory Arise" (1777)

Columbia, Columbia, to glory arise.
The queen of the world, and the child of the skies!
Thy genius commands thee; with rapture behold,
While ages on ages thy splendors unfold.
Thy reign is the last, and the noblest of time,

Most fruitful thy soil, most inviting thy clime;
Let the crimes of the east ne'er encrimson thy name,
Be freedom, and science, and virtue thy fame.

To conquest and slaughter let Europe aspire;
Whelm nations in blood, and wrap cities in fire;
Thy heroes the rights of mankind shall defend,
A world is thy realm: for a world be thy laws,
Enlarged as thine empire, and just as thy cause;
On Freedom's broad basis, that empire shall rise,
Extend with the main, and dissolve with the skies. . . .

- How does Dwight explain his belief in America's distinctive role in history?

- Do any of Dwight's themes continue to echo in our own time?

and thus offered convenient justification for whatever they believed necessary to do. This was not the last time Americans would make that dangerous equation.

By contrast, Loyalist clergy, such as Maryland's Jonathan Boucher, urged their parishioners to support the king as head of the Anglican church. During the months preceding independence, as the local Committee of Safety interrupted worship to harass him, Boucher carried a loaded pistol into the pulpit while he preached submission to royal authority.

Belief in the momentous importance of what they were doing increased the intensity of revolutionary politics. As independence was declared, people throughout the land raised toasts to the great event: "Liberty to those who have the spirit to preserve it," and "May Liberty expand sacred wings, and, in glorious effort, diffuse her influence o'er and o'er the

A Mock Parade Ordinary men and women took to the streets in political rallies, such as this mock parade of 1780 in Philadelphia, in which Benedict Arnold, an American general who deserted to the British, was burned in effigy. What do you suppose the two figures riding in the cart represent? (American Antiquarian Society)

globe." Inspired by the searing experience of rebellion, war, and nation building, Americans believed they held the future of human liberty in their hands. Small wonder that they took their politics so seriously.

The expanding array of extralegal crowds and committees that erupted during the 1770s and 1780s provided the most dramatic evidence of the people's new political commitment. Prior to independence, crowds had taken to the streets to protest measures like the Stamp Act. After 1776, direct political action increased as people gathered to administer rough-hewn justice to Loyalists and, as one individual protested, even direct "what we shall eat, drink, wear, speak, and think."

Patriots of more radical temperament defended these activities as legitimate expressions of the popular will. More conservative souls, however, worried that such behavior threatened political stability. Direct action by the people had been necessary in the struggle against England, but why such restlessness after the yoke of English tyranny had been thrown off? Even Thomas Paine expressed concern. "It is time to have done with tarring and feathering," he wrote in 1777. "I never did and never would encourage what may properly be called a mob, when any legal mode of redress can be had."

The expansion of popular politics resulted from an explosive combination of circumstances: the momentous events of revolution and war; the efforts of Patriot leaders to mobilize popular support for the struggle against England; and the determination of artisans, workers, farmers, and other common folk to apply the principles of liberty to the conditions of their own lives.

A Republican Ideology

As the American people moved from colonial subordination to independence, they struggled to establish their identity as a free and separate nation. What did it mean to be no longer English, but American? "Our style and manner of thinking," observed Thomas Paine, "have undergone a revolution. . . . We see with other eyes, we hear with other ears, and think with other thoughts than those we formerly used." The ideology of revolutionary republicanism, pieced together from English political ideas, Enlightenment theories, and religious beliefs, constituted that revolution in thought. Many of its central tenets were broadly shared among the American people, but its larger meanings were sharply contested throughout the Revolutionary era.

In addition to the rejection of monarchy that Paine had so eloquently expressed in *Common Sense*, the American people also rejected the system of hierarchical authority on which monarchy was based, a system that promised protection by the Crown in return for obedience by the people. Under a republican system, by contrast, the people contracting together created public authority for their own mutual good. In that fundamental change lay much of the American Revolution's radical promise.

Basic to republican belief was the notion that governmental power, when removed from the people's close oversight, threatened to expand at the expense of liberty. Recent experience with England had burned that lesson into people's consciousness. Although too much liberty could degenerate into political chaos, history seemed to demonstrate that

Tearing Down the Statue of George III
In celebration of American independence, Patriots and their slaves rushed to destroy symbols of British authority such as this statue of King George III that stood at Bowling Green in New York City. (*Library of Congress*)

trouble most often arose from too much, not too little government. "It is much easier to restrain the people from running into licentiousness," went a typical refrain, "than power from swelling into tyranny and oppression."

Given the need to limit governmental power, how could political order be maintained? The revolutionary generation offered an extraordinary answer to that question. Order was not to be imposed from above through traditional agencies of central control such as monarchies, standing armies, and state churches. In a republic, political discipline had to emerge from the self-regulated behavior of citizens, especially from their willingness to put the public good ahead of their private interests. In a republic, explained one pamphleteer, "each individual gives up all private interest that is not consistent with the general good." This radical principle of "public virtue" was an essential ingredient of republican belief.

By contrast, political "faction," or organized self-interest, was the "mortal disease" to which popular governments throughout history had succumbed. Given the absence in republics of a strong central government capable of imposing political order, factional conflict could easily spin out of control. This fear added to the intensity of political conflict in revolutionary America by encouraging people to attribute the worst motives to their opponents.

The idea of placing responsibility for political order with the people and counting on them to act selflessly for the good of the whole alarmed countless Americans. What if the people proved unworthy? If the attempt was made, warned one individual darkly, "the bands of society would be dissolved, the harmony of the world confused, and the order of nature subverted." A strong incentive to loyalty lurked in such concerns.

Few Patriots were so naive as to believe that the American people were altogether virtuous. During the first years of independence, when revolutionary enthusiasm ran high, many believed that public virtue was sufficiently widespread to support republican government. Others, however, argued that the American people would learn public virtue by its practice. The revolutionary struggle would serve as a "furnace of affliction," refining the American character as it strengthened people's capacity for virtuous behavior. It was an extraordinarily hopeful but risk-filled undertaking.

The principle of political equality was another controversial touchstone of republicanism. It was broadly assumed that republican governments must be grounded in popular consent, that elections must be frequent, and that citizens must be vigilant in defense of their liberties. But agreement often ended there.

Some Americans took the principle of political equality literally, arguing that every citizen should have an equal voice and that public office should be open to all. This position was most forcefully articulated by tenants and small farmers in the interior, as well as by workers and artisans in the coastal cities, who had long struggled to claim a political voice. More cautious citizens emphasized that individual liberty must be balanced by political order, arguing that stable republics required leadership by men of ability and experience, an "aristocracy of talent" that could give the people direction. Merchants, planters, and large commercial farmers who were used to providing such leadership saw no need for radical changes in the existing distribution of political power.

Forming New Governments

These differences of ideology and self-interest burst through the surface of American politics during the debates over new state constitutions. Fashioning new governments would not be easy, for the American people had no experience with government making on such a scale and had to undertake it in the midst of a disruptive war. In addition, there were sharp divisions over the kinds of governments they wanted to create. One person thought it the "most difficult and dangerous business" that was to be done. Events proved those words prophetic.

Rather than create new systems of government, Connecticut and Rhode Island continued under their colonial charters, simply deleting all reference to the British Crown. The other 11 states, however, set their charters aside and started anew. By 1778, all but Massachusetts had completed the task. Two years later it had done so as well.

Given their recent experience with England and the prompting of republican theory, constitution makers began with two overriding concerns: to limit the powers of government and to make public officials closely accountable. The only certain way of accomplishing these goals was by establishing a fundamental law, in the form of a written constitution, that could serve as a standard for controlling governmental behavior.

In most states, the provincial congresses, extra-legal successors to the defunct colonial assemblies, wrote the first constitutions. But this made people increasingly uneasy. If governmental bodies wrote the documents, they could change them as well, and what would then protect liberty against the abuse of governmental power? Some way had to be

Old Massachusetts Statehouse

Massachusetts was the first state to elect a special convention to draw up a new constitution and then return that constitution to the people for approval. The new government—along with Boston's officials, courts, and the Merchants' Exchange—met in the old colonial statehouse. (I. N. Phelps Stokes Collection, Miriam and Ira D. Wallach Division of Art, Prints and Photographs, The New York Public Library, Astor, Lenox and Tilden Foundations/Art Resource, NY)

found of grounding the fundamental law not in the actions of government, but directly in the people's sovereign will.

Massachusetts first perfected the new procedures. In 1779, its citizens elected a special convention for the sole purpose of preparing a new constitution, which was then returned to the people for ratification.

Through trial and argumentation, the revolutionary generation gradually worked out a clear understanding of what a constitution was and how it should be created. In the process, it established some of the most basic doctrines of American constitutionalism: that sovereignty resides in the people rather than government; that written constitutions embody the people's sovereign will; and that governments must function within clear constitutional limits. No principles have been more important to the preservation of American liberty.

The governments described by these new constitutions were considerably more democratic than the colonial regimes had been. Most state officials were now elected, many of them annually rather than every two or three years as before. The assemblies, moreover, were now larger and more representative than they had been prior to 1776, and many of the powers formerly exercised by colonial governors—control over the budget, veto power over legislation, and the right to appoint various state officials—were abolished or reallocated to the assemblies.

Different Paths to the Republican Goal

Constitution making generated heated controversy, especially over how democratic the new governments should be. In Pennsylvania, a coalition of western farmers, Philadelphia artisans, and radical leaders pushed through the most democratic state constitution of all. Drafted less than three months after independence, during the most intense period of political reform, it rejected the familiar English model of two legislative houses and an independent executive. Republican governments, the radicals insisted, should be simple and easily understood. The constitution thus provided for a single, all-powerful legislative house—its members annually elected, its debates open to the public.

DOCUMENT

Constitution of Pennsylvania (1776)

A truly radical assumption underlay this unitary design: that only the "common interest of society" and not "separate and jarring private interests" should be represented in public affairs. There was to be no governor; legislative committees would handle executive duties. Property-holding requirements for public office were abolished, and the franchise was opened to every white, tax-paying male over age 21. A bill of rights guaranteed every citizen religious freedom, trial by jury, and freedom of speech.

DOCUMENT

John Adams, Thoughts on Government (1776)

The most radical proposal called for the redistribution of property. "An enormous proportion of property vested in a few individuals," declared the proposed constitution, "is dangerous to the rights, and destructive of the common happiness of mankind." Alarmed conservatives just managed to fend off that radical proposal.

Debate over the proposed constitution polarized the state. Men of wealth condemned the document's supporters as "coffee-house demagogues"

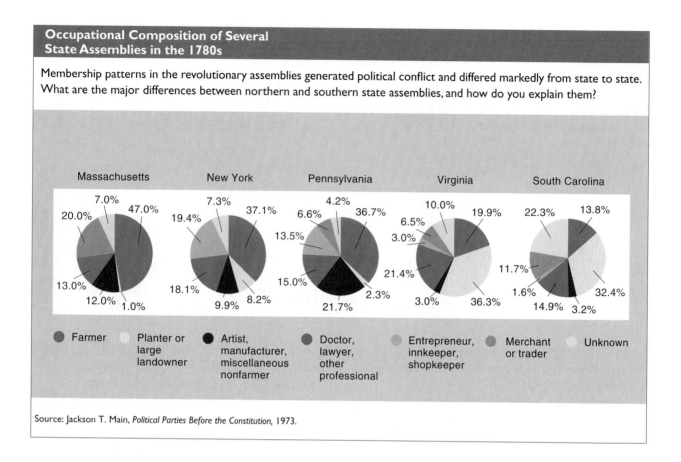

Occupational Composition of Several State Assemblies in the 1780s

Membership patterns in the revolutionary assemblies generated political conflict and differed markedly from state to state. What are the major differences between northern and southern state assemblies, and how do you explain them?

Source: Jackson T. Main, *Political Parties Before the Constitution*, 1973.

seeking to introduce a "tyranny of the people." The constitution's proponents—tradespeople, farmers, and other small producers—shot back that their critics were "the rich and great men" who had no "common interest with the body of the people."

In 1776, the radicals had their way, and the document was approved. The Pennsylvania constitution, together with its counterparts in Vermont and Georgia, represented the most radical thrust of revolutionary republicanism. Its guiding principle, declared Thomas Young, was that "the people at large [are] the true proprietors of governmental power." As later events would reveal, the struggle for political control in Pennsylvania was not over. For the moment, however, the lines of political power in Pennsylvania had been decisively redrawn.

In Massachusetts, constitution making followed a more cautious course. There the disruptions of war were less severe and the continuity of political leadership was greater. The constitution's main architect, John Adams, readily admitted that the new government must be firmly grounded in the people, yet he warned against "reckless experimentation" and regarded the Pennsylvania constitution as far too democratic. He thought a balance between two legislative houses and an independent executive was essential to preserving liberty.

Believing that society was inescapably divided between "democratic" and "aristocratic" forces, Adams sought to isolate each in separate legislative houses where they could guard against each other. Following Adams's advice, the Massachusetts convention provided for a popular, annually elected assembly and a senate apportioned on the basis of wealth. The constitution also provided for an independent governor empowered to veto legislation, make appointments, command the militia, and oversee state expenditures.

When the convention sent the document to the town meetings for approval on March 2, 1780, farmers and Boston artisans attacked it as "aristocratic," while the inhabitants of Petersham feared that "rich and powerful men" would control the proposed government. Despite such objections, the convention reconvened in June and declared the constitution approved, and the document went into effect four months later.

Women and the Limits of Republican Citizenship

While men of the revolutionary generation battled over sharing political power, they were virtually unanimous in the belief that women should be excluded from public affairs. Though women participated in revolutionary crowds and other political activities, they continued to be denied the franchise. Except on scattered occasions, women had neither voted nor held public office during the colonial period. Nor, with rare exceptions, did they do so in revolutionary America.

In New Jersey, the constitution of 1776 opened the franchise to "all free inhabitants" meeting property and residence requirements. During the 1780s, numerous women took advantage of that opening and cast their votes, leading one disgruntled male to

DOCUMENT

The New Jersey Constitution of 1776

protest, "It is evident that women, generally, are neither by nature, nor habit, nor education ... fitted to perform this duty with credit to themselves, or advantage to the public." Reflecting that widely held, male belief, the New Jersey Assembly in 1807 again disenfranchised women. The author of that law, John Condict, had narrowly escaped defeat several years earlier when women voted in conspicuous numbers for his opponent. In no other state did women even temporarily secure the vote. Not until the twentieth century would women secure the franchise, the most fundamental attribute of citizenship.

Prior to independence, most women had accepted the principle that political involvement fell outside the female sphere. Women, however, felt the urgency of the revolutionary crisis as intensely as men. "How shall I impose a silence upon myself," wondered Anne Emlen in 1777, "when the subject is so very interesting, so much engrossing conversation & what every member of the community is more or less concerned in?" With increasing frequency, women wrote and spoke to each other about public events, especially as they affected their own lives. Declared Eliza Wilkerson of South Carolina during the British invasion of 1780, "None were greater politicians than the several knots of ladies, who met together. All trifling discourses of fashions, and such low chat were thrown by, and we commenced perfect statesmen."

As the war progressed, growing numbers of women spoke out publicly. A few, such as Mercy Otis Warren and Esther DeBerdt Reed, published essays explaining women's urgent desire to contribute to the Patriot cause. In her 1780 broadside "The Sentiments of an American Woman," Reed declared that women wanted to serve like "those heroines of antiquity, who have rendered their sex illustrous," and called on women to renounce "vain ornament" as they had earlier renounced English tea. The money not spent on clothing and hairstyles would be the "offering of the Ladies" to Washington's army.

Mercy Otis Warren   Though women were discouraged from public writing, Mercy Otis Warren, related by birth and marriage to leading Massachusetts Patriots, published pamphlets and plays dealing with revolutionary politics. (*John Singleton Copley, Mrs. James Warren (Mercy Otis), about 1763. Courtesy, Museum of Fine Arts, Boston. Reproduced with permission © 1999 The Museum of Fine Arts, Boston. All Rights Reserved.*)

In Philadelphia, women responded by collecting $300,000 in continental currency from more than 1,600 individuals. Refusing Washington's proposal that the money be mixed with general funds in the national treasury, they insisted on using it to purchase materials for shirts so that each soldier might know he had received a contribution directly from the women.

Even women's traditional roles took on new political meaning. With English imports cut off and the army badly in need of clothing, spinning and weaving took on patriotic significance. Coming together as Daughters of Liberty, women made shirts and other items of clothing. Charity Clarke, a New York teenager, acknowledged that she "felt Nationaly" as she knitted stockings for the soldiers. Though "heroines may not distinguish themselves at the head of an army," she informed an English cousin, a "fighting army of amazons ... armed with spinning wheels" would emerge in America.

The most traditional female role, the care and nurture of children, took on special political resonance during the Revolutionary era. How could the republic be sustained once independence had been

Martha Ryan Copybook   Martha
Ryan, a young North Carolina girl, decorated
the cover of her copybook with political themes.
*(From the Ryan Cipher Book, #1940, Southern His-
torical Collection, The Library of the University of
North Carolina at Chapel Hill)*

won? Only by a rising generation of republican citizens schooled in the principles of public virtue and
ready to assume the task. How would they be prepared? During their formative years by their "Republican Mothers," the women of the Revolution.

Most women did not press for full political equality, since the idea flew in the face of long-standing social convention, and its advocacy exposed
a woman to public ridicule. Women, however, did speak out in defense of their
rights. Choosing words that had resonated
so powerfully during the protests against
England, Abigail Adams urged her husband, John, not to put "unlimited power"
into the hands of husbands. Remember,
she warned, "all men would be tyrants if they could."
John consulted Abigail on many things, but turned
this admonition quickly aside.

DOCUMENT

Adams Family
Letters (March,
April 1776)

While women developed new ties to the public
realm during the revolutionary years, the assumption
that politics was an exclusively male domain did not
easily die. Indeed, republican ideology, so effectively
invoked in support of American liberty against the
English king and Parliament, actually sharpened political distinctions between women and men. The independent judgment required of republican citizens assumed economic self-sufficiency, and that was denied
married women by the long-established principle of
coverture (a legal doctrine that transferred women's
property to their husbands, in effect designating them
economic as well as political dependents).

Republican virtue, moreover, was understood to
encompass such "manly" qualities as rationality,

self-discipline, and public sacrifice, qualities believed inconsistent with "feminine" attributes of emotion and self-indulgence. Finally, the desperate struggle against England strengthened patriarchal values by celebrating military heroism.

In time, new challenges to male political hegemony would emerge. When they did, women would find guidance in the universal principles enshrined in the Declaration of Independence that the women of the Revolution had helped to defend.

Conclusion

The Crucible of Revolution

When Congress launched its struggle for national liberation in July 1776, it steered the American people into uncharted seas. The break with England and accompanying war redrew the contours of American life and changed the destinies of countless people such as Long Bill Scott. Though the war ended in victory, liberty had its costs, as lives were lost, property destroyed, and local economies deranged. The conflict altered relationships between Native Americans and whites, for it left the Iroquois and Cherokee severely weakened and opened the floodgates of western expansion. Though women participated in revolutionary activities and achieved enhanced status as "Republican Mothers," they were still denied the vote.

By 1783, a new nation had come into being where none had existed before, a nation based not on age-encrusted principles of monarchy and aristocratic privilege but on the doctrines of republican liberty. That was the greatest change of all. However, the political transformations that were set in motion generated angry disputes whose outcome could be but dimly foreseen. How might individual liberty be reconciled with the need for public order? Who should be accorded full republican citizenship, and to whom should it be denied? How should constitutions be written and republican governments be organized? Thomas Paine put the matter succinctly: "The answer to the question, can America be happy under a government of her own, is short and simple—as happy as she pleases; she hath a blank sheet to write upon." The years immediately ahead would determine whether America's republican experiment, launched with such hopefulness in 1776, would succeed.

Success would depend as well on the new nation's position in a hostile Atlantic world. Though American independence had been acknowledged, the long-established web of connections tying the United States to England and Europe remained strong. Wartime alliances had revealed that North America remained an object of imperial ambition and European power politics, while the cutoff of Atlantic trade had made clear how dependent the nation still was on overseas commerce. The new American republic, moreover, served as a model and, on occasion, an asylum for political radicals intent on reforming the corrupt systems of England and France. At the same time, many Americans regarded their republic as a beacon for the struggles of oppressed people elsewhere. In these ways as well, the meaning of American independence remained to be worked out in the years ahead.

Questions for Review and Reflection

1. Why were England and its North American colonies unable to resolve their differences peacefully?

2. Wars often produce unintended consequences for their participants. How was that the case for the American people during the Revolutionary War?

3. Loyalists and Patriots both argued that they sought to uphold the rule of law. How could that be the case?

4. Many African Americans supported the struggle for American independence, but countless others did not. Explain the difference.

5. The conflict between the United States and England quickly became internationalized. Why was this so, and what difference did that make for the war's outcome?

Recommended Reading

Recommended Readings are posted on the Web site for this textbook. Visit www.ablongman.com/nash

Fiction and Film

The Broken Chain, a made-for-television historical drama produced and aired in 1994, tells the story of the Mohawk war chief Joseph Brant, who fought with England during the Revolutionary War and then led many of his people to Canada following the peace of 1783. *The Way of Duty,* a PBS documentary-drama based on a book by the historians Richard and Joy Buel, traces the challenging experiences of a Connecticut woman and her family during the American Revolution. James Fenimore Cooper's dramatic novel *The Pilot* (1824) offers an imaginative account of naval warfare and seafaring life during the Revolution. In the more recently published novel *Oliver Wiswell* (1940), Kenneth Roberts depicts the Revolution as seen through the eyes of an American Loyalist.

Discovering U.S. History Online

Articles of Confederation
www.yale.edu/lawweb/avalon/artconf.htm
The full text of the articles is presented, along with other relevant documents such as Benjamin Franklin's draft, John Dickinson's draft, and discussion of the Articles of Confederation in Jefferson's autobiography.

The American Revolution and Its Era: Maps and Charts of North America and the West Indies, 1750–1789
www.memory.loc.gov/ammem/gmdhtml/armhtml/armhome.html
This site gives geographical context to the American Revolution.

American Revolution
www.nps.gov/revwar/
This site includes a timeline of the war and links to all Revolutionary War national parks, as well as special exhibits.

North America Map Archive
www.uoregon.edu/~atlas/america/maps.html
This map collection includes an interactive map that shows America's configuration after the 1783 Treaty of Paris, including states and claimed territories.

Revolutionary Battles
www.wpi.edu/Academics/Depts/MilSci/BTSI
With an aim to instruct in military strategy, this site gives detailed information about four key revolutionary battles and their causes.

Oneida Indian Nation, 1777
www.one-web.org/1777.html
This site presents a several-part essay that explains the role the Oneida tribe played in the American Revolution. The discussion features quotes from Oneida oral history as well as contemporary publications.

Indians and the American Revolution
www.americanrevolution.org/ind1.html
This site presents the annotated text of a presentation by a former director of American Studies at the Smithsonian Institution in which he outlined the involvement of various Native American tribes in the American Revolution.

Spy Letters of the American Revolution
www.si.umich.edu/spies/
The story of the American Revolution is told through letters of its spies. This site gives context to the letters with a timeline, overall stories, maps of routes, and descriptions of their methods.

Archiving Early America
www.earlyamerica.com
Via this site, students can access writings, maps, and images of leading men and women reproduced from newspapers and magazines of the Revolutionary era.

Black Loyalists
www.collections.ic.gc.ca/blackloyalists
Using primary sources from various collections, this site explores the history of the African American Loyalists who earned their freedom by serving with the British and then fleeing to Canada to settle.

Intelligence in the War of Independence
www.cia.gov/cia/publications/warindep
This collection of primary documents explains how intelligence was organized, how it operated, and the techniques used during the War for Independence.

Was the American Revolution Inevitable?
www.bbc.co.uk/history/society_economy/empire/american_revolution_01.shtml
This essay explores the war from the British perspective.

The Army Medical Department, 1755–1818

www.armymedicine.army.mil/history/booksdocs/rev/gillett1/default.htm

An online complete, illustrated text of a volume describing the army's medical practices from the time of the Revolutionary War and the first quarter century of the nation.

The American Revolution: National Discussions of Our Revolutionary Origins

www.revolution.h-net.msu.edu

This site accompanies the PBS series *Liberty!* with essays and resource links to a rich array of sites containing information on the American Revolution. Included are the Bill of Rights, slave documents, and maps of the era.

Biographies of America's Founding Fathers

www.colonialhall.com

The biographical sketches of America's founding fathers are taken from the 1829 book *Lives of the Signers of the Declaration of Independence* by the Rev. Charles A. Goodrich.

Women in the American Revolution

www.rims.k12.ca.us/women_american_revolution/

Brief biographies of 25 women who played a role in the Revolutionary War. This site also includes a comprehensive bibliography of online sources.

The Charters of Freedom

www.archives.gov/exhibit_hall/charters_of_freedom/charters_of_freedom.html

This government site includes images and full text as well as background of three early documents: the Declaration of Independence, the Constitution, and the Bill of Rights.

Consolidating the Revolution

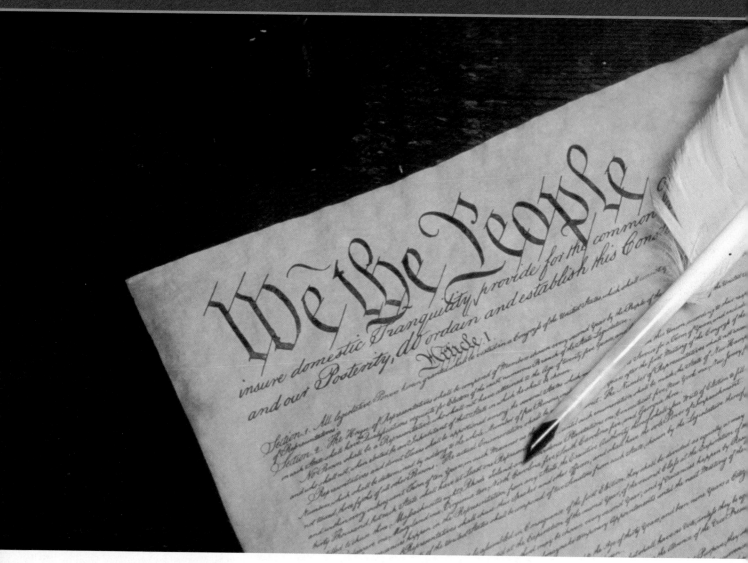

Ratification of the U.S. Constitution by the states in 1788 brought an end to the revolutionary years and ushered in a dramatically new era in the nation's history. *(John Feingersh/Stock, Boston)*

American Stories

Extending the Revolution

Timothy Bloodworth of New Hanover County, North Carolina, knew what the American Revolution was all about, for he had experienced it firsthand. A man of humble origins, Bloodworth had known poverty as a child. Lacking any formal education, he had worked hard during the middle decades of the eighteenth century as an innkeeper and ferry pilot, self-styled preacher and physician, blacksmith, and farmer. By the mid-1770s, he owned nine slaves and 4,200 acres of land, considerably more than most of his neighbors.

His unpretentious manner and commitment to political equality earned Bloodworth the confidence of his community. In 1758, at age 22, he was elected to the North Carolina colonial assembly. Over the next three decades, he was deeply involved in the political life of his home state.

When the colonies' troubles with England drew toward a crisis, Bloodworth spoke ardently of American rights and mobilized support for independence. In 1775, he helped form the Wilmington Committee of Safety. Filled with revolutionary fervor, he urged forward the process of republican political reform and, as commissioner of confiscated property for the district of Wilmington, pressed the attack on local Loyalists.

In 1784, shortly after the war ended, the North Carolina assembly named Bloodworth one of the state's delegates to the Confederation Congress. There he learned for the first time about the problems of governing a new nation. As the Congress struggled through the middle years of the 1780s with the intractable problems of foreign trade, war debt, and control of the trans-Appalachian interior, Bloodworth shared the growing conviction that the Articles of Confederation were too weak. He supported the Congress's call for a special convention to meet in Philadelphia in May 1787 for the purpose of taking action necessary "to render the constitution of the federal government adequate to the exigencies of the Union."

Like thousands of other Americans, Bloodworth eagerly awaited the convention's work. And like countless Americans, he was stunned by the result, for the proposed constitution described a government that seemed to him certain not to preserve republican liberty but to endanger it.

Once again sniffing political tyranny on the breeze, Bloodworth resigned his congressional seat and in August 1787 hurried back to North Carolina to help organize opposition to the proposed constitution. Over the next several years, he worked tirelessly for its defeat.

Alarmed by the prospect of such a powerful central government, Bloodworth protested that "we cannot consent to the adoption of a Constitution whose revenues lead to aristocratic tyranny, or monarchical despotism, and open a door wide as fancy can point, for the introduction of dissipation, bribery and corruption to the exclusion of public virtue." Had Americans so quickly forgotten the dangers of consolidated power? Were they already prepared to turn away from their brief experiment in republicanism?

Alarmed by a variety of provisions in the document, Bloodworth demanded the addition of a federal bill of rights to protect individual liberties. Echoing the language of revolutionary republicanism, he warned the North Carolina ratifying convention that "without the most express restrictions, Congress may trample on your rights. Every possible precaution should be taken when we grant powers," he continued, for "Rulers are always disposed to abuse them."

Bloodworth also feared the sweeping authority Congress would have to make "all laws which shall be necessary and proper" for carrying into execution "all other powers vested . . . in the government of the United States." That language, he insisted, "would result in the abolition of the state governments. Its sovereignty absolutely annihilates them."

In North Carolina, the arguments of Bloodworth and his Anti-Federalist colleagues carried the day. By a vote of 184 to 84, the ratifying convention declared that a bill of rights "asserting and securing from encroachment the great Principles of civil and religious Liberty, and the unalienable rights of the People" must be approved before North Carolina would concur. The convention was true to its word. Not until November 1789, well after the new government had gotten underway and Congress had forwarded a national bill of rights to the states for approval, did North Carolina, with Timothy Bloodworth's cautious endorsement, finally enter the new union.

Just as Timothy Bloodworth knew the difficulties of achieving American independence, so he learned the problems of preserving American liberty once independence had been won. This chapter examines the threats posed by the dangerous world surrounding the new nation: the continuing imperial ambitions of England and France in North America; Congress's inability to pay off the foreign-held war debt; the states' failure to join together in prying open foreign ports to American commerce; and continuing restrictions on free navigation of the Mississippi River, deemed essential to the development of the nation's interior.

Chapter 7 also discusses an array of domestic issues that troubled the nation's affairs. Disputes over taxation and paper money, slavery and the separation of church and state, and the extent of democratic political reform generated turmoil in the states, in some cases leading discontented citizens to openly challenge public authority.

By 1786, Timothy Bloodworth, like countless other Americans, was caught up in an escalating debate between Federalists, who believed that the Articles of Confederation were fatally deficient and must be replaced by a stronger national government, and the Anti-Federalists, who were deeply troubled by what they perceived to be the dangers to individual liberty posed by governmental power. That debate over the future of America's republican experiment, which constitutes the chapter's final topic, came to a head in the momentous Philadelphia convention of 1787, with its proposal for dramatic changes in the national government. With ratification of the new Constitution, the American people opened a portentous new era in their history and launched a dialogue over the very nature of American politics and government that continues to this day.

STRUGGLING WITH THE PEACETIME AGENDA

As the war ended, daunting problems of demobilization and adjustment to the novel conditions of independence troubled the new nation. Whether the Confederation Congress could effectively deal with the problems of the postwar era remained unclear.

Demobilizing the Army

Demobilizing the army presented the Confederation government with immediate challenges, for when

the fighting stopped, many of the troops refused to go home until Congress redressed their grievances. Trouble first arose in early 1783 when officers at the continental army camp in Newburgh, New York, sent a delegation to complain about arrears in pay and other benefits that Congress had promised them during the dark days of the war. When Congress called on the army to disband, an anonymous address circulated among the officers, attacking the "coldness and severity" of Congress and hinting darkly at more direct action if grievances were not addressed.

Several congressmen encouraged the officers' muttering, hoping the crisis would lend urgency to their own calls for a stronger central government. Most, however, found the challenge to Congress's authority alarming. Washington moved quickly to calm the situation. Promising that Congress would treat the officers justly, he counseled patience and urged his comrades not to tarnish the victory they had so recently won. His efforts succeeded, for the officers reaffirmed their confidence in the Congress and agreed to disband.

DOCUMENT

George Washington, The Newburgh Address (1783)

Officers were not the only ones to take action. In June, several hundred disgruntled continental soldiers and Pennsylvania militiamen gathered in front of Philadelphia's Independence Hall, where both Congress and Pennsylvania's Executive Council were meeting. When state authorities would not guarantee Congress's

The Resignation of General Washington, 1783 By resigning his commission in 1783 and returning to private life, Washington affirmed the supremacy of civilians over military authority. Note the women in the balcony observing the ceremony. Though distanced from the floor of Congress, they pay close attention to the proceedings. *(U.S. Capital Historical Society)* safety, it fled to Princeton, New Jersey. Once there, tension eased when Congress issued the soldiers three months' pay and furloughed them until they could be formally discharged. By early November, the crisis was over, but congressional authority had been seriously damaged.

Over the next several years, Congress shuffled between Princeton, Annapolis, Trenton, and New York City, its transience visible evidence of its steadily eroding authority. A hot-air balloon, scoffed the *Boston Evening Herald,* would "exactly accommodate the itinerant genius of Congress," because it could "float along from one end of the continent to the other . . . and when occasion requires . . . suddenly pop down into any of the states they please." Never had Congress been so openly mocked.

Opening the West

The Confederation Congress was not without significant accomplishments during the postwar years. Most notable were the two great land ordinances of 1785 and 1787. The first provided for the systematic survey and sale of the region west of Pennsylvania and north of the Ohio River. The area was to be laid out in townships six miles square, which were to be subdivided into lots of 640 acres each. Thus began the rectangular grid pattern of land survey and settlement that to this day characterizes the Midwest and distinguishes it so markedly from the irregular settlement patterns of the older, colonial areas to the east.

Two years later, Congress passed the Northwest Ordinance. It provided for the political organization of the same interior region, first under congressionally appointed officials, then under popularly elected territorial assemblies, and ultimately as new states to be incorporated into the Union. Together, the two ordinances represented a dramatic change from England's colonial administration. Rather than seeking to restrain white settlement as Parliament had attempted to do in the Proclamation Line of 1763, the central government in America's "Empire of Liberty" sought ways to promote settlement's expansion. In addition, settlements in the American West would not remain colonies subordinate to an imperial power, but would be fully incorporated as new states into the expanding American nation.

DOCUMENT

Northwest Ordinance (July 13, 1787)

Old Northwest Survey Patterns

The Land Ordinance passed by Congress in 1785 provided for the systematic, rectangular survey of lands west of Pennsylvania and north of the Ohio River. Townships were to be divided into lots of 640 acres. The purpose of the ordinance was to promote the rapid, orderly occupation of the Old Northwest. What differences might this new survey system have made in patterns of community settlement, land use, and social life compared to the random settlement patterns along the Atlantic coast?

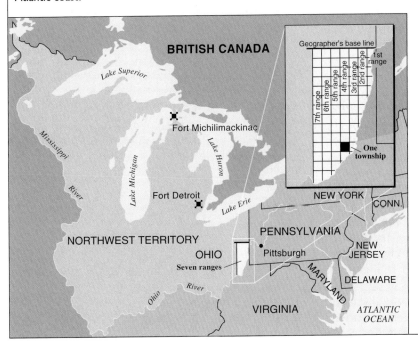

coexist with white society. Most whites simply argued that the Native Americans must be driven out of white settlers' way. "The gradual extension of our settlements," explained George Washington, "will as certainly cause the savage as the wolf to retire; both being beasts of prey though they differ in shape."

For a few years, the conquest strategy seemed to work. During the mid-1780s, Congress imposed land treaties on the interior tribes, among them the Iroquois. At the Treaty of Fort Stanwix in 1784, the Iroquois—their numbers sharply reduced by war, disease, and flight into Canada, and their once-proud confederation shattered—officially made peace, ceded most of their lands to the United States, and retreated to small reservations. By the 1790s, little remained of the once-imposing Iroquois domain but a few islands in a spreading sea of white settlement. On these "slums in the wilderness," the Iroquois

A Symbol for the New Nation Why was the figure of Columbia, symbolic of the new republic, represented as a woman? And why was she often portrayed as a Native American? *(Library of Congress)*

Both ordinances enjoyed broad political support, for they opened land to settlers and profits to speculators. Income from land sales, moreover, promised to help reduce the national debt. While permitting slave owners living north of the Ohio River to retain their chattels, the ordinance of 1787 prohibited the importation of new slaves into the region. This made the area more attractive to white farmers who worried about competing with slave labor and living among blacks. Southern delegates in Congress accepted the restriction because they could look forward to slavery's expansion south of the Ohio River. During the 1780s, the country's interior seemed large enough to accommodate everyone's needs. Despite these accomplishments, various events fueled doubts that the Confederation government was capable of ensuring westward expansion.

During the immediate postwar years, Congress operated as if the Native Americans of the interior were "conquered" peoples—allies of England who had lost the war and were now under U.S. control. Such claims were grounded in notions of the Native Americans' social and cultural inferiority. Even the most sympathetic whites believed that Native Americans must forgo their tribal ways before they could

A Plan for New States

During the 1780s, various people, Thomas Jefferson among them, devised imaginary maps of new states to be created west of the Appalachians. In his "Plan for Government of the Western Territory" (1784), Jefferson laid a rigidly symmetrical grid on the area rather than following the natural contours of the land. Why would he have done that? Where do you suppose he came up with the remarkable names for the projected new states?

North America After the Treaty of Paris, 1783

Though victorious in its struggle for independence, the United States was surrounded to the north, west, and south by British and Spanish possessions. Russia and France continued to harbor imperial ambitions in the Americas as well. **Reflecting on the Past** What problems and opportunities did European claims on areas of North America pose for the United States?

British	Disputed by United States and Britain
French	Disputed by United States and Spain
Russian	Disputed by Britain, Russia and Spain
Spanish	
United States	

struggled against disease and poverty, their traditional lifeways gone, their self-confidence broken. The Iroquois were not the only tribe to lose their land. In January 1785, representatives of the Wyandotte, Chippewa, Delaware, and Ottawa relinquished claim to most of present-day Ohio.

The treaties, often exacted under the threat of force, generated widespread resentment. Two years after the Fort Stanwix negotiations, the Iroquois repudiated the treaty, asserting that they were still sovereigns of their own soil and "equally free as . . . any nation under the sun."

By the mid-1780s, tribal groups north and south of the Ohio River were resisting white expansion into the interior. While the Creek resumed hostilities in Georgia, Native Americans north of the Ohio River strengthened their Western Confederacy, asserted that the river should serve as the boundary between them and the United States, and prepared for the defense of their homeland. As devastating Native American raids greeted settlers moving into the West, the entire region from the Great Lakes to the Gulf of Mexico was aflame with war. With the continental army disbanded, there was little that Congress could do.

The Revolution left behind a legacy of bitterness: among Native Americans because they had suffered defeat and faced a growing tide of white settlement,

HOW OTHERS SEE US

A View of Postwar America

North America . . . appears to be in a very distracted and broken condition. . . . Their Indian neighbors threaten them with hostilities. . . . The different States are at variance among themselves, disputing territories, removing boundaries, and contesting other questions of property! They are not less divided about . . . the proportion each State shall contribute to the support of their Government-general, the Congress; what degree of power this . . . body shall be invested with, or whether it shall be invested with any authority at all. . . . These, and many other important questions, agitate them exceedingly. To crown all, their boasted friends the French and they hate one another most cordially. . . .

Such are the blessed fruits of American Independency . . . ! How fatal has that chimera, that false light . . . that shining nothing, that IGNIS FATUUS, called INDEPENDENCY, been to you! How has it led you through all the paths of error and delusion, from your . . . safe dwelling, under the . . . protecting wing of British Government. . . . Generations yet unborn will lament your folly, and curse your false policy and base ingratitude to your parent country.

- Is this an accurate description of postwar conditions in the United States?

- What sources of information might have been available to the writer?

- What effect did the attitudes expressed here probably have on Anglo-American relations?

---

among white Americans because the Native Americans had sided with England and thus threatened the Revolution's success. Such bitterness would trouble Native American–white relations for years to come.

Congress's inability to open the interior to white settlement alarmed many groups of people. Speculators feared the loss of their investments. Farmers hoped to leave the crowded lands of the East for new open lands to the west. Revolutionary soldiers were eager to start afresh on the rich soil of Kentucky and Ohio that they had been promised as payment for military service. Even the new nation's leaders were concerned. Thomas Jefferson believed that America's "empire of liberty" depended on an expanding nation of yeoman farmers.

Congress also failed to resolve problems with European nations that continued to claim areas of the trans-Appalachian west. In June 1784, Spain—still in possession of Florida, the Gulf Coast, and vast areas west of the Mississippi—closed the mouth of the river to American shipping. The act outraged western settlers dependent on getting their produce to market by floating it downstream to New Orleans. Closure of the Mississippi alarmed land speculators as well, for it would discourage development of the southern backcountry and reduce their profits. Rumors spread that Spanish agents were urging American frontiersmen to break away from the new nation

and seek affiliation with Spain. Sensing the danger, Washington commented uneasily that settlers throughout the West were "on a pivot." "The touch of a feather," he warned, "would turn them away."

When Spain refused to reopen the Mississippi, Congress's secretary for foreign affairs, John Jay, offered to relinquish American claims to free transit of the river in return for a commercial treaty opening Spanish ports to American shipping. Though the bargain pleased merchants in the northeastern states, southern delegates in Congress were incensed at Jay's betrayal of their interests and opposed it. Stalemated, Congress could take no action at all.

Wrestling with the National Debt

A further indication of the Confederation's weakness was evident in Congress's inability to deal effectively with the nation's war debt, estimated at $35 million. French and Dutch bankers held much of the debt. Unable to make regular payments against the loan's principal, Congress had to borrow additional money just to pay the accumulating interest. Things were no better at home. In response to the incessant demands of its creditors, the government could only delay and try to borrow more.

In 1781, Congress appointed Robert Morris, a wealthy Philadelphia merchant, as superintendent of finance and gave him broad authority to deal with the nation's troubled affairs. Morris urged the states to stop issuing paper money and persuaded Congress to demand that the states pay their requisitions in specie (gold and silver coin). In addition, he persuaded Congress to charter the Bank of North America and took steps to make federal bonds more attractive to investors.

Though Morris made considerable progress, the government's finances remained shaky. Lacking authority to tax, Congress depended on the states' willingness to meet their financial obligations. This arrangement, however, proved unworkable. In October 1781, a desperate Congress requested $8 million from the states. Two and a half years later, less than $1.5 million had come in. In January 1784, Morris resigned. By 1786, federal revenue totaled $370,000 a year, not enough, one official lamented, to provide for "the bare maintenance of the federal government."

Not all Americans were alarmed. Some noted approvingly that several state governments, having brought their own financial affairs under control, were beginning to assume responsibility for portions of the national debt. Others, however, saw this as additional evidence of Congress's weakening condition and wondered how long a government unable to maintain its credit could endure.

Surviving in a Hostile Atlantic World

Congress's difficulties dealing with its creditors and failure to counter Spain's closure of the Mississippi pointed to a broader problem in American foreign relations. Even after the United States had formally won independence, Britain, France, and Spain continued to harbor imperial ambitions in North America. Before the century was over, France would regain vast areas west of the Mississippi River. Meanwhile, Great Britain's Union Jack still flew over Canada and British troops still occupied strategic outposts on American soil, while Spain continued to conjure up grim memories of past New World conquests.

The Revolutionary War had dramatically transformed America's relations with the outside world. England, once the nurturing "mother country," had become the enemy, while France, long the mortal foe of England and the colonies alike, had proven at best an uncertain friend. Given its imperial ambitions and entrenched monarchy, France feared colonial rebellions and regarded republicanism as deeply subversive. Moreover, French efforts to manipulate the peace process for its own advantage had taught the Americans a hard lesson in the dangers of power politics.

The reason for America's diplomatic troubles during the 1780s was clear: the country was new, weak, and republican in an Atlantic world dominated by strong, monarchical governments. Nothing revealed the difficulties of national survival more starkly than Congress's futile efforts to rebuild America's overseas commerce. When the Revolutionary War ended, familiar English goods once again flooded American markets. Few American goods, however, flowed the other way. John Adams learned why. In 1785, he arrived in London as the first American minister to England, carrying instructions to negotiate a commercial treaty. After endless rebuffs, he reported in frustration that England had no intention of reopening the empire's ports to American shipping. British officials testily reminded him that Americans had desired independence and must now live with its consequences.

While England remained intractable, wartime allies such as France and Spain returned to a policy of maritime restrictions against American commerce. Congressional efforts to secure authorization from the states to regulate foreign trade were unavailing because each state wanted to channel its trade for its own advantage. As a result, overseas trade continued to languish and economic hardship deepened.

By the late 1780s, the per capita value of American exports had fallen a startling 30 percent from the 1760s. No wonder that merchants and artisans, carpenters and shopkeepers, sailors and dock workers—all dependent on shipbuilding and overseas commerce—suffered. In an Atlantic world divided into exclusive, imperial trading spheres, the United States lacked the political unity and economic muscle to protect its basic interests.

SOURCES OF POLITICAL CONFLICT

Revolutionary politics took different forms in different states, depending on the impact of the war, the extent of Loyalism, patterns of social conflict, and the disruptions of economic life. Everywhere, though, citizens struggled with an often intractable array of issues.

Separating Church and State

Among the most explosive issues was deciding the proper relationship between church and state. Prior to 1776, only Rhode Island, New Jersey, Pennsylvania, and Delaware had allowed full religious liberty. In other colonies, established churches were endorsed by the government and supported by public

AMERICAN VOICES

During the Revolutionary era, many people assumed that being a Protestant Christian was a necessary qualification for American citizenship. Philadelphia's small Jewish community challenged that assumption, arguing, as in this Memorial to the Pennsylvania Assembly, that belief in the Old Testament alone, together with commitment to the Revolutionary cause, should qualify individuals for the full range of civil rights.

The Memorial of . . . the Synagogue of the Jews at Philadelphia . . . Most respectfully showeth, That by the tenth section of the Frame of Government of this Commonwealth, it is ordered that each member of the general assembly of . . . Pennsylvania . . . [shall] subscribe a declaration, which ends in these words, "I do acknowledge the Scriptures of the old and new Testament to be given by divine inspiration. . . ."

Your memorialists beg leave to observe, that this clause seems to limit the civil rights of your citizens . . . whereas by the second paragraph of the declaration of the rights of the inhabitants, it is asserted without any other limitation . . . "that no man who acknowledges the being of a God can be justly deprived . . . of any civil rights as a citizen on account of his religious sentiments. . . . "

Your memorialists . . . apprehend that a clause in the constitution, which disables them to be elected by their fellow citizens to represent them in assembly, is a stigma upon their nation and religion, and . . . [excludes them] from the most important and honorable part of the rights of a free citizen.

They have . . . contributed to the support of the militia, and of the government of this State; they have no inconsiderable property in lands and tenements . . . for which they pay taxes . . . and as a nation or a religious society, they stand unimpeached of any matter whatsoever, against the safety and happiness of the people.

- *What arguments does the Memorial make?*

- *Do you find those arguments convincing?*

- *Does the Memorial argue against all religious qualifications for citizenship?*

---

taxes. There, civil authorities grudgingly tolerated "dissenters" such as Methodists and Baptists. Yet their numbers were growing rapidly and they noisily pressed their case for full religious liberty.

With independence, pressure built for severing all ties between church and state. Isaac Backus, the most outspoken of New England's Baptists, protested that "many, who are filling the nation with the cry of *liberty* and against *oppressors* are at the same time themselves violating that dearest of all rights, *liberty of conscience.*" Such arguments were strengthened by the belief that throughout history, alliances between government and church authorities had brought religious oppression, and that voluntary choice was the only safe basis for religious association.

In Massachusetts, Congregationalists fought to preserve their long-established privileges. To separate church and state, they argued, was to risk infidelity and social disorder. Massachusetts's 1780 constitution guaranteed everyone the right to worship God "in the manner and season most agreeable to the dictates of his own conscience." But it also empowered the legislature to tax residents to support local ministers. A common religion and shared morality, avowed John Adams, were essential supports to liberty and republican government. Still unsatisfied, Backus argued that official support of religious worship should be ended completely. Religious toleration, he insisted, fell far short of true religious freedom. Not until 1833 were laws linking church and state finally repealed in Massachusetts.

In Virginia, Baptists pressed their cause against the Protestant Episcopal Church, successor to the Church of England. The adoption in 1786 of Thomas Jefferson's Bill for Establishing Religious Freedom, rejecting all connections between church and state and removing all religious tests for public office, decisively settled the issue. Three years later, that statute served as a model for the First Amendment to the new federal Constitution.

But even the most ardent supporters of religious freedom were not prepared to extend it universally. The wartime alliance with Catholic France together with congressional efforts to entice Catholic settlers in Québec to join the resistance against England had weakened long-established prejudices. Still, anti-Catholic biases remained strong, especially in

The Old Methodist Church, John Street, New York   This nineteenth-century print provides a view of the Old Methodist Church on John Street, New York. Founded in 1786, it was the first Methodist church erected in America. Methodists and Baptists were among the "dissenting" groups pressing for full religious freedom during the Revolutionary era. *(John Hill, A Correct View of the Old Methodist Church in John Street, New York, 1824. The Metropolitan Museum of Art. The Edward W. C. Arnold Collection of New York Prints, Maps and Pictures, Bequest of Edward W. C. Arnold [54.90.700])*

slave trade's permanent extinction. By 1790, every state except South Carolina and Georgia had outlawed slave importations.

Ending the slave trade had powerful implications, for it reduced the infusion of new Africans into the black population. As a result, an ever higher proportion of blacks was American born, thus speeding the cultural transformation by which Africans became African Americans.

Slavery itself came under attack during the Revolutionary era, with immense consequences for blacks and the nation's future. As the crisis with England heated up, catchwords such as *liberty* and *tyranny*, mobilized by colonists against British policies, reminded citizens that one-fifth of the colonial population was in chains. Samuel Hopkins, a New England clergyman, accosted his compatriots for "making a vain parade of being advocates for the liberties of mankind, while . . . continuing this lawless, cruel, inhuman, and abominable practice of enslaving your fellow creatures." Following independence, antislavery attacks intensified.

In Georgia and South Carolina, where blacks outnumbered whites more than two to one and where slave labor remained essential to the prosperous rice economy, slavery escaped significant challenge. Committed to the doctrine of racial superiority and fearing the black majority, whites shuddered at the prospect of black freedom and wound the local slave codes even tighter.

In Virginia and Maryland, by contrast, whites openly argued whether slavery was compatible with republicanism, and in these states significant change did occur. The weakened demand for slave labor in the depressed tobacco economy facilitated the debate. Though neither state abolished slavery, both passed laws making it easier for owners to free their slaves without continuing to be responsible for their behavior. Moreover, increasing numbers of blacks purchased their own or their families' freedom, or simply ran away. By 1800, more than one of every 10 blacks in

DOCUMENT

Marquis de Chastellux, Travels in North America (1786)

New England. The people of Northbridge, Massachusetts, wanted to exclude "Roman Catholics, pagons, or Mahomitents" from public office. The legal separation of church and state did not end religious discrimination, but it implanted the principle of religious freedom firmly in American law.

Slavery Under Attack

The place of slavery in a republican society also vexed the revolutionary generation. How, wondered many, could slavery be reconciled with the inalienable right to life, liberty, and the pursuit of happiness so boldly proclaimed in the nation's Declaration of Independence?

During the several decades preceding 1776, the trade in human chattels had flourished. The 1760s had witnessed the largest importation of slaves in colonial history. The Revolutionary War, however, halted the slave trade almost completely. Though southern planters talked of replacing their lost chattels once the war ended, a combination of revolutionary principles, a reduced need for field hands in the depressed Chesapeake tobacco economy, natural increase among the existing slave population, and anxiety over black rebelliousness argued for the

Elizabeth Freeman As the attack on slavery grew in the northern states, numerous blacks sued in state courts for their freedom. Among them was a woman named Mumbet, who argued that the "inherent liberty" cited by revolutionary leaders applied to all people, including black slaves. When she secured her own emancipation, she carefully chose a new name—Elizabeth Freeman. *(Portrait of Elizabeth Freeman, 1811, Courtesy of the Massachusetts Historical Society)*

the Chesapeake region was free, a dramatic increase from 30 years before. Even so, their freedom was limited, since many found themselves obligated to work for others as indentured servants.

The majority of free blacks lived and worked in towns such as Baltimore and Richmond where they formed communities that served as centers of African American society, as well as havens for slaves escaping from the countryside. In the Chesapeake region, the conditions of life for black Americans slowly changed for the better.

The most dramatic breakthrough occurred in northern states, where slavery was either abolished or put on the road to gradual extinction. Such actions were possible because blacks were a numerical minority—in most areas, they constituted less than 4 percent of the population—and slavery had neither the economic nor social importance that it did in the South. In 1780, the Pennsylvania assembly passed a law stipulating that all newborn blacks were to be free when they reached age 21. It was a

cautious but decisive step. Other northern states adopted similar policies of gradual emancipation.

Northern blacks joined in the attacks on slavery, eagerly petitioning state assemblies for their freedom. "Every Principle from which America has acted in the course of their unhappy difficulties with Great Britain," declared one group of Philadelphia blacks, "pleads stronger than a thousand arguments in favor of our petition."

In scattered instances, free blacks participated actively in revolutionary politics. When the first draft of the Massachusetts constitution, explicitly excluding blacks and mulattoes from the franchise, was made public, William Gordon, a white clergyman, voiced his protest. "Would it not be ridiculous . . . and unjust to exclude freemen from voting . . . though otherwise qualified, because their skins are black?" he questioned. "Why not . . . for being long-nosed, short-faced, or . . . lower than five feet nine?" In the end, Massachusetts's constitution made no mention of race, and there, as well as in Pennsylvania and New York, African Americans occasionally cast ballots.

If civic participation by blacks was scattered and temporary in the North, it was almost totally absent in the South. With the brief exception of North Carolina, free African Americans could neither vote nor enjoy the protection of their persons and property under the law. Southern blacks, the vast majority of them slaves, remained almost entirely without political voice other than the petitions against slavery and mistreatment that they pressed on the state regimes. Even if they were free, blacks continued to encounter pervasive discrimination.

DOCUMENT

Slave Petition to the General Assembly in Connecticut (1779)

Still, remarkable progress had been made. Prior to the Revolution, slavery had been an accepted fact of northern life. After the Revolution, it no longer was. That change made a vast difference in the lives of countless black Americans. The abolition of slavery in the North, moreover, widened the sectional divergence between North and South, with enormous consequences for the years ahead. In addition, there now existed a coherent, publicly proclaimed antislavery argument, closely linked in Americans' minds with the nation's founding. The first antislavery organizations had been created as well. Although another half century would pass before antislavery became a significant force in American politics, the groundwork for slavery's final abolition had been laid.

Politics and the Economy

The devastating economic effects of independence and war plagued the American economy throughout

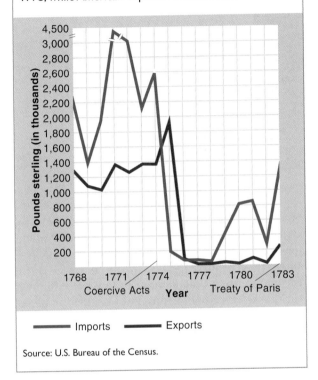

Exports and Imports, 1768–1783

Nonimportation affected colonial commerce during the late 1760s and early 1770s, but both exports and imports plummeted in 1774 and 1775. Why? Can you explain why imports recovered somewhat beginning in 1778, while American exports remained flat?

Pounds sterling (in thousands)

4,500 / 3,000 / 2,800 / 2,600 / 2,400 / 2,200 / 2,000 / 1,800 / 1,600 / 1,400 / 1,200 / 1,000 / 800 / 600 / 400 / 200

1768   1771 / 1774   1777   1780 / 1783
Coercive Acts   **Year**   Treaty of Paris

—— Imports   —— Exports

Source: U.S. Bureau of the Census.

from government contracts. Henry Knox, sometime merchant and commander of the continental artillery, observed that he was "exceedingly anxious to effect something in these fluctuating times, which may make . . . [me] easy for life." In the eighteenth century, as now, the boundary between private interest and public duty was often unclear.

But even as some prospered, countless others saw their affairs fall into disarray. Intractable issues such as price and wage inflation, skyrocketing taxation, and mushrooming debt set people sharply against each other. Heated debates arose as well over whether the states' war debts should be paid off at face value or at some reduced rate. Arguing for full value were the states' creditors—wealthy people who had loaned the states money and had bought up large amounts of government securities at deep discounts. Such people spoke earnestly of upholding the public honor and giving fair return to those who had risked their own resources in the revolutionary cause. Opposed were common folk angered by the speculators' profits. No one, they argued, should reap personal advantage from public distress.

The issue of taxation, seared into Americans' consciousness by their troubles with England, generated similarly heated controversy. As the costs of the war mounted, so did taxes. Between 1774 and 1778, Massachusetts levied more than £400,000 in taxes, a stunning increase over colonial days.

As taxes skyrocketed, farmers, artisans, and others of modest means argued that taxes should be payable in depreciated paper money or government securities. Lacking the hard money that states

the 1770s and 1780s. The cutoff of long-established patterns of overseas trade with England sent American commerce into a 20-year tailspin. While English warships prowled the coast, American vessels rocked idly at empty wharves, New England's once booming shipyards grew quiet, and communities whose livelihood depended on the sea sank into depression. Virginia tobacco planters, their British markets gone and their plantations open to seaborne attack, struggled to survive. Farmers in the middle and New England states often prospered when hungry armies were nearby, but their profits plummeted when the armies moved on.

Not everyone suffered equally. With the wearing of homespun clothes deemed patriotic, American artisans often prospered. (The slogan "Buy American" has a long tradition.) People with the right political connections, moreover, could make handsome profits

Women Petition for War Compensation

A City Devastated by War This view of Norfolk, Virginia, was painted by Benjamin Latrobe in 1796. It provides grim evidence of the war's ravages in many parts of the country. *(Henry Latrobe, "View of the part of the ruins of Norfolk," Undated [late March 1796], SKETCHBOOK I, No. 10 in Latrobe's View of America, 1795–1820, Maryland Historical Society, Baltimore)*

Continental Currency of the New Republic Lacking sufficient gold and silver to cover the escalating costs of war, Congress and the states printed massive amounts of paper money, which rapidly depreciated in value. Counterfeit currency produced by British agents and unscrupulous Americans added to the economic confusion. *(National Museum of American History, Smithsonian Institution)*

required in payment, they faced foreclosure of their property. Officials responded that allowing payment in depreciated paper would deprive governments of critically needed revenue.

Controversy swirled as well around efforts to control soaring prices. In Massachusetts, a bushel of corn that sold for less than a dollar in 1777 went for nearly $80 two years later, and in Maryland the price of wheat increased several thousandfold.

Every state experimented with price controls at one time or another. Seldom were such efforts effective; always they generated controversy. In Boston a crowd of women angered by the escalating cost of food tossed a merchant suspected of monopolizing commodities into a cart and dragged him through the city's streets, while "a large concourse of men stood amazed."

Individuals not yet integrated into the market economy supported price controls. They believed that goods should carry a "just price" that was fair to buyer and seller alike. In keeping with that principle, a crowd in New Windsor, New York, seized a shipment of tea bound for Albany in 1777 and sold it for what they deemed a fair offering.

Merchants, shopkeepers, and others accustomed to a commercial economy, however, believed that supply and demand should govern economic transactions. "It is contrary to the nature of commerce," observed Benjamin Franklin, "for government to interfere in the prices of commodities." Attempts to regulate prices only created a disincentive to labor, which was "the principal part of the wealth of every country."

Disputes over paper money also divided the American people. Faced with the uncontrollable escalation of wartime expenses, Congress and the states did what colonial governments had done before and American governments have done ever since: they printed money. In the first year of the war alone, they issued more than $400 million in various kinds of paper, and that was just the beginning. Citizens' willingness to accept such money at face value disappeared as the flood of paper increased. Congressional bills of credit that in 1776 were pegged against gold at the ratio of 1.5 to 1 had slipped five years later to 147 to 1. State currencies depreciated just as alarmingly.

Immense quantities of counterfeit currency produced by unscrupulous Americans out to make a profit, as well as by British agents intent on disrupting the American war effort, added to the confusion. So worthless did American currency become that a crowd paraded the streets of Philadelphia in 1781 with paper money stuck in their hats as cockades while leading a dog plastered with congressional dollars.

The social consequences of such depreciation were at times alarming. James Lovell reported nervously that "sailors with clubs" were parading the streets of Boston "instead of working for paper." With property values in disarray, it seemed at times as if the very foundations of society were coming unhinged. The war, wrote Thomas Paine, has "thrown property into channels where before it never was." While profiteers were "heaping up wealth," the rest of society was "jogging on in their old way, with few or no advantages."

The poor suffered most severely, for they were most vulnerable to losses in the purchasing power of wages and military pay. But they were not alone.

Farmers, merchants, planters, and artisans also faced growing debt and uncertainty.

Rarely has the American economy been in such disarray as at the nation's founding. Problems of debt, taxation, price control, and paper money seemed to exceed the capacity of politics for compromise and resolution.

POLITICAL TUMULT IN THE STATES

The many issues embroiling American politics came together with explosive force in the mid-1780s. The political crisis that resulted spurred demands for a new and more powerful national government.

The Limits of Republican Experimentation

In a pattern that would frequently recur in American history, the postwar era witnessed growing social and political conservatism. Exhausted by the war's ordeal, many Americans focused their energies on their personal lives. With the patriotic crusade against England successfully concluded, the initial surge of republican reform subsided. As a consequence, political leadership fell increasingly to men convinced that republican experimentation had gone too far, that individual liberty threatened to overbalance political order, and that the "better sort" of men, not democratic newcomers, should occupy public office.

The most dramatic change occurred in Pennsylvania, where the democratic constitution of 1776 was replaced in 1790 by a far more conservative document. The new constitution provided for a strong governor who could veto legislation and control the militia, and a conservative senate designed to balance the more democratic assembly. Gaining control even of the assembly by the mid-1780s, the conservatives proceeded to dismantle much of the radicals' program, stopped issuing paper money, and rechartered the Bank of North America. Pennsylvania's experiment in radical republicanism was over.

Shays's Rebellion

The conservative resurgence generated little controversy in Pennsylvania. Elsewhere, however, popular opposition to hard money and high-tax policies resulted in vigorous protest. Nowhere was the situation more volatile than in Massachusetts. The controversy that erupted there in 1786 echoed strongly of equal rights and popular consent, staples of the rhetoric of 1776.

Given the war's disruption, increasing numbers of Massachusetts citizens found by the mid-1780s that they had to borrow money simply to pay their taxes and support their families. Those who were better off borrowed to speculate in western land and government securities. Because there were no commercial banks in the state, people borrowed from one another in a complicated, highly unstable pyramid of credit that reached from wealthy merchants along the coast to shopkeepers and farmers in the interior.

Trouble began when English goods glutted the American market, forcing down prices. In 1785, a number of English banks, heavily overcommitted in the American trade, called in their American loans. When American merchants tried in turn to collect debts due them by local storekeepers, a credit crisis surged through the state's economy.

Citizens Petitioning the State Government for Relief This woodcut from *Bickerstaff's Genuine Boston Almanack* of 1787 depicts a county convention framing a petition for redress of grievances to the Massachusetts government. *(Library of Congress, LC-USZ62-45567)*

AMERICAN VOICES

Massachusetts Regulators Appeal to the People

In this document, consisting of excerpts from a letter to the Hampshire Herald, a newspaper published in Worcester, Massachusetts, an ordinary citizen sympathetic to the Shays rebels gives voice to a list of grievances.

Sir, it has . . . fallen to my lot to be employed . . . in stepping forth in defence of the rights and privileges of the people . . . of the county of Hampshire.

Upon the desire of the people now at arms, I take this method to publish to the world of mankind in general, particularly the people of this Commonwealth, some of the principal grievances we complain of . . . and mean to contend for, until a redress can be obtained . . . .

- The General Court, for certain obvious reasons, must be removed out of the town of Boston.
- A revision of the constitution is absolutely necessary. . . .
- Let the lands belonging to this Commonwealth . . . be sold at the best advantage, to pay . . . our domestic debt. . . .

- The total abolition of the Inferiour Court of Common Pleas and General Sessions of the Peace.
- Deputy Sheriffs totally set aside, as a useless set of officers in the community; and Constables . . . be empowered to do the duty, by which means a large swarm of lawyers will be banished from their wonted haunts, who have been more damage to the people at large, especially the common farmers, than the savage beasts of prey.

To this I boldly sign my proper name, as a hearty wellwisher to the real rights of the people.

Thomas Grover
Worcester, December 7, 1786

- *Why would each of the grievances listed here be of such importance to the Shaysites?*

Hardest hit were farmers and laboring people in the countryside and small towns. Caught in a tightening financial bind, they turned to the state government for "stay laws" suspending the collection of private debts and thus easing the threat of foreclosure against their farms and shops. They also demanded new issues of paper money with which to pay both debts and taxes. The largest creditors, most of whom lived in commercial towns along the coast, fought such relief proposals because they wanted repayment in hard money. They also feared that new paper money would quickly depreciate, further confounding economic affairs.

By 1786, Massachusetts farmers, desperate in the face of mounting debt and a lingering agricultural depression, were petitioning the Massachusetts assembly for relief in words that echoed the colonial protests of the 1760s. Their appeals, however, fell on deaf ears, for commercial and creditor interests now controlled the government. Turning aside appeals for tax relief, the government passed a law calling for full repayment of the state debt and levied a new round of taxes that would make payment possible. No matter that, as one angry citizen charged, "there was not . . . the money in possession or at command among

the people" to pay what was due. Between 1784 and 1786, 29 towns defaulted on their tax obligations.

As frustrated Americans had done before and would do again when the law proved unresponsive to their needs, Massachusetts farmers took matters into their own hands. A Hampshire County convention of delegates from 50 towns condemned the state senate, court fees, and tax system. It advised against violence, but crowds soon began to form.

The county courts drew much of the farmers' wrath, because they issued the writs of foreclosure that private creditors and state officials demanded. In September 1786, armed men closed down the court at Worcester. When farmers threatened similar actions elsewhere, an alarmed Governor James Bowdoin dispatched 600 militiamen to protect the state supreme court, then on circuit at Springfield.

About 500 insurgents had gathered nearby under the leadership of Daniel Shays, a popular Revolutionary War captain recently fallen on hard times. A "brave and good soldier," Shays had returned home in 1780, tired and frustrated, to await payment for his military service. Like thousands of others, he had a long wait. Meanwhile, his farming went badly, debts accumulated, and, as he later recalled, "the spector of debtor's

A Woman Petitions the North Carolina Assembly
Following the war, hundreds of women petitioned state legislatures to recover property and seek redress for other war-related grievances. In this petition, Mary Moore seeks compensation from the North Carolina Assembly. *(Courtesy of the North Carolina Division of Archives and History, Raleigh, North Carolina)*

jail . . . hovered close by." Most of the men who gathered around Shays were also debtors and veterans.

The Continental Congress, worried about a possible raid on the federal arsenal at Springfield and urged by the Massachusetts delegates to take action, authorized 1,300 troops, ostensibly for service against the Native Americans but actually to be ready for use against Shays and his supporters. For a few weeks, Massachusetts teetered on the brink of civil conflict.

The insurrection collapsed in eastern Massachusetts in late November, but it was far from over in the western part of the state. When several insurgent groups refused Governor James Bowdoin's order to disperse, he called out a force of 4,400 men, financed and led by worried eastern merchants. On January 26, 1787, Shays led 1,200 men toward the federal arsenal at Springfield. When they arrived, its frightened defenders opened

DOCUMENT
Military Reports of Shays's Rebellion (1787)

fire, killing four of the attackers and sending the Shaysites into retreat.

Over the next several weeks, the militia chased the remnants of Shays's followers across the state and sent Shays himself fleeing into Vermont for safety. By the end of February, the rebellion was over. In March, the legislature pardoned all but Shays and three other leaders; in another year, they too were forgiven.

Similar challenges to public authority, fired by personal troubles and frustration over unresponsive governments, erupted in other states. In Charles County, Maryland, a "tumultuary assemblage of the people" rushed into the courthouse, demanding more paper money and the suspension of debt collection. The governor condemned the "riotous and tumultuous" proceedings and warned against further "violence and outrages." In South Carolina, an incensed Hezekiah Mayham, being served by the sheriff with a writ of foreclosure, forced him to eat it on the spot. Warned Judge Aedanus Burke, not even "5,000 troops, the best in America" could enforce obedience to the court under such conditions.

Across the states, politics was in turmoil. While many felt betrayed by the Revolution's promise of equal rights and were angered by the "arrogant unresponsiveness" of government, others were alarmed by the "democratic excesses" that the Revolution appeared to have unleashed. What the immediate future held seemed exceedingly uncertain.

TOWARD A NEW NATIONAL GOVERNMENT

By 1786, belief was spreading among members of Congress that the nation was in crisis and that the republican experiment was in danger of foundering. Explanations for the crisis and prescriptions for its resolution varied, but attention focused on the inadequacies of the Articles of Confederation. Within two years, following a deeply divisive political struggle, a new constitution replaced the Articles, altering forever the course of American history.

The Rise of Federalism

The supporters of a stronger national government called themselves Federalists (leading their opponents to adopt the name Anti-Federalists). Led by men such as Washington, Hamilton, Madison, and Jay, whose experiences in the continental army and Congress had strengthened their national vision, Federalists believed that the nation's survival was at stake. Such men had never been comfortable with the more democratic impulses of the Revolution. While committed to moderate republicanism, they believed that democratic change had gone too far, property rights needed greater protection, and an "aristocracy of talent" should lead the country.

The Revolution, lamented John Jay, "laid open a wide field for the operation of ambition," especially for "men raised from low degrees to high stations and rendered giddy by elevation." It was time, he insisted, to find better ways of protecting "the worthy against the licentious."

Federalist leaders feared the loss of their own social and political power, but they were concerned as well about the collapse of the orderly world they believed essential to the preservation of republican liberty. In 1776, American liberty had required protection against unrestrained British power. Now, however, danger arose from excessive liberty that threatened to degenerate into license. "We have probably had too good an opinion of human nature," concluded Washington somberly. "Experience has taught us, that men will not adopt and carry into execution measures the best calculated for their own good, without the intervention of a coercive power." What America now needed was a "strong government, ably administered."

The Federalists regarded outbursts like Shays's uprising not as evidence of genuine social distress but as threats to social and political order. Although they were reassured by the speed with which the Shaysites had been dispatched, the episode persuaded them of the need for a stronger national government managed by the "better sort."

Congress's inability to handle the national debt, establish public credit, and restore overseas trade also troubled the Federalists. Sensitive to America's economic and military weakness, smarting from French and English arrogance, and aware of continuing European designs on North America, they called for a new national government capable of extending American trade, spurring economic recovery, and protecting the national interest.

Beyond that, the Federalists shared a vision of an expanding commercial republic, its people spreading across the rich lands of the interior, its merchant ships connecting America with the markets of Europe and beyond. That vision, so rich in national promise, seemed clearly at risk.

The Grand Convention

The first step toward governmental reform came in September 1786, when delegates from five states who were gathered in Annapolis, Maryland,

James Madison, Father of the U.S. Constitution
James Madison of Virginia, only 36 years old when the Philadelphia convention met, worked tirelessly between 1786 and 1788 to replace the Articles of Confederation with a new and more effective national constitution. (*Gilbert Stuart,* Portrait of James Madison, *1822. Mead Art Museum, Amherst Collection, Bequest of Herbert L. Pratt, Class of 1895*)

to discuss interstate commerce issued a call for a convention to revise the Articles of Confederation. In February, the Confederation Congress cautiously endorsed the idea. Before long, it became clear that far more than a revision of the Articles was afoot.

During May 1787, delegates representing every state except Rhode Island began assembling in Philadelphia. The city bustled with excitement as they gathered, for the roster read like an honor roll of the Revolution. From Virginia came the distinguished lawyer George Mason, chief author of Virginia's trailblazing bill of rights, and the already legendary George Washington. Proponents of the convention had held their breath while Washington considered whether to attend. His presence vastly increased the prospects of success. James Madison was there as well. No one, with perhaps the single exception of Alexander Hamilton, was more committed to nationalist reform. Certainly, no one had worked harder to prepare for the convention. Poring over treatises on republican government and natural law that his friend Thomas Jefferson had sent from France, Madison brought to Philadelphia a clear design for a new national government. That design, presented to the convention as the Virginia Plan, would serve as the basis for the new constitution. Nor did anyone rival the diminutive Madison's contributions to the convention's work. Tirelessly, he took the convention floor to argue the nationalist cause or buttonhole wavering delegates to strengthen their resolve. Somehow, he also found the energy to keep extensive notes of the debates in his personal shorthand. Those notes constitute the essential record of the convention's proceedings.

Two distinguished Virginians were conspicuously absent. Thomas Jefferson was in Paris as minister to France, and the old patriot Patrick Henry, an ardent champion of state supremacy, feared what the convention would do and wanted no part of it.

From Pennsylvania came the venerable Benjamin Franklin, too old to contribute significantly to the debates but still able to call quarreling members to account and reinspire them in their work. His colleagues from Pennsylvania included the erudite Scots lawyer James Wilson, whose nationalist sympathies had been inflamed when a democratic mob attacked his elegant Philadelphia townhouse in 1779. Robert Morris, probably the richest man in America, was there as well. Massachusetts was ably represented by Elbridge Gerry and Rufus King, while South Carolina sent John Rutledge and

Charles Pinckney. Roger Sherman led Connecticut's contingent.

The New York assembly sent a deeply divided delegation. Governor George Clinton, determined to protect New York's autonomy as well as his own political power, saw to it that several Anti-Federalist skeptics made the trip to Philadelphia. They were no match for Hamilton, however.

Born in the Leeward Islands, the "bastard brat of a Scots-peddlar" and a strong-willed woman with a troubled marriage, Hamilton used his intelligence and ingratiating charm to rise rapidly in the world. Sent to New York by wealthy sponsors, he quickly established himself as a favorite of the city's mercantile community. While still in his early twenties, he became Washington's wartime aide-de-camp. That relationship served Hamilton well for the next 20 years. Returning from the war, he married the wealthy Elizabeth Schuyler, thereby securing his personal fortune and strengthening his political connections. Together with Madison, Hamilton had promoted the abortive Annapolis convention. At Philadelphia, he was determined to drive his nationalist vision ahead.

Meeting in Independence Hall, where the Declaration of Independence had been proclaimed little more than a decade earlier, the convention elected Washington as its presiding officer, adopted rules of procedure, and, after spirited debate, voted to close the doors and conduct its business in secret.

Creating a New National Government This painting by Thomas Rossiter, done in the early nineteenth century, provides an imaginative portrayal of the Philadelphia convention, with George Washington presiding and a rising sun, symbolic of the new nation, shining behind him. *(Thomas Rossiter, Signing of the Constitution, ca. 1860–1870. Independence National Historical Park Collection)*

Drafting the Constitution

Debate focused first on the Virginia Plan, introduced on May 29 by Edmund Randolph. It outlined a potentially powerful national government and effectively set the convention's agenda. According to its provisions, there would be a bicameral Congress, with the lower house elected by the people and the upper house, or Senate, chosen by the lower house from nominees proposed by the state legislatures. The plan also called for a president who would be named by Congress, a national judiciary, and a Council of Revision, whose task was to review the constitutionality of federal laws.

DOCUMENT

James Madison,
The Virginia (or
Randolph) Plan
(1787)

The smaller states quickly objected to the Virginia Plan's call for proportional rather than equal representation of the states. On June 15, William Paterson introduced a counterproposal, the New Jersey Plan. It urged retention of the Articles of Confederation as the basic structure of government while conferring on Congress the long-sought powers to tax and regulate foreign and interstate commerce. After three days of heated debate, by a vote of seven states to three, the delegates adopted the Virginia Plan as the basis for further discussions. It was now clear that the convention would replace the Articles with a much stronger national government. The only question was how powerful the new government would be.

DOCUMENT

The New Jersey
Plan (1787)

At times over the next four months, it seemed that the Grand Convention would collapse under the weight of its own disagreements and the oppressive summer heat. How were the conflicting interests of large and small states to be reconciled? How should the balance of power between national and state governments be struck? How could an executive be created that was strong enough to govern but not so strong as to endanger republican liberty? And what, if anything, would the convention say about slavery and the slave trade, issues on which northerners and southerners, antislavery and proslavery advocates so passionately disagreed?

Hamilton presented an audaciously conservative proposal, calling for a Congress and president elected for life and a national government so powerful that the states would become little more than administrative agencies. Finding his plan under attack and his influence eroding, Hamilton withdrew from the convention in late June. He would return a month later but make few additional contributions to the convention's work.

At the other extreme stood the ardent Anti-Federalist Luther Martin of Maryland. Rude and unkempt, Martin opposed anything that threatened state sovereignty or smacked of aristocracy. Increasingly isolated by the convention's nationalist inclinations, Martin also returned home, in his case to spread the alarm.

By early July, with tempers frayed and frustration growing over the apparent deadlock, the delegates agreed to recess, ostensibly for Independence Day but actually to let Franklin, Roger Sherman of Connecticut, and several other delegates make a final effort at compromise. Everyone agreed that only a bold stroke could prevent a collapse.

That stroke came on July 12, as part of what has become known as the Great Compromise. The reassembled delegates settled one major point of controversy by agreeing that representation in the lower house should be based on the total of each state's white population plus three-fifths of its blacks. Though African Americans were not accorded citizenship and could not vote, the southern delegates argued that they should be fully counted for this purpose. Delegates from the northern states, where relatively few blacks lived, did not want them counted at all, but the bargain was struck. As part of this compromise, the convention agreed that direct taxes would also be apportioned on the basis of population and that blacks would be counted similarly in that calculation. On July 16, the convention accepted the principle that the states should have equal votes in the Senate. Thus the interests of both large states and small were effectively accommodated.

The convention then submitted its work to a committee of detail for drafting in proper constitutional form. That group reported on August 6, and for the next month the delegates hammered out the language of the document's seven articles. On several occasions, differences seemed so great that it was uncertain whether the convention could proceed. In each instance, however, agreement was reached, and the discussion continued.

Determined to give the new government the stability that state governments lacked, the delegates created an electoral process designed to bring people of wide experience and solid reputation into national office. An Electoral College of wise and experienced leaders, selected at the direction of state legislatures, would meet to choose the president. The process functioned exactly that way during the first several presidential elections.

Selection of the Senate would be similarly indirect, for its members were to be named by the state legislatures. (Not until 1913, with ratification of the Seventeenth Amendment, would the American people elect their senators directly.) Even the House of Representatives, the only popularly elected branch of the new government, was to be filled with people

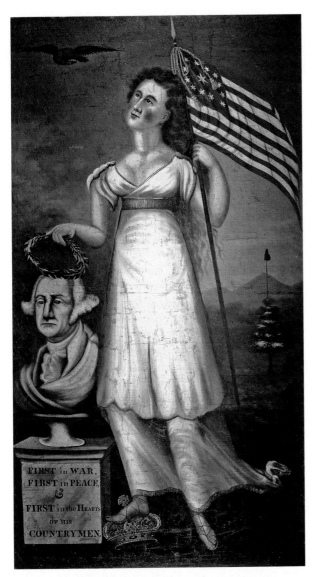

Symbols of the New Nation   This painting by an unknown artist is filled with political symbols whose meaning members
of the revolutionary generation would quickly have understood. How
many distinct symbols can you find in the painting? What messages
were they intended to convey? (Liberty and Washington, *1805,*
Fenimore Art Museum, Cooperstown, NY. Photo credit: Richard Walker)

of standing and wealth, for the Federalists were confident that only such men would be able to attract
the necessary votes.

The delegates' final set of compromises touched
the fate of black Americans. At the insistence of
southerners, the convention agreed that the slave
trade would not formally end for another 20 years.
As drafted, the Constitution did not contain the
words *slavery* or *slave trade,* but spoke more vaguely
about not prohibiting the "migration or importation
of such persons as any of the states now existing
shall think proper to admit." The meaning, however,
was entirely clear.

Despite Gouverneur Morris's impassioned charge
that slavery was a "nefarious institution" that would
bring "the curse of Heaven on the states where it pre-
vails," the delegates firmly rejected a proposal to
abolish slavery, thereby tacitly acknowledging its legitimacy. More than that, they guaranteed slavery's
protection, by writing in Section 2 of Article 4 that
"No person held to service or labour in one state, . . .
[and] escaping into another, shall, in consequence of
any law . . . therein, be discharged from such service,
but shall be delivered up on claim of the party to
whom such service or labour may be due." Through
such convoluted language, the delegates provided
federal sanction for the capture and return of runaway slaves. This fugitive slave clause would return
to haunt northern consciences in the years ahead. At
the time, however, it seemed a small price to pay for
sectional harmony and a new government.

Although the Constitution's unique federal system
of government called for shared responsibilities between the nation and the states, it decisively
strengthened the national government. Congress
would now have the authority to levy and collect
taxes, regulate commerce with foreign nations and
between the states, devise uniform rules for naturalization, administer national patents and copyrights,
and control the federal district in which it would
eventually be located. Conspicuously missing was
any statement reserving to the states all powers not
explicitly conferred on the central government. Such
language had proved crippling in the Articles of Confederation. On the contrary, the Constitution contained a number of clauses bestowing vaguely defined grants of power on the new government.
Section 8 of Article 1, for example, granted Congress
the authority to "provide for the . . . general welfare of
the United States" as well as to "make all laws . . . necessary and proper for carrying into execution . . . all
. . . powers vested by this Constitution in the government of the United States." Later generations would
call these phrases "elastic clauses" and would use
them to expand the federal government's activities.

In addition, Section 10 of Article 1 contained a
litany of powers denied to the states, among them issuing paper money and entering into agreements
with foreign powers without the consent of Congress.
A final measure of the Federalists' determination to
ensure the new government's supremacy over the
states, was the assertion in Article 6 that the Constitution and all laws and treaties passed under it were
to be regarded as the "supreme Law of the Land."

When the convention had finished its business, 3
of the 42 remaining delegates refused to sign the document. The other 39, however, affixed their names
and forwarded it to the Confederation Congress

RECOVERING THE PAST

Patriotic Paintings

The questions that historians ask are limited only by their own imagination and the evidence left behind for them to study. In addition to written documents such as household inventories and militia rolls, and material artifacts such as tombstones and the archaeological residue of burial mounds, historians also examine paintings and other forms of visual evidence for information about the past.

While showing the development of artistic styles and techniques, paintings also provide important windows into past eras for social and cultural historians by revealing how people looked and did their work, as well as what the landscape and built environment were like. Paintings also offer insights into the values and attitudes of past times, for they are often intended not only to please the viewer's eye but also to enlighten and instruct.

So it was with Charles Willson Peale, who as a member of the Pennsylvania militia carried paint kits and canvas along with his musket as he followed George Washington during the Revolutionary War. Before the war was over, he had completed four portraits of the general.

And so it was, even more spectacularly, with the artist John Trumbull, who recorded on canvas some of the most dramatic events of the nation's founding. Slighted for promotion during the Rhode Island campaign early in the war, Trumbull resigned his commission to become a painter. After a frustrating start, he sailed for London, where he studied with the artist Benjamin West, another transplanted American. Imprisoned briefly at the urging of angry American Loyalists, Trumbull was deported to the United States. Returning to England at the war's end, he was urged by West and Thomas Jefferson to paint an ambitious series of "national history" canvases. Over the next four decades, in addition to numerous portraits, religious subjects, and landscapes, Trumbull fashioned the most famous sequence of patriotic paintings ever undertaken by an American artist.

Included were four canvases, depicting crucial military and civil turning points in the struggle for American independence, commissioned by Congress in the early nineteenth century and now hanging in the capitol rotunda in Washington, D.C.—*The Surrender of General Burgoyne at Saratoga, The Surrender of Lord Cornwallis at Yorktown, The Declaration of Independence,* and *The Resignation of General Washington* as commander of the continental army. In addition to those monumental works, Trumbull fashioned a number of heroic battle scenes, including *The Death of General Warren at the Battle of Bunker Hill,* shown here.

Though Trumbull knew Warren and others who fought at Bunker Hill, he himself had witnessed the battle from a distance. Although Trumbull was familiar with the techniques of military combat from his own months in the army, he was not primarily concerned with literal accuracy as he composed his painting. Guided by the canons of classical aesthetics popular at the time, he was more interested in the power of artistic "invention" to impart "ideal" truths through the use of brush and pigment.

Examine the painting carefully. How has the artist arranged the figures in relationship to each other? What facial expressions and postures has he given to the people depicted? In what ways do the banners, clouds, and uses of light and color contribute to the painting's overall effect? What messages about the Revolutionary War did Trumbull want viewers to carry away from the canvas?

In all his historical canvases, Trumbull was intent on promoting national pride and constructing public memory. How does this painting serve those purposes? Why was the creation of a shared public memory so important during the early years of the new republic? Might Trumbull have had future generations of Americans as well as his own contemporaries in mind as he did his work?

Art and politics have been intimately related throughout our history, for painting, theater, music, and other forms of performance art have been employed to challenge as well as celebrate political leaders and their policies.

REFLECTING ON THE PAST   Think for a moment about the connections between art and politics in our own time. Why have controversies recently swirled around the National Endowments for the Arts and the Humanities? Should the government provide financial assistance for the arts? If so, should such assistance be accompanied by restrictions on the political messages such art might convey? Is art ever nonpolitical?

John Trumbull, *The Death of General Warren at the Battle of Bunker Hill.* *(Francis G. Mayer/CORBIS)*

along with the request that it be sent on to the states for approval. On September 17, the Grand Convention adjourned.

Federalists Versus Anti-Federalists

Ratification presented the Federalists with a more difficult problem than they had faced at Philadelphia, for the debate now shifted to the states, where sentiment was sharply divided and the political situation was more difficult to control. Recognizing the unlikelihood of gaining quick agreement by all 13 states, Federalists stipulated that the Constitution should go into effect when any 9 agreed to it. Other states could then enter the Union as they were ready. Ratification was to be decided by specially elected conventions rather than by the state assemblies. Approval by such conventions would give the new Constitution greater legitimacy by grounding it in the consent of the people.

In the Confederation Congress, opponents of the new Constitution charged that the Philadelphia Convention had grossly exceeded its authority. But after a few days' debate, Congress dutifully forwarded the document to the states for consideration. Word of the dramatic changes being proposed spread rapidly. In each state, Federalists and Anti-Federalists, the latter now actively opposing the Constitution, prepared to debate the new articles of government.

Opposition to the Constitution was widespread and vocal. Some critics warned of the threat to state interests. Others, like Timothy Blood-worth, charged the Federalists with betraying revolutionary republicanism. Like all "energetic" governments, the one being proposed would be corrupted by its own power. Far from the watchful eyes of the citizenry, its officials would behave as power wielders always had, and American liberty, so recently preserved at such high cost, would again come under attack.

Patrick Henry, Against Ratification of the Constitution (1788)

The Anti-Federalists were aghast at the Federalists' vision of an expanding "republican empire." "The idea of . . . [a] republic, on an average of 1,000 miles in length, and 800 in breadth, and containing 6 millions of white inhabitants all reduced to the same standards of morals, . . . habits . . . [and] laws," exclaimed one incredulous critic, is "contrary to the whole experience of mankind." Such an extended republic would quickly fall prey to factional conflict and internal disorder. Anti-Federalists continued to believe that republican liberty could be preserved only in small, homogeneous societies, where the seeds of faction were few and public virtue guided citizens' behavior.

Nor were Anti-Federalists persuaded that the proposed separation of executive, legislative, and judicial branches or the intended balance between state and national governments would prevent power's abuse. Government, they insisted, must be kept simple, for complexity only confused the people and cloaked selfish ambition.

Not all Anti-Federalists were democratic in sympathy. In the South, many opponents of the Constitution held slaves, and their appeals to local authority did not always mean support for political equality, even among whites. Yet along with their warnings against centralized power, many did speak fervently of democratic principles. Certainly they believed more firmly than their Federalist opponents that if government was to be safe, it must be tied closely to the people.

Federalist spokesmen moved quickly to counter the Anti-Federalists' attack, for many of the criticisms carried the sanction of the revolutionary past. Their most important effort was a series of essays penned by James Madison, Alexander Hamilton, and John Jay and published in New York under the pseudonym Publius. The *Federalist Papers,* as they were called, were written to promote ratification in New York but were quickly reprinted elsewhere.

Federalist No. 51 (Feb. 6, 1788)

Madison, Hamilton, and Jay moved systematically through the Constitution, explaining its virtues and responding to the Anti-Federalists' charges. In the process, they described a political vision fundamentally different from that of their Anti-Federalist opponents.

No difference was more dramatic than the Federalists' treatment of governmental power. Power, the Federalists argued, was not the enemy of liberty but its guarantor. Where government was not sufficiently "energetic" and "efficient" demagogues and disorganizers would find opportunity to do their nefarious work. It is far better, Hamilton wrote in *Federalist No. 26,* "to hazard the abuse of . . . confidence than to embarrass the government and endanger the public safety by impolitic restrictions of . . . authority."

The authors of the *Federalist Papers* also countered Anti-Federalist warnings that a single, extended republic would lead inevitably to factional conflict and the end of republican liberty. Turning the Anti-Federalists' argument on its head, they explained that political divisions were the inevitable accompaniment of human liberty. Madison wrote in *Federalist No. 10:* "Liberty is to faction what air is to fire, an aliment without which it instantly expires." To suppress faction would bring the destruction of liberty itself.

Publius (James Madison), Federalist No. 10 (1788)

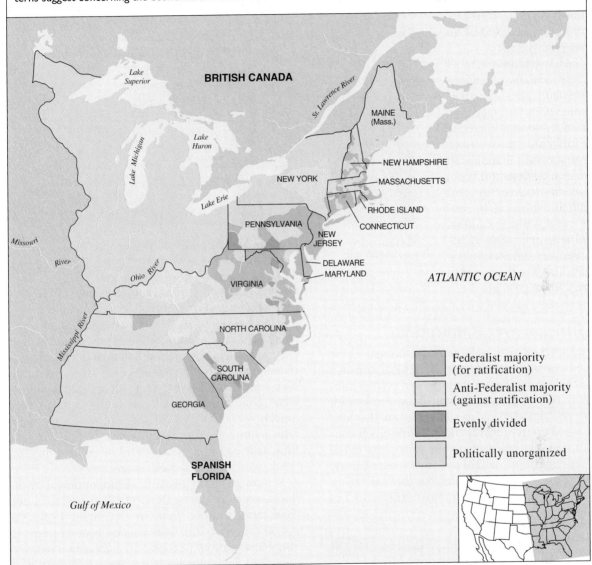

Federalist and Anti-Federalist Areas, 1787–1788

Distinct geographic patterns of Federalist and Anti-Federalist strength developed during the ratification debate. This map shows areas whose delegates to the state ratifying conventions voted for and against the Constitution. What do the patterns suggest concerning the economic and social bases of Federalist and Anti-Federalist support?

Earlier emphasis on public virtue as the guarantor of political order, Federalists affirmed, had been naive, for few people would consistently put the public good ahead of their own interests. Politics had to heed this harsh fact of human nature and provide for peaceful compromise among conflicting groups. That could be best accomplished by expanding the nation so that it included innumerable factions. Out of the clash and accommodation of social and economic interests would emerge the best possible approximation of the public good.

In that argument is to be found the basic rationale for modern democratic politics, but it left the Anti-Federalists sputtering in frustration. Where in the Federalists' scheme was there a place for that familiar abstraction, the public good? What would become of public virtue in a system built on the notion of competing, private interests? In such a free market of competition, the Anti-Federalists warned, the wealthy and powerful would thrive, while ordinary folk would suffer.

As the ratification debate revealed, the two camps held sharply different visions of the new republic. The Anti-Federalists remained much closer to the original republicanism of 1776, with its suspicion of power and wealth, its emphasis on the primacy of local government, and its fears of national development. They envisioned a decentralized republic filled with citizens who were self-reliant and guided by public virtue, and whose destiny was determined primarily by the states rather than the nation. Anxious about the future, they longed to preserve the political world of an idealized past.

The Federalists, on the other hand, persuaded that America's situation had changed dramatically since 1776, embraced the idea of nationhood and eagerly looked forward to the development of a rising "republican empire," fueled by commercial development and led by men of wealth and talent. Both Federalists and Anti-Federalists claimed to be heirs of the Revolution, yet they differed fundamentally in what they understood that heritage to be.

Celebrating Ratification　The federal ship *Hamilton* formed the centerpiece of a grand procession in New York City celebrating the successful ratification of the new Constitution.

The Struggle over Ratification

No one knows what most Americans thought of the proposed Constitution, for no national plebiscite on it was ever taken. Probably no more than several hundred thousand people participated in the elections for the state ratifying conventions, and many of the delegates carried no binding instructions from their constituents on how they should vote. A majority of the people probably opposed the document, out of either indifference or alarm. Fortunately for the Federalists, they did not have to persuade most Americans but

needed only to secure majorities in nine of the state ratifying conventions, a much less formidable task.

They set about that task with determination. As soon as the Philadelphia Convention adjourned, its members hurried home to organize the ratification movement in their states. In Delaware, Georgia, New Jersey, and Connecticut, where the Federalists were confident of their strength, they pressed quickly for a vote. Where the outcome was uncertain, as in New York, Massachusetts, and Virginia, they delayed, hoping that word of ratification elsewhere would work to their benefit.

It took less than a year to secure approval by the necessary nine states. Delaware, Pennsylvania, and New Jersey ratified first, in December 1787. Approval came a month later in Georgia and Connecticut. Massachusetts ratified in February 1788, but only after Federalist leaders agreed to forward a set of amendments outlining a federal bill of rights along with notice of ratification. The strategy worked, for it brought Samuel Adams and John Hancock into line, and with them the crucial convention votes that they controlled.

Maryland and South Carolina were the seventh and eighth states to approve. That left New Hampshire and Virginia vying for the honor of being ninth and putting the Constitution over the top. Sensing that they lacked the necessary votes, Federalists adjourned the New Hampshire convention and worked feverishly to build support. When the convention reconvened, it took but three days to secure a Federalist majority.

Two massive gaps in the new Union remained— Virginia and New York. Clearly, the nation could not

Ratification of the Constitution

Votes of State Ratifying Conventions

State	Date	For	Against
Delaware	December 1787	30	0
Pennsylvania	December 1787	46	23
New Jersey	December 1787	38	0
Georgia	January 1788	26	0
Connecticut	January 1788	128	40
Massachusetts	February 1788	187	168
Maryland	April 1788	63	11
South Carolina	May 1788	149	73
New Hampshire	June 1788	57	47
Virginia	June 1788	89	79
New York	July 1788	30	27
North Carolina	November 1789	194	77
Rhode Island	May 1790	34	32

endure without them. In Virginia, Madison gathered support by promising that the new Congress would immediately consider a federal bill of rights. Other Federalists spread the rumor that Patrick Henry, among the most influential Anti-Federalist leaders, had changed sides, a charge that Henry angrily denied. His oratory, however, proved no match for the careful politicking of Madison and others. On June 25, the Virginia convention voted to ratify by a narrow margin of 10 votes.

The New York convention gathered on June 17 at Poughkeepsie, with the Anti-Federalist followers of Governor Clinton firmly in command. Hamilton worked for delay, hoping that news of the results in New Hampshire and Virginia would turn the tide. For several weeks, approval hung in the balance. On July 27, approval squeaked through, 30 to 27. That left two states still uncommitted. North Carolina (with Timothy Bloodworth's skeptical approval) finally ratified in November 1789. Rhode Island did not enter the Union until May 1790, more than a year after the new government had gotten underway.

The Social Geography of Ratification

Federalist strength in the ratifying conventions was concentrated in areas along the coast and navigable rivers, and was strongest in cities and towns. Merchants and businessmen supported the Constitution most ardently. Enthusiasm also ran high among urban laborers, artisans, and shopkeepers—surprisingly so, given the Anti-Federalists' criticism of wealth and power and their emphasis on democratic equality. City artisans and workers, after all, had been in the vanguard of democratic reform during the Revolution. But in the troubled circumstances of the late 1780s, they worried primarily about their livelihoods and believed that a stronger government could better promote overseas trade and protect American artisans from foreign competition.

On July 4, 1788, a grand procession celebrating the Constitution's ratification wound through the streets of Philadelphia. Seventeen thousand strong, it graphically demonstrated the breadth of support for the Constitution. At the head of the line marched lawyers, merchants, and others of the city's elite. Close behind came representatives of virtually every trade in the city, from ship's carpenters to shoemakers, each trade carrying its own flags and banners. "May commerce flourish and industry be rewarded," declared the shipbuilders' banner. "Home-brewed is best," proclaimed the maltsters. For the moment, declared the democratic-minded physician Benjamin Rush in amazement, "rank . . . forgot all its claims." Within a few years, political disputes would divide merchants and artisans

once again. For the moment, however, people of all ranks joined in celebrating the new Constitution.

Outside the coastal cities, political alignments were more sharply divided. The Constitution found support among commercial farmers and southern planters eager for profit and anxious about overseas markets. But in the interior, Federalist enthusiasm waned and Anti-Federalist sentiment increased. Among ordinary farmers living outside the market economy, local loyalties and the republicanism of 1776 still held sway. They found Federalist visions of an expanding "American empire" alarming.

Why did the Federalists prevail when their opponents had only to tap into people's deep-seated fears of central government and appeal to their local loyalties? They won in part because of the widespread perception that the Articles of Confederation were inadequate and that America's experiment in republican independence was doomed unless decisive action was taken. More than anything, however, the Federalists succeeded because of their determination and political skill. Most of the Revolution's major leaders were Federalists. Time and again these worthies spoke out for the Constitution, and time and again their support proved decisive. Their experience in the continental army and as members of the Continental and Confederation Congresses fired their vision of what the nation might become. They brought that vision to the ratification process and asked others to share it. Their success turned the American republic in a new and fateful direction.

TIMELINE

1780s	Pennsylvania begins gradual abolition of slavery Virginia and Maryland debate abolition of slavery
1784	Treaty of Fort Stanwix with the Iroquois Spain closes the Mississippi River to American navigation
1785	Treaty of Hopewell with the Cherokee Land Ordinance for the Northwest Territory Jay–Gardoqui negotiations
1786	Virginia adopts Bill for Establishing Religious Freedom Annapolis Convention calls for revision of the Articles of Confederation
1786–1787	Shays's Rebellion
1787	Northwest Ordinance Constitutional Convention *Federalist Papers* published by Hamilton, Jay, and Madison
1788	Constitution ratified

Conclusion

Completing the Revolution

Only five years had passed between England's acknowledgment of American independence in 1783 and ratification of the new national Constitution, yet to many Americans it seemed far longer than that. At war's end, the difficulties of sustaining American liberty were already evident. The experience of the 1780s added to these difficulties as the American people struggled to survive in a hostile Atlantic environment and cope with troublesome issues of church and state, slavery and the slave trade, and an economy shattered by the cutoff of overseas trade and rampant inflation. Throughout the resulting political turmoil, Americans continued to argue over how democratic their experiment in republicanism could safely be, and even whether it could survive.

At the same time, the American people retained an immense reservoir of optimism about the future. Had they not defeated mighty England? Was not their Revolution destined to change the course of history and provide a model for all people? Did not America's wonderfully rich interior contain the promise of limitless economic and social opportunity? Though Timothy Bloodworth and others continued to worry, countless Americans, still filled with the enthusiasm of their new beginning, answered with a resounding "Yes." Much would depend, of course, on their new Constitution and the government soon to be created under it. As the ratification debate subsided and the Confederation Congress prepared to adjourn, the American people looked ahead—both eagerly and anxiously.

Questions for Review and Reflection

1. Under the terms of the peace treaty of 1783 ending the Revolutionary War, the western boundary of the United States was set at the Mississippi River. What problems did the new territory west of the Appalachian Mountains pose for the new nation, and how effectively did Congress handle those problems during the 1780s?

2. With independence, the United States had to develop its own ways of dealing with other nations, that is, its own foreign policy. What major foreign policy problems did Congress face during the 1780s, and how effectively did it deal with them?

3. Throughout the nation's history, wars have disrupted the American economy. To what extent was this true of the Revolutionary War and what were the consequences during the 1780s?

4. The successful struggle for American independence encouraged many Americans to apply the language of rights and equality used against England to the conditions of political, social, and religious life in the American states. Identify three examples of this pressure for democratic change and explain how successful they were during the 1780s.

5. The successful creation of the new American Constitution in 1787–1788 has often been interpreted as a conservative reaction to the more democratic tendencies of the American Revolution. Do you think this is an accurate judgment? Explain.

Recommended Reading

Recommended Readings are posted on the Web site for this textbook. Visit www.ablongman.com/nash

Fiction and Film

The visually lush commercial film *Jefferson in Paris* (1995) combines a depiction of Jefferson's years as U.S. minister to France (1785–1789) with commentaries on themes of liberty and slavery involving events leading to the French Revolution and Jefferson's controversial liaison with his slave girl Sally Hemmings. The documentary film *Unearthing the* *Slave Trade* (1994) uses the recent discovery and excavation of a black burying ground near Wall Street in New York City, where deceased slaves were interred from about 1712 to 1790, to depict the life of urban slaves in eighteenth-century America. Herman Melville's novel *Israel Potter* (1855) tells the story of a fictitious Revolutionary War sailor who encounters

Benjamin Franklin, Ethan Allen, and John Paul Jones during his adventures and ends up in England as a gardener to King George III. In *Those Who Love: A Biographical Novel of Abigail and John Adams* (1965),

Irving Stone traces the life story of this remarkable couple, largely through Abigail's eyes, as they move from early courtship through the end of John's presidency in 1800.

Discovering U.S. History Online

1777–1815: The Revolutionary War to the War of 1812
www.tax.org/Museum/1777-1815.htm
This essay explores by timeline the way the new nation dealt with finances, debt, and taxes.

Indian Affairs: Laws and Treaties
www.digital.library.okstate.edu/kappler
This site offers a digitized and searchable version of U.S. treaties, laws, and executive orders pertaining to Native American tribes. Volume two contains treaties from 1770–1890.

Colonial Currency
www.etext.lib.virginia.edu/users/brock/
This site includes informative primary and secondary sources on early American currency.

Evolution of Territories and States from the Old "Northwest Territory"
www.jlindquist.com/mapsupp1.html
This site includes a link to the full text of the Northwest Ordinance of 1787, tables and maps showing the geographical evolution of the territory, photos of the area, and an image of the map showing Jefferson's concept for the states to be carved out of the territory.

Religion and the American Revolution
www.lcweb.loc.gov/exhibits/religion/rel03.html
Providing an overview of eighteenth-century religion in the American colonies, this site draws on primary source material such as paintings of clergymen, title pages of published sermons, and other artifacts.

A Struggle from the Start
www.hartford-hwp.com/HBHP/exhibit/index.html
A local history, this site presents a virtual exhibit of the history of Hartford's African American community from 1638 to the present, including the post-Revolutionary period.

Shays' Rebellion
www.sjchs-history.org/shays.html
A brief, illustrated explanation of the rebellion and its participants.

Within These Walls
www.americanhistory.si.edu/house/default.asp
Part of the museum's "Hands on History," this virtual exhibit tells the story of five families who lived in one house over 200 years, including the Choate family (1757–1772).

You Be the Historian
www.americanhistory.si.edu/hohr/springer
Part of the Smithsonian's online museum, this exhibit enables students to examine artifacts from the home of New Castle, Delaware, residents Thomas and Elizabeth Springer and interpret the lives of a late eighteenth-century American family.

The Founders' Constitution
www.press-pubs.uchicago.edu/founders/
An online anthology of the five-volume print edition, this site presents the full text (searchable) of the Constitution and of such "fundamental documents" as the Northwest Ordinance. Many primary source letters revealing the formation of the ideas that would become the constitution are also available on the site.

A Procedural Guide to the Electoral College
www.archives.gov/federal_register/electoral_college/electoral_college.html
This site explains how the Electoral College works as well as how it was established.

The Federalist
www.law.emory.edu/FEDERAL/federalist
www.law.emory.edu/FEDERAL/usconst.html
This searchable site, which presents a collection of the most important *Federalist Papers* as well as the complete text of the Constitution, is especially useful for its information about the Bill of Rights and other constitutional amendments.

Documents from the Continental Congress and the Constitutional Convention, 1774–1789
www.memory.loc.gov/ammem/bdsds/bdsdhome.html
This site allows access to the Continental Congress Broadside Collection (253 titles) and the Constitutional Convention Broadside Collection (21 titles), containing documents relating to the work of Congress and the drafting and ratification of the Constitution. Items include extracts of the journals of Congress, resolutions, proclamations, committee reports, treaties, and early printed versions of the U.S. Constitution and the Declaration of Independence.

Independence Hall National Historical Park
www.nps.gov/inde/visit.html
This National Park Service site contains images and historical accounts of Independence Hall and other Philadelphia buildings closely associated with the founding of the United States.

CHAPTER 8

Creating a Nation

In December 1790, the national government moved from New York to Philadelphia, where it stayed until moving to the new capital in the District of Columbia in 1799. While in Philadelphia, the House and Senate met in Congress Hall, adjacent to the Philadelphia State House depicted here. In this image, a variety of people, including several Indians, mingle in the State House yard. *(The Historical Society of Pennsylvania (HSP), The State House, Philadelphia, 1800, William Birch, [Bd 61 B 531 plate 22])*

American Stories

In October 1789, David Brown arrived in Dedham, Massachusetts. Born about 50 years earlier in Bethlehem, Connecticut, Brown served in the Revolutionary army. After the war, he shipped out on an American merchantman to see the world. His travels, as he reported, took him to "nineteen different . . . Kingdoms in Europe, and nearly all the United States." For two years before settling in Dedham, he visited scores of Massachusetts towns, supporting himself as a day laborer while discussing the troubled state of public affairs with local townspeople.

Initially, the people of Dedham took little notice of Brown, but he soon made his presence felt. Though he had little formal schooling, he was a man of powerful opinions and considerable natural ability. His reading and personal experience had persuaded him that government was a conspiracy of the rich to exploit farmers, artisans, and other common folk, and he was quick to make his opinions known.

The object of his wrath was the central government recently established under the new national constitution. Though he could cite no evidence, he accused government leaders of engrossing the nation's western lands for themselves. "Five hundred [people] out of the union of five millions receive all the benefit of public property and live upon the ruins of the rest of the community," he fumed in one of his numerous pamphlets. Such a government, he warned, would soon lose the confidence of the people.

In the highly charged political climate of the 1790s, Brown's exaggerated attacks on the new government brought a sharp response. In 1798, John Davis, the federal district attorney in Boston, issued a warrant for Brown's arrest on charges of sedition, while government-supported newspapers attacked him as a "rallying point of insurrection and disorder." Fearing arrest, Brown fled to Salem, where he was caught and charged with intent to defame the government and aid the country's enemies. Lacking $400 bail, he was clapped in prison.

In June 1799, Brown came before the U.S. Circuit Court, Justice Samuel Chase presiding. Chase's behavior was anything but judicious. Convinced that critics of the administration were enemies of the republic, Chase was determined to make Brown an example. Confused and hoping for leniency, Brown pleaded guilty to the charges against him.

Ignoring Brown's plea, Chase directed the federal prosecutor to "examine the witness . . . so that the degree of his guilt might be duly ascertained." Before passing sentence, Chase demanded that Brown provide the names of his accomplices and a list of subscribers to his writings. When Brown refused, protesting that he would "lose all my friends," Chase sentenced him to a fine of $480 and 18 months in jail, no matter that Brown could not pay the fine and faced the prospect of indefinite imprisonment.

In rendering judgment, Chase castigated Brown for his "disorganizing doctrines and . . . falsehoods, and the very alarming and dangerous excesses to which he attempted to incite the uninformed part of the community." Not all citizens, Chase thought, should be allowed to comment so brashly on public affairs. For nearly two years, Brown languished in prison. Not until the Federalist party was defeated in the election of 1800 and the Jeffersonian Republicans had taken office was he freed.

David Brown discovered how easy it was for critics of the government to get into trouble in the early republic, one of the most tumultuous eras in American political history. Though independence had been won, the struggle over political power and control of the revolutionary heritage continued. As Benjamin Rush, Philadelphia physician and revolutionary patriot, explained: "The American War is over, but this is far from being the case with the American Revolution. On the contrary, nothing but the first act of the great drama is closed. It remains [for us] . . . to establish and perfect our new forms of government." Events would soon demonstrate how difficult, and how important to the nation's future, that task would be.

Controversy between Federalist supporters of the national government and the emerging Jeffersonian Republican opposition first erupted over domestic policies designed to stabilize the nation's finances and promote its economic development. Those policies revealed deep-seated conflicts between economic interests and raised urgent questions of how the new constitution should be interpreted. What was the proper balance of power between state and national governments? How should governing authority be allocated between the executive branch and Congress? Much depended on the answer to those troubling questions.

Within a few years, international events further roiled American politics. The French Revolution and a successful revolt by black Haitians against French colonial power in the Caribbean—the two most dramatic events in a larger web of democratic insurgencies against established authorities that reached from Europe to the Americas—inflamed congressional politics and roused the people at large. By the last years of the 1790s, the prospect of war with France and Federalist security measures such as the Alien and Sedition Acts brought the nation to the brink of political upheaval. That prospect was narrowly avoided by the Federalists' defeat and Thomas Jefferson's election as president in 1800.

Having captured the presidency and control of Congress, the Jeffersonian Republicans set about the task of refashioning the government. At home, they dismantled the Federalists' war program, reduced the national debt, promoted westward expansion, and emphasized state rather than national authority. Abroad, they struggled less successfully to protect American commerce on the high seas and avoid embroilment in European war.

Adding to the political crisis was widespread anxiety over the nation's novel and still unproven "experiment" in creating a sprawling, diverse republic. The absence of fully developed political parties skilled in forging compromise among leaders at the nation's capital and organizing the surging political energy among the people compounded the problem. By the time Thomas Jefferson left the presidency in 1809, it was apparent how fragile, and yet how resilient, America's new government was proving to be.

LAUNCHING THE NATIONAL REPUBLIC

Once the Constitution had been ratified, its Anti-Federalist critics seemed ready to give the experiment a chance. They were determined, however, to watch closely for the first signs of danger. It was not many months before they sounded the alarm.

Beginning the New Government

On April 16, 1789, George Washington, unanimously elected president by the Electoral College, started north from Virginia to be inaugurated first president of the United States. His feelings were mixed as he set forth. "I bade adieu to Mount Vernon, to private life, and to domestic felicity," he confided to his diary, "and with a mind oppressed with more anxious and painful sensations than I have words to express, set out for New York . . . with the best disposition to render service to my country in obedience to its call, but with less hope of answering its expectations." He had good reason for such foreboding.

The president-elect was the object of constant adulation as he journeyed north. In villages and towns, guns boomed their salutes, children danced in the streets, church bells pealed, and local dignitaries toasted his arrival. On April 23, he was rowed on an elegant, flower-festooned barge from the New Jersey shore to New York City, where throngs of citizens and newly elected members of Congress greeted the weary traveler. That evening, bonfires illuminated the city.

Inaugural day was April 30. Shortly after noon, on a small balcony overlooking Wall Street, Washington took the oath of office. "It is done," exulted New York's chancellor, Robert Livingston. "Long live George Washington, President of the United States!" With the crowd roaring its approval and 13 guns booming in the harbor, the president bowed his way off the balcony and into Federal Hall. Late into the night, celebrations filled the air.

Though hopefulness attended the new government's beginning, the first weeks were tense, because everyone knew how important it was that the government be set on a proper republican course. "Things which appear of little importance in themselves and at the beginning," the president warned, "may have great and durable consequences."

When Washington addressed the first Congress, republican purists complained that it smacked too much of the English monarch's speech from the throne at the opening of Parliament. Congress then had to decide whether it should accord him a title.

President-Elect Washington Travels to New York This imaginative scene of President-Elect Washington's reception in Trenton, New Jersey, during his trip from Virginia to New York City for his first inauguration depicts the popular adulation that surrounded him. What other messages can you find in the picture's details? *(Library of Congress)*

12 amendments and sent them to the states for approval. By December 1791, 10 had been ratified and became the national Bill of Rights. Among other things, they guaranteed freedom of speech, press, and religion; pledged the right of trial by jury and due process of law; forbade "unreasonable searches and seizures"; and protected individuals against self-incrimination in criminal cases. The Bill of Rights was the most important achievement of these early years, for it has protected citizens' democratic rights ever since.

Vice President Adams proposed "His Most Benign Highness," while others offered the even gaudier suggestion "His Highness, the President of the United States, and Protector of the Rights of the Same." Howls of outrage arose from those who thought titles had no place in a republic. Good sense finally prevailing, Congress settled on the now-familiar "Mr. President." The belief that such decisions might determine the new government's direction for years to come gave politics a special intensity.

The Bill of Rights

Among Congress's first tasks was consideration of the constitutional amendments that several states had made a condition of their ratification. Although Madison and other Federalists had argued that a national bill of rights was unnecessary, they were ready to keep their promise that such amendments would be considered. That would reassure the fearful, fend off calls for a second constitutional convention, and build support for the new regime. "We have in this way something to gain," Madison shrewdly observed, "and if we proceed with caution, nothing to lose."

From the variety of proposals offered by the states, Madison culled a set of specific propositions for Congress to consider. After extensive debate, Congress reached agreement in September 1789 on

DOCUMENT

James Madison, Defense of the Bill of Rights (June 8, 1789)

The People Divide

During its first months, Washington's administration enjoyed almost universal support. The honeymoon, however, did not last long. By the mid-1790s, opposition groups had formed a coalition known as the Jeffersonian Republicans, while the administration's supporters rallied under the name of Federalists.

Disagreement began in January 1790, when Secretary of the Treasury Alexander Hamilton submitted to Congress the first of several major policy statements on the country's economic future. Seldom in the nation's history has a single official so dominated public affairs as did Hamilton in these early years. A man of extraordinary intelligence and ambition, Hamilton preferred to act behind the scenes, out of public view. His instincts for locating and seizing the levers of political power were unerring.

An ardent proponent of America's economic development, Hamilton, perhaps more than any of the nation's founders, foresaw the country's future strength and was determined to promote its growth by encouraging domestic manufacturing and overseas trade. The United States, he was fond of saying, was a "Hercules in the cradle." Competitive self-interest, whether of nations or individuals, he thought the surest guide to behavior. He most admired ambitious entrepreneurs eager to tie their fortunes to America's rising empire, and he believed that a close alliance between them and government officials was essential to achieving American greatness.

At the same time, Hamilton's politics were profoundly conservative. He continued to be deeply

Alexander Hamilton Alexander Hamilton used the office of secretary of the treasury and his personal relationship with President Washington to shape national policy during the early 1790s. What personal qualities was the portraitist attempting to convey? *(Alexander Hamilton, The White House, © White House Historical Association)*

impressed by the stability of the British monarchy and confident governing style of the British upper class. Hamilton distrusted the people's wisdom and feared their purposes. "The people," he asserted, "are turbulent and changing; they seldom judge or determine right."

Believing the Constitution was not "high-toned" enough, Hamilton was eager to give it proper direction. His opportunity came when Washington named him secretary of the treasury. Recognizing the potential importance of his office, he determined to build the kind of nation he envisioned.

In his first "Report on the Public Credit," Hamilton recommended funding the remaining Revolutionary War debt by enabling the government's creditors to exchange their badly depreciated securities at face value for new, interest-bearing government bonds. Second, he proposed that the federal government assume responsibility for the $21.5 million in remaining state war debts. These actions, he hoped, would stabilize the government's finances, establish its credit, build confidence in the new nation at home and abroad, and tie business and commercial interests firmly to the new administration.

Consideration of Hamilton's economic program was interrupted by the new Congress's first debate over slavery. It was stimulated by petitions from

Quakers and the Pennsylvania Abolition Society lamenting the "licentious wickedness of the African trade for slaves" and calling on Congress to end the slave trade abroad and ameliorate the conditions of slavery at home.

In the House of Representatives, southern delegates warned that claims of congressional authority over domestic slavery threatened to "blow the trumpet of civil war." The slave trade they defended as rescuing blacks from African savagery. Alarmed and seeking to put the troublesome issue to rest, northern delegates agreed that Congress had "no authority to interfere in the emancipation of slaves, or in the treatment of them." The Philadelphia Quaker John Pemberton lamented that Hamilton's funding system was so much the darling of northerners that they were eager "to obtain the favor" of southern delegates by closing their eyes to slavery.

When debate on Hamilton's report resumed, the proposal to fund the foreign debt aroused little controversy, but Hamilton's plans for handling the government's domestic obligations generated immediate opposition. In the House of Representatives, James Madison, Hamilton's recent ally in the ratification process, protested the unfairness of funding depreciated securities at face value because speculators, some anticipating Hamilton's proposals, had acquired many of them at a fraction of their initial worth. Madison and his southern colleagues knew as well that northern businessmen held most of the securities and that funding would bring little benefit to the South.

Hamilton was not impressed. The speculators, he observed, "paid what the commodity was worth in the market, and took the risks." They should therefore "reap the benefit." If his plan served the interests of the wealthy, that was exactly as he intended, for it would further strengthen ties between wealth and national power. After considerable grumbling, Congress endorsed the funding plan.

Federal assumption of the remaining state debts aroused sharper criticism. States with the largest unpaid obligations, such as Massachusetts, thought assumption a splendid idea. But others that had already retired much of their debt, such as Virginia and Pennsylvania, were adamantly opposed. Critics also warned that assumption would strengthen the central government at the expense of the states, since wealthy individuals would now look to it rather than the states for a return on their investments. Moreover, with its increased need for revenue to pay off the accumulated debt, the federal government would have strong reason to exercise its newly acquired power of taxation. That was exactly what Hamilton intended.

Drawing Inspiration from the Republican Past
The revolutionary generation found inspiration in the republican eras of ancient Greece and Rome. This bust of Thomas Jefferson, cast in the classical style, was completed in 1789 by the French sculptor Jean-Antoine Houdon. *(Jean-Antoine Houdon,* Thomas Jefferson, *portrait bust, 1839.1, Collection of the New-York Historical Society)*

Once again, Congress endorsed Hamilton's bill, in good measure because Madison and Jefferson supported it as part of an agreement to move the seat of government from New York to Philadelphia, and eventually to a new federal district on the Potomac River. Southerners hoped that moving the government away from northern commercial centers would enable them to align it with their own agrarian interests.

Opposition to the funding and assumption scheme, however, did not die. In December 1790, the Virginia assembly passed a series of resolutions, framed by that old Anti-Federalist Patrick Henry, warning that southern agriculture was being subordinated to the interests of northern commerce, and that the national government's powers were expanding dangerously. In response, Hamilton confided privately that "This is the first symptom of a spirit which must either be killed, or will kill the Constitution."

As the controversy grew, Hamilton introduced the second phase of his financial program, a national bank capable of handling the government's financial affairs and pooling private investment capital for economic development. He had the Bank of England and its ties to the royal government in mind, though he was careful not to say so publicly.

Opposition to the bank came almost entirely from the South. The bank's southern critics protested that the Constitution did not authorize the creation of a national bank. The bank, moreover, would serve the needs of northern merchants and manufacturers far better than those of southern agrarians. Still, in February 1792, Congress approved the bank bill.

When Washington asked his cabinet whether he should sign the bill, Hamilton said yes. Following the constitutional doctrine of "implied powers"— the principle that the government had the authority to make any laws "necessary and proper" for exercising the powers specifically granted it by the Constitution—he argued that Congress could charter such a bank under its power to collect taxes and regulate trade. Secretary of State Jefferson, however, urged a veto. He saw in Hamilton's argument a blueprint for the indefinite expansion of federal authority and insisted that the government possessed only those powers specifically listed in the Constitution. Because the

DOCUMENT

Alexander Hamilton, "Bank" (1791)

Constitution said nothing about chartering banks, the bill was unconstitutional and should be rejected. To Jefferson's distress, Washington took Hamilton's advice and signed the bank bill into law.

In December 1790, in his second "Report on the Public Credit," Hamilton proposed a series of excise taxes, including one on the manufacture of distilled liquor. This so-called Whiskey Tax signaled the government's intention to use its taxing authority to increase federal revenue. The power to tax and spend, Hamilton knew, was the power to govern. The Whiskey Tax became law in March 1791.

Finally, in his "Report on Manufactures" issued in December 1791, Hamilton called for tariffs (taxes) on imported European goods as a way of protecting American industries; bounties to encourage the expansion of commercial agriculture; and a network of federally sponsored internal improvements such as roads and lighthouses. These were intended to stimulate commerce and bind the nation more tightly together. Neither northern merchants nor southern agrarians, however, wanted tariffs that might reduce overseas trade and raise the cost of living, so Congress never endorsed this report.

All the while, criticism of Hamilton's policies continued to grow. In October 1791, opposition leaders in Congress established a newspaper that vigorously attacked the administration's policies. Hamilton responded with a series of anonymous articles in the administration's paper accusing Jefferson (inaccurately) of having opposed the Constitution and (also inaccurately) of fomenting opposition to the government. Alarmed, Washington pleaded for restraint. The month-long debate revealed how acrimonious politics had become at the nation's capital.

Political conflict was now spreading beyond the circle of governing officials in Philadelphia. In northern towns and cities, artisans and other working people turned out in support of Hamilton's efforts to improve credit and stimulate economic development. With their economic circumstances improving, they seemed undisturbed by constitutional issues or the special benefits his policies brought to a privileged few. Within a few years, many of them would move into the Jeffersonian opposition, but for the moment their support of the administration was secure.

The Whiskey Rebellion

The farmers of western Pennsylvania voiced their opposition to government policies in dramatic fashion. Their anger focused on the Whiskey Tax. Ever since the trouble with England 30 years earlier, Americans had been suspicious of the connections between taxation and governmental power. Farmers had special

Whiskey Rebellion Tax Protest–1794

reason to dislike this particular tax. Their livelihood depended on transporting surplus grain over the Appalachians to eastern markets. Shipping it in bulk was prohibitively expensive, so they distilled the grain and moved it more efficiently as whiskey. The Whiskey Tax threatened to make this trade unprofitable. The farmers also protested that people charged with tax evasion had to stand trial in federal court hundreds of miles away in Philadelphia.

Westerners also sensed control of their local affairs slipping away, as the backcountry was increasingly absorbed in a market economy and system of politics dominated by the more populous, commercialized areas to the east. In southern states such as South Carolina, the integration of coastal and interior regions went smoothly because of similar agricultural interests and a shared anxiety over the region's black majority. In the more economically diverse and racially homogenous states of the north, however, conflicts between coastal and backcountry regions sharpened.

Hamilton cared little what western farmers thought about the Whiskey Tax. The government needed revenue, and the farmers would have to bear the cost. Angered by Federalist arrogance as much as by the tax, farmers quickly made their resentment known.

Trouble was brewing by the summer of 1792 as angry citizens gathered in mass meetings across

Washington and Hamilton Lead a Federal Army Against the Whiskey Rebels
President Washington and Treasury Secretary Hamilton led a federal army of nearly 13,000 troops into western Pennsylvania in 1794. Rebellious farmers, protesting the government's excise tax on whiskey, dispersed as the army approached. What political story is the artist trying to tell? *(Frederick Kemmelmeyer,* Washington Reviewing the Western Army at Fort Cumberland, Maryland. *The Metropolitan Museum of Art, Gift of Edgar William and Bernice Chrysler Garbisch, 1963 [63.201.2] Photograph © 1983 The Metropolitan Museum of Art)*

western Pennsylvania. In August, a convention at Pittsburgh denounced the Whiskey Tax and vowed to prevent its collection. Like opponents of the Stamp Act in 1765 and the Shays rebels in 1786, they decided that liberties would be lost if resistance did not soon begin. Alarmed, Washington issued a proclamation warning against such "unlawful" gatherings and insisting that the tax would be enforced. As collections began, the farmers took matters into their own hands.

In July 1794, when federal marshal David Lennox and John Neville, a local excise inspector, attempted to serve papers on several recalcitrant farmers near Pittsburgh, an angry crowd of 500 armed men cornered a dozen federal soldiers in Neville's home. After an exchange of gunfire, the soldiers surrendered and Neville's house was put to the torch. Similar episodes, some of them involving the erection of liberty poles reminiscent of the Revolution, erupted across the state. At Parkinson's Ferry, a convention of more than 200 delegates debated armed resistance.

Fearing that the protests might spread through the entire backcountry from Maine to Georgia, and concerned by rumors that Spanish emissaries and western adventurers were plotting secession in Kentucky and the western Carolinas, Washington called out federal troops to restore order. For more than a year, Hamilton had been urging the use of force against the protesters. To him, the insurrection was not evidence of an unjust policy needing change but a test of the administration's ability to govern. He eagerly volunteered to accompany the troops west.

DOCUMENT
George Washington, Proclamation Regarding the Whiskey Rebellion (1794)

In late August, a federal force of nearly 13,000 men, larger than the average strength of the continental army during the Revolutionary War, marched into western Pennsylvania. At its center was Colonel William McPherson's "Pennsylvania Blues," a strongly Federalist cavalry regiment. At its head rode the president and secretary of the treasury. Persuaded of the danger to his safety, Washington returned to Philadelphia, but Hamilton pressed ahead. When later criticized for accompanying the army to Pittsburgh, he replied that he had "long since . . . learned to hold public opinion of no value." The battle for which Hamilton hoped never materialized, however, for as the federal army approached, the "Whiskey Rebels" dispersed. Of 20 prisoners taken, two were convicted of treason and sentenced to death. Later, in a calmer mood, Washington pardoned them both.

As people soon realized, the "Whiskey Rebellion" had never threatened the government's safety. "An

insurrection was . . . proclaimed," Jefferson scoffed, "but could never be found." Even such an ardent Federalist as Fisher Ames was uneasy at the sight of federal troops marching against American citizens. "Elective rulers," he warned, "can scarcely ever employ the physical force of a democracy without turning the moral force, or the power of public opinion, against the government." The American people would have additional reason to ponder Ames's warning in the years immediately ahead.

DOCUMENT
George Washington, Whiskey Rebellion Address to Congress (1794)

THE REPUBLIC IN A THREATENING WORLD

Because the nation was so new and the outside world so threatening, foreign policy generated extraordinary excitement during the 1790s. This was especially so after the tumultuous events of the French and Haitian Revolutions burst onto the international scene. The revolution in France and the European war that accompanied it threatened to draw America in, while across Europe, Ireland, and the Caribbean, political insurgents, invoking the Declaration of Independence and America's colonial rebellion as inspiration for their own cause, joined in what historians call the age of democratic revolution.

The Promise and Peril of the French Revolution

France's revolution began in 1789 as an effort to reform an arbitrary but weakened monarchy. Pent-up demands for social justice, however, quickly outran attempts at moderate reform, and in 1793, when the recently proclaimed republican regime beheaded Louis XVI, France plunged into a genuinely radical revolution. By the end of 1793, Europe was locked in a deadly struggle between revolutionary France and a counterrevolutionary coalition led by Prussia and Great Britain.

For more than a decade, the French Revolution dominated European affairs. Before it was finished, it would transform the course of Western history. The revolution also cut like a plowshare through the surface of American politics, threatening the nation's security and dividing Americans deeply against each other.

The outbreak of European war posed thorny diplomatic problems for Washington's administration. By the mid-1790s, American merchants were earning handsome profits from neutral trade with both England and France, while American shipbuilding was

Urban Prosperity in the Late 1790s This scene of bustling commercial activity in New York City in 1797 reveals the benefits that expanded neutral trade brought to the nation's major seaports. On the right of the painting is the elegant Tontine Coffee House, which served as a tavern, housed the New York Stock Exchange, and boasted of such amenities as water closets, a bell system for communication between rooms, and an inside bath. *(Guy Francis, Tontine Coffee House, N.Y.C., oil on linen, 1907.32, Collection of the New-York Historical Society)*

booming. In 1800, American ships carried an astonishing 92 percent of all commerce between America and Europe. The economic benefits were most evident in cities along the Atlantic coast but radiated as well into the surrounding countryside, where cargoes of agricultural and forest goods, as well as the provisions required by ships' crews, were produced.

America's expanding commerce, however, generated problems. While England and France sought access to American goods, each was determined to prevent those goods from reaching the other, if necessary by stopping American ships and confiscating their cargoes. When locked in such a deadly struggle, neither belligerent was willing to bind itself by the formalities of international law guaranteeing neutral trade.

America's relations with England were additionally complicated by the Royal Navy's practice of impressing American sailors into service aboard its warships to meet the growing demand for seamen. This posed the difficult problem of protecting American citizens without getting drawn into the European conflict.

The French treaty of 1778 compounded the government's dilemma. It appeared to require that the United States aid France much as France had assisted the American states against England a decade and a half earlier. Americans sympathetic to the French cause argued that the commitment still held. Others, fearing the consequences of American involvement and the political infection that closer ties with revolutionary France might bring, insisted that the treaty had lapsed when the French king was overthrown.

The American people's intense reaction to the revolution in France further complicated the situation. At first, it seemed an extension of America's own struggle for liberty. Even the swing toward social revolution did not immediately dampen American enthusiasm. By the mid-1790s, however, especially after France's revolutionary regime launched its attack on organized Christianity, many Americans pulled back in alarm. What connection could there possibly be between the principles of 1776 and the chaos so evident in France? The differences were indeed profound.

For the Federalists, revolutionary France symbolized social anarchy and threatened the European order on which they believed the nation's commercial and diplomatic security depended. With increasing vehemence, they castigated the revolution, championed England as the defender of European civilization, and sought ways of linking England and the United States more closely together.

Many Americans, however, continued to support France. While decrying the revolution's excesses, they believed that liberty would ultimately emerge from the turmoil. Though Jefferson regretted the shedding of innocent blood, he thought it necessary if true liberty was to be achieved. John Bradford, editor of the *Kentucky Gazette,* thought similarly. "Instead of reviling the French republicans as monsters," he wrote, the "friends of royalty in this country" should admire their patience in suffering so long under their monarch. In Bradford's judgment, England was not a bastion of civilized order, but of political privilege and oppression.

The turmoil in France challenged American assumptions about the gendered basis of politics as well. There, women participated in revolutionary

Women Affirm Their Rights In this 1792 print from *The Lady's Magazine* of Philadelphia, a kneeling woman presents Columbia with a copy of Mary Wollstonecraft's "A Vindication of the Rights of Woman," one of the most outspokenly feminist writings of the time. Note the Liberty Cap on Columbia's pole. The cap was a potent political symbol in both the American and French revolutions. *(The Library Company of Philadelphia [Per: 5.7.51708.O])*

crowds and joined in arguments over issues of political equality. When word of radical feminist activity reached North American shores, it echoed loudly in the political consciousness of many American women.

In August 1794, Philadelphia citizens gathered to celebrate the progress of French liberty. Mimicking the public festivals popular in revolutionary France, a crowd of women and men paraded down Market Street to the French minister's residence. There, women dressed in gowns emblazoned with the French tricolor gathered around an "altar of liberty," reciting patriotic odes before finally dispersing.

Upper-class women such as Anne Willing Bingham, wife of a Federalist senator and daughter of a socially prominent Philadelphia family, opened their

dinner parties and social salons to political talk, a practice that became a common part of civic life at the nation's capital. In all of these ways, women explored the boundaries of American citizenship and claimed a wider presence in the public sphere.

Democratic Revolutions in Europe and the Atlantic World

The revolution in France was but the most dramatic among an array of political insurgencies that challenged aristocratic power and promoted democratic values throughout Europe and the Atlantic world during the 1790s. As with the French revolution, they generated dispute among the American people.

Supported by invading armies from revolutionary France and inspired by the doctrine of natural rights voiced during the American and French revolutions, rebellions against long-entrenched privilege erupted from the Netherlands to the Italian peninsula. Though some of these movements were repressed, others resulted in the creation of new states, such as the Batavian and Cisalpine Republics.

Toussaint L'Ouverture This swashbuckling portrait of the Haitian revolutionary Toussaint L'Ouverture appeared in *An Historical Account of the Black Empire of Haiti*, published in London in 1805. Is the portrayal intended to be complimentary or mocking? *(R Snark/Art Resource, NY).*

The Outbreak of Democratic Insurgencies

During the late eighteenth and early nineteenth centuries, numerous democratic insurgencies erupted in Europe and the Caribbean. **Reflecting on the Past** What connections did these insurgencies have with the American and French revolutions?

SWEDEN-NORWAY

RUSSIAN EMPIRE

Polish Revolution 1791, 1794

DENMARK

UNITED KINGDOM

NETH. 1784–1795

AUSTRIAN EMPIRE

Ireland 1798

BELGIUM 1789

GERMAN STATES

SWITZERLAND
Helvitic Republic 1799

BRITISH NORTH AMERICA

Republic 1792–99
Reign of Terror 1793–94
Napoleon 1799–1814

FRANCE
French Revolution 1789

OTTOMAN EMPIRE

Italian Revolutions 1796–99

UNITED STATES OF AMERICA

SPAIN

PORTUGAL

New Orleans

FLORIDA

CUBA (Sp.)

AFRICA

JAMAICA (Br.)

REPUBLIC OF HAITI 1791 1801

SOUTH AMERICA

1789   Dates of successful revolutions or declarations of independence

1789   Dates of unsuccessful or suppressed revolutions

Democratic insurgencies broke out as well in Latin America and the Caribbean. The most important occurred on the island of San Domingue, soon to be known as Haiti. Beginning in 1791, a multiracial coalition, emboldened by events in revolutionary France, rose in rebellion against French colonial rule. Conflict quickly developed between white landowners seeking to preserve their privileges while throwing off the colonial yoke, poor whites demanding access to land, mixed-race mulattoes chafing under years of discrimination, and black slaves angered by brutal repression. For more than a decade, black and white Haitians conducted a furious struggle against a combined French and British force of 30,000. (Though France's mortal

IMAGE
Slave Revolt,
Saint-
Domingue,
1791

enemy in Europe, England feared rebellion among the 300,000 slaves on Jamaica, its nearby possession, and offered military support.) The conflict devastated Haiti's sugar economy and caused more than 100,000 casualties among whites and blacks alike.

In 1798, the island's black majority, led by the charismatic Toussaint L'Ouverture, seized control of the rebellion, making the abolition of slavery its primary goal. Six years later, the victorious Haitian rebels established Haiti as the first black nation–state in the Americas.

While Haitian rebels celebrated the Declaration of Independence as a manifesto of universal freedom, North American whites followed events on that troubled island with a mixture of enthusiasm and dread. The Haitian revolt appeared to affirm the

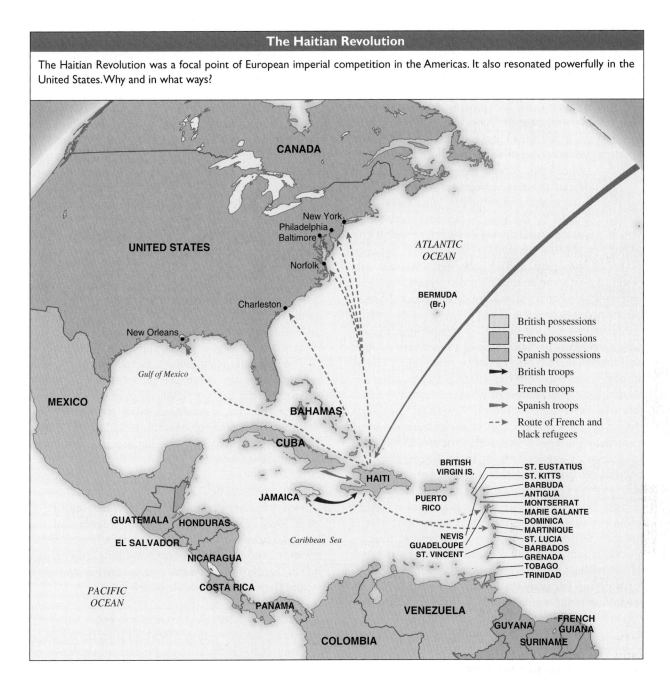

The Haitian Revolution

The Haitian Revolution was a focal point of European imperial competition in the Americas. It also resonated powerfully in the United States. Why and in what ways?

universal relevance of the U.S. struggle for liberty, and struck another blow against European colonialism in the New World. During the height of the Haitian insurgency, American warships ferried black troops from one part of the island to another in preparation for battle.

U.S. citizens, however, contemplated with dread the effect on North American slaves of a successful black rebellion so close by. The Haitian achievement, moreover, cast doubt on the racial assumption that blacks were incapable of comprehending liberty's true meaning. White southerners were especially anxious. The governor of North Carolina issued a proclamation warning Haitians fleeing the

island's chaos to stay away. When Haitian officials appealed in "the name of humanity" for "fraternal aid" in their liberation struggle, Congress demurred. If Haiti became an independent state, warned Pennsylvania senator Albert Gallatin, it might become "a dangerous neighbor" offering asylum to runaway slaves. When the Haitian republic was proclaimed in 1804, the U.S. government withheld recognition. Not until after the American Civil War were diplomatic relations finally established.

Though each of the democratic insurgencies that erupted during the 1790s was inspired by local experiences of injustice, they shared a common

RECOVERING THE PAST

Foreign Travel Journals

Historians utilize many different kinds of sources in their quest to recover the American past. Among the most revealing are travel accounts penned by foreign visitors eager to learn about the United States and record their impressions of it. From the days of earliest explorations to our own time, travelers have been fascinated by the people, customs, institutions, and physical setting of North America. Out of this continuing interaction between America and its foreign visitors has emerged a rich and fascinating travel literature that reveals much not only about America but about the travelers who have visited it as well.

DOCUMENT

Charles William Janson, *The Stranger in America* (1807)

During the second quarter of the nineteenth century, a stream of perceptive European visitors—Alexis de Tocqueville, Harriet Martineau, and Francis Grund among them—toured the United States, eager to record their impressions of what Jacksonian America was like. Fifty years earlier, the American Revolution fanned similar interest in the minds of Europeans fascinated by the newly independent nation and anxious to discern its implications for them. Among the most opinionated and engaging of these earlier commentators was the Frenchman Moreau de Saint Méry.

Born on the French island of Martinique in January 1750, de Saint Méry established a successful legal practice before moving to France, where relatives introduced him to polite Parisian society. In the late 1780s, he became an ardent champion of political reform during the early days of the French Revolution. As the revolution entered its radical phase, however, he was forced to flee to the United States for safety. Arriving at Norfolk, Virginia, with his wife and two children, de Saint Méry settled in Philadelphia, where he remained from October 1794 to August 1798. While there, he mingled with civic and cultural leaders, opened a bookstore that served as a rendezvous for French émigrés who also had fled the revolution's turmoil, and published a French-language paper that reported the latest news from home. In the late summer of 1798, de Saint Méry returned safely to France.

As with all such travel accounts, de Saint Méry's commentary must be read with a critical eye, for travelers disagreed over what they thought important and worth reporting, and interpreted what they saw in very different ways. In nearly 400 pages of commentary, de Saint Méry touched on numerous aspects of American life, but none in more frank and compelling fashion than relations between the sexes. The selections that follow (somewhat rearranged for greater continuity) provide tantalizing insights into the behavior and sexual mores of American men and women in the early years of the republic.

What did de Saint Méry find most interesting about gender relations in Philadelphia? How did religion, class, and ethnicity shape men's and women's behavior? of what forms of behavior did he approve and disapprove?

The explicit commentary of de Saint Méry is unique among the numerous accounts left by foreign travelers in the early republic, most of whom showed far more interest in America's racial makeup, political practices, and physical environment. Thus, de Saint Méry's observations may be idiosyncratic and should be approached with caution.

What other kinds of sources might enable us to evaluate the accuracy of such travel accounts? In what ways is a traveler's own nationality, gender, religion, or class likely to shape his or her impressions of the United States? Similarly, how important is it to know travelers' motives for coming, how long they stayed, which parts of the country they visited, and with whom they associated while here?

REFLECTING ON THE PAST Does the gendered world of late eighteenth-century Philadelphia, as described by de Saint Méry, seem strange or familiar, attractive or distasteful to your own sensibilities? If you were to visit another country today, how accurate do you think you could be in assessing the social behavior and cultural values of its people? To what extent would your values, perhaps like those of Moreau de Saint Méry, color your impressions? Might it be more difficult to understand some foreign cultures than others? Why?

Moreau de Saint Méry's American Journal

American men, generally speaking, are tall and thin . . . [and] seem to have no strength . . . . They are brave, but they lack drive. Indifferent toward almost everything, they sometimes behave in a manner that suggests real energy; then follow it with a "Oh-to-hell-with-it" attitude which shows that they seldom feel genuine enthusiasm.

Their dinner consists of . . . English roast surrounded by potatoes . . . baked or fried eggs, boiled or fried fish, salad which may be thinly sliced cabbage . . . [and] sweets to which they are excessively partial. . . . The entire meal is washed down with cider, weak or strong beer . . . [and] wine . . . which they keep drinking right through dessert, toward the end of which any ladies who are at the dinner leave the table and withdraw by themselves, leaving the men free to drink as much as they please . . . . Toasts are drunk, cigars are lighted, diners run to the corners of the room hunting night tables and vases which will enable them to hold a greater amount of liquor . . . . Finally the dinner table is deserted because of boredom, fatigue or drunkenness . . . .

American women are pretty, and those of Philadelphia are prettiest of all . . . . Girls ordinarily mature in Philadelphia at the age of fourteen, and reach that period without unusual symptoms . . . . But they soon grow pale . . . . After eighteen years old they lose their charms . . . . Their hair is scanty, their teeth bad . . . . In short, while charming and adorable at fifteen, they are faded at twenty-three, old at thirty-five, decrepit at forty or forty-five . . . .

American women carefully wash their faces and hands, but not their mouths, seldom their feet and even more seldom their bodies . . . . They are greatly addicted to finery and have a strong desire to display themselves—a desire . . . inflamed by their love of adornment. They cannot, however, imitate that elegance of style possessed by Frenchwomen . . . .

One is struck by the tall and pretty young girls one sees in the streets, going and coming from school. They wear their hair long, and skirts with closed seams. But when nubility has arrived they put up their hair with a comb, and the back of the skirt has a placket. At this time, they . . . become their own mistresses, and can go walking alone and have suitors . . . .

They invariably make their own choice of a suitor, and the parents raise no objection because that's the custom of the country. The suitor comes into the house when he wishes; goes on walks with his loved one whenever he desires. On Sunday he often takes her out in a cabriolet, and brings her back in the evening without anyone wanting to know where they went . . . . Although in general one is conscious of widespread modesty in Philadelphia, . . . the disregard . . . of some parents for the manner in which their daughters form relationships to which they . . . have not given their approval is an encouragement to indiscretions . . . .

A young woman trusts in her suitor's delicacy and charges him with maintaining for her a respect which she is not always able to command. Each day both of them are entrusted to no one but each other . . . . Her servant . . . leaves the house as soon as night has arrived . . . . Her father, her mother, her entire family have gone to bed. The suitor and his mistress remain alone; and sometimes, when the servant returns, she finds them asleep and the candle out, such is the frigidity of love in this country . . . .

When one considers the unlimited liberty which young ladies enjoy, one is astonished by their universal eagerness to be married . . . . When a young woman marries, she enters a wholly different existence. She is no longer a . . . butterfly who denies herself nothing and whose only laws are her whims and her suitor's wish. She now lives only for her husband, and to devote herself without surcease to the care of her household and her home . . . . The more her husband is capable of multiplying . . . the pleasures of matrimony . . . the more her health may suffer, most of all when she has a child; for sometimes while nursing it, or as soon as it is weaned, she has already conceived another . . . .

In spite of conjugal customs which would seem to indicate a state of happiness, they do not produce the happiness which would be expected to result . . . . This is evidenced by the multiplicity of second marriages . . . . The men in particular remarry oftenest . . . . Divorce is obtained with scandalous ease. From this alone one can judge the extent of loose habits . . . .

Bastards are extremely common in Philadelphia. There are two principal reasons for this. In the first place, the city is full of religious sects, but none of them give their clergymen any authority to enforce obedience. Consequently there is no way of inspiring shame in women who become mothers for no reason except the pleasure they get out of it. In the second place, once an illegitimate child is twelve months old, a mother can disembarrass herself of him by farming him out for twenty-one years. This makes it possible for her to commit the same sin for a second time. It never occurs to her that her child can never know her, and that the whole business is shameful . . . .

There are streetwalkers . . . in Philadelphia. These are very young and very pretty girls, elegantly dressed, who promenade two by two, arm in arm and walking very rapidly, at an hour which indicates that they aren't just out for a stroll . . . . Anyone who accosts them is taken to their home . . . [where] they fulfill every desire for two dollars, half of which is supposed to pay for the use of the room. Quaker youths are frequent visitors in the houses of ill fame, which have multiplied in Philadelphia and are frequented at all hours. There is even a well-known gentleman who leaves his horse tied to the post outside one of these houses, so that everyone knows when he is there and exactly how long he stays . . . .

Source: Moreau de St. Méry's American Journey, 1793–1798, trans. and ed. Kenneth Roberts and Anna M. Roberts (New York: Doubleday, 1947), 265, 281–283, 312–313.

American Voices

A Member of the Boston African Society, Celebrating the End of the African Slave Trade

Free blacks followed the Haitian Revolution and emergence of a black republic in Haiti with great interest. They also celebrated the official end of the slave trade in the United States, as the excerpts from this address reveal.

Did not America think it was a privilege truly desirable to be enjoyed, when her mother nation was about to invade her land, and bring her under her dominion; did she not greatly regret the thought of a deprivation of her freedom when she asked the assistance of her sister nation, France, to vindicate her cause against Britain with her? If desirable, I say, to America under such circumstances, why not to any or all the nations of the earth . . . ?

Slavery hath ever had a tendency to spread ignorance and darkness, poverty and distress in the world. Although it hath advanced a few, yet many have been the sufferers; it was first invented by men of the most malicious dispositions, and has been carried on by men of similar character . . . .

Freedom is desirable; if not, would men sacrifice their time, their property, and finally lose their lives in the pursuit of it? If it was not a thing that was truly valuable, should we see whole nations engaged in hostility, to procure it for their country, wives and children? Yea, I say there is something so dreadful in slavery that some had rather die than experience it.

- *Why did the North American slave trade officially end in 1808?*

- *Was the speaker primarily addressing the all-black audience of the Boston African Society, or the larger Boston community?*

dedication to human liberty and drew on principles articulated in revolutionary America and France. And though they were widely scattered across Europe and the Atlantic basin, news about them circulated in the United States via newspapers, networks of personal correspondence, and an expanding human traffic of soldiers, émigrés, and political idealists who crisscrossed the Atlantic during these tumultuous years.

During the mid-1790s, Joel Barlow and other Americans, motivated by curiosity and democratic principle, journeyed to France, eager to witness the further unfolding of universal liberty. The American expatriate Thomas Paine was granted honorary French citizenship and served briefly in the revolutionary Convention before running afoul of the Terror. At the same time, a stream of French émigrés (among them Moreau de Saint Méry (see the "Recovering the Past" essay, pp. 260–261), sought sanctuary in the United States.

As the 1790s progressed, growing numbers of English and Irish radicals fleeing the deepening political conservatism in Britain also took passage for North America. When they arrived, many joined the Jeffersonian opposition as newspaper editors and activists, adding to the party's democratic commitment and anti-British stance.

The emerging transatlantic web of radical dissent was strengthened as well by a multiracial underclass of sailors, runaway slaves, and other common folk—restive men, and occasionally women, from the far corners of the Atlantic world who circulated in and out of North American ports. Their rough appearance, vivid tales of injustice, and readiness to challenge local authorities added to the country's political clamor.

The Democratic–Republican Societies

Political clubs, providing safe havens where dissidents could gather to read political tracts and plot political change, served as weapons of democratic reform throughout the Atlantic world during the 1790s. The Jacobin clubs in France were the best known, but similar groups sprouted up in the United States.

As early as 1792, ordinary citizens began to form "constitutional societies" dedicated to "watching over the rights of the people" and giving the alarm in case of governmental encroachments on American liberty. Several dozen societies, modeled after the Sons of Liberty and Committees of Correspondence that had mobilized patriots against England 20 years earlier, formed in opposition to Hamilton's financial program. The French Revolution stoked the fires of democratic enthusiasm and spurred the societies' growth, as did the arrival in 1793 of Citizen Edmund Genêt, the French minister to the United States.

Genêt landed at Charleston, South Carolina, to a tumultuous reception. His instructions were to court popular support and negotiate a commercial treaty with the United States. Shortly after his arrival, however, he began commissioning American privateers to attack British shipping in the Caribbean and enlisting American seamen for expeditions against Spanish Florida, clear violations of American neutrality.

As he traveled north toward Philadelphia, Genêt generated more enthusiastic receptions. His popularity, however, soon led him into trouble. In open defiance of diplomatic protocol, he urged Congress to reject Washington's recently issued Neutrality Proclamation and side with revolutionary France. On August 2, the president demanded Genêt's recall, charging that his conduct threatened "war abroad and anarchy at home."

DOCUMENT
Proclamation
of Neutrality
(1793)

Though Genêt failed as a diplomat, he succeeded in fanning popular enthusiasm for revolutionary France. With his open encouragement, the Democratic Society of Pennsylvania, the largest and most influential of the new popular associations, called for the support of France abroad and the "spirit of freedom and equality" at home. President Washington and his Federalist colleagues might wonder whether that second challenge was aimed at them.

About 40 popular societies scattered from Maine to Georgia sprang up during the next several years. Working people—artisans and laborers in the cities, small farmers and tenants in the countryside—provided the bulk of membership. Federalist critics derided them as "the lowest orders of . . . draymen . . . broken hucksters, and trans-Atlantic traitors." That final canard referred to the growing tide of Irish immigrants, fleeing hard times and political repression at home, who combined demands for Irish independence from England with a

Cartoons as Newspaper Politics Cartoons became powerful weapons in the rapidly expanding, superheated political press of the 1790s. This Jeffersonian cartoon lampoons William Cobbett, one of the Federalists' most acid-penned pamphleteers who wrote under the pseudonym Peter Porcupine. While Columbia swoons over the political turmoil, the English Lion urges Cobbett to "sow the seeds of discord" and the Devil mutters "More scandal. Let us destroy this Idol Liberty." *(The Historical Society of Pennsylvania [HSP], "Caricature against William Cobbett, editor of the Porcupine Gazette," 1796, [Bb612Se31])*

commitment to political equality and a relish for rough-and-tumble politics.

The societies' leaders were most often doctors, tradesmen, and lawyers, men of acknowledged respectability. Leaders and followers alike were united by a common determination to preserve the "principles of '76" against the "royalizing" tendencies of Washington's administration. Committed to an awakened citizenry, the societies organized public celebrations, issued ringing addresses filled with democratic principles, and fired off petitions sharply critical of administration policies to the president and Congress. Washington's proclamation of neutrality they labeled a "pusillanimous truckling to Britain, despotically conceived and unconstitutionally promulgated." Several of the societies openly urged the United States to enter the war on France's behalf.

West of the Appalachians, local democratic societies agitated against England's continuing occupation of frontier posts south of the Great Lakes and berated Spain for closing the Mississippi River at New Orleans to American shipping. Everywhere they protested the Excise Tax, opposed the administration's overtures to England, and called for a press free from control by Federalist "aristocrats." William Manning, a Massachusetts farmer who had marched to the "Concord fight" in 1775 and who continued to praise the principles for which he had earlier fought, declared that a laboring man may as well "hunt for pins in a haymow" as try to collect accurate knowledge from the "promiscuous piles of contradictions" appearing in Federalist newspapers.

President Washington was incensed by the societies' support of Genêt and their sharp criticism of the government, while the arch-Federalist Fisher Ames thundered against these "nurseries of sedition" that threatened to revolutionize America as the Jacobins had revolutionized France. In January 1794, a Virginia Federalist berated Kentucky's Democratic Society as "that horrible sink of treason, that hateful synagogue of anarchy, that odious conclave of tumult, that frightful cathedral of discord, that poisonous garden of conspiracy, that hellish school of rebellion and opposition to all regular and well-balanced authority!" Such polemics indicated how inflamed public discourse had become.

As controversy escalated, another circumstance added to the anxiety gripping politicians at the Philadelphia capital. Through the summer of 1793, an unrelenting heat wave descended on southeastern Pennsylvania, searing trees and gardens, threatening supplies of potable water, and raising a stench in the refuse-filled streets. Even more alarming, from early August to mid-October a deadly epidemic of yellow fever gripped the city, sending wealthier citizens fleeing for safety to the countryside and taking a terrible toll on those forced to stay behind. The poor and elderly fared worst. Blacks also died in large numbers when the Free African Society, responding to appeals from the mayor, volunteered nurses to tend the sick and labor to bury the dead. The belief that blacks were naturally immune to the fever's ravages proved tragically false.

Before early frosts finally destroyed the swarms of mosquitoes that carried the deadly pestilence through the city's crowded streets, well over 4,000 black and white Philadelphians, more than 10 percent of the city's population, had died. Yellow fever would return before the decade was out, but never again did it reap such a deadly harvest.

Jay's Controversial Treaty

The uproar over Jay's Treaty with England further heightened political tensions at mid-decade. Alarmed by deteriorating relations with England, Washington sent Chief Justice John Jay to London in the spring of 1794 to negotiate a wide range of issues carried over from the Revolutionary War. The treaty that the chief justice brought home in early 1795 contained British promises to withdraw from the western posts and provide American ships selective access to British West Indian ports. However, it totally ignored a host of other lingering problems. When its terms were made public, they triggered an explosion of protest.

The administration's pleas that the agreement headed off an open breach with England and was the best that could be obtained failed to pacify its critics. In New York City, Hamilton was stoned while defending the treaty at a mass meeting. The "rabble," sniffed one Federalist, attempted "to knock out Hamilton's brains to reduce him to an equality with themselves." Southern planters were angry because the agreement brought no compensation for their lost slaves. Westerners complained that the British were not evacuating the military posts, while merchants and sailors railed against Jay's failure to stop impressment or open the West Indies to American trade. After a long and acrimonious debate, the Senate ratified the treaty by a narrow margin.

DOCUMENT

The Treaty of San Lorenzo (1796)

The administration made better progress on the still-volatile issue of free transit of the Mississippi River. In the Treaty of San Lorenzo, negotiated by Thomas Pinckney in 1795, Spain for the first time recognized the United States' boundaries under the peace treaty of 1783 (the Mississippi River to the west and the thirty-first parallel to the south) and gave up all claim to U.S. territory. Spain also granted Americans free navigation of the Mississippi and the right to unload goods for transshipment at New Orleans—but only for three years. What would happen after that remained uncertain.

By mid-decade, political harmony had disappeared as divisions deepened on virtually every important issue of foreign and domestic policy. Jefferson, increasingly estranged from the administration, resigned as secretary of state, joining Madison and others in open opposition to Washington's policies.

George Washington's Farewell Address (1796)

In September 1796, in what came to be called his Farewell Address, Washington deplored the deepening political divisions, warned against entangling alliances with foreign nations, and announced that he would not accept a third term. He had long been contemplating retirement, for he was 64 and wearied by political attacks. "As to you, sir," fumed Thomas Paine in a letter published in an opposition newspaper, "treacherous in private friendship . . . and a hypocrite in public life, the world will be puzzled to decide . . . whether you have abandoned good principles, or whether you ever had any." Few American presidents have been subjected to such public abuse.

THE POLITICAL CRISIS DEEPENS

By 1796, bitter controversy surrounded the national government. It intensified during the last half of the decade until the very stability of the country seemed threatened.

The Election of 1796

With Washington out of the picture, the presidential election quickly narrowed to John Adams versus Jefferson. They knew each other well. Both had played distinguished roles during the Revolution, when they had shared in the electrifying task of drafting the Declaration of Independence. They had joined forces again during the 1780s, when Adams served as first U.S. minister to Great Britain and Jefferson as minister to France. They had come together a third time in Washington's administration, Adams as vice president and Jefferson as secretary of state.

Though they had earned each other's respect, they now differed sharply in their visions of the nation's future. While fearing Hamilton's ambition and distrusting his infatuation with England, Adams was a committed Federalist. He believed in a vigorous

IMAGE

John Adams

national government, was appalled by the French Revolution, and feared "excessive democracy." Jefferson, while firmly supporting the Constitution, was alarmed by Hamilton's financial program, viewed France's revolution as a logical if chaotic extension of America's struggle for freedom, and hoped to expand democracy at home. By 1796, he had become the leader of an increasingly vocal opposition, the Jeffersonian Republican party.

The election of 1796 bound Jefferson and Adams together once again, this time in a deeply strained and ill-fated alliance. Adams received 71 electoral votes and became president. Jefferson came in second with 68 and, as then specified in the Constitution, assumed the vice presidency. The narrowness of Adams's majority—his enemies gleefully reminded him that he was only a "President of three votes"—foreshadowed the troubles that lay ahead.

Adams later recalled his inaugural day: "A solemn scene it was indeed, and it was made more affecting by the presence of the General [Washington], whose countenance was as serene and unclouded as the

John Adams John Adams, Washington's vice president, won a narrow victory over Jefferson for the presidency in 1796. His administration foundered on conflicts over foreign policy abroad and the suppression of political dissent at home. (Portrait of John Adams. *Adams National Historic Site/U.S. Department of the Interior, National Park Service*)

day. He seemed to enjoy a triumph over me. Methought I heard him say, 'Ay! I am fairly out and you fairly in! See which of us will be the happiest.'" The answer was not long in coming.

The War Crisis with France

Adams had no sooner taken office than he confronted a deepening crisis with France, generated by French naval vessels interfering with American merchant ships in the Caribbean. That crisis would push the nation to the brink of civil conflict.

Hoping to ease relations between the two countries, Adams sent three commissioners to Paris to negotiate an accord. When they arrived, agents of the French foreign minister Talleyrand (identified only as "X," "Y," and "Z") made it clear that the success of the American mission depended on a loan to the French government and a $240,000 "gratuity" (more accurately, a bribe) for themselves. The two staunchly Federalist commissioners, John Marshall and Charles Pinckney, indignantly sailed home. The third commissioner, Elbridge Gerry, alarmed by Talleyrand's intimation that France would declare war if all three Americans left, stayed on.

When Adams reported the so-called XYZ Affair to Congress, Federalists quickly exploited the French blunder. Secretary of State Pickering urged an immediate declaration of war, while Federalist congressmen thundered against the insult to American honor and promised "millions for defense, but not one cent for tribute." Caught up in the anti-French furor and emboldened by the petitions of support that flooded in from around the country, the president lashed out at "enemies" at home and abroad. Emotions were further inflamed by the so-called Quasi War, a series of encounters between American and French ships on the high seas.

For the moment, the Republicans were in disarray. Publicly, they deplored the French government's behavior and pledged to uphold the nation's honor. But among themselves, they voiced alarm over Federalist intentions—with good reason, because the Federalists soon mounted a crash program to repel foreign invaders and root out "traitors" at home.

The Alien and Sedition Acts

In May 1798, Congress called for a naval force capable of defending the American coast against French attack. In July, it moved closer to an open breach with France by repealing the treaty of 1778 and calling for the formation of a 10,000-man army. The army's stated mission was to repel a French invasion, but this seemed an unlikely danger given France's desperate struggle in Europe. The Jeffersonians, remembering the speed with which the Federalists had deployed troops against the Whiskey Rebels only a few years earlier, feared the army would be used against them.

As criticism of the army bill mounted, Adams had second thoughts. He was still enough of an old revolutionary to worry about the dangers of standing armies. "This damned army," he burst out, "will be the ruin of the country." He was further angered when members of his party sought to put Hamilton in command of the troops. To the dismay of hardline Federalists, Adams issued only a few of the officers' commissions that Congress had authorized. Without officers, the army could not be mobilized.

Fearful of foreign subversion and aware that French and Irish immigrants were active in the Jeffersonian opposition, the Federalist-dominated

Political Emotions Run High A fight erupted in the House of Representatives in 1798 when Matthew Lyon, a Jeffersonian from Vermont, spat on the Federalist Roger Griswold. As the two congressmen battle, other representatives and a dog look on. *(Print Collection, Miriam and Ira D. Wallach Division of Art, Prints and Photographs, The New York Public Library, Astor, Lenox and Tilden Foundations)*

AMERICAN VOICES

In this 1803 publication, Samuel Miller describes the remarkable transformation of American journalism in the early republic.

It is worthy of remark that newspapers have almost entirely changed their form and character. . . . For a long time . . . they were confined, in general, to the mere statement of facts. But they have gradually assumed an office more extensive, and risen to a more important station in society. They have become the vehicles of discussion, in which the principles of government, the interests of nations, the spirit and tendency of public measures, and the public and private characters of individuals, are all arraigned, tried, and decided. Instead, therefore, of being considered . . . of small moment in society, they have become immense moral and political engines, closely connected with the welfare of the state, and deeply involving both its peace and prosperity. . . .

By means of this powerful instrument, impressions on the public mind may be made with a celerity, and to an extent, of which our remote ancestors had no conception, and which cannot but give rise to the most important consequences in society. Never was there given to man a political engine of greater power; and never, assuredly, did this engine before operate on so large a scale. . . .

- *What is the revolution in print communication that Miller describes?*

- *What were the connections between this revolution in print and American politics of the late eighteenth century?*

Congress acted to curb the flow of aliens into the country. In June 1798, the Naturalization Act raised the residence requirement for citizenship from 5 to 14 years, while the Alien Act authorized the president to expel aliens whom he judged "dangerous to the peace and safety of the United States." Another bill, the Alien Enemies Act, empowered the president in time of war to arrest, imprison, or banish the subjects of any hostile nation without specifying charges against them or providing opportunity for appeal. The Federalist congressman Harrison Gray Otis explained that there was no need "to invite hordes of Wild Irishmen, or the turbulent and disorderly of all parts of the world, to come here with a view to distract our tranquility."

The implications of these acts for basic political liberties were ominous enough, but the Federalists had not yet finished. In mid-July, Congress passed the Sedition Act, aimed directly at the Jeffersonians. The bill made it punishable by fine and imprisonment for anyone to conspire in opposition to "any measure or measures of the government" or to aid "any insurrection, riot, unlawful assembly, or combination." Fines and imprisonment also awaited those who dared to "write, print, utter, or publish . . . any false, scandalous and malicious writing" bringing the government, Congress, or the president into disrepute. The Federalist moves stunned the Jeffersonians, for they threatened to smother all political opposition.

DOCUMENT

The Alien and Sedition Acts (1798)

Under the terms of the Alien Act, Secretary of State Pickering launched investigations intended to force foreigners to register with the government. The act's chilling effects were immediately apparent. Toward the end of July, Pickering noted approvingly that large numbers of aliens, especially people of French ancestry, were leaving the country. As prosecutions under the Sedition Act went forward, 25 people, among them David Brown of Dedham, were arrested. Fifteen were indicted, and ten were ultimately convicted, the majority of them Jeffersonian printers and editors.

Representative Matthew Lyon, a cantankerous, acid-tongued congressman from Vermont, learned the consequences of political indiscretion, even for members of Congress. Born in Ireland, Lyon had come to America as a young indentured servant, bringing with him undying enmity toward England and disrespect for privilege of every sort. A veteran of the war for American independence, he took his revolutionary principles seriously.

During a heated debate over the Sedition Act, Lyon spat in the face of Federalist congressman Roger Griswold of Connecticut, thus earning the derisive sobriquet of the "Spitting Lion." Two weeks later, Griswold exacted revenge by caning Lyon on the House floor. Later that year, Lyon was hauled into court, fined $1,000, and sentenced to four months in prison. His crime? Reference in a personal letter to President Adams's "unbounded thirst for ridiculous pomp, foolish adulation, and selfish avarice."

Local Reverberations

David Brown was not the only ordinary citizen to experience the enmity of Federalist authorities, for the simmering political conflict penetrated deep into American communities. On July 27, 1798, President and Mrs. Adams passed through Newark, New Jersey, on their way from Philadelphia to their home in Quincy, Massachusetts. As the nation's first couple moved along Broad Street around 11 o'clock that morning, they were greeted by firing cannon, ringing church bells, and cheering citizens.

Not all Newark's residents shared in the moment's enthusiasm. Luther Baldwin was in John Burnett's dram shop when one of the tavern's other customers, noting that the cannon continued to fire after the president had passed by, commented acidly, "There goes the President and they are firing at his a—." A "little merry with drink," Baldwin replied that "he did not care if they fired thro' his a—." Whereupon the Federalist tavern keeper cried out that

Baldwin had spoken sedition and must be punished. Within a year he was hauled before a federal circuit court, convicted of speaking "seditious words tending to defame the President and Government of the United States," fined, and committed to jail until both fine and court fees were paid.

Jeffersonian Republicans made a field day of Baldwin's trial. The New York *Argus* wondered in mock astonishment whether the "most enthusiastic Federalists and Tories" supposed that anyone "would feel . . . justification in firing at such a disgusting target as the a—of J. A.?" However, there was danger as well as humor in the Federalists' overreaction. When so much is made of such a "ridiculous expression" as Baldwin's, the *Argus* warned, the "malignancy of the federal faction" was plainly revealed.

The Virginia and Kentucky Resolutions

With little prospect of reversing the actions of the Federalist-dominated Congress, Jeffersonians turned to the states for redress. On November 16, 1798, the Kentucky Assembly passed a resolution declaring that the national government had violated the Bill of

Divisive Issues of the 1790s

Issues	Federalist Party	Jeffersonian Republican Party
Domestic Policy		
Paying the national debt	Favors—Fund remaining debt at face value.	Favors—But wants discrimination between original holders and speculators.
Assumption of remaining state debts	Favors—As way of strengthening central government.	Opposes—As unfair to Southern States and source of power for central government.
Bank of the United States	Favors—To stabilize national economy, promote economic growth, and enhance power of central government.	Opposes—As exceeding central government's constitutional authority, and adding to consolidation of central authority.
Whiskey Tax	Favors—To provide revenue for central government.	Opposes—Warns of dangers in taxing power of central government.
Whiskey Rebellion	Favors—Suppression of rebellion as challenge to central government.	Opposes—Use of federal force to suppress protest.
Alien and Sedition Acts	Favors—As necessary to protect national security.	Opposes—As infringement of constitutional rights and threat to political opposition.
Federal army	Favors—As necessary to defend against possible French invasion.	Opposes—As dangerous enhancement of federal authority and threat to political opposition.
Foreign Policy		
French Revolution	Initially endorses political reform in France, but alarmed by radicalism following 1793. Fears French influence in U.S. Cheers England as bastion of political order.	Endorses political reform in France. Continues cautious support following 1793. Suspicious of British motives.
Jay's Treaty	Supports as best agreement possible, and as promoting trade with England.	Opposes—Criticizes treaty's silence concerning impressment, return of confiscated slaves, etc.
XYZ Affair	Expresses outrage over affront to American dignity.	Also expresses outrage, though worries over domestic political fallout.
Declaration of war with France	Favors, following XYZ Affair—Badly divided when Adams opts for peace.	Opposes—As unnecessary and threatening dangerous domestic repercussions.

Rights. Faced with an arbitrary exercise of federal power, each state had "an equal right" to judge of infractions and decide on the proper "mode and measure of redress." Nullification (declaring a federal law invalid within a state's borders) was the "rightful remedy" for unconstitutional laws. Similar resolutions, written by Madison and passed the following month by the Virginia assembly, asserted that when the central government threatened the people's liberties, the states were "duty bound to interpose for arresting the progress of the evil." It would not be the last time in U.S. history that state leaders would claim authority to set aside a federal law.

The Kentucky and Virginia Resolutions received little support elsewhere and, as it turned out, the Alien and Sedition Acts were not enforced in the South. Still, the resolutions indicated the depth of popular opposition to the Federalist program.

As the Federalists pressed ahead, the Virginia assembly called for reorganization of the militia and formation of a state arsenal at Harpers Ferry. In Philadelphia, Federalist patrols walked the streets to protect government officials from angry crowds. As a precaution, President Adams smuggled arms into the White House. As 1799 began, the country seemed on the brink of upheaval.

The Kentucky and Virginia Resolutions (1798, 1799)

Within a year, however, the political cycle turned again, this time decisively against the Federalists. From Europe, the president's son, John Quincy Adams, sent assurances that Talleyrand was prepared to negotiate an honorable accord. Fearful that war with France "would convulse the attachments of the country," Adams seized the opening and determined to appoint new peace commissioners. "The end of war is peace," he explained, "and peace was offered me." He had also concluded that his only chance of reelection lay in fashioning a peace coalition from elements of both parties.

Adams's cabinet was enraged, for the Federalist war program depended for its legitimacy on continuation of the French crisis. After Secretary of State Pickering ignored the president's orders to dispatch the peace commissioners, Adams dismissed him and instructed them to depart. By year's end, the envoys secured an agreement releasing the United States from the 1778 alliance and restoring peaceful relations.

The "Revolution of 1800"

As the election of 1800 approached, the Federalists were in disarray, having squandered the political advantage handed them by the XYZ Affair. With peace a reality, they stood before the nation charged with exercising federal power unconstitutionally, suppressing political dissent, and threatening to use a federal army against American citizens. Adams's opponents within the Federalist party were furious at his "betrayal." When he announced his intention to seek reelection, they plotted his defeat.

Emotions ran high as the election approached. In Philadelphia, gangs of young Federalists and Jeffersonians clashed in the streets. "A fray ensued," one observer reported, "the light horse were called in, and the city was so filled with confusion . . . that it was dangerous going out."

The Federalist Fisher Ames berated the Jeffersonians as "fire-eating salamanders" and "poison-sucking toads," while they returned the abuse in kind. In Virginia, rumors of a slave insurrection briefly interrupted the political feuding, but the scare passed and Federalists and Jeffersonians were soon at each others' throats once again. This election, Jefferson declared, will "fix the national character" by determining whether "republicanism or aristocracy" will prevail.

Fisher Ames, "The Republican, No. II" (1804)

Election day was tense throughout the country, but passed without serious incident. As the results were tallied, it became clear that the Jeffersonians had handed the Federalists a decisive defeat. The two Jeffersonian candidates for president, Jefferson

The Presidential Election of 1800

Though the federal government was little more than a decade old, the electoral vote in 1800 revealed the sectional divisions that already troubled national politics.

NEW HAMPSHIRE (6)
MAINE (Mass.)
VERMONT (4)
NEW YORK (12)
MASSACHUSETTS (16)
INDIANA TERRITORY
NORTHWEST TERRITORY
PENNSYLVANIA (15)
RHODE ISLAND (4)
CONNECTICUT (9)
NEW JERSEY (7)
DELAWARE (3)
MARYLAND (10)
VIRGINIA (21)
KENTUCKY (4)
TENNESSEE (3)
NORTH CAROLINA (12)
MISSISSIPPI TERRITORY
SOUTH CAROLINA (8)
GEORGIA (4)

Electoral Votes for:
Jefferson (Republican)
Adams (Federalist)
Vote divided

The Death of Washington   Washington's death in 1799 generated a surge of public mourning as countless eulogies celebrated him as the "Father of his Country." The picture is rich in religious and patriotic symbols. How many can you identify, and what meanings are they intended to convey? *(Photograph Courtesy Peabody Essex Museum [AE81885])*

and Aaron Burr, each had 73 electoral votes. Adams trailed with 65.

Because of the tie vote, the election was thrown into the House of Representatives, as provided in the Constitution, where a deadlock quickly developed. After a bitter struggle, the House finally elected Jefferson, 10 states to 4, on the thirty-sixth ballot. (Seeking to prevent a recurrence of such a crisis, the next Congress passed and the states then ratified the Twelfth

Amendment, providing for separate Electoral College ballots for president and vice president.) The magnitude of the Federalists' defeat was even more evident in congressional elections, where they lost their majorities in both House and Senate.

The election's outcome revealed the strong sectional divisions now evident in the country's politics. The Federalists dominated New England because of regional loyalty to Adams, the area's commercial ties with England, and fears that their opponents intended to import social revolution from France. From Maryland south, political control by the Jeffersonians was almost as complete. In the middle states, the election was more closely contested.

The Federalist–Jeffersonian conflict was rooted as well in socioeconomic divisions among the American people. Federalist support was strongest among merchants, manufacturers, and commercial farmers situated within easy reach of the coast. In New York City and Philadelphia, Federalists were most numerous in wards where houses were largest and addresses most fashionable. All had supported the Constitution in 1787–1788.

The Jeffersonian coalition included most of the old Anti-Federalists but was broader than that. The Jeffersonians found support among urban workers and artisans, many of whom had once been staunch Federalists. The coalition, moreover, was led by individuals such as Madison and Jefferson who had helped create the Constitution and set the new government on its feet. Unlike the Anti-Federalists, the Jeffersonians were ardent supporters of the Constitution, but insisted that it be implemented in ways consistent with political liberty and a strong dependence on the states.

Not all Jeffersonians were democratic in sympathy. Some continued to argue the importance of leadership by a "natural aristocracy of talent." Most southern Jeffersonians found no inconsistency between black slavery and white liberty, and virtually all continued to believe that politics should remain an exclusively male domain. Still, the Jeffersonian coalition included countless individuals committed to the creation of a more democratic society. Motivated by a combination of electoral self-interest, political principle, and the determination of ordinary people to claim their rights as republican citizens, the Jeffersonian Republicans mounted elaborate parades, organized get-out-the-vote campaigns in New York City and other urban centers, and utilized the popular press to mobilize the people. In the process they contributed to a growing tide of popular politics.

AUDIO
Jefferson and Liberty

In the election of 1800, control of the federal government passed for the first time from one political party to another, not easily but peacefully and legally. The "Revolution of 1800," Jefferson claimed, was "as real a revolution in the principles of our government as that of 1776 was in its form." The years immediately ahead would reveal whether he was correct.

RESTORING AMERICAN LIBERTY

The Jeffersonians took office in 1801 determined to calm the political storms, consolidate their recent electoral victory, rescue the government from Federalist mismanagement, and set it on a proper republican course.

The Jeffersonians Take Control

In November 1800 the government had moved from Philadelphia to the District of Columbia, located on the Potomac River. To the consternation of the arriving politicians, the new capital was little more than a swampy village of 5,000 inhabitants. Little had yet materialized of the grand design of plazas and boulevards radiating outward from the Capitol that had been created by the Frenchman Pierre L'Enfant, aided by the black American mathematician and surveyor Benjamin Banneker. The wing of the Capitol building containing the House of Representatives was finished, but the Senate chamber and president's mansion were uncompleted.

IMAGE

The Pastoral Setting of Washington, D.C.

To rid the government of Federalist pomp, Jefferson planned a simple inauguration. Shortly before noon on March 4, he walked to the Capitol from his nearby boardinghouse. Dressed as a plain citizen, the president-elect read his short inaugural address, Chief Justice John Marshall (a fellow Virginian but staunch Federalist, recently appointed to the Supreme Court by John Adams) administered the oath of office, and a militia company fired a 16-gun salute.

IMAGE

A View of the Capitol in 1800 by William Russel Birch

Despite the modesty of the occasion, the moment was filled with significance. Mrs. Samuel Harrison Smith, Washington resident and political observer, described the moment's drama. "I have this morning witnessed one of the most interesting scenes a free people can ever witness," she wrote to a friend. "The changes of administration, which in every . . . age have most generally been epochs of confusion, villainy, and bloodshed, in this our happy country take place without any species of distraction or disorder." Countless Americans shared her sense of pride and relief.

In his inaugural speech, Jefferson enumerated the "essential principles" that would guide his administration: "equal and exact justice to all," support of the states as "the surest bulwarks against anti-republican tendencies," "absolute acquiescence" in the

The New Capital
Unlike highly commercial, cosmopolitan centers such as New York and Philadelphia that had served as earlier capitals, Washington seemed lost in the undeveloped countryside along the Potomac River. *(Library of Congress, LC-USZC4-530)*

Jefferson, First
Inaugural
Address (1801)

decisions of the majority, supremacy of civil over military authority, reduction of government spending, "honest payment" of the public debt, freedom of the press, and "freedom of the person under the protection of the habeas corpus." Though Jefferson never mentioned the Federalists by name, his litany of principles reverberated with the dark experience of the 1790s.

The president spoke also of political reconciliation, asserting that "every difference of opinion is not a difference of principle," and affirming that "we are all republicans—we are all federalists." Not all his followers welcomed that final flourish, for many were eager to scatter the Federalists to the political winds. Jefferson eventually agreed that a "general sweep" of Federalist officeholders was necessary. By 1808, virtually all government offices were in Jeffersonian hands.

Politics and the Federal Courts

Having lost Congress and the presidency, the Federalists turned to the federal judiciary for protection against the expected Jeffersonian onslaught. In the last months of the Adams administration, the Federalist-controlled Congress had passed a new Judiciary Act increasing the number of circuit courts, complete with judges, marshals, and clerks. Before leaving office, Adams filled many of those offices with staunch Federalists. When the new Jeffersonian-dominated

Congress convened, it challenged the Federalist hold on the judiciary. In January 1802, by a strict party vote, Congress repealed the Judiciary Act.

As Federalists sputtered in anger, exultant Jeffersonians prepared to purge several highly partisan Federalist judges. In March 1803, the House of Representatives impeached district judge John Pickering of New Hampshire. The grounds were not the "high crimes and misdemeanors" required by the Constitution, but the Federalist diatribes with which Pickering regularly assaulted defendants and juries. Impeachment, asserted Representative William Branch Giles of Virginia, is nothing more than a declaration by Congress that an individual holds "dangerous opinions," which if allowed to go into effect "will work the destruction of the Union." Although Giles's speech echoed the language of repression used by Federalists only a few years earlier, the Jeffersonian-controlled Senate convicted Pickering by a straight party vote.

Emboldened by their success, the Jeffersonians next impeached Supreme Court justice Samuel Chase, one of the most notorious Federalist partisans, charging him with "intemperate and inflammatory political harangues." When the trial revealed that Chase had committed no impeachable offense, he was acquitted and returned triumphantly to the bench.

Chase was a sorry hero, but constitutional principles are often established in the defense of less than heroic people. Had Chase's impeachment succeeded,

Federal Revenues and Expenditures, 1790–1810 (in thousands of dollars)				
Year	Revenues		Expenditures	
1790	Customs	4,399	Military	634
	Other	19	Interest on public debt	2,349
		4,418	Other	1,426
				4,409
1800	Customs	9,081	Military	6,010
	Internal revenue	809	Interest on public debt	3,375
	Other	793	Other	1,466
		10,683		10,851
1810	Customs	8,583	Military	3,948
	Internal revenue	7	Interest on public debt	2,845
	Sale of public lands	697	Other	1,447
	Other	793		8,240
		10,080		

Note: In constant dollars, the estimated revenue of the federal government in 2001 was $2,136 trillion and its estimated expenditures were $1,856 trillion.

Source: U.S. Bureau of the Census and *Statistical Abstract of the United States, 2001.*

Chief Justice Marshall would almost certainly have been next, and that would have precipitated a constitutional crisis. Sensing the danger, the Jeffersonians pulled back, content to allow time and attrition to cleanse the courts of Federalist control. The vital principle of judicial independence had been narrowly preserved.

Dismantling the Federalist War Program

The Jeffersonians quickly moved to dismantle the Federalists' war program. They ended prosecution of newspaper editors under the Sedition Act, freed its victims, and in 1802 let it lapse. While several Federalist editors felt the government's displeasure, the Jeffersonians never duplicated the Federalists' attempts to stifle political dissent. As a consequence, freedom of the press, among the bedrock principles of American liberty, was solidly affirmed. "Error of opinion may be tolerated," Jefferson explained in his first inaugural address, "where reason is left free to combat it." This was especially important at a time when the press was becoming an essential vehicle of democratic politics. In the years ahead the American people would often struggle to reaffirm that freedom.

Jefferson also undercut the Alien Acts by dismantling the hated inspection system. In 1802, Congress restored the requirement of 5 rather than 14 years of residence before a foreigner could become a citizen. The Federalists' provisional army was also quickly disbanded; no longer would federal troops intimidate American citizens.

Jefferson was determined as well to reduce the size of the federal government, even though it had fewer than 3,000 civilian employees, only 300 of them, including the cabinet and Congress, in Washington. (That amounted to 1 federal official for every 1,914 citizens, compared with 1 for approximately every 68 citizens today.) The "principal care of our persons and property," Jefferson declared, should be left to the states because they were more closely attuned to the needs of the people and could be held more closely accountable. The federal government should do little more than oversee foreign policy, deliver the mail, deal with Native Americans on federal land, and administer the public domain. Though the Jeffersonian Republicans may not have "revolutionized" the government as they claimed, they pointed it in a new direction.

BUILDING AN AGRARIAN NATION

The Jeffersonian Republicans did more than reverse Federalist initiatives, for they were determined to implement their own vision of an expanding, agrarian nation. That vision was mixed and inconsistent, because the Jeffersonian Party was made up of conflicting groups, as American political parties have always been. Among them were southern planters, like Jefferson himself, determined to maintain a slavery-based agrarian order; lower- and middle-class southerners committed to black servitude but ardent proponents of political equality

IMAGE
Statue of Jefferson

among whites; northern artisans harboring an aversion to slavery, though rarely a commitment to racial equality, and a fierce dedication to honest toil and their own economic interests; western farmers devoted to self-sufficiency on the land; and northern intellectuals committed to political democracy. In time, this diversity would splinter the Jeffersonian coalition. For the moment, however, these groups found unity not only in their common Federalist enemies, but also in a set of broadly shared principles that guided government policy through Jefferson's two administrations (1801–1809).

The Jeffersonian Vision

Political liberty, the Jeffersonians believed, could survive only under conditions of broad economic and social equality. Their strategy centered on the independent yeoman farmer—self-reliant, industrious, and concerned for the public good. Such qualities were deemed essential to democratic citizenship.

The Jeffersonian vision was clouded, however, because industriousness generated wealth, wealth bred social inequality, and inequality threatened to destroy the very foundation of a democratic society. The solution to that dilemma lay in rapid territorial expansion that would provide land for the nation's citizen farmers, draw restless people out of crowded eastern cities, preserve the social equality that democratic liberty required, and delay, perhaps even prevent, the cyclical process of political growth, maturity, and decay that had been the fate of past nations.

Calls for expanding white settlement were strengthened by the somber writings of an English clergyman and political economist named Thomas Malthus, who in 1798 published an essay that jolted Europeans and Americans alike. Observing the increasingly crowded conditions of his native England, Malthus argued that "the power of population" was "greater than the power in the earth to produce subsistence for man." Hopes for a steadily improving quality of life, he warned, were a delusion, for the future would be filled with increasing misery as population outran the supply of food.

Jefferson took Malthus's warnings seriously but believed that the Englishman failed to understand that the United States' vast reservoir of land would enable it to escape Europe's fate. In Europe, Jefferson explained, "the quantity of food is fixed ... [while] supernumerary births add ... to mortality." In America, however,

the immense extent of uncultivated, fertile lands would support families of any size. Food could increase geometrically with births. Territorial expansion was thus indispensable to the Jeffersonian vision of the nation's future.

There were other reasons for promoting expansion. Occupation of the West would secure the nation's borders against lingering threats from Britain, France, and Spain. Finally, the Jeffersonians calculated that newly created western states would strengthen their political control and ensure the Federalists' demise.

Time would reveal that the United States' ability to avoid Europe's woes by continental expansion, a basic tenet of American exceptionalism, was more limited than Jefferson imagined. Yet from the perspective of the early nineteenth century, the Jeffersonians offered a compelling and hopeful vision of the nation's future.

The Windfall Louisiana Purchase

The goal of securing agrarian democracy by territorial expansion explains Jefferson's most dramatic accomplishment, the Louisiana Purchase of 1803. It nearly doubled the nation's size.

In 1800, Spain ceded the vast trans-Mississippi region called Louisiana to France. Jefferson was disturbed at this evidence that European nations still coveted North American soil. His fears were well grounded, for in October 1802 the Spanish commander at New Orleans, which Spain had retained, closed the Mississippi River to American commerce.

New Orleans In this 1803 panorama by Boqueto de Woiserie, the American eagle extends its wings over New Orleans following the Louisiana Purchase. Why was New Orleans such an important and controversial place? *(Boquesto de Woiserie, A View of New Orleans taken from the Plantation of Marigny, 1803, Chicago Historical Society, P&S-1932. 0018)*

Exploring the Trans-Mississippi West, 1804–1807

During his two administrations, President Jefferson sent several exploring expeditions into the vast Louisiana Territory and beyond. Why did he send them, and what did they accomplish?

BRITISH POSSESSIONS

LEWIS
1806
1805
Fort Clatsop
OREGON
COUNTRY
Columbia River
Snake River
CLARK
Yellowstone River
Fort Mandan
ROCKY MOUNTAINS
Great Salt Lake
Colorado River
Platte River
LOUISIANA
Missouri River
1804
LEWIS & CLARK
GREAT PLAINS
St. Louis
PIKE
1805–1806
San Francisco
Pikes Peak
1806–1807
Taos
Santa Fé
PIKE
Arkansas River
Red River
FREEMAN
San Luis Obispo
Santa Barbara
Los Angeles
San Diego
SPANISH
El Paso
Rio Grande
POSSESSIONS
San Antonio
Natchitoches
1806
Fort Adams
New Orleans
Mobile
SPANISH FLORIDA
NEW HAMPSHIRE
VERMONT
MAINE
MASSACHUSETTS
NEW YORK
RHODE ISLAND
CONNECTICUT
NEW JERSEY
DELAWARE
MARYLAND
MICHIGAN TERRITORY
PENNSYLVANIA
OHIO
Ohio River
INDIANA TERRITORY
VIRGINIA
KENTUCKY
NORTH CAROLINA
TENNESSEE
SOUTH CAROLINA
Mississippi River
MISSISSIPPI TERRITORY
GEORGIA

✖ Forts
✝ Missions
☐ Louisiana Purchase, 1803

Spain's action raised consternation in Washington and the West.

In response, Jefferson instructed Robert Livingston, the American minister to France, to purchase a tract of land on the lower Mississippi that might serve as an American port, thus guaranteeing free transit for American shipping. By the time James Monroe arrived in Paris in April 1803 to assist in the negotiations, the French ruler, Napoleon Bonaparte, had decided to sell all of Louisiana. Faced with the threat of renewed war with England, as well as the successful black rebellion against French rule in Haiti, Napoleon feared American designs on Louisiana and knew he could not keep American settlers out. Soon the deal was struck. For $15 million, the United States obtained nearly 830,000 square miles of new territory.

DOCUMENT
Constitutionality of the Louisiana Purchase (1803)

Federalists reacted with alarm to the news, fearing correctly that the states to be carved from Louisiana would be staunchly Jeffersonian. They worried as well that a rapidly expanding frontier would "decivilize" the nation.

Territorial expansion did not stop with Louisiana. In 1810, American adventurers fomented a revolt in Spanish West Florida and proclaimed an independent republic. Two years later, over vigorous Spanish objections, Congress annexed the region. In the Adams-Onís (or Transcontinental) Treaty of 1819, Spain ceded East Florida. As part of the 1819 agreement, the United States also extended its territorial claims to the Pacific Northwest.

Opening the Trans-Mississippi West

If America's expanding domain was to serve the needs of the agrarian nation, it would have to be explored and prepared for white settlement. In the summer of 1803, Jefferson dispatched an expedition led by Meriwether Lewis and William Clark to explore the far Northwest, make contact with the Native Americans there, open the fur trade, and bring back scientific information about the area. For nearly two and a half years, the intrepid explorers, assisted by the Shoshone woman Sacagawea,

DOCUMENT
Lewis and Clark Meet the Shoshone (Aug. 17, 1805)

Meriwether
Lewis

made their way across thousands of miles of hostile and unmapped terrain—up the Missouri River, through the Rockies via the Bitterroot Valley and Lolo Pass, down the Columbia to the Pacific coast, and back again, finally reemerging at St. Louis in September 1806. Lewis and Clark's journey, which some have called the greatest wilderness trip ever recorded, fanned people's interest in the Trans-Mississippi West and demonstrated the feasibility of an overland route to the Pacific.

William Clark

In 1805 and 1806, Lieutenant Zebulon Pike explored the sources of the Mississippi River in northern Minnesota, then undertook an equally bold venture into the Rocky Mountains, where he surveyed the peak that still bears his name. In the following decade, the government established a string of military posts from Fort Snelling, at the confluence of the Minnesota and Mississippi Rivers, to Fort Smith on the Arkansas. They were intended to secure the nation's frontier, promote the fur trade, and support white settlement.

The Louisiana
Purchase

A FOREIGN POLICY FOR THE NEW NATION

While Jefferson was preoccupied with refashioning the government and extending American territory during his first term of office, his second term was dominated by foreign affairs. As Washington and John Adams had discovered and Jefferson soon learned, the Atlantic world was a dangerous place.

Jeffersonian Principles

During the early years of the nineteenth century, several goals guided the Jeffersonians' efforts to fashion a foreign policy appropriate for the expanding, agrarian nation. Chief among them were protecting American interests on the high seas, clearing the Great Lakes region of British troops, and breaking free of the country's historic dependence on Europe.

Jeffersonian foreign policy was based on the principle of "no entangling alliances" with Europe that Washington had articulated in his Farewell Address of 1796. England remained the principal enemy, but France, now that the revolution had ended in Napoleon Bonaparte's dictatorial rule, was suspect as well.

Second, Jeffersonians emphasized the importance of overseas commerce for the nation's well-being. Foreign trade would provide markets for America's

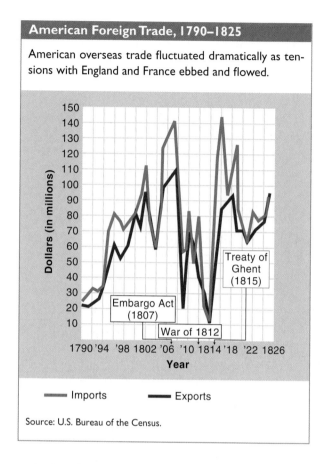

American Foreign Trade, 1790–1825

American overseas trade fluctuated dramatically as tensions with England and France ebbed and flowed.

Dollars (in millions)

150 140 130 120 110 100 90 80 70 60 50 40 30 20 10

Embargo Act (1807)

Treaty of Ghent (1815)

War of 1812

1790 '94 '98 1802 '06 '10 1814 '18 '22 1826
Year

—— Imports   —— Exports

Source: U.S. Bureau of the Census.

agricultural produce and bring manufactured goods in return. Unlike the Federalists, the Jeffersonians hoped to keep large-scale manufacturing in Europe. They feared the concentrations of wealth and dependent working classes that domestic manufacturing would bring.

Peace was the Jeffersonians' third goal. War was objectionable not only because people were killed and property destroyed, but also because it endangered liberty by inflaming politics, stifling free speech, swelling the public debt, and expanding governmental power. Jeffersonians understood the dangers lurking throughout the Atlantic world and knew that protecting the nation's interests might require force. Between 1801 and 1805, Jefferson dispatched naval vessels to defend U.S. commerce against the Barbary States (Algiers, Morocco, Tripoli, and Tunis) in the Mediterranean Sea. War, however, was to be a policy of last resort.

Struggling for Neutral Rights

After a brief interlude of peace, European war resumed in 1803. Once again Britain and France seized American shipping. Britain's naval superiority made its attacks especially serious. Its continuing refusal to stop impressment, vacate its posts south of the Great Lakes, and reopen the West Indies to American trade heightened Anglo-American tension.

In response to British seizures of U.S. shipping, Congress passed the Non-Importation Act in April 1806, banning British imports that could be produced domestically or acquired elsewhere. A month later, Britain blockaded the European coast. In retaliation, Napoleon forbade all commerce with the British Isles.

Tension between Britain and the United States reached the breaking point in June 1807, when the British warship *Leopard* stopped the American frigate *Chesapeake* off the Virginia coast and demanded that four crew members be handed over as British deserters. When the American commander refused, protesting that the sailors were U.S. citizens, the *Leopard* opened fire, killing 3 men and wounding 18. After the *Chesapeake* limped back into port with the story, cries of outrage rang across the land.

British Impressment, 1812

Knowing that the United States was not prepared to confront Britain, Jefferson proposed withdrawing American ships from the Atlantic. In December 1807, Congress passed the Embargo Act, forbidding American vessels from sailing for foreign ports. The embargo was one of Jefferson's most ill-fated decisions.

The embargo had relatively little effect on Britain, since British shipping profited from the withdrawal of American competition and British merchants found new sources of agricultural produce in Latin America. The embargo's impact at home, however, was far-reaching. U.S. exports plummeted 80 percent in a year, while imports dropped by more than half. New England was hardest hit. In ports such as Boston and Providence, ships lay idle and thousands of workers were unemployed as depression settled in.

Up and down the coast, communities openly violated the embargo. As attempts to police it failed, English goods were smuggled in across the Canadian border. Throughout the Federalist Northeast, bitterness threatened to escalate into open rebellion. When federal officials declared martial law and sent in troops in an effort to control the situation near Lake Champlain in upstate New York, local citizens fired on U.S. revenue boats and recaptured confiscated goods.

In language reminiscent of the Virginia and Kentucky Resolutions, Connecticut's Federalist governor declared that states were duty-bound "to interpose their protecting shield" between the liberties of the people and oppressive acts of the general government. Faced with the embargo's ineffectiveness abroad and disastrous political consequences at home, Congress repealed the measure in 1809.

As Jefferson's presidency ended, officials found themselves in a quandary. How could American rights on the high seas be protected and the country's honor upheld without being drawn into a European war and without further inflaming American politics? The nation would continue to struggle with that dilemma in the years immediately ahead.

The Embargo Stifles American Commerce The tranquility of Crowninshield Wharf in Salem, Massachusetts, reveals ships idled and docks emptied by Jefferson's embargo. *(George Ropes, Crowninshield's Wharf, 1806. Photograph courtesy Peabody Essex Museum, [M3459])*

Conclusion

A Period of Trial and Transition

The decade of the 1790s was a time of continuing political crisis. Scarcely had the new government been formed than divisions appeared, initially among political leaders at the capital, but increasingly among the people at large. Hamilton's domestic policies generated the initial conflict. It was the French Revolution, European war, Jay's Treaty, and the Federalist war program, however, that galvanized political energies and set Federalists and Jeffersonian Republicans so adamantly against each other. Countless citizens such as David Brown were caught up in the confusion. The Haitian rebellion together with other democratic insurgencies in Ireland, Europe, and the Americas further inflamed the country's politics.

In control of the federal government following the election of 1800, the Jeffersonians labored to set it on a more democratic course. At home, they fashioned domestic policies designed to redirect authority to the states and promote the country's agrarian expansion. Abroad they attempted, with more ambiguous results and at considerable political cost, to protect American rights in a hostile Atlantic world while avoiding European entanglements.

By the time Thomas Jefferson left the presidency and James Madison took office in 1809, politics at the seat of national government and in the states had drawn more closely together, as leaders perfected the techniques of democratic politics, utilizing a highly partisan press and organizing political parties better skilled in managing the expanding (white, male) electorate. These transitions, emerging in the midst of deep-seated controversy, would soon alter the very character of American political life.

Questions for Review and Reflection

1. Identify three foreign policy crises of the years 1790–1809, and explain why each was so controversial.

2. How did Federalists and Jeffersonians differ in their political principles? In the kind of economy they wished the nation to have?

3. Disputes over the proper balance of authority between the national government and the states have been a recurring theme of American history from 1790 to our own time. Why did the issue generate such controversy during the period covered in this chapter?

4. Tension between the demands of national security and the protection of citizens' basic rights has been another recurrent theme of our history. Why did that tension become so severe during the 1790s?

Recommended Reading

Recommended Readings are posted on the Web site for this textbook. Visit www.ablongman.com/nash

Fiction and Film

Adapted from Laurel Thatcher Ulrich's prize-winning book, the docudrama *A Midwife's Tale* (1997) depicts the daily life of nurse-midwife Martha Ballard, who delivered a thousand babies and served her New England community during the closing years of the eighteenth century. The initial installment of C-SPAN's *American Presidents: Life Portraits* series (1999) effectively portrays the challenges and accomplishments of the nation's first president, George Washington. In the novel *Fever* (1996), John Weidman offers a vivid account of the yellow fever plague that killed thousands of people and threatened social chaos in Philadelphia in 1793. The essayist and novelist Gore Vidal explores the tangled politics and personalities of the early republic via a largely sympathetic portrayal of Aaron Burr (who killed Alexander Hamilton in a duel in 1804) in *Burr: A Novel* (1973).

Discovering U.S. History Online

Birth of the Nation: The First Federal Congress 1789–1791

www.gwu.edu/~ffcp/

This online exhibit "provides an overview of the work of and issues faced by this seminal Congress."

The Bradford House—Whiskey Rebellion—Whiskey Insurrection

www.bradfordhouse.org

David Bradford was a prominent figure in the "Whiskey Insurrection." His home has been restored as a museum; its Web site includes a description of the rebellion, its causes, Bradford's role, and the end results.

George Washington's Mount Vernon Estate and Gardens

www.mountvernon.org

Pictures and documents from Mount Vernon, the home of the first president, George Washington.

The Papers of George Washington

http://gwpapers.virginia.edu

This richly illustrated site is the online home of George Washington's papers and includes the text of many of the documents, maps, images, and articles about Washington and his time.

The French Revolution

www.woodberry.org/acad/hist/FRWEB

This well-organized site provides an illustrated introduction to the French Revolution, its events, and its people.

John Adams

www.whitehouse.gov/WH/glimpse/presidents/html/ja2.html

This site contains biographical information about the second president and links to his inaugural address, his more quotable phrases, and information about his wife, Abigail.

The Haitian Revolution of 1791–1803

www.webster.edu/~corbetre/haiti/history/revolution/
revolution1.htm

This site presents a four-part historical essay on the Haitian Revolution and its significance.

Benjamin Rush, Yellow Fever, and the Birth of Modern Medicine

www.geocities.com/bobarnebeck/fever1793.html

An "online book with companion essays and primary documents," this site offers details on issues of disease and public health in Philadelphia during the 1790s.

Learning About the Senate: Series of Historical Minutes, 1790–1850

www.senate.gov/pagelayout/history/
b_three_sections_with_teasers/essays.htm

This government site details some of the key issues facing the Senate including Jay's Treaty, complaints from early constituents, and confirming Supreme Court justices.

The Alien and Sedition Acts

www.yale.edu/lawweb/avalon/alsedact.htm

The full text of these acts is available on this site.

Nullification Issues

www.jmu.edu/madison/nullification

This illustrated site presents the Virginia and Kentucky Resolutions, how James Madison responded to them, a letter from Andrew Jackson, and the Senate debate.

Building the Capitol for a New Nation

www.loc.gov/exhibits/us.capitol/s0.html

Compiled from holdings in the Library of Congress, this site contains detailed information on the design and early construction of the Capitol building in Washington, D.C.

Thomas Jefferson

www.ipl.org/div/potus/tjefferson.html

This site contains basic factual data about Jefferson's election and presidency, speeches, and online biographies.

The Louisiana Purchase Exhibit

www.sec.state.la.us/purchase/purchase-index.htm

A colorful, illustrated presentation of the details of the Louisiana Purchase, the negotiations, documents, and a series of historical maps.

Thomas Jefferson Digital Archive

www.etext.virginia.edu/jefferson/

This site is the virtual home for numerous resources about Jefferson and his times.

Monticello: The Home of Thomas Jefferson

www.monticello.org

This site explores Jefferson's ideas through an examination of Monticello, Jefferson's unique home.

Lewis and Clark: The Journey of the Corps of Discovery

www.pbs.org/lewisandclark

This is a companion site to Ken Burns's film, containing a timeline of the expedition, a collection of related links, a bibliography, and more than 800 minutes of unedited, full-length RealPlayer interviews with seven experts featured in the film.

British-American Diplomacy, 1782–1863

www.yale.edu/lawweb/avalon/diplomacy/britain/
brtreaty.htm

An online archive of important treaties and conventions between England and the United States.

Napoleonic War Series

www.wtj.com/wars/napoleonic

Exploration of this site gives context to America's relations with Europe during the early part of the nineteenth century.

Birth of the Navy, Prelude to the War of 1812

www.mariner.org/usnavy/08/08a.htm

This illustrated chapter of the online book includes "Impressment of American Soldiers," "The *Chesapeake* Affair of 1807," "American Reaction to the *Chesapeake* Affair," and "Entanglement in World Affairs," as well as the text of original documents.

War of 1812

www.city-net.com/~markd/roots/history/
us_war_of_1812.htm

A brief essay covering the foreign conflicts in the period leading up to the War of 1812.

Society and Politics in the Early Republic

Detail from Thomas Coke Ruckle, *Fairview Inn or Three Mile House on Old Frederick Road* (near Baltimore), 1829. At country inns, people on the move bought supplies, exchanged goods, and secured information about the routes that lay ahead. *(T. C. Ruckle, Fairview Inn, 1899. Maryland Historical Society, Baltimore, Maryland)*

American Stories

Creating New Lives

In May 1809, Mary and James Harrod gathered their five children, loaded a few belongings (tools, seeds for the summer planting, and several prized pieces of furniture) on a wagon, closed the door on their four-room cabin, fell in line with a dozen other families, and headed west from Spotsylvania County, Virginia, toward a new life in Kentucky. They left behind 15 years of wearying effort trying to wring a modest living from 10 acres of marginal upland, and a family cemetery that held two of their other children and Mary's parents.

Beyond the Appalachian Mountains, 450 difficult miles ahead, lay additional hard work and uncertainty. Though central Kentucky, where the Harrods would settle, contained few Indian villages, powerful tribes from north and south of the Ohio River hunted there and fought over its control. They also fought the growing tide of white settlers. The first years would be especially hard for James and Mary as they "opened up" the land, planted the first crops, and erected a cabin. They would be lonesome as well, for the Harrods would be unlikely to see even the chimney smoke of their nearest neighbors.

Yet James and Mary were hopeful as they trudged west. The land agent who had sold them their claim had promised rich, fertile soil that in time would support a good life. And they had been excited at the prospect of joining the swelling stream of migrants seeking new lives in the Trans-Appalachian West. They looked forward as well to escaping Virginia's slave society with its arrogant planters and oppressed slaves—no place for poor whites to live. Once in Kentucky, they settled on their own plot of land, joined with others in fashioning a new community, and took responsibility for their own lives.

In April 1795, Ben Thompson started north from Queen Anne's County, Maryland, for New York City. Ben knew little beyond farming, but he was ambitious, and when he arrived in New York he listened carefully to the ships' captains who talked about life at sea while they recruited men for their crews. Ben was lucky, for he arrived just as American overseas commerce, stimulated by renewed war in Europe, was entering a decade of unprecedented prosperity. Sailors were in demand, pay was good, and few questions were asked. For five years, Ben sailed the seas. Having enough of travel, he returned to New York and hired out as an apprentice to a ship's carpenter.

About the same time, Phyllis Sherman left her home in Norwalk, Connecticut. She also headed for New York, where she took a job as a maid in the household of one of the city's wealthy merchants. As fate would have it, Phyllis and Ben met, fell in love, and in the spring of 1802 were married.

There is little of note in this except that Ben and Phyllis were former slaves and were married in the African Methodist Episcopal Zion Church. Ben had cast off his slave name, Cato, as a sign of liberation, while Phyllis kept the name her master had given her. Ben was doubly fortunate, for he had purchased his freedom just as cotton production began to expand through the Old Southwest, creating a growing demand for field slaves shipped in from the Chesapeake. In another decade, he would have faced greater difficulty securing his independence. Phyllis had been freed as a child when slavery ended in Connecticut. As she grew up, she tired of living as a servant with her former owner's family and longed for the companionship of other blacks. She had heard that there were people of color in New York City, and she was correct. In 1800, it contained 6,300 African Americans, more than half of them free.

Though life in New York was better than either Ben or Phyllis had known before, it was hardly easy. They shared only marginally in the city's commercial prosperity. In 1804, they watched helplessly as yellow fever carried off their daughter and many of their friends. And while they found support in newly established African American churches and the expanding black community, they had to be constantly on guard because slave ships still moved in and out of the port and slave catchers pursued southern runaways in the city's streets.

In the early republic, thousands of Americans seized opportunities to improve their lives. Some, like Ben Thompson and Phyllis Sherman, moved from the countryside to the nation's burgeoning cities, while others, such as Mary and James Harrod, joined the swelling tide of westward expansion. Their actions helped strengthen American values of social equality, individual initiative, and personal autonomy.

They contributed as well to a process of social transformation that historians have called the "opening" of American society. That process was powered by the accelerating movement of people across the land, disrupting families, weakening long-established communities, and creating countless new settlements. It was fueled as well by an expanding market economy with its relentless discipline of supply and demand, pursuit of individual profit, and contractual relationships. This chapter examines the onset of these processes of social change that would continue to transform people's lives throughout the nineteenth century.

The chapter also explores the multiple ways in which America's diverse regions became knitted together into an increasingly coherent nation, as well as the tensions that resulted from those closer ties. Chapter 9 turns next to a variety of reform movements that sought to achieve social justice and bring the conditions of daily life into conformity with the nation's democratic ideals.

In the early republic, Indian-white relations continued to trouble the nation's affairs, as westward migration and newly fashioned Indian policies generated both peaceful accommodation and armed resistance. These complicated issues constitute an additional focus of the chapter.

The years of the early nineteenth century also brought important changes in the nation's foreign policy. With the War of 1812, the United States finally escaped the condition of neocolonialism that since independence had left it vulnerable to European wars and pressure. Just as important, the Monroe Doctrine of 1823 created a new framework for relations with other nations in the Americas.

Finally, we examine the collapse of the Federalist–Jeffersonian political system and the emergence of a distinctly new style of American politics that was increasingly democratic in temper and forms of party organization.

A NATION OF REGIONS

In the early republic, the vast majority of Americans drew their living from the land. As the nineteenth century began, 83 percent of the labor force was engaged in agriculture; that figure had hardly changed 25 years later. Yet across the nation, people occupied the land in very different ways.

The Northeast

In the Northeast, a region stretching from New Jersey and eastern Pennsylvania to New England, family farms dominated the landscape. On New England's rock-strewn land, farmers often abandoned field crops for the greater profits to be made from dairying and livestock. On the richer agricultural lands of New York and Pennsylvania, farmers cultivated the land intensively, planting crops year after year rather than following the time-honored practice of allowing worn-out fields to lie fallow and recover their fertility. Before 1776, the mid-Atlantic landscape had looked unkempt, with wide areas still covered by timber and fallow lands lapsing into brush. Fifty years later, the countryside looked increasingly orderly, its carefully cultivated fields marked by hedges and stone walls.

Farmers in southeastern Pennsylvania and along New York's Hudson River valley produced an

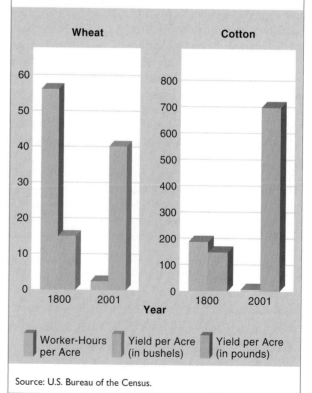

Agricultural Productivity in 1800 and 2001

As this figure indicates, American agricultural productivity soared during the nineteenth and twentieth centuries. Why was it so relatively low in 1800?

Source: U.S. Bureau of the Census.

agricultural surplus, the produce left over after meeting their families' needs, and exchanged it in nearby towns for commodities such as tea, window glass, and tools. Across much of the rural Northeast, however, cash played a small part in economic exchange. Noted an observant Frenchman, people "supply their needs in the countryside by direct reciprocal exchanges. The tailor and the bootmaker . . . do the work of their calling at the home of the farmer . . . who . . . provides the raw material for it and pays for the work in goods . . . . They write down what they give and receive on both sides, and at the end of the year . . . settle a large variety of exchanges with a very small quantity of coin."

Most farms were not large. By 1800, the average farm in longer-settled areas was no more than 100 to 150 acres, down substantially from half a century before. That was primarily a result of the continuing division of farm property from fathers to sons. Even

in southeastern Pennsylvania, the most productive agricultural region in the entire Northeast, economic opportunity was declining. Continuous planting had robbed the soil of fertility, forcing farmers to bring more marginal land under cultivation, thus bringing a steady decline in productivity.

By 1800, nearly 20 percent of male taxpayers in southeastern Pennsylvania were single, clear evidence that young men were delaying marriage until they could establish themselves financially. In some localities, as many as 30 percent of married taxpayers were landless.

Whereas the majority of northeasterners made their living from the land, growing numbers of rural folk also worked for wages as artisans or day laborers in nearby towns, or toiled in the small-scale manufactories—grain and saw mills, potash works, and iron forges—that dotted the rural landscape. Farm women contributed to the family economy by

Rural Industry in the North

Prior to the expansion of urban industrialization beginning in the 1830s, American manufacturing was small in scale and was often scattered across the countryside. What circumstances would be most likely to determine the location of the different industries included on this map?

An Agricultural Fair
This Pennsylvania scene reveals the interests of farmers and more elegantly attired gentlemen in the commercial benefits of "scientific" livestock breeding. Note what appear to be plowing contests in the background. *(John A. Woodside, A Country Fair in Pennsylvania, 1824, Private Collection, © Christie's Images/Bridgeman Art Library)*

helping with the livestock, preserving food, and making clothes for sale or exchange with neighbors. As the practice of men working for wages outside the family setting grew, women's unwaged domestic labor began to be regarded as less valuable.

Frustrated by the backwardness of American agriculture, reformers compiled agricultural libraries and issued publications promoting "scientific" techniques. One of them, Elkanah Watson, a prosperous businessman turned gentleman farmer, experimented with fine-fleeced merino sheep whose valuable wool promised new prosperity.

Watson was instrumental as well in creating the nation's first agricultural fairs in western Massachusetts. Part visionary and part huckster, Watson intended the fairs' displays of equipment, animals, and produce to educate farmers and "excite a lively spirit of competition" among them. His efforts succeeded beyond his fondest hopes, for within a few years rural folk by the thousands were converging on the annual Berkshire gatherings. In a short while, these precursors to the county fairs that have remained a staple of rural and small-town American life had spread from Maine to Virginia and as far west as Illinois.

By 1830, demands posed by the Northeast's expanding population for new agricultural land and a wide variety of wood products had transformed much of the region's once heavily forested landscape. The numerous iron

furnaces scattered across the countryside consumed firewood voraciously, while the production of potash and turpentine, planks for wooden houses, and fencing for fields further depleted forest ranges.

More than anything, though, it was the demand for heating fuel during the long winter months that made the woodcutter's ax ring. Rural households burned from 20 to 30 cords of firewood annually in highly inefficient open fireplaces. As the region's coastal cities increased in size and nearby wood lots

An Early Sawmill   As settlers moved west, they cleared the land of trees for agriculture and produced lumber for houses and fencing, as this sketch of a sawmill in upstate New York suggests. *(Library of Congress)*

were exhausted, fuel had to be fetched from inland areas as far as 100 miles away.

The South

Life was very different in the South, a region stretching from Maryland to Georgia along the coast, and west to the newly forming states of Alabama and Mississippi. In 1800, much of southern agriculture was in disarray. Low prices, land exhausted of its fertility, and the loss of slaves during the Revolutionary War had left the Chesapeake economy in shambles. One English traveler reported that in the Shenandoah Valley of Virginia, crops were "so intermixed with extensive tracts of waste land, worn out by the culture of tobacco . . . that on the whole the country had the appearance of barrenness."

In hopes of boosting their sagging fortunes, southern planters experimented with wheat and other grains. Regional recovery began in earnest, however, when they turned to a new staple crop—cotton. In 1790, the South had produced 3,135 bales of cotton; by 1820, output had mushroomed to 334,378 bales. In 1805, cotton accounted for 30 percent of the nation's agricultural exports; by 1820, it exceeded half. Across the old coastal South and the newly developing states of Alabama, Mississippi, and Tennessee, cotton was becoming king.

A fortuitous combination of circumstances fueled the transformation: the growing demand for raw cotton by textile mills in England and the American Northeast; wonderfully productive virgin soil; a long, steamy growing season; an ample supply of slave labor; and southern planters' long experience in producing and marketing staple crops.

Eli Whitney's cotton gin speeded the process as well. The silky fibers of long-staple cotton could be easily separated from the cotton's seeds. The delicate

Overseeing Enslaved Workers In this scene from near Fredericksburg, Maryland, female slaves grub tree stumps from a field while an overseer looks on. As tobacco cultivation gave way to a more diversified economy, male slaves were often assigned to other jobs. Slave labor, provided by women as well as men, followed the spread of cotton cultivation into new lands of the southern interior. *(Benjamin Latrobe, An Overseer Doing His Duty. Maryland Historical Society, Baltimore)*

long-staple plant, however, grew only in the hot, humid climate along the southern coast. The hardier, short-staple variety could be successfully cultivated in the southern interior, but its fibers clung tenaciously to the plant's sticky, green seeds. A slave could clean no more than a pound of short-staple cotton a day.

IMAGE

A Patent Drawing of Eli Whitney's Cotton Gin

A solution began to appear in 1793 when Eli Whitney, a Yankee schoolteacher living in the South, set his mind to the problem of short-staple cotton and its seeds. Within a few days, he had designed a functioning model of what he called a "cotton gin." It was disarmingly simple, nothing more than a box containing a roller equipped with wire teeth, designed to pull the fibers through a comblike barrier, thus stripping them from the seeds. A hand crank

View of Richmond, Virginia This 1804 etching reveals the bucolic setting of Richmond, Virginia, recently the new state capital. Note the dominating presence of the capitol building, designed by Thomas Jefferson. Modeled after an ancient Roman temple, the structure was intended to represent civic values of simplicity, proportion, and good order. *(Charles B.J. Févret de Saint-Mémin, (1770–1852), View of Richmond, Virginia. Miriam and Ira D. Wallach Division, The New York Public Library/Art Resource, NY)*

activated the mechanism. With this crude device a laborer could clean up to 50 pounds of short-staple cotton a day.

The swing to cotton marked a momentous turning point in the South's—and the nation's—history. It raised the value of southern land and opened economic opportunity for countless southern whites, but it also increased the demand for black field hands and breathed new life into slavery. Some of the escalating demand for slave labor was met from overseas. In 1803, Georgia and South Carolina alone imported 20,000 new slaves, as southern planters and northern suppliers rushed to meet the need before the slave trade ended in 1808. Much of the demand for agricultural labor, however, was met by the internal slave trade that moved black labor from the worn-out lands of the Chesapeake to the lush cotton fields of the southern interior.

Trans-Appalachia

West of the Appalachian Mountains, a third region of settlement was forming as the nineteenth century began. In the eighteenth century, British colonists had called the regions west of white settlement the "backcountry," the land that lay behind them as they faced east, toward the Atlantic and Europe. As attention shifted toward settlement of the Trans-Appalachian West, however, people spoke increasingly of an ever-expanding "frontier."

Trans-Appalachia, a broad and shifting "middle ground" of settlement and encounter, extended from the mountains to the Mississippi River and from the Great Lakes to the Gulf of Mexico. In 1790, scarcely 100,000 white settlers had lived there. By 1810, augmented by people like Mary and James Harrod, their number had swollen to nearly one million. A decade later, there were over a million more. They came by wagon through the Cumberland Gap and other tortuous routes into Kentucky and Tennessee, or clambered aboard flatboats at Pittsburgh to float down the Ohio River to destinations at Wheeling, Cincinnati, and Louisville.

The human tide appeared to grow with each passing year. The woods were full of new settlers, wrote an amazed observer near Batavia in western New York in 1805. "Axes are resounding, and the trees literally falling around us as we passed." America, he exclaimed, "is breaking up and going west!"

Settlers were drawn by the promotions of speculators seeking their fortunes in the sale of western land. By 1800, absentee landlords had engrossed much of present-day West Virginia, Tennessee, and the western Carolinas. Between 1790 and 1820, land companies hawked vast areas of New York, Ohio, and Kentucky to prospective settlers such as the Harrods. Many ventures failed, but countless others returned handsome profits to their investors. Individual settlers joined in the speculative fever, often going deeply into debt to buy extra land, expecting to resell it when population increased and land values rose.

North of the Ohio River, settlement followed the grid pattern prescribed in the Land Ordinance of 1785. There, free-labor agriculture took hold and towns such as Columbus and Cincinnati emerged as service and cultural centers for the surrounding population. South of the Ohio, white settlers and their black slaves distributed themselves more randomly across the land, much as their ancestors had done back east. In Kentucky and Tennessee, free-labor agriculture was soon challenged by the spread of slavery-based cotton.

In this constantly shifting "borderland," people of different ethnicity, race, class, and regional origin mingled together, their conflicting social, economic, and cultural values often generating tension. But as they built new communities, they fashioned new ways of life, in the process strengthening belief in America as a land of opportunity.

As people poured in, the newness and diversity of Trans-Appalachia gained it a reputation for rough

Marietta, Ohio The new town of Marietta, Ohio, located on the Ohio River, was laid out amid earthworks fashioned hundreds of years earlier by Indian Mound Builders. (Charles Sullivan, Painting of the Marietta Group of Prehistoric Earthworks Marietta, Ohio, showing Campus Martius and a log cabin of the Ohio Company . . . 1835–1845, Ohio Historical Society Museum)

HOW OTHERS SEE US

Frances Trollope, *Domestic Manners of the Americans*

Frances Trollope, born in England and wife of an English barrister, came to the United States in 1827. She settled for a few years in Cincinnati where she opened a lecture hall, had a shop for the sale of fancy goods, and made something of a name for herself. When her business venture failed, she returned to England where in 1832 she published Domestic Manners of the Americans, *one of the most acerbic and yet insightful of the many travel accounts penned by foreign visitors to the early republic.*

The "simple" manner of living in Western America was more distasteful to me from its leveling effects on the manners of the people than from the personal privations that it rendered necessary. . . . The total and universal want of manners, both in males and females, is so remarkable that I was constantly endeavouring to account for it. It certainly does not proceed from want of intellect . . . but there is no charm, no grace in their conversation. . . . There is always something either in the expression or the accent that jars the feelings and shocks the taste. . . . In America, that polish which removes the coarser and rougher parts of our nature is unknown and undreamed of. . . . Nothing can exceed their activity and perseverance in all kinds of speculation, handicraft, and enterprise which promises a profitable pecuniary result. I heard an Englishman . . . declare that he had never overheard Americans conversing without the word DOLLAR being pronounced between them. . . . Yet the Americans declare that "they are the most moral people upon earth". . . . My honest conviction is that the standard of moral character in the United States is greatly lower than in Europe. . . . It is amusing to observe how soothing the idea seems [to Americans] that they are more modern, more advanced than England. Our classic literature, our princely dignities, our noble institutions, are all [regarded as] bygone relics of the dark ages. . . .

■ *What was it about the American people that set Trollope's teeth on edge?*

---

and colorful ways. The transience of the population, together with large numbers of young, unattached males, kept society unsettled. In Louisville and similar towns along the Ohio River, boatmen, gamblers, con men, and speculators gave civic life a raucous quality, while the grandeur of the natural surroundings stoked people's imaginations. No characters were more famous in popular folklore than western adventurers such as Daniel Boone. None was more colorful than the mythical riverman Mike Fink, "half man, half alligator," who could "whip his weight in grizzly bears." And nothing revealed the West's rawness more graphically than the eye-gouging, ear-biting, no-holds-barred, "rough and tumble" brawls that regularly erupted.

As settlers arrived, they began the long process of transforming the region's heavily forested land. In mountainous areas of western Pennsylvania, hillsides were denuded of trees that anxious travelers dragged behind their wagons as makeshift brakes during the jolting ride downhill. Believing, erroneously, that open land was infertile, farmers staked their claims where the trees grew thickest and set about the arduous task of rooting them out by cutting off a girdle of bark then setting them on fire, or leaving them to die in place while planting crops around the decaying hulks. "The scene is truly savage," observed an English traveler used to the orderly landscape of his own country. "Immense trees stripped of their foliage, and half consumed by fire extend their sprawling limbs . . . now bleached by the weather." The relentless demand for wood added to the assault on the region's forests. As expanding areas of Trans-Appalachia came under the farmer's plow, forests and wildlife gave way.

The Nation's Cities

Though most Americans lived on the land or in small towns, increasing numbers dwelt in the nation's expanding cities. From 1790 to 1830, the nation's population increased by nearly 230 percent, but urban places of more than 2,500 residents grew almost twice as fast.

Patterns of urban development differed from region to region. The most dramatic growth occurred in the port cities of the Northeast. By 1830, the region contained four cities of more than 50,000. New York alone held over 100,000 people, while inland towns such as Springfield, Massachusetts, and Albany, New York, proliferated as service centers for their surrounding areas.

Five Points, New York This rather humorous depiction of a bustling intersection in New York City in 1827 suggests the increasing crowdedness of the country's largest cities. How many different kinds of people and activities can you identify? *(Five Points, New York, 1827, in Valentine's Manual, 1855. Museum of the City of New York Gift of Lou Sepersky and Leida Snow, [97.227.3])*

The cities of the Atlantic seaboard were ethnically diverse, even though the wars of the American and French revolutions sharply reduced European immigration between the 1770s and 1820s. In New York and Philadelphia, Irish, German, British, and African Americans, together with travelers from around the world, jostled for space on the cities' sidewalks. Sailors, often speaking strange tongues, added raucous behavior and at times an edge of danger to urban life.

As during the colonial era, economic life still centered on the wharves where sailing ships from distant ports docked, and the warehouses where cargoes were stored. Urban economies were changing, however, as manufacturing was beginning to transform urban life. Philadelphia was becoming a textile manufacturing center, while New York produced shoes and iron goods. As these enterprises expanded, artisan production slowly gave way to factory-based labor.

Such changes widened the gap between the cities' richer and poorer inhabitants. Prosperous merchants rested securely at the top of the social pyramid, their households graced by fine table linens and store-bought furniture, the artifacts of an expanding consumer economy. Below them came an aspiring middle class of artisans, shopkeepers, and professional men whose families shared modestly in the general prosperity. At the bottom spread a growing underclass of common laborers, dock workers, and the unemployed, their lives a continuous struggle for survival. Though rich and poor had lived close together in colonial cities, rising land values now forced the lower classes into crowded alleys and tenements,

while more prosperous urban dwellers began clustering in fashionable neighborhoods.

In the Southeast, urban development centered in long-established ports such as Charleston, Richmond, and Savannah. As during the colonial period, they continued to serve as commercial entrepots, exporting agricultural products and importing manufactured goods. Half their population was black, the vast majority of them slaves.

In Trans-Appalachia, fledgling towns such as Pittsburgh and Chicago dotted the region's rivers and lakes. Only small villages in 1790, these interior cities held 30 percent of the nation's urban population by 1830. New Orleans and St. Louis reflected their multinational origins. Established as a French colony in 1718, New Orleans came under Spanish rule in 1763. When the city became part of the United States in 1803, French and Spanish Creole families continued to dominate urban life. For several decades, U.S. citizens remained a minority among the white population. Of its 27,000 people, nearly 13,000 were black. Upriver from New Orleans, the smaller town of St. Louis—at different times part of French and Spanish North America—had a similarly diverse population. Enslaved blacks made up nearly one-third of the town's 1,000 residents.

Though increasing rapidly in population, America's urban places remained small in area. In these "walking cities," residents could easily stroll from one side of town to the other. Rapid growth, however, brought increasing congestion. Asa Greene, a New York physician, observed ruefully that to cross Broadway "you must button your coat tightly about you . . . settle your hat firmly on your head, look up street and down street . . . to see what carts and carriages are upon you, and then run for your life."

Philadelphia led the way in street paving, but dust in dry season and mud when it rained constantly plagued urban life. One alarmed citizen, finding a man embedded up to his neck in a mud hole following a violent downpour, offered to help pull him out. "No need to worry," replied the man, "I have a horse underneath me." So, at least, went a popular fable.

More than mud clogged urban streets in the early nineteenth century, for residents dumped their garbage there, privies leached into open drains, and livestock roamed freely, leaving their droppings behind. Though one urban dweller thought the scavenging hogs she encountered were "disgusting," she acknowledged that without them the streets would soon be choked with filth. Packs of stray dogs added to the confusion.

Under such conditions, typhoid and dysentery, spread by contaminated water, took a continuous toll. Not until 1832 with construction of the Croton Aqueduct did New York City establish a safe and adequate water supply.

Urban families had long maintained small garden plots and milk cows. As populations grew and land values increased, however, gardens and cows gradually disappeared, further weakening diet and health. The rigors of poor diet, frequent disease, and inadequate medical care often brought life to an early end. Scarcely half of urban dwellers reached age 45. Unlike today, women on average died sooner than men, their bodies weakened by frequent childbirth. While birthrates had begun a long term decline, white women could still expect to bear from four to eight children. Immigrant and black women averaged even more.

INDIAN–WHITE RELATIONS IN THE EARLY REPUBLIC

Indian–white relations took a dramatic turn in the early years of the nineteenth century. In 1790, vast areas of trans-Appalachia were still controlled by Native American tribes. North of the Ohio River, the Shawnee, Delaware, and Miami formed a western confederacy capable of mustering several thousand warriors. South of the river lived five major tribal groups: the Cherokee, Creek, Choctaw, Chickasaw, and Seminole. Together, they totaled nearly 60,000 people. By 1830, however, the balance of power throughout Trans-Appalachia had shifted decisively as white settlers, many of them bringing their black slaves with them south of the Ohio River, streamed into the region.

In response, tribal groups devised various strategies of resistance and survival. Among the Cherokee, many sought peaceful accommodation. Others, like the Shawnee and Creek, rose in armed resistance. Neither strategy was altogether successful, for by 1830 the Indians faced a future of continued acculturation, military defeat, or forced migration west of the Mississippi River.

Less dramatic but no less important, the social and cultural separation of Indians and white Americans sharpened during these years. As late as the 1780s, Indians still walked the streets of New York and Philadelphia, while countless Indians and white Americans interacted as traders or marriage partners. By 1830, such contacts were much less common and racial separation increased as Native Americans were confined on reservations or forced to move farther west.

The Goals of Indian Policy

During the years from 1790 to 1830, the federal government established policies that would govern Indian–white relations through much of the nineteenth century. Intended in part to promote the assimilation of Native Americans into white society, the policies actually speeded the transfer of Indian land to white settlers and set the stage for a later, more dramatic program of Indian removal.

Native American Land Cessions

With the government's initial "conquest" theory rendered obsolete by the Indians' refusal to regard themselves as a conquered people (see Chapter 7), U.S. officials shifted course by recognizing Indian rights to the land they inhabited and declaring that all future land transfers would come through treaty agreements.

Henry Knox, Washington's first secretary of war, laid out the government's new position in 1789. The Indians, he explained, "being the prior occupants of the soil, possess the right of the soil." It should not be taken from them "unless by their free consent, or by the right of conquest in case of just war." The Indian Intercourse Act of 1790 declared that public treaties, ratified by Congress, would henceforth be the only legal means of obtaining Indian land. Though it promised a more humane Indian policy, the acquisition of Indian land for white settlement remained the overarching goal.

The new, treaty-based strategy proved effective. Native American leaders frequently ceded land in return for trade goods, yearly annuity payments, and assurances that there would be no further demands. Reluctant tribal leaders could often be persuaded to

RECOVERING THE PAST

Census Returns

Throughout the nation's history, the American population has changed dramatically, not only in size and geographic distribution but also in birth and death rates, marriage age, and family size. In the early nineteenth century, for example, the average life expectancy of white Americans was about 45 years, and men tended to outlive women. In our own time, the average life expectancy has reached 74, and women on average live longer than men. Populations have differed as well across regions, in urban and rural settings, and among racial, ethnic, and class groups.

Changes in the demographic profile of the American population have powerful effects on the nation's economic, social, and political development. The changing size and makeup of the labor force shape economic activity, while changing proportions of older and younger Americans affect consumer habits and put different demands on health care and educational systems—as the aging of baby boomers in our own time is again making clear. When mortality rates were high, as was often the case in early American history, parents had more children in an effort to stabilize their families. As mortality declined during the nineteenth century, so too did birthrates and family size.

Demographic information can tell us a great deal about the life experiences of ordinary Americans. Indeed, demographic data is often the major source of information about otherwise anonymous individuals. For all these reasons, historians spend considerable time analyzing populations and the ways they change.

Two kinds of demographic data have proved most important. One consists of birth, death, and marriage records, often found in church or town registers. These records chronicle the basic demographic events in people's lives. If they are complete and continuous enough, they allow historians to trace the life course of individuals and to reconstruct patterns of family and community life.

Here we offer an example of the second kind of demographic data, a census. The material is from the federal census of 1820. Article 1, Section 2 of the Constitution called for an enumeration (or counting) of the nation's population every 10 years, "in such manner" as Congress required. The information was to be used in determining the periodic reapportionment of the House of Representatives and allocation of direct taxes to the states. The first decennial census was taken in 1790.

Compared with modern census inquiries, the first federal censuses collected limited information. The 1790s census, for example, gathered data under six headings: "Name of head of family," "Free white males, 16 years and upwards," "Free white males, under 16," "Free white females," "All other free persons," and "Slaves." As the nation grew, the demand for additional information increased. In 1820, Congress for the first time called for the collection of economic data. In the decades following, categories of social and economic data were gradually expanded.

The table provided here contains data from three cities—New York City; Charleston, South Carolina; and Cincinnati, Ohio—located in different sections of the country. What do the data tell you about the racial, gender, and age profiles of these cities? How do they differ? Do you find significant age and gender differences between white and black populations? Between free blacks and slaves? Can you explain the differences that you find? In making your calculations, be sure to take into account both absolute numbers and proportions of the total populations.

Why were there no slaves in Cincinnati, while there were still slaves in New York? What kinds of people might have been included under the heading "Foreigners not naturalized?" The economic data included in the 1820 census was very general. What conclusions are you able to draw concerning economic activities in the three cities? Can you explain the differences?

REFLECTING ON THE PAST How would the federal census of 2000 differ from the census displayed here? Why do disputes often arise over the kinds of information that should be gathered?

Data from the Federal Census of 1820

	New York City	Charleston	Cincinnati
Free white males, 25 and under	36,122	3,780	3,419
Free white males, 26 and over	21,331	2,119	1,672
Free white males, total	57,453 (44)	5,899 (23)	5,091 (51)
Free white females, 25 and under	37,438	3,297	3,137
Free white females, 26 and over	20,070	2,033	1,152
Free white females, total	57,508 (44)	5,330 (21)	4,289 (43)
Total white population	114,961 (88)	11,229 (44)	9,380 (93)
Free colored males, 25 and under	2,201	394	120
Free colored males, 26 and over	1,993	229	99
Free colored males, total	4,194 (3)	623 (2)	219 (2)
Free colored females, 25 and under	3,342	467	132
Free colored females, 26 and over	2,832	385	82
Free colored females, total	6,174 (5)	852 (3)	214 (2)
Male slaves, 25 and under	144	3,656	0
Male slaves, 26 and over	33	2,039	0
Male slaves, total	177 (1)	5,695 (22)	0 (0)
Female slaves, 25 and under	233	4,347	0
Female slaves, 26 and over	108	2,610	0
Female slaves, total	341 (1)	6,957 (27)	0 (0)
Total black population	10,886 (8)	14,127 (55)	433 (0)
Foreigners not naturalized	5,390 (4)	425 (2)	241 (2)
Total city population	131,237	25,781	10,054
Persons engaged in agriculture	386	164	29
Persons engaged in commerce	3,142	1,138	63
Persons engaged in manufacturing	9,523	887	211

Notes: New York City did not then include Kings, Queens, or Suffolk counties. Figures in parentheses represent percentages of each city's total population.

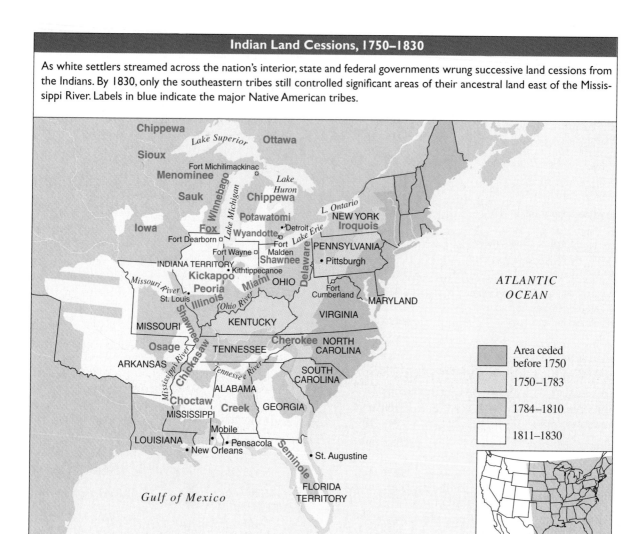

Indian Land Cessions, 1750–1830

As white settlers streamed across the nation's interior, state and federal governments wrung successive land cessions from the Indians. By 1830, only the southeastern tribes still controlled significant areas of their ancestral land east of the Mississippi River. Labels in blue indicate the major Native American tribes.

cooperate by warnings about the inevitable spread of white settlement, or more tractable chieftains could be found. In these ways, vast areas of tribal land passed to white settlers.

Federal policy also attempted to regulate the fur trade, in which both Native Americans and white traders eagerly participated. The Indians, in return for their abundant furs, secured the blankets, guns, and rum that they valued highly, while white traders acquired valuable furs in exchange for inexpensive trade goods.

The fur trade brought handsome profits to companies such as John Jacob Astor's American Fur Company (1808), but often worked to the Indians' disadvantage. Rum devastated Indian communities, while trade goods frequently transmitted diseases such as measles and smallpox. Indians often became dependent on the trade because it provided the only reliable supplies of coveted goods such as iron kettles and firearms. As the demand for furs and pelts increased, Native Americans frequently overtrapped

DOCUMENT

Treaty with the Sioux and Other Tribes (1825)

their hunting grounds, forcing them to compete with other tribes for new sources of furs farther west.

In an effort to reduce fraud and the resulting conflict, Congress created government trading posts, or "factories," where Indians could come for fairer treatment. Native Americans, however, frequently found themselves deeply in debt to government traders. In 1822, Congress abolished the factory system.

A third objective of federal Indian policy was to "civilize" and "Christianize" Native Americans, then assimilate them into white society. With the government's blessing, Moravians, Baptists, and other religious groups sent scores of missionaries to live among the Indians, preach the Gospel, and teach white ways. John Stewart, a freeborn, part-Indian mulatto, was one such missionary. From 1815 to his death in 1821, he preached to the Wyandotte near Sandusky, Ohio. Among the most selfless were Quakers who labored with the Iroquois in New York. In spite of the missionaries' best efforts, however, most Indians remained aloof. The chasm between Christianity and their own religions was too wide (see Chapter 2).

Education was the other weapon of assimilation. In 1793, Congress appropriated $20,000 to promote literacy, agriculture, and vocational instruction among Indians. Federal officials encouraged missionaries to establish schools where Indian children could learn the three Rs and vocational skills. But the vast majority of Indian children never attended, they and their parents distrusting the schools' alien environment.

Although white assimilationists cared deeply about the physical and spiritual fate of Native American people, they showed little sympathy for Indian culture, for they demanded that Native Americans give up their language, religion, and extended family arrangements and adopt the ways of white society. Assimilation or removal were the stark alternatives posed by even the most benevolent whites.

Strategies of Survival: The Iroquois and Cherokee

Faced with the loss of land and tribal autonomy, Native Americans devised various strategies of resistance and survival. Among the Iroquois, a prophet named Handsome Lake led his people through a religious renewal and cultural revitalization. As a young man, he had joined in the fight against American independence. His spirit broken by the American victory, he had watched helplessly as Indian land was taken and his people were confined on New York reservations. Handsome Lake's own life crumbled as well. On several occasions, alcohol and depression brought him close to death.

Following a series of visions in 1799, Handsome Lake began preaching a combination of Indian and white ways: temperance, peace, land retention, and a new religion combining elements of Christianity and traditional Iroquois belief. His vision offered hope and renewed pride in the midst of the Iroquois' radically changed lives.

Far to the south, the Cherokee followed a different path of accommodation. As the nineteenth century began, the Cherokee still controlled millions of acres in Tennessee, Georgia, and the western Carolinas. Their land base, however, was shrinking.

Southern state governments, responding to white demands for Indian land, undercut tribal autonomy. In 1801, Tennessee unilaterally brought Cherokee lands under the authority of state courts. The Cherokee, who had their own system of justice and distrusted the state courts as biased, rejected Tennessee's demands.

Soon a group of full-blood leaders called for armed resistance. Better to stand and fight, they argued, than follow the false path of accommodation. Others, including mixed-bloods such as John Ross, insisted that accommodation offered the best hope for survival.

After a bitter struggle, the accommodationists won out and brought the tribe's scattered villages under a common government, the better to protect their freedom and prevent the further loss of land. In 1808, the Cherokee National Council adopted a written legal code combining elements of U.S. and Indian law, and in 1827, it devised a written constitution patterned after those of nearby states. The council also issued a bold declaration that the Cherokee were an independent nation with full sovereignty over their lands. In 1829, the Cherokee government made it an offense punishable by death for any member of the tribe to transfer land to white ownership without the consent of tribal authorities.

Meanwhile, the process of social and cultural accommodation, encouraged by Cherokee leaders such as Ross and promoted by white missionaries and government agents, went forward. As the Cherokee turned from their traditional hunting, gathering, and farming economy to settled agriculture, many moved from village settlements onto individual farmsteads. Others established sawmills, country stores, and blacksmith shops. In contrast to traditional practices of communal ownership, the concept of private property took hold.

The majority of Cherokee people kept their crude log cabins and continued to live a hand-to-mouth existence. But some mixed-bloods who learned English and understood how to deal with white authorities accumulated hundreds of acres of fertile land and scores of black slaves.

Since the mid-eighteenth century, the Cherokee had held a few runaway blacks in slavelike conditions. During the early nineteenth century, Cherokee slavery expanded and became harsher. By 1820, there were nearly 1,300 black slaves in the Cherokee nation. A tribal law of 1824 forbade intermarriage with blacks. The accelerating spread of cotton cultivation increased the demand for slave labor among the Cherokee, as among southern whites. As accommodation increased, slave ownership became a mark of social standing.

By 1820, the strategy of peaceful accommodation had brought clear rewards. Tribal government was stronger and the sense of Cherokee identity was reasonably secure. But success would prove the Cherokee people's undoing. As their self-confidence grew, so did the hostility of neighboring whites impatient to acquire their land. That hostility would soon erupt in a campaign to drive the Cherokee from their land forever.

Patterns of Armed Resistance: The Shawnee and Creek

Not all tribes proved so accommodating to white expansion. The Shawnee and Creek, faced with growing threats to their political and cultural survival, rose in armed resistance. Conflict, smoldering as the nineteenth century began, burst into flame during the War of 1812.

In the late 1780s, chieftains such as Little Turtle of the Miami and Blue Jacket of the Shawnee had led devastating raids across Indiana, Ohio, and western Pennsylvania, panicking white settlers and openly challenging U.S. control of the Old Northwest. In 1794, President Washington, determined to smash the Indians' resistance once and for all, sent a federal army led by the old Revolutionary War general Anthony Wayne into the area. It won a decisive victory over 2,000 Indian warriors in the Battle of Fallen Timbers. Shortly after, in the Treaty of Greenville, the assembled chiefs ceded the southern two-thirds of Ohio. That cession opened the heart of the Old Northwest to white control. Subsequent treaties further reduced the Indians' land base, driving the tribes more tightly in on each other.

By 1809, two Shawnee leaders, the brothers Tecumseh and Tenskwatawa, the latter known to whites as "the Prophet," were traveling among the region's tribes warning of their common danger and forging an alliance against the invading whites. They established headquarters at an ancient Indian town named Kithtippecanoe in northern Indiana. Soon it became a gathering point for Native Americans from across the region responding to the messages of cultural pride, land retention, and pan-Indian resistance proclaimed by the Shawnee brothers.

Tenskwatawa, the Prophet

Between 1809 and 1811, Tecumseh carried his message south to the Creek and the Cherokee. His speeches rang with bitterness. "The white race is a wicked race," he told his listeners. "Since the days when the white race first came in contact with the red men, there has been a continual series of aggressions. The hunting grounds are fast disappearing, and they are driving the red men farther and farther to the west." The only hope was "a war of extermination against the paleface." Though the southern tribes refused to join, by 1811 more than 1,000 fighting men had gathered at Kithtippecanoe.

Alarmed, the governor of the Indiana Territory, William Henry Harrison, surrounded the Indian stronghold with a force of 1,000 soldiers. After a successful all-day battle, he burned Kithtippecanoe to the ground.

Tecumseh Though Tecumseh's vision of a Pan-Indian alliance reaching from the Great Lakes to the Gulf of Mexico never materialized, he led tribes of the Northwest in militant opposition to white territorial expansion. *(The Granger Collection, New York)*

The Indians, however, were not yet defeated. Tecumseh's followers, taking advantage of the recent outbreak of the War of 1812 with England and aided by British troops from Canada, mounted devastating raids across Indiana and southern Michigan. With the British, they crushed American armies at Detroit and followed up with forays against Fort Wayne. The tide turned, however, at the Battle of the Thames near Detroit, where Harrison inflicted a grievous defeat on a combined British and Indian force. Among those slain was Tecumseh.

The American victory at the Thames signaled the collapse of Tecumseh's confederacy and an end to Indian resistance in the Old Northwest. Beginning in 1815, American settlers surged once more across Ohio and Indiana, then into Illinois and Michigan. The balance of power in the Old Northwest had shifted decisively.

To the south, the Creek challenged white intruders with similar militancy. As the nineteenth century began, white settlers were pushing onto Creek lands in northwestern Georgia and central Alabama. Although some Creek leaders urged accommodation, others, called Red Sticks, prepared to fight. The embers of this conflict were fanned into flame by an aggressive Tennessee militia

Pennsylvania Gazette, "Indian Hostilities" (1812)

commander named Andrew Jackson. Citing Creek atrocities against "defenseless women and children," Jackson urged President Jefferson to endorse a campaign against the "ruthless foe."

Jackson got his chance in the summer of 1813, when the Red Sticks carried out a series of devastating raids and assaulted Fort Mims on the Alabama River, killing 500 men, women, and children. News of the tragedy elicited bitter cries for revenge.

At the head of 5,000 Tennessee and Kentucky militia, augmented by warriors from other tribes eager to punish their traditional Creek enemies, Jackson launched his long-awaited attack. As he moved south, the fighting grew more ferocious. Davey Crockett, one of Jackson's soldiers, later reported that the militia volunteers shot down the Red Sticks "like dogs." The Indians gave like measure in return.

The climactic battle of the Creek War came in March 1814 at Horseshoe Bend, on the Tallapoosa River in central Alabama. While American cannon fire raked the Red Sticks' fortified town of Tohopeka, Cherokee warriors cut off all hope of retreat. In the battle that followed, more than 800 Native Americans died, more than in any other Indian–white battle in American history. Jackson followed up his victory with a scorched-earth sweep through the remaining Red Stick towns.

After allowing the Red Stick chieftain and his followers to return home, Jackson exacted his final revenge by constructing Fort Jackson on the Hickory Ground, the most sacred spot of the Creek nation. During the following months, he seized 22 million acres, nearly two-thirds of the Creek domain. Before his Indian fighting days were over, Jackson would acquire for the United States, through treaty or conquest, nearly three-fourths of Alabama and Florida, a third of Tennessee, and a fifth of Georgia and Mississippi.

Indian–white conflict in the South did not end with the Creek defeat at Horseshoe Bend. For nearly a decade, the Second Seminole War, costly in lives and money, would ravage much of Florida. Just as Tecumseh's death had signaled the end of Indian resistance in the North, however, so Jackson's defeat of the Creek broke the back of Indian defenses in much of the South. With all possibility of armed resistance gone, Native Americans gave way before the swelling tide of white settlement.

PERFECTING A DEMOCRATIC SOCIETY

Throughout the nation's history, the American people have launched a variety of reform movements aimed at achieving social justice and bringing the conditions of daily life into conformity with democratic ideals. The first of those reform eras occurred in the early nineteenth century.

The Revolutionary Heritage

Reform was inspired by democratic ideals fostered during the Revolution and kept fresh in countless Americans' minds. Preeminent among them was the principle of social equality. In part, this meant equality of opportunity—the notion that people should have a chance to rise as far as ability and ambition would carry them. The doctrine of social equality had a powerful moral dimension as well, because it implied an equality of worth among individuals, no matter what their social standing might be.

The Revolution also fostered a belief in the "youthfulness" of America, in contrast to the "old" and "decadent" nations of Europe. This sense of America's uniqueness, combined with the seemingly limitless land of the interior, offered the promise of creating a nation unlike any that had existed before, one in which ordinary citizens could create new lives for themselves and their families, if given the chance.

The Evangelical Impulse

A surge of evangelical Christianity inspired the reform impulse as well. Throughout the nation's history, religion has been a major force in American public life. This was true in the early republic when a wave of Protestant enthusiasm in what has become known as the Second Great Awakening swept across the nation. From its beginnings in the 1790s through much of the nineteenth century, in settings ranging from the Cane Ridge district of backwoods Kentucky to the cities of the Northeast, Americans by the tens of thousands sought personal salvation and social belonging in the shared experience of religious revivalism.

Sacramental Scene in a Western Forest

Displayed most spectacularly at Methodist and Baptist camp meetings, the revivals crossed boundaries of class and race. Rough-hewn itinerant preachers, black as well as white, many of them theologically untrained but all of them afire with religious conviction, spread the Gospel message, in the process knitting networks of believers closely together.

In 1809, Benjamin Latrobe, principal architect of the new Capitol building in Washington, D.C., and a shrewd observer of the American scene, visited a Methodist camp meeting on the Leesburg Road in northern Virginia. Positioning himself at the head of

A Camp Meeting
Camp meetings were fundamental events during the Second Great Awakening. What does this depiction tell you about the kinds of people who attended and the activities that took place? *(Alexander Rider, Camp Meeting. Collection of the New-York Historical Society/ Bridgeman Art Library)*

the clearing, Latrobe watched in fascination as a blacksmith named Mr. Bunn "spoke with immense rapidity & exertion . . . of the judgement to come." As Bunn exhorted the assembled throng, "a general groaning & shrieking was . . . heard from all Quarters" while the preacher "threw out both his arms sideways at full length, & shook himself violently." Every time Bunn pronounced "the stroke of grace," Latrobe continued, he brought his hands together with an astonishing clap.

Perhaps no one represented the Awakening's religious fervor and egalitarian values more vividly than Lorenzo Dow. A self-declared "holy man" who claimed visionary powers and was an unabashed salesman of his own religious writings, Dow traveled the length and breadth of the land bringing a potent combination of Gospel message and Jeffersonian politics to frontier hamlets and eastern cities alike. During 1804 alone, he preached to as many as 800 gatherings while traveling as many as 10,000 miles. His boundless energy, communicative gifts, and common touch may have made him the most widely known American of his time.

Though the salvation of souls was the central purpose of revival camp meetings, they ministered to other human needs as well. "The novelty of a camp especially to the women and children, the dancing and singing, & the pleasure of a crowd," noted Latrobe, imparted a powerful sense of social belonging in a society undergoing rapid change.

Offering a simple message that ordinary folks could readily grasp, the Awakening emphasized the equality of all believers before God, held out the promise of universal salvation, and declared each individual responsible for his or her own soul. The Awakening also called on believers to demonstrate their faith by going into the world to lift up the downtrodden. That mandate would provide much of the energy for later reforms such as temperance and abolition. Its influence was evident as well in earlier efforts at perfecting American society.

Alleviating Poverty and Distress

In the early republic, as at other times in the nation's history, social ideals often jarred against social reality. One source of tension was the contrast between the affirmations of democratic equality and deepening social divisions.

As the nineteenth century began, women continued to hold far less property than men. For black slaves, ownership of anything more than the most basic personal possessions was unattainable. Though the condition of free blacks such as Ben Thompson and Phyllis Sherman was better, they, too, held little of the country's wealth.

Among white males, property was broadly shared in rural areas of the North, where free labor and family-farm agriculture predominated, and least so in the South, where planters' control of slave labor and the best land permitted them to monopolize the lion's share of the region's wealth. The most even distribution of property was to be found on the edges of white settlement in Trans-Appalachia, but it was often an

The Hot Corn Seller

A Street Peddler Among the urban poor, women as well as men peddled food and other commodities in an effort to make ends meet. *(Nicolino Calyo, The Hot Corn Seller, ca. 1840. Museum of the City of New York)*

equality of want. In some areas, such as southern Appalachia, well over 50 percent of settlers lived as tenants, unable to gain ownership of the land they worked from absentee landlords. Poor transportation often deprived frontier areas of access to outside markets, further depressing people's lives.

Though America contained no permanent and destitute underclass (at least among white citizens), poverty was real and increasing. In the South, it was most evident among poor whites living on the sandy pine barrens of the backcountry. In the North, port cities held growing numbers of the poor. Boston artisans and shopkeepers, who together had owned 20 percent of the city's wealth in 1700, held scarcely half as much a century later.

Recurring economic recessions hit the urban poor with particular force, while winter added to hard times as shipping slowed and jobs disappeared. During the winter of 1805, New York's Mayor DeWitt Clinton, worried about the potentially disruptive behavior of 10,000 impoverished New Yorkers, asked the state legislature for help. In the winter of 1814–1815, relief agencies assisted nearly one-fifth of the city's

population. Across rural New England and southeastern Pennsylvania, propertyless men and women, the "strolling poor," roamed the countryside searching for work.

Three other groups were conspicuous among the nation's poor. One consisted of old Revolutionary War veterans like Long Bill Scott, who had found poverty as well as adventure in the war. State and federal governments were peppered with petitions from grizzled veterans and their widows, describing their misery and seeking relief. Women and children also suffered disproportionately from poverty. Between 1816 and 1821, they outnumbered men in New York City's almshouses.

For every American who actually suffered poverty's effects, several others lived just beyond its reach. The thinness of their margin of safety became evident during the depression of 1819–1822. Triggered by a financial panic caused by the unsound practices of hundreds of newly chartered state banks, a deep depression settled over the land, generating bankruptcies and sending unemployment soaring. By the early 1820s, the depression was lifting, but it left behind broken fortunes and shattered dreams.

Alleviating poverty was one goal of the early reformers. In New York City, private and public authorities established more than 100 relief agencies to assist unfortunates from orphans to poverty-stricken seamen. Across the nation, a "charitable revolution" witnessed the increase of benevolent institutions from 50 in 1790 to nearly 2,000 by 1820. Most of these ventures drew a sharp distinction between the "worthy poor" who merited help and the "idle poor" who were deemed to lack character and thus deserve their fate. No matter that a New York commission in 1823 found only 46 able-bodied adults among the 851 inmates of the city's poorhouses.

Municipal authorities and private charities also established orphanages, insane asylums, and hospitals. Many such efforts were short-lived, but they attested to the continuing strength of revolutionary and religious ideals and provided a foundation for the more ambitious reforms that would come later in the century.

Women's Lives

Women's lives did not change dramatically during the early years of the nineteenth century. But developments occurred that set the stage for later, more significant breakthroughs.

Divorce was one area in which women achieved greater equality. When a neighbor asked John Backus, a silversmith in Great Barrington, Massachusetts, why he kicked and struck his wife, John replied that it was partly because his father had treated his mother in the same way. We do not know whether John's mother tolerated such abuse, but his wife did not. She complained of cruelty and secured a divorce. More and more women followed her example.

Securing a divorce was not easy, for most states allowed it only on grounds of adultery, and South Carolina did not permit it at all. Moreover, coverture laws required wives to transfer their property to their husbands, making divorce a risky economic proposition for women. New laws enabling women to file for divorce in court rather than having to secure legislative approval made the process easier. Even so, women faced the uncomfortable task of persuading all-male juries of their husbands' infidelities.

Young Women at School This painting captures a ceremony at the Raleigh Female Academy in Virginia about 1816. Examine the painting closely. What kinds of people are present? What does the painting tell you about the purposes and ideals of female education? *(Jacob Marling, The Crowning of Flora, 1816/The Chrysler Museum of Art, Norfolk, VA, Gift of Edgar William and Bernice Chrysler Garbisch 80.118.20)*

Still, divorce was becoming more available to women. In Massachusetts during the decade after independence, 50 percent more women than men filed for divorce, with an almost equal rate of success. Part of the explanation lay in the war's disruptions, which led some men to desert their families, thus encouraging their wives to take action. The Trans-Appalachian West lured men away as well. It seems just as certain, however, that women took to heart prevailing values of individualism and equality, leading them to expect more of marriage.

Changes also occurred in women's education. Young women would have to be properly prepared

DOCUMENT

"Early Habits of Industry," *Mother's Magazine* (1834)

for their prospective role as "Republican Mothers," having prime responsibility for training future citizens in principles of republican virtue. Some women, such as Judith Sargent Murray, demanded more of women's education. In the 1790s, Murray criticized parents who pointed their daughters exclusively toward marriage and dependence. "They should be enabled to procure for themselves the necessaries of life; independence should be placed within their grasp," she wrote. "A woman should reverence herself."

Between 1790 and 1830, a number of female academies were established, mostly in the northeastern states. Though some prescribed bookkeeping, reading,

geography, and history as proper elements of girls' as well as boys' education, traditionalists were decidedly more conservative, warning that undue intellectual activity would "unsex" women. Even the most ardent supporters of female learning, such as Murray, conceded that education was primarily important so that women might function more effectively within the domestic sphere. Still, by 1830, literacy for white females was at an all-time high.

DOCUMENT

Molly Wallace, Valedictory Address (1792)

Women were affected in various ways by changes in American religious life. Though women had long outnumbered men in church membership, the Second Great Awakening drew them into the churches in even greater numbers. Lacking public tax support as church and state drew apart, ministers relied on female volunteers to raise funds and promote missionary and charitable projects. In that way, churches offered women limited entrance into public life.

At the same time, the evangelical impulse, to which many women were drawn, actually reduced women's roles in the churches. Whereas women had previously served as religious exhorters and participated in Baptist and Methodist church governance, they found themselves increasingly marginalized as those rapidly growing denominations strove for social acceptance and adopted older denominations' rigidly gendered rules. In matters of church discipline, women were more frequently charged with "disorderliness" and condemned for "disobedience" than their male brethren. In these ways, a once-robust tradition of piety in which men and women shared spiritual truth and ministered equally to each other's souls gave way.

Race, Slavery, and the Limits of Reform

As we saw in Chapter 7, the Revolution initiated the end of slavery in the northern states and challenged it in the Upper South. As the new century began, however, private manumissions were declining in Maryland and Virginia, while antislavery sentiment was weakening, and more rigid categories of racial exclusiveness were appearing throughout the North. The gradual abolition of slavery there had soothed many white consciences.

In the South, the spread of cotton cultivation sent the value of slave labor soaring, just as revolutionary idealism was fading with the passage of time.

Equally important were two slave rebellions that generated alarm among southern whites. Panic-stricken refugees fleeing the successful revolt of black Haitians on the Caribbean island of St. Domingue (see Chapter 8) spread terror through the South. In response, southern legislatures tightened their "Black Codes," cut the importation of new slaves from the Caribbean, and weeded out malcontents among their chattels.

A second shock followed in the summer of 1800, when a rebellion just outside Richmond, Virginia, was nipped in the bud. A 24-year-old slave named Gabriel devised a plan to arm 1,000 slaves for an assault on the city. Gabriel and his accomplices were American-born blacks who spoke English and worked at skilled jobs that provided a good bit of personal autonomy. They fashioned their own ideology of liberation by appropriating the revolutionary tradition of Virginia's whites and applying it to the conditions of their own lives.

A drenching downpour delayed the attack, giving time for several house servants (subsequently granted freedom by the Virginia Assembly) to sound

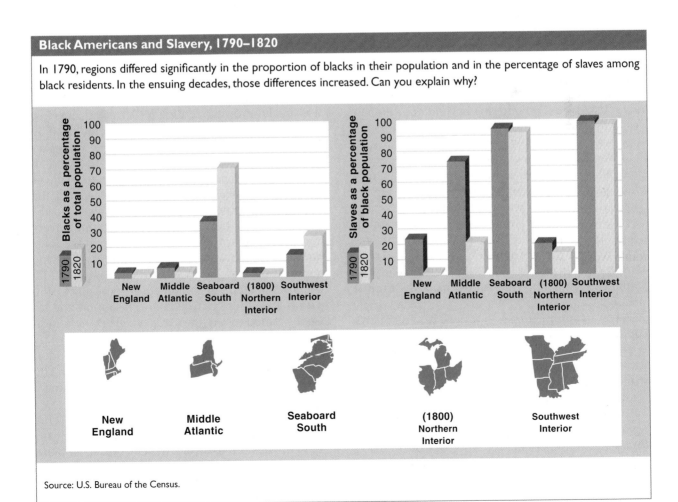

Black Americans and Slavery, 1790–1820

In 1790, regions differed significantly in the proportion of blacks in their population and in the percentage of slaves among black residents. In the ensuing decades, those differences increased. Can you explain why?

Source: U.S. Bureau of the Census.

AMERICAN VOICES

Abraham Camp Longs for True Freedom

The majority of black spokesmen argued against the colonization of American blacks outside the United States. Some, however, such as Abraham Camp, a free black living in Indiana, declared themselves willing to undertake the risks of emigration for the chance of true freedom. He made that clear in this letter of July 13, 1818, to the secretary of the American Colonization Society. In the years ahead, angrier black Americans would issue more strident calls for separation and black nationalism.

I am a free man of colour, have a family and a large connection of free people of colour residing on the Wabash (river), who are all willing to leave America whenever the way shall be opened. We love this country and its liberties, if we could share an equal right in them, but our freedom is partial, and we have no hope that it ever will be otherwise here; therefore we had rather be gone, though we should suffer hunger and nakedness for years.... Nothing shall be lacking on our part in complying with whatever provision shall be made by the United States, whether it be to go to Africa or some other place; we shall hold ourselves in readiness, praying that God (who made man free in the beginning, and who by his kind providence has broken the yoke from every white American) would inspire the heart of every true son of liberty with zeal and pity, to open the door of freedom for us also.

■ *Why has Camp turned his back on the promise of America?*

---

the alarm. No whites died in the abortive rebellion, but scores of slaves and free blacks were arrested, and 25 suspects, including Gabriel, were hanged at the order of Governor James Monroe. The carnage both alarmed and saddened Thomas Jefferson. "There is strong sentiment that there has been hanging enough," he confided to Monroe. "The other states and the world at large will forever condemn us if we . . . go one step beyond absolute necessity." In the midst of panic, however, the line between necessity and revenge was hard to find.

In the early nineteenth century, antislavery appeals all but disappeared from the South. Even religious groups that had once denounced slavery grew quiet. "A majority of the (white) people of the southern states," declared a Georgia congressman in 1806, deprecated slavery as a "political evil" but did not consider it a crime or believe it "immoral to hold human flesh in bondage." Confederate spokesmen would be saying much the same thing at the time of the Civil War.

Slavery continued to exist as well in the nation's capital, where Congress retained Maryland's slave code for the District of Columbia. There, black servants attended the needs of southern congressmen, while slave markets thrived in the shadow of the Capitol building.

In the Northeast, antislavery sentiment was also weakening. With racial domination no longer enforced by law, whites invoked the doctrine of black inferiority to justify racial exclusiveness and ensure their own continued control. The belief in immutable racial differences also encouraged conciliatory attitudes toward slave owners in the South. Compared to the eighteenth century, when ideas of racial exclusiveness had competed with Enlightenment beliefs in the common humanity of all mankind, rigid ideas of racial difference were becoming increasingly common.

The hardening of racial attitudes was evident as well in the growing sentiment for colonizing free blacks in western Africa (areas that would become Liberia and Sierra Leone). The American Colonization Society typified these attitudes. Founded in 1816 with the encouragement of leaders such as Henry Clay, James Madison, and John Marshall, the Society enjoyed widespread support among northern white men and women. While detesting slavery and proclaiming their own benevolent intentions, northern members were uneasy over the growing number of free blacks in their midst. White churches, wishing to combine Christian conversion with colonization, offered financial support and religious sanction for the Society's work. Southern slave owners saw in colonization a convenient way of reducing the South's free black population and ridding themselves of troublesome bondsmen. The Society never sent many American blacks abroad, but it did help allay white anxieties.

Although some black leaders, such as Paul Cuffe, were sympathetic to colonization, believing it offered the best promise of true freedom, most black spokesmen vigorously opposed it. They condemned the ideology of black inferiority on which colonization was based and demanded their full rights as Americans. In joining together to oppose colonization, American blacks gained experience in forging a more effective political voice. That experience would prove valuable training for the abolitionist crusade that lay ahead.

Not all northern whites succumbed to the new racism. The states of Massachusetts, Rhode Island, and Pennsylvania would soon become hotbeds of a resurgent, multiracial abolition movement. Blacks, moreover, enjoyed greater liberty in the cities of the Northeast than elsewhere in the nation.

Racism reared its ugly head in the West as well. In 1823, a proslavery mob in Illinois torched the state capital and threatened Governor Edward Coles for his efforts to end de facto slavery in the state. Proposals for a new state constitution included calls, ultimately unsuccessful, for legalizing slavery within the state's borders.

In Cincinnati, white citizens grew anxious as the city's black population grew. By 1829, one of every 10 residents was black. In July of that year, city leaders announced that they would begin enforcing Ohio's black laws by requiring black residents to carry certificates certifying their free status.

While whites debated the new policy, black leaders petitioned the state legislature for repeal of the "obnoxious black laws." Soon an antiblack coalition of city leaders, unskilled workers fearing competition for jobs, and members of the Cincinnati Colonization Society began to form. In late August, several hundred whites invaded the town's black neighborhoods. Several people were killed in the ensuing melee. In the months that followed, more than half the city's blacks fled, many seeking sanctuary in Canada.

Though the foreign slave trade officially ended in 1808, government efforts to suppress the continuing practice were sporadic. In addition, American diplomats continued to press England for the return of chattels confiscated during the Revolutionary War and the War of 1812. During the early years of the republic, the revolutionary promise of equality rang hollow for most black Americans.

Forming Free Black Communities

During the half century following independence, vibrant black communities appeared in port cities along the Atlantic coast. As the lives of Ben Thompson and Phyllis Sherman revealed, emancipation in the North and the increasing number of freed people in the Upper South enabled growing numbers of African Americans to seek the companionship of people of color in places such as New York, Philadelphia, and Baltimore. In 1776, some 4,000 slaves and several hundred free blacks had called the port cities home; 50 years later, 40,000 African Americans did so.

Black communities provided a measure of security, as well as better chances of finding a marriage partner and establishing a family. Family formation was eased by the fact that many of the urban migrants were women, thus correcting a long-standing gender imbalance in the black urban population. Initially, many blacks formed extended households that included relatives, friends, and boarders. As circumstances allowed, single-family units were formed. By 1820, most blacks in the northern cities lived in autonomous households.

As their numbers grew, African Americans created organizations independent of white control and capable of serving the needs of black communities. Schools educated black children excluded from white academies, mutual-aid societies offered help to the down-and-out, and fraternal associations such as African American Masonic Lodges provided fellowship and mutual support.

Black churches quickly emerged as the cornerstones of black community life. Following the Revolution, growing numbers of free blacks joined integrated Methodist and Baptist congregations, drawn by those churches' strongly biblical theology, enthusiastic worship, and antislavery stand. By 1790, 20 percent of Methodist church members were black. As the numbers of black communicants grew, however, they often found themselves segregated in church galleries, excluded from leadership roles, and even denied communion.

In 1794, a small group of black Methodists led by Richard Allen, a slave-born, itinerant preacher, organized the Bethel African American Methodist Church in Philadelphia. Originally established within American Methodism, Allen's congregation moved toward separatism by requiring that only "Africans and descendants of the African race" be admitted to membership. In 1815, it rejected all oversight by the white Methodist leadership, and a year later joined a similar congregation in Baltimore to form the African Methodist Episcopal Church—the first independent black denomination in the United States. Black Baptists also formed separate churches in Boston, Philadelphia, New Orleans, and St. Louis.

Located in the heart of black communities, these churches nurtured African American forms of worship and provided education for black children and burial sites for families excluded from white cemeteries. Equally important, they offered secure places where the basic rituals of family and community

Black Methodist Church "African" churches and other organizations were rare before 1800 but grew steadily in the ensuing decades. In this watercolor of a black Methodist church meeting, the Russian traveler and painter Paul Svinin offers his impression of the physical emotion often displayed by black worshipers. What do you make of his presentation? *(Pavel Petrovich Svinin, Negro Methodists Holding a Meeting. The Metropolitan Museum of Art, Rogers Fund, 1942. (42.95.19) Photograph © 1985 The Metropolitan Museum of Art)*

life—marriages and births, funerals and anniversaries—could be celebrated and where community norms could be enforced. By the 1830s, a rich cultural and institutional life had taken root in the black neighborhoods of American cities.

White hostility, however, remained a reality of black urban life, especially during hard times when free blacks competed with white laborers for scarce jobs and affordable housing. Though overt racial violence was infrequent during the early decades of the century, blacks found themselves increasingly segregated in residence, employment, and social life.

Black life was far different in southern cities, where the vast majority remained enslaved. Of Charleston's 14,127 blacks (over half the city's population), 90 percent were slaves. That circumstance, together with the South's rigid "Black Codes," frustrated black community building.

In New Orleans, on the other hand, policies established during Spanish colonial rule had produced the largest free black (*libre*) and mixed race (*mulatto*) population in North America. While racial hierarchies clearly existed, *libres*, their numbers augmented by manumitted slaves and refugees fleeing revolutionary Haiti, prospered. By 1820, *libres* accounted for 46 percent of the black population. They constituted a uniquely prosperous and independent black community.

Yet several developments threatened their privileges. Among them were the thousands of new slaves imported to provide labor for the burgeoning sugar economy (what one historian has called the "re-Africanization" of Louisiana), alarm over black rebellion in nearby Haiti, and the introduction of rigid racial ideologies by new white settlers.

THE END OF NEOCOLONIALISM

Following the election of 1808, James Madison, second in the "Virginia dynasty" of presidents, assumed office. As American ships once more ventured into the Atlantic following the embargo's collapse, and as the British navy renewed its depredations, war fever continued to mount. Within a few years, conflict with England erupted in the War of 1812. The war brought an end to a period of neocolonialism when the United States, though formally independent, was still vulnerable to the actions of England and other European powers. During the two administrations of James Monroe (1817–1825), the Jeffersonian Republicans also fashioned a momentous new role for the United States within the Americas.

The War of 1812

As tensions with England increased, the loudest shouts for war came from the West and South. The election of 1810 brought to Congress a new group of western and southern leaders, firmly Jeffersonian in party loyalty but impatient with the administration's bumbling foreign policy and demanding tougher measures. These War Hawks included such future political giants as Henry Clay of Kentucky and John C. Calhoun of South Carolina.

A Scene on the Frontiers as Practiced by the Humane British and Their Worthy Allies, 1812

For too long, cried the War Hawks, the United States had tolerated Britain's presence on American soil, encouragement of Indian raids, and attacks on American commerce. They talked freely of expanding the nation's boundaries north into Canada and south into Spanish Florida. Most of all, these young nationalists resented British arrogance and America's continuing humiliation. No government or political party, they warned, could long endure unless they protected the people's interests and upheld the nation's honor.

Responding to the growing pressure, President Madison finally asked Congress for a declaration of war on June 1, 1812. Opposition came entirely from the New England and mid-Atlantic states—ironically, the regions British policy affected most adversely—whereas the South and West voted solidly for war. Rarely had sectional alignments been more sharply drawn.

Rarely, either, had American foreign policy proven less effective. Madison decided to abandon economic for military coercion just as the British government, under domestic pressure to seek accommodation, suspended its European blockade. Three days later, unaware of Britain's action (it took three weeks for news to cross the Atlantic), Congress declared war.

Burning of the White House in 1814

The war proved a strange affair. Britain beat back several American forays into Canada and launched a series of attacks along the Gulf Coast. As it had done during the Revolutionary War, the British navy blockaded American coastal waters, while landing parties launched punishing attacks along the eastern seaboard. On August 24, 1814, a British force occupied Washington, torched the Capitol and president's mansion (soon to be called the White House after being repaired and whitewashed), and sent the president, Congress, and panic-stricken American troops fleeing into Virginia. Britain, however, did not press its advantage, for it was preoccupied with Napoleon's armies in Europe and wanted to end the American quarrel.

Letter from Dolley Payne Madison to Lucy Payne Todd (1814)

Emotions ran high among Federalist critics and Jeffersonian Republican supporters of the war. During bloody riots in Baltimore in June of 1812, several people, including an old Federalist Revolutionary War general, were badly beaten in the streets. In Federalist New England, opposition to the war veered toward outright disloyalty. In December 1814, delegates from the five New England states met at Hartford, Connecticut, to debate proposals for secession. Cooler heads prevailed, but before adjourning, the Hartford Convention asserted the right of a state to "interpose" its authority against "unconstitutional" acts of the government. Now it was New England's turn to play with the nullification fire. As the war dragged on, Federalist support soared in the Northeast, while elsewhere bitterness grew over New England's disloyalty.

Before the war ended, American forces won several impressive victories, among them Commander Oliver Hazard Perry's defeat of the British fleet on Lake Erie in 1813. That victory ended any threat of a British invasion from Canada and weakened the British–Indian alliance that had menaced American interests in the region. The most dramatic American triumph was Andrew Jackson's smashing victory in 1815 over an attacking British force at New Orleans. But it had little to do with the war's outcome, for it occurred after preliminary terms of peace had already been signed.

Increasingly concerned about Europe, the British government offered to begin peace negotiations. Madison eagerly accepted, and on Christmas Eve in 1814, at Ghent, Belgium, the two sides reached agreement. Britain agreed to evacuate the western posts, but the treaty ignored other outstanding issues, including impressment, neutral rights, and American access to

The Capitol Building Destroyed During the War of 1812, British troops set fire to the House and Senate wings of the Capitol in Washington, D.C., the only time in the nation's history when the building has been seriously damaged. *(Library of Congress, LC-DIG-ppmsca-02160)*

The War of 1812

The War of 1812 scarcely touched the lives of most Americans, but areas around the Great Lakes, Lake Champlain, Chesapeake Bay, and the Gulf Coast witnessed significant fighting. Why was the fighting almost entirely restricted to these areas?

Canadian fisheries. It simply declared the fighting over, called for the return of prisoners and captured territory, and provided for joint commissions to deal with lingering disputes.

Still, the war left its mark on the American nation. Four thousand African Americans, constituting nearly 20 percent of American seamen, fought in the war, demonstrating their patriotism and

DOCUMENT

The Treaty of Ghent (1814)

challenging white racial stereotypes. At least as many free and enslaved blacks took the opportunity to serve the British as spies, messengers, and guides, much as had occurred during the American Revolution. A hundred or so newly liberated slaves accompanied the troops that burned the Capitol and president's house in the summer of 1814.

The British attack on Fort McHenry in Baltimore harbor inspired a young officer, Francis Scott Key, to compose a poem titled "The Star Spangled Banner," which was then set to a familiar English tune. (In 1931, Congress designated it the official national anthem.) In addition, the war made Andrew Jackson a hero and established him as a major political figure. The American people, moreover, regarded the contest as a "Second War of American Independence" that finally secured the nation from outside interference. That belief fed a surge of postwar nationalism.

Following 1815, the nation focused its energies on the task of internal development—occupying the continent, building the economy, and reforming American society. At the same time, European countries entered what would prove to be almost a century free of general war. In the past, European wars had drawn America in; in the twentieth century, they would do so again. For the rest of the nineteenth century, however, that fateful link was broken. Finally, European colonialism was shifting to Africa and Asia, and that diverted European attention from the Americas as well.

The United States and the Americas

While disengaging from Europe, the president and Congress fashioned new policies for Latin America that would guide the nation's hemispheric relations for years to come. Many Americans cheered when Spain and Portugal's Latin American colonies, holding up the American Revolution as a model of liberation, began their struggle for independence in 1808. U.S. leaders were happy to see European colonialism weakened and held out hope that newly independent nations, no longer suffering under imperial control, would be open to increased trade. But they were skeptical that the racially mixed populations of Latin America, with their history of colonial oppression, could govern themselves effectively. There was concern as well that the newly independent countries might attempt to form a South American confederacy capable of challenging U.S. interests. Brought together "in a single mass," Jefferson mused, "they would be a very formidable neighbor."

After initial reluctance (primarily for fear of disrupting delicate efforts then under way to secure Florida from Spain), President Monroe sent Congress a message proposing formal recognition of the Latin American republics. Congress quickly agreed.

Trouble, however, arose in November 1822, when the major European powers talked of helping Spain regain its American empire. Such prospects alarmed Great Britain as well as the United States, and in August 1823, the British foreign secretary

broached the idea of Anglo-American cooperation to thwart Spain's intentions.

Secretary of State John Quincy Adams opposed the idea. John Adams's son had joined the Jeffersonian camp several years earlier as part of the continuing exodus from the Federalist party. Filled with the spirit of nationalism following the War of 1812 and suspicious of British intentions, Adams called for independent action based on two principles: a sharp separation between the Old World and the New, and U.S. dominance in the Western Hemisphere.

Monroe agreed that the United States should issue its own policy statement. In his annual message of December 1823, he outlined a new Latin American policy. Though known as the Monroe Doctrine, Adams had devised it.

The doctrine asserted four basic principles: (1) the American continents were closed to new European colonization, (2) the political systems of the Americas were separate from those of Europe, (3) the United States would consider as dangerous to its peace and safety any attempts to extend Europe's political influence in the Western Hemisphere, and (4) the United States would neither interfere with existing colonies in the New World nor meddle in Europe's affairs.

Monroe's bold declaration had little immediate effect, for the United States possessed neither the economic nor military power to enforce it. But by the end of the nineteenth century, when the nation's might had increased, it would become clear what a fateful moment in the history of the Western Hemisphere Monroe's declaration had been.

KNITTING THE NATION TOGETHER

At the Philadelphia convention of 1788, Federalists and Anti-Federalists had argued whether such a diverse and sprawling republic could long survive. After the vast area of Louisiana was added and white settlement surged into Trans-Appalachia, those concerns increased. Given the country's primitive modes of travel, limited forms of communication, and small central government, problems of national unity continued to bedevil the American people. Although the nation would not be securely unified until after the Civil War, progress was clearly evident in the early republic.

Conquering Distance

It has been estimated that within half an hour of President Kennedy's assassination in Dallas, Texas, in

1963, 68 percent of the American people had learned the news. By contrast, when George Washington died in December 1799 in Alexandria, Virginia, it took 5 days for word to reach Philadelphia (scarcely 140 miles away), 11 days to get as far as Boston, and more than 3 weeks to penetrate west to Lexington, Kentucky. In the absence of modern technologies such as telephones, television, and the Internet, human travel was the only way of communicating across space. By the 1820s, however, improvements in transportation and communication had begun to knit the nation more effectively together.

American Stage Wagon

A flurry of turnpike construction in the northeastern states contributed to the improvement. Most turnpikes consisted of little more than dirt roadways cut through the woods, with tree stumps sawed off just low enough to clear wagon axles. A trip of 25 miles often filled a day. Tolls, moreover, were high. People typically made their way on horseback along crude trails that wound across the countryside.

Still, when a turnpike between Philadelphia and Lancaster, Pennsylvania, proved profitable, dozens of others quickly followed. By 1811, the New York legislature had chartered 137 turnpike companies and the New England states 200 more. By 1830, improvements had cut travel time along these roadways in half.

In the first federal road building project, Congress in 1806 authorized construction of a National Road from Cumberland, Maryland, to the West. By 1818, it had reached Wheeling on the Ohio River and

The *Clermont*   This lithograph shows the *Clermont*, one of the earliest steamboats, passing West Point on the Hudson River about 1810. *(Charles Balthazar Julien Fevret de Saint-Mémin, Vue de l'Hudson à West-Point avec le bateau inventé par Fulton, 1818. Miriam and Ira D. Wallach Division, The New York Public Library/Art Resource, NY)*

had reduced travel time between its terminals from eight days to three.

Given the difficulties of overland routes, Americans traveled by water whenever possible. During the early years of the century, the first steamboats appeared along the Atlantic coast and began to ply the waters of the Ohio and Mississippi rivers. In 1807, Robert Fulton launched his 160-ton side-wheeler *Clermont*, demonstrating the feasibility of steam travel. Four years later, the *New Orleans* made the first successful run over the falls of the Ohio River at Cincinnati, then continued down the

The Difficulties of Travel   The turnpike system reduced travel time through the countryside. Here an express coach makes its way through the forest. *(Album of Western Sketches: Highways and Byeways of the Forest, a Scene on "the Road"; 1836 By: George Tattersall. English, 1817–1849 [active U.S. 1836]; Pen and brown ink with brush and brown wash, heightened with white gouache, over graphite pencil, on gray paper; Sheet: 21.0 x 29.8 cm [8¹/₄ x 11³/₄ in.] Museum of Fine Arts, Boston; Gift of Maxim Karolik; [56.400.11] ©2003 The Museum of Fine Arts, Boston)*

Advances in Communication and Transportation

Steamboats, railways, and steam-driven rotary presses would continue to revolutionize communication during the middle decades of the nineteenth century. The process, however, was well underway by 1830. Study the travel map carefully. Did travel rates improve more dramatically moving from east to west, or north to south? Can you explain the findings?

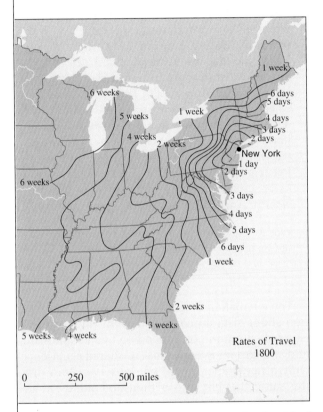

Rates of Travel
1800

0   250   500 miles

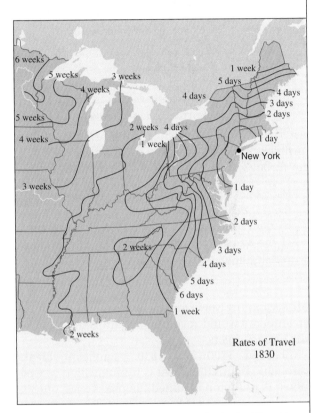

Rates of Travel
1830

Reprinted by permission of the publisher from *Urban Growth and the Circulation of Information* by Allan J. Pred, pp.176–177, Cambridge, Mass.: Harvard University Press, Copyright © 1973 by the President and Fellows of Harvard College.

Growth in Communication, 1790–1830

Compare the rates by which the population increased on the one hand and the increases in the number of post offices, miles of post routes, and newspapers on the other.

	1790	1810	Percent Increase, 1790–1810	1830	Percent Increase, 1810–1830
U.S. population (in thousands)	3,929	7,224	84%	12,901	79%
Post offices	75	2,300	297%	8,450	267%
Miles of post routes	1,875	36,406	185%	115,176	216%
Number of newspapers	108	390	261%	910[*]	133%[*]

[*]Estimated

Sources: *Historical Statistics of the United States*; Clarence Brigham, *Bibliography of American Newspapers, 1690–1820*; S. D. North, *History and Present Condition of the Newspaper and Periodical Press of the United States*.

AMERICAN VOICES

On First Viewing the *Clermont*

Americans have often been intrigued by new technologies but have also been made anxious by them. The author of this account describes local reactions to the first voyage of Robert Fulton's steamboat the Clermont in 1807.

A knot of villagers was gathered on a high bluff just opposite Poughkeepsie, on the west bank of the Hudson, attracted by the appearance of a strange, dark looking craft, which was slowly making its way up the river. Some imagined it to be a sea monster, while others did not hesitate to express their belief that it was a sign of the approaching judgment. What seemed strange in the vessel was the substitution of lofty and straight black smoke-pipes rising from the deck, instead of the gracefully tapered masts that commonly stood on the vessels navigating the stream, and, in place of the spars and rigging, the curious play of the working-beam and pistons and the slow turning and splashing of the huge and naked paddle wheels met the astonished gaze. The dense clouds of smoke, as they rose wave upon wave, added still more to the wonderment of the rustics. . . . The fishermen became terrified and rowed homewards, and they saw nothing but destruction devastating their fishing grounds, while the wreaths of black vapor and the rushing noise of the paddle-wheels, foaming with the stirred up waters, produced great excitement among the boatmen. . . . [Still,] who can doubt that Fulton . . . [believed] that his invention was carrying the message of freedom to every land, that no man could tell all its benefits, or describe all its wonders? What a wonderful achievement! What a splendid triumph!

■ *Why did the* Clermont *make such a powerful impression on people's imaginations?*

Mississippi to New Orleans. Within a few decades, steamboats would revolutionize transportation on the nation's rivers.

Between 1790 and 1830, significant breakthroughs occurred in print communication as well. When Washington assumed the presidency, only 92 newspapers existed. Most were weeklies, and virtually all were printed in cities along the Atlantic coast. The majority had no more than 600 subscribers. By 1830, the number of newspapers had increased to more than 1,000, about one-third of them dailies. Some were published in places as far inland as Pittsburgh and St. Louis.

By 1820, the ratio of newspapers to population was higher in the United States than in Great Britain. The English traveler Frances Trollope commented in amazement on Americans' "universal reading" of papers, while another visitor claimed that "there is scarcely a hamlet that has not its newspaper." The widespread practice of reading newspapers aloud in taverns, shops, and homes further extended their reach.

The swelling demand for newspapers was spurred by rising literacy rates (most notably among women and lower-class men), the demand for information generated by the nation's expanding market economy, the democratic belief in the importance of an informed citizenry, and the growing importance of newspapers as an instrument of party politics.

The circulation of newspapers brought information about distant people and events into formerly isolated communities, expanding people's horizons and strengthening their sense of shared experience. Only a newspaper, noted one observer, "can drop the same thought into a thousand minds at the same moment."

During these years, the American postal system expanded similarly. When Washington was inaugurated, there were only 75 post offices in the country. As late as 1792, there were none in the entire trans-Appalachian West. By 1820, nearly 8,500 post offices lay scattered throughout the nation, while the number of letters carried by the postal system increased ninefold. Though it cost 25 cents to send a letter 30 miles or more—a prohibitive sum for most folks when daily wages averaged only a dollar—the cost had declined by half.

Strengthening American Nationalism

If improvements in travel and communication, together with the sense of national pride fostered by the War of 1812, strengthened American nationalism, so, too, did the galvanizing experience of the Second Great Awakening. It reinforced belief in America as God's chosen nation and tied Americans together in networks of shared religious identity woven by the hundreds of itinerant ministers who carried the

Independence Day Celebration Americans found meaning in Fourth of July celebrations in the early republic, as they have throughout the nation's history. Identify the different people and activities depicted here. Why was the occasion so important in people's lives? *(The Historical Society of Pennsylvania (HSP),* Fourth of July Celebration, *India ink and watercolors on paper by Lewis Krimmel, [Bc 882 K897])*

Gospel message into communities in every part of the country. The flood of printed tracts circulated by religious organizations reinforced the sense of religious unity.

Rituals of patriotic celebration on occasions such as Washington's birthday and the Fourth of July also helped unify the country. Federalists and Jeffersonian Republicans, northerners and southerners, black and white Americans filled these occasions with their own, often conflicting meanings, yet all were eager to claim a voice in shaping the nation's heritage. Reports of these local celebrations, carried across the land via newspapers and correspondence, knitted communities together in a national conversation of patriotism.

National unity was further strengthened by several key decisions of the Supreme Court. In a series of trailblazing cases, the Court, led by Chief Justice John Marshall, laid down some of the most basic doctrines of American constitutional law. In *Marbury* v. *Madison* (1803), the Court established the principle of judicial review, the assertion that the Court had the authority to judge the constitutionality of congressional laws and executive actions. In the case of *Martin* v. *Hunter's Lessee* (1816), the Court claimed appellate jurisdiction over the decisions of state courts.

Three years later, in another landmark decision, *McCulloch* v. *Maryland,* the Court set aside claims that Congress had exceeded its authority in chartering the Second Bank of the United States in 1816. In a unanimous decision, Marshall issued a ringing endorsement of the doctrine of loose, as opposed to strict, construction of the Constitution. "Let the end [of a congressional law] be legitimate," he declared, "let it be within the scope of the constitution, and all means which are appropriate . . . to that end, which are not prohibited, but consist with the letter and spirit of the constitution, are constitutional." The bank's charter would thus stand.

No state, he further argued, possessed the right to tax a branch of a nationally chartered bank, as Maryland had attempted to do, because "the power to tax involves the power to destroy." The principle of national supremacy lay at the very

Martin v. Hunter's Lessee

McCulloch v. Maryland (1819)

DOCUMENT

Marbury v. Madison (1803)

John Marshall John Marshall, appointed chief justice of the United States by President Adams in 1801, served in that position for 34 years. Under his leadership, the Supreme Court established some of the most basic principles of American constitutional law. *(Boston Atheneum)*

center of Marshall's finding. The doctrines elaborated in these path-breaking decisions would continue to shape the nation's history in the years ahead.

The Specter of Sectionalism

Despite the surge of national spirit following the War of 1812, Federalist talk of disunion had revealed just how fragile national unity still was. That became starkly evident in the Missouri crisis of 1819–1820.

Since 1789, politicians had labored to keep the explosive issue of slavery tucked safely beneath the surface of political life, for they understood how quickly it could jeopardize the nation. Their fears were borne out in 1819 when Missouri's application for admission to the Union raised anew the question of slavery's expansion. The Northwest Ordinance of 1787 had prohibited slavery north of the Ohio River while allowing its expansion to the south. But Congress had said nothing about slavery's place in the vast Louisiana territory west of the Mississippi.

Though there were several thousand slaves in the Missouri Territory, Senator Rufus King of New York demanded that Missouri prohibit slavery before entering the Union. His proposal triggered a fierce debate over Congress's authority to regulate slavery in the Trans-Mississippi West. Southerners were adamant that the area must remain open to their slave property and were determined to preserve the equal balance of slave and free states in the Senate. Already by 1819, the more rapidly growing population of the free states had given

The House of Representatives The House of Representatives, depicted in this 1821 painting by Samuel F. B. Morse, later inventor of the telegraph, rang with debate over the Missouri Compromise and other explosive issues. *(Samuel F. B. Morse, The Old House of Representatives, 1882, 86½ x 130¾ in., oil on canvas. In the Collection of the Corcoran Gallery of Art, Washington, D.C., Museum Purchase, Gallery Fund 11.14)*

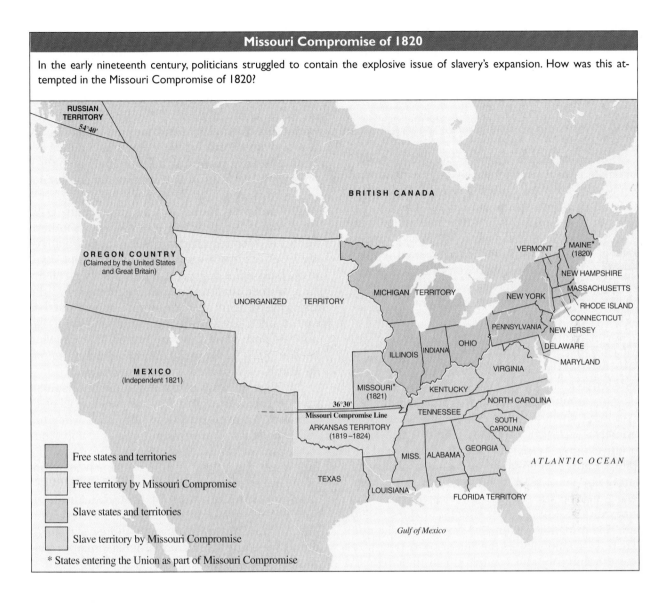

Missouri Compromise of 1820

In the early nineteenth century, politicians struggled to contain the explosive issue of slavery's expansion. How was this attempted in the Missouri Compromise of 1820?

Free states and territories

Free territory by Missouri Compromise

Slave states and territories

Slave territory by Missouri Compromise

* States entering the Union as part of Missouri Compromise

them a 105-to-81 advantage in the House of Representatives. Equality in the Senate offered the only sure protection for southern interests. Northerners, however, vowed to keep the territories west of the Mississippi open to free labor, which meant closing them to slavery.

For nearly three months, Congress debated the issue. During much of the time, free blacks, listening intently to northern antislavery speeches, filled the House gallery. "This momentous question," worried the aged Jefferson, "like a fire-bell in the night, [has] awakened and filled me with terror." Northerners were similarly alarmed. The Missouri question, declared the editor of the New York *Daily Advertiser,* "involves not only the future character of our nation, but the future weight and influence of the free states. If now lost—it is lost forever."

DOCUMENT

Missouri
Enabling Act
(March 6,
1820)

In the end, compromise prevailed. Missouri gained admission as a slave state, while Maine (formerly part of Massachusetts) came in as a counterbalancing free state. A line was drawn west from Missouri at latitude 36° 309 to the Rocky Mountains. Lands south of that line would be open to slavery; areas to the north of it would not.

Yet the issue would not die. Controversy erupted again when antislavery forces in Congress protested a clause in the Missouri constitution excluding free blacks and mulattoes from the state. They argued that the denial of citizenship and civil rights to free blacks in Missouri would set a precedent for similar denials in other states. The Missouri legislature assured Congress that the offending clause would not be used to abridge the rights of any U.S. citizens, thus assuaging congressional critics and ensuring Missouri's admission to the union. In spite of such assurances, free blacks continued to be excluded from the state.

For the moment, the issue of slavery's expansion had been put to rest. It would not be long, however, before the problem would set North and South even more violently against each other.

POLITICS IN TRANSITION

For two decades following the election of 1800, Jeffersonian Republicans monopolized the presidency and dominated Congress, while the Federalist party languished. By the late 1820s, however, the Jeffersonian ascendancy had ended, and the Federalist–Jeffersonian party system was in disarray. As that happened, new political alignments began to appear. When they did, America was poised on the threshold of a new political era.

James Madison, First Inaugural Address (1809)

The Collapse of the Federalist–Jeffersonian Party System

For a while following the election of 1800, Federalists had maintained a drumfire of attack on the Jeffersonians, including the charge published by a Federalist editor in 1803 that Jefferson had sired several children by his slave Sally Hemings. But Federalists were discredited by accusations of disloyalty during the War of 1812 and were tainted by their lingering aristocratic image. Some Federalists endorsed broad suffrage as essential to social stability and governmental legitimacy, but many did not. "There is a tendency in the majority to tyrannize over the minority and trample down their rights," asserted one New York Federalist," [and] in the indolent . . . to cast the burthens of society upon the industrious and the virtuous." Federalists continued to believe that political leadership should be exercised by "the wise and the good." Saddled with this outlook, the Federalist party gradually collapsed.

The Jeffersonians' overwhelming political success after the War of 1812, spurred by fresh recruits in the East and the admission of new states in the West, proved their undoing. No single party could contain the nation's swelling diversity of economic and social interests, deepening sectional divisions, and personal ambitions of newly emerging political leaders.

In response to growing pressures from the West and Northeast, as well as to nationalist sentiment stimulated by the War of 1812, Madison's administration launched a Federalist-like program of national development. In March 1816, the president signed a bill creating a second Bank of the United States (the first bank's charter had expired in 1811), intended to stimulate economic expansion and regulate the loose currency-issuing practices of countless state-chartered banks. At Madison's urging, Congress passed America's first protective tariff, a set of duties on imported goods intended to protect America's "infant industries" that had sprung up during the embargo. He also launched a federally subsidized network of roads and canals. By the early 1820s, Henry Clay and others, now calling themselves National Republicans, were proposing an even more ambitious program of tariffs and internal improvements, under the name of the American System.

The administration's policies drew sharp criticism from so-called Old Republicans, southern politicians who regarded themselves as guardians of the Jeffersonian conscience. Speaking in opposition to the bank bill, Congressman John Randolph of Virginia warned that "the question is whether . . . the state governments are to be swept away; or whether we . . . still . . . regard their integrity and preservation as part of our policy." Over the following decade, the Old Republicans continued to sound the alarm, even as their numbers dwindled.

The final collapse of the Federalist–Jeffersonian party system was triggered by the presidential election of 1824. For the first time since 1800, when the "Virginia dynasty" of Jefferson, Madison, and Monroe began, there was competition for the presidency from every major wing of the Jeffersonian coalition. Of the five candidates, John Quincy Adams of Massachusetts and Henry Clay of Kentucky advocated bold federal programs of economic development. William Crawford of Georgia and Andrew Jackson of Tennessee clung to traditional Jeffersonian principles of limited government, agrarianism, and states' rights. In between stood John Calhoun of South Carolina, just beginning his fateful passage from nationalism to southern nullification.

When none of the presidential candidates received an electoral majority, the election, as in 1800, moved into the House of Representatives. There, an alliance of Adams and Clay supporters gave the New Englander the election, even though he trailed Jackson in electoral votes, 84 to 99. The Jacksonians' charges of a "corrupt bargain" gained credence when Adams appointed Clay secretary of state.

Adams's ill-fated administration revealed the disarray in American politics. His stirring calls for federal road and canal building, standardization of weights and measures, a national university, and government support for science and the arts quickly fell victim to sectional conflicts, political factionalism, and his own scorn for the increasingly democratic politics of the time. Within a year of his inauguration,

John Quincy Adams, Inaugural Address (1825)

Adams's administration had foundered. For the rest of his term, politicians jockeyed for position in the political realignment that was underway.

Women at the Republican Court

Much as aristocratic women had long exerted influence at English and European courts, so elite American women such as Margaret Bayard Smith forged an American style of parlor politics. Initiated at Philadelphia in the 1790s when a national governing community was taking shape, parlor politics became an integral part of the Washington scene after 1800.

As political actors in their own right, women visited the Supreme Court and attended sessions of Congress, frequently circulating on the House and Senate floors and even sitting in members' seats. "The House of Representatives," observed Bayard Smith, "is a lounging place for both sexes, where acquaintance is as easily made as at public amusements." Women also filled the House galleries as electoral votes were counted in the 1808 presidential election, and listened intently to the debates over war in 1812.

DOCUMENT

James Wilson's Law Lecture to Women (1791)

They also utilized networks of friendship, dinner parties, and social gatherings to reinforce political alliances, lobby political appointments, and promote legislation. In the process, they contributed to the new government's effectiveness while challenging the lines separating public (male) and private (female) spheres.

No one participated in the capital's parlor politics with greater relish than Louisa Catherine Adams, who launched what she called "my campaign" for the candidacy of her husband, John Quincy Adams, in the disputed presidential election of 1824. During his term in office, she continued to work the Washington scene.

If privileged women found it possible to achieve political influence in Washington, however, other women continued to find themselves politically isolated. That was in part because of a conservative backlash against the radically feminist politics evident earlier during the French Revolution. The claims of American women for a greater political voice at home could easily be tarred with the brush of French "anarchy" by anxious American males. Also, American political democracy became more rigidly gendered as male-dominated political parties grew in importance and voting, still limited to men, became the defining act of political participation.

A New Style of Politics

While women, blacks, and Native Americans continued to be excluded from the franchise, white men now flocked to the polls in unprecedented numbers. In state elections, voter turnout at times reached as high as 80 percent of the qualifying electorate, far higher than previously.

The growing strength of democratic beliefs and decisions by state governments to abolish long-established property-owning requirements for the

John Lewis Krimmel, *Election Day at the State House, 1816* Election days were often raucous affairs in the increasingly democratic, male-dominated politics of the early republic, as this Philadelphia scene amply testifies. *(The Historical Society of Pennsylvania [HSP], India ink and watercolors on paper of* Election Day at the State House, 1816 *by John Lewis Krimmel, [Bc 47 K897])*

franchise helps explain the dramatic increase. In addition, state programs of road and canal building, bank regulation, temperance enforcement, and poor relief activated people's self-interest, thus drawing them into the political arena. And it was in the states that a new generation of political leaders such as Martin Van Buren and Henry Clay, skilled in party organization, sophisticated in the use of a partisan press, and uninhibited by the revolutionary genera-

tion's fear of political "faction" perfected the techniques of mass, democratic politics. By the 1820s, voter registration drives, party conventions, and popular campaigning had become commonplace.

The election of Andrew Jackson to the presidency in 1828 represented the culmination of these democratic changes. For the first time, the techniques of mass politics were applied to presidential electioneering, thus changing American politics forever.

TIMELINE

1790	Indian Intercourse Act
1790s	Second Great Awakening begins
1793	Invention of the cotton gin
1794	Battle of Fallen Timbers
1795	Treaty of Greenville
1800	Gabriel's Rebellion
1803	*Marbury* v. *Madison*
1806	National Road begun
1807	Fulton's steamboat *Clermont* launched
1808	James Madison elected president
	Official end of the slave trade
1811	Battle of Kithtippecanoe
1812	Madison reelected
	War declared against Great Britain
1813	Battle of the Thames
1813–1814	Creek War

1814	Treaty of Ghent
	Battle of Horseshoe Bend
1814–1815	Hartford Convention
1815	Battle of New Orleans
1816	James Monroe elected president
	Second Bank of the United States chartered
	American Colonization Society founded
	African Methodist Episcopal Church established
1819	Adams–Onís Treaty with Spain
	McCulloch v. *Maryland*
1819–1822	Bank panic and depression
1819–1820	Missouri Compromise
1822	Diplomatic recognition of Latin American republics
1823	Monroe Doctrine proclaimed
1824	John Quincy Adams elected president
1827	Cherokee adopt written constitution

Conclusion

The Passing of an Era

In the early nineteenth century, the United States consisted of diverse, often conflicting, and loosely connected regions. Within those regions ordinary citizens such as Mary and James Harrod, Ben Thompson, and Phyllis Sherman struggled to fashion new lives. Their efforts gave human expression to the nation's values of social equality, individual opportunity, and personal autonomy.

Those values, strengthened by the country's revolutionary heritage and the Great Awakening, inspired

reforms intended to improve the conditions of American life. Though the lives of many white women were bettered, gender restrictions continued to limit women's opportunities. The reinvigoration of chattel slavery in the South imperiled the lives of countless black slaves, while deepening racism in the North circumscribed the lives of free blacks. To the west, Native Americans, pursuing strategies of resistance and accommodation, gradually gave way in the face of expanding white settlement.

During these same years, American leaders fashioned important new relationships with the outside world. Following the War of 1812, the United States finally ended its neocolonial dependence on England and Europe. In the Monroe Doctrine, it defined a portentous new relationship with the emerging nations of Latin America.

As the country grew, American nationalism was strengthened by improvements in travel and print communication, the widely shared experience of the Great Awakening, and a series of path-breaking decisions handed down by the Supreme Court. At the same time, sectional tensions continued to simmer, breaking ominously through the surface of political life in the Missouri Crisis.

These years brought decisive changes to American politics. Privileged white women exerted influence in the nation's capital, though most women continued to find themselves politically marginalized.

Still, sophisticated political parties enlisted men by the tens of thousands in electoral politics.

By the 1820s, the American people had turned from an era of founding, when the nation was new and the outcome of the republican experiment uncertain, to a new era of national security and development. That transition was dramatized on July 4, 1826, the fiftieth anniversary of American independence, when two of the remaining revolutionary patriarchs, John Adams and Thomas Jefferson, died within a few hours of each other. "The sterling virtues of the Revolution are silently passing away," mused George McDuffie of South Carolina during that jubilee year, "and the period is not distant when there will be no living monument to remind us of those glorious days of trial." As the anniversary celebrations ended and the revolutionary founders faded into memory, the American people had reason to ponder what the future would bring.

Questions for Review and Reflection

1. How did the nation's regions differ in the early republic? To what extent were these differences of long standing, and to what extent did they reflect developments since the end of the Revolutionary War?

2. Why did some Indian tribes follow the path of accommodation to white expansion, while others rose in armed resistance? What differences resulted?

3. What circumstances promoted social reform in the early republic, and what circumstances inhibited it?

4. How and why did the United States refashion its relationship to the outside world in the early nineteenth century?

5. What circumstances served to unite and to divide the nation during these years?

Recommended Reading

Recommended Readings are posted on the Web site for this textbook. Visit www.ablongman.com/nash

Fiction and Film

In the classic American novel *Rip Van Winkle* (1829), Washington Irving explores the transience of historical memory via the story of an eighteenth-century New Yorker who mysteriously falls asleep during the American Revolution and awakes decades later to find his community radically changed and himself the object of intense curiosity. *Scandalmonger* (2000), a novel by *New York Times* columnist William Safire, describes personal intrigue within high political circles in the early

republic. *Tecumseh: The Last Warrior* (1995), a made-for-television historical drama, offers an imaginative rendering of the Shawnee leader who sought to unite tribes north and south of the Ohio River against invading white settlers in the early nineteenth century. *Lewis and Clark: The Journey of the Corps of Discovery* (1997), a PBS documentary by Ken Burns, tells the story of this path-breaking expedition and reveals the dramatic landscape through which it passed.

Discovering U.S. History Online ——————————————————————

Turns of the Centuries Exhibit

www.americancenturies.mass.edu/turns/index.jsp

Web site visitors can examine museum artifacts from three "turn-of-the-century" eras: 1680–1720, 1780–1820, and 1880–1920. The exhibits for each era demonstrate "Family Life," "Native American Indians," "African Americans," "Newcomers," and "The Land."

Birch's Views of Philadelphia in 1800

www.ushistory.org/birch

This site presents a facsimile of 29 engravings of Philadelphia at the beginning of the nineteenth century.

Nineteenth-Century Views of Manhattan

www.nypl.org/research/chss/spe/art/print/exhibits/
movingup/opening.htm

This site presents an annotated exhibition of nineteenth-century prints that demonstrate the urban growth in early nineteenth-century Manhattan.

Charlottesville: A Brief Urban History

www.iath.virginia.edu/schwartz/cville/
cville.history.html

This illustrated history focuses on development of Charlottesville in the nineteenth century.

The Seminole Tribe of Florida

www.seminoletribe.com/history/index.shtml

This site is dedicated to the rich history and culture of the Seminole, including the campaigns Andrew Jackson led against the tribe before and during his presidency.

The Iroquois of the Northeast

www.carnegiemuseums.org/cmnh/exhibits/
north-south-east-west/iroquois/index.html

A virtual exhibit of the Iroquois and their way of life.

Native Americans in North Georgia

www.ngeorgia.com/history/findex.html

This site presents a several-part history of Georgia's Native Americans, especially the Creek and Cherokee.

Divining America: Religion and the National Culture, the 19th Century

www.nhc.rtp.nc.us:8080/tserve/nineteen.htm

Using essays and contemporary photos and primary sources, this site includes several essays including "Evangelicalism, Revivalism, and Second Great Awakening" and "Evangelicalism as a Social Movement."

Colonization

www.loc.gov/exhibits/african/afam002.html

This site explores the roots of the colonization movement, including the American Colonization Society.

A History of African Americans of Delaware and Maryland's Eastern Shore

www.udel.edu/BlackHistory

This site offers a collection of several essays on blacks in these colonies, especially the growth of antebellum free black communities.

Judith Sargent Murray Society

www.hurdsmith.com/judith/

This site presents Murray's biography, an illustrated tour of her world, and several of her published essays.

Casebook: The War of 1812

http://warof1812.casebook.org/index.html

A detailed presentation of the War of 1812, this site presents the people, battles, press coverage contemporary to the war, primary source documents, and a timeline.

James Madison

www.jmu.edu/madison

This site explores many aspects of James Madison's career and the historical events and ideas he influenced.

Nationalism

www.fordham.edu/halsall/mod/modsbook17.html

This site has collected essays (public domain texts) on the surging global nationalism of the early nineteenth century, giving context to America's own rising patriotism during those years.

The Marshall Cases for the American Revolution

www.odur.let.rug.nl/~usa/D/1801-
1825/marshallcases/marxx.htm

This site presents thorough descriptions and text excerpts from court records of John Marshall's six best-known cases as well as a brief biography.

The Missouri Compromise

www.darien.k12.ct.us/jburt/approject/civilwar/1820/
per3/index.htm

Created for a class project, this site offers a topical presentation of the Missouri Compromise.

Thomas Jefferson

www.loc.gov/exhibits/jefferson

This extensive, illustrated exhibit presents Jefferson's life and ideas, including the progression of his ideas of federalism and his legacy.

Martin Van Buren—His Early Years

www.mindspring.com/~braniff/mvb-earl.htm

Part of a larger site on Martin Van Buren, this page gives a year-by-year description of his early years.

History of the Fourth of July

www.pbs.org/capitolfourth/history.html

This site presents a colorful illustrated history of Fourth of July celebrations.

Road Through the Wilderness

www.connerprairie.org/ntlroad.html

The National Road was a hot political topic in the early republic and was part of the beginning of the development of America's infrastucture. This site tells the history of the building of the National Road.

CHAPTER 10

Economic Transformations in the Northeast and the Old Northwest

This picture of an 1845 fair suggests the cornucopia of goods made available in the early stages of industrialization. *(B. J. Harrison, Fair of the American Institute at Niblo's Garden, 1845/Museum of the City of New York)*

American Stories

Discovering Success in the Midst of Financial Ruin

For her first 18 years, Susan Warner was little touched by the far-reaching economic and social changes that were transforming the character of the country and her own city of New York. Whereas some New Yorkers toiled to make a living by taking in piecework and others responded to unsettling new means of producing goods by joining trade unions to agitate for wages that would enable them to "live as comfortable as others," Susan was surrounded by luxuries and privilege. Much of the year was spent in the family's townhouse in St. Mark's Place, not far from the home of the enormously rich real estate investor and fur trader John Jacob Astor. There Susan acquired the social graces and skills appropriate for a girl of her position and background. She had dancing and singing lessons, studied Italian and French, and learned the etiquette involved in receiving visitors and making calls. When hot weather made life in New York unpleasant, the Warners escaped to the cooler airs of Canaan, where they had a summer house. Like any girl of her social class, Susan realized that her carefree existence could not last forever. With her marriage, which she confidently expected some time in the future, would come significant new responsibilities as a wife and mother but not the end of the comfortable life to which she was accustomed.

It was not marriage and motherhood that disrupted the pattern of Susan's life but financial disaster. Sheltered as she had been from the unsettling economic and social changes of the early nineteenth century, Susan discovered that she, too, was at the mercy of forces beyond her control. Her father, heretofore so successful a provider and parent, lost most of his fortune during the financial Panic of 1837. Like others experiencing a sharp economic reversal, the Warners had to make radical adjustments. The fashionable home in St. Mark's Place and the pleasures of New York were exchanged for a more modest existence on an island in the Hudson River. Susan turned "housekeeper" and learned how to do tasks once relegated to others: sewing and making butter, pudding sauces, and johnny cake.

The change of residence and Susan's attempt to master domestic skills did not halt the family's financial decline. Prized possessions, including the piano and engravings, all symbols of the life the Warners had once taken for granted, eventually went up for auction. "When at last the men and the confusion were gone," Susan's younger sister, Anna, recalled, "then we woke up to life."

Waking up to life meant facing the necessity of making money. But what could Susan do to reverse sliding family fortunes? True, some women labored as factory operatives, domestics, seamstresses, or schoolteachers, but it was doubtful Susan could even imagine herself in any of these occupations. Her Aunt Fanny, however, had a suggestion that was more congenial to the genteel young woman. Knowing that the steam-powered printing press had revolutionized the publishing world and created a mass readership, much of it female, Aunt Fanny told her niece, "Sue, I believe if you would try, you could write a story." "Whether she added 'that . . . would sell,' I am not sure," recalled Anna later, "but of course that was what she meant."

Taking Aunt Fanny's advice to heart, Susan started to write a novel that would sell. She constructed her story around the trials of a young orphan girl, Ellen Montgomery. As Ellen suffered one reverse after another, she learned the lessons that allowed her to survive and eventually triumph over adversity: piety, self-denial, discipline, and the power of a mother's love. Titled *The Wide, Wide World,* the novel was accepted for publication only after the mother of the publisher, George Putnam, read it and told her son, "If you never publish another book, you must make *The Wide, Wide World* available for your fellow men." A modest 750 copies were printed. Much to the surprise of the cautious Putnam, if not to his mother, 13 editions were published within two years. *The Wide, Wide World* became the first American novel to sell more than one million copies. It was one of the bestsellers of the century.

Long before she realized the book's success, Susan, who was now much aware of the need to make money, was working on a new story. Drawing on her own experience of economic and social reversal, Susan described the spiritual and intellectual life of a young girl thrust into poverty after an early life of luxury in New York. Titled *Queechy,* this novel was also a great success.

Though her fame as a writer made Susan Warner unusual, her books' popularity suggested how well they spoke to the concerns and interests of a broad readership. The background of social and financial uncertainty, with its sudden changes of fortune, so prominent in several of the novels, captured the reality and fears of a fluid society in the process of transformation. While one French writer was amazed that "in America a three-volume novel is devoted to the history of the moral progress of a girl of thirteen," pious heroines such as Ellen Montgomery, who struggled to master their passions and urges toward independence, were shining exemplars of the new norms for middle-class women. Their successful efforts to mold themselves heartened readers who believed that the future of the nation depended on virtuous mothers who struggled to live up to new ideals. Susan's novels validated their efforts and spoke to the importance of the domestic sphere. "I feel strongly impelled to pour out to you my most heartful thanks," wrote one woman. None of the other leading writers of the day had been able to minister "to the highest and noblest feelings of my nature *so much as yourself.*"

Susan Warner's life and novels serve as an introduction to the far-reaching changes that this chapter explores and that constitute one of the major themes of this text. Between 1820 and 1860, as Susan Warner discovered, economic transformations in the Northeast and the Old Northwest reshaped economic, social, cultural, and political life. Though most Americans still lived in rural settings, economic growth and the new industrial mode of production affected them through the creation of new goods, opportunities, and markets. In cities and factory towns, the new economic order ushered in new forms of work, new class arrangements, and new forms of social strife.

After placing American economic change in an international context, another focus of this text, and discussing the factors that fueled antebellum growth, the chapter turns to the industrial world, where so many of the new patterns of work and life appeared. An investigation of urbanization reveals shifting class arrangements and values as well as rising social and racial tensions. Finally, an examination of rural communities in the East and on the frontier in the Old Northwest highlights the transformation of these two sections of the country. Between 1840 and 1860, industrialization and economic growth increasingly knit them together.

ECONOMIC GROWTH

Between 1820 and 1860, the American economy entered a new and more complex phase as it shifted from reliance on agriculture as the major source of growth toward an industrial and technological future. Amid general national expansion, real per capita output grew an average of 2 percent annually between 1820 and 1840 and slightly less between 1840 and 1860. This doubling of per capita income over a 40-year period suggests that many Americans were enjoying a rising standard of living.

But the economy was also unstable, as the Warners discovered. Periods of boom (1822–1834, mid-1840s–1850s) alternated with periods of bust (1816–1821, 1837–1843). As never before, Americans faced dramatic and recurrent shifts in the availability of jobs and goods and in prices and wages. Particularly at risk were working-class Americans, a third of whom lost their jobs in depression years. And because regional economies were increasingly linked, problems in one area tended to affect conditions in others.

The Transatlantic Context for Growth

American economic growth was linked to and influenced by events elsewhere in the world, particularly in Great Britain. Britain was the home of the Industrial Revolution, the event that some historians believe to be among the most important of human history in terms of its impact on material life. For the first time, production of goods proceeded at a faster pace than the growth of population.

The Industrial Revolution beginning in Britain in the eighteenth century involved many technological innovations that spurred new developments and efficiencies. Among the most important developments was the discovery in the 1780s of a way to eliminate carbon and other substances from pig iron. This opened the way for cheap, durable iron machines that led to the increased production of goods. Another milestone, the improvement of the steam engine, originally used to pump water out of coal mines, eventually led to railroads and steamboats, thus revolutionizing transportation. Steam-powered machinery also transformed cloth production, moving it from cottages to factories. The British textile industry was the giant of the early Industrial Revolution. The use of machinery allowed the production of more and cheaper textiles. The industry became a prime market for American cotton as well as cotton from India and Brazil. British demand for raw cotton helped to cement the South's attachment to slavery.

By 1850, Great Britain was the most powerful country in the world, and its citizens were the richest.

Significant Factors Promoting Economic Growth, 1820–1860

Factor	Important Features	Contribution to Growth
Abundant natural resources	Acquisition of new territories (Louisiana Purchase, Florida, trans-Mississippi West); exploitation and discovery of eastern resources	Provided raw materials and energy vital to economic transformation
Substantial population growth	Increase from 9 million in 1820 to more than 30 million in 1860—due to natural increase of population and, especially after 1840, to rising immigration; importance of immigration from Ireland, Germany	Provided workers and consumers necessary for economic growth; immigration increased diversity of workforce with complex results, among them supply of capital and technological know-how
Transportation revolution	Improvement of roads; extensive canal building, 1817–1837; increasing importance of railroad construction thereafter; by 1860, 30,000 miles of tracks; steamboats facilitate travel on water	Facilitated movement of people, goods, and information; drew people into national economy market; stimulated agricultural expansion, regional crop specialization; decreased costs of shipping goods; strengthened ties between Northeast and Midwest
Capital investment	Investments by European investors and U.S. interests; importance of mercantile capital and banks, insurance companies in funneling capital to economic enterprises	Provided capital to support variety of new economic enterprises, improvements in transportation
Government support	Local, state, and national legislation; loans favoring enterprise; judicial decisions	Provided capital, privileges, and supportive climate for economic enterprises
Industrialization	New methods of producing goods, with and without involvement of machinery	Produced more numerous, cheaper goods for mass market; transformed classes and nature of work; affected distribution of wealth and individual opportunity

In the following decades, its factories and mines churned out most of the world's coal and more than half of its iron and textiles. Not surprisingly, Americans would look to England and English know-how as they embarked on their own course of industrialization. While American industrial development did not mimic that of the British, there were many similarities between the two countries' experiences.

Factors Fueling Economic Development

The United States enjoyed abundant natural resources that facilitated economic changes and, thanks to European immigration, the expanding population necessary for economic expansion. The size of American families was shrinking—in 1800, the average white woman bore seven children; by 1860, the number had declined to five. Thus immigration from Europe provided the new workers, new households, and new consumers so essential to economic development as well as the capital and technological ideas that helped shape American growth.

Improved transportation played a key role in bringing about economic and geographic expansion. Early in the century, high freight rates discouraged production for distant markets and the exploitation of resources, while primitive transportation hindered western settlement. Canal-building projects in the 1820s and 1830s dramatically transformed this situation. The 363-mile-long Erie Canal, the last link in a chain of waterways binding New York City to the Great Lakes and the Northwest, was the most impressive of these new canals. The volume of goods and people it carried at low cost as well as the economic advantages it conferred on those within its reach (suggested by both the figure on inland freight rates and the table on economic growth) prompted the construction of more than 3,000 miles of canals by 1840, primarily in eastern and midwestern states.

Even at the height of the canal boom, politicians, promoters, and others, impressed with Britain's success with steam-powered railways, also supported the construction of railroads. Unlike canals that might freeze during the winter, railroads could operate year-round and could be built almost anywhere. These advantages encouraged Baltimore merchants, envious of New York's water link to the Northwest, to begin the Baltimore & Ohio Railroad in 1828.

DOCUMENT

Albany *Daily Advertiser,* Opening of the Erie Canal (1819)

AUDIO

The Erie Canal

Despite the interest in and advantages of railroads, there were technical problems: the first trains jumped their tracks and spewed sparks, setting nearby fields ablaze. But such difficulties were quickly overcome. By 1840, there were 3,000 miles of track, more than in all the countries of Europe. Another 5,000 miles were laid during the 1840s, and by the end of the 1850s, total mileage soared to 30,000. Like the canals, the new railroads strengthened the links between the Old Northwest and the East.

Improved transportation so profoundly influenced American life that some historians use the term *transportation revolution* to refer to its impact. Canals and railroads bound the country together in a new way. They provided farmers, merchants, and manufacturers with cheap and reliable access to distant markets and goods and encouraged Americans to settle the frontier and cultivate virgin lands. The economic opportunities they opened fostered technological innovations that could increase production. Eventually, the strong economic and social ties the waterways and then the railways fostered between the Northwest and the East led people living in the two regions to share political outlooks.

Railroads exerted enormous influence, especially in terms of the pattern of western settlement. As the railroads followed—or led—settlers westward, their routes could determine whether a city, town, or even homestead survived. The railroad transformed Chicago from a small settlement into a bustling commercial and transportation center. In 1850, the city contained not one mile of track, but within five years, 2,200 miles of track serving 150,000 square miles terminated in Chicago.

The dramatic rise in railroad construction in the two decades before the Civil War contributed to faster economic growth after 1839. Goods, people, commercial information, and mail flowed ever more predictably, rapidly, and cheaply. In 1790, an order from Boston

IMAGE

Anti-Railroad Poster in Philadelphia, 1839

MAP

Expanding America and Internal Improvements

The Erie Canal This painting suggests the ambitious efforts that lay behind the construction of the 363-mile canal linking New York to the Great Lakes and the Northwest. Irish immigrants who flooded the country during the antebellum period provided the muscle power for this and other transportation projects. What does this picture suggest about the ways in which freight was moved along the canal? *(John William Hill, View on the Erie Canal. Phelp Stokes Collection of American Historical Prints, The New York Public Library/Art Resource, NY)*

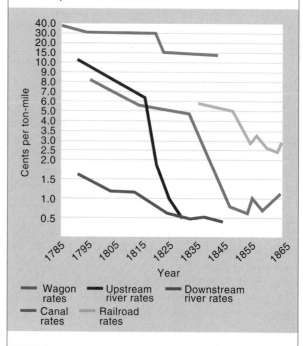

Inland Freight Rates

As this chart makes dramatically clear, the transportation revolution had a tremendous impact on the cost of shipping goods and materials to markets and factories. In what period did the cost of transporting goods by canal fall most significantly? What do you think caused the decline in upstream river rates?

Cents per ton-mile

Year

— Wagon rates
— Upstream river rates
— Downstream river rates
— Canal rates
— Railroad rates

The Transportation Revolution

This map shows the impact of the transportation revolution. Note the components of that revolution: roads, canals, and then railroad lines. What were the important regional connections opened up by transportation improvements? How would you compare northern and southern development? What were the commercial results of the new transportation networks?

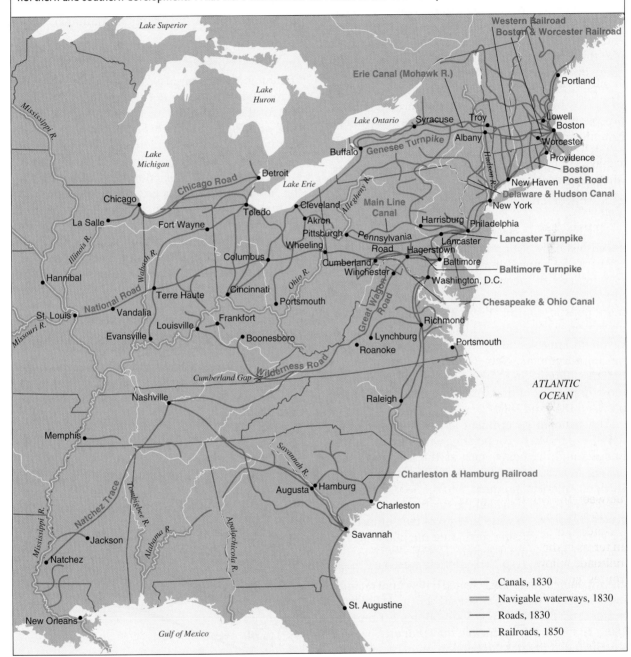

——	Canals, 1830
≡≡≡	Navigable waterways, 1830
——	Roads, 1830
——	Railroads, 1850

took two weeks to reach Philadelphia; in 1836, it took only 36 hours.

Improved transportation stimulated agricultural expansion and regional specialization. Farmers began to plant larger crops for the market, concentrating on those most suited to their soil and climate. By the late 1830s, the Old Northwest had become the country's granary, and New England farmers turned to dairy or produce farming. In 1860, American farmers were producing four to five times as much wheat, corn, cattle, and hogs as they had in 1810. Their achievements meant plentiful, cheap food for American workers and more income for farmers to spend on the new consumer goods.

Capital and Government Support

Internal improvements, the exploitation of natural resources, and the cultivation of new lands all demanded capital. Between 1790 and 1861, more than $500 million in foreign capital, most of it from Great Britain, was invested in state bonds, transportation, and land. Foreign investors financed as much as one-third of all canal construction and bought about one-quarter of all railroad bonds.

American mercantile capital fueled growth as well. As Chapter 8 suggested, the merchant class prospered in the half century after the Revolution. Now merchants invested in schemes ranging from canals to textile factories. Many ventured into the production of goods and became manufacturers themselves. Other prosperous Americans also eagerly sought opportunities to put their capital to work.

Local and state government played their part by enthusiastically supporting economic growth. States often helped new ventures raise capital by passing laws of incorporation; by awarding entrepreneurs special privileges such as tax breaks or monopolistic control; by underwriting bonds for improvement projects, which increased their investment appeal; and by providing loans for internal improvements. New York, Pennsylvania, Ohio, Indiana, Illinois, and Virginia publicly financed almost 75 percent of the canal systems in their states between 1815 and 1860.

The national government also encouraged economic expansion by cooperating with states on some internal improvements, such as the National Road linking Maryland and Illinois. Federal tariff policy shielded American products, and the Second Bank of the United States provided the financial stability investors required. So widespread was the enthusiasm for growth that the line separating the public sector from the private often became unclear.

The law also helped promote aggressive economic growth. Judicial decisions created a new understanding of property rights. The case of *Palmer* v. *Mulligan*, decided by the New York State Supreme Court in 1805, laid down the principle that property ownership included the right to develop property for business purposes. Land was increasingly defined as a productive asset for exploitation, not merely subsistence, as earlier judicial rulings had suggested.

Investors and business operators alike wanted to increase predictability in the conduct of business. Contracts lay at the heart of commercial relationships, but contract law hardly existed in 1800. A period of rapid development ensued. A series of important Supreme Court decisions between 1819 and 1824 established the basic principle that contracts were binding. In *Dartmouth College* v. *Woodward*, the Court held that a state charter could not be modified unless both parties agreed, and it declared in *Sturges* v. *Crowninshield* that a New York law allowing debtors to repudiate their debts was unconstitutional.

A New Mentality

Economic expansion also depended on intangible factors. When a farmer decided to specialize in apples for the New York market rather than to concentrate on raising food for his family, he was thinking in a new way. So was a merchant who invested in banks that would, in turn, finance a variety of economic enterprises. The entrepreneurial outlook—the *"universal desire,"* as one newspaper editor put it, *"to get forward"*—was shared by millions of Americans. By encouraging investment, new business and agricultural ventures, and land speculation, it played a vital role in antebellum development.

Europeans often recognized other intangible factors. As one Frenchman observed in 1834, Americans

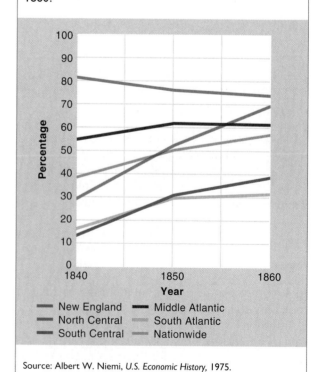

White Secondary School Enrollment, 1840–1860

Note the regional difference in school enrollment and changes over time. What area of the country made the biggest gains in school enrollment between 1840 and 1860?

Source: Albert W. Niemi, *U.S. Economic History*, 1975.

HOW OTHERS SEE US

Alexis de Tocqueville, An Analysis of the Lure of Commerce and Manufacturing

In 1831 a French magistrate, Alexis de Tocqueville, came to the United States to examine the American prison system. While the exploration of the penal system was his official reason for spending nine months in the United States, he was actually more interested in understanding how American democracy operated. His book Democracy in America, *published in 1835 and 1840, has become a classic study of this country in the 1830s.*

Agriculture is, perhaps, of all the useful arts, that which improves most slowly amongst democratic nations. Frequently, indeed, it would seem to be stationary, because other arts are making rapid strides toward perfection. On the other hand, almost all the tastes and habit which the equality of condition produces naturally lead men to commercial and industrial occupations.

Suppose an active, enlightened, and free man, enjoying a competency, but full of desires: he is too poor to live in idleness; he is rich enough to feel himself protected from the immediate fear of want, and he thinks how he can better his condition. . . . life is slipping away time is urgent. . . . The cultivation of the ground promises an almost certain result to his exertions, but a slow one; men are not enriched by it without patience and toil.

Agriculture is therefore only suited to those who have already larger superfluous wealth, or to those who penury bids them only seek a bare subsistence. The choice of such a man as we have supposed is soon made; he sells his plot of ground, leaves his dwelling, and embarks in some hazardous but lucrative calling.

Democratic communities abound in men of this kind. . . . Thus, democracy not only swells the number of working-men, but it leads men to prefer one kind of labor to another; and, whilst it diverts them from agriculture, it encourages their taste for commerce and manufactures.

- *What argument does de Tocqueville make to explain the American interest in commerce and manufacturing work?*

- *Does the discussion in this chapter support de Tocqueville's analysis about the supposed preference of Americans for industrial and commercial rather than agricultural pursuits?*

Source: Alexis de Tocqueville, *Democracy in America*, ed. Richard D. Heffner (New York: New American Library, 1956), 213.

---

were energetic and open to change. "All here is circulation, motion, and boiling agitation. Experiment follows experiment; enterprise succeeds to enterprise." Some saw an American mechanical "genius." "In Massachusetts and Connecticut," one Frenchman insisted, "there is not a labourer who had not invented a machine or tool." He exaggerated (many American innovations drew on British precedents and were introduced by immigrants familiar with the British originals), but every invention did attract scores of imitators.

Mechanically minded Americans prided themselves on developing efficient tools and machines. The McCormick harvester, the Colt revolver, Goodyear vulcanized rubber products, and the sewing machine—all were developed, refined, and developed further. Such improvements cut labor costs and increased efficiency. By 1840, the average American cotton textile mill was about 10 percent more efficient and 3 percent more profitable than its British counterpart.

Although the shortage of labor in the United States stimulated technological innovations that replaced humans with machines, the rapid spread of education after 1800 also spurred innovation and productivity. By 1840, most whites were literate, and public schools were educating 38.4 percent of white children between ages 5 and 19. The belief that education meant economic growth fostered enthusiasm for public education, particularly in the Northeast.

The development of the Massachusetts Common School illustrates the connections many saw between education and progress. Although several states had decided to use tax monies for education by 1800, Massachusetts was the first to move toward mass education. In 1827, it mandated that taxes pay the whole cost of the state's public schools, and in 1836 it forbade factory managers to hire children who had not spent 3 of the previous 12

DOCUMENT

Horace Mann, Report of the Massachusetts Board of Education (1848) months in school. Still, the Massachusetts school system limped along with run-down school buildings, nonexistent curricula, and students with nothing to do.

Under the leadership of Horace Mann, the reform of state education for white children began in earnest in 1837. He and others pressed for graded schools, uniform curricula, and teacher training, and fought the local control that often blocked progress. Mann's success inspired reformers everywhere. For the first time in American history, primary education became the rule for most children outside the South between ages 5 and 19. The expansion of education created a whole new career of schoolteaching, mostly attracting young women.

Mann believed that education promoted inventiveness. Businessmen often agreed. Prominent industrialists in the 1840s were convinced that education produced reliable workers who could handle complex machinery without undue supervision. Manufacturers valued education not merely because of its intellectual content, but also because it encouraged habits necessary for a disciplined and productive workforce

Ambivalence Toward Change

While supporting education as a means to economic growth, many Americans, like their European counterparts, also firmly believed in its social value. They expected the public schools to mold student character and promote "virtuous habits" and "rational self-governing" behavior. Many school activities sought to instill good habits. Students learned facts by rote because memory work and recitation taught them discipline and concentration. Nineteenth-century schoolbooks reinforced classroom goals. "It is a great sin to be idle," children read in one 1830 text, and another encouragingly pointed out, "He who rises early and is industrious and temperate will acquire health and riches."

The concern with education and character indicates that Americans both welcomed economic progress and feared its results. The improvements in transportation that encouraged trade and emigration, for example, created anxieties that civilization might disintegrate as people moved far from their place of birth and familiar institutions. Others worried that rapid change undermined the American family. Schools, which taught students to be deferential, obedient, and punctual, could counter the worst by-products of change. The schools served as much as a defense against change as they did its agent.

A Young Woman and Her Book This photograph of a young woman can be dated to the 1850s by the clothing she wears. What hints of her social status does this photograph provide? Can you discern the character of the book she is studying? How many signs of the impact of the Industrial Revolution can you find here? *(A sixth plate daguerreotype from the collection of Mark Koenigsberg)*

Other signs of cultural uneasiness appeared. In the eighteenth century, Benjamin Franklin emphasized the importance of hard work in his celebrated *Poor Richard's Almanack*. In the 1830s, popularizers restated Franklin's message. As the publishing revolution lowered costs and speeded the production of printed material, authors poured out tracts, stories, and manuals on how to get ahead. Claiming that hard work and good character led to success, they touted the virtues of diligence, punctuality, temperance, and thrift. These habits probably did assist economic growth. Slothful workers are seldom productive. Industry and perseverance often pay off. But the success of early nineteenth-century economic ventures frequently depended on the ability to take risks and to think daringly. The emphasis these publicists gave to the safe but stolid virtues and behavior suggests their fear of social disintegration. Their books and tracts aimed to counter unsettling effects of change and ensure the dominance of middle-class values.

The Advance of Industrialization

As had been true for Great Britain in the eighteenth century, the advance of industrialization in the

Julia Hieronymus, Trials of a Teacher

After her father's financial reversals, Julia Hieronymus left home in 1819 to "commence life's struggle in earnest." Deciding to teach school in the Virginia town of Wytheville, Hieronymus rented a room capable of holding up to 40 students. She discovered that her work was not all smooth sailing, however.

My first serious difficulty was with a little girl about ten years of age, the youngest child of a large family, who had been badly spoiled at home. She was noisy, indolent, and impatient under restraint. Continually teasing and annoying others, this little nettle-top went on from bad to worse, until endurance was no longer a virtue. I was anxious to keep her in school, as I had five from the same family, and it was quite to my interest to get along pleasantly with her. But it could not be. One afternoon her resistance to my authority reached its climax; so I quietly removed her from the school-room to an adjoining apartment and gave her the well-merited punishment with my slipper, the first she had ever had in her life. Her screams were terrific. There was an awful silence in the school-room, and you might have heard a pin drop, as I led her back, and, placing the bonnet on her head, ordered her to go home and never return. I then quietly resumed my seat, and the lessons proceeded as usual until the hour of dismissal.

■ *What does this passage reveal about Hieronymus's expectations about her students' behavior?*

■ *What does it reveal about the realities of teaching?*

■ *Hieronymus went on to explain that following this incident she wept and prayed. Why do you think she was so upset?*

United States fueled economic growth in the decades before the Civil War. As was also the case in Britain, economic changes spilled over to transform many other aspects of life. The types of work people did, the places where they labored, and the relationships they had with their bosses were all affected by new modes of production. The American class system was modified as a new working class dependent on wages emerged and as a new middle class took shape.

Factory production moved away from the decentralized system of artisan or family-based manufacturing using hand tools and reorganized work by breaking down the manufacture of an article into discrete steps. Initially, early manufacturers often relied on what came to be called the "putting-out" system. Their strategy was to gain control of the raw materials from which goods were fashioned—leather in the case of shoes; cotton, flax, and wool for textiles—and the arrangements for marketing the finished products. Some steps in the manufacturing process they farmed out to workers in shops and homes, paying them on a piecework basis, for the pieces they were able to "put out." Manufacturers consolidated other steps in their own central shops.

The putting-out system not only reorganized production but also entangled rural families in the market economy and affected their relationships with one another. Early pieceworkers might labor as a family unit, leaving men to exercise their power as fathers and husbands. But by the 1830s, men were moving into the workplace, while wives and daughters continued to take in piecework. Usually, the women worked only intermittently. They took in shoes or made palm-leaf hats to pay off a family debt or to earn some cash for a desirable new good like cotton cloth or an iron cookstove. While most outworkers were not highly paid, they enjoyed earning their own cash and store credit. Piecework provided them with a new kind of independence even as they continued to stay at home.

The putting-out system persisted even as some manufacturers moved to consolidate all the steps of production under one roof. Hand labor gradually gave way to power-driven machinery such as wooden "spinning jennies." Often manufacturers sought the help of British immigrants who had the practical experience and technical know-how that few Americans possessed. As factory workers replaced artisans and home manufacturers, the volume of goods rose, and prices dropped dramatically. The price of a yard of cotton cloth fell from 18 cents to 2 cents over the 45 years preceding the Civil War.

The transportation improvements that provided the opportunity to reach large markets encouraged the reorganization of the production process and the use of machinery. The simple tastes and rural

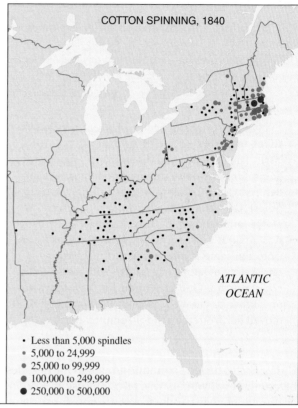

The Growth of Cotton Textile Manufacturing, 1810–1840

The concentration of textile manufacturing in New England suggests the changing economic and social trends in that region.

COTTON SPINNING, 1810

ATLANTIC OCEAN

• Less than 5,000 spindles
• 5,000 to 24,999
● 25,000 to 99,999

COTTON SPINNING, 1840

ATLANTIC OCEAN

• Less than 5,000 spindles
• 5,000 to 24,999
● 25,000 to 99,999
● 100,000 to 249,999
● 250,000 to 500,000

character of the American people suggested the wisdom of manufacturing inexpensive everyday goods such as cloth and shoes rather than luxuries for the rich.

Between 1820 and 1860, textile manufacturing became the country's leading industry. Textile mills sprang up across the New England and mid-Atlantic states, regions with swift-flowing streams to power the mills, capitalists eager to finance the ventures, children and women to tend the machines, and numerous cities and towns with ready markets for cheap textiles. Early mills were small affairs, containing only the machines for carding and spinning. The thread was then put out to home workers to be woven into cloth. The early mechanization of cloth production did not replace home manufacture but supplemented it.

Experiments were underway that would further transform the industry. Closeted in the attic of a Boston house in 1813, Francis Cabot Lowell, a merchant, and Paul Moody, a mechanic, worked to devise a power loom capable of weaving cloth. Lowell's study of mechanical looms during his earlier tour of English and Scottish cotton factories guided their work. Eventually, they succeeded, and the loom they devised was soon installed in a mill at Waltham,

Massachusetts, capitalized at $300,000 by Lowell and his Boston Associates.

The most important innovation of the Waltham operation was Lowell's decision to bring all the steps of cotton cloth production together under one roof. The Waltham mill thus differed from mills in Rhode Island and Great Britain, where spinning and weaving were separate operations. Through this centralizing of the entire manufacturing process and workforce in one factory, cloth for the mass market could be produced more cheaply and more profitably. The work of maintaining the equipment in good order encouraged machinists to improve existing machines. Constant innovation thus helped mills make cloth ever more cheaply and quickly. In 1823, the Boston Associates expanded their operations to East Chelmsford on the Merrimack River, a town they renamed Lowell.

Most New England mills followed the Lowell system. But in the mid-Atlantic states, the textile industry was more varied. Philadelphia became a center for fine textiles, and Rhode Island factories produced less expensive materials. Maryland manufacturers, like those in Philadelphia, focused on quality goods. The cumulative impact of the rise of the textile industry was to supplant the home production of cloth, even though some women would continue to spin and weave for their families for some years to come, and hand-loom weavers would survive for another generation. In the process, Americans were transformed from a people clad in earth-colored homespun into a nation decked out in more colorful clothing.

Textile mills were an important component of the increasingly industrial character of the Northeast. The majority of the South's cotton went to England,

DOCUMENT
Technology and the Shoe Industry

but an increasing share flowed to northeastern mills. Other manufacturing concerns, such as shoemaking, also contributed to the Northeast's economy. By 1860, fully 71 percent of all manufacturing workers lived in this region of the country. Still other important manufacturing operations reached west and south from New England. The processing of wheat, timber, and hides using power-driven machinery was common in most communities of 200 families or more. Although one-third of them were clustered in Philadelphia, paper mills were widespread. The ironworking and metalworking industry stretched from Albany, New York, south to Maryland, and west to Cincinnati.

Environmental Consequences

Although canals, railroads, steamboats, and the growth of industry undergirded economic growth,

their impact on the environment was far-reaching and often harmful. Steamboats and early railroads, for example, depended on wood for fuel. So, too, did home heating stoves. Armed with new steel axes, lumbermen and farmers kept up with the increased demand for wood, and the eastern forest and the wildlife that lived there rapidly disappeared. Better transportation, which encouraged western settlement, also promoted forest clearance as individual settlers cleared land for crops and cut wood for housing. Sawmills and milldams interfered with spawning habits of fish, clogged their gills with sawdust, and even changed the flow of rivers. The process of ecological change, spurred by the desire for wood, recurred as lumber companies and entrepreneurs moved from the East to exploit the forests of the Great Lakes and the Gulf states.

IMAGE
Mill in West Virginia

As late as 1840, wood was the main source for the country's energy needs. But the high price of wood and the discovery of anthracite coal in Pennsylvania signaled the beginning of a shift to coal as the major source of power. While the East gradually regained some of its forest cover, the heavy use of coal resulted in air pollution. Steam engines and heating stoves poured out dirty fumes into the air. In New York City, one could see the evidence of pollution everywhere—in the gray cloud hanging over the city; in the smoke rising from its machine shops, refineries, and private houses; and in the acrid smells

THE MANCHESTER PRINT WORKS, AT MANCHESTER, N. H.

A New Hampshire Printing Factory *Gleason's Pictorial,* one of the many modestly priced publications that the introduction of steam-powered printing presses put within reach of the reading public, pictures the Manchester Print Works in New Hampshire in 1854. How has the mill complex been depicted? What signs of pollution does the picture convey? Men appear in the foreground, but more than half the workers in this calico factory were female. *(Library of Congress)* and black soot that were a part of daily life. Pittsburgh, considered by some the dirtiest city in the United States, was surrounded by "a dense black smoke" and rained down "flakes of soot" on houses and people alike.

Textile mills located along rivers and streams might present a prettier picture than the shops and refineries of New York because they used water as the source of power. But mills also adversely affected the environment. Dams and canals supporting industrial activities contributed to soil erosion. "Industrial operations," declared the Vermont fish commissioner in 1857, are "destructive to fish that live or spawn in fresh water. . . . The thousand deleterious mineral substances, discharged into rivers from metallurgical, chemical, and manufacturing establishments, poison them by shoals."

Some Americans were aware of the environmental consequences of rapid growth and change. Author James Fenimore Cooper had one of his characters in his novel *The Pioneers* condemn those who destroyed nature "without remorse and without shame." The popularity in the 1820s of a song with the lines "Woodman, / Spare that tree / Touch not a single bough" suggested sympathy for that point of view. Yet most Americans accepted the changing environment as an inevitable part of progress.

EARLY MANUFACTURING

Industrialization created a more efficient means of producing more goods at much lower cost than had been possible in the homes and small shops of an earlier day. Philadelphian Samuel Breck's diary reveals some of the new profusion and range of goods. "Went to town principally to see the Exhibition of American Manufactures at the Masonic Hall," he noted in 1833. "More than 700 articles have been sent. . . . porcelains, beautiful Canton cotton . . . soft and capacious blankets, silver plate, cabinet ware, marble mantels, splendid pianos and centre tables, chymical drugs, hardware, saddlery, and the most beautiful black broadcloth I ever saw."

Two examples illustrate how industrialization transformed American life in both simple and complex ways. Before the nineteenth century, local printing shops depended on manual labor to produce books, newspapers, and journals. The cost of reading material was high enough to make a library a sign of wealth. Many literate families of moderate means had little in their homes to read other than a family Bible and an almanac.

Calico Factory,
1854

Between 1830 and 1850, however, adoption and improvement of British inventions revolutionized the printing and publishing industries. Like other changes in production, the transformation of publishing involved not only technological but also managerial and marketing innovations. A $2.5 million market in 1830, the book business quintupled by 1850.

As books and magazines dropped in cost and grew in number, far more people could afford them. Without this new mass market of readers, Susan Warner's literary success would hardly have been possible. But the implications of the changes in publishing went beyond best sellers. The presence of inexpensive reading material inspired and nourished literacy. Easy access to reading material also encouraged a new sort of independence. No longer needing to rely solely on the words of the "better sort" for information, people could form their own views on the basis of what they read. At the same time, however, readers everywhere were exposed repeatedly to the mainstream norms, values, and ideas expressed in magazines and books. Even on the frontier, pioneer women could study inexpensive ladies' magazines and books of domestic advice or be inspired by the pious example of Ellen Montgomery in *The Wide, Wide World.* Their husbands could follow the latest political news, market prices, or theories about scientific farming while the children learned their letters and the moral lesson in McGuffey readers. The proliferation of printed matter had an enormous impact on people's stock of information, values, tastes, and use of leisure time.

Just as printed materials wrought great changes in American life, the making of inexpensive timepieces affected its pace and rhythms. Before the 1830s, when few Americans could afford a clock, it was difficult to make exact plans or to establish rigid schedules. But the production of timepieces soared in the 1830s, and by midcentury, peddlers had carried inexpensive, mass-produced wooden clocks everywhere. Even on the frontier, "in cabins where there was not a chair to sit on," according to one observer, "there was sure to be a Connecticut clock." Free of nature's irregular divisions of the day, Americans could decide how to use their time and coordinate their activities. Clocks encouraged a more disciplined use of time and undergirded the economic changes taking place. Timepieces, for example, were essential for the successful operation of steamboats and railroads, which ran on schedules.

Clocks also imposed a new rhythm in many workplaces. For some Americans, the clock represented a form of oppression rather than liberation.

An early mill song put it directly: "The factory bell begins to ring / And we must all obey, / And to our old employment go / Or else be turned away."

A NEW ENGLAND TEXTILE TOWN

The process of industrialization and its impact on work and the workforce are well illustrated by Lowell, the "model" Massachusetts textile town, and Cincinnati, a bustling midwestern industrial center. Though the communities shared certain traits, there were also significant differences. Lowell reveals the importance of women in the early stages of industrialization while Cincinnati shows that industrialization was often an uneven and complex process.

Lowell was planned and built for industrial purposes in the 1820s. Planners focused on its shops, mills, and worker housing, but the bustling town had a charm that prompted visitors to see it as a model factory community. In 1836, Lowell, with 17,000 inhabitants, was the country's most important textile center.

Lowell's planners, understanding the difficulty of luring men away from farming, realized that they might recruit unmarried women relatively cheaply for a stint in the mills. Unlike factory owners farther south, they decided not to depend on child labor. By hiring women who would work only until marriage, they hoped to avoid the depraved and depressed workforce so evident in Great Britain. New England factory communities, they hoped, would become models for the world. By 1830, women composed nearly 70 percent of the Lowell textile workforce. As the first women to labor outside their homes in large numbers, they were also among the first Americans to experience the full impact of the factory system.

Working and Living in a Mill Town

At age 15, Mary Paul wrote to her father asking him "to consent to let me go to Lowell if you can." This young woman from Vermont was typical of those drawn to work in Lowell. In 1830, more than 63 percent of Lowell's population was female, and most were between ages 15 and 29.

Women workers came from New England's middling rural families and took jobs in the mills for a variety of reasons, but desperate poverty was not one of them. The decline of home manufacture deprived many women, especially daughters in farming families, of their traditional productive role. Some had already earned money at home by taking in piecework. Millwork offered them a chance for economic independence, better wages than domestic service, and an interesting environment. Few made a permanent commitment by coming to Lowell. They came to work for a few years, felt free to go home or to school for a few months, and then return to millwork. Once married—and the majority of women did marry—they left the mill workforce forever.

DOCUMENT

Letters of John and Elizabeth Hodgon (1840)

Millwork was regimented and exhausting. Six days a week, the workers began their 12-hour day at dawn or earlier with only a half hour for breakfast and lunch. Within the factory, the organization of space facilitated production. In the basement was the waterwheel, the source of power. Above,

Lowell Mill Workers

How does this engraving produced in the 1850s by the American Banknote Company picture the female workers tending their machines? The way in which these young women are concentrating on their task suggests that they had to pay close attention to their repetitive work. The engraving gives little idea of the tedium, noise, and other difficulties of millwork that the young women often mentioned in their letters. *(Print Collection, Miriam and Ira D. Wallach Division of Art, Prints and Photographs, The New York Public Library, Astor, Lenox and Tilden Foundations/Art Resource, NY)*

"A Week in the Mill," *Lowell Offering*, Vol. V (1845): 217-218

successive floors were completely open, each containing the machines necessary for the different steps of cloth making. Elevators moved materials from one floor to another. Under the watchful eyes of male overseers, the women tended their machines. Work spaces were noisy, poorly lit, and badly ventilated, the windows often nailed shut.

Millwork required the women to adapt to both new work and new living situations. Hoping to attract respectable and productive female workers, mill owners built company boardinghouses for them. Headed by female housekeepers, the boardinghouse maintained strict rules, including a 10 P.M. curfew, and afforded little personal privacy. The cramped quarters encouraged close ties and a sense of community. Group norms dictated acceptable behavior, clothing, and speech. Shared leisure activities included lectures, night classes, sewing and literary circles, and church.

The Harbinger, "Female Workers of Lowell" (1836)

Female Responses to Work

Although millwork offered better wages than other occupations open to women, all female workers had limited job mobility. The small number staying in the mills for more than a few years did receive increases in pay and promotions to more responsible positions. A top female wage earner took home 40 percent more than a newcomer. But she never could earn as much as male employees, who at the top of the job ladder earned 200 percent more than men at the bottom. Because only men could hold supervisory positions, economic and job discrimination characterized the early American industrial system.

Job discrimination generally went unquestioned, for most female operatives accepted gender differences as part of life. But the sense of sisterhood, so much a part of the Lowell work experience, supported open protest, most of it focused against a system that workers feared was turning them into a class of dependent wage earners. Lowell women's critique of the new industrial order drew on both the sense of female community and the revolutionary tradition and exposed the social gap between owners and operatives.

Trouble broke out when hard times hit Lowell in February 1834. Falling prices, poor sales, and rising inventories prompted managers to announce a 15 percent wage cut. This was their way of protecting profits—at the expense of their employees. The millworkers sprang into action. Petitions circulated,

threatening a strike. Meetings followed. At one lunchtime gathering, when the company agent fired an apparent ringleader, "she declared that every girl in the room should leave with her," then "made a signal, and . . . they all marched out & few returned the ensuing morning." The strikers roamed the streets, appealing to other workers, and they visited other mills. In all, about a sixth of the town's workforce turned out.

Though this work stoppage was brief, involved only a minority of workers, and failed to prevent the wage reduction, it demonstrated some women's concern about the impact of industrialization on the labor force. Strikers, taunted as unfeminine for their "amazonian display," refused to agree that workers were inferior to bosses. Pointing out that they were daughters of free men, strikers (as the words of their song suggest) sought to link their protest to their fathers' and grandfathers' efforts to throw off the bonds of British oppression during the Revolution.

> *Let oppression shrug her shoulders,*
> *And a haughty tyrant frown,*
> *And little upstart Ignorance,*
> *In mockery look down.*
> *Yet I value not the feeble threats*
> *Of Tories in disguise,*
> *While the flag of Independence*
> *O'er our noble nation flies.*

The women viewed threatened wage reductions as an unjust attack on their economic independence and also on their claim to equal status with their employers. Revolutionary rhetoric that once held only political meaning took on economic overtones as Lowell women confronted industrial work.

"A Second Peep at Factory Life," *Lowell Offering*, Vol. V (1845): 97-100

During the 1830s, wage cuts, long hours, increased workloads, and production speedups, mandated by owners' desires to protect profits, constantly reminded Lowell women and other textile workers of the possibility of "wage slavery." In Dover, New Hampshire, 800 women turned out and formed a union in 1834 to protest wage cuts. In the 1840s, women in several New England states agitated for the 10-hour day, and petitions from Lowell prompted the Massachusetts legislature to hold the first government hearing on industrial working conditions.

The Changing Character of the Workforce

Most protest efforts met with limited success. The short tenure of most female millworkers prevented permanent labor organizations. Protests mounted in hard times often failed because mill owners could easily replace striking workers. Increasingly, owners found that they could do without the Yankee women altogether. The waves of immigration in the 1840s and 1850s created a new pool of labor. The newcomers were desperate for jobs and would accept lower wages than New England farm girls. Gradually, the Irish began to replace Yankee women in the mills. Representing only 8 percent of the Lowell workforce in 1845, the Irish composed nearly half the workers by 1860.

As the example of Lowell suggests, the reality of massive immigration had a far-reaching effect on American life in the antebellum period. Immigration, of course, had been a constant part of the country's experience from the early seventeenth century. But it occurred on an unprecedented scale after 1845, as the nearby figure makes clear. What had been a trickle in the 1820s—some 128,502 foreigners came to U.S. shores during that decade—became a torrent in the 1850s, with more than 2.8 million migrants to the United States. Although families and single women emigrated, the majority of the newcomers were young European men of working age.

This vast movement of people, which began in the 1840s and continued throughout the nineteenth century, resulted from Europe's population explosion and the new farming and industrial practices that undermined or ended traditional means of livelihood. Poverty and the lack of opportunity heightened the appeal of leaving home. As one Scottish woman wrote to an American friend in 1847, "we can not mak it better [here]. All that we can duo is if you can give us any encouragement [is] to ama[grate?] to your Country."

Famine uprooted the largest group of immigrants: the Irish. In 1845, a terrible blight attacked and destroyed the potato crop, the staple of the Irish diet. Years of devastating hunger followed. One million Irish starved to death between 1841 and 1851; another million and a half emigrated. Although not all came to the United States, those who did arrived almost penniless in eastern port cities without the skills needed for good jobs. With only their raw labor to sell, employers, as one observer noted, "will engage Paddy as they would a dray horse." Yet, limited as their opportunities were, immigrants saved money to send home to help their families or to pay for their passage to the United States.

German immigrants, the second-largest group of newcomers during this period (1,361,506 arrived between 1840 and 1859), were not facing such drastic conditions. But as Henry Brokmeyer observed, "Hunger brought me . . . here [and] hunger is the

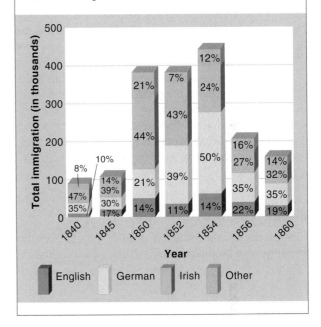

Immigration: Volume and Sources, 1840–1860

This chart captures the growing ethnic diversity of the country in the years before the Civil War. What is only implied is the element of religious diversity that immigration also introduced. Most of the Irish immigrants and half of the Germans were Roman Catholics. The presence of immigrants who differed so dramatically from Protestant Americans in background and culture contributed to the tensions of the period. Can you identify the period that witnessed the greatest influx of Roman Catholics?

cause of European immigration to this country." Some Germans, however, arrived with sufficient resources to go west and buy land. (The significance of this German midwestern presence is suggested by the fact that as late as 1940, German was one of the most common "street" languages in Minnesota.) Others like Brokmeyer had the training to join the urban working class as shoemakers, cabinetmakers, or tailors.

The arrival of so many non-British newcomers made American society more diverse than it had ever been. The consequences of this diversity were complex, as discussions in this and subsequent chapters will make clear. Because more than half of the Irish and German immigrants were Roman Catholics, a religion long feared and disliked by Protestants, religious differences acerbated economic and ethnic tensions.

The impact of the Irish presence in Lowell was far-reaching. As the ethnic makeup of the workforce changed in the city, so did its gender composition. More

DOCUMENT

Samuel F. B. Morse, Foreign Immigration (1835)

men came to work in the mills. By 1860, some 30 percent of the Lowell workers were male. All these changes made the Yankee women expendable and increased the costs of going "against the mill."

It was easy for New England women to blame the Irish for declining pay and deteriorating conditions. Gender no longer unified female workers, not only because there were more men in the mills but also because Irish women and New England women had little in common. The Irish mill girl who started working as early as age 13 to earn money for her family's survival had a different perspective on work from that of the older Yankee woman who was earning money for herself. Segregated living conditions further divided the workforce and undermined the likelihood of united worker actions in the 1850s.

Lowell itself changed as the Irish crowded into the city and New England women gradually left the mills. With owners no longer feeling the need to continue paternalistic practices, boardinghouses disappeared. A permanent workforce, once a nightmare to owners, had become a reality by 1860, and Lowell's reputation as a model factory town faded away.

Factories on the Frontier

Cincinnati, a small Ohio River settlement of 2,540 in 1810, grew to be the country's third-largest industrial center by 1840. With a population of 40,382, it contained a variety of industries at different stages of development. Cincinnati manufacturers who turned out machines, machine parts, hardware, and furniture were quick to mechanize for increased volume and profits. Other trades such as carriage making and cigar making moved far more slowly toward mechanization. Alongside these concerns, artisans such as coopers, blacksmiths, and riverboat builders still labored in small shops, using traditional hand tools. The new and the old ways coexisted in Cincinnati, as they did in most manufacturing communities.

No uniform work experience prevailed in Cincinnati. The size of the shop, the nature of work, the skills required, and the rewards all varied widely. In 1850, most Cincinnati workers toiled in small or medium-sized shops, but almost 20 percent labored in factories with more than 100 employees. Some artisans continued to use a wide array of skills as they produced goods in time-honored ways. Others used their skills in new factories, but they tended to focus on more specialized and limited tasks. In furniture factories, for example, machines did the rough work of cutting, boring, and planing, while some artisans worked exclusively as varnishers, others as carpenters, and still others as finishers. No single worker made a chair from start to finish. But all used some of their skills and earned steady

Cincinnati and the Ohio River In 1848, an unknown photographer took this picture of Cincinnati. The prominence of steamboats in the picture suggests the role that location and improvements in transportation played in the city's growth. Although the countryside is visible in the background, the rows of substantial commercial and industrial buildings make Cincinnati's status as a bustling urban center clear. *(Public Library of Cincinnati and Hamilton County, Ohio)*

wages. Though in the long run, machines threatened to replace them, these skilled factory workers often had reason in the short run to praise the factory's opportunities.

Less fortunate was the new class of unskilled factory laborers who performed limited tasks either with or without the assistance of machinery. In the meatpacking industry, for example, workers sat at long tables. Some cleaned the ears of the hogs, others scraped the bristles, others had the unenviable task of gutting the dead animals. Whereas owners in the industry profited from efficient new operations, workers received low wages and had little job security. Because they had no skills to sell, they were easily replaced and casually dismissed during business slowdowns.

The experience of Cincinnati's working women differed from that of their male counterparts. Cincinnati's large black community was so economically marginal that a majority of black women labored as washerwomen, cooks, or maids. Many white women were "outworkers" for the city's growing ready-to-wear clothing industry. Manufacturers purchased the cloth, cut it into basic patterns, and then contracted the work out to women to be finished in small workshops or at home. Like many other urban women, Cincinnati women sought this employment because husbands or fathers could not earn enough to support the family and because outwork often allowed them to labor at home. Middle-class domestic ideology prescribed that home was the proper sphere for women. Many working men supported this view because they feared that female labor would undercut their wages and destroy order in the family. Outwork, then, allowed poor married women to supplement their family income while honoring social norms.

Paid by the piece, female outworkers were among the most exploited of Cincinnati's workers. Long days spent sewing in darkened rooms not only often failed to bring an adequate financial reward but also led to health problems, including ruined eyes and curved spines. The successful marketing of sewing machines in the 1850s contributed to worsening working conditions and lower pay. The sewing machine made stitching easier, so the pool of potential workers increased and the volume of work that bosses expected grew. As tasks were further subdivided, work also became more monotonous. As one Cincinnati citizen observed, "As many as 17 hands" were employed on a single pair of pants.

Cincinnati employers claimed that the new industrial order offered great opportunities to most of the city's male citizens. Manufacturing work encouraged the "manly virtues" so necessary to the "republican citizen." Not all Cincinnati workers agreed. Like the Low-

workers in Lowell and other manufacturing communities, Cincinnati's laborers rose up against their bosses in the decades before the Civil War.

The working man's plight, as Cincinnati labor leaders analyzed it, stemmed from his loss of independence. Even though a manufacturing job provided a decent livelihood for some people, the new industrial order was changing the nature of the laboring class itself. A new kind of worker had emerged. Rather than selling the products of his skills, he had only his raw labor to sell. His "wage slavery," or dependence on wages, promised to be lifelong. The reorganization of work signaled the end of the progression from apprentice to journeyman to master and undermined traditional skills. Few workers could expect to rise to the position of independent artisan. Most would labor only for others, just as slaves labored for their masters. Nor would wages bring to most that other form of independence: the ownership of shop and home. The expression "wage slavery" contained a deep truth about the changed conditions of many American working men.

Workers also resented the masters' attempts to control their lives. In the new factories, owners insisted on a steady pace of work and uninterrupted production. Artisans who were used to working in spurts, stopping for a few moments of conversation or a drink, disliked the new routines. Those who took a dram or two at work found themselves discharged. Even outside the workplace, manufacturers attacked Cincinnati's working-class culture. Crusades to abolish volunteer fire companies and to close down saloons, both attacked as nonproductive activities, suggested how little equality the Cincinnati worker enjoyed in an industrializing society.

The fact that workers' wages in Cincinnati, as in other cities, rose more slowly than food and housing costs compounded discontent over changing working conditions. The working class sensed it was losing ground at the very time the city's rich were growing visibly richer. In 1817, the top tenth of the city's taxpayers owned more than half the wealth, whereas the bottom half possessed only 10 percent. In 1860, the share of the top tenth had increased to two-thirds, while the bottom half's share had shrunk to 2.4 percent. Cincinnati workers may not have known these exact percentages, but they could see growing social and economic inequality in the luxurious mansions that the city's rich were building and in the spreading blight of slums.

In the decades before the Civil War, Cincinnati workers formed unions, turned out for fair wages, and rallied in favor of the 10-hour day. Like the Lowell mill girls, they cloaked their protest with the mantle of the Revolution. Striking workers staged

Changing Occupational Distribution, 1820–1860

The decline of agriculture and the increased involvement in industrial pursuits are represented in this table. In what 20-year period did agriculture decline most dramatically? In what 20-year period did manufacturing increase most?

	1820	1840	1860
Agriculture	78.8%	63.1%	52.9%
Mining	0.4	0.6	1.6
Construction	—	5.1	4.7
Manufacturing	2.7	8.8	13.8
Trade	—	6.2	8.0
Transport	1.6	1.8	2.0
Service	4.1	5.0	6.4
Other	12.4	9.4	10.6

Source: U.S. Bureau of the Census

parades with fifes and drums and appropriated patriotic symbols to bolster their demands for justice and independence. Although they did not see their bosses as a separate or hostile class, labor activists insisted that masters were denying workers a fair share of profits. This unjust distribution doomed them to economic dependency. Because the republic depended on a free and independent citizenry, the male workers warned that their bosses' policies threatened to undermine the republic itself.

Only in the early 1850s did Cincinnati workers begin to suspect that their employers formed a distinct class of parasitic "nonproducers." Although most strikes still revolved around familiar issues of better hours and wages, signs appeared of the more hostile labor relations that would emerge after the Civil War.

As elsewhere, skilled workers were in the forefront of Cincinnati's labor protest and union activities. But their victories proved temporary. Depression and bad times always harmed labor organizations and canceled out employers' concessions. Furthermore, Cincinnati workers did not readily unite to protest new conditions. The uneven pace of industrialization meant that these workers, unlike the Lowell mill women, had no common working experience. Moreover, growing cultural, religious, and ethnic diversity compounded differences in the workplace. By 1850, almost half the people in the city were foreign born, most of them German, whereas only 22 percent had been in 1825.

As the heterogeneity of the American people increased, ethnic and religious tensions simmered. Immigrants, near the bottom of the occupational ladder, faced limited job choices and suspicion of their faith, habits, and culture. Protestant workers frequently felt that they had more in common with their Protestant bosses than with Catholic Irish or German fellow workers. These tensions exploded in Cincinnati in the spring of 1855. Americans attacked barricades erected in German neighborhoods, crying out death threats. Their wrath visited the Irish as well. Ethnic, cultural, and social differences often drove workers apart and concealed their common grievances. In many cases, disunity served economic progress by undermining workers' efforts for higher pay, shorter hours, and better working conditions, thus enabling businesses to maximize productivity and profits while minimizing the cost of labor.

URBAN LIFE

Americans experienced the impact of economic growth most dramatically in the cities. In the four decades before the Civil War, the rate of urbanization in the United States was faster than ever before or since. In 1820, about 9 percent of the American people lived in cities (defined as areas containing a population of 2,500 or more). Forty years later, almost 20 percent of them did. Older cities such as Philadelphia and New York mushroomed, while new cities such as Cincinnati, Columbus, and Chicago sprang up. Although urban growth was not confined to the East, it was most dramatic there. By 1860, more than one-third of the people living in the Northeast were urban residents, compared with only 14 percent of westerners and 7 percent of southerners. Although the majority of northerners still lived on farms or in small farm towns, the region was clearly urbanizing.

The Process of Urbanization

Three distinct types of cities—commercial centers, mill towns, and transportation hubs—emerged during these years of rapid economic growth. Although a lack of water power limited industrial development, commercial seaports such as Boston, Philadelphia, and Baltimore expanded steadily and developed diversified manufacturing to supplement the older functions of importing, exporting, and providing services and credit. New

IMAGE

Ships and Port at Mystic, CT

York replaced Philadelphia as the country's largest and most important city. The completion of the Erie Canal allowed New York merchants to gain control of much of the trade with the West. By 1840, they had also seized the largest share of the country's import and export trade.

A New Form of Building Construction The balloon frame, the most important technological improvement in building in the years before the Civil War, allowed the rapid construction of housing in new and old sections of the country. First introduced in 1839 in Chicago, the balloon frame was made of small, light, mill-cut pieces of lumber joined by factory-produced nails. Unlike the older forms of building construction that had used heavy timbers joined by handmade pegs and mortise-and-tenon joints, balloon frames were easy to put together and demanded only a few workers. Have you seen examples of a balloon frame house under construction today? *(W.W. Wilson, Constructing a Balloon Frame House, from Edward Shaw,* The Modern Architect, *1855. The Metropolitan Museum of Art, Harris Brisbane Dick Fund, 1934. [34.46.9])*

Access to water power spurred the development of a second kind of city, exemplified by Lowell, Massachusetts; Trenton, New Jersey; and Wilmington, Delaware. Situated inland along the waterfalls and rapids that provided the power to run their mills, these cities burgeoned.

A third type of city arose between 1820 and 1840, west of the Appalachian Mountains, where one-quarter of the nation's urban growth occurred. Louisville, Cleveland, and St. Louis typified cities that served as transportation and distribution centers from the earliest days of frontier settlement. In the 1850s, Chicago's most significant business was selling lumber to prairie farmers.

Until 1840, the people eagerly crowding into cities came mostly from the American countryside. Then ships began to spill their human cargoes into eastern seaports. Immigrants who could afford it, many of them Germans or Scandinavians, left crowded port cities for the interior. Those who were penniless sought work in eastern cities. By 1860,

fully 20 percent of those living in the Northeast were immigrants; in some of the largest cities, they and their children composed more than half the population. The Irish were the largest foreign group in the Northeast.

While a few cities, such as New York and Boston, provided parks where residents could escape from the sounds, noises, and smells of urban life, much about urban life was grimy and difficult, especially for those who belonged to the working class. Speculators, finding the grid pattern the cheapest and most efficient way to divide land for development, created miles of monotonous new streets and houses. Overwhelmed by rapid growth, city governments provided few of the services we consider essential today, and usually only to those who paid for them. Poor families devoted many hours to securing necessities, including water. The ability to pay for services determined not only comfort, but health.

Class Structure in the Cities

The drastic differences in the quality of urban life reflected social fluidity and the growing economic inequality that characterized many American cities. In contrast to the colonial period, the first half of the nineteenth century witnessed a dramatic rise in the concentration of wealth in the United States. The pattern was most extreme in cities.

Because Americans believed that capitalists deserved most of their profits, the well-to-do profited handsomely from this period of growth whereas workers lost ground. Philadelphia provides one example of these economic trends. The merchants, brokers, lawyers, bankers, and manufacturers of Philadelphia's upper class gained increasing control of the city's wealth. By the late 1840s, the wealthiest 4 percent of the population held about two-thirds of the wealth. Because more wealth was being generated, the widening gap between the upper class and the working class did not cause mass suffering. But growing inequality hardened class lines and contributed to labor protests.

Between 1820 and 1860, a new working and middle class took shape in Philadelphia and elsewhere. As preindustrial ways of producing goods yielded to factory production and as the pace of

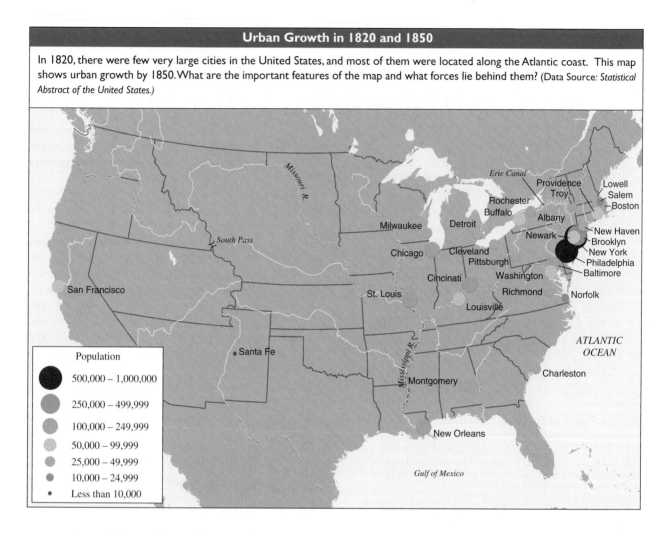

Urban Growth in 1820 and 1850

In 1820, there were few very large cities in the United States, and most of them were located along the Atlantic coast. This map shows urban growth by 1850. What are the important features of the map and what forces lie behind them? (Data Source: *Statistical Abstract of the United States.*)

Population

- 500,000 – 1,000,000
- 250,000 – 499,999
- 100,000 – 249,999
- 50,000 – 99,999
- 25,000 – 49,999
- 10,000 – 24,999
- Less than 10,000

economic activity quickened, some former artisans and skilled workers seized newly created opportunities. Perhaps 10 to 15 percent of Philadelphians in each decade before the Civil War improved their occupations and places of residence. Increasingly, membership in this middle class meant having a nonmanual occupation and a special place of work suited to activities depending on brainpower rather than brawn. But downward occupational mobility increased. Former artisans or journeymen became part of a new class of permanent manual workers, dependent on wages. Fed by waves of immigrants, the lower class grew at an accelerating rate. The percentage of unskilled wage earners living in poverty or on its brink increased from 17 to 24 percent between 1820 and 1860, while the proportion of artisans, once the heart of the laboring class, shrank from 56 to 47 percent.

The Urban Working Class

As with so much else in urban life, housing patterns reflected social and economic divisions. The poorest rented quarters in crowded shacks, shanties, and two-room houses. Because renters moved often, from one cramped lodging to another, it was difficult for them to create close-knit neighborhoods that might offer fellowship and assistance to offset the harsh conditions of daily life.

Substantial houses fronting the main streets concealed the worst urban housing, which was in back alleys or even in backyards. Many visitors did not even realize slums lay behind the rows of brick housing, nor did they know of the uncollected garbage, privy runoffs, and fetid decay in the dark, unpaved alleys. In his diary, Philadelphia shopkeeper Joseph Sill left a description of living conditions at the bottom. "In the afternoon," he wrote, "Mrs. S

Boston Slums

& I went to the lowest part of the City to see some poor persons who had call'd upon us for Charity. We found one woman, with two children, & expecting soon to be confined, living in a cellar, part of which was unfloored, & exhibited much wretchedness; but it was tolerably clean. Her husband is a Weaver, & had his loom in the Cellar, but has only occasional work."

What the Sills witnessed during their visit to the weaver's family was not just poverty but the transformation of working-class family life. Men could no longer be sure of supporting their wives and children, even when they were employed. Children as young as 10 might be working for wages or helping with piece-work. Women might be taking in work at home. Making ends meet colored family relations. Men felt they had lost much of their authority and power. Sons, earning their own money, did not necessarily respect their fathers. Husbands found themselves having to help with housework when wives were too busy. Observed one immigrant, "the idea of either husband or wife acknowledging one or the other to be 'Boss' [was] quite out of the question." With wives responsible for buying food at urban markets, husbands sometimes felt their wives were careless with their hard-earned money. When one woman failed to explain clearly what she had done with the grocery money, her angry husband "said if she did not give him a full account . . . he would kill her or something like that." The squabble ended in murder. This family was an extreme case, but family violence was not uncommon in working-class quarters.

Middle-Class Life and Ideals

Like the Sills, other members of the new middle class profited from the dramatic increase in wealth in antebellum America. They lived in pleasantly furnished houses, enjoying more peace, more privacy, and more comfort than the less affluent. Franklin stoves gave warmth in winter, and iron cookstoves made cooking easier. Conveniences such as Astral lamps made it possible to read after dark. Bathing stands and bowls ensured higher standards of cleanliness. Rugs muffled sounds and kept in the heat.

Material circumstances were one badge of middle-class status, but there were others as well. The acceptance of certain norms and values also identified a person as a member of the new middle class. Genteel behavior and the careful observance of elaborate rules of etiquette (for example, a gentleman was expected to back out of a parlor after making a call upon a lady), the appropriate clothes and conversation, an elegantly furnished parlor for the entertainment of visitors—all served to establish the standing of a middle-class family.

New expectations about the roles of men and women, prompted partly by economic change, also shaped middle-class life. In the seventeenth and eighteenth centuries, the labor of men and women, adults and children, all contributed to the family's economic welfare. But improved transportation, new products, and the rise of factory production and large businesses changed the family economy. Falling prices for processed and manufactured goods such as soap, candles, clothing, and even bread made it unnecessary for women, except on the frontier, to continue making these items at home.

As men increasingly involved themselves in a money economy, whether through commerce or

---

Wealth Distribution in Three Eastern Cities in the 1840s

Americans and foreign visitors often commented on the rough equality they believed characterized American life. What do these wealth distribution figures, although incomplete, suggest?

Level of Wealth	Percentage of Population	Approximate Noncorporate Wealth Owned	Percentage Noncorporate Wealth
Brooklyn in 1841			
$50,000 or more	1	$10,087,000	42
$15,000 to $50,000	2	$14,000,000	17
$4,500 to $15,000	9	$15,730,000	24
$1,000 to $4,500	15	$12,804,000	12
$100 to $1,000	7	$11,000,000	4
Under $100	66	—	—
New York City in 1845			
$50,000 or more	1	$85,804,000	40
$20,000 to $50,000	3	$55,000,000	26
Boston in 1848			
$90,000 or more	1	$47,778,500	37
$35,000 to $90,000	3	$34,781,800	27
$4,000 to $35,000	15	$40,636,400	32
Under $4,000	81	$16,000,000	4

Source: Edward Pessen, *Riches, Class, and Power Before the Civil War*, 1973.

market farming, women's and children's contributions to the family welfare became relatively less significant. Although middle-class women and children still worked in their homes as their husbands left to "bring home the bacon," they often neither produced vital goods nor earned money. Even the rhythm of their lives, oriented to housework rather than the demands of the clock, separated them from the bustling commercial world in which their husbands now labored. By 1820, the notion that the sexes occupied separate spheres emerged. Men's sphere was the public world, whereas women's was the domestic.

Men were charged with the task of financial support, a responsibility that (as Susan Warner's family experience suggested) was a heavy one in a changing economy. Women's duties included working at home—not as producer but as housekeeper. As the popular book *Whisper to a Bride* counseled readers, "For his sake . . . acquaint thyself with the knowledge that appertaineth unto a wife and housekeeper. If thou art deficient in this knowledge, rest not, till thou hast acquired it. It cometh readily to an attentive mind, and groweth with experience."

The role of housekeeper had both pleasure and frustration built into it. Susan Warner's celebration of domestic life in her novels suggested the satisfactions derived from a cozy household. Yet it was sometimes impossible to achieve the new standards of cleanliness, order, and beauty. Catharine Beecher's "Words of Comfort for a Discouraged Housekeeper" listed just a few of the problems—an inconvenient house, sick children, poor domestics—that undermined efforts to create a perfect, harmonious home.

Although women were expected to become "systematic, neat and thorough" housekeepers, whatever the personal costs might be, they were also given more elevated responsibilities as moral and cultural guardians of their own families and, by extension, of society as a whole. Believing that women were innately pious, virtuous, unselfish, and modest (all characteristics that men lacked), publicists built on the argument developed during the Revolutionary era. By training future citizens and workers to be obedient, moral, patriotic, and hardworking, mothers ensured the welfare of the republic. Just as important, they preserved important values in a time of rapid change. Because men had none of women's virtues and were daily caught up in the fast-paced world of business, wives were responsible for helping husbands cope with temptations and tensions. In the words of one preacher, a wife was the "guardian angel" who "watches over" her husband's interests, "warns him against dangers, comforts him

under trial; and by . . . pious, assiduous, and attractive deportment, constantly endeavors to render him more virtuous, more useful, more honourable, and more happy."

This view, characterizing women as morally superior to and different from men, had important consequences for female life. Although the concept of domesticity seemed to confine women to their homes, it actually prompted women to take on activities in the outside world. If women were the guardians of morality, why should they not carry out their tasks in the public sphere? "Woman," said Sarah Hale, editor of the popular magazine *Godey's Lady's Book*, was "God's appointed agent of *morality*." Such reasoning lay behind the tremendous growth of voluntary female associations in the early decades of the nineteenth century. Initially, most involved religious and charitable activities. Women supported orphanages, paid for and distributed religious tracts and Bibles, established Sunday schools, and ministered to the poor. The associations provided women with congenial companions and suitable tasks for their "moral character." In the 1830s, as we shall see in Chapter 12, women added specific moral concerns such as the abolition of slavery to their missionary and benevolent efforts. As these women took on more active and controversial tasks, they often clashed with men and with social conventions about "woman's place."

The notion of separate spheres established norms for middle-class men and women but were far more flexible than they appeared. Men played a much greater part in the household and in child rearing than gender proscriptions would suggest. Many women were active in the public world. Obviously, men were not always aggressive and rational nor were all women pious, disinterested, selfless, virtuous, cheerful, and loving. But these ideas influenced how men and women thought of themselves. It helped promote "male" and "female" behavior by encouraging particular choices, and it helped many men and women make psychological sense of their lives.

New norms, effectively spread by the publishing industry, also influenced rural and urban working women. The insistence on marriage and service to family discouraged married women from entering the workforce. Many took in piecework so that they could remain at home. Those who had to work often bore a burden of guilt. Though the new feminine ideal may have suited urban middle-class women, it created difficult tensions in the lives of working-class women.

As family roles were reformulated, a new view of childhood emerged. Working-class children still

Two Children This daguerreotype shows two children posed on an upholstered bench. Each child holds a book. While we do not know the identity of these children or even whether they were related, the image reveals new middle-class norms. The fact that the children are holding books suggests the importance now attached to primary education. Note the groomed hair styles and clothing. Neat appearance and cleanliness were also important middle-class values. The fact that the children are the subject of this picture hints at the importance attached to children in the middle-class family. (*The Library of Congress, LC-USZ6-1988 DLC*)

worked or scavenged for goods to sell or use at home, but middle-class children were no longer expected to contribute economically to the family. Middle-class parents now came to see childhood as a special stage of life, a period of preparation for adulthood. In a child's early years, mothers were to impart important values, including the necessity of behaving in accordance with gender prescriptions. Harsh punishments lost favor. As Catharine Beecher explained, "Affection can govern the human with a sway more powerful than the authority of reason or [even] the voices of conscience." Schooling also prepared a child for the future, and urban middle-class parents supported the public school movement.

Children's fiction, which poured off the printing presses, also socialized children. Stories pictured modest youngsters happily making the correct choices of playmates and activities, obeying their parents, and being dutiful, religious, loving, and industrious. Occasionally, as in *The Child at Home* (1833), the reader could discover the horrible consequences of wrongdoing. The young girl who refused to bring her sick mother a glass of water saw her promptly die. Heavy-handed moralizing made sure that children got the proper message.

The growing publishing industry helped spread new ideas about family roles and appropriate family behavior. Novels, magazines, etiquette and child rearing manuals, and schoolbooks all carried the message from northern and midwestern centers of publishing to the South, to the West, and to the frontier. Probably few Americans lived up to the new standards established for the model parent or child, but the standards increasingly influenced them.

New notions of family life supported the widespread use of contraception for the first time in American history. Because children required so much loving attention and needed careful preparation for adulthood, many parents desired smaller families. The declining birthrate was evident first in the Northeast, particularly in cities and among the middle class. Contraceptive methods included abortion, which was legal in many states until 1860. This medical procedure terminated perhaps as many as one-third of all pregnancies. Other birth control methods included coitus interruptus and abstinence. The success of these methods for family limitation suggests that many men and women adopted the new definitions of the female as naturally affectionate but passionless and sexually restrained.

Mounting Urban Tensions

The social and economic changes transforming American cities and festering ethnic and racial tensions in the half century before the Civil War produced unprecedented urban violence. Baltimore, Philadelphia, Boston, and New York experienced at least 35 major riots between 1830 and 1860, while cities whose populations reached 20,000 by 1850 also witnessed scenes of urban disorder. Mob actions sometimes lasted for days because there was no force strong enough to quell group disorder. American cities were slow to establish modern police forces. Traditional constables and night watches did not try to stop crimes, discover offenses, or "prevent a tumult."

An unsavory riot in Philadelphia in August 1834 revealed not only racial and social antagonisms but the inability of the city's police force to control the mob. Starting off with the destruction of a merry-go-round patronized by both blacks and whites, the riot turned into an orgy of destruction, looting, and intimidation of black residents. In the several days of violence, at least one black person was killed, and numerous others injured. As one shocked eyewitness reported, "The mob exhibited more than fiendish brutality, beating and mutilating some of the old, confiding and unoffending blacks with a savageness surpassing anything we could have believed men capable of."

This racial explanation overlooked the range of causes underlying the rampage of fury and destruction. The rioters were young and generally of low

RECOVERING THE PAST

Family Paintings

Although paintings are often admired and studied for artistic reasons alone, their value as historical documents should not be overlooked. In an age before the camera, paintings, sketches, and even pictures done in needlework captured Americans at different moments of life and memorialized their significant rituals. Paintings of American families in their homes, for example, reveal both an idealized conception of family life and the details of its reality. In addition, the paintings provide us with a sense of what the houses of the middle and upper classes (who could afford to commission art) were like.

Artists trained in the European tradition of realism painted family scenes and portraits, but so did many painters who lacked formal academic training, the so-called primitive artists. Their art was abstract in the sense that the artists tended to emphasize what they knew or felt rather than what they actually saw.

Some primitive artists were women who had received some drawing instruction at school. They often worked primarily for their own pleasure. Other artists were artisans, perhaps house or sign painters, who painted pictures in their leisure time. Some traveling house decorators made a living by making paintings and wall decorations. Many primitive paintings are unsigned, and even when we know the painter's identity, we rarely know more than a name and perhaps a date. Primitive artists flourished in the first three-quarters of the nineteenth century, eventually supplanted by the camera and inexpensive prints.

We see below a painting of the Sargent family done by an unknown artist around 1800. Though not an exact representation of reality, it does convey what the artist and the buyer considered important. Like any piece of historical evidence, this painting must be approached

Anonymous, *The Sargent Family*, 1800. *(The Sargent Family, gift of Edgar William and Bernice Chrysler Garbisch, Image © 2003 Board of Trustees, National Gallery of Art, Washington)*

H. Knight, *The Family at Home*, 1836. *(Private collection)*

critically and carefully. Our questions focus on four areas: (1) the individual family members and their treatment, (2) the objects associated with each, (3) the implied or apparent relationship between family members, and (4) the domestic environment. The painting gives us an idealized version of what both the painter and the subjects felt ought to be as well as what actually was. First, study the family itself. Describe what you see. How many family members are there, and what is each one doing? What seems to be the relationship between husband and wife? Why do you think Mr. Sargent is painted with his hat on? Who seems to dominate the painting, and how is this dominance conveyed (positioning, attitude or facial expression, eye contact, clothing)? What can you conclude about different "spheres" and roles for men and women?

Why do you think the artist painted two empty chairs and included a ball and a dog in this scene of family life? What do these choices suggest about attitudes toward children and their upbringing? What seems to be the role of the children in the family? What does the painting suggest about how this family

wished to be viewed? How do your conclusions relate to information discussed in this chapter?

Take a look at the room in which the Sargents are gathered. Make an inventory of the objects and furnishings in it. The room seems quite barren in comparison with present-day interiors. Why? Why do you think the chairs are placed near the window and door? What kind of scene does the window frame?

The *Family at Home,* painted by H. Knight in 1836, is a more detailed painting showing a larger family gathering almost 40 years later. Similar questions can be asked about this painting, particularly in relationship to the different treatment of boys and girls and the positioning and objects associated with each gender. There are many clues about the different socialization of male and female children. The family's living room can be contrasted with the Sargent family's room to reveal some of the changes brought about by industrialization.

REFLECTING ON THE PAST   How do these nineteenth-century homes and gender roles differ from those in colonial New England and the Chesapeake?

social standing. Many were Irish; some had criminal records. A number of those arrested, however, were from a "class of mechanics of whom better things are expected," and middle-class onlookers egged the mob on. The rioters revealed that in the event of an "attack by the city police, they confidently counted" on the assistance of these bystanders.

The mob's composition hints at some of the reasons for participation. Many of the rioters were newly arrived Irish immigrants at the bottom of the economic ladder who competed with blacks for jobs. Subsequent violence against blacks suggested that economic rivalry was an important component of the riot. But if blacks threatened the dream of advancement of some whites, this was not the complaint of the skilled workers. These men were more likely to have believed themselves injured by a changing economic system that undermined the small-scale mode of production. Dreams of a better life seemed increasingly illusory as declining wages pushed them closer to unskilled workers than to the middle class. Like other rioters, they were living in one of the poorest and most crowded parts of the city. Their immediate scapegoats were blacks, but the intangible villain was the economic system itself.

Urban expansion also figured as a factor in the racial violence. Most of the rioters lived either in the riot area or nearby. Racial tensions generated by squalid surroundings and social proximity go far to explain the outbreak of violence. The same area would later become the scene of race riots and election trouble and became infamous for harboring criminals and juvenile gangs. The absence of middle- or upper-class participants did not mean that these groups were untroubled during times of growth and change, but their material circumstances cushioned them from some of the more unsettling forces.

African Americans in Philadelphia This cartoon was one of a series titled "Life in Philadelphia." Philadelphia had a large, free African American community that often became the target for racial animosity. In what ways has the cartoonist presented a negative picture of the man and woman in the cartoon? Notice the exaggerated racial features of the two figures and the overelaborate clothing of the dandified man passing his card to the woman coming up from the basement. The verbal message reinforced the visual one. The man asks, "Is Miss Dinah at home?" The woman replies, "Yes sir but she bery potickly engaged in washing de dishes." He replies, "Ah! I'm sorry I cant have the honour to pay my devours to her. Give her my card." *(The Print & Picture Collection, The Free Library of Philadelphia)*

Finally, the character of the free black community itself was a factor in producing those gruesome August events. Not only was the community large and visible, but it also had created its own institutions and its own elite. The mob vented its rage against black affluence by targeting the solid brick houses of middle-class blacks and robbing them of silver and watches. Black wealth threatened the notion of the proper social order held by many white Philadelphians and seemed unspeakable when whites could not afford life's basic necessities or lacked jobs.

Ten years later another riot in Philadelphia illustrated the depth of religious and ethnic animosity in that city. Sparked by Catholic objections to the city's policy of using the St. James version of the Bible in the public schools, the controversy escalated from a disagreement over the use of the Protestant Bible to the accusation that Irish Catholics intended to "trample our free Protestant institutions in the dust." A mass rally organized by the nativists in an Irish immigrant neighborhood got out of hand and ended in violence. In the nights and days that followed, six people were killed and much immigrant property destroyed. Two Catholic churches were burned to the ground. As had been the case in 1834, the mob contained working-class men and boys. Also supporting the nativist cause, however, were middle-class men such as lawyers and doctors. Both groups resented the presence of Irish immigrants and feared that these outsiders threatened American culture, religion, and politics.

When the rioters torched St. Augustine's Catholic Church the second night of the disturbances, the city's mayor attempted to reason with the crowd. Rather than listen to the mayor, someone in the crowd threw a stone at him, knocking him down. Cheers went up as the church steeple toppled. Without an armed police force, city officials such as the mayor were powerless to stop mob actions. Each chaotic event made the London model more attractive, and eventually residents and city officials in Philadelphia (and in other large cities) supported an expanded, quasi-military, preventive, and uniformed police force. By 1855, most sizable eastern cities had established such forces.

The Black Underclass

Between 1800 and 1860, the number of free blacks in the United States grew dramatically, from 108,435 in 1800 to 488,070 in 1860. Most of these lived in northeastern cities, although Baltimore had the largest free African American population of all, and New Orleans also had a sizable free black community. While African Americans constituted a minority of urban residents, whites noted the increased numbers, often with negative feelings. As one African American woman confessed, white prejudice based on "dislike to the color of the skin" had "often embittered" her feelings.

Events in Philadelphia showed how hazardous life for free blacks could be. Although a small elite group of blacks emerged in Philadelphia and in other cities as well, most African Americans did not enjoy the rewards of economic expansion and industrial progress. Black men, often with little or no education, held transient and frequently dangerous jobs. Black women, many of whom headed their households because the men were away working or had died, held jobs before and after marriage. In Philadelphia in 1849, almost half of the black women washed clothes for a living. Others took boarders into their homes, thus adding to their domestic chores.

Northern whites, like southerners, believed in black inferiority and depravity and feared black competition. Although northern states had passed gradual abolition acts between 1780 and 1803 and the national government had banned slaves from entering new states to be formed out of the Northwest Territory, nowhere did any government extend equal rights and citizenship or economic opportunities to free blacks in their midst.

For a time in the early nineteenth century, some blacks living in the North were permitted to vote, but they soon lost that right. Beginning in the 1830s, in part because of the influx of fugitive slaves and manumitted blacks without property or jobs, Pennsylvania, Connecticut, and New Jersey disenfranchised blacks. New York allowed only those with three years' residence and property valued at $250 or more to vote. Only the New England states (with the exception of Connecticut), which had tiny black populations, preserved the right to vote regardless of color. By 1840, fully 93 percent of the northern free black population lived in states where law or custom prevented them from voting.

Other black civil rights were also restricted. In five northern states, blacks could not testify against whites or serve on juries. In most states, the two races were thoroughly segregated. Blacks increasingly endured separate and inferior facilities in railway cars, steamboats, hospitals, prisons, and other asylums. In some states, they could enter public buildings only as personal servants of white men. They sat in "Negro pews" in churches and took communion only after whites had left the church. Although most Protestant religious denominations in the antebellum period split into northern and southern branches over the issue of slavery, most northern churches were not disposed to welcome blacks as full members.

As the Philadelphia riot revealed, whites were driving blacks from their jobs. In 1839, *The Colored American* blamed the Irish. "These impoverished and destitute beings . . . are crowding themselves into every place of business . . . and driving the poor colored American citizen out." Increasingly after 1837, these "white niggers" became coachmen, stevedores, barbers, cooks, and house servants—all occupations blacks had once held.

Educational opportunities for blacks were also severely limited. Only a few school systems admitted blacks, in separate facilities. The case of Prudence Crandall illustrates the lengths to which northern whites would go to maintain racial segregation. In 1833, Crandall, a Quaker schoolmistress in Canterbury, Connecticut, announced that she would admit "young colored ladies and Misses" to her school. The outraged townspeople, fearful that New England would become the "Liberia of America," tried all sorts of persuasion and intimidation to stop Crandall.

Nonetheless, Crandall opened the school. Hostile citizens harassed and insulted students and teachers, refused to sell them provisions, and denied them medical care and admission to churches. Ministers preached against Crandall's efforts, and local residents poured manure in the school's well, set the school on fire, and knocked in walls with a battering ram. Crandall was arrested, and after two trials—in which free blacks were declared to have no citizenship rights—she finally gave up and moved to Illinois.

Crandall likely did not find the Old Northwest much more hospitable. The fast-growing western states were intensely committed to white supremacy and black exclusion. In Ohio, the response to talk of freeing the slaves was to pass "Black laws" excluding them from the state. Said one Ohioan, "The banks of the Ohio would be lined with men with muskets to keep off the emancipated slaves." In 1829 in Cincinnati, where evidence of freedom papers and $500 bond were demanded of blacks who wished to live in the city, white rioters ran nearly 2,000 blacks out of town.

As an Indiana newspaper editor observed in 1854, informal customs made life dangerous for blacks. They were "constantly subject to insults and annoyance in traveling and the daily avocations of life; [and] are practically excluded from all social privileges, and even from the Christian communion." An Indiana senator proclaimed in 1850 that a black could "never live together equally" with whites because "the same power that has given him a black skin, with less weight or volume of brain, has given us a white skin with greater volume of brain and intellect." A neighboring politician, Abraham Lincoln of Illinois, would not have disagreed with this assessment.

RURAL COMMUNITIES

Although the percentage of American workers involved in farming fell from 71 to 53 percent between 1830 and 1860, agriculture persisted as the country's most significant economic activity. The small family farm still characterized eastern and western agriculture, and farm products still made up most of the nation's exports.

Even though farming remained the dominant way of life, agriculture changed in the antebellum period. Vast new tracts of land came under cultivation in the West. Railroads, canals, and better roads pulled rural Americans into the orbit of the wider world. Some crops were shipped to regional markets; others, such as grain, hides, and pork, stimulated industrial processing. Manufactured goods, ranging from cloth to better tools, flowed in return to farm families. Like city dwellers, farmers and their families read books, magazines, and papers that exposed them to new ideas. Commercial farming encouraged different ways of thinking and acting and lessened the isolation so typical before 1820.

Farming in the East

Antebellum economic changes created new rural patterns in the Northeast. Marginal lands in New England, New York, and Pennsylvania, cultivated as more fertile lands ran out, yielded discouraging returns. Gradually, after 1830, farmers abandoned these farms, forest reclaimed farmland, and the New England hill country began a slow decline.

Those farmers who did not migrate west had to transform production. Unable to compete with western grain, they embraced new agricultural opportunities created by better transportation and growing urban markets. The extension of railroad lines into rural areas, for example, allowed farmers as far away as Vermont to ship cooled milk to the city. Other farmers used the new railroads to ship fruit and vegetables to the cities. By 1837, a Boston housewife could buy a wide variety of fresh vegetables and fruits, ranging from cauliflower to raspberries, at the central market. Cookbooks began to include recipes calling for fresh ingredients.

As northern farmers adopted new crops, they began to regard farming as a scientific endeavor. After 1800, northern farmers started using manure as fertilizer; by the 1820s, some farmers were rotating their crops and planting new grasses and clover to restore fertility to the soil. These techniques recovered worn-out wheat and tobacco lands in Maryland and Delaware for livestock farming. While farmers in the Delaware River valley were leaders in adopting new methods, interest in scientific farming was widespread. New journals informed readers of modern farming practices, and many states established agricultural agencies. Although wasteful farming practices did not disappear, they became less characteristic of the Northeast. Improved farming methods

Preparing for Market This 1856 print shows the farm as a center of human and animal activity and suggests the shifts in eastern agriculture that took place in the East as competition from the Midwest stimulated farmers to raise new crops for the market. The rise of commercial farming also encouraged technological innovation—the McCormick reaper was patented in 1834. *(Currier and Ives, Preparing for Market, 1856. Scala/Art Resource, NY)*

contributed to increased agricultural output and helped reverse a 200-year decline in farm productivity in some of the oldest areas of settlement. A "scientific" farmer in 1850 could often produce two to four times as much per acre as in 1820. Experimentation and the exchange of information also led to the development of thousands of special varieties of plants for local conditions by 1860.

Rural attitudes also changed. Cash transactions replaced the exchange of goods. Country stores became more reluctant to accept wood, rye, corn, oats, and butter as payment for goods instead of cash. As some farmers adopted the "get-ahead" ethic and entered the market economy, those who were content with just getting along fell behind. Wealth inequality increased throughout the rural Northeast.

Frontier Families

Many people who left the North during these years headed for the expanding frontier. After the War of 1812, Americans flooded into the Old Northwest. Early communities dotted the Ohio River, the link to the South. Concentrating on corn and pork, settlers sent their products down the Ohio and Mississippi rivers to southern buyers. In 1820, less than one-fifth of the American population lived west of the Appalachians; by 1860, almost half did, and Ohio and Illinois had become two of the nation's most populous states.

By 1830, Ohio, Indiana, and southern Illinois were heavily settled, but Michigan, northern Illinois,

Wisconsin, and parts of Iowa and Missouri were still frontier. During the next decade, land sales and settlement boomed in the Old Northwest. Changes in federal land policy, which reduced both prices and the minimum acreage a settler had to buy, helped stimulate migration. Eastern capital also contributed to the boom with loans, mortgages, and speculative buying. Speculators frequently bought up large tracts of land from the government and then subdivided them and sold parcels off to settlers.

DOCUMENT

"The Western Country," Letters in *Nile's Weekly Register*

Internal improvement schemes after 1830 also contributed to new settlement patterns and tied the Old Northwest firmly to the East. Wheat for the eastern market rather than corn and hogs for the southern market became increasingly important with the transportation links eastward. Between 1840 and 1860, Illinois, southern Wisconsin, and eastern Iowa turned into the country's most rapidly growing grain regions. In the 1850s, these three states accounted for 70 percent of the increase in national wheat production.

Although the Old Northwest passed rapidly through the frontier stage between 1830 and 1860, its farming families faced severe challenges. Catharine Skinner, who moved from New York to Indiana with her husband when she was 24, described her rigorous existence. "We are poor and live in the woods where deers roam plentifully and the wolf is occasionally heard," she wrote to her sister in 1849. "We are employed in honest business and trying to do the best we can; we have got 80 acres of land in the

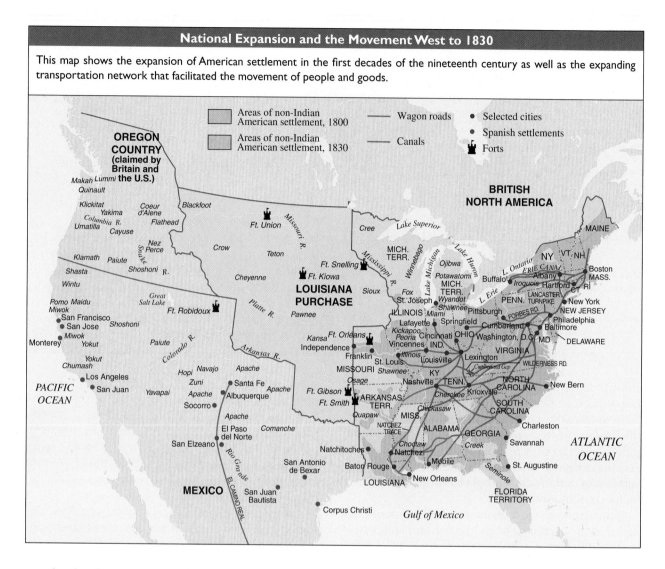

National Expansion and the Movement West to 1830

This map shows the expansion of American settlement in the first decades of the nineteenth century as well as the expanding transportation network that facilitated the movement of people and goods.

woods of Indiana, a very level country; we have got two acres cleared and fenced and four more pirty well under way; we have got about five acres of wheat in the ground; we raised corn enough for our use and to fat our pork . . . we have a cow so that we have milk and butter and plenty of corn bread but wheat is hard to be got in account of our not having mony."

The Skinners were typical. Western farms were small, for there were limits to what a family with hand tools could manage. A family with two healthy men could care for about 50 acres. In wooded areas, it took several years to get even that much land under cultivation, for only a few acres could be cleared in a year. Even on the prairies, the typical settler needed five years to get his farm in full operation.

Catharine Skinner mentioned the shortage of money and described her family as "poor." Although money was in short supply in the Northwest, she probably overstated her family's poverty. It took capital to begin farming—a minimum initial investment of perhaps $100 for 80 acres of government land,

$300 for basic farming equipment, and another $100 or $150 for livestock. To buy an already "improved" farm cost more, and free bidding at government auctions could drive the price of unimproved federal land far above the minimum price. Once farmers moved onto the prairies of Indiana and Illinois, they needed an initial investment of about $1,000 because they had to buy materials for fencing, housing, and expensive steel plows. If farmers invested in the new horse-drawn reapers, they could cultivate more land, but all their costs also increased.

Opportunities in the Old Northwest

It was possible to begin farming with less, however. Some farmers borrowed from relatives, banks, or insurance companies. Others rented land from farmers who had bought more acres than they could manage. Tenants who furnished their own seeds and animals could expect to keep about one-third of the yield. Within a few years, some saved enough to buy their own farms. Even those without any capital could work as hired hands. Labor was scarce, so they earned good wages. In Indiana, German settler Jacob Schramm hired men "to help with heavy labors of lumbering and field work, ditch-digging, and so on." Five to 10 years of frugal living and steady work for men like those hired by Schramm would bring the sum needed to get started.

Probably about one-quarter of the western farm population consisted of young men laboring as tenants or hired hands. Although they stood on the bottom rung of the agricultural ladder, their chances of moving up and joining the rural middle class were favorable. Widespread ownership of land characterized western rural communities. Lucinda Easteen knew as much when she told her younger sister to come to Illinois, where "you can have a home of your own, but never give your hand or heart to a lazy man."

Rural communities, unlike the cities, had no growing class of propertyless wage earners, but inequalities nevertheless existed in the Old Northwest. In Butler County, Ohio, for example, 16 percent of people leaving wills in the 1830s held half the wealth. By 1860, the wealthiest 8 percent held half the wealth. In a Wisconsin frontier county in 1860, the richest 10 percent owned 40 percent of all property. Although rural wealth was not as concentrated as urban, a few residents benefited more from rapid economic development than others.

Nevertheless, the Northwest offered many American families the chance to become independent producers and to enjoy a "pleasing competence." The rigors of frontier life faded with time. As Catharine Skinner wrote to her sister from her new Illinois home in 1850, "We here have meetings instead of hearing the hunters gun and the woo[d]man's ax on the sabbath."

Commercial farming brought new patterns of family life. As one Illinois farmer told his wife and daughter, "Store away your looms, wheels, [and] warping bars . . . all of your utensils for weaving cloth up in the loft. The boys and I can make enough by increasing our herds." Many farm families had money to spend on new goods. As early as 1836, the *Dubuque Visitor* was advertising the availability of ready-made clothing and "Calicoes, Ginghams, Muslins, Cambricks, Laces and Ribbands." The next year the *Iowa News* told of the arrival of "Ready Made Clothing from New York."

Agriculture and the Environment

Shifting agricultural patterns in the East and expanding settlement into the Old Northwest contributed to the changing character of the American landscape. As naturalist John Audubon mused in 1826, "A century hence," the rivers, swamps, and mountains "will not be here as I see them. Nature

---

TIMELINE

1805	*Palmer* v. *Mulligan*
1816	Second Bank of the United States chartered
1817	New York Stock Exchange established
1819	*Dartmouth College* v. *Woodward*
1820	Land Act of 1820 The expression "woman's sphere" becomes current
1823	City of Lowell, Massachusetts, founded by Boston Associates
1824	*Sturges* v. *Crowninshield*
1824–1850	Construction of canals in the Northeast
1825–1856	Construction of canals linking the Ohio, the Mississippi, and the Great Lakes
1828	Baltimore & Ohio Railroad begins operation
1830	Preemption Act facilitates western land acquisition by squatters
1830s	Boom in the Old Northwest Increasing discrimination against free blacks Public education movement spreads

1833	Philadelphia establishes small police force
1834	Philadelphia race riots Lowell work stoppage Cyrus McCormick patents his reaper
1837	Horace Mann becomes secretary of Massachusetts Board of Education
1837–1844	Financial panic and depression
1840	Agitation for 10-hour day
1840s–1850s	Rising tide of immigration Expansion of railroad system
1844	Anti-Catholic riots in Philadelphia
1849	Cholera epidemic in New York, St. Louis, and Cincinnati
1850s	Rise of urban police forces
1857	Financial Panic

will have been robbed of many brilliant charms, the rivers will be tormented and turned astray from their primitive course, the hills will be levelled with the swamps, and perhaps the swamps will have become a mount surmounted by a fortress of a thousand guns." His sense of the consequences of the movement of peoples and the exploitation of land was shared by one French visitor who remarked that Americans would never be satisfied until they had subdued nature.

More than the subjugation of nature was involved, however. When eastern farmers changed their agricultural practices as they became involved in the market economy, their decisions left an imprint on the land. Selling wood and potash stimulated clearing of forests, as did the desire for new tools, plow castings, threshing machines, and wagon boxes, which

were produced in furnaces fueled by charcoal. As forests disappeared, so, too, did their wildlife. Even using mineral manures such as gypsum or lime or organic fertilizers such as guano to revitalize worn-out soil and increase crop yields meant the depletion of land elsewhere.

When farmers moved into the Old Northwest, they used new steel plows, like the one developed in 1837 by Illinois blacksmith John Deere. Unlike older eastern plows, the new ones could cut through the dense, tough prairie cover. Deep plowing and the intensive cultivation of large cash crops had immediate benefits. But these practices could result in robbing the soil of necessary minerals such as phosphorus, carbon, and nitrogen. When farmers built new timber houses as frontier conditions receded, they helped fuel the destruction of the country's forests.

Conclusion

The Character of Progress

Between 1820 and 1860, the United States experienced tremendous growth and economic development. Transportation improvements facilitated the movement of people, goods, and ideas. Larger markets stimulated both agricultural and industrial production. There were more goods and ample food for the American people. Cities and towns were established and thrived. Visitors constantly remarked on the amazing bustle and rapid pace of American life. The United States was, in the words of one Frenchman, "one gigantic workshop, over the entrance of which there is the blazing inscription 'NO ADMISSION HERE, EXCEPT ON BUSINESS.'"

Although the wonders of American development dazzled foreigners and Americans alike, economic growth had its costs, as Susan Warner's novel made clear. Expansion was cyclic, and financial panics and depression punctuated the era. Industrial profits were based partly on low wages to workers. Time-

honored routes to economic independence disappeared, and a large class of unskilled, impoverished workers appeared in U.S. cities. Growing inequality characterized urban and rural life, prompting some labor activists to criticize new economic and social arrangements. But workers, still largely unorganized, did not speak with one voice. Ethnic, racial, and religious diversity divided Americans in new and troubling ways.

Yet a basic optimism and sense of pride also characterized the age. To observers, however, it frequently seemed as if the East and the Old Northwest were responsible for the country's achievements. During these decades, many noted that the paths between the East, Northwest, and South seemed to diverge. The rise of King Cotton in the South, where slave rather than free labor formed the foundation of the economy, created a new kind of tension in American life, as the next chapter will show.

Questions for Review and Reflection

1. List what you consider the most significant factors underlying American economic growth and explain why you think the factors you have chosen were so important.

2. Explain the ways in which Great Britain contributed to American economic development. How was American industry both similar to and different from British industry?

3. Compare and contrast industrialism in Lowell and Cincinnati.

4. How did economic changes transform the American class system and the relationship between classes?

5. What were the benefits and drawbacks of the economic and technological changes discussed in this chapter? Consider daily life, work, the division of wealth, gender roles, and community relations.

Recommended Reading

Recommended Readings are posted on the web site for this textbook. Visit www.ablongman.com/nash

Fiction and Film

Nathaniel Hawthorne's novel *The Scarlet Letter* (1850, but use any edition), although set in the Puritan period, reveals more about the attitudes and controversies of the antebellum period than it does about the seventeenth century. The novels of James Fenimore Cooper provide a picture of the impact of social and economic change on the frontier. Susan Warner's *The Wide, Wide World* (any edition) as well as her other popular novels provide an excellent picture of female interests and concerns in this period (although certainly not all her readers were women). The feature film *Little Women* (1994) presents a moving picture of the domestic and family life so idealized by the middle class. It also suggests the struggle of the middle class to maintain its status in difficult times. Some critics have pointed out that this adaptation of Louisa May Alcott's novel has strong overtones of contemporary feminism. *Out of Ireland: The Story of Irish Emigration to America* (1994) gives a vivid picture of Irish emigration between 1840 and 1920.

Discovering U.S. History Online

Whole Cloth: Discovering Science and Technology Through American History
www.si.edu.lemelson/centerpieces/whole_cloth/
The Jerome and Dorothy Lemelson Center for the Study of Invention and Innovation/Society for the History of Technology put together this site, which includes excellent activities and sources concerning early American manufacturing and industry.

19th-Century Scientific American Online
www.history.rochester.edu/Scientific_American/
Magazines and journals are windows through which we can view society. This site provides online editions of one of the more interesting nineteenth-century journals.

Jacksonian Medicine
www.connerprairie.org/historyonline/jmed.html
Survival was far from certain in the Jacksonian era. This site discusses some of the reasons for this as well as some of the possible cures of the times.

Penn 1830: A Virtual Tour
www.archives.upenn.edu/histy/features/1830
This "virtual tour" shows what a fairly typical campus looked like and what student life was like at one of the larger universities in the antebellum era.

A Brief History of Central Banking in the United States
http://odur.let.rug.nl/~usa/E/usbank/bankxx.htm
Of particular interest at this site is the section on the Second Bank of the United States (1816–1836).

The Erie Canal
www.syracuse.com/features/eriecanal/
This site features an overview of the history of the Erie Canal as well as the section "Life on the Erie Canal," built around the diary of a 14-year-old girl who traveled from Amsterdam to Syracuse, New York, in the early nineteenth century. It explores the construction and importance of the Erie Canal.

Inland Navigation: Connecting the New Republic, 1790–1840
www.xroads.virginia.edu/~HYPER/DETOC/transport/front.html
This illustrated site gives the history of American canals, rivers, railroads, and roads: "early systems of transportation [that] wove the new country together. . . ."

Lowell National Historic Park
www.nps.gov/lowe/home.htm
This well-illustrated site offers a detailed history of the Lowell textile mills and gives an overview of early manufacturing.

19th-Century Schoolbooks
http://digital.library.pitt.edu/nietz/
This site offers an insight into nineteenth-century education with full-text, digital reproductions of nineteenth-century textbooks as well as two texts on the history of textbooks.

The Gentleman's Page: A Practical Guide for the 19th-Century American Man
www.lahacal.org/gentleman/
Drawing from contemporary photographs and nineteenth-century etiquette books, this site lends insight to the attire and behavior expected of urban "gentlemen."

Common School Period
www.nd.edu/~rbarger/www7/common.html
This site presents several topics relevant to the 1840–1880 period in American education, including a brief illustrated biography of Horace Mann, information on the

"Catholic Controversy," compulsory attendance, and African American education.

Connor Prairie Living History Museum

www.connerprairie.org/historyonline/

This is the online counterpart to a nineteenth-century living history museum that offers illustrated essays such as "Clothing of the 1830s," "The American Woman of the Early Nineteenth Century" and "Jacksonian Medicine." The site also has a series of articles on "Life in the 1880s" and online versions of the museum's exhibits, including "Taming the Wilderness: Rivers, Roads, Canals, and Railroads."

A History of American Agriculture

www.usda.gov/history2/front.htm

This government Web site offers an interactive timeline of American agriculture that contains several topics, including "Economic Cycles," "Farm Machinery and Technology," "Life on the Farm," and "Government Programs and Policy."

Slavery and the Old South

The young Frederick Douglass, shown here in a photograph from about 1855, understood as well as any American the profound human, social, and political complexities and consequences of slavery. What qualities do you see in his face?
(Schomburg Center for Research in Black Culture/Art Resource, NY)

American Stories

A Young Slave Discovers the Path to Freedom

As a young slave, Frederick Douglass was sent by his master to live in Baltimore. When he first met his mistress, Sophia Auld, he was "astonished at her goodness" as she began to teach him to read. Her husband, however, ordered her to stop. Maryland law forbade teaching slaves to read. A literate slave was "unmanageable," "utterly unfit . . . to be a slave," he said. From this episode Douglass learned that "what he most dreaded, that I most desired . . . and the argument which he so warmly urged, against my learning to read, only served to inspire me with a desire and determination to learn."

In the seven years he lived with the Aulds, young Frederick used "various strata-gems" to teach himself to read and write. In the narrative of his early life, written after his dramatic escape to the North, Douglass acknowledged that his master's "bitter opposition" had helped him achieve his freedom as much as did Mrs. Auld's "kindly aid."

Most slaves did not, like Douglass, escape. But all were as tied to their masters as Douglass was to the Aulds. Nor could whites in antebellum America escape the influence of slavery. Otherwise decent people were often compelled by the "peculiar institution" to act inhumanely. After Sophia Auld's husband's interference, Douglass observed that she was transformed into a demon by the "fatal poison of irresponsible power." Her formerly tender heart turned to "stone" when she ceased teaching him. "Slavery proved as injurious to her," Douglass wrote, "as it did to me."

A slavebreaker, Mr. Covey, to whom Douglass was sent in 1833 to have his will broken, also paid the cost of slavery. Covey succeeded for a time, Douglass sadly reported, in breaking his "body, soul, and spirit" by brutal work and discipline. But one hot August day in 1833 he could stand it no longer; the two men fought a long, grueling battle. Douglass won. Victory, he said, "rekindled the few expiring embers of freedom, and revived within me a sense of my own manhood." Although it would be four more years before his escape north, the young man never again felt like a slave. The key to Douglass's resistance to Covey's power was not just his strong will, or even the magical root he carried, but rather his knowledge of how to challenge and jeopardize Covey's reputation and livelihood as a slavebreaker. The oppressed survive by knowing their oppressors.

As Mrs. Auld and Covey discovered, as long as some people were not free, no one was free. Douglass observed, "You cannot outlaw one part of the people without endangering the rights and liberties of all people. You cannot put a chain on the ankle of the bondsman without finding the other end of it about your own necks." After quarreling with a house servant, one plantation mistress complained that she "exercises dominion over me—or tries to do it. One would have thought . . . that I was the Servant, she the mistress." Many whites lived in constant fear of a slave revolt. A Louisiana planter recalled that he had "known times here when there was not a single planter who had a calm night's rest; they then never lay down to sleep without a brace of loaded pistols at their sides." In slave folktales, the clever Brer Rabbit usually outwitted the more powerful Brer Fox or Brer Wolf, thus reversing the roles of oppressed and oppressor.

Slavery in America was both an intricate web of human relationships and a labor system. Two large themes permeate this chapter. First, after tracing the economic development of the Old South in global context, in which slavery and cotton played vital roles, this chapter will emphasize the dreams, daily lives, and relationships of masters and slaves who, like Douglass and the Aulds, lived, loved, learned, worked, and struggled with one another in the years before the Civil War.

Perhaps no issue in American history has generated as many interpretations or as much emotional controversy as slavery. Three interpretive schools developed over the years, each adding to our knowledge of "the peculiar institution." The first saw slavery as a relatively humane institution in which plantation owners took care of helpless, childlike slaves. The second depicted slavery as a harsh and cruel system of exploitation. The third, and most recent, interpretation described slavery from the perspective of the slaves, who, like Douglass, did indeed suffer brutal treatment yet nevertheless survived with integrity, intelligence, and self-esteem supported by community and culture. While the first and second interpretive schools emphasized workaday interactions among powerful masters and seemingly passive, victimized slaves, the third focused on

357

the creative energies, agency, and vibrancy of life in the slave quarters from sundown to sunup.

In a unique structure, this chapter follows these masters and slaves through their day, from morning in the Big House through the hot afternoon in the fields to the slave cabins at night. Although slavery crucially defined the Old South, diverse social groups and international trade patterns contributed to the tremendous economic growth of the South from 1820 to 1860. We will look first at these socioeconomic aspects of antebellum southern life and then follow whites and blacks through a southern day from morning to noon to night.

BUILDING A DIVERSE COTTON KINGDOM

Many myths obscure our understanding of the antebellum South. It was not a monolithic society filled only with large cotton plantations worked by hundreds of slaves. The realities were much more complex. Large-plantation agriculture was dominant in the antebellum South, but most southern whites (75 percent) were not even slaveholders, much less large planters. Although rich slaveholding planters dominated the political and social life of the South, middling, yeoman "self-working farmers" with few or no slaves played a significant role. Most southern farmers lived not in imposing mansions but in modestly small or dark, cramped, two-room cabins. Cotton was a key cash crop in the South, but more acreage was actually planted in corn. Some masters were kindly, but many were not; some slaves were contented, but most were not.

There were many Souths, encompassing several geographic regions, each with different economic bases and social structures reflecting its own cultural values. The older Upper South of Virginia, Maryland, North Carolina, and Kentucky grew different staple crops from those grown in the newer Lower or "Black Belt" South, from South Carolina to eastern Texas. Within each state, moreover, the economies of flat coastal areas differed from inland upcountry forests and pine barrens. A still further diversity existed between these areas and the Appalachian highlands, running from northern Alabama to western Virginia. Southern cities, few in number—New Orleans, Savannah, Charleston, and Richmond—differed dramatically from rural areas.

Slavery in the South

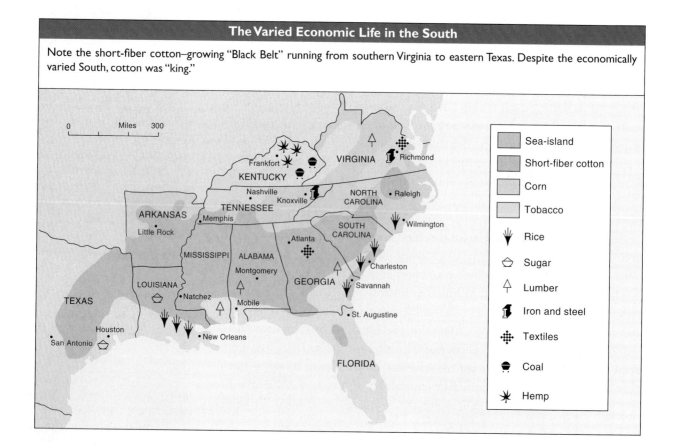

The Varied Economic Life in the South

Note the short-fiber cotton–growing "Black Belt" running from southern Virginia to eastern Texas. Despite the economically varied South, cotton was "king."

Although the South was diverse, agriculture dominated its industry and commerce. In 1859, a Virginia planter complained about a neighbor who was considering abandoning his farm to become a merchant. "To me it seems to be a wild idea," the planter wrote in his diary. Southerners placed a high value on agriculture. Slavery was primarily a labor system intended to produce wealth for landowners. Although slavery in older areas was paternalistic, with masters and slaves owing mutual obligations, increasingly it became a capitalistic enterprise intended to maximize profits. As such, it was tied into a growing international web of economic relations.

The Expansion of Slavery in a Global Economy

In the 20 years preceding the Civil War, the South's agricultural economy grew slightly faster than the North's. Personal income in 1860 was 15 percent higher in the South than in the prosperous states of the Old Northwest. If the South had become an independent nation in 1860, it would have ranked as one of the wealthiest countries in the world in per capita income, a wealth based mainly on cotton.

The world was deeply involved in the tremendous economic growth of the South in the early nineteenth century. The expansion of cotton depended on five factors: technological developments, land, labor, demand, and a global system of trade. The technological breakthrough was the cotton gin, invented by Eli Whitney in 1793, which allowed farmers to separate the cotton fibers from the sticky seeds in the hardier "short staple" cotton plant. The gin wedded the southern economy to cotton production, increased the need for more land and labor, and stimulated slavery's southwestward expansion into Alabama, Mississippi, western Tennessee and, with the Louisiana Purchase, into Louisiana, Arkansas, and eastern Texas. The opening up of vast new territories to cotton production brought the South into a global economy of trade.

Eli Whitney's Cotton Gin

For several centuries, British, Dutch, French, and Spanish merchants had been developing a worldwide system of trade, exchanging European manufactured goods for gold and silver from Latin America; silk, spices, cotton, and tea from China and India; and tobacco, coffee, sugar, and lumber from the Caribbean and North America. This international web of trade in turn motivated further technological developments, speeding the coming of the Industrial Revolution.

Starting in England in the late eighteenth century, the industrial factory system, made possible by an agricultural revolution providing surplus food and labor to cities, gradually replaced "putting out" various tasks to a cottage industry of rural people. Inventions of the spinning jenny, the flying shuttle, and the steam engine, which mechanized textile manufacturing, put textile production under one roof. Stimulating these developments was the demand by the British and other European nations' working classes to replace heavy linen and woolen clothes with lightweight, inexpensive cotton clothes. As British textile manufacturers sought to supply this demand, they eagerly bought all the cotton they could from the American South. Compared to the importation of only 22 million pounds of cotton from the United States in the pre–cotton gin year of 1787, by 1840, England imported 366 million pounds!

To meet this huge demand, southern farmers rushed westward to the fresh, fertile lands of the Gulf States to plant cotton as well as corn and other crops. Large-plantation owners, who alone could afford to purchase the gins, slaves, and vast lands needed to grow cotton, spread the plantation system southwestward. Despite the abolition of slavery in the North and occasional talk of emancipation in the South, slavery became more deeply entrenched in southern life. Thoughts of ending slavery were dispelled by one word: cotton.

Cotton Gin on a Plantation in Louisiana

Although more acreage was planted in corn, cotton was the largest cash crop and for that reason was called "king." In 1820, the South became the world's largest producer of cotton, and from 1815 to 1860 cotton represented more than half of all American exports. Cotton spurred economic growth not only in England but also throughout the United States. New England textile mills bought it; northern merchants profitably shipped, insured, and marketed it; northern bankers acquired capital from cotton sales; and western grain farmers found the South a major market for their foodstuffs.

The supply of cotton to Sheffield and Leeds in England, Brussels, and other European cities, as well as to Lowell and Lawrence, Massachusetts, grew at an astonishing rate. Cotton production soared from 461,000 bales in 1817 to 4.8 million bales in 1860, a more than tenfold jump.

Slavery in Latin America

Europeans depended on the slave-based economy in Latin America as well as in the American South. Africans were enslaved not only in Virginia and the

Carolinas but also in Jamaica, Barbados, Cuba, Martinique, and other European-owned islands in the West Indies, in Spanish Mexico and Central America, and throughout South America, including Portuguese Brazil, which at 1 million in 1800 had the largest slave population in all the Americas.

Historians used to argue that because of restraints of Catholicism, Roman legal codes, and the greater frequency of racial intermarriage, slavery was more benign and less barbaric in Spanish Latin America than in the United States, and that slaves enjoyed more dignity as people. Though it is true that Latin American slaves had more religious holidays and days of rest than in the North, and that caste distinctions based on gradations of color were more prevalent, it is now thought that slavery was just as harsh, if not more so, and that differences within Latin America and between Latin and North American slavery were more economic, demographic, and regional than religious and cultural.

Slavery emerged in Latin America out of economic necessity to provide labor where the indigenous population of Indians, decimated by both disease and intermarriage, could not be replaced. Sugar was to Latin America as cotton was to the southern United States, doubling in output at the beginning of the nineteenth century to meet growing European demands. In Cuba, Jamaica, and Barbados, and other Caribbean islands and in the Bahia region of Brazil, slaves were indispensable to the sugarcane industry, cutting, carting, milling, boiling, and refining sugar for a growing global market that included rum and other liquor distilleries. By 1840, Cuba was the world's largest producer of cane sugar.

Enslaved Africans also worked in Peruvian and Chilean vineyards and in cacao, coca, cotton, and tobacco fields throughout Central and South America. They toiled in Mexican, Colombian, Peruvian, Venezuelan, and Brazilian gold, silver, and copper mines; as construction menials, cowboys, tradespeople, dockworkers, teamsters, and muleteers for overland and maritime transportation; and as servants to royal and religious officials. Women were generally expected to perform the same physical labor as men.

The conditions of work in Bolivian mines and Brazilian sugar fields, for example, were as harsh as in southern Black Belt cotton fields, and perhaps even worse. Slaves labored in gangs yet were held accountable as individuals. As market demands for sugar increased in the nineteenth century, sugar growers pressured slaves to increase their productivity, which rose from 1,500 to 2,500 pounds per year. Since slaves could produce enough sugar within two years to equal the value of their purchase, they were

literally worked to debilitation and death, the average working life in the fields falling from 15 to 7 years and the death rate increasing from 6 to 10 percent. Whippings were used to enforce obedience, and strict supervision and control were maintained to prevent Africans from mixing with Indians and Europeans and from fleeing to nearby jungles to join communities of escaped slaves, called maroons.

Perhaps the most distinctive aspect of Latin American slavery was the heavy preponderance of enslaved African men and the absence of women and families compared to the United States. By the nineteenth century, the gender ratio was three men to every two women, with a 2:1 ratio on the sugar estates of Brazil and Cuba; as late as 1875, only one in six Brazilian slaves was recorded as married. The birthrate was lower in Latin America, 40 births per 1,000 compared to 50 per 1,000 in the United States, and the death rate was appalling, the result of hard work, tropical epidemic diseases, malnutrition, and an extremely high infant mortality rate. With low birthrates and lower life expectancy (age 23 in Brazil, 35 in the United States), the slave population in Latin America actually dropped in the nineteenth century. While Brazil's slave population climbed to just 1,510,000, numbers in the United States reached more than 4 million by 1860.

Unlike in the United States, where natural births increased the slave population, Latin Americans used the African slave trade to replenish lost labor. Between 1810 and 1870, after the 1807 abolition of the slave trade by Great Britain and the United States, nearly 2 million Africans were taken to the Americas, 60 percent to Brazil and 32 percent to Cuba and Puerto Rico, as compared to 2.7 percent smuggled illegally to the American South. The last American countries to abolish slavery were Cuba (1880) and Brazil (1888). Although official abolition of slavery was slow to occur, intermarriages among Europeans, Indians, and Africans in Latin America led to an increase in the population of free people of color, who by midcentury outnumbered slaves (80 percent in Brazil)—strikingly different from the United States, where free blacks constituted only 12 percent of the population.

Latin American slaves obtained their freedom by various means: through racial intermarriage, as payment for special favors and other contracts, in wills on a master's death, and by purchasing their own freedom by extra work and hiring out. Relative autonomy and incentives such as presents, privileges, extra rations, holidays, and their own gardens to supplement diet deficiencies were given to many Latin American slaves. One slaveholder manual said, "the slave who owns neither flees nor causes disorder." Thus, although conditions in Latin America were as harsh as or even harsher than in the American South, rights of slaves were more fluid, shifting with changing economic and demographic conditions.

White and Black Migrations in the South

Conditions changed in the United States, too. Seeking profits from the British and from the worldwide demand for cotton, southerners migrated southwestward in huge numbers between 1830 and 1860, pushing the southeastern Indians and Mexicans in Texas out of the way. Like northern grain farmers, southern farmers followed parallel migration paths westward. From the coastal states they trekked westward into the lower Midwest and into the Lower South. By the 1830s, the center of cotton production had shifted from the Carolinas and Georgia to Alabama and Mississippi. This process continued in the 1850s as southerners forged into Arkansas, Louisiana, and eastern Texas. A father and his sons would go first, find land and clear it, plant some corn and later some cotton, and begin to raise a cabin. Leaving the sons to finish, the father would return east, where his wife and daughters had been managing the farm, pack up the household, and bring it to the new home.

These migrating southern families were not only pulled by the prospect of fresh land, cheap labor, and new riches, but they were also pushed westward by deteriorating economic conditions. A long depression in the Upper South beginning in the 1820s affected tobacco and cotton prices, as years of constant use had exhausted formerly fertile lands. In a society that valued land ownership, farm families had several choices. One was to move west; another was to stay and diversify. Farmers of the Upper South therefore shifted to grains, mainly corn and wheat, which required less slave labor, and to selling slaves.

The internal slave trade from Virginia and the Upper South "down the river" to the Old Southwest thus became a multimillion-dollar "industry" in the 1830s. Between 1830 and 1860, an estimated 300,000 Virginia slaves were transported south for sale. One of the busiest routes was from Alexandria, Virginia, almost within view of the nation's capital, to a huge depot near Natchez, Mississippi, one of the richest large-plantation areas of the South, indeed a city with more millionaires than any other in the United States. Although southern states occasionally attempted to control the traffic in slaves, these efforts were poorly enforced. Besides, the reason for outlawing the slave trade was generally not humanitarian but rather reflected fear of a rapid increase in the slave population. Alabama, Mississippi, and Louisiana all banned the importation of slaves after the Nat Turner revolt in Virginia in 1831, resuming only in the profitable 1850s.

DOCUMENT

Frances E. W. Harper, "The Slave Auction" (1854)

Congress formally ended external slave imports on January 1, 1808, the earliest date permitted by the Constitution and the same year that Great Britain ended its slave trade. Enforcement by the United States was weak, and many thousands of Africans continued to be smuggled to North America until the end of the Civil War. The increase in the slave population was not the result of this illegal trade, however, but of natural reproduction, often encouraged by slave owners eager for more laborers and salable human property for higher profits.

A Slave Coffle This engraving of a group of slaves in chains depicts the stark inhumanity of the slave trade. Note the white man (in the right corner) raising the whip to hurry the slaves along. In front of him are a woman and child, and another woman stares at him in moral disbelief. What is your response to this engraving? *(Library of Congress)*

Southern Dependence on Slavery

The rapid increase in the number of slaves, from 1.5 million in 1820 to 4 million in 1860, marked southern economic growth and its dependence on both cotton and slavery. A Tennessee senator said that slavery was "sacred," the basis of civilization, and an English traveler noted that it would be easier to attack popery in Rome or Islam in Constantinople than slavery in the American South.

Although most slaves worked on plantations and medium-sized farms, just as in Latin America, they were found in all segments of the southern economy. In 1850, some 75 percent of all slaves were engaged in agricultural labor: 55 percent growing cotton, 10 percent tobacco, and 10 percent rice, sugar, and hemp. Of the remaining one-fourth, about 15 percent were domestic servants. The 300,000 slaves in 1850 who were not domestic or agricultural laborers worked as lumberjacks and turpentine producers in Carolina and Georgia forests; coal and salt miners in Virginia and Kentucky; boiler stokers and deckhands on Mississippi River steamships; textile laborers in Alabama cotton mills; dockworkers in Savannah and Charleston; and tobacco and iron workers in Richmond factories. A visitor to Natchez in 1835 saw slaves working as "mechanics, draymen, hostelers, labourers, hucksters, and washwomen."

Slave Dockworkers, 1860

Some southern industrialists, like William Gregg of South Carolina, argued that poor whites should be given preference for factory work. The Tredegar Iron Company of Richmond, which manufactured boilers and steam engines, axes and saws, and cannon and shot, decided in 1847 to shift from white labor "almost exclusively" to slave laborers, who were cheaper and not likely to organize. This strategy foreshadowed the many future companies that exploited black labor while putting an economic squeeze on organized white workers who, along with southern white artisans (blacksmiths, cabinetmakers, butchers, and tanners were threatened by black slave competition. Some even opposed slavery.

Tredegar Ironworks, Richmond

Whether in factories, mines, or cotton fields, slavery was profitable as a source of labor and capital investment. In 1859, the average plantation slave produced $78 in cotton earnings for his master annually while costing only about $32 to be fed, clothed, and housed. The "crop value per slave" increased from about $15 in 1800 to $125 in 1860. Enslaved women were likely to bear from two to six children, increasing their value. Slaves were a good

investment. In 1844, a "prime field hand" sold for $600. A cotton boom beginning in 1849 raised this price to $1,800 by 1860. A slave owner could prosper by buying slaves, working them for several years, and selling them for a profit.

The economic growth of the South was impressive, but the dependence on a cotton and slave economy was limiting. Generally, agricultural growth spurs the rise of cities and industry, but not in the Old South. In 1860, the South had 35 percent of the U.S. population but only 15 percent of its manufacturing. Just before the Civil War, one southerner in 14 was a city dweller, compared with one of every three northerners.

Some southerners were aware of the dangers of the single focus on cotton. De Bow's *Review,* an important journal published in New Orleans, called for more economic independence in the South through agricultural diversification, industrialization, and an improved transportation system. De Bow urged using slave labor in factories. But the planter class disagreed. As long as money could be made through a patriarchal, agricultural slave system that also valued honor and regulated race and gender relationships, plantation owners saw no reason to risk capital in new ventures.

De Bow's *Review,* "The Stability of the Union" (1850)

Paternalism and Honor in the Planter Class

The aversion to industrialism in the South stemmed from the fact that most southerners, inheriting traditions of medieval chivalry, Protestantism, and their Celtic Scots–Irish cultural heritage, espoused a lifestyle of refined paternalism based on a rigid sense of social-class hierarchy and obligations. Wealthy planters, emulating the aristocratic English landowning class, claimed a privileged status as social "betters" and insisted on being treated with deference by those below them. This was especially important for those living in elegant mansions in isolated areas surrounded by black slaves and envious poor whites, circumstances that led to a violent undercurrent throughout the South.

The head of the plantation had to care for his "inferiors," much like a kindly father. This meant providing the necessities of life to slaves (and white overseers), treating them as humanely as he could, and expecting faithful obedience, loyalty, and hard work in return. The plantation wife was an essential part of this culture. Placed on a pedestal and expected to uphold genteel values of sexual purity, spiritual piety, and submissive patience, she managed the household

ANALYZING HISTORY

Slavery Expands with the Cotton Boom

Although the South had a diverse agricultural economy, growing tobacco, rice, and sugar, cotton was the primary cash crop. Note the spectacular and simultaneous growth of cotton production and slave population between 1790 and 1860.

REFLECTING ON THE PAST   In what 20-year period did the greatest growth occur? By 1860, which states have the densest concentration of cotton production? Where are the most slaves? How do you explain any differences? Why, for example, were there so many slaves in Virginia and South Carolina? What were the implications of the increasing importance of cotton for U.S. exports for relations with other countries, especially England?

Cotton Production and Slave Population 1790–1860

= 200,000 slaves

= 200,000 bales of cotton production

= 1,000,000 bales of cotton production

1790
3,135
698,000

1820
334,000
1,500,000

1840
1,300,000
2,500,000

1860
4.8 million
4,000,000

In seventy years, the slave population quadrupled while cotton production increased more than 1,500 percent.

The cotton gin, invented by Eli Whitney in 1793, used a mechanized comb to remove the seeds from the cotton ball. Whitney's machine could clean the seeds out of the cotton faster than 50 people working by hand.

Cotton as a fraction of U.S. exports, 1800–1860

7.1% — 1800
32.0% — 1820
51.6% — 1840
57.5% — 1860

The demand for cotton came from Europe, especially England.

By 1860, slavery had extended throughout the South, with the greatest concentrations of slaves in the cotton-producing states (the "slave belt") of the Deep South.

● 500 slaves
● 1,000 bales

Southern Cotton Production and Concentration of Slavery, 1820 and 1860

1820

1860

and extended gracious hospitality to social equals. That she also had to put up with a double sexual standard and the hypermasculinity of plantation life made it all the more important that she reflect ladylike virtues and be fiercely protected.

This masculine code, which valued activities such as politics, war, hunting, and gambling, carried with it a rigid code of honor. Southern men enjoyed political and military ceremonies and reviews, as well as leisure activities of the hunt, cards, cockfighting, and horse racing. They were sensitive to lapses of appropriate, chivalrous behavior and to insults to their honor. Such slights led to duels, regulated by strict gentlemanly rules. One southern visitor said that the "smallest breach of courtesy" was "sufficient grounds for a challenge." Another described the life of the plantation elite in Natchez in 1847: "Many of the chivalric gentry whom I have been permitted to see dashing about here on highbred horses, seem to find their greatest enjoyment in recounting their bear hunts, 'great fights,' and occasional exploits with revolvers and Bowie knives." Although duels were outlawed in most states, the laws were routinely ignored. Ironically, the sometimes lawless and violent paternalistic code of honor in the Old South was intended to uphold law, order, and the plantation system.

Slavery, Class, and Yeoman Farmers

Slavery clearly served social as well as economic purposes. Although the proportion of southern white families that owned slaves slowly declined from 40 to 25 percent as some families sold slaves to cotton planters, the ideal of slave ownership permeated all classes and determined southern society's patriarchal and hierarchical character. At the top stood the paternalistic planter aristocracy, much of it new wealth, elbowing its way among old established families like the Byrds and Carters of Virginia. Some 10,000 rich families owned 50 or more slaves in 1860; about 3,000 of these owned more than 100. A slightly larger group of small planters held from 10 to 50 slaves. But the largest group, 70 percent of all slaveholders in 1860, comprised 270,000 middle-level, yeoman farm families with fewer than 10 slaves. The typical slaveholder worked a small family farm of about 100 acres with 8 or 9 slaves, who were perhaps members of the same family. The typical slave, however, was more likely to be one of 20 or more on a large farm or small plantation.

William Airs, a South Carolina low-country farmer, owned nine slaves and worked 130 acres of mostly cotton in 1850. A decade later, with the addition of

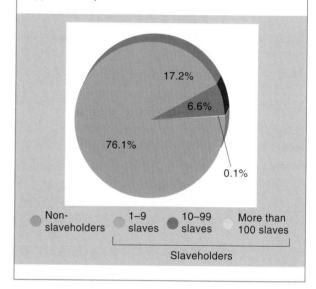

White Class Structure in the South, 1860

In a pyramidal class structure, the richest southerners were those few with the largest number of slaves. As the chart shows, three-fourths of antebellum southerners held no slaves at all. For what reasons did each class support slavery?

17.2%

6.6%

76.1%

0.1%

Non-slaveholders   1–9 slaves   10–99 slaves   More than 100 slaves

Slaveholders

one more slave, he was able to buy more land and produced 54 bushels of rice in addition to cotton. In 1841, a young white North Carolinian, John Flintoff, went to Mississippi dreaming of wealth and prestige. Beginning as an overseer managing an uncle's farm, he bought a "negro boy 7 years old" even before he owned any land. After several years of unrewarding struggle, Flintoff married and returned to North Carolina. There he finally bought 124 acres and a few cheap, young blacks, and by 1860, he had a modest farm with several slaves growing corn, wheat, and tobacco. Although he never realized his grand dreams, his son went to college, and his wife, he reported proudly, "has lived a Lady."

Slavery was a powerful force in the lives of middle-level farmers like Flintoff and Airs, who had only a few slaves. Economic, social, and political standing depended on owning slaves. Most white southerners thus supported slavery whether they owned slaves or not. They also defended the institution because it gave them feelings of superiority over blacks and of kinship, if not quite equality, with other whites. Although there was always a small element of southern society that believed in emancipation, most southerners did not. An Alabama farmer with a small farm told a northern visitor in the 1850s that if the slaves got their freedom, "they'd all think themselves just as

Plantation and Southern Commerce

good as we. . . . How would you like to hev a nigger feelin' just as good as a white man?"

Yeoman farmers also stoutly defended their independence and their property and lands as "self-working farmers." Small as it was, their land and household was indispensably important to their livelihood, self-esteem, and political rights in a region dominated by the privileged elite. Fiercely proud of their independence and jealously protective of their modest properties, the yeoman farmers struggled for a share of political power against the planters. Other than defending states' rights and their property against the national government (and sometimes against their powerful planter neighbors), yeoman political behavior focused on such local issues as militia organization and the election of sheriffs and tax collectors.

Yeoman farmers also defended their "households of faith," adamantly believing in an evangelical Christianity that endorsed the sanctity both of the family and of slavery. Acknowledging spiritual equality (slaves, one woman said, may have "souls as well as white people"), they practiced a measure of equality in their daily lives. The yeoman household economic

The Life of Yeoman Farm Families Southern yeoman farm families lived self-sufficient lives in cabins such as this one on the edge of a clearing. The isolation of the woman drawing water from a well was partly relieved by gatherings such as quilting parties, which created not only social contact but also a uniquely female American work of useful art. Note that men were also at the party, talking (politics, perhaps) by the stove, bouncing a baby, carrying food, and courting a young woman by the quilt. *(Above: Abby Aldrich Rockefeller Folk Art Museum, Williamsburg, VA; right: North Wind Picture Archives)*

system included wives, the older children, and perhaps a handful of slaves or one slave hired on weekends. A neighbor said of Ezekiel Stokes of South Carolina that his slaves "were but three or four for help, and he and his family worked with [them] in the fields."

The Nonslaveholding South

Below Airs, Flintoff, and other middling farmers lived the majority of white southerners who owned no slaves at all. Some 30 to 50 percent were landless. This nonslaveholding class, 75 percent of all southerners, was scattered throughout the South. Newton Knight, for example, worked a harsh piece of land cut out of the pines of southern Mississippi. He and his wife lived in a crude log cabin, scratching out their livelihood by growing corn and sweet potatoes and raising chickens and hogs. A staunch Baptist given to fits of violence, Knight had once killed a black.

Abner Ginn lived in the South Carolina low country, and although he had 560 acres in 1850, most of it was woodland and swamp, little of it cleared. On this land, worth only $1,000, he and his wife and nine children (six were under age 10) grew subsistence foodstuffs such as corn and sweet potatoes and managed a small herd of beef cattle and some dairy cows and pigs. He also managed to grow two bales of cotton for market. He had no slaves, though occasionally he would hire one to help him split rails, dig fence posts, and cut shingles. During the 1850s, as Ginn's children grew older and were able to help more, he brought more land under cultivation and added wheat, rye, rice, and some horses. More successful than most nonslaveholding whites, the "hard-working" Abner Ginn was called "a well-off poor man." Success mainly meant retaining his independence and land and increasing its value.

Living throughout the South but especially up-country in the Appalachian highlands, whites like

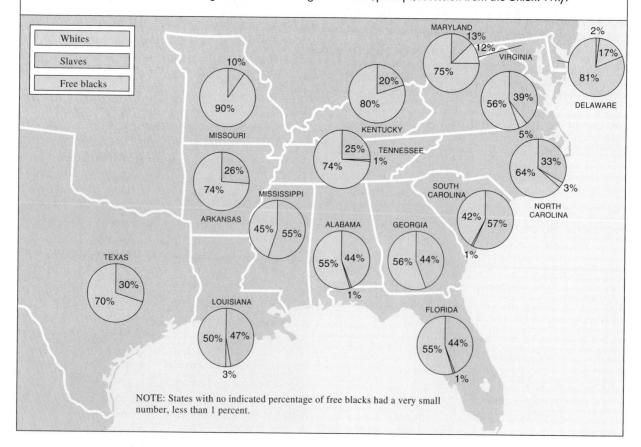

Population Patterns in the South: Whites, Slaves, and Free Blacks, by State, 1860

Where were most free blacks, and how would you explain their location? How do you explain the tiny percentage of free blacks in South Carolina, Florida, and Louisiana, and where do you think they were? Which two states had the largest percentage of slaves, and how do you think that affected the regulation of race relations? Given the data on this map, where would you predict the strongest sentiments among whites for states' rights and even, perhaps, secession from the Union? Why?

NOTE: States with no indicated percentage of free blacks had a very small number, less than 1 percent.

Ginn and Knight worked poorer lands than yeomen and planters. Far from commercial centers, they were largely self-sufficient, raising almost all their food and trading hogs, eggs, small game, or home-made items for cash and necessary manufactured items such as kettles and rifles. With the indispensable help of their wives and children, they maintained a subsistence household economy, making soap, shoes, candles, whiskey, coarse textiles, and ax handles. They lived in two-room log houses separated by a "dog run." Their drab, isolated life was brightened when neighbors and families gathered at corn huskings and quilting parties, logrolling and wrestling matches, and political stump and revivalist Baptist or Methodist camp meetings.

Nonslaveholding farmers were in the majority. In 1860 in North Carolina and even in the large plantation states of Mississippi and Louisiana, 60–70 percent of farms were less than 100 acres. Despite numerical majorities, these farmers were politically marginalized. Resenting the tradition of political deference to "betters," they were unable to challenge planters for political power. Most fought with the Confederacy during the Civil War; a few, such as those in southern Mississippi who organized a guerrilla band of Unionists, silently harbored Unionist views.

Another group was herdsmen raising hogs and other livestock, fed on corn or allowed to roam in the woods. These whites supplied bacon and pork to local slaveholders (who often thought hog raising beneath their dignity) and drove herds to stockyards in Nashville, Louisville, and Savannah. The South raised two-thirds of the nation's hogs. In 1860, the value of southern livestock was $500 million, twice that of cotton. However valuable the total size of the hog business, hog herdsmen were low on the southern social ladder.

Below them were the poorest whites of the South, about 10 percent of the population. Often sneeringly called "dirt eaters" and "crackers," they scraped out a living in isolated, inhospitable areas by growing vegetables, hunting small game, and raising a few pigs. Some made corn whiskey, and many hired out as farmhands for an average wage of $14 per month. Because of poor diet and bad living conditions, these poor whites often suffered from hookworm and malaria. This, along with the natural debilitation of heat and poverty, gave them a reputation as lazy, shiftless, and illiterate. An English visitor described them as "the most degraded race of human beings claiming an Anglo-Saxon origin that can be found on the face of the earth."

Poor whites stayed poor partly because the slave system allowed the planter class to accumulate a disproportionate amount of land and political power. High slave prices made entry into the planter class increasingly difficult, raising class tensions. Because large planters dominated southern life and owned the most slaves, slavery and the relations between slaves and masters is best understood by looking at plantation life during a typical day from morning to night.

MORNING: MASTER AND MISTRESS IN THE BIG HOUSE

It is early morning in the South. Imagine four scenes. In the first, William Waller of Virginia and a neighbor are preparing to leave with 20 choice slaves on a long trip to the slave market in Natchez, Mississippi. Waller is making this "intolerable" journey to sell some of his slaves in order to ease his heavy debts. Although he "loaths the vocation of slave trading," he must recover some money to see his family "freed from my bondage" of indebtedness. To ease his conscience, he intends to supervise the sale personally, thus securing the best possible deal not only for himself but also for his departing slaves.

On another plantation, owned by the wealthy James Hammond of South Carolina, the horn blows an hour before daylight to awaken slaves for field work. Hammond rises soon after, aware that to run an efficient plantation he must "draw the rein tighter and tighter" to hold his slaves "in complete check." In general, he says, "15 to 20 lashes will be sufficient flogging" for most offenses, but "in extreme cases" the punishment "must not exceed 100 lashes in one day."

On an Alabama plantation, Hugh Lawson is up early, writing a sorrowful letter telling about the death of a "devotedly attached and faithful" slave, Jim. "I feel desolate," Hugh writes, "my most devoted friend is gone." As Lawson pens his letter, a female slave, already awake, "walked across a frosty field in the early morning" to the big house to build a fire for her mistress. As the mistress wakes up, she says to the slave, a grown woman taking care of two families, "Well, how's my little nigger today?"

In a fourth household, a middling farm in up-country Georgia, Charles Brock awakens at dawn to join his two sons and four slaves digging up stumps and plowing fields of grains and sweet potatoes, while Brock's wife and a female slave tend the cows.

As these diverse scenes suggest, slavery thoroughly permeated the lives of southern slaveholders. For slaves, morning was a time for getting up early for work. But for white slaveholders, morning involved contact with slaves in many ways: as burdens of figuring profit and loss, as objects to be kept obedient and orderly, as intimates and fellow workers, and as ever-present reminders of fear, hate, and uncertainty.

The Burdens of Slaveholding

Robert Francis Withers Allston (1801–1864) was a major rice planter in a low, swampy, mosquito-infested tidal area of South Carolina where four rivers empty into Winyah Bay. It was a perfect spot for growing rice, but so unhealthy that few whites wanted to live there. The death rate among slaves was appallingly high. In 1840, a total of 18,274 slaves toiled there, but only 2,193 whites, many for only part of the year.

Robert was the fifth generation of Allstons to live in this inhospitable land. By 1860, he owned seven plantations along the Peedee River, totaling some 4,000 acres, in addition to 9,500 acres of pasture and timberland. He held nearly 600 slaves, 236 of whom worked at the home plantation, Chicora Wood. The total value of his land and slaves in the 1850s was approximately $300,000. Rich in land and labor, he had large mortgages and debts.

DOCUMENT

Overseer's Report from Chicora Wood Plantation (1858)

Allston was an enlightened, talented, public-spirited man. Educated at West Point and trained for the law, he did far more than practice agriculture. He served South Carolina for many years as state senator and governor. His political creed of "virtue and purity," he wrote in 1838, was based on "the principles of Thomas Jefferson." The core of his conviction was a "plain, honest, commonsense reading of the Constitution," which for Allston meant the constitutionality of slavery and nullification and the illegitimacy of abolitionism and the U.S. Bank. Allston also reflected Jefferson's humane side. Active in the Episcopal Church, he advocated liberalization of South Carolina's poor laws, an improved system of public education open to rich and poor, humanitarian care of disabled people, and the improvement of conditions for the Catawba Indians.

In 1832, Allston married the equally enlightened Adele Petigru. She participated fully in the management of the plantation and ran it while Robert was away on political business. In a letter to her husband in 1850, Adele demonstrated her diverse interests by reporting on family affairs and the children's learning, sickness among the slaves, the status of spring plowing, the building of a canal and causeway, the bottling of wine, and current politics. After Robert's death during the Civil War, she would assume control of the Allston plantations, abandoned when Union troops arrived.

Except during the worst periods of mosquitoes and heat, both Allstons were fully engaged in plantation operations. Managing thousands of acres of rice required not only an enormous investment in labor and equipment, but also careful supervision of both slaves and an elaborate irrigation system. Although working rice rather than cotton, Allston's concerns were typical of large planters.

His letters frequently expressed the burdens of owning slaves. Although Allston was careful to distribute enough cloth, blankets, and shoes to his slaves and to give them rest, the sickness and death of slaves, especially young fieldworkers, headed his list of concerns. "I lost in one year 28 negroes," he complained, "22 of whom were task hands." He tried to keep slave families together, but sold slaves when necessary. In a letter to his son Benjamin, he expressed concern over the bad example set by a slave driver who was "abandon'd by his hands" because he had not worked with them the previous Sunday. In the same letter, Allston urged Benjamin to keep up the "patrol duty," less to guard against runaway slaves, he said, than to restrain "vagabond whites." Clearly, the paternal planter class felt a duty to control lower-class whites as well as black slaves.

Other planters likewise saw slavery as both a duty and a burden. Many insisted that they worked harder than their slaves to feed and clothe them. R. L. Dabney of Virginia exclaimed, "there could be no greater curse inflicted on us than to be compelled to manage a parcel of Negroes." Curse or not, Dabney and other planters profited from their burdens, a point they seldom admitted.

The Plantation Mistress

Adele Allston and other plantation wives experienced other kinds of burdens. "The mistress of a plantation," wrote one, "was the most complete slave on it." Another complained, "It is the slaves who own me. Morning, noon, and night, I'm obliged to look after them," burdens that Adele Allston would have understood.

In accord with the southern code of honor, plantation mistresses were expected to adhere to domestic values by improving their husbands' morals, which often meant restraining them from excessive cruelty, and by beautifying their parlors for proper hospitality. They also suffered under a double standard of morality. Although they were expected to act as chaste ladies, their husbands had virtually unrestricted sexual access to slave women. "God forgive us, but ours is a monstrous system," Mary Boykin Chesnut wrote in her diary. "Any lady is ready to tell

George Fitzhugh, A Southern White Justification of Slavery

In his 1854 book, Sociology for the South, or the Failure of Free Society, *George Fitzhugh offered this among many defenses of slavery. What is your view of Fitzhugh's arguments?*

The negro race is inferior to the white race, and living in their midst, they would be far outstripped or outwitted in the chase of free competition. Gradual but certain extermination would be their fate. We presume the maddest abolitionist does not think the negro's providence of habits and money-making capacity at all to compare to those of the whites. This defect of character would alone justify enslaving him, if he is to remain here. In Africa or the West Indies, he would become idolatrous, savage and cannibal, or be devoured by savages and cannibals. At the North he would freeze or starve.

We would remind those who deprecate and sympathize with negro slavery, that his slavery here relieves him from a far more cruel slavery in Africa, or from idolatry and cannibalism, and every brutal vice and crime that can disgrace humanity; and that it Christianizes, protects, supports and civilizes him; that it governs him far better than free laborers at the North are governed. . . . Our negroes are not only better off as to physical comfort than free laborers, but their moral condition is better.

- *What assumptions does Fitzhugh make about enslaved Africans and about Africa itself?*

- *What is his view of Christianity?*

---

you who is the father of all the mulatto children in everybody's household but her own. Those, she seems to think, drop from the clouds." But plantation wives had their own double standard: a former slave woman said of her mistress, "though a warm-hearted woman, [she] was a violent advocate of slavery. I have . . . puzzled how to reconcile this with her otherwise Christian character."

Chesnut called the sexual dynamics of slavery "the sorest spot." But there were others. Together with enslaved black females, plantation mistresses had to tend to the food, clothing, health, and welfare of not just their husbands and children, but the slaves, too. A Tennessee planter's son remembered his mother and grandmother as "the busiest women I ever saw."

The plantation mistress, then, served many roles: as a potential humanizing influence on men; as a tough, resourceful, responsible manager of numerous plantation affairs; as a perpetuator of the system; and sometimes as a victim herself.

Justifying Slavery

The behavior of Douglass's mistress discussed at the beginning of this chapter suggests that slavery led otherwise good people to act inhumanely. Increasingly attacked as immoral, slaveholders felt compelled to justify the institution, not only to opponents of the system, but perhaps also to themselves. Until the 1830s, they explained away slavery as a "necessary evil." But unlike in England, where opposition to

slavery in the British West Indies succeeded in getting it abolished in 1834, in the United States, as abolitionists stepped up their attack in the 1830s, southerners shifted to justifying slavery in five arguments as, in John C. Calhoun's words, "a positive good."

A biblical justification was based in part on the curse that had fallen on the son of Ham, one of Noah's children, and in part on Old and New Testament admonitions to servants to obey their masters. In a historical justification, southerners claimed that slavery had always existed and all the great ancient civilizations—Egypt, Greece, Rome—were built on it. A leading southern economic magazine, De Bow's *Review*, said in 1851 that "civilization itself may almost be said to depend upon the continued servitude of blacks in America."

The legal justification rested on the U.S. Constitution's refusal to forbid slavery and on three passages clearly implying its legality: the "three-fifths" clause, the protection of the overseas slave trade for 20 years, and the mandate for returning fugitive slaves across state lines.

A fourth justification for slavery was pseudoscientific. Until the 1830s, most white southerners believed that blacks were degraded not by nature but by African climate and their slave condition. Claiming scientific authority, books were written to show black deficiency because of cranial shape and size. With the rise of the "positive good" defense in the 1830s, southerners began to argue that blacks had been created separately as an inherently inferior race, and therefore the destiny of the inferior

370   **PART 3** An Expanding People, 1820–1877

Africans was to work for the superior Caucasians. At best, the slave system would domesticate "uncivilized" blacks. As Allston put it, "The educated master is the negro's best friend upon earth."

A sociological defense of slavery was implicit in Allston's paternalistic statement. George Fitzhugh, a leading advocate of this view, argued, "the Negro is

George Fitzhugh, *Slavery Justified* (1854); *The Blessings of Slavery* (1857)

but a grown child and must be governed as a child," and so needed the paternal guidance, restraint, and protection of a white master. Many southerners believed that chaos and race mixing would ensue if slaves were freed. Allston wrote that emancipation was unthinkable because it would lead to "giving up our beautiful country to the ravages of the black race and amalgamation with savages." Fitzhugh compared the treatment of southern slaves favorably with that of free laborers working in northern factories. These "wage slaves," he argued, worked as hard as slaves, yet with their paltry wages they had to feed, clothe, and shelter themselves. Since southern masters took care of all these necessities, freeing their slaves would be a heartless burden to both blacks and whites.

Southern apologists for slavery faced the difficult intellectual task of justifying a system that ran against the main ideological directions of nineteenth-century American society: the expansion of individual liberty, mobility, economic opportunity, and democratic political participation. The southern defense of slavery had also to take into account the 75 percent of white families who owned no slaves but envied those who did. To deflect potential for class antagonisms among whites, wealthy planters developed a justification of slavery that emphasized white superiority regardless of class.

The underlying but rarely admitted motive behind all these justifications was that slavery was profitable, as it was in Latin America. As the southern defense of slavery intensified in the 1840s and 1850s, it aroused greater opposition from northerners and from slaves themselves. Perhaps slavery's worst cruelty was not physical but psychological: to be enslaved and barred from participation in a nation that espoused freedom and equality of opportunity.

NOON: SLAVES IN HOUSE AND FIELDS

It is two o'clock on a hot July afternoon on the plantation. The midday lunch break is over, and the slaves are returning to work in the fields. Lunch was the usual cornmeal and pork. The slaves now work

listlessly, their low stamina resulting from a deficient diet and suffocating heat and humidity. Douglass remembered that "we worked all weathers .... It was never too hot, or too cold." Mary Reynolds, a Louisiana slave, recalled that she hated most having to pick cotton "when the frost was on the bolls," which made her hands "git sore and crack open and bleed."

Daily Toil

The daily work schedule for most slaves, whether in the fields or the "Big House," was long and demanding. Awakened before daybreak, they worked on an average day 14 hours in the summer and 10 hours in the winter; during harvest, an 18-hour workday was not uncommon. Depending on the size of the workforce and the crop, the slaves were organized either in gangs or according to tasks. Gangs, usually of 20 to 25, worked the cotton rows under the watchful eye and quick whip of a driver. Ben Simpson, a Georgia slave, remembered vividly his master's "great, long whip platted out of rawhide" that struck any slave who would "fall behind or give out."

Under the task system, which slaves preferred and negotiated for cleverly, each slave had a specific task to complete daily. It gave slaves incentive to work hard enough to finish early, but their work was scrutinized constantly. An overseer's weekly report to Robert Allston in 1860 noted that he had "flogged for hoeing corn bad Fanny 12 lashes, Sylvia 12, Monday 12, Phoebee 12, Susanna 12, Salina 12, Celia 12, Iris 12." Black slave drivers were no less demanding. One reported to his master that because the slaves only got $1^1/_2$ acres plowed instead of 7, "I gave them ten licks a peace [sic] upon their skins [and] I gave Julyann eight or ten licks for misplacing her hoe."

An average slave was expected to pick 130 to 150 pounds of cotton per day; work on sugar and rice plantations was even harder. Sugar demanded constant cultivation, digging ditches in snake-infested fields. At harvest time, cutting, stripping, and carrying the cane to the sugar house for boiling was exhausting, as was cutting and hauling huge quantities of firewood. Working in the low-country rice fields was worse: slaves spent long hours standing in water up to their knees.

House slaves, mostly women, had relatively easier assignments, though they were usually called on to help with the harvest. Their usual work was in or near the Big House as maids, cooks, seamstresses, laundresses, coachmen, drivers, gardeners, and "mammies." Slaves did most of the skilled artisan work on the plantation as carpenters, stonemasons, blacksmiths, weavers, mechanics, and millers. House slaves ate and dressed better than those in

Scenes from the Life of the Enslaved Slaves survived nobly despite hard work, ill health, a deficient diet, and poor living conditions. Enslaved families had a double burden of work and caring for their families, as seen in the photographs (top) of women working in the fields, one picking cotton with a child and the other helping till rice, and in the drawing (bottom left) of the woman cooking in her cabin while her children look out from the doorway. But female slaves also managed to develop networks of support while working, as seen in the drawing (bottom right) of the three women winnowing rice. *(Top: Photographs from Photographs and Prints Division, Schomburg Center for Research in Black Culture, The New York Public Library, Astor, Lenox and Tilden Foundations/Art Resource, NY; bottom left: Private Collection; bottom right: From Down by the Riverside by Charles Joyner;)*

the fields, and there was more intimacy between whites and blacks. But there were disadvantages: close supervision, duty day and night, and conflicts with whites that could range from being given unpleasant jobs to insults, spontaneous angry whippings, and sexual assault. The most feared punishment, however, other than sale to the Deep South, was to be sent to the fields.

Slave Health and Punishments

Although slave owners had an interest in keeping their workforce healthy, slaves led sickly lives. Home was a crude, one-room log cabin with a dirt floor and a fireplace. Cracks and holes allowed mosquitoes easy entry, disturbing sleep. Typical furnishings included a table, some stools or boxes to sit on, an iron pot and wooden dishes, and perhaps a bed. Cabins were crowded, usually housing more than one family. Clothing, issued once or twice a year, was shabby and uncomfortable. Women often made their own and their children's clothes.

Studies on the adequacy of slave diet disagree. But compared with Latin American slaves, North American slaves were fed well. Once a week, each slave got an average ration of a peck of cornmeal,

---

An Overseer's Report

W. Sweet to Adele Petigru Allston N[ightin]gale hall, 14th September, 1864

Dear madam I comence my harvest on last saterday on Boath Plantations the weather is very fin for harvest so far I will Bring some Rice in to the Barn yard at N[ightin]gale hall to Day and at ganderloss to morrow. I think that I will make about 2 Barrels of Syrrup on Each Place I finish grinding at ganderloss to Day I will not finish at Nightingale hall until the last of next weeak. litle Dianah was confined with a boy child on the 9 I am very sorry to say to you that one of Prisilia children a boy name July Dide on 12th with fits a[nd] fever I have had a grea[t] deal of fever among the children But not much among the grone negroes. old Rose is Stil quite sick mr Belflowers sent toney to mee on friday last I have concluded to let toney wife stay whare she is for a while as I understand that she is Pregnant and will not Be much survice in the harvest if I am Rong for soe Doing Pleas let mee know. the negroes all sends thare love to you an family my self and family is very un well.

N[ightin]gale hall

8th September	all hands hoing Bancks and grinding shugar cain no sick
9th September	all hands hoing Bancks grind shugar cain no sick
10th September	all hands cu[tt]ing Rice grinding shugar cain no sick
12th September	all hands harvesting grinding shugar cain 3 women with sick children
13th September	all hands harvesting grinding shugar cain 3 women with sick children
14th September	all hands harvesting grinding shugar cain 1 woman with sick child

Source: J. H. Easterby, ed., *The South Carolina Rice Plantation as Revealed in the Papers of Robert F. W. Allston*, 1945.

---

three to four pounds of salt pork or bacon, some molasses, and perhaps some sweet potatoes. The mainstay was corn. While a few slaves were able to grow vegetables and to fish or hunt, most rarely enjoyed fresh meat, dairy products, fruits, or vegetables. The limitations of their diet led to theft of food and the practice of eating dirt, which caused worms. Deficient slave diet also resulted in skin disorders, cracked lips, sore eyes, vitamin deficiency diseases, and even mental illness.

Enslaved women especially suffered weaknesses caused by vitamin deficiency, hard work, and disease, as well as those associated with menstruation and childbirth. Women were expected to do the same tasks in the fields as the men, in addition to cooking, sewing, child care, and traditional female jobs in the quarters when the fieldwork was finished. "Pregnant women," the usual rule stated, "should not plough or lift" and had a three-week recovery period following birth. But these guidelines were often violated. Mortality of slave children under age 5 was twice as high as for white children.

Life expectancy for North American slaves was longer than for those in Latin America and the Caribbean, where the rigorous sugar industry used them up within a few years. However, because of poor diet and the climate, slaves in the United States were highly susceptible to epidemics. Despite some resistance as a result of the sickle-cell trait, many slaves died from malaria, yellow fever, cholera, and other diseases spread by mosquitoes or bad water. Slaves everywhere suffered and died from intestinal ailments in the summer and respiratory diseases in the winter. An average of 20 percent (and sometimes 50 to 60 percent) of the slaves on a given plantation would be sick at one time, and no overseer's report was complete without recording sicknesses and days of lost labor.

The relatively frequent incidence of whippings and other physical punishments aggravated the poor physical condition of the slaves. Many slaveholders offered rewards—a garden plot, an extra holiday, hiring out, and passes—as inducements for faithful labor, and they withheld these privileges as punishment. But southern court records, newspapers, plantation diaries, and slave memoirs reveal that sadistic punishments were frequent and harsh.

The slave William Wells Brown reported that on his plantation, the whip was used "very frequently and freely" for inadequate or uncompleted work, stealing, running away, and insolence and lying. Whippings ranged from 10 to 100 strokes of the lash. Former slaves described a good owner as one who did not "whip too much" and a bad owner as one who "whipped till he'd bloodied you and blistered you." Slaveholders had many theories on the appropriate kind of lash to inflict sufficient pain and punishment without damaging a valuable laborer. Other punishments included confinement in stocks and jails during leisure hours, chains, muzzling, salting lash wounds, branding, burning, castration, mauling by dogs, and having to do "women's work."

Nothing testifies better to the physical brutality of slavery than the advertisements for runaways that slaveholders printed in antebellum newspapers. In searching for the best way to describe the physical characteristics of a missing slave, slave owners unwittingly condemned their own behavior. A Mississippi runaway was

DOCUMENT
Runaway Slave Advertisements (1838–1839)

described as having "large raised scars . . . in the small of his back and on his abdomen nearly as large as a person's finger." A Georgia female was "considerably marked by the whip." Branding left even more vivid marks. One fugitive, Betty, was described as recently "burnt . . . with a hot iron on the left side of her face." "I tried to make the letter M," her master admitted in his diary.

Slave Law and the Family

Complicating master–slave relationships was the status of slaves as simultaneously human beings and property, a legal and psychological ambiguity the South never resolved. On the one hand, slaves had names, personalities, families, and wills of their own, making them fellow humans. On the other hand, they were items of property, purchased to perform specific profit-making tasks. As a Kentucky court put the problem in 1836, "Although the law of this state considers slaves as property, . . . it recognizes their personal existence."

This ambiguity led to confusion in the laws governing treatment of slaves. Until the early 1830s, some southern abolitionist activity persisted, primarily in the Upper South, and slaves had slight hopes of being freed. But they also suffered careless, often brutal treatment. This confusion changed with the convergence in 1831 of Nat Turner's revolt

and William Lloyd Garrison's attack on slavery in the *Liberator* (see Chapter 12). After 1831, the South tightened up the slave system. Laws prohibited manumission, and slaves' hopes of freedom other than by revolt or escape vanished. At the same time, laws protecting them from overly severe treatment were strengthened.

But laws were rarely enforced, and treatment varied with individual slaveholders, depending on their mood and other circumstances. Most planters, like Robert Allston, encouraged their slaves to marry and tried to keep families intact, believing that families made black males more docile and less inclined to run away. But some masters failed to respect slave marriages or broke them up because of financial problems, which southern law permitted them to do. A North Carolina Supreme Court justice said in 1853, "Our law required no solemnity or form in regard to the marriage of slaves."

Bill of Sale for Slaves, 1835

Adding to the pain of forced breakup of the slave family was the sexual abuse of enslaved women. Although the frequency of such abuse is unknown, the presence of thousands of mulattoes in the antebellum era points to the practice. White men in the South took advantage of slave women by offering gifts for sexual "favors," by threatening those who refused sex with physical punishment or the sale of

A Slave Market The breakup of families and friendships was an ever-present fear for slaves, who might be sold for economic reasons or in retribution for uncooperative behavior. Study this painting of a slave market by an unidentified artist. Note the varied colors of the African Americans (the light-skinned young woman in the center, the mulatto male in the left foreground staring longingly at her, and to the right dark-skinned women clutching their children) and the diversity of the whites (the suave merchant reclining in a chair on the porch, nattily attired slave auctioneers and buyers, and a gaudily dressed lower-class overseer cracking the whip over the separation of child from mother). All southern social classes perpetuated slavery, and African Americans of all hues were victimized by it. (Slave Market, ca. 1850–1860, Carnegie Museum of Art, Pittsburgh; Gift of Mrs. W. Fitch Ingersoll)

AMERICAN VOICES

When a North Carolina slave, Harriet Jacobs, is told by Dr. Flint, her master, who had been making obscene suggestions to her, that she must stop seeing a free black lover, she confronts Flint in this exchange from Incidents in the Life of a Slave Girl, *published in Boston in 1861.*

"So you want to be married, do you?" said he, "and to a free nigger."

"Yes, sir."

"Well, I'll soon convince you whether I am your master, or the nigger fellow you honor so highly. If you <u>must</u> have a husband, you may take up with one of my slaves."

What a situation to be in, as the wife of one of <u>his</u> slaves, even if my heart had been interested!

I replied, "Don't you suppose, sir, that a slave can have some preference about marrying? Do you suppose that all men are alike to her?"

"Do you love this nigger?" said he, abruptly.

"Yes, sir."

"How dare you tell me so!" he exclaimed, in great wrath. After a slight pause, he added, "I supposed you thought more of yourself; that you felt above the insults of such puppies."

I replied, "If he is a puppy I am a puppy, for we are both of the negro race. It is right and honorable for us to love each other. The man you call a puppy never insulted me, sir; and he would not love me if he did not believe me to be a virtuous woman."

He sprang upon me like a tiger, and gave me a stunning blow. It was the first time he had ever struck me; and fear did not enable me to control my anger. When I had recovered a little from the effects, I exclaimed, "You have struck me for answering you honestly. How I despise you!"

- *Who do you think "wins" the exchange?*
- *Why do you think so?*
- *What does this exchange suggest about the southern justification of slavery?*

---

a child or loved one, by purchasing concubines, and by outright rape. As Frederick Douglass put it, "The slave woman is at the mercy of the fathers, sons or brothers of her master."

To obtain cheap additional slaves for the workforce, slaveholders encouraged young slave women to bear children, whether married or not. If verbal prodding and inducements such as less work and more rations did not work, masters would force mates on slave women. "Massa" Hawkins, for example, chose Rufus to live with an unwilling 16-year-old Rose Williams. Years later, she recalled how she first repulsed him: "I puts de feet 'gainst him and give him a shove and out he go on de floor." When Rufus persisted, Rose took a poker and "lets him have it over de head." Hawkins then threatened Rose with a "whippin' at de stake" or sale away "from my folks." This was too much for her. "What am I's to do? So I 'cides to do as de massa wish and so I yields."

Slaves, however, usually chose their own mates on the basis of mutual attraction during a courtship complicated by threats of white interference. As among poor whites, premarital intercourse was frequent, but promiscuous behavior was rare. Most couples maintained affectionate, lasting relationships. This, too, led to numerous sorrows. Members of slave families, powerless to intervene, had to witness the flogging or physical abuse of loved ones. William Wells Brown remembered that "cold chills ran over me and I wept aloud" when he saw his mother whipped. For this reason, some slaves preferred to marry a spouse from another plantation.

Although motherhood was the key event in an enslaved woman's life, bearing children and the double burden of work and family responsibilities challenged her resourcefulness. Some masters provided time off for nursing mothers, but the more common practice was for them to work in the fields with their newborn infants lying nearby, wrapped in cloth for protection from the sun. Women developed support networks, looking after one another's children; meeting to sew, quilt, cook, or do laundry; and attending births, caring for the sick and dying, and praying together.

The worst trauma for slaves was the separation of families, a haunting fear rarely absent from slave consciousness. Although many slaveholders had

Notice for a Slave Sale Announcement of a slave sale in Charleston, 1860. What do you learn about the economics and morality of slavery from this poster? (*Five Slave Narratives: A Compendium*)

both moral and economic reasons to maintain families, inevitably they found themselves destroying them. One study of 30 years of data from the Deep South shows that masters dissolved one-third of all slave marriages. Even then, the slaves tried to maintain contact with loved ones sold elsewhere. "My Dear Wife for you and my Children my pen cannot Express the Griffe I feel to be parted from you all," wrote Abream Scriven.

There was a sound basis, in fact, for the abolitionists' contention that slavery was a harsh, brutal system. However, two points need to be emphasized. First, although slavery led otherwise decent human beings to commit inhumane acts, many slaveholders throughout the South were not cruel; they did what they could for their slaves, out of both economic self-interest and Christian morality. Second, whether under kind or cruel masters, the slaves endured with dignity, communal sensitivity, and occasional joy. If daytime in the fields describes slavery at its worst, nighttime in the quarters, as examined from the black perspective, reveals noble

survival powers and their capacity to mold an African American culture even under slavery.

NIGHT: SLAVES IN THEIR QUARTERS

It is near sundown, and the workday is almost over. Some slaves begin singing the gentle spiritual "Steal Away to Jesus," and others join in. To the unwary overseer or master, the song suggests happy slaves, content with their earthly lot and looking forward to heaven. To the slaves, however, the song is a signal that, as ex-slave Wash Wilson put it, they are to "steal away to Jesus" because "dere gwine be a 'ligious meetin' dat night."

In the slave quarters, away from whites and daily work, Wilson said, "sometimes us sing and pray all night." In the quarters, slaves preserved much of their African heritage and created an elaborate black community that helped them make sense out of their lives. In family life, religion, song, dance, the playing of musical instruments, and the telling of stories, the slaves both sought release from suffering and created a vibrant community and culture.

Slave Quarters, Hermitage Plantation, Savannah, Georgia

Black Christianity

As suggested by the scene Wash Wilson described, Christian worship was indispensable to life in the slave quarters, mixed with elements of Islamic and African religious practices. The revivals of the early nineteenth century led to an enormous growth of Christianity among black Americans. Black religious gatherings were usually forbidden unless white observers were present or white preachers led them. Independent black Baptist and Methodist churches, especially in the border states and cities, served slaves, free blacks, and occasionally even whites. These separate churches steered a careful path to maintain their freedom and avoid white interference, as did slave preachers, who occasionally administered baptisms and marriages.

The vast majority of southern black slaves attended plantation churches set up by their masters. These churches were rigidly segregated, either by a roped-off rear section for the blacks or, as one slave said, "us niggers sat on one side and de white folks sat on the other." Robert Allston built a prayer house for his slaves, reporting with pride that they were "attentive . . . and greatly improved in intelligence and morals." For the slaveholders, religion was a form of social control. Sermons emphasized the importance of work, obedience, and respect for the master's property. "All that preacher talked about," one slave remembered, "was for us slaves to obey our master and not to lie and steal." To enforce obedience, slaves were required to say catechisms that emphasized the masters' view of black inferiority and sinfulness: "Q. Who was the first Negro? A. Cain. Q. How did he become so? A. The Lord set a black mark upon him. Q. Did the Southern slave come from him? A. Yes."

DOCUMENT
A Catechism for
Slaves (1854)

There were limits, however, to white control. Although some slaves accommodated to the master's brand of Christianity and patiently waited for heavenly deliverance, others rebelled and sought earthly liberty. Not far from Allston's plantation, several slaves were discovered (and imprisoned) for singing "We'll soon be free / We'll fight for liberty / When de Lord will call us home." Douglass organized an illegal Sabbath school, "the sweetest engagement with which I was ever blessed," where he and others risked whippings while learning about Christianity and how to read. In religious schools and meetings like these, the slaves created an "invisible" church. On Sunday morning, they dutifully sat through the "white fo'ks service in de morning," Sarah, an Alabama slave recalled, waiting for the "real meetin'" and "real preachin'" later that night.

Long into the night, they would sing, dance, shout, and pray in the call-and-response pattern characteristic of black religion to this day. "Ya' see," Sarah explained, "niggers lack ta shout a whole lot an' wid de white fo'ks al'round 'em, dey couldn't shout jes' lack dey want to." But at night they could, taking care to deaden the sound to keep the whites away by hanging curtains from the trees or, in an African custom, to turn over a pot to "catch the sound." Another African practice, the ring shout, a dance forbidden by Methodists, was transformed into the "ecstatic shout," praising the Lord. The religious ceremony in "the hush arbor" relieved the day's burdens and expressed communal religious values. "At night," another slave recalled with pride, "was when the darkies really did have they freedom of spirit."

Although many of the practices were African, the messages reiterated over again in the invisible slave church were the Judeo-Christian themes of suffering

John Antrobus, *Plantation Burial* After sundown, when the work was done, slaves often gathered in "hush arbors" deep in the woods, away from the overseer's and master's interference. There they danced the "ring shout" and "praised de Lord" in ways that combined African and Christian forms of spiritual expression. This painting by John Antrobus shows a "Negro Burial." (*John Antrobus, A Plantation Burial, 1860. The Historic New Orleans Collection, accession no. 1960.46*)

and deliverance from bondage. "We prayed a lot to be free," Anderson Edwards said. "The folks would sing and pray and testify and clap their hands," recalled Simon Brown, "just as if God was right there in the midst of them." The freedom the slaves sought was a complex blend of a peaceful soul and an earthly escape from slavery, as reflected in spirituals.

The Power of Song

A group of slaves gathers at night in the woods behind their quarters to sing and shout together. Two moods are expressed. First, they mourn with "trebbled spirit" being stolen from Africa, their families "sold apart." But second, they sing: "There's a better day a-coming. / Will you go along with me? / There's a better day a-coming. / Go sound the jubilee."

AUDIO
Death Come a
Knockin'

Music was a crucial form of expression in the slave quarters on both secular and religious occasions. The slaves were adept at creating a song, as one woman recalled, "on de spurn of de moment." Jeanette Robinson Murphy described a process of spontaneous creation that, whether in rural gospels or urban jazz, describes black music to this day. "We'd all be at the 'prayer house' de Lord's day," she said, when all of a sudden in the midst of a white preacher's sermon, "de Lord would come a-shinin' thoo dem pages and revive dis ole nigger's heart." She continued, "I'd jump up dar and den and holler and shout and sing and pat, and dey would all cotch de words and I'd sing it to some ole shout song I'd heard 'em sing from Africa, and dey'd all take it up and keep at it, and keep a-addin' to it, and den it would be a spiritual."

Spirituals reiterated the basic Judeo-Christian theme: a chosen people, the children of God, were held in bondage but would be delivered: "To the Promised Land I'm Bound to Go," "Go Down Moses," and "Who Will Deliver Po' Me?" What they meant by deliverance often had a double meaning: freedom in heaven and freedom in the North. Where, exactly, was the desired destination of "Oh Canaan, sweet Canaan / I am bound for the land of Canaan"? Was it heaven? Freedom "anyplace else but here"? A literal reference to the terminus of the Underground Railroad in Canada? For different slaves, and at different times for the same person, it meant all of these.

AUDIO
Pharaoh's Host
Got Lost

Slave songs did not always contain double or hidden meanings. Sometimes slaves gathered simply for music, to play fiddles, drums, and other instruments fashioned on West African models. Slave musicians were invited to perform at white ceremonies and parties, but most played for the slave community. Weddings, funerals, holiday celebrations, family reunions, and a successful harvest were all occasions for a communal gathering, usually with music.

So, too, was news of external events that affected their lives—a crisis in the master's situation, a change in the slave code, a Civil War battle, or emancipation. "The songs of the slave," Douglass wrote, "represent the sorrows of his heart": broken families, burdens of work, trouble, toil, and homelessness. But they also expressed joy, triumph, and deliverance. Each expression of sorrow usually ended in an outburst of eventual liberation and justice. The deep sorrow of "sometimes I feel like a motherless chile" was transformed later in the song into "sometimes I feel like / A eagle in de air. . . . / Gonna spread my wings an' / Fly, fly, fly."

AUDIO
When the Roll
Is Called Up
Yonder

The Enduring Family

The role of music in all milestones of family life suggests that the family was central to life in the slave quarters. Although sexual abuse and family separation were all too real, so was the hope for family continuity. Naming practices, for example, show that children were connected to large extended families.

The benefits of family cohesion were those of any group: love, protection, education, moral guidance, cultural transmission, status, role models, and support. All these existed in the slave quarters. As the slaves gathered in the quarters at the end of the day, parents passed on to their children the family story, language patterns and words, recipes, folktales, musical traditions, and models of strength and beauty. Thus they preserved cultural traditions, which enhanced the identity and self-esteem of parents and children alike. Parents also taught their children how to cope with slavery and survive. As young ones neared the age for full-time fieldwork, their parents instructed them in the best ways to pick cotton or corn, how to avoid the overseer's whip, whom to trust and learn from, and ways of fooling the master.

Opportunities existed on many plantations for parents to perform extra work for money to buy sugar or clothing; to hunt and fish, thereby adding protein to their family's diet; or to tend a small garden to grow vegetables. In such small ways, they improved the welfare of their families. J. W. C. Pennington proudly recalled helping his "father at night in

RECOVERING THE PAST

Folktales

A frequent activity of family life in the slave quarters was telling stories. The folktale was an especially useful and indirect way in which older slaves could express hostility toward their masters, impart wisdom to the young, and teach them how to survive and gain a measure of freedom, while at the same time entertaining themselves. Folktales, cleverly indirect, reveal to historians a great deal about the enslaved Africans' view of their experience and aspirations.

Although the tales took many forms, perhaps the best known are the "Brer Rabbit" animal stories. The trickster rabbit, who existed originally in West African folklore (and in Brazilian fables as a tortoise), was weak and careless, often looked down on by the other animals. Like the slaves, he was a victim. But he was also boastful, outwardly happy, and full of mischief. More important, he knew how to use cleverness and cunning to outwit stronger foes (like Brer Wolf), usually by knowing them better than they knew him, a psychological necessity for all who are oppressed.

In one story, the powerful Brer Tiger took all the water and food for himself during a time of famine, leaving the weaker animals miserable. Brer Rabbit, however, turned things around. He played on Brer Tiger's fears that he would be blown away by a "big wind," which was secretly manufactured by the rabbit with the help of other creatures. The tiger was so afraid of the wind (perhaps the winds of revolt?) that he begged Brer Rabbit to tie him "tightly" to a tree to keep from being blown away. Brer Rabbit, although initially resistant in order to make Brer Tiger beg harder, was finally happy to oblige, after which all the creatures of the forest were able to share the cool water and juicy pears that the tiger had denied them.

In another folktale, Brer Rabbit fell into a well but then got out by tricking Brer Wolf into thinking it was better to be in the cool bottom of the well than outside where it was hot. As the wolf lowered himself down in one bucket, Brer Rabbit rose up in the other, laughingly saying as he passed Brer Wolf, "Dis am life; some go up and some go down." In these stories, the slaves vicariously outwitted their more powerful masters and usually reversed roles.

The accompanying story excerpt is from perhaps the most famous animal tale, "The Tar Baby Tricks Brer Rabbit." This version is by William J. Faulkner, who, after he retired as minister and dean of men at Fisk University, gathered and recorded the folktales he had heard in his youth in South Carolina from a former slave. Rev. Faulkner did not like to tell stories in dialect because he believed readers formed stereotyped judgments from the dialect and missed the significance of the tale itself. We enter the story as an angry Brer Wolf has decided on a plan to catch the lazy Brer Rabbit, who refused to help the wolf build a well and has been fooling him by drinking from the well while Brer Wolf was asleep.

When you have finished reading the story, ask yourself what you learned about slavery from this story. Did violence work for Brer Rabbit or did it only make things worse? What finally worked? How do you interpret the ending? Brer Rabbit returned to the briar patch, "the place where I was born." But is the briar patch, with all its thorns, scratches, and roots, more like Africa or slavery? Or what?

REFLECTING ON THE PAST Think about the stories you heard as a child or now find yourself telling others. How do they express the realities, flaws, values, and dreams of the American people? The same question applies to the songs we sing, the art we make, the rhythms we move to, and the jokes we tell: What do they tell us about ourselves and our values? In answering these questions, we deepen our knowledge of history.

Tar Baby

Brer Wolf studied and studied to find a way to catch Brer Rabbit. He scratched his head, and he pulled his chin whiskers until by and by he said, "I know what I'll do. I'll make me a tar baby, and I'll catch that good-for-nothing rabbit."*

And so Brer Wolf worked and worked until he had made a pretty little girl out of tar. He dressed the tar baby in a calico apron and carried her up to the well, where he stood her up and fastened her to a post in the ground so that nobody could move her. Then Brer Wolf hid in the bushes and waited for Brer Rabbit to come for some water. But three days passed before Brer Rabbit visited the well again. On the fourth day, he came with a bucket in his hand. When he saw the little girl, he stopped and looked at her. Then he said, "Hello. What's your name? What are you doing here, little girl?"

The little girl said nothing.

This made Brer Rabbit angry, and he shouted at her, "You no-mannered little snip, you! How come you don't speak to your elders?"

The little girl still said nothing.

"I know what to do with little children like you. I'll slap your face and teach you some manners if you don't speak to me," said Brer Rabbit.

Still the little girl said nothing.

And then Brer Rabbit lost his head and said, "Speak to me, I say. I'm going to slap you." With that, Brer Rabbit slapped the tar baby in the face, and his right hand stuck.

"A-ha, you hold my hand, do you? Turn me loose, I say. Turn me loose. If you don't, I'm going to slap you with my left hand. And if I hit you with my left hand, I'll knock the daylights out of you."

But the little girl said nothing. So Brer Rabbit drew back his left hand and slapped the little girl in her face, bim, and his left hand stuck.

"Oh, I see. You're going to hold both my hands, are you? You better turn me loose. If you don't, I'm going to kick you. And if I kick you, it's going to be like thunder and lightning!" With that, Brer Rabbit drew back his right foot and kicked the little girl in the shins with all his might, blap! Then his right foot stuck.

"Well, sir, isn't this something? You better turn my foot loose. If you don't, I've got another foot left, and I'm going to kick you with it, and you'll think a cyclone hit you." Then Brer Rabbit gave that little girl a powerful kick in the shins with his left foot, blip! With that, his left foot stuck, and there he hung off the ground, between the heavens and the earth. He was in an awful fix. But he still thought he could get loose.

So he said to the little girl, "You've got my feet and my hands all stuck up, but I've got one more weapon, and that's my head. If you don't turn me loose, I'm going to butt you! And if I butt you, I'll knock your brains out." Finally then, Brer Rabbit struck the little girl a powerful knock on the forehead with his head, and it stuck, and there he hung. Smart old Brer Rabbit, he couldn't move. He was held fast by the little tar baby.

Now, Brer Wolf was hiding under the bushes, watching all that was going on. And as soon as he was certain that Brer Rabbit was caught good by his little tar baby, he walked over to Brer Rabbit and said, "A-ha, you're the one who wouldn't dig a well. And you're the one who's going to catch his drinking water from the dew off the grass. A-ha, I caught the fellow who's been stealing my water. And he isn't anybody but you, Brer Rabbit. I'm going to fix you good."

"No, sir, Brer Wolf, I haven't been bothering your water. I was just going over to Brer Bear's house, and I stopped by here long enough to speak to this little no-manners girl," said Brer Rabbit.

"Yes, you're the one," said Brer Wolf. "You're the very one who's been stealing my drinking water all this time. And I'm going to kill you."

"Please, sir, Brer Wolf, don't kill me," begged Brer Rabbit. "I haven't done anything wrong."

"Yes, I'm going to kill you, but I don't know how I'm going to do it yet," growled Brer Wolf. "Oh, I know what I'll do. I'll throw you in the fire and burn you up."

"All right, Brer Wolf," said Brer Rabbit. "Throw me in the fire. That's a good way to die. That's the way my grandmother died, and she said it's a quick way to go. You can do anything with me, anything you want, but please, sir, don't throw me in the briar patch."

"No, I'm not going to throw you in the fire, and I'm not going to throw you in the briar patch. I'm going to throw you down the well and drown you," said Brer Wolf.

"All right, Brer Wolf, throw me down the well," said Brer Rabbit. "That's an easy way to die, but I'm surely going to smell up your drinking water, sir."

"No, I'm not going to drown you," said Brer Wolf. "Drowning is too good for you." Then Brer Wolf thought and thought and scratched his head and pulled his chin whiskers. Finally he said, "I know what I'm going to do with you. I'll throw you in the briar patch."

"Oh, no, Brer Wolf," cried Brer Rabbit. "Please, sir, don't throw me in the briar patch. Those briars will tear up my hide, pull out my hair, and scratch out my eyes. That'll be an awful way to die, Brer Wolf. Please, sir, don't do that to me."

"That's exactly what I'll do with you," said Brer Wolf all happy-like. Then he caught Brer Rabbit by his hind legs, whirled him around and around over his head, and threw him way over into the middle of the briar patch.

After a minute or two, Brer Rabbit stood up on his hind legs and laughed at Brer Wolf and said to him, "Thank you, Brer Wolf, thank you. This is the place where I was born. My grandmother and grandfather and all my family were born right here in the briar patch."

And that's the end of the story.

*Note: Masters often spread tar on fences to catch slaves who, when hungry, would sneak into fields and orchards to steal food. Tar stuck on the hands would betray the "guilty" slave.

making straw hats and willow-baskets, by which means we supplied our family with little articles of food, clothing and luxury."

Slaves were not always totally at the mercy of abusive masters and overseers. Mary Prince used sass to tell her Antigua mistress "not to use me so."

She told her Bermuda master, who struck her for dropping some plates, that "he was a very indecent man—very spiteful," and that "I would not live longer with him." Occasionally, one family member could intervene to prevent the abuse of another. Harriet Jacobs fended off her master's advances partly by her cleverness and sass ("I openly . . . expressed my contempt for him"), and partly by threats to use her free grandmother's considerable influence in the community against him. That enraged but stopped him.

When family intervention, appeals for mercy, or conjurers' magic did not work, some slaves resorted to force. In 1800, a slave named Ben shot dead a white man for living with Ben's wife, and another slave killed an overseer in 1859 for raping his wife. Female slaves risked serious consequences by protecting themselves or family members. When Cherry Loguen was attacked by a knife-wielding rapist, she knocked him out with a large branch. When an Arkansas overseer abused a slave woman named Lucy, her son reported that she "jumped on him and like to tore him up."

The love and affection that slaves had for each other was sometimes a liability. Many slaves, women especially, were reluctant to run away because they did not want to leave their families. Those who fled were easily caught because, as an

Slave Families in Their Quarters In these photographs of the quarters "at night," slave men, women, and children created a vibrant black community, socializing outdoors as they did house chores, and providing love, support, and self-esteem to family members. The 1862 photograph (top left) shows five generations of one family from a South Carolina plantation. What comment would you make about gender roles in these two photographs? (Top: Library of Congress; Bottom: Collection of the New-York Historical Society [PR-002-347.20])

DOCUMENT

Frances E. W. Harper, "The Slave Mother" (1854)

overseer near Natchez, Mississippi, told a northern visitor, they "almost always kept in the neighborhood, because they did not like to go where they could not sometimes get back and see their families." Others were reluctant to give up private means of supplementing their diet and resources by hiring out or growing food for trade.

As these episodes suggest, violence, sexual abuse, and separation constantly threatened slave families. Yet slave parents continued to serve as protectors, providers, comforters, transmitters of culture, and role models for their children.

RESISTANCE AND FREEDOM

Songs, folktales (as seen in this chapter's "Recovering the Past" feature), and other forms of cultural expression enabled slaves to articulate their resistance to slavery. For example, in the song "Ole Jim," on Jim's "journey" to the "kingdom," he invited others to "go 'long" with him, taunting his owner: "O blow, blow, Ole Massa, blow de cotton horn / Ole Jim'll neber wuck no mo' in de cotton an' de corn." From refusal to work, it was a short step to outright revolt. In another song, "Samson," the slaves clearly stated their determination to abolish the house of bondage: "An' if I had-'n my way / I'd tear the buildin' down! / . . . And now I got my way / And I'll tear this buildin' down." Every hostile song, story, or event, like Douglass's fight with Covey, was an act of resistance by which slaves asserted their dignity and gained a measure of mental freedom.

Forms of Black Protest

Slaves protested the burdensome demands of continuous forced labor in various "day-to-day" acts of resistance. These ranged from breaking tools to burning houses, from stealing food to defending fellow slaves from punishment, from self-mutilation to work slowdowns, and from poisoning masters to feigning illness.

Slave women, aware of their childbearing value, were adept at missing work on account of "disorders and irregularities." They established networks of support while winnowing and pounding rice or shucking corn, sharing miseries but also encouraging each other in private acts of sass and subtle defiance such as ruining the master's meals and faking sickness or painful menstrual cramps.

Overseers also suffered from these acts of disobedience, for their job depended on productivity, which in turn depended on the goodwill of the slave workers. Slaves adeptly played on the frequent struggles between overseer and master.

Many slaveholders resorted to using black drivers rather than overseers, but this created other problems. Slave drivers were "men between," charged with the tricky job of getting the master's work done without alienating fellow slaves or compromising their own loyalties. Although some drivers were as brutal as white overseers, many became leaders and role models for other slaves. A common practice of the drivers was to appear to punish without really doing so. Solomon Northrup reported that he "learned to handle the whip with marvelous dexterity and precision, throwing the lash within a hair's breadth of the back, the ear, the nose, without, however, touching either of them."

Another form of resistance was to run away. The typical runaway was a young male who ran off alone and hid out in a nearby wood or swamp. He left to avoid a whipping or because he had just been whipped, to protest excessive work demands, or, as one master put it, for "no cause" at all. But there was a cause—the need to experience a period of freedom away from the restraints and discipline of the plantation. Many runaways would sneak back to the quarters for food, and after a few days, if not tracked down by hounds, they would return, perhaps to be whipped, but also perhaps with some concessions for better treatment. Some slaves left again and again. Remus and his wife Patty ran away from their master in Alabama three times; after each jailing, they ran away again.

DOCUMENT

From the Narratives of Fugitive Slaves in Canada (1855)

Some runaways hid out for months and years in communities of escaped slaves known as *maroons,* especially in Florida, where Seminole and other Indians befriended them. In these maroons, blacks and Natives intermarried and shared a common hostility to whites. The Seminole resistance against the United States after the acquisition of Florida in 1819 was in fact a black–Seminole alliance, which succeeded for several years in evading American troops. Creek and other Indians were hired to track down runaways and eventually the black Seminole were re-enslaved and removed to the Indian Territory in Oklahoma, where some escaped again to the Texas–Mexico borderlands. Large maroon communities, also known as *cimarrons, quilombos,* and *palenques,* existed in the mountains of Mexico, Colombia, Peru, and Brazil, as well as on West Indian islands.

DOCUMENT

Levi Coffin, Reminiscences of the Underground Railroad in the 1850s

Slaves were ingenious in their means of escape: forging passes, posing as master and servant, disguising one's gender, sneaking aboard ships, and pretending loyalty until taken by the master on a trip to the North. One slave even had himself mailed to the North in a large box. The Underground Railroad, organized by abolitionists, was a series of safe houses and stations where runaway slaves could rest, eat, and spend the night before continuing. Harriet Tubman, who led some 300 slaves out of the South on 19 separate trips, was the railroad's most famous "conductor." It is difficult to know exactly how many slaves actually escaped to the North and Canada, but the numbers were not large. One estimate suggests that in 1850, about 1,000 slaves (out of more than 3 million) attempted to run away, and most of them were returned. Nightly patrols by whites reduced the chances for any slave to escape and probably deterred many slaves from even trying.

Harriet Tubman

Other ways in which slaves sought their freedom included petitioning Congress and state legislatures, bringing suit against their masters that they were being held in bondage illegally, and persuading masters to provide for emancipation in their wills. Many toiled to purchase their own freedom by hiring out to do extra work at night and on holidays.

Slave Revolts

The ultimate act of resistance was rebellion. Countless slaves committed individual acts of revolt. In addition, there were hundreds of conspiracies whereby slaves met to plan a group escape and often the massacre of whites. Most of these conspiracies never led to action, either because circumstances changed or the slaves lost the will to follow through or, more often, because some fellow slave—perhaps planted by the master—betrayed the plot. Such spies thwarted the elaborate conspiracies of Gabriel in Virginia in 1800 and Denmark Vesey in South Carolina in 1822. Both men were skilled, knowledgeable leaders who planned their revolts in hopes that larger events would support them—a possible war with France in 1800 and the Missouri debates in 1820. Both conspiracies were thwarted before revolts could begin, and both resulted in severe reprisals by whites, including mass executions of leaders and the random killing of innocent blacks. The severity of these responses indicated southern whites' enormous fear of slave revolt.

Only a few organized revolts ever actually took place, especially compared to Latin America where slaves revolted far more frequently: St. Domingue in 1791, Barbados in 1816, British Guiana (Demerara) in 1823, Jamaica in 1831–1832, Cuba in 1843–1844, and Brazil in 1810, 1814, 1835, 1843, and the 1880s. In Brazil, weaker military control, easier escape to rugged interior areas, the larger number of blacks to whites, the disproportionate ratio of males to females, and continued dependence on the African slave trade to replenish workers (rather than natural increase) explained these frequent revolts. Compared with the near 1:1 gender ratio of slaves in the United States, Latin American slaves had little family or female restraint on violent revolts.

The most famous slave revolt in North America, led by Nat Turner, occurred in Southampton County, Virginia, in 1831. Turner was an intelligent, skilled, unmarried, religious slave who had experienced many visions of "white spirits and black spirits engaged in battle." He believed himself "ordained for some great purpose in the hands of the Almighty." He and his followers intended, Turner said, "to carry terror and devastation" throughout the country. On a hot, August night, Turner and his followers crept into the home of Turner's master—a "kind master" with "the greatest confidence in me"—and killed the entire family. Before the insurrection was finally put down, 55 white men, women, and children had been murdered and twice as many blacks killed in the aftermath. Turner hid for two weeks before he was apprehended and executed, but not before dictating a chilling confession to a white lawyer.

DOCUMENT
The Confessions of Nat Turner (1831)

The Nat Turner revolt was a crucial moment for southern whites. A Virginia legislator suspected that there was "a Nat Turner ... in every family," and slaveholders throughout the South slept less securely. The fact that Turner was an intelligent and trusted slave and yet led such a terrible revolt suggests again how difficult it is to generalize about slavery and slave behavior. Slaves, like masters, had diverse personalities and changeable moods, and their behavior could not be predicted easily. Sometimes humble and deferential, at other times obstinate and rebellious, the slaves made the best of a bad situation and did what they needed to do to survive with a measure of self-worth.

Nat Turner Rebellion, 1831

Free Blacks: Becoming One's Own Master

Frederick Douglass said of the slave, "Give him a bad master, and he aspires to a good master; give him a good master, and he wishes to become his own master." In 1838, Douglass forged a free black's papers as a seaman and sailed from Baltimore to become his own master in the North, where he found "great insecurity and loneliness." Apart from the immediate difficulties of finding food, shelter, and

Slave Revolts, Maroons, and the Abolition of Slavery in the Americas, 1790–1888

Throughout the Americas, enslaved Africans found many ways to protest their enslavement, including revolt, escape, and petitioning the abolition of slavery altogether. Maroons were communities of successful runaway slaves who fled to dense forested and largely inaccessible areas where they often intermarried with Native groups. Some carried on a kind of guerrilla warfare with Europeans who tried to track them down. **Reflecting on the Past** Do you see any patterns in the outbreaks of this partial mapping of slave revolts, by either place or time? What relationships do you see, if any, between slave revolts and abolition? Between national independence movements and abolition? What other observations would you make about the data on this map?

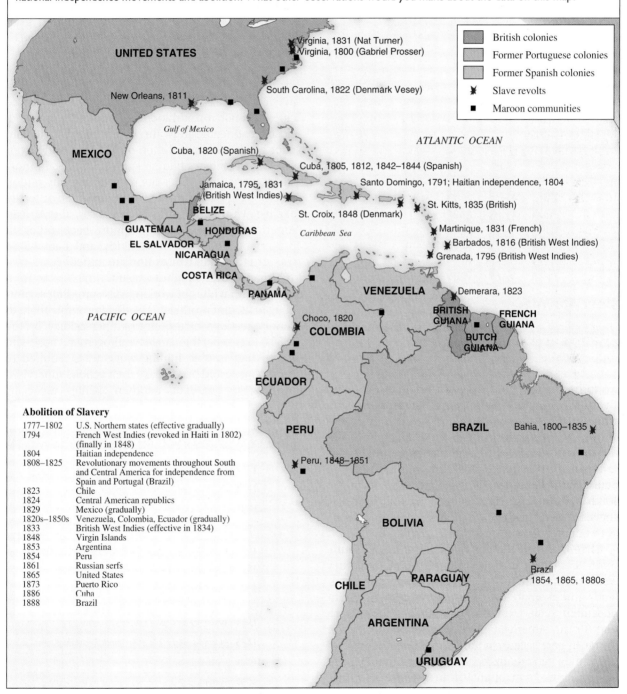

Legend:
- British colonies
- Former Portuguese colonies
- Former Spanish colonies
- ✱ Slave revolts
- ■ Maroon communities

Abolition of Slavery

1777–1802	U.S. Northern states (effective gradually)
1794	French West Indies (revoked in Haiti in 1802) (finally in 1848)
1804	Haitian independence
1808–1825	Revolutionary movements throughout South and Central America for independence from Spain and Portugal (Brazil)
1823	Chile
1824	Central American republics
1829	Mexico (gradually)
1820s–1850s	Venezuela, Colombia, Ecuador (gradually)
1833	British West Indies (effective in 1834)
1848	Virgin Islands
1853	Argentina
1854	Peru
1861	Russian serfs
1865	United States
1873	Puerto Rico
1886	Cuba
1888	Brazil

Growth of Black Population: Slave and Free, 1820–1860

Although the number of free African Americans doubled in size between 1820 and 1860, their proportion relative to the total black population actually decreased. Does this mean that southern whites were more or less likely to end slavery voluntarily?

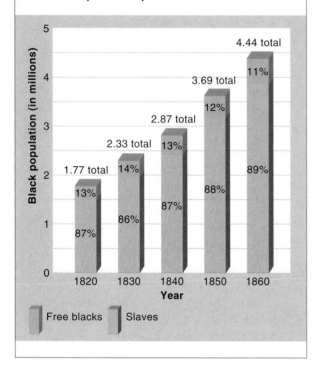

Free blacks   Slaves

American communities—their churches, schools, and benevolent societies flourishing in the midst of white hostility.

Most free African Americans in the antebellum South were poor farmhands, day laborers, or wood-cutters. In the cities, they worked in factories and lived in appalling poverty. A few skilled jobs, such as barbering, shoemaking, and plastering, were reserved for black men, but they were barred from more than 50 other trades. Women worked as cooks, laundresses, and domestics. The 15 percent of free African Americans who lived in the Lower South were divided into two distinct castes. Most were poor. But in New Orleans, Charleston, and other southern cities, a small, mixed-blood free black elite emerged, closely connected to white society and distant from poor blacks. A handful even owned land and slaves.

Most free blacks had no such privileges. In most states, they could not vote, bear arms, buy liquor, assemble, speak in public, form societies, or testify against whites in court. Nevertheless, the African American persistence to support each other in prayer meetings, burial societies, and back alleys was stronger than white efforts to impede it.

Urban whites sought to restrain free blacks from mixing with whites in working-class grogshops, gambling halls, and brothels, as well as to confine them to certain sections of the city or (increasingly by the 1850s) to compel them to leave altogether. Those who stayed had trouble finding work, were required to carry papers, and had to have their actions supervised by a white guardian. Southern whites especially

work, he realized that he was a fugitive in a land "whose inhabitants are legalized kidnappers" who could at any moment seize and return him to the South. Douglass thus joined the 12 percent of the African American population who were not slaves.

Between 1820 and 1860, the number of free blacks in the United States doubled, from 233,500 to 488,000. This rise resulted from natural increase, successful escapes, "passing" as whites, purchasing of freedom, and manumission.

More than half the free blacks lived in the South, most (85 percent in 1860) in the Upper South. They were found scattered on impoverished rural farm-lands and in small towns, feared by whites as an inducement to slave unrest. One-third of the southern free African American population lived in cities or towns. In part because it took a long time to buy free-dom, they tended to be older, more literate, and lighter-skinned than other African Americans. In 1860, more than 40 percent of free blacks were mulattoes (compared with 10 percent of the slaves). Free blacks in Baltimore, Richmond, Charleston, New Orleans, and other southern cities developed vibrant African

TIMELINE

1787	Constitution adopted with proslavery provisions
1793	Eli Whitney invents cotton gin
1800	Gabriel conspiracy in Virginia
1808	External slave trade prohibited by Congress
1820	South becomes world's largest cotton producer
1822	Denmark Vesey's conspiracy in Charleston
1830s	Southern justification of slavery changes from a necessary evil to a positive good
1831	Nat Turner's slave revolt in Virginia
1845	*Narrative of the Life of Frederick Douglass* published
1850s	Cotton boom
1852	Harriet Beecher Stowe publishes best-selling *Uncle Tom's Cabin*
1860	Cotton production and prices peak

HOW OTHERS SEE US

Frederick Douglass, "What to the Slave Is the 4th of July?"

Although Frederick Douglass lived in the United States, as a slave—and even as a free person—he was not considered a citizen and had no rights. Therefore, his view of America was definitely that of an outsider. Douglass's remarks were made in 1852 at a meeting of the Rochester, New York, Ladies Anti-Slavery Society. His title: "What to the Slave Is the 4th of July?"

What, to the American slave, is your Fourth of July? I answer: a day that reveals to him, more than all other days in the year, the gross injustice and cruelty to which he is the constant victim. To him, your celebration is a sham; your boasted liberty, an unholy license; your national greatness, swelling vanity; your sounds of rejoicing are empty and heartless; your denunciation of tyrants, brass-fronted impudence; your shouts of liberty and equality, hollow mockery; your prayers and hymns, your sermons and thanksgivings, with all your religious parade and solemnity, are to Him, mere bombast, fraud, deception, impiety, and hypocrisy—a thin veil to cover up crimes which would disgrace a nation of savages. There is not a nation on the earth guilty of practices more shocking and bloody than are the people of the United States at this very hour.

■ *How accurate and how fair do you think he was?*

---

feared contact between free blacks and slaves. A Baltimore black paper said in 1826 that "though we are not slaves, we are not free."

The key institution in these developments was the African American church, "the Alpha and Omega of all things," Martin Delaney wrote to Douglass. Welcoming the freedom from white control, independent urban black churches grew enormously in the two decades before the Civil War. The African Methodist Episcopal (AME) Church in Baltimore doubled its membership between 1836 and 1856. By 1860, Baltimore had 15 African American churches representing five different denominations, and in Virginia 14 new black Baptist churches were founded between 1841 and 1860. These institutions gave spiritual solace, set community standards, and offered a host of educational, insurance, self-help, and recreational opportunities.

Free Black Church

Nor were African American Catholics left out. Baltimore and New Orleans had strong black Catholic communities made up of Creoles, converts, former slaves, and refugees from Haiti. The first ordained black priests were three Georgia sons, born of a mulatto slave mother and an Irish immigrant father and educated at Holy Cross in the 1850s, though it would be three decades before another black was ordained. In the absence of African American priests, black sisterhoods took on special importance. The Sisters of the Holy Family and other communities of Catholic black women, begun in eastern

A Black Congregation at Prayer   Churches for free blacks, rare before 1800, became a major source of social as well as religious activity by the 1840s. *(Library of Congress)*

cities, started schools and ministered to the aged and infirm as they spread with black Catholic communities westward to Louisville and St. Louis.

African American churches were centers of vital urban black community activities and springboards for activist black preachers seeking larger changes in American society. The Reverend J. C. Pennington, an escaped slave, attended lectures at Yale Divinity School (though he was denied the right to enroll or borrow books). Licensed to preach in 1838, he headed prominent black churches in New Haven, Hartford, and New York City. Pennington started several schools, was an abolitionist leader of the National Negro Convention movement (described in Chapter 12), and founded a black missionary society focused on Africa. Charles Ray was educated at Wesleyan University in Connecticut and, as minister of a New York City black church for 20 years, was involved with the Underground Railroad and editor of *The Colored American.* Such black religious leaders prepared the way not only for civil war, but also for an unprecedented postwar growth of African American churches.

A young AME minister, Henry M. Turner, proudly proclaimed in the 1850s, "We, as a race, have a chance to be Somebody, and if we are ever going to be a people, now is the time." Turner's exhortations had been heralded 20 years earlier by Maria Stewart, the first African American woman to give published public speeches. Stewart's religious conversion gave her confidence to brave censure and ridicule in speaking out on behalf of abolitionism and equal rights for free blacks and women. She argued that had St. Paul known "of our wrongs and deprivations, . . . he would make no objections to our pleading in public for our rights."

In part because free blacks were becoming more of a "people" demanding their "rights," they faced a crisis in the 1850s. Growing prosperity and the deepening conflict between the North and South over slavery in the territories caused many white southerners to be even more concerned than usual with the presence of free blacks. Pressures increased in the late 1850s to either deport or enslave them. Not surprisingly, some black leaders began to look more favorably on migration to Africa. That quest was interrupted, however, by the outbreak of the Civil War, rekindling in Douglass the "expiring embers of freedom."

Conclusion

Douglass's Dream of Freedom

Frederick Douglass eventually won his freedom by forging a free black sailor's pass and escaping through Chesapeake Bay to New York. In a real sense, he wrote himself into freedom. The *Narrative of the Life of Frederick Douglass,* "written by himself" in 1845, was a way for Douglass both to expose the many evils of slavery and to create his own identity, even to the point of choosing his own name. Ironically, Douglass had learned to value reading and writing from his Baltimore masters, the Aulds.

DOCUMENT

Passages from *Narrative of the Life of Frederick Douglass* (1883)

This reminds us again of the intricate and subtle ways in which the lives of slaves and masters were tied together in the antebellum South. Our understanding of the complexities of this relationship is enhanced as we consider the variations of life in the Big House in the morning, in the fields during the afternoons, in the slave quarters at night, and in the degrees of freedom blacks achieved through resistance, revolt, and free status.

In a poignant moment in his *Narrative,* Douglass described his boyhood dreams of freedom as he looked out at the boats on the waters of Chesapeake Bay. Contrasting his own enslavement with the boats he saw as "freedom's swift-winged angels," Douglass vowed to escape: "This very bay shall yet bear me into freedom. . . . There is a better day coming." As we will see later, southern white planters also bemoaned their lack of freedom relative to the North and made their own plans to achieve independent status through secession. Meanwhile, as that struggle brewed beneath the surface of antebellum life, many other Americans were dismayed by various evil aspects in their society, slavery among them, and sought ways of shaping a better America to match ideal dreams with social realities. We turn to these other dreams in the next chapter.

Recommended Reading

Recommended Readings are posted on the Web site for this textbook. Visit www.ablongman.com/nash

Questions for Review and Reflection

1. In what ways—social and economic—was the South dependent on slavery and cotton, and in what ways was it not? How much variety—social and economic—existed in the Old South?

2. Compare and contrast North American with Latin American slavery.

3. Show your understanding of the morning, noon, and night structure of this chapter by explaining it to a

friend not in the course. How does this structure reflect three different interpretations of slavery?

4. List five or six different ways in which slaves resisted their enslavement and achieved a measure of autonomy, agency, and self-esteem.

5. What does the author of this chapter think was the worst thing about slavery? What do you think? What does the institution of slavery suggest about American values and how have they changed over time?

Fiction and Film

The Bondswoman's Narrative (2002) by Hannah Crafts, recently discovered and edited by Henry Louis Gates, Jr., is perhaps the earliest known novel by an African American woman. Written in the 1850s, hers is a captivating story of a light-skinned North Carolina slave, part fiction and part autobiography, whose escape to the North involved a series of horrifying experiences. Harriet Beecher Stowe's famous novel, *Uncle Tom's Cabin* (1852), follows various black and white lives in antebellum Kentucky and the Deep South. Charles Johnson's *Middle Passage* (1990) describes antebellum life in New Orleans and on slave trade ships between West Africa and the Caribbean. Toni Morrison's novel *Beloved* (1988) is a powerful and moving account of African American life both during and after slavery. Alice Randall's *The Wind Done Gone* (2001) is a parody of Margaret Mitchell's *Gone with the Wind* (1936). *Kindred* (1979), by Octavia Butler, a contemporary African American science fiction writer, is

about a black Los Angeles woman who is transported back to 1815, where she endures the brutality of slavery even as she seeks to save the life of the son of her slave-owning white ancestors. A recent novel about slavery is perhaps the best. Edward P. Jones's *The Known World* (2003) won the Pulitzer Prize for literature. His exquisitely written story examines all aspects of the morality of slavery and depicts the complex human dimensions of black and white relations going far beyond conventions of evil white slaveholders and victimized slaves. *Amistad* is a 1997 Hollywood film based on a successful mutiny on a slave ship in 1839 near Cuba and the subsequent capture and trial of the mutineers in Connecticut, where they were defended by former president John Quincy Adams. The film, featuring the rebel leader Cinque, contains vivid scenes aboard slave ships. *Beloved* is a heartbreaking but ultimately inspiring 1998 film version of Toni Morrison's novel.

Discovering U.S. History Online

Slave Culture
www.kingtisdell.org/exhibit.htm
This site offers an illustrated explanation of slavery culture in Savannah from antebellum Savannah to the end of the Reconstruction era.

Letters from the Slave States
www.fordham.edu/halsall/mod/1857stirling.html
This site provides a reprint of an article with interviews of plantation owners and former slaves.

Africans in America, 1791–1831
www.pbs.org/wgbh/aia/part3/index.html
These PBS images and documents (both primary source and modern commentaries) illustrate the growth and entrenchment of slavery, the rise of abolitionism (especially in Philadelphia), and the black church.

Songs of the Underground Railroad
www.appleseedrec.com/underground/sounds.html
This site presents samples of popular slavery songs and interpretations of the meaning of the lyrics.

Virginia Runaways
www.wise.virginia.edu/history/runaways
This site presents a "digital database" of the detailed "runaway and captured slave and servant advertisements from 18th-century Virginia newspapers."

North American Slave Narratives, Beginnings to 1920
http://www.metalab.unc.edu/docsouth
The University of North Carolina site offers a rich collection of narratives about slavery, edited by William Andrews, who has written widely and well about slave narratives.

CHAPTER 12

Shaping America in the Antebellum Age

This 1839 painting of a camp meeting captures the religious fervor that many Americans turned to in the face of social and economic upheavals. These mass conversions led some believers to individual salvation and others to social reform. *(J. Maze Burbank, Jr.,* Religious Camp Meeting, *c. 1839. Courtesy of The Whaling Museum)*

American Stories

Experiencing the Costs of a Commitment

On November 19, 1836, as the second term of President Andrew Jackson neared its end, 30-year-old Marius Robinson and Emily Rakestraw were married near Cincinnati, Ohio. Two months later, Marius went on the road to speak against slavery and organize abolitionist societies in Ohio. Emily stayed in Cincinnati to teach in a school for free blacks. During their 10-month separation, they exchanged affectionate letters that told of their love and work.

Writing to Emily after midnight from Concord, Ohio, Marius complained of the "desolation of loneliness" he felt without her. Emily responded that she felt "about our separation just as you do" and confessed that her "womanish nature" did not enjoy self-denial. In their letters, each imagined the "form and features" of the other and chided the other for not writing more often. Each voiced concern for the burdens of the other's work. Each expressed comfort and support, doubted his or her own abilities ("a miserable comforter I am"), and agreed that in their separation, as Marius put it, "we must look alone to God."

DOCUMENT
Charles Finney,
Lecture to
Converts

With such love for each other, what prompted this painful separation so early in their marriage? Emily wrote of their duty "to labor long in this cause so near and dear to us both," together if possible, but apart if so decreed by God. Marius, who had been converted by revivalist Charles G. Finney and his abolitionist disciple Theodore Weld, described the reason for their separation: "God and humanity bleeding and suffering demand our services apart." Driven by a strong religious commitment to serve others, these two young reformers dedicated themselves to several social causes: abolition of slavery, equal rights and education for free blacks, temperance, and women's rights.

Their commitments cost more than separation. When Emily went to Cincinnati to work with other young reformers, her parents disapproved. When she married Marius, who already had a reputation as a "rebel," her parents disowned her. Emily wrote with sadness that her sisters and friends also "love me less . . . than they did in by-gone days." Marius responded that he wished he could "dry your tears" and sought to heal the rift. Although Emily's family eventually accepted their marriage, there were other griefs. Teaching at the school in Cincinnati was demanding, and Emily could not get rid of a persistent cough. Furthermore, the white citizens of the city treated the school and the young abolitionists in their midst with contempt. Earlier in the year, Marius had escaped an angry mob by disguising himself and mingling with the crowd that came to sack the offices of a reformist journal edited by James G. Birney. Emily, meanwhile, tirelessly persisted in the work of "our school" while worrying about the health and safety of her husband.

She had good reason for concern, for Marius's letters were full of reports of mob attacks, disrupted meetings, stonings, and narrow escapes. At two lectures near Granville, Ohio, he was "mobbed thrice, once most rousingly," by crowds of "the veriest savages I ever saw," armed with clubs and intense hatred for those speaking against slavery. In June, he was dragged from his Quaker host's home, beaten, and tarred and feathered. Never quite recovering his health, Marius spent six months in bed, weak and dispirited. For nearly 10 years after that, the Robinsons lived quietly on an Ohio farm, only slightly involved in abolitionist activity. Despite the joyous birth of two daughters, they felt lonely, restless, and guilt-ridden, "tired of days blank of benevolent effort and almost of benevolent desires."

The work of Emily and Marius Robinson represents one response by the American people to the rapid social and economic changes of the antebellum era described in Chapters 10 and 11. In September 1835, a year before the Robinsons' marriage, the *Niles Register* commented on some 500 recent incidents of mob violence and social upheaval. "Society seems everywhere unhinged, and the demon of 'blood and slaughter' has been let loose upon us. . . . [The] character of our countrymen seems suddenly changed." How did Americans adapt to these changes? In a world that seemed everywhere "unhinged" and out of control, in which old rules and patterns no longer provided guidance, how did people maintain some sense of control over their lives? How did they seek to shape their altered world? How could they both adopt the benefits of change and reduce the accompanying disruptions?

One way was to embrace the changes fully. Thus, some Americans became entrepreneurs in new industries; invested in banks, canals, and railroads; bought more land and slaves; and invented new machines. Others went west or to the new textile mills, enrolled in Common Schools, joined trade unions, specialized their labor in both the workplace and the home, and celebrated modernization's practical benefits. Marius Robinson eventually went into life insurance, though he and Emily never fully abandoned their reformist efforts and idealism.

But many Americans were uncomfortable with the character of the new era. Some worried about the unrestrained power and selfish materialism symbolized by the slave master's control over his slaves. Others feared that institutions such as the U.S. Bank represented a "monied aristocracy" capable of undermining the country's honest producers. Seeking positions of leadership and authority, these critics of the new order tried to shape a nation that retained the benefits of economic change without sacrificing humane principles of liberty, equality of opportunity, and community virtue. This chapter examines four ways in which the American people responded to change by attempting to influence their country's development: religious revivalism, party politics, utopian communitarianism, and social reform.

RELIGIOUS REVIVAL AND REFORM PHILOSOPHY

When the Frenchman Alexis de Tocqueville visited the United States in 1831 and 1832, he observed that he could find "no country in the whole world in which the Christian religion retains a greater influence over the souls of men than in America." Tocqueville was describing a new and powerful religious enthusiasm among American Protestants. Religious rebirth gave some Americans a mooring in a fast-changing world, while others were inspired to refashion their society, working through new political parties to shape an agenda for the nation or through reform associations targeting a particular social evil. Although not all evangelicals agreed about politics or even about what needed reform, religion was the lens through which they viewed events and sought change.

Finney and the Second Great Awakening

From the late 1790s until the late 1830s, a wave of religious revivals that matched the intensity of the Great Awakening of the 1730s and 1740s swept through the United States. While there were many links between Protestant denominations in the United States and in Great Britain, the popular character of American revivalism gave it a distinctive stamp. British religion was becoming more conservative, while American Protestantism was becoming more democratic.

IMAGE
Sacramental Scene in a Western Forest

The turn-of-the-century frontier camp meeting revivals and the New England revivals sparked by Lyman Beecher took on a new emphasis and location after 1830. Led by the spellbinding Charles G. Finney, under whose influence Marius Robinson had been converted, revivalism shifted to upstate New York and the Old Northwest. Both areas had been gripped by profound economic and social changes.

Rochester, New York, was typical. Like Lowell and Cincinnati, by the 1830s it was booming. Located on the recently completed Erie Canal, it was changed by the canal from a sleepy village of 300 in 1815 to a bustling commercial and milling city of nearly 20,000 by 1830. As in other cities, economic growth affected relationships between masters and workers, distancing them both physically and psychologically. As the gulf widened, the masters' control over their laborers weakened. Saloons and unions sprang up in workingmen's neighborhoods, and workers became more transient, following opportunities westward.

In 1830, prompted partly by their concerns about poverty and absenteeism, both caused presumably by alcohol, prominent Rochester citizens invited Charles Finney to the city. He led what became one of the most successful revivals of the Second Great Awakening. Finney preached nearly every night and three times on Sundays, first converting the city's business elite, often through their wives with the help of his wife Lydia, and then converting many workers. For six

DOCUMENT
Richard McNemar, The Kentucky Revival (1808)

DOCUMENT
Charles Finney, What a Revival of Religion Is (1835)

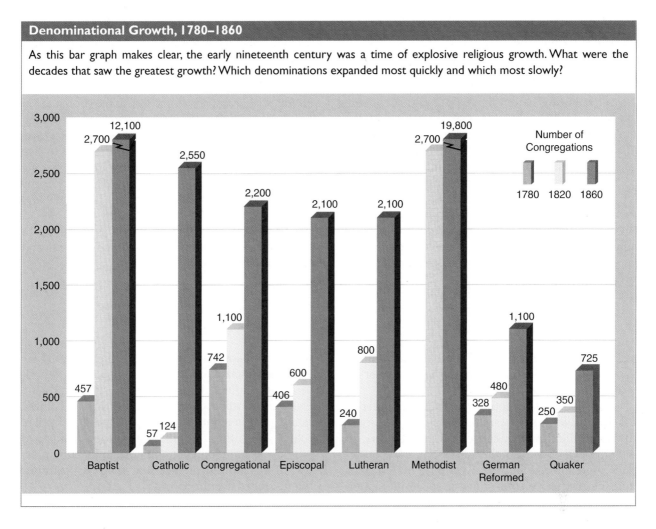

Denominational Growth, 1780–1860

As this bar graph makes clear, the early nineteenth century was a time of explosive religious growth. What were the decades that saw the greatest growth? Which denominations expanded most quickly and which most slowly?

months, Rochester experienced a citywide prayer meeting in which one conversion led to another.

The Rochester revival was part of a wave of religious enthusiasm in America that contributed to the tremendous growth of Methodists, Baptists, and other evangelical denominations in the first half of the nineteenth century. By 1844, Methodism became the country's largest denomination with more than a million members. Revivalist preachers emphasized emotion over doctrine, softening such Calvinist tenets as predestination that suggested that individual salvation resulted from God's decision rather than human effort and faith.

Jonathan Edwards had believed that revivals were God's miracles, but Finney understood that the human "agency" of the minister was crucial in causing a revival. "We must have exciting, powerful preaching," he said, "or the devil will have the people." He even published a do-it-yourself manual for other revivalists. But few could match Finney's powerful preaching style, which relied on both logic and emotions to trigger conversions. When he threw an imaginary brick at the Devil, people ducked. When

his finger pointed the descent of a sinner into hell, people in the back row stood up to see the final disappearance.

Other revivalists, especially in the South, sought personal conversion that brought with it the promise of salvation. American Catholics also caught the revival fervor in the 1830s. Scattered in small but growing numbers in the East and the Ohio River valley, urban Catholic leaders recognized that survival as a small, often despised religion depended on constant reinvigoration and evangelism. Focusing on the parish mission, energetic retreats and revivals gathered Catholics from miles around to preserve a religious heritage seriously threatened by life in Protestant America.

Finney believed that humans were not passive objects of God's predestined plan, but moral free agents who could choose good over evil and thereby eradicate sin. Unlike Catholic and southern revivalism, Finney revivals insisted that conversion and salvation were not the end of religious experience but the beginning. Finney encouraged not only individual reformation but also the commitment on the part of converted Christians to embrace the sacred duty of reforming society.

The Transcendentalists

No one knew this better than Ralph Waldo Emerson, a Concord, Massachusetts, essayist who was the era's foremost intellectual figure. Emerson's essays of the 1830s influenced the midcentury generation of reformist American thinkers, artists, and writers. New England intellectuals who lived near Emerson were called Transcendentalists because of their belief that truth was found in intuition beyond (that is, intuition that transcended) sense experience. Casting off the European intellectual tradition, Emerson urged Americans to look inward and to nature for self-knowledge, self-reliance, and the spark of divinity burning within them. "To acquaint a man with himself," he wrote, would inspire a "reverence" for self and others, which would then lead outward to social reform. "What is man born for," Emerson wrote, "but to be a Reformer?"

Ralph Waldo Emerson, "Self-Reliance" (1841)

Inspired by self-reflection, the Transcendentalists asked troublesome questions about the quality of American life. They challenged not only slavery, an obvious evil, but also the obsessive, competitive pace of economic life, the overriding materialism, and the restrictive conformity of social life. Emerson's friend, the brilliant Margaret Fuller, questioned the absence of women's voices, founded and edited *The Dial,* an influential Transcendentalist journal, and broke new ground by writing not just about women's rights but also about literature, prison reform, and the moral quality of American life. New York *Tribune* editor Horace Greeley called her "the most remarkable woman in America."

Although not considered Transcendentalists, Nathaniel Hawthorne and Herman Melville, two giants of midcentury American literature, also wrote of these many concerns and celebrated virtue over self-interest and emotion over reason. Hawthorne's great subject was the "truth of the human heart." In his greatest novel, *The Scarlet Letter* (1850), Hawthorne sympathetically told the story of a courageous Puritan woman's adultery and her eventual loving triumph over the narrowness of both cold intellect and intolerant conformity. Melville's epic novel *Moby Dick* (1851) was on one level a rousing story of whaling on the high seas in pursuit of the great white whale, and on another an allegory of good and evil, bravery and weakness, innocence and experience. Like Emerson and Fuller, Hawthorne and Melville

mirrored the tensions of the age as they explored issues of freedom and control.

When Emerson wrote, "Whoso would be a man, must be a nonconformist," he described his friend Henry David Thoreau. No one thought more deeply about the virtuous natural life than Thoreau. On July 4, 1845, he went to live in a small hut by Walden Pond, near Concord, to confront the "essential facts of life"—to discover who he was and how to live well. When Thoreau left Walden two years later, he protested against slavery and the Mexican War by refusing to pay his taxes. He went to jail briefly and wrote an essay, "Civil Disobedience" (1849), and a book, *Walden* (1854), both classic statements of what one person can do to protest unjust laws and wars and live a life of principle.

THE POLITICAL RESPONSE TO CHANGE

Although Transcendentalism touched only a few elite New Englanders, perhaps 40 percent of Americans were affected by evangelical Protestantism. Evangelical values and religious loyalties colored many people's understanding of the appropriate role of government and influenced their politics. As politics became more a popular than an elite interest, it was not surprising that religious commitments spilled over into it.

At the heart of American politics was the concern for the continued health of the democratic republican experiment. As American society changed, so did the understanding of what was needed to maintain that health. In the late 1850s, a Maine newspaper warned that the preservation of the nation's freedom depended on the willingness of its citizens to go to the polls. It was, in fact, the "positive duty of every citizen of a Republic to vote." This insistence on voting as crucial to the well-being of the country was a new emphasis in the United States and unique in the world at that time.

Before the 1820s, politics in both the United States and Europe was primarily an activity for the social and economic elite. In Europe, conservatives feared the political involvement of the lower classes and in both Great Britain and France resisted popular pressures to gain universal male suffrage. In the United States, however, the power of revolutionary ideas and the relative weakness of the country's upper classes led to a gradual extension of the franchise to all white men. During the early nineteenth century, many states were

Ralph Waldo Emerson, "The Concord Hymn" (1837)

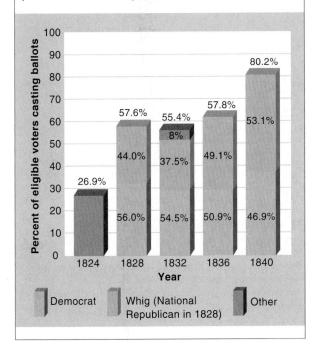

More Americans Vote for President, 1824–1840

The single-party system (Jeffersonian Democratic Republican) that existed in 1824 collapsed with the intense personal rivalries and ideological differences of the 1820s and 1830s. The emergence of a two-party system in the Jacksonian era dramatically increased (white male) voter participation to percentages far exceeding those of modern U.S. presidential elections. How do you explain this tremendous growth?

voluntarily removing voting restrictions even though the majority of white men did not trouble themselves with political matters. But the Panic of 1819 and the spirited presidential campaigns for Andrew Jackson helped create widespread interest in politics and a distinctive American style of politics. For many Americans, political participation became an important way of asserting and supporting important values and promoting their vision of the republic.

Changing Political Culture

Jackson's presidency was crucial in bringing politics to the center of many Americans' lives. Styling himself as the people's candidate in 1828, Andrew Jackson derided the Adams administration as corrupt and aristocratic and promised a more democratic political system. He told voters that he intended to "purify" and "reform the Government," purging all "who have been appointed from political considerations or against the

will of the people." Most Americans believed the campaign rhetoric. Four times more men turned out to vote in the election of 1828 than had four years earlier. They gave Jackson a resounding 56 percent of their ballots. No other president in the century would equal that percentage of popular support.

Despite his image as a democratic hero, Jackson was not personally very democratic, nor did the era he symbolized involve any significant redistribution of wealth. Jackson owned slaves, defended slavery, and condoned mob attacks on abolitionists like Marius Robinson. He disliked Native Americans and ordered the forcible removal of the southeastern tribal nations to west of the Mississippi River in blatant disregard of treaty rights and a Supreme Court decision. Belying promises of widening opportunity, the rich got richer during the Jacksonian era, and most farming and urban laboring families struggled.

But the nation's political life had changed in important ways. The old system of politics, based on elite coalitions bound by ties of family and friendship and dependent on voters deferring to their "betters," largely disappeared. In its place emerged a competitive party system, begun early in the republic but now oriented toward heavy voter participation. The major parties grew adept at raising money, selecting and promoting candidates, and bringing voters to the polls. A new "democratic" style of political life emerged as parties sponsored conventions, rallies (much like fervent evangelical revivals), and parades to encourage political participation and identification. Party politics became a central preoccupation for many adult white males. Even women, who were formally excluded from voting, were often caught up in party politics and turned up at rallies and speeches.

Political parties appealed to popular emotions, religious views, and ethnic prejudices. Party-subsidized newspapers regularly indulged in scurrilous attacks on rivals. The language of politics became contentious and militaristic. Jackson's rhetoric exemplified the new trends. He described an opponent as an "enemy" who waged "war against the cause of the people." Politicians talked of elections as battles and party members as their disciplined "rank and file." Strong party identification became part of the new national political culture.

DOCUMENT

Davy Crockett, Advice to Politicians (1835)

Jackson's Path to the White House

Andrew Jackson's early career gave few hints of his future political importance. Orphaned at 14, young

Jackson grew up in poverty and was often in trouble. As a law student, he was "a most roaring, rollicking, game-cocking, horse-racing, card-playing, mischievous fellow." Still, he passed the bar and set out at age 21 to seek his fortune in frontier Nashville. There he built up a successful law practice and went on to become state attorney general, a substantial landowner, and a prominent citizen.

Jackson's national reputation stemmed mainly from his military exploits, primarily against Native Americans. As major general of the Tennessee militia, he proved able and popular, winning the nickname of "Old Hickory" for his toughness. His victory over the Creek nation in the South in 1813 and 1814 brought notoriety and an appointment as major general in the U.S. Army. Victory at New Orleans in 1815 made him a national hero. Within two years, he was talked of as a presidential candidate. While aggressive military forays into Spanish Florida in 1818 bothered rival politicians and added to Jackson's reputation for scandal, they increased both his popularity and his interest in the presidency. Recognizing that his greatest appeal lay with ordinary people, Jackson cultivated their support. But he also secured effective political backing, and by 1824 he sought nomination for the presidency.

Jackson won both the popular and the electoral votes in 1824 but lost in the House of Representatives to John Quincy Adams. This failure highlighted the importance of political organization. Confident of his strength in the West and helped by Adams's vice president, John C. Calhoun, in the South, Jackson organized his campaign by setting up committees and newspapers in many states and by encouraging efforts to undermine Adams and Henry Clay.

A loose coalition promoting Jackson's candidacy began to call itself the Democratic party. Politicians of diverse views from all sections of the country were drawn to it, including Martin Van Buren of New York. Jackson masterfully waffled on controversial issues. He concealed his dislike of banks and paper money and vaguely advocated a "middle and just course" on the tariff. He promised to cleanse government of corruption and privileged interests.

The Jackson–Adams campaign in 1828 degenerated into a nasty but entertaining contest. The Democrats whipped up enthusiasm with barbecues, mass rallies, and parades and gave out buttons and hats with hickory leaves attached. Few people discussed issues, and both sides made slanderous personal attacks. Supporters of Adams and Clay, who called themselves National Republicans, branded Jackson "an adulterer, a gambler, a cockfighter, a brawler, a drunkard, and a murderer," and maligned his wife Rachel as immoral.

The Man of the People   Unlike rivals J. Q. Adams and Henry Clay, who deprived Jackson of the presidency in 1824, Jackson (nicknamed "Old Hickory" after America's toughest hardwood) claimed to honor the constitutional electoral system and the will of the people. What many historical events does this poster refer to? Was Jackson a man of the people? *(Collection of the New-York Historical Society, 8838)*

The Jacksonians, in turn, charged Adams with buying Clay's support in 1824 and described him as a "stingy, undemocratic" aristocrat determined to destroy the people's liberties. Worse yet, they said, Adams was an intellectual. Campaign slogans contrasted the hero of New Orleans, "a man who can fight," with a wimpy Adams, "a man who can write."

Jackson's supporters in Washington worked to ensure his election by devising a tariff bill to win necessary support in key states. Under the leadership of Van Buren, who hoped to replace Calhoun as Jackson's heir apparent, the Democrats in Congress managed to pass what opponents called the "Tariff of Abominations." It arbitrarily raised rates to protect New England textiles, Pennsylvania iron, and some agricultural goods, securing voters in those states where the Democrats needed more support. John Randolph of Virginia sneered that the tariff "referred to manufactures of no . . . kind but the manufacture of a President of the United States."

The efforts of Jackson and his party paid off as he won an astonishing 647,286 ballots, about 56 percent of the total. Organization, money, effective publicity, and a popular style of campaigning had brought the 60-year-old Jackson to the presidency. His inauguration, however, horrified many. Washington was packed for the ceremonies. When Jackson appeared to take the oath of office, wild cheering broke out. Few heard him, but many hoped to shake the new president's hand, and Jackson was all but mobbed. At the White House reception, the crowd got completely out of hand. As Justice Joseph Story observed, a throng of people, "from the highest and most polished, down to the most vulgar and gross," poured into the White House, overturning furniture in a rush for food and punch. As Jackson escaped through a side door, many guests dove out windows when the wine and ice cream were carried out to the lawn. The inauguration, to Story, meant the "reign of King Mob." But another observer called it a "proud day for the people." Their contrasting views on the inauguration captured the essence of the Jackson era.

Andrew Jackson's Inauguration

Old Hickory's Vigorous Presidency

Although Jackson adopted vague positions on important issues during the campaign, as president he needed to confront many of them. His decisions, often controversial, helped sharpen what it meant to be a Democrat.

A few key convictions, drawn from Jeffersonian principles—the limited power of the national government, the obligation of the national government to defend the interests of the nation's average people against the "monied aristocracy"—guided Jackson's actions as president. Seeing himself as the people's most authentic representative (only the president was elected by all the people), Jackson intended to be a vigorous executive. More than any predecessor, Jackson used presidential power in the name of the people and justified his actions by appeals to the voters. Jackson asserted his power most dramatically through the veto. His six predecessors had cast only nine vetoes, mostly against measures that they had believed unconstitutional. Jackson, however, vetoed 12 bills during his two terms, often because they conflicted with his political agenda.

Andrew Jackson Taking the Oath of Office in 1829

Jackson had promised to correct what he called an undemocratic and corrupt system of government officeholding. Too often, "unfaithful or incompetent" men clung to government jobs for years. Jackson proposed to throw these "scoundrels" out and establish a system of rotation of office. The duties of public office were so "plain and simple," he said, that ordinary men could fulfill them.

Jackson's rhetoric was more extreme than his actions. He did not replace officeholders wholesale. In the first year and a half of his presidency, he removed 919 officeholders of a total of 10,093, mostly for corruption or incompetence. Nor were the new Democratic appointees especially plain, untutored, or honest; they were in fact much like their predecessors. Still, Jackson's rhetoric helped create a new democratic political culture that would last for most of the nineteenth century.

His policy on internal improvements—roads, canals, and other forms of transportation—was less far-seeing. Like most Americans, Jackson recognized their economic importance and as president wished "to see them extended to every part of the country." But Jackson was against infringement of states' rights. When proposals for federal support for internal improvements seemed to rob local and state authorities of their proper function, he opposed them. In 1830, he vetoed the Maysville Road bill, which proposed federal funding for a road in Henry Clay's Kentucky. But projects of national significance, such as river improvements and lighthouses, were different. During his presidency, Jackson supported an annual average of $1.3 million in internal improvements.

In a period of rapid economic change, tariffs stirred heated debate. New England and the mid-Atlantic states, centers of manufacturing, favored protective tariffs. The South had long opposed them because they made it more expensive to buy manufactured goods from the North or abroad and threatened to provoke foreign retaliation against southern cotton and tobacco exports. Feelings ran particularly high in South Carolina. Some of that state's leaders mistakenly believed that the tariff was the prime reason for the depression that hung over their state. In addition, some worried that the federal government might eventually interfere with slavery, a frightening prospect in a state where slaves outnumbered whites.

Vice President Calhoun, a brilliant political thinker and opponent of the tariff, provided the appropriate theory to check federal power and to protect minority rights. "We are not a nation," he once remarked, "but a Union, a confederacy of equal and sovereign states." In 1828, the same year as the hateful "tariff of abominations," Calhoun anonymously published *Exposition and Protest,* presenting nullification as a means by which southern states could protect themselves from harmful national action by declaring legislation null and void.

Two years later, Calhoun's doctrine was aired in a Senate debate over public land policy. South Carolina's Robert Hayne defined nullification and, in the name of liberty, urged western states to adopt it. New

Andrew Jackson   This representation of Andrew Jackson was from his 1832 campaign for reelection. Study the depiction of Jackson carefully. What clothing is he wearing? What are the objects surrounding the oval portrait? Why is the eagle in the picture? What message and appeal does the image convey? *(Library of Congress, cph 3b37026)*

England's Daniel Webster responded. The federal government, he said, was no mere agent of the state legislatures. It was "made for the people, made by the people, and answerable to the people." No state legislature, therefore, could ever be sovereign over the people. Aware that nullification could mean a "once glorious Union . . . drenched . . . in fraternal blood," Webster cried out in his powerful closing words that the appropriate motto for the nation was not "Liberty first and Union afterwards, but Liberty and Union, now and forever, one and inseparable!"

The drama was repeated a month later in a dinner toast, when President Jackson declared his position. Despite his support of states' rights, Jackson did not believe that any state had the right to reject the will of the majority or to destroy the Union. Jackson rose for a toast, held high his glass, and said, "Our Union—it must be preserved." Thus challenged, Calhoun followed: "The Union—next to our liberty most dear." The split between them widened over personal as well as ideological issues, and in 1832, Calhoun resigned as vice president. Final rupture came in a collision over the tariff and nullification.

In 1832, hewing to Jackson's "middle course," Congress modified the tariff of 1828 by retaining

high duties on some goods but lowering other rates to an earlier level. A South Carolina convention later that year adopted an Ordinance of Nullification, voiding the tariffs of 1828 and 1832 in the state. The legislature funded a volunteer army and threatened secession if the federal government tried to force the state to comply. South Carolina had attacked the principles of federal union and majority rule. Jackson responded forcefully. To the "ambitious malcontents" in South Carolina, he proclaimed emphatically that "the laws of the United States must be executed. . . . The Union will be preserved and treason and rebellion promptly put down."

DOCUMENT

South Carolina's Ordinance of Nullification (1832)

Jackson's proclamation stimulated an outburst of patriotism all over the country, isolating South Carolina. Jackson asked Congress for legislation to enforce tariff duties (the Force Bill of 1833), and new tariff revisions, engineered by Clay and supported by Calhoun, called for reductions over a 10-year period. Its objective secured, South Carolina quickly repealed its nullification of the tariff laws but saved face by nullifying the Force Bill, which Jackson ignored. The crisis was over. Left unresolved, however, were the constitutional issues it raised. Was the Union permanent? Was secession a valid way to protect minority rights? Such questions would trouble Americans for three decades.

DOCUMENT

The Force Bill (1833)

Jackson's Native American Policy

Jackson not only threatened force on South Carolina, he used it on southeastern Native Americans. His policy of forcible relocation westward and on reservations defined white practice toward Native Americans for the rest of the century.

In the early nineteenth century, the vast lands of the five "civilized nations" of the Southeast (the Cherokee, Choctaw, Chickasaw, Seminole, and Creek) had been seriously eroded by land-hungry whites supported by military campaigns led by professional Native American fighters such as Jackson. The Creek lost 22 million acres in Georgia and Alabama after Jackson defeated them at Horseshoe Bend in 1814. Land cessions to the government and private sales accounted for even bigger losses: Cherokee holdings of more than 50 million acres in 1802 had dwindled to only 9 million acres 20 years later.

A Supreme Court decision in 1823 declaring that Native Americans could occupy but not hold title to land in the United States bolstered the trend. Seeing that their survival was threatened, Native American nations acted. By 1825, the Creek, Cherokee, and

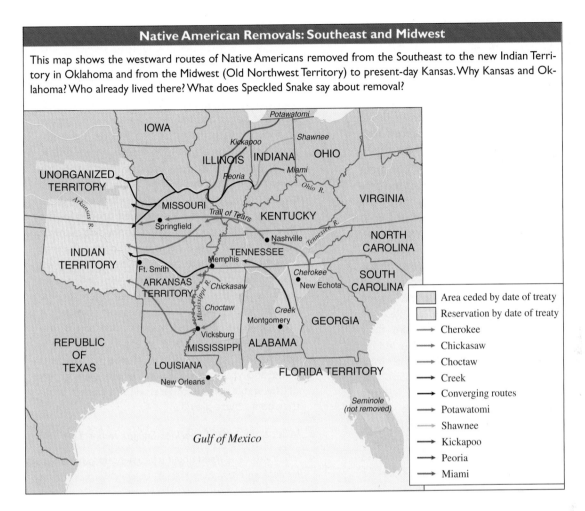

Native American Removals: Southeast and Midwest

This map shows the westward routes of Native Americans removed from the Southeast to the new Indian Territory in Oklahoma and from the Midwest (Old Northwest Territory) to present-day Kansas. Why Kansas and Oklahoma? Who already lived there? What does Speckled Snake say about removal?

Chickasaw restricted land sales to government agents. The Cherokee, having already assimilated such elements of white culture as agricultural practices and slaveholding (see Chapter 9), established a police force to prevent local leaders from selling off tribal lands. Native American determination to resist whites confronted white resolve to gain tribal lands for cotton. Jackson's election in 1828 boosted efforts to relocate the Native Americans west of the Mississippi.

In 1829, Jackson recommended to Congress removal of the southeastern tribes. Appealing at first to sympathy, Jackson argued that because the Native Americans were "surrounded by the whites with their arts of civilization," they were inevitably doomed to "weakness and decay." Removal was justified, Jackson claimed, by both "humanity and national honor." He also insisted that state laws should prevail over the claims of either Native Americans or the federal government (thus contradicting his tariff policy).

The crisis came to a head in Georgia that same year, when the Georgia legislature declared the Cherokee tribal council

DOCUMENT

Andrew Jackson, First Annual Message to Congress (1829)

illegal and claimed jurisdiction over both the tribe and its lands. In 1830, the Cherokee were forbidden to bring suits or testify against whites in the Georgia courts. The Cherokee protested to the Supreme Court. In two landmark cases in 1831 and 1832 (*Cherokee Nation* v. *Georgia* and *Worcester* v. *Georgia*), Chief Justice Marshall held that the Georgia law was "repugnant to the Constitution" with "no force" over the Cherokee, and that by inviolable treaty rights Native Americans were considered "domestic dependent nations" of the U.S. federal government, a ruling that would help restore Native American treaty rights.

Legal victory, however, did not suppress white land hunger. With Jackson's blessing, Georgians defied Marshall's decision. By 1835, harassment, intimidation, and bribery had persuaded a minority of chiefs to sign a removal treaty. That year, Jackson informed the Cherokee, "You cannot remain where you are. Circumstances . . . render it impossible that you can flourish in the midst of a civilized community." Many Cherokee refused to leave and the nation split into two factions. Chief John Ross protested to Congress that the treaty was illegitimate. "We are stripped

AMERICAN VOICES

Speckled Snake, A Native American Reply to Jackson's Removal Policy

A warrior chief of the Creek Nation, Speckled Snake, responded to President Jackson's mixed message declaring concern for Native Americans even as he recommended their removal to Oklahoma.

Brothers! We have heard the Talk of our great father; it is very kind. He says he loves his red children. Brothers! I have listened to many talks from our great father. When he first came over the wide waters, he was but a little man, and wore a red coat. Our chiefs met him on the banks of the Savannah, and smoked with him the pipe of peace. He was then very little. . . . The Muscogees gave the white man land, and kindled him a fire, that he might warm himself, and when his enemies, the pale faces of the South, made war on him, their young men drew the tomahawk, and protected his head from the scalping knife. But when the white man had warmed himself before the Indian's fire, and filled himself with their hominy, he became very large. With a step he bestrode the mountains, and his feet covered the plains and the vallies. His hands grasped the Eastern and the Western sea, and his head rested on the moon. Then he became our great father. He loves his red children, and he said, 'get a little farther, lest I tread on thee.' With one foot he pushed the red man over the Oconee [River], and with the other he trampled down the graves of his fathers, and the forests where he had so long hunted the deer. But our great father still loved his red children; and he soon made to them another talk, he said. 'get a little farther, you are too near me.' . . . Yet he continued to love his red children, and when he found them too slow in moving, he sent his great guns before him to sweep his path. Brothers! I have listened to a great many talks from our great father.—But they always began and ended in this—'get a little further, you are too near me . . . there is a pleasant country—it shall be yours forever.' I have listened to his present talk; he says the land where you now live is not yours—go beyond the Mississippi; there is game, and you may remain while the grass grows or the water runs. Brothers, will not our great father come there also?"

- What is the tone of Speckled Snake's remarks?

- What has he learned about white behavior and how does he deal with it?

The Trail of Tears
Their attempts at assimilating into white society having failed, the Cherokee finally succumbed to white pressures and their own internal divisions and were forced to travel along the "Trail of Tears" to Oklahoma in 1838. About 4,000 died along the way. The Cherokee removal was actually the last major Native American group east of the Mississippi forced west. Describe as much as you can about what is in this painting. What emotions does it arouse in you? (Robert Lindneaux, Trail of Tears. Woolaroc Museum, Bartlesville, Oklahoma)

Key Court Cases on Native American Rights

These Supreme Court cases decided in the nineteenth century have provided the legal basis for Native American activism in the twentieth century. Although Native American victories in court during the Jacksonian period did not halt the ability of whites to take over tribal lands, in the twentieth century, these court decisions allowed Native American tribes to win numerous court victories. What clauses in these decisions might provide the basis for those later victories?

Johnson & Graham's Lessee v. William Mcintosh (1823)

This case focused on the status of a land grant from a Native American tribe to an individual person. The decision recognized the tribes sovereignty and its rights to land. The court stated that only the federal government was competent to negotiate with tribes for their lands. "It has been contested that the Indian claims amounted to nothing. Their right of possession has never been questioned . . . the Court is decidedly of the opinion, that the plaintiffs do not exhibit a title which can be sustained in the Courts of the United States."

Cherokee Nation v. Georgia (1831)

This case involved the status of state law within the Cherokee nation. The court classified the Native American tribes as domestic dependent nations whose relationship was like that of a ward to a guardian.
"Though the Indians are acknowledged to have an unquestionable, and, heretofore, unquestioned right to the lands they occupy until that right shall be extinguished by a voluntary cession to our government, yet it may well be doubted whether those tribes . . . can, with strict accuracy, be denominated as foreign nations. They may more correctly, perhaps, be denominated as domestic dependent nations."

Worcester v. Georgia (1832)

This case was prompted by the state of Georgia's attempt to extend state law over the Cherokee nation. The decision reaffirmed Native American political rights, stating that Georgia laws had no force in Native American territories and that only the federal government had jurisdiction in tribal territories.
"The Indian nations had always been considered as distinct, independent, political communities . . . the settled doctrine of the law of nations is, that a weaker power does not surrender its independence—its rights to self-government—by associating with a stronger."

Mitchell v. United States (1835)

This decision affirmed the rights Native Americans have as occupants (not owners) of the land.
"It is enough to consider as a settled principle, that the right of occupancy is considered as sacred as the fee simple of the white."

---

of every attribute of freedom. . . . Our property may be plundered . . . our lives may be taken away."

His words did no good. In 1837 and 1838, the U.S. Army removed the Cherokee west to the Indian Territory in present-day Oklahoma. An eyewitness described how the Cherokee trek began: "families at dinner were startled by the sudden gleam of bayonets in the doorway and rose to be driven with blows and oaths along the weary miles of trail that led to the stockade. Men were seized in their fields . . . women were taken from their [spinning] wheels and children from their play." As they looked back, they saw "their homes in flames, fired by the lawless rabble that followed on the heels of the soldiers to loot and pillage."

IMAGE
Cherokee Trail of Tears

The removal, whose $6 million cost was deducted from the $9 million awarded the Cherokee for its eastern lands, killed perhaps a quarter of the 15,000 who set out. The Cherokee remember this as the "Trail of Tears." Despite resistance, especially by the Seminole in Florida, between 1821 and 1840, all southeastern tribes as well as those in the Old Northwest were forced westward to Kansas and Oklahoma. Although both Jackson and the Removal Act of 1830 had

DOCUMENT
Andrew Jackson, Second Annual Message to Congress (1830)

promised to protect and forever guarantee the Native American lands in the West, within a generation those promises, like others before and since, would be broken. Native American removal left the eastern United States open for the enormous economic expansion described in Chapter 10.

Jackson's Bank War and "Van Ruin's" Depression

As the (white) people's advocate, Jackson could not ignore the Second Bank of the United States, which in 1816 had received a charter for 20 years. The bank generated intense feelings. Jackson called it a "monster" that threatened the people's liberties. But it was not as irresponsible as Jacksonians imagined.

Guided since 1823 by the aristocratic Nicholas Biddle, the Philadelphia bank and its 29 branches generally played a responsible economic role in an expansionary period. As the nation's largest commercial bank, the "B.U.S." could shift funds around the country as needed. It influenced state banks by restraining them from making unwise loans by insisting that they back their notes with specie (gold or silver coin) and by calling in its own loans. The bank accepted federal deposits, made commercial loans, and bought and sold government bonds.

Businessmen, state bankers needing credit, and nationalist politicians such as Webster and Clay, who were on the bank's payroll, all favored it.

Other Americans, led by the president, distrusted the bank. Businessmen and speculators in western lands resented its control over state banking and wanted cheap, inflated money to finance new projects and expansion. Some state bankers resented its power over their actions. Southern and western farmers regarded it as immoral because it dealt with paper rather than landed property. Others simply thought it was unconstitutional.

Jackson had long opposed the B.U.S. He hated banks in general because of a near–financial disaster in his own past and also because he and his advisers considered the B.U.S. the chief example of a special privilege monopoly that hurt the common people—farmers, artisans, and debtors. Jackson called the bank an "irresponsible power," a threat to the republic. Its power and financial resources, he thought, made it a "vast electioneering engine" with "power to control the Government."

Aware of Jackson's hostility, Clay and Webster persuaded Biddle to ask Congress for a new charter in 1832, four years ahead of schedule. They reasoned that in an election year, Jackson would not risk a veto. The bill to recharter the bank swept through Congress. Jackson took up the challenge. "The bank . . . is trying to kill me," he told Van Buren, "but I will kill it." Jackson determined not only to veto the bill but also to carry his case to the public. His veto message, condemning the bank as undemocratic, un-American, and unconstitutional, was meant to stir up voters. He presented the bank as a dangerous monopoly that gave special privileges to the rich and harmed "the humble members of society." He also pointed to the high percentage of foreign investors in the bank. Jackson's veto message turned the issue into a struggle between the people and the aristocracy as he made the bank into a symbol of everything that worried Americans in a time of change.

DOCUMENT

Andrew Jackson, Veto of the Bank Bill (1832)

The bank furor helped clarify party differences. In the election of 1832, the National Republicans, now calling themselves Whigs, nominated Henry Clay, and they and Biddle spent thousands of dollars trying to defeat "King Andrew." Democratic campaign rhetoric pitted Jackson, the people, and democracy against Clay, the bank, and aristocracy. The Anti-Masons, the first third party in American political life, expressed popular resentments against the elitist Masonic order (Jackson was a member) and other secret societies.

Jackson won handsomely, with 124,000 more popular votes than the combined total for Clay and the Anti-Mason candidate, William Wirt. "He may be President for life if he chooses," said Wirt of Jackson.

Jackson, seeing the election as a victory for his bank policy, closed in on Biddle, even though the bank's charter had four years to run. He decided to weaken the B.U.S. by transferring $10 million in government funds to state banks. Although two secretaries of the treasury balked at the removal request as financially unsound, Jackson persisted until he found one, Roger Taney, willing to do it. Taney's reward was an appointment as chief justice of the Supreme Court when Marshall died.

Jackson's war with Biddle and the bank had serious economic consequences. A wave of speculation

A DEMOCRATIC VOTER

A Democratic Voter This print may date from the election of 1836. The artist was making fun of a split in the New York City Democratic party. What clues indicate the party of the artist, or his attitude toward the Irish? What do you learn about the voting process and political culture? How secret was the ballot? *(Library of Congress, cph 3a33207)* in western lands and ambitious new state internal improvement schemes in the mid-1830s produced inflated land prices and a flood of paper money. Even Jackson was concerned, and he tried to curtail irresponsible economic activity. In July 1836, he issued the Specie Circular, announcing that the government would accept only gold and silver in payment for public lands. Panicky investors rushed to change paper notes into specie, while banks started calling in loans. The result was the Panic of 1837. Jackson was blamed for this rapid monetary expansion followed by sudden deflation, but international trade problems with Britain and China probably contributed more to the panic and to the ensuing seven years of depression.

Whatever the primary cause, Jackson left his successor, Martin Van Buren (who was elected in 1836 over a trio of Whig opponents), with an economic crisis. Van Buren had barely taken the oath of office in 1837 when banks and businesses began to collapse. "Martin Van Ruin's" presidency was dominated by a severe depression. As New York banks suspended credit and began calling in loans, some $6 million was lost on defaulted debts. By the fall of 1837, one-third of America's workers were unemployed, and thousands of others had only part-time work. Those who kept their jobs saw wages fall by 30 to 50 percent within two years. The price of necessities such as flour and coal nearly doubled. As winter neared in late 1837, a journalist estimated that 200,000 New

Yorkers were "in utter hopeless distress with no means of surviving the winter but those provided by charity." They took to the streets demanding, "Bread! Meat! Rent! Fuel!," and mostly "for Work!"

Soup kitchens and bread lines grew faster than jobs. Laboring families found themselves defenseless, for the depression destroyed the trade union movement begun a decade earlier—a demise hastened by employers who imposed longer hours, cut wages and piece rates, and divided workers. As the hardships of the depression grew worse, violence increased. In 1842, when Philadelphia textile employers lowered wages below subsistence levels, angry hand-loom weavers broke machinery, destroyed cloth, and wrecked the homes of Irish strikebreakers.

Job competition, poverty, and ethnic animosities led to violent clashes in other eastern cities as well. "How is it," a Philadelphia mechanic asked in 1837, that in a country as rich as the United States so many people were "pinched for the common necessaries of life . . . [and] bowed down with gloom and despair?" President Van Buren's responses to the social misery behind this question were sympathetic but limited. An executive order in 1840 declaring a 10-hour workday for federal employees affected few workers.

The Second American Party System

By the mid-1830s, a new two-party system and a lively national political culture had emerged in the

The Second American Party System		
	Democrats	**Whigs**
Leaders	Andrew Jackson	Henry Clay
	John C. Calhoun	Daniel Webster
	Martin Van Buren	John Quincy Adams
	Thomas Hart Benton	William Henry Harrison
Political tradition	Republican party (Jefferson, Madison)	Federalist party (Hamilton, John Adams)
Major Political Beliefs		
	State and local autonomy	National power
	Opposition to monopoly and privilege	Support for U.S. Bank, high tariff
	Low land prices and tariffs	Internal improvements
	Freedom from government interference	Broad government role in reforming America
Primary Sources of Support		
Region	South and West	New England, mid-Atlantic, Upper Midwest
Class	Middle-class and small farmers, northeastern urban laborers and artisans	Big southern planters and wealthy businessmen, pockets of middling farmers in Midwest and South, artisans
Ethnicity	Scots–Irish, Irish, French, German, and Canadian immigrants	English, New England old stock
Religion	Catholics, frontier Baptists and Methodists, free thinkers	Presbyterians, Congregationalists, Quakers, moralists, reformers

Appealing to the Voters   (left) In the election of 1840, the Whigs "out-Jacksoned the Jacksonians" by playing to the popular political style of slogans, songs, and cider. How is Harrison portrayed? What does "Tippecanoe" refer to? (above) Louisiana Democrats responded to the Whig use of the log cabin and cider campaign with this cartoon, titled the "Federal-Abolition-Whig Trap to Catch Voters In." What dangers await this unwary voter by the promise of hard cider? "Just let him get a taste," the text said, "and they come down at once upon him, hard and heavy, swig after swig . . . " *(Left: Cincinnati Historical Society Library; above: Library of Congress)*

United States. The parties had taken shape amid the conflicts of Jackson's presidency and the religious fervor of the Second Great Awakening. Although both parties included wealthy and influential leaders and mirrored the nation's growing diversity, Democrats had the better claim to be "the party of the common man" with strength in all sections of the country.

Whigs represented greater wealth than Democrats and were strongest in New England and in areas settled by New Englanders across the Upper Midwest. Appealing to businessmen and manufacturers, Whigs generally endorsed Clay's American System: a national bank, federally supported internal improvements, and tariff protection for industry. Many large southern cotton planters joined the Whig party because of its position on bank credit and internal improvements. Whigs ran almost evenly with Democrats in the South for a decade, and artisans and laborers belonged equally to each party. The difficulty in drawing clear regional or class distinctions between Whigs and Democrats suggests that ethnic, religious, and cultural background also influenced party choice.

In the Jeffersonian tradition, the Democrats espoused liberty and local rule. They wanted freedom from those who legislated morality, from religious tyranny, from special privilege, and from too much government. For them, the best society was one in which all Americans were free to follow their own individual interests. The Democrats appealed to members of religious denominations that had suffered discrimination in colonies and states where there had been an established church. Scots–Irish, French, German, and Irish Catholic immigrants, as well as freethinkers and labor organizers, tended to be Jacksonians. Democrats were less moralistic than Whigs on matters such as drinking and slavery. Their religious background generally taught the inevitability of sin and evil, so Democrats sought to keep politics separate from moral issues.

By contrast, for many Whigs, religious and moral values shaped political goals and the way they understood issues. Calling themselves "the party of law and order," most Whigs did not think Americans needed more freedom; rather, they had to learn to use the freedom they already had. If all men were to vote, they should learn how to use their political privileges. Old-stock New England Yankee Congregationalists and Presbyterians were usually Whigs. So were Quakers and evangelical Protestants, who believed that positive government action could change moral behavior and eradicate sin. Whigs supported a wide variety of reforms, such as temperance, antislavery, public education, and strict observance of the Sabbath, as well as government action to promote economic development.

Party identification played an increasingly large part in the lives of American men. Gaudy new electioneering styles were designed to recruit new voters into the political process and ensure party loyalty. Politics offered excitement, camaraderie, and a way to shape the changing world.

The election of 1840 illustrated the new political culture. Passing over Henry Clay, the Whigs nominated William Henry Harrison of Indiana, the aging hero of the Battle of Tippecanoe of 1811. Virginian John Tyler was nominated as vice president to underline the regional diversity of the party. The Democrats had no choice but to renominate Van Buren, who conducted a quiet campaign. The Whig campaign, however, featured every form of popularized appeal: songs, cartoons, barbecues, and torchlight parades, posing Harrison (who lived in a mansion) in front of a rural log cabin and dispensing jugs of hard cider to grateful voters.

AUDIO

Martin Van Buren

The Whigs labeled Van Buren an aristocratic dandy, contrasting him with their humble candidate by his cabin. Harrison reminded voters of General Jackson, and they swept him into office, with 234 electoral votes to Van Buren's 60. In one of the largest turnouts in American history, more than 80 percent of eligible voters marched to the polls. A Democratic party journal acknowledged that "we taught them how to conquer us."

Concern over the new politics outlasted Harrison, who died only a month after taking office. One man complained during the campaign that he was tired of all the hoopla over "the Old Hero. Nothing but politics ... mass-meetings are held in every groggery." The implied criticism of the role that alcohol played in party politics highlights the moral and religious perspective many Americans, especially Whigs, brought to politics. Others, however, rejected politics and sought other means to impose order and morality on American society.

PERFECTIONIST REFORM AND UTOPIANISM

"Be ye therefore perfect even as your Father in heaven is perfect," commanded the Bible. Mid-nineteenth-century reformers, inspired by the Finney revivals, took the challenge seriously. Eventually, many believed, a perfected millennial era—1,000 years of

Motivations and Causes of Reform in America, 1830–1850

- Changing relationships between men and women, masters and workers as a result of the market economy, growth of cities, and increasing immigration
- Finney and other religious revivals in the Second Great Awakening
- Social activist and ethical impulses of the Whig party
- Psychological anxieties over shifting class and ethnic relationships
- Family traditions and youthful idealism
- Puritan and Revolutionary traditions of the American mission to remake the world
- Republican ideology and Enlightenment emphasis on virtue and good citizenship
- Romantic literary influences such as Transcendentalism

peace, harmony, and Christian brotherhood—would bring the Second Coming of Christ.

The perfectionist thrust in religion fit America's sense of itself as chosen by God to reform the world. The impulse to reform in the 1830s had deep-rooted causes: the Puritan idea of American mission; the secular examples of founding fathers such as Benjamin Franklin to do good, reinforced by Republican ideology and romantic beliefs in the natural goodness of human nature; the social activist tendencies in Whig political ideology; anxiety over shifting class relationships and socioeconomic change; family influence and the desire of young people to choose careers of principled service; and the direct influence of revivalism.

The International Character of Reform

Not all the forces leading to reform came from within. During the early decades of the nineteenth century, the Atlantic Ocean was a highway for reform ideas and reformers. Many of the conditions that troubled Americans, often spawned by industrialization, also troubled Europeans. Women organized in Britain and the United States to reform prostitutes. Societies to encourage temperance flourished in Germany, Ireland, and England as well as the United States. French and British liberals agitated to end the slave trade as did their American counterparts.

A steady stream of men and women traveled from one side of the Atlantic to the other, raising money, publicizing their ideas, studying what had been done outside their own country, and setting up social experiments. Abolitionists Frederick Douglass and William Lloyd Garrison visited England to gain support for their struggle against slavery, while English abolitionist George Thompson toured the northern states to assist abolitionists there. Scottish cotton mill owner Robert Owen came to the United States in the 1820s to set up a socialist community after creating a model factory town in Scotland.

There was cross-fertilization across national boundaries of ideas and reform strategies. Owen's book *The Book of the Moral World* (1820) inspired cooperative efforts of many kinds while the work of female antislavery societies in Britain and Scotland served as models for American women. Letters between reformers in different countries also helped strengthen the reform commitment and inspire action. Hearing of success elsewhere gave faith that change might come at home, while learning of failures prompted discussions of appropriate strategies.

The Dilemmas of Reform

Throughout the Atlantic world, reformers faced difficult dilemmas about how best to effect change. Is it more effective to appeal to people's minds in order to change bad institutions, or to change institutions first, assuming that altered behavior will then change attitudes? Taking the first path, the reformer relies on education, the moral suasion of sermons, tracts, literature, argument, and personal testimony. Following the second, the reformer acts politically and institutionally, seeking to pass laws, win elections, form unions, boycott goods, and create or abolish institutions. Reformers must also decide whether to attempt to bring about limited, piecemeal practical change on a single issue or go for ideal utopian perfection in eliminating all social evils. Should they use or recommend force, even violence, enter into coalitions with less principled potential allies, or maintain their values at all cost?

As Marius and Emily Robinson understood, promoting change has its costs. Advocates of change experience enormous pressures, recriminations, and economic or physical persecution. Moreover, reformers invariably disagree on appropriate ideology and tactics, and so they end up quarreling with one another. Although

reformers suffer pressure to conform, their duty to themselves, their society, and their God sustains their commitment.

Utopian Communities: Oneida and the Shakers

Thoreau tried to lead an ideal solitary life. Others tried to redeem a flawed society that was losing the cohesion and traditional values of small community life by creating miniature utopian societies—alternatives to a world of factories, foreigners, immorality, and entrepreneurs.

In 1831, as President Jackson and the South Carolina nullifiers squared off, as Nat Turner planned his revolt, and as the citizens of Rochester sought ways of controlling their workers' drinking habits, a young man in Putney, Vermont, heard Charles Finney preach on one of his whirlwind tours of New England. John Humphrey Noyes was an instant, if unorthodox, convert.

Noyes believed that final conversion led to absolute perfection and complete release from sin. But his earthly happiness was soon sorely tested when a woman he loved rejected both his doctrine and his marriage offer. Despondent, Noyes wrote to a friend, "when the will of God is done on earth as it is in heaven there will be no marriage." Among those who were perfect, he argued, all men and women belonged equally to each other. Others called his doctrines "free love" and socialism. Noyes recovered from his unhappy love affair and married

The Shakers   In this sacred Shaker dance, sin is being shaken out of the body through the fingertips. Note the separation of women and men. Why were they separated? What does their clothing indicate? *(Shaker Villages of Pleasant Hill, Harrodsburg, Kentucky)*

a loyal follower. When she bore four stillborn babies within six years, Noyes again revised his unconventional ideas about sex.

In 1848, Noyes and 51 devoted followers founded a "perfectionist" community at Oneida, New York. Under his strong leadership, it prospered, although many Americans found the community's rejection of middle-class marriage norms immoral. Sexual life at the commune was subject to many regulations, including male continence except under carefully prescribed conditions. Only certain spiritually advanced males (usually Noyes) could father children. Other controversial practices included communal child rearing, sexual equality in work, the removal of the competitive spirit from both work and play, and an elaborate program of "mutual criticism" at community meetings presided over by "Father" Noyes. In contrast to his sexual policies, Noyes made wise economic decisions that bound community members together in mutual prosperity. Forsaking the agricultural emphasis that typified most other communes, he opted for modern manufacturing, first producing steel animal traps and later silverware.

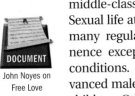

DOCUMENT

John Noyes on Free Love (1865) and Bible Communism (1845 and 1849)

Noyes greatly admired another group of communitarians, the Shakers, who also believed in perfectionism, communal property, and bringing on the millennial kingdom of heaven. Unlike the Oneidans, Shakers condemned sexuality and demanded absolute celibacy, so that only conversions could bring in new members. Founded by an Englishwoman, Mother Ann Lee, Shaker conversions grew during the Second Great Awakening, peaking around 6,000 souls by the 1850s, with communities from Maine to New York to Kentucky. Shakers believed that God had a dual personality, male and female, and that Ann Lee was the female counterpart to the masculine Christ. Shaker worship featured frenetic dancing intended to release (or "shake") sin out through the fingertips. Shaker communities, some of which survived long into the twentieth century, were known for their communal ownership of property, equality of women and men, simplicity, and beautifully crafted furniture.

IMAGE

Shaker Village at Alfred, Maine, 1845

Other Utopias

Over 100 utopian communities like Oneida and the Shaker colonies were founded. Some were religiously motivated; others were secular. Most were small and lasted only a few months or years. All eventually collapsed, though they gave birth to significant social ideas.

Pietist German-speaking immigrants founded the earliest utopian communities in America to preserve their language, spirituality, and ascetic lifestyle. The most notable of these were the Ephrata colonists in Pennsylvania, the Harmonists in Indiana, and the Amana Society in Iowa. Other antebellum reformers, however, founded on the secular principles of reason inherited from the Enlightenment, responded more directly to the social misery and wretched working conditions accompanying industrialization. Evil, these communities assumed, came from bad environments, not from individual sin.

MAP

Utopian Communities Before the Civil War

Robert Owen was the best known of the secular communalists. A Scottish industrialist who saw the miserable lives of cotton mill workers, he envisioned a society of small towns with good schools and healthy work. Unemployment, poverty, and vice would be unknown in Owen's model communities. In 1824, he established his first town in America at New Harmony, Indiana. But little harmony prevailed, and it failed within three years.

IMAGE

Robert Owen's Harmony Community

Brook Farm, founded by two Concord friends of Emerson, sought to integrate "intellectual and manual labor." Residents would hoe in the fields and shovel manure for a few hours each day and then study literature and recite poetry. Although the colony lasted less than three years, it produced some notable literature in Margaret Fuller's journal, *The Dial.* Nathaniel Hawthorne briefly lived at Brook Farm and wrote a novel, *The Blithedale Romance* (1852), criticizing the utopians' naive optimism.

The utopian communities all failed for similar reasons. Americans seemed ill-suited to communal living and were unwilling to share either their property or their spouses. Nor did celibacy arouse much enthusiasm. Other recurring problems included unstable leadership, financial bickering, local hostility toward sexual experimentation and other unorthodox practices, the indiscriminate admission of members, and waning enthusiasm. Emerson pinned the failure of the communities on their inability to combat individualism. As he said of Brook Farm, an epitaph suitable for all utopian communities: "It met every test but life itself."

DOCUMENT

Nathaniel Hawthorne, A Letter from Brook Farm (1841)

Millerites and Mormons

If utopian communities failed to bring about the peaceful millennium, an alternative hope was to leap directly to the Second Coming of Christ. William

Utopian Communities Before 1860

The Mormons retreated to the trans-Mississippi West to realize their vision of a better society, but most communitarians did not go so far away from "civilization" to establish their experiments. Why did they not flee more settled and ordinary communities? Why did they avoid the South?

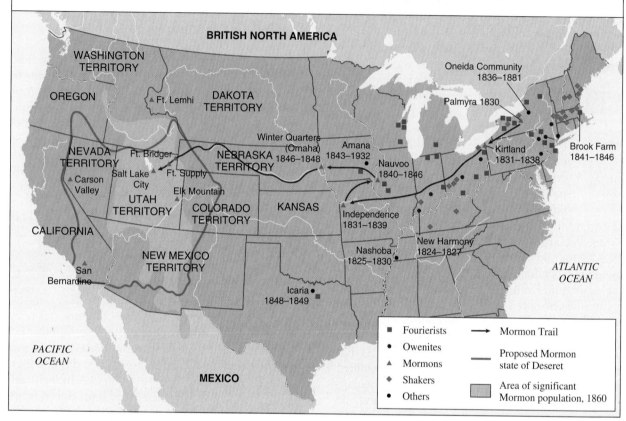

Miller, a shy farmer from upstate New York, figured out its exact time: 1843, probably in March. A sect gathered around him to prepare for Christ's return and the Day of Judgment. Excitement and fear grew as the day came closer. Some people gave away all their belongings, put on robes, and flocked to high hills and rooftops to be nearer to the blessed event. When 1843 passed without the end of the world, Miller recalculated. Each new disappointment diminished his followers, and he died discredited in 1848. A small Millerite sect, the Seventh-Day Adventists, gave up predicting the date of the Second Coming, choosing instead to live with the expectation that it will be "right soon." They continue to this day.

Other groups that emerged from the same religiously active area of upstate New York were more successful. As Palmyra, New York, was being swept by Finney revivalism, young Joseph Smith, a recent convert, claimed to be visited by the angel Moroni, who led him to golden tablets buried near his home. On these were inscribed *The Book of Mormon*, which described the one true church and a "lost tribe of Israel" missing for centuries. The book also

predicted the appearance of an American prophet who would establish a new and pure kingdom of Christ in America. Smith published his book in 1830 and soon founded the Church of Jesus Christ of Latter-Day Saints (the Mormons). His visionary leadership attracted thousands of ordinary people trying to escape what they viewed as social disorder, religious impurity, and commercial degradation in the 1830s.

Smith and a steadily growing band of converts migrated first to Ohio, next to Missouri, and then back to Illinois. The frequent migrations were one consequence of the ridicule, persecution, and violence that they encountered. Hostility stemmed in part from their missionary work, in part from their support for local Native American tribes, and in part from rumors of unorthodox sexual practices.

Despite external persecution and internal dissension over Smith's strong leadership style, the Mormons prospered. Converts from England and northern Europe added substantially to their numbers. By the mid-1840s, Nauvoo, Illinois, with a thriving population of nearly 15,000, was the showplace of Mormonism. Smith petitioned Congress for separate territorial status and ran for the presidency in 1844. This was too much for the citizens of nearby towns. Violence escalated and culminated first in a charge against Smith for treason and then in his murder. Under the brilliant leadership of Smith's successor, Brigham Young, the Mormons headed westward in 1846 in their continuing search for the "land of promise."

REFORMING SOCIETY

The Mormons and the utopian communitarians had as their common goal, in Young's words, "the spread of righteousness upon the earth." Most people, however, preferred to focus on a specific social evil.

"We are all a little wild here," Emerson wrote in 1840, "with numberless projects of social reform." Mobilized in part by their increased participation in the political parties of Jacksonian America, the reformers created and joined all kinds of social reform societies. Their ranks were swelled by thousands of women, stirred to action by the religious revivals and freed from domestic burdens by delayed marriage and smaller families. In hundreds of voluntary societies, people like Emily Rakestraw and Marius

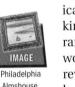

IMAGE

Philadelphia Almshouse, House of Employment, and Prison

Robinson tackled such issues as alcohol, diet and health, sexuality, the institutional treatment of the mentally ill and other social outcasts, the rights of labor, slavery, and women's rights.

Temperance

On New Year's Eve in 1831, a Finney disciple, Theodore Dwight Weld, delivered a four-hour temperance lecture in Rochester. Graphically, he described the awful fate of those who refused to stop drinking and urged his audience not only to cease their tippling but also to stop others. Several were converted on the spot. The next day, the largest providers of whiskey in Rochester rolled their barrels out onto the sidewalk and smashed them as Christians cheered.

Nineteenth-century Americans drank heavily. It was said that "a house could not be raised, a field of wheat cut down, nor could there be a log rolling, a husking, a quilting, a wedding, or a funeral without the aid of alcohol." With drinking came poverty, crime, illness, insanity, battered and broken families, and corrupt politics.

DOCUMENT

Henry Clay Work, "Come Home Father!" (1864)

Early efforts at curbing alcohol emphasized moderation. Local societies agreed to limit how much they drank or to imbibe only beer and wine. Some met in local taverns to toast moderation. But influenced by the revivals, the movement achieved better organization and clearer goals. The American Temperance Society, founded in 1826, aimed at the "teetotal" pledge, vowing to avoid all alcohol including communion wine. Within a few years thousands of local and state societies had formed.

Temperance advocates copied revival techniques. Fiery lecturers expounded on the evil consequences of drink and urged group pressure on the weak-willed. A deluge of graphic and sometimes gory and exaggerated temperance tracts poured out. "Some are killed instantly," one claimed, "some die a lingering, gradual death; some commit suicide in fits of intoxication; and some are actually burnt up."

Temperance Propaganda This piece of temperance propaganda is from a journal entitled *Cold Water Magazine.* Why that title? From the whole picture, what are the effects of drinking? *(The Library Company of Philadelphia [Pert 8, 51767.0, v. 1])*

Lyman Beecher, "Six Sermons on Intemperance" (1828)

In another, an "intemperate man," it was claimed, died when his "breath caught fire by coming in contact with a lighted candle."

By 1840, disagreements over goals and methods split the temperance movement into many separate organizations. In depression times, when jobs and stable families were harder to find than whiskey and beer, laboring men and women moved more by practical concerns than religious fervor joined the crusade. The Washington Temperance Society, founded in a Baltimore tavern in 1840, was enormously popular with unemployed young workers and grew to an estimated 600,000 members in three years. The Washingtonians, arguing that alcoholism was a disease rather than moral failure, changed the shape of the temperance movement. They replaced revivalist techniques with those of the new party politics by organizing parades, picnics, melodramas, and festivals to encourage people to take the pledge.

Tactics in the 1840s also shifted away from moral suasion to political action. Temperance societies lobbied for local option laws, which allowed communities to prohibit the sale, manufacture, and consumption of alcohol. The first such law in the nation was passed in Maine in 1851. Fifteen other states followed with similar laws before the Civil War. Despite weak enforcement, the per capita drinking rate fell dramatically in the 1850s. Interrupted by the Civil War, the movement reached its ultimate objective with passage of the Eighteenth Amendment in 1919.

The temperance crusade reveals the many practical motivations for Americans to join reform societies. For some, as in Rochester, temperance provided an opportunity for the Protestant middle classes to exert some control over laborers, immigrants, and Catholics. Perfectionists saw abstinence as a way of practicing self-control. For many women, the temperance effort represented a way to control abusive husbands and fathers. For many young men, especially after the onset of the depression of 1837, a temperance society provided entertainment, fellowship, and contacts to help their careers. In temperance societies as in political parties, Americans found jobs, purpose, support, spouses, and relief from the loneliness and uncertainty of a changing world.

Health and Sexuality

It was a short step from the physical and psychological ravages of drink to other potentially harmful effects on the body. Reformers were quick to attack too

much eating, too many stimulants, and, above all, too much sex. Many endorsed a variety of special diets and exercise programs for maintaining good health. Some promoted cure-all panaceas, including hydropathy (bathing and water purges to treat urogenital infections), hypnotism, phrenology (the study of bumps on the head), and "spiritualist" séances.

Sylvester Graham, inventor of the graham cracker, combined many of these enthusiasms into a focus on sexual purity. In 1834, he delivered a series of lectures on chastity, later published as an advice book. To those "troubled" by sexual desire, he recommended "cold baths" and "more active exercise in the open air." Women were advised to "have intercourse only for procreation." Although females learned to control sexuality for their own purposes, male "sexual purity" advocates urged sexual restraint to protect various male interests. One doctor argued that women ought not to be educated because blood needed for the womb would be diverted to the head, thus breeding "puny men." Men were warned not to "spend their seed" in unnatural acts.

The authors of antebellum "health" manuals advocated abstinence from sexual activity as vehemently as from alcohol. The body, they argued, was a closed energy system in which each organ had particular and limited functions to perform. Semen must be saved for reproductive purposes and should not be wasted in masturbation or intercourse only for pleasure. Such waste would cause enervation, disease, insanity, and death. Some argued further that the "expenditure" of sperm meant a loss of energy from the economy.

Humanizing the Asylum

Struggling to restore order to American society, some reformers preferred to work not to influence individuals but to change institutions such as asylums, almshouses, prisons, schools, and factories. Horace Mann, who led the struggle for common schools in Massachusetts, was a typical antebellum reformer. He blended idealism with a practical sense of how to make educational improvements in one state: teacher training schools, higher teachers' salaries, and compulsory attendance laws.

Other reformers were less successful in achieving their goals. Helping social outcasts presented special challenges. Colonial families and communities had looked after orphans, paupers, the mentally ill, and even criminals. Beginning early in the nineteenth century, states built various institutions to uplift and house social victims. In some, such as prisons and almshouses, the sane and insane, children and hardened adult criminals were thrown together in terrible conditions. In 1843, Dorothea Dix, a frail New Eng-lander, reported to a horrified Massachusetts legisla-ture that the state's imprisoned insane people lived in the "extremest state of degradation and misery," con-fined in "cages, closets, stalls, pens! Chained, naked, beaten with rods, and lashed into obedience!" Dix recommended special asylums where the insane could be "humanly and properly controlled" by trained attendants.

Many perfectionist reformers like Dix believed that asylums could reform society's outcasts. Convinced that bad institutions corrupted basically good human beings, they reasoned that reformed institutions could rehabilitate them. In 1853, Charles Loring Brace started a Children's Aid Society in New York City that was a model of change through effective educa-tion and self-help. Reformers like Dix and Brace, as well as Samuel Gridley Howe and Thomas Gallaudet, who founded institutions for the care and education of the blind and deaf, achieved remarkable results.

But all too often, results were disappointing. Prison reformers believed that a proper penitentiary could bring a hardened criminal "back to virtue." They argued intensely over the most appropriate structural design for rehabilitating criminals. Some preferred the rectangular prison at Auburn, New York, with its tiny cells and common workrooms. Others praised Pennsylvania's star-shaped system, where each inmate was in solitary con-finement in a fairly modern cell. All prison reformers assumed that "peni-tents" in isolated cells, studying the Bible and reflecting on their wrongdoing, would eventually decide to become good citizens. In fact, many criminals went mad or com-mitted suicide. Institutions built by well-inten-tioned reformers became dumping places for soci-ety's outcasts. By midcentury, American prisons and mental asylums had become what they remain: sadly impersonal, understaffed, and overcrowded.

IMAGE
Prisons

Working-Class Reform

Efforts to improve the institutional conditions of American life were not all top-down movements ini-tiated and led by middle-class reformers. For work-ing-class Americans, as in England, the institution most in need of transformation was the factory. Workers, many of them involved in other issues such as temperance, peace, and abolitionism, tried to im-prove their own lives. As labor leader Seth Luther told a meeting of New England mechanics and laborers, "We must take our business into our own hands. Let us awake." And awake they did, forming both trade unions and workingmen's parties.

A Minstrel Show Character A popular workingmen's form of entertainment was the minstrel show, in which whites would blacken their faces with burnt cork and perform songs and skits that negatively stereotyped blacks. Two oft-depicted types were thick-lipped, dim-witted slavish clowns and faithful "old Darkies." Another was the northern pseudosuave dandy like "Zip Coon," shown here, who despite his airs was always humiliated so as to reassure white workers that free blacks posed no threat to take either their women or their jobs. Compare this image to the pleading slave on page 411. Is one more stereotyped than the other? (The Harvard Theatre Collec-tion, The Houghton Library)

Between 1828 and 1832, dozens of workingmen's parties arose. They advocated free, tax-supported schools; free public lands in the West; equal rights for the poor; and elimination of monopolistic privilege. Trade union ac-tivity began in Philadelphia in 1827 as skilled workers organized journeymen carpenters, plasterers, printers, weavers, tailors, and other tradesmen. That same year, 15 unions combined into a citywide federation, a process followed in other cities. The National Trades Union, founded in 1834, was the first attempt at a national labor organization.

DOCUMENT

Preamble of the Mechanics Union of Trade Associations (1827)

Trade unions fared better than labor parties, as Jacksonian Democrats siphoned off workers' votes. Union programs set more practical goals, including shorter hours, wages that would keep pace with rising prices, and ways (such as the closed shop) of warding off the competitive threat of cheap labor. In addition, both workers and their middle-class supporters called for the abolition of imprisonment for debt and of compulsory militia duty (both of which often cost workers their jobs), free public education, improved living conditions for workers, and the right to organize. Discouraged by anti-union decisions of New York State courts, workers compared their protests to the rebels of the Boston Tea Party.

Fired by revolutionary tradition, rising political influence, and a union membership of near 300,000, workers struck some 168 times between 1834 and 1836. More than two-thirds of the strikes were over wages (see Chapter 10); the others were for shorter hours. Identifying with the "blood of our fathers" shed on the battlefields of the American Revolution, Boston tradesmen struck in 1835 for a 10-hour workday. They failed, but their attempt heralded the resurgence of a successful 10-hour workday movement in the 1850s. The Panic of 1837 ushered in a depression that dashed the hopes and efforts of American workers. But the organizational work of the 1830s promised that the labor movement would reemerge, strengthened, later in the century.

ABOLITIONISM AND THE WOMEN'S RIGHTS MOVEMENT

As American workers struggled in cities like Lowell for better wages and hours in 1834, Emily and Marius Robinson arrived in Cincinnati to fight for their causes. Along with many other young idealists, they were attracted by the newly founded Lane Seminary, a school to train abolitionist leaders. Financed by two wealthy New York brothers, Arthur and Lewis Tappan, Lane soon became a center of reformist activity. When nervous local residents persuaded president Lyman Beecher to crack down, 75 "Lane rebels" fled to Oberlin in northern Ohio. They turned Oberlin College into the first institution in the United States open both to women and men, blacks and whites. The movements to abolish slavery and for equal rights for women and free blacks coalesced.

The goals of the struggle against slavery and subtle forms of racism and sexism often seemed as distant and unrealizable as the millennium itself. Yet antislavery and feminist advocates persisted in their efforts to abolish what they believed were concrete, visible, ingrained social wrongs. Whether seeking to eliminate coercion in the cotton fields or in the kitchen, they faced the dual challenge of pursuing elusive goals while achieving practical changes in everyday life.

Tensions Within the Antislavery Movement

Although the antislavery movement was smaller than temperance advocacy, it revealed more clearly the difficulties of pursuing significant social change in America. William Lloyd Garrison passionately desired to improve, if not perfect, a flawed world. He was also ambitious and said that his name would "one day be known to the world." He was right. On January 1, 1831, eight months before Nat Turner's revolt, Garrison published the first issue of *The Liberator,* soon to become the leading antislavery journal in

 DOCUMENT
William Lloyd Garrison, First Issue of *The Liberator* (1831)

the United States. "I am in earnest," he wrote. "I will not equivocate—*and I will be heard.*" After organizing the New England Anti-Slavery Society with a group of blacks and whites in a church basement in Boston, in 1833 Garrison and 62 others established the American Anti-Slavery Society, which called for an immediate end to slavery.

Until then, most antislavery whites had advocated gradual emancipation by individual slave owners. Many joined the American Colonization Society, founded in 1816, which sent a few ex-slaves to Liberia. But these efforts proved inadequate and racist, the main goal being to rid the country of free blacks. Rejected by African Americans and attacked by Garrisonians, colonization lost much of its support.

Repudiating gradualism, Garrison and others in the American Anti-Slavery Society viewed slavery as a sin and called for immediate emancipation in uncompromising language. As Garrison declared, "I do not wish to think, or speak, or write, with moderation." There could be "no Union with slaveholders," he argued, condemning the Constitution that perpetuated slavery as "an agreement with Hell." Inspired by *The Liberator* and antislavery lecturers such as Garrison, Marius Robinson, and the African American activist Maria Stewart, dozens of local male and female abolitionist societies dedicated to the immediate emancipation of the slaves arose, mostly in the Northeast and Northwest. A society founded by free black women in Boston in 1831, the African-American Female Intelligence Society, was the first antislavery organization dedicated to immediate emancipation.

The determination to eliminate slavery was reinforced by victories in the antislavery movement elsewhere in the world. Agitation against the international

An Abolitionist Message This image of an imploring slave was one of the favorite abolitionist devices. Sometimes the caption asked, "Am I not a Man and a Brother?" In this case, the caption has been changed to encourage antislavery supporters to make weekly donations to the Massachusetts Anti-Slavery Society. What does the biblical text suggest? How do the objects portrayed reinforce the message? *(Boston Public Library/Rare Books Department. Courtesy of the Trustees)*

slave trade in several European countries and the abolition of slavery in the 1820s and 1830s in newly independent Latin American nations showed that change was possible. But it was the antislavery movement in Great Britain that most influenced American antislavery activists. British activists waged a decades-long campaign to persuade Parliament to emancipate slaves in Britain's Caribbean colonies. Antislavery societies of men and women provided an organizational basis for agitation, including massive petition campaigns. After achieving victory in 1833, these groups supported American efforts by providing advice, money, speakers, and an audience for traveling American abolitionists such as Frederick Douglass.

American antislavery reformers disagreed about tactics as well as goals. Their primary method was to convince slaveholders that slavery was a sin. They sought to overwhelm slaveholders with moral guilt. Slaveholding whites, black abolitionist David Walker declared, were guilty of hypocrisy in using Christianity to justify whippings. "Have not the Americans the Bible in their hands? Do they believe it?

Surely they do not. See how they treat us in open violation of the Bible!!" But as Marius wrote to Emily Robinson, "The spirit of slavery is not confined to the South." His Ohio trip suggests that northerners were equally guilty in providing the support necessary to maintain the slave system.

By 1837 abolitionists had flooded the nation with over a million pieces of antislavery literature. Their writing described slave owners as "mansteallers," men who, as Garrison wrote, led lives of "unbridled lust, . . . of haughty domination, of cowardly ruffianism, of boundless dissipation, of matchless insolence, of infinite self-conceit, of unequalled oppression, of more than savage cruelty." In 1839, Weld published *American Slavery as It Is,* which described in the goriest possible detail the inhumane treatment of slaves. Other abolitionists preferred more direct political and economic methods. Some brought antislavery petitions before Congress and formed third parties. Boycotting goods made by slave labor was another tactic.

Illustrations from the American Anti-Slavery Almanac for 1840

Still another approach, although rare, was to call for slave rebellion, as did two northern blacks, Walker in an 1829 pamphlet and Henry Highland Garnet in a speech at a convention of black Americans in 1843. Walker's powerful essay, "David Walker's Appeal," called on slaves to cease their submissiveness and rise up and throw off the yoke of slavery. "Now I ask you," Walker wrote, "had you not rather be killed than to be a slave to a tyrant, who takes the life of your mother, wife, and dear little children?" It was Walker, however, who was mysteriously found dead on a Boston street a year after the publication of his pamphlet. Garnet's call for rebellion was clear: "Brethren arise, arise! Strike for your lives and liberties. Now is the day and the hour. . . . You cannot be more oppressed than you have been—you cannot suffer greater cruelties than you have already. *Rather die freemen, than live to be slaves.* Remember that you are THREE MILLIONS!"

Abolitionists' tactical disagreements helped splinter the movement. Garrison's unyielding personal style and dedication to even less popular causes such as women's rights offended many abolitionists. In 1840, at its annual meeting in New York, the American Anti-Slavery Society split. Several delegates walked out when a woman, Abby Kelley, was elected to a previously all-male committee. One group, which supported multiple issues and moral suasion, stayed with Garrison; the other left to pursue political action and the Liberty party.

Class differences and race further divided abolitionists. Northern workers, though fearful of the potential job competition implicit in emancipation,

RECOVERING THE PAST

Slave Narratives

In the 1840s and 1850s, male and female abolitionists eagerly sought out and published book-length accounts of slavery written by runaway slaves themselves. These chilling stories of captivity and successful escapes, in the voices of former slaves, had enormous emotional power and were instrumental in the effort of abolitionists to influence public opinion and end slavery. According to one estimate, nearly 100 book-length "slave narratives" were published, selections from two of which are included here.

The slave narratives were derived from three American autobiographical traditions: spiritual confessionals characteristic of Puritans like Jonathan Edwards; the rags-to-riches individualistic success story of Benjamin Franklin; and Native American captivity narratives. The last tradition, popular reading in the early nineteenth century, described the three-part process of white captives (usually women) being dragged away from their villages by Indians, then suffering the trials, tortures, and coping adaptations of living in a Native American village, and finally returning home to white civilization. Some women refused to be "redeemed," preferring to stay, often with an Indian husband.

The African American slave narratives followed a similar three-stage pattern, beginning with either a childhood in a West African village or the relative innocence of childhood on a southern plantation. Aimed at northern white readers, the bulk of the story described, in vivid detail, the brutal oppressions of captivity and slavery, dwelling on the horrors of the slave ships, slave sales and the breakup of families, and the daily beatings, punishments, and harsh rigors of life on the plantation. But the narratives also described a creative and self-empowering will to survive: cunning strategies for avoiding work, sassing one's owner, connecting with loved ones, and learning how to read and write. The narratives concluded with the story of escape and the taking on of a new identity in freedom.

In fact, for many former slaves, the actual process of writing the narrative marked the attainment of their identity and freedom, often involving a ritual of self-naming. As William L. Andrews put it in *To Tell a Free Story,* for blacks to write their story was "in some ways uniquely self-liberating, the final, climactic act in the drama of their lifelong quests for freedom." Other themes included poignant appeals to white readers to agitate for the abolition of slavery; contrasts between the slaveholder's use of religion to justify slavery and the simple, spiritually based Christianity of the slaves themselves; and the supportive strength of the slave community and the white and black underground network in facilitating a successful runaway.

Although not the first, the prototypical slave narrative was that of Frederick Douglass, whose story is told in Chapter 11. Douglass grew up witnessing the horrors of slavery on a Maryland plantation and as an urban slave in Baltimore, learned to read and write, successfully defied the cruel Mr. Covey's efforts to break his will as a slave, and finally escaped to fight for abolitionism. Similar stories were told by Henry Bibb, William Wells Brown, Olaudah Equiano, Harriet Jacobs, Mattie Jackson, Solomon Northup, Sojourner Truth, and many, many others, all of which provided gory details of whippings and the wrenching loss of loved ones.

The two short selections here—from James W. C. Pennington's *Fugitive Blacksmith* (1849) and Harriet Jacobs's *Incidents in the Life of a Slave Girl* (1861)—focus not on white oppression but on the initial process of planning an escape. Note that Jacobs wrote under the pseudonym Linda Brent; as background to this passage, she discovers that her two children are to be brought to her master's plantation to be "broke in." As you read, look for restraints on running away, anticipated difficulties, sources of support, and the intelligent cleverness of the runaways.

REFLECTING ON THE PAST What role does religion play in their efforts? What about issues of family, trust, safety, and self-reliance? What do you learn about slavery in these brief descriptions of the first moments of self-emancipation? Can you imagine the impact they had on northern readers, and why abolitionists avidly used the narratives as part of their attack on slavery?

The Flight

It was the Sabbath: the holy day which God in his infinite wisdom gave for the rest of both man and beast. In the state of Maryland, the slaves generally have the Sabbath, except in those districts where the evil weed, tobacco, is cultivated; and then, when it is the season for setting the plant, they are liable to be robbed of this only rest.

It was in the month of November, somewhat past the middle of the month. It was a bright day, and all was quiet. Most of the slaves were resting about their quarters; others had leave to visit their friends on other plantations, and were absent. The evening previous I had arranged my little bundle of clothing, and had secreted it at some distance from the house. I had spent most of the forenoon in my workshop, engaged in deep and solemn thought.

It is impossible for me now to recollect all the perplexing thoughts that passed through my mind during that forenoon; it was a day of heartaching to me. But

I distinctly remember the two great difficulties that stood in the way of my flight: I had a father and mother whom I dearly loved,—I had also six sisters and four brothers on the plantation. The question was, shall I hide my purpose from them? moreover, how will my flight affect them when I am gone? Will they not be suspected? Will not the whole family be sold off as a disaffected family, as is generally the case when one of its members flies? But a still more trying question was, how can I expect to succeed, I have no knowledge of distance or direction. I know that Pennsylvania is a free state, but I know not where its soil begins, or where that of Maryland ends? Indeed, at this time there was no safety in Pennsylvania, New Jersey, or New York, for a fugitive, except in lurking-places, or under the care of judicious friends, who could be entrusted not only with liberty, but also with life itself.

With such difficulties before my mind, the day had rapidly worn away; and it was just past noon. One of my perplexing questions I had settled—I had resolved to let no one into my secret; but the other difficulty was now to be met. It was to be met without the least knowledge of its magnitude, except by imagination. Yet of one thing there could be no mistake, that the consequences of a failure would be most serious. Within my recollection no one had attempted to escape from my master; but I had many cases in my mind's eye, of slaves of other planters who had failed, and who had been made examples of the most cruel treatment, by flogging and selling to the far South, where they were never to see their friends more. I was not without serious apprehension that such would be my fate. The bare possibility was impressively solemn; but the hour was now come, and the man must act and be free, or remain a slave for ever. How the impression came to be upon my mind I cannot tell; but there was a strange and horrifying belief, that if I did not meet the crisis that day, I should be self-doomed—that my ear would be nailed to the door-post for ever. The emotions of that moment I cannot fully depict. Hope, fear, dread, terror, love, sorrow, and deep melancholy were mingled in my mind together; my mental state was one of most painful distraction. When I looked at my numerous family— a beloved father and mother, eleven brothers and sisters, &c.; but when I looked at slavery as such; when I looked at it in its mildest form, with all its annoyances; and above all, when I remembered that one of the chief annoyances of slavery, in the most mild form, is the liability of being at any moment sold into the worst form; it seemed that no consideration, not even that of life itself, could tempt me to give up the thought of flight. And then when I considered the difficulties of the way—the reward that would be offered—the human blood-hounds that would be set upon my track—the weariness— the hunger—the gloomy thought, of not only losing all one's friends in one day, but of having to seek and to make new friends in a strange world. But, as I have said, the hour was come, and the man must act, or for ever be a slave.

Harriet Jacobs—from *Incidents in the Life of a Slave Girl*

Again and again I had traversed those dreary twelve miles, to and from the town; and all the way, I was meditating upon some means of escape for myself and my children. My friends had made every effort that ingenuity could devise to effect our purchase, but all their plans had proved abortive. Dr. Flint was suspicious, and determined not to loosen his grasp upon us. I could have made my escape alone; but it was more for my helpless children than for myself that I longed for freedom. Though the boon would have been precious to me, above all price, I would not have taken it at the expense of leaving them in slavery. Every trial I endured, every sacrifice I made for their sakes, drew them closer to my heart, and gave me fresh courage to beat back the dark waves that rolled and rolled over me in a seemingly endless night of storms. . . .

My plan was to conceal myself at the house of a friend, and remain there a few weeks till the search was over. My hope was that the doctor would get discouraged, and, for fear of losing my value, and also of subsequently finding my children among the missing, he would consent to sell us; and I knew somebody would buy us. I had done all in my power to make my children comfortable during the time I expected to be separated from them. . . .

Mr. Flint was hard pushed for house servants, and rather than lose me he had restrained his malice. I did my work faithfully, though not, of course, with a willing mind. They were evidently afraid I should leave them. Mr. Flint wished that I should sleep in the great house instead of the servants' quarters. His wife agreed to the proposition, but said I mustn't bring my bed into the house, because it would scatter feathers on her carpet. I knew when I went there that they would never think of such a thing as furnishing a bed of any kind for me and my little one. I therefore carried my own bed, and now I was forbidden to use it. I did as I was ordered. But now that I was certain my children were to be put in their power, in order to give them a stronger hold on me, I resolved to leave them that night. I remembered the grief this step would bring upon my dear old grandmother; and nothing less than the freedom of my children would have induced me to disregard her advice. I went about my evening work with trembling steps. Mr. Flint twice called from his chamber door to inquire why the house was not locked up. I replied that I had not done my work. "You have had time enough to do it," said he. "Take care how you answer me!"

I shut all the windows, locked all the doors, and went up to the third story, to wait till midnight. How long those hours seemed, and how fervently I prayed that God would not forsake me in this hour of utmost need! I was about to risk every thing on the throw of a die; and if I failed, O what would become of me and my poor children? They would be made to suffer for my fault.

At half past twelve I stole softly down stairs. I stopped on the second floor, thinking I heard a noise. I felt my way down into the parlor, and looked out of the window. The night was so intensely dark that I could see nothing. I raised the window very softly and jumped out. Large drops of rain were falling, and the darkness bewildered me. I dropped on my knees, and breathed a short prayer to God for guidance and protection. I groped my way to the road, and rushed towards the town with almost lightning speed. I arrived at my grandmother's house, but dared not see her. She would say, "Linda, you are killing me;" and I knew that would unnerve me. I tapped softly at the window of a room, occupied by a woman, who had lived in the house several years. I knew she was a faithful friend, and could be trusted with my secret. I tapped several times before she heard me. . . . I told her I had a hiding-place, and that was all it was best for her to know.

. . . The tidings made the old doctor rave and storm at a furious rate. It was a busy day for them. My grandmother's house was searched from top to bottom. As my trunk was empty, they concluded I had taken my clothes with me. Before ten o'clock every vessel northward bound was thoroughly examined, and the law against harboring fugitives was read to all on board. At night a watch was set over the town. Knowing how distressed my grandmother would be, I wanted to send her a message; but it could not be done. Every one who went in or out of her house was closely watched. The doctor said he would take my children, unless she became responsible for them; which of course she willingly did. The next day was spent in searching. Before night, the following advertisement was posted at every corner, and in every public place for miles round:——

$300 Reward! Ran away from the subscriber, an intelligent, bright, mulatto girl, named Linda, 21 years of age. Five feet four inches high. Dark eyes, and black hair inclined to curl; but it can be made straight. Has a decayed spot on a front tooth. She can read and write, and in all probability will try to get to the Free States. All persons are forbidden, under penalty of law, to harbor or employ said slave. $150 will be given to whoever takes her in the state, and $300 if taken out of the state and delivered to me, or lodged in jail.

Dr. Flint

Note: James Pennington successfully escaped to New York, where he became a Presbyterian minister and later performed Frederick Douglass's marriage rites. Harriet Jacobs hid for seven years in a cramped, tiny garret in her grandmother's house before finally escaping in disguise by ship; she eventually was reunited with her children. To mislead Dr. Flint as to her location, she wrote letters to him secreted to and postmarked from the North begging him to free her children.

413

nevertheless saw their "wage slavery" as similar to chattel slavery. Strains between northern labor leaders and middle-class abolitionists, who minimized the seriousness of workingmen's concerns, were similar to those between white and black antislavery forces. Whites such as Wendell Phillips decried slavery as a moral blot on American society; blacks such as Douglass were more concerned with the effects of slavery and discrimination on African Americans. Moreover, white abolitionists tended to see slavery and freedom as absolute opposites: a person was either a slave or free. African Americans knew that there were degrees of freedom and that discriminatory restrictions on freedom existed for blacks in the North just as did relative degrees of servitude in the South.

Furthermore, black abolitionists themselves experienced prejudice, not just from ordinary northern citizens but also from white abolitionists. One free black, in fact, described a white abolitionist as one who hated slavery, "especially that slavery which is 1,000 to 1,500 miles away," but who hated even more "a man who wears a black skin." Many antislavery businessmen refused to hire blacks. The antislavery societies usually provided less than full membership rights for blacks, let them only do menial tasks rather than set policy, and perpetuated black stereotypes in their literature. Conflict between Garrison and Douglass reflected these tensions. The famous runaway was one of the most effective orators in the movement. But after a while, rather than simply describing his life as a slave, Douglass began skillfully to analyze abolitionist policies. Garrison warned him that if he sounded too smart, audiences would never believe he had been a slave; other whites told him to stick to the facts and let them take care of the philosophy.

Douglass gradually moved away from Garrison's views, endorsing political action and sometimes even slave rebellion. Garrison's response, particularly when Douglass came out for the Liberty party, was to denounce his independence as "ungrateful . . . and malevolent in spirit." In 1847, Douglass started his own journal, the *North Star*, later called *Frederick Douglass's Paper*. In it, he expressed his appreciation for the help of that "noble band of white laborers" but declared that it was time for those who "suffered the wrong" to lead the way in advocating liberty.

Moving beyond Garrison, a few black nationalists, such as the fiery Martin Delany, totally rejected white American society and advocated emigration to Africa. Most African Americans, however, agreed with Douglass to work to end slavery and discrimination in the United States, their home for many generations. David Ruggles in New York and William Still in Philadelphia led black vigilance groups that helped fugitive slaves escape to Canada or to safe northern black settlements. Ministers, writers, and orators such as Douglass, Garnet, Maria Stewart, William Wells Brown, Samuel Cornish, Lewis Hayden, and Sojourner Truth lectured and wrote journals and slave narratives on the evils of slavery. They also organized a National Negro Convention movement, which began holding annual meetings in 1830, meeting not only to condemn slavery but also to discuss issues of discrimination facing northern free blacks.

Flood Tide of Abolitionism

Black and white abolitionists, however, agreed more than they disagreed and usually worked together well. They supported each other's publications. The first subscribers to Garrison's *Liberator* were nearly all African American, and an estimated 80 percent of the readers of Douglass's paper were white. Weld and Garrison often stayed in the homes of black abolitionists when they traveled. In addition, black and white "stations" cooperated on the Underground Railroad, passing fugitives from one hiding place to the next, often from a black church to a white farmer's barn to a Quaker meetinghouse to a black carpenter's shop.

The two races worked together fighting discrimination as well as slavery. When David Ruggles was dragged from the "white car" of a New Bedford, Massachusetts, railway in 1841, Garrison, Douglass, and 40 other protesters organized what may have been the first successful integrated "sit-in" in American history. Blacks and whites also worked harmoniously in protesting segregated schools; after several years of boycotts and legal challenges, they forced Massachusetts in 1855 to become the first to outlaw segregated public education. Not for 99 years would the U.S. Supreme Court begin desegregating schools throughout the country.

White and black abolitionists were united perhaps most closely by defending themselves against the attacks by people who regarded them as dangerous fanatics bent on disrupting society. As abolitionists organized to rid the nation of slavery, they aroused many people—northerners as well as southerners—who were eager to rid the nation of abolitionists. Mob attacks, such as the one on Marius Robinson in Ohio occurred frequently in the mid-1830s. Abolitionists were stoned, dragged through streets, ousted

DOCUMENT

National Convention of Colored People, Report on Abolition (1847)

AMERICAN VOICES

Martha Wright's New York Family Helps a Fugitive Slave

As part of their commitment to abolitionism, antislavery families sometimes helped fugitive slaves who had escaped from the South. Martha and David Wright and their children, Tallman and Eliza, allowed a fugitive slave to spend the night in their Auburn, New York, home in January 1843. In this letter to her sister, Martha described the experience.

Before I go to bed I will write a few lines. Our slave returned about 9 last evening & sat alone in the kitchen & read till David came. He went down & talked with him—he said he was from Baltimore & had paid his master 300 dollars—he asked 800—being sold to go south he ran away ... & was on his way to Massachusetts where his people lived. As I didn't fancy having him go up stairs he had D's old cloak, & slept by the kitchen stove on my settee—how little I imagined to what use it was to be applied. After getting him to put a stick in the furnace D. left him & fastened the door at the head of the kitchen stairs he gave him 50¢ he wanted to get a ride part way—early this morning David saw him & got some bread & butter for him as he wished to be off before it was very light. So after putting in more wood & tying up a couple of shirts & bosoms that he gave him, he cleared. Tallman came down early to have some interesting conversation with him about the land of chains & was much disappointed to find he had left—he had to go to the Post Office then, but could not find his tippet which he knew he hung in the kitchen with his cap, and as David noticed it in the evening the inference was that early morning walks made warmer clothing desirable & the slave had taken ... the tippet.—but we didn't say so to Tallman, David sd. It ws. Give such a shock to his philanthropy & as to Eliza, she was afraid as could be of him before & hardly dared to go to bed & if she should know it she would hardly dare stay in the house if another came.

■ *What assistance did the Wrights give to the slave?*

■ *How did the different members of the family react to his presence? What do you think accounts for their reactions?*

■ *What is your response to the stolen tippet (scarf)? Why might the slave have taken it?*

---

from their jobs and homes, and reviled by northern mobs, often led by leading citizens. Weld, known as "the most mobbed man in the United States," could hardly finish a speech without disruption. Douglass endured similar attacks, and Garrison was saved from a Boston mob only by being put in jail. In 1837, Elijah Lovejoy, an antislavery editor in Illinois, was murdered.

Antiabolitionists were as fervid as the abolitionists. "I warn the abolitionists, ignorant and infatuated barbarians as they are," growled one South Carolinian, "that if chance shall throw any of them into our hands, they may expect a felon's death." One widely circulated book in 1836 described opponents of slavery, led by the "gloomy, wild, and malignant" Garrison, as "crack-brained enthusiasts" and "female fanatics" with "disturbed minds." President Jackson joined in, denouncing the abolitionists in his annual message in 1835 as "incendiaries" deserving to have their "unconstitutional and wicked" activities broken up by mobs, and he urged Congress to ban antislavery literature from the U.S. mails. A year later, southern Democratic congressmen, with support from Van Buren, passed a "gag rule" to stop the flood of abolitionist petitions in Congress.

By the 1840s, the antislavery movement had gained significant strength. Many northerners, including workers otherwise unsympathetic to the goal of ending slavery, decried the mob violence, supported free speech, and denounced the South and its northern defenders as undemocratic. The gag rule, interference with the mails, and the killing of Lovejoy seemed proof of the growing pernicious influence of slave power. Former president John Quincy Adams, now a congressman, devoted himself for several years to the repeal of the gag rule, which he finally achieved in 1844, keeping the matter alive until the question of slavery in the territories became the dominant national political issue of the 1850s. Meanwhile, black and white abolitionists struggled on using many different tactics without

Stopping a Debate on Abolition   It was dangerous to be a public abolitionist in this period. In this Winslow Homer engraving for *Harper's Weekly* titled "Expulsion of Negroes and Abolitionists from Tremont Temple, Boston, Massachusetts, on December 3, 1860," Homer shows Frederick Douglass being forced from the stage by pro-southern demonstrators, who interrupted the meeting called to debate "How can American slavery be Abolished?" With opposition like this in Boston, the heart of abolitionist sentiment, how *could* slavery be abolished? *(Expulsion of the Negroes and Abolitionists from Tremont Temple, Boston, Massachusetts, on December 3, 1860, 1860, Winslow Homer. The Museum of Fine Arts, Houston; The Mavis P. Wilson Kelsey Collection of Winslow Homer Graphics)*

yet knowing that the only one that would eventually work would be civil war.

Women Reformers and Women's Rights

In 1832, Maria Stewart said that she heard "a spiritual interrogation—'Who shall go forward, and take off the reproach that is cast upon the people of color? Shall it be a woman?'" As a young Quaker teacher in Massachusetts four years later, Abby Kelley circulated petitions for the local antislavery society. Like Stewart, she too came to reform through religious conviction, writing in 1837, "I think endeavors to improve mankind [are] the only object worth living for." Religiously motivated women such as Margaret Fuller, Ann Lee, Dix, Stewart, and Kelley, were active in the movements for abolitionism, utopianism, care of society's outcasts, black rights, and other moral and political reforms. They were also engaged in a struggle for their own rights as women, beginning with the right to speak in public.

In 1838, Kelley braved the threats of an angry crowd in Philadelphia by delivering an abolitionist speech to a convention of antislavery women so

eloquently that Weld told her that if she did not join the movement full-time, "God will smite you." Before the convention was over, incensed by both abolitionism and women speaking in public, a mob burned the hall to the ground.

After a soul-searching year, Kelley left teaching to devote all her efforts to antislavery and women's rights. When she married, she retained her own name and went on lecture tours of the West while her husband stayed home to care for their daughter. Other young women were also defining unconventional new relationships while illustrating the profound difficulty of both fulfilling traditional roles and speaking out for reform. Angelina and Sarah Grimké, outspoken Quaker sisters from Philadelphia who had grown up in slaveholding South Carolina, went to New England in 1837 to lecture on abolitionism. Criticized for speaking to audiences containing both men and women, Angelina defended women's rights to speak in public. After the tour, Angelina married Theodore Weld and stopped her public lectures to show that she could also be a good wife and mother. But she and Sarah, who moved in with her, undertook most of the research and writing for Weld's book attacking American slavery.

Young white couples like these, while pursuing reform, also experimented with equal relationships in an age that assigned distinctly unequal roles to husbands and wives. On the one hand, women were told that their sphere was the home, where they were to uphold piety and virtue and influence their husbands and children to lead morally upright lives. On the other hand, they were assured that their ethical influence would be "felt around the globe." Not surprisingly, many women joined the perfectionist movement to cleanse America of its sins, as well as to improve their own condition.

To achieve greater personal autonomy, antebellum American women, like their English sisters, pursued several paths depending on their class, cultural background, and situation. Thus, in 1834, the

Marriage Certificate

DOCUMENT

Catharine Beecher, "A Treatise on Domestic Economy" (1841)

Lowell textile workers went on strike against wage reductions while looking to marriage as an escape from millwork. Catharine Beecher argued that it was by accepting marriage and the home as a woman's sphere and by mastering domestic duties there that women could best achieve power and autonomy. In another form of "domestic feminism," American wives exerted considerable control over their own bodies by persuading their husbands to practice abstinence, coitus interruptus, and other forms of birth control.

Other women found an outlet for their role as moral guardians by attacking the sexual double standard. In 1834, a group of Presbyterian women formed the New York Female Moral Reform Society. Inspired by revivalism, they visited brothels, opened

Dress Reform One of the reforms proposed during the antebellum period was the reform of women's clothing. How would you describe the bloomer costume pictured here? What advantages did it offer compared to women's usual attire? Are there class implications to this costume? What reasons might a person have to oppose dress reform? *(Library of Congress)*

a refuge house to convert prostitutes, and even publicly identified brothel patrons. Within five years, there were 445 auxiliaries of the society.

Lowell mill workers and New York moral reformers generally accepted the duties—and attractions—of female domesticity. Other women, usually from upper-middle-class families, did not. They sought control over their lives by working directly for more legally protected rights. Campaigns to secure married women's control of their property and custody of their children involved many of them. Others gained from abolitionism a growing awareness of the similarities between the oppression of slaves and of women. Collecting antislavery signatures and speaking out publicly, they continued to face denials of their right to speak or act politically. American women "have good cause to be grateful to the slave," Kelley wrote, for in "striving to strike his iron off, we found most surely, that we were manacled *ourselves.*"

The more active women became in antislavery activities, the more hostility they encountered, especially from conservative clergymen quoting the Bible to justify female inferiority and servility. Sarah Grimké was criticized once too often. She struck back in 1837 with *Letters on the Condition of Women and the Equality of the Sexes,* concluding that "men and women were created equal" and that "whatever is right for man to do, is right for woman." Arguing that men ought to be satisfied with 6,000 years of dominion based on a false interpretation of the Creation story, Grimké concluded that she sought "no favors for my sex. I surrender not our claim to equality. All I ask of our brethren is, that they will take their feet from off our necks and permit us to stand upright on that ground which God designed us to occupy."

Grimké's strong message was soon translated into an active movement for women's rights. Illustrative of its international character, the American movement was born in London. At the World Anti-Slavery Convention in 1840, attended by many American abolitionists, male delegates refused to let women participate. Two of the women, Elizabeth Cady Stanton and Lucretia Mott, a Quaker minister, had to sit behind curtains and were forbidden to speak. "Mrs. Mott was to me an entirely new revelation of womanhood," Stanton wrote later, "I sought every opportunity to be at her side." When they returned home, they resolved to "form a society to advocate the rights of women." In 1848, in Seneca Falls, New York, their intentions, though delayed, were fulfilled in one of the most significant protest gatherings of the antebellum era.

In preparing for the meeting, Mott and Stanton drew up a list of women's grievances. Chief among

IMAGE

Elizabeth Cady Stanton

Elizabeth Cady Stanton, Declaration of Sentiments (1848)

them were the right to vote and the right for married women to control their own property and earnings. Modeling their "Declaration of Sentiments" on the Declaration of Independence, the women at Seneca Falls proclaimed it a self-evident truth that "all men and women are created equal" and that men had usurped women's freedom and dignity. The remedy was expressed in 11 resolutions calling for equal opportunities in education and work, equality before the law, and the right to appear on public platforms. The most controversial resolution called for women's "sacred right to the elective franchise." The convention approved Mott and Stanton's list of resolutions.

Throughout the 1850s, led by Stanton and Susan B. Anthony, women continued to meet in annual conventions, working by resolution, persuasion, and petition campaign to achieve equal political, legal, and property rights with men. The right to vote, however, was considered the cornerstone of the movement. It remained so for 72 years of struggle until 1920 with the passage of the Nineteenth Amendment. The Seneca Falls convention was crucial in beginning the campaign for equal public rights. The seeds of psychological autonomy and self-respect, however, were sown in the struggles of countless women like Abby Kelley, Sarah Grimké, Maria Stewart, and Emily Robinson. The struggle for that kind of liberation continues today.

TIMELINE

1824	New Harmony established
1825	John Quincy Adams chosen president by the House of Representatives
1826	American Temperance Society founded
1828	Calhoun publishes *Exposition and Protest* Jackson defeats Adams for the presidency Tariff of Abominations
1828–1832	Rise of workingmen's parties
1830	Webster–Hayne debate and Jackson–Calhoun toast Joseph Smith, *The Book of Mormon* Indian Removal Act
1830–1831	Charles Finney's religious revivals
1831	Garrison begins publishing *The Liberator*
1832	Jackson vetoes U.S. Bank charter Jackson re-elected *Worcester v. Georgia*
1832–1833	Nullification crisis
1832–1836	Removal of funds from U.S. Bank to state banks
1833	Force Bill Calhoun resigns as vice president American Anti-Slavery Society founded
1834	New York Female Moral Reform Society founded National Trades Union founded Whig party established
1835–1836	Countless incidents of mob violence
1836	"Gag rule" Specie Circular Van Buren elected president

1837	Financial panic and depression Sarah Grimké, *Letters on the Condition of Women and the Equality of the Sexes*
1837–1838	Cherokee "Trail of Tears"
1840	William Henry Harrison elected president American Anti-Slavery Society splits World Anti-Slavery Convention 10-hour day for federal employees Liberty party Formed
1840–1841	Transcendentalists found Hopedale and Brook Farm
1843	Dorothea Dix's report on treatment of the insane
1844	Joseph Smith murdered in Nauvoo, Illinois
1846–1848	Mormon migration to the Great Basin
1847	First issue of Frederick Douglass's *North Star*
1848	Oneida community founded First women's rights convention at Seneca Falls, New York
1850	Nathaniel Hawthorne's *Scarlet Letter* is published
1851	Maine prohibition law Herman Melville's *Moby Dick* is published
1853	Children's Aid Society established in New York City
1854	Thoreau's *Walden* is published
1855	Massachusetts bans segregated public schools

Conclusion

Perfecting America

Inspired by religious revivalism, advocates for women's rights and temperance, abolitionists, and other reformers carried on very different crusades from those waged by Andrew Jackson against Native Americans, nullificationists, and the U.S. Bank. In fact, Jacksonian politics and antebellum reform were often at odds. Most abolitionists and temperance reformers were anti-Jackson Whigs. Jackson and most Democrats repudiated the passionate moralism of reformers.

Yet both sides shared more than either side would admit. Reformers and political parties were both organized rationally. Both mirrored new tensions in a changing, growing society. Both had an abiding faith in change and the idea of progress, yet feared that sinister forces jeopardized that progress. Whether ridding the nation of alcohol or the national bank, slavery or nullification, mob violence or political opponents, both forces saw these responsibilities in terms of patriotic duty. Whether inspired by religious revivalism or political party loyalty, both believed that by stamping out evil forces, they could shape a better America. In this effort, they turned to politics, religion, reform, and new lifestyles. Whether politicians like Jackson and Clay, religious community leaders like Noyes and Ann Lee, or reformers like Garrison, the Grimkés, and Emily and Marius Robinson, these antebellum Americans sought to remake their country politically and morally as it underwent social and economic change.

As the United States neared midcentury, slavery emerged as the most divisive issue. Against much opposition, the reformers had made slavery a matter of national political debate by the 1840s. Although both major political parties tried to evade the question, westward expansion and the addition of new territories to the nation would soon make avoidance impossible. Would new states be slave or free? The question increasingly aroused the deepest passions of the American people. For the pioneer family, who formed the driving force behind the westward movement, however, questions involving their fears and dreams seemed more immediate. We turn to this family and that movement in the next chapter.

Questions for Review and Reflection

1. How does the story of Marius Robinson and Emily Rakestraw introduce the major themes and structure of the chapter?

2. What social, economic, and political forces motivated Americans to seek ways of controlling their lives? How did they try to shape both their own lives and also America?

3. What were the major issues of Jackson's presidential administration? Do you think he was primarily a unifier or a divider? Did he advance or set back the development of American democracy? Explain your response.

4. What were the key differences between Democrats and Whigs? Who supported each party and why? Which would you have supported, and why?

5. What was the role of religion in antebellum American life? How did revivalism affect social change? Do you agree that this was the proper function of religion?

6. What were the three (or four) major antebellum reform movements? What motivations, values, challenges, and resources were common to each of them? Would you have been a reformer? Why or why not?

Recommended Reading

Recommended Readings are posted on the Web site for this textbook. Visit www.ablongman.com/nash

Fiction and Film

Nathaniel Hawthorne's *Blithedale Romance* (1852), a novel set in a utopian community much like Brook Farm, reveals the challenges of perfecting America through socialistic communal experiments and other reforms such as woman suffrage, spiritualism, and prison reform. Hawthorne's *The Scarlet Letter* (1850) and *Celestial Railroad and Other Stories* (1963 edition, reprinting stories written in the 1830s and 1840s)—in particular, "The Birthmark," "Rappaccini's Daughter," and "Ethan Brand"—show the author's struggles to balance the head and the heart, scientific and romantic perfectionism. *Not for Ourselves Alone: The Story of Elizabeth Cady Stanton and Susan B. Anthony* is a superb documentary produced by Ken Burns for PBS in 1999. Other film possibilities include *Frederick Douglass: When the Lion Wrote History* (1994) and a dramatization of *Uncle Tom's Cabin* (1987). *The Journey of August King*, a 1996 film based on a 1971 novel, deals with the decision of a North Carolina frontiersman to help a female fugitive slave.

Discovering U.S. History Online

Women in America

www.xroads.virginia.edu/~HYPER/DETOC/FEM/home.htm

This University of Virginia site takes a look at women in antebellum America, 1820–1842.

Godey's Lady's Book Online Home Page

www.history.rochester.edu/godeys/

This site provides an online text of this interesting nineteenth-century journal.

Influence of Prominent Abolitionists

www.loc.gov/exhibits/african/influ.html

This Library of Congress exhibit site, with pictures and text, discusses some key African American abolitionists and their efforts to end slavery.

Transcendentalists

www.transcendentalists.com

This site has background information on Transcendentalists, interactive information on Thoreau and Emerson, and information on other Transcendentalists.

Religion and the National Culture in the Nineteenth Century

www.nhc.rtp.nc.us:8080/tserve/nineteen.htm

Using essays and contemporary photos and primary sources, this site was "designed to help teachers of American history bring their students to a greater understanding of the role religion has played in the development of the United States."

Andrew Jackson

www.ipl.org/ref/POTUS/ajackson.html

This site contains basic factual data about Jackson's election, presidency, and speeches, as well as online biographies.

The Trail of Tears

www.ourgeorgiahistory.com/indians/cherokee/trail_of_tears.html

A thorough interactive essay explains the history of the Trail of Tears. The site also presents information on Cherokee forts and a map of the various routes traveled during this period of Native American removal.

Social History of the Antebellum Period

www.moa.cit.cornell.edu/moa/index.html

This site contains primary sources in American social history from the antebellum period through Reconstruction.

Reform Movements

www.womhist.binghamton.edu/datelist.htm

This site includes many essays and primary sources relevant to the antebellum reform movements, including "The Appeal of Female Moral Reform," "The Nineteenth-Century Dress Reform Movement, 1838–1881," and "Lucretia Mott's Reform Networks, 1840–1860."

Moving West

This painting by Albert Bierstadt captures the majesty of the western landscape, which dwarfs the Native Americans depicted in the foreground. *(Albert Bierstadt,* The Rocky Mountains, Lander's Peak. *Geoffrey Clements/CORBIS)*

American Stories

The Surprises of a Missionary Life

It was July 4, 1836, but nothing in her 28 years had prepared Narcissa Whitman for the sights and sounds that marked this particular holiday. Earlier in the day, Narcissa and the party with which she was traveling had crossed over the South Pass of the Rocky Mountains, a memorable milestone for the nation's birthday. Now evening had come, and the caravan had set up camp for the night. Suddenly, wild cries and the sound of gunshots and galloping horses broke the silence. Fourteen or fifteen men, most dressed as Native Americans, advanced toward the camp. Frightened by the threatening appearance of the horsemen, the noise, and the bullets whizzing over her head, Narcissa may well have wondered if her journey and even her life were to end. But as the horsemen approached, the anxious travelers could make out a white flag tied to one of the riders' rifles. These were not foes but friends who had ridden out from the annual fur traders' rendezvous to greet the caravan.

Two days later Narcissa reached the rendezvous site, where hundreds of Indians as well as 200 whites, mostly traders and trappers, were gathered to exchange furs, tell stories, drink, and enjoy themselves. Some of the mounted Native Americans, "carrying their war weapons, wearing their war emblems and implements of music," put on a special display. The exhibition was a novelty for Narcissa as was her presence for the Native Americans. Narcissa found herself the center of attention "in the midst of [a] gazing throng" of curious Indians. The experience was not unpleasant, and Narcissa's impression of the natives was favorable: "They all like us and that we have come to live with them."

Narcissa Whitman was one of the first white women to cross the Rocky Mountains and live in Oregon Territory in the 1830s. While many more Americans would follow her, only a few would share her reasons for coming west. They would come to farm, dig for gold, speculate in land, open a store, or practice law. However, Narcissa and her husband, Dr. Marcus Whitman, did not go west to better their lives but to carry God's word to the Native Americans. Inspired by the revivals of the Second Great Awakening and convinced that all non-Christians were headed toward eternal damnation, Narcissa and her husband came to settle among the Native Americans in Oregon Territory and to convert them to Christianity and the American way of life.

This dream of becoming a missionary was one Narcissa had nourished since her early teens. But once the Whitmans had established their mission station in the Walla Walla valley, Narcissa slowly discovered that missionary work was nothing like her youthful fantasies. Although the Cayuse Indians listened to the missionaries and even adopted some Christian practices, they never lived up to the Whitmans' high standards. None of them had conversion experiences that the Whitmans judged necessary for admittance to the Presbyterian church nor were they quick to abandon Native American customs. They continued to consult their medicine men and refused to settle permanently next to the mission station. Cayuse women seemed little interested in the middle-class domestic skills Narcissa wished to teach them. Narcissa's positive impression of Native Americans disappeared. The Cayuse, she wrote, were "insolent, proud, domineering, arrogant, and ferocious."

There were other disappointments and personal tragedies as well. Marcus was often away from the mission on medical business, and Narcissa was lonely and sometimes frightened when he was absent. Her beloved daughter fell into the river and drowned. Often sick and unhappy, Narcissa did not conceive again.

DOCUMENT

Marcus Whitman to Rev. David Green (1844)

As time passed, however, Narcissa's dismay and depression over her lack of success faded as hopeful signs of new possibilities other than Indian missionary work appeared. As she wrote to her mother in 1840, "a tide of immigration appears to be moving this way rapidly." In the following years, more and more American families made their way past the mission station, headed for the Willamette valley. In one wagon train was a family of children who had been orphaned during their journey. The Whitmans took them in and adopted all seven children. Narcissa threw herself into caring for them and found herself too busy to work actively with the Cayuse.

The Native Americans were dismayed at the numbers of whites coming into the territory, but the Whitmans, convinced that the future of the West lay with the emigrants, welcomed them. The day of the Indians had passed. As a "hunted, despised and unprotected" people, the Whitmans believed that the Native Americans were headed toward "entire extinction." But in an unexpected turn of events, some of the Cayuse protested against this vision, turned against the Whitmans, and killed them both. Such violent actions did nothing to hold back the swarm of Americans heading west.

Narcissa Whitman and her husband, Marcus, were among thousands of Americans who played a part in the nation's expansion into the trans-Mississippi West. While the religious faith that drove them west differentiated them from many crossing the western plains and prairies, the Whitmans' cultural beliefs about the inferiority of the Native Americans and the necessity of American settlement were widely shared. Shared too was the conviction that American values and way of life were superior to those of the Native Americans and Mexicans who occupied the land.

This chapter concerns movement into the trans-Mississippi West between 1830 and 1865. First we will consider how and when Americans moved west, by what means the United States acquired the vast territories that in 1840 belonged to other nations, and the meaning of "Manifest Destiny," the slogan used to defend the conquest of the continent west of the Mississippi River. Then we explore the nature of life on the western farms; in western mining communities where Latin American, Chinese, and European adventurers mingled with American fortune seekers; and in western cities. Finally, the chapter examines responses of Native Americans and Mexican Americans to expansion and illuminates the ways different cultural traditions intersected in the West.

PROBING THE TRANS-MISSISSIPPI WEST

Until the 1840s, most Americans lived east of the Mississippi in a nation with fluid and changing boundaries. By 1860, however, some 4.3 million Americans had moved beyond the great river into the trans-Mississippi West, and the United States had acquired fixed boundaries with Canada and Mexico and reached the western edge of the continent.

The International Context for American Expansionism

When the Whitmans arrived in Oregon Territory, they stayed at a bustling British fur trading post with hundreds of workers, French Canadians, English, Scots, and many from mixed European–Indian backgrounds. The establishment symbolized the international setting within which American expansionism occurred. The shifting interests and fortunes of several European nations helped shape the character and timing of westward emigration even though individual settlers might not recognize the large forces affecting their experiences.

In 1815, except for Louisiana Territory, Spain held title to most of the trans-Mississippi West. For hundreds of years, Spaniards had marched north from Mexico to explore, settle, and spread Spanish culture to native peoples. Eventually, Spanish holdings included present-day Texas, Arizona, New Mexico, Nevada, Utah, western Colorado, California, and parts of Wyoming, Kansas, and Oklahoma. Spanish rulers tried to exclude foreigners from these frontier areas but increasingly found this policy difficult to enforce.

The area was vast, and Spain itself was experiencing internal difficulties that weakened its hold on its New World colonies. In 1820, the conservative Spanish monarch faced liberal revolt at home. Its ideas sparked liberation movements in the New World.

In 1821, Mexico declared its independence and acquired Spain's territories in the trans-Mississippi West with a population that included 75,000 Spanish-speaking inhabitants and numerous Native American tribes. While maintaining control of this distant region and its peoples would have been difficult under any circumstances, Mexico was not successful in forming a strong or a stable government until the 1860s. It was in a weak position to resist the avid American appetite for expansion.

North of California lay Oregon country, a vaguely defined area extending to Alaska. Russia, Spain, Great Britain, and Spain all had claims to Oregon, but negotiations with Russia and Spain in 1819 and 1824 left just the United States and Britain in contention for the territory. Joint British–American occupation, agreed on in 1818 and 1827, delayed settling the boundary question. With only a handful of Americans in the territory, Oregon's future would depend partly on how Britain, the world's richest and most powerful country, defined its interests there as Americans began to stream into Oregon in the 1840s.

Early Interest in the West

Some Americans penetrated the trans-Mississippi West long before the great migrations of the 1840s and 1850s. The fur business attracted American trappers and traders to Oregon by 1811 and a decade later to the Rockies. Many of these men married Native

North and South America, 1800–1836

Events in Europe had a dramatic impact on the Americas. the popularization of the ideas of the French Revolution and Napoleon's defeat of the Spanish king in 1808 contributed to ending Spanish rule in the Americas. Note how rapidly countries claimed their independence in the Southern Hemisphere and Latin America. **Reflecting on the Past** How did the changing political landscape of the Americas affect the power and influence of the United States in the region?

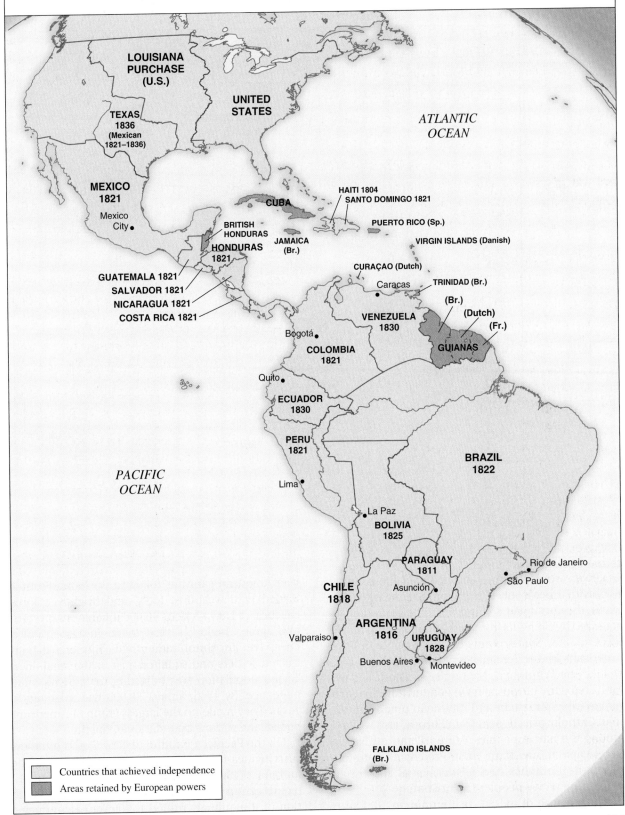

LOUISIANA PURCHASE (U.S.)

UNITED STATES

ATLANTIC OCEAN

TEXAS 1836 (Mexican 1821–1836)

MEXICO 1821

Mexico City

CUBA

HAITI 1804
SANTO DOMINGO 1821

PUERTO RICO (Sp.)

VIRGIN ISLANDS (Danish)

BRITISH HONDURAS

JAMAICA (Br.)

HONDURAS 1821

CURAÇAO (Dutch)

Caracas

TRINIDAD (Br.)

GUATEMALA 1821
SALVADOR 1821
NICARAGUA 1821
COSTA RICA 1821

(Br.)

(Dutch)

VENEZUELA 1830

(Fr.)

Bogotá

GUIANAS

COLOMBIA 1821

Quito

ECUADOR 1830

PERU 1821

BRAZIL 1822

PACIFIC OCEAN

Lima

La Paz

BOLIVIA 1825

PARAGUAY 1811

Rio de Janeiro

São Paulo

CHILE 1818

Asunción

ARGENTINA 1816

URUGUAY 1828

Valparaiso

Buenos Aires

Montevideo

FALKLAND ISLANDS (Br.)

☐ Countries that achieved independence
▨ Areas retained by European powers

425

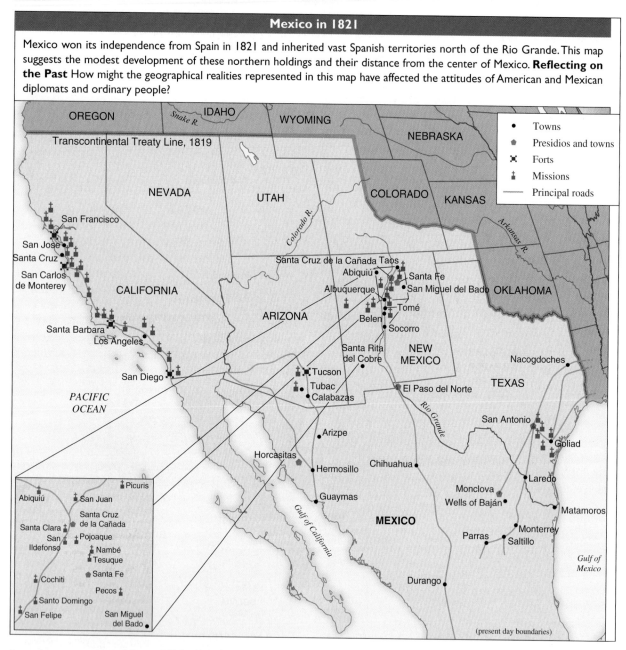

Mexico in 1821

Mexico won its independence from Spain in 1821 and inherited vast Spanish territories north of the Rio Grande. This map suggests the modest development of these northern holdings and their distance from the center of Mexico. **Reflecting on the Past** How might the geographical realities represented in this map have affected the attitudes of American and Mexican diplomats and ordinary people?

American women and established valuable connections with tribes involved in trapping. Along with their wives, they occupied a cultural middle ground characterized by elements from both American and native ways of life. Some ultimately became guides for Americans who emigrated later to the West.

Like the Whitmans, Methodist missionaries established early outposts in Oregon territory to teach native tribes Christian and American practices. Roman Catholic priests, sent from Europe, also worked among the native peoples. More tolerant of Native American culture than their Protestant counterparts, the Catholics had greater initial success in converting native peoples to Christianity.

The collapse of the Spanish Empire in 1821 provided Americans with a variety of opportunities. Each

year American caravans followed the Santa Fe Trail, loaded with weapons, tools, and brightly colored calicoes for New Mexico's 40,000 inhabitants. Eventually, some "Anglos" settled there. In Texas, it was cheap land for cotton rather than commerce that attracted settlers and squatters just as the small local Tejano population was adjusting to Mexico's independence. By 1835, almost 30,000 had migrated to Texas. They made up the largest group of Americans outside the nation's boundaries at that time.

On the Pacific, a handful of New England traders carrying sea-otter skins to China anchored in the harbors of Spanish California in the early nineteenth century. By the 1830s, as the near extermination of the animals ruined this trade, a commerce developed that exchanged California cowhides and tallow for clothes, boots, hardware, and furniture manufactured in the East.

Tribes driven from the South and the Old Northwest by the American government into present-day Oklahoma and Kansas were among the earliest easterners to settle in the trans-Mississippi West. Ironically, some of these tribes acted as agents of white civilization by introducing cotton, the plantation system, black slavery, and schools. Other tribes triggered conflicts that weakened the western tribes with whom they came into contact. These disruptions foreshadowed white incursions later in the century.

The fact that much of the trans-Mississippi West lay outside U.S. boundaries and that the government had guaranteed Indian tribes permanent possession of some western territories did not deter American economic or missionary activities. By the 1840s, a growing volume of published works detailed information that made emigration feasible. Lansford Hastings's *Emigrants' Guide to Oregon and California* (1845) provided both practical information and a rationale for emigration. American settlement would bring "genuine Republicanism and unsophisticated Democracy" to the West, replacing "ignorance, superstition, and despotism."

Territorial Expansion in the 1850s

Hastings's confidence that the future of the West lay with the United States was speedily realized. During the 1840s the United States, by war and diplomacy, acquired Mexico's possessions in the Southwest and on the Pacific and title to the Oregon country up to the 49th parallel. With the Gadsden Purchase in 1853, the country obtained another chunk of Mexican territory.

Manifest Destiny

Bursts of florid rhetoric accompanied territorial growth, and Americans used the slogan "Manifest Destiny" to justify and account for it. The phrase, coined in 1845 by John L. O'Sullivan, editor of the *Democratic Review,* expressed the conviction that the country's superior institutions and culture gave Americans a God-given right, even an obligation, to spread their civilization across the entire continent. This sense of uniqueness and mission was a legacy of early Puritan utopianism and Revolutionary republicanism. By the 1840s, the successful absorption of the Louisiana Territory, rapid population growth, and advances in transportation, communication, and industry bolstered the idea of national superiority. Publicists of Manifest Destiny proclaimed that the nation not only could but must absorb new territories.

DOCUMENT

John L. O'Sullivan, "Annexation" and "The Great Nation of Futurity" (1845)

WINNING THE TRANS-MISSISSIPPI WEST

Manifest Destiny justified expansion, but events in Texas triggered the government's determination to acquire territories west of the Mississippi River. The Texas question originated in the years when Spain held most of the Southwest. Although some settlements such as Santa Fe, founded in 1609, were almost

A Vision of the Westward Movement   This 1872 painting by John Gast—with its large, goddesslike figure trailing telegraph lines, its parade of settlers, and its depiction of technological progress—captures the confidence of white Americans that the acquisition of the West was a positive and inevitable event. What picture does this painting give of the emigration to the West? What emigrants moving into the West are omitted? *(John Gast, Westward, Ho! (American Progress). Museum of the American West Collection, Autry National Center)*

as old as Jamestown, the sparsely populated and underdeveloped Southwest acted primarily as a buffer zone for Mexico. The main centers of Spanish settlement were geographically distant from one another and thousands of miles from Mexico City. This weak defensive perimeter was increasingly vulnerable as Spain weakened, but its legal status was recognized internationally in the Transcontinental Treaty. Moreover, in its treaty negotiations with Spain in 1819, the United States, in return for Florida, accepted a southern border excluding Texas, to which the Americans had vague claims stemming from the Louisiana Purchase.

Annexing Texas, 1845

By the time the treaty was ratified in 1821, Mexico had won its independence from Spain but scarcely had an opportunity to cope with the borderlands, their people, and their problems or to achieve national stability. Mexicans soon had reason to wonder whether the American disavowal of any claim to Texas in the Transcontinental Treaty would last, for political leaders such as Henry Clay began to cry out for "reannexation." Fear about American expansionism, fueled by several attempts to buy Texas and by continuing aggressive American statements, permeated Mexican politics.

In 1823, the Mexican government resolved to strengthen border areas by increasing population. To attract settlers, it offered land in return for token payments and pledges to become Roman Catholics and Mexican citizens. Stephen F. Austin, whose father had gained rights from Spain to bring 200 families into Texas two years earlier, was among the first of the American impresarios, or contractors, to take advantage of this opportunity. His call for settlers brought an enthusiastic response, as Mary Austin Holley recalled. "I was a young thing then, but 5 months married, my husband . . . failed in Tennessee, proposed to commence business in New Orleans. I ready to go anywhere . . . freely consented. Just then Stephen Austin and Joe Hawkins were crying up Texas—beautiful country, land for nothing, etc.—Texas fever rose then . . . there we must go. There without much reflection, we did go." Like the Holleys, most of the American settlers came from the South, and some brought slaves. By the end of the decade, some 15,000 white Americans and 1,000 slaves lived in Texas, far outnumbering the 5,000 Tejano inhabitants.

Mexican officials soon had second thoughts. Although Stephen Austin converted to Roman Catholicism, few settlers gave signs of honoring their bargain with the Mexican government. Most

remained far more American than Mexican. Some were malcontents who disliked Mexican laws and customs and the limitations on their economic and commercial opportunities. In late 1826, a small group of them rebelled and declared the Republic of Fredonia. Although Stephen Austin and others assisted in putting down the brief uprising, American newspapers hailed the rebels as "apostles of democracy" and called Mexico an "alien civilization."

Mexican anxiety grew apace. Secretary of Foreign Relations Lucas Aláman accused American settlers of being advance agents of the United States. "They commence by introducing themselves into the territory which they covet," he told the Mexican Congress, "grow, multiply, become the predominant party in the population. . . . These pioneers excite . . . movements which disturb the political state of the country . . . and then follow discontents and dissatisfaction."

In 1829, the Mexican government altered its Texas policy. Determined to curb American influence, the government abolished slavery in Texas in 1830 and forbade further emigration from the United States. Officials began to collect customs duties on goods crossing the Louisiana border. But little changed in Texas. American slave owners freed their slaves and then forced them to sign life indenture contracts. Emigrants still crossed the border and outnumbered Mexicans.

Tensions escalated, and in October 1835, a skirmish between the colonial militia and Mexican forces opened hostilities. Sam Houston, onetime governor of Tennessee and army officer, became commander in chief of the Texas forces. Although Texans called the war with Mexico a revolution, a Vermont soldier perhaps more accurately observed, "It is in fact a rebellion."

The new Mexican dictator and general Antonio López de Santa Anna hurried north to crush the rebellion with an army of 6,000 conscripts. Although he had a numerical advantage, many of his soldiers were Mayan Indians who had been drafted unwillingly, spoke no Spanish, and were exhausted by the long march. Supply lines were spread thin. Nevertheless, Santa Anna and his men won the initial engagements of the war: the Alamo at San Antonio fell to him, as did the fortress of Goliad, to the southeast. All the Americans were killed, even though the Americans holding Goliad had surrendered.

DOCUMENT

William Barret Travis, Letter from the Alamo (1836)

As he pursued Houston and the Texans toward the San Jacinto River, carelessness proved Santa Anna's undoing. Although fully anticipating an American attack, the Mexican general and his men settled down to their usual siesta on April 21, 1836,

The Alamo

without posting an adequate guard. As the Mexicans dozed, the Americans attacked. With cries of "Remember the Alamo! Remember Goliad!" the Texans overcame the army, captured its commander in his slippers, and won the war within 20 minutes. Their casualties were minimal: 8 or 9 dead, 17 wounded. But 630 Mexicans lay dead.

With the victory at San Jacinto, Texas gained its independence. Threatened with lynching, Santa Anna saw little choice but to sign the treaty of independence setting the republic's boundary at the Rio Grande. When news of the disastrous events reached Mexico City, however, the Mexican Congress repudiated an "agreement carried out under the threat of death." Mexico maintained that Texas was still part of Mexico.

The new republic started off shakily, financially unstable, unrecognized by its enemy, rejected by its

friends. Although Texans immediately sought admission to the Union, their bid failed. Jackson, whose agent in Texas reported that the republic's "future security must depend more upon the weakness and imbecility of her enemy than upon her own strength," was reluctant to run the risk of war with Mexico. With the union precariously balanced with 13 free and 13 slave states, many northerners violently opposed annexation of another slave state. Petitions poured into Congress in 1837 opposing annexation, and John Quincy Adams repeatedly denounced the idea. Annexation was too explosive a political issue to pursue; debate finally died down and then disappeared.

For the next few years, the Lone Star Republic led a precarious existence. Mexico refused to recognize its independence but could send only an occasional raiding party across the border. Texans skirmished with Mexican bands, did their share of border raiding, and suffered an ignominious defeat in an ill-conceived attempt to capture Santa Fe in 1841. Diplomatic maneuvering in European capitals for financial aid and recognition was only moderately successful. Financial ties with the United States increased, however, as trade grew and many Americans invested in Texas bonds and lands.

Austin, Texas, 1840

Texas became headline news again in 1844. "It is the greatest question of the age," an Alabama expansionist declared, "and I predict will agitate the country more than all the other public questions ever have." He was right. Although President John Tyler (who assumed office after Harrison's sudden death) reopened the question of annexation hoping to ensure his re-election, the issue exploded. It brought to life powerful sectional, national, and political tensions and demonstrated the divisiveness of the questions connected to the western expansion of slavery. Southern Democrats claimed that the South's future hinged on the annexation of Texas. "Now is the time to vindicate and save our institutions," John C. Calhoun insisted.

Other wings of the Democratic party capitalized more successfully on the issue, however. Senators such as Lewis Cass of Michigan, Stephen Douglas of Illinois, and Robert Walker of Mississippi vigorously supported annexation, not because it would expand slavery, a topic they carefully avoided, but because it would spread the benefits of American civilization. Their arguments, classic examples of the basic tenets of Manifest Destiny, put the question into a national context of expanding American freedom. So powerfully did they link Texas to Manifest Destiny and avoid sectional issues that their candidate, James Polk of Tennessee, secured the Democratic nomination in 1844. Polk called for "the reannexation of Texas at the

The Texas Revolution, 1836

This map shows the significance of American settlement in Texas and the major military engagements of the war. The map also suggests how far the Mexican army had traveled before meeting the Texans on the battlefield.

earliest practicable period" and the occupation of the Oregon Territory. Manifest Destiny had come of age.

Whigs tended to oppose annexation, fearing slavery's expansion and the growth of southern power. They accused the Democrats of exploiting Manifest Destiny, more as a means of securing office than of bringing freedom to Texas.

The Whigs were right that the annexation issue would bring victory to the Democrats. Polk won a close election in 1844. But by the time he took the oath of office in March 1845, Tyler had resolved the question of annexation by pushing through Congress a joint resolution admitting Texas to the Union. Unlike a treaty, which required the approval of two-thirds of the Senate and which Tyler had already failed to win, a joint resolution needed only majority support. Nine years after its revolution, Texas finally joined the Union with the unusual right to divide into five states if it chose to do so.

War with Mexico, 1846–1848

When Mexico learned of Texas's annexation, it promptly severed diplomatic ties with the United States. It was easy for Mexicans to interpret the events from the 1820s on as part of an American plot to steal Texas. During the war for Texas independence, American newspapers, especially those in the South, had enthusiastically hailed the efforts of the rebels, while southern money and volunteers had aided the Texans in their struggle. Now that the Americans had gained Texas, would they want still more?

In his inaugural address in 1845, President Polk pointed out "that our system may easily be extended to the utmost bounds of our territorial limits, and that as it shall be extended the bonds of our Union, so far from being weakened will become stronger." What were those territorial limits? Did they extend into the territory the Mexican government considered its own?

Polk, like many other Americans, failed to appreciate how the annexation of Texas humiliated Mexico and increased pressures on its government to respond belligerently. Knowing that Mexico was weak, the president anticipated that it would grant his grandiose demands: a Texas boundary at the Rio Grande rather than the Nueces River 150 miles to the north, as well as California and New Mexico.

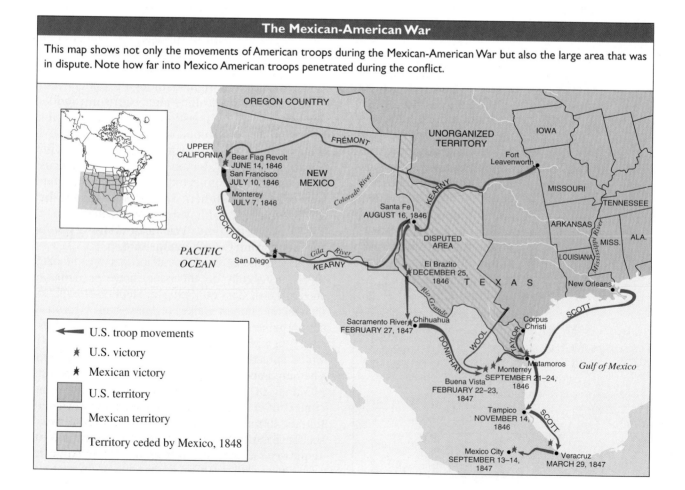

The Mexican-American War

This map shows not only the movements of American troops during the Mexican-American War but also the large area that was in dispute. Note how far into Mexico American troops penetrated during the conflict.

The Battle of Buena Vista   In February 1847, American forces, depleted by the departure of 9,000 troops for the Veracruz campaign, met Santa Anna's much larger army several miles north of the hacienda of Buena Vista. The Americans, largely inexperienced volunteers, dug themselves into the valley's gullies and ravines. After bitter conflict, the Americans won the day with far fewer casualties than their Mexican opponents. This victory secured northeastern Mexico for the Americans and helped make General Zachary Taylor into a popular hero and potential political candidate. *(Frances Flora Bond Palmer,* Battle of Buena Vista. View of the Battle-Ground of "The Angostura" fought near Buena Vista, Mexico February 23rd. 1847. [Looking S. West] *Toned lithograph (hand-colored), 1847, 19¹⁄₄ x 29¹⁄₂ inches. Amon Carter Museum, Fort Worth, Texas 1971.48)*

Even before the Texans could accept the invitation to join the Union, rumors of a Mexican invasion were afloat. As a precautionary move, Polk ordered General Zachary Taylor to move "on or near the Rio Grande." By October 1845, Taylor and 3,500 American troops had reached the Nueces River. The presence of the army did not mean that Polk actually expected war. Rather, he hoped that military might, coupled with secret diplomacy, would bring the desired concessions. In November, the president sent his agent, John L. Slidell, to Mexico City. When the Mexican government refused to receive Slidell, Polk angrily decided to force Mexico into accepting American terms. He ordered Taylor south to the Rio Grande. To the Mexicans, who insisted that the Nueces River was the legitimate boundary, their presence constituted an act of war. Democratic newspapers and expansionists enthusiastically hailed Polk's provocative decision; the Whigs opposed it.

IMAGE
The Storming
of Chapultepec

It was only a matter of time before an incident occurred to justify American hostilities. In late April, the Mexican government declared a state of defensive war. Two days later, a skirmish between Mexican and American troops resulted in 16 American casualties. When Polk received Taylor's report, he quickly drafted a war message for Congress. The president claimed that Mexico had "passed the boundary of the United States . . . invaded our territory and shed American blood upon American soil." "War exists," he claimed, adding untruthfully, "notwithstanding all our efforts to avoid it, exists by act of Mexico."

DOCUMENT
Thomas Corwin,
"Against the
Mexican War"
(1847)

Although Congress declared war, the conflict bitterly divided Americans. Many Whigs, including Abraham Lincoln, questioned the accuracy of Polk's initial account of the events, and their opposition grew more vocal as time passed. Lincoln called the war one "of conquest brought into existence to catch votes." The American Peace Society revealed sordid examples of army misbehavior in Mexico, and Frederick Douglass accused the country of "cupidity and love of dominion." Many workers also criticized the war.

Debate continued as American troops swept into Mexico and advanced toward the capital. Although the Mexicans were also fighting Native American tribes on their northern border, the government refused to admit defeat and end the hostilities. The war dragged on. The *American Review,* a Whig paper, proclaimed that the conflict was a "crime over which angels may weep." In 1847, a month after General Winfield Scott took Mexico City, Philadelphian Joseph Sills wrote in his diary, "There is a widely spread conviction . . . that it is a wicked & disgraceful war."

Yet Polk enjoyed the enthusiastic support of expansionists. Most soldiers were eager volunteers. Some expansionists even urged permanent occupation of Mexico. Illinois Democratic senator Sidney Breese told the Senate, "The avowed objects of the war . . . [were] to obtain redress of wrongs, a permanent and honorable peace, and indemnity for the past and security for the future." To secure these goals, Breese could even contemplate permanent occupation with "great ultimate good" to the United States, to Mexico, "and to humanity."

Inflated rhetoric did not win the war, however. In the end, chance helped draw hostilities to a close. Mexican moderates approached Polk's diplomatic representative, Nicholas Trist, who accompanied the American army in Mexico. In Trist's baggage were detailed though out-of-date instructions outlining Polk's requirements: the Rio Grande boundary, Upper California, and New Mexico. Although the president had lost confidence in Trist and had ordered him home, Trist stayed in Mexico to negotiate an end to the war. Having obtained most of Polk's objectives, he returned to Washington to an ungrateful president who fired him from his job at the State Department and denounced him as an "unqualified scoundrel."

General Winfield Scott in Mexico City

California and New Mexico

Although Texas and Mexico dominated the headlines, Polk considered California and New Mexico part of any resolution of the Mexico crisis. Serious American interest in California dated from the late 1830s. Before then, few Americans were living in California. Many had married into California families and taken Mexican citizenship. But gradual recognition of California's fine harbors, its favorable position for the China trade, and suspicion that Great Britain had designs on it, fed the conviction that California must

Richard Henry Dana, Jr., *Two Years Before the Mast* (1840)

become part of the United States. The arrival of 1,500 overland emigrants in the 1840s increased the likelihood that California would not long remain a Mexican outpost.

In 1845, Polk appointed Thomas Larkin, a successful American merchant in Monterey, as his confidential agent. "If the people [of California] should desire to unite their destiny with ours," wrote Polk's secretary of state, James Buchanan, to Larkin, "they would be received as brethren." Polk's efforts to buy California suggested that he was sensitive to the fragility of American claims to the region. But Santa Anna, carrying the burden of having lost Texas, was in no position to sell.

New Mexico was also on Polk's list. Profitable economic ties with the United States dating back to the 1820s stimulated American territorial ambitions. As part of the oldest and largest Mexican community in North America, however, most New Mexicans had little desire for annexation. The unsuccessful attempt by the Texans to capture Santa Fe in 1841 and border clashes in the two following years did not enhance the attractiveness of Anglo neighbors. But because New Mexico stood awkwardly in the path of westward expansion and was further isolated from Mexico by the annexation of Texas in 1846, its future was uncertain.

In June 1846, shortly after the declaration of war with Mexico, American troops led by Colonel Stephen W. Kearney left Fort Leavenworth, Kansas, for New Mexico. Kearney had orders to occupy Mexico's northern provinces and to protect the lucrative Santa Fe trade. Two months later, the army took Santa Fe without a shot, although one eyewitness noticed "surly" countenances and a "wail of grief." New Mexico's upper class, having already made strategic alliances with Americans, readily accepted the new rulers. However, ordinary Mexicans and Pueblo Indians did not take conquest so lightly. After Kearney departed for California, resistance erupted first in New Mexico and then in California. Kearney was wounded, and the first appointed American governor of New Mexico was killed. In the end, superior American military strength won the day. By January 1847, both California and New Mexico were firmly in American hands.

The Treaty of Guadalupe Hidalgo, 1848

Negotiated by Trist and signed on February 2, 1848, the Treaty of Guadalupe Hidalgo resolved the original issues by setting the Rio Grande as the boundary between Mexico and the United States

The Oregon Country

What does this map reveal about the claims to Oregon voiced during the election of 1844? How do the claims correspond to the eventual boundaries established with Great Britain? The major trails that brought American settlers to the West suggest the population movements that lay behind the Oregon controversy.

and by transferring the Southwest and California into American hands. At a cost of 13,000 American lives, mostly due to disease, the United States gained 75,000 Spanish-speaking inhabitants, 150,000 Native Americans, and 529,017 square miles, almost a third of prewar Mexico. It paid Mexico $15 million (and another $10 million in 1853 for the Gadsden Purchase), agreed to honor American claims against Mexico, and guaranteed the civil, political, and property rights of former Mexican citizens. Although sporadic violence would continue for years in the Southwest as Mexicans protested the outcome, the war was over, and the Americans had won.

The Oregon Question, 1844–1846

In the Pacific Northwest, the presence of mighty Great Britain suggested reliance on diplomacy rather than war. Glossing over the disputed nature of American claims to the Oregon Territory, Polk assured the inauguration day crowd that "our title to the country of Oregon is 'clear and unquestionable.'" The British did not agree.

Though the British considered the president's speech belligerent, Polk correctly noted that Americans had not hesitated to settle the disputed territories. Between 1842 and 1845, the number of Americans in Oregon grew from 400 to more than 5,000, mostly south of the Columbia River in the Willamette valley. By 1843, these settlers had written a constitution and soon after elected a legislature. At the same time, declining British interest in the area set the stage for an eventual compromise. The near destruction of the beaver had weakened the fur trade, and the riches produced in Britain by the Industrial Revolution made colonies appear less important than they had been in the eighteenth century. Britain had already granted Canada self-rule. Attractive commercial opportunities were opening up in other parts of the world such as India and China, while New Zealand, annexed in 1840, and Australia became magnets for British emigration.

Polk's flamboyant posture and the expansive American claims made mediation difficult, however. Polk's campaign slogan claimed a boundary of 54°40'. But Polk was not willing to go to war with Great Britain for Oregon. Privately, he considered reasonable a boundary at the forty-ninth parallel, which would extend the existing Canadian–American border to the Pacific.

Soon after his inauguration, Polk offered his compromise to Great Britain, but his tone antagonized the British. In his year-end address to Congress in 1845, the president increased diplomatic tensions by again claiming Oregon and giving the required one year's notice of American intention to cancel the joint occupation.

Despite slogans, most Americans did not want to fight for Oregon. As war with Mexico loomed, the task of resolving the disagreement became more urgent. The British, too, were eager to settle, and in June 1846 they agreed to the forty-ninth-parallel boundary if Vancouver Island remained British. Polk ended the crisis just weeks before the declaration of war with Mexico; he escaped some of the responsibility for retreating from slogans by sharing it with the Senate, who approved the compromise.

As these events show, Manifest Destiny was an idea that supported and justified expansionist policies. It corresponded to Americans' basic belief that expansion was necessary and right. As early as 1816, American geography books pictured the nation's western boundary at the Pacific and included Texas. Popular literature typically described Native Americans as a dying race and Mexicans as "injurious neighbor[s]."

IMAGE

Carl Nebel, "General Scott's Triumph," (1851)

HOW OTHERS SEE US

A French Newspaper Comments on President Polk's Oregon Policy

On December 30, 1845, the London Times *included an excerpt from the French newspaper* Journal des Debats *that commented on President's Polk message about Oregon.*

The message of the President of the United States respecting the Oregon question, is not of a tenour to indicate that Mr. Polk is animated by a spirit of conciliation. He dwells much upon his moderation, but he shows it so little, and his tone is such, that should a similar tone be assumed by the British Government, the affair must inevitably terminate in a war. Negotiations rejecting the Oregon territory have been pending since the year 1818. Both Powers wish to possess the river Columbia, the only important stream in the west of the New World. In the conferences which were held in 1818, 1824, and 1826, it was agreed that the navigation should be free for both countries, but the United States wished to possess both banks from the 49th degree of latitude to the ocean. England offered the left bank, preserving the other for herself, both countries having the free right of traffic with the Indians. Such is the convention which at present exists, and which Mr. Polk wishes to put an end to. The President, instead of exerting himself to bring the debate to a pacific termination, appears to have done all in his power to render it impossible. . . . The President breathes war, and his message in that respect is a novelty, even after those of General Jackson. Mr. Polk evidently belongs to a new school; and the American democracy, since the taking possession of Texas, abandons itself to an ambition which may prove fatal to it. His message is without precedent, not merely as regards the manner in which the Oregon question is treated, but on account of the general tone which characterizes it. Up to the present time, or at least up to the time of General Jackson, it was customary in the messages to speak in a differential tone to the European Powers. The Presidents were men who had seen Europe, and who duly appreciated the power of the great states of the old continent. In those solemn documents concocted principally for the multitude, they showed themselves proud of the republican institutions, they made a pompous parade of the prosperity sans egale (the favourite term of the country), but they carefully avoided anything which might be regarded at the other side of the Atlantic as vain and ridiculous bravadoes. . . . Mr. Polk, very different from his illustrious predecessors, reduces himself to the level of the rough cultivators of the valley of the Ohio, in whose opinion Europe is a collection of degraded beings groaning under the weight of monarchical government, and which it would be no difficult matter for the forces of the Union to overcome. It is impossible to explain the imprudent language contained in the President's message in any other manner. But England is not the only Power to which the arrogant message applies. France us likewise roughly handled with respect to the Texas affair. France is reproached with wishing to have Texas made an independent state instead of going to swell the American federation, and the incorporation of Texas is represented as a victory over the European monarchies.

■ *How does the French newspaper characterize Polk and American policy on the Oregon question?*

Source: *The London Times,* December 30, 1845, from "The Mexican-American War and the Media, 1845–1848, transcribed by 3a

Only whites could make the wilderness flower. Thus, as lands east of the Mississippi filled up, Americans automatically called on familiar ideas to justify expansion.

GOING WEST AND EAST

Americans lost little time in moving into the new territories. During the 1840s, 1850s, and 1860s, thousands of Americans left their homes for the West. By 1860, California alone had 380,000 settlers. At the same time, thousands of Chinese headed south and east to destinations such as Australia, Hawaii, and North and South America to escape the unrest caused by the opium wars in the 1840s with Great Britain, internal unrest, and poor economic conditions. Sixty-three thousand had come to the United States by 1870. Most were in California, the land of the "Gold Mountain."

One Chinese folk song depicted the "perilous journey" to the United States "sailing [in] a boat

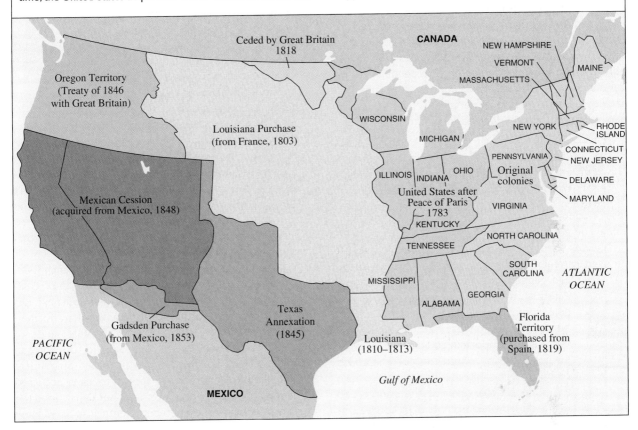

U.S. Territorial Expansion by 1860

This map reveals that it took more than 100 years for the United States to expand from the original 13 colonies to Mississippi. You can see the substantial gains Americans won as a result of the Revolution. Then, as the map shows, within the span of a lifetime, the United States acquired the vast territories across the Mississippi River.

with bamboo poles across the sea." The Chinese, of course, had little choice on their travel route to the American West, but American migrants did. Some chose the sea route; although the trip was expensive, one could sail from Atlantic or Gulf Coast ports around South America to the West Coast or embark for Panama, cross the isthmus by land, and then continue by sea. Most emigrants from the states, however, chose land routes. In 1843, the first large party succeeded in crossing the plains and mountains to Oregon. More followed. Between 1841 and 1867, some 350,000 traveled the overland trails to California or Oregon, while others trekked part of the way to intermediate points such as Colorado and Utah.

IMAGE
Oregon Trail Marker

The Emigrants

Most of the emigrants who headed for the Far West, where slavery was prohibited, were white and American born. They came from the Midwest and the Upper South. A few free blacks made the trip as well. Pioneer Margaret Frink remembered seeing a "Negro woman . . . tramping along through the heat and dust, carrying a cast iron black stove on her head, with her provisions and a blanket piled on top . . . bravely pushing on for California." Emigrants from the Deep South usually selected Arkansas or Texas as their destination, and many took their slaves with them. By 1840, more than 11,000 slaves toiled in Texas and 20,000 in Arkansas.

The many pioneers who kept journals during the five- to six-month overland trip captured the human dimension of emigrating. Their journals, usually their only contribution to the historical record, focused on day-to-day events and expressed some of the thoughts and emotions experienced on the long journey west. One migrant, Lodisa Frizzell, described her feelings at parting in 1852:

Who is there that does not recollect their first night when started on a long journey, the well known voices of our friends still ring in our ears, the parting kiss feels

RECOVERING THE PAST

Personal Diaries

Nineteenth-century journals kept by hundreds of ordinary men and women traveling west on the overland trails constitute a rich source for exploring the nature of the westward experience. They are also an example of how private sources can be used to deepen our understanding of the past. Diaries, journals, and letters all provide us with a personal perspective on major happenings. These sources tend to focus on the concrete, so they convey the texture of daily life in the nineteenth century, daily routines and amusements, clothing, habits, and interactions with family and friends. They also provide evidence of the varied concerns, attitudes, and prejudices of the writers, thus providing a test of commonly accepted generalizations about individual and group behavior.

Like any historical source, personal documents must be used carefully. It is important to note the writer's age, gender, class, and regional identification. Although this information may not be available, some of the writer's background can be deduced from what he or she has written. It is also important to consider for what purpose and for whom the document was composed. This information will help explain the tone or character of the source and what has been included or left out. It is, of course, important to avoid generalizing too much from one or even several similar sources. Only after reading many diaries, letters, and journals is it possible to make valid generalizations about life in the past.

Here we present excerpts from two travel journals of the 1850s. Few of the writers considered their journals strictly private. Often they were intended as a family record or as information for friends back home.

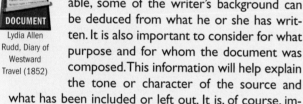

DOCUMENT
Lydia Allen Rudd, Diary of Westward Travel (1852)

Therefore, material of a personal nature has often been excluded. Nineteenth-century Americans referred to certain topics, such as pregnancy, only indirectly or not at all.

One excerpt comes from Mary Bailey's 1852 journal. Mary was 22 years old when she crossed the plains to California with her 32-year-old doctor husband. Originally a New Englander, Mary had lived in Ohio for six years before moving west. The Baileys were reasonably prosperous and were able to restock necessary supplies on the road west. The other writer, Robert Robe, was 30 years old when he crossed along the same route a year earlier than the Baileys, headed for Oregon. Robert was a native of Ohio and a Presbyterian minister.

As you read these excerpts, notice what each journal reveals about the trip west. What kinds of challenges did the emigrants face on their journey? Do these correspond to the picture you may have formed from novels, television, and movies? What kinds of work needed to be done, and who did it? Can you see any indication of a division of work based on gender? What kinds of interactions appear to have occurred between men and women on the trip? What does the pattern tell us about nineteenth-century society? How does the painting of the "emigrant train" reinforce the journal accounts of men's and women's roles?

REFLECTING ON THE PAST Even these short excerpts suggest that men and women, as they traveled west, may have had different concerns and different perspectives on the journey. In what ways do the two accounts differ, and in what ways are they similar?

DOCUMENT
Journal Entry of Francis Parkman (August 6–8, 1846)

(Benjamin Reinhardt, The Emigrant Train Bedding Down for the Night, 1867, 40 x 70 in. oil on canvas. In the Collection of the Corcoran Gallery of Art, Washington, D.C., Gift of Mr. and Mrs. Lansdell K. Christie, 59.21)

Journal of Mary Stuart Bailey

Wednesday, April 13, 1852 Left our hitherto happy home in Sylvania amid the tears of parting kisses of dear friends, many of whom were endeared to me by their kindness shown to me when I was a stranger in a strange land, when sickness and death visited our small family & removed our darling, our only child in a moment, as it were. Such kindness I can never forget. . . .

Friday, 21st [May] Rained last night. Slept in the tent for the first time. I was Yankee enough to protect myself by pinning up blankets over my head. I am quite at home in my tent.

12:00 Have traveled in the rain all day & we are stuck in the mud. I sit in the wagon writing while the men are at work doubling the teams to draw us out. . . .

Sunday, 23rd. Walked to the top of the hill where I could be quiet & commune with nature and nature's God. This afternoon I was annoyed by something very unpleasant & shed many tears and felt very unhappy. . . .

Thursday, 4th [June] Very cold this morning after the shower. . . . We stopped on the banks of the Platte to take dinner. I am sitting on the banks of the Platte with my feet almost in the water. Have been writing to my Mother. How I wish I had some of my own relations with me. . . .

Sunday, 4th [July] Started at 3 o'clock to find feed or know where it was. Had to go 4 or 5 miles off the road. Found water & good grass. Camped on the sand with sage roots for fuel. It is wintery, cold & somewhat inclined to rain, not pleasant. Rather a dreary Independence Day. We speak of our friends at home. We think they are thinking of us. . . .

Monday, 12th. Stayed in camp another day to get our horse better. He is much improved. It is cold enough. Washed in the morning & had the sick headache in the afternoon. . . .

Thursday, 12th [August] Very warm. Slept until we stopped to take breakfast. Mr. Patterson starts as soon as light & stops in the heat of the day to rest the animals. We do not have much time to do anything except 4 or 5 hours in the middle of the day. . . .

Friday, 17th [September] Have been confined ever since Monday with ague in my face which is very much swollen. Have suffered very much. We are now in Carson Valley. Plenty of trees but the country is very barren.

Saturday, 18th. Very pleasant, delightful weather. Feel much better today. We are not stirring this afternoon. We have heard to a great deal of suffering, people being thrown out on the desert to die & being picked up & brought to the hospital. . . .

Source: From Ho for California! Women's Overland Diaries, *Sandra L. Myers, ed., Reprinted with the permission of the Henry E. Huntington Library.*

Journal of Robert Robe

[May] 19, [1851] A fine day. The first spent in travelling on the plains of the Platte river.

20. Continue our journey up the Platte valley which I would judge to be here some 12 miles wide on this side of the river. The only game seen here are the antelope and wolf beside some wild fowl.

21. A rainy morning started early passed an old Pawnee village in ruins. The houses are constructed by placing timbers in forks and upon these without placing upright poles then rushes bound with [illegible] and finally earth. Chimney in center. Day became more & more rainy and wound up with a storm which beggared description.

22. Bluff approach the river—travelling less monotonous river finely skirted with timber.

23. Roads very muddy in afternoon. Today our wagon severed itself from our former companions & joined a company of Californians.

24. Before starting a trader direct from Ft. Kearney arrived at our camp. He informs us it is yet 25 miles thither. Travelling is by no means dangerous a waggon of provisions passing with only three guards. In the afternoon passed the entrance of the Independence Weston & St. Jo. roads. Emigrants became more numerous.

25. Passed Fort Kearney this morning and after a short drive encamped. Having conversed with some of the soldiers I find they consider life very monotonous.

26. Roads heavy—short drive—a storm.

27. High Bluffs on the opposite side of river approach and present a beautiful appearance. At night a fearful storm.

28. Roads heavy nothing singular.

29. Have arrived in the region abounding in Buffalo. At noon a considerable herd came in sight. The first any of us had ever seen. Thus now for the chase—the horsemen proved too swift in pursuit and frightened them into the Bluffs without capturing any—the footmen pursued however and killed three pretty good success for the first.

30. Nothing remarkable today.

31. Game being abundant we resolved to rest our stock and hunt today—Started in the morning on foot. Saw probably 1,000 Buffalo. Shot at several and killed one. Where ever we found them wolves were prowling around as if to guard them. Their real object is however no doubt to seize the calves as their prey. Saw a town of Prairie dogs, they are nearly as large as a gray squirrel. They bark fiercely when at a little distance but on near approach flee to their holes. Wherever they are we see numerous owls. After a very extensive ramble and having seen a variety of game we returned at sunset with most voracious appetites.

June 1. The Bluffs became beautifully undulating losing their precipitous aspect and the country further back is beautifully rolling prairie.

2. In the evening camped beside our old friends Miller and Dovey. They had met with a great loss this morning their 3 horses having taken fright at a drove of buffalo and ran entirely away. Some of our company killed more buffalo this evening & a company went in the night with teams to bring them in.

Source: Journal of Robert Robe (1851) from Washington Historic Quarterly, *January 1928. Reprinted with permission.*

still warm upon our lips, and that last separating word farewell! sinks deeply into the heart! It may be the last we ever hear from some or all of them, and to those who start . . . there can be no more solemn scene of parting only at death.

Most emigrants traveled with family and relatives. Only during the gold rush years did large numbers, usually young men, travel independently. Migration was a family experience, mostly involving men and women in their late 20s to early 40s. A sizable number of them had recently married. And for most, migration was a familiar experience. Like other geographically mobile Americans, emigrants to the Far West had earlier moved to other frontiers, often as children or as newlyweds. The difference was the vast distance to this frontier and the seemingly final separation from home.

Migrants' Motives

What led so many Americans to sell most of their possessions and embark on an unknown future thousands of miles away? Many believed that frontier life would offer rich opportunities. A popular folk song expressed this widespread conviction:

Since times has been hard, I'll tell you sweetheart,
I've a notion to leave off my plow and my cart,
Away to Californy a journey pursue,
To double my fortunes as other men do.

The kinds of opportunities emigrants expected varied widely. Thousands sought riches in the form of gold. Others anticipated making their fortune as merchants, shopkeepers, and peddlers. Some intended to speculate in land, acquiring large blocks of public lands and then selling them later to settlers at a handsome profit. The possibility of professional rewards gained from practicing law or medicine attracted still others.

Most migrants dreamed of bettering their life by cultivating the land. As one settler explained, "The motive that induced us to part with pleasant associates and dear friends of our childhood days, was to obtain from the government of the United States a grant of land that 'Uncle Sam' had promised." Federal and state land policies made the acquisition of land increasingly alluring. Preemption acts during the 1830s and 1840s gave "squatters" the right to settle public lands before the government offered them for sale and then allowed them to purchase these lands at the minimum price once they came on the market. At the same time, the amount of land a family had to

DOCUMENT

Letter from Mariah and Stephen King to Their Family

buy shrank to only 40 acres. In 1862, the Homestead Act went further by offering 160 acres of government land free to citizens or future citizens over 21 who lived on the property, improved it, and paid a small registration fee. Oregon's land policy, which predated the Homestead Act, was even more generous. It awarded a single man 320 acres of free land and a married man 640 acres, provided he occupied his claim for four years and made improvements.

Some emigrants hoped the West would restore them to health. Settlers from the Mississippi valley wished to escape the region's debilitating malarial fevers. Doctors advised those suffering the dreaded tuberculosis that the long out-of-doors trip and the western climate might cure them. Even invalids grasped at the advice offered by one doctor in 1850, who urged them to "attach themselves to the companies of emigrants bound for Oregon or Upper California."

Others pursued religious or cultural missions in the West. Missionary couples like David and Catherine Blaine, who settled in Seattle when it was a frontier outpost, were determined to bring Protestantism and education west. Stirred by tales of the "deplorable morals" on the frontier, they willingly left the comforts of home to evangelize and educate westerners. Still others, like the Mormons, made the long trek to Utah to establish a society in conformity with their religious beliefs.

Not everyone who dreamed of setting off for the frontier could do so, however. Unlike the moves to earlier frontiers, the trip to the Far West involved considerable expense. The sea route, while probably the most comfortable, was the most costly, an estimated $600 per person for the trip around Cape Horn. For the same sum, four people could travel overland. And if the emigrants sold their wagons and oxen at the journey's end, the final expenses might amount to only $220. Clearly, however, the initial financial outlay was considerable enough to rule out the trip for the very poor. Despite increasingly liberal land policies, American migration to the Far West (with the exception of group migration to Utah) was a movement of the middle class.

IMAGE

A Forty-Niner's Covered Wagon

Like Americans, Chinese migrants were also inspired by the dream of bettering their condition. Most were married men who faced limited opportunities in their villages. Labor circulars proclaimed that Americans "want the Chinaman to come and make him very welcome. . . . Money is in great plenty and to spare in America." The message was reinforced when emigrants to Hawaii and the United States returned with money in their pockets.

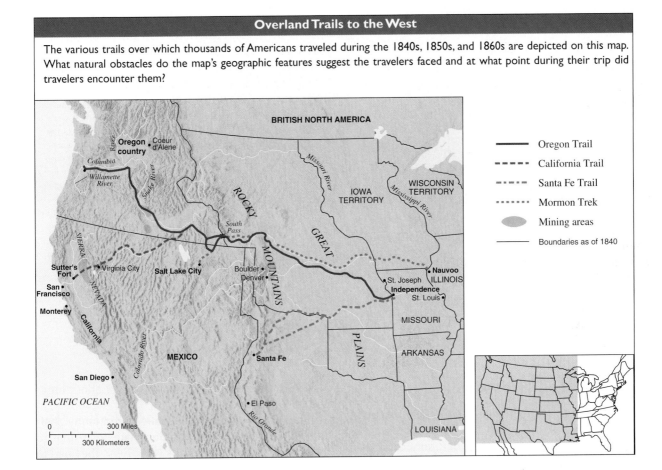

Overland Trails to the West

The various trails over which thousands of Americans traveled during the 1840s, 1850s, and 1860s are depicted on this map. What natural obstacles do the map's geographic features suggest the travelers faced and at what point during their trip did travelers encounter them?

In the 1860s, Chinese laborers could earn $30 a month working for the railroad, far more than the $3 to $5 they could expect if they stayed home.

The Overland Trails

The trip for American emigrants began in the late spring at starting points in Iowa and Missouri. By mid-May the grass was usually up for the stock, and the emigrant trains set out. Making only 15 miles a day, emigrants first followed the valley of the Platte River up to South Pass in the Rockies. This part of the trip seemed novel, even enjoyable. Until the 1850s, conflict with Native Americans was rare. The traditional division of labor persisted: Men did "outdoor" work such as driving and repairing wagons, and women handled domestic chores. Young children stayed out of the way in wagons, while older brothers and sisters walked alongside and lent a hand. Wagon trains might stop to observe the Sabbath, allowing for rest and laundry.

Later, difficulties multiplied. Cholera often took a heavy toll. Deserts and mountains replaced rolling prairies. Emigrants had to cross the final mountain ranges—the Sierras and the Cascades—before the first snowfall, so they pushed on relentlessly. Animals weakened by constant travel, poor feed, and bad water sickened, collapsed, and often died. Families had to lighten wagons by throwing out possessions lovingly brought from home. Food supplies dwindled, and the familiar division of responsibilities often collapsed. Women found themselves loading and driving wagons, even helping to drag them over rocky mountain trails. Their husbands worked frantically with the animals and the wagons as the time of the first snowfall

DOCUMENT

Elizabeth Dixon Smith Geer, Journal (1847, 1848)

drew closer. Tempers frayed. Family harmony often collapsed. Mary Power, who with her husband and three children crossed in 1853, revealed exasperation and depression in her journal: "I felt my courage must fail me, for there we were in a strange land, almost without anything to eat, [with] a team that was not able to pull an empty wagon."

Finally, five or six months after setting out, emigrants arrived, exhausted and often penniless, in Oregon or California. As one wrote at the end of her journey in 1854, its "care, fatigue, tediousness, perplexities and dangers of various kinds, can not be excelled."

A Mormon Wagon Train What does this view of a Mormon wagon train in the 1850s suggest about the terrain that emigrant families encountered as they went west? The Mormon migrations were the most organized of the migrations into the trans-Mississippi West, although not all Mormons were lucky enough to travel by wagon. Some emigrants to Utah pushed handcarts across the plains to their destination. *(Used by permission, Utah State Historical Society, all rights reserved. Photo no. 10077)*

LIVING IN THE WEST

Whether elated or depressed when they reached their destinations, emigrants had no choice but to start anew. As they did so, they naturally drew on their experiences back East. "Pioneers though we are, and proud of it, we are not content with the wilds . . . with the idleness of the land, the rudely construct[ed] log cabin," one Oregon settler explained.

Farming in the West

Pioneer farmers faced the urgent task of establishing homesteads and beginning farming. First, they had to locate a suitable claim, then clear land, and construct a shelter. Only then could they plant crops.

As farmers labored "to get the land subdued and the wilde nature out of it," they repeated a process that had occurred on earlier frontiers. Felling timber, pulling out native plants that seemed without value, and planting familiar crops began a transformation of the landscape. Results were often unanticipated. When they planted seed brought from home, farmers unknowingly also introduced weeds that did all too well, like the Canadian thistle that gradually displaced native grass and rendered land useless for grazing.

Emigrants did not recognize the ecological transformation they set in motion. The goal of taming nature was so central and difficult that there

was little time or inclination to wonder about long-range consequences.

The task of getting started presented many challenges. Since emigrant families had been able to bring only a few possessions with them, they had to work without familiar tools and implements. The Oregon bride who set up housekeeping in the 1840s with only a stew kettle and three knives was not unusual. Men often found themselves assisting wives in unfamiliar domestic chores while women helped men with their heavy outdoor work. After months of intense interaction with other travelers, families often felt lonely and thought longingly of friends and family back home. Although they might interact with nearby Native Americans, cultural biases made close friendships difficult.

One pioneer remembered that "in those days anyone residing within twenty miles was considered a neighbor." But the isolation usually ended within a few years as new emigrants arrived and old settlers sought better claims. As rural communities grew, settlers established schools, churches, and clubs. These organizations redefined acceptable forms of behavior and enforced conventional standards.

Determination to re-establish familiar institutions was most apparent in law and politics. In Oregon, pioneers set up a political system based on eastern models before territorial status was resolved. Before permanent schools or churches existed, men resumed familiar political rituals of electioneering, voting, and talking politics. They went to court to ensure law and order.

Setting up a Common School system and churches was more difficult and less urgent than beginning political life. Few settlers initially thought education important enough to tax themselves for permanent public schools. Schools operated sporadically and only for students paying at least part of the fees. While confirmed believers attended early church services, they often discovered that there were too few members of individual denominations to support separate churches. Nor were converts plentiful, for many settlers had lost the habit of regular churchgoing. David Blaine learned the "unwelcome lesson" that "separation from gospel influences" had left many "quite indifferent to gospel truth."

The chronic shortage of cash on the frontier hampered the growth of both schools and churches. Until farmers could send their goods to market, they had little cash to spare. Geographic mobility also contributed to institutional instability. Up to three-quarters of the population of a frontier county might vanish within a 10-year period. Some farmed in as many as four locations before finding a satisfactory claim. Institutions relying on continuing personal and financial support suffered accordingly.

Yet newspapers, journals, and books, which circulated early on the frontier, reinforced familiar norms and determination. As more settlers arrived, support for educational, religious, and cultural institutions grew. In the end, as one pioneer pointed out, "We have a telegraph line from the East, a daily rail road train, daily mail and I am beginning to feel quite civilized. And here ended my pioneer experience." Only 16 years had passed since she had crossed the plains.

Although the belief in special economic and social opportunities on the frontier encouraged emigration, the dream was often illusory. Western society rapidly acquired a social and economic structure similar to that of the East. Frontier newspapers referred to leading settlers as the "better" sort, and workers for hire and tenant farmers appeared. Widespread geographic mobility also suggests that many could not capitalize on the benefits of homesteading. Those who left communities were generally less successful than the core of stable residents, who became economic and social leaders. Those on the move believed that fortune would finally smile at their next stop. Said one wife when her husband announced another move: "I seemed to have heard all this before."

Mining Western Resources

The mineral riches of the trans-Mississippi West prompted people to leave their ordinary lives behind and set out to make their fortunes. News of the discovery of gold in 1848 in California swept the country like "wildfire," according to one Missouri emigrant. Thousands raced to cash in on the bonanza. Within a year, California's population ballooned from 14,000 to almost 100,000. By 1852, that figure had more than doubled.

Like migrants who planned to establish farms in the West, the "forty-niners" were mostly young (in

An Episcopal Church in Kansas

It was not easy for denominations to establish strong congregations in the West. How would you describe this church and what does its appearance suggest about the challenges of religion in the West? How many people attended this church on the day of the photograph? How many parishioners do you think would be necessary to establish a strong congregation? *(Kansas State Historical Society)*

AMERICAN VOICES

Mollie Dorsey Sanford, On Arriving in Denver, June 1860

Mollie Dorsey Sanford emigrated with her family from Indiana to Nebraska Territory in 1857. In 1860, at the age of 21, she married her older suitor, By Sanford. Mollie reported in her diary that she caught "Pikes Peak Fever" when she learned about the gold rush in Colorado and that she had encouraged her husband "to make arrangements to go" to Denver to try their luck. When the couple arrived in Denver in June 1860, Dora, Mollie's younger sister, and her husband were already there.

The Promised Land is gained and we are in Denver tonight. We entered the city of the plains at 10 o'clock A.M. We soon found Dora. They are camping on the banks of Cherry Creek, a dry, sandy channel. There are no houses to be had, and hundreds of families are living in wagons, tents, and shelters made of carpets and bedding. I like the looks of the place. Everybody seems glad to welcome the coming pilgrims, as we are called, anybody from "back in the States." It is estimated there are five thousand people in and around Denver. It seems so near the mountains that I thought I could easily walk over there, but Dora says they are 12 miles away. The atmosphere is so dry and clear it brings distant objects nearer. . . . By sees no chance to get work at his trade, as the place is overrun, a blacksmith shop on every corner. We have interviewed our mutual pocket-book and found less than five dollars left. But we are supplied with several months' provisions of staple articles. The luxuries we will dispense with.

- *What picture does Mollie give of Denver and its atmosphere?*

- *What is her mood?*

- *What challenges does Denver present to the Sanfords?*

1850, more than half the people in California were in their 20s). Unlike pioneers headed for rural homesteads, however, the gold seekers were unmarried, predominantly male, and heterogeneous. Of those pouring into California in 1849, about 80 percent came from the United States, 8 percent from Mexico, and 5 percent from South America. The rest came from Europe and Asia. California was thus one of the most diverse places in the country. Few of its residents, however, were as interested in settling the West as they were in extracting its precious metals and returning home rich.

California was the first and most dramatic of the western mining discoveries. But others followed. Rumors of gold propelled between 25,000 and 30,000 emigrants, many from California, to British Columbia in Canada in 1858. A year later, news of gold strikes in Colorado set off another rush for fortune. Precious metals unearthed in the Pacific Northwest early in the decade and in Montana and Idaho a few years later kept dreams alive and prospectors moving. In the mid-1870s, more gold, this time in the Black Hills of North Dakota, attracted hordes of fortune seekers.

In contrast to the agricultural settlements, where early residents were isolated and the community expanded gradually, the discovery of gold or silver spurred rapid, if usually short-lived, growth. Mining camps, ramshackle and often hastily constructed, soon housed hundreds or even thousands of miners and people serving them. Merchants, saloonkeepers, cooks, druggists, gamblers, and prostitutes hurried into boom areas as fast as prospectors. Usually, about half the residents of any mining camp were there to prospect the miners rather than the mines.

Given the motivation, character, and ethnic diversity of those flocking to boomtowns and the feeble attempts to set up local government in what were perceived as temporary communities, it was hardly surprising that mining life was often disorderly. Racial antagonism between American miners and foreigners, whom they labeled "greasers" (Mexicans), "chinks" (Chinese), "keskedees" (Frenchmen), and lesser "breeds," led to ugly riots and lynchings. Miners had few qualms about eliminating those who interfered with the race for riches. Fistfights, drunkenness, and murder occurred often enough to become part of the lore of the gold rush. Wrote one woman, "In the short space of twenty four days, we have had murders, fearful accidents, bloody deaths, a mob, whippings, a hanging, an attempt at suicide, and a fatal duel."

DOCUMENT

Edward Gould Burrum, Six Months in the Gold Mines (1850)

Chinese and American Miners This photograph captures some of the international character of the mining fields. American miners stand on the left and Chinese laborers on the right. How would you compare the two groups of men? Are there any signs of the racial animosity that was one of the realities of mining life? *(Courtesy of the California History Room, California State Library, Sacramento, California)*

and expensive machinery. Eventually, mining became a corporate industrial concern, with miners as wage earners. As early as 1852, the changing nature of mining in California had transformed most of the shaggy miners into wage workers.

Probably 5 percent of early gold rush emigrants to California were women and children. Many of the women also anticipated getting "rich in a hurry." Because there were so few of them, the cooking, nursing, laundry, and hotel services women provided had a high value. When Luzena Wilson arrived in Sacramento, a miner offered to pay her $10 for a biscuit. That night, Luzena dreamt she saw "crowds of bearded miners striking gold from the earth with every blow of the pick, each one seeming to leave a share for me." Yet it was wearying work. As Mary Ballou thought it over, she decided, "I would not advise any Lady to come out here and suffer to toil and fatigue I have suffered for the sake of a little gold." As men's profits shrank, so, too, did those of the women who served them.

Some of the first women to arrive were prostitutes. They rejected the hard labor of cooking and washing that "respectable" women performed, hoping that the gender ratio would make their profession especially profitable. Prostitutes may have constituted as much as 20 percent of California's female population in 1850, and they probably vastly outnumbered other women in early mining camps. During boom days, they made good money and sometimes won a recognized place in society. But prostitutes always ran risks in a disorderly environment and often were the victims of murder and violence.

If mining life was usually not this violent, it tolerated behavior unacceptable farther east. Miners were not trying to re-create eastern communities but to get rich. Married men, convinced of the raucous character of mining communities, hesitated to bring wives and families west. As one declared, "I would much prefer that a wife of mine should board in a respectable bawd house in the city of New York than live anywhere in the city of San Francisco."

Although a lucky few struck it rich or at least made enough money to return home with their pride intact, miners' journals and letters reveal that many made only enough to keep going. Wrote one, "Everybody in the States who has friends here is always writing for them to come home. Now they all long to go home. . . . But it is hard for a man to leave . . . with nothing. . . . I have no pile yet, but you can bet your life I will never come home until I have something more than when I started." The problem was that easily mined silver and gold deposits soon ran out. Chinese miners proved adept at finding what early miners overlooked. Working individually or in small companies, they became a familiar sight in their distinctive clothes, big hats, and pigtails. But even their patient efforts brought decreasing rewards. The remaining rich deposits lay deeply embedded in rock or gravel. Extraction required cooperative efforts, capital, technological experience,

The Mexicans, South Americans, Chinese, and small numbers of blacks seeking their fortunes in California soon discovered that although they contributed substantially to California's growth, racial discrimination flourished. At first, American miners hoped to force foreigners of color out of the goldfields altogether. But an attempt to declare mining illegal for foreigners failed. A high tax on foreign miners proved more successful. Thousands of Mexicans left the mines, while the Chinese found other jobs in San Francisco and Sacramento. As business stagnated in mining towns, however, white miners had second thoughts about the levy and reduced it. By 1870, when the tax was declared unconstitutional,

After the Rush   This picture of the near–ghost town of Ophir City, Nevada, taken in the 1870s, points to the way the mining frontier left its mark on the landscape and suggests the unstable nature of such a frontier. *(Photo by W.H. Jackson, The Denver Public Library, Western History Collection)*

the Chinese, who had paid 85 percent of it, had "contributed" $5 million to California for the right to prospect. The hostility that led to this legislation also fed widespread violence against the Chinese and Mexicans.

Black Americans found that their skin color placed them in a situation akin to that of foreigners. Deprived of the vote, forbidden to testify in civil or criminal cases involving whites, and excluded from the bounties of the homestead law, blacks led a precarious existence. When news arrived of the discovery of gold in British Columbia in the late 1850s, hundreds of blacks as well as thousands of Chinese left the state, hoping that Canada would be more hospitable than California.

For the Native American tribes of the interior, the mining rushes were disasters. Accustomed to foraging for food, they found fish and game increasingly scarce as miners diverted streams, hunted game, or drove it from mining areas altogether. When Native Americans responded by raiding mining camps, miners erupted with fury. They stalked and killed native men and women, sometimes collecting bounties offered by some mining communities for their scalps. Indian women were raped; children were kidnapped and offered as apprentices. As one miner pointed out, "Indians seven or eight years old are worth $100 . . . [and] it is a damn poor Indian that's not worth $50." Without legal recourse because of their skin color, Native Americans could

not withstand the onslaught of white society. Subjected not only to violence but to white disease, they died by the thousands. In 1849, there had been about 150,000 Native Americans in California. In just over 20 years, their numbers had tumbled to fewer than 30,000.

Although the mining experience was never as brutal for whites as for people of color, white men and women's fantasies of dazzling riches rarely came true. The ghost towns of the West testify to the typical pattern: boom, bust, decay, death. The empty streets and rotting buildings stood as symbols of dashed hopes and disappointed dreams. Also left behind were other physical signs recalling the presence and passing of mining operations. Forests had been decimated to provide timber for the flumes to divert rivers from their channels in the hopes of exposing rich gold deposits in the dry river beds. Slurries and ditches created mounds of debris that during floods or heavy rains oozed over fields and choked rivers and streams. Consumed by visions of glittering metal, miners had been blind to the realities of eroding soil, deforested mountains, diverted waterways, and silt.

It was difficult, however, to recognize some of the negative consequences of the discovery of gold, for it had many positive effects on the West as a whole. Between 1848 and 1883, California mines supplied two-thirds of the country's gold. Gold transformed San Francisco from a sleepy town into a bustling metropolis. It fueled the agricultural and commercial development of California and Oregon, as miners provided a market for goods and services. Gold built harbors, railroads, and irrigation systems not just in California and Oregon but all over the West. Though few people made large fortunes, both the region and the nation profited from gold.

Establishing God's Kingdom

In the decades before 1860, many emigrants heading for the Far West stopped to rest and buy supplies in Salt Lake City, the heart of the Mormon state of Deseret. There they encountered a society that seemed familiar, yet foreign and shocking. Visitors admired the attractively laid-out town with its irrigation ditches, gardens, and tidy houses. But as they noted the decorous nature of everyday life, they gossiped about polygamy and searched for signs of rebellion in the faces of Mormon women. Emigrants who opposed slavery were fond of comparing the Mormon wife to the black slave. They were amazed that so few Mormon women seemed interested in escaping from the bonds of plural marriage.

Violent events brought the Mormons to the arid Great Basin area. Two years after Joseph Smith's

Nauvoo, Illinois This photograph shows the Mormon settlement in Nauvoo, Illinois. In the background, you can see the Mormon temple, a dignified and substantial building that could almost be an academy or New England church. The town's development points to the organization and leadership of the new religion. When mobs chased the Mormons out of Nauvoo in the mid-1840s and killed Joseph Smith, the Mormons moved west and built up a new community in Utah. *(Courtesy of the Church archives, The Church of Jesus Christ of Latter-Day Saints)*

murder in 1844, angry mobs chased the last of the "Saints" out of Nauvoo, Illinois. As they struggled to join their advance groups at temporary camps in Iowa, Smith's successor, Brigham Young, realized that the Saints' best hope for survival lay in situating the kingdom of God somewhere in the West, far removed from the United States.

The Mexican-American War unexpectedly furthered Mormon plans. At first, most Mormons probably agreed with Hosea Stout, who hoped that the war "might never end until the States were entirely destroyed." But Brigham Young realized that war might provide desperately needed capital. By recruiting 500 young Mormons for Kearney's Army of the West, Young acquired vital resources. The battalion's advance pay bought wagonloads of supplies for starving and sick Mormons strung out along the trail between Missouri and Iowa and helped finance the impending great migration.

Young selected the Great Basin area, technically part of Mexico, as the best site for his future kingdom. It was arid and remote, 1,000 miles from its nearest "civilized" neighbors. But Mormon leaders concluded that if irrigated, the area might prove as fertile as the fields and vineyards of ancient Israel.

In April 1847, Young led an exploratory expedition of 143 men, 3 women, and 2 children to this promised land. In late July, after reaching Salt Lake, Young exclaimed, "This is the place." Before returning to Iowa to prepare Mormons for the trip to Utah, he announced his land policy. Settlers would receive virtually free land on the basis of a family's size and its ability to cultivate it. After Young left, the expeditionary group followed his directions to construct irrigation ditches and begin planting.

The following months and years tested Young's organizational talents and his followers' cooperative abilities. By September 1847, fully 566 wagons and 1,500 of the Saints had made the arduous trek to Salt Lake City. Still more Mormons came the next year, inspired by visions of a new Zion in the West. Their trip was also a collective venture, planned and directed by Church leaders. By 1850, the Mormon settlement had attracted more than 11,000 settlers. Missionary efforts in the United States and abroad, especially in Great Britain and Scandinavia, drew thousands of converts to the Great Basin. The Church emigration society and a loan fund facilitated the journey for many who could never have otherwise undertaken the trip. By the end of the decade, more than 30,000 Saints lived in Utah, not only in Salt Lake City but also in more than 90 village colonies Young had planned. Though hardship marked these early years, the Mormons thrived. As one early settler remarked, "We have everything around us we could ask."

Non-Mormon, or "Gentile," emigrants passing through Utah found much that was recognizable. The government had familiar characteristics. Most Mormons were farmers; many of them came originally from New England and the Midwest and shared mainstream customs and attitudes. But outsiders also perceived profound differences, for the heart of Mormon society was not the individual farmer on his own homestead but the cooperative village.

Years of persecution had nourished a strong sense of group identity and acceptance of Church leadership. Organized by Church leaders, who made the essential decisions, farming became a collective enterprise. All farmers were allotted land. All had irrigation rights, for water belonged to the community. During Sunday services, the local bishop might give farming instructions to his congregation along with his sermon. As Young explained, "I have looked upon the community of Latter-Day Saints in a vision and beheld them organized as the great family of heaven, each person performing his several duties in his line of industry, working for the good of the whole more than for individual aggrandizement." In this vast communal effort, every Mormon was expected to work for success, men and women alike. "We do not believe in having any drones in the hive," one woman said tartly.

The Church was omnipresent in Utah; in fact, nothing separated Church and state. Despite familiar government forms, Church leaders occupied all important political posts. Brigham Young's Governing Quorum contained the high priests of the Church, who made both religious and political decisions.

When it became clear that Utah would become a territory, Mormon leaders drew up a constitution dividing religious and political power. But once in place, powers overlapped. As one Gentile pointed out, "This intimate connection of church and state seems to pervade everything that is done. The supreme power in both being lodged in the hands of the same individuals, it is difficult to separate their two official characters, and to determine whether in any one instance they act as spiritual or merely temporal officers."

Although the Treaty of Guadalupe Hidalgo officially incorporated Utah into the United States, it had little effect on political and religious arrangements. Brigham Young became territorial governor. Local bishops continued as spiritual leaders and civil magistrates. Mormons had come to Utah to establish a kingdom rather than a republic. Their motives dictated the unique politico-religious nature of the Utah experience.

Other aspects of the Mormon frontier were distinctive. Mormon policy toward the Native American tribes was remarkably enlightened. As one prominent Mormon explained, "It has been our habit to shoot Indians with tobacco and bread biscuits rather than with powder and lead, and we are most successful with them." After two expeditions against the Timpanago and Shoshone in 1850, Mormons concentrated on converting rather than killing Native Americans. Mormon missionaries learned Bannock, Ute, Navajo, and Hopi languages to bring the faith to these tribes. They also encouraged Native Americans to ranch and farm.

Although most Gentiles could tolerate some of the differences they encountered in Utah, few could accept polygamy and the seemingly immoral extended family structure that plural marriage entailed. Although Joseph Smith and other Church leaders had secretly practiced polygamy in the early 1840s, Brigham Young publicly revealed the doctrine only in 1852, when the Saints were safely in Utah. Smith believed that the highest or "celestial" form of marriage brought special rewards in the afterlife. Because wives and children contributed to these rewards, polygamy was a means of sanctification. From a practical standpoint, polygamy served to incorporate into Mormon society single female converts who had left their families to come to Utah.

Although most Mormons accepted the doctrine and its religious justification, some found it hard to follow. One woman called it a "great trial of feelings." Actually, relatively few families were polygamous. During the 40-year period in which Mormons practiced plural marriage, only 10 to 20 percent of Mormon families were polygamous. Few men had more than two wives. Because of the expense of maintaining several families and the personal strains involved, usually only the most successful and visible Mormon leaders practiced polygamy.

Polygamous family life was a far cry from the lascivious arrangement outsiders fantasized. Jealousy among wives could destroy the institution of plural marriage, so Mormon leaders minimized the role of romantic love and sexual attraction in courtship and marriage. Instead, they encouraged marriages founded on mutual attachment, with sex for procreation rather than pleasure.

To the shock of outsiders, Mormon women did not consider themselves slaves but highly regarded members of the community. Whether plural wives or not, they saw polygamy as the cutting edge of their society and defended it to the outside world. Polygamy was preferable to monogamy, which left the single woman without the economic and social protection of family life and forced some of them into prostitution; as Brenda Pratt explained, "Polygamy . . . tends directly to the chastity of women, and the sound health and morals . . . of their children."

Although they faced obvious difficulties, many plural wives found rewards in polygamy. Without the constant presence of husbands, they had an unusual opportunity for independence. Many treated husbands when they visited as revered friends; their children, not their spouses, provided them with day-to-day emotional satisfaction. Occasionally, plural wives lived together and shared domestic work, becoming close friends. As one such wife put it, "We three . . . loved each other more than sisters" and would "go hand in hand together down till eternity."

Although the Mormon settlement seemed alien to outsiders, it succeeded in terms of its numbers, its growing economic prosperity, and its group unity. Long-term threats loomed, however, once the region became part of the United States. Attacks on Young's

power as well as heated verbal denunciations of polygamy proliferated. Efforts began in Congress to outlaw polygamy. In the years before the Civil War, Mormons withstood these assaults on their way of life. But as Utah became more connected to the rest of the country, the tide would turn against them.

Cities in the West

Many emigrants went west not to farm or pan for gold but to live in cities such as San Francisco, Denver, and Portland. There they pursued business and professional opportunities or perhaps speculated in real estate.

Cities were integral to frontier life. Some, like St. Joseph, Missouri, which catered to the emigrant trade, preceded agricultural settlement. Others, like Portland, were destinations for overland travelers or were market and supply centers for emigrant farmers. San Francisco and Denver were "instant cities," transformed as the discovery of precious metals sent thousands of miners to and through them. Once the strike ran out, many miners returned to these cities to make a new start. In San Francisco, a Chinese community took shape as Chinese laborers abandoned mining and railroad work. In 1860, almost 3,000 Chinese lived in Chinatown; 10 years later, that number grew to 12,022.

Bustling commercial life offered residents a wide range of occupations and services. As a Portland emigrant remarked in 1852, "In many ways life here . . . was more primitive than it was in the early times in Illinois and Missouri. But in others it was far more advanced. . . . We could get the world's commodities here which could not be had then, or scarcely at all, in the interior of Illinois or Missouri."

Young, single men seeking their fortunes made up a disproportionate share of urban populations. Frontier Portland had more than three men for every woman. Predictably, urban life was often noisy and rowdy, and occasionally violent. Some women tried to reform the atmosphere by attempting to close stores on Sunday or to prohibit drinking. Others, of course, enjoyed all the attention that came with the presence of so many young men. Eventually, the gender ratio became balanced, but as late as 1880, fully 18 of the 24 largest western cities had more men than women.

San Francisco in 1853 This view of San Francisco reveals the rapid transformation of the city. Brick buildings (several stories high, with elaborate cornices), board sidewalks, kerosene street lamps, and the inevitable grid street pattern give San Francisco the appearance of an eastern city rather than a raw western community, though it was only four years after the gold rush. How far from the San Francisco harbor are these buildings? *(Courtesy of The Bancroft Library, University of California, Berkeley)*

Western cities soon lost their distinctiveness. The history of Portland suggests the common pattern of development. In 1845, it was only a clearing in the forest, with lively speculation in town lots. By the early 1850s, Portland had become a small trading center with a few rough log structures and muddy tracks for streets. As farmers poured into Oregon, the city became a regional commercial center. More permanent structures were built, giving it an "eastern" appearance.

The belief that western cities offered special opportunities initially drew many young men to Portland and other urban areas. Success was greatest, however, for those arriving with assets. By the 1860s, when the city's population had reached 2,874, Portland's Social Club symbolized the emergence of an elite. Portland's businessmen, lawyers, and editors controlled an increasing share of the community's wealth and set its social standards, showing how rapidly and far Portland had traveled from its raw frontier beginnings.

CULTURES IN CONFLICT

Looking at westward expansion through the eyes of white emigrants provides only one view of the migration experience. In such a diverse region, many other views existed.

Some of those heading to the American West came from southern China. Mostly men, they planned to work for a few years and then return home to their families. Initially, California welcomed the Chinese. One San Francisco merchant reported in 1855 that the Chinese were "received like guests" and treated "with politeness. From far and near we came and were pleased." However, such tolerance soon disappeared as more Chinese arrived on the West Coast. Chinese workers met hostility, violence, and ridicule as they labored in mining camps, on the railroads, and in other jobs. A telegram from Chinese miners in the California mountains betrayed the anxieties many must have felt: "Am afraid there will be big fight." Increasingly perceived by whites as racial threats, called "nagurs" with an appearance supposedly "but a slight removal from the African race," Chinese workers faced many forms of harassment. In 1880, California legislators expressed white hostility by passing a law that made illegal any marriage between a white person and a "negro, mulatto, or Mongolian."

Confronting the Plains Tribes

Some whites likened the Chinese to the Native Americans, another group that would see the western

experience differently from white emigrants. An entry from an Oregon Trail journal hints at what one such perspective might be. On May 7, 1864, Mary Warner, a bride of only a few months, described a frightening event. That day, a "fine-looking" Indian had visited the wagon train and tried to buy her. Mary's husband, probably uncertain how to handle the situation, played along, agreeing to trade his wife for two ponies. The Indian generously offered three. "Then," wrote Mary, "he took hold of my shawl to make me understand to get out [of the wagon]. About this time I got frightened and really was so hysterical [that] I began to cry." Everyone laughed at her, she reported, though surely the Indian found the whole incident no more amusing than she had.

This ordinary encounter on the overland trail only begins to point to the social and cultural differences separating white Americans moving west and the native peoples with whom they came in contact. Confident of their values and rights, emigrants had little regard for those who had lived in the West for centuries and no compunction in seizing their lands. Like the Whitmans, many predicted that the

A Indian Child   This dark image, made in about 1851, provides a rare glimpse of one of California's Native American children. What do the boy's clothes suggest about the impact of white society on Native American culture during the gold rush? Generally, the gold rush was a disaster for Native American tribes in California, where violence against Native Americans was all too common. *(Oakland Museum of California, Gift of Anonymous Donor)*

Four Bears,
From His Last Speech

Four Bears was a Mandan warrior chief whose many exploits were depicted on a buffalo robe that he wore. In the late 1830s, smallpox spread to tribes on the upper Missouri River. Four Bears and his entire family, along with between 1,000 and 2,000 of his tribe, died of the disease. An American trader wrote down Four Bears' last speech.

Ever since I can remember, I have loved the Whites, I have lived With them ever since I was a Boy, and to the best of my Knowledge, I have never Wronged a White Man, on the Contrary, I have always Protected them from the insults of Others, Which they cannot deny.... I have done every thing that a red Skin could do for them, and how have they repaid it! With ingratitude! I have Never Called a White Man a Dog, but to day, I do Pronounce them to be a set of Black harted Dogs, they have deceived Me ... to day I am Wounded, and by Whom, by those same White Dogs that I have always Considered, and treated as Brothers.

■ *What is the implication of Four Bears' remarks?*

■ *What does this excerpt suggest about the consequences of the white advance into the West?*

Source: Colin G. Calloway, ed., *Our Hearts Fell to the Ground* (Boston: Bedford Books, 1996), 68–69.

Native American race would die out, a just reward for tribal "degeneracy."

During the 1840s, white Americans for the first time came into extensive contact with the powerful Plains tribes, whose culture differed from that of the more familiar eastern woodland tribes. Probably a quarter million Native Americans occupied the area from the Rocky Mountains to the Missouri River and from the Platte River to New Mexico. Nearest the Missouri and Iowa frontier lived the "border" tribes—the Pawnee, Omaha, Oto, Ponca, and Kansa. These groups, unlike other Plains tribes, lived in villages and raised crops, though they supplemented their diet with buffalo meat during the summer months. On the Central Plains lived the Brulé and Oglala Sioux, Cheyenne, Shoshone, and Arapaho, aggressive tribes who followed the buffalo and often raided the border tribes. In the Southwest were the Comanche, Ute, Navajo, and some Apache bands; the Kiowa, Wichita, Apache, and southern Comanche claimed northern and western Texas as their hunting grounds. Many of the southwestern tribes had adopted aspects of Spanish culture and European domestic animals such as cattle, sheep, and horses.

Although differences existed, the Plains tribes shared important similarities. Most had adopted a nomadic way of life after the introduction of Spanish horses in the sixteenth century increased their seasonal mobility from 50 to 500 miles. Horses allowed Native American braves to hunt the buffalo with such success that tribes (with the exclusion of the border groups) came to depend on the beasts

A Native American Captive   This illustration of a young woman being carried away by a Comanche chief came from a book entitled *Thrilling Adventures Among the Indians*, published in 1850. How might such a depiction color emigrants' views of the Native Americans they encountered in the trans-Mississippi West? How might the depiction have shaped the way newcomers dealt with the rights of Native Americans? *(Courtesy of The Newberry Library, Chicago)*

Native American Land Cessions in 1840

This map of Native American tribes and groupings reveals locations in 1840, but it presents too static a picture of tribal territories. Some of the Native American groups in the West had been forced across the Mississippi by events in the Midwest. What does the map show about the pace of Native American land cessions in the nineteenth century, especially in the trans-Mississippi West?

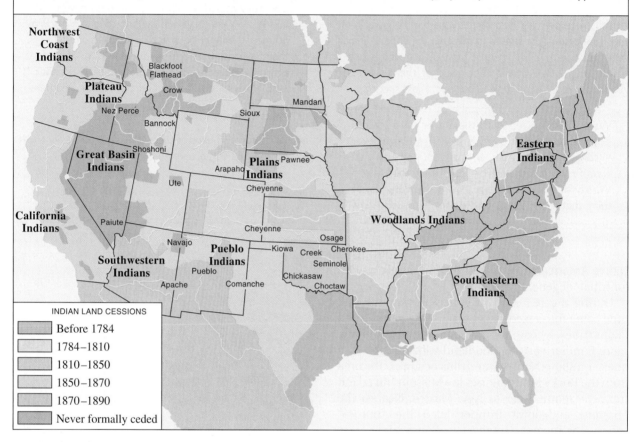

for food, clothing, fuel, teepee dwellings, and trading purposes. Because women were responsible for processing buffalo products, some men had more than one wife to tan skins for trading.

Mobility also increased tribal contact and conflict. War played a central part in the lives of the Plains tribes. No male became a fully accepted member of his tribe until he had proved himself in battle. But tribal warfare was not like the warfare of white men. Native Americans sought not to exterminate their enemies or to claim territory but rather to steal horses and to prove individual prowess. They considered it braver to touch an enemy than to kill or scalp him. Moreover, because individual tribes were loosely organized, chiefs had only limited authority. As Chief Low Horn, a Blackfoot, explained, chiefs "could not restrain their young men . . . their young men were wild, and ambitious, in their turn to be braves and chiefs. They wanted by some brave act to win the favor of their young women, and bring scalps and horses to show their prowess."

This pattern of conflict on the Great Plains discouraged political unity. But even so, armed with guns, mounted on fast ponies, and skilled in warfare and raiding, the Plains tribes posed a fearsome obstacle to white expansion. They had signed no treaties with the United States and had few friendly feelings toward whites. Their contact with white society had brought gains through trade in skins, but the trade had also introduced alcohol and destructive epidemics of smallpox and scarlet fever.

In the early 1840s, relations between Native Americans and whites were peaceable. But the intrusion of whites set in motion an environmental cycle that eventually caused conflict. Native American tribes depended on the buffalo but respected this source of life. The Teton Sioux performed rituals to ensure a continuing supply of the animals, while hunters often ritualistically apologized to the Great Unseen Buffalo for slaughtering what the tribe needed. The grasses that nourished the buffalo also sustained the Indians' own ponies and the animals that supported horse traders such as the Cheyenne.

Whites, however, put their stock to graze on the grass that both the Native Americans' ponies and the buffalo needed. And they adopted the "most exciting sport," the buffalo hunt. As the great herds began to shrink, Native American tribes began to battle one another for hunting grounds and food. The powerful Sioux swooped down into the hunting grounds of their enemies and mounted destructive raids against the Pawnee and other smaller tribes. In an 1846 petition to President Polk, the Sioux explained that "for several years past the Emigrants going over the Mountains from the United States, have been the cause that Buffalo have in great measure left our hunting grounds, thereby causing us to go into the Country of Our Enemies to hunt, exposing our lives daily for the necessary subsistence of our wives and Children and getting killed on several occasions." Despite their plight, the Sioux had "all along treated the Emigrants in the most friendly manner, giving them free passage through our hunting grounds."

The Sioux requested compensation for white damages. When the president denied their request, they tried to extract taxes from those passing over their lands. Emigrants were outraged. Frontier newspapers printed letters denouncing the Sioux, demanding adequate protection for travelers and some chastening of the "savages." However, little was done to relieve the suffering of the tribes bearing the brunt of Sioux aggression, the dismay of the Sioux at the white invasion, or the fears of the emigrants themselves.

The discovery of gold in California, which lured more than 20,000 across the Great Plains in 1849 alone, became the catalyst for federal action. The vast numbers of gold seekers and their animals wrought such devastation in the Platte valley that it rapidly became a wasteland for the Indians. The dreaded cholera that whites carried with them spread to the Indians, killing thousands.

To meet the crisis, government officials devised a two-pronged plan. The government would construct a chain of forts to protect emigrants and, simultaneously, call the tribes to a general conference. Officials expected that in return for generous presents, Native Americans would end tribal warfare and limit their movements to prescribed areas. They instructed tribes to select chiefs to speak for them at the conference.

The Fort Laramie Council, 1851

In 1851, the tribal council convened at Fort Laramie. As many as 10,000 Native Americans, hopeful of ending the destruction of their way of life and eager for the promised presents, gathered at the fort. Tribal animosities simmered, however. Skirmishes occurred on the way to the fort, and the border

A Cultural Contrast This drawing, done by an unknown Native American artist sometime in the 1840s, contrasts the traditionally clad Indians and the wild animals they hunted with the formally dressed white men and their stock animals. Has the artist depicted whites in a sympathetic manner? *(Archives de Jesuites, St. Jerome Quebec)*

tribes, fearful of the Sioux, declined to participate. The Comanche, Kiowa, and Apache also refused to come, because their enemies, the Sioux and the Crow, were to be there.

At the conference, whites told the gathered tribes that times had changed. In the past, "you had plenty of buffalo and game . . . and your Great Father well knows that war has always been your favorite amusement and pursuit. He then left the question of peace and war to yourselves. Now, since the settling of the districts West . . . by the white men, your condition has changed." There would be compensation for the destruction of their grass, timber, and buffalo and annual payments of goods and services. But in return, the

DOCUMENT

The Treaty of Fort Laramie (1851)

tribes had to give up their rights of free movement. The government drew tribal boundaries, and chiefs promised to stay within them. In most cases, some tribal lands were sold.

The Fort Laramie Treaty was the first agreement between the Plains tribes and the U.S. government. It expressed the conviction of whites that Indians must stay in clearly defined areas apart from white civilization.

But this system of isolation and its purported benefits were still in the future. During the conference, ominous signs appeared that more trouble would precede any "resolution" of Native American–white affairs. Sioux Chief Black Hawk told whites, "You have split the country and I do not like it." His powerful tribe refused to be restricted to lands north of the Platte, for south of the river lay their recently conquered lands. "These lands once belonged to the Kiowas and the Crows," one Sioux explained, "but we whipped those nations out of them and in this we did what the white men do when they want the lands of the Indians." The words suggested that Native Americans, despite agreements, would not willingly abandon their traditional way of life for confinement. In the following years, it would become evident that Americans and Sioux had conflicting interests south of the Platte. Elsewhere in the trans-Mississippi West, other tribes, like the fierce Navajo of New Mexico, also resisted white attempts to confine them.

DOCUMENT

Chief Seattle, Oration (1854)

Overwhelming the Mexican Settlers

In the Southwest, in Texas, and in California, Americans encountered a Spanish-speaking population and Hispanic culture. Expansionist senator Lewis Cass expressed Americans' scorn for both. Speaking in a congressional debate on the annexation of New Mexico, Cass stated, "We do not want the people of Mexico, either as citizens or as subjects. All we want is a portion of territory . . . with a population, which would soon recede, or identify itself with ours." Americans regarded Mexicans as lazy, ignorant, and cunning, the "dregs of society." Although Mexicans easily recognized such cultural arrogance, they lacked the numbers to fend off American aggression.

Although Anglo–Mexican interaction differed, few Anglos heeded the Treaty of Guadalupe Hidalgo's assurances that Mexicans would have citizens' rights and the "free enjoyment of their liberty and property." The greatest numbers of Spanish-speaking people lived in New Mexico, and, of all

former Mexican citizens, they probably fared the best. Most were of mixed blood, living marginally as ranch hands for rich landowners or as farmers and herdsmen in small villages dominated by a *patron*, or headman. As the century wore on, Americans produced legal titles and took over lands long occupied by peasant farmers and stock raisers. But despite economic reversals, New Mexicans survived, carrying their rural culture well into the twentieth century.

Light-skinned, upper-class landowners fared better. Even before the conquest, rich New Mexicans had protected their future by establishing contacts with American businessmen and by sending their sons east to American schools. When the United States annexed New Mexico, this substantial and powerful class contracted strategic marriage and business alliances with the Anglo men slowly trickling into the territory. Only rarely did they worry about their poorer countrymen. Class interests outweighed ethnic or cultural considerations.

A Hispanic Resident of California in the 1850s
This arresting daguerreotype of a young Hispanic woman gives few hints of the difficulties most Hispanics experienced during and after the gold rush. What clues do her clothes give as to her social and cultural background? How would you compare her clothing to that worn by the young American women depicted in Chapter 10 (see pp. 328 and 333)? *(Oakland Museum of California, Gift of Dr. Stanley B. Burns)*

In Texas, the Spanish-speaking residents, only 10 percent of the population in 1840, shrank to a mere 6 percent by 1860. Although the upper class also intermarried with Americans, they lost most of their power as Germans, Irish, French, and Americans poured into the state. Poor, dark-skinned Hispanics clustered in low-paying and largely unskilled jobs.

In California, the discovery of gold radically changed the situation for the Californios. In 1848, there were 7,000 Californios and about twice as many Anglos. By 1860, the Anglo population had ballooned to 360,000. Hispanic Americans were hard pressed to cope with the rapid influx of outsiders. At first, Californios and several thousand Mexicans from Sonora joined Anglos and others in the gold fields. But competition there fed antagonism and finally open conflict. Posters warned foreigners out of the gold fields. In Anglo eyes, one Hispanic was much like another, even if one claimed to be a Californio with political rights and another a Sonoran. Taxes and terrorism ultimately succeeded in forcing most Spanish speakers out of the mines and established the racial contours of the new California.

Other changes were even more disastrous. In 1851, Congress passed the Gwin Land Law, supposedly validating Spanish and Mexican land titles. But it violated the Treaty of Guadalupe Hidalgo because it forced California landowners to defend what was already theirs and encouraged squatters to settle on land in the hopes that the Californios' titles would prove false. It took an average of 17 years to establish clear title to land. Landowners found themselves paying American lawyers large fees, often in land, and borrowing at high interest rates to cover court proceedings. A victory at court often turned into a defeat when legal expenses forced owners to sell their lands to pay debts.

Working-class Hispanic Americans, laboring for Anglo farmers or for mining and later railroad companies, earned less money and did more unpleasant jobs than Anglo workers. By 1870, the average Hispanic American worker's property was worth only about a third of its value of 20 years earlier.

Various forms of resistance to American expansion emerged. Some, like Tiburcio Vásquez in southern California, became *bandidos*. As he explained, the American presence provoked a "spirit of hatred and revenge ... I believed we were unjustly and wrongfully deprived of the social rights that belonged to us." Others, like the members of Las Gorras Blancas in New Mexico, ripped up railroad ties and cut the barbed-wire fences of Anglo ranchers and farmers, while the religiously oriented Penitentes tried to work through the ballot box. Ordinary men, women, and children resisted efforts to convert them to Protestantism and held onto familiar customs and beliefs while learning some of the skills they hoped would enable them to flourish in a changing culture.

TIMELINE

1803–1806	Lewis and Clark expedition
1818	Treaty on joint U.S.–British occupation of Oregon
1819	Spain cedes Spanish territory in United States and sets transcontinental boundary of Louisiana Purchase, excluding Texas
1821	Mexican independence Opening of Santa Fe Trail Stephen Austin leads American settlement of Texas
1821–1840	Native American removals
1830	Mexico abolishes slavery in Texas
1836	Battles of the Alamo and San Jacinto Texas declares independence
1840s	Emigrant crossings of overland trails
1844	James Polk elected president
1845	"Manifest Destiny" coined United States annexes Texas and sends troops to the Rio Grande Americans attempt to buy Upper California and New Mexico
1846	Mexico declares defensive war United States declares war and takes Santa Fe Resolution of Oregon question
1847	Attacks on Veracruz and Mexico City Mormon migration to Utah begins
1848	Treaty of Guadalupe Hidalgo
1849	California gold rush begins
1850	California admitted to the Union
1851	Fort Laramie Treaty
1853	Gadsden Purchase
1862	Homestead Act

Conclusion

Fruits of Manifest Destiny

Like Narcissa Whitman and her husband, many nineteenth-century Americans decided that they had a unique right to settle the West and make it flower. They were not much concerned with the fate of those who had lived for centuries on the land. The process of acquiring the western half of the continent was so swift that there seemed little point in worrying about the losers. The tale of western expansion loomed large in the imagination of the American people for many years. Some western settlers became folk heroes. The Whitmans were remembered by the founding of Whitman College in Walla Walla, Washington. All white Americans could be thankful for the special opportunities and the new chance that the West seemed to hold out. Certainly, the nation did gain vast natural wealth in the trans-Mississippi West. But only a small fraction of the hopeful emigrants heading for the frontier realized their dreams of success. And the move west and east had a dark side, as the acquisition of new territories fueled the controversy over the future of slavery.

Questions for Review and Reflection

1. Explain how and why the westward movement entangled the United States in the affairs of foreign powers.

2. Compare and contrast the acquisition of Texas and the Southwest with the annexation of Oregon.

3. What racial and ethnic tensions emerged in the West because of American expansionism?

4. What factors caused problems and tensions between Native Americans and whites?

5. What important American beliefs and values were involved in the westward movement? How did they shape the westward experience?

Recommended Reading

Recommended Readings are posted on the Web site for this textbook. Visit www.ablongman.com/nash

Fiction and Film

Mark Twain's *Roughing It* (1872) is often humorous, but through the humor you can see Twain's insightful comments about westerners' values and standards. James C. Work's *Gunfight!* (1996) contains a selection of gunfight stories originally printed in popular magazines. For an example of an early "dime novel," see Ann Sophia Winterbotham Stephens's *Malaeska: Indian Wife of the White Hunter* (1861, but use any edition). *The West* (1996) is a nine-part series by Ken Burns that was first shown on television. The films provide a sympathetic and critical account of the settlement and its impact on Native Americans. *The Donner Party* (1992) is a PBS video of the disastrous experience of a party of emigrants caught in the Sierra Nevada during the winter of 1846–1847. One critic notes a dark tone to the film, which is characteristic of the new Western history.

Discovering U.S. History Online

Fort Scott National Historic Site
www.nps.gov/fosc/mandest.htm
This illustrated site recounts the role of dragoon soldiers from Fort Scott as armed escorts for settlers traveling over the Santa Fe and Oregon Trails.

The Mexican-American War
www.sunsite.unam.mx/revistas/1847/
This well-illustrated site offers several sections (each available in English or Spanish) that explain the causes, courses, and outcomes of the Mexican-American War.

Alamo History
www.drtl.org/History/
This site presents an illustrated timeline of the Alamo mission, including its role in the famous battle.

The Treaty of Guadalupe Hidalgo
www.loc.gov/exhibits/ghtreaty
This site gives background on the treaty and has an exhibit of digitized images of each page of the treaty, including the seals. A map of the area of negotiation is also presented.

The Oregon Trail
www.ukans.edu/carrie/kancoll/index.html
www.isu.edu/~trinmich/Oregontrail.html
The Kansas Collection site holds several good primary sources with images concerning the Oregon Trail and America's early movement westward. The second site is a companion to the PBS film *The Oregon Trail* in which the authors present audio clips from historians, illustrated essays, maps, and images about this famous trail.

The Donner Party
www.members.aol.com/danmrosen/donner/index.htm
This site includes logs recreated from primary sources from the infamous party that resorted to extreme measures to survive. It also has images of the region.

James Knox Polk
www.ipl.org/ref/POTUS/jkpolk.html
This site contains basic factual data about Polk, including his presidency, speeches, cabinet members, and election information.

American Mountain Men
www.xmission.com/~drudy/amm.html
Private letters can speak volumes about the concerns and environment of the writers and recipients. Letters from early settlers west of the Mississippi River are offered on this site, which is an online research center devoted to the trappers, explorers, and traders known as the Mountain Men.

California in the Gold Rush Decade
www.huntington.org/Education/GoldRush
www.museumca.org/goldrush
The first site is a presentation of the "Huntington Library's remarkable collection of Gold Rush manuscripts, drawings, and rare printed materials." The second is a well-illustrated interactive site on the Gold Rush exhibit formerly on display at the Oakland Museum of California.

The National Museum of the American Indian, Smithsonian Institution and The George Gustav Heye Center
www.conexus.si.edu/main.htm
A cooperative effort of these two institutions, this site hosts several virtual exhibits about Native American culture and history.

Native American Women
www.gowest.coalliance.org/exhib/gallery4/leadin.htm
This site is an annotated photographic gallery of Native American women.

CHAPTER 14

The Union in Peril

George Caleb Bingham's *Stump Speaking* (1856) captures the democratic energy of politics at midcentury. Note the Lincoln-like figure sitting to the right. *(Private Collection/Bridgeman Art Library)*

American Stories

Four Men Respond to the Union in Peril

The autumn of 1860 was a time of ominous rumors and expectations. The election was held on November 6 in an atmosphere of crisis. In Springfield, Illinois, Abraham Lincoln, taking coffee and sandwiches prepared by the "ladies of Springfield," waited as the telegraph brought in the returns. By 1 A.M., victory was certain. He reported later, "I went home, but not to get much sleep, for I then felt, as I never had before, the responsibility that was upon me." Indeed, he and the American people faced the most serious crisis since the founding of the Republic.

Lincoln won a four-party election with only 39 percent of the popular vote. He appealed almost exclusively to northern voters in a blatantly sectional campaign, defeating his three opponents by carrying every free state except New Jersey. Only Illinois senator Stephen Douglas campaigned actively in every section of the country. For his efforts, he received the second-highest number of votes. Douglas's appeal, especially in the closing days of the campaign, was "on behalf of the Union," which he feared—correctly—was in imminent danger of splitting apart.

That fall, other Americans sensed the crisis and faced their own fears and responsibilities. A month before the election, South Carolina plantation owner Robert Allston wrote his oldest son, Benjamin, that "disastrous consequences" would follow from a Lincoln victory. Although his letter mentioned the possibility of secession, he dealt mostly with plantation concerns: a new horse, the mood of the slaves, ordering supplies from the city, instructions for making trousers on a sewing machine. After Lincoln's election, Allston corresponded with a southern colleague about the need for an "effective military organization" to resist "Northern and Federal aggression." In his shift from sewing machines to military ones, Robert Allston prepared for what he called the "impending crisis."

Frederick Douglass greeted the election of 1860 with characteristic optimism. This was an opportunity to "educate . . . the people in their moral and political duties," he said, adding, "slaveholders know that the day of their power is over when a Republican President is elected." But no sooner had Lincoln's victory been determined than Douglass's hopes turned sour. He noted that Republican leaders, who were trying to keep border states from seceding, sounded more antiabolitionist than antislavery. They vowed not to touch slavery in areas where it already existed (including the District of Columbia), to enforce the hated Fugitive Slave Act, and to put down slave rebellions. In fact, Douglass bitterly contested, slavery would "be as safe, and safer" with Lincoln than with a Democrat.

Iowa farmer Michael Luark was not so sure. Born in Virginia, he was a typically mobile nineteenth-century American. Growing up in Indiana, he followed the mining booms of the 1850s to Colorado and California, then returned to the Midwest to farm. Luark sought a good living and resented the furor over slavery. He could not, however, avoid the issue. Writing in his diary on the last day of 1860, Luark looked ahead to 1861 with a deep sense of fear. "Startling" political changes would occur, he predicted, perhaps even the "Dissolution of the Union and Civil War with all its train of horrors." He blamed abolitionist agitators, perhaps reflecting his Virginia origins. On New Year's Day, he expressed his fears that Lincoln would let the "most ultra sectional and Abolition" men disturb the "vexed Slavery question" even further, as Frederick Douglass wanted. But if this happened, Luark warned, "then farewell to our beloved Union of States." Within four months of this diary entry, the guns of the Confederate States of America fired on a federal fort in South Carolina. The Civil War had begun.

The firing on Fort Sumter made real Luark's fears, Douglass's hopes, and Lincoln's and Allston's preparations for responsibility. America's shaky democratic political system faced its worst crisis. The explanation of the peril and dissolution of the Union forms the theme of this chapter.

Such calamitous events as Civil War had numerous causes, large and small. The reactions of Allston, Douglass, and Luark to Lincoln's election suggest some of them: moral duties, sectional politics, growing apprehensions over emotional agitators, and a concern for freedom and independence on the part of blacks, white southerners, and western farmers. But as Douglass understood, by 1860, it was clear that "slavery is the real issue, the single bone of contention between all parties and sections. It is the one disturbing force, and explains the confused and irregular motion of our political machine."

This chapter analyzes how the momentous issue of slavery disrupted the political system and eventually the Union itself. We will look at how four major developments between 1848 and 1861 contributed to the Civil War: first, a sectional dispute over the extension of slavery into the western territories; second, the breakdown of the political party system; third, growing cultural differences in the views and lifestyles of southerners and northerners; and fourth, intensifying emotional and ideological polarization between the two regions over losing their way of life and sacred republican rights at the hands of the other. A preview of civil war, bringing all four causes together, occurred in 1855–1856 in Kansas. Eventually, emotional events, mistrust, and irreconcilable differences made conflict inevitable. Lincoln's election was the spark that touched off the conflagration of civil war, with all its "train of horrors."

SLAVERY IN THE TERRITORIES

As Narcissa Whitman sadly discovered with the Cayuse Indians in eastern Washington (see Chapter 13), white migration westward was discouraging and downright dangerous. It was especially damaging to the freedom, safety, and cultural integrity of Native Americans and Mexicans, whose lands stood in the way. Moreover, the westward movement imperiled freedom and eventually the Union by causing a collision between Yankees and slaveholders.

The North and the South had mostly contained their differences over slavery for 60 years after the Constitutional Convention. Compromise in 1787 had resolved questions of the slave trade and how to count slaves for congressional representation. Although slavery threatened the uneasy sectional harmony in 1820 ("like a fire bell in the night," Jefferson had said), the Missouri Compromise had established a workable balance of free and slave states and had defined a geographic line (36°30') to determine future decisions. In 1833, compromise had defused South Carolina's attempt at nullification, and the gag rule in 1836 had kept abolitionist petitions off the floor of Congress.

Each apparent resolution, however, raised the level of emotional conflict between North and South and postponed ultimate settlement of the slavery question. One reason why these compromises temporarily worked was the two-party system, with Whigs and Democrats in both North and South. Party loyalties served as an "antidote," as Van Buren put it, to sectional allegiance. The parties differed over cultural and economic issues, but slavery was largely kept out of political campaigns and congressional debates. This changed in the late 1840s.

Free Soil or Constitutional Protection?

When war with Mexico broke out in 1846, Pennsylvania congressman David Wilmot added an amendment to an appropriations bill declaring that "neither slavery nor involuntary servitude shall ever exist" in any territories acquired from Mexico. Legislators debated the Wilmot Proviso not as Whigs and Democrats but as northerners and southerners.

A Boston newspaper prophetically observed that Wilmot's resolution "brought to a head the great question which is about to divide the American people." When the war ended, several solutions were presented to deal with this question of slavery in the territories. First was the "free soil" idea of preventing any extensions of slavery. Two precedents suggested that Congress could do this. One was the Northwest Ordinance, which had barred slaves from the Upper Midwest; the other was the Missouri Compromise.

Free soil had mixed motives. For some, slavery was a moral evil to be destroyed. But for many northern white farmers looking westward, the threat of economic competition with an expanding system of large-scale slave labor was even more serious. Nor did they wish to compete for land with free blacks. As Wilmot put it, his proviso was intended to preserve the area for the "sons of toil, of my own race and own color." Other northerners supported the proviso as a means of restraining the growing political power and "insufferable arrogance" of the "spirit and demands of the Slave Power."

Opposed to the free-soil position were the arguments of Senator John C. Calhoun of South Carolina, expressed in several resolutions introduced in the Senate in 1847. Congress not only lacked the constitutional right to exclude slavery from the territories, he argued, but actually had a duty to protect it. Therefore, the Wilmot Proviso was unconstitutional.

Popular Sovereignty and the Election of 1848

With such divisive potential, it was natural that many Americans sought a compromise solution to keep slavery out of politics. Polk's secretary of state, James Buchanan of Pennsylvania, proposed extending the Missouri Compromise line to the Pacific Ocean, thereby avoiding thorny questions about the morality of slavery and the constitutionality of congressional authority. So would "popular sovereignty," the proposal of Michigan senator Lewis Cass to leave decisions about permitting slavery to territorial legislatures. The idea appealed to the American democratic belief in local self-government but left many details unanswered. At what point in the progress toward statehood could a territorial legislature decide about slavery? Cass preferred to leave such questions ambiguous.

Democrats, liking popular sovereignty because it could mean all things to all people, nominated Cass for president in 1848. Cass denounced abolitionists and the Wilmot Proviso but otherwise avoided the issue of slavery. The Democrats, however, printed two campaign biographies of Cass, one for the South and one for the North.

The Whigs found an even better way to hold the party together by evading the slavery issue. Rejecting Henry Clay, they nominated the Mexican-American War hero General Zachary Taylor, a Louisiana slaveholder. Taylor compared himself with Washington as a "no party" man above politics. Standing for no party was about all he stood for. Southern Whigs supported Taylor because they thought he might understand the burdens of slaveholding, and northern Whigs were pleased that he took no stand on the Wilmot Proviso.

The evasions of the two major parties disappointed Calhoun, who tried to create a new, unified southern party. His "Address to the People of the Southern States" threatened secession and called for a united stand against further attempts to interfere with the southern right to extend slavery. Although only 48 of 121 southern representatives signed the address, Calhoun's argument raised the specter of secession and disunion.

Warnings also came from the North. A New York Democratic faction bolted to support Van Buren for president. At first, the split had more to do with

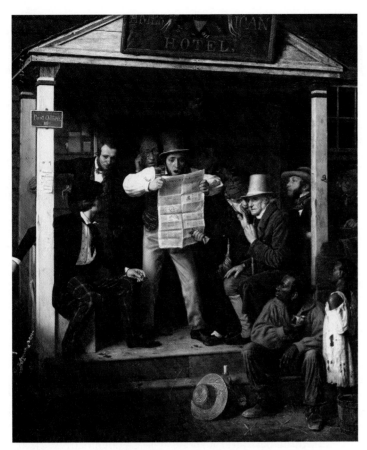

Getting the Latest News   This 1848 painting by Richard Caton Woodville, titled *War News from Mexico*, captures the mood of the period from the Mexican-American War through the Civil War; in towns across the country, outside countless "American Hotels," the American people listened eagerly to the latest news in an era of steadily worsening political, socioeconomic, and constitutional crises. Separate from the men on the porch, but clearly a part of the picture, are a black father and daughter in rags; they await the war news with special interest. What would explain their interest in the outcome of the Mexican war? *(Richard Caton Woodville, War News from Mexico. The Manoogian Collection, on loan to the National Gallery of Art, Washington, Image © 2005 Board of Trustees, National Gallery of Art, Washington, 1848, oil on canvas, .686 x .627 (27 x 24³/₄)*

So were the Missouri Compromise and other federal acts that prevented slaveholders from taking their slave property into U.S. territories.

Economic, political, and moral considerations stood behind Calhoun's position. Many southerners hungered for new cotton lands in the West and Southwest, even in Central America and the Caribbean. Southerners feared that northerners wanted to trample on their right to protect their institutions against abolitionism. Southern leaders saw the Wilmot Proviso as a moral issue touching basic republican principles. One congressman called it "treason to the Constitution," and Senator Robert Toombs of Georgia warned that if Congress passed the proviso, he would favor disunion rather than "degradation."

RECOVERING THE PAST

Senate Speeches

The history of ordinary Americans is recovered in letters, diaries, folktales, and other nontraditional sources. But in times of political conflict, as in the years before the Civil War, historians turn to more conventional sources such as congressional speeches. Recorded in the *Congressional Globe,* these speeches are a revealing means of recovering the substance, tone, and drama of political debate.

The mid-nineteenth century was an era of giants in the U.S. Senate: Daniel Webster, Henry Clay, Thomas Hart Benton, John C. Calhoun, William Seward, and Stephen Douglas. When Congress debated a major issue, such as the tariff, nullification, or the extension of slavery, large crowds packed the Senate galleries. The speeches were quickly printed and widely distributed. These spectacular oratorical encounters provided mass entertainment and political instruction. Such was the case with the Senate speeches over the Compromise of 1850. The three principal figures early in the debates were Clay (Kentucky), Calhoun (South Carolina), and Webster (Massachusetts), each of whom delivered memorable speeches to crown brilliant careers.

Born within five years of each other as the American Revolution was ending (1777–1782), each man began his political career in the House of Representatives in the War of 1812 era. Each served a term as secretary of state; in addition, Clay was speaker of the House and Calhoun secretary of war and vice president. Each served for more than a decade in the Senate (Clay, 13 years; Calhoun, 15 years; Webster, 19 years). Clay and Webster were leaders of the Whig party; Calhoun was a leader of the Democrats. During their 40 years of public service, they represented strong nationalistic positions as well as their various states and sections. All three were failing candidates for president between 1824 and 1844. All three spent most of their careers in the political shadow of Andrew Jackson, and all three clashed with him.

Forty years of political and ideological conflict with each other not only sharpened their oratorical skills but also led to mutual respect. Webster said of Calhoun that he was "the ablest man in the Senate. He could have demolished Newton, Calvin, or even John Locke as a logician." Calhoun said of Clay, "He is a bad man, but by god, I love him." And "Old Man Eloquent" himself, John Quincy Adams, said of Webster that he was "the most consummate orator of modern times."

DOCUMENT

Daniel Webster, Speech to the Senate (March 7, 1850)

It was therefore a momentous event when they each prepared speeches and met for one last encounter early in 1850. Clay was over 70 years old and in failing health, but he sought to keep the Union together by defending his compromise proposals in a four-hour speech spread over two days in February. The Senate galleries were so packed that listeners were pushed into hallways and even into the rotunda of the Capitol. Copies of his speech were in such demand that over 100,000 were printed.

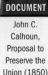

DOCUMENT

John C. Calhoun, Proposal to Preserve the Union (1850)

A month later, on March 7, Webster rose to join Clay in defending the compromise, three days after a seriously ill Calhoun had "tottered into the Senate" on the arm of a friend to hear James Mason of Virginia read his rejection of the compromise. Within a month, Calhoun was dead. Clay and Webster followed him to the grave two years later, and Senate leadership passed on to Seward, Douglas, and others.

REFLECTING ON THE PAST As you read these brief excerpts from each speech, try to imagine yourself sitting in the gallery overlooking the Senate floor absorbing the drama. What oratorical devices does each speaker use? How do they differ? To what extent does each man reflect his region, especially on the fugitive slave issue? To what extent do they appeal to an indivisible Union? On whom do you put the burden of resolving the conflicts? Which passages convey the most emotional power? Which speaker is most persuasive to you? Why?

Henry Clay

February 5–6, 1850

I have seen many periods of great anxiety, of peril, and of danger in this country, and I have never before risen to address any assemblage so oppressed, so appalled, and so anxious; and sir, I hope it will not be out of place to do here, what again and again I have done in my private chamber, to implore of Him who holds the destinies of nations and individuals in His hands, to bestow upon our country His blessing, to calm the violence and rage of party, to still passion, to allow reason once more to resume its empire. . . .

Mr. President, it is passion, passion-party, party, and intemperance—that is all I dread in the adjustment of the great questions which unhappily at this time divide our distracted country. Sir, at this moment we have in the legislative bodies of this Capitol and in the States, twenty old furnaces in full blast, emitting heat, and passion, and intemperance, and diffusing them throughout the whole extent of this broad land. Two months ago all was calm in comparison to the present moment. All now is uproar, confusion, and menace to the existence of the Union, and to the happiness and safety of this people. . . .

Sir, when I came to consider this subject, there were two or three general purposes which it seemed to me to be most desirable, if possible, to accomplish. The one was, to settle all the controverted questions arising out of the subject of slavery. . . . I therefore turned my attention to every subject connected with this institution of slavery, and out of which controverted questions had sprung, to see if it were possible or practicable to accommodate and adjust the whole of them. . . .

We are told now, and it is rung throughout this entire country, that the Union is threatened with subversion and destruction. Well, the first question which naturally rises is, supposing the Union to be dissolved,—having all the causes of grievance which are complained of,—How far will a dissolution furnish a remedy for those grievances? If the Union is to be dissolved for any existing causes, it will be dissolved because slavery is interdicted or not allowed to be introduced into the ceded territories; because slavery is threatened to be abolished in the District of Columbia, and because fugitive slaves are not returned, as in my opinion they ought to be, and restored to their masters. These, I believe, will be the causes; if there be any causes, which can lead to the direful event to which I have referred. . . .

Mr. President, I am directly opposed to any purpose of secession, of separation. I am for staying within the Union, and defying any portion of this Union to expel or drive me out of the Union.

John C. Calhoun

March 4, 1850

Having now, Senators, explained what it is that endangers the Union, and traced it to its cause, and explained its nature and character, the question again recurs—How can the Union be saved? To this I answer, there is but one way by which it can be—and that is—by adopting such measures as will satisfy the States belonging to the Southern section, that they can remain in the Union consistently with their honor and their safety. . . .

But will the North agree to this? It is for her to answer the question. But, I will say, she cannot refuse, if she has half the love of the Union which she professes to have, or without justly exposing herself to the charge that her love of power and aggrandizement is far greater than her love of the Union. At all events, the responsibility of saving the Union rests on the North, and not on the South. . . .

Daniel Webster

March 7, 1850

Mr. President: I wish to speak to-day, not as a Massachusetts man, nor as a Northern man, but as an American, and a member of the Senate of the United States. . . .

I speak to-day for the preservation of the Union. "Hear me for my cause." I speak to-day, out of a solicitous and anxious heart, for the restoration to the country of that quiet and that harmony which make the blessing of this Union so rich, and so dear to us all. . . . I shall bestow a little attention, Sir, upon these various grievances existing on the one side and on the other. I begin with complaints of the South . . . and especially to one which has in my opinion just foundation; and that is, that there has been found at the North, among individuals and among legislators, a disinclination to perform fully their constitutional duties in regard to the return of persons bound to service who have escaped into the free States. In that respect, the South, in my judgment, is right, and the North is wrong. Every member of every Northern legislature is bound by oath, like every other officer in the country, to support the Constitution of the United States; and the article of the Constitution which says to these States they shall deliver up fugitives from service is as binding in honor and conscience as any other article. . . .

Where is the line to be drawn? What States are to secede? What is to remain American? What am I to be? An American no longer? Am I to become a sectional man, a local man, a separatist, with no country in common with the gentlemen who sit around me here, or who fill the other house of Congress? Heaven forbid! Where is the flag of the republic to remain? Where is the eagle still to tower? or is he to cower, and shrink, and fall to the ground?

AMERICAN VOICES

Henry David Thoreau, as we saw in Chapter 12, went to jail to protest both slavery and the Mexican War. His essay on "Civil Disobedience" was—and is—a powerful argument for how one person of principle can stand up against tyranny and injustice.

When a sixth of the population of a nation which has undertaken to be the refuge of liberty are slaves, and a whole country is unjustly overrun and conquered by a foreign army, and subjected to military law, I think that it is not too soon for honest men to rebel and revolutionize. What makes this duty the more urgent is the fact that the country so overrun is not our own, but ours is the invading army.

. . . There are thousands who are *in opinion* opposed to slavery and to the war, and who yet in effect do nothing to put an end to them; who, esteeming themselves children of Washington and Franklin, sit down with their hands in their pockets, and say that they know not what to do, and do nothing. . . . Unjust laws exist: shall we be content to obey them, or shall we endeavor to amend them, and obey them until we have succeeded, or shall we transgress them at once?

- *What is the most powerful point in this passage for you?*

- *Can you apply Thoreau's argument to contemporary events in American life?*

---

state politics than moral principles, but it soon involved the question of slavery in the territories. Disaffected "conscience" Whigs from Massachusetts also explored a third-party alternative. These groups met in Buffalo, New York, to form the Free-Soil party and nominated Van Buren. The platform of the new party, an uneasy mixture of ardent abolitionists and opponents of free blacks moving into western lands, pledged to fight for "free soil, free speech, free labor and free men."

Taylor won easily, largely because defections from Cass to the Free-Soilers cost the Democrats New York and Pennsylvania. Although weakened, the two-party system survived. Purely sectional parties had failed. The Free-Soilers took only about 10 percent of the popular vote.

The Compromise of 1850

Taylor won the election by avoiding slavery questions. But as president, he had to deal with them. When he was inaugurated in 1849, four issues faced the nation. First, the rush of some 80,000 gold miners to California qualified it for statehood. But California's entry as a free state would upset the balance between slave and free states in the Senate that had prevailed since 1820. The unresolved status of the Mexican cession in the Southwest posed a second problem. The longer the area remained unorganized, the louder local inhabitants called for an application of either the Wilmot Proviso or the Calhoun doctrine. The Texas–New Mexico boundary was also disputed, with Texas claiming

everything east of Santa Fe. Northerners feared that Texas might split into five or six slave states. A third problem was the existence of slavery and one of the largest slave markets in North America in the nation's capital. Fourth, southerners resented the lax federal enforcement of the Fugitive Slave Act of 1793. They called for a stronger act that would end protection for runaways fleeing to Canada.

Taylor was a newcomer to politics (he had never voted in a presidential election before 1848), and he tackled these problems somewhat evasively. Sidestepping the issue of slavery in the territories, he invited California and New Mexico to seek statehood immediately, presumably as free states. But soon he alienated both southern supporters such as Calhoun and mainstream Whig leaders such as Clay and Webster.

Early in 1850, the old compromiser Henry Clay sought to regain control of the Whig party by proposing solutions to the divisive issues before the nation. With Webster's support, Clay introduced a series of resolutions in an omnibus package intended to settle these issues once and for all. The stormy debates, great speeches, and political maneuvering that followed made up a crucial and dramatic moment in American history. Yet after 70 speeches on behalf of the compromise, the Senate defeated Clay's Omnibus Bill. Tired and disheartened, the 73-year-old Clay left Washington and died two years later. Into the gap stepped Senator Stephen Douglas of Illinois, who saw that Clay's resolutions had a better chance of passing if voted on

DOCUMENT

Henry Clay, Speech to the Senate (Jan. 29, 1850)

Henry Clay Addresses the Senate Henry Clay argues for the compromise package of 1850 in this painting by R. Whitechurch, titled *The United States Senate, 1850.* Clay warned that failure to adopt his bill would lead to "furious" and "bloody" civil war. Was he right? *(Library of Congress, LC-USZ62-689)*

The Compromise of 1850

"I have seen many periods of great anxiety, of peril, and of danger in this country," Henry Clay told Congress in February 1850, "and I have never before risen to address any assemblage so oppressed, so appalled, and so anxious." What followed were the debates that led eventually to the passage of the Compromise of 1850. Can you find three of the four major parts of the bill on the map? What was the fourth?

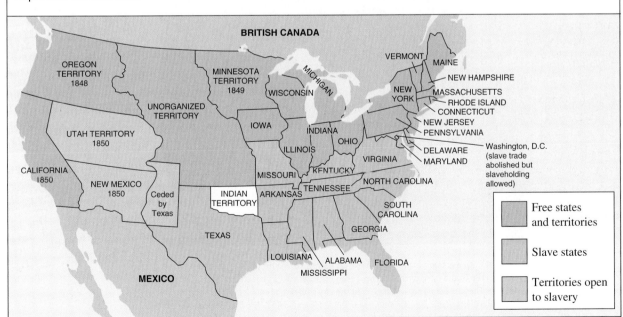

individually. Under Douglas's leadership, and with the support of President Millard Fillmore, who succeeded to the presidency upon Taylor's sudden death, a series of bills was finally passed.

The Compromise of 1850 put Clay's resolutions, slightly altered, into law. First, California entered the Union as a free state, ending the balance of free and slave states. Second, territorial governments were organized in New Mexico and Utah, letting local people decide whether to permit slavery. The Texas–New Mexico border was settled, denying Texas the disputed area. In return, the federal government gave Texas $10 million to pay debts owed to Mexico. Third, the slave trade, but not slavery, was abolished in the District of Columbia.

DOCUMENT

The Fugitive Slave Act (1850)

The fourth and most controversial part of the compromise was the Fugitive Slave Act, containing many provisions that offended northerners. One denied alleged fugitives a jury trial, leaving special cases for decision by commissioners (who were paid $5 for setting a fugitive free but $10 for returning a fugitive). An especially repugnant provision compelled northern citizens to help catch runaways.

Consequences of Compromise

The Compromise of 1850 was the last attempt to keep slavery out of politics. Voting on the different bills followed sectional lines on some issues and party lines on others. Douglas felt pleased with his "final settlement" of the slavery question.

But the compromise only delayed more serious sectional conflict, and it added two new ingredients to American politics. First, political realignment along sectional lines tightened. Second, although repudiated by most ordinary citizens, the ideas of secessionism, disunion, and a "higher law" than the Constitution entered political discussions. People wondered whether the question of slavery in the territories could be compromised away next time.

Others were immediately upset. The new fugitive slave law angered many northerners because it brought the evils of slavery right into their midst. Owners of runaway slaves hired agents (labeled "kidnappers" in the North) to hunt down fugitives. In a few dramatic episodes, notably in Boston, literary and religious intellectuals led mass protests to resist slave hunters. When Senator Webster supported the law, New England abolitionists denounced him as "indescribably base and wicked." Ralph Waldo Emerson said he would not obey the "filthy law."

Frederick Douglass would not obey it either. As a runaway slave, he faced arrest and return to the South until friends overcame his objections and purchased his freedom. Douglass still risked harm by his strong defiance of the Fugitive Slave Act.

The Dangers of Escape As a group of runaways makes its way north in this painting by Theodor Kaufmann entitled *On to Liberty* (1867), the peril of the journey, even if successful, is reflected in this broadside published by Boston abolitionist Theodore Parker, which alerted the city's black community in 1851 to the dangers posed by the Fugitive Slave Act. *(Left: Theodor Kaufmann, On to Liberty, 1867. The Metropolitan Museum of Art, Gift of Erving and Joyce Wolfe, 1982. (1982.443.3) Photograph © 1982 The Metropolitan Museum of Art; right: Harold Washington Library Center, Special Collections & Preservation Division, Chicago Public Library)*

Arguing the "rightfulness of forcible resistance," he urged free blacks to arm themselves. "The only way to make the Fugitive Slave Law a dead letter," he said in Pittsburgh in 1853, "is to make a half dozen or more dead kidnappers." Douglass raised money for black fugitives, hid runaways in his home, helped hundreds escape to Canada, and supported black organizations such as the League of Freedom in Boston.

Other northerners, white and black, stepped up work for the Underground Railroad and helped runaway slaves evade capture. Several states passed

IMAGE
Hypocrisy of the Fugitive Slave Act, 1851

"personal liberty laws" that prohibited using state officials and institutions in the recovery of fugitive slaves. But most northerners complied. Of some 200 blacks arrested in the first six years of the law, only 15 were rescued, and only 3 of these by force. Failed rescues, in fact, had more emotional impact than successful ones. In two cases in the early 1850s (Thomas Sims in 1851 and Anthony Burns in 1854), angry mobs of abolitionists in Boston failed to prevent the forcible return of blacks to the South. These celebrated cases aroused more antislavery emotions among northerners than the abolitionists had been able to do with all their tracts and speeches. Amos Lawrence, a textile tycoon in Massachusetts, wrote of the trial of Anthony Burns that sent him back to the South: "We went to bed one night old fashioned, conservative Compromise Union Whigs and waked up stark mad abolitionists."

Longtime abolitionists escalated their rhetoric, fueling emotions over slavery in the aftermath of 1850. In an Independence Day speech in 1852, Frederick Douglass wondered, "What, to the American slave, is your 4th of July?" (See "How Others See Us," p. 385) It was, he said, the day that revealed to the slave that American claims of national greatness were vain and empty; the "shouts of liberty and equality" were "fraud, deception, impiety, and hypocrisy." Douglass's speeches, like those of another ex-slave, Sojourner Truth, became increasingly strident.

DOCUMENT
Frederick Douglass, Independence Day Speech (1852)

At a women's rights convention in 1851 in Akron, Ohio, Truth made one of the decade's boldest statements for minority rights. Clergymen attending the convention heckled female speakers. Up stood Sojourner Truth to speak in words still debated by historians. She pointed to her many years of childbearing and hard, backbreaking work as a slave, crying out a refrain, "And ar'n't I a woman?" Referring to Jesus, she said he came "from God and a woman: Man

had nothing to do with Him." Referring to Eve, she concluded, "If the first woman God ever made was strong enough to turn the world upside down all alone, these women together ought to be able to turn it back, and get it right side up again! And now they is asking to do it, the men better let them." She silenced the hecklers.

As Truth spoke, another American woman, Harriet Beecher Stowe, was finishing a novel, *Uncle Tom's Cabin*, that would go far toward turning the world upside down. As politicians were hoping the American people would forget slavery, Stowe's novel brought it to the attention of thousands. She gave readers an absorbing indictment of the horrors of slavery and its impact on both northerners and southerners. Published initially as magazine serials, each month's chapter ended at a nail-biting dramatic moment. Readers throughout the North cheered Eliza's daring escape across the ice floes on the Ohio River, cried over Uncle Tom's humanity and Little Eva's death, suffered under the lash of Simon Legree, and rejoiced in the reuniting of black family members.

Although it outraged the South when published in full in 1852, *Uncle Tom's Cabin* became one of the all-time best-sellers in American history. In the first year, more than 300,000 copies were printed, and Stowe's novel was eventually published in 20 languages. When President Lincoln met Stowe in 1863, he is reported to have said to her: "So you're the little woman who wrote the book that made this great war!"

DOCUMENT
Harriet Beecher Stowe, *Uncle Tom's Cabin* (1852)

POLITICAL DISINTEGRATION

The response to *Uncle Tom's Cabin* and the Fugitive Slave Act indicated that politicians had congratulated themselves too soon for saving the Republic in 1850. Political developments, not all dealing with slavery, were already weakening the ability of political parties—and ultimately the nation—to withstand the passions slavery aroused.

Weakened Party Politics in the Early 1850s

As we see today, political parties seek to persuade voters that their party stands for moral values and economic policies crucially different from those of the opposition. In the period between 1850 and 1854 these differences were blurred, thereby undermining party loyalty.

Changing Political Party Systems and Leaders

It is characteristic of American politics that when the two major parties fail to respond to the pressing issues of the day, third parties are born and major party realignment occurs. This happened in the 1850s over the issue of slavery and its extension into the territories, which resulted in the collapse of the Whigs and the emergence of the Republican party. Note that the "Republican" party begins in one tradition and ends up in the other. Is political realignment happening again in American politics? What do the two parties stand for today?

First Party System: 1790s–1820s

Republican	Federalist
Jefferson	Hamilton
Madison	John Adams
Monroe	

Transition: 1824 and 1828

Democrat-Republican	National Republican
Jackson	J. Q. Adams

Second Party System: 1830s–1850s

Democrat	Whig
Jackson	Clay
Van Buren	Webster
Calhoun	W. H. Harrison
Polk	

Third Party System: 1856–1890s

Democrat	Republican
Douglas	Lincoln
Pierce	Seward
Buchanan	Grant

Both parties scrambled to convince voters that they had favored the Compromise of 1850. In addition, several states rewrote their constitutions and remodeled their laws. These changes reduced the number of patronage jobs that politicians could dispense and regularized the process for securing banking, railroad, and other corporate charters, ending the role formerly played by the legislature and undermining the importance of parties in citizens' lives. For almost a quarter of a century Whigs and Democrats had disagreed over the tariff, money and banking, and government-supported internal improvements. Now, in better times, party distinctions over economic policies seemed less important.

Political battles were fought over social rather than economic issues and locally rather than at the national level. Thus, Georgia voters in 1851 pitted "the jealousies of the poor who owned no slaves, against the rich slaveholder." In Indiana, where Congressman George Julian observed that people "hate the Negro with a perfect if not a supreme hatred," legislators rewrote the state constitution in 1851, depriving blacks of the rights to vote, attend white schools, and make contracts. Those who could not post a $500 bond were expelled from the state, and an 1852 law made it a crime for blacks to settle in Indiana. In Massachusetts, temperance reform and a law limiting the working day to 10 hours were hot issues. Fleeting political alliances developed around particular issues and local personalities. As a Baltimore businessman said, "The two old parties are fast melting away."

The election of 1852 illustrated the lessening significance of political parties. The Whigs nominated General Winfield Scott, another Mexican-American War hero, who they hoped would repeat Taylor's success four years earlier. With the deaths of Clay and Webster, party leadership passed to Senator William Seward of New York, who desired a president he could influence more successfully than the pro-southern Fillmore. Still, it took 52 ballots to nominate Scott over Fillmore, alienating southern Whigs. Democrats had their own problems. After 49 ballots, the party turned to a lackluster compromise candidate, Franklin Pierce of New Hampshire.

The two parties offered little choice and downplayed issues so as not to widen intraparty divisions. Voter interest diminished. "Genl. Apathy is the strongest candidate out here," was a typical report from Ohio, while the Baltimore *Sun* remarked, "there is no issue that much interests the people." Democratic leaders resorted to bribes and drinks to buy the support of thousands of new Catholic immigrants from Ireland and Germany, who could be naturalized and were eligible to vote after only three years. Pierce won easily, 254 to 42 electoral votes.

The Kansas–Nebraska Act

The Whig party's final disintegration came on a February day in 1854 when southern Whigs, choosing to be more southern than Whig, supported Stephen Douglas's Nebraska bill. The Illinois senator had many reasons for introducing a bill organizing the Nebraska Territory (which included Kansas). As an ardent nationalist, he was interested in the continuing development of the West. He wanted the eastern terminus for a transcontinental railroad in Chicago rather than in rival St. Louis. This meant organizing the lands west of Iowa and Missouri.

Politics also played a role. Douglas hoped to recapture the party leadership he had held in passing the Compromise of 1850 and aspired to the presidency. Although he had replaced Cass as the great advocate of popular sovereignty, thus winning favor among northern Democrats, he needed southern Democratic support. Many southerners, especially

Celebrating a Political Victory In George Caleb Bingham's *Verdict of the People* (after 1855), the American flag flies proudly over a happy throng celebrating the outcome of democratic politics. How well did the political process work in the 1850s? In an earlier version of this same painting, the women on a hotel balcony in the upper right display a banner announcing (ironically?) "Freedom for Virtue." What do you think that means? *(George Caleb Bingham, Verdict of the People, No. 2 (after 1855), Courtesy of the R.W. Norton Art Gallery, Shreveport, Louisiana)*

neighboring Missouri slaveholders, opposed organizing the Nebraska Territory unless open to slavery.

But the Nebraska Territory lay north of the Missouri Compromise line prohibiting slavery.

Stephen Douglas

Douglas's bill, introduced early in 1854, recommended using popular sovereignty in organizing the Kansas and Nebraska territories. Douglas reasoned that the climate and soil of the prairies in Kansas and Nebraska would never support slavery-based agriculture, and that people would choose to be a free state. Therefore, he could win the votes he needed for the railroad without also getting slavery. By stating that the states created out of the Nebraska Territory would enter the Union "with or without slavery, as their constitution may prescribe at the time of their admission," his bill in effect cancelled the Missouri Compromise.

Douglas miscalculated. Northerners from his own party immediately attacked him and his bill as a "criminal betrayal of precious rights" and as part of a plot promoting his own presidential ambitions by turning free Nebraska over to "slavery despotism." Whigs and abolitionists were even more outraged. Frederick Douglass branded the act a "hateful" attempt to extend slavery, the result of the "audacious villainy of the slave power."

The Compromise of 1850 and the Kansas-Nebraska Act

But the more Stephen Douglas was attacked, the harder he fought. What began

as a railroad measure ended in reopening the question of slavery in the territories, which Douglas had thought finally settled in 1850. What began as a way of avoiding conflict ended in violence over whether Kansas would enter the Union slave or free. What began as a way of strengthening party lines over issues ended up destroying one party (Whigs), planting deep, irreconcilable divisions in another (Democrats), and creating two new ones (Know-Nothings and Republicans).

Expansionist "Young America" in the Larger World

The Democratic party was weakened in the early 1850s not only by the Kansas–Nebraska Act but also by an expansive energy that led Americans to adventures far beyond Kansas. As republican revolutions erupted in 1848 in Europe (Austria-Hungary, France, Germany) and had initial successes, Americans hailed them as evidence that free republican institutions were the wave of the future. "Young America" was the label assumed by patriots eager to spread Americanism abroad; however, these ardent republican nationalists ironically also abetted the spread of slavery.

Song of the Open Road—Calamus

Pierce's platform in 1852 reflected this nationalism, declaring that the war with Mexico had been "just and necessary." Many Democrats took the overwhelming victory as a mandate to continue adding

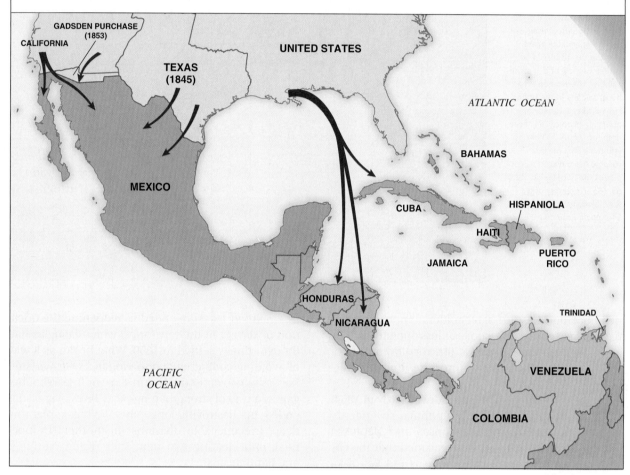

Expansionist "Young America" in the 1850s: Attempted Raids into Latin America

Note the flurry of expansionist American raids and forays southward into Mexico and the Caribbean between the mid-1840s and mid-1850s. **Reflecting on the Past** What major events and motives caused the expansionist interest? Why was Cuba a key target? Are there any similar events today?

territory. A Philadelphia newspaper in 1853 described the United States as a nation bound on the "East by sunrise, West by sunset, North by the Arctic Expedition, and South as far as we darn please."

Many of Pierce's diplomatic appointees were southerners interested in adding new cotton-growing lands to the Union, especially from Latin America where the newly independent nations were wracked by internal disputes over the distribution of land. Pierce's ambassador to Mexico, for example, South Carolinian James Gadsden, had instructions to negotiate with Mexican president Santa Anna for the acquisition of large parts of northern Mexico. Gadsden did not get all he wanted, but he did manage to purchase a strip of southwestern desert for a transcontinental railroad linking the Deep South with the Pacific Coast.

Failure to acquire more territory from Mexico legally did not discourage expansionist Americans

from pursuing illegal means. During the 1850s, Texans and Californians staged dozens of raids (called "filibusters") into Mexico. The most daring such adventurer was William Walker, a tiny Tennessean with a zest for danger and power. In 1853, he invaded Mexican Baja California with fewer than 300 men and declared himself president of the Republic of Sonora. Arrested and tried in the United States, he was acquitted in eight minutes. Two years later, he invaded Nicaragua, where he proclaimed himself an elected dictator and legalized slavery. When the Nicaraguans, with British help, regained control, the U.S. Navy rescued Walker. After a triumphant tour in the South, he tried twice more to conquer Nicaragua. Walker came to a fitting end in 1860 when, invading Honduras this time, he was captured and shot by a firing squad.

Undaunted by failures in the Southwest, the Pierce administration looked to the acquisition of

Cuba. Many Americans thought this Spanish colony was destined for U.S. annexation and would be an ideal place for expanding the slave-based economy. Some argued that Cuba belonged to the United States because it was physically connected by alluvial deposits from the Mississippi River. "What God has joined together let no man put asunder," one said. In the 1840s, the Polk administration had vainly offered Spain $10 million for Cuba. Unsuccessful efforts were then made to foment a revolution among Cuban sugar planters, who were expected to request annexation by the United States. Several plans, including one by Secretary of War Jefferson Davis of Mississippi, were made to invade Cuba and carve it into several slave states.

Although President Pierce did not support these illegal efforts, he wanted the island. Secretary of State William Marcy instructed the minister to Spain, Pierre Soulé, to offer $130 million for Cuba, upping the price. If that failed, Marcy suggested stronger measures. In 1854, the secretary arranged for Soulé and the American ministers to France and England to meet in Belgium, where they issued the Ostend Manifesto to pressure Spain to sell Cuba to the United States.

The manifesto argued that Cuba "belongs naturally" to the United States and that they were "one people with one destiny." Trade and commerce in the hemisphere would "never be secure" until Cuba was part of the United States. Moreover, southern slaveholders feared that a slave rebellion would "Africanize" Cuba, like Haiti, suggesting all kinds of "horrors to the white race" in the nearby southern United States. American acquisition of Cuba was necessary, therefore, to "preserve our rectitude and self-respect." If Spain refused to sell, the ministers at Ostend threatened a Cuban revolution with American support. If that failed, "we should be justified in wresting it from Spain."

Even Marcy was shocked when he received the document and he quickly repudiated the manifesto. Like the Kansas–Nebraska Act, Democrats supported the Ostend Manifesto in order to further the expansion of slavery. The outraged reaction of northerners in both cases divided and further weakened the Democratic party.

Nativism, Know-Nothings, and Republicans

Meanwhile, increasing immigration also damaged an already enfeebled Whig party and alarmed many native-born Americans. To the average hardworking Protestant American, the foreigners pouring into the cities and following the railroads westward spoke unfamiliar languages, wore funny clothes, drank alcohol

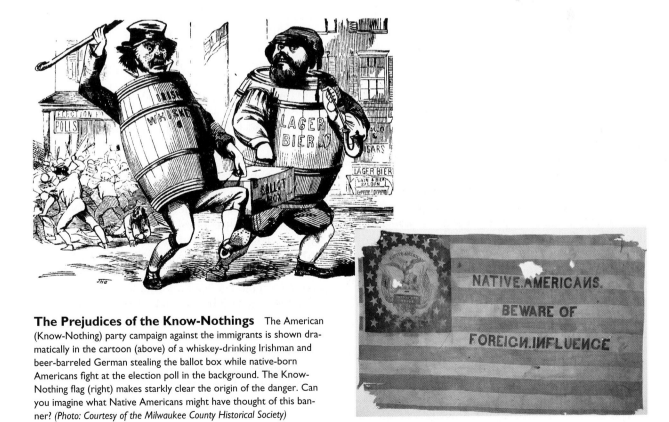

The Prejudices of the Know-Nothings The American (Know-Nothing) party campaign against the immigrants is shown dramatically in the cartoon (above) of a whiskey-drinking Irishman and beer-barreled German stealing the ballot box while native-born Americans fight at the election poll in the background. The Know-Nothing flag (right) makes starkly clear the origin of the danger. Can you imagine what Native Americans might have thought of this banner? *(Photo: Courtesy of the Milwaukee County Historical Society)*

AMERICAN VOICES

Henry Villard, born in Bavaria, emigrated to the United States in 1853 just in time for the intense political upheavals over the extension of slavery into the Kansas and Nebraska territories. In his Memoirs *(1904), he described his first "lesson in practical politics" shortly after he arrived.*

The deliberate attempts of the Democrats in the South, aided by the bulk of their Northern sympathizers, to secure an extension of the territory open to slavery [to Kansas] was the all-absorbing and all-exciting topic. . . . It was made the dividing line in the Chicago municipal election that spring [1856]. Of course, I had no right to vote, but that did not prevent me from enlisting as a violent partisan on the anti-Democratic side. The contest was fought directly over slavery. . . . On election day, I acted as a ticket-distributor, and had then my first sight of violent scenes and rioting at the polls. The 'right' and 'wrong' seemed to be so clearly defined that I could not understand how any intelligent mind could be at all in doubt. That

the ignorant, priest-ridden Irish should support the Democratic candidates was comprehensible, but it aroused my disgust and indignation that there were Germans on the Democratic ticket, a German newspaper and prominent Germans who actually supported it. I looked upon them as contemptible apostates. I was confident, too, that the unholy combination would be overwhelmingly defeated. My unutterable humiliation and grief may be imagined, therefore, when the Democrats obtained a decisive victory. Influenced by the predictions of the dire . . . evils that would befall the country if the Democrats carried the day, I felt wofully depressed in spirit. It seemed to me almost as if the world would come to an end.

- *What was Villard's lesson in "practical politics"?*

- *Have you had a similar lesson in politics, local or national?*

---

freely, and bred crime and pauperism. Moreover, they seemed content with a lower standard of living by working for lower wages and thus threatened to take jobs away from American workers.

Worst of all from the Protestant perspective, Irish and German immigrants spearheaded an unprecedented growth of American Catholicism. By the 1850s, there were nearly 3 million Catholics in the United States, not only in eastern cities but expanding westward into the Ohio valley (Germans in Wheeling, Cincinnati, and St. Louis) and along old French-Canadian trade routes through Detroit, Green Bay, and Vincennes. A surprising and, to many, disturbing development was Catholic success in converting Protestants. As one Catholic explained, it was "a time when great throngs of Americans began to flock to the Roman Catholic Church despite bitterly intense propaganda and overt opposition."

Two notable conversions in 1844 compelled Protestant Americans to take the threat seriously. Orestes Brownson, a Jacksonian Democrat and spiritual seeker, moved successively through Congregationalism, Presbyterianism, Unitarianism, and Transcendentalism until finally converting to a Catholicism he argued was fully compatible with democracy. His disciple, the Methodist German immigrant Isaac Hecker, converted to Catholicism two

months earlier in 1844, joining the Redemptorist order. Led by Jesuits and Redemptorists like Hecker, more than 400 parish mission revivals and retreats were held in the 1850s in an aggressive effort to convert urban American Protestants to Roman Catholicism. The opening of Catholic schools especially offended and threatened Protestants.

Many Protestants charged that Catholic immigrants corrupted American politics. Indeed, most Catholics did indeed prefer the Democratic party, which was less inclined than Whigs to interfere with religion, schooling, drinking, and other aspects of personal behavior and rights. It was mostly former Whigs, therefore, who in 1854 founded the American party to oppose the new immigrants. Members wanted a longer period of naturalization to guarantee the "vital principles of Republican Government" and pledged never to vote for Irish Catholics, whose highest loyalty was supposedly to the pope in Rome. They also agreed to keep information about their order secret. If asked, they would say, "I know nothing." Hence, they were dubbed the Know-Nothing party.

The Know-Nothings appealed to the middle and lower classes—to workers worried about their jobs and to farmers and small-town Americans nervous about change. A New Yorker said in 1854, "Roman Catholicism is feared more than American slavery."

It was widely believed that Catholics slavishly obeyed the orders of their priests, who represented a Church associated with European despotism. The Church's opposition to the European revolutionary movements of 1848 intensified nativist fears that Catholicism threatened the democratic order. In the 1854 and 1855 elections, the Know-Nothings gave anti-Catholicism a national, political focus for the first time.

To other northerners, however, the "slave power" seemed a more serious threat than the pope. No sooner had debates over Nebraska ended than the nucleus of another new party appeared: the Republican party. Drawn almost entirely from "conscience" Whigs and disaffected Democrats (including Free-Soilers), the Republicans combined four elements.

Moral fervor led the first group, headed by senators Seward (New York), Charles Sumner (Massachusetts) and Salmon P. Chase (Ohio), to demand prohibiting slavery in the territories, freeing slaves in the District of Columbia, repealing the Fugitive Slave Act, and banning the internal slave trade. There were, however, limits to most Republicans' idealism. A more moderate and larger group, typified by Abraham Lincoln of Illinois, opposed slavery in the western territories, but would not interfere with it where it already existed. This group also opposed equal rights for northern free blacks.

Many Republicans were anti-Catholic as well as antislavery. A third element of the party, true to traditional Whig reformist and revivalist impulses, wanted to cleanse America of intemperance, impiety, parochial schooling, and other forms of immorality—including voting for Democrats, who catered to the "grog shops, foreign vote, and Catholic brethren" and combined the "forces of Jesuitism and Slavery."

The fourth element of the Republican party, a Whig legacy from Henry Clay's American System, included those who wanted the federal government to promote economic development and the dignity of free labor, believing that both led to progress. At the heart of the new party and the American future, Republicans proclaimed, were hardworking, middle-class, mobile, free white laborers—farmers, small businessmen, and independent artisans. Lincoln's hometown paper, the Springfield *Republican,* said in 1856 that Republican strength came from "those who work with their hands, who live and act independently, who hold the stakes of home and family, of farm and workshop, of education and freedom."

These strengths were tested in a three-party race in 1856. The Know-Nothing (American) party nominated Fillmore, who had strong support in the Upper South. The Republicans chose John C. Frémont, an ardent Free-Soiler from Missouri with virtually no political experience but with fame as an explorer of the West and a military record against Mexicans in California. The Democrats nominated Pennsylvanian James Buchanan, a "northern man with southern principles." Frémont carried several free states, while Fillmore took only Maryland. Buchanan, benefiting from a divided opposition, won with only 45 percent of the popular vote.

After 1856, the Know-Nothings died out, largely because Republican leaders cleverly redirected nativist fears—and voters—to their broader program. Moreover, Know-Nothing secrecy, hatred, and occasional violent attacks on Catholic voters damaged their image. Still, the Know-Nothings represented a powerful current in American politics that would return each time social and economic changes seemed to threaten the nation. It became convenient to label certain people "un-American" and try to root them out. The Know-Nothing party disappeared but nativist hostility to new immigrants did not.

KANSAS AND THE TWO CULTURES

The slavery issue also would not go away. As Democrats sought to expand slavery and other American institutions westward across the plains and south into Cuba, Republicans wanted to halt the advance of slavery. In 1854, Lincoln worried that slavery "deprives our republican example of its just influence in the world." The specific cause of his concern was the likelihood that slavery might be extended into Kansas as a result of the passage that year of Stephen Douglas's Kansas–Nebraska Act.

Competing for Kansas

During the congressional debates over the Nebraska bill, Seward accepted the challenge of slave-state senators to "engage in competition for the virgin soil of Kansas." Soon after Congress passed the Kansas–Nebraska Act in 1854, the Massachusetts Emigrant Aid Society was founded to recruit free-soil settlers for Kansas. Frederick Douglass called for "companies of emigrants from the free states ... to possess the goodly land." By the summer of 1855, about 1,200 New England colonists had migrated to Kansas.

One migrant was Julia Louisa Lovejoy, a Vermont minister's wife. As a riverboat carried her into a slave state for the first time, she wrote of the dilapidated plantation homes on the monotonous Missouri

The Fight for Kansas   Led by Senator David Atchison, thousands of gun-toting Missourians crossed into Kansas in 1854 and 1855 to vote illegally for a proslavery territorial government. The ensuing bloodshed made Kansas a preview of the Civil War. Why in Kansas? *(Courtesy of The Newberry Library, Chicago)*

shore as the "blighting mildew of slavery." By the time she and her husband arrived in the Kansas Territory, Julia had concluded that the "morals" of the slave-holding Missourians moving into Kansas were of an "*undescribably repulsive* and undesirable character." To her, northerners came to bring the "energetic Yankee" virtues of morality and economic enterprise to drunken, unclean slaveholders.

Perhaps she had in mind David Atchison, Democratic senator from Missouri. Atchison believed that Congress must protect slavery in the territories, allowing Missouri slaveholders into Kansas. In 1853, he pledged "to extend the institutions of Missouri over the Territory at whatever sacrifice of blood or treasure." New England migrants, he said, were "negro thieves" and "abolition tyrants," and recommended that Missourians defend their property and interests "with the *bayonet*" and, if need be, "to kill every God-damned abolitionist in the district."

Under Atchison's inflammatory leadership, secret societies sprang up in the Missouri counties adjacent to Kansas dedicated to combating the Free-Soilers. One editor exclaimed that northerners came to Kansas "for the express purpose of stealing, running off and hiding runaway negroes from Missouri [and] taking to their own bed . . . a stinking negro wench." Not slaveholders, he said, but New Englanders were immoral, uncivilized, and hypocritical. Rumors of 20,000 such Massachusetts migrants

spurred Missourians to action. Thousands poured across the border late in 1854 to vote on permitting slavery in the territory. Twice as many ballots were cast as the number of registered voters; in one polling place only 20 of more than 600 voters were legal residents.

The proslavery forces overreacted. The permanent population of Kansas consisted primarily of migrants from Missouri and other border states—people more concerned with land titles than slavery. They opposed any blacks—slave or free—moving into their state. As one clergyman put it, "I kem to Kansas to live in a free state and I don't want niggers a-trampin' over my grave."

In March 1855, a second election was held to select a territorial legislature. The pattern of border crossings, intimidation, and illegal voting was repeated. Atchison himself, drinking "considerable whiskey," led an armed band across the state line to vote and frighten away would-be free-soil voters. Not surprisingly, swollen numbers of illegal voters elected a proslavery territorial legislature. Free-Soilers, meanwhile, held their own convention in Lawrence and created a free-soil government at Topeka. It banned blacks from the state. The proslavery legislature settled in Lecompton, giving Kansas two governments.

The struggle shifted to Washington. Although President Pierce could have nullified the illegal election, he did nothing. Congress debated and sent an investigating committee, further inflaming passions. Throughout 1855, the call to arms grew more strident. One proslavery newspaper invited southerners to bring their weapons and "send the scoundrels" from the North "back to whence they came, or . . . to hell, it matters not which." In South Carolina, Robert Allston wrote his son Benjamin that he was "raising men and money . . . to counteract the effect of the Northern hordes. . . . We are disposed to fight the battle of our rights . . . on the field of Kansas."

Both sides saw Kansas as a holy battleground. An Alabama colonel sold his slaves to raise money to hire an army of 300 men to fight for slavery in Kansas, promising free land to his recruits. A Baptist minister blessed their departure from Montgomery, promised them God's favor, and gave each man a Bible. Northern Christians responded in kind. At Yale University, the noted minister Henry Ward Beecher presented 25 Bibles and 25 Sharps rifles to young men who would go fight for the Lord in Kansas. "There are times," he said, "when self-defense is a religious duty. If that duty was ever imperative it is now, and in Kansas." Beecher suggested that rifles would be of greater use than Bibles. Missourians dubbed them "Beecher's Bibles" and vowed, as one newspaper put it, "Blood for Blood!"

"Bleeding Kansas"

As civil war threatened in Kansas, Brooklyn poet Walt Whitman heralded American democracy in his epic poem *Leaves of Grass* (1855). Whitman

DOCUMENT

Walt Whitman, Preface to *Leaves of Grass* (1855)

identified himself as the embodiment of average Americans "of every hue and caste, . . . of every rank and religion." His poems embraced urban mechanics, southern woodcutters, runaway slaves, mining camp prostitutes, and a long list of others in his poetic celebration of "the word Democratic, the word En-Masse." But Whitman's faith in the American masses faltered in the mid-1850s. He worried that a knife plunged into the "breast" of the Union would bring on the "red blood of civil war."

Blood indeed flowed in Kansas. In May 1856, supported by a pro-southern federal marshal, a mob entered Lawrence, smashed the offices and presses of a Free-Soil newspaper, fired several cannonballs into the Free State Hotel, and destroyed homes and shops. Three nights later, believing he was doing God's will, John Brown led a small New England band, including four of his sons, to a proslavery settlement near Pottawatomie Creek and hacked five men to death with swords.

Violence also entered the halls of Congress. That same week, abolitionist Senator Charles Sumner delivered a tirade known as "The Crime Against Kansas." He lashed out at the "incredible atrocities of the Assassins and . . . Thugs" from the South. He accused proslavery Senate leaders, especially Andrew Butler of South Carolina, of cavorting with the "harlot, Slavery." Two days later, Butler's nephew, Congressman Preston Brooks, avenged his honor by beating Sumner senseless with his cane as he sat at his Senate desk.

The sack of Lawrence, the Pottawatomie massacre, and the caning of Sumner set off serious civil disturbances in "Bleeding Kansas" that lasted throughout the summer. Crops were burned, homes were destroyed, fights broke out in saloons and streets, and night raiders tortured and murdered their enemies. For Charles Lines, who just wanted to farm his land in peace, it was impossible to remain neutral. Lines hoped his neighbors near Lawrence would avoid "involving themselves in trouble." But when proslavery forces tortured a mild-mannered neighbor to death, Lines joined the battle. "Blood," he wrote, "must end in the triumph of the right."

Even before the bleeding of Kansas began, the New York *Tribune* warned, "We are two peoples. We are a people for Freedom and a people for Slavery. Between the two, conflict is inevitable." As the rhetoric and violence in Kansas demonstrated, competing visions of two separate cultures for the future destiny of the United States were at stake. Despite many similarities between the North and the South, the gap between the two sides widened with the hostilities of the mid-1850s.

Northern Views and Visions

As Julia Lovejoy suggested, the North saw itself as a prosperous land of bustling commerce and expanding, independent agriculture. Northern farmers and workers were self-made free men and women who believed in individualism and democracy. The "free labor system" of the North, as both Seward and Lincoln often said, offered equality of opportunity and upward mobility. Both generated more wealth. Although the North contained many growing cities, northerners revered the values of the small towns that spread from New England across the Upper Midwest. These values included a respect for the rights of the people, tempered by the rule of law; individual enterprise, balanced by a concern for one's neighbors; and a fierce morality rooted in Protestantism. Northerners would regulate morality—by persuasion if possible but by legislation if necessary—to purge irreligion, illiteracy, and intemperance from American society. It was no accident that laws for universal public education and against the

A Northern City and a Southern Plantation These scenes illustrate the contrasting socioeconomic cultures of the antebellum North and South. Chicago (top) was a rapidly growing, bustling northern city in the 1850s; situated on the Great Lakes and a developing railroad hub, Chicago became the distribution center for industrial and agricultural goods throughout the Midwest. The vital unit of southern commerce was, by contrast, the individual plantation (bottom), with steamboats and flatboats carrying cotton and sugar to port cities for trade with Europe. Are there examples today of two sides portraying each other in such starkly contrasting ways? *(Top: Corbis; bottom: Library of Congress)*

sale and consumption of alcohol both began in New England.

Northerners valued the kind of republican government that guaranteed the rights of free men, enabling them to achieve economic progress. This belief supported government action to promote free labor, industrial growth, immigration, foreign trade (protected by tariffs), and the extension of railroads and free farm homesteads westward across the continent. Energetic mobility, both westward and upward, would dissolve state, regional, and class loyalties and increase the sense of nationhood. A strong

Union could achieve national and even international greatness. These were the conditions befitting a chosen people who would, as Seward put it, spread American institutions around the world and "renovate the condition of mankind." These were the principles of the Republican party.

Only free men could achieve economic progress and moral society. In northerners' eyes, therefore, the worst sin was the loss of one's freedom. Slavery was the root of all evil. It was, Seward said, "incompatible with all . . . the elements of the security, welfare, and greatness of nations." The South was the antithesis of everything that northerners saw as good. Southerners were unfree, backward, economically stagnant, uneducated, lawless, immoral, and in conflict with the values and ideals of the nineteenth century. Julia Lovejoy's denunciation of slaveholding Missourians was mild. Other Yankee migrants saw southerners as "wild beasts" who guzzled whiskey, ate dirt, swore, raped slave women, and fought or dueled at the slightest excuse. In the slang of the day, they were "Pukes."

The Southern Perspective

Southerners were a diverse people who, like northerners, shared certain broad values, generally those of the planter class. If in the North the values of economic enterprise were most important, southerners revered social values most. They admired the English gentry and saw themselves as courteous, refined, hospitable, and chivalrous. By contrast, they saw "Yankees" as coarse, ill-mannered, aggressive, and materialistic. In a society where one person in three was a black slave, racial distinctions and paternalistic relationships were crucial in maintaining order and white supremacy. Fear of slave revolt was ever-present. The South had five times as many military schools as the North. Northerners educated the many for economic utility; southerners educated the few for character. In short, the white South saw itself as an ordered society guided by the planters' genteel code.

Southerners agreed with northerners that sovereignty in a republic rested in the people, who created a government of laws to protect life, liberty, and property. But unlike northerners, southerners believed that the democratic principle of self-government was best preserved in local political units such as the states. They were ready to fight to resist any tyrannical encroachment on their liberty, as they had in 1776. They saw themselves as true revolutionary patriots. Like northerners, southerners cherished the Union. But they preferred the loose confederacy of the Jeffersonian past, not Seward's centralized nationalism.

To southerners, Yankees were in too much of a hurry—to make money, to reform others' behavior, to put dreamy theories (such as racial equality) into practice. Two images dominated the South's view of northerners: either they were stingy, hypocritical, moralizing Puritans, or they were grubby, slum-dwelling, Catholic immigrants. A Georgia paper combined both images in an 1856 editorial: "Free society! we sicken at the name. What is it but a conglomeration of greasy mechanics, filthy operatives, small-fisted farmers, and moon-struck theorists?" These northerners, the paper said, "are devoid of society fitted for well-bred gentlemen."

Each side saw the other threatening its freedom and degrading proper republican society. Each saw the other imposing barriers to its vision for America's future, which included the economic systems described in Chapters 10 and 11. As hostilities rose, the views each section had of the other grew steadily more rigid and conspiratorial. Northerners saw the South as a "slave power," determined to foist the slave system on free labor throughout the land. Southerners saw the North as full of "black Republicanism," determined to destroy their way of life.

POLARIZATION AND THE ROAD TO WAR

The struggle over Kansas solidified the image of the Republicans as a northern party and seriously weakened the Democrats. Further events, mostly over the question of slavery in the territories, soon split the Democratic party irrevocably into sectional halves: the *Dred Scott* decision of the Supreme Court (1857), the constitutional crisis in Kansas (1857), the Lincoln–Douglas debates in Illinois (1858), John Brown's raid in Virginia (1859), and Lincoln's election (1860). These incidents further polarized the negative images each culture held of the other and accelerated the nation down the road to civil war.

The *Dred Scott* Case

The events of 1857 reinforced the arguments of those who believed in a slave power conspiracy. Two days after James Buchanan's inauguration, the Supreme Court finally ruled in *Dred Scott* v. *Sanford*. The case had been before the Court for nearly three years, longer for the Scott slave family. Back in 1846, Dred and Harriet Scott had filed suit in Missouri for their freedom. They argued that their master had taken them into northern territories where the Missouri Compromise prohibited slavery, and therefore they should be freed. By the time the case reached the Supreme Court, the issue of slavery in the territories was a hot political issue.

DOCUMENT

Supreme Court Decision, *Dred Scott* v. *Sanford* (1857)

When the Court, with its southern majority, issued a 7–2 decision, it made three rulings. First, because blacks were, as Chief Justice Roger Taney put it, "beings of an inferior order [who] had no rights which white men were bound to respect," Dred Scott was not a citizen and had no right to sue in federal courts. Justice Peter Daniel of Virginia was even more indelicate in his consenting opinion, saying that the "African Negro race" did not belong "to the family of nations" but rather was a subject for "commerce or traffic." The second ruling stated that the Missouri Compromise was unconstitutional because Congress had no power to ban slavery in a territory. Third, the court decided that taking the Scotts into free states did not affect their status.

The implications of these decisions went far beyond the Scotts' personal freedom. The arguments about black citizenship infuriated many northerners. Frederick Douglass called the ruling "a most scandalous and devilish perversion of the Constitution, and a brazen misstatement of the facts of history." Many citizens worried about the few rights free blacks still held. Even more troubling, the decision hinted that slavery might be legal in the free states of the North. People who suspected a conspiracy were not calmed when Buchanan endorsed the *Dred Scott* decision as a final settlement of the right of citizens to take their "property of any kind, including slaves, into the common Territories . . . and to have it protected there under the Federal Constitution." Far from settling the issue of slavery in the territories, as Buchanan had hoped, *Dred Scott* threw it back into American politics, opened new questions, and increased sectional hostilities.

IMAGE
Dred Scott

Constitutional Crisis in Kansas

The *Dred Scott* decision and Buchanan's endorsement fed northern suspicions of a slave power conspiracy to impose slavery everywhere. Events in Kansas, which still had two governments, heightened these fears. In the summer of 1857, Kansas had yet another election, with so many irregularities that only 2,000 out of a possible 24,000 votes counted. A proslavery slate of delegates was elected to a constitutional convention meeting at Lecompton as a preparation for statehood. The convention barred free blacks from the state, guaranteed the property rights of the few slaveholders in Kansas, and asked voters to decide in a referendum whether to permit more slaves.

The proslavery Lecompton constitution, clearly unrepresentative of the wishes of the majority of the people of Kansas, was sent to Congress for approval. Eager to retain southern Democratic support, Buchanan endorsed it. Stephen Douglas challenged the president's power and jeopardized his standing with southern Democrats by opposing it. Facing reelection to the Senate from Illinois in 1858, Douglas needed to hold the support of the northern wing of his party. Congress sent the Lecompton constitution back to the people of Kansas for another referendum. This time they defeated it, which meant that Kansas remained a territory rather than becoming a slave state. While Kansas was left in an uncertain status, the larger political effect of the struggle was to split the Democratic party almost beyond repair.

No sooner had Douglas settled the Lecompton question than he faced re-election in Illinois. Douglas's opposition to the Lecompton constitution had restored his prestige in the North as an opponent of the slave power. This cut some ground out from under the Republican party's claim that only it could stop the spread of southern power. Party leaders from the West, however, had a candidate who understood the importance of distinguishing Republican moral and political views from those of the Democrats.

Lincoln and the Illinois Debates

Although relatively unknown nationally and out of elective office for several years, by 1858 Abraham Lincoln of Illinois was challenging William Seward for leadership of the Republican party. Lincoln's character was shaped on the midwestern frontier, where he had educated himself, developed mild abolitionist views, and dreamed of America's greatness.

Douglas was clearly the leading Democrat, so the 1858 election in Illinois gave a preview of the presidential election of 1860. The other Douglass, Frederick, observed that "the slave power idea was the ideological glue of the Republican party." Lincoln's handling of this idea would be crucial in distinguishing him from Stephen Douglas. The Illinois campaign featured a series of seven debates between Lincoln and Douglas, which took place in different cities. Addressing a national as well as a local audience, the debaters confronted the heated racial issues before the nation.

Lincoln set a solemn tone when he accepted the Republican senatorial nomination in Chicago. The American nation, he said, was in a "crisis" and building toward a worse one. "A House divided against itself cannot stand. I believe this government cannot endure, permanently half *slave* and half *free*." Lincoln said he did not expect the Union "to be dissolved" or "the house to fall," but rather that "it will become *all* one thing, or *all* the other." Then he rehearsed the history of the South's growing influence over national policy since the Kansas–Nebraska Act, which he blamed on Douglas. Lincoln stated his firm opposition to the *Dred Scott* decision, which he believed part of a conspiracy involving Pierce, Buchanan, Taney, and Douglas. He and others like him opposing this conspiracy wished to place slavery on a "course of ultimate extinction."

DOCUMENT
Lincoln, "A House Divided" (1858)

Debating Douglas, Lincoln reiterated these controversial themes. Although far from a radical abolitionist, in these debates Lincoln skillfully staked out a moral position on race and slavery not just in advance of Douglas but well ahead of his time.

Lincoln was also very much a part of his time. He believed in white superiority, opposed granting specific equal civil rights to free blacks, and said that physical and moral differences between whites and blacks would "forever forbid the two races from living together on terms of social and political equality." "Separation" and colonization in Liberia or Central America was the best solution. But Lincoln differed from most contemporaries in his deep commitment to the equality and dignity of all human beings.

DOCUMENT
Lincoln, Charleston Debate (1858)

Countering Douglas's racial slurs, Lincoln said that he believed not only that blacks were "entitled to all the natural rights . . . in the Declaration of Independence" but also that they had many specific economic rights as well, such as "the right to put into his mouth the bread that his own hands have earned." In these rights, blacks were "my equal and the equal of Judge Douglas, and the equal of every living man."

Unlike Douglas, Lincoln hated slavery. At Galesburg, he said, "I contemplate slavery as a moral, social, and political evil." In Quincy, he said that the difference between a Republican and a Democrat was quite simply whether one thought slavery wrong or right. Douglas was more equivocal and dodged the issue in Freeport, pointing out that slavery would not exist if favorable local legislation did not support it. But Douglas's moral indifference to slavery was clear: he did not care whether a territorial legislature voted it "up or down." Republicans did care, Lincoln answered, and said that stopping the expansion of slavery would set the course toward "ultimate extinction." Although barred by the Constitution from interfering with slavery where it already existed, Lincoln said that because Republicans believed slavery was wrong, "we propose a course of policy that shall deal with it as a wrong."

What Lincoln meant by "policy" was not yet clear, not even to himself. However, he did succeed in affirming that Republicans were the only moral and political force capable of stopping the slave power. It seems ironic now (though not then), that Douglas won

the election. Elsewhere in 1858, however, Democrats did poorly, losing 18 congressional seats.

DOCUMENT
Lincoln and Douglas, Galesburg Debate (1858)

John Brown's Raid

Unlike Lincoln, John Brown was prepared to act decisively against slavery. On October 16, 1859, he and a band of 22 men attacked a federal arsenal at Harpers Ferry, Virginia (now West Virginia). He hoped to provoke a general uprising of slaves throughout the Upper South or at least provide the arms for slaves to make their way to freedom. Although he seized the arsenal for a time, federal troops soon overcame him. Nearly half his men were killed, including two sons. Brown was captured, tried, and hanged for treason, ending a lifetime of failures.

IMAGE
John Brown, ca. 1850

In death, however, Brown was not a failure. His daring if foolhardy raid and his dignified behavior during his trial and speedy execution unleashed powerful passions. The North–South gap widened. Although Brown's death was widely condemned, many northerners responded to it with an outpouring of sympathy at memorial rallies, parades, and prayer meetings. Thoreau compared him to

John Brown as an Avenging Hero This modern mural captures both the madness and passionate larger-than-life commitment of John Brown against a backdrop of flag-covered wagon trains across the Great Plains, a raging tornado and angry sky (God's wrath?), struggling slaves (by his left knee), and a violent confrontation between those for and against slavery. How do you respond to these images? *(Kansas State Historical Society)*

Tarring and Feathering of a Southern Sympathizer   In the aftermath of John Brown's raid, passions fed by fear were unleashed throughout the South against northern sympathizers, and vice versa. A year later, the editor of a Massachusetts newspaper who expressed Democratic, southern sympathies found himself the victim of the time-honored mob punishment of tarring and feathering. *(Picture Collection, The New York Public Library, Astor, Lenox & Tilden Foundations)*

Christ, calling Brown an "angel of light." Abolitionist William Lloyd Garrison, a pacifist, wished "success to every slave insurrection" in the South. Ministers called slave revolt a "divine weapon" and glorified Brown's treason as "holy."

Brown's raid, Frederick Douglass pointed out, showed that slavery was a "system of brute force" that would be ended only when "met with its own weapons." Southerners were filled with "dread and terror" over the possibility of a wave of slave revolts led by hundreds of imaginary John Browns and Nat Turners, and concluded that northerners would stop at nothing to free the slaves. This suspicion further eroded freedom of thought and expression. A North Carolinian described a "spirit of terror, mobs, arrests, and violence" in his state. Twelve families in Berea, Kentucky, were evicted from the state for their mild abolitionist sentiments. A Texas minister who criticized the treatment of slaves in a sermon got 70 lashes.

DOCUMENT

John Brown, Address Before Sentencing (Nov. 2, 1859)

AUDIO

Battle Hymn of the Republic

With Brown's raid, southerners also became more convinced, as the governor of South Carolina put it, of a "black Republican" plot in the North "arrayed against the slaveholders." In this atmosphere of mistrust, southern Unionists lost their influence, and power became concentrated in the hands of those favoring secession. Only one step remained to complete the southern sense of having become a permanent minority within the United States: withdrawal to form a new nation. Senator Robert Toombs of Georgia, insistent that northern "enemies" were plotting the South's ruin, warned fellow southerners late in 1859, "Never permit this Federal government to pass into the traitorous hands of the black Republican party."

DOCUMENT

William Lloyd Garrison on John Brown's Raid (1859)

The Election of 1860

When the Democratic convention met in Charleston, South Carolina, a secessionist hotbed, it sat for a

Two Maps of the Presidential Election of 1860

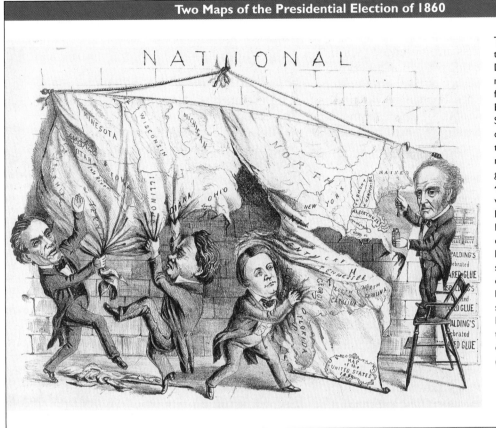

This 1860 pre-election cartoon shows Lincoln and Douglas (left) fighting for the midwestern states (and California and Oregon), while Breckinridge tears off the South, and the compromise candidate Bell, standing on the chair, tries to hold the nation together with a little glue. Lincoln won with only 40 percent of the popular vote. Note on the map below the states Lincoln and Breckinridge won: what does that suggest? Although he was second in many states, Douglas took only one, Missouri, perhaps for both real and symbolic reasons. Why do you think so? How do you explain the three states Bell won? Why did Lincoln win the election? *(Cartoon: Library of Congress)*

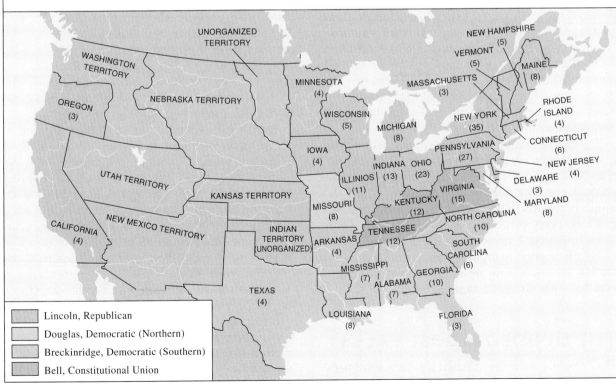

Lincoln, Republican
Douglas, Democratic (Northern)
Breckinridge, Democratic (Southern)
Bell, Constitutional Union

record 10 days and went through 59 ballots without being able to name a candidate. Southern delegates withdrew twice, forcing adjournments. Reconvening in Baltimore, the Democrats acknowledged their irreparable division by choosing two candidates at two separate conventions: Douglas for northern Democrats and John C. Breckinridge, Buchanan's vice president, for the proslavery South. The Constitutional Union party, made up of former southern Whigs and border-state nativists, claimed the middle ground and nominated John Bell, a slaveholder from Tennessee who favored compromise.

1860 Presidential Election Banner (Republican)

With Democrats split and a new party in contention, the Republican strategy aimed at keeping the states carried by Frémont in 1856 and adding Pennsylvania, Illinois, and Indiana. Seward, the leading candidate, had been tempering his antislavery views to appear more electable. So had Lincoln, who seemed more likely than Seward to carry those key states. After shrewd maneuvers emphasizing his "availability" as a moderate, Lincoln was nominated.

The Republican platform also exuded moderation, opposing only slavery's extension. Mostly it spoke of tariff protection, subsidized internal improvements, free labor, and a homestead bill. Republicans, like southern Democrats, defended their view of what republican values meant for America's future. It did not include the equal rights envisioned by Frederick Douglass. An English traveler in 1860 observed that in America "we see, in effect, two nations—one white and another black—growing up together within the same political circle, but never mingling on a principle of equality."

The Republican moderate strategy worked as planned. Lincoln was elected by sweeping the entire Northeast and Midwest. Although he got less than 40 percent of the popular vote nationwide, his triumph in the North was decisive. Even a united Democratic party could not have defeated him. With victory assured, Lincoln finished his sandwich and coffee on election night in Springfield and prepared for his awesome new responsibilities. They came even before his inauguration.

THE DIVIDED HOUSE FALLS

The Republicans overestimated Unionist sentiment in the South. A year earlier, some southern congressmen had walked out in protest when the House chose an antislavery speaker. A Republican leader, Carl Schurz, recalling this, said that the

southerners had taken a drink and then come back. Now, Schurz predicted, they would walk out, take two drinks, and come back again. He was wrong.

Secession and Uncertainty

On December 20, 1860, South Carolina seceded from the Union, declaring the "experiment" of putting people with "different pursuits and institutions" under one government a failure. By February 1, the other six Deep South states—Mississippi, Florida, Alabama, Georgia, Louisiana, and Texas— also left. A week later, delegates meeting in Montgomery, Alabama, created the Confederate States of America and elected Jefferson Davis, a Mississippi senator and cotton planter, its provisional president. The divided house had fallen, as Lincoln had predicted. But it was not yet certain whether the house could be put back together or whether there would be civil war.

DOCUMENT

South Carolina Declaration on the Causes of Secession

The government in Washington had three options. First was compromise, but the emotions of the time ruled that out, as the proposed compromises were mostly pro-southern. Second, as suggested by New York *Tribune* editor Horace Greeley, was to let the seven states "go in peace," taking care not to lose the border states. Northern businessmen, fearing the loss of profitable economic ties with the South, were opposed, as were those who believed in an indissoluble Union. The third option was to compel secessionist states to return, which probably meant war.

DOCUMENT

Jefferson Davis, Address to the Provisional Congress (1861)

Republican hopes that southern Unionism would assert itself and make none of these options necessary seemed possible in February 1861. No more states seceded. The nation waited, wondering what Virginia and the border states would do, what outgoing President Buchanan would do, and what Congress would do. Buchanan did nothing. Congress made some feeble efforts to pass compromise legislation, waiting in vain for the support of the president-elect. And as Union supporters struggled with secessionists, Virginia and the border states, like the entire nation, waited for Lincoln.

Frederick Douglass waited, too, without much hope. He wanted the "complete and universal *abolition* of the whole slave system," as well as equal suffrage and other rights for free blacks. His momentary expectation during the presidential campaign, that Lincoln and the Republicans had the will to do this, had been thoroughly dashed. In November, the voters of New York State had

The Causes of the Civil War

Using this chart as a summary, how would you explain the primary cause of the Civil War? Which four or five of the "issues and events" would you use to support your argument?

Date	Issues and Events	Deeper, Underlying Causes of Civil War
1600s–1860s	Slavery in the South	Major underlying pervasive cause
1700s–1860s	Development of two distinct socioeconomic systems and cultures	Further reinforced slavery as fundamental socioeconomic, cultural, moral issue
1787–1860s	States' rights, nullification doctrine	Ongoing political issue, less fundamental as cause
1820	Missouri Compromise (36°30′)	Background for conflict over slavery in territories
1828–1833	South Carolina tariff nullification crisis	Background for secession leadership in South Carolina
1831–1860s	Antislavery movements, southern justification	Thirty years of emotional preparation for conflict
1846–1848	War with Mexico (Wilmot Proviso, Calhoun, popular sovereignty)	Options for issue of slavery in territories

Date	Issues and Events	Specific Impact on the Road to War
1850	Compromise of 1850	Temporary and unsatisfactory "settlement" of divisive issue
1851–1854	Fugitive slaves returned and rescued in North; personal liberty laws passed in North; Harriet Beecher Stowe's *Uncle Tom's Cabin*	Heightened northern emotional reactions against the South and slavery
1852–1856	Breakdown of Whig party and national Democratic party; creation of a new party system with sectional basis	Made national politics an arena where sectional and cultural differences over slavery were fought
1854	Ostend Manifesto and other expansionist efforts in Central America	Reinforced image of Democratic party as favoring slavery
	Formation of Republican party	Major party identified as opposing the extension of slavery
	Kansas-Nebraska Act	Reopened "settled" issue of slavery in the territories
1856	"Bleeding Kansas"; Senator Sumner physically attacked in Senate	Foretaste of Civil War (200 killed, $2 million in property lost) inflamed emotions and polarized North and South
1857	Dred Scott decision; proslavery Lecompton constitution in Kansas	Made North fear a "slave power conspiracy," supported by President Buchanan and the Supreme Court
1858	Lincoln–Douglas debates in Illinois; Democrats lose 18 seats in Congress	Set stage for election of 1860
1859	John Brown's raid and reactions in North and South	Made South fear a "black Republican" plot against slavery; further polarization and irrationality
1860	Democratic party splits in half; Lincoln elected president; South Carolina secedes from Union	Final breakdown of national parties and election of "northern" president; no more compromises
1861	Six more southern states secede by February 1; Confederate Constitution adopted February 4; Lincoln inaugurated March 4; Fort Sumter attacked April 12	Civil War begins

defeated a referendum for black suffrage by more votes than a similar measure 14 years earlier. Moreover, Douglass saw northern politicians and businessmen "granting the most demoralizing concessions to the Slave Power."

In his despair, Douglass began to explore possibilities for emigration and colonization in Haiti, an idea he had long opposed. To achieve full freedom and citizenship in the United States for all blacks, he said in January 1861, he would "welcome the hardships consequent upon a dissolution of the Union." In February, Douglass said, "Let the conflict come." He opposed all compromises, hoping that with Lincoln's inauguration in March it would "be decided, and decided forever, which of the two, Freedom or Slavery, shall give law to this Republic."

Lincoln and Fort Sumter

As Douglass penned these thoughts, Lincoln began a long, slow train ride from Springfield, Illinois, to Washington, writing and rewriting his inaugural address. Lincoln's quietness in the period between his election and his inauguration led many to judge him weak and indecisive. He was not. Lincoln firmly opposed secession and any compromises with the principle of stopping the extension of slavery. He would neither conciliate secessionist southern states nor force their return.

Lincoln devoutly believed in his constitutional responsibility to uphold the laws of the land. The focus of his attention was a federal fort in the harbor of Charleston, South Carolina. Major Robert Anderson, the commander of Fort Sumter, was running out of provisions and had requested new supplies from Washington. Lincoln would enforce the laws and protect federal property at Fort Sumter.

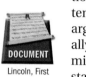

DOCUMENT

Lincoln, First Inaugural Address (1861)

As the new president delivered his inaugural address on March 4, he faced a tense and divided nation. Lincoln asserted his unequivocal intention to enforce the laws of the land, arguing that the Union was constitutionally "perpetual" and indissoluble. He reminded the nation that the "only substantial dispute" was that "one section of our country believes slavery is *right*, and ought to be extended, while the other believes it is *wrong*, and ought not to be extended." Still appealing to Unionist strength among southern moderates, Lincoln said he would make no attempts to interfere with existing slavery and would respect the law to return fugitive slaves. Nearing the end of his address, Lincoln put the burden of initiating a civil war on the "dissatisfied fellow-countrymen" who had seceded. As if foreseeing the horrible events that might follow, he closed his speech eloquently:

> I am loath to close. We are not enemies, but friends. We must not be enemies. Though passion may have strained, it must not break our bonds of affection. The mystic chords of memory, stretching from every battlefield, and patriot grave, to every living heart and hearthstone, all over this broad land, will yet swell the chorus of the Union, when again touched, as surely they will be, by the better angels of our nature.

Frederick Douglass was not impressed with Lincoln's "honied phrases" and accused him of "weakness, timidity and conciliation." Also unmoved, Robert Allston wrote his son from Charleston, where he was watching the developing crisis over Fort Sumter, that the Confederacy's "advantage" was in having a "much better president than they have."

On April 6, Lincoln notified the governor of South Carolina that he was sending "provisions only" to Fort Sumter. No effort would be made "to throw in men, arms, or ammunition" unless the fort was attacked. On April 10, Jefferson Davis directed General P. G. T. Beauregard to demand the surrender of Fort Sumter. Davis told Beauregard to reduce the fort if Major Anderson refused.

On April 12, as Lincoln's relief expedition neared Charleston, Beauregard's batteries began shelling Fort Sumter, and the Civil War began. Frederick Douglass was about to leave for Haiti when he heard the news. He immediately changed his plans: "This is no time . . . to leave the country." He announced his readiness to help end the war by aiding the Union to organize freed slaves "into a liberating army" to "make war upon . . . the savage barbarism of slavery." The Allstons had changed places, and it was Benjamin who described the events in Charleston harbor to his father. On April 14, Benjamin reported exuberantly the "glorious, and astonishing news that Sumter has fallen." With it fell America's divided house.

IMAGE

Fort Sumter— Lithograph

Conclusion

The "Irrepressible Conflict"

Lincoln had been right. The nation could no longer endure half-slave and half-free. The collision between North and South, William Seward said, was not an "accidental, unnecessary" event but an "irrepressible conflict between opposing and enduring forces." Those forces had been at work for many decades, but they developed with increasing intensity after 1848 in the conflict over the extension of slavery into the territories. Although economic, cultural, political, constitutional, and emotional forces all contributed to the developing opposition between North and South, slavery was the fundamental, enduring force that underlay all others, causing what Walt Whitman called the "red blood of civil war." Abraham Lincoln, Frederick Douglass, the Allston family, Michael Luark, and the American people all faced a radically altered national scene. All wondered whether the American democratic system would be able to withstand this challenge.

TIMELINE

1832	Nullification crisis
1835–1840	Intensification of abolitionist attacks on slavery Violent retaliatory attacks on abolitionists
1846	Wilmot Proviso
1848	Free-Soil party founded Zachary Taylor elected president
1850	Compromise of 1850, including Fugitive Slave Act
1850–1854	"Young America" movement
1851	Women's rights convention in Akron, Ohio
1852	Harriet Beecher Stowe publishes *Uncle Tom's Cabin* Franklin Pierce elected president
1854	Ostend Manifesto Kansas–Nebraska Act nullifies Missouri Compromise Republican and Know-Nothing parties formed

1855	Walt Whitman publishes *Leaves of Grass*
1855–1856	Thousands pour into Kansas, creating months of turmoil and violence
1856	John Brown's massacre in Kansas Sumner–Brooks incident in Senate James Buchanan elected president
1857	*Dred Scott* decision legalizes slavery in territories Lecompton constitution in Kansas
1858	Lincoln–Douglas debates
1859	John Brown's raid at Harpers Ferry
1860	Democratic party splits Four-party campaign Abraham Lincoln elected president
1860–1861	Seven southern states secede
1861	Confederate States of America founded Attack on Fort Sumter begins Civil War

Questions for Review and Reflection

1. What options existed for dealing with slavery in the territories, and what compromises did Congress propose? How well did they work?

2. How did political party alignments change in the 1850s and how did that affect the path to civil war?

3. Examine how southerners and northerners viewed each other, especially in Kansas. How did cultural stereotypes and emotional attitudes contribute to the outbreak of civil war?

4. Can you explain four basic, underlying causes of the American Civil War? Which do you think was most significant, and what specific events would you use to support your choice?

5. To what extent was the American democratic political system flexible enough to handle the issues of the 1850s? Could the Civil War have been avoided, or was it inevitable?

Recommended Reading

Recommended Readings are posted on the Web site for this textbook. Visit www.ablongman.com/nash

Fiction and Film

The most important novel about slavery during the antebellum era was Harriet Beecher Stowe's *Uncle Tom's Cabin* (1852). Written in serial form, each episode stopped at a nail-biting moment and aroused the conscience of the North. Walt Whitman's collection of poems, *Leaves of Grass* (1855), celebrates not only the poet's own ego but also the common people and democratic American values

in a decade that sorely tested those values. Russell Banks's *Cloudsplitter* (1998) is a long but riveting novel about John Brown and his activities during the 1850s, told through the eyes of one of his sons. *The Bondswoman's Daughter* by Hannah Crafts (2002), recently discovered by Henry Louis Gates, Jr., is a captivating story of a runaway slave woman in the 1850s. Toni Morrison's award-winning novel

Beloved (1988), later made into a feature film, tells the story, based on a true event in 1856, of an escaped slave mother who killed her child as bounty hunters were about to seize her family and return them to slavery. Part I of Ken Burns's PBS film series

The Civil War (1989) sets the slavery and 1850s background for his haunting documentary portrayal of the Civil War. Another fine video is *John Brown's Holy War* (1999) from the PBS series *The American Experience.*

Discovering U.S. History Online

Compromise of 1850

www.loc.gov/exhibits/treasures/trm043.html

This exhibit shows digitized images of compromise documents by John C. Calhoun and Daniel Webster's notes for introductory remarks.

Uncle Tom's Cabin and American Culture

www.iath.virginia.edu/utc/sitemap.html

Along with searchable access to the text of *Uncle Tom's Cabin,* this site contains an archive of primary material (texts, images, songs, 3-D objects, film clips, and so on), an interactive timeline, and virtual exhibits designed for exploring and understanding the primary material.

Bleeding Kansas

www.ukans.edu/carrie/kancoll/galbks.htm

Contemporary and later accounts of America's rehearsal for the Civil War make up this excellent University of Kansas site, filled with primary documents from the mid-1850s.

Africans in America, Judgment Day, 1831–1865

www.pbs.org/wgbh/aia/part4/index.html

A large collection of people and events, historical documents, and modern voices on antebellum slavery, abolitionism, slavery in the territories, John Brown's raid, and the Civil War.

Secession Era Editorials Project

http://history.furman.edu/~benson/docs/index.htm

This site presents a Furman University digital collection of northern and southern newspaper editorials on the Kansas–Nebraska Act, the *Dred Scott* case, John Brown's raid, and other issues form the 1850s. Excellent links and context.

The Dred Scott Case

www.library.wustl.edu/vlib/dredscott/

This site presents digital images and transcriptions of 85 original documents and a timeline of events surrounding the case.

John Brown's Holy War

www.pbs.org/wgbh/amex/brown

This companion Web site to the video contains primary source and biographical materials, a timeline, profiles of related people and events, information on the song "John Brown's Body," and a bibliography.

Crisis at Fort Sumter

www.tulane.edu/~latner/CrisisMain.html

This site presents "an interactive historical simulation and decision making program. Using text, images, and sound, it reconstructs the dilemmas of policy formation and decision making in the period between Abraham Lincoln's election in November 1860 and the battle of Fort Sumter in April 1861."

CHAPTER 15

The Union Severed

Images of a safe and happy homecoming fill the dreams of Union soldiers sleeping in their camp in this painting *The Soldier's Dream* (c. 1865) by an unknown artist. Soldiers—both Union and Confederate—often expressed their longing in their letters home. J. K. Street of the 9th Texas Infantry wrote to his wife: "I think of you so much and it is great pleasure to me to think of you and the many pleasant associations of home and it is endearments . . . I think of you so much thro' the day that I dream of you at night." In his letter of July 14, 1861—his last letter—to his wife Sarah, Major Sullivan Ballou of the 2nd Rhode Island Volunteers wrote: "The memories of the blissful moments I have spent with you come creeping over me . . . how hard it is for me to give them up and burn to ashes the hopes of future years when . . . we might still have lived and loved together." *(© Atwater Kent Museum of Philadelphia, Courtesy of Historical Society of Pennsylvania Collection/Bridgeman Art Library)*

American Stories

A War That Touched Lives

In his remarks to Congress in 1862, Abraham Lincoln reminded congressmen that "We cannot escape history. We of this Congress and this administration will be remembered in spite of ourselves. No personal significance, or insignificance, can spare . . . us. The fiery trial through which we pass, will light us down, in honor or dishonor, to the latest generation." Lincoln's conviction that Americans would long remember him and other major actors of the Civil War was correct. Jefferson Davis, Robert E. Lee, Ulysses S. Grant—these are the men whose characters, actions, and decisions have been the subject of continuing discussion and analysis, whose statues and memorials dot the American countryside and grace urban squares. Whether seen as heroes or villains, great men have dominated the story of the Civil War.

Yet from the earliest days, the war touched the lives of even the most uncelebrated Americans. From Indianapolis, 20-year-old Arthur Carpenter wrote to his parents in Massachusetts begging for permission to enlist in the volunteer army: "I have always longed for the time to come when I could enter the army and be a military man, and when this war broke out, I thought the time had come, but you would not permit me to enter the service . . . now I make one more appeal to you." The pleas worked, and Carpenter enlisted, spending most of the war fighting in Kentucky and Tennessee.

In that same year, in Tennessee, George and Ethie Eagleton faced anguishing decisions. Though not an abolitionist, George, a 30-year-old Presbyterian preacher, was unsympathetic to slavery and opposed to secession. But when his native state left the Union, George felt compelled to follow and enlisted in the 44th Tennessee Infantry. Ethie, his 26-year-old wife, despaired over the war, George's decision, and her own forlorn situation.

> Mr. Eagleton's school dismissed—and what for? O my God, must I write it? He has enlisted in the service of his country—to war—the most unrighteous war that ever was brought on any nation that ever lived. Pres. Lincoln has done what no other Pres. ever dared to do—he has divided these once peaceful and happy United States. And Oh! the dreadful dark cloud that is now hanging over our country—'tis enough to sicken the heart of any one. . . . Mr. E. is gone. . . . What will become of me, left here without a home and relatives, a babe just nine months old and no George.

Both Carpenter and the Eagletons survived the war, but the conflict transformed each of their lives. Carpenter had difficulty settling down. Filled with bitter memories of the war years in Tennessee, the Eagletons moved to Arkansas. Ordinary people such as Carpenter and the Eagletons are historically anonymous. Yet their actions on the battlefield and behind the lines helped to shape the course of events, as their leaders realized, even if today we tend to remember only the famous and influential.

For thousands of Americans, from Lincoln and Davis to Carpenter and the Eagletons, war was both a profoundly personal and a major national event. Its impact reached far beyond the four years of hostilities. The war that was fought to conserve two political, social, and economic visions ended by changing familiar ways of life in both North and South. War was a transforming force, both destructive and creative in its effect on the structure and social dynamics of society and on the lives of ordinary people. This theme underlies this chapter's analysis of the war's three stages: the initial months of preparation, the years of military stalemate between 1861 and 1865, and, finally, resolution.

ORGANIZING FOR WAR

The Confederate bombardment of Fort Sumter on April 12, 1861, and the surrender of Union troops the

Confederate Flag over Fort Sumter

next day ended the uncertainty of the secession winter. The North's response to Fort Sumter was a virtual declaration of war as President Lincoln called for state militia volunteers to crush southern "insurrection." His action pushed several slave states (Virginia, North Carolina, Tennessee, and Arkansas) off the fence and into the southern camp. Other states (Maryland, Kentucky, and Missouri) agonizingly debated which way to go. The "War Between the States" was now a reality.

Many Americans were unenthusiastic about the course of events. Southerners like George Eagleton reluctantly followed Tennessee out of the Union. When he enlisted, he complained of the "disgraceful cowardice of many who were last winter for secession and war . . . but are now refusing self and means for the prosecution of war." Robert E. Lee of Virginia also hesitated but finally decided that he could not "raise [a] hand against . . . relatives . . . children . . . home." Whites living in the southern uplands (where blacks were few and slaveholders were heartily disliked), yeoman farmers in the Deep South (who owned no slaves), and many border state residents were dismayed at secession and war. Many would eventually join the Union forces.

In the North, large numbers had supported neither the Republican party nor Lincoln. Irish immigrants fearing the competition of free black labor and southerners now living in Illinois, Indiana, and Ohio harbored misgivings. Indeed, northern Democrats at first blamed Lincoln and the Republicans almost as much as southern secessionists for the nation's crisis.

Nevertheless, the days following Fort Sumter and Lincoln's call for troops saw an outpouring of support on both sides, fueled in part by relief at decisive action, in part by patriotism and love of adventure, and in part by unemployment. Northern blacks and even some southern freedpeople proclaimed themselves "ready to go forth and do battle," while whites like Carpenter enthusiastically flocked to enlist. In some places, workers were so eager to join up that trade unions collapsed. Sisters, wives, and mothers set to work making uniforms. A New Yorker, Jane Woolsey, described the drama of those early days "of terrible excitement":

Outside the parlor windows the city is gay and brilliant with excited crowds, the incessant movement and music of marching regiments and all the thousands of flags, big and little, which suddenly came fluttering out of every window and door. . . . In our little circle of friends, one mother has just sent away an idolized son; another, two; another, four. . . . One sweet young wife is packing a regulation valise for her husband today, and doesn't let him see her cry.

The war fever produced so many volunteers that neither northern nor southern officials could handle the throng. Northern authorities turned aside offers from blacks to serve. Both sides sent thousands of white would-be soldiers home. The conviction that the conflict would rapidly come to a glorious conclusion fueled the eagerness to enlist. "We really did not think that there was going to be an actual war," remembered Mary Ward, a young Georgia woman. "We had an idea that when our soldiers got upon the ground and showed, unmistakably that they were really ready and willing to fight . . . the whole trouble would be declared at an end." Lincoln's call for 75,000 state militiamen for only 90 days of service, and a similar enlistment term for Confederate soldiers, supported the notion that the war would be short.

The Balance of Resources

The Civil War was one of several military conflicts during the nineteenth century that sought national independence. In Europe, Italian and German patriots struggled to create new nations out of individual states. Unlike their European counterparts, however, southern nationalists proclaimed their independence by withdrawing from an already unified state. Likening their struggle to that of the Revolutionary generation that had broken away from Great Britain's tyranny, southerners argued that they were "now enlisted in The Holy Cause of Liberty and Independence." While they legitimized secession by appealing to freedom, however, southerners were also preserving freedom's antithesis, slavery.

The outcome of the southern bid for autonomy was much in doubt. Although statistics of population and industrial development suggested a northern victory, Great Britain with similar advantages in 1775 had lost that war. Many northern assets would become effective only with time.

The North's white population greatly exceeded the South's, giving the appearance of a military advantage. Yet early in the war, the armies were more evenly matched. Almost 187,000 Union troops bore arms in July 1861, while just over 112,000 men marched under Confederate colors. Southerners believed that their army would prove to be superior fighters. Many northerners feared so, too. And slaves

Railroads in 1860

This map shows the railroads at the beginning of the Civil War. What does it reveal about the differences in the transportation systems in the North and the South? In what ways was the war effort of each side helped or hindered by the rail system? In what ways did the configuration of southern transportation benefit the South?

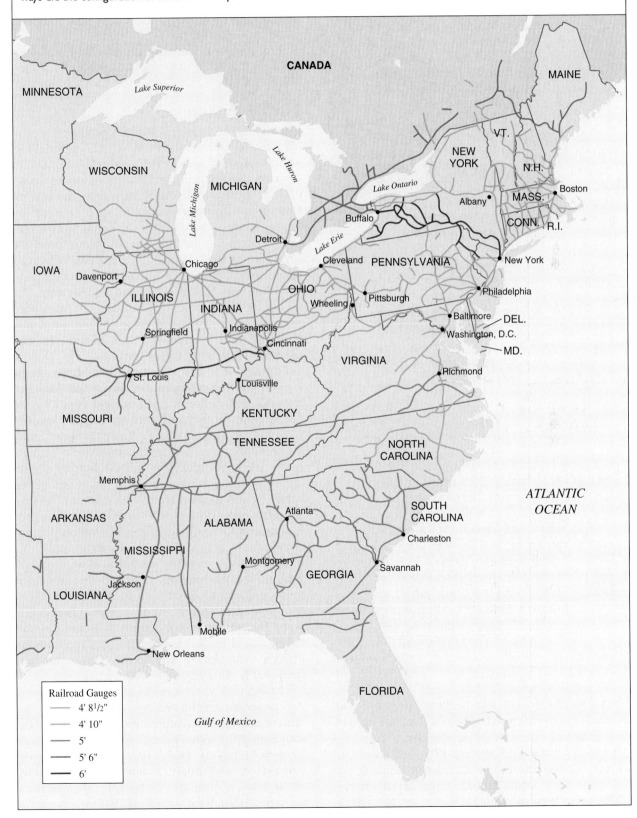

Railroad Gauges
— 4' 8¹/₂"
— 4' 10"
— 5'
— 5' 6"
— 6'

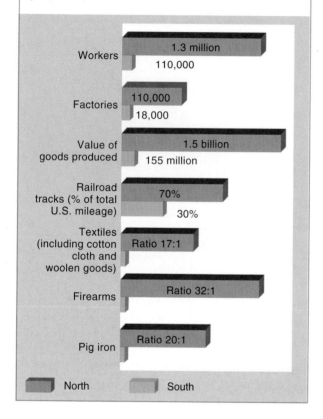

Resources for War: North Versus South

This chart shows the long-range advantages the North enjoyed in the war, but the length and destruction of the conflict suggest that the North was not able to capitalize on its strengths effectively to bring the war to a quick end.

	North	South
Workers	1.3 million	110,000
Factories	110,000	18,000
Value of goods produced	1.5 billion	155 million
Railroad tracks (% of total U.S. mileage)	70%	30%
Textiles (including cotton cloth and woolen goods)	Ratio 17:1	
Firearms	Ratio 32:1	
Pig iron	Ratio 20:1	

could carry on vital work behind the lines, freeing most adult white males to serve the Confederacy.

The Union also enjoyed impressive economic advantages. In the North, 1 million workers in 110,000 manufacturing concerns produced goods valued at $1.5 billion annually, while 110,000 southern workers in 18,000 manufacturing concerns produced goods valued at only $155 million a year. But northern industrial resources had to be mobilized. That would take time, especially because the government did not intend to direct production. A depleted northern treasury made the government's first task the raising of funds to pay for military necessities.

Workers in D.C. During the Civil War

The South depended on imported northern and European manufactured goods. If Lincoln cut off that trade, the South would have to create its industry almost from scratch. Its railroad system was organized to move cotton, not armies and supplies. Yet the agricultural South did have important resources of food, draft animals, and, of course, cotton, which southerners believed would secure British and French support. By waging a defensive war, the South could tap regional loyalty and enjoy protected lines. Because much of the South raised cotton and tobacco rather than food crops, Union armies could not live off the land, and extended supply lines were always vulnerable. The Union had to conquer and occupy; the South merely had to survive until its enemy gave up.

The Border States

Uncertainty and divided loyalties produced indecision in the border states. When the seven Deep South states seceded in 1860 and 1861, all the border states except Unionist Delaware adopted a wait-and-see attitude. Their decisions were critically important to both North and South.

The states of the Upper South could provide natural borders for the Confederacy along the Ohio River, access to its river traffic, and vital resources, wealth, and population. The major railroad link to the West ran through Maryland and western Virginia. Virginia boasted the South's largest ironworks, and Tennessee provided its principal source of grain. Missouri opened the road to the West and controlled Mississippi River traffic.

For the North, every border state remaining loyal was a psychological triumph. Nor was the North unaware of the economic and strategic advantages of keeping the border states with the Union. However, Lincoln's call for troops precipitated the secession of Virginia, Arkansas, Tennessee, and North Carolina between April 17 and May 20, 1861. Maryland, precariously balanced between the pro-Confederate southern and Eastern Shore counties and Unionist western and northern areas, and with pro-southern enthusiasts abounding in Baltimore, vividly demonstrated the significance of border state loyalty.

On April 19, the 6th Massachusetts Regiment, heading for Washington, marched through Baltimore and was attacked by a mob of some 10,000 southern sympathizers, some carrying Confederate flags. The bloody confrontation and confusion allowed would-be secessionists to burn the railroad bridges to the north and south. Washington was temporarily cut off from the rest of the Union.

Lincoln took stern measures to secure Maryland. The president agreed temporarily to route troops around Baltimore. In return, the governor called the state legislature into session at Frederick in Unionist western Maryland. This action and Lincoln's swift violation of civil liberties dampened secessionist enthusiasm. Hundreds of southern sympathizers, including 19 state legislators and Baltimore's mayor,

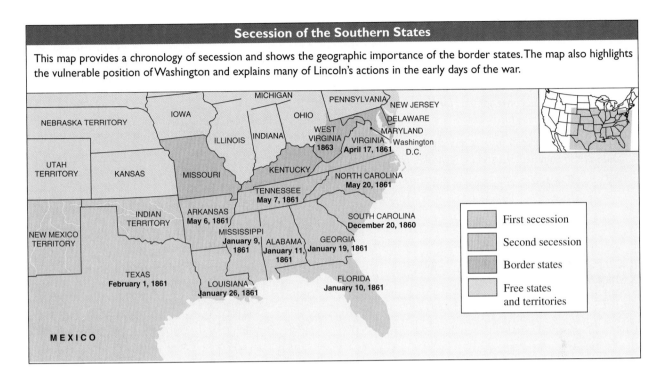

Secession of the Southern States

This map provides a chronology of secession and shows the geographic importance of the border states. The map also highlights the vulnerable position of Washington and explains many of Lincoln's actions in the early days of the war.

were imprisoned without trial. Although Chief Justice Roger B. Taney challenged the president's action and issued a writ of habeas corpus for the release of a southern supporter, Lincoln ignored him. A month later, Taney ruled in *Ex Parte Merryman* that if the public's safety was endangered, only Congress could suspend habeas corpus. By then, Lincoln had secured Maryland.

Although Lincoln's quick and harsh response ensured Maryland's loyalty, he was more cautious elsewhere. Above all, he had to deal with slavery prudently, for hasty action would push border states into the Confederacy. Thus, when General John C. Frémont issued an unauthorized declaration of emancipation in Missouri in August 1861, Lincoln revoked the order and recalled him. The president expected a chain reaction if certain key states seceded. After complex maneuvering, Kentucky and Missouri, like Maryland, remained in the Union.

Challenges of War

The tense weeks after Fort Sumter spilled over with unexpected challenges. Neither side could handle the floods of volunteers. Both faced enormous organizational problems as they readied for war. In the South, a nation–state had to be created and its apparatus set in motion. Everything from a constitution and government departments to a flag and postage stamps had to be devised. As one onlooker observed, "The whole country was new. Everything was to be done—and to be made."

In February 1861, the original seceding states sent delegates to Montgomery, Alabama, to work on a provisional framework and to select a provisional president and vice president. The delegates swiftly wrote a constitution resembling the federal

Owe Ever Pay Never This image, printed on an envelope, shows a design for a Confederate 50-cent piece. Who do you think the man on the right is? Who is the man on the left and what is he pointing at the man wearing the top hat? In the background, you can see a group of men hard at work and standing before them a man wielding a whip. What is the overall message of this design? *(Collection of the New-York Historical Society, (PR-022-3-91-38)*

How Others See Us

This English journal became famous for its cartoons. Here Lincoln appears without his beard.

- *What does this cartoon suggest about the ways in which some British commentators viewed Lincoln's racial views?*

- *How might an American respond to this view?*

The American Difficulty President Abe: "What a nice White House this would be, if it were not for the blacks!" (Source: *Punch Cartoon Library*).

DOCUMENT

Confederate Constitution (March 11, 1861)

constitution of 1787 except in its emphasis on the "sovereign and independent character" of the states and its explicit recognition of slavery. The provisional president, Jefferson Davis of Mississippi, tried to assemble a geographically and politically balanced cabinet of moderates. His cabinet was balanced but contained few of his friends and, more serious, few men of political stature. As time passed, it turned out to be unstable as well.

Davis's cabinet appointees faced the formidable challenge of creating government departments from scratch. They had to hire employees and initiate administrative procedures with woefully inadequate resources. The president's office was in a hotel parlor. The Confederate Treasury Department was merely a room in an Alabama bank "without furniture of any kind; empty . . . of desks, tables, chairs or other appliances for the conduct of business." Treasury Secretary Christopher G. Memminger bought furniture with his own money; operations lurched forward in fits and starts. In those early days, when an army captain came to the treasury with a warrant from Davis for blankets, he found only one clerk. After reading the warrant, the clerk offered the captain a few dollars of his own, explaining, "This, Captain, is all the money that I will certify as being in the Confederate Treasury at this moment." Other departments faced similar difficulties.

Despite such challenges, the new Confederate government could count on widespread civilian enthusiasm and a growing sense of nationalism. Ordinary people spoke proudly of the South as "our nation" and referred to themselves as the "southern people." Georgia's governor insisted that "poor and rich, have a common interest, a common destiny." Southern Protestant ministers encouraged a sense of collective identity and reminded southerners that they were God's chosen people. The conflict was a sacred one.

Unlike Davis, Lincoln did not have to establish a postal system or decide the status of laws passed before 1861. But he too faced organizational problems. Military officers and government clerks daily left the capital for the South. The treasury was empty. The Republicans had won their first presidential election, and floods of office seekers thronged the White House looking for rewards.

Nor was it easy for Lincoln, who knew few of the "prominent men of the day," to select a cabinet. Finally, he appointed important Republicans from different factions of the party to cabinet posts whether they agreed with him or not. Most were almost strangers. Several scorned him as a bumbling backwoods politician. Treasury Secretary Salmon P. Chase actually hoped to replace Lincoln as president in four years' time. Soon after the inauguration, Secretary of State William Seward sent Lincoln a memo condescendingly offering to oversee the formulation of presidential policy.

Lincoln and His Cabinet

Lincoln and Davis

A number of Lincoln's early actions illustrated his leadership skills. As his Illinois law partner, William Herndon, pointed out, Lincoln's "mind was tough—solid—knotty—gnarly, more or less like his body." In his reply to Seward's memo, the president firmly indicated that he intended to run his own administration. After Sumter, he swiftly called up the state militias, expanded the navy, and suspended habeas corpus. He ordered a naval blockade of the South and approved the expenditure of funds for military purposes, all without congressional sanction, because Congress was not in session. As Lincoln told legislators later, "The dogmas of the quiet past are inadequate to the stormy present. . . . As our case is new, so must we think anew, and act anew . . . and then we shall save our country." This willingness to "think anew" was a valuable personal asset, even though some regarded the expansion of presidential power as despotic.

By coincidence, Lincoln and his rival, Jefferson Davis, were born only 100 miles apart in Kentucky. However, the course of their lives diverged radically. Lincoln's father had migrated north and eked out a simple existence as a farmer in Indiana and Illinois. Lincoln's formal education was rudimentary; he was

largely self-taught. Davis's family had moved south to Mississippi and become cotton planters. Davis grew up in comfortable circumstances, went to Transylvania University and West Point, and

Jefferson Davis

fought in the Mexican-American War before his election to the U.S. Senate. His social, political, and economic prominence led to his appointment as secretary of war under Franklin Pierce (1853–1857). Tall, distinguished-looking, and very rich, he appeared every inch the aristocratic southerner.

Although Davis was not eager to accept the presidency, he loyally responded to the call of the provisional congress in 1861 and worked tirelessly until the war's end. His wife, Varina, observed that "the President hardly takes time to eat his meals and works late at night." Some contemporaries suggested that Davis's inability to let subordinates handle details explained this schedule. Others observed that he was sickly, reserved, humorless, too sensitive to criticism, and hard to get along with. But, like Lincoln, Davis found it necessary to "think anew." He reassured southerners in his inaugural address that his aims were conservative, "to preserve the Government of our fathers in spirit." Yet under the pressure of events, he moved toward creating a new kind of South.

CLASHING ON THE BATTLEFIELD, 1861–1862

The Civil War was the most brutal and destructive conflict in American history. Much of the bloodshed resulted from changing military technology coupled with inadequate communications. By 1861, the range of rifles had increased from 100 to 500 yards, in part owing to the new French minié bullet, which traveled with tremendous velocity and accuracy. The greater reach of the new rifles meant that it was no longer possible to position

Union Artillery at Yorktown

the artillery close enough to enemy lines to support an infantry charge. Therefore, during the Civil War, attacking infantry soldiers faced a final, often fatal, dash of 500 yards in the face of deadly enemy fire.

As it became clear that infantry charges resulted in horrible carnage, military leaders increasingly valued the importance of the strong defensive position. Although Confederate soldiers criticized General Lee as "King of Spades" when he first ordered them to construct earthworks, the epithet evolved into one of affection as it became obvious that earthworks saved lives. Union commanders followed suit. By the end of

1862, both armies dug defensive earthworks and trenches whenever they interrupted their march.

War in the East

The war's brutal character only gradually revealed itself. The Union's commanding general, 70-year-old Winfield Scott, at first pressed for a cautious, long-term strategy, the Anaconda Plan. Scott proposed weakening the South gradually through blockades on land and sea until the northern army was strong enough for the kill. The public, however, hungered for quick victory. So did Lincoln: He knew that the longer the war lasted, the more embittered the South and the North would both become, making reunion ever more difficult. So 35,000 partially trained men led by General Irwin McDowell left Washington in sweltering July weather, heading for Richmond.

The Civil War
Part I:
1861–1862

On July 21, 1861, only 25 miles from the capital at Manassas Creek (also called Bull Run), inexperienced northern troops confronted 25,000 raw Confederate soldiers commanded by Brigadier General

P. G. T. Beauregard, a West Point classmate of McDowell's. Although sightseers, journalists, and politicians gaily accompanied the Union troops, Bull Run was no picnic. The battle was inconclusive until the arrival of 2,300 fresh Confederate troops, brought by trains, decided the day. Terrified and bewildered Union soldiers and sightseers fled toward Washington. Defeated though the Union forces were, inexperienced Confederate troops failed to turn the rout into a quick, decisive victory. As General Joseph E. Johnston pointed out, his men were disorganized, confused by victory, and insufficiently supplied with food to chase the Union army back toward Washington.

In many ways, the Battle of Bull Run was prophetic. Victory would be neither quick nor easy. Both armies were unprofessional. Both sides faced problems with short-term enlistments and with the logistical problems involved in moving and supplying the largest American armies ever put in the field.

South Carolinian Robert Allston viewed the battlefield at Bull Run and decided it had been a "glorious tho bloody" day. For the Union, the loss was sobering. Lincoln began his search for a winning

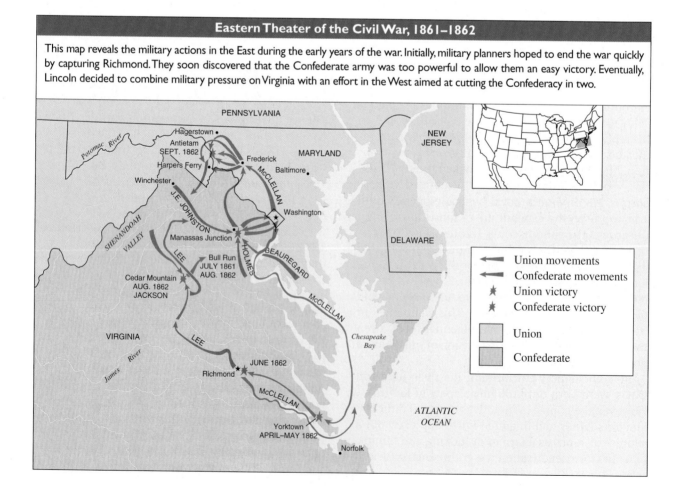

Eastern Theater of the Civil War, 1861–1862

This map reveals the military actions in the East during the early years of the war. Initially, military planners hoped to end the war quickly by capturing Richmond. They soon discovered that the Confederate army was too powerful to allow them an easy victory. Eventually, Lincoln decided to combine military pressure on Virginia with an effort in the West aimed at cutting the Confederacy in two.

DOCUMENT

George
McClellan to
Abraham
Lincoln (July 7,
1862)

commander by replacing McDowell with 34-year-old General George McClellan. Formerly an army engineer, McClellan began the process of transforming the Army of the Potomac into a fighting force. Short-term militias went home. In the fall of 1861, McClellan became general in chief of the Union armies.

McClellan had considerable organizational ability but no desire to be a daring battlefield leader. Convinced that the North must combine military victory with persuading the South to rejoin the Union, he sought to avoid embittering loss of life and property—to win "by maneuvering rather than fighting."

In March 1862, pushed by an impatient Lincoln, McClellan finally led his army of 130,000 toward Richmond, now the Confederate capital.

IMAGE

Battle of
Antietam

But just as it seemed that victory was within grasp, Lee drove the Union forces back. The Peninsula campaign was abandoned. For the Union, the campaign was a frustrating failure. For Lee, the success in repelling the invasion was one step in the process that was making him and the Army of Northern Virginia into a symbol of the spirit of the new nation.

Other Union defeats followed in 1862 as commanders came and went. In September, the South took

the offensive with a bold invasion of Maryland. But after a costly defeat at Antietam, in which more than 5,000 soldiers were slaughtered and another 17,000 wounded on the grisliest day of the war, Lee withdrew to Virginia. The war in the East was stalemated.

War in the West

The early struggle in the East focused on Richmond, the Confederacy's capital and one of the South's most important railroad, industrial, and munitions centers. But the East was only one of three theaters. Between the Appalachians and the Mississippi lay the western theater. The Mississippi River, with its vital river trade and its great port, New Orleans, was a major strategic objective. Here both George Eagleton and Arthur Carpenter served. Beyond lay the trans-Mississippi West—Louisiana, Arkansas, Missouri, Texas, and the Great Plains—where Native American tribes joined the conflict on both sides.

Union objectives in the West were twofold. The army sought to dominate Kentucky and eastern Tennessee, the avenues to the South and West, and to win control of the Mississippi in order to split the South in two.

In the western theater, Ulysses S. Grant rose to prominence. His modest military credentials included education at West Point, service in the Mexican-American War, and an undistinguished stint in the peacetime army. After his resignation, he went bankrupt. Shortly after Fort Sumter, Grant enlisted as a colonel in an Illinois militia regiment. Within two months, he was a brigadier general. He proved to be a military genius, able to see beyond individual battles to larger goals. In 1862, he realized that the Tennessee and Cumberland rivers offered pathways for the successful invasion of Tennessee. A premature Confederate invasion of Kentucky allowed Grant to bring his forces into that state without arousing sharp local opposition. Assisted by gunboats, Grant was largely responsible for the capture of Fort Henry and Fort Donelson, key points on the rivers, in February 1862. His successes there raised fears among Confederate leaders that southern mountaineers, loyal to the Union, would rush to Grant's support.

Despite Grant's grasp of strategy, his army was nearly destroyed by a surprise Confederate attack at Shiloh Church in Tennessee. The North won, but at enormous cost. In that two-day engagement, the Union suffered more than 13,000 casualties, while 10,000 Confederates lay dead or wounded. More American men fell in this single battle than in the American Revolution, the War of 1812, and the Mexican-American War combined. Because neither

A Toll of Death and Destruction   This dying horse, stripped of saddle and bridle, was the mount of a Confederate officer killed during the battle of Antietam. The stark character of the picture reveals the devastating nature of the Civil War battlefield. *(Library of Congress [LC-B8184-558])*

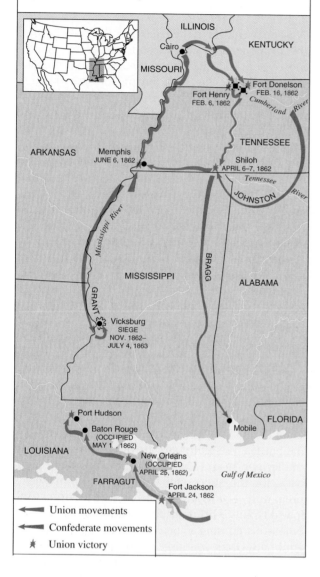

Trans-Mississippi Campaign of the Civil War

The military movements in the trans-Mississippi West appear here. Union forces operating in the Mississippi valley were attempting to separate Texas, Arkansas, and Louisiana from other southern states as part of an attempt to squeeze the Confederacy.

ILLINOIS
Cairo
KENTUCKY
MISSOURI
Fort Donelson
FEB. 16, 1862
Fort Henry
FEB. 6, 1862
Cumberland River
TENNESSEE
ARKANSAS
Memphis
JUNE 6, 1862
Shiloh
APRIL 6–7, 1862
Tennessee River
JOHNSTON
Mississippi River
MISSISSIPPI
BRAGG
ALABAMA
GRANT
Vicksburg
SIEGE
NOV. 1862–
JULY 4, 1863
Port Hudson
FLORIDA
Baton Rouge
(OCCUPIED
MAY 1 , 1862)
Mobile
LOUISIANA
New Orleans
(OCCUPIED
APRIL 25, 1862)
Gulf of Mexico
FARRAGUT
Fort Jackson
APRIL 24, 1862

◄━━ Union movements
◄━ Confederate movements
★ Union victory

army offered sufficient care on the battlefield, untreated wounds caused many of the deaths. A day after the battle ended, nine-tenths of the wounded still lay in the rain, many dying of exposure or drowning. Those who survived the downpour had infected wounds by the time they received medical attention.

Though more successful than efforts in the East, such devastating Union campaigns failed to bring decisive results. Western plans were never coordinated with eastern military activities. Victories there did not force the South to its knees.

The war in the trans-Mississippi West was a sporadic, far-flung struggle. California was the prize that lured both armies into the Southwest. Confederate Texan troops held Albuquerque and Santa Fe briefly in 1862, but a mixed force, including volunteer soldiers from the Colorado mining fields and Mexican Americans, drove them out. A Union force recruited in California arrived after the Confederates were gone. It spent the remainder of the Civil War years fighting the Apache and the Navajo and with brutal competence crushed both Native American nations.

Farther east was another prize, the Missouri River, which flowed into the Mississippi River, bordered Illinois, and affected military campaigns in Kentucky and Tennessee. Initially, Confederate troops were successful here, as they had been in New Mexico. But in March 1862, at Pea Ridge in northern Arkansas, Union forces whipped a Confederate army that included a brigade of Native Americans from the Five Civilized Nations. Missouri entered the Union camp for the first time in the war, but fierce guerrilla warfare continued.

Naval Warfare

At the beginning of the war, Lincoln decided to strangle the South with a naval blockade. But success was elusive. In 1861, the navy intercepted only about one blockade runner in ten and in 1862, one in eight.

More successful were operations to gain footholds along the southern coast. In November 1861, a Union expedition took Port Royal Sound, where it freed the first slaves, and the nearby South Carolina sea islands. By gaining these and other important coastal points, the navy increased the possibility of an effective blockade. The Union's major naval triumph in the early war years was the capture of the South's biggest port, New Orleans, in 1862. The success of this amphibious effort stimulated other joint attempts to cut the South in two.

The Confederates, recognizing that they could not match the Union fleet, concentrated on developing new weapons such as torpedoes and ironclad vessels. The *Merrimac* was one key to southern naval strategy. Originally a U.S. warship that had sunk as the federal navy hurriedly abandoned the Norfolk Navy Yard early in the war, the Confederates raised the vessel and covered it with heavy iron armor. Rechristened the *Virginia*, the ship steamed out of Norfolk in March 1862, heading directly for the Union ships blocking the harbor. Using its 1,500-pound ram and guns, the *Virginia* drove one-third of the vessels aground and destroyed the squadron's largest ships. But the victory was short-lived. The next day, the *Virginia* confronted the *Monitor,* a newly completed Union iron vessel. They dueled inconclusively, and the *Virginia* withdrew. It was burned during the evacuation of Norfolk that May. Southern attempts to buy ironclad ships abroad faded and, with them, southern hopes of escaping the northern noose.

Still, Confederate attacks on northern commerce brought some success. Southern raiders, many of them built in Britain, wreaked havoc on northern shipping. In its two-year career, the *Alabama* destroyed 69 Union merchant vessels valued at more than $6 million. But such blows did not seriously damage the North's war effort.

Thus the first two years brought victories to both sides, but the war remained deadlocked. The South was far from defeated; the North was equally far from giving up. Costs in manpower and supplies far exceeded what either side had expected.

Cotton Diplomacy

Both sides in the Civil War realized the critical importance of European attitudes to the outcome of the struggle. Diplomatic recognition of the Confederacy would legitimize the new nation in the eyes of the world. Furthermore, just as French and Dutch aid had helped the American colonies win their independence, European loans and assistance might bring the South victory. But if the European nations refused to recognize the South, the fiction of the Union was kept alive, undermining Confederate chances for long-term survival. The European powers, of course, consulted their own national interests. Neither England nor France, the two most important nations, wished to back the losing side. Nor did they wish to upset Europe's delicate balance of power by hasty intervention in American affairs. One by one, therefore, the European states declared a policy of neutrality.

Southerners were sure that cotton would be their trump card. English and French textile mills needed cotton, and southerners believed that their owners would eventually force government recognition of the Confederacy and an end to the North's blockade. But a glut of cotton in 1860 and 1861 left foreign mill owners oversupplied. As stockpiles dwindled, European industrialists found cotton in India and Egypt. The conviction that cotton was "the king who can shake the jewels in the crown of Queen Victoria" proved false.

Union secretary of state Seward sought above all else to prevent diplomatic recognition of the Confederacy. The North had its own economic ties with Europe, so the Union was not as disadvantaged as

southerners thought. Seward daringly threatened Great Britain with war if it interfered in what he insisted was an internal matter. Some called his boldness reckless, even mad. Nevertheless, his policy succeeded. Even though England allowed the construction of Confederate raiders in its ports, it did not intervene in American affairs in 1861 or 1862. Nor did the other European powers. Unless the military situation changed dramatically, the Europeans were willing to sit on the sidelines.

Common Problems, Novel Solutions

As the conflict dragged on into 1863, unanticipated problems appeared in both the Union and the Confederacy, and leaders devised novel approaches to solve them. War acted as a catalyst for changes that no one could have imagined in the heady spring days of 1861.

The problem of fighting a long war was partly monetary. Both treasuries had been empty initially, and the war proved extraordinarily expensive. Neither side considered trying to finance the war by imposing direct taxes. Such an approach violated custom and risked alienating support. Nevertheless, each side was so starved for funds that it initiated taxation on a small scale. Ultimately, taxes financed 21 percent of the North's war expenses (but only 1 percent of southern expenses). Both treasuries also tried borrowing. Northerners bought more than $2 billion worth of bonds, but southerners proved reluctant to buy their government's bonds.

As in the American Revolution, the unwelcome solution was to print paper money. In August 1861, the Confederacy put into circulation $100 million in crudely engraved bills. Millions more followed the next year. Five months later, the Union issued $150 million in paper money, soon nicknamed "greenbacks" because of their color. Although financing the war with paper money was unexpected, the resulting inflation was not. Inflation was particularly troublesome in the Confederacy, but a "modest" 80 percent increase in food prices brought southern city families near starvation and contributed to urban unhappiness during the war.

Both sides confronted similar manpower problems as initial enthusiasm for the war evaporated. Soldiering, it turned out, was nothing like the militia parades and outings familiar to most American males. Young men were shocked at the deadly diseases that accompanied the army and were unprepared for the boredom of camp life. As one North Carolina soldier explained, "If anyone wishes to become used to the crosses and trials of

AUDIO

When This Cruel
War Is Over

A Recruiting Poster How many different strategies does this poster use to persuade men to join the 36th Regiment of New York Volunteers? The central picture shows a soldier on the right who calls out, "Americans! Your country calls. Your cherished institutions and your Noble Flag are threatened by rebels and traitors." The man on the left replies, "We will come. We know our country's needs and will respond to the call." Who does the female figure in the center represent? (Collection of the New-York Historical Society [PR-055-3-149])

this life, let him enter camp life." None were prepared for the vast and impersonal destruction of the battlefield, which mocked values such as courage and honor. It was with anguish that Robert Carter of Massachusetts saw bodies tossed into trenches "with not a prayer, eulogy or tear to distinguish them from so many animals." Many in the service longed to go home. The swarm of volunteers disappeared. Rather than fill their military quotas from within, rich northern communities began offering bounties of $800 to $1,000 to outsiders who would join up.

Arthur Carpenter's letters give a good picture of life in the ranks and his growing disillusionment with the war. As Carpenter's regiment moved into Kentucky and Tennessee in the winter of 1862, his enthusiasm for army life evaporated. "Soldiering in Kentucky and Tennessee," he complained, "is not so pretty as it was in Indianapolis. . . . We have been half starved, half frozen, and half drowned. The mud in Kentucky is awful." Soldiering often meant marching over rutted roads carrying 50 or 60 pounds of equipment with insufficient food, water, or supplies. One blanket was not enough in the winter. In the summer, stifling woollen uniforms attracted lice and other vermin. Poor food, bugs, inadequate sanitation, and exposure invited disease. Carpenter marched through Tennessee suffering from diarrhea and then fever. His regiment left him behind in a convalescent barracks in Louisville. Fearing the hospital at least as much as the sickness, he fled as soon as he could.

DOCUMENT

Charles Harvey Brewster, Three Letters from the Front (1862)

Confederate soldiers, even less well supplied than their northern counterparts, complained similarly. In 1862, a Virginia captain described what General Lee called the best army "the world ever saw":

Men Present for Duty in the Civil War

This chart demonstrates the growing superiority of the North in terms of manpower and the impact of draft laws. After 1863, blacks, like native-born Americans and Irish and German immigrants, served in the armed forces.

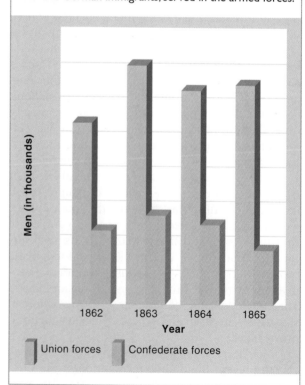

AMERICAN VOICES

Isaac Watts, A Description of Camp Life with the Vermont Heavy Artillery

Isaac Watts grew up in a farm family in Peacham, Vermont. When the war broke out, he was too young to serve, but in 1862, his half brother, Dustan, enlisted. The next year, Dustan wrote his sister that he had heard that Isaac was thinking of joining up, "but that Father would not here of it—I do not blame Father for not wanting him to go, as he seems to be all the one left him to see to things." When Isaac turned 21, however, he left Peacham and joined the Vermont Heavy Artillery, then stationed near Washington. His letter describes camp life and items he wants from home.

I[t] blew all the morning pretty hard and just before noon commenced blowing a perfect hurricanes. . . . quite a number of the tents blew down and though ours did not we expected every minute when it would and thought we would be on the safe side and move into the barracks. They are pretty much done except the bunks . . . I don't know but I can sleep just as sound and rest as well on the floor with a blanket under me as I used to at home on a good bed. There is nothing like getting used to a thing . . . I want my boots, a couple of pocket hdkfs. And a towel. . . . My clothes have been good, but will rip a little as every thing else that is sewn with machines. I want about 15 lbs. Of butter and 8 or 10 of sugar. . . . If you have or can get some cheese without too much trouble, put in two or three pounds . . . a hank of linen thread and a little ball of yarn. I want my razor strop put in, a quire of paper and a bunch of envelopes.

- How would you describe the tone of this letter?

- What does the list of things that Isaac wants suggest about army life?

During our forced marches and hard fights, the soldiers have been compelled to throw away their knapsacks and there is scarcely a private in the army who has a change of clothing of any kind. Hundreds of men are perfectly barefooted and there is no telling when they can be supplied with shoes.

Such circumstances prompted some to desert. An estimated one of every seven Union soldiers and one of every nine men enlisting in the Confederate armies deserted. The majority, however, stayed with their units. As one southern soldier explained, "I am determined to anything and do everything I can for my country."

Manpower needs led both governments to resort to the draft. Despite the sacrosanct notion of states' rights, the Confederate Congress passed the first conscription act in American history in March 1862. Four months later, the Union Congress approved a draft measure. Rather than forcing men to serve, both laws sought to encourage men already in the army to re-enlist and to attract volunteers. Ultimately, more than 30 percent of the Confederate army were drafted. But because the northern draft law allowed payment to secure volunteers, only 6 percent of the Union forces were draftees.

The Confederacy relied more heavily on the draft than the Union did because the North's initial manpower pool was larger and growing. During the war, 180,000 foreigners of military age poured into the northern states. Some came specifically to claim bounties and fight. Immigrants constituted at least 20 percent of the Union army.

Necessary though they were, draft laws were very unpopular. The first Confederate conscription declared all able-bodied men between 18 and 35 eligible for military service but allowed numerous exemptions and the purchase of substitutes. Critics complained that the provision entitling every planter with more than 20 slaves to one exemption from military service favored rich slave owners. Certainly, the legislation fed class tension in the South and undermined the loyalty of the poorer classes, particularly southern mountaineers. The advice one woman shouted after her husband as he was dragged off to the army was hardly unique. "You desert again, quick as you kin. . . . Desert, Jake!" The law, as one southerner pointed out, "aroused a spirit of rebellion." But as long as the South won battlefield victories, the discontent did not reach dangerous proportions.

Northern legislation was neither more popular nor fair. The 1863 draft allowed the hiring of substitutes, and $300 bought an exemption from military service. Already suffering from inflation, workers resented the ease with which moneyed citizens could avoid army duty. In July 1863, the resentment boiled over in New York City in the largest civil disturbance of the nineteenth century. The violence demonstrated that northern morale and support for the war also wavered as the conflict persisted.

The three-day riot was sparked by the process of selecting several thousand conscripts on an early July weekend. By Monday, workers opposed to the draft were parading through the streets. Several Irish members of the Black Joker Volunteer Fire Company, whose names had been listed, were determined to destroy draft records and the hated Enrollment Office. Events spun out of control as a mob torched the armory, plundered the houses of the rich, and looted jewelry stores. African Americans, whom the Irish hated as economic competitors and the cause of the war, became special targets. Crowds shouting "Vengeance on every nigger in New York" beat and lynched African Americans and even burned the Colored Orphan Asylum. More than 100 people died in the violence. There was much truth in the accusation that the war on both sides was a rich man's war but a poor man's fight.

Political Dissension, 1862

As the war continued, rumbles of dissension grew louder. On February 24, 1862, the *Richmond Examiner* summarized many southerners' frustration. "The Confederacy has had everything that was required for success but one, and that one thing it was and is supposed to possess more than anything else, namely Talent." As victory proved elusive, necessitating unpopular measures like the draft, criticism of Confederate leaders mounted. Jefferson Davis's vice president, Alexander Stephens of Georgia, became one of the administration's bitterest accusers. Public criticism reflected private disapproval. Wrote one southerner to a friend, "Impeach Jeff Davis for incompetency & call a convention of the States. . . . West Point is death to us & sick Presidents & Generals are equally fatal."

Because the South had no party system, dissatisfaction with Davis and his handling of the war tended to be factional, petty, and personal. No party mechanism channeled or curbed irresponsible criticism. Detractors rarely felt it necessary to offer programs in place of Davis's policies. Davis suffered personally from the carping comments of his detractors. More important, the Confederacy suffered. Without a party leader's traditional weapons and rewards, Davis had no mechanism to generate enthusiasm for his war policies.

Although Lincoln has since become a folk hero, at the time, many northerners derided his performance and eagerly looked forward to a new president in 1864. Peace Democrats, called Copperheads, claimed that Lincoln betrayed the Constitution and that working-class Americans bore the brunt of his conscription policy. New York Democrats warned the city's Irish residents that freed blacks would "steal the work and bread of honest Irish." Immigrant workers in eastern cities and those who lived in the southern parts of the Midwest had little sympathy for abolitionism or blacks, and they supported the antiwar stance of the Copperheads. Even Democrats favoring the war effort found Lincoln arbitrary and tyrannical. They also worried that extreme Republicans would push Lincoln into making the war a crusade for the abolition of slavery.

Republicans were themselves divided. Moderates favored a cautious approach toward winning the war, fearing the possible consequences of emancipating the slaves, confiscating Confederate property, or arming blacks. The radicals, however, urged Lincoln to make emancipation a wartime objective. They hoped for a victory that would revolutionize southern social and racial arrangements.

Before the war, Lincoln had advocated ending slavery's expansion in the West but not its abolition in the South. In the early stages of the conflict, he retained his moderate stance. He hoped that pro-Union sentiment would emerge in the South and compel its leaders to abandon their rebellion. He began changing his mind in early 1862. The reduction of the congressional Republican majority in the fall elections of 1862 made it imperative that Lincoln listen not only to both factions of his party but also to the Democratic opposition.

THE TIDE TURNS, 1863–1865

Hard political realities as well as Lincoln's sense of the public's mood help explain why he delayed an emancipation proclamation until 1863. Like congressional Democrats, many northerners supported a war for the Union but not one for emancipation. Not only did many, if not most, whites see blacks as inferior, but they also suspected that emancipation would trigger a massive influx of former slaves who would steal white men's jobs and political rights. Race riots in New York, Brooklyn, Philadelphia, and Buffalo dramatized white attitudes. In Cincinnati, Irish dockworkers attacked blacks who were offering to work for less pay with the cry, "Let's clear out the niggers." Arthur Carpenter's evaluation of blacks was typical of many northern soldiers confronting blacks for the first time. In December 1861, he wrote to his parents:

No one who has ever seen the nigger in all its glory on the southern plantations . . . will ever vote for emancipation. . . . If emancipation is to be the policy of the war (and I think it will not) I do not care how quick the country goes to pot. The negro never was intended to be equal with the white man.

The Emancipation Proclamation, 1863

If the president moved too fast on emancipation, he risked losing the allegiance of people like Carpenter, offending the border states, and increasing the Democrats' chances for political victory. But if Lincoln did not move at all, he would alienate abolitionists and lose the support of radical Republicans, which he could ill afford.

For these reasons, Lincoln proceeded cautiously. At first, he hoped the border states would take the initiative. In the early spring of 1862, he urged Congress to pass a joint resolution offering federal compensation to states beginning a "gradual abolishment of slavery." Border-state opposition killed the idea, for people there refused to believe, as Lincoln did, that the "friction and abrasion" of war would finally end slavery. Abolitionists and northern blacks, however, greeted Lincoln's proposal with a "thrill of joy."

That summer, Lincoln told his cabinet he intended to emancipate the slaves. Secretary of State Seward urged the president to delay any general proclamation until the North won a decisive military victory. Otherwise, he warned, Lincoln would appear to be urging racial insurrection behind the Confederate lines to compensate for northern military bungling.

Lincoln followed Seward's advice, using that summer and fall to prepare the North for the shift in the war's purpose. To counteract white racial fears of free blacks, he promoted various schemes for establishing free black communities in Haiti and Panama. Seizing unexpected opportunities, he lay the groundwork for the proclamation itself. In August, Horace Greeley, the influential abolitionist editor of the New York *Tribune,* printed an open letter to Lincoln attacking him for failing to act on slavery. In his reply, Lincoln linked the idea of emancipation to military necessity. His primary goal, he wrote, was to save the Union:

DOCUMENT

Abraham Lincoln to Horace Greeley (1862)

If I could save the Union without freeing any slave, I would do it; and if I could save it by freeing all the slaves, I would do it; and if I could do it by freeing some and leaving others alone, I would also do that. What I do about Slavery and the colored race, I do because I believe it helps to save this Union.

If Lincoln attacked slavery, then, it would be because emancipation would save white lives, preserve the democratic process, and bring victory.

In September 1862, the Union success at Antietam gave Lincoln the opportunity to issue a preliminary emancipation proclamation. It stated that unless rebellious states (or parts of states in rebellion) returned to the Union by January 1, 1863, the president would declare their slaves "forever free." Although the proclamation was supposedly aimed at bringing the southern states back into the Union, Lincoln no longer expected the South to lay down arms. Rather, he was preparing northerners to accept the eventuality of emancipation on the grounds of necessity. Frederick Douglass greeted the president's action with jubilation. "We shout for joy," he wrote, "that we live to record this righteous decree."

IMAGE

Lincoln Visiting General McClellan

Not all northerners shared Douglass's joy. In fact, the September proclamation probably harmed Lincoln's party in the fall elections. As one Democratic ditty put it:

"De Union!" used to be de cry—
For dat we want it strong;
But now de motto seems to be,
"De nigger, right or wrong."

Although the elections of 1862 weakened the Republicans' grasp on the national government, they did not destroy it. Still, cautious cabinet members begged Lincoln to forget about emancipation. His refusal demonstrated his vision and humanity, as did his efforts to reduce racial fears. "Is it dreaded that the freed people will swarm forth and cover the whole land?" he asked. "Are they not already in the land? Will liberation make them any more numerous? Equally distributed among the whites of the whole country, and there would be but one colored to seven whites. Could the one, in any way, greatly disturb the other?"

Finally, on New Year's Day 1863, Lincoln issued the promised Emancipation Proclamation. It was an "act of justice, warranted by the Constitution upon military necessity." Thus, what had started as a war to save the Union now also became a struggle that, if victorious, would free the slaves. Yet the proclamation had no immediate impact on slavery. It affected only slaves living in the unconquered portions of the Confederacy. It was silent about slaves in the border states and in parts of the South already in northern hands. These limitations led Elizabeth Cady Stanton and Susan B. Anthony to establish the women's Loyal

DOCUMENT

The Emancipation Proclamation

A French View of Emancipation This depiction of African Americans celebrating the Emancipation Proclamation appeared in the French publication *Le Monde Illustre*. How has the artist provided a triumphant and sympathetic picture of rejoicing freedpeople? What does this picture, published in France, suggest about the diplomatic importance to the Union cause of the Emancipation Proclamation?

National League to lobby Congress to emancipate all southern slaves.

Though the Emancipation Proclamation did not immediately liberate southern slaves from their masters, it had a tremendous symbolic importance and changed the nature of the war. On New Year's Day, blacks gathered outside the White House to cheer the president and tell him that if he would "come out of that palace, they would hug him to death." For the first time, the government had committed itself to freeing slaves. Jubilant blacks could only believe that the president's action heralded a new era for their race. More immediately, the proclamation sanctioned the policy of accepting blacks as soldiers. Blacks also hoped that the news would reach southern slaves, encouraging them either to flee to Union lines or to subvert the southern war effort by refusing to work for their masters.

Diplomatic concerns also lay behind the Emancipation Proclamation. Lincoln and his advisers anticipated that the commitment to abolish slavery would favorably impress foreign powers. European statesmen, however, remained cautious. The English prime minister called the proclamation "trash." But important segments of the English public who opposed slavery now regarded any attempt to help the South as immoral. Foreigners could better understand and sympathize with a war to free the slaves than they could with a war to save the Union. In diplomacy, where image is so important, Lincoln had created a more attractive picture of the North. The Emancipation Proclamation became the North's symbolic call for human freedom.

Unanticipated Consequences of War

The Emancipation Proclamation was but another example of the war's surprising consequences. Innovation was necessary for victory. In the final two years of the war, both North and South experimented on the battlefields and behind the lines in desperate efforts to conclude the conflict successfully.

One of the Union's experiments involved using black troops for combat duty. Blacks had offered themselves as soldiers in 1861 but had been rejected. They were serving as cooks, laborers, teamsters, and carpenters in the army, however, and composed as much as a quarter of the navy. But as white casualties mounted, so did the interest in black service on the battlefield. The Union government allowed states to escape draft quotas if they enlisted enough volunteers, and they allowed them to count southern black enlistees on their state rosters. Northern governors grew increasingly interested in black military service. One piece of doggerel reflected changing attitudes:

Some tell us 'tis a burnin' shame
To make the naygers fight;
And that the thrade of bein' kilt
Belongs but to the white:
But as for me, upon my soul!
So liberal are we here.
I'll let Sambo be murthered instead of myself
On every day in the year.

Beyond white self-interest lay the promises of the Emancipation Proclamation and the desire to prove blacks' value to the Union. Black leaders such as Frederick Douglass pressed for military service. "Once let the black man get upon his person the brass letter, U.S., let him get an eagle on his button, and a musket on his shoulder and bullets in his pocket," Douglass believed that "there is no power on earth that can deny that he has earned the right to citizenship." By the war's end, 186,000 blacks (10 percent of the army) had served the Union cause, 134,111 of them escapees from slave states.

DOCUMENT

James Henry Gooding, Letter to President Lincoln (1863); Letter from a Free Black Volunteer to *The Christian Recorder* (1864)

Enrolling blacks in the Union army was an important step toward citizenship and acceptance of blacks by white society. But the black experience in the army highlighted some of the obstacles to racial acceptance. Black soldiers, usually led by white officers, were second-class soldiers for most of the war, receiving lower pay ($10 a month as compared with $13), poorer food, often more menial work, and fewer benefits than whites. Even whites working to equalize black and white pay often considered blacks inferior. Many white soldiers, including an entire regiment from Illinois, quit the service rather than fight alongside blacks.

The army's racial experiment had mixed results. But the faithful and courageous service of black troops helped modify some of the most demeaning white racial stereotypes of blacks. The black soldiers, many former slaves, who conquered the South felt a sense of pride and dignity as they performed their duties. Wrote one, "We march through these fine thoroughfares where once the slave was forbid being out after nine P.M. . . . Negro soldiers!— with banners floating."

As the conflict continued, basic assumptions weakened about how it should be waged. One wartime casualty was the courtly idea that war involved only armies. Early in the war, many officers tried to protect civilians and their property. In the Richmond campaign, General McClellan actually posted guards to prevent stealing. Such concern for rebel property soon vanished, and along with it went chickens, corn, livestock, and, as George Eagleton

Contrabands This photograph was taken in the summer of 1862 in Cumberland Landing, Virginia. Sitting in front of the cabin are about 20 men and women who had fled to Union lines and freedom. The flight of slaves, called contrabands, had the potential of seriously undermining the southern war effort and southern morale, but their presence also posed difficulties for Union commanders and northern leaders who were often not sure what to do with them. What might be some of the reasons why there were more women than men in this picture? *(Library of Congress [LC-B811-0383])*

Black Troops Storm Fort Wagner   Newspaper engravings provided civilians with images of the conflict. This colored lithograph by Currier & Ives was produced a generation after the war, but it is very much like the journalistic images of the time. The picture shows a famous black regiment, the 54th Massachusetts, storming Fort Wagner, South Carolina. What specific elements of this depiction provide an interpretation of the behavior of the troops during the assault? The experiences of the 54th formed the basis for the Hollywood movie *Glory*. *(Library of Congress)*

noted with disgust, even the furnishings of churches, down to the binding of the Bible in the pulpit. Southern troops, on the few occasions when they came North, also lived off the land. War touched all of society, not just the battlefield participants.

Changing Military Strategies, 1863–1865

In the early war years, the South's military strategy combined defense with selective maneuvers. Until the summer of 1863, the strategy seemed to be succeeding, at least in the eastern theater. But an occasional victory over the invading northern army, such as at Fredericksburg in December 1862, did not change the course of the war. Realizing this, Lee reviewed his strategy and concluded, "There is nothing to be gained by this army remaining quietly on the defensive." Unless the South won

IMAGE

Robert E. Lee

victories in the North, he believed, civilian confidence would disintegrate, and the North would continue its efforts to crush the southern bid for independence. He was willing to take risks to gain peace and national recognition.

In the summer of 1863, Lee led the Confederate army of northern Virginia across the Potomac into Maryland and southern Pennsylvania. Hoping for a victory that would threaten both Philadelphia and Washington, he even dreamed of capturing a northern city. Such spectacular feats would surely bring diplomatic recognition and might even force the North to sue for peace. On a practical level, Lee sought provisions for his men and their animals.

At Gettysburg on a hot and humid July 1, Lee came abruptly face to face with a Union army led by General George Meade. During three days of fighting, Lee ordered costly infantry

MAP

The Civil War Part II: 1863–1865

AMERICAN VOICES

Susie King Taylor, From *Reminiscences of My Life in Camp*

In 1902, Susie King Taylor's account of her life as an army laundress during the Civil War was published. She was connected to the 33rd U.S. Colored Infantry, her husband's regiment. After escaping from slavery, she spent some time on St. Simon's, an island liberated by Union troops.

There were about six hundred men, women, and children on St. Simon's, the women and children being in the majority, and we were afraid to go very far from our own quarters in the daytime, and at night even to go out of the house for a long time, although the men were on the watch all the time; for there were not any soldiers on the island, only the marines who were on the gunboats along the coast. The rebels, knowing this, could steal by them under cover of the night, and getting on the island would capture any person venturing out alone and carry them to the mainland. Several of the men disappeared, and as they were never heard from we came to the conclusion they had been carried off in this way.

- *What does this account reveal about the realities and fears of former slaves?*

- *What does it suggest about the Confederate point of view?*

---

assaults that probably lost him the battle. On July 3, Lee sent three divisions, about 15,000 men in all, against the Union center. The assault, known as Pickett's Charge, was as futile as it was gallant. At 700 yards, the Union artillery opened fire. One southern officer described the scene: "Pickett's division just seemed to melt away in the blue musketry smoke which now covered the hill. Nothing but stragglers came back."

Despite his losses, Lee did procure the food and fodder he needed and captured thousands of prisoners. Gettysburg was a defeat, but neither Lee, nor his men, nor southern civilians regarded it as conclusive. Fighting would continue for another year and a half. In 1864, one high army officer revealed his continuing belief in the struggle's outcome. "Our hearts are full of hope," he wrote. "Oh! I do pray that we may be established as an independent people, . . . [and] recognized as God's Peculiar People!" While many remained hopeful, Lee's Gettysburg losses were so heavy that he could never mount another southern offensive.

DOCUMENT

John Dooley, Journal (1863)

Despite the Gettysburg victory, Lincoln was dissatisfied with General Meade, who had failed to finish off Lee's retreating army. His disappointment faded with news of a great victory on July 4 at Vicksburg in the western theater. The capture of the city completed the Union campaign to gain control of the Mississippi River and to divide the

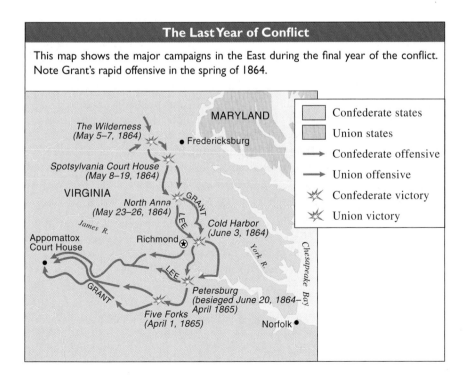

The Last Year of Conflict

This map shows the major campaigns in the East during the final year of the conflict. Note Grant's rapid offensive in the spring of 1864.

MARYLAND

The Wilderness (May 5–7, 1864)

Fredericksburg

Spotsylvania Court House (May 8–19, 1864)

VIRGINIA

North Anna (May 23–26, 1864)

GRANT

LEE

James R.

Appomattox Court House

Richmond

Cold Harbor (June 3, 1864)

York R.

Chesapeake Bay

LEE

GRANT

Petersburg (besieged June 20, 1864– April 1865)

Five Forks (April 1, 1865)

Norfolk

Confederate states
Union states
Confederate offensive
Union offensive
Confederate victory
Union victory

Gettysburg 1863 This albumen print by Timothy H. O'Sullivan is titled *A Harvest of Death, Gettysburg, Pennsylvania, July, 1863*. What did O'Sullivan wish to suggest with this picture of the battlefield? Civil War pictures made it clear that photography was starting to play an important role in recording the sweep of American life. *(Rare Books Division, The New York Public Library, Astor, Lenox and Tilden Foundations/Art Resource, NY)*

South. Ulysses S. Grant, who was responsible for the victory, demonstrated the boldness and flexibility that Lincoln had been looking for in a commander.

Lincoln, The Gettysburg Address (1863)

By the summer of 1863, the Union controlled much of Arkansas, Louisiana, Mississippi, Missouri, Kentucky, and Tennessee. The following spring, Lincoln appointed Grant general in chief of the Union armies. Grant planned for victory within a year. "The art of war is simple enough," he reasoned. "Find out where your enemy is. Get at him as soon as you can. Strike at him as hard as you can, and keep moving on."

As an outsider to the prewar military establishment, Grant easily rejected conventional military wisdom. "If men make war in slavish observance of rules, they will fail," he asserted. He anticipated no one decisive engagement but rather a grim campaign of annihilation, using the North's superior resources of men and supplies to wear down and defeat the South. Although Grant's plan entailed large casualties on both sides, he justified the strategy by arguing that "now the carnage was to be limited to a single year."

General Ulysses S. Grant at City Point, Virginia

A campaign of annihilation involved the destruction not only of enemy armies but also of the resources that fueled the southern war effort. Although the idea of cutting the enemy off from needed supplies was implicit in the naval blockade, economic or "total" warfare was a relatively new and shocking idea. Grant, however, "regarded it as humane to both sides to protect the persons of those found at their homes, but to consume everything that could be used to support or supply armies." Following this policy, he set out after Lee's army in Virginia. General William Tecumseh Sherman, who pursued General Joseph Johnston from Tennessee toward Atlanta, further refined this plan.

The war, Sherman believed, must also be waged in the minds of civilians, and he intended to make southerners "fear and dread" their foes. His campaign to seize Atlanta and his march to Savannah spread destruction and terror. Ordered to forage "liberally" on the land, his army left desolation in its wake. "Reduction to poverty," Sherman asserted, "brings prayers for peace." A Georgia woman described in her diary the impact of Sherman's march:

William T. Sherman, The March Through Georgia (1875)

There was hardly a fence left standing all the way from Sparta to Gordon. The fields were trampled down and the road was lined with carcasses of horses, hogs and cattle that the invaders, unable either to consume or to carry away with them, had wantonly shot down, to starve out the people. . . . The dwellings that were standing all showed signs of pillage, and on every plantation we saw . . . charred remains.

This destruction, with its goal of total victory, demonstrated once more how conflict produced

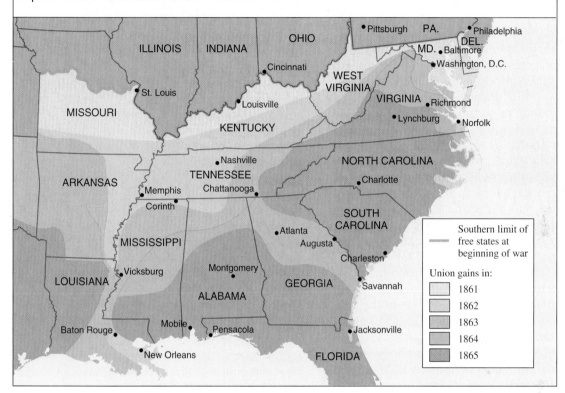

The Progress of War, 1861–1865

In this map you can see the very slow progression of the North's effort to conquer the South. For much of the war, the South controlled large areas of contiguous territory. This control of the southern homeland helped southerners to feel that it was possible for them to win the war. At what point in time might the realities depicted in this map have made southerners decide their cause was lost?

Legend: Southern limit of free states at beginning of war. Union gains in: 1861, 1862, 1863, 1864, 1865

the unexpected. The war that both North and South had hoped would be quick and relatively painless was ending after four long years with great cost to both sides. But the bitter nature of warfare during that final year threatened Lincoln's hopes for reconciliation.

CHANGES WROUGHT BY WAR

As bold new tactics emerged both on and off the battlefield, both governments took steps that changed their societies in surprising ways. Of the two, the South, which had left the Union to conserve a traditional way of life, experienced the more radical transformation.

A New South

The expansion of the central government's power in the South, starting with the passage of the 1862 Conscription Act, continued in the last years of the

war. Secession grew out of the concept of states' rights, but, ironically, winning the war depended on central direction and control. Many southerners denounced Davis because he recognized the need for the central government to take the lead. Despite the accusations, the Confederate Congress cooperated with him and established important precedents. In 1863, it enacted a comprehensive tax law and an impressment act that allowed government agents to requisition food, horses, wagons, and other necessary war materials, often for only about half their market price. These were prime examples of the central government's power to interfere with private property. Government impressment of slaves for war work in 1863 affected the very form of private property that had originally driven the South from the Union.

The Conscription Act of 1862 did not solve the Confederate army's manpower problems. By 1864, the southern armies were only one-third the size of the Union forces. Hence, in February 1864, an expanded conscription measure made all white males between ages 17 and 50 subject to the draft. By

1865, the necessities of war had led to the unthinkable: arming slaves as soldiers. Black companies were recruited in Richmond and other southern towns. However, because the war soon ended, no blacks actually fought for the Confederacy.

In a message sent to Congress in November 1864, Davis speculated on some of the issues involved in arming slaves. "Should a slave who had served his country" be retained in servitude, he wondered, "or should his emancipation be held out to him as a reward for faithful service, or should it be granted at once on the promise of such service . . . ?" The war fought by the South to preserve slavery ended in the contemplation of emancipation.

Southern agriculture also changed under the pressure of war. Earlier, the South had imported food from the North, concentrating on the production of staples such as cotton and tobacco for market. Now, more and more land was turned over to food crops. Some farmers voluntarily shifted crops, but others responded only to state laws reducing the acreage permitted for cotton and tobacco cultivation. These measures never succeeded in raising enough food to feed southerners adequately. But they contributed to a dramatic decline in the production of cotton, from 4.5 million bales in 1861 to 300,000 bales in 1864.

The South had always relied on imported manufactured goods. Even though some blockade runners were able to evade the Union ships, the noose tightened after 1862. The Confederacy could not, in any case, rely on blockade runners to arm and equip the army. Thus, war triggered the expansion of military-related industries in the South. Here, too, the government played a crucial role. The war and navy offices directed industrial development, awarding contracts to private manufacturing firms such as Richmond's Tredegar Iron Works and operating other factories themselves. The number of southern industrial workers rose dramatically. In 1861, the Tredegar Iron Works employed 700 workers; two years later, it employed 2,500, more than half of them black. The head of the Army Ordnance Bureau reflected on the amazing transformation: "Where three years ago we were not making a gun, pistol nor a sabre, no shot nor shell . . . we now make all these in quantities to meet the demands of our large armies." At the end of the war, the soldiers were better supplied with arms and munitions than with food.

Although the war did not transform the southern class structure, relations between the classes began to change. The pressures of the struggle undermined the solidarity of whites, which was based on racism and supposed political unanimity. Draft resistance and desertion reflected the alienation of

On the Home Front Appearing on a printed envelope, this image reveals several aspects of female experience during wartime. Why is this woman doing laundry? What is being suggested about the changes in her life that have occurred as a result of the war? What feelings does she express? This women's speculation about the possibilities of doing humble work in the military alerts us to the fact that washerwomen accompanied the armies wherever they went. *(Collection of the New-York Historical Society [PR-022-3-88-5])*

some southerners from a war perceived as serving only the interests of upper-class plantation owners. More and more yeoman families suffered grinding poverty as the men went off to war and government officials and armies requisitioned needed resources. Harlan Fuller, a poor farmer from Georgia, explained his family's situation in the spring of 1864. Even though Fuller was 50, he was now eligible for the draft. "I am liable at any time to be taken away from my little crops leaving my family almost without provisions & no hope of making any crop atal. I have sent six sons to the war & now the seventh enrolled he being the last I have no help left atal." This new poverty was an ominous hint of the decline of the yeoman farming class in postwar years.

The North

Although changes in the South were more noticeable, the Union's government and economy also responded to the demands of war. Like Davis, Lincoln was accused of being a dictator. Although he rarely tried to control Congress, veto its legislation, or direct government departments, Lincoln did use executive power freely. He violated the writ of habeas corpus by suspending the civil rights of more than 13,000 northerners, who languished in prison without trials; curbed the freedom of the press because of supposedly disloyal and inflammatory articles; established conscription; issued the Emancipation Proclamation; and removed army generals. Lincoln argued that this vast extension of presidential power was temporarily justified because, as president, he was responsible for defending and preserving the Constitution.

Many of the wartime changes in government proved more permanent than Lincoln imagined. The financial necessities of war helped revolutionize the country's banking system. Ever since Andrew Jackson's destruction of the Bank of the United States, state banks had served American financial needs. Treasury Secretary Chase found this banking system inadequate and proposed to replace it. In 1863 and 1864, Congress passed banking acts that established a national currency issued by federally chartered banks and backed by government bonds. The country had a federal banking system once again.

The northern economy also changed under wartime demands. The need to feed soldiers and civilians stimulated the expansion of agriculture and new investment in farm machinery. With so many men off soldiering, farmers were at first short of labor. McCormick reapers performed the work of four to six men, and farmers began to buy them. During the war, McCormick sold 165,000 of his machines. Northern farming, especially in the Midwest, was well on the way to becoming mechanized. Farmers not only succeeded in growing enough grain to feed civilians and soldiers but also gathered a surplus to export as well.

The war also selectively stimulated manufacturing. Although it is easy to imagine that northern industry as a whole expanded during the Civil War, in fact, the war retarded overall economic growth. War consumed rather than generated wealth. Between 1860 and 1870, the annual rate of increase in real manufacturing value added was only 2.3 percent, in contrast with 7.8 percent for the years between 1840 and 1860 and 6 percent for the period from 1870 to 1900. Some important prewar industries, such as cotton textiles, languished without a supply of southern cotton.

Effect of a 32-Pound Shell

However, industries that produced for the war machine, especially those with advantages of scale, expanded and made large profits. Each year, the Union army required 1.5 million uniforms and 3 million pairs of shoes; the woollen and leather industries grew accordingly. Meatpackers and producers of iron, steel, and pocket watches all profited from wartime opportunities. Cincinnati was one city that flourished from supplying soldiers with everything from pork to soap and candles.

On the Home Front, 1861–1865

Events on the battlefield were intimately connected to life behind the lines. As both northern and southern leaders realized, civilian morale was crucial to the war's outcome. If civilians lost faith, they would lack the will to continue the conflict.

The war stimulated religious efforts to generate enthusiasm and loyalty on the home front. On both sides, Protestant clergymen threw themselves behind the war effort. As northern preacher Henry Ward Beecher proclaimed, "God hates lukewarm patriotism as much as lukewarm religion, and we hate it too." Southern ministers gave similar messages and urged southerners to reform their lives, for victory could not come without moral change. In North and South, every defeat was a cause for soul searching. Fast days and revivals provided a spiritual dimension to the conflict and helped people deal with discouragement and death.

In numerous ways, the war transformed northern and southern society. The very fact of conflict established a new perspective for most civilians. War news vied with local events for their attention. They read newspapers and national weekly magazines with a new eagerness. The use of the mails increased dramatically as they corresponded with faraway relatives and friends. Wrote one North Carolina woman, "I never liked to write letters before, but it is a pleasure as well as a relief now." Distant events became almost as real and vivid as those at home. The war helped make Americans less parochial, integrating them into the larger world.

For some Americans, such as John D. Rockefeller and Andrew Carnegie, war brought army contracts and unanticipated riches. The New York *Herald* reported that New York City had never been "so gay, . . . so crowded, so prosperous," as it was in March 1864. Residents of Cincinnati noted people who "became suddenly immensely wealthy, and in their fine equipages, with liveried servants, rolled in magnificence along the city streets." In the South, blockade runners made fortunes slipping luxury goods past Union ships.

Women Working at U.S. Arsenal

For the majority of Americans, however, war meant deprivation. The war effort gobbled up a large part of each side's resources, and ultimately ordinary people suffered. To be sure, the demand for workers ended unemployment and changed employment patterns. Large numbers of women and blacks entered the workforce, a phenomenon that would be repeated in all future American wars. But whereas work was easy to get and wages appeared to increase, real income actually declined. Inflation, especially destructive in the South, was largely to blame. By 1864, eggs sold in Richmond for $6 a dozen; butter brought $25 a pound. Strikes and union organizing pointed to working-class discontent.

Low wages compounded the problem of declining income and particularly harmed women workers. Often forced into the labor market because husbands could save little from small army stipends, army wives and other women took what pay they could get. As more women entered the workforce, employers cut costs by slashing wages. In 1861, the Union government paid Philadelphia seamstresses 17 cents per shirt. At the height of inflation, three years later, the government reduced the piecework rate to 15 cents. Private employers paid even less, about 8 cents a shirt. Working women in the South fared no better. War may have brought prosperity to a few Americans in the North and South, but for most it meant trying to survive on an inadequate income.

Economic dislocation caused by the war reduced the standard of living for civilians. Shortages and hardships were severe in the South, which bore the brunt of the fighting. Most white southerners did without food, manufactured goods, and medicine during the war. Farming families without slaves to help with fieldwork fared poorly. As one Georgia woman explained, "I can't manage a farm well enough [alone] to make a suporte." Conditions were most dismal in cities, where carts brought in vital supplies, because trains were reserved for military use. Hunger was rampant. Food riots erupted in Richmond and other cities; crowds of hungry whites broke into stores to steal food. The very cleanliness of southern cities pointed to urban hunger. As one Richmond resident noted, everything was so "cleanly consumed that no garbage or filth can accumulate."

The Impact of the War in the South   The dislocations caused by the war were many. These southerners, forced to leave their home by invading troops, have packed what few belongings they could transport and stand ready to evacuate their homestead. How many children can you find in the picture? What does the fact that the woman in the foreground is smoking a pipe suggest about the social class of this group? *(Library of Congress)*

Thousands of southerners who fled as Union armies advanced suddenly found themselves homeless. "The country for miles around is filled with refugees," noted an army officer in 1862. "Every house is crowded and hundreds are living in churches, in barns and tents." Caught up in the effort of mere survival, refugees worried about what had happened to homes and possessions left behind and whether anything would remain when they returned. Life was probably just as agonizing for those who chose to stay put when Union troops arrived. Virginia Gray, an Arkansas woman, wrote in her diary of her fear of the "Feds" and the turmoil they caused when they suddenly appeared and then disappeared.

White flight also disrupted slave life. Even the arrival of Union forces could prove a mixed blessing. One slave described the upsetting behavior of the Yankees at his plantation in Arkansas: "Them folks stood round there all day. Killed hogs . . . killed cows. . . . Took all kinds of sugar and preserves. . . . Tore all the feathers out of the mattresses looking for money. Then they put Old Miss and her daughter in the kitchen to cooking." So frightened was this slave's mother that she hid in her bed, only to be roused by the lieutenant, who told her, "We ain't a-going to do you no hurt. . . . We are freeing you." But the next day, the Yanks were gone and the Confederates back. During Sherman's march through Georgia in 1864, his troops stole not only from whites but from slaves as well. Indeed some soldiers flogged blacks who tried to stop the looting.

Wartime Race Relations

The journal kept by Emily Harris in South Carolina conveys some of the character of life behind the lines. She revealed not only the predictable story of shortages, hardships, and the psychological burdens of those at home but also the subtle social changes the war stimulated. Emily and her husband, David, lived on a 500-acre farm with their seven young children and 10 slaves. When David went to war, Emily had to manage the farm, even though David worried that she would be "much at a loss with the . . . farm and the negroes."

Emily's early entries establish two themes that persist for the years she kept her diary. She worried about how David would survive the "privation and hardships" of army life and was also anxious about her own "load of responsibilities." Her December 1862 entry provides a poignant picture of a wife's thoughts. "All going well as far as I can judge but tonight it is raining and cold and a soldier's wife cannot be happy in bad weather and during a battle." The dozens of tasks she had to do depressed her. "I shall never get used to being left as the head of affairs," she wrote in January 1863. "I am not an independent woman nor ever shall be." As time passed and the war went badly, the dismal news and mounting list of casualties heightened her concern about David's safety.

Her relations with her slaves compounded Emily's problems. As so many southerners discovered, war transformed the master–slave relationship. Because Emily was not the master David had been, her slaves gradually claimed unaccustomed liberties. At Christmas in 1864, several left the farm without her permission; others stayed away longer than she allowed. "Old Will" boldly requested his freedom. Worse yet, she discovered that her slaves had helped three Yankees who had escaped from prison camp.

DOCUMENT

Annie L. Burton, "Memories of Childhood's Slavery Days" (1909)

The master–slave relationship was crumbling, and Emily reported in her journal the consequences for whites. "It seems people are getting afraid of negroes." Although not admitting to fear, she revealed that she could no longer control the blacks, who were increasingly unwilling to play a subservient role.

Understanding what was at stake, slaves, in their own way, often worked for their freedom. Said one later, "Us slaves worked den when we felt like it, which wasn't often." Emily's journal entry for February 22 confessed a "painful necessity." "I am reduced," she said, "to the use of a stick but the negroes are becoming so impudent and disrespectful that I cannot bear it." A mere two weeks later she added, "The Negroes are all expecting to be set free very soon and it causes them to be very troublesom."

Similar scenes occurred throughout the South. Insubordination, refusal to work, and refusal to accept punishment marked the behavior of black slaves, especially those who worked as field hands. Thousands of blacks (probably 20 percent of all slaves), many of them women who had been exploited as workers and as sexual objects, fled toward Union lines after the early months of the war. Their flight pointed to the changing nature of race relations and the harm slaves could do to the southern cause. Reflected one slaveowner, "The 'faithful slave' is about played out."

Women and the War

If Emily Harris's journal reveals that she was sometimes overwhelmed by her responsibilities and shocked by the changes in dealings with her slaves, it also illustrates how the war affected women's lives. Nineteenth-century ideology promoted women's domestic role and minimized their economic importance. But the war made it impossible for many women to live according to conventional norms. So many men on both sides had gone off to fight that, just like many of their grandmothers during the American Revolution, women had to find jobs and carry on farming operations. During the war years, southern women who had no slaves to help with the farmwork and northern farm wives who labored without the assistance of husbands or sons carried new physical and emotional burdens. For southern women, who faced shortages and even displacement, sanity sometimes seemed at stake. Emily Harris felt she was going crazy. Others found their patriotism waning and urged their men to come home.

Women supported the war effort by participating in numerous war-related activities. In both North and South, they entered government service in large numbers. In the North, hundreds of women became military nurses. Under the supervision of Drs. Emily and Elizabeth Blackwell; Dorothea Dix, superintendent of army nurses; and Clara Barton, northern women nursed the wounded and dying for low pay or even for none at all. They also attempted to improve hospital conditions by attacking red tape and bureaucracy. The diary of a volunteer, Harriet Whetten, revealed the activist attitude of many others:

DOCUMENT

Clara Barton, Medical Life on the Battlefield (1862)

RECOVERING THE PAST

Photography

The invention of photography in 1839 expanded the visual and imaginative world of nineteenth-century Americans. For the first time, Americans could visually record events in their own lives and see images of people and incidents from far away. Photographs, of course, also expand the boundaries of the historian's world. As photographic techniques became simpler, more and more visual information about the nineteenth century was captured. Historians can use photographs to discover what nineteenth-century Americans wore, how they celebrated weddings and funerals, and what their families, houses, and cities looked like. Pictures of election campaigns, parades, strikes, and wars show the texture of public life. But historians can also study photographs, as they do paintings, to glean information about attitudes and norms. The choice of subjects, the way people and objects are arranged and grouped, and the relationships between people in photographs are all clues to the social and cultural values of nineteenth-century Americans.

Some knowledge of the early history of photography helps place the visual evidence in the proper perspective. The earliest type of photograph, the daguerreotype, was not a print but the negative itself on a sheet of silver-plated copper. The first daguerreotype required between 15 and 30 minutes for the proper exposure. This accounts for the stiff and formal quality of many of these photographs. Glass ambrotypes (negatives on glass) and tintypes (negatives on gray iron bases), developed after the daguerreotype, were easier and cheaper to produce. But both techniques produced only one picture and required what to us would seem an interminable time for exposure.

A major breakthrough came in the 1850s with the development of the wet-plate process. In this process, the photographer coated a glass negative with a sensitive solution, exposed the negative (took the picture), and then quickly developed it. The new procedure required a relatively short exposure time of perhaps five seconds outdoors and one minute inside. Action shots, however, were still not feasible. The entire process tied the photographer to the darkroom. Traveling photographers carried their darkrooms with

Mathew Brady, *Confederate Captives, Gettysburg.* *(National Archives)*

512

them. The advantage of the wet-plate process was that it was possible to make many paper prints from one negative, opening new commercial vistas for professional photographers.

Mathew Brady, a fashionable Washington photographer, realized that the camera was the "eye of history" and asked Lincoln for permission to record the war with his camera. He and his team of photographers left about 8,000 glass negatives, currently stored in the Library of Congress and the National Archives, as their record of the Civil War. Shown here are two photographs, one of three Confederate soldiers captured at Gettysburg, the other of the battlefield of Cold Harbor in Virginia.

In the first photograph, study and describe the three soldiers. How are they posed? What kind of clothes are they wearing? What about their equipment? What seems to be their physical condition?

The second picture was taken in April 1865, about a year after the battle at Cold Harbor. In the background, you can see two Union soldiers digging graves. In the foreground are the grisly remains of the battle. What do you think is the intent of the photograph? The choice of subject matter shows clearly that photography reveals attitudes as well as facts. What attitude toward war and death is conveyed in this picture? Why is the burial taking place a full year after the battle? What does this tell us about the nature of civil warfare? Notice that the soldiers ordered to undertake this ghastly chore are black, as was customary. What might this scene suggest about the experience of black soldiers in the Union army?

REFLECTING ON THE PAST Using the photograph of Confederate captives as evidence, what might you conclude about the southern soldier—his equipment, uniforms, shoes? How well fed do the men in the picture appear? What attitudes are conveyed through their facial expressions and poses? What kind of mood was the northern photographer trying to create? What might a northern viewer conclude about the South's war effort after looking at this picture?

These photographs just begin to suggest what can be discovered from old photographs. Your local historical society and library probably have photograph collections available to you. In addition, at home or in a relative's attic, you may find visual records of your family and its history.

I have never seen such a dirty disorganized place as the Hospital. The neglect of cleanliness is inexcusable. All sorts of filth, standing water, and the embalming house near the Hospital. . . . No time had to be lost. Miss Gill and I set the contrabands at work making beds & cleaning.

Although men largely staffed southern military hospitals, Confederate women also cared for the sick and wounded in their homes and in makeshift hospitals behind the battle lines. Grim though the work was, many women felt that they were participating in the real world for the first time in their lives.

Women moved outside the domestic sphere in other forms of volunteer war work. Some women gained administrative experience in soldiers' aid societies and in the U.S. Sanitary Commission, which raised $50 million by the war's end for medical supplies, nurses' salaries, and other wartime necessities. Others made bandages and clothes, put together packages for soldiers at the front, and helped army wives and disabled soldiers find jobs.

DOCUMENT

U.S. Sanitary Commission, Sketch of Its Purposes (1864)

Many of the changes women experienced during the war years ended when peace returned. Jobs in industry and government disappeared when the men came to reclaim them. Women turned over the operation of farms to returning husbands. But for women whose men came home maimed or not at all, the work had not ended. Nor had the discrimination. Trying to pick up the threads of their former lives, they found it impossible to forget what they had done to help the war effort. At least some of them were sure they had equaled their men in courage and commitment.

The Election of 1864

In the North, the election of 1864 brought some of the transformations of wartime into the political arena. The Democrats, seeking to regain power by capitalizing on war weariness, nominated General George McClellan for president. The party proclaimed the war a failure and demanded an armistice with the South. During the campaign, Democrats accused Lincoln of arbitrarily expanding executive power and denounced sweeping economic measures such as the banking bills. Arguing that the president had transformed the war from one for Union into one for emancipation, they tried to inflame racial passions by insinuating that if the Republicans won, a fusion of blacks and whites would result.

Although Lincoln gained the Republican renomination because of his tight control over party machinery and patronage, his party did not unite behind him. Lincoln seemed to please no one. His veto of the radical reconstruction plan for the South, the Wade–Davis bill, led to cries of "usurpation." The Emancipation Proclamation did not sit well with conservatives. Union defeats during the summer encouraged those who wanted to make peace with the South. In August 1864, a gloomy Lincoln told his cabinet that he expected to lose the election. As late as September, some Republicans actually hoped to reconvene the convention and select another candidate.

Sherman's capture of Atlanta in September 1864 and the march through Georgia to Savannah helped swing voters to Lincoln. In the end, Republicans had no desire to see the Democrats oust their party. Lincoln won 55 percent of the popular vote and swept the electoral college.

Why the North Won

In the months after Lincoln's re-election, the war drew to an agonizing conclusion. Sherman moved north from Atlanta to North Carolina, while Grant pummeled Lee's forces in Virginia. The losses Grant sustained in Virginia were staggering: 18,000 in the Battle of the Wilderness, more than 8,000 at Spotsylvania, and another 12,000 at Cold Harbor. New recruits stepped forward to replace the dead. On April 9, 1865, Grant accepted Lee's surrender at Appomattox. Southern soldiers and officers were allowed to return home with their personal equipment after promising to remain there peaceably. The war was finally over.

IMAGE

Appomattox Court House

Technically, the war was won on the battlefield and at sea. But Grant's military strategy succeeded because the Union's manpower and economic resources could survive staggering losses of men and equipment while the Confederacy's could not. As Union armies pushed back the borders of the Confederacy, the South lost control of territories essential for its war effort. Finally, naval strategy eventually paid off because the North could build enough ships to make its blockade work. In 1861, fully 90 percent of the blockade runners were slipping through the naval cordon. By the war's end, only half made it.

The South had taken tremendous steps toward meeting war needs. But despite the impressive growth of manufacturing and the increasing acreage devoted to foodstuffs, the southern army and the southern people were poorly fed and poorly clothed. As one civilian realized, "The question of bread and meat . . . is beginning to be regarded as a more serious one even than that of War." Women working alone or with disgruntled slaves on farms could not produce enough food. Worn-out farm equipment was not replaced. The government's impressment of slaves and animals cut production. The half million blacks who fled to Union lines also played their part in pulling the South down in defeat.

New industries could not meet the extraordinary demands of wartime, and advancing Union forces destroyed many of them. A Confederate officer in

Destruction of the Confederacy

northern Virginia observed, "Many of our soldiers are thinly clothed and without shoes and in addition to this, very few of the infantry have tents. With this freezing weather, their sufferings are indescribable." Skimpy rations, only one-third of a pound of meat for each soldier a day by 1864, weakened the Confederate force, whose trail was "traceable by the deposit of dysenteric stool" it left behind. By that time, the Union armies were so well supplied that soldiers often threw away heavy blankets and coats as they advanced.

The South's woefully inadequate transportation system also contributed to defeat. Primitive roads deteriorated and became all but impassable without repairs. The railroad system, geared to the needs of cotton, not war, was inefficient. When tracks wore out or were destroyed, they were not replaced. Rails were too heavy for blockade runners to bother with, and as the Confederate railroad coordinator observed in 1865, "Not a single bar of railroad iron has been rolled in the Confederacy since the war, nor can we hope to do better." Thus, food intended for the army rotted awaiting shipment. Supplies were tied up in bottlenecks and soldiers went hungry. Food riots in southern cities pointed to the hunger, anger, and growing demoralization of civilians.

Ironically, measures the Confederacy took to strengthen its ability to win the war, as one Texan later observed, "weakened and paralyzed it." Conscription, impressment, and taxes all contributed to resentment and sometimes open resistance. They fueled class tensions already strained by the poverty that war brought to many yeoman farmers and led some of them to assist the invaders or to join the Union army. The proposal to use slaves as soldiers called into question the war's purpose. The many southern governors who refused to contribute men, money, and supplies on the scale Davis requested implicitly condoned disloyalty to the cause.

It is natural to compare Lincoln and Davis as war leaders. There is no doubt that Lincoln's humanity, his awareness of the terrible costs of war, his determination to save the Union, and his eloquence set

him apart as one of this country's most extraordinary presidents. Yet the men's personal characteristics were probably less important than the differences between the political and social systems of the two regions. Without the support of a party behind him, Davis failed to engender enthusiasm or loyalty. Even though the Republicans rarely united behind Lincoln, they uniformly wanted to keep the Democrats from office. Despite all the squabbles, Republicans tended to support Lincoln's policies in Congress and back in their home districts. Commanding considerable resources of patronage, Lincoln was able to line up federal, state, and local officials behind his party and administration.

Just as the northern political system provided Lincoln with more flexibility and support, its social system also proved more able to meet the war's extraordinary demands. Although both societies adopted innovations in an effort to secure victory, northerners were more cooperative, disciplined, and aggressive in meeting the organizational and production challenges of wartime. In the southern states, old attitudes, habits, and values impeded the war effort. Southern governors, wedded to states' rights, refused to cooperate with the Confederate government. North Carolina, the center of the southern textile industry, actually kept back most uniforms for its own regiments. At the war's end, 92,000 uniforms and thousands of blankets, shoes, and tents still lay in its warehouses. When Sherman approached Atlanta, Georgia's governor would not turn over the 10,000 men in the state army to Confederate commanders. Even slaveholders, whose property had been the cause for secession, resisted the impressment of their slaves for war work.

In the end, the Confederacy collapsed, exhausted and bleeding. Hungry soldiers received letters from their families revealing desperate situations at home. They worried and then slipped away. By December 1864, the Confederate desertion rate had passed 50 percent. Replacements could not be found. Farmers hid livestock and produce from tax collectors. Many southerners felt their cause was lost and resigned themselves to defeat. But some fought on till the end. One northerner described them as they surrendered at Appomattox:

> Before us in proud humiliation stood the embodiment of manhood: men whom neither toils and sufferings, nor the fact of death, nor disaster, nor hopelessness could bend from their resolve; standing before us now, thin, worn, and famished, but erect, and with eyes looking level into ours, waking memories that bound us together as no other bond.

The Costs of War

Field Hospital, Virginia, 1862

The long war was over, but the memories of that event would fester for years to come. About 3 million American men, one-third of all free males between ages 15 and 59, had served in the army. Each would remember his own personal history of the war. For George Eagleton, who had worked in army field hospitals, the history was one of "Death and destruction! Blood! Blood! Agony! Death! Gaping flesh wounds, broken bones, amputations, bullet and bomb fragment extractions." Of all wars Americans have fought, none has been more deadly. The death rate during this war was more than five times the death rate during World War II. About 360,000 Union soldiers and another 258,000 Confederate soldiers died, about one-third of them because their wounds were either improperly treated or not treated at all. Disease claimed more lives than combat. Despite the efforts of men such as Eagleton and the women army nurses, hospitals could not handle the scores of wounded and dying. "Glory is not for the private soldier, such as die in the hospitals," reflected one Tennessee soldier, "being eat up with the deadly gangrene, and being imperfectly waited on."

Amputation Being Performed, 1863

Thousands of men would be reminded of the human costs of war by the injuries they carried with them to the grave, by the missing limbs that marked them as Civil War veterans. About 275,000 on each side were maimed. Another 410,000 (195,000 northerners and 215,000 southerners) would remember wretchedly overcrowded and unsanitary prison camps. The lucky ones would recall only the dullness and boredom. The worst memory was of those who rotted in prison camps, such as Andersonville in Georgia, where 31,000 Union soldiers were confined. At the war's end, more than 12,000 graves were counted there.

Some Americans found it hard to throw off wartime experiences and adjust to peace. As Arthur Carpenter's letters suggest, he gradually grew accustomed to army life. War provided him with a sense of purpose. When it was over, he felt aimless. A full year after the war's end, he wrote, "Camp life agrees with me better than any other." Many others had difficulty returning to civilian routines and finding a new focus for life. Even those who adjusted successfully discovered that they looked at life from a different perspective. The experience of fighting, of mixing with all sorts of people from many places, and of traveling far from home had lifted former soldiers out of their familiar local world and widened their vision. Fighting the war made the concept of national union real.

Unanswered Questions

Richmond in Ruins

What, then, had the war accomplished? On the one hand, death and destruction. Physically, the war devastated the South. Historians have estimated a 43 percent decline in southern wealth during the war years, exclusive of the value of slaves. Great cities like Atlanta, Columbia, and Richmond lay in ruins. Fields lay weed-choked and uncultivated. Tools were worn out. One-third or more of the South's stock of mules, horses, and swine had disappeared. Two-thirds of the railroads had been destroyed. Thousands were hungry, homeless, and bitter about their four years of what now appeared a useless sacrifice. More than 4 million slaves, a vast financial investment, were free.

Charleston, South Carolina, in 1865 What does this picture suggest about the impact of the war on Charleston? *(Library of Congress, [LC-DIG-cwpb 02421 DLC])*

On the other hand, the war had resolved the question of union and ended the debate over the relationship of the states to the federal government. During the war, Republicans seized the opportunity to pass legislation that would foster national union and economic growth: the Pacific Railroad Act of 1862, which set aside huge tracts of public land to finance the transcontinental railroad; the Homestead Act of 1862, which was to provide yeoman farmers cheaper and easier access to the public domain; the Morrill Act of 1862, which established support for agricultural (land-grant) colleges; and the banking acts of 1863 and 1864.

The war had also resolved the issue of slavery, the thorny problem that had so long plagued American life. Yet uncertainties outnumbered certainties. What would happen to the former slaves? When blacks had fled to Union lines during the war, commanders had not known what to do with them. Now the problem became even more pressing. Were blacks to have the same civil and political rights as whites? In the Union army, they had been second-class soldiers. The behavior of Union forces toward liberated blacks in the South showed how deep the stain of racism went. One white soldier, caught stealing a quilt by a former slave, shouted, "I'm fighting for $14 a month and the Union"—not to end slavery. Would blacks be given land, the means for economic independence? What would be their relations with their former owners?

What, indeed, would be the status of the conquered South in the nation? Should it be punished for the rebellion? Some people thought so. Should southerners keep their property? Some people thought not. There were clues to Lincoln's intentions. As early as December 1863, the president had announced a generous plan of reconciliation. He was willing to recognize the government of former Confederate states established by a group of citizens equal to 10 percent of those voting in 1860, as long as the group swore to support the Constitution and to accept the abolition of slavery. He began to restore state governments in three former Confederate states on that basis. But not all northerners agreed with his leniency, and the debate continued.

In his 1865 inaugural address, Lincoln urged Americans to harbor "malice towards none . . . and charity for all." "Let us strive," he urged, "to finish the work we are in; to bind up the nation's wounds . . . to do all which may achieve a just and lasting peace." Privately, the president said the same thing. Generosity and goodwill would pave the way for reconciliation. On April 14, he pressed the point home to his cabinet. His wish was to avoid persecution and bloodshed. That same evening, only five days after the surrender at Appomattox, the president attended a play at Ford's Theatre. There, as one horrified eyewitness reported,

DOCUMENT

Lincoln, Second Inaugural Address (1865)

> a pistol was heard and a man . . . dressed in a black suit of clothes leaped onto the stage apparently from the President's box. He held in his right hand a dagger whose blade appeared about 10 inches long. . . . Every one leaped to his feet, and the cry of "the President is assassinated" was heard—Getting where I could see into the President's box, I saw Mrs. Lincoln . . . in apparent anguish.

DOCUMENT

Lincoln Assassination Reward Poster

John Wilkes Booth, a southern sympathizer, had killed the president.

TIMELINE

1861 Lincoln calls up state militia and suspends habeas corpus
First Battle of Bull Run
Union blockades the South

1862 Battles at Shiloh, Bull Run, and Antietam
Monitor and *Virginia* battle
First black regiment authorized by Union
Union issues greenbacks
South institutes military draft
Pacific Railroad Act
Homestead Act
Morrill Land-Grant College Act

1863 Lincoln issues Emancipation Proclamation
Congress adopts military draft

Battles of Gettysburg and Vicksburg
Union Banking Act
Southern tax laws and impressment act
New York draft riots
Southern food riots

1864 Sherman's march through Georgia
Lincoln re-elected
Union Banking Act

1865 Lee surrenders at Appomattox
Lincoln assassinated; Andrew Johnson becomes president

Conclusion

An Uncertain Future

As the war ended, many Americans grieved for the man whose decisions had so marked their lives for five years. "Strong men have wept tonight & the nation will mourn tomorrow," wrote one eyewitness to the assassination. Many more wept for friends and relations who had not survived the war, but whose actions had in one way or another contributed to its outcome. The lucky ones, like Arthur Carpenter and George and Ethie Eagleton, now faced the necessity of putting their lives back together and moving forward into an uncertain future. Perhaps not all Americans realized how drastically the war had altered their lives, their prospects, and their nation. It was only as time passed that the war's impact became clear to them. And it was only with time that they recognized how many problems the war had left unsolved. It is to these years of Reconstruction that we turn next.

Questions for Review and Reflection

1. Assess the strengths and weaknesses of the North and South at the beginning of the war. What northern strengths actually led to northern victory and what Confederate weaknesses explain southern defeat?

2. Describe the military campaigns in each region of the country over the course of the war.

3. What were the most important transformations in the Union and Confederacy during the war and why, in your opinion, were these changes so significant?

4. Compare and contrast Lincoln and Davis as war leaders and the two governments over which they presided.

5. What role did race play during the war?

6. Consider the Civil War as a struggle between differing beliefs and values and assess the importance of northern victory for this struggle. In what ways did the war's outcome realize or fail to realize the founding principles of this nation?

Recommended Reading

Recommended Readings are posted on the Web site for this textbook. Visit www.ablongman.com/nash

Fiction and Film

Stephen Crane's *The Red Badge of Courage* (1895) examines the soldier's experience during the war, while MacKinlay Kantor's novel *Andersonville* (1955) provides an insight into the Civil War's worst prison camp. *Enemy Women* (2002) by Paulette Jiles follows the journey of a young Missouri woman who tries to rescue her father who has been carried off by the Union militia to St. Louis. The feature film *Glory* (1989) focuses on a black regiment, the 54th Massachusetts, that demonstrated its heroism in the midst of battle. You will get a better sense of the character of warfare and race relations if you see this film. *Cold Mountain* (2003) follows a Confederate soldier as he tries to reach his home in 1864. The movie gives a good picture of the disintegration of southern society, but you will not find much indication of why the South went to war. The classic *Gone with the Wind* (1939) offers a romanticized but powerful picture of southern life before, during, and after the Civil War. Ken Burns's famous documentary series *The Civil War* (1990) is a powerful evocation of that period with ample use of period photographs and documents.

Discovering U.S. History Online

Index of Civil War Information on the Internet

www.cwc.lsu.edu

A good starting place for research, this index has as its mission to "locate, index, and make available all appropriate private and public data on the Internet regarding the Civil War" and to promote the study of the Civil War from the perspectives of all professions, occupations, and academic disciplines. It includes a guide on evaluating sources of information on the Internet.

Causes of the Civil War

www.members.aol.com/jfepperson/causes.html

The site offers a collection of "primary documents from the period of the secession crisis . . . with the goal of shedding light on the causes of secession, hence of the war." Document sections include "Party Platforms and Secession Documents," "Compromise Proposals," and "Abraham Lincoln's Speeches and Letters," as well as documents from individual states, other quotes, and political speeches and commentaries.

Crisis at Fort Sumter

www.tulane.edu/~latner/CrisisMain.html

This well-crafted use of hypermedia with assignments and problems explains and explores the events and causes leading to the Civil War.

Charleston

www.awod.com/gallery/probono/cwchas/
cwlayout.html

William Hamilton, the author, attorney and Civil War re-enactor, presents the history of the Civil War in and around Charleston, South Carolina, via timelines, biographies, primary sources, battleground information, and illustrations.

Abraham Lincoln

www.ipl.org/ref/POTUS/alincoln.html

This site contains basic factual data about Lincoln, including his presidency, speeches, cabinet members, and election information.

Black American Contributions to Union Intelligence During the Civil War

www.odci.gov/cia/publications/dispatches/

This illustrated article, reprinted from the CIA journal *Studies in Intelligence* (Winter 1998–1999) offers information about this little-known contribution to the Union war effort.

America's First Look into the Camera: Daguerreotype Portraits and Views, 1839–1864

www.memory.loc.gov/ammem/daghtml/dagpres.html

This exhibit presents samples of the major subjects of this searchable database of more than 650 daguerreotypes. Portraits, architectural views, and some street scenes make up most of the collection.

The Union Reconstructed

In a scene like that depicted in this **Winslow Homer** painting titled *A Visit from the Old Mistress,* imagine Adele Allston returning to her plantation to reunite with former slaves. **What sort of new relationships might they form in a world that had been profoundly changed by the wrenching Civil War?** *(Winslow Homer, A Visit from the Old Mistress, 1876. National Museum of American Art/Art Resource , NY)*

American Stories

Blacks and Whites Redefine Their Dreams and Relationships

In April 1864, a year before Lincoln's assassination, Robert Allston died, leaving his wife, Adele, and his daughter, Elizabeth, to manage their many rice plantations. Elizabeth felt a "sense of terrible desolation and sorrow" as the Civil War raged around her. With Union troops moving through coastal South Carolina in the winter of 1864–1865, Elizabeth's sorrow turned to "terror" as Union soldiers arrived and searched for liquor, firearms, and valuables, subjecting the Allston women to an insulting search. The women fled.

Later, Yankee troops encouraged the Allston slaves to take furniture, food, and other goods from the Big House. "My house at Chicora Wood plantation has been robbed of every article of furniture and much defaced," Adele complained to the local Union commander, adding, "all my provisions of meat, lard, coffee and tea [were] taken [and] distributed among the Negroes." Before they left, the liberating Union soldiers gave the keys to the crop barns to the semifree slaves.

After the war, Adele Allston swore allegiance to the United States and secured a written order for the newly freed African Americans to relinquish those keys. She and Elizabeth returned in the summer of 1865 to reclaim the plantations and reassert white authority. She was assured that although the blacks had guns, "no outrage has been committed against the whites except in the matter of property." But property was the issue. Possession of the keys to the barns, Elizabeth wrote, would be the "test case" of whether former masters or former slaves would control land, labor, and its fruits, as well as the subtle aspects of interpersonal relations.

Nervously, Adele and Elizabeth Allston confronted their former slaves at their old home. To their surprise, a pleasant reunion took place as the Allston women greeted the blacks by name, inquired after their children, and caught up on their lives. A trusted black foreman handed over the keys to the barns. This harmonious scene was repeated elsewhere.

But at one plantation, the Allston women met defiant and armed African Americans, who ominously lined both sides of the road as the carriage arrived. An old black driver, Uncle Jacob, was unsure whether to yield the keys to the barns full of rice and corn, put there by slave labor. Mrs. Allston insisted. As Uncle Jacob hesitated, an angry young man shouted out: "If you give up the key, blood'll flow." Uncle Jacob slowly slipped the keys back into his pocket.

The African Americans sang freedom songs and brandished hoes, pitchforks, and guns to discourage anyone from going to town for help. Two blacks, however, slipped away to find some Union officers. The Allston women spent the night safely, if restlessly, in their house. Early the next morning, they were awakened by a knock at the unlocked front door. There stood Uncle Jacob. Without a word, he gave back the keys.

The story of the keys reveals most of the essential human ingredients of the Reconstruction era. Defeated southern whites were determined to resume control of both land and labor. The law and federal enforcement generally supported the property owners. The Allston women were friendly to the blacks in a maternal way and insisted on restoring prewar deference in black–white relations. Adele and Elizabeth, in short, both feared and cared about their former slaves.

The African American freedpeople likewise revealed mixed feelings toward their former owners: anger, loyalty, love, resentment, and pride. They paid respect to the Allstons but not to their property and crops. They did not want revenge but rather economic independence and freedom.

In this encounter between former slaves and their mistresses, the role of the northern federal officials is most revealing. Union soldiers, literally and symbolically, gave the keys of freedom to the freedpeople but did not stay around long enough to guarantee that freedom. Despite initially encouraging blacks to plunder the master's house and seize the crops, in the crucial encounter after the war, northern officials had disappeared. Understanding the limits of northern help, Uncle Jacob ended up handing the keys to land and liberty back to his former owner. The blacks realized that if they wanted to ensure their freedom, they had to do it themselves.

This chapter describes what happened to the conflicting goals and dreams of three groups as they sought to redefine new social, economic, and political relationships during the postwar Reconstruction era. It also shows how America sought to re-establish stable democratic governments. Amid vast devastation and bitter race and class divisions, Civil War survivors sought to put their lives back together. Victorious but variously motivated northern officials, defeated but defiant southern planters, and impoverished but hopeful African Americans could not all fulfill their conflicting goals and dreams, yet each had to try. Reconstruction would be divisive, leaving a mixed legacy of human gains and losses.

THE BITTERSWEET AFTERMATH OF WAR

"There are sad changes in store for both races," the daughter of a Georgia planter wrote in her diary in the summer of 1865. To understand the bittersweet nature of Reconstruction, we must look at the state of the nation after the assassination of President Lincoln.

The United States in 1865

Constitutionally, the "Union" faced a crisis in April 1865. What was the status of the 11 former Confederate states? The North had denied the South's constitutional right to secede but needed four years of civil war and more than 600,000 deaths to win the point. Lincoln's official position had been that the southern states had never left the Union, which was "constitutionally indestructible," and were only "out of their proper relation" with the United States. The president, therefore, as commander in chief, had the authority to decide how to set relations right again.

Lincoln's congressional opponents argued that by declaring war on the Union, the Confederate states had broken their constitutional ties and reverted to a kind of pre-statehood status, like territories or "conquered provinces." Congress, therefore, should resolve the constitutional issues and direct Reconstruction.

Politically, differences between Congress and the White House mirrored a wider struggle between two branches of the national government. During war, as has usually been the case, the executive branch assumed broad powers necessary for rapid mobilization of resources and domestic security. Many believed, however, that Lincoln had far exceeded his constitutional authority and that his successor, Andrew Johnson, was worse. Would Congress reassert its authority?

In April 1865, the Republican party ruled virtually unchecked. Republicans had made immense achievements in the eyes of the northern public: winning the war, preserving the Union, and freeing the slaves. They had enacted sweeping economic programs on behalf of free labor and free enterprise, including a high protective tariff, a national banking system, broad use of the power to tax and to borrow and print money, generous federal appropriations for internal improvements, the Homestead Act, and an act to establish land-grant colleges to teach agricultural and mechanical skills. But the party remained an uneasy grouping of former Whigs, Know-Nothings, Unionist Democrats, and antislavery idealists.

The United States in 1865: Crises at the End of the Civil War

Given the enormous casualties, costs, and crises of the immediate aftermath of the Civil War, what attitudes and behaviors would you predict for the major combatants in the war?

Military Casualties

360,000 Union soldiers dead
260,000 Confederate soldiers dead
620,000 Total dead
375,000 Seriously wounded and maimed
995,000 Casualties nationwide in a total male population of 15 million (nearly 1 in 15)

Physical and Economic Crises

The South devastated; its railroads, industry, and some major cities in ruins; its fields and livestock wasted

Constitutional Crisis

Eleven former Confederate states not a part of the Union, their status unclear and future status uncertain

Political Crisis

Republican party (entirely of the North) dominant in Congress; a former Democratic slaveholder from Tennessee, Andrew Johnson, in the presidency

Social Crisis

Nearly 4 million black freedpeople throughout the South facing challenges of survival and freedom, along with thousands of hungry, demobilized Confederate soldiers and displaced white families

Psychological Crisis

Incalculable stores of resentment, bitterness, anger, and despair, North and South, white and black

Conflicting Goals During Reconstruction

Examine these conflicting goals, which, at a human level, were the challenge of Reconstruction. How could each group possibly fulfill its goals when so many of them conflict with those of other groups? You may find yourself referring back to this chart throughout the chapter. How can each group fulfill its goals?

Victorious Northern ("Radical") Republicans

- Justify the war by remaking southern society in the image of the North
- Inflict political but not physical or economic punishment on Confederate leaders
- Continue programs of economic progress begun during the war: high tariffs, railroad subsidies, national banking
- Maintain the Republican party in power
- Help the freedpeople make the transition to full freedom by providing them with the tools of citizenship (suffrage) and equal economic opportunity

Northern Moderates (Republicans and Democrats)

- Quickly establish peace and order, reconciliation between North and South
- Bestow on the southern states leniency, amnesty, and merciful readmission to the Union
- Perpetuate land ownership, free labor, market competition, and other capitalist ventures
- Promote local self-determination of economic and social issues; limit interference by the national government
- Provide limited support for black suffrage

Old Southern Planter Aristocracy (Former Confederates)

- Ensure protection from black uprising and prevent excessive freedom for former slaves
- Secure amnesty, pardon, and restoration of confiscated lands
- Restore traditional plantation-based, market-crop economy with blacks as cheap labor force
- Restore traditional political leaders in the states
- Restore traditional paternalistic race relations as basis of social order

New "Other South": Yeoman Farmers and Former Whigs (Unionists)

- Quickly establish peace and order, reconciliation between North and South
- Achieve recognition of loyalty and economic value of yeoman farmers
- Create greater diversity in southern economy: capital investments in railroads, factories, and the diversification of agriculture
- Displace the planter aristocracy with new leaders drawn from new economic interests
- Limit the rights and powers of freedpeople; extend suffrage only to the educated few

Black Freedpeople

- Secure physical protection from abuse and terror by local whites
- Achieve economic independence through land ownership (40 acres and a mule) and equal access to trades
- Receive educational opportunity and foster the development of family and cultural bonds
- Obtain equal civil rights and protection under the law
- Commence political participation through the right to vote

The Democrats were in shambles. Republicans depicted southern Democrats as rebels, murderers, and traitors, and they blasted northern Democrats as weak-willed, disloyal, and opposed to economic growth and progress. Nevertheless, in the election of 1864, needing to show that the war was a bipartisan effort, the Republicans had named a Unionist Tennessee Democrat, Andrew Johnson, as Lincoln's vice president. Now the tactless Johnson headed the government.

Economically, the United States in the spring of 1865 presented stark contrasts. Northern cities and railroads hummed with productive activity; southern cities and railroads lay in ruin. Northern banks flourished; southern financial institutions were bankrupt. Mechanized northern farms were more productive than ever; southern farms and plantations, especially those along Sherman's march, resembled a "howling waste." "The Yankees came through," a Georgian said, "and just tore up everything."

Socially, a half million southern whites faced starvation as soldiers, many with amputated arms and legs, returned home in April 1865. Yet, as a later southern writer explained, "If this war had smashed the Southern world, it had left the essential Southern mind and will . . . entirely unshaken." In this horrific context, nearly 4 million freedpeople faced the challenges of freedom. After initial joy and celebration in jubilee songs, freedmen and freedwomen quickly realized their continuing dependence on former owners. A Mississippian woman said:

AUDIO
Free at Last

I used to think if I could be free I should be the happiest of anybody in the world. But when my master come to me, and says—Lizzie, you is free! it seems like I was in a kind of daze. And when I would wake up in the morning I would think to myself, Is I free? Hasn't I got to get up before day light and go into the field of work?

For Lizzie and 4 million other blacks, everything—and nothing—had changed.

Hopes Among the Freedpeople

Throughout the South in the summer of 1865, optimism surged through the old slave quarters. As Union soldiers marched through Richmond, blacks chanted: "Slavery chain done broke at last! Gonna praise God till I die!" The slavery chain, however, broke slowly, link by link. After Union troops swept through an area, "we'd begin celebratin'," one man said, but Confederate soldiers would follow, or master and overseer would return, and "tell us to go back to work." A North Carolina slave recalled celebrating emancipation "about twelve times." The freedmen and

Suffering the Consequences of War This 1867 engraving shows two southern women and their children soon after the Civil War. In what ways are they similar and in what ways different? Is there a basis for sisterhood bonds? What separates them, if anything? From *Frank Leslie's Illustrated Newspaper*, February 23, 1867. *(The Granger Collection, New York)*

freedwomen learned, therefore, not to rejoice too quickly or openly.

Gradually, though, African Americans began to test the reality of freedom. Typically, their first step was to leave the plantation, if only for a few hours or days. "If I stay here I'll never know I am free," said a South Carolina woman, who went to work as a cook in a nearby town. Some freedpeople cut their ties entirely—returning to an earlier master, or, more often, going into towns and cities to find jobs, schools, churches, and association with other blacks, safe from whippings and retaliation.

Many freedpeople left the plantation in search of a spouse, parent, or child sold away years before. Advertisements detailing these sorrowful searches filled African

DOCUMENT

Jourdon Anderson to His Former Master (1865)

American newspapers. For those who found a spouse and those who had been living together in slave marriages, freedom meant getting married legally, sometimes in mass ceremonies common in the first months of emancipation. Legal marriage was important morally, but it also established the legitimacy of children and meant access to land titles and other economic opportunities. Marriage brought special burdens for black women who assumed the now-familiar double role of housekeeper and breadwinner. Their determination to create a traditional family life and care for their children resulted in the withdrawal of many women from plantation field labor.

Freedpeople also demonstrated their new status by choosing surnames. Names connoting independence, such as Washington, were common. Revealing their mixed feelings toward their former masters, some would adopt their master's name, while others would pick "any big name 'ceptin' their master's." Emancipation changed black manners around whites as well. Masks fell, and expressions of deference—tipping a hat, stepping aside, feigning happiness, calling whites "master" or "ma'am"—diminished. For the blacks, these changes were necessary expressions of selfhood, proving that race relations had changed, while whites saw such behaviors as acts of "insolence" and "insubordination."

The freedpeople made education a priority. A Mississippi farmer vowed to "give my children a chance to go to school, for I consider education next best ting to liberty." An official in Virginia echoed the observation of many when he said that the freedmen were "down right crazy to learn." A traveler throughout the South counted "at least five hundred" schools "taught by colored people." Another noted that blacks were "determined to be self-taught."

Other than the passion for education, the primary goal for most African Americans was getting land. "All I want is to git to own fo' or five acres ob land, dat I can build me a little house on and call my home," a Mississippi black said. Through a combination of educational and economic independence, basic means of controlling one's own life, labor and land, freedpeople like Lizzie would make sure that emancipation was real.

During the war, some Union generals had put liberated slaves in charge of confiscated and abandoned lands. In the Sea Islands of South Carolina and Georgia, African Americans had been working 40-acre plots of land and harvesting their own crops for several years. Farther inland, freed-people who received land were the former slaves of the Cherokee and Creek. Some blacks held title to these lands. Northern philanthropists had organized others to grow cotton for the Treasury Department to prove the superiority of free labor. In Mississippi, thousands of former slaves worked 40-acre tracts on leased lands that ironically had been previously owned by Jefferson Davis. In this highly successful experiment, they made profits sufficient to repay the government for initial costs, then lost the land to Davis's brother.

DOCUMENT

James C. Beecher, Report on Land Reform (1865, 1866)

Many freedpeople expected a new economic order as fair payment for their years of involuntary work. "It's de white man's turn ter labor now," a black preacher told a group of Florida field hands, saying, "de Guverment is gwine ter gie ter ev'ry Nigger forty acres of lan' an' a mule." One man was willing to settle for less, desiring only one acre of land— "Ef you make it de acre dat Marsa's house sets on." Another was more guarded, aware of how easy the power could shift back to white planters: "Gib us our

Tradition and Change In these two scenes from 1865, one an early photograph of a group of newly freed former slaves leaving the cotton fields after a day of gang labor carrying cotton on their heads, the other a painting titled *The Armed Slave*, everything—and nothing—had changed. What has changed and not changed from slavery times? What is the meaning of the painting? Note the position of gun and bayonet. Could you create a story about these two images? *(Top: © Collection of The New-York Historical Society; bottom: William Spang, The Armed Slave. The Civil War Library and Museum, Philadelphia)*

AMERICAN VOICES

Calvin Holly, A Black Union Soldier's Letter Protesting Conditions After the War

This December 16, 1865, letter from Calvin Holly ("colered Privt") to Major General O. O. Howard, head of the Freedmen's Bureau, describes the horrible conditions for freedpeople in Vicksburg, Mississippi, eight months after Appomattox.

Major General, O. O. Howard, Suffer me to address you a few lines in reguard to the colered people in this State, from all I can learn and see, I think the colered people are in a great many ways being outraged beyond humanity, houses have been tourn down from over the heades of women and Children—and the old Negroes after they have been worked there till they are 70 or 80 yers of age drive them off in the cold to frieze and starve to death.

One Woman come to (Col) Thomas, the coldest day that has been this winter and said that she and her eight children lay out last night, and come near friezing after She had paid some wrent on the house Some are being knocked down for saying they are free, while a great many are being worked just as they ust to be when Slaves, without any compensation. Report came in town this morning that two colered women was found dead side the Jackson road with their throats cot lying side by side. . . . So, General, to make short of a long story, I think the safety of this country depenes upon giving the Colered man all the rights of a white man, and especially the Rebs. and let him know that there is power enough in the arm of the Government to give Justice, to all her loyal citizens—

■ *Who won the Civil War? Who lost? How complex are these questions?*

Source: Records of the Bureau of Refugees, Freedmen, and Abandoned Lands, National Archives

own land and we take care ourselves; but widout land, de ole massas can hire us or starve us, as dey please." Cautions aside, freedpeople had every expectation of receiving the "forty acres and a mule" that had been promised. Once they obtained land, family unity, and education, some looked forward to civil rights and the vote—along with protection from vengeful defeated Confederates.

The White South's Fearful Response

White southerners had equally strong dreams and expectations. Middle-class (yeoman) farmers and poor whites stood beside rich planters in bread lines, all hoping to regain land and livelihood. Suffering from "extreme want and destitution," as a Cherokee County, Georgia, resident put it, southern whites responded to the immediate postwar crises with feelings of outrage, loss, and injustice. "My pa paid his own money for our niggers," one man said, "and that's not all they've robbed us of. They have taken our horses and cattle and sheep and everything." Others felt the loss more personally, as former faithful slaves suddenly left. "Something dreadful has happened," a Florida woman wrote in 1865. "My dear black mammy has left us. . . . I feel lost, I feel as if someone is dead in the house. Whatever will I do without my Mammy?"

DOCUMENT

"I'm a Good Old Rebel" (1866)

A more dominant emotion than sorrow was fear. The entire structure of southern society was shaken, and the semblance of racial peace and order that slavery had provided was shattered. Many white southerners could hardly imagine a society without blacks in bondage. Having lost control of

---

The Promise of Land: 40 Acres

Note the progression in various documents in this chapter from promised lands (this page), to lands restored to whites (p. 529), to work contracts (p. 535), to semiautonomous tenant farms (p. 536). Freedom came by degrees to freedpeople. Was this progress?

To All Whom It May Concern

Edisto Island, August 15th, 1865

George Owens, having selected for settlement forty acres of Land, on Theodore Belab's Place, pursuant to Special Field Orders, No. 15, Headquarters Military Division of the Mississippi, Savannah, Ga., Jan. 16, 1865; he has permission to hold and occupy the said Tract, subject to such regulations as may be established by proper authority; and all persons are prohibited from interfering with him in his possession of the same.

By command of   R. SAXTON
Brev't Maj. Gen.,
Ass't Comm.
S.C., Ga., and Fla.

The End of Slavery? The Black Codes, widespread violence against freedpeople, and President John-son's veto of the civil rights bill gave rise to the sardonic title "Slavery Is Dead?" in this Thomas Nast cartoon. What do you see in the two scenes? Describe the two images of justice. What is Nast saying? *(Courtesy of The Newberry Library, Chicago)*

all that was familiar and revered, whites feared everything—from losing their cheap labor supply to having blacks sit next to them on trains. Many feared the inconvenience of doing chores such as housework that they had rarely done before. A Georgia woman, Eliza Andrews, complained that it seemed to her a "waste of time for people who are capable of doing something better to spend their time sweeping and dusting while scores of lazy ne-groes that are fit for nothing else are lying around idle." Worse yet was the "impudent and presumin'" new manners of former slaves, a North Carolinian put it, worrying that blacks wanted social as well as civil equality.

Ironically, given the rape of black women during slavery, southern whites' worst fears were of rape and revenge. African American "impudence," some thought, would lead to legal intermarriage and "Africanization," the destruction of the purity of the white race. African American Union soldiers seemed especially ominous. These fears were greatly exagger-ated, as demobilization of black soldiers came

quickly, and rape and violence by blacks against whites was extremely rare.

Believing their world turned upside down, the for-mer planter aristocracy tried to set it right again. To reestablish white dominance, southern legislatures passed "Black Codes" in the first year after the war. Many of the codes granted freedpeople the right to marry, sue and be sued, testify in court, and hold property. But these rights were qualified. Complicated passages explained under exactly what circumstances blacks could testify against whites or own property (mostly they could not) or exercise other rights of free people. Forbidden were racial intermarriage, bearing arms, possessing alcoholic beverages, sitting on trains (except in baggage compartments), being on city streets at night, and congre-gating in large groups.

Many of the qualified rights guaranteed by the Black Codes were passed only to in-duce the federal government to withdraw

DOCUMENT

The Mississippi Black Code (1865)

DOCUMENT

"From the Colored Citizens of Norfolk" (1865)

AMERICAN VOICES

James A. Payne, A Southern White Man's Letter Protesting Conditions After the War

The September 1, 1867, letter of James A. Payne, a Baton Rouge, Louisiana, planter, to his stepdaughter describes his reasons for wanting to leave Louisiana.

Dear Kate,

. . . Perhaps all of you may think it strange that I should break up housekeeping so soon after getting them here but this country is changing is rapidly that it is Impossible to point out the future. My prejudices against Negroe equality can never be got over it is coming about here that equality is so far forced upon you that you may protest as much as you please but your Childrens Associates will be the Negroes The Schooles are equal. The Negroe have the ascendancy, and can <u>out vote</u> the Whites upon every thing Then it has always been my intention to put the Boys to boarding School Just as soon as they were old enough I would like to have Kept them with Grace one more year, she

was carrying them along well making them Little Gentlemen. but I became satisfied we were going to have yellow fever and I did not feel willing to Keep the Children here and risk their lives when there was nothing particular to be gained. . . . There is no yellow fever in Town yet but it is getting pretty Bad in New Orleans and we look for it every day.

- *What do you think is Payne's main reason for wanting to leave Louisiana?*

- *How do you reconcile Payne's "voice" and views with Calvin Holly's "voice" and views from nearby Mississippi two years earlier?*

- *What do these differences suggest about the complex difficulties of Reconstruction?*

its remaining troops from the South. This was a crucial issue, for in many places marauding groups of whites were terrorizing defenseless blacks. In one small district in Kentucky, for example, a government agent reported in 1865:

Twenty-three cases of severe and inhuman beating and whipping of men; four of beating and shooting; two of robbing and shooting; three of robbing; five men shot and killed; two shot and wounded; four beaten to death; one beaten and roasted; three women assaulted and ravished; four women beaten; two women tied up and whipped until insensible; two men and their families beaten and driven from their homes, and their property destroyed; two instances of burning of dwellings, and one of the inmates shot.

Freedpeople clearly needed protection and the right to testify in court against whites.

For white planters, the violence was another sign of social disorder that could be eased only by restoring a plantation-based society. Besides, they needed African American labor. Key provisions of the Black Codes regulated freedpeople's economic status. "Vagrancy" laws provided that any blacks not "lawfully employed" (by a white employer) could be arrested, jailed, fined, or hired out to a man who would assume responsibility for their debts and behavior. The codes regulated black laborers' work contracts with white

landowners, including severe penalties for leaving before the yearly contract was fulfilled and rules for proper behavior, attitude, and manners. A Kentucky newspaper was blunt: "The tune . . . will not be 'forty acres and a mule,' but . . . 'work nigger or starve.'"

NATIONAL RECONSTRUCTION POLITICS

The Black Codes directly challenged the national government in 1865. Would it use its power to uphold the codes, white property rights, and racial intimidation, or to defend the liberties of the freedpeople? Although the primary drama of Reconstruction pitted white landowners against black freedmen over land, labor, and liberties in the South, in the background of these local struggles lurked the debate over Reconstruction policy among politicians in Washington. This dual drama would extend well into the twentieth century.

Presidential Reconstruction by Proclamation

After initially demanding that the defeated Confederates be punished for "treason," President Johnson

Promised Land Restored to Whites

Richard H. Jenkins, an applicant for the restoration of his plantation on Wadmalaw Island, S. C., called "Rackett Hall," the same having been unoccupied during the past year and up to the 1st of Jan. 1866, except by one freedman who planted no crop, and being held by the Bureau of Refugees, Freedmen and Abandoned Lands, having conformed to the requirements of Circular No. 15 of said Bureau, dated Washington, D. C., Sept. 12, 1865, the aforesaid property is hereby restored to his possession.

. . . The Undersigned, Richard H. Jenkins, does hereby solemnly promise and engage, that he will secure to the Refugees and Freedmen now resident on his Wadmalaw Island Estate, the crops of the past year, harvested or unharvested; also, that the said Refugees and Freedmen shall be allowed to remain at their present houses or other homes on the island, so long as the responsible Refugees and Freedmen (embracing parents, guardians, and other natural protectors) shall enter into contracts, by leases or for wages, in terms satisfactory to the Supervising Board.

Also, that the undersigned will take the proper steps to enter into contracts with the above described responsible Refugees and Freedmen, the latter being required on their part to enter into said contracts on or before the 15th day of February, 1866, or surrender their right to remain on the said estate, it being understood that if they are unwilling to contract after the expiration of said period, the Supervising Board is to aid in getting them homes and employment elsewhere.

Andrew Johnson

soon adopted a more lenient policy. On May 29, 1865, he issued two proclamations setting forth his Reconstruction program. Like Lincoln's, it rested on the claim that the southern states had never left the Union.

Johnson's first proclamation continued Lincoln's policies by offering "amnesty and pardon, with restoration of all rights of property" to most former Confederates who would swear allegiance to the Constitution and the Union. Johnson revealed his Jacksonian hostility to "aristocratic" planters by exempting government leaders of the former Confederacy and rich rebels with taxable property valued over $20,000. They could, however, apply for individual pardons, which Johnson granted to nearly all applicants.

In his second proclamation, Johnson accepted the reconstructed government of North Carolina and prescribed the steps by which other southern states could reestablish state governments. First, the president would appoint a provisional governor, who would call a state convention representing those "who are loyal to the United States," including persons who took the oath of allegiance or were otherwise pardoned. The convention must ratify the Thirteenth Amendment, which abolished slavery; void secession; repudiate Confederate debts; and elect new state officials and members of Congress.

Under Johnson's plan, all southern states completed Reconstruction and sent representatives to Congress, which convened in December 1865. Defiant southern voters elected dozens of former officers and legislators of the Confederacy, including a few not yet pardoned. Some state conventions hedged on ratifying the Thirteenth Amendment, and some asserted former owners' right to compensation for lost slave property. No state convention provided for black suffrage, and most did nothing to guarantee civil rights, schooling, or economic protection for the freedpeople. Eight months after Appomattox, the southern states were back in the Union, freedpeople were working for former masters, and the new president seemed firmly in charge. Reconstruction seemed to be over. A young French reporter, Georges Clemenceau, wondered whether the North, having made so many "painful sacrifices," would "let itself be tricked out of what it had spent so much trouble and perseverance to win."

Congressional Reconstruction by Amendment

Late in 1865, northern leaders painfully saw that almost none of their postwar goals were being fulfilled and that the Republicans were likely to lose their political power. Would Democrats and the South gain by postwar elections what they had been unable to achieve by civil war?

A song popular in the North in 1866 posed the question, "Who shall rule this American Nation?"—those who would betray their country and "murder the innocent freedmen" or those "loyal millions" who had shed their "blood in battle"? The answer was obvious. Congressional Republicans, led by Congressman Thaddeus Stevens of Pennsylvania and Senator Charles Sumner of Massachusetts, decided to set their own policies for Reconstruction. Although labeled "radicals," the vast majority of Republicans were moderates on the economic and political rights of African Americans.

Thaddeus Stevens

Rejecting Johnson's position that the South had already been reconstructed, Congress exercised its constitutional authority to decide on its own membership. It refused to seat the new senators and

The Memphis Riot   A white mob burned this freedpeople's school during the Memphis riot of May 1866. What is your response to this image? What legal protections did the freedpeople have? *(The Library Company of Philadelphia)*

representatives from the former Confederate states. It also established the Joint Committee on Reconstruction to investigate conditions in the South. Its report documented white resistance, disorder, and the appalling treatment and conditions of freedpeople.

Congress passed a civil rights bill in 1866 to protect the fragile rights of African Americans and extended for two more years the Freedmen's Bureau, an agency providing emergency assistance at the end of the war. Johnson vetoed both bills and called his congressional opponents "traitors." His actions drove moderates into the radical camp, and Congress passed both bills over his veto—both, however, watered down by weakening the power of enforcement. Southern courts regularly disallowed black testimony against whites, acquitted whites of violence, and sentenced blacks to compulsory labor.

In such a climate, southern racial violence erupted. In a typical outbreak, in May 1866, white mobs in Memphis, encouraged by police violence against black Union soldiers stationed nearby, rampaged for over 40 hours of terror, killing, beating, robbing, and raping virtually helpless black residents and burning houses, schools, and churches. A Memphis newspaper said that the soldiers would

"do the country more good in the cotton field than in the camp," and prominent local officials urged the mob to "go ahead and kill the last damned one of the nigger race." Forty-eight people, all but two of them black, died. The local Union army commander took his time restoring order, arguing that his troops "hated Negroes too." A congressional inquiry concluded that Memphis blacks had "no protection from the law whatever."

A month later, Congress sent to the states for ratification the Fourteenth Amendment, the single most significant act of the Reconstruction era. The first section of the amendment promised permanent constitutional protection of the civil rights of blacks by defining them as citizens. States were prohibited from depriving "any person of life, liberty, or property, without due process of law," and all citizens were guaranteed the "equal protection of the laws." Section 2 granted black male suffrage in the South, inserting the word "male" into the Constitution for the first time, stating that those states denying the black vote would have their "basis of representation" reduced proportionally. Other sections of the amendment barred leaders of the Confederacy from national or state offices (except by act of Congress),

Reconstruction Amendments		
Constitutional Seeds of Dreams Deferred for 100 Years (or More)		
Substance	**Outcome of Ratification Process**	**Final Implementation and Enforcement**
Thirteenth Amendment—Passed by Congress January 1865		
Prohibited slavery in the United States	Ratified by 27 states, including 8 southern states, by December 1865	Immediate, although economic freedom came by degrees
Fourteenth Amendment—Passed by Congress June 1866		
(1) Defined equal national citizenship; (2) reduced state representation in Congress proportional to number of disfranchised voters; (3) denied former Confederates the right to hold office; (4) Confederate debts and lost property claims voided and illegal	Rejected by 12 southern and border states by February 1867; Congress made readmission depend on ratification; ratified in July 1868	Civil Rights Act of 1964
Fifteenth Amendment—Passed by Congress February 1869		
Prohibited denial of vote because of race, color, or previous servitude (but not sex)	Ratification by Virginia, Texas, Mississippi, and Georgia required for readmission; ratified in March 1870	Voting Rights Act of 1965

Note: See exact wording in U.S. Constitution in the Appendix.

repudiated the Confederate debt, and denied claims of compensation to former slave owners. Johnson urged the southern states to reject the Fourteenth Amendment, and 10 immediately did so.

The Fourteenth Amendment was the central issue of the 1866 midterm election. Johnson barnstormed the country asking voters to throw out the radical Republicans and trading insults with hecklers. Democrats north and south appealed openly to racial prejudice in attacking the Fourteenth Amendment, charging that the nation would be "Africanized," black equality threatening both the marketplace and the bedroom. Republicans responded by attacking Johnson personally and freely "waved the bloody shirt," reminding voters of Democrats' treason during the civil war. Governor Oliver P. Morton of Indiana described the Democratic party as a "common sewer and loathsome receptacle [for] inhumanity and barbarism." The result was an overwhelming Republican victory. The mandate was clear: presidential Reconstruction had not worked, and Congress could present its own.

Early in 1867, Congress passed three Reconstruction acts. The southern states were divided into five military districts, whose military commanders had broad powers to maintain order and protect civil and property rights. Congress also defined a new process for readmitting a state. Qualified voters—including blacks but excluding unreconstructed rebels—would elect delegates to state constitutional conventions that would write new

Reconstruction

constitutions guaranteeing black suffrage. After the new voters of the states had ratified these constitutions, elections would be held to choose governors and state legislatures. When a state ratified the Fourteenth Amendment, its representatives to Congress would be accepted, completing readmission to the Union.

The President Impeached

Congress also restricted presidential powers and established legislative dominance over the executive branch. The Tenure of Office Act, designed to prevent Johnson from firing the outspoken Secretary of War Edwin Stanton, limited the president's appointment powers. Other measures trimmed his power as commander in chief.

Johnson responded exactly as congressional Republicans had anticipated. He vetoed the Reconstruction acts, removed cabinet officers and other officials sympathetic to Congress, hindered the work of Freedmen's Bureau agents, and limited the activities of military commanders in the South. The House Judiciary Committee charged the president with "usurpations of power" and of acting in the "interests of the great criminals" who had led the rebellion. But moderate House Republicans defeated the impeachment resolutions.

Impeachment Trial of Andrew Johnson

In August 1867, Johnson dismissed Stanton and asked for Senate consent. When the Senate refused, the president ordered Stanton to surrender his office, which he refused, barricading himself inside. The House quickly approved impeachment resolutions, charging the president with "high crimes and misdemeanors." The three-month trial in the Senate early in 1868 featured impassioned oratory, similar to the trial of President Bill Clinton 131 years later. Evidence was skimpy, however, that Johnson, like Clinton, had committed any constitutional crime justifying his removal. With seven moderate Republicans joining Democrats against conviction, the effort to find the president guilty fell one vote short of the required two-thirds majority. Not until the late twentieth century (Nixon and Clinton) would an American president face removal from office through impeachment.

Moderate Republicans feared that by removing Johnson, they might get Ohio senator Benjamin Wade, a leading radical Republican, as president. Wade had endorsed woman suffrage, rights for labor unions, and civil rights for African Americans in both southern and northern states. As moderate Republicans gained strength in 1868 through their support of the eventual presidential election winner, Ulysses S. Grant, principled radicalism lost much of its power within Republican ranks.

What Congressional Moderation Meant for Rebels, Blacks, and Women

The impeachment crisis revealed that most Republicans were more interested in protecting themselves than blacks and in punishing Johnson rather than the South. Congress's political battle against the president was not matched by an idealistic resolve on behalf of the freedpeople. State and local elections of 1867 showed that voters preferred moderate Reconstruction policies. It is important to look not only at what Congress did during Reconstruction but also at what it did not do.

With the exception of Jefferson Davis, Congress did not imprison rebel Confederate leaders, and only one person, the commander of the infamous Andersonville prison camp, was executed. Congress did not insist on a long probation before southern states could be readmitted to the Union. It did not reorganize southern local governments. It did not mandate a national program of education for freedpeople. It did not confiscate and redistribute land to the freedmen, nor did it prevent Johnson from taking land away from those who had gained titles during the war. It did not, except indirectly and with great reluctance, provide economic help to black citizens.

Congress did, however, grant citizenship and suffrage to freedmen, but not to freedwomen. Northerners were no more prepared than southerners to make all African Americans fully equal citizens. Between 1865 and 1869, voters in seven northern states turned down referendums proposing black (male) suffrage; only in Iowa and Minnesota did northern whites grant the vote to blacks. Proposals to give black men the vote gained support in the North only after the election of 1868, when General Grant, the supposedly invincible military hero, barely won the popular vote in several states. To ensure grateful black votes, congressional Republicans, who had twice rejected a suffrage amendment, took another look at the idea. After a bitter fight, the Fifteenth Amendment, forbidding all states to deny the vote "on account of race, color, or previous condition of servitude," became part of the Constitution in 1870. A black preacher from Pittsburgh observed that "the Republican party had done the Negro good, but they were doing themselves good at the same time."

IMAGE
1868 Democratic National Convention

One casualty of the Fourteenth and Fifteenth Amendments was the goodwill of women who had worked for their suffrage for two decades. They had hoped that male legislators would recognize their wartime service in support of the Union and were shocked that black males got the vote rather than loyal white (or black) women. Elizabeth Cady Stanton and Susan B. Anthony, veteran suffragists and opponents of slavery, campaigned against the Fourteenth Amendment, breaking with abolitionist allies such as Frederick Douglass, who had long supported woman suffrage yet declared that this was "the Negro's hour." Anthony vowed to "cut off this right arm of mine before I will ever work for or demand the ballot for the Negro and not the woman."

Disappointment over the suffrage issue helped split the women's movement in 1869. Anthony and Stanton continued their fight for a national amendment for woman suffrage and a long list of property, educational, and sexual rights, while other women focused on securing the vote state by state. Abandoned by radical and moderate men alike, women had few champions in Congress and their efforts were put off for half a century.

Congress compromised the rights of African Americans as well as women. It gave blacks the vote but not land, the opposite of what they wanted first. Almost alone, Thaddeus Stevens argued that "forty acres . . . and a hut would be more valuable . . . than the . . . right to vote." But Congress never seriously considered his plan to confiscate the land of the "chief rebels" and give a small portion of it, divided into 40-acre plots, to freedpeople, an act that would have violated deeply held American beliefs on the sacredness of private property. Moreover, northern business interests looking to develop southern industry and invest in southern land liked the prospect of a large pool of propertyless black workers.

Congress did, however, pass the Southern Homestead Act of 1866 making public lands available to blacks and loyal whites in five southern states. But the land was poor and inaccessible; no transportation, tools, or seed were provided; and most blacks were bound by contracts that prevented them from making claims before the deadline. Only about 4,000 African American families even applied for the Homestead Act lands, and fewer than 20 percent of them saw their claims completed. White claimants did little better.

THE LIVES OF FREEDPEOPLE

Union army major George Reynolds boasted late in 1865 that in the area of Mississippi under his command, he had "kept the negroes at work, and in a good state of discipline." Clinton Fisk, a well-meaning white who helped found a black college in Tennessee, told freedmen in 1866 that they could be "as free and as happy" working again for their "old master . . . as any where else in the world." Such pronouncements reminded blacks of white preachers' exhortations during slavery to work hard and obey their masters. Ironically, Fisk and Reynolds were agents of the Freedmen's Bureau, the agency intended to aid the black transition from slavery to freedom.

The Freedmen's Bureau

Never before in American history has one small agency—underfinanced, understaffed, and undersupported—been given a harder task than the Bureau of Freedmen, Refugees and Abandoned Lands. Controlling less than 1 percent of southern lands, the bureau's name is telling; its fate epitomizes Reconstruction.

The Freedmen's Bureau performed many essential services. It issued emergency food rations, clothed and sheltered homeless victims of the war, and established medical and hospital facilities. It provided funds to relocate thousands of freedpeople. It helped blacks search for relatives and get legally married. It represented

African Americans in local civil courts to ensure that they got fair trials. Working with northern missionary aid societies and southern black churches, the bureau became responsible for an extensive education program, its greatest success.

IMAGE
Freedmen at Rest on a Levee

Many of the agency's earliest teachers were Quaker and Yankee "schoolmarms" who volunteered through the American Missionary Association to teach in the South. In October, 1865, Esther Douglass found "120 dirty, half naked, perfectly wild black children" in her schoolroom near Savannah, Georgia. Eight months later, she reported, "their progress was wonderful"; they could read, sing hymns, and repeat Bible verses. Bureau commissioner General O. O. Howard estimated that by 1868, one-third of southern black children had been educated by bureau schools. By 1870, when funds were discontinued, there were nearly 250,000 pupils in 4,329 agency schools.

The bureau's largest task was to promote African Americans' economic survival, serving as an employment agency. This included settling blacks on abandoned lands and getting them started with tools, seed, and draft animals, as well as arranging work contracts with white landowners. But in this area, the Freedmen's Bureau, although not intending to instill a new dependency, more often than not supported the needs of

DOCUMENT
Affidavit of Ex-Slave Enoch Braston (1866)

Freedmen's Bureau Agents and Clients The Freedmen's Bureau had fewer resources in relation to its purpose than any agency in the nation's history. *Harper's Weekly* published this engraving of freedpeople lining up for aid in Memphis in 1866. How empathetic do the agents look to you? *(Library of Congress [LC-USZ62-22120])*

whites to find cheap labor rather than blacks to become independent farmers.

Although a few agents were idealistic northerners eager to help freedpeople adjust to freedom, most were Union army officers more concerned with social order than social transformation. Working in a postwar climate of resentment and violence, Freedmen's Bureau agents were overworked, underpaid, spread too thin (at its peak only 900 agents were scattered across 11 states), and constantly harassed by local whites. Even the best-intentioned agents would have agreed with General Howard's belief in the nineteenth-century American values of self-help, minimal government interference in the marketplace, sanctity of private property, contractual obligations, and white superiority.

Southern Skepticism of the Freedmen's Bureau (1866)

On a typical day, overburdened agents would visit local courts and schools, file reports, supervise the signing of work contracts, and handle numerous complaints, most involving contract violations between whites and blacks or property and domestic disputes among blacks. A Georgia agent wrote that he was "*tired out* and *broke down.* . . . Every day for 6 months, day after day, I have had from 5 to 20 complaints, *generally trivial* and of no moment, yet requiring consideration & attention coming from both Black & White." Another, reflecting his growing frustrations, complained that the freedpeople were "disrespectful and greatly in need of instruction." In finding work for freedmen and imploring freedwomen to hold their husbands accountable as providers, agents complained of "disrespect" and often sided with white landowners by telling blacks to obey orders, trust employers, and accept disadvantageous contracts. One agent sent a man who had complained of a severe beating back to work with the advice, "Don't be sassy [and] don't be lazy when you've got work to do." By 1868, funding had stopped and the agents were gone.

Despite numerous constraints, the Freedmen's Bureau accomplished much. In little more than two years, the agency issued 20 million rations (nearly one-third to poor whites); reunited families and resettled some 30,000 displaced war refugees; treated some 450,000 people for illness and injury; built 40 hospitals and more than 4,000 schools; provided books, tools, and furnishings to the freedmen; and occasionally protected their civil rights. The great African American historian and leading black intellectual W. E. B. Du Bois wrote, "In a time of perfect calm, amid willing neighbors and streaming wealth," it "would have been a herculean task" for the bureau to fulfill its many purposes. But in the midst of hunger, hate, sorrow, suspicion, and cruelty, "the work of . . . social regeneration was in large part foredoomed to failure." But Du Bois, reflecting the varied views of freedpeople themselves, recognized that in laying the foundation for black labor, future land ownership, a public school system, and recognition before courts of law, the Freedmen's Bureau was "successful beyond the dreams of thoughtful men."

Economic Freedom by Degrees

Despite the best efforts of the Freedmen's Bureau, the failure of Congress to provide the promised 40 acres and a mule forced freedpeople into a new economic dependency on former masters. Blacks made some progress, however, in degrees of economic autonomy and were partly responsible, along with international economic developments, in forcing the white planter class into making major changes in southern agriculture.

First, a land-intensive system replaced the labor intensity of slavery. Land ownership was concentrated into fewer and even larger holdings than before the war. From South Carolina to Louisiana, the wealthiest tenth of the population owned about 60 percent of the real estate in the 1870s. Second, these large planters increasingly concentrated on one crop, usually cotton, and were tied into the international market. This resulted in a steady drop in food production (both grains and livestock). Third, one-crop farming created a new credit system whereby most farmers—black and white—were forced into dependence on local merchants for renting land, housing, provisions, seed, and farm implements and animals. These changes affected race relations and class tensions among whites.

This new system, however, took a few years to develop after emancipation. At first, most African Americans signed contracts with white landowners and worked fields in gangs very much as during slavery. Supervised by superintendents who still used the lash, they toiled from sunrise to sunset for a meager wage and a monthly allotment of bacon and meal. All members of the family had to work to receive their rations.

A Sharecrop Contract

Freedpeople resented this new semi-servitude, refused to sign the contracts, and sought a measure of independence working the land themselves. A South Carolina freedman said, "If I can't own de land, I'll hire or lease land, but I won't contract." Freedwomen especially wanted to send their children to school rather than to the fields and apprenticeships, and insisted on "no more outdoor work."

A Freedman's Work Contract

As you read this rather typical work contract defining the first economic relationship between whites and blacks in the early months of the postwar period, note the regulation of social behavior and deportment, as well as work and "pay" arrangements. How different is this from slavery? As a freedman or freedwoman, would you have signed such an agreement? Why or why not? What options would you have had?

State of South Carolina
Darlington District
Articles of Agreement

This Agreement entered into between Mrs. Adele Allston Exect of the one part, and the Freedmen and Women of The Upper Quarters plantation of the other part Witnesseth:

That the latter agree, for the remainder of the present year, to reside upon and devote their labor to the cultivation of the Plantation of the former. And they further agree, that they will in all respects, conform to such reasonable and necessary plantation rules and regulations as Mrs. Allston's Agent may prescribe; that they will not keep any gun, pistol, or other offensive weapon, or leave the plantation without permission from their employer; that in all things connected with their duties as laborers on said plantation, they will yield prompt obedience to all orders from Mrs. Allston or his [sic] agent; that they will be orderly and quiet in their conduct, avoiding drunkenness and other gross vices; that they will not misuse any of the Plantation Tools, or Agricultural Implements, or any Animals entrusted to their care, or any Boats, Flats, Carts or Wagons; that they will give up at the expiration of this Contract, all Tools & c., belonging to the Plantation, and in case any property, of any description belonging to the Plantation shall be willfully or through negligence destroyed or injured, the value of the Articles so destroyed, shall be deducted from the portion of the Crops which the person or persons, so offending, shall be entitled to receive under this Contract.

Any deviations from the condition of the foregoing Contract may, upon sufficient proof, be punished with dismissal from the Plantation, or in such other manner as may be determined by the Provost Court; and the person or persons so dismissed, shall forfeit the whole, or a part of his, her or their portion of the crop, as the Court may decide.

In consideration of the foregoing Services duly performed, Mrs. Allston agrees, after deducting Seventy five bushels of Corn for each work Animal, exclusively used in cultivating the Crops for the present year; to turn over to the said Freedmen and Women, one half of the remaining Corn, Peas, Potatoes, made this season. He [sic] further agrees to furnish the usual rations until the Contract is performed.

All Cotton Seed Produced on the Plantation is to be reserved for the use of the Plantation. The Freedmen, Women and Children are to be treated in a manner consistent with their freedom. Necessary medical attention will be furnished as heretofore.

Any deviation from the conditions of this Contract upon the part of the said Mrs. Allston or her Agent or Agents shall be punished in such manner as may be determined by a Provost Court, or a Military Commission. This agreement to continue till the first day of January 1866.

Witness our hand at The Upper Quarters this 28th day of July 1865.

A Sharecropper's Home and Family Sharecroppers and tenant farmers, though more autonomous than contract laborers, remained dependent on the landlord for their survival. Yet how different is this from the photograph at the top of p. 525? What are the differences, and how do you explain the change? *(Brown Brothers)*

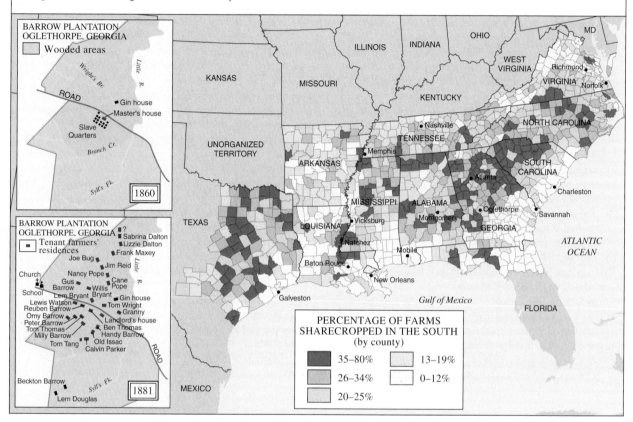

The Rise of Tenancy in the South, 1880

Although no longer slaves and after resisting labor contracts and the gang system of field labor, the freedpeople (as well as many poor whites) became tenant farmers, working on shares in the New South. The former slaves on the Barrow plantation in Georgia, for example, moved their households to individual 25-to 30-acre tenant farms, which they rented from the Barrow family in annual contracts requiring payment in cotton and other cash crops. Where was the highest percentage of tenant farms, and how do you explain it? How would you explain the low-percentage areas? What do you notice about how circumstances have changed—and not changed—on the Barrow plantation?

PERCENTAGE OF FARMS SHARECROPPED IN THE SOUTH (by county)

35–80%   13–19%
26–34%   0–12%
20–25%

A Georgia planter observed that freedpeople wanted "to get away from all overseers, to hire or purchase land, and work for themselves." Many broke contracts, haggled over wages, engaged in work slowdowns or strikes, burned barns, and otherwise expressed their displeasure with the contract labor system. In coastal rice-growing regions resistance was especially strong. The freedmen "refuse work at any price," a bureau agent reported, and the women "wish to stay in the house or the garden all the time." Even when offered livestock and other incentives, the Allstons' blacks refused to sign their contracts, and in 1869 Adele Allston was forced to sell much of her vast landholdings.

Blacks' insistence on autonomy and land of their own was the major impetus for the change from the contract system to tenancy and sharecropping. Families would hitch mules to their old slave cabin and drag it to their plot, as far from

IMAGE

Five Generations of a Slave Family

the Big House as possible. Sharecroppers received seed, fertilizer, implements, food, and clothing. In return, the landlord (or a local merchant) told them what and how much to grow, and he took a share—usually half—of the harvest. The croppers' half usually went to pay for goods bought on credit (at high interest rates) from the landlord. Thus, sharecroppers remained tied to the land.

Tenant farmers had only slightly more independence. Before a harvest, they promised to sell their crop to a local merchant in return for renting land, tools, and other necessities. From the merchant's store they also had to buy goods on credit (at higher prices than whites paid) against the harvest. At "settling up" time, income from sale of the crop was compared to accumulated debts. It was possible, especially after an unusually bountiful season, to come out ahead and eventually to own one's own land. But tenants rarely did; in debt at the end of each year, they had to pledge the next year's crop.

World cotton prices remained low, and whereas big landowners still generated profits through their large scale of operation, sharecroppers rarely made much money. When sharecroppers were able to pay their debts, landowners frequently altered loan agreements. Thus, debt peonage replaced slavery, ensuring a continuing cheap labor supply to grow cotton and other staples in the South.

Despite this bleak picture, painstaking, industrious work by African Americans helped many gradually accumulate a measure of income, personal property, and autonomy, especially in the household economy of producing eggs, butter, meat, food crops, and other staples. Debt did not necessarily mean a lack of subsistence. In Virginia the declining tobacco crop forced white planters to sell off small parcels of land to blacks. Throughout the South, a few African Americans became independent landowners—about 3–4 percent by 1880, but closer to 25 percent by 1900.

White Farmers During Reconstruction

Changes in southern agriculture affected yeoman and poor white farmers as well, and planters worried about a coalition between poor black and pro-Unionist white farmers. As a white Georgia farmer said in 1865, "We should tuk the land, as we did the niggers, and split it, and giv part to the niggers and part to me and t'other Union fellers." But confiscation and redistribution of land was no more likely for white farmers than for the freedpeople. Whites, too, had to concentrate on growing staples, pledging their crops against high-interest credit, and facing perpetual indebtedness. In the upcountry piedmont area of Georgia, for example, the number of whites working their own land dropped from nine in ten before the Civil War to seven in ten by 1880, while cotton production doubled.

Reliance on cotton meant fewer food crops and therefore greater dependence on merchants for provisions. In 1884, Jephta Dickson of Jackson County, Georgia, purchased more than $50 worth of flour, meal, meat, syrup, peas, and corn from a local store; 25 years earlier he had been almost completely self-sufficient. Fencing laws seriously curtailed the livelihood of poor whites raising pigs and hogs, and restrictions on hunting and fishing reduced the ability of poor whites and blacks alike to supplement incomes and diets.

In the worn-out flatlands and barren mountainous regions of the South, poor whites' antebellum poverty, health, and isolation worsened after the war. A Freedmen's Bureau agent in South Carolina described the poor whites in his area as "gaunt and ragged, ungainly, stooping and clumsy in build." They lived a marginal existence, hunting, fishing, and growing corn and potato crops that, as a North Carolinian put it, "come up puny, grow puny, and mature puny." Many poor white farmers, in fact, were even less productive than black sharecroppers. Some became farmhands at $6 a month (with board). Others fled to low-paying jobs in cotton mills, where they would not have to compete against blacks.

The cultural life of poor southern whites reflected both their lowly position and their pride. Their emotional religion centered on camp meeting religious revivals where, in backwoods clearings, men and women praised God, told tall tales of superhuman feats, and exchanged folk remedies for poor health. Their ballads and folklore told of debt, chain gangs, and deeds of drinking prowess. Their quilt making and house construction reflected a marginal culture in which everything was saved and reused.

In part because their lives were so hard, poor whites clung to their belief in white superiority. Many joined the Ku Klux Klan (founded by six Confederate veterans) and other southern white terrorist groups that emerged between 1866 and 1868. A federal officer reported, "The poorer classes of white people . . . have a most intense hatred of the Negro." Actually populated by a cross-section of southern whites, the Klan expressed its hatred in midnight raids on teachers in black schools, laborers who disputed their landlords' discipline, Republican voters, and any black whose "impudence" caused him not to "bow and scrape to a white man, as was done formerly."

Ku Klux Klan Members

Black Self-Help Institutions

Victimized by Klan intimidation and violence, African Americans found their hopes and dreams thwarted. A Texan, Felix Haywood, recalled:

> We thought we was goin' to be richer than white folks, 'cause we was stronger and knowed how to work, and the whites . . . didn't have us to work for them anymore. But it didn't turn out that way. We soon found out that freedom could make folks proud but it didn't make 'em rich.

It was clear to many black leaders, therefore, that because white institutions could not fulfill the promises of emancipation, blacks would have to do it themselves.

They began, significantly, with churches. Traditions of black community self-help survived in the organized churches and schools of the antebellum

Black Schoolchildren with Their Books and Teacher Along with land of their own and
equal civil rights, what freedpeople wanted most was education. Despite white opposition and limited funds
for black schools, one of the most positive outcomes of the Reconstruction era was education of the freedpeople. Contrast this photo with the drawing of the burning Memphis school. How do you explain the change?
(Valentine Museum, Richmond, Virginia)

free Negro communities and in the "invisible" cultural institutions of the slave quarters. As Union
troops liberated areas of the Confederacy, blacks
fled white churches for their own, causing a rapid
increase in the growth of membership in African
American churches. The Negro Baptist Church grew
from 150,000 members in 1850 to 500,000 in 1870,
while the membership of the African Methodist
Episcopal Church increased fourfold in the postwar
decade, from 100,000 to more than 400,000 members. Other denominations such as the Colored
(later Christian) Methodist Episcopal (CME)
Church, the Reformed Zion Union Apostolic
Church, and the Colored Presbyterian Church all
broke with their white counterparts to establish autonomous black churches in the first decade after
emancipation.

African American ministers continued to exert
community leadership. Many led efforts to oppose
discrimination, some by entering politics: more
than one-fifth of the black officeholders in South
Carolina were ministers. Most preachers, however,
focused on sin, salvation, and revivalist enthusiasm.

An English visitor to the South in 1867–1868, after
observing a revivalist preacher in Savannah arouse
nearly 1,000 people to "sway, and cry, and groan,"
noted the intensity of black "devoutness." Despite
some efforts urging blacks to pray more quietly,
most congregations preferred traditional forms of
religious expression. One woman said: "We make
noise 'bout ebery ting else … I want ter go ter
Heaben in de good ole way."

The freedpeople's desire for education was as
strong as for religion. Even before the Freedmen's
Bureau ceased operating schools, African Americans assumed more responsibility for their costs
and operation. Black South Carolinians contributed
$17,000, 16 percent of the cash cost of education,
and more in labor and supplies. Louisiana and Kentucky blacks contributed more to education than
the bureau itself. Georgia African Americans increased the number of "freedom schools" from 79 to
232 in 1866–1867, despite attacks by local whites
who stoned them on their way home and threatened to "kill every d——d nigger white man" who
worked in the schools.

Black teachers increasingly replaced whites. By 1868, 43 percent of the bureau's teachers were African American, working for four or five dollars a month and boarding with families. Although white teachers played a remarkable role in the education of freedpeople during Reconstruction, black teachers were more persistent and positive. Charlotte Forten, for example, who taught in a school in the Sea Islands, noted that even after a half day's "hard toil" in the fields, her older pupils were "as bright and as anxious to learn as ever." Despite the taunting degradation of "the haughty Anglo-Saxon race," she said, blacks showed "a desire for knowledge, and a capability for attaining it."

Indeed, by 1870 there was a 20 percent gain in freed black adult literacy, a figure that, against difficult odds, would continue to grow for all ages to the end of the century, when more than 1.5 million black children attended school with 28,560 black teachers. This achievement was remarkable in the face of crowded facilities, limited resources, local opposition, and absenteeism caused by the demands of fieldwork. In Georgia, for example, only 5 percent of black children went to school for part of any one year between 1865 and 1870, as opposed to 20 percent of white children. To train teachers such as Forten, northern philanthropists founded Fisk, Howard, Atlanta, and other black universities in the South between 1865 and 1867.

African American schools, like churches, became community centers. They published newspapers, provided training in trades and farming, and promoted political participation and land ownership. A black farmer in Mississippi founded both a school and a society to facilitate land acquisition and better agricultural methods. These efforts made black schools objects of local white hostility. A Virginia freedman told a congressional committee that in his county, anyone starting a school would be killed and blacks were "afraid to be caught with a book." In Alabama, the Klan hanged an Irish-born teacher and four black men. In 1869, in Tennessee alone, 37 black schools were burned to the ground.

Attempted KKK Lynching

White opposition to black education and land ownership stimulated African American nationalism and separatism. In the late 1860s, Benjamin "Pap" Singleton, a former Tennessee slave, urged freedpeople to abandon politics and migrate westward. He organized a land company in 1869, purchased public property in Kansas, and in the early 1870s took several groups from Tennessee and Kentucky to establish separate black towns in the prairie state. In following years, thousands of "exodusters"

"Exodustoers"

from the Lower South bought some 10,000 infertile acres in Kansas. But natural and human obstacles to self-sufficiency often proved insurmountable. By the 1880s, despairing of ever finding economic independence in the United States, Singleton and other nationalists advocated emigration to Canada and Liberia. Other black leaders such as Frederick Douglass continued to press for full citizenship rights within the United States.

RECONSTRUCTION IN THE SOUTHERN STATES

Douglass's confidence in the power of the ballot seemed warranted in the enthusiastic early months under the Reconstruction Acts of 1867. With President Johnson neutralized, national Republican leaders finally could prevail. Local Republicans, taking advantage of the inability or refusal of many southern whites to vote, overwhelmingly elected their delegates to state constitutional conventions in the fall of 1867. Guardedly optimistic and sensing the "sacred importance" of their work, black and white Republicans began creating new state governments.

Republican Rule

Contrary to early pro-southern historians, the southern state governments under Republican rule were not dominated by illiterate black majorities intent on "Africanizing" the South by passing compulsory racial intermarriage laws, as many whites feared. Nor were these governments unusually corrupt or extravagant, nor did they use massive numbers of federal troops to enforce their will. By 1869, only 1,100 federal soldiers remained in Virginia, and most federal troops in Texas were guarding the frontier against Mexico and hostile Native Americans. Lacking strong military backing, the new state governments faced economic distress and increasingly violent harassment.

Diverse coalitions made up the new governments elected under congressional Reconstruction. These "black and tan" governments (as opponents called them) were actually predominantly white, except for the lower house of the South Carolina legislature. Some new leaders came from the old Whig elite of bankers, industrialists, and others interested more in economic growth and sectional reconciliation than in radical social reforms. A second group consisted of northern Republican capitalists who headed south to invest in land, railroads, and new industries. Others included Union veterans, missionaries, and teachers inspired to work for the

Freedmen's Bureau schools, people unfairly labeled "carpetbaggers."

Moderate African Americans made up a third group in the Republican state governments. A large percentage of black officeholders were mulattos, many of them well-educated preachers, teachers, and soldiers from the North. Others were self-edu- cated tradesmen or representatives of the small landed class of southern blacks. In South Carolina, for example, of some 255 black state and federal officials elected between 1868 and 1876, two-thirds were literate and one-third owned real estate; only 15 percent owned no property at all.

Black Senator and Congressmen

This class composition meant that black leaders often supported policies that largely ignored the land redistribution needs of the black masses. Their goals fit squarely into the American republi- can tradition. African American leaders reminded whites that they, too, were southerners: "the dust of our fathers mingles with yours in the same grave yards," an 1865 petition put it, seeking only that "the same laws which govern white men shall govern black men . . . in equity and justice."

The primary accomplishment of Republican rule in the South was to eliminate undemocratic features from prewar state constitutions. All states provided universal male suffrage and loosened requirements for holding office. Underrepresented counties got more legislative seats. Automatic imprisonment for debt was ended, and laws were enacted to relieve poverty and to care for the disabled. Many southern states passed their first divorce laws and provisions granting property rights to married women. Lists of crimes punishable by death were shortened, in one state from 26 to 5.

Republican governments financially and physi- cally reconstructed the South by overhauling tax sys- tems and approving generous railroad and other capital investment bonds. Harbors, roads, and bridges were rebuilt; hospitals and asylums were es- tablished. Most important, the Republican govern- ments created the South's first public school systems. As in the North, these schools were largely segre- gated, but for the first time, rich and poor, black and white alike had access to education. By the 1880s, African American school attendance increased from 5 percent to more than 40 percent, and white atten- dance increased from 20 percent to more than 60 percent. All this cost money, and so the Republicans also increased tax rates and state debts.

These considerable achievements came in the face of opposition like that expressed at a conven- tion of Louisiana planters, which labeled the Re- publican leaders the "lowest and most corrupt body of men ever assembled in the South." There was some corruption, mostly in land sales, railway bonds, and construction contracts. Such graft had become a way of life in postwar American politics, South and North. But given their lack of experience with politics, the black role was remarkable. As Du Bois put it, "There was one thing that the White

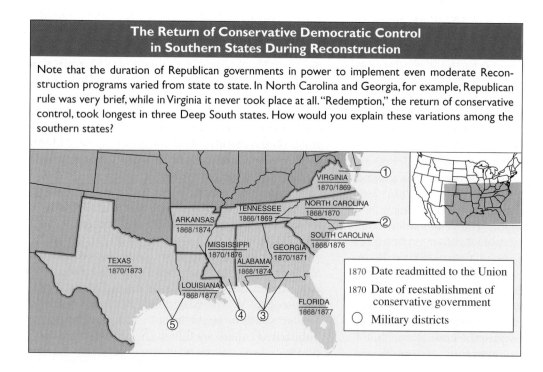

The Return of Conservative Democratic Control in Southern States During Reconstruction

Note that the duration of Republican governments in power to implement even moderate Recon- struction programs varied from state to state. In North Carolina and Georgia, for example, Republican rule was very brief, while in Virginia it never took place at all. "Redemption," the return of conservative control, took longest in three Deep South states. How would you explain these variations among the southern states?

VIRGINIA 1870/1869 — ①
TENNESSEE 1866/1869
NORTH CAROLINA 1868/1870
ARKANSAS 1868/1874
SOUTH CAROLINA 1868/1876 — ②
MISSISSIPPI 1870/1876
GEORGIA 1870/1871
TEXAS 1870/1873
ALABAMA 1868/1874
LOUISIANA 1868/1877
FLORIDA 1868/1877
④ ③
⑤

1870 Date readmitted to the Union
1870 Date of reestablishment of conservative government
○ Military districts

South feared more than negro dishonesty, ignorance, and incompetence, and that was negro honesty, knowledge, and efficiency."

Despite its effectiveness in modernizing southern state governments, the Republican coalition did not survive, lasting longest in the Deep South, where the black population was equal to or greater than the white. In Virginia, Republicans ruled hardly at all, as Democrats professed agreement with Congress's Reconstruction guidelines while doing as they pleased and encouraging northern investors to rebuild shattered cities. In South Carolina, African American leaders' unwillingness to use their power to help black laborers contributed to their loss of political control to the Democrats, and class divisions among blacks in Louisiana helped weaken the Republican regime there. In Alabama a flood of northern capital created a new industrial and merchant class to rival the old planter aristocracy. But the primary reason for the return of Democrats to power was the use of violence.

"From the Plantation to the Senate"

Violence and "Redemption"

A Mississippi paper said, "We must render this either a white man's government, or convert the land into a Negro man's cemetery." Although violence was pervasive throughout the South (led by many white supremacist groups in addition to the Ku Klux Klan), Mississippi and North Carolina typify the pattern.

"Worse Than Slavery"

After losing a close election in North Carolina in 1868, conservatives waged a concentrated terrorist campaign in several piedmont counties, areas of strong Unionist support. If the Democrats could win these counties in 1870, they would most likely win statewide. In the year before the election, several prominent Republicans were killed, including a white state senator, whose throat was cut, and a leading black Union League organizer, who was hanged in the courthouse square with a sign pinned to his breast: "Bewar, ye guilty, both white and black." Scores of citizens were flogged, tortured, fired from their jobs, or driven in the middle of the night from burning homes and barns. The courts consistently refused to prosecute anyone for these crimes, which local papers blamed on "disgusting negroes and white Radicals." The conservative campaign worked. In the election of 1870, some 12,000 fewer Republicans voted in the two crucial counties than had voted two years earlier, and the Democrats swept back into power.

Ku Klux Klan Warning

In Mississippi's state election in 1875, Democrats used similar tactics, openly announcing that "the thieves . . . robbers, and scoundrels" in power "deserve death and ought to be killed." In the "Mississippi Plan," local Democratic clubs formed armed militias, marching defiantly through black areas, breaking up Republican meetings, and provoking riots to justify killing hundreds. Armed men were posted during voter registration to intimidate Republicans. At the election itself, voters were either "helped" by gun-toting whites to cast a Democratic ballot, or chased away by clubs. Counties that had given Republican majorities in the thousands managed a total of less than a dozen votes in 1875.

Democrats called their victory "redemption." As conservative Democrats resumed control of each state government, Reconstruction ended. Redemption succeeded with a combination of persistent white southern resistance, including violence and coercion, and a failure of northern will. Albion Tourgée summed up the Reconstruction era in his novel *A Fool's Errand* (1879): "The spirit of the dead Confederacy was stronger than the mandate of the nation to which it had succumbed in battle."

Congress and President Grant did not totally ignore southern violence. Three Force Acts, passed in 1870 and 1871, gave the president strong powers to use federal supervisors to ensure that citizens were not prevented from voting by force or fraud. The third act, known as the Ku Klux Klan Act, declared illegal secret organizations that used disguise and coercion to deprive others of equal protection of the laws. Congress created a joint committee to investigate Klan violence, and in 1872 its report filled 13 huge volumes with horrifying testimony. Grant sent messages to Congress proclaiming the importance of the right to vote and condemning lawlessness, and dispatched troops to Hamburg, South Carolina, where violence against blacks was the worst. However, reform Republicans lost interest in defending African Americans, and regular Republicans decided that they could keep political power without black votes. In 1875, Grant's advisers told him that Republicans might lose important Ohio elections if he continued protecting blacks, so he rejected appeals by Mississippi blacks for troops to guarantee free elections. He and the nation, Grant said, "had tired of these annual autumnal outbreaks."

The success of the Democrats' Mississippi Plan in 1875, repeated a year later in South Carolina and Louisiana, indicated that congressional reports, presidential proclamations, and the Force Acts did little to stop the reign of terror against black and white Republicans throughout the South. Despite hundreds of arrests, all-white juries refused to find whites guilty

RECOVERING THE PAST

Novels

We usually read novels, short stories, and other forms of fiction for pleasure, that is, for the enjoyment of plot, style, symbolism, and character development. In addition to being well written, "classic" novels such as *Moby Dick, Huckleberry Finn, The Great Gatsby, The Invisible Man,* and *Beloved* explore timeless questions of good and evil, of innocence and knowledge, of noble dreams fulfilled and shattered. We enjoy novels because we often find ourselves identifying with one of the major characters. Through that person's problems, joys, relationships, and search for identity, we gain insights about our own.

Even though novels may be historically untrue, we can also read them as historical sources, for they reveal much about the attitudes, dreams, fears, and ordinary, everyday experiences of human beings in a particular period. They also show how people responded to the major events of that era. The novelist, like the historian, is a product of time and place and has an interpretive point of view. Consider the two novels about Reconstruction that are quoted here. Neither is reputed for great literary merit, yet both reveal much about the various interpretations and impassioned attitudes of the post–Civil War era. *A Fool's Errand* was written by Albion Tourgée, a northerner, while *The Clansman* was written by Thomas Dixon, Jr., a southerner.

Tourgée was a young northern teacher and lawyer who fought with the Union army and moved to North Carolina after the war, partly for health reasons and partly to begin a legal career. He became a judge and was an active Republican, supporting black suffrage and helping shape the new state constitution and the codification of North Carolina laws. Because he boldly criticized the Ku Klux Klan for its campaign of terror against blacks, his life was threatened many times. When he left North Carolina in 1879, he published an autobiographical novel about his experiences as a judge challenging the Klan's violence against the freedpeople.

DOCUMENT
Albion W. Tourgée, Letter on Ku Klux Klan Activities (1870)

The "fool's errand" in the novel is that of the northern veteran Comfort Servosse, who, like Tourgée, seeks to fulfill humane goals on behalf of both blacks and whites in post–Civil War North Carolina. His efforts are thwarted, however, by threats, intimidation, a campaign of violent "outrages" against Republican leaders in the county, and a lack of support from Congress. Historians have verified the accuracy of many of the events in Tourgée's novel. While exposing the brutality of the Klan, Tourgée features loyal southern Unionists, respectable planters ashamed of Klan violence, and even guilt-ridden, poor white Klansmen who try to protect or warn intended victims.

In 1905, the year of Tourgée's death, another North Carolinian published a novel with a very different analysis of Reconstruction and its fate. Thomas Dixon, Jr., was a lawyer, North Carolina state legislator, Baptist minister, pro-Klan lecturer, and novelist. *The Clansman,* subtitled *A Historical Romance of the Ku Klux Klan,* reflects turn-of-the-century attitudes most white southerners still had about Republican rule during Reconstruction. According to Dixon, once the "Great Heart" Lincoln was gone, a power-crazed, vindictive, radical Congress, led by scheming Austin Stoneman (Thaddeus Stevens), sought to impose corrupt carpetbagger and brutal black rule by bayonet on a helpless South. Only through the inspired leadership and redemptive role of the Ku Klux Klan was the South saved from the horrors of rape and revenge.

Dixon dedicated *The Clansman* to his uncle, who was a Grand Titan of the Klan in North Carolina during the time when two crucial counties were being transformed from Republican to Democratic through intimidation and terror. No such violence shows up in Dixon's novel. When the novel was made the basis of D. W. Griffith's film classic *Birth of a Nation* in 1915, the novel's attitudes were firmly imprinted on the twentieth-century American mind.

Both novels convey Reconstruction attitudes toward the freedpeople. Both create clearly defined heroes and villains. Both include exciting chase scenes, narrow escapes, daring rescues, and tragic deaths. Both include romantic subplots in which a southern man falls in love with a northern woman (both white). Yet the two novels are strikingly different.

REFLECTING ON THE PAST Even in these brief excerpts, what differences of style and attitude do you see in the descriptions of Uncle Jerry and Old Aleck? What emotional responses do you have to these passages? How do you think turn-of-the-twentieth-century Americans might have responded?

When the second Christmas came, Metta wrote again to her sister:

"The feeling is terribly bitter against Comfort on account of his course towards the colored people. There is quite a village of them on the lower end of the plantation. They have a church, a sabbath school, and are to have next year a school. You can not imagine how kind they have been to us, and how much they are attached to Comfort. . . . I got Comfort to go with me to one of their prayer-meetings a few nights ago. I had heard a great deal about them, but had never attended one before. It was strangely weird. There were, perhaps, fifty present, mostly middle-aged men and women. They were singing in a soft, low monotone, interspersed with prolonged exclamatory notes, a sort of rude hymn, which I was surprised to know was one of their old songs in slave times. How the chorus came to be endured in those days I can not imagine. It was

'Free! free! free, my Lord, free!
An' we walks de hebben-ly way!'

"A few looked around as we came in and seated ourselves; and Uncle Jerry, the saint of the settlement, came forward on his staves, and said, in his soft voice,

"'Ev'nin', Kunnel! Sarvant, Missus! Will you walk up, an' hev seats in front?'

"We told him we had just looked in, and might go in a short time; so we would stay in the back part of the audience.

"Uncle Jerry can not read nor write; but he is a man of strange intelligence and power. Unable to do work of any account, he is the faithful friend, monitor, and director of others. He has a house and piece of land, all paid for, a good horse and cow, and, with the aid of his wife and two boys, made a fine crop this season. He is one of the most promising colored men in the settlement: so Comfort says, at least. Everybody seems to have great respect for his character. I don't know how many people I have heard speak of his religion. Mr. Savage used to say he had rather hear him pray than any other man on earth. He was much prized by his master, even after he was disabled, on account of his faithfulness and character."

At noon Ben and Phil strolled to the polling-place to watch the progress of the first election under Negro rule. The Square was jammed with shouting, jostling, perspiring negroes, men, women, and children. The day was warm, and the African odour was supreme even in the open air. . . .

The negroes, under the drill of the League and the Freedman's Bureau, protected by the bayonet, were voting to enfranchise themselves, disfranchise their former masters, ratify a new constitution, and elect a legislature to do their will. Old Aleck was a candidate for the House, chief poll-holder, and seemed to be in charge of the movements of the voters outside the booth as well as inside. He appeared to be omnipresent, and his self-importance was a sight Phil had never dreamed. He could not keep his eyes off him. . . .

[Aleck] was a born African orator, undoubtedly descended from a long line of savage spell-binders, whose eloquence in the palaver houses of the jungle had made them native leaders. His thin spindle-shanks supported an oblong, protruding stomach, resembling an elderly monkey's, which seemed so heavy it swayed his back to carry it.

The animal vivacity of his small eyes and the flexibility of his eyebrows, which he worked up and down rapidly with every change of countenance, expressed his eager desires.

He had laid aside his new shoes, which hurt him, and went barefooted to facilitate his movements on the great occasion. His heels projected and his foot was so flat that what should have been the hollow of it made a hole in the dirt where he left his track.

He was already mellow with liquor, and was dressed in an old army uniform and cap, with two horse-pistols buckled around his waist. On a strap hanging from his shoulder were strung a half-dozen tin canteens filled with whiskey.

"The negroes of the South are free—
free as air," says the parliamentary Wat-
erson. This is what the *State*, a well-
known Democratic organ of Tennessee,
says, in huge capitals, on the subject:
'Let it be known before the election that
the farmers have agreed to spot every
leading Radical negro in the county, and
treat him as an enemy for all time to come.
The rotten ring must and shall be broken
at any and all costs. The Democrats have
determined to withdraw all employment
from their enemies. Let this fact be
known."

Ensuring a Vote for the Democratic Ticket Although the Fourteenth and Fifteenth Amendments gave African American males the right to vote in the late 1860s, by the 1870s white southerners opposed to black suffrage found many ways to influence that vote, thus returning white Democrats to office. In this cartoon, titled "Of course he wants to vote the Democratic Ticket," one of the two pistol-wielding men is saying: "You're as free as air, ain't you? Say you are, or I'll blow your black head off!" Note that another freedman is being led down the street to the polling place. Do you think he will also vote Democratic or for the party of Lincoln? *(CORBIS)*

of crimes against blacks. The U.S. Supreme Court backed them, in two 1874 decisions throwing out cases against whites convicted of preventing blacks from voting and declaring key parts of the Force Acts unconstitutional. Officially the Klan's power ended, but the attitudes (and tactics) of Klansmen would continue long into the next century.

Shifting National Priorities

The American people in the North, like their leaders, were tired of battles over freedpeople. Frustrated with the difficulties of trying to transform an unwilling South, the easiest course was to give citizenship and the vote to African Americans and leave them to fend for themselves. Americans of increasing ethnic diversity were primarily interested in starting families, finding work, and making money. Slovakian immigrants fired furnaces in Pittsburgh; Chinese men pounded in railroad ties for the Central Pacific over the Sierra Nevada mountains and across the Nevada desert; Yankee women taught in one-room schoolhouses in Vermont for $23 a month; Mexican vaqueros drove Texas cattle herds to Kansas; and Scandinavian families battled heat, locusts, and high railroad rates on farmsteads in the Dakotas.

American priorities had shifted at both the individual and national levels. Failing to effect a smooth transition from slavery to freedom for freedpeople, northern leaders focused their efforts on accelerating

and solidifying their program of economic growth and industrial and territorial expansion.

As North Carolina Klansmen convened in dark forests in North Carolina in 1869, the Central Pacific and Union Pacific railroads met in Utah, linking the Atlantic and Pacific. As southern cotton production revived, northern iron and steel manufacturing and western settlement of the mining, cattle, and agricultural frontiers also surged. As black farmers haggled over work contracts with landowners in Georgia, white workers were organizing the National Labor Union in Baltimore. As Elizabeth and Adele Allston demanded the keys to their crop barns in the summer of 1865, the Boston Labor Reform Association was demanding that "our ... education, morals, dwellings, and the whole Social System" needed to be "reconstructed." If the South would not be reconstructed, labor relations might be.

The years between 1865 and 1875 featured not only the rise (and fall) of Republican governments in the South but also a spectacular rise of working-class organizations. Stimulated by the Civil War to improve working conditions in northern factories, trade unions, labor reform associations, and labor parties flourished, culminating in the founding of the National Labor Union in 1866. Before the depression of 1873, an estimated 300,000 to 500,000 American workers enrolled in some 1,500 trade unions, the largest such increase in the nineteenth century. This growth inevitably stirred class tensions. In 1876, hundreds of freedmen in the rice region along the

Life in the Post–Civil War North and South What obvious contrasts in family life during Reconstruction do you see in these two pictures, the top a northern family in an 1868 Currier & Ives print, the bottom a southern family of free people? Can you list all the differences? *(Top: Museum of the City of New York, The Harry T. Peters Collection; bottom: The Granger Collection, New York).*

Combahee River in South Carolina went on strike to protest a 40-cent-per-day wage cut, clashing with local sheriffs and white Democratic rifle clubs. A year later, also fighting wage cuts, thousands of northern railroad workers went out in a nationwide wave of strikes, clashing with police and the National Guard.

As economic relations changed, so did the Republican party. Heralded by the moderate tone of state elections of 1867 and Grant's election in 1868, the Republicans changed from a party of moral reform to one of material interest. In the continuing struggle in American political values between "virtue and commerce," self-interest was again winning. Abandoning the Freedmen's Bureau as an inappropriate federal expense, Republican politicians had no difficulty handing out huge grants of money and land to the railroads. As freedpeople were told to help themselves, the Union Pacific was getting subsidies of between $16,000 and $48,000 for each mile of track it laid. As Susan B. Anthony and other suffragists tramped through the snows of upstate New York with petitions for the right to vote, Boss Tweed and other urban bosses defrauded New York taxpayers of millions of dollars. As Native Americans in the Great Plains struggled to preserve the sacred Black Hills from gold prospectors protected by U.S. soldiers, corrupt government officials in the East "mined" public treasuries.

By 1869, the year financier Jay Gould almost cornered the gold market, the nation was increasingly defined by its sordid, materialistic "go-getters." Henry Adams, descendant of two presidents, was living in Washington, D.C., during this era. As he wrote in his 1907 autobiography *The Education of Henry Adams,* he had had high expectations in 1869 that Grant, like George Washington, would restore moral order and peace. But when Grant announced his cabinet, a group of army cronies and rich friends to whom he owed favors, Adams felt betrayed, charging that Grant's administration "outraged every rule of decency."

Honest himself, Grant showed poor judgment of others. The scandals of his administration touched his relatives, his cabinet, and two vice presidents. Outright graft, loose prosecution, and generally negligent administration flourished in a half dozen departments. Most scandals involved large sums of public money. The Whiskey Ring affair, for example, cost the public millions of dollars in lost tax revenues siphoned off to government officials. Gould's gold scam received the unwitting aid of Grant's Treasury Department and the knowing help of the president's brother-in-law.

Nor was Congress pure. Crédit Mobilier, a dummy corporation supposedly building the transcontinental

The End of Reconstruction   Under a caption quoting a Democratic party newspaper, "This is a white man's government," this Thomas Nast cartoon from 1868 shows three white groups (stereotyped as apelike northern Irish workers, unrepentant former Confederates, and rich northern capitalist Democrats) joining hands to bring Republican Reconstruction to an end almost before it began. They stand on the back of a black Union soldier still clutching the flag and reaching in vain for a ballot box. What is each standing figure holding in his hands? What else do you see here? What's in the background? No single image better captures the story of the end of Reconstruction. (Harper's Weekly, *September 5, 1868/The Granger Collection, New York*)

railroad, received generous bonds and contracts in exchange for giving congressmen gifts of money, stocks, and railroad lands. An Ohio congressman described the House of Representatives in 1873 as an "auction room where more valuable considerations were disposed of under the speaker's hammer than any place on earth." In Henry Adams's 1880 novel *Democracy,* written about Washington life during this period, the answer to the question of whether "a respectable government" was possible in a democracy was that "no responsible government can long be much better or much worse than the society it represents."

The election of 1872 showed that the public was uninterested in moral issues. "Liberal" Republicans, disgusted with Grant, formed a third party calling for lower tariffs and fewer grants to railroads, civil service reform, and the removal of federal troops from the South. Their candidate, Horace Greeley, editor of the New York *Tribune,* was also nominated by the Democrats, whom he had spent much of his earlier career condemning. But despite his wretched record, Grant easily won a second term.

The End of Reconstruction

Soon after Grant's second inauguration, a financial panic, caused by commercial overexpansion into railroads, railroad mismanagement, and the collapse of some eastern banks, started a terrible depression that lasted throughout the mid-1870s. In these hard times, economic issues dominated politics, further diverting attention from southern blacks. As Democrats took control of the House of Representatives in 1874 and looked toward winning the White House in 1876, politicians talked about new Grant scandals, unemployment and public works, the currency, and tariffs. No one said much about freedpeople. In 1875, a guilt-ridden Congress did pass Senator Charles Sumner's civil rights bill to put teeth into the Fourteenth Amendment. But the act was not enforced, and eight years later the Supreme Court declared it unconstitutional. Congressional Reconstruction, long dormant, was over. The election of 1876, closest in American history until 2000, sealed the end.

"The Shackle Broken by the Genius of Freedom"

As their presidential candidate in 1876, the Republicans chose a former governor of Ohio, Rutherford B. Hayes, partly because of his reputation for honesty, partly because he had been a Union officer (a necessity for post–Civil War candidates), and partly because, as Henry Adams put it, he was "obnoxious to no one." The Democrats nominated Governor Samuel J. Tilden of New York, a well-known civil service reformer who had broken the corrupt Tweed ring.

Like Al Gore in 2000, Tilden won a popular-vote majority and appeared to have enough electoral votes (184 to 165) for victory—except for 20 disputed votes, all but one in the Deep South states of Florida, Louisiana, and South Carolina, where Republicans still controlled the voting apparatus despite Democratic intimidation. To settle the dispute, Congress created a commission of eight Republicans and seven Democrats who voted along party lines to give Hayes all 20 votes and a narrow electoral-college victory, 185 to 184.

Rutherford B. Hayes

Outraged Democrats protested the outcome and threatened to stop the Senate from officially counting the electoral votes, preventing Hayes's inauguration. There was talk of a new civil war. But unlike the

TIMELINE	
1865	Civil War ends
	Lincoln assassinated; Andrew Johnson becomes president
	Johnson proposes general amnesty and Reconstruction plan
	Racial confusion, widespread hunger, and demobilization
	Thirteenth Amendment ratified
	Freedmen's Bureau established
1865–1866	Black Codes
	Repossession of land by whites and freedpeople's contracts
1866	Freedmen's Bureau renewed and Civil Rights Act passed over Johnson's veto
	Southern Homestead Act
	Ku Klux Klan formed
1867	Reconstruction Acts passed over Johnson's veto
	Impeachment controversy
	Freedmen's Bureau ends
1868	Fourteenth Amendment ratified
	Senate fails to convict Johnson of impeachment charges
	Ulysses Grant elected president
1868–1870	Ten states readmitted under congressional plan
1869	Georgia and Virginia re-establish Democratic party control
1870	Fifteenth Amendment ratified
1870s–1880s	Black "exodusters" migrate to Kansas
1870–1871	Force Acts
	North Carolina and Georgia re-establish Democratic control
1872	Grant re-elected president
1873	Crédit Mobilier scandal
	Panic causes depression
1874	Alabama and Arkansas re-establish Democratic control
1875	Civil Rights Act passed
	Mississippi re-establishes Democratic control
1876	Hayes–Tilden election
1876–1877	South Carolina, Louisiana, and Florida re-establish Democratic control
1877	Compromise of 1877; Rutherford B. Hayes assumes presidency and ends Reconstruction
1880s	Tenancy and sharecropping prevail in the South
	Disfranchisement and segregation of southern blacks begins

1850s, a North–South compromise emerged. Northern investors wanted the government to subsidize a New Orleans-to-California railroad. Southerners wanted northern dollars but not northern political influence—no social agencies, no federal enforcement of the Fourteenth and Fifteenth Amendments, and no military occupation, not even the symbolic presence left in 1876.

As the March 4 inauguration date approached, under the Grant motto of "peace at any price," the forces of mutual self-interest concluded the "compromise of 1877." On March 2, Hayes was declared president-elect. After his inauguration, he ordered the last federal troops out of the South, sending them west to fight Native Americans; appointed a former Confederate general to his cabinet; supported federal aid for economic and railroad development in the South; and promised to let southerners handle race relations themselves. On a goodwill trip to the South, he told blacks that "your rights and interests would be safer if this great mass of intelligent white men were let alone by the general government." The message was clear: Hayes would not enforce the Fourteenth and Fifteenth Amendments, initiating a pattern of governmental inaction and white northern abandonment of African Americans that lasted to the 1960s. But the immediate crisis was averted, officially ending Reconstruction.

Conclusion

A Mixed Legacy

In the 12 years between Appomattox and Hayes's inauguration, victorious northern Republicans, defeated white southerners, and hopeful black freedpeople each dreamed of more than the others would give. Each got something. The compromise of 1877 cemented the reunion of South and North, providing new opportunities for economic development in both regions. The Republican party achieved its economic goals and generally held the White House, though not always Congress, until 1932. The ex-Confederate states came back into the Union, and southerners retained their grip on southern lands and black labor, though not without struggle and some changes. The Allstons' freedpeople refused to sign work contracts, even when offered livestock and other favors, and in 1869 Adele Allston had to sell much of her lands, albeit to whites.

In 1880, Frederick Douglass wrote: "Our Reconstruction measures were radically defective. . . . To the freedmen was given the machinery of liberty, but there was denied to them the steam to put it in motion. . . . The old master class . . . retained the power to starve them to death, and wherever this power is held there is the power of slavery." The wonder, Douglass said, was "not that freedmen have made so little progress, but, rather, that they have made so much; not that they have been standing still, but that they have been able to stand at all."

Freedpeople had made strong gains in education and in economic and family survival. Despite sharecropping and tenancy, black laborers organized themselves to achieve a measure of autonomy and opportunity in their lives. The three great Reconstruction amendments, despite flagrant violation over the next 100 years, held out the promise that the dreams of equal citizenship and political participation would yet be realized.

But there was still an underlying tragedy to Reconstruction, as a short story by W. E. B. Du Bois, written in 1903, makes sadly clear. Two boyhood playmates, both named John, one black and one white, are sent from the fictional town of Altamaha, Georgia, north to school to prepare for leadership of their respective communities, the black John as a teacher and the white John as a judge and possibly governor. After several years, both Johns returned to Altamaha, but a series of tragic events shattered their hopes. Both Johns misunderstood the people of the town, and each was in turn misunderstood. As black John walked through the forest after his school had been closed because he taught ideals of liberty, he came upon white John in an attempted rape of his sister. Without a word, he picked up a fallen limb, and with "all the pent-up hatred of his great black arm," killed his boyhood playmate. Within hours he was lynched.

Du Bois's story captures the human cost of the Reconstruction era. The black scholar's hope for reconciliation by a "union of intelligence and sympathy across the color-line" was smashed in the tragic encounter between the two Johns. Both young men, each once filled with glorious dreams, lay dead under the pines of the Georgia forest. Dying with them were hopes that interracial harmony, intersectional trust, and equal opportunities and rights for freedpeople might be the legacies of Reconstruction. Conspicuously absent in the forest scene was the presence of northerners. They had turned their attention to other, less noble, causes.

Questions for Review and Reflection

1. At the end of the Civil War, what were the goals and dreams of defeated southern whites, victorious northerners, and emancipated freedpeople? Can you name three for each group?

2. How did each group pursue its goals and dreams, what resources did each have, and how did they conflict with each other between 1865 and 1877?

3. What differences existed *within* each of the three major groups?

4. What was the relationship between northern presidential and congressional politics and southern daily life and race relations during Reconstruction?

5. What is your assessment of how well American democratic politics and values served the dreams of diverse American peoples in the postwar era?

Recommended Reading

Recommended Readings are posted on the Web site for this textbook. Visit www.ablongman.com/nash

Fiction and Film

W. E. B. Du Bois's *The Quest of the Silver Fleece* (1911) is a little-known novel by the sociologist–historian about the lives of sharecroppers during Reconstruction. Howard Fast's *Freedom Road* (1944) is a novel about the heroic but ultimately failed efforts of poor whites and blacks to unite for mutual benefit during the era. Ernest Gaines's *The Autobiography of Miss Jane Pittman* (1971) is a gripping fictional account of a proud centenarian black woman who lived from the time of the Civil War to the era of civil rights. In *A Fool's Errand* (1879), as described in this chapter's "Recovering the Past" essay, Albion Tourgée takes the viewpoint of a sympathetic white judge who helps the freedpeople in North Carolina during Reconstruction.

Margaret Walker's *Jubilee* (1966) is a black woman novelist's epic version of the African American experience in the Civil War era, and Alice Randall's *The Wind Done Gone* (2001) is a parody of Margaret

Mitchell's *Gone with the Wind* (1936); both follow black and white families from slavery to Reconstruction. Toni Morrison's *Beloved* (1988), an extraordinary novel set near Cincinnati in 1873 that includes flashbacks, is about the lasting traumas of slavery as black women especially seek to put their lives together and pursue their dreams of freedom. The film of the same name (1998), though slow moving, follows the time disconnections of the novel well with many moving scenes. *Birth of a Nation,* the classic 1913 film by D. W. Griffith that portrays the rise of the Ku Klux Klan as the defender of white supremacy and womanhood, is based on Thomas Dixon's *The Clansman* (1905) (also described in the "Recovering the Past" essay in this chapter). A quite different film portrayal is seen in Oscar Micheaux's *Within Our Gates* (1919), the first feature film by an African American, available from the Library of Congress early American film collection.

Discovering U.S. History Online

A Documentary History of Emancipation, 1861–1867
www.inform.umd.edu/ARHU/Depts/History/Freedman/home.html
This site presents a rich collection of primary sources from the Freedom and Southern Society Project of the University of Maryland, containing superb links to nine projected volumes of collected documents.

Freedmen's Bureau Online
www.freedmensbureau.com
This site offers an excellent collection of Freedmen's Bureau sites, including marriage records and accounts of "murders and other outrages," as well as links to other African American and Freedmen's Bureau sites.

Freedmen's Bureau in Augusta County, Virginia

www.vcdh.virginia.edu/afam/reconst.html

This student-made project traces the attempts by Augusta County African Americans and the U.S. Freedmen's Bureau to reunite families, establish fair labor practices, and build community institutions.

The Impeachment of Andrew Johnson

www.andrewjohnson.com

More than 200 excerpts from contemporary issues of *Harper's Weekly* (1865–1869) provide in-depth information about Andrew Johnson and the impeachment process.

**Images of African Americans
from the Nineteenth Century**

www.digital.nypl.org/schomburg/images_aa19/

This site contains a vast collection of visual images by artists, engravers, and photographers capturing elements of African American life in the nineteenth century.

Reports on Black America, 1857–1874

www.blackhistory.harpweek.com

Fascinating text and imagery found in the pages of *Harper's Weekly* magazine.

African American Perspectives, 1818–1907

www.memory.loc.gov/ammem/aap/aaphome.html

This searchable collection is filled with links to Reconstruction topics and political speeches and manuscripts from the Federal Writers' Project interviews with ex-slaves in the 1930s.

CHAPTER 17

Rural America: The West and the New South

The flat landscape disappearing into the horizon, the picture of a hardworking and determined woman—these suggest some of the geographic and physical realities of rural life in the West.
(Harvey Dunn The Homesteader's Wife, 1916/South Dakota Art Museum Collection)

American Stories

Realizing Dreams: Life on the Great Plains

In 1873, Milton Leeper, his wife, Hattie, and their baby, Anna, climbed into a wagon piled high with their possessions and set out to homestead in Boone County, Nebraska. Once on the claim, the Leepers dreamed confidently of their future. Hattie wrote to her sister in Iowa, "I like our place the best of any around here. When we get a fine house and 100 acres under cultivation," she added, "I wouldn't trade with any one." But Milton had broken only 13 acres when disaster struck. Hordes of grasshoppers appeared, and the Leepers fled their claim and took refuge in the nearby town of Fremont.

There they stayed for two years. Milton first worked at a store and then hired out to other farmers. Hattie sewed, kept a boarder, and cared for chickens and a milk cow. The family lived on the brink of poverty but never gave up hope. "Times are hard and we have had bad luck," Hattie acknowledged, but "I am going to hold that claim . . . there will [be] one gal that won't be out of a home." In 1876, the Leepers triumphantly returned to their claim with the modest sum of $27 to help them start over.

The grasshoppers were gone, there was enough rain, and preaching was only half a mile away. The Leepers, like others, began to prosper. Two more daughters were born and cared for in the comfortable sod house—"homely" on the outside but plastered and cozy within. As Hattie explained, the homesteaders lived "just as civilized as they would in Chicago."

Their luck did not last. Hattie, pregnant again, fell ill and died in childbirth along with her infant son. Heartbroken, Milton buried his wife and child and left the claim. The last frontier had momentarily defeated him, although he would try farming in at least four other locations before his death in 1905.

The same year that the Leepers established their Boone County homestead, another family tried their luck in a Danish settlement about 200 miles west of Omaha. Rasmus and Ane Ebbesen and their eight-year-old son, Peter, had arrived in the United States from Denmark in 1868, lured by the promise of an "abundance" of free land "for all willing to cultivate it." By 1870, they had made it as far west as Council Bluffs, Iowa. There they stopped to earn the capital that would be necessary to begin farming. Rasmus dug ditches for the railroad, Ane worked as a cleaning woman in a local boardinghouse, and young Peter brought drinking water to thirsty laborers who were digging ditches for the town gas works.

Like the Leepers, the Ebbesens eagerly settled on their homestead and began to cultivate the soil. Peter later recalled that the problems that the family had anticipated never materialized. Even the rumors that the Sioux, "flying demons" in the eyes of settlers, were on the rampage proved false. The real problems the family faced were unexpected: rattlesnakes, prairie fires, and an invasion of grasshoppers. The grasshoppers were just as devastating to the Ebbesen farm as they had been to the Leeper homestead. But unlike the Leepers, the Ebbesens stayed on the claim. Although the family "barely had enough" to eat, they survived the three years of grasshopper infestation.

In the following years, the Ebbesens thrived. Rasmus had almost all the original 80 acres under cultivation and purchased an additional 80 acres from the railroad. A succession of sod houses rose on the land and finally even a two-story frame house, paid for with money Peter earned teaching school. By the time they were in their 50s, they could look with pride at their "luxurient and promising crop." But once more natural disaster struck: a "violent hailstorm . . . which completely devastated the whole lot."

The Ebbesens were lucky, however. A banker offered to buy them out, although the amount was $1,000 less than what the family calculated as the farm's "real worth." But it was enough for the purchase of a "modest" house in town. Later, there was even a "dwelling of two stories and nine rooms . . . with adjacent park."

The stories of the Leepers and the Ebbesens, though different in their details and endings, hint at some of the problems confronting rural Americans in the last quarter of the nineteenth century. As a mature industrial economy transformed agriculture and shifted the balance of economic power permanently away from America's farmlands to the country's cities and factories, many farmers found it impossible to realize the traditional dream of rural independence and prosperity. Even bountiful harvests no longer guaranteed success. "We were told two years ago to go to work and raise a big crop; that was all we needed," said one farmer. "We went to work and plowed and planted; the rains fell, the sun shone, nature smiled, and we raised the big crop they told us to; and what came of it? Eight cent corn, ten cent oats, two cent beef and no price at all for butter and eggs—that's what came of it." Native Americans also discovered that changes in rural life threatened their values and dreams. As the Sioux leader Red Cloud told railroad surveyors in Wyoming, "We do not want you here. You are scaring away the buffalo."

This chapter explores several of this book's basic themes as it analyzes the agricultural transformation of the late nineteenth century. Highlighting the ways in which rural Americans—red, white, yellow, and black—joined the industrial world, it asks how diverse groups responded to new economic and social conditions. The rise of large-scale agriculture in the West, the exploitation of its natural resources, and the development of the Great Plains form a backdrop for discussing the impact of white settlement on western tribes and assessing how well native peoples were able to preserve their culture and traditions. In an analysis of the South, the efforts of whites to create a "New South" form a contrast to the underlying realities of race and cotton. Although the chapter shows that discrimination and economic peonage characterized the lives of most black southerners during this period, it also describes the rise of new black protest tactics and ideologies. Finally, the chapter highlights the ways in which agricultural problems of the late nineteenth century, which would continue to characterize much of agricultural life in the twentieth century, led American farmers to become reformers.

MODERNIZING AGRICULTURE

Between 1865 and 1900, the nation's farms more than doubled in number as Americans flocked west of the Mississippi. Farmers raised specialized crops with modern machinery and sped them to market over an expanding railroad system. And they became capitalists, and, as one farmer observed, had to "understand farming as a business."

While small family farms still typified American agriculture, vast mechanized operations devoted to the cultivation of one crop appeared, especially west of the Mississippi River. The bonanza farms, established in the late 1870s on the northern plains, symbolized the trend to large-scale agriculture. Thousands of acres in size, these wheat farms required large capital investments; corporations owned many of them. Like factories, they depended on machinery, hired hundreds of workers, and relied on efficient managers. Although bonanza farms were not typical, they dramatized the agricultural changes that were occurring everywhere on a smaller scale.

Despite their success in adapting farming to modern conditions, farmers were slipping from their dominant position in the workforce. In 1860, they represented almost 60 percent of the labor force; by 1900, less than 37 percent of employed Americans farmed. At the same time, farmers' contribution to the nation's wealth declined from one-third to one-quarter.

American Agriculture and the World

The expansion of American agriculture was tied to changing global patterns and demands. During the nineteenth century, the population of Europe exploded, growing from 175 million in 1800 to 435 million in 1910. While some Europeans continued to till the land, increasing numbers abandoned farming and drifted into cities to find industrial work. In Britain, farmers, who made up only 10 percent of the total workforce, could not produce nearly enough to feed the nation. Like other European countries, Great Britain had to import substantial supplies of food for its citizens. The growing demand prompted American farmers along with their counterparts in eastern Europe, Australia, and New Zealand to expand their operations for the European market.

In their attempts to improve crop yields and livestock, American farmers both benefited from and contributed to trends in agriculture elsewhere in the world. German scientists facilitated agricultural expansion after 1850 by developing better seeds, livestock, and chemical fertilizers. The land-grant university system in the United States, established during the Civil War, ensured that American agriculturists would continue to have access to research into and development of better strains of crops and animals and more effective farming methods. For their part, American farmers led the way in using farm machinery such as the horse-drawn harvester, showing farmers elsewhere in the world the way to raise bigger harvests.

Price of Wholesale Wheat Flour, 1865–1900

The plummeting price of wheat flour was just one indication of the difficulties farmers faced in the late nineteenth century. How much lower was the price of wheat flour in 1900 than in 1865?

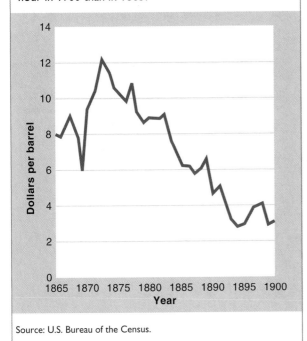

Source: U.S. Bureau of the Census.

This integration into the wider world depended on improved transportation at home and abroad. Reliable, cheap transportation in the United States allowed farmers to specialize: wheat on the Great Plains, corn in the Midwest. Eastern farmers turned to vegetable, fruit, and dairy farming—or sold out.

Cotton, tobacco, wheat, and rice dominated in the South, and grain, fruits, and vegetables were prevalent in the Far West. The development of steamships and an ever-expanding network of railroad systems in Europe ensured that American goods and products could move swiftly, efficiently, and cheaply across land and sea to distant markets.

As farmers specialized for national and international markets, their success depended increasingly on outside forces and demands. Bankers and investors, many of them European, provided the capital to improve transportation and expand operations; intermediaries stored and sometimes sold produce; and railroads and steamships carried it to market. A prosperous economy at home and abroad put money into laborers' pockets for food purchases. But when several European countries banned American pork imports between 1879 and 1883, fearing trichinosis, American stock raisers suffered. As Russian, Argentinean, and Canadian farmers turned to wheat cultivation, increased competition in the world market affected the United States' chief cash crop. Moreover, the worldwide deflation of prices for crops such as wheat and corn affected all who raised these crops for the international market, including American farmers.

The Character of American Agriculture

Technological innovation played a major role in facilitating American agricultural expansion. Harvesters, binders, and other new machines, pulled by work animals, diminished much of the drudgery of farming life, making the production of crops easier, more efficient, and cheaper. Moreover, they allowed

A Vision of the Lackawanna Valley   George Inness's *Lackawanna Valley*—with the reclining figure in the foreground, the train, and puffing smokestacks in the background—suggests that there need be no conflict between technology and agriculture. What other signs of technology besides the train can you see in this painting? *(George Inness, The Lackawanna Valley, Gift of Mrs. Huttleston Rogers, © 2000 Board of Trustees, National Gallery of Art, Washington, c. 1856, oil on canvas, .860 x 1.275 [33⁷/₈ x 50¹/₄])*

HOW OTHERS SEE US

A. Egmont Hake and O. E. Wesslau, "The American Tariff War"

This article, published in an English magazine in 1890, attacked the American tariff system. Great Britain pursued a free trade policy, so the criticism of American tariffs was hardly surprising. In this passage, the authors discuss the impact of tariffs on American farmers.

The wonder is, not that the American farmer has to struggle with mortgages, debts, and a profit-less business, but that he has been able to exist at all. The explanation is to be found in the enormous profit that farming actually yields, though the manufacturers and not the farmers pocket the money. The latter have no rent to pay. As civilization was pushed westward, they obtained farms, not to say estates and vast territories, for next to nothing. Most of the land was level and extremely suitable for cheap machine culture. The alluvial soil was deep, rich, and yielded splendid harvests, during ten to fifteen years, without the use of fertilizers. But the farmers had another source of profit which outweighed all the rest, namely, the rise in the value of the land which he had obtained almost for nothing. As the population thickened round the pioneer-farmers, as villages, communities, and towns arose, his land went up in value, and in millions of cases it was only a question of time for the poor settler to become a wealthy landowner. The protective system may, from the Protectionist point of view, be described as a mechanism for the sharing of the enormous profits of the farmer between a host of people unwilling to adopt the hard work and rough life of a farmer.

- *The authors suggest that tariffs protecting American manufacturers harm the farmers. Why?*

- *Would an American farmer agree with the picture of agricultural expansion given here?*

Source: A. Egmont Hake and O. E. Wesslau, "The American Tariff War," *Fortnightly Review*, 54 (1890), 565.

---

a farmer to cultivate far more land than was possible with hand tools. But machinery was expensive, and many American farmers borrowed to buy it. In the decade of the 1880s, mortgage indebtedness grew two and a half times as fast as agricultural wealth.

Only gradually did farmers realize the perils of their new situation in the world. Productivity rose 40 percent between 1869 and 1899. But the harvests for crops such as wheat were so large that the domestic market could not absorb them. Foreign competition and deflation further affected steadily declining prices. In 1867, corn sold for 78 cents a bushel; by 1889, it had tumbled to 23 cents. Wheat similarly plummeted from about $2 a bushel in 1867 to only 70 cents a bushel in 1889. Cotton profits also spiraled downward, the value of a bale depreciating from $43 in 1866 to $30 in the 1890s.

Falling prices did not automatically hurt all farmers. Because the supply of money rose more slowly than productivity, all prices declined—by more than half between the end of the Civil War and 1900 (for a discussion of the money issue, see Chapter 19). Farmers were receiving less for their crops but also paying less for their purchases. But deflation may have encouraged overproduction. To make the same amount of money, many farmers believed they had to raise larger and larger crops. As they did, prices fell even lower. Furthermore, deflation increased the real value of debts. In 1888, it took 174 bushels of wheat to pay the interest on a $2,000 mortgage at 8 percent. By 1895, it took 320 bushels. Falling prices thus affected most negatively farmers in newly settled areas who borrowed heavily to finance their new operations.

THE WEST

In 1893, the young American historian Frederick Jackson Turner addressed historians gathered at Chicago's World's Fair. Even though the hour was late, Turner's remarks must have galvanized some of his listeners. The age of the American frontier had ended, Turner declared, pointing to recent census data that suggested the disappearance of vacant land in the West. Although Turner overstated his case (for even in the twentieth century much of the West remained uninhabited), his analysis did reflect the rapid expansion into the trans-Mississippi West after the Civil War. Between 1870 and

MAP

Resources and Conflict in the West

1900, acreage devoted to farming tripled west of the Mississippi, while from 1880 to 1900, the western population grew at a faster rate than that of the nation as a whole.

The Frontier Thesis in National and Global Context

DOCUMENT

Frederick Jackson Turner, "The Significance of the Frontier" (1893)

Turner greeted the end of the frontier as a milestone in the nation's history. The frontier had played a central role, he argued, in shaping the American character and American institutions. Over the course of American history, the struggle to tame the wilderness had changed settlers from Europeans into Americans and created a rugged individualism that "promoted democracy." Turner's thesis, emphasizing the unique nature of the American experience and linking it to the frontier, won many supporters. His interpretation complemented long-held ideas about the exceptional nature of American society and character. It accorded with what many saw as a long struggle to conquer what Turner called the "wilderness."

But the American westward movement was less unusual than Turner suggested. The settlement of the trans-Mississippi West was part of a global pattern that redistributed European populations into new areas of the world. Paralleling their American counterparts, farmers, miners, and ranchers were claiming land in Argentina, Brazil, New Zealand, Australia, Canada, and South Africa. Like Americans, they argued that native occupants had failed to make the land productive, and they used their technological superiority to wrest the land from those they considered backward and inferior. Around the world, many native peoples were facing domination by settler societies or retreating as far away from "civilization" as they could.

Turner's frontier scheme gave the place of honor to the frontier farmer who transformed and civilized the wilderness. Before the Civil War, however, real farmers avoided settling many parts of the West. Few chose to try their luck on the Great Plains, an area from 200 to 700 miles wide, extending from Canada to Texas. Much of this region, especially beyond the ninety-eighth meridian, had little rain. The absence of trees seemed to symbolize the plains' unsuitability for agriculture.

The Cattleman's West, 1860–1890

While the region of the Great Plains initially discouraged farmers, its grasses provided the foundation for the cattle kingdom. Mining discoveries in California and the Rocky Mountains established a market for meat. When cattlemen discovered before the Civil

Ranching in the West Here a lone cowboy herds cattle. Although novels and movies often romanticize cowboys, their job was far from glamorous or financially rewarding. How would you describe the landscape in this photograph? How does it suggest some of the realities of herding cattle? *(Brown Brothers)*

War that their animals could graze throughout the year on bunchgrass that accommodatingly turned into hay on its own, the future of the Great Plains for cattle raising became clear.

Although cattle raising dated back to Spanish mission days, the realization of the commercial possibilities for cattle ranching was partly a by-product of Union military strategy. During the war, the North had split the South, cutting Texas off from Confederate cattle markets. By the war's end, millions of longhorns roamed the Texas range. The postwar burst of railroad construction provided a way of turning these cattle into dollars. If Texas ranchers drove their steers north to Abilene, Wichita, or Dodge City, they could be loaded on railroad cars for slaughtering and packinghouses in cities such as Chicago and Kansas City. In the cattle drives of the late 1860s and 1870s, cowboys herded thousands of longhorns north with hefty profits for owners and investors.

Perspectives on the American Cowboy (1884, 1886)

Ranchers on the Great Plains bought some of the cattle and bred them with Hereford and Angus cows to create cattle able to withstand the region's severe winters. In the late 1870s and early 1880s, huge ranches appeared in eastern Colorado, Wyoming, and Montana and in western Kansas, Nebraska, and the Dakotas. These ventures, many owned by outside investors, paid off handsomely. Because the cattle could roam at will over the public domain, they cost owners little as they fattened up but commanded good prices at the time of sale. The cowboys (one-third of them Mexican and black) who herded the steers, however, shared few of the profits. Their meager wages of $25 to $40 a month were just enough to pay for a fling in the saloons, dance halls, and gambling palaces in Dodge City or Abilene when taking the cattle to market.

By the mid-1880s, the first phase of the cattle frontier was ending as farmers moved onto the plains, bought up public lands once used for grazing, and fenced them in. But the competition between cattle ranchers and farmers was only one factor in the cattle frontier's collapse. Eager for profits, ranchers overstocked their herds in the mid-1880s. European investors added to the rush of capital into herding. Hungry cattle ate everything in sight, then weakened as grass became scarce. As was often the case on the plains, the weather played an important role. A winter of memorable blizzards followed the very hot summer of 1886. Cattle, usually able to forage for themselves during the winter months, could not dig through the deep snow to the grass and died from starvation. By spring, 90 percent of the cattle

were dead. One observer reported seeing "countless carcasses of cattle . . . going down [a stream] with the ice, rolling over and over as they went, sometimes with all four stiffened legs pointing skyward. For days on end, tearing down with the grinding ice cakes, went Death's cattle roundup." Frantic owners dumped their surviving cattle on the market, getting $8 or even less per animal.

In the aftermath, the ranchers who remained stock raisers adopted new techniques. Experimenting with new breeds, they began to fence in their herds and to feed them grain during the winter. Since consumers were hungering for tender beef, these new methods suited the market. Ranching, like farming, was becoming a modern business.

Ranching altered the western landscape in ways that had immediate and future ecological consequences. As one Texan realized, "Grass is what counts. It's what saves us all—as far as we get saved. . . . Grass is what holds the earth together." Seeing native species as either competing with cattle for nourishment or threatening them, ranchers hunted and killed antelope, elk, wolves, and other wildlife. When cattlemen overstocked the range, their herds devoured the perennial grasses. In their place, tough, less-nutritious annual grasses sprang up, and sometimes even these grasses disappeared. Lands once able to support large herds of cattle eventually were transformed into deserts of sagebrush, weeds, and dust.

Farmers on the Great Plains, 1865–1890s

Views of the agricultural possibilities of the Great Plains brightened after the Civil War, and railroads played a key role in transforming views of the region's potential. Now that rail lines crossed the continent, they needed customers, settlers, and freight to make a profit. Along with town boosters and land speculators, also hoping to capitalize on their investments, railroads joined in extravagant promotional campaigns. "This is the sole remaining section of paradise in the western world," promised one newspaper. "All the wild romances of the gorgeous orient dwindle into nothing when compared to the everyday realities of Dakota's progress." Propaganda reached beyond the United States to bring the message to Scandinavians, Germans, and others. Dismissing the fear that the plains lacked adequate rainfall to support cultivation, the promotional material assured readers that "All that is needed is to plow, plant, and attend to the crops properly; the rains are abundant." Above-average rainfall in the 1880s strengthened the case.

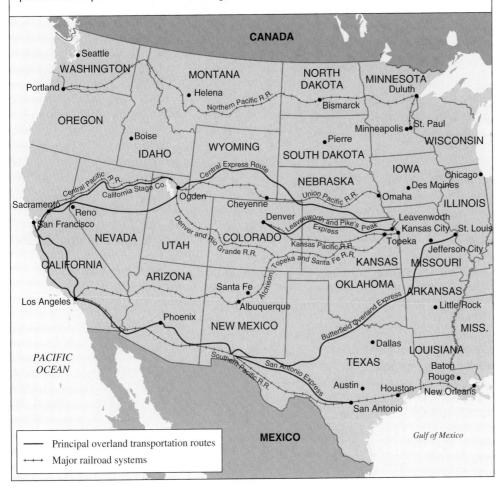

Routes West

On this map, you can trace the various overland routes to the West. How many railroad lines ran across the West? Notice how the railroads contributed to urban growth as trains made their way west. The transcontinental railroads also provided the basis for the economic and demographic expansion and helped to tie East and West together.

— Principal overland transportation routes

↤→ Major railroad systems

In the first boom period of settlement, lasting from 1879 to the early 1890s, tens of thousands of eager families moved onto the Great Plains and began farming. The majority came from Illinois, Iowa, and Missouri. But like the Ebbesens, a substantial number of settlers were immigrants, making the Great Plains the second most important destination for foreign immigration. The greatest numbers came from Germany, the British Isles, and Canada, joined by smaller groups of Scandinavians, Czechs, and Poles. Unlike the single immigrant men flocking to American cities for work, these newcomers came with their families. From the beginning, they intended to put down roots in the new country.

Some settlers established their farms by making claims under the provisions of the Homestead Act, which granted 160 acres to any family head or adult who lived on the claim for five years or who paid

$1.25 an acre after six months of residence. Because homestead land was frequently less desirable than land held by railroads and speculators, however, most settlers bought land outright rather than taking up claims. The costs of getting started were thus more substantial than the Homestead Act would suggest. Western land was cheap compared with farmland in the East, but an individual farmer was fortunate if he could buy a good quarter section for under $500. The costs of machinery would often reach $700. Although some farmers thought it made better economic sense to lease rather than buy land, many rented only because they lacked the capital to purchase land and set up operations. In 1880, some 20 percent of the plains farmers were tenants, and this percentage rose over time.

DOCUMENT

The Land Acts, 1862, 1873, 1894

Norwegian Settlers at Home   This sod house, surrounded by wooden planks, was the home of a Norwegian family. Note that the family are dressed in their good clothes. What objects have they decided to include in this photograph? What do the children on the left appear to be holding? Why do you think the family decided to be portrayed in this way, with these objects displayed with them? *(The Fred Hulstrand History in Pictures Collection, NDSU, Fargo, ND)*

Achieving success on a plains farm was much more difficult than promotional materials promised. Violent changes in the weather and temperature along with the scarcity of water and wood all demanded adjustments. Without firewood, farmers learned to burn corncobs and twisted straw for warmth. The log cabin, long the symbol of frontier life, was replaced by houses of sod "bricks." Although from a distance such houses often looked like mounds of earth—"homely old things," as Hattie Leeper described them—they frequently had glass windows, wooden shingles, and even plastered interiors. Dark and gloomy to our eyes, they were comfortable, cozy, and practical for the settlers. Walls two to three feet thick kept out the scorching summer heat and fierce cold of winter, the moaning winds, and the prairie fires. The solidity of the sod house provided a welcome contrast to the impersonal power and scale of nature.

Late-nineteenth-century industrial innovations helped settlers overcome some of the natural obstacles. The shortage of timber for fencing and housing had encouraged early emigrants to go elsewhere. But in the 1870s, Joseph Glidden developed barbed wire as a cheap alternative to timber fencing. Having seen a simple wooden device designed to keep animals away from fences at a country fair, Glidden thought of making fencing wire with similar protruding barbs. Before long, he and a partner were producing hundreds of miles of barbed-wire fencing that could be used to enclose fields on the plains. Other innovations overcame other challenges. Twine binders, which speeded up grain harvesting, reduced the threat of losing crops to the unpredictable weather. And mail-order steel windmills for pumping water from deep underground wells relieved some of the water shortages by the 1890s.

Industrial innovations, however, could not resolve all of the problems confronting Great Plains settlers. Miriam Peckham, a Kansas homesteader, wrote:

> I tell you Auntie no one can depend on farming for a living in this country. Henry is very industrious and this year had in over thirty acres of small grain, 8 acres of corn and about an acre of potatoes. We have sold our small grain . . . and it come to $100; now deduct $27.00 for cutting, $16.00 for threshing, $19.00 for hired help, say nothing of boarding our help, none of the trouble of drawing 25 miles to market and 25 cts on each head for ferriage over the river and where is your profit. I sometimes think this a God forsaken country, the [grass]hopper hurt our corn and we have 1/2 a crop and utterly destroyed our garden. If one wants trials, let them come to Kansas.

Peckham's letter highlights the uncertainties of frontier life: the costs of machinery, the vagaries of

The Wheat Harvest This 1880 photo highlights the role of machine and animal power rather than human power during the wheat harvest. With more land under cultivation, there was a strong impetus to develop larger and/or more efficient harvesting machines. *(CORBIS)*

crops and markets, the threat of pests and natural disasters, the shortage of cash. Unlike earlier emigrants to the Far West, who had to finance the six-month trip, many plains pioneers took up their homesteads with only a few dollars in their pockets. Survival often depended on how well families managed to do during the crucial first years and how much work each member of the family, including women and children, could perform. If they succeeded in raising and selling their crops, they might accumulate the capital needed to continue. But if nature was harsh or their luck or health bad, or if they were unable to adjust to new conditions or to do the hard labor that was necessary to get the farm going, the chances of failure grew.

Life on the plains had its compensations, however. Willa Cather, who grew up in Nebraska, showed both the harshness and the appeal of the prairie in her novels. Alexandra Bergson, the main character of *O Pioneers!* (1913), loves the land: "It seemed beautiful to her, rich and strong and glorious." The thousands of letters and diaries that survive from the period also provide a positive picture of farming life. One woman reflected on the way she had softened the harsh landscape. "Our flower garden was such a vision of beauty . . . the dreary, desolate place was blossoming in all the gorgeous beauty that God has promised to those who try."

In the late 1880s and early 1890s, the first boom on the Great Plains halted abruptly. Falling agricultural prices cut

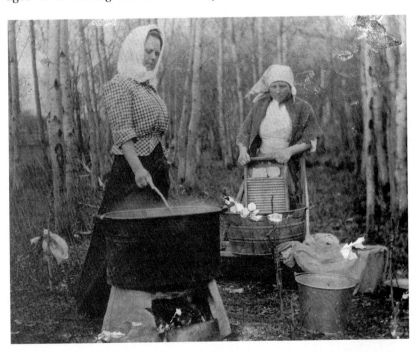

Domestic Work in the West This photograph shows some of the hard physical labor involved in homesteading. How many steps were involved in doing the family laundry? The clothing of these women, probably settlers in North Dakota, identifies them as immigrants. Their presence reminds us that the West was the home of diverse peoples including Asians, European newcomers, Native Americans, black migrants, and Hispanics whose families had lived in the West for generations. *(The Fred Hulstrand History in Pictures Collection, NDSU, Fargo, ND)*

profits. Then, the unusual rainfall that had lured farmers into the semiarid region near the 100th meridian vanished. A devastating drought followed.

DOCUMENT

John E. Read, *Farming for Profit* (1891)

One farmer reported in 1890 that he had earned $41.48 from his wheat crop, yet his expenses for seed and threshing amounted to $56.00. The destitute survived on boiled weeds, a few potatoes, and a little bread and butter. Many farmers had debts they now could not repay. Thousands lost their farms to creditors. Some stayed on as tenants. Homesteaders like the Leepers gave up. By 1900, two-thirds of homesteaded farms had failed. Many homesteaders fled east. In western Kansas, the population declined by half between 1888 and 1892. The wagons of those who retreated bore the epitaph of their experience: "In God We Trusted: In Kansas We Busted."

Whether individual farmers remained on the Great Plains or retreated to more promising climates, collectively these new agricultural efforts had a significant long-term impact on the region's environment. When farmers removed sod to build their sod houses and broke the prairies with their plows to plant their crops, they were removing the earth's protective covering. The heavy winds so common on the prairies could lift exposed topsoil and carry it miles away. Deep plowing, which was essential for dry farming techniques introduced after the drought of the 1880s, worsened this situation. The dust bowl of the 1930s was the eventual outcome of these agricultural interventions. Other less obvious consequences of farming and settlement on the Great Plains included a lowering of the water table level as mail-order steel windmills provided the power for pumping water from deep

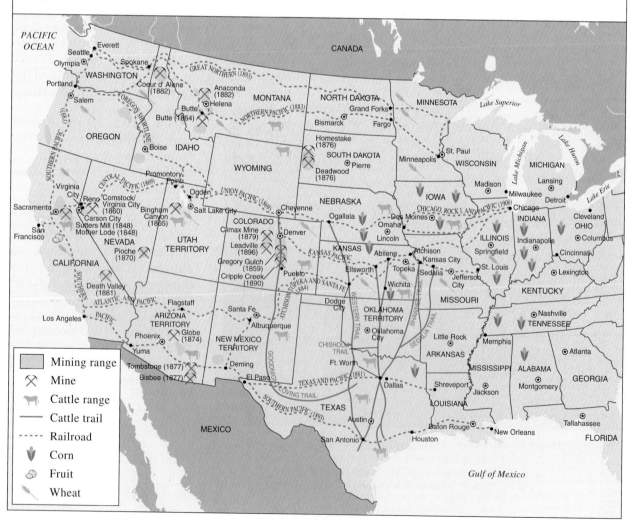

The New Economy of the West, 1850–1893

This map shows the importance of mining, ranching, and farming in the western part of the nation. Note the railroad links with the East.

underground. Far from the plains, the pine forests around the Great Lakes fell to satisfy the settlers' need for wood and the railroads' voracious appetite for railroad ties.

Cornucopia on the Pacific

When gold was discovered in California, Americans rushed west to find it. But as one father told his eager son, "Plant your lands; these be your best gold fields." He was right; with the completion of a national railroad system, farming eventually became California's greatest asset. But farming in California resembled neither romanticized depictions of rural life nor the vision of the framers of the Homestead Act. The state's agricultural success would rest on railroads, machinery, and irrigation.

Although federal and state land policies supposedly promoted "homes for the homeless," little of California's land was actually homesteaded or developed as small family farms. When California entered the Union, Mexican ranchers had vast landholdings that never became part of the public domain. Because most Mexican Americans impoverished themselves in legal efforts to establish the legitimacy of their claims, speculators eventually acquired much of their land. Consequently, farmers needed substantial sums to buy land.

By 1871, reformer Henry George described California as "not a country of farms but a country of plantations and estates." California farms were indeed substantially larger than farms in the rest of the country. In 1870, the average California farm was 482 acres, whereas the average farm size nationwide was only 153 acres. By 1900, farms of 1,000 acres or more made up two-thirds of the state's farmland. This landscape reflected the advent of large-scale farming. As one California visitor reported to the *New York Times* in 1887, "You go through miles and miles of wheat fields, you see the fertility of the land and the beauty of the scenery, but where are the hundreds of farm houses . . . that you would see in Ohio or Iowa?"

Small farmers and ranchers did exist, of course, but they found it difficult to compete with large, mechanized operators using cheap migrant laborers, usually Mexican or Chinese. One wheat farm in the San Joaquin Valley was so vast that workers started plowing in the morning at one end of the 17-mile field, ate lunch at its halfway point, and camped at its end that night.

The value of much of California's agricultural land, especially the southern half of the Central Valley, depended on water. By the 1870s, water, land, and railroad companies, using the labor and expertise of Chinese workers, were taking on the huge costs of building dams, headgates, and canals. They passed on the costs of construction to settlers now eager to acquire hitherto barren lands along with water rights. By 1890, more than a quarter of California's farms benefited from irrigation. The irrigation ditches were a fitting symbol of the importance of technology and a managerial attitude toward the land that characterized late-nineteenth-century agriculture, particularly in California.

Although grain was initially California's most valuable crop, it faced stiff competition from farmers on the plains and in other parts of the world. Some argued that land capable of raising luscious

Agricultural Productivity, 1800–1900

The astonishing gains in the productivity of wheat farmers point to the use of reapers that cut and bound the wheat and thrashers that knocked the grain off the stalks. The combine integrated both operations and also cleared and bagged the grain.

Crop and Productivity Indicator	1800	1840	1880	1900
Wheat				
Worker-hours/acre	56	35	30	15
Yield/acre (bushels)	15	15	13	14
Worker-hours/100 bushels	373	233	152	108
Corn				
Worker-hours/acre	86	69	46	38
Yield/acre (bushels)	25	25	26	26
Worker-hours/100 bushels	344	276	180	147
Cotton				
Worker-hours/acre	185	135	119	112
Yield/acre (bushels)	147	147	179	191
Worker-hours/bale	601	439	318	280

Source: U.S. Bureau of the Census.

fruits "in a climate surpassing that of Italy, is too valuable for the cultivation of simple cereals." But high railroad rates and lack of refrigeration limited the volume of fresh fruit and vegetables sent to market. As railroad managers in the 1880s realized the potential profitability of California produce, they lowered rates and introduced refrigerated railroad cars. In June 1888, fresh apricots and cherries successfully survived the trip from California to New York. Fruit and vegetable production rose, benefiting from the agricultural expertise of Chinese laborers, tenant farmers, and Chinese entrepreneurs. So important were their contributions that some have argued that Chinese know-how was mainly responsible for the shift to produce farming. By 1890, about 9,000 carloads of navel oranges were heading east. Before long, California fruit appeared in London markets and on English dining tables.

The Mining West

Mining hastened rapid western growth and development. The first and best-known mining rush occurred in 1848 when gold was discovered in California, but others followed as precious metals—silver, iron, copper, coal, lead, zinc, and tin—lured thousands west to Colorado, Montana, Idaho, and Nevada as well as to states such as Minnesota.

Mining discoveries were transformative events, for they attracted people and businesses west, often to places far away from agricultural settlements. Hastily built mining communities might be eyesores, but they had bustling urban characters. If and when the strike was over, however, residents abandoned the mining camps and towns as fast as they had rushed into them. The pattern of boom and bust characterized much of mining life.

While the image of the independent miner panning for gold has passed into the nation's memory, the reality of late-nineteenth-century mining was nothing like the popular stereotype. Retrieving minerals from rock was difficult, expensive, and dangerous. A successful mine required a large labor force, industrial tools, and railroad links. Miners worked way below the earth's surface in poorly ventilated tunnels, with no means for removing human or animal waste. Temperatures could reach as high as 120 degrees. Accidents were part of the job, which depended on blasting equipment and industrial machinery. In 1884, a Montana miner drilled into an unexploded dynamite charge and lost his eyes and ear. He received no compensation, for the court decided that the accident "was the result of an unforeseen and unavoidable accident incident to the risk of mining."

DOCUMENT

John Lester, "Hydraulic Mining" (1873)

Cripple Creek, Colorado   This photograph shows the houses and mining buildings at "The Summit," a mining camp at Cripple Creek, Colorado, in the 1880s. How does this picture suggest the impact of mining on the environment? What would it be like to live and work at The Summit? *(Photo by W. E. Hook, Denver Public Library, Western History Collection)*

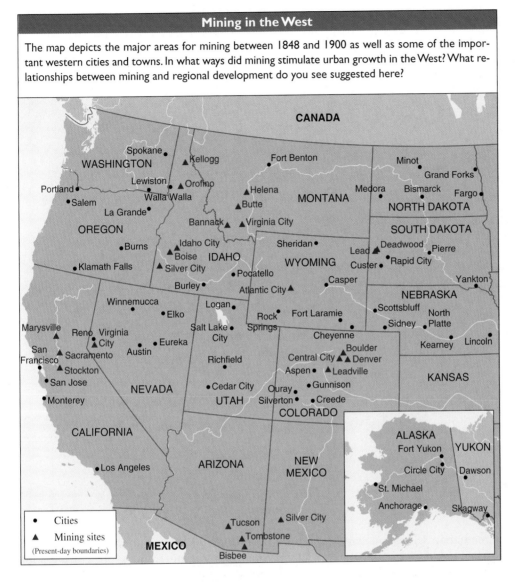

Mining in the West

The map depicts the major areas for mining between 1848 and 1900 as well as some of the important western cities and towns. In what ways did mining stimulate urban growth in the West? What relationships between mining and regional development do you see suggested here?

As the next chapter will show, in time, western miners became one of the most radical groups of industrial workers.

Exploiting Natural Resources

Mining was a big business with high costs and a basic dynamic that encouraged rapid and thorough exploitation of the earth's resources. The decimation of the nation's forests went hand in hand with large-scale mining and the railroads that provided the links to markets. Both railroads and mining depended on wood—railroads for wooden ties, mines for shaft timber and ore reduction. The impact of these demands is captured by the California State Board of Agriculture's estimate in the late 1860s that one-third of the state's forests had already disappeared.

When lumber companies cut down timber, they affected the flow of streams and destroyed the habitat supporting birds and animals. Like the activities of farmers and cattle owners, the companies that stripped the earth of its forest cover were also contributing to soil erosion. The idea that the public lands belonging to the federal government ought to be rapidly developed supported such exploitation of the nation's natural resources. Often, in return for royalties, the government leased parts of the public domain to companies that hoped to extract valuable minerals, not to own the land permanently. In other cases, companies bought land, but not always legally. In 1878, Congress passed the Timber and Stone Act, which initially applied to Nevada, Oregon, Washington, and California. This legislation allowed the sale of 160-acre parcels of the public domain that were "unfit for cultivation" and "valuable chiefly for timber." Timber companies were quick to see the possibilities in the new law. They hired men willing to register for claims and then to turn them over to timber interests.

The Natural Environment of the West

Study the patterns of rainfall and the natural features of the West, including rivers and mountain ranges. What do these patterns suggest about native vegetation and the prospects for farming? What is revealed about the role of water and irrigation in the West? What difficulties facing the settlers are revealed?

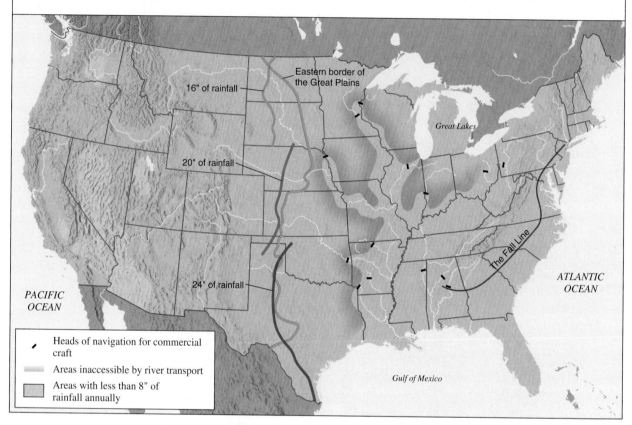

By the end of the century, more than 3.5 million acres of the public domain had been acquired under the legislation, and most of it was in corporate hands.

The rapacious and rapid exploitation of resources combined with the increasing pace of industrialization made some Americans uneasy. Many believed that forests played a part in causing rainfall and that their destruction would have an adverse impact on the climate. Others, such as John Muir, lamented the destruction of the country's great natural beauty. In 1868, Muir came upon the Great Valley of California, "all one sheet of plant gold, hazy and vanishing in the distance . . . one smooth, continuous bed of honey-bloom." He soon realized, however, that a "wild, restless agriculture" and "flocks of hoofed locusts, sweeping over the ground like a fire" would destroy this vision of loveliness. Muir became a preservation champion. He played a part in the creation of Yosemite National Park in 1890, participated in a successful effort to allow President Benjamin Harrison to classify certain parts of the public domain as forest reserves (the

Forest Reserve Act of 1891), and in 1892 established the Sierra Club. At the same time, conservation ideas were also emerging. Gifford Pinchot, who became a leading advocate of these ideas, was less interested in the preservation of the nation's wilderness areas than in careful management of its natural resources. "Conservation," he explained, "means the wise use of the earth and its resources for the lasting good of man." Both perspectives, however, were more popular in the East than in the West, where the seeming abundance of natural resources and the profit motive diminished support.

RESOLVING THE NATIVE AMERICAN QUESTION

Black Elk, an Oglala Sioux, listened to a story his father had heard from his father.

A long time ago . . . there was once a Lakota [Sioux] holy man, called Drinks Water, who dreamed what was to be; and this was long before the coming of the Wasichus [white men]. He dreamed . . . that a strange race had woven a spider's web all around the Lakotas. And he said: "When this happens, you shall live in square gray houses, in a barren land, and beside those square gray houses you shall starve."

Black Elk saw this strange dream come true.

As farmers settled the western frontier and became entangled in a national economy, they clashed with the Native American tribes who lived on the land. In California, disease and violence killed 90 percent of the Native American population in the 30 years following the gold rush. Elsewhere, the struggle among Native Americans, white settlers, the U.S. Army, and government officials and reformers was prolonged and bitter. Although some tribes moved onto government reservations with little protest, most tribes, including the Nez Percé in the Northwest, the Apache in the Southwest, and the Plains Indians, resisted the attempts to curb their way of life and to transform their culture.

Background to the Plains Wars

The lives of most Plains Indians revolved around the buffalo. Increased emigration to California and Oregon in the 1840s and 1850s disrupted tribal pursuits and animal migration patterns. Initially, the federal government tried, without much success, to persuade the Plains tribes to stay away from white wagon trains and white settlers. As Lone Horn, a Miniconjou chief, explained when American commissioners at the 1851 Fort Laramie Council asked him whether he would be satisfied to live on the Missouri River,

Sioux Encampment, Early 1890s

Feather Earring Pictured here is a mounted member of the Apache tribe, one of the Native American groups resisting white expansion. Probably taken in the 1860s, this picture shows both the strength of Native American culture and the impact of white culture. Can you pick out signs of both cultural traditions? (Photo by J. F. Mourer, Denver Public Library, Western History Collection)

"When the buffalo comes close to the river, we come close to it. When the buffaloes go off, we go off after them."

During the Civil War, the eastern tribes that were forced to relocate in Oklahoma divided: some tribes, especially the slaveholders, supported the Confederacy, while other tribes supported the Union. After the war, however, all were branded as "traitors." The federal government callously nullified earlier pledges and treaties, leaving Native Americans defenseless against further incursions on their lands. As settlers pushed into Kansas, the tribes living in Kansas were shunted into Oklahoma.

The White Perspective

When the Civil War ended, red and white people on the Great Plains were already at war. In 1864, the Colorado militia massacred a band of friendly Cheyenne at Sand Creek. Cheyenne, Sioux, and Arapaho soon responded in kind. The Great Plains wars had begun.

DOCUMENT

Congressional Report on the Sand Creek Massacre (1867)

Although not all whites condoned this butchery, the congressional commission authorized to make peace viewed Native Americans' future narrowly. The commissioners, including the commander of the army in the West, Civil War hero William T. Sherman, accepted as fact that the West belonged to an "industrious, thrifty, and enlightened population" of whites. Native Americans, the commission believed, must relocate to western South Dakota or Oklahoma to learn white ways. Annuities, food, and clothes would ease their transition to "civilized" life.

At two major conferences in 1867 and 1868, chiefs listened to these drastic proposals spelling the end of traditional native life. Some agreed; others, like one Kiowa chief, insisted, "I don't want to settle. I love to roam over the prairies." In any case, the agreements were not binding because no chief had authority to speak for his tribe. For its part, the U.S. Senate dragged its feet in approving the treaties. Supplies promised to Indians who settled in the arid reserved areas failed to materialize, and wildlife proved too sparse to support them. These tribes soon drifted back to their former hunting grounds.

Sherman warned, "All who cling to their old hunting ground are hostile and will remain so till killed off." When persuasion failed, the U.S. Army went to war. "The more we can kill this year," Sherman remarked, "the less will have to be killed the next war." In 1867, he ordered General Philip Sheridan to deal with the tribes. Sheridan introduced winter campaigning, aimed at seeking out Indians who divided

Recovering the Past

Weekly and monthly magazines constitute a rich primary source for the historian, offering a vivid picture of the issues of the day and useful insights into popular tastes and values. With advances in the publishing industry and an increasingly literate population, the number of these journals soared in the years following the Civil War. In 1865, only 700 periodicals were published. Twenty years later, there were 3,300. As the *National Magazine* grumbled, "Magazines, magazines, magazines! The newsstands are already groaning under the heavy load, and there are still more coming."

Some of these magazines were aimed at the mass market. *Frank Leslie's Illustrated Newspaper,* established in 1855, was one of the most successful. At its height, circulation reached 100,000. Making skillful use of pictures (sometimes as large as two by three feet and folded into the magazine), the weekly covered important news of the day as well as music, drama, sports, and books. Although Leslie relied more heavily on graphics and sensationalism than do modern news weeklies, his publication was a forerunner of *Newsweek* and *Time*.

Another kind of weekly magazine was aimed primarily at middle- and upper-class readers. Editors such as the oft-quoted Edwin Lawrence Godkin of *The Nation,* with a circulation of about 30,000, hoped to influence those in positions of authority and power by providing a forum for the discussion of reform issues. In contrast, *Scribner's* revealed a more conservative, middle-of-the-road point of view. Both magazines, however, exuded a confident, progressive tone that was characteristic of middle-class Americans.

Harper's Weekly was one of the most important magazines designed primarily for middle- and upper-class readers. Established in 1857, this publication continued in print until 1916. The success of *Harper's Weekly*, which called itself a "family newspaper," rested on a combination of its moderate point of view and an exciting use of illustrations and cartoons touching on contemporary events. The popular cartoons of Thomas Nast appeared in this magazine. In large part because of the use of graphics, the circulation of *Harper's Weekly* reached a peak of 160,000 in 1872.

Illustrated here is a page from the January 16, 1869, issue of *Harper's Weekly*. The layout immediately suggests the importance of graphics. Most of the page is taken up with the three pictures. The top and bottom pictures are wood engravings based on drawings by Theodore R. Davis, one of *Harper's* best-known illustrator-reporters. The center picture was derived from a photograph.

The story featured on this page concerns a victory of General George Custer in the war against the Cheyenne tribe that the U.S. Army was waging that winter. Davis had been a correspondent in the West covering Custer's actions in 1867. But when news of Custer's victory arrived, Davis was back in New York. He thus drew on his imagination for the two scenes reproduced on the next page. What kind of characterization of Native Americans does Davis give in the picture at the top of the page? What view of American soldiers does he suggest? At the bottom of the page, you can see soldiers slaughtering "worthless" horses while Cheyenne teepees burn in the background. Would the average viewer have any sympathy for the plight of the Cheyenne after looking at this picture? This "victory," in fact, involved the slaughter not only of horses but also of all males over age 8.

The editors' decision to insert a picture that had nothing to do with the incident being reported was obviously significant. As you can see, the subject in the center illustration is a white hunter who had been killed and scalped by Indians. By considering the choice of graphics and text, you can begin to discover how magazines provide insight, not only into the events of the day but also into the ways magazines shaped the values and perspectives of nineteenth-century men and women.

REFLECTING ON THE PAST   What kind of special relationship were the editors suggesting by placing the picture of one dead white hunter in the center of a page that primarily covered a specific conflict between the Indians and the U.S. Army? How might the reader respond to the group of pictures as a whole? How do you? How does the text contribute to the overall view of the Indian–white relationship that the pictures suggest?

CUSTER'S INDIAN SCOUTS CELEBRATING THE VICTORY OVER BLACK KETTLE.—[Sketched by Thos. R. Davis.]

THE INDIAN WAR.

THE SCALPED HUNTER.—[Photographed by Wm. S. Soule.]

Harper's Weekly delivered powerful messages about the Native Americans in its choice of illustrations.

AMERICAN VOICES

Sister Blandina Segale, From Her Diary, November 1882

Sister Blandina Segale, a member of the Cincinnati Sisters of Charity, had hoped to work in the West from the time she joined the Catholic order of nuns. In 1872, she was ordered to Colorado. After spending four years there, she went on to do mission work in New Mexico. The following excerpt is from her diary, which she kept for more than 20 years. The date on this entry is November 1882.

When I boarded the Lamy branch to the ancient city, I noticed a number of Pino Indians. Scarcely was I seated when a blanketed chief came to ask me in incorrect Spanish:

"Tu vas Carlisle, Santa Catalina escuola?" (Are you going to Carlisle, to Saint Catherine's School?)

"There is no Santa Catalina School in Carlisle."

"No Santa Catalina School, no papooses!"

With this the Indian agent, Thomas by name came to ask me if the atmosphere were too oppressive, meaning the nearness of the Indian to me. I retorted, "The oppression just now comes from another quarter." . . .

That English phrase, "The survival of the fittest," is being applied to the rightful owners of this country. Let us stretch our imagination and see ten million suddenly descend on us? Would we not, if given a new chance, be more considerate with the Indians? The money supplied by our government and misapplied by the agents helps the extermination.

■ *In what ways does this journal entry suggest the varying opinions of whites about Native Americans?*

---

into small groups during the winter and exterminating them.

Completion of the transcontinental railroad in 1869 added yet another pressure for "solving" the Indian question. Transcontinental railroads wanted rights-of-way through tribal lands and needed white settlers to make their operations profitable. Few whites considered Native Americans to have any right to lands they wanted.

In his 1872 annual report, the commissioner for Indian affairs, Francis Amasa Walker, addressed two fundamental questions: how to prevent Indians from blocking white migration to the Great Plains, and what to do with them over the long run. Walker suggested buying off the "savages" with promises of food and gifts, luring them onto reservations, and there imposing a "rigid reformatory discipline," necessary because Indians were "unused to manual labor." Though Walker wanted to save the Indians from destruction, he offered only one grim choice: "yield or perish."

The Tribal View

Native Americans defied such attacks on their ancient way of life and protested the wholesale violation of treaties. Black Elk remembered that, in 1863, when he was only three, his father had his leg broken in a fierce battle against the white men. "When I was older," he recalled,

I learned what the fighting was about. . . . Up on the Madison Fork the Wasichus had found much of the yellow metal that they worship and that makes them crazy, and they wanted to have a road up through our country to the place where the yellow metal was; but my people did not want the road. It would scare the bison and make them go away, and also it would let the other Wasichus come in like a river. They told us that they wanted only to use a little land, as much as a wagon would take between the wheels; but our people knew better.

DOCUMENT

Chief Red Cloud's Speech

Black Elk's father and many others soon realized that fighting was the only "way to keep our country." But "wherever we went, the soldiers came to kill us."

Broken promises fired Indian resistance. In 1875, the federal government allowed gold prospectors into the Black Hills, part of the Sioux reservation and one of their sacred places. Chiefs Sitting Bull, Crazy Horse, and Rain-in-the-Face led the angry Sioux on the warpath. At the Battle of Little Big Horn in 1876, they vanquished General George Custer. But their bravery and skill could not permanently withstand the power of the well-supplied, well-armed, and determined U.S. Army. Elsewhere, the pattern of resistance and ultimate defeat was repeated. In Texas,

IMAGE

Oglala Sioux Pictogram of the Battle of Little Big Horn

General Sherman vanquished Native American tribes, and in the Pacific Northwest, Nez Percé Chief Joseph surrendered in 1877.

The wholesale destruction of the buffalo was an important element in white victory. The animals were central to Native American life, culture, and religion. As one Pawnee chief explained, "Am afraid when we have no meat to offer, Great Spirit ... will be angry & punish us." Although Plains Indians could be wasteful of buffalo in areas where the animals were abundant, white miners and hunters ultimately destroyed the herds. Sportsmen shot the beasts from train windows. Railroad crews ate the meat. Ranchers' cattle competed for grass. And demand for buffalo bones for fertilizer and hides for robes and shoes encouraged the decimation.

IMAGE
Bison Grazing

The slaughter, which had claimed 13 million animals by 1883, was disgraceful in retrospect. The Indians considered white men demented. "They just killed and killed because they like to do that," said one, whereas when "we hunted the bison ... [we] killed only what we needed." But the destruction of the herds pleased whites who were determined to curb the movements of Native Americans. As Secretary of the Interior Columbus Delano explained in

1872, "I cannot regard the rapid disappearance of the game from its former haunts as a matter prejudicial to our management of the Indians." Rather, he said, "as they become convinced that they can no longer rely upon the supply of game for their support, they will return to the more reliable source of subsistence furnished at their agencies."

The 1887 Dawes Act

Changing federal policy was aimed at ending Native American power and culture. In 1871, Congress abandoned the practice, in effect since the 1790s, of treating the tribes as sovereign nations. Other measures supplemented this attempt to undermine both tribal integrity and the prestige of tribal leaders, whom negotiators would no longer recognize as speaking for their tribes. The government urged tribes to replace tribal justice with a court system and extended federal jurisdiction to the reservations. Tribes were also warned not to gather for religious ceremonies.

DOCUMENT
The Dawes Act
(1887)

The Dawes Severalty Act of 1887 pulled together the strands of federal Indian policy that emerged after the Civil War and set its course for the rest of the century. Believing that tribal bonds kept Indians in savagery, reformers intended to destroy them. As Theodore Roosevelt noted approvingly, the bill was a "mighty pulverizing engine to break up the tribal mass." The reservation policy was, in effect, abandoned. Rather than allotting reservation lands to tribal groups, the act allowed the president to distribute these lands to individuals. Private property, the framers of the bill reasoned, would undermine communal norms and tribal identity and encourage tribes to settle down and farm as white men did. Although Indian agents explained that Native Americans opposed the Dawes Act, Congress, convinced that white people knew what was best for Indians, did not hesitate to legislate on their behalf.

The fact that speculators as well as reformers lobbied for

Buffalo Bill's Wild West As the plains and prairies of the trans-Mississippi West filled up with farms and rural communities, Americans became nostalgic for the recent past. Buffalo Bill's Wild West show offered a colorful but inaccurate picture of the migration west. Native Americans were hired for the show to take part in scenes in which they attacked "innocent settlers" and travelers. White audiences loved the clear picture the show provided of villains and heroes, while ironically Native Americans were often grateful for the opportunity to escape the confines of reservation life and to earn money. Can you identify the different flags in the poster and the different groups that participated in the show? *(The Granger Collection, New York)*

A Indian School These girls, attending a Indian school, are neatly dressed in identical dresses and aprons, with hair pulled into buns rather than braided. What does this picture reveal about the objective of this education for young Indian girls? *(Bettmann/CORBIS)*

the legislation betrayed another motive at work. Even if each Indian family head claimed a typical share of 160 acres, millions of "surplus" acres would remain for sale to white settlers. Within 20 years of the Dawes Act, Native Americans had lost 60 percent of their lands. The federal government held the profits from land sales "in trust" and used them for the "civilizing" mission.

The Ghost Dance: An Indian Renewal Ritual

By the 1890s, the grim reality of their plight made many Native Americans responsive to a new religious revitalization movement. Like other prophets before him, the Paiute holy man, Wovoka, held out hope that history would reverse itself. He assured his followers that a natural disaster would eliminate the white race and that their ancestors and wild game would return to earth. If Indians performed a special dance called the Ghost Dance and observed traditional customs, this transformation would come more quickly. Wovoka's prophecies spread rapidly. Believers expressed their faith and hope through the new rituals of ghost or spirit dancing, hypnosis, and meditation.

Although Wovoka's prophecies discouraged hostile actions against whites, American settlers were uneasy. Indian agents tried to prevent the ghost dances and filed hysterical reports. "Indians are dancing in the snow and are wild and crazy. . . . We need protection, and we need it now." One agent identified the Sioux medicine man Sitting Bull, who had strenuously opposed American expansion, as a leading troublemaker and decided to arrest him. In the confusion of arrest, Indian police killed Sitting Bull.

Bands of Sioux fled the reservation with the army in swift pursuit. In late December 1890, the army overtook the Sioux at Wounded Knee Creek. Although the Sioux had raised a flag of truce, a scuffle that ensued as they were turning over their weapons led to a bloody massacre. Using the most up-to-date machine guns and Hotchkiss cannons, the army killed more than 200 men, women, and children. An eyewitness described the desolate scene a few days later. "Among the fragments of burned tents . . . we saw the frozen bodies lying close together or piled one upon another."

DOCUMENT

Accounts of the Wounded Knee Massacre (1890s)

Thus arose the lament of Black Elk, who saw his people diminished, starving, despairing:

Once we were happy in our own country and we were seldom hungry, for then the two-leggeds and the four-leggeds lived together like relatives, and there was plenty for them and for us. But then the Wasichus came, and they have made little islands for us . . . , and always these islands are becoming smaller, for around them surges the gnawing flood of the Wasichus; . . . dirty with lies and greed.

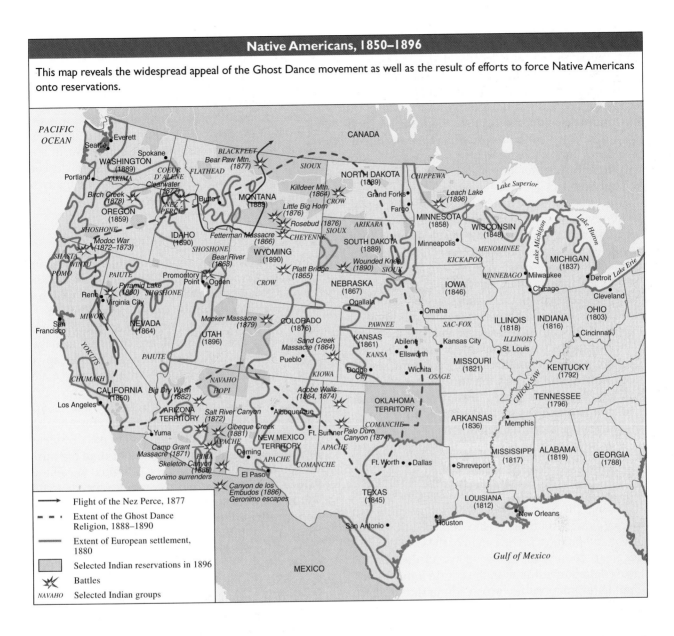

Native Americans, 1850–1896

This map reveals the widespread appeal of the Ghost Dance movement as well as the result of efforts to force Native Americans onto reservations.

As Black Elk recognized, white Americans had finally defeated the western tribes. Once independent, proud, and strong, Native Americans suffered dependency, poverty, and social and cultural disorganization on the reservations, in grim Indian schools, and in city slums. The country's original inhabitants seemed to have no place in the American nation.

THE NEW SOUTH

The trans-Mississippi West was transformed as native peoples were subdued, the Great Plains were settled, and commercial agriculture helped knit the region into the larger world. Mining camps turned into industrial centers. Western cities grew at a fast

pace; by 1900, nearly 40 percent of westerners lived in cities. The large number of itinerant workers who worked in mines, forests, and fields provided a flexible workforce that supported economic growth.

In contrast to this pattern, the southern economy sputtered. Of all the nation's agricultural regions, the South was the poorest. In 1880, southerners' yearly earnings were only half the national average. The agricultural labor force was neither efficient, nor mobile, nor prosperous enough to invest in needed improvements. And while some southerners dreamed of making the agricultural South rival the industrial North, their dreams were never realized. The region remained dependent on the North. Southern industrial workers were poorly paid, caught in dead-end jobs with little hope of advancement.

Postwar Southerners Face the Future

After the painful war and Reconstruction, compelling arguments for regional self-sufficiency rang out. Those who wanted a "New South" argued that southern backwardness did not stem from the war itself, but from basic conditions in southern life—a rural economy based on cotton foremost among them. The defeat only made clearer the reality of the nineteenth century. Power and wealth came not from cotton but from factories, machines, and cities.

The effort to create a New South was far-ranging. In hundreds of speeches, editorials, pamphlets, articles, and books, spokesmen for the New South, such as Atlanta newspaper publisher Henry Grady, encouraged fellow southerners to change—to abandon prewar ideals that glorified leisure and gentility and adopt new entrepreneurial values. To lure northern investment, critical because the South was short of capital, New South advocates also held out the possibility of "fabulous" profits. In a bid to encourage manufacturers, several southern state governments offered tax exemptions and the cheap labor of leased convicts. Texas and Florida awarded the railroads land grants, and cities such as Atlanta and Louisville mounted huge industrial exhibitions. The most startling example of commitment to the vision of a New South may have come in 1886 when southern railroad companies, in a crash effort, relaid railroad tracks and adjusted rolling stock to fit the northern gauges.

During the late nineteenth century, northern money flowed south as dollars replaced the moral fervor and political involvement of the Civil War and Reconstruction years. In the 1880s, northerners increased their investment in the cotton industry sevenfold and financed the expansion of the southern railroad system. Northern capital fueled southern urban expansion. By 1900, some 15 percent of all southerners lived in cities, whereas only 7 percent had in 1860. (The national averages for these years were 40 and 20 percent, respectively.)

Birmingham, Alabama, symbolized the New South. In 1870, the site was a peaceful cornfield. The next year, two northern real estate speculators arrived on the scene, attracted by the area's rich iron deposits. Despite a siege of cholera and the depression of the 1870s, Birmingham rapidly became the center of the southern iron and steel industry. By 1890, a total of 38,414 people lived in the city. Coke ovens, blast furnaces, rolling mills, iron foundries, and machine shops belched forth polluting smoke into the air where once there had been only fields. Millions of dollars' worth of finished goods poured forth from the city's mills and factories, and eight railroad lines carried them away.

Other southern cities flourished as well. Memphis prospered from its lumber industry and the manufacturing of cottonseed products, and Richmond became the country's tobacco capital even as its flour mills and iron and steel foundries continued to produce wealth. Augusta, Georgia, was the "Lowell of the South," a leader in the emerging textile industry that blossomed in Georgia, North and South Carolina, and Alabama. Augusta's eight cotton mills employed about 2,800 workers, many of them women and children.

The Other Side of Progress

New South leaders—a small group of merchants, industrialists, and planters—bragged about the growth of the iron and textile industries and paraded statistics to prove the success of efforts to modernize. The South, one writer boasted, was "throbbing with industrial and railroad activity." Middle-class southerners increasingly accepted new entrepreneurial values. But the South made slow progress.

Older values persisted. Indeed, New South spokesmen paradoxically kept older, chivalric values alive by romanticizing the recent past. By viewing "all Confederate veterans" rather than big businessmen as "heroes" and by clinging to genteel values that did not glorify getting ahead, many southerners resisted the demands of the new economic order. Despite the interest in modernization, southerners did not invest in a modern workforce. The southern school system lagged far behind that of the North.

Although new industries and signs of progress abounded, two of the new industries depended on tobacco and cotton—traditional crops long at the center of rural life. As they had before the war, commerce and government work drove urban growth. Moreover, the South did not better its position relative to the North. Whereas in 1860, the South had 17 percent of the country's manufacturing concerns, by 1904, it had only 15 percent. The South's achievements were not insignificant during a period in which northern industry and cities rapidly expanded, but they could not make the South the equal of the North.

Moreover, the South failed to reap many benefits from industrialization. As in the antebellum period, the South remained an economic vassal of the North. Southern businessmen grew in number, but with the exception of the American Tobacco Company, no great southern corporations arose. Instead, southerners worked for northern companies and corporations, which absorbed southern businesses or dominated them financially. Profits flowed north. "Our capitalists are going into your country," the Lowell *Manufacturers' Record* noted, "because they see a chance to make money there, but you must not think that they will give your people the benefit of the money they make. That will come North and enrich their heirs, or set up public libraries in our country towns." As dollars fled north, so, too, went the power to make critical decisions. In many cases, northern directors determined that southern mills and factories could handle only the early stages of processing, while northern factories finished the goods. Thus, southern cotton mills sent yarn and coarse cloth north for completion. Southern manufacturers who did finish their products, hoping to compete in the marketplace, found that railroad rate discrimination robbed their goods of any competitive edge.

Individual workers in the new industries may have found factory life preferable to sharecropping, but their rewards were meager. Caught in low-skill jobs with little chance for advancement, workers earned lower wages and worked longer hours in the South than elsewhere. Per capita income was the same in 1900 as it had been in 1860—and only half the national average. In North Carolina in the 1890s, workers were paid an average of 50 cents a day and toiled 70 hours a week. Black workers, who made up 6 percent of the southern manufacturing force in 1890 (but were excluded from textile mills), usually had the worst jobs and the lowest pay.

The thousands of women and children who labored gave silent testimony to the fact that their husbands and fathers could not earn enough to support their families. As usual, women and children earned lower wages than men. Justifying these policies, one Augusta factory president claimed that the employment of children was "a matter of charity with us; some of them would starve if they were not given employment. . . . Ours are not overworked. The work we give children is very light." Actually, many children at his factory were doing the same work as adults, but for children's pay.

Cotton Still King

Although New South advocates envisioned the South's transformation from a rural to an industrial society, they always recognized the need for agricultural change. "It's time for an agricultural revolution," proclaimed Henry Grady, the New South's most vocal spokesman. Overdependence on "King Cotton" hobbled southern agriculture by making farmers the victims of faraway market forces and an oppressive credit system. Subdivide old cotton

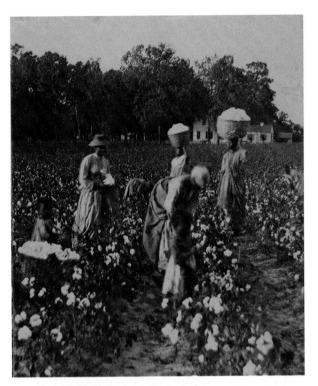

The South Carolina Cotton Fields What evidence does this photograph, taken in the 1870s, provide for understanding the character of black life after the Civil War and the limitations of the New South's effort to transform southern life? *(Photography Collection, Robert N. Dennis Collection of Stereoscopic Views, The New York Public Library/Art Resource, NY)*

plantations into small diversified farms, Grady urged. Raising choice produce for urban markets could result in "simply wonderful profits."

A new agricultural South with new class and economic arrangements did emerge, but not the one Grady envisioned. Despite the breakup of some plantations, large landowners were resourceful in keeping their property and dealing with postwar conditions, as Chapter 16 showed. As they adopted new agricultural arrangements, former slaves sank into peonage.

White farmers on small and medium-size holdings fared only slightly better than black tenants and sharecroppers. Immediately after the war, high cotton prices tempted them to raise as much cotton as they could. Then prices began a disastrous decline, from 11 cents a pound in 1875 to less than 5 cents in 1894. Yeoman farmers became entangled in debt. Each year, farmers bought supplies on credit from merchants so they could plant the next year's crop and support their families until harvest. In return, merchants demanded their exclusive business and acquired a lien (claim) on their crops. But when farmers sold their crops at declining prices, they usually discovered that they had not earned enough to settle with the merchant, who had charged dearly for store goods and whose annual interest rates might exceed 100 percent. Each year, thousands of farmers fell further behind. By 1900, more than half of the South's white farmers and three-quarters of its black farmers were tenants. Tenancy increased all over rural America, but nowhere faster than in the Deep South.

These patterns had baneful results for individual southerners and for the South as a whole. Caught in a cycle of debt and poverty, few farmers could think of improving techniques or diversifying crops. Desperate to pay debts, they concentrated on cotton despite falling prices. Landowners pressured tenants to raise a market crop. Far from diversifying, farmers increasingly limited their crops. By 1880, the South was not growing enough food to feed its people adequately. Poor nutrition contributed to chronic bad health.

The Nadir of Black Life

Grady and other New South advocates painted a picture of a strong, prosperous, and industrialized South, a region that could deal with the troublesome race issue without interference. Grady had few regrets over the end of slavery, which he thought had contributed to southern economic backwardness. Realizing that black labor would be crucial to the transformation he sought, he advocated racial cooperation. But racial cooperation did not mean equality. Grady assumed that blacks were racially inferior and supported an informal system of segregation. "The negro is entitled to his freedom, his franchise, to full and equal legal rights," Grady wrote in 1883. But "social equality he can never have."

By the time of Grady's death in 1889, a much harsher perspective on southern race relations was replacing his view. In 1891, at a national assembly of women's clubs in Washington, D.C., Frances Watkins Harper, a black speaker, writer, and former abolitionist, anticipated efforts to strip the vote from blacks and appealed to the white women at the meeting not to abandon black suffrage. "I deem it a privilege to present the negro," she said, "not as a mere dependent asking for Northern sympathy or Southern compassion, but as a member of the body politic who has a claim upon the nation for justice, simple justice." Women, of all people, should not seek to achieve their own right to vote at the expense of the vote for black men, she explained. "Instead of taking the ballot from his hands, teach him how to use it, and add his quota to the progress, strength, and durability of the nation."

The decision by congressional leaders in 1890 to shelve a proposed act for protecting black civil rights and the defeat of the Blair bill providing federal assistance for educational institutions left black Americans vulnerable, as Harper realized. The traditional sponsor of the rights of freedpeople, the Republican party, left blacks to fend for themselves as a minority in the white South. The courts also abandoned blacks. In 1878, the Supreme Court declared unconstitutional a Louisiana statute banning discrimination in transportation. In 1882, the Court voided the Ku Klux Klan Act of 1871, which had been passed to break the power of the Klan. In 1883, the provisions of the Civil Rights Act of 1875, which assured blacks of equal rights in public places, were declared unconstitutional on the grounds that the federal government did not have the right to involve itself in racial relations between individuals.

Northern leaders did not oppose these actions. In fact, northerners increasingly promulgated negative stereotypes in magazines, newspapers, cartoons, advertisements, "coon songs," serious art and theater, and the minstrel shows that dominated northern entertainment. The *Atlantic Monthly* in 1890 anticipated a strong current in magazine literature when it expressed doubts that this "lowly variety of man" could ever be brought up to the intellectual and moral standards of whites. Other magazines openly opposed suffrage as wasted on people too "ignorant, weak, lazy and incompetent" to make good use of it. *Forum* magazine suggested that "American Negroes" had "too much liberty." When this freedom was combined with natural "race traits" of stealing and hankering after white women, the *Forum* advised in 1893, black crime increased. Only lynching and burning would deter the "barbarous" rapist and other "sadly degenerated" Negroes corrupted since the Civil War by independence and too much education.

Encouraged by northern public opinion, and with the blessing of Congress and the Supreme Court, southern citizens and legislatures sought to make blacks permanently second-class members of southern society. In the political sphere, white southerners amended state constitutions to disfranchise black voters. By various legal devices—the poll tax, literacy tests, "good character" and "understanding" clauses administered by white voter registrars, and all-white primary elections—blacks lost the right to vote. The most ingenious method was the "grandfather clause," which specified that only citizens whose grandfathers were registered to vote on January 1, 1867, could cast their ballots. This virtually excluded blacks. Although the Supreme Court outlawed blatantly discriminatory laws such as grandfather clauses, a series of other constitutional changes such as those just mentioned, beginning in

Mississippi in 1890 and spreading to all 11 former Confederate states by 1910, effectively excluded the black vote. The results were dramatic. Louisiana, for example, contained 130,334 registered black voters in 1896. Eight years later, there were only 1,342.

In a second tactic in the 1890s, state and local laws legalized informal segregation in public facilities. Beginning with railroads and schools, "Jim Crow" laws were extended to libraries, restaurants, hospitals, prisons, parks and playgrounds, cemeteries, toilets, drinking fountains, and nearly every other place where blacks and whites might mingle. The Supreme Court upheld these laws in 1896 in *Plessy* v. *Ferguson* by declaring that "separate but equal" facilities did not violate the equal protection clause of the Fourteenth Amendment because separation did not necessarily mean the inferiority of a group. The Court's decision opened the way for as many forms of legal segregation as southern lawmakers could devise.

DOCUMENT

Opinion of the Supreme Court in *Plessy* v. *Ferguson* (1896)

Political and social discrimination made it ever more possible to keep blacks permanently confined to agricultural and unskilled labor. While extended families—aunts, uncles, cousins, and other kin—all helped blacks cope with their dire situation, the truth was that all too often blacks depended on whites for their material welfare. In 1900, nearly 84 percent of black workers nationwide engaged in some form of agricultural labor as farmhands, overseers, sharecroppers, or tenant or independent farmers or in service jobs, primarily domestic service and laundry work. These had been the primary slave occupations. The remaining 16 percent worked in forests, sawmills, mines, and, with northward migration, northern cities.

Gone were the skilled black tradesmen of slavery days. At the end of the Civil War, at least half of all skilled artisans in the South had been black. But by the 1890s, the percentage had decreased to less than 10 percent, as whites systematically excluded blacks from the trades. The factory work that blacks had been doing was also reduced, largely to drive a wedge between poor blacks and whites in order to prevent unionization. In Greensboro, North Carolina, for example, where in 1870 some 30 percent of all blacks worked in skilled trades or factory occupations, by 1910, blacks in the skilled trades had been reduced to 8 percent, and not a single black worked in a Greensboro factory. The exclusion of blacks from industry prevented them from acquiring the skills and habits that would enable them to rise into the middle class as would many European immigrants and their children by the mid-twentieth century.

Lynching In 1896, an African American named William Biggerstaff was hanged for what was labeled the murder of a white man. The picture cannot reveal the innocence or guilt of the accused. Lynching and violence aimed at blacks became common in the late nineteenth century. What does the presence of the people in the background suggest about lynchings? *(Montana Historical Society, Helena, MT)*

Blacks did not accept their declining position passively. In the mid-1880s, they enthusiastically joined the mass worker organization the Knights of Labor (discussed in Chapter 18), first in cities such as Richmond and Atlanta and then in rural areas. But southern whites feared that the Knights' policies of racial and economic cooperation might lead to social equality. The Charleston *News and Courier* warned of the dangers of "miscegenation" and the possibility that the South would be left "in the possession of . . . mongrels and hybrids." As blacks continued to join it, whites abandoned the order in growing numbers. The flight of whites weakened the organization in the South, and a backlash of white violence finally smashed it.

Against this backdrop, incidents of lynchings and other forms of violence against blacks increased. Lynching was a way to show both black men and white women the dire consequences of stepping out of line. On February 21, 1891, the *New York Times* reported that in Texarkana, Arkansas, a mob apprehended Ed Coy, a 32-year-old black man who was charged with the rape of a white woman. He was tied to a stake and then burned alive. As Coy proclaimed his innocence to a large crowd, his alleged victim somewhat hesitatingly put the torch to his oil-soaked body. The *Times* report concluded that only by the "terrible death such as fire . . . can inflict" could other blacks "be deterred from the commission of like crimes." Ed Coy was one of more than 1,400 black men lynched or burned alive during the 1890s. About one-third were charged with sex crimes. The rest were accused of a variety of "crimes" related to not knowing their place; this included marrying or insulting a white woman, testifying in court against whites, or having a "bad reputation."

Paris, Texas, Lynching, 1893

Diverging Black Responses

White discrimination and exploitation nourished new protest tactics and ideologies among blacks. For years, Frederick Douglass had been proclaiming that blacks should remain loyal Americans and count on the promises of the Republican party. But on his deathbed in 1895, his last words were allegedly, "Agitate! Agitate! Agitate!"

Agitation had its costs. In Memphis, Tennessee, Ida B. Wells, the first female editor of an important newspaper, launched an antilynching campaign in 1892. So hostile was the response from the white community that Wells carried a gun to protect herself. When white citizens finally destroyed the press and threatened her partner, Wells left Memphis to pursue her activism elsewhere.

Ida B. Wells, Events in Paris, Texas (1895)

Some black leaders called for black separatism within white America. T. Thomas Fortune wrote in the black New York *Freeman* in 1887 that "there will one day be an African Empire." Three years later, he organized the Afro-American League (a precursor of the NAACP), insisting that blacks must join together to fight the rising tide of discrimination. "Let us stand up," he urged, "in our own organization where color will not be a brand of odium." The league encouraged independent voting, opposed segregation and lynching, and urged the establishment of black institutions such as banks to support black businesses. As a sympathetic journalist explained, "The solution of the problem is in our own hands. . . . The Negro must preserve his identity."

Although some promoted black nationalism, most blacks worked patiently but persistently within white society for equality and social justice. In 1887, J. C. Price formed the Citizens Equal Rights

Association, which supported various petitions and direct-action campaigns to protest segregation. The association also called for state laws to guarantee equal rights in the aftermath of the Supreme Court's 1883 ruling. Other blacks boycotted streetcars in southern cities and petitioned Congress, demanding reparations for unpaid labor as slaves.

Efforts to escape oppression in the South, such as "Pap" Singleton's movement to found black towns in Tennessee and Kansas, continued. In the 1890s, black leaders lobbied to make the Oklahoma Territory, recently opened to white settlement, an all-black state. Blacks founded 25 towns there as well as many towns in other states and even in Mexico. But these attempts, like earlier ones, were short-lived, for they were crippled by limited funds and by the hostility of white neighbors. Singleton eventually recommended migration to Canada or Liberia as a final solution, and later black nationalist leaders also looked increasingly to Africa. Bishop Henry McNeal Turner, a former Union soldier and prominent black leader, despaired of ever securing equal rights for American blacks. He described the Constitution as "a dirty rag, a cheat, a libel" and said that it ought to be "spit upon by every Negro in the land." In 1894, he organized the International Migration Society to return blacks to Africa, arguing that "this country owes us forty billions of dollars" to help. He succeeded in sending two boatloads of emigrants to Liberia, but this colonization effort worked no more successfully than those earlier in the century.

As Frederick Douglass had long argued, no matter how important African roots might be, blacks had been in the Americas for generations and would have to win justice and equal rights here. W. E. B. Du Bois, the first black to receive a Ph.D. from Harvard, agreed. Yet in 1900, he attended the first Pan-African Conference in London, where he argued that blacks must lead the struggle for liberation both in Africa and in the United States. It was at this conference that Du Bois first made his prophetic comment that "the problem of the Twentieth Century" would be "the problem of the color line."

Despite these vigorous voices of militant anger and nationalistic fervor, most black Americans continued to follow the slow, moderate, self-help program of Booker T. Washington, the best-known black leader in America. Born a slave, Washington had risen through hard and faithful work to become the founder (in 1881) and principal of Tuskegee Institute in Alabama, which he personally and dramatically built into the nation's largest and best-known industrial training school. At Tuskegee, young blacks received a highly disciplined

Booker T. Washington

education in scientific agricultural techniques and vocational skilled trades. Washington believed that economic self-help and the familiar Puritan virtues of hard work, frugality, cleanliness, and moderation would lead to success for African Americans despite the realities of racism. He spent much of his time traveling through the North to secure philanthropic gifts to support Tuskegee. In time, he became a favorite of the American entrepreneurial elite whose capitalist assumptions he shared.

DOCUMENT

Booker T. Washington, Atlanta Exposition Address (1895)

In 1895, Washington was asked to deliver a speech at the Cotton States and International Exposition in Atlanta, celebrating three decades of industrial and agricultural progress since the Civil War. He took advantage of that invitation, a rare honor for a former slave, to make a significant statement about the position of blacks in the South. Without a hint of protest, Washington decided "to say something that would cement the friendship of the races." He therefore proclaimed black loyalty to the economic development of the South while accepting the lowly status of southern blacks. "It is at the bottom of life we must begin, and not at the top," he declared. "In all things that are purely social we can be as separate as the fingers, yet one as the hand in all things essential to mutual progress." Although Washington worked actively behind the scenes for black civil rights, in Atlanta, he publicly renounced black interest in either the vote or civil rights as well as social equality with whites. Whites throughout the country enthusiastically acclaimed Washington's address, but many blacks called his "Atlanta Compromise" a serious setback in the struggle for black rights.

Washington has often been charged with conceding too quickly that political rights should follow rather than precede economic well-being. In 1903, Du Bois confronted Washington directly in *The Souls of Black Folk*, arguing instead for the "manly assertion" of a program of equal civil rights, suffrage, and higher education in the ideals of liberal learning. A trip through the Black Belt of Dougherty County, Georgia, showed Du Bois the "forlorn and forsaken" condition of southern blacks. The young sociologist saw that most blacks were confined to dependent agricultural labor, "fighting a hard battle with debt" year after year. Although "here and there a man has raised his head above these murky waters . . . a pall of debt hangs over the beautiful land." Beneath all others was the cotton picker, who, with his wife and children,

DOCUMENT

W. E. B. Du Bois, "Of Mr. Booker T. Washington and Others" (1903)

would have to work from sunup to sundown to pick 100 pounds of cotton to make 50 cents. The lives of most blacks were still tied to the land of the South. If they were to improve their lives, rural blacks would have to organize.

FARM PROTEST

During the post–Civil War period, many farmers, black and white, began to realize that only through collective action could they improve rural life. Not all were dissatisfied; midwestern farmers and those near city markets adjusted to changing economic conditions. Southern and western farmers, however, faced new problems that led to the first mass organization of farmers in American history.

The Grange in the 1860s and 1870s

The earliest effort to organize white farmers came in 1867 when Oliver Kelley founded the Order of the Patrons of Husbandry. Originally a social and cultural organization, it soon was protesting the powerlessness of the "immense helpless mob" of farmers, victims of "human vampires." The depression of the 1870s (discussed in Chapter 18) sharpened discontent. By 1875, an estimated 800,000 had joined Kelley's organization, now known as the National Grange.

IMAGE

The Purposes of the Grange

The Grangers recognized some, but not all, of the complex changes that had created rural problems. Some of their "reforms" attempted to bypass intermediaries by establishing buying and selling cooperatives. Although many cooperatives failed, they indicated that farmers realized the need for unified action. Midwestern farmers also accused grain elevator operators of cheating them, and they pointed to the railroads, America's first big business, as the worst offenders. As Chapter 18 will show, cutthroat competition among railroad companies generally brought lower rates. But even though charges dropped nationwide, railroads often set high rates in rural areas, and their rebates to large shippers discriminated against small operators.

DOCUMENT

Proceedings of the 13th Session of the Grange (1879)

Farmers recognized that confronting the mighty railroads demanded cooperation with others, like western businessmen whose interests railroads also hurt, and political action. Between 1869 and 1874, businessmen and farmers successfully pressed Illinois, Iowa, Wisconsin, and Minnesota to pass so-called Granger laws (an inaccurate name, for the

Grangers did not deserve complete credit for them) establishing maximum rates that railroads and grain elevators could charge. Other states set up railroad commissions to regulate railroad rates, or outlawed railroad pools, rebates, passes, and other practices that seemed to represent "unjust discrimination and distortion."

Railroad companies and grain elevators quickly challenged the new laws. In 1877, the Supreme Court upheld them in *Munn* v. *Illinois*. Even so, it soon became apparent that state commissions might control local rates but not long-haul rates. While Granger laws did not control the railroads and raised questions difficult to resolve on the local level, they established an important principle. The Supreme Court had made it clear that state legislatures could regulate businesses of a public nature such as the railroads. When the Court reversed its ruling in *Wabash* v. *Illinois* in 1886, pressure increased on Congress to continue the struggle.

The Interstate Commerce Act of 1887

In 1887, Congress responded to farmers, railroad managers who wished to control the fierce competition that threatened to bankrupt their companies, and shippers who objected to transportation rates by passing the Interstate Commerce Act. That legislation required that railroad rates be "reasonable and just," that rate schedules be made public, and that practices such as rebates be discontinued. The act also set up the first federal regulatory agency, the Interstate Commerce Commission (ICC). The ICC had the power to investigate and prosecute lawbreakers, but the legislation limited its authority to control over commerce conducted between states.

DOCUMENT

The Interstate Commerce Act, 1887

Like state railroad commissions, the ICC found it difficult to define a reasonable rate. Moreover, thousands of cases overwhelmed the tiny staff in the early months of operation. In the long run, the lack of enforcement power was most serious. The ICC's only recourse was to bring offenders into the federal courts and engage in lengthy legal proceedings. Few railroads worried about defying ICC directions on rates. When they appeared in court four or five years later, they often won their cases from judges suspicious of new federal authority. Between 1887 and 1906, a total of 16 cases made their way to the Supreme Court, which decided 15 of them in the railroads' favor. As one railroad executive candidly admitted, "There is not a road in the country that can be accused of living up to the rules of the Interstate Commerce Law."

The Southern Farmers' Alliance in the 1880s and 1890s

The Grange declined in the late 1870s as the nation recovered from depression. But farm protest did not die. Depression struck farmers once again in the late 1880s and worsened in the early 1890s. Official statistics told the familiar, dismal story of falling grain prices on the plains and prairies. The national currency shortage, which usually reached critical proportions at harvest time, helped drive agricultural prices ever lower. Debt and shipping costs, however, climbed. It sometimes cost a farmer as much as one bushel of corn to send another bushel to market. Distraught farmers again tried organization, education, and cooperation.

The Southern Farmers' Alliance became one of the most important reform organizations of the 1880s. Its ambitious organizational drive sent lecturers across the South and onto the Plains. Alliance lecturers proposed programs that would help realize their slogan: "Equal rights to all, special privileges to none." Among the Alliance's efforts were experiments with cooperatives to free farmers from the clutches of supply merchants, banks, and other credit agencies. While cooperatives often failed, the Alliance also supported legislative efforts to regulate powerful monopolies and corporations that, they believed, gouged farmers. Many Alliance members believed that increasing the money supply was critical to improving the position of farmers and supported a national banking system empowered to issue paper money. Finally, the Alliance called for a variety of measures to improve the quality of rural life. Better rural public schools, state agricultural colleges, and improvements in the status of women were all on its agenda.

DOCUMENT

N. A. Dunning, Ed., *Alliance's Vision of Community* (1891)

By 1890, rural discontent swept more than a million farmers into the Alliance. Included in this burst of organization growth were black as well as white farmers. Organized in 1888, the Colored Farmers' Alliance recognized that farmers of both races shared common economic problems and therefore must cooperate. But many southern cotton farmers, depending on black labor, disagreed. In 1891, black cotton pickers on plantations near Memphis went on strike. Revealing the racial tensions simmering just below the surface, white posses chased the strikers and lynched 15 of them.

The Ocala Platform, 1890

In December 1890, the National Alliance gathered in Ocala, Florida, to develop a platform. Most delegates believed that the federal government had failed to address the farmers' problems. They attacked both parties as too subservient to the "will of corporation and money power."

Much of the Alliance's program was radical in the context of late-nineteenth-century political life. It called for the direct election of U.S. senators and supported lowering the tariff (a topic much debated in Congress) with the dangerous-sounding justification that prices must be reduced for the sake of the "poor of our land." The money plank went far beyond what any national legislator would consider, boldly envisioning a new banking system controlled by the federal government. The platform called for the government to take an active economic role by increasing the amount of money in circulation in the form of treasury notes and silver. More money would cause inflation and help debtors pay off loans.

The platform also called for subtreasuries (federal warehouses) in agricultural regions where farmers could store their produce at low interest rates until market prices favored selling. To tide farmers over, the federal government would lend farmers up to 80 percent of the current local price for their produce. Other demands included a graduated income tax and the regulation of transportation and communication networks—or, if regulation failed, their nationalization.

Even though a minority of farmers belonged to the Alliance, many Americans feared it. The New York *Sun* reported that the Alliance had caused a "panic" in the two major parties.

Although the Alliance was not formally in politics, it supported sympathetic candidates in the fall elections of 1890. A surprising number of them won. Alliance victories in the West hurt the Republican party enough to cause President Harrison to refer to "our election disaster." Before long, many Alliance members were pressing for an independent political party. Legislators elected with Alliance support did not necessarily bring action on issues of interest to farmers, or even respect. On the national level, no one had much interest in the Ocala platform. But among rural spokesmen, the first to realize the necessity of forming an independent third party was Georgia's Tom Watson, who also knew that success in the South would depend on unity between white and black farmers.

TIMELINE

1860s	Cattle drives from Texas begin		**1886**	Severe winter ends cattle boom
				Wabash v. Illinois
1865–1867	Sioux wars on the Great Plains		**1887**	Dawes Severalty Act
1867	National Grange founded			Interstate Commerce Act
1869	Transcontinental railroad completed			Farm prices plummet
1869–1874	Granger laws		**1888**	Colored Farmers' Alliance founded
1873	Financial panic triggers economic depression		**1890**	Afro-American League founded
1874	Barbed wire patented			Sioux ghost dance movement
1875	Black Hills gold rush incites Sioux war			Massacre at Wounded Knee
1876	Custer's last stand at Little Big Horn			Ocala platform
1877	*Munn v. Illinois*			Yosemite National Park established
	Bonanza farms in the Great Plains		**1890s**	Black disfranchisement in the South
1878	Timber and Stone Act			Jim Crow laws passed in the South
1880s	Attempts to create a "New South"			Declining farm prices
1881	Tuskegee Institute founded		**1891**	Forest Reserve Act
1883–1885	Depression		**1892**	Sierra Club founded
1884	Southern Farmers' Alliance founded		**1895**	Booker T. Washington's "Atlanta Compromise" address
			1896	*Plessy v. Ferguson*

Conclusion

Farming in the Industrial Age

The late nineteenth century brought turbulence to rural America. The "Indian problem," which had plagued Americans for 200 years, was tragically solved for a while, but not without resistance and bloodshed. Few whites found these events troubling. Most were caught up in the challenge of responding to a fast-changing world. Believing themselves to be the backbone of the nation, white farmers brought Native American lands into cultivation, modernized their farms, and raised bumper crops. But success and a comfortable competency eluded many of them. Some, like Milton Leeper, never gave up hope or farming. Many were caught in a cycle of poverty and debt. Others fled to towns and cities as did the Ebbesen family. Once there, many joined the industrial workforce, described in the next chapter. Some turned to collective action and politics. Their actions demonstrate that they did not merely react to events but attempted to shape them.

Questions for Review and Reflection

1. Compare and contrast farming on the Great Plains with farming in California.

2. How did technology affect agriculture and mining in the West?

3. Describe the differing viewpoints of Native Americans and whites and the differing cultural values lying behind these viewpoints.

4. What were the reasons that the New South did not achieve its goals?

5. Compare and contrast the treatment of Native Americans and African Americans in this period. Are there any similarities?

6. In what ways did agricultural life in the West and South create conditions that did not mesh with the ideals of American life?

Recommended Reading

Recommended Readings are posted on the Web site for this textbook. Visit www.ablongman.com/nash

Fiction and Film

Willa Cather's novels *My Antonia* (1918) and *O Pioneers!* (1913) emphasize the energy and determination of those farming in the post–Civil War West as well as the presence of immigrants there. O. E. Rölvaag's *Giants in the Earth* (1927) deals with immigrant families but gives a very grim picture of their adjustment to farming life in the United States. Written in 1885 by Maria Amparo Ruiz de Burton, *The Squatter and the Don* provides insights into the views of Mexican Americans. *The Searchers* (1956), *Stagecoach* (1939), and *She Wore a Yellow Ribbon* (1949) come from the heyday of western films and reveal mid-twentieth century (and John Wayne's) views of the late frontier. *Dances with Wolves* (1990) is Kevin Costner's indictment of the white assault on Native American life and culture. His sympathetic depiction of Native American life bears marks of the consciousness of the 1990s. *Ethnic Notions* (1987), an Emmy-winning documentary by Marlon Riggs, traces the evolution of negative stereotypes of African Americans and the ways these stereotypes have been embodied in popular culture.

Discovering U.S. History Online

McCormick Farm

www.vaes.vt.edu/steeles/mccormick/harvest.html

Cyrus Hall McCormick invented the McCormick reaper, and his former farm is now owned by Virginia Polytechnic Institute and State University. This site chronicles various stages of harvesting technological development via an interactive photo essay.

Heroes and Villains

www.ukans.edu/carrie/kancoll

Part of the Kansas Collection Gallery, this site offers glimpses of heroes and villains of the West via books, letters, diaries, photos, and other materials from the past.

Fort Larned National Historic Site

www.nps.gov/fols/home.html

The companion Web site for Fort Larned, a preserved fort from the "Indian Wars Period," offers a virtual tour of the fort, information about the Buffalo Soldiers, soldier equipment, Plains Indians, and other learning tools and facts.

Yosemite History

www.yosemite.ca.us/history

This site presents articles contemporary to Yosemite's creation and biographies of key figures, maps, and photos.

Native American Documents

www.csusm.edu/projects/nadp/nadp.htm

Several documents relating to Native Americans have been transcribed and indexed for use on this site. The documents include indexed published reports of the commissioner of Indian affairs and the Board of Indian Commissioners for 1871, "allotment" data, and more than 100 documents from the Rogue River War and Siletz Reservation.

Lynching in America

www.journale.com/withoutsanctuary/index.html

This site presents a stark visual history of lynching in the South. The site includes a flash movie with narration.

The Grange Society

www.indianhill.org/History/Hist018.htm

This local historical site gives an example of an agricultural society that became an increasingly "commercialized industry."

Farmers' Alliance and Colored Farmers' Alliance

www.tsha.utexas.edu/handbook/online/articles/view/FF/aaf2.html

www.tsha.utexas.edu/handbook/online/articles/view/CC/aac1.html

These two articles from this online "multidisciplinary encyclopedia of Texas history" give more detail about these allied farm-protest organizations.

CHAPTER 18

The Rise of Smokestack America

This anxious scene of a strike hints at the tensions between workers and owners during the industrial era. *(Robert Koehler, The Strike, 1886. Deutsches Historisches Museum, Berlin, Germany/Bridgeman Art Library)*

American Stories

Telling His Story: O'Donnell and the Senators

By 1883, Thomas O'Donnell, an Irish immigrant, had lived in the United States for more than a decade. He was 30 years old, married, with two young children. His third child had died in 1882, and O'Donnell was still in debt for the funeral. Money was scarce, for O'Donnell was a textile worker in Fall River, Massachusetts, and not well educated. "I went to work when I was young," he explained, "and have been working ever since."

However, O'Donnell worked only sporadically at the mill. New machines needed "a good deal of small help," and the mill owners preferred to hire man-and-boy teams. Because O'Donnell's children were very young, he often saw others preferred for day work. Once, when he was passed over, he asked the boss "what am I to do; I have got two little boys at home . . . how am I to get something for them to eat; I can't get a turn when I come here. . . . I says, 'Have I got to starve; ain't I to have any work?'"

O'Donnell and his family were barely getting by, even though he worked with pick and shovel when he could. He estimated that he had earned only $133 the previous year. Rent came to $72. The family spent $2 for a little coal but depended for heat on driftwood that O'Donnell picked up on the beach. Clams were a major part of the family diet, but on some days there was nothing to eat at all.

The children "got along very nicely all summer," but it was now November, and they were beginning to "feel quite sickly." It was hardly surprising. "One has one shoe on, a very poor one, and a slipper, that was picked up somewhere. The other has two odd shoes on, with the heel out." His wife was healthy, but not ready for winter. She had two dresses, one saved for church, and an "undershirt that she got given to her, and . . . an old wrapper, which is about a mile too big for her; somebody gave it to her."

O'Donnell was describing his family's marginal existence to a Senate committee gathering testimony in Boston in 1883 on the relations between labor and capital. As the senators heard the tale, they asked him why he did not go west. "It would not cost you over $1,500," said one senator. The gap between the worlds of the senator and the worker could not have been more dramatic. O'Donnell replied, "Well, I never saw over a $20 bill . . . if some one would give me $1,500 I will go." Asked by the senator if he had friends who could provide him with the funds, O'Donnell sadly replied no.

The senators, of course, were far better acquainted with the world of comfort and leisure than with the poverty of families like the O'Donnells. From their vantage point, the fruits of industrial progress were clear. As the United States became a world industrial leader in the years after the Civil War, its factories poured forth an abundance of ever-cheaper goods ranging from steel rails and farm reapers to mass-produced parlor sets. These were years of tremendous growth and broad economic and social change. Manufacturing replaced agriculture as the leading source of economic growth between 1860 and 1900. By 1890, a majority of the American workforce held nonagricultural jobs; more than a third lived in cities. A rural nation of farmers was becoming a nation of industrial workers and city dwellers.

As O'Donnell's appearance before the Senate committee illustrates, industrial and technological advances profoundly changed the nature of American life. For O'Donnell and others like him, the benefits of this transformation were hard to see. Although no nationwide studies of poverty existed, estimates suggest that perhaps half of the American population was too poor to take advantage of the new goods of the age. Eventually, the disparity between the reality of life for humble families like the O'Donnells and American ideals would give rise to attempts to improve conditions for working-class Americans, but it is unlikely that O'Donnell ever profited from such efforts.

This chapter examines the maturing of the American industrial economy, a phenomenon that affected all facets of American life, from the rhythms of daily life and work to the allocation of wealth. Focusing on the years between 1865 and 1900, it describes the rise of heavy industry, the organization and character of the new industrial workplace, and the emergence of big business. It then examines the locus of industrial life, the fast-growing city; its peoples, whom heavy immigration had made ever more diverse; its social classes; and its communities. The chapter's central theme grows out of O'Donnell's story: As the United States built up its railroads, cities, and factories, its production and profit orientation resulted in unequal distribution of wealth and power. Although many Americans were too exhausted by life's daily struggles to protest new inequalities, strikes and other forms of working-class resistance sought to return dignity and power to working people and to compensate them more generously for the labor they performed. The ineffectiveness of these protests points to the many obstacles confronting those who wished to change the status quo.

THE TEXTURE OF INDUSTRIAL PROGRESS

When Americans went to war in 1861, agriculture was the country's leading source of economic growth. Forty years later, manufacturing had taken its place. During these years, the production of manufactured goods outpaced population growth. By 1900, three times as many goods per person existed as in 1860. Per capita income increased by more than 2 percent a year. But these aggregate figures disguise the fact that many people gained not at all.

As the nature of the American economy changed, big businesses became the characteristic form of economic organization. They could raise the capital to build huge factories, acquire expensive and efficient machinery, hire hundreds of workers, and use the most up-to-date methods. The result was more goods at lower prices.

New regions grew in industrial importance. From New England to the Midwest lay the country's industrial heartland. New England remained a center of light industry, while the Midwest still processed natural resources. Now, however, the production of iron, steel, and transportation equipment joined older manufacturing operations there. In the Far West, manufacturers concentrated on processing the region's natural resources, but heavy industry made strides as well. In the South, the textile industry put down roots by the 1890s.

Although many factors contributed to dramatically rising industrial productivity, the changing character of the industrial sector explains many of the gains. Pre–Civil War manufacturers had concentrated either on producing textiles, clothing, and leather products or on processing agricultural and natural resources such as grain, logs, and lumber. Although these operations remained important, heavy industry grew rapidly after the war. The manufacturing of steel, iron, and machinery meant for other producers rather than consumers fueled economic growth.

Technological Innovations

An accelerating pace of technological change contributed to and was shaped by the industrial transformation of the late nineteenth century. Technological breakthroughs allowed more efficient production that, in turn, helped generate new needs and further innovation. Developments in the steel and electric industries exemplify this interdependent process and highlight the contributions of entrepreneurs and new ways of organizing research and innovation.

Before the Civil War, skilled workers produced iron in a slow and expensive process. The iron was so soft that trains wore out rails in a matter of years. The need for a harder metal supported the development and introduction of new technologies. The Bessemer converter (named after its English inventor) transformed iron into steel by forcing air through the liquid iron, thus reducing the carbon (see "Analyzing History" on p. 587). The process contributed to the rapid expansion of the steel industry and had the added advantage of reducing the need for highly paid skilled workers.

Neither an inventor nor an engineer, Andrew Carnegie recognized the promise not only of new processes but also of new ways of organizing industry. Steel companies such as Carnegie's acquired access to raw materials and markets and brought all stages of steel manufacturing, from smelting to rolling, into one mill. Output soared, and prices fell. When Andrew Carnegie introduced the Bessemer process in his plant in the mid-1870s, the price of steel plummeted from $100 a ton to $12 a ton by 1900.

In turn, the production of a cheaper, stronger, more durable material than iron created new goods, new demands, and new markets, and it stimulated further technological change. Bessemer furnaces, geared toward making steel rails, did not produce steel for building. Experimentation with the open-hearth process, which used very high temperatures, resulted in steel for bridge and ship builders, engineers, architects, and even designers of subways. Countless Americans bought steel in more humble forms: wire, nails, bolts, needles, and screws.

New power sources facilitated American industry's shift to mass production

Genuine Connellsville Coke. National Bureau of Engraving

ANALYZING HISTORY

Steel: The Engine of Industrial Growth

Innovations in the steel industry affected many aspects of American life. They helped make an efficient national transportation network a reality through the production of steel rails, stimulated urban growth and a new urban character with steel girders for bridges and high buildings, and provided working-class jobs in many different urban hubs.

REFLECTING ON THE PAST   What was the relationship between production and prices? How does this relationship explain business attitudes and practices? What is its relationship to the growth of the large industrial firms? The stock market? In what ways does the information contained here relate to the creation of a mass market in the United States?

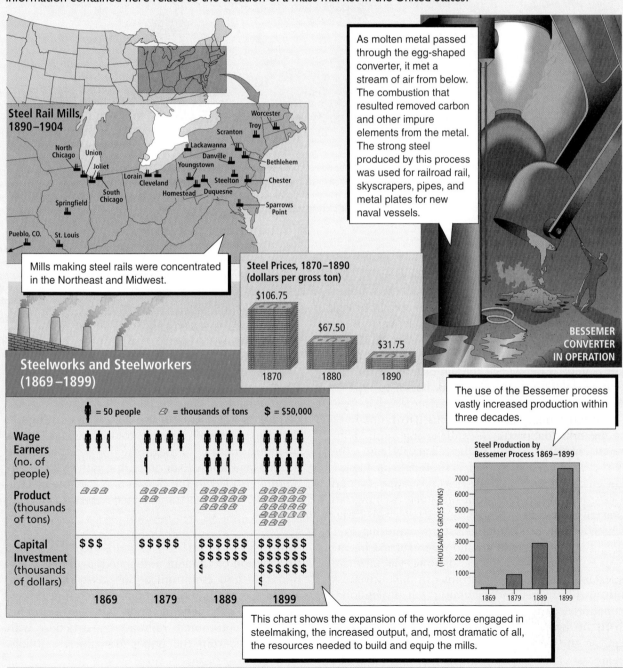

Steel Rail Mills, 1890–1904

Worcester, Troy, Scranton, Lackawanna, Danville, Youngstown, Bethlehem, North Chicago, Union, Joliet, Lorain, Cleveland, Steelton, Chester, South Chicago, Homestead, Duquesne, Springfield, Sparrows Point, Pueblo, CO., St. Louis

Mills making steel rails were concentrated in the Northeast and Midwest.

As molten metal passed through the egg-shaped converter, it met a stream of air from below. The combustion that resulted removed carbon and other impure elements from the metal. The strong steel produced by this process was used for railroad rail, skyscrapers, pipes, and metal plates for new naval vessels.

BESSEMER CONVERTER IN OPERATION

Steel Prices, 1870–1890 (dollars per gross ton)

$106.75 — 1870
$67.50 — 1880
$31.75 — 1890

The use of the Bessemer process vastly increased production within three decades.

Steelworks and Steelworkers (1869–1899)

👤 = 50 people   ✏ = thousands of tons $ = $50,000

	1869	1879	1889	1899
Wage Earners (no. of people)				
Product (thousands of tons)				
Capital Investment (thousands of dollars)	$ $ $	$ $ $ $ $	$ $ $ $ $ $ / $ $ $ $ $ $ / $	$ $ $ $ $ $ / $ $ $ $ $ $ / $ $ $ $ $ $ / $

Steel Production by Bessemer Process 1869–1899

(THOUSANDS GROSS TONS)
7000, 6000, 5000, 4000, 3000, 2000, 1000

1869, 1879, 1889, 1899

This chart shows the expansion of the workforce engaged in steelmaking, the increased output, and, most dramatic of all, the resources needed to build and equip the mills.

The Homestead Steel Works   The Homestead Steel Works, pictured here in about 1890, was located near Pittsburgh, Pennsylvania. The vast scale of the enterprise suggests the ways in which technological innovation stimulated the expansion of the steel industry in the late nineteenth century. Although the two small figures in the foreground humanize the picture, what does this picture suggest about the character of work in the steel mills? *(Courtesy of Rivers of Steel Archives)*

and also suggest the importance of new ways of organizing research and innovation. In 1869, about half of the nation's industrial power came from water. The opening of new anthracite deposits, however, cut the cost of coal, and American industry rapidly converted to steam. By 1900, steam engines generated 80 percent of the nation's industrial energy supply. But soon electricity began to replace steam as a power source.

Experiments in generating electricity dated back to the middle of the eighteenth century and facilitated the development of the telegraph before the Civil War. In 1878, Thomas Edison, having already developed the ticker tape (to send information from the stock exchange to investors' offices) and a telegraph capable of simultaneously transmitting four messages along the wires, turned his attention to electric lighting. His ultimate success came not only from his own inventiveness but also from his understanding that professional collaboration could foster successful innovation. In 1876, he set up a research lab with a range of specialists and facilities. His work with the ticker tape

IMAGE
Edison in His Lab, 1898

ensured generous support from the business and financial community.

By 1880, Edison had not only developed a workable and safe lightbulb but also created a company in New York to build the electric generating station to provide electricity to the city's customers. Since people used their electric lights mainly at night, there was a built-in incentive to find a way to use generators during the day. Electric traction trolley cars using steel tracks provided one way to maximize the potential of the generating station. Experimenting with electric generators also led to the development of the electric machine, which has transformed American life.

DOCUMENT
Thomas Edison, The Success of the Electric Light (October 1880)

Railroads: Pioneers of Big Business

Completion of efficient and speedy national transportation and communications networks encouraged mass production and mass marketing. Beginning in 1862, federal and state governments vigorously promoted railroad construction with land grants from the public domain. Eventually, railroads received lands one and a half times the size of Texas. Local governments gave everything from land for stations to tax breaks.

With such incentives, the first transcontinental railroad was finished in 1869. Four additional transcontinental lines and miles of feeder and branch roads were laid down in the 1870s and 1880s. By 1890, trains rumbled across 165,000 miles of tracks. Telegraph lines arose alongside them.

Railroads, the pioneers of big business, were a great modernizing force. After the Civil War, railroad companies expanded in size and complexity. The costs of construction required unprecedented amounts of capital, while the numbers of workers and the operation of the business demanded new management techniques. No single person could finance a railroad, supervise its vast operations, or resolve the questions such a large enterprise raised. How should the operations and employees be organized? What were long- and short-term needs? What were proper rates? What share of the profits did workers deserve?

Unlike small businesses, railroads' high costs and heavy indebtedness encouraged aggressive business practices. When several lines competed, railroads often offered lower rates or secret rebates (cheaper fares in exchange for all of a company's business). Rate wars caused freight rates to drop steadily but could also plunge a railroad into bankruptcy. Instability plagued the industry.

In the 1870s, railroad leaders sought to eliminate this ruinous competition. They established "pools"—informal agreements that set uniform rates or divided up the traffic. Yet these deals never completely succeeded. Too often, companies broke them, especially during business downturns.

Railroad leaders often tried to control costs and counter late-nineteenth-century falling prices by slashing wages. Owners justified this practice by reasoning that they had taken all the risks. As a result, railroads faced powerful worker unrest.

The huge scale and complexity of railroads called for innovative management techniques. In 1854, the Erie Railroad hired engineer and inventor Daniel McCallum to discover how to make managers and employees more accountable. McCallum pointed out that large organizations needed to be handled differently from small ones. He worked out a system that divided responsibilities and ensured a regular flow of information. It attracted widespread interest. Other large-scale businesses copied the new procedures that effectively distributed work and separated management from operations. They also learned lessons from the railroads' competitiveness,

their efforts to underprice one another, and their drive to cut workers' wages.

Growth in Other Industries

By the last quarter of the century, the textile, metal, and machinery industries equaled the railroads in size. In 1870, the typical iron and steel firm employed fewer than 100 workers. Thirty years later, the average workforce was four times as large. By 1900, more than 1,000 American factories had giant labor forces ranging between 500 and 1,000 workers. Almost 450 others employed more than 1,000 workers. Big business had come of age.

Business expansion was accomplished in one of two ways (or a combination of both). Some owners, like steel magnate Andrew Carnegie, integrated their businesses vertically. Vertical integration meant adding operations either before or after the production process. Even though he had introduced the most up-to-date innovations in his steel mills, Carnegie realized he needed his own sources of pig iron, coal, and coke. This was "backward" integration, away from the consumer, to avoid dependence on suppliers. When Carnegie acquired steamships and railroads to transport his finished products, he was integrating "forward," toward the consumer. Companies that integrated vertically frequently achieved economies of scale through more-efficient management techniques.

Other companies copied the railroads and integrated horizontally by combining similar businesses. They did not intend to control the various stages of production, as was the case with vertical integration, but rather to gain a monopoly of the market to eliminate competition and to stabilize prices. Horizontal integration sometimes, though not always, brought economies and thus greater profits. But by controlling prices, monopolies did boost earnings.

John D. Rockefeller used the strategy of horizontal integration to gain control of the oil market. By a combination of astute and ruthless techniques, Rockefeller bought or drove out competitors of his Standard Oil of New Jersey. Although the company never achieved a complete monopoly, by 1898 it was refining 84 percent of the nation's oil. Rockefeller reflected, "The day of individual competition [in the oil business] . . . is past and gone."

Rockefeller accurately characterized the new economic climate. As giant businesses competed intensely, often cutting wages and prices, they absorbed or eliminated smaller and weaker producers.

IMAGE

John D. Rockefeller— Cartoon

Business ownership became increasingly concentrated. In 1870, some 808 American iron and steel firms competed in the marketplace. By 1900, fewer than 70 were left.

Like the railroads, many big businesses saw the wisdom of incorporation. Corporations had many advantages. By selling stock, they could raise funds for large-scale operations. Limited liability protected investors' personal assets while the corporation's legal identity allowed it to survive the death of original and subsequent shareholders. Longevity suggested a measure of stability that made corporations attractive to investors.

Financing Postwar Growth

Such changes demanded huge amounts of capital along with the willingness to accept financial risks. The creation of the railroad system alone cost more than $1 billion by 1859 (the canal system's modest price tag was less than $2 million). The completion of the national railroad network required another $10 billion. British, French, and German investors saw American railroads as a good investment; ultimately, foreigners contributed one-third of the sum needed to complete the system. Americans also eagerly supported new ventures and began to devote an increasing percentage of the national income to investment rather than consumption.

Although savings and commercial banks continued to invest their depositors' capital, investment banking houses such as Morgan & Co. played a new and significant role in transferring resources to economic enterprises. Investment bankers marketed investment opportunities. They bought up blocks of corporate bonds (which offered set interest rates and eventually the repayment of principal) at a discount for interested investors and also sold stocks (which paid dividends only if the company made a profit). Because stocks were riskier investments than bonds, buyers were cautious at first. But when John Pierpont Morgan, a respected investment banker, began to market stocks, they became more popular. The market for industrial securities expanded rapidly in the 1880s and 1890s. Although some Americans feared the power of investment bankers and distrusted the financial market, both were integral to the economic expansion of the late nineteenth century.

J. P. Morgan

American Industry and the World

The industrialization of the late nineteenth century represented the second stage of the great transformation that began in Great Britain in the eighteenth century. By reorganizing production, often through the use of machinery, early manufacturers were able to turn out more and cheaper goods than at any time in human history. Innovation created the textile, mining, and metal industries and stimulated changes in transportation and communications. From Britain, industrialization spread to other countries in Europe as well as to the United States.

The second stage of the Industrial Revolution was marked by the application of science and technology to manufacturing and by the creation of new ways to mass-produce goods. The United States was the leader in developing techniques of mass production, while Germany excelled in using science and technology to reshape production. Technological innovations transformed German industry. As in the United States, giant firms turned out goods (especially heavy machinery and chemicals) for ever-lower prices. Along with Great Britain, Germany and the United States produced two-thirds of the world's manufactured products between 1870 and 1930.

Great Britain, the world's most powerful nation during the nineteenth century, had long been its economic leader. But now the balance of power began to shift as German and American businesses developed large new enterprises, introduced new ways of organizing and efficiently managing them, invested heavily in equipment, and promoted research. Great Britain lost ground, preferring traditional ways of organizing businesses rather than the new corporate structure. British manufacturing continued to be centered in older industries such as textiles, while British investors channeled their capital away from domestic industries toward investment opportunities abroad. American railroads and subways were constructed partly with the assistance of British investors.

The full impact of the changed position of the United States in the world triggered by its industrial might became fully apparent only in the twentieth century. But the importance of connections with other nations was obvious. Standard Oil sent two-thirds of the kerosene it refined to overseas markets. Firms manufacturing sewing machines, office machines such as typewriters, and farm machinery dominated the world market. Singer Sewing Machine had a factory in Scotland in the 1880s and two decades later manufactured more than 400,000 machines in Moscow, employing 2,500 workers and 300 managers. American locomotives were exported to South America, parts of Africa and Europe, the Middle East, and Asia. The Baldwin Locomotive Works of Philadelphia produced as many engines as any other locomotive company in the world. These connections between American business and other nations

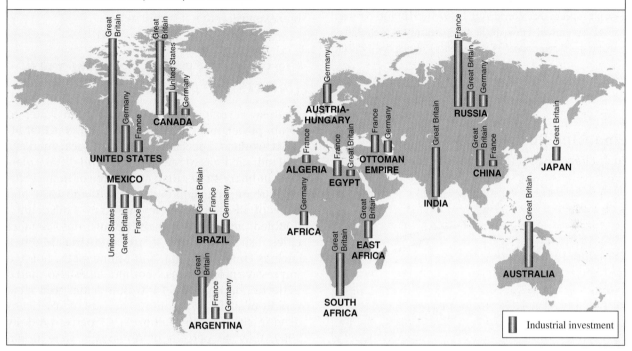

European and American Industrial Investment, 1900

Here we can see the broad impact that industrialized countries had on the rest of the world. Although industrialization was initially centered in western Europe and the United States, its influence was global. Industrial countries sought new markets, new sources of raw material, and new places for investment and development. **Reflecting on the Past** In what places was the United States most interested? Where did individual European countries invest heavily? How would you compare the global impact of the United States to that of major European countries?

meant that events elsewhere in the world could affect the American economy. Furthermore, they suggested the intricate ties binding American business to other parts of the world. American industrial production contributed to the economic development of other countries around the globe, while American business also competed with foreign producers. John D. Rockefeller told a congressional committee that Standard Oil "spared no expense in forcing its products into the markets of the world among people civilized and uncivilized," and that the company was "holding its market against the competition of Russia and all the many countries which are producers of oil and competitors against American oil."

An Erratic Global Economy

Affected by national and worldwide economic trends, the transformation of the American economy was neither smooth nor steady. Rockefeller, describing his years in the oil business as "hazardous," confessed that he did not know "how we came through them."

Two depressions, one from 1873 to 1879 and the other from 1893 to 1897, surpassed the severity of economic downturns before the Civil War. Collapsing land values, unsound banking practices, and changes in the supply of money had caused the earlier depressions. The depressions of the late nineteenth century, when the economy was larger and more interdependent, were industrial, intense, and accompanied by widespread unemployment, a phenomenon new to American life. They were also related to economic declines in European industrial nations.

During expansionary years, manufacturers flooded markets with goods. The global pattern of falling prices that characterized the postwar period and fierce competition between producers combined to encourage overproduction. When the market was finally saturated, sales and profits declined, and the economy spiraled downward. Owners slowed production and laid off workers. Industrial workers, now an increasing percentage of the American workforce, depended solely on wages for their livelihood. As they economized and bought less food, farm prices also plummeted. Farmers, like wage workers, cut back on purchases. Business and trade stagnated, and the railroads were finally affected. Eventually, the cycle bottomed out, but in the meantime, millions of workers lost employment,

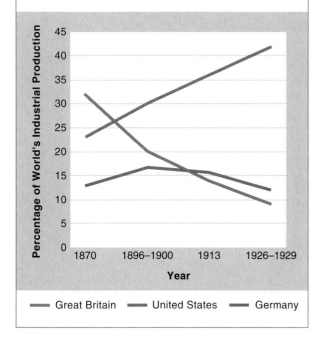

World's Industrial Output

This graph shows the changing pattern of industrial production among the world's most significant manufacturing nations. **Reflecting on the Past** In which period did American industry make its greatest gains? What lies behind these rapid gains? What economic impact does the graph suggest that World War I (1914–1918) had on the three countries? How might the patterns of the 1920s shape the three countries' experiences during the 1930s?

Percentage of World's Industrial Production — **Year**: 1870, 1896–1900, 1913, 1926–1929

— Great Britain — United States — Germany

thousands of businesses went bankrupt, and many Americans suffered.

Pollution

Widespread pollution, another by-product of the industrial age, worried most Americans less than the fluctuations of the economic cycle. But industrial processes everywhere adversely affected the environment. In the iron and steel city of Birmingham, Alabama, for example, the coke ovens poured smoke, soot, and ashes into the air. Coal tar, a by-product of the coking process, was dumped, making the soil so acid that nothing would grow on it.

When industrial, human, and animal wastes were channeled into rivers, they killed fish and other forms of marine life and plants that were part of that ecosystem. By the late nineteenth century, the pollution of eastern and midwestern rivers as well as lakes had become pronounced.

The intellectual rationale stressed growth, development, and the rapid exploitation of the country's resources—not conservation. As the last chapter

pointed out, small steps were taken toward protecting the environment. Presidents Grover Cleveland and Benjamin Harrison both set aside forest reserves, and there was growing interest in creating national parks. But such activities were limited in scope and did not begin to touch the problems created by the rise of heavy industry and the rapid urban expansion that it stimulated.

URBAN EXPANSION IN THE INDUSTRIAL AGE

As postwar manufacturers shifted from water to steam power, most favored urban locations that offered workers, specialized services, local markets, and railroad links to raw materials and distant markets. Industry, rather than commerce or finance, fueled urban expansion between 1870 and 1900, and cities of all sizes grew. New York and Philadelphia doubled and tripled their populations. Smaller cities, especially those in the industrial Midwest such as Omaha, Duluth, and Minneapolis, boasted impressive growth rates. Southern cities also shared in the dramatic growth. Far western cities grew most rapidly of all. In 1870, some 25 percent of Americans lived in cities, but in California, 37 percent did. By 1900, fully 40 percent of Americans were urban dwellers.

A Growing Population

The American population grew about 2 percent a year, but cities expanded far more rapidly. Although more people were born than died in American cities, births contributed only modestly to the urban explosion. Urban families tended to have fewer children than rural ones, and the host of urban health hazards meant that the death rate for infants was twice as high in cities as in the countryside. In the 1880s, half the children born in Chicago did not live to celebrate their fifth birthdays.

The real cause of rapid urban growth was the spectacular ability of the cities to attract newcomers from the nation's small towns and farms and abroad. For rural Americans, the "push" came from agricultural modernization: farm machines were replacing human hands. The "pull" was the promise of employment. Although urban jobs were often dirty, dangerous, and exhausting, so was farm work. Furthermore, by 1890 manufacturing workers were earning hundreds of

DOCUMENT

Adna Weber, The Growth of Cities in the 19th Century (1899)

dollars more a year than farm laborers. Higher urban living costs gobbled up some of the differential

Falling Birthrates

This chart shows the falling birthrate over the course of almost 200 years. By 1860, the average size of an American family was 5.3 members as compared to 5.8 in 1800. In what 20-year period during the nineteenth century did the largest decline in birthrates occur?

While the American birthrate was falling, it was higher than in Europe. By 1860, natural increase and immigration combined to make the American population as a whole larger than the British population. It was not long before the United States was also larger than Germany and France.

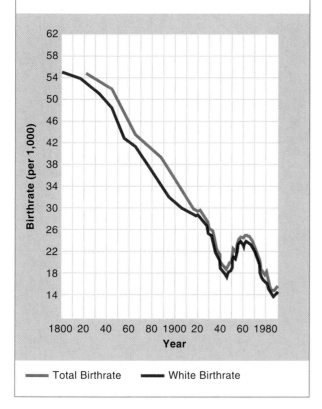

— Total Birthrate   ▬ White Birthrate

between rural and urban wages but not all of it. The "gilded metropolis" also offered a host of "marvels" absent from rural life. Shops, theaters, restaurants, department stores, baseball games, and the crowds amazed and amused young people coming from towns and farms. Although technological innovations such as electric lights (invented in 1879) and telephones (1876) were still not widespread, they further increased the desirability of cities.

Southern blacks, often single and young, also joined the migratory stream into the cities. In the West and North, blacks formed only a tiny part of the population, but in southern cities they were more numerous. About 44 percent of late-nineteenth-century Atlanta's residents were black, and so were 38

percent of Nashville's. But all cities offered them few rewards as well as many dangers.

The New Immigration, 1880–1900

Sadie Frowne was born in a small village in Poland, where her mother ran a small grocery store and her father farmed. After her father died, times were hard, and mother and daughter came by steerage to New York, where they had relatives. Although she was only 13 years old, Sadie went to work, first as a domestic servant and then in a sweatshop. Her mother found a job in an underwear factory. Mother and daughter were part of a mass migration from Europe that sent 40 million people to the United States between 1815 and 1915 and another 20 million to Canada and Latin America. Like the Frownes, three-quarters of the newcomers arriving in the United States in the last quarter century stayed in the Northeast. Many of the rest settled in cities across the nation, where they soon outnumbered native-born whites.

Over the course of the century, the major sources of immigration to the United States changed. Until 1880, three-quarters of those coming to the United States, often called the "old immigrants," hailed from the British Isles, Germany, and Scandinavia. Irish and Germans were the largest groups. By 1890, however, these nationalities composed only 60 percent of the total number of newcomers. "New immigrants" such as the Frownes from southern and eastern Europe (Italy, Poland, Russia, Austria-Hungary, Greece, Turkey, and Syria) made up most of the rest. Italian Catholics were by far the most numerous (8 million came between 1876 and 1915),

Recipients of European Migration, 1846–1932

While most migration from Europe was headed toward the United States, immigrants flocked to South America, Canada, and Australia and New Zealand as well. In Argentina, Italian immigrants made up a larger percentage of the population than they did in the United States and thus influenced Argentinean culture more profoundly than they affected American culture. **Reflecting on the Past** What does this table suggest about the push–pull factors in the process of migration?

(Estimates in millions)

United States	34.2
Argentina and Uruguay	7.1
Canada	5.2
Brazil	4.4
Australia and New Zealand	3.5
Cuba	.9

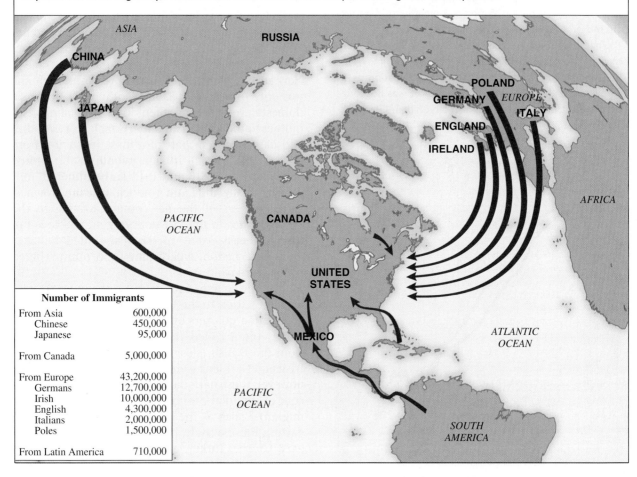

Migration to the United States, 1860–1910

This map makes clear the many parts of the world that sent population to the United States. Many of those who came were dislodged by economic changes in their home countries. **Reflecting on the Past** What were the most important short-term consequences of these migratory streams? What have been the most important long-term consequences?

Number of Immigrants	
From Asia	600,000
Chinese	450,000
Japanese	95,000
From Canada	5,000,000
From Europe	43,200,000
Germans	12,700,000
Irish	10,000,000
English	4,300,000
Italians	2,000,000
Poles	1,500,000
From Latin America	710,000

followed by eastern European Jews and then Slavs (Russians and Poles).

The large numbers were the result of cheaper, faster, and better transportation. Trains reached far into eastern and southern Europe. On transatlantic vessels, even steerage passengers could now expect a bed with blankets, cooked meals, and a communal washroom. But dissatisfaction with life at home was basic to the decision to migrate. Overpopulation, famine, and disease drove people to leave. "We could have eaten each other had we stayed," explained one Italian immigrant.

Efforts to modernize European economies also stimulated immigration. New agricultural techniques led landlords to consolidate their land, evicting longtime tenants. Younger European farmers traveled in increasingly wide circles searching for work. Some emigrated to cities elsewhere in Europe,

IMAGE
Immigrants at Ellis Island

others to Canada or South America. The largest share went to the United States. Similarly, artisans whose skills were made obsolete by the introduction of machinery pulled up stakes and headed for the United States and other destinations.

Government policies pushed others to leave. Up until 1881, most Jews coming to the United States were Germans who had integrated successfully into American society. Many became Reform Jews, which they considered a "distinctively American" form of Judaism, quite different from "the boneless Orthodoxy of the old World." After 1881, however, Orthodox Jews fled to the United States from Russia, Lithuania, and Poland. Following the assassination of the Russian czar in 1881, a harsh policy toward Jews was implemented. Jews were barred from most occupations, forced to relocate their homes, and restricted in the practice of their religion.

DOCUMENT
Letters to the *Jewish Daily Forward* (1906–1907)

had few skills. Jews, however, came most often in family groups, and women predominated among the Irish. When times were good and American industry needed large numbers of unskilled laborers, migration was heavy. When times were bad and letters warned that "work is dull all over . . . no work to be got except by chance or influence," numbers fell off. Many immigrants hoped to earn enough money in America to realize their ambitions at home. Italians were particularly likely to return to Italy. Between 20 and 30 percent did. But others, like the Jews, had little interest in going back to their former homelands.

Although the greatest influx of Mexicans would come in the twentieth century, Mexican laborers added to the stream of migrants. Like many European countries, Mexico was in the throes of modernization. Overpopulation and new land policies uprooted many inhabitants, while the construction of a railroad from the Texas border 900 miles into Mexico in 1895 facilitated migration. Many Mexicans ended up in the Southwest and West, working for the railroads and in mines.

Life in the Old Country Here we see a village street in Russia in the late nineteenth century. What is the condition of the street? What signs of utilities are there? How are the children clothed? In what ways might immigrants who came from this village think about the urban conditions they encountered in the United States? *(Keystone-Mast Collection, URL/California Museum of Photography, University of California, Riverside)*

Foreign-born Population, 1890

Vicious persecution threatened life itself as the following eyewitness account makes clear: "From their hiding places in cellars and garrets the Jews were dragged forth and tortured to death. . . . Babies were thrown from the higher stories to the street pavement. . . . The local bishop drove in a carriage and passed through the crowd, giving them his blessing as he passed." In the first 10 years of persecution, 150,000 Jews left Russia, the vast majority headed for the United States. By 1914, 2 million had made the journey.

Opportunity also lured thousands to American shores. State commissioners of immigration and American railroad and steamship companies, eager for workers and customers, wooed potential immigrants. Friends and relatives wrote letters describing favorable living and working conditions and promising to help newcomers find work. American cities were great places for "blast frnises and Rolen milles," explained one unskilled worker. Often money for the passage or pictures of friends in alluringly fashionable clothes were slipped between the pages of letters. The phenomenon of immigrants being recruited through the reports and efforts of their predecessors has come to be known as "chain migration."

Like rural and small-town Americans, Europeans came primarily to work. Most were young, single men who, in contrast to pre–Civil War immigrants,

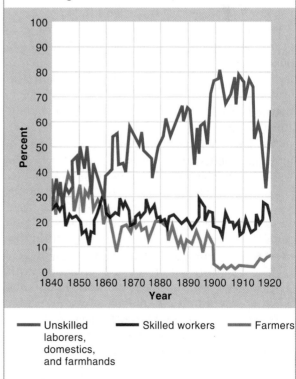

Working-Class Immigration, 1840–1920

The large numbers of unskilled workers coming to the United States were responding to the need for unskilled labor during the second Industrial Revolution.

——— Unskilled laborers, domestics, and farmhands   ——— Skilled workers   ——— Farmers

Source: U.S. Bureau of the Census.

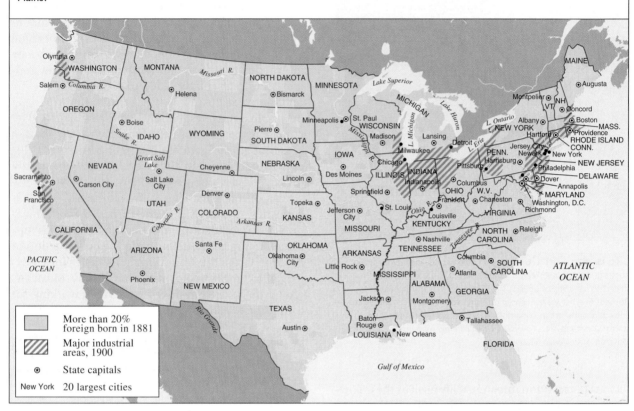

Foreign Immigration, 1880–1920

This map shows how immigrants favored industrial areas as well as the West and areas along American borders. As you can see, the South did not attract large numbers of foreigners. What factors deterred immigration to the South and the southern Great Plains?

Legend:
- More than 20% foreign born in 1881
- Major industrial areas, 1900
- ⊛ State capitals
- New York   20 largest cities

Writing to his son in the United States, a Chinese father pointed out, "Men go abroad so that they might make money for support of their families, but you have sent neither money nor a letter since you left." Overpopulation, depressed conditions, unemployment, and crop failures drove 264,000 Chinese to the United States between 1860 and 1900. Most stayed on the West Coast, where they constituted a significant minority. As unskilled male contract laborers who planned to work for a number of years and then return to their wives and families at home, they performed some of the hardest, dirtiest, and least desirable jobs in the West. They worked in mining and agriculture and on railroad and levee construction, and labored in factory and laundry work. To serve these men, often away from their wives for years, contractors also brought in a limited number of Chinese women to serve as prostitutes. Virtually enslaved, few of these women could pay off the costs of their passage or escape from brothel life.

The importance of migration from Europe, Mexico, and Asia can hardly be overestimated. Immigrants

DOCUMENT

Memorial of the Chinese Six Companies to U. S. Grant (1876)

contributed to the country's rapid urbanization and provided much of the labor needed to accomplish the economic transformation of the late nineteenth century. Their presence also helped transform American society. The American population became far more heterogeneous in terms of ethnicity and religion than any other industrial nation. Since most immigrants were workers, they altered the character of the laboring class. Differences between immigrant groups and between immigrants and American workers weakened immigrants' ability to respond to employers with one voice. The presence of those who spoke little or no English and had values and experiences very different from those of native-born Americans challenged American ideals, beliefs, and practices.

THE INDUSTRIAL CITY, 1880–1900

The late-nineteenth-century industrial city had new physical and social arrangements that attracted widespread comment. Slums, not new, seemed disturbing because so many people lived in them. Yet

Lower East Side, New York Here is a picture of life on Hester Street on New York's Lower East Side. Study the photograph to see what it reveals about living conditions in New York City. What indications are there of commercial activity? Why are there so many women on the street and so few men? What is suggested about children? What does the picture suggest about city services to this poor neighborhood? What are the major contrasts between this part of New York and the downtown scene shown on p. 600? *(New York City Views, Milstein Division of U.S. History, Local History & Genealogy, The New York Public Library/Art Resource, NY)*

cities also contained grand mansions, handsome business and industrial buildings, grandiose civic monuments, parks, and acres of substantial middle-class homes.

By the last quarter of the nineteenth century, the antebellum "walking city," whose size and configuration had been limited by the necessity of walking to work, disappeared. Where once substantial houses, businesses, and small artisan dwellings had stood side by side, central business districts emerged. Here were banks, shops, theaters, professional firms, and businesses. Few people lived downtown, although many worked or shopped there. Surrounding the

business center were areas of light manufacturing and wholesale activity with housing for workers. Beyond these working-class neighborhoods stretched middle-class residential areas. Then came the suburbs, with "pure air, peacefulness," and "natural scenery." Scattered throughout the city were pockets of industrial activity surrounded by crowded working-class housing.

This new pattern, with the poorest city residents clustered near the center, reversed the early nineteenth-century urban form in which much of the most desirable housing was in the heart of the city. New living arrangements were also more segregated by race and class than those in the preindustrial walking city. Homogeneous social and economic neighborhoods emerged, and it became more unusual than before for a poor, working-class family to live near a middle- or upper-class family.

Transportation improvements enormously affected the development of American cities. The revolution started modestly in the 1820s and 1830s with slow, horse-drawn "omnibuses" accommodating only 10 to 12 passengers. Expensive fares meant most people still walked to work. In the 1850s, many cities introduced faster and bigger horse railways, allowing the city to expand outward about four miles. The cost of a fare, however, limited ridership to the prosperous classes. Cable cars, trolleys, and subways after 1880 further extended city boundaries, enabling the middle class to escape grimy industrial districts.

Neighborhoods and Neighborhood Life

Working-class neighborhoods clustered near the center of most industrial cities. Here lived newcomers from the American countryside and, because most immigrants settled in cities, crowds of foreigners as well.

Ethnic groups frequently gathered in particular neighborhoods, often located near industries requiring their labor. In Detroit in 1880, for example, 37 percent of the city's native-born families lived in one area, whereas 40 percent of the Irish inhabited

Chinese Immigrants on Shipboard   Although not one of the largest immigrant groups in the late nineteenth century, Chinese made up a sizable proportion of foreign workers in California. Who is in the picture and how are they dressed? Because of the male nature of Chinese immigration, many of the Chinese women coming to the United States were prostitutes. In 1873 Congress passed a law curtailing Asian female immigration on moral grounds. *(Asian American Studies Library, UC-Berkeley)*

DOCUMENT

William B. Farwell, *The Chinese at Home and Abroad* (1885)

the "Irish West Side." More than half of the Germans and almost three-quarters of the Poles settled on the city's east side. Although such neighborhoods often had an ethnic flavor, with small specialty shops and foreign-language signs, they were not ethnic ghettos. Immigrants and native-born Americans often lived in the same neighborhoods, on the same streets, and even in the same houses. The Chinatowns that sprang up in western cities and in places like New York were exceptions to this pattern. Hostility from whites kept most Chinese secluded in Chinatowns where they felt safe among their own people.

Working-class neighborhoods were often what would be called slums today. They were crowded and unsanitary with inadequate public services. Many workers lived in houses once occupied by middle- and upper-class residents, now divided and subdivided to accommodate more people than the original builders had intended. Others squeezed into tenements, which were specially constructed to house as many families as possible. Small apartments were dark and stuffy and often had windowless rooms. Outdoor privies, shared by several families, were the rule. Water came from outdoor hydrants, and women had to carry it inside for cooking, washing, and cleaning. When there were indoor fixtures, they frequently emptied waste directly into unpaved alleys and courts served by inadequate sewage systems or none at all. Piles of garbage and waste

IMAGE

New York City Tenements

stank in the summer and froze in the winter. Even when people kept their own living quarters clean, their outside environment was unsanitary and unhealthy. It was no surprise that urban death rates were so high. Only at the turn of the century did the public health movement, particularly the efforts to treat water supplies with germ-killing chemicals, begin to ameliorate these living conditions.

Not every working-class family lived in abject circumstances. Skilled workers might rent comfortable quarters, and a few even owned their own homes. A study of working-class families in Massachusetts found the family of one skilled worker living "in a tenement of five rooms in a pleasant and healthy locality, with good surroundings. The apartments are well furnished and [the] parlor carpeted." The family even had a sewing machine. But unskilled and semiskilled workers were not so fortunate. The Massachusetts survey describes the family of an unskilled ironworker crammed into a tenement of four rooms,

in an overcrowded block, to which belong only two privies for about fifty people. When this place was visited the vault had overflowed in the yard and the sink-water was also running in the same place, and created a stench that was really frightful. . . . The house inside, was badly furnished and dirty, and a disgrace to Worcester.

Drab as their neighborhoods usually were, working families created a community life that helped alleviate some of their dreary physical surroundings.

The expense of moving around the city helped encourage a neighborhood and family focus. Long working hours meant that precious free time was apt to be spent close to home.

The wide range of institutions and associations that came to life in urban neighborhoods demonstrates that working-class men and women were not just victims of their environment. Frequently rooted in religious and ethnic identities, these organizations helped residents feel at home in the city. But they also could separate ethnic groups from one another and from native-born Americans. A Lithuanian worker in Chicago found companionship in a Lithuanian Concertina Club and a Lithuanian society that gave two picnics and two balls each year. Irish collective life focused around the Roman Catholic parish church, Irish nationalist organizations, ward politics, and Irish saloons. Jews gathered in their synagogues, Hebrew schools, and Hebrew- and Yiddish-speaking literary groups. Germans had their family saloons and educational and singing societies. Various Chinese organizations provided benefits, including education, health, and religious services. Although such activities may have slowed assimilation into American society and discouraged intergroup contact, they provided companionship, a social network, spiritual consolation, and a bridge between life in the "old country" and life in America.

African Americans faced the most wretched living conditions of any group in the city. In the North, they often lived in segregated black neighborhoods. In southern cities, they gathered in back alleys and small streets. Many could afford only rented rooms. However, a rich religious and associational life tempered the suffering. African American churches enjoyed phenomenal growth. Black members of mainline Protestant denominations separated from their white counterparts to establish autonomy and self-respect. The African Methodist Episcopal Church, with a membership of 20,000 in 1856, founded churches in every city and sizable town, and by 1900 claimed more than 400,000 members. African American worship continued to express the emotional exuberance that had characterized slave religion. Energetic preaching and expressive music helped make churchgoing a fulfilling spiritual experience. Often associated with churches were mutual-aid and benevolent societies that helped needy members of the community. Outreach activities also included support for missionaries in Africa.

Some urban African Americans in the late nineteenth century rose into the middle class. In spite of the heavy odds against them, they created the nucleus of professional life. Ministers, businessmen, doctors, and lawyers became leaders of their communities.

Beyond working-class neighborhoods and pockets of black housing lay streets of middle-class houses. Here lived the urban lower middle class: clerks, shopkeepers, bookkeepers, salespeople, and small tradespeople. Their salaries allowed them to buy or rent houses with some privacy and comfort. Separate spaces for cooking and laundry work kept hot and often odorous housekeeping tasks away from other living areas. Many houses boasted up-to-date gas lighting and bathrooms. Outside, the neighborhoods were cleaner and more attractive than in the inner city. Residents could pay for garbage collection, gaslights, and other improvements.

Streetcar Suburbs

On the fringes of the city were houses for the substantial middle class and the rich, who made their money in business, commerce, and the professions or inherited family fortunes. Public transportation sped them downtown to their offices and then home. Robert Work, a modestly successful cap and hat merchant, moved his family to a $5,500 house in West Philadelphia in 1865 and commuted more than four miles to work.

The 1880 census revealed the Work family's comfortable lifestyle. The household contained two servants, two boarders, Robert's wife, and their son, who was still in school. The Works' house had running hot and cold water, indoor bathrooms, central heating, and other modern conveniences of the age. Elaborately carved furniture, rugs, draperies, and lace curtains probably graced the downstairs, where the family entertained and gathered for meals. Upstairs, comfortable bedrooms provided a maximum of privacy for family members. The live-in servants, who did most of the housework, shared little of this space or privacy, however. They were restricted to the kitchen, the pantry, and bedrooms in the attic.

The Social Geography of the Cities

In industrial cities of this era, people were sorted by class, income, occupation, and race. Their circumstances not only dictated who would live comfortably with access to some of the conveniences and improvements that industrial development had made possible but also affected family size and domestic life. Although the size of the middle-class family was shrinking over the course of the century, working-class and immigrant families remained large. For example, in Buffalo, New York, in 1900,

New York City Downtown New York City in 1890 hosted a mixture of horse-drawn vehicles and the new "horseless carriages." The nonresidential character of the central business district gave a special character to the late-nineteenth-century city. What sorts of people appear in the picture? What signs of their social class does the picture provide? *(Brown Brothers)*

middle-class families had an average of 3.5 children, while laboring families had an average of 5.7 children. Because working-class children went out to work, large families made economic sense and represented one means of improving a family's well-being.

Upper- and middle-class neighborhoods and working-class neighborhoods were physically separated, so city dwellers often had little firsthand knowledge of people different from themselves. Ignorance led to distorted views and social disapproval. Reformers criticized working-class families for encouraging their children to leave school and work. Middle-class newspapers unsympathetically described laboring men as "loafing" and criticized the "crowds of idlers, who, day and night, infect Main Street." Yet those "idlers" were often men who could not find employment. The comments of a working-class woman to her temperance visitors in 1874 suggest the critical view from the bottom of society up: "When the rich stopped drinking, it would be time to speak to the poor about it."

THE LIFE OF THE MIDDLE CLASS

The sharp comments made by different classes of Americans suggest the economic and social polarization that late-nineteenth-century industrialization spawned. For middle-class Americans, there was much to value in the new age. Between 1865 and 1890, average middle-class income rose about 30 percent.

By 1900, fully 36 percent of urban families owned their homes.

Industrial expansion raised living standards for the increasing numbers of Americans. They were able to purchase dozens of products, manufactured, packaged, and promoted in an explosion of technological inventions and shrewd marketing techniques. Among still-familiar products and brands invented or mass-produced for the first time in the 1890s are Jell-O, Wesson oil, the Hershey bar, Aunt Jemima pancake mix, and Coca-Cola.

More leisure time and greater access to consumer goods signaled industrialism's power to transform

Middle-Class Comfort This photograph of a middle-class house in River Forest, Illinois, suggests the comfort available to those who could afford it and the ways suburban life shielded the middle class from the squalor and ugliness of industrial life. What does the exterior of the house suggest about what the inside might be like? How are the porch and garden treated? Why was the porch so large? *(Culver Pictures)*

the lives of middle-class Americans. Plentiful immigrant servant girls relieved urban middle-class wives of many housekeeping chores, and smaller families lightened the burdens of motherhood. New department stores began to appear in the central business districts in the 1870s, feeding the desire for material possessions and revolutionizing retailing. Shopping for home furnishings and clothes became integral to many middle-class women's lives.

New Freedoms for Middle-Class Women

As many middle-class women acquired leisure time and enhanced purchasing power, they also won new freedoms. Several states granted women more property rights in marriage, adding to their growing sense of independence. Casting off confining crinolines, they now wore a shirtwaist blouse and ankle-length skirt that was more comfortable for working, school, and sports. The "new woman" was celebrated as *Life* magazine's attractively active, slightly rebellious "Gibson girl."

Using their new freedom, women joined organizations of all kinds—literary societies, charity groups, reform clubs. There they gained organizational experience, awareness of their talents, and contact with people and problems outside their traditional family roles. The depression of 1893 stimulated many women to investigate slum and factory conditions, and some began even earlier. Jane Addams, who told her college classmates in 1881 to lead lives "filled with good works and honest toil," went on to found Hull House, a famous social settlement.

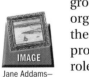
Jane Addams— Portrait

Job opportunities for these educated middle-class women were generally limited to the social services and teaching. Still regarded as a suitable female occupation, teaching was a highly demanding but poorly paying field that grew as urban schools expanded under the pressure of a burgeoning population. By the 1890s, the willingness of middle-class women to work for low pay opened up new forms of employment in office work, nursing, and department stores. But moving up to high-status jobs proved difficult, even for middle-class women.

After the Civil War, educational opportunities for women expanded. New women's colleges offered programs similar to those at competitive men's colleges, while midwestern and western state schools dropped prohibitions against women. In 1890, some 13 percent of all college graduates were women; by 1900, nearly 20 percent were.

Medical College for Women

Higher education prepared middle-class women for conventional female roles as well as for work and public service. A few courageous graduates overcame many barriers to enter the professions. By the early twentieth century, the number of women professionals (including teachers) was increasing at three times the rate for men.

One reason for the greater independence of American women was that they were having fewer babies. This was especially true of educated women. In 1900, nearly one married woman in five was childless. Advances in birth control technology (the modern diaphragm was developed in 1880) helped make new patterns possible. Decreasing family size and an increase in the divorce rate (1 out of 12 marriages in 1905) fueled male fears. Arguments against the new woman intensified as many men reaffirmed Victorian stereotypes of "woman's sphere." One male orator in 1896 inveighed against the new woman's public role because "a woman's brain involves emotions rather than intellect." Male campaigns against prostitution and for sex hygiene, as well as efforts to reinforce traditional sex roles, reflected deep fears that female passions might weaken male vigor.

Male Mobility and the Success Ethic

As middle-class women's lives were changing, so were men's. Expansion of the postwar economy and changes in the structure of American business opened up many new job opportunities for middle-class men. The growing complexity of census classifications reveals some of these new jobs. Where the census taker had once noted only the occupation of "clerk," now were listed "accountant," "salesman," and "shipping clerk." As the lower ranks of the white-collar world became more specialized, the number of middle-class jobs increased.

To prepare for these new careers, Americans required more education. The number of public high schools in the United States increased from 160 in 1870 to 6,000 in 1900. By 1900, a majority of states and territories had compulsory school-attendance laws.

Higher education also expanded in this period. The number of students in colleges and universities nearly doubled, from 53,000 in 1870 to 101,000 in 1900. Charles Eliot, president of Harvard from 1869 to 1909, led that university through a period of dynamic growth, introducing reforms such as higher faculty salaries and sabbatical leaves as well as the elective system of course selection for students. Harvard's growth reflected the rise of the university to a new stature in American life. As the land-grant state universities (made possible by the Morrill Act

HOW OTHERS SEE US

Herbert Spencer, "The Americans"

Herbert Spencer was an English intellectual who adapted Charles Darwin's theory of the survival of the fittest to human society. These remarks come from a speech he made at a New York dinner during his visit to this country in 1882.

Everywhere I have been struck with the number of faces which told in strong lines of the burdens that had to be borne. I have been struck, too, with the large proportion of gray-haired men; and inquiries have brought out the fact, that with you the hair begins to turn some ten years earlier than with us. Moreover, in every circle I have met men who had themselves suffered from nervous collapse due to stress of business, or named friends who had either killed themselves by overwork, or had been permanently incapacitated, or wasted long periods in endeavors to recover health. I do but echo the opinion of all the observant persons I have spoken to that immense injury is being done by this high-pressure life—the physique is being undermined. . . . Beyond these immediate mischiefs there are remoter mischiefs. Exclusive devotion to work has the result that amusements cease to please; and, when relaxation becomes imperative, life becomes dreary from lack of its sole interest—the interest in business. The remark current in England, that, when the American travels, his aim is to do the greatest amount of sight-seeing in the shortest time, I find current here also.

- *What social class is Spencer talking about?*

- *How do his comments reflect the values of English society?*

- *How seriously should we take them?*

Source: Herbert Spencer, "The Americans," *Living Age*, 41 (1883), 327–328.

---

of 1862) continued to expand, generous gifts from wealthy businessmen helped found leading research universities such as Stanford, Johns Hopkins, and the University of Chicago.

These developments led to greater specialization and professionalism in education, medicine, law, and business. Before the Civil War, a Swedish pioneer in Wisconsin described a young mason who "laid aside the trowel, got himself some medical books, and assumed the title of doctor." But by the 1890s, with government licensing and the rise of professional schools, the word *career* began to take on its modern meaning. No longer were tradespeople likely to read up on medicine and become doctors. In this period, organizations such as the American Medical Association and the American Bar Association were regulating and professionalizing membership. The number of law schools doubled in the last quarter of the century, and 86 new medical schools were founded in the same period. Dental schools increased from 9 to 56 between 1875 and 1900.

The need for lawyers, bankers, architects, and insurance agents to serve business and industry expanded career opportunities. Between 1870 and 1900, the number of engineers, chemists, metallurgists, and architects grew rapidly. As large companies formed and became bureaucratized, business required many more managerial positions. As the public sector expanded, new careers in social services and government opened up as well. Young professional experts with graduate training in the social sciences filled many of them. The professional disciplines of history, economics, sociology, psychology, and political science all date from the last 20 years of the nineteenth century.

The social ethic of the age stressed that economic rewards were available to anyone who fervently sought them. Many people argued that, unlike in Europe, where family background and social class determined social rank, in America, few barriers held back those of good character and diligent work habits. Anyone doubting this opportunity needed only be reminded of the rise of two giants of industry. John D. Rockefeller had worked for a neighboring farmer and raised turkeys as a boy. Andrew Carnegie's mother was a washerwoman, and his father had worked himself to death in the mills within five years of reaching the United States. Both had risen spectacularly through their own efforts. Writers, lecturers, clergymen, and politicians zealously propagated the rags-to-riches tradition of upward mobility. Self-help manuals that outlined the steps to success for self-made men became widely available.

The best-known popularizer of the myth of the self-made man was Horatio Alger, Jr. Millions of boys read his 119 novels, with titles such as *Strive and Succeed* and *Bound to Rise*. In a typical Alger novel, *Ragged Dick*, the story opens with the hero leading the low life of a shoeshine boy in the streets. Dressed in rags, he sleeps in packing crates and unwisely spends his money on tobacco, liquor, gambling, and the theater. A chance opportunity to foil an attempt to cheat a gentleman results in the reward of a new suit of clothes for Dick. Before long, Dick aspires to become an office boy, "learn the business and grow up 'spectable." As he begins the process of becoming respectable, good fortune intervenes again. Dick rescues a child who tumbles into the icy waters of the harbor. Her father completes the hero's transformation from Ragged Dick to Richard Hunter, Esq., by offering him a job as a clerk in his counting house. Although moralists pointed to virtuous habits as crucial in Alger's heroes, success often depended as much on luck as on pluck.

Unlimited and equal opportunity for upward advancement in America has never been as easy as the "bootstraps" ethic maintains. But the persistence of the success myth owes something to the fact that many Americans, particularly those who began well, did rise rapidly. Native-born, middle-class whites tended to have the skills, resources, and connections that opened up the most desirable jobs. Financier Jay Gould overstated the case in maintaining that "nearly every one that occupies a prominent position has come up from the ranks." In fact, the typical big businessman was a white, Anglo-Saxon Protestant from a middle- or upper-class family whose father was most likely in business, banking, or commerce.

INDUSTRIAL WORK AND THE LABORING CLASS

David Lawlor, an Irish immigrant who came to the United States in 1872, might have agreed with Jay Gould on the opportunities for mobility. As a child, he worked in the Fall River textile mills and read Horatio Alger in his free time. Like Alger's heroes, he went to night school and rose in the business world, eventually becoming an advertising executive.

But Lawlor's success was exceptional. Most working-class Americans labored long hours on dangerous factory floors, in cramped sweatshops, or in steamy basement kitchens for meager wages. As industrialization transformed the nature of work and the composition of the workforce, traditional opportunities for mobility and even for a secure livelihood slipped from the grasp of many working-class Americans.

The Impact of Ethnic Diversity

Immigrants made up a sizable portion of the urban working class in the late nineteenth century. They formed 20 percent of the labor force and more than 40 percent of laborers in the manufacturing and extractive industries. In cities, where they tended to settle, they accounted for more than half the working-class population.

Industrial Work What can you say about the work of a puddler based on this photograph? While we might be dismayed by the nature of the puddler's job, puddling was an occupation that demanded skill and paid well. *(Courtesy of Rivers of Steel Archives)*

Industrial work, urban life, labor protest, and local politics were influenced by the fact that more than half the urban industrial class was foreign, unskilled, perhaps illiterate, and often possessed only a limited command of the English language. Eager for the unskilled positions rapidly being created as mechanization and mass production took hold, immigrants often shared little with native-born workers or even with one another. Because of immigration, American working-class society was a mosaic of nationalities, cultures, religions, and interests.

The ethnic diversity of the industrial workforce helps explain its occupational patterns. Generally occupation was related to ethnic background and experience. At the top of the working-class hierarchy, native-born Protestant whites held a disproportionate share of well-paying skilled jobs. They were the aristocrats of the working class. Their jobs demanded expertise and training, as had been true of skilled industrial workers in the pre–Civil War period. But their occupations bore the mark of late-nineteenth-century industrialism. They were machinists, iron puddlers and rollers, engineers, foremen, mechanics, and printers.

Skilled northern European immigrants filled most of the middle-rank positions. Often they had held similar jobs in their homeland. The Germans found work as tailors, bakers, brewers, and shoemakers, while Cornish and Irish miners secured skilled jobs in midwestern and western mines. The Jews, who had tailoring experience in their homelands, became the backbone of the garment industry (where they faced little competition from American male workers, who considered it unmanly to work on women's clothes).

But most of the "new immigrants" from southern and central Europe had no urban industrial experience. They labored in the unskilled, dirty jobs near the bottom of the occupational ladder. They relined blast furnaces in steel mills, carried raw materials or finished products from place to place, or cleaned up after skilled workers. Often, they were carmen or day laborers on the docks, ditchdiggers, or construction workers. Hiring was often on a daily basis, arranged through intermediaries such as the Italian padrone. Unskilled work provided little in the way of either job stability or income.

At the bottom, blacks occupied the most marginal positions as janitors, servants, porters, and laborers. Racial discrimination generally excluded them from industrial jobs, even though their occupational background differed little from that of rural white immigrants. There were always plenty of whites eager to work, so it was not necessary to hire blacks except occasionally as scabs during a labor strike. "It is an exceptional case where you find any colored labor in the factories, except as porters," observed one white. "Neither colored female . . . nor male laborer is engaged in the mechanical arts."

The Changing Nature of Work

The rise of big business, characterized by mechanization and mass production, changed the size and shape of the workforce and the nature of work itself. More and more Americans became wage earners. The number of manufacturing workers doubled between 1880 and 1900, with the fastest expansion in the unskilled and semiskilled ranks.

But the need for skilled workers remained. New positions, as in steam fitting and structural ironwork, appeared as industries expanded and changed. Increasingly, older skills became obsolete, however. And all skilled workers faced the possibility that technical advances would eliminate their favored jobs or that employers would hire unskilled helpers to take over parts of their jobs. In industries as different as shoemaking, cigar making, and iron puddling, new methods of

Increase in Size of Industries, 1860–1900

This table highlights the dramatic changes in the workplace over a 40-year period. Think about what the figures suggest about the experience of work. What industries typically had the largest workforces in 1900? What industries had the most dramatic increases in the size of their workforces between 1860 and 1900?

Industry	Average Number of Workers per Establishment	
	1860	1900
Cotton goods	112	287
Glass	81	149
Iron and steel	65	333
Hosiery and knit goods	46	91
Silk and silk goods	39	135
Woollen goods	33	67
Carpets and rugs	31	213
Tobacco	30	67
Slaughtering and meatpacking	20	61
Paper and wood pulp	15	65
Shipbuilding	15	42
Agricultural implements	8	65
Leather	5	40
Malt liquors	5	26

Source: U.S. Bureau of the Census.

production and organization undermined the position of skilled workers.

Work Settings and Experiences

The workplace could be a dock or cluttered factory yard, a multistoried textile mill, a huge, barnlike steel mill with all the latest machinery, or a mine tunnel hundreds of feet underground. A majority of American manufacturing workers now labored in factories, and the numbers of those working in large plants dominated by the unceasing rhythms of machinery increased steadily.

Some Americans, however, still toiled in small shops and sweatshops tucked away in basements, lofts, or immigrant apartments. Even in these smaller settings, the pressure to produce was relentless, for volume, not hours, determined pay. When contractors cut wages, workers had to speed up to earn the same pay.

IMAGE

Families Working in Sweatshops

The organization of work divided workers. Those paid by the piece competed against the speed, agility, and output of other workers. It was hard to feel bonds with unknown and unseen competitors. In large factories, workers separated into small work groups and mingled only rarely with the rest of the workforce. The clustering of ethnic groups in certain types of work also undermined working-class solidarity.

All workers had a very long working day in common. Although the factory day had fallen from the 12 hours expected before the Civil War, people still spent more than half their waking hours on the job—usually 10 hours a day, six days a week. Different occupations had specific demands. Bakers worked 65 hours a week; canners worked 77. Sweatshop workers might labor far into the night, long after factory workers had gone home.

Work was usually unhealthy, dangerous, and comfortless. Although a few states passed laws to regulate work conditions, enforcement was spotty. Few owners observed regulations about toilets, drinking facilities, or washing areas. Nor did they concern themselves with the health or safety of their employees. Women, bent over sewing machines, developed digestive illnesses and curved spines. Poorly ventilated mines stank of human waste and spoiled garbage, with temperatures sometimes rising above 120 degrees. Miners worked with dynamite and all too often died in cave-ins caused by inadequate timber supports in the mine shafts. When new drilling machinery was introduced into western mines, it produced tiny stone particles that caused lung disease.

Accident rates in the United States far exceeded those of Europe's industrial nations. Each year, 35,000 workers died from industrial mishaps. Iron and steel mills were the big killers, although the railroads alone accounted for 6,000 fatalities a year during the 1890s. Nationwide, nearly one-quarter of the men reaching age 20 in 1880 would not live to see 44 (compared with 7 percent today). American business owners had little legal responsibility—and some felt none—for employees' safety or health. The law placed the burden of avoiding accidents on the workers, who were expected to quit if they thought conditions were unsafe.

Industrial workers labored at jobs that were also increasingly specialized and monotonous. The size of many firms allowed a kind of specialization that was impossible in a small enterprise. Even skilled workers did not produce a complete product, and the range of their skills was narrowing. "A man never learns the machinist's trade now," one New Yorker grumbled. "The different branches of

A Garment Factory Many young Jewish women worked in the garment industry. You see an example of their working conditions here. How would you describe these women's workplace? How safe is it? How comfortable is it? What might it be like to work here in the summer? Who are the men in the background? *(Brown Brothers)*

the trade are divided and subdivided so that one man may make just a particular part of a machine and may not know anything whatever about another part of the same machine." Cabinetmakers found themselves not crafting cabinets but putting together and finishing pieces made by others. In such circumstances, many skilled workers complained that they were being reduced to drudges and wage slaves.

Still, industrial work provided some personal benefits. New arrangements helped humanize the workplace. Workers who obtained jobs through family and friends labored alongside them. In most industries, the foreman controlled day-to-day activities. He chose workers from the crowds at the gate, fired those who proved unsatisfactory, selected appropriate materials and equipment, and determined the order and pace of production. Because the foreman was himself a member of the working class who had climbed his way up, he might sympathize with subordinates. Yet the foreman could also be authoritarian and harsh, especially if the workers he supervised were unskilled or belonged to another ethnic group.

The Worker's Share in Industrial Progress

The huge fortunes accumulated by famous industrialists such as Andrew Carnegie and John D. Rockefeller during the late nineteenth century dramatized the pattern of wealth concentration that had begun in the early period of industrialization. In 1890, the top 1 percent of American families possessed more than a quarter of the wealth, whereas the share held by the top 10 percent was about 73 percent. Economic growth still benefited people who influenced its path, and they claimed the lion's share of the rewards.

But what of the workers who tended the machines that lay at the base of industrial wealth? Working-class Americans made up the largest segment of the labor force (more than 50 percent), so their experience reveals important facets of the American social and economic systems and American values.

Statistics of increasing production, of ever more goods, tell part of the story. Figures on real wages also reveal something important. Industry still needed skilled workers and paid them well. Average real wages rose more than 50 percent between 1860 and 1900. Skilled manufacturing workers, about one-tenth of the nonagricultural working class in the late nineteenth century, saw their wages rise by about 74 percent. But wages for the unskilled increased by only 31 percent. The differential was substantial and widened as the century drew to a close.

Taken as a whole, the working class accrued substantial benefits in the late nineteenth century, even

---

Two Nineteenth-Century Budgets

What do these two monthly family budgets reveal about different standards of living and different consumption choices? What do you consider the most significant differences between the lives of these two families? In 2001 dollars, the laborer took home $448 a month while the accountant earned about $1,259 a month. The laborer spent about $530 on his monthly expenses while the accountant's budgeted expenses came to about $817.

	Monthly budget of a laborer, his wife, and one child in 1891; his income is $23.67	Monthly budget of a married bank accountant with no children in 1892; his income is about $66.50
Food	$6.51	$13.22
Rent	9.02	9.88
Furniture	3.61	0.30
Taxes and insurance	3.32	7.11
Utilities	2.94	4.99
Sundries	1.09	2.10
Liquor and tobacco	0.66	0.42
Medicine	0.29	0.27
Clothes	0.21	0.19
Dry goods	0.16	2.45
Postage	0.10	—
Transportation	0.08	1.71
Reading material	—	0.53
	$27.99	$43.17

Source: Chart from *The Changing Face of Inequality* by Oliver Zunz © University of Chicago Press. Reprinted with permission.

Labor Force Distribution, 1890

Whereas a majority of Americans in the twentieth century defined themselves as middle class, in the nineteenth century, most Americans held working-class jobs. Approximately what percentage of workers held middle- or upper-class jobs?

1890

- 54.3%
- 26.3%
- 12.4%
- 3.1%
- 1.4%
- 2.5%

- ● Upper-class occupations
- ● Upper- or middle-class occupations
- ● Middle-class occupations
- ● Farmer
- ● Working-class occupations
- ● Other occupations

Source: U.S. Bureau of the Census.

if its share of the total wealth did not increase. American workers had more material comforts than their European counterparts. But the general picture conceals the realities of working-class economic life. A U.S. Bureau of Labor study of working-class families in 1889 revealed great disparities of income: a young girl in a silk mill made $130 a year; a laborer earned $384 a year; a carpenter took home $686. The carpenter's family lived in a four-room house. Their breakfast usually included meat or eggs, hotcakes, butter, cake, and coffee. The silk worker and the laborer, by contrast, ate bread and butter as the main portion of two of their three daily meals. Their yearly income fell far short of the $600 to $800 that was necessary for a family to survive in any comfort.

For workers without steady employment, rising real wages were meaningless. Workers, especially those who were unskilled, often found work only sporadically. When times were slow or conditions depressed, as they were between 1873 and 1879 and 1893 and 1897, employers, especially in small firms, laid off both skilled and unskilled workers and reduced wages. Even in a good year like 1890, one out of every five men outside agriculture had been unemployed at least a month. One-quarter lost four months or more.

Unemployment insurance did not exist, so workers had no cushion against losing their jobs. One woman grimly recalled, "If the factory shuts down without warning, as it did last year for six weeks, we have a growing expense with nothing to counterbalance." Older workers who had no social security or those who had accidents on the job but no disability insurance had severely reduced incomes. Occasionally, kindhearted employers offered assistance in hard times, but it was rarely enough. The Lawrence Manufacturing Company compensated one of its workers $50 for the loss of a hand and awarded another $66.71 for a severed arm.

Although nineteenth-century ideology pictured men as breadwinners, many working-class married men could not earn enough to support their families. A working-class family's standard of living thus often depended on its number of workers. Today, two-income families are common. But in the nineteenth century, married women did not usually take outside employment, although they contributed to family income by taking in sewing, laundry, and boarders. In 1890, only 3.3 percent of married women worked in the paid labor force.

The Family Economy

If married women did not work for pay outside their homes, their children did. The laborer whose annual earnings amounted to only $384 depended on his 13-year-old son, not his wife, to go out and earn an extra $196, critical to the family's welfare. Sending children into the labor market was an essential survival strategy for many working-class Americans. In 1880, one-fifth of the nation's children between ages 10 and 14 held jobs.

Child labor was closely linked to a father's income, which in turn depended on skill, ethnic background, and occupation. Immigrant families more frequently sent their young children out to work (and also had more children) than native-born families. Middle-class reformers who sentimentalized childhood disapproved of parents who put their children to work. As one investigator of working-class life reported, "Father never attended school, and thinks his children will have sufficient schooling before they reach their tenth year, thinks no advantage will be gained from longer attendance at school, so children will be put to work as soon as able." Reformers believed that such fathers condemned their children to future destitution by denying them education. Actually, sending children to work was a means of coping with the immediate threat of poverty, financing the education of one of the children, or paying off the mortgage.

Many more young people over age 14 were working for wages than was the case for children. Half of

IMAGE

Child Glass Factory Worker, 1911

Young Workers Children and young adults worked, although the pattern of employment differed based on gender, ethnic background, and economic circumstances. Here three boys enter the Hill Manufacturing Company in Lewiston, Maine. The boys' workday began at 5:30 A.M. How old would you estimate the different boys are? *(Library of Congress [LC-USZ62-91570])*

VIDEO

Women in the Work Place, 1904

all Philadelphia's students had quit school by that age. Daughters as well as sons were expected to take positions, although young women from immigrant families were more likely to work than young American women. As *Arthur's Home Magazine* for women pointed out, a girl's earnings would help "to relieve her hardworking father of the burden of her support, to supply home with comforts and refinements, to educate a younger brother." By 1900, nearly 20 percent of American women were in the labor force.

Employed women earned far less than men. An experienced female factory worker might be paid between $5 and $6 a week, whereas an unskilled male laborer could make about $8. Discrimination, present from women's earliest days in the workforce, persisted. Still, factory jobs were desirable because they often paid better than other kinds of work open to women.

By the 1890s, new forms of employment in office work, nursing, and clerking in department stores offered some young women attractive opportunities.

IMAGE

Women in the Work Place, Late 19th Century

In San Francisco, the number of clerical jobs doubled between 1852 and 1880. But most women faced limited employment options, and ethnic taboos and cultural traditions helped shape choices. About a quarter of working women secured factory jobs. Italian and Jewish women (whose cultural backgrounds virtually forbade their going into domestic service) clustered in the garment industry, and Poles and Slavs went into textiles, food processing, and meatpacking. In some industries, such as textiles and tobacco, women composed an important segment of the workforce. But about 40 percent of them, especially those from Irish, Scandinavian, and black families, took jobs as maids, cooks, laundresses, and nurses.

Domestic service was arduous, with few machines to lighten the labor. A Minneapolis housemaid described an exhausting routine. "I used to get up at four o'clock every morning and work till ten P.M. every day of the week. Mondays and Tuesdays, when the washing and ironing was to be done, I used to get up at two o'clock and wash or iron until breakfast time." Nor could domestics count on much sympathy from their employers. "Do not think it necessary to give a hired girl as good a room as that used by members of the family," said one lady of the house. "She should sleep near the kitchen and not go up the front stairs or through the front hall to reach her room." Live-in servants received room and board plus $2 to $5 a week. The fact that so many women took domestic work despite the job's disadvantages speaks clearly of their limited opportunities.

The dismal situation facing working women drove some, such as Rose Haggerty, into prostitution. Burdened with a widowed and sickly mother and four young brothers and sisters, Rose was only 14 years old when she started work at a New York

Number of Women Employed in Selected Industries, 1870–1910

This chart shows the growth of women workers in several key industries. Although far fewer women had paid jobs than men, they were never absent from the workplace.

Year	Industry					
	Chemical	Electrical	Paper	Printing	Food	Metal
1870	403	—	6,242	4,397	2,460	5,217
1880	862	—	14,126	9,322	4,503	7,668
1890	2,140	—	22,444	24,640	10,169	15,232
1900	3,427	—	27,261	32,938	19,713	21,335
1910	15,198	12,093	33,419	47,640	48,099	56,208

Source: U.S. Department of Labor, Women's Bureau, *Women's Occupations Through Seven Decades*, Bulletin no. 218 (Washington, D.C.: Government Printing Office, 1947), 95, 120, 121, 123, 130, 133.

DOCUMENT

Massachusetts Bureau of Statistics of Labor, *The Working Girls of Boston* (1884)

paper-bag factory. She earned $10 a month, with $6 going for rent. Her fortunes improved when a friend helped her buy a sewing machine. Rose then sewed shirts at home, often working as long as 14 hours a day, to support her family. Suddenly, the piecework rate for shirts was slashed in half. In desperation, Rose contemplated suicide. But when a sailor offered her money for spending the night with him, she realized she had an alternative. Prostitution meant food, rent, and heat for her family. "Let God Almighty judge who's to blame most," the 20-year-old Rose reflected, "I that was driven, or them that drove me to the pass I'm in."

Prostitution appears to have increased in the late nineteenth century, although there is no way of knowing the actual numbers of women involved. Probably most single women accepted the respectable jobs open to them. They tolerated discrimination and low wages because their families depended on their contributions. They also knew that when they married, they would probably leave the paid workforce forever.

Marriage hardly ended women's work, however. Like colonial families, late-nineteenth-century working-class families operated as cooperative economic units. The unpaid domestic labor of working-class wives was critical to family survival. With husbands away for 10 to 11 hours a day, women bore

Domestic Servants

Wearing their best clothes, these domestics pose for the camera. What do the women appear to be holding and why? In what room does the picture appear to have been taken? Although there is no way to ascertain the background of these young women, a majority of domestic servants were Irish or Irish American. Domestic work was often exhausting and provided little privacy or free time, but many women were attracted by the opportunity to live in a middle-class home and have regular meals. In addition, domestic work often paid better than factory work. Still, some young women avoided service, explaining that "it's freedom that we want when the day's work is done." *(Historical Society of Wisconsin, #WHi [V22] 1387)*

RECOVERING THE PAST

Congressional Hearings

Students of history can discover fascinating materials on nineteenth-century life by exploring the published records of the American political system. Privately published from 1833 to 1873, the *Congressional Globe* details the proceedings of the Senate and the House, revealing the nature of congressional deliberations in an era when debate, such as that over the Compromise of 1850 in the Senate, was the focus of the national political process. After 1873, the government published these proceedings in the *Congressional Record*. The *Record* is not a literal transcription of debate, for members can edit their remarks, insert speeches, and add supporting materials. Still, it gives a good sense of the proceedings of both the Senate and the House.

Much of the serious work of government, past and present, takes place in congressional committees. One foreign observer called Congress "not so much a legislative assembly as a huge panel from which committees are selected." The committee system is almost as old as the constitutional system itself and is rooted in the Constitution's granting of lawmaking power to Congress. From the start, Congress divided into assorted committees to gather information, enabling members to evaluate legislative proposals intelligently.

Two kinds of committees existed in the House and Senate. Standing committees had permanent responsibility for reviewing legislative proposals on a host of financial, judicial, foreign, and other affairs. By 1892, the Senate had 44 standing committees and the House had 50. Select committees were temporary, often charged with investigating specific problems. In the late nineteenth century, congressional committees investigated such problems as Ku Klux Klan terrorism, the sweatshop system, tenement house conditions, and relations between labor and capital. In each case, extensive hearings were held.

Congressional hearings have become increasingly important sources of historical evidence in recent years. They show the Senate and the House of Representatives in action as they seek to translate popular sentiment into law. But they also reveal public attitudes as they record the voices of Americans testifying in committee halls. Because one function of legislative hearings is to enable diverse groups to express their frustrations and desires, they often contain the testimony of witnesses drawn from many different social and economic backgrounds. Included here is the partial testimony of a Massachusetts laborer who appeared before the Senate Committee on Education and Labor in 1883. Because working-class witnesses like this man usually left no other record of their experiences or thoughts, committee reports and hearings provide valuable insight into the lives and attitudes of ordinary people.

Hearings also reveal the attitudes and social values of committee members. Hence, caution is needed in the use of hearings. Witnesses often have vested interests and are frequently coached and cautious in what they communicate on the stand. Rather than seeking to illuminate issues, committee members often speak and explore questions for other—usually political—reasons.

Despite these limitations, committee hearings are rich sources of information. In this excerpt, what can you learn about the life of the witness testifying before the committee? In what way do the values of the committee members conflict with those of the witness? Why is the chairman so harsh toward the witness? Is he entirely unsympathetic? Why do you think the questioner overemphasizes the relationship between moral beliefs and economic realities? What kind of social tensions does the passage reveal?

REFLECTING ON THE PAST Have you observed any recent hearings of congressional investigating committees on television? Are moral behavior and hunger still topics of concern for Americans? How is the interaction between modern "haves" and "have-nots" similar to and different from the interaction between this laborer and the committee members in 1883? Do ethical beliefs and economic realities still separate social classes?

Hearings on the Relations Between Labor and Capital

Q. You get a dollar a day, wages?—A. That is the average pay that men receive. The rents, especially in Somerville, are so high that it is almost impossible for the working men to live in a house.

Q. What rent do you pay?—A. For the last year I have been paying $10 a month, and most of the men out there have to pay about that amount for a house—$10 a month for rooms.

Q. For a full house, or for rooms only?—A. For rooms in a house.

Q. How many rooms?—A. Four or five.

Q. How much of your time have you been out of work, or idle, for the last full year, say?—A. I have not been out of work more than three weeks altogether, because I have been making a dollar or two peddling or doing something, when I was out of work, in the currying line.

Q. Making about the same that you made at your trade?—A. Well, I have made at my trade a little more than that, but that is the average.

Q. Are you a common drunkard?—A. No, sir.

Q. Do you smoke a great deal?—A. Well, yes, sir; I smoke as much as any man.

The CHAIRMAN. I want to know how much you have got together in the course of a year, and what you have spent your money for, so that folks can see whether you have had pay enough to get rich on.

The WITNESS. A good idea.

The CHAIRMAN. That is precisely the sort of idea that people ought to know. How much money do you think you have earned during this last year; has it averaged a dollar a day for three hundred days?

The WITNESS. I have averaged more than that; I have averaged $350 or $400. I will say, for the year.

Q. You pay $10 a month rent; that makes $120 a year?—A. Yes, sir.

The CHAIRMAN. I have asked you these questions in this abrupt way because I want to find out whether you have spent much for practices that might have been dispensed with. You say you smoke?

The WITNESS. Yes, sir.

Q. How much a week do you spend for that?—A. I get 20 cents worth of tobacco a week.

Q. That is $10.40 a year?—A. Yes, sir.

Q. And you say you are not a common drunkard?—A. No, sir.

Q. Do you imagine that you have spent as much more for any form of beer, or ale, or anything of that kind, that you could have got along without?—A. No, sir.

Q. How much do you think has gone in that way?—A. About $1 or $2.

Q. During the whole year?—A. Yes, sir.

Q. That would make $11.40 or $12.40—we will call it $12—gone for wickedness. Now, what else, besides your living, besides the support of your wife and children?—A. Well, I don't know as there is anything else.

Q. Can you not think of anything else that was wrong?—A. No, sir.

Q. Twelve dollars have gone for sin and iniquity; and $120 for rent; that makes $132?—A. Yes.

Q. How many children have you?—A. Two.

Q. Your family consists of yourself, your wife, and two children?—A. Yes.

Q. One hundred and thirty-two dollars from $400 leaves you $268, does it not?—A. Yes, sir.

Q. And with that amount you have furnished your family?—A. Yes, sir.

Q. You have been as economical as you could, I suppose?—A. Yes.

Q. How much money have you left?—A. Sixty dollars in debt.

Q. How did you do that?—A. I don't know, sir.

Q. Can you not think of something more that you have wasted?—A. No, sir.

Q. Have you been as careful as you could?—A. Yes, sir.

Q. And you have come out at the end of the year $60 in debt?—A. Yes, sir.

Q. Have you been extravagant in your family expenses?—A. No, sir; a man can't be very extravagant on that much money. . . .

Q. And there are four of you in the family?—A. Yes, sir.

Q. How many pounds of beefsteak have you had in your family, that you bought for your own home consumption within this year that we have been speaking of?—A. I don't think there has been five pounds of beefsteak.

Q. You have had a little pork steak?—A. We had a half a pound of pork steak yesterday; I don't know when we had any before.

Q. What other kinds of meat have you had within a year?—A. Well, we have had corn beef twice I think that I can remember this year—on Sunday, for dinner.

Q. Twice is all that you can remember within a year?—A. Yes—and some cabbage.

Q. What have you eaten?—A. Well, bread mostly, when we could get it; we sometimes couldn't make out to get that, and have had to go without a meal.

Q. Has there been any day in the year that you have had to go without anything to eat?—A. Yes, sir, several days.

Q. More than one day at a time?—A. No.

Q. How about the children and your wife—did they go without anything to eat too?—A. My wife went out this morning and went to a neighbor's and got a loaf of bread and fetched it home, and when she got home the children were crying for something to eat.

Q. Have the children had anything to eat to-day except that, do you think?—A. They had that loaf of bread—I don't know what they have had since then, if they have had anything.

Q. Did you leave any money at home?—A. No, sir.

Q. If that loaf is gone, is there anything in the house?—A. No, sir; unless my wife goes out and gets something; and I don't know who would mind the children while she goes out.

AMERICAN VOICES

Helen Campbell, Interview with a Domestic Servant

In the 1880s, a journalist, Helen Campbell, interviewed domestic servants as part of her investigation of "prisoners of poverty," women who had been unable to earn enough in industrial jobs to support themselves. The woman who speaks here had worked in a cotton mill and had accepted a position as a chambermaid in the household of one of the owners.

We were poor at home, and four of us worked in the mill, but I had a little room all my own, even if it didn't hold much. In that splendid big house the servants' room was over the kitchen,—hot and close in summer, and cold in winter, and four beds in it. We five had to live there together, with only two bureaus and a bit of a closet, and one washstand for all. There was no chance to keep clean or your things in nice order, or anything by yourself, and I gave up. Then I went into a little family, and tried general housework, and the mistress taught me a great deal, and was good and kind, only there the kitchen was a dark little place and, my room like it, and I hadn't an hour in anything that was pleasant and warm.

- *What does this young woman value?*

- *What are the differences and similarities between those whom the servant considers good and bad mistresses?*

- *Why does the servant stay in domestic service?*

the burden of child care and the domestic chores. Because working-class families could not afford labor-saving conveniences, housework was time-consuming and arduous. Without an icebox, a working-class woman spent part of each day shopping for food (more expensive in small quantities). Doing laundry entailed carrying water from outside pumps, heating it on the stove, washing the clothes, rinsing them with fresh water, and hanging them up to dry. Ironing was a hot and unpleasant job in small and stuffy quarters. Keeping an apartment or house clean when the atmosphere was grimy and unpaved roads were littered with refuse and horse dung was a challenge.

Home Washing Machine and Wringer, 1869

As managers of family resources, married women bore important responsibilities. What American families had once produced for themselves now had to be bought. It was up to the working-class wife to scour secondhand shops to find cheap clothes for her family. Domestic economies were vital to survival. "In summer and winter alike," one woman explained, "I must try to buy the food that will sustain us the greatest number of meals at the lowest price."

Women also supplemented family income by taking in work. Jewish and Italian women frequently did piecework and sewing at home. In the Northeast and the Midwest, between 10 and 40 percent of all working-class families kept boarders. Immigrant families in particular often made ends meet by taking single, young countrymen into their homes. Having borders meant providing meals and clean laundry, juggling different work schedules, and sacrificing privacy. But the advantages of extra income far outweighed the disadvantages for many working-class families.

Black women's working lives reflected the obstacles African Americans faced in late-nineteenth-century cities. Although only about 7 percent of married white women worked outside the home, African American women did so both before and after marriage. In southern cities in 1880, about three-quarters of single black women and one-third of married black women worked outside the home. Because industrial employers would not hire African American women, most of them had to work as domestics or laundresses. The high percentage of married black women in the labor force reflected the marginal wages their husbands earned. But it may also be explained in part by the lesson learned during slavery that children could thrive without the constant attention of their mothers.

CAPITAL VERSUS LABOR

Class conflict characterized late-nineteenth-century industrial life. Although workers welcomed the progress that factories made possible, many rejected their employers' values, which emphasized individual gain at the expense of collective good. While owners reaped most of the profits, workers were turning into wage slaves. Fashioning their arguments from their republican legacy,

The Protectors of Our Industry, 1883

workers claimed that the degradation of the country's citizen laborers threatened to undermine the republic itself.

On-the-Job Protests

Workers and employers engaged in a struggle over who would control the workplace. Many workers staunchly resisted unsatisfactory working conditions and the tendency of bosses to treat them "like any other piece of machinery, to be made to do the maximum amount of work with the minimum expenditure of fuel." Skilled workers, such as iron puddlers and glassblowers, had indispensable knowledge about the production process as well as practical experience and were in a key position to direct on-the-job actions. Sometimes they struggled to retain control over critical work decisions. Detroit printers, for example, tried to retain the right to distribute headlines and white space (the "fat") rather than letting their bosses hand out the fat as a special reward and means of increasing competition among workers. Others hoped to humanize work. Cigar makers clung to their custom of having one worker read to others as they performed their tedious chores.

Workers sought to control the pace of production. Too many goods meant an inhuman pace of work and might result in overproduction, massive layoffs, and a reduction in the prices paid for piecework. So an experienced worker might whisper to a new hand, "See here, young fellow, you're working too fast. You'll spoil our job for us if you don't go slower."

A newspaper account of a glassblowers' strike in 1884 illustrates the clash between capital and labor. With an eye toward bigger profits, the boss tried to increase output. "He knew if the limit was taken off, the men could work ten or twelve hours every day in the week; that in their thirst for the mighty dollar they would kill themselves with labor; they would 'black sheep' their fellows by doing the labor of two men." But his employees resisted his proposal, refusing to drive themselves to exhaustion for a few dollars more. "They thundered out no. They even offered to take a reduction that would average ten percent all around, but they said, 'We will keep the forty-eight box limit.' Threats and curses would not move them." For these workers, a decent pace of work and a respectable wage was more important than promises of extra money.

In attempting to protect themselves and the dignity of their labor, workers devised ways of combating employer attempts to speed up the production process. Denouncing fellow workers who refused to honor production codes as "hogs," "runners," "chasers," and "job wreckers," they ostracized and even injured them. As the banner of the Detroit Coopers' Union proudly proclaimed at a parade in 1880: "Each for himself is the bosses' plea / [but] Union for all will make you free."

Absenteeism, drunkenness at work, and general inefficiency were other widespread worker practices that contained elements of protest. In three industrial firms in the late nineteenth century, one-quarter of the workers stayed home at least one day a week. Some of these lost days were due to layoffs, but not all. The efforts of employers to impose stiff fines on absent workers suggested their frustration with uncooperative workers.

To a surprising extent, workers made the final protest by quitting their jobs altogether. Most employers responded by penalizing workers who left without giving sufficient notice—but to little avail. A Massachusetts labor study in 1878 found that although two-thirds of the workers surveyed had been in the same occupation for more than 10 years, only 15 percent of them were in the same job. A similar rate of turnover occurred in the industrial workforce in the early twentieth century. Workers unmistakably and clearly voted with their feet.

Strike Activity After 1876

The most direct and strenuous attempts to change conditions in the workplace came in the form of thousands of strikes punctuating the late nineteenth century. In 1877, railroad workers staged the first and most violent nationwide industrial strike of the nineteenth century. The immediate cause of the disturbance was the railroad owners' decision to reduce wages. But the rapid spread of the strike from Baltimore to Pittsburgh and then to cities as distant as San Francisco, Chicago, and Omaha, as well as the violence of the strikers, who destroyed railroad property and kept trains idle, indicated more fundamental discontent.

Organizing American Labor in the Late 19th Century

An erratic economy, high unemployment rates, and the lack of job security all contributed to the conflagration. More than 100 people died before federal troops ended the strike. The frenzied response of the propertied class, which saw the strike as the beginning of revolution and favored the intervention of the military, forecast the pattern of later conflicts. Time and time again, middle- and upper-class Americans would turn to the power of the state to crush labor activism.

Labor Unrest   This depiction of working-class unrest appeared in *Harper's Weekly* in 1894. Why does the artist give a prominent place to the National Guardsmen and the destruction wrought during the trouble? Contrast the individualized guardsmen with the faceless mob in the background and draw some general conclusions about the artist's choices and intent. *(The Granger Collection, New York)*

A wave of confrontations followed the strike of 1877. Between 1881 and 1905, a total of 36,757 strikes erupted, involving more than 6 million workers—three times the strike activity in France.

These numbers indicate that far more than the "poorest part" of the workers were involved. Many investigations of this era found evidence of widespread working-class discontent. When Samuel M. Hotchkiss, commissioner of the Connecticut Bureau of Labor Statistics, informally surveyed the state's workers in 1887, he was shocked by the "feeling of bitterness," the "distrust of employers," and the "discontent and unrest." These sentiments exploded into strikes, sabotage, and violence, most often linked to demands for higher wages and shorter hours.

Nineteenth-century strike activity underwent important changes, however, as the consciousness of American workers expanded. In the period of early industrialization, discontented laborers rioted in their neighborhoods rather than at their workplaces. Between 1845 and the Civil War, however, strikes at the workplace began to replace neighborhood riots. Although workers showed their anger against their employers by turning out and often calling for higher wages, they had only a murky sense that the strike could be a weapon to force employers to improve working conditions.

As industrialization transformed work and an increasing percentage of the workforce entered factories, collective actions at the workplace spread. Local and national unions played a more important role in organizing protest, conducting 60 percent of the strikes between 1881 and 1905. As working-class leaders realized more clearly the importance of collective action and perceived that transportation had knit the nation together, they worked to coordinate local and national efforts. By 1891, more than one-tenth of the strikes called by unionized workers were sympathy strikes. Coordination among strikers employed by different companies improved as workers made similar wage demands. Finally, pay among the most highly unionized workers became less of an issue. Workers sought more humane conditions. Some attempted to end subcontracting and the degradation of skills. Others, such as the glassblowers, struggled to enforce work rules. Indeed, by the early 1890s, more than one-fifth of strikes involved the rules governing the workplace.

Labor Organizing, 1865–1900

Civil War experience colored postwar labor organizing. As one working-class song pointed out, workers had borne the brunt of that struggle. "You gave your son to the war / The rich man loaned his gold / And the rich man's son is happy to-day, / And yours is under the mold." Workers who had fought to save the Union argued that wartime sacrifices justified efforts for justice and equality in the workplace.

Labor leaders quickly realized the need for national as well as local organizations to protect the laboring class against "despotic employers." In 1866, several craft unions and reform groups formed the National Labor Union (NLU). Claiming 300,000 members by the early 1870s, the organization supported a range of causes including temperance, women's rights, and the establishment of cooperatives to bring the "wealth of the land" into "the hands of those who produce it."

The call for an eight-hour day reveals some of the basic assumptions of the organized labor movement. Few workers saw employers as a hostile class or wanted to destroy the economic system. But they did believe bosses were often dangerous tyrants whose demands for their time threatened to turn citizens into slaves. The eight-hour day would curb the power of owners and allow workers the time to cultivate the qualities necessary for republican citizenship.

Many of the NLU's specific goals survived, although the organization did not. An unsuccessful attempt to create a political party and the depression of 1873 decimated the NLU. Survival and job searches took precedence over union causes.

The Knights of Labor and the AFL

As the depression wound down, a new mass organization, the Noble and Holy Order of the Knights of Labor, rose to prominence. Founded as a secret society in 1869, the order became public and national when Terence V. Powderly was elected Grand Master Workman in 1879. The Knights of Labor sought "to secure to the workers the full enjoyment of the wealth they create." Because the industrial system denied workers their fair share as producers, the Knights of Labor proposed a cooperative system of production paralleling the existing system. Cooperative efforts would provide workers with the economic independence necessary for citizenship, and an eight-hour day would allow them time for moral, intellectual, and political pursuits.

Terence Powderly at Knights of Labor Convention

The Knights of Labor was open to all American "producers," defined as all contributing members of society—skilled and unskilled, black and white, men and women, even merchants and manufacturers. Only the idle and the corrupt (gamblers, saloonkeepers, speculators, bankers, lawyers) were excluded.

Many shopkeepers joined, advertising themselves as a "friend of the workingman." This inclusive membership policy provided the organization with the potential power of great numbers. The organization grew in spurts, attracting miners between 1874 and 1879, skilled urban tradespeople between 1879 and 1885, and unskilled workers thereafter.

Women Delegates, National Meeting of Knights of Labor, 1886

Although Powderly frowned on strikes, the organization reaped the benefit of grassroots strike activity. Local struggles proliferated after 1883. In 1884, unorganized workers of the Union Pacific Railroad walked off the job when management announced a wage cut. Within two days, the company caved in, and the men joined the Knights. The next year, a successful strike against the Missouri Pacific Railroad brought in another wave of members. Then, in 1886, the Haymarket Riot in Chicago caused such a growth in labor militancy that in that single year the membership of the Knights of Labor ballooned from 100,000 to 700,000.

The "riot" at Haymarket was, in fact, a peaceful protest meeting connected with a lockout at the McCormick Reaper Works. When the Chicago police arrived to disperse the crowd, a bomb exploded. Seven policemen died. Although no one knows who planted the bomb, eight anarchists were tried and convicted. Three were executed, one committed suicide, and the others served prison terms.

George Engel, Address by a Condemned Haymarket Anarchist (1886)

Labor agitation and turbulence spilled over into politics. In 1884 and 1885, the Knights lobbied for a national contract labor law that would demand work contracts and state laws outlawing convict labor. The organization also pressed successfully for the creation of a federal Department of Labor. As new members poured in, however, direct political action became increasingly attractive. Despite many local successes, no national labor party emerged.

The Knights could not sustain momentum. Alarmed by the Haymarket Riot, employers determined to break the organization. A strike against Jay Gould's southwestern railroad system in 1886 collapsed. Consumer and producer cooperatives fizzled; the policy of accepting both black and white workers led to strife and discord in the South. The two major political parties co-opted labor politicians. Furthermore, national leaders of the organization also failed. Powderly could neither unify his diverse following nor control militants opposing him. By 1890, membership plummeted to 100,000, although the Knights continued to play a role well into the 1890s.

The American Federation of Labor (AFL), founded in 1886, became the nation's dominant union in the 1890s. The history of the Knights pointed up the problems of a national union that admitted all who worked for wages, but officially rejected strikes in favor of the ballot box and arbitration. The leader of the AFL, Samuel Gompers, had a different notion of effective worker organization. He was convinced that skilled workers should put their specific occupational interests first, so that they could control the supply of skilled labor and keep wages up.

Gompers organized the AFL as a federation of skilled trades—cigar makers, iron molders, iron-workers, carpenters, and others—each one autonomous, yet linked through an executive council to work together for prolabor national legislation and mutual support during boycott and strike actions. He repudiated dreams of a cooperative commonwealth or of ending the wage system, instead focusing on immediate "bread and butter" issues—higher wages, shorter hours, industrial safety, and the right to organize. Although Gompers rejected direct political action as a means of obtaining labor's goals, he believed in the value of the strike. A shrewd organizer, he knew from bitter experience the importance of dues high enough to sustain a strike fund through a long, tough fight.

Under Gompers's leadership, the AFL grew from 140,000 in 1886 to nearly 1 million by 1900. Although his notion of a labor organization was elitist, he steered his union through a series of crises, fending off challenges from socialists on his left and corporate opposition to strikes on his right. But there was no room in his organization for the unskilled or for blacks. The AFL did make a brief, halfhearted attempt to unionize women in 1892, but men resented women as coworkers and preferred them to stay in the home. The AFL agreed. In 1900, the International Ladies' Garment Workers Union (ILGWU) was established. Although women were its backbone, men dominated the leadership.

Working-Class Setbacks

Despite the growth of working-class organizations, workers lost many battles. Some of the more spectacular clashes reveal why working-class activism often failed and why so many workers lived precariously.

In 1892, silver miners in Coeur d'Alene, Idaho, struck when their employers installed machine drills in the mines, reduced skilled workers to shovelmen, and cut wages. The owners, supported by state militiamen and the federal government, successfully broke the strike by using scabs, but not without fighting. Several hundred union men were eventually tried and found guilty of a wide variety of charges. Out of the defeat emerged the Western Federation of Miners (WFM), whose chief goal was an eight-hour law for miners.

The Coeur d'Alene struggle set the pattern for many subsequent strikes. Mine owners fought strikes by shutting off credit to union men, hiring strikebreakers and armed guards, and infiltrating unions with spies. Violence was frequent, usually ending with the arrival of state militia, arrests or intimidation, legal action, and blacklisting. Despite this, the WFM won as many strikes as it lost.

The Homestead and Pullman Strikes of 1892 and 1894

Labor's worst setback came in 1892 at the Homestead steel mills near Pittsburgh. Carnegie had purchased the Homestead plant and put Henry Clay Frick in charge. Together, they wanted to break the union that threatened to extend its organization of the steel industry. After three months of stalemated negotiations over a new wage contract, Frick issued an ultimatum. Workers must accept wage cuts or be replaced. Frick barricaded the entire plant and hired 300 armed Pinkerton guards. As they arrived on July 6, they and armed steelworkers fought a daylong gun battle. Several men on both sides were killed, and the Pinkertons retreated. Then, at Frick's request, the governor of Pennsylvania sent 8,000 troops to crush the strike and the union. Two and a half weeks later, a New York anarchist tried to assassinate Frick.

The Homestead strike dramatized the lengths to which both labor and capital would go. Eugene Debs, for many years an ardent organizer of railroad workers, wrote, "If the year 1892 taught the workingmen any lesson worthy of heed, it was that the capitalist class, like a devilfish, had grasped them with its tentacles and was dragging them down to fathomless depths of degradation."

Homestead Strikers Surrendering

Debs saw 1893 as the year in which organized labor would "escape the prehensile clutch of these monsters." Instead, 1893 brought a serious depression and more setbacks for labor. Undaunted, Debs combined several of the separate railroad brotherhoods into a united American Railway Union (ARU). Within a year, more than 150,000 railroadmen joined the ARU, and Debs won a strike against the Great Northern Railroad, which had attempted to slash wages.

Debs faced his toughest crisis at the Pullman Palace Car Company in Chicago. The company maintained a model company town near Chicago—naturally, called Pullman—where management controlled all aspects of workers' lives. Late in 1893, as the depression worsened, the Pullman Company cut wages by one-third and laid off many workers, without reducing rents or prices in its stores. Forced to pay in rent what they could not earn in wages, working families struggled through the winter. Those working experienced speedups, threats, and further wage cuts. Desperate Pullman workers joined the ARU in the spring of 1894 and struck.

In late June, after Pullman refused to submit the dispute to arbitration, Debs led the ARU into a sympathy strike in support of the striking Pullman workers. Remembering the ill-fated railroad strike of 1877, Debs advised his lieutenants to "use no violence" and "stop no trains." Rather, he sought to boycott trains handling Pullman cars throughout the West. As the boycott spread, the General Managers Association (GMA), which ran the 24 railroads centered in Chicago, came to Pullman's support. Hiring 2,500 strikebreakers, the GMA appealed to the state and federal governments for military and judicial support in stopping the strike.

Governor Richard Altgeld of Illinois, sympathizing with the workers and believing that local law enforcement was sufficient, opposed using federal troops. But U.S. attorney general Richard Olney, a former railroad lawyer, obtained a court injunction on July 2 to end the strike as a "conspiracy in restraint of trade." Two days later, President Cleveland ordered federal troops to crush the strikers. Violence escalated rapidly. Local and federal officials hired armed guards, and the railroads paid them to help the troops. Within two days, strikers and guards were fighting bitterly. As troops poured into Chicago, the violence worsened, leaving scores of workers dead.

Debs's resources would run out unless he could enlist wider labor support. "We must all stand together or go down in hopeless defeat," he warned other unions. When Gompers refused support, the strike collapsed. Debs and several other leaders were found guilty of contempt of court. Hitherto a lifelong Democrat, Debs became a staunch socialist. His arrest and the defeat of the Pullman strike killed the American Railway Union. In 1895, in *In re Debs*, the Supreme Court upheld the legality of using an injunction to stop a strike, giving management a powerful weapon against unions. Most unions survived the difficult days of the 1890s, but the labor movement emerged as a distinct underdog in its conflicts with organized capital.

Although in smaller communities strikes against outside owners might win local middle-class support, most labor conflicts encountered the widespread

Chinatown This 1898 photograph shows a crowded street in San Francisco's Chinatown. Violent outbreaks against Chinese immigrants must have made some of them wary of leaving Chinatown. What does this picture suggest about the character of Chinese immigration to the United States? *(Library of Congress [LC-USZ62-41901])*

Lee Chew Protests the Treatment of the Chinese in the United States

Lee Chew came from China to the United States when he was 20. He worked as a household servant, laundry operator, miner, and railroad laborer. He ended up in New York, opening a store in Chinatown.

The treatment of the Chinese in this country is all wrong and mean. It is persisted in merely because China is not a fighting nation. The Americans would not dare to treat Germans, English, Italians or even Japanese as they treat the Chinese, because if they did there would be a war.

There is no reason for the prejudice against the Chinese. . . . The trouble is that the Chinese are such excellent and faithful workers that bosses will have no others when they can get them. . . . It was the jealousy of laboring men of other nationalities—especially the Irish—that raised all the outcry against the Chinese. No one would hire an Irishman, German, Englishman or Italian when he could get a Chinese because our countrymen are so much more honest, industrious, steady, sober, and painstaking.

- *What insights does this passage provide about the Chinese experience in the United States?*

- *What strains among immigrants are suggested?*

Source: Hamilton Holt, ed., *The Life Stories of Undistinguished Americans as Told by Themselves* (New York: Routledge, 2000), 184.

---

middle- and upper-class conviction that unions were un-American. Many people claimed to accept the idea of worker organizations, but would not concede that unions should participate in making economic or work decisions. Most employers violently resisted union demands as infringements of their right to manage their business. The sharp competition of the late nineteenth century, combined with a pattern of falling prices, stiffened employers' resistance to workers' demands. State and local governments and the courts frequently supported them.

The severe depressions of the 1870s and 1890s further undermined working-class activism. Workers could not focus on union issues when survival itself was in question. Many unions collapsed during hard times.

A fundamental problem was the reluctance of most workers to organize even in favorable times. In 1870, less than one-tenth of the industrial workforce belonged to unions, about the same as on the eve of the Civil War. Thirty years later, despite the expansion of the workforce, only 8.4 percent (mostly skilled workers) were union members. Why were workers so slow to join unions? Certainly, diverse work settings and ethnic differences made it difficult for workers to recognize common bonds. Many unskilled workers sensed that labor "aristocrats" did not have their interests at heart. Moreover, many native-born American workers still clung to the tradition of individualism or dreamed of entering the middle class.

An Irish woman highlighted another important point. "There should be a law . . . to give a job to every decent man that's out of work," she declared, "and another law to keep all them I-talians from comin' in and takin' the bread out of the mouths of honest people." Ethnic and religious diversity complicated forging a common front. Many foreigners, planning to return to their homeland, had limited interest in changing conditions in the United States—and because their goal was to work, they took jobs as scabs. Much of the violence that accompanied working-class actions erupted when owners brought in strikebreakers. Some Americans blamed immigrants for both low wages and failed worker actions.

Tension within laboring ranks appeared most dramatically in the anti-Chinese campaign of the 1870s and 1880s as white workers in the West began to blame the Chinese for economic hardships. A meeting of San Francisco workers in 1877 in favor of the eight-hour day exploded into a rampage against the Chinese. In following years, angry mobs killed Chinese workers in Tacoma, Seattle, Denver, and Rock Springs, Wyoming. Local hostility was expressed at the national level when, in 1882, Congress passed the Chinese Exclusion Act with the support of the Knights of Labor, prohibiting the immigration of Chinese workers for a 10-year period. It was extended in 1892 and made permanent in 1902.

DOCUMENT

Chinese Exclusion Act (1882)

Yet many immigrants, especially skilled ones, supported unions and cooperated with native-born Americans. Often ethnic bonds tied members to one another and to the community. For example, in the 1860s and 1870s, as the Molders' Union in Troy, New York, battled with manufacturers, its Irish membership won sympathy and support from the Irish-dominated police force, the Roman Catholic Church, fraternal orders, and public officials.

The importance of workers' organizations lay not so much in their successful struggles and protests as in the implicit criticism they offered of American society. Using the language of republicanism, many workers lashed out at an economic order that robbed them of their dignity and humanity. As producers of wealth, they protested that so little of it was theirs. As members of the working class, they rejected the middle-class belief in individualism and social mobility.

The Balance Sheet

Except for skilled workers, most laboring people found it impossible to earn much of a share in the material bounty that industrialization created. Newly arrived immigrants especially suffered from low pay and economic uncertainty. Long hours on the job and the necessity of walking to and from work left workers with little free time. Family budgets could include, at best, only small amounts for recreation. Even a ticket to a baseball game was a luxury.

Yet this view of the harshness of working-class life partly grows out of our own standards of what is acceptable today. Because so few working-class men or women recorded their thoughts and reactions, it is hard to know just what they expected or how they viewed their experiences. But culture and background influenced their perspectives. The family tenement, one Polish immigrant remarked, "seemed quite advanced when compared with our home" in Poland. A Lithuanian agreed. "Even though the toilet was in the hall, and the whole floor used it, yet it was a toilet. There was no such thing in Lithuania." A 10-hour job in the steel mill might be an improvement over dawn-to-dusk farmwork that brought no wages.

Studies of several cities show that nineteenth-century workers achieved some occupational mobility. One worker in five in Los Angeles and Atlanta during the 1890s, for example, managed to climb into the middle class. Most immigrant workers were stuck in ill-paid, insecure jobs, but their children ended up doing better. The son of an unskilled laborer might move on to become a semiskilled or skilled worker as new immigrants took the jobs at the bottom. Second-generation Irish made progress, especially in the West and the Midwest.

Even in Boston, 40 percent of the children of Irish immigrants obtained white-collar jobs.

Mobility, like occupation, was related to background. Native-born whites, Jews, and Germans rose more swiftly and fell less often than Irish, Italians, or Poles. Cultural attitudes, family size, education, and group leadership all contributed to different ethnic mobility patterns. Jews, for example, valued education and sacrificed to keep children in school. By 1915, Jews represented 85 percent of the free City College student body in New York City, 20 percent of New York University's student body, and one-sixth of those studying at Columbia University. With an education, they moved upward. The Slavs, however, who valued a steady income over mobility and education, took their children out of school and sent them to work at an early age. They believed that this course of action not only helped the family but gave the child a head start in securing reliable, stable employment. The southern Italian proverb "Do not make your child better than you are" suggests the value Italians placed on family rather than individual success. Differing attitudes and values led to different aspirations and career patterns.

Two groups enjoyed little mobility: African Americans and Hispanic Americans. African Americans were largely excluded from the industrial occupational structure and were restricted to unskilled jobs. Unlike immigrant industrial workers, they did not have the opportunity to move to better jobs as new, unskilled workers took the positions at the bottom. A study in Los Angeles suggests that Hispanic residents made minimal gains. Their experiences elsewhere may have been much the same.

Although immigrants' occupational mobility was limited, other kinds of rewards often compensated for the lack of success at the workplace. Home ownership for groups such as the Irish, who in their homeland had rarely owned their own homes, was an achievement that also could bring in extra income from boarders and provide some cushion against the uncertainties of industrial life and old age. Adept politicians, the Irish came to dominate big-city government in the late nineteenth century, filling many city jobs, particularly in the police force. The Irish were also successful in the construction industry and dominated the hierarchy of the Catholic church. Irish who did not share this upward mobility could nevertheless benefit from ethnic connections and take pride in their group's achievements.

Likewise, participation in social clubs and fraternal orders compensated in part for lack of advancement at work. Ethnic associations, parades, and holidays provided a sense of identity and security that offset the limitations of the job world.

Moreover, a few rags-to-riches stories always encouraged those who struggled. For example, the family of John Kearney in Poughkeepsie, New York, achieved modest success. After 20 years as a laborer, John started his own business as a junk dealer and even bought a simple house. His sons started off in better jobs than their father. One became a grocery store clerk and then later a baker, a policeman, and, finally, at age 40, an inspector at the waterworks. Another was an iron molder, and the third son was a post office worker and eventually the superintendent of city streets. If this success paled next to that of industrial giants such as Andrew Carnegie and John D. Rockefeller, it was still enough to keep the American dream alive.

TIMELINE

1843–1884	"Old immigration"
1844	Telegraph invented
1850s	Steam power widely used in manufacturing
1859	Value of U.S. industrial production exceeds value of agricultural production
1866	National Labor Union founded
1869	Transcontinental railroad completed
Knights of Labor organized
1870	Standard Oil of Ohio formed
1870s–1880s	Consolidation of continental railroad network
1873	Bethlehem Steel begins using Bessemer process
1873–1879	Depression
1876	Alexander G. Bell invents telephone
Thomas Edison establishes his "invention factory" at Menlo Park, New Jersey
1877	Railroad workers hold first nationwide industrial strike

1879	Thomas Edison invents incandescent light
1882	Chinese Exclusion Act
1885–1914	"New immigration"
1886	American Federation of Labor founded
Haymarket Riot in Chicago
1887	Interstate Commerce Act
1890	Sherman Anti-Trust Act
1892	Standard Oil of New Jersey formed
Coeur d'Alene strike
Homestead steelworkers strike
1893	Chicago World's Fair
1893–1897	Depression
1894	Pullman railroad workers strike
1900	International Ladies' Garment Workers Union founded
Corporations responsible for two-thirds of U.S. manufacturing

Conclusion

The Complexity of Industrial Capitalism

The rapid growth of the late nineteenth century made the United States one of the world's industrial giants. Many factors contributed to the "wonderful accomplishments" of the age. They ranged from sympathetic government policies to the rise of big business and the emergence of a cheap industrial workforce. But it was also a turbulent period. Many Americans benefited only marginally from the new wealth. Some of them protested by joining unions, walking out on strike, or initiating on-the-job actions. Most lived their lives more quietly and never had the opportunity that Thomas O'Donnell did of telling their story to others. But middle-class Americans began to wonder about the O'Donnells of the country. It is to their concerns, worries, and aspirations that we now turn.

Recommended Readings

Recommended Readings are posted on the Web site for this textbook. Visit www.ablongman.com/nash

Fiction and Film

In *Sister Carrie* (1900), Theodore Dreiser tells the story of a young rural woman who comes to Chicago and violates its social norms to acquire some of the city's offerings. Stephen Crane's novel *Maggie: A Girl of the Streets* (1893) gives a grim picture of life in the urban slums. Thomas Bell follows several generations of the same immigrant family whose American life is entwined with steel in *Out of This Furnace* (1976 ed.). *The Richest Man in the World: Andrew Carnegie*, a 1997 film made for PBS, analyzes the personal and professional life of Carnegie and makes good use of interviews with business and labor historians. It offers extended treatment of the Homestead strike, for which the film holds Carnegie largely responsible. *The Age of Innocence*, which takes place in 1870s New York, offers a splendid picture of the sumptuous lives of the rich and the norms and values to which they were supposed to adhere. This 1993 Martin Scorsese film is based on the novel of the same name by Edith Wharton.

Questions for Review and Reflection

1. What explains the United States' rise to industrial and economic prominence in the late nineteenth century?

2. In what ways did American cities change in this period?

3. Explain which groups were able to realize the American dream of success and which were not and why.

4. Compare and contrast the experiences of middle-class and working-class women.

5. What factors undermined the working-class efforts at collective action and which promoted them? In your opinion, which were the most important factors underlying the failures of the working class?

Discovering U.S. History Online

Andrew Carnegie

www.pbs.org/wgbh/pages/amex/carnegie/

The online companion to the PBS film *The Richest Man in the World: Andrew Carnegie*, this Web site provides an outline of the film, a biography, a photo gallery, and information about the Homestead strike.

The Rockefellers

www.pbs.org/wgbh/amex/rockefellers/index.html

Companion to the PBS film of the same title, the site presents audio clips from historians, illustrated essays, maps, and images about this famous industrialist family.

John D. Rockefeller and the Standard Oil Company

www.micheloud.com/FXM/SC

This study, with accompanying images, tells of the rise of Rockefeller's mammoth company.

Enarco

www.enarco.com/home.htm

This positive history of the company reflects the industrial changes of late-nineteenth-century America.

Angel Island: The Pacific Gateway

www.internationalchannel.com/education/angelisland

Angel Island was the principal gateway for Chinese immigrants. This site documents and illustrates the experiences of these immigrants as they entered the United States.

The Great Chicago Fire

www.chicagohs.org/fire/index.html

This site examines the Chicago fire from contemporary accounts and photographs as well as from personal artifacts and memories. Since Chicago was emblematic of the urban industrialization of the country, the story of its great fire and reconstruction provide a window on the nature of cities of this era.

Lower East Side Tenement Museum

www.thirteen.org/tenement/index.html

The goal of this museum is "to preserve and interpret the history of the immigrant experience on the Lower East Side." This site presents digital exhibits from the museum.

Ellis Island

www.ellisisland.com/indexHistory.html

This official museum site presents a timeline and an overview of the Ellis Island immigration experience.

Nineteenth-Century American Children and What They Read

www.merrycoz.org/kids.htm

The author of this site presents text and author information from several nineteenth-century contemporary children's books and magazines, giving an insight to the culture of the times.

Jane Addams

www.hullhouse.org/website

This site presents a biography of Jane Addams as well as the history of the association as "the direct descendent of the settlement house founded by Jane Addams in 1889."

Anarchism

www.Pitzer.edu/~dward/Anarchist_Archives/archivehome.html

This site offers classic anarchist texts, including information and graphics for the Haymarket Riot.

Haymarket

www.chicagohistory.org/dramas

This illustrated site, drawing extensively from the "Haymarket Affair Digital Collection," thoroughly examines the Haymarket bombing in seven sections: a Prologue, five "Acts," and the Epilogue. The material examines the national as well as the local political context of the incident.

American Labor History

www.geocities.com/CollegePark/Quad/6460/AmLabHist/

This site provides a general chronological survey of the history of labor in America. The author also has included with each section an extensive list of Internet references on labor history.

The Samuel Gompers Papers: A Documentary History of the American Working Class

www.inform.umd.edu/EdRes/Colleges/ARHU/Depts/History/Gompers/web1.html

This site includes information about the papers project and also has a photo gallery, selected documents, and a brief history of the first president of the American Federation of Labor (AFL).

The Strike at Homestead, 1892

www.history.ohio-state.edu/projects/HomesteadStrike1892/

Drawing from contemporary sources, this site provides an overview of the town and the strike. A photographic essay is also included.

CHAPTER 19

Politics and Reform

Although this 1892 painting by John Klir shows the outcome of a "Lost Bet" in the election that year, note the ethnic, racial, and class diversity of the street crowds, momentarily united in the enjoyment of watching the humiliated loser pulling his victorious opponent (and a wagon full of American flags). What kind of diversity do you see in the painting? Will a more diverse America hold together? *(Library of Congress [LC-USZC4-2113])*

American Stories

A Utopian Novelist Warns of Two Americas

At the start of his best-seller *Looking Backward* (1888), Edward Bellamy likened the American society of his day to a huge stagecoach. Dragging the coach along sandy roads and over steep hills were the "masses of humanity." While they strained desperately "under the pitiless lashing of hunger" to pull the coach, at the top sat the favored

624

few, riding in breezy comfort but still fearful that they might fall from their seats and have to pull the coach themselves.

Bellamy's famous coach allegory began a utopian novel in which the class divisions and pitiless competition of the nineteenth century were replaced by a classless, caring, cooperative new society. Economic anxieties and hardships were supplanted by satisfying labor and leisure. In place of the coach, all citizens in the year 2000 walked together and shopped in equal comfort and security under a huge umbrella (not unlike modern malls) over the sidewalks of the city.

The novel opens in 1887. The hero, a wealthy Bostonian, falls asleep worrying about the effect local labor struggles might have on his upcoming wedding. When he wakes up, it is the year 2000. Utopia has been achieved peacefully through the development of one gigantic trust, owned and operated by the national government. All citizens between ages 21 and 45 work in an industrial army with equalized pay and work difficulty. Retirement after 45 is devoted to hobbies, reading, culture, and the minimal leadership necessary in a society without crime, corruption, poverty, or war.

DOCUMENT

Edward Bellamy, *Looking Backward* (1888)

Bellamy's book was popular with educated middle-class Americans, who were attracted by his vision of a society in which humans were both morally good and materially well off—and in which core values of the 1880s survived intact, including individual taste and incentive, private property, and rags-to-riches presidents. He filled the novel with futuristic technological wonders, such as television and credit cards, a double-dream surprise ending, and a love story. Bellamy's treatment of the role of women reflected his era's struggle with changing gender. Women in 2000 were relieved of housework by labor-saving gadgets, married for love, and worked in the industrial army, albeit in "lighter occupations." They did not participate in government, and their primary role was still to supervise domestic affairs, nurture the young, and beautify culture.

Like most middle-class Americans of his day, Bellamy disapproved of European socialism. Although some features of his utopia were socialistic, he and his admirers called his system "nationalism." This appealed to a new generation of Americans who had put aside Civil War antagonisms to embrace the greatness of a growing, if now economically divided, nation. In the early 1890s, with Americans buying nearly 10,000 copies of *Looking Backward* every week, more than 160 Nationalist clubs were formed to crusade for the adoption of Bellamy's ideas.

The inequalities of wealth described in Bellamy's coach scene reflected a political life in which many participated but only a few benefited. The wealthiest 10 percent, who rode high on the coach, dominated national politics, while untutored bosses held sway in governing cities. Except for token expressions of support, national political leaders ignored the cries of factory workers, immigrants, farmers, African Americans, Native Americans, and other victims of the vast transformation of American industrial, urban, and agrarian life in the late nineteenth century. But as the century closed, middle-class Americans like Bellamy, as well as labor, agrarian, and ethnic leaders themselves, proposed various reforms. Their concern was never more appropriate than during the depression of the mid-1890s, a real-life social upheaval that mirrored the worst features and fears of Bellamy's fictional coach.

In this chapter, we will examine American politics at the national and local level from the end of Reconstruction to the 1890s, a period that in the United States as well as in Europe bolstered the rich and neglected the corrosive human problems of urban industrial life. Then we will look at the growing social and political involvement of educated middle-class reformers who, despite their distaste for mass politics, were inspired by a religious social gospel to work for social change both locally and nationally. We will conclude with an account of the pivotal importance of the 1890s, highlighted by the Populist revolt, the depression of 1893–1897, and the election of 1896. In an age of strong national identity and pride, the events of the 1890s shook many comfortable citizens out of their apathy and began the reshaping of American politics.

POLITICS IN THE GILDED AGE

Mark Twain,
The Gilded Age
(1873)

Co-authoring a satirical book in 1873, Mark Twain coined the expression "Gilded Age" to describe Grant's corrupt presidency. The phrase, with its suggestion of shallow glitter, characterized social and political life in the last quarter of the nineteenth century. Although politics was marred by corruption, and politicians avoided fundamental issues in favor of a politics of mass entertainment—pomp, parades, pennants, and penny beer—voter participation in national elections between 1876 and 1896 hovered at an all-time high of 73 to 82 percent of all registered voters.

Behind the glitter, two gradual changes occurred that would greatly affect twentieth-century politics. First was the development of a professional bureaucracy of elite specialists in congressional committees and executive offices. These experts emerged as a counterfoil to the perceived dangers of majority rule represented by high voter participation, especially by new immigrants, "millions of newcomers alien to our traditions," according to New England poet James Russell Lowell. Second, after a period of close elections and Republican–Democratic party stalemate, new issues, concerns, and parties fostered a political realignment in the 1890s.

Politics, Parties, Patronage, and Presidents

American government in the 1870s and 1880s clearly supported the interests of riders atop Bellamy's coach. Few nineteenth-century Americans would have agreed that the national government should tackle problems of poverty, unemployment, and trusts. They mistrusted organized power and believed that all would benefit from an economic life free of government interference. After the traumas of the Civil War era, when a strong centralized state pursued high moral causes, political leaders of the late nineteenth century favored a period of government passivity, permitting the free pursuit of industrial expansion and wealth. As Republican leader Roscoe Conkling explained, the role of government was "to clear the way of impediments and dangers, and leave every class and every individual free and safe in the exertions and pursuits of life."

The Gilded Age, Henry Adams observed, was the most "thoroughly ordinary" period ever in American politics. "One might search the whole list of Congress, Judiciary, and Executive during the twenty-five years 1870–95 and find little but damaged reputation." Few eras of American government were so corrupt, and Adams was especially sensitive to the low quality of democratic politics compared to the exalted morality of his grandfather John Quincy Adams and great-grandfather John Adams.

During the weak presidencies of Andrew Johnson and Ulysses Grant, Congress emerged as the dominant branch of government with power centered in the committee system. Senators James G. Blaine (R-Maine) and Roscoe Conkling (R-New York) typified the moral quality of legislative leadership. Despite lying about having been paid off by favors to railroads, Blaine was probably the most popular Republican politician of the era. Charming, intelligent, witty, and able, he served twice as secretary of state and was a serious contender for the presidency in every election from 1876 to 1892. Conkling dispensed lucrative jobs at the New York customhouse and spent most of his career rewarding the party faithful with government jobs. In more than two decades in Congress, he never drafted a bill.

Legislation was not Congress's primary purpose. In 1879, a disgusted student of legislative politics, Woodrow Wilson, wrote: "No leaders, no principles; no principles, no parties." A British observer, Lord Bryce, concluded that the most cohesive force in American politics was not principle but patronage: the "desire for office and for office as a means of gain." The two parties, like two bottles of liquor, Bryce said, bore different labels, yet "each was empty."

Yet these characterizations were not entirely accurate. There were differences, as party professionals solidified their popular base to achieve political ends. Party affiliation, as today, generally reflected not just economic but also cultural, social, and religious questions. Republican votes came from northeastern Yankee industrial interests along with New England and

Keep the Ball
Rolling, 1888

Scandinavian Lutheran farming migrants across the Upper Midwest. Democrats depended on southern whites, northern workers, and urban immigrants. Because the Republican party had proved its willingness in the past to mobilize the power of the state to reshape society, people who wanted to regulate moral as well as economic power were attracted to it. White southerners and Irish and German Catholics preferred the Democratic party because it opposed government efforts to regulate morals. Said one Chicago Democrat, "A Republican is a man who wants you t' go t' church every Sunday. A Democrat says if a man wants t' have a glass of beer on Sunday he can have it."

For a few years, Civil War and Reconstruction issues generated party differences. But after 1876, the two parties were evenly matched, and they avoided controversial stands on national issues. In three of the five presidential elections between 1876 and 1892, a mere 1 percent of the vote separated the two major candidates. In 1880, James Garfield won by only 7,018 votes; in 1884, Grover Cleveland squeaked past Blaine by a popular-vote margin of 48.5 to 48.2 percent. In two elections (1876 and 1888), the electoral-vote winner had fewer popular votes. Further evidence of political stalemate was that only twice, each time for only

two years, did one party control the White House and both houses of Congress. Although all the presidents in the era except Cleveland were Republicans, the Democrats controlled the House of Representatives in 8 of the 10 sessions of Congress between 1875 and 1895.

Gilded Age presidents were undistinguished and, like Washington, D.C., itself, played a minor role in national life. None of them—Hayes (1877–1881), Garfield (1881), Chester A. Arthur (1881–1885), Cleveland (1885–1889 and 1893–1897), and Benjamin Harrison (1889–1893)—served two consecutive terms. None was strongly identified with any particular issue. None has been highly regarded by historians. Garfield is remembered primarily for being shot by a disappointed office seeker and by hanging on for two and a half months before he died. The only Democrat in the group, Cleveland, differed little from the Republicans. Upon his election in 1884, financier Jay Gould sent him a telegram stating that "the vast business interests of the country will be entirely safe in your hands." When Cleveland violated the expectation that presidents should not initiate ideas by devoting his annual message in 1887 to calling for a lower tariff, Congress did nothing. Voters turned him out of office a year later.

Grover Cleveland

Presidential Elections, 1872–1892

A British observer of American politics, James Bryce, said in 1888 that "the American usually votes with his party, right or wrong, and the fact that there is little distinction of view between the parties makes it easier to stick to your old friends." To what extent does this chart show that American voters stuck to their party? How close were the elections? What was the usual percent difference? In which two elections did the popular-vote winner, as in 2000, lose the election? Are parties today more like or unlike those from the late nineteenth century?

Year	Candidate	Party	Popular Vote	Electoral Vote
1872	ULYSSES S. GRANT	Republican	3,596,745 (56%)	286
	Horace Greeley*	Democrat	2,843,446 (44%)	0*
1876	Samuel J. Tilden	Democrat	4,284,020 (51%)	184
	RUTHERFORD B. HAYES	Republican	4,036,572 (48%)	185
1880	JAMES A. GARFIELD	Republican	4,449,053 (48.5%)	214
	Winfield S. Hancock	Democrat	4,442,035 (48.1%)	155
	James B. Weaver	Greenback-Labor	308,578	0
1884	GROVER CLEVELAND	Democrat	4,911,017 (48.5%)	219
	James G. Blaine	Republican	4,848,334 (48.2%)	182
	Minor parties		325,739 (03.3%)	0
1888	Grover Cleveland	Democrat	5,540,050 (48.6%)	168
	BENJAMIN HARRISON	Republican	5,444,337 (47.9%)	233
	Minor parties		396,441 (03.5%)	0
1892	GROVER CLEVELAND	Democrat	5,554,414 (46%)	277
	Benjamin Harrison	Republican	5,190,802 (43%)	145
	James B. Weaver	Populist	1,027,329 (9%)	22

*Greeley died before the Electoral College met.

Note: Winners' names are in capital letters.

National Issues

Four issues were important at the national level in the Gilded Age: the tariff, currency, civil service, and government regulation of railroads. In confronting these issues, legislators tried to serve both their own self-interest and the national interest of an efficient, productive, growing economy.

The tariff was one issue in which party, as well as regional attitudes toward the use of government power, made some difference. Republicans wanted government to support business interests and stood for a high tariff to protect businesspeople, wage earners, and farmers from foreign competition. Democrats demanded a low tariff because "the government is best which governs least." But politicians accommodated local interests when it came to tariffs. Democratic senator Daniel Vorhees of Indiana explained, "I am a protectionist for every interest which I am sent here by my constituents to protect."

Tariff revisions were bewilderingly complex as legislators catered to many special interests that one senator described as "not far from disgusting." Most tariffs included a jumble of higher and lower rates that defied understanding. The federal government depended on tariffs and excise taxes (primarily on tobacco and liquor) for most of its revenue, so there was little chance that the tariff would be abolished or substantially lowered. Surpluses produced by the tariff during the Gilded Age helped the parties finance patronage jobs and government programs.

The currency question was even more complicated. During the Civil War, the federal government had circulated paper money (greenbacks) that could not be exchanged for gold or silver (specie). In the late 1860s and 1870s, politicians debated whether the United States should return to a metallic standard, which would allow paper money to be exchanged for specie. "Hard-money" advocates supported either withdrawing all paper money from circulation or making it convertible to specie. They opposed increasing the volume of money, fearing inflation. "Soft money" Greenbackers argued that there was not enough currency in circulation for an expanding economy and urged increasing the supply of paper money in order to raise farm prices and cut interest rates.

Hard-money interests had more clout. In 1873, Congress demonetized silver. In 1875, it passed the

Political Advertisements of the 1880s Although the tariff protectionist Harrison defeated Cleveland in 1888 (the results were reversed in 1892), all Gilded Age presidents were essentially "preservers" rather than innovators. None had approached the greatness of Washington, Lincoln, and the other presidents hovering over Harrison and Morton in this illustration. In a second image from 1888, titled *The Presidential B.B. Club*, politics and business are merged in a tobacco advertisement, which shows Cleveland the fielder tagging out Harrison the batter—true enough for the election of 1892 but not for 1888, which Harrison won. Why baseball? What other images do you see in these two campaign visuals? (*Left: Library of Congress [LC-USZ62-7177]; right: From the collection of David J. and Janice L. Frent*)

Specie Resumption Act, gradually retiring greenbacks from circulation and putting the nation firmly on the gold standard. But as large supplies of silver were mined in the West, pressure resumed for increasing the money supply by coining silver. Soft-money advocates pushed for the unlimited coinage of silver in addition to gold. In an 1878 compromise, the Treasury was required to buy between $2 million and $4 million of silver each month and to coin it as silver dollars. Despite this increase in the money supply, the period was not inflationary. Prices fell, disappointing supporters of soft money. They pushed for more silver, continuing the controversy into the 1890s.

The issue of civil service reform was, as Henry Adams observed, a "subject almost as dangerous in political conversation in Washington as slavery itself in the old days before the war." The worst feature of the spoils system was that parties financed themselves by assessing holders of patronage jobs often as much as 1 percent of their annual salaries. Reformers, mostly middle-class, native-born, white Protestants, demanded competitive examinations to create an honest and professional civil service—but also one that would bar immigrants and their urban political machine bosses from the spoils of office.

Most Americans expected their presidents to reward the faithful with government jobs. Garfield's assassination by a crazed office seeker created a public backlash. When he died, even a loyal Republican said of his successor, "My God! Chet Arthur in the White House!" But Arthur surprised doubters by being a capable and dignified president, responsive to growing demands for civil service reform. Congress passed the Pendleton Act of 1883, mandating merit examinations for about one-tenth of federal offices. Gradually, more bureaucrats fell under its coverage, but parties became no more honest. As campaign contributions from government employees dried up, parties turned to huge corporate contributions, which in 1888 helped elect Benjamin Harrison.

DOCUMENT

Pendleton Civil Service Act (1883)

The Lure of Local Politics

The fact that the major parties did not disagree substantially on issues such as money and civil service does not mean that nineteenth-century Americans found politics dull. Far more eligible voters turned out in the late nineteenth century than at any time since. The 78.5 percent average turnout to vote for president in the 1880s contrasts sharply with the near 50 percent of eligible Americans who voted in recent elections.

American men were drawn to the polls in part by the hoopla of party parades, buttons, and banners, but also by local issues. Voters expressed strong interest in emotional social values issues of race, religion, nationality, and alcohol, which often overrode economic self-interest. Iowa farmers favored curbing the power of the railroads to set high grain-shipping rates, but they also turned out to vote for temperance and compulsory education laws. Irish Catholics in New York wanted support for parochial schools, while third-generation, middle-class American Protestants from Illinois and Connecticut voted for laws compelling attendance at public schools. Nashville whites supported laws that established segregated railroad cars and other public facilities. Ohio and Indiana Protestants urged laws against drinking to protect social order and morality against hard-drinking Catholics, while German–Catholic Milwaukee brewery workers, cherishing both their jobs and their beer, voted against local temperance laws.

The new urban immigrants played a large role in stimulating political participation. As traditional native-born elites left local government for more-lucrative and higher-status business careers, urban bosses stepped in. Their control rested on their ability to deliver the immigrant vote, which they secured by operating informal welfare systems. Bosses such as "Big Tim" Sullivan of New York and Michael "Hinky Dink" Kenna of Chicago handed out jobs and money for rent, fuel, and bail. Sullivan gave birthday shoes to poor children in his district and turkeys to poor families at Thanksgiving. New York City's Tammany Hall boss, George Washington Plunkitt, attended Jewish weddings, Irish Catholic confirmations, and Italian funerals; prevented evictions; posted bail; and otherwise provided favors to the members of his district, all in exchange for votes. As he explained, "I think that there's got to be in every ward somebody that any bloke can come to—no matter what he's done—and get help."

Party leaders also won votes by making politics exciting. The parades, rallies, buttons, songs, and oratory of late-nineteenth-century campaigns generated excitement as a substitute for substantive issues. In the election of 1884, for example, emotions ran high over the moral lapses of the opposing candidates—Blaine's corruption and Cleveland's illegitimate child. Democrats chanted in election eve rallies: "Blaine! Blaine! James G. Blaine! / Continental liar from the state of Maine!" while Republicans responded: "Ma! Ma! Where's my pa? / Gone to the White House, Ha! Ha! Ha!" Cleveland won in part because an unwise Republican clergyman called the Democrats the party of "rum, Romanism, and rebellion," ensuring Cleveland an outpouring of Catholic support in crucial New York.

A Warning to the House Judiciary Committee Women, often targets of drunken male violence, campaigned for temperance as well as for equal rights. Here Victoria Claflin Woodhull reads a suffrage proposal to the House Judiciary Committee in 1871. If denied the vote, she vowed that women were "plotting a revolution; we will overthrow this bogus Republic and plant a government of righteousness in its stead." How do you think the male congressmen responded to Ms. Woodhull? What do you imagine the other women are doing and thinking in this picture? (*Library of Congress [LC-USZ62-2023]*)

Party leaders used local and ethnic issues for their benefit. In New Mexico, for example, the Santa Fe ring, a small group of Anglo-Protestant Republican bankers, lawyers, and politicians, had long exploited local anti-Mexican feelings to grab lands. The ring controlled judges, legislators, and the business interests of the state, including many Spanish-speaking voters. When desperate Mexican-American tenant farmers turned to violence in the 1880s, the ring used the situation to dispossess Mexican Americans, Native Americans, and poor white squatters from enormous tracts of land.

Prohibition also provoked spirited local contests. Many Americans considered drinking a serious social problem. Annual consumption of brewery beer had risen from 2.7 gallons per capita in 1850 to 17.9 gallons in 1880. In one city, saloons outnumbered churches 31 to 1. Such statistics shocked those who believed that drinking would destroy character; corrupt politics; and cause poverty, crime, and unrestrained sexuality. Because they were often the targets of violent, drunken men, women especially supported temperance. Rather than try to persuade individuals to give up drink, as the pre–Civil War temperance movement had done, many now sought to ban drinking by making it illegal.

The battle in San Jose, California, illustrates the strong passions such efforts aroused. In the 1870s, temperance reformers put on the ballot a local option referendum to ban the sale of liquor in San Jose. Women erected a temperance tent where they held daily meetings. Despite denunciations from clergymen and heckling from some local drinkers, the women refused to retreat to their homes. On election eve, a large crowd appeared at the temperance tent, but a larger one turned up at a pro-liquor rally. In the morning, women roamed the streets, urging men to adopt the referendum. Children marched to the polls and saloons, singing, "Father, dear father,

A Political Cartoon Grover Cleveland's hypocrisy as "Grover the Good" is lampooned by this cartoon from the election of 1884 showing a tearful mother with Cleveland's "illegitimate" child. The people elected him anyway. Why do you think so? (*The Granger Collection, New York*)

come home with me now." By afternoon, the mood grew ugly; the women were harassed and threatened by drunken men, and the proposal lost by a vote of 1,430 to 918.

Emotional conflicts boiled in the 1880s at the state level over education and other issues. As Catholics in Boston and New York sought political support for parochial schools, Protestant Republicans in Iowa, Illinois, and Wisconsin sponsored laws mandating that children attend "some public or private day school" where instruction was in English, an early (but not the last) movement for English-only education. These laws aimed to undermine parochial schools, which taught in the language of the immigrants. In Iowa, where a state prohibition law also passed, the Republican slogan was "A schoolhouse on every hill, and no saloon in the valley." Local Republicans bragged that "Iowa will go Democratic when hell goes Methodist," and indeed they won. But in Wisconsin, a law for compulsory school attendance was so strongly anti-Catholic that it backfired. Many voters, disillusioned with pious Republican moralism, shifted to the Democratic party.

MIDDLE-CLASS REFORM

Most middle-class Americans avoided reformist politics. But urban corruption, poverty, and labor violence frightened many out of their aversion to politics.

Frances Willard and the Women's Christian Temperance Union (WCTU) is an example. As president of the WCTU from 1879 until 1898, Willard headed the largest women's organization in the country. Most WCTU members were churchgoing, white, Protestant women who believed drunkenness caused poverty and family violence. But after 1886, the WCTU reversed its position, attributing drunkenness to poverty, unemployment, and bad labor conditions. Willard joined the Knights of Labor in 1887 and by the 1890s had influenced the WCTU to extend its programs to alleviate the problems of workers, particularly women and children.

The Gospel of Wealth and Social Darwinism

Willard called herself a Christian socialist because she believed in applying the ethical principles of Jesus to economic life. For Willard and many other educated, middle-class reformers, Christianity called for a cooperative social order that would reduce inequalities of wealth. But for most Gilded Age Americans, Christianity supported the competitive individualistic

ethic. Leading ministers preached sermons and wrote treatises justifying class divisions and the moral superiority of the wealthy. Episcopal Bishop William Lawrence wrote that it was "God's will that some men should attain great wealth." Philadelphia Baptist preacher Russell Conwell's famous sermon "Acres of Diamonds," delivered 6,000 times to an estimated 13 million listeners, praised riches as a sure sign of "godliness" and stressed the power of money to "do good."

Industrialist Andrew Carnegie expressed the ethic most clearly. In an article titled "The Gospel of Wealth" (1889), Carnegie celebrated competition for producing better goods at lower prices. The concentration of wealth in a few hands, he concluded, was "not only beneficial but essential to the future of the race." The fittest would bring order and efficiency out of the chaos of rapid industrialization. Carnegie's defense of the

DOCUMENT

Andrew Carnegie, "Wealth" (June 1889)

new economic order in his book *Triumphant Democracy* (1886) found as many supporters as Bellamy's *Looking Backward*, partly because Carnegie insisted that the rich must spend some of their wealth to benefit their "poorer brethren." Carnegie built hundreds of libraries, many still operating in large and small towns throughout the United States, and in later years turned his philanthropic attentions to world peace.

Carnegie's ideas reflected an ideology known as social Darwinism, based on the work of the English naturalist Charles Darwin, whose *Origin of Species* was published in 1859. Darwin had concluded that plant and animal species evolved through natural selection. In the struggle for existence, some species managed to adapt to their environment and survived; others failed to adapt and perished. Herbert Spencer, an English social philosopher, applied this "survival of the fittest" notion to human society. Progress, Spencer said, resulted from relentless competition in which the weak were eliminated and the strong climbed to the top, as in Bellamy's coach. Spencer warned against any interference in the economic world by tampering with the natural laws of selection: "The whole effort of nature is to get rid of such as are unfit, to clear the world of them, and make room for better."

When Spencer visited the United States in 1882, leading men of business, science, religion, and politics thronged to honor him with a lavish banquet in New York City. Here was the man whose theories justified their amassed fortunes as men of "superior ability, foresight, and adaptability," and they praised him as the founder not only of a new sociology but also of a new religion. Spencer's American followers, Carnegie and Yale political economist William Graham Sumner, insisted

DOCUMENT

William Graham Sumner, *What the Social Classes Owe to Each Other* (1883)

The Gap Between Rich and Poor   Describe what you see in these two photographs. Note the contrasts between them, one the bedroom in Alexander Stewart's Fifth Avenue mansion, representing society's "fittest" element. The other is a one-room immigrant tenement on New York's Lower East Side. How would the inhabitants of these two dwellings differ in their social and political views? *(Left: Brown Brothers; right: International Museum of Photography/George Eastman House)*

that poverty resulted from the struggle for existence. Attempts to end it were pointless, if not immoral. To take power or money away from millionaires, Sumner scoffed, was "like killing off our generals in war." It was "absurd," he wrote, to pass laws permitting society's "worst members" to survive, or to "sit down with a slate and pencil to plan out a new social world."

The scientific vocabulary of social Darwinism injected scientific rationality into what often seemed a baffling economic order. Sumner and Spencer argued that underlying laws of political economy, like those of the natural world, dictated economic affairs. Social Darwinists also believed in the superiority of the Anglo-Saxon race, which they maintained had reached the highest stage of evolution. Their theories were used to justify race supremacy and imperialism (see Chapter 20) as well as the monopolistic efforts of American businessmen. "The growth of a large business," John D. Rockefeller, Jr., told a YMCA class in Cleveland, like the growth of "the American beauty rose," happens "only by sacrificing the early buds which grow up around it." This was, he said, "merely the working out of a law of nature and a law of God."

Reform Darwinism and Pragmatism

Others questioned social Darwinism. Brooks Adams, Henry's brother, wrote that social philosophers such

as Spencer and Sumner were "hired by the comfortable classes to prove that everything was all right." Fading aristocrats such as the Adams family, increasingly displaced by a new industrial elite, may have felt a touch of envy for the new rich. But intellectual reformers directly challenged the gloomy social Darwinian notion that nothing could be done to alleviate poverty and injustice. With roots in antebellum abolitionism, women's rights, and other crusades for social justice, men such as Wendell Phillips, Frederick Douglass, and Franklin Sanborn and women such as Elizabeth Cady Stanton and Susan B. Anthony transferred their reform fervor to postbellum issues. Sanborn, for example, an inspector of charities in Massachusetts, founded the American Social Science Association in 1865 to "treat wisely the great social problems of the day." An early advocate of doing social scientific research on society's problems, Sanborn was known as the "leading social worker of his day."

Reformer Henry George, an amateur social scientist, observed that wherever the highest degree of "material progress" had been realized, "we find the deepest poverty." George's book *Progress and Poverty* (1879) dramatically showed the contradictions of American life. With Bellamy's *Looking Backward*, it was the most influential book of the age, selling 2 million copies by 1905. George admitted that economic growth had produced wonders, but he pointed out the social costs and the loss of Christian values. His remedy was to break up land-holding monopolists who profited from the increasing value of their land, which they rented to those who actually did the work. He proposed a "single tax" on the unearned increases in land value received by landlords.

George's solution may seem simplistic, but his religious tone and optimistic faith in the capacity of humans to effect change appealed to many middle-class intellectuals. Some went further. Sociologist Lester Frank Ward and economist Richard T. Ely both found examples of cooperation in nature and demonstrated that competition and laissez-faire had proved both wasteful and inhumane. Reform Darwinists urged an economic order marked by cooperation and regulation.

Two pragmatists, John Dewey and William James, established a philosophical foundation for reform. James, a professor at Harvard, argued that while environment was important, so was human will. People could influence the course of human events. "What is the 'cash value' of a thought, idea, or belief?" James asked. What was its result? "The ultimate test for us of what a truth means," he suggested, was in the "consequences" of a particular idea and what kind of moral "conduct it dictates."

James and young social scientists including Ward and Ely gathered statistics documenting social wrongs and rejected the social determinism of Spencer and Sumner. They argued that the application of intelligence and human agency could change the "survival of the fittest" into the "fitting of as many

as possible to survive." Their position encouraged educators, economists, and reformers of every stripe, giving them an intellectual justification to struggle against misery and inequalities of wealth.

Settlements and Social Gospel

Jane Addams saw the gap between progress and poverty in the streets of Chicago in the winter of 1893. "The stream of laboring people goes past you," she wrote, and "your heart sinks with a sudden sense of futility." Born in rural Illinois, Addams founded Hull House in Chicago in 1889 "to aid in the solution of the social and industrial problems which are engendered by the modern conditions of life in a great city." Also in 1889, Wellesley literature professor Vida Scudder, feeling "the agitating and painful vibrations" of urban poverty, joined six other Smith College graduates to form an organization of college women to work in settlement houses.

Middle-class activists such as Addams and Scudder worried in particular about the degradation of life and labor in America's cities, factories, and farms. They were influenced by middle-class English socialists; by European social prophets such as Karl Marx, Leo Tolstoy, and Victor Hugo; by Americans such as Emerson, Whitman, George, and Bellamy; and by the ethical teachings of Jesus. Their message was highly idealistic, ethical, and Christian. They preferred a society marked by cooperation rather than competition in which, as they liked to say, people were guided by the "golden rule rather

Lessons and Services of the Settlement House What is being taught to immigrant women in this typical settlement house poster? The public health clinic is in Vida Scudder's Denison House in Boston. Settlement house work, Scudder wrote, fulfilled "a biting curiosity about the way the Other Half lived, and a strange hunger for fellowship with them." Do you see evidence of cross-cultural, cross-class bonding? (*Left: U.S. Government Education Bureau of the National Geographic Image Collection; right: Schlesinger Library, Radcliffe Institute, Harvard University*)

than the rule of gold." Like Frances Willard, they meant to apply the ethics of Jesus to industrial and urban life in order to bring about the kingdom of heaven on earth. Some preferred to put their goals in more secular terms, speaking of radically transforming American society. Most, however, worked within existing institutions. As middle-class intellectuals and professionals, they tended to stress an educational approach to problems. But they were also practical, seeking tangible improvements by crusading for tenement-house and factory-conditions legislation, mediating labor disputes, and living among the poor people they helped.

The settlement house movement typified 1890s middle-class reformers' blend of idealism and practicality. The primary purpose of settlement houses was to help immigrant families, especially women, adapt Old World rural styles of childbearing, child care, and housekeeping to American urban life. They launched day nurseries, kindergartens, and boarding rooms for immigrant working women; they offered classes in sewing, cooking, nutrition, health care, and English; and they tried to keep young people out of saloons by organizing sports clubs and coffeehouses.

A second purpose of the settlement house movement was to give college-educated women meaningful work at a time when they faced professional barriers and to allow them to preserve the strong feelings of sacrifice and sisterhood they had experienced at college. As Scudder explained, settlement house workers were like "early Christians" in their renunciation of worldly goods and dedication to a life of service. A third goal was to gather data exposing social misery in order to spur legislative action—developing city building codes for tenements, abolishing child labor, and improving factory safety. Hull House, Addams said, was intended in part "to investigate and improve the conditions in the industrial districts of Chicago." Settlement houses and organizations such as the Christian Social Union, with their dual emphasis on the scientific gathering of facts and Christian commitment, helped nourish the new discipline of sociology, first taught in divinity schools.

Jane Addams, *Twenty Years at Hull House* (1910)

Meanwhile, Dwight Moody preached a more traditional Christianity in American cities, leading hundreds of urban revivals in the 1870s. Discovering his mission while in England for the YMCA, Moody mastered the art of the folksy sermon filled with Bible and family stories, the easy path from sin to salvation by filling out a decision card, and the importance of music in making converts. The revivals appealed to lower-class, rural folk who were both drawn to the city by their hopes and pushed there by economic ruin. Supported by business-people who felt that religion would make workers and immigrants more docile, Moody's revivalist "passion for souls" provided a safe community in the midst of urban confusion. Revivalism helped to nearly double evangelical Protestant church membership in the last two decades of the century. Although some urban workers drifted into secular faiths such as socialism, most embraced the "old-time" religion.

Unlike Moody, many Protestant ministers preferred the Social Gospel movement of the 1890s, which tied salvation to social betterment. Like the settlement house workers, these religious leaders sought to make Christianity relevant to urban problems. In books such as *Working Men and Their Employers* and *Applied Christianity*, Congregational minister Washington Gladden advocated collective bargaining and corporate profit sharing. Walter Rauschenbusch, a young Baptist minister in the notorious Hell's Kitchen area of New York City, raised an even louder voice. Often called on to conduct funeral services for children killed by the airless, diseased tenements and sweatshops, Rauschenbusch scathingly attacked capitalism and church ignorance of socioeconomic issues. His progressive ideas for social justice and a welfare state were later published in two landmark books: *Christianity and the Social Crisis* (1907) and *Christianizing the Social Order* (1912).

Perhaps the most influential book promoting social Christianity was the best-selling novel *In His Steps*, published in 1896 by Charles Sheldon. The novel portrayed the dramatic changes made possible by a few community leaders who resolved to base all their actions on a single question: "What would Jesus do?" For a minister, this meant seeking to "bridge the chasm between the church and labor." For the idle rich, it meant settlement house work and reforming prostitutes. For landlords and factory owners, it meant improving the living and working conditions of tenants and laborers. Although filled with naive sentimentality characteristic of much of the Social Gospel, *In His Steps* prepared thousands of influential, middle-class Americans for progressive civic leadership.

Reforming the City

No late-nineteenth-century institution needed reforming more than urban government, called by the president of Cornell "the worst in Christendom—the most expensive, the most inefficient, and the most corrupt." A Philadelphia committee pointed to years of "inefficiency, waste, badly paved and filthy

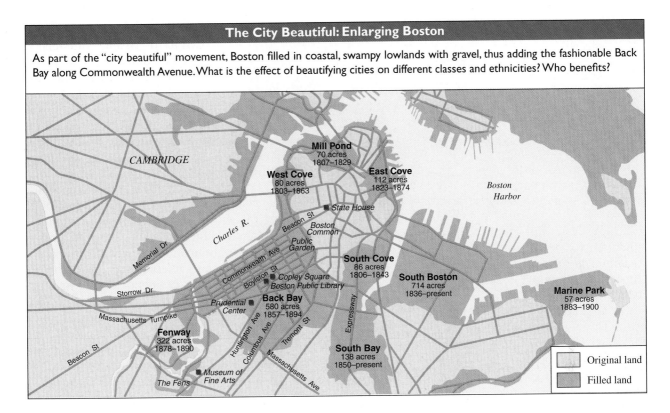

The City Beautiful: Enlarging Boston

As part of the "city beautiful" movement, Boston filled in coastal, swampy lowlands with gravel, thus adding the fashionable Back Bay along Commonwealth Avenue. What is the effect of beautifying cities on different classes and ethnicities? Who benefits?

streets, unwholesome and offensive water, and slovenly and costly management." New York and Chicago, where cholera and typhoid epidemics resulted from raw sewage poured into Lake Michigan, were even worse, rivaling the appalling sewage, water, and health conditions in European cities such as London, Frankfurt, and Rome.

Creating a "city beautiful" through environmental remedies was one approach to cleaning up dirty cities. Urban planners put in water mains and sewers and landscape architects built city parks and planted trees along broadened boulevards lined by elegant homes and public buildings—libraries, museums, theaters, and music halls. Boston filled in more than 500 acres of tidal flats in the Back Bay and elsewhere around the core of the city and created an elegant upper-class neighborhood along tree-lined Commonwealth Avenue. But the transformation of urban space rarely reached the squalid sections of the city inhabited by recent immigrants and rural transplants packed into crowded tenement houses along filthy streets filled with milling people, garbage, and animals.

Rapid urban growth swamped city leaders with new demands for service. Flush toilets, thirsty horses pulling street railways, and industrial users of water, for example, all exhausted the capacity of municipal waterworks built for an earlier age. As city governments struggled, they raised taxes and incurred vast debts, which bred graft and gave rise

to the boss. In addition to dispensing jobs and favors in return for votes, urban bosses awarded street railway, gas line, and other utility franchises and construction contracts to local businesses in return for kickbacks and other favors. Bosses tipped off friendly real estate agents about the location of projected city improvements and received favors from the owners of saloons, brothels, and gambling clubs in return for help with police protection, bail, and influence with judges. These institutions were vital to the urban economy and played an important role in easing the immigrants' way into American life. For many young women, prostitution meant economic survival. For men, the saloon was the center of social life and a source of cheap meals and job leads.

Boss Tweed

Bossism deeply offended middle-class urban reformers, unkindly dubbed "goo-goos" for their advocacy of good government. They opposed not only graft and vice but also the perversion of democracy by the exploitation of ignorant immigrants. The immigrants, said one, "follow blindly leaders of their own race, are not moved by discussion, and exercise no judgment of their own"—and so were "not fit for the suffrage."

Urban reformers' programs were similar in most cities. They not only advocated the "Americanization" of immigrants in public schools (and opposed parochial schooling) but also formed clubs

PUCK

HOW IS IT IN YOUR CITY?

Favors from a Party Boss Reformers wanted to eliminate the rule of urban party bosses. What in this *Puck* magazine cartoon would they criticize and want to change? What good did bosses do? Did the good outweigh the bad? What is local politics like in *your* city? *(Courtesy of The Newberry Library, Chicago)*

and voters' leagues to discuss the failings of municipal government. They delighted in exposing electoral irregularities and large-scale graft. These discoveries led to strident calls for replacing the mayor, often an Irish Catholic, with an Anglo-Saxon Protestant reformer.

Politics colored every reform issue. Anglo-Saxon men favored prohibition partly to remove ethnic saloon-owner influence from politics and supported woman suffrage partly to gain a middle-class political advantage against male immigrant voters. Most urban reformers could barely hide their distaste for the "city proletariat mob," as one put it. They proposed to replace bosses with expert city managers, who would bring honest professionalism to city government. They hoped to make government cheaper and thereby lower taxes, which ironically ended up cutting services to the poor. Another unexpected consequence was to disfranchise working-class and ethnic groups, whose political participation depended on the boss system.

Not all urban reformers were elitist. Samuel Jones, for example, opposed bossism and passionately advocated political participation by urban immigrants. He himself had begun as a poor Welsh immigrant in the Pennsylvania oil fields but worked his way up in the rags-to-riches tradition to ownership of several oil fields and a factory in Toledo, Ohio. Once successful, however, Jones espoused a

different ethic from Carnegie's "Gospel of Wealth." Influenced by a combination of firsthand contact with the "piteous appeals" of unemployed workers and by his reading of social reformers and the New Testament, in 1894 Jones resolved that he would "apply the Golden Rule as a rule of conduct" in his factory. He instituted an eight-hour workday, a $2 minimum daily wage (50 to 75 cents higher than the local average for 10 hours), a cooperative insurance program, and an annual 5 percent Christmas dividend. Plastering the Golden Rule over his factory walls, Jones hired former criminals and social outcasts. He anticipated twentieth-century industrial reforms by creating a company cafeteria offering a hot lunch for 15 cents, a Golden Rule Park for workers and their families, employee music groups, and a Golden Rule Hall, where he invited social visionaries to speak.

In 1897, Jones was elected to the first of an unprecedented four terms as mayor of Toledo. A maverick Republican who antagonized prominent citizens, Jones was adored by ordinary people. He advocated municipal ownership of utilities; public-works jobs and housing for the unemployed; more civic parks and playgrounds with free pools, skating rinks, and sleigh rides; and free vocational education and kindergartens. A pacifist, he took away policemen's sidearms and heavy clubs. In police court, Jones regularly dismissed most cases of petty theft and drunkenness on grounds that the accused were victims of social injustice, and he often released prostitutes after fining every man in the room 10 cents—and himself a dollar—for condoning prostitution. Crime in notoriously sinful Toledo fell during his term. When "Golden Rule" Jones died in 1904, nearly 55,000 people, "tears streaming down their faces," filed past his coffin.

The Struggle for Woman Suffrage

Women served, in Jane Addams's phrase, as "urban housekeepers" in the settlement house and good-government movements, precursors of welfare programs in the twentieth century. They also reflected the tension many women felt between their public

Jane Addams of Hull House   The young Jane Addams was one of the college-educated women who chose to remain unmarried and pursue a career as an "urban housekeeper" and social reformer, serving immigrant families in the Chicago neighborhood near her Hull House. (*Jane Addams Memorial Collection, [JAMC neg. 21], Special Collections, University Library, University of Illinois at Chicago*)

and private lives, that is, between their obligations to self, family, and society. This tension was seldom expressed openly. A few women writers, however, began to vent the frustrations of middle-class domestic life. In her novel *The Awakening* (1899), Kate Chopin told the story of a young woman who, in discovering her own sexuality and life's possibilities beyond being a "mother-woman," defied conventional expectations of a woman's role. Her sexual affair and eventual suicide prompted a St. Louis newspaper to label the novel "poison."

Some middle-class women—Addams and Scudder, for example—avoided marriage, preferring the nurturing relationships found in the female settlement house community. "Married life looks to me . . . terribly impoverished for women," a Smith College graduate observed, adding, "most of my deeper friendships have been with women." A few women boldly advocated free love or, less openly, formed lesbian relationships. Although most preferred traditional marriages and chose not to work outside the home, the generation of women that came of age in

the 1890s married less—and later—than any other in American history.

Many women reconciled the conflicting pressures between their private and public lives and deflected male criticism by seeing their work as maternal. Addams called Hull House the "great mother breast of our common humanity." Frances Willard told Susan B. Anthony in 1898 that "government is only housekeeping on the broadest scale," a job men had botched, requiring women's saving participation. A leading labor organizer was Mary Harris "Mother" Jones, and the fiery feminist anarchist Emma Goldman titled her monthly journal *Mother Earth.* By using nurturant language to describe their work, women furthered the very arguments used against them. Many remained economically dependent on men, and all women still lacked the essential rights of citizenship. How could they be municipal housekeepers if they could not yet even vote?

After the Seneca Falls Convention in 1848, women's civil and political rights advanced very slowly. Although several western states gave women the right to vote in municipal and school board elections, before 1890 only the territory of Wyoming (1869) granted full political equality. Colorado, Utah, and Idaho enfranchised women in the 1890s, but no other states granted suffrage until 1910. This slow pace resulted in part from an antisuffrage movement led by an odd combination of ministers, saloon interests, and men threatened in various ways by women's voting rights. "Equal suffrage," said a Texas senator, "is a repudiation of manhood."

In the 1890s, leading suffragists reexamined their situation. The two wings of the women's rights movement, split since 1869, combined in 1890 as the National American Woman Suffrage Association (NAWSA). Elizabeth Cady Stanton and Susan B. Anthony, both in their 70s, continued to head the association. But in 1895, Stanton's *Woman's Bible,* a devastating attack on the religious argument against woman suffrage, embarrassed many younger women. At the NAWSA convention in 1896, despite the pleas of Anthony not to "sit in judgment" on her good friend, a resolution renouncing any NAWSA connection with Stanton's book passed by a vote of 53 to 41. That vote signaled the passage of leadership to younger, more moderate women who, unlike Stanton and Anthony, concentrated on the single issue of the vote.

IMAGE

Suffragist Speaking

Changing leadership meant a shift in the arguments for suffrage. Since 1848, suffragists had argued primarily from the principle of "our republican idea, individual citizenship," as Stanton put it in 1892. But younger leaders shifted to three expedient

AMERICAN VOICES

Elizabeth Cady Stanton
Speaks Out for a "Woman's Bible"

In 1895, Elizabeth Cady Stanton published her highly controversial Woman's Bible *in order to protest male theologians' centuries-long revisions and interpretations of the Bible that attempted to justify putting women into an inferior "sphere."*

We have the usual array of objectors to meet and answer. One correspondent conjures us to suspend the work, as it is "ridiculous" for "women to attempt the revision of the Scriptures." I wonder if any man wrote to the late revising committee of Divines to stop their work on the ground that it was ridiculous for men to revise the Bible. Why is it more ridiculous for women to protest against her present status in the Old and New Testament, in the ordinances and discipline of the church, than in the statutes and constitution of the state? Why is it more ridiculous to arraign ecclesiastics for their false teaching and acts of injustice to women, than members of Congress and the House of Commons? Why is it more audacious to review Moses than Blackstone, the Jewish code of laws, than the English system of jurisprudence? Women have compelled their legislators in every state in this Union to so modify their statutes for women that the old common law is now almost a dead letter.

Why not compel Bishops and Revising Committees to modify their creeds and dogmas? Forty years ago it seemed as ridiculous to timid, time-serving and retrograde folk for women to demand an expurgated edition of the laws, as it now does to demand an expurgated edition of the Liturgies and the Scriptures.

Come, come, my conservative friend, wipe the dew off your spectacles, and see that the world is moving. Whatever your views may be as to the importance of the proposed work, your political and social degradation are but an outgrowth of your status in the Bible.

. . . How can woman's position be changed from that of a subordinate to an equal, without opposition, without the broadest discussion of all the questions involved in her present degradation? For so far-reaching and momentous a reform as her complete independence, an entire revolution in all existing institutions is inevitable.

Let us remember that all reforms are interdependent, and that whatever is done to establish one principle on a solid basis, strengthens all. Reformers who are always compromising, have not yet grasped the idea that truth is the only safe ground to stand upon. The object of an individual life is not to carry one fragmentary measure in human progress, but to utter the highest truth clearly seen in all directions, and thus to round out and perfect a well balanced character. . . . We have many women abundantly endowed with capabilities to understand and revise what men have thus far written.

- *From this short passage from Stanton's introduction, what do you think of her arguments?*

- *Is it more difficult to change churches or politics?*

---

arguments. The first was that women needed the vote to pass self-protection laws to guard against rapists and unsafe industrial work. The second argument, Addams's notion of urban housekeeping, pointed out that political enfranchisement would further women's role in cleaning up immoral cities and corrupt politics.

The third expedient argument reflected urban middle-class reformers' prejudice against non-Protestant immigrants. Machine bosses saw to it that immigrant men got to vote, sometimes several times in a day. Suffragists argued that educated, native-born American women should get the vote to counteract the undesirable influence of illiterate male immigrants. In a speech in Iowa in 1894, Carrie Chapman Catt, who would succeed Anthony as president of NAWSA in 1900, argued that the "Government is menaced with great danger . . . in the votes possessed by the males in the slums of the cities," a danger that could be averted only by cutting off that vote and giving it to women. In the new century, under the leadership of women such as Catt, woman suffrage would finally be secured.

POLITICS IN THE PIVOTAL 1890S

Americans mistakenly think of the last decade of the nineteenth century as the "gay nineties," symbolized by mustached baseball players, sporty Gibson girls,

From the Depths The contrasts between rich and poor and the threat of social upheaval are dramatically illustrated in this turn-of-the-century work titled *From the Depths*. *(Culver Pictures)*

and the opulent dinners of rich entrepreneurs. The 1890s was, indeed, a decade of baseball and bicycles, urban electrification, and the enormous wealth of the few. But it was also a decade of dark tenements, grinding work, desperate unemployment, and debilitating poverty. The early 1890s included protesting farmers; Wounded Knee and the "second great removal" of Native Americans; segregation, disfranchisement, and lynchings for blacks; and the "new immigration," a changing workplace, and devastating labor defeats at Coeur d'Alene, Homestead, and Pullman.

Gibson Girl, 1899

The 1890s, far from gay, were years of contrasts and crises. The obvious contrast, as Bellamy had anticipated, was between the rich and the poor. Supreme Court justice John Harlan saw a "deep feeling of unrest" everywhere among people worrying that the nation was in "real danger from . . . the slavery that would result from aggregations of capital in the hands of a few." Populist "Sockless" Jerry Simpson simply saw a struggle between "the robbers and

the robbed." And between them, he said, "there is no middle ground."

The gap was indeed huge between Kansas orator Mary E. Lease, who in 1890 said, "What you farmers need to do is to raise less corn, and more Hell," and the wealthy Indianapolis woman who told her husband, "I'm going to Europe and spend my money before these crazy people take it." The pivotal nature of the 1890s hinged on this feeling of polarizing unrest and upheaval as the nation underwent the traumas of change from a rural to an urban society. The new immigration from Europe and the internal migrations of African Americans and farmers added to the "great danger" against which Carrie Catt warned. The depression of 1893 widened the gap between rich and poor, accelerating demands for reform. The federal bureaucracy slowly began to adapt to the needs of governing a complex specialized society, and Congress purposefully moved to confront national problems.

DOCUMENT

Mary Elizabeth Lease, from *Populist Crusader* (1892)

Republican Legislation in the Early 1890s

Harrison's election in 1888 was accompanied by Republican control of both houses of Congress. As the English and Germans were enacting national health, housing, and social insurance laws, American legislators in 1890 inched forward on five areas: Civil War veterans' pensions, trusts, tariffs, the money question, and rights for blacks. On the first issue, a bill providing generous support of $160 million a year for Union veterans and their dependents sailed through Congress.

The Sherman Anti-Trust Act passed with only one nay vote. It declared illegal "every contract, combination . . . or conspiracy in restraint of trade or commerce." Although the Sherman Act was vague and not really intended to break up big corporations, it was an initial attempt to restrain large business combinations. But in *United States* v. *E. C. Knight* (1895), the Supreme Court ruled that the American Sugar Refining Company, which controlled more than 90 percent of the nation's sugar-refining capacity, was not in violation of the Sherman Act.

A tariff bill introduced in 1890 by Ohio Republican William McKinley stirred more controversy. McKinley's bill raised tariffs higher than ever. As European nations moved away from a commitment to free trade and experienced heightened feelings of nationalism, they put in place protective measures that affected American interests. Despite heated opposition from agrarian interests, whose products

Major Legislative Activity of the Gilded Age

In the table, notice the kinds of issues dealt with at the national level as opposed to state and local arenas. What does this suggest about the interests of the American people and how federalism worked in the late nineteenth century? Do you think the apparent division of governmental responsibilities made sense? How is it the same or different today?

Date	National
1871	National Civil Service Commission created
1873	Coinage Act demonetizes silver
	"Salary Grab" Act (increased salaries of Congress and top federal officials) partly repealed
1875	Specie Resumption Act retires greenback dollars
1878	Bland-Allison Act permits partial coining of silver
1882	Chinese Exclusion Act
	Federal Immigration Law restricts certain categories of immigrants and requires head tax of all immigrants
1883	Standard time (four time zones) established for the entire country
	Pendleton Civil Service Act
1887	Interstate Commerce Act sets up Interstate Commerce Commission
	Dawes Act divides Indian tribal lands into individual allotments
1890	Dependent Pension Act grants pensions to Union army veterans
	Sherman Anti-Trust Act
	Sherman Silver Purchase Act has government buy more silver
	McKinley Tariff sets high protective tariff
	Federal elections bill to protect black voting rights in South fails in Senate
	Blair bill to provide support for education defeated
1891	Immigration law gives federal government control of overseas immigration
1893	Sherman Silver Purchase Act repealed
1894	Wilson-Gorman Tariff lowers duties slightly
1900	Currency Act puts United States on gold standard

Date	State and Local
1850s–1880s	State and local laws intended to restrict or prohibit consumption of alcoholic beverages
1871	Illinois Railroad Act sets up railroad commission to fix rates and prohibit discrimination
1874	Railroad regulatory laws in Wisconsin and Iowa
1881	Kansas adopts statewide prohibition
1882	Iowa passes state prohibition amendment
1880s	Massachusetts, Connecticut, Rhode Island, Montana, Michigan, Ohio, and Missouri all pass local laws prohibiting consumption of alcohol
	Santa Fe ring dominates New Mexico politics and land grabbing
1889	New Jersey repeals a county-option prohibition law of 1888
	Laws in Wisconsin and Illinois mandate compulsory attendance of children at schools in which instruction is in English
	Kansas, Maine, Michigan, and Tennessee pass antitrust laws
1889–1890	Massachusetts debates bill on compulsory schooling in English
1890–1910	Eleven former Confederate states pass segregation laws
1891	Nebraska passes eight-hour workday law
1893	Colorado adopts woman suffrage
1894–1896	Woman suffrage referenda defeated in Kansas and California
1899–1902	Eleven former Confederate states amend state constitutions and pass statutes restricting the voting rights of blacks

were generally not protected, McKinley's bill passed the House and, after nearly 500 amendments, also the Senate.

Silver was trickier. Recognizing the appeal of free silver to agrarian debtors and organized farmers, Republican leaders feared their party might be hurt by the issue. Senator John Sherman (R-Ohio), the brother of Union general William Sherman, proposed a compromise that momentarily satisfied almost everyone. The Sherman Silver Purchase Act ordered the Treasury to buy 4.5 million ounces of silver monthly and to issue Treasury notes for it. Silverites were pleased by the proposed increase in the money supply. Opponents felt they had averted the worst—free coinage of silver. The gold standard still stood.

Republicans were also prepared to confront violations of the voting rights of southern blacks in 1890. As usual, political considerations trumped moral ones. Since 1877, the South had become a Democratic stronghold, where party victories could be traced to fraud and intimidation of black Republican voters. "To be a Republican . . . in the South," one Georgian noted, "is to be a foolish martyr." Republican legislation, then, was intended to honor old commitments to freed male voters and improve party fortunes in the South. An elections bill proposed by Massachusetts senator Henry Cabot Lodge sought to ensure African American voter registration and fair elections. But a storm of Democratic disapproval arose, branding Lodge's measure the "Force Bill." Former president Cleveland called it a "dark blow at the freedom of the ballot," and the Mobile *Daily Register* claimed that it "would deluge the South in blood." Senate Democrats delayed action with a filibuster.

Meanwhile, in order to secure passage of the McKinley Tariff, Republican leaders bargained away the elections bill, ending major-party efforts to protect African American voting rights in the South until the 1960s. In a second setback for black southerners, the Senate, fearful of giving the federal government a role in education, defeated a bill to provide federal aid to black schools in the South that received a disproportionately small share of local and state funds. "The plain truth is," said the New York *Herald*, "the North has got tired of the negro," foreshadowing a similar retreat from civil rights legislation 100 years later.

The legislative efforts of the summer of 1890, impressive by nineteenth-century standards, fell far short of solving the nation's problems. Trusts grew more rapidly after the Sherman Act than before. Union veterans were pleased with their pensions, but southerners were incensed that Confederate veterans were left out. Others, seeing the pension measure as extravagant, labeled the fifty-first Congress the "billion-dollar Congress." Despite efforts to please farmers, many still viewed tariff protection as a benefit primarily for eastern manufacturers. Farm prices continued to slide, and gold and silver advocates were only momentarily silenced. African American rights were put off to another time. Polarizing inequalities of wealth remained. Voters abandoned the GOP in droves in the 1890 congressional elections, dropping the number of Republicans in the House from 168 to 88.

Two years later, Cleveland won a presidential rematch with Harrison. "The lessons of paternalism ought to be unlearned," he said in his inaugural address, "and the better lesson taught that while the people should . . . support their government, its functions do not include the support of the people."

Formation of the People's Party, 1892

Farmers knew all too well that government did not support them. In February 1892, the People's, or Populist, party was established with Leonidas Polk, president of the National Farmers Alliance, as its presidential candidate. "The time has arrived," he thundered, "for the great West, the great South, and the great Northwest, to link their hands and hearts together and march to the ballot box and take possession of the government . . . and run it in the interest of the people." But by July, at the party convention in Omaha, Polk had died. Reflecting its Midwestern and southern alliance roots, the party nominated James B. Weaver, a Union army veteran from Iowa, as its standard bearer, and James G. Field, a former Confederate soldier, for vice president.

The platform preamble, written by Ignatius Donnelly, a Minnesota farmer–politician, blazed with the urgent spirit of the agrarian protest movement, proclaiming that in the midst of political and corporate corruption "the people are demoralized. . . . The fruits of the toil of millions are boldly stolen to build up colossal fortunes . . . we breed two great classes—paupers and millionaires." To heal that divide, Donnelly advocated ending "the controlling influences dominating the old political parties."

The Omaha demands expanded the Ocala platform of 1890 (see Chapter 17). They included more direct democracy (popular election of senators, direct primaries, the initiative and referendum, and the secret ballot) and several pro-labor planks (the eight-hour workday, immigration restriction, and condemnation of the use of Pinkerton agents as an "army of mercenaries . . . a menace to our liberties"). The Populists also endorsed a graduated income tax, free and unlimited coinage of silver at a ratio of 16 to 1 (meaning that the U.S. Mint would have to buy silver for coinage at one-sixteenth the current, official price of the equivalent amount of gold), and government ownership of railroads and telephone and telegraph companies. "The time has come," the platform said, "when the railroad corporations will either own the people or the people must own the railroads."

DOCUMENT

The People's Party Platform (1892)

Although Populists attempted to widen political debate by promoting a new vision of government activism to resolve farmers' problems, the obstacles the new party faced were monumental: weaning the South from the Democrats, encouraging southern

AMERICAN VOICES

Ignatius Donnelly, A Minnesota Farmer Issues an Angry Call for Reform

The preamble to the National People's (Populist) Party plat-form adopted in Omaha on July 4, 1892, was written by Ignatius Donnelly, a Minnesota farmer, lawyer, writer, and activist.

We meet in the midst of a nation brought to the verge of moral, political, and material ruin. Corruption dominates the ballot-box, the Legislatures, the Congress, and touches even the ermine of the bench. The people are demoralized; most of the States have been compelled to isolate the voters at the polling places to prevent universal intimidation and bribery. The newspapers are largely subsidized or muzzled, public opinion silenced, business prostrated, homes covered with mortgages, labor impoverished, and the land concentrating in the hands of capitalists. The urban workmen are denied the right to organize for self-protection, imported pauperized labor beats down their wages, a hireling standing army, unrecognized by our laws, is established to shoot them down, and they are rapidly degenerating into European conditions. The fruits of the toil of millions are boldly stolen to build up colossal fortunes for a few, unprecedented in the history of mankind; and the possessors of those, in turn, despise the republic and endanger liberty. From the same prolific womb of governmental injustice we breed the two great classes—tramps and millionaires.

. . . We have witnessed for more than a quarter of a century the struggles of the two great political parties for power and plunder, while grievous wrongs have been inflicted upon the suffering people. We charge that the controlling influences dominating both these parties have permitted the existing dreadful conditions to develop without serious effort to prevent or restrain them. Neither do they now promise us any substantial reform. They have agreed together to ignore, in the coming campaign, every issue but one. They propose to drown the outcries of a plundered people with the uproar of a sham battle over the tariff, so that capitalists, corporations, national banks, rings, trusts, watered stock, the demonetization of silver and the oppressions of the usurers may all be lost sight of. They propose to sacrifice our homes, lives, and children on the altar of mammon; to destroy the multitude in order to secure corruption funds from the millionaires.

. . . Assembled on the anniversary of the birthday of the nation, and filled with the spirit of the grand general and chief who established our independence, we seek to restore the government of the Republic to the hands of "the plain people," with which class it originated . . .

We believe that the power of government—in other words, of the people—should be expanded . . . as rapidly and as far as the good sense of an intelligent people and the teachings of experience shall justify, to the end that oppression, injustice, and poverty shall eventually cease in the land.

- *In this excerpt, what is Donnelly's assessment of the American socioeconomic and political situation?*
- *What values does he espouse?*
- *Could a similar assessment be made in America today?*

A Party of Patches, 1891

whites to work with blacks, and persuading voters of both parties to abandon familiar political ties. But the new party pressed ahead. Weaver campaigned actively in the South, where he faced egg- and rock-throwing Democrats, who fanned racial fears in opposing his efforts to include blacks in the People's party. Despite hostile opposition, Weaver won more than 1 million popular votes (the first third-party candidate to do so), and he carried four states (Kansas, Colorado, Idaho, and Nevada) and parts of two others (Oregon and North Dakota), for a total of 22 electoral votes.

The Populists' support was substantial but regional, coming from western miners and mine owners who favored the demand for silver coinage and from rural Americans from the Great Plains. But the People's party failed to break the Democratic stranglehold on the South, nor did it appeal to city workers of the Northeast who were suspicious of the party's anti-urban tone and its desire for higher agricultural prices (which meant higher food prices). Perhaps most damaging, the Populists made few inroads with Midwestern farmers, who owed fewer debts and were relatively more prosperous than farmers elsewhere and saw little value in the Omaha platform. Although the Populists were not yet finished, most discontented farmers in 1892 voted for Cleveland and the Democrats, not for the Populists.

The Depression of 1893

Though winning the election, Cleveland soon faced a difficult test. No sooner had he taken office than began one of the worst depressions ever to grip the American economy, lasting from 1893 to 1897. Its severity was heightened by the growth of a national economy and global economic interdependence. The depression started in Europe and spread to the United States as overseas buyers cut back on their purchases of American products. Shrinking markets abroad soon crippled American manufacturing.

Foreign investors, worried about the stability of American currency after passage of the Sherman Silver Purchase Act, dumped some $300 million of their securities in the United States. As gold left the country to pay for these securities, the nation's money supply declined. At the same time, falling prices hurt farmers, many of whom discovered that it cost more to raise their crops and livestock than they could make in the market. Workers fared no better: wages fell faster than the price of food and rent.

The collapse in 1893 was also caused by overextensions in railroad construction and crops. Farmers, troubled by falling prices, planted more, hoping the market would pick up. As the realization of overextension spread, confidence faltered, then gave way to financial panic. When Wall Street

A City of Contrasts in 1893 The depression of 1893 accentuated contrasts between rich and poor. While middle-class Americans enjoyed visiting the Palace of Electricity and boating on the lagoons of the Chicago World's Columbian Exposition (above), slum children played in filthy streets nearby, with Jane Addams's Hull House less than a mile away (left). *(Above: Bettman/CORBIS; left, Library of Congress)*

crashed early in 1893, investors frantically sold their shares, companies plunged into bankruptcy, and disaster spread. People rushed to exchange paper notes for gold, further reducing gold reserves and confidence in the economy. Banks called in loans, which by the end of the year led to 16,000 business bankruptcies and 500 bank failures.

The capital crunch and diminished buying power of rural and small-town Americans (still half the population) forced massive factory closings. Within a year, an estimated 3 million Americans—20 percent of the workforce—lost jobs. People fearfully watched tramps wandering from city to city looking for work. "There are thousands of homeless and starving men in the streets," one young man reported from Chicago, indicating that he had seen "more misery in this last week than I ever saw in my life before."

As in Bellamy's coach image, the misery of the many was not shared by the few, which only increased discontent. While unemployed men foraged in garbage dumps for food, the wealthy gave lavish parties—at one, dining while seated on horses—sometimes costing as much as $100,000. While poor families shivered in poorly heated tenements, the very rich built million-dollar summer resorts at Newport, Rhode Island, or grand mansions on New York's Fifth Avenue and Chicago's Gold Coast. While Lithuanian immigrants walked or rode packed streetcars to work, wealthy men luxuriated on huge pleasure yachts. J. P. Morgan owned three, one with a crew of 85 sailors.

Nowhere were these inequalities more apparent than in Chicago during the World's Columbian Exposition, which opened on May 1, 1893, five days before a plummeting stock market began the depression. The Chicago World's Fair showcased, as President Cleveland said in an opening-day speech, the "stupendous results of American enterprise." When he pressed an ivory telegraph key, he started electric current that unfurled flags, spouted water through gigantic fountains, lit 10,000 electric lights, and powered huge steam engines. For six months, some 27 million visitors strolled around the White City, admiring its wide lagoons, its neoclassical white plaster buildings, and its exhibit halls filled with inventions. Built at a cost of $31 million, the fair celebrated the marvelous mechanical accomplishments of American enterprise and of the "city beautiful" movement to make cities more livable.

But as fairgoers celebrated by sipping pink champagne, Americans in immigrant wards less than a mile away drank contaminated water, crowded into packed tenements, and looked in vain for jobs. The area around Hull House was especially disreputable,

with saloons, gambling halls, brothels, and pawnshops dotting the neighborhood. "If Christ came to Chicago," British journalist W. T. Stead wrote in a book of that title in 1894, this would be "one of the last precincts into which we should care to take Him." Stead's book showed readers the "ugly sight" of corruption, poverty, and wasted lives in a city with 200 millionaires and 200,000 unemployed men.

Despite the magnitude of despair during the depression, national politicians and leaders were reluctant to respond. Mass demonstrations forced some city authorities to provide soup kitchens and places for the homeless to sleep. When an army of unemployed led by Jacob Coxey marched on Washington in the spring of 1894 to press for public work relief, its leaders were arrested for walking on the Capitol grass. Cleveland's reputation for callousness worsened later that summer when he sent federal troops to Chicago to crush the Pullman strike.

Jacob Coxey's Arrest

The president focused on tariff reform and repeal of the Silver Purchase Act, which he blamed for the depression. Although repeal was ultimately necessary to re-establish business confidence, in the short run Cleveland only worsened the financial crisis, highlighted the silver panacea, and hurt conservative Democrats. With workers, farmers, and wealthy silver miners alienated, voters abandoned the Democrats in the midterm elections of 1894, giving both Populists and Republicans high hopes for 1896.

The Crucial Election of 1896

The 1896 presidential campaign, waged during a depression and featuring a climactic battle over the currency, was one of the most critical in American history. Although Cleveland was in disgrace for ignoring depression woes, few leaders in either major party thought the federal government was responsible for alleviating the suffering of the people. But unemployed Polish meatpackers in Chicago; railway firemen in Terre Haute, Indiana; unskilled Slavic workers in Pennsylvania blast furnaces; Italian immigrant women in New Haven tenements; and desperate white and black tenant farmers in Georgia all wondered where relief might be found. Would either major party respond to the pressing human needs of the depression? Would the People's party set a new national agenda for politics? Would the established order prevail? These questions were raised and largely resolved in the election of 1896.

As the election approached, Populist leaders emphasized the silver issue and debated whether to fuse

A Dynamic Orator William Jennings Bryan, a surprise nominee at the 1896 Democratic Convention, was a vigorous proponent of the "cause of humanity." His nomination threw the country into a frenzy of fear. Would you have voted for Bryan or William McKinley in 1896? *(Library of Congress)*

with one of the major parties by agreeing on a joint ticket, which meant abandoning much of the Populist platform. Influenced by silver mine owners, many Populists became convinced that they must make a single-issue commitment to the free and unlimited coinage of silver at the ratio of 16 to 1.

In the throes of the depression in the mid-1890s, silver took on enormous importance as the symbol of the many grievances of downtrodden Americans. Popular literature captured the rural, moral dimensions of the silver movement. Some argue that L. Frank Baum's *Wonderful Wizard of Oz* (1900) was a free-silver moral allegory of rural values (Kansas, Auntie Em, the uneducated but wise scarecrow, and the good-hearted tin woodsman) and Populist attitudes and policies (the wicked witch of the East, and the magical silver shoes in harmony with the yellow brick road, in "Oz"—ounces).

The Republicans nominated William McKinley. As a congressman and twice governor of Ohio, McKinley was happily identified with the high protective tariff that bore his name. Citing the familiar argument that prosperity depended on the gold standard and protection, Republicans blamed the depression on Cleveland's attempt to lower the tariff.

The excitement of the Democratic convention in July contrasted with the staid, smoothly organized Republican gathering. With Cleveland already repudiated by his party, state after state elected delegates pledged to silver. Gold Democrats, however, had enough power to wage a close battle for the platform plank on money. Leading

the silver forces was an ardent young silverite, William Jennings Bryan, a 36-year-old former congressman from Nebraska. Few saw him as presidential material, but Bryan arranged to give the closing argument for a silver plank himself. His dramatic speech swept the convention for silver and ensured his own nomination. "I come to speak to you," Bryan cried out, "in defense of a cause as holy as the cause of liberty—the cause of humanity." Concluding one of the most famous political speeches in American history, Bryan attacked the "goldbugs":

DOCUMENT

William Jennings Bryan, "Cross of Gold" Speech (1896)

> Having behind us the producing masses of this nation . . . and toilers everywhere, we will answer their demand for a gold standard by saying to them: "You shall not press down upon the brow of labor this crown of thorns, you shall not crucify mankind upon a cross of gold."

Bryan stretched out his arms as if on a cross, and the convention exploded with applause.

Populist strategy lay in shambles when the Democrats named a silver candidate. Some party leaders favored fusion with the Democratic ticket (whose vice-presidential candidate was a goldbug), but antifusionists were outraged. Unwisely, the Populists also nominated Bryan, with Georgia Populist Tom Watson for vice president. Running on competing silver slates damaged Bryan's chances.

During the campaign, McKinley stayed at his home in Canton, Ohio, where some 750,000 admirers came to visit him, brought by low excursion rates

RECOVERING THE PAST

Political Campaign Artifacts: Buttons and Posters

Historians recover the past in printed sources such as books, diaries, magazines, and government documents as well as in visual records such as paintings, photographs, and the artifacts of material culture. Throughout American history, presidential political campaigns have produced, in addition to the streams of speeches, words, and sound bites, mountains of material objects: buttons, badges, banners, bumper stickers, yard signs, posters, cartoons, and other campaign paraphernalia to persuade voters to support one candidate or another.

The election of 1896 was no exception and, in fact, produced a plethora of political campaign artifacts on behalf of William McKinley and William Jennings Bryan. The fervor of that pivotal political contest led to the production of thousands of lapel pins, buttons, ribbons, bandanas, shirts, teacups, paper and soap dolls, posters, and other articles intended to influence American voters to cast their ballot for Bryan or McKinley. Although some of it seems silly, symbolic imagery was important. The examination of just two kinds of material paraphernalia—buttons and posters—reveals a great deal

about the issues, values, symbolism, and style of the election of 1896.

REFLECTING ON THE PAST Examine the buttons pictured here (as well as the "goldbug" and other stickpins). What issues are voters reminded of, and how complex is the message? How many different ways is the message, reinforced by recurring symbols, repeated on these buttons? Now compare the buttons and pins with the two posters. Do not worry that you cannot read most of the words; focus instead on the visual imagery and such words as you can make out. How do the posters reinforce key symbols, slogans, and substantive issues associated with each candidate? What visual images do the posters add? What audience do you think these campaign artifacts had in mind? What summary statements would you make about the 1896 campaign on the basis of these material items? Do these artifacts suggest that voters were more or less involved with political issues and party identification than they are today? What artifacts would best reflect an early twenty-first-century presidential campaign, and what would future historians learn from them?

Artifacts from the McKinley and Bryan campaigns. (Left: Courtesy Michael Kelly; right: © David J. and Janice L. Frent Collection/Corbis)

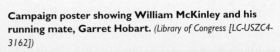

Campaign poster showing William McKinley and his running mate, Garret Hobart. *(Library of Congress [LC-USZC4-3162])*

Campaign poster showing William Jennings Bryan, his wife and children, and the text of the "Cross of Gold" speech. *(The Granger Collection, New York)*

The Presidential Election of 1896

In his sweep of the densely populated urban Northeast and Midwest, McKinley beat Bryan by the largest popular-vote margin since 1872. In his cabled congratulations (the first ever by a loser), Bryan, ever the "democrat," said: "We have submitted the issues to the American people and their will is law." Note that California's nine electoral votes (few compared with today) were split. As was then legal, one elector, from the Imperial Valley bordering the Arizona Territory, voted for Bryan and the Democrats.

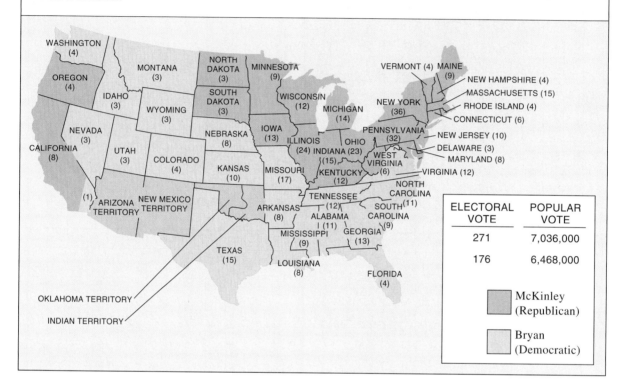

ELECTORAL VOTE	POPULAR VOTE
271	7,036,000
176	6,468,000

■ McKinley (Republican)

□ Bryan (Democratic)

offered by the railroads. The Republicans made an unprecedented effort to reach voters through a highly sophisticated media campaign, heavily financed by such major corporations as Standard Oil and the railroads. Party leaders hired thousands of speakers to support McKinley and distributed more than 200 million pamphlets in 14 languages to a voting population of 15 million, all advertising McKinley as the "advance agent of prosperity."

McKinley appealed not only to the business classes but also to unemployed workers, to whom he promised a "full dinner pail." He also spoke about the money issue, declaring that "our currency today is . . . as good as gold." Free silver, he warned, would cause inflation and more economic disaster. Recovery depended not on money, but on tariff reform to stimulate industry and provide jobs—"not open mints for the unlimited coinage of the silver of the world," he said, "but open mills for the full and unrestricted labor of American workingmen."

Bryan took his case directly to the people. Three million Americans in 27 states heard him speak as he traveled more than 18,000 miles, giving as many as 30 speeches a day. Bryan's message was simple:

prosperity required free coinage of silver. Government policies should attend to the needs of the producing classes rather than the vested interests. But the rhetoric favored rural toilers. "The great cities rest upon our broad and fertile prairies," he said in the "Cross of Gold" speech, "destroy our farms and the grass will grow in the streets of every city in the country." Urban workers were not inspired by this rhetoric, nor were immigrants influenced by Bryan's prairie moralizing.

To influential easterners, the brash young Nebraskan represented a threat. Theodore Roosevelt wrote, "This silver craze surpasses belief. Bryan's election would be a great calamity." A Brooklyn minister declared that the Democratic platform was "made in Hell." One newspaper editor said of Bryan that he was just like Nebraska's Platte River: "six inches deep and six miles wide at the mouth." Others branded him a "madman" and an "anarchist."

With such intense interest in the election, voters turned out in record numbers. In the key states of Illinois, Indiana, and Ohio, 95 percent of those eligible to vote

IMAGE

The Sacrilegious Candidate, 1896

went to the polls. McKinley won with 271 electoral votes to Bryan's 176, the largest popular majority since Grant trounced Greeley in 1872. Millionaire Mark Hanna jubilantly wired McKinley: "God's in his heaven, all's right with the world."

Although Bryan won more than 6 million votes (47 percent of the total), more than any previous Democratic winner, he failed to carry the Midwest or the urban middle classes and industrial masses, who had little confidence that the Democrats could stimulate economic growth or cope with industrialism. McKinley's promise of a "full dinner pail" was more convincing than the untested formula for free silver. Northern laborers feared that inflation would leave them even poorer—that prices and rents would rise faster than their wages. Catholic immigrants distrusted Populist Protestantism. In the Great Lakes states, prosperous farmers felt less discontent than farmers elsewhere. But the realities of an increasingly global network of production, prices, and markets also played a part in Bryan's defeat. Poor wheat harvests in India, Australia, and Argentina drove up world grain prices, and many of the complaints of American farmers evaporated with a better price for their crops.

The New Shape of American Politics

The landslide Republican victory broke the stalemate in post–Civil War American politics. Republicans dropped their identification with the politics of piety and strengthened their image as the party of prosperity and national greatness, which gave them a party dominance that lasted until the 1930s. The Democrats, under Bryan's leadership until 1912, put on the mantle of Populist agrarian morals but were largely reduced to a sectional party, reflecting southern views on money, race, and national power. The 1896 election demonstrated that the Northeast and the Great Lakes states had acquired so many immigrants that they now controlled the nation's political destiny. The demoralized Populists disappeared, yet within the next 20 years, many Populist issues (direct election of senators, direct primaries, graduated income tax, woman suffrage, and others) were adopted by the two major parties.

Another result of the election of 1896 was a change in the pattern of political participation. Because the Republicans were so dominant outside the South, and Democrats were so powerful in the South, few states had vigorous two-party political battles and therefore had less reason to mobilize large numbers of voters. With results so often a foregone conclusion, voters had little motivation to cast a ballot. Many black voters in the South, moreover, were disfranchised, and middle-class good-government reformers

were not as effective as party bosses in turning out urban voters. The tremendous rate of political participation that had characterized the nineteenth century since the Jackson era gradually declined. In the twentieth century, political involvement among poorer Americans declined considerably, a phenomenon unique among western democracies.

McKinley had promised that Republican rule meant prosperity, and as soon as he took office, the

TIMELINE	
1873	Congress demonetizes silver
1875	Specie Resumption Act
1877	Rutherford B. Hayes becomes president
1878	Bland–Allison Act
1879	Henry George, *Progress and Poverty*
1880	James A. Garfield elected president
1881	Garfield assassinated Chester A. Arthur succeeds to presidency
1883	Pendleton Civil Service Act
1884	Grover Cleveland elected president W. D. Howells, *The Rise of Silas Lapham*
1887	College Settlement House Association founded
1888	Edward Bellamy, *Looking Backward* Benjamin Harrison elected president
1889	Jane Addams establishes Hull House Andrew Carnegie promulgates "The Gospel of Wealth"
1890	Sherman Anti-Trust Act Sherman Silver Purchase Act McKinley Tariff Elections bill defeated
1890s	Wyoming, Colorado, Utah, and Idaho grant woman suffrage
1892	Cleveland elected president for the second time Populist party wins more than 1 million votes Homestead steel strike
1893	World's Columbian Exposition, Chicago
1893–1897	Financial panic and depression
1894	Pullman strike Coxey's march on Washington
1895	*United States* v. *E. C. Knight*
1896	Charles Sheldon, *In His Steps* Populist party fuses with Democrats William McKinley elected president
1897	"Golden Rule" Jones elected mayor of Toledo, Ohio Economic recovery begins

economy recovered. Discoveries of gold in the Yukon and the Alaskan Klondike increased the money supply, ending the silver mania until the next great depression in the early 1930s. Industrial production returned to full capacity. Touring the Midwest in 1898, McKinley spoke to cheering crowds about the hopeful shift from "industrial depression to industrial activity."

McKinley's election marked not only the return of economic health but also the emergence of the executive as the dominant focus of the American political system. Just as McKinley's campaign (like Benjamin Harrison's in 1888) set the pattern for the extravagant corporate contributions in presidential campaigns that have marked modern times, his conduct as president foreshadowed the twentieth-century presidency. McKinley rejected traditional views of the president as the passive executor of laws, instead playing an active role in dealing with Congress and the press. His frequent trips away from Washington showed an increasing regard for gathering public opinion in the interests of advancing federal and national power. As we shall see in Chapter 20, McKinley began the transformation of the presidency into a potent force in world affairs as well.

Conclusion

Looking Forward

This chapter began with Edward Bellamy's imaginary look backward from the year 2000 at the grim economic realities and unresponsive politics of American life in the late nineteenth century. McKinley's triumph in 1896 indicated that in a decade marked by depression, Populist revolt, and cries for action to close the inequalities of wealth—represented by Bellamy's coach—the established order remained intact. Calls for change did not necessarily lead to change. But in the areas of personal action and the philosophical bases for social change, intellectual middle-class reformers such as Edward Bellamy, Henry George, Frances Willard, Jane Addams, and "Golden Rule" Jones were showing the way to progressive reforms in the new century. More Americans were able to look forward to the kind of cooperative, caring, and cleaner world envisioned in Bellamy's utopian novel.

As 1900 approached, people took a predictably intense interest in what the new century would be like. Henry Adams, still the pessimist, saw an ominous future, predicting the explosive and ultimately destructive energy of unrestrained industrial development, symbolized by the "dynamo" and other engines of American and European power. Such forces, he warned, would overwhelm the gentler, moral forces represented by art, woman, and religious symbols. But others were more optimistic, preferring to place their confidence in America's self-image as an exemplary nation, demonstrating to the world the moral superiority of its economic system, democratic institutions, and middle-class Protestant values. Surely the new century, most thought, would see not only the continued perfection of these values and institutions but also the spread of the American model around the globe. Such confidence resulted in foreign expansion by the American people even before the old century had ended. We turn to that next.

Questions for Review and Reflection

1. How would you characterize the politics of the Gilded Age? How does it compare to present-day politics?

2. What political issues concerned the American people in the late nineteenth century, and do you think they were the appropriate ones?

3. What role did middle-class reformers, especially women, play in dealing with social and political problems in the Gilded Age? How did religion influence reform?

4. Why was the election of 1896 such a crucial and pivotal one in the development of American political parties? How were the policies and areas of support of the two major parties similar to and different from those of the present?

5. Was the American democratic system responsive to the needs of the American people in the Gilded Age? Was it even "democratic"? How well did politics reflect national ideals and values?

Recommended Reading

Recommended Readings are posted on the Web site for this textbook. Visit www.ablongman.com/nash

Fiction and Film

Mark Twain and Charles D. Warner's *The Gilded Age* (1873) spares no one in its satirical critique of the social, political, and economic life of late-nineteenth-century America. Henry Adams's *Democracy: An American Novel* (1880) uses an ironic title to capture the elitist nature of politics and life in Washington in the Gilded Age. Two novels by William Dean Howells, *A Hazard of New Fortunes* (1889) and *The Rise of Silas Lapham* (1885), portray the social life of the new rich in the 1880s. Edward Bellamy's *Looking Backward* (1888) is the utopian novel that began this chapter and that stimulated much late-nineteenth-century reform, rivaled only by Charles Sheldon's social gospel novel *In His Steps* (1896). Kate Chopin's *The Awakening* (1899), set in New Orleans in the 1890s, tells the story of a woman's discovery of self. Theodore Dreiser's *Sister Carrie* (1900), influenced by social Darwinian determinism and set in Chicago and New York, shows the life of a young farm girl who rises to fame and fortune in the city.

Frank Norris's immense novel *The Octopus* (1901), set in the San Joaquin Valley of California, shows struggles not only between ranchers and railroads but also between rich and poor, city and country, commercial wheat farmers and sheep herders, and native-born and immigrant Americans. Anzia Yezierska's *Bread Givers* (1925) reveals the struggles between an Old World Jewish father and his Americanized daughter. *Hester Street* (1975) is a wonderfully teachable video about Jewish immigrants in New York City and, like *Bread Givers,* the process of Americanization. Ed. L. Doctorow's *Ragtime* (1975) is an innovative novel that plays fast and loose with the history and historical figures of turn-of-the-century America; it was also made into a Broadway play. Upper-class life in the late nineteenth century is portrayed in the Hollywood film *The Bostonians* (1998), based on a novel by Henry James. Gore Vidal's *1876: A Novel* (1976) takes a playful, imaginative look at America in its centennial year.

Discovering U.S. History Online

Gilded Age Presidents

www.potus.com/rbhayes.html
www.potus.com/jagarfield.html
www.potus.com/caarthur.html
www.potus.com/gcleveland.html
www.potus.com/bharrison.html

These sites contain basic factual data about Gilded Age presidents Hayes, Garfield, Arthur, Cleveland, and Harrison, including speeches and online biographies.

Late Nineteenth-Century Articles

www.boondocksnet.com

This site includes several exhibitions with links to contemporary articles, art, and cartoons about the late nineteenth century and early twentieth century, including "World's Fairs and Expositions: Defining America and the World, 1876–1916" and "Mark Twain on War and Imperialism."

The Gilded Age

www.wm.edu/~srnels/gilded.html

This site offers links to Gilded Age documents and sources, especially literature.

The Rich in the Gilded Age

www.newportmansions.org

This site presents a virtual tour of Newport mansions along with background information.

The Life of William Jennings Bryan

www.mission.lib.tx.us/exhibits/bryan/bryan.htm

This site offers an online presentation of Hidalgo County Historical Museum's exhibit on William Jennings Bryan as well as digitized sources on his life and campaign for president.

The Election of 1896

www.iath.virginia.edu/seminar/unit8/home.htm

This fine University of Virginia site contains biographical information, images, great cartoons, and related links about the pivotal election of 1896.

1896: The Presidential Campaign: Cartoons and Commentary

www.iberia.vassar.edu/1896/

The site contains several sections: "Cartoons," "Parties and Platforms," "Leaders," "Campaign Themes," and "Special Features," as well as background on the depression of 1893.

World's Columbian Exhibition

www.boondocksnet.com/expos/columbian.html

Part of a larger site, "World's Fairs and Expositions: Defining America and the World, 1876–1916," superbly edited by Jim Zwick, this site is full of links to contemporary articles, art, and cartoons about the Columbian Exhibition in Chicago in 1893, with attention to architecture, art and literature, race relations, religion, social issues, and technology. A virtual visit to the fair.

CHAPTER 20

Becoming a World Power

Dewey at Manila Bay, May 1, 1898 (painting by Rufus Zogbaum): American Expansionism Triumphant. What artistic elements make this a heroic painting? *(CORBIS)*

American Stories

Private Grayson Kills a Soldier in the Philippines

In January 1899, the U.S. Senate was locked in a dramatic debate over whether to ratify the Treaty of Paris concluding the recent war with Spain over Cuban independence. At the same time, American soldiers uneasily faced Filipino rebels across a neutral zone around the outskirts of Manila, the capital of the Philippines. Until recent weeks, the Americans and Filipinos had been allies, together defeating the Spanish to liberate the Philippines. The American fleet under Admiral George Dewey had destroyed the Spanish naval squadron in Manila Bay on May 1, 1898. Three weeks later, an American ship brought from exile the native Filipino insurrectionary leader Emilio Aguinaldo to lead rebel forces on land, while U.S. gunboats patrolled the seas.

At first, the Filipinos looked on the Americans as liberators. Although the intentions of the United States were never clear, as in a later intervention in Iraq, Aguinaldo believed that, as in Cuba, the Americans had no territorial ambitions. They would simply drive the Spanish out and then leave. In June, therefore, Aguinaldo declared the independence of the Philippines and began setting up a constitutional government. American officials pointedly ignored the independence ceremonies. When an armistice ended the war in August, American troops denied Aguinaldo's Filipino soldiers an opportunity to liberate their own capital city and shunted them off to the suburbs. The armistice agreement recognized American rights to the "harbor, city, and bay of Manila," while the proposed Treaty of Paris gave the United States the entire Philippine Islands archipelago.

Consequently, tension mounted in the streets of Manila and along 14 miles of trenches separating American and Filipino soldiers. Taunts, obscenities, and racial epithets were shouted across the neutral zone. Barroom skirmishes and knifings filled the nights; American soldiers searched houses without warrants and looted stores. Their behavior was not unlike that of English soldiers in Boston in the 1770s.

On the night of February 4, 1899, Privates William Grayson and David Miller of Company B, 1st Nebraska Volunteers, were on patrol in Santa Mesa, a Manila suburb surrounded on three sides by insurgent trenches. The Americans had orders to shoot any Filipino soldiers in the neutral area. As the two Americans cautiously worked their way to a bridge over the San Juan River, they heard a Filipino signal whistle, answered by another. Then a red lantern flashed from a nearby blockhouse. The two froze as four Filipinos emerged from the darkness on the road ahead. "Halt!" Grayson shouted. The native lieutenant in charge answered, "Halto!"—either mockingly or because he had similar orders. Standing less than 15 feet apart, the two men repeated their commands. After a moment's hesitation, Grayson fired, killing his opponent with one bullet. As the other Filipinos jumped out at them, Grayson and Miller shot two more. Then they turned and ran back to their own lines shouting warnings of attack. A full-scale battle followed.

The next day, Commodore Dewey cabled Washington that the "insurgents have inaugurated general engagement" and promised a hasty suppression of the insurrection. The outbreak of hostilities ended the Senate debates. On February 6, the Senate ratified the Treaty of Paris, thus formally annexing the Philippines and sparking a war between the United States and Aguinaldo's Filipino nationalist revolutionaries, who represented a small but growing percentage of the population.

In a guerrilla war similar to those that Americans would fight later in the twentieth century in eastern Asia and the Middle East, Filipino nationalists tried to undermine the American will by hit-and-run attacks. American soldiers, meanwhile, remained in heavily garrisoned cities and undertook search-and-destroy missions to root out rebels and pacify the countryside. The Filipino-American War lasted until July 1902, three years longer than the Spanish-American War that caused it and involving far more troops, casualties, and monetary and moral costs.

How did all this happen? What brought Private Grayson to "shoot my first nigger," as he put it, halfway around the world? For the first time in history, regular American soldiers found themselves fighting outside North America. The "champion of oppressed nations," as Aguinaldo said, had turned into an oppressor nation itself, imposing the American way of life and American institutions on faraway peoples against their will. It would not be the last time.

The war in the Philippines marked a critical transformation of America's role in the world. As the United States exerted its influence on the world, so also did global events influence the American people. Within a few years at the turn of the century, the United States acquired an empire, however small by European standards, and established itself as a world power. In this chapter, we will review the historical dilemmas of America's role in the world in the late nineteenth century when expansionism was increasing worldwide. In this global context, we will examine the motivations for intensified expansionism by the United States in the 1890s and how they were manifested in Cuba, the Philippines, and elsewhere. Finally, we will look at how the fundamental patterns of American foreign policy to this day were established for Latin America, eastern Asia and the Middle East, and Europe. Throughout, we will see that the tension between idealism and self-interest that has permeated America's domestic history has also guided its foreign policy.

STEPS TOWARD EMPIRE

The circumstances that brought Privates Grayson and Miller from Nebraska to the Philippines originated deep in American history. As early as the seventeenth-century Puritan migration, Americans worried about how to do good in a sinful world. John Winthrop sought to set up a "city on a hill" in the New World, a model community of righteous living for the rest of the world to imitate. "Let the eyes of the world be upon us," Winthrop had said. That wish, reaffirmed during the American Revolution, became a permanent goal of American policy toward the outside world.

America as a Model Society

Nineteenth-century Americans, like the Russians, French, English, and Chinese, continued to believe in their nation's special mission in the world. But only the United States claimed a mission of democratic representative government. The Monroe Doctrine in 1823, pointing out the differences between autocratic Europe and republican America, warned Europe's monarchies to keep out of the New World and not to interfere with emerging Latin American independence movements. In succeeding decades, distinguished European visitors came to observe the "great social revolution" in the United States. They found representative and responsive democratic political and legal institutions, vibrant Protestantism, boundless energy, and an ability to apply unregulated economic activity and inventive genius to stupendous achievements of production.

In an evil world, Americans then, as now, believed that they stood as a transforming force for good. But how could a nation committed to isolationism—to avoiding entanglements with European nations—do the transforming? One way was to encourage other countries to observe and imitate the good example set by the United States. Other nations, however, were often attracted to competing models of modernization, such as socialism, or preferred their own religious traditions, such as Islam. Such differences often led to a more aggressive American foreign policy, as seen in the aftermath of the September 11, 2001, attacks on New York City and the Pentagon.

Patience and passivity are not characteristic traits of the American people. Therefore, throughout the country's history, American leaders have actively and sometimes forcefully sought to impose their ideas and institutions on others. These unclearly intentioned international crusades, as in recent years in the Caribbean, Somalia, Afghanistan, and Iraq, have not always been well received. Hence, the effort to spread the American model to an imperfect world has been both a blessing and a burden—for others as well as for the American people.

Early Expansionism

Persistent expansionism marked the first century of American independence. Jefferson's purchase of Louisiana in 1803, the taking of Indian lands during the War of 1812, and the midcentury pursuit of "Manifest Destiny" spread the United States across North America. In the 1850s, Americans began to look beyond their own continent as Commodore Perry in 1853 "opened" Japan, and southerners sought more cotton lands in the Caribbean. Although generally not entangled with European affairs for most of the century (as Washington and Jefferson had advised), the American people and government were very much entangled elsewhere. To the Mexicans, and to the Cherokee, Creek, Iroquois, Shawnee, Lakota, Navajo, Nez Percé, and other Native American nations, the United States was far from isolationist, a concept that referred only to Europe.

After the Civil War, Secretary of State William Seward spoke of an America that would hold a "commanding sway in the world," destined to exert

Waging War in the Philippines When the United States went to war against Spain in 1898, partly to help the Cubans win their independence from imperial Spanish rule, no one could have imagined the ironic outcome. Within a year, Americans would impose imperial rule over the Philippines, marching through and burning villages (as the Twentieth Kansas Volunteers are doing here) and waging war against civilians in a faraway Asian land. How did that happen? *(Above: Courtesy of The Newberry Library, Chicago; right: Keystone-Mast Collection [24039], URL/California Museum of Photography, University of California at Riverside)*

commercial domination "on the Pacific ocean, and its islands and continents." He purchased Alaska from Russia in 1867 for $7.2 million and acquired a coaling station in the Midway Islands near Hawaii, where missionaries and merchants were already active. He advocated annexing Cuba and other Caribbean islands, tried to negotiate a treaty for an American-built canal through Panama, and dreamed of "possession" of the entire North and Central American continent and ultimately "control of the world."

In 1870, foreshadowing the Philippines debates 30 years later, supporters of President Grant, arguing the strategic and economic importance of the Caribbean, tried to persuade the Senate to annex Santo Domingo on the island of Hispaniola. Opponents responded that annexation violated American principles of self-determination and government by consent. They also claimed that brown-skinned Caribbean peoples were unassimilable. Expansionism, moreover, might involve foreign entanglements, a large and expensive navy,

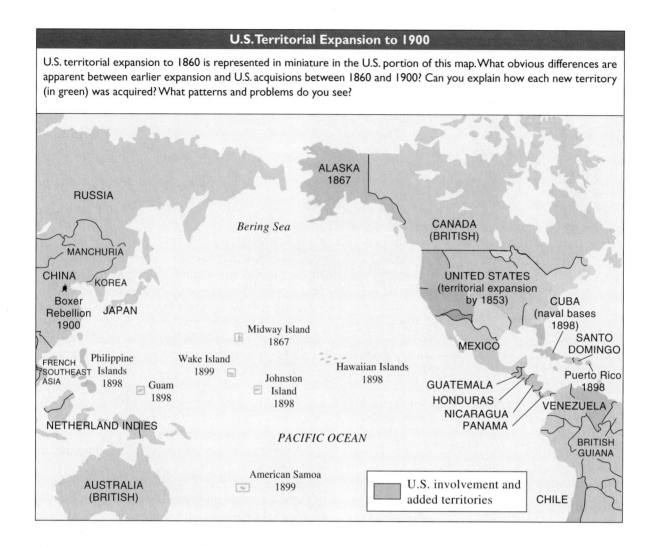

U.S. Territorial Expansion to 1900

U.S. territorial expansion to 1860 is represented in miniature in the U.S. portion of this map. What obvious differences are apparent between earlier expansion and U.S. acquisions between 1860 and 1900? Can you explain how each new territory (in green) was acquired? What patterns and problems do you see?

RUSSIA

Bering Sea

ALASKA
1867

MANCHURIA

CANADA
(BRITISH)

CHINA
KOREA

★

Boxer
Rebellion
1900

JAPAN

UNITED STATES
(territorial expansion
by 1853)

CUBA
(naval bases
1898)

Midway Island
1867

MEXICO

SANTO
DOMINGO

FRENCH
SOUTHEAST
ASIA

Philippine
Islands
1898

Wake Island
1899

Guam
1898

Johnston
Island
1898

Hawaiian Islands
1898

GUATEMALA
HONDURAS
NICARAGUA
PANAMA

Puerto Rico
1898

VENEZUELA

NETHERLAND INDIES

PACIFIC OCEAN

BRITISH
GUIANA

AUSTRALIA
(BRITISH)

American Samoa
1899

U.S. involvement and
added territories

CHILE

bigger government, and higher taxes; the Senate rejected annexation.

Although reluctant to add territory outright, Americans eagerly sought commercial dominance in Latin America and Asia, with a canal through Central America to facilitate interocean traffic. But American talk of building a canal across Nicaragua produced only Nicaraguan suspicions. In 1881, secretary of state James G. Blaine sought to convene a conference of American nations to promote hemispheric peace and trade. Latin Americans may have wondered what Blaine intended, for in 1881 he intervened in three separate border disputes in Central and South America, in each case at the cost of goodwill. Conditions worsened in 1889. A barroom brawl in Chile resulted in the death of two American sailors, and President Harrison threatened war, demanding "prompt and full reparation." After Chile complied, Blaine held the first Pan-American Conference to improve economic ties among the nations of the Americas.

U.S. economic influence spread to the Pacific. In the mid-1870s, American sugar-growing interests in

the Hawaiian Islands were strong enough to put whites in positions of influence over the monarchy. In 1875, they obtained a treaty admitting Hawaiian sugar duty-free to the United States, and in 1887, the United States also won exclusive rights to build a naval base at Pearl Harbor. Native Hawaiians resented the influence of American sugar interests, especially as they brought in Japanese to replace native people in the sugarcane fields, with some 200,000 arriving between 1885 and 1924.

In 1891, the nationalistic queen Liliuokalani assumed the throne and pursued a policy of "Hawaii for the Hawaiians." Two years later, white planters, fearful that the queen might turn to Japan for support, staged a coup with the help of U.S. gunboats and marines and imprisoned the queen. With the success of their bloodless coup, called by one journalist a revolution "of sugar, by sugar, for sugar," the whites sought formal annexation by the friendly Harrison administration. But when Grover Cleveland, who opposed imperial

IMAGE

Queen
Liliuokalani–
Portrait, 1887

expansion, returned to the presidency for his second term, he stopped the move. The sugar growers waited patiently for a more desirable time for annexation, which came during the war in 1898.

American Expansionism in Global Context

American forays into the Pacific and Latin America brought the United States increasingly into contact and conflict with European nations. The nineteenth century was marked by European imperial expansionism throughout much of the world. In southern and southeastern Asia, the British were in India, Burma, and Malaya; the French in Cambodia, Vietnam, and Laos; the Dutch in Singapore and the East Indies; and the Spanish in the Philippines. These and other colonial powers divided China—its Manchu dynasty weakened by the opium trade, internal conflicts, and European pressure—into spheres of economic influence. A Chinese newspaper editorial complained that other nations "all want to satisfy their ambitions to nibble at China and swallow it." The Russians wrested away Manchuria, and Japan took Korea after intervention in a Korean peasant rebellion in 1894. In addition, China was forced to cede Taiwan and southern Manchuria to Japanese influence and control.

In Africa, Europeans scrambled to gain control of both coastal and interior areas, with England,

World Colonial Empires, 1900

France, Germany, Portugal, and Belgium grabbing the most land and exploiting African peoples. Only two independent African nations existed in the late nineteenth century: Liberia, founded in 1822 by Americans to resettle free blacks, and the fragmented kingdom of Ethiopia, which thrashed the Italians when they invaded in 1896. With nearly all of Africa divided, the only way imperial powers could acquire more land was to fight one another. Thus, in 1899, war broke out in southern Africa between the British and the Boers, descendants of Dutch settlers—a war waged with a savagery Europeans usually reserved for black indigenous peoples. The English killed cattle, destroyed Boer farms, and drove civilians into camps where an estimated 20,000 women and children perished from starvation and malnutrition. The British won, but at a horrific cost.

Africa was not then of interest to the United States, but in the Pacific and the Caribbean, it was inevitable that the United States, a late arrival to imperialism, would collide with European rivals. Moving outward from Hawaii closer to the markets of eastern Asia, the United States acquired a naval and coaling station in the Samoan Islands in 1878, sharing the port with Great Britain and Germany. American and German naval forces almost fought each other there in 1889—before a typhoon ended the crisis by wiping out both navies. Troubles in the Pacific also occurred in the late 1880s over the American seizure of several Canadian ships in fur seal and fishing disputes in the Bering Sea, settled only by the threat of British naval action and an international arbitration ruling, which ordered the United States to pay damages.

Closer to home, the United States sought to replace Great Britain as the most influential nation in Central America and northern South America. In 1895, a boundary dispute between Venezuela and British Guyana threatened to bring British intervention against the Venezuelans. President Cleveland, needing a popular political issue during the depression, asked Secretary of State Richard Olney to send a message to Great Britain. Invoking the Monroe Doctrine, Olney's note (stronger than Cleveland intended) called the United States "practically sovereign on this continent" and demanded international arbitration to settle the dispute. The British ignored the note, and war loomed. Both sides realized that war between two English-speaking nations would be an "absurdity," and the boundary dispute was settled.

Despite expansionist bluster, these encounters showed that the United States in 1895 had neither the means nor a consistent policy for enlarging its role in the world. The diplomatic service was small and unprofessional. No U.S. embassy official in Beijing spoke Chinese. The U.S. Army, with about 28,000 men, was smaller than Bulgaria's. The navy, dismantled after the Civil War and partly rebuilt under President Arthur, still had many obsolete ships and ranked no higher than tenth in the world. By 1898, things would change.

EXPANSIONISM IN THE 1890S

In 1893, the historian Frederick Jackson Turner wrote that for three centuries "the dominant fact in American life has been expansion." The "extension of American influence to outlying islands and adjoining countries," he thought, indicated still more expansionism. Turner struck a responsive chord in a country that had always been restless and optimistic. With the western frontier declared closed, Americans would surely look for new frontiers, for mobility and markets as well as for morality and missionary activity. The motivations for the expansionist impulse of the late 1890s resembled those that had prompted Europeans to settle the New World in the first place: greed, glory, and God. We will examine expansionism as a reflection of profits, patriotism, piety, and politics.

Profits: Searching for Overseas Markets

Senator Albert Beveridge of Indiana bragged in 1898 that "American factories are making more than the American people can use; American soil is producing more than they can consume. Fate has written our policy for us; the trade of the world must and shall be ours." Americans such as Beveridge revived older dreams of an American commercial empire in the Caribbean Sea and the Pacific Ocean. American businessmen saw huge profits beckoning in heavily populated Latin America and Asia, and they wanted to get their share of these markets, as well as access to the sugar, coffee, fruits, oil, rubber, and minerals that were abundant in these lands.

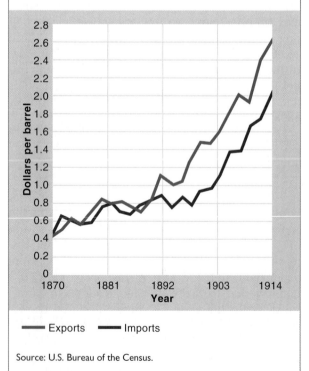

American Foreign Trade, 1870–1914

After a rather gradual increase in trade through the boom-and-bust cycles of the 1870s and 1880s and an actual dip during the depression of 1893–1895, American foreign trade saw spectacular increases during the Republican era of Presidents McKinley, Roosevelt, and Taft. What is the relationship between foreign trade and imperial expansion?

Source: U.S. Bureau of the Census.

Understanding that commercial expansion required a stronger navy and coaling stations and colonies, business interests began to shape diplomatic and military strategy. Senator Orville Platt of Connecticut said in 1893: "A policy of isolationism did well enough when we were an embryo nation, but today things are different." But not all businesspeople in the 1890s liked commercial expansion or a vigorous foreign policy. Some preferred traditional trade with Canada and Europe rather than risky new ventures in Asia and Latin America. Some thought it more important to recover from the depression than to annex distant islands.

But the drop in domestic consumption during the depression prompted businesses to expand into new markets to sell surplus goods. The tremendous growth of American production in the post–Civil War years made expansionism more attractive than drowning in overproduction, cutting prices, or laying off workers, which would increase social unrest. The newly formed National Association of Manufacturers, which led the way, proclaimed in 1896 that "the trade centers of Central and South America are natural markets for American products."

Despite the 1890s depression, products spewed from American factories at a staggering rate. The United States moved from fourth place in the world in manufacturing in 1870 to first place in 1900, doubling the number of factories and tripling the value of farm output. The United States led the world in railroad construction and such mass-produced technological products as agricultural machinery, sewing machines, electrical implements, cash registers, and telephones. Manufactured goods grew nearly fivefold between 1895 and 1914. The total value of American exports tripled, from $434 million in 1866 to nearly $1.5 billion in 1900. By 1914, exports had risen to $2.5 billion, a 67 percent increase over 1900. The increased trade continued to go mainly to Europe rather than Asia. In 1900, for example, only 3 to 4 percent of U.S. exports went to China and Japan. But interest in Asian markets continued to grow (the number of American firms in China rose from 50 in 1870 to 550 by 1930), especially as agricultural output continued to increase and prices stayed low.

Investments followed a similar pattern. American direct investments abroad increased from about $634 million to $2.6 billion between 1897 and 1914. Although the greatest activity was in Britain, Canada, and Mexico, most attention focused on actual and potential investment in Latin America and Eastern Asia. Central American investment increased from $21 million in 1897 to $93 million by 1914, mainly in mines, railroads, and banana and coffee plantations. At the turn of the century came the formation and growth of America's largest multinational corporations: the United Fruit Company, Alcoa Aluminum, Du Pont, American Tobacco, and others. Initially slow to respond to investment and market opportunities abroad, these companies soon supported an aggressive foreign policy.

Patriotism: Asserting National Power

In 1898, a State Department memorandum stated that "we can no longer afford to disregard international rivalries now that we ourselves have become a competitor in the worldwide struggle for trade." The national state, then, should support commercial interests.

Americans, therefore, also saw expansion in terms of national glory and greatness. In the late 1890s, a group formed around assistant secretary of the navy Theodore Roosevelt and Massachusetts senator Henry Cabot Lodge emerged as highly influential leaders of a changing American foreign policy.

Uncle Sam's Imperial Stretch   Citing the Monroe Doctrine and the Roosevelt–Lodge "large policy" as justification, U.S. imperial interests at the turn of the century spread American economic, political, and military influence from Alaska across the Caribbean to South America. Uncle Sam is looking westward. Why?
(Bettmann/Corbis)

These intensely nationalistic young men shifted to what Lodge called the "large policy" by which economic interests would take second place to questions of what he and Roosevelt called "national honor." By 1899, a State Department official wrote that the United States had become "a world power. . . . Where formerly we had only commercial interests, now we have territorial and political interests as well."

Naval strategist Alfred Thayer Mahan greatly influenced the new foreign policy elite. Mahan's books argued that in a world of Darwinian struggle for survival, national power depended on naval supremacy, control of sea lanes, and vigorous development of domestic resources and foreign markets. He advocated colonies in both the Caribbean and the Pacific, linked by a canal built and controlled by the United States. In a world of constant "strife" where "everywhere nation is arrayed against nation," he said, it was imperative that Americans develop sea power and "look outward."

Piety: The Missionary Impulse

As Mahan's statements suggest, a strong sense of duty and the missionary ideal of doing good for others also motivated expansionism—and sometimes rationalized the exploitation and oppression of weaker peoples. Roosevelt, Lodge, Mahan, and other Americans (such as George W. Bush in a later age) all would have agreed with the following summary of expansionist arguments:

> Certain nations are more civilized than others, especially those peopled by English-speaking, white, Protestant Anglo-Saxons. They enjoy free enterprise and democratic political institutions, which means representative government, distributive power, and the rule of law. Further evidence of the civilized nature of such nations includes their advanced technological and industrial development, large middle classes, and a high degree of education and literacy. The prime examples in the world are England and the United States.
>
> In the natural struggle for existence, those races and nations that survive and prosper prove their fitness and superiority. The United States, as a matter of history, geographic location, and political genius, is so favored and fit that God has chosen it to uplift less favored peoples. This responsibility cannot be avoided. It is a national duty, or burden—the "white man's burden"—that civilized nations undertake to bring peace, progressive values, and ordered liberty to the world.

The argument begins with principles of modernization and ends in statements of America's pious sense of itself as morally exceptional. A missionary put it more crudely in 1885: "The Christian nations are subduing the world in order to make mankind free."

Josiah Strong, a Congregationalist minister, was perhaps the most ardent advocate of American missionary expansionism. In a book titled *Our Country* (1885), he argued that in the struggle for survival among nations, the United States had emerged as the center of Anglo-Saxonism and was "divinely commissioned" to spread political liberty, Protestant Christianity, and civilized values over the earth. "This powerful race," he wrote, "will move down upon Mexico, down upon Central and South America, out upon the islands of the sea, over upon Africa and beyond." Indiana senator Albert Beveridge agreed, saying in 1899 that God had prepared English-speaking Anglo-Saxons to become "the master organizers of the world to establish and administer governments among savages and senile peoples."

DOCUMENT

Josiah Strong, *Our Country* (1885)

Missionaries carried Western values to non-Christian lands around the world, especially China. The number of American Protestant missionaries in China increased from 436 in 1874 to 5,462 in 1914, and the estimated number of Christian converts in China jumped from 5,000 in 1870 to nearly 100,000 in 1900. Although the number of converts was much less than missionaries hoped, this tiny fraction of the Chinese population included young reformist intellectuals who, steeped in Western ideas, helped overthrow the Manchu dynasty in 1912. Economic relations between China and the United States increased roughly at the same rate as missionary activity.

DOCUMENT

Albert Beveridge, "The March of the Flag" (1898)

Politics: Manipulating Public Opinion

Although less significant than the other factors, politics also played a role. As in the past, public opinion on international issues shaped presidential politics. The psychological tensions and economic hardships of the 1890s depression jarred national self-confidence. Foreign adventures then, as now, provided a distraction from domestic turmoil and promised to restore patriotic pride and win votes.

This process was helped by the growth of a highly competitive popular press, the penny daily newspapers, which brought international issues before a mass readership. When New York City newspapers, notably William Randolph Hearst's *Journal* and Joseph Pulitzer's *World*, competed in stirring up public support for the Cuban rebels against Spain, politicians dared not ignore the outcry. Daily reports of

Spanish atrocities in 1896 and 1897 kept public moral outrage constantly before President McKinley. His Democratic opponent, William Jennings Bryan, entered the fray, advocating American intervention in Cuba on moral grounds of a holy war to help the oppressed. Bryan even raised a regiment of Nebraska volunteers for war, but the Republican administration kept him far from battle and therefore far from the headlines.

Politics, then, joined profits, patriotism, and piety in motivating the expansionism of the 1890s. These four impulses interacted to produce the Spanish-American War, the annexation of the Philippine Islands and subsequent war, and the energetic foreign policy of President Theodore Roosevelt.

WAR IN CUBA AND THE PHILIPPINES

Lying 90 miles off Florida, Cuba had been the object of intense American interest for a half century. Spain could not halt the continuing struggle of the Cuban people for a measure of autonomy and relief from exploitive labor in the sugar plantations, even after slavery itself ended. Cuban uprisings and pressure for complete independence raised tensions between Spain and the United States.

The Road to War

When the Cuban revolt flared up anew in 1895, the Madrid government again failed to implement reforms. Instead, it sent General Valeriano Weyler y Nicolau, dubbed "the butcher" by the American press, with 50,000 troops to quell the disturbance. When Weyler began herding rural Cubans into "reconcentration" camps, Americans were outraged. An outpouring of sympathy swept the nation, especially as sensationalist reports of horrible suffering and the deaths of thousands in the camps filled American newspapers. "The old, the young, the weak, the crippled," wrote the New York *World*, "all are butchered without mercy."

The Cuban struggle appealed to a country convinced of its role as protector of the weak and defender of the right of self-determination. One editorial deplored Spanish "injustice, oppression, extortion, and demoralization," while describing the Cubans as heroic freedom fighters "inspired by our glorious example of beneficent free institutions and successful self-government." Motivated in part by genuine humanitarian concern and a sense of duty, many Americans held rallies to raise money and food for famine relief, called for land reform

The *Maine* Blows Up in Havana Harbor The artist has captured here the horror of the sinking of the *Maine*, with scenes before and after the explosion. What actions did Assistant Secretary of the Navy Theodore Roosevelt take after the sinking of the *Maine* that caused Secretary John Long to write in his diary, "I find that Roosevelt has come very near causing more of an explosion than happened to the *Maine*." *(Chicago Historical Society [ICHi-08428])*

and, for some, armed intervention. But neither Cleveland nor McKinley wanted war.

Self-interest also played a role. For many years, Americans had noted the profitable resources and strategic location of the island. American companies had invested extensively in Cuban sugar plantations. Appeals for reform had much to do with ensuring a stable environment for further investments and trade ($27 million in 1897), as well as for protecting the sugar fields against the ravages of civil war.

The election of 1896 only temporarily diverted attention from Cuba. A new government in Madrid recalled Weyler and made halfhearted concessions. But conditions worsened in the reconcentration camps, and the American press kept harping on the plight of the Cuban people. McKinley, eager not to upset recovery from the depression, skillfully resisted war pressures. But he could not control Spanish misrule or Cuban aspirations for freedom.

Events early in 1898 sparked the outbreak of hostilities. Rioting in Havana intensified both Spanish repression and American outrage. A letter from the Spanish minister to the United States, Dupuy de Lôme, calling McKinley a "weak," hypocritical politician, was intercepted and made public. Americans fumed. Hearst's New York *Journal* called de Lôme's letter "the worst insult to the United States in its history."

A second event was more serious. When the rioting broke out, the U.S. battleship *Maine* was sent to Havana harbor to protect American citizens. On February 15, a tremendous explosion blew up the *Maine*, killing 262 men. Advocates of American intervention blamed the Spanish. Newspapers trumpeted slogans like "Remember the *Maine!* To hell with Spain!"

Assistant Secretary of the Navy Theodore Roosevelt had been preparing for war for many years. He said that he believed the *Maine* had been sunk "by an act of dirty treachery on the part of the Spaniards" and would "give anything if President McKinley would order the fleet to Havana tomorrow." When the president did not, Roosevelt privately declared that McKinley had "no more backbone than a chocolate éclair" and continued readying the navy for action. A board of inquiry at the time concluded that an external submarine mine caused the disaster, but later studies showed that a faulty boiler or some other internal defect set off the explosion, a possibility even Roosevelt later conceded.

After the sinking of the *Maine*, Roosevelt took advantage of the secretary of the navy's absence from the office one day to cable Commodore George Dewey, commander of the U.S. Pacific fleet at Hong Kong. Roosevelt ordered Dewey to fill his ships with coal and, "in the event" of a declaration of war with Spain, to sail to the Philippines and make sure "the Spanish squadron does not leave the Asiatic coast." "The Secretary is away and I am having immense fun running the Navy," Roosevelt wrote in his diary that night.

Roosevelt's act was consistent with policies he had been urging on his more cautious superior for more than a year. As early as 1895, the navy had contingency plans for attacking the Philippines. Influenced by Mahan, Roosevelt wanted to enlarge the navy. He also believed that the United States should construct an interoceanic canal, acquire the Danish West Indies (the Virgin Islands), annex Hawaii, and oust Spain from Cuba. As Roosevelt told McKinley late in 1897, he was putting the navy in "the best possible shape" for the day "when war began."

The public outcry over the *Maine* drowned out McKinley's efforts to avoid war. With the issues politicized, McKinley pressured the Madrid government to make further concessions. Spain did, though refusing to grant full independence to Cuba, and the president finally acted. On April 11, 1898, he sent an ambiguous message to Congress that seemed to call for war. Two weeks later, Congress authorized using troops against Spain and recognized Cuban independence, actions amounting to a declaration of war. In a significant additional resolution, the Teller Amendment, Congress stated that the United States had no intention of annexing Cuba. Massachusetts senator George Hoar, who later assailed the United States for its war against the Filipinos, declared that intervention in Cuba

Maine Explosion, 1898

Burial of the *Maine* Victims

would be "the most honorable single war in all history," undertaken without "the slightest thought or desire of foreign conquest or of national gain." A Cuban revolutionary general was more realistic, saying, "I expect nothing from the Americans. We should trust everything to our efforts. It is better to rise or fall without help than to contract debts of gratitude with such a powerful neighbor."

"A Splendid Little War": Various Views

The outbreak of war between Spain and the United States did not go unnoticed in Europe. Kaiser Wilhelm II of Germany sarcastically offered to join with other European monarchs to help Spain resist the efforts of "the American-British Society for International Theft and Warmongering . . . to snatch Cuba from Spain." But Spain was left to face the United States alone, fully expecting a defeat. When war broke out, a Spanish rear admiral said that the ruptured relations with the United States "would surely be fatal."

Indeed, the war was short and relatively easy for the Americans, and "fatal" for the Spanish, who at the war's conclusion were left with "only two major combat vessels." The Americans won naval battles almost without return fire. At both major engagements, Manila Bay and Santiago Bay in Cuba,

Our Victorious Fleet in Cuban Waters

The Spanish-American War

Refer to the map on p. 656 to see how far apart these two war zones were. How could the United States more easily manage a widely separated two-ocean empire? What did it need to do?

The Cuban Arena

The Philippine Arena

Teddy's Charge and African American Troops in Cuba The celebrated charge of "Teddy's Rough Riders" up Kettle Hill, shown in the painting (left), was made possible (and safe) because Spanish resistance was neutralized by African American troops like these from the Ninth U.S. Cavalry (above). What is your comment on these two visual images? *(The Granger Collection, New York)*

only two Americans died, one of them from heat prostration while stoking coal. Guam and Puerto Rico were taken virtually without a shot. Only 385 men died from Spanish bullets, but more than 5,000 succumbed to tropical diseases. As the four-month war neared its end in August, Secretary of State John Hay wrote Roosevelt that "it has been a splendid little war; begun with the highest motives, carried on with magnificent intelligence and spirit."

The Spanish-American War seemed splendid in other ways, as letters from American soldiers suggest. One young man wrote that his comrades were all "in good spirits" because oranges and coconuts were plentiful and "every trooper has his canteen full of lemonade all the time." Another wrote his brother that he was having "a lot of fun chasing Spaniards."

But the war was not much fun for other soldiers. One said, "Words are inadequate to express the feeling of pain and sickness when one has the fever. For about a week every bone in my body ached and I did not care much whether I lived or not." Another described "a man shot while loading his gun," noting

that "the Spanish Mauser bullet struck the magazine of his carbine and split, a part of it going through his scalp and a part through his neck. . . . He was a mass of blood."

Nor was the war splendid for African American soldiers, who fought in segregated units and noted stark differences between their rude treatment in the American South and warm, grateful greetings in Cuba and Puerto Rico. African Americans were especially sympathetic to the Cuban people's struggle against unjust treatment. One wrote in his journal, "At last we have taken up the sword to enforce the divine rights of a people who have been unjustly treated," an understandable sentiment during a decade marked by the restricting of rights for African Americans by southern state legislatures.

VIDEO
Roosevelt's Rough Riders

For Colonel Roosevelt, who resigned from the navy to lead a cavalry unit as soon as war was declared, the war was excitement and political opportunity. After a close brush with death in Cuba, Roosevelt declared with delight that he felt "the wolf rise in the heart" during "the power of joy in battle." But ironically, he

Teddy Roosevelt– Rough Rider

needed help from African American soldiers to achieve his goals. His celebrated charge up Kettle Hill near Santiago was made possible by black troops first clearing the hill and then protecting his flank. The "charge" made three-inch headlines and propelled him toward the New York governor's mansion. "I would rather have led that charge," he said later, "than served three terms in the U.S. Senate." More than anyone, Roosevelt used the war to advance not only his political career but also the glory of national expansionism.

The Philippines Debates and War

Roosevelt's ordering Admiral Dewey to Manila initiated a chain of events that led to the annexation of the Philippines. The most crucial battle of the Spanish-American War occurred on May 1, 1898, when Dewey destroyed the Spanish fleet in Manila Bay and cabled McKinley for additional troops. Although the president admitted later that he was uncertain "within two thousand miles" where "those darned islands were," he sent twice as many troops as Dewey had asked for and immediately began shaping American public opinion to accept the "political, commercial [and] humanitarian" reasons for annexing the Philippines, a policy he called "Benevolent Assimilation." The Treaty of Paris gave the United States all 7,000 islands in the archipelago in exchange for a $20 million payment to Spain.

The treaty went to the Senate for ratification during the winter of 1898–1899. Senators hurled arguments across the floor of the Senate as American soldiers hurled oaths and taunts across the neutral zone at Aguinaldo's insurgents near Manila. Private Grayson's encounter, described at the beginning of

DOCUMENT

William McKinley, "Decision on the Philippines" (1901)

this chapter, led to the passage of the treaty in a close Senate vote—and began the Filipino-American War and the debates over what to do with the Philippines.

The entire nation joined the argument. At stake were two very different views of foreign policy and of America's vision of itself. After several months seeking advice and listening to public opinion, McKinley finally recommended annexation on the grounds of international politics, commercial advantage, Filipino incapacity for self-rule, and the American responsibility to create Christian, civilized order. Many Democrats supported the president out of fear of being labeled disloyal. At a time when

openly racist thought flourished in the United States, Filipinos were described as childlike, dirty, and backward and were compared to blacks and Native Americans. "The country won't be pacified," a Kansas veteran of the Sioux wars told a reporter, "until the niggers are killed off like the Indians." Roosevelt called Aguinaldo a "renegade Pawnee" and said that the Filipinos had no right "to administer the country which they happen to be occupying."

A small but prominent and vocal Anti-Imperialist League vigorously opposed war and annexation. These dignitaries included former presidents Harrison and Cleveland, Samuel Gompers, Andrew Carnegie, Jane Addams, and Mark Twain. In arguments heard more recently about Iraq, anti-imperialists argued that taking over other countries contradicted American ideals. First, the annexation of territory without

DOCUMENT

Carl Schurz, *Platform of the Anti-Imperialist League* (1899)

postwar planning or steps toward statehood was unwise, unprecedented, and unconstitutional. Second, to occupy and govern a foreign people without their consent violated the ideals of the Declaration of Independence. Third, social reforms needed at home demanded American energies and money. "Before we attempt to teach house-keeping to the world," one writer put it, we needed "to set our own house in order."

Not all anti-imperialist arguments were so noble. A racist position alleged that Filipinos were nonwhite, Catholic, inferior in size and intelligence, and therefore unassimilable. Annexation would lead to miscegenation and contamination of Anglo-Saxon blood, said South Carolina senator Ben Tillman, who opposed "incorporating any more colored men into the body politic." A practical argument suggested that once in possession of the Philippines, the United States would have to defend them, necessitating acquiring more territories—in turn leading to higher taxes and bigger government, and perhaps calling for American troops to fight distant Asian wars.

The last argument became fact when Private Grayson's encounter started the Filipino-American War. Before it ended in 1902, some 126,500 American troops served in the Philippines, 4,234 died there, and 2,800 more were wounded. The cost was $400 million. Filipino casualties were much higher. In addition to 18,000 killed in combat, an estimated 200,000— and perhaps many more—Filipinos died of famine and disease as American soldiers burned villages and destroyed crops and livestock to deny the rebels their food

DOCUMENT

Congressional Speeches on Imperialism (1900)

AMERICAN VOICES

Jane Addams Speaks Out Against Imperialism, War, and Violence

Jane Addams, founder of Hull House in Chicago, gave this address on "Democracy or Militarism" at a Chicago Liberty meeting on April 30, 1899. An opponent of the Spanish-American War, Addams served as vice president of the national Anti-Imperialist League and was a co-founder and first president of the Women's International League for Peace and Freedom in 1919.

Let us not make the mistake of confusing moral issues sometimes involved in warfare with warfare itself. Let us not glorify the brutality. The same strenuous endeavor, the same heroic self-sacrifice, the same fine courage and readiness to meet death, may be displayed without the accompaniment of killing our fellow men. With all [British poet] Kipling's insight he has, over and over, failed to distinguish between war and imperialism on the one hand and the advance of civilization on the other.

. . . Some of us were beginning to hope that we were getting away from the ideals set by the civil war, that we had made all the presidents we could from men who had distinguished themselves in that war, and were coming to seek another type of man. That we were ready to accept the peace ideal, to be proud of our title as a peace nation; to recognize that the man who cleans a city is greater than he who bombards it, and the man who irrigates a plain greater than he who lays it waste. Then came the Spanish war, with its gilt and lace and tinsel, and again the moral issues are confused with exhibitions of brutality.

For ten years I have lived in a neighborhood which is by no means criminal, and yet during last October and November we were startled by seven murders within a radius of ten blocks. A little investigation of details and motives, the accident of a personal acquaintance with two of the criminals, made it not in the least difficult to trace the murders back to the influence of war.

. . . Psychologists intimate that action is determined by the selection of the subject upon which the attention is habitually fixed. The newspapers, the theatrical posters, the street conversations for weeks had to do with war and bloodshed. The little children on the street played at war, day after day, killing Spaniards. The humane instinct, which keeps in abeyance the tendency to cruelty, the growing belief that the life of each human being—however hopeless or degraded, is still sacred—gives way, and the barbaric instinct asserts itself.

It is doubtless only during a time of war that the men and women of Chicago could tolerate whipping for children in our city prison, and it is only during such a time that the introduction in the legislature of a bill for the re-establishment of the whipping post could be possible. National events determine our ideals, as much as our ideals determine national events.

- *What is the basis of Addams's arguments against violence and war?*
- *To what extent do they apply in our world today?*
- *Do you agree that wars abroad lead to violence at home?*
- *Do you agree that national events influence our ideals?*

---

supply. General Jacob H. Smith told his troops that "the more you kill and burn, the better you will please me." Insurgent ineptness, Aguinaldo's inability to extend the fight across ethnic boundaries, and atrocities on both sides increased the frustrations of a lengthening war. The American "water cure" and other tortures were especially brutal.

As U.S. treatment of the Filipinos became more and more like Spanish treatment of the Cubans, the hypocrisy of American behavior became even more evident. This was especially true for African American soldiers. They identified with the dark-skinned insurgents, whom they saw as tied to the land, burdened by debt, and pressed by poverty like themselves. "I feel sorry for these people," a sergeant in the Twenty-Fourth Infantry wrote. "You have no idea the way these people are treated by the Americans here."

The war starkly exposed the hypocrisies of shouldering the white man's burden. After the war, Aguinaldo wrote that Americans made "vague verbal

DOCUMENT

Mark Twain, "Incident in the Philippines" (1924)

RECOVERING THE PAST

Political Cartoons

One of the most enjoyable ways of recovering the values and attitudes of the past is through political cartoons. Ralph Waldo Emerson once said, "Caricatures are often the truest history of the times." A deft drawing of a popular or unpopular politician can freeze ideas and events in time, conveying more effectively than columns of print the central issues—and especially the hypocrisies and misbehaviors of an era. Cartoonists are often at their best when they are critical, exaggerating a physical feature of a political figure or capturing public sentiment against the government.

The history of political cartoons in the United States goes back to Benjamin Franklin's "Join or Die" cartoon calling for colonial cooperation against the French in 1754. But political cartoons were rare until Andrew Jackson's presidency. Even after such cartoons as "King Andrew the First" in the 1830s, they did not gain notoriety until the advent of Thomas Nast's cartoons in *Harper's Weekly* in the 1870s. Nast drew scathing cartoons exposing the corruption of William "Boss" Tweed's Tammany Hall, depicting Tweed and his men as vultures and smiling deceivers. "Stop them damn pictures," Tweed ordered. "I don't care so much what the papers write about me. My constituents can't read. But, damn it, they can see pictures." Tweed sent some of his men to Nast with an offer of $100,000 to "study art" in Europe. The $5,000-a-year artist negotiated up to a half million dollars before refusing Tweed's offer. "I made up my mind not long ago to put some of those fellows behind bars," Nast said, "and I'm going to put them there." His cartoons helped drive Tweed out of office.

The emergence of the United States as a world power and the rise of Theodore Roosevelt gave cartoonists plenty to draw about. At the same time, the rise of cheap newspapers such as William Randolph Hearst's *Journal* and Joseph Pulitzer's *World* provided a rich opportunity for cartoonists, whose clever images attracted more readers. When the Spanish-American War broke out, newspapers whipped up public sentiment by having artists draw fake pictures of fierce Spaniards stripping American women at sea and killing helpless Cubans. Hearst used these tactics to increase his paper's daily circulation to 1 million copies.

By the time of the debates over Philippine annexation, many cartoonists took an anti-imperialist stance, pointing out American hypocrisy. Within a year, cartoonists shifted from depicting "The Spanish Brute Adds Mutilation to Murder" (1898) to "Liberty Halts

"The Spanish Brute Adds Mutilation to Murder," by Grant Hamilton in *Judge*, July 9, 1898. *(Culver Pictures)*

American Butchery in the Philippines" (1899), both included here. Note the similarities in that both cartoons condemn the "butchery" of native peoples. But the villain has changed. Although Uncle Sam as a killer is not nearly as menacing as the figure of Spain as an ugly gorilla, both cartoons share a similarity of stance, blood-covered swords, and a trail of bodies behind.

Theodore Roosevelt's rise to the presidency and his broad grin, eyeglasses, and walrus mustache gave cartoonists a perfect target for caricature, as did his energetic style and such distinctive aspects as the "big stick" symbol and the "rough rider" image. To understand and appreciate the meaning of any cartoon, certain facts must be ascertained, such as the date, artist, and source of the cartoon; the particular historical characters, events, and context depicted in it; the significance of the caption; and the master symbols employed by the cartoonist. The Roosevelt cartoons "Panama or Bust" (1903) and "For President!" (1904), filled with symbols and images, were both printed in American daily newspapers.

REFLECTING ON THE PAST   What symbols and images do you see in these cartoons? How many can you identify, and how are they used? Who is the female figure, and what does she represent? How would you explain the change of bloodied sword bearer? What is the attitude of the Roosevelt cartoonists toward the president? In addition to these cartoons, look at the others in this chapter reflecting the widening reach of American expansionism. How do the images and symbols used in these reflect the cartoonist's point of view? How are various nationalities depicted in the cartoons? Check some recent newspapers: Who is criticized and stereotyped today, and how do cartoonists reveal their attitudes and political positions? What do contemporary cartoons reveal about American attitudes?

L. C. Gregg in the *Atlanta Constitution.*

FOR PRESIDENT!

"Panama or Bust," from the *New York Times,* 1903 (above); "For President!" by L. C. Gregg, in the *Atlanta Constitution,* 1904 (right).

Two Views of War's Results   Compare the photograph with the cartoon from 1898–1899. The photo shows American soldiers standing guard over captured Filipino guerrillas in 1899. The cartoon, by Charles L. (Bart) Batholomew of the *Minneapolis Journal* (July 2, 1898), presents a happier, if stereotyped, view of three new Americans, including one labeled "Philippines" on the skirt to the right. Or are they happier? What is the cartoonist's message? What similarities and differences do you see in these two visual images? *(Photo: Library of Congress)*

offers of friendship and aid and then fairly drowned them out with the boom of cannons and the rattle of Gatling guns." On reading a report that 8,000 Filipinos had been killed in the first year of the war, Carnegie wrote a letter, dripping with sarcasm, congratulating McKinley for "civilizing the Filipinos. . . . About 8,000 of them have been completely civilized and sent to Heaven. I hope you like it." An ardent anti-imperialist poet, Ernest Howard Crosby, wrote a parody of Rudyard Kipling's "White Man's Burden," which he titled "The Real 'White Man's Burden'":

DOCUMENT
Rudyard Kipling, "The White Man's Burden" (1899)

Take up the White Man's burden.
Send forth your sturdy kin,

And load them down with Bibles
And cannon-balls and gin.
Throw in a few diseases
To spread the tropic climes,
For there the healthy niggers
Are quite behind the times.
They need our labor question too.
And politics and fraud—
We've made a pretty mess at home,
Let's make a mess abroad.

Another writer penned a devastating one-liner: "Dewey took Manila with the loss of one man—and all our institutions."

The anti-imperialists failed either to prevent annexation or to interfere with

DOCUMENT
Ernest Howard Crosby, "The Real 'White Man's Burden'" (1899)

DOCUMENT
William Graham Sumner, "On Empire and the Philippines" (1898)

the war effort. However prestigious and principled, they had little or no political power. An older elite, they were out of tune with the period of exuberant expansionist national pride, prosperity, and promise.

Expansionism Triumphant

By 1900, Americans had ample reason to be patriotic. Within a year, the United States had acquired several island territories in the Pacific and Caribbean. But several questions arose over what to do with the new territories. What was their status? Were they colonies? Would they be granted statehood, or would they develop gradually from colonies to constitutional parts of the United States? Did Hawaiians, Puerto Ricans, and Filipinos have the same rights as American citizens on the mainland? Were they protected by the U.S. Constitution?

Bill of Fare, 1901

Although slightly different governing systems were worked out for each new territory, the solution in each case was to define its status as somewhere between a colony and a candidate for statehood. The indigenous people were usually allowed to elect their own legislature, but had governors and other judicial and administrative officials appointed by the American president. The first full governor of the Philippines, McKinley appointee William Howard Taft, effectively moved the Filipinos toward self-government, which came finally in 1946.

The question of constitutional rights was resolved by deciding that Hawaiians and Puerto Ricans, for example, would be treated differently from Texans and Oregonians. In the "insular cases" of 1901, the Supreme Court ruled that these people would achieve citizenship and constitutional rights only when Congress said they were ready. To the question, "Does the Constitution follow the flag?" the answer, as Secretary of State Elihu Root put it, was that "Ye-es . . . the Constitution follows the flag—but doesn't quite catch up with it."

Uncle Sam Teaching the World

In the election of 1900, Bryan was again the Democratic nominee and tried to make imperialism

Republican Campaign Poster   What is the persuasive political point of this 1900 campaign poster to reelect William McKinley? What was life like under the Democrats in 1896 and what has changed? Why would voters want to vote again for McKinley? *(David J. and Janice L. Frent Collection/CORBIS)*

the "paramount issue" of the campaign. He failed, in part because the country strongly favored annexing the Philippines. In the closing weeks of the campaign, Bryan shied away from imperialism and focused on domestic issues—trusts, the labor question, and free silver.

Changing strategies did Bryan no good either. Prosperity returned with the discovery of gold in Alaska, and cries for reform fell on deaf ears. The McKinley forces rightly claimed that four years of Republican rule had brought more money, jobs, thriving factories, and manufactured goods, as well as tremendous growth in American prestige abroad. Spain had been ejected from Cuba, and the American flag flew in many places around the globe. As Tom Watson put it, noting the end of the Populist revolt with the war fervor over Cuba, "The blare of the bugle drowned out the voice of the reformer."

He was more right than he knew. Within a year, Theodore Roosevelt rose from assistant secretary of the navy to colonel of the Rough Riders to governor of New York. For some Republican politicos, who thought he was too vigorous and independent, this quick rise as McKinley's potential rival came too fast. One way to eliminate Roosevelt politically, or at least slow him down, was to make him vice president, which they did in 1900. But six months into McKinley's second term, an anarchist killed him, the third presidential assassination in less than 40 years. "Now look," exclaimed party boss Mark Hanna, who had opposed putting Roosevelt on the ticket, "that damned cowboy is President of the United States!"

THEODORE ROOSEVELT'S ENERGETIC DIPLOMACY

At a White House dinner party in 1905, a guest told a story about visiting the Roosevelt home when "Teedie" was a baby. "You were in your bassinet, making a good deal of fuss and noise," the guest reported, "and your father lifted you out and asked me to hold you." Secretary of State Elihu Root looked up and asked, "Was he hard to hold?" Whether true or not, the story reveals much about President Roosevelt's principles and policies on foreign affairs. As president from 1901 to 1909, and as the most dominating American personality for the 15 years between 1897 and 1912, Roosevelt made much fuss and noise about the activist role he thought the United States should play in the world. As he implemented his policies, he often seemed "hard to hold." Yet Roosevelt's energetic foreign policy in Latin America, eastern Asia, and Europe paved the way

for the vital role as a world power that the United States would play for the next century.

Foreign Policy as Darwinian Struggle

Roosevelt advocated both individual physical fitness and collective national strength. An undersized boy, he had pursued a rigorous bodybuilding program, and as a young man on his North Dakota ranch, he learned to value the "strenuous life." Reading Darwin taught him that life was a constant struggle for survival. When he became president, his ideal was a "nation of men, not weaklings." "All the great masterful races," he said, "have been fighting races." Although he believed in Anglo-Saxon superiority, he admired—and feared—Japanese military prowess. Powerful nations, like individuals, Roosevelt believed, had a duty to cultivate vigor, strength, courage, and moral commitment to civilized values. In practical terms, this meant developing natural resources, building large navies, and being ever-prepared to fight.

Although famous for saying "speak softly and carry a big stick," Roosevelt often not only wielded a large stick but spoke loudly as well. In a speech in 1897, he used the word *war* 62 times, saying, "no triumph of peace is quite so great as the supreme triumphs of war." But despite his bluster, Roosevelt was usually restrained in exercising force. He won the Nobel Peace Prize in 1906 for helping end the Russo-Japanese War. The big stick and the loud talk were meant to preserve order and peace.

Roosevelt divided the world into civilized and uncivilized nations, the former usually defined as Anglo-Saxon and English-speaking. Civilized nations had a responsibility to "police" the uncivilized, not only maintaining order but also spreading superior values and institutions. Taking on the "white man's burden," civilized nations sometimes had to wage war on the uncivilized—justly so, he argued, because the victors bestowed the blessings of culture and racial superiority on the vanquished. But a war between two civilized nations (for example, Germany and Great Britain) would be foolish. Above all, Roosevelt believed in the balance of power. Strong, advanced nations had a duty to use their power to preserve order and peace. The United States had "no choice," Roosevelt said, "but to "play a great part in the world." With a 1900 population of 75 million, more than that of Great Britain, Germany, or France, the United States could no longer "avoid responsibilities" to exercise a greater role in world affairs.

Roosevelt developed a highly personal style of diplomacy. Bypassing the State Department, he preferred face-to-face contact and personal exchanges of letters with foreign diplomats and heads of state. He made foreign policy while horseback riding with the German ambassador and while discussing history with a French minister. A British emissary observed that Roosevelt had a "powerful personality" and a commanding knowledge of the world. Ministries from London to Tokyo respected him.

When threats failed to accomplish his goals, Roosevelt used direct personal intervention. "In a crisis the duty of a leader is to lead," he said, noting that Congress was too slow. When he wanted Panama, Roosevelt bragged later, "I took the Canal Zone" rather than submitting a long "dignified State Paper" for congressional debate. And while Congress debated, he gloated, the building of the canal began. Roosevelt's energetic executive activism in foreign affairs, for better or worse, influenced presidents from Woodrow Wilson to George W. Bush.

Taking the Panama Canal

To justify the intervention of 2,600 American troops in Honduras and Nicaragua in 1906, Philander Knox, later a secretary of state, said that "because of the Monroe Doctrine" the United States is "held responsible for the order of Central America." The closeness of the canal, he said, "makes the preservation of peace in that neighborhood particularly necessary." The Panama Canal was not yet finished when Knox spoke, but it had already become a cornerstone of U.S. policy.

Three problems had to be surmounted in order to dig an interoceanic connection. First, an 1850 treaty bound the United States to build a canal jointly with Great Britain, a problem resolved in 1901 when the British canceled the treaty in exchange for an American guarantee that the canal would be open to all nations. A second problem was where to dig it. American engineers rejected a long route through Nicaragua in favor of a shorter, more rugged path across Panama, where a French firm had already begun work. This raised the third problem: Panama was a province of Colombia, which rejected the terms the United States offered. The refusal angered Roosevelt, who called the Colombians "Dagoes" who tried to "hold us up" like highway robbers.

Building the Panama Canal

Aware of Roosevelt's fury, encouraged by hints of American support, and eager for the economic benefits that a canal would bring, Panamanian nationalists in 1903 staged a revolution led by several rich families and Philippe Bunau-Varilla of the French canal company. An American warship deterred Colombian intervention, and local troops were separated from their officers, who were bought off. A bloodless revolution occurred on November 3; on November 4, Panama declared its independence; and on November 6, the United States recognized it. Two weeks later, a treaty established the American right to build and operate a canal through Panama and to exercise "titular sovereignty" over the 10-mile-wide Canal Zone. The Panamanian government protested, and a later government called it the "treaty that no Panamanian signed." Roosevelt later claimed that the diplomatic and engineering achievement, completed in 1914, would "rank . . . with the Louisiana Purchase and the acquisition of Texas."

Theodore Roosevelt, Third Annual Message to Congress (1903)

Policing the Caribbean

As late as 1901, the Monroe Doctrine was still regarded, according to Roosevelt, as the "equivalent to an open door in South America." To the United States, this meant that although no nation had a right "to get territorial possessions," all nations had equal commercial rights in the Western Hemisphere south of the Rio

Building the Panama Canal In 1903, despite protests from the Panamanian government, the United States acquired the right to begin the enormous engineering feat of building the Panama Canal. *(The Granger Collection, New York)*

Grande. But as American investments poured into Central America and the Caribbean, the policy changed to one of asserting U.S. dominance in the Caribbean basin.

This change was demonstrated in 1902 when Germany and Great Britain blockaded Venezuela's ports to force the government to pay defaulted debts. Roosevelt was especially worried that German influence would replace the British. He insisted that the European powers accept arbitration and threatened to "move Dewey's ships" to the Venezuelan coast. The crisis passed, largely for other reasons, but Roosevelt's threat of force made very clear the paramount presence and self-interest of the United States in the Caribbean.

IMAGE

His Foresight, 1901

The United States kept liberated Cuba under a military governor, Leonard Wood, until 1902, when the Cubans elected a congress and president. The United States honored Cuban independence, as it had promised to do, but in the Platt Amendment, which Cubans reluctantly added to their constitution in 1901, the United States obtained many economic rights in Cuba, a naval base at Guantanamo Bay, and the right to intervene if Cuban sovereignty were ever threatened. Newspapers in Havana assailed this violation of their newfound independence. A cartoon titled "The Cuban Calvary" showed a figure

DOCUMENT

Platt Amendment (1901)

representing "the Cuban people" crucified between two thieves, Wood and McKinley.

American policy intended to make Cuba a model of how a newly independent nation could achieve orderly self-government with only minimal guidance. Cuban self-government, however, was shaky. When in 1906 a political crisis threatened to spiral into civil war, Roosevelt expressed his fury with "that infernal little Cuban republic." He sent warships to patrol the coastline and special commissioners and troops "to restore order and peace and public confidence." As he left office in 1909, Roosevelt proudly proclaimed, "we have done our best to put Cuba on the road to stable and orderly government." The road was paved with sugar, as U.S. trade with Cuba increased from $27 million to $43 million in the decade following 1898. Along with economic development, which mostly benefited American companies, American political and military involvement in Cuban affairs would continue throughout the century.

The pattern was repeated throughout the Caribbean. The Dominican Republic, for example, suffered from unstable governments and great poverty. In 1904, as a revolt erupted, European creditors pressured the Dominican government for payment of $40 million in defaulted bonds. Sending its warships to discourage European intervention, the United States took over the collection of customs in the republic. Two years later, the United

TR as Caribbean Policeman The "big stick" became a memorable image in American diplomacy as Teddy Roosevelt sought to make the United States a "policeman" not only of the Caribbean basin but also of the whole world. What image does Roosevelt convey, and how are the people of the world responding to him? *(Puck, 1901)*

States intervened in Guatemala and Nicaragua, where American bankers controlled nearly 50 percent of all trade, the first of several twentieth-century interventions in those countries.

In a policy known as the Roosevelt Corollary to the Monroe Doctrine, the president announced in his annual message to Congress in 1904 that civilized nations should "insist on the proper policing of the world." The goal of the United States, he said, was to have "stable, orderly and prosperous neighbors." A country that paid its debts and kept order "need fear no interference." But "chronic wrong-doing" would require the United States to intervene as an "international police power." Whereas the Monroe Doctrine had warned European nations not to intervene in the Western Hemisphere, the Roosevelt Corollary justified American intervention. Starting with a desire to protect property, loans, and investments, the United States wound up supporting the tyrannical regimes of elites who owned most of the land, suppressed the poor, blocked reforms, and acted as American surrogates.

After 1904, the Roosevelt Corollary was invoked in several Caribbean countries. Intervention usually

Activities of the United States in the Caribbean, 1898–1930s

required the landing of U.S. Marines to counter a threat to American property. Occupying capital cities and major seaports, Marines, bankers, and customs officials usually remained for several years, until they were satisfied that stability had been re-established. Roosevelt's successors, William Howard Taft and Woodrow Wilson, pursued the same interventionist policy. So would late-twentieth-century presidents: Ronald Reagan (Grenada and Nicaragua), George H. W. Bush (Panama), and Bill Clinton (Haiti).

Opening Doors to China and Closing Doors to America

Throughout the nineteenth century, American relations with China were restricted to a small but profitable trade. Britain, in competition with France, Germany, and Russia, took advantage of the crumbling Manchu dynasty to force treaties on China, creating "treaty ports" and granting exclusive trading privileges in various parts of the country. After 1898, the United States, with dreams of exploiting the seemingly unlimited markets of China, wanted to join the competition and enlarge its share. Those with moral interests, however, including many missionaries, reminded Americans of their revolutionary tradition against European imperialism. They opposed U.S. commercial exploitation of a weak nation and supported the preservation of China's political integrity

as the other imperial powers moved toward partitioning the country.

American attitudes toward the Chinese people reflected this confusion of motives. Although some admired China's ancient culture, the dominant American attitude viewed the Chinese as heathen, exotic, and backward. Nativist workingmen's riots against the competition of Chinese workers in the 1870s and 1880s and the Chinese Exclusion Act of 1882 barring further immigration to the United States reflected this negative stereotype. The Chinese, in turn, regarded the United States with a mixture of admiration, curiosity, resentment, suspicion, and disdain.

The annexation of Hawaii and the Philippines in 1898 convinced Secretary of State Hay that the United States should announce a China policy. He did so in the Open Door notes of 1899–1900, which became the cornerstone of U.S. policy in eastern Asia for more than half a century. The first note demanded an open door for American trade by declaring the principle of equal access to commercial rights in China by all nations. The second note, addressing Russian movement into Manchuria, called on all countries to respect the "territorial and administrative integrity" of China. This second principle announced a larger American role in Asia, offering China protection and preserving an East Asian balance of power.

An early test of this new role came during the Boxer Rebellion in 1900. The Boxers were a society of young traditionalist Chinese in revolt against both the Manchu dynasty and the growing Western presence in China. During the summer of 1900, Boxers killed some 242 missionaries and other foreigners and besieged the western quarter of Beijing. Eventually an international military force of 19,000 troops, including some 3,000 Americans, marched on Beijing to end the siege.

The relationship with China was plagued by the exclusionist immigration policy of the United States and by laws inhibiting Chinese in America from becoming naturalized citizens. Educated at Yale, Yung Wing had been living in the United States since the 1850s and headed an educational mission to bring Chinese students to the United States. But while he was visiting China in 1898, his American citizenship was revoked and he was allowed to re-enter the country only as an alien. Wing denounced American discriminatory laws, pointing out "how far this Republic has departed from its high ideal." But despite unjust laws, barriers, and riots, Chinese students and workers kept coming to the United States, entering illegally through Mexico and British Columbia. In 1905, Chinese nationalists at home boycotted

U.S. Involvement in the Pacific and Eastern Asia, 1898–1909

By 1898, the United States expanded far into eastern Asia and the Pacific. **Reflecting on the Past** Which motivations do you think were most important for U.S. involvement in the Pacific and eastern Asia at the turn of the twentieth century: profits, patriotism, piety, or politics? What major twentieth-century events followed the acquisition of territories in the Pacific and the development of greater trade with East Asian countries? Where is there a strong American presence still today?

American goods and called for a change in immigration policy. Roosevelt, contemptuous of what he called "backward" Chinese, bristled and sent troops to the Philippines as a threat. Halfheartedly, he also asked Congress for a modified immigration bill, but nothing came of it.

Despite exclusion and insults, the idea that the United States had a unique guardian relationship with China persisted into the twentieth century. Japan had ambitions in China, which created a rivalry between Japan and the United States, testing the American commitment to the Open Door in China and the balance of power in eastern Asia.

Tensions were reduced because investments developed very slowly, and the dream of the "great China market" for American grains and textiles always remained larger in imagination than in reality.

Balancing Japan in the Pacific from California to Manchuria

Population pressures, war, and a quest for economic opportunities dramatically increased Japanese immigration to the United States around the turn of the century. Some immigrants came from Hawaii, where they had "worked like machines" in the sugarcane

West Coast Japanese Immigrants Japanese immigrants to the West Coast of the United States around the turn of the century worked hard, irrigated the valleys of California, Oregon, and Washington, and became independent and highly productive farmers. What obstacles did they face? *(Pat Hathaway Collection of California Views)*

fields, many dying from overwork and white diseases. "Hawaii, Hawaii," a sorrowful poet wrote: "Like a dream / So I came / But my tears / Are flowing now / In the canefields." Pursuing "huge dreams of fortune . . . across the ocean," some 200,000 Japanese went directly to the West Coast of the United States, coming first to work on railroads and in West Coast canneries, mines, and logging camps.

Others worked on farms in the valleys of California, Oregon, and Washington, many successfully rising to own their own lands and turning marginal farmlands into productive agricultural businesses. Japanese-owned farms increased from 4,698 acres in 1900 to 194,742 by 1910, when Japanese-owned farms produced 70 percent of the California strawberry crop. Kinji Ushijima, for example, developed 10,000 acres of potato lands worth $500,000 in the fertile deltas between Stockton and Sacramento. By 1912, known then as George Shima, the "Potato King," he was praised by the *San Francisco Chronicle*. But when Shima moved to a well-to-do neighborhood in Berkeley, local newspapers and protesting professors complained of the "Yellow Peril in College Town." Shima refused to move.

Another success story was Abiko Kyutaro, who built several successful service businesses and in 1906 founded a model Japanese farming community in the San Joaquin Valley, with 42 families turning desert land into bountiful orchards, grape vineyards, and alfalfa fields. In discussing the Yamato (or "new Japan") Colony, Kyutaro proclaimed, "The Japanese must settle permanently with their countrymen on large pieces of land if they are to succeed in America."

Threatened by this competitive success, native white Californians sought ways to exclude Japanese immigrants, discriminate against them, and limit their ability to own or lease land. Japanese workers were barred from factory jobs and shunted off to agricultural labor in California fields and orchards. In 1906, the San Francisco school board, claiming that Japanese children were "crowding the whites out of the schools," segregated them into separate schools. Californians passed an anti-Japanese resolution and asked Roosevelt to persuade Japan to stop the emigration. Calling the California legislators "idiots" for their actions and denouncing anti-Japanese rioting in San Francisco, Roosevelt favored restriction rather than exclusion. In the "Gentlemen's Agreement" notes of 1907–1908, the Japanese, while insulted, agreed to limit the migration of unskilled workers to the United States. In return, Californians repealed some of their anti-Japanese laws. Tensions continued.

It was one thing to check Japanese power in California but quite another to stop it in eastern Asia, where Roosevelt was determined to maintain the balance of power. The Boxer Rebellion of 1900 left Russia with 50,000 troops in Manchuria, making it the strongest regional power. Roosevelt's admiration for the Japanese as a "fighting" people and valuable factor in the "civilization of the future" contrasted with his low regard for the Russians, whom he described as "corrupt," "treacherous," and "incompetent." As Japan moved into Korea and Russia into Manchuria, Roosevelt hoped that each would check the growing power of the other.

Roosevelt welcomed news in 1904 that Japan had successfully mounted a surprise attack on Port Arthur in Manchuria, beginning the Russo-Japanese War. He was "well pleased with the Japanese victory," he told his son, "for Japan is playing our game," but as Japanese victories continued, he worried that Japan might play the game too well, shutting the United States out of Asian markets. Roosevelt tilted toward Russia. When the Japanese expressed an interest in ending the war, the American president was pleased to exert his influence.

Roosevelt's goal was to achieve peace and leave a balanced situation. "It is best," he wrote, that Russia be left "face to face with Japan so that each may have a moderative action on the other." Nothing better symbolized the new American presence in the world than the 1905 negotiation and signing of a peace treaty in Portsmouth, New Hampshire, ending a war between Russia and Japan halfway around the globe in Manchuria. The Treaty of Portsmouth left Japan dominant in Manchuria (and Korea) with the United States as the major balance to Japan's power. In the Root-Takahira Agreement of 1908, in return for recognizing the Japanese entrenched presence in Manchuria, Roosevelt got Japan's promise to honor U.S. control in the Philippines and to make no further encroachments into China.

The agreement barely papered over Japanese-American tensions. Some Japanese blamed Roosevelt for the fact that the Treaty of Portsmouth had not given them indemnities from Russia. American insensitivity on the immigration issue left bad feelings. In Manchuria, the U.S. consul general aggressively pushed an anti-Japanese program of financing capital investment projects in banking and railroads. This policy, known as "dollar diplomacy" under Roosevelt's successor, William Howard Taft, like the pursuit of markets, was larger in prospect than results. Nevertheless, the United States was in Japan's way, and rumors of war circulated.

It was clearly a moment for Roosevelt's "big stick." In 1907, he told Secretary of State Root that he was "more concerned over the Japanese situation than almost any other. Thank Heaven we have the navy in good shape." Although the naval buildup had begun over a decade earlier, under Roosevelt the U.S. Navy developed into a formidable force. From 1900 to 1905, outlays to the navy rose from $56 to $117 million, a naval binge unprecedented in peacetime. In 1907, to make it clear that "the Pacific was as much our home waters as the Atlantic," Roosevelt sent his new, modernized "Great White Fleet" on a goodwill world tour. Pointedly, the first stop was Yokohama, Japan. Although American sailors were greeted warmly, the act may have stimulated a naval buildup

in Japan, which came back to haunt the United States at Pearl Harbor in 1941. But for the time being, the balance of power in eastern Asia was preserved.

Preventing War in Europe

The United States had stretched the Monroe Doctrine to justify sending Marines and engineers to Latin America and the navy and dollars to East Asia. Treaties, agreements, and the protection of territories and interests entangled the United States with foreign nations from Panama and Nicaragua to the Philippines and Japan. Toward European nations, however, traditional neutrality continued.

Roosevelt believed that the most serious threats to world peace and civilized order lay in the relationships among Germany, Great Britain, and France, especially as these nations collided with one another over colonies in Asia and Africa and engaged in a naval arms race. Roosevelt established two fundamental policies toward Europe that would define the U.S. role throughout the century. The first was to make friendship with Great Britain the cornerstone of U.S. policy. The second was to prevent a general war in Europe. Toward this end, Roosevelt depended on his personal negotiating skills and began the twentieth-century practice of a kind of summit diplomacy with leaders of major European nations.

The Venezuelan crisis of 1895 shocked the United States and Britain into an awareness of their mutual interests. Both nations appreciated the neutrality of the other in their respective colonial wars in the Philippines and South Africa. Roosevelt supported British imperialism because he favored the dominance of the "English-speaking race" and believed that Britain was "fighting the battle of civilization." Both nations, moreover, were worried about Germany. Roosevelt wrote to Lodge in 1901 that the United States had "not the least particle of danger to fear" from Britain but that German ambitions and militarism represented the major threat to peace in Europe. As German naval power increased, Britain had to bring its fleet closer to home. Friendly allies were needed to police parts of the world formerly patrolled by the British navy. Great Britain therefore concluded a mutual-protection treaty with Japan in 1902 and willingly let the United States police Central America and the Caribbean Sea.

Language, cultural traditions, and strategic self-interest drew the two countries together. Roosevelt was unashamedly pro-British, and his most intimate circle of friends included many English. In 1905, he told King Edward VII that "the English people are more apt to be friendly to us than any other." As Roosevelt left the presidency in 1909, one of his

Global Imperial Activities, 1893–1904

Reflecting on the Past Note the growing role of the United States and the global nature of imperialism. Can you locate on a map or globe the many places mentioned in this chart? What conclusions can you draw about the racial composition of the "where" and the "who"? What larger conclusions might you make about this era of history? Who benefited? Who did not?

Year	Where	Who	What
1893	Hawaii	United States	U.S.-backed annexationists overthrow Hawaiian queen.
1893	Laos	France	Laos becomes a French protectorate.
1893	French Guyana; Ivory Coast	France	France establishes two colonies on two continents.
1894–1895	China	Japan	Japan starts and wins war with China. Japan acquires Taiwan and gets an indemnity for war costs.
1895	South Africa	Britain	British annex Tongaland.
1895	Venezuela	United States; Britain	Tensions over boundary dispute with British Guyana.
1896	Ethiopia	Italy	Italy invades Ethiopia and is defeated by the Ethiopian army.
1896	Rhodesia (Zimbabwe)	Britain	A revolt begins in Rhodesia and is suppressed.
1896–1897	Madagascar	France	French claim Madagascar and depose the queen.
1896–1898	Sudan	Britain	British reconquer Sudan.
1897–1898	Hawaii	United States	United States annexes Hawaii.
1897	China	Germany	Germans occupy Shandong Province.
1898–1899	Philippines	Spain; United States	Annexed by United States after Spanish-American War.
1898–1902	Guam; Puerto Rico; Cuba	Spain; United States	Islands become U.S. territories or protectorates after Spanish-American War.
1899	China	United States	United States establishes Open Door policy.
1899–1902	South Africa; Philippines	Britain; Boers; United States; Philippines	Wars pass control of indigenous peoples to British and Americans.
1899	Ghana	Britain	Ashanti rebellion suppressed.
1900–1901	China	United States; Japan; Britain; Germany and others	Boxer Rebellion suppressed.
1902	Venezuela	United States; Britain; Germany	Blockade ports and compete with one another over Venezuelan debt crisis.
1903	Colombia/Panama	United States	United States backs Panamanian revolutionaries for independence from Colombia.
1904	Manchuria	Japan; Russia	Japan attacks Port Arthur, starting the Russo-Japanese War.

final acts was to proclaim the special friendship between the United States and Great Britain.

Kaiser Wilhelm II of Germany underestimated the Anglo-American friendship and thought that Roosevelt was really pro-German, an illusion Roosevelt cultivated when the kaiser sought his support on several diplomatic issues between 1905 and 1909. In each case, Roosevelt flattered Wilhelm while cleverly rejecting his overtures. The relationship gave Roosevelt a unique advantage in trying to prevent war in Europe, most notably during the Moroccan crisis in 1905 and 1906. When Germany and France threatened to go to war over the control of Morocco, Roosevelt intervened at the kaiser's bidding and arranged a conference in Algeciras, Spain, to head off conflict. The treaty signed in 1906 peacefully settled the Moroccan issue, though favorably for the French.

Roosevelt continued to counter meddlesome German policies. When the kaiser sought to promote a German-Chinese-American agreement to balance the Anglo-Japanese Treaty in Asia, Roosevelt rebuffed him. Touring Europe in 1910, the former president was warmly entertained by Wilhelm, who continued to misunderstand him. Roosevelt, meanwhile, kept urging his British friends to counter the German naval buildup in order to maintain peace in Europe.

In 1911, Roosevelt wrote that nothing would be worse than if "Germany should ever overthrow England and establish the supremacy in Europe she aims at." Roosevelt's European policy included cementing friendship with Britain and, while maintaining official neutrality, using diplomacy to prevent European hostilities. The relationship between Great Britain and Germany continued to deteriorate, however, and by 1914, a new American president, Woodrow Wilson, faced the terrible reality that Roosevelt had sought to prevent. When World War I finally broke out, no American was more eager to fight on the British side against the Germans than Colonel Roosevelt of the Rough Riders.

Conclusion

The Responsibilities of Power

The realities of power in the 1890s brought increasing international responsibilities. Roosevelt said in 1910 that because of "strength and geographical situation," the United States had itself become "more and more, the balance of power of the whole world." This ominous responsibility was also an opportunity to extend American economic, political, and moral influence (and some would say muscle) around the globe even while insulting new and would-be immigrants at home.

As president in the first decade of the twentieth century, Roosevelt established aggressive American policies toward the rest of the world. The United States dominated and policed Central America and the Caribbean Sea to maintain order and protect its investments and other economic interests. In eastern Asia, Americans marched through Hay's Open Door with treaties, troops, navies, missionaries, and dollars to protect the newly annexed Philippine Islands, to develop markets and investments, and to preserve the balance of power in Asia. In Europe, the United States sought to remain neutral and uninvolved in European affairs and at the same time to cement Anglo-American friendship and prevent "civilized" nations from going to war.

How well these policies worked would be seen over the next 100 years. Torn between being an isolationist model and an interventionist savior, the fundamental ambivalence of America's sense of itself as an example to others has persisted. As questionable actions around the world—Private Grayson's and others' in the Filipino-American War, for example—

painfully demonstrated, it was increasingly difficult for the United States to be both responsible and good, both powerful and loved. The American people experienced, therefore, both the satisfactions and burdens, both the profits and costs, of their increasing international role, as they have to this day.

Questions for Review and Reflection

1. What is the fundamental dilemma of American foreign policy inherited from the Puritans, and to what extent do you think it fits historical events?

2. What are the four P's (or the three G's) that explain the motivations for American expansionism in the 1890s?

3. Compare and contrast the causes and consequences of the Spanish-American and Filipino-American wars. What are the major differences between these two conflicts?

4. Give three to four justifications for annexing the Philippine Islands and three to four reasons opposing annexation. Which set of arguments do you think is most compelling?

5. Outline the major principles, with examples, of President Roosevelt's foreign policy in the Caribbean, eastern Asia, and Europe. How well have these policies worked in the 100 years since Roosevelt's time?

6. Do you think that U.S. foreign policy has been primarily as an interventionist savior of other nations or as an interfering expansionist into the affairs of other nations? Or some of both? Give examples.

Recommended Reading

Recommended Readings are posted on the Web site for this textbook. Visit www.ablongman.com/nash

Fiction and Film

William Schroeder's *Cousins of Color* (2004), a historical novel about an African American soldier in the Philippines in 1899 who defects to the insurgent Filipino side, has obvious parallels to the American war against Iraq. Ernest Howard Crosby's *Captain Jinks, Hero* (1902), a delight if you can find it, is an earlier anti-imperialist novel set in the Philippines. James Michener's *Hawaii* (1959) is an immense saga of the multicultural history of the islands annexed by the United States in 1898. *The Woman Warrior* by Maxine Hong Kingston (1975) faithfully reflects Chinese culture in the coming-of-age story of a young Chinese American woman in California. Frank Chin's *Donald Duk* (1911) is a fanciful story of San Francisco's Chinatown, with flashbacks to the history of Chinese railroad workers in the late nineteenth century. The PBS video *Crucible of Empire: The Spanish-American War* (1999) uses rare archival materials, photos, motion pictures, newspapers, and popular songs to recreate the war. Two PBS videos from *The American Experience* series depict the history of the era: *Hawaii's Last Queen* (1997) describes the clash between native Hawaiians and U.S. business interests and Marines, and *America, 1900* (1998) focuses on the year 1900, including the second presidential race between McKinley and Bryan. *In Our Image*, a history of America in the Philippines from 1898 to 1946, is a video produced to accompany Stanley Karnow's *In Our Image: America's Empire in the Philippines* (1989). The first tape covers the Filipino-American War.

Discovering U.S. History Online

Imperialism in the Making of America
www.boondocksnet.com/moa/
This site by Jim Zwick is a rich source of nineteenth-century articles and visual materials about imperialism from archival sites at the University of Michigan and Cornell University.

Anti-Imperialism in the United States, 1898–1935
www.boondocksnet.com/ai
This site presents an extensive collection of primary written and visual documents about anti-imperialism in America, put together by Jim Zwick.

The Age of Imperialism

www.smplanet.com/imperialism/toc.html

This site offers an online history of U.S. imperialism with teaching resources and links.

Images from the Philippine–United States War

www.historicaltextarchive.com/USA/twenty/filipino.html

This site contains an archive of historical photos from the war.

William McKinley

www.history.ohio-state.edu/projects/McKinley/SpanAmWar.htm

The Ohio State University site contains a collection of essays, photos, and cartoons about McKinley and the Spanish-American War.

The Panama Canal

www.pancanal.com/eng

This English version of the Panama Canal Web site includes a colorful, interactive section on the history of the canal.

America, 1900

www.pbs.org/wgbh/amex/1900

A companion to the documentary video, this site contains information on more than 20 key figures from the period and many key events from the early 1900s.

CHAPTER 21

The Progressives Confront Industrial Capitalism

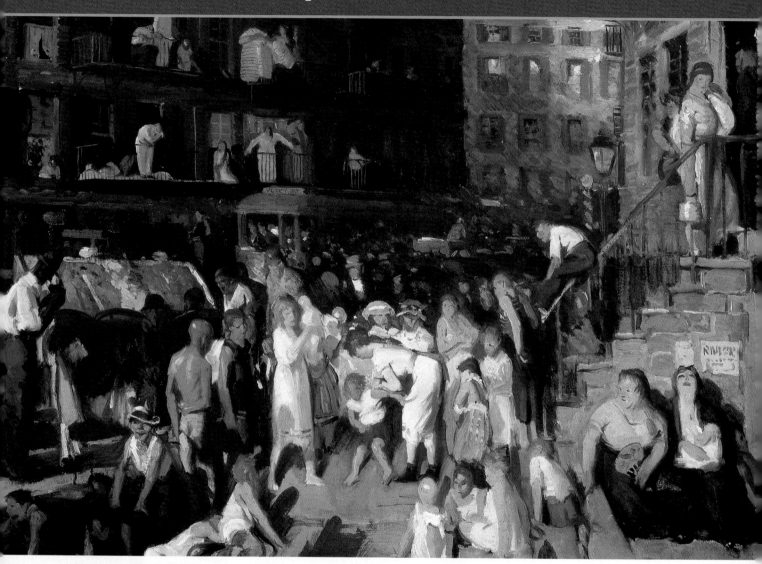

George Bellows, *Cliff Dwellers*, 1913 Bellows was one of many talented artists who migrated from the Midwest to New York early in the century. In this painting, he captures some of the life and excitement in a tenement district on a hot summer night. To Bellows, this was romantic; to the progressive reformers, it was a problem to be solved. How have cities changed in the nearly one hundred years since Bellows painted this scene? *(George Bellows, Cliff Dwellers, 1913. Los Angeles County Museum of Art, Los Angeles County Funds)*

American Stories

A Professional Woman Joins the Progressive Crusade

Frances Kellor, a young woman who grew up in Ohio and Michigan, received her law degree in 1897 from Cornell University and became one of the small but growing group of professionally trained women in the United States. Deciding that she was more interested in solving the nation's social problems than in practicing law, she moved to Chicago, studied sociology, and trained herself as a social reformer. Kellor believed passionately that poverty and inequality could be eliminated in America. She also had the progressive faith that if Americans could only hear the truth about the millions of people living in urban slums, they would rise up and make changes. She was one of the experts who provided the evidence to document what was wrong in industrial America.

Like many progressives, Kellor believed that environment was more important than heredity in determining ability, prosperity, and happiness. Better schools and better housing, she thought, would produce better citizens. While a small group of progressives advocated the sterilization of criminals and the mentally defective, Kellor argued that even criminals were victims of their environment. Kellor demonstrated that poor health and deprived childhoods explained the only differences between criminals and college students. If it were impossible to define a criminal type, then it must be possible to reduce crime by improving the environment.

Kellor was an efficient professional. Like the majority of the professional women of her generation, she never married but devoted her life to social research and social reform. She lived for a time at Hull House in Chicago and at the College Settlement in New York, centers not only of social research and reform but also of lively community. For many young people, the settlement, with its sense of commitment and its exciting conversation around the dinner table, provided an alternative to the nuclear family or the single apartment.

While staying at the College Settlement, Kellor researched and wrote a muckraking study of employment agencies, published in 1904 as *Out of Work*. She revealed how employment agencies exploited immigrants, blacks, and other recent arrivals in the city. Kellor's book, like the writing of most progressives, spilled over with moral outrage. But Kellor went beyond moralism to suggest corrective legislation at the state and national

VIDEO
Ellis Island
Immigrants,
1903

levels. She became one of the leaders of the movement to Americanize the immigrants pouring into the country in unprecedented numbers. Between 1899 and 1920, more than 8 million people came to the United States, most from southern and eastern Europe. Many Americans feared that this flood of immigrants threatened the very basis of American democracy. Kellor and her coworkers represented the side of progressivism that sought state and federal laws to protect the new arrivals from exploitation and to establish agencies and facilities to educate and Americanize them. Another group of progressives, often allied with organized labor, tried to pass laws to restrict immigration. Kellor did not entirely escape the ethnocentrism that was a part of her generation's worldview, and like most progressives she tried to teach middle-class values to the new arrivals, but she did believe that all immigrants could be made into useful citizens.

Convinced of the need for a national movement to promote reform legislation, Kellor helped found the National Committee for Immigrants in America, which tried to promote a national policy "to make all these people Americans," and a federal bureau to organize the campaign. Eventually, she helped establish the Division of Immigrant Education within the Department of Labor. But a political movement led by Theodore Roosevelt excited her most. More than almost any other single person, Kellor had been responsible for alerting Roosevelt to the problems the immigrants faced in American cities. When Roosevelt formed the new Progressive party in 1912, she was one of the many social workers and social researchers who joined him. She campaigned for Roosevelt and directed the Progressive Service Organization, intended to educate voters in all areas of social justice and welfare after the election. After Roosevelt's defeat and the collapse of the Progressive party in 1914, Kellor continued to work for Americanization. She spent the rest of her life promoting justice, order, and efficiency as well as trying to find ways of resolving industrial and international disputes.

While no one person can represent all facets of a complex movement, Frances Kellor's life illustrates two important aspects of progressivism, the first nationwide reform movement of the modern era: first, a commitment to promote social justice, ensure equal opportunity, and preserve democracy; second, a search for order and efficiency in a world complicated by rapid industrialization, immigration, and spectacular urban growth. Like many progressive leaders, Kellor was a part of a global movement to confront these problems, and she was influenced by writers and reformers in England and Germany as well as those in the United States. Progressivism reached its height in the years between 1900 and 1914. Like most American reform movements, the progressive movement did not plot to overthrow the government; rather, it sought to use the government to promote American ideals and to ensure the survival of the American way of life.

This chapter traces the important aspects of progressivism. It examines the social justice movement, which sought to promote reform among the poor and to improve life for those who had fallen victim to an urban and industrial civilization. It surveys life among workers, a group the reformers sometimes helped but often misunderstood. Then it traces the reform movements in the cities and states, where countless officials and experts tried to reduce chaos and promote order and democracy. Finally, it examines progressivism at the national level during the administrations of Theodore Roosevelt and Woodrow Wilson, the first thoroughly modern presidents.

THE SOCIAL JUSTICE MOVEMENT

Historians write of a "progressive movement," but actually there were a number of movements, some of them contradictory, but all focusing on the problems created by a rapidly expanding urban and industrial world. Some reformers, often from the middle class, sought to humanize the modern city. They hoped to improve housing and schools and to provide a better life for the poor and recent immigrants. Others were concerned with the conditions of work and the rights of labor. Still others pressed for changes in the political system to make it more responsive to the people. Progressivism had roots in the 1890s, when many reformers were shocked by the devastation caused by the depression of 1893, and they read Henry George's *Progress and Poverty* (1879) and Edward Bellamy's *Looking Backward* (1888). They were also influenced by John Ruskin, the strange and eccentric British reformer and art historian, who hated the industrial city. Like the British, they were appalled by a pamphlet titled *The Bitter Cry of Outcast London*, which revealed the horrors of the slums of East London. They were also influenced by the British and American Social Gospel movement, which sought to build the kingdom of God on earth by eliminating poverty and promoting equality (see Chapter 19).

The Progressive Movement in Global Context

Most progressives saw their movement in a global context with a particular focus on an Atlantic world. Many had studied at European universities. They attended conferences on urban and industrial problems held at the Paris Exposition of 1900, and they belonged to organizations such as the International Association for Labor Legislation, which tried to promote legislation to aid workers. They read the latest sociological studies from Britain, France, and Germany. Many were introduced to the problems of the modern industrial city by walking through the streets of East London or the slums of Berlin. Others were inspired by visiting Toynbee Hall, the pioneer social settlement in London, and by observing the municipal housing and government-owned streetcar lines in Glasgow, Scotland, and Dresden, Germany. John R. Commons, the economist from the University of Wisconsin who trained many progressive experts, kept a chart of labor legislation from around the world on the wall of his seminar room as a constant reminder of the global reform network. At the same time, European reformers visited American cities and took part in American conferences.

The United States lagged behind much of the industrialized world in passing social legislation, perhaps because it lacked the strong labor and socialist movements present in most European countries. Many European countries, along with Australia, New Zealand, and Brazil, passed laws regulating hours and wages and creating pensions for the elderly. Germany enacted sickness, accident, and disability insurance in the 1880s. Great Britain had workers' compensation by the late 1890s, and old age, sickness, and unemployment insurance by 1911, all paid for with public funds. But American cities, unlike those in Europe, were filled with immigrants from a dozen countries who had cultural adjustments and a language barrier to overcome. The American federal system meant that most reform

John Sloan, *Women Drying Their Hair*, 1912 Sloan (1871–1951) was one of the leading members of the "ash can school," a group of artists who experimented with new techniques and painted ordinary scenes of urban life, such as that shown here. His paintings offended many because he flouted genteel codes of propriety and decorum, and he showed working-class women in ways that were just as shocking as progressive-era reports on child labor and prostitution. Why was this painting shocking to Americans in 1912? *(John Sloan,* Sunday, Women Dry Their Hair, *1912. © Addison Gallery of American Art, Phillips Academy, Andover, Massachusetts. All Rights Reserved.)*

battles had to be fought first at the local and state levels before they could reach the national scene. A unique mix of religion, politics, and moral outrage imparted a particular character to the progressive movement in the United States.

The Progressive Worldview

Intellectually, the progressives were influenced by Darwinism. They believed that the world was in flux, and they rebelled against the fixed and the formal in every field. One of the philosophers of the movement, John Dewey, wrote that ideas could become instruments for change. In his philosophy of pragmatism, William James tried to explain all ideas in terms of their consequences. Most progressives were convinced that environment was much more important than heredity in forming character. Thus, if one could build better schools and houses, one could make better people and a more perfect society. Yet even the more advanced reformers thought in racial and ethnic categories. They believed that some groups could be molded and changed more easily than others. Thus, progressivism did not usually mean progress for blacks.

In many ways, progressivism was the first modern reform movement. It sought to bring order and efficiency to a world that had been transformed by rapid growth and new technology. Yet elements of nostalgia infected the movement as reformers tried to preserve the handicrafts of a preindustrial age and to promote small-town and farm values in the city. The progressive leaders were almost always middle class, and they quite consciously tried to teach their middle-class values to the immigrants and the working class. Often, the progressives seemed more interested in control than in reform; frequently, their efforts to help smacked of paternalism.

The progressives were part of a statistics-minded generation. They conducted surveys, gathered facts, wrote reports, and usually believed that their reports would lead to change. The haunting photographs of young workers taken by Lewis Hine, the stark and beautiful city paintings by John Sloan, and the realist novels of Theodore Dreiser and William Dean Howells reflect the progressives' drive to document and record.

The progressives were optimistic about human nature, and they believed that change was possible. In retrospect, they may seem naive or bigoted, but they wrestled with many social questions, some of them old but fraught with new urgency in an industrialized society. What is the proper relation of government to society? In a world of large corporations, huge cities, and massive transportation systems, how much should the government regulate and control? How much responsibility does society have to care for the poor and needy? The progressives could not agree on the answers, but they struggled with the questions.

RECOVERING THE PAST

Documentary Photographs

Photographs are a revealing way of recovering the past visually. But when looking at a photograph, especially an old one, it is easy to assume that it is an accurate representation of the past. However, much like novelists and historians, photographers have a point of view. They take their pictures for a reason—often to prove a point. As one photographer remarked, "Photographs don't lie, but liars take photographs."

To document the need for reform in the cities, progressives collected statistics, made surveys, described settlement house life, and even wrote novels. But they discovered that the photograph was often more effective than words. Jacob Riis, the Danish-born author of *How the Other Half Lives* (1890), a devastating exposure of conditions in New York City tenement house slums, was also a pioneer in urban photography. Others had taken pictures of dank alleys and street urchins before, but Riis was the first to photograph slum conditions with the express purpose of promoting reform. At first he hired photographers, but then he bought a camera and taught himself how to use it. He even tried a new German flash powder to illuminate dark alleys and tenement rooms to record the horror of slum life.

Riis made many of his photographs into lantern slides and used them to illustrate his lectures on the need for housing reform. Although he was a creative and innovative photographer, his pictures were often far from objective. His equipment was awkward, his film slow. He had to set up and prepare carefully before snapping the shutter. His views of tenement ghetto streets and poor children now seem like clichés, but they were designed to make Americans angry and to arouse them to reform.

Another important progressive photographer was Lewis Hine. Although trained as a sociologist, he taught himself photography. Hine used his camera to illustrate his lectures at the Ethical Culture School in New York. In 1908, he was hired as a full-time investigator by the National Child Labor Committee. His haunting photographs of children in factories helped convince many Americans of the need to abolish child labor. Hine's chil-

IMAGE

Little Spinner in Globe Cotton Mill, 1909— Lewis Hine Photo

Lewis Hine, *Carolina Cotton Mill,* 1908. *(Lewis Hine,* Carolina Cotton Mill, *1908. George Eastman House)*

dren were appealing human beings. He showed them eating, running, working, and staring wistfully out factory windows. His photographs avoided the pathos that Riis was so fond of recording, but just as surely they documented the need for reform.

Another technique that the reform photographer used was the before-and-after shot. The two photographs shown opposite of a one-room apartment in Philadelphia early in the century illustrate how progressive reformers tried to teach immigrants to imitate middle-class manners. The "before" photograph shows a room cluttered with washtubs, laundry, cooking utensils, clothes, tools, even an old Christmas decoration. In the "after" picture, much of the clutter has been cleaned up. A window has been installed to let in light and fresh air. The wallpaper, presumably a haven

The reality of one-room tenement apartments (above) contrasted with the tidiness that reformers saw as the ideal (right). *(Urban Archives, Temple University, Philadelphia, PA)*

for hidden bugs and germs, has been torn off. The cooking utensils and laundry have been put away. The woodwork has been stained, and some ceremonial objects have been gathered on a shelf.

What else can you find that has been changed? How well do you think the message of the photographic combinations like this one worked? Would the immigrant family be happy with the new look and condition of their room? Could anyone live in one room and keep it so neat?

REFLECTING ON THE PAST   As you look at these, or any photographs, ask yourself: What is the photographer's purpose and point of view? Why was this particular angle chosen for the picture? And why center on these particular people or objects? What does the photographer reveal about his or her purpose? What does the photographer reveal unintentionally? How have fast film and new camera styles changed photography? On what subjects do reform-minded photographers train their cameras today?

The Muckrakers

Writers who exposed corruption and other social evils were labeled "muckrakers" by Theodore Roosevelt. Not all muckrakers were reformers—some wrote just for the money—but reformers learned from their techniques of exposé. In part, the muckrakers were a product of a journalistic revolution in the 1890s. The older magazines often had elite audiences and few illustrations. The new magazines had slick formats, more advertising, and wide sales. Competing for readers, editors eagerly published articles telling the public what was wrong in America.

Lincoln Steffens, a young California journalist, wrote articles exposing the connections between respectable businessmen and corrupt politicians. When published as a book in 1904, *The Shame of the Cities* became a battle cry for people determined to clean up city government. Ida Tarbell, a teacher turned journalist, revealed the ruthlessness of John D. Rockefeller's Standard Oil Company. David Graham Phillips uncovered the alliance of politics and business in *The Treason of the Senate* (1906). Robert Hunter, a young settlement worker, shocked Americans in 1904 with his book *Poverty*. In his compelling novel *The Octopus,* Frank Norris dramatized the railroads' stranglehold on the farmers, while Upton Sinclair's novel *The Jungle* (1906) described the horrors of the Chicago meatpacking industry.

DOCUMENT

Lincoln Steffens, *The Shame of the Cities* (1904)

Child Labor

Nothing disturbed the social justice progressives more than the sight of children, sometimes as young as 8 or 10, working long hours in dangerous and depressing factories. Young people had worked in factories since the beginning of the Industrial Revolution, but that did not make the practice any less repugnant to the reformers. "Children are put into industry very much as we put in raw material," Jane Addams objected, "and the product we look for is not better men and women, but better manufactured goods."

The crusade against child labor was a typical social justice reform effort. Its origins lay in the moral indignation of middle-class reformers. But reform went beyond moral outrage as reformers gathered statistics, took photographs documenting the abuse of children, and used their evidence to push for legislation first on the local level, then in the states, and eventually in Washington.

Florence Kelley was one of the most important leaders in the crusade against child

DOCUMENT

John Spargo, *The Bitter Cry of Children* (1906)

Newsboys Nothing disturbed the reformers more than the sight of little children, sullen and stunted, working long hours in factory, farm, and mine. But of all child laborers perhaps the newsboys caused the most concern. They often had to pick up their papers late at night or very early in the morning. They sometimes were homeless and slept wherever they could find a place. But even more troubling, they associated with unsavory characters and fell prey to bad habits. In this photo Lewis Hine captures three young newsboys in St. Louis in 1910. Why were reformers upset by photos like this? If you had to work, would you prefer the mine or the factory or would you become a newsboy? (*Lewis Hine,* Newsies at Skeeter Branch, St. Louis, MO, 11 AM, May 9, 1910. *The Metropolitan Museum of Art, Gift of Phyllis D. Massar, 1970. (1970.727.1) All Rights Reserved, The Metropolitan Museum of Art.*)

labor. Kelley had grown up in an upper-class Philadelphia family and graduated from Cornell in 1882—like Addams and Kellor she was a member of the first generation of college women in the United States. When the University of Pennsylvania refused her admission as a graduate student because she was a woman, she went to the University of Zurich in Switzerland. Her European experience was crucial in her development. It transformed her from an upper-class dilettante into a committed reformer. She married a Polish-Russian scholar and became a socialist. The marriage failed, and some years later, Kelley moved to Chicago with her children, became a Hull House resident, and poured her considerable energies into the campaign against child labor. A friend described her as "explosive, hot-tempered, determined ... a smoking volcano that at any moment would burst into flames." When she could find no attorney in Chicago to argue child labor cases against some of the prominent corporations, she went to law school, passed the bar exam, and argued the cases herself.

Kelley and the other child labor reformers quickly recognized the need for state laws. Marshaling their evidence about the tragic effects on growing children of working long hours in dark and damp factories, they pressured the Illinois state legislature into passing an anti–child labor law. A few years later, however, the state supreme court ruled it unconstitutional, convincing reformers that national action was necessary.

Edgar Gardner Murphy, an Alabama clergyman, suggested the formation of the National Child Labor Committee. Like many other Social Gospel ministers, Murphy believed that the church should reform society as well as save souls. He was appalled by the number of young children working in southern textile mills, where they were exposed to great danger and condemned to "compulsory ignorance" (because they dropped out of school).

The National Child Labor Committee, headquartered in New York, drew up a model state child labor law, encouraged state and city campaigns, and coordinated the movement around the country. Although two-thirds of the states passed some form of child labor law between 1905 and 1907, many had loopholes that exempted a large number of children, including newsboys and youngsters who worked in the theater. A national bill was defeated in 1906, but in 1912 the child labor reformers convinced Congress to establish a children's bureau in the Department of Labor. Despite these efforts, compulsory school attendance laws did more to reduce the number of children who worked than federal and state laws, which proved difficult to pass and even more difficult to enforce. Although American child labor reformers borrowed their tactics and research methods from European reformers, the movement to restrict the labor of children was much more successful in Europe. In most European countries, legislation quickly restricted the hours of all workers including men. This did not happen consistently in the United States until the 1930s.

Like other progressive reform efforts, the battle against child labor was only partly successful. Too many businesses, both small and large, were profiting from employing children at low wages. Too many politicians and judges were reluctant to regulate the work of children or adults because work seemed such an individual and personal matter. And some parents, who often desperately needed the money their children earned in the factories, opposed the reformers and even broke the law to allow their children to work.

DOCUMENT

Mother Jones, "The March of the Mill Children" (1903)

The reformers also worried over the young people who got into trouble with the law, often for pranks that in rural areas would have seemed harmless. They feared for young people tried by adult courts and thrown into jail with hardened criminals. Reformers organized juvenile courts, in which judges had the authority to put delinquent youths on probation, take them from their families and make them wards of the state, or assign them to an institution. A uniquely American invention, the juvenile court often helped prevent young delinquents from adopting a life of crime. Yet the juvenile offender was frequently deprived of all rights of due process, a fact that the Supreme Court finally recognized in 1967, when it ruled that children were entitled to procedural rights when accused of a crime.

Working Women and Woman Suffrage

Closely connected with the anti–child labor movement was the effort to limit the hours of women's work. The most important court case on women's work came before the U.S. Supreme Court in 1908. Josephine Goldmark, research director of the National Consumer's League, an organization dedicated to seeking protective legislation for workers and the safe and sanitary manufacturing of consumer productions, wrote the brief for *Muller* v. *Oregon*. Goldmark's brother-in-law, Louis Brandeis, argued the case before the Court. The Court upheld the Oregon law limiting the workday of women in factories and laundries to 10 hours largely because Goldmark's sociological argument detailed the danger and disease that these women workers faced. Most states fell into line with the Supreme Court decision and passed protective legislation for women, though many companies found ways to circumvent the laws. Even the work permitted by the law seemed too long to some women. "I think ten hours is too much for a woman," one factory worker stated. "I have four children and have to work hard at home. Make me awful tired. I would like nine hours. I get up at 5:30. When I wash, I have to stay up till one or two o'clock."

By contending that "women are fundamentally weaker than men in all that makes for endurance: in muscular strength, in nervous energy, in the powers of persistent attention and application," the reformers won some protection for women workers. But their arguments that women were weaker than men would eventually be used to reinforce gender segregation of the workforce for the next half century.

In addition to working for protective legislation for working women, the social justice progressives also campaigned for woman suffrage. The early battles for the right of women to vote were fought at the state level, with the greatest success coming in the West. Wyoming (1869), Utah (1870), Colorado (1893), Idaho (1896), Washington (1910), California (1911), Arizona and Oregon (1912), and Montana and Nevada (1914) gave women

DOCUMENT

Helen M. Todd, "Getting Out the Vote" (1911)

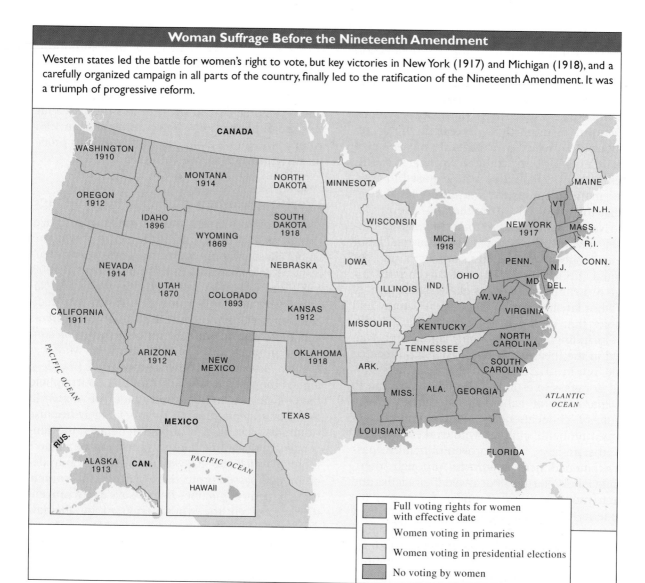

Woman Suffrage Before the Nineteenth Amendment

Western states led the battle for women's right to vote, but key victories in New York (1917) and Michigan (1918), and a carefully organized campaign in all parts of the country, finally led to the ratification of the Nineteenth Amendment. It was a triumph of progressive reform.

Legend:
- Full voting rights for women with effective date
- Women voting in primaries
- Women voting in presidential elections
- No voting by women

MAP

Woman Suffrage Before the Nineteenth Amendment

the right to vote in at least some elections. But this did not mean that the western states were more enlightened on gender issues. In the East and Midwest, both with large immigrant populations, suffrage and prohibition were often tied closely together. Many men believed that women, if given the vote, would support prohibition. The campaign to win the vote for women was a global movement, and the suffrage leaders in the United States were in touch with women in other countries. They often met their foreign counterparts at meetings of the International Woman Suffrage Alliance. The United States lagged behind New Zealand, Finland, Norway, and several other countries in granting female suffrage. Women in Great Britain were allowed to vote in 1918, but not until 1938 could they vote on an equal basis with men.

The political process that eventually led to woman suffrage in the United States was slowed by the difficulty of amending the Constitution and the need to fight the battle one state at a time. But the progressives pressed on. Some suffrage advocates argued that middle-class women would offset the votes of ignorant and corrupt immigrant men, but many progressives supported votes for all women. Jane Addams argued that urban women not only could vote intelligently but also needed the vote to protect, clothe, and feed their families. Women in an urban age, she suggested, needed to be municipal housekeepers. Through suffrage, they would ensure that elected officials provided adequate services—pure water, uncontaminated food, proper sanitation, and police protection. The progressive

DOCUMENT

Jane Addams, "Ballots Necessary for Women" (1906)

insistence that all women needed the vote helped ensure the victory for woman suffrage that would come after World War I.

Much more controversial than either votes for women or protective legislation was the movement for birth control. Even many advanced progressives could not imagine themselves teaching immigrant women how to prevent conception, especially because the Comstock Law of 1873 made it illegal to promote or even write about contraceptive devices.

Margaret Sanger, a nurse who had watched poor women suffer from too many births and even die from dangerous, illegal abortions, was one of the founders of the modern American birth control movement. Middle-class Americans had limited family size in the nineteenth century through abstinence, withdrawal, and abortion, as well as through the use of primitive birth control devices, but much ignorance and misinformation remained, even among middle-class women. Sanger obtained the latest medical and scientific European studies and in 1914 explained in her magazine, *The Woman Rebel*, and in a pamphlet, *Family Limitation*, that women could separate sex from procreation. She was promptly indicted for violation of the postal code and fled to Europe to avoid arrest.

IMAGE

Margaret Sanger's Newspaper, 1914

Birth control remained controversial, and in most states illegal, for many years. Yet Sanger helped bring the topic of sexuality and contraception out into the open. When she returned to the United States in 1921, she founded the American Birth Control League, which became the Planned Parenthood Federation in 1942.

Reforming Home and School

The reformers believed that better housing and education could transform the lives of the poor and create a better world. Books such as Jacob Riis's *How the Other Half Lives* (1890) horrified them. With vivid language and haunting photographs, Riis had documented the misery of New York's slums.

In the first decade of the twentieth century, the progressives took a new approach toward housing problems. They combined their vision of what needed to be done to improve society with their practical ability to organize public opinion and gets laws passed. They collected statistics, conducted surveys, organized committees, and constructed exhibits to demonstrate the effect of urban overcrowding. Then they worked for the passage of tenement house laws in several cities. These laws set fire codes and regulated the number of windows and bathrooms and the size of apartments, but the laws were often evaded or modified. In 1910, the progressives organized the National Housing Association, and some of them looked ahead to federal laws and even to government-subsidized housing. American housing reformers were inspired by model working-class dwellings in London, municipal housing in Glasgow, and various experiments in government-constructed housing in France, Belgium, and Germany, but they realized that in the United States, they had to start with regulation at the local level.

Ironically, many middle-class women reformers who tried to teach working-class families how to live in their tenement flats had never organized their own homes. Often they lived in settlement houses, where they ate in a dining hall and never had to worry about cleaning, cooking, or doing laundry. Some of them, however, began to realize that the domestic tasks expected of women of all classes kept many of them from taking their full place in society. Charlotte Perkins Gilman, author of *Women and Economics* (1898), dismantled the traditional view of "woman's sphere" and sketched an alternative. Suggesting that entrepreneurs ought to build apartment houses designed to allow women to combine motherhood with careers, she advocated shared kitchen facilities and a common dining room, a laundry run by efficient workers, and a roof-garden day nursery with a professional teacher.

DOCUMENT

Charlotte Gilman Perkins, "If I Were a Man" (1914)

Gilman, who criticized private homes as "bloated buildings, filled with a thousand superfluities," was joined by a few radicals in promoting new living arrangements. However, most Americans of all political persuasions continued to view the home as sacred space where the mother ruled supreme and created an atmosphere of domestic tranquility for the husband and children. Many reformers disapproved of the clutter and lack of privacy in immigrant tenements. But often immigrant family ideals and values differed from those of the middle-class reformers.

Next to better housing, the progressives stressed better schools as a way to produce better citizens. Public school systems were often rigid and corrupt. Far from producing citizens who would help transform society, the schools seemed to reinforce the conservative habits that blocked change. A reporter who traveled around the country in 1892 encountered teachers who drilled pupils through repetitious rote learning. A Chicago teacher advised her students, "Don't stop to think; tell me what you know." When asked why the students were not allowed to move their heads, a New York teacher replied, "Why should they look behind when the teacher is in front of them?"

AMERICAN VOICES

Rosa, An Italian Immigrant Learns English at a Settlement House in Chicago

Most accounts of the settlement movement were written by settlement workers and reformers. This is a rare first person description recalled by an Italian woman who left an abusive husband and moved to Chicago to start a new life.

In the first beginning we always came in the club and made two circles in the room. One circle was for those ladies who could talk English and the other circle was for the ladies who talked German. Mis' Reuter talked German to the German ladies, and Miss Gray talked English to the other ladies. But I guess they both did some preaching. They used to tell us that it's not nice to drink the beer, and we must not let the baby do this, and this. Me, I was the only Italian woman—where were they going to put me? I couldn't talk German, so I went in the English circle. So after we had about an hour, or an hour and a half of preaching, they would pull up the circle and we'd play the games together. All together we played the games—the Norwegian, the German, the English and me. Then we would have some cake and coffee and the goodnight song. . . .

Pretty soon they started the classes to teach us poor people to talk and write in English. The talk of the people in the settlement house was different entirely than what I used to hear. I used to love those American people, and I was listening and listening how they talked. That's how I learned to talk some good English. Oh, I was glad when I learned enough English to go by the priest in the Irish church and confess myself and make the priest understand what was the sin! But I never learned to do the writing in English. I all the time used to come to that class so tired and so sleepy after scrubbing and washing the whole day—I went to sleep when they started the writing. I couldn't learn it. They had clubs for the children too; my little girls loved to go. And after a few years when they started the kindergarten, my Luie was one of the first children to go in. . . .

- *Critics charged that the settlement workers betrayed a paternalism and class bias. Do you see any of that in Rosa's account?*

- *What was her attitude toward the settlement house and her experiences there?*

Progressive education, like many other aspects of progressivism, opposed the rigid and the formal in favor of flexibility and change. John Dewey was the key philosopher of progressive education. In his laboratory school at the University of Chicago, he experimented with new educational methods. He replaced the school desks, which were bolted down and always faced the front, with seats that could be moved into circles and arranged in small groups. The movable seat, in fact, became one of the symbols of the progressive education movement.

Dewey insisted that the schools be child-centered, not subject-oriented. Teachers should teach children rather than teach history or mathematics. He did not mean that history and math should not be taught but that those subjects should be related to the students' experience. Students should learn by doing. They should not just learn about democracy; the school itself should operate like a democracy.

Dewey also maintained that schools should become instruments for social reform. But like most progressives, Dewey was never quite clear whether he wanted schools to help students adjust to the existing society or to turn out graduates who would change the world. Although he wavered on that point, the spirit of progressive education, like the spirit of progressivism in general, was optimistic. Dewey's progressive education, which sought to educate all Americans, stood in sharp contrast to European models, in which educating the intellectual and social elite took precedence over schooling the masses.

Crusades Against Saloons, Theaters, and Prostitution

Progressives often displayed a moral outrage when it came to the behavior of the working class that surprised and confused foreign observers. American attitudes toward prostitution and prohibition especially baffled many Europeans. Most social justice progressives opposed the sale of alcohol. Some came from Protestant homes in which consumption

IMAGE

George Bellows, *The Drunk*, 1923–1924

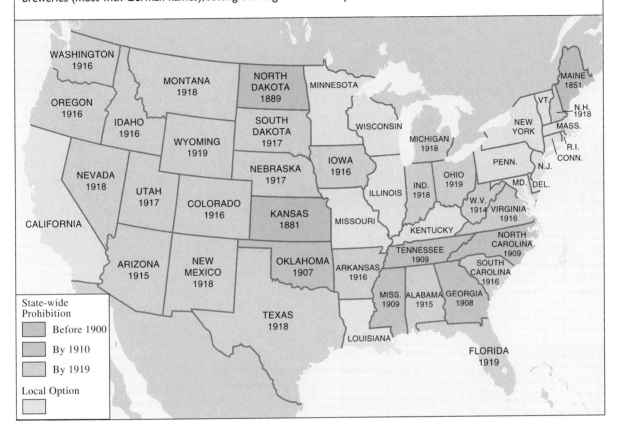

State Prohibition by 1919

Temperance reform had achieved considerable success before the adoption of the Eighteenth Amendment in 1919. Some states, such as Maine, Kansas, and North Dakota, had voted dry since the middle of the nineteenth century, while other states joined the antiliquor crusade during the progressive era. Anti-German hysteria during World War I helped close breweries (most with German names), setting the stage for national prohibition in 1919.

State-wide Prohibition
- Before 1900
- By 1910
- By 1919
- Local Option

of liquor was considered a sin, but most advocated prohibition because they saw eliminating the sale of alcohol as part of the process of reforming the city and conserving human resources.

Americans did drink great quantities of beer, wine, and hard liquor, and the amount they consumed rose rapidly after 1900, peaking between 1911 and 1915. An earlier temperance movement had achieved some success in the 1840s and 1850s, but only three states still had prohibition laws in force. The modern antiliquor movement was spearheaded in the 1880s and 1890s by the Women's Christian Temperance Union and after 1900 by the Anti-Saloon League and a coalition of religious leaders and social reformers. During the progressive era, temperance forces had considerable success in influencing legislation. Seven states passed temperance laws between 1906 and 1912.

The reformers were appalled to see young children going into saloons to bring home a pail of beer for the family and horrified by tales of alcoholic fathers beating wives and children. But most often

progressives focused on the saloon, which they not only viewed as a place for drinking but also linked to drug traffic, prostitution, and political corruption. Although they never quite understood the role that alcohol played in the social life of many ethnic groups, Jane Addams and other settlement workers appreciated the saloon's importance as a neighborhood social center. Addams started a coffeehouse at Hull House in an attempt to lure people away from the saloon. The progressives never found an adequate substitute for the saloon, but they set to work to pass local and state prohibition laws. Joining forces with diverse groups to push for change, they achieved victory when, on December 22, 1917, Congress sent to the states for ratification a constitutional amendment prohibiting the sale, manufacture, and import of intoxicating liquor within the United States. The spirit of sacrifice for the war effort facilitated rapid ratification of the amendment.

In addition to the saloon, progressives saw the urban dance hall and the movie theater as threats to the morals and well-being of young people, especially

The Musketeers of Pig Alley Lillian Gish was one of the stars of the silent film *The Musketeers of Pig Alley* (1912), which was directed by D. W. Griffith three years before he made *Birth of a Nation*. The film shows Gish and other characters trapped in a ghetto but at the same time enjoying the pleasures of the saloons and dance halls—hardly the message that the progressive reformers were trying to get across. Why were movies so exciting to young people in 1912? Do you react in a similar way to movies today? *(Photofest)*

young women. The motion picture, invented in 1889, developed as an important form of entertainment during the first decade of the twentieth century. At first, the "nickelodeons," as the early movie theaters were called, appealed mainly to a lower-class and largely ethnic audience. In 1902, New York City had 50 theaters; by 1908, there were more than 400 showing 30-minute dramas and romances.

Not until World War I, when D. W. Griffith produced long feature films, did the movies begin to attract a middle-class audience. The most popular of these early films was Griffith's *Birth of a Nation* (1915), a blatantly racist and distorted epic of black debauchery during Reconstruction. Many early films were imported from France, Italy, and Germany; because they were silent, it was easy to use subtitles in any language. But one did not need to know the language, or even be able to read, to enjoy the action. That was part of the attraction of the early films. Some films stressed slapstick humor or romance and adventure; others bordered on pornography. The reformers objected not only to the plots and content of the films but also to the location of the theaters (near saloons and burlesque houses) and to their dark interiors. But for young immigrant women, who made up the bulk of the audience at most urban movie theaters, the films provided rare exciting moments in their lives. One daughter of strict Italian parents remarked, "The one

place I was allowed to go by myself was the movies. I went to the movies for fun. My parents wouldn't let me go anywhere else, even when I was twenty-four."

Saloons, dance halls, and movie theaters all seemed dangerous to progressives interested in improving life in the city, because all appeared to be somehow connected with the worst evil of all, prostitution. Campaigns against prostitution had been waged since the early nineteenth century, but they were nothing compared with the progressives' crusade to wipe out what they called the "social evil." All major cities and many smaller ones appointed vice commissions and made elaborate studies of prostitution. The reports, which often ran to several thick volumes, were typical progressive documents, compiled by experts, filled with elaborate statistical studies, and laced with moral outrage.

DOCUMENT

Report of the Vice Commission, Louisville, Kentucky (1915)

The progressive crusade against prostitution attracted many kinds of people, for often contradictory reasons. Racists and immigration restrictionists maintained that inferior people—blacks and recent immigrants, especially those from southern and eastern Europe—became prostitutes and pimps. Most progressives, however, stressed environmental causes. They viewed prostitution, along with child labor and poor housing, as evils that education and reform could eliminate.

Progressive reformers also considered economic causes of prostitution. "Is it any wonder," the Chicago Vice Commission asked, "that a tempted girl who receives only six dollars per week working with her hands sells her body for twenty-five dollars per week when she learns there is a demand for it and men are willing to pay the price?" "Do you suppose I am going back to earn five or six dollars a week in a factory," one prostitute asked an investigator, "when I can earn that amount any night and often much more?"

Despite all their efforts, the progressives failed to end prostitution and did virtually nothing to address its roots in poverty. They wiped out a few red-light districts, closed a number of brothels, and managed to push a bill through Congress (the Mann Act of 1910) that prohibited the interstate transport of women for immoral purposes. Perhaps more important, they persuaded several states to raise the age of consent for women and in 20 states they made the Wassermann test for syphilis mandatory for both men and women before a marriage license could be issued.

THE WORKER IN THE PROGRESSIVE ERA

Progressive reformers sympathized with industrial workers who struggled to earn a living for themselves and their families. The progressives sought protective legislation (particularly for women and children), unemployment insurance, and workers' compensation. But often they had little understanding of what it was really like to sell one's strength by the hour. For example, they supported labor's right to organize at a time when labor had few friends, yet they often opposed the strike as a weapon against management. And neither organized labor nor the reformers, individually or in shaky partnership, had power over industry. Control was in the hands of the owners and managers, who were determined to strengthen their grip on the workplace as the nature of industrial work was being transformed.

The Changing Nature of Industrial Labor

John Mekras arrived in New York from Greece in 1912 and traveled immediately to Manchester, New Hampshire, where he found a job in the giant Amoskeag textile mill. He did not speak a word of English. "The man who hands out the jobs sent me to the spinning room," he later remembered. "There I don't know anything about the spinning. I'm a farmer .... I don't know what the boss is talking about." Mekras didn't last long at the mill. He was one of the many industrial workers who had difficulty adjusting to factory work in the early twentieth century.

Many workers—whether from Greece, eastern Europe, rural Vermont, or Michigan—confronted a bewildering world based on order and routine. Unlike farm or craft work, factory life was dominated by the clock, the bell tower, and the boss. The workers continued to resist the mindless routine and relentless pace of factory work, and they subtly sabotaged the employers' efforts to control the workplace. They stayed at home on holidays when they were supposed to work, took unauthorized breaks, and set their own informal productivity schedules. Often they were fired or quit. In the woollen industry, for example, the annual turnover of workers between 1907 and 1910 was more than 100 percent. In New York needleworker shops in 1912 and 1913, the turnover rate was more than 250 percent.

VIDEO
Punching the Clock

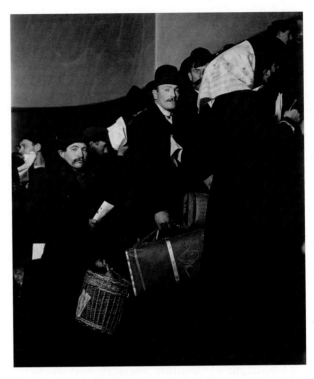

Climbing into the Promised Land Immigrants from eastern and southern Europe came to the United States in great numbers from 1890 to 1914. Many of them were detained at Ellis Island in New York. There usually was a long wait, embarrassing questions to answer, forms to fill out, a complicated bureaucracy to get past. There was also a medical exam to endure. Some immigrants failed the exam and were rejected and sent back to Europe. Still they came with hope and determination. Lewis Hine titled this photo *Climbing into the promised land, Ellis Island, 1908.* Did the United States live up to the hopes of most immigrants? What emotions, thoughts, and concerns can you read on the faces of these immigrants? *(Lewis Hine,* Climbing into the Promised Land, Ellis Island, 1908. © *Brooklyn Museum of Art, New York, USA, Gift of Mr. and Mrs. Walter Rosenblum/Bridgeman Art Library.)*

Overall in American industry, one-third of the workers stayed at their jobs less than a year.

The nature of work continued to change in the early twentieth century as industrialists extended late-nineteenth-century efforts to make their factories and their workforces more efficient, productive, and profitable. In some industries, the introduction of new machines revolutionized work and eliminated highly paid, skilled jobs. For example, glassblowing machines (invented about 1900) replaced thousands of glassblowers or reduced them from artisans to workers. Power-driven machines, better-organized operations, and finally the moving assembly line, perfected by Henry Ford, transformed the nature of work and turned many laborers into unskilled tenders of machines.

It was not just machines that changed the nature of industrial work. The principles of scientific

VIDEO
Westinghouse Air Brake Co., Westinghouse Works

management, which set out new rules for organizing work, were also important. The key figure was Frederick Taylor, the son of a prominent Philadelphia family. After Taylor had a nervous breakdown while at a private school, his physicians prescribed manual labor as a cure, and he went to work as a laborer at the Midvale Steel Company in Philadelphia. Working his way up rapidly while studying engineering at night, he became chief engineer at the factory in the 1880s. Later he used this experience to develop his four principles of scientific management: centralized planning, systematic analysis of each job, detailed instructions to and close supervision of each worker, and an incentive wage system to encourage laborers to work harder and faster.

Frederick W. Taylor, *The Principles of Scientific Management* (1911)

Taylor studied all kinds of workers and timed the various components of their jobs with a stopwatch in order to determine the fastest way of performing a task. Many owners enthusiastically adopted Taylor's concepts of scientific management, seeing an opportunity to increase their profits and shift control of the workplace from the skilled workers to the managers. Not surprisingly, many workers resented the emphasis on higher productivity and tighter control. "We don't want to work as fast as we are able to," one machinist remarked. "We want to work as fast as we think it comfortable for us to work."

Samuel Gompers, head of the American Federation of Labor (AFL), however, was quick to recognize that Taylorism would reduce workers to "mere machines." Under Gompers, the AFL prospered during the progressive era. Between 1897 and 1904, union membership grew from 447,000 to more than 2 million, with three out of every four union members claimed by the AFL. By 1914, the AFL alone had more than 2 million members. Gompers's "pure and simple unionism" was most successful among coal miners, railroad workers, and the building trades. As we saw in Chapter 18, Gompers ignored the growing army of unskilled and immigrant workers and concentrated on raising the wages and improving the working conditions of the skilled artisans who were members of unions affiliated with the AFL.

Samuel Gompers, *The American Labor Movement* (1914)

For a time, Gompers's strategy seemed to work. Several industries negotiated with the AFL as a way of avoiding disruptive strikes. But cooperation was short-lived. Labor unions were defeated in a number of disastrous strikes, and the National Association of Manufacturers (NAM) launched an aggressive counterattack. NAM and other employer associations provided strikebreakers, used industrial spies, and blacklisted union members to prevent them from obtaining other jobs.

Early in the century, courts at all levels sided overwhelmingly with employers. They often declared strikes illegal and were quick to issue restraining orders, making it impossible for workers to interfere with the operation of a business. The Supreme Court came down squarely on management's side, ruling in the Danbury Hatters case (*Loewe* v. *Lawler,* 1908) that the boycott of an industry by a labor union violated the Sherman Anti-Trust Act. The boycott had been a valuable tool for striking workers, enabling them to picket and pressure companies doing business with their employers during a strike.

Although many social justice progressives sympathized with the working class, they spent more time promoting protective legislation than strengthening organized labor. Often cast in the role of mediators during industrial disputes, they found it difficult to comprehend what life was really like for people who had to work six days a week.

Working women and their problems aroused more sympathy among progressive reformers than the plight of working men. The number of women working outside the home increased steadily during the progressive era, from more than 5 million in 1900 to nearly 8.5 million in 1920. But few belonged to unions.

Many upper-class women reformers tried to help working women in a variety of ways. The settlement houses organized day-care centers, clubs, and classes, and many reformers tried to pass protective legislation. Tension and misunderstanding often cropped up between the reformers and the working women, but one organization in which there was genuine cooperation was the Women's Trade Union League. Founded in 1903, the league was organized by Mary Kenney and William English Walling, a socialist and reformer, but it also drew local leaders from the working class, such as Rose Schneiderman, a Jewish immigrant cap maker, and Leonora O'Reilly, a collar maker. The league established branches in most large eastern and midwestern cities and served for more than a decade as an important force in helping organize women into unions. The league forced the AFL to pay more attention to women, helped out in time of strikes, and publicized the plight of working women.

Garment Workers and the Triangle Fire

Thousands of young women, most of them Jewish and Italian, were employed in the garment industry

AMERICAN VOICES

Pauline Newman, Conditions in a Garment Factory

Many children of immigrants went to work in factories to help support their families. Most accounts of child labor were constructed by investigators and reformers. This is a rare personal experience recalled many years later by a woman who became a labor leader.

A cousin of mine worked for the Triangle Shirtwaist Company and she got me on there in October of 1901. It was probably the largest shirtwaist factory in the city of New York then. They had more than two hundred operators, cutters, examiners, finishers. Altogether more than four hundred people on two floors. The fire took place on one floor, the floor where we worked. You've probably heard about that. But that was years later. . . .

What I had to do was not really very difficult. It was just monotonous. When the shirtwaists were finished at the machine there were some threads that were left, and all the youngsters—we had a corner on the floor that resembled a kindergarten—we were given little scissors to cut the threads off. It wasn't heavy work, but it was monotonous, because you did the same thing from seven-thirty in the morning till nine at night.

Well, of course, there were [child labor] laws on the books, but no one bothered to enforce them. The employers were always tipped off if there was going to be an inspection. "Quick," they'd say, "into the boxes!" And we children would climb into the big boxes the finished shirts were stored in. Then some shirts were piled on top of us, and when the inspector came—no children. The factory always got an okay from the inspector, and I suppose someone at City Hall got a little something, too.

The employers didn't recognize anyone working for them as a human being. You were not allowed to sing. Operators would have like to have sung, because they, too, had the same thing to do and weren't allowed to sing. We weren't allowed to talk to each other. Oh, no, they would sneak up behind if you were found talking to your next colleague. You were admonished: "If you keep on you'll be fired." If you went to the toilet and you were there longer than the floor lady thought you should be, you would be laid off for half a day and sent home. And, of course, that meant no pay. You were not allowed to have your lunch on the fire escape in the summertime. The door was locked to keep us in. That's why so many people were trapped when the fire broke out.

My pay was $1.50 a week no matter how many hours I worked. My sisters made $6.00 a week; and the cutters, they were skilled workers, they might get as much as $12.00. The employers had a sign in the elevator that said: "If you don't come in on Sunday, don't come in on Monday." You were expected to work every day if they need you and the pay was the same whether you worked extra or not. You had to be there at seven-thirty, so you got up at five-thirty, took the horse car, then the electric trolley to Greene Street, to be there on time. . . .

- *What was the most difficult thing about working in the factory?*

- *How did the owners evade the child labor laws and other laws?*

---

in New York City. Most were between ages 16 and 25; some lived with their families, and others lived alone or with a roommate. They worked a 56-hour, six-day week and made about $6 a week for their efforts. New York was the center of the garment industry, with more than 600 shirtwaist (blouse) and dress factories employing more than 30,000 workers.

Like other industries, garment manufacturing had changed in the first decade of the twentieth century. Once conducted in thousands of dark and dingy tenement rooms, now operations were centralized in large loft buildings in lower Manhattan. These buildings were an improvement over the tenements, but many were overcrowded, and they had few fire escapes or safety features. The owners applied scientific management techniques to heighten productivity and thereby increase their profits. But conditions for the workers were miserable. Most of the women had to rent their sewing machines and pay for the electricity they used. They were penalized for making

Triangle Fire Victims The Triangle fire shocked the nation, and dramatic photographs, such as this candid shot showing bodies and bystanders waiting for more young women to jump, helped stimulate the investigation that followed. What event in your lifetime was as shocking as this photo? *(Brown Brothers)*

mistakes or talking too loudly. They were usually supervised by a male contractor who badgered and sometimes even sexually harassed them.

In 1909, some of the women went out on strike to protest the working conditions. The International Ladies' Garment Workers Union (ILGWU) and the Women's Trade Union League supported them. But strikers were beaten and sometimes arrested by unsympathetic policemen and by strikebreakers on the picket lines. At a mass meeting held at Cooper Union in New York on November 22, 1909, Clara Lemlich, a young shirtwaist worker who had been injured on the picket line and was angered by the long speeches and lack of action, rose and in an emotional speech in Yiddish demanded a general strike. The entire audience pledged its agreement. The next day, all over the city, the shirtwaist workers went out on strike.

"The uprising of the twenty thousand," as the strike was called, startled the nation. One young worker wrote in her diary, "It is a good thing, that strike is. It makes you feel like a grown-up person." The Jews learned a little Italian and the Italians a little Yiddish so that they could communicate. Many social reformers, ministers, priests, and rabbis urged the strikers on. Mary Dreier, an upper-class reformer and president of the New York branch of the Women's Trade Union League, was arrested for marching with the strikers. A young state legislator, Fiorello La Guardia, later to become a congressman and mayor of New York, was one of the many public officials to aid the strikers.

The shirtwaist workers won, recognition for their union and some improvements in the factories, but their victory was limited. The young women went back to work amid still oppressive and unsafe conditions. On Saturday, March 25, 1911, a fire broke out on the eighth floor of the 10-story loft building housing the Triangle Shirtwaist Company near Washington Square in New York. There had been several small fires in the factory in previous weeks, so no one thought much about another one. But this fire was different. Within minutes, the top three floors of the factory were ablaze. The owners had locked most of the exit doors. The elevators broke down. There were no fire escapes. Forty-six women jumped to their deaths, some of them in groups of three and four holding hands. More than 100 died in the flames.

Shocked by the Triangle fire, the state legislature appointed a commission to investigate working conditions in the state. One investigator for the commission was a young social worker named Frances Perkins, who in the 1930s would become secretary of labor. She led the politicians through the dark lofts, filthy tenements, and unsafe factories around the state to show them the conditions under which young women worked. The result was state legislation limiting the work of women to 54 hours a week, prohibiting labor by children under age 14, and improving safety regulations in factories. One supporter of the bills in Albany was a young state senator named Franklin Delano Roosevelt.

The investigative commission was a favorite progressive tactic. When there was a problem, reformers often got a city council, a state legislature, or the federal government to appoint a commission. If they could not find a government body to give them a mandate, they conducted their own studies. They brought in experts, compiled statistics, and published reports.

The federal Industrial Relations Commission, created in 1912 to study the causes of industrial unrest and violence, conducted one of the most important investigations, a study of the labor–management conflict at the Colorado Fuel and Iron Industry near Ludlow, Colorado. In the fall of 1913, miners at the company, which was largely owned by the Rockefeller family, went on strike demanding an eight-hour workday, better safety precautions, and the removal of armed guards. Colorado Fuel and Iron was a paternalistic empire in which workers lived in company towns, were paid in company scrip, and were forced to shop at the company store. When the company refused to negotiate with the striking workers, the strike turned violent. In the spring of 1914, strikebreakers and national guardsmen armed with machine guns fired on the workers, killing 11 children and 2 women in an incident that became known as the Ludlow Massacre.

The Industrial Relations Commission called John D. Rockefeller, Jr., to testify and implied that he was personally guilty of the murders. The commission decided in its report that violent class conflict could be avoided only by limiting the use of armed guards and detectives, by restricting monopoly, by protecting the right of the workers to organize, and, most dramatically, by redistributing wealth through taxation. The commission's report, not surprisingly, fell on deaf ears. Most progressives, like most Americans, denied the commission's conclusion that class conflict was inevitable.

Radical Labor

Not everyone accepted the progressives' faith in investigations and protective labor legislation. Nor did everyone approve of Samuel Gompers's conservative tactics or his emphasis on getting higher wages for skilled workers. A group of about 200 radicals met in Chicago in 1905 to form a new union as an alternative to the AFL. They called it the Industrial Workers of the World (IWW) and talked of one big union.

Logo for Industrial Workers of the World

Like the Knights of Labor in the 1880s, the IWW would welcome all workers: the unskilled and even the unemployed, women, African Americans, Asians, and all other ethnic groups.

Daniel De Leon of the Socialist Labor Party attended the organizational meeting, and so did Eugene Debs. Debs, who had been converted to socialism

after the Pullman strike of 1894, had already emerged by 1905 as one of the outstanding radical leaders in the country. Also attending was Mary Harris "Mother" Jones, who dressed like a society matron but attacked labor leaders "who sit on velvet chairs in conferences with labor's oppressors." "Mother" Jones had been a dressmaker, a Populist, and a member of the Knights of Labor. During the 1890s, she had marched with miners' wives on the picket line in western Pennsylvania.

Presiding at the Chicago meeting was "Big Bill" Haywood, the president of the Western Federation of Miners. He had been a cowboy, a miner, and a prospector. Somewhere along the way, he had lost an eye and mangled a hand, but he had a booming

An IWW Performance The way art and politics sometimes combined in the progressive era is illustrated by this poster for a performance by a group of political radicals at Madison Square Garden in New York. They re-enacted the IWW-supported silk workers' strike, which was then going on in Paterson, New Jersey. Many of the actual strikers took part in the performance. But the play lost money, and the strike ultimately failed. Still, this impressively designed program cover recalls a time when radical artists and labor leaders sought to transform the world. Why do many Americans even today have a romantic view of the IWW? *(The Tamiment Institute Library, New York University)*

voice and a passionate commitment to the workers. Denouncing Gompers and the AFL, he talked of class conflict. "The purpose of the IWW," he proclaimed, "is to bring the workers of this country into the possession of the full value of the product of their toil."

Haywood dominated the movement, which played an important role in organizing the militant strike of textile workers in Lawrence, Massachusetts, in 1912 and the following year in Paterson, New Jersey, and Akron, Ohio. The IWW had its greatest success organizing itinerant lumbermen and migratory workers in the Northwest. But in other places, especially in times of high unemployment, the Wobblies (as they were called) helped unskilled workers vent their anger against their employers.

Yet the IWW remained a small organization, troubled by internal squabbles and disagreements. Most American workers did not feel, as European workers did, that they were involved in a perpetual class struggle with their capitalist employers, but that did not mean that they were docile and passive. Many American workers struggled with their managers over control of the workplace, and workers occasionally went on strike for better wages and working conditions. Immigrants often did not join in these actions. Some immigrant workers, intent on earning enough money to go back home, had no time to join the conflict. Most of those who stayed in the United States held fast to the dream of a better job or moving up into the middle class. They avoided organized labor militancy. They knew that even if they failed, their sons and daughters would profit from the American way. The AFL, not the IWW, became the dominant American labor movement. But for a few, the IWW represented a dream of what might have been. For others, its presence, though small and largely ineffective, meant that perhaps someday a European-style labor movement might develop in America.

REFORM IN THE CITIES AND STATES

The reform movements of the progressive era usually started at the local level, then moved to the state, and finally to the nation's capital. Progressivism in the cities and states had roots in the depression and discontent of the 1890s. The reform banners called for more democracy, more power for the people, and legislation regulating railroads and other businesses. Yet often the professional and business classes were the movement's leaders. They intended to bring order out of chaos and to modernize the city and the state during a time of rapid growth.

Municipal Reformers

American cities grew rapidly in the last part of the nineteenth and the first part of the twentieth century. New York, which had a population of 1.2 million in 1880, grew to 3.4 million by 1900 and 5.6 million in 1920. Chicago expanded even more dramatically, from 500,000 in 1880 to 1.7 million in 1900 and 2.7 million in 1920. Los Angeles was a town of 11,000 in 1880 but multiplied 10 times by 1900, and then increased another 5 times, to more than a half million, by 1920.

The spectacular and continuing growth of the cities caused problems and created a need for housing, transportation, and municipal services. But it was the kind of people who were moving into the cities that worried many observers. Americans from small towns and farms continued to throng to the urban centers, as they had throughout the nineteenth century, but immigration produced the greatest surge in population. Fully 40 percent of New York's population and 36 percent of Chicago's was foreign born in 1910; if one included the children of the immigrants, the percentage approached 80 percent in some cities. To many Protestant Americans, the new immigrants seemed to threaten the American way of life and the very tenets of democracy.

The presence of large immigrant populations was the most important difference between American and European cities, and it made attempts to reform the city different in the United States. Twentieth-century reformers, mostly middle-class citizens like those in the nineteenth century, wanted to regulate and control the sprawling metropolis, restore democracy, reduce corruption, and limit the power of the political bosses and their immigrant allies. When these reformers talked of restoring power to the people, they usually meant ensuring control for people like themselves. The chief aim of municipal reform was to make the city more organized and efficient for the business and professional classes who were to control its workings.

Municipal reform movements varied from city to city, but everywhere the reformers tried to limit the power of the city bosses, whom they saw as corrupt and antidemocratic. In Boston, the reformers tried to strengthen the power of the mayor, break the hold of the city council, and eliminate council corruption. They succeeded in removing all party designations from city election ballots, and they extended the term of the mayor from two to four years. But to their chagrin, in the election of 1910,

A Traffic Jam in Chicago in 1909
Cities grew so rapidly that they often ceased to work. This 1909 photograph shows Dearborn Street looking south from Randolph Street in Chicago. Horse-drawn vehicles, streetcars, pedestrians, and even a few early autos clogged the intersection and created the urban inefficiency that angered municipal reformers. How have urban centers changed today? Have we solved the problem of urban transportation and crowding? *(Chicago Historical Society, [ICHi-04151])*

John Fitzgerald, grandfather of John F. Kennedy and foe of reform, defeated their candidate.

The most dramatic innovation in municipal reform was the replacement of both mayor and council with a nonpartisan commission of administrators. This scheme began quite accidentally when a hurricane devastated Galveston, Texas, in September 1900. More than 6,000 people died in the worst natural disaster in the nation's history. The existing government was helpless to deal with the crisis, so the state legislature appointed five commissioners to run the city during the emergency.

DOCUMENT

Walker Percy, "Birmingham Under the Commission Plan" (1911)

The idea spread to Houston, Dallas, and Austin and to cities in other states. It proved most popular in small to medium-sized cities in the Midwest and the Pacific Northwest. By World War I, more than 400 cities had adopted the commission form. Dayton, Ohio, went one step further: after a disastrous flood in 1913, the city hired a manager to run the city and to report to the elected council. Appointed, not elected, the city manager was more a businessman or technician than a politician. Government by experts was the perfect symbol of what most municipal reformers had in mind.

The commission and the expert manager did not replace the mayor in most large cities. One of the most flamboyant and successful of the progressive mayors was Tom Johnson of Cleveland. Johnson had made a fortune by investing in utility and railroad franchises before he was 40. But Henry George's *Progress and Poverty* so influenced him that he began a second career as a reformer. Elected mayor of Cleveland in 1901, he reduced transit fares and built parks and municipal bathhouses throughout the city. Johnson also broke the connection between the police and prostitution in the city by promising the madams and the brothel owners that he would not bother them if they would be orderly and not steal from their customers or pay off the police.

His most controversial move, however, was advocating city ownership of the street railroads and utilities. Like many American urban reformers, Johnson had always admired the municipally owned transportation systems in European cities. "Only through municipal ownership," he argued, "can the gulf which divides the community into a small dominant class on one side and the unorganized people on the other be bridged." Johnson was defeated in 1909 in part because he alienated many powerful business interests, but one of his lieutenants, Newton D. Baker, was elected mayor in 1911 and carried on many of his programs. Cleveland was one of many cities that began to regulate municipal utilities or take them over from the private owners.

The Global Adoption of the Telephone

The United States and Europe led the way in adopting the telephone during the progressive era. But the small towns and the farms lagged behind the cities everywhere in the world. **Reflecting on the Past** How did the telephone change business and personal habits for those who could afford the new device?

1912

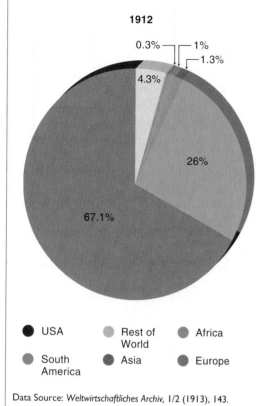

0.3% · 1% · 1.3% · 4.3% · 26% · 67.1%

- ● USA
- ● South America
- ● Rest of World
- ● Asia
- ● Africa
- ● Europe

Telephones per 100 Inhabitants

	1895	Rank	1911	Rank
Stockholm	4.1	1	19.9	2
Christiania (Oslo)	3	2	6.9	8
Los Angeles	2	3	24	1
Berlin	1.6	4	5.3	9
Hamburg	1.5	5	4.7	10
Copenhagen	1.2	6	7	7
Boston	1	7	9.2	4
Chicago	0.8	8	11	3
Paris	0.7	9	2.7	12
New York	0.6	10	8.3	6
Vienna	0.5	11	2.3	13
Philadelphia	0.3	12	8.6	5
London	0.2	13	2.8	11
St. Petersburg	0.2	14	2.2	14

Data Source: *Weltwirtschaftliches Archiv*, I/2 (1913), 143.

In Cleveland, both Tom Johnson and Newton Baker promoted the arts, music, and adult education. They also supervised the construction of a civic center, a library, and a museum. Most other American cities during the progressive era set out to bring culture and beauty to their centers. They were influenced at least in part by the great, classical White City constructed for the Chicago World's Fair of 1893, but even more by the grand European boulevards, especially the Champs-Élysées in Paris.

The architects of the "city beautiful" movement, strongly influenced by European city planners, preferred the impressive and ceremonial architecture of Rome or the Renaissance for libraries, museums, railroad stations, and other public buildings. The huge Pennsylvania Station in New York (now replaced by Madison Square Garden) was modeled after the imperial Roman baths of Caracalla, and the Free Library in Philadelphia was an almost exact copy of a building in Paris. The city beautiful leaders tried to make the city more attractive and meaningful for the middle and upper classes. The museums

and the libraries were closed on Sundays, the only day the working class could possibly visit them.

The social justice progressives, especially those connected with the social settlements, were more concerned with neighborhood parks and playgrounds than with the ceremonial boulevards and grand buildings. Hull House established the first public playground in Chicago. Jacob Riis, the housing reformer, and Lillian Wald of the Henry Street Settlement campaigned in New York for small parks and for the opening of schoolyards on weekends. Some progressives looked back nostalgically to their rural childhoods and desperately tried to get urban children out of the city in the summertime to attend rural camps. But they also tried to make the city more livable as well as more beautiful.

Most progressives had an ambivalent attitude toward the city. They feared it, and they loved it. Some saw the great urban areas filled with immigrants as a threat to American democracy, but one of Tom Johnson's young assistants, Frederic C. Howe, who had traveled and studied in Europe, wrote a book titled

The City: The Hope of Democracy (1905). Hope or threat, the progressives realized that the United States had become an urban nation and that the problems of the city had to be faced.

Reform in the States

The progressive movements in the states had many roots and took many forms, but because of the American federal system, the states took on an importance that confused observers from other parts of the world. In some states, especially in the West, progressive attempts to regulate railroads and utilities were simply an extension of Populism. In other states, the reform drive emerged from municipal reform efforts. Most states passed laws during the progressive era designed to extend democracy and give more authority to the people. Initiative and referendum laws allowed citizens to originate legislation and to overturn laws passed by the legislature, and recall laws gave the people a way to remove elected officials. Oregon was one of the leaders in this kind of legislation and, as in other western states, the progressives in Oregon tried to limit the power of the public utilities and the railroads. A notable success for progressive reform was the ratification in 1913 of the Seventeenth Amendment to the Constitution, which provided for the direct election of U.S. senators rather than their appointment by the legislatures.

Much progressive state legislation promoted order and efficiency, but many states passed social justice measures as well. Maryland enacted the first workers' compensation law in 1902, paying employees for days missed because of job-related injuries. By 1917, 37 states (almost all outside the South) had passed workers' compensation laws and 28 states had set maximum hours for women working in industry. Illinois approved a law aiding mothers with dependent children. Several states passed anti–child labor bills, and Oregon's 10-hour law restricting women's labor became a model for other states.

The states with the most successful reform movements elected strong and aggressive governors: Charles Evans Hughes in New York, Hoke Smith in Georgia, Hiram Johnson in California, Woodrow Wilson in New Jersey, and Robert La Follette in Wisconsin. After Wilson, La Follette was the most famous and in many ways the model progressive governor. Born in a small town in Wisconsin, he graduated from the University of Wisconsin in 1879 and was admitted to the bar. Practicing law during the 1890s in Madison, the state capital, he received a large retainer from the Milwaukee Railroad and defended

Landmark Social Legislation in the States	
1902	Maryland passed the first state worker's compensation law.
1903	Oregon adopted a law limiting women's work to ten hours a day in factories (upheld by the United States Supreme Court in *Muller v. Oregon*, 1908).
1911	Illinois enacted the first state law providing public assistance to mothers with dependent children.
1912	Massachusetts passed the first minimum-wage law. A commission fixed wage rates for women and children. This and other similar state laws were overturned by the United States Supreme Court in *Atkins v. Children's Hospital*, 1923.

the railroad against both riders and laborers who sued the company.

The depression of 1893 hit Wisconsin hard. More than one-third of the state's citizens were out of work, farmers lost their farms, and many small businesses went bankrupt. At the same time, the rich seemed to be getting richer. As grassroots discontent spread, a group of Milwaukee reformers attacked the giant corporations and the street railways. Several newspapers joined the battle and denounced special privilege and corruption. Everyone could agree on the need for tax reform, railroad regulation, and more participation of the people in government.

La Follette, who had had little interest in reform, took advantage of the general mood of discontent to win the governorship in 1901. It seemed ironic that La Follette, who had once taken a retainer from a railroad, owed his victory to his attack on the railroads. But La Follette was a shrewd politician. He used professors from the University of Wisconsin (in the capital) to prepare reports and do statistical studies. Then he worked with the legislature to pass a state primary law and an act regulating the railroads. "Go back to the first principles of democracy; go back to the people" was his battle cry. The "Wisconsin idea" attracted the attention of journalists such as Lincoln Steffens and Ray Stannard Baker, and they helped popularize the "laboratory of democracy" around the country. La Follette won national recognition and was elected to the Senate in 1906.

The progressive movement did improve government and made it more responsible to the people in Wisconsin and other states. For example, the railroads were brought under the control of a railroad commission. But by 1910, the railroads no longer complained about the new taxes and restrictions. They had discovered that it was to their advantage to make their operations more efficient, and often they were able to convince the commission that they should raise rates or abandon the operation of unprofitable lines.

Progressivism in the states, like progressivism everywhere, had mixed results. But the spirit of reform that swept the country was real, and progressive movements on the local level did eventually have an impact on Washington, especially during the administrations of Theodore Roosevelt and Woodrow Wilson.

THEODORE ROOSEVELT AND THE SQUARE DEAL

President William McKinley was shot in Buffalo, New York, on September 6, 1901, by Leon Czolgosz, an anarchist. McKinley died eight days later, making Theodore Roosevelt, at age 42, the youngest man ever to become president.

No one knew what to expect from Roosevelt. Some politicians thought he was too radical; a few social justice progressives remembered his suggestion that the soldiers should fire on the strikers during the 1894 Pullman strike. Nonetheless, under his leadership, progressivism reshaped the national political agenda. Although early progressive reformers had attacked problems that they saw in their own communities, they gradually understood that some problems could not be solved at the state or local level. The emergence of a national industrial economy had spawned conditions that demanded national solutions. Roosevelt began the process that would continue, sometimes with setbacks, throughout the twentieth century—a process that would regulate business, move beyond the states, and promote reform.

Progressives at the national level turned their attention to the workings of the economic system. They scrutinized the operation and organization of the railroads and other large corporations. They examined the threats to the natural environment. They reviewed the quality of the products of American industry. As they fashioned legislation to remedy the flaws in the economic

system, they vastly expanded the power of the national government.

A Strong and Controversial President

Roosevelt came to the presidency with considerable experience. He had run unsuccessfully for mayor of New York, served a term in the New York state assembly, spent four years as a U.S. civil service commissioner, and served two years as the police commissioner of New York City. His exploits in the Spanish-American War brought him to the public's attention, but he had also been an effective assistant secretary of the navy and a reform governor of New York. While police commissioner and governor, he had been influenced by a number of progressives. He had supported conservation, an eight-hour workday, and other progressive measures in New York. But no one was sure how he would act as president. He came from an upper-class family, had traveled widely in Europe, and had associated with the important and the powerful all over the world. He had written a number of books and was one of the most intellectual and cosmopolitan presidents since Thomas Jefferson. But there was no guarantee that he would be a progressive in office.

Roosevelt loved being president. He called the office a "bully pulpit," and he enjoyed talking to the

TR's Bully Pulpit Theodore Roosevelt was a dynamic public speaker who used his position to influence public opinion. Despite his high-pitched voice, he could be heard at the back of the crowd in the days before microphones. Note the row of reporters decked out in their summer straw hats writing their stories as the president speaks How have presidential speeches and the role of reporters changed since Roosevelt's time? *(Brown Brothers)*

Collage Celebrating the Career of Teddy Roosevelt

people and the press. His appealing personality and sense of humor made him a good subject for the new mass-market newspapers and magazines. The American people quickly adopted him as their favorite. They called him "Teddy" and named a stuffed bear after him. Sometimes his exuberance got a little out of hand. On one occasion, he took a foreign diplomat on a nude swim in the Potomac River. You have to understand, another observer remarked, that "the president is really only six years old."

Roosevelt was much more than an exuberant six-year-old. He was the strongest president since Lincoln. By revitalizing the executive branch, reorganizing the army command structure, and modernizing the consular service, he made many aspects of the federal government more efficient. He established the Bureau of Corporations, appointed independent commissions staffed with experts, and enlisted talented and well-trained men to work for the government. "TR," as he became known, called a White House conference on the care of dependent children, and in 1905, he even summoned college presidents and football coaches to the White House to discuss ways to limit violence in football. Although he angered many social justice progressives who felt he did not go far enough, he was the first president to listen to the pleas of the progressives and to invite them to the White House. Learning from experts such as Frances Kellor, he gradually became more concerned with social justice. In 1904, running on a platform of a "Square Deal" for the American people, he was reelected by an overwhelming margin.

Theodore Roosevelt

Dealing with the Trusts

One of Roosevelt's first actions as president was to attempt to control the large industrial corporations. He took office in the middle of an unprecedented wave of business consolidation. Between 1897 and 1904, some 4,227 companies combined to form 257 large corporations. U.S. Steel, the first billion-dollar corporation, was formed in 1901 by joining Carnegie Steel with its eight main competitors. The new company controlled two-thirds of the market, and financier J. P. Morgan made $7 million on the deal.

"The Verdict"— Anti-Monopoly Cartoon, 1899

The Sherman Anti-Trust Act of 1890 had been virtually useless in controlling the trusts, but muckrakers and progressives called for new regulation. Some even demanded a return to the age of small

business. Roosevelt opposed neither bigness nor the right of businessmen to make money. "We draw the line against misconduct, not against wealth," he said.

To the shock of much of the business community, he directed his attorney general to file suit to dissolve the Northern Securities Company, a giant railroad monopoly put together by James J. Hill and J. P. Morgan. Morgan came to the White House to tell Roosevelt, "If we have done anything wrong, send your man to my man and they can fix it up." A furious Roosevelt let Morgan and other businessmen know that they could not deal with the president of the United States as just another tycoon. The government won its case and proceeded to prosecute some of the largest corporations, including Standard Oil of New Jersey and the American Tobacco Company.

Roosevelt's antitrust policy did not end the power of the giant corporations or even alter their methods of doing business, nor did it force down the price of kerosene, cigars, or railroad tickets. But it did breathe some life into the Sherman Anti-Trust Act and increased the role of the federal government as regulator. It also caused large firms such as U.S. Steel to diversify to avoid antitrust suits.

TR as "Jack the Giant Killer"— *Puck* Cartoon

Roosevelt sought to strengthen the regulatory powers of the federal government in other ways. He steered the Elkins Act through Congress in 1903 and the Hepburn Act in 1906, which together increased the power of the Interstate Commerce Commission (ICC). The first act eliminated the use of rebates by railroads, a method that many large corporations had used to get favored treatment. The second act broadened the power of the ICC and gave it the right to investigate and enforce rates. Opponents in Congress weakened both bills, however, and the legislation neither ended abuses nor satisfied the farmers and small-business owners who had always been the railroads' chief critics.

Roosevelt firmly believed in corporate capitalism. He detested socialism and felt much more comfortable around business executives than labor leaders. Yet he saw his role as mediator and regulator. His view of the power of the presidency was illustrated in 1902 during the anthracite coal strike. Led by John Mitchell of the United Mine Workers, the coal miners went on strike to protest low wages, long hours, and unsafe working conditions. In 1901, a total of 513 coal miners had died in industrial accidents. The mine owners refused to talk to the miners. They hired

TR and His "Big Stick"

strikebreakers and used private security forces to threaten and intimidate the workers.

Roosevelt had no particular sympathy for labor, but in the fall of 1902, schools began closing for lack of coal, and it looked as if many citizens would suffer through the winter. Coal, which usually sold for $5 a ton, rose to $14. Roosevelt called the owners and representatives of the union to the White House, even though the mine owners protested that they would not deal with "outlaws." Finally, the president appointed a commission that included representatives of the union as well as the community. Within weeks, the miners went back to work with a 10 percent raise, back pay, and a nine-hour day. But the agreement failed to recognize the union. Neither side was entirely happy with the agreement. Roosevelt often compromised and sought the middle ground; in fact, one of his critics called him "a man on two horsebacks."

Meat Inspection and Pure Food and Drugs

Roosevelt's first major legislative reform began almost accidentally in 1904 when Upton Sinclair, a 26-year-old muckraking journalist, started research on the Chicago stockyards. Born in Baltimore, Sinclair had grown up in New York, where he wrote dime novels to pay his tuition at City College. He was converted to socialism, but it was more a romantic, Christian socialism than a Marxist-style European radicalism. Though he knew little about Chicago, he wanted to expose the exploitation of the poor and oppressed in America. He boarded at the University of Chicago Settlement while he did research, conducted interviews, and wrote the story of the meat industry that was published in 1906 as *The Jungle*. Sinclair documented exploitation in his fictional account, but his description of contaminated meat drew more attention. He described spoiled hams treated with formaldehyde and sausages made from rotten meat scraps, rats, and other refuse. Hoping to convert his readers to socialism, Sinclair instead turned their stomachs and caused a public outcry for better regulation of the meatpacking industry.

Roosevelt ordered a study of the meatpacking industry and then used the report to pressure Congress and the meatpackers to accept a bill introduced by Albert Beveridge, the progressive senator from Indiana. In the end, the Meat Inspection Act of 1906 was a compromise. It enforced some federal inspection and mandated sanitary conditions in all companies selling meat in interstate commerce.

DOCUMENT

Upton Sinclair, *The Jungle* (1906)

The meatpackers defeated a provision that would have required the dating of all meat. Some of the large companies supported the compromise because it gave them an advantage in their battle with the smaller firms. But the act was a beginning and an example of how muckrakers, social justice progressives, and public outcry eventually led to reform legislation. Passage of the act also shows how Roosevelt used the public mood and manipulated the political process to achieve his goals. Many of the progressive reformers were disappointed with the final result, but Roosevelt was always willing to settle for half a loaf rather than none at all. Ironically, the Meat Inspection Act restored the public's confidence in the meat industry and helped the industry increase its profits.

Taking advantage of the publicity that circulated around *The Jungle*, a group of reformers, writers, and government officials supported legislation to regulate the sale of food and drugs. Americans consumed an enormous quantity of patent medicines, which they purchased through the mail, from traveling salesmen, and from local stores. Many packaged and canned foods contained dangerous chemicals and impurities. One popular remedy, Hosteter's Stomach Bitters, was revealed on analysis to contain 44 percent alcohol. Coca-Cola, a popular soft drink, contained a small amount of cocaine, and many medicines were laced with opium. Many people, including women and children, became alcoholics or drug addicts in their quest to feel better. The Pure Food and Drug Act, which Congress passed on the same day in 1906 as the Meat Inspection Act, was not a perfect bill, but it corrected some of the worst abuses, including eliminating the cocaine from Coca-Cola.

Conservation

Although Roosevelt was pleased with the new legislation for regulating the food and drug industries, he always considered his conservation program his most important domestic achievement. An outdoorsman, hunter, and amateur naturalist since his youth, he announced soon after he became president that the planned protection of the nation's forests and water resources would be one of his most vital concerns. Using his executive authority, he more than tripled the land set aside for national forests, bringing the total to more than 150 million acres.

Because he had traveled widely in the West, Roosevelt understood, as few easterners did, the problems created by limited water in the western states. In 1902, with his enthusiastic support, Congress passed the Newlands Act, named for its chief

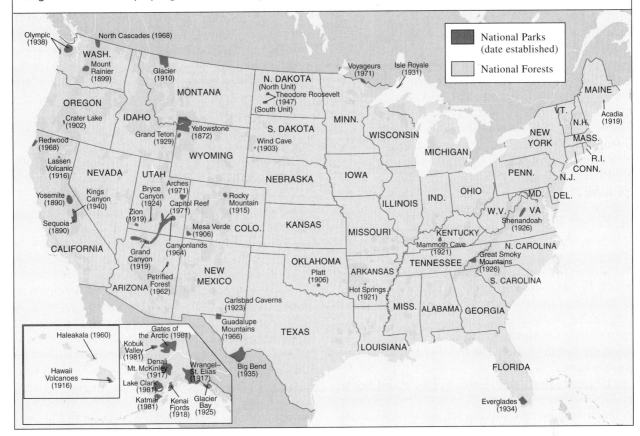

National Parks and Forests

Yellowstone, Yosemite, and a few other national parks were established before Theodore Roosevelt became president, but his passionate interest in conservation led to a movement to set aside and preserve thousands of acres of the public domain. Despite disagreements over the proper goals for the management of federal land, the movement continues to this day.

sponsor, Congressman Francis Newlands of Nevada. The National Reclamation Act (as it was officially called) set aside the proceeds from the sale of public land in 16 western states to pay for the construction of irrigation projects in those states. Although it tended to help big farmers more than small producers, the Newlands Act federalized irrigation for the first time.

More important than the conservation bills passed during Roosevelt's presidency, however, were his efforts to raise the public consciousness about the need to save the nation's natural resources. He convened a White House Conservation Conference in 1908 that included among its delegates most of the governors and representatives of 70 national organizations. A direct result of the conference was Roosevelt's appointment of a National Conservation Commission charged with making an inventory of the natural resources in the entire country. To chair the commission, Roosevelt appointed Gifford Pinchot, probably the most important conservation advocate in the country.

A graduate of Yale, Pinchot had studied scientific forestry management in Germany and France before becoming the forest manager of the Vanderbilts' Biltmore estate in North Carolina. In 1898, he was appointed chief of the U.S. Division of Forestry, and in 1900, he became the head of the Bureau of Forestry in the Department of Agriculture. An advocate of selective logging, fire control, and limited grazing on public lands, he became a friend and adviser to Roosevelt.

Pinchot's conservation policies pleased many in the timber and cattle industries; at the same time, they angered those who simply wanted to exploit the land. But his policies were denounced by the followers of John Muir, who believed passionately in preserving the land in a wilderness state. Muir had founded the Sierra Club in 1862 and had led a successful campaign to create Yosemite National Park in California. With his shaggy gray beard, his rough blue work clothes, and his black slouch hat, Muir seemed like an eccentric to many, but thousands agreed with him when he argued that preserving the

American wilderness was a spiritual and psychological necessity for overcivilized and overstimulated urban dwellers. Muir was one of the leaders in a "back to nature" movement at the turn of the century. Many middle-class Americans took up hiking, camping, and other outdoor activities, and children joined the Boy Scouts (founded in 1910) and the Camp Fire Girls (1912). The "back to nature movement" was not strictly American. The Boy Scouts were patterned after the British Boy Scouts, and hiking and mountain climbing were popular activities in many countries early in the twentieth century.

The conflicting philosophies of conservationist Pinchot and preservationist Muir were most dramatically demonstrated by the controversy over Hetch-Hetchy, a remote valley deep within Yosemite National Park. It was a pristine wilderness area, and Muir and his followers wanted to keep it that way. But in 1901, the mayor of San Francisco decided the valley would make a perfect place for a dam and reservoir to supply his growing city with water for decades to come. Muir argued that wilderness soon would be scarcer than water and more important for the moral strength of the nation. Pinchot, on the other hand, maintained that it was foolish to pander to the aesthetic enjoyment of a tiny group of people when the comfort and welfare of the great majority were at stake.

The Hetch-Hetchy affair was fought in the newspapers and magazines as well as in the halls of Congress, but in the end, the conservationists won out over the preservationists. Roosevelt and Congress sided with Pinchot and eventually the dam was built, turning the valley into a lake. But the debate over how to use the nation's land and water would continue throughout the twentieth century.

Progressivism for Whites Only

Like most of his generation, Roosevelt thought in stereotyped racial terms. He called Native Americans "savages" and once remarked that blacks were "wholly unfit for the suffrage." He believed that blacks, Asians, and Native Americans were inferior, and he feared that massive migrations from southern and eastern Europe threatened the United States. This kind of racism was supported by scientific theories accepted by many experts in the universities. Supporters of eugenics, who believed that selective breeding would improve the human race, advocated the forced sterilization of criminals, mental patients, and other undesirable types. Roosevelt was influenced by these theories, but he was first of all a

Booker T. Washington

politician, so he made gestures of goodwill to most groups. He even invited Booker T. Washington to the White House in 1901, though many southerners viciously attacked the president for this breach of etiquette. Roosevelt also appointed several qualified blacks to minor federal posts, notably Dr. William D. Crum to head the Charleston, South Carolina, customs house in 1905.

At other times, however, Roosevelt seemed insensitive to the needs and feelings of black Americans. This was especially true in his handling of the Brownsville, Texas, riot of 1906. Members of a black army unit stationed there, angered by discrimination against them, rioted one hot August night. Exactly what happened no one was sure, but one white man was killed and several wounded. Waiting until after the midterm elections of 1906, Roosevelt ordered all 167 members of three companies dishonorably discharged. It was an unjust punishment for an unproven crime, and 66 years later, the secretary of the army granted honorable discharges to the men, although most of them were by that time dead.

Theodore Roosevelt, ca. 1901

The progressive era coincided with the years of greatest segregation in the South, and in southern states, progressivism meant keeping blacks outside the political process. Even the most advanced progressives seldom included blacks in their reform schemes. Like most social settlements, Hull House was segregated, although Jane Addams (more than most progressives) struggled to overcome the racist attitudes of her day. She helped found a settlement that served a black neighborhood in Chicago, and she spoke out repeatedly against lynching. Addams also supported the founding of the National Association for the Advancement of Colored People (NAACP) in 1909, the most important organization of the progressive era aimed at promoting equality and justice for blacks.

The founding of the NAACP is the story of cooperation between a group of white social justice progressives and a number of courageous black leaders. Even in the age of segregation and lynching, blacks in all parts of the country—through churches, clubs, and schools—sought to promote a better life for themselves. In Boston, William Monroe Trotter used his newspaper to oppose Booker T. Washington's policy of accommodation. In Chicago, Ida B. Wells, an ardent crusader against lynching, organized a women's club for blacks and founded the Negro Fellowship League to help black migrants. The most important black leader who argued for equality and opportunity for his people was W. E. B. Du Bois. He differed dramatically from Washington on the proper position of

An American History Class Tuskegee Institute followed Booker T. Washington's philosophy of black advancement through accommodation to the white status quo. Here students study white American history, but most of their time was spent on more practical subjects. This photo was taken in 1902 by Frances Benjamin Johnson, a pioneer woman photographer. How have classrooms changed in the last hundred years? How have they stayed the same? *(Library of Congress)*

blacks in American life (see Chapter 17). Whereas Washington advocated vocational education, Du Bois argued for the best education possible for the most talented tenth of the black population. Whereas Washington preached compromise and accommodation to the dominant white society, Du Bois increasingly urged aggressive action to ensure equality.

Denouncing Washington for accepting the "alleged inferiority of the Negro," Du Bois called a meeting of young and militant blacks in 1905. They met in Canada, not far from Niagara Falls, and issued an angry statement. "We want to pull down nothing but we don't propose to be pulled down," the platform announced. "We believe in taking what we can get but we don't believe in being satisfied with it and in permitting anybody for a moment to imagine we're satisfied." The Niagara movement, as it came to be called, was small, but it was soon augmented by a group of white liberals concerned with violence against blacks and race riots in Atlanta and even in Springfield, Illinois, the home of Abraham Lincoln. Jane Addams joined the new organization,

as did Oswald Garrison Villard, grandson of abolitionist William Lloyd Garrison.

In 1910, the Niagara movement combined with the NAACP, and Du Bois became editor of its journal, *The Crisis.* He toned down his rhetoric, but he tried to promote equality for all blacks. The NAACP was a typical progressive organization, seeking to work within the American system to promote reform. But to Roosevelt and many others who called themselves progressives, the NAACP seemed dangerously radical.

William Howard Taft

After two terms as president, Roosevelt decided to step down. But he soon regretted his decision. Only 50 years old, he was at the peak of his popularity and power. Because the U.S. system of government provides little creative function for former presidents, Roosevelt decided to travel and to go big-game hunting in Africa. But before he left, he personally selected his successor.

William Howard Taft, Roosevelt's personal choice for the Republican nomination and winner over Democratic candidate William Jennings Bryan in 1908, was a distinguished lawyer, federal judge, and public servant. Born in Cincinnati, Taft had been the first civil governor of the Philippines and Roosevelt's secretary of war. In some ways, he seemed more progressive than Roosevelt. His administration instituted more suits against monopolies in one term than Roosevelt had in two. He supported the eight-hour workday and legislation to make mining safer, and he urged the passage of the Mann–Elkins Act in 1910, which strengthened the ICC by giving it more power to set railroad rates and extending its jurisdiction over telephone and telegraph companies. Taft and Congress also authorized the first tax on corporate profits. He also encouraged the process that eventually led to the passage of the federal income tax, which was authorized under the Sixteenth Amendment, ratified in 1913. That probably did more to transform the relationship of the government to the people than all other progressive measures combined.

But Taft soon ran into difficulties. His biggest problem was his style. He was a huge man, weighing more than 300 pounds. (Rumors circulated that he had to have a special, oversize bathtub installed in the White House.) Easily made fun of, the president wrote ponderous prose and spoke uninspiringly. He also lacked Roosevelt's political skills and angered many of the progressives in the Republican party, especially the midwestern insurgents led by Senator Robert La Follette of Wisconsin. Many progressives were annoyed when he signed the Payne–Aldrich Tariff, which midwesterners thought left rates on cotton and wool cloth and other items too high and played into the hands of the eastern industrial interests.

Taft's Inefficient—*Puck* Cartoon

Even Roosevelt was infuriated when his successor reversed many of his conservation policies and fired chief forester Gifford Pinchot, who had attacked secretary of the interior Richard A. Ballinger for giving away rich coal lands in Alaska to mining interests. Roosevelt broke with Taft, letting it be known that he was willing to run again for president. This set up one of the most exciting and significant elections in American history.

The Election of 1912

Woodrow Wilson won the Democratic nomination for president in 1912. The son and grandson of Presbyterian ministers, Wilson grew up in a comfortable and intellectual southern household and early on seemed more interested in politics than in religion. He graduated from Princeton University in 1879, studied law at the University of Virginia, and practiced law briefly before entering graduate school at the Johns Hopkins University in Baltimore. His book, *Congressional Government* (1885), established his reputation as a shrewd analyst of American politics. Less flamboyant than Roosevelt, he was an excellent public speaker, possessing the power to convince people with his words. In 1902 Wilson was elected president of Princeton University, and during the next few years he established a national reputation as an educational leader. Wilson had never lost interest in politics, however, so when offered a chance by the Democratic machine to run for governor of New Jersey, he took it eagerly. In his two years as governor, he showed courage as he quickly alienated some of the conservatives who had helped elect him. Building a coalition of reformers, he worked with them to pass a direct primary law and a workers' compensation law. He also created a commission to regulate transportation and public utility companies. By 1912, Wilson not only was an expert on government and politics but had also acquired the reputation of a progressive.

Roosevelt, who had been speaking out on a variety of issues since 1910, competed with Taft for the Republican nomination, but Taft, as the incumbent president and party leader, was able to win it. Roosevelt then startled the nation by walking out of the convention and forming a new political party, the Progressive party. The new party would not have been formed without Roosevelt, but it was always more than Roosevelt. It appealed to progressives from all over the country who had become frustrated with the conservative leadership in both major parties.

William Howard Taft

Many social workers and social justice progressives supported the Progressive party because of its platform, which contained provisions they had been advocating for years. The Progressives supported an eight-hour workday, a six-day workweek, the abolition of child labor under age 16, and a federal system of accident, old age, and unemployment insurance. Unlike the Democrats, the Progressives also endorsed woman suffrage.

Herbert Croly, *Progressive Democracy* (1914)

Most supporters of the Progressives in 1912 did not realistically think they could win, but they were convinced that they could organize a new political movement that would replace the Republican party, just as the Republicans had replaced the Whigs after 1856. To this end, Progressive leaders led by Frances Kellor set up the Progressive Service, designed to apply the principles of social research to educating voters between elections.

The Progressive party convention in Chicago seemed to many observers more like a religious revival meeting or a social work conference than a political gathering. The delegates sang "Onward Christian Soldiers," "The Battle Hymn of the Republic," and "Roosevelt, Oh Roosevelt" (to the tune of "Maryland, My Maryland"). They waved their bandannas, and when Jane Addams rose to second Roosevelt's nomination, a large group of women marched around the auditorium with a banner that read "Votes for Women."

The enthusiasm for Roosevelt and the Progressive party was misleading, for behind the unified facade lurked many disagreements. Roosevelt had become more progressive on many issues since leaving the presidency. He even attacked the financiers "to whom the acquisition of untold millions is the supreme goal of life, and who are too often utterly indifferent as to how these millions are obtained." But he was not as committed to social reform as some of the delegates. Perhaps the most divisive issue was the controversy over seating black delegates from several southern states. A number of social justice progressives fought hard to include a plank in the platform supporting equality for blacks and for seating the black delegation. Roosevelt, however, thought he had a realistic chance to carry several southern states, and he was not convinced that black equality was an important progressive issue. In the end, no blacks sat with the southern delegates, and the platform made no mention of black equality.

The political campaign in 1912 became a contest primarily between Roosevelt and Wilson; Taft, the Republican candidate and incumbent, was ignored by most reporters who covered the campaign. On one level, the campaign became a debate over political philosophy. What is the proper relationship of government to society in a modern industrial age? Roosevelt spoke of a "New Nationalism." In a modern industrial society, he argued, large corporations were "inevitable and necessary." What was needed was not the breakup of the trusts but a strong president and increased power in the hands of the federal government to regulate business and industry and to ensure the rights of labor, women and children, and other groups. The government should be the "steward of the public welfare." He argued for using Hamiltonian means to ensure Jeffersonian ends, for using strong central government to guarantee the rights of the people.

Wilson responded with a program he called the "New Freedom." Drawing on the ideas of Louis Brandeis, he emphasized the need for the Jeffersonian tradition of limited government with open competition. He spoke of the "curse of bigness" and argued against too much federal power.

The level of debate during the campaign was impressive, making this one of the few elections in American history in which important ideas were actually discussed. It also

Fernand Léger, *La Ville (The City)*, 1919 The Armory Show held in New York in 1913 introduced modern art, most of it European and much of it abstract, to the American public. It was a cultural moment of great importance during the progressive era. Many Europeans (as well as many Americans) viewed the United States as a country with little culture, but French artist Fernand Léger was enthralled by New York, especially at night. "I was struck by the illuminated advertisements that swept the streets," he wrote. "You were there talking to someone, and suddenly he became blue. Then the colour disappeared and another came, and he became red, yellow. That kind of projected colour is free, it is in space. I wanted to do the same thing in my canvases." What do you make of this painting? Is the United States still viewed by foreign visitors as a land of little culture? *(Fernand Léger, La Ville, 1919. Digital Image © The Museum of Modern Art/Licensed by SCALA/Art Resource, NY. © 2007 Artists Rights Society (ARS), New York/ADAGP, Paris)*

		Presidential Elections of the Progressive Era		
Year	**Candidate**	**Party**	**Popular Vote**	**Electoral Vote**
1900	WILLIAM MCKINLEY	Republican	7,218,039 (51.7%)	292
	William Jennings Bryan	Democratic, Populist	6,358,345 (45.5%)	155
1904	THEODORE ROOSEVELT	Republican	7,628,834 (56.4%)	336
	Alton B. Parker	Democratic	5,084,401 (37.6%)	140
	Eugene V. Debs	Socialist	402,460 (3.0%)	0
1908	WILLIAM H. TAFT	Republican	7,679,006 (51.6%)	321
	William J. Bryan	Democratic	6,409,106 (43.1%)	162
	Eugene V. Debs	Socialist	420,820 (2.8%)	0
1912	WOODROW WILSON	Democratic	6,296,547 (41.9%)	435
	Theodore Roosevelt	Progressive	4,118,571 (27.4%)	88
	William H. Taft	Republican	3,486,720 (23.2%)	8
	Eugene V. Debs	Socialist	897,011 (6.0%)	0
1916	WOODROW WILSON	Democratic	9,129,606 (49.4%)	277
	Charles E. Hughes	Republican	8,538,221 (46.2%)	254
	Allan L. Benson	Socialist	585,113 (3.2%)	0

Note: Winners' names appear in capital letters.

marked a watershed for political thought for liberals who rejected Jefferson's distrust of a strong central government. It is easy to exaggerate the differences between Roosevelt and Wilson. There was some truth in the charge of William Allen White, the editor of the Emporia, Kansas, *Gazette,* when he remarked, "Between the New Nationalism and the New Freedom was that fantastic imaginary gulf that always had existed between Tweedle-dum and Tweedle-dee." Certainly, in the end, the things that Roosevelt and Wilson could agree on were more important than the issues that divided them. Both Roosevelt and Wilson urged reform within the American system. Both defended corporate capitalism, and both opposed socialism and radical labor organizations such as the IWW. Both wanted to promote more democracy and to strengthen conservative labor unions. And both were very different in style and substance from the fourth candidate, Eugene Debs, who ran on the Socialist party ticket in 1912.

In 1912, Debs was the most important socialist leader in the country. Socialism has always been a minority movement in the United States, but it reached its greatest success in the United States in the first decade of the twentieth century. Thirty-three cities, including Milwaukee, Wisconsin; Reading, Pennsylvania; Butte, Montana; Jackson, Michigan; and Berkeley, California, chose socialist mayors. Socialists Victor Berger from Wisconsin and Meyer London from New York were elected to Congress. The most important socialist periodical, *Appeal to Reason,* published in

Eugene V. Debs, "The Outlook for Socialism in the United States" (1900)

Girard, Kansas, increased its circulation from about 30,000 in 1900 to nearly 300,000 in 1906. Socialism appealed to a diverse group. In the cities, some who called themselves socialists merely favored municipal ownership of street railways. Some reformers, such as Florence Kelley and William English Walling, joined the party because of their frustration with the slow progress of reform. The party also attracted many recent immigrants, who brought with them a European sense of class and loyalty to socialism.

A tremendously appealing figure and a great orator, Debs had run for president in 1900, 1904, and 1908, but in 1912 he reached much wider audiences in more parts of the country. His message differed radically from that of Wilson or Roosevelt. Unlike the progressives, socialists argued for fundamental change in the American system. Debs polled almost 900,000 votes in 1912 (6 percent of the popular vote), the best showing ever for a socialist in the United States. Wilson received 6.3 million votes; Roosevelt, a little more than 4 million; and Taft, 3.5 million. Wilson garnered 435 electoral votes; Roosevelt, 88; and Taft, only 8.

WOODROW WILSON AND THE NEW FREEDOM

Wilson was elected largely because Roosevelt and the Progressive party split the Republican vote. But once elected, Wilson became a vigorous and aggressive chief executive who set out to translate his ideas about progressive government into legislation. Wilson was the first southerner elected president since the Civil War, but Wilson, like Roosevelt, had to work within his party, and that restricted how progressive he could be. But he was also constrained by his own background and inclinations. Still, like Roosevelt, Wilson became more progressive during his presidency.

Tariff and Banking Reform

Wilson was not as charismatic as Roosevelt. He had a more difficult time relating to people in small groups, but he was an excellent public speaker who dominated through the force of his intellect. He probably had an exaggerated belief in his ability to persuade and a tendency to trust his own intuition too much. Ironically, his early success in getting his legislative agenda through Congress contributed to the overconfidence that would get him into difficulty later in foreign affairs. But his ability to push his legislative program through Congress during his first two years in office was matched only by Franklin Roosevelt during the first months of the New Deal and by Lyndon Johnson in 1965.

Within a month of his inauguration, Wilson went before a joint session of Congress to outline his legislative program. He recommended reducing the tariff to eliminate favoritism, freeing the banking system from Wall Street control, and restoring competition in industry. By appearing in person before Congress, he broke a precedent established by Thomas Jefferson.

The first item on Wilson's agenda was tariff reform. The Underwood Tariff, passed in 1913, was not a free-trade bill, but it did reduce tariff rates on hundreds of items for the first time in many years. Attached to the Underwood bill was a provision for a small and slightly graduated income tax, which had been made possible by the passage of the Sixteenth Amendment. It imposed a modest rate of 1 percent on income over $4,000 (thus exempting a large portion of the population), with a surtax rising to 6 percent on high incomes. The income tax was enacted to replace the money lost from lowering the tariff. Wilson seemed to have no interest in using it to redistribute wealth in America.

The next item on Wilson's agenda was reform of the banking system. A financial panic in 1907 had revealed the need for a central bank, but few people could agree on the exact nature of the reforms. A congressional committee, led by Arsène Pujo of Louisiana, had revealed a massive consolidation of banks and trust companies and a system of interlocking directorates and informal arrangements that concentrated resources and power in the hands of a few firms, such as the J. P. Morgan Company. The progressive faction of the Democratic party, armed with the Pujo Committee's findings, argued for a banking system and a currency controlled by the federal government. But talk of banking reform raised the specter among conservative Democrats and the business community of socialism, populism, and the monetary ideas of William Jennings Bryan.

The bill that passed Congress was a compromise. In creating the Federal Reserve System, it was the

DOCUMENT

Louis Brandeis, *Other People's Money and How Banks Use It* (1913)

Opposing Woman Suffrage Many men opposed suffrage for women because they feared the vote would change gender roles and destroy women's feminine ways. They also believed that women with the vote would support prohibition and other dangerous reforms. They often argued that women had no place in the masculine and corrupt world of politics. Many women also opposed suffrage because they believed their husbands and fathers or because they feared change. Would you have supported the vote for women if you had been alive in 1920? How have women's votes changed America? *(Library of Congress [LC-USZ62-25338])*

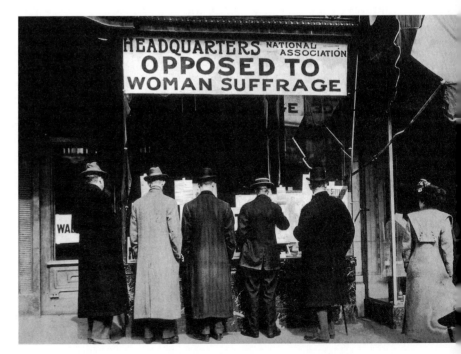

Key Progressive Legislation

National Reclamations Act (Newlands Act), 1902

Used proceeds from sale of public lands in the western states to finance construction and maintenance of irrigation projects.

Elkins Act, 1903

Strengthened the Interstate Commerce Commission Act primarily by eliminating rebates to selected corporations.

Hepburn Act, 1906

Strengthened the Interstate Commerce Commission by giving it power to fix rates and broadening its jurisdiction to include express companies, oil pipelines, terminals, and bridges.

Meat Inspection Act, 1906

Provide for federal inspection of all companies selling meat in interstate commerce.

Pure Food and Drug Act, 1906

Prohibited the manufacture, sale, or transportation of adulterated or fraudulently labeled foods or drugs in interstate commerce.

Mann–Elkins Act, 1910

Put telephone, telegraph, cable, and wireless companies under the jurisdiction of the Interstate Commerce Commission.

Mann Act, 1910

Prohibited interstate transportation of women for immoral purposes.

Sixteenth Amendment to the Constitution, 1913 (proposed in 1909)

Gave Congress the power to impose a federal tax on income from all sources. An inheritance tax was added in 1916.

Federal Child Labor Law (Keatings–Owen Act), 1916

Barred products of child labor from interstate commerce; declared unconstitutional in 1918. Another act passed in 1919 was declared unconstitutional in 1920. In 1924 a child labor amendment to the Constitution was submitted to the states, but was never ratified.

Adamson Act, 1916

Provided for an eight-hour day and time and a half for overtime on interstate railroads.

Federal Farm Loan Act, 1916

Provided farmers with long-term credit.

Eighteenth Amendment to the Constitution, 1919 (proposed in 1917)

Prohibited the manufacture, sale, or transportation of intoxicating beverages; repealed by the Twenty-First Amendment in 1933.

Nineteenth Amendment to the Constitution, 1920 (proposed in 1919)

Provided that the right of citizens of the United States to vote should not be denied or abridged by the United States or any state on account of sex.

first reorganization of the banking system since the Civil War. The bill provided for 12 Federal Reserve banks and a Federal Reserve Board appointed by the president. The bill also created a flexible currency, based on Federal Reserve notes, that could be expanded or contracted as the situation required. The Federal Reserve System was not without its flaws, as later developments would show, and it did not end the power of the large eastern banks; but it was an improvement, and it appealed to the part of the progressive movement that sought order and efficiency.

Despite these reform measures, Wilson was not very progressive in some of his actions during his first two years in office. In the spring of 1914, he failed to support a bill that would have provided long-term rural credit financed by the federal government. He opposed a woman suffrage amendment, arguing that the states should decide who could vote. He also failed to support an anti–child labor bill after it had passed the House. Most distressing to some progressives, he ordered the segregation of blacks in several federal departments. When southern Democrats, suddenly in control in many departments, began dismissing black federal office-holders, especially those "who boss white girls," Wilson did nothing. When the NAACP complained that the shops, offices, restrooms, and lunchrooms of the post office and treasury departments and the Bureau of Engraving were segregated, Wilson replied, "I sincerely believe it to be in [the blacks'] best interest." When the president endorsed the blatantly racist movie *Birth of a Nation*, others doubted that he believed in justice for the African American people. "Have you a 'new freedom' for white Americans and a new slavery for your African-American fellow citizens?" Boston journalist William Monroe Trotter asked.

Moving Closer to a New Nationalism

How to control the great corporations in America was a question Wilson and Roosevelt had debated extensively during the 1912 campaign. Wilson's solution was the Clayton Act, submitted to Congress in 1914. The bill prohibited a number of unfair trading practices, outlawed the interlocking directorate, and made it illegal for corporations to purchase stock in other corporations if doing so tended to reduce competition. It was not clear how the government would enforce these provisions and ensure the competition that Wilson's New Freedom doctrine called for. Labor leaders protested that the bill had no provision exempting labor organizations from prosecution under the Sherman Anti-Trust Act. When a section was added exempting both labor and agricultural organizations, Samuel Gompers hailed it as labor's Magna Carta. It was hardly that, because the courts interpreted the provision so that labor unions remained subject to court injunctions during strikes despite the Clayton Act.

More important than the Clayton Act, which both supporters and opponents realized was too vague to be enforced, was the creation of the Federal Trade Commission (FTC), modeled after the ICC, with enough power to move directly against corporations accused of restricting competition. The FTC was the idea of Louis Brandeis, but Wilson accepted it even though it seemed closer to the philosophy of New Nationalism than to Wilson's New Freedom.

The Federal Trade Commission and the Clayton Act did not end monopoly, and the courts in the next two decades did not increase the government's power to regulate business. The success of Wilson's reform agenda appeared minimal in 1914, but the outbreak of war in Europe and the need to win the election of 1916 would influence him in becoming more progressive in the next years (see Chapter 22).

Neither Wilson nor Roosevelt satisfied the demands of the advanced progressives. These two progressive presidents spent most of their efforts on trying to regulate economic power rather than promoting social justice. Yet the most important legacy of these two powerful politicians was their attempts to strengthen the office of president and the executive branch of the federal government. The nineteenth-century American presidents after Lincoln had been relatively weak, and much of the federal power had resided with Congress. The progressive presidents reasserted presidential authority, modernized the executive branch, and began the creation of the federal bureaucracy, which has had a major impact on the lives of Americans.

Both Wilson and Roosevelt used the presidency as a bully pulpit to make pronouncements, create news, and influence policy. Roosevelt strengthened the Interstate Commerce Commission and Wilson created

TIMELINE

1901	McKinley assassinated; Theodore Roosevelt becomes president
	Robert La Follette elected governor of Wisconsin
	Tom Johnson elected mayor of Cleveland
	Model tenement house bill passed in New York
	U.S. Steel formed
1902	Anthracite coal strike
1903	Women's Trade Union League founded
	Elkins Act
1904	Roosevelt re-elected
	Lincoln Steffens writes *The Shame of the Cities*
1905	Frederic C. Howe writes *The City: The Hope of Democracy*
	Industrial Workers of the World (IWW) formed
1906	Upton Sinclair writes *The Jungle*
	Hepburn Act
	Meat Inspection Act
	Pure Food and Drug Act
1907	Financial panic
1908	*Muller v. Oregon*
	Danbury Hatters case (*Loewe v. Lawler*)
	William Howard Taft elected president
1909	National Association for the Advancement of Colored People (NAACP) founded
1910	Ballinger–Pinchot controversy
	Mann Act
1911	Frederick Taylor writes *The Principles of Scientific Management*
	Triangle Shirtwaist Company fire
1912	Progressive party founded by Theodore Roosevelt
	Woodrow Wilson elected president
	Children's Bureau established
	Industrial Relations Commission founded
1913	Sixteenth Amendment (income tax) ratified
	Underwood Tariff
	Federal Reserve System established
	Seventeenth Amendment (direct election of senators) passed
1914	Clayton Act
	Federal Trade Commission Act
	AFL has more than 2 million members
	Ludlow Massacre in Colorado

the Federal Trade Commission, both of which were the forerunners of many other federal regulatory bodies. By breaking precedent and delivering his annual message in person before a joint session of Congress, Wilson symbolized the new power of the presidency.

The nature of politics was changed by more than just the increased power of the executive branch. The new bureaus, committees, and commissions brought to Washington a new kind of expert, trained in the universities, at the state and local level, and in voluntary organizations. Julia Lathrop, a coworker of Jane Addams at Hull House, was one such expert.

Appointed by President Taft in 1912 to become chief of the newly created Children's Bureau, she was the first woman ever appointed to such a position. She used her post not only to work for better child labor laws but also to train a new generation of women experts who would take their positions in state, federal, and private agencies in the 1920s and 1930s. Other experts emerged in Washington during the progressive era to influence policy in subtle and important ways. The expert, the commission, the statistical survey, and the increased power of the executive branch were all legacies of the progressive era.

Conclusion

The Limits of Progressivism

The progressive era was a time when many Americans set out to promote reform because they saw poverty, despair, and disorder in the country transformed by immigration, urbanism, and industrialism. But unlike the socialists, the progressives saw nothing fundamentally wrong with the American system. Progressivism, part of a global movement to regulate and control rampaging industrialism, was largely a middle-class movement that sought to help the poor, the immigrants, and the working class. Yet the poor were rarely consulted about policy, and many groups, especially African Americans, were almost entirely left out of reform plans. Progressives had an optimistic view of human nature and an exaggerated faith in statistics, commissions, and committees. They talked of the need for more democracy, but they often succeeded in promoting bureaucracy and a government run by experts. They believed there was a need to regulate business, promote efficiency, and spread social justice, but these were often contradictory goals. In the end, their regulatory laws tended to aid business and strengthen corporate capitalism, while social justice and equal opportunity remained difficult to achieve. By contrast, most of the industrialized nations of western Europe, especially Germany, Denmark, and Great Britain, passed

legislation during this period providing for old-age pensions and health and unemployment insurance.

Progressivism was a broad, diverse, and sometimes contradictory movement that had its roots in the 1890s and reached its height in the early twentieth century. It began with many local movements and voluntary efforts to deal with the problems created by urban industrialism and then moved to the state and finally the national level, where it enlisted government to regulate the private sector and to promote reform. Women played important roles in organizing reform, and many became experts at gathering statistics and writing reports. Eventually, they began to fill positions in the new agencies in the state capitals and in Washington. Frances Kellor was one of those professional women who devoted her life to reform and to helping immigrants. Neither Theodore Roosevelt nor Woodrow Wilson was an advanced progressive, but during both their administrations, progressivism achieved some success. Both presidents strengthened the power of the presidency, and both promoted the idea that the federal government had the responsibility to regulate and control and to promote social justice. Progressivism would be altered by World War I, but it survived, with its strengths and weaknesses, to affect American society through most of the twentieth century.

Questions for Review and Reflection

1. What contributions did women make to the Progressive movement?

2. Why did the United States lag behind several European countries in passing social legislation?

3. Was Prohibition a Progressive measure?

4. How did progressivism differ from socialism?

5. What was the long-range legacy of the Progressive movement?

Recommended Reading

Recommended Readings are posted on the Web site for this textbook. Visit www.ablongman.com/nash

Fiction and Film

Three books written in the early 1900s help readers understand what life was like during the progressive era. Theodore Dreiser's *Sister Carrie* (1900) is a classic of social realism that was controversial at the time it was published. Upton Sinclair's *The Jungle* (1906) is about the meatpacking industry and the failure of the American dream. *Susan Lenox* (1917), written by David Graham Phillips, is an epic of slum life and political corruption. *Birth of a Nation* (1915) is an important film not only because of its innovative technique but also because it is a mirror of the racism of the progressive era. *Hester Street* (1975), a later film, creates a realistic picture of the immigrant experience and the conflict between husbands and wives created by assimilation. According to some critics, *Citizen Kane* (1941) is the best American film ever made. Based loosely on the life of newspaper magnate William Randolph Hearst, the film deals with much of the history of the early twentieth century. The documentary *Unforgivable Blackness: The Rise and Fall of Jack Johnson* (2005) deals with the racism and popular culture (especially boxing) in the progressive era.

Discovering U.S. History Online

How the Other Half Lives: Studies Among the Tenements of New York
www.cis.yale.edu/amstud/inforev/riis/title.html
This site presents the full text, including illustrations, of this classic work.

Turn-of-the-Century America, 1880–1920
http://lcweb2.loc.gov/ammem/detroit/dethome.htm
This Library of Congress collection has thousands of photographs from turn-of-the-century America.

American Sweatshops
www.americanhistory.si.edu/sweatshops/
This site presents a history of American sweatshops from 1820 to 1997 through images and text.

The Triangle Factory Fire
www.ilr.cornell.edu/trianglefire/
The Kheel Center has put together this site composed of oral histories, cartoons, images, and essays about the shirtwaist factory fire of March 1911.

The Westinghouse World
http://memory.loc.gov/ammem/papr/west/westgorg.html
Part of the Westinghouse Works Collection, this special exhibition presents an overview of this turn of-the-century factory, the working conditions, projects, and a brief biography of the founder.

The Trial of Bill Haywood

www.law.umkc.edu/faculty/projects/ftrials/haywood/haywood.htm

Bill Haywood was a labor radical accused of ordering the assassination of former governor of Idaho Frank Steunenberg in 1907. This site contains images, chronology, and court and official documents.

Memories of the Industrial Workers of the World (IWW)

www.geocities.com/CapitolHill/5202/rebelgirl.html

Elizabeth Gurley Flynn gave this speech presenting her memoirs of IWW two years before her death.

IWW Historical Reclamation Project

http://parsons.iww.org/~iw/info/books/

A cooperative effort of present union members to preserve the history of IWW, this site presents a collection of pamphlets, writings, Web references, and so on.

Arts and Crafts Archives

www.arts-crafts.com/archive/archive.shtml

This site serves as a guide to materials on the arts and crafts movement, which lasted roughly from 1890 to 1929.

The Evolution of the Conservation Movement, 1850–1920

http://memory.loc.gov/ammem/amrvhtml/conshome.html

This Library of Congress site brings together scores of primary sources and photographs about "the historical formation and cultural foundations of the movement to conserve and protect America's natural heritage."

America 1900

www.pbs.org/wgbh/pages/amex/1900

This is the companion site to the PBS documentary *America 1900.* It includes audio clips of respected historians on the economics, politics, and culture of 1900; a primary-source database; a timeline of the year; downloadable software to compile your family tree; and other materials.

Chicago in 1900

www.chipublib.org/004chicago/1900/intro.html

This site presents a sketch of Chicago in 1900, including its architecture, commerce, crime, education, family, economics, amusements, geography, government, health, population, and transportation.

The Anthracite Coal Strike, 1902

www.history.ohio-state.edu/projects/coal/1902anthracitestrike/

As an example of turn-of-the-century strikes, this site presents the anthracite strike of 1902, including a chronology of the strike, primary documents, a description of the issues, and political cartoons.

The Wright Brothers in Photographs

www.libraries.wright.edu/special/wright_brothers/dmc.html

This image database "provides thorough coverage of the Wrights' early inventive period documenting their experimental gliders and flight testing in both North Carolina and Ohio."

Theodore Roosevelt Association

www.theodoreroosevelt.org

Chartered by Congress in 1920 to "preserve the memory and ideals of the 26th President of the United States," the Theodore Roosevelt Association presents a thorough site containing much biographical and research information.

Theodore Roosevelt

www.potus.com/troosevelt.html

This site contains basic factual data about Roosevelt's election and presidency, speeches, and online biographies.

William Howard Taft

www.potus.com/whtaft.html

This site contains basic factual data about Taft's election and presidency, speeches, and online biographies.

Woodrow Wilson

www.potus.com/wwilson.html

This site contains basic factual data about Wilson's election and presidency, speeches, and online biographies.

CHAPTER 22

The Great War

Harvey Dunn, *Prisoners and Wounded*, 1918   This 1918 painting of German and American wounded and exhausted soldiers after the Meuse-Argonne offensive captures some of the horror and pathos of war. How does this image contrast with the war memorials? Where are the heroes?
(Harvey Dunn, Prisoners and Wounded, *1918. National Museum of American History, Smithsonian Institution)*

American Stories

A Young Man Enlists in the Great Adventure

On April 7, 1917, the day after the United States officially declared war on Germany, Edmund P. Arpin, Jr., a young man of 22 from Grand Rapids, Wisconsin, decided to enlist in the army. The war seemed to provide a solution for his aimless drifting. It was not patriotism that led him to join the army but his craving for adventure and excitement. A month later, he was at Fort Sheridan, Illinois, along with hundreds of other eager young men, preparing to become an army officer. He felt a certain pride and sense of purpose, and especially a feeling of comradeship with the other men, but the war was a long way off.

Arpin finally arrived with his unit in Liverpool on December 23, 1917, aboard the *Leviathan,* a German luxury liner that the United States had interned when war was declared and then pressed into service as a troop transport. In England, he discovered that American troops were not greeted as saviors. Hostility against the Americans simmered partly because of the previous unit's drunken brawls. Despite the efforts of the U.S. government to protect its soldiers from the sins of Europe, drinking seems to have been a preoccupation of the soldiers in Arpin's outfit. Arpin also learned something about French wine and women, but he spent most of the endless waiting time learning to play contract bridge.

Arpin saw some of the horror of war when he went to the front with a French regiment as an observer, but his own unit did not engage in combat until October 1918, when the war was almost over. He took part in the bloody Meuse-Argonne offensive, which helped end the war. But he discovered that war was not the heroic struggle of carefully planned campaigns that newspapers and books described. War was filled with misfired weapons, mix-ups, and erroneous attacks. Wounded in the leg in an assault on an unnamed hill and awarded a Distinguished Service Cross for his bravery, Arpin later learned that the order to attack had been recalled, but word had not reached him in time.

When the armistice came, Arpin was recovering in a field hospital. He was disappointed that the war had ended so soon, but he was well enough to go to Paris to take part in the victory celebration and to explore some of the famous Paris restaurants and nightclubs. In many ways, the highlight of his war experiences was not a battle or his medal but his adventure after the war was over. With a friend, he went absent without leave and set out to explore Germany. They avoided the military police, traveled on a train illegally, and had many narrow escapes, but they made it back to the hospital without being arrested.

Edmund Arpin was in the army for two years. He was one of 4,791,172 Americans who served in the army, navy, and marines. He was one of the 2 million who went overseas and one of the 230,074 who were wounded. Some of his friends were among the 48,909 who were killed. When he was mustered out of the army in March 1919, he felt lost and confused. Being a civilian was not nearly as exciting as being in the army and visiting new and exotic places.

In time, Arpin settled down. He became a successful businessman, married, and raised a family. A member of the American Legion, he periodically went to conventions and reminisced with men from his division about their escapades in France. Although the war changed their lives in many ways, most would never again feel the same sense of common purpose and adventure. "I don't suppose any of us felt, before or since, so necessary to God and man," one veteran recalled.

For Edmund P. Arpin, Jr., the Great War was the most important event of a lifetime. Just as war changed his life, so, too, did it alter the lives of most Americans. Trends begun during the progressive era accelerated. The power and influence of the federal government increased. Not only did the war promote woman suffrage, prohibition, and public housing, but it also helped create an administrative bureaucracy that blurred the lines between public and private, between government and business—a trend that would continue into the twenty-first century.

In this chapter, we examine the complicated circumstances that led the United States into the war and share the wartime experiences of American men and women overseas and at home. We will study not only military actions but also the impact of the war on domestic policies and on the lives of ordinary Americans, including the migration of African Americans into northern cities. The war cut off immigration from Europe and led to a policy of immigrant restriction in the next decade. The war left a legacy of prejudice and hate and raised the basic question, could the tenets of American democracy, such as freedom of speech, survive participation in a major war? The chapter concludes with a look at the idealistic efforts to promote peace at the end of the war and the disillusion that followed. Woodrow Wilson's foreign policy, which sought to make the world safe for democracy, marked a watershed in the relationship of the United States to the world. The Great War was global war in every sense, and it thrust the United States into the role of leadership on the world scene as an interventionist savior of democratic values, but many Americans were reluctant to accept that role. But whether they liked it or not, the world was a different place in 1919 than it had been in 1914 and that would have a profound influence on American lives.

THE EARLY WAR YEARS

Few Americans expected the Great War that erupted in Europe in the summer of 1914 to affect their lives or alter their comfortable world. When a Serbian student terrorist assassinated Archduke Franz Ferdinand of Austria-Hungary in Sarajevo, the capital of the province of Bosnia, a place most Americans had never heard of, the act precipitated a series of events leading to the most destructive war the world had ever known.

The Causes of War

The Great War, as everyone called it at the time, seemed to begin accidentally, but its root causes reached back many years and involved intense rivalry over trade, empire, and military strength. The Great War, which would cost at least 10 million lives and have a profound influence on every aspect of culture and society, did not seem inevitable in 1914. There had been wars throughout the nineteenth century, including the Boer War, the Franco-Prussian War, and the American Civil War, but these wars, though bloody, were mostly local. There had not been a major global conflict since the end of the Napoleonic Wars in 1815. In fact, there were many signs of international cooperation, with agreements on telegraphs in 1865, postage in 1875, and copyright in 1880. Most nations in the world had even agreed on international time zones by the 1890s. An international conference at The Hague in the Netherlands in 1899 had set up a World Court to settle disputes before they led to war. Peace advocates and politicians alike promoted disarmament conferences and predicted that better technology and improved communication would lead to permanent peace. "It looks as though we are going to be the age of treaties rather than the age of wars, the century of reason rather than the century of force," a leader of the American peace movement announced.

However, the same forces of improved technology and communication that seemed to be bringing nations closer together also helped create a rising tide of nationalism—a pride in being French or English or German. There was also a growing European rivalry over trade, colonies, and spheres of influence in Africa and Asia. Theodore Roosevelt had tried to arbitrate differences between Germany, France, and Great Britain over trade at a conference in Morocco in 1905 and 1906, but the tension and disagreements remained. At the same time, Austria and Russia clashed over territory and influence in the Balkans, where there was a rising sense of Slavic nationalism. Modern Germany, which was created from a number of small states in 1871, emerged as a powerful industrial giant. About 1900, Germany began to build a navy large enough to compete with the British fleet, the most powerful in the world. Great Britain, in turn, built even more battleships. As European nations armed, they drew up a complex series of treaties. Austria-Hungary and Germany (the Central Powers) became military allies, and Britain, France, and Russia (the Allied Powers) agreed to assist one another in case of attack. Despite peace conferences and international agreements, many promoted by the United States, the European balance of power rested precariously on layers of treaties that barely obscured years of jealousy and distrust.

The incident in Sarajevo destroyed that balance. The leaders of Austria-Hungary were determined to punish Serbia for the assassination. Russia mobilized to aid Serbia. Germany, supporting Austria-Hungary, declared war on Russia and France. Britain hesitated, but when Germany invaded Belgium to attack France, Britain declared war on Germany. Within a few months, the Ottoman Empire (Turkey) and Bulgaria joined the Central Powers.

European Empires in 1914

In 1914, European countries had colonies or "spheres of influence" in all parts of the world. Although the United States got into the imperialism game late, it also had an empire and an interest in global trade. European imperialism and competition over trade was very much a factor in the origins of World War I. The war would alter the economic and political map of the world. **Reflecting on the Past** Which European nations were most powerful in Asia and Africa in 1914? How has this map changed today?

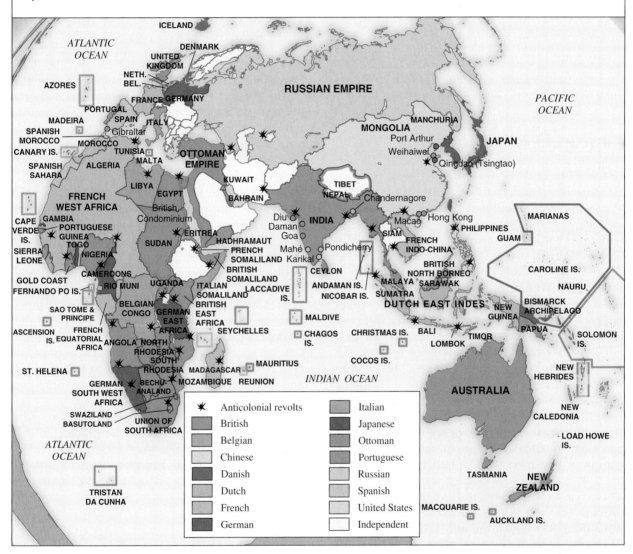

Italy joined the Allies after being secretly promised additional territory after the war. Japan declared war on Germany not because of an interest in the European struggle but in order to acquire German rights in China's Shantung province and a number of Pacific Islands. Spain, Switzerland, the Netherlands, Denmark, Norway, Sweden, and initially the United States, remained neutral. In August 1914, as Europe rushed toward war, British foreign secretary Sir Edward Grey remarked: "The lamps are going out all over Europe. We shall not see them lit again in our lifetime." His prediction proved to be deadly accurate.

When news of the German invasion of Belgium and reports of the first bloody battles began to reach the United States in late summer, most Americans believed that madness had replaced reason. Europeans "have reverted to the condition of savage tribes roaming the forests and falling upon each other in a fury of blood and carnage," the *New York Times* announced. The American sense that the nation would never succumb to the barbarism of war, combined with the knowledge that the Atlantic Ocean separated Europe from the United States, contributed to a great sense of relief after the first shock of the war began to wear off. Woodrow Wilson's official proclamation of neutrality on August 4, 1914, reinforced the belief that the United States had no major stake in the outcome of the war. The president was preoccupied with his own personal tragedy. His wife, Ellen Axson Wilson, died of Bright's disease the day after his proclamation. Two weeks later, still engulfed by his own grief, he urged all Americans to "be neutral in fact as well as in name, . . . impartial in thought as well as in action." The United States, he argued, must preserve itself "fit and free" to do what "is honest and disinterested . . . for the peace of the world." But remaining uninvolved, at least emotionally, was going to be difficult.

American Reactions

Many social reformers despaired when they heard the news from Europe. Even during its first months, the war seemed to deflect energy away from reform. "We are three thousand miles away from the smoke and flames of combat, and have not a single regiment or battleship involved," remarked John Haynes Holmes, a liberal New York minister. "Yet who in the United States is thinking of recreation centers, improved housing or the minimum wage?" Settlement worker Lillian Wald responded to the threat of war by helping lead 1,500 women in a "woman's peace" parade down New York's Fifth Avenue. Jane Addams of Hull House helped organize the American Woman's Peace party. Drawing on traditional conceptions of female character, she argued that women had a special responsibility to work for peace and to speak out against the blasphemy of war because women and children suffered most in any war, especially in a modern war in which civilians as well as soldiers became targets.

IMAGE

Leaders of Women's International League for Peace and Freedom

Although many people worked to promote an international plan to end the war through mediation, others could hardly wait to take part in the great adventure. Hundreds of young American men, most of them students or recent college graduates, volunteered to join ambulance units in order to take part in the war effort without actually fighting. Among these men were Ernest Hemingway, John Dos Passos, and E. E. Cummings, who later turned their wartime adventures into literary masterpieces. Others volunteered for service with the French Foreign Legion or joined the Lafayette Escadrille, a unit of pilots made up of well-to-do American volunteers attached to the French army. Many of these young men were inspired by an older generation who pictured war as a romantic and manly adventure. One college president talked of the chastening and purifying effect of

armed conflict, and Theodore Roosevelt projected an image of war that was something like a football game in which red-blooded American men could test their idealism and manhood.

Alan Seeger, a 1910 graduate of Harvard, was one of those who believed in the romantic and noble purpose of the war. He had been living in Paris since 1912, and when the war broke out, he quickly joined the French Foreign Legion. For the next two years, he wrote sentimental poetry, articles, and letters describing his adventures. "You have no idea how beautiful it is to see the troops undulating along the road . . . with the captains and lieutenants on horse back at the head of the companies," he wrote his mother. When Seeger was killed in 1916, he became an instant hero. Some called him "America's Rupert Brooke," after the gallant British poet who died early in the war.

Many Americans visualized war as a romantic struggle for honor and glory because the only conflict they remembered was the "splendid little war" of 1898. For them, war meant Theodore Roosevelt leading the charge in Cuba and Commodore Dewey destroying the Spanish fleet in Manila harbor without the loss of an American life. Many older Americans recalled the Civil War, but the horrors of those years had faded, leaving only the memory of heroic triumphs. As Oliver Wendell Holmes, the Supreme Court justice who had been wounded in the Civil War, remarked, "War, when you are at it, is horrible and dull. It is only when time has passed that you see that its message was divine."

The reports from the battlefields, even during the first months of the war, should have indicated that the message was anything but divine. This would be a modern war in which men died by the thousands, cut down by an improved and efficient technology of killing.

The New Military Technology

Military planners had not anticipated the stalemate that quickly developed. The German Schlieffen plan called for a rapid strike through Belgium to attack Paris and the French army from the rear. However, the French stopped the German advance at the Battle of the Marne in September 1914, and the fighting soon bogged down in a costly and bloody routine. Soldiers on both sides dug miles of trenches and strung out barbed wire to protect them. Thousands died in battles that gained only a few yards or nothing at all. At the Battle of the Somme in the summer of 1916, the German casualties were 600,000 men killed or wounded. The British lost 419,000 and the French 194,000, and the battle did not change the course of the war. Rapid-firing rifles, improved explosives, incendiary shells, and tracer bullets all added to the destruction. Most devastating of all, however, was the improved artillery, sometimes mounted on trucks and directed by spotters using wireless radios, that could fire over the horizon and hit targets many miles behind the lines. The technology of defense, especially the machine gun, neutralized the frontal assault, the most popular military tactic since the American Civil War. As one writer explained: "Three men and a machine gun can stop a battalion of heroes." But the generals on both sides continued to order their men to charge to their almost certain deaths.

The war was both a traditional and a revolutionary struggle. It was the last war in which cavalry was used and the first to employ a new generation of military technologies. By 1918, airplanes, initially used only for observation, were creating terror below with their bombs. Tanks made their first appearance in 1916, but it was not until the last days of the war that this new offensive weapon began to neutralize the machine gun. Trucks hauled men and equipment, but hundreds of thousands of horses were also used on the battlefields; for some soldiers, the sight of great numbers of dead horses on the battlefields was more depressing than the presence of dead men. Wireless radio and the telephone were indispensable, but carrier pigeons sometimes provided the only link between the front line and the command post in the rear. In the spring of 1915, the Germans introduced a terrible new weapon—poison gas. Chlorine gas blinded its victims, caused acid burns on the skin, and consumed the lungs. Gas masks provided some protection but were never entirely effective. Poison gas attacks, used by both sides after 1915, were one of the most terrifying aspects of trench warfare.

For most Americans, the western front, which stretched from Belgium through France, was the most important battleground of the war. But along the eastern front, Russian troops engaged German and Austrian armies in bitter fighting. After Italy joined the conflict in 1915, a third front developed along the northern Italian and Austrian border, while submarines and battleships carried the fight around the world.

The Great War was truly a global struggle. Soldiers from the British Empire, New Zealand, Australia, Canada, and India fought on the western front alongside French-speaking black Africans. The British and the French battled in Africa to capture Germany's African colonies, and the struggle continued until 1918, especially in East Africa. The British, who initially thought they were only going to support the French on the western front, found themselves in the Middle East, in Mesopotamia (Iraq), and fighting Turks in the Dardanelles between the Aegean and the Black Sea. In one of the great disasters of the war, the British attacked Gallipoli, first with battleships and then with hundreds of thousands of men. After losing one-third of their fleet and more than a quarter of a million men, many of them Australians and New Zealanders, the British withdrew. Reports of carnage, on and off the battlefield, poured in. After they entered the war, the Turks systematically massacred an estimated 800,000 Armenians in one of the worst acts of genocide in the world's history. Yet the United States and the European countries stood by and did nothing.

Some Americans could hardly wait to join the fighting. Theodore Roosevelt and his friend Leonard

A War Victim The Great War, despite the new technology of trucks, tanks, and airplanes, was also a war that used hundreds of thousands of horses to drag and carry men and equipment. Many horses were killed and many more got stuck in the mud. This photo shows a British unit with one horse stuck so badly that it was probably shot rather than rescued. In World War I soldiers like these spent more time waiting than they did fighting and every break meant time for a smoke. What else can you learn about the military experience during World War I by studying this photo? *(The Art Archive/Imperial War Museum)*

The Great War in Europe and the Middle East

The Great War had an impact not only on Europe but also on North Africa and the Middle East. Even the countries that remained neutral felt the influence of global war. **Reflecting on the Past** For most Americans, the war was in France on the western front. Where else were major battles fought?

Wood, the army chief of staff, led a movement to prepare American men for war. In 1913, Wood established a camp for college men at Plattsburgh, New York, to give them some experience with military life, order, discipline, and command. By 1915, thousands had crowded into the camp; even the mayor of New York enrolled. The young men learned to shoot rifles and to endure long marches and field exercises. But most of all, they associated with one another. Gathered around the campfire at night, they heard Wood and other veterans tell of winning glory and honor on

the battlefield. In their minds at least, they were already leading a bayonet charge against the enemy, and the enemy was Germany.

Difficulties of Neutrality

Not all Americans were so eager to enter the fray, but many sympathized with one side or the other. Some Americans favored the Central Powers. About 8 million Austrian Americans and German Americans lived in the United States. Some supported their homeland. They viewed Kaiser Wilhelm II's Germany as a progressive parliamentary democracy. The anti-British sentiment of some Irish Americans led them to take sides not so much for Germany as against England. A few Swedish Americans distrusted Russia so vehemently that they had difficulty supporting the Allies. A number of American scholars, physicians, and intellectuals fondly remembered studying in Germany. To them, Germany meant great universities and cathedrals, music, and culture. It also represented social planning, health insurance, unemployment compensation, and many programs for which the progressives had been fighting.

Despite Wilson's efforts to promote neutrality, for most Americans, the ties of language and culture tipped the balance toward the Allies. After all, did not the English-speaking people of the world have special bonds and special responsibilities to promote civilization and ensure justice in the world? American connections with the French were not so close, but they were even more sentimental. The French, everyone remembered, had supported the American Revolution, and the French people had given the Statue of Liberty, the very symbol of American opportunity and democracy, to the United States.

Other reasons made real neutrality nearly impossible. The fact that export and import trade with the Allies was much more important than with the Central Powers favored the Allies. Wilson's advisers, especially Robert Lansing and Edward House, openly supported the French and the British. Most newspaper owners and editors had close ethnic, cultural, and sometimes economic ties to the British and the French. The newspapers were quick to picture the Germans as barbaric Huns and to accept and embellish the atrocity stories that came from the front, some of them planted by British propaganda experts. Gradually for Wilson, and probably for most Americans, the perception that England and France were fighting to preserve civilization from the forces of Prussian evil replaced the idea that all Europeans were barbaric and decadent. But the American people were not yet willing to go to war to save civilization. Let France and England do that.

Woodrow Wilson also sympathized with the Allies for practical and idealistic reasons. He wanted to keep the United States out of the war, but he did not object to using force to promote diplomatic ends. He believed that by keeping the United States out of the war, he might control the peace. The war, he hoped, would show the futility of imperialism and would usher in a world of free trade in products and ideas. Remaining neutral while maintaining trade with the belligerents became increasingly difficult. Remaining neutral while speaking out about the peace eventually became impossible. The need to trade and the desire to control the peace finally led the United States into the Great War.

World Trade and Neutrality Rights

The United States was part of an international economic community in 1914 and the outbreak of war in the summer of 1914 caused an immediate economic panic. On July 31, 1914, the Wilson administration closed the stock exchange to prevent the unloading of European securities and panic selling. It also adopted a policy discouraging loans by American banks to belligerent nations. Most difficult was the matter of neutral trade. Wilson insisted on the rights of Americans to trade with both the Allies and the Central Powers, but Great Britain instituted an illegal naval blockade, mined the North Sea, and began seizing American ships, even those carrying food and raw materials to Italy, the Netherlands, and other neutral nations. The first crisis that Wilson faced was whether to accept the illicit British blockade. To do so would be to surrender one of the rights he supported most ardently, the right of free trade.

Wilson eventually backed down and accepted British control of the sea. His conviction that the destinies of the United States and Great Britain were intertwined outweighed his idealistic belief in free trade and caused him to react more harshly to German violations of international law than he did to British violators. Consequently, American trade with the Central Powers declined between 1914 and 1916 from $169 million to just over $1 million, whereas trade with the Allies increased during the same period from $825 million to more than $3 billion. At the same time, the U.S. government eased restrictions on private loans to belligerents. In March 1915, the House of Morgan loaned the French government $50 million, and in the fall of 1915, the French and British obtained an unsecured loan of $500 million from American banks. With dollars as well as sentiments, the United States gradually ceased to be neutral.

Germany retaliated against British control of the seas with submarine warfare, using its new weapon, the U-boat *(Unterseeboot)*. International law required a belligerent warship to warn a passenger or merchant ship before attacking, but a U-boat rising to the surface to issue a warning would have meant being blown out of the water by an armed merchant ship. On February 4, 1915, Germany announced a submarine blockade of the British Isles. Until Britain gave up its campaign to starve the German population, the Germans would

DOCUMENT

Adolf K.G.E. von Spiegel, U-Boat 202 (1919)

Unterseeboot A German U-boat sinking a fishing ship somewhere in the Atlantic. The German submarine revolutionized the war at sea, and the sinking of the British ocean liner *Lusitania* and various American ships led directly to the United States entering the war. At first the submarines had the advantage, but by 1918, anti-submarine technology had been developed to enable the United States and Great Britain to win the battle of the Atlantic. Germany lost 178 submarines with 5,400 men. How did the submarine change the nature of the war at sea? *(Erich Lessing/Art Resource, NY)*

sink even neutral ships. Wilson warned Germany that it would be held to "strict accountability" for illegal destruction of American ships or lives.

In March 1915, a German U-boat sank a British liner en route to Africa, killing 103 people, including one American. How should the United States respond? Wilson's advisers could not agree. Robert Lansing, a legal counsel at the State Department, urged the president to issue a strong protest, charging a breach of international law. William Jennings Bryan, the secretary of state, argued that an American traveling on a British ship was guilty of "contributory negligence" and urged Wilson to prohibit Americans from traveling on belligerent ships in the war zone. Wilson never did settle the dispute, for on May 7, 1915, a greater crisis erupted. A German U-boat torpedoed the British luxury liner *Lusitania* off the Irish coast. The liner, which was not armed but was carrying war supplies, sank in 18 minutes. Nearly 1,200 people, including many women and children, drowned. Among the dead were 128 Americans. Suddenly Americans confronted the horror of total war fought with modern weapons, a war that killed civilians, including women and children, just as easily as it killed soldiers.

The tragedy horrified most Americans. Despite earlier warnings by the Germans in American newspapers that it was dangerous to travel in war zones, the same newspapers denounced the act as "mass murder." Some called for a declaration of war. Wilson

and most Americans had no idea of going to war in the spring of 1915, but the president refused to take Bryan's advice and prevent further loss of American lives by simply prohibiting all Americans from traveling on belligerent ships. Instead, he sent a series of protest notes demanding reparation for the loss of American lives and a pledge from Germany that it would cease attacking ocean liners without warning.

Sinking of the *Lusitania*—New York *Tribune*

Bryan resigned as secretary of state over the tone of the notes and charged that the United States was not being truly neutral. Some denounced Bryan as a traitor, but others charged that if the United States really wanted to stay out of the war, Bryan's position was more logical, consistent, and humane than Wilson's. The president replaced Bryan with Robert Lansing, who was much more eager than Bryan to oppose Germany, even at the risk of war.

The tense situation eased late in 1915. After a German U-boat sank the British steamer *Arabic*, which claimed two American lives, the German ambassador promised that Germany would not attack ocean liners without warning (the *Arabic* pledge). But the *Lusitania* crisis caused an outpouring of books and articles urging the nation to prepare for war. The National Security League, the most effective of the preparedness groups, called for a bigger army and navy, a system of universal military training, and "patriotic education and national sentiment and service among the people of the United States."

Organizing on the other side was a group of progressive reformers who formed the American Union Against Militarism. They feared that those urging preparedness were deliberately setting out to destroy liberal social reform at home and to promote imperialism abroad.

Wilson sympathized with the preparedness groups to the extent of asking Congress on November 4, 1915, for an enlarged and reorganized army. The bill met with great opposition, especially from southern and western congressmen, but the Army Reorganization Bill that Wilson signed in June 1916 increased the regular army to just over 200,000 and integrated the National Guard into the defense structure. Few Americans, however, expected those young men to go to war. Even before American soldiers arrived in France, however, Wilson used the army and the marines in Mexico and Central America.

Intervening in Mexico and Central America

Wilson envisioned a world purged of imperialism, a world of free trade, but a world where American ideas and products would find their way. Combining the zeal of a Christian missionary with the conviction of a college professor, he spoke of "releasing the intelligence of America for the service of mankind." Although Wilson denounced the "big stick" and "dollar diplomacy" of the Roosevelt and Taft years, Wilson's administration used force more systematically than did his predecessors. The rhetoric was different, yet just as much as Roosevelt, Wilson tried to maintain stability in the countries to the south in order to promote American economic and strategic interests.

At first, Wilson's foreign policy seemed to reverse some of the most callous aspects of dollar diplomacy in Central America. Secretary of State Bryan signed a treaty with Colombia in 1913 in which the United States agreed to pay $5 million for the loss of Panama and virtually apologized for the Roosevelt administration's treatment of Colombia. The Senate, not so willing to admit that the United States had been wrong, refused to ratify the treaty.

The change in spirit proved illusory. After a disastrous civil war in the Dominican Republic, the United States offered in 1915 to take over the country's finances and police force. When the Dominican leaders rejected a treaty making their country virtually a protectorate of the United States, Wilson ordered in the marines. They took control of the government in May 1916. Although Americans built roads, schools, and hospitals, people resented their presence. The United States intervened in Haiti with similar results. In Nicaragua, the Wilson administration kept the marines sent by Taft in 1912 to prop up a pro-American regime and acquired the right, through treaty, to intervene at any time to preserve order and protect American property. Except for a brief period in the mid-1920s, the marines remained until 1933.

Wilson's policy of intervention ran into the greatest difficulty in Mexico, a country that had been ruled by dictator Porfirio Díaz, who had long welcomed American investors. By 1910, more than 40,000 American citizens lived in Mexico, and more than $1 billion of American money was invested there. In 1911, however, Francisco Madero, a reformer who wanted to destroy the privileges of the upper classes, overthrew Díaz. Two years later, Madero was deposed and murdered by order of Victoriano Huerta, the head of the army.

Wilson refused to recognize the Huerta government. Everyone admitted that Huerta was a ruthless dictator, but diplomatic recognition, the exchange of ambassadors, and the regulation of trade and communication had never meant approval. In the world of business and diplomacy, it merely meant that a particular government was in power. But Wilson set out to remove what he called a "government of butchers."

At first, Wilson applied diplomatic pressure. Then, using a minor incident as an excuse, he asked Congress for power to involve American troops if necessary. Few Mexicans liked Huerta, but they liked the idea of North American interference even less, and they rallied around the dictator. The United States landed troops at Veracruz, Mexico. Wilson's action outraged many Europeans and Latin Americans as well as Americans.

Wilson's military intervention drove Huerta out of office, but a civil war between forces led by Venustiano Carranza and those led by General Francisco "Pancho" Villa ensued. The United States sent arms to Carranza, who was considered less radical than Villa, and Carranza's soldiers defeated Villa's. When an angry Villa led what was left of his army in a raid on Columbus, New Mexico, in March 1916, Wilson sent an expedition commanded by Brigadier General John Pershing to track down Villa and his men. The strange and comic scene developed of an American army charging 300 miles into Mexico unable to catch the retreating villain. The Mexicans feared that Pershing's army was planning to occupy northern Mexico. Carranza shot off a bitter note to Wilson, accusing him of threatening war, but Wilson refused to withdraw the troops. Tensions rose. An

Pancho Villa This photograph shows Pancho Villa on horseback leading the rebel Mexican army that clashed with the American army in Mexico in 1916. President Wilson sent American forces more than 300 miles into Mexico to arrest Villa, who allegedly had murdered a number of Americans, but they were not able to catch him. What impact do you think the American invasion of Mexico had on America's relation with Mexico and Latin America? *(Brown Brothers)*

American patrol attacked a Mexican garrison, with loss of life on both sides. In January 1917, just as war seemed inevitable, Wilson agreed to recall the troops and to recognize the Carranza government. Had it not been for the growing crisis in Europe, it is likely that war with Mexico would have resulted.

THE UNITED STATES ENTERS THE WAR

A significant minority of Americans opposed joining the European war in 1917, and that decision would remain controversial when it was re-examined in the 1930s. But once involved, the government and the American people made the war into a patriotic crusade that influenced all aspects of American life.

The Election of 1916

American political campaigns do not stop even in times of international crisis. As 1915 turned to 1916, Wilson had to think of re-election as well as of preparedness, submarine warfare, and the Mexican campaign. At first glance, the president's chances of re-election seemed poor. He had won in 1912 only because Theodore Roosevelt and the Progressive party had split the Republican vote. If supporters of the Progressives in 1912 returned to the Republican fold, Wilson's chances were slim indeed. Because the Progressive party had done very badly in the 1914 congressional elections, Roosevelt seemed ready to seek the Republican nomination.

Wilson was aware that he had to win over voters who had favored Roosevelt in 1912. In January 1916, he appointed Louis D. Brandeis to the Supreme Court. The first Jew ever to sit on the Court, Brandeis was confirmed over the strong opposition of many legal organizations. His appointment pleased the social justice progressives because he had always championed reform causes. They made it clear to Wilson that the real test for them was whether he supported the anti–child labor and workers' compensation bills pending in Congress.

In August, Wilson put heavy pressure on Congress and obtained passage of the Worker's Compensation Bill, which gave some protection to federal employees, and the Keatings–Owen Child Labor Bill, which prohibited the shipment in interstate commerce of goods produced by children under age 14 and in some cases under 16. This bill, later declared unconstitutional, was a far-reaching proposal that for the first time used federal control over interstate commerce to dictate the conditions under which businesspeople could manufacture products.

To attract farm support, Wilson pushed for passage of the Federal Farm Loan Act, which created 12 Federal Farm Loan banks to extend long-term credit to farmers. Urged on by organized labor as well as by many progressives, he supported the Adamson Act, which established an eight-hour workday for all interstate railway workers. Within a few months, Wilson reversed the New Freedom doctrines he had earlier supported and brought the force of the federal government into play on the side of reform. The flurry of legislation early in 1916 provided one triumph for the progressive movement. The strategy seemed to work, for progressives of all kinds enthusiastically endorsed the president.

The election of 1916, however, turned as much on foreign affairs as on domestic policy. The Republicans ignored Theodore Roosevelt and nominated instead the staid and respectable Charles Evans Hughes, a former governor of New York and future Supreme Court justice. Their platform called for "straight and honest neutrality" and "adequate preparedness." In a bitter campaign, Hughes attacked Wilson for not promoting American rights in Mexico more vigorously and for giving in to the unreasonable demands of labor. Wilson, on his part, implied that electing Hughes would guarantee war with both Mexico and Germany and that his opponents were somehow not "100 percent Americans." As the campaign progressed, the peace issue became more and more important, and the cry "He kept us out of war" echoed through every Democratic rally. It was a slogan that would soon seem strangely ironic.

VIDEO

Charles E. Hughes 1916 Presidential Campaign Speech

The election was extremely close. In fact, Wilson went to bed on election night thinking he had lost the presidency. The election was not finally decided until the Democrats carried California (by fewer than 4,000 votes). Wilson won by carrying the West as well as the South.

Deciding for War

Wilson's victory in 1916 seemed to be a mandate for staying out of the European war. Those who supported Wilson as a peace candidate applauded in January 1917 when he went before the Senate to clarify the American position on a negotiated settlement of the war. The German government had earlier indicated that it might be willing to go to the conference table. Wilson outlined a plan for a negotiated settlement before either side had achieved victory. It would be a peace among equals, "a peace without victory," a peace without indemnities and annexations. The agreement Wilson outlined contained his idealistic vision of the postwar world as an open marketplace, and it could have worked only if Germany and the Allies were willing to settle for a draw. But neither side was interested in such a conclusion after years of bitter and costly conflict.

The German government refused to accept a peace without victory, probably because early in 1917, the German leaders thought they could win. On January 31, 1917, the Germans announced that they would sink on sight any ship, belligerent or neutral, sailing toward England or France. A few days later, in retaliation, the United States broke diplomatic relations with Germany. But Wilson—and probably most Americans—still hoped to avert war without shutting off American trade. As goods began to pile

DOCUMENT

The Zimmermann Telegram (1917)

up in warehouses and American ships stayed idly in port, however, pressure mounted to arm American merchant ships. An intercepted telegram from the German foreign secretary, Arthur Zimmermann, to the German minister in Mexico increased anti-German feeling. If war broke out, the German minister was to offer Mexico the territory it had lost in Texas, New Mexico, and Arizona in 1848. In return, Mexico would join Germany in a war against the United States. When the Zimmermann note was released to the press on March 1, 1917, many Americans demanded war against Germany. Wilson still hesitated.

As the country waited on the brink of war, news of revolution in Russia reached Washington. That event would prove as important as the war itself. The March 1917 revolution in Russia was a spontaneous uprising of workers, housewives, and soldiers against the government of Czar Nicholas II and its conduct of the war. The army had suffered staggering losses at the front. The civilian population was in desperate condition. Food was scarce, and the railroads and industry had nearly collapsed. At first, Wilson and other Americans were enthusiastic about the new republic led by Alexander Kerensky. The overthrow of the feudal aristocracy seemed in the spirit of the American Revolution. Kerensky promised to continue the struggle against Germany. But on November 6, 1917, the revolution took a more extreme turn. Vladimir Ilyich Ulyanov, known as Lenin, returned from exile in Switzerland and led the radical Bolsheviks to victory over the Kerensky regime. He immediately signed an armistice with Germany that released thousands of German troops, who had been fighting the Russians, to join the battle against the Allies on the western front.

Lenin, a brilliant lawyer and revolutionary tactician, was a follower of Karl Marx (1818–1883). Marx was a German intellectual and radical philosopher who had described the alienation of the working class under capitalism and predicted a growing split between the proletariat (the unpropertied workers) and the capitalists. Lenin extended Marx's ideas and argued that capitalist nations eventually would be forced to go to war over raw materials and markets. Believing that capitalism and imperialism went hand in hand, Lenin argued that the only way to end imperialism was to end capitalism. Communism, Lenin predicted, would eventually dominate the globe, and the new Soviet Union, not the United States, would be the model for the rest of the world to follow. The Russian Revolution threatened Wilson's vision of the world and his plan to bring the United States into the war "to make the world safe for democracy."

More disturbing than the revolution in Russia, however, was the situation in the North Atlantic, where German U-boats sank five American ships between March 12 and March 21, 1917. Wilson no longer hesitated. On April 2, he urged Congress to declare war. His words conveyed a sense of mission about the country's entry into the war, but Wilson's voice was low and somber. "It is a fearful thing," he concluded, "to lead this great, peaceful people into war, into the most terrible and disastrous of all wars." The war resolution swept the Senate 82 to 6 and the House of Representatives 373 to 50.

DOCUMENT

President Wilson's War Message (1917)

Once war was declared, most Americans forgot their doubts. Young men rushed to enlist; women volunteered to become nurses or to serve in other ways. Towns were united by patriotism.

A Patriotic Crusade

Not all Americans applauded the declaration of war. Some pacifists and socialists and a few others opposed America's entry into the war. "To whom does war bring prosperity?" Senator George Norris of Nebraska asked on the Senate floor. "Not to the soldier, . . . not to the broken hearted widow, . . . not to the mother who weeps at the death of her brave boy. . . . I feel that we are about to put the dollar sign on the American flag."

For most Americans in the spring of 1917, the war seemed remote. A few days after war was declared, a Senate committee listened to a member of the War Department staff list the vast quantities of materials needed to supply an American army in France. One of the senators, jolted awake, exclaimed, "Good Lord! You're not going to send soldiers over there, are you?"

To convince senators and citizens alike that the war was real and that American participation was just, Wilson appointed a Committee on Public Information, headed by George Creel, a muckraking journalist from Denver. The Creel Committee launched a gigantic propaganda campaign to persuade the American public that the United States had gone to war to promote the cause of freedom and democracy and to prevent the barbarous hordes from overrunning Europe and eventually the Western Hemisphere.

DOCUMENT

"Boy Scouts Support the War Effort" (1917)

The patriotic crusade soon became stridently anti-German and anti-immigrant. Most school districts banned the teaching of German. Sauerkraut was renamed "liberty cabbage," and German measles became "liberty measles." Many families Americanized their German surnames. Several

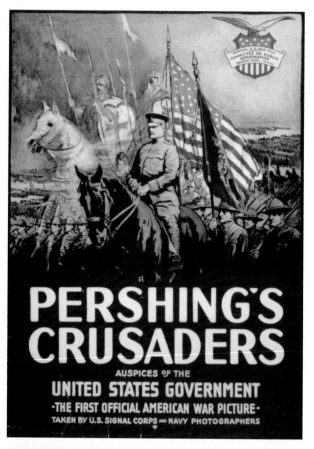

PERSHING'S CRUSADERS

AUSPICES OF THE

UNITED STATES GOVERNMENT

-THE FIRST OFFICIAL AMERICAN WAR PICTURE-

TAKEN BY U.S. SIGNAL CORPS AND NAVY PHOTOGRAPHERS

Pershing's Crusaders This official 1917 U.S. government publication compares American soldiers to medieval knights. It makes explicit the American belief that by entering World War I they were joining not only a war but also a crusade to make the world safe for democracy. They were not just supporting the Allied cause, but they had a special mission to rescue the old world and to spread the American way of life. How do you suppose Europeans reacted to this American sense of mission and superiority? *(Library of Congress, LC-USZC4-1539)*

cities banned music by German composers from symphony concerts. South Dakota prohibited the use of German on the telephone, and in Iowa, a state official announced, "If their language is disloyal, they should be imprisoned. If their acts are disloyal, they should be shot." Occasionally, the patriotic fever led to violence. The most notorious incident occurred in East St. Louis, Illinois, which had a large German population. A mob seized Robert Prager, a young German American, in April 1918, stripped off his clothes, dressed him in an American flag, marched him through the streets, and lynched him. The eventual trial led to the acquittal of the ringleaders on the grounds that the lynching was a "patriotic murder."

AUDIO

Immigrants and the Great War

The Wilson administration did not condone domestic violence and murder, but heated patriotism led to irrational hatreds and fears. Suspect were not only German Americans but also radicals, pacifists, and anyone who raised doubts about the American war efforts or the government's policies. The Los Angeles police ignored complaints that Mexicans were being harassed, because after learning of the Zimmermann telegram they believed that all Mexicans were pro-German. In Wisconsin, Senator Robert La Follette, who had voted against the war resolution, was burned in effigy and censured by the faculty of the University of Wisconsin. At a number of universities, professors were dismissed, sometimes for as little as questioning the morality or the necessity of America's participation in the war.

DOCUMENT
Newton D. Baker, Treatment of German Americans (1918)

On June 15, 1917, Congress, at Wilson's behest, passed the Espionage Act, which provided imprisonment of up to 20 years or a fine of up to $10,000, or both, for people who aided the enemy or who "willfully cause . . . insubordination, disloyalty, mutiny or refusal of duty in the military . . . forces of the United States." The act also authorized the postmaster general to prohibit from the mails any matter he thought advocated treason or forcible resistance to U.S. laws. The act was used to stamp out dissent, even to discipline anyone who questioned the administration's policies. Using the act, Postmaster General Albert S. Burleson banned the magazines *American Socialist* and *The Masses* from the mails.

DOCUMENT
Espionage Act (1917)

Congress later added the Trading with the Enemy Act and a Sedition Act. The latter prohibited disloyal, profane, scurrilous, and abusive remarks about the form of government, flag, or uniform of the United States. It even prohibited citizens from opposing the purchase of war bonds. For delivering a speech denouncing capitalism and the war, Socialist party leader Eugene Debs was convicted of violating the Sedition Act and sentenced to 10 years in prison. In 1919, the Supreme Court upheld the conviction, even though Debs had not explicitly urged violation of the draft laws. Not all Americans agreed with the decision, for while still in prison, Debs polled close to 1 million votes in the presidential election of 1920. Ultimately, the government prosecuted 2,168 people under the Espionage and Sedition Acts and convicted about half of them. But these figures do not include the thousands who were informally persecuted and deprived of their liberties and their right of free speech.

AUDIO
"The Speech That Sent Debs to Jail"

One woman was sentenced to prison for writing, "I am for the people and the government is for the profiteers." Ricardo Flores Magon, a leading Mexican American labor organizer and radical in the Southwest, was sentenced to 20 years in prison for criticizing Wilson's Mexican policy and violating the Neutrality Acts. In Cincinnati, a pacifist minister, Herbert S. Bigelow, was dragged from the stage where he was about to give a speech, taken to a wooded area by a mob, bound and gagged, and whipped. In Bisbee, Arizona, where wartime demand for copper had increased the population to 20,000, the miners went on strike in June 1917 to protest low wages and unsafe conditions in the mines. The owners blamed the strike on the IWW, which they claimed was controlled by the Germans. The IWW had little to do with the strike, but the local sheriff led a posse of men into the miners' homes, where they rounded up 1,200 "undesirables" and shipped them in boxcars into Mexico. The mine owners then quickly hired strikebreakers so the production of copper to support the war effort could continue.

DOCUMENT
Abrams v. United States (1919)

Army Medical Examiner: "At last a perfect soldier!"

"At Last a Perfect Soldier" This antiwar, antimilitary cartoon appeared in the American radical magazine *The Masses* in July 1916. *The Masses* was an irreverent journal that for a few years published important articles and illustrations by leading artists. It was shut down as subversive during the war by the U.S. government. How does this image contrast to the usual depiction of the soldier as hero? Do you agree with this image of the soldier today? (*The Masses*, 8, July 1916, [back cover]/The Tamiment Institute Library, New York University)

The Civil Liberties Bureau, an outgrowth of the American Union Against Militarism, protested the blatant abridgment of freedom of speech during the war, but the protests fell on deaf ears at the Justice Department and in the White House. Rights and freedoms have been reduced or suspended during all wars, but the massive disregard for basic rights was greater during World War I than during the Civil War. This was ironic because Wilson had often written and spoken of the need to preserve freedom of speech and civil liberties. During the war, however, he tolerated the vigilante tactics of his own Justice Department, offering no more than feeble protest. Wilson was so convinced his cause was just that he ignored the rights of those who opposed him.

Raising an Army

Debate over a volunteer army versus the draft had been going on for several years before the United States entered the war. People who favored some form of universal military service argued that college graduates, farmers, and young men from the slums of eastern cities could learn from one another as they trained together. Opponents of a draft pointed out that people making such claims were most often the college graduates, who assumed they would command the boys from the slums. The draft was not democratic, they argued, but the tool of an imperialist power bent on ending dissent. "Back of the cry that America must have compulsory service or perish," one opponent charged, "is a clearly thought out and heavily backed project to mold the United States into an efficient, orderly nation, economically and politically controlled by those who know what is good for the people." Memories of massive draft riots during the Civil War also led some to fear a draft.

Wilson and his secretary of war, Newton Baker, both initially opposed the draft. In the end, both concluded that it was the most efficient way to organize military personnel. Ironically, it was Theodore Roosevelt who tipped Wilson in favor of the draft. Even though his health was failing and he was blind in one eye, the old Rough Rider was determined to recruit a volunteer division and lead it personally against the Germans. The thought of his old enemy Theodore Roosevelt blustering about Europe so frightened Wilson that he supported the Selective Service Act in part, at least, to prevent such volunteer outfits as Roosevelt planned. Congress argued over the bill, the House insisting that the minimum age for draftees should be 21, not 18. On June 5, 1917, some 9.5 million men between

IMAGE

Recruiting Poster for the Marines

ages 21 and 31 registered, with little protest. In August 1918, Congress extended the act to men between ages 18 and 45. In all, more than 24 million men registered and more than 2.8 million were inducted, making up more than 75 percent of soldiers who served in the war.

The draft worked well, but it was not quite the perfect system that Wilson claimed. Draft protests erupted in a few places, the largest in Oklahoma, where a group of tenant farmers planned a march on Washington to take over the government and end the "rich man's war." But the Green Corn Rebellion, as it came to be called, died before it got started. A local posse arrested about 900 rebels and took them off to jail.

Some men escaped the draft. Some were deferred because of war-related jobs, and others resisted by claiming exemption for reasons of conscience. The Selective Service Act did exempt men who belonged to religious groups that forbade members from engaging in war, but religious motivation was often difficult to define, and nonreligious conscientious objection was even more complicated. Thousands of conscientious objectors were inducted. Some served in noncombat positions; others went to prison.

THE MILITARY EXPERIENCE

Family albums in millions of American homes contain photographs of those who were drafted or volunteered: young men in uniform, some of them stiff and formal, some of them candid shots of soldiers on leave in Paris or Washington or Chicago. These photographs testify to the importance of the war to a generation of Americans. For years afterward, the men and women who lived through the war sang "Tipperary," "There's a Long, Long Trail," and "Pack Up Your Troubles" and remembered rather sentimentally what the war had meant to them. For some, the war was a tragic event, as they saw the horrors of the battlefield firsthand. For others, it was a liberating experience and the most exciting period of their lives.

The American Soldier

The typical soldier, according to the U.S. Medical Department, stood 5 feet $7\frac{1}{2}$ inches tall, weighed $141\frac{1}{2}$ pounds, and was 22 years old. He took a physical exam, an intelligence test, and a psychological test, and he probably watched a movie called *Fit to Fight,* which warned him about the dangers of venereal disease. The majority of American soldiers had not attended high school. The median level of education

Soldiers Taking
an IQ Test
During WWI

for native whites was 6.9 years, 4.7 years for immigrants, and just 2.6 years for southern blacks. As many as 31 percent of the recruits were declared illiterate, but the intelligence tests were so primitive that they probably tested social class more than anything else. More than half the recent immigrants from eastern Europe ranked in the "inferior" category. Fully 29 percent of the recruits were rejected as physically unfit for service, a finding that shocked health experts.

Most World War I soldiers were ill-educated and unsophisticated young men from farms, small towns, and urban neighborhoods. They came from all social classes and ethnic groups, yet most were transformed into soldiers. The military experience

"Feminine
Patriotism"

changed the lives and often the attitudes of many young men and some women. Women contributed to the war effort as telephone operators and clerk typists in the navy and the marines. Some went overseas as army and navy nurses. Others volunteered for a tour of duty with the Red Cross, the Salvation Army, or the YMCA. Yet the military experience in World War I was predominantly male. Even going to training camp was a new and often frightening experience. A leave in Paris or London, or even in New York or New Orleans, was an adventure to remember for a lifetime. Even those

who never got overseas or who never saw a battle experienced subtle changes. Many soldiers saw their first movie in the army or had their first contact with trucks and cars. Military service changed the shaving habits of a generation because the new safety razor was standard issue. The war also led to the growing popularity of the cigarette rather than the pipe or cigar because a pack of cigarettes fit comfortably into a shirt pocket and a cigarette could be smoked during a short break. The war experience also caused many men to abandon the pocket watch for the more convenient wristwatch, which had been considered effeminate before the war.

The Black Soldier

Blacks had served in all American wars, and many fought valiantly in the Civil War and the Spanish-American War. Yet black soldiers had most often performed menial work and belonged to segregated units. Most black leaders supported American participation in the war. An exception was Boston journalist William Monroe Trotter, who argued that German atrocities were no worse than the lynching of black men in America. Instead of making the world safe for democracy, he suggested, the government should make "the South safe for Negroes." But W. E. B. Du Bois, the editor of *The Crisis*, urged blacks to close ranks and support the war. He predicted that

Entertaining Black Servicemen Assigned to segregated units, black soldiers were also excluded from white recreation facilities. Here black women from Newark, New Jersey, aided by white social workers, entertain black servicemen. How do you think black men felt about fighting for freedom in a segregated army? *(National Archives)*

Government Propaganda

All governments produce propaganda. Especially in time of war, governments try to convince their citizens that the cause is important and worthwhile even if it means sacrifice. Before the United States entered the World War I, both Great Britain and Germany presented their side of the conflict through stories planted in newspapers, photographs, and other devices. Some historians argue that the British propaganda depicting the Germans as barbaric Huns who killed little boys and Catholic nuns played a large role in convincing Americans of the righteousness of the Allied cause.

When the United States entered the war, a special committee under the direction of George Creel did its best to persuade Americans that the war was a crusade against evil. The committee organized a national network of "four-minute men," local citizens with the proper political views who could be used to whip up a crowd into a patriotic frenzy. These local rallies, enlivened by bands and parades, urged people of all ages to support the war effort and buy war bonds. The Creel Committee also produced literature for the schools, much of it prepared by college professors who volunteered their services. One pamphlet, titled *Why America Fights Germany,* described in lurid detail a possible German invasion of the United States. The committee also used the new technology of motion pictures, which proved to be the most effective propaganda device of all.

IMAGE

Visual of the Enemy, ca. 1917–1918

There is a narrow line between education and propaganda. As early as 1910, Thomas Edison made films instructing the public about the dangers of tuberculosis, and others produced movies that demonstrated how to avoid everything from typhoid to tooth decay. However, during the war, the government quickly realized the power of the new medium and adopted it to train soldiers, instill patriotism, and help the troops avoid the temptations of alcohol and sex.

After the United States entered World War I, the Commission of Training Camp Activities made a film called *Fit to Fight* that was shown to almost all male servicemen. It was an hour-long drama following the careers of five young recruits. Four of them, by associating with the wrong people and through lack of willpower, caught venereal disease. The film interspersed a simplistic plot with grotesque shots of men with various kinds of venereal disease. The film also glorified athletics,

Liberty Bond propaganda. *(The Granger Collection, New York)*

especially football and boxing, as a substitute for sex. It emphasized the importance of patriotism and purity for America's fighting force. In one scene, Bill Hale, the only soldier in the film to remain pure, breaks up a peace rally and beats up the speaker. "It serves you right," the pacifist's sister remarks, "I'm glad Billy punched you."

Fit to Fight was so successful that the government commissioned another film, *The End of the Road,* to be shown to women who lived near military bases. The film is the story of Vera and Mary. Although still reflecting progressive attitudes, the film's message is somewhat different from that of *Fit to Fight.* Vera's strict mother tells her daughter that sex is dirty, leaving Vera to pick up "distorted and obscene" information about sex on the street. She falls victim to the first man who comes

Anti-VD poster issued by the U.S. Commission on Training Camp Activities. *(Army Educational Commission)*

Scene from *Fit to Fight*. *(War Department, Commission on Training Camps)*

along and contracts a venereal disease. Mary, in contrast, has an enlightened mother who explains where babies come from. When Mary grows up, she rejects marriage and becomes a professional woman, a nurse. In the end, she falls in love with a doctor and gets married. *The End of the Road* has a number of subplots and many frightening shots of syphilitic sores. Several illustrations show the dangers of indiscriminate sex. Among other things, the film preached the importance of science and sex education and the need for self-control.

REFLECTING ON THE PAST What do the anti-VD films tell us about the attitudes, ideas, and prejudices of the World War I period? What images do they project about men, women, and gender roles? Would you find the same kind of moralism, patriotism, and fear of VD today? How have attitudes toward sex changed? Were you shown sex education films in school? Were they like these? Who sponsored them? What can historians learn from such films? Does the government produce propaganda today?

the war experience would cause the "walls of prejudice" to crumble gradually before the "onslaught of common sense." But the walls did not crumble, and the black soldier never received equal or fair treatment during the war.

The Selective Service Act made no mention of race, and African Americans in most cases registered

African American Recruiting Poster

without protest. Many whites, especially in the South, feared having too many blacks trained in the use of arms. In some areas, draft boards exempted single white men but drafted black fathers. The most notorious situation existed in Atlanta, where one draft board inducted 97 percent of the African Americans registered but exempted 85 percent of the whites. Still, most southern whites found it difficult to imagine a black man in the uniform of the U.S. Army.

White attitudes toward African Americans sometimes led to conflict. In August 1917, violence erupted in Houston, Texas, involving soldiers from the regular army's all-black Twenty-Fourth Infantry Division. Harassed by the Jim Crow laws, which had been tightened for their benefit, a group of soldiers went on a rampage, killing 17 white civilians. More than 100 soldiers were court-martialed; 13 were condemned to death. Those convicted were hanged three days later before any appeals could be filed.

This violence, coming only a month after the race riot in East St. Louis, Illinois, brought on in part by the migration of southern blacks to the area, caused great concern about the handling of African American soldiers. Secretary of War Baker made it clear that the army had no intention of upsetting the status quo. The basic government policy was complete segregation and careful distribution of black units throughout the country.

African Americans were prohibited from joining the marines and restricted to menial jobs in the navy. A great many black nurses volunteered to go

DOCUMENT

Statement to French Authorities Concerning Black American Troops (1918)

to France, but only six actually went— and they were assigned to black units. In 1918, official policy and American prejudice would not allow black women to care for white men. While some African Americans were trained as junior officers in the army, they were assigned to the all-black Ninety-Second Division, where the high-ranking officers were white. But few black officers or enlisted men would see

action. A staff report decided that "the mass of colored drafted men cannot be used for combatant troops." Most of the black soldiers, including about 80 percent of those sent to France, worked as stevedores and common laborers under the supervision of white, noncommissioned officers. "Everyone who has handled colored labor knows that the gang bosses must be white if any work is to be done," remarked Lieutenant Colonel U. S. Grant, the grandson of the Civil War general. Other black soldiers acted as servants, drivers, and porters for the white officers. It was a demeaning and ironic policy for a government that advertised itself as standing for justice, honor, and democracy.

Over There

The conflict that Wilson called the war "to make the world safe for democracy" had become a contest of stalemate and slaughter. To this ghastly war, Americans made important contributions. In fact, without their help, the Allies might have lost. But the American contribution was most significant only in the war's final months. When the United States entered the conflict in the spring of 1917, the fighting had dragged on for nearly three years. After a few rapid advances and retreats, the war in western Europe had settled down to a tactical and bloody stalemate. The human costs of trench warfare were horrifying. In one battle in 1916, a total of 60,000 British soldiers were killed or wounded in a single day, yet the battle lines did not move

AUDIO

Over There

an inch. By the spring of 1917, the British and French armies were down to their last reserves. Italy's army had nearly collapsed. In the East, the Russians were engaged in a bitter internal struggle, and in November, the Bolshevik Revolution would cause them to sue for a separate peace, freeing the German divisions on the eastern front to join in one final assault in the West. The Allies desperately needed fresh American troops, but those troops had to be trained, equipped, and transported to the front. That took time.

A few token American regiments arrived in France in the summer of 1917 under the command of General John J. "Black Jack" Pershing, a tall, serious, Missouri-born graduate of West Point. He had fought in the Spanish-American War and led the expedition to track down Pancho Villa in Mexico in 1916. When the first troops marched in a parade in Paris on July 4, 1917, the emotional French crowd shouted, *"Vive les Américains"* and showered them with flowers, hugs, and kisses. But the American commanders worried that many of their soldiers were so inexperienced they did not even know how to march, let alone fight. The first Americans saw action near Verdun in October 1917. By March 1918, more than 300,000 American soldiers had reached France, and by November 1918, more than 2 million.

IMAGE

African American Soldiers Under French Command

One reason that the U.S. forces were slow to see actual combat was Pershing's insistence that they be kept separate from the French and British divisions. An exception was made for four regiments of black soldiers who were assigned to the French army. Despite the American warning to the French not to "spoil the Negroes" by allowing them to mix with the French civilian population, these soldiers fought so well that the French later awarded three of the regiments the Croix de Guerre, their highest unit citation.

In the spring of 1918, with Russia out of the war and the British blockade becoming more and more effective, the Germans launched an all-out, desperate offensive to win the war before full American military and industrial power became a factor in the contest. By late May, the Germans had pushed to within 50 miles of Paris. American troops were thrown into the line and helped stem the German advance at Château-Thierry, Belleau Wood, and Cantigny, place names that proud survivors would later endow with almost sacred significance. Americans also took part in the Allied offensive led by General Ferdinand Foch of France in the summer of 1918.

In September, more than half a million American troops fought near St. Mihiel; this was the first battle in which large numbers of Americans were pressed into action. One enlisted man remembered that he "saw a sight which I shall never forget. It was zero hour and in one instant the entire front as far as the eye could reach in either direction was a sheet of flame, while the heavy artillery made the earth quake." The Americans suffered more than 7,000 casualties, but they captured more than 16,000 German soldiers. The victory, even if it came against exhausted and retreating German troops, seemed to vindicate Pershing's insistence on a separate American army. British and French commanders were critical of what they considered the disorganized, inexperienced, and ill-equipped American forces.

DOCUMENT

Eugene Kennedy, A "Doughboy" Describes the Fighting Front (1918)

In the fall of 1918, the combined British, French, and American armies drove the Germans back. Faced with low morale among the German soldiers, the mutiny of the German fleet, and the surrender of Austria, Kaiser Wilhelm II abdicated on November 8, and the armistice was signed on November 11. More than 1 million American soldiers took part in the final Allied offensive near the Meuse River and the Argonne forest. It was in this battle that Edmund Arpin was wounded. Many of the men were inexperienced, and some, who had been rushed through training as "90-day wonders," had never handled a rifle before arriving in France. There were many disastrous mistakes and bungled situations. The most famous blunder was the "lost battalion." An American unit advanced beyond its support and was cut off and surrounded. The battalion suffered 70 percent casualties before being rescued.

The performance of the all-black Ninety-Second Division was also controversial. The Ninety-Second had been deliberately dispersed around the United States and had never trained as a unit. Its higher officers were white, and they repeatedly asked to be transferred. Many of its men were only partly trained and poorly equipped, and they were continually being called away from their military duties to work as stevedores and common laborers. At the last

Deadly Weapons of the Great War   New technology made the Great War more horrible in some ways than past wars. British soldiers wearing primitive gas masks operate a Vickers machine gun. The machine gun effectively neutralized the tactic of massive infantry charges, while poison gas attacks increased the number of soldiers with "shell shock" or mental illness. How has war changed since 1918? Is mental illness still a factor among soldiers in time of war? *(Imperial War Museum, London)*

AMERICAN VOICES

Private John Figarovsky, American Soldiers Get a Warm Welcome in France

The United States entered the war late, but when American soldiers finally arrived in France they were greeted with enthusiasm by French soldiers and civilians who were tired of the terrible war. The American soldiers thought of the war as a great adventure.

When we landed, one of the first things we did was to parade through the town of St. Nazaire. The French people were just delirious with joy, because in the Americans they saw hope for the future. As we marched through town, the sidewalks and even the gutters on both sides were full of people and we felt so proud and important that such a fuss was being made over us. The mayor even proclaimed a holiday.

Most of us were young fellows, and we must have made a good impression because the French girls would jump in the ranks and throw flowers at us and scream and even kiss some of the soldiers. But we kept on, you know, with army discipline, we tried not to notice too much of that. It was such a wonderful reception, we never imagined anything like that would happen, that we'd be welcomed so warmly. They must have admired us a lot, and of course we were looking forward to the great adventure ahead of us. We were looking forward to the fight—we didn't know how serious it was because we'd never been to war before. But we didn't stay in St. Nazaire for long, we were marched about three miles out of town where they had some cantonments.

When we trained with the French troops they were very cooperative. Most of them were short, and it seemed they'd had their clothes on for a year—they hardly ever changed their clothes. But they were very nonchalant about everything. I guess they were tired after four years of warfare. And they were surprised to see that we were so eager to get into the fight.

- *How long do you suppose the Americans' eagerness to get into the fight lasted?*

- *Have the French always seen Americans as the hope of the future?*

---

minute during the Meuse-Argonne offensive, the Ninety-Second was assigned to a particularly difficult position on the line. They had no maps and no wire-cutting equipment. Battalion commanders lost contact with their men, and on several occasions, the men broke and ran in the face of enemy fire. The division was withdrawn in disgrace, and for years politicians and military leaders used this incident to point out that black soldiers would never make good fighting men, ignoring the difficulties under which the Ninety-Second fought and the valor shown by black troops assigned to the French army.

The war produced a few American heroes. Joseph Oklahombie, a Choctaw, overran several German machine gun nests and captured more than 100 German soldiers. Sergeant Alvin York, a former conscientious objector from Tennessee, single-handedly killed or captured 160 Germans using only his rifle and pistol. The press made him a celebrity, but his heroics were not typical. Artillery, machine guns, and, near the end, tanks, trucks, and airplanes won the war. "To be shelled when you are in the open is one of the most terrible of human experiences," one American soldier wrote. "You hear this rushing, tearing sound as the thing comes toward you, and then the huge explosion as it strikes, and infinitely worse, you see its hideous work as men stagger, fall, struggle, or lie quiet and unrecognizable."

With few exceptions, the Americans fought hard and well. Although the French and British criticized American inexperience and disarray, they admired their exuberance, their "pep," and their ability to move large numbers of men and equipment efficiently. Sometimes it seemed that Americans simply overwhelmed the enemy with their numbers. They suffered more than 120,000 casualties in the Meuse-Argonne campaign alone. One officer estimated that he lost 10 soldiers for every German his men killed in the final offensive.

French Couple Welcomes Two U.S. Soldiers

The United States entered the war late but still lost more than 48,000 service personnel and had many more wounded. Disease claimed 15 of every 1,000 soldiers each year (compared with 65 per 1,000 in the Civil War). But American losses were tiny compared to those suffered by the European

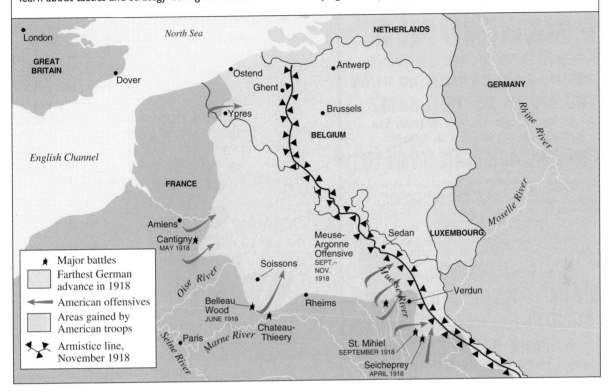

Western Front of the Great War, 1918

For more than three years, the war settled down to a bloody stalemate on the western front. But in 1918, American soldiers played important roles in the Allied offensive that finally ended the war. **Reflecting on the Past** What can you learn about tactics and strategy during the Great War from studying this map?

* Major battles
▢ Farthest German advance in 1918
← American offensives
▢ Areas gained by American troops
◄ Armistice line, November 1918

armies. The British lost 900,000 men, the French 1.4 million, and the Russians 1.7 million. Nor was the financial burden as costly for the United States as for its Allies. American units fired French artillery pieces; American soldiers were usually transported in British ships and wore helmets and other equipment modeled after the British. The United States

purchased clothing and blankets, even horses, in Europe. American fliers, including heroes such as Eddie Rickenbacker, flew French and British planes. The United States contributed huge amounts of men and supplies in the last months of the war, and that finally tipped the balance. But it had entered late and sacrificed little compared with France and England. That would influence the peace settlement.

IMAGE

Temporary Shelter for U.S. Wounded

World War I Losses

The total cost of the war was estimated at more than $330 billion. The cost in human life was even more horrible. The number of known dead was placed at about 10 million men and the wounded at about 20 million, distributed among chief combatants as follows (round numbers). **Reflecting on the Past** Which countries bore the brunt of dead and wounded? How did this influence the peace settlement?

	Dead	Wounded	Prisoner
Great Britain	947,000	2,122,000	192,000
France	1,385,000	3,044,000	446,000
Russia	1,700,000	4,950,000	500,000
Italy	460,000	947,000	530,000
United States	115,000	206,000	4,500
Germany	1,808,000	4,247,000	618,000
Austria-Hungary	1,200,000	3,620,000	200,000
Turkey	325,000	400,000	—

A Global Pandemic

The end of the Great War brought relief and joy to many, but in the fall of 1918 an influenza pandemic swept around the world, killing an estimated 50 million people, with 675,000 deaths in the United States in a little more than a year. The Spanish Flu, as it was called (although there is no evidence that it originated in Spain), seems to have started at about the same time in Europe, Asia, America, and even in remote Eskimo villages. Only a small percentage of those who caught the disease died from it, but unlike most epidemics, it hit hardest among young adults. More than 43,000 American servicemen died from

INFLUENZA

FREQUENTLY COMPLICATED WITH

PNEUMONIA

IS PREVALENT AT THIS TIME THROUGHOUT AMERICA.

THIS THEATRE IS CO-OPERATING WITH THE DEPARTMENT OF HEALTH.

YOU MUST DO THE SAME

IF YOU HAVE A COLD AND ARE COUGHING AND SNEEZING. DO NOT ENTER THIS THEATRE

GO HOME AND GO TO BED UNTIL YOU ARE WELL

Coughing, Sneezing or Spitting Will Not Be Permitted In The Theatre. In case you must cough or Sneeze, do so in your own hand-kerchief, and if the Coughing or Sneezing Persists Leave The Theatre At Once.

This Theatre has agreed to co-operate with the Department Of Health in disseminating the truth about Influenza, and thus serve a great educational purpose.

HELP US TO KEEP CHICAGO THE HEALTHIEST CITY IN THE WORLD

JOHN DILL ROBERTSON
COMMISSIONER OF HEALTH

A Warning about the Influenza Pandemic   This poster was distributed in 1918 to movie theaters in Chicago by the Commissioner of Health. The language of the poster reveals the fear and near panic that many Americans felt in the face of the deadly flu epidemic. Do posters like this do any good? (National Library of Medicine)

the flu (almost as many as died on the battlefield). Early in the epidemic, rumors blamed German germ warfare for the disease, but the German army was infected as well. No antibiotics or shots could prevent or cure the disease, and the surgical masks required in some cities did no good. Even President Wilson came near death from the disease in the spring of 1919. The flu of 1918–1919 killed more people in a short time than any event in human history, perhaps 20 million worldwide. The speed with which the disease spread around the world was another reminder of how the modern world was interconnected and isolation was impossible. The virus that caused the outbreak has never been identified.

DOMESTIC IMPACT OF THE WAR

For at least 30 years before the United States entered the Great War, a debate raged over the proper role of the federal government in regulating industry and protecting people who could not protect themselves. Controversy also centered on the question of how much power the federal government should have to tax and control individuals and corporations and the proper relation of the federal government to state and local governments. The war and the problems it raised increased the power of the federal government in a variety of ways. The wartime experience did not end the debate, but the United States emerged from the war a more modern nation, with more power residing in Washington. At the same time, the federal government with its huge expenditures provided immense economic advantage to businesses engaged in war production and to the cities where those businesses were located.

Financing the War

The war, by one calculation, cost the United States more than $33 billion. Interest and veterans' benefits bring the total to nearly $112 billion. Early on, when an economist suggested that the war might cost the United States $10 billion, everyone laughed. Yet many in the Wilson administration knew the war was going to be expensive, and they set out to raise the money by borrowing and by increasing taxes.

Secretary of the Treasury William McAdoo was in charge of financing the war. Studying the policies that treasury secretary Salmon Chase had followed during the Civil War, he decided that Chase had made a mistake in not appealing to the emotions of the people. A war must be a "kind of crusade," he remarked. He also learned from the British, French, and German propaganda campaigns. McAdoo's campaign to sell liberty bonds to ordinary American citizens at a very low interest rate appealed to American loyalty. "Lick a Stamp and Lick the Kaiser," one poster urged. Celebrities such as film stars Mary Pickford and Douglas Fairbanks promoted the bonds, and McAdoo employed the Boy Scouts to sell them. "Every Scout to Save a Soldier" was the slogan. He even implied that people who did not buy bonds were traitors. "A man who can't lend his government $1.25 per week at the rate of 4% interest is not entitled to be an American citizen," he announced. A banner flew over the main street in Gary, Indiana, that made the point of the campaign clear: "ARE YOU WORTHY TO BE FOUGHT AND DIED FOR? BUY LIBERTY BONDS."

The public responded enthusiastically, but they discovered after the war that their bonds had dropped to about 80 percent of face value. Because the interest on the bonds was tax exempt, well-to-do

"Buy War Bonds" Poster

citizens profited more from buying the bonds than did ordinary men, women, and children. But the wealthy were not as pleased with McAdoo's other plan to finance the war: raising taxes. The War Revenue Act of 1917 boosted the tax rate sharply, levied a tax on excess profits, and increased estate taxes. The next year, another bill raised the tax on the largest incomes to 77 percent. The wealthy protested, but a number of progressives were just as unhappy with the bill, for they wanted to confiscate all income over $100,000 a year. Despite taxes and liberty bonds, however, World War I, like the Civil War, was financed in large part by inflation. Food prices, for example, nearly doubled between 1917 and 1919.

Mrs. Hearst Reviews a Liberty Loan Parade

Increasing Federal Power

The major wars of the twentieth century made huge demands on the nations that fought them and helped transform their governments. The United States was no exception. At first, Wilson tried to work through a variety of state agencies to mobilize the nation's resources. The need for more centralized control and authority soon led Wilson to create a series of federal agencies to deal with the war emergency. The first crisis was food. Poor grain crops for two years and an increasing demand for American food in Europe caused shortages. Wilson appointed Herbert Hoover, a young engineer who had won great prestige as head of the Commission for Relief of Belgium, to direct the Food Administration. Hoover instituted a series of "wheatless" and "meatless" days and urged housewives to cooperate. Women emerged during the war as the most important group of consumers. The government urged them to save, just as later it would urge them to buy.

The Wilson administration used the authority of the federal government to organize resources for the war effort. The National Research Council and the National Advisory Committee on Aeronautics helped mobilize scientists in industry and the universities to produce strategic materials formerly imported from Germany, especially optical glass and chemicals to combat poison-gas warfare. American companies also tried to reproduce German color lithography, which had dominated the market for postcards, posters, and magazine illustrations before the war. Perhaps most valuable were the efforts of scientists in industry to improve radio, airplanes, and instruments to predict the weather and detect submarines. The war stimulated research and development and made the

"Join a Sheep Club" Poster, ca. 1917-1919

United States less dependent on European science and technology.

The War Industries Board, led by Bernard Baruch, a shrewd Wall Street broker, used the power of the government to control scarce materials and, on occasion, to set prices and priorities. Cooperation among government, business, and university scientists to promote research and develop new products was one legacy of the war. The government itself went into the shipbuilding business. The largest shipyard, at Hog Island near Philadelphia, employed as many as 35,000 workers but did not launch its first ship until the late summer of 1918. San Francisco and Seattle also became major shipbuilding centers, while San Diego owed its rapid growth to the presence of a major naval base.

The government also got into the business of running the railroads. When a severe winter and a lack of coordination brought the rail system near collapse in December 1917, Wilson put all the nation's railroads under the control of the United Railway Administration. The government spent more than $500 million to improve the rails and equipment, and in 1918, the railroads did run more efficiently than they had under private control. Some businessmen complained of "war socialism" and of increased rules and regulations. Like it or not, the war increased the influence of the federal government.

War Workers

The Wilson administration sought to protect and extend the rights of organized labor during the war, while mobilizing the workers necessary to keep the factories running. The National War Labor Board insisted on adequate wages and reduced hours, and it tried to prevent exploitation of women and children working under government contracts. On one occasion, when a munitions plant refused to accept the War Labor Board's decision, the government simply took over the factory. When workers threatened to strike for better wages or hours or for greater control over the workplace, the board often ruled that they either work or be drafted into the army.

The Wilson administration favored the conservative labor movement of Samuel Gompers and the AFL, and the Justice Department put the radical Industrial Workers of the World "out of business." Beginning in September 1917, federal agents conducted massive raids on IWW offices and arrested most of its leaders.

Samuel Gompers took advantage of the crisis to strengthen the AFL's position to speak for labor. He supported the administration policies by making it

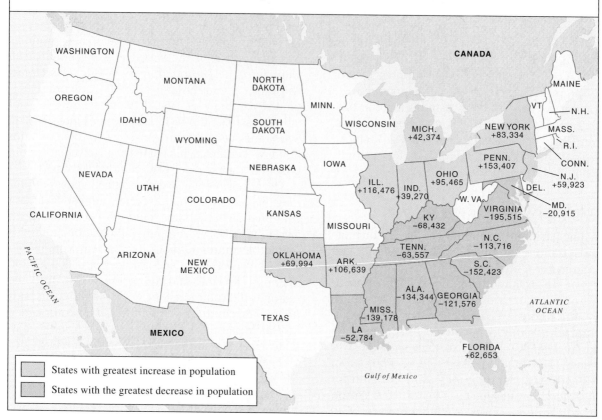

African American Migration, 1910–1920

This map illustrates the massive migration of African Americans from the South to the North during the Great War. Most moved to find better jobs, but in the process they changed the dynamics of race relations in the country. **Reflecting on the Past** What other changes resulted from this migration?

MICH. +42,374
NEW YORK +83,334
PENN. +153,407
OHIO +95,465
ILL. +116,476
IND. +39,270
N.J. +59,923
W. VA.
VIRGINIA –195,515
MD. –20,915
KY –68,432
N.C. –113,716
TENN. –63,557
S.C. –152,423
OKLAHOMA +69,994
ARK. +106,639
ALA. –134,344
GEORGIA –121,576
MISS. –139,178
LA –52,784
FLORIDA +62,653

States with greatest increase in population
States with the greatest decrease in population

---

clear that he opposed the IWW as well as socialists and communists. Convincing Wilson that it was important to protect the rights of organized labor during wartime, he announced that "no other policy is compatible with the spirit and methods of democracy." As the AFL won a voice in home-front policy, its membership increased from 2.7 million in 1916 to more than 4 million in 1917. Organized labor's wartime gains, however, would prove only temporary.

The war opened up industrial employment opportunities for black men. With 4 million men in the armed forces and the flow of immigrants interrupted by the war, American manufacturers for the first time hired African Americans in large numbers. In Chicago before the war, only 3,000 black men held factory jobs; in 1920, more than 15,000 did.

MAP
African American Population, 1910 and 1950

Northern labor agents and the railroads actively recruited southern blacks, but the news of jobs in northern cities spread by word of mouth as well. By 1920, more than 300,000 blacks had joined the "great migration" north. This massive movement of people, which continued into the 1920s, had a permanent impact on the South as well as on the northern cities. Like African Americans, thousands of Mexicans headed north into the United States, as immigration officials relaxed the regulations because of the need for labor in the farms and factories of the Southwest.

IMAGE
African American Women Workers

The war also created new employment opportunities for women. Posters and patriotic speeches urged women to do their duty for the war effort. One poster showed a woman at her typewriter, the shadow of a soldier in the background, with the message: "STENOGRAPHERS, WASHINGTON NEEDS YOU." Women responded to these appeals out of patriotism, as well as out of a need to increase their earnings and to make up for inflation, which diminished real wages. Women went into every kind of industry. They labored in brickyards and in heavy industry, became conductors on the railroad,

DOCUMENT
Letters from the Great Migration

AMERICAN VOICES

An African American Woman Decides to Move North

Many African Americans wrote to the Chicago Defender, *an African American newspaper, during the war seeking information about transportation to the North.*

Mobile, Ala., April 25, 1917

Sir: I was reading in that paper about the Colored race and while reading it I seen in it where cars [the railroad] would be here for the 15 of May which is one month from to day. Will you be so kind as to let me know where they are coming to and I will be glad to know because I am a poor woman and have a husband and five children living and three dead one single and two twin girls six months old today and my husband only get $1.50 a day and the mother of 8 children 25 years old and I want to get out of this dog hold because I don't know what I am raising they up for in this place and I want to get to Chicago where I know they will be raised and my husband crazy to get there because he know he can get more to raise his children and will you please let me know where the cars is going to stop to so that he can come where he can take care of me and my children. He get there a while and then he send for me. . . .

- *Why were African Americans so eager to move to the North during the war?*

- *Did they find the promised land in Chicago, Detroit, New York, and Philadelphia?*

Source: "Letters of Negro Migrants of 1916–1918," Collected under the direction of Emmett J. Scott, *Journal of Negro History* (July and October 1919). Copyright The Association for the Study of Negro History and Life.

Icewomen Women proved during the war that they could do "men's work." These two young women deliver ice, a backbreaking task, but one that was necessary in the days before electric refrigerators. Despite women like these, the war did not change the American ideal that women's proper place was in the home. Has that ideal changed since 1918? *(National Archives)*

and turned out shells in munitions plants. They even organized the Woman's Land Army to mobilize female labor for the farms. They demonstrated that women could do any kind of job, whatever the physical or intellectual demands. Black women left domestic service for jobs in textile mills, even in the stockyards. However, racial discrimination, even in the North, prevented them from moving too far up the occupational ladder.

Even though women demonstrated that they could take over jobs once thought suitable only for men, their progress during the war proved temporary. Only about 5 percent of the women employed during the war were new to the workforce, and almost all of them were unmarried. For most, it meant a shift of occupations or a move up to a better-paying position. Moreover, the war accelerated trends already underway. It increased the need for telephone operators, sales personnel, secretaries, and other white-collar workers, and in these occupations, women soon became a majority. Telephone operator, for example, became an almost exclusively female job. By 1917, women represented 99 percent of all operators as the telephone network spanned the nation.

In the end, the war did provide limited opportunities for some women, but it did not change the dominant perception that a woman's place was in the home. After the war was over, the men returned, and the gains made by women almost disappeared. There were 8 million women in the workforce in 1910 but only 8.5 million in 1920.

The Climax of Progressivism

Many progressives, especially the social justice progressives, opposed U.S. entry into the war until a few months before the nation declared war. But after April 1917, many began to see the "social possibilities of war." They deplored the death and destruction, the abridgment of freedom of speech, and the patriotic spirit that accompanied the war. But they praised the social planning the conflict stimulated. They approved of the Wilson administration's support for collective bargaining, the eight-hour workday, and protection for women and children in industry. They applauded Secretary of War Baker when he announced, "We cannot afford, when we are losing boys in France, to lose children in the United States at the same time." They welcomed the experiments with government-owned housing projects, woman suffrage, and Prohibition. Many endorsed the government takeover of the railroads and control of business during the war.

One of the best examples of the progressives' influence on wartime activities was the Commission on Training Camp Activities, set up early in the war to solve the problem of mobilizing, entertaining, and protecting American servicemen at home and abroad. This experiment was a uniquely American effort; no other country tried anything like it. The chairman of the commission was Raymond Fosdick, a former settlement worker. He appointed a number of experts from the Playground Association, the YMCA, and social work agencies. They set out to organize community singing and baseball, establish post exchanges and theaters, and even provide university extension lectures to educate the servicemen. The overriding assumption was that the military experience would help produce better citizens, people who would be ready to vote for social reform once they returned to civilian life.

The Commission on Training Camp Activities also incorporated the progressive crusades against alcohol and prostitution. The Military Draft Act prohibited the sale of liquor to men in uniform and gave the president power to establish zones around military bases where prostitution and alcohol would be prohibited. Some military commanders protested, and at least one city official argued that prostitutes were "God-provided means for the prevention of the violation of innocent girls, by men who are exercising their 'God-given passions.'" Yet the commission, with the full cooperation of the Wilson administration, set out to wipe out sin, or at least to put it out of the reach of servicemen. "Fit to fight" became the motto. "Men must live straight if they would shoot straight," one official announced.

It was a typical progressive effort combining moral indignation with the use of the latest scientific prophylaxis. The commissioners prided themselves on having eliminated all the red-light districts near the training camps by 1918. When the boys go to France, the secretary of war remarked, "I want them to have invisible armour to take with them. I want them to have armour made up of a set of social habits replacing those of their homes and communities."

France tested the "invisible armour." The government, despite hundreds of letters of protest from American mothers, decided that it could not prevent the soldiers from drinking wine in France, but it could forbid them to buy or accept as gifts anything but light wine and beer. If Arpin's outfit is typical, the soldiers often ignored the rules.

Sex was even more difficult to regulate in France than liquor. Both the British and the French armies had tried to solve the problem of venereal disease by licensing and inspecting prostitutes. Georges Clemenceau, the French premier, found the American attitude toward prostitution difficult to comprehend. On one occasion, he accused the Americans of spreading disease throughout the French civilian population and graciously offered to provide the Americans with licensed prostitutes. General Pershing considered the letter containing the offer "too hot to handle." So he gave it to Fosdick, who showed it to Baker, who remarked, "For God's sake, Raymond, don't show this to the President or he'll stop the war." The Americans never accepted Clemenceau's offer, and he continued to be baffled by the American progressive mentality.

Suffrage for Women

In the fall of 1918, while American soldiers were mobilizing for the final offensive in France and hundreds of thousands of women were working in factories and serving as Red Cross and Salvation Army volunteers near the army bases, Woodrow Wilson spoke before the Senate to ask its support for the vote for women. He argued that woman suffrage was "vital to the winning of the war." Although Wilson had earlier opposed the vote for women and his positive statement at this late date was not necessary, his voice was a welcome addition to a rising chorus of support for an amendment to the Constitution that would permit the female half of the population to vote.

Many still opposed woman suffrage. Some argued that the vote would make women less feminine, more worldly, and less able to perform their primary tasks as wives and mothers. The National Association Opposed to Woman Suffrage protested that only radicals wanted the vote and declared that woman suffrage, socialism, and feminism were "three branches of the same Social Revolution."

Carrie Chapman Catt, an efficient administrator and tireless organizer, devised the strategy that finally secured the vote for women. Catt, who grew up in Iowa, joined the Iowa Woman Suffrage Association at age 28 shortly after her first husband died. Before remarrying, she insisted on a legal agreement giving her four months a year away from her husband to work for the suffrage cause. In 1915, she became president of the National American Woman Suffrage Association (NAWSA), the organization founded in 1890 and based in part on the society organized by Elizabeth Cady Stanton and Susan B. Anthony in 1869.

Catt coordinated the state campaigns with the office in Washington, directing a growing army of dedicated workers. The Washington headquarters sent precise information to the states on ways to pressure congressmen in local districts. In Washington, they maintained a file on each congressman and senator. "There were facts supplied by our members in the states about his personal, political, business and religious affiliations; there were reports of interviews; . . . there was everything that could be discovered about his stand on woman suffrage."

The careful planning began to produce results, but a group of more militant reformers, impatient with the slow progress, broke off from NAWSA to form the National Women's Party (NWP) in 1916. This group was led by Alice Paul, a Quaker from New Jersey, who had participated in some of the suffrage battles in England. Paul and her group, using tactics borrowed from the militant British suffragettes, picketed the White House, chained themselves to the fence, and blocked the streets. They carried banners that asked, "MR. PRESIDENT, HOW LONG MUST WOMEN WAIT FOR LIBERTY?" In the summer of 1917, the government arrested more than 200 women and charged them with "obstructing the sidewalk." That was just the kind of publicity the militants sought, and they made the most of it. Wilson, fearing even more embarrassment, began to cooperate with the more moderate reformers.

The careful organizing of NAWSA and the more militant tactics of the NWP both contributed to the final success of the woman suffrage crusade. The war did not cause the passage of the Nineteenth Amendment, but it did accelerate the process. Fourteen state legislatures petitioned Congress in 1917 and 26 in 1919, urging the enactment of the amendment. Early in 1919, the House of Representatives passed the suffrage amendment 304 to 90, and the Senate approved by a vote of 56 to 25. Fourteen months later, the required 36 states had ratified the amendment, and women at last had the vote. "We are no longer petitioners," Catt announced in celebration. "We are not wards of the nation, but free and equal citizens." But the achievement of votes for women would not prove the triumph of feminism, nor the signal for the beginning of a new reform movement that the women leaders expected to occur.

PLANNING FOR PEACE

Woodrow Wilson turned U.S. participation in the war into a religious crusade to change the nature of international relations. It was a war to make the world safe for democracy—and more. On January 8, 1918, in part to counteract the Bolshevik charge that the war was merely a struggle among imperialist powers, he announced his plan to organize the peace. Called the Fourteen Points, it argued for

President Wilson's Fourteen Points

"open covenants of peace openly arrived at," freedom of the seas, equality of trade, and the self-determination of all peoples. But his most important point, the fourteenth, called for an international organization, a "league of nations," to preserve peace. The victorious Allies, who had suffered grievously in the conflict, had less idealistic goals than did Wilson for peacemaking.

The Versailles Peace Conference

Late in 1918, Wilson announced that he would head the American delegation at Versailles, near Paris, symbolizing his belief that he alone could overcome the forces of greed and imperialism in Europe and bring peace to the world. Wilson and his entourage of college professors, technical experts, and advisers set sail for Paris on the *George Washington* on December 4, 1918. Secretary of State Lansing, Edward House, and a number of other advisers were there; conspicuously missing, however, was Henry Cabot Lodge, chairman of the Senate Foreign Relations Committee and the most powerful man in the Senate, or any other Republican senator.

Lodge's absence would prove a serious blunder, for the Republican-controlled Senate would have to approve any treaty negotiated in Paris. It is difficult to explain Wilson's lack of political insight, except that he disliked Lodge intensely and hated political bargaining and compromise. Preferring to announce great principles, he had supreme confidence in his ability to persuade and to get his way by appealing to the people.

Wilson's self-confidence grew during a triumphant tour through Europe before the conference. The ordinary people greeted him as a savior who had ended the tragic war. But the American president had greater difficulty convincing the political leaders at the peace conference of his genius. In Paris, he faced the reality of European power politics and ambitions and the personalities of David Lloyd George of Great Britain, Vittorio Orlando of Italy, and Georges Clemenceau of France.

Though Wilson was more naive and idealistic than his European counterparts, he was a clever negotiator who won many concessions at the peace table, sometimes by threatening to go home if his counterparts would not compromise. The European leaders were determined to punish Germany and enlarge their empires. Wilson, however, pressed for a new kind of international relations based on his Fourteen Points. He achieved limited acceptance of the idea of self-determination, his dream that each national group could have its own country and that the people should decide in what country they wanted to live.

Blowing Bubbles, 1919

From what had been the Austro-Hungarian empire, the peacemakers carved the new countries of Austria, Hungary, and Yugoslavia. In addition, they created Poland, Czechoslovakia, Finland, Estonia, Latvia, and Lithuania, in part to help contain the threat of bolshevism in eastern Europe. France was to occupy the industrial Saar region of Germany for 15 years, after which a plebiscite would then determine whether the people wanted to become a part of Germany or France. Italy gained the port city of Trieste, but not the neighboring city of Fiume, with its largely Italian-speaking population. Dividing up the map of Europe was difficult at best, but perhaps the biggest mistake that Wilson and other major leaders made was to give the small nations little power at the negotiating table and to exclude Soviet Russia entirely.

While Wilson won some points at the peace negotiations, he also had to make major concessions. He was forced to give in to the Allied demand that Germany pay reparations (later set at $56 billion),

Celebrating the Armistice　Gaspard Maillol, a French artist, captures some of the joy and celebration when the Great War finally came to an end on November 11, 1918. That date, Armistice Day, became an important holiday in the United States, a time to honor those who had served and those who had died in World War I. Armistice Day has now been replaced by Veterans Day and has lost some of its special meaning. This painting depicts the harmony and happiness among the various Allies. Did that spirit last? Is it important to have holidays to honor soldiers and their sacrifices? (*Gaspard Maillol,* Armistice Day in Paris, France, November 11, 1918. *The Art Archive/Musée des 2 Guerres Mondiales Paris/Dagli Orti.*)

lose much of its oil- and coal-rich territory, and admit to its war guilt. He accepted a mandate system, to be supervised by the League of Nations, that allowed France and Britain to take over portions of the Middle East and Japan to occupy Germany's colonies in the Pacific as well as China's Shantung province. And he acquiesced when the Allies turned Germany's African colonies into "mandate possessions" because they did not want to allow self-determination of blacks in areas they had colonized.

France Demands War Reparations— Cartoon

Although Wilson yielded to the Allies on the fate of Germany's former colonies in Africa, he did not envision a reordering of global race relations. He opposed and finally defeated a measure introduced by Japan to include a clause in the league covenant to support racial equality in all parts of the world. W. E. B. Du Bois, who was in Paris as part of the American delegation at the first Pan-African Congress, supported the Japanese resolution for racial equality. He also spoke against colonialism and criticized "white civilization" for subjugating blacks in various parts of the world. He hoped that the Pan-African movement would become a global effort to unite

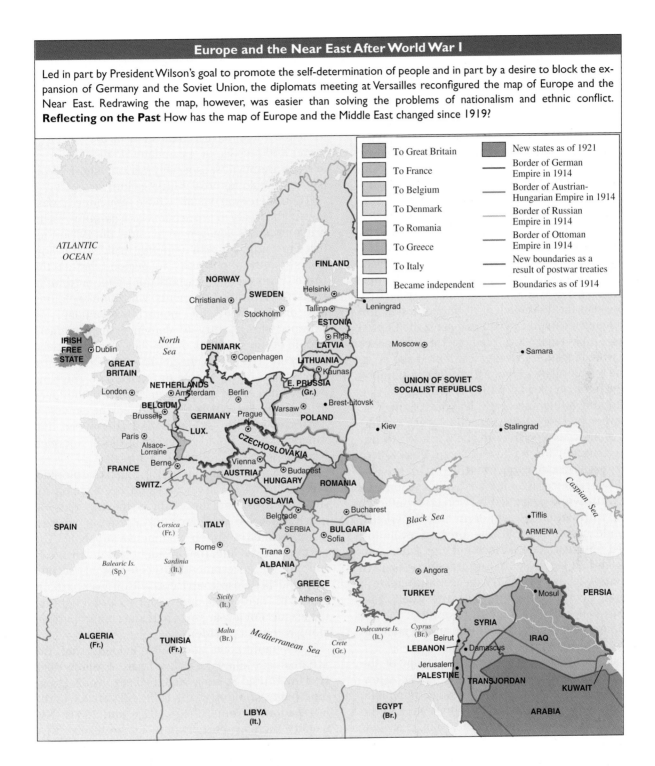

Europe and the Near East After World War I

Led in part by President Wilson's goal to promote the self-determination of people and in part by a desire to block the expansion of Germany and the Soviet Union, the diplomats meeting at Versailles reconfigured the map of Europe and the Near East. Redrawing the map, however, was easier than solving the problems of nationalism and ethnic conflict. **Reflecting on the Past** How has the map of Europe and the Middle East changed since 1919?

Legend	
To Great Britain	New states as of 1921
To France	Border of German Empire in 1914
To Belgium	Border of Austrian-Hungarian Empire in 1914
To Denmark	Border of Russian Empire in 1914
To Romania	Border of Ottoman Empire in 1914
To Greece	New boundaries as a result of postwar treaties
To Italy	Boundaries as of 1914
Became independent	

people of color around the world. But Wilson and the other leaders at Versailles ignored Du Bois.

The Versailles treaty did not represent "peace without victory." The German people felt betrayed. Japan, which had expected to play a larger role in the peace conference, felt slighted. The Italians were angry because they received less territory than they expected. These resentments would later have grave consequences. Wilson also did not win approval for

freedom of the seas or the abolition of trade barriers, but he did gain endorsement for the League of Nations, the organization he hoped would prevent all future wars. The league consisted of a council of the five great powers, elected delegates from the smaller countries, and a World Court to settle disputes. But the key to collective security was contained in Article 10 of the league covenant, which pledged all members "to respect and preserve against external aggression the territorial integrity" of all other members.

Wilson's Failed Dream

While the statesmen met at Versailles to sign the peace treaty hammered out in Paris and to divide up Europe, a group of prominent and successful women—lawyers, physicians, administrators, and writers from all over the world, including many from the Central Powers—met in Zurich, Switzerland. Jane Addams led the American delegation that included Jeannette Rankin, a congresswoman from Montana (one of the few states where women could vote). They formed the Women's International League for Peace and Freedom. Electing Addams president of the new organization, they denounced the harsh peace terms, which called for disarmament of only one side and exacted great economic penalties against the Central Powers. Prophetically, they predicted that the peace treaty would result in the spread of hatred and anarchy and "create all over Europe discords and animosities which can only lead to future wars."

Hate and intolerance were legacies of the war. They were present at the Versailles peace conference, where Clemenceau especially wanted to humiliate Germany for the destruction of French lives and property. Also hanging over the conference was the Bolshevik success in Russia. Lenin's vision of a communist world order, led by workers, conflicted sharply with Wilson's dream of an anti-imperialist, free-trade, capitalist world. The threat of revolution seemed so great that Wilson and the Allies sent American and Japanese troops into Siberia in 1919 to attempt to defeat the Bolsheviks and create a moderate republic. But by 1920, the troops had failed in their mission. They withdrew, but the Soviet Union never forgot the American intervention and the threat of bolshevism remained.

Most Americans supported the concept of the League of Nations in the summer of 1919. A few, such as former senator Albert Beveridge of Indiana, an ardent nationalist, denounced the league as the work of "amiable old male grannies who, over their afternoon tea, are planning to denationalize America and denationalize the nation's manhood." But 33 governors endorsed the plan. Yet in the end, the Senate refused to accept American membership in the league. The League of Nations treaty, one commentator has suggested, was killed by its friends and not by its enemies.

First there was Lodge, who had earlier endorsed the idea of some kind of international peacekeeping organization but who objected to Article 10, which obligated all members to come to the defense of the others in case of attack. He claimed that it would force Americans to fight the wars of foreigners. Lodge, like Wilson, was a lawyer and a scholar as well as a politician. But in background and personality, he was very different from Wilson. A Republican senator since 1893, he had great faith in the power and prestige of the Senate. He disliked all Democrats, especially Wilson, whose idealism and missionary zeal infuriated him.

DOCUMENT

Henry Cabot Lodge's Objections to Article 10 (1919)

Then there was Wilson, whose only hope of passage of the treaty in the Senate was a compromise to bring moderate senators to his side. But Wilson refused to compromise or to modify Article 10 to allow Congress the opportunity to decide whether the United States would support the league in time of crisis. Angry at his opponents, who were exploiting the disagreement for political advantage, he stumped the country to convince the American people of the rightness of his plan. The people did not need to be convinced. They greeted Wilson much the way the people of France had. Traveling by train, he gave 37 speeches in 29 cities in the space of three weeks. When he described the graves of American soldiers in France and announced that American boys would never again die in a foreign war, the people responded with applause.

After one dramatic speech in Pueblo, Colorado, Wilson collapsed. His health had been failing for some months, and the strain of the trip was too much. He was rushed back to Washington, where a few days later he suffered a massive stroke. For the next year and a half, the president was incapable of running the government. Protected by his second wife and his closest advisers, Wilson was partially paralyzed, depressed, and unable to lead a fight for the league. For a year and a half, the country limped along without a president.

After many votes and much maneuvering, the Senate finally killed the league treaty in March 1920. Had the United States joined the League of Nations, it probably would have made little difference in the international events of the 1920s and 1930s. Nor would American participation in the league have prevented World War II. The United States did not resign from the world of diplomacy or trade, nor did the United States become isolated from the rest of the world by refusing to join the league. But the rejection of the league treaty was symbolic of the refusal of many Americans to admit that the world and America's place in it had changed dramatically since 1914. The United States was now one of the world's most powerful countries, but the American people had not yet integrated that reality into their sense of themselves as a people and a nation.

TIMELINE

1914	Archduke Ferdinand assassinated; World War I begins
	United States declares neutrality
	American troops invade Mexico and occupy Veracruz
1915	Germany announces submarine blockade of Great Britain
	Lusitania sunk
	Arabic pledge
	Marines land in Haiti
1916	Army Reorganization Bill
	Expedition into Mexico
	Wilson re-elected
	Workmen's Compensation Bill
	Keatings–Owen Child Labor Bill
	Federal Farm Loan Act
	National Women's Party (NWP) founded
1917	Germany resumes unrestricted submarine warfare
	United States breaks relations with Germany

	Zimmermann telegram
	Russian Revolution
	United States declares war on Germany
	War Revenue Act
	Espionage Act
	Committee on Public Information established
	Trading with the Enemy Act
	Selective Service Act
	War Industries Board formed
1918	Sedition Act
	Flu epidemic sweeps nation
	Wilson's Fourteen Points
	American troops intervene in Russian Revolution
1919	Paris peace conference
	Eighteenth Amendment prohibits alcoholic beverages
	Senate rejects Treaty of Versailles
1920	Nineteenth Amendment grants suffrage for women

Conclusion

The Divided Legacy of the Great War

For Edmund Arpin and many of his friends, who left small towns and urban neighborhoods to join the military forces, the war was a great adventure. For the next decades at American Legion conventions and Armistice Day parades, they continued to celebrate their days of glory. For others who served, the war's results were more tragic. Many died. Some came home injured, disabled by poison gas, or unable to cope with the complex world that had opened up to them.

In a larger sense, the war was both a triumph and a tragedy for the American people. The war created opportunities for blacks who migrated to the North, for women who found more rewarding jobs, and for farmers who suddenly discovered a demand for their products. But much of the promise and the hope proved temporary.

The war provided a certain climax to the progressive movement. The passage of the woman suffrage amendment and the use of federal power in a variety of ways to promote justice and order pleased reformers, who had been working toward these ends for many decades. But the results were often disappointing. Once the war ended, much federal legislation was dismantled or reduced in effectiveness and

woman suffrage had little initial impact on social legislation. Yet the power of the federal government did increase during the war in a variety of ways. From taking control of the railroads to building ships and public housing, to regulating the economy, the government took an active role. Much of that role would diminish in the next decade, but a strong, active government during the war would become a model during the 1930s for those who tried to solve the problem of a major depression.

The Great War marked the coming of age of the United States as a world power. At the end of the war, the United States had become the world's largest creditor and an important factor in international trade and diplomacy. But the country seemed reluctant to accept the new responsibility. The war and the settlement were at least in part responsible for the global depression of the 1930s, and the problems created by the war led directly to another global war, thus causing the next generation to label the conflict of 1914–1918 World War I. The war stimulated patriotism and pride in the country, but it also increased intolerance, cut off immigration from Europe, and led to disillusionment. With this mixed legacy from the war, the country entered the new era of the 1920s.

Questions for Review and Reflection

1. Why did the United States, so determined to stay out of the Great War in 1914, join the Allied cause enthusiastically in 1917?

2. Why did the war lead to hate, prejudice, and the abridgment of civil liberties?

3. How did the war affect women and minorities in America?

4. Why did Wilson's idealistic peace plan fail?

5. What were the long-range consequences of World War I? For the United States? For the world?

Recommended Reading

Recommended Readings are posted on the Web site for this textbook. Visit www.ablongman.com/nash

Fiction and Film

Erich Maria Remarque highlights the horror of the war in his classic *All Quiet on the Western Front* (1929), which is told from the German point of view; John Dos Passos describes the war as a bitter experience in *Three Soldiers* (1921); and Ernest Hemingway portrays its futility in *A Farewell to Arms* (1929). *All Quiet on the Western Front* was made into a powerful movie (1930) from Remarque's novel. Told from the German point of view, it became an antiwar classic in the 1930s. *Reds* (1981) is a Hollywood film about socialists, feminists, and communists. It tells the story of John Reed, Louise Bryant, and their radical friends in Greenwich Village before the war and their support of the Russian Revolution after 1917. *Lawrence of Arabia* (1962) is the epic story of how British writer, soldier, and eccentric T. E. Lawrence enlisted the desert tribes of Africa to fight against the Turks during World War I. *Paths of Glory* (1957), a fictionalized version of the Battle of Verdun, gives a good sense of the horrors of trench warfare.

Discovering U.S. History Online

The World War I Document Archive
www.llb.byu.edu/~rdh/wwi/
This archive contains sources about World War I in general, not just America's involvement.

Lusitania Online
www.lusitania.net
This site presents a background of the luxury liner, information about its crew and its passengers, and accounts of its sinking by a German submarine.

Letters of World War I
www.news.bbc.co.uk/1/hi/special_report/1998/10/98/world_war_1/197437.stm
A special collection of illustrated articles on World War I, including "The War to End All Wars," "War Revolution in Russia," "The Christmas Truce," and many others. Several collections of letters home are included as well.

Great War Series
www.wtj.com/wars/greatwar
This online journal has a collection of World War I archives and several World War I articles, including "The Western Front" and "The Eastern Front."

The Balkan Causes of World War I
www.firstworldwar.com/features/balkan_causes.htm
This illustrated essay on the role of the Balkan events in precipitating World War I also includes links to a year-by-year timeline of the war.

World War I Trenches
www.worldwar1.com
Presented and maintained by a WWI enthusiast, this site provides information on armory, war maps, photos, documents, timelines, and other data concerning the prosecution of the world's first global war.

Election of 1916

www.presidency.ucsb.edu/site/elections/1916.htm

Along with the official counts, this site has several sections: "Mandates," "president's party in House elections," "voter turnout," "financing," and "popularity."

Influenza, 1918

www.pbs.org/wgbh/pages/amex/influenza

Companion to the PBS film of the same title, this site reveals the impact of the great flu epidemic of 1918.

Art of the First World War

www.art-ww1.com/gb/index2.html

A cooperative effort of major history museums, this site presents more than 100 paintings depicting scenes from World War I.

Women's Suffrage

www.rochester.edu/SBA/history.html

This site includes a chronology, important texts relating to woman suffrage, and biographical information on Susan B. Anthony and Elizabeth Cady Stanton.

The Versailles Treaty

http://history.acusd.edu/gen/text/versaillestreaty/vercontents.html

The complete treaty is presented on the site along with links to relevant maps, photos, and political cartoons.

CHAPTER 23

Affluence and Anxiety

The movies, illegal liquor, the stock market, and the new jazz dances all appear in Thomas Hart Benton's painting of the pleasures of urban life in the 1920s. Can you find any other symbols of the 1920s in this painting? *(Thomas Hart Benton,* City Activities with Dance Hall, *from* America Today, *1930, Distemper and egg tempera on gessoed linen with oil glaze, 92 x 134 ¹/₂ in. Collection, AXA Financial, Inc.)*

American Stories

A Black Sharecropper and His Family Move North

John and Lizzie Parker were black sharecroppers who lived in a "stubborn, ageless hut squatted on a little hill" in central Alabama. They had two daughters—one age 6, the other already married. The whole family worked hard in the cotton fields, but they had little to show for their labor. One day in 1917, Lizzie straightened her shoulders and declared, "I'm through. I've picked my last sack of cotton. I've cleared my last field." Like many southern African Americans, the Parkers sought opportunity and a better life in the North. World War I cut off the flow of immigrants from Europe, and suddenly there was a shortage of workers. Some companies sent special trains into the South to recruit African Americans. John Parker signed up with a mining company in West Virginia. The company offered free transportation for his family. "You will be allowed to get your food at the company store and there are houses awaiting for you," the agent promised.

The sound of the train whistle seemed to promise better days ahead for her family as Lizzie gathered her possessions and headed north. But it turned out that the houses in the company town in West Virginia were little better than those they left in Alabama. After deducting for rent and for supplies from the company store, almost no money was left at the end of the week. John hated the dirty and dangerous work in the mine and realized that he would never get ahead by staying there. But instead of venting his anger on his white boss, he ran away, leaving his family in West Virginia.

John drifted to Detroit, where he got a job with the American Car and Foundry Company. It was 1918, and the pay was good, more than he had ever made before. After a few weeks, he rented an apartment and sent for his family. For the first time, Lizzie had a gas stove and an indoor toilet, and Sally, who was now 7, started school. It seemed as if their dream had come true. John had always believed that if he worked hard and treated people fairly, he would succeed.

Detroit was not quite the dream, however. It was crowded with all kinds of migrants, many attracted by the wartime jobs at the Ford Motor Company and other factories. The new arrivals increased the racial tension already present in the city. Sally was beaten up by a gang of white youths at school. Even in their neighborhood, which had been solidly Jewish before their arrival, the shopkeeper and the old residents made it clear that they did not like blacks moving into their community. The Ku Klux Klan, which gained many new members in Detroit, also made life uncomfortable for the blacks who had moved north to seek jobs and opportunity. Suddenly the war ended, and almost immediately John lost his job. Then the landlord raised the rent, and the Parkers were forced to leave their apartment for housing in a section just outside the city near Eight Mile Road. The surrounding suburbs had paved streets, wide lawns, and elegant houses, but this black ghetto had dirt streets and shacks that reminded the Parkers of the company town where they had lived in West Virginia. Lizzie had to get along without her bathroom, for here there was no indoor plumbing and no electricity, only a pump in the yard and an outhouse.

The recession winter of 1921–1922 was particularly difficult. The auto industry and other companies laid off most of their workers. John could find only part-time employment, while Lizzie worked as a domestic servant for white families. Because no bus route connected the black community to surrounding suburbs, she often had to trek miles through the snow. The shack they called home was freezing cold, and it was cramped because their married daughter and her husband had joined them in Detroit.

Lizzie did not give up her dream, however. With strength, determination, and a sense of humor, she kept the family together. In 1924, Sally entered high school. By the end of the decade, Sally had graduated from high school, and the Parkers finally had electricity and indoor plumbing in the house, though the streets were still unpaved. Those unpaved streets stood as a symbol of their unfulfilled dream. The Parkers, like most of the African Americans who moved north in the decade after World War I, had improved their lot, but they still lived outside Detroit—and, in many ways, outside America.

Like most Americans in the 1920s, the Parkers pursued the American dream of success. For them, a comfortable house and a steady job, a new bathroom, and an education for their younger daughter constituted that dream.

For others during the decade, the symbol of success might be owning a new automobile or a new suburban house, or perhaps making a killing on the stock market. The Parkers, like all Americans, whether they realized it or not, were influenced by a global market beyond their control. The 1920s, the decade between the end of World War I and the stock market crash, has often been referred to as the "jazz age," a time when the American people had one long party complete with flappers, speakeasies, illegal bathtub gin, and young people dancing the Charleston late into the night. This frivolous interpretation has some basis in fact, but most Americans did not share in the party, for they were too busy struggling to make a living.

In this chapter, we will explore some of the conflicting trends of an exciting decade. First, we will examine the currents of intolerance that influenced almost all the events and social movements of the time. We will also look at some developments in technology, especially the automobile, which changed life for almost everyone during the 1920s and created the illusion of prosperity for all. We will then focus on groups—women, blacks, industrial workers, and farmers—who had their hopes and dreams raised but not always fulfilled during the decade. We will conclude by looking at the way business, politics, and foreign policy were intertwined during the age of Harding, Coolidge, and Hoover.

POSTWAR PROBLEMS

The enthusiasm for social progress that marked the war years evaporated in 1919. Public housing, social insurance, government ownership of the railroads, and many other experiments quickly ended. The sense of progress and purpose that the war had fostered withered. The year following the end of the war was marked by strikes and violence and by fear that Bolsheviks, blacks, foreigners, and others were destroying the American way of life. Some of the fear and intolerance resulted from wartime patriotism, while some arose from the postwar economic and political turmoil that forced Americans to deal with new and immensely troubling situations.

The Red Scare

Americans have often feared radicals and other groups that seem to be conspiring to overthrow the American way of life. In the 1840s, in the 1890s, and at other times in the past, Catholics, Mormons, Populists, immigrants, and holders of many political views have all been attacked as dangerous and "un-American." But before 1917, anarchists seemed to pose the worst threat. The Russian Revolution changed that. *Bolshevik* suddenly became the most dangerous and devious radical, while *Communist* was transformed from a member of a utopian community to a dreaded, threatening subversive. For some Americans, *Bolshevik* and *German* became somehow mixed together, especially after the Treaty of Brest–Litovsk in 1918 removed the new Soviet state from the war. In the spring of 1919, with the Russian announcement of a policy of worldwide

revolution and with Communist uprisings in Hungary and Bavaria, many Americans feared that the Communists planned to take over the United States.

Immediately after the war, there were perhaps 25,000 American Communists, but they never threatened the United States. Some were idealists, such as John Reed, the son of a wealthy businessman, who had been converted to socialism in New York's Greenwich Village.

Appalled by the carnage in what he considered a capitalistic war, Reed went to Russia as a journalist, just in time to witness the bloody Bolshevik takeover. His eyewitness account, *Ten Days That Shook the World*, optimistically predicted a worldwide revolution. Seeing little hope for that revolution in postwar America, he returned to Moscow, where he died in 1920, disillusioned by the new regime's authoritarian nature.

The "Red Menace" and the Palmer Raids

Reed was one of the romantic American intellectuals who saw great hope for the future in the Russian Revolution. His mentor Lincoln Steffens, the muckraking journalist, remarked after a visit to the Soviet Union a few years later, "I have been over into the future and it works." But relatively few Americans, even among those who had been Socialists, and fewer still among the workers, joined the Communist party. The threat to the American system of government was very slight. But in 1919, the Communists seemed to be a threat, particularly as a series of devastating strikes erupted across the country. Workers in the United States had suffered from wartime inflation, which had almost doubled prices between 1914 and 1919, while most wages remained the same. During 1919, more than 4 million workers took part in 4,000 strikes. Few wanted to overthrow the government; rather, they demanded higher wages, shorter hours, and in some cases more control over the workplace.

On January 21, 1919, some 35,000 shipyard workers went on strike in Seattle, Washington. Within a few days, a general strike paralyzed the city; transportation and business stopped. The mayor of Seattle called for federal troops. Within five days, using strong-arm tactics, the mayor put down the strike and was hailed across the country as a "red-blooded patriot."

Yet the strikes continued elsewhere. In September 1919, all 343,000 employees of U.S. Steel walked out in an attempt to win an eight-hour workday and an "American living wage." The average workweek in the steel industry in 1919 was 68.7 hours; the unskilled worker averaged $1,400 per year, while the minimum subsistence for a family of five that same year was estimated at $1,575. Within days, the strike spread to Bethlehem Steel.

From the beginning, the owners blamed the strikes on the Bolsheviks. They put ads in the newspapers urging workers to "Stand by America, Show Up the Red Agitator." They also imported strikebreakers, provoked riots, broke up union meetings, and finally used police and soldiers to end the strike. Eighteen strikers were killed. Because most people believed that the Communists had inspired the strike, the issue of long hours and poor pay got lost, and eventually the union surrendered.

While the steel strike was still in progress, the police in Boston went on strike. Like most other workers, the police were struggling to survive on prewar salaries in inflationary times. The Boston newspapers blamed the strike on Communist influence. College students and army veterans volunteered to replace the police and prevent looting in the city. The president of Harvard assured the students that their grades would not suffer. The government quickly broke the strike and fired the policemen. When Samuel Gompers urged Governor Calvin Coolidge to ask the Boston authorities to reinstate them, Coolidge responded with the laconic statement that made him famous and eventually helped him win the presidency: "There is no right to strike against the public safety by anybody, anywhere, anytime."

To many Americans, strikes were bad enough, especially strikes that dangerous radicals seemingly inspired, but bombs were even worse. The "bomb-throwing radical" was almost a cliché, probably stemming from the hysteria over the Haymarket Riot of 1886. On April 28, 1919, a bomb was discovered in a small package delivered to the home of the mayor of Seattle. The next day, the maid of a former senator from Georgia opened a package, and a bomb blew her hands off. Other bombings occurred in June, including one that shattered the front of Attorney General A. Mitchell Palmer's home in Washington. The bombings seem to have been the work of misguided radicals who thought they might spark a genuine revolution in America. But their effect was to provide substantial evidence that revolution was around the corner, even though most American workers wanted only shorter hours, better working conditions, and a chance to realize the American dream.

The strikes and bombs, combined with the general postwar mood of distrust and suspicion, persuaded many people of a real and immediate threat to the nation. No one was more convinced than A. Mitchell Palmer. From a Quaker family in a small Pennsylvania town, the attorney general had graduated from Swarthmore College and had been admitted to the Pennsylvania bar in 1893 at age 21. After serving three terms as a congressman, he helped swing the Pennsylvania delegation to Wilson at the 1912 convention.

Wilson offered him the post of secretary of war, but Palmer's pacifism led him to refuse. He did support the United States' entry into the war, however, and served as alien property custodian, a job created by the Trading with the Enemy Act. This position apparently convinced him of the danger of radical subversive activities in America. The bombing of his home intensified his fears, and in the summer of 1919, he determined to find and destroy the Red network. He organized a special antiradical division within the Justice Department and put a young man named J. Edgar Hoover in charge of coordinating information on domestic radical activities.

Obsessed with the "Red Menace," Palmer instituted a series of raids, beginning in November 1919. Simultaneously, in several cities, his men rounded up 250 members of the Union of Russian Workers, many of whom were beaten and roughed up in the process. In December, 249 aliens, including the famous anarchist Emma Goldman, were deported, although very few were Communists and even fewer had any desire to overthrow the government of the United States. Palmer's men arrested 500 people in Detroit and 800 in Boston.

DOCUMENT

A. Mitchell Palmer on the Menace of Communism (1920)

The Palmer raids, one of the most massive violations of civil liberties in American history to this date, found few dangerous radicals but did fan the flames of fear and intolerance in the country. In Indiana, a jury quickly acquitted a man who had killed an alien for yelling, "To hell with the United States." Billy Sunday, a Christian evangelist, suggested that the best solution was to shoot aliens rather than to deport them.

Palmer became a national hero for ferreting out Communists, but in the end, only about 600 were deported out of the more than 5,000 arrested. The worst of the "Red Scare" was over by the end of 1920, but the fear of radicals and the emotional patriotism survived throughout the decade to color almost every aspect of politics, daily life, and social legislation.

The Red Scare promoted many patriotic organizations and societies determined to eliminate Communism from American life. The best known was the American Legion, but there were also the American Defense Society, the Sentinels of the Republic, the United States Flag Association, and the Daughters of the American Revolution. Such groups provided a sense of purpose and a feeling of belonging in a rapidly changing America. But often what united their efforts was an obsessive fear of Communists and radicals.

Some organizations targeted women social reformers. One group attacked the "Hot-House, Hull House Variety of Parlor Bolshevists" and during the 1920s circulated a number of "spider-web charts" that purported to connect liberals and progressives, especially progressive women, to communism. Protesting those charges did little good, for the accusers claimed to know the "truth" and would not be deflected from their purpose of exterminating dangerous radicals.

Charles Dana Gibson, "Like a Moth, It Works in the Dark," 1923

anti-Catholic. As an increasing number of second- and third-generation American Catholics began to achieve some success, even winning elections at the state and municipal level, many Protestants began to worry. The Klan declared that "America is Protestant and so it must remain." It opposed the teaching of evolution; glorified old-time religion; supported immigration restriction; denounced short skirts, petting, and "demon rum"; and upheld patriotism and the purity of women. The Klan was also militantly antiblack and its members took as their special mission the task of keeping blacks in their "proper place." They often used peaceful measures to accomplish their aim, but if those failed, they resorted to violence, kidnapping, and lynching.

The Klan grew slowly until after the war. Aggressive recruiting as well as the fear and confusion of the postwar period led to rapid growth in the 1920s. A great many women joined the Klan. In some states Women of the Ku Klux Klan (WKKK) made up more than half the membership. Although women shared the ideology of their male counterparts, they also campaigned for women's rights and for equal treatment of all white, Protestant women. For both men and women, the Klan served as a social club—a club that kept out all who were different and therefore dangerous.

The Creed of Klanswomen (1924)

The Ku Klux Klan

Among the superpatriotic organizations claiming to protect the American way of life, the Ku Klux Klan (KKK) was the most extreme. The Klan was organized in Georgia by William J. Simmons, a lay preacher, salesman, and member of many fraternal organizations. He adopted the name and white-sheet uniform of the old antiblack Reconstruction organization that was glorified in 1915 in the immensely popular but racist feature film *Birth of a Nation*. Simmons appointed himself head ("Imperial Wizard") of the new Klan.

Unlike the original organization, which took almost anyone who was white, the new Klan was thoroughly Protestant and explicitly antiforeign, anti-Semitic, and

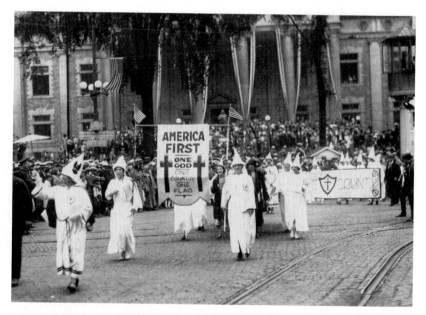

Women of the Ku Klux Klan The Klan, with its elaborate rituals and uniforms, exploited the fear of blacks, Jews, liberals, and Catholics while preaching "traditional" values. The appeal of the Klan was not limited to the South, and many women joined. This is a photo of women Klan members marching in an America First Parade in Binghamton, New York. Why did so many women join the Klan? Is there anything like it today? *(Bettmann/CORBIS)*

The Klan flourished in small towns and rural areas in the South, where it set out to keep the returning black soldiers in their "proper place," but it soon spread throughout the country; at least half the members came from urban areas. The Klan was especially strong in the working-class neighborhoods of Detroit, Indianapolis, Atlanta, and Chicago, where the migration of African Americans and other ethnic groups increased fear of everything "un-American." At the peak of its power, the Klan had several million members, many of them from the middle class. In some states, especially Indiana, Colorado, Oregon, Oklahoma, Louisiana, and Texas, it influenced politics and determined some elections. The Klan's power declined after 1925 because of a series of internal power struggles and several scandals. The Klan survived in some areas into the 1930s, but it had all but disappeared by the outbreak of World War II. Yet the end of the Klan did not mean the end of prejudice.

Ethnic and Religious Intolerance

One result of the Red Scare and the unreasoned fear of foreigners and radicals, which dragged on through much of the decade, was the conviction and sentencing of two Italian anarchists, Nicola Sacco and Bartolomeo Vanzetti. Arrested in 1920 for allegedly murdering a guard during a robbery of the shoe factory in South Braintree, Massachusetts, the two were convicted and sentenced to die in the summer of 1921 on what many liberals considered circumstantial and flimsy evidence. Indeed, it seemed to many that the two Italians, who spoke in broken English and were admitted anarchists, were punished because of their radicalism and their foreign appearance.

The case took on symbolic significance as many intellectuals in Europe and America rallied to their defense and to the defense of civil liberties. Appeal after appeal failed, but finally the governor of Massachusetts appointed a commission to re-examine the evidence in the case. The commission reaffirmed the verdict, and the two were executed in the electric chair on August 23, 1927, despite massive protests and midnight vigils around the country. Recent evidence, including ballistic tests, suggests that they may have been guilty, but the trial and its aftermath nevertheless pointed to the ethnic prejudice and divisions in American society.

The KKK and well-publicized cases such as Sacco–Vanzetti touched a relatively small number of people, but a general spirit of intolerance permeated

DOCUMENT
Court Statements of Nicola Sacco and Bartolomeo Vanzetti (1927)

the decade and influenced the lives of millions. In Dearborn, Michigan, Henry Ford published anti-Semitic diatribes in the *Dearborn Independent,* and many country clubs and resort hotels prohibited Jews from even entering the doors. Unable to frequent the fashionable resorts, Jews built their own in the Catskills in New York State, Long Branch in New Jersey, and other areas. Many colleges, private academies, and medical schools had Jewish quotas, some openly and others informally, and many suburbs explicitly limited residents to "Christians." Catholics, too, were prohibited from many fashionable and fraternal organizations as well as many country clubs, but unlike Jews, Catholics created their own schools and colleges. Few Catholics even tried to enroll in the elite colleges in which bias against Catholics and Catholicism remained. There had always been a great deal of prejudice and intolerance in the United States, but during the decade of the 1920s, much of that intolerance became more fixed and formal.

A PROSPERING ECONOMY

A time of intolerance and anxiety for many Americans, the decade after World War I was a time of industrial expansion and widespread prosperity for numerous others. Recovering from a postwar depression in 1921 and 1922, the economy soared. Fueled by new technology, more efficient planning and management, and innovative advertising, industrial production almost doubled during the decade, and the gross national product rose by an astonishing 40 percent. A construction boom created new suburbs around American cities, and a new generation of skyscrapers transformed the cities themselves. However, the benefits of this prosperity fell unevenly on the many social groups that formed American society.

While the American economy boomed, much of the rest of the world suffered in the aftermath of the war. Germany, wracked by inflation so great that it took millions of marks to buy a loaf of bread, sank into depression and was unable to make reparations payments. Great Britain and France recovered slowly from the war's devastation. Although it was not clear at the time, it became obvious later that the United States was part of a global economy and eventually would be affected by the economic difficulties of the rest of the world.

The Rising Standard of Living

Signs of the new prosperity appeared in many forms. Millions of homes and apartments were built

Burning Money for Fuel A German woman in 1923 uses the devalued mark to light a fire because it was cheaper to use paper currency than to purchase kindling wood or even a newspaper. Women used baby carriages to carry enough money to buy a loaf of bread. A postage stamp cost a million marks. Most European countries faced inflation in the postwar years, but it was worst in Germany. In 1918, a mark was worth about a dollar. By January 1923, it took 7,000 marks to buy a dollar; by February, 18,000; by July, 160,000; by August, 1 million; and by December, 4 trillion marks to equal a dollar. The hyperinflation, caused by the war and by the harsh peace settlement, wiped out the savings of the middle class, led to depression, and contributed directly to the rise of Hitler. Do Americans in the twenty-first century still fear inflation? *(Bettman/CORBIS)*

fixtures annually. The bathroom, with unlimited hot water, privacy, and clean white fixtures, symbolized American affluence.

In sharp contrast to people in European countries, middle-class Americans had more leisure time, a shorter workweek, and more paid vacation time. The American diet also improved during the decade. Health improved and life expectancy increased. Educational opportunities also expanded. In 1900, only 1 in 10 young people of high-school age remained in school; by 1930, that number had grown to 6 in 10, and much of the increase came in the 1920s. In 1900, only 1 college-age person in 33 attended an institution of higher learning; by 1930, the ratio was 1 in 7, and more than a million people were enrolled in the nation's colleges.

The Rise of the Modern Corporation

The structure and practice of American business were transformed in the 1920s. Mergers increased during the decade at a rate greater than at any time since the end of the 1890s—there were more than 1,200 mergers in 1929 alone—creating such giants as General Electric, General Motors, Sears Roebuck, Du Pont, and U.S. Rubber. These were not monopolies but oligopolies (industry domination spread among a few large firms). By 1930, the 200 largest corporations controlled almost half the corporate wealth in the country.

Perhaps the most important business trend of the decade was the emergence of a new kind of manager like Alfred P. Sloan, Jr., an engineer who reorganized General Motors. Sloan divided the company into components, freeing top managers to concentrate on planning new products, controlling inventory, and integrating the whole operation. Marketing and advertising became as important as production, and many businesses began to spend more money on research. The new manager often had a large staff but owned no part of the company. He was usually an expert at cost accounting and analyzing data. Increasingly, he was a graduate of one of the new business colleges.

Continuing and extending the trends started by Frederick Taylor before World War I, the new managers tried to keep employees working efficiently, but they used more than the stopwatch and the assembly line. They introduced pensions, recreation facilities, cafeterias, and, in some cases, paid vacations and profit-sharing plans. But the managers were not being altruistic; rather, "welfare capitalism" was designed to reduce worker discontent and to discourage labor unions.

Planning was the key to the new corporate structure, and planning often meant a continuation of

and equipped with the latest conveniences. The number of telephones installed nearly doubled between 1915 and 1930. Plastics, rayon, and cellophane altered the habits of millions of Americans, and new products, such as cigarette lighters, reinforced concrete, dry ice, and Pyrex glass created new demands unheard of a decade before.

Perhaps the most tangible sign of the new prosperity was the modern American bathroom. Hotels and the urban upper class began to install cast-iron bathtubs and primitive flush toilets in the late nineteenth century, but not until the early 1920s did the enameled tub, toilet, and washbasin become standard. By 1925, American factories turned out 5 million enameled bathroom

IMAGE

The Living Room, 1916

HOW OTHERS SEE US

Luigi Barzini, Jr., An Italian Student Falls in Love with the United States

Luigi Barzini, Jr., an Italian writer and journalist, first came to the United States in August 1925 to enroll as a student at Columbia University. He was impressed with how everything seemed modern and constantly changing. "The restlessness, mobility, the unceasing quest for something better impressed me," he wrote.

I was pleased with almost everything, from the new gadgets in the bathroom and kitchen to the taste of the chemical substitute for vanilla. I liked Americans' pride in their country, their common-sense acceptance of obvious ideas, their admiration for their old bourgeoisie, the style of their lives and their houses. I thought American girls were more beautiful than any in Europe. I could put up with American coffee and liked home-cooked American food. I loved American architecture, music, literature, jokes. I was charmed by the lean, silent men who smoked pipes, lived outdoors, wore tweeds, and said disagreeable ironic things almost without opening their mouths; they charmed me, of course, because there were no such people in Italy. I liked the obvious waste of precious materials, the heavy bronze doors of banks and movie theaters, the bronze cuspidors, the excessively heavy steel beams supporting bridges, the large bumpers on automobiles, all the unmistakable signs of wealth—even to the use of cream instead of milk in tea.

- Like many foreign visitors, Barzini was impressed by American wealth and American restlessness. Is there anything he didn't like about the United States?

- Do visitors have similar reactions to the United States today?

---

the business–government cooperation that had developed during World War I. Experts from philanthropic foundations, the National Bureau of Economic Research, and the U.S. Department of Commerce worked together, hoping that they could provide a middle ground between collectivism and laissez-faire economy. All the planning and the new managerial authority failed to prevent the economic collapse of 1929, but the modern corporation survived the depression to exert a growing influence on American life in the 1930s and after.

Electrification

The 1920s also marked the climax of the "second Industrial Revolution," powered by electricity and producing a growing array of consumer goods. By 1929, electrical generators provided 80 percent of the power used in industry. Less than one of every ten American homes had electricity in 1907; by 1919 more than two-thirds did.

Electricity brought dozens of gadgets and labor-saving devices into the home. Washing machines and electric irons gradually reduced the drudgery of washday for women, and vacuum cleaners, electric toasters, and sewing machines lightened housework. But the new machines still needed human direction and did not reduce the time the average housewife spent doing housework. For many poor urban and rural women, the traditional female tasks of carrying, pushing, pulling, and lifting went on as they had for centuries. In many ways, the success of the electric revolution increased the contrast in American life. The "great white ways" of the cities, lit by electric lights, symbolized progress, but they also made the darkness of slums and hamlets seem even more forbidding.

A Global Automobile Culture

Automobile manufacturing, like electrification, underwent spectacular growth in the 1920s, and the United States led the way. The automobile was one major factor in the postwar economic boom. It stimulated and transformed the petroleum, steel, and rubber industries. The auto forced the construction and improvement of streets and highways and led to millions of dollars of expenditures on labor and concrete. In 1925, the secretary of agriculture approved the first uniform numbering system for the nation's highways, but it was still an adventure to drive from one city to another.

The best known transcontinental road was the Lincoln Highway. It started in New York; continued to Philadelphia, Pittsburgh, Fort Wayne, and Joliet;

IMAGE

Scranton, Pennsylvania, 1911— Streetlights at Night

and then roughly traced the route of the first transcontinental railroad to Omaha, Cheyenne, Salt Lake City, Reno, and San Francisco (paralleling today's Route 80.) The Lincoln Highway was marked using existing roads in 1913, but large sections were barely passable until well into the 1920s. Beginning in 1916, with the Federal Highway Act, the government began to aid road building, but the great majority of roads remained under state or local control. In Europe, where the national governments built the roads, the highways were superior in the 1920s, but there were far fewer cars in Europe and the distance between cities much shorter than in the United States.

The auto created new suburbs and allowed families to live many miles from their work. The filling station, the diner, and the overnight cabin became familiar and eventually standardized objects on the American scene. Traffic lights, stop signs, billboards, and parking lots appeared. Hitching posts and watering troughs became rarer, and gradually the garage replaced the livery stable. The auto changed the look of the American landscape and threatened the environment as well. Oil and gasoline contaminated streams, and piles of old tires and rusting hulks of discarded cars became a familiar eyesore along highways. At the same time, emissions from thousands and then millions of internal combustion engines polluted the air. The increasing use of nonrenewable fossil fuels was already apparent in the 1920s, and it was a trend that would continue. In 1916, American oil refineries produced 50 million barrels of gasoline; in 1929, production had increased to 425 million barrels. But there was no turning back. The age of the auto had replaced the age of the horse.

The auto changed American life in other ways. It led to the decline of the small crossroads store as well

IMAGE

Downtown Scene with Cars

as many small churches because the rural family could now drive to the larger city or town. The tractor changed methods of farming. Trucks replaced the horse and wagon and altered the marketing of farm products. Buses began to eliminate the one-room schoolhouse, because it was now possible to transport students to larger schools. The automobile allowed young people for the first time to escape the chaperoning of parents.

Gradually, as the decade progressed, the automobile became not just transportation but a sign of status. Advertising helped create the impression that it was the symbol of the good life, of sex, freedom, and speed. The auto in turn transformed advertising and design. It even altered the way products were purchased. By 1926, three-fourths of the cars sold were

bought on some kind of deferred-payment plan. Installment credit, first tried by a group of businessmen in Toledo, Ohio, in 1915 to sell more autos, was soon used to promote sewing machines, refrigerators, and other consumer products. "Buy now, pay later" became the American way.

The United States had a love affair with the auto from the beginning. There were 8,000 motor vehicles registered in the country in 1900, and nearly a million in 1912. But only in the 1920s did the auto come within the reach of middle-class consumers. In 1929, Americans purchased 4.5 million cars, and by the end of that year, nearly 27 million were registered.

In part because of Henry Ford and the development of the inexpensive car, and because the United States had a much larger middle class who could afford a car, the ownership of automobiles expanded rapidly in the United States. Most European autos were custom-made. Morris Motors, the most important British company, did not adopt the assembly line method of production until 1934. France, Germany, and England all subsidized auto manufacture for military purposes, further delaying the development of an inexpensive car. But because of their strong central governments, European countries adopted safety standards and required national licenses for vehicles and drivers before such measures were adopted in the United States.

In America, the states created the rules, and in the beginning it was assumed that anyone could drive a car. The world agreed on time zones, postage regulations, and other things, but not on which side of the road to drive on. In Great Britain, Australia, Japan, and a few other countries, cars were driven on the left side, while in the United States and most of Europe, driving on the right side was the proper thing to do. Eventually most of the world, following the American lead, was transformed by automobile culture, but in many countries, that did not happen until after World War II.

Henry Ford

Many men contributed to the development and production of the auto—William Durant organized General Motors; Charles Kettering, an engineering genius, developed the electric self-starter; and Ransom E. Olds built the first mass-produced, moderately priced, light car. Above all the others loomed a name that would become synonymous with the automobile itself—Henry Ford.

Ford had the reputation of being a progressive industrial leader and a champion of the common people. As with all men and women who take on symbolic significance, the truth is less dramatic than the stories.

Automobile Assembly Line The automobile changed life in the United States in many ways. In 1929, 27 million cars were registered in the United States, up from 1 million in 1900. Hundreds of thousands of people were employed in the auto industry, in manufacturing, sales, and service. The assembly line, first used by Henry Ford in 1913, transformed not only the auto industry, but also the way other products were manufactured. In addition, it changed the nature of work and altered the lives of those who worked on the line. Can you imagine working in a factory like this? In what other ways did the auto change life for Americans in the 1920s? *(From the Collections of The Henry Ford Museum)*

Henry Ford and His First Car, 1918

industrial fascist—the Mussolini of Detroit." He ruthlessly pressured his dealers and used them to bail him out of difficult financial situations. Instead of borrowing money from a bank, he forced dealers to buy extra cars, trucks, and tractors. He used spies on the assembly lines and fired workers and executives at the least provocation. But he did produce a car that transformed America.

The Model T, which cost $600 in 1912, was reduced gradually in price until it sold for only $290 in 1924. The "Tin Lizzie," as it was affectionately called, was light and easily repaired. Some owners claimed all one needed were a pair of pliers and some baling wire to keep it running. If it got stuck on bad roads, as it often did, a reasonably healthy man could lift it. Replacement parts were standardized and widely available.

The Model T did not change from year to year, nor did it deviate from its one color, black. Except for adding a self-starter, offering a closed model, and making a few minor face-lift changes, Ford kept the Model T in 1927 much as he had introduced it in 1909. By that time, its popularity had declined as many people traded up to sleeker, more colorful, and, they thought, more prestigious autos put out by Ford's competitors; as a result, wages at Ford dipped below the industry average.

The Model A, introduced in 1927, did not dominate the market as the Model T had done, but the gigantic River Rouge factory, spreading over a thousand acres in Dearborn, Michigan, was built especially to produce the new model. It became the symbol of mass production in the new era. The auto industry, like most American business, went through a period of consolidation in the 1920s. In 1908, more than 250 companies were producing cars in the United States. By 1929, only 44 remained.

For example, Ford is often credited with inventing the assembly line. What he actually did (along with a team of engineers) was adapt the assembly line and the concept of interchangeable parts to the production of autos. Introduced in 1913, the new method reduced the time it took to produce a car from 14 hours to an hour and a half. The product of the carefully planned system, the Model T was the prototype of the inexpensive family car.

Automobile Assembly Line, 1925

In 1914, Ford startled the country by announcing that he was increasing the minimum pay of the Ford assembly-line worker to $5 a day (almost twice the national average pay for factory workers). Ford was not a humanitarian. He wanted a dependable workforce and realized that skilled workers were less likely to quit if they received good pay. Ford was one of the first to recognize that workers were consumers as well as producers and that they might buy Model T Fords. But work in the Ford factory had its disadvantages. Work on the assembly line was repetitive and numbing. "You could drop over dead," one worker recalled, "and they wouldn't stop the line." And when the line closed down, as it did periodically, the workers were released without compensation.

Henry Ford was not an easy man for whom to work. One newspaper account in 1928 called him "an

The Exploding Metropolis

The automobile transformed the city and led to the gradual decline of the streetcar and the interurban trolley. In the late nineteenth century, railroads and streetcars had created suburbs near the major cities, but the great expansion of suburban population occurred in the 1920s. Shaker Heights, a Cleveland suburb, was in some ways a typical development. Built on the site of a former Shaker community, the new suburb was planned and developed by two

Ten Largest Cities in 1900 and 1930*

What trends are revealed by this chart? Why are some cities growing faster than others?

	1900			1930	
1. New York	4,023,000		1. New York	9,423,000	
2. Chicago	1,768,000		2. Chicago	3,870,000	
3. Philadelphia	1,458,000		3. Philadelphia	2,399,000	
4. Boston	905,000		4. Detroit	1,837,000	
5. Pittsburgh	622,000		5. Los Angeles	1,778,000	
6. St. Louis	612,000		6. Boston	1,545,000	
7. Baltimore	543,000		7. Pittsburgh	1,312,000	
8. San Francisco	444,000		8. San Francisco	1,104,000	
9. Cincinnati	414,000		9. St. Louis	1,094,000	
10. Cleveland	402,000		10. Cleveland	1,048,000	

*Figures are for the entire metropolitan areas, including suburbs.

Source: U.S. Bureau of the Census.

businessmen. They controlled the size and style of the homes and restricted buyers. No blacks were allowed. Curving roads led off the main auto boulevards, and landscaping and natural areas contributed to a parklike atmosphere. The suburb increased in population from 1,700 in 1919 to more than 15,000 in 1929, and the price of lots multiplied by 10 during the decade.

Other suburbs grew in an equally spectacular manner. Beverly Hills, near Los Angeles, increased in population by 2,485 percent during the decade. Grosse Point Park, near Detroit, grew by 725 percent, and Elmwood Park, near Chicago, increased by 716 percent. The automobile also allowed industry to move to the suburbs. The number of employees in manufacturing establishments in the suburbs of the 11 largest cities increased from 365,000 in 1919 to 1.2 million in 1937.

The biggest land boom of all occurred in Florida, where the city of Miami mushroomed from 30,000 in 1920 to 75,000 in 1925. One plot of land in West Palm Beach sold for $800,000 in 1923; two years later, it was worth $4 million. A hurricane in 1926 ended the Florida land boom temporarily, but most cities and their suburbs continued to grow during the decade.

The most spectacular growth of all took place in two cities that the auto virtually created. Detroit grew from 300,000 in 1900 to 1,837,000 in 1930, and Los Angeles expanded from 114,000 in 1900 to 1,778,000 in 1930. With sprawling subdivisions connected by a growing network of roads, Los Angeles was the city of the future.

Cities expanded horizontally during the 1920s, sprawling into the countryside, but city centers grew vertically. A building boom that peaked near the end of the decade created new skylines for most urban centers. Even cities such as Tulsa, Dallas, Kansas City, Memphis, and Syracuse built skyscrapers. By 1929, there were 377 buildings of more than 20 stories in American cities. Many were started just before the stock market crash ended the building boom, and the empty offices stood as a stark reminder of the limits of expansion. The most famous skyscraper of all, the Empire State Building in New York, which towers 102 stories in the air, was finished in 1931 but not completely occupied until after World War II.

A Communications Revolution

Changing communications altered the way many Americans lived as well as the way they conducted business. The telephone was first demonstrated in 1876. By 1899, more than 1 million phones were in operation. During the 1920s, the number of homes with phones increased from 9 million to 13 million. Still, by the end of the decade, more than half of American homes were without phones.

Even more than the telephone, the radio symbolized the technological and communicational changes of the 1920s. Department stores quickly began to stock radios, or crystal sets as they were called, but many Americans in the 1920s built their own receivers. The first station to begin commercial broadcasting was WWJ in Detroit in the summer of 1920. When WWJ and KDKA in Pittsburgh broadcast the election returns in 1920, they ushered in a new era in politics. The next year, WJZ of Newark, New Jersey, broadcast the World Series, beginning a process that would transform baseball and

VIDEO

College Football, 1903

AMERICAN VOICES

Babe Ruth Homers in the 1927 World Series

The 1920s produced a number of sports heroes, but none were as famous or as flamboyant as Babe Ruth, who led the New York Yankees to the American League Pennant and then to victory over the Pittsburgh Pirates in the World Series. He hit .356 with 164 RBIs and 60 home runs (a record that stood until 1961). Following is the account of game three of the World Series that appeared in the New York Times *on September 8, 1927.*

The big time came in the seventh. The Yanks had the game safely stowed away and the suspense was over after six innings of sturdy batting, but the fans still stood up and demanded that Mr. Ruth get busy and do something for home and country.... "A homer, Babe! Give us a homer!" ran the burden of the plea, and the big fellow pulled his cap on tighter, took a reef in his belt, dug spikes into the ground and grimly faced little Mike Cvengros, the southpaw, who had just relieved Lee Meadows.

... Upward and onward, gaining speed and height with every foot, the little white ball winged with terrific speed until it dashed itself against the seats of the right-field bleachers, more than a quarter of the way up the peopled slope.

And now the populace had its homer and it stood up and gave the glad, joyous howl that must have rang out in the Roman arenas of old....

Suddenly the Pirates looked very old and weary and *oppressed*, and life seemed to lean very heavily on their shoulders.

■ *Has the language of sports journalism changed since 1927?*

■ *Are any sports heroes today the equal of Babe Ruth in the 1920s?*

Source: "From Babe Ruth Homers in the 1927 World Series" *New York Times*, September 8, 1927. Copyright © 1927 by The New York Times Co. Reprinted with Permission.

---

eventually football and basketball as well. Five hundred stations took to the airwaves in 1922 alone, many of them sponsored by department stores and others by newspapers and colleges. In the same year, a radio station in New York broadcast the first commercial, an indication that the airways would be used to increase the demand for the goods the factories were producing.

Much early broadcasting consisted of classical music, but soon came news analysis and coverage of presidential inaugurals and important events. Some stations produced live dramas, but it was the serials such as *Amos 'n' Andy* that more than any other programs made radio a national medium. Millions of people scattered across the country could sit in their living rooms (and after 1927, in their cars) listening to the same program. But until about 1924 one needed earphones to hear the radio. The record industry grew just as rapidly. By the end of the decade, people in all sections of the country were humming the same popular songs. Actors and announcers became celebrities. The radio, even more than the automobile, marked the end of silence and, to a certain extent, the end of privacy.

AUDIO
Hungarian Rag

A New Machine of Sound Most farmers did not own a radio until the end of the 1930s when they finally got electricity, although a few had battery-powered models. The radio altered lives and brought a new magic of sound into 2 million to 3 million households during the 1920s. Until about 1924, one had to use headsets to hear the sound. This man is using a battery-powered set with a wire connected to an outside antenna. The reception on such sets was often poor. Can you imagine a world without radio? How did the radio alter lives?

RECOVERING THE PAST

Advertising

Have you ever noticed that television commercials can often be more interesting and creative than the programs? One authority has suggested that the best way for a foreign visitor to understand the American character and popular culture is to study television commercials. Television advertising, the thesis goes, appeals to basic cultural assumptions. The nature of advertising not only reveals for historians the prejudices, fears, values, and aspirations of a people but also makes an impact on historical development itself, influencing patterns of taste and purchasing habits. One modern critic calls advertising a "peculiarly American force that now compares with such long-standing institutions as the school and church in the magnitude of its social impact."

As long as manufacturing was local and limited, there was no need to advertise. Before the Civil War, for example, the local area could usually absorb all that was produced; therefore, a simple announcement in a local paper was sufficient to let people know that a particular product was available. But when factories began producing more than the local market could ordinarily consume, advertising came into play to create a larger demand.

Although national advertising began with the emergence of "name brands" in the late nineteenth century, it did not achieve the importance it now holds until the 1920s. In 1918, the total gross advertising revenue in magazines was $58.5 million. By 1920, it had more than doubled to $129.5 million, and by 1929, it was nearly $200 million. These figures should not be surprising in a decade that often equated advertising with religion. The biblical Moses was called the "ad-writer for the Deity," and in a best-selling book, Bruce Barton, a Madison Avenue advertiser, reinterpreted Jesus, the "man nobody knows," as a master salesman. Wrote Barton: "He would be a national advertiser today."

The designers of ads began to study psychology to determine what motives, conscious or unconscious, influenced consumers. One psychologist concluded that the appeal to the human instinct for "gaining social prestige" would sell the most goods. Another way to sell products, many learned, was to create anxiety in the mind of the consumer over body odor, bad breath, oily hair, dandruff,

DOCUMENT
Advertisements from 1925 and 1927

"...and Jane, dear... Jack just raved about my teeth."

"I just smiled my prettiest smile... and let him rave. I could have said 'Of course I have beautiful teeth... I've used Colgate's all my life'. But I didn't want Jack to think I was a living advertisement for Colgate's tooth paste."

* * * * *

Beautiful teeth glisten gloriously. They compel the admiration of all who see them. And there is health as well as beauty in gleaming teeth, for when they are scrupulously kept clean, germs and poisons of decay can't lurk and breed around them.

Remove Those Causes of Decay

Save yourself the embarrassment so often caused by poor teeth. Fight the germs of tooth decay.

Colgate's will keep your teeth scrupulously clean. It reaches all the hard-to-get-at places between the teeth and around the edges of the gums, and so *removes causes* of tooth decay. It is the dependable tooth paste for you to use.

Washes—Polishes—Protects

The principal ingredients of Colgate's are mild soap and fine chalk, the two

things that dental authorities say a safe dental cream should contain. The combined action of these ingredients washes, polishes and protects the delicate enamel of your teeth.

Use Colgate's Regularly

Just remember that beautiful, healthy teeth are more a matter of good care than of good luck. Use Colgate's after meals and at bedtime. It will keep your teeth clean and gloriously attractive.

And you'll like its taste... even children love to use it regularly.

Priced right too! Large tube 25c.

Colgate's
Established 1806

COLGATE'S RIBBON DENTAL CREAM

Toothpaste advertisement.

pimples, and other embarrassing ailments. In 1921, the Lambert Company used the term *halitosis* for bad breath in an ad for Listerine. Within six years, sales of Listerine had increased from a little more than 100,000 bottles a year to more than 4 million.

The appeal to sex also sold products, advertisers soon found, as did the desire for the latest style or invention. But perhaps the most important thing advertisers marketed was youth. "We are going to sell

Automobile advertisement (1929). *(CORBIS)*

For Clean-up King
I Nominate . . .

by LOU GEHRIG

New York Yankees' Clean-up Ace Makes
Novel Choice for All-Time Honor

I DON'T need to tell baseball fans how important the "clean-up" (number four) man is in the batting line-up. With three reliable hitters batting ahead of him, it is his wallops that bring in the runs.

In my thirteen years of big league baseball I have watched some of the most famous "clean-up" men in the history of the game. But the other day in Boston I had the pleasure of seeing the "clean-up" king that gets my vote for the "all-time" honors. Strangely enough, this "clean-up" king isn't a slugger at all. Instead of cleaning up the bases, this one's specialty is cleaning up faces.

Here's how it happened. While in Boston playing the Red Sox, I made an inspection trip through the Gillette Safety Razor factory. There I discovered that what is true of baseball is also true of Gillette Blades. In baseball, the pick of the raw material is tried out, tested, and trained for the big league teams. At the Gillette factory I found that they buy only the finest steel, and put it through gruelling tests before it is made into Gillette Blades.

For instance, like a rookie baseball player, Gillette Blade steel has to be hardened and tempered.

To do this, Gillette uses electric furnaces, each one controlled by a device which can tell in an instant if the steel passing through the furnaces requires more heat or less heat. Faster than a speedball, the signal is flashed from the box to a great battery of switches, and the heat is raised or lowered accordingly. Then to make doubly sure that there is no possibility of error, they X-ray the steel with an electro-magnetic tester to detect hidden flaws.

A good ball player has to have precision and accuracy, too . . . and that's where Gillette chalks up a winning score. Grinding machines, adjustable to 1/10,000 of an inch give Gillette Blades shaving edges so keen you can't see them, even with the most powerful microscope.

These are some of the reasons why I nominate the Gillette Blade for all-time Clean-up King. For when it comes to cleaning up on stubborn bristles—with the greatest of ease and comfort—Gillette hits a home run with the bases loaded. Yes, Sir!—if baseball could only train players as accurately and efficiently as Gillette makes razor blades, we'd all find it easy to bat 1000.

With these important facts before you, why let anyone deprive you of shaving comfort by selling you a substitute! Ask for Gillette Blades and be sure to get them.

GILLETTE SAFETY RAZOR COMPANY, BOSTON, MASS.

Razor blade advertisement.

every artificial thing there is," a cosmetics salesman wrote in 1926, "and above all it is going to be young-young-young! We make women feel young." A great portion of the ads were aimed at women. As one trade journal announced: "The proper study of mankind is man . . . , but the proper study of markets is woman."

REFLECTING ON THE PAST Look at the accompanying advertisements carefully. What do they tell you about American culture in the 1920s? What do they suggest about attitudes toward women? Do they reveal any special anxieties? How are they similar to and different from advertising today?

Even more dramatic was the phenomenon of the movies. Forty million viewers a week went to the movies in 1922, and by 1929 that number had increased to more than 100 million. Early movies were made in New York, Chicago, and a few other cities, but by the mid-1920s, the village of Hollywood, near Los Angeles, had become the movie capital of the world. Giant firms such as Metro-Goldwyn-Mayer, created in 1924, dominated the industry, which ranked first among all industries in California. Men, women, and children flocked to small theaters in the towns and to movie palaces in the cities, where they could dream of romance or adventure. Charlie Chaplin, Rudolph Valentino, Lillian Gish, and Greta Garbo were more famous and more important to millions of Americans than were most government officials. The motion pictures, which before the war had attracted mostly the working class, now seemed to appeal across class, regional, and generational lines.

A New Form of Entertainment   This photograph shows opening night, October 6, 1927, at a theater in Times Square, New York. *The Jazz Singer* with Al Jolson, the first commercially successful film with sound, attracted large audiences. The silent film continued to survive for a few years, but gradually the sound film took over, forcing theaters to buy new equipment and actors to change their style. Some silent-film stars with unattractive voices were forced to retire. Are movies as important today as they were in 1927? *(Warner Brothers/First National/The Kobal Collection)*

The movies had the power to influence attitudes and ideas. In the 1920s, many parents feared that the movies would dictate ideas about sex and life. One young college woman remembered, "One day I went to see Viola Dana in *The Five Dollar Baby*. The scenes which showed her as a baby fascinated me so that I stayed to see it over four times. I forgot home, dinner and everything. About eight o'clock mother came after me." She also admitted that the movies taught her how to smoke, and in some of the movies "there were some lovely scenes which just got me all hot 'n' bothered."

Not only movie stars became celebrities in the 1920s. Sports figures such as Babe Ruth, Bobby Jones, Jack Dempsey, and Red Grange were just as famous. The great spectator sports of the decade owed much to the increase in leisure time and to the automobile, the radio, and the mass-circulation newspaper. Thousands drove autos to college towns to watch football heroes perform. Millions listened for scores or read about the results the next day.

The year 1927 seemed to mark the beginning of the new age of mechanization and progress. That was the year Henry Ford produced his 15 millionth car and introduced the Model A. During that year, radio-telephone service was established between San Francisco and Manila. The first radio network was organized (CBS), and the first talking movie (*The Jazz Singer*) was released. In 1927, the Holland Tunnel, the first underwater vehicular roadway, connected New York and New Jersey. It was also the year that Charles Lindbergh flew from New York to Paris in his single-engine plane in $33\frac{1}{2}$ hours. Lindbergh was not the first to fly the Atlantic, but he was the first to fly it alone, an accomplishment that won him $25,000 in prize money and captured the world's imagination. He was young and handsome, and his feat seemed to represent not only the triumph

Charles Lindbergh and *Spirit of St. Louis*

of an individual but also the triumph of the machine. Lindbergh never talked of his accomplishments in the first person; he always said "we," meaning his airplane as well. He was greeted by 4 million people when he returned to New York for a triumphant ticker-tape parade. Like many movie stars and sports heroes, he had become an instant celebrity. When Americans cheered Lindbergh, they were reaffirming their belief in the American dream and their faith in individual initiative as well as in technology.

HOPES RAISED, PROMISES DEFERRED

The 1920s was a time when all kinds of hopes seemed realizable. "Don't envy successful salesmen—be one!" one advertisement screamed. Buy a car. Build a house. Start a career. Invest in land. Invest in stocks. Make a fortune.

Not all Americans, of course, were intent on making a stock-market killing or expected to win a huge fortune. Some merely wished to retain traditional values in a society that seemed to question them. Others wanted a steady job and a little respect. Still others hungered for the new appliances so alluringly described in ads and on the radio. Many discovered, however, that no matter how modest their hopes might be, they lay tantalizingly out of reach.

Clash of Values

During the 1920s, radio, movies, advertising, and mass-circulation magazines promoted a national, secular culture. But this new culture, which emphasized consumption, pleasure, upward mobility, and even sex, clashed with the traditional values of hard work, thrift, church, family, and home. Although it would be easy to see these cultural differences as a reflection of an urban–rural conflict, in fact, many people clinging to the old ways had moved into the cities. Still, many Americans feared that new cultural values, scientific breakthroughs, and new ideas such as bolshevism, relativism, Freudianism, and biblical criticism threatened their familiar way of life. A trial over the teaching of evolutionary ideas in high school in the little town of Dayton, Tennessee, symbolized, even as it exaggerated, the clash of the old versus the new, the traditional versus the modern, the city versus the country.

The scientific community and most educated people had long accepted the basic concepts of evolution, if not all the details of Charles Darwin's theories. But many Christians, especially those from Protestant evangelical churches, accepted the Bible as the literal truth. They believed that faith in the Gospel message was crucial to living a virtuous life on earth and, more important, going to heaven. Many of these faithful saw a major spiritual crisis in the dramatic changes of the 1920s. Resistance to the concept of evolution resulted in legislative efforts in several states to forbid its teaching.

IMAGE

Clarence Darrow at the Scopes Trial, 1925

John Scopes, a young biology teacher, broke the law by teaching evolutionary theory to his class, and the state of Tennessee brought him to trial. The American Civil Liberties Union hired Clarence Darrow, perhaps the country's most famous defense lawyer, to defend Scopes; the World Christian Fundamentalist Association engaged William Jennings Bryan, former presidential candidate and secretary of state, to assist the prosecution. Bryan was old and tired (he died only a few days after the trial), but he was still an eloquent and deeply religious man. In cross-examination, Darrow reduced Bryan's statements to intellectual rubble and also revealed that Bryan was at a loss to explain much of the Bible. He could not explain how Eve was created from Adam's rib or where Cain got his wife. Nevertheless, the jury declared Scopes guilty, for he had clearly broken the law.

The press from all over the country covered the trial and upheld science and academic freedom. Journalists such as H. L. Mencken had a field day poking fun at Bryan and the fundamentalists. "Heave an egg out a Pullman window," Mencken wrote, "and you will hit a Fundamentalist almost anywhere in the United States today. . . . They are everywhere where learning is too heavy a burden for mortal minds to carry."

Religious Fundamentalism

Some observers, including Mencken, thought that the Scopes trial ended what one writer in 1926 called "the fundamentalist menace." Yet religious fundamentalism continued to survive in a world fast becoming urban, modern, and sophisticated. Fundamentalism cut across many denominations and covered over many differences, but all fundamentalists believed in the literal interpretation and the infallibility of the Bible and that Jesus Christ was the only road to salvation. They rejected secularism, liberal theology, pluralism, the Social Gospel, and any sense that reform on earth could lead to perfection. They had a strong and unshakable belief in what they knew was the truth, and they were willing to fight for their belief.

Throughout the 1920s and the 1930s, attendance at Christian colleges and the circulation of fundamentalist periodicals and newspapers increased dramatically, and evangelical ministers reached large audiences. One of the most popular and flamboyant of the ministers was Billy Sunday, a former baseball player who jumped about the stage as he pitched his brand of Christianity. For Sunday, Christianity and patriotism were synonymous. Another popular preacher was Aimee Semple McPherson, a faith healer who founded her own church, the International Church of the Four Square Gospel, in Los Angeles in 1927. Dressed as a University of Southern California football player, she ran across the stage

John Steuart Curry, *Baptism in Kansas* Curry was one of the 1920s regionalist painters who found inspiration in the American heartland. In this painting, he depicts a religious ritual that underscores the conflict between rural and urban values. Is there still a religious split today between urban and rural America? Or is the cultural divide defined differently today? *(John Steuart Curry, [1897–1946], Baptism in Kansas, 1928. Oil on canvas, 40 x 50 in. [101.6 x 127 cm]. Gift of Gertrude Vanderbilt Whitney © 1996 Whitney Museum of American Art, New York [31.159])*

"carrying the ball for Christ"; wielding a pitchfork, she drove the devil out of the auditorium.

Sunday and McPherson may have been flamboyant performers, but it was the radio that extended the reach of the fundamentalist preachers even more dramatically. McPherson was the first woman to hold a radio license, and she had the second most popular radio show in Los Angeles in the late 1920s. In the 1930s, *The Old Fashioned Revival Hour* was carried on 356 stations and reached an audience of more than 20 million people, more than any other prime-time broadcast. For many, the period between the wars was a time when people drifted away from organized religion, an age of technological marvels, and modernism in all fields, but for many others, it was a time when fundamentalist religion and old-fashioned values not only survived but also prospered. Yet many fundamentalist sects succeeded in winning numerous converts because their leaders were skilled at using modern technology.

Immigration and Migration

Immigrants and anyone else perceived as "un-American" seemed to threaten the old ways. A movement to restrict immigration had existed for decades. An act passed in 1882 prohibited the entry of criminals, paupers, and the insane, and special agreements between 1880 and 1908 restricted both Chinese and Japanese immigration. But the fear and

intolerance of the war years and the period right after the war resulted in major restrictive legislation.

The first strongly restrictive immigration law passed in 1917 over President Wilson's veto. It required a literacy test for the first time (an immigrant had to read a passage in one of a number of languages). The bill also prohibited the immigration of certain political radicals. However, the literacy test did not stop the more than 1 million immigrants who poured into the country in 1920 and 1921.

Eye Examination at Ellis Island, ca. 1913

In 1921, Congress limited European immigration in any one year to 3 percent of the number of each nationality present in the country in 1910. In order to limit immigration from southern and eastern Europe and to ban all immigration from Asia, Congress in 1924 changed the quota to 2 percent of those in the country in 1890. The National Origins Act of 1927 set an overall limit of 150,000 European immigrants a year, with more than 60 percent coming from Great Britain and Germany, but fewer than 4 percent from Italy.

Ethnicity increasingly became a factor in political alignments during the 1920s. Restrictive immigration laws, sponsored by Republicans, helped attract American Jews, Italians, and Poles to the Democratic party. By 1924, the Democratic party was so evenly divided between northern urban Catholics and southern rural Protestants that the

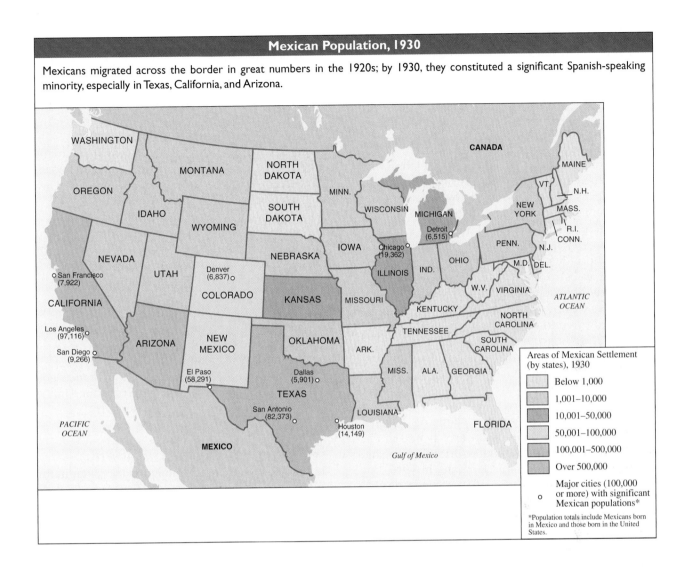

Mexican Population, 1930

Mexicans migrated across the border in great numbers in the 1920s; by 1930, they constituted a significant Spanish-speaking minority, especially in Texas, California, and Arizona.

Areas of Mexican Settlement (by states), 1930

- Below 1,000
- 1,001–10,000
- 10,001–50,000
- 50,001–100,000
- 100,001–500,000
- Over 500,000

o Major cities (100,000 or more) with significant Mexican populations*

*Population totals include Mexicans born in Mexico and those born in the United States.

party voted, by a very small margin, to condemn the Ku Klux Klan.

The immigration acts of 1921, 1924, and 1927 sharply limited European immigration and virtually banned Asian immigrants. The 1924 law contained a provision prohibiting the entry of aliens ineligible for citizenship. This provision was aimed directly at the Japanese, for the Chinese had already been excluded; but even without this provision, only a small number could have entered the United States. "We try hard to be American," one California resident remarked, "But Americans always say you always Japanese." Denied both citizenship and the right to own land, the first-generation issei placed all of their hope in their children, but the second-generation nisei often felt trapped between the land of their parents and the America they lived in, and they still were treated as second-class citizens.

DOCUMENT

1924 Immigration Law

The immigration laws of the 1920s cut off the streams of cheap labor that had provided muscle for an industrializing country since the early nineteenth century. At the same time, by exempting immigrants from the Western Hemisphere, the new laws opened the country to Mexican laborers who were eager to escape poverty in their own land and to work in the fields and farms of California and the Southwest. Though they never matched the flood of eastern and southern Europeans who entered the country before World War I, Mexican immigrants soon became the country's largest first-generation immigrant group. Nearly half a million arrived in the 1920s, in contrast to only 31,000 in the first decade of the century. Mexican farm workers often lived in primitive camps, where conditions were unsanitary and health care was nonexistent.

Mexicans also migrated to industrial cities such as Detroit, St. Louis, and Kansas City. Northern companies recruited them and paid their transportation. The Bethlehem Steel Corporation brought 1,000 Mexicans into its Pennsylvania plant in 1923, and U.S. Steel imported 1,500 as strikebreakers to Lorain, Ohio, about the same time. During the 1920s, the population of El Paso, Texas, became more than 50 percent Mexican, and that of San Antonio a little less than 50 percent Mexican. In California, the Mexican population reached 368,000 in 1929, and in Los Angeles, the population was about 20 percent Mexican. Like African Americans, the Mexicans found opportunity by migrating, but they did not escape prejudice or hardship.

African Americans migrated north in great numbers from 1915 to 1920. Reduced European immigration and industrial growth caused many northern companies to recruit southern blacks. Trains stopped at the depots in small southern towns, sometimes picking up hundreds of blacks in a single day. Lured by editorials and advertisements placed by industries in northern black newspapers such as the Chicago *Defender* and driven out of the South by an agricultural depression, many African Americans eagerly headed north.

Most black migrants were unskilled. They found work in the huge meatpacking plants of Chicago, East St. Louis, Omaha, and Kansas City and in the shipyards and steel mills. Only 50 African Americans worked for the Ford Motor Company in 1916, but 2,500 worked there in 1920 and 10,000 in 1926. The black population of Chicago increased from 44,000 in 1910 to 234,000 by 1930. Cleveland's black population grew eightfold between 1910 and 1930.

African Americans unquestionably improved their lives by moving north. But most were like the Parkers, whom we met at the beginning of this chapter—their dreams were only partly fulfilled. Most crowded into segregated housing and faced prejudice and hate.

Often the young black men moved first, and only later brought their wives and children, putting great pressure on many black families. Some young men, like John Parker, restrained their anger, but others like Richard Wright's fictional Bigger Thomas, portrayed movingly in *Native Son* (1940), struck out violently against white society. The presence of more African Americans in the industrial cities of the North led to the development of black ghettos and increased the racial tension that occasionally flared into violence.

One of the worst race riots took place in Chicago in 1919. The riot began at a beach on a hot July day. A black youth drowned in a white swimming area. Blacks claimed he had been hit by stones, but the police refused to arrest any of the

DOCUMENT

The Chicago *Defender*, The Chicago Riot (1919)

white men. A group of African Americans attacked the police, and the riot was on. It lasted four days. White youths drove through the black sections of the city, shooting blacks from car windows. Blacks returned the fire. Several dozen were killed, and hundreds were wounded. The tension between the races did not die when the riot was over.

Race riots broke out in other places as well. In the early 1920s, few cities escaped racial tension and violence. Riots exploded in Knoxville, Tennessee; Omaha, Nebraska; and Tulsa, Oklahoma. Racial conflict in Elaine, Arkansas, demonstrated that not even the rural South was immune.

The wave of violence and racism angered and disillusioned W. E. B. Du Bois, who had urged African Americans to close ranks and support the American cause during the war. In an angry editorial for *The Crisis,* he announced: "We return from fighting. We return fighting. Make way for Democracy; we saved it in France, and by the Great Jehovah, we will save it in the United States of America, or know the reason why."

DOCUMENT

F. J. Grimke, Address to African American Soldiers Returning from War (1919)

Marcus Garvey: Black Messiah

Du Bois was not the only militant black leader in the postwar years. A flamboyant Jamaican fed a growing sense of black pride during that time. Marcus Garvey arrived in New York at age 29. Largely self-taught, he was an admirer of Booker T. Washington. Although he never abandoned Washington's philosophy of self-help, he thoroughly transformed it. Washington focused on economic betterment through self-help; Garvey saw self-help as a means of political empowerment by which African peoples would reclaim their homelands from European powers.

In Jamaica, Garvey had founded the Universal Negro Improvement Association. By 1919, he had established 30 branches in the United States and the Caribbean. He also set up the newspaper *The Negro World,* the Black Cross Nurses, and a chain of grocery stores, millinery shops, and restaurants. His biggest project was the Black Star Line, a steamship company that was to be owned and operated by African Americans. Advocating the return of blacks to Africa, he declared himself the "provisional president of Africa," a title he adopted from Eamon De Valera, the first "provisional president of Ireland." Garvey glorified the African past and preached that God and Jesus were black.

Garvey won converts, mostly among lower-middle-class blacks, through the force of his oratory and the power of his personality, but especially through

The Harlem Renaissance

A group of black writers, artists, and intellectuals who settled in Harlem after the war led a movement related in some ways to Garvey's black nationalism crusade. It was less flamboyant but in the end more important. They studied anthropology, art, history, and music, and they wrote novels and poetry that explored the ambivalent role of blacks in America. Like Garvey, they expressed their pride in being black and sought their African roots and the folk tradition of blacks in America. But unlike Garvey, they had no desire to go back to Africa; instead, they sought a way to be both black and American.

Alain Locke, the first black Rhodes scholar and a dapper professor of philosophy at Howard University, was in one sense the father of the movement called the Harlem Renaissance. His collection of essays and art, *The New Negro* (1925), announced the movement to the outside world. Langston Hughes, a poet and

Black Messiah Marcus Garvey (second from the right), shown dressed in his favorite uniform, became a hero for many black Americans. How did his appeal differ from that of other African American leaders? *(Hulton Archive/Getty Images)*

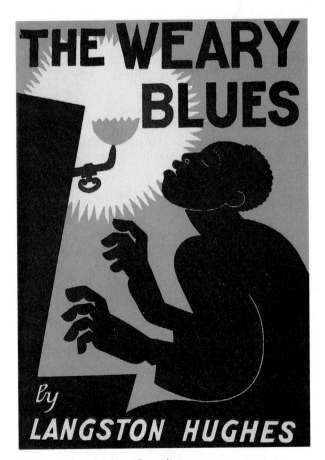

Poet of the Harlem Renaissance Langston Hughes was one of the most important Harlem Renaissance writers. Like many other African American writers, he sought out his African roots. But he later wrote: "I was only an American Negro who loved the surface of Africa and the rhythms of Africa, but I was not Africa. I was Chicago and Kansas City and Broadway and Harlem." What was the larger impact of the Harlem Renaissance? *(Fales Library/Special Collections, New York University)*

his message that blacks should be proud of being black. "Up you mighty race, you can accomplish what you will," Garvey thundered. Thousands of blacks cheered as his Universal African Legions, dressed in blue and red uniforms, marched by. They waved the red, black, and green flag and sang "Ethiopia, the Land of Our Fathers," while thousands invested their money in the Black Star Line. The line soon collapsed, however, in part because white entrepreneurs sold Garvey inferior ships and equipment. Garvey was arrested for using the mails to defraud shareholders and was sentenced to five years in prison. Although President Coolidge commuted the sentence, Garvey was ordered deported as an undesirable alien and left America in 1927. Despite his failures, he convinced thousands of black Americans, especially the poor and discouraged, that they could join together and accomplish something and that they should feel pride in their heritage and their future.

novelist born in Missouri, went to high school in Cleveland, lived in Mexico, and traveled in Europe and Africa before settling in Harlem. He wrote bitter but humorous poems, using black vernacular to describe the pathos and the pride of African Americans. In *Weary Blues,* he adapted the rhythm and beat of black jazz and the blues to his poetry.

Jazz was an important force in Harlem in the 1920s, and many prosperous whites came from downtown to listen to Louis Armstrong, Fletcher Henderson, Duke Ellington, and other black musicians. The promise of expressing primitive emotions, the erotic atmosphere, the music, and the illegal sex, drugs, and liquor made Harlem an intriguing place for many brought up in Victorian white America.

Harlem jazz was also exported to Europe, especially to Paris. Returning black servicemen reported that African Americans were treated without prejudice in France, and black musicians began to drift to the Montmartre section of Paris, where American jazz and jazz singers such as the seductive Josephine Baker, star of *Revue Nègre,* became the toast of the town. Ironically, many American tourists in the 1920s first heard an African American jazz band in Paris. Many Europeans criticized the United States for its materialism and for its innocent exuberance. They were not impressed with American literature or American art, but they loved American jazz. It was the beginning of the export of American popular culture that would impress most of the rest of the world in the decades after World War II.

The Jamaican Claude McKay, who came to Harlem by way of Tuskegee and Kansas, wrote about the underside of life in Harlem in *Home to Harlem* (1925), one of the most popular of the "new Negro" novels. McKay portrayed two black men—one, named Jake, who has deserted the white man's army and finds a life of simple and erotic pleasure in Harlem's cabarets, the other an intellectual who is unable to make such an easy choice. "My damned white education has robbed me of much of the primitive vitality, the pure stamina, the simple unwaggering strength of the Jakes of the negro race," he laments.

This was the dilemma of many of the Harlem writers: how to be both black and intellectual. They worried that they depended on white patrons, who introduced them to writers and artists in Greenwich Village and made contacts for them at New York publishing houses. Many of the white patrons pressured the black writers to conform to the white elite idea of black authenticity. The black writers resented this intrusion, but it was their only hope to be recognized. Jean Toomer, more self-consciously avant-garde than many of the other black writers, wrote haunting poems trying to explore the difficulty of black identity; in the novel *Cane* (1923), he sketched maladjusted, almost grotesque characters who expressed some of the alienation that many writers felt in the 1920s.

Many African American writers felt alienated from American society. They tried living in Paris or in Greenwich Village, but most felt drawn to Harlem, which in the 1920s was rapidly becoming the center of black population in New York City. More than 117,000 white people left the neighborhood during the decade, while more than 87,000 blacks moved in. Countee Cullen, the only writer in the group actually born in New York, remarked, "In spite of myself I find that I am activated by a strong sense of race consciousness." So, too, was Zora Neale Hurston activated—born in Florida, she went to New York to study at Barnard College, earned an advanced degree in anthropology from Columbia University, and used her interest in folklore to write stories of robust and passionate rural blacks. Much of the work of the Harlem writers was read by very small numbers, but another generation of young black intellectuals in the 1960s still struggling with the dilemma of how to be both black and American would rediscover it.

The Lost Generation

One did not need to be black to be disillusioned with society. Many white intellectuals, writers, and artists also felt alienated from what they perceived as the materialism, conformity, and provincial prejudice that dominated American life. Many writers, including F. Scott Fitzgerald, Ernest Hemingway, E. E. Cummings, and T. S. Eliot, moved to Europe. They wanted to divorce themselves from the country they pretended to detest, but cheap rents and inexpensive food in Paris also influenced their decisions. Many of those who gathered at European cafés, drinking the wine that was illegal in the United States, wrote novels, plays, and poems about America. Like so many American intellectuals in all periods, they had a love–hate relationship with their country.

For many writers, the disillusionment began with the war itself. Hemingway eagerly volunteered to go to Europe as an ambulance driver. But when he was wounded on the Italian front, he re-evaluated the purpose of the war and the meaning of all the slaughter. His novel *The Sun Also Rises* (1926) is the story of the purposeless European wanderings of a group of Americans. But it is also the story of Jake Barnes, who was made impotent by a war injury. His "unreasonable wound" is a symbol of the futility of life in the postwar period.

F. Scott Fitzgerald, who loved to frequent the cafés and parties in Paris, became a celebrity during the 1920s. He was sometimes confused, even in his own mind, with the dashing heroes about whom he wrote. He epitomized some of the despair of his generation, which had "grown up to find all Gods dead, all wars fought, all faiths in man shaken." His best novel, *The Great Gatsby* (1925), was a critique of the American success myth. The book describes the elaborate parties given by a mysterious business-man, who, it turns out, has made his money illegally as a bootlegger. Gatsby hopes to win back a beautiful woman who has forsaken him for another man. But wealth does not buy happiness, and Gatsby's life ends tragically, as so many lives seemed to end in the novels written during this decade.

Paris was the place to which many American writers flocked, but it was not necessary to live in France to criticize American society. Sherwood Anderson, born in Camden, Ohio, created a fictional midwestern town in *Winesburg, Ohio* (1919) as a way to describe the dull, narrow, warped lives that seemed to provide a metaphor for American culture. Sinclair Lewis, another midwesterner, created scathing parodies of middle-class, small-town life in *Main Street* (1920) and *Babbitt* (1922). The "hero" of the latter novel is a salesman from the town of Zenith. He is a "he-man," a "regular guy" who distrusts "red professors," foreign-born people, and anyone from New York.

But no one had more fun laughing at the American middle class than H. L. Mencken, who edited the *American Mercury* in Baltimore and denounced what he called the "booboisie." He labeled Woodrow Wilson a "self-bamboozled Presbyterian" and poked fun at Warren Harding's prose, which he said reminded him of "a string of wet sponges, . . . of stale bean soup, of college yells, of dogs barking idiotically through endless nights."

Ironically, while intellectuals despaired over American society and complained that art could not

Ernest Hemingway on Safari

survive in a business-dominated civilization, literature flourished. The novels of Hemingway, Fitzgerald, Lewis, William Faulkner, and Gertrude Stein; the plays of Eugene O'Neill and Maxwell Anderson; the poetry of T. S. Eliot, Hart Crane, E. E. Cummings, and Marianne Moore; and the work of many black writers, such as Langston Hughes, Claude McKay, and Zora Neale Hurston, marked the 1920s as one of the most creative decades in American literature.

Women Struggle for Equality

Any mention of the role of women in the 1920s brings to mind the image of the flapper—a young woman with a short skirt, bobbed hair, and a boyish

figure dancing the Charleston, smoking, drinking, and enjoying sexual encounters. F. Scott Fitzgerald's heroines in novels such as *This Side of Paradise* (1920) and *The Great Gatsby* (1925) provided the role models for young people to imitate, and movie stars such as Clara Bow and Gloria Swanson, aggressively seductive on the screen, supplied even more dramatic examples of flirtatious and provocative behavior.

IMAGE
Clara Bow, the "It" Girl, 1927

Without question, women acquired more sexual freedom in the 1920s. "None of the Victorian mothers had any idea how casually their daughters were accustomed to being kissed," F. Scott Fitzgerald wrote. However, it is difficult, if not impossible, to know how accustomed those daughters (and their mothers) were to kissing and enjoying other sexual activity. Contraceptives, especially the diaphragm, became more readily available during the decade, and Margaret Sanger, who had been indicted for sending birth control information through the mail in 1914, organized the first American birth control conference in 1921. Still, most states made the selling or prescribing of birth control devices illegal, and federal laws prohibited sending literature discussing birth control through the mail.

DOCUMENT
Eleanor Rowland Wembridge, "Petting and the Campus" (1925)

Family size declined during the decade (from 3.6 children in 1900 to 2.5 in 1930), and young people were apparently more inclined to marry for love than for security. More women expected sexual satisfaction in marriage (nearly 60 percent in one poll) and felt that divorce was the best solution for an unhappy marriage. In another poll, nearly 85 percent approved of sexual intercourse as an expression of love and affection and not simply for procreation. But the polls were hardly scientific and tended to be biased toward the attitudes of the urban middle class. Despite more freedom for women, the double standard persisted.

DOCUMENT
Margaret Sanger, "Happiness in Marriage" (1926)

Women's lives were shaped by other innovations of the 1920s. Electricity, running water, washing machines, vacuum cleaners, and other labor-saving devices made housework easier for the middle class. Yet these developments did not touch large numbers of rural and urban working-class women. Even middle-class women discovered that new appliances did not reduce time spent doing housework. Standards of cleanliness rose, and women were urged to make their houses more spotless than any nineteenth-century housekeeper would have felt

Women in the Labor Force, 1900–1930

Why is the percentage of women working gradually increasing between 1900 and 1930? Why are more married women working?

Year	Women in Labor Force	Percentage of Women in Total Labor Force	Percentage of Total Women of Working Age	Single	Married	Widowed
1900	4,997,000	18.1	20.6	66.2	15.4	18.4
1910*	7,640,000	NA	25.4	60.2	24.7	15.0
1920	8,347,000	20.4	23.7	77.0†	23.0	—†
1930	10,632,000	21.9	24.8	53.9	28.9	17.2

*Data not comparable with other censuses due to a difference in the basis of enumeration.
† Single includes widowed and divorced.

Source: U.S. Bureau of the Census.

necessary. At the same time, magazines and newspapers bombarded women with advertising urging them to buy products to make themselves better housekeepers yet still be beautiful. It must have been frustrating for those who could not afford the magic new products or whose hands and teeth and skin failed to look youthful despite all their efforts. The ads also promoted new dress styles, shorter skirts, and no corsets. The young adopted them quickly, and they also learned to swim (and to display more of their bodies on the beach), to play tennis (but only if they belonged to a tennis club), and to ride a bicycle.

More women worked outside the home. Whereas in 1890, only 17 percent of women were employed, by 1933, some 22 percent were. But their share of manufacturing jobs fell from 19 percent to 16 percent between 1900 and 1930. The greatest expansion of jobs was in white-collar occupations that were being feminized—for example, secretary, bookkeeper, clerk, and telephone operator. In 1930, fully 96 percent of stenographers were women. Although more married women had jobs (an increase of 25 percent during the decade), most of them held low-paying jobs, and most single women assumed that marriage would terminate their employment.

For some working women—secretaries and teachers, for example—marriage often led to dismissal from their jobs. Married women are "very unstable in their work; their first claim is to home and children," a businessman concluded. Although women might not be able to work after their weddings (in one poll of college men, only one in nine said he would allow

DOCUMENT

Caroline Manning, *The Immigrant Woman and Her Job* (1930)

his wife to work after marriage), a job as a secretary could be good preparation for marriage. A business office was a good place to meet eligible men, but more than that, a secretary learned endurance, self-effacement, and obedience, traits that would make her a good wife. Considering these attitudes, it is not surprising that the disparity between male and female wages widened during the decade. By 1930, women earned only 57 percent of what men were paid.

The image of the flapper in the 1920s promised more freedom and equality for women than they actually achieved. The flapper was young, white, slender, and upper class (Fitzgerald fixed her ideal age at 19), and most women did not fit those categories. The flapper was frivolous and daring, not professional and competent. Although the proportion of

Working Women of the 1920s Although the flapper look of short skirts and bobbed hair appeared in the workplace in the 1920s, for most working women of the era, employed in low-paying jobs as file clerks, typists, and telephone operators, the flapper lifestyle of freedom and equality was more illusion than reality. *(Bettmann-CORBIS)*

women lawyers and bankers increased slightly during the decade, the rate of growth declined, and the number of women doctors and scientists dropped. In the 1920s, women acquired some sexual freedom and a limited amount of opportunity outside the home, but the promise of the prewar feminist movement and the hopes that accompanied the suffrage amendment remained unfulfilled.

Winning the vote for women did not ensure equality. Women could vote, but often they could not serve on juries. In some states, women could not hold office, own a business, or sign a contract without their husbands' permission. Women were usually held responsible for an illegitimate birth, and divorce laws almost always favored men. Many women leaders were disappointed in the small turnout of women in the presidential election of 1920. To educate women in the reality of politics, they organized the National League of Women Voters to "finish the fight." A nonpartisan organization, it became an important educational organization for middle-class women, but it did little to eliminate inequality.

Alice Paul, who had led the militant National Women's Party in 1916, chained herself to the White House fence once again to promote an equal rights amendment to the Constitution. The amendment got support in Wisconsin and in several other states, but many women opposed it on the grounds that such an amendment would cancel the special legislation to protect women in industry that had taken so long to enact in the two preceding decades. Feminists disagreed in the 1920s on the proper way to promote equality and rights for women, but the political and social climate was not conducive to feminist causes.

Rural America in the 1920s

Most farmers did not share in the prosperity of the 1920s. Responding to worldwide demands and rising prices for wheat, cotton, and other products, many farmers invested in additional land, tractors, and farm equipment during the war. Then prices tumbled. By 1921, the price of wheat had dropped 40 percent, corn 32 percent, and hogs 50 percent. Total farm income fell from $10 million to $4 million in the postwar depression. Many farmers could not make payments on their tractors. Because the value of land fell, they often lost both mortgage and land and still owed the bank money.

The changing nature of farming was part of the problem. The use of chemical fertilizers and new hybrid seeds, some developed by government experiment stations and land-grant colleges, increased the yield per acre. By 1930, some 920,000 tractors and 900,000 trucks were in use on American farms. They not only made farming more efficient, but they also allowed land formerly used to raise feed for horses and mules to be planted in cash crops. Production increased at the very time that worldwide demand for American farm products declined. In 1929, the United States shipped abroad only one-third the wheat it had exported in 1919, and only one-ninth the meat. Farmers, especially in North America and Europe, had prospered during the war because of the great demand for food. Expecting the demand to continue, many farmers borrowed to purchase new equipment and to increase the number of acres they cultivated. But the demand for produce did not last, leading to a worldwide decline in prices and making debts difficult to repay.

Victims not only of the global marketplace, American farmers were also vulnerable to the power of nature. This became apparent in the spring of 1927 when the worst flood in the nation's history devastated the Mississippi River valley, flooding more than 27,000 square miles of land and making a million people homeless.

Not all farmers suffered. Large commercial operations, using mechanized equipment, produced most of the cash crops. At the same time, many small farmers found themselves unable to compete with agribusiness. Some of them, along with many farm laborers, solved the problem of declining rural profitability by leaving the farms. In 1900, fully 40 percent of the labor force worked on farms; by 1930, only 21 percent earned their living from the land.

Few farmers could afford the products of the new technology. Although many middle-class urban families were more prosperous than they had ever been—buying new cars, radios, and bathrooms—only one farm family in ten had electricity in the 1920s. The lot of the farm wife had not changed for centuries. She ran a domestic factory, did all the household chores, and helped on the farm as well.

Farmers tried to improve their position by supporting legislation in the state capitals and in Washington. Most of their efforts went into the McNary–Haugen Farm Relief Bill, which would have provided government price support for key agricultural products. The bill was introduced a number of times between 1924 and 1928 without success, but farm organizations in all parts of the country learned how to work together to influence Congress. That would have important ramifications for the future.

The Workers' Share of Prosperity

Hundreds of thousands of workers improved their standard of living in the 1920s, yet inequality grew.

Real wages increased 21 percent between 1923 and 1929, but corporate dividends went up by nearly two-thirds in the same period. The workers did not profit from the increased production they helped create, and that boded ill for the future. The richest 5 percent of the population increased their share of the wealth from a quarter to a third, and the wealthiest 1 percent controlled a whopping 19 percent of all income.

Even among workers there was great disparity. Those employed on the auto assembly lines or in the new factories producing radios saw their wages go up, and many saw their hours decline. Yet the majority of American working-class families did not earn enough to move them much beyond subsistence level. One study suggested that a family needed $2,000 to $2,400 in 1924 to maintain an "American standard of living." But in that year, 16 million families earned less than $2,000. For the chambermaids in New York hotels who worked seven days a week or the itinerant Mexican migrant laborers in the Southwest, labor was so exhausting that at the end of the day, it was impossible to take advantage of new consumer products and modern lifestyles, even if they had the money.

Organized labor fell on hard times in the 1920s. Labor union membership fell from about 5 million in 1921 to less than 3.5 million in 1929. Although a majority of American workers had never supported unions, unions now faced competition from employers' new policies. A number of large employers lured workers away from unions with promises that seemed to equal union benefits: profit-sharing plans, pensions, and their own company unions. The National Association of Manufacturers and individual businesses carried on a vigorous campaign to restore the open shop. The leadership of the AFL became increasingly conservative during the decade and had little interest in launching movements to organize laborers in the large industries.

The more aggressive unions such as the United Mine Workers, led by the flamboyant John L. Lewis, also encountered difficulties. The union's attempt to organize miners in West Virginia had led to violent clashes between union members and imported guards. President Harding called out troops in 1921 to put down an "army organized by the strikers." The next year, Lewis called the greatest coal strike in history and further violence erupted, especially in Williamson County, Illinois. Internal strife also weakened the union, and Lewis had to accept wage reductions in the negotiations of 1927.

Organized labor, like so many other groups, struggled desperately during the decade to take advantage of the prosperity. It won some victories, and it made some progress. But American affluence was beyond the reach of many groups during the decade. Eventually, the inequality would lead to disaster.

THE BUSINESS OF POLITICS

"Among the nations of the earth today America stands for one idea: *Business*," a popular writer announced in 1921. "Through business, properly conceived, managed and conducted, the human race is finally to be redeemed." Bruce Barton, the head of the largest advertising firm in the country, was the author of one of the most popular nonfiction books of the decade. In *The Man Nobody Knows* (1925), he depicted Christ as "the founder of modern business." He took 12 men from the bottom ranks of society and forged them into a successful organization. "All work is worship; all useful service prayer," Barton argued. If the businessman would just copy Christ, he could become a supersalesman.

Business, especially big business, prospered in the 1920s, and the image of businessmen, enhanced by their important role in World War I, rose further. The government reduced regulation, lowered taxes, and cooperated to aid business expansion at home and abroad. Business and politics, always intertwined, were especially allied during the decade. Wealthy financiers such as Andrew Mellon and Charles Dawes participated in formulating both domestic and foreign policy. Even more significant, a new kind of businessman was elected president in 1928. Herbert Hoover, international engineer and efficiency expert,

DOCUMENT
Edward Earle Purinton, "Big Ideas from Big Business" (1921)

was the very symbol of the modern techniques and practices that many people confidently expected to transform the United States and the world. Business leaders wielded power in other countries, but in no country were business and politics so closely intertwined as in the United States.

Harding and Coolidge

The Republicans, almost assured of victory in 1920 because of bitter reaction against Woodrow Wilson, might have preferred nominating their old standard-bearer, Theodore Roosevelt, but he had died the year before. Warren G. Harding, a former newspaper editor from Ohio, captured the nomination after meeting late at night with some of the party's most powerful men in a hotel room in Chicago. No one ever discovered what Harding promised, but the meeting in the "smoke-filled

VIDEO
Warren G. Harding

room" became legendary. To balance the ticket, the Republicans chose as their vice presidential candidate Calvin Coolidge of Massachusetts, who had gained attention by his firm stand during the Boston police strike. The Democrats seemed equally unimaginative. After 44 roll calls, they finally nominated Governor James Cox of Ohio and picked Franklin D. Roosevelt, a young politician from New York, to run as vice president. Roosevelt had been the assistant secretary of the navy but otherwise had not distinguished himself.

Harding won in a landslide. His 60.4 percent of the vote was the widest margin yet recorded in a presidential election. More significant, fewer than 50 percent of the eligible voters went to the polls. The newly enfranchised women, especially in working-class neighborhoods, stayed away from the voting booths. So did large numbers of men. To many people, it did not seem to matter who was president.

Presidents Harding and Coolidge

In contrast to the reform-minded presidents Roosevelt and Wilson, Harding reflected the conservatism of the 1920s. He was a jovial man who brought many Ohio friends to Washington and placed them in positions of power. A visitor to the White House described Harding and his cohorts discussing the problems of the day, with "the air heavy with tobacco smoke, trays with bottles containing every imaginable brand of whiskey" near at hand.

At a little house a few blocks from the White House on K Street, Harry Daugherty, Harding's attorney general and longtime associate, held forth with a group of friends. Amid bootleg liquor and the atmosphere of a brothel, they did a brisk business in selling favors, taking bribes, and organizing illegal schemes. Harding, however, was not personally corrupt, and the nation's leading businessmen approved of his policies of higher tariffs and lower taxes. Nor did Harding spend all his time drinking with his cronies. He called a conference on disarmament and another to deal with the problems of unemployment, and he pardoned Eugene Debs, who had been in prison since the war. Harding once remarked that he could never be considered one of the great presidents, but he thought perhaps he might be "one of the best loved." He was probably right. When he died suddenly in August 1923, the American people genuinely mourned him.

Executive Orders and Senate Resolutions on the Teapot Dome Scandal (1920)

Only after Calvin Coolidge became president did the full extent of the corruption and scandals of the Harding administration come to light. A Senate committee discovered that the secretary of the interior, Albert Fall, had illegally leased government-owned oil reserves in the Teapot Dome section of Wyoming to private business interests in return for over $300,000 in bribes. Illegal activities were also discovered in the Veterans Administration and elsewhere in government. Daugherty resigned in disgrace, the secretary of the navy barely avoided prison, two of Harding's advisers committed suicide, and Fall was sentenced to jail.

Though dour and taciturn, Coolidge was honest. No hint of scandal infected his administration or his personal life. Born in a little town in Vermont, he was sworn in as president by his father, a justice of the peace, in a ceremony conducted by the light of kerosene lamps at his ancestral home. To many, Coolidge represented old-fashioned rural values, simple religious faith, and personal integrity—a world fast disappearing in the 1920s.

Coolidge ran for re-election in 1924 with the financier Charles Dawes as his running mate. There was little question that he would win. The Democrats were so equally divided between northern urban Catholics and southern rural Protestants that it took 103 ballots before they nominated John Davis, an affable corporate lawyer with little national following.

A group of dissidents, mostly representing the farmers and the laborers dissatisfied with both nominees, formed a new Progressive party. They adopted the name, but little else, from Theodore Roosevelt's party of 1912. Nominating Robert La Follette of Wisconsin for president, they drafted a platform calling for government ownership of railroads and ratification of the child labor amendment. La Follette attacked the "control of government and industry by private monopoly." He received nearly 5 million votes, only 3.5 million short of Davis's total. But Coolidge and prosperity won easily.

Like Harding, Coolidge was a popular president. Symbolizing his administration was his wealthy secretary of the treasury, Andrew Mellon, who set out to lower individual and corporate taxes. In 1922, Congress, with Mellon's endorsement, repealed the wartime excess profits tax. Although it raised some taxes slightly, it exempted most families from any tax at all by giving everyone a $2,500 exemption, plus $400 for each dependent. In 1926, the rate was lowered to 5 percent and the maximum surtax to 40 percent. Only families with incomes above $3,500 paid any taxes at all. In 1928, Congress reduced taxes further, removed most excise taxes, and lowered the corporate tax rate. The 200 largest corporations increased their assets during the decade from $43 to $81 billion.

Businessmen and the President Beginning in 1920, Henry Ford, Thomas Edison, and Harvey Firestone went on auto trips together in part to celebrate the new automobile culture. In the summer of 1924, they stopped in Plymouth, Vermont, to visit with President Calvin Coolidge, who was vacationing at the family homestead. A local photographer took this photograph and made it into a postcard, which he sold as a souvenir. The president is autographing a sap bucket to be placed in Henry Ford's new museum near Detroit. From left to right: Harvey Firestone, President Coolidge, Henry Ford, Thomas Edison, Russell Firestone, Grace Coolidge, and John Coolidge, the president's father. Coolidge often pretended he was a simple Vermonter, but actually he was much more comfortable around the corporate elite than he was dealing with ordinary Americans. What was the danger of the close relationship between the presidents and business leaders in the 1920s? Does that close relationship still exist? *(Allen F. Davis Collection)*

"The chief business of the American people is business," Coolidge announced. "The man who builds a factory builds a temple. . . . The man who works there worships there." Coolidge's idea of the proper role of the federal government was to have as little as possible to do with the functioning of business and the lives of the people. Not everyone approved of his policies, or his personality. "No other president in my time slept so much," a White House usher remembered. But most Americans approved of his inactivity.

Herbert Hoover

One bright light in the lackluster Harding and Coolidge administrations was Herbert Hoover. Born in Iowa, raised in Oregon, and educated in California, he served as secretary of commerce under both presidents. Hoover had made a fortune as an international mining engineer before 1914 and then earned a reputation as a great humanitarian for his work managing the Belgian Relief Committee and directing the Food Administration during World War I. He was mentioned as a candidate for president in 1920, when he had the support of such

progressives as Jane Addams, Louis Brandeis, and Walter Lippmann.

Hoover was a dynamo of energy and efficiency. He expanded his department to control and regulate the airlines, radio, and other new industries. By directing the Bureau of Standards to work with the trade associations and with individual businesses, Hoover managed to standardize the size of almost everything manufactured in the United States, from nuts and bolts and bottles to automobile tires, mattresses, and electric fixtures. He supported zoning codes, the eight-hour workday in major industries, better nutrition for children, and the conservation of national resources. He pushed through the Pollution Act of 1924, which represented the first attempt to control oil pollution along the American coastline.

As secretary of commerce, Hoover used the force of the federal government to regulate, stimulate, and promote, but he believed first of all in free enterprise and local volunteer action to solve problems. In 1921, he convinced Harding of the need to do something about unemployment during the postwar recession. The president's conference on unemployment, convened in September 1921, marked the first time the national government had admitted any responsibility to the unemployed. The result of the conference (the first of many on a variety of topics that Hoover was to organize) was a flood of publicity, pamphlets, and advice from experts. Most of all, the conference urged state and local governments and businesses to cooperate on a volunteer basis to solve the problem. The primary responsibility of the federal government, Hoover believed, was to educate and promote. With all his activity and his organizing, Hoover earned a reputation during the Harding and Coolidge years as an efficient and progressive administrator and as a humanitarian who could organize flood relief. He became one of the most popular figures in government service.

Global Expansion

The decade of the 1920s is often remembered as a time of isolation, when the United States rejected the League of Nations treaty and turned its back on the rest of the world. It is true that many Americans had little interest in what was going on in Paris, Moscow, or Rio de Janeiro, and it is also true that a bloc of congressmen was determined that the United States would never again enter another European war. But the United States remained involved—indeed, increased its involvement—in international affairs during the decade. Although the United States never joined the League of Nations, and a few dedicated isolationists, led by Senator William Borah, blocked membership in the World Court, the United States cooperated with many league agencies and conferences and took the lead in trying to reduce naval armaments and to solve the problems of international finance caused in part by the war.

Looking back from the vantage point of World War II, the decade of the 1920s seemed happy, productive, and normal in most parts of the world. But there were ominous clouds on the horizon. Great Britain and France were slow to recover from the war, while Germany was mired in economic and political chaos. Japan and Italy were unhappy with the peace settlement. Germany's African colonies had been split between France and Great Britain, but imperialism and colonial empires had not diminished. Fascism was establishing a foothold in Spain and Italy, while Soviet communism was becoming more firmly entrenched in Russia. The collapse of the Ottoman Empire had led to the establishment of a new Turkish republic, but the rest of the Middle East was fragmented both economically and politically and presented problems that would persist for the rest of the twentieth century and beyond.

Business, trade, and finance marked the decade as one of international expansion for the United States. With American corporate investments overseas growing sevenfold during the decade, the United States was transformed from a debtor to a creditor nation. The continued involvement of the United States in the affairs of South and Central American countries also indicated that the country had growing interests beyond its national boundaries. The United States also increased its international position in cable communication, wireless telegraphy, news services, and motion pictures. In some areas, such as film, the United States led the world. In 1925, 95 percent of the films shown in Great Britain and Canada and 70 percent of those shown in France were American made.

Despite growing global expansion in many areas, the U.S. government took up its role of international power reluctantly and with a number of contradictory and disastrous results. "We seek no part in directing the destiny of the world," Harding announced in his inaugural address, but even Harding discovered that international problems would not disappear. One that required immediate attention was the naval arms race. Since the late nineteenth century, the battleship had become the symbol of national power and pride. Although the aircraft carrier would be more important than the battleship in World War II, the battleship retained its prestige between the wars. A navy was important for protecting trade and empire, but the race to build battleships was caused by something more than practical economics.

The United States called the first international conference to discuss disarmament. At the Washington Conference on Naval Disarmament, which convened in November 1921, Secretary of State Charles Evans Hughes startled the delegates by proposing a 10-year "holiday" on the construction of warships and by offering to sink or scrap 845,000 tons of American ships, including 30 battleships. He urged Britain and Japan to do the same. The delegates greeted Hughes's speech with enthusiastic cheering and applause, and they set about the task of sinking more ships than the admirals of all their countries had managed to do in a century.

The conference participants ultimately agreed to fix the tonnage of capital ships at a ratio of the United States and Great Britain, 5; Japan, 3; and France and Italy, 1.67. Japan agreed only reluctantly, but when the United States promised not to fortify its Pacific Island possessions, Japan yielded. In light of what happened in 1941, the Washington Naval Conference has often been criticized, but in 1921, it was appropriately hailed as the first time in history that the major nations of the world had agreed to disarm. The conference did not cause World War II; neither, as it turned out, did it prevent it. But it was a creative start to reducing tensions and to meeting the challenges of the modern arms race. And it was the United States that took the lead by offering to be the first to scrap its battleships.

American foreign policy in the 1920s tried to reduce the risk of international conflict, resist revolution, and make the world safe for trade and investment. In its dealings with Latin America, the United States continued its policy of intervention. By the end of the decade, the United States controlled the financial affairs of 10 Latin American nations. The marines were withdrawn from the Dominican Republic in 1924, but that country remained a virtual protectorate of the United States until 1941. The government ordered the marines out of Nicaragua in 1925 but sent them back the next year when a liberal insurrection threatened the conservative government. But the U.S. Marines, and the Nicaraguan troops they had trained, had a difficult time containing a guerrilla band led by Augusto Sandino, a charismatic leader and one of Latin America's greatest heroes. The Sandinistas, supported by the great majority of peasants, came out of the hills to attack the politicians and their American supporters. In 1934, Sandino was murdered by General Anastasio Somoza, a ruthless leader supported by the United States. For more than 40 years, Somoza and his two sons ruled Nicaragua as a private fiefdom, a legacy not yet resolved in that strife-torn country.

Mexico frightened American businessmen in the mid-1920s by beginning to nationalize foreign holdings in oil and mineral rights. Fearing that further military activity would "injure American interests," businessmen and bankers urged Coolidge not to send marines but to negotiate instead. Coolidge appointed Dwight W. Morrow of the J. P. Morgan Company as ambassador, and his conciliatory attitude led to agreements protecting American investments. Throughout the decade, the goal of U.S. policy toward Central and South America, whether in the form of negotiations or intervention, was to maintain a special sphere of influence.

The U.S. policy of promoting peace, stability, and trade was not always consistent or carefully thought out, and this was especially true in its relationships with Europe. At the end of the war, European countries owed the United States more than $10 billion, with Great Britain and France responsible for about three-fourths of that amount. Both countries, mired in postwar economic problems, suggested that the United States forgive the debts, arguing that they had paid for the war in lives and property destroyed. But the United States, although adjusting the interest and the payment schedule, refused to forget the debt. "They hired the money, didn't they?" Coolidge supposedly remarked.

The only way European nations could repay the United States was by exporting products, but in a series of tariff acts, especially the Fordney–McCumber Tariff of 1922, Congress erected a protective barrier to trade. This act also gave the president power to lower or raise individual rates; in almost every case, both Harding and Coolidge used the power to raise them. Finally, in 1930, the Hawley–Smoot Tariff raised rates even further, despite the protests of many economists. American policy of high tariffs (a counterproductive policy for a creditor nation) caused retaliation and restrictions on American trade, which American corporations were trying to increase.

The inability of the European countries to export products to the United States and to repay their loans was intertwined with the reparations agreement made with Germany. Germany's economy was in disarray after the war, with inflation raging and its industrial plant throttled by the peace treaty. By 1921, Germany was defaulting on its payments. The United States, which believed a healthy Germany important to European stability and world trade, instituted a plan engineered by Charles Dawes whereby the German debt would be renegotiated and spread over a longer period. In the meantime, American bankers and the American government lent Germany hundreds of millions of dollars. In the end, the United States lent money to Germany so it could make payments to Britain and France so that those countries could continue their payments to the United States.

The United States had replaced Great Britain as the dominant force in international finance, but the nation in the 1920s was a reluctant and inconsistent world leader. The United States had stayed out of the League of Nations and was hesitant to get involved in multinational agreements. However, some agreements seemed proper to sign; the most idealistic of all was the Kellogg–Briand pact to outlaw war. The French foreign minister, Aristide Briand, suggested a treaty between the United States and France in large part to commemorate long years of friendship between the two countries, but secretary of state Frank B. Kellogg in 1928 expanded the idea to a multinational treaty to outlaw war. Fourteen nations agreed to sign the treaty, and eventually 62 nations signed, but the only power behind the treaty was moral force rather than economic or military sanctions.

The Survival of Progressivism

The decade of the 1920s was a time of reaction against reform, but progressivism did not simply die. It survived in many forms through the period that Jane Addams called a time of "political and social sag."

The greatest success of the social justice movement was the 1921 Sheppard–Towner Maternity Act, one of the first pieces of federal social welfare legislation and the product of long progressive agitation. A study conducted by the Children's Bureau discovered that more than 3,000 mothers died in childbirth in 1918 and that more than 250,000 infants also died. The United States ranked eighteenth out of 20 countries in maternal mortality and eleventh in infant deaths. The low rank of the United States was caused in part by the poor conditions in urban slums and by rural poverty, especially among southern blacks. But it was also the result of the lack of government intervention to improve health care while many European countries provided health insurance and government-supported medical clinics. Sara Josephine Baker, the pioneer physician and founder of the American Child Health Association, was not being ironic when she remarked, "It's six times safer to be a soldier in the trenches in France than to be born a baby in the United States."

The maternity bill called for $1 million a year to assist the states in providing medical aid and visiting nurses to teach expectant mothers how to care for themselves and their babies. The bill was controversial from the beginning. The American Medical Association, which had supported pure food and drug legislation and laws to protect against health quacks and to enforce standards for medical schools, attacked this bill as leading to socialism and interfering with the relationship between doctor and patient.

Despite the opposition, the bill passed Congress and was signed by President Harding in 1921. The appropriation for the bill was for only six years, and the opposition, again raising the specter of a feminist-Socialist-Communist plot, succeeded in repealing the law in 1929. Yet the Sheppard-Towner Act, promoted and fought for by a group of progressive women, indicated that concern for social justice was not dead in the age of Harding and Coolidge.

Temperance Triumphant

For one large group of progressives, Prohibition, like child labor reform and maternity benefits, was an important effort to conserve human resources. By 1918, more than three-fourths of the people in the country lived in dry states or counties, but it was the war that allowed the antisaloon advocates to associate Prohibition with patriotism. "We have German enemies across the water," one prohibitionist announced. "We have German enemies in this country too. And the worst of all our German enemies, the most treacherous, the most menacing are Pabst, Schlitz, Blatz and Miller." In 1919, Congress passed the Volstead Act, banning the brewing and selling of beverages containing more than one-half of one percent alcohol. In June 1919, the thirty-sixth state ratified the Eighteenth Amendment, prohibiting the manufacture, sale, and transport of intoxicating liquors. But the country had, for all practical purposes, been dry since 1917.

The Prohibition experiment probably did reduce the total consumption of alcohol in the country, especially in rural areas and urban working-class neighborhoods. Fewer arrests for drunkenness occurred, and deaths from alcoholism declined. But the legislation showed the difficulty of using law to promote moral reform. Most people who wanted to

Presidential Elections, 1920–1928

What political trends are revealed in this chart?

Year	Candidate	Party	Popular Vote	Electoral Vote
1920	WARREN G. HARDING	Republican	16,152,200 (60.4%)	404
	James M. Cox	Democratic	9,147,353 (34.2%)	127
	Eugene V. Debs	Socialist	919,799 (3.4%)	0
1924	CALVIN COOLIDGE	Republican	15,725,016 (54.0%)	382
	John W. Davis	Democratic	8,385,586 (28.8%)	136
	Robert M. La Follette	Progressive	4,822,856 (16.6%)	13
1928	HERBERT C. HOOVER	Republican	21,392,190 (58.2%)	444
	Alfred E. Smith	Democratic	15,016,443 (40.9%)	87

Note: Winners' names appear in capital letters.

drink during the "noble experiment" found a way. Speakeasies replaced saloons, and people consumed bathtub gin, home brew, and many strange and dangerous concoctions. Bartenders invented the cocktail to disguise the poor quality of liquor, and women, at least middle- and upper-class women, began to drink in public for the first time.

Prohibition also created great bootlegging rings, which were tied to organized crime in many cities.

AUDIO
Prohibition Is a Failure

Al Capone of Chicago was the most famous underworld figure whose power and wealth were based on the sale of illegal alcohol. His organization alone grossed an estimated $60 million in 1927; ironically, most of the profit came from distributing beer. Many supporters of Prohibition slowly came to favor its repeal, some because it reduced the power of the states, others because it stimulated too much illegal activity and because it did not seem to be worth the social and political costs.

The Election of 1928

On August 2, 1927, President Coolidge announced simply, "I do not choose to run for President in 1928." Hoover immediately became the logical Republican candidate. Hoover and Coolidge were not especially close. Coolidge resented what he considered Hoover's spendthrift ways. "That man has offered me unsolicited advice for six years, all of it bad," Coolidge once remarked. Though lacking an

IMAGE
A Heavy Load for Al, 1928

enthusiastic endorsement from the president and opposed by some Republicans who thought him to be too progressive, Hoover easily won the nomination. In a year when the country was buoyant with optimism and when prosperity seemed as if it would go on forever, few doubted that Hoover would be elected.

The Democrats nominated Alfred Smith, a Catholic Irish American from New York. With his New York accent, his opposition to Prohibition, and his flamboyant style, he contrasted sharply with the more sedate Hoover. On one level, it was a bitter contest between Catholic "wets" and Protestant "drys," between the urban, ethnic Tammany politician and former governor of New York against the rural-born but sophisticated secretary of commerce. Religious prejudice, especially a persistent anti-Catholicism, played an important role in the campaign. But looked at more closely, the two candidates differed little. Both were self-made men, both were "progressives." Social justice reformers campaigned for each candidate. Both candidates tried to attract women voters, both were favorable to organized labor, both defended capitalism, and both had millionaires and corporate executives among their advisers.

Hoover won in a landslide, 444 electoral votes to 76 for Smith, who carried only Massachusetts and Rhode Island outside the Deep South. But the 1928 campaign revitalized the Democratic party. Smith polled nearly twice as many votes as the Democratic

"Black Thursday"   Cars, mounted policemen, frantic bankers, worried stock brokers, and investors on Wall Street on October 24, 1929—"Black Thursday." The stock market crash in the United States would have a global impact. It revealed weaknesses in the world economy and helped trigger a global depression. *(CORBIS)*

candidate in 1924, and for the first time, the Democrats carried the 12 largest cities.

Stock Market Crash

Hoover, as it turned out, had only six months to apply his progressive and efficient methods to running the country; in the fall of 1929, the prosperity that seemed endless suddenly came to a halt. In 1928 and 1929, rampant speculation made the stock market boom. Money could be made everywhere—in real estate and business ventures, but especially in the stock market. "Everybody ought to be Rich," Al Smith's campaign manager argued in an article in *Ladies' Home Journal* early in 1929. Just save $15 a month and buy good common stock with it, and that money would turn into $80,000 in 20 years (a considerable fortune in 1929). Good common stock seemed to be easy to find in 1929.

Only a small percentage of the American people invested in the stock market, for many had no way of saving even $15 a month. But a large number got into the game in the late 1920s because it seemed a safe and sure way to make money. For many, the stock market came to represent the American economy, and the economy was booming. The *New York Times* index of 25 industrial stocks reached 100 in 1924, moved up to 181 in 1925, dropped a bit in 1926, and rose again to 245 by the end of 1927.

Then the orgy started. During 1928, the market rose to 331. Many investors and speculators began to buy on margin (borrowing to invest). Businessmen and others began to invest in the market money that would ordinarily have gone into houses, cars, and other goods. Yet even at the peak of the boom, probably only about 1.5 million Americans owned stock.

In early September 1929, the *New York Times* index peaked at 452 and then began to drift downward. On October 23, the market lost 31 points. The next day ("Black Thursday"), it first seemed that everyone was trying to sell, but at the end of the day, the panic appeared to be over. It was not. By mid-November, the market had plummeted to 224, about half what it had been two months before. This represented a loss on paper of over $26 billion. Still, a month later, the chairman of the board of Bethlehem Steel could announce, "Never before has American business been

TIMELINE

1900–1930	Electricity powers the "second Industrial Revolution"
1917	Race riot in East St. Louis, Illinois
1918	World War I ends
1919	Treaty of Versailles
	Strikes in Seattle, Boston, and elsewhere
	Red Scare and Palmer raids
	Race riots in Chicago and other cities
	Marcus Garvey's Universal Negro Improvement Association spreads
1920	Warren Harding elected president
	Women vote in national elections
	First commercial radio broadcast
	Sacco and Vanzetti arrested
	Sinclair Lewis, *Main Street*
1921	Immigration Quota Law
	Naval Disarmament Conference
	First birth control conference
	Sheppard–Towner Maternity Act
1921–1922	Postwar depression
1922	Fordney–McCumber Tariff
	Sinclair Lewis, *Babbitt*
1923	Harding dies; Calvin Coolidge becomes president
	Teapot Dome scandal

1924	Coolidge reelected president
	Peak of Ku Klux Klan activity
	Immigration Quota Law
1925	Scopes trial in Dayton, Tennessee
	F. Scott Fitzgerald, *The Great Gatsby*
	Bruce Barton, *The Man Nobody Knows*
	Alain Locke, *The New Negro*
	Claude McKay, *Home to Harlem*
	5 million enameled bathroom fixtures produced
1926	Ernest Hemingway, *The Sun Also Rises*
1927	National Origins Act
	McNary–Haugen Farm Relief Bill
	Sacco and Vanzetti executed
	Lindbergh flies solo from New York to Paris
	First talking movie, *The Jazz Singer*
	Henry Ford produces 15 millionth car
1928	Herbert Hoover elected president
	Kellogg–Briand Treaty
	Stock market soars
1929	27 million registered autos in country
	10 million households own radios
	100 million people attend movies
	Stock market crash

as firmly entrenched for prosperity as it is today." Some businessmen even got back into the market, thinking that it had reached its low point. But it continued to go down. Tens of thousands of investors lost everything. Those who had bought on margin had to keep coming up with money to pay off their loans as the value of their holdings declined. There was panic and despair, but the legendary stories of executives jumping out of windows were grossly exaggerated.

The stock market crash was more symptom than cause of the economic collapse. Weak banking systems in both Europe and America, the rise of protectionism, the drop in farm prices, and the decline of purchasing power all foreshadowed the economic disaster that would follow the stock market debacle.

Conclusion

A New Era of Prosperity and Problems

The stock market crash ended the decade of prosperity. The crash did not cause the Depression, but the stock market debacle revealed the weakness of the economy. The fruits of economic expansion had been unevenly distributed. The Parker family, introduced at the beginning of this chapter, and many other families in both rural and urban America did not share in the prosperity. Not enough people could afford to buy the autos, refrigerators, and other products pouring from American factories. Prosperity had been built on a shaky foundation. When that foundation crumbled in 1929, the nation slid into a major depression. But the Depression was related to global financial trends and to economic problems created by World War I and the peace settlement. High tariffs and reparations that wrecked the German economy and a weakened banking system all contributed to the economic collapse. Looking back from the vantage point of the 1930s or later, the 1920s seemed a golden era—an age of flappers, bootleg gin, constant parties, literary masterpieces, sports heroes, and easy wealth. The truth is much more complicated. More than most decades, the 1920s was a time of paradox and contradictions.

The 1920s was a time of prosperity, yet a great many people, including farmers, blacks, and other ordinary Americans, did not prosper. The 1920s was a time of modernization, but only about 10 percent of rural families had electricity. It was a time when women achieved more sexual freedom, but the feminist movement declined. It was a time of Prohibition, but many Americans increased their consumption of alcohol. It was a time of reaction against reform, yet progressivism survived. It was a time when intellectuals felt disillusioned with America, yet it was one of the most creative and innovative periods for American writers. It was a time of flamboyant heroes, yet the American people elected the lackluster Harding and Coolidge as their presidents. It was a time of progress, when almost every year saw a new technological breakthrough, but it was also a decade of hate and intolerance. The complex and contradictory legacy of the 1920s continues to fascinate and to influence our time.

Questions for Review and Reflection

1. What was the Harlem Renaissance?
2. Did the Prohibition experiment succeed or fail?
3. In foreign policy during the 1920s did the United States try to isolate itself from the rest of the world?
4. What groups did not share in the prosperity of the decade?
5. Why are Harding and Coolidge often considered among our worst presidents?

Recommended Reading

Recommended Readings are posted on the Web site for this textbook. Visit www.ablongman.com/nash

Fiction and Film

Sinclair Lewis's novel *Babbitt* (1922) depicts the narrowness of small-town life in the Midwest. F. Scott Fitzgerald describes the reckless lives of the very rich in *The Great Gatsby* (1925). Claude McKay's novel *Home to Harlem* (1928) is one of the best fictional works to come out of the Harlem Renaissance. *Front Page* (1931) is a movie that depicts the world of corrupt politicians and cynical newspapermen in Chicago during the roaring twenties. The 1974 film version of *The Great Gatsby* is not entirely faithful to the novel, but it still captures some of the opulence and pathos of the lives of the very rich in the 1920s. To appreciate two of the great actors and comics of the silent film era, check out Charles Chaplin in *City Lights* (1931) and Buster Keaton in *The General* (1927).

Discovering U.S. History Online

Red Scare (1918–1921)

www.newman.baruch.cuny.edu/digital/redscare/default.htm

The site presents an extensive database of post–World War I images, mostly taken from *Literary Digest,* a weekly compendium of news from various newspapers and magazines contemporary to the period.

The Trial of Sacco and Vanzetti

www.courttv.com/greatesttrials/sacco.vanzetti/

An illustrated summary of the trial, commentary by experts, and video clips from the companion film.

Automotive History

www.mel.lib.mi.us/business/autos-history.html

This site, from the Michigan Electronic Library, has several links to sites about automotive history in America.

Emergence of Advertising in America

http://scriptorium.lib.duke.edu/eaa

The images presented in this exhibit "illustrate the rise of consumer culture, especially after the American Civil War, and the birth of a professionalized advertising industry in the United States."

Chicago: Destination for the Great Migration

www.loc.gov/exhibits/african/afam011.html

This Library of Congress site looks at the black experience of the great migration through the lens of one prominent destination.

Titanic

www.nationalgeographic.com/society/ngo/explorer/titanic/movie.html

This site offers historical perspective via photos from the wreckage of the *Titanic,* a first-person account from a survivor, and a discussion forum.

Ernest Hemingway

www.npg.si.edu/exh/hemingway/

This site presents a biography of author Ernest Hemingway, illustrated with various paintings.

Tennessee vs. John Scopes

www.law.umkc.edu/faculty/projects/ftrials/scopes/scopes.htm

This site contains images, chronology, and court and official documents of the so-called Monkey Trial of 1925.

The 1920s

www.louisville.edu/~kprayb01/1920s.html

This site is divided into three sections: a descriptive timeline, essays and biographies, and an opinion essay.

The Marcus Garvey and Universal Negro Improvement Association Papers Project

www.isop.ucla.edu/mgpp

This site presents a biography of Garvey, sample documents from the volumes of his papers, and photo and sound archives.

Harlem 1900–1940: An African-American Community

www.si.umich.edu/CHICO/Harlem

A timeline of the Harlem Renaissance along with an exhibit that covers such topics as the "Schomburg Center itself, political movements, education, sports, social organizations, religion, the Harlem Hospital theater, business and music."

Photographs from the Golden Age of Jazz

http://lcweb2.loc.gov/ammem/wghtml/wghome.html

A searchable database of Gottlieb's photographs of jazz pioneers, audio commentary on some of the photographs, and scanned articles from the 1940s in which his photographs appeared.

Negro League Baseball

www.negroleaguebaseball.com

This site has articles about desegregation, baseball, and Jim Crow, as well as images of teams and players.

Urban Leisure

www.suba.com/~scottn/explore/mainmenu.htm

An exploration of the jazz culture in Chicago and its influence on the multi-ethnic commercial culture in that city, the "groundwork for the spread of mass culture across the nation during the twentieth century."

The Harlem Renaissance

www.nku.edu/~diesmanj/harlem_intro.html

This site provides an overview of writing and painting from the Harlem Renaissance, with a gallery of paintings by Loïs Mailou, William H. Johnson, and Palmer Hayden and the full text of several poems and short stories by various authors.

Temperance and Prohibition

http://prohibition.history.ohio-state.edu

This site looks at the temperance movement over time and contains many information links.

The Coolidge Era and the Consumer Economy, 1921–1929

http://lcweb2.loc.gov/ammem/coolhtml/ccpres00.html

This site "assembles a wide array of Library of Congress source materials from the 1920s that document the widespread prosperity of the Coolidge years, the nation's transition to a mass consumer economy, and the role of government in this transition."

Calvin Coolidge

www.potus.com/ccoolidge.html

This site contains basic factual data about Coolidge's election and presidency, speeches, and online biographies.

Herbert C. Hoover

www.potus.com/hhoover.html

This site contains basic factual data about Hoover's election and presidency, speeches, and online biographies.

October 24, 1929

www.arts.unimelb.edu.au/amu/ucr/student/1997/Yee/ny.html

An overview of "Black Thursday" and the events leading up to it by way of headlines that appeared in the *New York Times.*

CHAPTER 24

The Great Depression and the New Deal

The WPA (Works Progress Administration) hired artists from 1935 to 1943 to create murals for public buildings. The assumption was not only that "artists need to eat too," as Harry Hopkins announced, but also that art was an important part of culture and should be supported by the federal government. Here Moses Soyer, a Philadelphia artist, depicts WPA artists creating a mural. Do you think it is appropriate for the government to subsidize artists? *(Moses Soyer, Artists on WPA, 1935. Smithsonian American Art Museum, Washington DC/Art Resource, New York)*

American Stories

Coming of Age and Riding the Rails During the Depression

Flickering in a Seattle movie theater in the depths of the Great Depression, the Hollywood production *Wild Boys of the Road* captivated 13-year-old Robert Symmonds. The film, released in 1933, told the story of boys hitching rides on trains and tramping around the country. It was supposed to warn teenagers of the dangers of rail riding, but for some it had the opposite effect. Robert, a boy from a middle-class home, already had a fascination with hobos. He had watched his mother give sand-wiches to the transient men who sometimes knocked on the back door. He had taken to hanging around the "Hooverville" shantytown south of the King Street railroad station, where he would sit next to the fires and listen to the rail riders' stories. Stoked for adventure, when school let out in 1934, Robert and a school friend hopped onto a moving boxcar on a train headed out of town. Hands reached out to pull them aboard the car, which already held 20 men. The two boys journeyed as far as Vancouver, Washington, and home to Seattle again. It was frightening, and exhilarating.

Seattle, WA, Shantytown

In 1938, under the weight of the Depression, the Symmonds family's security business failed. Years later, Robert recalled the effects on his father: "It hurt him bad when he went broke and all his friends deserted him. He did the best he could but never recovered his self-esteem and his pride." The loss of income forced Robert's family to accept a relative's offer of shelter in a three-room mountain cabin without electricity. Because of the move, Robert could no longer attend high school in Seattle. Once again, this time out of necessity, he turned to the rails, leaving his parents and three sisters behind.

Robert faced a personal challenge of surviving difficult times, but he also was part of a looming problem that troubled the administration of Franklin D. Roosevelt. Thousands of young people were graduating from high school or leaving school early, with very few jobs open to them. An estimated 250,000 young people were among the drifters who resorted to the often dangerous practice of hitching rides on trains around the country. Robert rode the rails during summers to find work harvesting fruit up and down the West Coast. In 1939, his travels took him to Montana, where he encountered the Roo-sevelt administration's solution for the "youth problem": the Civilian Conservation Corps (CCC). When he enlisted in the CCC, Robert became one of nearly 3 million young men age 17 and older who found work in government-sponsored conservation projects between 1933 and 1942. In exchange for their work, CCC workers earned $25 a month for their families back home plus $5 a month spending money for themselves.

The CCC was known as Roosevelt's "tree army" because the corps planted trees covering more than 2 million acres, improved more than 4 million acres of existing forest, and fought forest fires. In addition, the CCC worked on a wide variety of conservation-related projects in a nation suffering from deforestation, erosion, drought, dust storms, and other environmental problems. They improved parks and recreation areas and even Civil War historic sites, including the notorious Andersonville prison camp in Georgia. In many ways, the CCC operated like a military organization, with workers wearing surplus World War I uniforms and following a fixed regimen of work and recreation that began with a bugler's call at 6 A.M. Many of its veterans credited the corps with transforming them from boys into men, although others chafed under the discipline of the camps.

One historian has called the CCC the greatest peacetime mobilization in U.S. history, and it set the stage for the wartime mobilization that followed. By the time Robert Symmonds joined the CCC in 1939, war loomed in Europe. Like many CCC veterans, Robert's next stop in life was military service. He joined the navy and after the war became a merchant seaman. In later years, like many Americans of his generation, Robert remembered his experiences of the Great Depression grimly, but with some nostalgia. He even returned to hopping rides on railroad cars again during his retirement years, out of a sense of adventure rather than necessity. "It's something that got into my blood years ago," he explained. "I guess it is a freedom thing."

The Great Depression changed the lives of all Americans, separating that generation from the one that followed. An exaggerated need for security, the fear of failure, a nagging sense of guilt, and a real sense that it might happen all over again divided the Depression generation from everyone born after 1940. Like Robert Symmonds, they never forgot those bleak years.

This chapter explores the causes and consequences of the Great Depression, which had an impact around the world. We will look at Herbert Hoover and his efforts to combat the Depression and then turn to Franklin Roosevelt, the dominant personality of the 1930s. We will examine the New Deal and Roosevelt's program to bring relief, recovery, and reform to the nation. The New Deal legislation, some of which continued reforms started during the progressive era, did not end the Depression. But this legislation was based on the idea that the federal government had some responsibility for the economy and for promoting the welfare of all the people. We will also look at the other side of the 1930s, for the decade did not consist only of crippling unemployment and New Deal agencies. It was also a time of great strides in technology, when innovative developments in radio, movies, and the automobile affected the lives of most Americans.

THE GREAT DEPRESSION

There had been recessions and depressions in American history, notably in the 1830s, 1870s, and 1890s, but nothing compared with the devastating economic collapse of the 1930s. The Great Depression was all the more shocking because it came after a decade of unprecedented prosperity, when most experts assumed that the United States was immune to a downturn in the business cycle. The Great Depression had an impact on all areas of American life; perhaps most important, it destroyed American confidence in the future.

The Depression Begins

Few people anticipated the stock market crash in the fall of 1929. But even after the collapse of the stock market, few expected the entire economy to go into a tailspin. General Electric stock, selling for 396 in 1929, fell to 34 in 1932; U.S. Steel declined from 261 to 21. By 1932, the median income had plunged to half of what it had been in 1929. Construction spending fell to one-sixth of the 1929 level. By 1932, at least one of every four American breadwinners was out of work, and industrial production had almost ground to a halt.

Why did the nation sink deeper and deeper into depression? The answer is complex, but it appears in retrospect that the prosperity of the 1920s was superficial. Farmers and coal and textile workers had suffered all through the 1920s from low prices, and the farmers were the first group in the 1930s to plunge into depression. But other aspects of the economy also lurched out of balance. Two percent of the population received about 28 percent of the national income, but the lower 60 percent got only 24 percent. Businesses increased profits while holding down wages and the prices of raw materials. This pattern depressed consumer purchasing power. American workers, like American farmers, did not have the money to buy the goods they helped to produce. There was a relative decline in purchasing power in the late 1920s, unemployment was high in some industries, and the housing and automobile industries were already beginning to slacken before the crash.

VIDEO
Prosperity of the 1920s and the Great Depression

Well-to-do Americans were speculating a significant portion of their money in the stock market. Their illusion of permanent prosperity helped fire the boom of the 1920s, just as their pessimism and lack of confidence helped exaggerate the Depression in 1931 and 1932.

Other factors were also involved. The stock market crash revealed serious structural weaknesses in the financial and banking systems (7,000 banks had failed during the 1920s). The Federal Reserve Board, fearing inflation, tightened credit—exactly the opposite of the action it should have taken to fight a slowdown in purchasing. But the Depression was also caused by global economic problems created by World War I and the peace settlement. Large reparations exacted against Germany had led to the collapse of the German economy, and high tariffs had reduced international trade. When American investment in Europe slowed in 1928 and 1929, European economies declined. Americans purchased fewer European goods, and Europeans got along without American products. As the European financial situation worsened, the American economy spiraled downward.

IMAGE
John Baer, "We Demand a New Deal!" 1931

The federal government might have prevented the stock market crash and the Depression by more careful regulation of business and the stock market. Central planning might have ensured a more equitable distribution of income. But that kind of policy would have taken more foresight than most people had in the 1920s. It certainly would have required different people to be in power, and it is unlikely that the Democrats, had they been in control, would have altered the government's policies in fundamental ways.

Hoover and the Great Depression

Initial business and government reactions to the stock market crash were optimistic. "All the evidence indicates that the worst effects of the crash upon unemployment will have been passed during the next sixty days," Herbert Hoover reported. Hoover, the great planner and progressive efficiency expert, did not sit idly by and watch the country drift toward disorder. His upbeat first statements were calculated to prevent further panic.

Hoover acted aggressively to stem the economic collapse. More than any president before him, he used the power of the federal government and the office of the president to deal with an economic crisis. Nobody called it a depression for the first year at least, for the economic problems seemed very much like earlier cyclic recessions. Hoover called conferences of businessmen and labor leaders. He met with mayors and governors and encouraged them to speed up public works projects. He created agencies and boards, such as the National Credit Corporation and the Emergency Committee for Employment, to obtain voluntary action to solve the problem. Hoover even supported a tax cut, which Congress enacted in December 1929, but it did little to stimulate spending.

ECONOMIC DECLINE

Voluntary action and psychological campaigns could not stop the Depression. The stock market, after appearing to bottom out in the winter of 1930–1931, continued its decline, responding in part to the European economic collapse that undermined international finance and trade. Of course, not everyone lost money in the market. William Danforth, founder of Ralston Purina, and Joseph Kennedy, film magnate, entrepreneur, and the father of a future president, were among those who made millions of dollars by selling short as the market went down.

More than a collapsing market afflicted the economy; an additional 1,300 banks failed in 1930. Despite Hoover's pleas, many factories cut back on production, and some simply closed. U.S. Steel announced a 10 percent wage cut in 1931. As the auto industry laid off workers, the unemployment rate rose to more

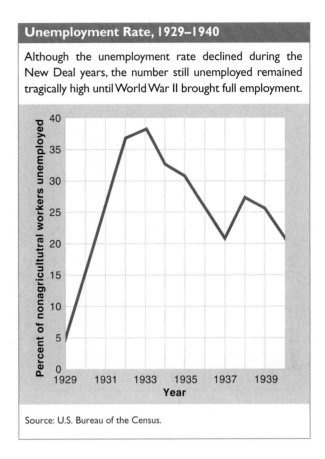

Unemployment Rate, 1929–1940

Although the unemployment rate declined during the New Deal years, the number still unemployed remained tragically high until World War II brought full employment.

Source: U.S. Bureau of the Census.

than 40 percent in Detroit. More than 4 million Americans were out of work in 1930, and at least 12 million were unemployed by 1932. Foreclosures and evictions created thousands of personal tragedies. While the middle class watched in horror as their life savings and their dreams disappeared, the rich were increasingly concerned as the price of government bonds (the symbol of safety and security) dropped. They began to hoard gold and fear revolution.

There was never any real danger of revolution. Some farmers organized to dump their milk to protest low prices, and when a neighbor's farm was sold, they gathered to hold a penny auction, bidding only a few cents for equipment and returning it to their dispossessed neighbor. But everywhere, people despaired as the Depression deepened in 1931 and 1932. For unemployed blacks and for many tenant farmers, the Depression had little immediate effect because their lives were already so depressed. Most Americans (the 98 percent who did not own stock) hardly noticed the stock market crash; for them, the Depression meant the loss of a job or a bank foreclosure. For Robert Symmonds it meant the failure of his father's business and being forced to drop out of high school. For some farmers, it was burning corn rather than coal because the price of corn had fallen so low that it was not worth marketing.

Out of Work   The worst result of the Depression was hopelessness and despair. Those emotions are captured in this painting by Isaac Soyer of an unemployment office. When did the unemployment crisis finally end? *(Isaac Soyer, Employment Agency, 1937, Oil on canvas, 34¹⁄₄ x 45 in. [87 x 114.3 cm]. Collection of Whitney Museum of American Art, Purchase, 37.44, Photograph © 2000: Whitney Museum of American Art)*

For some in the cities, the Depression meant not having enough money to feed the children. In Chicago, children fought with men and women over the garbage dumped by the city trucks. In Toledo, when municipal and private charity funds were drying up (as they did in all cities), those granted assistance were given only 2.14 cents per meal per person. In Philadelphia a social worker noticed that the children were playing a game called "Eviction." "Sometimes they play 'Relief,'" she remarked, "but 'Eviction' has more action and all of them know how to play."

Not everyone went hungry, stood in bread lines, or lost jobs during the Depression, but almost everyone was affected, and many victims tended to blame themselves. A businessman who lost his job and had to stand in a relief line remembered years later how he would bend his head low so nobody would recognize him. A 28-year-old teacher in New Orleans was released because of a cut in funds, and in desperation she took a job as a domestic servant. "If with all the advantages I've had," she remarked, "I can't make a living, I'm just no good, I guess. I've given up ever amounting to anything. It's no use."

The Depression probably disrupted women's lives less than men's. When men lost their jobs, their identity and sense of purpose as the family breadwinner were shattered. Some helped out with

IMAGE
Depression Era
Breadline

family chores, but usually with bitterness and resentment. For women, however, even when money was short, there was still cooking, cleaning, and mending, and women were still in command of their households. Yet many women were forced to do extra work. They took in laundry, found room for a boarder, and made the clothes they formerly would have bought. Women also bore the psychological burden of unemployed husbands, hungry children, and unpaid bills. The Depression altered patterns of family life, and many families were forced to move in with relatives. The marriage rate, the divorce rate, and the birthrate all dropped during the decade. Many of these changes created tension that statistics cannot capture.

A Global Depression

Hoover reacted to growing despair by urging more voluntary action. He insisted on maintaining the gold standard, believing it to be the only responsible currency, and a balanced budget, but so did almost everyone else. He blamed the Depression on international economic problems, and he was at least partly right. The legacy of the war and the global economic policies of the 1920s had been one cause of the economic downturn in the United States, and as the United States sank into depression, the world followed. In May 1931, the leading Austrian bank collapsed; by June, the German financial system, which had gone from hyperinflation to false stability, was in chaos. In September, England abandoned the gold standard, precipitating a decline in international lending and trade. Soon most of the industrialized world, including Argentina, Brazil, and Japan, was caught in the Great Depression. In some countries, the social safety net of health and unemployment insurance helped, but there were hungry and unemployed people in much of the world. That a stock market crash in the United States triggered a worldwide depression indicated that by 1930 the United States was an economic world power, but that was little solace as the global depression exaggerated and extended the Depression at home.

Children with "Hoover's Poor Farm" Sign

Despite the worldwide depression, Americans began to blame Hoover for some of the disaster. The president became isolated and bitter. The shanties that grew near all the large cities were called "Hoovervilles," and the privies "Hoover villas." Unable to admit mistakes and to take a new tack, he could not communicate personal empathy for the poor and the unemployed.

Hoover did try innovative schemes. More public works projects were built during his administration than in the previous 30 years. In the summer of 1931, he attempted to organize a pool of private money to rescue banks and businesses that were near failure. When the private effort failed, he turned reluctantly to Congress, which passed a bill early in 1932 authorizing the Reconstruction Finance Corporation. The RFC was capitalized at $500 million, but a short time later that was increased to $3 billion. It was authorized to make loans to banks, insurance companies, farm mortgage companies, and railroads. Some critics charged that it was simply another trickle-down measure whereby businessmen and bankers would be given aid while the unemployed were ignored. Hoover, however, correctly understood the immense costs to individuals and to communities when a bank or mortgage company failed. The RFC did help shore up a number of shaky financial institutions and remained the major government finance agency until World War II. But it became much more effective under Roosevelt because it lent directly to industry.

Hoover also asked Congress for a Home Financing Corporation to make mortgages more readily available. The Federal Home Loan Bank Act of 1932 became the basis for the Federal Housing Administration of the New Deal years. He supported the passage of the Glass–Steagall Banking Act of 1932, which expanded credit to make more loans available to businesses and individuals. But Hoover rejected calls for the federal government to restrict production in hopes of raising farm prices—that, he believed, was too much government intervention. He maintained that the federal government should promote cooperation and even create public works. But he firmly believed in loans, not direct subsidies, and he thought it was the responsibility of state and local governments, as well as of private charity, to provide direct relief to the unemployed and the needy.

The Bonus Army

Many World War I veterans lost their jobs during the Great Depression, and beginning in 1930, they lobbied for the payment of their veterans' bonuses, which were not due until 1945. A bill passed Congress in 1931, over Hoover's veto, allowing them to borrow up to 50 percent of the bonus due them, but this concession did not satisfy the destitute veterans. In May 1932, about 17,000 veterans marched on Washington. Some took up residence in a shantytown called Bonus City that was located in the Anacostia flats outside the city.

In mid-June, the Senate defeated the bonus bill, and most of the veterans, disappointed but resigned, accepted a free railroad ticket home. Several thousand remained, however, along with some wives and children, in the unsanitary shacks during the steaming summer heat. Among them were a small group of committed Communists and other radicals. Hoover, who exaggerated the subversive elements among those still camped out in Washington, refused to talk to the leaders and finally called out the U.S. army.

Bonus Expeditionary Force March on Washington

General Douglas MacArthur, the army chief of staff, ordered the army to disperse the veterans. He described the Bonus marchers as a "mob . . . animated by the essence of revolution." With tanks, guns, and tear gas, the army routed veterans who 15 years before had worn the same uniform as their attackers. Two Bonus marchers were killed, and several others were injured. "What a pitiful spectacle is that of the great American Government, mightiest in the world, chasing unarmed men, women and children with Army tanks," commented a Washington newspaper. "If the Army must be called out to make war on unarmed citizens, this is no longer America." The army was not attacking revolutionaries in the streets of Washington but was routing bewildered, confused, unemployed men who had seen their American dream collapse.

The Bonus army fiasco, bread lines, and Hoovervilles became the symbols of Hoover's presidency. He deserved better because he tried to use

Bonus Army Shacks U.S. soldiers burn the Bonus army shacks within sight of the Capitol in the summer of 1932. This image of the failure of the American dream was published widely around the world. Who do you blame for the Bonus Army fiasco? *(National Archives)*

the power of the federal government to solve growing and increasingly complex economic problems. But in the end, his personality and background limited him. He could not understand why army veterans marched on Washington to ask for a handout when he thought they should all be back home working hard, practicing self-reliance, and cooperating "to avert the terrible situation in which we are today." He believed that the greatest problem besetting Americans was a lack of confidence. Yet he could not communicate with these people or inspire their confidence. Willing to use the federal government to support business, he could not accept federal aid for the unemployed. He feared an unbalanced budget and a large federal bureaucracy that would interfere with the "American way." Ironically, his actions and his inactions led in the next years to a massive increase in federal power and in the federal bureaucracy.

ROOSEVELT AND THE FIRST NEW DEAL

The first New Deal, lasting from 1933 to early 1935, focused mainly on recovery from the Depression and relief for the poor and unemployed. Some of the programs were borrowed from the Hoover administration, and some had their origin in the progressive period. Others were inspired by the nation's experiences in mobilizing for World War I. No single ideological position united all the legislation, for Franklin Roosevelt was a pragmatist who was willing to try a variety of programs. More than Hoover, however, he

believed in economic planning and in government spending to help the poor.

Roosevelt's caution and conservatism shaped the first New Deal. He did not promote socialism or suggest nationalizing the banks. He was even careful in authorizing public works projects to stimulate the economy. The New Deal was based on the assumption that it was possible to create a just society by superimposing a welfare state on the capitalist system, leaving the profit motive undisturbed. While the progressives believed in voluntary action and only reluctantly concluded that the federal government needed to intervene to promote a just society, the New Dealers, from the beginning, believed in an active role for the government. Roosevelt was confident he could achieve his goals through cooperation with the business community. Later he would move more toward reform, but at first his primary concern was simply relief and recovery.

The Election of 1932

The Republicans nominated Herbert Hoover for a second term, but in the summer of 1932, the Depression and Hoover's unpopularity opened the way for the Democrats. After a shrewd campaign, Franklin D. Roosevelt, governor of New York, emerged from the pack and won the nomination. Journalist Walter Lippmann's comment during the campaign that Roosevelt was a "pleasant man who, without any important qualifications for office, would like very much to be President" was exaggerated at the time and

IMAGE

FDR with Leg Braces

The Disabled President   This is a rare photograph of Franklin Roosevelt in his wheelchair taken in a private moment with his dog, Fala, and a young friend. Usually FDR's advisers carefully arranged to have the president photographed only when he was seated or propped up behind a podium. Despite being paralyzed from the waist down, the president gave the impression of health and vitality until near the end of his life. Did his physical disability restrict his ability to be president? *(Margaret Suckley Collection, Franklin Delano Roosevelt Library)*

seemed absurd later. Roosevelt, distantly related to Theodore Roosevelt, had served as an assistant secretary of the navy during World War I and had been the Democratic vice presidential candidate in 1920. Crippled by polio not long after, he had recovered enough to serve as governor of New York for two terms, although he was not especially well-known by the general public in 1932.

As governor, Roosevelt had promoted cheaper electric power, conservation, and old-age pensions. He became the first governor to support state aid for the unemployed, "not as a matter of charity, but as a matter of social duty." But it was difficult to tell during the presidential campaign exactly what he stood for. He did announce that the government must do something for the "forgotten man at the bottom of the economic pyramid," yet he also mentioned the need for balancing the budget and maintaining the gold standard. Ambiguity was probably the best strategy in 1932, but the truth was that Roosevelt did not have a master plan to save the country. But

he won the election overwhelmingly, carrying more than 57 percent of the popular vote.

During the campaign, Roosevelt had promised a "new deal for the American people." But the New Deal had to wait for four months because the Constitution provided that the new president be inaugurated on March 4 (this was changed to January 20 by the Twentieth Amendment, ratified in 1933). During the long interregnum, the state of the nation deteriorated badly. The banking system seemed near collapse, and the hardship increased. Despite his bitter defeat, Hoover tried to cooperate with the president-elect and with a hostile Congress, but he could accomplish little. Everyone waited for the new president to take office and to act.

VIDEO
FDR's Inauguration

In his inaugural address, Roosevelt announced confidently, "The only thing we have to fear is fear itself." This, of course, was not true, for the country faced the worst crisis since the Civil War, but Roosevelt's confidence and his ability to communicate with ordinary Americans were obvious early in his presidency. He had clever speechwriters, a sense of pace and rhythm in his speeches, and an ability, when he spoke on the radio, to convince listeners that he was speaking directly to them. Recognizing the possibilities of the new media, he instituted a series of radio "fireside chats" to explain to the American people what he was doing to solve the nation's problems. When he said "my friends," millions believed that he meant it, and they wrote letters to him in unprecedented numbers to explain their needs.

DOCUMENT
FDR, Radio Address (1933)

Roosevelt's Advisers

During the interregnum, Roosevelt surrounded himself with intelligent and innovative advisers. Some, such as James A. Farley, a former New York State boxing commissioner with a genius for remembering names, and Louis Howe, Roosevelt's secretary and confidant since 1912, had helped plan his successful campaign. His cabinet was made up of a mixture of people from different backgrounds who often did not agree with one another. Harold Ickes, the secretary of the interior, was a Republican lawyer from Chicago and a one-time supporter of Theodore Roosevelt. Another Republican, Henry Wallace of Iowa, a plant geneticist and agricultural statistician, became the secretary of agriculture. Frances Perkins, the first woman ever appointed to a cabinet post, became the secretary of labor. A disciple of Jane Addams and Florence Kelley, she had

AMERICAN VOICES

Mrs. Ivan G. Martin, "What Is to Become of Us?" An Oregon Woman Writes to Eleanor and Franklin Roosevelt

President Roosevelt, and especially his wife Eleanor, received hundreds of thousands of letters from ordinary citizens asking for help or explaining their troubles. The first lady finally had to hire several people to answer the letters. But in the end, there was little she could do.

July 15, 1939
Dear Sir and Madam,

Hardly expect this to reach you personally but I simply have to write to someone about the hopelessness of our trying to earn an honest living.

We are a family of four, one boy to enter high school this fall, the other boy in junior high. We've been married sixteen years, happily in spite of the terrific struggle trying to make both ends meet.

Our problem is the same as hundreds, more likely thousands of others. We started out with doctor and hospital bills the first few years of our married life and are still trying to pay them off. We make a fair living wage but can't live even comfortably on it as most of it goes to pay these old bills, all drawing interest now. We have tried to get on a cash basis but then the creditors press us. No matter how we try the future hasn't a sign of a rose tint. Is there a solution?

The whole family needs dental and eye care but how can it be managed? Husband's insurance even had to be dropped and his work is far from safe, but what else to do? We don't ask for charity or relief, but just help to get on our feet and free of debt.

Isn't there aid of some sort for the honest people, trying to get along? How can people be happy, contented and good Americans when every cent is needed for old accounts? I personally know dozens of families struggling just as we are. What is to become of us? We can't save for a rainy day because every cent is needed for bills.... I wonder if it's worth the struggle. Can you yourselves realize the fight we're making to live decently and honestly? In this glorious land of plenty of ours how can a common person get a start when he's burdened with old doctor bills and other small accounts . . . ?

Very Sincerely,
Mrs. Ivan G. Martin
Foster, Oregon

- *If you were Mrs. Roosevelt's secretary, how would you answer this letter?*

- *What does it reveal about the lot of the working poor at the end of the 1930s?*

---

been a settlement resident, secretary of the New York Consumers League, and an adviser to Al Smith.

In addition to the formal cabinet, Roosevelt appointed an informal "Brain Trust," including Adolph Berle, Jr., a young expert on corporation law, and Rexford Tugwell, a Columbia University authority on agricultural economics and a committed national planner. Roosevelt also appointed Raymond Moley, another Columbia professor, who later became one of the president's severest critics, and Harry Hopkins, a nervous, energetic man who loved to bet on horse races and had left Iowa to be a social worker in New York. Hopkins's passionate concern for the poor and unemployed would play a large role in the formulation of New Deal policy.

Eleanor Roosevelt, the president's wife, was a controversial first lady. She wrote a newspaper column and made a great many speeches and radio broadcasts. She traveled widely and was constantly listening to the concerns of women, minorities, and ordinary Americans. Attacked by critics who thought she had too much power and mocked for her protruding front teeth, her awkward ways, and her upper-class accent, she courageously took stands on issues of social justice and civil rights. She helped push the president toward social reform.

Roosevelt proved to be an adept politician. He was not well read, especially on economic matters, but he had the ability to learn from his advisers and yet not be dominated by them. He took ideas, plans, and suggestions from conflicting sources and combined them. He had a "flypaper mind," one of his advisers

IMAGE

Eleanor Roosevelt Visiting WPA Nursery

decided. There was no overall plan, no master strategy. An improviser and a pragmatist who once likened himself to a football quarterback who called one play and if it did not work called a different one, Roosevelt was an optimist by nature. And he believed in action.

ONE HUNDRED DAYS

Because Roosevelt took office in the middle of a major crisis, a cooperative Congress was willing to pass almost any legislation that he put before it. Not since Woodrow Wilson's first term had a president orchestrated Congress so effectively. In three months, numerous bills were rushed through. Some of them were hastily drafted and not well thought out, and some contradicted other legislation. But many of the laws passed during Roosevelt's first 100 days would have far-reaching implications for the relationship of government to society. Roosevelt was an opportunist, but unlike Hoover, he was willing to use direct government action to solve the problems of depression and unemployment. As it turned out, none of the bills passed during the first 100 days cured the Depression, but taken together, the legislation constituted one of the most innovative periods in American political history.

The Banking Crisis

The most immediate problem Roosevelt faced was the condition of the banks. Many had closed, and American citizens, no longer trusting the financial institutions, were hoarding money and putting their assets into gold. Roosevelt immediately declared a four-day bank holiday. Three days later, an emergency session of Congress approved his action and within hours gave the president broad powers over financial transactions, prohibited the hoarding of gold, and allowed for the reopening of sound banks, sometimes with loans from the Reconstruction Finance Corporation.

Within the next few years, Congress passed additional legislation that gave the federal government more regulatory power over the stock market and over the process by which corporations issued stock. It also passed the Banking Act of 1933, which strengthened the Federal Reserve System, established the Federal Deposit Insurance Corporation (FDIC), and insured individual deposits up to $5,000. Although the American Bankers Association opposed the plan as "unsound, unscientific, unjust and dangerous," banks were soon attracting depositors by advertising that they were protected by government insurance.

The American Dream Margaret Bourke-White, one of the outstanding documentary photographers of the 1930s, captured the disjunction between the ideal and the real in the Depression era. This photograph, depicting African American flood victims lining up for food in Louisville, Kentucky, underneath a propaganda billboard erected by the National Association of Manufacturers, contrasts the American Dream with the reality of racism and poverty. Does this famous photograph depict the contrast in American life unfairly? (*Margaret Bourke-White, The Louisville Flood, 1937. Photograph Copyright © 1966: Whitney Museum of American Art, New York, Gift of Sean Callahan [92.58]*)

The Democratic platform in 1932 called for reduced government spending and an end to Prohibition. Roosevelt moved quickly on both. The Economy Act, which passed Congress easily, called for a 15 percent reduction in government salaries as well as a reorganization of federal agencies to save money. The bill also cut veterans' pensions, despite their protests. However, the Economy Act's small savings were dwarfed by other bills passed the same week, which called for increased spending. The Beer-Wine Revenue Act legalized beer that had an alcohol content of 3.2 percent and light wines and levied a tax on both. The Twenty-First Amendment, ratified on December 5, 1933, repealed the Eighteenth Amendment and ended the Prohibition experiment. The veterans and the antiliquor forces, two of the strongest lobbying groups in the nation, were both overwhelmed by a Congress that seemed ready to give the president free rein.

Congress granted Roosevelt great power to devalue the dollar and to manipulate inflation. Some members argued for the old Populist solution of free and unlimited coinage of silver, while others called for issuing billions of dollars in paper currency. Bankers and businessmen feared inflation, but farmers and debtors favored an inflationary policy as a way to raise prices and put more money in their pockets. "I have always favored sound money," Roosevelt announced, "and I do now, but it is 'too darned sound' when it takes so much of farm products to buy a dollar." He rejected the more extreme inflationary plans supported by many congressmen from the agricultural states, but he did take the country off the gold standard. No longer would paper currency be redeemable in gold. The action terrified some conservative businessmen, who argued that it would lead to "uncontrolled inflation and complete chaos." Even Roosevelt's director of the budget announced solemnly that going off the gold standard "meant the end of Western Civilization."

Devaluation did not end Western civilization, but neither did it lead to instant recovery. After experimenting with pushing the price of gold up by buying it in the open market, Roosevelt and his advisers fixed the price at $35 an ounce in January 1934 (against the old price of $20.63). This inflated the dollar by about 40 percent. Roosevelt also tried briefly to induce inflation through the purchase of silver, but soon the country settled down to a slightly inflated currency and a dollar based on both gold and silver.

Relief Measures

Roosevelt believed in economy in government and in a balanced budget, but he also wanted to help the unemployed and the homeless. One survey estimated in 1933 that 1.5 million Americans were homeless. One man with a wife and six children from Latrobe, Pennsylvania, who was being evicted wrote, "I have 10 days to get another house, no job, no means of paying rent, can you advise me as to which would be the most humane way to dispose of myself and family, as this is about the only thing that I see left to do."

Roosevelt's answer was the Federal Emergency Relief Administration (FERA), which Congress authorized with an appropriation of $500 million in direct grants to cities and states. A few months later, Roosevelt created a Civil Works Administration (CWA) to put more than 4 million people to work on various state, municipal, and federal projects. Hopkins, who ran both agencies, had experimented with work relief programs in New York. Like most social workers, he believed it was much better to pay people to work than to give them charity. An accountant working on a road project said, "I'd rather stay out here in that ditch the rest of my life than take one cent of direct relief."

The CWA was not always effective, but in just over a year, the agency built or restored half a million miles of roads and constructed 40,000 schools and 1,000 airports. It hired 50,000 teachers to keep rural schools open and others to teach adult education courses in the cities. It also put more than a billion dollars of purchasing power into the economy. Roosevelt, who later would be accused of deficit spending, feared that the program was costing too much and might create a permanent class of relief recipients. In the spring of 1934, he ordered the CWA closed down.

The Public Works Administration (PWA), directed by Harold Ickes, in some respects overlapped the work of the CWA, but it lasted longer. Between 1933 and 1939, the PWA built hospitals, courthouses, and school buildings. It helped construct structures as diverse as the port of Brownsville, Texas, a bridge that linked Key West to the Florida mainland, and the library at the University of New Mexico. It built the aircraft carriers *Yorktown* and *Enterprise*, planes for the Army Air Corps, and low-cost housing for slum dwellers.

IMAGE

"PWA in Action" Poster

One purpose of the PWA was economic pump priming—the stimulation of the economy and consumer spending through the investment of government funds. Afraid that there might be scandals in the agency, Ickes spent money slowly and carefully. Thus, during the first years, PWA projects, worthwhile as most of them were, did little to stimulate the economy.

Agricultural Adjustment Act

In 1933, most farmers were desperate, as mounting surpluses and falling prices drastically cut their incomes. Some in the Midwest talked of open rebellion, even of revolution. But most observers saw only hopelessness and despair in farmers who had worked hard but were still losing their farms.

Congress passed a number of bills in 1933 and 1934 to deal with the agricultural crisis. But the New Deal's principal solution to the farm problem was

DOCUMENT

Henry A. Wallace Explains the Farm Act (1933)

the Agricultural Adjustment Act (AAA), which sought to control the overproduction of basic commodities so that farmers might regain the purchasing power they had enjoyed before World War I. To guarantee these "parity prices" (the average prices in the years 1909–1914), the production of major agricultural staples— wheat, cotton, corn, hogs, rice, tobacco, and milk—would be controlled by paying the farmers to reduce their acreage under cultivation. The AAA levied a tax at the processing stage to pay for the program.

The act aroused great disagreement among farm leaders and economists, but the controversy was nothing compared with the outcry from the public over the initial action of the AAA in the summer of 1933. To prevent a glut on the cotton and pork markets, the agency ordered 10 million acres of cotton plowed up and 6 million young pigs slaughtered. It seemed unnatural, even immoral, to kill pigs and plow up cotton when millions of people were underfed and in need of clothes. The story circulated that in the South, mules trained for many years to walk between the rows of cotton now refused to walk on the cotton plants. Some suggested that those mules were more intelligent than the government bureaucrats who had ordered the action.

The Agricultural Adjustment Act did raise the prices of some agricultural products. But it helped the larger farmers more than the small operators, and it was often disastrous for the tenant farmers and sharecroppers. Landowners often discharged tenant families when they reduced the acres under cultivation. Many sharecroppers were simply cast out on the road with a few possessions and nowhere to go. Large farmers cultivated their fewer acres more intensely, so that the total crop was little reduced. In the end, the prolonged drought that hit the Southwest in 1934 did more than the AAA to limit production and raise agricultural prices. But the long-range significance of the AAA, which was later declared unconstitutional,

was the establishment of the idea that the government should subsidize farmers for limiting production.

Industrial Recovery

The legislation during the first days of the Roosevelt administration contained something for almost every group. The National Industrial Recovery Act (NIRA) was designed to help business, raise prices, control production, and put people back to work. The act established the National Recovery Administration (NRA), with the power to set fair competition codes in all industries. For a time, everyone forgot about antitrust laws and talked of cooperation and planning rather than competition. There were parades and rallies, even a postage stamp, and industries that cooperated could display a blue eagle, the symbol of the NRA, designed to symbolize patriotic cooperation. "We Do Our Part," the posters and banners proclaimed, but the results were somewhat less than the promise.

Section 7a of the NIRA, included at the insistence of organized labor, guaranteed labor's right to organize and to bargain collectively and established the National Labor Board to see that their rights were respected. But the board, usually dominated by businesspeople, often interpreted the labor provisions of the contracts loosely. In addition, small-business

CCC in Action The Civilian Conservation Corps was one of the most popular of all the New Deal programs. The CCC put unemployed men (and a few women) to work restoring forests and building recreation facilities. Could we use a CCC today? *(Courtesy Franklin D. Roosevelt Library, [7420(273)])*

owners complained that the NIRA was unfair to their interests. Any attempt to set prices led to controversy.

Many consumers suspected that the codes and contracts were raising prices, while others feared the return of monopoly in some industries. One woman wrote the president that she was taking down her blue eagle because she had lost her job; another wrote from Tennessee to denounce the NIRA as a joke because it helped only the chain stores. The booster campaign for New Deal legislation backfired in the end because anyone with a complaint about a New Deal agency seemed to take it out on the NRA symbol of the blue eagle. When the Supreme Court declared the NIRA unconstitutional in 1935, few people complained. Still, the NIRA was an ambitious attempt to bring some order into a confused business situation, and the labor provisions of the act were picked up later by the National Labor Relations Act.

Civilian Conservation Corps

One of the most popular and successful of the New Deal programs, the Civilian Conservation Corps (CCC), combined work relief with the preservation of natural resources. It put young unemployed white men, such as Robert Symmonds, between ages 17 and 25 to work on reforestation, road and park construction, flood control, and other projects. There were a few carefully segregated black units. The men lived in work camps (more than 1,500 camps in all) and earned $30 a month, $25 of which had to be sent home to their families. Some complained that the CCC camps, run by the U.S. army, were too military, and one woman wrote from Minnesota to point out that all the best young men were at CCC camps when they ought to be home looking for real jobs and finding brides. Others complained that the CCC did nothing for unemployed young women, so a few special camps were organized for them, but only 8,000 women took part in a program that by 1941 had nearly 3 million participants. Overall, the CCC was one of the most successful and least controversial of all the New Deal programs.

Tennessee Valley Authority

Franklin Roosevelt, like his distant Republican relative Theodore, believed in conservation. He promoted flood-control projects and added millions of acres to the country's national forests, wildlife refuges, and fish and game sanctuaries. But the most important New Deal conservation project, the Tennessee Valley Authority (TVA), owed more to

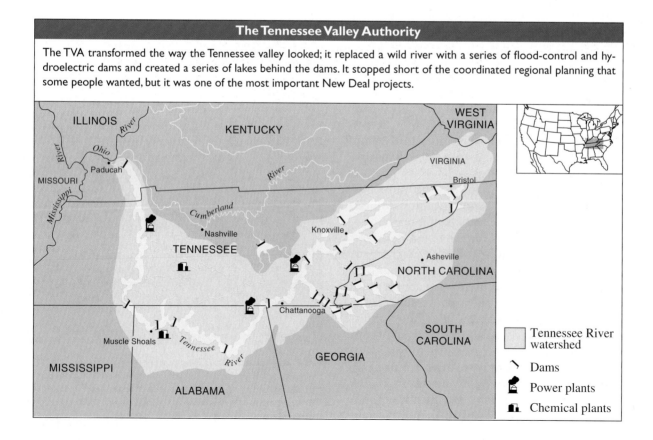

The Tennessee Valley Authority

The TVA transformed the way the Tennessee valley looked; it replaced a wild river with a series of flood-control and hydroelectric dams and created a series of lakes behind the dams. It stopped short of the coordinated regional planning that some people wanted, but it was one of the most important New Deal projects.

Republican George Norris, a progressive senator from Nebraska, than to Roosevelt.

During World War I, the federal government had built a hydroelectric plant and two munitions factories at Muscle Shoals, on the Tennessee River in Alabama. The government tried unsuccessfully to sell these facilities to private industry, but all through the 1920s, Norris campaigned to have the federal government operate them for the benefit of the valley's residents. Twice Republican presidents vetoed bills that would have allowed federal operation, but Roosevelt endorsed Norris's idea and expanded it into a regional development plan.

Congress authorized the TVA as an independent public corporation with the power to sell electricity and fertilizer and to promote flood control and land reclamation. The TVA built nine major dams and many minor ones between 1933 and 1944, affecting parts of Virginia, North Carolina, Georgia, Alabama, Mississippi, Tennessee, and Kentucky. Some private utility companies claimed that the TVA offered unfair competition to private industry, but it was an imaginative experiment in regional planning. It promoted everything from flood control to library bookmobiles. For residents of the valley, it meant cheaper electricity and changed lifestyles. The TVA meant radios, electric irons, washing machines, and other appliances for the first time. The largest federal construction project ever launched, it also created jobs for many thousands who helped build the dams. But government officials and businessmen who feared that the experiment would lead to socialism curbed the regional planning possibilities of the TVA.

The Tennessee Valley Authority

Critics of the New Deal

The furious legislative activity during the first 100 days of the New Deal helped alleviate the pessimism and despair hanging over the country. Stock market prices rose slightly, and industrial production was up 11 percent at the end of 1933. Still, the country remained locked in depression, and nearly 12 million Americans were without jobs. Yet Roosevelt captured the imagination of ordinary Americans everywhere. But conservatives were not so sure that Roosevelt was a savior; in fact, many businesspeople, after being impressed with Roosevelt's early economy measures and approving programs such as the NIRA, began to fear that the president was leading the country toward socialism. Appalled by work relief programs, regional planning such as the TVA, and the abandonment of the gold standard, many businesspeople were also annoyed by the

style of the president, whom they called "that man in the White House."

The conservative revolt against Roosevelt surfaced in the summer of 1934 as the congressional elections approached. A group of disgruntled politicians and businesspeople formed the Liberty League. The league supported conservative or at least anti–New Deal candidates for Congress, but it had little influence. In the election of 1934, the Democrats increased their majority from 310 to 319 in the House and from 60 to 69 in the Senate (only the second time in the twentieth century that the party in power had increased its control of Congress in the midterm election). A few people were learning to hate Roosevelt, but it was obvious that most Americans approved of what he was doing.

While some thought the New Deal was too radical, others maintained that the government had not done enough to help the poor. One source of criticism was the Communist party. Attracting supporters from all walks of life during a time when capitalism seemed to have failed, the Communist party increased its membership from 7,500 in 1930 to 75,000 in 1938. The Communists organized protest marches and tried to reach out to the oppressed and unemployed. While a majority who joined the party came from the working class, communism had a special appeal to writers, intellectuals, and some

The Radio Priest Father Charles E. Coughlin from Royal Oak, Michigan, was a flamboyant Catholic priest who was just as much the master of the radio as the president himself. At first he supported Roosevelt, but in 1935 he became one of FDR's most caustic critics. His impassioned anti-Semitic remarks finally caused the Catholic church to take him off the air. In what other ways was the radio important in the 1920s? *(Library of Congress [LC-USZ6-2-111027])*

college students during a decade when the American dream had turned into a nightmare.

A larger number of Americans, however, were influenced by other movements promising easy solutions to poverty and unemployment. In Minnesota, Governor Floyd Olson, elected on a Farm–Labor ticket, accused capitalism of causing the Depression and startled some listeners when he thundered, "I hope the present system of government goes right to hell." In California, Upton Sinclair, the muckraking socialist and author of *The Jungle,* ran for governor on the platform "End Poverty in California." He promised to pay everyone over age 60 a pension of $50 a month using higher income and inheritance taxes to finance the program. He won in the primary but lost the election, and his program collapsed.

California also produced Dr. Francis E. Townsend, who claimed he had a national following of more than 5 million people. His supporters backed the Townsend Old Age Revolving Pension Plan, which promised $200 a month to all unemployed citizens over age 60 on the condition that they spend it in the same month they received it. Economists laughed at the utopian scheme, but followers organized thousands of Townsend Pension Clubs across the country.

More threatening to Roosevelt and the New Deal were the protest movements led by Father Charles E. Coughlin and Senator Huey P. Long. Father

DOCUMENT

Father Charles E. Coughlin, "A Third Party" (1936)

Coughlin, a Roman Catholic priest from a Detroit suburb, attracted an audience of 30 million to 45 million to his national radio show. At first, he supported Roosevelt's policies, but later he savagely attacked the New Deal as excessively probusiness. Mixing religious commentary with visions of a society operating without bankers and big businessmen, he roused his audience with blatantly anti-Semitic appeals. Most often the "evil" bankers he described were Jewish—the Rothschilds, Warburgs, and Kuhn-Loebs. Anti-Semitism reached a peak in the 1930s, so Jews bore the brunt of nativist fury.

Huey Long, like Coughlin, had a charisma that won support from the millions still trying to survive

DOCUMENT

Huey Long, "Share Our Wealth" (1935)

in a country where the continuing depression made day-to-day existence a struggle. Elected governor of Louisiana in 1928, Long promoted a "Share the Wealth" program. He taxed the oil refineries and built hospitals, schools, and thousands of miles of new highways. By 1934, he was the virtual dictator of his state, personally controlling the police and the courts. Long talked about a guaranteed $2,000 to

$3,000 income for all American families (18.3 million families earned less than $1,000 per year in 1936) and promised pensions for the elderly and college educations for the young. He would pay for these programs by taxing the rich and liquidating the great fortunes. Had not an assassin's bullet cut Long down in September 1935, he might have mounted a third-party challenge to Roosevelt.

THE SECOND NEW DEAL

Responding in part to the discontent of the lower middle class but also to the threat of various utopian schemes, Roosevelt moved his programs in 1935 toward the goals of social reform and social justice. At the same time, he departed from attempts to cooperate with the business community. "We find our population suffering from old inequalities," Roosevelt announced in his annual message to Congress in January 1935. "In spite of our efforts and in spite of our talk, we have not weeded out the overprivileged and we have not effectively lifted up the underprivileged."

Work Relief and Social Security

The Works Progress Administration (WPA), authorized by Congress in April 1935, was the first massive attempt to deal with unemployment and its demoralizing effect on millions of Americans. The WPA employed about 3 million people a year on a variety of socially useful projects. The WPA workers, who earned wages lower than private industry paid, built bridges, airports, libraries, roads, and golf courses. Nearly 85 percent of the funds went directly into salaries and wages.

A minor but important part of the WPA funding supported writers, artists, actors, and musicians. Richard Wright, Jack Conroy, and Saul Bellow were among the 10,000 writers who were paid less than $100 a month. Experimental theater, innovative and well-written guides to all the states, murals painted in municipal and state buildings, and the Historical Records Survey were among the long-lasting results of these projects.

IMAGE

WPA's Federal Art Project

Only one member of a family could qualify for a WPA job, and first choice always went to the man. A woman could qualify only if she headed the household. But eventually more than 13 percent of the people who worked for the WPA were women, although their most common employment was in the sewing room, where old clothes were made over. "For unskilled men we have the shovel. For unskilled

WPA Workers The WPA (which some wags said stood for "We Putter Around") employed many people for a great variety of jobs. This is an unusual photograph because it is in color. A few photographers who worked for government agencies were beginning to experiment with color film, but most of the photographs that survive from the 1930s are black and white. Does the government have a responsibility to create jobs for the unemployed during a depression? *(Bettmann-CORBIS)*

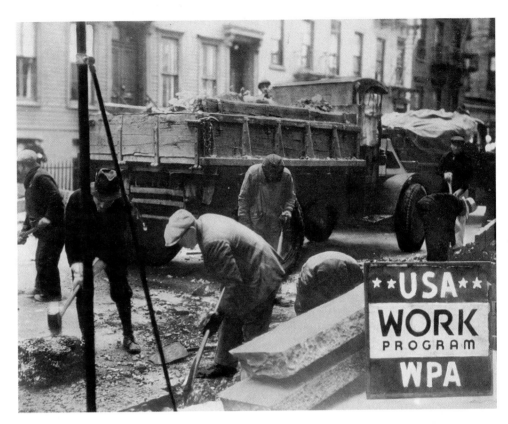

women we have only the needle," one official remarked.

The WPA was controversial from the beginning. Critics charged that the agency had hired Communists to paint murals or work on the state guides. For others, a "lazy good-for-nothing" leaning on a shovel symbolized the WPA. The initials WPA, some wags charged, stood for "We Pay for All" or "We Putter Around." Yet for all the criticism, the WPA did useful work; the program built nearly 6,000 schools, more than 2,500 hospitals, and 13,000 playgrounds. More important, it restored the morale of millions of unemployed Americans.

The National Youth Administration (NYA) supplemented the work of the WPA and assisted young men and women between ages 16 and 25, many of them students. A young law student named Richard Nixon earned 35 cents an hour working for the NYA while he was at Duke University, and Lyndon Johnson began his political career as director of the Texas NYA.

VIDEO

President Roosevelt Focuses on America's Youth

By far the most enduring reform came with the passage of the Social Security Act of 1935. Since the progressive period, social workers and reformers had argued for a national system of health insurance, old-age pensions, and unemployment insurance. By the 1930s,

the United States remained the only major industrial country without such programs. Within the Roosevelt circle, Frances Perkins argued most strongly for social insurance, but the popularity of the Townsend Plan and other schemes to aid the elderly helped convince Roosevelt of the need to act. The number of people over age 65 in the country increased from 5.7 million in 1925 to 7.8 million in 1935, and that group demanded action.

DOCUMENT

Frances Perkins and the Social Security Act (1935, 1960)

The Social Security Act of 1935 was a compromise. Congress quickly dropped a plan for federal health insurance because of opposition from the medical profession. The most important provision of the act was old-age and survivor insurance to be paid for by a tax of 1 percent on both employers and employees. The benefits initially ranged from $10 to $85 a month. The act also established a cooperative federal–state system of unemployment compensation. Other provisions authorized federal grants to the states to help care for the disabled and the blind. Finally, the Social Security Act provided some aid to dependent children. This provision would eventually expand to become the largest federal welfare program.

The National Association of Manufacturers denounced social security as a program that would regiment the people and destroy individual self-reliance.

Social Security
Act Poster

Yet in no other country was social insurance paid for in part by a regressive tax on workers' wages. "We put those payroll contributions there so as to give the contributors a legal, moral, and political right to collect their pensions and unemployment benefits," Roosevelt later explained. "With those taxes in there, no damn politician can ever scrap my social security program." It was never intended as a traditional pension program, but rather as a social contract whereby one generation helped to pay for the previous generation's retirement. But the law also excluded many people, including those who needed it the most, such as farm laborers and domestic servants. It discriminated against married women who were wage earners, and it failed to protect against sickness. Yet for all its weaknesses, it was one of the most important New Deal measures. A landmark in American social legislation, it marked the beginning of the welfare state that would expand significantly after World War II.

Aiding the Farmers

The Social Security Act and the Works Progress Administration were only two signs of Roosevelt's greater concern for social reform. The flurry of legislation in 1935 and early 1936, often called the "second New Deal," also included an effort to help American farmers. More than 1.7 million farm families had annual incomes of less than $500 in 1935, and 42 percent of all those who lived on farms were tenants. The Resettlement Administration (RA), motivated in part by a Jeffersonian ideal of yeoman farmers working their own land, set out to relocate tenant farmers on land purchased by the government. Lack of funds and fears that the Roosevelt administration was trying to establish Soviet-style collective farms limited the effectiveness of the RA program.

Much more important in improving the lives of farm families was the Rural Electrification Administration (REA), which was authorized in 1935 to lend money to cooperatives to generate and distribute electricity in isolated rural areas not served by private utilities. Only 10 percent of the nation's farms had electricity in 1936. When the REA's lines were finally attached, they dramatically changed the lives of millions of farm families who had been able only to dream about the radios, washing machines, and farm equipment advertised in magazines.

In the hill country west of Austin, Texas, for example, there was no electricity until the end of the 1930s. Houses were illuminated by kerosene lamps, whose wicks had to be trimmed just right or the lamp smoked or went out, but even with perfect adjustment, it was

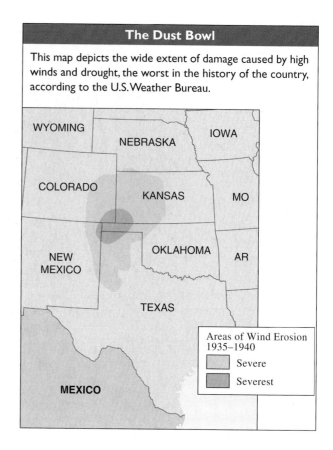

The Dust Bowl

This map depicts the wide extent of damage caused by high winds and drought, the worst in the history of the country, according to the U.S. Weather Bureau.

Areas of Wind Erosion
1935–1940
Severe
Severest

difficult to read by them. There were no bathrooms, because bathrooms required running water, and running water depended on an electric pump.

Women and children hauled water constantly—for infrequent baths, for continuous canning (because without a refrigerator, fruits and vegetables had to be put up almost immediately or they spoiled), and for wash day. Wash day, always Monday, meant scrubbing clothes by hand with harsh soap on a washboard; it meant boiling clothes in a large copper vat over a woodstove and stirring them with a wooden fork. It was a hot, backbreaking job, especially in summer.

It was memory of life in the hill country and personal knowledge of how hard his mother and grandmother toiled that inspired a young congressman from Texas, Lyndon Johnson, to work to bring rural electrification to the area. In November 1939, the lights finally came on in the hill country, plugging the area into the twentieth century.

The Dust Bowl: An Ecological Disaster

Those who tried to farm on the Great Plains fell victim to years of drought and dust storms. Record heat waves and below-average rainfall in the 1930s turned an area from the Oklahoma panhandle to western Kansas into a giant dust bowl. A single storm on May

Dust Bowl Family Thousands of families fled the dust bowl in old cars and headed for California. With no place to sleep, they used sheets and blankets to turn their cars into tents. John Steinbeck wrote about these migrants in *The Grapes of Wrath*. Do the dust bowl migrants represent a failure of the American dream? *(Courtesy Franklin D. Roosevelt Library [53227(575)])*

11, 1934, removed 300 million tons of topsoil and turned day into night. Between 1932 and 1939, there was an average of 50 storms a year. Cities kept their streetlights on for 24 hours a day. Dust covered everything from food to bedspreads and piled up in dunes in city streets and barnyards. Thousands died of "dust pneumonia." One woman remembered what it was like at night: "A trip for water to rinse the grit from our lips, and then back to bed with washcloths over our noses, we try to lie still, because every turn stirs the dust on the blankets." By the end of the decade, 10,000 farm homes were abandoned to the elements, and 9 million acres of farmland were reduced to a wasteland. By the end of the decade, 3.5 million people had abandoned their farms and joined a massive migration to find better lives.

More than 350,000 left Oklahoma during the decade and moved to California, a place that seemed to many like the promised land. But the name *Okie* came to mean any farm migrant. The plight of these wayfarers was immortalized by John Steinbeck in his novel about the Joad family, *The Grapes of Wrath* (1939). The next year, John Ford made a powerful movie based on the book, starring Henry Fonda as Tom Joad. Many Americans sympathized with the plight of the embattled farm family trying to escape the dust bowl and find a better life in California; others interpreted their defeat as a symbol of the failure of the American dream.

IMAGE
Family in a Dust Storm

The dust bowl was a natural disaster, but it was aided and exaggerated by human actions and inactions. The semiarid plains west of the ninety-eighth meridian were not suitable for intensive agriculture. Overgrazing, too much plowing, and indiscriminate planting over a period of 60 years exposed the thin soil to the elements. When the winds came in the 1930s, much of the land simply blew away. In the end, it was a matter of too little government planning and regulation and too many farmers using new technology to exploit natural resources for their own gain.

The Roosevelt administration did try to deal with the problem. The Taylor Grazing Act of 1934 restricted the use of the public range in an attempt to prevent overgrazing, and it ended an era of unregulated use of natural resources in the West. Before 1934, anyone could use public land, but the 1934 act required a permit and a fee. The Taylor Act established the principle that the remaining public domain was under federal control and not for sale. The Civilian Conservation Corps and other New Deal agencies planted trees, and the Soil Conservation Service promoted drought-resistant crops and contour plowing, but it was too little and too late. Even worse, according to some authorities, government measures applied after the disaster of 1930 encouraged farmers to return to raising wheat and other inappropriate crops, leading to more dust bowl crises in the 1950s and 1970s.

DOCUMENT

FDR Fireside Chat, September 6, 1936

The New Deal and the West

The New Deal probably aided the West more than any other region. The CCC, AAA, drought relief measures,

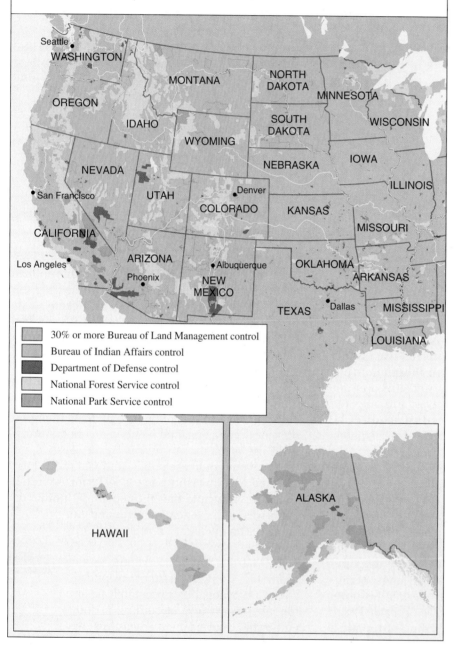

Taylor Grazing Act, 1934

The Taylor Grazing Act of 1934 marked the end of an era when the federal government transferred public land to private ownership. The federal ownership or control of vast amounts of land in the West set up a conflict between rugged individualism and government planning and management. Should the government own or control this amount of land?

	30% or more Bureau of Land Management control
	Bureau of Indian Affairs control
	Department of Defense control
	National Forest Service control
	National Park Service control

and various federal agencies helped the region to an extent that was out of proportion to the people who lived there. In fact, the top 14 states in per capita expenditure by federal agencies during the 1930s were all in the West. Most important were the large-scale water projects. The Boulder Dam (later renamed the Hoover Dam) on the Colorado River not only provided massive amounts of hydroelectric power but, with the construction of a 259-mile aqueduct, also provided the water that caused the city of Los Angeles to boom.

The largest power project of all was the Grand Coulee Dam on the Columbia River northwest of Spokane, Washington. Employing tens of thousands of men and pouring millions of dollars into the economy, the dam, finally completed in 1941, provided cheap electricity for the Pacific Northwest and eventually irrigated more than a million acres of arid land.

Despite all the federal aid to the region, many westerners, holding fast to the myth of frontier individualism, bitterly criticized the regulation and the bureaucracy that went with the grants. Cattlemen in Wyoming, Colorado, and Montana desperately needed the help of the federal government, but even as they accepted the aid, they denounced Roosevelt and the New Deal.

Controlling Corporate Power and Taxing the Wealthy

In the summer of 1935, Roosevelt set out to control the large corporations, and he even toyed with radical plans to tax the well-to-do heavily and redistribute wealth in the United States. The Public Utility Holding Company Act, passed in 1935, attempted to restrict the power of the giant utility companies, the 12 largest of which controlled more than half the country's power. The act gave various government commissions the authority to regulate and control the power companies and included a "death sentence"

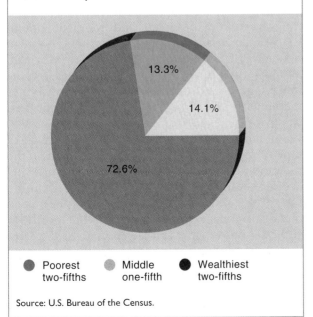

Distribution of Income, 1935–1936

Roosevelt and the New Deal never sought consistently to redistribute wealth in America, and a great disparity in income and assets remained. Why didn't Roosevelt and his advisors try to redistribute wealth?

13.3%

14.1%

72.6%

● Poorest two-fifths ● Middle one-fifth ● Wealthiest two-fifths

Source: U.S. Bureau of the Census.

clause that gave each company five years to demonstrate that its services were efficient. If it could not demonstrate this, the government could dissolve the company. This was one of the most radical attempts to control corporate power in American history.

In his message to Congress in 1935, Roosevelt also pointed out that the federal revenue laws had "done little to prevent an unjust concentration of wealth and economic power." He suggested steeper income taxes for wealthy groups and a much larger inheritance tax. When Congress dropped the inheritance tax provision, however, Roosevelt did not fight to have it restored. Even the weakened bill, increasing estate and gift taxes and raising the income tax rates at the top, angered many in the business community who thought that Roosevelt had sold out to Huey Long's "Share the Wealth" scheme.

The New Deal for Labor

Like many progressive reformers, Roosevelt was more interested in improving the lot of working people by passing social legislation than by strengthening the bargaining position of organized labor. Yet he saw labor as an important balance to the power of industry, and he listened to his advisers, especially Frances Perkins and Senator Robert Wagner of New York, who persistently brought up the needs of organized labor.

Roosevelt supported the National Labor Relations Act. Passed in 1935, it outlawed blacklisting and a number of other practices and reasserted labor's right to organize and to bargain collectively. The act also established a Labor Relations Board with the power to certify a properly elected bargaining unit. The act did not require workers to join unions, but it made the federal government a regulator, or at least a neutral force, in management–labor relations. That alone made the National Labor Relations Act one of the most important New Deal reform measures.

The Roosevelt administration's friendly attitude toward organized labor helped increase union membership from less than 3 million in 1933 to 4.5 million by 1935. Many groups, however, were left out, including farm laborers, unskilled workers, and women. Only about 3 percent of working women belonged to unions, and women earned only about 60 percent of wages paid to men for equivalent work. Still, many people resented that women were employed at all. The Brotherhood of Railway and Steamship Clerks ruled that no married woman whose husband could support her was eligible for a job.

The American Federation of Labor (AFL) had little interest in organizing unskilled workers, but a new group of committed and militant labor leaders emerged in the 1930s to take up that task. John L. Lewis, the eloquent head of the United Mine Workers, was the most aggressive. He was joined by David Dubinsky of the International Ladies' Garment Workers, and Sidney Hillman, president of the Amalgamated Clothing Workers. Dubinsky and Hillman were socialists who believed in economic planning, but both had worked closely with social justice progressives. These new progressive labor leaders formed the Committee of Industrial Organization (CIO) within the AFL and set out to organize workers in the steel, auto, and rubber industries. Rather than separating workers by skill or craft as the AFL preferred, they organized everyone into an industry-wide union much as the Knights of Labor had done in the 1880s. They also used new and aggressive tactics.

In 1936, the workers at three rubber plants in Akron, Ohio, went on unauthorized strikes. Instead of picketing outside the factory, they occupied the buildings and took them over, preventing the owners from running the factory with non-union workers. The "sit-down strike" became a new protest technique. Sometimes the workers occupied a factory for a week or more. After sit-down strikes against General Motors plants in Atlanta, Georgia, and Flint, Michigan, General Motors finally accepted the United Auto Workers (UAW) as their employees' bargaining agent. The General Motors strike was the most important event in a critical period of labor upheaval. Labor's voice now began to be heard in the decision-making process in major industries in which labor had long been denied any role. The strikes at General Motors also helped raise the status of organized labor in the eyes of many Americans.

Violence spread along with the sit-down strike. Chrysler capitulated, but the Ford Motor Company used hired gunmen to discourage the strikers. A bloody struggle ensued before Ford agreed to accept the UAW as the bargaining agent. Even U.S. Steel, which had been militantly anti-union, signed an agreement with the Steel Workers Organizing Committee calling for a 40-hour workweek and an eight-hour workday. But other steel companies refused to go along. In Chicago on Memorial Day in 1937, a confrontation between the police and peaceful picketers at the Republic Steel plant resulted in 10 deaths. In the "Memorial Day Massacre," as it came to be called, the police fired without provocation into a crowd of workers and their families, who had gathered near the plant in a holiday mood. All 10 of the dead were shot in the back.

The CIO's aggressive tactics gained many new members, to the horror of AFL leaders. They expelled the CIO leaders from the AFL, only to see

them form a separate Congress of Industrial Organization (the initials stayed the same). By accepting unskilled workers, African Americans, and others who had never belonged to a union before, the CIO infused the labor movement with a new spirit.

America's Minorities in the 1930s

Half a million African Americans joined unions through the CIO during the 1930s, and many blacks were aided by various New Deal agencies. Yet the familiar pattern of discrimination, low-paying jobs, and intimidation through violence persisted. Lynchings in the South actually increased in the New Deal years, rising from 8 in 1932 to 28 in 1933 and 20 in 1935.

One particular case came to symbolize and dramatize discrimination against African Americans in the 1930s. On March 25, 1931, in Scottsboro, Alabama, two young white women accused nine black men of raping them in a railroad boxcar as they all hitched a free ride. A jury of white men found all nine blacks guilty, and the court sentenced eight to die. The U.S. Supreme Court ordered new trials in 1933, on the grounds that the accused rapists had not received proper legal counsel. The case garnered much publicity in the United States and abroad. The youth of the defendants, their quick trial, and the harsh sentences made the "Scottsboro boys" a popular cause for many northern liberals and especially the Communist party.

For many southerners, however, it was a matter of defending the honor of white women. As one observer remarked of one of the accusers, she "might be a fallen woman, but by God she is a white woman." However, evidence supporting the alleged rapes was never presented, and eventually one of the women recanted. Yet the case dragged on. In new trials, five of the young men were convicted and given long prison terms. Charges against the other four were dropped in 1937. Four of the remaining five were paroled by 1946, and the fifth escaped to Michigan.

African Americans did not have to be accused of rape to want to flee to the North, however, and the migration of blacks to northern cities, which had accelerated during World War I, continued during the 1930s. The collapse of cotton prices forced black farmers and farm laborers to flee north for survival. But since most were poorly educated, they soon became trapped in northern ghettos, where they were eligible for only the most menial jobs. The black unemployment rate was triple that of whites, and blacks often received less per person in welfare payments.

Sharecroppers Despite the black migration North during World War I and the 1920s, more than 80 percent of African Americans lived in the South during the 1930s. Most were sharecroppers, tenant farmers who often were in debt to the landlord. They were trapped by prejudice, unable to vote, and oppressed by poverty. The New Deal policies often made their situation worse. Many were kicked off the land and became homeless drifters. Can you imagine what it was like to be a sharecropper? Why did the nation tolerate such inequality? *(Library of Congress, LC-USF34T01-9575)*

Black leaders attacked the Roosevelt administration for supporting or allowing segregation in government-sponsored facilities. The TVA model town of Norris, Tennessee, was off limits for blacks, and AAA policies actually drove blacks off the land in the South. The CCC segregated black and white workers, and the PWA financed segregated housing projects. Some charged that NRA stood for "Negroes Rarely Allowed." Blacks ought to realize, a writer in the NAACP journal *The Crisis* warned in 1935, "that the powers-that-be in the Roosevelt administration have nothing for them." Roosevelt, fearing that he might antagonize southern congressmen whose backing he needed, refused to support the two major civil rights bills of the era, an antilynching bill and a bill to abolish the poll tax. Yet Harold Ickes and Harry Hopkins worked to ensure that blacks were given opportunities in New Deal agencies. By 1941, black federal employees totaled 150,000, more than three times the number during the Hoover administration. Most worked in the lower ranks, but some were lawyers, architects, office managers, and engineers.

Partly responsible for the presence of more black employees was the "black cabinet," a group of more than 50 young blacks who had appointments in various New Deal agencies and were led by Mary McLeod Bethune, the daughter of a

Dr. William H. Hastie—"Black Cabinet" Member

sharecropper. She had founded a black primary school in Florida and then transformed it into Bethune-Cookman College. In the 1920s, she had organized the National Council of Negro Women. In 1934, Harry Hopkins, following the advice of Eleanor Roosevelt, appointed her to the advisory committee of the National Youth Administration. Bethune had some impact on New Deal policy and on the black cabinet. She spoke out forcefully, she picketed and protested, and she intervened shrewdly to obtain civil rights and more jobs for African Americans, but in the end the gains for blacks during the New Deal were very limited.

W. E. B. Du Bois, in the meantime, had become increasingly discouraged with token appointments and the reform of race relations through integration with white society. In the 1920s, he supported a series of pan-African conferences designed to unite black people from around the world. He resigned from the NAACP and from his position as editor of *The Crisis* in 1934 and devoted his time to promoting "voluntary segregation" and a "Negro Nation within a nation." Eventually, he joined the Communist party and moved to Ghana, where he died in 1963.

Although Roosevelt appointed a number of blacks to government positions, he was never particularly committed to civil rights. That was not true of Eleanor Roosevelt, who was educated in part by Mary McLeod Bethune. In 1939, when the Daughters of the American Revolution refused to allow Marian Anderson, a black concert singer, to use their stage, Mrs. Roosevelt publicly protested and resigned her membership in the DAR. She also arranged for Anderson to sing from the steps of the Lincoln Memorial, where 75,000 people gathered to listen and to support civil rights for all black citizens.

DOCUMENT

Mrs. Henry Weddington, Letter to FDR (1938)

Hundreds of thousands of Mexicans, brought to the United States to work in the 1920s, lost their jobs in the Depression. Drifting to the Southwest or settling in the urban *barrios* and the small towns and farms in the Southwest, they met signs such as "Only White Labor Employed" and "No Niggers, Mexicans, or Dogs Allowed." Some New Deal agencies helped destitute Mexicans. A few worked for the CCC and the WPA, but to be employed, an applicant had to qualify for state relief, and that eliminated most migrants. The primary solution was not to provide aid for Mexicans but to ship them back to Mexico. In Los Angeles and other cities, the police and immigration authorities rounded up aliens and held them illegally. A trainload of repatriates left Los Angeles

IMAGE

Mexican Workers and Their Cars

every month during 1933, and officials deported thousands from other cities. One estimate placed the number sent back in 1932 at 200,000, including some American citizens.

Not all the Mexicans were repatriated, however, and some who remained adopted militant tactics to obtain fair treatment. Mexican strawberry pickers went on strike in El Monte, California, and 18,000 cotton pickers walked away from their jobs in the San Joaquin valley in 1933. On August 31, 1939, during a record-breaking heat wave, nearly all of the 430 workers, most of them Mexican American women, staged a massive walkout at one of the largest food processing plants in Los Angeles. In Gallup, New Mexico, several thousand Mexican coal miners walked out on strike. They constructed a village of shacks and planned to wait out the strike. The miners, who were aided by writers and artists from Santa Fe and Taos, were evicted from their village by the city authorities. Federal agents arrested their leader, Jesus Pallares, and deported him to Mexico.

Asians (Chinese, Japanese, and a smaller number of Koreans and Asian Indians) also suffered during the Depression. Most lived in ethnic enclaves, lost their jobs, and were treated as foreigners—not quite black, but not white either. Asians, especially the second generation who were automatically citizens if they were born in the United States, were troubled by a "twoness." They were both Chinese or Japanese and American. At least their parents wanted them to retain ties to the old country and the old culture. One young Chinese student from San Francisco had to go to Chinese school after her regular school. "We never became proficient in reading or writing Chinese," she recalled, "probably because we never thought of ourselves as needing Chinese. After all, weren't we Americans?" A Japanese nisei remembered the "queer mixture of Occident and the Orient. I sat down to American breakfast and Japanese lunch. My palate developed a fondness for rice along with corned beef and cabbage. I became equally adept with knife and fork and with chopsticks. I said grace at mealtime in Japanese, and recited the Lord's prayer in English." But one Japanese father told his son to learn Japanese because there was no future for him in the United States. Most American failed to appreciate the sense of "twoness" that the Asians suffered with; indeed, they treated all Asians as aliens, and they had great difficulty distinguishing a Chinese from a Japanese from a Korean.

Native Americans also experienced alienation, disease, and despair during the Depression, and their plight was compounded by years of exploitation. Since the Dawes Act of 1887 (described in

Chapter 17), government policy had sought to make the Indian into a property-owning farmer and to limit tribal rights. Native Americans lost more than 60 percent of the 138 million acres granted them in 1887. The government declared some of the land surplus and encouraged individuals to settle on 160 acres and adopt the "habits of civilized life." Few Native Americans profited from this system, but many whites did.

Just as other progressives sought the quick assimilation of immigrants, the progressive-era Indian commissioners sped up the allotment process to increase Indian detribalization. But many Native Americans who remained on the reservations were not even citizens. Finally, in 1924, Congress granted citizenship to all Indians born in the United States. The original Americans became U.S. citizens, but that did not end their suffering.

Franklin Roosevelt brought a new spirit to Indian policy by appointing John Collier as commissioner of Indian affairs. Collier was primarily responsible for the passage of the Indian Reorganization Act of 1934, which sought to restore the political independence of the tribes and to end the allotment policy of the Dawes Act. "Even where a tribal group is split into factions, where leadership has broken down, where Indians clamor to distribute the tribal property, even there deep forces of cohesion persist and can be evoked," Collier wrote. The bill also sought to promote the "study of Indian civilization" and to "preserve and develop the special cultural contributions and achievements of such civilization, including Indian arts, crafts, skills and traditions."

IMAGE
WPA Project at Tonawanda Reservation

Not all Indians agreed with the new policies. Some chose to become members of the dominant culture, and the Navajos voted to reject the Reorganization Act. Some Americans charged that the act was inspired by communism. Others argued that its principal result would be to increase government bureaucracy, while missionaries claimed that the government was promoting paganism by allowing the Indians to practice their native religions.

The paradox and contradictions of U.S. policy toward the Indians can be illustrated by Collier's attempt to solve the Navajo problem. The Navajo lands, like most of the West, were overgrazed, and soil erosion threatened to fill the new lake behind the Hoover Dam with silt. By supporting a policy of reducing the herds of sheep and goats on Indian land and by promoting soil conservation, Collier contributed to the change in the Navajo lifestyle and to the end of their self-sufficiency, something he wanted to support.

Women and the New Deal

Women made some gains during the 1930s, and more women occupied high government positions than in any previous administration. Besides Frances Perkins, the secretary of labor, there was Molly Dewson, a social worker with the Massachusetts Girls Parole Department and the National Consumers League before becoming head of the Women's Division of the Democratic Committee and then an adviser to Roosevelt. Working closely with Eleanor Roosevelt to promote women's causes, she helped achieve a number of firsts: two women appointed ambassadors, a judge on the U.S. Court of Appeals, the director of the mint, and many women in government agencies.

Katharine Lenroot, director of the Children's Bureau, and Mary Anderson, head of the Women's Bureau, selected many other women to serve in their agencies. Some of these women had collaborated as social workers and now joined government bureaus to continue the fight for social justice. But they were usually in offices in which they did not threaten male prerogatives.

Despite some gains, the early New Deal programs did nothing for an estimated 140,000 homeless women, or the 2 million to 4 million unemployed women. Married women often were fired from their jobs on the grounds that they should be home caring for their families rather than depriving men of employment. Single, divorced, and widowed women were usually ignored. Eleanor Roosevelt was genuinely concerned over the plight of poor women. She sponsored a White House Conference in November 1933 on the Emergency Needs of Women. She also advocated including more women in the CCC, the WPA, and

IMAGE
Giving Her a Lift to Town, 1933

other programs, but in the end the New Deal did little for poor women.

THE LAST YEARS OF THE NEW DEAL

The New Deal was neither a consistent nor a well-organized effort to end the Depression and restructure society. Roosevelt was a politician and a pragmatist, unconcerned about ideological or programmatic consistency. The first New Deal of 1933–1934 concentrated on relief and recovery, while the legislation passed in 1935 and 1936 was more involved with social reform. In many ways, the election of 1936 marked the high point of Roosevelt's power and influence. After 1937, in part because of the growing threat of war but also because of increasing opposition in Congress, the pace of social legislation slowed. Yet several measures passed in 1937 and 1938 had such far-reaching significance that some historians refer to a third New Deal. Among the new measures were bills that provided for a minimum wage and for housing reform.

The Election of 1936

The Republicans in 1936 nominated a moderate, Governor Alfred Landon of Kansas. Although he attacked the New Deal, charging that new government programs were wasteful and created a dangerous federal bureaucracy, Landon only promised to do the same thing more cheaply and efficiently. Two-thirds of the newspapers in the country supported him, and the *Literary Digest* predicted his victory on the basis of a "scientific" telephone poll.

Roosevelt, helped by signs that the economy was recovering and supported by a coalition of the

FDR's Successful Presidential Campaigns, 1932–1944				
Year	**Candidate**	**Party**	**Popular Vote**	**Electoral Vote**
1932	FRANKLIN D. ROOSEVELT	Democratic	22,809,638 (57.4%)	472
	Herbert C. Hoover	Republican	15,758,901 (39.7%)	59
	Norman Thomas	Socialist	881,951 (2.2%)	0
1936	FRANKLIN D. ROOSEVELT	Democratic	27,751,612 (60.8%)	523
	Alfred M. Landon	Republican	16,681,913 (36.5%)	8
	William Lemke	Union	891,858 (1.9%)	0
1940	FRANKLIN D. ROOSEVELT	Democratic	27,243,466 (54.8%)	449
	Wendell L. Willkie	Republican	22,304,755 (44.8%)	82
1944	FRANKLIN D. ROOSEVELT	Democratic	25,602,505 (53.5%)	432
	Thomas E. Dewey	Republican	22,006,278 (46.0%)	99

Note: Winners' names appear in capital letters.

Democratic South, organized labor, farmers, and urban voters, won easily. A majority of African Americans for the first time deserted the party of

Lincoln, not because of Roosevelt's interest in civil rights for blacks but because New Deal relief programs assisted many poor blacks. A viable candidate to the left of the New Deal failed to materialize. In fact, the Socialist party candidate, Norman Thomas, polled fewer than 200,000 votes. Roosevelt won by more than 10 million votes, carrying every state except Maine and Vermont. Even the traditionally Republican states of Pennsylvania, Delaware, and Connecticut, which had voted Republican in almost every election since 1856, went for Roosevelt.

The Battle of the Supreme Court

"I see one-third of a nation ill-housed, ill-clad, ill-nourished," Roosevelt declared in his second inaugural address, and he vowed to alter that situation. But the president's first action in 1937 did not call for legislation to alleviate poverty. Instead, he announced a plan to reform the Supreme Court and the judicial system. The Court had invali-

dated not only a number of New Deal measures—including the NIRA and the first version of the AAA—but other measures as well.

Increasingly angry at the "nine old men" who seemed to be destroying New Deal initiatives and defying Congress's will, Roosevelt determined to create a more sympathetic Court. He hoped to gain power to appoint an extra justice for each justice over age 70, of whom there were six. His plan also called for modernizing the court system at all levels, but that plan got lost in the public outcry over the Court-packing scheme.

Roosevelt's plan to nullify the influence of the older and more reactionary justices foundered. Republicans accused him of being a dictator and of subverting the Constitution. Many congressmen from his own party refused to support him. Led by Vice President John Nance Garner of Texas, a number of southern Democrats broke with the president and formed a coalition with conservative Republicans that lasted for more than 30 years. After months of controversy, Roosevelt withdrew the legislation and admitted defeat. He had perhaps misunderstood his mandate, and he certainly underestimated the respect, even the reverence, that most Americans felt for the Supreme Court.

Ironically, though he lost the battle of the Supreme Court, Roosevelt won the war. By the spring of 1937,

the Court began to reverse its position and in a 5–4 decision upheld the National Labor Relations Act. When Justice Willis Van Devanter retired, Roosevelt was able to make his first Supreme Court appointment, thus ensuring at least a shaky liberal majority on the Court. After 1937 a series of court cases established the principle that Congress and federal power trumped states' rights and local control. But Roosevelt triumphed at great cost. His attempt to reorganize the Court dissipated energy and slowed the momentum of his legislative program. Seen as the most unpopular action he took as president, it made him vulnerable to criticism from opponents of the New Deal, and even some of his supporters were dismayed by what they regarded as an attack on the principle of separation of powers.

The economy improved in late 1936 and early 1937, but in August, the fragile prosperity collapsed. Unemployment shot back up, industrial production fell, and the stock market plummeted. Facing an embarrassing economic slump that evoked charges that the New Deal had failed, Roosevelt resorted to "deficit spending," as recommended by John Maynard Keynes, the British economist. Keynes argued that to get out of a depression, the government must spend massive amounts of money on goods and services to increase demand and revive production. The economy responded slowly but never fully recovered until wartime expenditures, beginning in 1940, stimulated it, reduced unemployment, and ended the Depression.

Completing the New Deal

Despite increasing hostility, Congress passed a number of important bills in 1937 and 1938 that completed the New Deal reform legislation. The Bankhead–Jones Farm Tenancy Act of 1937 created the Farm Security Administration (FSA) to aid tenant farmers, sharecroppers, and farm owners who had lost their farms. The FSA, which provided loans to grain collectives, also set up camps for migratory workers. Some people saw such policies as the first step toward Communist collectives, but the FSA in fact never had enough money to make a real difference.

Congress passed a new Agricultural Adjustment Act in 1938 that tried to solve the problem of farm surpluses, which persisted even after hundreds of thousands of farmers had lost their farms. The new act replaced the processing tax (which the Supreme Court had declared unconstitutional) with direct

Key 1930s Reform Legislation

Year	Legislation	Provisions
1932	Reconstruction Finance Corporation (RFC)	Granted emergency loans to banks, life insurance companies, and railroads (passed during Hoover administration)
1933	Civilian Conservation Corps (CCC)	Employed young men (and a few women) in reforestation, road construction, and flood control projects
1933	Agricultural Adjustment Act (AAA)	Granted farmers direct payments for reducing production of certain products; funds for payments provided by a processing tax, which was later declared unconstitutional
1933	Tennessee Valley Authority (TVA)	Created independent public corporation to construct dams and power projects and to develop the economy of a nine-state area in the Tennessee River valley
1933	National Industrial Recovery Act (NIRA)	Sought to revive business through a series of fair-competition codes; Section 7a guaranteed labor's right to organize (later declared unconstitutional)
1933	Public Works Administration (PWA)	Sought to increase employment and business activity through construction of roads, buildings, and other projects
1934	National Housing Act—created Federal Housing Administration (FHA)	Insured loans made by banks for construction of new homes and repair of old homes
1935	Emergency Relief Appropriation Act—created Works Progress Administration (WPA)	Employed more than 8 million people to repair roads, build bridges, and work on other projects; also hired artists and writers
1935	Social Security Act	Established unemployment compensation and old-age and survivors' insurance paid for by a joint tax on employers and employees
1935	National Labor Relations Act (Wagner-Connery Act)	Recognized the right of employees to join labor unions and to bargain collectively; created a National Labor Relations Board to supervise elections and to prevent unfair labor practices
1935	Public Utility Holding Act	Outlawed pyramiding of gas and electric companies through the use of holding companies and restricted these companies to activity in one area; a "death sentence" clause gave companies five years to prove local, useful, and efficient operation or be dissolved
1937	National Housing Act (Wagner-Steagall Act)	Authorized low-rent public housing projects
1938	Agricultural Adjustment Act (AAA)	Continued price supports and payments to farmers to limit production, as in 1933 act, but replaced processing tax with direct federal payment
1938	Fair Labor Standards Act	Established minimum wage of 40 cents an hour and maximum workweek of 40 hours in enterprises engaged in interstate commerce

payments from the federal treasury to farmers; added a soil conservation program; and provided for the marketing of surplus crops. Like its predecessor, the new act tried to stabilize farm prices by controlling production. But only the outbreak of World War II would end the problem of farm surplus, and then only temporarily.

In the cities, housing continued to be a problem. Progressive reformers had dreamed of providing better housing for the urban poor. They had campaigned for city ordinances and state laws and had built model tenements, but the first experiment with federal housing occurred during World War I. That brief experience encouraged a number of social reformers, who later became advisers to Roosevelt. They convinced him that federal low-cost housing should be part of New Deal reform.

The Reconstruction Finance Corporation made low-interest loans to housing projects, and the Public Works Administration constructed some apartment buildings. But not until the National Housing Act of 1937 did Roosevelt and his advisers try to develop a comprehensive housing policy for the poor. The act provided federal funds for slum clearance projects and for the construction of low-cost housing. By 1939, however, only 117,000 units had been built.

In the long run, New Deal housing legislation had a greater impact on middle-class housing policies and patterns. During the first 100 days of the New Deal, at Roosevelt's urging, Congress passed a bill creating the Home Owners Loan Corporation (HOLC), which over the next two years made more than $3 billion in low-interest loans and helped more than a million people save their homes from foreclosure. The HOLC also had a strong impact on housing policy by introducing the first long-term, fixed-rate mortgages. Formerly, all mortgages were for periods of no more than five years and were subject to frequent renegotiation.

The HOLC also introduced a uniform system of real estate appraisal that tended to undervalue urban property, especially in neighborhoods that were old, crowded, and ethnically mixed. The system gave the highest ratings to suburban developments where, according to the HOLC, there had been no "infiltration of Jews" or other undesirable groups. This was the beginning of the practice later called "redlining," in which lending agencies drew lines around neighborhoods and made it nearly impossible for prospective home buyers of certain ethnic or racial backgrounds to obtain a mortgage.

The Federal Housing Administration (FHA), created in 1934 by the National Housing Act, expanded and extended many of these HOLC policies. The FHA insured mortgages, many of them for 25 or 30 years; reduced the down payment required from 30 percent to less than 10 percent; and allowed more than 11 million families to buy homes between 1934 and 1972. The system, however, tended to favor purchasing new suburban homes rather than repairing older urban residences. New Deal housing policies helped make the suburban home with the long FHA mortgage part of the American way of life, but the policies also contributed to the decline of many urban neighborhoods.

Just as important as housing legislation was the Fair Labor Standards Act, which Congress passed in June 1938. Roosevelt's bill proposed for all industries engaged in interstate commerce a minimum wage of 25 cents an hour, to rise in two years to 40 cents an hour, and a maximum workweek of 44 hours, to be reduced to 40 hours. The act covered only 20 percent of the labor force and only 14 percent of working women. Nevertheless, when it went into effect, 750,000 workers immediately received raises, and by 1940, some 12 million had received pay increases. The law also prohibited child labor in interstate commerce, making it the first permanent federal law to prohibit youngsters under age 16 from working. And without emphasizing the matter, the law made no distinction between men and women, thus diminishing, if not completely ending, the need for special legislation for women.

The Fair Labor Standards Act was the last New Deal measure passed. The New Deal had many weaknesses, but it did dramatically increase government support for the needy. In 1913, local, state, and federal governments spent $21 million on public assistance. By 1932, that had risen to $218 million; by 1939, it was $4.9 billion.

THE OTHER SIDE OF THE 1930S

The Great Depression and the New Deal so dominate the history of the 1930s that it is easy to conclude that nothing else happened, that there were only bread lines and relief agencies. But there is another side of the decade, for a communications revolution changed the lives of middle-class Americans. The sale of radios and attendance at movies increased during the 1930s, and literature flourished. Americans were fascinated by technology, especially automobiles. Many people traveled during the decade; they stayed in motor courts and looked ahead to a brighter future dominated by streamlined appliances and gadgets that would mean an easier life.

Taking to the Road

"People give up everything in the world but their car," a banker in Muncie, Indiana, remarked during the Depression, and that seems to have been true all over the country. Although automobile production

A Streamlined Age   The age of the Great Depression was also a time of modern, streamlined design. There were streamlined trains, cars, and planes. There were even streamlined refrigerators, radios, and pencil sharpeners. The 1939 New York World's Fair was marked by modern design and exhibits that depicted a streamlined future based on technology. Even during the nation's greatest economic crisis, some Americans planned for a better future. How do you explain the irony of looking ahead to a streamlined future during a decade of despair? *(Underwood & Underwood/CORBIS)*

dropped off after 1929 and did not recover until the end of the 1930s, the number of motor vehicles registered, which declined from 26.7 million in 1930 to just over 24 million in 1933, increased to more than 32 million by 1940. People who could not afford new cars drove used ones. Even the "Okies" fleeing the dust bowl of the Southwest traveled in cars. They were secondhand, run-down cars to be sure, but the fact that even many poor Americans owned cars shocked visitors from Europe, where automobiles were still only for the rich.

The American middle class traveled at an increasing rate after the low point of 1932 and 1933. In 1938, the tourist industry was the third largest in the United States, behind only steel and automobile production. More than 4 million Americans traveled every year, and four out of five went by car. Many dragged a trailer for sleeping or stopped at the growing number of tourist courts and overnight cabins. In these predecessors of the motel, there were no doormen, no bellhops, no register to sign. The tourist court was much more informal than the hotel, and you could park your car next to your cabin.

The Electric Home

If the 1920s was the age of the bathroom, the 1930s was the era of the modern kitchen. The sale of

Washday Although the washing machine dates from the mid-nineteenth century, it did not end the drudgery of wash day; even the introduction of electric washers did not eliminate the constant wringing and rinsing that made wash day (usually Monday) a day to dread. The first automatic washing machines were introduced in the late 1930s but did not become commonplace until after World War II. This advertisement promotes the convenience of a machine that will spin-dry as well as wash. Notice the gender roles in the advertisement. The husband appreciates the saving but apparently does not put the clothes in the machine. "The Bendix" was a great improvement, but it was not until the 1950s that electric and gas dryers finally ended the task of hanging clothes on the line. How do you do your laundry today? Have things changed much since the 1930s? *(Bendix Home Appliances, Inc.)*

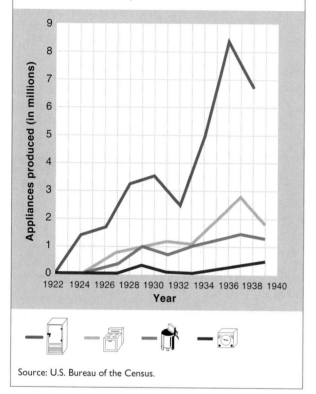

Household Appliance Production, 1922–1939

Electric appliances altered the lives of many American middle-class families during the 1930s. The replacement of the icebox with the electric refrigerator was especially dramatic. How did these appliances change the lifestyle of those who purchased them?

Source: U.S. Bureau of the Census.

electrical appliances increased throughout the decade, with refrigerators leading the way. In 1930, the number of refrigerators produced exceeded the number of iceboxes for the first time. Refrigerator production continued to rise throughout the decade, reaching a peak of 2.3 million in 1937. At first, the refrigerator was boxy and looked very much like an icebox with a motor sitting on top. In 1935, however, the refrigerator, like most other appliances, became streamlined. Sears, Roebuck advertised "The New 1935 Super Six Coldspot … Stunning in Its Streamlined Beauty." The Coldspot, which quickly influenced the look of all other models, was designed by Raymond Loewy, one of a group of industrial designers who emphasized sweeping horizontal lines, rounded corners, and a slick modern look. They hoped modern design would stimulate an optimistic attitude and, of course, increase sales. At the end of the decade, in 1939, the World's Fair in New York glorified the theme of a streamlined future, carefully planned and based on new technology.

This reverence for technological progress contrasted with the economic despair in the 1930s, but people adapted to it selectively. For example, the electric washing machine and electric iron revolutionized wash day. Yet even with labor-saving machines, most women continued to do their wash on Monday and their ironing on Tuesday. Packaged and canned goods became more widely available during the decade, and many women discovered that it was easier, and in some cases cheaper, to serve Kellogg's Corn Flakes or Nabisco Shredded Wheat than to make oatmeal, to heat Van Camp's pork and beans or Heinz spaghetti from a can than to prepare a meal, or to use commercially baked bread than to bake their own.

Ironically, despite these new conveniences, a great many middle-class families maintained their standard of living during the 1930s only because the women in the family learned to stretch and save and make do, and most wives spent as much time on housework as before. Some also took jobs outside the home to maintain their level of consumption. The number of married women who worked increased substantially during the decade. At the same time, many rural women, such as those in the hill country of Texas and other remote areas, and many wives of the unemployed simply made do. They continued to cook, clean, and sew as their ancestors had for generations.

The Age of Leisure

During the Depression, many middle-class people found themselves with time on their hands and sought out ways of spending it. The 1920s had been a time of spectator sports, of football and baseball heroes, of huge crowds that turned out to see boxing matches. Those sports continued during the Depression decade, although attendance suffered. Softball and miniature golf, which were cheap forms of entertainment and did not require expensive travel, also became popular. But leisure in the 1930s actually grew to be a problem, and professionals published some 450 new books on the subject. Leisure was mechanized; millions put their nickels in a slot and listened to a record played on a jukebox. Millions more played a pinball machine, a mechanized device that had no practical use other than entertainment and could end the game with one word: "Tilt."

Many popular games of the period had elaborate rules and directions. Contract bridge swept the country during the decade, and Monopoly was the most popular game of all. Produced by Parker Brothers, Monopoly was a fantasy of real estate

Georges Duhamel, A French Writer Visits the United States and Finds Nothing to Admire

Georges Duhamel, a French novelist, traveled in the United States at the beginning of the Great Depression. He used Chicago to symbolize all that he disliked about America. As much as he hated everything he saw, he feared that American culture was going to spread around the world.

O painters, my friends and brothers, you can never make anything of Chicago! You will never paint this world, for it is beyond the human grasp. Chicago is no more paintable than the desert. It is prodigious and untamed; it is not a living thing. . . .

America is devoted to its ephemeral works. It erects, not monuments, but merely buildings. Should it fall into ruins tomorrow, we should seek in its ashes in vain for the bronze statuette that is enough to immortalize a little Greek village. Ruins of Chicago!—prodigious heap of iron-work, concrete, and old plaster, the sole beauty of which will be gay plants and moss—I evoke you with horror and weariness of spirit. . . .

In that ridiculous moral atmosphere in which swarms not a great nation, but a confusion of races, how can one possibly find that sublime serenity which art must have if it is to quicken and flower . . . ? North America, which has not inspired painters—which has not raised up any sculptors, which has prompted the song of no musicians, unless it be that of the monotonous Negro, and whose barbarously industrial architecture seems to care not at all for the judgment of future times, has yet produced poets and writers. Almost all of them—oh mockery!—have turned from their native soil, in bitterness of spirit. . . .

But to paint Chicago? How can one do it with mere words or colors? Music alone, it seems to me, could accomplish the task. And rather than any imitative rhythm, soon lost in this tumult, it should be bitter chords, a heavy prelude to chaos.

- *Is Duhamel's criticism fair?*

- *Is it perhaps influenced by the time he visited?*

- *Is this kind of attack (that The United States has no culture, no tradition) still common among European visitors?*

---

speculation in which chance, luck, and the roll of the dice determined the winner. But one still had to obey the rules: "Go Directly to Jail. Do Not Pass Go. Do Not Collect $200." During a depression brought on in part by frenzied speculation, Americans were fascinated by a game whose purpose was to obtain real estate and utility monopolies and drive one's opponents into bankruptcy.

The 1930s was also a time of fads and instant celebrities, created by radio, newsreels, and businesspeople ready to turn almost anything to commercial advantage. The leading box office attraction between 1935 and 1938 was Shirley Temple, a blond and adorable child star. She inspired dolls, dishes, books, and clothes. Even stranger was the excitement created by the birth of five girl babies to a couple in northern Ontario in 1934. The Dionne quintuplets appeared on dozens of magazine covers and endorsed every imaginable product. Millions of people waited eagerly for the latest news about the babies, and more than 3 million traveled to see their home in Canada. The crazes over Shirley Temple and the Dionne quintuplets were products of the new technology, especially radio and the movies.

Literary Reflections of the 1930s

Though much of the literature of the 1930s reflected the decade's troubled currents, reading continued to be a popular and cheap entertainment. John Steinbeck, whose later novel *The Grapes of Wrath* (1939) followed the fortunes of the Joad family, described the plight of Mexican migrant workers in *Tortilla Flat* (1935). His novels expressed his belief that there was in American life a "crime . . . that goes beyond denunciation." He warned, "In the eyes of the hungry there is a growing wrath."

Other writers also questioned the American dream. John Dos Passos's trilogy *U.S.A.* (1930–1936) conveyed a deep pessimism about American capitalism that many other intellectuals shared. Less political were the novels of Thomas Wolfe and William Faulkner, who more sympathetically portrayed Americans caught up in the web of local life

RECOVERING THE PAST

The Movies

Just as some historians have used fiction to help define the cultural history of a decade, others in the twentieth century have turned to film to describe the "spirit of an age." On an elementary level, the movies help us appreciate changing styles in dress, furniture, and automobiles. We can even get some sense of how a particular time defined a beautiful woman or a handsome man, and we can learn about ethnic and racial stereotypes and assumptions about gender and class.

The decade of the 1930s is sometimes called the "golden age of the movies." Careful selection among the 500 or so feature films Hollywood produced each year during the decade—ranging from gangster and cowboy movies to Marx Brothers comedies, from historical romances to Busby Berkeley musical extravaganzas—could support a number of interpretations about the special myths and assumptions of the era. But one historian has argued that, especially after 1934, "not only did the movies amuse and entertain the nation through its most severe economic and social disorder, holding it together by their capacity to create unifying myths and dreams, but movie culture in the 1930s became a dominant culture for many

Americans, providing new values and social ideals to replace shattered old traditions."

The year 1934 was a dividing line for two reasons. The motion picture industry, like all other industries, had suffered during the Depression; 1933 marked the low point in attendance, with more than one-third of the theaters in the country shut down. The next year, however, attendance picked up, heralding a revival that lasted until 1946. Also in 1934, the movie industry adopted a code for which the Catholic Legion of Decency and other religious groups had lobbied. The new code prohibited the depiction of "sex perversion, interracial sex, abortion, incest, drugs and profanity." Even married couples could not be shown together in a double bed. Although a movie could depict immoral behavior, sin always had to be punished. "Evil and good should never be confused," the code announced.

Before the code, Hollywood had indeed produced graphic films, such as *The Public Enemy* (1931) and *Scarface* (1932), with a considerable amount of violence; musicals, such as *Gold Diggers of 1933,* filled with scantily clad young women; films featuring prostitutes, such as Jean Harlow in *Red Dust* (1932) and

A scene from It Happened One Night, 1934. (*Photofest*)

A scene from *Drums Along the Mohawk*, 1939. *(20th Century Fox/The Kobal Collection)*

Marlene Dietrich in *Blond Venus* (1930); and other films that confronted the problems of real life. But after 1934, Hollywood concentrated on movies that created a mythical world in which evil was always punished, family moral values won out in the end, and patriotism and American democracy were never questioned. Although the code was modified from time to time, it was not abandoned until 1966, when it was replaced by a rating system.

It Happened One Night (1934) and *Drums Along the Mohawk* (1939), two films out of thousands, illustrate some of the myths the movies created and sustained. Frank Capra, one of Hollywood's masters at entertaining without disturbing, directed *It Happened One Night*, a comedy-romance. A rich girl (played by Claudette Colbert) dives from her father's yacht off the coast of Florida and takes a bus for New York. She meets a newspaper reporter (Clark Gable), and they have a series of madcap adventures and fall in love. But mix-ups and misunderstandings make it appear that she will marry her old boyfriend. In the end, however, they are reunited and marry in an elaborate outdoor ceremony. Afterward, they presumably live happily ever after. The movie is funny and entertaining and presents a variation on the poor-boy-marries-rich-girl theme. Like so many movies of the time, this one suggests that life is fulfilled for a woman only if she can find the right man to marry.

Claudette Colbert also stars in *Drums Along the Mohawk,* this time with Henry Fonda. Based on a

1936 novel by Walter Edmonds, *Drums* is a sentimental story about a man who builds a house in the wilderness, marries a pretty girl, fights off the Indians, and works with the simple country folk to create a satisfying life in the very year the American colonies rebel against Great Britain. *Drums* was one of a number of films based on historical themes that Hollywood released just before World War II. *The Howards of Virginia* (1940), *Northwest Passage* (1939), and, most popular of all, *Gone with the Wind* (1939) were others in the same genre. Historical themes had been popular before, but with the world on the brink of war, the story of men and women in the wilderness struggling for family and country against Native Americans (stereotyped as savages) proved comforting as well as entertaining.

REFLECTING ON THE PAST Can a historian use movies to describe the values and myths of a particular time, or are the complexities and exaggerations too great? Are the most popular or most critically acclaimed films more useful than others in getting at the "spirit of an age"? Which films that are popular today tell us the most about our time and culture? Is there too much sex and violence in movies today? Should the government control the language, themes, and values depicted in movies? Are movies as important today as they were in the 1930s in defining and influencing the country's myths and values?

The Power of Radio The radio played an important role in the 1930s. Here a family crowds around a typical floor model to listen to the latest news or a favorite program. Has the impact of the radio changed since the 1930s? Is the radio still important in your life? (*Bettmann-CORBIS*)

and facing the complex problems of the modern era. Faulkner's fictional Yoknapatawpha County, brought to life in *The Sound and the Fury, As I Lay Dying, Sanctuary,* and *Light in August* (1929–1932), documented the South's racial problems and its poverty as well as its stubborn pride. But the book about the South that became one of the decade's best-sellers was far more optimistic and far less complex than Faulkner's work—Margaret Mitchell's *Gone with the Wind* (1936). Its success suggested that many Americans read to escape, not to explore their problems.

John Steinbeck

Radio's Finest Hour

The number of radios purchased increased steadily during the decade. In 1929, slightly more than 10 million households owned radios; by 1939, more than 27.5 million households had radios. Not just a source of music and news, the radio was a focal point of the living room. In many homes, the top of the radio became the symbolic mantel where cherished photos were displayed. Families gathered around the radio at night to listen to and laugh at Jack Benny or Edgar Bergen and Charlie McCarthy

or to try to solve a murder mystery with Mr. and Mrs. North. *The Lone Ranger,* another popular program, had 20 million listeners by 1939.

During the day there were soap operas. "Between thick slices of advertising," wrote James Thurber, "spread twelve minutes of dialogue, add predicament, villainy, and female suffering in equal measure, throw in a dash of nobility, sprinkle with tears, season with organ music, cover with a rich announcer sauce and serve five times a week." After school, teenagers and younger children argued over whether to listen to *Jack Armstrong, the All-American Boy* and *Captain Midnight* or *Stella Dallas* and *The Young Widder Brown.*

Most families had only one radio. The reception was sometimes poor, especially in rural areas and small towns. Voices faded in and out and disappeared during storms. But the magic of radio allowed many people to feel connected to distant places and to believe they knew the radio performers personally. Radio was also responsible for one of the most widespread episodes of mass hysteria of all time. On October 31, 1938, Orson Welles broadcast *The War of the Worlds* so realistically that thousands of listeners really believed that Martians had landed in New Jersey. If anyone needed proof, that single program demonstrated the power of the radio.

The Silver Screen

The 1930s were the golden decade of the movies. Between 60 million and 90 million Americans went to the movies every week. The medium was not entirely Depression-proof, but talking films had replaced the silent variety in the late 1920s, and attendance soared. Though it fell off slightly in the early 1930s, by 1934 movie viewing was climbing again. For many families, even in the depth of the Depression, movie money was almost as important as food money.

In the cities, one could go to an elaborate movie palace and live in a fantasy world far removed from the reality of Depression America. In small towns across the country, for 25 cents (10 cents for those under age 12) one could go to at least four movies during the week. There was a Sunday–Monday feature film (except in communities where the churches had prevented Sunday movies), a different feature of somewhat lesser prominence on Tuesday–Wednesday, and another on Thursday–Friday. On Saturday, there was a cowboy or detective movie. Sometimes a double feature played, and there were always short subjects, a cartoon, and a newsreel. On Saturday, there was usually a serial that left the heroine or hero in such a dire predicament that one just had to come back the next week to see how she or he survived.

The movies were a place to take a date, to go with friends, or to go as a family. Movies would be talked about for days. Young women tried to speak like Greta Garbo and to hold a cigarette like Joan Crawford. Jean Harlow and Mae West so popularized blond hair that sales of peroxide shot up. Young men tried to emulate Clark Gable and Cary Grant, and one young man admitted that it was "directly through the movies that I learned to kiss a girl on her ears, neck, and cheeks, as well as on the mouth." The animated cartoons of Walt Disney, one of the

true geniuses of the movie industry, were so popular that Mickey Mouse was more famous and familiar than most human celebrities. In May 1933, halfway into Roosevelt's first 100 days, Disney released *The Three Little Pigs,* whose theme song "Who's Afraid of the Big Bad Wolf?" became a national hit overnight. Some people felt it boosted the nation's morale as much as New Deal legislation. One critic suggested that the moral of the story, as retold by Disney, was that the little pig survived because he was conservative, diligent, and hardworking; others felt that it was the pig who used modern tools and planned ahead who won out.

TIMELINE

1929	Stock market crashes
1930	Depression worsens
1932	Reconstruction Finance Corporation established
	Federal Home Loan Bank Act
	Glass–Steagall Banking Act
	Federal Emergency Relief Act
	Bonus march on Washington
	Franklin D. Roosevelt elected president
1933	Emergency Banking Relief Act
	Home Owners Loan Corporation
	Twenty-first Amendment repeals Eighteenth Amendment, ending Prohibition
	Agricultural Adjustment Act
	National Industrial Recovery Act
	Civilian Conservation Corps
	Tennessee Valley Authority established
	Public Works Administration established
1934	Unemployment peaks
	Federal Housing Administration established
	Indian Reorganization Act

1935	Second New Deal begins
	Works Progress Administration established
	Social Security Act
	Rural Electrification Act
	National Labor Relations Act
	Public Utility Holding Company Act
	Committee of Industrial Organization (CIO) formed
1936	United Auto Workers hold sit-down strikes against General Motors
	Roosevelt re-elected president
	Economy begins to rebound
	Margaret Mitchell, *Gone with the Wind*
1937	Attempt to expand the Supreme Court
	Economic collapse
	Farm Security Administration established
	National Housing Act
1938	Fair Labor Standards Act
	Agricultural Adjustment Act
1939	John Steinbeck, *The Grapes of Wrath*

Conclusion

The Mixed Legacy of the Great Depression and the New Deal

The New Deal, despite its great variety of legislation, did not end the Depression, nor did it solve the problem of unemployment. For many Americans looking back on the decade of the 1930s, the most vivid memory was the shame and guilt of being unemployed, the despair and fear that came from losing a business or being evicted from a home or an apartment. For Robert Symmonds's generation, the experience of the Depression would influence their lives and their attitude toward money for the rest of

their lives. Parents who lived through the decade urged their children to find a secure job, to get married, and to settle down. "Every time I've encountered the Depression it has been used as a barrier and a club," one daughter of Depression parents remembered; "older people use it to explain to me that I can't understand anything: I didn't live through the Depression."

New Deal legislation did not solve the country's problems, but it did strengthen the federal government, especially the executive branch. Federal agencies such as the Federal Deposit Insurance Corporation and programs such as social security influenced the daily lives of most Americans, and rural electrification, the WPA, and the CCC changed the lives of millions. The New Deal also established the principle of federal responsibility for the health of the economy, initiated the concept of the welfare state, and dramatically increased government spending to help the poor. Federally subsidized housing, minimum-wage laws, and a policy for paying farmers to limit production, all aspects of these principles, had far-reaching implications. The shift of responsibility for the nation's welfare to Washington marked the New Deal as a landmark in the continuing story of the relationship of government to society.

The New Deal was as important for what it did not do as for what it did. It did not promote socialism or redistribute income or property. It promoted social justice and social reform, but it provided little for people at the bottom of American society, and less for African Americans and other minorities. The New Deal did not prevent business consolidation,

and, in the end, it probably strengthened corporate capitalism.

Roosevelt, with his colorful personality and his dramatic response to the nation's crisis, dominated his times in a way few presidents have done. Yet for some people who lived through the decade, neither Roosevelt nor bread lines but a new streamlined refrigerator or a Walt Disney movie symbolized the Depression decade. It is easy to study the United States in the 1930s without reference to what was going on in the rest of the world. But the United States was influenced by international economic and political trends during the decade. The Depression was global in its impact, and it was at least in part responsible for the rise of Hitler in Germany, for economic and military expansionism in Japan, and for encouraging Mussolini to undertake foreign adventures. Great Britain, France, the United States, and other countries, faced with economic disaster, passed high tariffs that in turn increased international tensions and led to aggressive nationalism. These global trends would eventually involve the United States in World War II.

Questions for Review and Reflection

1. Explain the origins of the Great Depression. How was the Depression in the United States related to global economic factors?

2. Explain the two major phases of the New Deal. What programs were enacted in each phase, and what did they seek to accomplish?

3. Who criticized the New Deal and why?

4. How did communication technologies and popular culture change during the 1930s?

5. Why are the Depression and the New Deal considered to have a mixed legacy?

Recommended Reading

Recommended Readings are posted on the Web site for this textbook. Visit www.ablongman.com/nash

Fiction and Film

James Farrell describes growing up in Depression Chicago in *Studs Lonigan* (1932–1935). John Steinbeck shows Oklahomans trying to escape the dust bowl in his novel *The Grapes of Wrath* (1939). Richard Wright details the trials of a young black man in *Native Son* (1940). *Modern Times* (1936) is a classic film that features Charlie Chaplin at his best as he depicts the impersonality of industrial civilization, in which machines dominate people. *The Grapes of Wrath* (1940) is another classic film.

Although it doesn't exhibit the despair and anger of the book, it is still a powerful depiction of the human cost of the dust bowl and the Depression. To appreciate how people in the 1930s were entertained by the movies, check out *Gone with the Wind* (1939), Fred Astaire and Ginger Rogers in *Top Hat* (1935) and *Swing Time* (1936), and *The Wizard of Oz* (1939). To see the genius of Walt Disney, watch *Snow White and the Seven Dwarfs* (1937).

Discovering U.S. History Online

Riding the Rails
www.pbs.org/wgbh/amex/rails
"At the height of the Great Depression, more than 250,000 teenagers were living on the road in America." This site, a companion to the PBS film, includes stories from real "hobos" and an examination of racial factors in the hobo lifestyle, hobo songs, a timeline, and maps.

Americans React to the Great Depression
http://lcweb2.loc.gov/ammem/ndlpedu/features/timeline/deprwwii/depress.depress.html
Documents and photographs illustrate aftereffects of the Great Depression, including a pushcart peddlers' colony, a photo collage of Hoovervilles, and photos of protests and demonstrations during this time period.

The Hoover Dam
http://xroads.virginia.edu/~MA98/haven/hoover
The site describes the construction of Hoover Dam in the context of the Great Depression.

Hooverville
www.realchangenews.org/pastarticles/features/articles/fea_hooverville1.html
www.realchangenews.org/pastarticles/features/articles/fea_hooverville2.html
www.realchangenews.org/pastarticles/features/articles/fea_hooverville3.html
These sites present illustrated articles on Seattle's Hooverville.

Migrant Labor Camps
www.lib.utexas.edu/photodraw/sanchez/migrant_camps.html
Annotated photographs document the conditions in Texas migrant camps during the 1930s.

New Deal
www.newdeal.feri.org
This database includes photographs, political cartoons, and texts—including speeches, letters, and other historic documents—from the New Deal period.

A New Deal for the Arts
www.archives.gov/exhibit_hall/new_deal_for_the_arts/index.html
Artwork, documents, and photographs recount the federal government's efforts to fund artists in the 1930s in this National Archives site.

Franklin D. Roosevelt Library and Digital Archives
www.fdrlibrary.marist.edu
The library presents more than 13,000 digitized documents in an effort to fulfill "Franklin Roosevelt's dream of making the records of the past available" to the general public.

A Short History of the Tennessee Valley Authority
www.tva.gov/abouttva/history.htm
This official history of the agency includes the complete text of the act that founded it.

One Hundred Days
www.nps.gov/fdrm/home.htm
This illustrated site presents information on Roosevelt's presidency, including the "one hundred days," arranged in "rooms."

Franklin Delano Roosevelt
www.potus.com/fdroosevelt.html
This site contains basic factual data about Roosevelt's election and presidency, speeches, and online biographies.

Voices from the Dust Bowl
www.memory.loc.gov/ammem/afctshtml/tshome.html
Farm Security Administration (FSA) studies of migrant work camps in central California in 1940 and 1941 compose the bulk of this site. The collection includes audio recordings, photographs, manuscript materials, and publications.

Weedpatch Camp
www.weedpatchcamp.com
History and personal reminiscences of life at the real-life migrant labor camp Arvin Federal Government Camp, portrayed as "Weedpatch Camp" in a John Steinbeck novel.

Taxation in War and Depression, 1933–1946
www.tax.org/THP/Civilization/Default.htm
This site is an online tax information resource. It includes thousands of searchable pages of documents and analysis on tax issues during the Depression and World War II and is part of a larger site that contains a cartoon gallery and World War II–era posters.

America from the Great Depression to World War II
http://lcweb2.loc.gov/ammem/fsahtml/fahome.html
This extensive, searchable database includes the special collections "Documenting America: Photographers on Assignment" and "Selected FSA Images: Popular Requests and Staff Selections."

Los Angeles at Work, 1920–1939
www.lapl.org/photo/laatwork
This archive contains promotional photographs created by the Los Angeles Chamber of Commerce during the "economic heyday" of the 1920s along with follow-up photos that were taken of business innovations during the Depression years.

America in the 1930s
www.xroads.virginia.edu/~1930s/home_1.html
A timeline of the 1930s along with a cultural overview of the decade in film, print, on radio, and by other displays.

World War II

Reading Right to Left—FIRST ROW: Britain, Canada, Australia, New Zealand, SECOND ROW: Southern Rhodesia, Newfoundland, South Africa, THIRD ROW: India, FOURTH ROW: The Colonial Empire

Reading Left to Right—FIRST ROW: U.S.A., China, U.S.S.R., Yugoslavia, SECOND ROW: Holland, France, Poland, Czechoslovakia, THIRD ROW: Greece, Norway, Belgium

FREEDOM SHALL PREVAIL!

PRINTED IN ENGLAND BY FOSH & CROSS LTD., LONDON. (31-

This World War II poster depicts the many nations united in the fight against the Axis powers. In reality there were often disagreements. Notice that to the right, the American sailor is marching next to Chinese and Soviet soldiers. Within a few years after victory, they would be enemies. (*University of Georgia Libraries, Hargrett Rare Book and Manuscript Library*)

American Stories

A Native American Boy Plays at War

N. Scott Momaday, a Kiowa Indian born in Lawton, Oklahoma, in 1934, grew up on Navajo, Apache, and Pueblo reservations. He was only 11 years old when World War II ended, yet the war had changed his life. Shortly after the United States entered the war, Momaday's parents moved to New Mexico, where his father got a job with an oil company and his mother worked in the civilian personnel office at an army air force base. Like many couples, they had struggled through the hard times of the Depression. The war meant jobs.

Momaday's best friend was Billy Don Johnson, a "reddish, robust boy of great good humor and intense loyalty." Together they played war, digging trenches and dragging themselves through imaginary minefields. They hurled grenades and fired endless rounds from their imaginary machine guns, pausing only to drink Kool-Aid from their canteens. At school, they were taught history and math and also how to hate the enemy and be proud of America. They recited the Pledge of Allegiance to the flag and sang "God Bless America," "The Star-Spangled Banner," and "Remember Pearl Harbor." Like most Americans, they believed that World War II was a good war fought against evil empires. The United States was always right, the enemy always wrong. It was an attitude that would influence Momaday and his generation for the rest of their lives.

Momaday's only difficulty was that his Native American face was often mistaken for that of an Asian. Almost every day on the playground, someone would yell, "Hi ya, Jap," and a fight was on. Billy Don always came to his friend's defense, but it was disconcerting to be taken for the enemy. His father read old Kiowa tales to Momaday, who was proud to be an Indian but prouder still to be an American. On Saturday, he and his friends would go to the local theater to cheer as they watched a Japanese Zero or a German ME-109 go down in flames. They pretended that they were P-40 pilots. "The whole field of vision shuddered with our fire: the 50-caliber tracers curved out, fixing brilliant arcs upon the span, and struck; then there was a black burst of smoke, and the target went spinning down to death."

Near the end of the war, his family moved again, as so many families did, so that his father might get a better job. This time they lived right next door to an air force base, and Momaday fell in love with the B-17 "Flying Fortress," the bomber that military strategists thought would win the war in the Pacific and in Europe. He felt a real sense of resentment and loss when the B-17 was replaced by the larger but not nearly so glamorous B-29.

Looking back on his early years, Momaday reflected on the importance of the war in his growing up. "I see now that one experiences easily the ordinary things of life," he decided, "the things which cast familiar shadows upon the sheer, transparent panels of time, and he perceives his experience in the only way he can, according to his age." Though Momaday's life during the war differed from the lives of boys old enough to join the armed forces, the war was no less real for him. Though his youth was affected by the fact that he was male, was an Indian, and lived in the Southwest, the most important influence was that he was an American growing up during the war. Ironically, his parents had been made U.S. citizens by an act of Congress in 1924, but like all Native Americans living in Arizona and New Mexico, they were denied the right to vote by state law.

The Momadays fared better than most Native Americans, who found prejudice against them undiminished and jobs, even in wartime, hard to find. Native American servicemen returning from the war discovered that they were still treated like "Indians." They were prohibited from buying liquor in many states, and those who returned to the reservations learned that they were ineligible for veterans' benefits. Still, Momaday thought of himself not so much as an Indian as an American, and that too was a product of his generation. But as he grew to maturity, he became a successful writer and spokesman for his people. In 1969, he won the Pulitzer Prize for his novel *House Made of Dawn*. He also recorded his experiences and memories in a book called *The Names* (1976). In his writing, he stresses the Native American's close identification with the land. Writing about his grandmother, he says: "The immense landscape of the continental interior lay like memory in her blood."

Momaday was just a child during World War II, but it had a profound effect on his life as it did on all of those who remembered the conflict. His generation would judge the global events of the rest of the twentieth century in terms of their sense of patriotism and valor acquired during the war. Although no American cities were bombed and the mainland was never invaded, World War II influenced almost every aspect of American life. The war ended the Depression. Industrial jobs were plentiful, and even though prejudice and discrimination did not disappear, blacks, Hispanics, women, and other minorities had new opportunities. Like World War I, the second war expanded cooperation between government and industry and increased the influence of government in all areas of American life. The war also ended the last remnants of American isolationism. The United States emerged from the war in 1945 as the most powerful and prosperous nation in the world.

This chapter traces the gradual involvement of the United States in the international events during the 1930s that finally led to participation in the most devastating war the world had seen. It recounts the diplomatic and military struggles of the war and the search for a secure peace. It also seeks to explain the impact of the war on ordinary people and on American attitudes about the world, as well as its effect on patriotism and the American way of life. Even those, like N. Scott Momaday, who grew up during the war and were too young to fight, were influenced by the war—and the sense of moral certainty that the war inspired—for the rest of their lives. The war brought prosperity to some as it brought death to others. It left the American people the most affluent in the world and the United States the most powerful nation.

THE TWISTING ROAD TO WAR

Looking back on the events between 1933 and 1941 that eventually led to American involvement in World War II, it is easy either to be critical of decisions made or actions not taken or to see everything that happened during the period as inevitable. Historical events are never inevitable, and leaders who must make decisions never have the advantage of retrospective vision; they have to deal with situations as they find them, and they never have all the facts.

Foreign Policy in a Global Age

In March 1933, Roosevelt faced not only overwhelming domestic difficulties but also an international crisis. The worldwide depression had caused near financial disaster in Europe. Germany had defaulted on its reparations installments, and most European countries were unable to keep up the payments on their debts to the United States.

Roosevelt had no master plan in foreign policy, just as he had none in the domestic sphere. In the first days of his administration, he gave conflicting signals as he groped to respond to the international situation. At first, it seemed that the president would cooperate in some kind of international economic agreement on tariffs and currency. But then he undercut the American delegation in London by refusing to go along with any international agreement. Solving the American domestic economic crisis seemed more important to

Roosevelt in 1933 than international economic cooperation. His actions signaled a decision to go it alone in foreign policy in the 1930s.

Roosevelt did, however, alter some of the foreign policy decisions of previous administrations. He recognized the Soviet government, hoping to gain a market for surplus American grain. Although the expected trade bonanza never materialized, the Soviet Union agreed to pay the old debts and to extend rights to American citizens living in the Soviet Union. Diplomatic recognition opened communications between the two emerging world powers.

The United States continued to support dictators, especially in Central America, because they promised to promote stability and preserve American economic interests. But Roosevelt completed the removal of American military forces from Haiti and Nicaragua in 1934, and in a series of pan-American conferences, he joined in pledging that no country in the hemisphere would intervene in the "internal or external affairs" of any other.

The first test case came in Cuba, where a revolution threatened American investments of more than $1 billion. But the United States did not send troops. Instead, Roosevelt dispatched special envoys to work out a conciliatory agreement with the revolutionary government. A short time later, when a coup led by Fulgencio Batista overthrew the revolutionary government, the United States not only recognized the Batista government but also offered a large loan and agreed to abrogate the Platt Amendment (which made Cuba a virtual protectorate of the United States) in return for the rights to the Guantanamo naval base on the island.

The Trade Agreements Act of 1934 gave the president power to lower tariff rates by as much as 50 percent. Using this act, the Roosevelt administration negotiated a series of agreements that improved trade. By 1935, half of American cotton exports and a large proportion of other products were going to Latin America. The Good Neighbor policy was good business for the United States, but increased trade did not solve the economic problems for either the United States or Latin America.

Another test of Latin American policy came in 1938 when Mexico nationalized the property of a number of American oil companies. Instead of intervening, as many businessmen urged, the State Department patiently worked out an agreement that included some compensation for the companies. The American government might have acted differently, however, if the threat of war in Europe in 1938 had not suggested that all the Western Hemisphere nations would have to cooperate to resist the growing power of Germany and Italy. At a pan-American conference held that year, the United States and most Latin American countries agreed to resist all foreign intervention in the hemisphere.

Europe on the Brink of War

Around the time that Roosevelt was first elected president, Adolf Hitler came to power in Germany. Born in Austria in 1889, Hitler had served as a corporal in the German army during World War I. Like many other Germans, he was angered by the Treaty of Versailles, and he blamed Germany's defeat on the Communists and the Jews. World War II in Europe was caused by World War I and by Germany's attempt to reverse the peace settlement.

Hitler became the leader of the National Socialist party of the German workers (*Nazi* is short for the German <u>Na</u>tional So<u>zi</u>alist), and in 1923, after leading an unsuccessful coup, he was sentenced to

German Painting Idealizing Hitler

prison. While in jail he wrote *Mein Kampf* ("My Struggle"), a long, rambling book spelling out his theories of racial purity, his hopes for Germany, and his venomous hatred of the Jews. After his release from prison, Hitler's following grew. He had a charismatic style and a plan. On January 30, 1933, he became chancellor of Germany, and within months the Reichstag (parliament) suspended the constitution, making Hitler Fuehrer (leader) and dictator. His Fascist regime concentrated political and economic power in a centralized state. He intended to conquer Europe and to make the German Third Reich (empire) the center of a new civilization.

Under Hitler's leadership, Germany prospered and recovered from the Depression faster than any other country except Japan. Economic recovery was caused in part by military spending, but Hitler also provided money for public works, autobahns (superhighways), and the development of the Volkswagen ("people's car"). He raised the quality of workers' lives and provided free recreational facilities and better health care. Many Germans were so grateful for restored prosperity and national pride that they failed to notice the dark side of his regime, which included concentration camps and virulent anti-Semitism.

Hitler at Nuremberg Rally, ca. 1928

In 1934, Hitler announced a program of German rearmament, violating the Versailles Treaty of 1919. Meanwhile, in Italy, the Fascist dictator Benito Mussolini was building a powerful military force; in 1934, he threatened to invade the East African country of Ethiopia. These ominous rumblings in Europe frightened Americans at the very time they were reexamining American entry into the Great War and vowing that they would never again get involved in a European conflict.

Senator Gerald P. Nye of North Dakota, who had helped expose the Teapot Dome scandal in 1924, turned to an investigation of the connection between corporate profits and American participation in World War I. His committee's public hearings revealed that many American businessmen had close relationships with the War Department. Businesses producing war materials had made huge profits. Though the committee failed to prove a conspiracy, it was easy to conclude that the United States had been tricked into going to war by the people who profited the most from it.

On many college campuses, students demonstrated against war. On April 13, 1934, a day of protest around the country, students at Smith College placed white crosses on the campus as a memorial to the people killed in the Great War and those who would die in the next one. The next year, even more students went on strike for a day. Students joined organizations such as Veterans of Future Wars and Future Gold Star Mothers and protested the presence of the Reserve Officers Training Corps (ROTC) on their campuses. One college president, who supported the peace movement, announced, "We will be called cowards . . . [but] I say that war must be banished from civilized society if democratic civilization and culture are to be perpetuated." Not all students supported the peace movement, but in the mid-1930s, many young people as well as adults joined peace societies such as the Fellowship of Reconciliation and the Women's International League for Peace and

Freedom. They were determined never again to support a foreign war. But in Europe, Asia, and Africa, there were already rumblings of another great international conflict.

Ethiopia and Spain

In May 1935, Italy invaded Ethiopia after rejecting the League of Nations' offer to mediate the difficulties between the two countries. Italian dive bombers and machine guns made quick work of the small and poorly equipped Ethiopian army. The Ethiopian war, remote as it seemed, frightened Congress, which passed a Neutrality Act authorizing the president to prohibit all arms shipments to nations at war and to advise all U.S. citizens not to travel on belligerents' ships except at their own risk. Remembering the process that had led the United States into World War I, Congress was determined that it would not happen again.

The League of Nations condemned Italy as the aggressor in the war, and Great Britain moved its fleet to the Mediterranean. Roosevelt used the authority of the Neutrality Act of 1935 to impose an arms embargo. But, in the midst of depression, neither Britain nor the United States wanted to stop shipments of oil to Italy or to commit its own soldiers to the fight. The embargo on arms had little impact on Italy, but it was disastrous for Ethiopia.

Many African Americans were disappointed and angry as they watched Europe and the United States fail to intervene to stop the invasion of Ethiopia, which for many symbolized black African freedom and independence.

"We shun political commitments which might entangle us in foreign war," Roosevelt announced in 1936. "We are not isolationist except in so far as we seek to isolate ourselves completely from war." But isolation became more difficult when a civil war broke out in Spain in 1936. General Francisco Franco, supported by the Catholic church and large landowners, revolted against the republican government. Mussolini had joined forces with Germany to form the Rome–Berlin Axis in 1936, and Germany and Italy aided Franco, sending planes and other weapons, while the Soviet Union came to the support of the anti-Franco Loyalists. On April 26, 1937, German airplanes bombed and machine-gunned the historic Basque capital city of Guernica, killing over 1,600 people. It was a preview of the massive destruction of cities and the death of hundreds of thousands of civilians during World War II.

The war in Spain polarized the United States. Most Catholics and many anti-Communists sided with Franco. But many American radicals, even those opposed to all war a few months before, found the Loyalist cause worth fighting and dying for. More than 3,000 Americans joined the Abraham

Picasso's *Guernica* On April 26, 1937, German airplanes supporting Franco's soldiers bombed and machine-gunned the historic Basque capital city of Guernica, killing more than 1,600 people and foreshadowing the massive destruction of civilians during World War II. Pablo Picasso, probably the most famous artist of the twentieth century, painted this black-and-white mural to denounce the attack. After the defeat of the Republican forces in Spain, Picasso refused to allow the painting to be displayed in the country. Only in 1975, after the end of the Franco regime, did the painting return to Madrid. What kind of symbols and images can you find in the painting? *(Pablo Picasso, Guernica, 1937. Art Resource, NY/© 2007 The Estate of Pablo Picasso/Artists Rights Society [ARS], New York)*

Lincoln Brigade, and hundreds were killed fighting fascism in Spain. "If this were a Spanish matter, I'd let it alone," Sam Levenger, a student at Ohio State, wrote. "But the rebellion would not last a week if it weren't for the Germans and the Italians. And if Hitler and Mussolini can send troops to Spain to attack the government elected by the people, why can't they do so in France? And after France?" Levenger was killed in Spain in 1937 at age 20.

Not everyone agreed that the moral issues in Spain were worth dying for. The U.S. government tried to stay neutral and to ship arms and equipment to neither side. While the United States, along with Britain and France, carefully protected its neutrality, Franco consolidated his dictatorship with the active aid of Germany and Italy. Meanwhile, Congress in 1937 passed another Neutrality Act, this time making it illegal for American citizens to travel on belligerents' ships. The act extended the embargo on arms and made even nonmilitary items available to belligerents only on a cash-and-carry basis.

Hitler and Mussolini in Munich, 1940

In a variety of ways, the United States tried to avoid repeating the mistakes that had led it into World War I. Unfortunately, World War II, which moved closer each day, would be a different kind of war, and the lessons of the first war would be of little use.

War in Europe

Roosevelt was by no means an isolationist, but he wanted to keep the United States out of the European conflagration. When he announced, "I hate war," he was expressing a deep personal belief that wars solve few problems. Unlike his distant cousin Theodore Roosevelt, he did not view war as a test of one's manhood. In foreign policy, just as in domestic affairs, FDR responded to events, but he moved reluctantly toward more and more American involvement in the war.

In March 1938, Hitler's Germany annexed Austria and then in September, as a result of the Munich Conference, occupied the Sudetenland, a part of Czechoslovakia. Within six months, Hitler's armies had overrun the rest of Czechoslovakia. Little protest came from the United States. Most Americans sympathized with the victims of Hitler's aggression, and at first, almost everyone hoped that compromises could be worked out and that Europe could settle its own problems. But that notion was destroyed on August 23, 1939, by the news of a Nazi–Soviet pact. Fascism and communism were political philosophies supposedly in deadly opposition. Many Americans had secretly hoped that Nazi Germany and Soviet Russia would fight it out, neutralizing each other. Now they had signed a nonaggression pact. A week later, Hitler's army attacked Poland, marking the official beginning of World War II. Britain and France honored their treaties and came to Poland's defense. "This nation will remain a neutral nation," Roosevelt announced, "but I cannot ask that every American remain neutral in thought as well."

Roosevelt asked for a repeal of the embargo section of the Neutrality Act and for the approval of the sale of arms on a cash-and-carry basis to France and Britain. The United States would help the countries struggling against Hitler, but not at the risk of entering the war or even at the threat of disrupting the civilian economy. Yet Roosevelt did take some secret risks. In August 1939, Albert Einstein, a Jewish refugee from Nazi Germany, and other distinguished scientists warned the president that German researchers were at work on an atomic bomb. Fearing the consequences of a powerful new weapon in Hitler's hands, Roosevelt authorized funds for a top-secret project to build an American bomb first. Only a few advisers and key members of Congress knew of the project, which was officially organized in 1941 and would ultimately change the course of human history.

Albert Einstein, Letter to President Roosevelt (1939)

The war in Poland ended quickly. With Germany attacking from the west and the Soviet Union from the east, the Poles were overwhelmed in a month. The fall of Poland in September 1939 brought a lull in the fighting. A number of Americans, who feared communist Russia more than fascist Germany, urged the United States to take the lead in negotiating a peace settlement that would recognize the German and Russian occupation of Poland. The British and French, however, were not interested in such a solution, and neither was Roosevelt.

Great Britain sent several divisions to aid the French against the expected German attack, but for months nothing happened. This interlude, sometimes called the "phony war," dramatically ended on April 9, 1940, when Germany attacked Norway and Denmark with a furious air and sea assault. A few weeks later, using armored vehicles supported by massive air strikes, the German *Blitzkrieg* ("lightning war") swept through Belgium, Luxembourg, and the Netherlands. A week later, the Germans stormed into France.

The famed Maginot line, a series of fortifications designed to repulse a German invasion, was useless, as German mechanized forces swept around the

Military Expenditures and the National Debt, 1929–1945

Increased taxes, the sale of war bonds, and price controls kept inflation under relative control during the war. Still, the war industry not only stimulated the economy but also increased the national debt. In what other ways do wars influence the economy?

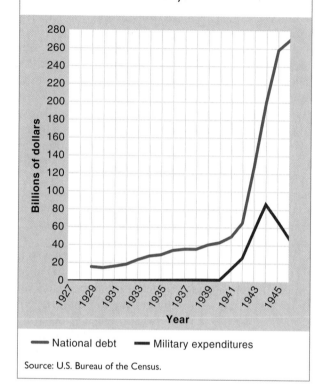

— National debt   — Military expenditures

Source: U.S. Bureau of the Census.

Winston Churchill, prime minister of Great Britain, asked for much more, but Roosevelt hesitated. In July 1940, the president did sign a measure authorizing $4 billion to increase the number of American naval warships. In September, Congress passed the Selective Service Act, which provided for the first peacetime draft in the history of the United States. More than a million men were to serve in the army for one year, but only in the Western Hemisphere. As the war in Europe reached a crisis in the fall of 1940, the American people were still undecided about the proper response.

The Election of 1940

Part of Roosevelt's reluctance to aid Great Britain more energetically came from his genuine desire to keep the United States out of the war, but it was also related to the presidential campaign waged during the crisis months of the summer and fall of 1940. Roosevelt broke a long tradition by seeking a third term. He marked the increasing support he was drawing from the liberal wing of the Democratic party by selecting liberal farm economist Henry Wallace of Iowa as his running mate.

The Republicans nominated Wendell Willkie of Indiana. Despite his big-business ties, Willkie approved of most New Deal legislation and supported aid to Great Britain. Energetic and attractive, Willkie was the most persuasive and exciting Republican candidate since Theodore Roosevelt, and he appealed to many people who distrusted or disliked Roosevelt. Yet in an atmosphere of international crisis, most voters chose to stay with Roosevelt. He won, 27 million to 22 million, and carried 38 of 48 states.

Lend-Lease

After the election, Roosevelt invented a scheme for sending aid to Britain without demanding payment. He called it "lend-lease." He compared the situation to lending a garden hose to a neighbor whose house was on fire. Senator Robert Taft of Ohio, however, thought the idea of lending military equipment and expecting it back was absurd. He decided it was more like lending chewing gum to a friend: "Once it had been used you did not want it back." Senator Burton K. Wheeler, an extreme isolationist, branded lend-lease "Roosevelt's triple A foreign policy" (after the Agricultural Adjustment Act) because it was designed to "plow under every fourth American boy."

The Lend-Lease Act, which Congress passed in March 1941, destroyed the fiction of neutrality. By that time, German submarines were sinking half a

DOCUMENT

Charles Lindbergh, Radio Address (1941)

end of the line and attacked from the rear. The French guns, solidly fixed in concrete and pointing toward Germany, were never fired. France surrendered in June as the British army fled back across the English Channel from Dunkirk.

How should the United States respond to the new and desperate situation in Europe? William Allen White, journalist and editor, and other concerned Americans organized the Committee to Defend America by Aiding the Allies, but others, including Charles Lindbergh, the hero of the 1920s, supported a group called America First. They argued that the United States should forget about England and concentrate on defending America. Roosevelt steered a cautious course. He approved the shipment to Britain of 50 overage American destroyers. In return, the United States received the right to establish naval and air bases on British territory from Newfoundland to Bermuda and British Guiana.

million tons of shipping each month in the Atlantic. In June, Roosevelt proclaimed a national emergency and ordered the closing of German and Italian consulates in the United States. On June 22, Germany suddenly attacked the Soviet Union. It was one of Hitler's biggest blunders of the war, forcing his armies to fight on two fronts.

When Roosevelt extended lend-lease aid to Russia in November 1941, most Americans accepted the Soviet Union as a friend and ally. By the autumn of 1941, the United States was virtually at war with Germany in the Atlantic. On September 11, Roosevelt issued a "shoot on sight" order for all American ships operating in the Atlantic, and on October 30, a German submarine sank an American destroyer off the coast of Newfoundland. The war in the Atlantic, however, was undeclared. Eventually, the sinking of enough American ships or another crisis would probably have provided the excuse for a formal declaration of war against Germany. It was not Germany, however, but Japan that catapulted the United States into World War II.

The Path to Pearl Harbor

Japan, controlled by ambitious military leaders, was the aggressor in the Far East as Hitler's Germany was in Europe. Intent on becoming a major world power yet desperately needing natural resources, especially oil, Japan was willing to risk war with China, the Soviet Union, and even the United States to get those resources. Japan invaded Manchuria in 1931 and launched an all-out assault on China in 1937. This was the beginning of what the Japanese would call "the Pacific War." The Japanese leaders assumed that at some point the United States would go to war if Japan tried to take the Philippines, but the Japanese attempted to delay that moment as long as possible by diplomatic means. The United States feared a two-front war and was willing to delay the confrontation with Japan until it had dealt with the German threat. Thus, between 1938 and 1941, the United States and Japan engaged in a kind of diplomatic shadow boxing.

The United States began to apply economic pressure in July 1939, giving Japan the required six months' notice regarding cancellation of the 1911 commercial agreement between the two countries. In September 1940, the Roosevelt administration forbade the shipment of airplane fuel and scrap metal to Japan. Other items were added to the embargo until by the spring of 1941, the United States allowed only oil to be shipped to Japan, hoping that the threat of cutting off this important resource would lead to negotiations and avert a crisis. Japan did open negotiations with the United States, but there was little to discuss. Japan would not withdraw from China as the United States demanded. Indeed, Japan, taking advantage of the situation in Europe, occupied French Indochina in 1940 and 1941. In July 1941, Roosevelt froze all Japanese assets in the United States, effectively embargoing trade with Japan.

Pearl Harbor An exploding American destroyer at Pearl Harbor, December 7, 1941. The attack on Pearl Harbor united the country and came to symbolize Japanese treachery and American lack of preparedness. Photographs such as this were published throughout the war to inspire Americans to work harder. Does Pearl Harbor still have meaning in our society today? (© SuperStock, Inc./SuperStock)

Roosevelt had an advantage in the negotiations with Japan, for the United States had broken the Japanese secret diplomatic code. But Japanese intentions were hard to decipher from the intercepted messages. The American leaders knew that Japan planned to attack, but they didn't know where. In September 1941, the Japanese decided to strike sometime after November unless the United States offered real concessions. The strike came not in the Philippines but at Pearl Harbor, the main American Pacific naval base, in Hawaii.

On the morning of December 7, 1941, Japanese airplanes launched from aircraft carriers attacked the U.S. fleet at Pearl Harbor. The surprise attack destroyed or disabled 19 ships (including 5 battleships) and 150 planes and killed 2,335 soldiers and sailors and 68 civilians. On the same day, the Japanese launched attacks on the Philippines, Guam, and the Midway Islands, as well as on the British colonies of Hong Kong and Malaya. The next day, with only one dissenting vote, Congress declared war on Japan.

Corporal John J. "Ted" Kohl, a 25-year-old from Springfield, Ohio, was standing guard that Sunday morning near an ammunition warehouse at Hickam Field, near Pearl Harbor. He had joined the army two years before when his marriage failed and he could not find work. A Japanese bomb hit nearby, and Ted Kohl blew up with the warehouse. It was not until Wednesday evening, December 10, that the telegram arrived in Springfield. "The Secretary of War desires to express his deep regrets that your son Cpl. John J. Kohl was killed in action in defense of his country." There would be hundreds of thousands of telegrams and even more tears before the war was over.

December 7, 1941, was a date that would "live in infamy," in the words of Franklin Roosevelt. It was also a day that would have far-reaching implications for American foreign policy and for American attitudes toward the world. The surprise attack united the country as nothing else could have. Even isolationists and America First advocates quickly rallied behind the war effort.

After the shock and anger subsided, Americans searched for a villain. Someone must have blundered, someone must have betrayed the country to have allowed the "inferior" Japanese to have carried out such a successful and devastating attack. A myth persists to this day that the villain was Roosevelt, who, the story goes, knew of the Japanese attack but failed to warn the military commanders so that the American people might unite behind the war effort against Germany. But Roosevelt did not know. There was no specific warning that the attack

was coming against Pearl Harbor, and the American ability to read the Japanese coded messages was of no help because the fleet kept radio silence.

The irony was that the Americans, partly because of racial prejudice against the Japanese, underestimated their ability. They ignored many warning signals because they did not believe that the Japanese could launch an attack on a target as far away as Hawaii. Most of the experts, including Roosevelt, expected the Japanese to attack the Philippines or perhaps Thailand. Many people blundered, but there was no conspiracy.

Even more important in the long run than the way the attack on Pearl Harbor united the American people was its effect on a generation of military and political leaders. Pearl Harbor became the symbol of unpreparedness. For a generation that experienced the anger and frustration of the attack on Pearl Harbor by an unscrupulous enemy, the lesson was to be prepared and ready to stop an aggressor before it had a chance to strike. The smoldering remains of the sinking battleships at Pearl Harbor on the morning of December 7, 1941, and the history lesson learned there would influence American policy not only during World War II but also in Korea, Vietnam, and the international confrontations thereafter.

THE HOME FRONT

Too often wars are described in terms of presidents and generals, emperors and kings, in terms of grand strategy and elaborate campaigns. But wars affect the lives of all people—the soldiers who fight and the women and children and men who stay home. World War II especially had an impact on all aspects of society—the economy, the movies and radio, even attitudes toward women and blacks. For many people, the war represented opportunity and the end of the Depression. For others, the excitement of faraway places meant that they could never return home again. For still others, the war left lasting scars.

Mobilizing for War

Converting American industry to war production was a complex task. Shortly after Pearl Harbor, Roosevelt created the War Production Board (WPB) and appointed Donald Nelson, executive vice president of Sears, Roebuck, to mobilize the nation's resources for an all-out war effort. The WPB offered businesses cost-plus contracts, guaranteeing a fixed and generous profit. Often the government also financed new plants and equipment. Secretary of War Henry Stimson explained: "If you . . . go to

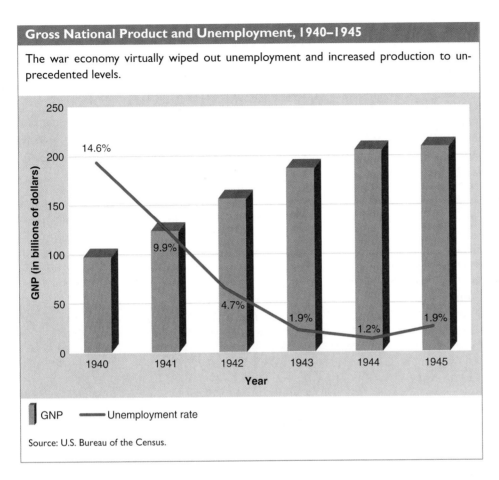

Gross National Product and Unemployment, 1940–1945

The war economy virtually wiped out unemployment and increased production to unprecedented levels.

GNP (in billions of dollars)

14.6%
9.9%
4.7%
1.9%
1.2%
1.9%

1940 1941 1942 1943 1944 1945
Year

GNP — Unemployment rate

Source: U.S. Bureau of the Census.

war . . . in a capitalist country, you have to let business make money out of the process or business won't work."

Roosevelt set up the Office of Scientific Research and Development (OSRD) to perfect new weapons and other products. The most important science and technology project carried on during the war was the development of the atomic bomb, but OSRD also improved radar and developed high-altitude bomb sights, jet engines, pressurized cabins for airplanes, and penicillin and other miracle drugs. Scientists under contract to the government also developed DDT and other effective insecticides, but none of the scientists recognized the dangerous side effects that DDT would have on the environment. The wartime collaboration of science, industry, and the government would lay the groundwork for massive projects in the postwar years.

The Roosevelt administration tried hard to gain the cooperation of businesspeople, many of them alienated by New Deal policies. The president appointed many business leaders to key positions and abandoned antitrust actions in any industry that was remotely related to the war effort. The policy worked. Industrial production and net corporate profits nearly doubled during the war. Large commercial

farmers also profited. The war years accelerated the mechanization of the farm and dramatically increased the use of fertilizer, but between 1940 and 1945 the farm population declined by 17 percent.

Many government agencies in addition to the War Production Board helped monitor the war effort. The Office of Price Administration (OPA) set prices and rationed products—and because it affected so many lives so disagreeably, many Americans regarded it as oppressive. The National War Labor Board (NWLB) had the authority to set wages and hours and to regulate working conditions, and it could seize factories whose owners refused to cooperate.

Union membership grew rapidly during the war, from 10.5 million in 1941 to 14.7 million in 1945. In return for a "no-strike pledge," the NWLB allowed agreements that required workers to retain their union membership through the life of a contract. Labor leaders, however, complained about increased government regulations and argued that wage controls coupled with wartime inflation were unfair. The NWLB finally allowed a 15 percent cost-of-living increase on some contracts, but that did not apply to overtime pay, which helped drive up wages in some industries during the war by about 70 percent.

In addition to wage and price controls and rationing, the government tried to reduce inflation by selling war bonds and by increasing taxes. The Revenue Act of 1942 raised tax rates, broadened the tax base, increased corporate taxes to 40 percent, and raised the excess-profits tax to 90 percent. In addition, the government initiated a payroll deduction for income taxes. The war made the income tax a reality for most Americans for the first time.

Despite some unfairness and much confusion, the American economy responded to the wartime crisis and produced the equipment and supplies that eventually won the war. American industries built 300,000 airplanes, 88,140 tanks, and 3,000 merchant ships. In 1944 alone, American factories produced 800,000 tons of synthetic rubber to replace the supply of natural rubber captured by the Japanese. Although the national debt grew from about $143 billion in 1943 to $260 billion in 1945, the government policy of taxation paid for about 40 percent of the war's cost. At the same time, full employment and the increase in two-income families, together with forced savings, helped provide capital for postwar expansion. In a limited way, the tax policy also tended to redistribute wealth, which the New Deal had failed to do. The top 5 percent income bracket, which controlled 23 percent of the disposable income in 1939, accounted for only 17 percent in 1945.

Women in an Airplane Factory

The war stimulated the growth of the federal bureaucracy and accelerated the trend, begun during World War I and extended in the 1920s and 1930s, toward the government's central role in the economy. The war also increased the cooperation between industry and government, creating what would later be called a military-industrial complex. But for most Americans, despite anger at the OPA and the income tax, the war meant the end of the Depression.

Patriotic Fervor

The war, so horrible elsewhere, was remote in the United States—except for the families that received the official telegram informing them that a loved one had been killed. The government tried to keep the conflict alive in the minds of Americans and to keep the country united behind the war effort. The Office of War Information controlled the news the American public received about the war and promoted patriotism. The government also sold war bonds, not only to help pay for the war and reduce inflation but also to sell the war to the American people. School-children purchased war stamps and faithfully pasted them in an album until they had accumulated stamps worth $18.75, enough to buy a $25 bond (redeemable 10 years later). Their bonds, they were told, would purchase bullets or a part for an airplane to kill "Japs" and Germans and defend the American way of life. "For Freedom's Sake, Buy War Bonds," one poster announced. Working men and women purchased

"Buy Victory Bonds" Poster

The Enemy   During the war American magazines and newspapers often depicted the Japanese as monkeys, insects, or rodents. Germans were rarely pictured this way. This December 12, 1942, issue of *Collier's* magazine pictures Japanese prime minister Hideki Tojo as a vampire bat carrying a bomb to drop on the United States. The Japanese, on the other hand, often pictured Americans and British as bloated capitalists and imperialists. What effect, do you suppose, did these caricatures have on attitudes and actions during the war? *(akg-images)*

bonds through payroll deduction plans and looked forward to spending the money on consumer goods after the war. In the end, the government sold more than $135 billion in war bonds. While the bond drives did help control inflation, they were most important in making millions of Americans feel that they were contributing to the war effort.

Those too old or too young to join the armed forces became air raid wardens or civilian defense and Red Cross volunteers. They raised victory gardens and took part in scrap drives. Even small children could join the war effort by collecting old rubber, wastepaper, and kitchen fats. Some items, including gasoline, sugar, butter, and meat, were rationed, but few people complained. Even horsemeat hamburgers seemed edible if they helped win the war. Newspaper and magazine advertising characterized ordinary actions as either speeding victory or impeding the war effort.

"Get in the Scrap" Poster, 1941-1945

Internment of Japanese Americans

Wartime campaigns not only stimulated patriotism but also promoted hatred for the enemy. The Nazis, especially Hitler and his Gestapo, had become synonymous with evil even before 1941. At the beginning of the war there was little animosity toward the German people, but before long most Americans ceased to make distinctions. All Germans seemed evil, although the anti-German hysteria that had swept the country during World War I never developed.

The Japanese were easier to hate than the Germans. The attack on Pearl Harbor created a special animosity toward the Japanese, but the depiction of the Japanese as warlike and subhuman owed something to a long tradition of fear of the so-called yellow peril and a distrust of all Asians. Movies, magazine articles, cartoons, and posters added to the image of the Japanese soldier or pilot with a toothy grin murdering innocent women and children or shooting down helpless Americans. Two weeks after Pearl Harbor, *Time* magazine explained to Americans how they could distinguish our Asian friends the Chinese "from the Japs." "Virtually all Japanese are short, Japanese are seldom fat; they often dry up with age," *Time* declared. "Most Chinese avoid horn-rimmed spectacles. Japanese walk stiffly erect, hard-heeled. Chinese, more relaxed, have an easy gait. The Chinese expression is likely to be more kindly, placid, open; the Japanese more positive,

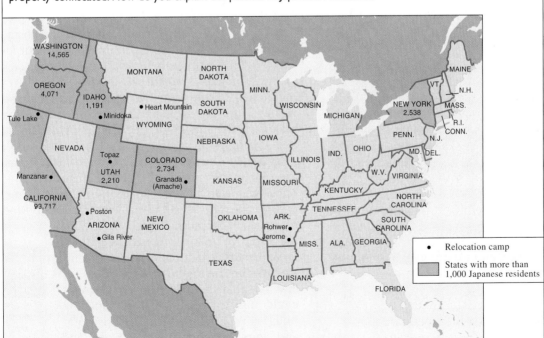

Relocation Camps

Early in 1942, responding to the hysterical fear that Japanese Americans living on the West Coast might engage in sabotage, the government ordered more than 100,000 Japanese Americans (many of them citizens) into relocation camps. A larger group of Japanese Americans living in Hawaii did not have their lives disrupted or their property confiscated. How do you explain the pattern of Japanese relocation?

dogmatic, arrogant." But Americans were not very good at distinguishing one Asian face from another. The Chinese and the Koreans tried to help by putting up signs that read, "We Are Not Japs," or "This Is a Chinese Shop."

The racial stereotype of the Japanese played a role in the treatment of Japanese Americans during the war. Some prejudice was shown against German and Italian Americans and some were relocated, but Japanese Americans were the only group confined in internment camps in large numbers and for the duration of the war. It was the greatest mass abridgment of civil liberties in American history.

At the time of Pearl Harbor, about 127,000 Japanese Americans lived in the United States, most on the West Coast. About 80,000 were nisei (Japanese born in the United States and holding American citizenship) and sansei (the sons and daughters of nisei); the rest were issei (aliens born in Japan who were ineligible for U.S. citizenship). The Japanese had long suffered from racial discrimination and

prejudice in the United States. They were barred from intermarriage with other groups and excluded from many clubs, restaurants, and recreation facilities. Many worked as tenant farmers, fishermen, and small-business owners. Others made up a small professional class of lawyers, teachers, and doctors and a large number of landowning farmers.

Although many retained cultural and linguistic ties to Japan, they posed no more threat to the country than did the much larger groups of Italian Americans and German Americans. But their appearance made them stand out as the others did not. After Pearl Harbor, an anti-Japanese panic seized the West Coast. A Los Angeles newspaper reported that armed Japanese were in Baja, California, ready to attack. Rumors suggested that Japanese fishermen were preparing to mine the harbor, blow up tunnels, and poison the water supply.

West Coast politicians and ordinary citizens urged the War Department and the president to evacuate the Japanese. The president capitulated and issued Executive Order 9066 authorizing the evacuation in February 1942. "The continued pressure of a largely unassimilated, tightly knit racial group, bound to an enemy nation by strong ties of race, culture, custom and religion, constituted a menace which had to be dealt with," General John De Witt argued, justifying the removal on military grounds. But racial fear and animosity, not military necessity, stood behind the order.

Japanese Americans at Santa Anita Racetrack in 1942

Eventually, the government built the "relocation centers" in remote, often arid, sections of the West. "The Japs live like rats, breed like rats, and act like rats. We don't want them," the governor of Idaho announced. The camps were primitive and unattractive. "When I first entered our room, I became sick to my stomach," a Japanese American woman remembered. "There were seven beds in the room and no furniture nor any partitions to separate the males and the females of the family. I just sat on the bed, staring at the bare wall."

The government evacuated about 110,000 Japanese, including about 60,000 American citizens. Those who were forced to leave their homes, farms, and businesses lost almost all their property and possessions. Farmers left their crops to be harvested by their American neighbors. Store owners sold out for a small percentage of what their goods were worth. Very few personal items or household goods could be transported. The Japanese Americans lost their worldly possessions, and something more—their pride and

A Young Nisei and Her Family's Belongings

Relocation Japanese American children on their way to a "relocation center." For many Japanese Americans, but especially for the children, the nightmare of the relocation camp experience would stay with them all their lives. Was the relocation of Japanese Americans necessary? *(Library of Congress)*

respect. One 6-year-old kept asking his mother to "take him back to America." He thought his relocation center was in Japan.

The evacuation of the Japanese Americans was unjustified. Even in Hawaii, where a much larger Japanese population existed, the government evacuated only a few (in part because the Japanese were so vital to the economy of the Islands), and no sabotage and little disloyalty occurred. The government allowed Japanese American men to volunteer for military service, and many served bravely in Europe. The 442nd Infantry Combat Team, made up entirely of nisei, became the most decorated unit in all the military service—another indication of the loyalty and patriotism of most Japanese Americans.

After January 1944, the United States government began drafting nisei men who were being retained in the relocation centers, but a few, as many as 10 percent in some camps, refused and became draft resisters and were sent to prison. They appreciated the irony and the injustice of being asked to register for the draft as citizens while being deprived of the rights of citizenship in relocation centers. At the same time that Japanese American citizens were confined to relocation centers, more than 400,000 German prisoners were confined to prison camps, usually in small towns across America. In some cases, they were treated better than Japanese American citizens. In 1988, Congress belatedly voted limited compensation for the Japanese Americans relocated during World War II.

IMAGE

Japanese American Family in Internment Camp

Asian, African, and Hispanic Americans at War

The Pacific War made China an ally of the United States, but Congress did not repeal the Chinese Exclusion Act until 1943, and then only 105 Chinese a year were allowed to enter the United States legally. Despite this affront, Chinese communities in the United States joined the war effort enthusiastically. They bought war bonds, collected scrap metal, and in other ways tried to show that they were loyal citizens. Almost 13,500 Chinese men enlisted or were drafted into the army. Many others took jobs in war industries. Formerly restricted to jobs in laundries or restaurants, they eagerly sought employment in factories. In fact, so many waiters left their jobs that four restaurants in New York's Chinatown had to close in 1942.

The Korean, Filipino, and Asian Indian population also contributed to the war effort. In California, 16,000 Filipinos registered for the first draft, and

many served behind enemy lines in the battle to recapture the Philippine Islands. As members of the United States Armed Forces, they were allowed to become citizens, but the Koreans were classified as enemy aliens. Still, many served in the army and proved valuable because they often could speak Japanese. The 1923 Supreme Court decision that had denied citizenship to Asian Indians was altered during the war in part because the United States needed India as an ally in the Pacific War. Despite increased acceptance during the war, Asians still faced prejudice and were often denied service in restaurants or refused admittance to theaters. Many Americans hated the Japanese; to them, all Asians looked like the enemy.

Even in much of the North, the United States remained a segregated society in 1941. African Americans could not live, eat, travel, work, or go to school with the same freedom that whites enjoyed. Black Americans profited little from the revival of prosperity and the expansion of jobs early in the war. Those who joined the military were usually assigned to menial jobs as cooks or laborers and were always assigned to segregated units with whites as the high-ranking officers. The myth that black soldiers had failed to perform well in World War I persisted. "Leadership is not embedded in the negro race yet," Secretary of War Henry Stimson wrote, "and to try to make commissioned officers . . . lead men into battle—colored men—is only to work a disaster to both."

DOCUMENT

Sterling A. Brown, "Out of Their Mouths" (1942)

Some black leaders found it especially ironic that as the country prepared to fight Hitler and his racist policies, the United States persisted in its own brand of racism. "A jim crow Army cannot fight for a free world," announced *The Crisis,* the journal of the NAACP. A. Philip Randolph decided to act rather than talk. The son of a Methodist minister, Randolph had worked with the first wave of African Americans migrating from the South to the northern cities during and just after World War I. He spent years trying "to carry the gospel of unionism to the colored world." He organized and led the Brotherhood of Sleeping Car Porters, and in 1937, he finally won grudging recognition of the union from the Pullman Company.

Respected and admired by black leaders of all political persuasions, Randolph convinced many of them in 1941 to join him in a march on Washington to demand equal rights. The threat of as many as 100,000 African Americans marching in protest in the nation's capital alarmed Roosevelt. At first, he sent his assistants, including his wife, Eleanor (who was greatly admired in the black community), to

"Rosie the Riveter"   Many African Americans moved north, lured by jobs in war industries. Prejudice remained even in the North, and some blacks were denied employment or were given the most menial tasks. Others, like these welders, found good jobs, improved their lives, and helped change the dynamics of race relations in the United States. What other developments resulted from the wartime employment of women and minorities? *(Library of Congress, [LCUSW3-34282-CC])*

barred from hotels and restaurants. Years later, one former black soldier recalled being refused service in a restaurant in Salina, Kansas, while the same restaurant served German prisoners from a camp nearby. "We continued to stare," he recalled. "This was really happening. . . . The people of Salina would serve these enemy soldiers and turn away black American G.I.'s."

Jobs in war industries helped many African Americans improve their economic conditions. Continuing the migration that had begun during World War I, about 1 million southern blacks moved to northern and western cities. The new arrivals increased pressure on overcrowded housing, aggravating tension among all hard-pressed groups. In Detroit, a race riot broke out in the summer of 1943 after Polish Americans protested a public housing development that promised to bring blacks into the neighborhood. Before federal and state troops could restore order, 25 blacks and 9 whites had been killed and more than $2 million worth of property was destroyed. Groups of white men roamed the city attacking blacks, overturning cars and setting fires. Other riots broke out in Mobile, Los Angeles, New York, and Beaumont, Texas. In all these cities, and in others, the legacy of hate lasted long after the war.

Mexican Americans, like most minority groups, profited during the war from the increased job opportunities provided by wartime industry, but they, too, faced racial prejudice. In California and in many parts of the Southwest, Mexicans could not use public swimming pools. Often lumped together with blacks, they were excluded from certain restaurants. Usually they were limited to menial jobs and were constantly harassed by the police, picked up for minor offenses, and jailed on the smallest excuse.

In Los Angeles, anti-Mexican prejudice flared into violence. The increased migration of Mexicans into the city as well as old hatreds created a volatile situation. Most of the hostility and anger focused on Mexican gang members, or *pachuchos*, especially those wearing zoot suits. The suits consisted of long, loose coats with padded shoulders, ballooned pants pegged at the ankles, and a wide-brimmed hat. A watch chain and a ducktail haircut completed the uniform. The zoot suit had originated in the black sections of northern cities and became a national craze during the war. It was a look some teenage males adopted to call attention to themselves and shock conventional society.

The zoot-suiters especially angered soldiers and sailors who were stationed in or on leave in Los Angeles. After a number of provocative incidents, violence broke out between the Mexican American youths and the servicemen in the spring of 1943.

dissuade Randolph from such drastic action. Finally, he talked to Randolph in person on June 18, 1941. Randolph and Roosevelt struck a bargain. Roosevelt refused to desegregate the armed forces, but in return for Randolph's calling off the march, the president issued Executive Order 8802, which stated that it was the policy of the United States that "there shall be no discrimination in the employment of workers in defense industries or government because of race, creed, color or national origin." He also established the Fair Employment Practices Commission (FEPC) to enforce the order.

DOCUMENT

A. Philip Randolph, "Why Should We March" (1942)

By threatening militant action, the black leaders wrested a major concession from the president. But the executive order did not end prejudice, and the FEPC, which its chairman described as the "most hated agency in Washington," had limited success in erasing the color line. Many black soldiers were angered and humiliated throughout the war by being made to sit in the back of buses and being

The servicemen, joined by others, beat up the Mexicans, stripped them of their offensive clothes, and then gave them haircuts. The police, both civilian and military, looked the other way, and when they did move in, they arrested the victims rather than their attackers.

SOCIAL IMPACT OF THE WAR

Modern wars have been incredibly destructive of human lives and property, but they have social results as well. The Civil War ended slavery and ensured the triumph of the industrial North for years to come; in so doing, it left a legacy of bitterness and transformed the race question from a sectional to a national problem. World War I ensured the success of woman suffrage and prohibition, caused a migration of blacks to northern cities, and ushered in a time of intolerance. World War II also had many social results. It altered patterns of work, leisure, education, and family life; caused a massive migration of people; created jobs; and changed lifestyles. It is difficult to overemphasize the impact of the war on the generation that lived through it.

Wartime Opportunities

More than 15 million American civilians moved during the war. Like the Momadays, many left home to find better jobs. In fact, for many Native Americans, wartime opportunities led to a migration from rural areas and reservations into cities. Americans moved off farms and away from small towns, flocking to cities, where defense jobs were readily available. They moved west: California alone gained more than 2 million people during the war. But they also moved out of the South into northern cities, while a smaller number moved from the North to the South. Late in the war, when a shortage of farm labor developed, some reversed the trend and moved back onto the farms. But a great many people moved somewhere. One observer, noticing the heavily packed cars heading west, decided that it was just like *The Grapes of Wrath,* without the poverty and the hopelessness.

The World War II migrants poured into industrial centers: 200,000 came to the Detroit area, nearly half a million to Los Angeles, and about 100,000 to Mobile, Alabama. They put pressure on schools, housing, and other services. Often they had to live in new Hoovervilles, trailer parks, or temporary housing. In San Pablo, California, a family of four adults and seven children lived in an 8-by-10-foot shack.

Nowhere was the change more dramatic than in the West, and especially in California, where the wartime boom transformed the region more dramatically than any development since the nineteenth-century economic revolution created by the railroads and mining. The federal government spent more than $70 billion in the state (one-tenth of the total for the entire country) to build army bases, shipyards, supply depots, and testing sites. In addition, private industry constructed so many facilities that the region became the center of a growing military-industrial complex. San Diego, for example, was transformed from a sleepy port and naval base into a sprawling metropolis. The population grew by 147 percent between 1941 and 1945, from 202,000 to 380,000. Vallezo, a small city near Oakland, grew from 20,000 to more than 100,000 in just two years. The U.S. Navy's Mare Island Shipyard, which was nearby, increased its workforce from 5,000 to 45,000. Vanport, just north of Portland, Oregon, was an empty mud flat in 1940; three years later, it was a bustling city of more than 40,000. Almost everyone in the new town worked for the Kaiser Ship Yards.

This spectacular growth created problems. There was a housing shortage, schools were overcrowded, and hospitals and municipal services could not keep up with the demand. Crime and prostitution increased as did racial tensions. Some migrants had never lived in a city and were homesick. On one occasion in a Willow Grove, Michigan, school, the children were all instructed to sing "Michigan, My Michigan"; no one knew the words because they all came from other states.

For the first time in years, many families had money to spend, but they had nothing to spend it on. The last new car rolled off the assembly line in February 1942. There were no washing machines, refrigerators, or radios in the stores, no gasoline and no tires to permit weekend trips. Even when people had time off, they tended to stay at home or in the neighborhood. Some of the new housing developments had the atmosphere of a mining camp, complete with drinking, prostitution, and barroom brawls.

The war required major adjustments in American family life. With several million men in the service and others far away working at defense jobs, the number of households headed by a woman increased dramatically. The number of marriages also rose sharply. Early in the war, a young man could be deferred if he had a dependent, and a wife qualified as a dependent. Later, many servicemen got married, often to women they barely knew, because they wanted a little excitement and perhaps someone to come home to. The birthrate also began to rise in 1940, as young couples started families as fast as they could. The number of births outside marriage also rose, and from the outset of the war, the divorce rate began to climb sharply. Yet most of the wartime marriages survived, and many of the women left at home looked ahead to a time after the war when they could settle down to a normal life.

Women Workers for Victory

Thousands of women took jobs in heavy industry that formerly would have been considered unladylike. They built tanks, airplanes, and ships, but they still earned less than men. At first, women were rarely hired because as the war in Europe pulled American industry out of its long slump, unemployed men snapped up the newly available positions. But by 1943, with many men drafted and male unemployment virtually nonexistent, the government was quick to suggest that it was women's patriotic duty to take their place on the assembly line. Nearly 3 million women served in the Women's Land Army to replace farm laborers who were in the army, but it was the woman factory worker who captured the public's imagination. A popular song was "Rosie the Riveter," who was "making history working for victory." She also helped her marine boyfriend by "working overtime on the riveting machine."

VIDEO

Rosie the Riveter

At the end of the war, the labor force included 19.5 million women, but three-fourths of them had been working before the conflict, and some of the additional ones might have sought work in normal times. The new women war workers tended to be older, and they were more often married than single. Some worked for patriotic reasons. "Every time I test a batch of rubber, I know it's going to help bring my three sons home quicker," a woman worker in a rubber plant remarked. But others worked for the money or to have something useful to do. Yet in 1944, women's weekly wages averaged $31.21, compared with $54.65 for men, reflecting women's more menial tasks and their low seniority as well as outright discrimination. Still, many women enjoyed factory work. "Boy have the men been getting away with murder all these years," exclaimed a Pittsburgh housewife. "Why I worked twice as hard selling in a department store and got half the pay."

IMAGE

"Women in War" Poster

Black women faced the most difficult situation during the war, and often when they applied for work, they were told, "We have not yet installed separate toilet facilities" or "We can't put a Negro in the front office." Not until 1944 did the telephone company in New York City hire a black telephone operator. Still, some black women moved during the war from domestic jobs to higher-paying factory work. Married women with young children also found it difficult to obtain work. There were few day-care facilities, and women were often informed that they should be home with their children.

Women workers often had to endure catcalls, whistles, and more overt sexual harassment on the job. Still, most persisted, and they tried to look feminine despite the heavy work clothes. In one Boston factory, a woman was hooted at for carrying a lunch box. Only men, it seemed, carried lunch boxes; women brought their lunch in a paper bag.

Many women war workers quickly left their jobs after the war ended. Some left by choice, but dismissals ran twice as high for women as for men. The war had barely shaken the notion that a woman's place was at home. Some women would have preferred to keep working. But most women, and an even larger percentage of men, agreed at the end of the war that women did not deserve an "equal chance with men" for jobs. For most Americans, a woman's place was still in the home.

Entertaining the People

According to one survey, Americans listened to the radio an average of $4^{1}/_{2}$ hours a day during the war. The major networks increased their news programs from less than 4 percent to nearly 30 percent of broadcasting time. Americans heard Edward R. Murrow broadcasting from London during the German air blitz with the sound of the air raid sirens in the background. They listened to Eric Sevareid cover the battle of Burma and describe the sensation of jumping out of an airplane. Often the signal faded out and the static made listening difficult, but the live broadcasts had drama and authenticity never before possible.

Even more than the reporters, the commentators became celebrities on whom the American people depended to explain what was going on around the world. Millions listened to the clipped, authoritative voice of H. V. Kaltenborn or to Gabriel Heatter, whose trademark was "Ah, there's good news tonight." But the war also intruded on almost all other programming. Music, which took up a large proportion of radio programming, also conveyed a war theme. There were "Goodbye, Mama (I'm Off to Yokohama)" and "Praise the Lord and Pass the Ammunition," but more numerous were songs of romance and love, songs about separation and hope for a better time after the war. The danceable tunes of Glenn Miller and Tommy Dorsey became just as much a part of wartime memories as ration books and far-off battlefields.

For many Americans, the motion picture became the most important leisure activity and a part of their fantasy life during the war. Attendance at the movies averaged about 100 million viewers a week. There might not be gasoline for weekend trips or Sunday drives, but the whole family could go to the movies. Even those in the military service could watch American movies on board ship or at a remote outpost. "Pinup" photographs of Hollywood stars decorated the barracks and even tanks and planes wherever American troops were stationed.

Musical comedies, cowboy movies, and historical romances remained popular during the war, but the conflict intruded even on Hollywood. Newsreels that offered a visual synopsis of the war news, always with an upbeat message and a touch of human interest, preceded most movies. Their theme was that the Americans were winning the war, even if early in the conflict there was little evidence to that effect. Many feature films also had a wartime theme, picturing the war in the Pacific complete with grinning, vicious Japanese villains (usually played by Chinese or Korean character actors). In the beginning of these films, the Japanese were always victorious, but in the end, they always got "what they deserved."

The movies set in Europe differed from those depicting the Far Eastern war. British and Americans, sometimes spies, sometimes downed airmen, could dress up like Germans and get away with it. They outwitted the Germans at every turn, sabotaging important installations, and made daring escapes from prison camps. Many wartime movies featured a multicultural platoon led by a veteran sergeant with a Protestant, a Catholic, a Jew, a black, a farmer, and a city resident. In several movies, the army was integrated, but in the real army, blacks served in segregated platoons.

Religion in Time of War

One of the four freedoms threatened by German and Japanese aggression was the "freedom to worship," and Roosevelt continually emphasized that the enemy was opposed to all religion. According to one estimate in 1940, 65 million Americans belonged to 250,000 churches and other religious institutions. There were about 23 million Catholics and 5 million Jews, and the rest were of one Protestant denomination or another. Most Americans thought of the United States as a Christian nation, and by that they usually meant a Protestant nation. While the war did lead to a measure of religious tolerance, anti-Semitism and anti-Catholicism did not

disappear. According to one poll, although 18 percent of Americans never went to church, more than 30 percent said that the war had strengthened their religious faith.

Those who joined the armed forces were given three choices under religion: They were asked to check Protestant, Catholic, or Jew, and their "dog tags" were marked *P, C,* or *H* (for *Hebrew*). There was no room for Hindu, Buddhist, Muslim, or atheist. Some men refused to fight on religious grounds. During World War I, only members of the traditional peace churches (Quaker, Brethren, and Mennonite) were deferred from military service as conscientious objectors. In World War II, the criterion was broadened to include those who opposed war because of "religious training and belief." More than 70,000 claimed exemption on those grounds, and the government honored about half those claims. Twenty-five thousand were assigned to noncombat military service.

A few clergymen remained pacifists and opposed the war, but far fewer than in World War I. A great many more volunteered to serve as chaplains, and like the men, they were categorized as Protestant, Catholic, or Jew. One of the most influential of the ministers who supported the use of force to combat evil was the Protestant theologian and clergyman Reinhold Niebuhr. In a series of books including *Moral Man and Immoral Society* (1932) and *Children of Light and Children of Darkness* (1944), he struck out against what he saw as a naive faith in the goodness of men, a faith that permeated the Social Gospel movement, the Progressive movement, and the New Deal. In a world gone mad, he interpreted all men as sinful, and he stressed the "evil that good men do." He argued for the use of force against evil. Neibhur's Christian Realism had little impact on most Americans, but he influenced the continuing debate in the 1930s, 1940s, and 1950s over the proper American response to evil around the world.

The GIs' War

GI, the abbreviation for *government issue,* became the affectionate designation for the ordinary soldier in World War II. The GIs came from every background and ethnic group. Some served reluctantly, some eagerly. A few became genuine heroes. All were turned into heroes by the press and the public, who seemed to believe that one American could easily defeat at least 20 Japanese or Germans. Ernie Pyle, one of the war correspondents who chronicled the authentic story of the ordinary GI, wrote of soldiers "just toiling from day to day in a world full of insecurity, discomfort, homesickness, and a dulled sense of danger."

In the midst of battle, the war was no fun, but only one soldier in eight who served ever saw combat, and even for many of those, the war was a great adventure (just as World War I had been). "When World War II broke out I was delighted," Mario Puzo, author of *The Godfather,* remembered. "There is no other word, terrible as it may sound. My country called. I was delivered from my mother, my family, and delivered *without* guilt." World War II catapulted young men and women out of their small towns and urban neighborhoods into exotic places, where they met new people and did new things.

The war was important for Mexican Americans, who were drafted and volunteered in great numbers. One-third of a million served in all branches of the military, a larger percentage than for many other ethnic groups. Although they encountered prejudice, they probably found less in the armed forces than they had at home, and many returned to civilian life with new ambitions and a new sense of self-esteem.

Many Native Americans also served. In fact, many were recruited for special service in the Marine Signal Corps. One group of Navajo completely befuddled the Japanese with a code based on their native language. But the Navajo code talkers and all other Native Americans who chose to return to the reservations after the war were ineligible for veterans' loans, hospitalization, and other benefits. They lived on federal land, and that, according to the law, canceled all the advantages that other veterans enjoyed after the war.

IMAGE

Navajo Indians Aiding the U.S. War Effort

For African Americans, who served throughout the war in segregated units and faced prejudice wherever they went, the military experience also had much to teach. Fewer blacks were sent overseas (about 79,000 of 504,000 blacks in the service in 1943), and fewer were in combat outfits, so the percentage of black soldiers killed and wounded was low. Many illiterate blacks, especially from the South, learned to read and write in the service. Blacks who went overseas began to realize that not everyone viewed them as inferior. One black army officer said, "What the hell do we want to fight the Japs for anyhow?

IMAGE

African American Fighter Pilots

"*Joe, yestiddy ya saved my life an' I swore I'd pay ya back. Here's my last pair of dry socks.*"

Willie and Joe Sergeant Bill Mauldin's biting cartoons published in *Stars and Stripes,* the army newspaper, depicted two GIs, Willie and Joe, as they slogged their way across Europe. Willie and Joe, sloppy, unshaven, and often insubordinate and cynical, contrasted sharply with the image of the American soldier promoted by the war department. General George S. Patton accused Mauldin of "undermining the morale of the army," but troops loved Willie and Joe. In this cartoon dry socks are more important to the soldier than patriotism and honor. Why did Mauldin anger the top army officers so much? *(Copyright 1944 by Bill Mauldin. Reprinted courtesy of the WIlliam Mauldin Estate.)*

They couldn't possibly treat us any worse than these 'crackers' right here at home." Most realized the paradox of fighting for freedom when they themselves had little freedom; they hoped things would improve after the war.

Because the war lasted longer than World War I, its impact was greater. In all, more than 16 million men and women served in some branch of the military service. About 322,000 were killed in the war, and more than 800,000 were wounded. The 12,000 listed as missing just disappeared. The war claimed many more lives than World War I and was the nation's costliest after the Civil War. But because of penicillin, blood plasma, sulfa drugs, and rapid

American Dead More than 300,000 American servicemen died during the war, but the government tried to protect the American people from learning the real cost of the battles. This photograph, published in 1943, was the first to show dead American soldiers. Why did the government protect the American people from seeing dead American soldiers? *(Time/Life Pictures/Getty Images.)*

war in the Philippines as prisoners of the Japanese. Most nurses, however, served far behind the lines tending the sick and wounded. Army nurses who were given officer rank were forbidden to date enlisted men. "Not permitting nurses and enlisted men to be seen together is certainly not American," one soldier decided.

Though nobody objected to women's serving as nurses, not until April 1943 did women physicians win the right to join the Army and Navy Medical Corps. Some people questioned whether it was right for women to serve in other capacities, but Congress authorized full military participation for women (except for combat) because of the military emergency and the argument that women could free men for combat duty. About 350,000 women joined the military service, most in the Women's Army Corps (WAC) and the women's branch of the Navy (WAVES), but others served in the coast guard and the marines. More than 1,000 women trained as pilots. As members of Women's Airforce Service Pilots (WASP), they flew bombers from the factories to landing fields in Great Britain.

Many recruiting posters suggested that the services needed women "for the precision work at which women are so adept" or for work in hospitals to comfort and attend to the wounded "as only women can do." Most women served in traditional female roles, doing office work, cooking, and cleaning. But others were engineers and pilots. Still, men and women were not treated equally. Women were explicitly kept out of combat situations and were often underused by male officers who found it difficult to view women in nontraditional roles.

Men were informed about contraceptives and encouraged to use them, but information about birth control was explicitly prohibited for women. Rumors charged many servicewomen with sexual promiscuity. On one occasion, the secretary of war defended the morality and the loyalty of the women in the service, but the rumors continued, spread apparently by men made uncomfortable by women's invasion of the male military domain. One cause for immediate discharge was pregnancy; yet

battlefield evacuation, the wounded in World War II were twice as likely to survive as those wounded in World War I. Penicillin also minimized the threat of venereal disease, but all men who served saw an anti-VD film, just as their predecessors had in World War I.

Women in Uniform

Women had served in all wars as nurses and cooks and in other support capacities, and during World War II many continued in these traditional roles. A few nurses landed in France just days after the Normandy invasion. Nurses served with the army and the marines in the Pacific. They dug their own foxholes and treated men under enemy fire. Sixty-six nurses spent the entire

IMAGE
"It's a Woman's War, Too" Poster

AMERICAN VOICES

Robert Kotlowitz, of Polish-Jewish background, grew up in Baltimore. After high school he started college at the Johns Hopkins University, but in 1943 at age 18 he dropped out and was drafted into the army. "I believed in the war," he wrote. "It seemed just and righteous to me." The war didn't seem so righteous on October 12, 1944, when Kotlowitz's platoon, led by Lieutenant Francis Gallagher, not much older than his men, was ordered to attack a hill in Northeastern France.

Within a few moments, . . . a lot had happened. Lieutenant Gallagher, for one, was already dead. We saw him die, quickly. A bullet pierced his scrawny boy's neck . . . as he moved forward ahead of us, just over the top of the rise. . . . Someone yelled Kaputt! as though it was an order. Gallagher stood there, upright and motionless, his ferret's face full of surprise, when the German's began to fire their Maussers. At the same moment, perfectly synchronized, a 180-degree sweep of machine-gun fire, which at first I mistook for our own, took us from right to left . . . dropping the platoon where it stood. It then came around in a second sweep.

I saw a hole open up in the back of Lieutenant Gallagher's neck, when the bullet passed through the front—surprised at how large and black it was, clean, too, as though it had been drilled by a mechanic's precision tool. There was a surge of surface blood at first, then a gurgle, like a tap being turned on, then a sudden torrent as he fell without a sound. Both of his carotid arteries must have poured in one stream through the wound. All of this took perhaps a dozen seconds: Gallagher's death, the machine-gun assault, and the paralysis of the third platoon.

We lay on the ground without moving. It was no light. . . . The sounds. . . . never before heard, swelling over the noise of small-arms and machine-gun fire, of boys' voices calling for help or screaming in pain or terror—our own boys' voices, unrecognizable at first, weird in pitch and timbre.

. . . There was no response from the rest of C Company behind us, no answering artillery or heavy weapons fire, and no supporting troops to help us slip out of the . . . rise that we had trapped ourselves in. . . . Slowly then, as the morning wore on, and the knowledge began to sink in, I came to realize that for us there was nothing to do but wait, flat out as we were, for our own deaths.

■ *Did the brutal reality of war cancel out the patriotism and the idealism that made many young men join the army?*

---

the pregnancy rate for both married and unmarried women remained low.

Thus, despite difficulties, women played important roles during the war, and when they left the service (unlike the women who had served in other wars), they had the same rights and privileges as the male veterans. The women in the service did not permanently alter the military or the public's perception of women's proper role, but they did change a few minds, and many of the women who served had their lives changed and their horizons broadened.

A WAR OF DIPLOMATS AND GENERALS

Pearl Harbor catapulted the country into war with Japan, and on December 11, 1941, Hitler declared war on the United States. Why he did so has never been fully explained; he was perhaps impressed by the apparent weakness of America that was demonstrated at Pearl Harbor. He was not required by his treaty with Japan to go to war with the United States, and without his declaration, the United States might have concentrated on the war against Japan. But Hitler forced the United States into the war against the Axis powers in both Europe and Asia.

War Aims

Why was the United States fighting the war? What did it hope to accomplish in a peace settlement once the war was over? Roosevelt and the other American leaders never really decided. In a speech before Congress in January 1941, Roosevelt had mentioned the four freedoms: freedom of speech and expression,

CHAPTER 25 World War II 847

freedom of worship, freedom from want, and freedom from fear. For many Americans, especially after Norman Rockwell expressed those freedoms in four sentimental paintings, this was what they were fighting for. Roosevelt spoke vaguely of the need to extend democracy and to establish a peacekeeping organization, but in direct contrast to Woodrow Wilson's Fourteen Points, he never spelled out in any detail the political purposes for fighting. There were some other implied reasons for going to war. Henry Luce, the editor of *Life* magazine, made those reasons explicit in an editorial written nine months before Pearl Harbor. He called his essay "The American Century," and he argued that the United States had the responsibility to spread the American way of life around the world.

DOCUMENT

FDR, "The Four Freedoms" (1941)

Roosevelt and his advisers, realizing that it would be impossible to mount an all-out war against both Japan and Germany, decided to fight a holding action in the Pacific while concentrating efforts against Hitler in Europe, where the immediate danger seemed greater. But the United States was not fighting alone. It joined the Soviet Union and Great Britain in what became a difficult, but ultimately effective alliance to defeat Nazi Germany. Churchill and Roosevelt got along well, although they often disagreed on strategy and tactics. Roosevelt's relationship with Stalin was much more strained, but he often agreed with the Russian leader about the way to fight the war. Stalin, a ruthless leader who had maintained his position of power only after eliminating hundreds of thousands of opponents, distrusted both the British and the Americans, but he needed them, just as they depended on him. Without the tremendous sacrifices of the Russian army and the Russian people in 1941 and 1942, Germany would have won the war before the vast American military and industrial might could be mobilized.

A Year of Disaster

The first half of 1942 was disastrous for the Allied cause. In the Pacific, the Japanese captured the Dutch East Indies with their vast riches in rubber, oil, and other resources. They swept into Burma, took Wake Island and Guam, and invaded the Aleutian Islands of Alaska. They pushed the American garrison on the Philippines onto the Bataan peninsula and finally onto the tiny island of Corregidor, where U.S. General Jonathan Wainwright surrendered more than 11,000 men to the Japanese. American reporters tried to play down the disasters, concentrating their stories on the few American victories and tales of American heroism against overwhelming odds. One of the soldiers on a

Pacific island picked up an American broadcast one night. "The news commentators in the States had us all winning the war," he discovered, "their buoyant cheerful voices talking of victory. We were out here where we would see these victories. They were all Japanese."

In Europe, the Germans pushed deep into Russia, threatening to capture all the industrial centers and the valuable oil fields. For a time, it appeared that they would even take Moscow. In North Africa, General Erwin Rommel and his mechanized divisions, the Afrika Korps, drove the British forces almost to Cairo in Egypt and threatened the Suez Canal. In contrast to World War I, which had been a war of stalemate, the opening phase of World War II was marked by air strikes and troops supported by trucks and tanks covering many miles each day. In the Atlantic, German submarines sank British and American ships more rapidly than they could be replaced. For a few dark months in 1942, it seemed that the Berlin–Tokyo Axis would win the war before the United States was ready to fight.

The Allies could not agree on the proper military strategy in Europe. Churchill advocated tightening the ring around Germany, using bombing raids to weaken the enemy and encouraging resistance among the occupied countries but avoiding any direct assault on the continent until success was ensured. Remembering the vast loss of British lives during World War I, he was determined to avoid similar casualties in this conflict. Stalin demanded a second front, an invasion of Europe in 1942, to relieve the pressure on the Russian army, which faced 200 German divisions along a 2,000-mile front. Roosevelt agreed to an offensive in 1942. But in the end, the invasion in 1942 came not in France but in North Africa. The decision was probably right from a military point of view; it would have been impossible to launch an invasion of France in 1942, and landing in Morocco helped relieve the pressure on the British army, which was fighting desperately to keep Cairo and the Suez Canal out of German hands. But Stalin never forgave Churchill and Roosevelt for not coming to the aid of the beleaguered Soviet troops.

IMAGE

Eisenhower and Paratroopers in World War II

Attacking in North Africa in November 1942, American and British troops tried to link up with a beleaguered British army. The American army, enthusiastic but inexperienced, met little resistance in the beginning. At Kasserine Pass in Tunisia, the Germans counterattacked and destroyed a large American force, inflicting 5,000 casualties. Roosevelt, who launched the invasion in part to give the American people a victory to relieve the dreary news from the

Buchenwald   Only at the end of the war did most Americans learn about the horrors of Nazi concentration camps and gas chambers. Senator Alben Barkley of Kentucky looks in disbelief at dead Jews stacked like wood at Buchenwald on April 24, 1945. Why didn't Americans learn about the Holocaust sooner? (*National Archives [RG-111-SC-204745, Box 63]*)

Far East, learned that victories often came with long casualty lists.

He also learned the necessity of political compromise. To gain a cease-fire in conquered French territory in North Africa, the United States recognized Admiral Jean Darlan as head of its provisional government. Darlan persecuted the Jews, exploited the Arabs, imprisoned his opponents, and collaborated with the Nazis. He seemed diametrically opposed to the principles the Americans said they were fighting for. Did the Darlan deal mean the United States would negotiate with Mussolini? Or with Hitler? The Darlan compromise reinforced Soviet distrust of the Americans and angered many Americans as well.

Roosevelt never compromised or made a deal with Hitler, but he did aid General Francisco Franco, the Fascist dictator in Spain, in return for safe passage of American shipping into the Mediterranean. But the United States did not aid only right-wing dictators. It also supplied arms to the left-wing resistance in France, to the Communist Tito in Yugoslavia, and to Ho Chi Minh, the anti-French resistance leader in Indochina. Roosevelt also authorized large-scale lend-lease aid to the Soviet Union. Although liberals criticized his support of dictators, Roosevelt was willing to do almost anything to win the war. Military expediency often dictated his political decisions.

Even on one of the most sensitive issues of the war, the plight of the Jews in occupied Europe, Roosevelt's solution was to win the war as quickly as possible. By November 1942, confirmed information had reached the United States that the Nazis were systematically exterminating Jews, but that evidence got little attention in the United States. The Roosevelt administration did nothing for more than a year, and even then it did scandalously little to rescue European Jews from the gas chambers. Only 21,000 refugees were allowed to enter the United States over a period of $3^{1}/_{2}$ years, just 10 percent of those who could have been admitted under immigration quotas.

Nazi Murder Mills

The U.S. War Department rejected suggestions that the gas chambers and railway lines be bombed. That might not have worked, but anti-Semitic feelings in the United States in the 1940s and the fear of massive Jewish immigration help explain the failure of the Roosevelt administration to act. The fact that the mass media, Christian leaders, and even American Jews failed to mount effective pressure on the government does not excuse the president for his indifference to the systematic murder of millions of people. Roosevelt could not have prevented the Holocaust, but vigorous action on his part might have saved many thousands of lives during the war.

A Strategy for Ending the War

The commanding general of the Allied armies in the North African campaign emerged as a genuine

World War II: Pacific Theater

After the surprise attack on Pearl Harbor, the Japanese extended their control in the Pacific from Burma to the Aleutian Islands and almost to Australia. But after American naval and air victories at Coral Sea and Midway in 1942, the Japanese were increasingly on the defensive. **Reflecting on the Past** How did the great distances in the Pacific influence military plans for both sides? Why was the aircraft carrier more important than the battleship in the Pacific War? Was there any alternative to the American strategy of moving slowly from one Japanese-occupied island to another? Why did China play such a crucial role in the war against Japan?

leader. Born in Texas, Dwight D. Eisenhower spent his boyhood in Abilene, Kansas. His small-town background made it easy for biographers and newspaper reporters to make him into an American hero. Eisenhower, however, had not come to hero status easily. In World War I, he trained soldiers in Texas and never got to France. He was only a lieutenant colonel when World War II erupted. George Marshall, the army's top general, had discovered Eisenhower's talents even before the war began. Eisenhower was quickly promoted to general and achieved a reputation as an expert planner and

organizer. Gregarious and outgoing, he had a broad smile that made most people like him instantly. He was not a brilliant field commander and made many mistakes in the African campaign, but he had the ability to get diverse people to work together, which was crucial in situations in which British and American units had to cooperate.

The American army moved slowly across North Africa, linked up with the British, invaded Sicily in July 1943, and finally stormed ashore in Italy in September. The Italian campaign proved long and bitter. Although the Italians overthrew Mussolini and surrendered in September 1943, the Germans occupied the peninsula and gave ground only after bloody fighting. The whole American army seemed bogged down for months. The Allies did not reach Rome until June 1944, and they never controlled all of Italy.

Despite the decision to make the war in Europe the first priority, American ships and planes halted the Japanese advance in the spring of 1942. In the Battle of Coral Sea in May 1942, American carrier-based planes inflicted heavy damage on the Japanese fleet and prevented the invasion of the southern tip of New Guinea and probably of Australia as well. It was the first naval battle in history in which no guns were fired from one surface ship against another; airplanes caused all the damage. In World War II, the aircraft carrier proved more important than the battleship. A month later, at the Battle of Midway, American planes sank four Japanese aircraft carriers and destroyed nearly 300 planes. This was the first major Japanese defeat; it restored some balance of power in the Pacific and ended the threat to Hawaii.

In 1943, the American sea and land forces leapfrogged from island to island, gradually retaking territory from the Japanese and building bases to attack the Philippines and eventually Japan itself. Progress often had terrible costs, however. In November 1943, about 5,000 marines landed on the coral beaches of the tiny island of Tarawa. Despite heavy naval bombardment and the support of hundreds of planes, the marines met fierce opposition. The four-day battle left more than 1,000 Americans dead and more than 3,000 wounded. One marine general thought it was all wasted effort and believed that the island should have been bypassed. Others disagreed. And no one asked the marines who stormed the beaches; less than half of the first wave survived.

World War II in the Pacific

The Pacific War was often brutal and dehumanizing. American soldiers often collected Japanese ears, skulls, and other body parts as souvenirs, something unheard of on the European battlegrounds. "In Europe we felt that our enemies, horrible and deadly as they were, were still people," Ernie Pyle, the American war correspondent, remarked. "But out here I soon gathered that the Japanese were looked upon as something subhuman or repulsive, the way some people feel about cockroaches or mice."

The Invasion of France

Operation Overlord, the code name for the largest amphibious invasion in history, the invasion Stalin

had wanted in 1942, finally began on June 6, 1944. It was, according to Churchill, "the most difficult and complicated operation that has ever taken place." The initial assault along a 60-mile stretch of the Normandy coast was conducted with 175,000 men supported by 600 warships and 11,000 planes. Within a month, more than a million troops and more than 170,000 vehicles had landed. Such an invasion would have been impossible during World War I.

Operation Overlord, Normandy, 1944

British and American forces, with some units from other countries, worked together, but Overlord was made possible by American industry, which, by the war's end, was turning out an astonishing 50 percent of all the world's goods. During the first few hours of the invasion, there seemed to be too many supplies. "Everything was confusing," one soldier remembered. It cost 2,245 killed and 1,670 wounded to secure the beachhead. "It was much lighter than anybody expected," one observer remarked. "But if you saw faces instead of numbers on the casualty list, it wasn't light at all."

For months before the invasion, American and British planes had bombed German transportation lines, industrial plants, and even cities. In all, more than 1.5 million tons of bombs were dropped on Europe. The massive bombing raids helped make the invasion a success, but evidence gathered after the war suggests that the bombs did not disrupt German war production as seriously as Allied strategists believed at the time. Often a factory or a rail center would be back in operation within a matter of days, sometimes within hours, after an attack. In the end, the bombing of the cities, rather than destroying morale, may have strengthened the resolve of the German people to fight to the bitter end. And the destruction of German cities did not come cheaply. German fighters and antiaircraft guns shot down 22 of 60 B-17s on June 23, 1943, and in July 1943, 100 planes and 1,000 airmen were lost and an additional 75 men had mental breakdowns.

The most destructive bombing raid of the war, carried out against Dresden on the nights of February 13 and 14, 1945, had no strategic purpose. It was launched by the British and Americans to help demonstrate to Stalin that they were aiding the Russian offensive. Dresden, a city of 630,000, was a communications center. Three waves of 1,200 planes dropped more than 4,000 tons of bombs, causing a firestorm that swept over eight square miles, destroyed everything in its path, and killed an estimated 25,000 to 40,000 civilians. One of the American pilots remarked, "For the first time I felt sorry for the population below." The fire-bombing

World War II: European and North African Theaters

The German war machine swept across Europe and North Africa and almost captured Cairo and Moscow, but after major defeats at Stalingrad and El Alamein in 1943, the Axis powers were in retreat. Many lives were lost on both sides before the Allied victory in 1945. **Reflecting on the Past** How was the African campaign important to the Allies' strategy to defeat Germany and Italy? Why was the invasion of France necessary even after the capture of North Africa and a portion of Italy? Why was the Soviet Union crucial to the war in Europe? Why was the war in Europe very different from the war in the Pacific?

of Tokyo on March 9, 1945, also killed an estimated 100,000 people. The massive "strategic" bombing of European and Asian cities for the purpose of breaking the morale of the civilian population introduced terror as a strategy and eventually made the decision to drop the atomic bomb on two Japanese cities easier.

With the dashing and eccentric General George Patton leading the charge and the more staid General Omar Bradley in command, the American army broke out of the Normandy beachhead in July 1944. Led by the tank battalions, it swept across France. American productive capacity and the ability to supply a mobile and motorized army eventually

brought victory. But not all American equipment was superior. The American fighter plane, the P-40, could not compete early in the war with the German ME-109. The United States was also far behind Germany in the development of rockets, but that was not as important in the actual fighting as was the inability of the United States, until the end of the war, to develop a tank that could compete in armament or firepower with the German tanks. But the American army made up for the deficiency of its tanks in part by having superior artillery. Perhaps even more important, most of the American soldiers had grown up tinkering with cars and radios. Children of the machine age, they managed to make repairs and to keep tanks, trucks, and guns functioning under difficult circumstances. They helped give the American army the superior mobility that eventually led to the defeat of Germany.

By late 1944, the American and British armies had swept across France, while the Russians had pushed the German forces out of much of eastern Europe. The war seemed nearly over. However, just before Christmas in 1944, the Germans launched a massive counterattack along an 80-mile front, much of it held by thinly dispersed and inexperienced American troops. The Germans drove 50 miles inside the American lines before they were checked.

World War II in Europe

During the Battle of the Bulge, as it was called, Eisenhower was so desperate for additional infantry that he offered to pardon any military prisoners in Europe who would take up a rifle and go into battle. Most of the prisoners, who were serving short sentences, declined the opportunity to clear their record. Eisenhower also promised any black soldiers in the service and supply outfits an opportunity to become infantrymen in the white units, though usually with a lower rank. However, his chief of staff, pointed out that this was against War Department regulations and was the "most dangerous thing I have seen in regard to race relations." Eisenhower recanted, not wishing to start a social revolution. Black soldiers who volunteered to join the battle fought in segregated platoons commanded by white officers.

The Politics of Victory

As the American and British armies raced across France into Germany in the winter and spring of 1945, the political and diplomatic aspects of the war began to overshadow military concerns. It became a matter not only of defeating Germany but also of determining who was going to control Germany and the rest of Europe once Hitler fell. The relationship between the Soviet Union and the other Allies had been badly strained during the war; with victory in sight, the tension became even greater. Although the American press pictured Stalin as a wise and democratic leader and the Russian people as quaint and heroic, a number of high-level American diplomats and presidential advisers distrusted the Russians and looked ahead to a confrontation with Soviet communism after the war. These men urged Roosevelt to make military decisions with the postwar political situation in mind.

The most pressing concern in the spring of 1945 was who should capture Berlin. The British wanted to beat the Russians to the capital city. Eisenhower,

however, fearing that the Germans might barricade themselves in the Austrian Alps and hold out indefinitely, ordered the armies south rather than toward Berlin. He also wanted to avoid unnecessary American casualties, and he planned to meet the Russian army at an easily marked spot to avoid any unfortunate incidents. The British and American forces could probably not have arrived in Berlin before the Russians in any case, but Eisenhower's decision generated controversy after the war. Russian and American troops met on April 25, 1945, at the Elbe River. On May 2, the Russians took Berlin. Hitler committed suicide. The long war in Europe finally came to an end on May 8, 1945, but political problems remained.

VIDEO

Truman on the End of World War II in Europe

In 1944, the United States continued to tighten the noose on Japan. American long-range B-29 bombers began sustained strikes on the Japanese mainland in June 1944. In a series of naval and air engagements, especially at the Battle of Leyte Gulf, American planes destroyed most of the remaining Japanese navy. By the end of 1944, an American victory in the Pacific was all but ensured. American forces recaptured the Philippines early the next year, yet it might take years to conquer the Japanese on their home islands.

While the military campaigns reached a critical stage in both Europe and the Pacific, Roosevelt took time off to run for an unprecedented fourth term. He agreed to drop Vice President Henry Wallace from the ticket because some thought him too radical and impetuous. To replace him, the Democratic convention selected a relatively unknown senator from Missouri. Harry S Truman, a World War I veteran, had been a judge in Kansas City before being elected to the Senate in 1934. His only fame came when, as chairman of the Senate Committee to Investigate the National Defense Program, he had insisted on honesty and efficiency in war contracts. He got some publicity for saving the taxpayers' dollars.

The Republicans nominated Thomas Dewey, the colorless and politically moderate governor of New York, who had a difficult time criticizing Roosevelt without appearing unpatriotic. Roosevelt seemed haggard and ill during much of the campaign, but he won the election easily. He would need all his strength to deal with the difficult political problems of ending the war and constructing a peace settlement.

The Big Three at Yalta

Roosevelt, Churchill, and Stalin, together with many of their advisers, met at Yalta in the Crimea in February 1945 to discuss the problems of the peace settlements.

Most of the agreements reached at Yalta were secret, and in the atmosphere of the subsequent Cold War, many would become controversial. Roosevelt wanted the help of the Soviet Union in ending the war in the Pacific to avoid the needless slaughter of American men in an invasion of the Japanese mainland. In return for a promise to enter the war within three months after the war in Europe was over, the Soviet Union was granted the Kurile Islands, the southern half of Sakhalin, and railroads and port facilities in North Korea, Manchuria, and Outer Mongolia. Later that seemed like a heavy price to pay for the promise, but realistically the Soviet Union controlled most of this territory and could not have been dislodged short of going to war.

The Big Three at Yalta

When the provisions of the secret treaties were revealed much later, many people would accuse Roosevelt of trusting the Russians too much. But Roosevelt wanted to retain a working relationship with the Soviet Union. If the peace was to be preserved, the major powers of the Grand Alliance would have to work together. Moreover, Roosevelt hoped to get the Soviet Union's agreement to cooperate with a new peace-preserving United Nations organization after the war.

VIDEO

The Yalta Conference

The European section of the Yalta agreement proved even more controversial. The diplomats decided to partition Germany and to divide the city of Berlin. The Polish agreements were even more difficult to swallow, in part because the invasion of Poland in 1939 had precipitated the war. The Polish government in exile in London was militantly anti-Communist and looked forward to returning to Poland after the war. Stalin demanded that the eastern half of Poland be given to the Soviet Union. Churchill and Roosevelt finally agreed to the Russian demands with the proviso that Poland be compensated with German territory on its western border. Stalin also agreed to include some members of the London-based Polish group in the new Polish government. He also promised to carry out "free and unfettered elections as soon as possible."

The Polish settlement would prove divisive after the war, and it quickly became clear that what the British and Americans wanted in eastern Europe contrasted with what the Soviet Union intended. Yet at the time it seemed imperative that Russia enter the war in the Pacific, and the reality was that in 1945 the Soviet army occupied most of eastern Europe.

The most potentially valuable accomplishment at Yalta was Stalin's agreement to join Roosevelt and Churchill in calling a conference in San Francisco in April 1945 to draft a United Nations charter. The charter gave primary responsibility for keeping global peace to the Security Council, composed of five permanent members (the United States, the Soviet Union, Great Britain, France, and China) and six other nations elected for two-year terms.

Perhaps just as important as Yalta for structuring the postwar world was the Bretton Woods Conference, held at a resort hotel in the White Mountains of New Hampshire in the summer of 1944 and attended by delegates from 44 nations (the Soviet Union refused to participate). The economists and politicians established a Bank for Reconstruction and Development (the World Bank) and the International Monetary Fund. They also decided on a fixed rate of exchange among the world's currencies using the dollar rather than the pound as the standard. The Bretton Woods agreement lasted for 25 years and established that the United States, not Great Britain, would be the dominant economic power in the postwar world.

The Atomic Age Begins

Two months after Yalta, on April 12, 1945, as the United Nations charter was being drafted, Roosevelt died suddenly of a massive cerebral hemorrhage. Hated and loved to the end, he was replaced by Harry Truman, who was both more difficult to hate and harder to love. In the beginning, Truman seemed tentative and unsure of himself. Yet it fell to the new president to make some of the most difficult decisions of all time. The most momentous of all was the decision to drop the atomic bomb.

The Manhattan Project, first organized in 1941, was one of the best-kept secrets of the war. A distinguished group of scientists, whose work on the project was centered in Los Alamos, New Mexico, set out to perfect and manufacture an atomic bomb before Germany did. But by the time the bomb was successfully tested in the New Mexico desert on July 16, 1945, the war in Europe had ended. The scientists working on the bomb assumed that they were perfecting a military weapon. Yet when they saw the ghastly power of that first bomb, J. Robert Oppenheimer, a leading scientist on the project, remembered that "some wept, a few cheered. Most stood silently." Some opposed the military use of the bomb. They realized its revolutionary power and worried about the future reputation of the United States if it unleashed this new force. But a presidential committee made up of scientists, military leaders, and politicians recommended that it be used on a military target in Japan as soon as possible.

"The final decision of where and when to use the atomic bomb was up to me," Truman later remembered. "Let there be no doubt about it. I regarded

RECOVERING THE PAST

History, Memory, and Monuments

In recent years, historians have been studying collective memory—the stories people tell about the past. Collective memory is closely related to national regional identity and is often associated with patriotism and war. But memory is usually selective and often contested. The generation that lived through World War II is getting older, and often these people fear that few remember or care about their war. One veteran of the Italian campaign recently remarked: "Today they don't even know what Anzio was. Most people aren't interested." The collective memory of World War II may include letters, photos, old uniforms, and stories told to grandchildren (oral history), but the collective memory of war often includes monuments as well.

Almost every small town and city in the Northeast, the Midwest, and the South has monuments to the soldiers who fought and died in the Civil War; often it is a statue of a common soldier with rifle at rest. In the South, a statue of Robert E. Lee on horseback came to symbolize the "Lost Cause." Usually monuments to war symbolize triumph or fighting for a just cause, even in defeat.

A large monument to World War II veterans finally opened on the mall in Washington in 2004 after years of controversy. There have been many other attempts to honor the World War II generation. The Air and Space Museum of the Smithsonian Institution in Washington, D.C., planned a major exhibit for 1995 to commemorate the fiftieth anniversary of the dropping of the first atomic bomb on Hiroshima and the end of World War II. The *Enola Gay,* the B-29 that dropped the bomb, was to be the centerpiece of the exhibit, but the historians and curators who organized the exhibit also planned to raise a number of questions that historians had been debating for years. Would the war have ended in days or weeks without the bomb? How was the decision to drop the bomb made? Was there a racial component to the decision? Would the United States have dropped the bomb on Germany? Was the bomb dropped more to impress the Soviet Union than to force the Japanese to surrender? What was the impact of the bomb on the ground? What implications did dropping the bomb have on the world after 1945?

The exhibit (except in greatly modified form) never took place. Many veterans of World War II and other Americans denounced it as traitorous and un-American. For these critics the decision to drop the bomb was not something to debate. For them, World War II was a contest between good and evil, and the bomb was simply a way to defeat the evil empire and save American lives. The controversy over the *Enola Gay* exhibit demonstrated that 50 years later, memory and history were at odds and that the memory of the war was still contested. The main reason the exhibit did not satisfy those who remembered the war was

Dedication of the Iwo Jima Memorial Monument in Washington, D.C., November 10, 1954. *(National Archives [127-GRA-A409861])*

854

that it did not commemorate triumph but instead seemed to question the motives of those who fought and died.

The Vietnam Veterans Memorial erected in Washington in 1982 was initially controversial for similar reasons. Designed by Maya Lin, a young artist and sculptor, it consists of a wall of polished granite inscribed with the names of 58,000 dead. There are no soldiers on horseback; in fact, there are no figures at all, not even a flag. Critics called it a "black gash of shame." Even the addition of a sculpture of three "fighting men" did not satisfy many. But to almost everyone's surprise, hundreds of thousands of veterans and friends of veterans found the monument deeply moving, and they left photos, flowers, poems, and other objects. For them, the memorial successfully represented collective memory. Still the critics were dissatisfied; they wanted something more like the Iwo Jima monument.

Iwo Jima was a tiny, desolate island 640 miles from Tokyo, important only because it was a base for Japanese fighters to attack American bombers on their way to the Japanese mainland. The Fourth and Fifth Marine Divisions invaded the island on February 17, 1945. After bitter fighting, the marines captured Mt. Suribachi, the highest point on the island, on February 23 and completed the conquest of the island on March 17. But it was a costly victory—there were 4,189 Americans killed, 15,000 wounded, and 419 missing.

Associated Press photographer Joe Rosenthal was one of several journalists who went ashore with the marines and one of three photographers assigned to record the raising of the American flag on top of Mt. Suribachi. A group of marines raised the flag twice so the photographers could get their pictures. It was Rosenthal's photograph of the second flag raising that became famous. On February 25, 1945, his photograph of the five marines and a navy corpsman raising the flag was on the front page of Sunday newspapers across the country. "Stars and Stripes on Iwo," "Old Glory over Volcano," the captions read. Within months, the image of the flag raising appeared on a War Bond poster with the caption: "Now All Together" and also on a postage stamp. Three of the six flag raisers were killed in the battle for Iwo Jima, but those who survived became heroes, and their images were used to sell war bonds. Clearly, the flag-raising image had touched American emotions and quickly became part of the collective memory of the war, a

Official poster for the 1945 war bond drive using the image of the Iwo Jima flag raising. *(Courtesy of the Virginia War Museum)*

symbol of the country pulling together to defeat the enemy.

In November 1954, a giant statue of the flag raising, designed by Felix De Weldon, was dedicated as a memorial to the U.S. Marine Corps on the edge of Arlington National Cemetery. Vice President Richard Nixon, speaking at the dedication, said that the statue symbolized "the hopes and dreams of the American people and the real purpose of our foreign policy." The flag-raising image played an important role in two movies: *The Sands of Iwo Jima* (1949), starring John Wayne, and *The Outsider* (1960), starring Tony Curtis. During the 1988 presidential campaign, George H. W. Bush chose to make a speech in front of the marine monument urging a constitutional amendment to ban the desecration of the flag. The image of the flag raising in photograph, drawing, film, and cartoon remains part of the collective memory of World War II.

REFLECTING ON THE PAST Why did the Iwo Jima monument mean so much to the World War II generation? Was the monument more important than the photograph? What makes a monument meaningful? Is it the size? The accuracy? The ability to arouse emotion? Why do some monuments and symbols become part of collective memory, while others become controversial or forgotten? There are more than 15,000 outdoor sculptures and monuments in the country, most created since the Civil War. What monuments can you locate in your community? What collective memory do they symbolize?

HOW OTHERS SEE US

Yamaoka Michiko, on the Ground at Hiroshima

Yamaoka Michiko, a young Japanese high school student, was 15 on August 6, 1945, when the Enola Gay dropped the first atomic bomb. She survived, but she was horribly burned and disfigured. After the war she was one of 25 victims brought to the United States to receive treatment and plastic surgery.

That morning I left the house at about seven forty-five. I heard that the B-29s had already gone home. Mom told me, "Watch out, the B-29s might come again." My house was one point three kilometers from hypocenter. . . . I heard the faint sound of planes as I approached the river. The planes were tricky. Sometimes they only pretended to leave. I could still hear the very faint sound of planes. Today, I have no hearing in my left ear because of the blast. I thought, how strange, so I put my right hand above my eyes and looked up to see if I could spot them. The sun was dazzling. That was the moment. . . .

They say temperatures of seven thousand degrees centigrade hit me. You can't really say it washed over me. It is hard to describe. I simply fainted. I remember my body floating in the air. That was probably the blast, but I don't know how far I was blown. When I came to my senses, my surroundings were silent. . . .

The only medicine was tempura oil, I put it on my body myself. I lay on the concrete for hours. My skin was now flat, not puffed up anymore. A scorching sky was overhead. The flies swarmed over me and covered my wounds, which were already festering. People were simply left lying around. When their faint breathing became silent, they'd say, "This one's dead," and put the body in a pile of corpses. Some called for water, and if they got it, they died immediately. . . .

When I went to America I had a deep hatred toward America. I asked myself why they ended the war by means which destroyed human beings. When I talked about how I suffered, I was told, "Well, you attacked Pearl Harbor!" I didn't understand much English then, and it's probably just as well. From the American point of view, they dropped that bomb in order to end the war faster, in order to create more damage faster. But it's inexcusable to harm human beings in this way. I wonder what kind of education there is now in America about atomic bombs. They're still making them, aren't they?

- Can you answer Yamaoka Michiko's question?

- Does the plastic surgery she received in America make up for her pain and suffering?

---

the bomb as a military weapon and never had any doubt that it should be used." But the decision had both military and political ramifications. Even though Japan had lost most of its empire by the summer of 1945, it still had a military force of several million men and thousands of kamikaze planes that had already wreaked havoc on the American fleet. The kamikaze pilots gave up their own lives to make sure that their planes, heavily laden with bombs, crashed on American ships. In the Battle of Okinawa, kamikaze pilots destroyed or disabled 28 American ships and killed 5,000 American sailors. There was little defense against such fanaticism.

Even with the Russian promise to enter the war, it appeared that an amphibious landing on the Japanese mainland would be necessary to end the war.

The monthlong battle for Iwo Jima, only 750 miles from Tokyo, had resulted in more than 4,000 American dead and 15,000 wounded, and the battle for Okinawa was even more costly. An invasion of the Japanese mainland would presumably be even more expensive in human lives. The bomb, many thought, could end the war without an invasion. But some people involved in the decision wanted to retaliate for Pearl Harbor, and still others needed to justify spending more than $2 billion on the project in the first place. The timing of the first bomb, however, indicates to some that the decision was intended to impress the Russians and ensure that they had little to do with the peace settlement in the Far East. One British scientist later charged that the decision to drop the bomb on Hiroshima was the "first

Total War Even before the destruction of Hiroshima and Nagasaki by atomic bombs, American fire-bombing raids destroyed many Japanese cities. A raid on Tokyo on March 9, 1945 (shown here a few days later), killed at least 100,000 people and left more than a million homeless. Was this kind of destruction of civilians justifiable even in a brutal war? *(National Archives [80-G-490421])*

TIMELINE

1931–1932	Japan seizes Manchuria
1933	Hitler becomes German chancellor United States recognizes the Soviet Union Roosevelt extends Good Neighbor policy
1934	Germany begins rearmament
1935	Italy invades Ethiopia First Neutrality Act
1936	Spanish civil war begins Second Neutrality Act Roosevelt re-elected
1938	Hitler annexes Austria, occupies Sudetenland German persecution of Jews intensifies
1939	Nazi–Soviet Pact German invasion of Poland; World War II begins
1940	Roosevelt elected for a third term Selective Service Act
1941	FDR's "Four Freedoms" speech Proposed black march on Washington Executive Order 8802 outlaws discrimination in defense industries

	Lend-Lease Act Germany attacks Russia Japanese assets in United States frozen Japanese attack Pearl Harbor; United States declares war on Japan Germany declares war on United States
1942	Internment of Japanese Americans Second Allied front in Africa launched
1943	Invasion of Sicily Italian campaign; Italy surrenders Race riots in Detroit and other cities
1944	Normandy invasion (Operation Overlord) Roosevelt elected for a fourth term
1945	Yalta Conference Roosevelt dies; Harry Truman becomes president Germany surrenders Successful test of atomic bomb Hiroshima and Nagasaki bombed; Japan surrenders

major operation of the cold diplomatic war with Russia."

Historians still debate whether the use of the atomic bomb on the Japanese cities was necessary to end the war, but for the hundreds of thousands of American troops waiting on board ships and on island bases (even in Europe) to invade the Japanese mainland, there was no question about the rightness of the decision. They believed that the bombs ended the war and saved their lives. On August 6, 1945, two days before the Soviet Union had promised to enter the war against Japan, a B-29 bomber, the *Enola Gay*, dropped a single atomic bomb over Hiroshima. It killed or severely wounded 160,000 civilians and destroyed four square miles of the city. One of the men on the plane saw the thick cloud of smoke and thought that they had missed their target. "It looked like it had landed on a forest. I didn't see any sign of the city." The Soviet Union entered the war on August 8. When Japan refused to surrender, a bomb was dropped on Nagasaki on August 9. The Japanese surrendered five days later. The war was finally over. The problems of the atomic age and the postwar world were just beginning.

Nagasaki Atomic Bomb Attack, August 1945

Conclusion

Peace, Prosperity, and International Responsibilities

The United States emerged from World War II with an enhanced reputation as the world's most powerful industrial and military nation. The war had finally ended the Great Depression and brought prosperity to most Americans. Even N. Scott Momaday's family secured better jobs because of the war, but, like many Americans, they had to move to take those jobs. The war also increased the power of the federal government. The payroll deduction of federal income taxes, begun during the war, symbolized the growth of a federal bureaucracy that affected the lives of all Americans. Ironically the war to preserve liberty and freedom was fought with segregated armed forces, and some American citizens, including many Japanese Americans, were deprived of their freedom. The war had also ended American isolationism and made the United States into the dominant global power. Of all the nations that fought in the war, the United States had suffered the least. No bombs were dropped on American factories, and no cities were destroyed. Although more than 300,000 Americans lost their lives, even this carnage seemed minimal when compared with more than 20 million Russian soldiers and civilians who died or the 6 million Jews and millions of others systematically exterminated by Hitler.

Americans greeted the end of the war with joy and relief. But those who lived through the war years, even those too young to fight, like N. Scott Momaday, recalled the war as a time when all Americans were united to achieve victory. They looked forward to the peace and prosperity for which they had fought. Yet within two years, the peace would be jeopardized by the Cold War, and the United States would be rearming its former enemies, Japan and Germany, to oppose its former friend, the Soviet Union. The irony of that situation reduced the joy of the hard-won peace and made the American people more suspicious of their government and its foreign policy. Yet the memory of World War II and the perception that the country was united against evil enemies, indeed that World War II was a "good war," would have an impact on American foreign policy, and even on Americans' perception of themselves, for decades to come.

Questions for Review and Reflection

1. Trace the series of international events that led to the United States' entry into World War II. Could the United States have stayed neutral?

2. Explain why and how the United States interned Japanese Americans in the aftermath of the attack on Pearl Harbor. Was the internment justified?

3. How did the war change the lives of women, African Americans, and Hispanic Americans?

4. What were the war aims of the United States, and how were they achieved?

5. What led the United States to develop the atomic bomb? What were the consequences of this new weapon for the Japanese, for Americans, and for the outcome of World War II?

Recommended Reading

Recommended Readings are posted on the Web site for this textbook. Visit www.ablongman.com/nash

Fiction and Film

In *The Dollmaker* (1954), Harriette Arnow tells the fictionalized story of a young woman from Kentucky who finds herself in wartime Detroit. Two powerful novels that tell the story of the battlefield experience are Norman Mailer's *The Naked and the Dead* (1948) and Irwin Shaw's *The Young Lions* (1948). Alan Furst has written a series of novels including *Night Soldiers* (1996) and *Red Gold* (1999) that capture the look and feel of Europe in the early days of the war. *Pearl Harbor* (2001) is a blockbuster film worth seeing for the special effects, but more interesting is *Tora! Tora! Tora!* (1970), a film that tells the story of the attack on Pearl Harbor from both the American and the Japanese points of view. It is compelling even as it oversimplifies history. *Saving Private Ryan* (1998), a film about one platoon's adventures on D-Day and after, is sentimental and romantic in spots but contains some graphic and violent scenes of the invasion of Normandy. *Memphis Belle* (1990) tells the story of one bomber crew. *Schindler's List* (1993) uses the Holocaust as background and subject. It is important to sample some of the movies produced during the war even though they are often filled with propaganda. *Bataan* (1943) was the first movie featuring an ethnic platoon. *Casablanca* (1943) and *Lifeboat* (1944) are classics.

Discovering U.S. History Online

World War II Timeline
http://history.acusd.edu/gen/WW2Timeline/start.html
This interactive timeline includes the years prior to American involvement in World War II.

Resource Listing for World War II
www.sunsite.unc.edu/pha/index.html
This site presents an extensive, categorized listing of World War II primary documents available on the Web.

World War II Museum
www.thedropzone.org
A virtual museum of World War II, this site covers the European and Pacific theaters, training, Axis accounts, and an innovative collection of oral histories.

Remembering Pearl Harbor
www.nationalgeographic.com/pearlharbor/
This site includes a detailed account of the attack, illustrated with maps and photographs, as well as a searchable archive of survivors' stories.

A People at War
www.archives.gov/exhibit_hall/a_people_at_war/a_people_at_war.html
This National Archives exhibit takes a close look at the contributions that millions of Americans made to the war effort.

Poster Art of World War II
www.archives.gov/exhibit_hall/powers_of_persuasion/powers_of_persuasion_home.html
These powerful posters at the National Archives were part of the battle for the hearts and minds of the American people during World War II.

Fighters on the Farm Front
http://arcweb.sos.state.or.us/osu/osuhomepage.html
This site offers an illustrated presentation of the efforts to replace the labor force lost by men going into military service.

Tuskegee Airmen
www.wpafb.af.mil/museum/history/prewwii/ta.htm
The Air Force Museum at Wright-Patterson Air Force Base maintains this site about the African American pilots of World War II.

African Americans in World War II
www.coax.net/people/lwf/ww2.htm
This site presents an extensive compilation of links to essays, some internal and some external to the site, which detail the experience of African Americans during World War II.

A. Philip Randolph
www.georgemeany.org/archives/apr.html
A biography of Randolph, emphasizing his beliefs and his work in civil and labor rights.

Japanese Americans

www.lib.washington.edu/exhibits/harmony

This site deals with all aspects of the Japanese wartime internment, relocation centers, and the human stories behind the massive removal of Japanese Americans from the West Coast.

Japanese Relocation Sites

www.cr.nps.gov/history/online_books/
anthropology74/

This book describes every relocation site used during the war and includes photographs, architectural drawings, and personal accounts. The full text is presented online.

Japanese American Relocation Photographs

www.usc.edu/isd/archives/arc/digarchives/jarda

This site presents a searchable archive of photos taken from the *Los Angeles Examiner.* The photos document "the relocation of Japanese Americans in California principally during the period 1941–1946. Many of the photographs show daily life in the camps."

Latinos and Latinas & World War II

www.utexas.edu/projects/latinoarchives

This site presents a background of Hispanic involvement in World War II as well as reprints of its publication, *Narratives,* with individual accounts of Hispanic services in the war and on the home front.

An Oral History of Rhode Island Women During World War II

www.stg.brown.edu/projects/WWII_Women/
tocCS.html

This site presents oral histories by students in the Honors English Program at South Kingstown High School as well as an explanation of oral history, essays on women and the war, and a timeline of World War II.

"Flygirls"

www.pbs.org/wgbh/amex/flygirls

This site presents the "largely unknown story of the Women Airforce Service Pilots (WASP)" with photos, sound clips, essays, profiles, a timeline, and a transcript of the companion film with a teacher's guide.

United States Holocaust Memorial Museum

www.ushmm.org

This official Web site of the Holocaust Museum in Washington, D.C., includes more than 15 online exhibitions.

A-Bomb

http://www.csi.ad.jp/ABOMB

This site offers information about the impact of the first atomic bomb as well as the background and context of weapons of total destruction.

Fifty Years from Trinity

http://seattletimes.nwsource.com/trinity/

A complete reprint of an anniversary special section of the newspaper that "detailed the history, impacts and future of atomic weapons and nuclear power." The site also includes teaching and discussion materials.

The U.S. Army Campaigns of World War II: Normandy

www.army.mil/cmh-pg/brochures/normandy/nor-
pam.htm

An online version of a 45-page brochure covering the assault, including maps and photographs.

Postwar America at Home, 1945–1960

The post–World War II years saw tremendous suburban development, which reflected the more general economic growth and economic prosperity of the period. *(Robert Bechtle, '58 Rambler, 1967. Gift of Mrs. McCauley Conner in memory of her father, Barklie McK. Henry, Brauer Museum of Art, 72.03, Valparaiso University)*

American Stories

An Entrepreneur Franchises the American Dream

Ray Kroc, an ambitious salesman, headed toward San Bernardino, California, on a business trip in 1954. For more than a decade he had been selling "multimixers"—stainless steel machines that could make six milkshakes at once—to restaurants and soda shops around the United States. On this trip, he was particularly interested in checking out a hamburger stand run by Richard and Maurice McDonald, who had bought eight of his "contraptions" and could therefore make 48 shakes at the same time.

Always eager to increase sales, Kroc wanted to see the McDonalds' operation for himself. The 52-year-old son of Bohemian parents had sold everything from real estate to radio time to paper cups before peddling the multimixers but had enjoyed no stunning success. Yet he was still on the alert for the key to the fortune that was part of the American dream. As he watched the lines of people at the San Bernardino McDonald's restaurant, the answer seemed at hand.

The McDonald brothers sold only standard hamburgers, french fries, and milkshakes, but they had developed a system that was fast, efficient, and clean. It drew on the automobile traffic that moved along Route 66. And it was profitable indeed. Sensing the possibilities, Kroc proposed that the two owners open other establishments as well. When they balked, he negotiated a 99-year contract that allowed him to sell the fast-food idea and the name—and their golden arches design—wherever he could.

On April 15, 1955, Kroc opened his first McDonald's restaurant in Des Plaines, a suburb of Chicago. Three months later, he sold his first franchise in Fresno, California. Others soon followed. Kroc scouted out new locations, almost always on highway "strips"; persuaded people to put up the capital; and provided them with specifications guaranteed to ensure future success. For his efforts, he received a percentage of the gross take.

From the start, Kroc insisted on standardization. Every McDonald's restaurant was the same—from the two functional arches supporting the glass enclosure that housed the kitchen and take-out window to the single arch near the road bearing a sign indicating how many 15-cent hamburgers had already been sold. All menus and prices were exactly the same, and Kroc demanded that everything from hamburger size to cooking time be constant. He insisted, too, that the establishments be clean. No pinball games or cigarette machines were permitted; the premium was on a good, inexpensive hamburger, quickly served, at a nice place.

McDonald's, of course, was an enormous success. In 1962, total sales exceeded $76 million. In 1964, before the company had been in operation for 10 years, it had sold more than 400 million hamburgers and 120 million pounds of french fries. By the end of the next year, there were 710 McDonald's stands in 44 states. In 1974, only 20 years after Kroc's vision of the hamburger's future, McDonald's did $2 billion worth of business. When Kroc died in 1984, a total of 45 billion burgers had been sold at 7,500 outlets in 32 countries. Ronald McDonald, the clown who came to represent the company, became known to children around the globe after his Washington, D.C., debut in November 1963. When McDonald's began to advertise, it became the country's first restaurant to buy television time. Musical slogans such as "You deserve a break today" and "We do it all for you" became better known than some popular songs.

The success of McDonald's provides an example of the development of new economic and technological trends in the United States in the post–World War II years. Ray Kroc capitalized on the changes of the automobile age. He understood that a restaurant had a better chance of success not in the city but along the highways, where it could draw on heavier traffic. Kroc understood, too, that the franchise notion provided the key to rapid economic growth. Finally, he sensed the importance of standardization and uniformity. He understood the mood of the time—the quiet conformity of people searching for the key to the American dream of prosperity and stability. The McDonald's image may have been monotonous, but that was part of its appeal. Customers always knew what they would get wherever they found the golden arches. If the atmosphere was "bland," that too was deliberate. As Kroc said, "Our theme is kind of synonymous with Sunday school, the Girl Scouts and the YMCA. McDonald's is clean and wholesome." It was a symbol of the age.

This chapter describes the structural and political changes in American society in the 25 years following World War II. Even as the nation became involved in the global confrontations of the Cold War with the Soviet Union (a story taken up in Chapter 27), Americans were preoccupied with the shifts in social and economic patterns that were taking place. This chapter examines how economic growth, spurred by technological advances, transformed the patterns of work and daily life in the United States. Self-interest triumphed over idealism, as most people gained a level of material comfort previously unknown. Comforted by a renewed commitment to organized religion that involved people of all persuasions, they felt confident in the patterns of their lives. The political world reflected the prosperity and affluence that followed years of depression and war. Building on the impact

of the New Deal and the American role as the "arsenal of democracy" in World War II, government was larger and more involved in people's lives than ever before, despite Republican resistance in the 1950s. Political commitments in the decade and a half after the war laid the groundwork for the welfare state that emerged in the 1960s.

But even as the nation prospered, it experienced serious social and economic divisions among its diverse peoples. This chapter also shows the enormous gaps that existed between rich and poor, even in the best of times. It shows the continuing presence of what one critic eloquently called "the other America" and documents the considerable income disparity and persistent prejudice that African Americans (like members of other minority groups) encountered in their efforts to share in the postwar prosperity. The frustrations they experienced highlighted the limits of the postwar American dream and led to the reform movements that changed American society.

ECONOMIC BOOM

Most Americans were optimistic after 1945. As servicemen returned home from fighting in World War II, their very presence caused a change in family patterns. A baby boom brought unprecedented population growth. The simultaneous and unexpected economic boom had an even greater impact. Large corporations increasingly dominated the business world, but unions grew as well, and most workers improved their lives. Technology appeared triumphant, with new products flooding the market and finding their way into most American homes. Prosperity convinced the growing middle class that all was well in the United States.

The Thriving Peacetime Economy

The wartime return of prosperity after the Great Depression continued in the postwar years, relieving fears of another depression. The next several decades saw one of the longest sustained economic expansions the country had ever known, as the United States solidified its position as the richest nation in the world. Other nations struggled with the aftereffects of World War II. Yet in the United States, prosperity was the norm.

The statistical evidence of economic success was impressive. The gross national product (GNP) jumped dramatically between 1945 and 1960, while

per capita personal income likewise rose—from $1,087 in 1945 to $2,026 in 1960. Almost 60 percent of all families in the country were now part of the middle class, a dramatic change from the class structure in the nineteenth and early twentieth centuries.

Personal resources fueled economic growth. During World War II, American consumers had

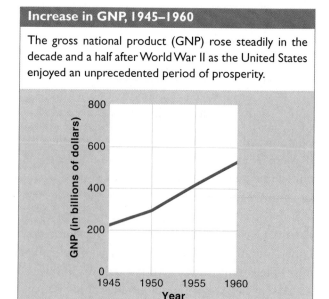

Increase in GNP, 1945–1960

The gross national product (GNP) rose steadily in the decade and a half after World War II as the United States enjoyed an unprecedented period of prosperity.

Source: National Income and Product Accounts, 1929–1994.

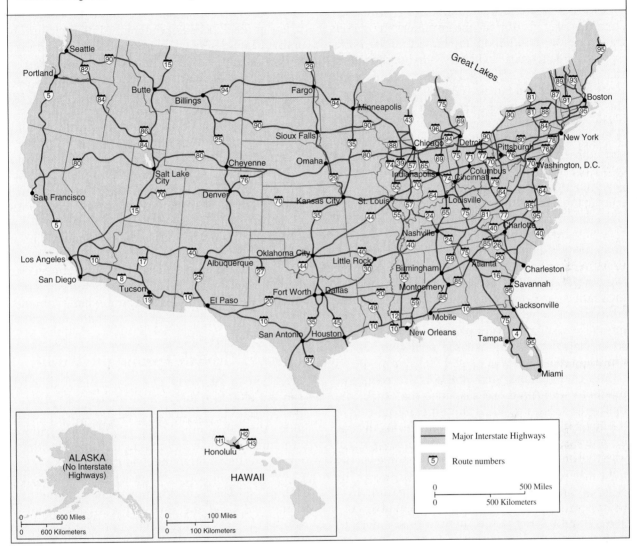

U.S. Interstate Highway System

The interstate highway system, established by legislative action in 1956, created an extensive network of roads that changed the landscape and living patterns of people throughout the United States. While the network was most extensive in the East, it extended throughout the entire country.

been unable to spend all they earned because factories were producing for war. With accumulated savings of $140 billion at the end of the struggle, consumers were ready to buy whatever they could. Equally important was the 22 percent rise in real purchasing power between 1946 and 1960. Families now had far more discretionary income—money to satisfy wants as well as needs—than before. At the end of the Great Depression, fewer than one-quarter of all households had any discretionary income; in 1960, three of every five did.

This new consumer power, in contrast to the underconsumption of the 1920s and 1930s, spurred the economy. Most homes now had an automobile, a television set, a refrigerator, a washing machine,

and a vacuum cleaner. But consumers could also indulge themselves with electric can openers, electric pencil sharpeners, electric toothbrushes, aerosol cans, and automatic transmissions for their cars.

The automobile industry played a key part in the boom. Just as cars and roads transformed America in the 1920s when mass production came of age, so they contributed to the equally great transformation three decades later. Limited to the production of military vehicles during World War II, the auto industry expanded dramatically in the postwar period. Seventy thousand cars were made in 1945; 8 million were manufactured in 1955; and not quite 7 million were produced in 1960. Customers now chose from a wide variety of engines, colors, and optional accessories. Fancy grilles and tail fins distinguished each year's models.

The development of a massive interstate highway system also stimulated auto production and so contributed to prosperity. Rather than encourage the growth of a mass transit system, through the Interstate Highway Act of 1956, the Eisenhower administration poured $26 billion, the largest public works expenditure in American history, into building more than 40,000 miles of federal highways, linking all parts of the United States. Federal officials claimed the system would make evacuation quicker in the event of nuclear attack. President Eisenhower boasted that "the amount of concrete poured to form these roadways would build . . . six sidewalks to the moon. . . . More than any single action by the government since the end of the war, this one would change the face of America." Significantly, this massive effort helped create a nation dependent on oil.

A housing boom also fed economic growth as home-ownership rates rose from 53 percent in 1945 to 62 percent in 1960. Much of the stimulus came from the GI Bill of 1944. In addition to giving returning servicemen priority for many jobs and providing educational benefits, it offered low-interest home mortgages. Millions of former servicemen from all social classes eagerly purchased their share of the American dream.

The government's increasingly active economic role both stimulated and sustained the expansion. Businesses were allowed to buy almost 80 percent of the factories built by the government during the war for much less than they cost. Even more important was the dramatic rise in defense spending as the Cold War escalated. In 1947, Congress passed the National Security Act creating the Department of Defense and authorized an initial budget of $13 billion. With the onset of the Korean War, the defense budget rose to $22 billion in 1951 and to about $47 billion in 1953. Approximately half of the total federal budget went to the armed forces. This spending, in turn, helped stimulate the aircraft and electronic industries. The government underwrote 90 percent of aviation and space research, 65 percent of electricity and electronics work, and 42 percent of scientific instrument development. Meanwhile, the close business–government ties of World War II grew stronger.

Most citizens welcomed the huge expenditures, not only because they supported the American stance in the struggle against communism but also because they understood the economic impact of military spending. Columnist David Lawrence noted in 1950, "Government planners figure they have found the magic formula for almost endless good times. Cold war is an automatic pump primer. Turn a spigot, and the public clamors for more arms spending."

Postwar American growth avoided some of the major problems that often bedevil periods of economic expansion—inflation and the enrichment of a few at the expense of the many. Inflation, a problem in the immediate postwar period, slowed from an average of 7 percent per year in the 1940s to a gentle 2 to 3 percent per year in the 1950s. And though the concentration of income remained the same—the bottom half of the population still earned less than the top tenth—the ranks of middle-class Americans grew.

American products were sold around the world. People in other countries had developed a taste for Coca-Cola during the war. Now numerous other goods became available overseas. American books, magazines, movies, and records promoted the spread of American culture and provided still more profits for American entrepreneurs.

A major economic transformation had occurred in the United States. Peaceful, prosperous, and productive, the nation had became what economist John Kenneth Galbraith called the "affluent society."

Postwar Growth Around the World

Elsewhere in the world, postwar reconstruction began but affluence took longer to arrive. Both European and Asian countries had suffered greater casualties than the United States, and some nations, even those on the winning side, had to deal with the enormous devastation that had taken place.

Great Britain was ravaged by the war. German bombs had fallen on downtown London, and residents had used the underground—the extensive subway system—to take shelter from the attacks. Rationing in England, necessary to provide the equitable distribution of scarce resources, lasted until the early 1950s. British factories, which had been the first to industrialize, were now inefficient and outdated. Home of the Industrial Revolution, England now failed to keep up with the rapid pace of technological innovation. The British automobile industry, for example, yielded part of its share of the world market to other nations, such as Germany, which introduced the inexpensive and reliable Volkswagen Beetle that was soon sold around the world. Meanwhile, Britain lagged behind other European nations in developing a modern superhighway system that could spur industrial development.

In the general election of 1945, British voters ousted Winston Churchill and the Conservative party in favor of the Labour party, which was committed to social change. It took over the coal and railroad industries and began to nationalize the steel industry. While owners were compensated, some critics argued that the government's actions stifled industrial progress. Nevertheless, Great Britain began an economic and social recovery. It even provided a system of socialized medicine far in advance of anything in the United States.

While France was on the winning side of the war, it had suffered the indignity of occupation. It, too, experienced recovery, thanks in part to a rising birthrate, which was also occurring in the United States. At the same time, France, like Britain, was struggling with the demands of its colonial empire to be free. Brutal struggles in Indochina and Algeria caused financial instability and helped undermine economic development until France pulled out of both areas in the 1950s.

Defeated nations showed the most dramatic development of all. As the United States decided that a strong West Germany was necessary as a buffer against the Soviet Union, it helped cause what came to be known as "the German miracle." Because much of German industrial capacity had been destroyed by the war, new factories could be built with the newest technological equipment. The Allied High Commission, responsible for governing Germany, provided economic aid, scaled down German debts, and eliminated controls over German industry. In the early 1950s, the West German rate of growth reached 10 percent a year, while the gross national product rose from $23 billion in 1950 to $103 billion in 1964.

Japan likewise revived quickly. Like Germany, it suffered tremendous wartime destruction, due to both conventional bombing and to the new atomic bombs that devastated Hiroshima and Nagasaki in 1945. Under the direction of General Douglas MacArthur, the United States directed the reconstruction effort. A new constitution created a democratic framework and led to the signing of a peace treaty in 1952. As political change occurred, the economy grew rapidly, and Japan overtook France and West Germany, soon ranking third in the world behind the United States and the Soviet Union.

So too did the Soviet Union rebuild. Reparations from West Germany and industrial extractions from Eastern Europe helped promote the reconstruction effort. The totalitarian structure of the Soviet state eliminated public debate about the allocation of resources, and the nation embarked on a series of initiatives that led to the development of a Soviet atomic bomb and an increase in the size of collective farms.

The Corporate Impact on American Life

After 1945, the major corporations in the United States tightened their hold on the American economy. Government policy in World War II had produced tremendous industrial concentration. The government suspended antitrust actions that might impede the war effort, while government contracts spurred expansion of the big corporations at the expense of smaller firms.

Industrial concentration continued after the war, making oligopoly—domination of a given industry by a few firms—a feature of American capitalism. Several waves of mergers had taken place in the past, including one in the 1890s and another in the 1920s. Still another occurred in the 1950s. At the same time, the booming economy encouraged the development of conglomerates—firms with holdings in a variety of industries in order to protect themselves against instability in one particular area.

McDonald's Golden Arches   McDonald's provided a model for other franchisers in the 1950s and the years that followed. The golden arches, shown here in an early version, were virtually the same wherever they appeared. Initially found along highways around the country, they were later built within cities and towns as well. How did the golden arches contribute to McDonald's popularity? *(Sandy Felsenthal/CORBIS)*

Expansion took other forms as well. Even as the major corporations grew, so did smaller franchise operations such as McDonald's, Kentucky Fried Chicken, and Burger King. Ray Kroc, introduced at the start of this chapter, provided a widely imitated pattern.

While expanding at home, large corporations also moved increasingly into foreign markets, as they had in the 1890s. But at the same time, they began to build plants overseas, where labor costs were cheaper. In the decade after 1957, General Electric built 61 plants abroad, and numerous other firms did the same. Corporate planning, meanwhile, developed rapidly, as firms sought managers who could assess information, weigh marketing trends, and make rational decisions to maximize profit.

Changing Work Patterns

As corporations changed, so did the world of work. Reversing a 150-year trend after World War II, the United States became less a goods producer and more a service provider. Between 1947 and 1957, the number of factory workers fell by 4 percent, while the number of clerical workers increased 23 percent and the number of salaried, middle-class employees rose 61 percent. By 1956, a majority of American workers held white-collar jobs, and the percentage rose in the years that followed. These new white-collar workers, paid by salary rather than by the hour, served as corporate managers, office workers, salespeople, and teachers.

Yet white-collar employees paid a price for comfort. Work in the huge corporations became ever more impersonal and bureaucratic, and white-collar employees seemed to dress, think, and act the same (as depicted in a popular novel and film of the 1950s, *The Man in the Gray Flannel Suit*). Corporations, preaching that teamwork was all-important, indoctrinated employees with the appropriate standards of conduct. RCA issued company neckties. IBM had training programs to teach employees the company line. Social critic C. Wright Mills observed,

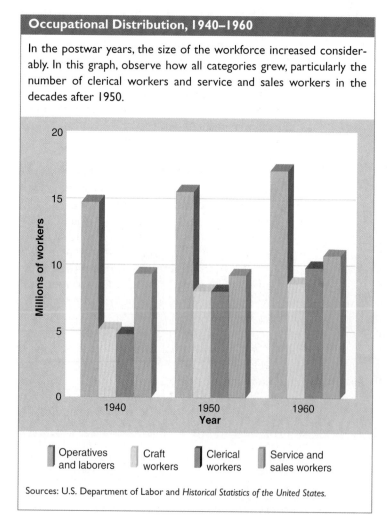

Occupational Distribution, 1940–1960

In the postwar years, the size of the workforce increased considerably. In this graph, observe how all categories grew, particularly the number of clerical workers and service and sales workers in the decades after 1950.

Operatives and laborers · Craft workers · Clerical workers · Service and sales workers

Sources: U.S. Department of Labor and *Historical Statistics of the United States.*

Suburban Commuters Commuters, such as these people in Park Forest, Illinois, in 1953, traveled from the suburbs to offices in the city every day. How would you describe the appearance of these commuters? Are there more men or women? How closely do they resemble one another? *(Time Life Pictures/Getty Images)*

"When white-collar people get jobs, they sell not only their time and energy but their personalities as well."

But not all Americans held white-collar jobs. Many were still blue-collar assembly line workers, who made the goods others enjoyed. They too dreamed of owning a suburban home and several cars and providing more for their children than they had enjoyed while growing up. Their lives were now more comfortable than ever before, as the union movement brought substantial gains. These were the more fortunate members of the working class. Millions of others, perhaps totaling 40 percent of the workforce, held less appealing and less well-paying positions. More and more worked as taxi drivers, farm laborers, or dime-store sales clerks. For them, jobs were less stable, less secure, and less interesting.

The Union Movement at High Tide

The union movement had come of age during the New Deal, and the end of World War II found it even stronger. There were more union members—14.5 million—than ever before. Ten million belonged to the American Federation of Labor (AFL); the other 4.5 million belonged to the Congress of Industrial Organizations (CIO). Having taken a wartime no-strike pledge and given their full support to the war effort, they now looked forward to better pay and a greater voice in workplace management.

The immediate postwar period was difficult. Cancellation of defense orders laid off war workers and prompted fears of a depression, like the one that had followed World War I. Even workers who held their jobs lost the overtime pay they had enjoyed during the war. Many responded by striking. In 1946 alone, 4.6 million workers went out on strike—more than ever before in U.S. history. There were work stoppages in the automobile, coal, steel, and electrical industries and a threatened strike by railway workers. These disruptions alienated middle-class Americans and outraged conservative Republicans who felt that unionization had gone too far.

In the late 1940s, a new equilibrium emerged. In many industries, big business at last recognized the basic rights of industrial workers, and union leaders and members in turn acknowledged the prerogatives of management and accepted the principle of fair profit. Corporations in the same industry agreed to cooperate rather than compete with one another over labor costs. This meant that once a leading firm reached agreement with the union, the other firms in that area adopted similar terms, and the costs of the new contract would be met by a general increase in prices.

At the same time, companies made material concessions to workers—for example, adjusting their pay to protect them against inflation. In 1948, General Motors offered the United Auto Workers a contract that included a cost-of-living adjustment (COLA) and a 2 percent "annual improvement factor" wage increase intended to share GM's productivity gains with workers. In 1950, GM again took the lead, this time with a five-year agreement providing pensions along with a cost-of-living adjustment and wage increase. Five years later, automobile workers won a guaranteed annual wage. The merger of the AFL and CIO in 1955 ratified the changes that had occurred in the labor movement, as the new organization, led by building trade unionist George Meany, represented more than 90 percent of the country's now larger group of 17.5 million union members. By the end of the 1950s, the COLA principle was built into most union contracts.

Union gains, like middle-class affluence, came at a price. Co-opted by the materialistic benefits big business provided, workers fell increasingly under the control of middle-level managers and watched anxiously as companies automated at home or expanded abroad, where labor was cheaper. But the agreements they had reached often precluded any response. The anti-Communist crusade, described in the next chapter, also undermined union radicalism. And throughout the period, in unions, as in other institutions, women and blacks faced continued discrimination.

Agricultural Workers in Trouble

The agricultural world changed even more than the industrial world in the postwar United States. On the eve of World War II, agriculture had supported one of every five Americans. Now, in one generation, mechanization and consolidation forced that figure down to one of every 20. Altogether, some 15 million rural jobs disappeared.

New technology revolutionized farming. Improved planting and harvesting machines and better fertilizers and pesticides brought massive gains in productivity. Increasing profitability led to agricultural consolidation. In the 25 years after 1945, average farm size almost doubled. Farms specialized more in cash crops, such as corn or soybeans, that were more profitable than hay or oats used to feed animals. Demanding large-scale investment, farming became a big business—often called "agribusiness." Family farms found it difficult to compete with the technologically superior corporations and watched their share of the market fall.

In response, farmers left the land in increasing numbers. Some were midwestern whites who generally found jobs in offices and factories. In the South, the upheaval was more disruptive. Many of the uprooted agricultural workers were African Americans, who became part of the huge migration north that had been going on since World War I. Overall, from 1910 to 1970, more than 6.5 million African Americans left the South; of these, 5 million moved north after 1940. Most of them gravitated to cities, where they faced problems of poverty and discrimination in housing and employment. The agricultural life, as it had been known for decades, even centuries, was over.

DEMOGRAPHIC AND TECHNOLOGICAL SHIFTS

The postwar economic boom was intertwined with a series of demographic changes. The population grew dramatically and continued to move west, while at the same time, millions of white Americans left the

cities for the suburbs that began to grow exponentially in the postwar years. New patterns, revolving around television and other gadgets provided by the advances of technology, came to characterize the consumer culture that dominated suburban life.

Population Growth

In post–World War II America, a growing population testified to prosperity's return. The birthrate soared in the postwar years as millions of Americans began families. The "baby boom" peaked in 1957, with a rate of more than 25 births per 1,000. In that year, 4.3 million babies were born, one every seven seconds. While the population growth of 19 million in the 1940s was double the rise of the decade before, that increase paled against the increase in the 1950s, which totaled 29 million.

The rising birthrate was the dominant factor affecting population growth, but the death rate was also declining. Miracle drugs such as penicillin and streptomycin, now widely available, helped cure strep throat and other bacterial infections, intestinal ailments, and more serious illnesses such as tuberculosis. A polio vaccine introduced a decade after the war virtually eliminated that dreaded disease. Life expectancy rose: midway through the 1950s, the

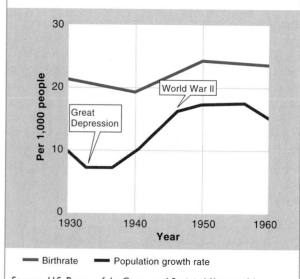

Birth and Population Growth Rates, 1900–1960

Both birth and population growth rates increased dramatically after the difficult years of the Great Depression. Note the baby boom that began at the end of World War II and continued for the next decade.

Sources: U.S. Bureau of the Census and *Statistical Abstract of the United States.*

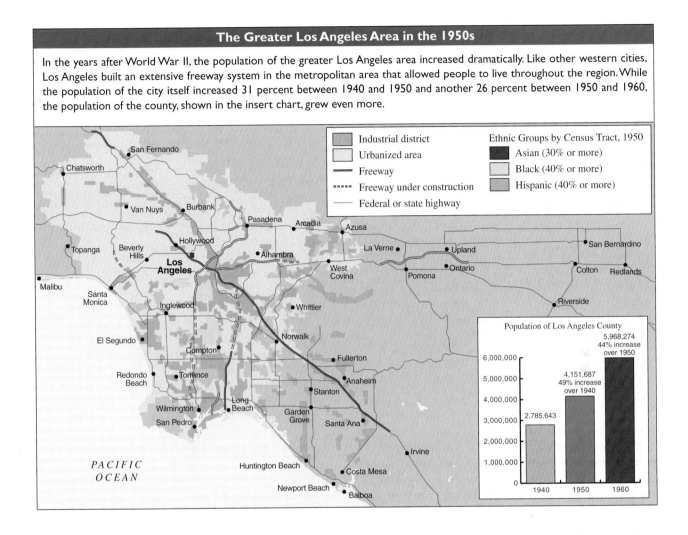

The Greater Los Angeles Area in the 1950s

In the years after World War II, the population of the greater Los Angeles area increased dramatically. Like other western cities, Los Angeles built an extensive freeway system in the metropolitan area that allowed people to live throughout the region. While the population of the city itself increased 31 percent between 1940 and 1950 and another 26 percent between 1950 and 1960, the population of the county, shown in the insert chart, grew even more.

average was 70 years for whites and 64 for blacks, compared with 55 for whites and 45 for blacks in 1920.

The baby boom shaped family and social patterns. Many women who had taken jobs during the war now left the workforce to rear their children and care for their homes. Their lives changed considerably as they substituted housework for paid work. Demand grew for diaper services and baby foods. Entering school, the baby-boom generation strained the educational system. Between 1946 and 1956, enrollment in grades 1 through 8 soared from 20 million to 30 million. Because school construction had slowed during the Depression and had virtually halted during the Second World War, classrooms were needed. Teachers, too, were in short supply.

Movement West

As the population grew, Americans became more mobile, and much of the movement was westward.

For many generations, working-class Americans had been the most likely to move; now geographic mobility spread to the middle class. Each year in the 1950s, more than a million farmers left their farms in search of new employment. Other Americans pulled up stakes and headed on as well, some moving to look for better jobs, others simply wandering for a while after returning home from the war and then settling down.

Population Increases in Selected Sun Belt Cities, 1940–1960 (in thousands)			
	1940	1950	1960
Los Angeles, California	1,504	1,970	2,479
Miami, Florida	172	249	292
Atlanta, Georgia	302	331	487
Dallas, Texas	295	434	680
Phoenix, Arizona	65	107	439

Source: U.S. Bureau of the Census.

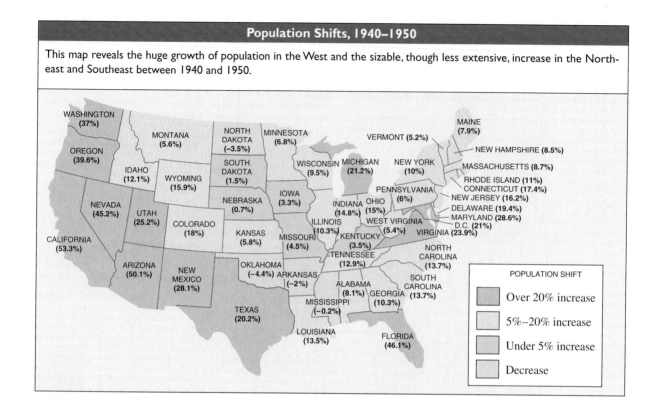

Population Shifts, 1940–1950

This map reveals the huge growth of population in the West and the sizable, though less extensive, increase in the Northeast and Southeast between 1940 and 1950.

WASHINGTON (37%)
OREGON (39.6%)
MONTANA (5.6%)
IDAHO (12.1%)
WYOMING (15.9%)
NEVADA (45.2%)
UTAH (25.2%)
COLORADO (18%)
CALIFORNIA (53.3%)
ARIZONA (50.1%)
NEW MEXICO (28.1%)
NORTH DAKOTA (−3.5%)
SOUTH DAKOTA (1.5%)
NEBRASKA (0.7%)
KANSAS (5.8%)
OKLAHOMA (−4.4%)
TEXAS (20.2%)
MINNESOTA (6.8%)
IOWA (3.3%)
MISSOURI (4.5%)
ARKANSAS (−2%)
LOUISIANA (13.5%)
WISCONSIN (9.5%)
MICHIGAN (21.2%)
ILLINOIS (10.3%)
INDIANA (14.8%)
KENTUCKY (3.5%)
TENNESSEE (12.9%)
MISSISSIPPI (−0.2%)
ALABAMA (8.1%)
GEORGIA (10.3%)
FLORIDA (46.1%)
OHIO (15%)
WEST VIRGINIA (5.4%)
VIRGINIA (23.9%)
NORTH CAROLINA (13.7%)
SOUTH CAROLINA (13.7%)
VERMONT (5.2%)
NEW YORK (10%)
PENNSYLVANIA (6%)
MAINE (7.9%)
NEW HAMPSHIRE (8.5%)
MASSACHUSETTS (8.7%)
RHODE ISLAND (11%)
CONNECTICUT (17.4%)
NEW JERSEY (16.2%)
DELAWARE (19.4%)
MARYLAND (28.6%)
D.C. (21%)

POPULATION SHIFT
Over 20% increase
5%–20% increase
Under 5% increase
Decrease

Population Shifts, 1940-1950

MAP

Wartime mobility encouraged the development of the West. Although the scarcity of water in the western states required massive water projects to support population growth, war workers and their families streamed to western cities where shipyards, airplane factories, and other industrial plants were located. After the war, this migration pattern persisted. The Sun Belt—the region stretching along the southern tier of the United States from Florida to California—attracted numerous new arrivals. Cities such as Houston, Albuquerque, Tucson, and Phoenix expanded phenomenally. The population of Phoenix soared from 65,000 in 1940 to 439,000 in 1960. In the 1950s, Los Angeles pulled ahead of Philadelphia as the third-largest city in the United States.

One-fifth of all the growth in the period took place in California. Even baseball teams—the Brooklyn Dodgers and the New York Giants—left the East Coast for western shores. By 1963, in a dramatic illustration of the importance of the West, California passed New York as the nation's most populous state.

The migration west occurred for a number of reasons. Servicemen who had been stationed in the West liked the scenery, climate, and pace of life. Many returned with their families after the war. With funds from the Federal Housing Administration or Veterans Administration, they could afford to borrow money and buy new homes. That spending, in turn, helped fuel the region's economic growth.

In addition, Cold War spending promoted economic development, and much of that expansion occurred in the West. Once the Korean War sparked increased military expenditures, California's economic growth outpaced that of the country as a whole. Aircraft production in the state accounted for more than 40 percent of the total increase in manufacturing employment there between 1949 and 1953. In the 1950s, rocket research further stimulated the aerospace industry. In 1959, California had nearly one-quarter of all prime military contracts in the nation. By 1962, the Pacific Coast as a whole held almost half of all Defense Department research and development contracts.

Finally, the West benefited from the boom in the service economy. Many western workers in postwar America were part of the growing service sector. The percentage of workers in such jobs was higher in virtually all western states than in eastern counterparts. Denver became a major regional center of the federal bureaucracy in the postwar years. From 14,000 people on the payroll in 1951, the number rose to 23,000 in 1961. Albuquerque likewise gained numerous federal offices and became known as "little Washington." The old West of cowboys, farmers, and miners was turning into a new West of bureaucrats, lawyers, and clerks.

The New Suburbs

As the population shifted westward after World War II, another form of movement was taking place. Millions of white Americans fled the inner city to suburban fringes, intensifying a movement that had begun before the war. Fourteen of the nation's largest cities, including New York, Boston, Chicago, Philadelphia, and Detroit, actually lost population in the 1950s. As central cities became places where poor nonwhites clustered, new urban and racial problems emerged.

For people of means, cities were places to work in but then to leave at five o'clock. In Manhattan, south of the New York borough's City Hall, the noontime population of 1.5 million dropped to 2,000 overnight. "It was becoming a part-time city," according to writer John Brooks, "tidally swamped with bustling humanity every weekday morning when the cars and commuter trains arrived, and abandoned again at nightfall when the wave sucked back—left pretty much to thieves, policemen, and rats."

As the cities declined, new suburbs blossomed. If the decade after World War I had witnessed a rural-to-urban shift, the decades after World War II saw a reverse shift to the regions outside the central cities, usually accessible only by car. By the end of the 1950s, one-third of all Americans resided in suburbs that promised fulfillment of the American dream and seemed insulated from the troubles of the world outside.

The pioneer of the postwar suburbanization movement was William J. Levitt, a builder eager to gamble and reap the rewards of a growing demand. Levitt had recognized the advantages of mass production during World War II, when his firm constructed housing for war workers. Aware that the GI Bill made mortgage money readily available, he saw the possibilities of suburban development. But to cash in, Levitt had to use new construction methods.

Mass production was the key. Individually designed houses were a thing of the past, he believed. "The reason we have it so good in this country," he said, "is that we can produce lots of things at low prices through mass production." Houses were among them. Working on a careful schedule, Levitt's team brought precut and preassembled materials to each site, put them together, and then moved on to the next location.

Levitt proved that his system worked. Construction costs at Levittown, New York, a new community of 17,000 homes built in the late 1940s, were only $10 per square foot, compared with the $12 to $15 common elsewhere. The next Levittown appeared in Bucks County, Pennsylvania, several years after the first, and another went up in Willingboro, New Jersey, at the end of the 1950s. Levitt's success provided a model for other developers.

Levitt argued that his homes helped underscore American values. "No man who owns his own house and lot can be a Communist," he once said. "He has too much to do." Levitt also helped perpetuate segregation by refusing to sell homes to blacks. "We can solve a housing problem, or we can try to solve a racial problem but we cannot combine the two," he declared in the early 1950s.

Government-insured mortgages, especially for veterans, fueled the housing boom. So did fairly low postwar interest rates. With many American families vividly remembering the Depression and saving significant parts of their paychecks, the nation had a pool of savings large enough to keep mortgage interest rates in the affordable 5 percent range.

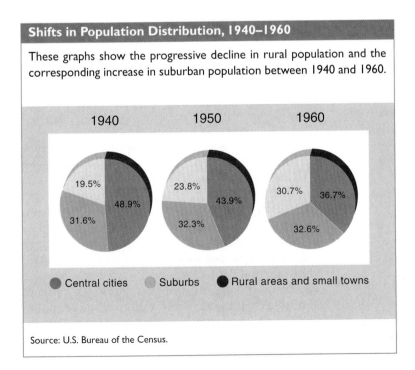

Shifts in Population Distribution, 1940–1960

These graphs show the progressive decline in rural population and the corresponding increase in suburban population between 1940 and 1960.

1940	1950	1960
19.5% / 31.6% / 48.9%	23.8% / 32.3% / 43.9%	30.7% / 32.6% / 36.7%

● Central cities   ● Suburbs   ● Rural areas and small towns

Source: U.S. Bureau of the Census.

Levittown Step-by-step mass production, with units completed in assembly line fashion, was the key to William Levitt's approach to housing. But the suburban developments he and others created were marked by street after street of houses that all looked the same. The Levittown in this picture was built on 1,200 acres of potato fields on Long Island in New York. How did the pattern you see here reflect the overall culture of the 1950s? *(Cornell Capa/Magnum Photos, Inc.)*

Suburbanization transformed the American landscape. Huge tracts of former fields, pastures, and forests were now divided into tiny standardized squares, each bearing a small house with a two-car garage and a manicured lawn. Stands of trees disappeared, for it was cheaper to cut them down than to work around them. Folksinger Malvina Reynolds described the new developments she saw:

AUDIO
Little Boxes

Little boxes on the hillside
Little boxes made of ticky tacky
Little boxes on the hillside
Little boxes all the same.
There's a green one and a pink one
And a blue one and a yellow one
And they're all made out of ticky tacky
And they all look just the same.

As suburbs flourished, businesses followed their customers out of the cities. Shopping centers led the way. At the end of World War II, there were eight, but the number multiplied rapidly in the 1950s. In a single three-month period in 1957, 17 new centers opened; by 1960, there were 3,840 in the United States. Developers such as Don M. Casto, who built the Miracle Mile near Columbus, Ohio, understood the importance of location as Americans moved out of the cities. "People have path-habits," he said, "like ants." Shopping centers catered to the suburban clientele and transformed consumer patterns. They allowed shoppers to avoid the cities entirely and further eroded urban health.

The Environmental Impact

Suburbanization had environmental consequences. Rapid expansion often took place without extensive planning and encroached on some of the nation's most attractive rural areas. Before long, virtually every American city was ringed by an ugly highway sporting garish neon signs. Billboard advertisements filled whatever space was not yet developed.

Responding to the increasingly cluttered terrain, architect Peter Blake ruthlessly attacked the practices of the 1950s in his muckraking book *God's Own Junkyard: The Planned Deterioration of America's Landscape*, published in 1964. He condemned the careless attitudes toward the environment that led to the "uglification" of a once lovely land. After describing breathtaking natural resources, Blake deplored the unconscionable desecration of the American landscape:

> Our suburbs are interminable wastelands dotted with millions of monotonous little houses on monotonous little lots and crisscrossed by highways lined with billboards, jazzed-up diners, used-car lots, drive-in movies, beflagged gas stations, and garish motels. Even the relatively unspoiled countryside beyond these suburban fringes has begun to sprout more telephone poles than trees, more trailer camps than national parks.

Despite occasional accounts like Blake's, there was little real consciousness of environmental issues in the early post–World War II years. The term *environment* itself was hardly used prior to the war. Yet the very prosperity that created the dismal highway strips in the late 1940s and 1950s was leading more and more Americans to appreciate natural environments as treasured parts of their rising standard of living. The shorter workweek provided more free time, and many Americans now had the means for longer vacations. They began to explore mountains and rivers and ocean shores and to ponder how to protect them. In 1958, Congress established the National Outdoor Recreation Review Commission, a first step toward consideration of environmental issues that became far more common in the next decade. Americans also began to recognize the need for open space in their communities in order to compensate for the urban overdevelopment.

Technology Supreme

A technological revolution transformed postwar America. Some developments—the use of atomic energy, for example—flowed directly from war research. Federal support for scientific activity increased dramatically, as the pattern of wartime collaboration continued. The government established the National Institutes of Health in 1948 to coordinate medical research and the National Science Foundation in 1950 to fund basic scientific research.

The advent of the Cold War led to ever-greater government involvement. The Atomic Energy Commission, created in 1946, and the Department of Defense, established in 1949, provided rapidly increasing funding for research and development. Support for the Los Alamos Scientific Laboratory, where the atomic bomb had been assembled, continued, while the government contracted with the University of California to open the new Livermore Laboratory near San Francisco. Money went to other large research universities as well and fueled their growth. Scientists engaged in both basic and applied research and helped develop nuclear weapons, jet planes, satellites, and consumer goods that were often the side products of military research. At the same time, other innovations came from the research and development activities sponsored by big business.

Computers both reflected and assisted the process of technological development. Prior to World War II, Vannevar Bush, an electrical engineer at the Massachusetts Institute of Technology, had built a machine filled with gears and shafts, along with electronic tubes in place of some mechanical parts, to solve differential equations. Wartime advances brought large but workable calculators, such as the Mark I electromechanical computer developed by engineer Howard Aiken and installed by IBM at Harvard in 1944. It was huge—55 feet long and 8 feet high—and had a million components.

Even more complicated was the Electronic Numerical Integrator and Calculator, called ENIAC, built in 1946 at the University of Pennsylvania. Like the Mark I, it was large, containing 18,000 electronic tubes and requiring tremendous amounts of electricity and special cooling procedures. It also needed to be "debugged" to remove insects attracted to the heat and light, giving rise to the term still used today by computer scientists for solving

The ENIAC Computer The ENIAC computer, first used in 1946, was a huge machine that took up an entire room. Yet it was far slower and far less powerful than the tiny desktop computers that became popular several decades later. How easy would it have been to use the machine pictured here? *(US Army Photo)*

software glitches. In a widely publicized test conducted soon after installation, operators set out to multiply 97,367 by itself 5,000 times. A reporter pushed the necessary button, and the task was completed in less than half a second. In the years that followed, new machines with their own internal instructions and memories were developed.

A key breakthrough in making computers faster and more reliable was the development of the transistor by three scientists at Bell Laboratories in 1948. Computers transformed American society as surely as industrialization had changed it a century before, and computer programmers and operators were in increasing demand as computers contributed dramatically to the centralization and interdependence of American life.

Computers were essential for space exploration. They helped scientists perform the mathematical calculations that let astronauts venture beyond the confines of the earth. In the postwar years, increasingly sophisticated forms of space flight became possible. Rocketry had developed during World War II but came of age after the war. Rockets could deliver nuclear weapons but could also launch satellites and provide the means to venture millions of miles into outer space.

Tiny transistors powered not only computers but also a wide variety of new appliances and gadgets designed for personal use. A transistorized miniature hearing aid, for example, could fit into the frame of a pair of eyeglasses. Stereophonic high-fidelity systems, using new transistor components, provided better sound.

An ominous technological trend related to computerization was the advent of automation. Mechanization was not new, but now it became far more widespread, threatening both skilled and unskilled workers. In 1952, the Ford Motor Company began using automatic drilling machines in an engine plant and found that now 41 workers could do a job that had previously required 117 workers. The implications of falling purchasing power as machines replaced workers were serious for an economy dependent on consumer demand.

The Consumer Culture

Americans maintained an ardent love affair with the appliances and gadgets produced by modern technology. By the end of the 1950s, most families had at least one automobile, as well as the staple appliances they had begun to purchase earlier—refrigerator, washing machine, television, and vacuum cleaner. Dozens of less-essential items also became popular. There were electric can openers, electric pencil sharpeners, and electric toothbrushes, as well as push-button phones, aerosol bombs, and automatic transmissions to eliminate the manual shifting of car gears.

The Mouseketeers   *The Mickey Mouse Club* was a popular daily feature on television in the 1950s. Millions of American children were glued to their television sets each day after school, as they shared a common experience and absorbed the values promoted by the television networks. What does this picture tell you about the composition of the cast? *(Photofest)*

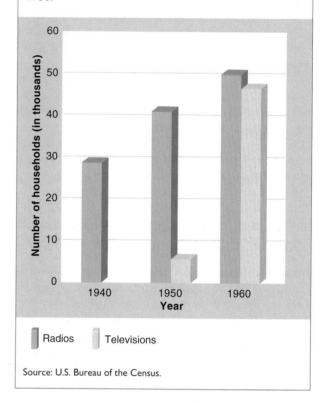

Households Owning Radios and Televisions, 1940–1960

Radio became increasingly popular in the postwar years, but observe the astronomical increase in the number of households owning television sets in the decade after 1950.

Radios   Televisions

Source: U.S. Bureau of the Census.

Television, developed in the 1930s, became a major influence on American life after World War II. In 1946, there were fewer than 17,000 television sets, but by 1960, three-quarters of all American families owned at least one set. In 1955, the average American family tuned in four to five hours each day. Some studies predicted that an American student, on graduating from high school, would have spent 11,000 hours in class and 15,000 hours before the "tube." Young Americans grew up to the strains of "Winky Dink and You," "The Mickey Mouse Club," and "Howdy Doody Time" in the 1950s. Older viewers watched situation comedies such as *I Love Lucy* and *Father Knows Best* and live dramas such as *Playhouse 90*.

Television highlighted the rock-and-roll music that developed in the 1950s. Americans watched Elvis Presley play his guitar and sing, gyrating his hips in a sexually suggestive way that terrified parents, who worried about the influence of this new music, based on black rhythm and blues songs, on their children. Young people eagerly watched their

IMAGE

Cover Illustration for "The Desi–Lucy Love Story," 1956

Dick Clark's American Bandstand, 1958

counterparts dance to the music of Bill Haley and the Comets, Little Richard, Chuck Berry, and Elvis himself on *American Bandstand* every afternoon.

Consumption, increasingly a pillar of the American economy, required a vast expansion of consumer credit. Installment plans facilitated buying a new car, while credit cards encouraged the purchase of smaller items such as television sets and household appliances. Eating out became easier when meals could be charged on a card. The first of the consumer credit cards—the Diner's Club card—appeared in 1950, followed at the end of the decade by the American Express card and the BankAmericard (later renamed Visa). By the end of the 1960s, about 50 million credit cards of all kinds were in use in the United States. Consumer credit—total private indebtedness—increased from $8.4 billion in 1946 to nearly $45 billion in 1958.

For consumers momentarily unsure about new purchases, a revitalized advertising industry was ready to persuade them to go ahead and buy. Advertising had come of age in the 1920s, as businesses persuaded customers that buying new products brought status and satisfaction. It had faltered when the economy collapsed in the 1930s but began to revive during the war, as firms kept the public aware of consumer goods, even those in short supply. With the postwar boom, advertisers again began to hawk their wares, this time even more aggressively than before.

Having weathered the poverty and unemployment of the 1930s and made sacrifices during a long war, Americans now regarded abundance and leisure as their due, sometimes neglecting to look beyond the immediate objects of their desire. As journalist William Shannon wrote, the decade was one of "self-satisfaction and gross materialism. . . . The loudest sound in the land has been the oink and grunt of private hoggishness. . . . It has been the age of the slob."

CONSENSUS AND CONFORMITY

As the economy expanded, an increasing sense of sameness pervaded American society. Third- and fourth-generation ethnic Americans became much more alike. As immigration slowed to a trickle after 1924, ties to Europe weakened, assimilation speeded up, and interethnic marriage skyrocketed. Television gave young and old a shared, visually seductive experience. Escaping the homogenizing tendencies was difficult. Sociologist David Riesman pointed out that in the classic nursery rhyme "This Little Pig

Went to Market," each pig went his own way. "Today, however, all little pigs go to market; none stay home; all have roast beef, if any do; and all say 'we-we.' "

Contours of Religious Life

Postwar Americans discovered a shared religious sense and returned to their churches in record numbers. By the end of the 1950s, fully 95 percent of all Americans identified with some religious denomination.

Ecumenical activities—worldwide efforts on the part of different Christian churches—promoted greater religious involvement. A first World Council of Churches meeting in 1948 in Amsterdam, the Netherlands, helped draw attention to the place of religion in modern life. Evangelical revivalism, led by Southern Baptist Billy Graham and others, became increasingly popular.

At the same time, Catholicism sought to broaden its appeal. This effort succeeded as Pope John XXIII convened the Vatican Ecumenical Council in 1962 to make the Catholic church's traditions and practices

Preacher Billy Graham Evangelist Billy Graham preached a fiery message to millions of Americans in the 1950s. On the radio, on television, and in huge revivals, he urged sinners to embrace God and so save their nation from the perils of the Communist threat. How did the religious message Graham preached fit into the contours of the Cold War? *(Bettmann/CORBIS)*

more accessible—for example, substituting modern languages for Latin in the liturgy.

Judaism likewise broadened its appeal. As assimilation occurred, quotas that had kept many out of more exclusive universities and other institutions began to disappear. Jews, like others, relied on the GI Bill to move to the suburbs, where they bought new homes and built new synagogues, most of which followed the more casual patterns of Reform or Conservative, rather than Orthodox, Judaism.

The religious revival drew in part on the power of suggestion that led Americans to do what others did. Religion could reinforce the importance of family life, for, according to one slogan, "The family that prays together stays together." The renewal of interest in religion also offered an acceptable means of escape from the anxieties of a middle-class executive's life. In the 1950s, the Full Gospel Businessmen's Fellowship not only provided religious camaraderie but also enjoyed access to the White House. In 1953, President Dwight D. Eisenhower began the tradition of opening the inaugural ceremony with a prayer.

Eisenhower reflected the national mood when he observed that "our government makes no sense unless it is founded in a deeply felt religious faith—and I don't care what it is." In 1954, Congress added the words "under God" to the pledge to the flag and the next year voted to require the phrase "In God We Trust" on all U.S. currency. Yet the revival sometimes seemed to rest on a shallow base of religious knowledge. In one public opinion poll, 80 percent of the respondents indicated that the Bible was God's revealed word, but only 35 percent were able to name the four Gospels and more than half were unable to name even one.

A challenge to religious conformity came from members of the so-called Beat Generation who embraced Buddhism. They helped promote the Buddhist vogue that emerged in the 1950s and 1960s, with Zen centers opening in Los Angeles in 1956, San Francisco in 1959, and New York in 1966. Zen stressed Buddha's emphasis on meditation that led to his enlightenment. In the next decade, the counterculture reached out to a variety of alternative religions, including some related to Buddhism (see Chapter 28).

Traditional Roles for Men and Women

World War II had interrupted traditional patterns of behavior for both men and women. As servicemen went overseas, women left their homes to work. After 1945, women faced tremendous pressure to leave their jobs and to conform to accepted prewar gender patterns, even though, paradoxically, more women entered the workforce than ever before.

Men and women had different postwar expectations. Most men expected to go to school and then find jobs to support their families. Viewing themselves as the primary breadwinners, they wanted their jobs waiting for them after the war. For women, the situation was more complex. While they wanted to resume patterns of family life that had been disrupted by the war, many had enjoyed working in the military plants and were reluctant to retreat to the home, despite pressure to do so.

In 1947, *Life* magazine ran a long photo essay called "The American Woman's Dilemma" that summed up the problem. The essay observed that women were caught in a conflict between the traditional expectation to stay home and the desire to have a paid job. A 1946 *Fortune* magazine poll also captured the discontent of some women. Asked whether they would prefer to be born again as men or as women, 25 percent of the women interviewed said they would prefer to be men. That dissatisfaction was strongest among white, well-educated, middle-class women, which was understandable, since family economic circumstances usually required black and lower-class white women to continue working outside the home.

By the 1950s, middle-class doubts and questions had largely receded. The baby boom increased average family size and made the decision to remain home easier. The flight to the suburbs gave women more to do, and they settled into the routines of redecorating their homes and gardens and transporting children to and from activities and schools.

In 1956, when *Life* produced a special issue on women, the message differed strikingly from that of nine years before. Profiling Marjorie Sutton, the magazine spoke of the "Busy Wife's Achievements" as "Home Manager, Mother, Hostess, and Useful Civic Worker." Married at age 16, Marjorie was now involved with the PTA, Camp Fire Girls, and charity causes. She cooked and sewed for her family of four children, supported her husband by entertaining 1,500 guests a year, and worked out on the trampoline "to keep her size 12 figure."

DOCUMENT

Ladies' Home Journal, "Young Mother" (1956)

Marjorie Sutton reflected the widespread social emphasis on marriage and home. Many women went to college to find husbands—and dropped out if they succeeded. Almost two-thirds of the women in college, but less than half the men, left before completing a degree. Women were expected to marry young, have children early, and encourage their husbands' careers. An article in *Esquire* magazine in 1954 called working wives a "menace."

Adlai Stevenson, Democratic presidential candidate in 1952 and 1956, defined the female role in

AMERICAN VOICES

Betty Friedan, From *The Feminine Mystique*

Betty Friedan was a journalist who first was active in union work, then wrote articles for popular women's magazines. After conducting a survey of her Smith College classmates, she wrote The Feminine Mystique, *which became widely popular after its publication in 1963.*

The problem lay buried, unspoken, for many years in the minds of American women. It was a strange stirring, a sense of dissatisfaction, a yearning that women suffered in the middle of the twentieth century in the United States. Each suburban wife struggled with it alone. As she made the beds, shopped for groceries, matched slipcover material, ate peanut butter sandwiches with her children, chauffeured Cub Scouts and Brownies, lay beside her husband at night—she was afraid to ask even of herself the silent question—Is this all?" . . .

If a woman had a problem in the 1950s and 1960s, she knew that something must be wrong with her marriage, or with herself. Other women were satisfied with their lives, she thought. What kind of a woman was she if she did not feel this mysterious fulfillment waxing the kitchen floor? She was so ashamed to admit her dissatisfaction that she never knew how many other women shared it. . . .

In 1960, the problem that has no name burst like a boil through the image of the happy American housewife. . . . We can no longer ignore that voice within women that says: "I want something more than my husband and my children and my home."

- *What is the problem Betty Friedan highlights here?*

- *Why do suburban women seem to be unhappy?*

- *How widespread does the problem seem to be to Friedan?*

---

politics. "The assignment for you, as wives and mothers," he told a group of women, "you can do in the living room with a baby in your lap or in the kitchen with a can opener in your hand." As in much of the nineteenth century, a woman was "to influence man and boy" in her "humble role of housewife" and mother.

Pediatrician Benjamin Spock agreed. In 1946 he published *Baby and Child Care,* the book most responsible for the child-rearing patterns of the postwar generation. In it, he advised mothers to stay at home if they wanted to raise stable and secure youngsters. Working outside the home might jeopardize their children's mental and emotional health.

Popular culture highlighted the stereotype of the woman concerned only about marriage and family. Author Betty Friedan described these patterns in her explosive 1963 critique, *The Feminine Mystique.* Shifting her attention away from the working-class and union issues that had concerned her before, she now profiled women in the 1950s and early 1960s. They "could desire no greater destiny than to glory in their own femininity. . . . All they had to do was to devote their lives from earliest girlhood to finding a husband and bearing children." Their role was clear. "It was unquestioned gospel," she wrote, "that women could identify with *nothing* beyond the home—not politics, not art, not science, not events large or small, war or peace, in the United States or the world, unless it could be approached through female experience as a wife or mother or translated into domestic detail."

Movies reinforced conventional images. Doris Day, charming and wholesome, was a favorite heroine. In film after film, she showed how an attractive woman who played her cards right could land her man.

The family was all-important in this scenario. Fewer than 10 percent of all Americans felt that an unmarried person could be happy. In a pattern endlessly reiterated by popular television programs, the family was meant to provide all satisfaction and contentment. The single-story ranch house that became so popular in this period reflected the focus on the family as the source of recreation and fun. No longer were kitchen and den private, as they had been earlier in a reflection of the notion of separate spheres. Now houses, with far more shared and open space, stressed livability and family comfort.

Sexuality was a troublesome if compelling postwar concern. In 1948, Alfred C. Kinsey published *Sexual Behavior in the Human Male.* Kinsey was an Indiana University zoologist who had previously studied the gall wasp. When asked to teach a course on marriage problems, he found little published material about human sexual activity and decided to collect his own. He compiled case histories of 5,300 white males and recorded patterns of sexual behavior.

RECOVERING THE PAST

Clothing can be an important source of information about the past. The clothes people wear often announce their age, gender, and class and frequently transmit some sense of their origin, occupation, and even their politics. The vocabulary of dress includes more than garments alone: hairstyles, jewelry, and makeup all contribute to the way people choose to present themselves. Clothing can signal strong emotions; a torn, unbuttoned shirt, for example, can indicate that a person who seldom dresses that way is really upset. Bright colors can demonstrate a daring sense and a willingness to make a strong statement. By examining clothing styles in a number of different decades, we can begin to understand something of the changing patterns of people's lives.

In the 1920s, flappers and other women often dressed like children, with loose dresses usually in pastel colors ending just below the knee. Large trimmings, such as huge artificial flowers, accentuated the effect. A "boyish" figure was considered most attractive. The clothes conveyed a feeling of playfulness and a willingness to embrace the freedom of the young. Men's suits in the same period were now made out of lighter materials and looked less padded than before. As the tall, stiff collar of an earlier age disappeared

Frances Perkins with laborers in the 1930s. *(Brown Brothers)*

and trousers became more high-waisted, men too had a more youthful look.

The Great Depression of the 1930s brought a change in style. Flappers now looked silly, especially as millions of people were starving. Advertisements and films promoted a new maturity and sophistication, more appropriate to hard times. Men's suits became heavier and darker, as if symbolically to provide protection in a bread line. Trousers were wider, and jackets were frequently double-breasted. Overcoats became longer. Women's clothes were likewise made out of heavier fabrics and used darker colors. Skirts fell almost to the ankles on occasion and were covered by longer coats. Clothes indicated that there was no place for the playfulness of the decade before.

As conditions improved during and after World War II, styles changed once more. In the 1940s, young teenage girls frequently wore bobby socks rolled down to their ankles. Working women wore overalls, but with their own adornments to maintain their femininity. Rosie the Riveter, drawn by noted artist Norman Rockwell, wore her overalls proudly as she sat with a riveting gun in her lap and an attractive scarf around her hair. In the postwar years, the "Man in the Gray Flannel Suit" looked serious, sober, and

Harlem women in the 1920s. *(Photographs and Prints Division, Schomburg Center for Research in Black Culture, The New York Public Library, Astor, Lenox and Tilden Foundations/Art Resources, NY)*

880

World War II women at work. (Oregon Historical Society, OrHi 37401)

A woman and child in the 1950s. (© The Dorothea Lange Collection, The Oakland Museum of California, City of Oakland, Gift of Paul S. Taylor)

well tailored, ready to go work for corporate America. His female partner wanted to look equally worldly and sophisticated and wore carefully tailored adult clothing, with the waist drawn in (often by a girdle) and heels as tall as three inches, when going out. The fashion industry helped define the decorative role women were supposed to play in supporting men as they advanced their business careers.

Then came the 1960s and an entirely new look. Casual clothing became a kind of uniform. The counterculture was a movement of the young, and clothing took on an increasingly youthful look. Skirts rose above the knee in 1963 and a few years later climbed to mid-thigh. Women began to wear pants and trouser suits. Men and women both favored jeans and informal shirts and let their hair grow longer. Men broke away from the gray suits of the preceding decade and indulged themselves in bright colors in what has been called the "peacock revolution."

REFLECTING ON THE PAST Look carefully at the pictures on these pages. They show fashions from different periods and can tell us a good deal about how these people defined themselves. Examine first the photo of the three black women from the 1920s. What kinds of adornments do you notice? What impression do these women convey?

Look at the photograph of Frances Perkins, secretary of labor in the 1930s. What kind of dress is she wearing? How do her clothes differ from those of the women in the 1920s? In the picture, she is talking to a number of working men. What do their clothes tell you about the kind of work they might be doing?

In the picture of two drill press operators during World War II, the women are dressed to handle the heavy machinery. Are their clothes different from those of the laborers in the preceding picture? How have the women accommodated themselves to their work, while still maintaining their individuality?

Now look at the picture of a woman in the 1950s. What kind of work might she do? What kind of flexibility do these clothes give her? What do the stylistic touches convey?

Finally, examine the photograph of the man and woman at an outdoor music festival in the 1960s. What does their clothing remind you of? Where might it come from? What impression are these people trying to create by their dress?

Countercultural dress in the 1960s. (Ken Heyman/Woodfin Camp & Associates)

Sex Symbol Marilyn Monroe   Sex goddess Marilyn Monroe—shown here in a widely distributed promotional photo for *The Seven Year Itch*—stirred the fantasies of American males in the 1950s. Despite the family orientation of suburban America, millions were captivated by her seductive appeal. What messages were conveyed by this picture? *(AP/World Wide Photos)*

Kinsey shocked the country with his statistics on premarital, extramarital, and otherwise illicit sexual acts. Among males who went to college, he concluded, 67 percent had engaged in sexual intercourse before marriage, as had 84 percent of those who went to high school but not beyond. Thirty-seven percent of the total male population had experienced some kind of overt homosexual activity. Five years later, Kinsey published a companion volume, *Sexual Behavior in the Human Female*, which detailed many of the same sexual patterns. Although critics denounced Kinsey for what they considered his unscientific methodology and challenged his results, both books sold widely, for they opened the door to a subject previously considered taboo.

Interest in sexuality was reflected in the fascination with sex goddesses such as Marilyn Monroe. With her blond hair, breathy voice, and raw sexuality, she personified the forbidden side of the good life and became one of Hollywood's most popular stars. The images of such film goddesses corresponded to male fantasies of women, visible in *Playboy* magazine, which first appeared in 1953 and soon achieved a huge readership. As for men's

wives, they were expected to manage their suburban homes and to be cheerful and willing objects of their husbands' desire.

Despite reaffirming the old ideology that a woman's place was in the home, the 1950s were years of unnoticed but important change. Because the supply of single women workers fell as a result of the low birthrate of the Depression years and increased schooling and early marriage, older married women continued the pattern begun during the war and entered the labor force in larger numbers than before. In 1940, only 15 percent of American wives had jobs. By 1950, 21 percent were employed, and 10 years later, the figure had risen to 30 percent. Moreover, more than half of all working women were married, a dramatic reversal of pre–World War II patterns. Although the media hailed those women who primarily tended to their families, some magazine articles, in fact, did stress the achievements of women outside the home.

While many working women were poor, divorced, or widowed, many others worked to acquire the desirable new products that were badges of middle-class status. They stepped into the new jobs created by economic expansion, clustering in office, sales, and service positions, occupations already defined as female. They and their employers considered their work subordinate to their primary role as wives and mothers. The conviction that women's main role was homemaking justified low wages and the denial of promotions. Comparatively few women entered professions where they would have challenged traditional notions of a woman's place.

African American women worked as always but often lost the jobs they had held during the war. For example, as the percentage of women in the Detroit automobile industry dropped from 25 percent to 7.5 percent in the immediate postwar period, black women who had held some of the jobs were the first to go. Bernice McCannon, an African American employee at a Virginia military base, observed, "I have always done domestic work for families. When war came, I made the same move many domestics did. I took a higher paying job in a government cafeteria as a junior baker. If domestic work offers a good living, I see no reason why most of us will not return to our old jobs. We will have no alternative." These jobs, however, did not pay well at all. In the 1950s, the employment picture improved somewhat. African American women succeeded both in moving into white-collar positions and in increasing their income. By 1960, more than one-third of all black women held clerical, sales, service, or professional jobs. The income gap between white women and black women holding similar jobs dropped from about 50 percent in 1940 to about 30 percent in 1960.

Cultural Rebels

Not all Americans fit the 1950s stereotypes. Some were alienated from the culture and rebelled against its values. As young people struggled to meet the standards and expectations of their peers, they were intrigued by Holden Caulfield, the main figure in J. D. Salinger's popular novel *The Catcher in the Rye* (1951). Holden, a boarding-school misfit, rebelled against the "phonies" around him who threatened his individuality and independence.

Writers of the "Beat Generation" espoused unconventional values in their stories and poems. Challenging the apathy and conformity of the period, they stressed spontaneity and spirituality and claimed that intuition was more important than reason, Eastern mysticism (with its Buddhist influence) more valuable than Western faith. The "Beats" deliberately outraged respectability by sneering at materialism, flaunting unconventional sex lives, and smoking marijuana.

Their literary work reflected their approach to life. Finding conventional academic forms confining, they rejected them. Jack Kerouac typed his best-selling novel *On the Road* (1957), describing freewheeling trips across country, on a 250-foot roll of

"Beat" Poet Allen Ginsberg Allen Ginsberg was one of the most influential "Beats" who went out of his way to protest what he considered the stultifying patterns of American life. His poetry challenged more conventional norms. How does this photograph relate to the things that troubled Ginsberg about modern American culture? *(Allen Ginsberg/CORBIS)*

paper. Dispensing with conventional punctuation and paragraphing, the book was a song of praise to the free lifestyle the "Beats" espoused.

Poet Allen Ginsberg, who, like Kerouac, was a Columbia University dropout, became equally well known for his poem "Howl." Written during a wild weekend in 1955, the poem was a scathing critique of modern, mechanized culture. The poem became a cult piece, particularly after the police seized it on the grounds that it was obscene. When the work survived a court test, national acclaim followed for Ginsberg. He and the other "Beats" furnished a model for rebellion in the 1960s.

The signs of cultural rebellion also appeared in popular

Rock-and-Roll Star Elvis Presley Elvis Presley, a truck driver from Memphis, Tennessee, turned rock and roll into a kind of teenage religion. In appearances such as this one at a state fair in Memphis, Tennessee, in 1956, his fans worked themselves into a frenzy. How did Elvis's popularity help a new youth culture develop? *(Getty Images)*

AMERICAN VOICES

Allen Ginsberg, "Howl"

Allen Ginsberg became part of the group known as the "Beat Generation" after he dropped out of Columbia University. Critical of modern American society, he articulated his complaints in his scathing poem "Howl" in 1955.

I saw the best minds of my generation destroyed by
    madness, starving hysterical naked,
dragging themselves through the negro streets at
    dawn looking for an angry fix,
angelheaded hipsters burning for the ancient
    heavenly connection to the starry dynamo in the
    machinery of night,
who poverty and tatters and hollow-eyed and high sat
    up smoking in the supernatural darkness of cold-
    water flats floating across the tops of cities
    contemplating jazz, . . .

who were burned alive in their innocent flannel suits
    on Madison Avenue amid blasts of leaden verse &
    the tanked-up clatter of the iron regiments of
    fashion & the nitroglycerine shrieks of the fairies
    of advertising & the mustard gas of sinister

intelligent editors, or were run down by the
    drunken taxicabs of Absolute Reality, . . .

What sphinx of cement and aluminum bashed open
    their skulls and ate up their brains and
    imagination?
Moloch! Solitude! Filth! Ugliness! Ashcans and
    unobtainable dollars! Children screaming under
    the stairways! Boys sobbing in armies! Old men
    weeping in the parks!
Moloch! Moloch! Nightmare of Moloch! Moloch the
    loveless! Mental Moloch! Moloch the heavy judger
    of men! . . .

- *What do you think Allen Ginsberg means in the first line of this poem?*

- *What kinds of things bother him about American society?*

- *Moloch was an evil sun god in ancient Palestine centuries ago, usually represented as a bronze statue with the head of a bull, to whom children were sacrificed. What do you think the poet means by invoking Moloch in the last lines above?*

music. Parents recoiled as their children flocked to hear a young Tennessee singer named Elvis Presley belt out rock-and-roll songs. Presley's sexy voice, gyrating hips, and other techniques borrowed from black singers made him the undisputed "king of rock and roll." A multimedia blitz of movies, television, and radio helped make songs such as "Heartbreak Hotel," "Don't Be Cruel," and "Hound Dog" smash singles. Eighteen Presley hits sold more than a million copies in the last four years of the 1950s. His black leather jacket and ducktail haircut became standard dress for rebellious male teenagers.

American painters, shucking off European influences that had shaped American artists for two centuries, also became a part of the cultural rebellion. Led by Jackson Pollock and the "New York school," some artists discarded the easel, laid gigantic canvases on the floor, and then used trowels, putty knives, and sticks to apply paint, glass shards, sand, and other materials in wild explosions of color. Known as abstract expressionists, these painters regarded the unconscious as the source of their artistic creations. "I am not aware of what is taking place [as I paint]," Pollock explained; "it is only after that I see what I have done." Like much of the literature of rebellion, abstract expressionism reflected the

Abstract Expressionist Artist Jackson Pollock at Work Jackson Pollock often stood over the canvas and flung the paint around him as he moved across the painting in progress. Here he is shown in 1951 dripping the paint on the work that became *Autumn Rhythm.* What does the painting represent to you? What does it say about Pollock's assessment of American society? *(Photo by Hans Namuth/Courtesy, Center for Creative Photography, The University of Arizona. © 1991 Hans Namuth Estate)*

artist's alienation from a world filled with nuclear threats, computerization, and materialism.

ORIGINS OF THE WELFARE STATE

The modern American welfare state originated in the New Deal. Franklin D. Roosevelt's efforts to deal with the ravages of the Great Depression and protect Americans from the problems stemming from industrial capitalism provided the basis for subsequent efforts to commit the government to help those who could not help themselves, even in prosperous times. Harry Truman's Fair Deal built squarely on Roosevelt's New Deal. Truman's Republican successor, Dwight Eisenhower, sought to scale down spending but made no effort to roll back the most important initiatives of the welfare state.

Harry S Truman

Harry S Truman, America's first postwar president, was an unpretentious man who took a straightforward approach to public affairs. He was, however, ill prepared for the office he assumed in the final months of World War II. His three months as vice president had done little to school him in the complexity of postwar issues. Nor had Franklin Roosevelt confided in Truman. It was no wonder that the new president felt insecure. To a former colleague in the Senate, he groaned, "I'm not big enough for this job." Critics agreed.

Yet Truman matured rapidly. A sign on the president's White House desk read, "The Buck Stops Here," and he was willing to make quick decisions on issues, even if associates sometimes wondered whether he understood all the implications.

Truman took the same feisty approach to public policy that characterized his conduct of foreign affairs (see Chapter 27). He stated his position clearly and simply, often in black-and-white terms. Believing in plain speaking, he seldom hesitated to let others know exactly where he stood. He attacked his political enemies vigorously when they resisted his initiatives and often took his case to the American people. He was, in many ways, an old-style Democratic politician who hoped to use his authority to benefit the middle-class and working-class Americans who made up his political base.

Truman's Struggles with a Conservative Congress

Like Roosevelt, Harry Truman believed that the federal government had the responsibility for ensuring the social welfare of all Americans. He shared his predecessor's commitment to assisting less-prosperous inhabitants of the country in a systematic, rational way. Truman wanted his administration to embrace and act on a series of carefully defined social and economic goals to extend New Deal initiatives even further.

Less than a week after the end of World War II, Truman called on Congress to pass a 21-point program. He wanted housing assistance, a higher minimum wage, more unemployment compensation, and a national commitment to maintaining full employment. During the next 10 weeks, Truman sent blueprints of further proposals to Congress, including health insurance and atomic energy legislation. But this liberal program soon ran into fierce political opposition.

The debate surrounding the Employment Act of 1946 hinted at the fate of Truman's proposals. This measure was a deliberate effort to apply the theory of English economist John Maynard Keynes to preserve economic equilibrium and prevent depression. A decade earlier Keynes had argued that massive spending was necessary to extricate a nation from depression. The money spent during World War II caused the economy to respond precisely as Keynes had predicted. Now economists wanted to institutionalize his ideas to forestall further problems. The initial bill, which enjoyed the strong support of labor, committed the government to maintaining full employment by monitoring the economy and taking remedial action in case of decline. Responses to a downturn included tax cuts and spending programs to stimulate the economy and reduce unemployment.

While liberals and labor leaders hailed the measure, business groups such as the National Association of Manufacturers condemned it. They claimed that government intervention would undermine free enterprise and promote socialism. Responding to the business community, Congress cut the proposal to bits. As finally passed, the act created a Council of Economic Advisers to make recommendations to the president, who was to report annually to Congress and the nation on the state of the economy. But it stopped short of committing the government to using fiscal tools to maintain full employment when economic indicators turned downward.

As the midterm elections of 1946 approached, Truman knew he was vulnerable. As more and more people questioned his competence as president, his support dropped from 87 percent of those polled after he assumed the office to 32 percent in November 1946. Gleeful Republicans asked the voters, "Had enough?"

They had. Republicans won majorities in both houses of Congress for the first time since the 1928 elections and gained a majority of the governorships as well. In Atlantic City, New Jersey, even a Republican candidate for justice of the peace who had died a week before the election was victorious.

After the 1946 elections, Truman faced an unsympathetic Eightieth Congress. Republicans and conservative Democrats, dominating both houses, planned to reverse the liberal policies of the Roosevelt years. Hoping to re-establish congressional authority and cut the power of the executive branch, they insisted on less government intervention in business and private affairs. They also demanded tax cuts and curtailment of the privileged position they felt labor had come to enjoy.

When the new Congress met, it slashed federal spending and taxes. In 1947, Congress twice passed tax-cut measures, which Truman vetoed. In 1948, another election year, Congress overrode the veto.

Congress also struck at Democratic labor policies. Angry at the gains won by labor in the 1930s and 1940s, Republicans wanted to check unions and to circumscribe their right to engage in the kind of disruptive strikes that had occurred immediately after the war. Early in Truman's presidency, Congress had passed a bill requiring notice for strikes as well as a cooling-off period if a strike occurred. Truman vetoed it. But in 1947, commanding more votes, the Republicans passed the Taft–Hartley Act, which sought to limit the power of unions by restricting the weapons they could employ. It spelled out unfair labor practices (such as preventing nonunion workers from working if they wished) and outlawed the closed shop, whereby an employee had to join a union before getting a job. The law likewise allowed states to prohibit the union shop, which forced workers to join the union after they had been hired. It gave the president the right to call for an 80-day cooling-off period in strikes affecting national security and required union officials to sign non-Communist oaths.

Union leaders and members were furious. They called the measure a "slave-labor law" and argued vigorously that it eliminated many of their hard-won rights and left labor–management relations the way they had been in pre–New Deal days. Vetoing the measure, Truman claimed that it was unworkable and unfair and went on nationwide radio to seek public approval. This move regained him some of the support he had lost earlier when he had sought to force strikers to go back to work immediately after the war. Congress, however, passed the Taft–Hartley measure over Truman's veto.

The Fair Deal and Its Fate

In 1948, Truman wanted a chance to consolidate a liberal program and decided to seek the presidency in his own right. Aware that he was an accidental occupant of the White House, he won what most people thought was a worthless nomination. Not only was his own popularity waning, but the Democratic party itself seemed to be falling apart.

The civil rights issue split the Democrats. When liberals defeated a moderate platform proposal and pressed for a stronger commitment to African American rights, angry delegates from Mississippi and Alabama stormed out of the convention. They later formed the States' Rights, or Dixiecrat, party. At their own convention, delegates from 13 states nominated Governor J. Strom Thurmond of South Carolina as their presidential candidate and affirmed their support for continued racial segregation.

Meanwhile, Henry A. Wallace, first secretary of agriculture, then vice president during Roosevelt's third term, and finally secretary of commerce, mounted his own challenge. Truman had fired Wallace from his cabinet for supporting a more temperate approach to the Soviet Union. Now Wallace became the presidential candidate of the Progressive party. Initially, he attracted widespread liberal interest because of his moderate position on Soviet–American affairs, his promotion of desegregation, and his promise to nationalize the railroads and major industries, but then support dropped off.

In that fragmented state, the Democrats took on the Republicans, who coveted the White House after 16 years out of power. Once again, the GOP nominated New York Governor Thomas E. Dewey, the unsuccessful candidate in 1944. Even though he was stiff and egocentric, the polls uniformly picked the Republicans to win. Dewey saw little value in brawling with his opponent and campaigned, in the words of one commentator, "with the humorless calculation of a Certified Public Accountant in pursuit of the Holy Grail."

Truman, as the underdog, conducted a two-fisted campaign. He appealed to ordinary Americans as an unpretentious man engaged in an uphill fight. Believing that everyone was against him but the people, he addressed Americans in familiar language. He called the Republicans a "bunch of old mossbacks" out to destroy the New Deal as he attacked the "do nothing" Eightieth Congress. Speaking informally in

Harry Truman Celebrating His Unexpected Victory In one of the nation's extraordinary political upsets, Harry Truman beat Thomas E. Dewey in 1948. Here an exuberant Truman holds a newspaper headline printed while he slept, before the vote turned his way. Why is Truman so gleeful? *(Bettmann/CORBIS)*

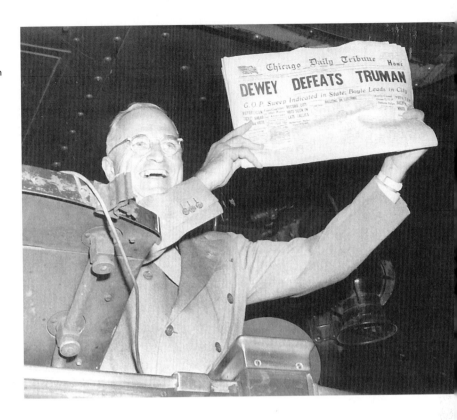

his choppy, aggressive style, he appealed to crowds that yelled, "Give 'em hell, Harry!" He did.

The pollsters predicting a Republican victory were wrong. On election day, disproving the bold headline "Dewey Defeats Truman" in the *Chicago Daily Tribune,* the incumbent president scored one of the most unexpected political upsets in American history, winning 303–189 in the Electoral College. Democrats also swept both houses of Congress.

Truman won primarily because he was able to revive the major elements of the Democratic coalition that Franklin Roosevelt had constructed more than a decade before. Despite the rocky days of 1946, Truman managed to hold on to labor, farm, and black votes. Labor's support was crucial. Working men and women had been irritated by his response to the strikes in the immediate postwar period but had been buoyed by his veto, even though unsuccessful, of the Taft–Hartley Act. In the end, wary of Wallace, they backed Truman.

The fragmentation of the Democratic party, which had threatened to hurt the president severely, helped him instead. The splinter parties drew off some votes but allowed Truman to make a more aggressive, direct appeal to the center.

With the election behind him, Truman pursued his liberal program. In his 1949 State of the Union message, he declared, "Every segment of our population and every individual has a right to expect from our Government a fair deal." The Fair Deal became the name for his domestic program, which included the measures he had proposed since 1945.

Parts of Truman's Fair Deal worked; others did not. Lawmakers raised the minimum wage and expanded social security programs. A housing program brought modest gains but did not really meet housing needs. A farm program, aimed at providing income support to farmers if prices fell, never made it through Congress. Although he desegregated the military, other parts of his civil rights program failed to win congressional support. The American Medical Association undermined the effort to provide national health insurance, and Congress rejected a measure to provide federal aid to education.

The mixed record was not entirely Truman's fault. Conservative legislators were largely responsible for sabotaging his efforts. At the same time, critics charged correctly that Truman was often unpragmatic and shrill in his struggles with an unsympathetic Congress. They argued that he sometimes seemed to provoke the confrontations that became a hallmark of his presidency. They also claimed that he was most concerned with foreign policy as he strove to secure bipartisan support for Cold War initiatives (see Chapter 27) and allowed his domestic program to suffer. Rising defense expenditures meant less money for projects at home.

Presidential Elections, 1948–1956				
Year	Candidate	Party	Popular Vote	Electoral Vote
1948	HARRY S TRUMAN	Democratic	24,105,812 (49.5%)	303
	Thomas E. Dewey	Republican	21,970,065 (45.1%)	189
	J. Strom Thurmond	States' Rights	1,169,063 (12.4%)	39
	Henry A. Wallace	Progressive	1,157,172 (12.4%)	0
1952	DWIGHT D. EISENHOWER	Republican	33,936,234 (55.1%)	442
	Adlai E. Stevenson	Democratic	27,314,992 (44.4%)	89
1956	DWIGHT D. EISENHOWER	Republican	35,590,472 (57.4%)	457
	Adlai E. Stevenson	Democratic	26,022,752 (42.0%)	73

Note: Winners' names appear in capital letters.

Still, Truman kept the liberal vision alive. The Fair Deal ratified many of the initiatives begun during the New Deal and led Americans to take programs such as social security for granted. Truman had not achieved everything he wanted—he had not even come close—but the nation had taken another step toward endorsing liberal goals.

The Election of Ike

Acceptance of the liberal state continued in the 1950s, even as the Republicans took control. By 1952, Truman's popularity had plummeted to 23 percent of the American people, and all indicators pointed to a political shift. The Democrats nominated Adlai Stevenson, Illinois's articulate and moderately liberal governor. The Republicans turned to Dwight Eisenhower, the World War II hero known as Ike.

Stevenson approached political issues in intellectual terms. "Let's talk sense to the American people," he said. "Let's tell them the truth." While liberals loved his approach, Stevenson himself anticipated the probable outcome. How, he wondered, could a man named Adlai beat a soldier called Ike?

The Republicans focused on communism, corruption, and Korea as major issues. They called the Democrats "soft on communism" and demanded a more aggressive approach at home and abroad. They criticized scandals involving Truman's cronies and friends. The Republicans also promised to end the unpopular Korean War.

VIDEO

Ike for President: Eisenhower Campaign Ad, 1952

Eisenhower proved to be a highly effective campaigner. He had a natural talent for taking his case to the American people, speaking in simple, reassuring terms they could understand. He struck a grandfatherly pose, unified the various wings of his party, and went on to victory at the polls. He received 55 percent of the vote and carried 41 states. The new president took office with a Republican Congress as well and had little difficulty winning a second term in 1956.

Dwight D. Eisenhower

Eisenhower stood in stark contrast to Truman. His easy manner and warm smile made him widely popular. As British field marshal Bernard Montgomery observed, "He has the power of drawing the hearts of men towards him as a magnet attracts bits of metal."

Eisenhower had not taken the typical route to the presidency. After World War II, he served successively as army chief of staff, president of Columbia University, and head of the North Atlantic Treaty Organization (NATO). Despite his lack of formal political background, he had a real ability to get people to compromise and work together.

Ike's limited experience with everyday politics conditioned his sense of the presidential role. Whereas Truman loved political infighting and wanted to take charge, Eisenhower was more restrained. The presidency for him was no "bully pulpit," as it had been for Theodore Roosevelt and even FDR. "I am not one of those desk-pounding types that likes to stick out his jaw and look like he is bossing the show," he said. "You do not lead by hitting people over the head. Any damn fool can do that, but it's usually called 'assault'—not 'leadership.' "

"Modern Republicanism"

Eisenhower wanted to limit the presidential role. He was uncomfortable with the growth of the executive office over the past 20 years. Like the Republicans in Congress with whom Truman had tangled, he wanted to restore the balance between the branches of government and to reduce the authority of the national government. He recognized, however, that it was impossible to scale back federal power to the limited levels of the 1920s, and he wanted to preserve social gains that even Republicans now accepted. Eisenhower sometimes termed his approach "dynamic conservatism" or "modern Republicanism," which, he explained, meant "conservative when it comes to money, liberal when it comes to human beings." Liberals quipped that his approach meant endorsing social projects and then failing to authorize the funds.

Economic concerns dominated the Eisenhower years. The president and his chief aides wanted desperately to preserve the value of the dollar, pare down levels of funding, cut taxes, and balance the budget after years of deficit spending. Eisenhower's administration also supported business interests. This orientation became obvious when defense secretary Charles E. Wilson, former president of General Motors, declared at his confirmation hearing, "What is good for our country is good for General Motors, and vice versa."

Eisenhower fulfilled his promise to reduce government's economic role. After Republicans received financial support from oil companies during the campaign, the new Congress, with a strong endorsement from the president, passed the Submerged Lands Act in 1953, transferring control of about $40 billion worth of oil lands from the federal government to the states. The *New York Times* called it "one of the greatest and surely the most unjustified give-away programs in all the history of the United States."

The administration also sought to reduce federal activity in the electric power field. Eisenhower favored private rather than public development of power, and once said about the Tennessee Valley Authority (TVA), the extensive public power and development project begun during the New Deal, "I'd like to see us sell the whole thing, but I suppose we can't go that far." He opposed a TVA proposal for expansion to provide power to the Atomic Energy Commission and instead authorized a private group, the Dixon–Yates syndicate, to build a plant in Arkansas for that purpose. Later, when charges of scandal arose, the administration canceled the agreement, but the basic preference for private development remained.

Committed to supporting business interests, the administration sometimes saw its program backfire. As a result of Eisenhower's reluctance to stimulate the economy too much, the annual rate of economic growth declined from 4.3 percent between 1947 and 1952 to 2.5 percent between 1953 and 1960. The economy was still growing, but more slowly than

before. The country also suffered three recessions—in 1953–1954, 1957–1958, and 1960–1961—in Eisenhower's eight years. During the slumps, tax revenues fell and the deficits that Eisenhower so wanted to avoid increased.

Eisenhower's understated approach led to a legislative stalemate, particularly when the Democrats regained control of Congress in 1954. Opponents gibed at Ike's restrained stance and laughed about limited White House leadership. One observed that Eisenhower proved that the country did not "need" a president. Another spoke of the Eisenhower doll— you wound it up and it did nothing for eight years.

Yet Eisenhower understood just what he was doing; he had a better grasp of public policy than his critics realized. Beneath his casual approach lay real shrewdness. "Don't worry," he once assured his aides as they briefed him for a press conference. "If that question comes up, I'll just confuse them." He worked quietly to create the consensus that he believed was necessary for legislative progress and practiced what later observers called a "hidden hand" presidency, unobtrusively orchestrating support for his own ends.

Dwight D. Eisenhower

Even more important was his role in ratifying the welfare state. By 1960, the government had become a major factor in ordinary people's lives. It had grown enormously, employing close to 2.5 million people throughout the 1950s. Federal expenditures,

A Popular and Personable President Dwight Eisenhower provided a reassuring presence in the White House in the 1950s. His very presence conveyed the impression that everything was going to be all right. How did his wide smile, pictured here, make Americans feel good about themselves and their country? *(Hulton Archive/Getty Images)*

which had stood at $3.5 billion in 1927, rose to $97 billion in 1960. The White House now took the lead in initiating legislation and in steering bills through Congress. Individuals had come to expect old-age pensions, unemployment payments, and a minimum wage. By accepting the fundamental features of the national state that the Democrats had created, Eisenhower ensured its survival.

DOCUMENT

Dwight D. Eisenhower, Farewell to the Nation (January 17, 1961)

For all the jokes at his expense, Eisenhower remained popular with the voters. He accomplished most of his goals, and he was one of the few presidents to leave office as highly regarded by the people as when he entered it. He was the kind of leader Americans wanted in prosperous times.

THE OTHER AMERICA

Not all Americans shared postwar middle-class affluence. Although most white Americans were barely conscious of poverty, it clearly existed in inner cities and rural areas. African Americans, uprooted from rural patterns and transplanted into urban slums, were among the hardest hit. But members of other minority groups, as well as less fortunate whites, suffered similar dislocations, unknown to the middle class.

Poverty amid Affluence

Many people in the "affluent society" lived in poverty. Economic growth favored the upper and middle classes. Although the popular "trickle-down" theory argued that economic expansion benefited all classes, little wealth reached the citizens at the bottom. In 1960, according to the Federal Bureau of Labor Statistics, a yearly subsistence-level income for a family of four was $3,000 and for a family of six was $4,000. The bureau reported that 40 million people (almost one-quarter of the population) lived below those levels, with nearly the same number only marginally above the line. Two million migrant workers labored long hours for a subsistence wage. Many less-mobile people were hardly better off. According to the 1960 census, 27 percent of the residential units in the United States were substandard.

Michael Harrington, socialist author and critic, shocked the country with his 1962 study *The Other America*. The poor, Harrington showed, were everywhere. He described New York City's "economic underworld," where "Puerto Ricans and Negroes, alcoholics, drifters, and disturbed people" haunted employment agencies for temporary positions as "dishwashers and day workers, the fly-by-night jobs." In the afternoon, he continued, "the jobs have all been handed out, yet the people still mill around. Some of them sit on benches in the larger offices. There is no real point to their waiting, yet they have nothing else to do."

Harrington also described the conditions faced by the rural poor. Despite the prosperity that surrounded them, the mountain folk of Appalachia, the tenant farmers of Mississippi, and the migrant farmers of Florida, Texas, and California were all caught in poverty's relentless cycle.

Hard Times for African Americans

African Americans were among the postwar nation's least prosperous citizens. In the South, agricultural workers continued to fall victim to foreign competition, mechanization, and eviction as white farmers turned to less labor-intensive crops such as soybeans and peanuts.

The southern agricultural population declined dramatically as millions of blacks moved to southern cities, where they found better jobs, better schooling, and freedom from landlords. Some achieved middle-class status; many more did not. They remained poor, with even less of a support system than they had known before.

Millions of African Americans also headed for northern cities after 1940. In the 1950s, Detroit's black population increased from 16 percent to 29 percent, Chicago's from 14 percent to 23 percent. At one point in this decade, Chicago's black population rose by more than 2,200 people each week. The new arrivals congregated in urban slums, where the growth of social services failed to keep pace with population growth.

MAP

African American Migration, 1915-1970

The black ghetto that had begun to develop earlier in the twentieth century became a permanent fixture in the post–World War II years. African Americans attempting to move elsewhere often found the way blocked. In 1951, a black couple purchasing a home in Cicero, Illinois, was driven away when an angry crowd broke the house's windows, defaced the walls, and shouted vile insults. This pattern was repeated around the country—in Birmingham, Chicago, Detroit, and countless other cities.

The experiences of African Americans in the cities often proved different from what they had expected. As author Claude Brown recalled, blacks were told that in the North, "Negroes lived in houses with bathrooms, electricity, running water, and indoor toilets. To them, this was the 'promised land'

Independence in Africa

In the 1950s and 1960s, most African nations threw off their colonial rulers and achieved independence. **Reflecting on the Past** During which decade did more nations become free? How did attaining independence change social and economic patterns in the African nations? What effect did it have on the patterns of the Cold War? What effect did it have on the civil rights struggle in the United States?

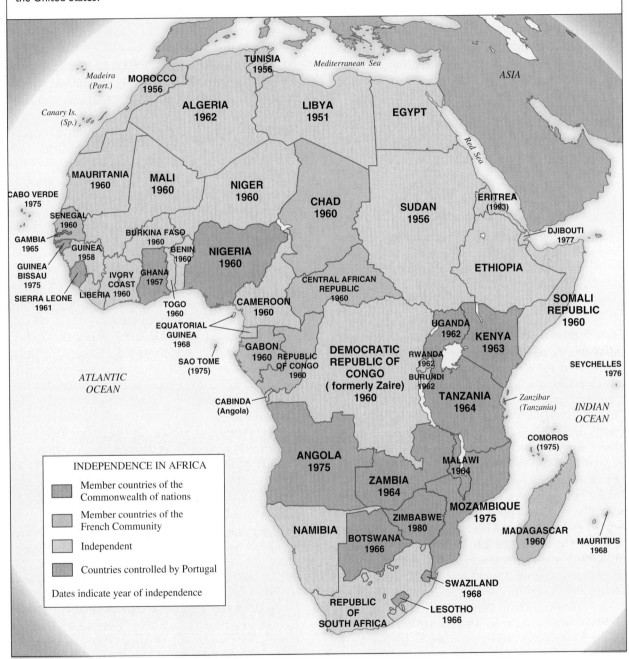

INDEPENDENCE IN AFRICA

- Member countries of the Commonwealth of nations
- Member countries of the French Community
- Independent
- Countries controlled by Portugal

Dates indicate year of independence

that Mammy had been singing about in the cotton fields for many years." But no one had told them "about one of the most important aspects of the promised land: it was a slum ghetto. . . . There were too many people full of hate and bitterness crowded into a dirty, stinky, uncared-for closet-size section of a great city."

Novelist and essayist James Baldwin likewise described slum conditions and their corrosive effect on American blacks in his 1961 book *Nobody Knows My Name:*

> They work in the white man's world all day and come home in the evening to this fetid block. They struggle to instill in their children some private sense of honor or dignity, which will help the child to survive. This means, of course, that they must struggle, stolidly, incessantly, to keep this sense alive in themselves, in spite of the insults, the indifference, and the cruelty they are certain to encounter in their working day. They patiently browbeat the landlord into fixing the heat, the plaster, the plumbing; this demands prodigious patience, nor is patience usually enough. . . . Such frustration, so long endured, is driving many strong and admirable men and women whose only crime is color to the very gates of paranoia.

Such conditions, and the constant slights that accompanied segregation in both the North and the South, took a toll. African Americans learned how, in the words of a turn-of-the-century poem by Paul Laurence Dunbar, to "wear the mask."

Still, the black community remained intact. Chicago's South Side neighborhood was a vibrant place, replacing New York's Harlem as black America's cultural capital in the 1950s. This section of the city included such figures as boxing champion Joe Louis, gospel singer Mahalia Jackson, and Representative William Dawson, one of the few African American members of Congress.

Here and elsewhere, the black church played an important role in sustaining African American life. Blacks moving into the cities retained churchgoing habits and a commitment to religious institutions from their rural days. Older, established churches assisted newcomers in the transition to urban America, while new religious groups began to form. The churches offered more than religious sustenance alone. Many provided day-care facilities, ran Boy Scout and Girl Scout troops, and sponsored a variety of other social services.

The growth of the black urban population fostered the increased growth of businesses catering to the African American community. Black newspapers now provided a more regional, rather than a national, focus, but magazines such as *Jet*, a pocket-size

weekly with a large, countrywide circulation, filled the void. Black-owned and black-operated banks and other financial institutions increased in number.

Yet most African Americans remained second-class citizens. Escape from the slums was difficult for many and impossible for most. Persistent poverty remained a dismal fact of life.

African American Gains

African Americans had made significant gains during World War II. Black servicemen returning from the war vowed to reject second-class citizenship and helped mobilize a grassroots movement to counter discrimination. In the postwar years, African struggles for independence, such as the Kenyan Mau Mau revolt against the British, inspired African American leaders who now saw the quest for black equality in a broader context. They took enormous pride in the achievement of independence by a number of

Baseball Superstar Jackie Robinson Jackie Robinson's electrifying play as the first African American in the major leagues led to acceptance of the integration of baseball. A spectacular rookie season in 1947 opened the way for other African Americans who had earlier been limited to the Negro leagues. In this photo, taken at Ebbets Field in Brooklyn during the 1957 World Series, Robinson is about to steal home. What impression do you have of Robinson here? *(Time Life Pictures/Getty Images)*

African nations and demanded comparable change at home. As Adam Clayton Powell, a Harlem preacher (and later congressman), warned, the black man "is ready to throw himself into the struggle to make the dream of America become flesh and blood, bread and butter, freedom and equality. He walks conscious of the fact that he is no longer alone—no longer a minority."

The racial question was dramatized in 1947 when Jackie Robinson broke the color line and began playing major league baseball with the Brooklyn Dodgers. Sometimes teammates were hostile, sometimes opponents crashed into him with spikes high, but Robinson kept his frustrations to himself. A splendid first season helped ease the way and resulted in his selection as Rookie of the Year. African Americans flocked to the ballpark and followed his exploits on the radio. As Charles Jones of Charlotte, North Carolina, noted, "Robinson was knocking a ball everywhere on a *white man's* baseball field. . . . I mean the entire community would be glued to listening, and inevitably Jackie would steal a base or knock a home run, and we'd be rooting." After Robinson's trailblazing effort, other blacks, formerly confined to the old Negro leagues, moved into the major leagues in baseball and then into other sports.

Some Americans were embarrassed as racial discrimination became entangled with Cold War politics. The appeal for support in Africa and Asia seemed hollow with segregation at home.

Somewhat reluctantly, Truman supported the civil rights movement. A moderate on questions of race, who believed in political, not social, equality, he responded to the growing strength of the African American vote. In 1946, he appointed a Committee on Civil Rights to investigate the problem of lynching and other brutalities against blacks and recommend remedies. The committee's report, released in October 1947, showed that black Americans remained second-class citizens in every area of American life and called for change.

Though Truman hedged at first, in February 1948, he sent a 10-point civil rights program to Congress, the first presidential civil rights plan since Reconstruction. When the southern wing of the Democratic party bolted later that year, he moved forward even more aggressively. First he issued an executive order barring discrimination in the federal establishment. Then he ordered equality of treatment in the military services. Personnel needs in the Korean War broke down the last restrictions, particularly when the army found that integrated units performed well.

DOCUMENT
Executive Order 9981 (1948)

Elsewhere, the administration pushed other reforms. The Justice Department, not previously supportive of litigation from the National Association for the Advancement of Colored People (NAACP) on behalf of equal rights for African Americans, now entered the battle against segregation and filed briefs challenging the constitutionality of restrictions in housing, education, and interstate transportation. These actions helped build the pressure for change that influenced the Supreme Court. Congress, however, took little action.

As the civil rights struggle gained momentum during the 1950s, the judicial system played a crucial role. The NAACP was determined to overturn the 1896 Supreme Court decision *Plessy* v. *Ferguson*, in which the Court had declared that segregation of the black and white races was constitutional if the facilities used by each were "separate but equal." The decree had been used for generations to sanction rigid segregation, primarily in the South, even though separate facilities were seldom, if ever, equal.

A direct challenge came in 1951. Oliver Brown, the father of 8-year-old Linda Brown, sued the school board of Topeka, Kansas, to allow his daughter to attend a school for white children that she passed as she walked to the bus that carried her to a black school farther away. The case reached the Supreme Court, which grouped several school segregation cases together.

On May 17, 1954, the Supreme Court released its bombshell ruling in *Brown* v. *Board of Education*. For more than a decade, Supreme Court decisions had gradually expanded black civil rights. Now the Court unanimously decreed that "separate facilities are inherently unequal" and concluded that the "separate but equal" doctrine had no place in public education. African Americans were elated. "The Supreme Court decision is the greatest victory for the Negro people since the Emancipation Proclamation," Harlem's *Amsterdam News* proclaimed. Author Ralph Ellison observed, "What a wonderful world of possibilities are unfolded for the children." A year later, the Court turned to the question of implementation and declared that local school boards, acting with the guidance of lower courts, should move "with all deliberate speed" to desegregate their facilities.

DOCUMENT
Brown v. Board of Education (1954)

President Eisenhower had the ultimate responsibility for executing the law. Doubting that simple changes in the law could improve race relations, he once observed, "I don't believe you can change the hearts of men with laws or decisions." While he thought privately that the *Brown* ruling was wrong, he knew that it was his constitutional duty to see that the decision was carried out. Even while urging sympathy for the South in its period of transition, he acted immediately to desegregate the Washington, D.C., schools as a model for the rest of the country. He also ordered desegregation in navy yards and veterans' hospitals.

The South resisted. The crucial confrontation came in Little Rock, Arkansas, in 1957. A desegregation plan, beginning with the token admission of a few black students to Central High School, was ready to go into effect. Just before the school year began, Governor Orval Faubus declared on television that it would not be possible to maintain order if integration took place. National Guardsmen, posted by the governor to keep the peace and armed with bayonets, turned away nine black students as they tried to enter the school. After three weeks, a federal court ordered the troops to leave. When the black children entered the building, the white students, spurred on by their elders, belligerently opposed them, chanting such slogans as "Two, four, six, eight, we ain't gonna integrate." In the face of hostile mobs, the black children left the school.

The Southern Manifesto (1956)

With the lines drawn, Ike knew that such resistance could not be tolerated, and he finally took the one action he had earlier called unthinkable. For the first time since the end of Reconstruction, an American president called out federal troops to protect the rights of black citizens. Eisenhower ordered paratroopers to Little Rock and placed National Guardsmen under federal command. The black children entered the school and attended classes with the military protecting their rights. Thus desegregation began.

Cooper v. Aaron (1958)

Meanwhile, African Americans, encouraged by their churches, began organizing themselves to take direct action, and their efforts significantly advanced the civil rights movement. In the 1930s and 1940s, some had joined demonstrations protesting job discrimination and segregation. All were horrified by the brutal murder of Emmett Till, a 14-year-old boy from Chicago visiting Mississippi, who offended a white woman at a country store. Pictures of his mangled body in an open casket helped energize the effort.

The catalyzing event occurred in Montgomery, Alabama, in December 1955. Rosa Parks, a 42-year-old

Integrating Little Rock's Central High School National Guardsmen, under federal command, escorted African American students into Central High School in Little Rock, Arkansas, in 1957. Observe the number of students and the number of soldiers as forcible integration began. How must the students have felt to have had such an armed escort? *(Burt Glinn/Magnum Photos, Inc.)*

get tired . . . of being kicked about by the brutal feet of oppression," he declared. It was time to be more assertive, to cease being "patient with anything less than freedom and justice."

Although King, like others, was arrested on the trumped-up charge of speeding and jailed, grassroots support bubbled up. In Montgomery, 50,000 African Americans walked or formed car pools to avoid the transit system. Their actions cut gross revenue on city buses by 65 percent. Almost a year later, the Supreme Court ruled that bus segregation, like school segregation, violated the Constitution, and the boycott ended. But the mood it fostered continued, as ordinary black men and women challenged the racial status quo and forced both white and black leaders to respond.

DOCUMENT

Voting Literacy Test

Meanwhile, a concerted effort developed to guarantee black voting rights. The provisions of the Fifteenth Amendment notwithstanding, many states had circumvented the law for decades. Some states required a poll tax or a literacy test or an examination of constitutional understanding. Blacks often found themselves excluded from the polls.

Largely because of the legislative genius of Senate majority leader Lyndon B. Johnson of Texas, a civil rights bill, the first since Reconstruction, moved toward passage. Paring the bill down to the provisions he felt would pass, Johnson pushed the measure through.

The Civil Rights Act of 1957 created a Civil Rights Commission and empowered the Justice Department to go to court in cases in which blacks were denied the right to vote. The bill was a compromise measure, yet it was the first successful effort to protect civil rights in 82 years.

Again led by Johnson, Congress passed the Civil Rights Act of 1960. This new measure set stiffer penalties for people who interfered with the right to vote but again stopped short of authorizing federal registrars to register blacks to vote and so, like its predecessor, was generally ineffective.

Latinos on the Fringe

Latinos, like other groups, had similar difficulties in the postwar United States. Latino immigrants from Cuba, Puerto Rico, Mexico, and Central America, often unskilled and illiterate, followed other less fortunate Americans to the cities. The conditions they encountered there were similar to those faced by blacks. Author Piri Thomas, born of Puerto Rican and Cuban parents in New York City's Spanish Harlem, described his neighborhood in his memoir *Down These Mean Streets:*

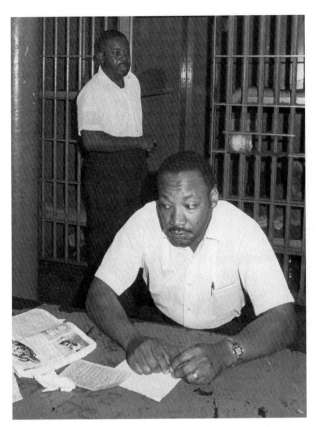

Civil Rights Leaders Martin Luther King, Jr., and Ralph Abernathy Baptist minister Martin Luther King, Jr., emerged as the black spokesman in the Montgomery, Alabama, bus boycott and soon became the most eloquent African American leader of the entire civil rights movement. He was often jailed for his efforts, as shown in this picture of him sharing a cell with Ralph Abernathy, another civil rights leader. What effect did the jailing of King have on the larger movement? *(Bettmann/CORBIS)*

black seamstress who was also secretary of the Montgomery branch of the NAACP, sat down in the front of a bus in a section reserved by custom for whites. When ordered to move back, the longtime activist refused to budge. The bus driver called the police at the next stop, and Parks was arrested for violating the segregation laws.

That episode had an enormous impact. "Somewhere in the universe, a gear in the machinery shifted," black activist Eldridge Cleaver observed, as African American civil rights officials seized the issue. E. D. Nixon, state NAACP president, told Parks, "This is the case we've been looking for. We can break this situation on the bus with your case." Fifty black leaders met to discuss the case and decided to organize a massive boycott of the bus system.

Martin Luther King, Jr., the 27-year-old minister of the Baptist church where the meeting was held, soon emerged as the preeminent spokesman of the protest. King was an impressive figure and an inspiring speaker. "There comes a time when people

Deportees Mexicans who entered the United States illegally were often arrested and deported. The men in this picture, waiting in a border patrol jail at Calexico, California, in 1951, walked 50 miles across the desert without adequate food and water, only to be apprehended and sent back. What image does this photograph convey about their state of mind? *(Time Life Pictures/Getty Images)*

Man! How many times have I stood on the rooftop of my
broken-down building at night and watched the bulb-
lit world below.
Like somehow it's different at night, this my Harlem.
There ain't no bright sunlight to reveal the stark naked
truth of garbage-lepered streets.
Gone is the drabness and hurt, covered by a friendly
night.
It makes clean the dirty-faced kids.

In the face of recurring discrimination, Spanish-speaking groups maintained a strong sense of group identity. The urban *barrios* where they settled preserved a sense of community and close-knit cohesive culture, even in the midst of pervasive poverty. The ties fostered in these communities provided a strong base for a growing political consciousness.

Chicanos, or Mexican Americans, were the most numerous of the newcomers and faced peculiar difficulties. During World War II, as the country experienced a labor shortage at home, American farmers sought Mexican *braceros* (helping hands) to harvest their crops. A program to encourage the seasonal immigration of farm workers continued after the war when the government signed a Migratory Labor Agreement with Mexico. Between 1948 and 1964, some 4.5 million Mexicans were brought to the United States for temporary work. *Braceros* were expected to return to Mexico at the end of their labor contract, but often they stayed. Joining them were millions more who entered the country illegally.

Conditions were harsh for the *braceros* in the best of times, but in periods of economic difficulty, troubles worsened. During a serious recession in 1953–1954, the government mounted Operation Wetback to deport illegal entrants and *braceros* who had remained in the country illegally and expelled 1.1 million. As immigration officials searched out illegal workers, all Chicanos found themselves vulnerable.

Operation Wetback did not end the reliance on poor Mexican farm laborers. A coalition of southern Democrats and conservative Republicans, mostly representing farm states, extended the Migratory Labor Agreement with Mexico, for the legislators wanted to continue to take advantage of the cheap labor. Two years after the massive deportations of 1954, a record 445,000 *braceros* crossed the border.

Puerto Ricans were numerous in other parts of the country. A steady stream of immigrants had been coming to New York from Puerto Rico since the 1920s. As the island's sugarcane economy became more mechanized, nearly 40 percent of the inhabitants left their homes. By the end of the 1960s, New York City had more Puerto Ricans than San Juan, the island's capital. El Barrio, in East Harlem, became the center of Puerto Rican activity, the home of *salsa* music and small *bodegas,* grocery stores that served the neighborhood. Author Guillermo Cotto-Thorner described the place fondly in his autobiographical novel, *Trópico en Manhattan,* through the words of Antonio, an older resident.

This . . . is our neighborhood, El Barrio. . . . It's said that
we Latins run things here. And that's how we see ourselves. While the Americans take most of the money

that circulates around here, we consider this part of the city to be ours. . . . The stores, barbershops, restaurants, butcher shops, churches, funeral parlors, greasy spoons, pool halls, everything is all Latino. Every now and then you see a business run by a Jew or an Irishman or an Italian, but you'll also see that even these people know a little Spanish.

Puerto Ricans, like many other immigrants, hoped to earn money in America and then return home. Some did; others stayed. Like countless Latinos, most failed to enjoy the promise of the American dream.

Like African Americans, Latinos fought for their own rights. The roots of the Latino struggle dated back to the World War II years. Chicanos established the American GI Forum because a Texas funeral home refused to bury a Mexican American casualty of World War II. When the group's protest led to a burial in Arlington National Cemetery, the possibilities of concerted action became clear. In the waning months of the war, a court case challenged Mexican American segregation in the schools. Gonzalo Méndez, an asparagus grower and a U.S. citizen who had lived in Orange County, California, for 25 years, filed suit to permit his children to attend the school reserved for Anglo-Americans, which was far more attractive than the Mexican one to which they had been assigned. A federal district court upheld his claim in the spring of 1945, and two years later, the circuit court affirmed the original ruling. With the favorable decision, other communities filed similar suits and began to press for integration of their schools. Meanwhile, Mexican American veterans chafed under continuing discrimination at home.

New organizations arose to struggle for equal rights. The Community Service Organization mobilized Chicanos against discrimination, as did the more radical Associación Nacional México-Americana. And the League of United Latin American Citizens continued reform efforts.

Confrontations continued. Los Angeles, with its large number of Chicanos, was the scene of numerous unsavory racial episodes. In mid-1951, on receiving a complaint about a loud record player, police officers raided a baptismal gathering at the home of Simon Fuentes. Breaking into the house without a warrant, they assaulted the members of the party. In the "Bloody Christmas" case at the end of the year, officers removed seven Mexican Americans from jail cells and beat them severely.

Chicano activism in the 1950s was fragmented. Some Mexican Americans considered their situation hopeless. More effective mobilization had to await another day.

The Native American Struggle

Native Americans likewise remained outsiders in the postwar years. Years of persistent discrimination made it even harder to cope with the changes they faced. As power lines reached their reservations, Indians purchased televisions, refrigerators, washing machines, and automobiles. As they partook of the consumer culture, old patterns inevitably changed. Reservation life lost its cohesiveness, and alcohol became a major problem. With good jobs unavailable on the reservations, more and more Indians gravitated to the cities. Bennie Bearskin, a Winnebago, left home for Chicago in 1947, explaining: "The most important reason was that I could at least feel confident that [I could get] perhaps fifty paychecks a year here. . . . Even though it might be more pleasant to be back home, for instance, Nebraska." But Indians who moved to the cities often had difficulty adjusting to urban life and frequently faced hostility from white Americans.

Native Americans, like Latinos, began their own struggle for equality. They achieved an important victory just after the end of World War II when Congress established the Indian Claims Commission. Hundreds of tribal suits charging that ancestral lands had been illegally seized could now be filed against the government in federal courts. Many of them led to large settlements of cash—a form of

Troubles for Native American Veterans After returning home at the end of World War II, many Native American veterans found it difficult to fit into either Native American or white society. Alcoholism—which sometimes led to confrontations with the law—became a problem, as reflected in this sketch by Native American artist Aaron Yava, who drew what he saw in what he called the "border towns of the Navajo Nation." What might have caused such confrontations? *(Courtesy of the family of Aaron Yava)*

TIMELINE

1946	4.6 million workers on strike ENIAC computer built Benjamin Spock, *Baby and Child Care* Employment Act
1947	Defense budget of $13 billion Taft–Hartley Act Jackie Robinson breaks the color line in major league baseball
1948	GM offers UAW cost-of-living adjustment Transistor developed at Bell Laboratories Alfred C. Kinsey, *Sexual Behavior in the Human* *Male* "Dixiecrat" party formed Truman defeats Dewey
1949	Truman launches Fair Deal
1950s	Each year a million farmers leave farms
1950	Diner's Club card inaugurated Associación Nacional México-Americana formed
1951	J. D. Salinger, *The Catcher in the Rye*
1952	Dwight D. Eisenhower elected president
1953	Defense budget of $47 billion Operation Wetback begins Submerged Lands Act

1954	Congress adds "under God" to pledge to flag *Brown* v. *Board of Education*
1955	First McDonald's opens in Illinois Merger of AFL and CIO Congress adds "In God We Trust" to currency Montgomery, Alabama, bus boycott begins Allen Ginsberg, "Howl"—written and read
1956	Interstate Highway Act Majority of U.S. workers hold white-collar jobs Eisenhower reelected
1957	Baby boom peaks Jack Kerouac, *On the Road* Little Rock, Arkansas, school integration crisis Civil Rights Act
1960	Three-quarters of all American families own a TV set Civil Rights Act
1962	Michael Harrington, *The Other America*
1963	California passes New York as most populous state Betty Friedan, *The Feminine Mystique*
1964	Peter Blake, *God's Own Junkyard*

reparation for past injustices—and sometimes the return of long-lost lands.

In the 1950s, federal Indian policy shifted course. As part of its effort to limit the role of the national government, the Eisenhower administration turned away from the New Deal policy of government support for tribal autonomy. In 1953, instead of trying to encourage Native American self-government, the administration adopted a new approach, known as "termination." The government proposed settling all outstanding claims and eliminating reservations as legitimate political entities. To encourage their assimilation into mainstream society, families who would leave the reservations and move to cities were offered small subsidies by the government.

The new policy infuriated Native Americans. Earl Old Person, a Blackfoot elder, declared: "It is important to note that in our Indian language the only translation for termination is to 'wipe out' or 'kill off' . . . How can we plan our future when the Indian Bureau threatens to wipe us out as a race? It is like trying to cook a meal in your tipi when someone is standing outside trying to burn the tipi down." With their lands no longer federally protected and their members deprived of treaty rights, many tribes became unwitting victims of people who wanted to seize their land. Though promising more freedom,

the new policy caused great disruption as the government terminated tribes such as the Klamath in Oregon, the Menominee in Wisconsin, the Alabama and Coushatta in Texas, and bands of Paiute in Utah.

The policy increased Indian activism. The National Congress of American Indians mobilized opposition to the federal program. A Seminole petition to the president in 1954 summed up a general view:

> We do not say that we are superior or inferior to the White Man and we do not say that the White Man is superior or inferior to us. We do say that we are not White Men but Indians, do not wish to become White Men but wish to remain Indians, and have an outlook on all things different from the outlook of the White Man.

Not only did the termination policy foster a sense of Indian identity, but it also sparked a dawning awareness among whites of the Indians' right to maintain their heritage. In 1958, the Eisenhower administration changed the policy of termination so that it required a tribe's consent. The policy continued to have the force of law, but implementation ceased.

Asian American Advances

For Asian Americans, conditions improved somewhat in the aftermath of World War II. The war against Nazism eroded the racism that proclaimed a commitment to white superiority. Japanese Americans, ravaged by their devastating internment during the war, fought back after the struggle. In 1946, a measure supporting a wartime law confiscating Japanese American property appeared on the ballot in California. But a spirited campaign by the Japanese American Citizens League reminding voters of the contributions of Japanese American soldiers during the war led to the measure's overwhelming defeat. Two years later, the Supreme Court, noting that the law was "nothing more than outright racial discrimination," declared it unconstitutional.

In 1952, the Immigration and Nationality Act, also known as the McCarran–Walter Act, eased immigration quotas. Although the basic framework of the National Origins Act of 1924 remained intact, it removed the longstanding ban on Japanese immigration and made first-generation Japanese immigrants eligible for citizenship. It also established a quota of 100 immigrants a year from each Asian country. While that number was tiny compared to those admitted annually from northern and western Europe, the measure was a first step in ending the discriminatory exclusion of the past.

By the 1950s, many second-and third-generation Chinese, Japanese, and Koreans had moved into white-collar work. Promoting education for their children, they became part of the growing middle class, hoping like others to enjoy the benefits of the American dream.

Conclusion

Qualms amid Affluence

In general, the United States during the decade and a half after World War II was stable and secure. Structural adjustments caused occasional moments of friction but were seldom visible in prosperous times. Recessions occurred periodically, but the economy righted itself after short downturns. For the most part, business boomed. The standard of living for many of the nation's citizens reached new heights, especially compared with standards in other parts of the world. Millions of middle-class Americans joined the ranks of suburban property owners, enjoying the benefits of shopping centers, fast-food establishments, and other material manifestations of what they considered the good life. Workers found themselves savoring the materialistic advantages of the era. The political world reflected prosperous times.

Some Americans did not share in the prosperity, but they were not visible in the affluent suburbs. Many African Americans and members of other minority groups were seriously disadvantaged, although they still believed they could share in the American dream and remained confident that deeply rooted patterns of discrimination could be changed. Even when they began to mobilize, their protest was peaceful at first.

Beneath the calm surface, though, there were signs of discontent. The seeds for the protest movements of the 1960s had already been sown. Disquieting signs were likewise evident on other fronts. The divorce rate increased as one-third of all marriages in the 1950s broke apart. Americans increasingly used newly developed tranquilizers in an effort to cope with problems in their lives. Some Americans began to criticize the materialism that seemed to undermine American efforts in the Cold War. Such criticisms in turn legitimized challenges by other groups, in the continuing struggle to make the realities of American life match the nation's ideals.

Criticisms and anxieties notwithstanding, the United States—for most whites and some people of color—continued to develop according to Ray Kroc's dreams as he first envisioned McDonald's establishments across the land. Healthy and comfortable, upper- and middle-class Americans expected prosperity and growth to continue in the years ahead.

Questions for Review and Reflection

1. What were the sources of American prosperity?
2. Who prospered most in postwar America?
3. Who was left out?
4. Why did conformity become the norm in the postwar United States?
5. How would you characterize the broad social and economic changes that took place in America in the years after World War II?

Recommended Reading

Recommended Readings are posted on the Web site for this textbook. Visit www.ablongman.com/nash

Fiction and Film

Guillermo Cotto-Thorner's, *Trópico en Manhattan* (1967) is an autobiographical novel about the Puerto Rican community in New York City. Allen Drury's, *Advise and Consent* (1959) is a novel about Washington politics, complete with blackmail and demagoguery. Ralph Ellison's *Invisible Man* (1952) is a powerful fictional account of an African American's journey through the 1950s. Allen Ginsberg's, *Howl and Other Poems* (1956) is a collection of iconoclastic poetry challenging the materialism of contemporary life. Jack Kerouac's *On the Road* (1957) is a stream-of-consciousness novel that questions the values of the 1950s. Arthur Miller's *Death of a Salesman* (1949) is the Pulitzer Prize–winning play about the shallow values of postwar American culture. J. D. Salinger's, *Catcher in the Rye* (1951) is the story of Holden Caulfield, a troubled adolescent who is overwhelmed by the phoniness of contemporary life. Sloan Wilson's, *The Man in the Gray Flannel Suit* (1955) is a novel challenging the conformity of corporate America in the 1950s.

The Best Years of Our Lives (1946), the Academy Award–winning story of three servicemen returning home after World War II, captures the values of the immediate postwar era. *To Kill a Mockingbird* (1962) is a film based on Harper Lee's novel by the same title about children learning about racism—and about how to deal with it—in the South. *Kinsey* (2004) describes the life and work of Alfred Kinsey, the controversial sex researcher. *The Man in the Gray Flannel Suit* (1956), the film made from the novel of the same name, critiques the lifestyle of corporate America in the 1950s. *The Murder of Emmett Till* (2003) is a powerful documentary film about the episode that helped mobilize African Americans. *The Untold Story of the Murder of Emmett Louis Till* (2004) is another vivid documentary that led the Justice Department to reopen the case. *No Down Payment* (1957) deals with life in the suburbs, as does the much more recent *Pleasantville* (1998), as it looks back at an earlier era.

Discovering U.S. History Online

The Postwar United States

http://lcweb2.loc.gov/ammem/ndlpedu/features/timeline/postwar/postwar.html

By way of primary documents, interviews, and artifacts, this site presents two sections: Arts and Entertainment: 1945–1968 and The Presidential Election of 1960.

Creating the Interstate System

www.tfhrc.gov/pubrds/summer96/p96su10.htm

An illustrated article from the U.S. Department of Transportation, Federal Highway Administration's "Public Roads Website."

Levittown: Documents of an Ideal American Suburb

www.uic.edu/~pbhales/Levittown/

The postwar boom in housing made suburban living the cultural norm in America and shaped a generation. The story of the classic suburb, Levittown, is told on this site in pictures and text.

Computer History Museum

www.computerhistory.org

Choose from an interactive timeline, an image gallery, a video gallery, and a "guided" tour of the exhibits to explore the history of computers.

Fifties Web

www.fiftiesweb.com

This entertaining personal site tells about and samples music and television from the 1950s. It also includes a related links page.

American Cultural History: 1950–1959

http://kclibrary.nhmccd.edu/decade50.html

This site presents facts about the decade and a comprehensive overview of several cultural subtopics.

Religion in Post–World War II America

www.nhc.rtp.nc.us:8080/tserve/twenty/tkeyinfo/trelww2.htm

An essay on religion along with links to online resources.

Rachel Carson

www.rachelcarson.org

An illustrated biography and bibliography of this pioneering ecologist.

Harry S Truman

http://www.ipl.org/div/potus/hstruman.html

This site contains basic factual data about Truman's election and presidency, speeches, and online biographies.

Harry S Truman Library and Museum

www.trumanlibrary.org

This presidential library site has numerous photos and various important primary documents relating to Truman.

Dwight David Eisenhower

http://www.ipl.org/div/potus/ddeisenhower.html

This site contains basic factual data about Eisenhower's election and presidency, including speeches and other materials.

The Dwight D. Eisenhower Library and Museum

www.eisenhower.utexas.edu

This site contains mainly photos of the president.

The Central High Crisis, Little Rock 1957

www.ardemgaz.com/prev/central/

Using articles and photographs from Arkansas newspapers, the site explores the 1957 Little Rock events.

Massive Resistance

www.vcdh.virginia.edu/vahistory/massive.resistance/index.html

This site documents Virginia's resistance to segregation of schools with photographs, interview clips, documents, and a timeline of events.

Civil Rights

www.museum.tv/education/unit1.shtml

This site includes three online video documentaries. *As We See It: Little Rock Central High School* is a remarkable story of growth at the once infamous Little Rock Central High School as seen through the eyes of three sets of students from each period of change: the late 1950s, the late 1960s, and the late 1970s. This show was narrated and produced by the class of 1979 at Central High (1979). In *Corner of the Carpet,* Frank McGee examines the economic and moral cost of slums in Montgomery, Alabama (1956). *Malcolm X: City Desk* is an interview featuring Malcolm X that centers on civil rights and the Black Muslim movement (1963).

CHAPTER 27

Chills and Fever During the Cold War, 1945–1960

The Cold War was closely connected to the nuclear arms race. The spectacular mushroom cloud, like the one created by this hydrogen blast at Eniwetok in the Pacific in 1952, was beautiful but frightening at the same time. *(National Archives)*

American Stories

A Government Employee Confronts the Anti-Communist Crusade

Val Lorwin was in France in November 1950 when he learned of the charges against him. A State Department employee on leave of absence after 16 years of government service, he was in Paris working on a book. Now he had to return to the United States to defend himself against the accusation that he was a member of the Communist party and thus a loyalty and security risk. It seemed to him a tasteless joke. Yet communism was no laughing matter in the United States. Suspicions of the Soviet Union had escalated after 1945, and a wave of paranoia swept through the United States.

Lorwin was an unlikely candidate to be caught up in the fallout of the Cold War. He had begun to work for the government in 1935, serving in a number of New Deal agencies, then in the Labor Department and on the War Production Board before he was drafted during World War II. While in the army, he was assigned to the Office of Strategic Services, an early intelligence agency, and he was frequently granted security clearances in the United States and abroad.

Lorwin, however, did have a left-wing past as an active socialist in the 1930s. His social life then had revolved around Socialist party causes, particularly the unionization of southern tenant farmers and the provision of aid to the unemployed. He and his wife, Madge, drafted statements and stuffed envelopes to support their goals. But that activity was wholly open and legal, and Lorwin had from the start been aggressively anti-Communist in political affairs.

Suddenly, Lorwin, like others in the period, faced a nightmare. Despite his spotless record, Lorwin was told that an unnamed accuser had identified him as a Communist. The burden of proof was entirely on him, and the chance of clearing his name was slim. He was entitled to a hearing if he chose, or he could resign.

Lorwin requested a hearing, and one was held late in 1950. Still struck by the absurdity of the situation, he refuted all accusations but made little effort to cite his own positive achievements. At the conclusion, he was informed that the government no longer doubted his loyalty but considered him a security risk, likewise grounds for dismissal from his job.

When he appealed the judgment, Lorwin was again denied access to the identity of his accuser. This time, however, he thoroughly prepared his defense. At the hearing, 97 witnesses either spoke under oath on Lorwin's behalf or left sworn written depositions testifying to his good character and meritorious service.

The issues in the hearings might have been considered comic in view of Lorwin's record, had not a man's reputation been at stake. The accuser had once lived with the Lorwins in Washington, D.C. Fifteen years later, he claimed that in 1935 Lorwin had revealed that he was holding a Communist party meeting in his home and had even shown him a party card.

Lorwin proved all the charges groundless. He also showed that in 1935 the Socialist party card was red, the color the accuser reported seeing, while the Communist party card was black. In March 1952, Lorwin was finally cleared for both loyalty and security.

Lorwin's troubles were not yet over. His name appeared on one of the lists produced by Senator Joseph McCarthy of Wisconsin, the most aggressive anti-Communist of the era, and Lorwin was again victimized. The next year, he was indicted for making false statements to the State Department Loyalty-Security Board. The charges this time proved as specious as before. Finally, in May 1954, admitting that its special prosecutor had deliberately lied to the grand jury and had no legitimate case, the Justice Department asked for dismissal of the indictment. Cleared at last, Lorwin went on to become a distinguished labor historian.

Val Lorwin was more fortunate than some victims of the anti-Communist crusade. Caught up in a global conflict that engulfed most of the world, he managed to weather a catastrophe that threatened to shatter his life. People rallied around him and gave him valuable support. Despite considerable emotional cost, he survived the witch hunt of the early 1950s, but his case still reflected vividly the ugly domestic consequences of the breakdown in relations between the Soviet Union and the United States.

The Cold War, which unfolded soon after the end of World War II and lasted for nearly 50 years, powerfully affected all aspects of American life. Rejecting for good the isolationist impulse that had governed foreign policy in the 1920s and 1930s, the United States began to play a major role in the world in the postwar years. Doubts about intervention in other lands faded as the nation acknowledged its dominant international position and resolved to do whatever was necessary to maintain it. The same sense of mission that had infused the United States in the Spanish-American War, World War I, and World War II now appeared in a revived evangelical faith and committed most Americans to the struggle against communism at home and abroad.

This chapter explores that continuing sense of mission and its consequences. It examines the roots of the Cold War both in the idealistic aim to keep the world safe for democracy and in the pursuit of economic self-interest that had long fueled American capitalism. It records how the determination to prevent the spread of communism led American policymakers to consider vast parts of the world as pivotal to American security and to act accordingly, particularly in Korea and Vietnam. It notes the impact on economic development, particularly in the West, where the mighty defense industry flourished. And it considers the tragic consequences of the effort to promote ideological unity in a rigid and doctrinaire version of the American dream that led to excesses threatening the principles of democracy itself.

ORIGINS OF THE COLD WAR

The Cold War developed by degrees. It stemmed from divergent views about the shape of the post–World War II world as the colonial empires in Asia, Africa, and the Middle East began to crumble. The United States, strong and secure, was intent on spreading its vision of freedom and free trade around the world to maintain its economic hegemony. The Soviet Union, concerned about security after a devastating war, demanded politically sympathetic neighbors on its borders to preserve its own autonomy. Suppressed during World War II, these differences now surfaced in a Soviet–American confrontation. As tensions rose, the two nations behaved, according to Senator J. William Fulbright, "like two big dogs, chewing on a bone."

The American Stance

The United States emerged from World War II more powerful than any nation ever before, and it sought to use that might to achieve a world order that could sustain American aims. American policymakers, following in Woodrow Wilson's footsteps, hoped to spread the values—liberty, equality, and democracy—underpinning the American dream. They assumed that they could furnish the stability that postwar reconstruction required. They did not always recognize that what they considered universal truths were rooted in specific historical circumstances in their own country and might not flourish elsewhere.

At the same time, American leaders sought a world where economic enterprise could thrive. Recollections of the Great Depression haunted leaders. With the American economy operating at full speed as a result of the war, world markets were needed once the fighting stopped. Government officials wanted to eliminate trade barriers—imposed by the Soviet Union and other nations—to provide outlets for industrial products and for surplus farm commodities such as wheat, cotton, and tobacco. As the largest source of goods for world markets, with exports totaling $14 billion in 1947, the United States required open channels for growth to continue.

Conflicting Aims During the Cold War	
United States	**Soviet Union**
Spread ideological values of liberty, equality, and democracy	Spread ideological values of class struggle, triumph of the proletariat
Extend the tradition of representative government	Extend the tradition of strong centralized government
Maintain stability around the world	Support revolutionary movements around the world
Fill vacuum created by the end of imperialism with regimes sympathetic to Western ideals	Support regimes sympathetic to the Soviet Union, particularly to avoid attack on its western flank
Maintain a world free for economic enterprise by eliminating trade barriers and providing markets for American exports	Rebuild the devastated Soviet economy by creating preferential trading arrangements in the region of Soviet dominance

Americans assumed that their prosperity would benefit the rest of the world, even when other nations disagreed.

Soviet Aims

The Soviet Union formulated its own goals after World War II. Russia had usually been governed in the past by a strongly centralized, sometimes autocratic, government, and that tradition—as much as Communist ideology, with its stress on class struggle and the inevitable triumph of a proletarian state—guided Soviet policy.

During the war, the Russians had played down talk of world revolution, which they knew their allies found threatening, and had mobilized domestic support with nationalistic appeals. As the struggle drew to a close, the Soviets still said little about world conquest, emphasizing socialism within the nation itself.

Rebuilding was the first priority. Devastated by the war, Soviet agriculture and industry lay in shambles. But revival required internal security. At the same time, the Russians felt vulnerable along their western flank. Such anxieties had a historical basis, for in the early nineteenth century, Napoleon had reached the gates of Moscow. Twice in the twentieth century, invasions had come from the west, most recently when Hitler had attacked in 1941. Haunted by fears of a quick German recovery, the Soviets demanded defensible borders and neighboring regimes sympathetic to Russian aims. They insisted on military and political stability in the regions closest to them.

Early Cold War Leadership

Both the United States and the Soviet Union had strong leadership in the early years of the Cold War. On the American side, presidents Harry Truman and Dwight Eisenhower accepted the centralization of authority Franklin Roosevelt had begun, as the executive branch became increasingly powerful in guiding foreign policy. In the Soviet Union, first Joseph Stalin, then Nikita Khrushchev provided equally forceful direction.

Truman and Eisenhower paid close attention to the Cold War struggle with the Soviet Union. Though their personal styles differed, both subscribed to traditional American attitudes about self-determination and the superiority of American political institutions and values. Both were determined to stand firm in the face of the Soviet threat. If accommodation was not possible, they were willing to take whatever steps were necessary to achieve American diplomatic aims.

As World War II drew to an end, Truman grew increasingly hostile to Soviet actions. Viewing collaboration as a wartime necessity, he was uncomfortable with what he felt were Soviet designs in Eastern Europe and Asia as the struggle wound down. It was now time, he said, "to stand up to the Russians" before they solidified positions in various parts of the world.

Soviet Propaganda
Joseph Stalin's autocratic approach to foreign and domestic affairs affronted American sensibilities. The Russian caption on this Soviet propaganda poster reads: "Under the Leadership of the Great Stalin—Forward to Communism!" What image does Stalin convey in this image? *(Hoover Institution Archives, Stanford, CA Russian & Soviet Poster Collection)*

Like Truman, Eisenhower saw communism as a monolithic force struggling for world supremacy and agreed that the Kremlin in Moscow was orchestrating subversive activity around the globe. Yet Eisenhower was more willing than Truman to practice accommodation when it served his ends.

Joseph Stalin, the Soviet leader at war's end, possessed almost absolute powers. He looked, in the words of one American diplomat, like "an old battle-scarred tiger." Though quiet and unassuming in appearance, he had presided over ruthless purges against his opponents in the 1930s. Now he was determined to do whatever was necessary to rebuild Soviet society, if possible with Western assistance, and to keep Eastern Europe within the Russian sphere of influence.

Stalin's death in March 1953 left a power vacuum in Soviet political affairs that was eventually filled by Nikita Khrushchev, who by 1958 held the offices of both prime minister and party secretary. A crude man, Khrushchev once used his shoe to pound a table at the United Nations while the British prime minister was speaking. During Khrushchev's regime, the Cold War continued, but for brief periods of time Soviet–American relations became less hostile.

Disillusionment with the USSR

American support for the Soviet Union faded quickly after the war. In September 1945, 54 percent of a national sample trusted the Russians to cooperate with the Americans in the postwar years. Two months later, the figure dropped to 44 percent, and by February 1946, to 35 percent.

As Americans soured on Russia, they began to equate the Nazi and Soviet systems. Just as they had in the 1930s, authors, journalists, and public officials pointed to similarities, some of them legitimate, between the regimes. Both states, they contended, maintained total control over communications and could eliminate political opposition whenever they chose. Both states used terror to silence dissidents, and Stalin's labor camps in

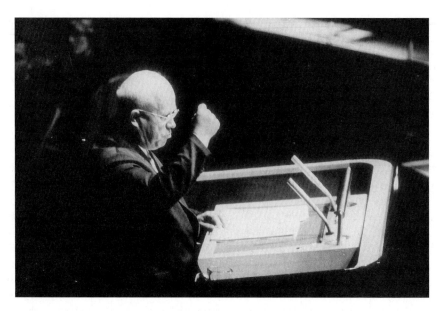

A New Soviet Leader　Soviet leader Nikita Khrushchev was an aggressive leader who sometimes spoke out belligerently in defense of his country's interests. Here he appears on the podium at the United Nations delivering a speech. What do you think Khrushchev hoped to accomplish by his often abrasive approach? *(Getty Images)*

Siberia could be compared with Hitler's concentration camps. After the U.S. publication in 1949 of George Orwell's frightening novel *1984, Life* magazine noted in an editorial that the ominous figure Big Brother was but a "mating" of Hitler and Stalin. Truman spoke for many Americans when he said in 1950 that "there isn't any difference between the totalitarian Russian government and the Hitler government. . . . They are all alike. They are . . . police state governments."

The lingering sense that the nation had not been quick enough to resist totalitarian aggression in the 1930s heightened American fears. Many believed that the free world had not responded promptly when the Germans, Italians, and Japanese first caused international trouble and were determined never to repeat the same mistake.

The Troublesome Polish Question

The first clash between East and West came, even before the war ended, over Poland. Soviet demands for a government willing to accept Russian influence clashed with American hopes for a more representative structure patterned after the Western model. The Yalta Conference of February 1945 attempted to resolve the issue (see Chapter 25), yet when Truman assumed office, the Polish situation remained unresolved.

Truman's unbending stance on Poland was made clear in an April 1945 meeting with Soviet foreign minister Vyacheslav Molotov. Concerned that the Russians were breaking the Yalta agreements, imprecise as they were, the American leader demanded a new democratic government there. Though Molotov appeared conciliatory, Truman insisted on Russian acquiescence. Truman later recalled that when Molotov protested, "I have never been talked to like that in my life," he himself retorted bluntly, "Carry out your agreements and you won't get talked to like that." Such bluntness contributed to the deterioration of Soviet–American relations.

Truman and Stalin met face-to-face for the first (and last) time at the Potsdam Conference in July 1945, the final wartime meeting of the United States, the Soviet Union, and Great Britain. There, outside devastated Berlin, the U.S. and Soviet leaders sized each other up as they considered the Russian–Polish boundary, the fate of Germany, and the American desire to obtain an unconditional surrender from Japan. It was Truman's first exposure to international diplomacy at the highest level, and it left him confident of his abilities. When he learned during the meeting of the first successful atomic bomb test in New Mexico, he became even more determined to insist that the Soviets behave in the ways he wished.

Economic Pressure on the USSR

One major source of controversy in the last stages of World War II was the question of U.S. aid to its allies. Responding to congressional pressure at home to limit foreign assistance as hostilities ended, Truman acted impulsively. Six days after V-E Day signaled the end of the European war in May 1945, he issued an executive order cutting off lend-lease supplies to the Allies. Ships heading for allied ports had to turn back in the middle of the ocean. Though the policy affected all nations receiving aid, it hurt the Soviet Union most of all and caused serious resentment.

The United States intended to use economic pressure in other ways as well. The USSR desperately needed financial assistance to rebuild after the war and, in January 1945, had requested a $6 billion loan. Roosevelt hedged, hoping to win concessions in return. In August, four months after FDR's death, the Russians renewed their application, but this time for only $1 billion. Truman, like his predecessor, dragged his heels, seeking to use the loan as a lever to gain access to markets in areas traditionally dominated by the Soviet Union. The United States first claimed to have lost the Soviet request, then in March 1946 indicated a willingness to consider the matter—but only if Russia pledged "nondiscrimination in world commerce." Stalin refused the offer and launched his own five-year plan instead.

Declaring the Cold War

As Soviet–American relations deteriorated, both sides stepped up their rhetorical attacks. In 1946, Stalin spoke out first, arguing that capitalism and communism were on a collision course, that a series of cataclysmic disturbances would tear the capitalist world apart, and that the Soviet system would inevitably triumph. "The Soviet social system has successfully stood the test in the fire of war," he declared, and would win the struggle ahead. Stalin's speech was a stark and ominous statement that worried the West. Supreme Court justice William O. Douglas called it the "declaration of World War III."

The response to Stalin's speech came not from an American but from England's former prime minister, Winston Churchill, long suspicious of the Soviet state. Speaking in Fulton, Missouri, in 1946, with Truman on the platform during the address, Churchill declared that "from Stettin in the Baltic to Trieste in the Adriatic, an iron curtain has descended across the Continent." To counter the threat, he urged that a vigilant association of English-speaking peoples work to contain Soviet designs. Such a coalition was the only way the Soviet Union could be stopped.

DOCUMENT

Winston Churchill, "Iron Curtain Speech" (March 5, 1946)

CONTAINING THE SOVIET UNION

Containment formed the basis of postwar American policy. While the fledgling United Nations, established in 1945, might have provided a forum to ease tensions, both the United States and the Soviet Union acted unilaterally, and with the aid of allies, in pursuit of their own ends. Within the United States, both Democrats and Republicans were determined to check Soviet expansion wherever threats appeared. The Soviet Union responded in an equally uncompromising way.

Containment Defined

George F. Kennan, chargé d'affaires at the American embassy in the Soviet Union and an expert on Soviet matters, was primarily responsible for defining the new policy of containment. After Stalin's speech in February 1946, Kennan sent an 8,000-word telegram to the State Department. In it he argued that Soviet

DOCUMENT

George F. Kennan, The Long Telegram (1946)

hostility stemmed from the "Kremlin's neurotic view of world affairs," which in turn came from the "traditional and instinctive Russian sense of insecurity." The stiff Soviet stance was not so much a response to American actions as a reflection of the Russian leaders' own efforts to maintain their autocratic rule. Russian fanaticism would not soften, regardless of how accommodating American policy became. Therefore, it had to be opposed at every turn.

Kennan's "long telegram" struck a resonant chord in Washington. Soon he published an extended analysis, under the pseudonym "Mr. X," in the prominent journal *Foreign Affairs*. "The whole Soviet governmental machine, including the mechanism of diplomacy," he wrote, "moves inexorably along the prescribed path, like a persistent toy automobile wound up and headed in a given direction, stopping only when it meets with some unanswerable force." Many Americans agreed with Kennan that Soviet pressure had to "be contained by the adroit and vigilant application of counter-force at a series of constantly shifting geographical and political points."

The concept of containment provided the philosophical justification for the hard-line stance that Americans, both in and out of government, adopted. Containment created the framework for military and economic assistance to countries that seemed threatened by the perceived Communist menace around the globe.

The First Step: The Truman Doctrine

The Truman Doctrine represented the first major application of containment policy. The Soviet Union was pressuring Turkey for joint control of the Dardanelles, the passage between the Black Sea and the Mediterranean. Meanwhile, a civil war in Greece pitted Communist elements against the ruling English-aided right-wing monarchy. Revolutionary pressures threatened to topple the Greek government.

In February 1947, Britain, still reeling from the war, informed the State Department that it could no longer give Greece and Turkey economic and military aid. Truman administration officials, who were willing to move into the void, knew they needed bipartisan support to accomplish such a major policy shift. A conservative Congress wanted smaller budgets and lower taxes rather than massive and expensive aid programs. Senator Arthur Vandenberg of Michigan, a key Republican, aware of the need for bipartisanship, told top policymakers that they had

The Authors of the Containment Policy   Harry Truman relied heavily on Dean Acheson, pictured here on the right, who served first as undersecretary of state and from 1949 on as secretary of state. Together Truman and Acheson helped develop the outlines of the containment policy that sought to limit the advances of the Soviet Union. What were the contours of that approach? *(Harry S. Truman Library)*

to begin "scaring hell out of the country" if they wanted support for a bold new containment policy.

Undersecretary of State Dean Acheson took the lead. Meeting with congressional leaders, he declared that "like apples in a barrel infected by one rotten one, the corruption of Greece would infect Iran and all to the east." He warned ominously that a Communist victory would "open three continents to Soviet penetration." The major powers were now "met at Armageddon," as the Soviet Union pressed forward. Only the United States had the power to resist.

Truman likewise played on the Soviet threat. On March 12, 1947, he told Congress, in a statement that came to be known as the Truman Doctrine, "I believe that it must be the policy of the United States to support free peoples who are resisting subjugation by armed minorities or by outside pressures." Unless the United States acted, the free world might not survive. "If we falter in our leadership," Truman said, "we may endanger the peace of the world—and we shall surely endanger the welfare of our own nation." To avert that calamity, he urged Congress to appropriate $400 million for military and economic aid to Turkey and Greece.

VIDEO

President Truman and the Threat of Communism

Not everyone approved of Truman's request. Autocratic regimes controlled Greece and Turkey, some observers pointed out. And where was the proof that Stalin had a hand in the Greek conflict? Others warned that the United States could not by itself stop communist encroachment in all parts of the world. Nonetheless, Congress passed Truman's foreign aid bill.

In assuming that Americans could police the globe, the Truman Doctrine was a major step in the advent of the Cold War. Journalist Walter Lippmann ominously termed the new containment policy a "strategic monstrosity" that could embroil the United States in disputes around the world. Events of the two succeeding decades proved Lippmann correct.

The Next Steps: The Marshall Plan, NATO, and NSC-68

The next step for American policymakers involved sending extensive economic aid for postwar recovery in Western Europe. At the war's end, most of Europe was economically and politically unstable, thereby offering inviting opportunities for communism to take hold. In France and Italy, large Communist parties grew stronger and refused to cooperate with established governments. In such circumstances, U.S. officials believed, the Soviet Union might easily intervene. Decisive action was needed, for as the new secretary of state, George Marshall, declared, "The patient is sinking while the doctors deliberate." Bolstering the European economy to provide markets for American goods provided another motive for action. Excellent customers earlier, Western Europeans in the aftermath of the war were able to purchase less at a time when the United States was producing more.

Marshall revealed the administration's willingness to assist European recovery in a Harvard University commencement address in June 1947. He asked all troubled European nations to draw up an aid program that the United States could support, a program "directed not against any country or doctrine but against hunger, poverty, desperation, and chaos." Soviet-bloc countries were welcome to participate, Marshall announced, aware that their involvement was unlikely since they would have to disclose economic records to join, and Communist nations maintained rigorous secrecy about their internal affairs.

DOCUMENT
George Marshall, The Marshall Plan (1947)

The proposed program would assist the ravaged nations, provide the United States with needed markets, and advance the nation's ideological aims. American aid, Marshall pointed out, would permit the "emergence of political and social conditions in which free institutions can exist." The Marshall Plan and the Truman Doctrine, Truman noted, were "two halves of the same walnut."

Responding quickly to Marshall's invitation, the Western European nations worked out the details of massive requests. In early 1948, Congress committed $13 billion over a period of four years to 16 cooperating nations. But not all Americans supported the Marshall Plan. Henry A. Wallace, former vice president and secretary of agriculture, called the scheme the "Martial Plan" and argued that it was another step toward war. Some members of Congress feared spreading American resources too thin.

The Contagion of Communism   Americans in the early postwar years were afraid that communism was a contagious disease spreading around the globe. In this picture from the spring of 1946, *Time* magazine pictured the relentless spread of an infection that would need to be contained. Why would such a map seem frightening to people who looked at it? (© 1946 Time, Inc. Reprinted by permission.)

HOW OTHERS SEE US

A West German Poster on the Marshall Plan

European nations welcomed the assistance provided by the Marshall Plan that could help them maintain their independence and avoid communism. This poster from West Germany hails freedom, which it calls the "free way" (freie bahn), in a play on the German word for "highway"—autobahn.

- *Why was communism a threat in postwar Europe?*

- *How could the Marshall Plan help European nations remain free?*

- *How effectively does this poster underscore the idea of freedom?*

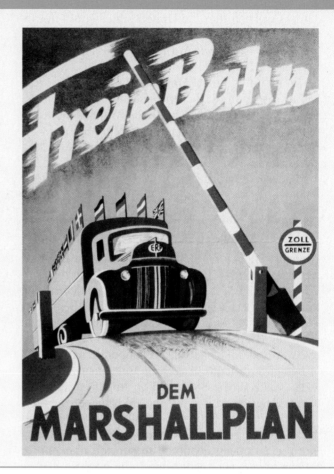

freie Bahn

ZOLL
GRENZE

DEM
MARSHALLPLAN

(The Art Archive)

But most legislators approved, and the containment policy moved forward another step.

Closely related to the Marshall Plan was a concerted Western effort to integrate a rebuilt Germany into a reviving Europe. At the war's end, Allied leaders had agreed to divide the defeated Nazi nation and its capital, Berlin, into four occupation zones (Soviet, American, British, and French). Allied leaders intended the division of both Germany and Berlin to be temporary, until a permanent peace treaty could be signed, but the lines of demarcation became rigid. With the onset of the Cold War and the growing Soviet domination of Eastern Europe, the West became worried and moved to fill the vacuum in Central Europe to counter the Russian threat. In late 1946, the Americans and British merged their zones for economic purposes and began assigning administrative duties to Germans. By mid-1947, the process of rebuilding German industry in the combined Western sector was underway.

Meanwhile, increasingly rigid separation divided Berlin into two separate cities.

Despite French fears, the United States sought to make Germany strong enough to anchor Europe. Secretary Marshall cautiously laid out the connections for Congress:

> The restoration of Europe involves the restoration of Germany. Without a revival of German production there can be no revival of Europe's economy. But we must be very careful to see that a revived Germany cannot again threaten the European community.

The Soviet Union was furious at what it regarded as a violation of the wartime agreement to act together. In mid-1948, the Soviets became irritated at an effort to introduce a new currency for the combined Western zones, a first step toward the creation of a separate West German nation, that would include the western part of divided Berlin, located within the Soviet-controlled eastern part of

The Berlin Airlift An American and British airlift in 1948 brought badly needed supplies to West Berliners isolated by a Soviet blockade of the city. By refusing to allow the Western powers to reach the city, located within the Soviet zone, the Russians hoped to drive them from Berlin, but the airlift broke the blockade. Why was an airplane more effective than a truck in providing supplies to West Berlin? *(Bettmann/CORBIS)*

Germany. A crisis erupted when the Soviets attempted to force the Western powers out of Berlin by refusing to allow them land access to their part of the city and banning all shipments through eastern Germany. In what became known as the Berlin airlift, the United States and the British Royal Air Force flew supplies to the beleaguered Berliners. Over the next year, more than 200,000 flights provided 13,000 tons daily of food, fuel, and other necessary materials. The airlift proved to be a public relations disaster for the Soviet Union and a triumph for the West. The Soviets finally ended the blockade, but Berlin remained a focal point of conflict, and there were now two separate German states: the Federal Republic of Germany, or West Germany, and the German Democratic Republic, or East Germany. The episode also highlighted for the Western powers the need for a more cohesive way of working together to meet the Soviet threat.

The next major link in the containment strategy was the creation of a military alliance in Europe in 1949 to complement the economic program. After the Soviets tightened their control of Hungary and Czechoslovakia, the United States took the lead in establishing the North Atlantic Treaty Organization (NATO). Twelve nations formed the alliance, vowing that an attack against any one member would be considered an attack against all, to be met by appropriate armed force.

The Senate, long opposed to such military pacts, approved this time. In his presidential farewell address in 1796, George Washington had warned against "entangling alliances," and the United States had long heeded his warning. Now the nation established its first military treaty ties with Europe since the American Revolution. Congress also voted military aid for its NATO allies. The Cold War had softened long-standing American reluctance to become closely involved in European affairs.

Two dramatic events in 1949—the Communist victory in the Chinese civil war and the Russian detonation of an atomic device—shocked the United States. The Communist victory in China was frightening enough, but the erosion of the American atomic monopoly was horrifying. Although American scientists had understood that, once the secret of the atom had been unlocked, the Soviets would be able to create a bomb of their own in several years, many top policymakers believed it would take the less technologically advanced Russians at least a decade and a half to do so. President Truman thought they might never be able to accomplish such a feat at all. In September 1949, an air force reconnaissance plane picked up air samples with a radioactivity content that revealed the Soviets had tested their own bomb, just four years after the United States had ushered in the atomic age. Now a nuclear arms race beckoned. Physical chemist

Cold War Europe in 1950

This map shows the rigid demarcation between East and West during the Cold War. Although there were a number of neutral countries in Europe, the other nations found themselves in a standoff, as each side tried to contain the possible advances of the other. The small insert map in the upper right-hand corner shows the division of Berlin that paralleled the division of Germany itself after World War II. **Reflecting on the Past** How widespread was the policy of neutrality in Cold War Europe? How powerful was the NATO bloc? How easily could one side move against the other in divided Europe?

Harold Urey observed on hearing the news: "There is only one thing worse than one nation having the atomic bomb—that's two nations having it."

The Chinese Communist victory and the Soviet bomb led the United States to define its aims still more specifically. Responding to Truman's request for a full-fledged review of U.S. foreign and defense policy, the National Security Council, organized in 1947 to provide policy coordination, produced a document called NSC-68, which shaped U.S. policy for the next 20 years.

NSC-68 built on the Cold War rhetoric of the Truman Doctrine, describing challenges facing the United States in cataclysmic terms. "The issues that face us are momentous," the paper said, "involving the fulfillment or destruction not only of this Republic but of civilization itself." Conflict between East

DOCUMENT

NSC-68
(1950)

and West, the document assumed, was unavoidable, for amoral Soviet objectives ran totally counter to U.S. aims. Negotiation was useless, for the Soviets could never be trusted to bargain in good faith.

NSC-68 then argued that if the United States hoped to meet the Soviet challenge, it must increase defense spending from the $13 billion set for 1950 to as much as $50 billion per year and increase the percentage of its budget allotted to defense from 5 percent to 20 percent. The costs were huge but necessary if the free world was to survive. "In summary," the document declared, "we must . . . wrest the initiative from the Soviet Union, [and] confront it with convincing evidence of the determination and ability of the free world to frustrate the Kremlin design of a world dominated by its will."

Containment in the 1950s

Containment, the keystone of American policy throughout the Truman years, was the rationale for the Truman Doctrine, the Marshall Plan, NATO, and NSC-68. Because this policy required detailed and up-to-date information about Communist moves, the government relied increasingly on the Central Intelligence Agency (CIA). Established by the National Security Act of 1947, the CIA conducted espionage in foreign lands, some of it visible, an increasing amount of it secret. With President Eisenhower's approval, by 1957, 80 percent of the CIA's budget went toward covert activities. More and more, Eisenhower relied on clandestine CIA actions to undermine foreign governments, subsidize friendly newspapers in distant lands, and assist those who supported the U.S. stance in the Cold War.

The civil rights movement that was gaining momentum in the 1950s also affected Cold War policy. American policymakers were aware of the impact of stories about racial discrimination in other nations, particularly nations moving toward independence in sub-Saharan Africa. In propaganda aimed abroad, U.S. leaders sought to portray the domestic civil rights movement in the best possible light.

At the same time, the administration reassessed the impact of the containment policy itself, especially in light of criticism that it was too cautious to counter the threat of communism. For most of Eisenhower's two terms, John Foster Dulles was secretary of state. A devout Presbyterian, he sought to move beyond containment and to counter the "Godless terrorism" of communism with a holy crusade to promote democracy and to free the countries under Soviet domination. Instead of advocating containment, the United States should make it "publicly known that it wants and expects liberation

An Anti-Communist Crusader Secretary of State John Foster Dulles viewed the Cold War as a moral struggle between good and evil. Opposed to "godless communism," he often appeared as a religious crusader for measures he believed were necessary for the survival of the free world. How does this picture capture Dulles's stern approach? *(Bettmann/CORBIS)*

to occur." Dulles favored immediate retaliation in the face of hostile Soviet ventures: "There is one solution and only one: that is for the free world to develop the will and organize the means to retaliate instantly against open aggression by Red armies, so that, if it occurred anywhere, we could and would strike back where it hurts, by means of our own choosing."

Eisenhower's own rhetoric was equally strong. In his 1953 inaugural address, he declared, "Forces of good and evil are massed and armed and opposed as rarely before in history. Freedom is pitted against slavery, lightness against the dark." Yet he was more conciliatory than Dulles and recognized the impossibility of changing the governments of the USSR's satellites. In mid-1953, when East Germans mounted anti-Soviet demonstrations, in a challenge that foreshadowed the revolt against communism three and a half decades later, the United States maintained its distance. In 1956, when Hungarian "freedom fighters" rose up against Russian domination, the United States again stood back as Soviet forces smashed the rebels and kept control of their

RECOVERING THE PAST

Public Opinion Polls

In recent years, historians have used a new source of evidence: the public opinion poll. People have always been concerned with what others think, and leaders have often sought to frame their behavior according to the preferences of the populace. As techniques of assessing the mind of the public have become more sophisticated, the poll has emerged as an integral part of the analysis of social and political life. Polls now measure opinion on many questions—social, cultural, intellectual, political, and diplomatic. Because of polls' increasing importance, it is useful to know how to use them in an effort to understand and recover the past.

The principle of polling is not new. In 1824, the *Harrisburg Pennsylvanian* sought to predict the winner of that year's presidential race, and in the 1880s, the *Boston Globe* sent reporters to selected precincts on election night to forecast final returns. In 1916, *Literary Digest* began conducting postcard polls to predict political results. By the 1930s, Elmo Roper and George Gallup had further developed the field of market research and public opinion polling. Notwithstanding an embarrassing mistake by *Literary Digest* in predicting a Landon victory over FDR in 1936, polling had become a scientific enterprise by World War II.

According to Gallup, a poll is not magic but "merely an instrument for gauging public opinion," especially the views of those often unheard. As Elmo Roper said, the poll is "one of the few ways through which the so-called common man can be articulate." Polling, therefore, is a valuable way to recover the attitudes, beliefs, and voices of ordinary people.

Yet certain cautions should be observed. Like all instruments of human activity, polls are imperfect and may even be dangerous. Historians using information from polls need to be aware of how large the samples were, when the interviewing was done, and how opinions might have been molded by the form of the poll itself. Questions can be poorly phrased. Some hint at the desirable answer or plant ideas in the minds of those interviewed. Polls sometimes provide ambiguous responses that can be interpreted many ways.

More seriously, some critics worry that human freedom itself is threatened by the pollsters' manipulative and increasingly accurate predictive techniques.

Despite these limitations, polls have become an ever-present part of American life. In the late 1940s and early 1950s, Americans were polled frequently about topics ranging from foreign aid, the United Nations, and the occupation of Germany and Japan to labor legislation, child punishment, and whether women should wear slacks in public (39 percent of men said no, as did 49 percent of women). Such topics as the first use of nuclear arms, presidential popularity, national defense, and U.S. troop intervention in a troubled area of the world remain as pertinent today as they were then.

REFLECTING ON THE PAST   A number of the polls included here deal with foreign policy during the Cold War in the early 1950s. How did people respond to Soviet nuclear capability? How did they regard Russian intentions and the appropriate American response? How do you analyze the results of these polls? What do you think is the significance of rating responses by levels of education? In what ways are the questions "loaded"? How might the results of these polls influence American foreign policy? What do you think is significant about the Indochina poll? These polls show the challenge-and-response nature of the Cold War. How do you think Americans would respond today to these questions?

Polls also shed light on domestic issues. Consider the poll on professions for young men and women taken in 1950. What does it tell us about the attitudes of the pollster on appropriate careers for men and women? Why do you think both men and women had nearly identical views on this subject? How do you think people today would answer these questions? Would they be presented in the same way? Also observe the poll on women in politics. To what extent have attitudes on this issue changed in the intervening years?

Foreign Policy Polls

December 2, 1949—Atom Bomb

Now that Russia has the atom bomb, do you think another war is more likely or less likely?

More likely	45%
Less likely	28%
Will make no difference	17%
No opinion	10%

BY EDUCATION
College

More likely	36%	Will make no difference	23%
Less likely	35%	No opinion	6%

High School

More likely	44%	Will make no difference	19%
Less likely	28%	No opinion	9%

Grade School

More likely	50%	Will make no difference	12%
Less likely	26%	No opinion	12%

May 1, 1950—National Defense

Do you think United States Government spending on national defense should be increased, decreased, or remain about the same?

Increased	63%
Same	24%
Decreased	7%
No opinion	6%

September 18, 1953—Indochina

The United States is now sending war materials to help the French fight the Communists in Indochina. Would you approve or disapprove of sending United States soldiers to take part in the fighting there?

Approve	8%
Disapprove	85%
No opinion	7%

January 11, 1950—Russia

As you hear and read about Russia these days, do you believe Russia is trying to build herself up to be the ruling power of the world—or is Russia just building up protection against being attacked in another war?

Rule the world	70%
Protect herself	18%
No opinion	12%

BY EDUCATION
College

Rule the world	73%
Protect herself	21%
No opinion	6%

High School

Rule the world	72%
Protect herself	18%
No opinion	10%

Grade School

Rule the world	67%
Protect herself	17%
No opinion	16%

February 12, 1951—Atomic Warfare

If the United States gets into an all-out war with Russia, do you think we should drop atom bombs on Russia first—or do you think we should use the atom bomb only if it is used on us?

Drop A-bomb first	66%
Only if used on us	19%
No opinion	15%

The greatest difference was between men and women—72% of the men questioned favored our dropping the bomb first, compared to 61% of the women.

Domestic Policy Polls

October 29, 1949—Women in Politics

If the party whose candidate you most often support nominated a woman for President of the United States, would you vote for her if she seemed qualified for the job?

Yes	48%
No	48%
No opinion	4%

BY SEX
Men

Yes	45%
No	50%
No opinion	5%

Women

Yes	51%
No	46%
No opinion	3%

BY POLITICAL AFFILIATION
Democrats

Yes	50%
No	48%
No opinion	2%

Republicans

Yes	46%
No	50%
No opinion	4%

Would you vote for a woman for Vice President of the United States if she seemed qualified for the job?

Yes	53%
No	43%
No opinion	4%

May 5, 1950—Most Important Problem

What do you think is the most important problem facing the entire country today?

War, threat of war	40%
Atomic bomb control	6%
Economic problems, living costs, inflation, taxes	15%
Strikes and labor troubles	4%
Corruption in government	3%
Unemployment	10%
Housing	3%
Communism	8%
Others	11%

July 12, 1950—Professions

Suppose a young man came to you and asked your advice about taking up a profession. Assuming that he was qualified to enter any of these professions, which one of them would you first recommend to him?

Doctor of medicine	29%
Government worker	6%
Engineer, builder	16%
Professor, teacher	5%
Business executive	8%
Banker	4%
Clergyman	8%
Dentist	4%
Lawyer	8%
Veterinarian	3%
None, don't know	9%

July 15, 1950—Professions

Suppose a young girl came to you and asked your advice about taking up a profession. Assuming that she was qualified to enter any of these professions, which one of them would you first recommend?

CHOICE OF WOMEN

Nurse	33%
Teacher	15%
Secretary	8%
Social service worker	8%
Dietitian	7%
Dressmaker	4%
Beautician	4%
Airline stewardess	3%
Actress	3%
Journalist	2%
Musician	2%
Model	2%
Librarian	2%
Medical, dental technician	1%
Others	2%
Don't know	4%

The views of men on this subject were nearly identical with those of women.

satellite. Because Western action could have precipitated a more general conflict, Eisenhower refused to translate rhetoric into action. Throughout the 1950s, the policy of containment, largely as it had been defined earlier, remained in effect.

CONTAINMENT IN ASIA, THE MIDDLE EAST, AND LATIN AMERICA

In a dramatic departure from its history of noninvolvement, the United States extended the policy of containment to meet challenges around the globe. Colonial empires were disintegrating, and countries seeking and attaining their independence now found themselves caught in the midst of the superpower struggle. In Asia, the Middle East, and Latin America, the United States discovered the tremendous appeal of communism as a social and political system in emerging nations and found that ever-greater efforts were required to advance American aims.

The Shock of the Chinese Revolution

The Communist victory in the Chinese civil war in 1949 strengthened U.S. commitment to global containment. An ally during World War II, China had struggled against the Japanese, while simultaneously fighting a bitter civil war deeply rooted in the Chinese past—in widespread poverty, disease, oppression by the landlord class, and national humiliation at the hands of foreign powers. Mao Zedong (Mao Tse-tung)*, founder of a branch of the Communist party, gathered followers who wished to reshape China in a distinctive Marxist mold. Opposing the Communists were the Nationalists, led by Jiang Jieshi (Chiang Kai-shek) who wanted to preserve their power and governmental leadership. By the early 1940s, the corrupt and inefficient Nationalist regime was exhausted. The Communist movement, meanwhile, grew stronger during the Second World War as Mao opposed the Japanese invaders and won the loyalty of Chinese peasants. Mao finally prevailed, as Jiang fled in 1949 to the island of Taiwan (Formosa), where he nursed the improbable belief that he was still the rightful ruler of all China and would one day return.

The United States failed to understand issues that were part of the long internal conflict in China or the immense popular support Mao had garnered.

---

*Chinese names are rendered in their modern *pinyin* spelling. At first occurrence, the older but perhaps more familiar spelling (usually Wade-Giles) is given in parentheses.

A New Chinese Leader   Mao Zedong, chairman of the Chinese Communist party, was a powerful and popular leader who drove Jiang Jieshi from power in 1949 and established a stronghold over the People's Republic of China he created at that time. How was Mao able to defeat his opponents and win the revolutionary war? *(Bettmann/CORBIS)*

As the Communist army moved toward victory, the *New York Times* termed Mao's party a "nauseous force," a "compact little oligarchy dominated by Moscow's nominees." Mao's proclamation of the People's Republic of China on October 1, 1949, fanned fears of Russian domination, for he had already announced his regime's support for the Soviet Union against the "imperialist" United States.

Events in China caused near hysteria in America. Even before Mao's victory, the State Department issued a 1,000-page document entitled *The China White Paper*, which outlined the background of the struggle and argued that the United States was powerless to alter the results. "The unfortunate but inescapable fact is that the ominous result of the civil war in China was beyond the control of the government of the United States," the *White Paper* declared. Staunch anti-Communists argued that Truman and the United States were to blame for the Nationalist defeat because they failed to provide Jiang with sufficient support. Four senators called the *White Paper* a

Chairman Mao Casts His Vote, 1953

"whitewash of a wishful, do-nothing policy which has succeeded only in placing Asia in danger of Soviet conquest with its ultimate threat to the peace of the world and our own national security." Secretary of State Dean Acheson briefly considered granting diplomatic recognition to the new Chinese government but backed off after the Communists seized American property, harassed American citizens, and openly allied China with the USSR. Like other Americans, Acheson mistakenly viewed the Chinese as Soviet puppets.

Tension with China increased during the Korean War (1950–1953) and again in 1954 when Mao's government began shelling Nationalist positions on the offshore islands of Quemoy and Matsu. Eisenhower, elected U.S. president in 1952, was committed to defending the Nationalists on Taiwan from a Communist attack, but he was unwilling to risk war over the islands. Again he showed an understanding of the need to proceed with caution.

Stalemate in the Korean War

The Korean War highlighted growing U.S. intervention in Asia. Concern about China and determination to contain communism led the United States into a bloody foreign struggle. But American objectives were not always clear and after three years of war remained largely unrealized.

The conflict in Korea stemmed from tensions lingering after World War II. Korea, long under Japanese control, hoped for independence after Japan's defeat. But after the atomic bombs dropped on Japan, the Allies, seeking to bring a rapid end to the Pacific struggle and expedite the transition to peace, temporarily divided Korea along the thirty-eighth parallel. The arrangement allowed Soviet troops to accept Japanese surrender in the north while American forces did the same in the south. The Soviet–American line, initially intended as a matter of military convenience, hardened after 1945, just as a similar division became rigid in Germany. In time, the Soviets set up a Korean government in the north and the Americans a second Korean government in the south. Though the major powers left Korea by the end of the decade, they continued to support the regimes they had created. Each Korean government hoped to reunify the country on its own terms.

The Korean War, 1950-1953

North Korea moved first. On June 25, 1950, North Korean forces crossed the thirty-eighth parallel and invaded South Korea. While the North Koreans used Soviet-built tanks, they operated on their own initiative. Kim Il

Sung, the North Korean leader, had visited Moscow earlier and gained Soviet acquiescence for an attack, but both the planning and the implementation occurred in Korea.

Taken by surprise and certain that Russia had masterminded the North Korean offensive to test the U.S. containment policy, Truman told the American public that "the attack upon Korea makes it plain beyond all doubt that communism has passed beyond the use of subversion to conquer independent nations and will now use armed invasion and war." He later reflected in his memoirs: "If this was allowed to go unchallenged it would mean a third world war, just as similar incidents had brought on the second world war."

Truman readied American naval and air forces and directed General Douglas MacArthur, head of the American occupation forces in Japan, to supply South Korea. The United States also went to the UN Security Council. With the Soviet Union absent in

General MacArthur General Douglas MacArthur was a superb tactician but a supremely egotistical commander of UN forces in Korea, where this picture was taken in the first year of the Korean War. Eventually his arrogance led him to challenge Truman's policy, whereupon the president relieved him of his command. How does this image convey MacArthur's strong-willed approach? *(Time Life Pictures/Getty Images)*

AMERICAN VOICES

Speech to Troops by Colonel Lewis "Chesty" Puller, Commanding Officer of the 1st Regiment of the Marine Corps in Korea in 1950

On November 10, 1950, the Marine Corps celebrated the anniversary of its founding. Colonel Puller sliced a 100-pound cake, decorated with radishes and jelly since candles were not available, with a captured North Korean sword. Then, after offering a tribute to the Marine Corps, he gave a brief speech to his troops in which he talked about the need to fight hard and complained about the lack of awareness of the nature of the conflict back home in the United States.

Now that's complied with, and I want to tell you something straight. Just do one thing for me—write your people back home and tell 'em there's one hell of a damned war on out here, and that the raggedy-tailed North Koreans have been shipping a lot of so-called good American troops, and may do it again. Tell 'em there's no secret weapon for our country but to get hard, to get in there and fight.

I want you to make 'em understand: Our country won't go on forever, if we stay as soft as we are now. There won't be an America—because some foreign soldiery will invade us and take our women and breed a hardier race.

- What did Colonel Puller want Americans at home to understand?

- What was Colonel Puller's overriding fear about what was happening in the war?

- How does he characterize the North Koreans?

- Why were Americans at home ambivalent about the conflict going on in Korea?

---

protest of the UN's refusal to admit the People's Republic of China, despite its victory in the Chinese civil war, the United States secured a unanimous resolution branding North Korea an aggressor, then another resolution calling on members of the organization to assist South Korea in repelling aggression and restoring peace. MacArthur became leader of all UN forces in this largest UN operation to date. The United States and South Korea provided more than 90 percent of the personnel, but 15 other nations participated in the UN effort.

Air and naval forces, then ground forces, went into battle south of the thirty-eighth parallel. Following a daring amphibious invasion that pushed the North Koreans back to the former boundary line, UN troops crossed the thirty-eighth parallel, hoping to reunify Korea under an American-backed government. Despite Chinese signals that this movement toward their border threatened their security, the UN troops pressed on. In October, Chinese troops appeared briefly in battle, then disappeared. The next month, the Chinese mounted a full-fledged counterattack, which pushed the UN forces back below the dividing line.

The resulting stalemate provoked a bitter struggle between MacArthur and Truman. The brilliant

IMAGE

U.S. Marines—1950

but arrogant general called for retaliatory air strikes against China. He faced opposition from General Omar Bradley, chairman of the Joint Chiefs of Staff, who declared, "Frankly, in the opinion of the Joint Chiefs of Staff, this strategy would involve us in the wrong war, at the wrong place, at the wrong time, with the wrong enemy," and from President Truman, who remained committed to conducting a limited war. MacArthur finally went too far. In April 1951, he argued that the American approach in Korea was wrong and asserted publicly that "there is no substitute for victory." Truman had no choice but to relieve the general for insubordination. The decision outraged many Americans. After the stunning victories of World War II, limited war was frustrating and difficult to understand.

The Korean War dragged on into Eisenhower's presidency. Campaigning in 1952, Ike promised to go to Korea, and three weeks after his election, he did so. When UN truce talks bogged down in May 1953, the fighting intensified and the new administration privately threatened the Chinese with the use of atomic weapons. This threat prompted the renewal of negotiations, and on July 27, 1953, an armistice was signed. After three long years, the unpopular war ended.

VIDEO

The Korean War Armistice

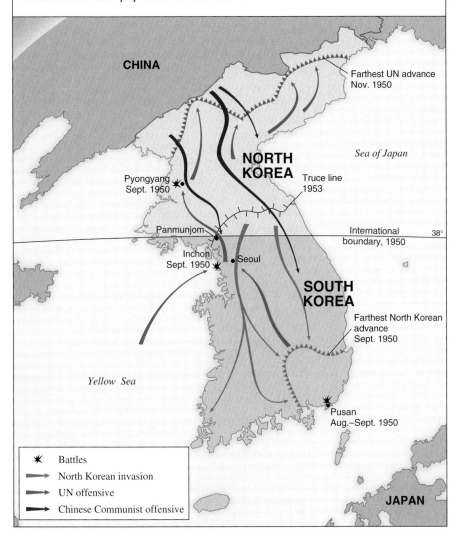

The Korean War

This map shows the ebb and flow of the Korean War. North Korea crossed the thirty-eighth parallel first, then the UN offensive drove the North Koreans close to the Chinese border, and finally the Chinese Communists entered the war and drove the UN forces back below the thirty-eighth parallel. The armistice signed at Panmunjom in 1953 provided a dividing line very close to the prewar line. **Reflecting on the Past** How far did both North Korea and South Korea penetrate into the territory of the other nation? What role did China play in the Korean War?

American involvement carried a heavy price: more than 33,000 Americans killed in action and more than 142,000 American casualties in all. The other 15 UN nations involved in the struggle accounted for another 17,000 casualties. But those figures paled in comparison to Korean casualties: as many as 2 million Koreans dead and countless others wounded and maimed.

The war significantly changed American attitudes and institutions. For the first time, American forces fought in racially integrated units. As commander in chief, Truman had ordered the integration of the armed forces in 1948, over the opposition of many generals, and African Americans became part of all military units. Their successful performance led to acceptance of military integration.

During the Korean War military expenditures soared from $13 billion in 1950 to about $47 billion three years later, as defense spending followed the guidelines proposed in NSC-68. In the process, the United States accepted the demands of permanent mobilization. Whereas the military absorbed less than one-third of the federal budget in 1950, a decade later, it took half. More than a million military

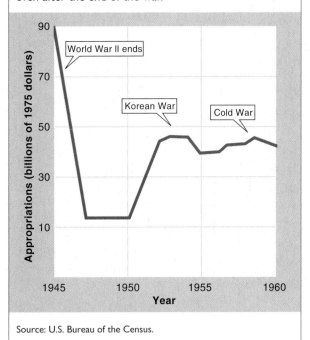

Defense Expenditures, 1945–1960

Defense spending plummeted after World War II, only to quadruple with the onset of the Korean War. After that increase, spending levels never dropped dramatically, even after the end of the war.

Source: U.S. Bureau of the Census.

During World War II, Japan occupied the region but allowed French collaborators to administer internal affairs. An independence movement, led by the Communist organizer and revolutionary Ho Chi Minh, sought to expel the Japanese conquerors from Vietnam. In 1945, the Allied powers faced the decision of how to deal with Ho and his nationalist movement.

Franklin Roosevelt, like Woodrow Wilson, believed in self-determination and wanted to end colonialism. But France was determined to regain its colony as a way of preserving its status as a great power, and by the time of his death, Roosevelt had backed down. Meanwhile, Ho Chi Minh established the Democratic Republic of Vietnam in 1945. The new government's declaration of independence echoed its American counterpart, declaring: "All men are created equal. They are endowed by their Creator with certain inalienable rights, among these are Life, Liberty and the pursuit of Happiness." Although the new government enjoyed widespread popular support, the United States refused to recognize it.

DOCUMENT

Ho Chi Minh, Declaration of Independence for the Democratic Republic of Vietnam (1945)

A long, bitter struggle broke out between French and Vietnamese forces, which became entangled with the larger Cold War. President Truman was less concerned about ending colonialism than with checking Soviet power. He needed France to balance the Soviets in Europe, where he wanted French support for America's policy in Germany and as a member of NATO, and that meant cooperating with France in Vietnam.

DOCUMENT

American Objectives in Southeast Asia (June 25, 1952)

Although Ho did not have close ties to the Soviet Union and was committed to his independent nationalist crusade, Truman and his advisers, who saw communism as a monolithic force, assumed wrongly that Ho took orders from Moscow. Hence, in 1950, the United States formally recognized the French puppet government in Vietnam, and by 1954, the United States was paying more than three-quarters of the cost of France's Indochina war.

After Eisenhower took office, France's position in Southeast Asia deteriorated. Secretary of State Dulles was eager to assist the French, and the chairman of the Joint Chiefs of Staff even contemplated using nuclear weapons, but Eisenhower refused to intervene directly. He understood the lack of American support for intervention in that far-off land. Senator John F. Kennedy spoke for many of his congressional colleagues when he declared in 1954: "I am frankly of the belief that no amount of American

personnel were stationed around the world. At home, an increasingly powerful military establishment became closely tied to corporate and scientific communities and created a military–industrial complex that employed 3.5 million Americans by 1960.

The Korean War had significant political effects as well. In September 1951, the United States signed a peace treaty with Japan and came to rely on the Japanese to maintain the balance of power in the Pacific. At the same time, the struggle poisoned relations with the People's Republic of China, which remained unrecognized by the United States, and ensured a diplomatic standoff that lasted more than 20 years.

Vietnam: The Roots of Conflict

The commitment to stopping the spread of communism led to the massive U.S. involvement in Vietnam. That struggle tore the United States apart, wrought enormous damage in Southeast Asia, and finally forced a re-evaluation of U.S. Cold War policies.

The roots of the war extended far back in the past. Indochina—the part of Southeast Asia that included Vietnam, Laos, and Cambodia—had been a French colony since the mid-nineteenth century.

Father Ho   Ho Chi Minh waged a long struggle first against France, then Japan, and finally the United States for the independence of Vietnam. The Vietnamese people viewed him as the father of the country. How does this picture of him with children contribute to that impression? *(Library of Congress [LC-USZ62-126864])*

military assistance in Indochina can conquer an enemy which is everywhere and at the same time nowhere, 'an enemy of the people' which has the sympathy and covert support of the people." As a French fortress at Dien Bien Phu in the north of Vietnam finally fell to Ho's forces, an international conference in Geneva sought to prevent Ho Chi Minh from gaining control of the entire country. The final declaration of the conference divided Vietnam along the seventeenth parallel, with elections promised in 1956 to unify the country and determine its political fate.

DOCUMENT

Eisenhower, Decision Not to Intervene at Dien Bien Phu (1954)

Two separate Vietnamese states emerged. Ho Chi Minh held power in the north, while in the south, Ngo Dinh Diem, a fierce anti-Communist who had been in exile in the United States, returned to form a government. Diem, a Vietnamese nationalist who had served in the colonial bureaucracy earlier, had proclaimed his support for Vietnamese independence while in America. Now he enjoyed the full support of the United States, which saw him as a

way of securing stability in Southeast Asia and avoiding further communist incursions. When he decided not to hold the elections mandated in the Geneva accord, the United States backed him in that decision. In the next few years, American aid increased and military advisers—675 by the time Eisenhower left office—began to assist the South Vietnamese. The United States had taken its first steps toward direct involvement in a ruinous war halfway around the world that would escalate out of control.

The Creation of Israel and Its Impact on the Middle East

The creation of the state of Israel became intertwined with larger Cold War issues. Jews had longed for a homeland for years, and the Zionist movement had sought a place in Palestine, in the Middle East, since the latter part of the nineteenth century. Jewish settlers who began to gravitate to Palestine were not welcomed by the Turks, who dominated the region, or by the British, who exercised control after World War I.

Then the Holocaust—and the slaughter of 6 million Jews—during World War II created new pressure for a Jewish state. The unwillingness—and inability—of the Western powers to intervene in time to stop the Nazi genocide created a groundswell of support, particularly among American Jews, for a Jewish homeland in the Arab-dominated Middle East.

In 1948, the United Nations attempted to partition Palestine into an Arab state and a Jewish state. Truman officially recognized the new state of Israel 15 minutes after it was proclaimed. But American recognition could not end bitter animosities between Arabs, who believed they had been robbed of their territory, and Jews, who felt they had finally regained a homeland after the horrors of the Holocaust. As Americans looked on, Arab forces from Egypt, Trans-Jordan, Syria, Lebanon, and Iraq invaded Israel, in the first of a continuing series of conflicts that continues to dominate the Middle East to the present day. The Israelis, fighting for the survival of their new nation, won the war and added territory to what the UN had given them. But struggles erupted in 1967 and again in 1973 with adversaries who did not recognize Israel's right to exist.

While sympathetic to Israel, the United States tried at the same time to maintain stability in the rest of the region. The Middle East had tremendous strategic importance as the supplier of oil for industrialized nations. In 1953, the CIA helped the Iranian army overthrow the government of Mohammed Mossadegh, which had nationalized oil wells formerly under

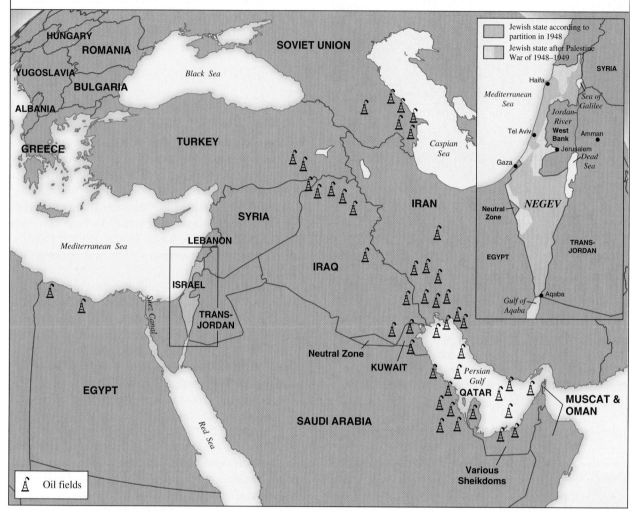

The Middle East in 1949

This map shows the extensive oil reserves that made the Middle East such an important region; it also shows the shifting boundaries of Israel as a result of the war following its independence in 1948. Notice how Israel's size increased after its victory in the first of a series of Middle Eastern conflicts. **Reflecting on the Past** Why was Middle Eastern oil such an important commodity to the rest of the world? How secure was Israel as it confronted the other Middle Eastern nations? How much territory did Israel gain in the conflict after the partition in 1948?

British control, and placed the shah of Iran securely on the throne. After the coup, British and American companies regained command of the wells, and thereafter the U.S. government provided military assistance to the shah.

As it cultivated close ties with Israel, the United States also tried to maintain the friendship of oil-rich Arab states or, at the very least, to prevent them from falling into the Soviet orbit of influence. In Egypt, the policy ran into trouble when Arab nationalist General Gamal Abdel Nasser planned a huge dam on the Nile River to produce electric power. Nasser hoped to follow a middle course by proclaiming his country's neutrality in the Cold War. Although Secretary of State Dulles offered U.S. financial support for the Aswan Dam project, Nasser also began discussions with the Soviet Union. An irate Dulles, who believed that neutralism was immoral, withdrew the American offer. Left without funds for the dam, in July 1956, Nasser seized and nationalized the British-controlled Suez Canal and closed it to Israeli ships. Now Great Britain was enraged. All of Europe feared that Nasser would disrupt the flow of oil from the Middle East.

In the fall, Israeli, British, and French military forces invaded Egypt. Eisenhower, who had not been consulted, was furious. When told that paratroopers were about to land near the canal, he said, "I

VIDEO

Eisenhower, Special Message to Congress on the Middle East, 1957 think it's the biggest error of our time, outside of losing China." Realizing that the attack might push Nasser into Moscow's arms, the United States sponsored a UN resolution condemning the attack and Dulles persuaded other nations not to send petroleum to England and France as long as they remained in Egypt. These actions persuaded the invaders to withdraw.

Before long, the United States again intervened in the Middle East. Concerned about the region's stability, the president declared in 1957, in what came to be called the Eisenhower Doctrine, that "the existing vacuum in the Middle East must be filled by the United States before it is filled by Russia." A year later, he authorized the landing of 14,000 soldiers in Lebanon to prop up a right-wing government challenged from within.

Restricting Revolt in Latin America

The Cold War also led to intervention in Latin America. In 1954, Dulles sniffed Communist activity in Guatemala, and Eisenhower ordered CIA support

A Case History of Communist Penetration in Guatemala, 1957

for a coup aimed at ousting the elected government of reform-minded Colonel Jacobo Arbenz Guzmán. It trained and equipped Guatemalans to overthrow the legitimate regime, which had appropriated property of the American-owned United Fruit Company. The right-wing takeover succeeded, established a military dictatorship that responded to U.S. wishes, and restored the property of the United Fruit Company. These actions demonstrated again the shortsighted American commitment to stability and private investment, whatever the internal effect or ultimate cost. The interference in Guatemala fed anti-American sentiment throughout Latin America.

In 1959, when Fidel Castro overthrew the dictatorship of Fulgencio Batista in Cuba, the shortsightedness of American policy became even clearer. Nationalism and the thrust for social reform were powerful forces in Latin America, as in the rest of the third world formerly dominated by European powers. As Milton Eisenhower, Ike's brother and adviser, pointed out: "Revolution is inevitable in Latin America. The people are angry. They are shackled to the past with bonds of ignorance, injustice, and poverty. And they no longer accept as universal or inevitable the oppressive prevailing order." But when Castro confiscated American property in Cuba, the Eisenhower administration cut off exports and severed diplomatic ties. In response, Cuba turned to the Soviet Union for support.

ATOMIC WEAPONS AND THE COLD WAR

Throughout the Cold War, the atomic bomb cast an ominous cloud over all diplomatic discussions and military initiatives. Atomic weapons were destructive enough, but the development of hydrogen bombs in both the United States and the Soviet Union ushered in an age of overkill.

Sharing the Secret of the Bomb

The United States, with British aid, had built the first atomic bomb and attempted to conceal the project from its wartime ally, the Soviet Union. Soviet spies, however, discovered that the Americans were working on the bomb, and, even before the war was over, the Soviets had initiated a program to create a bomb of their own.

The idea of sharing the atomic secret was considered in the immediate postwar years. Just before he retired, Secretary of War Henry L. Stimson favored cooperating with the Soviet Union rather than acting unilaterally. Recognizing the futility of trying to cajole the Russians while "having this weapon ostentatiously on our hip," he warned that "their suspicions and their distrust of our purposes and motives will increase." Only mutual accommodation could bring international cooperation.

For a time, the administration contemplated a system of international arms control. Realizing by early 1946 that mere possession of the bomb by the United States did not make the Russians more cooperative, Truman proposed to the United Nations the creation of an international agency to control atomic energy. When the Russians balked at a proposal that they argued favored the United States, the plan fizzled.

The United States gave up on the idea of sharing atomic secrets. Intent on retaining the technological advantage until the creation of a "foolproof method of control," Truman endorsed the Atomic Energy Act, passed by Congress in 1946. It established the Atomic Energy Commission (AEC) to supervise all atomic energy development in the United States and, under the tightest security, to authorize all nuclear activity in the nation at large. It also opened the way to a nuclear arms race once Russia developed its own bomb.

Nuclear Proliferation

As the atomic bomb found its way into popular culture, Americans at first showed more excitement than fear. In Los Angeles, the "Atombomb Dancers"

THURSDAY, AUGUST 9, 1945   "BABY, PLAY WITH NICE BALL?"   (Copyright in All Countries)

A New Plaything   The atom was a source of both hopes and fears for people around the world. Scientists and others realized that they faced serious choices as they struggled to deal with the consequences of atomic energy. British cartoonist David Low captured their concerns as they weighed their options. What were their hopes? What were their fears? *(Solo Syndication/Associated Newspapers)*

VIDEO

Duck and Cover

wiggled at the Burbank Burlesque Theater. In 1946, the Buchanan Brothers released a record called "Atomic Power," noting the brimstone fire from heaven that was "given by the mighty hand of God." David E. Lilienthal, first chairman of the AEC, recalled that the atom "had us bewitched. It was so gigantic, so terrible, so beyond the power of the imagination to embrace, that it seemed to be the ultimate fact. It would either destroy us all or it would bring about the millennium."

Anxiety lurked beneath the exuberance, though it did not surface dramatically as long as the United States held a nuclear monopoly. Then, in September 1949, when Americans learned that the Soviet Union had tested its own bomb, the American public was shocked. Suddenly the security of being the world's only atomic power had vanished. People wondered whether the Soviet test foreshadowed a nuclear attack and speculated when it might come. At the Capitol in Washington, D.C., members of the Joint Committee on Atomic Energy struggled over what to do about the announcement of the Soviet bomb.

When a thunderclap startled them, someone in the room said, "My God, that must be Number Two!" The editors of the *Bulletin of the Atomic Scientists*, the nation's foremost publication dealing with nuclear affairs, moved the minute hand of the "doomsday clock," on the journal's cover from seven minutes before midnight to three minutes before midnight. The clock, which was meant to indicate the global level of nuclear danger and the state of international security, reflected the editors' fear of proliferation.

In early 1950, Truman authorized the development of a new hydrogen superbomb, and by 1953, both the United States and the Soviet Union had unlocked the secret of the hydrogen bomb. This new fearsome weapon raised the stakes of the arms race ever higher. The government remained quiet about MIKE, the first test of a hydrogen device in the Pacific Ocean in 1952, but rumors circulated that it had created a hole in the ocean floor 175 feet deep and a mile wide. Later, after the 1954 BRAVO test, AEC chairman Lewis Strauss admitted that "an H-bomb can be made . . . large enough to take out a city," even New York. Then, in 1957, shortly after the news that the Soviets had successfully tested their first intercontinental ballistic missile (ICBM), Americans learned that the Soviets had launched into outer space *Sputnik*, the first artificial satellite—with a rocket that could also deliver a hydrogen bomb.

IMAGE

U.S. Hydrogen Bomb Test in the Pacific, 1952

Sputnik   The Cold War moved into space when the Soviet Union launched the first artificial satellite, known as *Sputnik* ("fellow traveler"). Shown here is a model of the satellite, which weighed 184 pounds and traveled in an elliptical orbit, ranging from about 140 to 560 miles above the earth. Americans, who prided themselves on their technological expertise, were stunned. Why do you think they were frightened as well as shocked? *(Bettmann/CORBIS)*

The discovery of radioactive fallout added another dimension to the nuclear dilemma. Fallout became publicly known after the BRAVO blast in 1954 showered Japanese fishermen on a ship called the *Lucky Dragon* 85 miles away with radioactive dust. They became ill with radiation sickness, and several months later, one of the seamen died. The Japanese, who had been the first to experience the effects of atomic weapons, were outraged and alarmed to be the first victims of the hydrogen bomb. Despite the contention of AEC Chairman Strauss that the *Lucky Dragon* was not a fishing boat but a "Red spy outfit" monitoring the test, the American ambassador to Japan apologized to the Japanese and the United States eventually provided financial compensation. But the damage was done. Everywhere people began to realize the terrible consequences of nuclear proliferation. Fallout had become a serious international problem—in the words of physicist Ralph Lapp, "a peril to humanity."

Both the scientific and the popular press focused attention on radioactive fallout. Radiation, Lapp observed, "cannot be felt and possesses all the terror of the unknown. It is something which evokes revulsion and helplessness—like a bubonic plague." Nevil Shute's best-selling 1957 novel *On the Beach,* and the film that followed, also sparked public awareness and fear. The story described a war that released so much radioactive waste that all life in the Northern Hemisphere disappeared, while the Southern Hemisphere awaited the same deadly fate.

In 1959, when *Consumer Reports,* the popular magazine that tested and compared various products, warned of the contamination of milk with the radioactive isotope strontium-90, the public grew even more alarmed.

The discovery of fallout provoked a shelter craze. Bob Russell, a Michigan sheriff, declared that "to build a new home in this day and age without including such an obvious necessity as a fallout shelter would be like leaving out the bathroom 20 years ago." *Good Housekeeping* magazine carried a full-page editorial in November 1958 urging the construction of family shelters. More and more companies advertised ready-made shelters. A firm in Miami reported numerous inquiries about shelters costing between $1,795 and $3,895, depending on capacity, and planned 900 franchises. *Life* magazine in 1955 featured an "H-Bomb Hideaway" for $3,000. By late 1960, the Office of Civil and Defense Mobilization estimated that a million family shelters had been built.

The Nuclear West

The new nuclear weapons sparked an enormous increase in defense spending and created a huge nuclear industry, located primarily in the West. Contractors liked the region because of its anti-union attitudes; labor stability, they argued, would make it easier to meet government deadlines.

During World War II, a number of the Manhattan Project's major centers were located in the West. The plant at Hanford, Washington, was one of the most important producers of fissionable material, and the first atomic weapon had been produced at Los Alamos, New Mexico. Development in this area expanded after the war. Hanford continued to produce plutonium, a facility outside Denver made plutonium triggers for thermonuclear bombs, the new Sandia National Laboratory in Albuquerque provided the production engineering of nuclear bombs, and the Los Alamos laboratory remained a major atomic research center. In 1951, the United States opened the Nevada Test Site, 65 miles north of Las Vegas, to try out nuclear weapons. The 1,350-square-mile tract of uninhabited land—an area largerer than the

Seeking Safety Americans sought protection from fallout in shelters that civil defense authorities told them would be just like home. Here a typical family in 1955 practices in the Kiddie Kokoon, which had beds and supplies of food and water to last for several weeks. Do you think family members would appear as happy as they seem here after a few days? *(Walter P. Reuther Library, Wayne State University)* state of Rhode Island—was the site of approximately 100 aboveground tests. The Las Vegas Chamber of Commerce offered schedules of test shots, and the mushroom cloud became the logo for the Southern Nevada telephone directory. Utah residents often rose early to watch atomic flashes and years later recalled "the beautiful mushroom as it'd come up, [and] change colors." Californians could sometimes see the light.

Satirist and songwriter Tom Lehrer highlighted the West in the song "The Wild West Is Where I Want to Be" in his first album in 1953. The first verse went:

> *Along the trail you'll find me lopin'*
> *Where the spaces are wide open,*
> *In the land of the old A.E.C.*
> *Where the scenery's attractive,*
> *And the air is radioactive,*
> *Oh, the wild west is where I want to be.*

Defense spending promoted other development as well. Naval commands had headquarters in Seattle, San Francisco, San Diego, and Honolulu. Radar sites, aimed at tracking incoming missiles, stretched all the way up to Alaska. The Boeing Company, located in Seattle, stimulated tremendous development in that city as it produced B-47 and B-52 airplanes that were the U.S. Air Force's main delivery vehicles for nuclear bombs.

"Massive Retaliation"

As Americans grappled with the implications of nuclear weapons, government policy came to depend increasingly on an atomic shield. The Soviet Union's success in building its own bomb encouraged the conviction that the United States had to increase its atomic forces. Truman authorized the development of a nuclear arsenal but also stressed conventional forms of defense. Eisenhower, however, found the effort fragmented and wasteful. Concerned with controlling the budget and cutting taxes, his administration decided to rely on atomic weapons rather than combat forces as the key to American defense.

Secretary of State Dulles developed the policy of threatening "massive retaliation." The United States, he declared, was willing and ready to use nuclear weapons against Communist aggression on whatever targets it chose. The policy allowed troop cutbacks and promised to be cost-effective by giving "more bang for the buck."

Massive retaliation provided for an all-or-nothing response, leaving no middle course, no alternatives between nuclear war and retreat. Still, it reflected Dulles's willingness to threaten direct retaliation to deter Soviet challenges around the world. "The ability

to get to the verge without getting into war is the necessary art," he said. "If you cannot master it you inevitably get into war." Critics called the policy "brinkmanship" and wondered what would happen if the line was crossed in the new atomic age. Eisenhower himself was horrified when he saw reports indicating that a coordinated atomic attack could leave a nation "a smoking, radiating ruin at the end of two hours." With characteristic caution, he did his best to ensure that the rhetoric of massive retaliation did not lead to war.

Atomic Protest

As the arms race spiraled, critics demanded that it end. In 1956, Democratic presidential candidate Adlai Stevenson pointed to "the danger of poisoning the atmosphere" and called for a halt to nuclear tests. Eisenhower did not respond, but Vice President Richard Nixon called Stevenson's suggestion

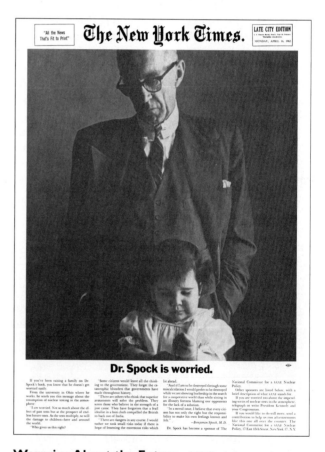

Worrying About the Future   SANE tried to get the United States, and the rest of the world, to stop testing nuclear weapons and dumping huge amounts of fallout in the atmosphere. This newspaper advertisement, which appeared in 1962, was part of the larger effort to make the world a safer place. How does this picture of noted pediatrician Dr. Benjamin Spock underscore a sense of fear? (Records of SANE, Inc., Swarthmore College Peace Collection)

"catastrophic nonsense," while Dulles minimized the hazards of radiation by arguing, "From a health standpoint, there is greater danger from wearing a wrist watch with a luminous dial."

In 1957, activists organized SANE, the National Committee for a Sane Nuclear Policy. One of its most effective advertisements featured internationally known pediatrician Benjamin Spock, looking down at a little girl with a frown on his face. "Dr. Spock is worried," the caption read, and the text below amplified on his concern. "I *am* worried," he said, "not so much about the effect of past tests but at the prospect of endless future ones. As the tests multiply, so will the damage to children—here and around the world."

Several years later, women who had worked with SANE took the protest movement a step further. To challenge continued testing, which dropped lethal radiation on all inhabitants of the globe, the protesters called on women throughout the country to suspend normal activities for a day and strike for peace. An estimated 50,000 women marched in 60 communities around the nation. Their slogans proclaimed "Let the Children Grow" and "End the Arms Race—Not the Human Race."

Pressure from many groups produced a political breakthrough and sustained it for a time. The superpowers began a voluntary moratorium on testing in the fall of 1958. It lasted until the Soviet Union resumed testing in September 1961 and the United States began again the following March.

THE COLD WAR AT HOME

The Cold War's effects on domestic affairs led to the creation of an internal loyalty program that seriously violated civil liberties. Maps (such as the one on p. 909) showed half the world colored red to dramatize the spread of communism. As Americans began to suspect Communist infiltration at home, some determined to root out all traces of communism inside the United States.

Truman's Loyalty Program

The Truman administration used increasingly shrill rhetoric in its drive to mobilize support for its containment program in the immediate postwar years. Spokespeople contrasted American virtues with diabolical Russian designs. For Truman, the issue confronting the world was one of "tyranny or freedom." Attorney general J. Howard McGrath spoke of "many Communists in America," each bearing the "germ of death for society."

When administration officials perceived an internal threat to security after the discovery of classified documents in the offices of the allegedly pro-Communist *Amerasia* magazine, Truman appointed a Temporary Commission on Employee Loyalty. Republican gains in the midterm elections of 1946 led him to try to head off a congressional loyalty probe that could be used for partisan ends, especially since Republicans had accused the Democrats of being "soft on communism."

On the basis of the report from his temporary commission, Truman in 1947 issued an executive decree establishing a new Federal Employee Loyalty Program. In the same week that he announced his containment policy, Truman ordered the FBI to check its files for evidence of subversive activity and to bring suspects before a new Civil Service Commission Loyalty Review Board. Initially, the program included safeguards and assumed that a challenged employee was innocent until proven guilty. But as the Loyalty Review Board assumed more power, it ignored individual rights. Employees about whom there was any doubt, regardless of proof, found themselves under attack, with little chance to fight back. Val Lorwin, whose story was told at the start of the chapter, was just one of many victims.

The Truman loyalty program examined several million employees but found grounds for dismissing only several hundred. Nonetheless, it bred the unwarranted fear of subversion, led to the assumption that absolute loyalty could be achieved, and legitimized investigative tactics that were used irresponsibly to harm innocent individuals.

The Congressional Loyalty Program

While Truman's loyalty probe investigated government employees, Congress launched its own program. In the early years of the Cold War, the law became increasingly explicit about what was illegal in the United States. The Smith Act of 1940 made it a crime to advocate or teach the forcible overthrow of the U.S. government. The McCarran Internal Security Act of 1950, passed over Truman's veto, further circumscribed Communist activity by declaring that it was illegal to conspire to act in a way that would "substantially contribute" to establishing a totalitarian dictatorship in America and by requiring members of Communist organizations to register with the attorney general. The American Communist party, which had never been large, even in the Depression, declined still further. Membership, numbering about 80,000 in 1947, fell to 55,000 in 1950 and to 25,000 in 1954.

AMERICAN VOICES

Interrogation of Writer Ring Lardner, Jr., by the House Un-American Activities Committee (HUAC) in 1947

In 1947, HUAC began an investigation of the motion picture industry, on the grounds that the left-wing sympathies of writers, actors, and directors compromised their work and could corrupt the American public. Well-publicized hearings became contentious, and the nation became familiar with the refrain: "Are you now or have you ever been a member of the Communist Party?" In the following selection, committee chairman J. Parnell Thomas and chief investigator Robert E. Stripling question Lardner and seek to find out about his involvement with the Screen Writers Guild, which HUAC considered subversive.

MR. LARDNER. Mr. Chairman, I have a short statement I would like to make....

THE CHAIRMAN. Mr. Lardner, the committee is unanimous in the fact that after you testify you may read your statement.

MR. LARDNER. Thank you....

MR. STRIPLING. Mr. Lardner, are you a member of the Screen Writers Guild?

MR. LARDNER. Mr. Stripling, I want to be cooperative about this, but there are certain limits to my cooperation. I don't want to help you divide or smash this particular guild, or to infiltrate the motion-picture business in any way for the purpose which seems to me to be to try to control that business, to control what the American people can see and hear in their motion-picture theaters.

THE CHAIRMAN. Now, Mr. Lardner, don't do like the others, if I were you, or you will never read your statement. I would suggest ——

MR. LARDNER. Mr. Chairman, let me ——

THE CHAIRMAN. You be responsive to the question.

MR. LARDNER: I am ——

THE CHAIRMAN. The question is: Are you a member of the Screen Writers Guild?

MR. LARDNER. But I understood you to say that I would be permitted to read the statement, Mr. Chairman.

THE CHAIRMAN. Yes; after you are finished with the questions and answers ——

MR. LARDNER. Yes....

THE CHAIRMAN. All right, then, a congressional committee is asking you: Are you a member of the Screen Writers Guild? Now you answer it "yes" or "no."

MR. LARDNER. Well, I am saying that in order to answer that ——

THE CHAIRMAN. All right, put the next question. Go to the $64 question.

THE WITNESS. I haven't ——

THE CHAIRMAN. Go to the next question.

MR. STRIPLING. Mr. Lardner, are you now or have you ever been a member of the Communist Party?

MR. LARDNER. Well, I would like to answer that question, too.

MR. STRIPLING. Mr. Lardner, the charge has been made before this committee that the Screen Writers Guild, which, according to the record, you are a member of, whether you admit it or not, has a number of individuals in it who are members of the Communist Party. The committee is seeking to determine the extent of Communist infiltration in the Screen Writers Guild and in other guilds within the motion-picture industry.

MR. LARDNER. Yes.

MR. STRIPLING. And certainly the question of whether or not you are a member of the Communist Party is very pertinent. Now, are you a member or have you ever been a member of the Communist Party?

MR. LARDNER. It seems to me you are trying to discredit the Screen Writers Guild through me and the motion-picture industry through the Screen Writers Guild and our whole practice of freedom of expression.

MR. STRIPLING. If you and others are members of the Communist Party you are the ones who are discrediting the Screen Writers Guild.

■ *Why do you think the interchange between Stripling and Lardner was so contentious?*

■ *What was Stripling trying to find out?*

■ *Why was Lardner reluctant to answer?*

Source: House Committee on Un-American Activities, *Hearings Regarding the Communist Infiltration of the Motion Picture Industry*, 80th Cong., 1st Sess., October 27, 1947, pp. 479–482.

The investigations of the House Un-American Activities Committee (HUAC) contributed to that decline. Intent on rooting out subversion, HUAC probed the motion picture industry in 1947, claiming that left-wing sympathies of writers, actors, directors, and producers were corrupting the American public. A frequent refrain in congressional hearings was "Are you now or have you ever been a member of the Communist party?" Altogether, HUAC called 19 Hollywood figures to testify. When 10 of them—including noted writers Ring Lardner, Jr., and Dalton Trumbo—refused to answer such accusatory questions by invoking their constitutional right to remain silent, Congress issued contempt citations. Members of the "Hollywood Ten" served prison sentences ranging from six months to one year and were blacklisted for years afterward. The movie industry knuckled under to HUAC and blacklisted anyone with even a marginally questionable past. Hollywood executives issued a statement that declared: "We will not knowingly employ a Communist nor a member of any party or groups which advocates the overthrow Government of the United States by force or by illegal or unconstitutional means."

Ronald Reagan, Testimony Before HUAC (1947)

Congress made a greater splash with the Hiss–Chambers case. Whittaker Chambers, a former Communist who had broken with the party in 1938 and had become a successful editor of *Time* magazine, charged that Alger Hiss had been a Communist in the 1930s. Hiss was a distinguished New Dealer who had served in the Agriculture Department before becoming assistant secretary of state. Now out of the government, he was president of the Carnegie Endowment for International Peace. He denied Chambers's charge, and the matter might have died there had not freshman congressman Richard Nixon taken up the case. Nixon finally extracted from Hiss an admission that he had once known Chambers, though by a different name. Hiss then sued Chambers for libel, whereupon Chambers charged that Hiss was a Soviet spy and during the 1930s had given Chambers military secrets to be passed on to the Soviets. Dramatically, Chambers produced rolls of microfilm that had been hidden in a hollowed-out pumpkin on his farm. The microfilm contained several State Department documents that had been typed on a typewriter Hiss had once owned.

Hiss was indicted for perjury for lying under oath about his former relationship with Chambers, the statute of limitations on prosecution for espionage having expired. The case made front-page news around the nation. Millions of Americans read about the case at around the same time they

An Anti-Communist Message from Hollywood As Hollywood implemented its blacklist of anyone deemed sympathetic to communism, filmmakers also began to make a number of anti-Communist films, such as *The Red Menace* in 1949, to show their own loyalty. How does this poster highlight the problems facing the United States? *(Michael Barson Collection)*

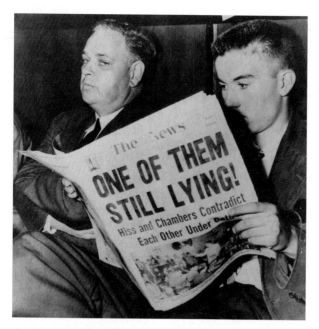

Seeking the Truth in the Alger Hiss Case As Whittaker Chambers (sitting on the left) confronted Alger Hiss, members of Congress as well as other Americans wondered which one of them was lying and which one was telling the truth. Newspaper headlines dramatized the confrontation, as the public followed the case with rapt attention. Why was this case so controversial? *(Library of Congress [LC-USZ62-126777])*

learned of Russia's first atomic explosion and the final victory of the Communist revolution in China. Chambers changed his story several times, but Hiss, too, seemed contradictory in his testimony and never adequately explained how he had such close ties with members of the Communist party or how some copies of stolen State Department documents had been typed on his typewriter. The first trial ended in a hung jury; in a second trial in January 1950 Hiss was convicted, sentenced to a five-year prison term, and fined $10,000.

For years, Americans debated whether Hiss was guilty as charged. He continued to assert his innocence for the remainder of his life, although evidence made available much later tends to substantiate Chambers's charges.

For many Americans, the Hiss case proved that a Communist threat indeed existed in the United States. It "forcibly demonstrated to the American people that domestic Communism was a real and present danger to the security of the nation," Richard Nixon declared after using the case to win a Senate seat from California and then the Republican vice presidential nomination in 1952. The case also led people to question the Democratic approach to the problem. Critics attacked Secretary of State Dean Acheson for supporting Hiss, who was his friend. They likewise questioned Truman's own

commitment to protect the nation from internal subversion. The dramatic Hiss case helped justify the even worse witch hunts that followed.

Congress also charged that homosexuals posed a security risk. The issue surfaced in February 1950, when Undersecretary of State John Peurifoy mentioned in testimony before the Senate Appropriations Committee that most of the 91 employees the State Department had dismissed for reasons of "moral turpitude" were homosexuals. This led to a press campaign against "sexual perverts." Then, in December, the Senate released a report that painted a threatening picture of the problems of homosexuals in the civil service. They lacked moral and emotional stability, the report suggested, and were therefore likely candidates for blackmail, which threatened national security. No one was safe from the intrusions of the Cold War crusade.

Senator Joe McCarthy

The key anti-Communist warrior in the 1950s was Joseph R. McCarthy, Republican senator from Wisconsin. He capitalized on the fear sparked by congressional and executive investigations and made the entire country cognizant of the Communist threat.

McCarthy came to the Communist issue almost accidentally. Elected to the U.S. Senate in 1946, McCarthy had an undistinguished career for much of his first term. As he began to contemplate re-election two years later, he was worried, for Truman had carried Wisconsin in 1948. McCarthy saw in the Communist question a way of mobilizing Republican support. He first gained national attention with a speech before the Wheeling, West Virginia, Women's Club in February 1950, not long after the conviction of Alger Hiss. In that address, McCarthy brandished in his hand what he said was a list of 205 known Communists in the State Department. Pressed for details, McCarthy first said that he would release his list only to the president, then reduced the number of names to 57.

DOCUMENT

Sen. Joseph P. McCarthy, Speech to Women's Club of Wheeling, WV (1950)

Early reactions to McCarthy were mixed. A subcommittee of the Senate Foreign Relations Committee, after investigating, called his charge a "fraud and a hoax." Even other Republicans, including Robert Taft and Richard Nixon, questioned his effectiveness. As his support grew, however, Republicans realized his partisan value and egged him on. Senator John Bricker of Ohio allegedly told him, "Joe, you're a dirty s.o.b., but there are times when you've got to have an s.o.b. around, and this is one of them."

McCarthy selected assorted targets in his crusade to wipe out communism. In the elections of 1950, he attacked Millard Tydings, the Democrat from Maryland who had chaired the subcommittee that dismissed McCarthy's first accusations. A doctored photograph showing Tydings with deposed American Communist party head Earl Browder helped bring about Tydings's defeat. McCarthy blasted Dean Acheson as the "Red Dean of the State Department" and slandered George C. Marshall, the architect of victory in World War II and the Marshall Plan for European recovery, as a "man steeped in falsehood . . . who has recourse to the lie whenever it suits his convenience."

McCarthy Telegram and Truman Draft Response (1950)

A demagogue throughout his career, McCarthy gained visibility through extensive press and television coverage. He knew how to issue press releases just before newspaper deadlines and to provide reporters with leaks that became the basis for stories. Playing on his tough reputation, he did not mind appearing disheveled, unshaven, and half sober. He used obscenity and vulgarity freely as he lashed out against his "vile and scurrilous" enemies as part of his effort to appeal for popular support by appearing as an ordinary man of the people.

McCarthy's tactics worked because of public alarm about the Communist threat. The Korean War revealed the aggressiveness of Communists in Asia. The arrest in 1950 of Julius and Ethel Rosenberg fed fears of internal subversion. The Rosenbergs, a seemingly ordinary American couple with two small children, were charged with stealing and transmitting atomic secrets to the Russians. To many Americans, it was inconceivable that the Soviets could have developed the bomb on their own. Treachery helped explain the Soviet explosion of an atomic device.

The next year, the Rosenbergs were found guilty of espionage. Judge Irving Kaufman expressed the rage of an insecure nation as he sentenced them to death. "I consider your crime worse than murder," he said. "Your conduct in putting into the hands of the Russians the A-bomb years before our best scientists predicted Russia would perfect the bomb has already caused, in my opinion, the Communist aggression in Korea, . . . and who knows but that millions more of innocent people may pay the price of your treason." Their execution in the electric chair after numerous appeals were turned down reflected a national commitment to respond to the Communist threat. For years, supporters of the Rosenbergs claimed that they were innocent victims of the anti-Communist crusade. More recent evidence indicates that Julius was guilty. Ethel, cognizant of his activities but not involved herself, was arrested, convicted, and executed in a futile government attempt to make Julius talk. Their deaths underscored the intensity of anti-Communist feeling in the United States.

When the Republicans won control of the Senate in 1952, McCarthy's power grew. He became chairman of the Government Operations Committee and head of the Senate Permanent Investigations Subcommittee. He now had a stronger base and two dedicated assistants, Roy Cohn and G. David Schine, who helped keep attention focused on the ostensible Communist threat. They assisted him in his domestic investigations and

AUDIO

Joseph P. McCarthy Speech

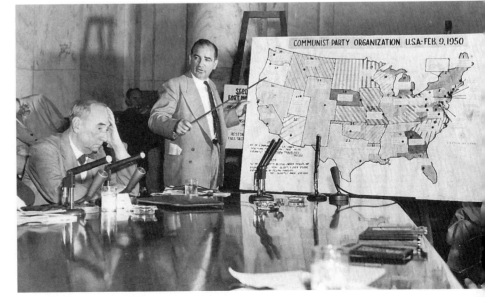

McCarthy's Anti-Communist Campaign Senator Joseph McCarthy's spurious charges inflamed anti-Communist sentiment in the 1950s. Here he uses a chart of Communist party organization in the United States to suggest that the nation would be at risk unless subversives were rooted out. How does the chart contribute to the impression McCarthy wanted to convey? *(Bettmann/CORBIS)*

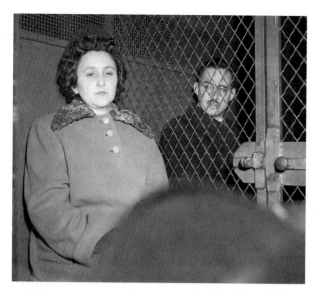

The Rosenbergs Convicted of Espionage Julius and Ethel Rosenberg proclaimed their innocence when charged with passing on secrets about the atomic bomb, but were found guilty and executed. Here they are going back to prison in a patrol car after hearing the verdict. Why did this case arouse such an uproar? *(Bettmann/CORBIS)*

even traveled abroad, ripping books off the shelves of American embassy libraries that they deemed subversive. The lists of suspects, including Val Lorwin (introduced at the start of this chapter), grew ever larger.

As McCarthy's anti-Communist witch hunt continued, Eisenhower became uneasy. He disliked the

senator but, recognizing his popularity, was reluctant to challenge him. At the height of his influence, polls showed that McCarthy had half the public behind him. With the country so inclined, Eisenhower compromised by voicing his disapproval quietly and privately.

Some allies of the United States were likewise concerned. The British, for example, had faced their own spy scandals in recent years but had dealt with disclosures of espionage more quietly and gracefully. They were uncomfortable with the hysterical American anti-Communist crusade.

With the help of Cohn and Schine, McCarthy pushed on, but finally he pushed too hard. In 1953, the army drafted Schine and then refused to allow the preferential treatment that Cohn insisted his colleague deserved. Angered, McCarthy began to investigate army security and even top-level army leaders. When the army charged that McCarthy was going too far, the Senate investigated the complaint.

The Army–McCarthy hearings began in April 1954 and lasted 36 days. Beamed to a captivated nationwide audience, they demonstrated the power of television to shape people's opinions. Americans saw McCarthy's savage tactics on screen. He came across to viewers as irresponsible and destructive, particularly in contrast to Boston lawyer Joseph Welch, who argued the army's case with quiet eloquence and showed McCarthy as the demagogue he was. At one point in the hearings, when McCarthy

Major Events of the Cold War

Year	Event	Effect
1946	Winston Churchill's "Iron Curtain" speech	First Western "declaration" of the Cold War
	George F. Kennan's long telegram	Spoke of Soviet insecurity and the need for containment
1947	George F. Kennan's article signed "Mr. X"	Elaborated on arguments in the telegram
	Truman Doctrine	Provided economic and military aid to Greece and Turkey
	Federal Employee Loyalty Program	Sought to root out subversion in the U.S. government
	HUAC investigation of the motion picture industry	Sought to expose Communist influences in the movies
1948	Marshall Plan	Provided massive American economic aid in rebuilding postwar Europe
	Berlin airlift	Brought in supplies when USSR closed off land access to the divided city
1949	NATO	Created a military alliance to withstand a possible Soviet attack
	First Soviet atomic bomb	Ended the American nuclear monopoly
	Communist victory in China	Made Americans fear the worldwide spread of communism
1950	Conviction of Alger Hiss	Seemed to bear out Communist danger at home
	Joseph McCarthy's first charges	Launched aggressive anti-Communist campaign in the United States
	NSC-68	Called for vigilance and increased military spending to counter the Communist threat
	Outbreak of the Korean War	North Korean invasion of South Korea viewed as part of Soviet conspiracy
1953	Armistice in Korea	Brought little change after years of bitter fighting
1954	Vietnamese victory over French at Dien Bien Phu	Early triumph for nationalism in Southeast Asia
	Army–McCarthy hearings	Brought downfall of Joseph McCarthy

accused a member of Welch's staff of being involved with an organization sympathetic to the Communist party, despite an earlier agreement not to raise the issue, Welch exploded. "Little did I dream you could be so reckless and so cruel as to do an injury to that lad," he said with a carefully controlled fury. "Have you no sense of decency, sir, at long last? Have you left no sense of decency?"

The hearings shattered McCarthy's mystical appeal. His ruthless tactics, patently visible to the national television audience, offended millions. The Senate, which had earlier backed off confronting McCarthy, finally censured him for his conduct. Even conservatives turned against McCarthy because he was no longer limiting his venom to Democrats and liberals. Although McCarthy remained in office, his influence disappeared. Three years later, at age 48, he died a broken man.

Yet for a time he had exerted a powerful hold in the United States. "To many Americans," radio commentator Fulton Lewis, Jr., said, "McCarthyism is Americanism." Seizing on the frustrations and anxieties of the Cold War, McCarthy struck a resonant chord. As his appeal grew, he put together a following that included both lower-class ethnic groups, who responded to the charges against established

elites, and conservative midwestern Republicans. But his real power base was the Senate, where, particularly after 1952, conservative Republicans saw McCarthy as a means of reasserting their own authority. Their support encouraged the vicious crusade.

The Casualties of Fear

The anti-Communist campaign kindled pervasive suspicion in American society. In the late 1940s and early 1950s, dissent no longer seemed safe. Civil servants, government workers, academics, and actors all came under attack and found that the right of due process often evaporated amid the Cold War Red Scare. Seasoned China experts lost their positions in the diplomatic service, and social justice legislation faltered.

This paranoia affected American life in countless ways. In New York, subway workers were fired when they refused to answer questions about their own political activities and beliefs. In Seattle, a fire department officer who denied current membership in the Communist party but refused to speak of his past was dismissed just 40 days before he reached the 25 years of service that would have qualified him for

TIMELINE

1945	Yalta Conference Roosevelt dies; Harry Truman becomes president Potsdam Conference
1946	American plan for control of atomic energy fails Atomic Energy Act Iran crisis in which U.S. forces USSR to leave Churchill's "Iron Curtain" speech
1947	Truman Doctrine Federal Employee Loyalty Program House Un-American Activities Committee (HUAC) investigates the movie industry
1948	Marshall Plan launched Berlin airlift Israel created by the United Nations Hiss–Chambers case Truman elected president
1949	Soviet Union tests atomic bomb North Atlantic Treaty Organization (NATO) established George Orwell, *1984* Mao Zedong's forces win Chinese civil war; Jiang Jieshi flees to Taiwan
1950	Truman authorizes development of the hydrogen bomb Alger Hiss convicted Joseph McCarthy's Wheeling (W. Va.) speech on subversion

	NSC-68 McCarran Internal Security Act
1950–1953	Korean War
1951	Japanese–American treaty
1952	Dwight D. Eisenhower elected president McCarthy heads Senate Permanent Investigations Subcommittee
1953	Stalin dies; Khrushchev consolidates power East Germans stage anti-Soviet demonstrations Shah of Iran returns to power in CIA-supported coup
1954	Fall of Dien Bien Phu ends French control of Indochina Geneva Conference on Vietnam Guatemalan government overthrown with CIA help Mao's forces shell Quemoy and Matsu Army–McCarthy hearings
1956	Suez incident Hungarian "freedom fighters" suppressed Eisenhower reelected
1957	Russians launch *Sputnik* satellite
1958	U.S. troops sent to support Lebanese government
1959	Castro deposes Batista in Cuba

retirement benefits. Navajo in Arizona and New Mexico, facing starvation in the bitter winter of 1947–1948, were denied government relief because of charges that their communal way of life was communistic and therefore un-American. Racism became intertwined with the anti-Communist crusade when African American actor Paul Robeson was accused of Communist leanings for criticizing American foreign policy and denied opportunities to perform. Subsequently the State Department revoked his passport. Black author W. E. B. Du Bois, who actually joined the Communist party, faced even more virulent attacks and likewise lost his passport. Hispanic laborers faced deportation for membership in unions with left-wing sympathies. In 1949, the Congress of Industrial Organizations (CIO) expelled 11 unions with a total membership of more than 1 million for alleged domination by Communists. Val Lorwin weathered the storm of malicious accusations and was finally vindicated, but others were less lucky. They were the unfortunate victims as the United States became consumed by the passions of the Cold War.

Conclusion

The Cold War in Perspective

The Cold War dominated international relations in the post–World War II years. Tensions grew after 1945 as the United States and the Soviet Union found themselves engaged in a bitter standoff that affected all diplomatic exchanges, encouraged an expensive arms race, and limited the resources available for reform at home. For the United States, it was a first experience with the fiercely competitive international relations that had long plagued the nations of Europe. And while there was seldom actual shooting, the struggle required warlike measures and imposed costs on all countries involved.

What caused the Cold War? Historians have long argued over the question of where responsibility should be placed. In the early years after the Second World War, policymakers and commentators who supported their actions justified the American stance as a bold and courageous effort to meet the Communist threat. Later, particularly in the 1960s, as the war in Vietnam eroded confidence in American foreign policy, revisionist historians began to argue that American actions were misguided, insensitive to Soviet needs, and at least partially responsible for escalating friction. As with most historical questions, there are no easy answers, but both sides must be weighed.

The Cold War stemmed from a competition for international influence between the two great world powers. After World War II, the U.S. goal was to exercise economic and political leadership in the world and thus to establish capitalist economies and democratic political institutions throughout Europe and in nations emerging from colonial rule. But these goals put the United States on a collision course with nations such as the Soviet Union that had a different vision of what the postwar world should be like and with anticolonial movements in emerging countries around the globe. Perceiving threats from the Soviet Union, China, and other Communist countries, the United States clung to its deep-rooted sense of mission and embarked on an increasingly aggressive effort at containment, based on its reading of the lessons of the past. American efforts culminated in the ill-fated war in Vietnam as the Communist nations of the world defended their own interests with equal force. The Cold War, with its profound effects at home and abroad, was the unfortunate result.

Questions for Review and Reflection

1. What were the roots of the conflict that turned into the Cold War?

2. Why did the United States and Soviet Union find it so difficult to get along in the years after World War II?

3. How did Cold War policy change in the 1950s from what it had been in the late 1940s?

4. What impact did the Cold War have on American society at home?

5. Could the Cold War have been avoided?

Recommended Reading

Recommended Readings are posted on the Web site for this textbook. Visit www.ablongman.com/nash

Fiction and Film

Fail-Safe by Eugene Burdick and Harvey Wheeler (1962) is a novel about an accidental nuclear war. *The Bridges at Toko-Ri* (1953) by James A. Michener is a novel about the frustrations of fighting the Korean War when people at home do not seem to care. Walter M. Miller, Jr.'s *A Canticle for Leibowitz* (1959) is about the devastation following a nuclear war that reduces civilization to a primitive state. Nevil Shute's *On the Beach* (1957) is a novel about a nuclear war that wiped out most life and created a radioactive cloud that is killing the rest.

Dr. Strangelove or: How I Learned to Stop Worrying and Love the Bomb (1964) is a movie made by Stanley Kubrick about the absurdity of nuclear war. *Fail-Safe* (1964) is the film from the novel of the same name about an accidental nuclear war that destroyed both Moscow and New York. *High Noon* (1952) is a Western dramatizing the need to stand up to outlaws and reflecting the need to resist the excesses of the anti-Communist crusade. *On the Beach* (1959) is the film from the novel of the same name about a nuclear war that ended all life on earth.

Discovering U.S. History Online

Cold War

www.learningcurve.gov.uk/coldwar/default.htm
www.cnn.com/SPECIALS/cold.war

The first URL is the address for a British site that uses primary sources from the United States and Europe to examine such questions as "Did the Cold War really start in 1919–39?" "Who caused the Cold War?" and "How did the Cold War work?" The second URL is the address for the companion site to the CNN series on the Cold War. It contains a good deal of information about a wide variety of issues.

The Marshall Plan

www.lcweb.loc.gov/exhibits/marshall

This site examines the Marshall Plan speech, reactions to the speech, and implementation of the European Recovery Program during the next 50 years. The site includes a photo exhibit of reconstruction projects at midpoint.

NATO

www.cnn.com/SPECIALS/1999/nato/

This site from CNN has an excellent timeline and images telling the history of the North Atlantic Treaty Organization.

The Truman Doctrine

www.trumanlibrary.org/whistlestop/study_collections/
doctrine/large/doctrine.htm

Part of the Truman presidential library Web site, this site offers images of primary sources dealing with what came to be known as the Truman Doctrine.

Korean War

www.trumanlibrary.org/korea/index.html
www.koreanwar.org

A joint project of two presidential libraries, the first site listed presents many of the archival resources (documents and photographs) from the two administrations involved in the Korean War. The second site has information about the Korean War and is a guide to resources on the struggle.

Vietnam War

http://vietnam.vassar.edu
www.pbs.org/wgbh/amex/vietnam/

The overview section of the first site gives a good background to the Vietnam War and the origins of American involvement under Eisenhower. The second site contains a detailed, interactive timeline of the war, interpretive essays, and autobiographical reflections.

Atomic Weapons

www.atomicarchive.com/index.shtml

A companion to a CD-ROM of the same name, this site offers biographies, documents, treaties, an atomic timeline, and more.

Nuclear Age Peace Foundation

www.nuclearfiles.org

The stated aim of this site is to create an "informed citizenry" regarding nuclear power and weapons. To achieve this goal, the site presents an interactive timeline, an image and audio archive, a database of nuclear treaties, various other primary documents, and a collection of essays.

Oak Ridge National Laboratory

www.ornl.gov/timeline/index.html

An interactive and illustrated timeline explains the projects of this governmental laboratory, from the first nuclear reactor (1940) to electron microscope images of the silicon crystal (1999).

Alger Hiss

http://homepages.nyu.edu/~th15/

Funded by grants from The Alger Hiss Research and Publication Project of the Nation Institute and from a Donor Advised Fund at the Community Foundation for Southern Arizona, this site seeks vindication for Hiss and also provides an array of information and sources on this key episode in the Cold War on the home front.

Senator Joe McCarthy

www.webcorp.com/mccarthy/mccarthypage.htm

This site includes audio and visual clips of McCarthy's speeches.

CHAPTER 28

Reform and Rebellion in the Turbulent Sixties, 1960–1969

The United States was comfortable and confident as the 1960s began. There was a basic consensus about the responsibility of the government to help those who could not help themselves. Then that consensus fragmented in the turbulence that accompanied the Vietnam War. *(Romare Bearden, The Dove, 1964. Digital Image Photo Credit: The Museum of Modern Art/Licensed by SCALA/Art Resource, NY. Art © Romare Bearden Foundation/Licensed by VAGA, New York, NY)*

American Stories

A Young Liberal Questions the Welfare State

Paul Cowan was an idealist in the 1960s. Like many students who came of age in these years, he believed in the possibility of social change and plunged into the struggle for liberal reform. He shared the hopes and dreams of other members of his generation, who felt that their government could make a difference in people's lives.

Cowan's commitment had developed slowly. He was a child of the 1950s, when most Americans were caught up in the consumer culture and paid little attention to the problems of people less fortunate than themselves. His grandfather had sold used cement bags in Chicago, but his father had become an executive at CBS television, and Cowan grew up in comfortable surroundings. He graduated from the Choate School (where John Kennedy had gone) in 1958, and then from Harvard University (where Kennedy had also been a student) in 1963.

When he entered college, Cowan was interested in politically conscious writers such as John Dos Passos, John Steinbeck, and James Agee and folk singers such as Pete Seeger and Woody Guthrie. They offered him entrance, he later recalled, into a "nation that seemed to be filled with energy and decency," one that lurked "beneath the dull, conformist facade of the Eisenhower years." While at Harvard, he was excited by antinuclear campaigns in New England and civil rights demonstrations in the South.

After college, he made good on his commitment to civil rights by going to Mississippi to work in the Freedom Summer Project of 1964. He was inspired by the example of John Kennedy, the liberal president whose administration promised "a new kind of politics" that could make the nation, and the world, a better place. During that summer, he wrote, "it was possible to believe that by changing ourselves we could change, and redeem, our America."

The Peace Corps came next. Paul and his wife, Rachel, were convinced that this organization, the idea of the young president, "really was a unique government agency, permanently protected by the lingering magic of John F. Kennedy's name." They were assigned to the city of Guayaquil, in Ecuador, in South America. Their task was to serve as mediators between administrators of the city hall and residents of the slums. They wanted to try to raise the standard of living by encouraging local governments to provide basic services such as garbage disposal and clean water.

But the work proved more frustrating than they had imagined. They bristled at the restrictions imposed by the Peace Corps bureaucracy. They despaired at the inadequate resources local government officials had to accomplish their aims. They wondered whether they were simply new imperialists, trying to impose their values on others who had priorities of their own. "From the day we moved into the *barrio*," Cowan later recalled, "the question we were most frequently asked by the people we were supposed to be organizing was whether we would leave them our clothes when we returned to the States."

Cowan came home disillusioned. "I saw that even the liberals I had wanted to emulate, men who seemed to be devoting their lives to fighting injustice, were unable to accept people from alien cultures on any terms but their own." He called his account of his own odyssey *The Making of an Un-American.*

Paul Cowan's passage through the 1960s mirrored the passage of American society as a whole. Millions of Americans shared his views of the possibilities of democracy as the period began. Mostly comfortable and confident, they supported the liberal agenda advanced by the Democratic party of John Kennedy and Lyndon Johnson. They endorsed the proposition that the government had responsibility for the welfare of all its citizens and accepted the need for a more active government role to help those of its diverse peoples who were unable to help themselves. That commitment lay behind the legislative achievements of the "Great Society," the last wave of twentieth-century reform that built on the gains of the Progressive era and the New Deal years before.

Then political reaction set in as the nation was torn apart by the ravages of the Vietnam War. The escalation of the war, which led to charges that the United States was engaging in an imperialistic crusade like those of other nations in the past, sent more than half a million American soldiers to fight in a far-off land and provoked a protest movement that ripped apart the society. Young Americans, espousing different values and a different version of the American dream, challenged the priorities of their parents. At the same time, they paraded their sexuality more openly, experimented with different forms of mystical religious faith, and enjoyed readily available drugs. In the end, their challenges helped reverse the course of the war. But in the process, liberal assumptions eroded as conservatives argued that an activist approach was responsible for the social and political chaos that consumed the country.

This chapter describes both the climax of twentieth-century liberalism and the turbulence that led to its decline. It focuses on the effort of the government, begun in the New Deal of Franklin Roosevelt, to help those caught short by the advances of industrial capitalism. It first examines the democratic commitment in the 1960s to provide necessary assistance to the less fortunate members of American society and then describes the turmoil that undermined the possibility of such aid. In pondering the possibilities of reform, this chapter outlines the various attempts to devise an effective political response to the major structural changes in the post–World War II economy described in Chapter 26. And then it shows how the Cold War assumptions outlined in Chapter 27 led to the rifts that ripped the nation apart.

JOHN F. KENNEDY: THE CAMELOT YEARS

The commitment to an American welfare state reached its high-water point in the 1960s. As the left-wing Labour Party in Great Britain played a more and more influential role and occasionally assumed power, and social democratic coalitions were equally active in other European nations, Americans took note. Democrats wanted to follow their example and broaden the role of government even further than Franklin D. Roosevelt and Harry S Truman had done in the 1930s and 1940s, in an effort to address the problems of poverty, unemployment, and racism. John F. Kennedy, a senator from Massachusetts, demanded that the United States move in the direction of what he called a "New Frontier."

The Election of 1960

In the 1960 presidential campaign, Kennedy argued that the government in general, and the president in particular, had to play an even more active role than they had in the Eisenhower years. He charged that the country had become lazy as it reveled in the prosperity of the 1950s. There were, in fact, serious problems that needed to be solved.

VIDEO

JFK Presidential Campaign Ad: It's Up to You

Kennedy ran against Vice President Richard Nixon, who had served as second-in-command to Eisenhower for eight years and who clearly had more executive experience than Kennedy. The two candidates squared off against one another in the first televised presidential debates. Seventy million Americans tuned in to watch the two men in the first contest. Kennedy appeared tanned and rested. Nixon, who had recently been hospitalized with an infection, looked tired and gaunt. Even worse, the makeup he applied to hide his heavy beard growth only accentuated it and gave him a swarthy complexion on screen. The debates made a major difference in the campaign (see the "Recovering the Past" essay, pp. 940–941). Kennedy himself admitted, "It was TV more than anything else that turned the tide." From this point on, television would play a major role in the political process and reshape its character.

Kennedy overcame seemingly insuperable odds to become the first Catholic in the White House. Al Smith had gained the Democratic nomination in 1928 but had then lost to Herbert Hoover, and the conventional wisdom held that a Catholic could not be elected. Yet Kennedy's victory was razor-thin. The electoral margin of 303 to 219 concealed the close popular tally, in which he triumphed by fewer than 120,000 of 68 million votes cast. If only a few thousand people had voted differently in Illinois and Texas, the election would have gone to Nixon. While Kennedy had Democratic majorities in Congress, many members of his party came from the South and were less sympathetic to liberal causes.

JFK

John Kennedy served as a symbol of the early 1960s. He was far younger than his predecessor; at age 43, he was the youngest man ever elected to the presidency. He came from an Irish Catholic family from Massachusetts that saw politics as a means of acceptance in Protestant America. Raised in comfort, he graduated from Harvard University and went on

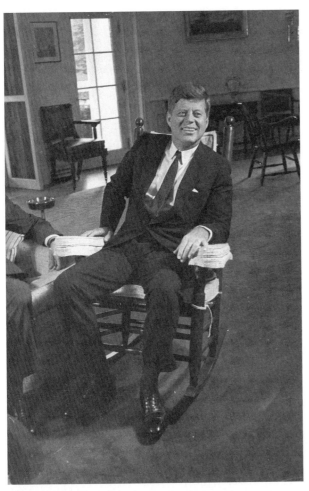

An Energetic Young Leader John Kennedy's energy and enthusiasm captured the imagination of Americans and people around the world, though few were aware of the physical ailments that affected him. He was fond of using this rocking chair in the White House, which he found comfortable for his ailing back. How did Kennedy's appearance contribute to his popularity and appeal? *(Bettmann/CORBIS)*

point even more movingly in his inaugural address: "The torch has been passed to a new generation of Americans—born in this century, tempered by war, disciplined by a hard and bitter peace, proud of our ancient heritage." Many Americans, like Paul Cowan, whom we met at the start of the chapter, were inspired by Kennedy's concluding call to action: "And so, my fellow Americans: Ask not what your country can do for you—ask what you can do for your country."

For Kennedy, strong leadership was all-important. The president, he believed, "must serve as a catalyst, an energizer." He must be able and willing to perform "in the very thick of the fight." Viewing himself as "tough-minded" and "hard-nosed," he was determined to provide firm direction and play a leading role in creating the national agenda, just as Franklin Roosevelt had done.

Kennedy surrounded himself with talented assistants. On his staff were 15 Rhodes scholars and several famous authors. The secretary of state was Dean Rusk, a former member of the State Department who had then served as president of the Rockefeller Foundation. The secretary of defense was Robert S. McNamara, the highly successful president of the Ford Motor Company.

Further contributing to Kennedy's attractive image were his glamorous wife, Jacqueline, and the glittering social occasions the couple hosted. Nobel Prize winners, musicians, and artists attended White House dinners. The Kennedys and their friends played touch football on the White House lawn and charged off on 50-mile hikes. Energy, exuberance, and excitement filled the air. The administration seemed like the Camelot of King Arthur's day, popularized in a Broadway musical in 1960.

DOCUMENT

JFK, Inaugural
Address
(1961)

to serve heroically in the navy during World War II, saving the lives of a number of his men when his boat—*PT 109*—was hit. He was elected first to the House of Representatives in 1946, then to the Senate in 1952, and was re-elected six years later by the largest majority in the history of the state.

The new president had a charismatic public presence. He was able to voice his aims in eloquent yet understandable language that motivated his followers. During the campaign, he pointed to "uncharted areas of science and space, unsolved problems of peace and war, unconquered pockets of ignorance and prejudice, unanswered questions of poverty and surplus" that Americans must confront, for "the New Frontier is here whether we seek it or not." He made the same

The New Frontier in Action

In office, Kennedy was committed to extending the welfare state. He sought to maintain an expanding economic system and to enlarge social welfare programs. In particular, he wanted to end the lingering recession that began in Eisenhower's last year by working with the business community while controlling price inflation.

These two goals conflicted when, in the spring of 1962, the large steel companies decided on a major price increase after steel unions had accepted a modest wage package. The angry president termed the price increases unjustifiable and pressed for executive and congressional action to force the steel companies to their knees. The large companies capitulated, but they disliked Kennedy's heavy-handed approach and decided that this Democratic

RECOVERING THE PAST

Television

In the last 50 years, television has played an increasingly important part in American life, providing historians with another source of evidence about American culture and society in the recent past. Television's popularity by the 1950s was the result of decades of experimentation dating back to the nineteenth century. In the 1930s, NBC installed a television station in the new Empire State Building in New York. Wearing green makeup and purple lipstick to provide better visual contrast, actors began to perform before live cameras in studios. At the end of the decade, *Amos 'n' Andy,* a popular radio show, was telecast, and as the 1940s began, Franklin D. Roosevelt became the first president to appear on television. World War II interrupted the development of television, and Americans relied on radio to bring them news. After the war, however, the commercial development of television quickly resumed. Assembly lines that had made electronic implements of war were now converted to consumer production, and thousands of new sets appeared on the market. The opening of Congress could be seen live in 1947; baseball coverage improved that same year owing to the zoom lens; children's shows such as *Howdy Doody* made their debut; and *Meet the Press,* a radio interview program, made the transition to television.

Although sports programs, variety shows hosted by Ed Sullivan and Milton Berle, TV dramas, and episodic series (*I Love Lucy* and *Gunsmoke,* for example) dominated TV broadcasting in the 1950s, television soon became entwined with politics and public affairs. Americans saw Senator Joseph McCarthy for themselves in the televised Army–McCarthy hearings in 1954; his malevolent behavior on camera contributed to his downfall. The 1948 presidential nominating conventions were the first to be televised, but the use of TV to enhance the public image of politicians was most thoroughly developed by the fatherly Dwight D. Eisenhower and the charismatic John F. Kennedy.

VIDEO
Kennedy-Nixon Debate

In November 1963, people throughout the United States shared the tragedy of John Kennedy's assassination, sitting stunned before their sets trying to understand the events of his fateful Texas trip. The shock and sorrow of the American people was repeated in the spring of 1968 as they gazed in disbelief at the funerals of Martin Luther King, Jr., and Robert Kennedy. A year later, a quarter of the world's population watched as Neil Armstrong became the first man to set foot on the moon. In that same era, television played an important part in shaping impressions of the war in Vietnam. More and more Americans began to understand the nature and impact of the conflict from what they saw on TV.

The candidates squaring off in their debate. (*AP/Wide World Photos*)

This combination of visual entertainment and enlightenment made owning a television set virtually a necessity. By 1970, fully 95 percent of American households owned a TV set, a staggering increase from the 9 percent only 20 years earlier. In fact, fewer families owned refrigerators or indoor toilets.

REFLECTING ON THE PAST   The implications of the impact of television on American society are of obvious interest to historians. How has television affected other communications and entertainment industries, such as radio, newspapers, and movies? Look at the "Television Tonight" listings shown here. What does the content of TV programming tell us about the values, interests, and tastes of the American people?

Perhaps most significant, what impact has TV had on the course of historical events like presidential campaigns, human relations, and wars? The pictures shown here are from the Kennedy–Nixon debates in the presidential campaign of 1960. The first picture shows the two candidates in the studio. The second picture shows a relaxed and energetic Kennedy staring directly into the TV camera. The third picture shows a taut and

John Kennedy (above) and Richard Nixon (right). (AP/Wide World Photos)

tense Nixon challenging the points made by his opponent. Which candidate seems to be speaking directly to the American people? Which candidate makes the better impression? Why? Polls of radio listeners taken after the first debate showed Nixon the winner; surveys of television viewers placed Kennedy in front. How do you account for this discrepancy?

Television Tonight

6:00—WTTV 4: Leave It to Beaver. Beaver tries to help a friend who has run away from home. Repeat.

6:30—WLTW-I 13: Cheyenne has a Laramie adventure in which Slim, Jess, and Jonesy work on a cattle drive. Repeat.

7:30—WTTV 4: The Untouchables. Eliot Ness tries to deal with a late gangster's niece who has a record of the murdered hood's career. Repeat.

7:30—WLW-I 13: Voyage to the Bottom of the Sea presents "Mutiny," in which Admiral Nelson shows signs of a mental breakdown during the search for a giant jellyfish which supposedly consumed a submarine.

7:30—WFBM-TV 6: Members of the Indianapolis Rotary Club discuss the 1965 business outlook with former U.S. Sen. Homer Capehart.

8:00—WFBM-TV 6: The Man from UNCLE is in at a new time and night. Thrush agents try to recapture one of their leaders before Napoleon Solo can deliver him to the Central Intelligence Agency. Ralph Taeger is guest star.

8:00—WISH-TV 8: I've Got a Secret welcomes the panel from To Tell the Truth: Tom Poston, Peggy Cass, Kitty Carlisle, and Orson Bean.

8:30—WLW-I 13: Basketball, I.U. vs. Iowa.

8:30—WISH-TV 8: Andy Griffith's comedy involves Goober's attempts to fill in at the sheriff's office.

9:00—WFBM-TV 6: Andy Williams is visited by composer Henry Mancini, Bobby Darin, and Vic Damone. Musical selections include "Charade," "Hello Dolly," and "Moon River."

9:00—WTTV 4: Lloyd Thaxton welcomes vocal group Herman's Hermits.

9:30—WISH-TV 8: Many Happy Returns. Walter's plan for currying favor with the store's boss hits a snag.

10:00—WFBM-TV 6: Alfred Hitchcock presents Margaret Leighton as a spinster who goes mad when she cannot cope with the strain of rearing an orphaned niece in "Where the Woodbine Twineth."

10:00—WLW-I 13: Ben Casey gets help in diagnosing a boy's illness from an Australian veterinarian with terminal leukemia. The vet's knowledge of bats provides the key.

10:00—WISH-TV 8: "Viet Nam: How We Got In—Can We Get Out?" is the topic of CBS Reports.

Source: Indianapolis News, January 11, 1965.

administration, like all the others, was hostile to business. In late May, six weeks after the steel crisis, the stock market plunged in the greatest drop since the Great Crash of 1929. Kennedy received the blame. "When Eisenhower had a heart attack," Wall Street analysts joked, "the market broke. If Kennedy would have a heart attack, the market would go up."

It now seemed doubly urgent to end the recession. Earlier a proponent of a balanced budget, Kennedy began to listen to his liberal advisers who proposed a Keynesian approach to economic growth. Budget deficits had promoted prosperity during the Second World War and might work in the same way in peacetime, too. A tax cut could put money in people's pockets, and their spending could stimulate the economy. In early 1963, the president called for a $13.5 billion cut in corporate taxes over the next three years. While that cut would cause a large deficit, it would also provide capital that business leaders could spend to revive the economy and ultimately increase tax revenues.

Opposition mounted. Conservatives refused to accept the basic premise that deficits would stimulate economic growth and argued, in Eisenhower's words, that "no family, no business, no nation can spend itself into prosperity." Some liberals claimed that it would be better to stimulate the economy by spending money to improve society rather than by cutting taxes and putting money in people's pockets. What good would it do, economist John Kenneth Galbraith wondered, to have "a few more dollars to spend if the air is too dirty to breathe, the water is too polluted to drink, the commuters are losing out in the struggle to get in and out of cities, the streets are filthy, and the schools are so bad that the young, perhaps wisely, stay away?" Congress pigeonholed the proposal in committee, and there it remained.

On other issues on the liberal agenda, Kennedy met similar resistance. Though he proposed legislation increasing the minimum wage and providing for federal aid for education, medical care for the elderly, housing subsidies, and urban renewal, the results were meager. His new minimum-wage measure passed Congress in pared-down form, but Kennedy did not have the votes in Congress to achieve most of his legislative program.

His inability to win necessary congressional support was most evident in the struggle to aid public education. Soon after taking office, Kennedy proposed a $2.3 billion program of grants to the states over a three-year period to help build schools and raise teachers' salaries. Immediately, a series of prickly questions emerged. Was it appropriate to spend large sums of money for social goals? Would federal aid bring federal control of school policies and curriculum? Should assistance go to segregated schools? Should it go to parochial schools? The administration proved willing to allow assistance to segregated schools, thereby easing white southern minds. On the Catholic question, however, it stumbled to a halt. Kennedy at first insisted, as he had throughout the campaign, that he would not allow his religion to influence his actions, and he opposed aid for parochial schools. But as Catholic pressure mounted and the administration realized that Catholic votes were necessary for passage, Kennedy began to reconsider. In the end, compromise proved impossible and the school aid measure died in committee.

Kennedy was more successful in securing funding for the exploration of space. The space program was caught up in the competition of the Cold War, and with the Soviet launching of *Sputnik* and then shots with first dogs, then astronauts, the USSR clearly had the lead. Finally, the American space program got off the ground. As first Alan Shepard and then John Glenn flew in space, Kennedy proposed that the United States commit itself to landing a man on the moon and returning him to earth before the end of the decade. Congress, caught up in the glamour of the proposal and worried about Soviet space achievements, assented and increased funding of the National Aeronautics and Space Administration (NASA).

DOCUMENT

JFK, Space Program Speech (1961)

Kennedy also established the Peace Corps, which sent young men and women overseas to assist developing countries. According to Kennedy aide Arthur M. Schlesinger, Jr., the Peace Corps was an effort "to replace protocol-minded, striped-pants officials by reform-minded missionaries of democracy who mixed with the people, spoke the native dialects, ate the food, and involved themselves in local struggles against ignorance and want." Paul Cowan, introduced at the start of this chapter, was one of thousands of volunteers who hoped to share their liberal dreams.

If Kennedy's successes were modest, he had at least made commitments that could be broadened later. He had reaffirmed the importance of executive leadership in the effort to extend the boundaries of the welfare state. And he had committed himself to using modern economics to maintain fiscal stability. The nation was poised to achieve liberal goals.

Civil Rights and Kennedy's Response

So it was with civil rights. The pressures that had mounted in the decade and a half after World War II

Sitting-In In violation of southern law, black college students refused to leave a lunch counter, launching a new campaign in the struggle for civil rights. Here the students wait patiently for service, or forcible eviction, as a way of dramatizing their determination to end segregation. What did the students hope to achieve by their actions? *(Bruce Roberts/Photo Researchers)*

had brought significant change in eliminating segregation in American society. As the effort continued, a spectrum of organizations, some old, some new, carried the fight forward.

DOCUMENT
SNCC, Statement of Purpose (1960)

The NAACP, founded in 1910, remained committed to overturning the legal bases for segregation in the aftermath of its victory in the *Brown* v. *Board of Education* case of 1954 (see Chapter 26). The Congress of Racial Equality (CORE), an interracial group established in 1942, promoted change through peaceful confrontation. In 1957, after their victory in the bus boycott in Montgomery, Alabama, Martin Luther King, Jr., and others formed the Southern Christian Leadership Conference (SCLC), an organization of southern black clergy. Far more militant was the Student Nonviolent Coordinating Committee (SNCC, pronounced "snick"), which began to operate in 1960 and recruited young Americans who had not been involved in the civil rights struggle.

Confrontations continued in the 1960s. On January 31, 1960, four black college students from the Agricultural and Technical College in Greensboro, North Carolina, protested continuing patterns of segregation, despite the Supreme Court's important rulings. Frustrated that they were permitted to shop but not to eat at a Woolworth's, a popular department store chain specializing in household goods, they sat down at the lunch counter and refused to leave. When a reporter inquired how long they had been planning the protest, the students responded, "All our lives!" They left at the end of the day, but the

next day more students showed up, and the following day still more. The sit-ins, which spread to other cities, captured media attention and eventually included as many as 70,000 participants. Those protesting often met with a brutal response. John Lewis, an African American activist who participated in a sit-in in Nashville, Tennessee, described his experience:

> A group of young white men came in and they started pulling and beating primarily the young women. They put lighted cigarettes down their backs, in their hair, and they were really beating people. In a short time police officials came in and placed all of us under arrest, and not a single member of the white group, the people that were opposing our sit-in, was arrested.

The following year, sit-ins gave rise to freedom rides, aimed at testing southern transportation facilities that recently had been desegregated by a Supreme Court decision. Organized initially by CORE and aided by SNCC, the program sent groups of blacks and whites together on buses heading south and stopping at terminals along the way. The riders, peaceful themselves, anticipated confrontations that would publicize their cause and generate political support. In Anniston, Alabama, a mob of white men attacked a bus that was

IMAGE
A 1960s March for Civil Rights

preparing to leave, slashing tires and throwing a firebomb inside a window they smashed. In Birmingham, police made an agreement with the Ku Klux Klan to give Klansmen 15 minutes alone to beat the Freedom Riders. Although the FBI knew

James Meredith's Achievement James Meredith refused to be driven from the University of Mississippi, despite the opposition of the governor and a campus riot. His perseverance paid off, as he ultimately earned his degree. What do you think it would have felt like to be black at the university during that time? (Bettmann/CORBIS)

happened." Participating in sit-ins, where she was thrashed and jailed for her activities, she remained deeply involved in the movement.

Many whites also joined the movement in the South. Mimi Feingold, a white student at Swarthmore College in Pennsylvania, helped picket the Woolworth's in Chester, Pennsylvania, and worked to unionize Swarthmore's black dining-hall workers. In 1961, after her sophomore year, she headed south to join the freedom rides sponsored by CORE. Like many others, Feingold found herself in the midst of often-violent confrontations and went to jail as an act of conscience.

In 1962, the civil rights movement accelerated. James Meredith, a black air force veteran and student at Jackson State College, applied to the all-white University of Mississippi, only to be rejected on racial grounds, although the Supreme Court affirmed his right to attend. Governor Ross Barnett, an adamant racist, announced defiantly that Meredith would not be admitted, and on one occasion personally blocked the way. A major riot followed; tear gas covered the

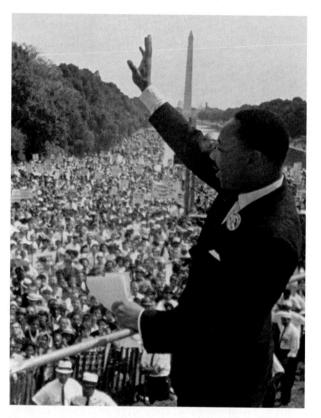

The March on Washington The 1963 march on Washington was a high point in the civil rights movement. Several hundred thousand demonstrators lined the reflecting pool leading out from the Washington Monument and heard Martin Luther King, Jr., shown here, and other black leaders eloquently plead for racial equality. How might such a march on the nation's capital advance the cause? (AP/Wide World Photos)

about the plan, the federal agency did nothing to stop it. Individual blacks and whites did work together to eliminate racial barriers, however, as the civil rights movement became the most powerful moral campaign since the abolitionist crusade before the Civil War.

Anne Moody, who grew up in a small town in Mississippi, personified the awakening of black consciousness. As a child, she had watched the murder of friends and acquaintances who had somehow transgressed the limits set for blacks. Overcoming the hardships of growing up poor and black in the rural South, Moody became the first member of her family to go to college, enrolling at Tougaloo College, near Jackson, Mississippi. Once there, she found her own place in the civil rights movement. She joined the NAACP and became involved in the activities of SNCC and CORE. Slowly, she noted, "I could feel myself beginning to change. For the first time I began to think something would be done about whites killing, beating, and misusing Negroes. I knew I was going to be a part of whatever

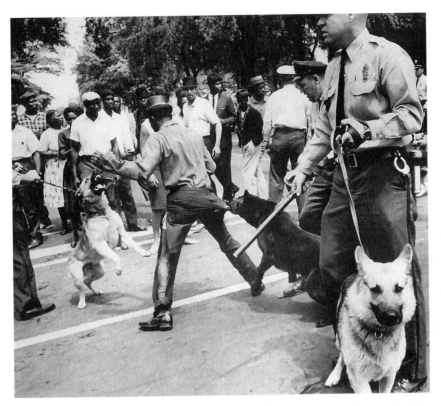

Attacks on Demonstrators in Birmingham   In Birmingham, city officials responded to peaceful demonstrators with brutal force. Here city police use trained dogs to drive marchers back. Televised nationally, the police response appalled the American public. As newsman Eric Sevareid observed, "A newspaper or television picture of a snarling police dog set upon a human being is recorded on the permanent photoelectric file of every human brain." What did the Birmingham authorities hope to achieve by use of these dogs? *(Charles Moore/Black Star)*

nothing, even though he had sought and won black support in 1960. The narrowness of his electoral victory made him reluctant to press white southerners on civil rights when he needed their votes on other issues. Kennedy initially failed to propose any civil rights legislation and ignored a campaign promise to end housing discrimination by presidential order. Not until November 1962, after the midterm elections, did he take a modest action—an executive order ending segregation in federally financed housing.

Events finally forced Kennedy to act more boldly. In the James Meredith confrontation, the president, like his predecessor in the Little Rock crisis, had to send federal troops to restore control and to guarantee Meredith's right to attend the university. The administration also forced the desegregation of the University of Alabama and helped arrange a compromise that eased discrimination in Birmingham's municipal facilities and hiring practices. And when white bombings aimed at eliminating black leaders in Birmingham caused thousands of blacks to abandon nonviolence and rampage through the streets, Kennedy readied federal troops to intervene.

He also spoke out more forcefully than before. In a nationally televised address, he called the quest for equal rights a "moral issue" and asked, "Are we to say to the world, and, much more importantly, to each other that this is a land of the free except for the Negroes." Just hours after the president spoke, assassins killed Medgar Evers, a black NAACP official, in his own driveway in Jackson, Mississippi.

Kennedy sent Congress a new and stronger civil rights bill, outlawing segregation in public places, banning discrimination wherever federal money was involved, and advancing the process of school integration. Polls showed that 63 percent of the nation supported his stand.

To lobby for passage of this measure, civil rights leaders, pressed from below by black activists, arranged a massive march on Washington in August 1963. More than 200,000 people gathered from

university grounds; and by the riot's end, two men lay dead and hundreds were hurt.

Other governors were equally aggressive. In his 1963 inaugural address, George C. Wallace of Alabama declared boldly, "Segregation now! Segregation tomorrow! Segregation forever!" as he voiced his opposition to integration.

Alabama became a national focus that year as a violent confrontation unfolded in Birmingham. Local black leaders encouraged Martin Luther King, Jr., to launch another attack on southern segregation in the city. Though the demonstrations were nonviolent, the responses were not. City officials declared that protest marches violated city regulations against parading without a license, and, over a five-week period, they arrested 2,200 blacks, some of them schoolchildren. Police Commissioner Eugene "Bull" Connor used high-pressure fire hoses, electric cattle prods, and trained police dogs to force the protesters back. As the media recorded the events, Americans watching television and reading newspapers were horrified.

Kennedy claimed to be sickened by the pictures from Birmingham but insisted that he could do across the country and demonstrated enthusiastically. Celebrities present included diplomat Ralph Bunche, writer James Baldwin, entertainers Sammy Davis, Jr., Harry Belafonte, and Lena Horne, and former baseball player Jackie Robinson. The folk music artists of the early 1960s were there as well. Joan Baez, Bob Dylan, and Peter, Paul, and Mary led the crowd in songs associated with the movement, such as "Blowin' in the Wind" and "We Shall Overcome."

VIDEO

Civil Rights March on Washington

The high point of the day was the address by Martin Luther King, Jr., the nation's preeminent spokesman for civil rights and proponent of nonviolent protest. King proclaimed his faith in the decency of his fellow citizens and in their ability to extend the promises of the Constitution and the Declaration of Independence to every American. With all the power of a southern preacher, he implored his audience to share his faith.

VIDEO

Rev. Martin Luther King, Jr., Speech at the March on Washington

"I have a dream," King declared, "that one day this nation will rise up and live out the true meaning of its creed: 'We hold these truths to be self-evident, that all men are created equal.' I have a dream that one day on the red hills of Georgia, the sons of former slaves and the sons of former slave-owners will be able to sit together at the table of brotherhood." It was a fervent appeal, and one to which the crowd responded. Each time King used the refrain "I have a

dream," thousands of blacks and whites roared together. King concluded by quoting from an old hymn: "Free at last! Free at last! Thank God almighty, we are free at last!"

Not all were moved. Anne Moody, who had come up from her activist work in Mississippi to attend the event, sat on the grass by the Lincoln Memorial as the speaker's words rang out. "Martin Luther King went on and on talking about his dream," she said. "I sat there thinking that . . . we never had time to sleep, much less dream." Nor was Congress prompted to do much. Despite large Democratic majorities, strong white southern resistance to the cause of civil rights continued, and the bill was bottled up in committee.

DOCUMENT

John L. Lewis, Address at the March on Washington (1963)

LYNDON B. JOHNSON AND THE GREAT SOCIETY

Kennedy knew he faced a difficult re-election battle in 1964. He wanted not only to win the presidency for a second term but also to increase liberal Democratic strength in Congress. Instead, an assassin's attack took his life and brought a new leader to the helm.

Change of Command

In November 1963, Kennedy traveled to Texas, where he hoped to unite the state's Democratic

A New President Kennedy's assassination thrust Lyndon Johnson into the presidency in an atmosphere of shocked grief and loss. Here, with Jacqueline Kennedy by his side, he takes the oath of office as he flies back from Dallas to Washington on the presidential plane. What were Johnson's immediate concerns as he assumed the presidency? (Bettmann/CORBIS)

party for the upcoming election. Dallas, one of the stops on the trip, was reputed to be hostile to the administration. Four weeks before, a conservative mob had abused Adlai Stevenson, ambassador to the United Nations. Now, on November 22, Kennedy had a chance to feel the pulse of the city for himself. Arriving at the airport, Henry González, a congressman accompanying the president in Texas, remarked jokingly, "Well, I'm taking my risks. I haven't got my steel vest yet." As the party entered the city in an open car, the president encountered friendly crowds. Suddenly shots rang out, and Kennedy slumped forward as bullets ripped through his head and throat. Mortally wounded, he died a short time later at a Dallas hospital. Lee Harvey Oswald, the accused assassin, was shot and killed a few days later by a minor underworld figure as he was being moved within the jail.

Americans were stunned. For days, people stayed at home and watched endless television replays of the assassination and its aftermath. The images of the handsome president felled by bullets, the funeral cortege, and the president's young son saluting his father's casket as it rolled by on the way to final burial at Arlington National Cemetery were all imprinted on people's minds. United around the event, members of an entire generation remembered where they had been when Kennedy was shot, just as an earlier generation recalled Pearl Harbor.

Vice President Lyndon Johnson succeeded Kennedy as president. Though less polished, Johnson was a more effective political leader than Kennedy and brought his own special skills and vision to the presidency.

LBJ

Johnson had taken a different road to the White House. He came from a far more humble background than Kennedy. He had begun his public career as a legislative assistant in the House of Representatives in Washington, D.C., then served as a New Deal official in Texas. He won election first to the House in 1937 and then to the Senate in 1948. Eager to be president, he accepted the vice presidential nomination when it became clear in 1960 that Kennedy was going to win.

Johnson was a man of elemental force. Always manipulative, he was often difficult to like. There was a streak of vulgarity that contributed to his earthy appeal but was frequently offensive. Those qualities notwithstanding, he was successful in the passion of his life—politics. Schooled in Congress and influenced by FDR, Johnson was the most able legislator of the postwar years. As Senate majority leader, he became famous for his ability to get things done. Ceaseless in his search for information, tireless in his attention to detail, he knew the strengths and weaknesses of everyone he faced. When he approached someone in the hall, one senator remarked, he was like a "great overpowering thunderstorm that consumed you as it closed in on you." He could flatter and cajole, and became famous for what came to be called the "Johnson treatment." According to columnists Rowland Evans, Jr., and Robert Novak, he zeroed in, "his face a scant millimeter from his target, his eyes widening and narrowing, his eyebrows rising and falling." He grabbed people by the lapels, made them listen, and usually got his way (see the series of illustrations on this page).

Lyndon Johnson

Lyndon Johnson in Action   Lyndon Johnson kept tight control of the Senate in the 1950s and was known for his ability to get his way. Here he is shown giving the famous "Johnson treatment" to Senator Theodore Francis Green in 1957. Note the way Green is bending backward in an unsuccessful effort to keep his distance from LBJ. Why do you think LBJ usually got his way? *(George Tames/The New York Times)*

Johnson ran the Senate with tight control and later tried to broaden his own appeal in his quest for the presidency. When that proved unsuccessful, he helped Kennedy win the election by serving in the second slot on the ticket, then went into a state of eclipse as vice president. He felt uncomfortable with the Kennedy crowd, useless and stifled in his new role. He told friends that he agreed with John Nance Garner, a vice president under FDR, who once observed that the vice presidency "wasn't worth a pitcher of warm spit."

Despite his own ambivalence about Kennedy, Johnson sensed the profound shock that gripped the United States after the assassination and was determined to utilize Kennedy's memory to achieve legislative success. Even more than Kennedy, he was willing to wield presidential power aggressively and to use the media to shape public opinion in pursuit of his vision of a society in which the comforts of life would be more widely shared and poverty would be eliminated once and for all.

The Great Society in Action

Lyndon Johnson had an expansive vision of the possibilities of reform. Using his considerable political skills, he succeeded in pushing through Congress the most extensive reform program in American history. Johnson began to develop the support he needed the day he took office. In his first public address, delivered to Congress and televised nationwide, he sought to dispel the image of impostor as he embraced Kennedy's liberal program. He began, in a measured tone, with the words, "All I have, I would have given gladly not to be standing here today." He asked members of Congress to work with him, and he underscored the theme "Let us continue" throughout his speech.

VIDEO
President Johnson Responds to the Death of JFK

As a first step, Johnson resolved to secure the measures Kennedy had been unable to extract from Congress. Bills to reduce taxes and ensure civil rights were his first and most pressing priorities, but he was interested too in aiding public education, providing medical care for the aged, and eliminating poverty. By the spring of 1964, he began to use the phrase "Great Society" to describe his expansive reform program.

Johnson's landslide victory over conservative Republican challenger Barry Goldwater of Arizona in the 1964 election validated LBJ's Great Society program. The 1964 race marked the first time in recent history that a conservative had gained the Republican nomination. Goldwater, however, frightened even members of his own party by proclaiming that

"extremism in the defense of liberty is no vice," and by speaking out against such popular programs as social security. LBJ received 61 percent of the popular vote and 486 electoral votes to Goldwater's 52. Democrats controlled both the Senate (68–32) and the House (295–140). Despite his defeat, Goldwater's candidacy reflected the growing power of conservatism within the Republican party and the ability of a grassroots group to organize a successful campaign in party primaries. It also drove moderate Republicans to vote for the Democratic party this time and gave Johnson a far more impressive mandate than Kennedy had ever enjoyed.

VIDEO
LBJ Presidential Campaign Ad: Little Girl vs. Mushroom Cloud

Johnson knew how to get laws passed. He appointed task forces that included legislators to study problems and suggest solutions, worked with them to draft bills, and maintained close contact with congressional leaders through a sophisticated liaison staff. Not since the FDR years had there been such a coordinated effort.

Civil rights reform was LBJ's first legislative priority and an integral part of the Great Society program, but other measures were equally important. Following Kennedy's lead, Johnson pressed for a tax cut. He accepted the Keynesian theory that deficits, properly managed, could promote prosperity. If people had more money to spend, then their purchases could stimulate the economy. Soon the tax bill passed.

With the tax cut in hand, the president pressed for the antipoverty program that Kennedy had begun to plan. Such an effort was bold and unprecedented in the United States, even though social democracy had a long history in European nations and other countries around the world. During the Progressive era at the turn of the century, some legislation had attempted to alleviate conditions associated with poverty. During the New Deal, Franklin Roosevelt had proposed programs to assist the one-third of the nation that could not help itself. Now Johnson took a step that no president had taken before; in his 1964 State of the Union message, he declared an "unconditional war on poverty in America."

DOCUMENT
LBJ, "The War on Poverty" (1964)

The center of this utopian effort to eradicate poverty was the Economic Opportunity Act of 1964. It created an Office of Economic Opportunity (OEO) to provide education and training through programs such as the Job Corps for unskilled young people trapped in the poverty cycle. VISTA (Volunteers in Service to America), patterned after the Peace Corps, offered assistance to the poor at home, while Head Start tried to give disadvantaged children a chance to succeed in school. Assorted community action programs gave the poor a voice in improving housing, health, and education in their own neighborhoods. Two agencies responded to Native American pressure by allowing Indians to devise programs and budgets and then administer programs themselves.

Aware of the escalating costs of medical care, Johnson also proposed a medical assistance plan. Both Truman and Kennedy had supported such an initiative but had failed to win congressional approval. Johnson succeeded. To head off conservative attacks, the administration tied the Medicare measure to the social security system and limited the program to the elderly. The new Medicaid program met the needs of those on welfare and certain other groups who could not afford private insurance. The Medicare–Medicaid initiative was the most important extension of federally directed social benefits since the Social Security Act of 1935. By the middle of the next decade, the two programs were paying for the medical costs of 20 percent of the American people.

Johnson was similarly successful in his effort to provide aid for elementary and secondary schools. Kennedy had met defeat when Catholics had insisted on assistance to parochial schools. Johnson, a Protestant, was able to deal with the ticklish religious question without charges of favoritism. His legislation allocated education money to the states based on the number of children from low-income families. Those

funds would then be distributed to assist deprived children in public as well as private schools.

In LBJ's expansive vision, the federal government would ensure that everyone shared in the promise of American life. Under his prodding, Congress passed a new housing act to give rent supplements to the poor and created a Cabinet Department of Housing and Urban Development. The federal government provided new forms of aid, such as legal assistance for those who could not afford to pay for it themselves. It moved further in funding higher education, including colleges and universities in its financial grants. Congress also provided artists and scholars with assistance through the National Endowments for the Arts and Humanities, created in 1965. Not since the Works Progress Administration in the New Deal had such groups been granted government aid.

At the same time, Johnson's administration provided much-needed immigration reform. The Immigration Act of 1965 replaced previously restrictive policy, in place since 1924, with a measure that vastly increased the ceiling on immigration and opened the door to immigrants from Asia and Latin America. By the late 1960s, some 350,000 immigrants were entering the United States annually, compared to the average of 47,000 per year between 1931 and 1945. This new stream of immigration created a population more

DOCUMENT

LBJ, Remarks on Signing the Immigration Bill (1965)

Roots of Selected Great Society Programs		
Progressive Period	**New Deal**	**Great Society**
Settlement house activity of Jane Addams and others	Relief efforts to ease unemployment (FERA, WPA)	Poverty programs (OEO)
Efforts to clean up slums (tenement house laws)	Housing program	Rehabilitation of slums through Model Cities program
Progressive party platform calling for federal accident, old-age, and unemployment insurance	Social security system providing unemployment compensation and old-age pensions	Medical care for the aged through social security (Medicare)
Activity to break up monopolies and regulate business	Regulation of utility companies	Regulation of highway safety and transportation
Efforts to regulate working conditions and benefits	Establishment of standards for working conditions and minimum wage	Raising of minimum wage
Efforts to increase literacy and spread education at all levels	Efforts to keep college students in school through NYA	Assistance to elementary, secondary, and higher education
Theodore Roosevelt's efforts at wilderness preservation	Conservation efforts (CCC, TVA planning)	Safeguarding of wilderness lands
Establishment of federal income tax	Tax reform to close loopholes and increase taxes for the wealthy	Tax cut to stimulate business activity
Theodore Roosevelt's overtures to Booker T. Washington	Discussion (but not passage) of antilynching legislation	Civil rights measures to ban discrimination in public accommodations and to guarantee right to vote

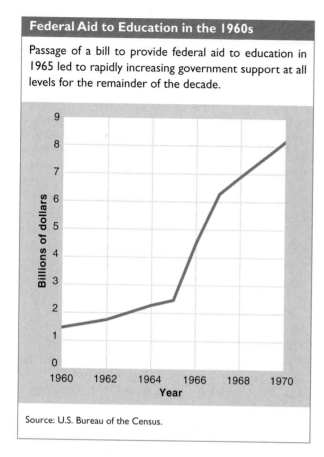

Federal Aid to Education in the 1960s

Passage of a bill to provide federal aid to education in 1965 led to rapidly increasing government support at all levels for the remainder of the decade.

Source: U.S. Bureau of the Census.

The National Wilderness Preservation Act of 1964 set aside 9.1 million acres of wilderness, and Congress passed other measures to limit air and water pollution. In addition, Lady Bird Johnson, the president's wife, led a beautification campaign to eliminate unsightly billboards and junkyards along the nation's highways.

Achievements and Challenges in Civil Rights

Lyndon Johnson was enormously successful in advancing the cause of civil rights. Seizing the opportunity provided by Kennedy's assassination, Johnson told Congress, "No memorial oration or eulogy could more eloquently honor President Kennedy's memory than the earliest possible passage of the civil rights bill." He pushed the bill through Congress, heading off a Senate filibuster by persuading

diverse than it had been since the early decades of the twentieth century. The consequences of this new diversity were far-ranging and affected many areas of American life, from politics, radio programming, and consumer products to street signs and public school classrooms.

The Great Society also reflected the stirring of the environmental movement. In 1962, naturalist Rachel Carson alerted the public to the dangers of pesticide poisoning and environmental pollution in her book *Silent Spring*. She took aim at chemical pesticides, especially DDT, which had increased crop yields but had brought disastrous side effects:

The most alarming of all man's assaults upon the environment is the contamination of air, earth, rivers, and sea with dangerous and even lethal materials. This pollution is for the most part irrecoverable; the chain of evil it initiates not only in the world that must support life but in living tissues is for the most part irreversible. In this now universal contamination of the environment, chemicals are the sinister and little-recognized partners of radiation in changing the very nature of the world—the very nature of its life.

Johnson was determined to deal with caustic fumes in the air, lethal sludge in rivers and streams, and the steady disappearance of wildlife.

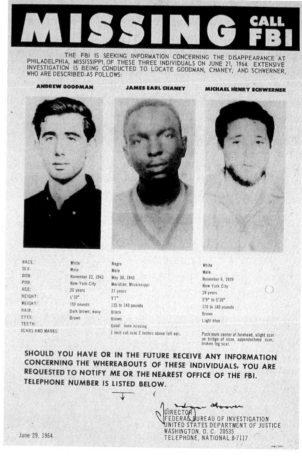

Three Missing Civil Rights Volunteers This poster shows pictures of the three civil rights workers who were missing soon after their arrival in Mississippi in the summer of 1964. What do the pictures tell you about the volunteers? What do you think people at the time would have thought when they saw this poster? *(Getty Images)*

his old colleague, minority leader Everett Dirksen of Illinois, to work for cloture—a two-thirds vote to cut off debate.

The Civil Rights Act of 1964 outlawed racial discrimination in all public accommodations and authorized the Justice Department to act with greater authority in school and voting matters. In addition, an equal-opportunity provision prohibited discriminatory hiring on grounds of race, gender, religion, or national origin in firms with more than 25 employees.

VIDEO

LBJ Signing the Civil Rights Bill

Although the law was one of the great achievements of the 1960s, Johnson realized that it was only a starting point, for widespread discrimination still existed in American society. Even with the voting rights measures of 1957 and 1960, African Americans in large areas of the South still found it difficult to vote. Freedom Summer, sponsored by SNCC and other civil rights groups in 1964, focused attention on the problem by sending black and white students to Mississippi to work for black rights. Early in the summer, two whites, Michael Schwerner and Andrew Goodman, and one black, James Chaney, were murdered. By the end of the summer, 80 workers had been beaten, 1,000 arrests had been made, and 37 churches had been bombed.

DOCUMENT

LBJ, Commencement Address at Howard University (1965)

Early in 1965, another confrontation made national headlines. Alabama police clubbed and tear-gassed demonstrators in an aborted march from Selma to the state capital at Montgomery. President Johnson sent the National Guard to protect another march to Montgomery and then asked Congress for a voting bill that would close the loopholes of the previous two acts.

The Voting Rights Act of 1965, perhaps the most important law of the decade, singled out the South for its restrictive practices and authorized the U.S. attorney general to appoint federal examiners to register voters where local officials were obstructing the registration of blacks. In the year after passage of the act, 400,000 blacks registered to vote in the Deep South; by 1968, the number reached 1 million.

MAP

Impact of the Voting Rights Act of 1965

Despite passage of the Civil Rights Act of 1964 and the Voting Rights Act of 1965, racial discrimination remained throughout the country. Still-segregated schools, wretched housing, and inadequate job opportunities were continuing problems. As the struggle for civil rights moved north, dramatic divisions within the movement emerged.

Initially, the civil rights campaign had been integrated and nonviolent. Its acknowledged leader was Martin Luther King, Jr. But now tensions between blacks and whites flared within organizations, and younger black leaders began to challenge King's nonviolent approach. They were tired of beatings, jailings, church bombings, and the slow pace of change when dependent on white liberal support and government action. Anne Moody, the stalwart activist in Mississippi, voiced the doubts so many blacks harbored about the possibility of real change. Discouraged after months of struggle, she boarded a bus taking civil rights workers north to testify about the abuses that still remained. As she listened to the others singing the movement's songs, she was overwhelmed by the suffering she had so often seen. "We Shall Overcome" reverberated around her, but all she could think was, "I wonder. I really wonder."

One episode that contributed to many blacks' suspicion of white liberals occurred at the Democratic national convention of 1964 in Atlantic City. SNCC, active in the Freedom Summer project in Mississippi, had founded the Freedom Democratic party as an alternative to the all-white delegation that was to represent the state. Testifying before the credentials committee, black activist Fannie Lou Hamer reported that she had been beaten, jailed, and denied the right to vote. Yet the committee's final compromise, pressed by President Johnson, who worried about losing southern support in the coming election, was that the white delegation would still be seated, with two members of the protest organization offered seats at large. That response hardly satisfied those who had risked their lives and families to try to vote in Mississippi. As civil rights leader James Forman observed, "Atlantic City was a powerful lesson, not only for the black people from Mississippi, but for all of SNCC. . . . No longer was there any hope . . . that the federal government would change the situation in the Deep South." SNCC, once a religious, integrated organization, began to change into an all-black cadre that could mobilize poor blacks for militant action. "Liberation" replaced civil rights as a goal.

Increasingly, angry blacks argued that the nation must no longer withhold the rights pledged in its founding credo. Black author James Baldwin wrote in one of his eloquent essays that unless change came soon, the worst could be expected: "If we do not now dare everything, the fulfillment of that prophecy, recreated from the Bible in song by a slave, is upon us: God gave Noah the rainbow sign, No more water, the fire next time!"

Even more responsible for channeling black frustration into a new set of goals and tactics was Malcolm X. Born Malcolm Little and reared in ghettos

American Voices

Anne Moody, From
Coming of Age in Mississippi

Anne Moody grew up in a poor black family in Mississippi. A bright student, she graduated from high school and won a scholarship to Natchez College, then went on to Tougaloo College. While in secondary school, she became aware of the National Association for the Advancement of Colored People (NAACP), and then in college, she did volunteer work for the Student Nonviolent Coordinating Committee (SNCC).

Things didn't seem to be coming along too well in the Delta. On Saturdays we would spend all day canvassing and often at night we would have mass rallies. But these were usually poorly attended. Many Negroes were afraid to come. In the beginning some were even afraid to talk to us. Most of these old plantation Negroes had been brainwashed so by the whites, they really thought that only whites were supposed to vote. There were even a few who had never heard of voting. The only thing most of them knew was how to handle a hoe. For years they had demonstrated how well they could do that. Some of them had calluses on their hands so thick they would hide them if they noticed you looking at them. . . .

As the work continued that summer, people began to come around. I guess they saw that our intentions were good. But some began getting fired from their jobs, thrown off plantations and left homeless. They could often find somewhere else to stay, but food and clothing became a problem. SNCC started to send representatives to Northern college campuses. They went begging for food, clothing and money for the people in Mississippi, and the food, clothing and money started coming in. The Delta Negroes still didn't understand the voting, but they knew they had found friends, friends they could trust.

That summer I could feel myself beginning to change. For the first time I began to think something would be done about whites killing, beating, and misusing Negroes. I knew I was going to be a part of whatever happened.

- *Why were some African Americans afraid to become too friendly with the civil rights workers, black or white?*

- *Why were some Mississippi blacks afraid to vote?*

- *What gave Anne Moody a sense of confidence that conditions could change?*

---

from Detroit to New York, he hustled numbers and prostitutes in the big cities. Arrested and imprisoned, he became a convert to the Nation of Islam and a disciple of black leader Elijah Muhammad. He began to preach that the white man was responsible for the black man's condition and that blacks had to help themselves.

Malcolm was impatient with the moderate civil rights movement. He grew tired of hearing "all of this non-violent, begging-the-white-man kind of dying . . . all of this sitting-in, sliding-in, wading-in, eating-in, diving-in, and all the rest." Espousing black separatism and black nationalism for most of his public career, he argued for black control of black communities, preached an international perspective embracing African peoples in diaspora, and appealed to blacks to fight racism "by any means necessary."

Malcolm X became the most dynamic spokesman for poor northern blacks since Marcus Garvey in the 1920s. Though he was assassinated by black antagonists in 1965, his African-centered, uncompromising perspective helped shape the struggle against racism.

One man influenced by Malcolm's message was Stokely Carmichael. Born in Trinidad, he came to the United States at age 11, where he grew up with an interest in political affairs and black protest. While at Howard University, he participated in pickets and demonstrations and was beaten and jailed. Frustrated with the strategy of civil disobedience as he became active in SNCC, he urged fieldworkers to carry weapons for self-defense. It was time for blacks to cease depending on whites, he argued, and to make SNCC into a black organization. His election as head of the student group reflected SNCC's growing radicalism.

The split in the black movement was dramatized in June 1966 when Carmichael's followers challenged those of Martin Luther King, Jr., during a march in Mississippi. King still adhered to nonviolence and

VIDEO

Malcolm X

Malcolm X at the Lectern "The day of nonviolence is over," Malcolm X proclaimed, as many African Americans listened enthusiastically. A compelling speaker, Malcolm made a powerful case for a more aggressive campaign for black rights. What image does Malcolm X convey in this photograph? *(Bettmann/CORBIS)*

interracial cooperation. Just out of jail after being arrested for his protest activities, Carmichael jumped onto a flatbed truck to address the group. "This is the twenty-seventh time I have been arrested—and I ain't going to jail no more!" he shouted. "The only way we gonna stop them white men from whippin' us is to take over. We been saying freedom for six years and we ain't got nothing. What we gonna start saying now is Black Power!" Carmichael had the audience in his hand as he repeated, and the crowd shouted back, "We . . . want . . . Black . . . Power!"

DOCUMENT

Stokely Carmichael, Black Power (1967)

Black Power was a call to build independent institutions in the African American community and to end the physical and sexual abuse of black women. It also fostered a powerful sense of black pride. The movement included a wide variety of different figures: cultural nationalists such as Maulana Ron Karenga, an activist scholar and early authority on Black Studies; advocates of black capitalism such as Nathan Wright, Jr., chairman of the 1967 and 1968 National and International Conferences on Black

Power; and revolutionary nationalists such as Huey P. Newton, a proponent of aggressive liberation measures. Its most enduring legacy was political and cultural mobilization at the grassroots level, even if it only partially realized its goals.

Black Power led to demands for more drastic action. The Black Panthers, radical activists who organized first in Oakland, California, and then in other cities, formed a militant organization that vowed to eradicate not only racial discrimination but capitalism as well. H. Rap Brown, who succeeded Carmichael as head of SNCC, became known for his statement that "violence is as American as cherry pie."

DOCUMENT

Reports from the Commission on the Los Angeles (Watts) Riots (1965)

Violence accompanied the more militant calls for reform and showed that racial injustice was not a southern problem but an American one. Riots erupted in Rochester, New York City, and several New Jersey cities in 1964. In 1965, in the Watts neighborhood of Los Angeles, a massive uprising lasting five days left 34 dead, more than 1,000 injured, and hundreds of structures burned to the ground. Violence broke out again in other cities in 1966, 1967, and 1968.

A Sympathetic Supreme Court

With the addition of four new liberal justices appointed by Kennedy and Johnson, the Supreme Court supported and promoted the liberal agenda. Under the leadership of chief justice Earl Warren, the Court followed the lead it had taken in *Brown* v. *Board of Education* outlawing school segregation by moving against Jim Crow practices in other public establishments.

The Court also supported civil liberties by beginning to protect the rights of individuals with radical political views. Similarly, the Court sought to protect accused suspects from police harassment. In *Gideon* v. *Wainwright* (1963), the justices decided that poor defendants in serious cases had the right to free legal counsel. In *Escobedo* v. *Illinois* (1964), they ruled that a suspect had to be given access to an attorney during questioning. In *Miranda* v. *Arizona* (1966), they argued that offenders had to be warned that statements extracted by the police could be used against them and that they could remain silent.

Other decisions similarly broke new ground. *Baker* v. *Carr* (1962) opened the way to reapportionment of state legislative bodies according to the standard, defined a year later in Justice William O. Douglas's words, of "one person, one vote." This crucial ruling helped break the political control of lightly populated rural districts in many state assemblies and made the U.S. House of Representatives much more responsive to urban and suburban issues. Meanwhile, the Court outraged conservatives by ruling that prayer could not be required in the public schools and that obscenity laws could no longer restrict allegedly pornographic material that might have some "redeeming social value."

The Great Society Under Attack

Supported by healthy economic growth, the Great Society worked for a few years as Johnson had hoped. The tax cut proved effective, and the consumer and business spending that it promoted led to a steady increase in the gross national product (GNP) of 7.1 percent in 1964, 8.1 percent in 1965, and 9.5 percent in 1966. As the economy improved, the budget deficit dropped just as predicted. Unemployment fell, and inflation remained under control. Medical programs provided basic security for the old and the poor. Education flourished as schools were built, and teachers' salaries increased as a result of the influx of federal aid.

Yet Johnson's dream of the Great Society proved illusory. Some programs promised too much; others were simply ill conceived or were underfunded. Factionalism was also a problem. Lyndon Johnson had reconstituted the old Democratic coalition in his triumph in 1964, with urban Catholics and southern whites joining organized labor, the black electorate, and the middle class. But diverse interests within the coalition soon clashed. Conservative white southerners and blue-collar white northerners felt threatened by the government's support of civil rights. Local urban bosses, long the backbone of the Democratic party, objected to grassroots participation of the urban poor, which threatened their own political control.

Criticisms of the Great Society and its liberal underpinnings came from across the political spectrum. There had never been widespread popular enthusiasm for much of the effort. Conservatives disliked the centralization of authority and the government's increased role in defining the national welfare. They also questioned involving the poor in reform programs, arguing that poor people lacked a broad vision of the nation's needs. Even middle-class Americans, generally supportive of liberal goals, sometimes grumbled that the government was paying too much attention to the underprivileged and neglecting the needs of the middle class.

Radicals, meanwhile, attacked the Great Society for not going far enough. They challenged its assumption that the American system was basically sound. "The welfare state is more machinery than substance," activist Tom Hayden declared, in suggesting that it was just a warmed-over version of the New Deal. It made no real effort to redistribute income which, in the radicals' view, was the only way to transform American life.

The Vietnam War dealt the Great Society a fatal blow. LBJ wanted to maintain both the war and his treasured domestic reform programs, but his effort to pursue these goals simultaneously produced serious inflation. The economy was already booming as a result of the tax cut and the spending for reform. As military expenditures increased, the productive system of the country could not keep up with demand. When Johnson refused to raise taxes, in an effort to hide the costs of the war, inflation spiraled out of control. Congress finally got into the act and slashed Great Society programs. As hard economic choices became increasingly necessary, many decided the country could no longer afford social reform on the scale that Johnson had proposed.

CONTINUING CONFRONTATIONS WITH COMMUNISTS

The Cold War continued throughout the 1960s. Presidents John F. Kennedy and Lyndon B. Johnson were both aggressive cold warriors who subscribed to the policies of their predecessors. Their commitment to stopping the spread of communism kept the nation locked in the same bitter conflict that had dominated foreign policy in the 1950s and led to continuing global confrontations that sometimes threatened the stability of the entire world.

The Bay of Pigs Fiasco and Its Consequences

Kennedy was intensely interested in foreign affairs. In his ringing inaugural address, his major focus was on diplomacy, and he barely mentioned domestic issues. In the midst of the Cold War, he was determined to stand firm in the face of Russian power. During the campaign, he had declared: "The enemy is the communist system itself—implacable, insatiable, unceasing in its drive for world domination." In his inaugural address, he eloquently described the dangers and challenges the United States faced. "In the long history of the world," he cried out, "only a few generations have been granted the role of defending freedom in its hour of maximum danger." The United States would "pay any price, bear any burden, meet any hardship, support any friend, oppose any foe, to assure the survival and success of liberty."

Kennedy perceived direct challenges from the Soviet Union almost from the beginning of his presidency. The first came at the Bay of Pigs in Cuba in the spring of 1961. Cuban–American relations had been strained since Fidel Castro's revolutionary army had seized power in 1959. A radical regime in Cuba, leaning toward the Soviet Union, could provide a model for upheaval elsewhere in Latin America and threaten the venerable Monroe Doctrine. One initiative to counter the Communist threat was the Alliance for Progress, which provided social and economic assistance to the less-developed nations of the hemisphere. But other, more aggressive, responses were deemed necessary as well.

Just before Kennedy assumed office, the United States broke diplomatic relations with Cuba. The CIA, meanwhile, was covertly training anti-Castro exiles to storm the Cuban coast at the Bay of Pigs. The American planners assumed the invasion would lead to an uprising of the Cuban people against Castro. While some top officials resisted the scheme, Kennedy approved the plan.

The invasion, which took place on April 17, 1961, was an unmitigated disaster. When an early air strike failed to destroy Cuban air power, Castro was able to hold off the troops coming ashore. Urged to use American planes for air cover, Kennedy refused, for by that time failure was clear. Rather than supporting the exiles, the Cubans had followed Castro instead, and the predicted popular uprising never materialized. The United States stood exposed to the world, attempting to overthrow a sovereign government. It had broken agreements not to interfere in the internal affairs of hemispheric neighbors and had intervened clumsily and unsuccessfully.

Although chastened by the debacle at the Bay of Pigs, Kennedy remained determined to deal sternly with the perceived Communist threat. Germany became the next battleground. For more than a decade, the nation had been divided (see Chapter 27). The Western powers had promoted the industrial development of West Germany, which was prospering and which stood in stark contrast to the drab, Soviet-controlled East Germany. Berlin, likewise divided, remained an irritant to the Russians, particularly since some 2.6 million East Germans had fled to West Germany, many of them making their escape through the city. Following a hostile

The Berlin Wall   The wall built by the Soviet Union bifurcated Berlin. Here, in this photograph taken in 1961, a hand rises from the eastern side of the wall. What is the impact of seeing the hand at the top of the wall? How hard or easy does it appear to have been to cross the wall and get to the other side? *(Time Life Pictures/Getty Images)*

meeting with Soviet leader Nikita Khrushchev in Vienna in June 1961 (where discussion centered on the question of a permanent settlement for the bifurcated city of Berlin to prevent the flow of East Germany refugees), Kennedy reacted aggressively. He asked Congress for $3 billion more in defense appropriations, for more personnel in the armed forces, and for funds for a civil defense fallout-shelter program, explicitly warning of the threat of nuclear war. The USSR responded in August by erecting a wall in Berlin to seal off its section of the city entirely. The concrete structure, topped by barbed wife, was 96 miles long and an average of 11.8 feet high. Menacing machine-gun emplacements made escape difficult. People who were caught scaling the wall were shot. Families were separated as the wall became a dramatic symbol of the division between East and West.

DOCUMENT

JFK, Address to the People of Berlin (June 28, 1963)

The Cuban Missile Face-Off

The next year, a new crisis arose. Understandably fearful of the American threat to Cuban independence after the Bay of Pigs invasion, Fidel Castro sought and secured Soviet assistance. American aerial photographs taken in October 1962 revealed that the USSR had begun to place what Kennedy considered offensive missiles on Cuban soil, although Cuba insisted they were defensive. The missiles did not

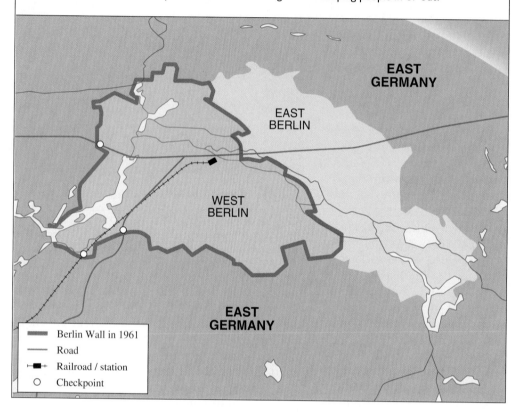

The Berlin Wall

The Berlin Wall effectively sealed West Berlin off both from the eastern sector of the city and from East Germany itself. Now people could only enter and exit West Berlin through a number of carefully monitored checkpoints. **Reflecting on the Past** Why was it so important for East Germany to prevent people from going into West Berlin? Why would people in West Berlin have wanted to go into East Berlin? How effective do you think such a wall might be in keeping people in or out?

Legend:
- Berlin Wall in 1961
- Road
- Railroad / station
- ○ Checkpoint

change the strategic balance significantly, for the Soviets could still wreak untold damage on American targets from more distant bases. But with Russian weapons installed just 90 miles from American shores, appearance was more important than reality. This time Kennedy was determined to win a confrontation with the Soviet Union over Cuba.

Top administration officials discussed various alternatives. Some members of the Executive Committee of the National Security Council wanted an air strike to knock out the sites; others, including Attorney General Robert Kennedy, the president's brother, opposed such a move. Still, the United States moved to a state of full alert. Bombers and missiles were armed with nuclear weapons and readied to go. The fleet prepared to move toward Cuba, and troops geared up to invade the island.

Kennedy went on nationwide television to tell the American people about the missiles and to demand their removal. He declared that the United States would not shrink from the risk of nuclear war and announced what he had decided to do: impose a naval "quarantine"—not a blockade, which would have been an act of war— around Cuba to prevent Soviet ships from bringing in additional missiles.

As the Soviet ships steamed toward the blockade and the nations stood "eyeball to eyeball" at the brink, the world held its breath. After several days, the tension broke, but only because Khrushchev called the Soviet ships back. Khrushchev then sent a long letter, transmitted by teletype, to Kennedy pledging to remove the missiles if the United States lifted the quarantine and promised to stay out of Cuba altogether. A second letter demanded that America remove its missiles from Turkey as well. The United States agreed to the first letter, ignored the second, and said nothing about its intention, already voiced, of removing its own missiles from Turkey. With that, the crisis ended. Secretary of State Dean Rusk observed, "We have won a considerable victory. You and I are still alive."

DOCUMENT

Executive Decisions on the Cuban Missile Crisis (1962)

VIDEO

President Kennedy and the Cuban Missile Crisis

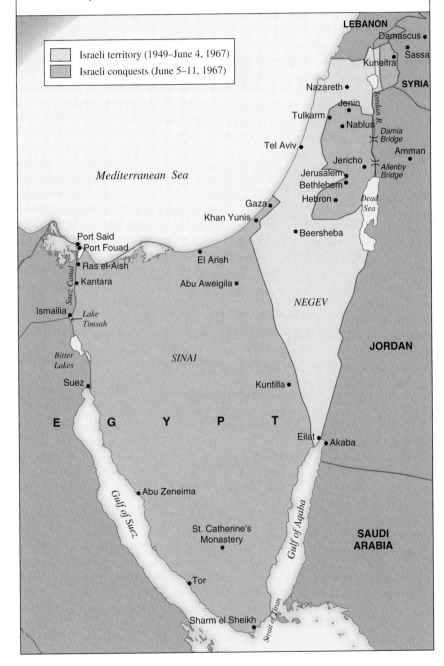

Israeli Conquests in 1967

The Six-Day War of 1967 ended in huge Israeli territorial gains, both in the Sinai and on the West Bank of the Jordan River. **Reflecting on the Past** How did the new territory compare with the size of the state of Israel prior to 1967? What effect did the Israeli victory have on the stability of the Middle East? How would the Arab nations have responded to the defeat?

Israeli territory (1949–June 4, 1967)
Israeli conquests (June 5–11, 1967)

VIDEO

The Cuban
Missile Crisis

The Cuban missile crisis was the most terrifying confrontation of the Cold War. The world was closer than it had ever been to nuclear war. Yet the president emerged from it as a hero who had stood firm. His reputation was enhanced, and his party benefited a few weeks later in the congressional elections. As the relief began to fade, however, critics charged that what Kennedy saw as his finest hour was in fact an unnecessary crisis. One consequence of the affair was the installation of a Soviet–American hotline to avoid similar episodes in the future. Another consequence was the USSR's determination to increase its nuclear arsenal so that it would never again be exposed as inferior to the United States. Despite the Limited Test Ban Treaty of 1963, which prohibited atmospheric testing, the nuclear arms race continued.

Confrontation and Containment Under Johnson

Johnson shared many of Kennedy's assumptions about the threat of communism. His understanding of the onset of World War II led him to believe that aggressors had to be stopped before they committed more aggression, for "if you let a bully come into your front yard one day, the next day he'll be up on your porch and the day after that he'll rape your wife in your own bed." Like Eisenhower and Kennedy, Johnson believed in the domino theory: if one country in a region fell, others were bound to follow. He assumed he could treat foreign adversaries just as he treated political opponents in the United States, and he was frustrated with what he called "piddly little piss-ant" countries that caused trouble.

In 1965, Johnson dispatched more than 20,000 troops to the Dominican Republic to counter "Castro-type elements" that were, in fact, engaged in a democratic revolution. His credibility suffered badly from the episode.

In the Middle East, the United States sought to use its influence to temper the violence that erupted in the area. In 1967, Israeli forces defeated the Egyptian army in the Six-Day War and seized the West Bank and Jerusalem, the Golan Heights, and the Sinai Peninsula. Americans pressed for a quick end to the fighting to maintain regional equilibrium and uninterrupted supplies of oil.

WAR IN VIETNAM AND TURMOIL AT HOME

The commitment to stopping the spread of communism led to the massive U.S. involvement in Vietnam. The roots of the conflict, described in Chapter 26, extended back to the early post–World War II years, but American participation remained relatively limited until Kennedy took office. Then the United States became increasingly engaged in the effort to resist a Communist takeover. That struggle wrought enormous damage in Southeast Asia, tore the United States apart, and finally forced a full-fledged re-evaluation of America's Cold War policies.

Escalation in Vietnam

JFK's commitment to Cold War victory led him to expand the American role in Vietnam, the country

A Protest in Vietnam In 1963, Buddhist priests in Vietnam burned themselves to death in Saigon to dramatize their opposition to the Diem government. Photographs in American newspapers horrified readers and created suspicion that South Vietnam was led by a corrupt and autocratic leader. Why would this photograph have affected people who saw it so strongly? *(Bettmann/CORBIS)*

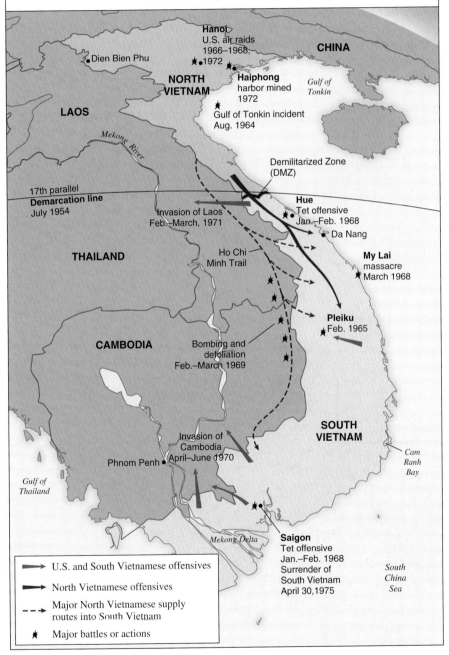

The Vietnam War

This map shows the major campaigns of the Vietnam War. The North Vietnamese Tet offensive of early 1968, pictured with red arrows, turned the tide against U.S. participation in the war and led to peace talks. The U.S. invasion of Cambodia in 1970, pictured with blue arrows, provoked serious opposition. **Reflecting on the Past** What role did North Vietnam play in the war? How far did American air power penetrate? Why did the United States and South Vietnam attack neighboring nations, such as Cambodia?

Dien Bien Phu

Hanoi
U.S. air raids
1966–1968,
★●1972

CHINA

NORTH
VIETNAM

Haiphong
harbor mined
1972

Gulf of
Tonkin

LAOS

Mekong River

Gulf of Tonkin incident
Aug. 1964

Demilitarized Zone
(DMZ)

17th parallel
Demarcation line
July 1954

Invasion of Laos
Feb.–March, 1971

Hue
Tet offensive
Jan.–Feb. 1968

Da Nang

THAILAND

Ho Chi
Minh Trail

My Lai
massacre
★ March 1968

CAMBODIA

Bombing and
defoliation
Feb.–March 1969

Pleiku
★ Feb. 1965

SOUTH
VIETNAM

Cam
Ranh
Bay

Invasion of
Cambodia
April–June 1970

Phnom Penh

Gulf of
Thailand

Mekong Delta

Saigon
Tet offensive
Jan.–Feb. 1968
Surrender of
South Vietnam
April 30,1975

South
China
Sea

➤ U.S. and South Vietnamese offensives

➤ North Vietnamese offensives

--➤ Major North Vietnamese supply
routes into South Vietnam

★ Major battles or actions

Analyzing History

The Vietnam War

The war in Vietnam consumed both soldiers and resources. The rapid escalation was accompanied by a mounting protest movement back in the United States that peaked when the troop involvement was greatest. Meanwhile, American planes and helicopters did devastating damage to the rice paddies and palm groves of this faraway land.

REFLECTING ON THE PAST   Why did the rapid buildup cause such intense protest at home? What effects did the bombs have on the Vietnamese? Why did the number of troops diminish after 1968?

BOMBING OF NORTH VIETNAM (BOMBING TONNAGE DROPPED)

659	892	1,842	218,561	15,347
1969	1970	1971	1972	1973

6,162,000 tons

2,150,000 tons

WWII (1941–45)   VIETNAM WAR (1965–73)

BOMBS DROPPED BY U.S. AIRCRAFT IN WORLD WAR II VS. VIETNAM WAR

The United States launched a massive bombing campaign aimed at targets in both North and South Vietnam. Note how the tonnage dropped in the Vietnam War compared to the tonnage dropped in World War II.

U.S. TROOPS IN VIETNAM, 1965–1973

Number of Troops (in 100,000s)

Peace talks begin

Nixon takes office

U.S. Pullout

1965 1966 1967 1968 1969 1970 1971 1972 1973

The number of American troops in Vietnam increased quickly once escalation began. By the time there were more than half a million U.S. soldiers involved, many Americans were actively engaged in protesting the war.

American policy was to stop the spread of communism from North Vietnam to South Vietnam.

960

he once called the "cornerstone of the free world in Southeast Asia." Now resolved to resist the spread of communism, Kennedy and his closest associates were confident of success. As Secretary of Defense Robert McNamara observed, "North Vietnam will never beat us. They can't even make ice cubes." During the Kennedy administration, the number of advisers rose from 675 to more than 16,000, and American soldiers were already losing their lives.

Despite American backing, South Vietnamese leader Ngo Dinh Diem, a Catholic, was rapidly losing support in his own country. Buddhist priests burned themselves alive in the capital of Saigon to protest the corruption and arbitrariness of Diem's regime. With the approval of the United States, South Vietnamese military leaders assassinated Diem and seized the government. Kennedy understood the importance of popular support for the South Vietnamese government if that country was to maintain its independence. But he was reluctant to withdraw and let the Vietnamese solve their own problems.

Lyndon Johnson shared the same reservations and, soon after assuming the presidency, he made a fundamental decision that guided policy for the next four years. South Vietnam was more unstable than ever after the assassination of Diem. Guerrillas, known as Viet Cong, challenged the regime, sometimes covertly and sometimes through the National Liberation Front, their political arm. Aided by Ho Chi Minh and the North Vietnamese, the insurgent Viet Cong slowly gained ground, but Johnson chose to stand firm. "I am not going to lose Vietnam," he said. "I am not going to be the President who saw Southeast Asia go the way China went."

In the 1964 election campaign, Johnson posed as a man of peace. "We don't want our American boys to do the fighting for Asian boys," he declared. "We are not going to send American boys nine or ten thousand miles away from home to do what Asian boys ought to be doing for themselves." He criticized those who suggested moving in with American bombs. But secretly he was planning to escalate the American role.

In August 1964, Johnson cleverly obtained congressional authorization for the war by announcing that North Vietnamese torpedo boats had made unprovoked attacks on American destroyers in the international waters of the Gulf of Tonkin, 30 miles from North Vietnam. Only later did it become clear that the American ships had violated the territorial waters of North Vietnam by assisting South Vietnamese commando raids in offshore combat zones. With the details of the attack still unclear, Johnson used the episode to obtain from Congress a resolution giving him authority to "take all necessary measures to repel any armed attack against the forces of the United States and to prevent further aggression." The Gulf of Tonkin resolution gave Johnson the leverage he sought. As he noted, it was "like grandma's nightshirt—it covered everything."

DOCUMENT
LBJ, Gulf of Tonkin Resolution (1964)

Military escalation began in earnest in February 1965, after Johnson's landslide electoral victory, when Viet Cong forces killed 7 Americans and wounded 109 in an attack on an American base at Pleiku. In response, Johnson authorized retaliatory bombing of North Vietnam to cut off the flow of supplies and to ease pressure on South Vietnam. He personally authorized every raid, boasting that the air force "can't even bomb an outhouse without my approval." A few months later, the president sent American ground troops into action. This marked the crucial turning point in the Americanization of the Vietnam War. Only 25,000 American soldiers were in Vietnam at the start of 1965; by the end of the year, there were 184,000. The number swelled to 385,000 in 1966, to 485,000 in 1967, and to 543,000 in 1968.

DOCUMENT
LBJ's Defense of the U.S. Presence in Vietnam (1965)

As escalation occurred, Johnson recognized his dilemma. He understood that the war was probably unwinnable, but he feared the loss of both American power and personal prestige if he pulled out. "Vietnam is getting worse every day," he told his wife in mid-1965. "It's like being in an airplane and I have to choose between crashing the plane or jumping out. I do not have a parachute."

And so American forces became direct participants in the fight to prop up a dictatorial regime in faraway South Vietnam. Although a somewhat more effective government headed by Nguyen Van Thieu and Nguyen Cao Ky was finally established, the level of violence increased. Saturation bombing of North Vietnam continued. Fragmentation bombs, killing and maiming countless civilians, and napalm, which seared off human flesh, were used extensively. Similar destruction wracked South Vietnam. And still, despite the repeatedly expressed contention of military commander William Westmoreland that there was "light at the end of the tunnel," the violence continued without pause.

IMAGE
LBJ in Vietnam, 1966

The Horror of Napalm
Napalm, a jellylike chemical dropped by American planes, stuck to people as it burned. In this picture, widely circulated throughout the world, a small girl whose skin was seared off by napalm tries unsuccessfully to escape the ravages of war. Why was this image so powerful? What do you feel when you look at it? *(AP/Wide World Photos)*

Student Activism and Antiwar Protest

Americans began to protest U.S. involvement in the war. Their protest had roots in a deeper disaffection, based in large part on post–World War II demographic patterns. Members of the baby boom generation came of age in the 1960s, and many of them, especially from the large middle class, moved on to some form of higher education. Between 1950 and 1964, the number of students in college more than doubled. By the end of the 1960s, college enrollment was more than four times what it had been in the 1940s. College served as a training ground for industry and corporate life; more important, it gave students time to experiment and grow before they had to make a living. In college, some students joined the struggle for civil rights. Hopeful at first, they gradually became discouraged by the gap between Kennedy's New Frontier rhetoric and the government's actual commitment.

Out of that disillusionment arose the radical spirit of the New Left. Civil rights activists were among those who in 1960 organized Students for a Democratic Society (SDS). In 1962, SDS issued a manifesto, the *Port Huron Statement,* written largely by Tom Hayden of the University of Michigan, which outlined both complaints and goals for a participatory democracy.

The first blow of the growing student rebellion came at the University of California in Berkeley. There, civil rights activists became involved in a confrontation soon known as the Free Speech Movement. It began in September 1964 when the university refused to allow students to distribute protest material outside the main campus gate. The students, many of whom had worked in the movement in the South, argued that their tables were off campus and therefore not subject to university restrictions on political activity. When police arrested one of the leaders, students surrounded the police car and kept it from moving all night. The university regents brought charges against the student leaders, and when the regents refused to drop the charges, the students occupied the administration building. The police stormed in and arrested the students. A strike, with faculty aid, mobilized wider support for the right to free speech.

The Free Speech Movement at Berkeley was basically a plea for traditional liberal reform. Students sought only the reaffirmation of the long-standing right to express themselves as they chose, and they aimed their attacks at the university, not at society as a whole. Later, in other institutions, the attack broadened. Students sought greater involvement in university affairs, argued for curriculum reform, and demanded admission of more minority students. Their success in gaining their demands changed the governance of American higher education.

AMERICAN VOICES

Tom Hayden and Other Members of Students for a Democratic Society, *Port Huron Statement*

Tom Hayden was a leader of the radical group, Students for a Democratic Society, one of the major New Left organizations of the 1960s. This manifesto, issued in 1962, summed up the critique of modern American society and outlined the kind of approach to government the students wanted.

We are people of this generation, bred in at least modest comfort, housed now in universities, looking uncomfortably to the world we inherit.

When we were kids the United States was the wealthiest and strongest country in the world; . . .

As we grew, however, our comfort was penetrated by events too troubling to dismiss. First, the permeating and victimizing fact of human degradation, symbolized by the Southern struggle against racial bigotry, compelled most of us from silence to activism. Second, the enclosing fact of the Cold War, symbolized by the presence of the Bomb, brought awareness that we ourselves, and our friends, and millions of abstract "others" we knew more directly because of our common peril, might die at any time. . . .

Loneliness, estrangement, isolation describe the vast distance between man and man today. . . .

We would replace power rooted in possession, privilege, or circumstance by power and uniqueness rooted in love, reflectiveness, reason, and creativity. As a *social system* we seek the establishment of a democracy of individual participation, governed by two central aims: that the individual share in those social decisions determining the quality and direction of his life; that society be organized to encourage independence in men and provide the media for their common participation. . . .

- According to Tom Hayden, what issues troubled young people as they grew up in the 1950s and 1960s?

- Why does Hayden suggest that isolation and estrangement are such powerful forces?

- What does Hayden mean by a "democracy of individual participation"?

The mounting protest against the escalation of the Vietnam War fueled and refocused the youth movement. The first antiwar teach-in took place in March 1965 at the University of Michigan. Others soon followed. Initially, both supporters and opponents of the war appeared at the teach-ins, but soon the sessions became more like antiwar rallies than instructional affairs.

VIDEO
Protests Against the Vietnam War

Boxer Muhammad Ali legitimated draft resistance when he declared, "I ain't got no quarrel with them Viet Cong," and refused military induction. Working through SDS and other organizations, radical activists campaigned against the draft, attacked ROTC units on campus, and sought to discredit firms that produced the destructive tools of war. "Make love, not war," students proclaimed.

The antiwar movement expanded. Women Strike for Peace, the most forceful women's antiwar organization, mobilized support by saying, "Stop! Don't drench the jungles of Asia with the blood of our sons. Don't force our sons to kill women and children whose only crime is to live in a country ripped by civil war." Students became even more shrill. "Hey, hey, LBJ. How many kids did you kill today?" they chanted. In 1967, some 300,000 people marched in New York City. In Washington, D.C., 100,000 tried to close down the Pentagon.

Working-class and middle-class Americans began to sour on the war at the time of the Tet offensive, celebrating the lunar new year in early 1968. The North Vietnamese mounted a massive attack on provincial capitals and district towns in South Vietnam. In Saigon, they struck the American embassy, Tan Son Nhut air base, and the presidential palace. Though beaten back, they won a psychological victory. American audiences watched the fighting on television, as they had for several years, seeing images of burning huts and wounded soldiers each evening as they ate dinner.

IMAGE
Protestors and Military Police, 1967

During the Tet offensive, American television networks showed scenes of a kind never screened before. One such clip, from NBC News, appears here in still photograph form. Viewers who watched the television clip saw the corpse drop to the ground, blood spouting from his head. Gazing at such graphic representations of death and destruction, many Americans wondered about their nation's purposes and actions—indeed, about whether the war could be won.

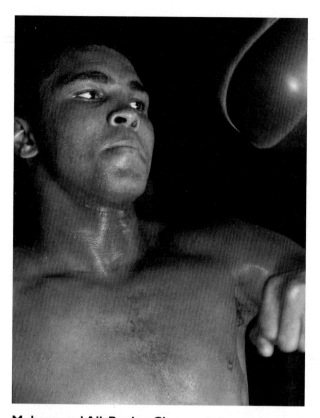

Muhammad Ali: Boxing Champ Muhammad Ali, one of the best boxers in history, liked to say he could "float like a butterfly, sting like a bee." When he refused army induction on the basis of his religious beliefs, the case eventually reached the Supreme Court, which decided in his favor. Allowed to box again, he regained his heavyweight title and served as a model to many African Americans. Why was Ali's resistance so important to the black community? *(Thomas Hoepker/Magnum Photos)*

Protest became a way of life. Between January 1 and June 15, 1968, hundreds of thousands of students staged 221 major demonstrations at more than 100 educational institutions. One of the most dramatic episodes came in April 1968 at Columbia University, where the issues of civil rights and war were tightly intertwined. A strong SDS chapter urged the university to break ties with the Institute of Defense Analysis, which specialized in military research. The Students' Afro-American Society tried to stop the building of a new gymnasium, which it claimed encroached on the Harlem community and disrupted life there. Whites occupied one building, blacks another. Finally, the president of the university called in the police. Hundreds of students were arrested; many were hurt. A student sympathy strike followed, and Columbia closed for the summer several weeks early.

The student protests in the United States were part of a worldwide wave of student activism. French students demonstrated in the streets of Paris. In Germany, young radicals such as Rudi Dutschke and Ulrike Meinhof were equally vocal in challenging conventional norms. In Japan, students waged armed battles with police.

The Counterculture

Cultural change accompanied political upheaval. In the 1960s, many Americans, particularly young people, lost faith in the sanctity of the American system.

Death of a Viet Cong Suspect In this picture, General Nguyen Ngoc Loan, the chief of the South Vietnamese National Police, looks at a Viet Cong prisoner, lifts his gun, and calmly blows out the captive's brains. This prize-winning photograph captured the horror of the war for many Americans. What impressions do you think this picture conveyed to people who saw it? *(AP/Wide World Photos)*

Pop Art Andy Warhol's painting of a Campbell's soup can was one of the best-known examples of "pop" art in the 1960s. Warhol and other artists drew on advertising images, comic strips, and other elements of popular culture in their painting and sculpture. What does this image tell you about the changing art world? *(Andy Warhol,* Campbell's Soup Can. *© SuperStock, Inc./SuperStock/© 2007 Andy Warhol Foundation/ARS, NY/™ Licensed by Campbell's Soup Co. All Rights Reserved.)*

"There was," observed Joseph Heller, the irreverent author of *Catch-22* (1961), "a general feeling that the platitudes of Americanism were horseshit." Many Americans—some politically active, some not—found new ways to assert their individuality and independence. As in the political sphere, the young led the way, often drawing on the example of the Beats of the 1950s as they sought new means of self-gratification and self-expression.

Surface appearances were most visible and, to older Americans, most troubling. The "hippies" of the 1960s carried themselves in different ways. Men let their hair grow and sprouted beards; men and women both donned jeans, muslin shirts, and other simple garments. Stressing spontaneity above all else, some rejected traditional marital customs and gravitated to communal living groups. Their example, shocking to some, soon found its way into the culture at large, both in the United States and among young people around the world.

Sexual norms underwent a revolution as more people separated sex from its traditional ties to family life. A generation of young women came of age with access to "the pill"—an oral contraceptive that was effortless to use and freed sexual experimentation from the threat of pregnancy. In 1960, the Food and Drug Administration approved Enovid, the first oral contraceptive available on the market. Within three years of its introduction, more than 2 million women were on the pill, and as the cost dropped, millions more began to use it.

Americans of all social classes became more open to exploring, and enjoying, their sexuality. Scholarly findings supported natural inclinations. In 1966, William H. Masters and Virginia E. Johnson published *Human Sexual Response,* based on intensive laboratory observation of couples engaged in sexual activities. Describing the kinds of response that women, as well as men, could experience, they destroyed the myth of the sexually passive woman.

Author and editor Nora Ephron summed up the sexual changes in the 1960s as she reflected on her own experiences. Initially she had "a hangover from the whole Fifties virgin thing," she recalled. "The first man I went to bed with, I was in love with and wanted to marry. The second one I was in love with, but I didn't have to marry him. With the third one, I thought I might fall in love."

The arts reflected the sexual revolution. Federal courts ruled that books like D. H. Lawrence's *Lady Chatterley's Lover* and other suppressed works could not be banned. Nudity became more common on stage and screen. In *Hair,* a rock musical, one scene featured the disrobing of performers of both genders in the course of an erotic celebration.

Paintings reflected both the mood of dissent and the urge to innovate, apparent in the larger society. "Op" artists painted sharply defined geometric figures in clear, vibrant colors, starkly different from the flowing, chaotic work of the abstract expressionists. "Pop" artists such as Andy Warhol, Roy Lichtenstein, and Jasper Johns broke with formalistic artistic conventions as they made ironic comments on American materialism and taste with their representations of everyday objects such as soup cans, comic strips, and pictures of Marilyn Monroe.

Hallucinogenic drugs also became a part of the counterculture. One prophet of the drug scene was Timothy Leary, a scientific researcher experimenting with LSD at Harvard University. Fired for violating a pledge not to use undergraduates as subjects, Leary aggressively asserted that drugs were necessary to free the mind. Working through his group, the League for Spiritual Discovery, he dressed in long robes and preached his message, "Tune in, turn on, drop out."

AUDIO
"Going Out"

Another apostle of life with drugs was Ken Kesey. While writing his first novel, *One Flew Over the Cuckoo's Nest,* he began participating in medical experiments at a hospital where he was introduced to

LSD. With the profits from his novel, Kesey established a commune of "Merry Pranksters" near Palo Alto, California. In 1964, the group headed east in a converted school bus painted in psychedelic Day-Glo colors, wired for sound, and stocked with enough orange juice and "acid" (LSD) to sustain the Pranksters across the continent.

Drug use was no longer confined to urban subcultures of musicians, artists, and the streetwise. Soldiers brought experience with drugs back from Vietnam. Young professionals began experimenting with cocaine as a stimulant. Taking a "tab" of LSD became part of the coming-of-age ritual for many middle-class college students. Marijuana became phenomenally popular in the 1960s. "Joints" of "grass" were passed around at high school, neighborhood, and college parties as readily as cans of beer had been in the previous generation.

Music became intimately connected with these cultural changes. The rock and roll of the 1950s and the gentle strains of folk music gave way to a new kind of rock that swept the country—and the world (see the "Recovering the Past" essay in Chapter 29, pp. 982–983, for a discussion of the music of the 1960s).

Rock festivals became popular throughout the 1960s. Held all over the country, the most dramatic such event occurred at the end of the decade. On an August weekend in 1969, some 400,000 people gathered in a large pasture in upstate New York for the Woodstock rock festival. This exuberant celebration, which featured earsplitting, around-the-clock entertainment and endlessly available marijuana,

went off without a hitch and seemed to the young to herald a new era. Another festival four months later at a stock car raceway in Altamont, California, was less fortunate. Four people died when audience members clashed with members of Hell's Angels, a motorcycle gang that had been hired to provide security for the Rolling Stones, one of the world's best-known rock groups.

The underside of the counterculture was most visible in the Haight-Ashbury section of San Francisco, where runaway "flower children" mingled with "burned-out" drug users and radical activists. For all the spontaneity and exuberance, the counterculture's darker side could not be ignored.

An Age of Assassination

In 1968, American society seemed to be tearing apart. The generation gap caused major rifts between parents and children. Political protest was growing increasingly violent. Yet there was still a basic confidence that the democratic process could bring meaningful change. John Kennedy had fallen to an assassin's bullet five years before and the nation had survived that trauma. Then two more killings of highly prominent figures undermined any sense of hope.

Martin Luther King, Jr., was the most visible spokesman for African Americans in the years after 1955. By the mid-1960s, he had broadened his crusade to attack poverty and economic injustice and had also begun to speak out against the war in Vietnam, which included a disproportionate number of

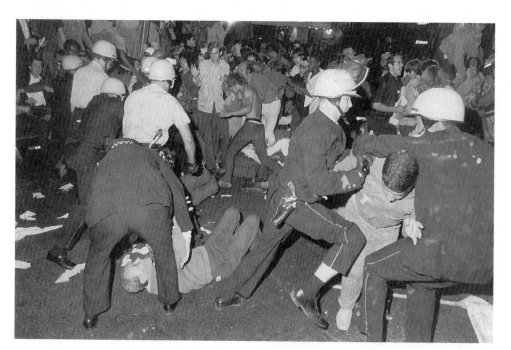

Chaos in Chicago
Policemen attacked demonstrators and bystanders alike at the turbulent Democratic convention of 1968. The senseless violence, pictured in graphic detail on national television, revealed serious rifts in the Democratic party and underscored the inability of political leaders to bridge the gaps. The horrifying chaos destroyed support for Democratic candidates and helped Nixon win the election. What reactions do you think people had to this image of the police clubbing protesters?
(Bettmann/CORBIS)

black soldiers serving in combat roles and losing their lives.

King knew he was a target. On April 3, 1968, he spoke eloquently at a church service, making reference to threats on his life. "We've got some difficult days ahead," he said. "But it doesn't matter with me now, because I've been to the mountain top . . . and I've seen the promised land."

The next day, as King stood on the balcony of his motel in Memphis, Tennessee, a bullet from a high-powered rifle ripped through his jaw and killed him. King's assassination sparked a wave of violence throughout the United States. In a spontaneous outburst of rage, African Americans in 124 cities rioted, setting fires and looting stores. For all Americans, King's death eroded faith in the possibility of nonviolent change.

Several months later, Robert F. Kennedy was also assassinated. Elected to the Senate from New York in 1964, he was running for the 1968 Democratic presidential nomination. Kennedy had spoken out eloquently to the poor and had persuaded antiwar activists that he could bring the Vietnam conflict to an end. In June, he had just finished delivering his victory speech after winning the California primary when he was shot by an assassin. Civil rights leader John Lewis, working on Kennedy's campaign, said, "Something was taken from us. The type of leadership that we had in a sense invested in, that we had helped to make and to nourish, was taken from us." Kennedy's death ended many people's hopes for reconciliation or reform.

The Chaotic Election of 1968

The turbulent 1968 Democratic convention, held in Chicago, undermined any hopes the party had for victory. The city's mayor, Richard Daley, was incensed at the radicals, peace activists, and hippies who had come to Chicago to protest the war and ordered law

DOCUMENT

LBJ, Decision Not to Seek Reelection (1968)

enforcement officers to clear out the demonstrators. Confrontations turned violent as police attacked protesters in the streets. Much of the violence took place in front of television cameras as crowds chanted, "The whole world is watching." Hubert Humphrey, Johnson's vice president, who ran for the Democratic nomination after Johnson refused to do so in the face of mounting antiwar protest, won what most people viewed as a worthless nomination.

Humphrey faced former vice president Richard Nixon, who had long dreamed of holding the nation's highest office. He had failed in his first bid in 1960 and later lost a race for governor of California. Written off by most politicians, he staged a comeback after the Goldwater debacle of 1964, and by 1968, he seemed to have a good shot at the presidency again.

VIDEO

Richard Nixon Presidential Campaign Ad: A Wavering Hubert Humphrey

Governor George C. Wallace of Alabama, a third-party candidate, exploited social and racial tensions in his campaign. Appealing to northern working-class voters as well as southern whites, Wallace characterized those who wanted to reform American life as "left-wing theoreticians, briefcase-totin' bureaucrats, ivory-tower guideline writers, bearded anarchists, smart-aleck editorial writers and pointy-headed professors." He hoped to ride into office on blue-collar resentment of social disorder and liberal aims.

Nixon addressed the same constituency, calling it the "silent majority." Capitalizing on the dismay these Americans felt over campus disruptions and inner-city riots and appealing to latent racism, he promised law and order if elected. He also called the Great Society a costly mistake, declaring that it was "time to quit pouring billions of dollars into programs that have failed." Heeding the advice of public-relations advisers, Nixon took the high ground and avoided shrill criticism himself. He gave Governor Spiro Agnew of Maryland, his

Presidential Elections of the 1960s			
Candidate	**Party**	**Popular Vote**	**Electoral Vote**
JOHN F. KENNEDY	Democratic	34,227,096 (49.9%)	303
Richard M. Nixon	Republican	34,108,546 (49.6%)	219
Harry F. Byrd	Independent	501,643 (0.7%)	15
LYNDON B. JOHNSON	Democratic	43,126,584 (61.1%)	486
Barry M. Goldwater	Republican	27,177,838 (38.5%)	52
RICHARD M. NIXON	Republican	31,783,783 (43.4%)	301
Hubert M. Humphrey	Democratic	31,271,839 (42.7%)	191
George C. Wallace	American Independent	9,899,557 (13.5%)	46

Note: Winners' names appear in capital letters.

vice presidential running mate, the task of leading the attack, just as he had done for Eisenhower in 1952. Agnew, much like the Nixon of old, responded aggressively, calling Hubert Humphrey "squishy soft on communism" and declaring that "if you've seen one city slum, you've seen them all."

Nixon received 43 percent of the popular vote, not quite 1 percent more than Humphrey, with Wallace capturing the rest. But it was enough to give the Republicans a majority in the Electoral College and Nixon the presidency at last. Sixty-two percent of all white voters (but only 12 percent of black voters) had cast their votes for either Nixon or Wallace, suggesting that the covert racial appeal had worked. Because many Americans split their tickets, the Democrats won both houses of Congress.

Continuing Protest

Meanwhile, protests continued. In October 1969, the Weathermen, a militant fringe group of SDS, sought to show that the revolution had arrived with a frontal attack on Chicago, scene of the violent Democratic convention of 1968. The Weathermen, taking their name from a line in a Bob Dylan song—"You don't need a weatherman to know which way the wind blows"— came from all over the country. Dressed in hard hats, jackboots, work gloves, and other padding, they rampaged through the streets with clubs, pipes, chains, and rocks. They ran into the police, as they had expected and hoped, and continued the attack. Some were arrested, others were shot, and the rest withdrew to regroup. For the next two days, they plotted strategy, engaged in minor skirmishes, and prepared for a final thrust. It came on the fourth day, once again pitting aggressive Weathermen against hostile police.

Why had the Weathermen launched their attack? "The status quo meant to us war, poverty, inequality, ignorance, famine and disease in most of the world," Bo Burlingham, a participant from Ohio, reflected. "To accept it was to condone and help perpetuate it. We felt like miners trapped in a terrible poisonous shaft with no light to guide us out. We resolved to destroy the tunnel even if we risked destroying ourselves in the process." The rationale of the Chicago "national action" may have been clear to the participants, but it convinced few other Americans. Citizens around the country were infuriated at what they saw.

TIMELINE

1960	John F. Kennedy elected president Birth control pill becomes available Sit-ins begin Students for a Democratic Society (SDS) founded
1961	Freedom rides Joseph Heller, *Catch-22* Ken Kesey, *One Flew Over the Cuckoo's Nest* Bay of Pigs invasion fails Khrushchev and Kennedy meet in Berlin Berlin Wall constructed JFK confronts steel companies
1962	Cuban missile crisis James Meredith crisis at the University of Mississippi SDS's *Port Huron Statement* Rachel Carson, *Silent Spring*
1963	Buddhist demonstrations in Vietnam Birmingham demonstration Civil rights march on Washington Kennedy assassinated; Lyndon B. Johnson becomes president Betty Friedan, *The Feminine Mystique*
1964	Economic Opportunity Act initiates War on Poverty Gulf of Tonkin resolution Johnson elected president Civil Rights Act Free Speech Movement, Berkeley
1965	Department of Housing and Urban Development established Elementary and Secondary Education Act Medicare established Martin Luther King, Jr., leads march from Selma to Montgomery Voting Rights Act United Farm Workers grape boycott Malcolm X assassinated Riot in Watts section of Los Angeles Ralph Nader, *Unsafe at Any Speed* Vietnam conflict escalates Marines sent to Dominican Republic
1966	Stokely Carmichael becomes head of SNCC and calls for "Black Power" Black Panthers founded Masters and Johnson, *Human Sexual Response*
1967	Urban riots in 22 cities
1967–1968	Antiwar demonstrations
1968	Student demonstrations at Columbia University and elsewhere Tet offensive in Vietnam Martin Luther King, Jr., assassinated Robert F. Kennedy assassinated Police and protesters clash at Democratic national convention Richard Nixon elected president
1969	Woodstock and Altamont rock festivals Weathermen's "Days of Rage" in Chicago

Conclusion

Political and Social Upheaval

The 1960s were turbulent years. In the first part of the decade, the United States was relatively calm. Liberal Democrats went even further than Franklin Roosevelt and Harry Truman as they pressed for large-scale government intervention to meet the social and economic problems that accompanied the modern industrial age. They were inspired by John Kennedy's rhetoric and saw the triumph of their approach in Lyndon Johnson's Great Society, as the nation strengthened its commitment to a capitalist welfare state. Then the Democratic party became impaled on the Vietnam War, and opposition to the conflict created more turbulence than the nation had known since the Civil War.

American society was in a state of upheaval. Young radicals challenged basic assumptions about how the government worked. They railed against social injustice at home, and they protested a foreign policy that they regarded as wrong. Their efforts faltered at first but then succeeded when they seized on the war in Vietnam as a primary focus and began to attack the Cold War policy that led to massive American military involvement in that faraway land. Student leaders, who often came from

politically active families, soon found hundreds of thousands of followers who joined in the marches and demonstrations that finally forced the nation to reconsider its aims. Meanwhile, members of the counterculture promoted their own more fluid values, challenged the patterns of conformity so important in the 1950s, and led millions of other Americans, some politically active, some not, to dress and act differently than in the past. The two strands of political activism and countercultural action were independent but intertwined, and they left the nation at the end of the decade very different than it had been before.

Most Americans, like Paul Cowan who was introduced at the start of this chapter, embraced the message of John Kennedy and the New Frontier in the early 1960s and endorsed the liberal approach. But over time, they began to question the tenets of liberalism as the economy faltered, as hard economic choices had to be made, and as the country became mired in an unwinnable war in Vietnam. Conservatives deplored the chaos, while disillusioned liberals like Paul Cowan wondered if their approach could ever succeed.

Questions for Review and Reflection

1. How did John F. Kennedy represent the hopes and ideals of Americans in the early 1960s?

2. How successful was Lyndon Johnson's Great Society?

3. What impact did the war in Vietnam have on protest at home?

4. What were the most important changes experienced by the United States in the late 1960s?

5. What was the lasting impact of the protest that rocked America in the 1960s?

Recommended Reading

Recommended Readings are posted on the Web site for this textbook. Visit www.ablongman.com/nash

Fiction and Film

Richard Fariña's *Been Down So Long It Looks Like Up to Me* (1966) is a novel about hallucinatory life in the 1960s. Barbara Garson's *MacBird* (1966), a play patterned loosely after *Macbeth,* pokes fun at the overarching ambitions of Lyndon Johnson. Vaughn

Meader's two record albums about *The First Family* (1962 and 1963—reissued on CD) provide a fictional glimpse at the Kennedy family. Bao Ninh's *The Sorrow of War* (1991) is a North Vietnamese novel (English version by Frank Palmos, from the original translation by Phan Thanh Hao) about the impact of the war; Tim O'Brien's *Going After Cacciato* (1978) is a novel about Vietnam in which one soldier simply decides to lay down his gun and walk home. O'Brien's *The Things They Carried* (1990) is a collection of short stories about the war. Robert Stone's *Dog Soldiers* (1974) is an older novel about the military side of the war in Vietnam.

Born on the Fourth of July (1989) is a film that tells Ron Kovic's story about being wounded in Vietnam and then returning home; Oliver Stone's film *The Doors* (1991) deals with Jim Morrison and his rock group in the 1960s. *Eyes on the Prize* (1987) is a superb, multipart documentary about the civil

rights movement. *The Graduate* (1967) became a cult film as it challenged the values of the 1950s and mocked the priorities of the world in which "plastics" were most important. *JFK* (1991) is Oliver Stone's film about the Kennedy assassination, in which he suggests a conspiracy killed the president. *Malcolm X* (1992) is Spike Lee's movie about the dramatic and outspoken black rights spokesman. *Mississippi Burning* (1988) is a film about three civil rights volunteers killed in Mississippi in 1964. Oliver Stone's movie *Platoon* (1986) deals with soldiers in the field in the war in Vietnam. *Thirteen Days* (2001) is a feature film about the Cuban missile crisis.

Discovering U.S. History Online

John Fitzgerald Kennedy

www.ipl.org/div/potus/jfkennedy.html

This site contains basic factual data about Kennedy's election and presidency, speeches, and online biographies.

The Kennedy Assassination

http://mcadams.posc.mu.edu/home.htm

This well-organized site has images, essays, and photos on the assassination.

Lyndon Baines Johnson

www.ipl.org/div/potus/lbjohnson.html

This site contains basic factual data about Johnson's election and presidency, speeches, and online biographies.

Voices of the Civil Rights Era

www.webcorp.com/civilrights/index.htm

This site provides audio clips about the civil rights movement from Martin Luther King, Jr., and Malcolm X.

Martin Luther King, Jr., Papers Project

www.stanford.edu/group/King/

This site has links and selected digital documents by and about Martin Luther King, Jr.

Civil Rights Timeline

www.infoplease.com/spot/civilrightstimeline1.html

This site contains a timeline of events in the 1950s and 1960s with pictures and links to related sites

Cold War Policies

http://history.acusd.edu/gen/20th/coldwar0.html

This site is an illustrated and annotated outline of the Cold War through the Johnson and Kennedy years.

The Cuban Missile Crisis

www.gwu.edu/~nsarchiv/nsa/cuba_mis_cri/

Declassified intelligence reports, photographs, audio, and essays shed new light on the Cuban missile crisis.

CIA and the Vietnam Policymakers: 1962–1968

www.odci.gov/csi/books/vietnam/index.html

Based on now-declassified material, this site offers a detailed account of CIA intelligence assessments during the Vietnam War and how U.S. policymakers used these assessments.

Battlefield Vietnam

www.pbs.org/battlefieldvietnam

This site presents an overview of the history of the Vietnam War; battle methods used, including guerrilla tactics and the air war; and the story of the Khe Sanh base.

Free Speech Movement: Student Protest—U.C. Berkeley, 1964–65

http://bancroft.berkeley.edu/FSM/

This site describes student protest through oral histories, documents, and a chronology.

The Sixties Project

http://lists.village.virginia.edu/sixties

This site has extensive exhibits, documents, and personal narratives from the 1960s.

The Digger Archives

www.diggers.org

This site provides information about the San Francisco Diggers, who became one of the legendary anarchist guerrilla street theater groups in Haight-Ashbury during the years 1966–1968.

1969 Woodstock Festival and Concert

www.woodstock69.com/index.htm

This site provides pictures and lists of songs from the famous rock festival.

CHAPTER 29

Disorder and Discontent, 1969–1980

Latinos, like women and members of other groups, worked to mobilize their communities behind the campaign for equal rights. This mural in an East Los Angeles housing project helped foster a sense of Chicano pride. *(Craig Aurness/Woodfin Camp & Associates)*

American Stories

Ann Clarke—as she chooses to call herself now—always wanted to go to college. But girls from Italian families rarely did when she was growing up. Her mother, a Sicilian immigrant and widow, asked her brother for advice: "Should Antonina go to college?" "What's the point?" he replied. "She's just going to get married."

Life had not been easy for Antonina Rose Rumore. As a child in the 1920s, her Italian-speaking grandmother cared for her while her mother worked to support the family, first in the sweatshops, then as a seamstress. Even as she dreamed about the future, Ann accommodated her culture's demands for dutiful daughters. Responsive to family needs, Ann finished the high school commercial course in three years. She struggled with ethnic prejudice as a legal secretary on Wall Street but still believed in the American dream and the Puritan work ethic. She was proud of her ability to bring money home to her family.

When World War II began, Ann wanted to join the WACs. "Better you should be a prostitute," her mother said. Ann went off to California instead, where she worked at a number of resorts. When she left California, she vowed to return to that land of freedom and opportunity.

After the war, Ann married Gerard Clarke, a college man with an English background. Her children would grow up accepted with Anglo-Saxon names. Over the next 15 years, Ann devoted herself to her family. She was a mother first and foremost, and that took all her time. But she still waited for her own chance. "I had this hunger to learn, this curiosity," she later recalled. By the early 1960s, her three children were all in school. Promising her husband to have dinner on the table every night at six, she enrolled at Pasadena City College. It was not easy, for family still came first, but Ann proved creative in finding time to study. When doing dishes or cleaning house, she memorized lists of dates, historical events, and other material for school. Holidays, however, complicated her efforts to complete assignments. Ann occasionally felt compelled to give everything up "to make Christmas." Forgetting about a whole semester's work two weeks before finals one year, she sewed nightgowns instead of writing her art history paper.

Her conflict over her studies was intensified by her position as one of the first older women to go back to college. "Sometimes I felt like I wanted to hide in the woodwork," she admitted. Often her teachers were younger than she was. It took four years to complete the two-year program. But she was not yet done, for she really wanted a bachelor's degree. Back she went, this time to California State College at Los Angeles.

As the years passed and the credits piled up, Ann became an honors student. Her children, now in college themselves, were proud and supportive; dinners became arguments over Faulkner and foreign policy. Even so, Ann still felt caught between her world at home and the world outside. Since she was at the top of her class, graduation should have been a special occasion. But she was only embarrassed when a letter from the school invited her parents to attend the final ceremonies. Ann could not bring herself to go.

With a college degree in hand, Ann returned to school for a teaching credential. Receiving her certificate at age 50, she faced the irony of social change. Once denied opportunities, Italians had assimilated into American society. Now she was just another Anglo in Los Angeles, caught in a changing immigration wave; now the city sought Latinos and other minorities to teach in the schools. Jobs in education were scarce, and she was close to retirement age, so she became a substitute teacher in Mexican American areas for the next 10 years, specializing in bilingual education.

Meanwhile, Ann was troubled by the Vietnam War. "For every boy that died, one of us should lie down," she told fellow workers. She was not an activist, but rather one of the millions of quieter Americans who ultimately helped bring about change. The social adjustments caused by the war affected her. Her son grew long hair and a beard and attended protest rallies. She worried that he would antagonize the ladies in Pasadena. Her daughter came home from college in boots and a leather miniskirt designed to shock. Ann accepted her children's changes as relatively superficial, confident in their fundamental values; they were "good kids," she knew. She trusted them, even as she worried about them.

Ann Clarke's experience paralleled that of millions of women in the post–World War II years. Caught up in traditional patterns of family life, these women began to recognize their need for something more against a backdrop of continuing political turbulence that sometimes seemed to undermine the nation's stability. They worried about both the global and the domestic consequences of the war in Vietnam and the constitutional issues in the Watergate scandal that threatened the American democratic system and eventually brought President Richard Nixon down. Meanwhile, American women, like blacks, Latinos and Latinas, Native Americans, and members of other groups, struggled to transform the conditions of their lives and the rights they enjoyed within American society. Building on the successes of the past several decades, these diverse groups demanded their own right to equality and equitable treatment in fulfillment of their own American dreams. In the course of their struggle, they changed the nation itself.

This chapter describes the continuing upheaval that shook American society in the 1970s. It shows the ongoing impact of global events as the Nixon administration struggled to find a way of ending the devastating struggle in Vietnam. Its effort to extricate American soldiers eased domestic protest, but then its decision to widen the war with incursions into other parts of Southeast Asia created further chaos in the United States. The chapter chronicles the most serious political scandal in American history, which led the president to resign. It records the growing agitation of environmental and consumer activists as they learned how to make their voices heard. And it describes the ongoing effort to provide liberty and equality in racial, gender, and social relations. While political challenges came from middle-class activists, social complaints came from often marginalized Americans who finally spoke out in an attempt to make the nation live up to its professed values. This chapter highlights the diverse voices that continued to echo throughout the 1970s in a heated debate about the distribution of social, political, and economic power in the United States.

THE DECLINE OF LIBERALISM

After eight years of Democratic rule, many Americans were frustrated with the liberal approach. They questioned the liberal agenda and the government's ability to solve social problems. As the war in Vietnam polarized the country, critics argued that the government was trying to do too much. Capitalizing on the alienation sparked by the war, the Republican administration of Richard Nixon resolved to scale down the commitment to social change. Like Dwight Eisenhower a decade and a half before, Nixon accepted some social programs as necessary but still wanted to cut spending and trim the federal bureaucracy. Furthermore, he and his political colleagues were determined to pay more attention to the needs of white, middle-class Americans who disliked the social disorder they saw as a consequence of rapid social change and resented the government's perceived favoritism toward the poor and dispossessed.

Richard Nixon and His Team

In and out of office, Nixon was a complex, remote man who carefully concealed his private self. Born poor, he was determined to be successful and accomplished that aim in the political sphere. Yet the setbacks he suffered hurt him, and he constantly appeared to be scheming to right himself again. There was, one of his aides noted, "a mean side to his nature" that he sought to keep from public view. Physically awkward and humorless, he was most comfortable alone or with a few wealthy friends. Even at work he insulated himself, preferring written contacts to personal ones, and he often retreated to a small room in the executive office building to be alone.

Nixon was keenly aware of the psychology of politics in the electronic age. He believed that "in the modern presidency, concern for image must rank with concern for substance." Thus, he posed in public as the defender of American morality, though in private he was frequently coarse and profane. Earlier in his career he had been labeled "Tricky Dick" for his apparent willingness to do anything to advance his career. In subsequent years, he had tried to create the appearance of a "new Nixon," but to many he still appeared to be a mechanical man, always calculating his next step. As author and columnist Garry Wills pointed out, "He is the least 'authentic' man alive, . . . A survivor. There is one Nixon only, though there seem to be new ones all the time—he will try to be what people want."

Philosophically, Nixon disagreed with the liberal faith in federal planning and wanted to decentralize social policy. But he agreed with his liberal

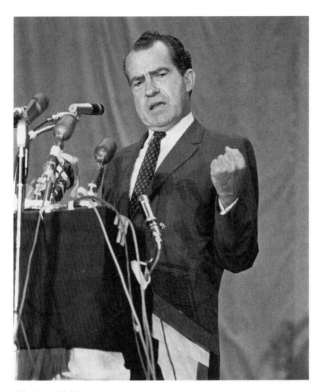

Richard Nixon Speaking to the "silent majority," Nixon promised to reinstitute traditional values and restore law and order. A private man, Nixon tried to insulate himself from the public and present a carefully crafted image through the national media. What impression does Nixon convey in this photograph? How does his body language communicate his intentions? *(Hiroji Kubota/Magnum Photos)*

predecessors that the presidency ought to be the engine of the political system. Faced with a Congress dominated by Democrats and their allocations of money for programs he opposed, he simply impounded (refused to spend) funds authorized by Congress. Later commentators saw the Nixon years as the height of what they came to call the "imperial presidency."

Nixon's cabinet appointees were white, male Republicans. For the most part, however, the president worked around his cabinet, relying on other White House staff members. In domestic affairs, Arthur Burns, a former chairman of the Council of Economic Advisers, and Daniel Patrick Moynihan, a Harvard professor of government (and a Democrat) were the most important. In foreign affairs, the talented and ambitious Henry A. Kissinger, another Harvard government professor, directed the National Security Council staff and later became secretary of state.

Another tier of White House officials—none with public-policy experience but all intensely loyal—insulated the president from the outside world and carried out his commands. Advertising executive

H. R. Haldeman, a tireless Nixon campaigner, became chief of staff. Of his relationship with the president, Haldeman remarked, "I get done what he wants done and I take the heat instead of him." Working with Haldeman was lawyer John Ehrlichman. Starting as a legal counselor, he rose to the post of chief domestic adviser. Haldeman and Ehrlichman framed issues and narrowed options for Nixon. They came to be called the "Berlin Wall" for the way they guarded the president's privacy. John Mitchell was known as "El Supremo" by the staff, as the "Big Enchilada" by Ehrlichman. A tough, successful bond lawyer from Nixon's New York law office, Mitchell became a fast friend and managed Nixon's 1968 campaign. In the new administration, he became attorney general and gave the president daily advice.

The Republican Agenda at Home

Although Nixon had come to political maturity in Republican circles, he understood that it was impossible to roll back the government's expanded role altogether. Accepting the basic contours of the welfare state, as other countries around the world did, he sought instead to systematize and scale back its programs. He was particularly determined "to reverse the flow of power and resources" away from the federal government and channel them to state and local governments, where he believed they belonged.

Despite initial reservations, Nixon proved willing to use economic tools to maintain stability. The economy was faltering when he assumed office. Inflation had risen from 2.2 percent in 1965 to 4.5 percent in 1968, largely as a result of the Vietnam War. Nixon responded by reducing government spending and pressing the Federal Reserve Board to raise interest rates. Although parts of the conservative plan worked, a mild recession occurred in 1969–1970, and inflation continued to rise. Realizing the political dangers of pursuing this policy, Nixon shifted course, imposed wage and price controls to stop inflation, and used monetary and fiscal policies to stimulate the economy. After his re-election in 1972, however, he lifted wage and price controls, and inflation resumed.

A number of factors besides the Vietnam War contributed to the troubling price spiral. Eager to court the farm vote, the administration made a large wheat sale to Russia in 1972. The sale proved to be a major miscalculation. With insufficient wheat left for the American market, grain prices shot up. Between 1971 and 1974, farm prices rose 66 percent, as agricultural inflation accompanied industrial inflation.

The Yom Kippur War of 1973

The Arab attack during the Yom Kippur observance took Israel by surprise. Initially, Egypt and Syria regained some of their lost territory, but then the Israeli counterattack cut back many of the gains. In the end, UN troops were stationed on borders of the Sinai Peninsula and Golan Heights to help stabilize those regions. **Reflecting on the Past** How had the map of the Middle East changed in the years after the establishment of the state of Israel in 1948? Who was the victor in the 1973 Yom Kippur War? Why could UN forces help maintain stability?

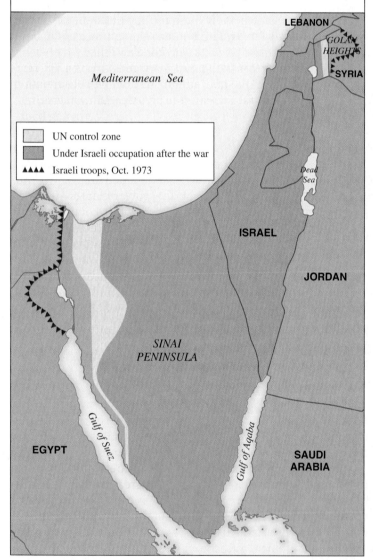

LEBANON

GOLAN HEIGHTS

Mediterranean Sea

SYRIA

☐ UN control zone
■ Under Israeli occupation after the war
▲▲▲▲ Israeli troops, Oct. 1973

Dead Sea

ISRAEL

JORDAN

SINAI PENINSULA

Gulf of Suez

Gulf of Aqaba

EGYPT

SAUDI ARABIA

Conflict in the Middle East, 1945–1997

The most critical factor in disrupting the economy, though, was the Arab oil embargo. American economic expansion had rested on cheap energy just as American patterns of life had depended on inexpensive gasoline. Turbulence in the Middle East intruded on the economic stability of the Western world.

The Six-Day War in 1967 made it clear that the Middle East was still a battleground. In 1967, anticipating an attack and launching a preemptive strike, Israeli forces defeated the Egyptian army and seized the West Bank and the Golan Heights, as well as the Arab sector of Jerusalem, which was reunited with the Israeli part of the city for the first time since 1948.

In the aftermath of the Six-Day War, the Organization of Petroleum Exporting Countries (OPEC) slowly raised oil prices in the early 1970s. Then another Arab-Israeli war in 1973 further disrupted the region. This conflict—the Yom Kippur War—came as Jews celebrated their holiest holiday, the Day of Atonement, and took them by surprise. The war pitted Israel against Egypt, Syria, Iraq, and Jordan. Initially Egypt, in the Sinai peninsula, and Syria, in the Golan Heights, were successful, but then the Israelis fought back. In the end, after several weeks of fighting, ceasefires went into effect, leaving Egypt and Syria with modest gains but the Israelis largely in control.

Meanwhile, in the midst of the fighting, Saudi Arabia, an economic leader of the Arab nations, imposed an embargo on oil shipped to Israel's ally, the United States. Other OPEC nations continued to supply oil but quadrupled their prices. Dependent on imports for one-third of their energy needs, Americans faced shortages and skyrocketing prices. When the embargo ended in 1974, prices remained high. Even though oil prices around the world increased, the United States was hardest hit because of the huge amounts of oil it used.

The oil crisis affected all aspects of American economic life. Manufacturers, farmers, homeowners—all were touched by high energy prices. A loaf of bread that had cost 28 cents in the early 1970s jumped to 89 cents, and automobiles cost 72 percent more in 1978 than they had in 1973. Accustomed to filling up their cars' tanks for only a few dollars, Americans were shocked at paying 65 cents a gallon. In 1974, inflation reached 11 percent. But then, as higher energy prices encouraged consumers to cut back on their purchases, the nation entered a recession as well. Unemployment climbed to 9 percent for several months in 1975, the highest level since the 1930s.

The United States faced fierce economic competition from abroad. The auto industry provided a good example. Large American cars, which gobbled up gasoline, now were challenged by smaller Japanese imports that were far more fuel-efficient. The tiny German Volkswagen Beetle was already popular with cost-conscious drivers. Now they had their choice of smaller cars from Honda, Datsun (later called Nissan), and Toyota, too.

As economic growth and stability eluded the nation, Nixon also tried to reorganize rapidly expanding and expensive welfare programs. Critics claimed that welfare was inefficient and that benefits discouraged people from seeking work. Nixon faced a political dilemma. He recognized the conservative tide growing in the Sun Belt regions of the country from Florida to Texas to California, where many voters wanted cutbacks in what they viewed as excessive government programs. At the same time, he wanted to create a new Republican coalition by winning over traditionally Democratic blue-collar

workers with reassurances that the Republicans would not dismantle the parts of the welfare state on which they relied.

Nixon endorsed the Family Assistance Plan, which would have guaranteed a minimum yearly stipend of $1,600 to a family of four, with food stamps providing about $800 more. The program, aiming to cut "welfare cheaters" who took unfair advantage of the system and to encourage recipients to work, was promising but it was attacked by both liberals, who felt it was too limited, and conservatives, who claimed it tried to do too much. It died in the Senate.

Nixon irritated liberals still further in his effort to restore "law and order." Political protest, rising crime rates, increased drug use, and more permissive attitudes toward sex all created a growing backlash among working-class and many middle-class Americans. Nixon decided to use government power to silence disruption and thereby strengthen his conservative political constituency.

Part of the administration's campaign involved denouncing disruptive elements. Nixon lashed out at demonstrators, at one point calling student activists "bums." More and more, however, he relied on his vice president to play the part of hatchet man. As he had demonstrated during the 1968 campaign, Spiro Agnew had a gift for jugular attack. He branded opposition elements, students in particular, as "ideological eunuchs" who made up an "effete corps of impudent snobs." At the same time, Nixon and Agnew appealed for support to blue-collar youth, whom they described as patriotic supporters of the Vietnam War.

The strongest part of Nixon's plan to circumscribe the liberal approach was Attorney General John Mitchell's campaign on crime, sometimes waged at the expense of individuals' constitutional rights. Mitchell's plan included reshaping the Supreme Court, which had rendered increasingly liberal decisions on the rights of defendants in the past decade and a half. That shift, Republican leaders argued, had resulted in moral and ethical laxity. During his first term, Nixon had the opportunity to name four judges to the Court, and he nominated men who shared his views. His first choice was Warren E. Burger as chief justice to replace the liberal Earl Warren, who was retiring. Burger, a moderate, was confirmed quickly. Other appointments, however, were more partisan and reflected Nixon's aggressively conservative approach. Intent on appealing to white southerners, he first selected Clement Haynesworth of South Carolina, then G. Harold Carswell of Florida. Both men on examination showed such racial biases or limitations that the Senate refused to

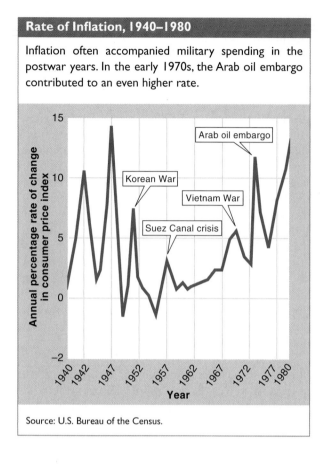

Rate of Inflation, 1940–1980

Inflation often accompanied military spending in the postwar years. In the early 1970s, the Arab oil embargo contributed to an even higher rate.

Source: U.S. Bureau of the Census.

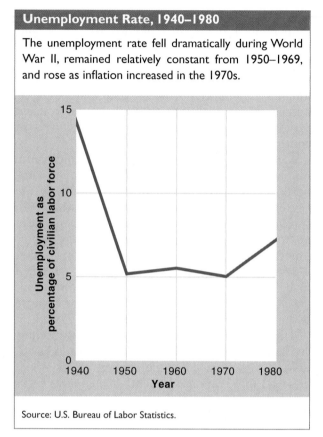

Unemployment Rate, 1940–1980

The unemployment rate fell dramatically during World War II, remained relatively constant from 1950–1969, and rose as inflation increased in the 1970s.

Source: U.S. Bureau of Labor Statistics.

confirm them. Nixon then appointed Harry Blackmun, Lewis F. Powell, Jr., and William Rehnquist, all able and qualified, and all inclined to tilt the Court in a more conservative direction.

Not surprisingly, the Court gradually shifted to the right. It narrowed defendants' rights in an attempt to ease the burden of the prosecution in its cases and slowed liberalizing of pornography laws. It supported Nixon's assault on the media by ruling that journalists did not have the right to refuse to answer questions for a grand jury, even if they had promised sources confidentiality. On other questions, however, the Court did not always act as the president had hoped. In the controversial 1973 *Roe* v. *Wade* decision, the Court legalized abortion, stating that women's rights included the right to control their own bodies. This decision was one that feminists, a group hardly supported by the president, had ardently sought.

DOCUMENT

Roe v. Wade (January 22, 1973)

Continuing Confrontations in Civil Rights

Richard Nixon was less sympathetic to the cause of civil rights than his predecessors. In 1968, the

Republicans won only 12 percent of the black vote, leading Nixon to conclude that any effort to woo the black electorate would endanger his attempt to obtain white southern support.

From the start, the Nixon administration sought to scale back the federal commitment to civil rights. It first moved to reduce appropriations for fair-housing enforcement, then tried to block an extension of the Voting Rights Act of 1965. Although Congress approved the extension, the administration's position on racial issues was clear. When South Carolina senator Strom Thurmond and others tried to suspend federal school desegregation guidelines, the Justice Department lent support by urging a delay in meeting desegregation deadlines in 33 of Mississippi's school districts. While a unanimous Supreme Court rebuffed the effort, the president disagreed publicly with the decision.

Nixon also faced the growing controversy over busing as a means of desegregation, a highly charged issue in the 1970s. Transporting students from one area to another to attend school was nothing new. By 1970, more than 18 million students, almost 40 percent of those in the United States, rode buses to school. Yet when busing became tangled with the question of integration, it inflamed passions.

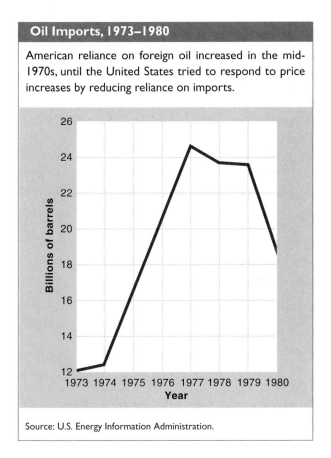

Oil Imports, 1973–1980

American reliance on foreign oil increased in the mid-1970s, until the United States tried to respond to price increases by reducing reliance on imports.

Source: U.S. Energy Information Administration.

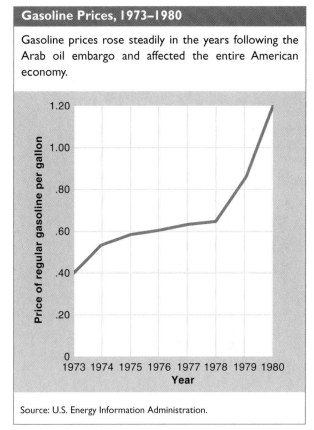

Gasoline Prices, 1973–1980

Gasoline prices rose steadily in the years following the Arab oil embargo and affected the entire American economy.

Source: U.S. Energy Information Administration.

In the South, before the Supreme Court endorsed integration, busing had long been used to maintain segregated schools. Some black students in Selma, Alabama, for example, traveled 50 miles by bus to an entirely black trade school in Montgomery, even though a similar school for whites stood nearby. Now, however, busing was a means of breaking down racial barriers.

The issue came to a head in North Carolina, in the Charlotte–Mecklenburg school system. A desegregation plan involving voluntary transfer was in effect, but many blacks still attended largely segregated schools. A federal judge ruled that the district was not in compliance with the latest Supreme Court decisions, and in 1971, the Supreme Court ruled that district courts had broad authority to order the desegregation of school systems—by busing, if necessary.

Earlier, Nixon had opposed such busing. Now he proposed a moratorium or even a restriction on busing and went on television to denounce it. Although Congress did not accede to his request, southerners knew where the president stood. So did northerners, for the issue became a national one. Schools in many of the nation's largest northern cities were as rigidly segregated as those in the

South, largely because of residential patterns. This segregation was called *de facto* to differentiate it from the *de jure,* or legal, segregation that had existed in the South. Mississippi senator John C. Stennis, a bitter foe of busing, hoped to stir up northerners by subjecting northern schools to the same busing standards as southern schools. He proposed requiring the government to enforce federal desegregation guidelines uniformly throughout the country or not use them at all. Court decisions subsequently ordered many northern cities to desegregate their schools.

Northern resistance to integration was fiercest in Boston, but the situation there was typical. In 1973, 85 percent of the blacks in the city attended schools that had a black majority. More than half of the African American students were in schools that were 90 percent black. In June 1974, a federal judge ordered busing to begin. The first phase, involving 17,000 pupils, was to start in the fall of that year.

For many younger students, attendance at different elementary schools went smoothly. Reassigned high school students were less fortunate. A white boycott at South Boston High cut attendance from the anticipated 1,500 to fewer than 100 on the first day. Buses bringing in black students were stoned,

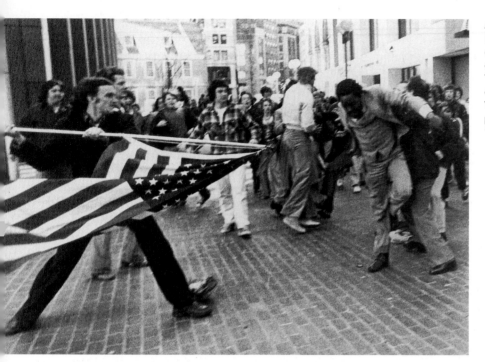

An Angry Confrontation in Boston When busing was mandated to end de facto school segregation in the North, the order frequently prompted fierce resistance. This photograph shows a bitter antibusing demonstration unfolding in Boston in 1976. What gives this prize-winning picture its special power? *(Stanley J. Forman, Pulitzer Prize 1977, "The Soiling of Old Glory")*

and some children were injured. White, working-class South Bostonians felt that they were being asked to carry the burden of middle-class liberals' racial views. Similar resentments triggered racial episodes elsewhere. In many cases, white families either enrolled their children in private schools or fled the city.

DOCUMENT

Ione Malloy, *Southie Won't Go* (1975)

The Republicans managed to slow down the school desegregation movement. Nixon openly catered to his conservative constituents and demonstrated he was on their side. His successor, Gerald Ford, never came out squarely against civil rights, but his lukewarm approach to desegregation demonstrated a further weakening of the federal commitment.

Integration at the postsecondary level came easier as federal affirmative action guidelines seeking to provide opportunities for groups discriminated against in the past brought more blacks into colleges and universities. Black enrollment in colleges reached 9.3 percent of the college population in 1976, then dropped back slightly to 9.1 percent in 1980, just what it had been in 1973.

As blacks struggled on the educational and occupational fronts, some whites protested that gains came at their expense and amounted to "reverse discrimination." In 1973 and 1974, for example, Allan Bakke, a white, applied to the medical school at the University of California at Davis. Twice rejected, he sued on the grounds that a racial quota reserving

Ratio of Median Black-to-White Family Income, 1940–1980

This chart shows the substantial difference between family income for blacks and whites and reveals that the percentage has risen slowly since World War II. Observe, however, the downturn in the 1970s.

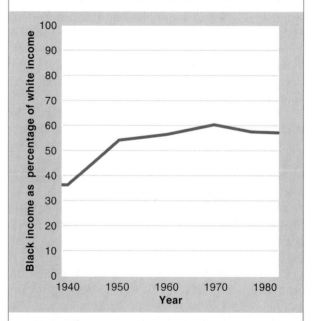

Source: Data from U.S. Department of Labor and *Statistical Abstract of the United States,* 1991.

16 of 100 places for minority-group applicants was a form of reverse discrimination that violated the Civil Rights Act of 1964. In 1978, the Supreme Court ordered Bakke's admission to the medical school, but in a complex ruling including six separate opinions, the Court allowed "consideration" of race in admissions policies, but not quotas.

The civil rights movement underscored the democratic values on which the nation was based, but the gap between rhetoric and reality remained. In an era when industrial and farming employment shrank and rents rose at a highly inflationary rate, most black families remained poor. African American income was substantially lower than white income, as the accompanying chart shows. After early optimism in the years when the movement made its greatest strides, black Americans and sympathetic whites were troubled by the direction of public policy. Given a wavering national commitment to reform in the 1970s, only pressures from reform groups kept the faltering civil rights movement alive.

THE ONGOING EFFORT IN VIETNAM

The war in Vietnam continued into the 1970s. When Nixon assumed office in 1969, he understood the need to heal the rifts that the struggle created in American society. During the campaign, he had spoken about a plan to end involvement in the war without specifying details. Once in office, he embarked on an effort to bring American troops home as a way of defusing opposition to the struggle. Unfortunately, his decision to try to avoid losing the war led to even further chaos at home.

Vietnamization—Bringing the Soldiers Home

A politician who had gained prominence as one of the nation's most aggressive anti-Communists, Nixon promised to bring the nation together. He gave top priority to extricating the United States from Vietnam while still seeking a way to win the war. To that end, he announced the Nixon Doctrine, which asserted that the United States would aid friends and allies but would not undertake the full burden of troop defense. The policy of Vietnamization entailed removing American forces and replacing them with Vietnamese troops. Between 1968 and 1972, American troop strength dropped from 543,000 to 39,000, and the reduction

won political support for Nixon at home. Yet as the transition occurred, the South Vietnamese steadily lost ground to the Viet Cong.

At the same time, Americans launched ferocious air attacks on North Vietnam. "Let's blow the hell out of them," Nixon instructed the Joint Chiefs of Staff. Nixon used the bombing campaign to portray himself to the North Vietnamese as an anti-Communist zealot with his hand on the nuclear trigger, assuming that fear of annihilation would bring the enemy to the peace table. But peace proved elusive, and war protests multiplied in 1969 and 1970.

DOCUMENT
Testimony, Winter Soldier Investigation (1971)

In November 1969, as a massive protest demonstration took place in Washington, D.C., stories surfaced about a horrifying massacre of civilians in Vietnam the year before at a place called My Lai (see the accompanying "American Voices" feature). Descriptions of the senseless violence on the part of American troops increased pressure for the United States to get out of Vietnam.

Widening the War

As much as Nixon wanted to defuse opposition to the war, he was determined not to lose the struggle either. Realizing that the Vietnamese relied on supplies funneled through Cambodia, Nixon announced in mid-1970 that American and Vietnamese troops were invading that country to clear out Communist enclaves there. The United States, he said, would not stand by as a "pitiful helpless giant" when there were actions it could take to stem the Communist advance.

IMAGE
Kent State Demonstrations

Nixon's invasion of Cambodia brought renewed demonstrations on college campuses, some with tragic results. At Kent State University in Ohio, the antiwar response was fierce. Soon after the president announced his moves, disgruntled students gathered downtown. Worried about the crowd, the local police called in sheriff's deputies to disperse the students. The next evening, groups of students collected on the college grounds. Assembling around the ROTC building, they began throwing firecrackers and rocks at the structure, which had become a hated symbol of the war. Then they set it on fire and watched it burn to the ground.

DOCUMENT
Report of the President's Commission on Campus Unrest (September 1970)

Governor James Rhodes of Ohio ordered the National Guard to the university.

RECOVERING THE PAST

Popular Music

One way to recover the past is through music. Popular songs not only provide insight into attitudes and beliefs but also quickly convey the mood and feelings of an era. Through their lyrics, songwriters express the hopes and fears of a people and the emotional tone of an age. Consider, for example, the powerful message conveyed in the Democratic party adoption of "Happy Days Are Here Again" as a campaign theme during the Great Depression. The decline of pop music and the rise of rock and roll in the 1950s tell historians a great deal about the mood of that period. Similarly, the popularity of both folk music and rock in the 1960s provides another way of following social change in that turbulent decade.

The music of the 1960s and 1970s moved beyond the syrupy ballads of the early 1950s and the rock-and-roll movement that Elvis Presley helped launch in the middle of the decade. As the United States confronted the challenges of the counterculture and the crosscurrents of political and social reform, new kinds of music began to be played.

Folk music took off at the start of the period. Building on a tradition launched by Woody Guthrie, Pete Seeger, and the Weavers, Joan Baez was one of the first folk singers to become popular. Accompanying herself on a guitar as she performed at coffee shops in Harvard Square and at the Newport Folk Festival, she soon overwhelmed audiences with her crystal-clear voice. She sang ballads, laments, and spir-

Bob Dylan. *(AP/Wide World Photos)*

ituals such as "We Shall Overcome" and became caught up in the protest activities of the period.

Equally active was Bob Dylan, who grew up playing rock and roll in high school, then folk music in college at the University of Minnesota. Disheveled and gravelly voiced, he wrote remarkable songs such as "Blowin' in the Wind" that were soon sung by other artists such as Peter, Paul, and Mary as well. His song "The Times They Are A-Changin'" (excerpted here) captured the inexorable force of the student protest movement best of all. Dylan, who alienated some of his folk music fans when he began playing the electric guitar, continued performing for decades.

The Times They Are A-Changin'

BY BOB DYLAN

Come mothers and fathers
Throughout the land
And don't criticize
What you can't understand

Joan Baez. *(John Launois/Stockphoto)*

982

*Your sons and your daughters
Are beyond your command
Your old road is
Rapidly agin'.
Please get out of the new one
If you can't lend your hand
For the times they are a-changin'.*

But these years were marked by far more than folk music alone. In the early part of the decade, an English group from Liverpool began to build a following in Great Britain. At the start of 1964, the Beatles released "I Want to Hold Your Hand" in the United States and appeared on the popular Ed Sullivan television show. Within weeks, Beatles songs held the first, second, third, fourth, and fifth positions on the *Billboard* singles chart, and *Meet the Beatles* became the best-selling LP record to date. With the release of *Sergeant Pepper's Lonely Hearts Club Band* a few years later, the Beatles branched out in new musical directions and reflected the influence of the counterculture with songs such as "Lucy in the Sky with Diamonds" (which some people said referred to the hallucinogenic drug LSD).

Mick Jagger and the Rolling Stones followed at the end of the 1960s. Another English group that changed the nature of American music, the Stones played a blues-based rock music that proclaimed a commitment to drugs, sex, and a decadent life of social upheaval. Jagger was an aggressive, sometimes violent

The Supremes. *(Brown Brothers)*

showman on stage, whose androgynous style showed his contempt for conventional sexual norms. Other artists, such as Jim Morrison of the Doors and Janis Joplin, reflected the same intensity of the new rock world, and both died from drug overdoses. This music too continued into the 1970s.

Meanwhile, other groups were setting off in different directions. On the pop scene, Motown Records in Detroit popularized a new kind of black rhythm and blues. By 1960, the gospel-pop-soul fusion was gaining followers. By the late 1960s, Motown Records was one of the largest black-owned companies in America and one of the most successful independent recording ventures in the business. Stevie Wonder, the Temptations, and the Supremes were among the groups who became enormously popular. The Supremes, led by Diana Ross, epitomized the Motown sound with such hits as "Where Did Our Love Go."

REFLECTING ON THE PAST What songs come to your mind when you think of the 1960s and 1970s? How is the music different from that of the 1950s? What do the lyrics tell you about the period?

Look at the verse from "The Times They Are A-Changin'" that is reprinted here. What does it tell you about the turbulence of the time? What, if anything, do these lyrics imply can be done about the changes in the air? What other songs can you think of that give you a similar handle on these turbulent years?

The Beatles. *(Getty Images)*

AMERICAN VOICES

Interview with Paul Meadlo on the My Lai Massacre

In 1968, an American infantry company entered My Lai, a small village in South Vietnam, to clear out members of the Viet Cong believed to be there. Instead of soldiers, the company found civilians. The American forces lost control and massacred several hundred women, children, and old men. Paul Meadlo was one of the soldiers involved in the slaughter. Lieutenant William Calley was the officer in charge. When news of the episode surfaced late in 1969, it underscored the futility—and failure—of the United States effort in the Vietnam War.

Q: How many people did you round up?

A: Well, there was about 40–50 people that we gathered in the center of the village. . . .

Q: What kind of people—men, women, children?

A: Men, women, children.

Q: Babies?

A: Babies. And we all huddled them up. We made them squat down, and Lieutenant Calley came over and said you know what to do with them, don't you. . . . And he told me to start shooting. So I poured about four clips into the group. . . .

Q: And you killed how many? At that time?

A: Well, I fired them on automatic, so you can't—you just spray the area on them and so you can't know how many you killed 'cause they were going fast. So I might have killed ten or fifteen of them.

Q: Men, women and children?

A: Men, women and children.

Q: And babies?

A: And babies. . . .

Q: Why did you do it?

A: Why did I do it? Because I felt like I was ordered to do it, and it seemed like that, at the time I felt like I was doing the right thing, because like I said I lost buddies. . . .

Q: Do you ever dream about all of this? . . .

A: Yes I did . . . and I still dream about it. . . . Some days . . . some nights, I can't even sleep. I just lay there thinking about it.

- *Why did Paul Meadlo fire on the men, women, and children in My Lai?*

- *Why were the troops willing to participate in such a massacre?*

- *How do you think the American public responded to this interview?*

Source: Interview with Paul Meadlo, *New York Times*, November 25, 1969. Copyright © 1969 by The New York Times Co. Reprinted with permission.

Tension grew, and finally the situation exploded as the guardsmen fired without provocation on students gathered on the campus. When the shooting stopped, four students lay dead, nine wounded. Two of the dead had been demonstrators who were more than 250 feet away when shot. The other two were innocent bystanders, almost 400 feet from the troops.

Students around the country, as well as other Americans, were outraged by the attack. Many were equally disturbed about a similar attack at Jackson State University in Mississippi, where a few students taunted police and National Guardsmen. The troops responded without warning by firing 460 rounds of automatic-weapon fire into a women's dormitory. When the gunfire ceased, two people were dead, more wounded. The dead, however, were black students at a black institution, and white America paid less attention to this attack.

In 1971, the Vietnam War made major headlines once more when the *New York Times* began publishing a secret Department of Defense account of American involvement. The so-called Pentagon Papers, leaked by Daniel Ellsberg, a defense analyst, gave Americans a firsthand look at the fabrications and faulty assumptions that had guided the steady expansion of the struggle. Even though the study stopped with the Johnson years, the Nixon administration was furious and tried, without success, to block publication.

The End of the War and Détente

Vietnam remained a political football when Nixon ran for re-election in 1972. Negotiations aimed at a settlement were underway, and just days before the election, Secretary of State Henry Kissinger announced, "Peace is at hand." When South Vietnam seemed to balk at the proposed settlement, however, the administration responded with the most intensive bombing campaign of the war. Hanoi, the capital of North Vietnam, was hit hard, and North

HOW OTHERS SEE US

French and German Posters on the American War in Vietnam

Nations around the world opposed the American intervention in Vietnam. As the war dragged on and more and more people died, posters highlighted the growing anger at American policy. The French poster below calls for "Peace in Vietnam" and demands an end to American aggression while highlighting the right of the Vietnamese people to choose their own destiny. The German poster asks for "Solidarity with Vietnam" and declares that the members of the community organization of Querfurt in Germany have donated money for the heroically fighting Vietnamese people.

Source: Museum of War Atrocities, Ho Chi Minh City, Vietnam.

- Why did other nations oppose American involvement in Vietnam?

- Who was responsible for the French poster, and what does that tell you about the dynamics of the struggle?

- What kind of tone do you detect in the two posters you see here?

Vietnamese harbors were mined. Only in the new year was a ceasefire finally signed.

The conflict in Vietnam lingered on into the spring of 1975. When the North Vietnamese finally consolidated their control over the entire country, Gerald Ford, who had succeeded Nixon as president, called for another $1 billion in aid, even as the South Vietnamese were abandoning arms and supplies in chaotic retreat. But Congress refused, leaving South Vietnam's crumbling government to fend for itself. Republicans hailed Kissinger for having finally freed the United States from the Southeast Asian quagmire. Antiwar critics condemned him for remaining involved for so long. The *New Republic* wryly observed that Kissinger brought peace to Vietnam in the same way Napoleon brought peace to Europe: by losing.

The long conflict had enormous consequences. Disillusionment with the war undermined assumptions about America's role in world affairs. In the longest war in its history, the United States lost almost 58,000 men, with far more wounded or maimed. Blacks and Chicanos were disproportionately represented in combat units and consequently suffered greater numbers of deaths and injuries. Many minority men saw military service as a means of advancement. In 1965, 24 percent of all soldiers killed in Vietnam were African American—a figure far higher than their percentage of the population as a whole. Financially, the nation spent more than $150 billion on the unsuccessful war. Domestic reform slowed, then stopped. Cynicism about the government increased, and American society was deeply divided. Only time would heal the wounds.

The Vietnam War

If the Republicans' Vietnam policy was a questionable success, accomplishments in other areas were impressive. Nixon, the consummate Red-baiter of the past, dealt imaginatively and successfully with the major Communist powers, reversing the direction of American policy since World War II.

Nixon's most dramatic step was establishing better relations with the People's Republic of China. In the two decades since Mao Zedong's victory in the Chinese revolution in 1949, the United States had refused to recognize the Communist government on the mainland, insisting that Jiang Jieshi's rump regime on Taiwan was the rightful government of the Chinese people. In 1971, with an eye on the upcoming elections, Nixon began softening his administration's rigid stance by announcing that he intended to visit China the following year. He suspected that he could use Chinese friendship as a bargaining chip in dealing with the Soviet Union. He acknowledged what most nations already knew: communism was not monolithic. Nixon also recognized that the press and television coverage of a dramatic trip could boost his image, as indeed it did.

Nixon went to China in February 1972. He met with Chinese leaders Mao Zedong and Zou Enlai (Chou En-lai), talked about international problems, exchanged toasts, and saw the Great Wall and other major sights. Wherever he went, American television cameras followed, helping introduce to the American public a nation about which it knew little. Though formal diplomatic relations were not yet restored, détente between the two countries had begun.

Seeking to play one Communist state against the other, Nixon also visited Russia, where he was likewise warmly welcomed. At a cordial summit meeting, the president and Soviet premier Leonid Brezhnev signed the first Strategic Arms Limitation Treaty (SALT I), which included a five-year agreement setting ceilings on intercontinental and other ballistic missiles, and an antiballistic missile treaty restricting the number of systems each nation could develop and deploy. At the same time, the two nations agreed to cooperate in space and to ease long-standing restrictions on trade. Business applauded the new approach, and most Americans approved of détente.

Nixon also recognized the need to promote peace in the Middle East. Henry Kissinger engaged in shuttle diplomacy—moving from one nation to another—to help arrange a ceasefire in the Yom Kippur War. In the aftermath of that war, recognizing the need for oil, Nixon and Kissinger worked to establish better relations with the Arab nations, even if doing so intruded on American support of Israel.

When Gerald Ford assumed office, he followed the policies begun under Nixon, although he ceased calling the approach détente. He continued the strategic arms limitation talks that provided hope for eventual nuclear disarmament, which culminated in the even more comprehensive SALT II agreement, signed but never ratified during Jimmy Carter's presidency.

CONSTITUTIONAL CONFLICT AND ITS CONSEQUENCES

As he dealt with chaos at home and abroad, Nixon worried about maintaining his political base. In his quest for re-election, he went too far and embroiled himself in a devastating political scandal that undermined his administration.

The Watergate Affair

Faced with a solidly Democratic Congress, the Nixon administration found many of its legislative initiatives blocked. Nixon was determined to end the stalemate by winning a second term and sweeping Republican majorities into both houses of Congress in 1972. His efforts to gain a decisive Republican victory at the polls led to serious abuses of power.

Nixon's re-election campaign was even better organized than the effort four years earlier. His fiercely loyal aides were prepared to do anything to win. Special counsel Charles W. Colson described himself as a "flag-waving, kick-'em-in-the-nuts, anti-press, anti-liberal Nixon fanatic." He had earlier played an important part in developing an "enemies list" of prominent figures judged to be unsympathetic to the administration. White House counsel John Dean defined his task as finding a way to "use the available federal machinery to screw our political enemies." One way was by authorizing tax audits of political opponents. Active in carrying out commands were E. Howard Hunt, a former CIA agent and a specialist in "dirty tricks," and G. Gordon Liddy, a onetime member of the FBI, who prided himself on his willingness to do anything without flinching.

The Committee to Re-Elect the President (CREEP), headed by John Mitchell, who resigned as attorney general, launched a massive fund-raising drive, aimed at collecting as much money as it could before a new campaign-finance law took effect. That money could be used for any purpose, including payments for the performance of dirty tricks aimed at disrupting the opposition's campaign. Other funds financed an intelligence branch within CREEP that had Liddy at its head and included Hunt.

Early in 1972, Liddy and his lieutenants proposed an elaborate scheme to wiretap the phones of various Democrats and to disrupt their nominating convention. Twice Mitchell refused to go along, arguing that the proposal was too risky and expensive. Finally, he approved a modified version of the plan to tap the phones of the Democratic National Committee at its headquarters in the Watergate apartment complex in Washington, D.C. Mitchell, formerly the top justice official in the land, had authorized breaking the law.

The wiretapping attempt took place on the evening of June 16, 1972, and ended with the arrest of those involved. Nixon's aides played down the matter and used federal resources to head off any investigation. When the FBI traced the money carried by the burglars to CREEP, the president authorized the CIA

DOCUMENT

House Judiciary Committee's Assessment of Nixon's Activities (1974)

to call off the FBI on the grounds that national security was at stake. Though not involved in the planning of the break-in, the president was now party to the cover-up. In the succeeding months, he authorized payment of hush money to silence Hunt and others. Members of the administration, including Mitchell, perjured themselves in court to shield the top officials who were involved.

Nixon trounced Democrat George McGovern in the election of 1972, receiving 61 percent of the popular vote. In a clear indication of the collapse of the Democratic coalition, 70 percent of southern voters cast their ballots for Nixon. The president, however, failed to gain the congressional majorities he sought.

When the Watergate burglars were brought to trial, they pleaded guilty and were sentenced to jail, but the case refused to die. The evidence indicated that others had played a part and the investigation of two zealous reporters, Bob Woodward and Carl Bernstein of the *Washington Post*, uncovered others involved. On one occasion, when they reached Mitchell and asked him about a story tying him to Watergate, he turned on them in fury. "All that crap you're putting in the paper?" he said. "It's all been denied."

Meanwhile, the Senate Select Committee on Presidential Campaign Activities undertook its own investigation, and one of the convicted burglars testified that the White House had been involved in the episode. Newspaper stories generated further leads, and the Senate hearings in turn provided new material for the press. Faced with rumors that the White

DOONESBURY   **by Garry Trudeau**

A Cartoonist Comments on Watergate   Although Nixon steadfastly denied his complicity in the Watergate affair, his tape recordings of White House conversations told a different story. In this classic *Doonesbury* cartoon from September 17, 1973, Garry Trudeau notes Nixon's efforts to head off the investigation. What do you think the cartoonist is trying to say here? *(Doonesbury © 1973 G. B. Trudeau. Reprinted with permission of Universal Press Syndicate. All rights reserved.)*

Presidential Elections of the 1970s				
Year	**Candidate**	**Party**	**Popular Vote**	**Electoral Vote**
1972	RICHARD M. NIXON	Republican	45,767,218 (60.7%)	520
	George S. McGovern	Democratic	28,357,668 (37.5%)	17
1976	JIMMY CARTER	Democratic	40,830,763 (50.0%)	297
	Gerald R. Ford	Republican	39,147,793 (48.0%)	240

Note: Winners' names appear in capital letters.

House was actively involved, Nixon decided that he had to release Haldeman and Ehrlichman, his two closest aides, to save his own neck, claiming on nationwide television, "there can be no whitewash at the White House."

In May 1973, the Senate committee began televised public hearings, reminiscent of the McCarthy hearings of the 1950s. As millions of Americans watched, the drama built. John Dean, seeking to save himself, testified that Nixon knew about the cover-up, and other staffers revealed a host of illegal activities undertaken at the White House: money had been paid to the burglars to silence them; State Department documents had been forged to smear a previous administration; wiretaps had been used to prevent top-level leaks. The most electrifying moment was the disclosure by another aide that the president had installed a secret taping system in his office that recorded all conversations. Tapes could verify or disprove the growing rumors that Nixon had in fact been party to the cover-up all along.

Nixon Releases Transcripts of the Oval Office Tapes

To show his own honesty, Nixon appointed Harvard law professor Archibald Cox as a special prosecutor in the Department of Justice. But when Cox tried to gain access to the tapes, Nixon resisted and finally fired him. Nixon's own popularity plummeted, and even the appointment of another special prosecutor, Leon Jaworski, did not help. More and more Americans now believed that the president had played at least some part in the cover-up and should take responsibility for his acts. *Time* magazine ran an editorial headlined, "The President Should Resign," and Congress considered impeachment.

Richard Nixon, "I Am Not a Crook"

The first steps, in accordance with constitutional mandate, took place in the House of Representatives. The House Judiciary Committee, made up of 21 Democrats and 17 Republicans, began to debate the impeachment case in late July 1974. By sizable tallies, it voted to impeach the president on the grounds of obstruction of justice, abuse of power, and refusal to obey a congressional subpoena to turn over his tapes. A full House of Representatives vote still had to occur, and the Senate would have to preside over a trial and convict the president of the charges before he could be removed from office. But for Nixon, the handwriting was on the wall.

After a brief delay, on August 5, Nixon obeyed a Supreme Court ruling and released the tapes. Despite a suspicious 18½ silence, they contained the "smoking gun"—clear evidence of his complicity in the cover-up. His ultimate resignation became but a matter of time. Four days later, on August 9, 1974, the extraordinary episode came to an end, as Nixon became the first American president ever to resign.

House Judiciary Committee's Conclusion on Impeachment (1974)

As other nations around the world watched the Watergate affair with interest, they did not always understand the stakes involved. In a parliamentary democracy, such as the British system, a prime minister resigns whenever a vote of no confidence occurs. Scandals or simply serious political opposition can trigger this result. In the United States, however, a presidential resignation had never occurred in the nation's 200-year past, and so such a step loomed large.

Watergate Special Prosecution Force Memorandum (August 9, 1974)

The Watergate affair seemed to be disturbing evidence that the appropriate balance of power in the federal government had disappeared. As the scandal wound down, many began to question the centralization of power in the American political system and to cite the "imperial presidency" as the cause of recent abuses. Others simply lost faith in the presidency altogether. A 1974 survey showed that trust in the presidency had declined by 50 percent in a two-year period. Coming on the heels of Lyndon Johnson's lying to the American people about involvement in Vietnam, the Watergate affair contributed to the cumulative disillusionment with politics in Washington and to the steady decrease in political participation. Barely half of those eligible to vote bothered to go to the polls in the presidential elections of 1976, 1980, and 1984. Even fewer cast ballots in nonpresidential contests.

Gerald Ford: Caretaker President

When Nixon resigned in disgrace midway through his second term, he was succeeded by Gerald Ford. An unpretentious, middle-American Republican who believed in traditional virtues, Ford had been appointed vice president in 1973 when Spiro Agnew resigned in disgrace for accepting bribes. After the appointment, Richard Rovere, a noted journalist, wrote in the *New Yorker:* "That he is thoroughly equipped to serve as Vice President seems unarguable; the office requires only a warm body and occasionally a nimble tongue. However . . . neither Richard Nixon nor anyone else has come forward to explain Gerald Ford's qualifications to serve as Chief Executive." The new president acknowledged his own limitations, declaring, "I am a Ford, not a Lincoln."

IMAGE

Gerald Ford

More important than his limitations were his views about public policy. Throughout a long tenure in the House of Representatives, Ford had had opposed federal aid to education, the poverty program, and mass transit. He had voted for civil rights measures only when weaker substitutes he had favored had gone down to defeat. Like his predecessor, he was determined to stop the liberal advances promoted by the Democrats in the 1960s.

Ford faced a daunting task. After Watergate, Washington was in turmoil. Americans wondered whether any politician could be trusted to guide public affairs. Ford worked quickly to restore trust in the presidency. He emphasized conciliation and compromise, and he promised to cooperate both with Congress and with American citizens. The nation responded gratefully. *Time* magazine pointed to a "mood of good feeling and even exhilaration in Washington that the city had not experienced for many years."

The new feeling did not last long. Ford weakened his base of support by pardoning Richard Nixon barely a month after his resignation. Ford's decidedly conservative bent in domestic policy often threw him into confrontation with a Democratic Congress. Economic problems proved most pressing in 1974, as inflation, fueled by oil price increases, hit 11 percent, unemployment reached 6.6 percent at the end of the year, and GNP declined. Home construction slackened and interest rates rose, while stock prices fell. Nixon, preoccupied with the Watergate crisis, had been unable to curb rising inflation and unemployment. Not since

A President by Appointment Gerald Ford, a genial man, sought to re-establish confidence in the government after succeeding Nixon as president. Far different from his predecessor, he served just over two years, as his bid for election to the presidency in 1976 ended in defeat. *(Bettmann/CORBIS)*

Franklin Roosevelt took office in the depths of the Great Depression had a new president faced economic difficulties so severe.

Like Herbert Hoover 45 years before, the conservative Ford hoped to restore confidence and persuade the public that conditions would improve with patience and goodwill. But his campaign to cajole Americans to "Whip Inflation Now" voluntarily failed dismally. At last convinced of the need for strong government action, the administration introduced a tight-money policy as a means of curbing inflation. It led to the most severe recession since the Depression, with unemployment peaking at 9 percent in early 1975. In response, Congress pushed for an antirecession spending program. Recognizing political reality, Ford endorsed a multibillion-dollar tax cut coupled with higher unemployment benefits. The economy made a modest recovery, although inflation and unemployment remained high, and federal budget deficits soared. Despite such improvement, Ford found himself at odds with Congress over the economy as well as efforts to expand the welfare state.

The Carter Interlude

In the election of 1976, the nation's bicentennial year, Ford faced Jimmy Carter, former governor of

Georgia. Carter, appealing to voters distrustful of political leadership, portrayed himself as an out-

sider. He stressed that he was not from Washington and observed that, unlike many of those mired in recent scandals, he was not a lawyer. Carter's quest for the Democratic nomination benefited from reforms that increased the significance of primary elections in selecting a presidential candidate and decreased the influence of party professionals. Assisted by public relations experts, he effectively utilized the media, especially television, which allowed him to bypass party machines and establish a direct electronic relationship with voters.

In the election, most elements of the old Democratic coalition came together once again, as the Democrats profited from the fallout of the Watergate affair. Carter won a 50-to-48-percent majority of the popular vote and a 297-to-240 tally in the Electoral College. He did well with members of the working class, African Americans, and Catholics. He won most of the South, heartening to the Democrats after Nixon's gains there. Racial voting differences continued, however, as Carter attracted less than half of all white voters but an overwhelming majority of black voters.

Carter stood in stark contrast to his recent predecessors in the White House. Rooted in the rural South, he was a peanut farmer who shared the values of the region. He

was also a graduate of the Naval Academy, trained as a manager and an engineer. A modest man, he was uncomfortable with the pomp and incessant political activity in Washington. He hoped to take a more restrained approach to the presidency and thereby defuse its imperial stamp.

Initially, voters saw Carter as a reform Democrat committed to his party's liberal goals. When he had accepted the Democratic nomination, he had called for an end to race and sex discrimination. He had challenged the "political and economic elite" in America and sought a new approach to providing for the poor, old, and weak.

But Carter was hardly the old-line liberal some Democrats had hoped for. Though he called himself a populist, his political philosophy and priorities were never clear. Critics charged that he had no legislative strategy. Rather, they said with some truth, he responded to problems in a haphazard way and failed to provide firm direction. His status as an outsider led him to ignore traditional political channels. He also seemed to become mired in detail and to lose sight of larger issues. Like Herbert Hoover, he was a technocrat in the White House when liberals wanted a visionary to help them overcome hard times.

In economic affairs, Carter gave liberals some hope at first as he accepted deficit spending. But when record deficits led to an increase in the money supply and brought inflation to about 10 percent a year, Carter slowed down the economy by reducing spending and cutting the deficit slightly. These budget cuts fell largely on social programs and distanced Carter from reform-minded Democrats who had supported him three years before. Yet even that effort to arrest growing deficits was not enough. When the budget released in early 1980 still showed high spending levels, the financial community reacted strongly. Bond prices fell, and interest rates rose dramatically.

Similarly, Carter disappointed liberals by failing to construct an effective energy policy. OPEC's

Celebrating a Triumph at Camp David One of Jimmy Carter's greatest achievements was taking the first steps toward peace in the Middle East. Here he celebrates the Camp David Agreement of September 1978, in which Anwar al-Sadat of Egypt, on the left, and Menachem Begin, on the right, shook hands and agreed to work together. What do the faces of these three leaders convey about the moment captured in this photograph? *(Black Star)*

increase of oil prices led many Americans to resent their dependence on foreign oil—more than 40 percent was being imported by the end of the decade—and to clamor for energy self-sufficiency. Carter responded in April 1977 with a comprehensive energy program, which he called the "moral equivalent of war." Critics seized on the acronym of that expression, MEOW, to ridicule the plan and had a field day attacking the president. Never an effective leader in working with the legislative branch, Carter watched his proposals bog down in Congress for 26 months. Eventually, the program committed the nation to move from oil dependence to reliance on coal, possibly even on sun and wind, and established a new synthetic-fuel corporation. Nuclear power, another alternative, seemed less attractive as costs rose and accidents occurred.

Jimmy Carter and the "Crisis of Confidence"

Carter further upset liberals by beginning deregulation—the removal of government controls in economic life. Arguing that certain restrictions established over the past century stifled competition and increased consumer costs, he supported decontrol of oil and natural gas prices to spur production. He also deregulated the railroad, trucking, and airline industries.

One of the high points in Carter's administration came with his involvement in the ever-turbulent Middle East. In the aftermath of the Yom Kippur War, Egyptian leader Anwar al-Sadat was disappointed in the ultimate failure of the struggle and was aware that his people needed relief from the incessant conflict. Dramatically, he flew to Israel and addressed the Knesset—the Israeli parliament—and committed himself to peace. At that point, Carter intervened and invited Sadat and Israeli leader Menachem Begin to come to a retreat at Camp David, in Maryland (not far from Washington, D.C.), where he helped the two leaders work out an accord in September 1978. It led to a formal peace treaty the next March. Egypt recognized Israel—and the Israeli right to exist—for the first time, and the Israelis gave up part of the occupied Sinai Peninsula. The United States promised substantial military aid to both parties, which led to a closer relationship with Egypt that continues to this day. As the United States superseded the Soviet Union as an ally of Egypt, the Russians countered by arming the radical Palestine Liberation Organization (PLO) and helped encourage leader Yasir Arafat in the ongoing guerrilla war.

Carter puzzled people overseas by his passionate commitment to human rights. It became a hallmark of his administration, especially when he ordered the United States to pull out of the Olympics in Moscow in 1980 in protest of the Soviet invasion of neighboring Afghanistan. Some Americans wondered how this commitment squared with the long-standing American approach of supporting dictators and overlooking human rights abuses in countries whose support the United States wanted in the Cold War.

As the 1970s ended, liberals were disappointed. Their hopes for a stronger commitment to a welfare state had been dashed, and conservatives had the upper hand. Despite a tenuous Democratic hold on the presidency at the end of the decade, liberalism was in trouble. And the turbulence that had marked the beginning of the decade had not disappeared.

THE CONTINUING QUEST FOR SOCIAL REFORM

A struggle for social reform was one more factor contributing to the turbulence of the 1970s. The black struggle for equality in the 1950s and 1960s helped spark a women's movement that soon developed a life of its own. This struggle, like the struggles of Latinos and Native Americans, employed the confrontational approach and the vocabulary of the civil rights movement to create pressure for change. In time, other groups appropriated the same strategies and kept reform efforts alive. While these movements had preexisting roots and usually began in the 1960s, they came of age in the 1970s, and in these years achieved their greatest gains.

Attacking the Feminine Mystique

Many white women joined the civil rights movement only to find that they were second-class activists. Men, black and white, held the policy positions and relegated women to menial chores when not actually involved in demonstrations or voter drives. Many women also felt sexually exploited by male leaders. Stokely Carmichael's comment underscored their point. "The only position for women in SNCC," he said, "is prone."

Although the civil rights movement helped spark the women's movement, broad social changes provided the preconditions. During the 1950s and 1960s, increasing numbers of married women entered the labor force (see Chapter 26). Equally important, many more young women were attending college. By 1970, women earned 41 percent of all B.A. degrees awarded, in comparison with only 25 percent in 1950. These educated young women held high hopes for themselves, even if they still earned substantially less than men.

This healthy, normal baby has a handicap. She was born female.

A Message from NOW on Gender Discrimination Awareness of racial discrimination led women to speak out against discrimination based on gender, as shown in this pointed advertisement sponsored by the National Organization for Women. What is the tone of the message? What does it imply should be done? (*Sponsored by Legal Momentum [then known as NOW Legal Defense and Education Fund]*)

The women's movement, which came into its own in the 1970s, depended on reform legislation to help end gender discrimination. Title VII of the 1964 Civil Rights bill, as originally drafted, prohibited discrimination on the grounds of race. During legislative debate, conservatives opposed to black civil rights seized on an amendment to include discrimination on the basis of gender, in the hope of defeating the entire bill. But the amendment passed, and then the full measure was approved, giving women a legal tool for attacking discrimination. They discovered, however, that the Equal Employment Opportunities Commission regarded women's complaints of discrimination as far less important than those of blacks.

DOCUMENT

NOW,
Statement of
Purpose
(1966)

Women's organizations played an important role in bringing about change in the 1970s. In 1966, a group of 28 professional women, including author Betty Friedan, established the National Organization for Women (NOW) "to take action to bring American women into full participation in the mainstream of American society now." By full participation, the founders meant not only fair pay and equal opportunity but a new, more egalitarian form of marriage. NOW also attacked the "false image of women . . . in the media." By 1967, some 1,000 women had joined the organization; four years later its membership reached 15,000.

NOW was a pressure group that sought to reform American society by promoting equal opportunity for women. To radical feminists, who had come up through the civil rights movement, NOW's agenda failed to confront adequately the problem of gender discrimination. Jo Freeman, a radical activist, observed, "Women's liberation does not mean equality with men . . . [because] equality in an unjust society is meaningless." These feminists wanted to educate millions of discontented but unpoliticized women about the oppression they faced. They tried, through the technique of consciousness raising, to help women understand the extent of their oppression and to analyze their experience as a political phenomenon. They wanted to demonstrate, in their phrase, that the personal was political.

The radicals gained mass-media attention at the Miss America pageant in Atlantic City, New Jersey, in September 1968. On the boardwalk, a hundred women nominated a sheep as their candidate for Miss America. They also set up a "freedom trash can" and placed in it "instruments of torture": bras, girdles, hair curlers, high heels, and copies of *Playboy* and *Cosmopolitan* magazines. In the pageant hall, they chanted "Freedom for women" and unfurled banners reading "Women's Liberation" in a public relations campaign that continued in the following years.

The women's movement hit its stride in the 1970s. In 1971, Helen Reddy expressed the energy of the movement in a song called "I Am Woman" that rose to the top of the charts:

I am woman, hear me roar
In numbers too big to ignore
And I know too much to go back and pretend
'Cause I've heard it all before
And I've been down there on the floor,
No one's ever gonna keep me down again.
Oh, yes, I am wise
But it's wisdom born of pain.
Yes, I've paid the price
But look how much I gained
If I have to
I can do anything.
I am strong,
I am invincible,
I am woman.

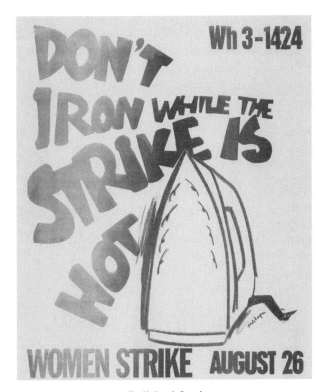

Urging Women to Political Action   This poster comes from Women's Equality Day—August 26, 1970—which was the fiftieth anniversary of the passage of the Nineteenth Amendment to the Constitution granting women the right to vote. Thousands of women put aside household chores and left their jobs to protest the lack of equality in the United States. How does the caption capture the mood of the protest? What could such a strike hope to achieve? *(Mary-Ann Lupa, courtesy Schlesinger Library, Radcliffe Institute for Advanced Study, Harvard University.)*

barred gender bias in federally assisted educational activities and programs, made easier the admission of women to colleges and changed the nature of intercollegiate athletics by requiring schools to fund sports teams for women. By 1980, fully 30 percent of the participants in intercollegiate sports were women, compared with 15 percent before Title IX became law.

A flurry of publications spread the principles of the women's movement. In 1972, journalist Gloria Steinem and several other women founded a new magazine, *Ms.,* which succeeded beyond their wildest dreams. By 1973, there were almost 200,000 subscribers. *Our Bodies, Ourselves,* a handbook published by a women's health collective, encouraged women to understand and control their bodies; it sold 850,000 copies between 1971 and 1976. Unlike older women's magazines, these publications dealt with abortion, employment, discrimination, and other feminist issues, such as the Equal Rights Amendment.

Reddy's song reflected a new militancy and sense of self-confidence among women.

Real changes were underway. A 1970 survey of first-year college students showed that men interested in such fields as business, medicine, engineering, and law outnumbered women eight to one; by 1975, the ratio had dropped to three to one. The proportion of women beginning law school quadrupled between 1969 and 1973. Women gained access to the military academies and entered senior officer ranks, although they were still restricted from combat command ranks. According to the Census Bureau, 45 percent of mothers with preschool children held jobs outside the home in 1980. That figure was four times as high as it had been 30 years before. To be sure, many employers systematically excluded women from certain positions, but the progress was still unmistakable.

Legal changes brought women more benefits and opportunities. Title IX of the Education Amendments of 1972 broadened the provisions of the Civil Rights Act of 1964. The new legislation, which

New Publications for Women   The women's movement spawned a number of publications that attempted to give women greater control over various aspects of their own lives. The book *Our Bodies, Ourselves* and *Ms.* magazine were two important sources in that effort. What do you think this cover picture was trying to convey? Is it successful? *(Reprinted by permission of Ms. Magazine, © 1982)*

Women in the Workforce, 1920–1980

This graph shows the dramatic increase in the number of women in the workforce over the years. Note particularly the rise in the number of working women 25–44 years old in the 1970s.

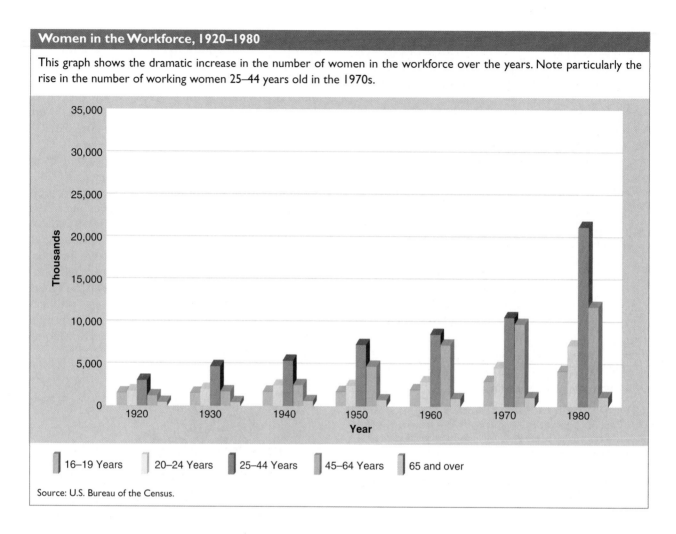

16–19 Years   20–24 Years   25–44 Years   45–64 Years   65 and over

Source: U.S. Bureau of the Census.

Women both in and out of NOW worked for congressional passage, then ratification, of the Equal Rights Amendment (ERA) to the Constitution. Passed by Congress in 1972, with ratification seemingly assured, it stated simply, "Equality of rights under the law shall not be denied or abridged by the United States or by any State on account of sex."

More radical feminists insisted that legal changes were not sufficient. Traditional gender and family roles would have to be discarded to end social exploitation. Socialist feminists claimed that it was not enough to strike out at male domination, for capitalist society itself was responsible for women's plight. Only through revolution could women be free.

Jimmy Carter Signs the ERA Resolution, 1972

Black women frequently viewed the women's movement with ambivalence. Some, like attorney Pauli Murray, became feminists. She worked closely with bureaucrats and legislators in Washington on legal measures to end gender discrimination. Others felt that the struggle for racial equality took precedence, and they were reluctant to divert

energy and attention from it. Members of NOW and similar organizations, they claimed, "suffered little more than boredom, gentle repression, and dishpan hands" and were hardly confronting the most important issues when they burned their bras and insisted on using the title Ms. rather than Mrs. or Miss.

Not all women were feminists. Many felt the women's movement was contemptuous of women who stayed at home to perform traditional tasks. Marabel Morgan was one who still insisted that the woman had a place at home by her husband's side. The wife of a Florida attorney, she argued that "it is only when a woman surrenders her life to her husband, reveres and worships him, and is willing to serve him, that she becomes really beautiful to him." In her book *The Total Woman* (1973), she counseled others to follow the 4A approach: accept, admire, adapt, appreciate. As of 1975, some 500,000 copies of the hardcover volume had been sold.

In politics, Phyllis Schlafly headed a nationwide campaign to block ratification of the ERA. "It won't do anything to help women," she said, "and it will take away from women the rights they already have, such as the right of a wife to be supported by her husband, the right of a woman to be exempted from military combat, and the right, if you wanted it, to go to a single-sex college." The ERA, she predicted, would lead to the establishment of coed bathrooms, the elimination of alimony, and the legalization of homosexual marriage.

Schlafly and her allies had their way. Within a few years after passage of the ERA, 35 states had agreed to the measure, but then the momentum disappeared. Even with an extension of the deadline granted in 1979, the amendment could not win support of the necessary 38 states. By mid-1982, the ERA was dead.

Despite the counterattacks, the women's movement flourished in the late 1960s and 1970s. In the tenth-anniversary issue of *Ms.* magazine in 1982, founding editor Gloria Steinem noted the differences a decade had made. "Now, we have words like 'sexual harassment' and 'battered women,'" she wrote. "Ten years ago, it was just called 'life.'" She also observed that "now, we are becoming the men we wanted to marry. Ten years ago, we were trained to marry a doctor, not be one."

Latino Mobilization

Latinos, like women, profited from the example of blacks in their struggle for equality that came of age in the 1970s. Long denied equal access to the American dream, they became more vocal and confrontational as their numbers increased dramatically in the postwar years. In 1970, some 9 million residents of the United States declared they were of Spanish origin; in 1980, the figure was 14.6 million. But their median household income remained less than three-fourths that of Anglos, and inferior education and political weakness reinforced social and cultural separation. Latinos comprised Puerto Ricans in the Northeast, Cubans in Florida, and Chicanos—Mexican Americans—in the West and Southwest. Chicanos took the lead in the protest struggle, though all groups developed a heightened sense of solidarity and group pride as they began to assert their own rights.

In the 1960s and 1970s, Mexican Americans became more active politically. In 1960, Chicanos supported Kennedy, helping him win Texas, and began to see the benefits of such support. In 1961, Henry B. González was elected to Congress from San Antonio. Three years later, Elizo ("Kika") de la Garza of Texas won election to the House and Joseph Montoya of New Mexico went to the Senate. Chicanos were gaining a political voice.

More important than political representation, which came only slowly, was direct action, which triumphed in the 1970s. César Chávez, founder of

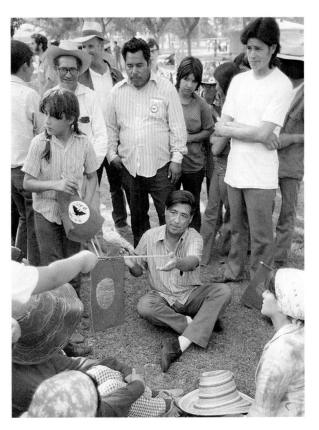

An Advocate for Migrant Workers César Chávez organized the United Farm Workers to give migrant Mexican workers representation in their struggle for better wages and working conditions. Here he works with laborers in his tireless campaign for their support. What kind of a leader do you think Chávez was on the basis of his appearance in this picture? *(Bob Fitch/Take Stock/Black Star)*

the United Farm Workers, proved what could be done by organizing one of the most exploited and ignored groups of laboring people in the country, the migrant farm workers of the West. Chávez (who came from a family whose members were "the first ones to leave the fields if anyone shouted 'Huelga!'—which is Spanish for 'Strike!'") concentrated on migrant Mexican field hands, who worked long hours for meager pay. By 1965, his organization had recruited 1,700 people and was beginning to attract volunteer help.

Latina women played an important part in the organizing effort. Dolores Huerta, a third-generation Mexican American, who became vice president of the United Farm Workers, observed how entire families were involved:

Excluding women, protecting them, keeping women at home, that's the middle-class way. Poor people's movements have always had whole families on the line, ready to move at a moment's notice, with more courage because that's all we had. It's a class not an ethnic thing.

AMERICAN VOICES

Helen Chávez, Reflections on the Family's Struggle

The Chávez family faced considerable difficulties as César Chávez left his leadership position with a Community Service Organization project in California and dedicated himself to organizing Chicano field workers. Often, César Chávez had to depend on his wife to support the family.

When we packed up in San Jose, we were so busy we forgot to go to the bank and get any money. The night before, Cesar had gotten sick and was just burning up with fever. I said, "Let's wait." But we had everything packed, and he had a house meeting that evening. He said, "No, we have to go."

I don't drive, so he had to. Here we get into our beat-up station wagon loaded with this huge rented trailer with all our belongings in it and the kids, and I just had maybe a few dollars.

We had to stop along the way because he was really burning up with fever, and I got a little something for the kids. Then the car stopped completely. We really didn't know what to do. Somebody stopped and helped us, so we gave them our last two dollars. The kids were hungry, but we didn't have any money to buy any food for them....

We went up to the little house we had rented, but it was dark, and there was no electricity. I think we had a flashlight. We just threw a few mattresses on the floor so the kids could sleep. I fed them and put them to bed.

Cesar went up to this meeting, sick as he was....

Cesar had always talked about organizing farm workers, ... After all, we were both farm workers, and my parents and his parents and our whole families.

Finally, he just made a decision that that's what he was going to do. He did discuss it and say that it would be a lot of work and a lot of sacrifice because we wouldn't have any income coming in. But it didn't worry me. It didn't frighten me. I figured we'd manage some way as long as one of us was able to work.

I never had any doubts that he would succeed. I thought a lot of people felt the way we did.

- *According to Helen Chávez, why did César Chávez become a labor organizer?*

- *What was life like for the Chávez family once that decision was made?*

- *What gave Helen Chávez the confidence that this effort would succeed?*

Chávez first took on the grape growers of California. Calling the grape workers out on strike, the union demanded better pay and working conditions as well as recognition of the union. When the growers did not concede, Chávez launched a nationwide consumer boycott of their products. Although the Schenley Corporation and several wine companies came to terms, others held out. In 1966, the DiGiorgio Corporation agreed to permit a union election but then rigged the results. When California governor Edmund G. Brown launched an investigation that resulted in another election, he became the first major political figure to support the long-powerless Chicano field hands. This time, the United Farm Workers won. Similar boycotts of lettuce and other products harvested by exploited labor also ended in success.

In 1975, César Chávez's long struggle for farmworkers won passage in California of a measure that required growers to bargain collectively with the elected representatives of the workers. Farmworkers had never been covered by the National Labor Relations Board. Now they had achieved the legal basis for representation that could help bring higher wages and improved working conditions. And Chávez had become a national figure.

Meanwhile, Mexican Americans pressed for reform in other areas. In the West and Southwest, Mexican American studies programs flourished. In 1969, at least 50 were available in California alone. Colleges and universities offered degrees, built library collections, and gave Chicanos access to their own past. The campuses also provided a network linking students together and mobilizing them for political action.

Beginning in 1968, Mexican American students began to protest conditions in secondary schools. They pointed to overcrowded and run-down institutions and to the 50 percent dropout rate that came from expulsion, transfer, or failure because students had never been taught to read. School walkouts took place in Colorado, Texas, and other parts of California and led to successful demands for Latino teachers, counselors, and courses as well as better facilities.

At the same time, new organizations emerged. Young Citizens for Community Action, founded by teenager David Sánchez and four Chicanos in East Los Angeles, began as a service club to assist the neighborhood. Later, the organization adopted a paramilitary stance and evolved into a defensive patrol, now known as Young Chicanos for Community Action, which tried to protect local residents. Its members became identified as the Brown Berets and formed chapters throughout the Midwest and Southwest.

Other Latinos followed a more political path. In Texas, José Angel Gutiérrez formed a citizens' organization that developed into the La Raza Unida political party and successfully promoted Mexican American candidates for political offices. Throughout the 1970s, it gained strength in the West and Southwest.

Among the new Chicano leaders was the charismatic Reies López Tijerina, or "El Tigre." A preacher, he became interested in land-grant issues and argued that the U.S. government had fraudulently deprived Chicanos of village lands. He formed an organization, La Alianza Federal de Mercedes (the Federal Alliance of Land Grants), which marched on the New Mexico state capital and occupied a number of national forests. Arrested, he stood trial and eventually served time in prison, where he became a symbol of political repression.

Rodolfo "Corky" Gonzáles was another such leader. A Golden Gloves boxing champion as a youth, he later served as a district captain for the Democratic party in Denver. He helped direct Denver poverty programs until he was fired for being overly zealous in his support of the Chicano community. Eloquently he described the despair many Chicanos felt:

I am Joaquin,
lost in a world of confusion,
caught up in the whirl of a gringo society,
confused by the rules,
scorned by attitudes,
suppressed by manipulation
and destroyed by modern society.

Gonzáles founded the Crusade for Justice to advance the Chicano cause through community organization. Like Tijerina, he was arrested for his part in a demonstration but was subsequently acquitted.

Latinos made a particular point of protesting the Vietnam War. Because the draft drew most heavily from the poorer segments of society, the Latino casualty rate was far higher than that of the population at large. In 1969, the Brown Berets organized the National Chicano Moratorium Committee and demonstrated against what they argued was a racial war, with black and brown Americans being used against their third world compatriots. Some of the rallies ended in confrontations with the police. News reporter Rubén Salazar, active in exposing questionable police activity, was killed in one such episode in 1970, and his death brought renewed charges of police brutality.

Aware of the growing numbers and growing demands of Latinos, the Nixon administration sought to defuse their anger and win their support. Cuban American refugees, strongly opposed to communism, shifted toward the Republican party, which they assumed was more likely eventually to intervene against Fidel Castro. Meanwhile, Nixon courted Chicanos by dangling political positions, government jobs, and promises of better programs for Mexican Americans. The effort paid off; Nixon received 31 percent of the Latino vote in 1972. Rather than reward his Latino followers, however, the president moved to cut back the poverty program, begun under Johnson, that assisted many of them.

Despite occasional gains in the 1970s, Latinos from all groups faced continuing problems. Discrimination persisted in housing, education, and employment. Activists had laid the groundwork for a campaign for equal rights, but the struggle had just begun.

Native American Protest

Like Latinos, Native Americans continued to suffer second-class status in the 1960s and 1970s. But, partly inspired by the confrontational tactics of other groups, they became more aggressive in their efforts to claim their rights and improve their living and working conditions. Their soaring numbers—the census put them at 550,000 in 1960 and 1,480,000 in 1980—gave them greater visibility and political clout.

In the 1960s, Native Americans had begun to assert themselves even more. Several hundred Indians meeting together in 1961 asked the government for

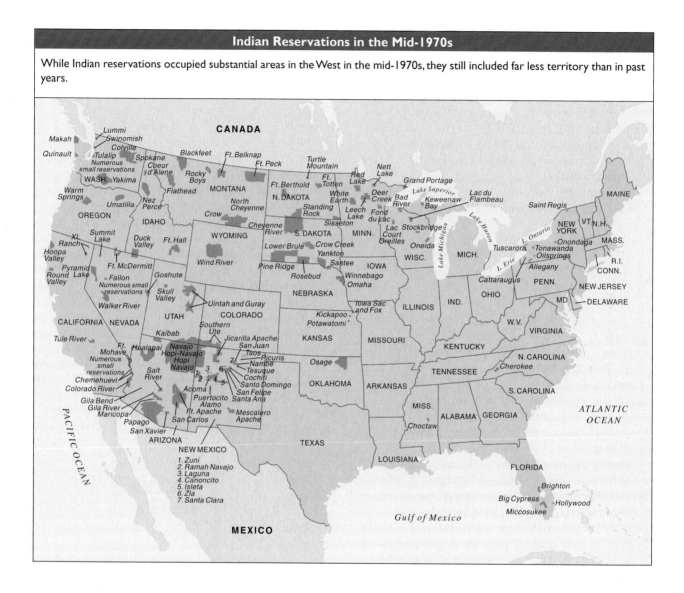

Indian Reservations in the Mid-1970s

While Indian reservations occupied substantial areas in the West in the mid-1970s, they still included far less territory than in past years.

the right to help make decisions about programs and budgets for the tribes. A group of college-educated Indians at the conference formed a National Indian Youth Council aimed at reestablishing national pride. Over the next several decades, the council helped change the attitudes of tribal leaders, who were frequently called "Uncle Tomahawks" and "apples" (red outside, white inside) for their willingness to sacrifice their people's needs to white demands.

American Indians learned from the examples of protest they saw around them in rising third world nationalism and, even more important, in the civil rights revolution. They too came to understand the place of interest-group politics in a diverse society. Finally, they were chastened by the excesses of the Vietnam War. They recognized a pattern of killing people of color that connected Indian–white rela-

tions to the excesses in the Philippines at the turn of the century and to atrocities in Korea and Vietnam.

Indians in the late 1960s and 1970s successfully promoted their own values and designs. Indian fashions became more common, museums and galleries displayed Indian art, and Indian jewelry found a new market. The larger culture came to appreciate important work by Native Americans. In 1968, N. Scott Momaday won the Pulitzer Prize for his book *House Made of Dawn*. Vine Deloria, Jr.'s *Custer Died for Your Sins* (1969) had even wider readership. Meanwhile, popular films such as *Little Big Man* (1970) provided sympathetic portrayals of Indian history. Indian-studies programs developed in colleges and universities. Organizations like the American Indian Historical Society protested traditional textbook treatment of Indians and demanded more honest portrayals.

At the same time, Native Americans became more confrontational. Like other groups, they worked through the courts when they could but also challenged authority more aggressively when necessary.

Led by a new generation of leaders, American Indians tried to protect what was left of their tribal lands. Elders reminded young people, "Once we owned all the land." For generations, federal and state governments had steadily encroached on Native American territory. That intrusion had to cease. Indian activists echoed the words of D'Arcy McNickle, a Flathead anthropologist, who had declared in 1961, "Everything is tied to our homeland."

The protest spirit was apparent on the Seneca Nation's Allegany reservation in New York State. Although a 1794 treaty had established the Seneca's right to the land, the federal government had planned since 1928 to build a flood-control dam there. In 1956, after hearings to which the Indians were not invited and about which they were not informed, Congress appropriated funds for the project. Court appeals failed to block the scheme, and the dam was eventually built. The government belatedly passed a $15 million reparations bill, but money did not compensate for the loss of 10,000 acres of land that contained sacred sites, hunting and fishing grounds, and homes.

The Seneca did somewhat better in the 1970s. When New York State tried to condemn a section of Seneca land to build a superhighway to run through part of the Allegany reservation, the Indians again went to court. In 1981, the state finally agreed to an exchange: state land elsewhere in addition to a cash settlement in return for an easement through the reservation. That decision encouraged tribal efforts in Montana, Wyoming, Utah, New Mexico, and Arizona to resist similar incursions on reservation lands.

Native American leaders found that lawsuits charging violations of treaty rights could give them powerful leverage. In 1967, in the first of many subsequent decisions upholding the Indian side, the U.S. Court of Claims ruled that the government in 1823 had forced the Seminole in Florida to cede their land for an unreasonably low price. The court directed the government to pay additional funds 144 years later. Legal assaults continued in the 1970s.

American Indians also vigorously protested a new assault on their long-abused water rights. On the northern plains, large conglomerates, responding to the international oil shortage, vastly extended their coal strip-mining operations. Fierce legal

The Occupation at Wounded Knee The Native American movement's armed occupation of Wounded Knee, South Dakota, the site of a late-nineteenth-century massacre of the Sioux, resulted in bloodshed that dramatized unfair government treatment of Native Americans. What elements of this scene convey the determination behind this episode? *(AP/Wide World Photos)*

struggles over possession of limited water resources resulted. Litigating tribes gained some legal ammunition in a landmark case involving the water rights of the Paiute on the Nevada–California border; in 1973, a federal court ruled that the government must carry out its obligation as trustee to protect Indian property.

Another effort involved the reassertion of fishing rights. In various parts of the nation, the Nisqually, Puyallup, Muckleshoot, Chippewa, and other tribes argued that they had treaty rights to fish where they chose, without worrying about the intrusive regulatory efforts of the states. Despite pressure from other fishermen, a series of court cases provided the tribes with some of the protection they claimed by ruling that nineteenth-century treaties allowing

Indians fishing rights "in common with" whites meant that Indians could take up to 50 percent of allowable limits.

Urban Indian activism became highly visible in 1968 when George Mitchell and Dennis Banks, Chippewa living in Minneapolis, founded the activist American Indian Movement (AIM). AIM got Office of Economic Opportunity funds channeled to Indian–controlled organizations. It also established patrols to protect drunken Indians from harassment by the police. As its successes became known, chapters formed in other cities.

An incident in November 1969 dramatized Native American militancy. A landing party of 78 Indians seized Alcatraz Island in San Francisco Bay in an effort to protest symbolically the inability of the Bureau of Indian Affairs to "deal practically" with questions of Indian welfare. The Indians converted the island, with its defunct federal prison, into a cultural and educational center. As author Vine Deloria, Jr., noted, "By making Alcatraz an experimental Indian center operated and planned by Indian people, we would be given a chance to see what we could do toward developing answers to modern social problems. . . . It just seems to a lot of Indians that this continent was a lot better off when we were running it." In 1971, federal officials removed the Indians from Alcatraz.

Similar protests followed. In 1972, militants launched the Broken Treaties Caravan to Washington. For six days, insurgents occupied the Bureau of Indian Affairs. In 1973, AIM took over the South Dakota village of Wounded Knee, where in 1890 the U.S. Seventh Cavalry had massacred the Sioux. The reservation surrounding the town was mired in poverty. Half the families were on welfare, alcoholism was widespread, and 81 percent of the student population had dropped out of school. The occupation was meant to dramatize these conditions and to draw attention to the 371 treaties AIM leaders claimed the government had broken. Federal officials responded by encircling the area and, when AIM tried to bring in supplies, killed one Indian and wounded another. The confrontation ended with a government agreement to re-examine the treaty rights of the Indians, although little of substance was subsequently done.

As they protested social and political abuses, Native Americans devoted increasing attention to providing education and developing legal skills. Because roughly half of the Indian population continued to live on reservations, many tribal communities founded their own colleges. In 1971, the Oglala Sioux established Oglala Lakota College on the Pine Ridge Reservation in South Dakota. The

motto "Wa Wo Ici Ya" ("We can do it ourselves") revealed the college's goal. Nearby Sinte Gleska College on the Rosebud Reservation was the first to offer accredited four-year and graduate programs. The number of Indians in college increased from a few hundred in the early 1960s to tens of thousands by 1980. Many of these graduates studied law and acted as legal advocates for their own people in the court cases they filed.

Indian protest brought results. The outcry against termination in the 1950s (see Chapter 26) had led the Kennedy and Johnson administrations in the 1960s to steer a middle course, neither endorsing nor disavowing the policy. Instead, they tried to bolster reservation economies and raise standards of living by persuading private industries to locate on reservations and by promoting the leasing of reservation lands to energy and development corporations. In the 1970s, the Navajo, Northern Cheyenne, Crow, and other tribes tried to cancel or renegotiate such leases, fearing "termination by corporation." Meanwhile the Menominee of Wisconsin confronted the hated policy head on. Activist Ada Deer became a major figure in the effort to restore reservation status. She and others organized new protest groups, secured political support from the state's senators, and in 1973 had the satisfaction of seeing President Richard Nixon sign the Menominee Restoration Act.

Legislation likewise disavowed the termination policy. In 1975, Congress passed an Indian Self-Determination Act. An Education Assistance Act that same year involved subcontracting federal services to tribal groups. Both laws reflected the government's decision to respond to Indian pressure and created a framework to guide federal policy in the decades ahead.

Gay and Lesbian Rights

Closely tied to the revolution in sexual norms that affected sexual relations, marriage, and family life was a fast-growing and increasingly militant gay liberation movement. There had always been people who accepted the "gay" lifestyle, but American society as a whole was unsympathetic, and many homosexuals kept their orientation to themselves. The climate of the 1970s encouraged gays to "come out of the closet." A nightlong riot in 1969, in response to a police raid on the Stonewall Inn, a homosexual bar in Greenwich Village in New York, helped spark a new consciousness and a movement for gay rights. Throughout the 1970s, homosexuals successfully fought the most blatant forms of

Sign at a Gay Pride March

discrimination. In 1973, the American Psychiatric Association ruled that homosexuality should no longer be classified as a mental illness, and that decision was overwhelmingly supported in a vote by the membership the next year. In 1975, the U.S. Civil Service Commission lifted its ban on employment of homosexuals.

In this new climate of acceptance, many gay men who had hidden or suppressed their sexuality revealed their secret. Women, too, became more open about their sexual orientation and demanded not to be penalized for choosing other females as partners. A lesbian movement developed, sometimes involving women active in the more radical wing of the women's movement. But many Americans and some churches remained unsympathetic—occasionally vehemently so—to anyone who challenged traditional sexual norms.

Environmental and Consumer Agitation

Although many of the social movements of the 1960s and 1970s were defined by race, gender, and sexual orientation, one cut across all boundaries. Emerging in the early 1960s but not flourishing until the 1970s, a powerful movement of Americans concerned with the environment began to revive issues raised in the Progressive era and to push them further. In the mid-1960s, a Gallup poll revealed that only 17 percent of the public considered air and water pollution to be one of the three major government problems. By 1970, that figure had risen to 53 percent.

The modern environmental movement stemmed in part from post–World War II yearnings for a better "quality of life." Many Americans began to recognize that clear air, unpolluted waters, and unspoiled wilderness were indispensable to a decent existence. They worried about threats to their natural surroundings, particularly after naturalist Rachel Carson published her brilliant book *Silent Spring* in 1962.

Public concern focused on a variety of targets. In 1969, Americans were troubled to learn that thermal pollution from nuclear power plants was killing fish in both eastern and western rivers. An article in *Sports Illustrated* aroused fishing enthusiasts, sailors, and other recreational activists who had not been previously concerned. A massive oil spill off the coast of southern California turned white beaches black and wiped out much of the marine life in the immediate area. Concern about the deterioration of the environment increased as people learned more about substances they had once taken for granted. In 1978, the public became alarmed

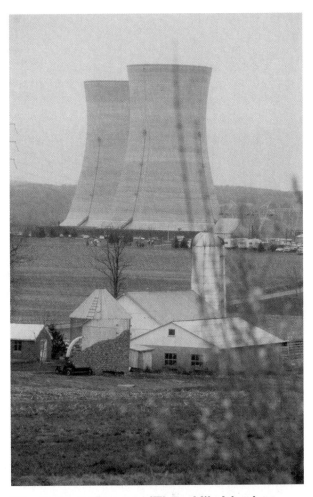

The Ominous Towers of Three Mile Island The accident at the reactor on Three Mile Island helped spark opposition to nuclear power. For people around the world, the cooling towers pictured here came to represent the horrifying possibilities of a nuclear reaction out of control. Why do the towers appear ominous? What might happen if a reaction went out of control? *(Bettmann/CORBIS)*

about the lethal effects of toxic chemicals dumped in the Love Canal neighborhood of Niagara Falls, New York. A few years later, attention focused on dioxin, one of the most deadly substances ever made, which surfaced in the Love Canal and other areas in concentrated form.

Equally frightening was the potential environmental damage from a nuclear accident. Such a calamity occurred at Three Mile Island near Harrisburg, Pennsylvania, in 1979. There, a faulty pressure-relief valve led to a loss of coolant. Initially, plant operators refused to believe indicators showing a serious malfunction. Part of the nuclear core became uncovered, part began to disintegrate, and the surrounding steam and water became highly radioactive. An explosion releasing radioactivity into the atmosphere appeared possible, and thousands of area residents fled. The scenario of nuclear disaster

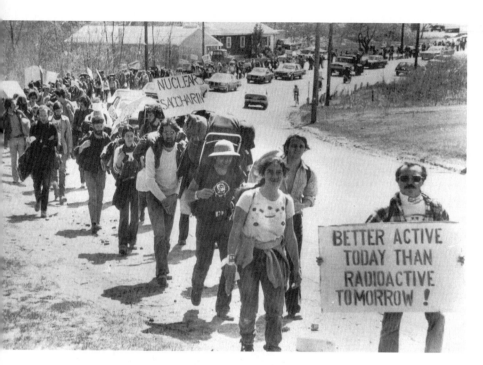

Protesting Nuclear Power
Antinuclear activists protested the proliferation of both atomic weapons and atomic power plants. Here members of the Clamshell Alliance agitate in 1977 against construction of a nuclear power plant in Seabrook, New Hampshire. How do the posters capture the mood and intention of the demonstrators? *(AP/Wide World Photos)*

depicted in the film *The China Syndrome* (1979) seemed frighteningly real. *Mad* magazine's Alfred E. Newman posed in front of the now-famous cooling towers and said, "Yes, me worry!" The worst never occurred and the danger period passed, but the plant remained shut down, filled with radioactive debris, a monument to a form of energy that was once hailed as the wave of the future but now appeared more destructive than any ever known.

The threat of a nuclear catastrophe underscored the arguments of grassroots environmental activists. Groups such as the Clamshell Alliance in New Hampshire and the Abalone Alliance in northern California campaigned aggressively against licensing new nuclear plants at Seabrook, New Hampshire, and Diablo Canyon, California. While activist tactics did not always succeed in their immediate goals, they mobilized opinion sufficiently so that no new plants were authorized after 1978. This pattern was at variance with the pattern in many other countries around the world, which continued to rely on nuclear power.

Western environmentalists were particularly worried about excessive use of water. The American West, one critic observed, had become "the greatest hydraulic society ever built in history." Massive irrigation systems had boosted the nation's use of water from 40 billion gallons a day in 1900 to 393 billion gallons by 1975, though the population had only tripled. Americans used three times as much water per capita as the world's average, and far more than other industrialized societies.

One serious source of concern was the Ogallala aquifer in the Great Plains. The drawing of enormous amounts of water in the 1950s and 1960s to make arid areas productive for farming had by the mid-1970s dramatically depleted the water stored in the aquifer. Conservation measures might delay, but not prevent, the day of reckoning.

The situation was similar in California. Because the state was naturally dry, its prosperity rested on massive irrigation projects, and in the late 1970s, it had 1,251 major reservoirs. Virtually every large river had at least one dam. Almost as much water was pumped from the ground, with little natural replenishment and even less regulation. Pointing to the destruction of the nation's rivers and streams and the severe lowering of the water table in many areas, environmentalists argued that something needed to be done before it was too late. Slowly, they made themselves heard. Critic Marc Reisner later noted, "Forty years ago, only a handful of heretics, howling at wilderness, challenged the notion that the West needed hundreds of new dams. Today they are almost vindicated."

Environmental agitation produced legislative results in the 1960s and 1970s. Lyndon Johnson's Great Society was responsible for basic legislation to halt the depletion of the country's natural resources. In the next few years, environmentalists went further, pressuring legislative and administrative bodies to regulate polluters. During Richard Nixon's presidency, Congress passed the Clean Air Act, the Water Quality Improvement Act, and the Resource Recovery Act and mandated a new Environmental Protection Agency (EPA) to spearhead the effort to control abuses. Initially, these measures aimed at controlling the toxic by-products of the modern industrial order. In subsequent years, environmentalists broadened the effort to include occupational health and social justice issues.

One such effort developed into an extraordinarily bitter economic and ecological debate. The Endangered Species Act of 1973 prohibited the federal government from supporting any projects that might jeopardize species threatened with extinction. It ran into direct conflict with commercial imperatives in the Pacific Northwest. Loggers in the Olympic Peninsula had long exploited the land by clear-cutting (cutting down all trees in a region, without leaving any standing). Environmentalists claimed that the forests they cut provided the last refuge for the spotted owl. Scientists and members of the U.S. Forest Service pushed to set aside timberland so that the owl could survive. Loggers protested that this action jeopardized their livelihood. As the issue wound its way through the courts, logging fell off drastically.

Another protest against regulation in the late 1970s and early 1980s came to be called the Sagebrush Rebellion. Critics argued that large federal landholdings in the West put that region at a disadvantage in economic competition with the East. They demanded that the national government cede the lands to states, which could sell or lease them for local gain. Conservative state legislatures in the Rocky Mountain states supported the scheme. Ranchers applauded the notion. In the end, it went nowhere,

though the agitation did persuade federal authorities to endorse a less restrictive policy on grazing.

Related to the environmental movement was a consumer movement. As Americans bought fashionable clothes, house furnishings, and electrical and electronic gadgets, they began to worry about unscrupulous sellers, just as they had earlier in the twentieth century. Over the years, Congress had established a variety of regulatory efforts as it started to safeguard citizens from marketplace abuse. In the 1970s, a stronger consumer movement developed, aimed at protecting the interests of the purchasing public and making business more responsible to consumers.

Ralph Nader led the movement. He had become interested in the issue of automobile safety while studying law at Harvard and had pursued that interest as a consultant to the Department of Labor. His book *Unsafe at Any Speed: The Designed-In Dangers of the American Automobile* (1965) argued that many cars were coffins on wheels. Head-on collisions, even at low speeds, could easily kill, for cosmetic bumpers could not withstand modest shocks. His efforts paved the way for the National Traffic and Motor Vehicle Safety Act of 1966, which set minimum safety standards for vehicles on public highways, provided for inspection to ensure compliance, and created a National Motor Vehicle Safety Advisory Council.

The consumer movement developed into a full-fledged campaign in the 1970s. Nader's efforts attracted scores of volunteers, called "Nader's Raiders." They turned out critiques and reports and, more important, inspired consumers to become more vocal in defending their rights.

TIMELINE

1968 Richard Nixon elected president	**1974** OPEC price increases
1969 Native Americans seize Alcatraz	Inflation hits 11 percent
La Raza Unida founded	Nixon resigns; Gerald Ford becomes president
1970 U.S. invasion of Cambodia	Ford pardons Nixon
Shootings at Kent State and Jackson State Universities	**1975** South Vietnam falls to the Communists
1971 *New York Times* publishes Pentagon Papers	End of the Vietnam War
1971–1975 School busing controversies in North and South	Unemployment reaches 9 percent
1972 Nixon visits People's Republic of China	Farmworkers win right to bargain collectively with growers
Nixon re-elected	Indian Self-Determination and Education Assistance Acts
SALT I agreement on nuclear arms	**1976** Jimmy Carter elected president
Ms. magazine founded	**1977** Carter energy program
Congress passes Equal Rights Amendment	**1978** *Bakke v. Regents of the University of California*
1973 Vietnam ceasefire agreement	**1979** Accident at Three Mile Island nuclear power plant
Watergate hearings in Congress	SALT II agreement signed
Spiro Agnew resigns as vice president	**1982** Ratification of ERA fails
AIM occupies Wounded Knee, South Dakota	

Conclusion

Sorting Out the Pieces

The late 1960s and 1970s were turbulent years. The chaos that seemed to reach a peak in 1968 continued, even as American participation in the war in Vietnam wound down. Richard Nixon recognized that he could contain the protest movement by bringing American soldiers home. He understood too the growing frustration with liberal reform and the wish of some Americans to dispense with the excesses they attributed to the young. For a time, he managed to silence protest and to promote a measure of harmony by his policy of Vietnamization, which cut back on the number of Americans dying in battle. But his desire to avoid losing the war led him to expand the conflict into neighboring parts of Indochina, and that move sparked even greater opposition than before.

Meanwhile, his own overarching ambition and need for electoral support led to the worst political scandal in American history. At just the time that the nation was trying to pick up the pieces from the unpopular war, he found himself embroiled in the Watergate affair, which threatened the United States with a real constitutional crisis that ended only when the president resigned.

During this entire time, disadvantaged groups demanded that the nation expand the meaning of equality. Building on the accomplishments of the civil rights movement in the 1950s and 1960s, women such as Ann Clarke, introduced at the start of the chapter, returned to school in ever-increasing numbers and found jobs and sometimes independence after years of being told that their place was at home. Native Americans and Latinos mobilized too and could see the stirrings of change. Gay rights activists made their voices heard. Environmentalists created a new awareness of the global dangers the nation and the world faced. Slowly, reformers succeeded in pressuring the government to help the nation fulfill its promise and ensure the realization of the ideals of American life.

But the course of change was ragged. Reform efforts suffered from the disillusionment with liberalism. Some movements were circumscribed by the changing political climate; others simply ran out of steam. Still, the various efforts left a legacy of ferment that could help spark further change in future years.

Questions for Review and Reflection

1. What were Richard Nixon's social and political priorities in the presidency?

2. How did Nixon propose to end the war in Vietnam?

3. What impact did the Watergate crisis have on American political life?

4. What advances did the women's movement make in the 1970s?

5. How successful was the quest for social reform in the 1970s?

Recommended Reading

Recommended Readings are posted on the Web site for this textbook. Visit www.ablongman.com/nash

Fiction and Film

Sara Davidson's *Loose Change* (1977) is a novel about the lives of three young women at the University of California at Berkeley. Marilyn French's *The Women's Room* (1977) is a novel about the impact of the women's movement on a circle of women. *House Made of Dawn* (1968) is N. Scott Momaday's Pulitzer Prize–winning novel about a young Indian living in both the white and Indian worlds. Alix Kates Shulman's *Memoirs of an Ex-Prom Queen* (1972) is the story of a young midwestern woman and her awakening during and after college.

All the President's Men (1976) is a film (based on the book of the same name) about the effort by *Washington Post* reporters Bob Woodward and Carl Bernstein to find the truth about the Watergate scandal. *Annie Hall* (1977) is Woody Allen's film about the problems of relationships. *Nixon* (1995) is Oliver Stone's movie examining the president's life. *The Times of Harvey Milk* (1984), which won the Academy Award for best documentary feature, tells the story of California's first openly gay politician, who was assassinated in 1978.

Discovering U.S. History Online

Nixon, Ford, and Carter

www.ipl.org/div/potus/rmnixon.html
www.ipl.org/div/potus/grford.html
www.ipl.org/div/potus/jecarter.html

These sites contain basic factual data about Nixon's and Carter's election and each president's presidency, speeches, and online biographies.

Vietnam: Yesterday and Today

http://servercc.oakton.edu/~wittman

The author, a librarian, presents a thorough topical bibliography on the Vietnam War.

Reflections, Memories, and Images of Vietnam Past

www.vietvet.org/thepast.htm

This site presents a gallery of "imagery, stories, poems, songs, maps, and narratives from or about the Vietnam War era."

Vietnam, A Different War

www.nytimes.com/library/world/asia/
vietnam-war-index.html

Drawing on its extensive coverage of the Vietnam War, this *New York Times* site offers both a contemporary perspective and a retrospective view of the events as a whole.

The Vietnam Veterans Memorial Wall Page

www.thewall-usa.com

A memorial for Vietnam casualties, this site gives personal insights into the individual effects of the war. A photo gallery is also included.

The My Lai Courts Martial, 1970

www.law.umkc.edu/faculty/projects/ftrials/mylai/
mylai.htm

This site contains chronology, images, and court documents describing the massacre of Vietnamese civilians at My Lai.

Watergate

www.washingtonpost.com/
wp-srv/national/longterm/watergate/front.htm

From the newspaper that broke the story, this site features a chronology, images, searchable articles, and a good deal of background information about the burglary and its consequences.

Watergate and the Constitution

www.archives.gov/digital_classroom/lessons/
watergate_and_constitution/watergate_and_
constitution.html

From the National Archives teaching materials, this site has a good chronology of Watergate and documents describing the pros and cons of seeking an indictment against former president Richard Nixon.

Three Mile Island

www.pbs.org/wgbh/amex/three/

This site provides a chronology and description of the 1969 nuclear accident.

The 1977 Women's Conference in Houston, Texas

www.lindagriffith.com/IWYcaptionsmain.html

This site offers a photographic history of this key national women's conference.

Latinos in History

http://teacher.scholastic.com/activities/hispanic/
history.htm

This site contains biographies of a variety of prominent Latino and Latina figures.

CHAPTER 30
The Revival of Conservatism, 1980–1992

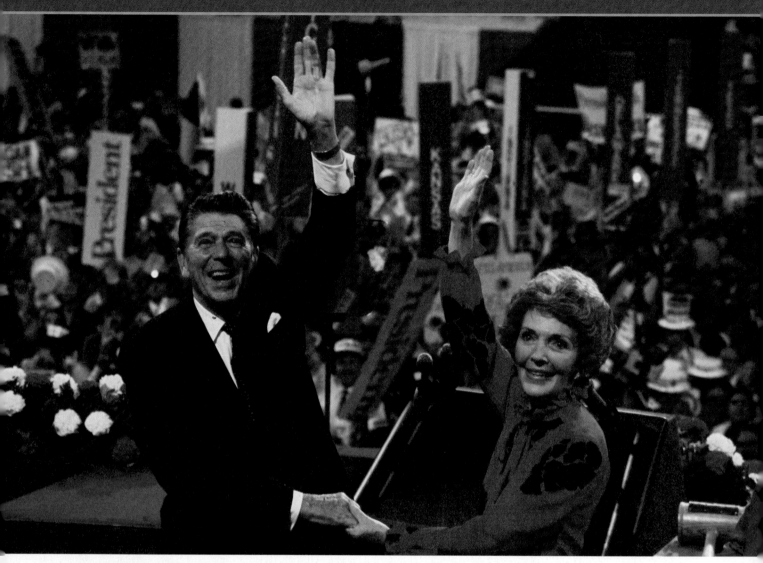

Ronald Reagan appealed to millions of Americans with his vision of a heroic national past. Working closely with his wife Nancy, he helped revive conservatism and created a new political consensus in the United States. *(Bettmann/CORBIS)*

American Stories

A Young Woman Embraces Republican Values

Leslie Maeby, a Republican political staffer in New York State in the 1980s, came from an immigrant family that had long been sympathetic to the Democratic party. Her great-grandfather, Aleksander Obrycki, had come to Baltimore from Poland in 1895. A common laborer who became a naturalized citizen in 1907, he worked for the Democratic

1006

party, meeting new immigrants on their arrival and introducing them to Democrats who could help them.

Leslie's grandfather Joe Obrycki became a numbers runner, collecting bets for local gamblers. More successful than his father, he survived the Great Depression of the 1930s with little difficulty. He too was a member of the Democratic party, a cog in the machine. As New Deal programs undermined machine rule, Joe, a ward heeler and professional gambler, ran for city council but lost. Defeat notwithstanding, he remained a loyal Democrat.

Leslie's mother, Vilma, was likewise a Democrat. Leslie's father, Jack Maeby, came from a working-class background in Baltimore and was raised as a Democrat. But as his football exploits took him to college at Bucknell University in Pennsylvania, he began to see the possibility of upward mobility. His own father, a factory worker, counseled him to "use this," pointing to his head, "instead of these," looking at his hands. Turning down an offer to go to graduate school, he entered a management training program with Montgomery Ward. The Maebys moved to Chicago first, then to the Albany, New York area, where they settled in the suburb of Colonie. While Albany, like most big cities, voted Democratic, Colonie was Republican.

Leslie Maeby was raised in the 1950s in a home where her mother remained Democratic, though frustrated with the Albany machine, and her father was Republican. The suburb, in the midst of a housing boom, developed quickly, as whites fled the larger city—and its black population—and sought safety in the standardized tract houses that were going up everywhere. Nelson Rockefeller, the liberal Republican governor of New York, garnered the support of both of Leslie's parents and many of their neighbors. Yet besides voting, neither Jack nor Vilma was very active politically.

Leslie drifted into politics in 1968, at age 15, without thinking about it. A cheerleader, she was drafted into a congressional campaign by the wife of Fred Field, the Republican candidate, who wanted her to wave pom-poms for her husband and greet supporters. Like the other "Field Girls," she dressed in a blue felt skirt, a white blouse, and suspenders that were striped like the flag. Several nights a week, the group rang doorbells and passed out campaign literature to voters. Leslie often made the first overtures in a household, to be followed by the candidate himself. She found the experience intoxicating, even more so when Fred Field won.

Leslie had followed an increasingly common course into the Republican fold. In a second-grade classroom, she had supported Republican presidential candidate Richard Nixon in 1960. In a mock presidential debate in 1964, she had represented conservative Republican presidential nominee Barry Goldwater. And even though Leslie talked about current events with her mother, a liberal Democrat, she was also influenced by her increasingly conservative Republican father as well as by the Republican community in which she lived. She followed her father's political inclinations and became Republican, as she put it, "almost by default." Race riots, first in Detroit, later in Albany and other American cities, troubled her and others. The chaos in Vietnam led to the rifts in the nation that helped elect Richard Nixon—along with Fred Field—in 1968. By the time she went to the State University of New York at Albany in 1971, she was a solid Republican.

In college, she joined a sorority, where she found women of a similar personal and political bent. Her group drank beer, rather than smoking pot, and wore evening gowns to formal dances, rather than wearing tattered jeans to a rock concert. A sorority sister recommended her for a position as a page in the State Senate in Albany, and Leslie found herself immersed in the political world.

Leslie saw first hand the underside of politics, including the ways those in power manipulated issues to their own advantage. Yet she decided to set aside her idealism and to work within the system. She rose quickly, serving in 1974 on the state platform committee. She worked for John Dunne, a Republican state senator, after graduating from college in 1975, and attended the Republican National Convention as a delegate at large in 1976. When Dunne sought the office of executive of Nassau County, Leslie ran his campaign. He lost and Leslie left the United States and backpacked through Europe. Yet everywhere she went, she was interested in what she could find about American politics. She wanted to be part of the process as the United States—under the leadership of Ronald Reagan—moved away from the welfare state.

Returning to the United States, in 1984 Leslie took the job of salvaging the re-election campaign of a Republican state senator. She succeeded in that effort, served for four years as executive assistant to the Republican state comptroller, and in 1989 became finance director of the state Republican party.

Leslie was a rock-ribbed Republican, who, like many Americans, reacted with frustration to chaos in national life and moved right as the party moved right. "It's like if you decide to be a nurse when you're eighteen, and stay one for twenty years," she said. "It becomes who you are. How you read the paper. How you watch the news. Your whole outlook."

The experience of Leslie Maeby mirrored that of countless Americans in the 1980s who left the Democratic party and supported the Republican agenda instead. At a time when people were disturbed by continuing racial conflict, troubled by changes in the welfare state that seemed to help disadvantaged citizens at the expense of middle- and upper-class Americans, and upset at the chaos caused by the Vietnam War, they began to reassess priorities within the democratic political system. In a time of flux, the Republican party seized the initiative and consolidated its own political power. In a process that began in the 1960s (as Jack Maeby left his Democratic roots and became a Republican), a new majority

emerged in the United States. Millions of Americans, including members of groups who had long considered themselves Democrats, voiced their frustration by voting Republican, some for the first time. Relying on a fervent religious faith, they succeeded in transforming their vision of the American dream into national policy, and in the 1980s and early 1990s, they watched the economy improve, though often to the benefit of the most affluent Americans. At the same time, members of a variety of minority groups continued to have difficulty finding jobs, the national debt skyrocketed, and finally, the stock market crashed. Meanwhile, harsh Cold War rhetoric led to fears that the continuing confrontation on the global stage between the Soviet Union and the United States might end in nuclear war.

This chapter describes the enormous changes that occurred in the 1980s and early 1990s. It highlights the role of people like Leslie Maeby in bringing to power a new political force that altered the landscape of the United States. It describes the economic and technological shifts that affected the daily lives of millions of Americans, bringing unprecedented prosperity to people at the top of the economic pyramid but leaving millions of less fortunate Americans behind. It explores the efforts of the Republican administrations of Ronald Reagan and George Bush to redefine—and limit—the government's role in the economy, and it assesses the impact such constriction had on ordinary Americans. And finally, it examines how foreign policy initiatives brought a successful end to the long and costly Cold War.

THE CONSERVATIVE TRANSFORMATION

In the 1980s and early 1990s, the Republican party re-established itself as the dominant force in national politics. The Republican ascendancy that had begun in the Nixon era was now largely complete. The liberal agenda that had governed national affairs ever since the New Deal of Franklin Roosevelt gave way to a new Republican coalition determined to scale back the welfare state and prevent what it perceived as the erosion of the nation's moral values. Firmly in control of the presidency, sometimes in control of the Senate and later the

whole Congress, the Republican party set the new national agenda.

The New Politics

Conservatism gained respect in the 1980s, not just in the United States but in other parts of the world as well. In Great Britain, for example, the Labour Party had gained power in the latter part of the 1960s, as the nation underscored its commitment to the welfare state. A national health plan provided medical care for all, and a comprehensive educational system opened up opportunities for people limited by the class-bound strictures of the past. But problems with both inflation and unemployment plagued Britain, like other nations, and in the 1980s, the Conservative party was back in power, with Margaret Thatcher as prime minister. Elsewhere in the late 1980s, particularly as communism began to crumble in Eastern and Central Europe, Christian Democratic movements became increasingly popular. Founded in the early twentieth century to capture the middle ground of moderate conservatism, midway between the left and the right, they occasionally came to power, sometimes alone and sometimes in coalitions with other groups. Now, as socialism deteriorated, they seemed a more viable alternative.

In the United States, conservatism attracted countless new adherents after the turbulence of the 1960s and the backlash of the Vietnam War. Innovative advertising and fund-raising techniques capitalized on national disaffection with liberal solutions to continuing social problems and made the conservative movement almost unstoppable.

Conservatives seized on Thomas Jefferson's maxim: "That government is best which governs least." The dramatic economic growth of the 1960s and 1970s, they believed, left a legacy of rising inflation, falling productivity, enormous waste, and out-of-control entitlements. The liberal solution of "throwing money at social problems" no longer worked, conservatives argued. Therefore, they sought to downsize government, reduce taxes, and roll back regulations that they claimed hampered business competition. They wanted to restore the focus on individual initiative and private enterprise, which they believed had made the nation strong.

The conservative philosophy had tremendous appeal. It promised profitability to those who worked hard and showed initiative. It attracted middle-class Americans, who were troubled that they were being forgotten in the commitment to assist minorities and the poor. It also offered hope for the revival of basic social and religious values that many citizens worried had been eaten away by rising divorce rates, legalized abortion, homosexuality, and media preoccupation with violence and sex.

The new conservative coalition covered a broad spectrum. Some followers embraced the economic doctrines of University of Chicago economist Milton Friedman, who promoted the free play of market forces and a sharp restriction of governmental activism in regulating the economy. Others applauded the social and political conservatism of North Carolina senator Jesse Helms, a tireless foe of anything he deemed pornographic and a fervent campaigner for a limited federal role. Still others flocked to the Republican fold because of their conviction that civil rights activists and "bleeding-heart liberals" practiced "reverse racism" with affirmative action, job quotas, and busing to promote equal opportunity.

The conservative coalition also drew deeply from religious fundamentalists who advocated a literal interpretation of Scriptures. Millions—devout Catholics, orthodox Jews, evangelical Protestants—demanded a return to stricter standards of morality.

Muslim Students in New York
Islam became increasingly popular in the United States in the 1980s and 1990s. This picture shows girls at the Al Iman School in Queens, New York City, wearing the long, shapeless robes and head scarves traditional in the Muslim world. Boys and girls are separated, but all study Arabic and English and learn Muslim rituals and prayers. How does the clothing shown in this picture reinforce Islamic values? *(William Lopez/New York Times Picture Collection)*

The Moral Majority The Reverend Jerry Falwell, founder of the Moral Majority, called for a crusade to revive moral values in the United States. His constituency was an important part of the new conservative movement. Which values became most important in the political world of the 1980s and early 1990s? *(Bettmann/CORBIS)*

Muslims, relying on the Qur'an, took an equally fundamentalist approach. All groups worried about sexual permissiveness, gay rights, drugs, crime, and women working outside the home, a practice they believed eroded family life. In short, fundamentalists objected to liberalizing tendencies and sought to refashion society by reaffirming scriptural morality and the centrality of religion in American life.

Many of these activists belonged to the so-called Moral Majority. The Reverend Jerry Falwell of Virginia and other television evangelists who focused on the concerns of religious fundamentalism attracted large followings in the 1980s. Emulating Father Charles E. Coughlin, the radio priest of the 1930s, they used electronic means to preach fiery sermons to enormous audiences and focused their television congregations on specific political ends. They also used their fund-raising ability to support candidates sympathetic to their cause. Moral Majority money began to fund politicians who demanded reinstituting school prayer, ending legalized abortion, and defeating the Equal Rights Amendment. Later

a group calling itself the Christian Coalition became even more powerful in supporting—and electing—candidates who met its litmus test on conservative values. The Christian Coalition and other similar groups believed strongly that a religious framework was the best way to assess candidates running for office. According to Evangelicals for Social Action, "To proclaim Christ's lordship in politics means evaluating political candidates by their commitment to biblical principles, rather than by their pragmatism, patriotism, or personality."

Conservatives from all camps capitalized on changing political techniques more successfully than their liberal opponents. They understood the importance of television in providing instant access to the American public. Politicians became increasingly adept at using "sound bites," often lasting no more than 15 or 30 seconds, to state their views. As the 1990s unfolded, they also relied on new electronic systems such as e-mail, fax machines, and the Internet to mobilize their followers.

Similarly, conservatives outdid liberals in using negative political advertising. Mudslinging has always been a part of the American political tradition, but now carefully crafted television ads concentrated not so much on conveying a positive image of a candidate's platform but on subtly attacking an

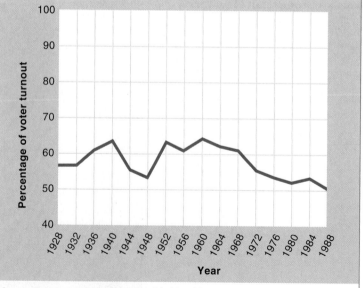

Voter Turnout, 1928–1988

Voter turnout was far lower in the twentieth century than it had been in the nineteenth century. The fact that barely 50 percent of the electorate voted in the 1980s reflects a pervasive sense of disillusionment with the political process.

Source: Data from *Historical Statistics of the United States* and *Statistical Abstract of the United States.*

opponent's character in order to create fundamental doubt in a voter's mind. It was small wonder that Americans became increasingly cynical about politics and avoided voting booths in record numbers.

Conservatives also were most successful in raising unprecedented sums of money for their campaigns. Richard Viguerie, the New Right mastermind, understood how to tap the huge conservative constituency for political ends and developed direct-mail appeals that assisted conservative candidates around the country.

At the same time, conservatives understood the need to provide an intellectual grounding for their positions. Conservative scholars worked in "think tanks" and other research organizations, such as the Hoover Institution at Stanford University and the American Enterprise Institute in Washington, D.C., that gave conservatism a solid institutional base. Their books, articles, and reports helped elect Ronald Reagan and other conservative politicians.

Conservative Leadership

More than any other Republican, Ronald Reagan was responsible for the success of the conservative cause. An actor turned politician, he had been a radio broadcaster in his native Midwest, then gravitated to California, where he began a movie career. Initially drawn to the Democratic party and impressed with the accomplishments of Franklin D. Roosevelt's New Deal, he was also sympathetic to union causes and served as president of the Screen Actors Guild in Hollywood. But his success on the silver screen affected his political inclinations, and he changed his affiliation from Democrat to Republican in the early 1960s. As his film career came to an end, he went to work as a public spokesman for General Electric, where his visibility and ability to articulate corporate values attracted the attention of conservatives who recognized his political potential and helped him win election as governor of California in 1966. He failed in his first bid for the presidency in 1976 but consolidated his strength over the next four years. By 1980, he had the firm support of the growing Right, which applauded his promise to reduce the size of the federal government but bolster military might.

Running against incumbent Jimmy Carter in 1980, Reagan scored a landslide victory, gaining a popular vote of 51 to 41 percent and a 489 to 49 Electoral College advantage. He also led the Republican party to control of the Senate for the first time since 1955. In 1984, he was re-elected

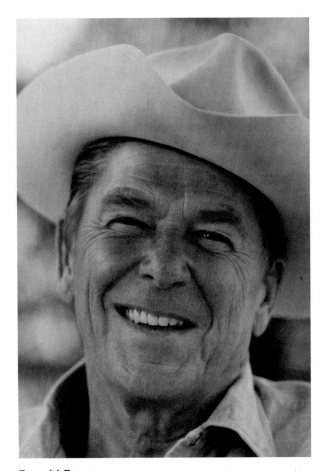

Ronald Reagan Ronald Reagan was fond of projecting an old-fashioned cowboy image. This picture captured the sense of rugged individualism he valued and appeared on the covers of both *Time* and *Newsweek* magazines when he died in 2004. What qualities seem to come across in this photograph? Why did this image have such a powerful appeal? *(Courtesy Ronald Reagan Library)*

Jimmy Carter Presidential Campaign Ad: Burning the Midnight Oil; Ronald Reagan Presidential Campaign Ad: A Bear in the Woods

by an even larger margin. He received 59 percent of the popular vote and swamped Democratic candidate Walter Mondale in the Electoral College 525 to 13, losing only Minnesota, Mondale's home state, and the District of Columbia. The Democrats, however, netted two additional seats in the Senate and maintained superiority in the House of Representatives.

Reagan had a pleasing manner and a special skill as a media communicator. Relying on his acting experience, he used television as Franklin D. Roosevelt had used radio in the 1930s. He was a gifted storyteller who loved using anecdotes and one-liners to make his point. In 1980, for example, he quibbled playfully with Carter over definitions of economic doldrums. "I'm talking in human terms and he is hiding behind a dictionary," Reagan said. "If he wants a definition, I'll give him one. A recession is when your neighbor loses his job. A depression is when you lose yours. A recovery is when Jimmy Carter loses his."

As president, Reagan managed to convey his sense of vision to the American people. He spoke of the United States as "the last best hope of man on earth," and, echoing John Winthrop's sermon to Puritans coming to the New World in 1630, he referred to America as a "shining city on a hill." He was fond of invoking images of Pilgrims coming ashore in New England, American prisoners of war returning from Vietnam, and astronauts landing on the moon, and he argued that history still had a place for the nation and its ideals. In response to those who spoke of a "national malaise," he retorted, "I find nothing wrong with the American people."

Ronald Reagan, First Inaugural Address (1981)

Throughout his eight years in office, Reagan enjoyed enormous popularity. People talked about a "Teflon" presidency, making a comparison with nonstick frying pans, for even serious criticisms failed to stick and disagreements over policy never diminished his personal-approval ratings. When he left the White House, an overwhelming 68 percent of the American public approved of his performance over the past eight years.

But Reagan had a number of liabilities that surfaced over time. He was the oldest president the nation had ever had; his attention often drifted, and he occasionally fell asleep during meetings, including one with the pope. While he could speak eloquently with a script in front of him, he was frequently unsure about what was being asked in press conferences. Uninterested in governing, he delegated a great deal of authority, even if that left him unclear about policy decisions. Worst of all, he suffered from charges of "sleaze" in his administration, with several aides and even his attorney general forced from office for improprieties ranging from perjury to influence peddling.

George Bush Presidential Campaign Ad: The Revolving Door

In 1988, Republican George H. W. Bush, who served eight years as Reagan's vice president, ran for the presidency.

George H. W. Bush George H. W. Bush capitalized on his position as vice president under Ronald Reagan and won a resounding victory in the election of 1988. Even so, he did not have the solid conservative mandate that Reagan enjoyed. How does the flag contribute to the impression Bush hoped to convey? *(CORBIS)*

Though a New Englander, he had prospered in the Texas oil industry, then served in Congress, as top envoy to China, and as head of the CIA. Termed a preppy wimp by the press, he became a pit bull who ran a mudslinging campaign against his Democratic opponent, Governor Michael Dukakis of Massachusetts. On election day, Bush swamped Dukakis, winning a 54–46 percent popular-vote majority and carrying 40 states. But conservatives who admired Reagan were suspicious of Bush, and he did not

Presidential Elections, 1980–1988

Year	Candidate	Party	Popular Vote	Electoral Vote
1980	RONALD REAGAN	Republican	43,899,248 (50.8%)	489
	Jimmy Carter	Democratic	36,481,435 (41.0%)	49
	John B. Anderson	Independent	5,719,437 (6.6%)	0
1984	RONALD REAGAN	Republican	53,428,357 (58.7%)	525
	Walter F. Mondale	Democratic	36,930,923 (40.6%)	13
1988	GEORGE BUSH	Republican	47,946,422 (53.9%)	426
	Michael Dukakis	Democratic	41,016,429 (46.1%)	112

Note: Winners' names appear in capital letters.

have the kind of mandate Reagan had enjoyed in 1980 and again in 1984. Even worse from the Republican point of view, Democrats controlled both houses of Congress.

Bush quickly put his own imprint on the presidency. Despite his upper-crust background, he was an unpretentious man who made a point of trying to appear down-to-earth. He also maintained his own network of friends and political contacts through handwritten notes, telephone calls, and personal visits. More than a year and a half into his term, he was still on his political honeymoon, with a personal approval rating of 67 percent. Support grew even stronger as he presided over the Persian Gulf War in 1991. Then, as the economy faltered and the results of the war seemed suspect, approval levels began to drop, and he failed in his bid for re-election in 1992.

Republican Policies at Home

Republicans in the 1980s and early 1990s aimed to reverse the economic stagnation of the Carter years and to provide new opportunities for business to

prosper. The United States, like industrialized nations around the world, had suffered from the Arab oil embargo of 1973, which had vastly increased energy prices. As the cost of driving cars and heating homes skyrocketed, the entire economy was knocked out of kilter. In an increasingly globalized economy, in which multinational firms had interests around the world, a downturn in one area—or one country—affected business efforts around the globe. Republicans wanted to provide American business interests with the ability to prosper at home and wherever else they operated.

VIDEO

Ronald Reagan on the Wisdom of Tax Cuts

To that end, Reagan proposed and implemented an economic recovery program that rested on the theory of supply-side economics. According to this much-criticized theory, reduction of taxes would encourage business expansion, which in turn would lead to a larger supply of goods to help stimulate the system as a whole. Even George Bush, during his brief run for the Republican nomination in 1980, was critical, charging that Reagan was promoting

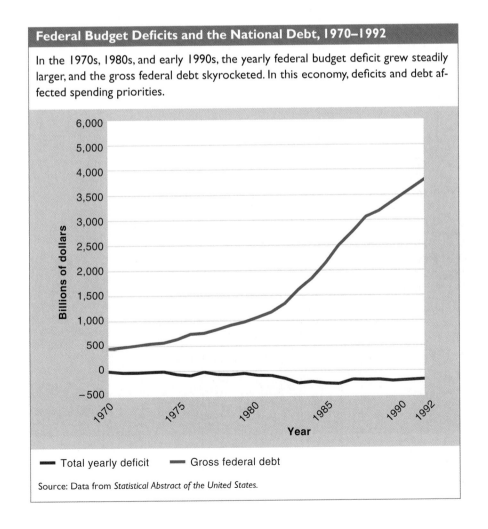

Federal Budget Deficits and the National Debt, 1970–1992

In the 1970s, 1980s, and early 1990s, the yearly federal budget deficit grew steadily larger, and the gross federal debt skyrocketed. In this economy, deficits and debt affected spending priorities.

— Total yearly deficit   — Gross federal debt

Source: Data from *Statistical Abstract of the United States.*

"voodoo economics." Despite such criticism, Republicans followed the president's lead and endorsed "Reaganomics," with its promise of a revitalized economy.

One early initiative involved tax reductions. A 5 percent cut in the tax rate was enacted to go into effect on October 1, 1981, followed by 10 percent cuts in 1982 and 1983. Although all taxpayers received some tax relief, the rich gained far more than middle- and lower-income Americans. Poverty-level Americans did not benefit at all. Tax cuts and enormous defense expenditures increased the budget deficit. From $74 billion in 1980, it jumped to $290 billion in 1992. Such massive deficits drove the gross federal debt—the total national indebtedness—upward from $909 billion in 1980 to $4.4 trillion in 1992. When Reagan assumed office, the per capita national debt was $4,035; 10 years later, in 1990, it was about $12,400.

Paul Craig Roberts, *The Supply-Side Revolution* (1984)

Faced with the need to raise more money and rectify an increasingly skewed tax code, in 1986 Congress passed and Reagan signed the most sweeping tax reform since the federal income tax began in 1913. It lowered rates, consolidated brackets, and closed loopholes to expand the tax base.

Though it ended up neither increasing nor decreasing the government's tax take, the measure was an important step toward treating low-income Americans more equitably. Still, most of the benefits went to the richest 5 percent of Americans.

At the same time, Reagan embarked on a major program of deregulation. In a campaign more comprehensive than Jimmy Carter's, he focused on agencies of the 1970s such as the Environmental Protection Agency (EPA), the Consumer Product Safety Commission, and the Occupational Safety and Health Administration (OSHA). The Republican administration argued that regulations pertaining to the consumer, the workplace, and the environment were inefficient, paternalistic, and excessively expensive. They impeded business growth and needed to be eliminated.

The Federal Communications Commission (FCC), which had effectively regulated the airwaves in the past, now shifted course. The head of the agency under Reagan scoffed at the idea that television had a public-service role. "Television is just another appliance," he declared. "It's just a toaster with pictures." The FCC increased the amount of time allotted to commercials and eliminated the rule that some programming had to be in the area of public-service broadcasts.

An American Family   In 1988, and again in 1992, George Bush and the Republicans emphasized traditional family values as a way of healing the social ills of the nation. In this campaign picture, Bush poses with his family at their home in Maine as a way of showing that he was a good family man. How effective do you think this photograph was in underscoring Bush's commitment to family issues? *(Sipa Press)*

Meanwhile, Reagan challenged the New Deal consensus that the federal government should monitor the economy and assist the least fortunate citizens. He had played by the rules of the system and had won fame and fortune. Others could do the same. He charged that government intruded too deeply into American life. It was time to eliminate "waste, fraud, and abuse" by cutting unnecessary programs.

Reagan needed to curtail social programs both because of sizable tax cuts and because of enormous military expenditures. Committed to a massive arms buildup, over a five-year period the administration sought an unprecedented military budget of $1.5 trillion. By 1985, with an allocation of $300 billion, the United States was spending half a million dollars a minute on defense and four times as much as at the height of the Vietnam War.

The huge cuts in social programs reversed the approach of liberals over the past 50 years. Republicans and conservative Democrats eliminated public-service jobs and reduced other aid to the cities, where the poor congregated. They cut back unemployment compensation and required Medicare patients to pay more for treatment. They lowered welfare benefits and food stamp allocations. They slashed the Legal Services Corporation, which provided legal services for the poor. They replaced grants for college students with loans. Spending on human resources fell by $101 billion between 1980 and 1982. The process continued even after Reagan left office. Between 1981 and 1992, federal spending (adjusted for inflation) fell 82 percent for subsidized housing, 63 percent for job training and employment services, and 40 percent for community services. Middle-class Americans, benefiting from the tax cuts, were not hurt by the slashes in social programs. But for millions of the nation's poorest citizens, the administration's approach caused real suffering.

Ironically, despite the huge cuts, overall federal spending for social welfare rose from $313 billion in 1980 to $533 billion in 1988. The increase came about because of growth in the payments of entitlement programs such as social security and Medicare, which provided benefits automatically to citizens in need. Even the most aggressive efforts of the Republicans could not wholly dismantle the welfare state.

As a political conservative distrustful of centralized government, Reagan wanted to place more power in the hands of state and local governments and to reduce the involvement of the federal government in people's lives. His "New Federalism" attempted to shift responsibilities from the federal to the state level. By eliminating federal funding and instead making grants to the states, which could spend the money as they saw fit, he hoped to fortify local initiative. Critics charged, with some justification, that the proposal was merely a way of moving programs from one place to another while eliminating federal funding. When a prolonged recession began in 1990, the administration's policy contributed to the near-bankruptcy of a number of states and municipalities, which now bore responsibility for programs formerly funded in Washington.

Reagan took a conservative approach to social issues as well. Accepting the support of the New Right, he strongly endorsed conservative social goals. To avoid compromising his economic program, however, he provided only symbolic support at first. He spoke out for public prayer in the schools without expending political capital in Congress to support the issue. In the same way, he showed his opposition to abortion by making sure that the first nongovernmental group to receive an audience at the White House was an antiabortion March for Life contingent.

George Bush followed directly in his predecessor's footsteps. Having forsworn his objection to "voodoo economics" as soon as he received the vice presidential nomination, Bush faithfully adhered to Reagan's general economic policy even after he became president. Running for president in 1988, he promised "no new taxes," although he later backed down from that pledge to join a bipartisan effort to bring the budget deficit under control.

Like Reagan, Bush wanted deep cuts in social programs. Tireless in his criticism of the Democratic majorities in the Senate and House of Representatives, he vetoed measure after measure to assist those caught in the ravages of a troubling recession that sent unemployment rates up to 8 percent and left one of every four urban children living in poverty.

Bush was more outspoken than Reagan in his support of conservative social goals. At the start of the 1980s, conservatives had questioned Bush's commitment to their social agenda, and, indeed, Bush had been sympathetic to a woman's right to choice in the abortion issue. As president, however, he firmly opposed abortion, and his Supreme Court appointments, like Reagan's, guaranteed that the effort to roll back or overturn *Roe* v. *Wade* would continue.

The Republican philosophy under Reagan and Bush dramatically reversed the nation's domestic agenda. Liberalism in the 1960s had reached a high-water mark in a time of steady growth, but in the 1980s decisions about social programs became

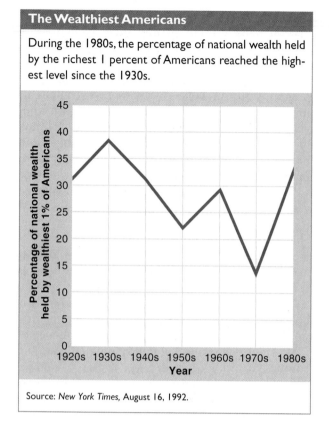

The Wealthiest Americans

During the 1980s, the percentage of national wealth held by the richest 1 percent of Americans reached the highest level since the 1930s.

Source: *New York Times*, August 16, 1992.

The 1980s, it became clear, produced "a decade of money fever," as author Tom Wolfe put it. Analyst Kevin Phillips called this period "the triumph of upper America," with "an ostentatious celebration of wealth, the political ascendancy of the rich and a glorification of capitalism, free markets and finance." The concentration of capital—an amassing of wealth at the top levels—produced dekamillionaires, centimillionaires, half-billionaires, and billionaires. "Garden-variety millionaires," Phillips noted, "had become so common that there were about 1.5 million of them by 1989." According to one study, the share of national wealth of the richest 1 percent of the nation rose from about 18 percent in 1976 to 36 percent in 1989. The net worth of the *Forbes* magazine 400 richest Americans nearly tripled between 1981 and 1989.

DOCUMENT

Patricia Morrisroe, "Yuppies" (1985)

Meanwhile, less-fortunate Americans suffered more than they had since the Great Depression. In 1987, one out of every five American children lived in poverty, up 24 percent since 1979. And millions of people, ranging from foreclosed farmers to laid-off industrial workers, were struggling to make ends meet.

more difficult, and millions of Americans like Leslie Maeby, introduced at the start of the chapter, came to believe that most of the Great Society programs had failed to conquer poverty and in fact had created lifelong welfare dependency. Conservatism offered a more attractive answer, particularly to Americans in the middle and upper classes who were already comfortable.

But the transformation was accompanied by a number of serious problems that emerged in the early 1990s. Bush faced a bankruptcy crisis in the savings and loan industry, which had taken advantage of the Republican deregulation policy to make unwise, high-risk investments that resulted in tremendous losses. Congress was forced to approve a $166 billion rescue plan (that soon reached more than $250 billion) committing taxpayers to bail out the industry.

DOCUMENT

T. Boone Pickens, "My Case for Reagan" (1984)

Republican policy also widened the gap between rich and poor. Tax breaks for the wealthy, deregulation initiatives, high interest rates for investors, permissiveness toward mergers, and enormous growth in the salaries of top business executives all contributed to the disparity. So did more lenient antitrust enforcement and a general sympathy for speculative finance.

AN END TO SOCIAL REFORM

The Republican attack on the welfare state included an effort to limit the commitment to social reform. Enough had been done already, conservatives argued, and gains for less fortunate Americans came at the expense of the middle class. It was time to end federal "intrusion" in this area.

Slowdown in the Struggle for Civil Rights

Republican policies slowed the civil rights movement. Reagan opposed busing to achieve racial balance, and his attorney general worked to dismantle affirmative action programs. Initially reluctant to support extension of the enormously successful Voting Rights Act of 1965, Reagan relented only under severe bipartisan criticism. He directed the Internal Revenue Service to cease banning tax exemptions for private schools that discriminated against blacks, only to see that move overturned by the Supreme Court in 1983. He also launched an assault on the Civil Rights Commission and hampered its effectiveness by appointing members who did not support its main goals.

The courts similarly weakened commitments to equal rights. As a result of Reagan's and Bush's judicial

Jesse Jackson Jesse Jackson demonstrated that an African American could attract a substantial level of support as he ran for president in 1984 and 1988. Here he is shown on the campaign trail in Chicago in 1988. Why were Jackson's campaigns so important? Who do you think his strongest supporters were? *(Marc Pokempner)*

Coalition in 1984 and ran for the presidency. Though he lost his bid for the Democratic nomination, he had the support of nearly 400 delegates, and in a nationally televised speech at the convention, he vowed not to forget his constituency. Four years later, in 1988, he sought the Democratic nomination again, this time with the support of 1,200 delegates at the convention, before falling short of his goal once more.

Despite significant victories in mayoral elections in major cities and other electoral gains, black–white relations remained tense. As Joseph Lattimore, an African American from Chicago, observed, "As far as integrating with you—we have sang 'We Shall Overcome,' we have prayed at the courthouse steps, we have made all these gestures, and the door is not open." Sylvia Matthews, also from Chicago, noted, "Today it seems more acceptable to be racist. Just in the kinds of things you hear people say."

appointments, federal courts stopped pushing for school integration. The Supreme Court's *Freeman* v. *Pitts* decision in 1992 granted a suburban Atlanta school board relief from a desegregation order on the grounds that it was not possible to counteract massive demographic shifts.

Yet African Americans kept the struggle alive. The Reverend Jesse Jackson, a longtime civil rights activist, established what he called the Rainbow

A riot in Los Angeles in 1992 revealed the continuing racial polarization. The year before, Americans had watched a videotaped, savage beating of black motorist Rodney King by white police officers, the

Los Angeles Burning While many Americans prospered in the 1980s and early 1990s, others found themselves left behind. The riot in Los Angeles in 1992, following the acquittal of the police officers accused of beating black motorist Rodney King, reflected the pent-up frustrations that could no longer be ignored. How does this picture capture the horror of the riot? *(Ed Carreon/Sipa Press)*

AMERICAN VOICES

Jesse Jackson was a civil rights activist who later moved into politics and ran for the presidency in 1984 and 1988. In his first campaign, he made a passionate speech before the Democratic National Convention in San Francisco, California, in which he called for the inclusion of all people in what he called a Rainbow Coalition that would guide American life.

Tonight we come together bound by our faith in a mighty God, with genuine respect and love for our country, and inheriting the legacy of a great party, the Democratic Party, which is the best hope for redirecting our nation on a more humane, just and peaceful course.

This is not a perfect party. We are not a perfect people. Yet, we are called to a perfect mission: our mission to feed the hungry; to clothe the naked; to house the homeless; to teach the illiterate; to provide jobs for the jobless; and to choose the human race over the nuclear race. . . .

My constituency is the desperate, the damned, the disinherited, the disrespected, and the despised. They are restless and seek relief. They've voted in record numbers. They have invested faith, hope and trust that they have in us. The Democratic Party must send them a signal that we care. I pledge my best to not let them down. . . .

America is not like a blanket—one piece of unbroken cloth, the same color, the same texture, the same size. America is more like a quilt—many patches, many pieces, many colors, many sizes, all woven and held together by a common thread. The white, the Hispanic, the black, the Arab, the Jew, the woman, the native American, the small farmer, the businessperson, the environmentalist, the peace activist, the young, the old, the lesbian, the gay and the disabled make up the American quilt.

Even in our fractured state, all of us count and all of us fit somewhere. We have proven that we can survive without each other. But we have not proven that we can win and progress without each other. We must come together.

- *What did Jesse Jackson see as his personal mission?*

- *Who made up Jackson's constituency?*

- *How did Jesse Jackson envision the various groups in America fitting together?*

---

most dramatic of a long string of incidents involving police brutality. When a California jury that did not include any African Americans acquitted the policemen, many people throughout the country became convinced that people of color could not obtain equal justice under the law. In Los Angeles, thousands reacted with uncontrolled fury, targeting supermarkets, drug stores, Korean businesses, restaurants, and mini-malls. Much of the chaos was orchestrated by gang members, but it also involved hundreds of ordinary citizens who acted irresponsibly, yet with a sense that the social contract had been broken by politicians and the rich who were unresponsive to their plight. Several days later, after the riot had run its course, 51 people (most of them black and Hispanic) lay dead, 2,000 were injured, and $1 billion in damage had been done to the city. It was the worst riot in decades, more deadly even than the Watts riot 27 years earlier. The upheaval served notice that racial injustice, social inequality, and poverty could no longer be ignored.

Obstacles to Women's Rights

Women had a similar experience in the 1980s and early 1990s. They, too, made significant electoral gains at the local, state, and national levels. In 1981, President Reagan named Sandra Day O'Connor as the first woman Supreme Court justice, and in 1984 Democrat Geraldine Ferraro became the first major-party female vice presidential nominee.

Yet women still faced problems that were compounded by conservative social policies. Access to new positions did not change their concentration in lower-paying jobs. In 1985, most working women were still secretaries, cashiers, bookkeepers, registered nurses, and waitresses—the same jobs most frequently held 10 years before. Even when women

Sandra Day O'Connor Sandra Day O'Connor became the first woman justice to sit on the U.S. Supreme Court. Her pre-Court career was similar to that of many other women, as she was denied numerous jobs when she emerged from law school. A decade later, Ruth Bader Ginsburg joined O'Connor on the nation's highest court. Here O'Connor testified at her confirmation hearings. What impression does she convey as she answered senators' questions? *(Getty Images)*

moved into positions traditionally held by men, their progress often stopped at the lower and middle levels. Interruptions of work—to bear children or assume family responsibilities—impeded advancement. In virtually all areas, American women had less support juggling family, home, and work than women in many European countries. And for those who managed to do everything on their own, a "glass ceiling" seemed to prevent them from moving up.

Wage differentials between women and men continued to exist. In 1985, full-time working women still earned only 59 cents for every dollar earned by men. Comparable-worth arguments that women should receive equal pay for different jobs of similar value met conservative resistance.

Conservatives also waged a dedicated campaign against the right to legal abortion. Despite the 1973 Supreme Court decision legalizing abortion, the issue remained very much alive. The number of abortions increased dramatically in the decade after the decision. In response, "pro-life" forces mobilized. Opponents lobbied to cut off federal funds that allowed the poor to obtain the abortions that the better-off could pay for themselves; they insisted that abortions should be performed in hospitals and not in less-expensive clinics; and they worked to reverse the original decision itself.

Though the Supreme Court underscored its judgment in 1983, the pro-life movement was not deterred. In 1989, a solidifying conservative majority on the Court ruled in *Webster* v. *Reproductive Health Services* that while women's right to abortion remained intact, state legislatures could impose limitations if they chose. With that judgment, a major legislative debate over the issue began, and numerous states began to mandate restrictions.

In 1992, in *Planned Parenthood* v. *Casey*, the Supreme Court reaffirmed what it termed the essence of the right to abortion, while permitting further state restrictions. It declared that a 24-hour waiting period for women seeking abortions was acceptable and required teenage girls to secure the permission of a parent (or a judge) before ending a pregnancy. The ruling clearly gave states greater latitude in the overall restrictive effort and made an abortion harder to obtain, particularly for poor women and young women.

In response to a conservative backlash, the women's movement became more racially inclusive. Black women now found more common ground with white feminists. While black women in the early 1990s still earned less on a weekly basis than white men and white women, that situation began to improve.

Women and men became more sensitive to the issue of sexual harassment. The dramatic confrontation between Supreme Court nominee Clarence Thomas and lawyer Anita Hill during confirmation hearings in 1991 dramatized both racial questions and the problem of sexual harassment. After the retirement of Thurgood Marshall, the only African American on the Supreme Court, President Bush sought to replace him with the much more conservative Clarence Thomas, putting African Americans, who wanted one of their own on the court, in a political bind. Then, during nationally televised confirmation hearings, Anita Hill accused Thomas of harassing her when she had worked for him earlier. Thomas furiously countered with charges of a "high-tech lynching." The Bush administration managed to garner the necessary votes for confirmation, and Thomas followed a conservative agenda in the years that followed. In the aftermath of the turbulent confirmation hearings, Americans in Congress, in the business community, and in the larger workplace all became more aware of inappropriate behavior that could no longer be tolerated.

The Limited Commitment to Latino Rights

Latinos likewise faced continuing concerns in the 1980s and early 1990s as the commitment to reform eroded. The Latino population increased substantially as a result of immigration reform during the Great Society of the 1960s (see Chapter 28). In the 1980s, 47 percent of all legal American immigration came from Mexico, the Caribbean, and Latin America. Many other immigrants arrived illegally. As the populations of Latin American nations soared and economic conditions deteriorated, more and more people looked to the United States for relief. In the mid-1970s, Leonard Chapman, commissioner of the Immigration and Naturalization Service, estimated that there might be 12 million foreigners in the nation illegally. While official estimates were lower, Attorney General William French Smith declared in 1983, "Simply put, we've lost control of our own borders."

Many of the new arrivals were skilled workers or professionals, who still had to retool after arriving in the United States. But even more prevalent were laborers, service sector workers, and semiskilled employees, who needed the benefit of social services at just the time they were being cut back.

Spanish-speaking students often found it difficult to finish school. In 1987, 40 percent of all Latino high school students did not graduate, and only 31 percent of Latino seniors were enrolled in college-preparatory courses; those who were in such classes frequently received little help from guidance counselors. Anel Albarran, a Mexican immigrant who arrived in East Los Angeles when she was 11 years old, applied to UCLA when a special high school teacher encouraged her and made sure that she received help in choosing the necessary courses. By contrast, her regular counselor took little interest in her; he waited until only two months before graduation to ask her if she had considered going onto college. "All he had wanted to do during high school," Anel observed, "was give me my classes and get me out of the room."

Like other groups, Latinos slowly extended their political gains. In the 1980s, Henry Cisneros became mayor of San Antonio and Federico Peña was elected mayor of Denver. In New Mexico, Governor Toney Anaya called himself the nation's highest-elected Hispanic. The number of Latinos holding elective offices nationwide increased 3.5 percent between 1986 and 1987, and the number of Latina women in such offices increased 20 percent in that time. The number of Latino public officials nationwide increased 73 percent between 1985 and 1994, and Lauro Cavazos became the first Latino Cabinet official when he was appointed secretary of education in 1988.

Latino workers, however, continued to have a hard time in the employment market. Even as the nation's overall unemployment rate dropped, the rate for the 12 million Latino workers barely budged—and worsened in relation to the rate for African Americans. Many found themselves suffering from outdated skills and weak educational backgrounds that limited economic opportunities.

Continuing Problems for Native Americans

Native Americans likewise experienced the waning commitment to reform, but they made some gains as a result of their own efforts. Some tribal communities developed business skills, although traditional Indian attitudes hardly fostered the capitalist perspective. As Dale Old Horn, an MIT graduate and department head at Little Big Horn College in Crow Agency, Montana, explained:

> The Crow Indian child is taught that he is part of a harmonious circle of kin relations, clans and nature. The white child is taught that he is the center of the circle. The Crow believe in sharing wealth, and whites believe in accumulating wealth.

Some Indian groups did adapt to the capitalist ethos. "Now we're beginning to realize that, if we want to be self-sufficient, we're going to have to become entrepreneurs ourselves," observed Iola Hayden, the Comanche executive director of Oklahomans for Indian Opportunity. The Choctaw in Mississippi were among the most successful. Before they began a drive toward self-sufficiency in 1979, their unemployment rate was 50 percent. By the middle of the 1980s, Choctaw owned all or part of three businesses on the reservation, employed 1,000 people, generated $30 million in work annually, and cut the unemployment rate in half. After Congress approved Native American gambling in 1988, an increasing number of tribes became involved in this industry. The Pequot in Connecticut built a casino in the southeastern part of the state that became the most profitable one in the nation.

American Voices

Sherman Alexie was just out of college when he published his first book of poems. In that collection, The Business of Fancy Dancing, *he captured some of the special moments and the serious difficulties of Native American life.*

Indian Boy Love Song (#1)

Everyone I have lost
in the closing of a door
the click of the lock

is not forgotten, they
do not die but remain
within the soft edges
of the earth, the ash

of house fires and cancer
in sin and forgiveness
huddled under old blankets

dreaming their way into
my hands, my heart
closing tight like fists.

Indian Boy Love Song (#2)

I never spoke
the language
of the old women

visiting my mother
in winters so cold
they could freeze
the tongue whole.

I never held my head
to their thin chests
believing in the heart.

Indian women, forgive me.
I grew up distant
and always afraid.

Indian Boy Love Song (#3)

I remember when I told
my cousin
she was more beautiful

than any white girl
I had ever seen.
She kissed me then
with both lips, a tongue

that tasted clean and un-
clean at the same time
like the river which divides

the heart of my heart, all
the beautiful white girls on one side,
my beautiful cousin on the other.

Indian Boy Love Song (#4)

I remember when my father would leave,
drinking,
for weeks. My mother would tell me

the dream he needed
most
Was the dream that frightened him
more

than any stranger ever could.
I
would wait by my window, dreaming

bottles
familiar in my hands, not my father's, always
empty.

- According to Sherman Alexie, what happens to the spirits of Indians who have died?

- What part does Alexie suggest old women play in maintaining traditions?

- How does Alexie compare the beauty of whites and Native Americans?

- How does Alexie feel about drinking in Native American life?

Despite entrepreneurial gains, Indians still remained (as the 1990 census showed) the nation's poorest group. As Ben Nighthorse Campbell, Republican senator from Colorado, noted in 1995, average Indian household income fell by 5 percent in the 1980s, while it rose for all other ethnic and racial groups. According to the 1990 census, median Indian household income was less than $20,000 a year.

Asian American Gains

Asian Americans climbed the social and economic ladder one rung at a time. The Asian American population increased dramatically with the influx of refugees at the end of the Vietnam War, with more than half a million arriving after 1975. In the 1980s, 37 percent of all immigrants to the United States came from Asia. In Los Angeles and other cities, Samoans, Taiwanese, Koreans, Vietnamese, Filipinos, and Cambodians competed for jobs and apartments with Mexicans, African Americans, and Anglos, just as newcomers had contended with one another in New York City a century earlier.

Immigrants from India, the Philippines, China, and Korea often brought skills and professional expertise, although Southeast Asian refugees were frequently less well-off when they arrived. Many of these unskilled immigrants provided the labor for the rapidly expanding West Coast electronics industry, though Indians provided impressive engineering and scientific talent. Asian immigrants, following a pattern established decades before, sought better and better opportunities for their children, and in California they became the largest group of entering students at a number of college campuses.

A Sweatshop of the Late Twentieth Century   Asian workers often found themselves trapped in low-paying jobs with little hope of advancement. Here Chinese women work at sewing machines in a cluttered factory, in conditions similar to those earlier in the twentieth century. How would you assess the working environment shown in this picture? *(Mark Peterson/CORBIS)*

Sometimes the media highlighted the successes of Asian immigrants, particularly in contrast to the problems encountered by other groups. In 1986, *U.S. News & World Report* noted Asian-American advances in a cover story, while *Newsweek* ran a lead article on "Asian Americans: A 'Model Minority,'" and *Fortune* called them "America's Super Minority." Asian Americans were proud of the exposure but pointed out that many members of the working class still struggled for a foothold. In the Chinatowns of San Francisco and Los Angeles, 40 to 50 percent of the workers were employed in the ill-paid service sector or garment industry; in New York's Chinatown, the figure was close to 70 percent. Chinese immigrant women, in particular, often had little choice but to work as seamstresses, just as women from other nationalities had earlier in the century.

Each group, each family, had its own story. Nguyen Ninh and Nguyen Viet, two brothers who remained in Vietnam after the victory of the North Vietnamese in 1975, were among the many who finally fled their war-torn country by boat. The boat sank, but they were rescued, only to be shuttled to Kuwait, then Greece, and finally to the United States, where another brother had arrived a few years before. Though they spoke no English, they immediately began to look for work. One became a carpenter's helper; the other worked as an attendant at a valet parking firm. With the money they earned,

they helped other members of their family emigrate. Slowly they learned English, obtained better jobs, and saved enough money to purchase a home.

Professionals from some countries had a hard time. One Vietnamese physician who resettled in Oklahoma noted, "When I come here, I am told that I must be a beginner again and serve like an apprentice for two years. I have no choice, so I will do it, but I have been wronged to be asked to do this." Professionals from other nations, with programs recognized in the United States, made the transition more easily.

Violent episodes sometimes highlighted discrimination. In 1982, in Detroit, Chinese American Vincent Chin was about to get married. At a strip club with friends the week before his wedding, he encountered two auto workers who thought that Chin was Japanese, and they regarded Japan as responsible for the crisis in the American auto industry as Japanese cars flooded the market. They followed Chin out the door and killed him with a baseball bat. In response to a guilty plea, both murderers received three years probation and $3,780 in fines. Detroit's Asian Americans were incensed but were reluctant to jeopardize what they considered their already vulnerable role in America.

Pressures on the Environmental Movement

Environmentalists, too, were discouraged by the direction of public policy in the 1980s and early 1990s.

Activists found that they faced fierce opposition in the Republican years. Reagan systematically restrained the EPA in his avowed effort to promote economic growth. Under the leadership of James Watt of Colorado, the Department of the Interior opened forest lands, wilderness areas, and coastal waters to economic development, with no concern for preserving the natural environment. When asked whether he believed it was important to protect the environment for future generations, Watt, a devout Christian, responded that he did not know how many generations there were before the Second Coming. Bush initially proved more sympathetic to environmental causes and delighted environmentalists by signing new clean-air legislation. Later, as the economy faltered, he was less willing to support environmental action that he claimed might slow economic growth. In 1992, he accommodated business by easing clean-air restrictions. That same year, at a United Nations–sponsored Earth Summit in Rio de Janeiro, Brazil, with 100 other heads of state, Bush stood alone in his refusal to sign a biological diversity treaty framed to conserve plant and animal species.

ECONOMIC AND DEMOGRAPHIC CHANGE

Republicans sought to reorganize the government against the backdrop of an economy that was volatile in the 1980s and early 1990s. As patterns of employment changed in an increasingly mechanized workplace, millions of workers struggled to survive the shocks. Under Republican supply-side economics, the business cycle moved from recession to boom and back to recession again. When Reagan took office in 1980, the economy was reeling under the impact of declining productivity, galloping inflation, oil shortages, and high unemployment. It revived in the early 1980s, then gave way to a deep recession that lasted from 1990 to 1992, underscoring the need for renewed productivity, full employment, and a more equitable distribution of wealth.

The Changing Nature of Work

Automation and other technological advances had a powerful impact on the American workplace. The *New York Times* reported in 1990 that "Some factories look as if they have been hit by a kind of economic neutron bomb, which left assembly lines running at full speed but eliminated most of the people who worked on them." Formerly profitable jobs disappeared. One pulp-mill worker voiced gloom about the future: "I think the country has a problem. The managers want everything run by computers. But if no one has a job, no one will know how to do anything anymore. Who will pay the taxes? What kind of society will it be when people have lost their knowledge and depend on computers for everything?"

In human terms, the introduction of the computer had other consequences as well. Now workers sat for hours before their screens. Some described the feeling of "floating in space" as they worked, or of being "lost behind the screen." Others worried about radiation from the monitor or muscular fatigue from sitting at a keyboard all day. Still others complained that they could no longer touch their work. As more Americans began to use computers, people who did not work with them complained about a growing "digital divide" that further increased the gap between rich and poor. Members of the middle and upper classes had easy access to computer technology, while less fortunate individuals, many of whom belonged to minority groups, found themselves left behind.

Yet even as the nature of work changed, people seemed to be working more. In past decades, leisure time had seemed to expand, and there was talk of a four-day workweek in the 1950s. In subsequent years, however, the amount of time Americans worked steadily rose so that in the mid-1990s, American employees worked many more hours each year than their counterparts in Germany or France. More time spent at work increased stress as workers attempted to juggle the pressures between employment and family life. Problems were particularly severe for women, still trying to cope with the pressures of a double load, as they maintained responsibility for the home even when working outside. Marriages came under significant strain.

The Shift to a Service Economy

The scarcity of good jobs stemmed in part from the restructuring of the economy that occurred in the 1980s. In a trend that had been underway for more than half a century, the United States continued its shift from an industrial base, in which most workers actually produced things, to a service base, in which most provided expertise or service to others in the workforce. By the mid-1980s, three-fourths of the 113 million employees in the country worked in the service sector as fast-food workers, clerks, computer programmers, doctors, lawyers, bankers, teachers, and bureaucrats. That shift, in turn, had its roots in the decline of the country's industrial sector. The United States had been the world's industrial leader since the late nineteenth century. By the 1980s and

RECOVERING THE PAST

The Internet and the World Wide Web

The Internet has become an integral part of our daily lives. More and more people use e-mail to communicate quickly with friends and colleagues around the world. Many Americans use the World Wide Web to make purchases ranging from books to automobiles. Others buy stocks online and rely on the Web to manage their portfolios. Historians and other scholars have come to depend on huge databases on the Web that are accessible from computers anywhere around the world.

The Internet has become an important tool for historical research. Historians can acquire census data on the Web. They can find essential statistical files, from both government offices and the private sector. They can examine huge collections of historical images. They can read the text of vital speeches. They can look at moving-picture clips from the Spanish-American War and listen to songs of the 1960s. But they need to be cautious in what they do. While the Internet provides access to a huge amount of material, the historian must evaluate it as if it was a more traditional source. But with that caution, it can be an extraordinarily useful tool.

While the Internet has only recently become an important source of historical information, it is not new. Its roots extend back 30 years, to the mid-1960s, when Americans were worried about the nuclear arms race with the Soviet Union at the height of the Cold War. After the Russians launched their *Sputnik* satellite in 1957 with a rocket that demonstrated the ability to send atomic weapons from one continent to another, American scientists dedicated themselves to catching up with and then surpassing the Soviets in space. To do so, they needed to develop their computer technology.

Scientists were also interested in figuring out how to maintain communication in the aftermath of a nuclear attack. As both the United States and the Soviet Union developed bigger and better atomic bombs and then in the 1950s began to create even more potent hydrogen weapons, it became clear that a full-scale nuclear war could wipe out a nation's ability to communicate with its distant military bases. The Department of Defense wanted to create a decentralized communication system that could continue to function even if part of it was wiped out.

In the early 1960s, scientists at the Massachusetts Institute of Technology developed the concept of time-sharing, in which different users at widely separated sites could use the same central computer at the same time. Another step forward came in the mid-1960s with the development of "packet-switching" technology, which broke down data into small, discrete packets that could be transmitted over telephone lines, using modems to connect the computers to the phone lines, and then reassembled when received by another computer at the other end.

Building on those steps, the Department of Defense established the Advanced Research Projects Agency Network, known as ARPANET, in 1969. It linked the computers of four institutions—the University of California campuses at Los Angeles and Santa Barbara, the Stanford Research Institute, and the University of Utah. Two years later, the system had expanded to include 23 universities and research centers around the country.

The system was hardly user-friendly in these early days. In an age before the advent of personal computers at home, or even office computers at work, only computer professionals, engineers, and other scientists mastered the intricacies of what were very complex systems. Once they did, however, they were able to communicate with one another through what became known as electronic mail, or e-mail.

The term *Internet* was first used to describe this decentralized network in 1982, and in 1986 the National Science Foundation created a network called NSFNET with a better-organized backbone for the

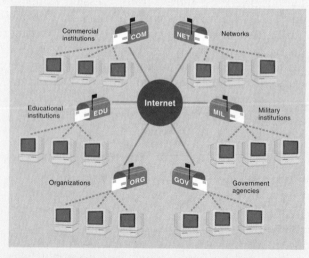

Internet and World Wide Web addresses are organized into domains, each indicated by a different three-letter suffix. Colleges and universities, for example, all use the "edu" designation.

The World Wide Web links numerous Web pages together. By clicking the computer mouse on a highlighted item, a user can move easily from one linked page to another.

entire system. This new infrastructure had different *domains,* each marked by a different suffix at the end of an e-mail address, such as "edu" for educational establishments, "com" for commercial enterprises, and "gov" for government offices.

But even with improvements, the Internet remained hard to use. While computer experts could find all kinds of information, others found it difficult to access what they wanted. Then, in 1991, the University of Minnesota developed a system for finding information by accessing a huge number of databases, and they named it after the university mascot—the golden gopher.

At about the same time, another development made an even greater impact on Internet use. In 1989, Tim Berners-Lee and others at the European Laboratory for Particle Physics (known as CERN) in Geneva, Switzerland, developed a new system for information distribution. It was based on the concept of hypertext, which involved embedding links to other documents or pieces of information in the text of a document itself. While reading an article or essay on the computer, you could simply move to another document by selecting the appropriate link. This system became the basis for what came to be called the World Wide Web in 1991; over the next few years, it supplanted the gophers as the easiest way to maneuver the masses of information in cyberspace. In 1993, Mark Andreessen and others at the National Center for Superconducting Applications at the University of Illinois at Champaign–Urbana went a step further when they developed what they called Mosaic, which was a graphical Web browser. It was an easy-to-use piece of computer software that enabled the user to click the mouse on graphics or icons as well as text in a document to move to another document or Web site. Andreessen and others then formed the Netscape Communications Corporation, a private company, which marketed Netscape Navigator to browse the Web. Microsoft's Internet Explorer provides another browser.

REFLECTING ON THE PAST Today, the World Wide Web is more accessible than ever before. But as more and more adults and children use the Web, legal issues remain to be resolved. What kinds of censorship are acceptable on the Web? How can writers, artists, and musicians maintain copyright protection for their work when the materials they produce are frequently instantly accessible on the Web? How can high-speed connections be made available to people with limited resources? How can systems be protected from "hackers" who use their ingenuity to break into commercial or government computer systems and disrupt the flow of information?

What kind of historical research might you do on the Web? How can you assess the veracity of the material you find on the Internet? What cautions are essential if you are to make the best use of Web sources?

Each chapter in this book contains a section at the end entitled "Discovering U.S. History Online." Look at the section in this chapter and try the various links. Which ones provide you with the most useful material? Look at the site on "The Gulf War." How could you use information here in pursuing a project on the struggle? What materials would be helpful that are not found here? What other sites can you find that provide additional material on this subject?

ANALYZING HISTORY

The Computer

The computer changed American life, just as the radio changed patterns in the 1920s and the television changed patterns in the 1950s. Dropping prices made computers increasingly accessible, and soon more and more Americans—and people around the world—began to use computers to work and play.

REFLECTING ON THE PAST   How has the computer changed American life? How has the increase in the number of computers changed relationships between America and the rest of the world? What different professions have been created by the growth of the computer?

WORLDWIDE SHIPMENTS OF PCs, 1985–2000

(MILLIONS)

1985   1990   1995   2000

The availability of computers rose dramatically in the years after 1985. Note how the figure tripled in the first decade and continued to rise after that.

MILESTONES IN COMPUTER DEVELOPMENT

☛ Vacuum tube
☛ Transistor
☛ Integrated circuit
☛ Microprocessor (computer on a chip)
☛ Internet
☛ World Wide Web

Personal Computers in American Homes (in millions)

0.75   17.38   22.60   35.53
1984   1989   1993   1997

Growth of World Wide Web sites in three years (6/93–6/96)

Web sites (in thousands)

240 200 160 120 80 40 0

6/93   6/94   6/95   6/96

The development of computer technology created an entirely new profession of people who made their living by writing the programs that made computers work.

As the number of PCs increased and as millions learned how to surf the Internet, the number of Web sites spiked dramatically.

Employment of Computer Programmers, 1984–1996

Employment (in thousands)

600 500 400 300 0

1984   1988   1992   1996

At first, the computer was a luxury, available only to experts or people with money. But in the 1980s and 1990s, computers, like televisions several decades earlier, moved into more American homes.

early 1990s, productivity had slowed in virtually all American industries.

The causes of this decline in productivity were complex. The most important factor was a widespread and systematic failure on the part of the United States to invest sufficiently in its basic productive capacity.

During the Reagan years, capital investment in real plants and equipment within the United States gave way to speculation, mergers, and spending abroad. At the end of the 1980s, domestic investment was down—5.7 percent in 1990 and 9.5 percent in 1991. The energy crisis and rising oil prices also contributed to the industrial decline. Finally, the war in Vietnam diverted federal funds from research and development with consequences that continued even after the conflict ended.

While American industry became less productive, other industrial nations moved forward. German and Japanese industries, rebuilt after World War II with U.S. aid and aggressively modernized thereafter, reached new heights of efficiency. As a result, the United States began to lose its share of the world market for industrial goods. In 1946, the country had provided 60 percent of the world's iron and steel. In 1978, it provided a mere 16 percent. By 1980, Japanese car manufacturers had captured nearly one-quarter of the American automobile market. The auto industry, which had been a mainstay of economic growth for much of the twentieth century, suffered plant shutdowns and massive layoffs. In 1991, its worst year ever, Ford lost a staggering $2.3 billion.

Workers in Transition

In the 1980s and early 1990s, American labor struggled to hold on to the gains realized by the post–World War II generation of blue-collar workers. The shift to a service economy, while providing new jobs, was difficult for many American workers. Millions of men and women who lost positions as a result of mergers, plant closings, and permanent economic contractions now found themselves in low-paying jobs with few opportunities for advancement. Entry-level posts were seldom located in the central cities, where most of the poor lived. Even when new jobs were created in the cities, minority residents often lacked the skills to acquire or hold them.

Meanwhile, the trade union movement faltered as the economy moved from an industrial to a service base. Unions had been most successful in organizing the nation's industrial workers in the years since the 1930s, and the United States emerged from World War II with unions strong. In the years that followed, the percentage of workers belonging to unions dropped, from just over 25 percent in 1980 to barely over 16 percent a decade later. As the total number of wage and salary workers rose substantially between 1983 and 1993, the overall number of union members dropped from 17.7 million to 16.6 million.

Union membership declined for a number of reasons. The shift from blue-collar to white-collar work contributed to the contraction. The increase in the workforce in the numbers of women and young people (groups that have historically been difficult to

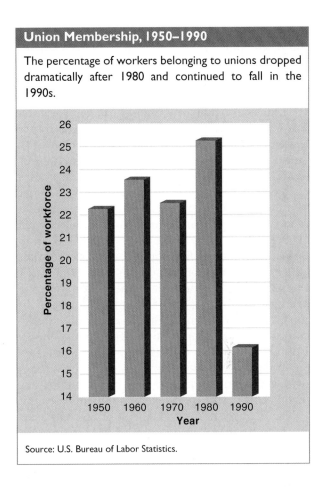

Union Membership, 1950–1990

The percentage of workers belonging to unions dropped dramatically after 1980 and continued to fall in the 1990s.

Source: U.S. Bureau of Labor Statistics.

organize) was another factor, as was the more forceful opposition to unions by managers applying the provisions of the Taft–Hartley Act of 1947, which restricted the tactics labor leaders could use. At the same time, union organizing efforts fell off significantly.

Union vulnerability was visible early in Reagan's first term, when members of the Professional Air Traffic Controllers Organization (PATCO) went on strike. Charging that the strike violated the law, the president—who had once been a union leader himself—fired the strikers, decertified the union, and ordered the training of new controllers at a cost of $1.3 billion. The message was clear: government employees could not challenge the public interest.

DOCUMENT

Ronald Reagan, The Air Traffic Controllers Strike (August 3, 1981)

Anti-union sentiments reverberated throughout the nongovernment sector as well, as many companies across the nation—confronted by falling prices and losses in revenue—sought to dissolve union agreements about hiring, wages, and benefits. Workers who kept their jobs found that their unions could not get favorable contracts. For example, in 1984 the United Auto Workers (UAW) ended a strike at General Motors by trading a pledge that GM would guarantee up to 70 percent of the production workers' lifetime jobs for a smaller wage increase than the union sought and a modification of the cost-of-living allowance that had been a part of UAW contracts since 1948.

Farmers also had to adjust as the larger workforce was reconstituted. Continuing a trend that began in the early twentieth century, the number of farms and farmers declined steadily. When Franklin Roosevelt took office in 1933, some 6.7 million farms covered the American landscape. Fifty years later, there were only 2.4 million. In 1980, farm residents made up 2.7 percent of the total population; by 1989, that figure had fallen to 1.9 percent. As family farms disappeared, farming income became more concentrated in the hands of the largest operators. In 1983, the top 1 percent of the nation's farmers produced 30 percent of all farm products, while the top 12 percent generated 90 percent of all farm income. The top 1 percent of the growers in the United States had average annual incomes of $572,000, but the small and medium-sized farmers who were being forced off the land frequently had incomes below the official government poverty line.

The extraordinary productivity of the most successful American farmers derived in part from the

Work Stoppages, 1960–1990	
Year	**Number of Stoppages**
1960	222
1970	381
1980	187
1990	44

use of chemical fertilizers, irrigation, pesticides, and scientific management. Government price-support programs helped, too. Yet that very productivity caused unexpected setbacks. In the 1970s, food shortages abroad made the United States the "breadbasket of the world." Farmers increased their output to meet multibillion-bushel grain export orders and profited handsomely from high prices in India, China, Russia, and other countries. To increase production, farmers often borrowed heavily at high interest rates. When a worldwide economic slump began in 1980, overseas demand for American farm products declined sharply and farm prices dropped.

Thousands of farmers, caught in the cycle of overproduction, heavy indebtedness, and falling prices, watched helplessly as banks and federal agencies foreclosed on their mortgages and drove them out of business. Dale Christensen, an Iowa corn grower, faced foreclosure in 1983 when the Farmers Home Administration called in his overdue payments on debts totaling $300,000. "I am 58 years old," he said. "My whole life has gone into this farm." He was one of many struggling farmers who, in spite of government crop-support programs that cost more in 1982 than all welfare programs for the poor, could not make ends meet.

The Roller-Coaster Economy

The economy shifted back and forth during the 1980s and early 1990s. The Reagan years began with a recession that lasted for several years. An economic boom between 1983 and 1990 gave way to a punishing recession as the new decade began. It appeared that the United States had embarked on another boom-and-bust cycle as unsettling as that which had prevailed in the early years of the twentieth century.

The recession of 1980 to 1982 began during the Carter administration, when the Federal Reserve Board tried to deal with mounting deficits by increasing the money supply. Program cuts to counter inflation brought substantial unemployment in the workforce. During Reagan's first year, the job situation deteriorated further, and by the end of 1982, the unemployment rate had climbed to 10.8 percent (and

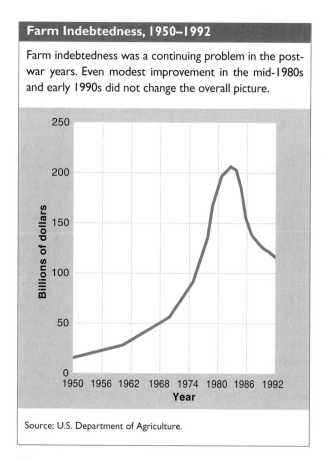

Farm Indebtedness, 1950–1992

Farm indebtedness was a continuing problem in the postwar years. Even modest improvement in the mid-1980s and early 1990s did not change the overall picture.

Source: U.S. Department of Agriculture.

more than 20 percent among African Americans). Nearly one-third of the nation's industrial capacity lay idle, and 12 million Americans were out of work.

Inflation, accompanied by heavy unemployment, continued to be a problem. The inflation rate, which reached 12.4 percent a year under Carter in 1980, fell after Reagan assumed office, to 8.9 percent in his first year and to about 5 percent during the remainder of his first term. But even the lower rate eroded the purchasing power of people already in difficulty.

The recession of 1980 to 1982 afflicted every region of the country. Business failures proliferated in every city and state, as large and small businesses closed their doors and fired employees. In 1982, business bankruptcies rose 50 percent from the previous year. In one week in June 1982, a total of 548 businesses failed, close to the 1932 weekly record of 612. In auto-making Detroit, Japanese competition and high interest rates sent car sales plummeting. The Detroit unemployment rate rose to more than 19 percent and affected the entire city.

Even the Sun Belt—the vast southern region stretching from coast to coast—showed the effects of the recession. It had enjoyed economic growth fostered by the availability of cheap, nonunion labor, tax advantages that state governments offered

corporations willing to locate plants there, and a favorable climate. Now it, too, began to suffer economic problems, and large areas began to stagnate. Overexpansion in the oil industry led to a collapse in prices that disrupted the economy in Texas, Oklahoma, Louisiana, and other oil-producing regions. Worldwide gluts of some minerals, copper for example, added to unemployment elsewhere in the Southwest.

Economic conditions improved in late 1983 and early 1984, particularly for Americans in the middle- and upper-income ranges. The federal tax cut Reagan pushed through encouraged consumer spending, and huge defense expenditures had a stimulating effect. The Republican effort to reduce restrictions and cut waste sparked business confidence. A voluntary Japanese quota on car exports assisted the ailing automobile industry. The stock market climbed as it reflected the optimistic buying spree. Inflation remained low, about 3 to 4 percent annually from 1982 to 1988. Interest rates likewise fell from 16.5 percent to 10.5 percent in the same period and remained thereafter below 11 percent. The unemployment rate at the end of the 1980s fell to below 6 percent nationally (though many of the new jobs that were created paid less than $13,000

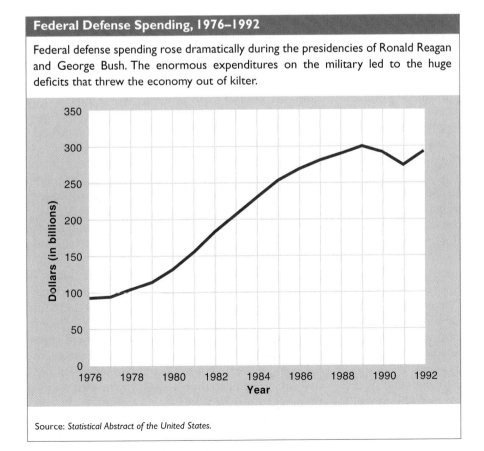

Federal Defense Spending, 1976–1992

Federal defense spending rose dramatically during the presidencies of Ronald Reagan and George Bush. The enormous expenditures on the military led to the huge deficits that threw the economy out of kilter.

Source: *Statistical Abstract of the United States.*

per year). Between the start of the recovery and 1988, real GNP grew at an annual rate of 4.2 percent.

But the economic upswing masked a number of problems. Millions of Americans remained poor. Many families continued to earn a middle-class income, but only by having two full-time income earners. They also went deeply into debt. To buy homes, young people accepted vastly higher mortgage interest rates than their parents had. Stiff credit card debts, often at 20 percent interest, were common. Under such circumstances, some young families struggled to remain in the middle class. Blue-collar workers had to accept lower standards of living. Single mothers were hit hardest of all.

The huge and growing budget deficits reflected the fundamental economic instability. Those deficits provoked doubts that resulted in the stock market crash of 1987. Six weeks of falling prices culminated with a 22.6 percent drop on Monday, October 19, almost double the plunge of "Black Tuesday," October 29, 1929. The deficits, negative trade balances, and exposures of Wall Street fraud all combined to puncture the bubble. The stock market revived, but the crash foreshadowed further problems.

Those problems surfaced in the early 1990s, as the country experienced another recession. A combination of massive military spending, growth of entitlement programs, and tax cuts sent budget deficits skyward. As bond traders in the 1980s speculated recklessly and pocketed huge profits, the basic productive structure of the country continued to decline. The huge increase in the national debt eroded business confidence, and this time the effects were felt not simply in the stock market but in the economy as a whole.

American firms suffered a serious decline, and to cope with shrinking profits and decreased consumer demand, companies scaled back dramatically. In late 1991, General Motors announced that it would close 21 plants, lay off 9,000 white-collar employees the next year, and eliminate more than 70,000 jobs in the next several years. Hundreds of other companies did the same thing, trimming corporate fat but also cutting thousands of jobs.

The unemployment rate rose once again. In mid-1991, it reached 7 percent, the highest level in nearly five years. About 8.7 million Americans were without jobs, up 2 million since the recession began.

Around the nation, state governments found it impossible to balance their budgets without resorting to massive spending cuts. Reagan's efforts to move programs from the federal to the state level worked as long as funding lasted, but as national support dropped and state tax revenues declined, states found themselves in a budgetary gridlock.

Most had constitutional prohibitions against running deficits, and so they had to slash spending for social services and education, even after yearly budgets had been approved.

After a number of false starts, the economy began to recover in mid-1992. The unemployment rate dropped, the productivity index rose, and a concerted effort began to bring the federal deficit down.

Population Shifts

As the American people dealt with the swings of the economy, demographic patterns changed significantly. The nation's population increased from 228 million to approximately 250 million between 1980 and 1990—a rise of 9.6 percent (as opposed to 11.5 percent in the 1970s) that was one of the lowest rates of growth in American history. At the same time, the complexion of the country changed. In 1992, the country's nonwhite population—African Americans, Latinos, Asians, and Native Americans—stood at an all-time high of 25 percent, the result of increased immigration and of minority birthrates significantly above the white birthrate.

The population shifted geographically as well. American cities increasingly filled with members of the nation's minorities. White families continued to leave for the steadily growing suburbs, which by 1990 contained almost half the population, more than ever before. In 15 of the nation's 28 largest cities—New York, Chicago, and Houston among them—minorities made up at least half the population. Minority representation varied by urban region. In Detroit, Washington, New Orleans, and Chicago, African Americans were the largest minority; in Phoenix, El Paso, San Antonio, and Los Angeles, Latinos held that position; in San Francisco, Asians outnumbered other groups.

The cities also grew steadily poorer. In Houston, for example, although increasing numbers of African Americans, Latinos, and Asians lived in the suburbs, most of the poorest minority families were concentrated in the city itself. As had been the case since World War II, commuters from the suburbs took the better-paying jobs, while people living in the cities held lower-paying positions. Mario Perez, a 27-year-old Latino immigrant, noted in 1991 that the increase in the number of Spanish-speaking immigrants in the nine years since he arrived in Houston made it easier to find a job but harder to secure well-paying work. Perez himself worked seven days a week sweeping streets downtown and tending plants for $5.50 an hour.

At the same time, the population was moving west. In 1900, the Mountain and Pacific states contained

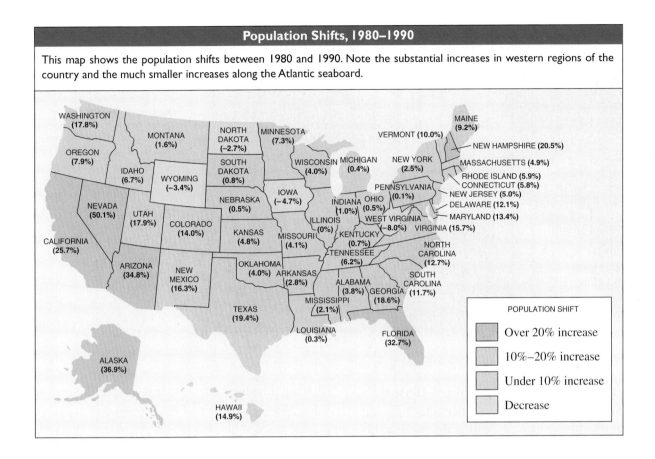

Population Shifts, 1980–1990

This map shows the population shifts between 1980 and 1990. Note the substantial increases in western regions of the country and the much smaller increases along the Atlantic seaboard.

POPULATION SHIFT

Over 20% increase

10%–20% increase

Under 10% increase

Decrease

about 5 percent of the nation's population. By 1990, that figure stood at 21 percent. The population of the nation as a whole rose by less than 10 percent in the 1980s, but the population of the West increased by 22 percent.

That population was becoming much more urbanized. In the 50 years following 1940, the six largest metropolitan areas in the West grew by 380 percent; the six largest in the East expanded by only 64 percent. By 1990, 80 percent of all westerners lived in metropolitan areas, compared to 76 percent of the people in the rest of the United States. As writer Wallace Stegner observed, the West "*is* urban; it's an oasis civilization."

With its urban development, the West became a pacesetter for the rest of the country. If the New England village was a symbol of the eighteenth century and the midwestern town was a similar symbol of the nineteenth century, then the western metropolis had special symbolic importance in the late twentieth century. Western cities were unbounded, open-ended, and sprawling in all directions. They seemed capable of expanding indefinitely. Horizontal, low-slung homes made western neighborhoods look very different from those in the Northeast. Tourism became a dynamic industry, with the West in the forefront. The motel, a western invention,

made automobile travel easier. Western cities were among the most popular tourist destinations, drawing visitors from all over the world.

California was the nation's fastest-growing state, its population increasing in the 1980s by nearly 26 percent. Responding to a question about California's impact on the rest of the country, Wallace Stegner replied, "We *are* the national culture, at its most energetic end." Los Angeles became the most dynamic example of American vitality and creativity. The motion picture industry exerted a worldwide impact. The city became a capital of consumption and served as a symbol of a dynamic national life.

FOREIGN POLICY AND THE END OF THE COLD WAR

In the early 1990s, the United States emerged triumphant in the Cold War that had dominated international politics since the end of World War II. In one of the most momentous turns in modern world history, communism collapsed in Eastern Europe and in the Soviet Union, and the various republics in the Soviet orbit moved toward capitalism and democracy. Other regions—the Middle East and Africa—experienced equally breathtaking change.

Reagan's "Star Wars" Program Reagan's Star Wars proposal drew tremendous criticism. Opponents argued that the program would be excessively expensive and would never work. This Department of Defense picture sought to demonstrate the potential of the program, officially known as the Strategic Defense Initiative. How do you think this picture conveys the high-tech aims of the program? *(U.S. Department of Defense)*

Reagan, Bush, and the Soviet Union

The Cold War was very much alive when Ronald Reagan assumed power in 1981. Like most of his compatriots, Reagan believed in large defense budgets and a militant approach toward the Soviet Union. He wanted to cripple the USSR economically by forcing it to spend more than it could afford on defense.

Viewing the Soviet Union as an "evil empire" in his first term, Reagan promoted a larger atomic arsenal by arguing that a nuclear war could be fought and won. The administration dropped efforts to obtain Senate ratification of SALT II, the arms reduction plan negotiated under Carter, although it observed the pact's restrictions. Then Reagan proposed the enormously expensive and bitterly criticized Strategic Defense Initiative, popularly known as "Star Wars" after a 1977 movie, to intercept Soviet missiles in outer space.

In his second term, Reagan softened his belligerence. Mikhail Gorbachev, the new Soviet leader, watching his own economy collapse under the pressure of the superheated arms race, realized the need for greater accommodation with the West. He understood that the only way the Soviet Union could survive was through arms negotiations with the United States that would help reduce his overextended budget. He therefore proposed a policy of *perestroika* (restructuring the economy) and *glasnost* (political openness to encourage

DOCUMENT

Ronald Reagan, "Evil Empire" Speech (1983)

VIDEO

Ronald Reagan at the Berlin Wall

personal initiative). His overtures opened the way to better relations with the United States.

Concerned with his own place in history, Reagan met with Gorbachev, and the two developed a close working relationship. Summit meetings led to an Intermediate-Range Nuclear Forces Treaty in 1987 that provided for the withdrawal and destruction of 2,500 Soviet and American nuclear missiles in Europe.

George Bush maintained Reagan's comfortable relationship with Gorbachev. At several summit meetings in 1989 and 1990, the two leaders signed agreements reducing the number of long-range nuclear weapons, ending the manufacture of chemical weapons, and easing trade restrictions. The Strategic Arms Reduction Treaty (START) signed in 1991 dramatically cut stockpiles of long-range weapons.

The End of the Cold War

The Cold War ended with astonishing speed. Gorbachev's efforts to restructure Soviet society and to work with the United States brought him acclaim around the world but led to trouble at home. In mid-1991, he faced an old-guard Communist coup, led by those who opposed *glasnost* and *perestroika*. He survived this right-wing challenge, but he could not resist those who wanted to go even further to establish democracy and capitalism. The forces he had unleashed finally destroyed the Soviet system and tore the USSR apart.

Boris Yeltsin, president of Russia, the strongest and largest of the Soviet republics, emerged as the dominant leader, but even he could not contain the forces of disintegration. Movements in the tiny Baltic republics of Latvia, Lithuania, and Estonia, culminating with independence in 1991, began the dismantling of the Soviet Union. The once-powerful superpower was now a collection of separate states. Although the republics coalesced loosely in a Commonwealth of Independent States, led by Russia, they retained their autonomy—and independent leadership—in domestic and foreign affairs.

Meanwhile, Communist regimes throughout Europe collapsed. In a series of remarkable developments that occurred at the same time and intertwined with the turbulence in the Soviet Union, many of the Communist satellites broke loose, rejected communism, and proclaimed a new commitment to democracy.

The most dramatic chapter in this story unfolded in Germany in November 1989. Responding to Gorbachev's softening stance toward the West, East Germany's Communist party boss announced unexpectedly that citizens of his country would be free to leave East Germany. Within hours, thousands of people gathered on both sides of the 28-mile Berlin Wall—the symbol of the Cold War that divided

President of a New Russia Boris Yeltsin, president of Russia, the largest of the republics in what had been the Soviet Union, became the most influential leader after Gorbachev's fall. But Yeltsin's efforts at economic reform met with serious opposition and led to his resignation as the century came to an end. How is Yeltsin conveying his confidence in this picture? What did he hope to achieve? *(Reuters/CORBIS)*

Berlin into East and West sectors. As the border guards stepped aside, East Germans flooded into West Berlin amid dancing, shouting, and fireworks. Within days, sledgehammer-wielding Germans pulverized the Berlin Wall, and soon the Communist government itself came tumbling down. By October 1990, the two Germanys were reunited.

The fall of the Berlin Wall reverberated all over Eastern Europe. Everywhere it brought in its wake the pell-mell overthrow of Communist regimes. In Poland, the 10-year-old Solidarity movement led by Lech Walesa triumphed in its long struggle against Soviet domination and found itself in power in December 1990, with Walesa as president. Governing, however, sometimes proved more difficult than leading the revolt. In Czechoslovakia, two decades after Soviet tanks had rolled into the streets of Prague to suppress a policy of liberalization, the forces of freedom were likewise victorious. Like Poland, Czechoslovakia sought and received aid from the United States. But not even economic assistance could keep the nation intact, as turbulence led to the creation of separate and independent Czech and Slovak republics. The same forces that culminated in the independence of Czechoslovakia brought new regimes in Bulgaria, Hungary, Romania, and Albania.

Yugoslavia, held together by a Communist dictatorship since 1945, proved to be the extreme case of

The Last Premier of the Soviet Union Mikhail Gorbachev was the Soviet leader who initiated the process that helped ease tensions with the United States and ultimately ended the Cold War. Gorbachev's policies provided for major readjustments in Soviet society, but those eventually tore the Soviet Union apart. Why was Gorbachev willing to work with the United States? What image does he convey in this photograph? *(AP/Wide World Photos)*

The Fall of Communism

In the late 1980s and early 1990s, the Soviet Union fragmented and lost control of its satellites in Eastern Europe. As many countries shown here declared their independence, Czechoslovakia broke into two nations, while Yugoslavia ruptured into a group of feuding states. **Reflecting on the Past** How widespread was the turbulence that led to the fall of communism? How quickly did the process take place? How did events in one country influence events in another country?

Largest and strongest of the former Soviet republics after 1991

Lithuania, Latvia and Estonia gained independence, 1991

German reunited, 1990

Elections held, 1989

Wall breached, 1989

Czechoslovakia split into Czech Republic and Slovakia, 1993

Communist regimes dismantled, 1989

Dissolution into warring states, 1991

ethnic hostility resurging amid collapsing central authority. In 1991, Yugoslavia splintered into its ethnic components. In Bosnia, the decision of the Muslim and Croatian majority to secede from Serbian-dominated Yugoslavia led Bosnian Serbs, backed by the Serbian republic, to embark on a brutal siege of the city of Sarajevo and an even more ruthless "ethnic cleansing" campaign to liquidate opponents. The United States remained out of the conflict, unsure about what to do.

Early in 1992, Bush and Yeltsin proclaimed a new era of "friendship and partnership" and formally declared an end to the Cold War. After half a century of confrontation, the United States had won. Yeltsin abandoned the quest for nuclear parity—maintaining an arsenal equal to that of the United States—and agreed to cut back Russian conventional forces. The United States then extended aid to the former Soviet republics, which needed help in reorganizing their economies as free enterprise systems.

Dismantling the Berlin Wall The destruction of the Berlin Wall in November 1989 was a symbolic blow to the entire Cold War structure that had solidified in Europe in the postwar years. People grabbed hammers and joined together in tearing down the hated wall. Joyous celebrations marked the reunification of a city that had been divided for decades. How does this dramatic picture convey the exuberant mood of the time? *(Alexandria Avakian/Woodfin Camp & Associates)*

Removing a Statue of Lenin As communism fell, authorities in Eastern Europe removed statues of Lenin, one of the dominant figures in creating the Soviet state after the Russian Revolution. Here, a statue in Bucharest, Romania, is readied for removal with a metal cable that looks like a hangman's noose. What impression do you get from this photograph? *(Sipa Press)*

American Involvement Overseas

As the United States struggled to keep abreast of the momentous changes in Eastern Europe, it was equally involved with events in the rest of the world. Here again the nation sought to preserve stability as the Cold War drew to an end.

In Latin America, the United States intervened frequently as it had in the past, hoping to impose stability on the volatile region. Viewing Central America as a Cold War battlefield early in his presidency, Reagan openly opposed left-wing guerrillas in El Salvador who fought to overthrow a repressive right-wing regime. He was fearful that still another nation might follow the Marxist examples of Cuba and Nicaragua. The United States increased its assistance to the antirevolutionary Salvadoran government, heedless of a similar course followed years before in Vietnam. Efforts to destroy the radical forces failed, but in 1989, a far-right faction won the Salvadoran elections and polarized the country.

MAP

Conflict in Central America, 1970-1998

Nicaragua became an even bloodier battleground in the effort to promote stability. In 1979, revolutionaries calling themselves Sandinistas (after César Sandino, who fought in the 1920s against U.S. occupation troops) overthrew the repressive Somoza family, which had ruled for three decades. President Carter initially extended aid to the Sandinistas and recognized the new regime, then cut off support to show his disapproval of their curbs on civil liberties and their alleged efforts to assist rebels in El Salvador. The Republicans adopted a far stronger position. Their 1980 platform pledged to replace the Sandinistas with a "free and independent" government. Once in office, Reagan circumvented congressional opposition to his efforts to defeat the revolutionary reformers and signed a National Security directive in November 1981 authorizing the CIA to arm and train counterrevolutionaries known as *contras.*

DOCUMENT

Ronald Reagan, Iran-*Contra* Address (March 4, 1987)

Nicaragua became enmeshed in a bitter civil war. When the war went badly for the *contras,* the CIA assumed the military initiative and mined Nicaraguan harbors, violating international law. Upon discovering these secret missions, Congress cut off military aid to the *contras.* Peaceful elections in early 1990 finally drove the Sandinistas out and brought the fighting to an end. Though the economy remained in desperate straits, the new regime seemed to offer the best hope of healing the wounds of the bloody conflict.

Reagan found it easier to maintain stability on the tiny Caribbean island of Grenada. The president ordered marines there in October 1983 after a coup installed a government sympathetic to Fidel Castro's Cuba. Concerned about the construction of a large airfield, 2,000 marines invaded the island, rescued a number of American medical students, and claimed triumph. Though the United Nations condemned it, Americans cheered what the administration called its "rescue mission."

Middle Eastern and Central American concerns became entangled in the Iran–*contra* affair. In 1987, Congress learned that the National Security Council had launched an effort to free American hostages in the Middle East by selling arms to Iran and then using the funds to aid the *contras,* in direct violation of both the law and congressional will. The trial of Oliver North, the National Security Council official responsible for the policy, focused on his distortions and falsifications before congressional committees and on his destruction of official documents that could have substantiated charges of wrongdoing by top officials. Convicted in 1989, North received a light sentence requiring no time in prison from a judge who recognized that North was not acting entirely on his own.

VIDEO

Oliver North Hearing

Bush, too, was involved in a variety of episodes abroad. Despite memories of past imperialism, the United States invaded Panama in 1989; the reasons it gave were to protect the canal, defend American citizens, and stop drug traffic. The campaign resulted in

Nelson Mandela Nelson Mandela served as a source of inspiration to black South Africans, as the long struggle against apartheid finally brought that system of rigid segregation to an end and led to the setting up of a biracial democracy with Mandela himself as president. How did Mandela manage to convey his own sense of confidence, commitment, and reconciliation? *(AP/Wide World Photos)*

the capture of military leader Manuel Noriega, notorious for his involvement in the drug trade. Noriega was brought to the United States, tried, and after a lengthy trial, convicted of drug-trafficking charges.

The United States likewise found itself drawn into turbulent African affairs. In South Africa, the United States supported the long and ultimately successful struggle against apartheid. This policy, whereby the white minority (only 15 percent of the population) segregated, suppressed, and denied basic human rights to the black majority, was part of South African law. A resistance movement, spearheaded by the African National Congress (ANC) sought to end apartheid. Nelson Mandela and other ANC leaders refused to give up, despite fierce resistance to their efforts to achieve freedom. While the United States had long expressed its dislike of this ruthless system of segregation, economic and political ties to South Africa kept the United States from taking steps to weaken it. Then, in 1986, bowing to increased domestic pressure, Congress imposed sanctions, including a rule prohibiting new American investments. The economic pressure damaged the South African economy and persuaded more than half of the 300 American firms doing business there to leave.

The final blow to apartheid came from the efforts of Nelson Mandela. The black ANC activist, who had become a symbol of the militant resistant movement during his 27 years in prison, steered his nation through a stunning transformation. In 1990, during Bush's presidency, South African prime minister Frederik W. de Klerk succumbed to pressure

Anti-American Demonstrators in Baghdad A multinational coalition freed Kuwait after Iraqi leader Saddam Hussein—whose image appears on the signs at the anti-American demonstration in Baghdad—annexed the oil-rich land in 1990. The Persian Gulf War gave George Bush a quick victory, but the long-range results of U.S. involvement were questionable. What impression do the multiple pictures of Saddam Hussein convey? *(Chris Morris/Black Star)*

from the United States and the rest of the world, which finally embraced the ANC cause. He freed Mandela and announced plans by which apartheid would be gradually overturned. Talks between South Africa's white government and the ANC that Mandela led laid the groundwork for a smooth transition to a biracial democracy. Mandela and de Klerk worked together to ensure peaceful elections in 1994, in which blacks voted for the first time. After years of struggle, the ANC assumed power and dismantled the apartheid system. Mandela himself became president of a South Africa that was building itself anew. American aid provided support in transitional times.

The Gulf War

When Iraqi leader Saddam Hussein invaded Kuwait in the summer of 1990, the United States led a coalition to drive Iraq out. Operation Desert Storm began in early 1991 and routed Iraqi forces, while leaving Kuwait's extensive oil fields in flames. **Reflecting on the Past** How many Middle Eastern countries were involved in the Gulf War? What role did oil play in the events that unfolded during the war? Why was Israel vulnerable during the conflict?

Elsewhere in Africa, U.S. policymakers had greater difficulty in maintaining post–Cold War stability. Somalia, an impoverished East African nation, suffered from a devastating famine, compounded by struggles between warlords that led to an almost total disintegration of order. In 1992, Bush sent U.S. troops to assist a UN effort to relieve the starvation and stabilize the country, but those efforts proved unsuccessful in a struggle that continued into the twenty-first century.

A dramatic crisis occurred in the Middle East in 1990 when Saddam Hussein, the dictator of Iraq, invaded and annexed oil-rich neighboring Kuwait. Hussein seemed intent on unifying Arab nations, threatening Israel, and dominating the Middle Eastern oil on which the West, including the United States, relied.

The Middle East in the 1980s and 1990s

President Bush reacted vigorously. Working through the UN, as Harry Truman had done in Korea, the United States persuaded the UN Security Council to vote unanimously to condemn the attack and impose an embargo on Iraq. After Hussein refused to relinquish Kuwait, in mid-January 1991 a U.S.-led multinational army of nearly half a million troops from 28 nations struck at Iraq. In Operation Desert Storm, the coalition forces' sophisticated missiles, aircraft, and tanks swiftly overwhelmed the Iraqis. Americans were initially jubilant. Then the euphoria faded as Saddam turned his remaining military power against minorities in Iraq. Bush's unwillingness to become bogged down in an Iraqi civil war and his eagerness to return U.S. troops home left the conflict unfinished. A year after his defeat, Hussein was as strongly entrenched as ever.

President Bush on the Gulf War

Meanwhile, the United States was involved in a larger, and ultimately more important, effort to bring peace to the Middle East. In the early 1990s, Secretary of State James Baker finally secured agreement from the major parties in the region to speak to one another face to face. A victory in the Israeli parliamentary elections in mid-1992 for Yitzhak Rabin, a soldier who recognized the need for peace and was ready to compromise, offered further hope for the talks.

TIMELINE

1980	Ronald Reagan elected president
1980–1982	Recession
1981	Reagan breaks air controllers' strike AIDS (acquired immune deficiency syndrome) discovered
1981–1983	Tax cuts; deficit spending increases
1983	Reagan proposes Strategic Defense Initiative ("Star Wars")
1984	Reagan re-elected
1986	Tax reform measure passed Immigration Reform and Control Act
1987	Iran–*contra* affair becomes public Stock market crashes Intermediate-Range Nuclear Forces Treaty signed
1988	George H. W. Bush elected president
1989	Federal bailout of savings and loan industry Fall of the Berlin Wall
1990	National debt reaches $3.1 trillion Sandinistas driven from power in Nicaragua Nelson Mandela freed in South Africa U.S. population reaches 250 million
1990–1992	Recession
1991	Persian Gulf War Failed coup in Soviet Union Disintegration of the Soviet Union Strategic Arms Reduction Treaty (START) signed Ethnic turbulence in fragmented former Yugoslavia
1992	Declaration of the end of the Cold War

Conclusion

Conservatism in Context

In the 1980s and early 1990s, the United States witnessed the resurgence of conservatism. The assault on the welfare state, dubbed the "Reagan Revolution," created a less-regulated economy, whatever the implications for less-fortunate Americans. The policies of Ronald Reagan and George Bush continued the trend begun by Richard Nixon in the 1970s. They reshaped the political agenda and reversed the liberal approach that had held sway since the New Deal of Franklin Roosevelt in the 1930s. In foreign affairs, Republican administrations likewise shifted course. Reagan first assumed a steel-ribbed posture toward the Soviet Union, then moved toward détente, and watched as his successor declared victory in the Cold War.

To be sure, there were limits to the transformation. Such fundamental programs as social security and Medicare remained securely in place, accepted by all but the most implacable splinter groups. Even the most conservative presidents of the past half century could not return to an imagined era of unbridled individualism and puny federal government. On the international front, despite the end of the Cold War, the nation's defense budget remained far higher than many Americans wished, and the nuclear arsenal continued to pose a threat to the human race.

Nor was the transformation beneficial to everyone. Periods of deep recession wrought havoc on the lives of blue-collar and white-collar workers alike. Working-class Americans were caught in the spiral of downward mobility that made them question the ability of the nation's economy to reward hard work. Liberals and conservatives both worried about the mounting national debt and the capacity of the economy to compete with Japan, South Korea, Germany, and other countries. Countless Americans fretted about the growing gaps between rich and poor. They fought with one another over what rules should govern a woman's right to an abortion. For the first time in American history, many children could not hope to do better than their parents had done. Reluctantly they tried to prepare themselves to accept a scaled-down version of the American dream.

Questions for Review and Reflection

1. How did the conservative movement become a major force in American life?

2. How successful was Reagan in implementing his conservative program?

3. What was the fate of social reform movements in the 1980s?

4. How did economic issues affect American life in the 1980s?

5. How did the Cold War finally come to an end?

Recommended Reading

Recommended Readings are posted on the Web site for this textbook. Visit www.ablongman.com/nash

Fiction and Film

Sherman Alexie's first book, *The Business of Fancydancing* (1992) is a collection of poems and short stories about American Indian life. Julia Alvarez's *How the Garcia Girls Lost Their Accents* (1992) is the fictional account of four young women from the Dominican Republic and their transition to American life. Tom Wolfe's *The Bonfire of the Vanities* (1987) is a novel about the arrogance of the upper class in New York—the masters of the universe—and the consequences when an accident occurs.

The film *Bedtime for Bonzo* (1951) shows Ronald Reagan the actor playing the part of a professor trying to teach morals to a chimpanzee. *Knute Rockne, All American* (1940) is another of Reagan's films in which he plays the part of George Gipp (the Gipper), a Notre Dame football player. *The Life and Times of Harvey Milk* (1984) is an Academy Award–winning documentary about the gay San Francisco city supervisor who was murdered. *Wall Street* (1987) captures the sense of greed and corporate arrogance that created the tone for the 1980s. *When Harry Met Sally* (1989) is a film about the difficulties of relationships between men and women.

Discovering U.S. History Online ——————————————————

Ronald Wilson Reagan
www.ipl.org/div/potus/rwreagan.html
This site contains basic factual data about Reagan's election and presidency, speeches, and online biographies.

Ronald Reagan Presidential Library
www.reagan.utexas.edu
This site offers selected pictures and written documents from the Reagan years.

Media, Advertising, and the 1984 Presidential Election
http://it.stlawu.edu/~quack/seminar/home.htm
This site presents a study of "the Reagan campaign's use of media, in the form of paid advertising and news coverage . . . [and contrasts it] with Mondale's approach, in order to demonstrate how different the campaigns truly were."

The Reagan Years
www.cnn.com/SPECIALS/2001/reagan.years
This site includes photos and speeches from Reagan's life, especially from key issues and events of his presidency such as Reaganomics, the Iran–*contra* affair, and his views on the Communist empire in an attempt to contribute to the "debate [on] the legacy of [his] two-term presidency."

George Herbert Walker Bush
www.ipl.org/div/potus/ghwbush.html
This site contains basic factual data about George H. W. Bush's election and presidency, speeches, and online biographies.

Divining America: Religion and the National Culture in the Twentieth Century
www.nhc.rtp.nc.us:8080/tserve/twenty.htm
Using essays and primary sources, the site was "designed to help teachers of American history bring their students to a greater understanding of the role religion has played in the development of the United States."

U.S. Forest Service History
www.lib.duke.edu/forest/Research/usfscoll/
Incorporating original documents and photographs as well as bibliographic references, this site presents "information about the history of the United States Forest Service, in the Department of Agriculture."

United States Environmental Protection Agency
www.epa.gov/history
A history of the agency, including a timeline from 1970 to the present, topical information, publications, collection search, and photographs.

The Forgotten Americans
www.pbs.org/klru/forgottenamericans/
Companion site to the film, this site offers a portrait of the "Third World conditions" experienced by the mostly Latino residents of U.S. neighborhoods outside the city limits in Texas, California, Arizona, and New Mexico, called *colonias*.

American Cultural History: 1980–1989
http://kclibrary.nhmccd.edu/decade80.html
An informative breakdown of various cultural and economic trends during the 1980s, including Art and Architecture, Books and Literature, Fashion and Fads, Education, Events and Technology, Music and Media, Theater, and Film and Television.

Global Economy
www.pbs.org/wgbh/commandingheights/lo
This site examines the "forces, values, events, and ideas that have shaped the present global economic system, including Reagan's introduction of 'supply-side' economics."

An Outline of the U.S. Economy
http://usinfo.state.gov/products/pubs/oecon/
This text-based Web site presents the basics of the American economy as well as a brief history of major economic events.

Foreign Policy
http://globetrotter.berkeley.edu/clips/
This site has a three-part series, "The End of the Cold War," that includes extensive news quotes on "The Search for a U.S. Strategy," "Europe's Search for a New Identity," and "The Collapse of Communism in Eastern Europe and the Shaping of a Western Response."

The Cold War
www.cnn.com/SPECIALS/cold.war
This is the companion site to the CNN series on the Cold War. It contains some material on the end of the struggle.

The Gulf War
www.pbs.org/pages/frontline/gulf
This site combines personal accounts with a chronology and general information about the war.

The Post–Cold War World, 1992–2005

American society became more and more aware of its multicultural past and present in the 1990s. Different groups competed with each other for positions in the marketplace and other public spaces as the gap between rich and poor continued to grow greater. *(Billy Morrow Jackson, Station, 1981–1982, Beloit College Collection, Beloit, WI)*

American Stories

An Immigrant Family Struggles as the Economy Improves

In 1997, Marlene Garrett bundled up her three sleepy children—ages 4, 3, and 1—and took them to the babysitter's home every morning at 5 A.M. "Mama has to go to work so she can buy you shoes," she told them as she left for a job behind the counter at a bagel café in Fort Lauderdale, Florida, that began at 6 A.M. This was a new position and she did not want to be late.

Marlene had come to the United States from Jamaica eight years earlier. She and her husband, Rod, had high hopes for a better life in the United States, and they were fortunate enough to be employed. But both of them held entry-level jobs and had to struggle to make ends meet. Rod worked in a factory making hospital curtains and brought home about $250 a week. Marlene had just left a $5.25-an-hour job selling sneakers for her $6-an-hour job at the bagel café. It was a small improvement, but the $200 she earned weekly made it possible to pay the monthly rent of $400 and buy groceries. With luck, they could repair or replace the car, which had recently died, and perhaps begin to pay off their $5,000 debt from medical bills. They had no health insurance and could only hope that no one got sick.

Marlene was not happy about her babysitting arrangements. Her real preference was to stay at home. "Who's a better caretaker than mom?" she asked. But remaining at home was out of the question. Welfare might have been a possibility in the past, but the United States was in the process of cutting back drastically on its welfare rolls, and, in any event, Marlene was not comfortable with that alternative. "I don't want to plant that seed in my children," she said. "I want to work."

Marlene had few day-care options. She would have liked to have taken Scherrod, Angelique, and Hasia to the Holy Temple Christian Academy—her church's day-care center and preschool—but it cost $180 a week for three children and was beyond reach. Several months before, when she had been earning $8 an hour as a home health aide for the elderly, she had thought she could afford the church center and had even put money down for school uniforms for the kids. Then her car gave out and made it impossible to continue that job.

Instead of the Holy Temple Christian Academy, Marlene took the children to the home of Vivienne, a woman from the Bahamas who worked nights at the self-service laundry where Marlene did her wash. Vivienne's apartment was simple and clean but had no toys or books anywhere in sight. Most days, the children watched television during the 10 hours that Marlene was away.

The Garretts knew how important it was to stimulate their children. Reflecting longingly on the church center and what it offered, Marlene said, "The children play games. They go on field trips. They teach them, they train them. My children are bright. You would be amazed at what they would acquire in a year." But instead of a stimulating center, the Garretts had to settle for a place that was simply safe.

At a time when the administration of Bill Clinton was trying to reconfigure the welfare system, people like the Garretts found themselves left out. Florida, like many states, budgeted most of its child-care money for families moving off welfare to jobs. People who had never been on welfare received nothing. As the executive director of a Florida child-care referral agency observed, "Many of these parents have no choice but to leave their children in substandard arrangements that are rotting their brains, and jeopardizing their futures."

Marlene refused to give up hope. Her children were on a waiting list for help from the state that might make the Holy Temple Christian Academy accessible. Meanwhile, she took a second job working nights at the local Marriott Hotel. She had to pay Vivienne more money for the extra hours, and she worried even more about the additional time away from the children, but felt she had no choice. "It is temporary," she said. "I am doing what I have to do."

Marlene and Rod Garrett were like millions of poor Americans who found themselves left out of the prosperity that returned to the United States in the mid-1990s. Despite rosy economic indicators, more than 35 million Americans still lived below the federally defined poverty line. Life was hardly easy for the Garretts or for other families who found themselves on the bottom side of the line. Then, soon after George W. Bush succeeded Bill Clinton as president in 2001, the economy faltered. Now even more Americans found themselves in the same straits as the Garretts.

The Garretts' struggle to care for their children—and for themselves—unfolded against the backdrop of the longest period of economic growth in

American history. As a deep recession in the early 1990s lifted, the economy went on a tear. American corporations, increasingly operating in a multinational context, dominated the global economy. Taking advantage of remarkable advances in communications technology, corporations found it easy to do business in a world smaller than ever before. The easy availability of money encouraged middle- and upper-class Americans to invest in the stock market and mutual funds, often enabling them to realize large gains, at least on paper. The troubling budget deficit that had soared in the Reagan administration disappeared as the government, guided by Democratic president Bill Clinton, ran a surplus for the first time in years. The unemployment level dropped, yet for Americans at the bottom of the economic ladder, some of them immigrants from abroad, conditions remained difficult. Many of the jobs now available as a result of the relentless shift toward a service economy paid little more than the minimum wage, and people like the Garretts, who dreamed of a better life, still found themselves struggling to survive.

Meanwhile, the global scene shifted abruptly. The cataclysmic events in Europe that ended nearly a half century of Cold War required the United States to redefine its international role. This led to substantial debate as both Republicans, who controlled Congress for most of the 1990s, and Democrats, who controlled the White House for the same period, voiced reservations about playing an interventionist, and potentially expensive, role abroad. Then, as the new decade began, the United States confronted the menace of terrorism on a scale never known before. The attacks that destroyed the World Trade Center towers in New York City and left a gaping hole in the Pentagon in Washington, D.C., led to a war on terrorism and a fundamental reconfiguration of American foreign policy.

This chapter describes demographic shifts, reflected in the census of 2000, that changed the face of the American people. It highlights the revival of the economy that brought unprecedented prosperity for many but still failed to accommodate the needs of less fortunate Americans like the Garretts, and then records the even greater suffering as the economy fell apart. It examines the political struggle between Democrats and Republicans that led to a debate about democratic values and brought the second presidential impeachment in American history. It notes the bitterly contested national election of 2000 and its conservative aftermath. Finally, it explores the continuing effort to define the tensions surrounding the American role in the turbulent and terrorist-dominated post–Cold War world.

THE CHANGING FACE OF THE AMERICAN PEOPLE

The United States changed dramatically in the 1990s, as the continuing influx of new immigrants reshaped demographic patterns. The overall population, as reported in the census of 2000, grew more rapidly than it had in the past several decades and reflected the steady increase in the number of nonwhite Americans.

The New Pilgrims

The second great wave of immigrants in the twentieth century changed the face of America. The number of immigrants to the United States in the 20-year period from 1981 to 2000 was approximately 17.5 million, making it the most voluminous period of immigration in American history. In the decade of the 1990s, close to 10 million immigrants were counted, just less than the 10.1 million immigrants recorded in the 10 years from 1905 to 1914, which stands as the all-time record for that span of time. Altogether, nearly one-third of the population growth in the 1990s stemmed from immigration.

Immigrants settled in the 1990s and the early part of the new century in a pattern resembling that of the previous several decades. Whereas most immigrants around the turn of the preceding century remained near the East Coast, or in contiguous states, in 2000, 39.9 percent of the foreign born settled in western states, with only 22.6 percent of the foreign born living in the Northeast. The shift was a result of larger demographic shifts in the United States. As the twentieth century began, the Northeast still dominated the economic and cultural life of the nation. A hundred years later, the West was increasingly dominant. California had surpassed New York as the most populous state, and Los Angeles International Airport, known as LAX, had replaced Ellis Island as the port of entry for many immigrants.

Immigration, 1970–1998

This chart shows the significant rise in immigration after 1970, as the tightly restricted quotas in force from the 1920s to 1965 were liberalized. The steady rise in the 1970s and 1980s reflected the arrival of Asian and Latin Americans, while the spike in the early 1990s occurred because of the amnesty that legalized the status of many illegal immigrants who were now officially counted.

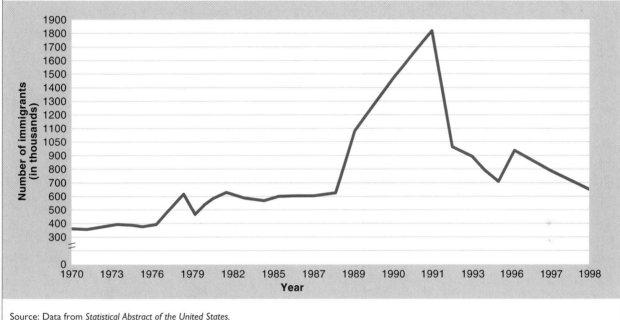

Source: Data from *Statistical Abstract of the United States.*

The sources of recent immigration were similar to those of the 1970s and 1980s. In 2000, just over one-third of all immigrants—legal and illegal—came from Central America, and just over one-quarter came from Asia. Faltering economies in many countries in Latin America led people living on the fringe to look toward the United States, where a better life might be possible. Some Asian immigrants came in response to similar disruptions at home. Hispanic and Asian growth increased even more rapidly in the first years of the twenty-first century. Between 2000 and 2003, the Hispanic population increased 13 percent, while the Asian population rose 12.6 percent, according to a Census Bureau report released in 2004. These increases far exceeded the overall rise of 3 percent during the same period.

Immigrants continued to arrive from other parts of the world as well. Inhabitants of African nations, often as poor as their Latin American and Asian counterparts and similarly faced with deteriorating living conditions, saw hope for a brighter future in America, just as earlier immigrants had. Meanwhile, Europe continued to experience its own wave of immigration, largely from former colonies.

Illegal immigration remained a problem. Of the 33.5 million foreigners that the Census Bureau estimated lived in America in 2004, between 8 million and 12 million, perhaps even more, were illegal entrants. People talked about the nation's "broken borders" as record numbers of immigrants lost their lives in the desert while trying to cross into the United States from Mexico.

The influx of new arrivals was spurred by the Immigration Act of 1965, which was aimed at curbing illegal immigration while offering amnesty to aliens who had lived in the United States prior to 1982. Part of Lyndon Johnson's Great Society program, this act authorized the impartial acceptance of immigrants from all parts of the world and was directly responsible for the greater numbers of Asians and Latin Americans. In 1986, Congress passed the Immigration Reform and Control Act, aimed at curbing illegal immigration while offering amnesty to aliens living in the United States. The Immigration Act of 1990 opened the doors wider, raising immigration quotas while cutting back on restrictions that had limited entry in the past. It also provided for swift deportation of aliens who committed crimes. Two other measures in 1992 expanded eligibility slightly. In 2001, the United States and

MAP

Immigration to the United States, 1945–1990

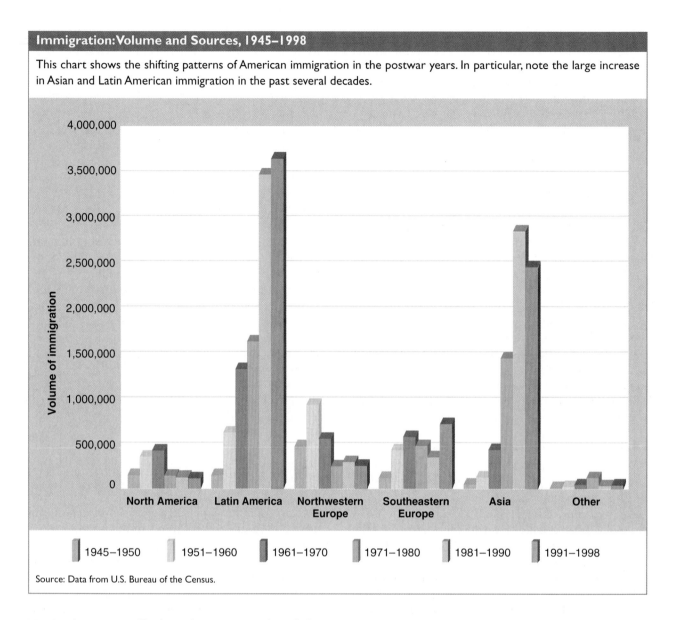

Immigration: Volume and Sources, 1945–1998

This chart shows the shifting patterns of American immigration in the postwar years. In particular, note the large increase in Asian and Latin American immigration in the past several decades.

Source: Data from U.S. Bureau of the Census.

Mexico began to talk about how to ease the plight of Mexican immigrants and permit illegal arrivals to stay.

The rise in the number of immigrants fueled anti-immigrant feeling in some quarters. In the 1970s and 1980s, America's efforts to help immigrants coincided with still-intact social-assistance programs of the liberal welfare state. Affirmative action programs aided both legal and illegal arrivals. Bilingual classrooms became more common, and multiculturalism, stressing the different values that made up a larger American identity, became a dominant theme in many schools.

Yet those efforts brought increasing resistance from Americans already here, particularly as the structure of the economy changed and good jobs became scarcer. At the same time, there was a cultural

backlash, just as there had been in earlier eras. Opponents to immigration also worried about the challenge to America's character posed by new arrivals who clung to social patterns of their own. Americans were not alone in their fears. Europeans, too, were apprehensive at the threats to their way of life. Opposition to German *gastsarbeiter*—guestworkers—became a political issue. In the Netherlands, Pim Fortuyn, a right-wing politician who had argued for extreme restrictions on immigration, was assassinated just before the 2002 general election in which his party had expected to do well and he had hopes of becoming prime minister.

That opposition, which echoed the anti-immigrant feeling of the past, included strenuous efforts to restrict illegal immigration. Resistance came to a head in 1994 in California, where voters passed

Proposition 187, denying illegal aliens access to public education and medical clinics. Just days after the election, a federal judge issued a preliminary injunction to prevent implementation of the ballot measure, which she made permanent several years later. Yet Proposition 187 provided a model for other states to follow and caught the attention of members of Congress, especially Republicans, who gained control of the legislature in 1994. Two years later, Congress passed legislation barring legal immigrants (who were not yet citizens) from receiving food stamps and disability assistance from the federal government. Meanwhile, toward the end of the decade, California ended its support for bilingual education, mandating English immersion instead and sparking a similar drive throughout the nation.

DOCUMENT

Illegal Immigration Reform and Immigrant Responsibility Act of 1996

Economic improvement, and the move toward full employment in the latter part of the 1990s, brought a political shift in the immigration debate. In 2000, pressure mounted to increase the number of visas for high-tech workers abroad, while a coalition of business groups and immigrant-rights organizations pressed for admitting more unskilled workers who could take the unfilled jobs in the service sector. Political considerations also played a part in the shift. Both Democrats and Republicans recognized the voting power of Latinos in particular and wanted to win their support.

Immigration issues became headline news at the end of the 1990s in the highly publicized case of six-year-old Elián Gonzales. In November 1999, he was miraculously pulled out of the water near Florida when a group of Cuban boat people trying to reach the United States drowned. His father, still back in Cuba, had not given permission for the boy to leave and wanted him back. The Miami Cuban community, which hated Fidel Castro and his Communist regime, wanted the boy to receive asylum and stay in the United States. Others, including the Immigration and Naturalization Service (INS), argued that the boy should be returned to his father in Cuba. In the end, the INS seized the boy and returned him to Cuba.

The INS, already unpopular, attracted fierce criticism in the face of the terrorist attacks of September 11, 2001. It had allowed into the country immigrants from Saudi Arabia and elsewhere who had orchestrated the airplane hijackings that shocked the world. Now Americans began to look askance at Arabs or Muslims elsewhere in the country and to condemn the INS for its laxity in screening out potential terrorists. In the years that

followed, legal and illegal immigrants faced increased pressure from restrictive laws aimed at countering terrorism.

The Census of 2000

The 2000 census reported a 13 percent increase in the nation's population, as the United States gained 32.7 million people in the 1990s to reach a total of 281.4 million inhabitants. This expansion surpassed the record 10-year increase of 28 million people in the 1950s, in the midst of the baby boom after World War II. The rate of growth, which had slowed down over the next three decades, accelerated in the 1990s as a result of both increased immigration and longer life expectancy. By 2003, the total population of the United States reached 290.8 million.

While every state had a net increase in population, growth was greatest in the West, an increasingly important area in the nation's economic, social, and cultural life. Altogether, the West as a whole gained 10.4 million people and expanded by 19 percent. Some areas showed extraordinary expansion. The Phoenix, Arizona, metropolitan area grew by 45 percent, while the Las Vegas, Nevada, metropolitan region expanded by 83 percent.

MAP

Population Density of the United States, 1998

The United States remained about 69 percent white, with a 12 percent African American and 11 percent Latino population. Latinos continued to flock to southern California, the Texas border region, and the south of Florida, and they also began to congregate in increasing numbers in Chicago and Denver and other, more central locations. Overall, their numbers increased by 38.8 percent. African Americans maintained their dominance in older northern cities such as Detroit and in Washington, D.C., while continuing to move into metropolitan suburbs, where they found changing employment and housing opportunities.

Nationally, the Asian and Pacific Islander population increased by 43 percent. In California, Asians showed the largest increase of any group. They now made up nearly 13 percent of the state population and maintained their position as the third-largest population group, after whites and Latinos. Much of the Asian population growth occurred in the suburbs, where the more affluent moved, though large pockets of the poor remained in Chinatown in Los Angeles, Little Phnom Penh in Long Beach, and similar areas.

The 2000 census revealed that the combination of Latinos, African Americans, and Asians now outnumbered whites in California. This was the first time since 1860, when California began to provide

Portrait of a Nation

The 2000 census documented changing population patterns and reported where different groups resided in the United States. Note the concentration of African Americans in the Southeast and the concentration of Hispanics in the Southwest. The Asian American population was greatest in the West, while Native Americans, who had once roamed the continent, were now confined to a number of much smaller western areas.

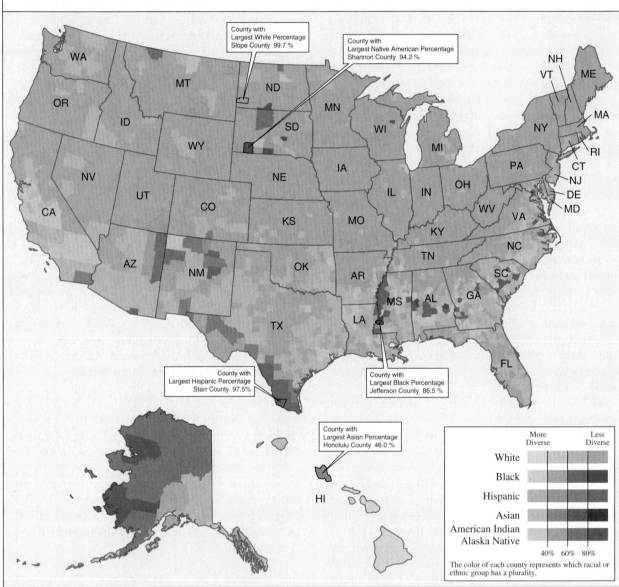

County with Largest White Percentage
Slope County 99.7 %

County with Largest Native American Percentage
Shannon County 94.2 %

County with Largest Hispanic Percentage
Starr County 97.5 %

County with Largest Black Percentage
Jefferson County 86.5 %

County with Largest Asian Percentage
Honolulu County 46.0 %

More Diverse   Less Diverse

White
Black
Hispanic
Asian
American Indian Alaska Native

40%   60%   80%

The color of each county represents which racial or ethnic group has a plurality.

Source: "Portrait of a Nation" *New York Times*, April 1, 2001. Copyright © 2001 by The New York Times Co. Reprinted with permission.

accurate census data, that whites did not have a majority. State politics already began to reflect the shift. In 1998, Cruz Bustamante became the first Latino elected to statewide office in California since 1871, when he became lieutenant governor. This shift had enormous social and political implications. The United States, founded as a white man's country, had now developed into a nation where people of color were increasingly numerous and influential.

One new feature of the 2000 census revealed the desire of large numbers of Americans to identify themselves as part of more than one racial or ethnic group. Nationwide, 2.4 percent of the American people identified themselves as multiracial. In Hawaii, 21 percent of all residents traced their heritage to two or more racial or ethnic groups. At long last, the United States was beginning to embrace its multicultural and multiracial heritage.

Population Change for the Ten Largest Cities, 1990–2000				
Most American cities grew in the 1990s, although some old industrial centers such as Philadelphia and Detroit lost population.				
	Population		**Change, 1990–2000**	
City and State	**April 1, 1990**	**April 1, 2000**	**Number**	**Percent**
New York, NY	7,322,564	8,008,278	685,714	9.4
Los Angeles, CA	3,485,398	3,694,820	209,422	6.0
Chicago, IL	2,783,726	2,896,016	112,290	4.0
Houston, TX	1,630,553	1,953,631	323,078	19.8
Philadelphia, PA	1,585,577	1,517,550	-68,027	-4.3
Phoenix, AZ	983,403	1,321,045	337,642	34.3
San Diego, CA	1,110,549	1,223,400	112,851	10.2
Dallas, TX	1,006,877	1,188,580	181,703	18.0
San Antonio, TX	935,933	1,144,646	208,713	22.3
Detroit, MI	1,027,974	951,270	-76,704	-7.5

Source: U.S. Census Bureau, Census 2000; 1990 Census, *Population and Housing Unit Counts, United States* (1990 CPH-2-1).

ECONOMIC AND SOCIAL CHANGE

The American economy improved dramatically in the 1990s. Yet despite the revival, millions of Americans remained poor, and homelessness became an increasingly visible problem. Meanwhile, groups pushing for equality made significant gains, but they still faced resistance in their long, continuing struggle for fair treatment in the United States.

Boom and Bust

American economic recovery began in mid-1992, even as other parts of the world found themselves facing industrial problems. In Germany, where extraordinary economic growth had occurred in the post–World War II years, the economy—the largest in Europe—faltered. As the growth rate slowed, the unemployment rate, which was 5.2 percent in 1990, rose steadily over the course of the decade, reaching 10 percent in 1997 (and going even higher in the new millennium). Reunification of East Germany and West Germany came at a heavy cost. The Japanese economy, the second-largest in the world (after the United States), likewise encountered trouble. Japan had revived dramatically after World War II, and growth had continued into the 1970s and 1980s, when productivity was higher than in the United States. Then the American productivity rate caught up, as Japan found itself hemmed in with excessive bureaucratic regulation and a system of lifetime employment for workers that made it difficult for companies to compete.

Against that backdrop, the American revival was even more remarkable. The promotion of big business in the Reagan era spurred investment and led to significant economic expansion as large firms grew larger still and became even more involved in the global economy. The lowering of interest rates by the Federal Reserve Board revived confidence and promoted consumer spending. Productivity rose steadily throughout the decade, though not quite as quickly as it had in the 1950s and 1960s. Similarly, the national economic growth rate began to rise again, reaching 3.9 percent in 1997, while averaging 3 percent in the years since the recovery began. Growth, like productivity, was not as dramatic as it had sometimes been in the golden years of industrial development, but it was sustained in what became the longest expansion in American history. Inflation fell to a 30-year low. The unemployment rate also declined, dropping from 7.8 percent in 1992 to 4.6 percent in 1997. Taking credit for the recovery, President Bill Clinton declared that the drop in unemployment was "the latest evidence that our economy is growing, steady and strong, that the American dream is in fact alive and well."

One reflection of the return of prosperity was the soaring stock market. A willingness to invest in the market is often a good indicator of confidence in the nation's economic health. In the 1990s, millions of Americans became emboldened by the positive economic indicators and invested billions of dollars in mutual funds and stocks. This period was marked by a dramatic increase in the number of investors, reaching approximately 50 percent of the population in 2000. Some purchased stocks for themselves, often working on their own computers, without using a stockbroker. Others purchased mutual funds, in which experts took the money invested and used their advice to put together a diversified portfolio. Much of the investment was in the high-tech area, in which people poured billions of dollars into start-up companies not yet making a profit, in the hope that they would take off. The market soared, with the Dow Jones average topping the once-unimaginable 10,000 barrier in 1999 and quickly moving past the 11,000 mark. Investors, most from the middle and upper classes, made considerable amounts of money in the market.

An even more important sign of economic health was the dramatic reduction in the budget deficit. A Democratic effort to preempt a Republican issue and hold down spending paid off, particularly as low interest rates encouraged economic expansion. In 1998, the United States finished with a budget surplus for the first time in 29 years. With $70 billion—the largest surplus ever—left over at the end of the fiscal year, Democrats and Republicans began arguing about how the money should be used. Most Democrats favored using funds to bolster the social security system, while Republicans, who controlled Congress, preferred a politically attractive tax cut. Forgotten in the euphoria was the fact that the national debt—the total of all past deficits—remained more than $5.4 trillion.

In these prosperous times, American companies embarked on a wave of mergers similar to those of the late nineteenth and early twentieth centuries that had created the great oil and steel corporations. In the defense industry, for example, Lockheed and Martin Marietta merged in 1994, while Boeing merged with McDonnell Douglas in 1996. In 1997, a record $1 trillion in mergers involving American companies took place as huge conglomerates swallowed up smaller competitors in the interests of efficiency and ever-larger profits. One consequence of the mergers, however, was layoffs of workers who duplicated tasks and seemed superfluous. The jobs available to those looking for other work were often low-paying positions such as those held by Marlene Garrett and her husband, introduced at the beginning of this chapter.

Then, all too quickly, the economy faltered. The bullish stock market reminded some observers of the speculative bubble of the 1920s. Alan Greenspan, chairman of the Federal Reserve Board, cautioned in 1996 against "irrational exuberance" in the market, but most investors, especially those making millions of dollars, ignored the warning. In 2000, the stock market began to slide, as investors realized that many of the financial gains did not reflect commensurate gains in productivity. The year ended with the major stock indexes—the Dow Jones Industrial Average and the Nasdaq Composite—showing their

worst performance in decades, and in 2001 and 2002, the market continued to fall, wiping out the paper gains of millions of large and small investors.

The nation's overall growth rate began to slow as investment declined. Lack of confidence in the market, particularly in the high-tech area that had fueled the boom, led to a corresponding lack of confidence in the economy. As a recession began in 2000, a tax cut further undermined the stability of the economy. Promoted by Republican George W. Bush after his victory in the 2000 presidential election, the tax cut was skewed in favor of wealthy Americans and not only failed to provide a necessary stimulus but contributed to the decline.

By early 2001, it was clear that the economy was slumping. In February, manufacturing fell to its lowest point in 10 years. Unemployment rolls increased and applications for state unemployment benefits surged. Outsourcing—moving jobs overseas and thereby displacing American workers—increased at an alarming rate. *Newsweek* magazine ran a story asking the question everyone feared: "How Safe Is Your Job?"

Confidence in the economy was further eroded by growing reports of corporate greed and managerial fraud. Emboldened by deregulation in the 1980s, many corporations had taken advantage of lax oversight practices and made huge—and sometimes illegal—profits. Toward the end of 2001, the Enron Corporation, a company that bought and sold energy, admitted that it had filed five years of misleading reports and declared bankruptcy. As the scandal grew, it became clear that the Arthur Andersen accounting firm had participated in providing cover for financial irregularities and faced an indictment for its role in the process. As the corporate empire began to tumble, the top executives cashed in their stock and made millions of dollars, while the company's workers, unaware of the looming catastrophe and prohibited from unloading stock, lost not just their jobs but their life savings as well.

Some people argued that the Enron case was an anomaly—a bad apple in the barrel—and contended that the rest of corporate America was in good shape. As 2002 unfolded, it became clear that many other companies had been falsifying their books. Just as Americans had discovered the abuses of big business during the Progressive period of the late nineteenth and early twentieth centuries, now they found themselves troubled by the corporate scandals in the daily news as the twenty-first century began. Worse still, millions who had prospered in the booming market of the 1990s found their gains wiped out and their jobs at risk, while those who had never had much remained marginalized.

Meanwhile overall union membership continued to fall. The AFL–CIO, which had about 16.6 million members in 1993, had only 13 million members a decade later. One important shift, however, was the increase in membership in public employee unions. That figure, only 400,000 in the mid-1950s, soared to more than 4 million in the 1970s and continued to increase even as unions in the private sector lost members. In the 1990s, the National Educational Association, which was not affiliated with the AFL–CIO, was the largest union in the nation, with about 2 million members. These shifts reflected the changing nature of the workforce and the continuing effort to look out for the interests of the working population.

Poverty and Homelessness

Poverty was a problem even in boom times. The Census Bureau reported in 1997 that 35.6 million people in the United States—the richest country in the world—still lived below what was defined as the poverty line of about $16,000 a year for a family of four. The percentage—13.3 percent—had fallen slightly in each of the past few years, but it was still sizable, especially considering that it included one out of every three *working* Americans. Worse still was the fact that in 1998, there were 900,000 more Americans living below the poverty line than in 1990. Nor did the situation improve in the new century. In 2004, the Department of Agriculture reported that more than 12 million American families struggled—sometimes without success—to feed themselves. Meanwhile, record levels of Americans lacked health insurance. A Census Bureau report in 2004 showed a figure of 45 million in 2003, up from 43.6 million the year before. Looking at the same period, the Congressional Budget Office reported that nearly 60 million people found themselves without health coverage at some point during the year.

Poverty in the United States was different than in other parts of the world, to be sure. People in American slums had more material benefits than many of the residents of Soweto, the huge slum just outside Johannesburg in South Africa. Homeless Americans were more fortunate than Cambodian beggars who were often incapacitated by the explosions of land mines that still dotted their country years after the Vietnam War. Yet the American poor, like the poor in most other industrialized nations, still found themselves on the fringes of society, unable to cope on their own.

Urban Americans had the toughest time of all. Even as population shifts led more and more people to live in cities, government programs often failed to provide fully for urban needs. As cities lost population to the suburbs in the last half of the twentieth century, they lost their tax base at the same time and could not easily meet the demand for services. Near the end of the twentieth century, the poverty

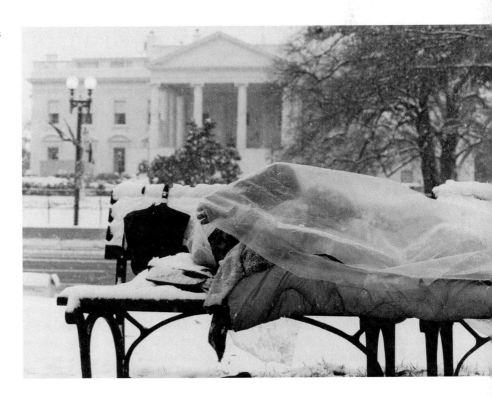

Homeless in America The homeless became far more visible in the 1990s. Here a man lies sleeping under a thin sheet of plastic, serving as his blanket, right in front of the White House in Washington, D.C. What impression does the proximity to the White House convey? *(Bettmann/CORBIS)*

American Voices

Michelle Kennedy, "Mothering Without a Net"

Michelle Kennedy was a college-educated mother of three children who found herself homeless, living in a car. After leaving her husband, who insisted that the family live alone in the woods, she found herself with very few assets to provide for the necessities of life. Her account, first published online, then expanded into a book, was a devastating indictment of conditions for those at the lower end of the socioeconomic scale.

The click of the door handle is entirely too loud as I pull it to peer in and check on my three sleeping children. They are all breathing. In fact, they look peaceful, sleeping there in the back of the station wagon, under the yellowy light of a street lamp.

I smooth the curls on my daughter's face and gently close the door. Walking through the back door of the kitchen, I look back once and then, all right just once more. I smile at the cooks—they'll keep an eye out the door for me—as I rush through the kitchen and grab the food for my customers from under the warmers....

I tip out the bartender and head for the small parking lot behind the restaurant, where, I am told, my children are still blissfully asleep. Again, I open the door, ever so carefully, and collapse into the front seat.

"Hi, Mom." Startled, I whip around to find Matthew, the eldest, who is 5, blinking his eyes awake. "How was work?" he asks.

"It was fine," I reply. "Very busy. It's late, though, you should go back to sleep. We'll talk in the morning."

"OK." Within seconds he is out again.

Living in the car doesn't seem to faze him. Oh sure, he asks why we have to keep sleeping in the car, but my answer—plain and simple—that I don't have the money yet to get us an apartment, seems to suffice, and he doesn't whine about not having a television. Well, we do have a television, actually. It was a graduation present from years before and it's tucked in front of the passenger seat. I tried to sell it, but it wasn't worth much, so I decided to keep it. A last vestige of middle-class life. I was a middle-class housewife once upon a time....

Tonight I wince as I start up the car (I need a new muffler); I don't want the kids to wake up. My plan is to stay down at the beach tonight. The police know me—I wait on them all the time—and they let me park here as long as I leave early. On the weekends we stay in the campground, where there's a playground and a shower included in the deal. We also cook out and roast marshmallows (a truly cheap source of entertainment at 79 cents a bag)....

While I am optimistic for the future and set on getting through this (there's a reason for everything, right?), I cannot contain my anger sometimes. Sitting on an old log, watching the kids play in the surf, I am almost shaking with pain and fear and rage. How is it possible that this is what my life is supposed to be like? I went to American University, damn it! I worked in the U.S. Senate! I am smarter than this—I have to be.

- Why do Michelle Kennedy and her children live in the car?

- Who helps Kennedy and her family survive, and what kind of assistance do they provide?

- Why is Kennedy so angry about the situation in which she finds herself?

Source: This article first appeared in Salon.com at http://www.Salon.com. An online version remains in the Salon archives. Reprinted with permission.

rate in New York, Los Angeles, and Chicago hovered around 20 percent. In Cleveland, Detroit, Miami, and New Orleans, it was closer to 30 percent.

The gap between rich and poor increased significantly in the last two decades of the twentieth century. The efforts of the Reagan and Bush administrations in the 1980s and early 1990s to cut back on government spending and eliminate social programs that had provided services for the poor had a powerful effect in causing the growing gap. In 1999, it took 100 million people to equal the wealth of the top 1 percent. As always, minorities fared worse than whites. The net worth of a typical white household at the beginning of the 1990s was 12 times that of the net worth of a typical black household and 8 times that of the net worth of a typical Latino household. Minorities and women continued to lose ground faster than the rest of the population as the decade unfolded. That trend continued in the first years of the new century. Even as the Internal Revenue Service was reporting that overall income fell between 2000 and 2002, the wealthy increased their share, so that a white household now had a net worth 14 times that of a black household and 11 times that of a Latino household. A 2005 study indicated that profound gaps between blacks and whites persisted.

Just as the United States rediscovered its poor in the 1960s, so it rediscovered its homeless in the 1980s and 1990s. Even as unemployment dropped in the 1980s, the number of homeless quadrupled during that time. Numbers were hard to ascertain, for the homeless had no fixed addresses, but one estimate in 1990 calculated that 6 million to 7 million people had been homeless at some point in the past five years. A federal report in 2000 noted that approximately 3.5 million people would become homeless at least once during the year, with 1.35 million of those children.

People became homeless for a variety of reasons. Some started life in disturbed families. Others fell prey to alcohol and drugs. Still others had health or learning problems that eroded the possibility of a stable life. For millions of working Americans, homelessness was just a serious and unaffordable illness away. While families in the past had felt a responsibility for taking care of their own, increased mobility in the twentieth century created a fragmentation that led more and more people to fall through the cracks. Though many Americans initially regarded the homeless as "bag ladies, winos, and junkies," they gradually came to realize that the underclass category included others as well.

Red, a homeless man in Las Vegas, Nevada, described his plight in 2000:

> I've been homeless for five years. It's getting worse. All they do at the shelter is give us food and a place to stay. I'm just maintaining. I can't get out of it at this rate. If I find a job and I put down the shelter address, they won't give you a job. At the blood blank, if they find out you're living at the shelter, they won't even let you donate blood. So I can't get money by donating blood.

As the federal government cut back on relief programs in an effort that had begun in the 1980s, private agencies had to pick up the slack. Goodwill Industries International reported a steady climb in the number of people it assisted with incomes well above the poverty line who still could not make ends meet.

Aging and Illness

The American population was older than ever before as the century came to an end. Between 1900 and 1994, when the population of the country

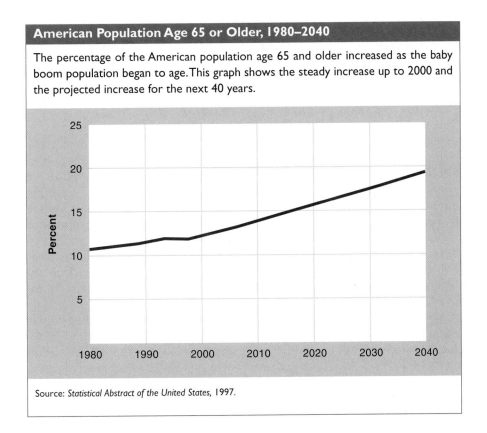

American Population Age 65 or Older, 1980–2040

The percentage of the American population age 65 and older increased as the baby boom population began to age. This graph shows the steady increase up to 2000 and the projected increase for the next 40 years.

Source: *Statistical Abstract of the United States*, 1997.

tripled, the number of people over age 65 rose elevenfold and continued to rise in the next decade, reaching 33 million, or just about 12 percent of the population, in 2001. Underlying the rapid increase was the steady advance in medical care, which in the twentieth century had increased life expectancy in the United States from 47 to 74 years as the elderly were healthier than ever before. People once considered themselves old when they reached age 65; now, many Americans in their 80s continued to lead productive lives—participating in activities such as writing books, teaching classes, and consulting with corporate clients.

Changes in the United States were somewhat different than those elsewhere, particularly in the developing world. According to one estimate, the entire population of the globe age 65 and over was likely to more than double in the 1998–2025 period, while the youth population under age 15 would grow by only 6 percent. Even so, most dependents in the world were likely to be children in the coming quarter century. Only in the United States and other developed countries would elderly dependents outnumber those under age 15.

One component of the aging revolution was Viagra, a new drug designed to help men with impotence that came on the market in the 1990s. Whether sexual dysfunction was a result of prostate illness, common among older males, or emotional distress, Viagra helped ailing men enjoy normal sex lives. Americans, including the elderly, now talked frankly about erectile dysfunction, just as they had talked openly about birth control when the birth control pill was introduced three and a half decades before. *Newsweek* magazine noted in 1998 that Viagra was the fastest-selling drug in history.

The elderly raised new issues in a nation suffering periodic recessions. Many wanted to continue working and opposed mandatory retirement rules that drove them from their jobs. Legislation in 1978 that raised the mandatory retirement age from 65 to 70 helped older workers but decreased employment opportunities for younger workers seeking jobs. In 1986, federal legislation amending the Age Discrimination in Employment Act prohibited mandatory retirement on the basis of age for virtually all workers and created continuing problems for younger employees in the 1990s. A Supreme Court ruling in 2005 held that a worker suing to reverse age discrimination did not need to prove that the employer had acted intentionally. The political power of the elderly became increasingly visible.

Generational resentment over jobs was compounded by the knotty problems faced by the social security system, which had been established a half

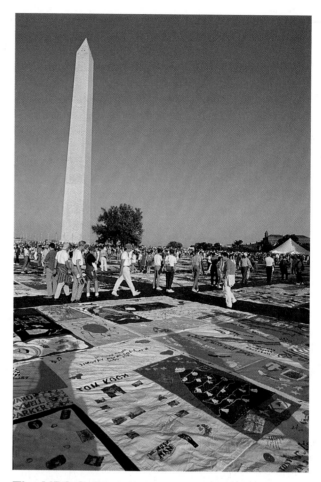

The AIDS Quilt As the AIDS epidemic caused more and more deaths, family members and friends began to create a huge quilt to celebrate the lives of those who had died. Each panel represented a different person. The quilt, shown here in Washington, D.C., was on display around the country and drew millions of viewers who came to remember those lost to the disease. How do the various portions of the quilt create a larger statement? What statement do you think the quilt is making? *(Black Star)*

century earlier. Other parts of the world—Scandinavia, for example—provided social services out of general revenues and took such expenditures for granted. However, in the United States, contributions to the system were necessary to keep it solvent, and that became a problem as the population aged. As more and more Americans retired, the system had difficulty generating sufficient revenue to make the payments due without assistance from the trust fund made up of surpluses in the past. In the early 1980s, it appeared that the entire system might collapse. A government solution involving higher taxes for those still employed and a later age for qualifying for benefits rescued the fund for a time, but many Americans in the 1990s and early years of the twenty-first century feared that system would run out of money entirely within several decades. Meanwhile, millions of elderly people wondered how they could afford the rapidly increasing cost of prescription drugs, even with a drug benefit plan passed in 2003 that seemed to help people in only a limited way at a huge cost to the government.

As Americans lived longer, they increasingly developed Alzheimer's disease, which gradually destroys a patient's memory and brings on infantile behavior. Diagnosis is difficult, and there is no treatment to reverse the ailment's course. The illness gained exposure in 1995 when the family of Ronald Reagan disclosed that the former president had the incurable disease.

Other illnesses affected old and young alike. The discovery of AIDS (acquired immune deficiency syndrome) in 1981 marked the start of one of the most serious diseases in the history of the United States—and the world. Some nations found themselves decimated by AIDS. In China, for example, entire villages were infected with HIV (the human immunodeficiency virus that causes AIDS) as a result of unsterile practices in blood stations. In 2002, Russia faced a spiraling rate of infection and had 70,000 full-blown cases of AIDS, compared with 5,500 the previous year. Africa was hit even harder. One estimate from the United Nations, the World Bank, and the World Health Organization found that 34.3 million people in the world had AIDS, with 24.5 million of them in sub-Saharan Africa. Of the 13.2 million children in the world orphaned by the disease, 12.1 million came from the sub-Saharan region. In Kenya, some schools lost a teacher a month to AIDS. In Zimbabwe, estimates of life expectancy were expected to fall from age 61 in 2005 to age 33 in 2010.

While health conditions in the United States were better than those in many parts of the world, AIDS still had a corrosive effect. The sexual revolution of the 1960s had brought a major change in sexual patterns, particularly among the young, but now sexual experimentation was threatened by this deadly new disease. Although it seemed to strike intravenous drug users and homosexuals with numerous partners more than other groups at first, it soon spread to the heterosexual population as well. Babies with AIDS were born to mothers with the illness. AIDS became the leading cause of death in Americans between ages 25 and 44. The growing number of deaths—approximately 458,000 in 2001—suggested that the disease would reach epic proportions. That same year, some 800,000 to 900,000 Americans of all ages and ethnicities were living with HIV, which could burst into full-blown AIDS at any time. Advertisements in the national media advised the use of condoms, and the U.S. surgeon general mailed a brochure, *Understanding AIDS,* to every household in the United States. New

drugs, taken in combination, extended the lifespan of those with the HIV virus and reduced the death rate in the 1990s, but AIDS remained a lethal, and ultimately fatal, disease. Despite medical advances, a cure remained elusive.

Recognizing the devastating worldwide impact of the disease, President Bush announced a major new effort in 2003. He committed the United States to triple its commitment to $15 billion over the next five years to try to counter AIDS in Africa. It was a bold attempt both to head off new infections and to care for those already experiencing the effects of the virus in one of the hardest-hit areas of the globe.

Minorities and Women Face the Twenty-First Century

Americans fighting for equality made gains in the 1990s. But efforts at reform often encountered resistance.

African Americans   For African Americans, home ownership and employment figures rose. The numbers of murders and other violent crimes that involved blacks dropped. A record 40 percent of African Americans attended college in 1997, up from 32 percent in 1991. Yet African Americans faced constant reminders that Martin Luther King, Jr.'s dream of a color-blind America was not yet a reality. A report in 2002 revealed that more than 70 percent of all black and Latino students attended predominantly minority schools in the 2000–2001 school year. Fifty years after the landmark *Brown* v. *Board of Education* decision of 1954, two-thirds of the public school students in the Cincinnati, Ohio, area attended schools that were at least 90 percent black or 90 percent white. Meanwhile, incidents such as the beating of black motorist Rodney King in Los Angeles in 1991 and the rioting that occurred the next year made many people wonder just how much progress the civil rights movement had made. A survey in San Diego noted that the police there stopped African American and Latino motorists more than whites and Asian Americans—a pattern that was common around the country. The 2000 census revealed that the nation was more racially and ethnically diverse than ever before, yet it pointed out that people still lived in neighborhoods inhabited by people like themselves. African American historian John Hope Franklin, looking back in 1995 at the eight decades of his life, summed up common frustrations when he said: "Just about the time you sit down or sit back and say, 'Oh, yes, we're really moving,' you get slapped back down."

Affirmative action was one area in which blacks faced a backlash. Energized by their political victories in 1994, conservatives launched a powerful attack on the policy of giving preferential treatment to groups that had suffered discrimination in the past. Arguing that government leaders had never intended affirmative action to be a permanent policy, they pushed ballot initiatives and pressured public agencies to bring the practice to an end. The most visible of those was Proposition 209 in California, approved by voters in the election of 1996, which prohibited the use of gender or race in awarding state government contracts or admitting students to state colleges and universities. The increasingly conservative Supreme Court also waded into the controversy. In 1995, the Court let stand a lower court ruling prohibiting colleges and universities from awarding special scholarships to African Americans or other minorities. In 1996, it declined to hear an appeal of a U.S. District Court decision two years before in *Hopwood* v. *Texas* that prohibited the use of affirmative action in higher education. Meanwhile, other cases moved through the legal system. In late 2003, the Supreme Court ruled in two cases involving the University of Michigan that affirmative action was acceptable, even as it rejected a point system the university used in carrying out the policy in undergraduate admissions. Before that ruling, the Texas legislature sought to craft an alternative policy guaranteeing admission to the top 10 percent of the graduating class from any Texas high school in a Texas college. That plan helped maintain diversity but aroused the ire of white parents who once again felt their children were suffering from the effort.

The booming job market in the late 1990s was the most important factor in fostering better race relations. It provided new opportunities for people who had been unable to find jobs. A survey in 1999 reported that young black men in particular were moving back into the economic mainstream at a faster rate than their white counterparts, and crime levels were falling in areas where joblessness was declining. The jobless rate for young black men was still twice that for young white men, but the improvement was encouraging.

Even so, tensions that had existed throughout the twentieth century persisted. Issues stemming from continuing discrimination in finding jobs and persistent antagonism by the police erupted in the spring of 2001 in Cincinnati, Ohio. When a white policeman killed an unarmed black youth, confrontations around the city provided a bitter reminder of riots in the past. While many whites had good reason to feel safe and optimistic about the future, many blacks worried about daily survival and persistent discrimination.

In early 2002, African American television correspondent Ed Bradley pointed to changes he had seen in the course of his career. "When asked about progress," he said, "I'm often reminded of the old lady sitting in the church who says, 'It ain't what it ought to be, but thank God it ain't what it used to be.'" Bradley was right, but many African Americans wondered when further change would come.

Women   Women likewise made steady progress in the 1990s. They were increasingly involved in academic programs and professions that had been closed to them several decades earlier. In 2001, for example, women made up 49.4 percent of all first-year law students, compared to 10 percent in 1970; that pattern was reflected in other segments of society as well. In the academic world that same year, women held 44 percent of all entry-level college teaching jobs, though they had only 14 percent of the most senior positions, revealing another common pattern. In addition, women worked as pilots on commercial planes and served on the front lines fighting the forest fires that broke out in the West in the summer of 2002. At the same time that there was substantial gender change in nearly every segment of the job market, there was still continuing resistance to inclusion at the top. Women started to become the heads of major firms as the glass ceiling, preventing women from rising to the top of the corporate ladder, began to crack in the 1990s, yet most leaders were still men.

IMAGE

First Ladies in 1994

Abortion remained a polarizing issue, particularly as antiabortion activists sought to disrupt abortion clinics. They launched around-the-clock pickets, aimed at frightening away women seeking abortions. Physicians performing abortions found their lives at risk; Barnet Slepian, a Buffalo doctor, was killed in 1998 in his own home by a sniper shooting through a window. Abortion opponents also took aim at a seldom used, late-term procedure they called "partial birth abortion." Congress passed a measure banning the procedure, but President Clinton vetoed it. When some states passed their own restrictive measure, the courts stepped into the controversy, and in mid-2000, the Supreme Court, by a narrow 5–4 vote margin, declared that a Nebraska law banning the practice (and by implication, similar laws in 30 other states) were unconstitutional. That same year, when the Food and Drug Administration finally approved a drug known as RU-486, the so-called abortion pill, abortion opponents jumped into the controversy and sought—unsuccessfully—to attach conditions that would effectively eliminate its use. Then in 2003 President Bush signed the Partial Birth Abortion Ban Act. Clinton had twice vetoed an earlier version of the measure, but passage this time indicated the growing strength of abortion opponents in one of the most divisive issues facing the American people.

The abortion debate was just one measure that created a backlash against the feminist label, even as men and women both accepted the changes brought by the women's movement. Women hesitated to be associated with what they still considered a radical fringe, and that affected how they identified themselves. In 1998, only 26 percent of working women said, "To me, a career is as important as being a wife and mother," down from 36 percent in 1979. While young women took for granted the gains fought for and won by their mothers and grandmothers, fewer wanted to call themselves feminists.

Yet the feminist movement persisted and brought continued improvements in the lives of women. American feminists looked to their counterparts in Europe, where advances had been even greater. Nations seeking to join the European Union had to accept its equal rights provisions. The French government considered the issue of gender parity in political representation and in 2000 passed a measure mandating that in certain cases, there needed to be an equal number of male and female candidates. Backlash was much less common in Europe. Progress in the United States did not always come easily, particularly as demographic patterns changed. The 2000 census revealed that the number of families headed by single mothers had risen to 7.5 million, an increase of 25 percent since 1990. Still, despite problems, efforts to bring about equal rights continued.

Latinos Latinos likewise pushed for greater equality and had demographic change on their side. The 2000 census and subsequent studies based on the data provided noted that the Latino population spread farther and faster than any previous immigrant wave, even exceeding the influx of eastern Europeans in the early twentieth century. The Latino population increase of 38 percent since 1990 dwarfed the national rise. In 2000, 46 percent of all Latinos owned their own homes, compared to 42 percent a decade before, though that figure still lagged behind the national number of 66 percent. In 2003, Hispanics edged past African Americans and became the nation's largest minority group.

The emergence of a sturdy middle class gave Latinos a greater voice in social and political affairs. In 1993, Henry Cisneros became secretary of housing and urban development, and Federico Peña became secretary of transportation in Bill Clinton's administration. At the end of the decade, Latino political figures became even more numerous and visible. In California, for example, both the lieutenant governor and the speaker of the assembly were Chicano, as was the mayor of San Jose. Democrat Loretta Sanchez, who defeated eight-term congressman Robert Dornan in Orange County, served in the U.S. House of Representatives. In the George W. Bush administration, White House counsel Alberto Gonzales played a major role in advising the president during the first term and became attorney general in the second.

As the nation's overall unemployment rate dropped in the mid-1990s, the rate for the 12 million Latino workers likewise fell—from 9.8 percent in 1992 to 7.3 percent in 1997. Then it rose again during the recession that hit in the early part of the new century, moving to about 8.5 percent in 2002, with only 40 percent of the 1.26 million unemployed Latinos eligible for unemployment benefits. And as had long been the case, the rate remained higher than the rate for white workers. Meanwhile, median Hispanic household income fell, even as it rose for every other ethnic and racial group. Many Latinos found it difficult to make ends meet.

Latinos nevertheless had a growing impact on American culture. Merengue music could often be heard in music stores or on the radio. Argentine steakhouses could be found in many cities. Use of the Spanish language became more and more common around the country. President George W. Bush himself used Spanish in appealing to this important electoral bloc. In 2004, *Newsweek* reported: "Some say Hispanics are forming their own cultural havens. To others, they're simply the new mainstream."

As both numbers and influence increased, Latinos faced many of the same difficulties as blacks. Proposition 209 in California, ending affirmative action at the state level, led to a drop in the percentage of Latino students in the first-year class at the University of California at Berkeley from 13 percent in 1997 to 7 percent in 1998. But aggressive efforts by university administrators to look more carefully at a variety of issues and to minimize the value attached to standardized tests brought an increase of Latino students in subsequent years.

Native Americans Native Americans found they had less influence, in part because of their smaller numbers. In the 2000 census, only 4.1 million people, or 1.5 percent of the population, identified themselves as American Indian or Alaska Native. Yet

Diminishing Tribal Lands

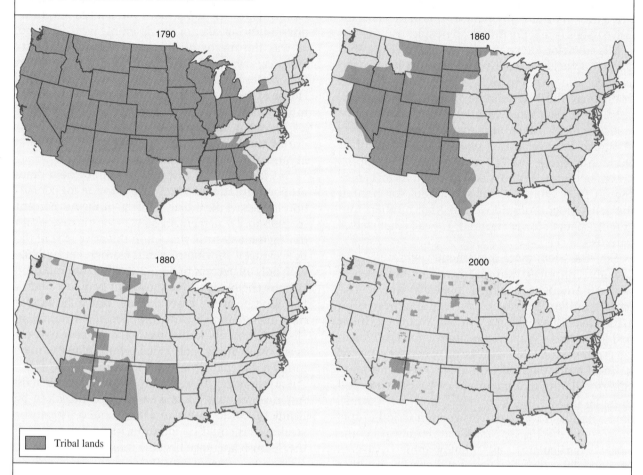

While Native Americans steadily lost their territory over a period of 200 years, in the 1990s, Indians filed lawsuits to regain tribal lands and were successful in some of their claims.

1790

1860

1880

2000

Tribal lands

Source: *"Mending a Trail of Broken Treaties" The Nation, New York Times,* June 25, 2002. Copyright © 2002 by The New York Times Co. Reprinted with permission.

Indians still managed to keep the causes that concerned them before the public.

Indians continued their legal efforts to regain lost land. In 1999, the federal government joined the Oneida Indians in a lawsuit demanding restitution for the 270,000 acres of land in central New York that they claimed state and local governments had illegally acquired from them in the late eighteenth and early nineteenth centuries. Other New York tribes made similar claims. In early 2000, the federal government returned 84,000 acres in northern Utah that it had taken from the Ute in 1916 when it sought to secure the rights to valuable reserves of oil shale. "We're trying to do the right thing, returning land to its rightful owners," energy secretary Bill Richardson declared.

Indians also pressed successfully for the return of their ancestors' skeletal remains, removed by white scientists and museum officials over the course of the last century. With passage of the Native American Graves Protection and Repatriation Act of 1990, skeletons and sacred objects were returned to the tribes to which they belonged. In 1997, Harvard's Peabody Museum sent back the bones of nearly 2,000 Pueblo Indians in the largest single return of these remains.

Underrepresented at many universities, a number of Indian high school students participated in a summer program in 2004 aimed at helping them apply to selective schools and then succeed once admitted. Cultural problems often complicated the effort to get a college education. "It's like navigating with a foot in two canoes," said Norbert Hill, executive director of

A Native American Senator Native Americans became more politically active in the 1990s. In the election of 1992, Ben Nighthorse Campbell was elected to the Senate from his home state of Colorado. What does Campbell's election tell you about the changing nature of American politics? *(AP/Wide World Photos)*

the American Indian Graduate Center of Albuquerque, New Mexico. With the proper support, new opportunities became available.

Native American women became increasingly active in the larger reform effort. Ada Deer, who had successfully fought the government's termination policy in the 1970s, served as assistant secretary of the interior in the 1990s. Winona LaDuke, an environmental activist, directed the Honor the Earth Fund and the White Earth Land Recovery Project, fought needless hydroelectric development, and was singled out by *Time* magazine as one of the nation's 50 most promising leaders under age 40. In 2000, she served as Ralph Nader's vice presidential running mate on the Green party ticket.

Many Indians still felt a sense of dislocation, captured by novelist Sherman Alexie in 1993. Asked what it was like to return from the city to the reservation, he responded through the narrator in one of the stories in *The Lone Ranger and Tonto Fistfight in Heaven:*

"It's like a bad dream you never wake up from," I said, and it's true. Sometimes I still feel like half of me is lost

in the city, with its foot wedged into a steam grate or something. Stuck in one of those revolving doors, going round and round while all the white people are laughing. Standing completely still on an escalator that will not move, but I didn't have the courage to climb the stairs by myself.

An important symbolic gesture occurred in the last months of the Clinton administration. As the Bureau of Indian Affairs celebrated its 175th anniversary, Kevin Gover, head of the agency, reversed the pattern that had been so predominant in the past when he apologized for the nation's repressive treatment of Native Americans. "In truth, this is no occasion for celebration," he said. It was, rather, a time "for sorrowful truths to be spoken, a time for contrition." He spoke of "the decimation of the mighty bison herds, the use of the poison alcohol to destroy minds and body, and the cowardly killing of women and children." The suffering inflicted on the Indians "made for tragedy on a scale so ghastly that it cannot be dismissed as merely the inevitable consequence of the clash of competing cultures." Secretary of the Interior Bruce Babbitt called the bureau "a work in progress" and noted that now most of its 10,000 employees were Native Americans themselves.

Asian Americans Asian Americans enjoyed real success in the 1990s. The nearly 11 million people—approximately 4 percent of the national population—of Asian descent in the United States in 2000 created a critical mass. They came from a variety of cultures, to be sure, and Filipinos often had different experiences from those of Chinese or Koreans or Japanese, yet together they had an increasingly important impact on American society. Many of the children enjoyed remarkable educational achievements, making up a disproportionate share of the students at the most prestigious universities. In 2000, President Clinton appointed Norman Y. Mineta as secretary of commerce, making him the first Asian American to hold a cabinet position.

Yet Asian Americans in the 1990s found themselves in an ambiguous position. While they had higher median incomes than whites, due in part to a dedicated work ethic, newcomers faced serious economic problems. Older assumptions also persisted. A report in 2000 observed that many Americans still saw Asian Americans as secretive and inscrutable. That kind of reaction was frustrating. "Too many people in this country continue to see us in simple stereotypes," complained Paul M. Ong, a social policy professor at the University of California at Los Angeles.

Asian American efforts to secure their own rights were complicated by the fact that two-thirds were

AMERICAN VOICES

Marilyn Chin, "How I Got That Name"

Marilyn Chin, a prize-winning poet, uses images from Chinese stories and tales in telling the story of her own life and in so doing captures a sense of the difficulties of growing up in a foreign land.

How I Got That Name
an essay on assimilation

I am Marilyn Mei Ling Chin.
Oh, how I love the resoluteness
of that first person singular
followed by that stalwart indicative
of "be," without the certain i-n-g
of "becoming." Of course,
the name had been changed
somewhere between Angel Island and the sea,
when my father the paperson
in the late 1950s
obsessed with a bombshell blonde
transliterated "Mei Ling" to "Marilyn." . . .
My mother couldn't pronounce the "r."
She dubbed me "Numba one female offshoot"
for brevity: . . .

Oh, how trustworthy our daughters,
how thrifty our sons!
How we've managed to fool the experts
in education, statistics and demography—
We're not very creative but not adverse to rote-learning.
Indeed, they can *use* us.
But the "Model Minority" is a tease.
We know you are watching now,
so we refuse to give you any! . . .

So here lies Marilyn Mei Ling Chin,
married once, twice to so-and-so, a Lee
and a Wong,
Granddaughter of Jack "the patriarch"
and the brooding Sulin Fong,
daughter of the virtuous Yuet Kuen Wong
and G. G. Chin the infamous,
sister of a dozen, cousin of a million,
survived by everybody and forgotten by all.
She was neither black nor white,
neither cherished nor vanquished,
just another squatter in her own bamboo grove
minding her poetry—
when one day heaven was unmerciful,
and a chasm opened where she stood.
Like the jowls of a mighty white whale,
or the jaws of a metaphysical Godzilla,
it swallowed her whole.
She did not flinch nor writhe,
nor fret about the afterlife,
but stayed! Solid as wood, happily
a little gnawed, tattered, mesmerized
by all that was lavished upon her
and all that was taken away!

■ *How did Marilyn Chin get her name?*

■ *How does Chin feel about the perception that Asian Americans make up a "Model Minority" in American life?*

■ *How has Chin made peace with the elements of her own life?*

---

immigrants, and most came to the United States after 1965. As the leader of one Chinese American civil rights group noted, "Most don't know civil rights history. They may not understand the struggles of other minorities. But the fact is we are still seen as minorities in this country, no ifs, ands or buts about it."

Gays The struggle for gay rights also continued, and slowly gays began to achieve their demands. In a major change in 2000, the Big Three automakers—General Motors, Ford, and Chrysler—announced health-care benefits for partners of gay employees, in a move that covered 465,000 workers. That same year, Vermont recognized same-sex relationships through civil unions, though stopped short of permitting gay marriages. In 2002, the American Academy of Pediatricians announced its support of the right of gay men and women to adopt the children of their partners. Gay activism helped broaden the definition of family. As the gay rights movement celebrated the 30-year anniversary of the gay rights parade commemorating the 1969 riot at the Stonewall Inn in Greenwich Village that had sparked gay resistance, proponents noted that the event had changed from a protest to a party. As the *New York Times* observed, "that in itself is a sign of success."

Yet resistance to gays playing a more visible role in American society persisted. In 1998, 21-year-old University of Wyoming student Matthew Shepard

A New Civil Rights Demonstrator Asian Americans followed the example of civil rights activists to demand appropriate treatment. In an effort to counter decades of discrimination—and violence—some marched in 1993 to commemorate the thirtieth anniversary of the March on Washington in which Martin Luther King, Jr., and other activists demanded equality. How do you think the struggle of Asian Americans for equality resembled the African American struggle? (© Corky Lee)

died after being brutally beaten and tortured by two men troubled by his lifestyle. When actress Ellen DeGeneres came out as lesbian on television, both as a character in her sitcom and in real life, some viewers wondered whether her public decision accounted for the eventual canceling of her show. While most American cities had thriving gay communities, there was still deep-seated resistance to gays living openly in some quarters.

The polarization over the acceptance of gays was most visible in a 5–4 Supreme Court ruling in mid-2000 that the Boy Scouts could bar gay troop leaders and even gay boys from the organization. The case began when the Boy Scouts ousted James Dale, an assistant scoutmaster, after the organization discovered he was gay. After a series of appeals, the Court declared that forcing the Scouts to accept gays violated the organization's First Amendment rights of free expression and free association.

Some Americans supported the ruling. But a growing number began to speak out in opposition. "I think discrimination within the Boy Scouts gets rid of the whole concept of what the Boy Scouts are all about," said Kevin Elliot, a 13-year-old eighth grader who was a scout himself. In the spring of 2001, filmmaker Steven Spielberg, a former Eagle Scout, resigned from an advisory group after 10 years of service, saying he could not serve a group practicing "intolerance and discrimination."

The gay issue surfaced again as the 2004 election loomed. In 2003, the Supreme Court struck down a Texas law banning gay sex, arguing that it violated privacy rights. Then in 2004, Massachusetts courts ruled that gay marriage was constitutional, and San Francisco permitted gay couples to marry there. The backlash helped mobilize conservatives around the country, and voters in a number of states approved constitutional bans on gay marriage.

DEMOCRATIC REVIVAL

The 1990s saw a Democratic revival in politics. After the success of conservative Republicans in the 1980s in challenging the assumptions of the liberal welfare state and advancing a more limited conception of the role of government, Democrats regrouped, reformulated their message, and followed the lead of the Republicans in relying on new forms of media to broadcast political appeals. The pattern in the United States reflected similar shifts in the rest of the world as more liberal politicians asserted that government needed to play a greater role in advancing public welfare. Politicians in a number of countries tried to recast their appeal in different ways, rather than trotting out tarnished notions from the past, to win office and then implement their plans. In Great Britain, the Labour party headed by Tony Blair took over from the

RECOVERING THE PAST

As we reach our own time, the historical past perhaps most worth recovering is our own. Our own story is as valid a part of the story of American history as the tale of Revolutionary War soldiers, frontier women, reform politicians, and immigrant grandparents. In this computerized age, the person we need to recover is ourself, a self that has been formed, at least in part, by the entire American experience we have been studying.

Autobiography is the form of writing in which people tell their own life's history. Although written autobiographies are at least as old as the literature of the early Christians (for example, *The Confessions of St. Augustine*), the word *autobiography* dates from the late eighteenth century, around the time of the French and American revolutions. That is no accident. These momentous events represented the triumph of individual liberty and the sovereignty of the self. *The Autobiography of Benjamin Franklin,* written between 1771 and Franklin's death in 1790 (and excerpted here), is a classic celebration of the American success story. Franklin's work set the standard for one autobiographical form, the memoir of one's public achievements and success. The other brief autobiographical memoir, from the reminiscences of Elizabeth Cady Stanton, also reflects the tone and range of this tradition.

Not all autobiographies are written late in life to celebrate one's accomplishments. The confessional

---

Autobiographical Memoirs

Benjamin Franklin

DEAR SON,

I have ever had a pleasure in obtaining any little anecdotes of my ancestors. You may remember the enquiries I made among the remains of my relations when you were with me in England and the journey I undertook for that purpose. Imagining it may be equally agreeable to you to know the circumstances of my life—many of which you are yet unacquainted with—and expecting a week's uninterrupted leisure in my present country retirement, I sit down to write them for you. Besides, there are some other inducements that excite me to this undertaking. From the poverty and obscurity in which I was born and in which I passed my earliest years, I have raised myself to a state of affluence and some degree of celebrity in the world. As constant good fortune has accompanied me even to an advanced period of life, my posterity will perhaps be desirous of learning the means, which I employed, and which, thanks to Providence, so well succeeded with me. They may also deem them fit to be imitated, should any of them find themselves in similar circumstances.

Source: *The Autobiography of Benjamin Franklin* (1771).

Elizabeth Cady Stanton

Elizabeth Cady Stanton

It was 'mid such exhilarating scenes that Miss Anthony and I wrote addresses for temperance, anti-slavery, educational and woman's rights conventions. Here we forged resolutions, protests, appeals, petitions, agricultural reports, and constitutional arguments; for we made it a matter of conscience to accept every invitation to speak on every question, in order to maintain woman's right to do so. To this end we took turns on the domestic watchtowers, directing amusements, settling disputes, protecting the weak against the strong, and trying to secure equal rights to all in the home as well as the nation.

It is often said, by those who know Miss Anthony best, that she has been my good angel, always pushing and goading me to work, and that but for her pertinacity I should never have accomplished the little I have. On the other hand it has been said that I forged the thunderbolts and she fired them. Perhaps all this is, in a measure, true. With the cares of a large family I might, in time, like too many women, have become wholly absorbed in a narrow family selfishness, had not my friend been continually exploring new fields for missionary labors. Her description of a body of men on any platform, complacently deciding questions in which women had an equal interest, without an equal voice, readily aroused me to a determination to throw a firebrand into the midst of their assembly.

Source: Elizabeth Cady Stanton, *Eighty Years and More: Reminiscences, 1815–1897* (1898).

Confessional Autobiographies

Black Elk

And so it was all over.

I did not know then how much was ended. When I look back now from this high hill of my old age, I can still see the butchered women and children lying heaped and scattered all along the crooked gulch as plain as when I saw them with eyes still young. And I can see that something else died there in the bloody mud, and was buried in the blizzard. A people's dream died there. It was a beautiful dream.

And I, to whom so great a vision was given in my youth,—you see me now a pitiful old man who has done nothing, for the nation's hoop is broken and scattered. There is no center any longer, and the sacred tree is dead.

Source: *Black Elk Speaks,* as told through John G. Neihardt (1932).

Malcolm X

I want to say before I go on that I have never previously told anyone my sordid past in detail. I haven't done it now to sound as though I might be proud of how bad, how evil, I was.

But people are always speculating—why am I as I am? To understand that of any person, his whole life, from birth, must be reviewed. All of our experiences fuse into our personality. Everything that ever happened to us is an ingredient.

Today, when everything that I do has an urgency, I would not spend one hour in the preparation of a book which has the ambition to perhaps titillate some readers. But I am spending many hours because the full story is the best way that I know to have it seen, and understood, that I had sunk to the very bottom of the American white man's society when—soon now, in prison—I found Allah and the religion of Islam and it completely transformed my life.

Source: *The Autobiography of Malcolm X,* with the assistance of Alex Haley (1964).

---

autobiography, unlike most memoirs, explores the author's interior life, acknowledging flaws and failures as well as successes; it may be written at any age. The purpose of this type of autobiography is not just to reconstruct one's past to preserve it for posterity, but to find from one's past an identity in order to know better how to live one's future. The story of religious confessions and conversions is an obvious example. This form also includes secular self-examinations such as those by Maxine Hong Kingston in *The Woman Warrior* (1976), Piri Thomas in *Down These Mean Streets* (1967), or Maya Angelou in a series of five autobiographical sketches beginning with *I Know Why the Caged Bird Sings* (1969). The other two excerpts presented here are among the finest examples of confessional autobiography and suggest its variety.

These examples hardly convey the full range of the autobiographical form or how available to all people is the opportunity to tell the story of one's life. In 1909, William Dean Howells called autobiography the "most democratic province in the republic of letters." A recent critic agrees, pointing out:

To this genre have been drawn public and private figures: poets, philosophers, prizefighters; actresses, artists, political activists; statesmen and penitentiary prisoners; financiers and football players; Quakers and Black Muslims; immigrants and Indians. The range of personality, experience, and profession reflected in the forms of American autobiography is as varied as American life itself.

Your story, too, is a legitimate part of American history. But writing an autobiography, while open to all, is deceptively difficult. Like historians, autobiographers face problems of sources, selection, interpretation, and style. As in the writing of any history, the account of one's past must be objective, not only in the verifiable accuracy of details but also in the honest selection of representative events to be described. Moreover, in fiction as well as history, the autobiographer must provide a structured form, an organizing principle, literary merit, and thematic coherence to the story. Many other challenges face the would-be autobiographer, such as finding a balance between one's public life and the private self and handling problems of memory, ego (should one, for example, use the first or third person?), and death.

REFLECTING ON THE PAST To get an idea of the difficulties of writing an autobiography, try writing your own. Limit yourself to 1,000 words. Good luck.

Conservative party of Margaret Thatcher. In Germany, Gerhard Schroeder of the Social Democratic party unseated the more conservative Helmut Kohl of the Christian Democratic Union, who had served as chancellor for 16 years. But in the United States, for much of the decade, even as the Democrats regained the White House, the Republicans maintained control of Congress and bitter partisan fighting was the result.

Democratic Victory

In 1992, the Democratic party mounted an aggressive challenge to Republican rule. After a fierce primary campaign, Governor Bill Clinton of Arkansas triumphed over a crowded field of candidates. Overcoming allegations of marital instability, marijuana use, and draft evasion, he argued that it was time for a new generation to take command. Forty-six years old, he had reached maturity in the 1960s and stood in stark contrast to President George H. W. Bush, now running for re-election, who had come of age during World War II. The third candidate in what became a three-way race was H. Ross Perot, a billionaire businessman from Texas who had made a fortune in the computer data-processing field. Stressing his independence from both political parties, he declared that he alone could provide the business experience and leadership the nation needed.

This campaign, more than any in the past, was fought on television. In addition to three televised presidential debates, the candidates appeared on talk shows and interview programs. Perot energized his campaign with appearances on *Larry King Live*. Bill Clinton used a post–Super Bowl appearance on *60 Minutes* to answer charges questioning his character and later played his saxophone on *The Arsenio Hall Show* and appeared on MTV. This reliance on the electronic marketplace reoriented American campaign politics. Although Bush's popularity rating was high after the success of the Persian Gulf War, many Americans soured on him when he reneged on his campaign promise of "no new taxes."

On election day, Clinton won 43 percent of the popular vote to 38 percent for Bush and 19 percent for Perot. The electoral vote margin was even larger: 357 for Clinton, 168 for Bush, 0 for Perot. The Democrats retained control of both houses of Congress, with more women and minority members than ever before.

The president-elect wanted to check the cynicism that was poisoning political life. In 1964,

The "Hip" Candidate Bill Clinton was an exuberant campaigner who used his musical talent to attract support when he ran for president in 1992. Here he plays his saxophone on nationwide television on *The Arsenio Hall Show* in Los Angeles. What kind of image was Clinton trying to convey in this photograph? *(AP/Wide World Photos)*

three-quarters of the American public trusted the government to do the right thing most of the time. Three decades later, after the deception of leaders in the Vietnam War and the Watergate affair, the number was closer to one-quarter. Clinton sought to shift the nation's course after 12 years of Republican rule with Cabinet nominations that included four women, four African Americans, and two Latinos. He held a televised "economic summit" to explore national options and demonstrated a keen grasp of the details of policy. In his inaugural address, Clinton declared that "a new season of American renewal has begun."

Clinton soon found his hands full at home. Although the economy finally began to improve, the public gave the president little credit for the upturn. He gained Senate ratification of the North American Free Trade Agreement (NAFTA)—aimed at promoting free trade between Canada, Mexico, and the United States—in November 1993 after a bitter battle in which opponents argued that American workers would lose their jobs to less well-paid Mexicans. He secured passage of a crime bill banning the manufacture, sale, or possession of assault weapons. But he failed to win approval of his major legislative initiative: health-care reform. The United States lagged behind most other industrialized countries in the way it provided for public health. A national health-care system in Great Britain provided universal coverage. An even more extensive system in Scandinavia met all health needs. In the United States, people were largely expected to deal with their health needs on their own. Medicare took care of the elderly, and Medicaid provided some re-

DOCUMENT

Statements on the Clinton Health Care Plan (1993)

lief for the poor, but both were limited when compared to the coverage provided by other nations. "This health-care system of ours is badly broken," Clinton said in September 1993, "and it's time to fix it." Particularly troublesome were escalating costs and the lack of universal medical care, which left 35 million Americans with no medical insurance. Clinton's complicated proposal for a system of health alliances in each state provoked intense opposition from the health-care and insurance industries and from politicians with plans of their own. In the end, he was unable to persuade Congress either to accept his approach or adopt a workable alternative.

Republican Resurgence

Voters demonstrated their dissatisfaction in the midterm elections of 1994. Republicans argued that government regulations were hampering business and costing too much. They challenged the notion that the federal government was primarily responsible for health care and other such services. Capitalizing on the continuing appeal of the leadership of Ronald Reagan in the 1980s, they demanded a scaled-down role for the government. Republicans swept control of both the Senate and the House of Representatives for the first time in more than 40 years. At the state level, Republicans picked up 12 governorships and took control in seven of the eight largest states.

The election marked the end of the commitment to the welfare state. The 104th Congress moved aggressively to make good on its promises—outlined during the campaign in the Republicans' Contract with America—to scale back the role of the federal government, eliminate environmental regulations, cut funding for educational programs such as Head Start, reduce taxes, and balance the budget. Under the leadership of Newt Gingrich, the new speaker of the House of Representatives, Congress launched a frontal attack on the budget, proposing massive cuts in virtually all social services. It demanded the elimination of three Cabinet departments and insisted on gutting the National Endowment for the

Humanities, the National Endowment for the Arts, and the Public Broadcasting System. When, at the end of 1995, President Clinton and Speaker Gingrich tangled with one another on the size of the cuts and refused to compromise on a budget, the government shut down and 800,000 federal employees found themselves temporarily "furloughed."

While the House of Representatives passed most of the measures proposed in the Contract with America, only a few of them became law. The Senate balked at some; the president vetoed others. After all the attention it received, voters lost interest in the Contract with America. As the election of 1996 approached, Newt Gingrich found himself out of favor, as millions of Americans began to realize that they would suffer from the cuts more aggressive Republicans sought.

A Second Term for Clinton

As Bill Clinton sought a second term in 1996, the Republicans nominated Senate minority leader Robert

A Confident Clinton Bill Clinton was an astute politician and an energetic campaigner. What impression does he convey in this photograph of him on the campaign trail? As he looked back on his presidency in his memoir *My Life*, Clinton was satisfied with his achievements and sorry about the scandals that marred his tenure in office. How do you assess the Clinton presidency? How did the confidence exhibited in this picture sometimes get him in trouble? *(Peter Turnley/CORBIS)*

Dole as their presidential candidate. The 73-year-old Dole ran a lackluster campaign. His pledge to push through a sweeping 15 percent tax reduction failed to excite voter interest. Even supporters wondered how he would balance the budget at the same time. Stung by Democratic congressional defeats two years before, Clinton reshaped his own image and announced that the "era of big government is over." Like Tony Blair in Great Britain, who spoke repeatedly of a New Labour approach, Clinton co-opted Republican issues, pledging to balance the budget himself and enraging liberal supporters by signing a welfare reform bill that slashed benefits and removed millions of people from the rolls. At the same time, he posed as the protector of Medicare and other programs that were threatened by proposed Republican cuts.

Clinton's strategy worked. On election day, he won a resounding victory over Dole. He received 49 percent of the popular vote to 41 percent for Dole and 8 percent for H. Ross Perot, who ran again, though this time less successfully than four years before. In the electoral tally, Clinton received 379 votes to 159 for Dole. Yet the Republicans kept control of Congress. In the House of Representatives, they lost a number of seats but retained a majority. In the Senate, they added two seats to what they had won in 1994. Voters seemed willing to support Clinton, but not to give him the mandate he sought.

Partisan Politics and Impeachment

Democrats made small gains in the midterm elections of 1998. They worried about their prospects as election day approached, for Clinton had been accused by an independent prosecutor, appointed by the Justice Department, of having engaged in an improper sexual relationship with Monica Lewinsky, a White House intern. While Clinton denied the relationship at first, the lengthy report presented to Congress left little doubt that such a connection existed, and Clinton finally admitted to the relationship in a nationally televised address.

As Republicans in Congress began to consider impeachment, Americans outside Washington felt differently. Disturbed at what Clinton had done in his personal life, they nonetheless approved overwhelmingly of the job he was doing as president; in fact, his approval ratings were higher than any of his presidential predecessors in the recent past.

Those sentiments were reflected in the 1998 midterm election. Republicans, who had hoped to score sizable gains in both house of Congress, maintained their 55–45 margin in the Senate, but lost five seats in the House of Representatives, ending up

with a 223–211 margin that made it even more difficult to pursue their own agenda.

Despite that clear signal from the voters, House Republicans continued their efforts to remove the president. Just weeks after the election, a majority impeached him on counts of perjury and obstruction of justice. At the start of 1999, the case moved to the Senate for a trial, in which Clinton fought to retain his office, just as Andrew Johnson had done 131 years before. In the Senate, presided over by the chief justice of the Supreme Court, a two-thirds vote was necessary to find the president guilty and remove him from office. After weeks of testimony, despite universal condemnation of Clinton's personal behavior, the Senate voted for acquittal. Democrats, joined by a number of Republicans, stood by the president, and with that coalition, neither charge managed to muster even a majority. The count of perjury was decided by a 45–55 vote, while the count of obstruction of justice failed on a 50–50 vote. The distraction of the impeachment and trial were finally over, and the country could once again turn its attention to more pressing issues.

DOCUMENT

Articles of Impeachment Against William Jefferson Clinton

An enormously successful politician, Clinton not only escaped conviction in the highly visible—and embarrassing—impeachment case, but he also managed to co-opt Republican issues and seize the political center. When he moved to reconfigure the national welfare system, to limit the number of years a person could receive benefits and to pare down the number of people on welfare rolls, conservatives were pleased while liberals were furious. Yet in other ways, he quietly advanced liberal goals, with incremental appropriations, even when he was unable to push major programs, such as his medical insurance scheme, through Congress. His administration's antitrust suit against the Microsoft Corporation aroused controversy. Although it was initially successful in court, it was partially overturned on appeal and eventually dropped after Clinton left the White House. Suits against the nation's tobacco companies for deliberately misleading advertising in the face of known health risks were more popular with the public. In 1997 in a landmark settlement, tobacco companies were assessed $368 billion to cover liability claims and reimburse the states for medical costs related to smoking.

DOCUMENT

Bill Clinton, Answers to Articles of Impeachment (January 11, 1999)

Polls taken throughout both his terms indicated that Clinton remained popular (even when people disapproved of his personal conduct). Overall, in the words of the *New York Times,* Clinton demonstrated "striking strengths, glaring shortcomings."

He came into office wanting to be a Roosevelt-like figure, with dreams of reconfiguring the role of government, but after the health-care debacle, he ended up instead quietly endorsing and implementing a variety of more modest causes. He faced more criticism—from the right—than virtually any other politician, and it led to his impeachment. Yet he brought some of his troubles on himself and paid a heavy price for his misdeeds.

THE SECOND BUSH PRESIDENCY

Republicans regained control of the White House in the election of 2000. Unable to oust Bill Clinton from the presidency by impeachment, they were determined to win back what they considered to be rightfully theirs in the conservative resurgence of the past 20 years. Texas governor George W. Bush (son of former president George H. W. Bush—the first father–son combination since John Adams and John Quincy Adams) promised to return morality and respect to the White House and appealed to those disturbed by Clinton's behavior.

The Election of 2000

The election of 2000 promised to be close. The strong economy gave Vice President Al Gore, the Democratic nominee, an initial advantage. Yet the Republicans, led by the younger Bush, insisted the country needed a change. The campaign revolved around what the government should do with the federal budget surplus, with Republicans arguing that much of the money should be returned to the public in the form of a tax cut and Democrats countering that the surplus should be used to bolster the ailing social security program and to pay down the national debt. In the weeks before the election, polls showed that the race was virtually tied.

On election night, as the returns trickled in, neither Bush nor Gore had captured the 270 electoral votes necessary to win the presidency. The electoral vote in Florida, one of the undecided states, was large enough to give the winner a victory. A recount, required by law, began, and Florida became a battleground as lawyers for both sides swarmed to the state to monitor the counting. Democrats and Republicans argued bitterly, in court and in the media, about how the recount should proceed. They also argued about which ballots should be counted.

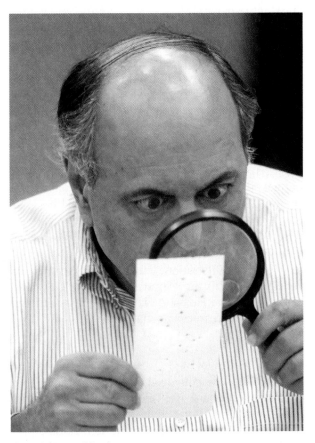

Checking a Chad In Florida—and other states—punch card ballots were sometimes defective, and if the little stubs of cardboard—called chads—were not pushed out entirely, the vote might be counted inaccurately. Here Judge Robert Rosenberg looks carefully at a disputed ballot during the manual recount in Florida. What does this image convey about the election and the possibility of a genuinely accurate count? *(AP/Wide World Photos)*

Some punch-card ballots, where a voter punched a hole next to the name of the candidate chosen, proved defective, and the particle of paper—called a chad—failed to drop off. Should such a ballot be counted if the intent of the voter was clear, even if the chad still hung by a thread to the card? And how could that intent be ascertained? Democrats also contended that in certain African American precincts, voters had been turned away from the polls. That charge was all the more significant because black voters around the country favored Gore by a 9–1 margin.

In December, more than five weeks after the election, after suits and countersuits by both sides, the case reached the Supreme Court. In *Bush* v. *Gore,* the justices overturned a Florida Supreme Court decision allowing the recount to proceed, and ruled, by a 5–4 vote, with the most conservative justices voting in a bloc, that the recount should be curtailed, leaving Bush the winner. Although Gore won the popular vote by about 450,000 votes, Bush triumphed in the

Electoral College by a 271–266 majority. Ill feelings persisted as a result of the partisan ruling. Supreme Court justice John Paul Stevens wrote a scathing dissent, in which he argued: "Although we may never know with complete certainty the identity of the winner of this year's presidential election, the identity of the loser is perfectly clear. It is the nation's confidence in the judge as an impartial guardian of the law."

The voting in congressional races was equally close. The new Senate was evenly split, with each party holding 50 seats. Republicans organized the chamber and gained all committee chairs, because Vice President Dick Cheney broke the tie. Yet five months after the new session began, Senator James Jeffords of Vermont, frustrated with the approach of the Bush administration, left the Republican party, giving control to the Democrats. Republicans also lost seats in the House of Representatives, leaving them with but a nine-vote majority.

The New Leader

George W. Bush had enjoyed an eclectic career before becoming president. Born into a political family, he had shown little interest in politics himself, gravitating into the Texas oil business and then gaining part ownership of a professional baseball team before running successfully for governor of Texas.

Bush was very different from Clinton. Whereas his predecessor was sometimes called a "policy wonk" who understood all the details of his assorted initiatives, Bush saw himself as a corporate chief executive officer (CEO) who established the broad outlines of policy but then left the details to others. Ronald Reagan had taken that approach, but his communication skills were better than Bush's. Yet

Bush had a dogged tenacity that served him well and helped him overcome the early image of incompetence. Author Gail Sheehy observed that "the blind drive to win is a hallmark of the Bush family clan." The new president, she said "has to win, he absolutely has to win and if he thinks he's going to lose, he will change the rules or extend the play. Or if it really is bad he'll take his bat and ball and go home." Bush often seemed to ignore criticism and to push ahead with a resolute persistence, no matter what. His religious faith gave him the support he needed, and when once asked if he relied on his father in hard times, he responded that his father "is the wrong father to appeal to in terms of strength. There is a higher father that I appeal to."

Bush used propaganda skillfully. He was aware of the importance of public opinion and made the most of appearances. Dressed in a flight jacket, he landed on an aircraft carrier to announce—prematurely it turned out—the successful end of an incursion into the Middle East. Photographers always sought to capture him in the best possible light. And his administration made payments to people posing as reporters and experts in prepackaged segments purporting to be real news stories distributed to local news outlets around the country to create support for his programs.

Promoting the Private Sector

As president, Bush had the interests of corporate America at heart. During the campaign, he talked about a tax cut, and this became his first priority. Supply-side economists, who argued successfully in the 1980s that lower tax rates were necessary to promote economic growth, became more influential in his administration.

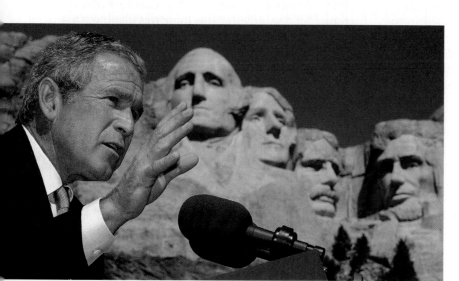

Looking for a Place in History?
George Bush paid close attention to the image conveyed to the American people, and photographers constantly captured him in ways that underscored his importance. Here he stands in front of Mt. Rushmore, with its famous rock sculptures of several of America's best-known presidents. What impression does the juxtaposition in this photograph convey to you? *(AP/World Wide Photos)*

Presidential Elections, 1992–2004

Year	Candidate	Party	Popular Vote		Electoral Vote
1992	BILL CLINTON	Democratic	43,728,275	(43.2%)	357
	George Bush	Republican	38,167,416	(37.7%)	168
	H. Ross Perot	Independent	19,237,245	(19.0%)	0
1996	BILL CLINTON	Democratic	47,401,185	(49.2%)	379
	Robert Dole	Republican	39,197,469	(40.7%)	159
	H. Ross Perot	Reform	8,085,294	(8.4%)	0
2000	GEORGE W. BUSH	Republican	50,546,002	(47.87%)	271
	Albert Gore	Democratic	50,999,897	(48.38%)	266
	Ralph Nader	Green	2,882,955	(2.74%)	0
2004	GEORGE W. BUSH	Republican	60,934,251	(51%)	286
	John F. Kerry	Democratic	57,765,291	(48%)	252
	Ralph Nader	Independent	405,933	(0%)	0

Note: Winners' names appear in capital letters.

By mid-2001, the tax cut became law. It lowered tax rates for everyone, allowed more tax-free saving for education, and reduced estate taxes. The measure promised to save every taxpayer at least several hundred dollars a year, though it was heavily skewed in favor of the wealthy. Meanwhile, the economy continued to falter as the growth rate slowed and a full-blown recession ensued.

Like his father and Reagan, Bush wanted to reduce the size of government and squelch its intrusions into private affairs, but at the same time, he sought to bolster the military. His first budget, for example, proposed deep cuts in health programs for people without access to health insurance. But his proposals for defense called for far greater spending, even before the terrorist attacks of September 11, 2001. Military spending increased dramatically in the years that followed, providing the administration already dealing with smaller revenue as a result of the tax cut with an even stronger argument to cut back social programs that conservatives had never liked.

Bush infuriated environmentalists. Soon after it assumed power, the new administration moved to allow road building in national forests and reversed the phasing in of bans on snowmobiles in national parks. Under pressure from real estate interests, the administration sought to shrink legal protection of endangered species. It eased environmental restrictions that coal industry officials claimed threatened mining jobs. It proposed looser standards for mercury emissions than Bill Clinton had sought and issued new rules easing the requirements for pollution controls when utilities built new plants. Bush made his own priorities crystal clear. When his own Environmental Protection Agency (EPA) issued a report in mid-2002 linking the use of fossil fuel (such as coal and oil) to global warming, he simply dismissed the study, indicating that he had no confidence in the judgments of the scientists working for the EPA.

Gone was a commitment to the public interest that had increased over the course of the twentieth century. In the spring of 2003, the Interior Department announced that large swaths of public land would no longer be designated as wilderness and protected from development. That policy shift removed more than 200 million acres of land from wilderness study and opened them to mining, logging, drilling, and road building. And, catering to the interests of oil companies, the administration fought to promote drilling in the protected Arctic National Wildlife Refuge, even in the face of estimates that very little oil was there to be found. Opponents managed to stymie that effort during Bush's first term, but kept up the pressure.

A Second Term for Bush

The election of 2004 was bitter and contentious. Running for re-election, Bush faced Massachusetts senator John Kerry, a Vietnam War hero who attacked Republican efforts in the foreign policy sphere, questioned its ability to protect the nation from terrorist attacks, and charged that tax cuts had done little to revive a still-sluggish economy. Both candidates raised huge amounts of money, far more than had been solicited in the past, and both parties ended up running attack ads that questioned the integrity of the candidates. Republican groups tore into Kerry's service record; Democratic groups called attention to Bush's successful effort to avoid the war in Vietnam by serving in the National Guard. Civility sometimes seemed to disappear. As former senator Warren B. Rudman observed, "I don't recall the hatred—not just dislike and disagreement, but hatred—that a lot of Republicans had for Clinton and a lot of Democrats now have for President Bush." But even though Bush seemed vulnerable, Kerry failed to arouse the interest of voters. He seemed to be, according to *The Economist* magazine, "the political equivalent of Valium." In a race that remained close to the end, Bush prevailed with 51 percent of the popular vote and a modest Electoral College majority. Republicans added to their majorities in both the Senate and the House of Representatives, as voters in the heartland of American agreed with the Republican party's conservative moral values.

At the start of his second term, Bush moved quickly to demand reform of Social Security. The program, which had run surpluses in the past, faced increasing pressures as the baby boom generation born just after World War II approached retirement. Experts disagreed on just when the system would run short of money, but it was clear that problems were imminent in the next few decades. Bush called for an overhaul that would allow workers to invest part of their contributions in private retirement accounts that would depend on gains in the stock market. Critics charged that the new proposal would undermine the policy of guaranteed pensions and could make millions of workers vulnerable if the market dropped, as it had just a few years before. They argued that the system could be made more secure by increasing payroll taxes, raising the amount on which such taxes were levied, or mandating that workers retire a year or two later. Even as Bush pushed ahead, members of both political parties resisted the effort.

The budget that Bush submitted to Congress in early 2005 reflected the administration's priorities. As the surplus of the Clinton years turned into an ever-larger deficit under Bush—estimated to be almost $400 billion in the year ahead—the budget still contained tax cuts of $100 billion over the next five years. Critics charged that the underlying intention was to make it impossible to support programs aimed at assisting the poor, people like Rod and Marlene Garrett. They also noted the irony that this budget was the largest ever in the nation's history and pointed out that an administration that claimed to want to scale down big government was playing an ever-increasing role when it came to regulation of social issues such as faith-based initiatives and abortion.

FOREIGN POLICY IN THE POST–COLD WAR WORLD

As the Cold War ended, the United States had to examine its own assumptions about its international role. The world was now a different place. With extraordinary communications advances, it was more closely linked than ever before. Violence and upheaval in one part of the globe now had an almost immediate impact on other areas. In this setting, new questions arose: What kind of leadership would the United States exert as the one remaining superpower on the globe? How involved would it become in peacekeeping missions in violence-wracked lands? What kind of assistance would it extend to developing nations now that the competition with the Soviet Union that had fueled foreign aid was over? How would it deal with the threat of terrorism? These questions, asked in different forms over the course of past centuries, helped shape foreign policy in transitional times.

The Balkan Crisis

In the Balkans, in Eastern Europe, ethnic and religious violence worsened in the mid-1990s. Yugoslavia—a collection of different ethnic constituencies held together by a Communist dictatorship—had collapsed in 1991. Muslims and Croats had fought bitterly with Serbs in the province of Bosnia. The world watched the Bosnian Serbs liquidate opponents in a process that came to be called "ethnic cleansing" during the siege of the city of Sarajevo. Brutal killing escalated out of control, rape became commonplace, and civilians suffered most from the uncurbed violence. As the region became increasingly volatile, the United States remained out of the conflict, while the United Nations proved unable to bring about peace. In mid-1995, a North Atlantic Treaty Organization (NATO) bombing campaign forced the Bosnian Serbs into negotiations, and a peace conference held in Dayton, Ohio, led to the commitment of American troops, along with soldiers from other countries, to stabilize the region.

DOCUMENT

The Balkan Proximity Peace Talks Agreement (1995)

In 1999, a smoldering conflict in Kosovo, another of the provinces of the former Yugoslavia, led to war. In an effort to stop Slobodan Milosevic, the Serbian leader responsible for the devastation of Bosnia, from squelching a movement for autonomy in Kosovo, NATO launched an American-led bombing campaign. Even without the introduction of ground troops, this air assault was the largest allied operation in Europe since World War II. Milosevic responded with an even more violent "ethnic cleansing" campaign that drove hundreds of thousands of Kosovars from their homes.

Milosevic finally succumbed. After refusing to recognize the election victory of the opposition leader in 2000, he was arrested in 2001 and brought to the Netherlands to stand trial for crimes against humanity at the International Court of Justice in The Hague.

The Middle East in Flames

In the Middle East, Clinton tried to play the part of peacemaker, just as Jimmy Carter had done 15 years before. On September 13, 1993, in a dramatic ceremony on the White House lawn, Palestine Liberation Organization leader Yasir Arafat and Israeli Prime Minister Yitzhak Rabin took the first public step toward ending years of conflict as they shook hands and signed a peace agreement that led to Palestinian self-rule in the Gaza strip. In 1995, Israel and the PLO signed a further agreement, and the Israelis handed over control of the West Bank of the Jordan River to the Palestinians. A treaty between Jordan and Israel brought peace on still another border. While extremists tried to destroy the peace process by assassinating Rabin, the effort to heal old animosities continued.

In 1998, Clinton once again played the role of mediator, this time facilitating an agreement leading to the return of land in the West Bank area to the Palestinians in return for peace between Arafat and Israeli leader Benjamin Netanyahu. As Clinton prepared to leave office, he sought to seal a final agreement between the Israelis and the Palestinians, but this time he was not successful, as the Palestinians rejected a generous settlement offer, and the smoldering Middle Eastern tensions burst once more in flames that threatened to engulf the entire region.

The level of Mideast violence in the early twenty-first century was worse than it had ever been before. The shortsighted Israeli policy of building settlements in occupied Arab land, and the Palestinian unwillingness to compromise at the negotiating table, culminated in a horrifying escalation of bloodshed following an intrusive Israeli visit to a holy Palestinian religious site in Jerusalem, a city claimed by both sides. Palestinian suicide bombers, some of them adolescents, wrought havoc on Israeli buses and in Jewish shops. A bomb exploded at Hebrew University in mid-2002, killing not just Israelis but Americans as well. Each time a deadly attack occurred, the Israelis counterattacked with equal violence in a never-ending spiral.

Bush was at first reluctant to intervene. Eventually, as the killing cycle continued, he moved from inattention to fumbling attention, becoming increasingly sympathetic to Israel as the suicide attacks continued. He lashed out at Yasir Arafat for not speaking out against the bombings, but was unable to bring the adversaries to the negotiating table. Meanwhile, many of the European nations, feeling that only the United States could help bring peace to the region, voiced dismay at American policy.

African Struggles

Africa also remained a source of concern to American policymakers who struggled to deal with a series of never-ending crises. Left behind as other parts of the world industrialized and moved ahead, the continent was also ravaged by the AIDS epidemic, which infected and killed far more people than

A Historic Handshake President Bill Clinton helped orchestrate this famous handshake between Israeli prime minister Yitzhak Rabin and Palestine Liberation Organization chairman Yasir Arafat in 1993. Though the two men had long been adversaries, they now began to work together to settle the bitter conflicts in the Middle East. How do Clinton's actions in the picture give a sense of his role? How do the two longtime adversaries appear to react to one another? *(AP/Wide World Photos)*

Siege in the West Bank

As Middle Eastern violence escalated out of control, Israeli forces in early 2002 responded to suicide bombings by mounting a massive siege of Yasir Arafat's headquarters in the West Bank—the area located on the West Bank of the Jordan River. Though the siege left Arafat unhurt, it undermined his authority and left the question of Palestinian leadership in doubt. **Reflecting on the Past** Why was the West Bank such a volatile area? Why did Israel mount a siege in the West Bank? Why did the siege undermine Arafat's authority?

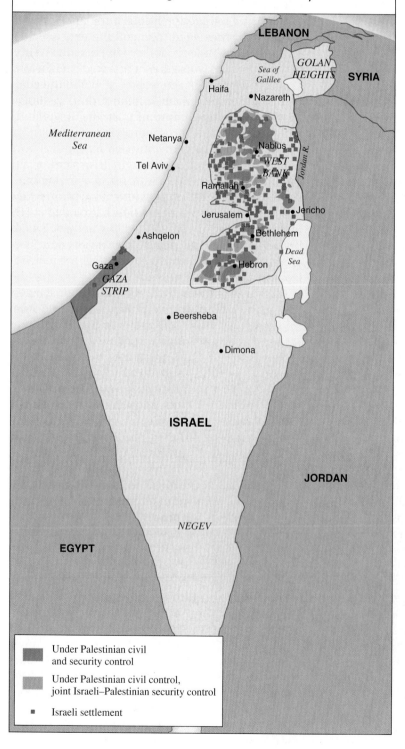

Under Palestinian civil and security control

Under Palestinian civil control, joint Israeli–Palestinian security control

■ Israeli settlement

in other parts of the world. Meanwhile, most other nations paid little attention to the region. During the Cold War, the United States and the Soviet Union had competed for the allegiance of African nations, but with the end of the conflict, that focus faded. Bill Clinton became the first American president to make an extended trip to Africa, as he sought to dramatize international responsibility for assisting the continent, and he watched with satisfaction as Nelson Mandela handed over power in South Africa to his successor in a peaceful transition. But other areas proved more problematical. Six months after Clinton became president, a fire-fight with one faction in war-ravaged Somalia, in East Africa, resulted in several dozen American casualties. The shooting prompted some Americans, still haunted by the memory of Vietnam, to demand withdrawal. Reluctant to back down as he groped to define his policy, Clinton first increased the number of U.S. troops, then in 1993, recalled the soldiers without having restored order.

Present-Day Africa and the Middle East

The United States was similarly baffled by a crisis in Rwanda, in central Africa. There a fragile balance of power between two ethnic groups—the Tutsis and the Hutus—broke down. When the Hutu president died in a suspicious plane crash in 1994, hard-line Hutus blamed Tutsi rebels and embarked on a massive genocidal campaign that resulted in the slaughter of hundreds of thousands of innocent Tutsis and moderate Hutus. As the world followed the carnage on television, the United States, like many European nations, debated the possibility of intervention on humanitarian grounds but decided to do nothing. Eventually the killing stopped, although the friction between the rival groups remained.

George W. Bush was much less interested in Africa than his predecessor. He chose not to attend a conference on sustainable development held in South Africa in the summer of 2002, thus sending a clear signal that the United States was more interested in its own business interests than in the economic problems of the less-developed world. When Robert Mugabe, the longtime ruler of Zimbabwe, appropriated the land of white farmers to give it to blacks and precipitated a major economic crisis that threatened starvation for many in the country, the United States did little. Bush visited five African nations in 2003, but it was a whirlwind trip aimed at supporting areas sympathetic to the United States.

Relations with Russia

In the area that formerly had been the Soviet Union, the United States continued to try to promote both democracy and free-market capitalism. It worked closely with Boris Yeltsin in Russia, and then with his successor, Vladimir Putin, who assumed power on the last day of the twentieth century and was then elected president in his own right in 2001. But Russia remained unstable, still caught up in the complications of a huge political, social, and economic transformation that was far from over.

George W. Bush recognized the need to work with Putin. In a series of meetings, both in Russia and in the United States, Bush developed a close working relationship with the Russian leader, whose assistance he needed in maintaining European stability. The Soviet Union had ceased to exist, but the component parts still remained important in the larger international scene.

Terror on September 11

On September 11, 2001, three hijacked airplanes slammed into the World Trade Center towers in New York City and the Pentagon in Washington, D.C. The fires in New York from exploding jet fuel caused the towers to crumble, altering the skyline forever. Altogether about 3,000 people died in the terrorist attacks. A fourth plane, probably headed for either the White House or the Capitol, crashed in Pennsylvania when passengers fought back against the attackers.

The hijackers were Muslim extremists, most from Saudi Arabia, trained at flight schools in the United States, who belonged to the al Qaeda network headed by a Saudi exile named Osama bin Laden. Osama bin Laden and his organization were head-quartered in Afghanistan, ruled by the extremely conservative Muslim Taliban group that was seeking to impose the law of the Qur'an, the Muslim holy book, on civil society. Osama bin Laden and his associates were furious at the United States for its Middle Eastern policy of support for Israel, and they also hated its affluent and materialistic values that often conflicted with their religious values and values elsewhere in the world.

The terrorist attacks shattered America's sense of security within its own borders. Irate at the unprovoked strikes, President Bush vowed to find and punish the terrorists. Like his father in the Gulf War a decade earlier, he put together a worldwide coalition to assist the United States, and he quickly launched a bombing campaign to smoke out Osama bin Laden and his network. Although the bombing, followed by attacks by ground troops in Afghanistan, defeated the Taliban and drove its members from power, the campaign failed to find Osama bin

George W. Bush, Address to Congress (September 20, 2001)

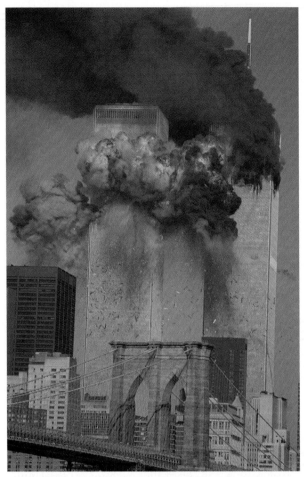

An Indelible Image of September 11, 2001   The World Trade Center towers in New York City once dominated the skyline on the Hudson River. As two hijacked commercial airplanes crashed into the tall structures on September 11, 2001, both towers burst into flames and later collapsed, killing most of the people who were still inside. What impression does this photograph of the burning towers convey? *(Steve Ludlum/The New York Times)*

Laden. An international coalition attempted to assist in rebuilding Afghanistan, and Bush, who had spoken out vigorously against nation building in his own electoral campaign, now found himself a reluctant participant in the process. Hamid Karzai became head of a new government, but the instability of his regime was reflected in threats—and attempts—on his life.

Terrorism, the United States discovered, was a complicated enemy. It was, of course, nothing new. For the last couple of decades, terrorism had been a constant source of concern as the nation sought to thwart hijackings, kidnappings, and bombings before they occurred. Sometimes these efforts were successful; sometimes (as in the 1993 bombing at the World Trade Center) they were not. But

nothing compared to the attacks of September 11, 2001.

As Bush's approval ratings soared to more than 90 percent, he vowed a lengthy campaign to root out terrorism wherever it surfaced in the world. He embarked on a massive governmental reorganization to create a new Department of Homeland Security to help prevent future attacks. In the Patriot Act, he invoked terrorism as a reason to allow the government to encroach on individual liberties—in the interest of security—more extensively than in the past. Ironically, a president dedicated to smaller government now found himself in the forefront of an effort to give government a much larger role.

American Muslims were often the victims of the government effort. Some faced attacks by Americans angry at the terrorist strikes. Others were held, often without being charged with a crime, on the suspicion that they were somehow involved.

The antiterrorism campaign escalated. In early 2002, Bush spoke out forcefully against what he called an "axis of evil," as he referred to Iraq, Iran, and North Korea. He was particularly intent on driving Iraqi leader Saddam Hussein from power. Hussein had launched the attack on Kuwait that had led to the Gulf War during the administration of Bush's father. While the United States and the coalition it had put together had won that war, the military had called off the campaign before toppling Hussein. Now Bush, arguing that Hussein was creating weapons of mass destruction, vowed to complete the task. Bush's secretary of state, Colin Powell, who was inclined to a more restrained foreign policy, opposed Secretary of Defense Donald Rumsfeld and Vice President Dick Cheney, who enthusiastically supported an attack. Bush's argument that he could invade Iraq even without the support of Congress aroused a firestorm of protest both in the United States and around the world.

The war in Iraq, fought with British but not United Nations support, began in March 2003. American forces were successful, and just a month and a half later, Bush declared that the major phase of combat operations was over. In December, U.S. soldiers captured Saddam Hussein hiding in a hole in the ground. But even the capture of the Iraqi dictator could not quell increasing opposition to the American occupation, which led to fierce fighting in the months that followed. As the deadline for handing sovereignty over to Iraq in mid-2004 approached, Sunnis, Shiites, and Kurds fought with each other for a share of power, but were united in their opposition to the continuing

How Others See Us

Many Europeans opposed the U.S. invasion of Iraq in 2002. President George W. Bush lashed out equally angrily at his European opponents as he proceeded with the war. Europeans continued to view the American government with suspicion at the start of his second term, but still hoped for a thaw in relations. This piece by Elfriede Jelinek of Austria, winner of the 2004 Nobel Prize in Literature, reflects a prevalent European view.

President Bush needs Europe. He knows it himself by now. He started a war in defiance of international law and didn't pay any attention to the Europeans, and with that he split the continent into a "new" (good) Europe and an "old" (bad) one.

Now he ought to convince Europeans that he is not planning another war (for example against Syria or Iran), while at the same time professing to think highly of the opinion of European nations and to value them. The freedom that Mr. Bush proclaimed in his inauguration speech cannot be achieved and maintained without the help of the Europeans. First and foremost he has to convince Europe that he is not planning a new war, which shouldn't be difficult.

After all, his troops can only with the greatest difficulty halfway pacify Iraq.

- *Why does Elfriede Jelinek suggest that Europeans opposed President Bush earlier?*

- *Why does Jelinek feel that Bush needs the assistance of Europe now?*

- *What does Jelinek believe Bush should do to reassure the Europeans?*

American presence. Insurgent attacks against American troops and Iraqis in new official positions also continued. Photographs of American abuse of prisoners in the notorious Abu Ghraib prison aroused resentment in the Middle East and among people around the world. By mid-2005, the American death toll in Iraq had surpassed 1,800 and mounting opposition reflected the sense that the war was spiraling out of control. Though the United States made good on its commitment to turn over authority to an interim Iraqi government, as elections took place in early 2005, serious, and perhaps intractable, problems remained. Violence in Iraq continued without an end in sight.

TIMELINE

1991–1999	Ethnic turbulence in fragmented former Yugoslavia
1992	Bill Clinton elected president Czechoslovakia splits into separate Czech and Slovak Republics Riots erupt in Los Angeles
1993	North American Free Trade Agreement (NAFTA) ratified Palestine Liberation Organization and Israel sign peace treaty
1994	Nelson Mandela elected president of South Africa
1996	Bill Clinton re-elected
1998	Budget surplus announced Bill Clinton impeached by the House of Representatives
1999	Bill Clinton acquitted by the Senate Stock market soars as Dow Jones average passes 10,000
2000	George W. Bush elected president
2001	Economy falters Stock market dips below 10,000 Tax cut passed Terrorists strike New York City and Washington, D.C.
2002	Recession continues and Dow Jones average drops below 8,000
2003	U.S. and coalition forces invade Iraq
2004	George W. Bush re-elected
2005	Bush calls for a major overhaul of social security

Conclusion

The Recent Past in Perspective

In the 1990s, the United States prospered in a period of economic growth longer than any in its history. After weathering a recession at the start of the decade, the economy began to boom, and the boom continued for the next 10 years. Most middle- and upper-class Americans prospered. The budget deficit disappeared, and the government ran a sizable surplus. Yet not all Americans shared in the prosperity. Despite the drop in the unemployment level, many of the available jobs paid little more than the minimum wage, and people like Marlene and Rod Garrett, met at the start of the chapter, had trouble making ends meet. Members of minority groups, whose numbers grew throughout the decade, had the toughest time of all.

Meanwhile, Americans worried about their role in the outside world. As they enjoyed their newfound prosperity, some were reluctant to spend money in an activist role abroad. They debated what to do about the defense establishment, which had begun to deteriorate, and were hesitant to become deeply involved in foreign conflicts where they had trouble ascertaining American interests. Then, in 2001, the brutal terrorist attacks on New York City and Washington, D.C., mobilized the nation. Recognizing at long last that terrorism threatened the entire globe, including the United States, they prepared themselves for an extended effort to try to bring it under control and to make the world a safer place. As they had in years past, in both World War I and World War II, the United States again sought to protect the democratic way of life for the American people and for people elsewhere as well.

Questions for Review and Reflection

1. What happened to the economy in the 1990s, and how did economic developments affect political action?

2. How were the Democrats able to regain power in 1992 after more than a decade of Republican rule?

3. How successful was Bill Clinton's presidency?

4. What did the closeness of the elections of 2000 and 2004 indicate about divisions in American society?

5. How did the terrorist attacks of September 11, 2001, affect the course of American foreign policy?

Recommended Reading

Recommended Readings are posted on the Web site for this textbook. Visit www.ablongman.com/nash

Fiction and Film

Sherman Alexie's *The Lone Ranger and Tonto Fistfight in Heaven* (1993) is a collection of stories about contemporary Native American life; *Ten Little Indians* (2003) is an even more recent collection of Alexie's stories. Robert Olen Butler's *A Good Scent from a Strange Mountain* (1992) is a Pulitzer Prize–winning collection of short stories about Vietnamese immigrants in the United States. Joe Klein's *Primary Colors: A Novel of Politics* (1996), originally published anonymously, provides a vivid portrait of a politician very much like Bill Clinton. Alice Mattison's *Men Giving Money, Women Yelling* (1997) is a series of intersecting stories about the complexities of people's lives and relationships. Lorrie Moore's *Birds of America: Stories* (1998) is another collection of stories about modern culture and life, including one about a nuclear family involved in a meltdown.

Americanos: Latino Life in the United States (1999) is a documentary film about the impact of Hispanics around the country. *The Contender* (2000) is a movie about partisan political bickering; *Black Hawk Down* (2001) is a film about the bitter fighting in Somalia; *Philadelphia* (1993) is a movie about a lawyer who contracts the AIDS virus; *Lone Star* (1996) is a movie set in Rio County, Texas, that provides a vivid portrait of the frictions between Mexicans, Anglos, and African Americans; *Primary Colors* (1998) is the lively film made from the novel of the same name.

Discovering U.S. History Online

United States Census 2000

www.census.gov/main/www/cen2000.html

This site includes searchable data using the "American Factfinder" and "State and Country Quick Facts."

The Landscape of Asian America

www.asian-nation.org/index.shtml

This site presents a broad look at the history of Asians in America up to the present time as well as details of immigration and present-day enclaves of Asians in the United States.

U.S. Department of Labor, Bureau of Labor Statistics

www.bls.gov

This site contains recent economic information about wages, inflation, employment, and industrial activity.

Homelessness: Programs and the People They Serve

www.huduser.org/publications/homeless/homeless_tech.html

The full text of this detailed report on the state of homelessness at the end of the twentieth century is available online in PDF format.

William Jefferson Clinton

www.ipl.org/div/potus/wjclinton.html

This site contains basic factual data about Clinton's election and presidency, speeches, and online biographies.

William J. Clinton Presidential Library & Museum

www.clintonlibrary.gov

This is the site of the new Clinton library, which contains all of his official papers and materials.

Investigating the President: The Trial

www.cnn.com/ALLPOLITICS/resources/1998/lewinsky

This site from CNN provides information and documents about the scandals surrounding President Clinton and his impeachment.

Election Collection 2000

web.archive.org/collections/e2k.html

This site contains links to 797 candidate Web sites and other sites covering election day and its aftermath. The sites are presented in their archived state—that is, as they were at the time of the election.

George Walker Bush

www.ipl.org/div/potus/gwbush.html

This site contains basic factual data about Bush's election and presidency, speeches, and online biographies.

A Nation Challenged

www.nytimes.com/pages/national/dayofterror

This site from the *New York Times* contains archives for six months of stories and accounts, including video images and pictures, of the September 11, 2001, terrorist attacks on the World Trade Center towers in New York City and the Pentagon in Washington, D.C.

Understanding Afghanistan: A Land in Crisis

www.nationalgeographic.com/landincrisis/

This site presents current news from *National Geographic,* including maps, recent photographs, and lesson plans. The site also makes available online a few of the magazine's articles about Afghanistan, terrorist attacks, Islam, rescue work, and an archived Webcast of "National Geographic Explores a Changing World," a film screening and panel discussion on the Middle East and Afghanistan after the events of September 11, 2001, accompanied by a discussion forum.

War in Iraq

www.cnn.com/SPECIALS/2003/iraq/

This site, which includes maps and video selections, deals with the events of the war and its impact on the world.

Picturing the Century: One Hundred Years of Photography from the National Archives

www.archives.gov/exhibit_hall/picturing_the_century

The photographs in this selection "depict both the mundane and high political drama, society's failings as well as its triumphs, war's ugliness as well as its bravery."

The Twentieth Century

www.cnn.com/SPECIALS/1999/century

A decade-by-decade look at the twentieth century via headlines, innovation, culture, and personalities.

Appendix

For additional reference material, go to
www.ablongman.com/nash7e/appendix
The online appendix includes the following:

THE DECLARATION OF INDEPENDENCE IN CONGRESS, JULY 4, 1776

The Unanimous Declaration of the Thirteen United States of America

When, in the course of human events, it becomes necessary for one people to dissolve the political bonds which have connected them with another, and to assume, among the powers of the earth, the separate and equal station to which the laws of nature and of nature's God entitle them, a decent respect to the opinions of mankind requires that they should declare the causes which impel them to the separation.

We hold these truths to be self-evident: That all men are created equal; that they are endowed by their Creator with certain unalienable rights; that among these are life, liberty, and the pursuit of happiness; that, to secure these rights, governments are instituted among men, deriving their just powers from the consent of the governed; that whenever any form of government becomes destructive of these ends, it is the right of the people to alter or to abolish it, and to institute new government, laying its foundation on such principles, and organizing its powers in such form, as to them shall seem most likely to effect their safety and happiness. Prudence, indeed, will dictate that governments long established should not be changed for light and transient causes; and accordingly all experience hath shown that mankind are more disposed to suffer, while evils are sufferable, than to right themselves by abolishing the forms to which they are accustomed. But when a long train of abuses and usurpations, pursuing invariably the same object, evinces a design to reduce them under absolute despotism, it is their right, it is their duty, to throw off such government, and to provide new guards for their future security. Such has been the patient sufferance of these colonies; and such is now the necessity which constrains them to alter their former systems of government. The history of the present King of Great Britain is a history of repeated injuries and usurpations, all having in direct object the establishment of an absolute tyranny over these states. To prove this, let facts be submitted to a candid world.

He has refused his assent to laws, the most wholesome and necessary for the public good.

He has forbidden his governors to pass laws of immediate and pressing importance, unless suspended in their operation till his assent should be obtained; and, when so suspended, he has utterly neglected to attend to them.

He has refused to pass other laws for the accommodation of large districts of people, unless those people would relinquish the right of representation in the legislature, a right inestimable to them, and formidable to tyrants only.

He has called together legislative bodies at places unusual, uncomfortable, and distant from the depository of their public records, for the sole purpose of fatiguing them into compliance with his measures.

He has dissolved representative houses repeatedly, for opposing, with manly firmness, his invasions on the rights of the people.

He has refused for a long time, after such dissolutions, to cause others to be elected; whereby the legislative powers, incapable of annihilation, have returned to the people at large for their exercise; the state remaining, in the mean time, exposed to all the dangers of invasions from without and convulsions within.

He has endeavored to prevent the population of these states; for that purpose obstructing the laws for naturalization of foreigners; refusing to pass others to encourage their migration hither, and raising the conditions of new appropriations of lands.

He has obstructed the administration of justice, by refusing his assent to laws for establishing judiciary powers.

He has made judges dependent on his will alone, for the tenure of their offices, and the amount and payment of their salaries.

He has erected a multitude of new offices, and sent hither swarms of officers to harass our people and eat out their substance.

He has kept among us, in times of peace, standing armies, without the consent of our legislatures.

He has affected to render the military independent of, and superior to, the civil power.

He has combined with others to subject us to a jurisdiction foreign to our constitution, and unacknowledged by our laws, giving his assent to their acts of pretended legislation:

For quartering large bodies of armed troops among us;

For protecting them, by a mock trial, from punishment for any murder which they should commit on the inhabitants of these states;

For cutting off our trade with all parts of the world;

For imposing taxes on us without our consent;

For depriving us, in many cases, of the benefits of trial by jury;

For transporting us beyond seas, to be tried for pretended offenses;

For abolishing the free system of English laws in a neighboring province, establishing therein an arbitrary government, and enlarging its boundaries, so as to render it at once an example and fit instrument for introducing the same absolute rule into these colonies;

For taking away our charters abolishing our most valuable laws, and altering fundamentally the forms of our governments;

For suspending our own legislatures, and declaring themselves invested with power to legislate for us in all cases whatsoever.

He has abdicated government here, by declaring us out of his protection and waging war against us.

He has plundered our seas, ravaged our coasts, burned our towns, and destroyed the lives of our people.

He is at this time transporting large armies of foreign mercenaries to complete the works of death, desolation, and tyranny already begun with circumstances of cruelty and perfidy scarcely paralleled in the most barbarous ages, and totally unworthy the head of a civilized nation.

He has constrained our fellow-citizens, taken captive on the high seas, to bear arms against their country, to become the executioners of their friends and brethren, or to fall themselves by their hands.

He has excited domestic insurrection among us, and has endeavored to bring on the inhabitants of our frontiers the merciless Indian savages, whose known rule of warfare is an undistinguished destruction of all ages, sexes, and conditions.

In every stage of these oppressions we have petitioned for redress in the most humble terms; our repeated petitions have been answered only by repeated injury. A prince, whose character is thus marked by every act which may define a tyrant, is unfit to be the ruler of a free people.

Nor have we been wanting in our attentions to our British brethren. We have warned them, from time to time, of attempts by their legislature to extend an unwarrantable jurisdiction over us. We have reminded them of the circumstances of our emigration and settlement here. We have appealed to their native justice and magnanimity; and we have conjured them, by the ties of our common kindred, to disavow these usurpations, which would inevitably interrupt our connections and correspondence. They, too, have been deaf to the voice of justice and of consanguinity. We must, therefore, acquiesce in the necessity which denounces our separation, and hold them, as we hold the rest of mankind, enemies in war, in peace friends.

We, therefore, the representatives of the United States of America, in General Congress assembled, appealing to the Supreme Judge of the world for the rectitude of our intentions, do, in the name and by the authority of the good people of these colonies, solemnly publish and declare, that these United Colonies are, and of right, ought to be, FREE AND INDEPENDENT STATES; that they are absolved from all allegiance to the British crown, and that all political connection between them and the state of Great Britain is, and ought to be, totally dissolved; and that, as free and independent states, they have full power to levy war, conclude peace, contract alliances, establish commerce, and do all other acts and things which independent states may of right do. And for the support of this declaration, with a firm reliance on the protection of Devine Providence, we mutually pledge to each other our lives, our fortunes, and our sacred honor.

JOHN HANCOCK

BUTTON GWENNETT
LYMAN HALL
GEO. WALTON
WM. HOOPER
JOSEPH HEWES
JOHN PENN
EDWARD RUTLEDGE
THOS. HEYWARD, JUNR.
THOMAS LYNCH, JUNR.
ARTHUR MIDDLETON
SAMUEL CHASE
WM. PACA
THOS. STONE
CHARLES CARROLL OF CARROLLTON
GEORGE WYTHE
RICHARD HENRY LEE
TH. JEFFERSON
BENJA. HARRISON
THS. NELSON, JR.

FRANCIS LIGHTFOOT LEE
CARTER BRAXTON
ROBT. MORRIS
BENJAMIN RUSH
BENJA. FRANKLIN
JOHN MORTON
GEO. CLYMER
JAS. SMITH
GEO. TAYLOR
JAMES WILSON
GEO. ROSS
CAESAR RODNEY
GEO. READ
THO. MÍKEAN
WM. FLOYD
PHIL. LIVINGSTON
FRANS. LEWIS
LEWIS MORRIS
RICHD. STOCKTON

JNO. WITHERSPOON
FRAS. HOPKINSON
JOHN HART
ABRA. CLARK
JOSIAH BARTLETT
WM. WHIPPLE
SAML. ADAMS
JOHN ADAMS
ROBT. TREAT PAINE
ELBRIDGE GERRY
STEP. HOPKINS
WILLIAM ELLERY
ROGER SHERMAN
SAMÍEL. HUNTINGTON
WM. WILLIAMS
OLIVER WOLCOTT
MATHEW THORNTON

THE CONSTITUTION OF THE UNITED STATES OF AMERICA

PREAMBLE

We the People of the United States, in Order to form a more perfect Union, establish Justice, insure domestic Tranquility, provide for the common defence, promote the general Welfare, and secure the Blessings of Liberty to ourselves and our Posterity, do ordain and establish this Constitution for the United States of America.

ARTICLE I.

Section 1   All legislative Powers herein granted shall be vested in a Congress of the United States, which shall consist of a Senate and House of Representatives.

Section 2   The House of Representatives shall be composed of Members chosen every second Year by the People of the several States, and the Electors in each State shall have the Qualifications requisite for Electors of the most numerous Branch of the State Legislature.

No Person shall be a Representative who shall not have attained to the Age of twenty five Years, and been seven Years a Citizen of the United States, and who shall not, when elected, be an Inhabitant of that State in which he shall be chosen.

Representatives and direct Taxes shall be apportioned among the several States which may be included within this Union, according to their respective Numbers, *which shall be determined by adding to the whole Number of free Persons, including those bound to Service for a Term of Years, and excluding Indians not taxed, three fifths of all other Persons.* The actual Enumeration shall be made within three Years after the first Meeting of the Congress of the United States, and within every subsequent Term of ten Years, in such Manner as they shall by Law direct. The Number of Representatives shall not exceed one for every thirty Thousand, but each State shall have at Least one Representative; *and until such enumeration shall be made, the State of New Hampshire shall be entitled to chuse three, Massachusetts eight, Rhode-Island and Providence Plantations one, Connecticut five, New-York six, New Jersey four, Pennsylvania eight, Delaware one, Maryland six, Virginia ten, North Carolina five, South Carolina five, and Georgia three.*

When vacancies happen in the Representation from any State, the Executive Authority thereof shall issue Writs of Election to fill such Vacancies.

The House of Representatives shall chuse their Speaker and other Officers; and shall have the sole Power of Impeachment.

Section 3   The Senate of the United States shall be composed of two Senators from each State, chosen by the Legislature thereof, for six Years; and each Senator shall have one Vote.

Immediately after they shall be assembled in Consequence of the first Election, they shall be divided as equally as may be into three Classes. The Seats of the Senators of the first Class shall be vacated at the Expiration of the second Year, of the second Class at the Expiration of the fourth Year, and of the third Class at the Expiration of the sixth Year, so that one third may be chosen every second Year; and if Vacancies happen by Resignation, or otherwise, during the Recess of the Legislature of any State, the Executive thereof may make temporary Appointments until the next Meeting of the Legislature, which shall then fill such Vacancies.

No Person shall be a Senator who shall not have attained to the Age of thirty Years, and been nine Years a Citizen of the United States, and who shall not, when elected, be an Inhabitant of that State for which he shall be chosen.

The Vice President of the United States shall be President of the Senate, but shall have no Vote, unless they be equally divided.

The Senate shall choose their other Officers, and also a President *pro tempore,* in the Absence of the Vice President, or when he shall exercise the Office of President of the United States.

The Senate shall have the sole Power to try all Impeachments. When sitting for that Purpose, they shall be on Oath or Affirmation. When the President of the United States is tried the Chief Justice shall preside: And no Person shall be convicted without the Concurrence of two thirds of the Members present.

Judgment in Cases of Impeachment shall not extend further than to removal from Office, and disqualification to hold and enjoy any Office of honor, Trust or Profit under the United States: but the Party convicted shall nevertheless be liable and subject to Indictment, Trial, Judgment and Punishment, according to Law.

Section 4   The Times, Places and Manner of holding Elections for Senators and Representatives, shall be prescribed in each State by the Legislature thereof; but the Congress may at any time by Law make or alter such Regulations, except as to the Places of chusing Senators.

The Congress shall assemble at least once in every Year, and such Meeting *shall be on the first Monday in December, unless they shall by Law appoint a different Day.*

Section 5   Each House shall be the Judge of the Elections, Returns and Qualifications of its own Members, and a Majority of each shall constitute a Quorum to do Business; but a smaller Number may adjourn from day to day, and may be authorized to compel the Attendance of absent Members, in such Manner, and under such Penalties as each House may provide.

Each House may determine the Rules of its Proceedings, punish its Members for disorderly

---

The Constitution became effective March 4, 1789. Any portion of the text that has been amended is printed in italics.

Behaviour, and, with the Concurrence of two thirds, expel a Member.

Each House shall keep a Journal of its Proceedings, and from time to time publish the same, excepting such Parts as may in their Judgment require Secrecy; and the Yeas and Nays of the Members of either House on any question shall, at the Desire of one fifth of those Present, be entered on the Journal.

Neither House, during the Session of Congress, shall, without the Consent of the other, adjourn for more than three days, nor to any other Place than that in which the two Houses shall be sitting.

Section 6   The Senators and Representatives shall receive a Compensation for their Services, to be ascertained by Law, and paid out of the Treasury of the United States. They shall in all Cases, except Treason, Felony and Breach of the Peace, be privileged from Arrest during their Attendance at the Session of their respective Houses, and in going to and returning from the same; and for any Speech or Debate in either House, they shall not be questioned in any other Place.

No Senator or Representative shall, during the Time for which he was elected, be appointed to any civil Office under the Authority of the United States, which shall have been created, or the Emoluments whereof shall have been encreased during such time; and no Person holding any Office under the United States, shall be a Member of either House during his Continuance in Office.

Section 7   All Bills for raising Revenue shall originate in the House of Representatives; but the Senate may propose or concur with Amendments as on other Bills.

Every Bill which shall have passed the House of Representatives and the Senate, shall, before it become a Law, be presented to the President of the United States; If he approve he shall sign it, but if not he shall return it, with his Objections to that House in which it shall have originated, who shall enter the Objections at large on their Journal, and proceed to reconsider it. If after such Reconsideration two thirds of that House shall agree to pass the Bill, it shall be sent, together with the Objections, to the other House, by which it shall likewise be reconsidered, and if approved by two thirds of that House, it shall become a Law. But in all such Cases the Votes of both Houses shall be determined by yeas and Nays, and the Names of the Persons voting for and against the Bill shall be entered on the Journal of each House respectively. If any Bill shall not be returned by the President within ten Days (Sundays excepted) after it shall have been presented to him, the Same shall be a Law, in like Manner as if he had signed it, unless the Congress by their Adjournment prevent its Return, in which Case it shall not be a Law.

Every Order, Resolution, or Vote to which the Concurrence of the Senate and House of Representatives may be necessary (except on a question of Adjournment) shall be presented to the President of the United States; and before the Same shall take Effect, shall be approved by him, or being disapproved by him, shall be repassed by two thirds of the Senate and House of Representatives, according to the Rules and Limitations prescribed in the Case of a Bill.

Section 8   The Congress shall have Power:

To lay and collect Taxes, Duties, Imposts and Excises, to pay the Debts and provide for the common Defence and general Welfare of the United States; but all Duties, Imposts and Excises shall be uniform throughout the United States;

To borrow Money on the credit of the United States;

To regulate Commerce with foreign Nations, and among the several States, and with the Indian Tribes;

To establish an uniform Rule of Naturalization, and uniform Laws on the subject of Bankruptcies throughout the United States;

To coin Money, regulate the Value thereof, and of foreign Coin, and fix the Standard of Weights and Measures;

To provide for the Punishment of counterfeiting the Securities and current Coin of the United States;

To establish Post Offices and post Roads;

To promote the Progress of Science and useful Arts, by securing for limited Times to Authors and Inventors the exclusive Right to their respective Writings and Discoveries;

To constitute Tribunals inferior to the supreme Court;

To define and punish Piracies and Felonies committed on the high Seas, and Offences against the Law of Nations;

To declare War, grant Letters of Marque and Reprisal, and make Rules concerning Captures on Land and Water;

To raise and support Armies, but no Appropriation of Money to that Use shall be for a longer Term than two Years;

To provide and maintain a Navy;

To make Rules for the Government and Regulation of the land and naval Forces;

To provide for calling forth the Militia to execute the Laws of the Union, suppress Insurrections and repel Invasions;

To provide for organizing, arming, and disciplining, the Militia, and for governing such Part of them as may be employed in the Service of the United States, reserving to the States respectively, the Appointment of the Officers, and the Authority of training the Militia according to the discipline prescribed by Congress;

To exercise exclusive Legislation in all Cases whatsoever, over such District (not exceeding ten Miles square) as may, by Cession of particular States, and the Acceptance of Congress, become the Seat of the Government of the United States, and to exercise like Authority over all Places purchased by the Consent of the Legislature of the State in which the Same shall be, for the Erection of Forts, Magazines, Arsenals, dock-Yards, and other needful Buildings;

To make all Laws which shall be necessary and proper for carrying into Execution the foregoing

Powers, and all other Powers vested by this Constitution in the Government of the United States, or in any Department or Officer thereof.

Section 9 *The Migration or Importation of such Persons as any of the States now existing shall think proper to admit, shall not be prohibited by the Congress prior to the Year one thousand eight hundred and eight, but a Tax or duty may be imposed on such Importation, not exceeding ten dollars for each Person.*

The Privilege of the Writ of Habeas Corpus shall not be suspended, unless when in Cases of Rebellion or Invasion the public Safety may require it.

No Bill of Attainder or ex post facto Law shall be passed.

No Capitation, or other direct, Tax shall be laid, unless in Proportion to the Census or Enumeration herein before directed to be taken.

No Tax or Duty shall be laid on Articles exported from any State.

No Preference shall be given by any Regulation of Commerce or Revenue to the Ports of one State over those of another: nor shall Vessels bound to, or from, one State, be obliged to enter, clear, or pay Duties in another.

No Money shall be drawn from the Treasury, but in Consequence of Appropriations made by Law; and a regular Statement and Account of the Receipts and Expenditures of all public Money shall be published from time to time.

No Title of Nobility shall be granted by the United States: And no Person holding any Office of Profit or Trust under them, shall, without the Consent of the Congress, accept of any present, Emolument, Office, or Title, of any kind whatever, from any King, Prince, or foreign State.

Section 10 No State shall enter into any Treaty, Alliance, or Confederation; grant Letters of Marque and Reprisal; coin Money; emit Bills of Credit; make any Thing but gold and silver Coin a Tender in Payment of Debts; pass any Bill of Attainder, ex post facto Law, or Law impairing the Obligation of Contracts, or grant any Title of Nobility.

No State shall, without the Consent of the Congress, lay any Imposts or Duties on Imports or Exports, except what may be absolutely necessary for executing it's inspection Laws: and the net Produce of all Duties and Imposts, laid by any State on Imports or Exports, shall be for the Use of the Treasury of the United States; and all such Laws shall be subject to the Revision and Controul of the Congress.

No State shall, without the Consent of Congress, lay any Duty of Tonnage, keep Troops, or Ships of War in time of Peace, enter into any Agreement or Compact with another State, or with a foreign Power, or engage in War, unless actually invaded, or in such imminent Danger as will not admit of delay.

ARTICLE II.

Section 1 The executive Power shall be vested in a President of the United States of America. He shall hold his Office during the Term of four Years, and, together with the Vice President, chosen for the same Term, be elected, as follows

Each State shall appoint, in such Manner as the Legislature thereof may direct, a Number of Electors, equal to the whole Number of Senators and Representatives to which the State may be entitled in the Congress: but no Senator or Representative, or Person holding an Office of Trust or Profit under the United States, shall be appointed an Elector.

The Electors shall meet in their respective States, and vote by Ballot for two Persons, of whom one at least shall not be an Inhabitant of the same State with themselves. And they shall make a List of all the Persons voted for, and of the Number of Votes for each; which List they shall sign and certify, and transmit sealed to the Seat of Government of the United States, directed to the President of the Senate. The President of the Senate shall, in the Presence of the Senate and House of Representatives, open all the Certificates, and the Votes shall then be counted. The Person having the greatest Number of Votes shall be the President, if such Number be a Majority of the whole Number of Electors appointed; and if there be more than one who have such Majority, and have an equal Number of Votes, then the House of Representatives shall immediately chuse by Ballot one of them for President; and if no Person have a Majority, then from the five highest on the List the said House shall in like Manner chuse the President. But in chusing the President, the Votes shall be taken by States, the Representation from each State having one Vote; A quorum for this Purpose shall consist of a Member or Members from two thirds of the States, and a Majority of all the States shall be necessary to a Choice. In every Case, after the Choice of the President, the Person having the greatest Number of Votes of the Electors shall be the Vice President. But if there should remain two or more who have equal Votes, the Senate shall chuse from them by Ballot the Vice President. The Congress may determine the Time of chusing the Electors, and the Day on which they shall give their Votes; which Day shall be the same throughout the United States.

No Person except a natural born Citizen, *or a Citizen of the United States, at the time of the Adoption of this Constitution,* shall be eligible to the Office of President; neither shall any Person be eligible to that Office who shall not have attained to the Age of thirty five Years, and been fourteen Years a Resident within the United States.

In Case of the Removal of the President from Office, or of his Death, Resignation, or Inability to discharge the Powers and Duties of the said Office, the Same shall devolve on the Vice President, and the Congress may by Law provide for the Case of Removal, Death, Resignation or Inability, both of the President and Vice President declaring what Officer shall then act as President, and such Officer shall act accordingly, until the Disability be removed, or a President shall be elected.

The President shall, at stated Times, receive for his Services, a Compensation, which shall neither be increased nor diminished during the Period for which he shall have been elected, and he shall not receive within that Period any other Emolument from the United States, or any of them.

Before he enter on the Execution of his Office, he shall take the following Oath or Affirmation: "I do solemnly swear (or affirm) that I will faithfully execute the Office of President of the United States, and will to the best of my Ability, preserve, protect and defend the Constitution of the United States."

Section 2   The President shall be Commander in Chief of the Army and Navy of the United States, and of the Militia of the several States, when called into the actual Service of the United States; he may require the Opinion, in writing, of the principal Officer in each of the executive Departments, upon any Subject relating to the Duties of their respective Offices, and he shall have Power to grant Reprieves and Pardons for Offences against the United States, except in Cases of Impeachment.

He shall have Power, by and with the Advice and Consent of the Senate, to make Treaties, provided two thirds of the Senators present concur; and he shall nominate, and by and with the Advice and Consent of the Senate, shall appoint Ambassadors, other public Ministers and Consuls, Judges of the supreme Court, and all other Officers of the United States, whose Appointments are not herein otherwise provided for, and which shall be established by Law: but the Congress may by Law vest the Appointment of such inferior Officers, as they think proper, in the President alone, in the Courts of Law, or in the Heads of Departments.

The President shall have Power to fill up all Vacancies that may happen during the Recess of the Senate, by granting Commissions which shall expire at the End of their next Session.

Section 3   He shall from time to time give to the Congress Information of the State of the Union, and recommend to their Consideration such Measures as he shall judge necessary and expedient; he may, on extraordinary Occasions, convene both Houses, or either of them, and in Case of Disagreement between them, with Respect to the Time of Adjournment, he may adjourn them to such Time as he shall think proper; he shall receive Ambassadors and other public Ministers; he shall take Care that the Laws be faithfully executed, and shall Commission all the Officers of the United States.

Section 4   The President, Vice President and all civil Officers of the United States, shall be removed from Office on Impeachment for, and Conviction of, Treason, Bribery, or other high Crimes and Misdemeanors.

ARTICLE III.

Section 1   The judicial Power of the United States, shall be vested in one supreme Court, and in such inferior Courts as the Congress may from time to time ordain and establish. The Judges, both of the supreme and inferior Courts, shall hold their Offices during good Behaviour, and shall, at stated Times, receive for their Services, a Compensation which shall not be diminished during their Continuance in Office.

Section 2   The judicial Power shall extend to all Cases, in Law and Equity, arising under this Constitution, the Laws of the United States, and Treaties made, or which shall be made, under their Authority;—to all Cases affecting Ambassadors, other public Ministers and Consuls;—to all Cases of admiralty and maritime Jurisdiction;—to Controversies to which the United States shall be a Party;—to Controversies between two or more States;—*between a State and Citizens of another State;*—between Citizens of different States;—between Citizens of the same State claiming Lands under Grants of different States, and between a State, or the Citizens thereof, and foreign States, Citizens or Subjects.

In all Cases affecting Ambassadors, other public Ministers and Consuls, and those in which a State shall be Party, the supreme Court shall have original Jurisdiction. In all the other Cases before mentioned, the supreme Court shall have appellate Jurisdiction, both as to Law and Fact, with such Exceptions, and under such Regulations as the Congress shall make.

The Trial of all Crimes, except in Cases of Impeachment, shall be by Jury; and such Trial shall be held in the State where the said Crimes shall have been committed; but when not committed within any State, the Trial shall be at such Place or Places as the Congress may by Law have directed.

Section 3   Treason against the United States, shall consist only in levying War against them, or in adhering to their Enemies, giving them Aid and Comfort. No Person shall be convicted of Treason unless on the Testimony of two Witnesses to the same overt Act, or on Confession in open Court.

The Congress shall have Power to declare the Punishment of Treason, but no Attainder of Treason shall work Corruption of Blood, or Forfeiture except during the Life of the Person attainted.

ARTICLE IV.

Section 1   Full Faith and Credit shall be given in each State to the public Acts, Records, and judicial Proceedings of every other State. And the Congress may by general Laws prescribe the Manner in which such Acts, Records and Proceedings shall be proved, and the Effect thereof.

Section 2   The Citizens of each State shall be entitled to all Privileges and Immunities of Citizens in the several States.

A Person charged in any State with Treason, Felony, or other Crime, who shall flee from Justice, and be found in another State, shall on Demand of the executive Authority of the State from which he fled, be delivered up, to be removed to the State having Jurisdiction of the Crime.

No Person held to Service or Labour in one State, under the Laws thereof, escaping into another, shall, in

Consequence of any Law or Regulation therein, be discharged from such Service or Labour, but shall be delivered up on Claim of the Party to whom such Service or Labour may be due.

Section 3 New States may be admitted by the Congress into this Union; but no new State shall be formed or erected within the Jurisdiction of any other State; nor any State be formed by the Junction of two or more States, or Parts of States, without the Consent of the Legislatures of the States concerned as well as of the Congress.

The Congress shall have Power to dispose of and make all needful Rules and Regulations respecting the Territory or other Property belonging to the United States; and nothing in this Constitution shall be so construed as to Prejudice any Claims of the United States, or of any particular State.

Section 4 The United States shall guarantee to every State in this Union a Republican Form of Government, and shall protect each of them against Invasion; and on Application of the Legislature, or of the Executive (when the Legislature cannot be convened) against domestic Violence.

ARTICLE V.

The Congress, whenever two thirds of both Houses shall deem it necessary, shall propose Amendments to this Constitution, or, on the Application of the Legislatures of two thirds of the several States, shall call a Convention for proposing Amendments, which, in either Case, shall be valid to all Intents and Purposes, as Part of this Constitution, when ratified by the Legislatures of three fourths of the several States, or by Conventions in three fourths thereof, as the one or the other Mode of Ratification may be proposed by the Congress; Provided that *no Amendment which may be* made prior to the Year One thousand eight hundred and eight shall in any Manner affect the first and fourth Clauses in the Ninth Section of the first Article; *and that* no State, without its Consent, shall be deprived of its equal Suffrage in the Senate.

ARTICLE VI.

All Debts contracted and Engagements entered into, before the Adoption of this Constitution, shall be as valid against the United States under this Constitution, as under the Confederation.

This Constitution, and the Laws of the United States which shall be made in Pursuance thereof; and all Treaties made or which shall be made, under the Authority of the United States, shall be the supreme Law of the Land; and the Judges in every State shall be bound thereby, any Thing in the Constitution or Laws of any State to the Contrary notwithstanding.

The Senators and Representatives before mentioned, and the Members of the several State Legislatures, and all executive and judicial Officers, both of the United States and of the several States, shall be bound by Oath or Affirmation, to support this Constitution; but no religious Test shall ever be required as a Qualification to any Office or public Trust under the United States.

ARTICLE VII.

The Ratification of the Conventions of nine States, shall be sufficient for the Establishment of this Constitution between the States so ratifying the Same.

Done in Convention by the Unanimous Consent of the States present the Seventeenth Day of September in the Year of our Lord one thousand seven hundred and Eighty seven and of the Independence of the United States of America the Twelfth IN WITNESS whereof We have hereunto subscribed our Names,

GEORGE WASHINGTON,
President and Deputy from Virginia

North Carolina

WILLIAM BLOUNT
RICHARD DOBBS SPRAIGHT
HU WILLIAMSON

Pennsylvania

BENJAMIN FRANKLIN
THOMAS MIFFLIN
ROBERT MORRIS
GEORGE CLYMER
THOMAS FITZSIMONS
JARED INGERSOLL
JAMES WILSON
GOUVERNEUR MORRIS

Delaware

GEORGE READ
GUNNING BEDFORD, JR.
JOHN DICKINSON
RICHARD BASSETT
JACOB BROOM

South Carolina

J. RUTLEDGE
CHARLES C. PINCKNEY
PIERCE BUTLER

Virginia

JOHN BLAIR
JAMES MADISON, JR.

New Jersey

WILLIAM LIVINGSTON
DAVID BREARLEY
WILLIAM PATERSON
JONATHAN DAYTON

Maryland

JAMES MCHENRY
DANIEL OF ST. THOMAS JENIFER
DANIEL CARROLL

Massachusetts

NATHANIEL GORHAM
RUFUS KING

Connecticut

WILLIAM S. JOHNSON
ROGER SHERMAN

New York

ALEXANDER HAMILTON

New Hampshire

JOHN LANGDON
NICHOLAS GILMAN

Georgia

WILLIAM FEW
ABRAHAM BALDWIN

AMENDMENTS TO THE CONSTITUTION

The first ten amendments (the Bill of Rights) were adopted in 1791.

AMENDMENT I

Congress shall make no law respecting an establishment of religion, or prohibiting the free exercise thereof; or abridging the freedom of speech, or of the press; or the right of the people peaceably to assemble, and to petition the Government for a redress of grievances.

AMENDMENT II

A well regulated Militia, being necessary to the security of a free State, the right of the people to keep and bear Arms, shall not be infringed.

AMENDMENT III

No Soldier shall, in time of peace be quartered in any house, without the consent of the Owner, nor in time of war, but in a manner to be prescribed by law.

AMENDMENT IV

The right of the people to be secure in their persons, houses, papers, and effects, against unreasonable searches and seizures, shall not be violated, and no Warrants shall issue, but upon probable cause, supported by Oath or affirmation, and particularly describing the place to be searched, and the persons or things to be seized.

AMENDMENT V

No person shall be held to answer for a capital, or otherwise infamous crime, unless on a presentment or indictment of a Grand Jury, except in cases arising in the land or naval forces, or in the Militia, when in actual service in time of War or public danger; nor shall any person be subject for the same offence to be twice put in jeopardy of life or limb; nor shall be compelled in any criminal case to be a witness against himself, nor be deprived of life, liberty, or property, without due process of law; nor shall private property be taken for public use, without just compensation.

AMENDMENT VI

In all criminal prosecutions, the accused shall enjoy the right to a speedy and public trial, by an impartial jury of the State and district wherein the crime shall have been committed, which district shall have been previously ascertained by law, and to be informed of the nature and cause of the accusation; to be confronted with the witnesses against him; to have compulsory process for obtaining witnesses in his favor, and to have the Assistance of Counsel for his defence.

AMENDMENT VII

In Suits at common law, where the value in controversy shall exceed twenty dollars, the right of trial by jury shall be preserved, and no fact tried by a jury, shall be otherwise re-examined in any Court of the United States, than according to the rules of the common law.

AMENDMENT VIII

Excessive bail shall not be required, nor excessive fines imposed, nor cruel and unusual punishments inflicted.

AMENDMENT IX

The enumeration in the Constitution, of certain rights, shall not be construed to deny or disparage others retained by the people.

AMENDMENT X

The powers not delegated to the United States by the Constitution, nor prohibited by it to the States, are reserved to the States respectively, or to the people.

AMENDMENT XI [ADOPTED 1798]

The Judicial power of the United States shall not be construed to extend to any suit in law or equity, commenced or prosecuted against one of the United States by Citizens of another State, or by Citizens or Subjects of any Foreign State.

AMENDMENT XII [ADOPTED 1804]

The Electors shall meet in their respective states, and vote by ballot for President and Vice-President, one of whom, at least, shall not be an inhabitant of the same state with themselves; they shall name in their ballots the person voted for as President, and in distinct ballots the person voted for as Vice-President, and they shall make distinct lists of all persons voted for as President, and of all persons voted for as Vice-President, and of the number of votes for each, which list they shall sign and certify, and transmit sealed to the seat of the government of the United States, directed to the President of the Senate;—The President of the Senate shall, in the presence of the Senate and House of Representatives, open all the certificates and the votes shall then be counted;—The person having the greatest number of votes for President, shall be the President, if such number be a majority of the whole number of Electors appointed; and if no person have such majority, then from the persons having the highest numbers not exceeding three on the list of those voted for as President, the House of Representatives shall choose immediately, by ballot, the President. But in choosing the President, the votes shall be taken by states, the representation from each state having one vote; a quorum for this purpose shall consist of a member or members from two thirds of the states, and a majority of all the states shall be necessary to a choice. And if the House of Representatives shall not choose a President whenever the right of choice shall devolve upon them, before the *fourth day of March* next following, then the Vice-President shall act as President, as in the case of the death or other constitutional disability of the President.

The person having the greatest number of votes as Vice-President, shall be the Vice-President, if such number be a majority of the whole number of Electors appointed, and if no person have a majority, then from the two highest numbers on the list, the Senate shall choose the Vice-President; a quorum for the purpose shall consist of two thirds of the whole number of Senators, and a majority of the whole number shall be necessary to a choice. But no person constitutionally ineligible to the office of President shall be eligible to that of Vice-President of the United States.

AMENDMENT XIII [ADOPTED 1865]

Section 1 Neither slavery nor involuntary servitude, except as a punishment for crime whereof the party shall have been duly convicted, shall exist within the United States, or any place subject to their jurisdiction.

Section 2 Congress shall have power to enforce this article by appropriate legislation.

AMENDMENT XIV [ADOPTED 1868]

Section 1 All persons born or naturalized in the United States, and subject to the jurisdiction thereof, are citizens of the United States and of the State wherein they reside. No State shall make or enforce any law which shall abridge the privileges or immunities of citizens of the United States; nor shall any State deprive any person of life, liberty, or property, without due process of law; nor deny to any person within its jurisdiction the equal protection of the laws.

Section 2 Representatives shall be apportioned among the several States according to their respective numbers, counting the whole number of persons in each State, excluding Indians not taxed. But when the right to vote at any election for the choice of electors for President and Vice-President of the United States, Representatives in Congress, the Executive and Judicial officers of a State, or the members of the Legislature thereof, is denied to any of the male inhabitants of such State, being twenty-one years of age, and citizens of the United States, or in any way abridged, except for participation in rebellion, or other crime, the basis of representation therein shall be reduced in the proportion which the number of such male citizens shall bear to the whole number of male citizens twenty-one years of age in such State.

Section 3 No person shall be a Senator or Representative in Congress, or elector of President and Vice-President, or hold any office, civil or military, under the United States, or under any State, who, having previously taken an oath, as a member of Congress, or as an officer of the United States, or as a member of any State legislature, or as an executive or judicial officer of any State, to support the Constitution of the United States, shall have engaged in insurrection or rebellion against the same, or given aid or comfort to the enemies

thereof. But Congress may by a vote of two thirds of each House, remove such disability.

Section 4 The validity of the public debt of the United States, authorized by law, including debts incurred for payment of pensions and bounties for services in suppressing insurrection or rebellion, shall not be questioned. But neither the United States nor any State shall assume or pay any debt or obligation incurred in aid of insurrection or rebellion against the United States, or any claim for the loss or emancipation of any slave; but all such debts, obligations and claims shall be held illegal and void.

Section 5 The Congress shall have power to enforce, by appropriate legislation, the provisions of this article.

AMENDMENT XV [ADOPTED 1870]

Section 1 The right of citizens of the United States to vote shall not be denied or abridged by the United States or by any State on account of race, color, or previous condition of servitude.

Section 2 The Congress shall have power to enforce this article by appropriate legislation.

AMENDMENT XVI [ADOPTED 1913]

The Congress shall have power to lay and collect taxes on incomes, from whatever source derived, without apportionment among the several States, and without regard to any census or enumeration.

AMENDMENT XVII [ADOPTED 1913]

The Senate of the United States shall be composed of two Senators from each State, elected by the people thereof, for six years; and each Senator shall have one vote. The electors in each State shall have the qualifications requisite for electors of the most numerous branch of the State legislatures.

When vacancies happen in the representation of any State in the Senate, the executive authority of such State shall issue writs of election to fill such vacancies: *Provided,* That the legislature of any State may empower the executive thereof to make temporary appointments until the people fill the vacancies by election as the legislature may direct.

This amendment shall not be so construed as to affect the election or term of any Senator chosen before it becomes valid as part of the Constitution.

AMENDMENT XVIII [ADOPTED 1919; REPEALED 1933]

Section 1 After one year from the ratification of this article the manufacture, sale, or transportation of intoxicating liquors within, the importation thereof into, or the exportation thereof from the United States and all territory subject to the jurisdiction thereof for beverage purposes is hereby prohibited.

Section 2 The Congress and the several States shall have concurrent power to enforce this article by appropriate legislation.

Section 3 This article shall be inoperative unless it shall have been ratified as an amendment to the Constitution by the legislatures of the several States, as provided in the Constitution, within seven years from the date of the submission hereof to the States by the Congress.

AMENDMENT XIX [ADOPTED 1920]

Section 1 The right of citizens of the United States to vote shall not be denied or abridged by the United States or by any State on account of sex.

Section 2 Congress shall have power to enforce this article by appropriate legislation.

AMENDMENT XX [ADOPTED 1933]

Section 1 The terms of the President and Vice-President shall end at noon on the 20th day of January, and the terms of Senators and Representatives at noon on the third day of January, of the years in which such terms would have ended if this article had not been ratified; and the terms of their successors shall then begin.

Section 2 The Congress shall assemble at least once in every year, and such meeting shall begin at noon on the third day of January, unless they shall by law appoint a different day.

Section 3 If, at the time fixed for the beginning of the term of the President, the President elect shall have died, the Vice-President elect shall become President. If a President shall not have been chosen before the time fixed for the beginning of his term, or if the President elect shall have failed to qualify, then the Vice-President elect shall act as President until a President shall have qualified; and the Congress may by law provide for the case wherein neither a President elect nor a Vice-President elect shall have qualified, declaring who shall then act as President, or the manner in which one who is to act shall be selected, and such person shall act accordingly until a President or Vice-President shall have qualified.

Section 4 The Congress may by law provide for the case of the death of any of the persons from whom the House of Representatives may choose a President whenever the right of choice shall have devolved upon them, and for the case of the death of any of the persons from whom the Senate may choose a Vice-President whenever the right of choice shall have devolved upon them.

Section 5 Sections 1 and 2 shall take effect on the 15th day of October following the ratification of this article.

Section 6 This article shall be inoperative unless it shall have been ratified as an amendment to the Constitution by the legislatures of three fourths of the several States within seven years from the date of its submission.

AMENDMENT XXI [ADOPTED 1933]

Section 1 The eighteenth article of amendment to the Constitution of the United States is hereby repealed.

Section 2 The transportation or importation into any State, Territory, or possession of the United States for delivery or use therein of intoxicating liquors, in violation of the laws thereof, is hereby prohibited.

Section 3 This article shall be inoperative unless it shall have been ratified as an amendment to the Constitution by conventions in the several States, as provided in the Constitution, within seven years from the date of the submission hereof to the States by the Congress.

AMENDMENT XXII [ADOPTED 1951]

Section 1 No person shall be elected to the office of the President more than twice, and no person who has held the office of President, or acted as President, for more than two years of a term to which some other person was elected President shall be elected to the office of the President more than once. But this Article shall not apply to any person holding the office of President when this Article was proposed by the Congress, and shall not prevent any person who may be holding the office of President, or acting as President, during the term within which this Article becomes operative from holding the office of President or acting as President during the remainder of such term.

Section 2 This article shall be inoperative unless it shall have been ratified as an amendment to the Constitution by the legislatures of three fourths of the several States within seven years from the date of its submission to the States by the Congress.

AMENDMENT XXIII [ADOPTED 1961]

Section 1 The District constituting the seat of Government of the United States shall appoint in such manner as the Congress may direct:

A number of electors of President and Vice-President equal to the whole number of Senators and Representatives in Congress to which the District would be entitled if it were a State, but in no event more than the least populous State; they shall be in addition to those appointed by the States, but they shall be considered, for the purposes of the election of President and Vice-President, to be electors appointed by a State; and they shall meet in the District and perform such duties as provided by the twelfth article of amendment.

Section 2 The Congress shall have power to enforce this article by appropriate legislation.

AMENDMENT XXIV [ADOPTED 1964]

Section 1 The right of citizens of the United States to vote in any primary or other election for President or Vice-President, for electors for President or Vice-President, or for Senator or Representative in Congress, shall not be denied or abridged by the United States or any State by reason of failure to pay any poll tax or other tax.

Section 2 The Congress shall have power to enforce this article by appropriate legislation.

AMENDMENT XXV [ADOPTED 1967]

Section 1 In case of the removal of the President from office or his death or resignation, the Vice-President shall become President.

Section 2 Whenever there is a vacancy in the office of the Vice-President, the President shall nominate a Vice-President who shall take the office upon confirmation by a majority vote of both houses of Congress.

Section 3 Whenever the President transmits to the President pro tempore of the Senate and the Speaker of the House of Representatives his written declaration that he is unable to discharge the powers and duties of his office, and until he transmits to them a written declaration to the contrary, such powers and duties shall be discharged by the Vice-President as Acting President.

Section 4 Whenever the Vice-President and a majority of either the principal officers of the executive departments, or of such other body as Congress may by law provide, transmit to the President pro tempore of the Senate and the Speaker of the House of Representatives their written declaration that the President is unable to discharge the powers and duties of his office, the Vice-President shall immediately assume the powers and duties of the office as Acting President.

Thereafter, when the President transmits to the President pro tempore of the Senate and the Speaker of the House of Representatives his written declaration that no inability exists, he shall resume the powers and duties of his office unless the Vice-President and a majority of either the principal officers of the executive department, or of such other body as Congress may by law provide, transmit within four days to the President pro tempore of the Senate and the Speaker of the House of Representatives their written declaration that the President is unable to discharge the powers and duties of his office. Thereupon Congress shall decide the issue, assembling within 48 hours for that purpose if not in session. If the Congress, within 21 days after receipt of the latter written declaration, or, if Congress is not in session, within 21 days after Congress is required to assemble, determines by two-thirds vote of both houses that the President is unable to discharge the powers and duties of his office, the Vice-President shall continue to discharge the same as Acting President; otherwise, the President shall resume the powers and duties of his office.

AMENDMENT XXVI [ADOPTED 1971]

Section 1 The right of citizens of the United States, who are eighteen years of age or older, to vote shall not be denied or abridged by the United States or any state on account of age.

Section 2 The Congress shall have power to enforce this article by appropriate legislation.

AMENDMENT XXVII [ADOPTED 1992]

No law, varying the compensation for the services of Senators and Representatives, shall take effect until an election of Representatives have intervened.

PRESIDENTIAL ELECTIONS

Year	Candidates	Parties	Popular Vote	Electoral Vote	Voter Participation
1789	GEORGE WASHINGTON		*	69	
	John Adams			34	
	Others			35	
1792	GEORGE WASHINGTON		*	132	
	John Adams			77	
	George Clinton			50	
	Others			5	
1796	JOHN ADAMS	Federalist	*	71	
	Thomas Jefferson	Democratic-Republican		68	
	Thomas Pinckney	Federalist		59	
	Aaron Burr	Dem.-Rep.		30	
	Others			48	
1800	THOMAS JEFFERSON	Dem.-Rep.	*	73	
	Aaron Burr	Dem.-Rep.		73	
	C. C. Pinckney	Federalist		64	
	John Jay	Federalist		1	
1804	THOMAS JEFFERSON	Dem.-Rep.	*	122	
	C. C. Pinckney	Federalist		14	
1808	JAMES MADISON	Dem.-Rep.	*	122	
	C. C. Pinckney	Federalist		47	
	George Clinton	Dem.-Rep.		6	
1812	JAMES MADISON	Dem.-Rep.	*	128	
	De Witt Clinton	Federalist		89	
1816	JAMES MONROE	Dem.-Rep.	*	183	
	Rufus King	Federalist		34	
1820	JAMES MONROE	Dem.-Rep.	*	231	
	John Quincy Adams	Dem.-Rep.		1	
1824	JOHN Q. ADAMS	Dem.-Rep.	108,740 (10.5%)	84	26.9%
	Andrew Jackson	Dem.-Rep.	153,544 (43.1%)	99	
	William H. Crawford	Dem.-Rep.	46,618 (13.1%)	41	
	Henry Clay	Dem.-Rep.	47,136 (13.2%)	37	
1828	ANDREW JACKSON	Democratic	647,286 (56.0%)	178	57.6%
	John Quincy Adams	National Republican	508,064 (44.0%)	83	
1832	ANDREW JACKSON	Democratic	687,502 (55.0%)	219	55.4%
	Henry Clay	National Republican	530,189 (42.4%)	49	
	John Floyd	Independent		11	
	William Wirt	Anti-Mason	33,108 (2.6%)	7	
1836	MARTIN VAN BUREN	Democratic	765,483 (50.9%)	170	57.8%
	W. H. Harrison	Whig		73	
	Hugh L. White	Whig	739,795 (49.1%)	26	
	Daniel Webster	Whig		14	
	W. P. Magnum	Independent		11	
1840	WILLIAM H. HARRISON	Whig	1,274,624 (53.1%)	234	80.2%
	Martin Van Buren	Democratic	1,127,781 (46.9%)	60	
	J. G. Birney	Liberty	7,069	—	
1844	JAMES K. POLK	Democratic	1,338,464 (49.6%)	170	78.9%
	Henry Clay	Whig	1,300,097 (48.1%)	105	
	J. G. Birney	Liberty	62,300 (2.3%)	—	
1848	ZACHARY TAYLOR	Whig	1,360,967 (47.4%)	163	72.7%
	Lewis Cass	Democratic	1,222,342 (42.5%)	127	
	Martin Van Buren	Free-Soil	291,263 (10.1%)	—	

*Electors elected by state legislators.

Year	Candidates	Parties	Popular Vote	Electoral Vote	Voter Participation
1852	FRANKLIN PIERCE	Democratic	1,601,117 (50.9%)	254	69.6%
	Winfield Scott	Whig	1,385,453 (44.1%)	42	
	John P. Hale	Free-Soil	155,825 (5.0%)	—	
1856	JAMES BUCHANAN	Democratic	1,832,955 (45.3%)	174	78.9%
	John C. Fremont	Republican	1,339,932 (33.1%)	114	
	Millard Fillmore	American	871,731 (21.6%)	8	
1860	ABRAHAM LINCOLN	Republican	1,865,593 (39.8%)	180	81.2%
	Stephen A. Douglas	Democratic	1,382,713 (29.5%)	12	
	John C. Breckinridge	Democratic	848,356 (18.1%)	72	
	John Bell	Union	592,906 (12.6%)	39	
1864	ABRAHAM LINCOLN	Republican	2,213,655 (55.0%)	212	73.8%
	George B. McClellan	Democratic	1,805,237 (45.0%)	21	
1868	ULYSSES S. GRANT	Republican	3,012,833 (52.7%)	214	78.1%
	Horatio Seymour	Democratic	2,703,249 (47.3%)	80	
1872	ULYSSES S. GRANT	Republican	3,597,132 (55.6%)	286	71.3%
	Horace Greeley	Democratic; Liberal Republican	2,834,125 (43.9%)	66	
1876	RUTHERFORD B. HAYES	Republican	4,036,298 (48.0%)	185	81.8%
	Samuel J. Tilden	Democratic	4,300,590 (51.0%)	184	
1880	JAMES A. GARFIELD	Republican	4,454,416 (48.5%)	214	79.4%
	Winfield S. Hancock	Democratic	4,444,952 (48.1%)	155	
1884	GROVER CLEVELAND	Democratic	4,874,986 (48.5%)	219	77.5%
	James G. Blaine	Republican	4,851,981 (48.2%)	182	
1888	BENJAMIN HARRISON	Republican	5,439,853 (47.9%)	233	79.3%
	Grover Cleveland	Democratic	5,540,309 (48.6%)	168	
1892	GROVER CLEVELAND	Democratic	5,556,918 (46.1%)	277	74.7%
	Benjamin Harrison	Republican	5,176,108 (43.0%)	145	
	James B. Weaver	People's	1,041,028 (8.5%)	22	
1896	WILLIAM McKINLEY	Republican	7,104,779 (51.1%)	271	79.3%
	William J. Bryan	Democratic People's	6,502,925 (47.7%)	176	
1900	WILLIAM McKINLEY	Republican	7,207,923 (51.7%)	292	73.2%
	William J. Bryan	Dem.-Populist	6,358,133 (45.5%)	155	
1904	THEODORE ROOSEVELT	Republican	7,623,486 (57.9%)	336	65.2%
	Alton B. Parker	Democratic	5,077,911 (37.6%)	140	
	Eugene V. Debs	Socialist	402,283 (3.0%)	—	
1908	WILLIAM H. TAFT	Republican	7,678,908 (51.6%)	321	65.4%
	William J. Bryan	Democratic	6,409,104 (43.1%)	162	
	Eugene V. Debs	Socialist	420,793 (2.8%)	—	
1912	WOODROW WILSON	Democratic	6,293,454 (41.9%)	435	58.8%
	Theodore Roosevelt	Progressive	4,119,538 (27.4%)	88	
	William H. Taft	Republican	3,484,980 (23.2%)	8	
	Eugene V. Debs	Socialist	900,672 (6.0%)	—	
1916	WOODROW WILSON	Democratic	9,129,606 (49.4%)	277	61.6%
	Charles E. Hughes	Republican	8,538,221 (46.2%)	254	
	A. L. Benson	Socialist	585,113 (3.2%)	—	
1920	WARREN G. HARDING	Republican	16,152,200 (60.4%)	404	49.2%
	James M. Cox	Democratic	9,147,353 (34.2%)	127	
	Eugene V. Debs	Socialist	919,799 (3.4%)	—	
1924	CALVIN COOLIDGE	Republican	15,725,016 (54.0%)	382	48.9%
	John W. Davis	Democratic	8,386,503 (28.8%)	136	
	Robert M. La Follette	Progressive	4,822,856 (16.6%)	13	
1928	HERBERT HOOVER	Republican	21,391,381 (58.2%)	444	56.9%
	Alfred E. Smith	Democratic	15,016,443 (40.9%)	87	
	Norman Thomas	Socialist	267,835 (0.7%)	—	

Year	Candidates	Parties	Popular Vote	Electoral Vote	Voter Participation
1932	FRANKLIN D. ROOSEVELT	Democratic	22,821,857 (57.4%)	472	56.9%
	Herbert Hoover	Republican	15,761,841 (39.7%)	59	
	Norman Thomas	Socialist	881,951 (2.2%)	—	
1936	FRANKLIN D. ROOSEVELT	Democratic	27,751,597 (60.8%)	523	61.0%
	Alfred M. Landon	Republican	16,679,583 (36.5%)	8	
	William Lemke	Union	882,479 (1.9%)	—	
1940	FRANKLIN D. ROOSEVELT	Democratic	27,244,160 (54.8%)	449	62.5%
	Wendell L. Willkie	Republican	22,305,198 (44.8%)	82	
1944	FRANKLIN D. ROOSEVELT	Democrat	25,602,504 (53.5%)	432	55.9%
	Thomas E. Dewey	Republican	22,006,285 (46.0%)	99	
1948	HARRY S TRUMAN	Democratic	24,105,695 (49.5%)	304	53.0%
	Thomas E. Dewey	Republican	21,969,170 (45.1%)	189	
	J. Strom Thurmond	State-Rights Democratic	1,169,021 (2.4%)	38	
	Henry A. Wallace	Progressive	1,156,103 (2.4%)	—	
1952	DWIGHT D. EISENHOWER	Republican	33,936,252 (55.1%)	442	63.3%
	Adlai E. Stevenson	Democratic	27,314,992 (44.4%)	89	
1956	DWIGHT D. EISENHOWER	Republican	35,575,420 (57.6%)	457	60.5%
	Adlai E. Stevenson	Democratic	26,033,066 (42.1%)	73	
	Other	—	—	1	
1960	JOHN F. KENNEDY	Democratic	34,227,096 (49.9%)	303	62.8%
	Richard M. Nixon	Republican	34,108,546 (49.6%)	219	
	Other	—	—	15	
1964	LYNDON B. JOHNSON	Democratic	43,126,506 (61.1%)	486	61.7%
	Barry M. Goldwater	Republican	27,176,799 (38.5%)	52	
1968	RICHARD M. NIXON	Republican	31,770,237 (43.4.%)	301	60.6%
	Hubert H. Humphrey	Democratic	31,270,633 (42.7%)	191	
	George Wallace	American Indep.	9,906,141 (13.5%)	46	
1972	RICHARD M. NIXON	Republican	47,169,911 (60.7%)	520	55.2%
	George S. McGovern	Democratic	29,170,383 (37.5%)	17	
	Other	—	—	1	
1976	JIMMY CARTER	Democratic	40,828,587 (50.0%)	297	53.5%
	Gerald R. Ford	Republican	39,147,613 (47.9%)	241	
	Other	—	1,575,459 (2.1%)	—	
1980	RONALD REAGAN	Republican	43,901,812 (50.7%)	489	52.6%
	Jimmy Carter	Democratic	35,483,820 (41.0%)	49	
	John B. Anderson	Independent	5,719,722 (6.6%)	—	
	Ed Clark	Libertarian	921,188 (1.1%)	—	
1984	RONALD REAGAN	Republican	54,455,075 (59.0%)	525	53.3%
	Walter Mondale	Democratic	37,577,185 (41.0%)	13	
1988	GEORGE H. W. BUSH	Republican	48,886,000 (45.6%)	426	57.4%
	Michael S. Dukakis	Democratic	41,809,000 (45.6%)	111	
1992	WILLIAM J. CLINTON	Democratic	43,728,375 (43%)	370	55.0%
	George H. W. Bush	Republican	38,167,416 (38%)	168	
	Ross Perot	—	19,237,247 (19%)	—	
1996	WILLIAM J. CLINTON	Democratic	45,590,703 (50%)	379	48.8%
	Robert Dole	Republican	37,816,307 (41%)	159	
	Ross Perot	Independent	7,866,284 (9%)		
2000	GEORGE W. BUSH	Republican	50,456,062 (47%)	271	51.0%
	Albert Gore	Democratic	50,996,582 (49%)	267	
	Ralph Nader	Independent	2,858,843 (3%)	—	
2004	GEORGE W. BUSH	Republican	60,934,251 (51%)	286	
	John F. Kerry	Democrat	57,765,291 (48%)	252	
	Ralph Nader	Independent	405,933 (0%)	—	

STATES OF THE UNITED STATES

State	Date of Admission	State	Date of Admission
Delaware	December 7, 1787	Michigan	January 16, 1837
Pennsylvania	December 12, 1787	Florida	March 3, 1845
New Jersey	December 18, 1787	Texas	December 29, 1845
Georgia	January 2, 1788	Iowa	December 28, 1846
Connecticut	January 9, 1788	Wisconsin	May 29, 1848
Massachusetts	February 6, 1788	California	September 9, 1850
Maryland	April 28, 1788	Minnesota	May 11, 1858
South Carolina	May 23, 1788	Oregon	February 14, 1859
New Hampshire	June 21, 1788	Kansas	January 29, 1861
Virginia	June 25, 1788	West Virginia	June 19, 1863
New York	July 26, 1788	Nevada	October 31, 1864
North Carolina	November 21, 1789	Nebraska	March 1, 1867
Rhode Island	May 29, 1790	Colorado	August 1, 1876
Vermont	March 4, 1791	North Dakota	November 2, 1889
Kentucky	June 1, 1792	South Dakota	November 2, 1889
Tennessee	June 1, 1796	Montana	November 8, 1889
Ohio	March 1, 1803	Washington	November 11, 1889
Louisiana	April 30, 1812	Idaho	July 3, 1890
Indiana	December 11, 1816	Wyoming	July 10, 1890
Mississippi	December 10, 1817	Utah	January 4, 1896
Illinois	December 3, 1818	Oklahoma	November 16, 1907
Alabama	December 14, 1819	New Mexico	January 6, 1912
Maine	March 15, 1820	Arizona	February 14, 1912
Missouri	August 10, 1821	Alaska	January 3, 1959
Arkansas	June 15, 1836	Hawaii	August 21, 1959

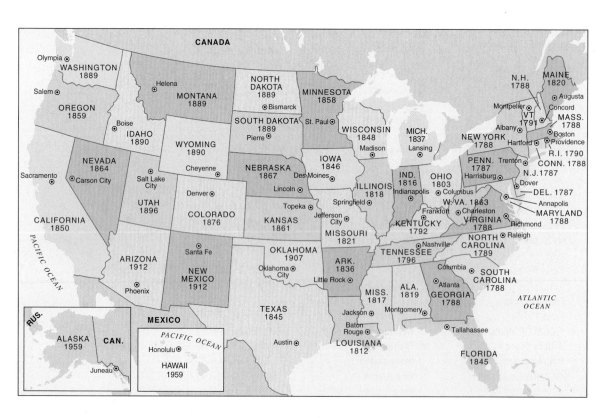

POPULATION OF THE UNITED STATES

Year	Number of States	Population	Percent Increase	Population per Square Mile
1790	13	3,929,214		4.5
1800	16	5,308,483	35.1	6.1
1810	17	7,239,881	36.4	4.3
1820	23	9,638,453	33.1	5.5
1830	24	12,866,020	33.5	7.4
1840	26	17,069,453	32.7	9.8
1850	31	23,191,876	35.9	7.9
1860	33	31,443,321	35.6	10.6
1870	37	39,818,449	26.6	13.4
1880	38	50,155,783	26.0	16.9
1890	44	62,947,714	25.5	21.2
1900	45	75,994,575	20.7	25.6
1910	46	91,972,266	21.0	31.0
1920	48	105,710,620	14.9	35.6
1930	48	122,775,046	16.1	41.2
1940	48	131,669,275	7.2	44.2
1950	48	150,697,361	14.5	50.7
1960	50	179,323,175	19.0	50.6
1970	50	203,235,298	13.3	57.5
1980	50	226,545,805	11.5	64.1
1990	50	248,709,873	9.8	70.3
2000	50	281,421,906	13.0	77.0

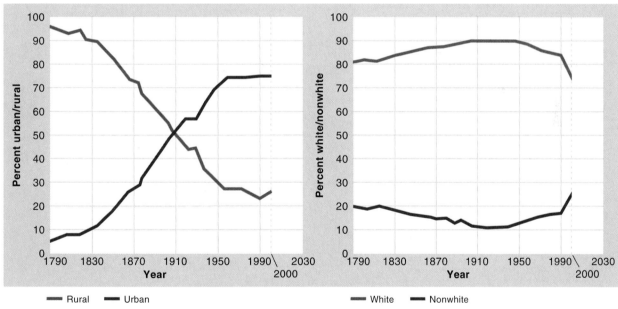

Source: U.S. Bureau of the Census estimates

Credits

Chapter 1

p. 15, The Legend of the Great League of the Iroquois, from *The Death and Rebirth of Seneca*, Anthony F. C. Wallace, New York, NY: Alfred A. Knopf, 1970.

p. 31, Gomes Eannes de Zurara, The Arrival of a Slave Ship at Lagos, Portugal, from *Chronicle of the Discovery and Conquest of Guinea*.

Chapter 2

p. 40, Christopher Columbus, The Encounter with the Taíno, From *Journals of Christopher Columbus* in *Major Problems in American Indian History*, Albert L. Hurtado and Peter Iverson, Lexington, MA: D.C. Heath, 1994.

p. 46, "Titu Cusi's account of Manco's rebellion," trans. by the editors, in John H. Parry and Robert G. Keith, eds., *New Iberian World*, Vol. III (New York: Times Books, 1984), pp. 143, 144.

Chapter 3

p. 101, William Penn, Letter to the Delaware Indians, From "Letter from William Penn to Delaware Indian Chiefs," October 18, 1681, London. Historical Society of Pennsylvania, Stauffer Collection. Reprinted with permission.

Chapter 4

p. 123, Charles Woodmason, A Congregation in the Southern Backcountry, from *The Carolina Backcountry on the Eve of the Revolution: The Journal and Other Writings of Charles Woodmason, Anglican Itinerant*, Richard J. Hooker. Chapel Hill, NC: University of North Carolina Press, 1953.

Chapter 5

p. 181, George Sims, "Address to the Inhabitants of Granville County," From *Some Eighteenth Century Tracts Concerning North Carolina*, William K. Boyd, ed. Raleigh, NC: Edwards and Broughton, 1927.

Chapter 10

p. 329, Julia Hieronymus, Trials of a Teacher, from *60 Years in a Schoolroom*, Julia A. Trevis. Cincinnati: 1878.

Chapter 11

p. 379, "Tar Baby," "The Tar Baby Tricks Brer Rabbit" from *Days When the Animals Talked: Black American Folktales and How They Came to Be* by William J. Faulkner, ed. Copyright © 1993 Africa World Press. Reprinted by permission.

Chapter 12

p. 398, Speckled Snake, A Native American Reply to Jackson's Removal Policy, From "Speech of Speckled Snake," *Cherokee Phoenix and Indian's Advocate*, July 8, 1829, vol. II, no. 14, p. 2, Special Collections, Hunter Library, Western Carolina University. Reprinted by permission.

p. 415, Martha Wright's New York Family Helps a Fugitive Slave, From "Letter of Martha Coffin Wright to Lucretia Mott" January 18–19, 1843. Garrison Family Papers, Sophia Smith Collection, Smith College, Northampton, MA. Reprinted by permission of James Livingston, author of "A Very Dangerous Woman: Martha Wright and Women's Rights."

Chapter 13

p. 442, Mollie Dorsey Sanford, On Arriving in Denver, June 1860, Reprinted from *Mollie: The Journal of Mollie Dorsey Sanford* by permission of the University of Nebraska Press. © 1959 by the University of Nebraska Press. © renewed 1987 by the University of Nebraska Press.

Chapter 15

p. 499, Isaac Watts, A Description of Camp Life with the Vermont Heavy Artillery, By permission of University of Massachusetts Press, from "Roxana's Children," copyright 1995 Lynn A. Bonfield & Mary C. Morrison.

p. 505, Susie King Taylor, *Reminiscences of My Life in Camp*, from *Reminiscences of My Life in Camp with the 33rd United States Colored Troops*, Susie King Taylor. Boston, 1902.

Chapter 16

p. 528, James A. Payne, A Southern White Man Protests Conditions in the South After the Civil War, From "Letter from James A. Payne," September 1, 1867, from Lilly Library's Barnhart Mss. Collection. Reprinted courtesy Lilly Library, Indiana University, Bloomington, IN

Chapter 17

p. 570, Sister Blandina Segale, from her Diary, November 1882, From "Sister Blandina Segale Diary Entry Nov. 1882" from *So Much to Be Done: Women Settlers on the Mining and Ranching Frontier*, by R. B. Moynihan, S. Armitage, C. Fischer Dichamp, eds. Copyright © 1990. Reprinted by permission of Archives Sisters of Charity of Cincinnati.

Chapter 18

p. 612, Helen Campbell, Interview with a Domestic Servant, From *Documents of the Social History of American Women*, Nancy F. Cott, ed. Boston, MA: Northeastern University Press, 1996.

Chapter 20

p. 665, Jane Addams Speaks Out Against Imperialism, War, and Violence, Democracy or Militarism, Jane Addams. Chicago: Central Anti-Imperialist League, 1899.

Chapter 21

p. 692, Rosa: An Italian Immigrant Learns English at a Settlement House in Chicago, From Rosa: *The Life of an Italian Immigrant*, Marie Hall, ets. Copyright © 1999.

Reprinted by permission of the University of Wisconsin Press.

p. 697, Pauline Newman, Conditions in a Garment Factory, From Pauline Newman from Lithuania, 1901" reprinted from *American Mosaic: The Immigrant Experience in the Words of Those Who Lived It*, by Joan Morrison and Charlotte Fox Zabusky, © 1980, 1993, by permission of the University of Pittsburgh Press.

Chapter 22

p. 740, Private John Figarovsky, American Soldiers Get a Warm Welcome in France, From "Private John Figarovsky" from *Forgotten Voices of the Great War* by Max Arthur. Copyright © 2002 by Max Arthur. Reprinted by permission of Globe Pequot Press/Lyons Press.

Chapter 23

p. 761, Luigi Barzini, Jr., An Italian Student Falls in Love with the United States, From *As Others See Us: The United States Through Foreign Eyes*, Franz M. Joseph, ed. Princeton, NJ: Princeton University Press, 1959.

Chapter 24

p. 798, Mrs. Ivan G. Martin, "What is to become of us?" An Oregon Woman Writes to Eleanor and Franklin Roosevelt, From the book *Dear Mrs. Roosevelt: Letters to Eleanor Roosevelt Through Depression and War* edited by Cathy D. Knepper. Copyright © 2004 by Cathy D. Knepper. Appears by permission of the publisher, Carroll and Graf, a division of Avalon Publishing Group.

p. 819, Georges Duhamel, A French Writer Visits the United States and Finds Nothing to Admire, From *America: The Menace: Scenes from the Life of the Future*, George Duhamel. London, England: George Allen & Unwin, 1931.

Chapter 25

p. 846, PFC Robert Kotlowitz Faces Battle, From *Before Their Time* by Robert Kotlowitz, copyright © 1997 by Robert Kotlowitz. Used by permission of Alfred A. Knopf, a division of Random House, Inc.

p. 856, Yamaoka Michiko, On the Ground at Hiroshima, From Yamaoka Michiko, "Eight Hundred Meters from Hypocenter," in *Japan at War: An Oral History* by Haruko Taya Cook and Theodore F. Cook. Copyright © 1993 New Press. Reprinted by permission of The New Press.

Chapter 26

p. 874, Verse from "Little Boxes" lyrics by Malvina Reynolds, Verse from "Little Boxes" by Malvina Reynolds © 1962 Schroeder Music Co. (ASCAP).

p. 879, Betty Friedan, from *The Feminine Mystique*, Betty Friedan. New York, NY: W.W. Norton, 1963.

p. 884, Allen Ginsberg, "Howl." Three excerpts (22 l. in total) from *'Howl'* from *Collected Poems 1947–1980 by Allen Ginsberg*. Copyright © 1955 by Allen Ginsberg. Reprinted by permission of HarperCollins Publishers.

Chapter 27

p. 915, The Gallop Poll, George C. Gallop: The Gallop Poll: Public Opinion, 1935–1971, vol. 2 (New York: Random House, 1972).

p. 918, Colonel Lewis Puller, Speech to the Troops, From *Korea: The Untold Story of the War*, Joseph C. Goulden. New York, NY: Times Books, 1982.

Chapter 28

p. 952, Anne Moody, from *Coming of Age in Mississippi*, From Coming of Age in Mississippi, Anne Moody. New York, NY: Dell Publishing Company, 1968.

Chapter 29

pp. 982–983, Bob Dylan, lyrics to "The Times They Are A-Changin," From "Times They Are A-Changin" by Bob Dylan. Copyright © 1963 by Warner Bros. Inc. Copyright renewed 1991 by Special Rider Music. All rights reserved. International copyright secured. Reprinted by permission.

p. 992, "I Am Woman" lyrics by Helen Reddy, "I Am Woman" lyrics by Helen Reddy © 1971 by Irving Music Inc. and BMA.

p. 997, Rodolfo "Corky" Gonzales, "I am Joaquim" From "I am Joaquim" by Rodolfo Gonzales. Copyright © by Rodolfo Gonzales. Reprinted by permission.

p. 996, Helen Chávez, Reflections on the Family's Struggle From *Cesar Chavez: Autobiography of La Causa*, Jacques Levy. New York, NY: W.W. Norton, 1975.

Chapter 30

p. 1018, Jesse Jackson, Speech Before the Democratic National Convention, July 18, 1984.

p. 1021, Sherman Alexie, Four Related Poems, From "The Business of Fancy Dancing" by Sherman Alexie. Copyright © 1991 Sherman Alexie. Reprinted by permission of Hanging Loose Press.

Chapter 31

p. 1060, Marilyn Chin, "How I Got That Name," Marilyn Chin, "How I Got That Name" in *The Phoenix Gone, the Terrace Empty* (Minneapolis: Milkweed Editions, 1994). Copyright © 1994 by Marilyn Chin. Reprinted with permission from Milkweed Editions.

p. 1075, Elfriede Jelinek, "No New Wars," "No New Wars" by Elfriede Jelinek. *New York Times*, February 20, 2005. Copyright © 2005 by The New York Times Co. Reprinted with permission.

Price(s)
  agricultural, 555, 555 (illus.), 556
  farm, 1028
  in 1970s, 975, 977
  production and, 587
  after Revolution, 231–232
Price, J. C., 578
Price revolution, silver circulation
  and, 51
Price-support programs, for farmers,
  1028
Priests, African American, 385
Priest state, Cherokee, 134
Primary education, 328
Prince, Mary, 380
Princeton, 146
  battle at, 192
Printing industry, 331 (illus.), 332
Printing press, in Massachusetts, 86
Prison camps, in Civil War, 516
Prisoners and Wounded, 1918 (Dunn),
  720 (illus.)
Prisons, 408, 409
Privateers, during Seven Years' War,
  163
Private property, Indians and, 295, 571
Proclamation Line (1763), 197, 223
Proclamation of 1763, 162, 163
Production. *See also* Manufacturing
  agricultural, 563 (illus.), 777
  after Civil War, 658
  pace of, 613
  prices and, 587
Productivity
  agricultural, 556
  decline in, 1026–1027
  of farms, 1028
  in 1990s, 1049
  in sugar industry, 360
Products (American), worldwide sales
  of, 866
Professional Air Traffic Controllers
  Organization (PATCO), 1027
Professionals and professionalism, 602
  immigrants as, 1022
  women and, 601, 682–684
Profit(s)
  from colonies, 57
  overseas markets for, 658–659
  pursuit of, 140
  from war production, 829
Profiteers, after Revolution, 232–233
Progress, Spencer on, 631
Progress and Poverty (George),
  632–633, 684, 701
Progressive education, 692
Progressive party
  of 1912, 683, 710–711, 730
  in 1924, 779
  of 1948, 886
Progressive Service Organization, 684
Progressivism
  African Americans and, 708–709
  global context of, 684–685
  home and school reforms and,
    691–692

Kellor, Frances, and, 682–684
  legislation under, 714
  limits of, 716
  municipal reform and, 700–703
  in 1920s, 782–783
  presidential elections and, 712
  of Roosevelt, Theodore, 704–709
  social justice movement and,
    684–695
  state reform and, 703–704
  Taft and, 710
  Wilson and, 730
  women's rights and, 689–691
  workers and, 695–700
  worldview of, 685–688
  World War I and, 746
Prohibition, 630, 714
  amendment for, 693
  Anglo-Saxons and, 636
  end to, 800
  in 1920s, 783–784
  in states (1919), 693 (map)
Propaganda
  Soviet, 905 (illus.)
  of temperance movement, 407–408,
    407 (illus.)
  in World War I, 736–737, 736 (illus.),
    737 (illus.)
Property
  acquisition of, 137
  Indian vs. European concept of, 19
  inheritance of, 118
  redistribution of, 213
  slaves as, 373
  among whites, 298–299
  of women, 216
  of yeoman farmers, 365
Property rights, 326
Prophet, the. *See* Tenskwatawa (the
  Prophet, Shawnee)
Proposition 187 (California), 1047
Proposition 209 (California), 1056,
  1058
Proprietary colonies
  Carolina as, 96–98
  Maryland as, 76, 106
Prosperity
  in 1990s, 1049–1051
  during Seven Years' War, 163
  stock market crash and, 786
  urban, 256 (illus.)
  for workers, 777–778
  after World War I, 759–760
Prostitution, 417, 601, 635, 694
  Chinese women and, 598 (illus.)
  poverty and, 608–609
  in West, 443
  in World War I, 746
  in World War II, 841
Protective tariff, 314
Protest(s). *See also* Revolts and
  rebellions; specific groups
  by abolitionists, 414
  anti-American, 1037 (illus.)
  civil rights, 944–945, 945 (illus.)
  clergy and, 175

at Democratic National Convention
    (1968), 967
  against draft, 734
  farm, 579–581
  during Gilded Age, 644
  in interior colonies, 180–182
  labor, 612–614, 614 (illus.)
  by Latinos, 995–997
  in Maryland, 81
  by Mexican American students, 997
  Native American, 997–1000
  Nixon on, 977
  in North Carolina, 81
  against nuclear power, 926–927,
    1002, 1002 (illus.)
  against Roosevelt, Franklin D., 803
  by SDS, 968
  against segregation, 578
  by slaves, 381–382
  against Stamp Act, 166–168
  against Stamp Tax, 155
  against Tea Act, 171
  in Vietnam War, 962–964, 981
Protestants and Protestantism. *See
  also* Great Awakening; Puritans
  in Americas, 43
  Calvin and, 42–43
  colonial benefits to, 56
  denominational growth in, 391
    (illus.)
  Elizabeth I and, 54
  in England, 3, 104–105
  Great Awakening and, 143–146
  Klan and, 758
  Luther and, 41–42
  in Maryland, 76, 81
  missionary impulse and, 659–660
  nativism and, 469–471, 604
  in World War II, 843
Provincial congresses, after
  Revolution, 212–213
Provisional governors, in
  Reconstruction, 529
PT-109 (boat), 939
Ptolemy (astronomer), 30
Public aid, 816
Public Broadcasting System, 1065
Public employee unions, 1051
Public health movement, 598
Public land. *See* Land
Public officials, Latino, 1020, 1057
Public opinion, 660
  polls, 914–915
Public schools. *See* Schools
Public Utility Holding Company Act
    (1935), 809, 815
Public virtue
  Anti-Federalists on, 244
  Federalists on, 243
  principle of, 212
  women's roles and, 216
Public Works Administration (PWA,
    1933), 800, 815
Public works projects, under Hoover,
  795
Publishing, 332, 343

The World

ARCTIC OCEAN

Greenland
(DENMARK)

Arctic Circle
Alaska
(U.S.)

CANADA

**NORTH
AMERICA**

UNITED STATES

Azores
(PORT.)

Bermuda (U.K.)

ATLANTIC
OCEAN

PACIFIC
OCEAN

40°North Longitude

Midway Is.
(U.S.)

Tropic of Cancer

Hawaii (U.S.)

20°N

MEXICO

See inset below

CUBA
HAITI
BELIZE
HONDURAS
GUATEMALA
EL SALVADOR
COSTA RICA
PANAMA

DOMINICAN
REPUBLIC

CAPE VERDE

NICARAGUA

VENEZUELA

GUYANA
SURINAM
FR. GUIANA

Galápagos
Islands
(ECUADOR)

COLOMBIA

0° Equator

KIRIBATI

ECUADOR

SOUTH
AMERICA

WESTERN
SAMOA

American
Samoa (U.S.)

French
Polynesia
(FRANCE)

PERU

BRAZIL

TONGA

20°S

BOLIVIA

PARAGUAY

Tropic of Capricorn

Easter Island
(CHILE)

CHILE

40°S

ARGENTINA
URUGUAY

PACIFIC
OCEAN

Falkland Islands
(U.K.)

South Georgia
(Falkland Is.)

60°S

Antarctic Circle

80°S

ANTARCTICA

Central America
and the Caribbean

UNITED STATES

30°N

110°W

100°W

90°W

80°W

Gulf of Mexico

NORTH AMERICA

BAHAMAS

ATLANTIC OCEAN

20°N

MEXICO

CUBA

Cayman Is.
(U.K.)

JAMAICA

HAITI

Turks and Caicos Is. (U.K.)

DOMINICAN
REPUBLIC

Puerto Rico
(U.S.)

Virgin Is. (U.S. – U.K.)

ANTIGUA-BARBUDA

ST. KITTS AND NEVIS

West Indies

Guadeloupe (Fr.)
DOMINICA
Martinique (Fr.)
ST. LUCIA

BELIZE

HONDURAS

GUATEMALA
EL SALVADOR

**Central
America**

NICARAGUA

CARIBBEAN SEA

ST. VINCENT AND
THE GRENADINES

BARBADOS

GRENADA

PACIFIC OCEAN

Panama
Canal

TRINIDAD
AND TOBAGO

10°N

0   500 Miles

N
W   E
S

COSTA
RICA

PANAMA

COLOMBIA

VENEZUELA

SOUTH AMERICA

GUYANA

SURINAM

0   500 Kilometers